Ordnance Survey

STREET

Surrey

Contents

III   *Key to map symbols*

IV-V   *Key to map pages*

VI   *Administrative and post code boundaries*

1   *Street maps*

219   *Town plans of Guildford and Kingston*

220   *Town plans of Dorking, Epsom, Leatherhead and Woking*

221   *Explanation of street index reference system*

221   *Key to town, village and rural locality abbreviations in index*

223   *Index of hospitals, railway stations, schools, shopping centres, street names and universities*

PHILIP'S

First colour edition published 1996
Reprinted 1997, 1998 by

Ordnance Survey® and   George Philip Ltd., a division of
Romsey Road   Octopus Publishing Group Ltd
Maybush   Michelin House
Southampton   81 Fulham Road
SO16 4GU   London SW3 6RB

ISBN 0-540-06438-6 (pocket)

© Crown copyright 1996
© George Philip Ltd 1996

All rights reserved. No part of this publication may be reproduced,
stored in a retrieval system or transmitted, in any form or by any
means, electronic, mechanical, photocopying, recording or
otherwise, without the permission of the Publishers and the
copyright owner.

To the best of the Publishers' knowledge, the information in this
atlas was correct at the time of going to press. No responsibility
can be accepted for any errors or their consequences.

The representation in this atlas of a road, track or path is no
evidence of the existence of a right of way.

**The mapping between pages 1 and 220 (inclusive) in this
atlas is derived from Ordnance Survey® OSCAR® and Land-
Line® data, and Landranger® mapping.**

Ordnance Survey, OSCAR, Land-Line and Landranger are
registered trade marks of Ordnance Survey, the national mapping
agency of Great Britain.

Printed and bound in Spain by Cayfosa

Also available in various formats

- ◆ Berkshire
- ◆ Bristol and Avon
- ◆ Buckinghamshire
- ◆ Birmingham and
  West Midlands
  Cannock, Lichfield
  Rugeley
- ◆ Cardiff, Swansea
  and Glamorgan
- ◆ Cheshire
- ◆ Derbyshire
  Derby and Belper
- ◆ Durham
- ◆ Edinburgh & East
  Central Scotland

- ◆ East Essex
- ◆ West Essex
- ◆ Glasgow & West
  Central Scotland
- ◆ Greater Manchester
- ◆ North Hampshire
- ◆ South Hampshire
- ◆ Hertfordshire
- ◆ East Kent
- ◆ West Kent
- ◆ Lancashire
- ◆ Merseyside
  Northwich, Winsford
  Middlewich
- ◆ Nottinghamshire

- ◆ Oxfordshire
  Peak District Towns
- ◆ Staffordshire
  Stafford, Stone
  Uttoxeter
- ◆ East Sussex
- ◆ West Sussex
- ◆ Tyne and Wear
  Warrington, Widnes
  Runcorn
- ◆ Warwickshire
- ◆ South Yorkshire
- ◆ West Yorkshire

◆ Colour regional atlases (hardback, spiral, wire-o, pocket)   ● Colour local atlases (paperback)
◆ Black and white regional atlases (hardback, softback, pocket)

Key to map symbols

Motorway (with junction number)	
Primary route (dual carriageway and single)	
A Road (dual carriageway and single)	
B Road (dual carriageway and single)	
Minor road (dual carriageway and single)	
Other minor road	
Road under construction	
County boundaries	
Railway	
Rural track, private road or narrow road in urban area	
Gate or obstruction to traffic (restrictions may not apply at all times or to all vehicles)	
Path, bridleway, byway open to all traffic, road used as a public path, dismantled railways, etc.	
The representation in this atlas of a road, track or path is no evidence of the existence of a right of way	

174 Adjoining page indicator

Acad	**Academy**	Mon	**Monument**
Cemy	**Cemetery**	Mus	**Museum**
C Ctr	**Civic Centre**	Obsy	**Observatory**
CH	**Club House**	Pal	**Royal Palace**
Coll	**College**	PH	**Public House**
Ex H	**Exhibition Hall**	Resr	**Reservoir**
Ind Est	**Industrial Estate**	Ret Pk	**Retail Park**
Inst	**Institute**	Sch	**School**
Ct	**Law Court**	Sh Ctr	**Shopping Centre**
L Ctr	**Leisure Centre**	Sta	**Station**
LC	**Level Crossing**	TH	**Town Hall/House**
Liby	**Library**	Trad Est	**Trading Estate**
Mkt	**Market**	Univ	**University**
Meml	**Memorial**	YH	**Youth Hostel**

British Rail station	
Underground station	
Private Railway station	
Bus, coach station	
Ambulance station	
Coastguard station	
Fire station	
Police station	
Casualty entrance to hospital	
Churches, Place of worship	
H	**Hospital**
i	**Information Centre**
P	**Parking**
PO	**Post Office**
●	**Public Convenience**
	Important buildings, schools, colleges, universities and hospitals
Guildford City Sch	
River Wey	**Water Name**
	Stream
	River or canal (minor and major)
	Water Fill
	Tidal Water
	Woods

Scale bars:

0 — ¼ — ½ — ¾ — 1 mile

0 — 250m — 500m — 750m — 1 Kilometre

The scale of the maps is 3.92 cm to 1 km (2½ inches to 1 mile)

The small numbers around the edges of the maps identify the 1 kilometre National Grid lines

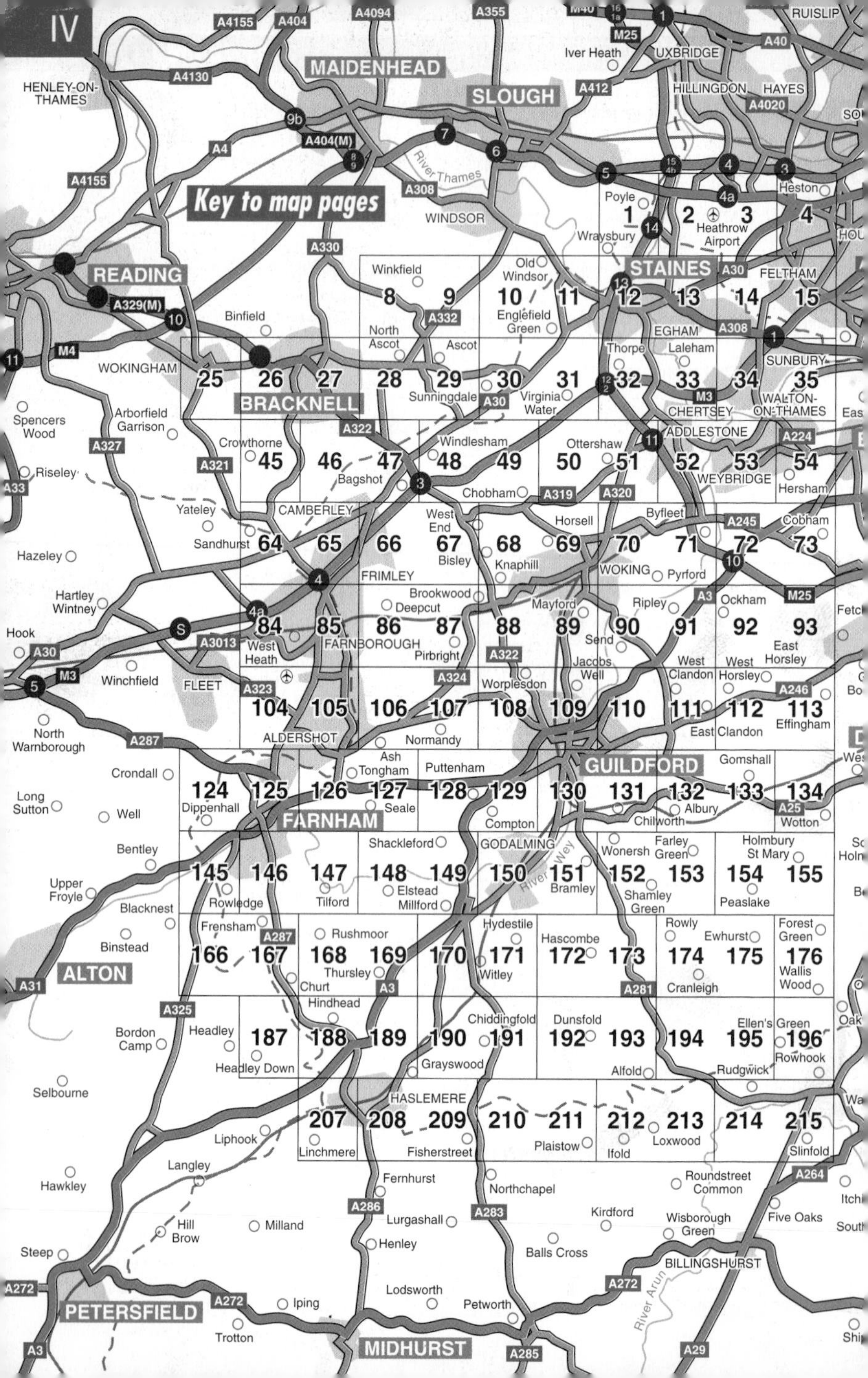
Key to map pages
A4155
A404
A4094
A355
M40
16
1a
M25
1
RUISLIP
MAIDENHEAD
Iver Heath
UXBRIDGE
A40
A4130
HENLEY-ON-THAMES
SLOUGH
A412
HILLINGDON
HAYES
A4020
9b
A404(M)
8/9
7
6
A4
A4155
River Thames
A308
5
15/4b
4
3
Poyle
4a
Heston
WINDSOR
1
2
Heathrow Airport
3
4
A330
Wraysbury
14
READING
Winkfield
Old Windsor
STAINES
A30
FELTHAM
A329(M)
8
9
10
11
13
12
13
14
15
10
Binfield
A332
Englefield Green
EGHAM
A308
1
11
M4
North Ascot
Ascot
Thorpe
Laleham
SUNBURY
WOKINGHAM
25
26
27
28
29
30
31
12/2
32
33
34
35
BRACKNELL
Sunningdale
A30
Virginia Water
M3
WALTON-ON-THAMES
Spencers Wood
Arborfield Garrison
CHERTSEY
A322
Windlesham
Ottershaw
11
ADDLESTONE
A224
A327
Crowthorne
45
46
47
48
49
50
51
52
53
54
A321
Riseley
Bagshot
3
WEYBRIDGE
Hersham
A33
Chobham
A319
A320
Yateley
CAMBERLEY
West End
Horsell
Byfleet
A245
Cobham
Sandhurst
64
65
66
67
68
69
70
71
72
73
Hazeley
Bisley
Knaphill
WOKING
Pyrford
10
4
FRIMLEY
Hartley Wintney
Brookwood
Deepcut
Mayford
Ripley
A3
Ockham
M25
4a
84
85
86
87
88
89
90
91
92
93
S
A3013
Hook
A30
West Heath
FARNBOROUGH
Pirbright
Send
East Horsley
A322
Jacobs Well
West Clandon
West Horsley
5
M3
Winchfield
FLEET
A324
A323
Worplesdon
A246
104
105
106
107
108
109
110
111
112
113
North Warnborough
A287
ALDERSHOT
Normandy
East Clandon
Effingham
Ash
GUILDFORD
Gomshall
Crondall
Tongham
Puttenham
124
125
126
127
128
129
130
131
132
133
134
Long Sutton
Well
Dippenhall
Seale
Albury
FARNHAM
Compton
Chilworth
A25
Wotton
Bentley
Shackleford
GODALMING
Farley Green
Wonersh
Holmbury St Mary
145
146
147
148
149
150
151
152
153
154
155
Upper Froyle
River Wey
Rowledge
Tilford
Elstead
Millford
Bramley
Shamley Green
Peaslake
Blacknest
Frensham
Hydestile
Rowly
Forest Green
Binstead
A287
Rushmoor
Hascombe
Ewhurst
166
167
168
169
170
171
172
173
174
175
176
ALTON
Thursley
Witley
Cranleigh
Wallis Wood
A31
Churt
A3
A281
A325
Hindhead
Chiddingfold
Dunsfold
Ellen's Green
Bordon Camp
Headley
187
188
189
190
191
192
193
194
195
196
Headley Down
Grayswood
Alfold
Rudgwick
Rowhook
Selbourne
HASLEMERE
207
208
209
210
211
212
213
214
215
Liphook
Linchmere
Fisherstreet
Plaistow
Ifold
Loxwood
Slinfold
Langley
Fernhurst
Roundstreet Common
A264
Hawkley
Northchapel
A286
Lurgashall
A283
Kirdford
Wisborough Green
Five Oaks
Hill Brow
Milland
Henley
Steep
Balls Cross
BILLINGSHURST
A272
A272
Lodsworth
River Arun
PETERSFIELD
A272
Iping
Petworth
Trotton
MIDHURST
A3
A285
A29

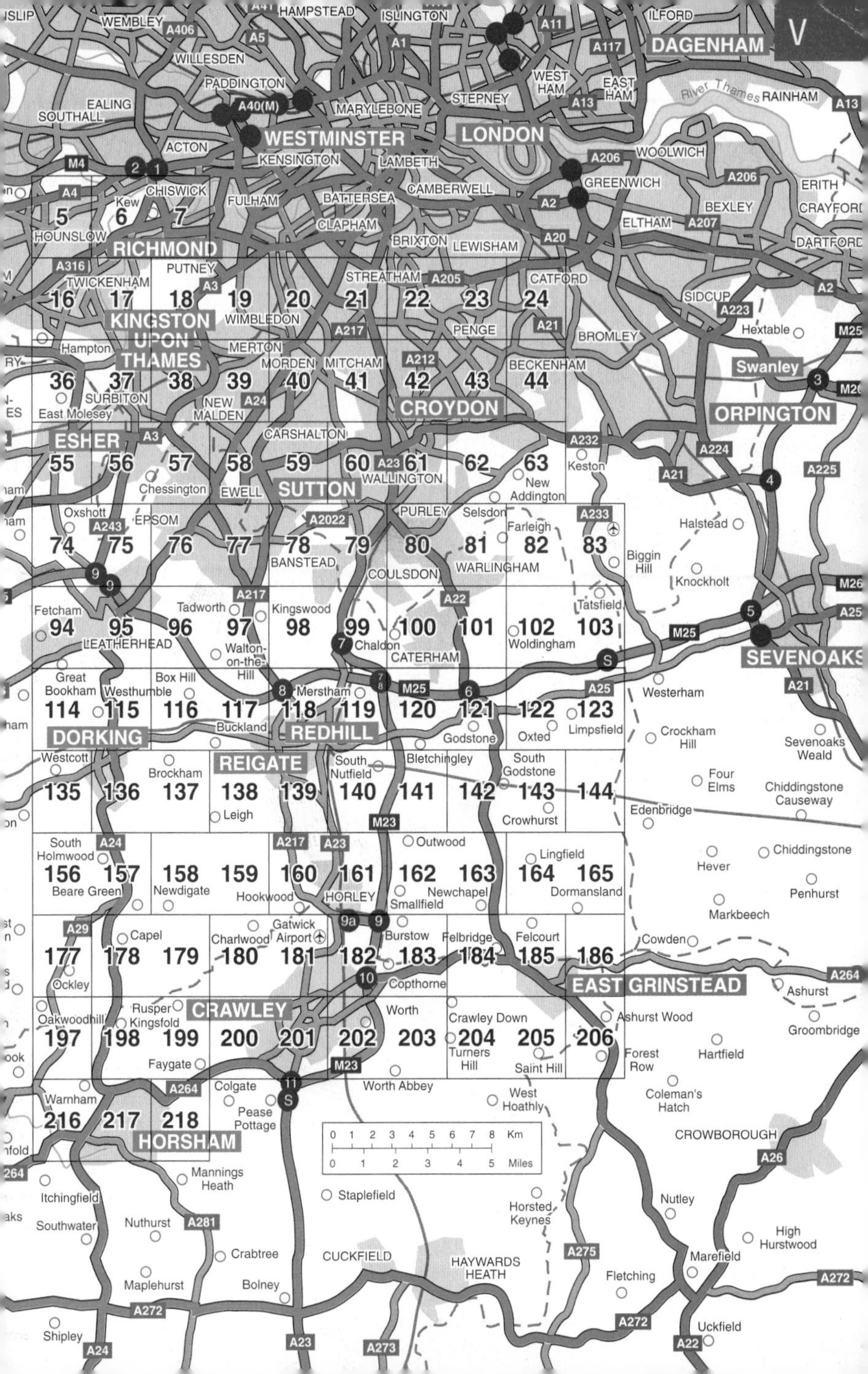

V
HAMPSTEAD
ISLINGTON
ILFORD
DAGENHAM
WEMBLEY
WILLESDEN
PADDINGTON
MARYLEBONE
STEPNEY
WEST HAM
EAST HAM
RAINHAM
River Thames
EALING
SOUTHALL
WESTMINSTER
LONDON
ACTON
KENSINGTON
LAMBETH
WOOLWICH
CHISWICK
CAMBERWELL
GREENWICH
ERITH
Kew
FULHAM
BATTERSEA
BEXLEY
CRAYFORD
HOUNSLOW
CLAPHAM
ELTHAM
DARTFORD
RICHMOND
BRIXTON
LEWISHAM
PUTNEY
STREATHAM
CATFORD
TWICKENHAM
SIDCUP
KINGSTON UPON THAMES
WIMBLEDON
PENGE
Hextable
BROMLEY
Hampton
MERTON
MORDEN
MITCHAM
Swanley
BECKENHAM
SURBITON
NEW MALDEN
CROYDON
ORPINGTON
East Molesey
ESHER
CARSHALTON
Keston
WALLINGTON
Chessington
EWELL
SUTTON
New Addington
Oxshott
EPSOM
PURLEY
Selsdon
Farleigh
Halstead
BANSTEAD
COULSDON
WARLINGHAM
Biggin Hill
Knockholt
Tatsfield
Fetcham
Tadworth
Kingswood
LEATHERHEAD
Walton-on-the-Hill
Chaldon
CATERHAM
Woldingham
SEVENOAKS
Great Bookham
Westhumble
Box Hill
Merstham
Westerham
DORKING
Buckland
REDHILL
Godstone
Oxted
Limpsfield
Crockham Hill
Sevenoaks Weald
Westcott
Brockham
REIGATE
South Nutfield
Bletchingley
South Godstone
Four Elms
Chiddingstone Causeway
Leigh
Crowhurst
Edenbridge
South Holmwood
Outwood
Lingfield
Hever
Chiddingstone
Beare Green
Newdigate
Hookwood
HORLEY
Newchapel
Smallfield
Dormansland
Penhurst
Markbeech
Capel
Gatwick Airport
Charlwood
Burstow
Felbridge
Felcourt
Cowden
Ockley
Copthorne
EAST GRINSTEAD
Ashurst
Rusper
Kingsfold
Oakwoodhill
CRAWLEY
Worth
Crawley Down
Ashurst Wood
Groombridge
Turners Hill
Saint Hill
Forest Row
Hartfield
Faygate
Worth Abbey
Colgate
Pease Pottage
West Hoathly
Coleman's Hatch
Warnham
HORSHAM
CROWBOROUGH
Km
Miles
Mannings Heath
Itchingfield
Staplefield
Horsted Keynes
Nutley
Southwater
Nuthurst
High Hurstwood
Crabtree
CUCKFIELD
HAYWARDS HEATH
Marefield
Fletching
Maplehurst
Bolney
Shipley
Uckfield

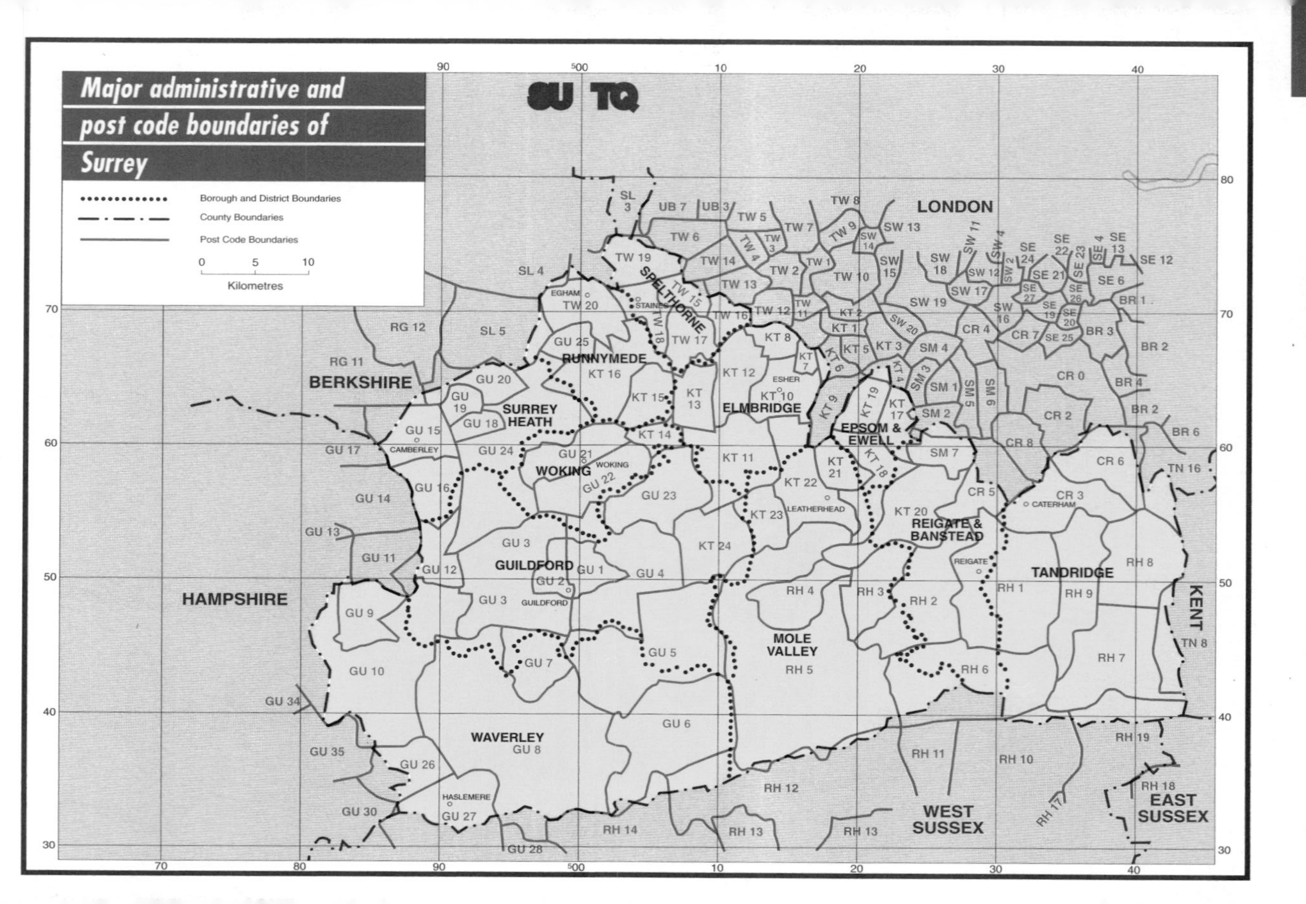

Major administrative and post code boundaries of Surrey

Borough and District Boundaries
County Boundaries
Post Code Boundaries

0   5   10
Kilometres

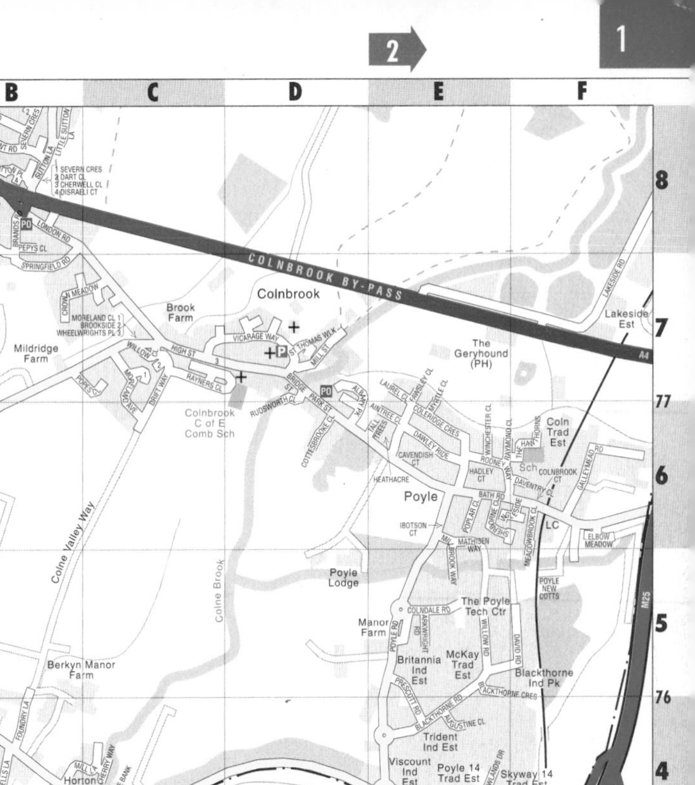

A   B   C   D   E   F

8

B470

MAJOR'S FARM RD

MALVERN CT

Brands Hill

LONDON RD

COLNBROOK BY-PASS

Colnbrook

SEVERN CRES
DART CL
CHERWELL CL
DISRAELI CT

Brook Farm

VICARAGE WAY

ST THOMAS WALK

The Greyhound (PH)

Lakeside Est

7

77

Mildridge Farm

The Queen Mother Resr

HIGH ST

Colnbrook C of E Comb Sch

Coln Trad Est

Poyle

Sch

COLNBROOK DR

LC

ELBOW MEADOW

6

Horton Lodge

Colne Valley Way

Colne Brook

Poyle Lodge

POYLE NEW COTTS

5

Rectory

Ashgood Farm

Berkyn Manor Farm

Manor Farm

Britannia Ind Est

McKay Trad Est

Blackthorne Ind Pk

PICKINS PIECE

HORTON RD

76

DATCHET RD

The Five Bells (PH)

Horton

HORTON TRAD EST

STANWELL RD

Wraysbury River

Trident Ind Est

Viscount Ind Est

Poyle 14 Trad Est

Skyway 14 Trad Est

M25

5

4

A3113
AIRPORT WAY

14

3

75

MEADOWVIEW

Stanwell Manor

2

Whitehall Nurseries

STATION RD

Wraysbury Sta

Wraysbury Resr

M25

RIVER COLNE

RUSSET CL

Lower Mill Farm

King George VI Resr

1

74

01   A   B   02   C   D   03   E   F

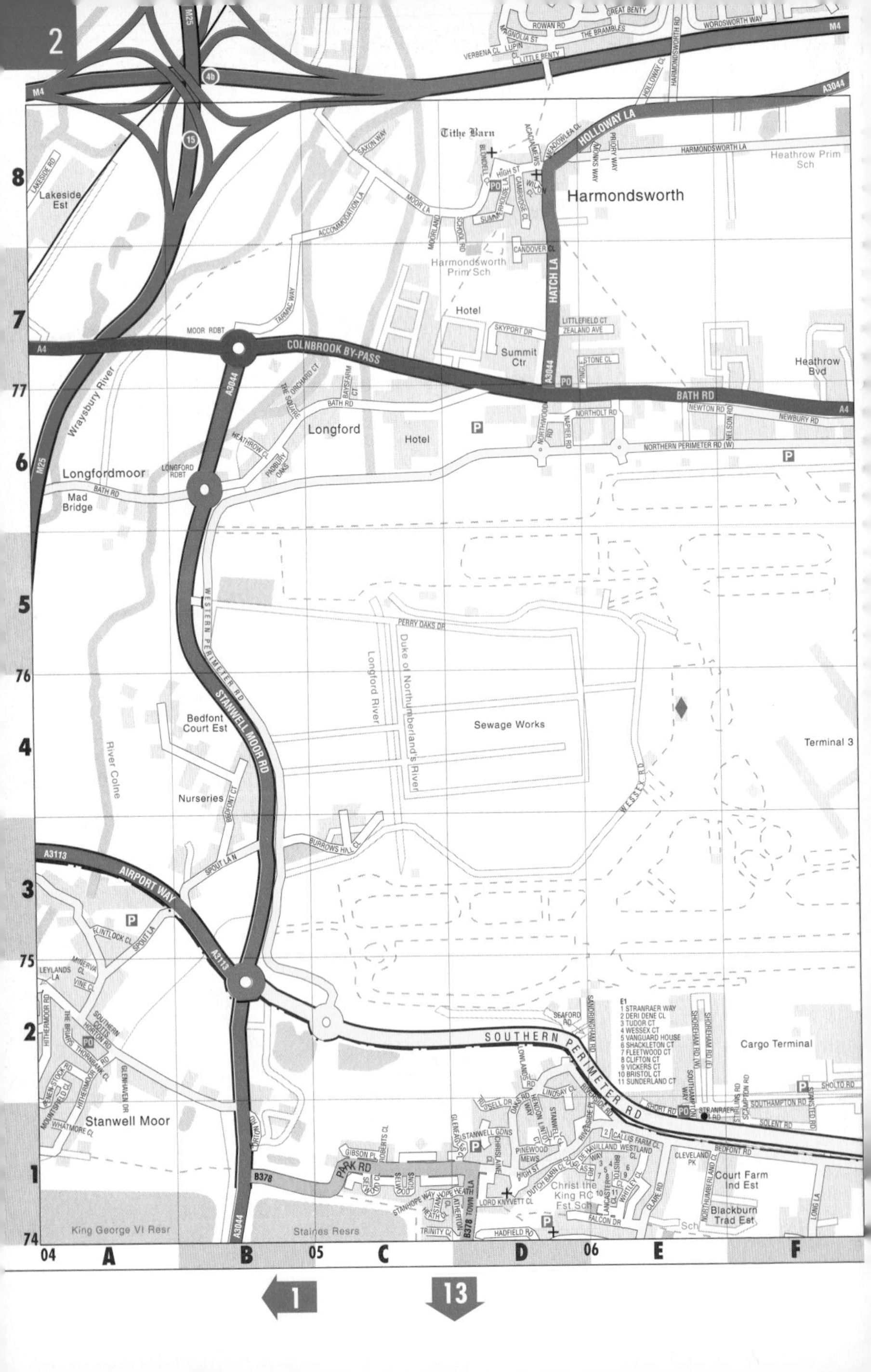
M4
M25
Harmondsworth
Tithe Barn
Lakeside Est
Harmondsworth Prim Sch
Hotel
Summit Ctr
Heathrow Prim Sch
Heathrow Bvd
COLNBROOK BY-PASS
BATH RD
HOLLOWAY LA
HATCH LA
MOOR RDBT
Longford
Longfordmoor
Mad Bridge
LONGFORD RDBT
Wraysbury River
NORTHERN PERIMETER RD (W)
WESTERN PERIMETER RD
STANWELL MOOR RD
PERRY OAKS DR
Longford River
Duke of Northumberland's River
Sewage Works
Bedfont Court Est
Nurseries
River Colne
Terminal 3
WESSEX RD
A3113
AIRPORT WAY
SOUTHERN PERIMETER RD
Cargo Terminal
Stanwell Moor
E1
1 STRANRAER WAY
2 DERI DENE CL
3 TUDOR CT
4 WESSEX CT
5 VANGUARD HOUSE
6 SHACKLETON CT
7 FLEETWOOD CT
8 CLIFTON CT
9 VICKERS CT
10 BRISTOL CT
11 SUNDERLAND CT
Christ the King RC Fst Sch
Court Farm Ind Est
Blackburn Trad Est
King George VI Resr
Staines Resrs
B378
A3044
04 A B 05 C D 06 E F
8 7 77 6 5 76 4 3 75 2 1 74

1
13

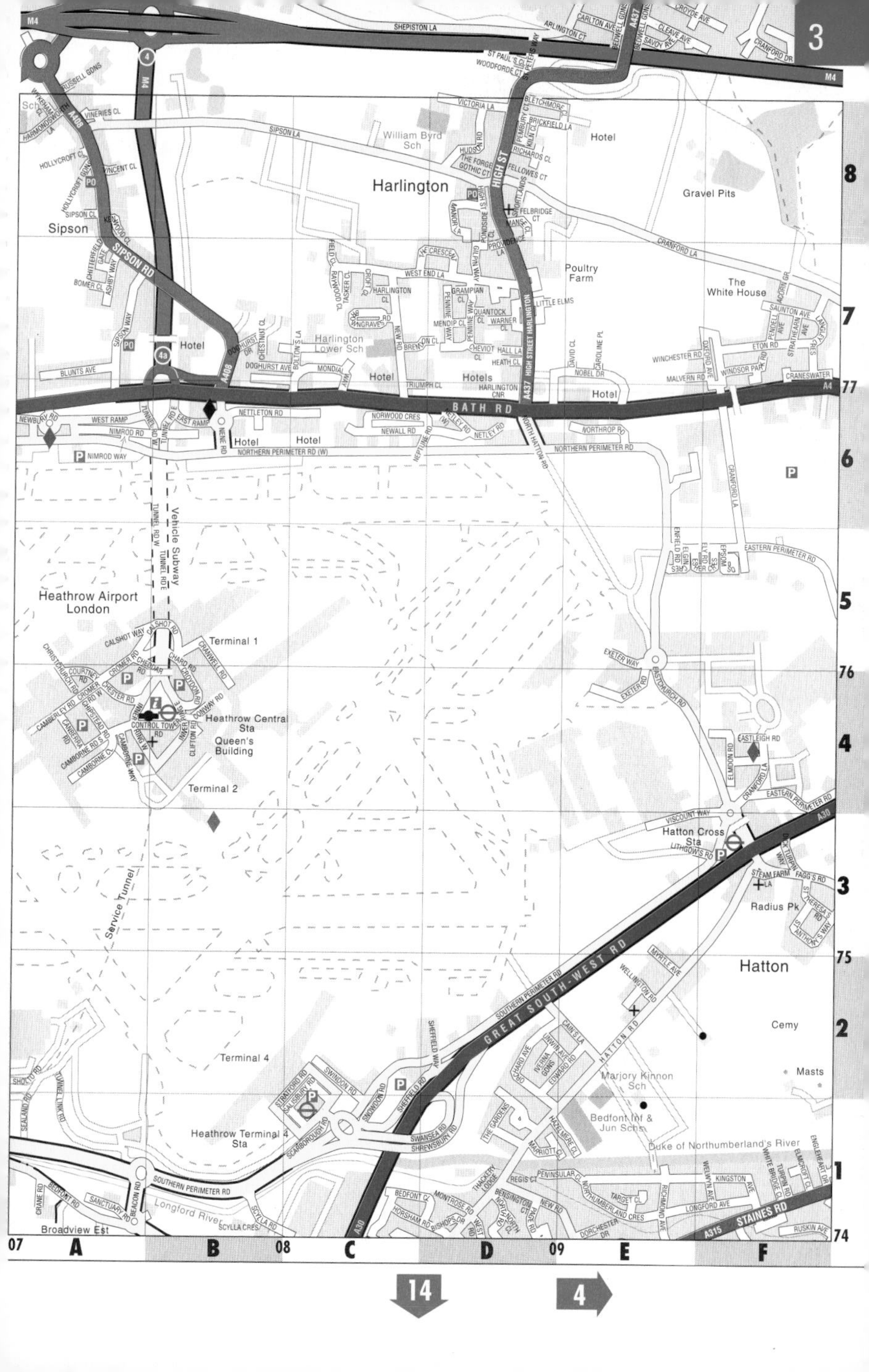
M4
SHEPISTON LA
ARLINGTON CT
CARLTON AVE
BEDWELL GDNS
CROYDE AVE
CLEAVE AVE
SAVOY AVE
CRANFORD DR
ST PAUL'S CL
WOODFORDE CT
ST PETERS WAY
A437
RUSSELL GDNS
WYKEHAM CL
HARMONDSWORTH LA
A408
VINERIES CL
Sch
VICTORIA LA
BLETCHMORE CL
BRICKFIELD LA
PEMBURY CT
KILN CT
RICHARDS CL
FELLOWES CT
SIPSON LA
William Byrd Sch
HUDSON RD
THE FORGE
GOTHIC CT
HIGH ST
Hotel
HOLLYCROFT CL
HOLLYCROFT GDNS
VINCENT CL
PO
Harlington
Gravel Pits
SIPSON CL
KENWOOD CL
Sipson
SIPSON RD
MANOR LA
HIGH ST
PONDSIDE CL
SHORTLANDS
MANSE CL
FELBRIDGE CT
PROVIDENCE LA
CRANFORD LA
GILPIN WAY
THE CRESCENT
FIELD CL
RAYWOOD CL
TASKER CL
CROFT CL
WEST END LA
HARLINGTON CL
Poultry Farm
The White House
CHITTERFIELD GATE
ASHBY WAY
BOMER CL
GRAMPIAN
PENNINE WAY
QUANTOCK CL
WARNER CL
LITTLE ELMS
A437 HIGH STREET HARLINGTON
ACORN GR
SAUNTON AVE
PENDELL AVE
STRATHEARN AVE
LANGLEY CRES
SIPSON WAY
DOGHURST DR
CHESTNUT CL
BOLTON'S LA
WINGRAVES RD
Harlington Lower Sch
NEW RD
MENDIP CL
BRENDON CL
CHEVIOT CL
HALL LA
HEATH CL
DAVID CL
CAROLINE PL
NOBEL DR
OXFORD AVE
WINCHESTER RD
ETON RD
WINDSOR PARK RD
MALVERN RD
CRANESWATER
BLUNTS AVE
DOGHURST AVE
MONDIAL WAY
Hotel
Hotels
TRIUMPH CL
HARLINGTON CNR
Hotel
A4
BATH RD
NEWBURY RD
WEST RAMP
NIMROD RD
TUNNEL RD W
TUNNEL RD E
EAST RAMP
NETTLETON RD
NORWOOD CRES
NEWALL RD
NETLEY RD (W)
NETLEY RD
NORTHROP RD
NENE RD
Hotel
Hotel
NEPTUNE RD
NORTH HATTON RD
NIMROD WAY
NORTHERN PERIMETER RD (W)
NORTHERN PERIMETER RD
CRANFORD LA
P
TUNNEL RD W
Vehicle Subway
TUNNEL RD E
ENFIELD RD
ELGIN CRES
ELY RD
ESHER CRES
EPSOM SQ
ESSEX RD
EASTERN PERIMETER RD
Heathrow Airport London
CALSHOT WAY
CALSHOT RD
Terminal 1
CRANWELL RD
CHRISTCHURCH RD
COURTNEY RD
CROMER RD
CHEDDAR
CHARD RD
CROYDON RD
EXETER WAY
EXETER RD
EASTCHURCH RD
CAMBERLEY RD
CHESTER RD
CHIPSTEAD RD
CONWAY RD
CANBERRA RD
CONTROL TOWER RD
Heathrow Central Sta
Queen's Building
CLIFTON RD
CAMBORNE RD S
CAMBORNE CL
CAMBORNE WAY
INNER RING W
EASTLEIGH RD
ELMDON RD
CRANFORD LA
Terminal 2
EASTERN PERIMETER RD
A30
VISCOUNT WAY
Hatton Cross Sta
LITHGOW'S RD
DICK TURPIN WAY
STEAM FARM LA
FAGG'S RD
Service Tunnel
ST THERESA'S RD
ST ANTHONY'S WAY
Radius Pk
GREAT SOUTH-WEST RD
Hatton
MYRTLE AVE
WELLINGTON RD
SOUTHERN PERIMETER RD
CAIN'S LA
UNWIN AVE
ORCHARD AVE
IVERNA GDNS
EDWARD RD
HATTON RD
Cemy
Terminal 4
SHEFFIELD WAY
SHOLTO RD
TUNNEL LINK RD
SWINDON RD
STRATFORD RD
SALISBURY RD
SNOWDON RD
SHEFFIELD RD
Masts
Marjory Kinnon Sch
SEALAND RD
SWANSEA RD
SHREWSBURY RD
THE GARDENS
HAZELMERE CL
Bedfont Inf & Jun Schs
Heathrow Terminal 4 Sta
SCARBOROUGH RD
MARRIOTT CL
Duke of Northumberland's River
ENGLEHEART DR
ELMCROFT CL
TURPIN RD
WHITE BRIDGE CL
PENINSULAR CL
REGIS CT
KINGSTON AVE
WELWYN AVE
CRANE RD
BEDFONT RD
SOUTHERN PERIMETER RD
BEACON RD
SANCTUARY RD
BEDFONT CL
MONTROSE RD
THACKERY LODGE
BENSINGTON CT
NORTHUMBERLAND CRES
TARGET CL
LONGFORD AVE
STAINES RD
A315
Longford River
HORSHAM RD
BISHOPS DR
WEST RD
NORTH RD
PAGE RD
NEW RD
RICHMOND AVE
RUSKIN AVE
Broadview Est
SCYLLA RD
SCYLLA CRES
DORCHESTER DR
A30
8
7
77
6
5
76
4
3
75
2
1
74
07
A
B
08
C
D
09
E
F

3

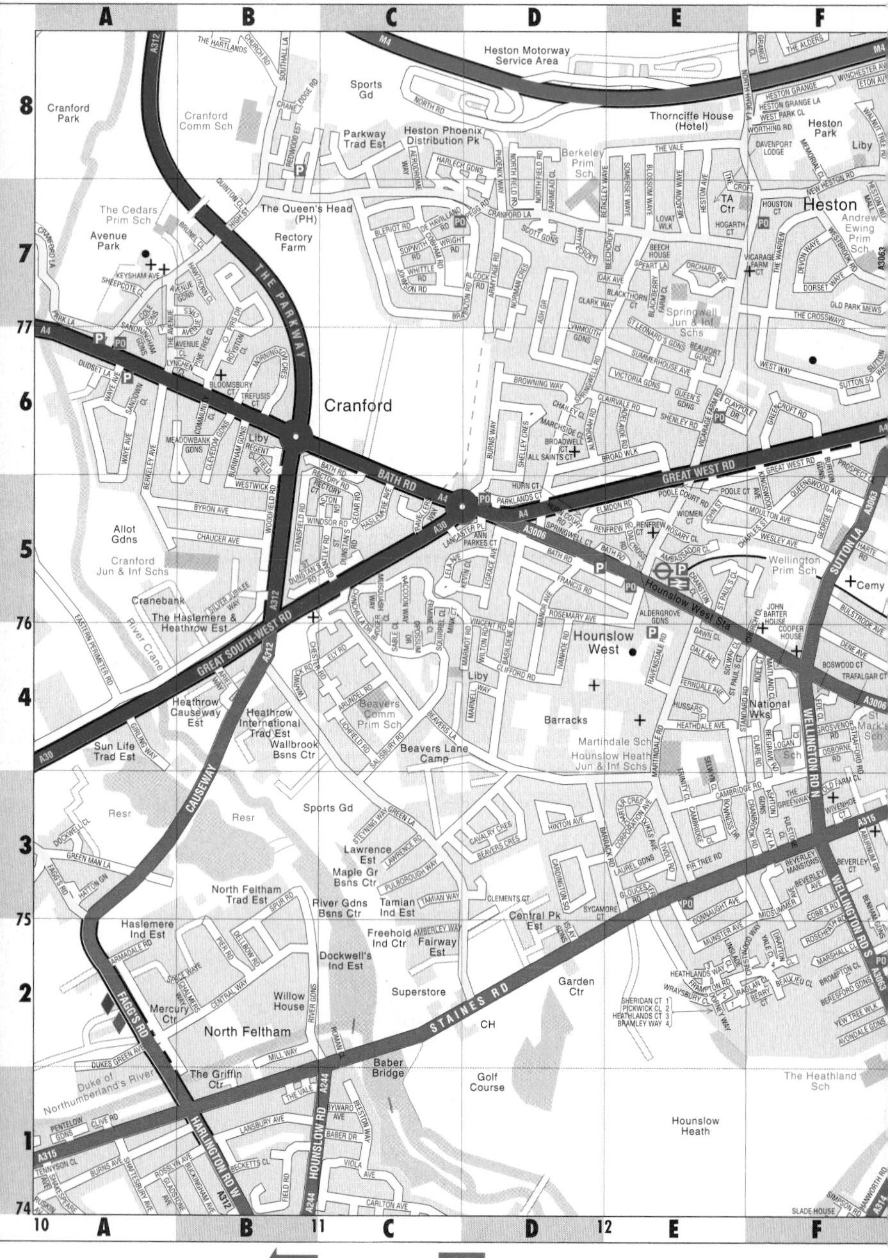
A
B
C
D
E
F
M4
Heston Motorway
Service Area
Sports
Gd
Cranford
Park
Cranford
Comm Sch
Parkway
Trad Est
Heston Phoenix
Distribution Pk
Thorncliffe House
(Hotel)
Heston
Park
Liby
Berkeley
Prim
Sch
The Cedars
Prim Sch
Avenue
Park
The Queen's Head
(PH)
Rectory
Farm
TA
Ctr
Heston
Andrew
Ewing
Prim
Sch
THE PARKWAY
Springwell
Jun & Inf
Schs
Cranford
Liby
BATH RD
GREAT WEST RD
Allot
Gdns
Cranford
Jun & Inf Schs
Cranebank
The Haslemere &
Heathrow Est
River Crane
Wellington
Prim Sch
Cemy
Hounslow West Sta
Hounslow
West
GREAT SOUTH-WEST RD
Heathrow
Causeway
Est
Heathrow
International
Trad Est
Wallbrook
Bsns Ctr
Beavers
Comm
Prim Sch
Beavers Lane
Camp
Liby
Barracks
Martindale Sch
Hounslow Heath
Jun & Inf Schs
National
Wks
St
Mark's
Sch
Sun Life
Trad Est
WELLINGTON RD N
CAUSEWAY
Resr
Resr
Sports Gd
Lawrence
Est
Maple Gr
Bsns Ctr
North Feltham
Trad Est
River Gdns
Bsns Ctr
Tamian
Ind Est
Central Pk
Est
Haslemere
Ind Est
Freehold
Ind Ctr
Fairway
Est
Dockwell's
Ind Est
Garden
Ctr
WELLINGTON RD S
Mercury
Ctr
Willow
House
Superstore
STAINES RD
CH
North Feltham
FAGG'S RD
Duke of
Northumberland's River
The Griffin
Ctr
Baber
Bridge
Golf
Course
The Heathland
Sch
Hounslow
Heath
HARLINGTON RD W
HOUNSLOW RD
A315
A30
A4
A312
A3006
A3063
A244
10
11
12

3
15

6

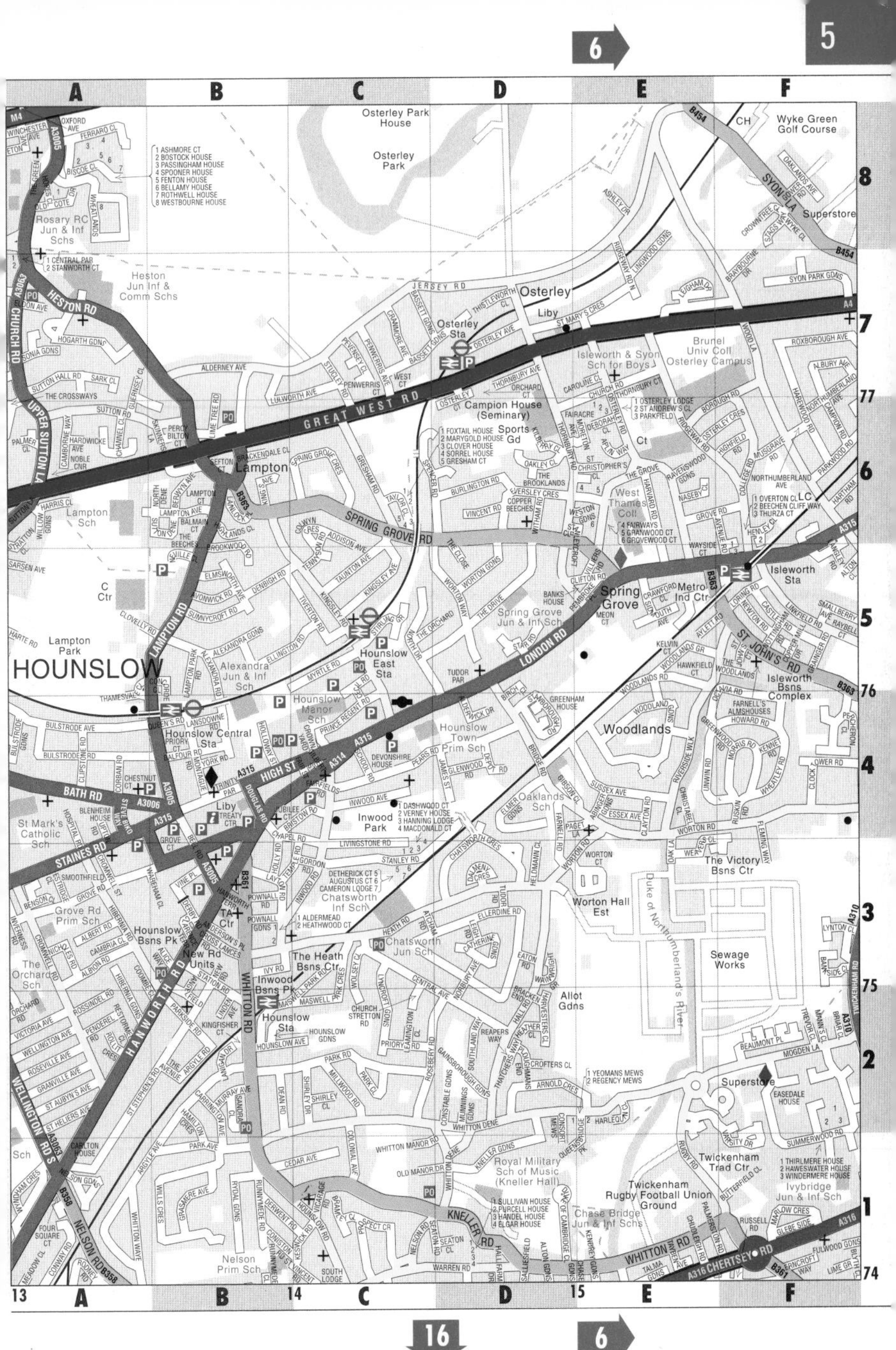
A
B
C
D
E
F
Osterley Park House
Osterley Park
Wyke Green Golf Course
Superstore
Rosary RC Jun & Inf Schs
Heston Jun Inf & Comm Schs
1 ASHMORE CT
2 BOSTOCK HOUSE
3 PASSINGHAM HOUSE
4 SPOONER HOUSE
5 FENTON HOUSE
6 BELLAMY HOUSE
7 ROTHWELL HOUSE
8 WESTBOURNE HOUSE
1 CENTRAL PAR
2 STANWORTH CT
HESTON RD
CHURCH RD
UPPER SUTTON LA
GREAT WEST RD
JERSEY RD
Osterley
Liby
Osterley Sta
ST MARY'S CRES
Brunel Univ Coll Osterley Campus
Isleworth & Syon Sch for Boys
SYON LA
SYON PARK GDNS
ROXBOROUGH AVE
Campion House (Seminary)
Sports Gd
1 FOXTAIL HOUSE
2 MARYGOLD HOUSE
3 CLOVER HOUSE
4 SORREL HOUSE
5 GRESHAM CT
1 OSTERLEY LODGE
2 ST ANDREW'S CL
3 PARKFIELD
Lampton
Lampton Sch
SPRING GROVE RD
West Thames Coll
4 FAIRWAYS
5 GRANWOOD CT
6 GROVEWOOD CT
1 OVERTON CL
2 BEECHEN CLIFF WAY
3 THURZA CT
Isleworth Sta
Spring Grove
Metro Ind Ctr
Spring Grove Jun & Inf Sch
LONDON RD
C Ctr
Lampton Park
HOUNSLOW
Alexandra Jun & Inf Sch
Hounslow East Sta
ST JOHN'S RD
Isleworth Bsns Complex
Hounslow Manor Sch
Hounslow Central Sta
Hounslow Town Prim Sch
Woodlands
FARNELL'S ALMSHOUSES
HIGH ST
BATH RD
St Mark's Catholic Sch
Liby
Inwood Park
1 DASHWOOD CT
2 VERNEY HOUSE
3 HANNING LODGE
4 MACDONALD CT
Oaklands Sch
STAINES RD
The Victory Bsns Ctr
DETHERICK CT 5
AUGUSTUS CT 6
CAMERON LODGE 7
Chatsworth Inf Sch
Grove Rd Prim Sch
Hounslow Bsns Pk
TA Ctr
New Rd Units
1 ALDERMEAD
2 HEATHWOOD CT
Worton Hall Est
Duke of Northumberland's River
Chatsworth Jun Sch
The Orchard Sch
The Heath Bsns Ctr
Inwood Bsns Pk
Sewage Works
Hounslow Sta
Allot Gdns
HANWORTH RD
WHITTON RD
1 YEOMANS MEWS
2 REGENCY MEWS
Superstore
WELLINGTON RD S
Royal Military Sch of Music (Kneller Hall)
Twickenham Trad Ctr
1 THIRLMERE HOUSE
2 HAWESWATER HOUSE
3 WINDERMERE HOUSE
Twickenham Rugby Football Union Ground
Ivybridge Jun & Inf Sch
1 SULLIVAN HOUSE
2 PURCELL HOUSE
3 HANDEL HOUSE
4 ELGAR HOUSE
Chase Bridge Jun & Inf Schs
KNELLER RD
WHITTON RD
CHERTSEY RD
Nelson Prim Sch
NELSON RD
South Lodge
13
14
15
74
75
76
77
1
2
3
4
5
6
7
8

16
6

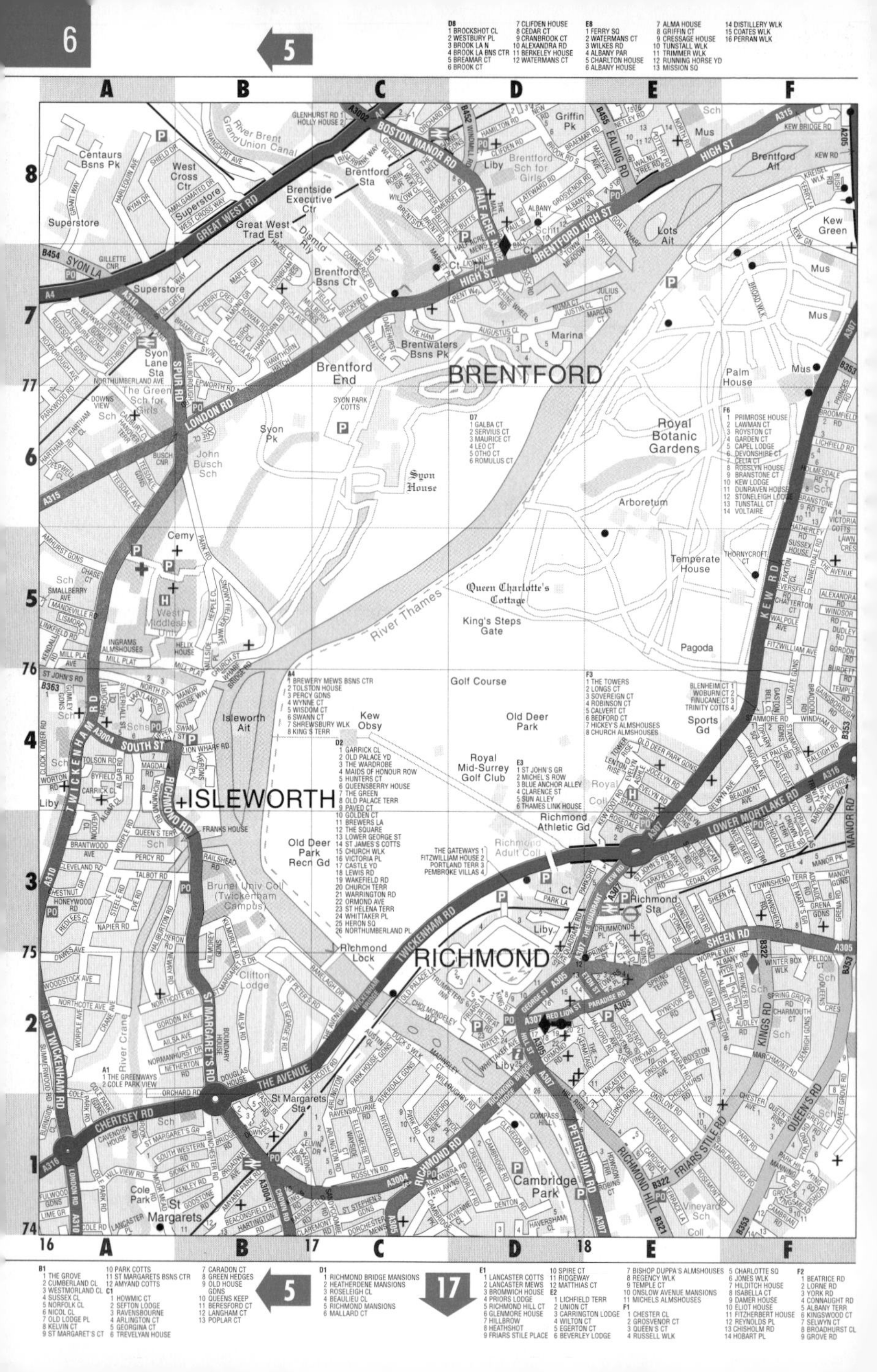

6
5
D8
1 BROCKSHOT CL
2 WESTBURY PL
3 BROOK LA N
4 BROOK LA BNS CTR
5 BREAMAR CT
6 BROOK CT
7 CLIFDEN HOUSE
8 CEDAR CT
9 CRANBROOK CT
10 ALEXANDRA RD
11 BERKELEY HOUSE
12 WATERMANS CT
E8
1 FERRY SQ
2 WATERMANS CT
3 WILKES RD
4 ALBANY PAR
5 CHARLTON HOUSE
6 ALBANY HOUSE
7 ALMA HOUSE
8 GRIFFIN CT
9 CRESSAGE HOUSE
10 TUNSTALL WLK
11 TRIMMER WLK
12 RUNNING HORSE YD
13 MISSION SQ
14 DISTILLERY WLK
15 COATES WLK
16 PERRAN WLK
BRENTFORD
ISLEWORTH
RICHMOND
Syon Pk
Syon House
Royal Botanic Gardens
Old Deer Park
River Thames
Kew Green
Brentford Ait
Lots Ait
Isleworth Ait
Queen Charlotte's Cottage
King's Steps Gate
Golf Course
Kew Obsy
Royal Mid-Surrey Golf Club
Richmond Lock
Cambridge Park
St Margarets
Cole Park
Palm House
Temperate House
Pagoda
Arboretum
D7
1 GALBA CT
2 SERVIUS CT
3 MAURICE CT
4 LEO CT
5 OTHO CT
6 ROMULUS CT
F6
1 PRIMROSE HOUSE
2 LAWMAN CT
3 ROYSTON CT
4 GARDEN CT
5 CAPEL LODGE
6 DEVONSHIRE CT
7 CELIA CT
8 ROSSLYN HOUSE
9 BRANSTONE CT
10 KEW LODGE
11 DUNRAVEN HOUSE
12 STONELEIGH LODGE
13 TUNSTALL CT
14 VOLTAIRE
A4
1 BREWERY MEWS BSNS CTR
2 TOLSTON HOUSE
3 PERCY GDNS
4 WYNNE CT
5 WISDOM CT
6 SWANN CT
7 SHREWSBURY WLK
8 KING'S TERR
F3
1 THE TOWERS
2 LONGS CT
3 SOVEREIGN CT
4 ROBINSON CT
5 CALVERT CT
6 BEDFORD CT
7 HICKEY'S ALMSHOUSES
8 CHURCH ALMSHOUSES
D2
1 GARRICK CL
2 OLD PALACE YD
3 THE WARDROBE
4 MAIDS OF HONOUR ROW
5 HUNTERS CT
6 QUEENSBERRY HOUSE
7 THE GREEN
8 OLD PALACE TERR
9 PAVED CT
10 GOLDEN CT
11 BREWERS LA
12 THE SQUARE
13 LOWER GEORGE ST
14 ST JAMES'S COTTS
15 CHURCH WLK
16 VICTORIA PL
17 CASTLE YD
18 LEWIS RD
19 WAKEFIELD RD
20 CHURCH TERR
21 WARRINGTON RD
22 ORMOND AVE
23 ST HELENA TERR
24 WHITTAKER PL
25 HERON SQ
26 NORTHUMBERLAND PL
E3
1 ST JOHN'S GR
2 MICHEL'S ROW
3 BLUE ANCHOR ALLEY
4 CLARENCE ST
5 SUN ALLEY
6 THAMES LINK HOUSE
A1
1 THE GREENWAYS
2 COLE PARK VIEW
B1
1 THE GROVE
2 CUMBERLAND CL
3 WESTMORLAND CL
4 SUSSEX CL
5 NORFOLK CL
6 NICOL CL
7 OLD LODGE PL
8 KELVIN CT
9 ST MARGARET'S CT
10 PARK COTTS
11 ST MARGARETS BSNS CTR
12 AMYAND COTTS
C1
1 HOWMIC CT
2 SEFTON LODGE
3 RAVENSBOURNE
4 ARLINGTON CT
5 GEORGINA CT
6 TREVELYAN HOUSE
7 CARADON CT
8 GREEN HEDGES
9 OLD HOUSE GDNS
10 QUEENS KEEP
11 BERESFORD CT
12 LANGHAM CT
13 POPLAR CT
D1
1 RICHMOND BRIDGE MANSIONS
2 HEATHERDENE MANSIONS
3 ROSELEIGH CL
4 BEAULIEU CL
5 RICHMOND MANSIONS
6 MALLARD CT
17
E1
1 LANCASTER COTTS
2 LANCASTER MEWS
3 BROMWICH HOUSE
4 PRIORS LODGE
5 RICHMOND HILL CT
6 GLENMORE HOUSE
7 HILLBROW
8 HEATHSHOT
9 FRIARS STILE PLACE
10 SPIRE CT
11 RIDGEWAY
12 MATTHIAS CT
E2
1 LICHFIELD TERR
2 UNION CT
3 CARRINGTON LODGE
4 WILTON CT
5 EGERTON CT
6 BEVERLEY LODGE
7 BISHOP DUPPA'S ALMSHOUSES
8 REGENCY WLK
9 TEMPLE CT
10 ONSLOW AVENUE MANSIONS
11 MICHELS ALMSHOUSES
F1
1 CHESTER CL
2 GROSVENOR CT
3 QUEEN'S CT
4 RUSSELL WLK
5 CHARLOTTE SQ
6 JONES WLK
7 HILDITCH HOUSE
8 ISABELLA CT
9 DAMER HOUSE
10 ELIOT HOUSE
11 FITZHERBERT HOUSE
12 REYNOLDS PL
13 CHISHOLM RD
14 HOBART PL
F2
1 BEATRICE RD
2 LORNE RD
3 YORK RD
4 CONNAUGHT RD
5 ALBANY TERR
6 KINGSWOOD CT
7 SELWYN CT
8 BROADHURST CL
9 GROVE RD

18

A6
1 CLARENDON CT
2 QUINTOCK HOUSE
3 BROOME CT
4 LONSDALE MEWS
5 CAMBRIDGE COTTS
6 SANDWAYS
7 VICTORIA COTTS
8 NORTH AVE
9 GROVEWOOD
10 HAMILTON HOUSE
11 MELVIN CT

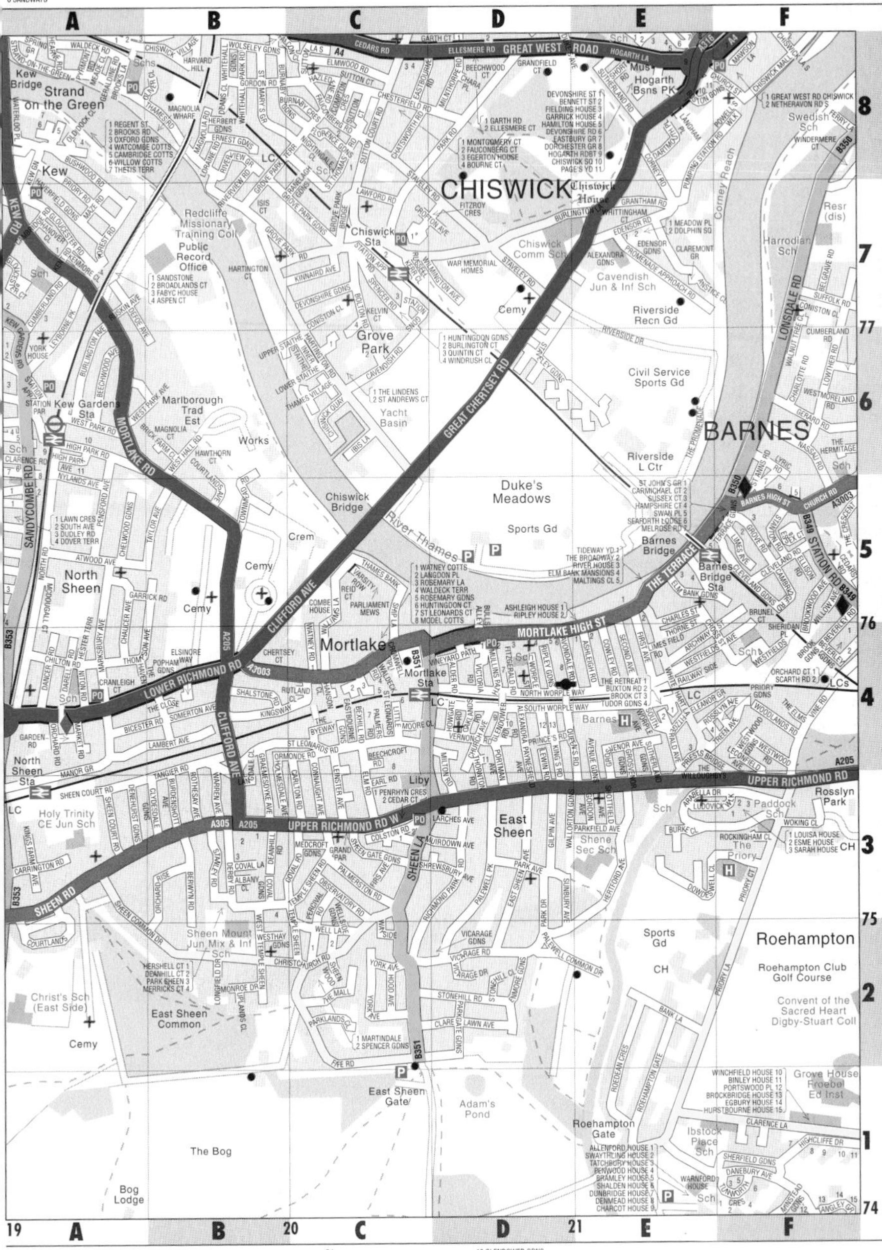

D4
1 RANN HOUSE
2 CRAVEN HOUSE
3 JOHN DEE HOUSE
4 KINDELL HOUSE
5 MONTGOMERY HOUSE
6 AVONDALE HOUSE
7 ADDINGTON CT
8 DOVECOTE GDNS
9 FIRMSTON HOUSE
10 GLENDOWER GDNS
11 CHESTNUT AVE
12 TREHERN RD
13 ROCK AVE

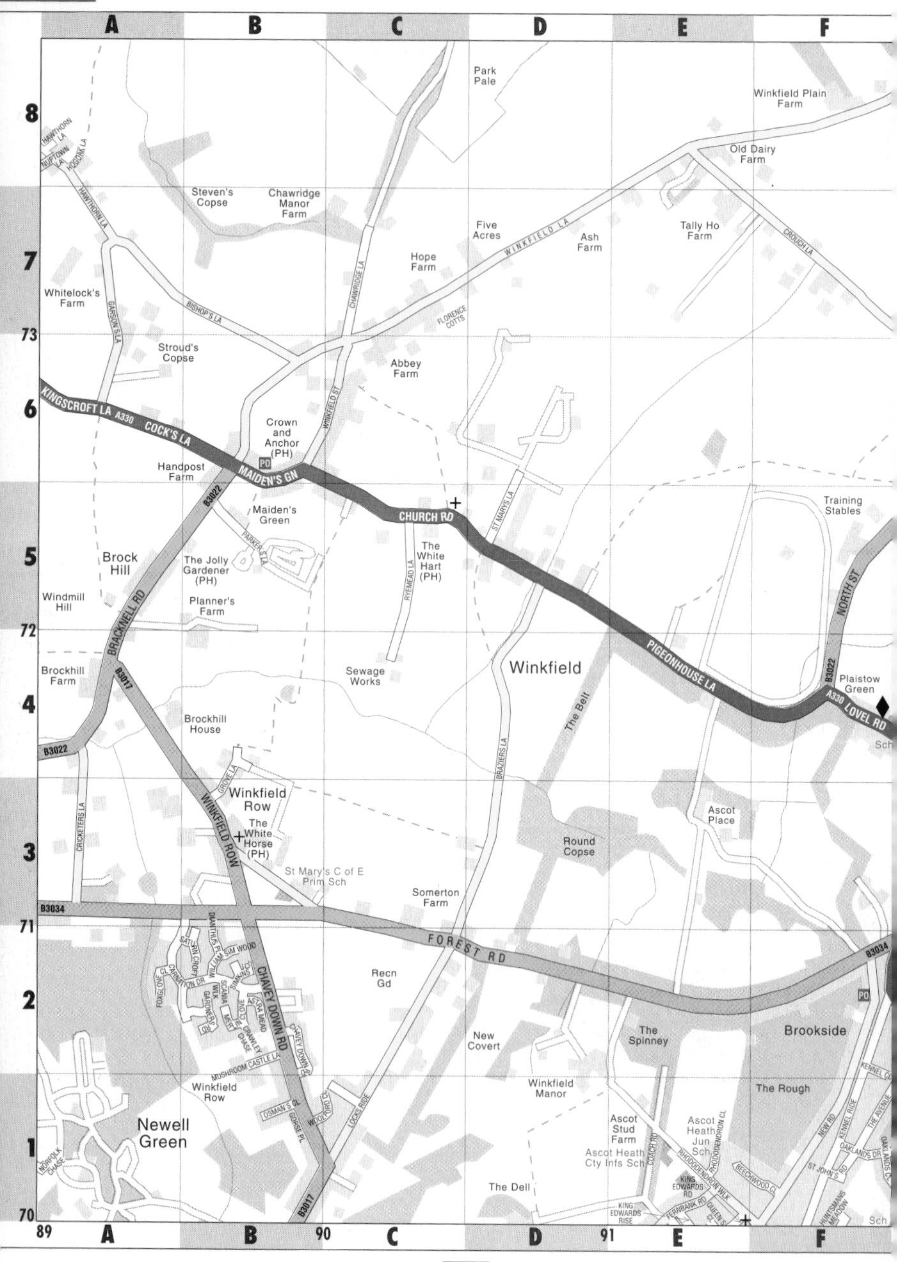

Park Pale
Winkfield Plain Farm
Old Dairy Farm
Steven's Copse
Chawridge Manor Farm
Five Acres
Ash Farm
Tally Ho Farm
Hope Farm
Whitelock's Farm
Stroud's Copse
Abbey Farm
Crown and Anchor (PH)
Handpost Farm
Maiden's Green
The Jolly Gardener (PH)
Brock Hill
Windmill Hill
Planner's Farm
The White Hart (PH)
Training Stables
Brockhill Farm
Sewage Works
Winkfield
Plaistow Green
Brockhill House
Winkfield Row
The White Horse (PH)
St Mary's C of E Prim Sch
Somerton Farm
Round Copse
Ascot Place
Recn Gd
The Spinney
Brookside
New Covert
The Rough
Winkfield Row
Winkfield Manor
Newell Green
Ascot Stud Farm
Ascot Heath Jun Sch
Ascot Heath Cty Infs Sch
The Dell
The Belt
KINGSCROFT LA
A330
COCK'S LA
MAIDEN'S GN
CHURCH RD
PIGEONHOUSE LA
LOVEL RD
NORTH ST
B3022
B3017
B3034
BRACKNELL RD
WINKFIELD ROW
CHAVEY DOWN RD
FOREST RD
WINKFIELD LA
CHAWRIDGE LA
WINKFIELD ST
BISHOP'S LA
GARSON'S LA
HAWTHORN LA
CROUCH LA
ST MARY'S LA
RYEMEAD LA
PARKER'S LA
BRAZIERS LA
GROVE LA
CRICKETERS LA
LOCKS RIDE
MUSHROOM CASTLE LA
COACH RD
RHODODENDRON WLK
NEW RD
KENNEL RIDE
ST JOHN'S RD
OAKLANDS DR
FLORENCE COTTS
Sch
A B C D E F
8 7 6 5 4 3 2 1
73 72 71 70
89 90 91

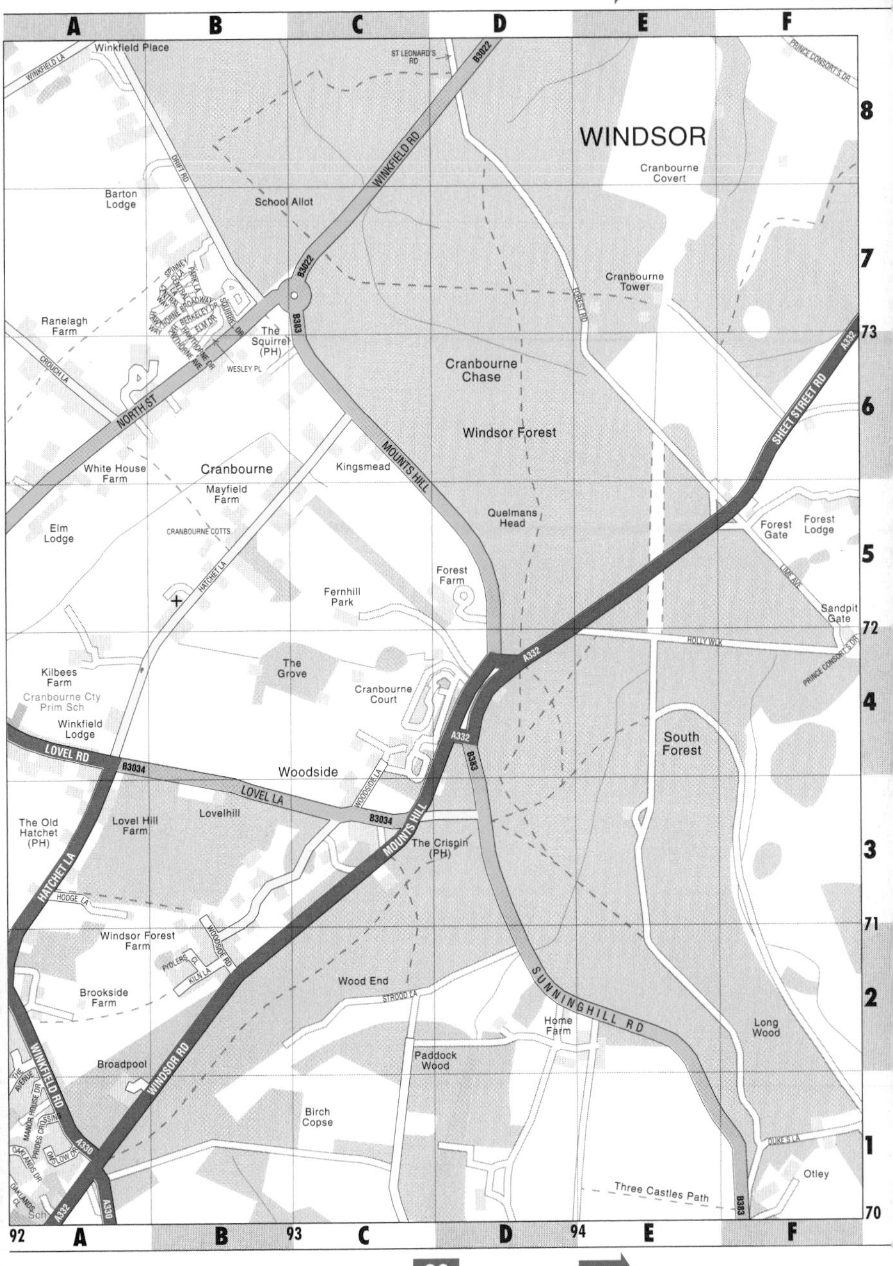

WINDSOR

A B C D E F

8
7
73
6
5
72
4
71
3
2
1
70

Winkfield Place
St LEONARD'S RD
B3022
PRINCE CONSORT'S DR.
Cranbourne Covert
WINKFIELD RD
Barton Lodge
School Allot
Cranbourne Tower
B3022
Ranelagh Farm
B383
The Squirrel (PH)
WESLEY PL
Cranbourne Chase
SHEET STREET RD
A332
CROSS RD
NORTH ST
White House Farm
Cranbourne
Mayfield Farm
CRANBOURNE COTTS.
Kingsmead
MOUNTS HILL
Windsor Forest
Quelmans Head
Forest Gate
Forest Lodge
Elm Lodge
HATCHET LA
Fernhill Park
Forest Farm
Sandpit Gate
LIME AV
72
Kilbees Farm
The Grove
Cranbourne Court
A332
HOLLY WALK
PRINCE CONSORT'S DTR.
Cranbourne Cty Prim Sch
Winkfield Lodge
LOVEL RD
B3034
LOVEL LA
Woodside
MOUNTS HILL
A332
B383
South Forest
The Old Hatchet (PH)
Lovel Hill Farm
Lovelhill
B3034
WINDSOR RD
HATCHET LA
HODGE LA
The Crispin (PH)
Windsor Forest Farm
PYGLERO
KILN LA
Wood End
STROOD LA
SUNNINGHILL RD
Long Wood
Brookside Farm
WINKFIELD RD
Broadpool
WINDSOR RD
Paddock Wood
Home Farm
Birch Copse
A332
Three Castles Path
B383
Otley

A   **B**   **C**   **D**   **E**   **F**

Flemish Farm

8

Bear's Rails

Cemy

Rush Pond

Prince of Wales Pond

King Edward VII (Old Windsor Unit)

H +

SHEET STREET RD

A332

Pickleherring Pond

7

Ranger's Lodge

Beehive Hill

Battle Bourne

The Gallop

Seymours Plantation

Bear's Rails Pond

THE LONG WALK

73

PRINCE CONSORT'S DR

Russel's Pond

Fiddle Covert

6

Statue

Snow Hill

Spring Hill

Cookes Hill

Richardson's Lawn

Three Castles Path

BISHOPSGATE RD

Isle Of Wight Pond

The Village

PO

THE VILLAGE

QUEEN ANNE'S GT

5

Deepstrood

Royal Lodge

The Fox & Hounds (PH)

Poets Lawn

+

72

Queen Anne's Ride

Windsor Great Park

Bishopsgate

4

Dark Wood

Royal School

Cow Pond

Chapel Wood

PARK CLOSE COTTS

MEZEL HILL COTTS

CUMBERLAND LODGE

DUKE'S LA

The Sun (PH)

3

Hilton's Covert

Mezel Hill

BISHOPSGATE RD

Wilderness

Park Close

WICK LA

Square Covert

71

Parkside House

Slans Hill

The Savill Gardens

2

Leiper Hill

Great Meadow Pond

Temple Hill

●

●

P

Norfolk Plantation

Norfolk Farm

Mill Pond

Statue

Smith's Lawn

Obelisk

1

Rosy Bottom

Obelisk Pond

70

Polo Gds

95   **A**   **B**   96   **C**   **D**   97   **E**   **F**

12

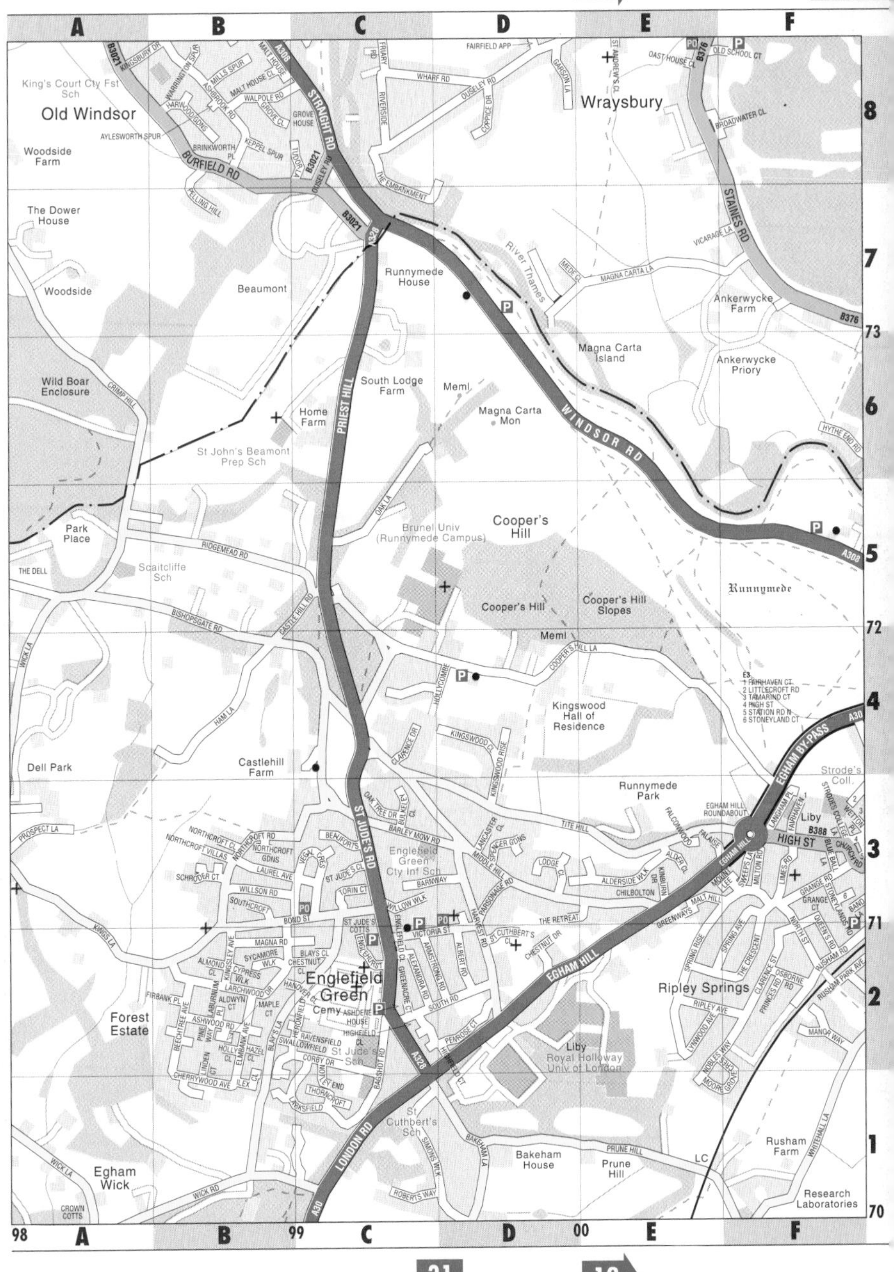
A
B
C
D
E
F
8
7
73
6
5
72
4
3
71
2
1
70
98
99
00
Old Windsor
King's Court Cty Fst Sch
Woodside Farm
The Dower House
Woodside
Wild Boar Enclosure
Park Place
THE DELL
Dell Park
Forest Estate
Egham Wick
CROWN COTTS
Beaumont
St John's Beaumont Prep Sch
Home Farm
Scaitcliffe Sch
Castlehill Farm
Runnymede House
South Lodge Farm
Meml
Magna Carta Mon
Brunel Univ (Runnymede Campus)
Cooper's Hill
Cooper's Hill Slopes
Kingswood Hall of Residence
Runnymede Park
Wraysbury
River Thames
Magna Carta Island
Ankerwycke Farm
Ankerwycke Priory
Runnymede
Strode's Coll.
Liby
Englefield Green
Englefield Green Cty Inf Sch
Cemy
St Jude's Sch
St Cuthbert's Sch
Royal Holloway Univ of London
Bakeham House
Prune Hill
Ripley Springs
Rusham Farm
Research Laboratories
LC
STRAIGHT RD
PRIEST HILL
ST JUDE'S RD
WINDSOR RD
BURFIELD RD
STAINES RD
EGHAM HILL
EGHAM BY-PASS
LONDON RD
HIGH ST
RIDGEMEAD RD
BISHOPSGATE RD
CASTLE HILL RD
WICK LA
HAM LA
CRIMP HILL
KINGS LA
PROSPECT LA
WICK RD
OAK LA
COOPER'S HILL LA
HOLLYCOMBE
KINGSWOOD CL
KINGSWOOD RISE
CLARENCE DR
TITE HILL
BARLEY MOW RD
BOND ST
HARVEST RD
PARSONAGE RD
THE RETREAT
BAKEHAM LA
PRUNE HILL
WHITEHALL LA
MANOR WAY
FAIRFIELD APP
WHARF RD
OUSELEY RD
FRIARY RD
RIVERSIDE
THE EMBANKMENT
COPPICE DR
GARSON LA
ST ANDREW'S CL
OAST HOUSE CL
OLD SCHOOL CT
BROADWATER CL
VICARAGE LA
MEDE CL
MAGNA CARTA LA
HYTHE END RD
KINGSBURY DR
WARRINGTON SPUR
MILLS SPUR
MALT HOUSE
MALT HOUSE CL
ASHBROOK RD
WALPOLE RD
GROVE CL
HARWOOD GDNS
AYLESWORTH SPUR
BRINKWORTH PL
KEPPEL SPUR
TUDOR LA
GROVE HOUSE
PELLING HILL
A308
A328
A30
B3021
B376
B388
E3
1 FAIRHAVEN CT
2 LITTLECROFT RD
3 TAMARIND CT
4 HIGH ST
5 STATION RD N
6 STONEYLAND CT
EGHAM HILL ROUNDABOUT

31
12

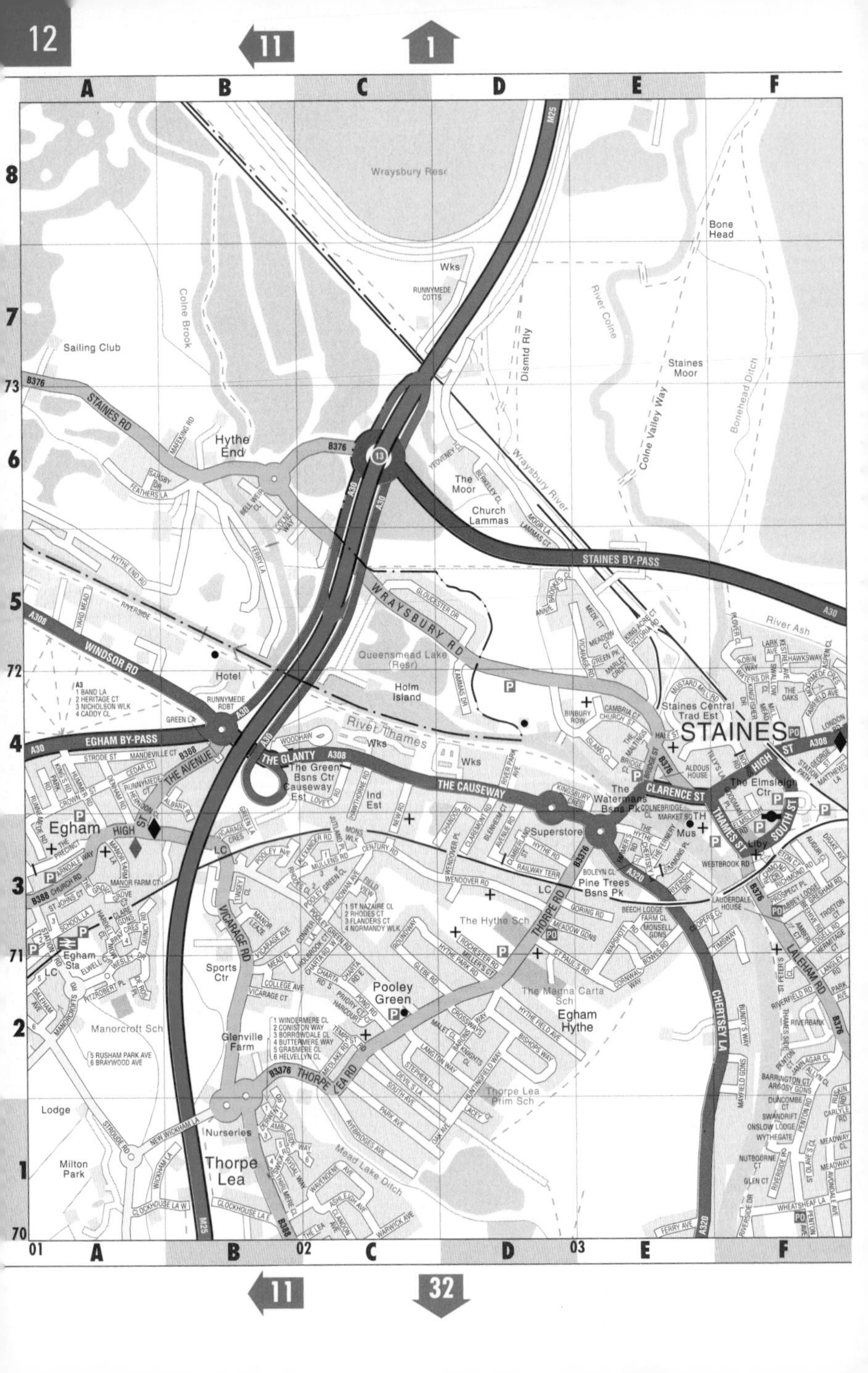
11
1
A
B
C
D
E
F
8
7
73
6
5
72
4
3
71
2
1
70
01
02
03
Wraysbury Resr
M25
Bone Head
Wks
RUNNYMEDE COTTS
Colne Brook
River Colne
Dismtd Rly
Staines Moor
Colne Valley Way
Bonehead Ditch
Sailing Club
B376
STAINES RD
MAFEKING RD
Hythe End
SARSBY DR
FEATHERS LA
BELL WEIR CL
COLNE WAY
FERRY LA
YEOVENEY CL
The Moor
BERKELEY CL
Church Lammas
Wraysbury River
MOOR LA
LAMMAS CT
STAINES BY-PASS
A30
HYTHE END RD
RIVERSIDE
YARD MEAD
A308
WINDSOR RD
GLOUCESTER DR
WRAYSBURY RD
Queensmead Lake (Resr)
Holm Island
LAMMAS DR
Hotel
RUNNYMEDE RDBT
GREEN LA
A3
1 BAND LA
2 HERITAGE CT
3 NICHOLSON WLK
4 CADDY CL
ANNIE BROOKES CL
MEDE CT
MEADOW CT
GREEN PK
VICARAGE RD
MARLEY CROFT
KING ACRE CT
VICTORIA RD
River Ash
PLOVER CL
ROBIN WAY
LARK AVE
KESTREL AVE
HAWKSWAY
WATERS DR
SWALLOW CL
KINGFISHER DR
MILL MEAD
THE OAKS
FAIRFIELD AVE
MUSTARD MILL RD
Staines Central Trad Est
BINBURY ROW
CAMBRIA CT
CHURCH ST
STAINES
River Thames
WOODHAW
Wks
EGHAM BY-PASS
STRODE ST
MANDEVILLE CT
THE GLANTY
The Green Bsns Ctr
Causeway Est
LOVETT RD
HAWTHORNE RD
Ind Est
NEW RD
RIVER PARK AVE
THE CAUSEWAY
KINGSBURY CRES
The Watermans Bsns Pk
CLARENCE ST
HALE ST
BRIDGE ST
ALDOUS HOUSE
THE MALTINGS
ISLAND CL
HIGH ST
STATION PATH
LONDON RD
ST GEORGE CT
ST MATTHEWS LA
The Elmsleigh Ctr
THAMES ST
SOUTH ST
Liby
Mus
TH
MARKET SQ
COLNEBRIDGE CL
B388
THE AVENUE
CEDAR CT
RUNNYMEDE CT
HUMMER RD
KINGS RD
PARK RD
CROWN ST
DENHAM RD
ALBANY RD
Egham
HIGH ST
THE PRECINCT
ARNDALE WAY
MANOR FARM LA
MANOR FARM CT
CHURCH RD
ST JOHNS CT
THE GROVE
SCHOOL LA
GROVE CL
CLARE GDNS
GREEN LA
VICARAGE CRES
LC
POOLEY AVE
ALEXANDER RD
MONS WLK
MULLENS RD
CENTURY RD
JUTLAND PL
WENDOVER PL
CHANDOS RD
CLAREMONT RD
BLENHEIM CT
AVENUE RD
Superstore
CUMBERLAND ST
HYTHE RD
RAILWAY TERR
WENDOVER RD
BOLEYN CL
Pine Trees Bsns Pk
GORING RD
B376
A320
THORPE RD
SIMMONS PL
RIVERSIDE DR
WESTBROOK RD
LAUDERDALE HOUSE
BEECH LODGE
FARM CL
MONSELL GDNS
COOPERS CL
TIMSWAY
DRAKE AVE
AUGUR CL
RICHMOND RD
PROSPECT PL
ABBEY LODGE
GRESHAM RD
TROSTON CT
EDGELL RD
HERMITAGE CT
LALEHAM RD
LANGLEY RD
PARK AVE
TIMSEY
MANOR LEAZE
VICARAGE AVE
POOLEY GREEN CL
ROWAN AVE
FIELD VIEW
1 ST NAZAIRE CL
2 RHODES CT
3 FLANDERS CT
4 NORMANDY WLK
The Hythe Sch
MEADOW GDNS
WAPSHOTT RD
BOWES RD
CORNWALL WAY
ST PAUL'S RD
ROCHESTER RD
MILLER'S CT
HYTHE PARK RD
GLEBE RD
ROUNDWAY
POOLEY GREEN RD
HOLBROOK CT
CHARTA RD
VICARAGE RD
Egham Sta
ELWELL CL
WESLEY DR
FITZROBERT PL
MANORCROFTS RD
DALEHAM AVE
Sports Ctr
COLLEGE AVE
VICARAGE CT
MEAD CL
The Magna Carta Sch
Egham Hythe
HYTHE FIELD AVE
BISHOPS WAY
CROSSWAYS
MIKLET CL
BARONS WAY
KNIGHTS CL
HUNTINGFIELD WAY
LANGTON WAY
STEPHEN CL
DEVIL'S LA
SOUTH AVE
PARK AVE
OAK AVE
LACEY CL
Pooley Green
PRIORY CT
HARCOURT
POND RD
1 WINDERMERE CL
2 CONISTON WAY
3 BORROWDALE CL
4 BUTTERMERE WAY
5 GRASMERE CL
6 HELVELLYN CL
Manorcroft Sch
5 RUSHAM PARK AVE
6 BRAYWOOD AVE
Glenville Farm
MEDLAKE RD
TEMPEST RD
B3376
THORPE LEA RD
Thorpe Lea Prim Sch
CHERTSEY LA
BUNDY'S WAY
MAYFIELD GDNS
RIVERFIELD RD
RIVERBANK
THAMES SIDE
PENTON RD
JANNAGAR CL
ALLYN CL
BARRINGTON CT
ARGOSY GDNS
DUNCOMBE CT
SWANDRIFT
ONSLOW LODGE
WYTHEGATE
NUTBOURNE CT
GLEN CT
RIVERSIDE RD
ST OLAVE'S CL
MEADWAY
AVONDALE AVE
WHEATSHEAF LA
PENTON AVE
RUSKIN RD
CARLYLE RD
Lodge
Milton Park
STROUDE RD
NEW WICKHAM LA
WICKHAM LA
CLOCKHOUSE LA W
Nurseries
Thorpe Lea
AYEBRIDGES AVE
Mead Lake Ditch
WAVENDENE AVE
ASHLEIGH AVE
CLANDON AVE
THE LEA
WARWICK AVE
CLOCKHOUSE LA E
B388
FERRY AVE
A320
11
32

2
14

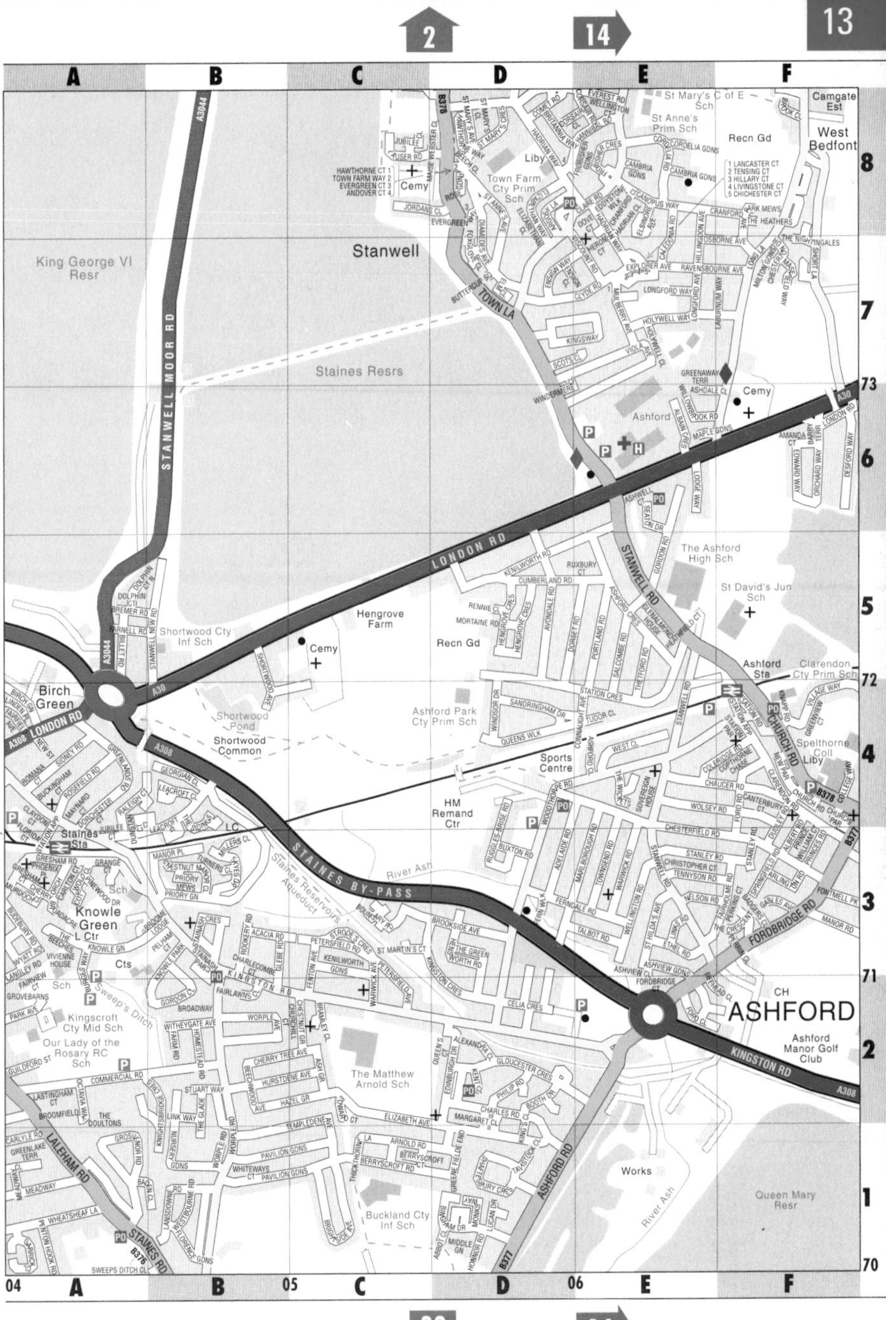
A
B
C
D
E
F
8
7
73
6
5
72
4
3
71
2
1
70
04
05
06
King George VI Resr
STANWELL MOOR RD
A3044
Staines Resrs
Stanwell
B378
TOWN LA
Town Farm Cty Prim Sch
Liby
Cemy
JUBILEE CL
FUSER RD
HAWTHORNE CT 1
TOWN FARM WAY 2
EVERGREEN CT 3
ANDOVER CT 4
JORDANS CL
EVERGREEN
BUTTERCUP CL
St Mary's C of E Sch
St Anne's Prim Sch
Recn Gd
Camgate Est
West Bedfont
EVEREST RD
WELLINGTON
COMET RD
BRITANNIA WAY
HADRIAN WAY
CAMBRIA GDNS
CAMBRIA GDNS
CORDELIA RD
CORDELIA GDNS
1 LANCASTER CT
2 TENSING CT
3 HILLARY CT
4 LIVINGSTONE CT
5 CHICHESTER CT
CANOPUS WAY
CRANFORD AVE
PARK MEWS
THE HEATHERS
THE NIGHTINGALES
OSBORNE AVE
EXPLORER AVE
RAVENSBOURNE AVE
LONGFORD WAY
HOLYWELL WAY
KINGSWAY
SCOTS CL
VIOLA AVE
HOLYWELL CL
MULBERRY AVE
LONGFORD AVE
LABURNUM WAY
HILLINGDON AVE
CALEDONIA RD
ENSIGN WAY
CLYDE RD
SHORT LA
LONG LA
WINDERMERE CL
GREENAWAY TERR
ASHDALE CL
Cemy
Ashford
MAPLE GDNS
ALBAIN CRES
AMANDA CT
EDWARD WAY
ORCHARD WAY
DESFORD WAY
LONDON RD
LODGE WAY
ASHWELL CT
SEATON DR
A30
LONDON RD
The Ashford High Sch
St David's Jun Sch
STANWELL RD
GORDON RD
KENILWORTH RD
RUXBURY CT
CUMBERLAND RD
HENGROVE CRES
RENNIE CL
MORTAINE RD
AVONDALE RD
DORSET RD
PORTLAND RD
SALCOMBE RD
THETFORD RD
ASHFORD CRES
GLENALMOND HOUSE
HEATHFIELD CT
Hengrove Farm
Recn Gd
Cemy
Shortwood Cty Inf Sch
SHORTWOOD AVE
DOLPHIN CT
DOLPHIN CL
BREMER RD
FARNELL RD
BILLET RD
STANWELL NEW RD
Birch Green
A308
LONDON RD
Ashford Sta
Clarendon Cty Prim Sch
STATION CRES
SANDRINGHAM DR
TUDOR CL
WINDSOR DR
QUEENS WLK
Ashford Park Cty Prim Sch
Shortwood Pond
Shortwood Common
A308
GEORGIAN CL
LEACROFT CL
Sports Centre
CONNAUGHT AVE
WEST CL
CHURCH RD
VILLAGE WAY
GREENVIEW CT
Spelthorne Coll
Liby
COLLEGE WAY
COPTHORNE CHASE
CHAUCER RD
CANTERBURY CT
WOLSEY RD
CHESTERFIELD RD
HM Remand Ctr
WOODTHORPE RD
BUXTON RD
ADELAIDE RD
MARLBOROUGH RD
TOWNSEND RD
WARWICK RD
STANWELL RD
STANLEY RD
CHRISTOPHER CT
TENNYSON RD
NELSON RD
B378
B377
ALBERT RD
PRINCE WILLIAM CT
PRINCES RD
ARLINGTON RD
SPRINGFIELD RD
FONTMELL PK
MANOR RD
FORDBRIDGE RD
STAINES BY-PASS
River Ash
Staines Reservoirs Aqueduct
Staines Sta
MANOR PL
MILLERS CL
PRIORY MEWS
PRIORY GN
GRESHAM RD
GRANGE
JUBILEE
LEACROFT
Knowle Green
L Ctr
KNOWLE GN
VIVIENNE HOUSE
Cts
Sch
Sch
KNOWLE PARK
BROOKSIDE AVE
ACACIA RD
KINGSTON RD
PETERSFIELD RD
PETERSFIELD AVE
KENILWORTH GDNS
ST MARTIN'S CT
KINGSTON CRES
CELIA CRES
FAIRLAWNS
BROADWAY
WORPLE AVE
FERNDALE RD
TALBOT RD
ETHEL RD
ASHVIEW CL
ASHVIEW GDNS
FORDBRIDGE CT
CH
ASHFORD
Ashford Manor Golf Club
KINGSTON RD
A308
Sweep's Ditch
Kingscroft Cty Mid Sch
Our Lady of the Rosary RC Sch
GUILDFORD ST
COMMERCIAL RD
WITHEYGATE AVE
HOMESTEAD RD
FARM RD
STUART WAY
CHERRY TREE AVE
HURSTDENE AVE
HAZEL GR
The Matthew Arnold Sch
ALEXANDRA CL
GLOUCESTER CRES
PHILIP RD
BOOTH RD
CHARLES RD
MARGARET CL
ELIZABETH AVE
LASTINGHAM CT
BROOMFIELD
THE DOULTONS
LINK WAY
THE GLADE
WORPLE RD
TEMPLEDENE AVE
ARNOLD RD
BERRYSCROFT RD
PAVILION GDNS
WHITEWAYS CT
CARLYLE RD
GREENLAKE TERR
MEADWAY
WHEATSHEAF LA
LALEHAM RD
STAINES RD
B376
SWEEPS DITCH CL
PENTON HOOK RD
Buckland Cty Inf Sch
BRIGHTSIDE AVE
ABBOT CL
MIDDLE GN
HONNOR RD
LUCAN DR
ASHFORD RD
B377
Works
River Ash
Queen Mary Resr

33
14

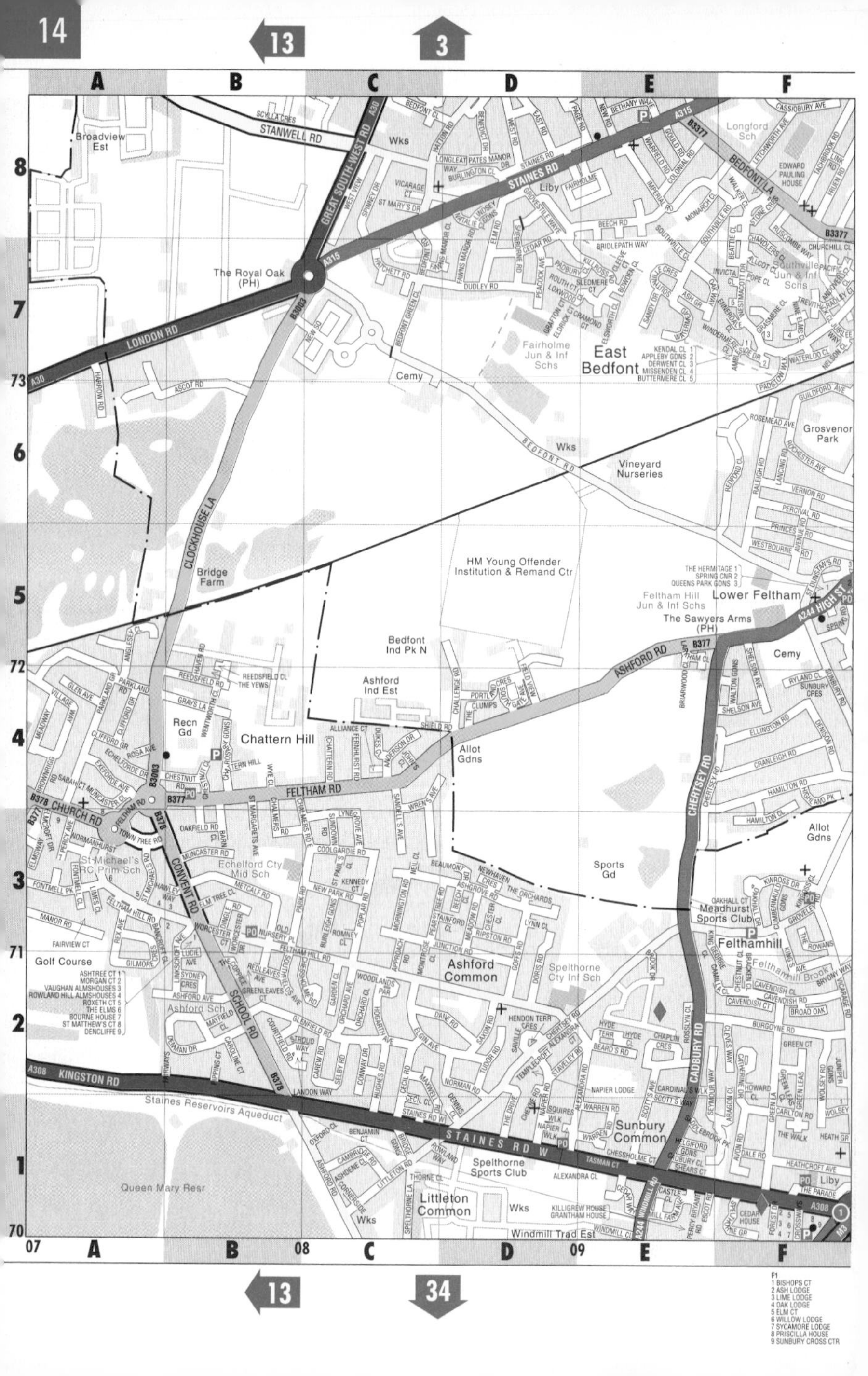

13
3
A
B
C
D
E
F
Broadview Est
STANWELL RD
SCYLLA CRES
GREAT SOUTH-WEST RD
A30
Wks
BEDFONT CL
HATTON RD
BENEDICT DR
WEST RD
EAST RD
PAGE RD
NEW RD
BETHANY WAYE
A315
B3377
Longford Sch
CASSIOBURY AVE
LETCHWORTH AVE
TACHBROOK RD
LINK RD
FRUEN RD
BEDFONT LA
EDWARD PAULING HOUSE
B3377
STAINES RD
Liby
FAIRHOLME
LONGLEAT WAY
PATES MANOR DR
BURLINGTON CL
VICARAGE CT
ST MARY'S DR
SPINNEY DR
WEST VIEW
IMPERIAL RD
COLONIAL RD
WARFIELD RD
GOULD RD
MONARCH CL
SOUTHVILLE RD
WALKER CL
STONE CRES
RUSCOMBE WAY
CHURCHILL CL
BEECH RD
BRIDLEPATH WAY
SOUTHVILLE CL
CHANDLERS CL
INVICTA CL
ALLCOT CL
POPE CL
Southville Jun & Inf Schs
PACIFIC CL
The Royal Oak (PH)
A315
HATCHETT RD
BEDFONT CL
DUDLEY RD
PEACOCK AVE
CEDAR RD
ELM RD
SHERBORNE RD
PADBURY CL
KILROSS RD
CLEEVE CT
SLEDMERE CT
BOWDEN CL
ROUTH CT
LOXWOOD CL
GRAYTON CL
ELDRICK CT
CRAMOND CT
ELLSWORTH CL
ASH GR
WATERMANS
WINDERMERE CL
GRASMERE CL
WATERLOO CL
NELSON CL
PADSTOW WALK
7
8
LONDON RD
B3003
BEDFONT GREEN CL
NEW SQ
Fairholme Jun & Inf Schs
East Bedfont
KENDAL CL 1
APPLEBY GDNS 2
DERWENT CL 3
MISSENDEN CL 4
BUTTERMERE CL 5
73
A30
HARROW RD
ASCOT RD
Cem
GUILDFORD AVE
ROSEMEAD AVE
Grosvenor Park
ROCHESTER AVE
6
Wks
BEDFONT RD
Vineyard Nurseries
REDFORD CL
RALEIGH RD
LANCING RD
VERNON RD
PERCIVAL RD
PRINCES RD
AVENUE RD
WESTBOURNE RD
CLOCKHOUSE LA
HM Young Offender Institution & Remand Ctr
Bridge Farm
THE HERMITAGE 1
SPRING CNR 2
QUEENS PARK GDNS 3
ST DUNSTAN'S RD
5
Feltham Hill Jun & Inf Schs
Lower Feltham
The Sawyers Arms (PH)
A244 HIGH ST
SPRING
Bedfont Ind Pk N
72
ANGLESEY CL
HAVEN RD
REEDSFIELD RD
REEDSFIELD CL
THE YEWS
GRAYS LA
PARKLAND GR
PARKLAND RD
GLEN AVE
VILLAGE WAY
MEADWAY
CLIFFORD GR
WENTWORTH CL
Ashford Ind Est
CHALLENGE RD
PORTLAND CRES
THE CLUMPS
SOUTH GATE AVE
FIELD VIEW
ASHFORD RD
B377
LARKHAM CL
BRIARWOOD CL
WALTON GDNS
SHELSON AVE
Cem
RYLAND CL
SUNBURY CRES
SUNBURY RD
Recn Gd
Chattern Hill
ALLIANCE CT
SHIELD RD
DUKES CL
ANDERSON DR
JOHNS CL
Allot Gdns
ELLINGTON RD
DENISON RD
4
CLIFFORD GR
ROSA AVE
ECHELFORDE DR
EXEFORDE AVE
BROWNRIGG RD
SABAH CT
MUNCASTER CL
CHESTNUT RD
TERN HILL
WYE CL
CHATTERN RD
FERNHURST RD
FELTHAM RD
B3003
B377
B378 CHURCH RD
B377
ELMCROFT DR
PERCY AVE
NORMANHURST
FELTHAM RD
TOWN TREE RD
OAKFIELD RD
B378
ST MARGARETS AVE
CHALMERS RD
CHESTNUT CL
LYNEGROVE AVE
SANDELL'S AVE
WREN'S AVE
CHERTSEY RD
CRANLEIGH RD
HAMILTON RD
HIGHLAND PK
HAMILTON CL
Allot Gdns
St Michael's RC Prim Sch
ELMSWAY
FONTMELL CL
CONVENT RD
MUNCASTER RD
Echelford Cty Mid Sch
COOLGARDIE RD
KENNEDY CT
BEAUMONT DR
NEWHAVEN CRES
THE ORCHARDS
ASHGROVE RD
Sports Gd
KINROSS DR
3
FONTMELL PK
LIMES CL
HAWLEY WAY
METCALF RD
ELM TREE CL
NEW PARK RD
POPLAR RD
MORNINGTON RD
NEIL CL
PEARTREE RD
BEECH CL
STAINFORD CL
MEADOW RD
CHESTER CL
LYNN CL
OAKHALL CT
Meadhurst Sports Club
CUMBERLAND GDNS
GROVELEY RD
THE ROWANS
MANOR RD
FELTHAM HILL RD
REX AVE
BANCROFT CT
WORCESTER CT
DINGLE RD
OLD NURSERY PL
BURLEIGH GDNS
ROMNEY CL
RIPSTON RD
JUNCTION RD
KING GEORGE CL
Felthamhill
FAIRVIEW CT
71
Golf Course
ASHTREE CT 1
MORGAN CT 2
VAUGHAN ALMSHOUSES 3
ROWLAND HILL ALMSHOUSES 4
ROXETH CT 5
THE ELMS 6
BOURNE HOUSE 7
ST MATTHEW'S CT 8
DENCLIFFE 9
GILMORE CRES
SYDNEY CRES
LUCIE AVE
THE COPPICE
REDLEAVES AVE
GREENLEAVES CT
FELTHAM HILL RD
WOODLANDS PAR
APPROACH RD
MONTROSE CL
Ashford Common
GOFFS RD
DORIS RD
Spelthorne Cty Inf Sch
BROOK DR
CHESTNUT CL
BRACKEN CL
Felthamhill Brook
BRYONY WAY
CAVENDISH CL
CAVENDISH RD
CAVENDISH CT
BROAD OAK
VICARAGE RD
ASHFORD AVE
Ashford Sch
MAYFIELD CL
SCHOOL RD
ORCHARD AVE
ORCHARD CL
HOGARTH AVE
GLENFIELD RD
DANE RD
HENDON TERR
CRES
SAXON RD
CHERTSEY RD
ALEXANDRA CT
HYDE TERR
HYDE CL
CHAPLIN CRES
ROSSLYN CL
BURGOYNE RD
2
DENMAN DR
CAROLINE CT
EPPING CT
FAIRWAYS
COURTFIELD RD
STROUD WAY
CAREW RD
SELBY RD
CONWAY DR
HUGHES RD
ELGIN AVE
CECIL RD
MAXWELL RD
NORMAN RD
TUDOR RD
SAVILLE
TEMPLECROFT
STAVELEY RD
BEARD'S RD
CADBURY RD
CLEVES WAY
CATHERINE DR
GREEN CT
JUNIPER GDNS
A308 KINGSTON RD
B378
LANDON WAY
CECIL CL
STAINES RD W
DENNIS CL
THE DRIVE
CHEYNE RD
NAPIER RD
SQUIRES WLK
NAPIER WLK
ALEXANDRA RD
WARREN RD
NAPIER LODGE
CARDINAL'S WLK
SCOTT'S WAY
SCOTT'S AVE
SEYMOUR WAY
ARAGON CL
HOWARD CL
GREEN LA
GREEN LEAS
WOLSEY RD
WOLSEY
CARLTON RD
THE WALK
HEATH GR
Staines Reservoirs Aqueduct
BENJAMIN CT
OXFORD CL
STAINES RD W
ROWLAND WAY
WARREN RD
Sunbury Common
HELGIFORD GDNS
BURY CL
SPEARS CT
AVON RD
DALE RD
HEATHCROFT AVE
1
CAMBRIDGE RD
ASHDENE CL
LITTLETON RD
Spelthorne Sports Club
ALEXANDRA CL
TASMAN CT
CHESSHOLME CT
Liby
THE PARADE
Queen Mary Resr
ASHFORD RD
CORNERSIDE
THORNE CL
Littleton Common
Wks
KILLIGREW HOUSE
GRANTHAM HOUSE
CASTLE CL
MILL FARM AVE
PERCY BRYANT RD
ESCOT RD
CEDAR HOUSE
FOREST DR
A308
A244 WINDMILL RD
WINDMILL CL
Windmill Trad Est
Wks
SPELTHORNE LA
70
07
08
09
A
B
C
D
E
F
13
34
F1
1 BISHOPS CT
2 ASH LODGE
3 LIME LODGE
4 OAK LODGE
5 ELM CT
6 WILLOW LODGE
7 SYCAMORE LODGE
8 PRISCILLA HOUSE
9 SUNBURY CROSS CTR

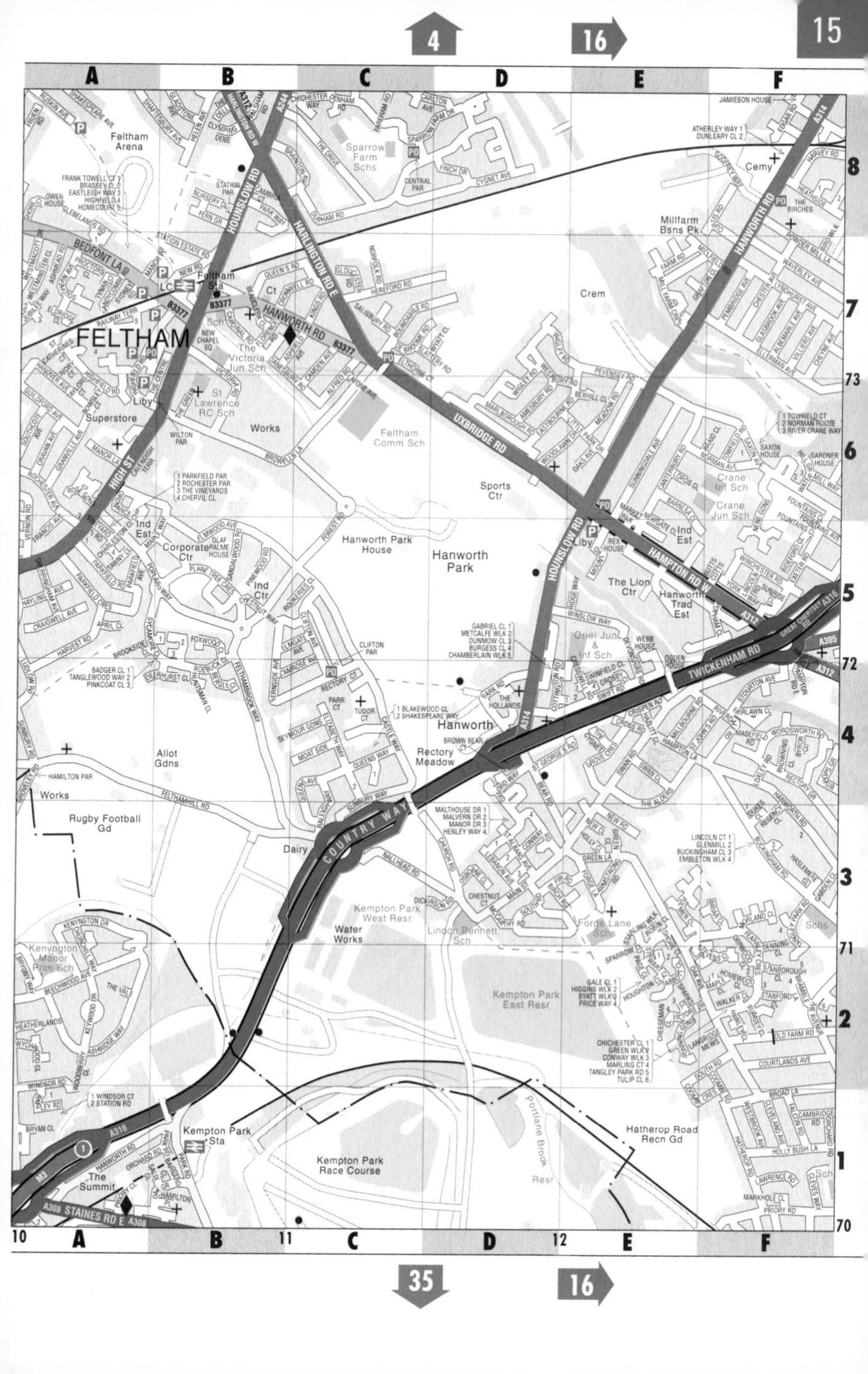
4
16
A
B
C
D
E
F
8
7
73
6
5
72
4
3
71
2
1
70
10
11
12
Feltham Arena
FELTHAM
Feltham Sta
Sparrow Farm Schs
Millfarm Bsns Pk
Cemy
Crem
The Victoria Jun Sch
St Lawrence RC Sch
Superstore
Liby
Works
Feltham Comm Sch
Sports Ctr
Corporate Ctr
Ind Est
Ind Ctr
Hanworth Park House
Hanworth Park
Crane Inf Sch
Crane Jun Sch
The Lion Ctr
Hanworth Trad Est
Oriel Jun & Inf Sch
Hanworth
Rectory Meadow
Allot Gdns
Rugby Football Gd
Dairy
Kempton Park West Resr
Water Works
Lindon Bennett Sch
Forge Lane Schs
Kempton Park East Resr
Kenyngton Manor Prim Sch
Kempton Park Sta
Kempton Park Race Course
Portlane Brook
Resr
Hatherop Road Recn Gd
The Summit
HOUNSLOW RD
HARLINGTON RD E
HANWORTH RD
UXBRIDGE RD
HAMPTON RD W
TWICKENHAM RD
COUNTRY WAY
HIGH ST
BEDFONT LA
STAINES RD E
A316
A314
A312
A244
A305
A308
B3377
M3

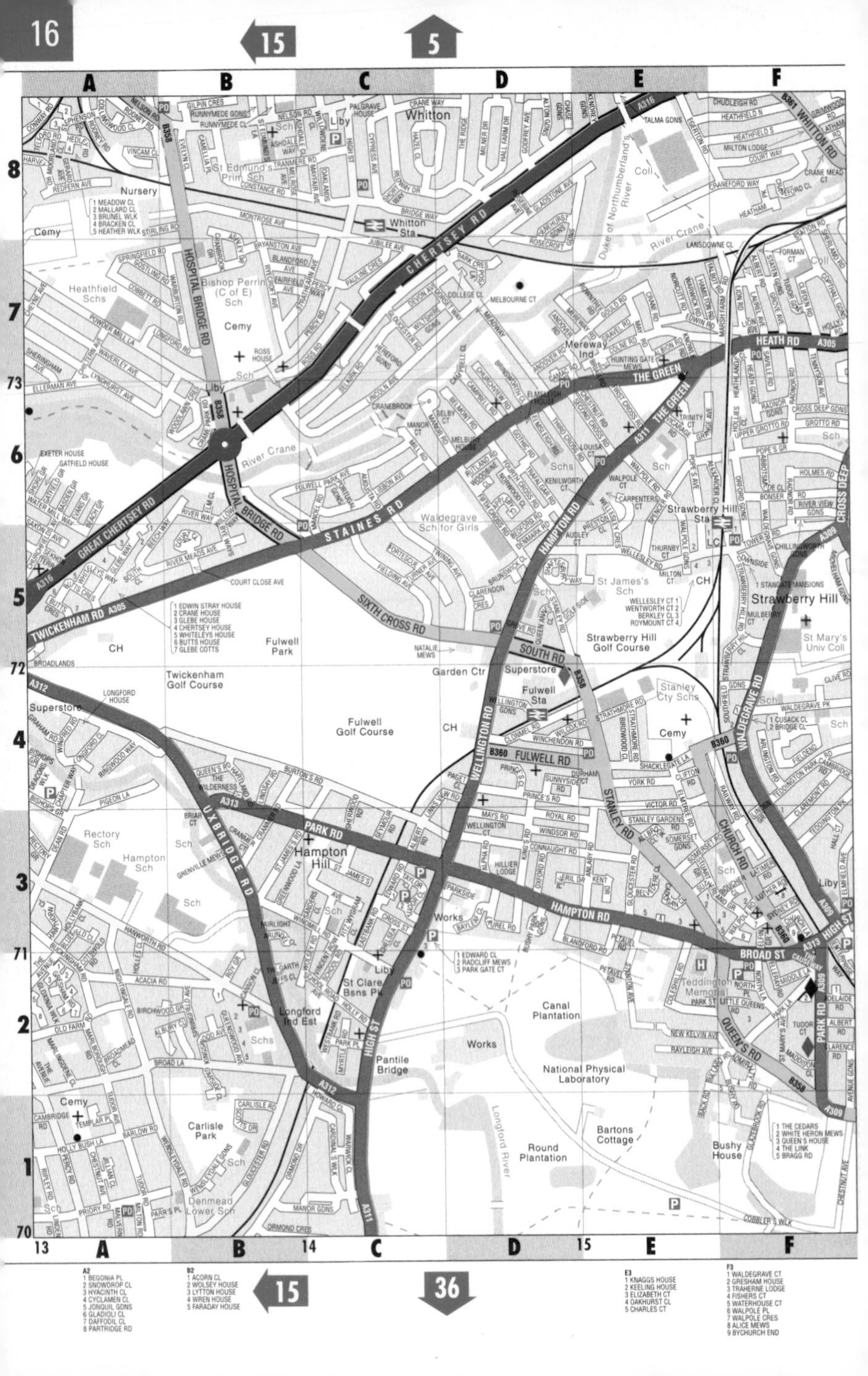
16
15
5
A B C D E F
Whitton
Whitton Sta
CHERTSEY RD
GREAT CHERTSEY RD
HOSPITAL BRIDGE RD
STAINES RD
TWICKENHAM RD
SIXTH CROSS RD
SOUTH RD
THE GREEN
HEATH RD
HAMPTON RD
WELLINGTON RD
STANLEY RD
FULWELL RD
UXBRIDGE RD
PARK RD
HIGH ST
CHURCH RD
WALDEGRAVE RD
BROAD ST
QUEEN'S RD
CROSS DEEP
Heathfield Schs
Bishop Perrin (C of E) Sch
Mereway Ind
Waldegrave Sch for Girls
Strawberry Hill Sta
Strawberry Hill
St Mary's Univ Coll
St James's Sch
Strawberry Hill Golf Course
Fulwell Park
Twickenham Golf Course
Fulwell Golf Course
Fulwell Sta
Garden Ctr
Superstore
Stanley Cty Schs
Rectory Sch
Hampton Sch
Hampton Hill
St Clare Bsns Pk
Longford Ind Est
Pantile Bridge
Works
Canal Plantation
National Physical Laboratory
Teddington Memorial
Bartons Cottage
Round Plantation
Longford River
Bushy House
Carlisle Park
Denmead Lower Sch
River Crane
Duke of Northumberland's River
COBBLER'S WLK
13 A B 14 C D 15 E F
A2
1 BEGONIA PL
2 SNOWDROP CL
3 HYACINTH CL
4 CYCLAMEN CL
5 JONQUIL GDNS
6 GLADIOLI CL
7 DAFFODIL CL
8 PARTRIDGE RD
B2
1 ACORN CL
2 WOLSEY HOUSE
3 LYTTON HOUSE
4 WREN HOUSE
5 FARADAY HOUSE
15
36
E3
1 KNAGGS HOUSE
2 KEELING HOUSE
3 ELIZABETH CT
4 OAKHURST CL
5 CHARLES CT
F3
1 WALDEGRAVE CT
2 GRESHAM HOUSE
3 TRAHERNE LODGE
4 FISHERS CT
5 WATERHOUSE CT
6 WALPOLE PL
7 WALPOLE CRES
8 ALICE MEWS
9 BYCHURCH END

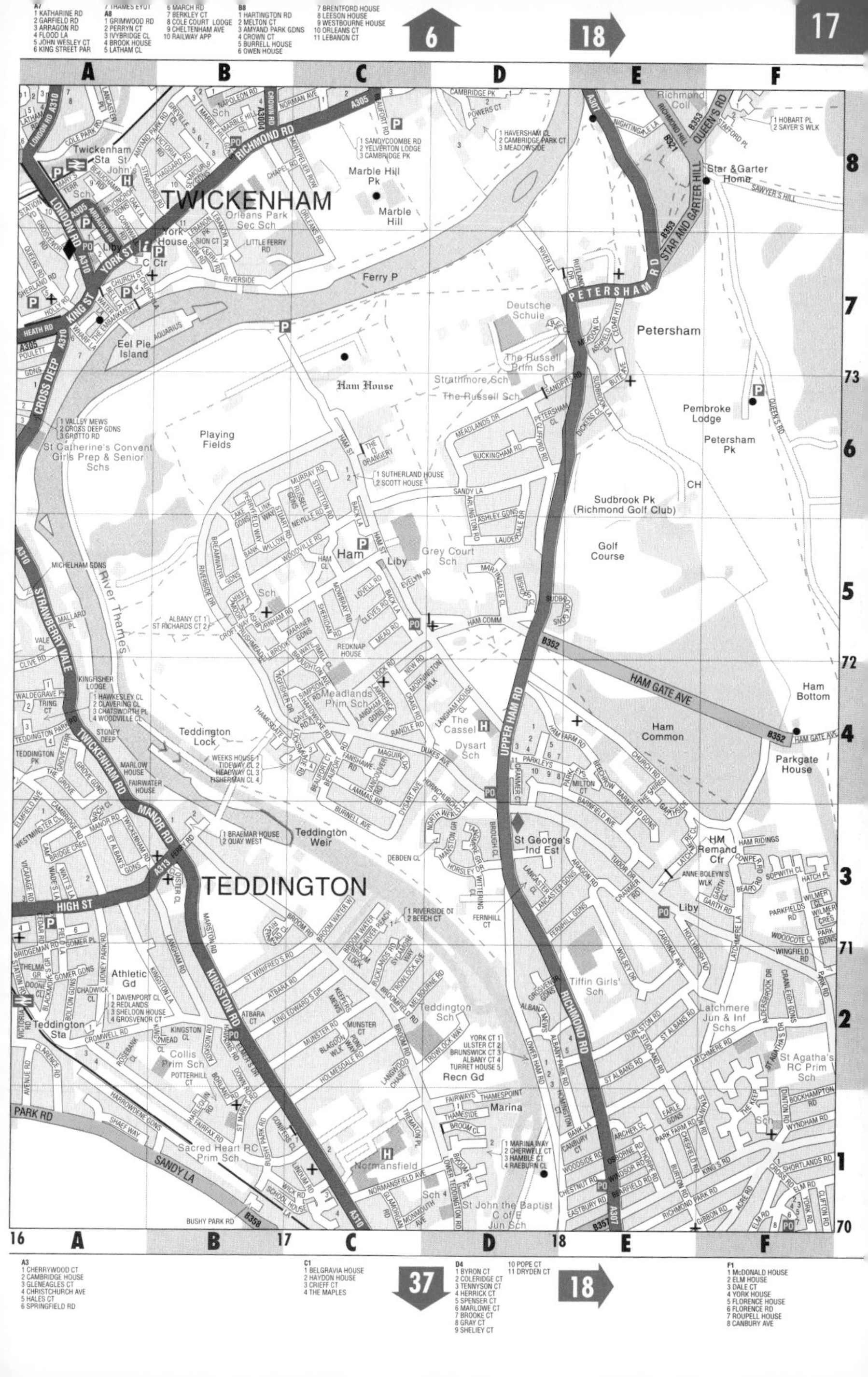
A7
1 KATHARINE RD
2 GARFIELD RD
3 ARRAGON RD
4 FLOOD LA
5 JOHN WESLEY CT
6 KING STREET PAR
7 THAMES EYOT
A8
1 GRIMWOOD RD
2 PERRYN CT
3 IVYBRIDGE CL
4 BROOK HOUSE
5 LATHAM CL
6 MARCH RD
7 BERKLEY CT
8 COLE COURT LODGE
9 CHELTENHAM AVE
10 RAILWAY APP
B8
1 HARTINGTON RD
2 MELTON CT
3 AMYAND PARK GDNS
4 CROWN CT
5 BURRELL HOUSE
6 OWEN HOUSE
7 BRENTFORD HOUSE
8 LEESON HOUSE
9 WESTBOURNE HOUSE
10 ORLEANS CT
11 LEBANON CT
6
18
A
B
C
D
E
F
8
7
73
6
5
72
4
3
71
2
1
70
16
17
18
TWICKENHAM
TEDDINGTON
Twickenham Sta
Marble Hill Pk
Marble Hill
Orleans Park Sec Sch
York House
Eel Pie Island
Ham House
Playing Fields
St Catherine's Convent Girls Prep & Senior Schs
Petersham
Deutsche Schule
Pembroke Lodge
Petersham Pk
Sudbrook Pk (Richmond Golf Club)
Golf Course
Star & Garter Home
Richmond Coll
Ham
Grey Court Sch
River Thames
Teddington Lock
Teddington Weir
Meadlands Prim Sch
The Cassel
Dysart Sch
Ham Common
Ham Bottom
Parkgate House
St George's Ind Est
HM Remand Ctr
Tiffin Girls' Sch
Latchmere Jun & Inf Schs
St Agatha's RC Prim Sch
Athletic Gd
Teddington Sta
Collis Prim Sch
Teddington Sch
Recn Gd
Marina
Sacred Heart RC Prim Sch
Normansfield
St John the Baptist C of E Jun Sch
RICHMOND RD
UPPER HAM RD
HAM GATE AVE
PETERSHAM RD
STAR AND GARTER HILL
KINGSTON RD
STRAWBERRY VALE
CROSS DEEP
TWICKENHAM RD
MANOR RD
HIGH ST
SANDY LA
PARK RD
A3
1 CHERRYWOOD CT
2 CAMBRIDGE HOUSE
3 GLENEAGLES CT
4 CHRISTCHURCH AVE
5 HALES CT
6 SPRINGFIELD RD
C1
1 BELGRAVIA HOUSE
2 HAYDON HOUSE
3 CRIEFF CT
4 THE MAPLES
37
D4
1 BYRON CT
2 COLERIDGE CT
3 TENNYSON CT
4 HERRICK CT
5 SPENSER CT
6 MARLOWE CT
7 BROOKE CT
8 GRAY CT
9 SHELIEY CT
10 POPE CT
11 DRYDEN CT
18
F1
1 McDONALD HOUSE
2 ELM HOUSE
3 DALE CT
4 YORK HOUSE
5 FLORENCE HOUSE
6 FLORENCE RD
7 ROUPELL HOUSE
8 CANBURY AVE

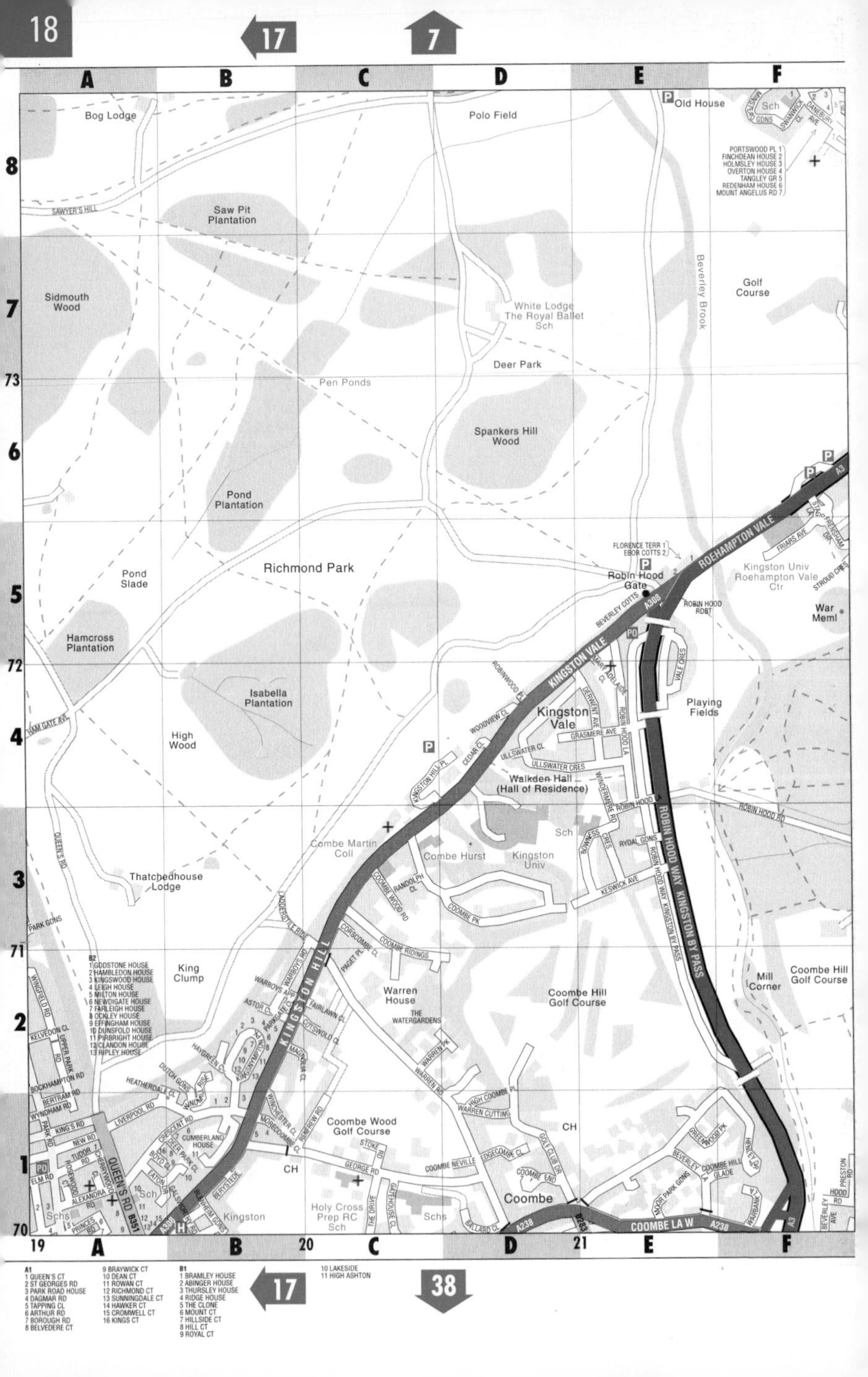

A B C D E F

Bog Lodge

Polo Field

Old House Sch

PORTSWOOD PL 1
FINCHDEAN HOUSE 2
HOLMSLEY HOUSE 3
OVERTON HOUSE 4
TANGLEY GR 5
REDENHAM HOUSE 6
MOUNT ANGELUS RD 7

8

SAWYER'S HILL

Saw Pit Plantation

7 Sidmouth Wood

White Lodge The Royal Ballet Sch

Golf Course

Beverley Brook

73 Pen Ponds

Deer Park

Spankers Hill Wood

6 Pond Plantation

A3

5 Pond Slade

Richmond Park

FLORENCE TERR 1
EBOR COTTS 2
Robin Hood Gate

ROEHAMPTON VALE

Kingston Univ Roehampton Vale Ctr

BEVERLEY COTTS

A308

ROBIN HOOD ROAD

War Meml

72 Hamcross Plantation

Isabella Plantation

KINGSTON VALE

Kingston Vale

Playing Fields

4 High Wood

ADAM GATE AVE

P

KINGSTON HILL RD

WOODBINE CT

CEDAR CL

ULLSWATER CL

GRASMERE AVE

ULLSWATER CRES

CRASMERE AVE

RODULA

Walkden Hall (Hall of Residence)

ROBIN HOOD RD

ROBIN HOOD WAY

ROBIN HOOD RD

Sch

RYDAL GDNS

KESWICK AVE

3 Thatchedhouse Lodge

PARK GDNS

Combe Martin Coll

Combe Hurst

Kingston Univ

ROBIN HOOD WAY KINGSTON BY PASS A3

71

QUEEN'S RD

82
TIGGOSTONE HOUSE
1 HAMBLEDON HOUSE
2 KINGSWOOD HOUSE
3 LEIGH HOUSE
4 MILTON HOUSE
5 NEWDIGATE HOUSE
6 OCKLEY HOUSE
7 EFFINGHAM HOUSE
8 PURBRIGHT HOUSE
10 DUNSFOLD HOUSE
11 CLANDON HOUSE
12 RIPLEY HOUSE

King Clump

KINGSTON HILL

CROSSCOMBE CL

PARKE PL

COOMBE RIDINGS

RANDOLPH CL

COOMBE BROOK

COOMBE PK

Warren House

THE WATERGARDENS

Coombe Hill Golf Course

Mill Corner

Coombe Hill Golf Course

2 WHEATFIELD WAY
KELVEDON CL
BOCKHAMPTON RD
BERTRAM RD
WYNDHAM RD

HEATHERDALE RD

CUMBERLAND HOUSE

WARREN RD

WARREN COOMBE

WARREN CUTTING

CH

1 KINGS RD
NEW RD
TUDOR
ALEXANDRA
Schs
Schs
QUEEN'S RD
LIVERPOOL RD
CUMBERLAND RD
GEORGE RD
STONE
COOMBE NEVILLE
EDGECOMBE CL
CH
Coombe
COOMBE END
BEVERLEY
COOMBE HILL GLADE
A3
PRESTON RD

Kingston

Coombe Wood Golf Course

Holy Cross Prep RC Sch

Schs

COOMBE LA W A238 A238

OAK PARK GDNS

BEVERLEY

A3

ROBIN HOOD LA

A1
1 QUEEN'S CT
2 ST GEORGES RD
3 PARK ROAD HOUSE
4 DAGMAR RD
5 TAPPING CL
6 ARTHUR RD
7 BOROUGH RD
8 BELVEDERE CT

9 BRAYWICK CT
10 DEAN CT
11 ROWAN CT
12 RICHMOND CT
13 SUNNINGDALE CT
14 HAWKER CT
15 CROMWELL CT
16 KINGS CT

B1
1 BRAMLEY HOUSE
2 ABINGER HOUSE
3 THURSLEY HOUSE
4 RIDGE HOUSE
5 THE CLONE
6 MOUNT CT
7 HILLSIDE CT
8 HILL CT
9 ROYAL CT

10 LAKESIDE
11 HIGH ASHTON

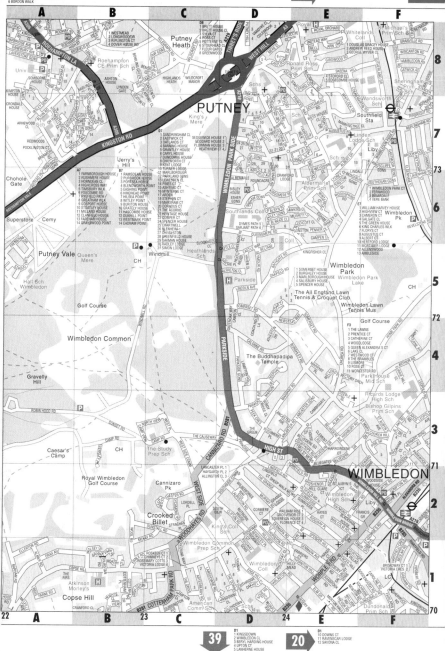

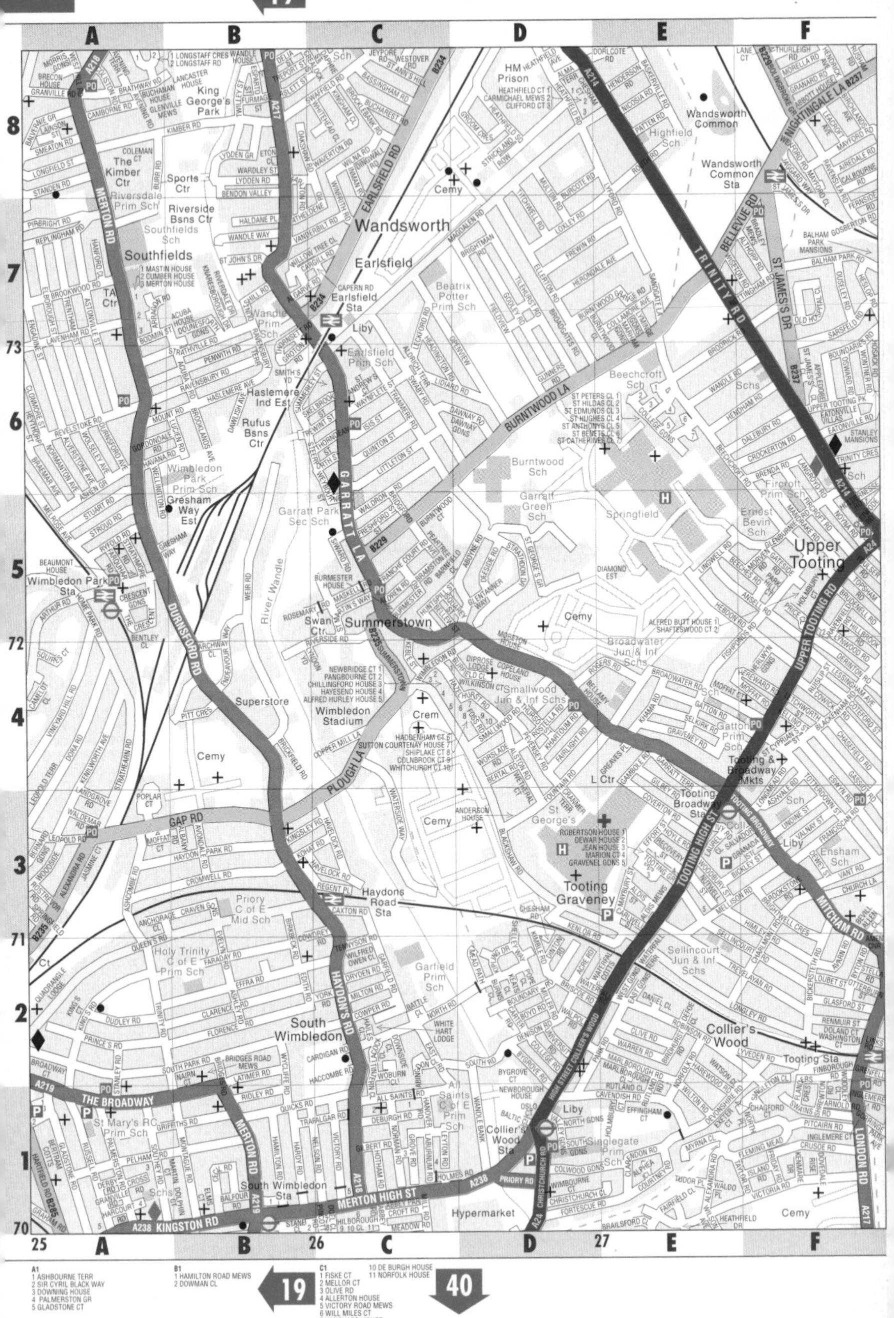

A1
1 ASHBOURNE TERR
2 SIR CYRIL BLACK WAY
3 DOWNING HOUSE
4 PALMERSTON GR
5 GLADSTONE CT

B1
1 HAMILTON ROAD MEWS
2 DOWMAN CL

C1
1 FISKE CT
2 MELLOR CT
3 OLD HO
4 ALLERTON HOUSE
5 VICTORY ROAD MEWS
6 WILL MILES CT
7 VANGUARD HOUSE
8 MYCHELL HOUSE
9 MERTON PL

10 DE BURGH HOUSE
11 NORFOLK HOUSE

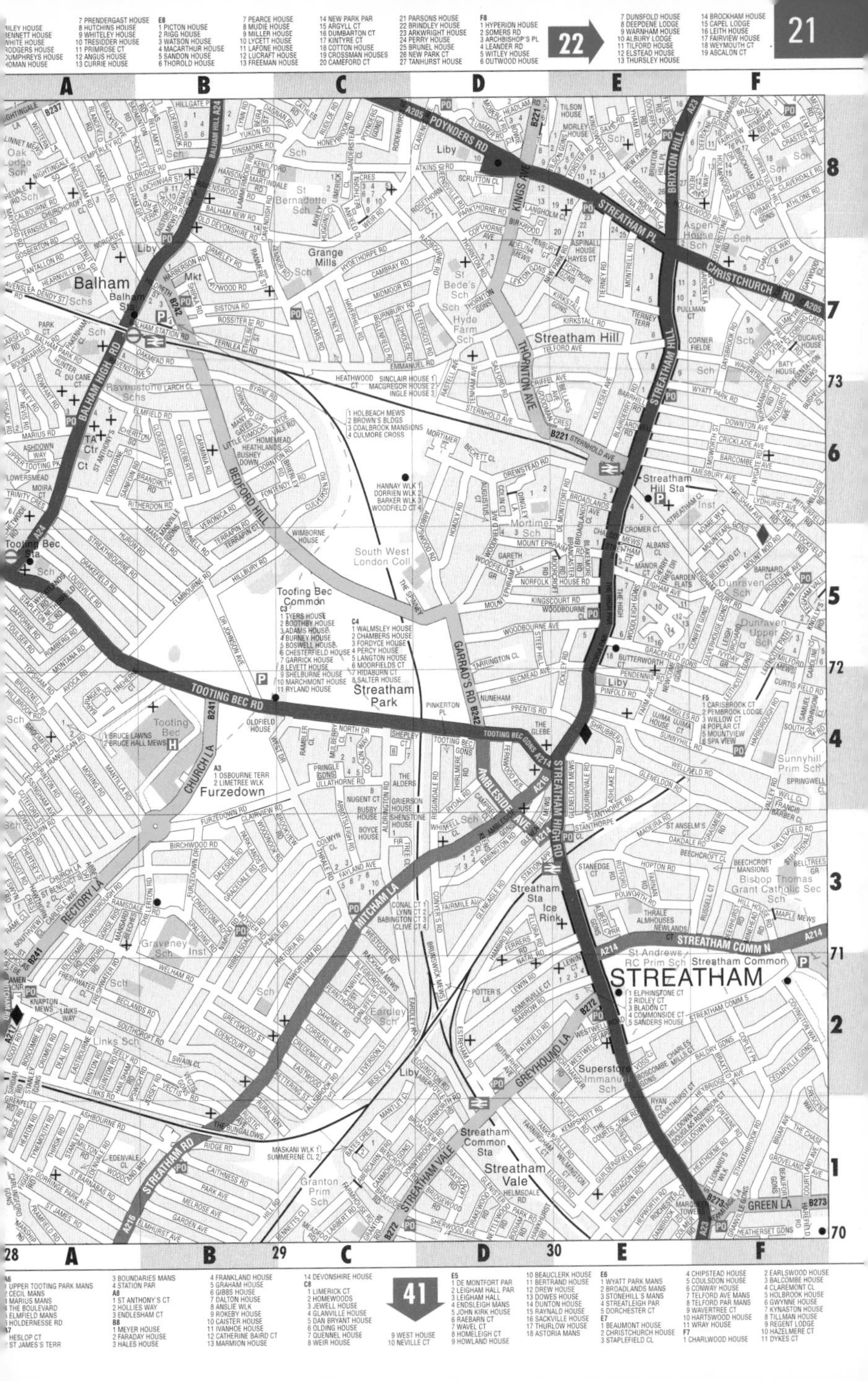

RILEY HOUSE
BENNETT HOUSE
WHITE HOUSE
RODGERS HOUSE
DUMPHREYS HOUSE
HOMAN HOUSE
7 PRENDERGAST HOUSE
8 HUTCHINS HOUSE
9 WHITELEY HOUSE
10 TRESIDDER HOUSE
11 PRIMROSE CT
12 ANGUS HOUSE
13 CURRIE HOUSE
E8
1 PICTON HOUSE
2 RIGG HOUSE
3 WATSON HOUSE
4 MACARTHUR HOUSE
5 SANDON HOUSE
6 THOROLD HOUSE
7 PEARCE HOUSE
8 MUDIE HOUSE
9 MILLER HOUSE
10 LYCETT HOUSE
11 LAFONE HOUSE
12 LUCRAFT HOUSE
13 FREEMAN HOUSE
14 NEW PARK PAR
15 ARGYLL CT
16 DUMBARTON CT
17 KINTYRE CT
18 COTTON HOUSE
19 CROSSMAN HOUSES
20 CAMEFORD CT
21 PARSONS HOUSE
22 BRINDLEY HOUSE
23 ARKWRIGHT HOUSE
24 PERRY HOUSE
25 BRUNEL HOUSE
26 NEW PARK CT
27 TANHURST HOUSE
F8
1 HYPERION HOUSE
2 SOMERS RD
3 ARCHBISHOP'S PL
4 LEANDER RD
5 WITLEY HOUSE
6 OUTWOOD HOUSE
22
7 DUNSFOLD HOUSE
8 DEEPDENE LODGE
9 WARNHAM HOUSE
10 ALBURY LODGE
11 TILFORD HOUSE
12 ELSTEAD HOUSE
13 THURSLEY HOUSE
14 BROCKHAM HOUSE
15 CAPEL LODGE
16 LEITH HOUSE
17 FAIRVIEW HOUSE
18 WEYMOUTH CT
19 ASCALON CT
21
A B C D E F
8 7 73 6 5 72 4 3 71 2 1 70
28 29 30
Balham
Balham Sta
Mkt
Liby
Grange Mills
St Bernadette Sch
St Bede's Sch
Hyde Farm Sch
Streatham Hill
Streatham Hill Sta
Aspen House Sch
Ravenstone Schs
TA Ctr
Tooting Bec Sta
Tooting Bec Common
South West London Coll
Mortimer Sch
Dunraven Sch
Dunraven Upper Sch
Streatham Park
Tooting Bec
Furzedown
Sunnyhill Prim Sch
Bishop Thomas Grant Catholic Sec Sch
Streatham Sta
Ice Rink
St Andrews RC Prim Sch
Streatham Common
STREATHAM
Graveney Sch
Eardley Sch
Links Sch
Superstore
Immanuel Sch
Streatham Common Sta
Streatham Vale
Granton Prim Sch
POYNDERS RD
STREATHAM PL
CHRISTCHURCH RD
BRIXTON HILL
STREATHAM HILL
KINGS AVE
THORNTON AVE
BALHAM HIGH RD
BEDFORD HILL
TOOTING BEC RD
GARRAD'S RD
STREATHAM HIGH RD
MITCHAM LA
RECTORY LA
STREATHAM RD
STREATHAM VALE
GREYHOUND LA
STREATHAM COMM N
GREEN LA
A205 A23 A24 A214 A216 A217 B221 B237 B241 B242 B272 B273
41
A6
1 UPPER TOOTING PARK MANS
2 CECIL MANS
3 MARIUS MANS
4 THE BOULEVARD
5 ELMFIELD MANS
6 HOLDERNESSE RD
A7
1 HESLOP CT
2 ST JAMES'S TERR
3 BOUNDARIES MANS
4 STATION PAR
A8
1 ST ANTHONY'S CT
2 HOLLIES WAY
3 ENDLESHAM CT
B8
1 MEYER HOUSE
2 FARADAY HOUSE
3 HALES HOUSE
4 FRANKLAND HOUSE
5 GRAHAM HOUSE
6 GIBBS HOUSE
7 DALTON HOUSE
8 ANSLIE WLK
9 ROKEBY HOUSE
10 CAISTER HOUSE
11 IVANHOE HOUSE
12 CATHERINE BAIRD CT
13 MARMION HOUSE
14 DEVONSHIRE HOUSE
C8
1 LIMERICK CT
2 HOMEWOODS
3 JEWELL HOUSE
4 GLANVILLE HOUSE
5 DAN BRYANT HOUSE
6 OLDING HOUSE
7 QUENNEL HOUSE
8 WEIR HOUSE
9 WEST HOUSE
10 NEVILLE CT
E5
1 DE MONTFORT PAR
2 LEIGHAM HALL PAR
3 LEIGHAM HALL
4 ENDSLEIGH MANS
5 JOHN KIRK HOUSE
6 RAEBARN CT
7 WAVEL CT
8 HOMELEIGH CT
9 HOWLAND HOUSE
10 BEAUCLERK HOUSE
11 BERTRAND HOUSE
12 DREW HOUSE
13 DOWES HOUSE
14 DUNTON HOUSE
15 RAYNALD HOUSE
16 SACKVILLE HOUSE
17 THURLOW HOUSE
18 ASTORIA MANS
E6
1 WYATT PARK MANS
2 BROADLANDS MANS
3 STONEHILL'S MANS
4 STREATLEIGH PAR
5 DORCHESTER CT
E7
1 BEAUMONT HOUSE
2 CHRISTCHURCH HOUSE
3 STAPLEFIELD CL
4 CHIPSTEAD HOUSE
5 COULSDON HOUSE
6 CONWAY HOUSE
7 TELFORD AVE MANS
8 TELFORD PAR MANS
9 WAVERTREE CT
10 HARTSWOOD HOUSE
11 WRAY HOUSE
F7
1 CHARLWOOD HOUSE
2 EARLSWOOD HOUSE
3 BALCOMBE HOUSE
4 CLAREMONT CL
5 HOLBROOK HOUSE
6 GWYNNE HOUSE
7 KYNASTON HOUSE
8 TILLMAN HOUSE
9 REGENT LODGE
10 HAZELMERE CT
11 DYKES CT

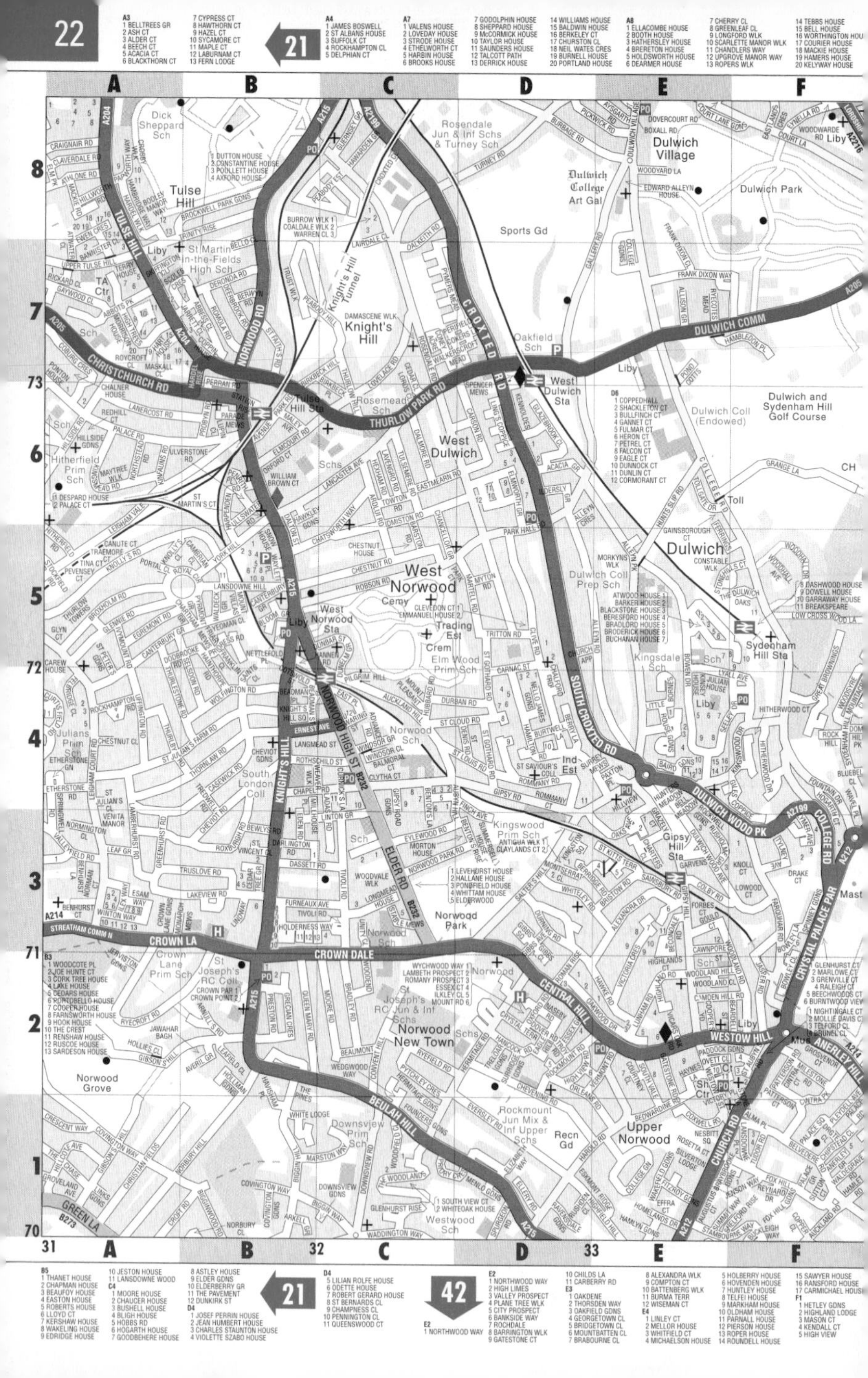

22
A3
1 BELLTREES GR
2 ASH CT
3 ALDER CT
4 BEECH CT
5 ACACIA CT
6 BLACKTHORN CT
7 CYPRESS CT
8 HAWTHORN CT
9 HAZEL CT
10 SYCAMORE CT
11 MAPLE CT
12 LABURNAM CT
13 FERN LODGE
21
A4
1 JAMES BOSWELL
2 ST ALBANS HOUSE
3 SUFFOLK CT
4 ROCKHAMPTON CL
5 DELPHIAN CT
A7
1 VALENS HOUSE
2 LOVEDAY HOUSE
3 STRODE HOUSE
4 ETHELWORTH CT
5 HARBIN HOUSE
6 BROOKS HOUSE
7 GODOLPHIN HOUSE
8 SHEPPARD HOUSE
9 McCORMICK HOUSE
10 TAYLOR HOUSE
11 SAUNDERS HOUSE
12 TALCOTT PATH
13 DERRICK HOUSE
14 WILLIAMS HOUSE
15 BALDWIN HOUSE
16 BERKELEY CT
17 CHURSTON CL
18 NEIL WATES CRES
19 BURNELL HOUSE
20 PORTLAND HOUSE
A8
1 ELLACOMBE HOUSE
2 BOOTH HOUSE
3 HATHERSLEY HOUSE
4 BRERETON HOUSE
5 HOLDSWORTH HOUSE
6 DEARMER HOUSE
7 CHERRY CL
8 GREENLEAF CL
9 LONGFORD WLK
10 SCARLETTE MANOR WLK
11 CHANDLERS WAY
12 UPGROVE MANOR WAY
13 ROPERS WLK
14 TEBBS HOUSE
15 BELL HOUSE
16 WORTHINGTON HOU
17 COURIER HOUSE
18 MACKIE HOUSE
19 HAMERS HOUSE
20 KELYWAY HOUSE
A
B
C
D
E
F
8
7
73
6
5
72
4
3
71
2
1
70
Dick Sheppard Sch
Rosendale Jun & Inf Schs & Turney Sch
Dulwich Village
Dulwich College Art Gal
Dulwich Park
Tulse Hill
Sports Gd
Knight's Hill Tunnel
Knight's Hill
Oakfield Sch
West Dulwich Sta
Tulse Hill Sta
Rosemead Sch
Dulwich Coll (Endowed)
Dulwich and Sydenham Hill Golf Course
West Dulwich
Hitherfield Prim Sch
Dulwich
West Norwood
Cemy
Dulwich Coll Prep Sch
West Norwood Sta
Trading Est
Crem
Elm Wood Prim Sch
Kingsdale Sch
Sydenham Hill Sta
Julians Prim Sch
Norwood Sch
South London Coll
Kingswood Prim Sch
Gipsy Hill Sta
Norwood Park
Crown Lane Prim Sch
St Joseph's RC Coll
St Joseph's RC Jun & Inf Schs
Norwood New Town
Norwood Grove
Downsview Prim Sch
Rockmount Jun Mix & Inf Upper Schs
Recn Gd
Upper Norwood
Westwood Sch
TULSE HILL
NORWOOD RD
CHRISTCHURCH RD
THURLOW PARK RD
CROXTED RD
DULWICH COMM
SOUTH CROXTED RD
KNIGHT'S HILL
NORWOOD HIGH ST
ELDER RD
DULWICH WOOD PK
COLLEGE RD
CROWN LA
CROWN DALE
CENTRAL HILL
WESTOW HILL
BEULAH HILL
CHURCH RD
CRYSTAL PALACE PAR
ANERLEY HILL
STREATHAM COMM N
GREEN LA
31
32
33
B5
1 THANET HOUSE
2 CHAPMAN HOUSE
3 BEAUFOY HOUSE
4 EASTON HOUSE
5 ROBERTS HOUSE
6 LLOYD CT
7 KERSHAW HOUSE
8 WAKELING HOUSE
9 EDRIDGE HOUSE
10 JESTON HOUSE
11 LANSDOWNE WOOD
C4
1 MOORE HOUSE
2 CHAUCER HOUSE
3 BUSHELL HOUSE
4 BLIGH HOUSE
5 HOBBS RD
6 HOGARTH HOUSE
7 GOODBEHERE HOUSE
8 ASTLEY HOUSE
9 ELDER GDNS
10 ELDERBERRY GR
11 THE PAVEMENT
12 DUNKIRK ST
D4
1 JOSEF PERRIN HOUSE
2 JEAN HUMBERT HOUSE
3 CHARLES STAUNTON HOUSE
4 VIOLETTE SZABO HOUSE
21
D4
5 LILIAN ROLFE HOUSE
6 ODETTE HOUSE
7 ROBERT GERARD HOUSE
8 ST BERNARDS CL
9 CHAMPNESS CL
10 PENNINGTON CL
11 QUEENSWOOD CT
42
E2
1 NORTHWOOD WAY
E2
1 NORTHWOOD WAY
2 HIGH LIMES
3 VALLEY PROSPECT
4 PLANE TREE WLK
5 CITY PROSPECT
6 BANKSIDE WAY
7 ROCHDALE
8 BARRINGTON WLK
9 GATESTONE CT
10 CHILDS LA
11 CARBERRY RD
E3
1 OAKDENE
2 THORSDEN WAY
3 OAKFIELD GDNS
4 GEORGETOWN CL
5 BRIDGETOWN CL
6 MOUNTBATTEN CL
7 BRABOURNE CL
8 ALEXANDRA WLK
9 COMPTON CT
10 BATTENBERG WLK
11 BURMA TERR
12 WISEMAN CT
E4
1 LINLEY CT
2 MELLOR HOUSE
3 WHITFIELD CT
4 MICHAELSON HOUSE
5 HOLBERRY HOUSE
6 HOVENDEN HOUSE
7 HUNTLEY HOUSE
8 TELFEI HOUSE
9 MARKHAM HOUSE
10 OLDHAM HOUSE
11 PARNALL HOUSE
12 PIERSON HOUSE
13 ROPER HOUSE
14 ROUNDELL HOUSE
15 SAWYER HOUSE
16 RANSFORD HOUSE
17 CARMICHAEL HOUSE
F1
1 HETLEY GDNS
2 HIGHLAND LODGE
3 MASON CT
4 KENDALL CT
5 HIGH VIEW

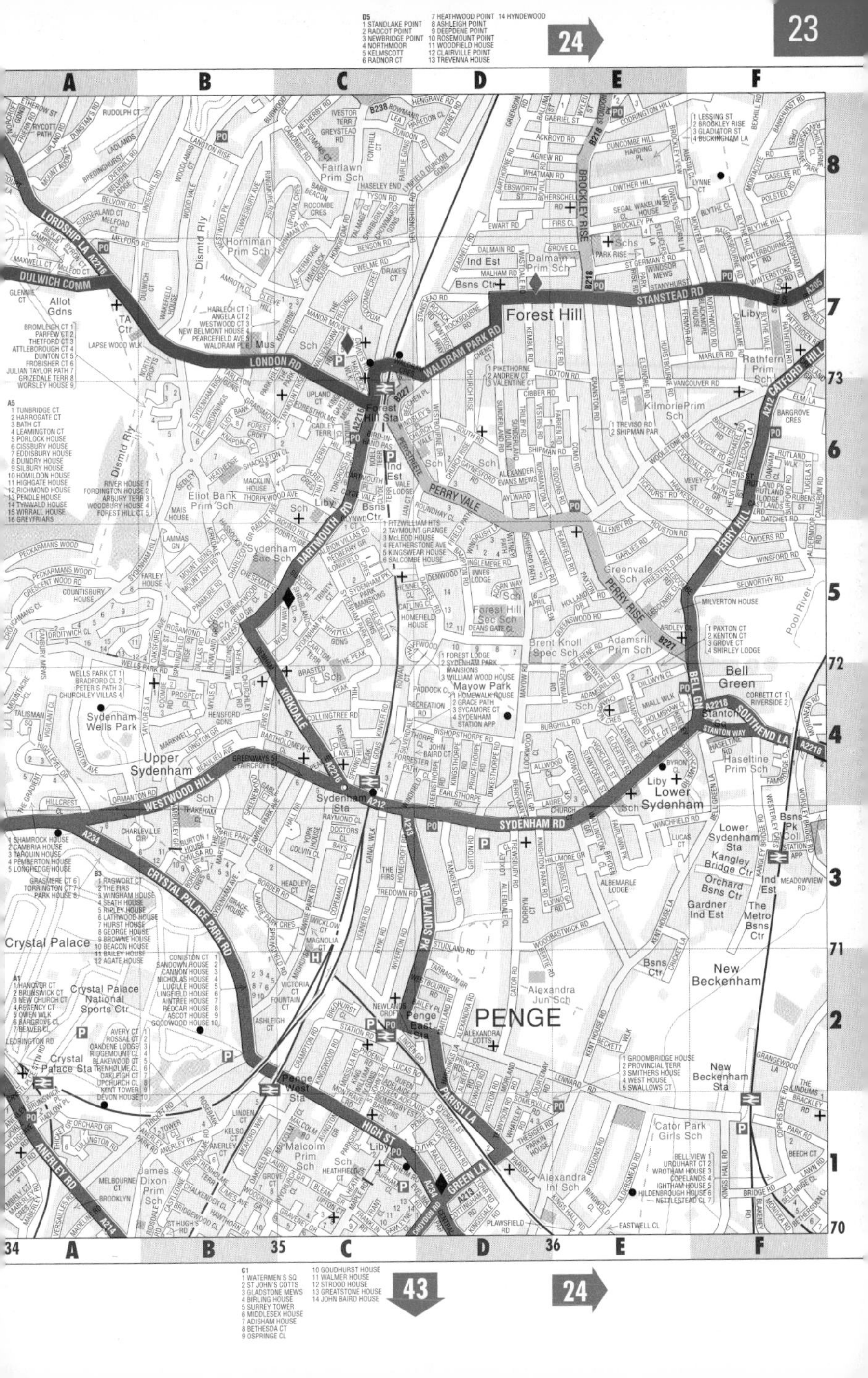

D5
1 STANDLAKE POINT
2 RADCOT POINT
3 NEWBRIDGE POINT
4 NORTHMOOR
5 KELMSCOTT
6 RADNOR CT
7 HEATHWOOD POINT
8 ASHLEIGH POINT
9 DEEPDENE POINT
10 ROSEMOUNT POINT
11 WOODFIELD HOUSE
12 CLAIRVILLE POINT
13 TREVENNA HOUSE
14 HYNDEWOOD
24
A
B
C
D
E
F
8
7
73
6
5
72
4
3
71
2
1
70
34
35
36
LORDSHIP LA
A2216
DULWICH COMM
Allot Gdns
TA Ctr
Dismtd Rly
Horniman Prim Sch
Fairlawn Prim Sch
LONDON RD
Mus
Sch
Forest Hill Sta
WALDRAM PARK RD
Forest Hill
Ind Est
Bsns Ctr
Dalmain Prim Sch
BROCKLEY RISE
B218
STANSTEAD RD
A205
Schs
Liby
Rathfern Prim Sch
CATFORD HILL
A212
KilmoriePrim Sch
PERRY VALE
DARTMOUTH RD
Eliot Bank Prim Sch
Sydenham Sec Sch
Forest Hill Sec Sch
Greenvale Sch
PERRY RISE
B227
Brent Knoll Spec Sch
Adamsrill Prim Sch
PERRY HILL
Bell Green
BELL GN
Stanton Sq
STANTON WAY
SOUTHEND LA
A2218
Haseltine Prim Sch
Mayow Park
KIRKDALE
Sydenham Wells Park
Upper Sydenham
WESTWOOD HILL
Sydenham Sta
A212
SYDENHAM RD
Lower Sydenham
Lower Sydenham Sta
Kangley Bridge Ctr
Orchard Bsns Ctr
Gardner Ind Est
The Metro Bsns Ctr
Ind Est
A234
CRYSTAL PALACE PARK RD
Crystal Palace
Crystal Palace National Sports Ctr
Crystal Palace Sta
NEWLANDS PK
A213
Alexandra Jun Sch
PENGE
Penge East Sta
Penge West Sta
New Beckenham
New Beckenham Sta
Cator Park Girls Sch
HIGH ST
Malcolm Prim Sch
James Dixon Prim Sch
Alexandra Inf Sch
GREEN LA
ANERLEY RD
A214
Pool River

C1
1 WATERMEN'S SQ
2 ST JOHN'S COTTS
3 GLADSTONE MEWS
4 BIRLING HOUSE
5 SURREY TOWER
6 MIDDLESEX HOUSE
7 ADISHAM HOUSE
8 BETHESDA CT
9 OSPRINGE CL
10 GOUDHURST HOUSE
11 WALMER HOUSE
12 STROOD HOUSE
13 GREATSTONE HOUSE
14 JOHN BAIRD CT
43
24

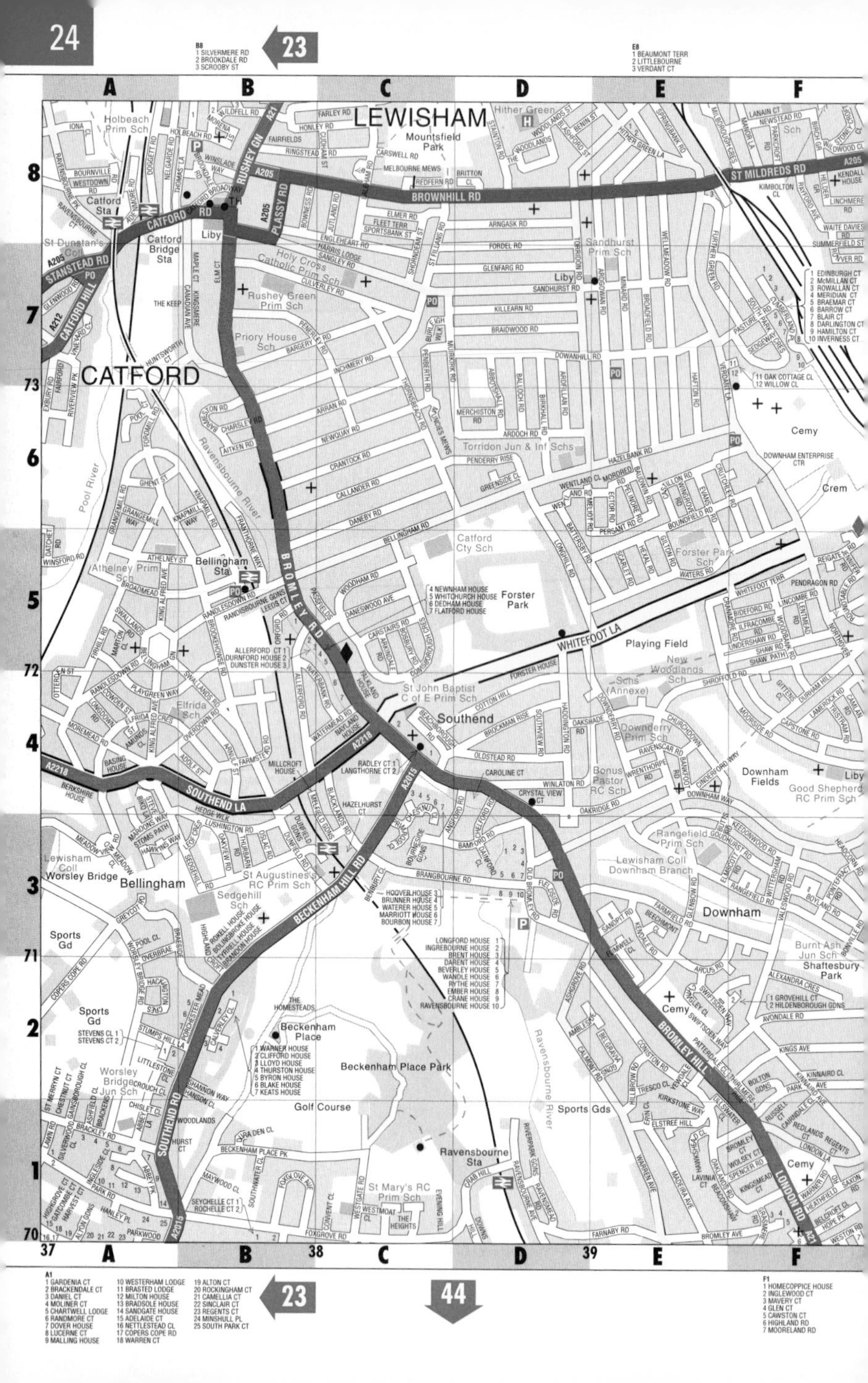

24
23
B8
1 SILVERMERE RD
2 BROOKDALE RD
3 SCROOBY ST
E8
1 BEAUMONT TERR
2 LITTLEBOURNE
3 VERDANT CT
A B C D E F
LEWISHAM
CATFORD
Hither Green
Mountsfield Park
Holbeach Prim Sch
Catford Sta
Catford Bridge Sta
St Dunstan's Coll
Holy Cross Catholic Prim Sch
Rushey Green Prim Sch
Priory House Sch
Sandhurst Prim Sch
Torridon Jun & Inf Schs
Catford Cty Sch
Forster Park
Forster Park Sch
Playing Field
New Woodlands Sch
Schs (Annexe)
Bellingham Sta
Athelney Prim Sch
Elfrida Sch
St John Baptist C of E Prim Sch
Southend
Downderry Prim Sch
Bonus Pastor RC Sch
Downham Fields
Good Shepherd RC Prim Sch
Rangefield Prim Sch
Lewisham Coll Downham Branch
Downham
Lewisham Coll
Worsley Bridge
Bellingham
St Augustine's RC Prim Sch
Sedgehill Sch
Sports Gd
Burnt Ash Jun Sch
Shaftesbury Park
Cemy
Crem
Beckenham Place
Beckenham Place Park
Golf Course
Ravensbourne Sta
St Mary's RC Prim Sch
Worsley Bridge Jun Sch
Sports Gds
Ravensbourne River
Pool River
BROWNHILL RD
ST MILDREDS RD
BROMLEY RD
BROMLEY HILL
BECKENHAM HILL RD
SOUTHEND LA
SOUTHEND RD
WHITEFOOT LA
LONDON RD
CATFORD HILL
STANSTEAD RD
RUSHEY GN
PLASSY RD
1 EDINBURGH CT
2 McMILLAN CT
3 ROWALLAN CT
4 MERIDIAN CT
5 BRAEMAR CT
6 BARROW CT
7 BLAIR CT
8 DARLINGTON CT
9 HAMILTON CT
10 INVERNESS CT
11 OAK COTTAGE CL
12 WILLOW CL
4 NEWNHAM HOUSE
5 WHITCHURCH HOUSE
6 DEDHAM HOUSE
7 FLATFORD HOUSE
ALLERFORD CT 1
DURNFORD HOUSE 2
DUNSTER HOUSE 3
RADLEY CT 1
LANGTHORNE CT 2
HOOVER HOUSE 3
BRUNNER HOUSE 4
WATERER HOUSE 5
MARRIOTT HOUSE 6
BOURBON HOUSE 7
LONGFORD HOUSE 1
INGREBOURNE HOUSE 2
BRENT HOUSE 3
DARENT HOUSE 4
BEVERLEY HOUSE 5
WANDLE HOUSE 6
RYTHE HOUSE 7
EMBER HOUSE 8
CRANE HOUSE 9
RAVENSBOURNE HOUSE 10
1 WARNER HOUSE
2 CLIFFORD HOUSE
3 LLOYD HOUSE
4 THURSTON HOUSE
5 BYRON HOUSE
6 BLAKE HOUSE
7 KEATS HOUSE
STEVENS CL 1
STEVENS CT 2
1 GROVEHILL CT
2 HILDENBOROUGH GDNS
SEYCHELLE CT 1
ROCHELLE CT 2
37 38 39
A1
1 GARDENIA CT
2 BRACKENDALE CT
3 DANIEL CT
4 MOLINER CT
5 CHARTWELL LODGE
6 RANDMORE CT
7 DOVER HOUSE
8 LUCERNE CT
9 MALLING HOUSE
10 WESTERHAM LODGE
11 BRASTED LODGE
12 MILTON HOUSE
13 BRADSOLE HOUSE
14 SANDGATE HOUSE
15 ADELAIDE CT
16 NETTLESTEAD CL
17 COPERS COPE RD
18 WARREN CT
19 ALTON CT
20 ROCKINGHAM CT
21 CAMELLIA CT
22 SINCLAIR CT
23 REGENTS CT
24 MINSHULL PL
25 SOUTH PARK CT
23
44
F1
1 HOMECOPPICE HOUSE
2 INGLEWOOD CT
3 MAVERY CT
4 GLEN CT
5 CAWSTON CT
6 HIGHLAND RD
7 MOORELAND RD

26

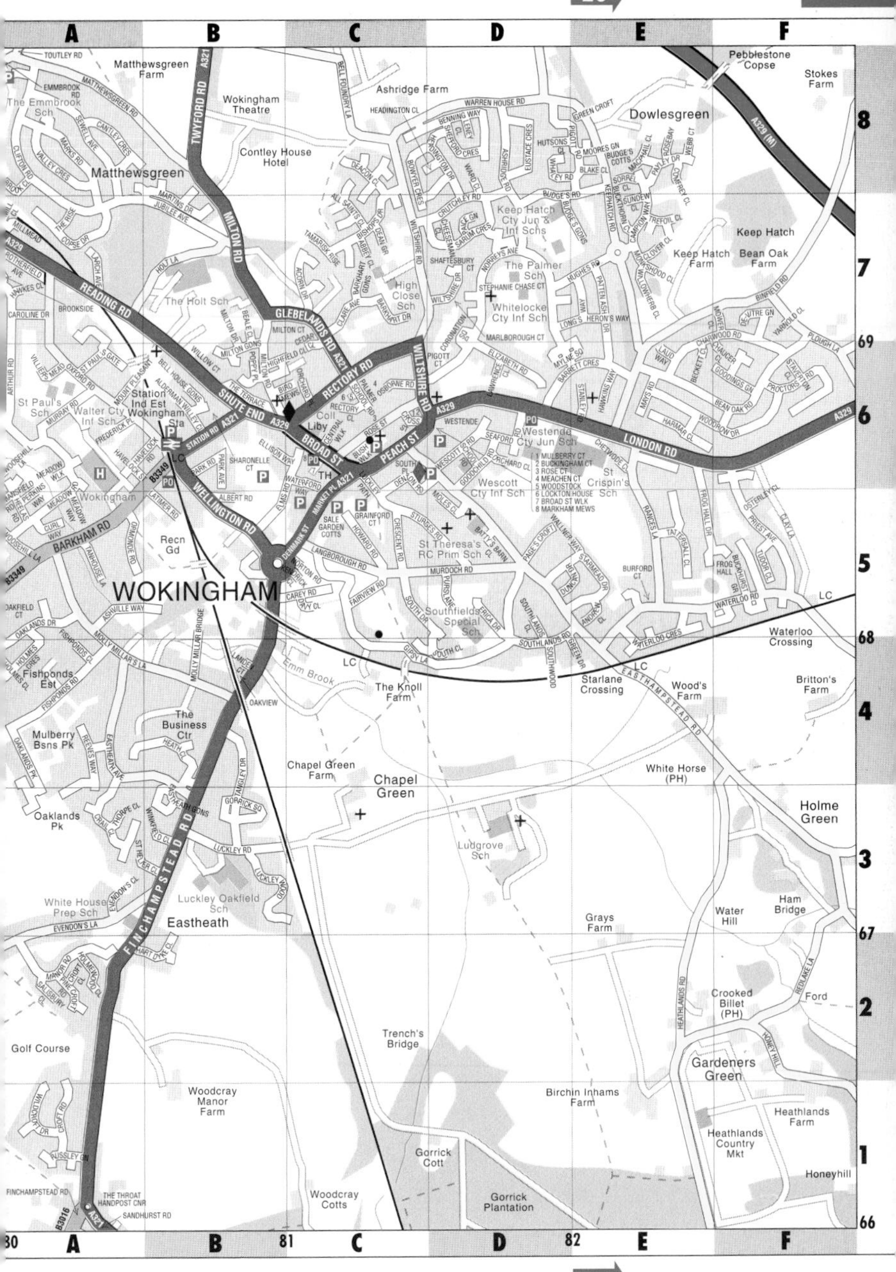

A
B
C
D
E
F
8
7
69
6
5
68
4
3
67
2
1
66
80
81
82
Matthewsgreen Farm
Ashridge Farm
Pebblestone Copse
Stokes Farm
Dowlesgreen
The Emmbrook Sch
Wokingham Theatre
Contley House Hotel
Matthewsgreen
Keep Hatch Cty Jun & Inf Schs
Keep Hatch
Keep Hatch Farm
Bean Oak Farm
The Palmer Sch
High Close Sch
The Holt Sch
Whitelocke Cty Inf Sch
Station Ind Est
Wokingham Sta
St Paul's Sch
Walter Cty Inf Sch
Coll
Liby
Westende Cty Jun Sch
St Crispin's Sch
Wescott Cty Inf Sch
TH
Recn Gd
St Theresa's RC Prim Sch
WOKINGHAM
Southfields Special Sch
Waterloo Crossing
Fishponds Est
Emm Brook
The Knoll Farm
Starlane Crossing
Wood's Farm
Britton's Farm
Mulberry Bsns Pk
The Business Ctr
Chapel Green Farm
Chapel Green
White Horse (PH)
Holme Green
Oaklands Pk
Ludgrove Sch
White House Prep Sch
Luckley Oakfield Sch
Eastheath
Grays Farm
Water Hill
Ham Bridge
Crooked Billet (PH)
Ford
Golf Course
Trench's Bridge
Gardeners Green
Woodcray Manor Farm
Birchin Inhams Farm
Heathlands Farm
Heathlands Country Mkt
Gorrick Cott
Honeyhill
Woodcray Cotts
Gorrick Plantation
TWYFORD RD
MILTON RD
READING RD
GLEBELANDS RD
RECTORY RD
WILTSHIRE RD
SHUTE END
BROAD ST
PEACH ST
LONDON RD
STATION RD
WELLINGTON RD
BARKHAM RD
FINCHAMPSTEAD RD
EASTHAMPSTEAD RD
LUCKLEY RD
MOLLY MILLAR'S LA
MURDOCH RD
WATERLOO RD
HEATHLANDS RD
REDLAKE LA
HONEY HILL
SANDHURST RD
THE THROAT
HANDPOST CNR
A329
A321
A329 (M)
B3349
B3016
LC
1 MULBERRY CT
2 BUCKINGHAM CT
3 ROSE CT
4 MEACHEN CT
5 WOODSTOCK
6 LOCKTON HOUSE
7 BROAD ST WLK
8 MARKHAM MEWS

26

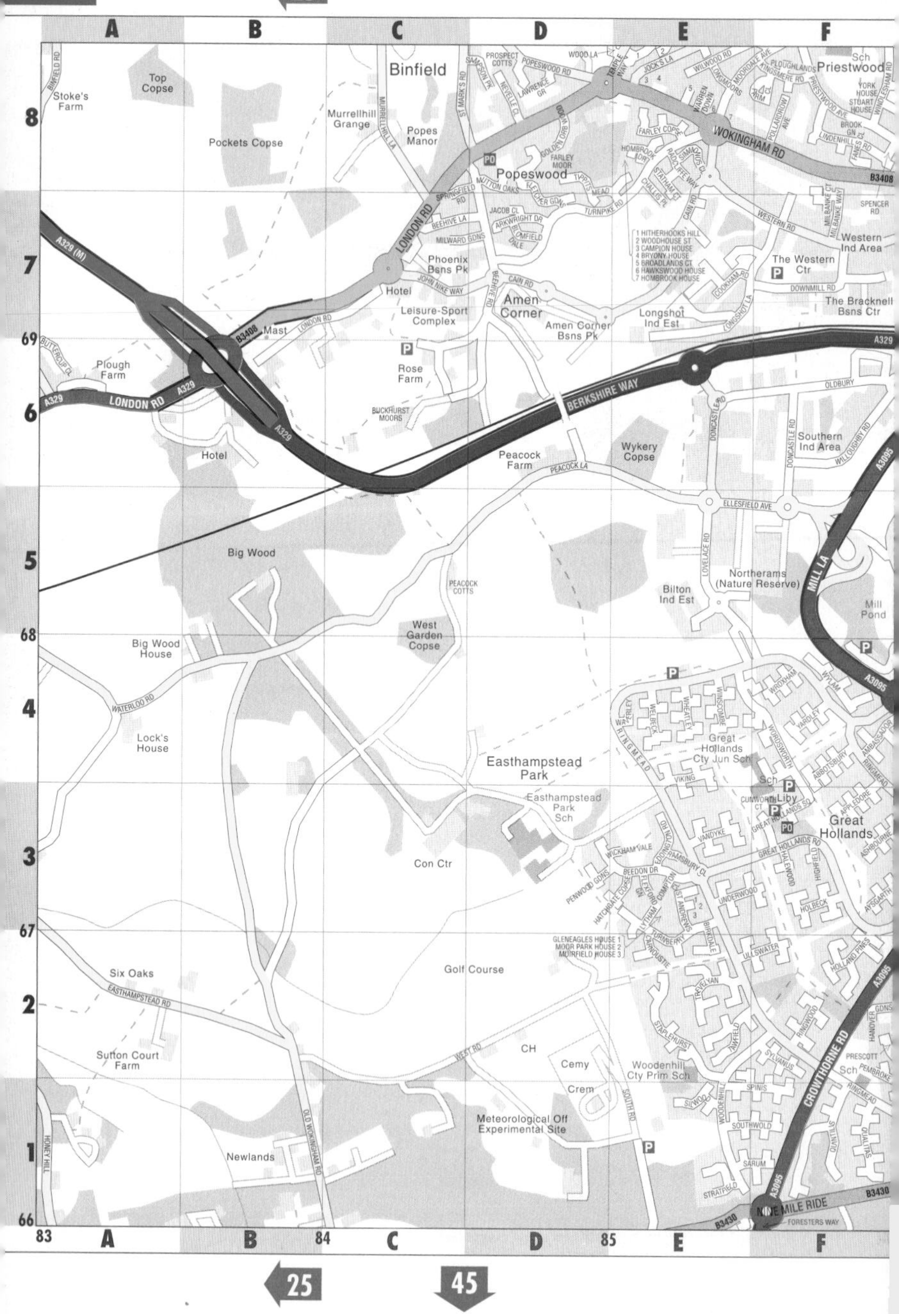

25

Binfield

A B C D E F

8

Stoke's Farm

Top Copse

Pockets Copse

Murrellhill Grange

Popes Manor

PROSPECT COTTS

POPESWOOD RD

WOOD LA

Sch
Priestwood

YORK HOUSE

WOKINGHAM RD

B3408

7

A329 (M)

LONDON RD

Mast

Phoenix Bsns Pk

Hotel

Leisure-Sport Complex

Amen Corner

Popeswood

FARLEY COPSE

HOMBROOK

1 HITHERHOOKS HILL
2 WOODHOUSE ST
3 CAMPION HOUSE
4 BRYONY HOUSE
5 BROADLANDS CT
6 HAWKSWOOD HOUSE
7 HOMBROOK HOUSE

WESTERN RD

The Western Ctr

SPENCER RD

Western Ind Area

The Bracknell Bsns Ctr

69

B3408

Plough Farm

Rose Farm

Amen Corner Bsns Pk

Longshot Ind Est

DOWNMILL RD

A329

OLDBURY

6

A329

LONDON RD

A329

Hotel

BUCKHURST MOORS

BERKSHIRE WAY

Peacock Farm

PEACOCK LA

Wykery Copse

ELLESFIELD AVE

Southern Ind Area

A3095

5

Big Wood

PEACOCK COTTS

Bilton Ind Est

Northerams (Nature Reserve)

MILL LA

Mill Pond

68

Big Wood House

WATERLOO RD

West Garden Copse

4

Lock's House

Easthampstead Park

Easthampstead Park Sch

Great Hollands Cty Jun Sch

Sch

Liby

Great Hollands

PO

3

Con Ctr

WICKHAM VALE

BEEDON DR

GREAT HOLLANDS RD

67

Six Oaks

EASTHAMPSTEAD RD

Golf Course

GLENEAGLES HOUSE 1
MOOR PARK HOUSE 2
MORFIELD HOUSE 3

ULLSWATER

2

Sutton Court Farm

WEST RD

CH

Cemy

Crem

Woodenhill Cty Prim Sch

CROWTHORNE RD

Sch

PRESCOTT

PEMBROKE

1

HONEY HILL

OLD WOKINGHAM RD

Newlands

SOUTH RD

Meteorological Off Experimental Site

SARUM

STRATFIELD

THREE MILE RIDE

B3430

FORESTERS WAY

66

83 A B 84 C D 85 E F

25

45

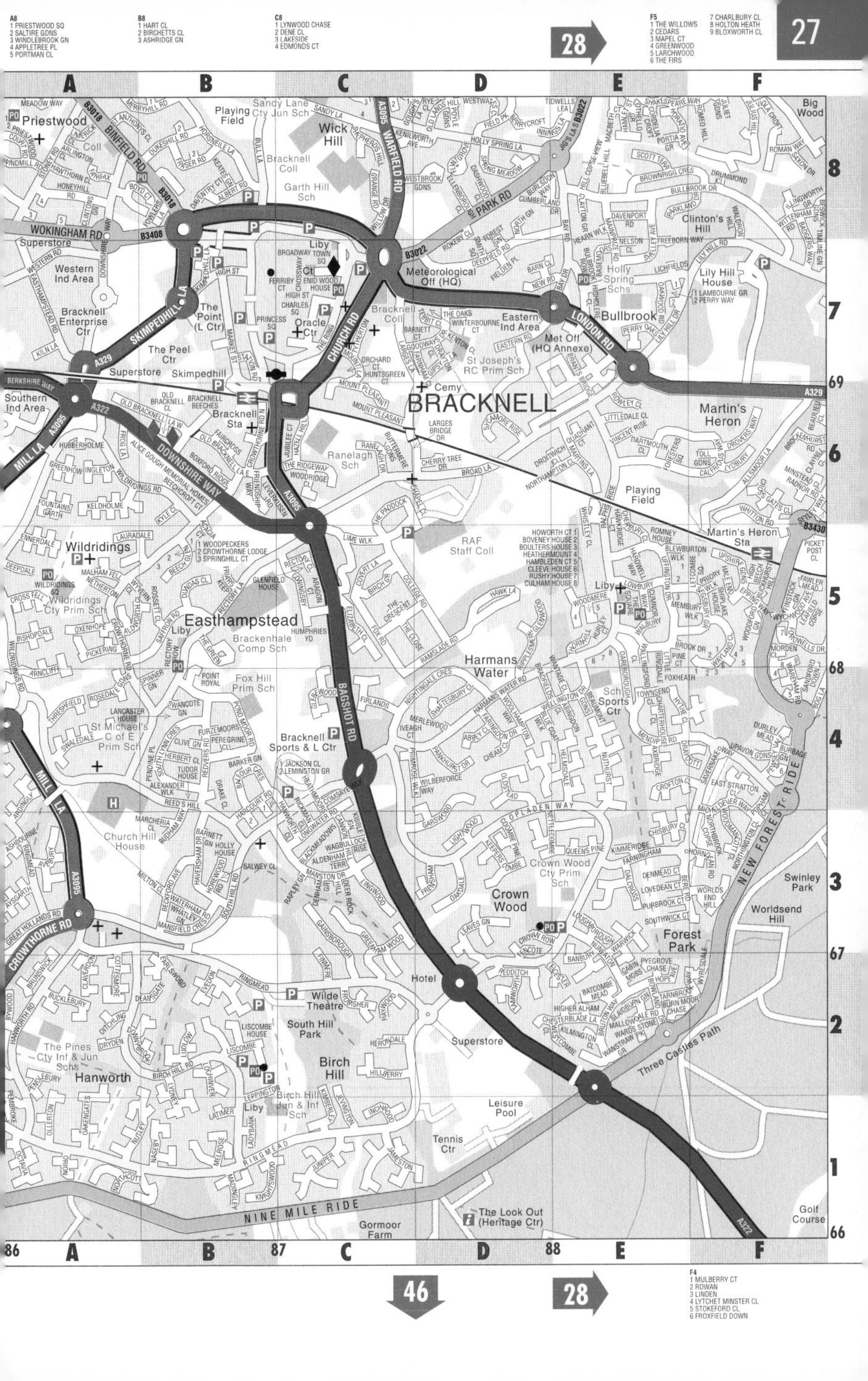
A8
1 PRIESTWOOD SQ
2 SALTIRE GDNS
3 WINDLEBROOK GN
4 APPLETREE PL
5 PORTMAN CL
B8
1 HART CL
2 BIRCHETTS CL
3 ASHRIDGE GN
C8
1 LYNWOOD CHASE
2 DENE CL
3 LAKESIDE
4 EDMONDS CT
28
F5
1 THE WILLOWS
2 CEDARS
3 MAPEL CT
4 GREENWOOD
5 LARCHWOOD
6 THE FIRS
7 CHARLBURY CL
8 HOLTON HEATH
9 BLOXWORTH CL
A
B
C
D
E
F
Priestwood
Playing Field
Sandy Lane Cty Jun Sch
Wick Hill
Bracknell Coll
Garth Hill Sch
Big Wood
WARFIELD RD
BINFIELD RD
WOKINGHAM RD
Superstore
Western Ind Area
Bracknell Enterprise Ctr
SKIMPEDHILL LA
The Point (L Ctr)
The Peel Ctr
Liby
Oracle Ctr
CHURCH RD
Meteorological Off (HQ)
PARK RD
Clinton's Hill
Lily Hill House
Holly Spring Schs
Bullbrook
LONDON RD
Eastern Ind Area
Met Off (HQ Annexe)
St Joseph's RC Prim Sch
Cemy
BRACKNELL
Bracknell Sta
Southern Ind Area
DOWNSHIRE WAY
MILL LA
Ranelagh Sch
Martin's Heron
Playing Field
Martin's Heron Sta
RAF Staff Coll
Wildridings
Wildridings Cty Prim Sch
Easthampstead
Brackenhale Comp Sch
Harmans Water
Fox Hill Prim Sch
Sch Sports Ctr
St Michael's C of E Prim Sch
Bracknell Sports & L Ctr
BAGSHOT RD
Church Hill House
Crown Wood Cty Prim Sch
Crown Wood
NEW FOREST RIDE
Swinley Park
Worldsend Hill
Forest Park
CROWTHORNE RD
Wilde Theatre
South Hill Park
Hotel
Superstore
Three Castles Path
The Pines Cty Inf & Jun Schs
Hanworth
Birch Hill
Birch Hill Jun & Inf Sch
Leisure Pool
Tennis Ctr
NINE MILE RIDE
Gormoor Farm
The Look Out (Heritage Ctr)
Golf Course
8
7
69
6
5
68
4
3
67
2
1
66
86
87
88
46
28
F4
1 MULBERRY CT
2 ROWAN
3 LINDEN
4 LYTCHET MINSTER CL
5 STOKEFORD CL
6 FROXFIELD DOWN

27
8

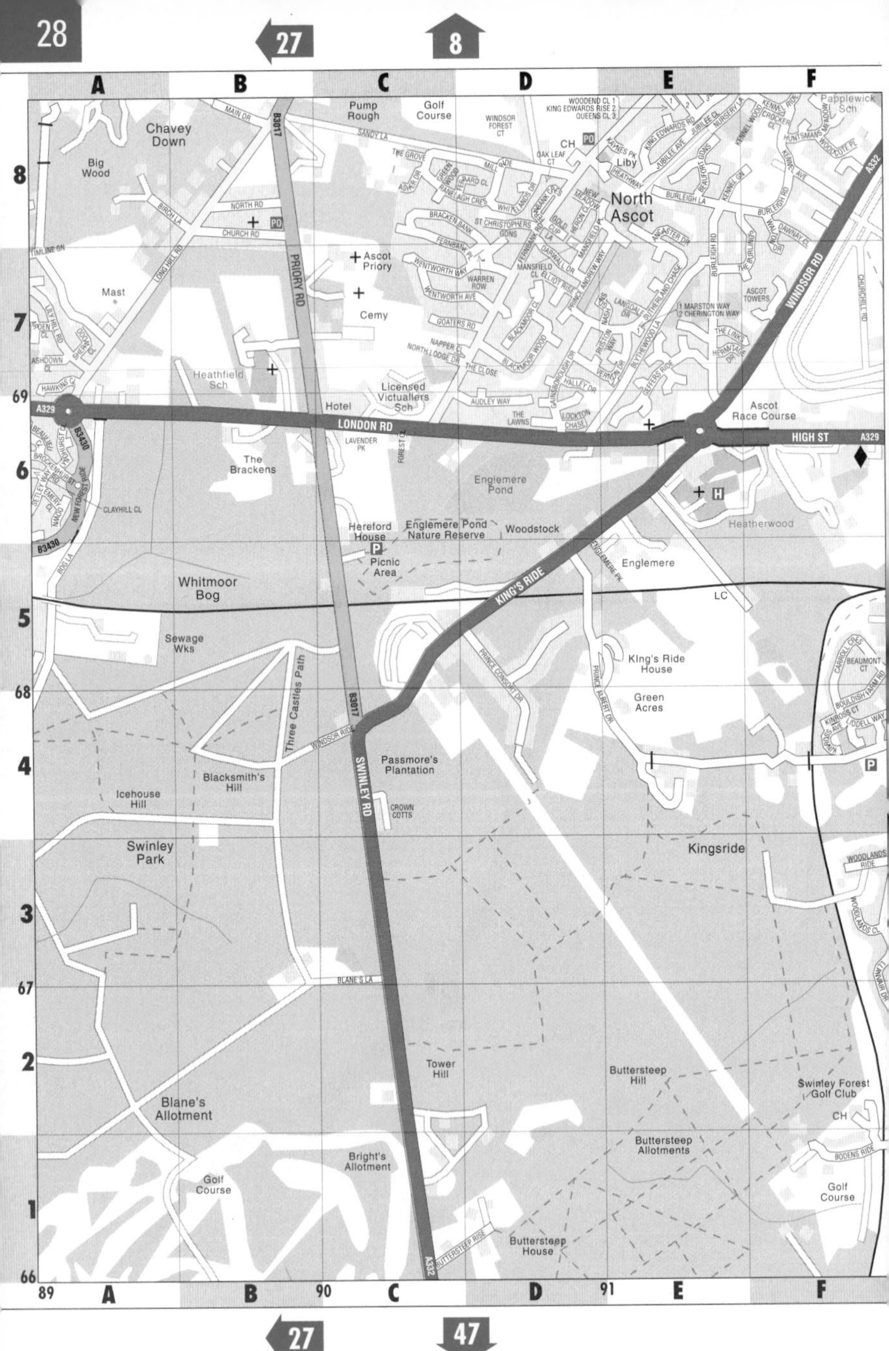
Chavey Down
Big Wood
Pump Rough
Golf Course
North Ascot
Ascot Priory
Cemy
Mast
Heathfield Sch
Licensed Victuallers Sch
Hotel
The Brackens
Englemere Pond
Hereford House
Englemere Pond Nature Reserve
Woodstock
Picnic Area
Englemere
Heatherwood
Ascot Race Course
Whitmoor Bog
Sewage Wks
King's Ride House
Green Acres
Passmore's Plantation
Blacksmith's Hill
Icehouse Hill
Swinley Park
Kingsride
Tower Hill
Buttersteep Hill
Blane's Allotment
Buttersteep Allotments
Bright's Allotment
Golf Course
Buttersteep House
Swinley Forest Golf Club
Papplewick Sch
LONDON RD
PRIORY RD
SWINLEY RD
KING'S RIDE
WINDSOR RD
HIGH ST
Three Castles Path
A329
A332
B3017
B3430
LC

27
47

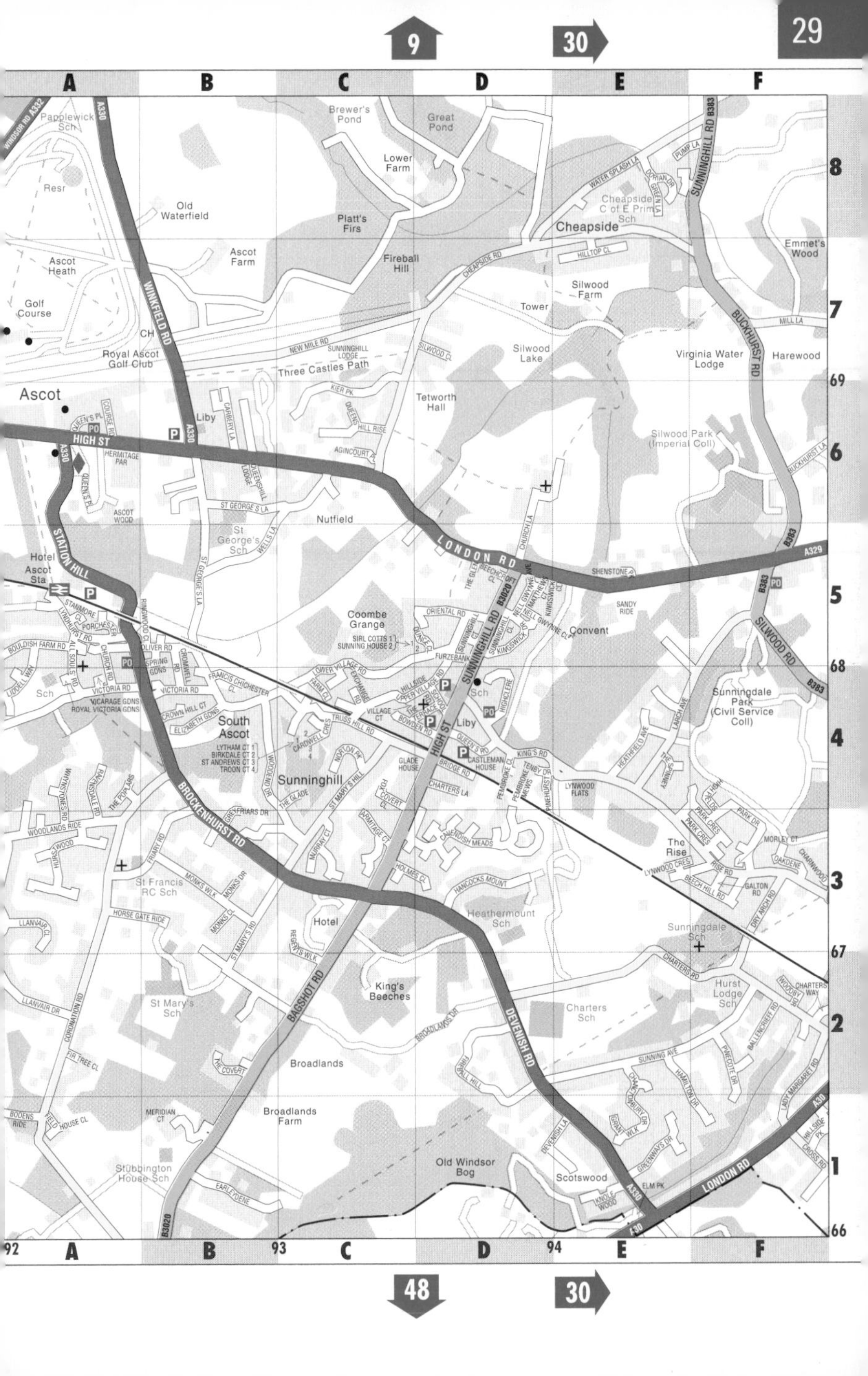
9
30
A
B
C
D
E
F
Papplewick Sch
Resr
Old Waterfield
Ascot Heath
Golf Course
Ascot Farm
Royal Ascot Golf Club
Ascot
Brewer's Pond
Great Pond
Lower Farm
Platt's Firs
Fireball Hill
Cheapside
Cheapside C of E Prim Sch
Silwood Farm
Tower
Silwood Lake
Three Castles Path
Tetworth Hall
Virginia Water Lodge
Harewood
Emmet's Wood
Silwood Park (Imperial Coll)
WINKFIELD RD
HIGH ST
LONDON RD
STATION HILL
Nutfield
St George's Sch
Hotel
Ascot Sta
Coombe Grange
Convent
Sunningdale Park (Civil Service Coll)
South Ascot
Sunninghill
SUNNINGHILL RD
BROCKENHURST RD
The Rise
St Francis RC Sch
Heathermount Sch
Sunningdale Sch
Hotel
King's Beeches
Hurst Lodge Sch
Charters Sch
St Mary's Sch
BAGSHOT RD
DEVENISH RD
Broadlands
Broadlands Farm
Old Windsor Bog
Scotswood
Stubbington House Sch
BUCKHURST RD
SILWOOD RD
92
93
94
66
67
68
69
1
2
3
4
5
6
7
8
48
30

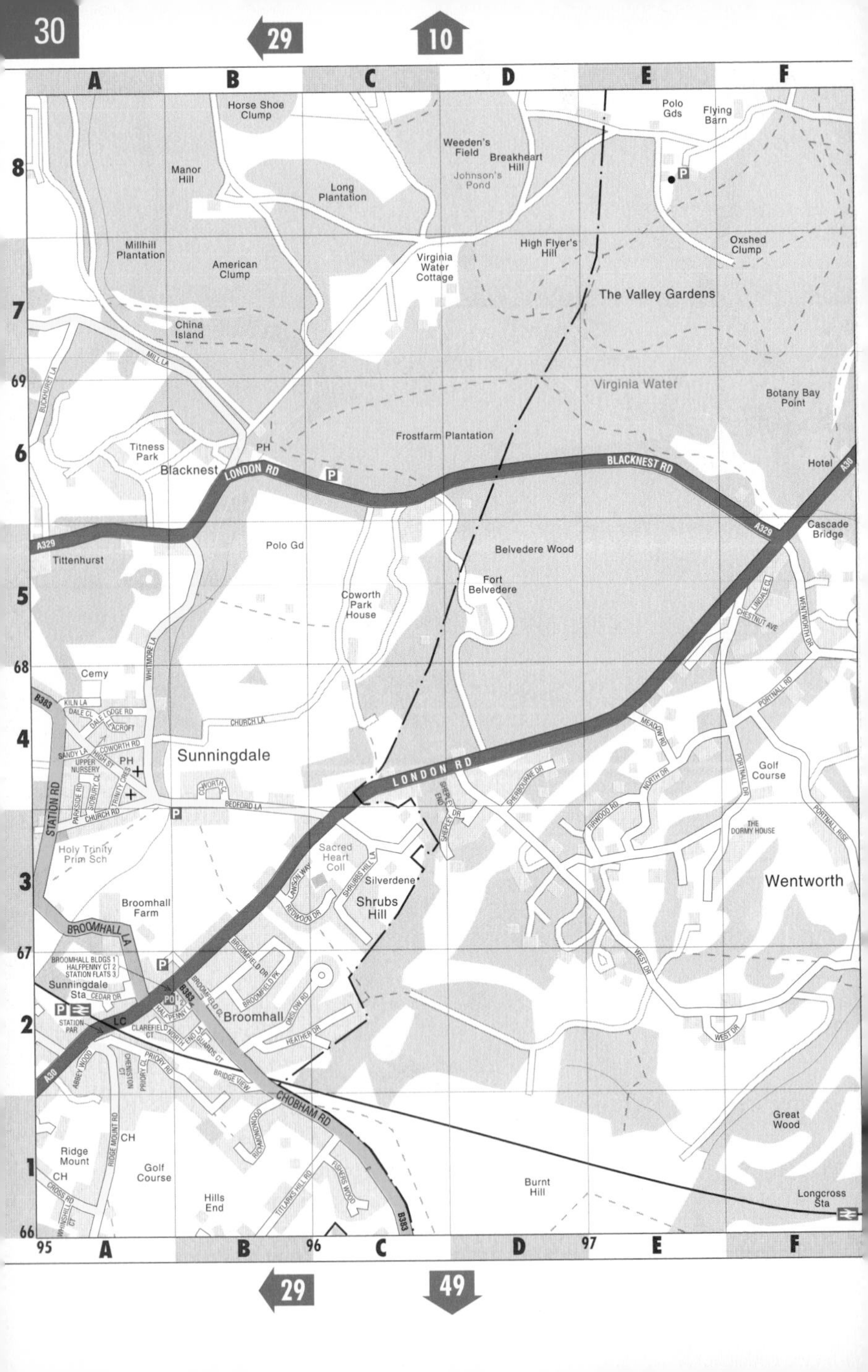
29
10
A
B
C
D
E
F
Horse Shoe Clump
Polo Gds
Flying Barn
Weeden's Field
Breakheart Hill
Johnson's Pond
Manor Hill
Long Plantation
Millhill Plantation
American Clump
Virginia Water Cottage
High Flyer's Hill
Oxshed Clump
The Valley Gardens
China Island
MILL LA
BUCKHURST LA
Virginia Water
Botany Bay Point
Titness Park
PH
Frostfarm Plantation
Blacknest
LONDON RD
BLACKNEST RD
Hotel
A30
A329
Tittenhurst
Polo Gd
Belvedere Wood
Cascade Bridge
Fort Belvedere
Coworth Park House
LINDALE CL
CHESTNUT AVE
WENTWORTH DR
WHITMORE LA
Cemy
PORTNALL RD
KILN LA
DALE CL
LODGE RD
ACROFT
B383
CHURCH LA
MEADOW RD
COWORTH RD
SANDY LA
HIGH ST
Sunningdale
UPPER NURSERY
SIDBURY CL
TRINITY CRES
PARKSIDE RD
CHURCH RD
COWORTH CL
BEDFORD LA
LONDON RD
SHERBOURNE DR
NORTH DR
PORTNALL DR
Golf Course
SHEPLEY END
SHEPLEY DR
FIRWOOD RD
THE DORMY HOUSE
PORTNALL RISE
STATION RD
Holy Trinity Prim Sch
Sacred Heart Coll
LAWSON WAY
SHRUBS HILL LA
Silverdene
Shrubs Hill
Wentworth
Broomhall Farm
REDWOOD DR
BROOMHALL LA
BROOMFIELD DR
BROOMFIELD PK
WEST DR
BROOMHALL BLDGS 1
HALFPENNY CT 2
STATION FLATS 3
Sunningdale Sta
CEDAR DR
ONSLOW RD
BROOMFIELD CL
PO
HALFPENNY LA
Broomhall
LC
STATION PAR
CLAREFIELD CT
NORTH END LA
HEATHER DR
GUARDS CT
WEST DR
ABBEY WOOD
CHENISTON CT
PRIORY RD
PRIORY CL
BRIDGE VIEW
CHOBHAM RD
RIDGE MOUNT RD
RICHMONDWOOD
CH
Great Wood
Ridge Mount
Golf Course
TITLARKS HILL RD
FISHERS WOOD
Burnt Hill
Longcross Sta
Hills End
WHINSHILL CT
CROSS RD
8
7
69
6
5
68
4
3
67
2
1
66
95
96
97
49

11
32

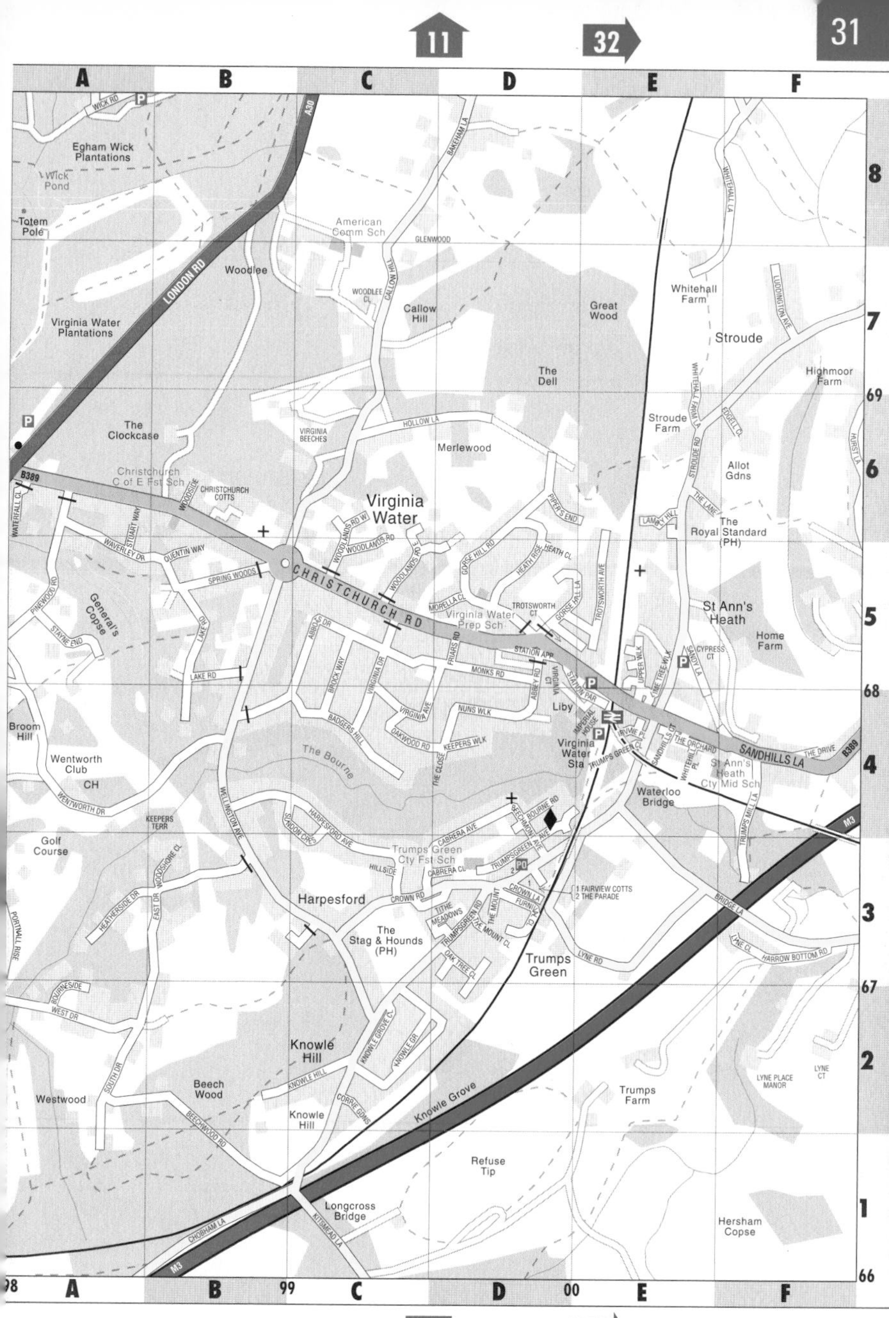
A
B
C
D
E
F
8
7
69
6
5
68
4
3
67
2
1
66
98
99
00
WICK RD
Egham Wick Plantations
Wick Pond
Totem Pole
A30
LONDON RD
Woodlee
Virginia Water Plantations
American Comm Sch
GLENWOOD
WOODLEE CL
CALLOW HILL
BAKEHAM LA
Callow Hill
Great Wood
WHITEHALL LA
Whitehall Farm
LUDDINGTON AVE
Stroude
Highmoor Farm
The Dell
The Clockcase
VIRGINIA BEECHES
HOLLOW LA
Merlewood
Stroude Farm
WHITEHALL FARM LA
EDGELL CL
STROUDE RD
HURST LA
Allot Gdns
B389
WATERFALL CL
Christchurch C of E Fst Sch
WOODSIDE
CHRISTCHURCH COTTS
Virginia Water
PIPER'S END
LAMBLY HILL
THE LANE
The Royal Standard (PH)
STUART WAY
WAVERLEY DR
QUENTIN WAY
WOODLANDS RD W
WOODLANDS RD
WOODLANDS RD E
GORSE HILL RD
HEATH RISE
HEATH CL
TROTSWORTH AVE
SPRING WOODS
CHRISTCHURCH RD
PINEWOOD RD
General's Copse
STAYNE END
LAKE RD
MORELLA CL
Virginia Water Prep Sch
TROTSWORTH CT
GORSE HILL LA
St Ann's Heath
Home Farm
ABBOTS DR
BROCK WAY
VIRGINIA DR
FRIARS RD
STATION APP
MONKS RD
VIRGINIA CT
STATION PAR
UPPER WLK
LIME TREE WLK
CYPRESS CT
SANDY LA
Broom Hill
Liby
BADGERS HILL
VIRGINIA AVE
NUNS WLK
ABBEY RD
IMPERIAL HOUSE
IVY PL
SANDHILLS CT
THE ORCHARD
SANDHILLS LA
THE DRIVE
Wentworth Club
CH
OAKWOOD RD
KEEPERS WLK
Virginia Water Sta
TRUMPS GREEN CL
WHITEHILL PL
St Ann's Heath Cty Mid Sch
The Bourne
THE CLOSE
WENTWORTH DR
WELLINGTON AVE
KEEPERS TERR
SANDON CRES
HARPESFORD AVE
CABRERA AVE
BOURNE RD
BEECHMONT AVE
Waterloo Bridge
TRUMPS MILL LA
M3
Golf Course
WOODSHORE CL
Trumps Green Cty Fst Sch
HILLSIDE
CABRERA CL
TRUMPSGREEN AVE
PO
1 FAIRVIEW COTTS
2 THE PARADE
CROWN LA
FURNIVAL CL
PORTNALL RISE
HEATHERSIDE DR
EAST DR
Harpesford
CROWN RD
TITHE MEADOWS
TRUMPSGREEN RD
THE MOUNT
THE MOUNT CL
BRIDGE LA
The Stag & Hounds (PH)
OAK TREE CL
Trumps Green
LYNE RD
LYNE CL
HARROW BOTTOM RD
BOURNESIDE
WEST DR
KNOWLE GROVE CL
KNOWLE GR
Knowle Hill
LYNE PLACE MANOR
LYNE CT
SOUTH DR
Beech Wood
KNOWLE HILL
Knowle Grove
Trumps Farm
Westwood
CORRIE GDNS
Knowle Hill
BEECHWOOD RD
Refuse Tip
Longcross Bridge
KITSMEAD LA
Hersham Copse
CHOBHAM LA

50
32

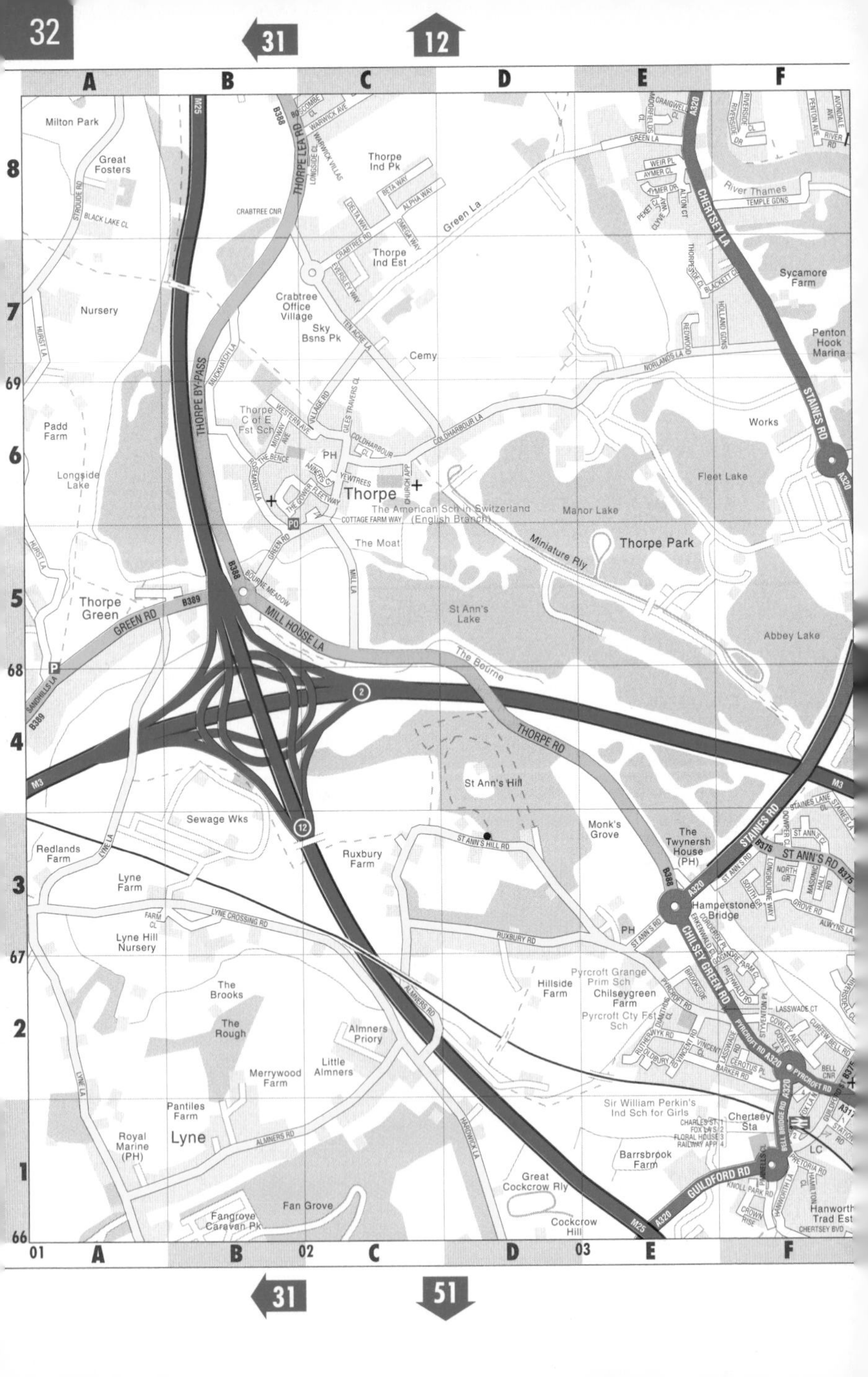
32
31
12
A
B
C
D
E
F
8
7
69
6
5
68
4
3
67
2
1
66
01
02
03
Milton Park
Great Fosters
STROUDE RD
BLACK LAKE CL
M25
B388
THORPE LEA RD
LONGSIDE CL
WARWICK AVE
WARWICK VILLAS
Thorpe Ind Pk
BETA WAY
ALPHA WAY
DELTA WAY
OMEGA WAY
CRABTREE CNR
CRABTREE RD
Thorpe Ind Est
EVERSLEY RD
EVERSLEY WAY
Green La
GREEN LA
CRAIGWELL CL
MOORFIELDS CL
A320
RIVERSIDE
RIVERSIDE DR
PENTON AVE
AVONDALE AVE
RIVER RD
WEIR PL
AYMER CL
AYMER DR
PEKET CL
ALTON CT
River Thames
TEMPLE GDNS
CHERTSEY LA
THORPESIDE CL
BLACKETT CL
HOLLAND GDNS
REDWOOD
Sycamore Farm
Penton Hook Marina
Nursery
HURST LA
Crabtree Office Village
Sky Bsns Pk
TEN ACRE LA
Cemy
NORLANDS LA
MUCKHATCH LA
THORPE BY-PASS
Thorpe C of E Fst Sch
WESTERN AVE
VILLAGE RD
GILES TRAVERS CL
MIDWAY AVE
THE BENCE
ROSEMARY LA
COLDHARBOUR LA
COLDHARBOUR CL
PH
CHURCH APP
YEWTREES
THE GOWER
FLEETWAY
Thorpe
PO
COTTAGE FARM WAY
The American Sch in Switzerland (English Branch)
GREEN RD
The Moat
MILL LA
Padd Farm
Longside Lake
Works
STAINES RD
Fleet Lake
Manor Lake
Thorpe Park
Miniature Rly
St Ann's Lake
Abbey Lake
Thorpe Green
B389
GREEN RD
BOURNE MEADOW
MILL HOUSE LA
The Bourne
P
SANDHILLS LA
2
M3
THORPE RD
St Ann's Hill
Sewage Wks
12
Redlands Farm
LYNE LA
Ruxbury Farm
ST ANN'S HILL RD
Monk's Grove
The Twynersh House (PH)
STAINES LANE CL
COWPER CL
ST ANN'S CL
B375
ST ANN'S RD
NORTH GR
MASONIC HALL RD
SOUTH GR
LONGBOURNE WAY
GROVE RD
ALWYNS LA
Lyne Farm
FARM CL
LYNE CROSSING RD
Hamperstone Bridge
Lyne Hill Nursery
RUXBURY RD
PH
CHILSEY GREEN RD
The Brooks
Hillside Farm
Pyrcroft Grange Prim Sch
Chilseygreen Farm
Pyrcroft Cty Fst Sch
PYRCROFT RD
BROOKSIDE
LASSWADE CT
COWLEY AVE
CURFEW BELL RD
The Rough
ALMNERS RD
Almners Priory
Little Almners
Merrywood Farm
VINCENT RD
VINCENT CL
LASSWADE RD
CEROTUS PL
BARKER RD
OLDBURY RD
BELL CNR
Pantiles Farm
Sir William Perkin's Ind Sch for Girls
CHARLES ST 1
FOX LA S 2
FLORAL HOUSE 3
RAILWAY APP 4
Chertsey Sta
BELL BRIDGE RD
GUILDFORD ST
Royal Marine (PH)
Lyne
HARDWICK LA
Barrsbrook Farm
LC
PRETORIA RD
GUILDFORD RD
KNOLL PARK RD
HANWORTH LA
HAMILTON CL
Great Cockcrow Rly
Fan Grove
Fangrove Caravan Pk
Cockcrow Hill
M25
CROWN RISE
Hanworth Trad Est
CHERTSEY BVD
31
51

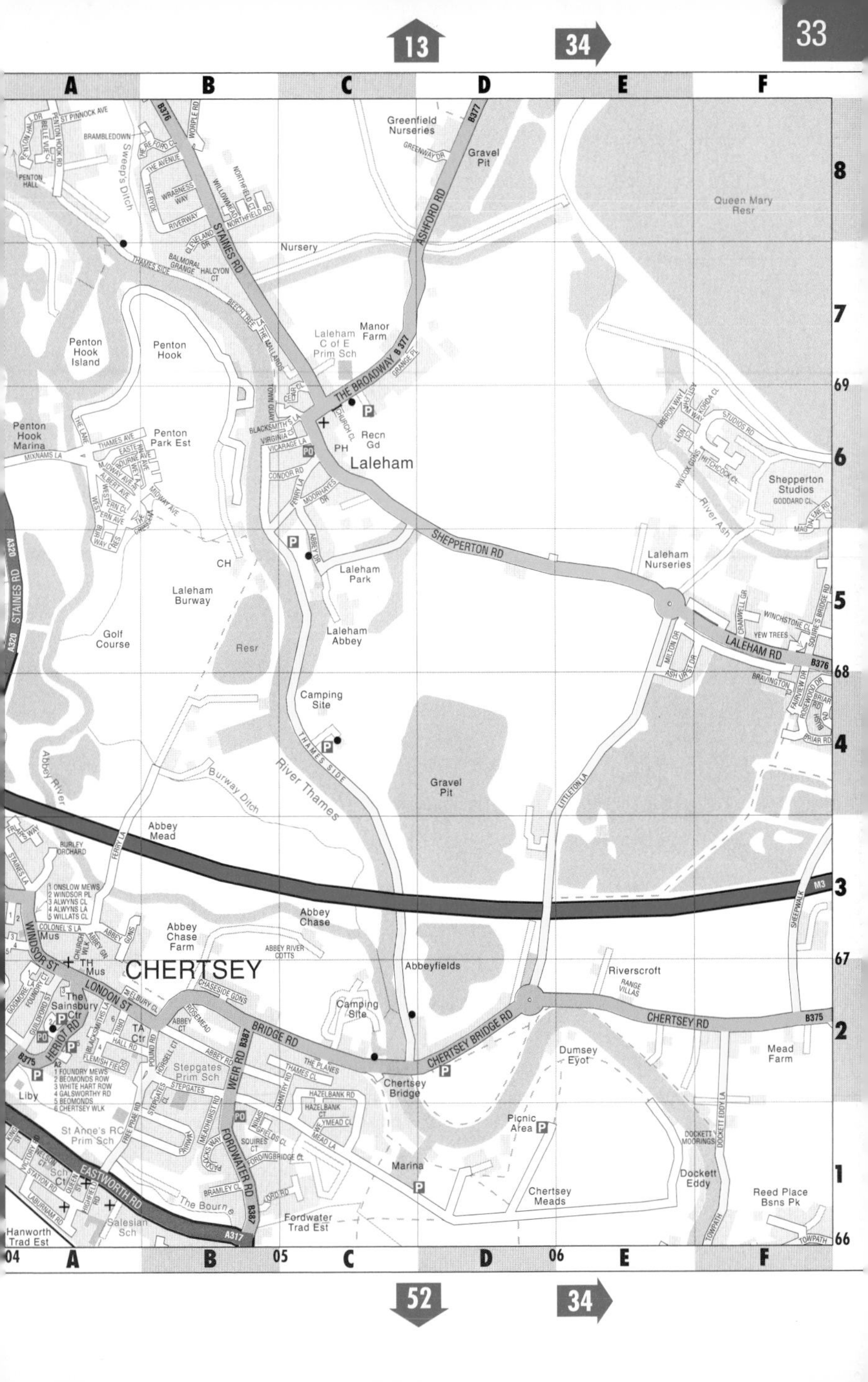

13
34
A
B
C
D
E
F
8
7
69
6
5
68
4
3
67
2
1
66
04
05
06
Greenfield Nurseries
Gravel Pit
Queen Mary Resr
Nursery
Sweep's Ditch
STAINES RD
ASHFORD RD
B376
B377
Penton Hook Island
Penton Hook
Laleham C of E Prim Sch
Manor Farm
THE BROADWAY
Penton Hook Marina
Penton Park Est
Recn Gd
PH
Laleham
SHEPPERTON RD
Shepperton Studios
River Ash
Laleham Nurseries
CH
Laleham Burway
Laleham Park
Golf Course
Resr
Laleham Abbey
LALEHAM RD
Camping Site
Gravel Pit
River Thames
THAMES SIDE
Burway Ditch
Abbey River
Abbey Mead
FERRY LA
LITTLETON LA
M3
Abbey Chase
Abbey Chase Farm
CHERTSEY
Abbeyfields
Riverscroft
CHERTSEY RD
B375
Camping Site
CHERTSEY BRIDGE RD
BRIDGE RD
LONDON ST
WINDSOR ST
Mus
TH
The Sainsbury Ctr
TA Ctr
Stepgates Prim Sch
WEIR RD
B387
Dumsey Eyot
Mead Farm
Chertsey Bridge
Liby
St Anne's RC Prim Sch
Picnic Area
Dockett Eddy
Marina
Chertsey Meads
Reed Place Bsns Pk
EASTWORTH RD
A317
FORDWATER RD
The Bourne
Salesian Sch
Fordwater Trad Est
Hanworth Trad Est
A320
52
34

33
14

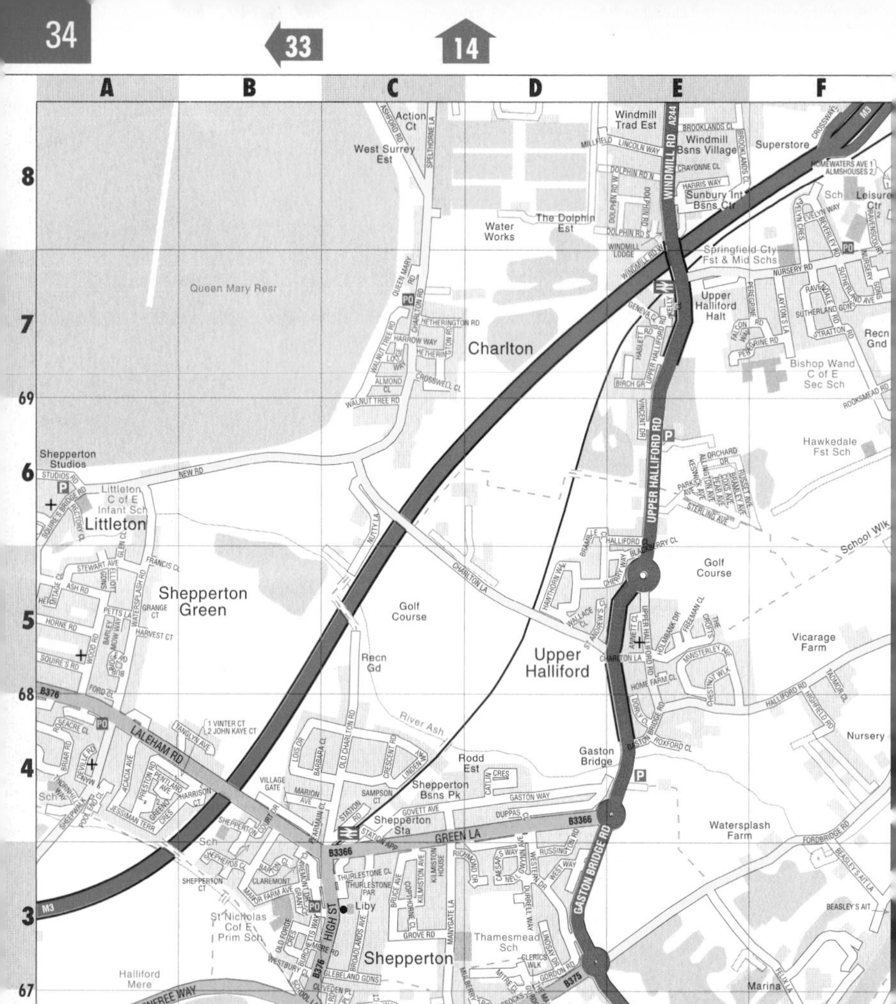
A
B
C
D
E
F
8
7
69
6
5
68
4
3
67
2
1
66
07
08
09
Action Ct
West Surrey Est
Windmill Trad Est
Windmill Bsns Village
Superstore
Sunbury Int Bsns Ctr
The Dolphin Est
Water Works
Queen Mary Resr
Springfield Cty Fst & Mid Schs
Upper Halliford Halt
Charlton
Bishop Wand C of E Sec Sch
Recn Gnd
Leisure Ctr
Sch
Hawkedale Fst Sch
Shepperton Studios
Littleton C of E Infant Sch
Littleton
Shepperton Green
Golf Course
Recn Gd
Upper Halliford
Vicarage Farm
School Wlk
River Ash
Rodd Est
Gaston Bridge
Shepperton Bsns Pk
Shepperton Sta
Nursery
Watersplash Farm
St Nicholas C of E Prim Sch
Liby
Thamesmead Sch
Shepperton
Halliford Mere
Halliford Sch
Lower Halliford
Marina
Gravel Pit
Cemy
Las Palmas Est
Playing Field
Desborough Island
PH
Walton Bridge
Thames Meadow
Desborough Sailing Club
River Thames
Works
Engine River
Desborough Channel
Ferry Wks
M3
A244
B376
B3366
B375
A3050
WINDMILL RD
UPPER HALLIFORD RD
GASTON BRIDGE RD
WALTON BRIDGE RD
OATLANDS DR
NEW ZEALAND AVE
LALEHAM RD
GREEN LA
HIGH ST
RUSSELL RD
RENFREE WAY
WALTON LA
CHARLTON LA
NEW RD
GASTON WAY
NURSERY RD
HALLIFORD RD
FORDBRIDGE RD
BRIDGE ST
HEPWORTH WAY

33
53

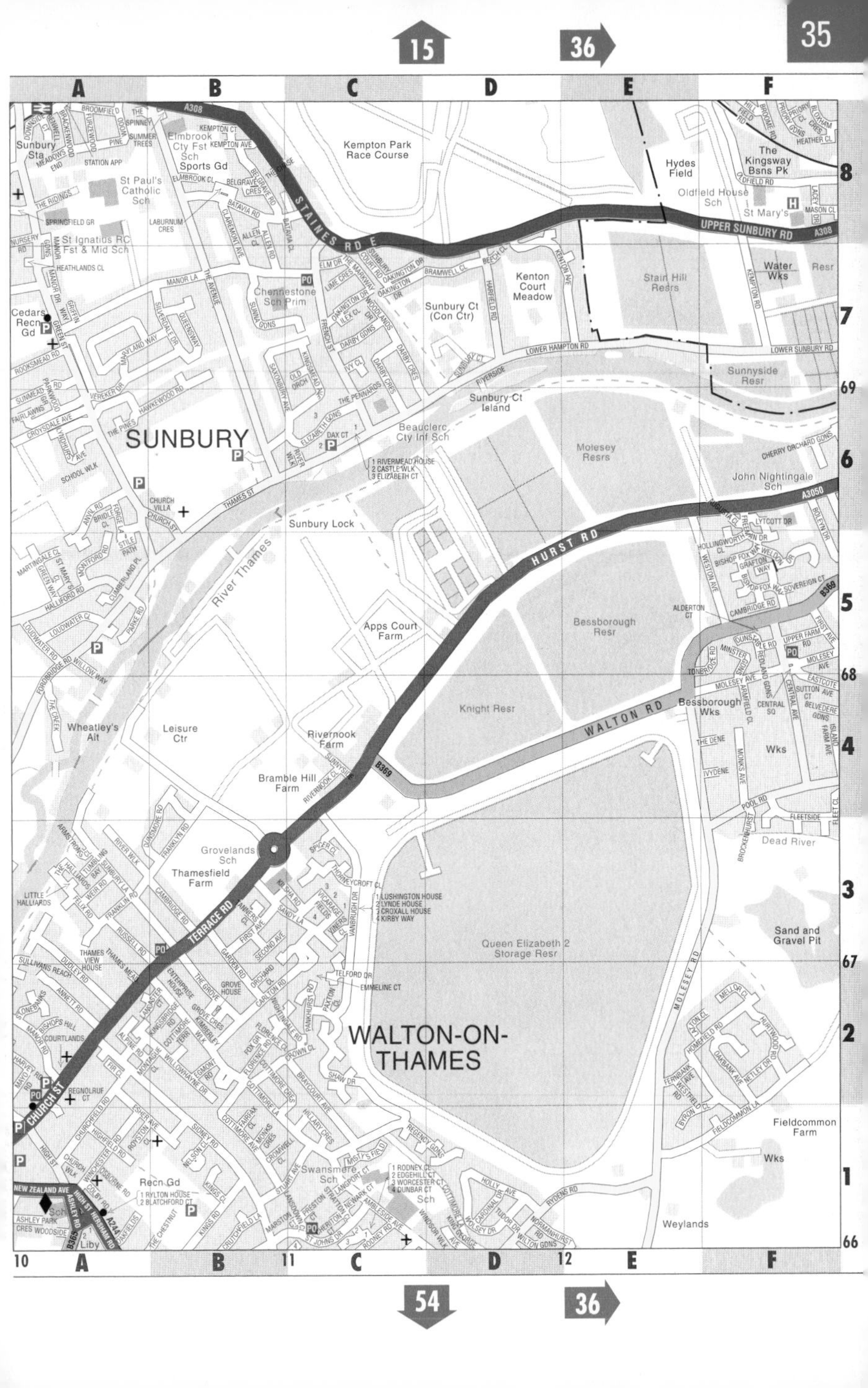
15
36
A
B
C
D
E
F
8
7
69
6
5
68
4
3
67
2
1
66
10
11
12
Sunbury Sta
Elmbrook Cty Fst Sch
Sports Gd
St Paul's Catholic Sch
St Ignatius RC Fst & Mid Sch
Kempton Park Race Course
Hydes Field
The Kingsway Bsns Pk
Oldfield House Sch
St Mary's
UPPER SUNBURY RD
A308
STAINES RD E
Stain Hill Resrs
Water Wks
Resr
Kenton Court Meadow
Sunbury Ct (Con Ctr)
Chennestone Sch Prim
Cedars Recn Gd
LOWER HAMPTON RD
LOWER SUNBURY RD
Sunnyside Resr
Sunbury Ct Island
Beauclerc Cty Inf Sch
SUNBURY
Molesey Resrs
1 RIVERMEAD HOUSE
2 CASTLE WLK
3 ELIZABETH CT
John Nightingale Sch
A3050
THAMES ST
Sunbury Lock
HURST RD
River Thames
Bessborough Resr
Apps Court Farm
B369
Knight Resr
WALTON RD
Bessborough Wks
Wheatley's Ait
Leisure Ctr
Rivernook Farm
Bramble Hill Farm
Wks
Dead River
Grovelands Sch
Thamesfield Farm
TERRACE RD
1 LUSHINGTON HOUSE
2 LYNDE HOUSE
3 CROXALL HOUSE
4 KIRBY WAY
Sand and Gravel Pit
Queen Elizabeth 2 Storage Resr
MOLESEY RD
WALTON-ON-THAMES
CHURCH ST
Fieldcommon Farm
Swansmere Sch
1 RODNEY CL
2 EDGEHILL CT
3 WORCESTER CT
4 DUNBAR CT
Recn Gd
1 RYLTON HOUSE
2 BLATCHFORD CT
Weylands
NEW ZEALAND AVE
A244
B365
Liby
54
36

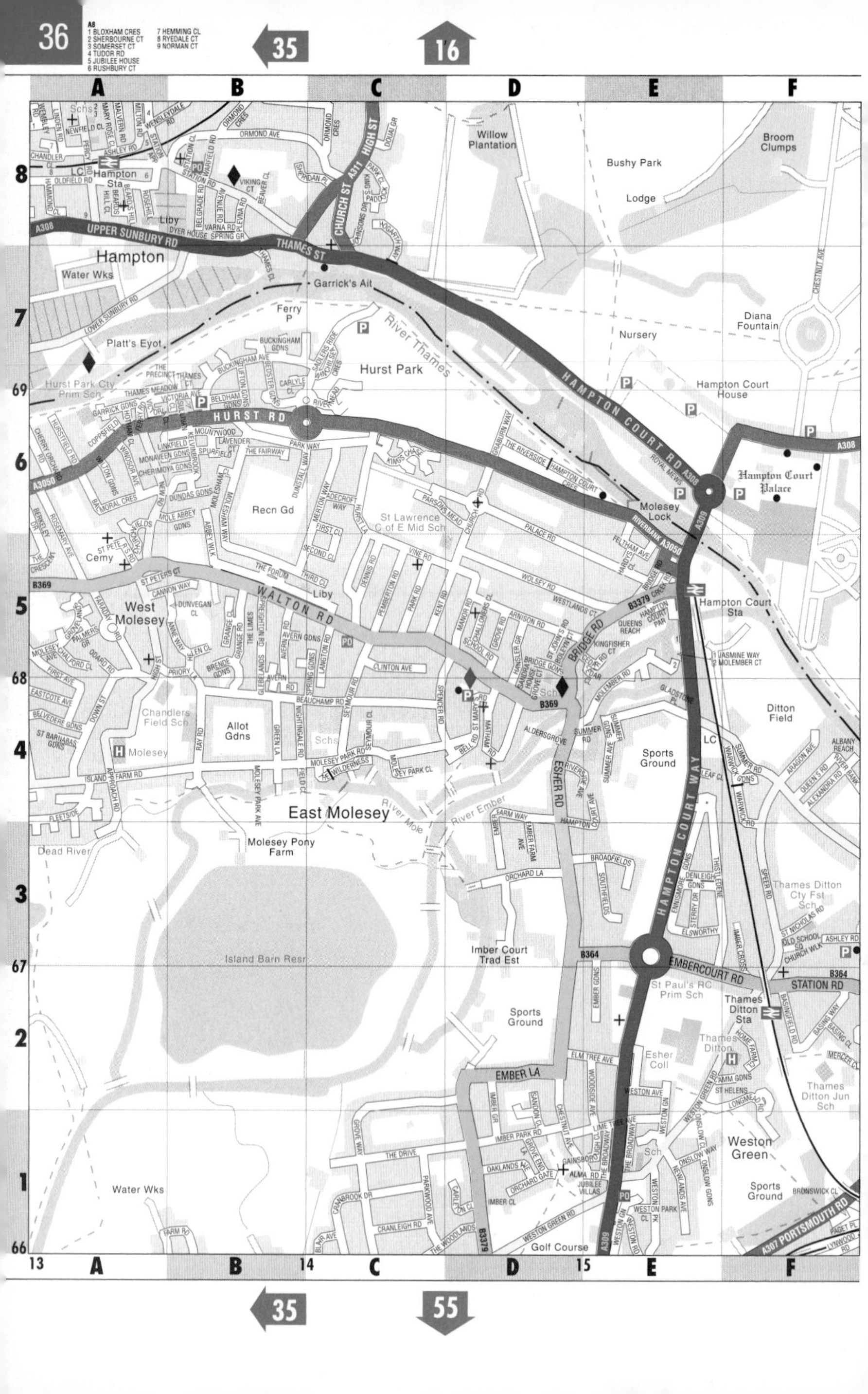

36
A8
1 BLOXHAM CRES
2 SHERBOURNE CT
3 SOMERSET CT
4 TUDOR RD
5 JUBILEE HOUSE
6 RUSHBURY CT
7 HEMMING CL
8 RYEDALE CT
9 NORMAN CT
35
16
A
B
C
D
E
F
8
7
69
6
5
68
4
3
67
2
1
66
13
14
15
Hampton
Hampton Sta
Willow Plantation
Bushy Park
Lodge
Broom Clumps
UPPER SUNBURY RD
THAMES ST
CHURCH ST
HIGH ST
Water Wks
Garrick's Ait
Ferry
Platt's Eyot
Hurst Park
River Thames
Nursery
Diana Fountain
Hurst Park Cty Prim Sch
HURST RD
HAMPTON COURT RD
Hampton Court House
Hampton Court Palace
Molesey Lock
Recn Gd
St Lawrence C of E Mid Sch
Cemy
West Molesey
WALTON RD
Liby
Hampton Court Sta
1 JASMINE WAY
2 MOLEMBER CT
Ditton Field
Chandlers Field Sch
Allot Gdns
Molesey
Sports Ground
East Molesey
River Mole
River Ember
HAMPTON COURT WAY
ESHER RD
Dead River
Molesey Pony Farm
Thames Ditton Cty Fst Sch
Island Barn Resr
Imber Court Trad Est
EMBERCOURT RD
STATION RD
St Paul's RC Prim Sch
Thames Ditton Sta
Thames Ditton
Esher Coll
EMBER LA
Thames Ditton Jun Sch
Weston Green
Water Wks
Golf Course
A307 PORTSMOUTH RD
A
B
C
D
E
F
35
55

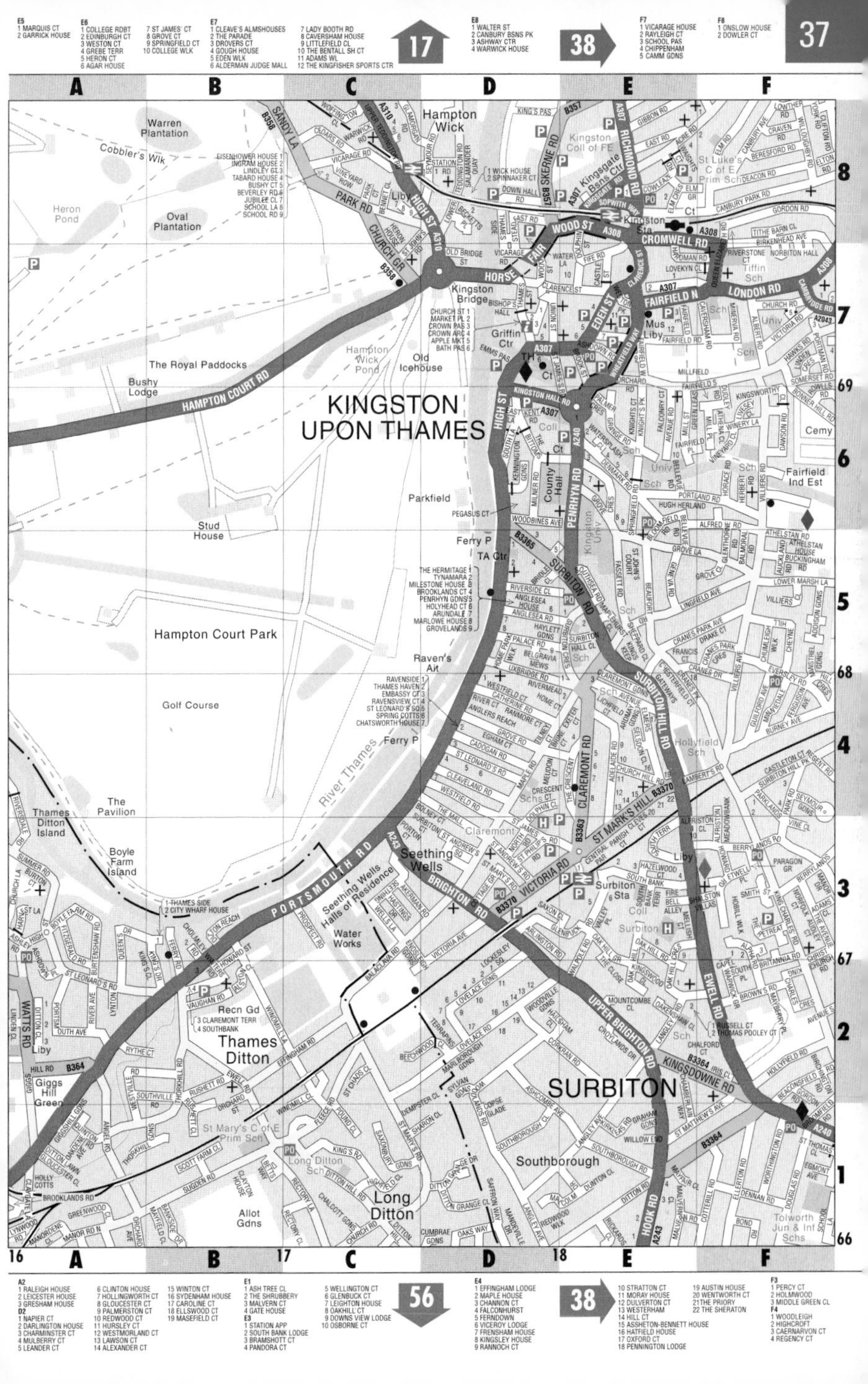
37
E5
1 MARQUIS CT
2 GARRICK HOUSE
E6
1 COLLEGE RDBT
2 EDINBURGH CT
3 WESTON CT
4 GREBE TERR
5 HERON CT
6 AGAR HOUSE
7 ST JAMES' CT
8 GROVE CT
9 SPRINGFIELD CT
10 COLLEGE WLK
E7
1 CLEAVE'S ALMSHOUSES
2 THE PARADE
3 DROVERS CT
4 GOUGH HOUSE
5 EDEN WLK
6 ALDERMAN JUDGE MALL
7 LADY BOOTH RD
8 CAVERSHAM HOUSE
9 LITTLEFIELD CL
10 THE BENTALL SH CTR
11 ADAMS WL
12 THE KINGFISHER SPORTS CTR
17
E8
1 WALTER ST
2 CANBURY BSNS PK
3 ASHWAY CTR
4 WARWICK HOUSE
38
F7
1 VICARAGE HOUSE
2 RAYLEIGH CT
3 SCHOOL PAS
4 CHIPPENHAM
5 CAMM GDNS
F8
1 ONSLOW HOUSE
2 DOWLER CT
A B C D E F
8 7 69 6 5 68 4 3 67 2 1 66
16 17 18
Warren Plantation
Cobbler's Wlk
Heron Pond
Oval Plantation
Hampton Wick
Kingston Coll of FE
Kingsgate Bsns Ctr
Kingston Sta
St Luke's C of E Prim Sch
Kingston Bridge
Griffin Ctr
Hampton Wick Pond
Old Icehouse
The Royal Paddocks
Bushy Lodge
HAMPTON COURT RD
KINGSTON UPON THAMES
Tiffin Sch
Mus Liby
Cemy
Fairfield Ind Est
Parkfield
Stud House
Ferry P
TA Ctr
County Hall
Kingston Univ
Hampton Court Park
Raven's Ait
Golf Course
River Thames
Ferry P
Hollyfield Sch
The Pavilion
Thames Ditton Island
Boyle Farm Island
Seething Wells
Seething Wells Halls of Residence
Water Works
Surbiton Sta
Surbiton Coll
PORTSMOUTH RD
BRIGHTON RD
VICTORIA RD
ST MARK'S HILL
SURBITON HILL RD
EWELL RD
UPPER BRIGHTON RD
KINGSDOWNE RD
CLAREMONT RD
PENRHYN RD
HIGH ST
RICHMOND RD
CROMWELL RD
LONDON RD
FAIRFIELD N
WOOD ST
HORSE FAIR
EDEN ST
SANDY LA
PARK RD
CHURCH GR
Recn Gd
Thames Ditton
Giggs Hill Green
Liby
WATTS RD
St Mary's C of E Prim Sch
Long Ditton Sch
Long Ditton
Allot Gdns
SURBITON
Southborough
HOOK RD
Tolworth Jun & Inf Schs
A2
1 RALEIGH HOUSE
2 LEICESTER HOUSE
3 GRESHAM HOUSE
D2
1 NAPIER CT
2 DARLINGTON HOUSE
3 CHARMINSTER CT
4 MULBERRY CT
5 LEANDER CT
6 CLINTON HOUSE
7 HOLLINGWORTH CT
8 GLOUCESTER CT
9 PALMERSTON CT
10 REDWOOD CT
11 HURSLEY CT
12 WESTMORLAND CT
13 LAWSON CT
14 ALEXANDER CT
15 WINTON CT
16 SYDENHAM HOUSE
17 CAROLINE CT
18 ELLSWOOD CT
19 MASEFIELD CT
E1
1 ASH TREE CL
2 THE SHRUBBERY
3 MALVERN CT
4 GATE HOUSE
E3
1 STATION APP
2 SOUTH BANK LODGE
3 BRAMSHOTT CT
4 PANDORA CT
5 WELLINGTON CT
6 GLENBUCK CT
7 LEIGHTON HOUSE
8 OAKHILL CT
9 DOWNS VIEW LODGE
10 OSBORNE CT
56
E4
1 EFFINGHAM LODGE
2 MAPLE HOUSE
3 CHANNON CT
4 FALCONHURST
5 FERNDOWN
6 VICEROY LODGE
7 FRENSHAM HOUSE
8 KINGSLEY HOUSE
9 RANNOCH CT
38
10 STRATTON CT
11 MORAY HOUSE
12 DULVERTON CT
13 WESTERHAM
14 HILL CT
15 ASSHETON-BENNETT HOUSE
16 HATFIELD HOUSE
17 OXFORD CT
18 PENNINGTON LODGE
19 AUSTIN HOUSE
20 WENTWORTH CT
21 THE PRIORY
22 THE SHERATON
F3
1 PERCY CT
2 HOLMWOOD
3 MIDDLE GREEN CL
F4
1 WOODLEIGH
2 HIGHCROFT
3 CAERNARVON CT
4 REGENCY CT

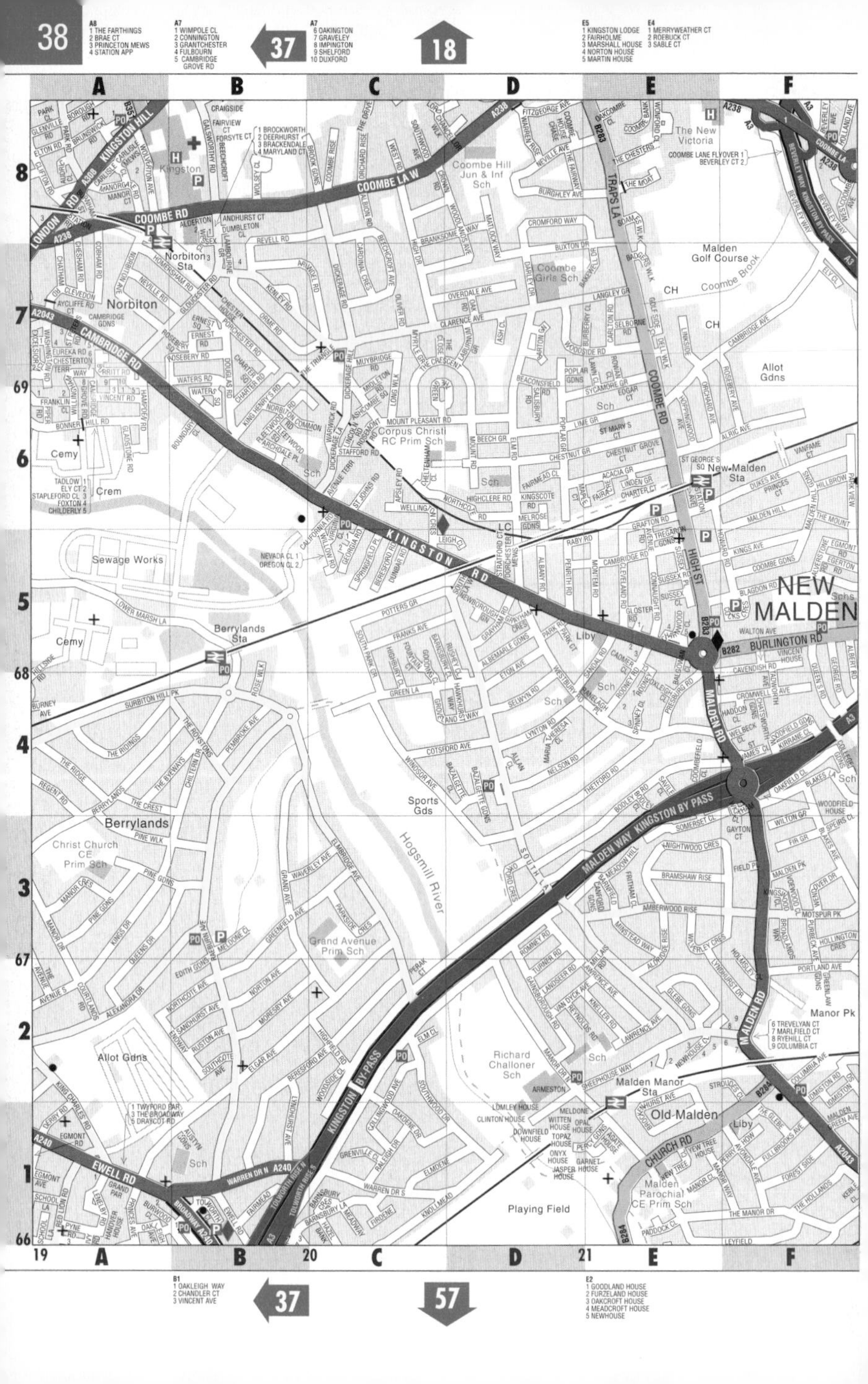

38
A8
1 THE FARTHINGS
2 BRAE CT
3 PRINCETON MEWS
4 STATION APP
A7
1 WIMPOLE CL
2 CONNINGTON
3 GRANTCHESTER
4 FULBOURN
5 CAMBRIDGE GROVE RD
37
A7
6 OAKINGTON
7 GRAVELEY
8 IMPINGTON
9 SHELFORD
10 DUXFORD
18
E5
1 KINGSTON LODGE
2 FAIRHOLME
3 MARSHALL HOUSE
4 NORTON HOUSE
5 MARTIN HOUSE
E4
1 MERRYWEATHER CT
2 ROEBUCK CT
3 SABLE CT
A
B
C
D
E
F
8
7
69
6
5
68
4
3
67
2
1
66
19
20
21
Kingston
Coombe Hill Jun & Inf Sch
The New Victoria
COOMBE LANE FLYOVER 1
BEVERLEY CT 2
COOMBE LA W
COOMBE RD
KINGSTON HILL
LONDON RD
Norbiton Sta
Norbiton
Malden Golf Course
Coombe Brook
Coombe Girls Sch
TRAPS LA
COOMBE RD
CAMBRIDGE RD
Allot Gdns
Corpus Christi RC Prim Sch
Cemy
Crem
TADLOW 1
ELY CT 2
STAPLEFORD CL 3
FOXTON 4
CHILDERLY 5
New Malden Sta
Sewage Works
KINGSTON RD
NEVADA CL 1
OREGON CL 2
NEW MALDEN
HIGH ST
BURLINGTON RD
Berrylands Sta
Liby
MALDEN RD
Sports Gds
Berrylands
Christ Church CE Prim Sch
Hogsmill River
KINGSTON BY PASS
MALDEN WAY
Grand Avenue Prim Sch
Manor Pk
6 TREVELYAN CT
7 MARLFIELD CT
8 RYEHILL CT
9 COLUMBIA CT
Allot Gdns
Richard Challoner Sch
Malden Manor Sta
Old Malden
1 TWYFORD PAR
3 THE BROADWAY
5 DRAYCOT RD
EWELL RD
KINGSTON BY-PASS
CHURCH RD
Malden Parochial CE Prim Sch
Playing Field
B1
1 OAKLEIGH WAY
2 CHANDLER CT
3 VINCENT AVE
37
57
E2
1 GOODLAND HOUSE
2 FURZELAND HOUSE
3 OAKCROFT HOUSE
4 MEADCROFT HOUSE
5 NEWHOUSE

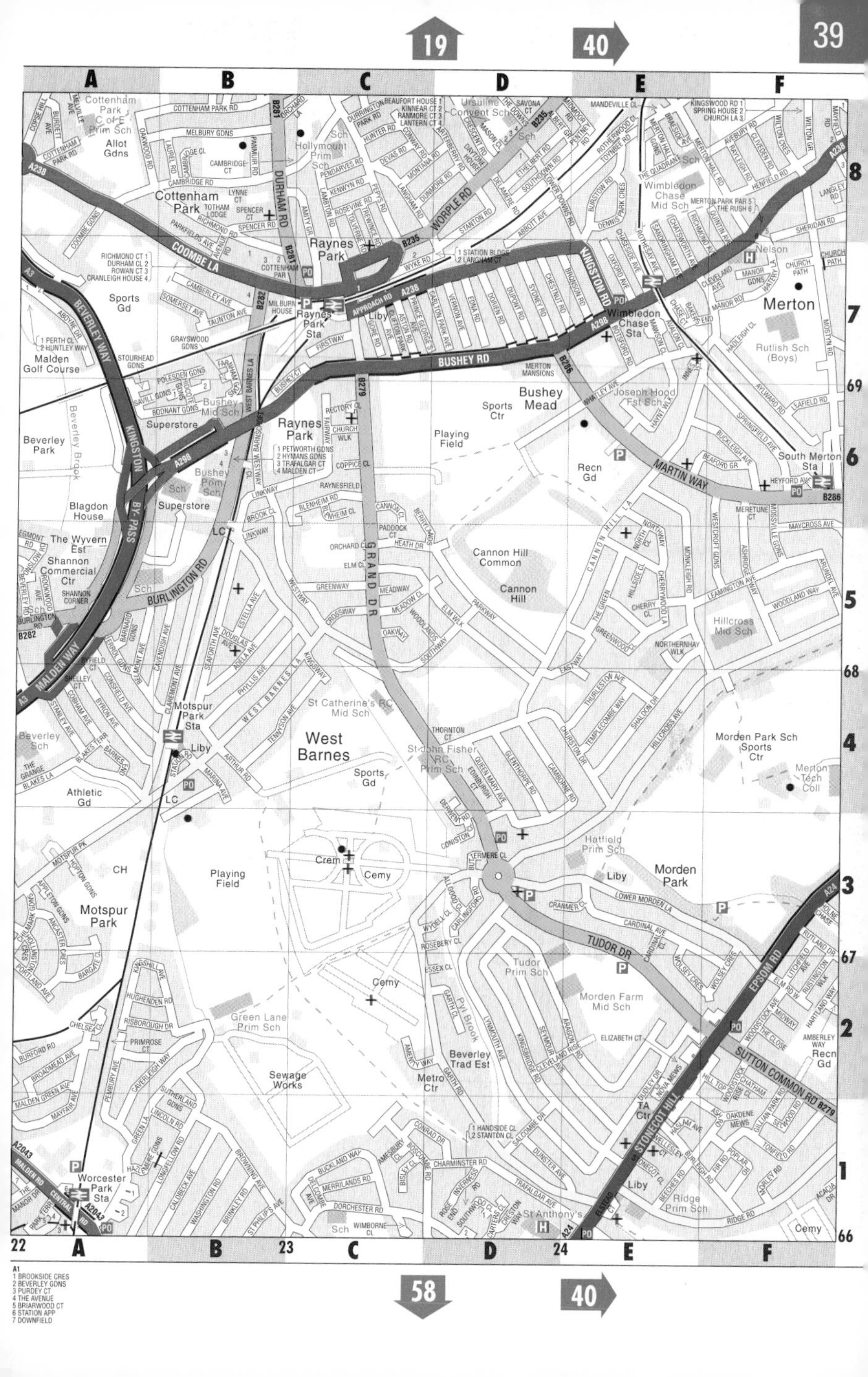

39
19
40
A B C D E F
8
7
69
6
5
68
4
3
67
2
1
66
22 A B 23 C D 24 E F
Cottenham Park C of E Prim Sch
Allot Gdns
Cottenham Park
Hollymount Prim Sch
Ursuline Convent Sch
Raynes Park
Wimbledon Chase Mid Sch
Merton
Nelson
COOMBE LA
WORPLE RD
KINGSTON RD
BUSHEY RD
DURHAM RD
BEVERLEY WAY
KINGSTON BY-PASS
Sports Gd
Raynes Park Sta
Wimbledon Chase Sta
Rutlish Sch (Boys)
Malden Golf Course
Bushey Mid Sch
Superstore
Beverley Park
Beverley Brook
Bushey Mead
Sports Ctr
Playing Field
Joseph Hood Fst Sch
Recn Gd
MARTIN WAY
South Merton Sta
Bushey Prim Sch
Blagdon House
The Wyvern Est
Shannon Commercial Ctr
BURLINGTON RD
Cannon Hill Common
Cannon Hill
GRAND DR
Hillcross Mid Sch
MALDEN WAY
Beverley Sch
Motspur Park Sta
Liby
St Catherine's RC Mid Sch
West Barnes
St John Fisher RC Prim Sch
Morden Park Sch Sports Ctr
Merton Tech Coll
Athletic Gd
Sports Gd
Playing Field
CH
Motspur Park
Crem
Cemy
Hatfield Prim Sch
Morden Park
TUDOR DR
Tudor Prim Sch
Morden Farm Mid Sch
EPSOM RD
Green Lane Prim Sch
Pyl Brook
Sewage Works
Beverley Trad Est
Metro Ctr
SUTTON COMMON RD
STONECOT HILL
TA Ctr
Ridge Prim Sch
Recn Gd
Worcester Park Sta
St Anthony's
Cemy
A1
1 BROOKSIDE CRES
2 BEVERLEY GDNS
3 PURDEY CT
4 THE AVENUE
5 BRIARWOOD CT
6 STATION APP
7 DOWNFIELD
58
40

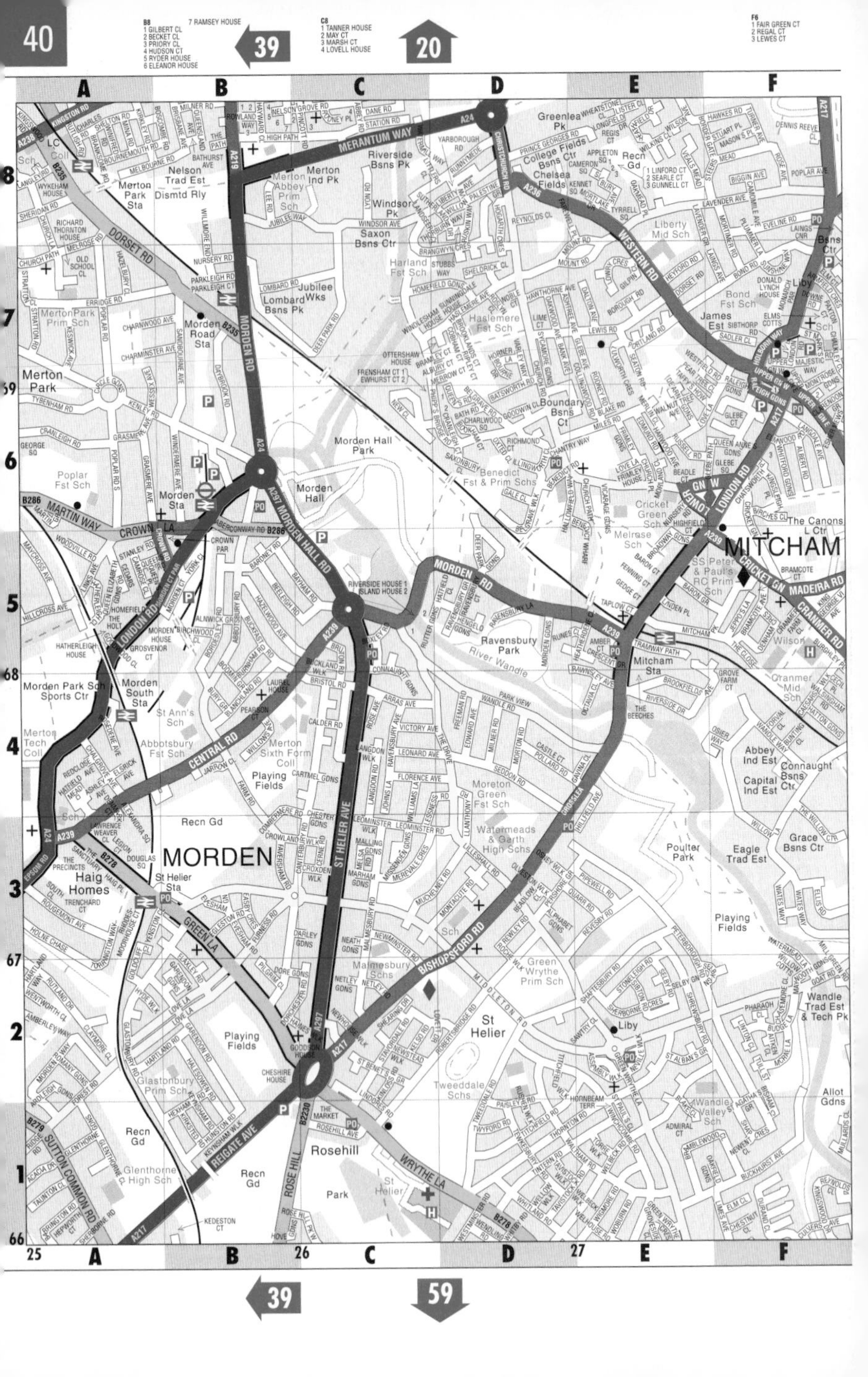

B8
1 GILBERT CL
2 BECKET CL
3 PRIORY CL
4 HUDSON CT
5 RYDER HOUSE
6 ELEANOR HOUSE
7 RAMSEY HOUSE
39
C8
1 TANNER HOUSE
2 MAY CT
3 MARSH CT
4 LOVELL HOUSE
20
F6
1 FAIR GREEN CT
2 REGAL CT
3 LEWES CT
A
B
C
D
E
F
Merton Park Sta
Nelson Trad Est
Dismtd Rly
Merton Ind Pk
Riverside Bsns Pk
MERANTUM WAY
Greenlea Pk
College Fields Bsns Ctr
Chelsea Fields
Recn Gd
Windsor Pk
Saxon Bsns Ctr
Liberty Mid Sch
WESTERN RD
DORSET RD
Harland Fst Sch
Jubilee Wks
Lombard Bsns Pk
Merton Park Prim Sch
Morden Road Sta
MORDEN RD
Haslemere Fst Sch
Bond Fst Sch
James Est
Merton Park
Boundary Bsns Ct
Morden Hall Park
Poplar Fst Sch
Morden Sta
Morden Hall
Benedict Fst & Prim Schs
Cricket Green Sch
Melrose Sch
MITCHAM
The Canons L Ctr
SS Peter & Paul's RC Prim Sch
MORDEN RD
Ravensbury Park
River Wandle
Mitcham Sta
Wilson
Morden Park Sch Sports Ctr
Morden South Sta
St Ann's Sch
Merton Sixth Form Coll
Cranmer Mid Sch
Merton Tech Coll
Abbotsbury Fst Sch
CENTRAL RD
Playing Fields
Moreton Green Fst Sch
Abbey Ind Est
Connaught Bsns Ctr
Capital Ind Est
Recn Gd
Watermeads & Garth High Schs
Poulter Park
Eagle Trad Est
Grace Bsns Ctr
MORDEN
Haig Homes
St Helier Sta
ST HELIER AVE
Playing Fields
Malmesbury Schs
BISHOPSFORD RD
Green Wrythe Prim Sch
St Helier
Liby
Wandle Trad Est & Tech Pk
Playing Fields
Glastonbury Prim Sch
Tweeddale Schs
Wandle Valley Sch
Allot Gdns
Recn Gd
REIGATE AVE
Rosehill
SUTTON COMMON RD
Glenthorne High Sch
Recn Gd
ROSE HILL
Park
WRYTHE LA
St Helier
25
26
27
39
59

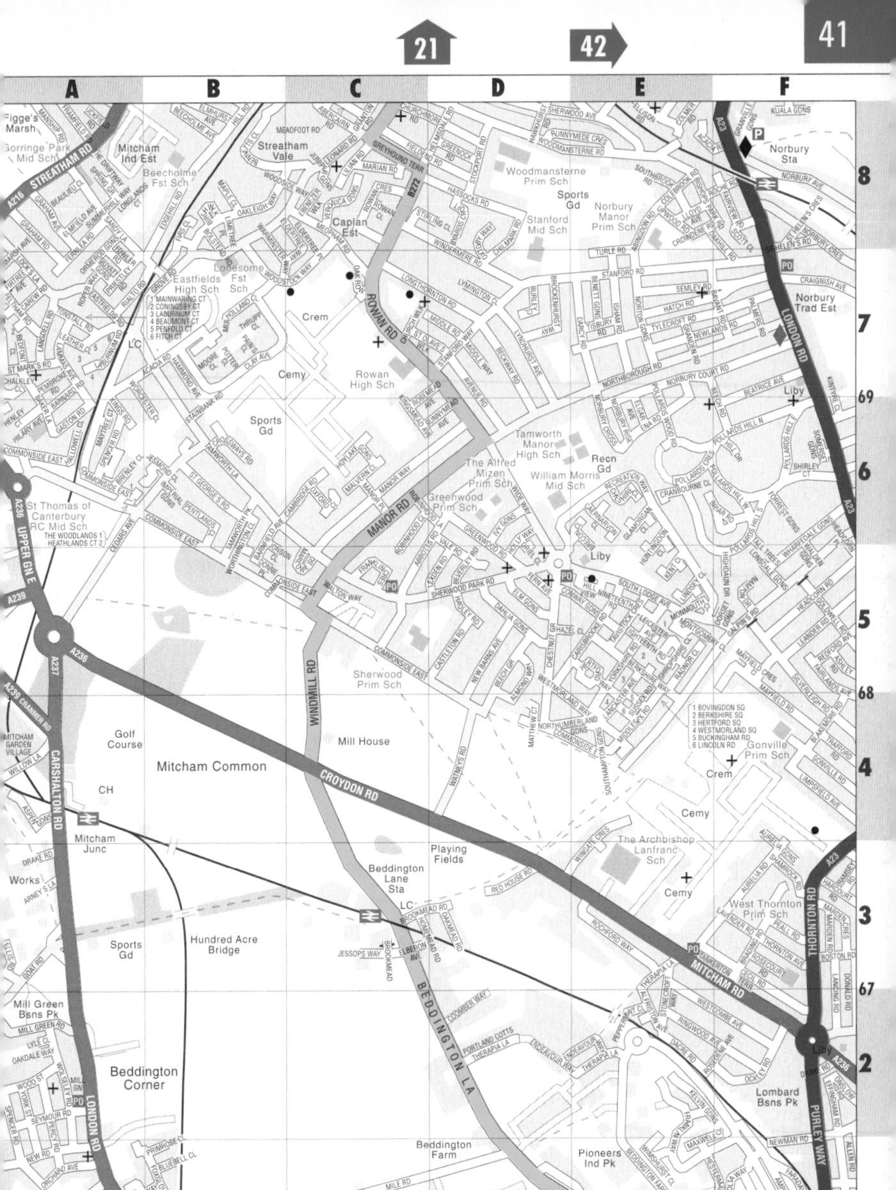
A
B
C
D
E
F
8
7
69
6
5
68
4
3
67
2
1
66
28
29
30
Figge's Marsh
Mitcham Ind Est
Beecholme Fst Sch
Streatham Vale
Caplan Est
Woodmansterne Prim Sch
Sports Gd
Stanford Mid Sch
Norbury Manor Prim Sch
Norbury Sta
Norbury Trad Est
Eastfields High Sch
Lonesome Fst Sch
1 MAINWARING CT
2 CONINGSBY CT
3 LABURNUM CT
4 BEAUMONT CT
5 PENFOLD CT
6 FITCH CT
Crem
Cemy
Rowan High Sch
Sports Gd
LC
STREATHAM RD
ROWAN RD
MANOR RD
LONDON RD
NORTHBOROUGH RD
Tamworth Manor High Sch
The Alfred Mizen Prim Sch
William Morris Mid Sch
Greenwood Prim Sch
Recn Gd
Liby
St Thomas of Canterbury RC Mid Sch
THE WOODLANDS 1
HEATHLANDS CT 2
UPPER GN E
COMMONSIDE EAST
Sherwood Prim Sch
1 BOVINGDON SQ
2 BERKSHIRE SQ
3 HERTFORD SQ
4 WESTMORLAND SQ
5 BUCKINGHAM RD
6 LINCOLN RD
Gonville Prim Sch
Crem
Cemy
Golf Course
Mitcham Common
Mill House
WINDMILL RD
CROYDON RD
CH
Mitcham Junc
CARSHALTON RD
Playing Fields
Beddington Lane Sta
The Archbishop Lanfranc Sch
Cemy
West Thornton Prim Sch
THORNTON RD
Works
Sports Gd
Hundred Acre Bridge
MITCHAM RD
BEDDINGTON LA
Mill Green Bsns Pk
Beddington Corner
Lombard Bsns Pk
PURLEY WAY
Beddington Farm
Pioneers Ind Pk
Sewage Works
Ind Est
Superstore
Waddon Marsh Sta
Soho Mills
MILE RD

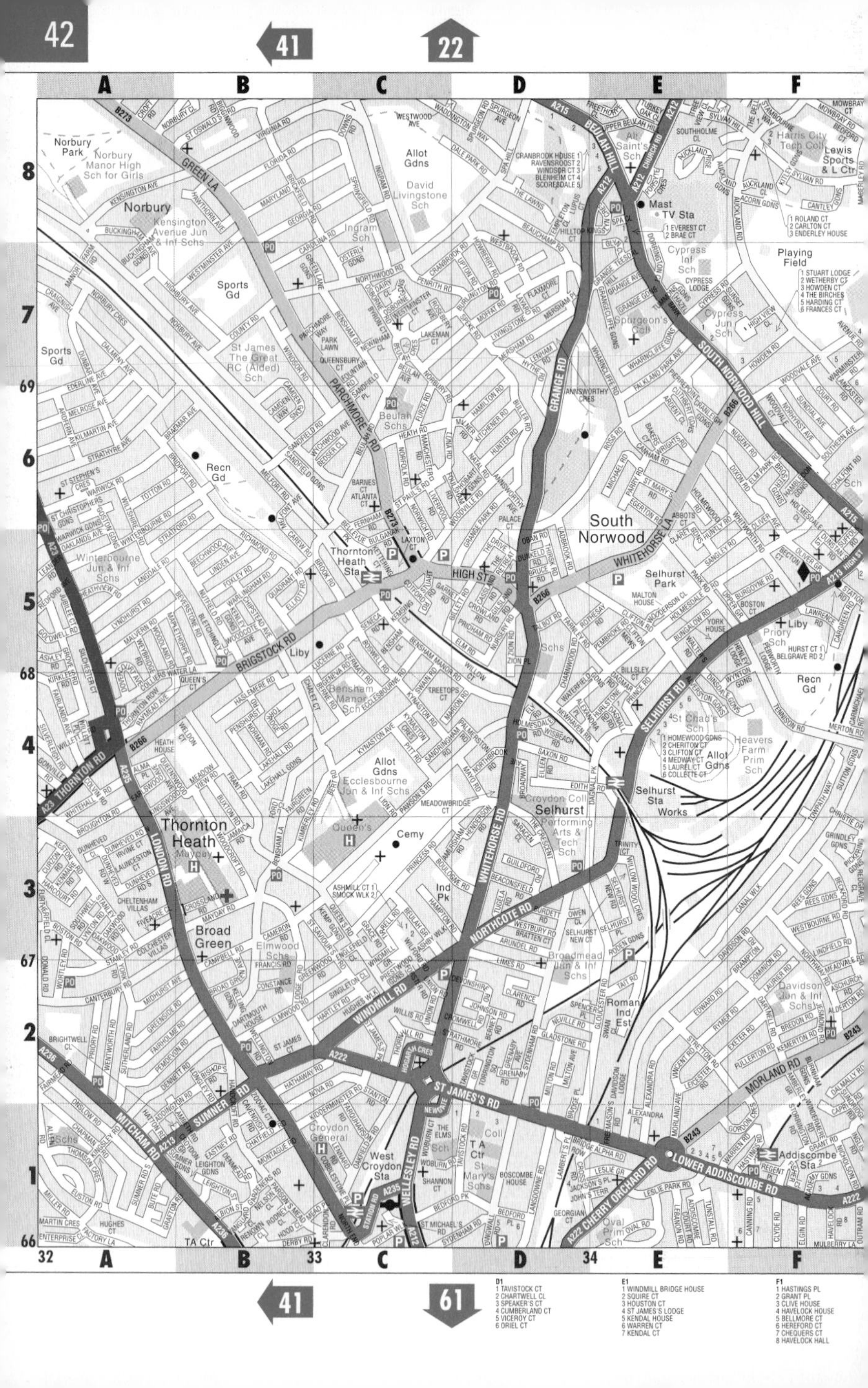

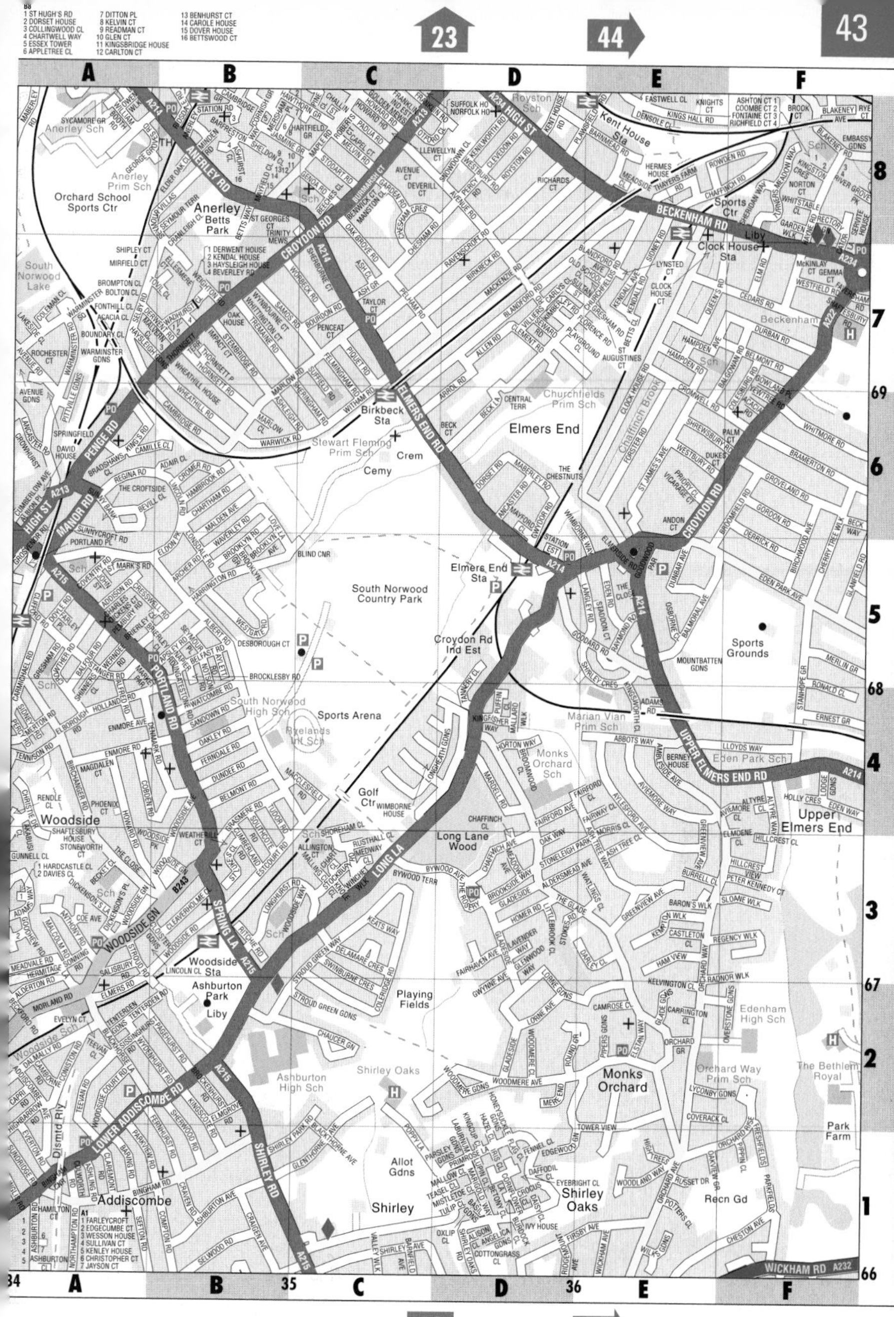
B8
1 ST HUGH'S RD
2 DORSET HOUSE
3 COLLINGWOOD CL
4 CHARTWELL WAY
5 ESSEX TOWER
6 APPLETREE CL
7 DITTON PL
8 KELVIN CT
9 READMAN CT
10 GLEN CT
11 KINGSBRIDGE HOUSE
12 CARLTON CT
13 BENHURST CT
14 CAROLE HOUSE
15 DOVER HOUSE
16 BETTSWOOD CT
23
44
A
B
C
D
E
F
8
7
6
5
4
3
2
1
69
68
67
66
34
35
36
Anerley Sch
Anerley Prim Sch
Orchard School Sports Ctr
Anerley
Betts Park
South Norwood Lake
ANERLEY RD
CROYDON RD
BECKENHAM RD
HIGH ST
PENGE RD
MANOR RD
Kent House Sta
Royston Sch
Sports Ctr
Clock House Sta
Liby
Beckenham
Birkbeck Sta
Stewart Fleming Prim Sch
Crem
Cemy
Churchfields Prim Sch
Elmers End
ELMERS END RD
Elmers End Sta
South Norwood Country Park
Croydon Rd Ind Est
Sports Grounds
Chaffinch Brook
South Norwood High Sch
Sports Arena
Ryelands Inf Sch
Marian Vian Prim Sch
Monks Orchard Sch
Eden Park Sch
UPPER ELMERS END RD
Upper Elmers End
Golf Ctr
Long Lane Wood
LONG LA
Woodside
PORTLAND RD
SPRING LA
WOODSIDE GN
Woodside Sta
Ashburton Park
Playing Fields
Edenham High Sch
Orchard Way Prim Sch
The Bethlem Royal
Park Farm
Ashburton High Sch
Shirley Oaks
Monks Orchard
LOWER ADDISCOMBE RD
SHIRLEY RD
Allot Gdns
Shirley
Shirley Oaks
Recn Gd
Addiscombe
Dismtd Rly
Woodside Sch
WICKHAM RD
A1
1 FARLEYCROFT
2 EDGECUMBE CT
3 WESSON HOUSE
4 SULLIVAN CT
5 KENLEY HOUSE
6 CHRISTOPHER CT
7 JAYSON CT

62
44

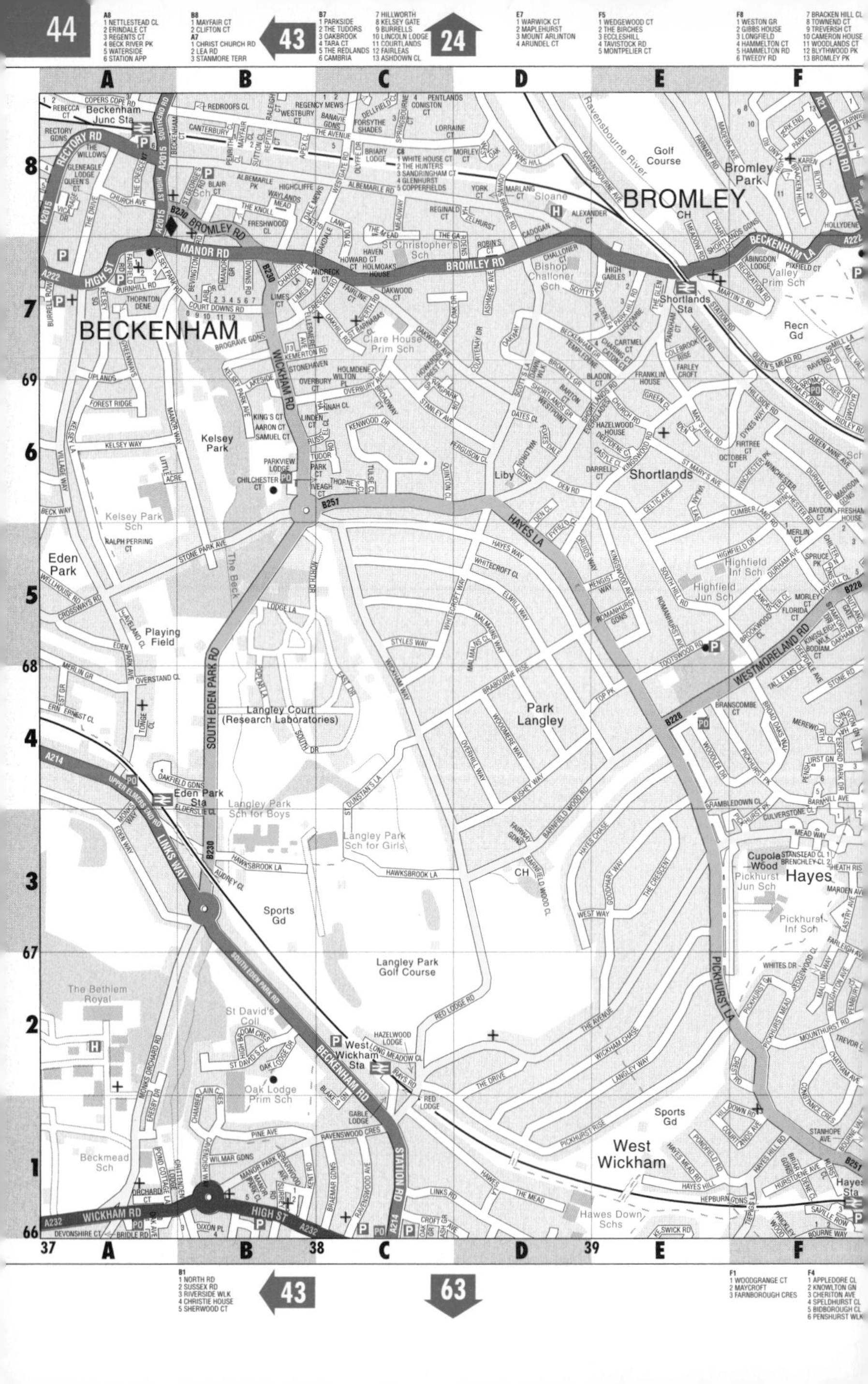

44
A8
1 NETTLESTEAD CL
2 ERINDALE CT
3 REGENTS CT
4 BECK RIVER PK
5 WATERSIDE
6 STATION APP
B8
1 MAYFAIR CT
2 CLIFTON CT
A7
1 CHRIST CHURCH RD
2 LEA RD
3 STANMORE TERR
43
B7
1 PARKSIDE
2 THE TUDORS
3 OAKBROOK
4 TARA CT
5 THE REDLANDS
6 CAMBRIA
7 HILLWORTH
8 KELSEY GATE
9 BURRELLS
10 LINCOLN LODGE
11 COURTLANDS
12 FAIRLEAS
13 ASHDOWN CL
24
E7
1 WARWICK CT
2 MAPLEHURST
3 MOUNT ARLINTON
4 ARUNDEL CT
F5
1 WEDGEWOOD CT
2 THE BIRCHES
3 ECCLESHILL
4 TAVISTOCK RD
5 MONTPELIER CT
F8
1 WESTON GR
2 GIBBS HOUSE
3 LONGFIELD
4 HAMMELTON CT
5 HAMMELTON RD
6 TWEEDY RD
7 BRACKEN HILL CL
8 TOWNEND CT
9 TREVERSH CT
10 CAMERON HOUSE
11 WOODLANDS CT
12 BLYTHWOOD PK
13 BROMLEY PK
C8
1 WHITE HOUSE CT
2 THE HUNTERS
3 SANDRINGHAM CT
4 GLENHURST
5 COPPERFIELDS
Beckenham Junc Sta
BECKENHAM
BROMLEY
Bromley Park
Golf Course
Ravensbourne River
Shortlands Sta
Shortlands
Kelsey Park
Kelsey Park Sch
Eden Park
Playing Field
Eden Park Sta
Langley Court (Research Laboratories)
Langley Park Sch for Boys
Langley Park Sch for Girls
Park Langley
Sports Gd
Langley Park Golf Course
The Bethlem Royal
St David's Coll
Oak Lodge Prim Sch
Beckmead Sch
West Wickham Sta
West Wickham
Hawes Down Schs
Hayes
Hayes Sta
Cupola Wood
Pickhurst Jun Sch
Pickhurst Inf Sch
Highfield Inf Sch
Highfield Jun Sch
Clare House Prim Sch
St Christopher's Sch
Bishop Challoner Sch
Valley Prim Sch
Recn Gd
Sloane
MANOR RD
BROMLEY RD
WICKHAM RD
SOUTH EDEN PARK RD
HAYES LA
PICKHURST LA
WESTMORELAND RD
BECKENHAM RD
STATION RD
WICKHAM RD
HIGH ST
LINKS WAY
BECKENHAM LA
LONDON RD
37
38
39
A B C D E F
8 7 69 6 5 68 4 3 67 2 1 66
B1
1 NORTH RD
2 SUSSEX RD
3 RIVERSIDE WLK
4 CHRISTIE HOUSE
5 SHERWOOD CT
43
63
F1
1 WOODGRANGE CT
2 MAYCROFT
3 FARNBOROUGH CRES
F4
1 APPLEDORE CL
2 KNOWLTON GN
3 CHERITON AVE
4 SPELDHURST CL
5 BIDBOROUGH CL
6 PENSHURST WLK

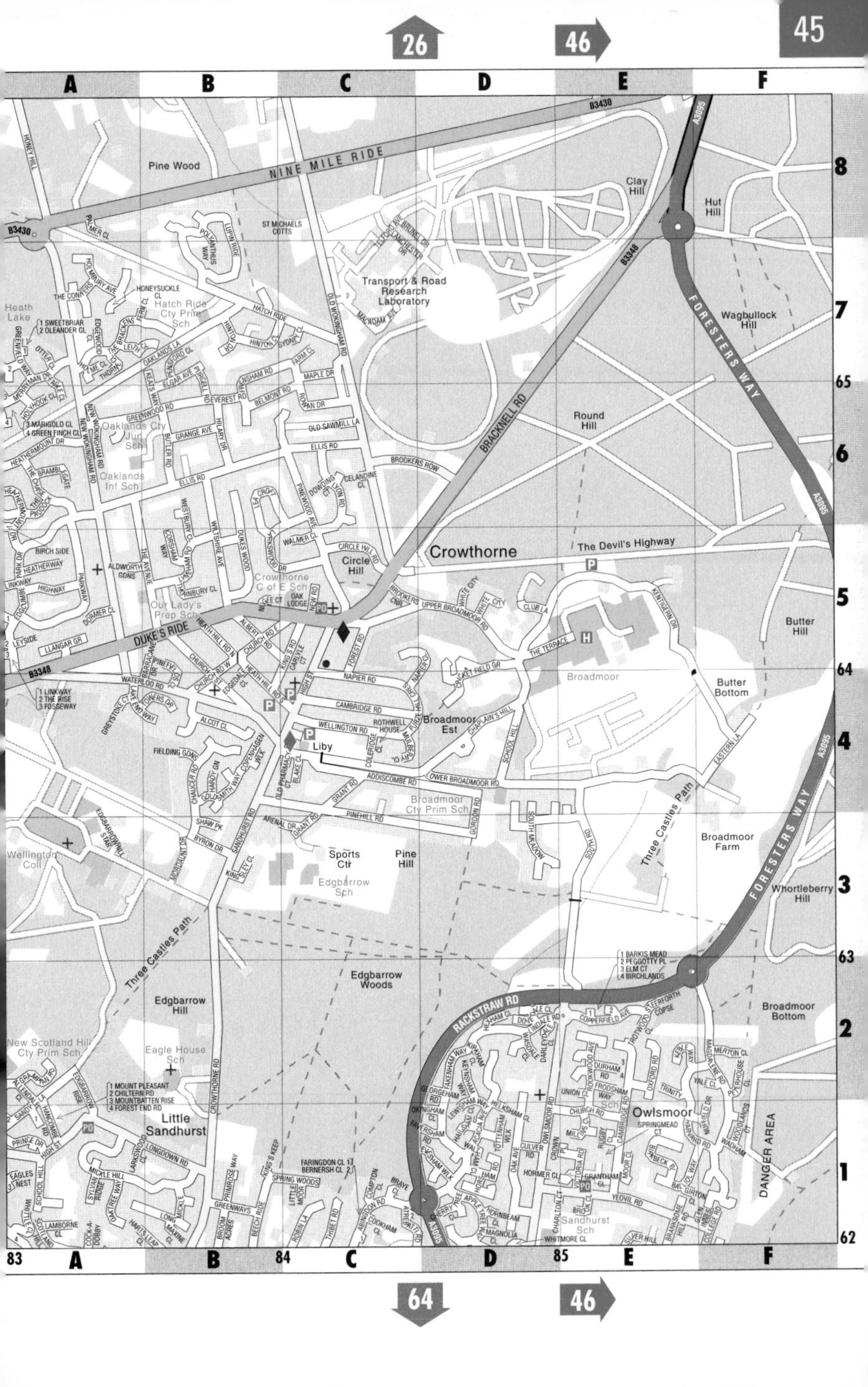
26
46
A
B
C
D
E
F
8
7
65
6
5
64
4
3
63
2
1
62
83
84
85
64
46
B3430
NINE MILE RIDE
Pine Wood
ST MICHAELS COTTS
Transport & Road Research Laboratory
Clay Hill
Hut Hill
A3095
B3348
FORESTERS WAY
Wagbullock Hill
Heath Lake
Hatch Ride Cty Prim Sch
Oaklands Cty Jun Sch
Oaklands Inf Sch
Round Hill
BRACKNELL RD
Crowthorne
The Devil's Highway
Circle Hill
Crowthorne C of E Sch
Our Lady's Prep Sch
DUKE'S RIDE
Butter Hill
Broadmoor
Butter Bottom
Broadmoor Est
Liby
Broadmoor Cty Prim Sch
Three Castles Path
Broadmoor Farm
Whortleberry Hill
Wellington Coll
Sports Ctr
Pine Hill
Edgbarrow Sch
Edgbarrow Woods
Edgbarrow Hill
Eagle House Sch
New Scotland Hill Cty Prim Sch
Little Sandhurst
RACKSTRAW RD
Owlsmoor
Broadmoor Bottom
DANGER AREA
Sandhurst Sch
CROWTHORNE RD
SANDHURST RD
OWLSMOOR RD
HONEY HILL
1 SWEETBRIAR
2 OLEANDER CL
3 MARIGOLD CL
4 GREEN FINCH CL
1 LINKWAY
2 THE RISE
3 FOSSEWAY
1 MOUNT PLEASANT
2 CHILTERN RD
3 MOUNTBATTEN RISE
4 FOREST END RD
1 BARKIS MEAD
2 PEGGOTTY PL
3 ELM CT
4 BIRCHLANDS
FARINGDON CL 1
BERNERSH CL 2

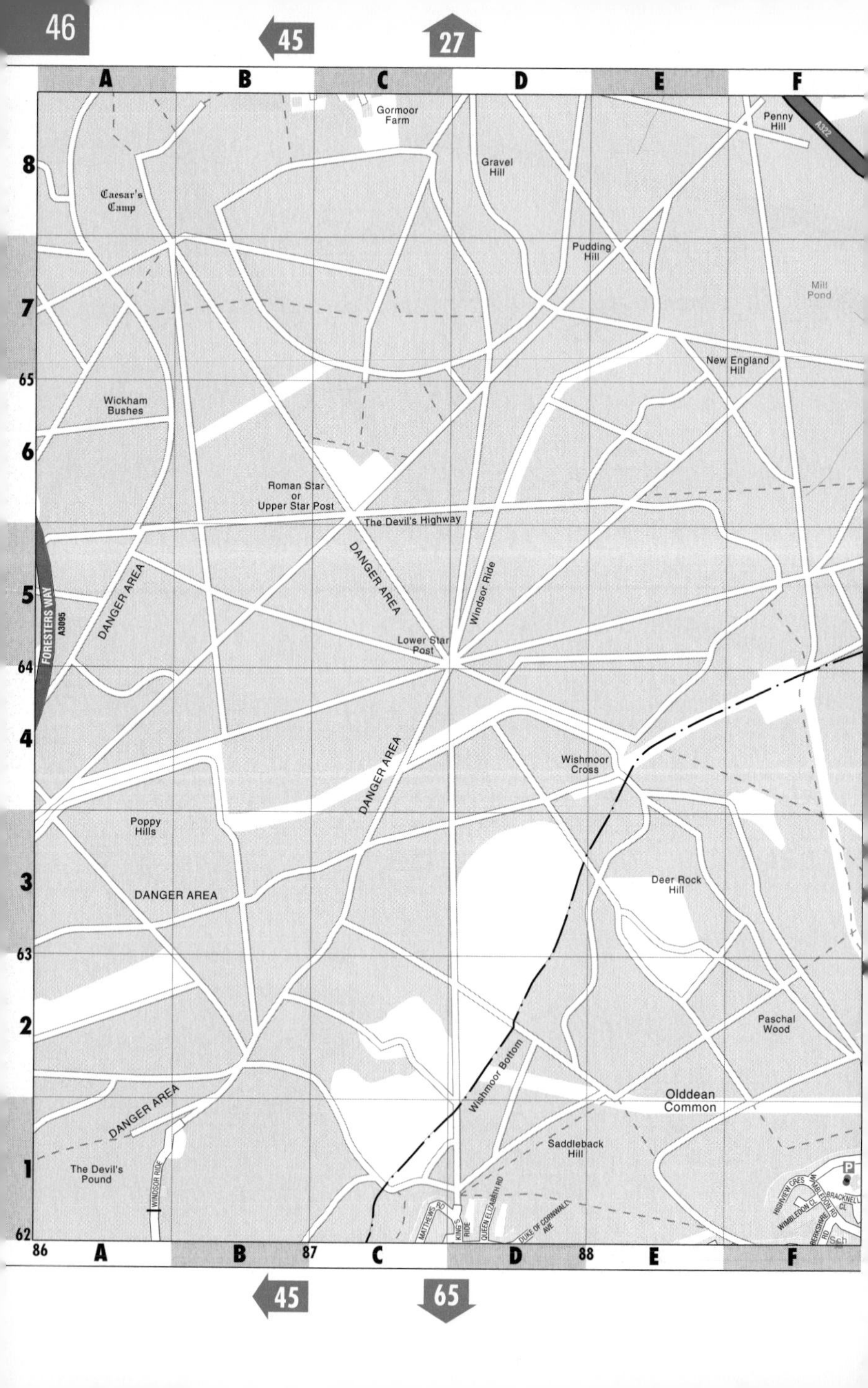
45
27
A
B
C
D
E
F
Gormoor Farm
Penny Hill
A322
Gravel Hill
Caesar's Camp
Pudding Hill
Mill Pond
New England Hill
Wickham Bushes
Roman Star or Upper Star Post
The Devil's Highway
DANGER AREA
DANGER AREA
Windsor Ride
FORESTERS WAY
A3095
Lower Star Post
DANGER AREA
Wishmoor Cross
Poppy Hills
DANGER AREA
Deer Rock Hill
Paschal Wood
Wishmoor Bottom
Olddean Common
DANGER AREA
Saddleback Hill
The Devil's Pound
WINDSOR RIDE
MATTHEWS RD
KING'S RIDE
QUEEN ELIZABETH RD
DUKE OF CORNWALL AVE
HIGHVIEW CRES
WIMBLEDON RD
WIMBLEDON CL
BRACKNELL CL
BERKSHIRE RD
Sch
P
8
7
65
6
5
64
4
3
63
2
1
62
86
87
88
45
65

28 48

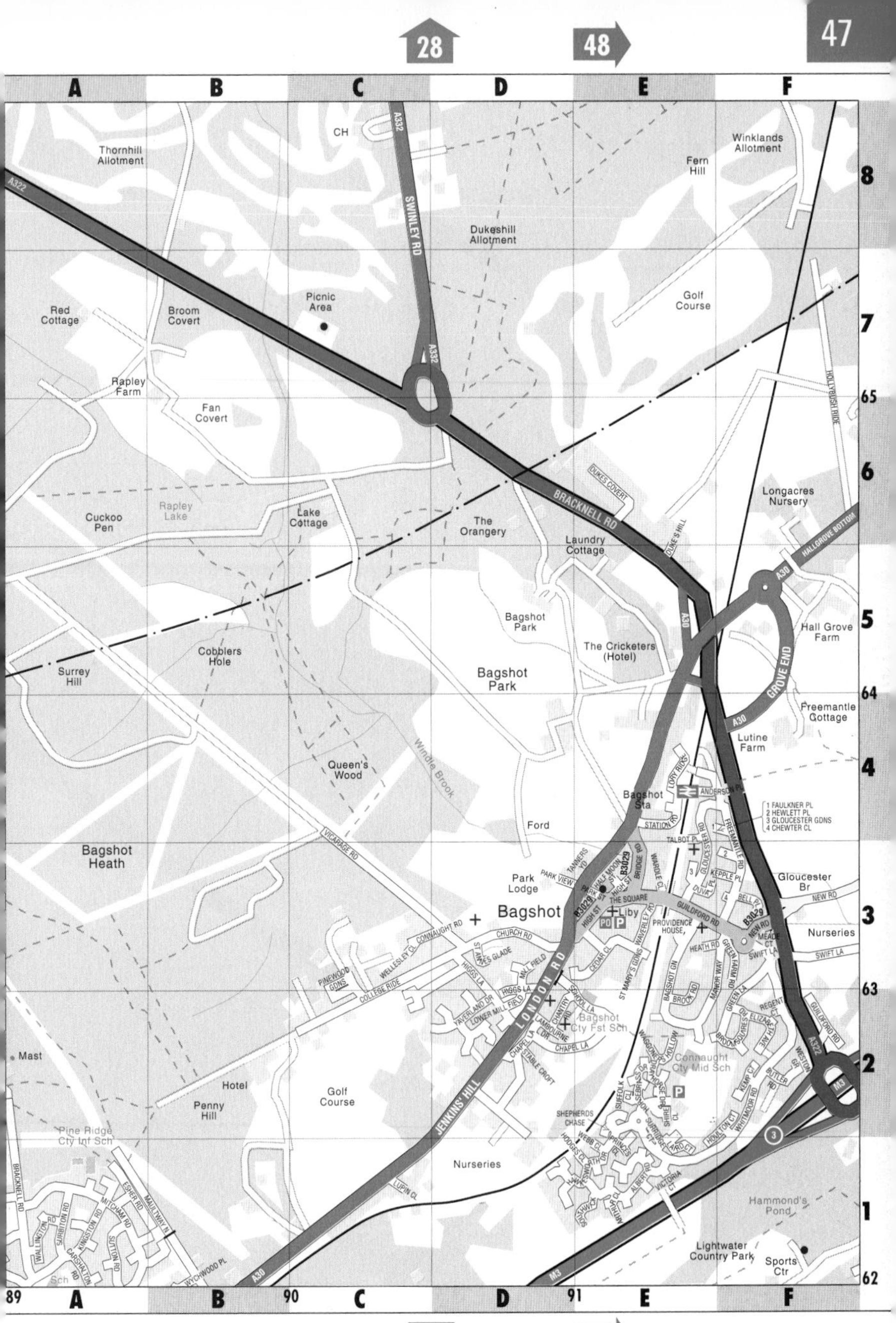
A B C D E F
8
7
65
6
5
64
4
3
63
2
1
62
89 90 91
A322
A332
SWINLEY RD
CH
Thornhill Allotment
Winklands Allotment
Fern Hill
Dukeshill Allotment
Golf Course
Red Cottage
Broom Covert
Picnic Area
Rapley Farm
Fan Covert
HOLLYBUSH RIDE
DUKES COVERT
BRACKNELL RD
Longacres Nursery
Cuckoo Pen
Rapley Lake
Lake Cottage
The Orangery
Laundry Cottage
DUKE'S HILL
HALLGROVE BOTTOM
A30
Bagshot Park
The Cricketers (Hotel)
Hall Grove Farm
Cobblers Hole
Surrey Hill
GROVE END
Freemantle Cottage
Lutine Farm
Windle Brook
Queen's Wood
Bagshot Sta
LORY RIDGE
ANDERSON PL
1 FAULKNER PL
2 HEWLETT PL
3 GLOUCESTER GDNS
4 CHEWTER CL
STATION RD
Ford
TALBOT PL
GLOUCESTER RD
FREEMANTLE RD
VICARAGE RD
Bagshot Heath
TANNERS YD
HALF MOON ST
B3029
BRIDGE RD
WARDLE CL
KEPPLE PL
Gloucester Br
Park Lodge
PARK VIEW
PARK ST
HIGH ST
THE SQUARE
DUNVA PL
BELL PL
NEW RD
Bagshot
Liby
GUILDFORD RD
PROVIDENCE HOUSE
MEADE CT
Nurseries
CONNAUGHT RD
CHURCH RD
PD P
HEATH RD
SWIFT LA
WELLESLEY CL
ST ANNES GLADE
CEDAR CL
GREEN FARM RD
PINEWOOD GDNS
HIGGS LA
MILL FIELD
ST MARY'S GDNS
WAVERLEY RD
MANOR WAY
COLLEGE RIDE
LONDON RD
SCHOOL LA
BAGSHOT GN
BROCK RD
GREEN LA
REGENT CT
GUILDFORD RD
YAVERLAND DR
LOWER MILL FIELD
CHANTRY RD
ELIZABETH AVE
LAMBOURNE DR
Bagshot Cty Fst Sch
BROOK SQUARE
A322
CHAPEL LA
Connaught Cty Mid Sch
HOLLOW
WESTON GR
BUTLER RD
Mast
STABLE CROFT
KEMP CT
JENKINS' HILL
Hotel
Golf Course
P
M3
Penny Hill
SUFFOLK CL
SHIRE CL
WHITMOOR RD
SHEPHERDS CHASE
HOULTON CT
LARK CT
3
Pine Ridge Cty Inf Sch
WEBB CL
PRINCES
Nurseries
HODGES CL
VICTORIA CT
BRACKNELL RD
ESHER RD
MAULTWAY N
LUPIN CL
ALBERT RD
Hammond's Pond
MITCHAM RD
SURBITON RD
KINGSTON RD
WALLINGTON RD
SUTTON RD
CARSHALTON RD
WYCHWOOD PL
Lightwater Country Park
Sports Ctr
Sch

66 48

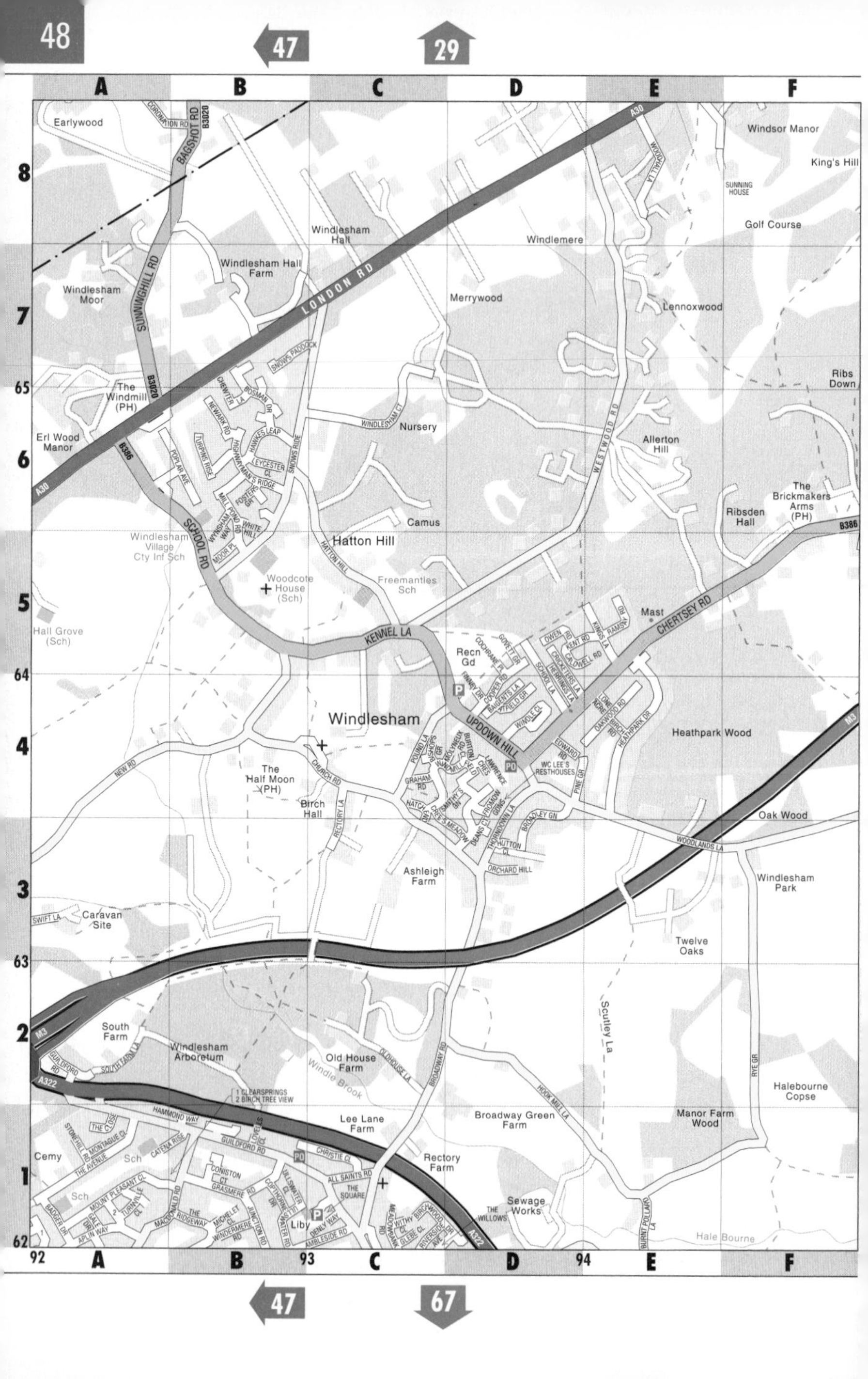
47
29
A
B
C
D
E
F
Earlywood
CORONATION RD
BAGSHOT RD
B3020
A30
WOODHALL LA
Windsor Manor
King's Hill
SUNNING HOUSE
Golf Course
Windlesham Hall
Windlemere
Windlesham Hall Farm
LONDON RD
Windlesham Moor
SUNNINGHILL RD
Merrywood
Lennoxwood
SNOWS PADDOCK
The Windmill (PH)
B3020
Ribs Down
CHEWTER LA
BOSMAN DR
NEWARK RD
WINDLESHAM CT
Nursery
Erl Wood Manor
HAWKES LEAP
TURPINS RISE
POPLAR AVE
LEYCESTER CL
SNOWS RIDE
WESTWOOD RD
Allerton Hill
B386
HIGHWAYMAN'S RIDGE
A30
FOSTERS GR
MILL POND RD
The Brickmakers Arms (PH)
Ribsden Hall
WYNSHAM WAY
WHITE HILL
Camus
B386
SCHOOL RD
Windlesham Village Cty Inf Sch
MOOR PL
Hatton Hill
HATTON HILL
Woodcote House (Sch)
Freemantles Sch
Mast
Hall Grove (Sch)
KENNEL LA
CHERTSEY RD
COCHRANE PL
GOVETT GR
OWEN RD
KENT RD
KINGS LA
RAMSAY RD
Recn Gd
CALDWELL RD
CRICKETERS LA
HERRINGS LA
SCHOOL LA
FINNEY DR
COOPER RD
BAIGENTS LA
FIELD GR
WINDLE CL
ONE ACRE
OAKWOOD RD
BIRCH RD
HEATHPARK DR
Windlesham
UPDOWN HILL
P
Heathpark Wood
M3
NEW RD
POUND LA
BISHOPS GR
MOLYNEUX RD
BURTON CL
LAWRENCE CRES
EDWARD RD
WC LEE'S RESTHOUSES
PINE GR
The Half Moon (PH)
CHURCH RD
GRAHAM RD
SMITH'S GN
FROMOW GDNS
Birch Hall
RECTORY LA
HATCH CL
CREY'S MEADOW
BROADLEY GN
DEANS CT
THORNDOWN LA
Oak Wood
HUTTON CL
WOODLANDS LA
ORCHARD HILL
Ashleigh Farm
Windlesham Park
SWIFT LA
Caravan Site
Twelve Oaks
Scutley La
M3
South Farm
SOUTH FARM LA
Windlesham Arboretum
Old House Farm
GUILDFORD RD
OLDHOUSE LA
BROADWAY RD
Windle Brook
RYE GR
Halebourne Copse
A322
HOOK MILL LA
1 CLEARSPRINGS
2 BIRCH TREE VIEW
HAMMOND WAY
Lee Lane Farm
Broadway Green Farm
Manor Farm Wood
THE CLOSE
STONEHILL RD
MONTAGUE CL
CATENA RISE
GUILDFORD RD
LOVELLS CL
P
CHRISTIE CL
Cemy
Sch
THE AVENUE
CONISTON CT
Rectory Farm
GRASMERE RD
ALL SAINTS RD
ULLSWATER CL
Sch
MOUNT PLEASANT CL
COPTHORNE DR
THE SQUARE
TURNVILLE CL
MACDONALD RD
THE RIDGEWAY
MICHELET CL
JUNCTION RD
WATER RD
P
Liby
DENLY WAY
MEADOWBANK RD
WITHY CL
BIRCHWOOD DR
GLEBE CL
RIVERSIDE AVE
THE WILLOWS
Sewage Works
BURNT POLLARD LA
Hale Bourne
BADGER DR
APLIN WAY
WINDERMERE RD
AMBLESIDE RD
A322
8
7
65
6
5
64
4
3
63
2
1
62
92
93
94
47
67

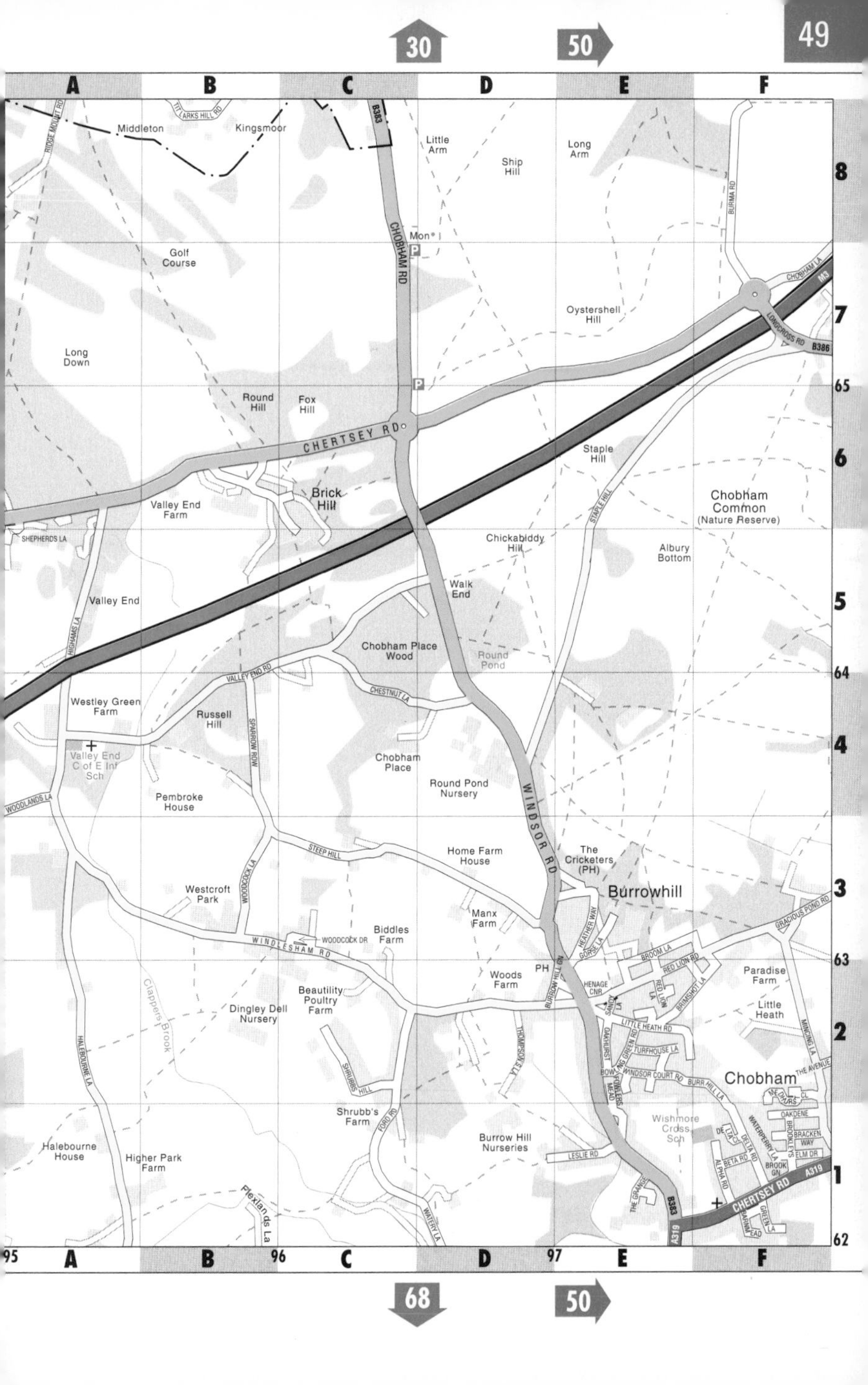
49
30
50
68
50
Middleton
Kingsmoor
Little Arm
Ship Hill
Long Arm
CHOBHAM RD
Mon
Golf Course
Oystershell Hill
Long Down
Round Hill
Fox Hill
CHERTSEY RD
Staple Hill
Brick Hill
Valley End Farm
SHEPHERDS LA
Chobham Common (Nature Reserve)
Chickabiddy Hill
Albury Bottom
STAPLE HILL
Walk End
Valley End
HIGHAMS LA
Chobham Place Wood
Round Pond
VALLEY END RD
CHESTNUT LA
Westley Green Farm
Russell Hill
SPARROW ROW
Valley End C of E Inf Sch
Chobham Place
Round Pond Nursery
WOODLANDS LA
Pembroke House
WINDSOR RD
STEEP HILL
Home Farm House
The Cricketers (PH)
Westcroft Park
WOODCOCK LA
Burrowhill
Manx Farm
WOODCOCK DR
Biddles Farm
WINDLESHAM RD
HEATHER WAY
GORSE LA
BROOM LA
RED LION RD
GRACIOUS POND RD
PH
Woods Farm
BURROW HILL GN
HENAGE CNR
RED LION LA
BRIMSHOT LA
Paradise Farm
Beautility Poultry Farm
Dingley Dell Nursery
Clappers Brook
LITTLE HEATH RD
Little Heath
THOMPSON'S LA
OAKHURST
TURFHOUSE LA
MINCING LA
HALEBOURNE LA
SHRUBBS HILL
WINDSOR COURT RD
BURR HILL LA
Chobham
THE AVENUE
MEAD
FOWLERS
Shrubb's Farm
FORD RD
Wishmore Cross Sch
OAKDENE
BRACKEN WAY
ELM DR
WATERPERRY LA
DELTA RD
ALPHA RD
BETA RD
Burrow Hill Nurseries
LESLIE RD
Halebourne House
Higher Park Farm
THE GRANGE
CHERTSEY RD
Plexlands La
WATERY LA
BURMA RD
CHOBHAM LA
LONGCROSS RD
B386
B383
A319
M3

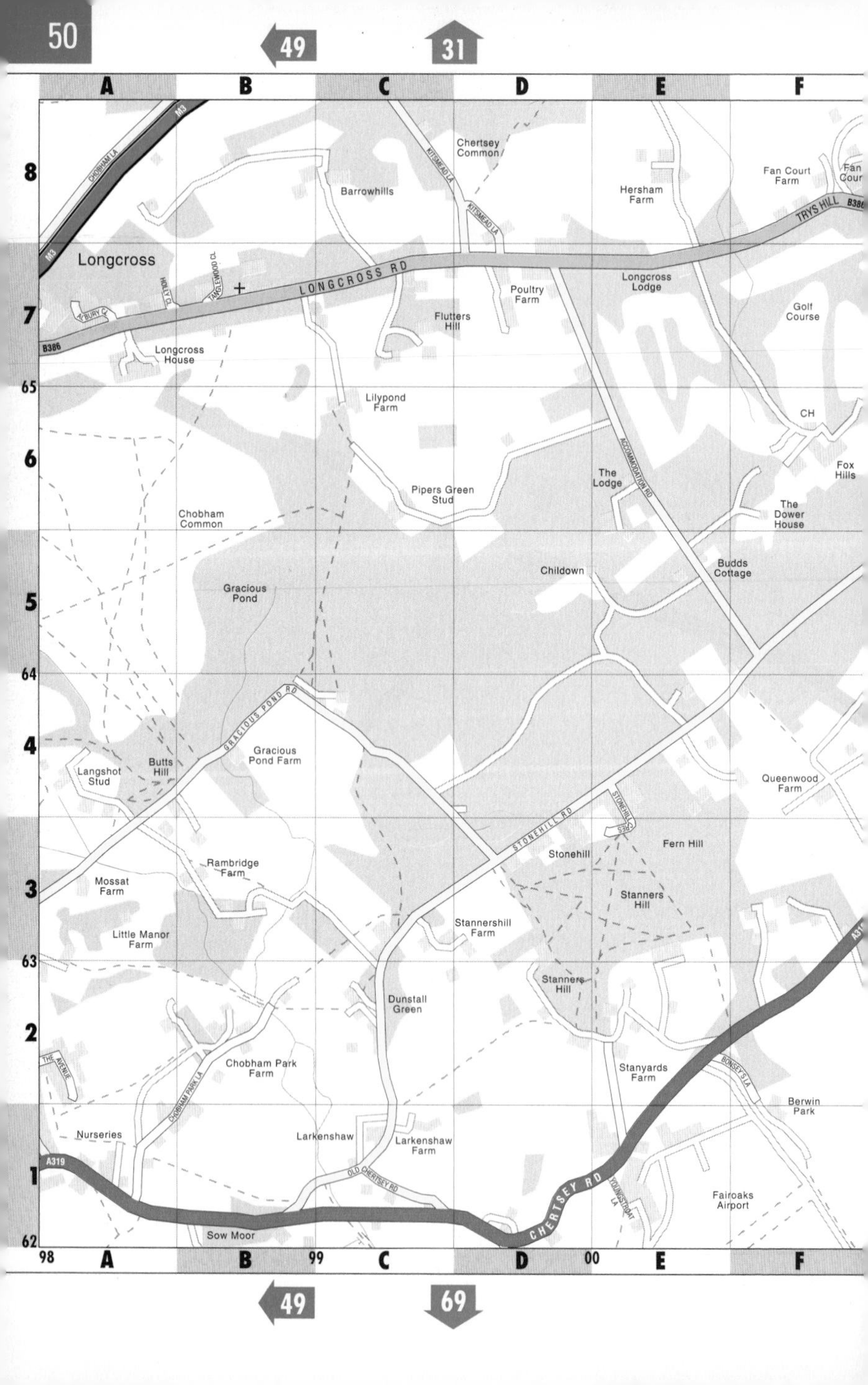
49
31
A
B
C
D
E
F
8
7
65
6
5
64
4
3
63
2
1
62
98
99
00
M3
CHOBHAM LA
Chertsey Common
KITSMEAD LA
Barrowhills
Hersham Farm
Fan Court Farm
TRYS HILL
B386
Longcross
HOLLY CL
TANGLEWOOD CL
LONGCROSS RD
ALBURY CL
Poultry Farm
Longcross Lodge
Golf Course
Flutters Hill
Longcross House
Lilypond Farm
CH
Fox Hills
The Lodge
ACCOMMODATION RD
Pipers Green Stud
The Dower House
Chobham Common
Childown
Budds Cottage
Gracious Pond
GRACIOUS POND RD
Gracious Pond Farm
Langshot Stud
Butts Hill
Queenwood Farm
STONEHILL CRES
STONEHILL RD
Stonehill
Fern Hill
Rambridge Farm
Mossat Farm
Stanners Hill
Little Manor Farm
Stannershill Farm
A319
Dunstall Green
THE AVENUE
Chobham Park Farm
CHOBHAM PARK LA
Stanyards Farm
BONSEY'S LA
Berwin Park
Nurseries
Larkenshaw
Larkenshaw Farm
OLD CHERTSEY RD
CHERTSEY RD
YOUNGSTROAT LA
Fairoaks Airport
Sow Moor
69

32

52

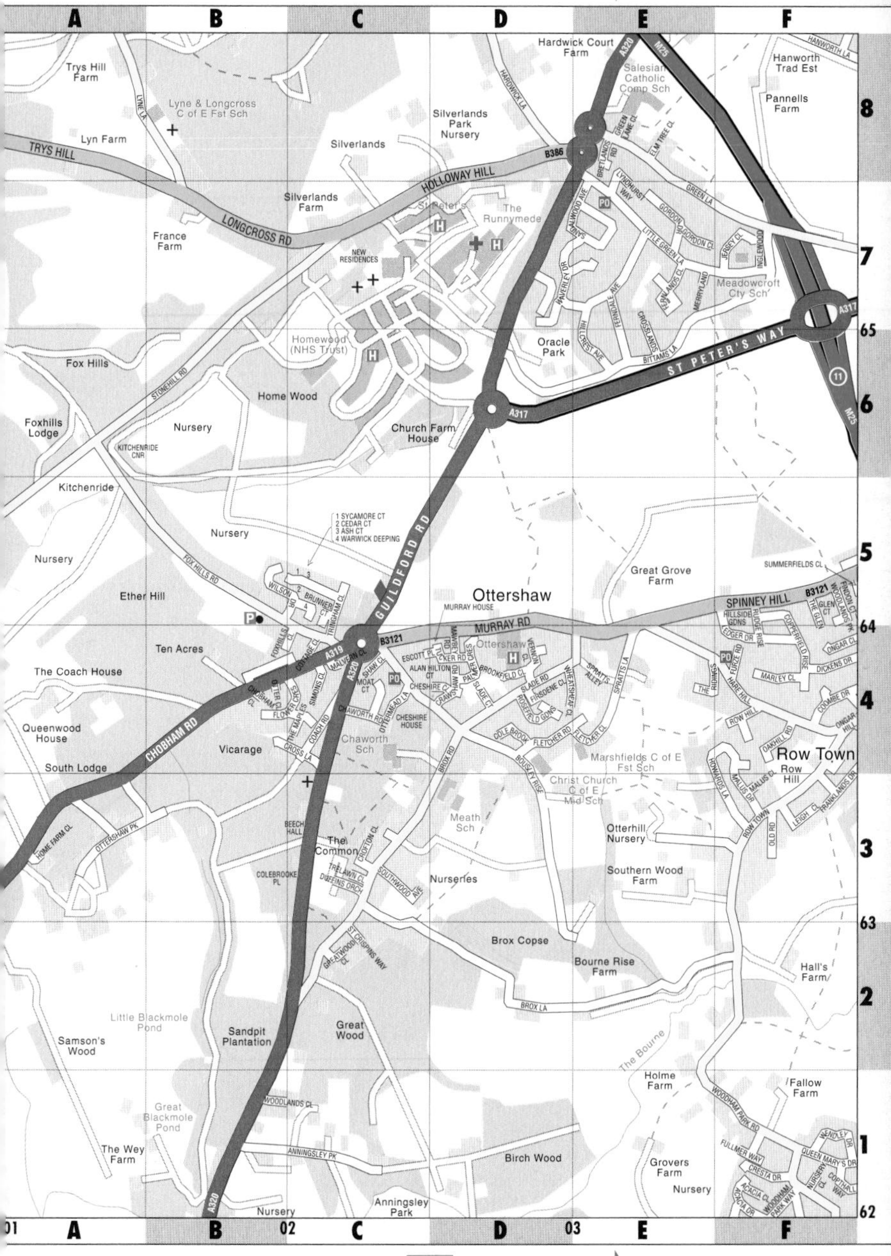

A
B
C
D
E
F
8
7
65
6
5
64
4
3
63
2
1
62
01
02
03
Trys Hill Farm
Hardwick Court Farm
Salesian Catholic Comp Sch
Hanworth Trad Est
Pannells Farm
Lyne & Longcross C of E Fst Sch
Lyn Farm
TRYS HILL
Silverlands Park Nursery
Silverlands
HOLLOWAY HILL
LONGCROSS RD
Silverlands Farm
St Peter's
The Runnymede
France Farm
NEW RESIDENCES
Meadowcroft Cty Sch
Homewood (NHS Trust)
Oracle Park
ST PETER'S WAY
Fox Hills
Home Wood
Foxhills Lodge
Nursery
Church Farm House
KITCHENRIDE CNR
Kitchenride
1 SYCAMORE CT
2 CEDAR CT
3 ASH CT
4 WARWICK DEEPING
Nursery
Nursery
GUILDFORD RD
Great Grove Farm
SUMMERFIELDS CL
Ether Hill
Ottershaw
MURRAY HOUSE
SPINNEY HILL
MURRAY RD
Ten Acres
The Coach House
CHOBHAM RD
Queenwood House
Vicarage
Chaworth Sch
Marshfields C of E Fst Sch
Row Town
Row Hill
South Lodge
Christ Church C of E Mid Sch
Meath Sch
The Common
Otterhill Nursery
Southern Wood Farm
Nurseries
Brox Copse
Bourne Rise Farm
Hall's Farm
BROX LA
Little Blackmole Pond
Samson's Wood
Sandpit Plantation
Great Wood
The Bourne
Holme Farm
Fallow Farm
Great Blackmole Pond
The Wey Farm
Birch Wood
Grovers Farm
Nursery
Nursery
Anningsley Park

70
52

51
33

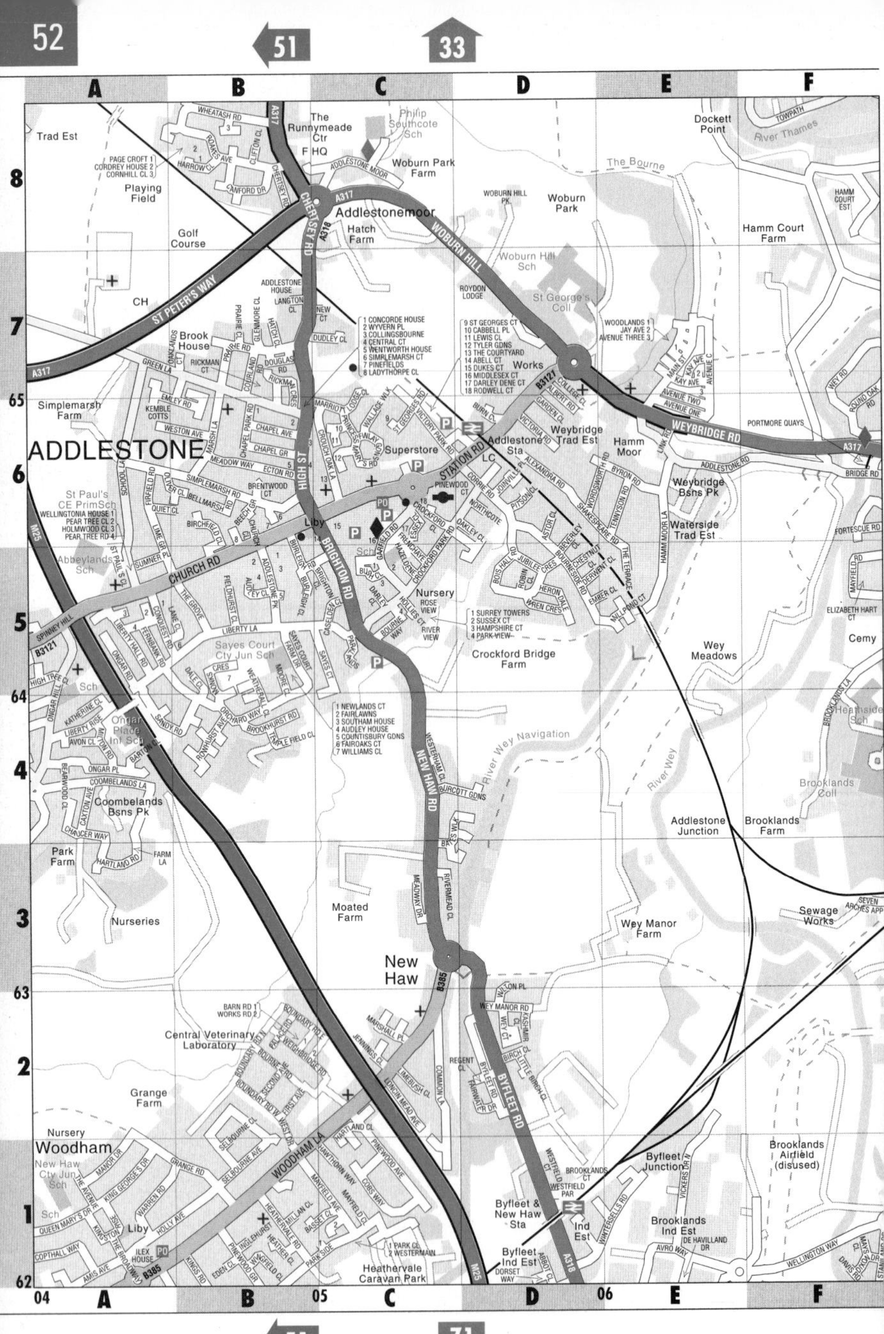
A
B
C
D
E
F
8
7
65
6
5
64
4
3
63
2
1
62
04
05
06
Trad Est
The Runnymeade Ctr
F HQ
Philip Southcote Sch
Woburn Park Farm
Dockett Point
River Thames
The Bourne
TOWPATH
Playing Field
Golf Course
Addlestonemoor
Hatch Farm
Woburn Park
WOBURN HILL
Woburn Hill Sch
St George's Coll
Hamm Court Farm
HAMM COURT EST
ROYDON LODGE
CH
ST PETER'S WAY
A317
A318
CHERTSEY RD
WHEATASH RD
ROAKES AVE
CLIFTON CL
HARROW CL
CANFORD DR
ADDLESTONE MOOR
PAGE CROFT 1
CORDREY HOUSE 2
CORNHILL CL 3
ADDLESTONE HOUSE
Brook House
ADDLESTONE
Simplemarsh Farm
KEMBLE COTTS
EMLEY RD
WESTON AVE
GREEN LA
OAKLANDS CT
PRAIRIE CL
PRAIRIE RD
GLENMORE CL
HATCH CL
LANGTON CL
NEW CT
DUDLEY CL
RICKMAN CT
COURLAND RD
DOUGLAS RD
MARSH LA
CHAPEL PARK RD
CHAPEL AVE
CHAPEL GR
MEADOW WAY
ECTON RD
SIMPLEMARSH RD
BELLMARSH RD
BRENTWOOD CT
1 CONCORDE HOUSE
2 WYVERN PL
3 COLLINGSBOURNE
4 CENTRAL CT
5 WENTWORTH HOUSE
6 SIMPLEMARSH CT
7 PINEFIELDS
8 LADYTHORPE CL
9 ST GEORGES CT
10 CABBELL PL
11 LEWIS CL
12 TYLER GDNS
13 THE COURTYARD
14 ABELL CT
15 DUKES CT
16 MIDDLESEX CT
17 DARLEY DENE CT
18 RODWELL CT
WOODLANDS 1
JAY AVE 2
AVENUE THREE 3
Works
MAIN ST
KAY AVE
AVENUE C
AVENUE TWO
AVENUE ONE
WEYBRIDGE RD
PORTMORE QUAYS
WEY RD
ROUND OAK RD
HIGH ST
Superstore
STATION RD
B3121
Addlestone Sta
LC
Weybridge Trad Est
Hamm Moor
COLLEGE CL
ALBERT RD
GARDEN CL
VICTORIA RD
ALEXANDRA RD
BURN CL
ADDLESTONE RD
BRIDGE RD
BYRON RD
WORDSWORTH RD
SHAKESPEARE RD
TENNYSON RD
Weybridge Bsns Pk
Waterside Trad Est
HAMM MOOR LA
FORTESCUE RD
St Paul's CE PrimSch
WELLINGTONIA HOUSE 1
PEAR TREE CL 2
HOLMWOOD CL 3
PEAR TREE RD 4
SCHOOL LA
FIRFIELD RD
QUIET CL
BIRCHFIELD CL
BEECH GR
CHURCH CL
Liby
CHURCH RD
Abbeylands Sch
SUMNER PL
LIME GR
ST PAUL'S CL
BRIGHTON RD
BURLEIGH RD
BURLEIGH CL
PINEWOOD CT
CROCKFORD CL
CROCKFORD PARK RD
NORTHCOTE
OAKLEY CL
CORRIE RD
JOINVILLE PL
PITSON CL
GARFIELD RD
FRENCHAYE
HAZELDENE
BUSH CL
DARLEY CL
Sch
Nursery
ROSE VIEW
RIVER VIEW
HOLLIES CT
BOURNE WAY
PARK LANDS
1 SURREY TOWERS
2 SUSSEX CT
3 HAMPSHIRE CT
4 PARK VIEW
BOIS HALL RD
JUBILEE CRES
ROBIN CL
HERON DALE
WREN CRES
ASTOR CL
BEVERLEY CL
BOURNESIDE RD
CHESTNUT CL
DERWENT CL
THE TERRACE
EMBER CL
MILLPOND CT
MAYFIELD RD
ELIZABETH HART CT
Cemy
Wey Meadows
SPINNEY HILL
B3121
M25
LIBERTY HALL RD
FERNBANK RD
CONQUEST RD
LANE CL
THE GROVE
FIELDHURST CL
AUDLEY CL
ADDLESTONE PK
LIBERTY LA
Sayes Court Cty Jun Sch
SAYES COURT FARM DR
SAYES CT
CASELDEA CL
Crockford Bridge Farm
ONGAR RD
DALE CL
SWANS CRES
WEATHERALL CL
MOORE CL
ORCHARD WAY
BROOKHURST RD
TEMPLE FIELD CL
ROWHURST AVE
SANDY RD
HIGH TREE CL
ONGAR HILL
KATHERINE CL
LIBERTY RISE
AVON CL
MILTON RD
Ongar Place Inf Sch
BARTON CL
ONGAR PL
1 NEWLANDS CT
2 FAIRLAWNS
3 SOUTHAM HOUSE
4 AUDLEY HOUSE
5 COUNTISBURY GDNS
6 FAIROAKS CT
7 WILLIAMS CL
WESTERHAM CL
NEW HAW RD
BURCOTT GDNS
River Wey Navigation
River Wey
BROOKLANDS LA
Heathside Sch
Brooklands Coll
BEARWOOD CL
COOMBELANDS LA
Coombelands Bsns Pk
CAXTON AVE
CHAUCER WAY
HARTLAND RD
FARM LA
Park Farm
Addlestone Junction
Brooklands Farm
BATES WLK
Moated Farm
MEADWAY DR
RIVERMEAD CL
Nurseries
Wey Manor Farm
Sewage Works
SEVEN ARCHES APP
New Haw
B385
WILTON PL
WEY MANOR RD
KASHMIR CL
WEY CT
BIRCH CL
LITTLE BIRCH CL
BARN RD 1
WORKS RD 2
Central Veterinary Laboratory
BOUNDARY RD E
WEYBRIDGE RD
MARSHALL PL
JENNINGS CL
LIMEBUSH CL
LINCOLN MEAD AVE
COMMON LA
REGENT CL
BYFLEET RD
FAIRWATER DR
Grange Farm
BOUNDARY RD N
PALACE RD
BOURNE RD
SECOND AVE
FIRST AVE
BOUNDARY RD W
WEST DR
SELBOURNE CL
SELBOURNE AVE
Nursery
Woodham
New Haw Cty Jun Sch
MANOR DR
THE AVENUE
KING GEORGE'S DR
GRANGE RD
WARREN RD
WOODHAM LA
HARTLAND CL
HAWTHORN WAY
PINEWOOD AVE
MAYFIELD AVE
MAYFIELD CL
COBS WAY
Sch
QUEEN MARY'S DR
KINGSTON AVE
THE BROADWAY
Liby
HOLLY AVE
COPTHALL WAY
AMIS AVE
ILEX HOUSE
PO
B385
KINGS RD
EDEN CL
PINEWOOD GR
INGLEHURST
WINGFIELD CL
HEATHER CL
HEATHERVALE RD
MILLAN CL
BASSET CL
PARK SIDE
1 PARK CL
2 WESTERMAIN
Heathervale Caravan Park
WESTFIELD CT
BROOKLANDS CT
WESTFIELD PAR
Byfleet & New Haw Sta
Ind Est
Byfleet Ind Est
DORSET WAY
ABBOT CL
A318
Byfleet Junction
VICKERS DR N
WINTERSELLS RD
Brooklands Ind Est
DE HAVILLAND DR
AVRO WAY
WELLINGTON WAY
Brooklands Airfield (disused)

51
71

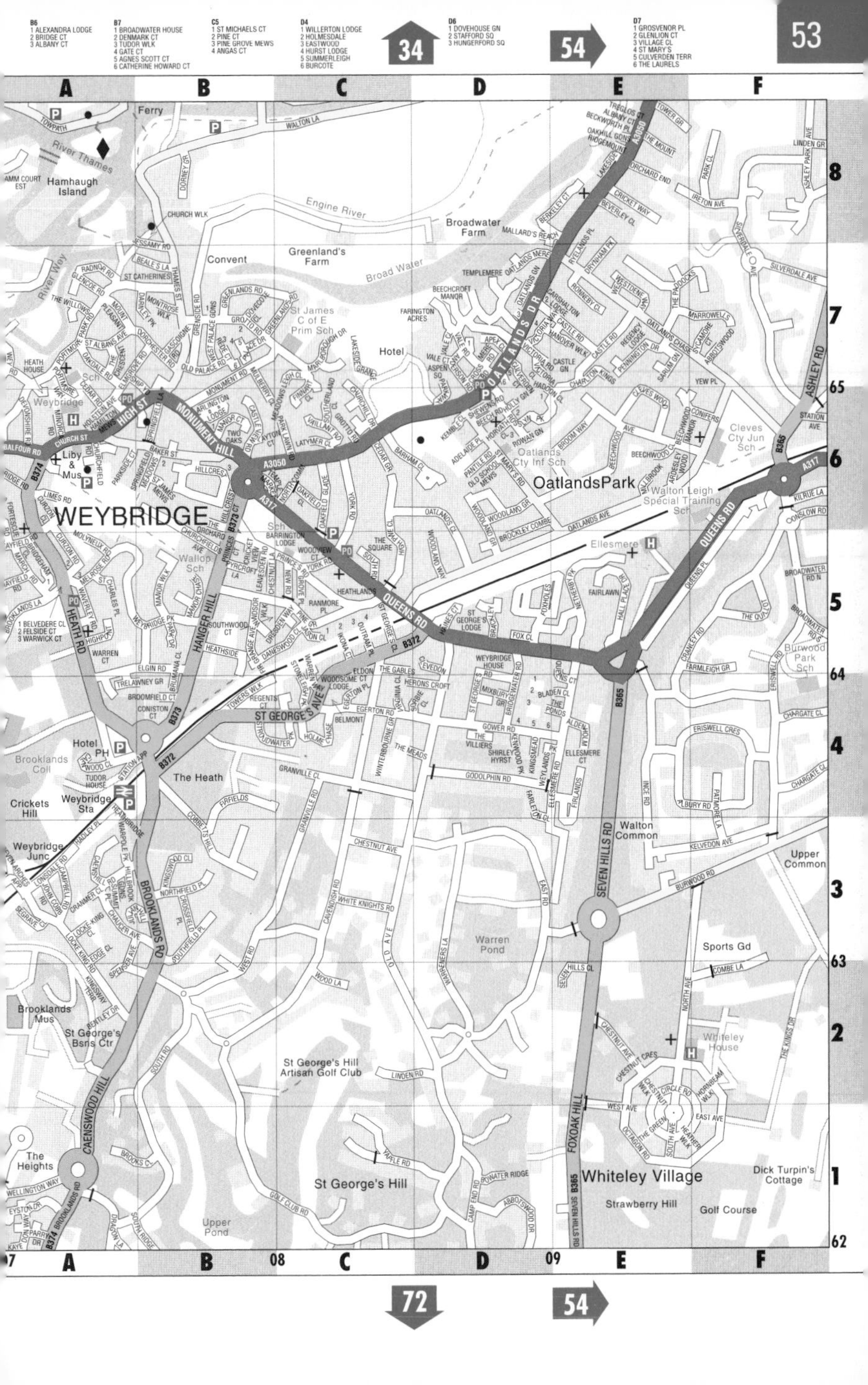
B6
1 ALEXANDRA LODGE
2 BRIDGE CT
3 ALBANY CT
B7
1 BROADWATER HOUSE
2 DENMARK CT
3 TUDOR WLK
4 GATE CT
5 AGNES SCOTT CT
6 CATHERINE HOWARD CT
C5
1 ST MICHAELS CT
2 PINE CT
3 PINE GROVE MEWS
4 ANGAS CT
D4
1 WILLERTON LODGE
2 HOLMESDALE
3 EASTWOOD
4 HURST LODGE
5 SUMMERLEIGH
6 BURCOTE
34
D6
1 DOVEHOUSE GN
2 STAFFORD SQ
3 HUNGERFORD SQ
54
D7
1 GROSVENOR PL
2 GLENLION CT
3 VILLAGE CL
4 ST MARY'S
5 CULVERDEN TERR
6 THE LAURELS
A
B
C
D
E
F
Ferry
River Thames
Hamhaugh Island
Engine River
Broadwater Farm
Convent
Greenland's Farm
Broad Water
River Wey
St James C of E Prim Sch
Hotel
OATLANDS DR
WEYBRIDGE
MONUMENT HILL
HIGH ST
QUEENS RD
OatlandsPark
Oatlands Cty Inf Sch
Walton Leigh Special Training Sch
Cleves Cty Jun Sch
Ellesmere
Wallop Sch
HANGER HILL
HEATH RD
ST GEORGE'S AVE
Burwood Park Sch
Brooklands Coll
The Heath
Weybridge Sta
Crickets Hill
Weybridge Junc
Walton Common
Upper Common
SEVEN HILLS RD
BROOKLANDS RD
Warren Pond
Sports Gd
Brooklands Mus
St George's Bsns Ctr
St George's Hill Artisan Golf Club
Whiteley House
CAENSWOOD HILL
The Heights
FOXOAK HILL
St George's Hill
Whiteley Village
Strawberry Hill
Dick Turpin's Cottage
Golf Course
Upper Pond
8
7
65
6
5
64
4
3
63
2
1
62
08
09
72
54

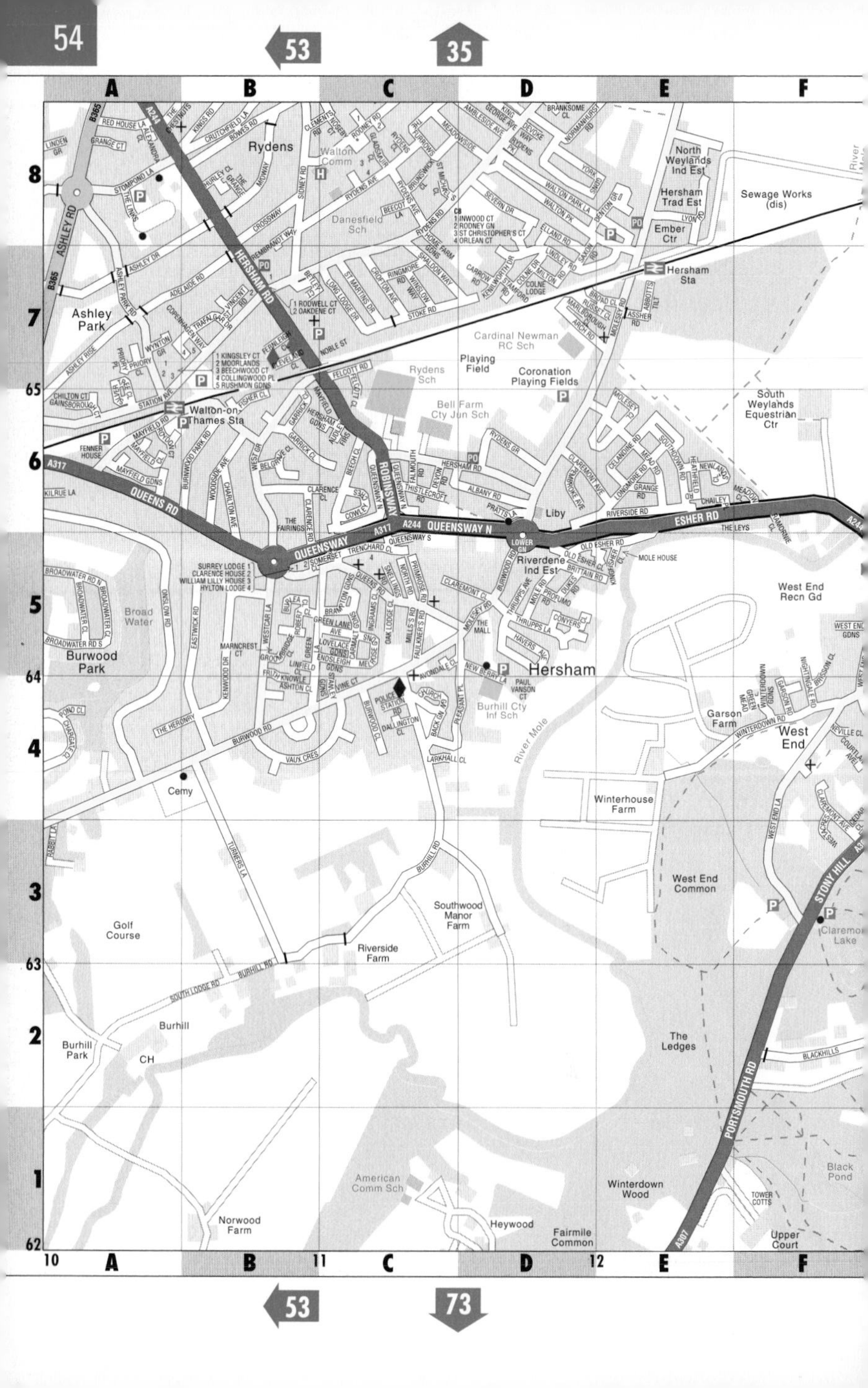

54
53
35
73
53
A
B
C
D
E
F
8
7
65
6
5
64
4
3
63
2
1
62
10
11
12
Rydens
Walton Comm
Danesfield Sch
North Weylands Ind Est
Hersham Trad Est
Ember Ctr
Sewage Works (dis)
Hersham Sta
Ashley Park
Cardinal Newman RC Sch
Playing Field
Rydens Sch
Coronation Playing Fields
Bell Farm Cty Jun Sch
Walton-on-Thames Sta
South Weylands Equestrian Ctr
Fenner House
Liby
Lower Gn
Riverdene Ind Est
West End Recn Gd
Broad Water
Burwood Park
Hersham
Burhill Cty Inf Sch
Garson Farm
West End
River Mole
Cemy
Winterhouse Farm
West End Common
Golf Course
Southwood Manor Farm
Riverside Farm
Claremont Lake
Burhill
Burhill Park
CH
The Ledges
American Comm Sch
Winterdown Wood
Black Pond
Tower Cotts
Norwood Farm
Heywood
Fairmile Common
Upper Court
HERSHAM RD
ROBINSWAY
QUEENS RD
QUEENSWAY
QUEENSWAY N
ESHER RD
ASHLEY RD
PORTSMOUTH RD
STONY HILL
BURWOOD RD
BURHILL RD
SOUTH LODGE RD
TURNERS LA
BLACKHILLS
MOLESEY RD
WINTERDOWN RD
A244
A317
A307
B365
CB
1 INWOOD CT
2 RODNEY GN
3 ST CHRISTOPHER'S CT
4 ORLEAN CT
1 RODWELL CT
2 OAKDENE CT
1 KINGSLEY CT
2 MOORLANDS
3 BEECHWOOD CT
4 COLLINGWOOD PL
5 RUSHMON GDNS
SURREY LODGE 1
CLARENCE HOUSE 2
WILLIAM LILLY HOUSE 3
HYLTON LODGE 4

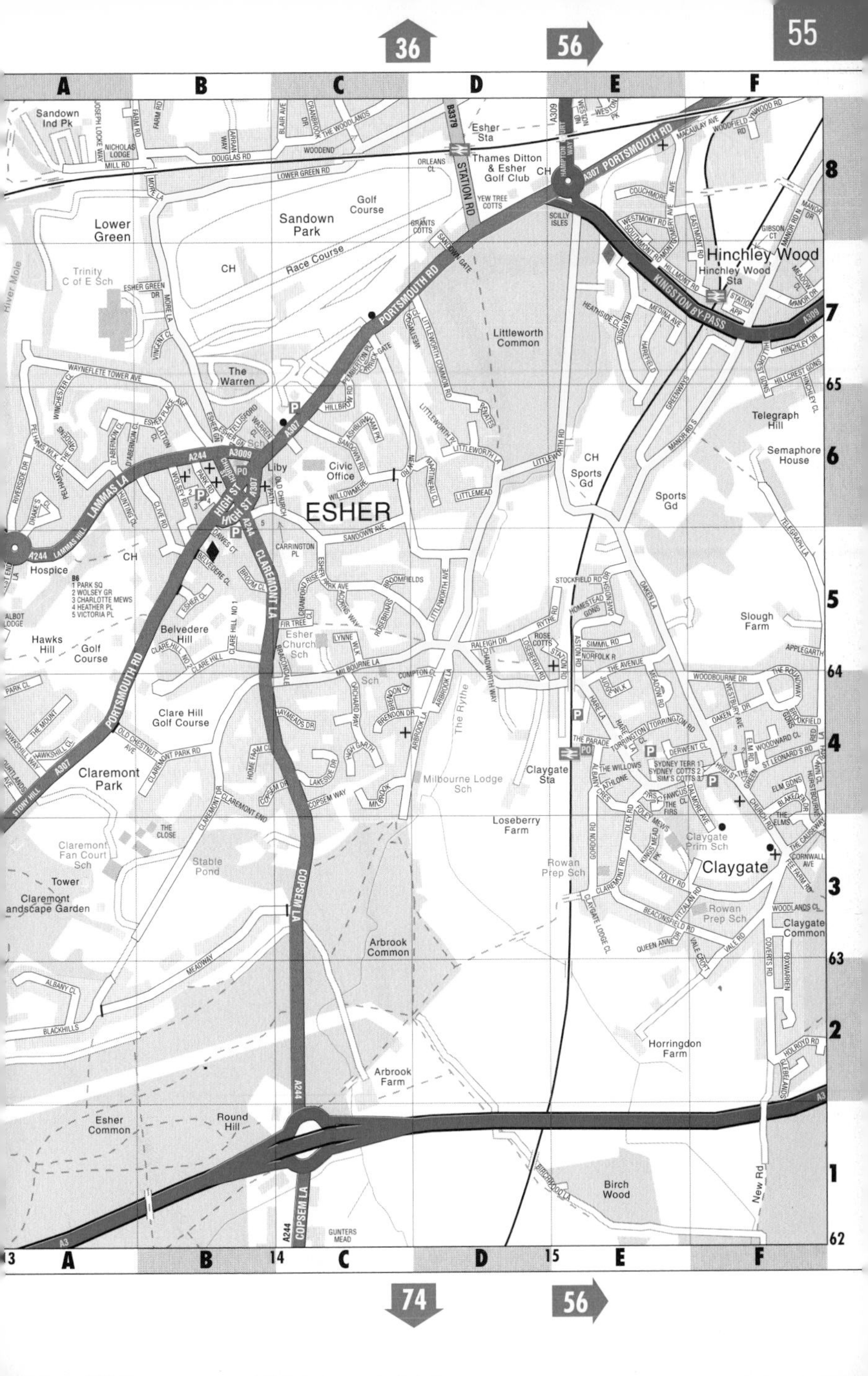

A B C D E F

8

7

65

6

5

64

4

3

63

2

1

62

A B C D E F
3 14 15

Sandown Ind Pk
Lower Green
Trinity C of E Sch
River Mole
Sandown Park
Golf Course
Race Course
CH
Esher Green Dr
Douglas Rd
Lower Green Rd
Woodend
The Woodlands
Blair Ave
Farm Rd
Mill Rd
Nicholab Lodge
Station Rd
Orleans Cl
Grants Cotts
Esher Sta
Thames Ditton & Esher Golf Club
Portsmouth Rd
Scilly Isles
Kingston By-Pass
Hinchley Wood
Hinchley Wood Sta
Yew Tree Cotts
Couchmore Ave
Westmont Rd
Telegraph Hill
Semaphore House
Littleworth Common
Littleworth
Littlemead
CH Sports Gd
Sports Gd
Slough Farm
Applegarth
The Warren
Waynflete Tower Ave
High St
Lammas La
Civic Office
ESHER
Carrington Pl
Bloomfields
Park Ave
The Firs
Lynne
Esher Church Sch
Milbourne La
Raleigh Dr
Rose Cotts
Norfolk Rd
Simm Rd
The Avenue
Stockfield Rd
The Parade
Woodbourne Dr
The Ridgeway
Oxfield
Hospice
Hawks Hill
Golf Course
Belvedere Hill
Clare Hill Golf Course
Clare Hill
The Rythe
Compton Cl
Brendon Dr
Copsem Way
Milbourne Lodge Sch
Claygate Sta
Loseberry Farm
The Firs
Torrington Rd
Derwent Rd
St Leonards Rd
Elm Grove
Woodland Cl
Claygate
Claygate Prim Sch
Cornwall Ave
Claremont Park
The Close
Stable Pond
Claremont Fan Court Sch
Tower
Claremont Landscape Garden
Albany Cl
Blackhills
Meadway
Copsem La
Arbrook Common
Rowan Prep Sch
Queen Annes
Rowan Prep Sch
Woodlands Cl
Claygate Common
Foxwarren
Esher Common
Round Hill
Arbrook Farm
Gunters Mead
Horringdon Farm
Birch Wood
New Rd
A3

1 Park Sq
2 Wolsey Gr
3 Charlotte Mews
4 Heather Pl
5 Victoria Pl

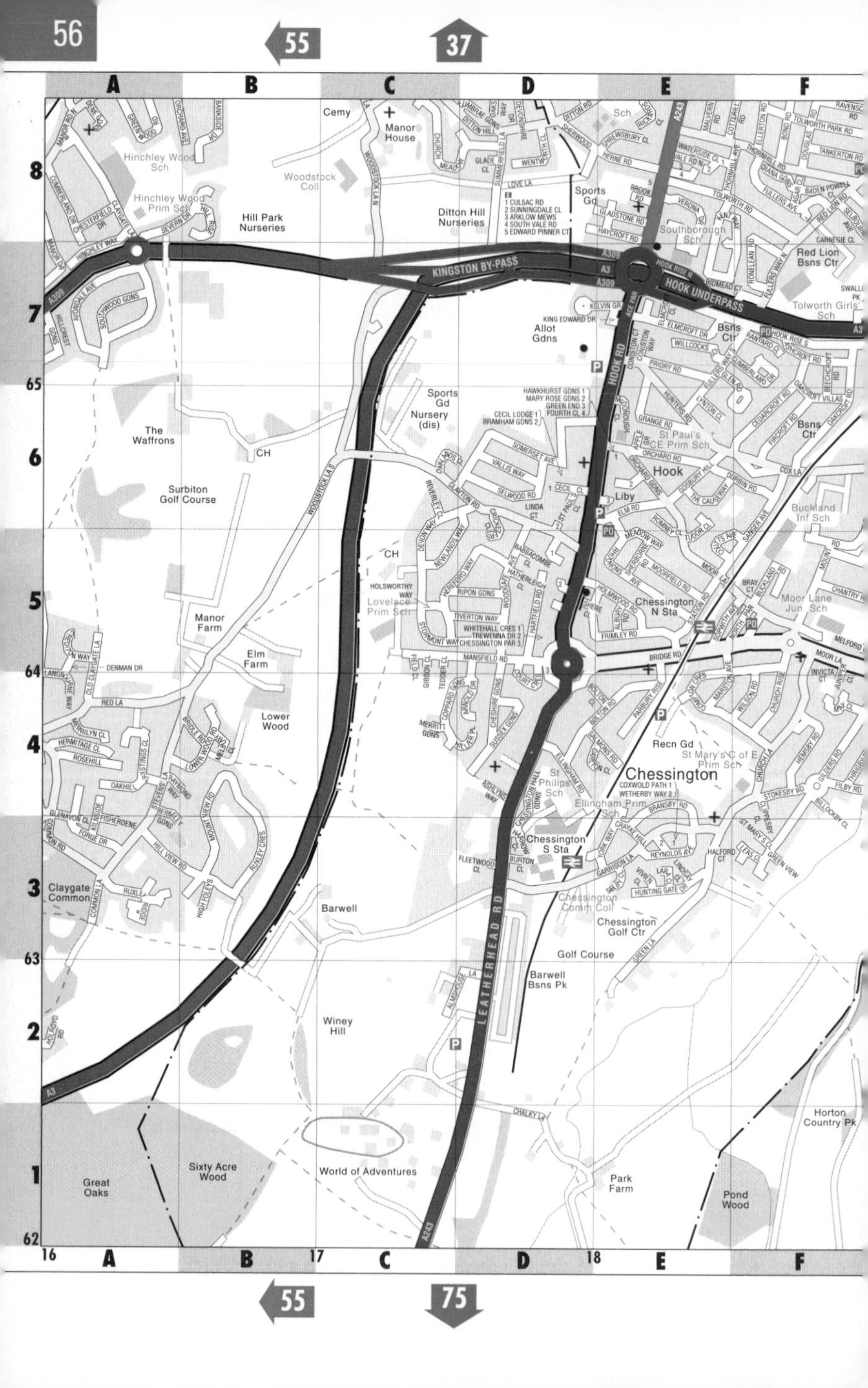

55
37
A
B
C
D
E
F
8
7
65
6
5
64
4
3
63
2
1
62
16
17
18
Cemy
Manor House
Hinchley Wood Sch
Hinchley Wood Prim Sch
Woodstock Coll
Hill Park Nurseries
Ditton Hill Nurseries
Sch
Sports Gd
Southborough Sch
Red Lion Bsns Ctr
Tolworth Girls' Sch
KINGSTON BY-PASS
HOOK UNDERPASS
HOOK RISE N
HOOK RISE S
A309
A3
A243
E8
1 CULSAC RD
2 SUNNINGDALE CL
3 ARKLOW MEWS
4 SOUTH VALE RD
5 EDWARD PINNER CT
Allot Gdns
KING EDWARD DR
KELVIN GR
HOOK RD
Bsns Ctr
HAWKHURST GDNS 1
MARY ROSE GDNS 2
GREEN END 3
FOURTH CL 4
CECIL LODGE 1
BRAMHAM GDNS 2
Sports Gd Nursery (dis)
The Waffrons
CH
Surbiton Golf Course
St Paul's CE Prim Sch
Hook
Liby
Buckland Inf Sch
Moor Lane Jun Sch
HOLSWORTHY WAY
Lovelace Prim Sch
WHITEHALL CRES 1
TREWENNA DR 2
CHESSINGTON PAR 3
Chessington N Sta
Manor Farm
Elm Farm
Lower Wood
MOOR LA
BRIDGE RD
MANSFIELD RD
RED LA
DENMAN DR
Recn Gd
St Mary's C of E Prim Sch
Chessington
COXWOLD PATH 1
WETHERBY WAY 2
St Philips Sch
Ellingham Prim Sch
Chessington S Sta
Claygate Common
Barwell
Chessington Comm Coll
Chessington Golf Ctr
Golf Course
Barwell Bsns Pk
LEATHERHEAD RD
Winey Hill
CHALKY LA
Horton Country Pk
Great Oaks
Sixty Acre Wood
World of Adventures
Park Farm
Pond Wood
55
75

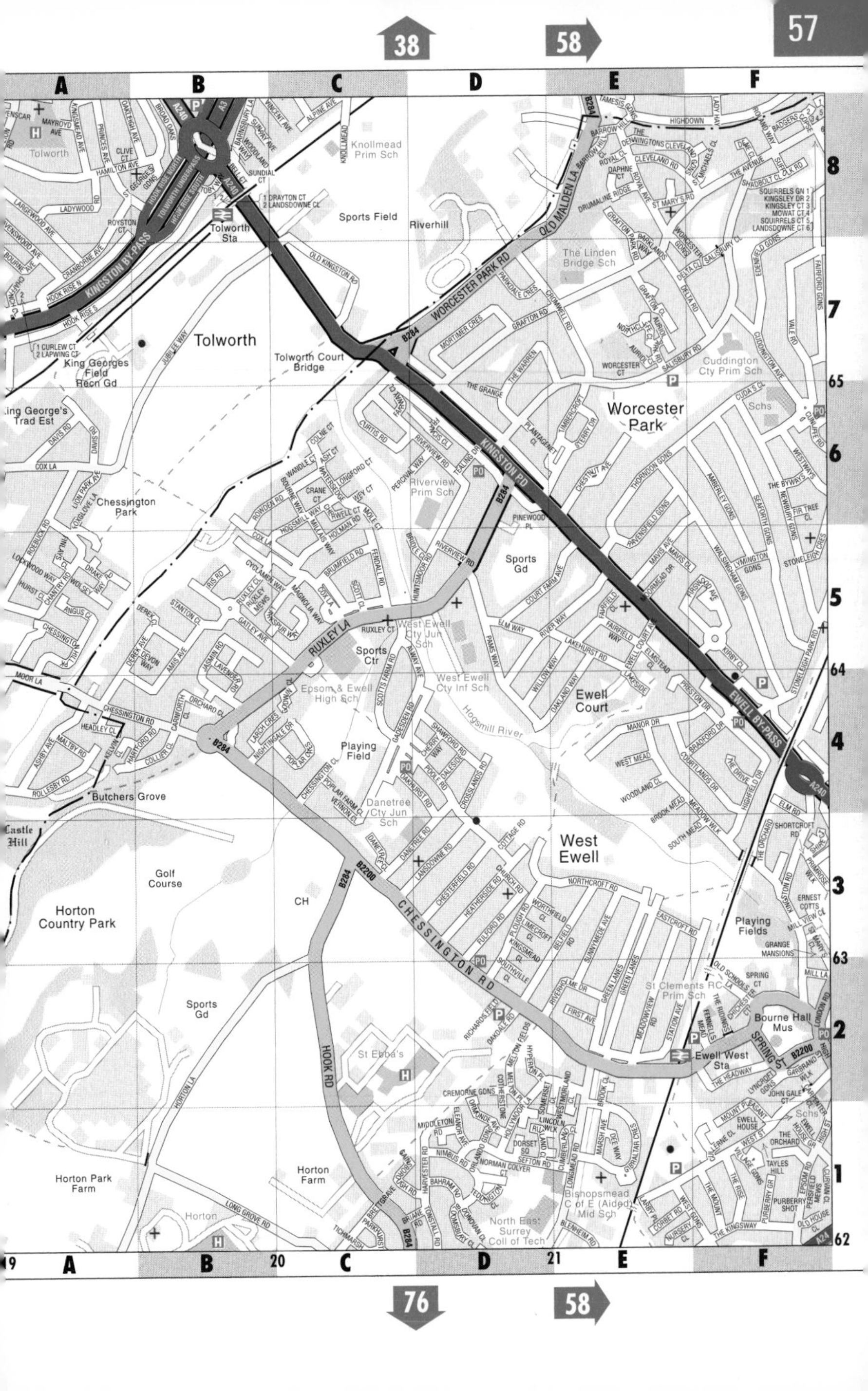
38
58
A
B
C
D
E
F
Tolworth
Tolworth Sta
Knollmead Prim Sch
Sports Field
Riverhill
KINGSTON BY-PASS
WORCESTER PARK RD
OLD MALDEN LA
The Linden Bridge Sch
Tolworth Court Bridge
King Georges Field Recn Gd
King George's Trad Est
Cuddington Cty Prim Sch
Worcester Park
Chessington Park
KINGSTON RD
Riverview Prim Sch
Sports Gd
RUXLEY LA
West Ewell Cty Jun Sch
Sports Ctr
West Ewell Cty Inf Sch
Epsom & Ewell High Sch
Ewell Court
Hogsmill River
EWELL BY-PASS
Playing Field
Butchers Grove
Castle Hill
Danetree Cty Jun Sch
West Ewell
Golf Course
Horton Country Park
CH
CHESSINGTON RD
Playing Fields
Sports Gd
St Clements RC Prim Sch
Bourne Hall Mus
Ewell West Sta
SPRING ST
HOOK RD
St Ebba's
Horton Farm
Horton Park Farm
Horton
Bishopsmead C of E (Aided) Mid Sch
North East Surrey Coll of Tech
8
7
65
6
5
64
4
3
63
2
1
62
19
20
21
76
58

57
39

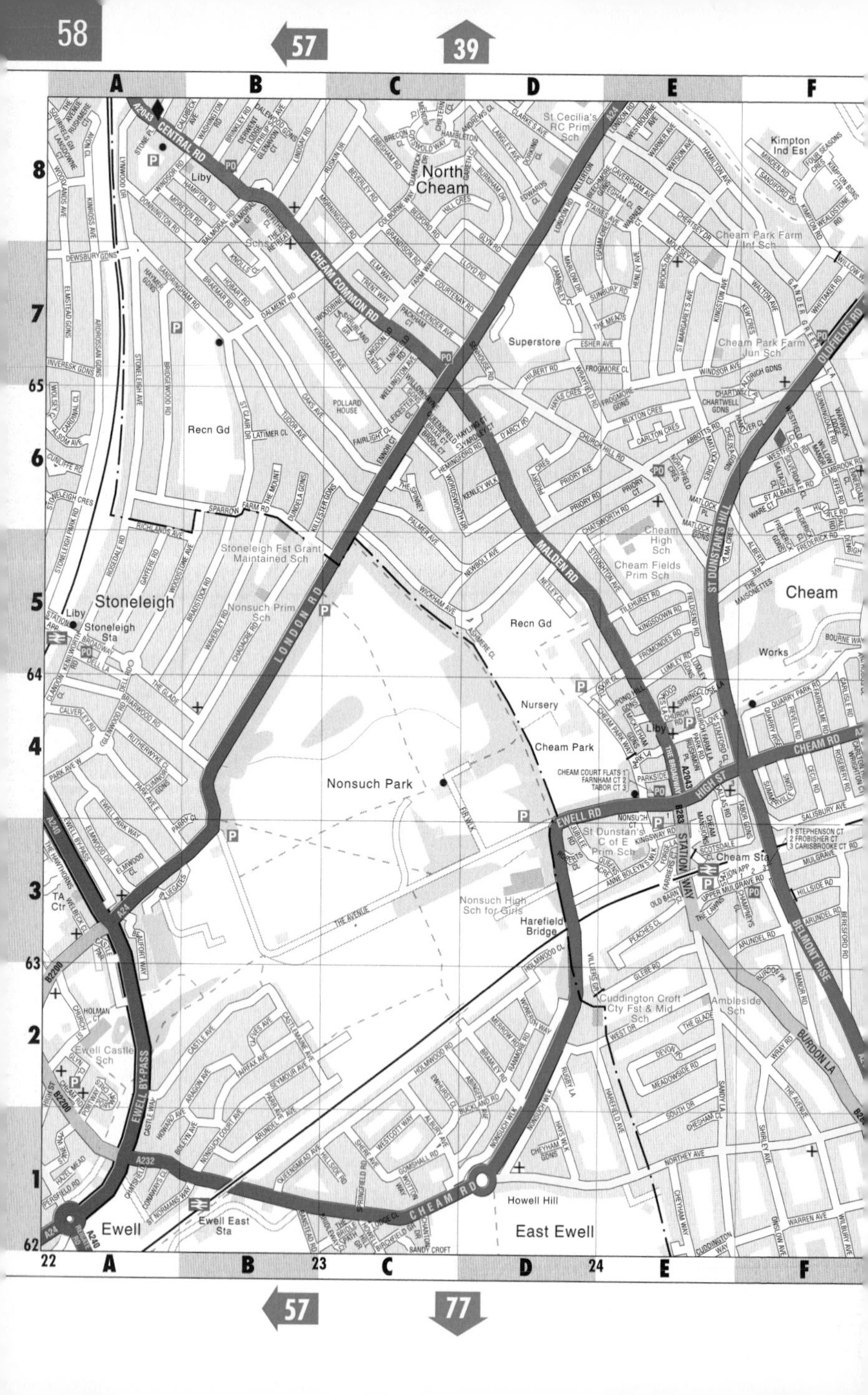
A
B
C
D
E
F
8
7
65
6
5
64
4
3
63
2
1
62
22
23
24
North Cheam
Kimpton Ind Est
St Cecilia's RC Prim Sch
CENTRAL RD
A2043
CHEAM COMMON RD
LONDON RD
A24
Liby
Schs
Superstore
Cheam Park Farm Inf Sch
Cheam Park Farm Jun Sch
Recn Gd
POLLARD HOUSE
MALDEN RD
ST DUNSTAN'S HILL
OLDFIELDS RD
Stoneleigh
Stoneleigh Sta
Stoneleigh Fst Grant Maintained Sch
Nonsuch Prim Sch
Cheam High Sch
Cheam Fields Prim Sch
Cheam
Works
Nursery
Cheam Park
Nonsuch Park
CHEAM RD
HIGH ST
EWELL RD
STATION WAY
St Dunstan's C of E Prim Sch
Cheam Sta
CHEAM COURT FLATS 1
FARNHAM CT 2
TABOR CT 3
1 STEPHENSON CT
2 FROBISHER CT
3 CARISBROOKE CT RD
Nonsuch High Sch for Girls
Harefield Bridge
Cuddington Croft Cty Fst & Mid Sch
Ambleside Sch
BELMONT RISE
BURDON LA
TA Ctr
Ewell Castle Sch
EWELL BY-PASS
A240
B2200
A232
Ewell
Ewell East Sta
Howell Hill
East Ewell
THE AVENUE

57
77

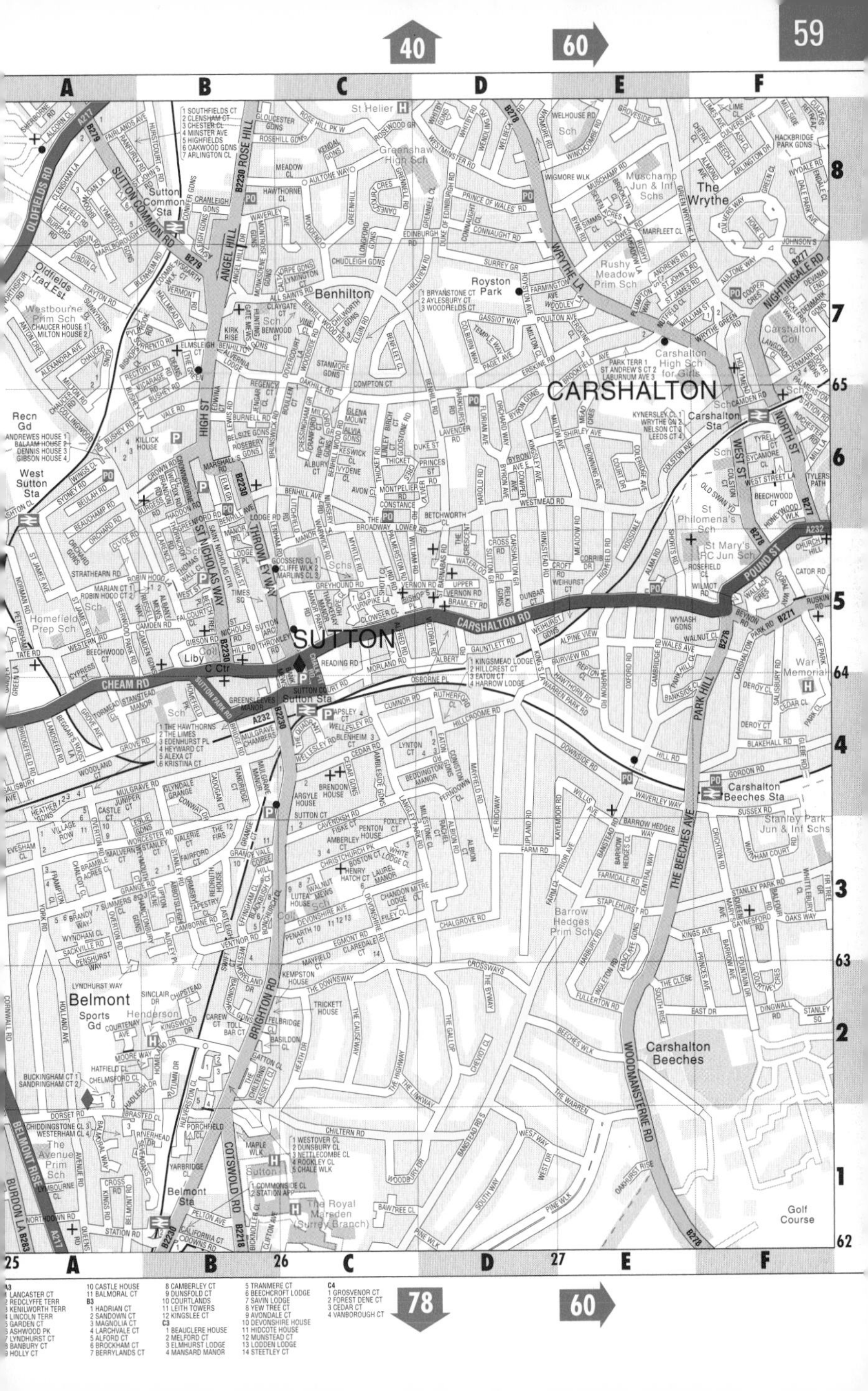
40
60
A B C D E F
8
7
65
6
64
5
4
3
63
2
1
62
CARSHALTON
SUTTON
Benhilton
The Wrythe
Royston Park
Belmont
Carshalton Beeches
Sutton Common Sta
West Sutton Sta
Sutton Sta
Carshalton Sta
Carshalton Beeches Sta
Belmont Sta
St Helier
Greenshaw High Sch
Muschamp Jun & Inf Schs
Rushy Meadow Prim Sch
Carshalton High Sch for Girls
Carshalton Coll
Westbourne Prim Sch
Oldfields Trad Est
Recn Gd
Homefield Prep Sch
St Philomena's Sch
St Mary's RC Jun Sch
War Memorial
Stanley Park Jun & Inf Schs
Barrow Hedges Prim Sch
Belmont Sports Gd
The Avenue Prim Sch
The Royal Marsden (Surrey Branch)
Golf Course
CHEAM RD
CARSHALTON RD
THROWLEY WAY
ST NICHOLAS WAY
HIGH ST
ANGEL HILL
B2230 ROSE HILL
SUTTON COMMON RD
WRYTHE LA
NIGHTINGALE RD
POUND ST
WEST ST
NORTH ST
PARK HILL
THE BEECHES AVE
WOODMANSTERNE RD
BRIGHTON RD
COTSWOLD RD
BELMONT RISE
BURDON LA
OLDFIELDS RD
25
26
27
A B C D E F
A3
1 LANCASTER CT
2 REDCLYFFE TERR
3 KENILWORTH TERR
4 LINCOLN TERR
5 GARDEN CT
6 ASHWOOD PK
7 LYNDHURST CT
8 BANBURY CT
9 HOLLY CT
10 CASTLE HOUSE
11 BALMORAL CT
B3
1 HADRIAN CT
2 SANDOWN CT
3 MAGNOLIA CT
4 LARCHVALE CT
5 ALFORD CT
6 BROCKHAM CT
7 BERRYLANDS CT
8 CAMBERLEY CT
9 DUNSFOLD CT
10 COURTLANDS
11 LEITH TOWERS
12 KINGSLEE CT
C3
1 BEAUCLERE HOUSE
2 MELFORD CT
3 ELMHURST LODGE
4 MANSARD MANOR
5 TRANMERE CT
6 BEECHCROFT LODGE
7 SAVIN LODGE
8 YEW TREE CT
9 AVONDALE CT
10 DEVONSHIRE HOUSE
11 HIDCOTE HOUSE
12 MUNSTEAD CT
13 LODDEN LODGE
14 STEETLEY CT
C4
1 GROSVENOR CT
2 FOREST DENE CT
3 CEDAR CT
4 VANBOROUGH CT
78
60

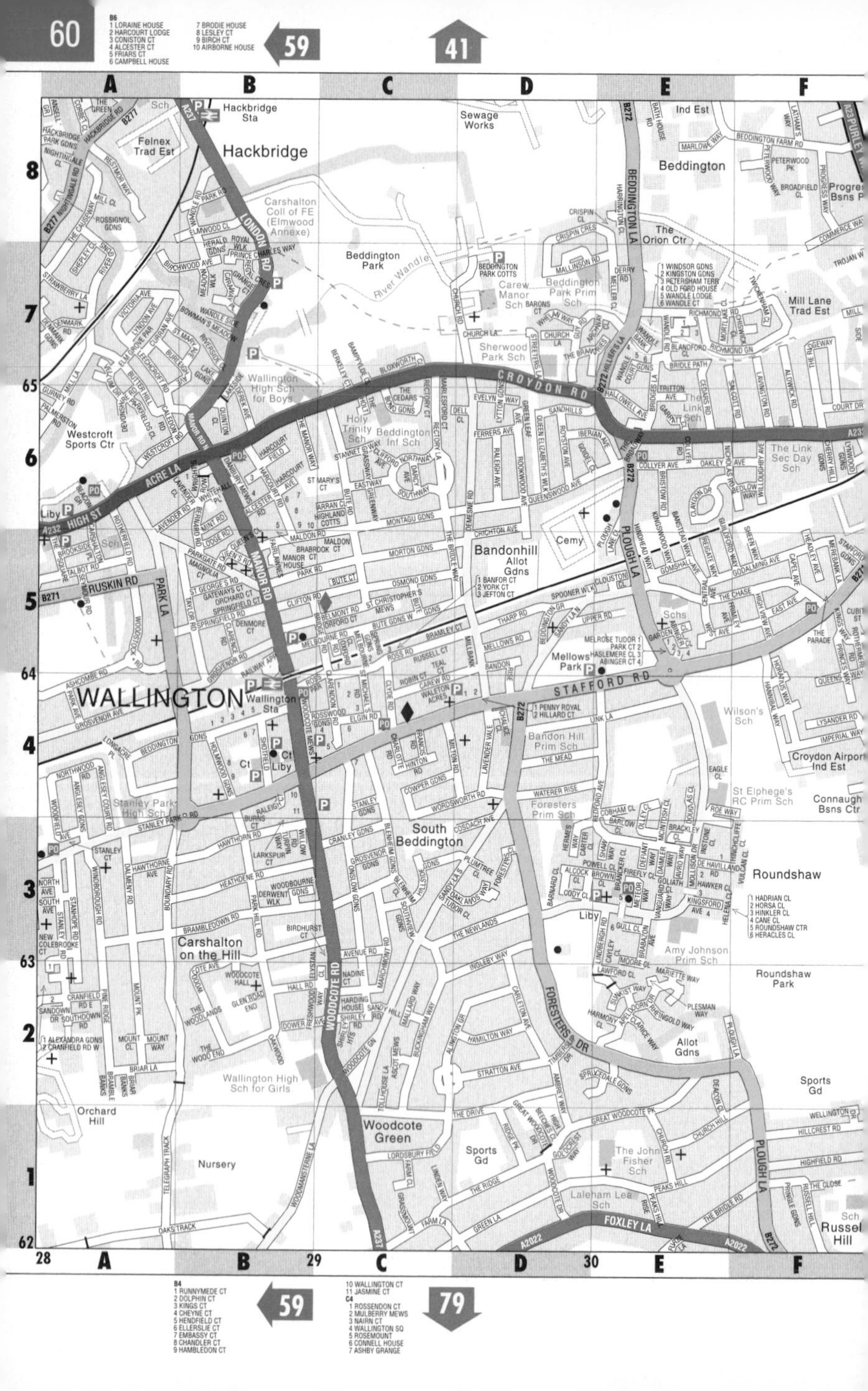

60

B6
1 LORAINE HOUSE
2 HARCOURT LODGE
3 CONISTON CT
4 ALCESTER CT
5 FRIARS CT
6 CAMPBELL HOUSE

7 BRODIE HOUSE
8 LESLEY CT
9 BIRCH CT
10 AIRBORNE HOUSE

59

41

59

79

B4
1 RUNNYMEDE CT
2 DOLPHIN CT
3 KINGS CT
4 CHEYNE CT
5 HENDFIELD CT
6 ELLERSLIE CT
7 EMBASSY CT
8 CHANDLER CT
9 HAMBLEDON CT

10 WALLINGTON CT
11 JASMINE CT

C4
1 ROSSENDON CT
2 MULBERRY MEWS
3 NAIRN CT
4 WALLINGTON SQ
5 ROSEMOUNT
6 CONNELL HOUSE
7 ASHBY GRANGE

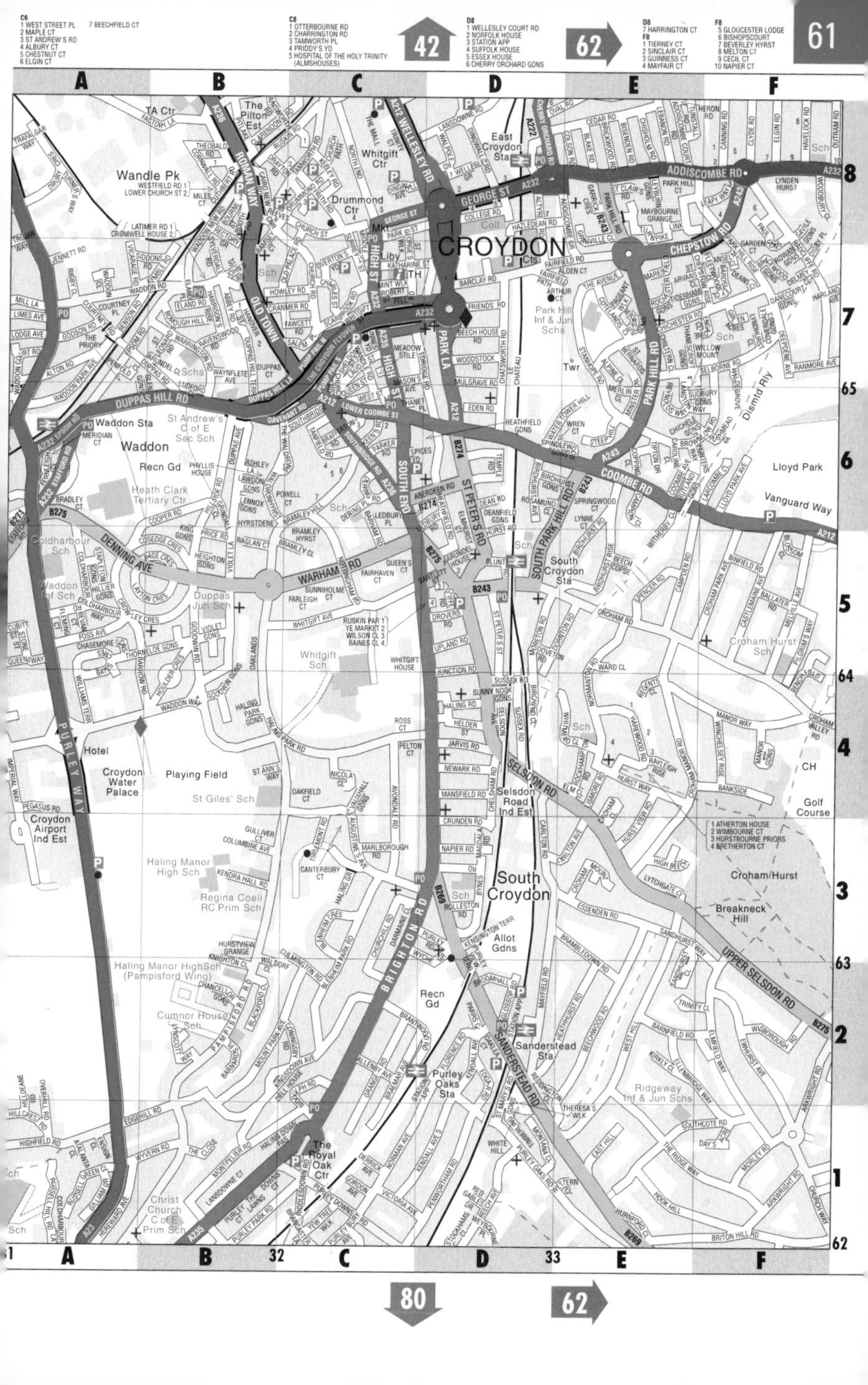
C6
1 WEST STREET PL
2 MAPLE CT
3 ST ANDREW'S RD
4 ALBURY CT
5 CHESTNUT CT
6 ELGIN CT
7 BEECHFIELD CT
C8
1 OTTERBOURNE RD
2 CHARRINGTON RD
3 TAMWORTH PL
4 PRIDDY'S YD
5 HOSPITAL OF THE HOLY TRINITY (ALMSHOUSES)
42
D8
1 WELLESLEY COURT RD
2 NORFOLK HOUSE
3 STATION APP
4 SUFFOLK HOUSE
5 ESSEX HOUSE
6 CHERRY ORCHARD GDNS
62
D8
7 HARRINGTON CT
F8
1 TIERNEY CT
2 SINCLAIR CT
3 GUINNESS CT
4 MAYFAIR CT
F8
5 GLOUCESTER LODGE
6 BISHOPSCOURT
7 BEVERLEY HYRST
8 MELTON CT
9 CECIL CT
10 NAPIER CT
61
A
B
C
D
E
F
CROYDON
East Croydon Sta
Whitgift Ctr
Drummond Ctr
Wandle Pk
The Pilton Est
TA Ctr
Waddon Sta
Waddon
Recn Gd
Heath Clark Tertiary Ctr
St Andrew's C of E Sec Sch
Coldharbour Sch
Waddon Inf Sch
Duppas Jun Sch
Whitgift Sch
Park Hill Inf & Jun Schs
Lloyd Park
Vanguard Way
South Croydon Sta
Croham Hurst Sch
Croham Hurst
Breakneck Hill
Golf Course
Hotel
Croydon Water Palace
Playing Field
St Giles' Sch
Croydon Airport Ind Est
Haling Manor High Sch
Regina Coeli RC Prim Sch
Haling Manor HighSch (Pampisford Wing)
Cumnor House Sch
Selsdon Road Ind Est
South Croydon
Allot Gdns
Recn Gd
Sanderstead Sta
Purley Oaks Sta
Ridgeway Inf & Jun Schs
The Royal Oak Ctr
Christ Church C of E Prim Sch
PURLEY WAY
DUPPAS HILL RD
DENNING AVE
WARHAM RD
COOMBE RD
ADDISCOMBE RD
GEORGE ST
WELLESLEY RD
PARK LA
HIGH ST
SOUTH END
BRIGHTON RD
SELSDON RD
UPPER SELSDON RD
SANDERSTEAD RD
SOUTH PARK HILL RD
PARK HILL RD
CHEPSTOW RD
RUSKIN PAR 1
YE MARKET 2
WILSON CL 3
BAINES CL 4
1 ATHERTON HOUSE
2 WIMBOURNE CT
3 HURSTBOURNE PRIORS
4 BRETHERTON CT
8
7
6
5
4
3
2
1
65
64
63
62
32
33
80
62

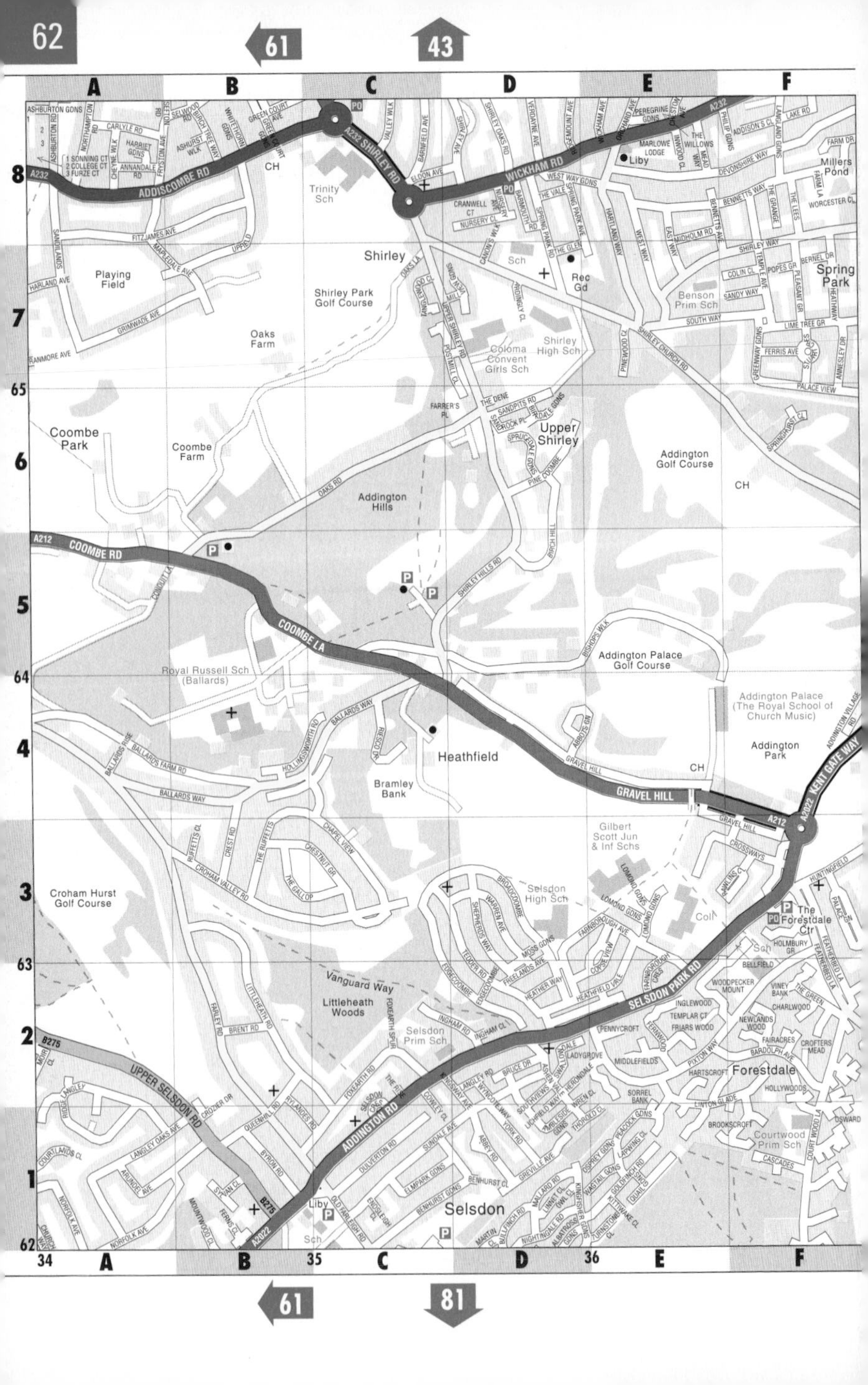

61
43
A
B
C
D
E
F
8
7
65
6
5
64
4
3
63
2
1
62
34
35
36
A232
ADDISCOMBE RD
A232 SHIRLEY RD
WICKHAM RD
Trinity Sch
Shirley
Playing Field
Shirley Park Golf Course
Oaks Farm
Coloma Convent Girls Sch
Shirley High Sch
Benson Prim Sch
Spring Park
Millers Pond
Rec Gd
Sch
Liby
CH
Coombe Park
Coombe Farm
Upper Shirley
Addington Golf Course
Addington Hills
A212
COOMBE RD
COOMBE LA
Royal Russell Sch (Ballards)
Addington Palace Golf Course
Addington Palace (The Royal School of Church Music)
Addington Park
Heathfield
Bramley Bank
GRAVEL HILL
A2022
KENT GATE WAY
Gilbert Scott Jun & Inf Schs
Selsdon High Sch
Coll
Croham Hurst Golf Course
Vanguard Way
Littleheath Woods
Selsdon Prim Sch
SELSDON PARK RD
The Forestdale Ctr
Forestdale
Courtwood Prim Sch
B275
UPPER SELSDON RD
ADDINGTON RD
Selsdon
Sch

44

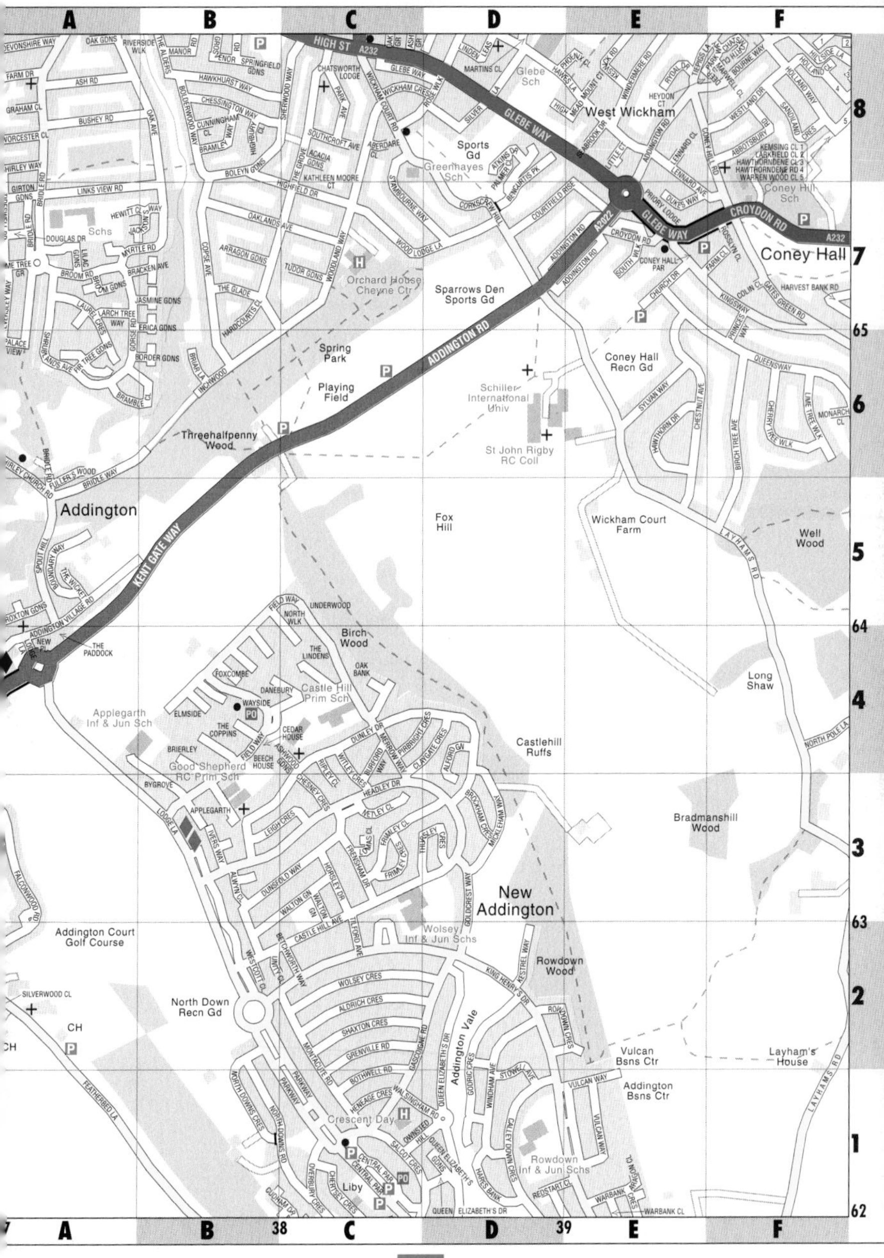
A
B
C
D
E
F
HIGH ST
A232
GLEBE WAY
CROYDON RD
ADDINGTON RD
A2022
KENT GATE WAY
Glebe Sch
West Wickham
Sports Gd
Greenhayes Sch
Coney Hill Sch
Coney Hall
Schs
Orchard House Cheyne Ctr
Sparrows Den Sports Gd
Spring Park
Playing Field
Coney Hall Recn Gd
Schiller International Univ
St John Rigby RC Coll
Threehalfpenny Wood
Addington
Fox Hill
Wickham Court Farm
Well Wood
Birch Wood
Castle Hill Prim Sch
Applegarth Inf & Jun Sch
Long Shaw
Castlehill Ruffs
Good Shepherd RC Prim Sch
Bradmanshill Wood
New Addington
Addington Court Golf Course
Wolsey Inf & Jun Schs
Rowdown Wood
North Down Recn Gd
Addington Vale
Vulcan Bsns Ctr
Layham's House
Addington Bsns Ctr
Crescent Day
Rowdown Inf & Jun Schs
Liby
LAYHAMS RD
8
7
65
6
5
64
4
3
63
2
1
62
38
39

82

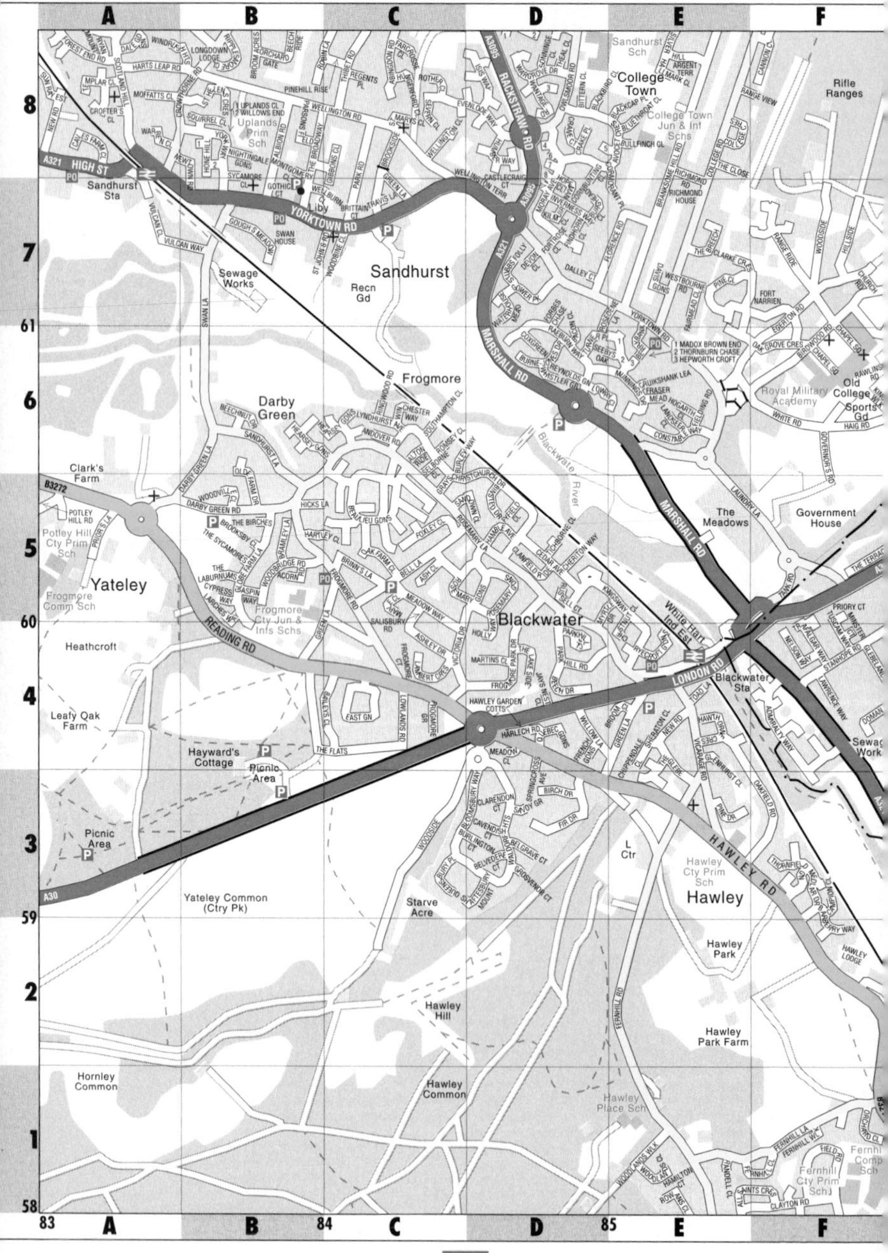

D8
1 MULBERRY CL
2 MAY CL
3 SHRIVENHAM CL
4 CENTURION CL
5 CHAFFINCH CL
6 TARBAT CT

7 ROCKFIELD WAY
8 BALINTORE CT

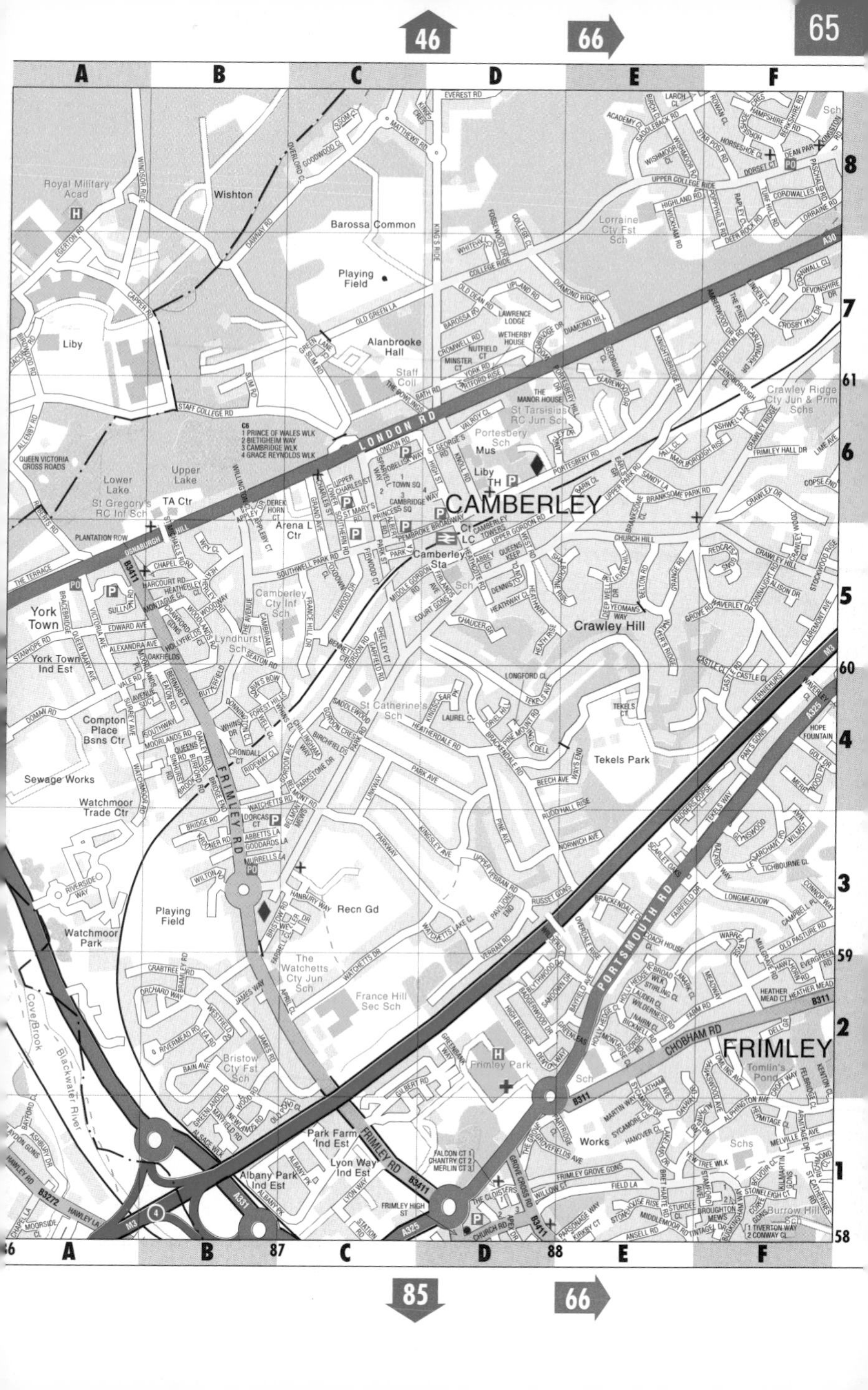

46
66
A
B
C
D
E
F
Royal Military Acad
Wishton
Barossa Common
Playing Field
Alanbrooke Hall
Staff Coll
Liby
Lower Lake
Upper Lake
St Gregory's RC Inf Sch
TA Ctr
Arena L Ctr
CAMBERLEY
Camberley Sta
Portesbery Sch
Mus
St Tarsisius RC Jun Sch
THE MANOR HOUSE
Lorraine Cty Fst Sch
Crawley Ridge Cty Jun & Prim Schs
York Town
York Town Ind Est
Compton Place Bsns Ctr
Sewage Works
Watchmoor Trade Ctr
Watchmoor Park
Camberley Cty Inf Sch
Lyndhurst Sch
Crawley Hill
St Catherine's Sch
Tekels Park
Playing Field
Recn Gd
The Watchetts Cty Jun Sch
France Hill Sec Sch
Bristow Cty Fst Sch
Frimley Park
Park Farm Ind Est
Lyon Way Ind Est
Albany Park Ind Est
Works
FRIMLEY
Tomlin's Pond
Burrow Hill Sch
Cove Brook
Blackwater River
LONDON RD
PORTSMOUTH RD
FRIMLEY RD
CHOBHAM RD
OSNABURGH HILL
A30
M3
A325
A331
B3411
B311
B3272
C6
1 PRINCE OF WALES WLK
2 BIETIGHEIM WAY
3 CAMBRIDGE WLK
4 GRACE REYNOLDS WLK
FALCON CT 1
CHANTRY CT 2
MERLIN CT 3
1 TIVERTON WAY
2 CONWAY CL
61
60
59
58
86
87
88
85
66

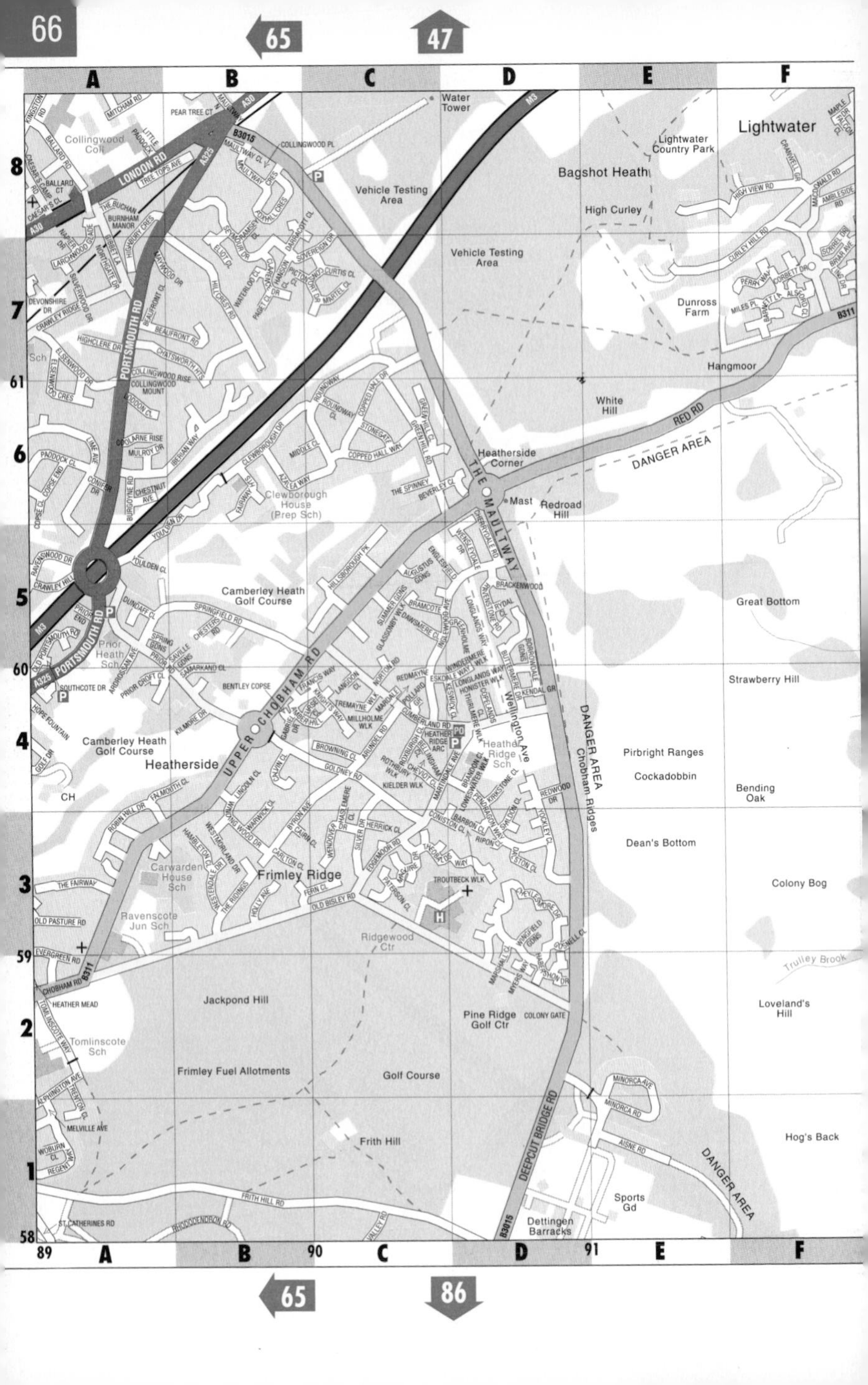
65
47
A
B
C
D
E
F
8
7
61
6
5
60
4
3
59
2
1
58
89
90
91
Water Tower
Lightwater
Lightwater Country Park
Bagshot Heath
High Curley
Vehicle Testing Area
Vehicle Testing Area
Collingwood Coll
LONDON RD
PORTSMOUTH RD
A30
A325
M3
B3015
B311
Dunross Farm
Hangmoor
White Hill
RED RD
DANGER AREA
Heatherside Corner
Mast
Redroad Hill
THE MAULTWAY
Clewborough House (Prep Sch)
Camberley Heath Golf Course
Great Bottom
Strawberry Hill
Prior Heath Sch
UPPER CHOBHAM RD
Wellington Ave
Heather Ridge Sch
DANGER AREA
Chobham Ridges
Pirbright Ranges
Cockadobbin
Bending Oak
Camberley Heath Golf Course
Heatherside
CH
Dean's Bottom
Carwarden House Sch
Frimley Ridge
Colony Bog
Ravenscote Jun Sch
Ridgewood Ctr
Trulley Brook
Jackpond Hill
Pine Ridge Golf Ctr
Loveland's Hill
Tomlinscote Sch
Frimley Fuel Allotments
Golf Course
DEEPCUT BRIDGE RD
Frith Hill
Hog's Back
DANGER AREA
Sports Gd
Dettingen Barracks
FRITH HILL RD
CHOBHAM RD
HEATHER MEAD
MINORCA AVE
MINORCA RD
AISNE RD
OLD BISLEY RD
COLONY GATE

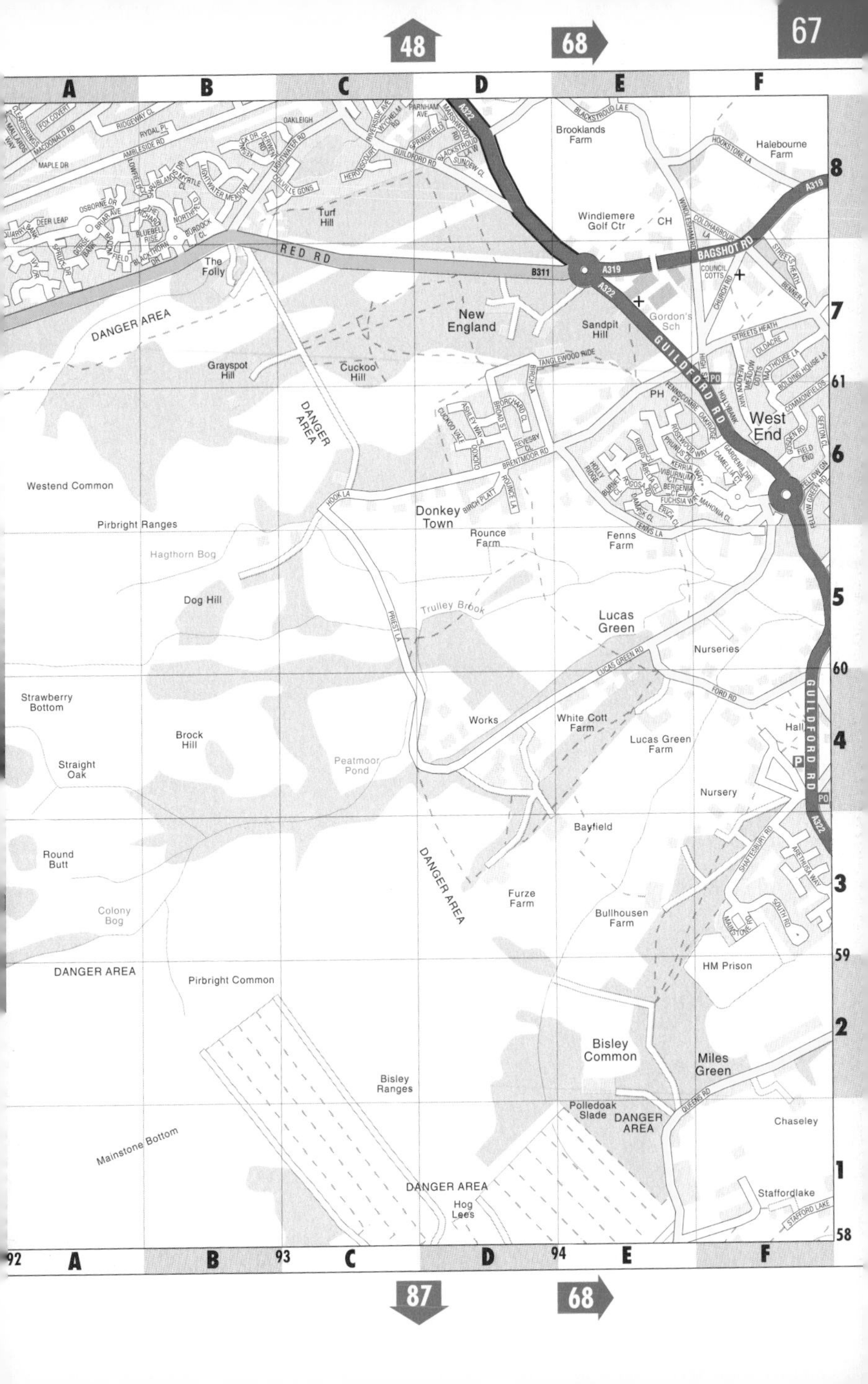
48
68
A
B
C
D
E
F
Brooklands Farm
Halebourne Farm
Turf Hill
Windlemere Golf Ctr
CH
RED RD
B311
A319
A322
BAGSHOT RD
The Folly
DANGER AREA
New England
Sandpit Hill
Gordon's Sch
COUNCIL COTTS
GUILDFORD RD
Grayspot Hill
Cuckoo Hill
PH
West End
PO
DANGER AREA
Westend Common
Pirbright Ranges
Donkey Town
Rounce Farm
Fenns Farm
Hagthorn Bog
Dog Hill
Trulley Brook
Lucas Green
Nurseries
LUCAS GREEN RD
FORD RD
PRIEST LA
Strawberry Bottom
Brock Hill
Works
White Cott Farm
Lucas Green Farm
Hall
Straight Oak
Peatmoor Pond
Nursery
Bayfield
Round Butt
DANGER AREA
Furze Farm
Colony Bog
Bullhousen Farm
HM Prison
DANGER AREA
Pirbright Common
Bisley Common
Miles Green
Bisley Ranges
Polledoak Slade
DANGER AREA
Chaseley
Mainstone Bottom
DANGER AREA
Hog Lees
Staffordlake
STAFFORD LAKE
QUEENS RD
8
7
61
6
5
60
4
3
59
2
1
58
92
93
94
87
68

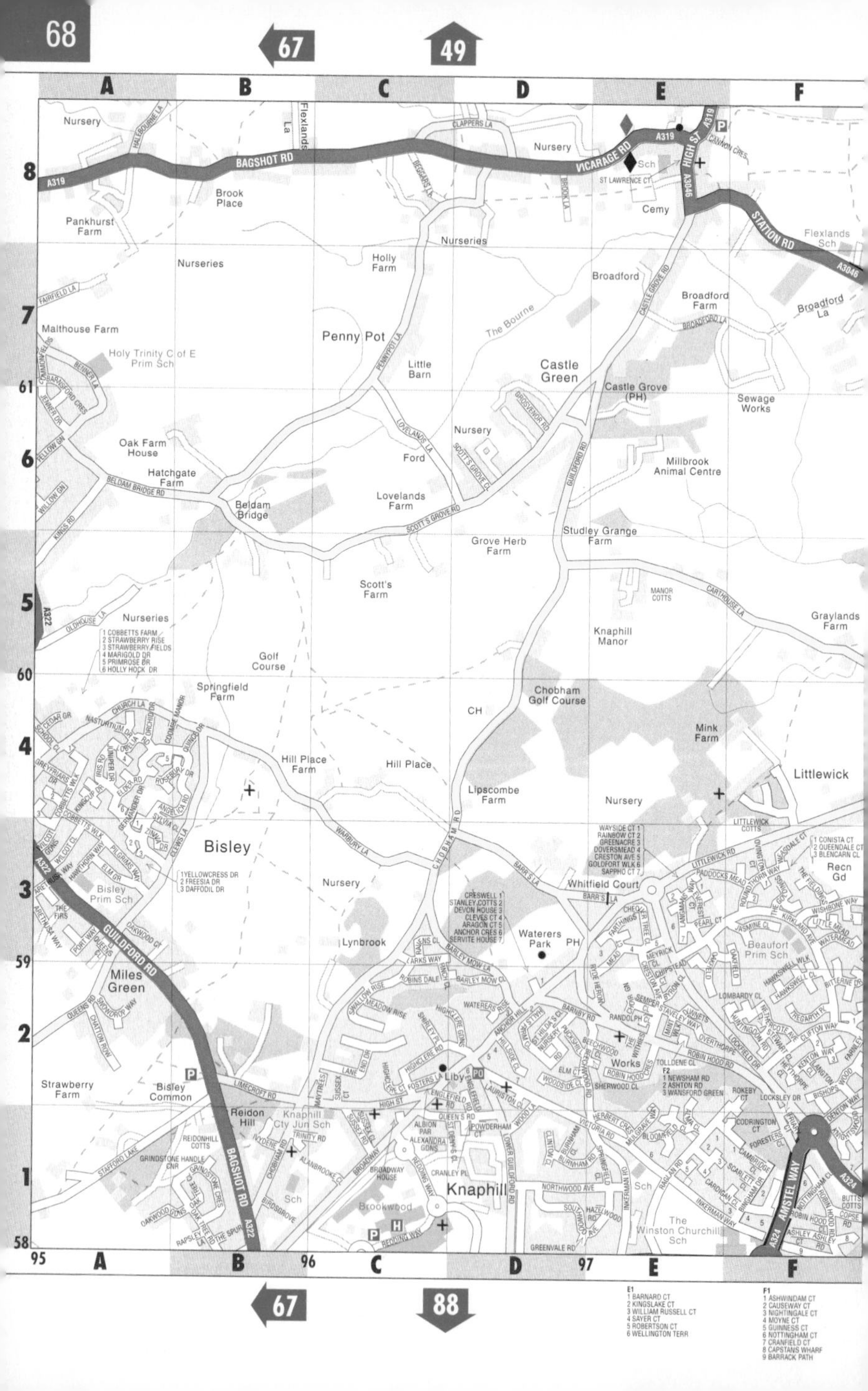

68
67
49
A
B
C
D
E
F
8
7
61
6
5
60
4
3
59
2
1
58
95
96
97
Nursery
Flexlands La
BAGSHOT RD
A319
CLAPPERS LA
VICARAGE RD
HIGH ST
CANNON CRES
A3046
Sch
ST LAWRENCE CT
Cemy
STATION RD
Flexlands Sch
Brook Place
Pankhurst Farm
Nurseries
Holly Farm
Broadford
Broadford Farm
Broadford La
BROADFORD LA
CASTLE GROVE RD
FAIRFIELD LA
Malthouse Farm
Holy Trinity C of E Prim Sch
Penny Pot
PENNYPOT LA
Little Barn
The Bourne
Castle Green
Castle Grove (PH)
Sewage Works
Oak Farm House
Hatchgate Farm
BELDAM BRIDGE RD
Beldam Bridge
LOVELANDS LA
Nursery
Ford
GROSVENOR RD
SCOTT'S GROVE CL
SCOTT'S GROVE RD
GUILDFORD RD
Millbrook Animal Centre
Lovelands Farm
Grove Herb Farm
Studley Grange Farm
KINGS RD
Scott's Farm
MANOR COTTS
CARTHOUSE LA
Graylands Farm
A322
OLDHOUSE LA
Nurseries
1 COBBETTS FARM
2 STRAWBERRY RISE
3 STRAWBERRY FIELDS
4 MARIGOLD DR
5 PRIMROSE DR
6 HOLLY HOCK DR
Golf Course
Knaphill Manor
Springfield Farm
Chobham Golf Course
CH
Mink Farm
Hill Place Farm
Hill Place
Littlewick
Lipscombe Farm
Nursery
CHOBHAM RD
LITTLEWICK COTTS
WARBURY LA
Bisley
WAYSIDE CT 1
RAINBOW CT 2
GREENACRE 3
DOVERSMEAD 4
CRESTON AVE 5
GOLDFORT WLK 6
SAPPHO CT 7
LITTLEWICK RD
1 CONISTA CT
2 QUEENDALE CT
3 BLENCARN CL
Recn Gd
1 YELLOWCRESS DR
2 FREESIA DR
3 DAFFODIL DR
Nursery
BARR'S LA
Whitfield Court
Bisley Prim Sch
CRESWELL 1
STANLEY COTTS 2
DEVON HOUSE 3
CLEVES CT 4
ARAGON CT 5
ANCHOR CRES 6
SERVITE HOUSE 7
GUILDFORD RD
Lynbrook
Waterers Park
PH
Beaufort Prim Sch
Miles Green
BARLEY MOW LA
BARLEY MOW CL
RANDOLPH CL
LOMBARDY CL
Works
Strawberry Farm
Bisley Common
LIMECROFT RD
Liby
PO
Reidon Hill
Knaphill Cty Jun Sch
HIGH ST
ROBIN HOOD RD
F2
1 NEWSHAM RD
2 ASHTON RD
3 WANSFORD GREEN
SHERWOOD CL
VICTORIA RD
LOCKSLEY DR
REIDONHILL COTTS
GRINDSTONE HANDLE CNR
STAFFORD LAKE
BAGSHOT RD
BROADWAY HOUSE
Knaphill
Sch
Brookwood
Sch
NORTHWOOD AVE
The Winston Churchill Sch
AMSTEL WAY
A324
OAKWOOD GDNS
RAPSLEY LA
THE SPUR
BIRDSGROVE
REDDING WAY
GREENVALE RD
INKERMAN WAY
88
E1
1 BARNARD CT
2 KINGSLAKE CT
3 WILLIAM RUSSELL CT
4 SAYER CT
5 ROBERTSON CT
6 WELLINGTON TERR
F1
1 ASHWINDAM CT
2 CAUSEWAY CT
3 NIGHTINGALE CT
4 MOYNE CT
5 GUINNESS CT
6 NOTTINGHAM CT
7 CRANFIELD CT
8 CAPSTANS WHARF
9 BARRACK PATH

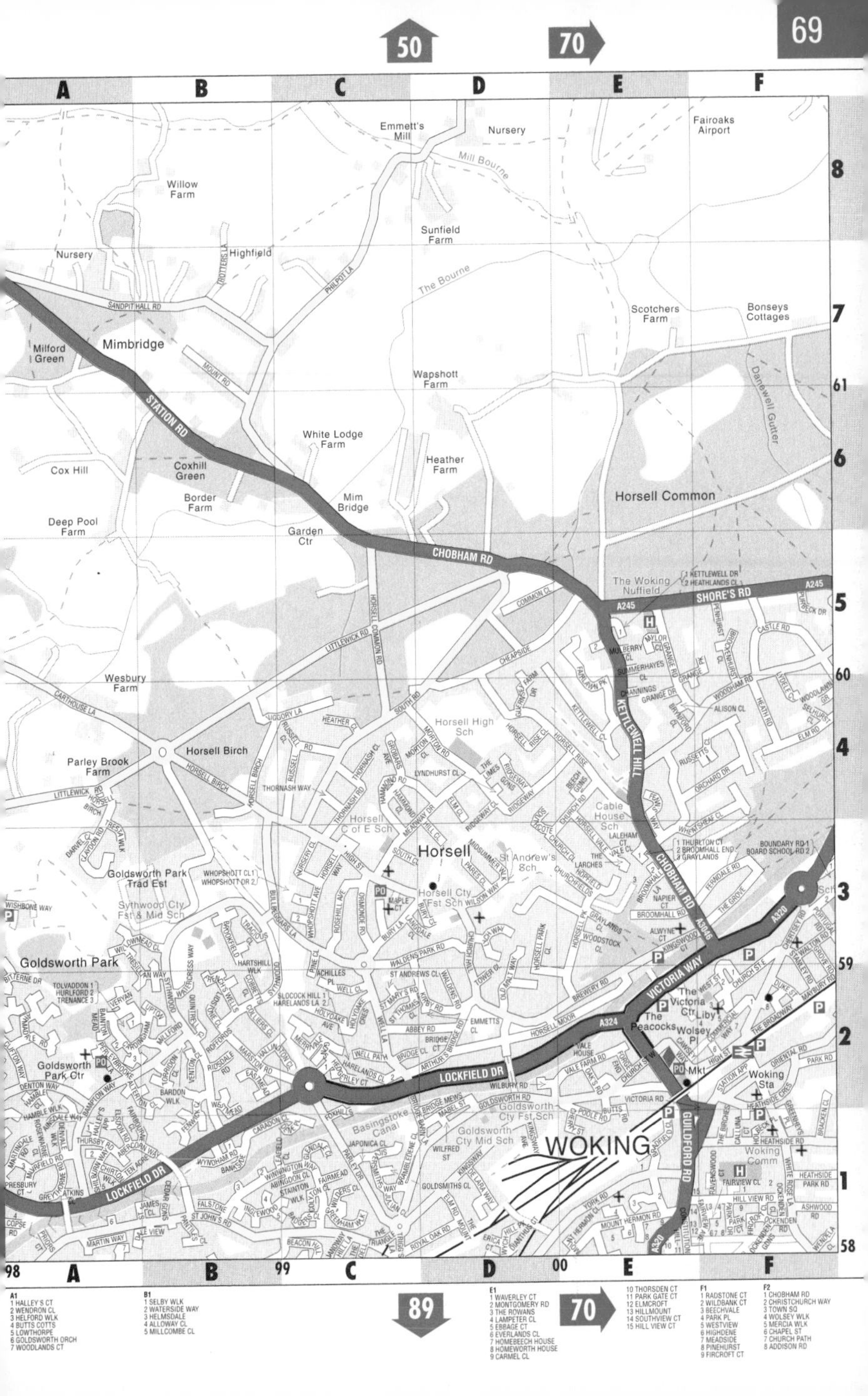

A1
1 HALLEY'S CT
2 WENDRON CL
3 HELFORD WLK
4 BUTTS COTTS
5 LOWTHORPE
6 GOLDSWORTH ORCH
7 WOODLANDS CT

B1
1 SELBY WLK
2 WATERSIDE WAY
3 HELMSDALE
4 ALLOWAY CL
5 MILLCOMBE CL

E1
1 WAVERLEY CT
2 MONTGOMERY RD
3 THE ROWANS
4 LAMPETER CL
5 EBBAGE CT
6 EVERLANDS CL
7 HOMEBEECH HOUSE
8 HOMEWORTH HOUSE
9 CARMEL CL

10 THORSDEN CT
11 PARK GATE CT
12 ELMCROFT
13 HELLMOUNT
14 SOUTHVIEW CT
15 HILL VIEW CT

F1
1 RADSTONE CT
2 WILDBANK CT
3 BEECHVALE
4 PARK PL
5 WESTVIEW
6 HIGHDENE
7 MEADSIDE
8 PINEHURST
9 FIRCROFT CT

F2
1 CHOBHAM RD
2 CHRISTCHURCH WAY
3 TOWN SQ
4 WOLSEY WLK
5 MERCIA WLK
6 CHAPEL ST
7 CHURCH PATH
8 ADDISON RD

69
51

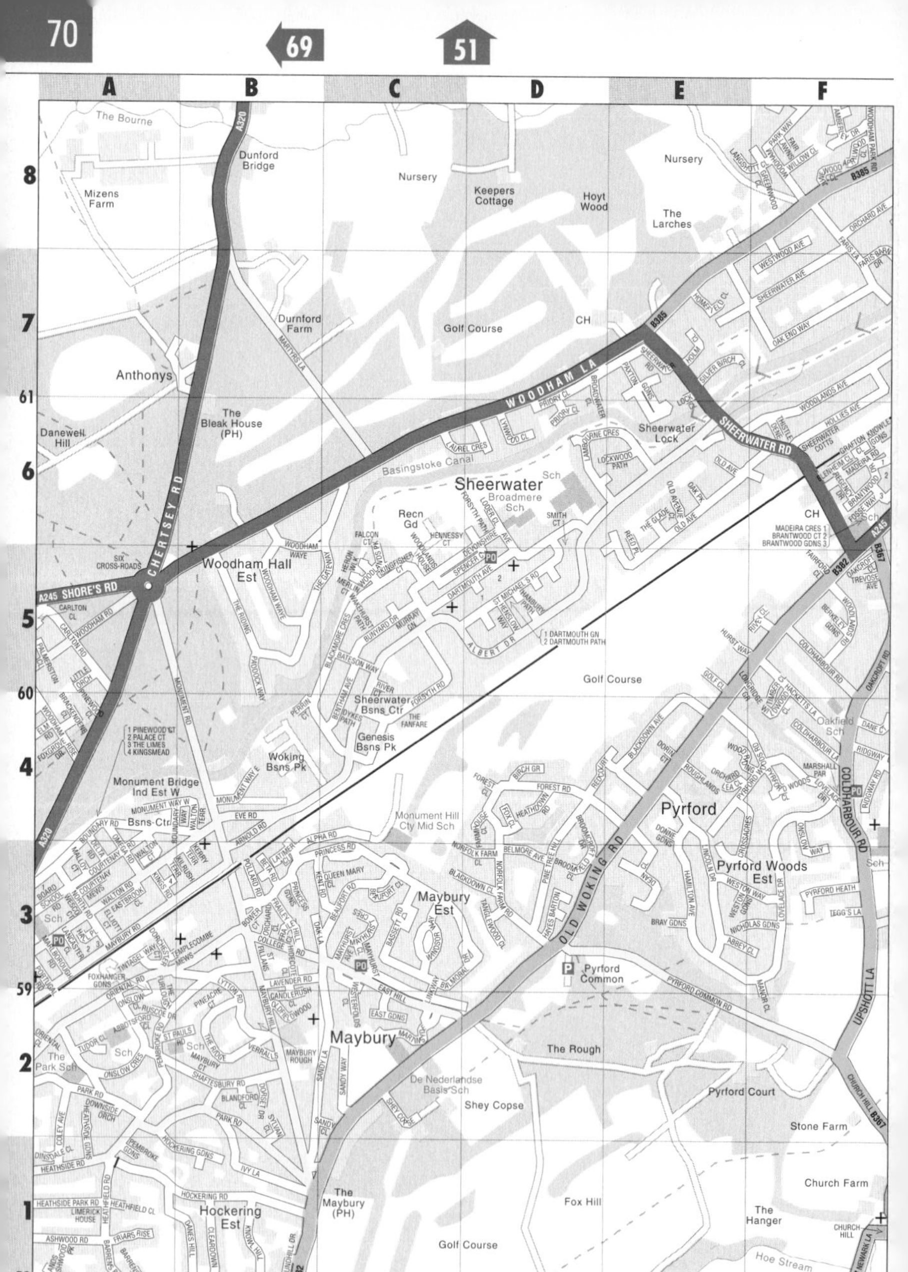
A
B
C
D
E
F
The Bourne
Dunford Bridge
Mizens Farm
Nursery
Keepers Cottage
Hoyt Wood
The Larches
Durnford Farm
Golf Course
CH
Anthonys
The Bleak House (PH)
Danewell Hill
WOODHAM LA
SHEERWATER RD
Sheerwater Lock
Basingstoke Canal
Sheerwater
Broadmere Sch
Recn Gd
CHERTSEY RD
SIX CROSS-ROADS
A245 SHORE'S RD
Woodham Hall Est
Golf Course
Sheerwater Bsns Ctr
Genesis Bsns Pk
Woking Bsns Pk
Monument Bridge Ind Est W
Bsns Ctr
Monument Hill Cty Mid Sch
Pyrford
Pyrford Woods Est
Oakfield Sch
COLDHARBOUR RD
OLD WOKING RD
Maybury Est
Pyrford Common
Maybury
The Park Sch
The Rough
De Nederlandse Basis Sch
Shey Copse
Pyrford Court
Stone Farm
UPSHOTT LA
Church Farm
The Maybury (PH)
Hockering Est
Fox Hill
The Hanger
Golf Course
Hoe Stream
8
7
61
6
5
60
4
3
59
2
1
58
01
02
03

69
90

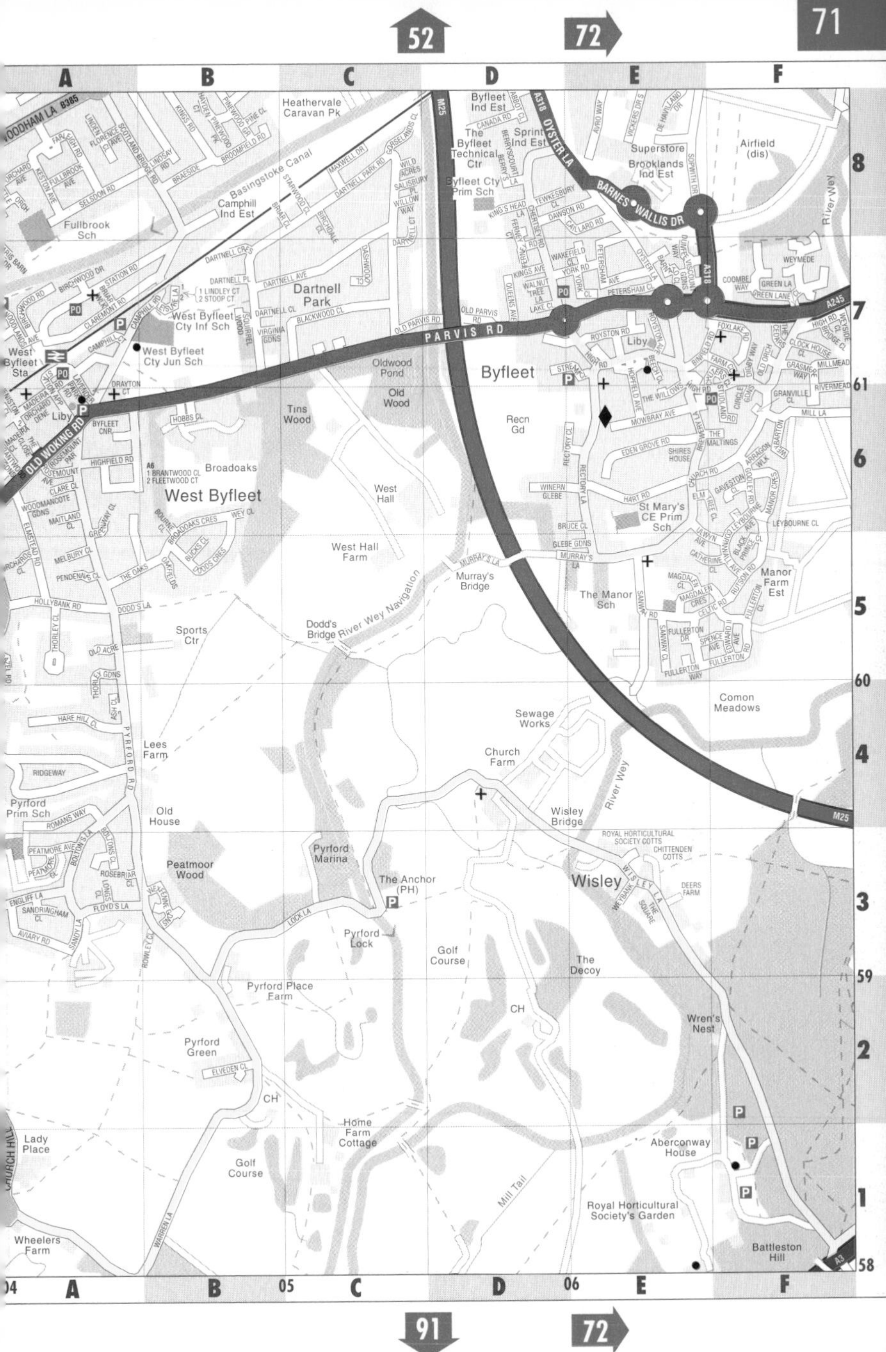

A　B　C　D　E　F

8

7

61

6

5

60

4

59

2

1

58

OODHAM LA B365

Fullbrook Sch

West Byfleet Sta

Liby

OLD WOKING RD

West Byfleet Cty Inf Sch

Camphill Ind Est

West Byfleet Cty Jun Sch

Dartnell Park

West Byfleet

Broadoaks

West Hall

West Hall Farm

Sports Ctr

Lees Farm

Pyrford Prim Sch

Old House

Peatmoor Wood

Pyrford Green

Lady Place

Golf Course

Wheelers Farm

Heathervale Caravan Pk

Basingstoke Canal

Tins Wood

Oldwood Pond

Old Wood

Dodd's Bridge River Way Navigation

Murray's Bridge

Pyrford Marina

The Anchor (PH)

Pyrford Lock

Pyrford Place Farm

Home Farm Cottage

Golf Course

Mill Tail

Byfleet Ind Est

The Byfleet Technical Ctr

Byfleet Cty Prim Sch

Spring Ind Est

A318 OYSTER LA

M25

Superstore

Brooklands Ind Est

BARNES · WALLIS DR

Airfield (dis)

River Way

A245

PARVIS RD

Byfleet

Liby

Recn Gd

Winery Glebe

St Mary's CE Prim Sch

The Manor Sch

Church Farm

Sewage Works

Wisley Bridge

River Way

Wisley

Royal Horticultural Society Cotts

Chittenden Cotts

Deers Farm

The Decoy

CH

Wren's Nest

Aberconway House

Royal Horticultural Society's Garden

Battleston Hill

Common Meadows

Manor Farm Est

The Haltings

M25

59

91　72

71
53

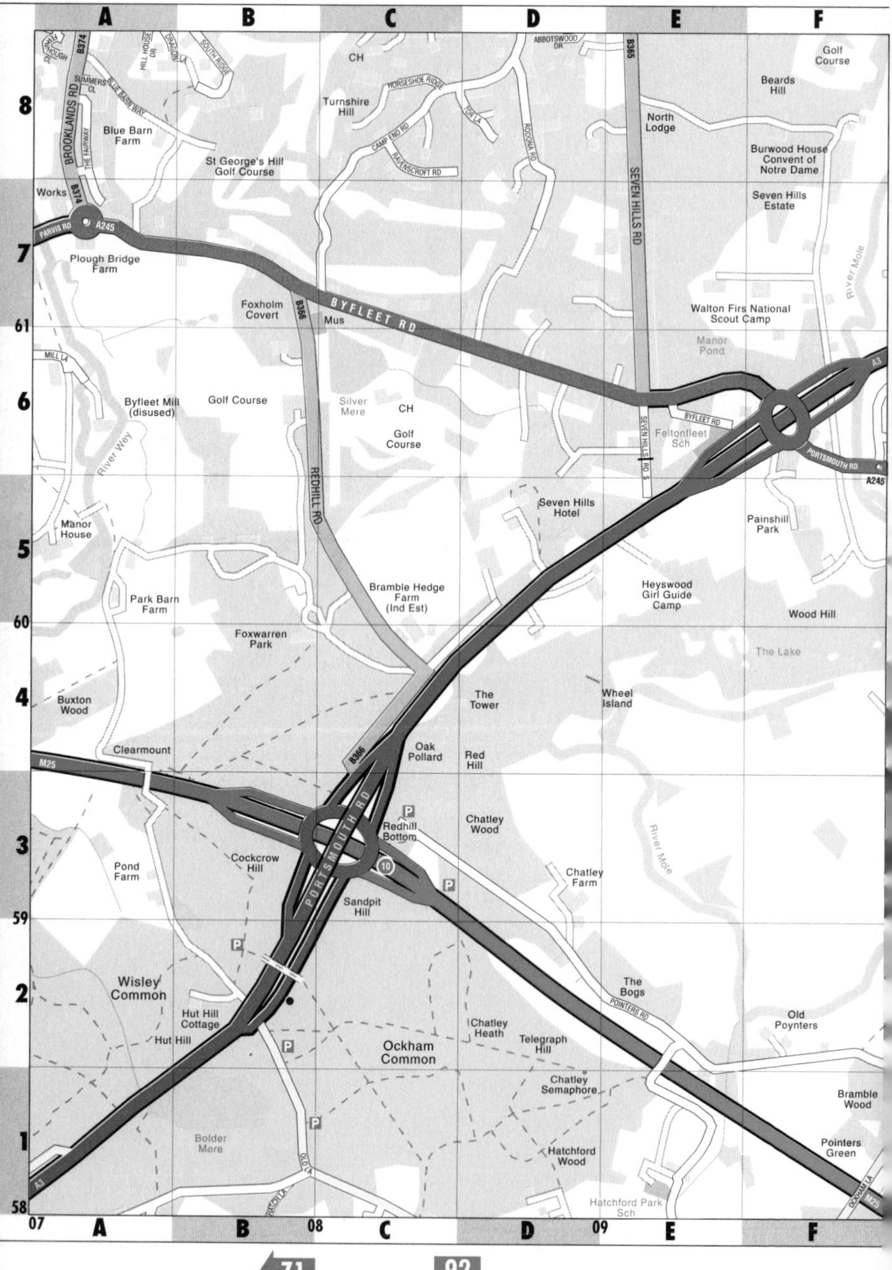
A
B
C
D
E
F
8
7
61
6
5
60
4
3
59
2
1
58
07
08
09
BROOKLANDS RD
B374
SUMMERS CL
BLUE BARN WAY
THE FAIRWAY
HILL HOUSE DR
DRAGON LA
SOUTH RIDGE
CH
Turnshire Hill
HORSESHOE RIDGE
CAMP END RD
RAVENSCROFT RD
TOR LA
RODONA RD
ABBOTSWOOD DR
B365
SEVEN HILLS RD
Golf Course
Beards Hill
North Lodge
Burwood House Convent of Notre Dame
Seven Hills Estate
Blue Barn Farm
St George's Hill Golf Course
Works
PARVIS RD
A245
Plough Bridge Farm
Foxholm Covert
B366
BYFLEET RD
Mus
Walton Firs National Scout Camp
Manor Pond
River Mole
MILL LA
A3
Byfleet Mill (disused)
Golf Course
Silver Mere
CH
Golf Course
Feltonfleet Sch
PORTSMOUTH RD
A245
River Wey
REDHILL RD
Seven Hills Hotel
Painshill Park
Manor House
Park Barn Farm
Bramble Hedge Farm (Ind Est)
Heyswood Girl Guide Camp
Wood Hill
Foxwarren Park
The Lake
Buxton Wood
The Tower
Wheel Island
Clearmount
M25
B366
Oak Pollard
Red Hill
Redhill Bottom
Chatley Wood
Pond Farm
Cockcrow Hill
PORTSMOUTH RD
10
Sandpit Hill
Chatley Farm
River Mole
Wisley Common
Hut Hill Cottage
Hut Hill
Chatley Heath
Telegraph Hill
Ockham Common
The Bogs
POINTERS RD
Old Poynters
Chatley Semaphore
Bramble Wood
Bolder Mere
OLD LA
Hatchford Wood
Pointers Green
HATCH LA
Hatchford Park Sch
OCKHAM LA
M25
P

71
92

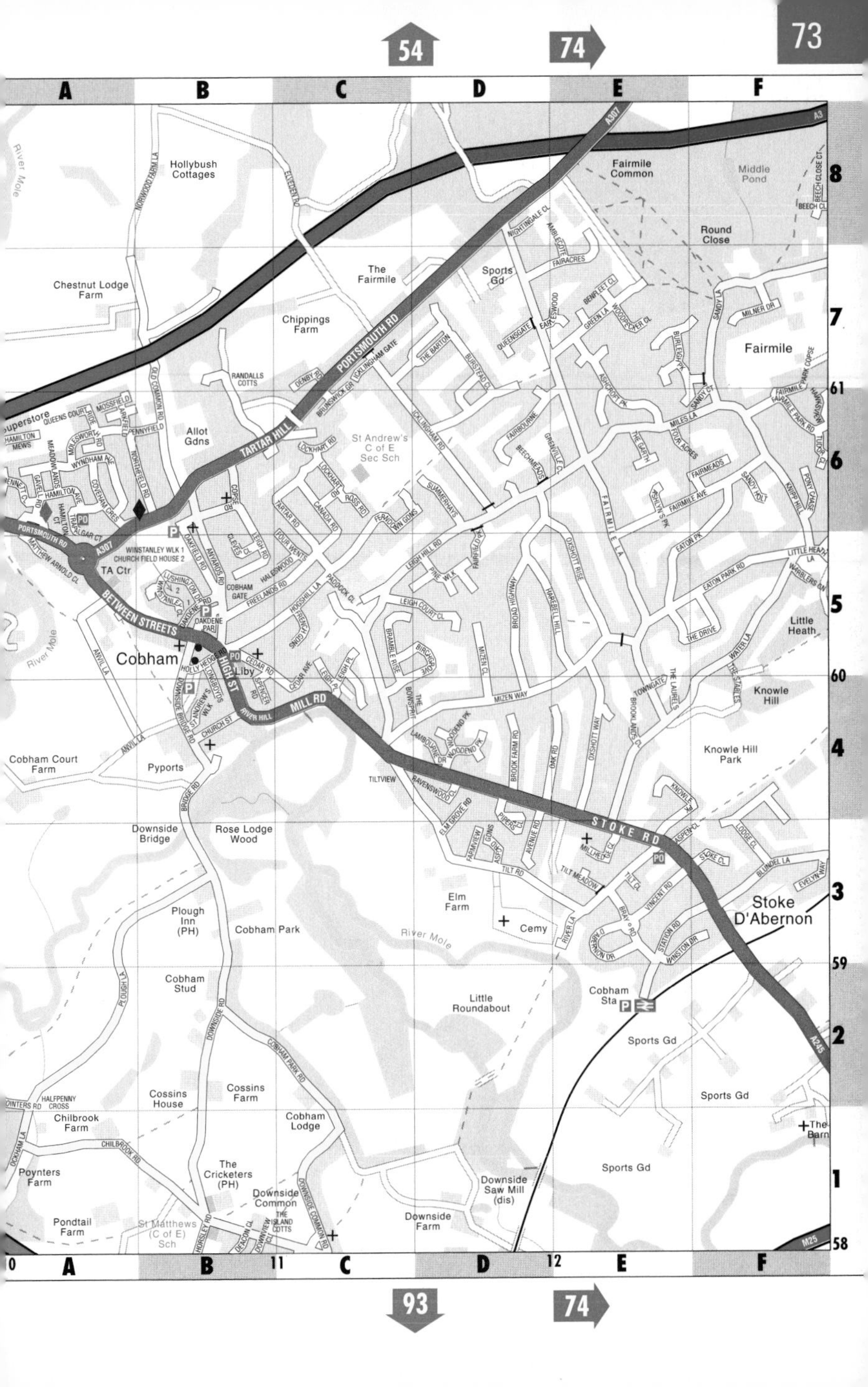
73
54
74
A
B
C
D
E
F
Hollybush Cottages
Chestnut Lodge Farm
Chippings Farm
The Fairmile
Sports Gd
Fairmile Common
Middle Pond
Round Close
Fairmile
RANDALLS COTTS
Allot Gdns
St Andrew's C of E Sec Sch
PORTSMOUTH RD
TARTAR HILL
A307
A3
Superstore
QUEENS COURT
MOSSFIELD
HAMILTON MEWS
MEADOWLANDS
WYNDHAM AVE
NORTHFIELD RD
OLD COMMON RD
NORWOOD FARM LA
ELVEDEN RD
LARKFIELD
PENNYFIELD
HAMILTON AVE
HAMILTON CT
TRAFALGAR CT
COVENHAM CRES
GAVELL RD
MATTHEW ARNOLD CL
WINSTANLEY WLK 1
CHURCH FIELD HOUSE 2
TA Ctr
BETWEEN STREETS
OAKFIELD RD
ANYARDS RD
CLEVES CL
LEIGH RD
COBHAM GATE
FREELANDS RD
HALESWOOD
FOUR WENTS
TARTAR RD
CANADA RD
LOCKHART RD
ROSS RD
HOGSHILL LA
FRENCH GDNS
PADDOCK CL
FERNDOWN GDNS
DENBY RD
BRUNSWICK GR
ICKLINGHAM GATE
ICKLINGHAM RD
THE BARTON
BURSTEAD CL
SUMMERHAYS
LEIGH HILL RD
PINE WLK
FAIRFIELD CL
LEIGH COURT CL
BRAMBLE RISE
BIRCHGROVE
THE BOWSPRIT
MIZEN CL
MIZEN WAY
BROAD HIGHWAY
HAREBELL HILL
OXSHOTT RISE
FAIRBOURNE
BEECHMEADS
GRENVILLE CL
NIGHTINGALE CL
AMBLESIDE
FAIRACRES
QUEENSGATE
EARLESWOOD
BENFLEET CL
GREEN LA
WOODPECKER CL
ASHCROFT PK
THE GARTH
FAIRMILE LA
MILES LA
FOUR ACRES
BURLEIGH PK
SANDY LA
SANDY CT
MILNER DR
FAIRMILE PARK COPSE
FAIRMILE PARK RD
HAWKSWAY
TUDOR CL
FAIRMEADS
ASHLEY'S PK
FAIRMILE AVE
SANDY HOLT
KNIPP HILL
PONY CHASE
EATON PK
EATON PARK RD
LITTLE HEATH LA
WARBLERS GN
Little Heath
THE DRIVE
TOWNGATE
THE LAURELS
WATER LA
THE STABLES
Knowle Hill
BROOKLANDS CL
Knowle Hill Park
BEECH CLOSE CT
BEECH CL
Cobham
HIGH ST
HOLLY HEDGE RD
OAKDENE PAR
LONGBOYDS
ST ANDREW'S WLK
DOWNSIDE BRIDGE RD
CHURCH ST
RIVER HILL
MILL RD
CEDAR RD
SPENCER RD
CEDAR AVE
LEIGH PL
Liby
PO
ANVIL LA
River Mole
Cobham Court Farm
Pyports
TILTVIEW
RAVENSWOOD CL
LAMBOURNE DR
WOODEND PK
BROOK FARM RD
OAK RD
OXSHOTT WAY
ELM GROVE RD
FARMVIEW
ASPEN GDNS
PIPERS CL
AVENUE RD
MILLHEDGE CL
STOKE RD
TILT RD
TILT MEADOW
TILT CL
VINCENT RD
BRAY RD
STATION RD
WINSTON DR
D'ABERNON DR
RIVER LA
KNOWLE PK
ASPEN CL
STOKE CL
LODGE CL
BLUNDEL LA
EVELYN WAY
Stoke D'Abernon
Downside Bridge
Rose Lodge Wood
BRIDGE RD
Elm Farm
Cemy
Plough Inn (PH)
Cobham Park
Cobham Stud
Little Roundabout
Cobham Sta
Sports Gd
A245
PLOUGH LA
DOWNSIDE RD
COBHAM PARK RD
Cossins House
Cossins Farm
Cobham Lodge
POINTERS RD
HALFPENNY CROSS
Chilbrook Farm
CHILBROOK RD
OCKHAM LA
Poyntersn Farm
The Cricketers (PH)
Downside Common
THE ISLAND COTTS
DOWNSIDE COMMON RD
Downside Saw Mill (dis)
Downside Farm
St Matthews (C of E) Sch
Pondtail Farm
HORSLEY RD
DEACON CL
DOWNVIEW CL
The Barn
M25
8
7
61
6
5
60
4
3
59
2
1
58
10
11
12
93
74

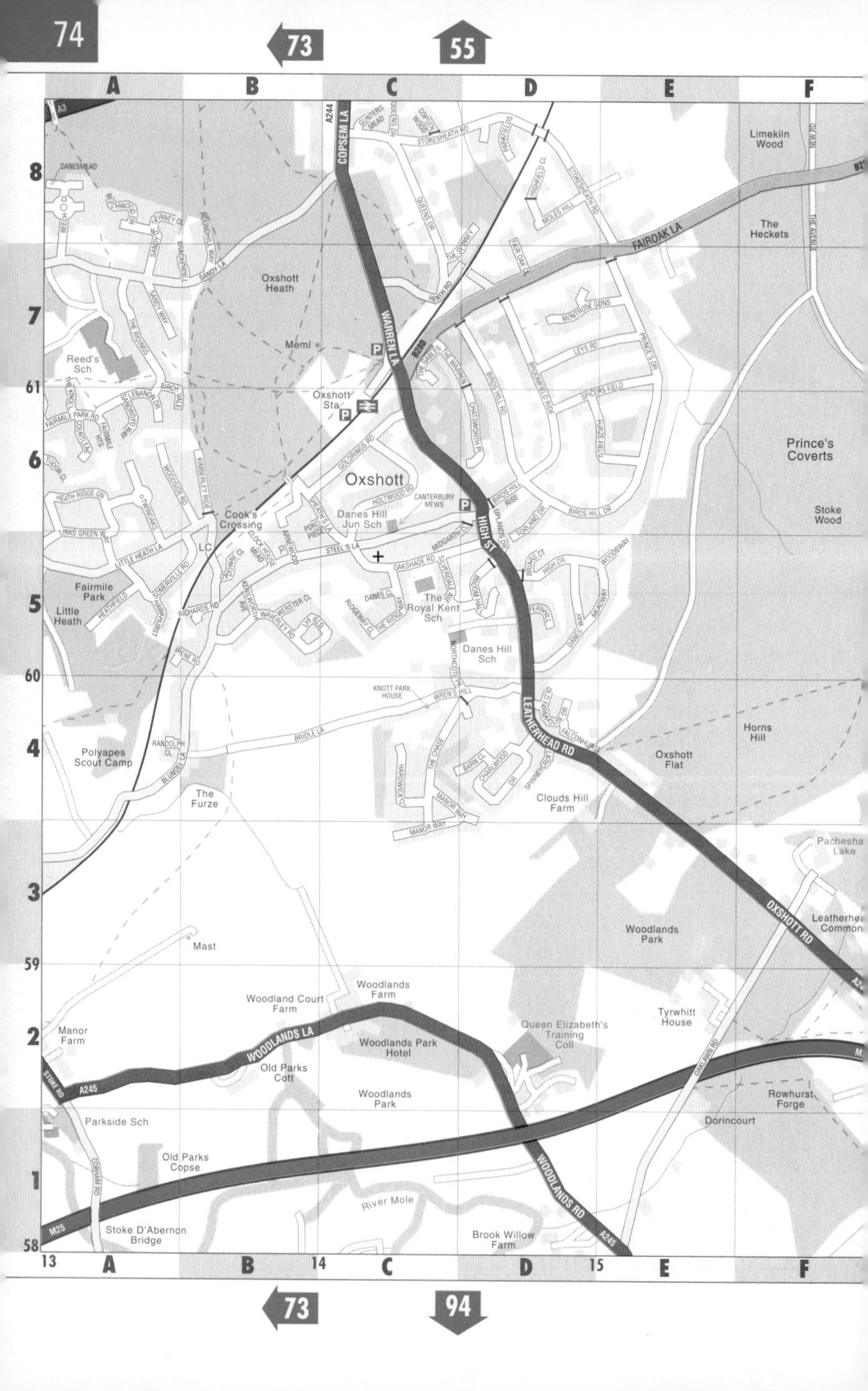

73
55
A
B
C
D
E
F
8
7
61
6
5
60
4
3
59
2
1
58
13
14
15
A3
DANESMEAD
BEECH CL
BEECHWOOD DR
SANDY CL
WINEY CL
BRACKENHILL
ROUNDHILL WAY
SANDY LA
SANDY WAY
Oxshott Heath
COPSEM LA
A244
GUNTERS MEAD
QUEENS DR
COPSEM WOOD
STOKESHEATH RD
PARKFIELDS
HIGHFIELD CL
MOLES HILL
Limekiln Wood
NEW RD
B2
The Heckets
THE AVENUE
FAIROAK LA
FAIR OAK CL
THE SPINNEY
HEATH RD
MONTROSE GDNS
WARREN LA
B280
Meml
P
Reed's Sch
THE RIDINGS
BIRCH VALE
THE KNOLL
LEBANON DR
SANDROYD WAY
FAIRMILE PARK RD
COURTLEAS
FAIRMILE HTS
TIVOLI CL
Oxshott Sta
THE GABLES
THE WARREN
CHATSWORTH PL
BIRDS HILL RD
BROOMFIELD RIDE
LEYS RD
SPICERS FIELD
FURZE FIELD
PRINCE'S DR
Prince's Coverts
GOLDRINGS RD
HOLTWOOD RD
Oxshott
CANTERBURY MEWS
Danes Hill Jun Sch
BIRDS HILL RISE
UPLANDS DR
TORLAND DR
BIRDS HILL DR
Stoke Wood
HEATH RIDGE GN
TWINOAKS
WOODSIDE RD
KIMBERLEY RIDE
Cook's Crossing
LINKS GREEN WAY
LITTLE HEATH LA
LC
CLOCK HOUSE MEAD
ARNEWOOD CL
SHEATH'S LA
POND PIECE
STEEL'S LA
MIDGARTH CL
HIGH ST
OAKSHADE RD
SILVERDALE AV
BROOM HALL
BRIARS CT
HIGH DR
WOODSWAY
Fairmile Park
Little Heath
HEATHFIELD
SOMERVILLE RD
HAWKHURST
RICHARDS RD
KENILWORTH AVE
WEBSTER CL
WAVERLEY RD
LYFIELD
DANES CL
RIDGEWAY CL
THE RIDGE
The Royal Kent Sch
FERNHILL
DANES WAY
MEADWAY
Danes Hill Sch
IRENE RD
NORTHCOTE RD
KNOTT PARK HOUSE
WREN'S HILL
LEATHERHEAD RD
FARMHOUSE CL
FALCONHURST
BRIDLE LA
RANDOLPH CL
Polyapes Scout Camp
BLUNDEL LA
THE CHASE
BARN CL
CHARLWOOD DR
SPINNEYCROFT
HARDWICK CL
MANOR WAY
Horns Hill
Oxshott Flat
Clouds Hill Farm
The Furze
Pachesham Lake
OXSHOTT RD
Leatherhead Common
Mast
Woodlands Park
Woodland Court Farm
Woodlands Farm
Tyrwhitt House
Queen Elizabeth's Training Coll
Manor Farm
WOODLANDS LA
Woodlands Park Hotel
Old Parks Cott
STOKE RD
A245
OAKLAWN RD
Rowhurst Forge
Woodlands Park
Parkside Sch
Dorincourt
Old Parks Copse
COBHAM RD
WOODLANDS RD
River Mole
M25
Stoke D'Abernon Bridge
Brook Willow Farm

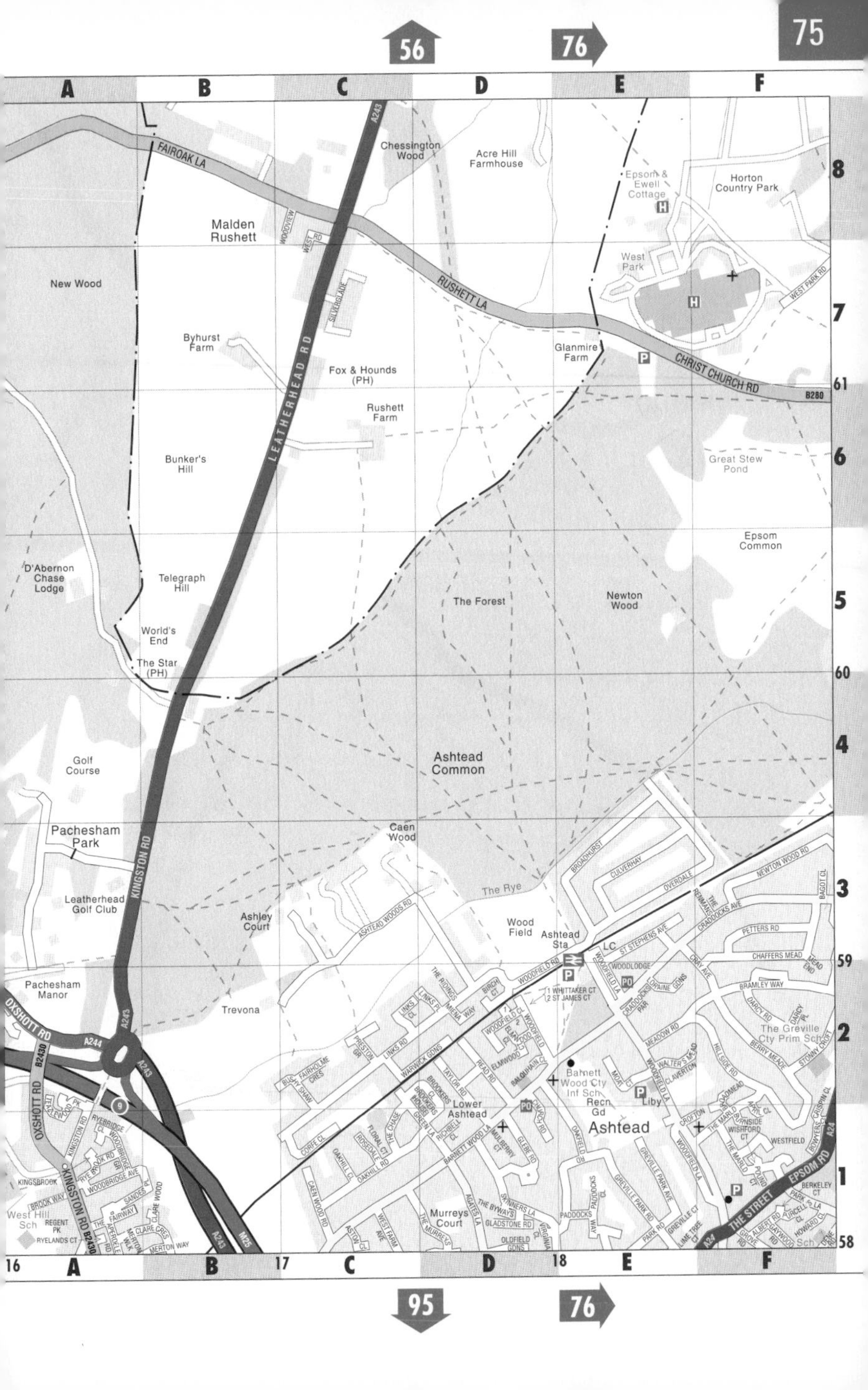
56
76
A
B
C
D
E
F
FAIROAK LA
A243
Chessington Wood
Acre Hill Farmhouse
Epsom & Ewell Cottage
Horton Country Park
Malden Rushett
WOODVIEW
WEST RD
New Wood
SILVERGLADE
RUSHETT LA
West Park
WEST PARK RD
Byhurst Farm
LEATHERHEAD RD
Fox & Hounds (PH)
Glanmire Farm
CHRIST CHURCH RD
B280
Rushett Farm
Bunker's Hill
Great Stew Pond
Epsom Common
D'Abernon Chase Lodge
Telegraph Hill
The Forest
Newton Wood
World's End
The Star (PH)
Golf Course
Ashtead Common
Pachesham Park
KINGSTON RD
Caen Wood
NEWTON WOOD RD
BROADHURST
CULVERHAY
OVERDALE
The Rye
BAGOT CL
Leatherhead Golf Club
THE REMNANTS
CRADDOCKS AVE
PETTERS RD
Ashley Court
ASHTEAD WOODS RD
Wood Field
Ashtead Sta
LC
ST STEPHENS AVE
CHAFFERS MEAD
MEAD END
WOODFIELD RD
WOODFIELD LA
WOODLODGE
CRAY AVE
Pachesham Manor
THE RIDINGS
LINKS PL
BIRCH CT
1 WHITTAKER CT
2 ST JAMES CT
LORAINE GDNS
BRAMLEY WAY
CRADDOCKS PAR
DARCY RD
DARCY PL
Trevona
OXSHOTT RD
A244
PRESTON GR
LINKS RD
MIENA WAY
WOODFIELD CL
ELM RD
WOODFIELD
MEADOW RD
The Greville Cty Prim Sch
BERRY MEADE
STONNY CROFT
B2430
FAIRHOLME CRES
WARWICK GDNS
READ RD
ELMWOOD
BALQUHAIN CL
WALTER'S MEAD
CLAVERTON
HILLSIDE RD
BUSHY SHAW
TAYLOR RD
Barnett Wood Cty Inf Sch
MOAT CT
Liby
CRISPIN CL
LEATHERWOOD PK
BROOKERS CL
Lower Ashtead
CHURCH RD
Recn Gd
ROADMEAD
APRIL CL
RYEBRIDGE CL
WOODBRIDGE GR
KINGSTON RD
CORFE CL
THE CHASE
GREEN LA
RICHBELL CL
Ashtead
CROFTON
THE MARLD
BURNSIDE
WISHFORD CT
WESTFIELD
ROWHURST
RYE BROOK RD
FLORAL CT
ROSEDALE
BARNETT WOOD LA
MULBERRY CT
GLEBE RD
OAKFIELD RD
GREVILLE PARK AVE
WOODFIELD LA
POUND CT
KINGSBROOK
WOODBRIDGE AVE
OAKHILL CL
OAKHILL RD
EPSOM RD
A24
BERKELEY CT
BROOK WAY
SANDES PL
CLARE WOOD
CAEN WOOD RD
AGATES LA
THE BYWAYS
SKINNERS LA
PADDOCKS CL
GREVILLE PARK RD
THE STREET
PARK LA
PURCELL CL
West Hill Sch
REGENT PK
THE FAIRWAY
THE AVERDELLE
MERTON WALK
CLARE CRES
WEST FARM AVE
Murreys Court
GLADSTONE RD
PADDOCKS WAY
PARK RD
GREVILLE CT
LIME TREE CT
ALBERT RD
GAYWOOD RD
HOWARD CL
RYELANDS CT
ASTON CL
THE MURREYS
OLDFIELD GDNS
VIRGINIA CL
GROVE RD
MERTON WAY
A243
M25
8
7
61
6
5
60
4
3
59
2
1
58
16
17
18
95
76

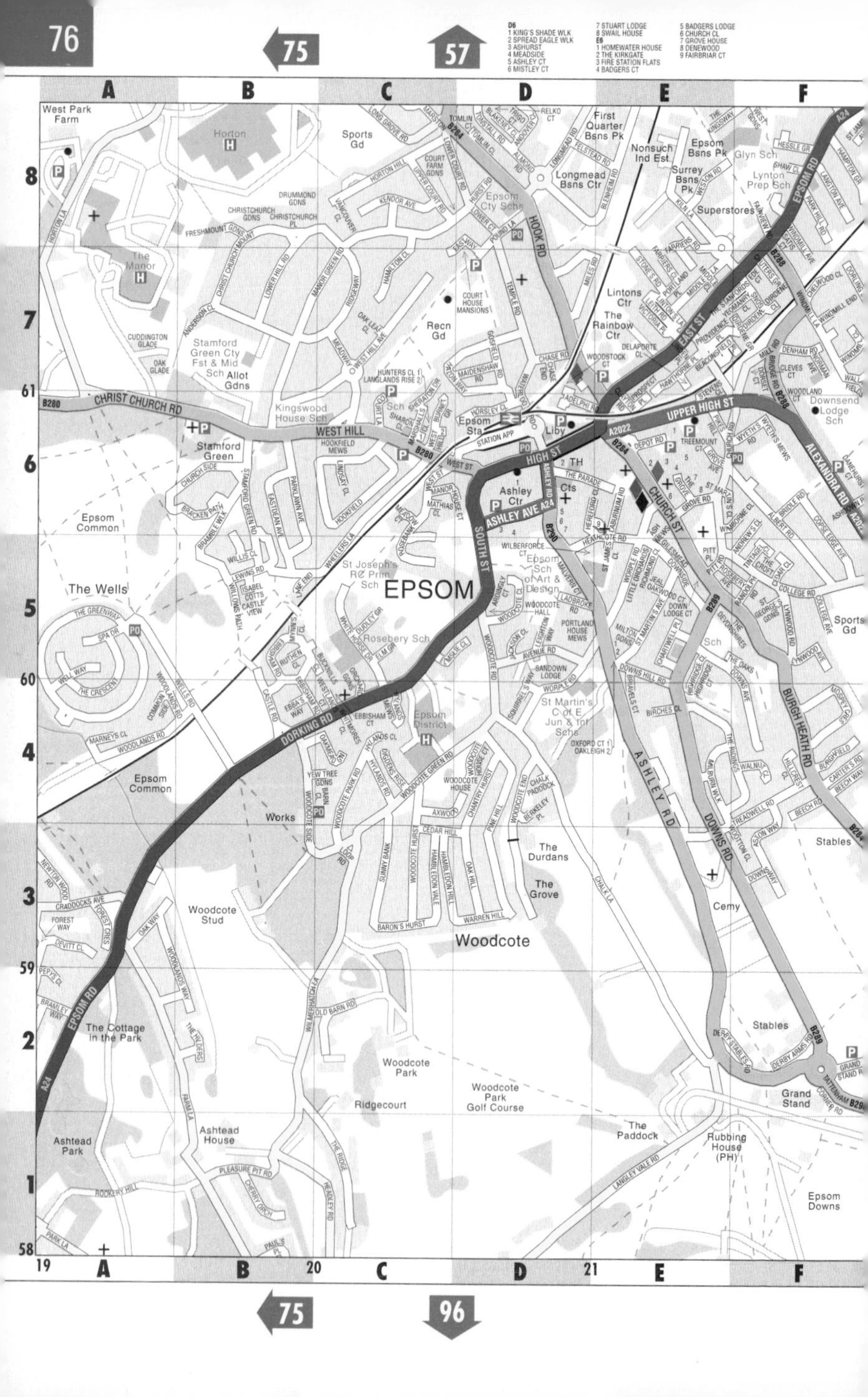
76
75
57
D6
1 KING'S SHADE WLK
2 SPREAD EAGLE WLK
3 ASHURST
4 MEADSIDE
5 ASHLEY CT
6 MISTLEY CT
7 STUART LODGE
8 SWAIL HOUSE
E6
1 HOMEWATER HOUSE
2 THE KIRKGATE
3 FIRE STATION FLATS
4 BADGERS CT
5 BADGERS LODGE
6 CHURCH CL
7 GROVE HOUSE
8 DENEWOOD
9 FAIRBRIAR CT
A
B
C
D
E
F
8
7
61
6
5
60
4
3
59
2
1
58
19
20
21
West Park Farm
Horton
Sports Gd
First Quarter Bsns Pk
Nonsuch Ind Est
Epsom Bsns Pk
Glyn Sch
Surrey Bsns Pk
Longmead Bsns Ctr
Lynton Prep Sch
Superstores
Epsom Cty Sch
HOOK RD
The Manor
Lintons Ctr
The Rainbow Ctr
Recn Gd
Stamford Green Cty Fst & Mid Sch
Allot Gdns
CHRIST CHURCH RD
Kingswood House Sch
WEST HILL
Epsom Sta
Liby
UPPER HIGH ST
Downsend Lodge Sch
Stamford Green
HIGH ST
EAST ST
Ashley Ctr
ASHLEY AVE
TH
Cts
CHURCH ST
Epsom Common
SOUTH ST
ALEXANDRA RD
St Joseph's RC Prim Sch
EPSOM
Epsom Sch of Art & Design
The Wells
Rosebery Sch
Sch
Sports Gd
St Martin's C of E Jun & Inf Schs
DORKING RD
Epsom District
ASHLEY RD
BURGH HEATH RD
Epsom Common
Works
DOWNS RD
Stables
The Durdans
The Grove
Cemy
Woodcote Stud
Woodcote
EPSOM RD
The Cottage in the Park
Stables
Woodcote Park
Woodcote Park Golf Course
Ridgecourt
Grand Stand
Ashtead Park
Ashtead House
The Paddock
Rubbing House (PH)
Epsom Downs
75
96

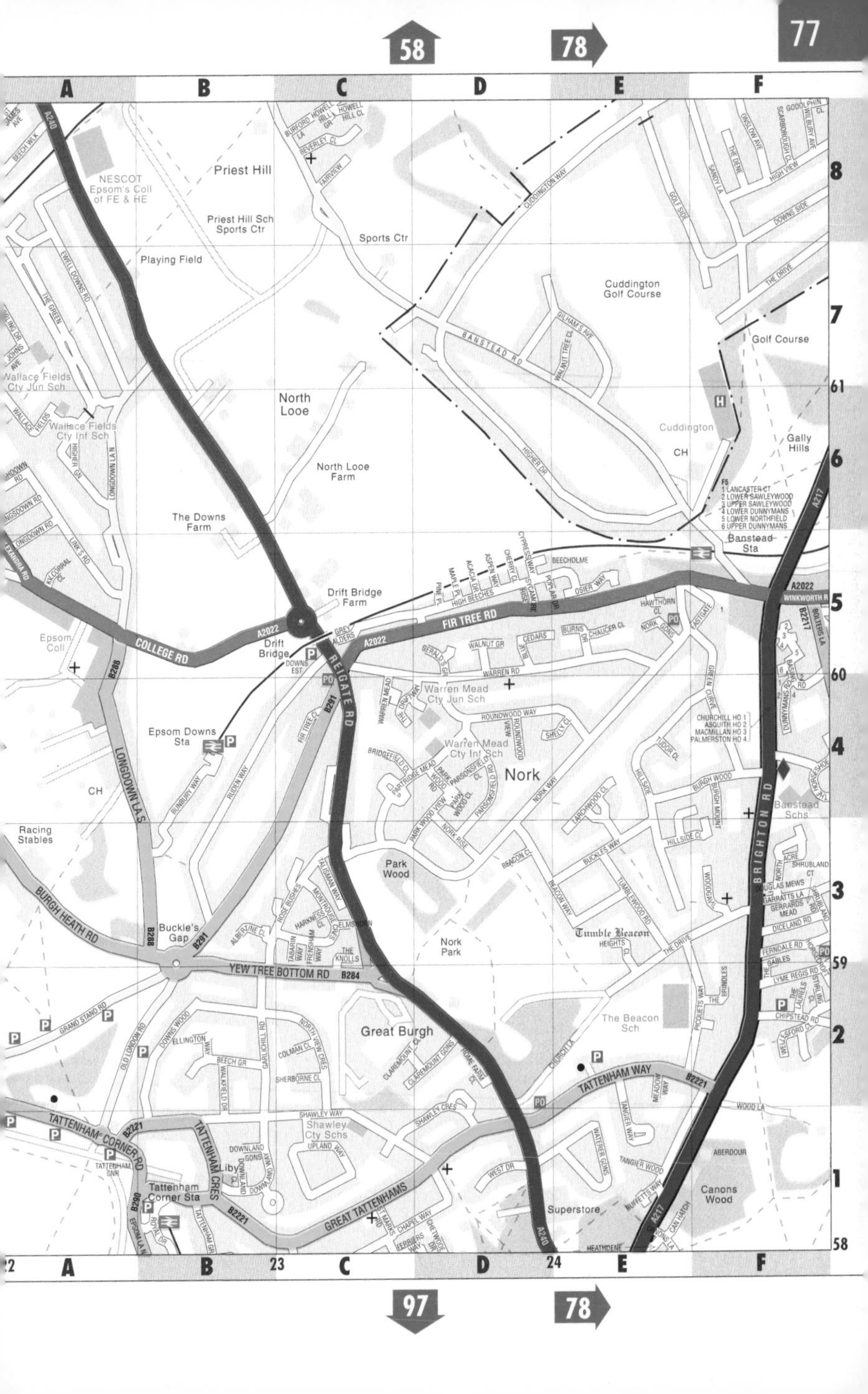
58
78
Priest Hill
NESCOT
Epsom's Coll of FE & HE
Priest Hill Sch Sports Ctr
Sports Ctr
Playing Field
Cuddington Golf Course
Golf Course
North Looe
North Looe Farm
Wallace Fields Cty Jun Sch
Wallace Fields Cty Inf Sch
Cuddington
Gally Hills
The Downs Farm
Banstead Sta
Drift Bridge Farm
Drift Bridge
Epsom Coll
COLLEGE RD
FIR TREE RD
REIGATE RD
Warren Mead Cty Jun Sch
Warren Mead Cty Inf Sch
Nork
Epsom Downs Sta
LONGDOWN LA S
Racing Stables
BRIGHTON RD
Banstead Schs
Park Wood
BURGH HEATH RD
Buckle's Gap
Nork Park
Tumble Beacon
YEW TREE BOTTOM RD
The Beacon Sch
Great Burgh
TATTENHAM WAY
Shawley Cty Schs
TATTENHAM CORNER RD
TATTENHAM CRES
Tattenham Corner Sta
GREAT TATTENHAMS
Superstore
Canons Wood
97
78

77
59

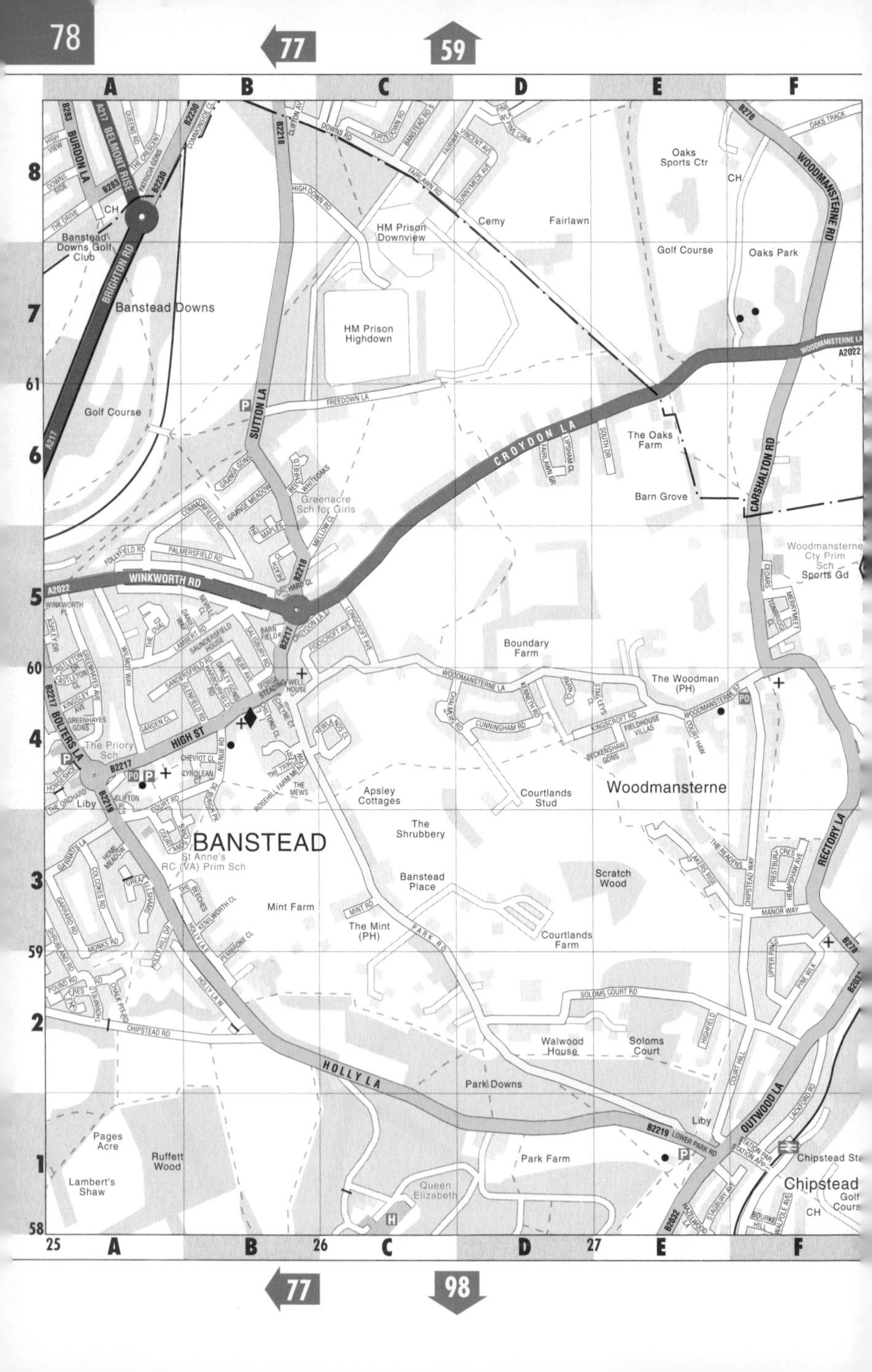
A
B
C
D
E
F
8
7
61
6
5
60
4
3
59
2
1
58
25
26
27
BANSTEAD
Woodmansterne
Banstead Downs
Banstead Downs Golf Club
Golf Course
HM Prison Downview
HM Prison Highdown
Cemy
Fairlawn
Oaks Sports Ctr
Golf Course
Oaks Park
CH
Greenacre Sch for Girls
The Oaks Farm
Barn Grove
Woodmansterne Cty Prim Sch
Sports Gd
Boundary Farm
The Woodman (PH)
Well House
The Priory Sch
Liby
Apsley Cottages
Courtlands Stud
The Shrubbery
St Anne's RC (VA) Prim Sch
Banstead Place
Scratch Wood
Mint Farm
The Mint (PH)
Courtlands Farm
Walwood House
Soloms Court
Park Downs
Liby
Pages Acre
Ruffett Wood
Lambert's Shaw
Park Farm
Queen Elizabeth
Chipstead Sta
Chipstead
Golf Course
CH
WINKWORTH RD
CROYDON LA
SUTTON LA
HIGH ST
HOLLY LA
BOLTERS LA
BRIGHTON RD
BELMONT RISE
BURDON LA
WOODMANSTERNE RD
WOODMANSTERNE LA
CARSHALTON RD
RECTORY LA
OUTWOOD LA
PARK RD
LOWER PARK RD
CHIPSTEAD RD
CHIPSTEAD WAY
FREEDOWN LA
SOLOMS COURT RD
A2022
A217
B2217
B2218
B2219
B2230
B2032
B278
B283

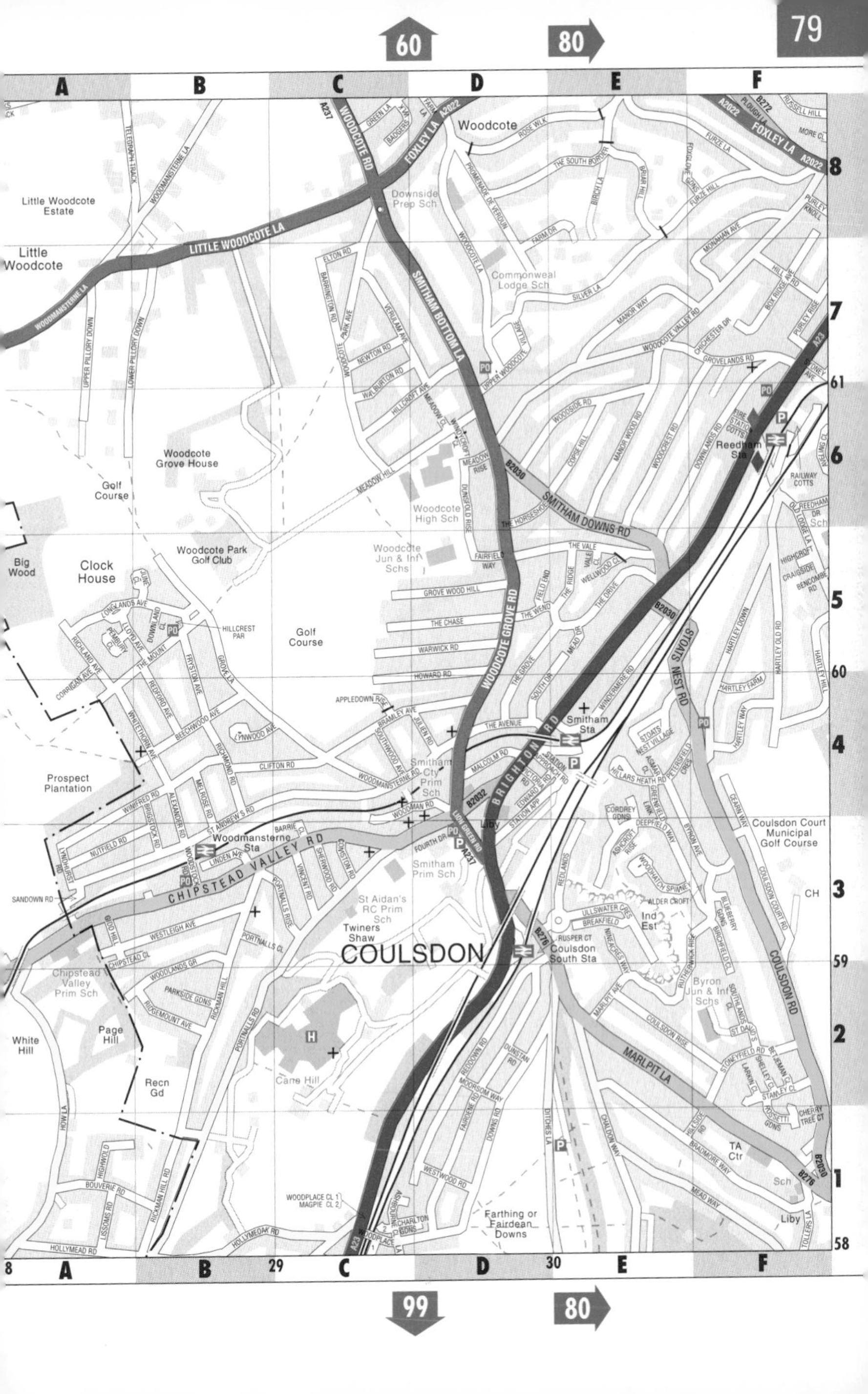
60
80
A
B
C
D
E
F
8
7
6
5
4
3
2
1
61
60
59
58
29
30
Little Woodcote Estate
Little Woodcote
LITTLE WOODCOTE LA
WOODMANSTERNE LA
TELEGRAPH TRACK
UPPER PILLORY DOWN
LOWER PILLORY DOWN
Woodcote
WOODCOTE RD
A237
FOXLEY LA
A2022
GREEN LA
BADGERS WLK
FARM LA
ROSE WLK
THE SOUTH BORDER
PROMENADE DE VERDUN
BIRCH LA
BRIAR HILL
FOXGLOVE GDNS
FURZE HILL
FURZE LA
PLOUGH LA
B272
RUSSELL HILL
MORE CL
PURLEY KNOLL
Downside Prep Sch
FARM DR
WOODCOTE LA
Commonweal Lodge Sch
SILVER LA
MONAHAN AVE
HILL RD
BOX RIDGE AVE
PURLEY RISE
MANOR WAY
WOODCOTE VALLEY RD
CHICHESTER DR
GROVELANDS RD
A23
UPPER WOODCOTE VILLAGE
ELTON RD
BARRINGTON RD
WOODCOTE PARK AVE
VERULAM AVE
NEWTON RD
WALBURTON RD
HILLCROFT AVE
MEADOW CL
WINDYCROFT CL
SMITHAM BOTTOM LA
WOODSIDE RD
COPSE HILL
MANOR WOOD RD
WOODCREST RD
DOWNLANDS RD
FIRE STATION COTTS
Reedham Sta
RAILWAY COTTS
OLD REEDHAM DR
LODGE LA
Sch
HIGHCROFT
CRAIGSIDE
BENCOMBE RD
Woodcote Grove House
Golf Course
MEADOW HILL
MEADOW RISE
DUNSFOLD RISE
B2030
SMITHAM DOWNS RD
THE HORSESHOE
Woodcote High Sch
Woodcote Jun & Inf Schs
FAIRFIELD WAY
THE VALE
VALE CL
WELLWOOD CL
Big Wood
Clock House
Woodcote Park Golf Club
JUNE CL
LONGLANDS AVE
LLOYD AVE
PEMBURY CL
DOWNLAND CL
HILLCREST PAR
RICHLAND AVE
THE MOUNT
FRYSTON AVE
GROVE LA
CORRIGAN AVE
REDFORD AVE
WHITETHORN AVE
BEECHWOOD AVE
LYNWOOD AVE
RICHMOND RD
GROVE WOOD HILL
THE CHASE
WARWICK RD
HOWARD RD
APPLEDOWN RISE
BRAMLEY AVE
JULIEN RD
WOODCOTE GROVE RD
FIELD END
THE RIDGE
THE WEND
THE DRIVE
MEAD DR
THE GROVE
SOUTH DR
WINDERMERE RD
THE AVENUE
Smitham Sta
STOATS NEST RD
HARTLEY DOWN
HARTLEY OLD RD
HARTLEY HILL
HARTLEY FARM
HARTLEY WAY
STOATS NEST VILLAGE
Prospect Plantation
CLIFTON RD
SOUTHWOOD AVE
WOODMANSTERNE RD
MALCOLM RD
BRIGHTON RD
STATION APPROACH RD
VICTORIA RD
EDWARD RD
Smitham Cty Prim Sch
B2032
ASMAR CL
PETERSFIELD CRES
HILLARS HEATH RD
GREENFIELD LINK
WINIFRED RD
BRIGSTOCK RD
ALEXANDER RD
MELROSE RD
ST ANDREW'S RD
WOODMAN RD
LION GREEN RD
STATION APP
Liby
CORDREY GDNS
DEEPFIELD WAY
BYRON AVE
GEARN WAY
Coulsdon Court Municipal Golf Course
LYNDHURST RD
NUTFIELD RD
Woodmansterne Sta
BARRIE CL
LINDEN AVE
WOODSTOCK
CHIPSTEAD VALLEY RD
VINCENT RD
SHERWOOD RD
CONISTON RD
FOURTH DR
Smitham Prim Sch
REDLANDS
ASHCROFT RISE
WOODHATCH SPINNEY
ALDER CROFT
BLUEBERRY GDNS
BIRCHFIELD CL
COULSDON COURT RD
SANDOWN RD
PORTNALLS RISE
St Aidan's RC Prim Sch
Twiners Shaw
ULLSWATER CRES
BREAKFIELD
Ind Est
CH
GIDD HILL
WESTLEIGH AVE
PORTNALLS CL
COULSDON
B276
RUSPER CT
Coulsdon South Sta
NINEACRES WAY
RUTHERWICK RISE
COULSDON RD
CHIPSTEAD CL
Chipstead Valley Prim Sch
WOODLANDS GR
PARKSIDE GDNS
RICKMAN HILL
PORTNALLS RD
RIDGEMOUNT AVE
MARLPIT AVE
Byron Jun & Inf Schs
SOUTHLANDS CL
COULSDON RISE
ST DAVID'S
White Hill
Page Hill
H
Cane Hill
REDDOWN RD
DUNSTAN RD
MARLPIT LA
STONEYFIELD RD
BETJEMAN CL
SHELLEY CL
LARKIN CL
STANLEY CL
Recn Gd
MOORSOM WAY
FAIRDENE RD
DOWNS RD
DITCHES LA
CHALDON WAY
HILLSIDE RD
ROSSETTI GDNS
CHERRY TREE CT
HOW LA
HIGHWOLD
P
TA Ctr
BRADMORE WAY
B2030
BOUVERIE RD
LISSOMS RD
RICKMAN HILL RD
WESTWOOD RD
MEAD WAY
Sch
WOODPLACE CL 1
MAGPIE CL 2
ASHBOURNE CL
CHARLTON GDNS
Farthing or Fairdean Downs
Liby
TOLLERS LA
HOLLYMEAD RD
HOLLYMEADE RD
WOODPLACE LA
99

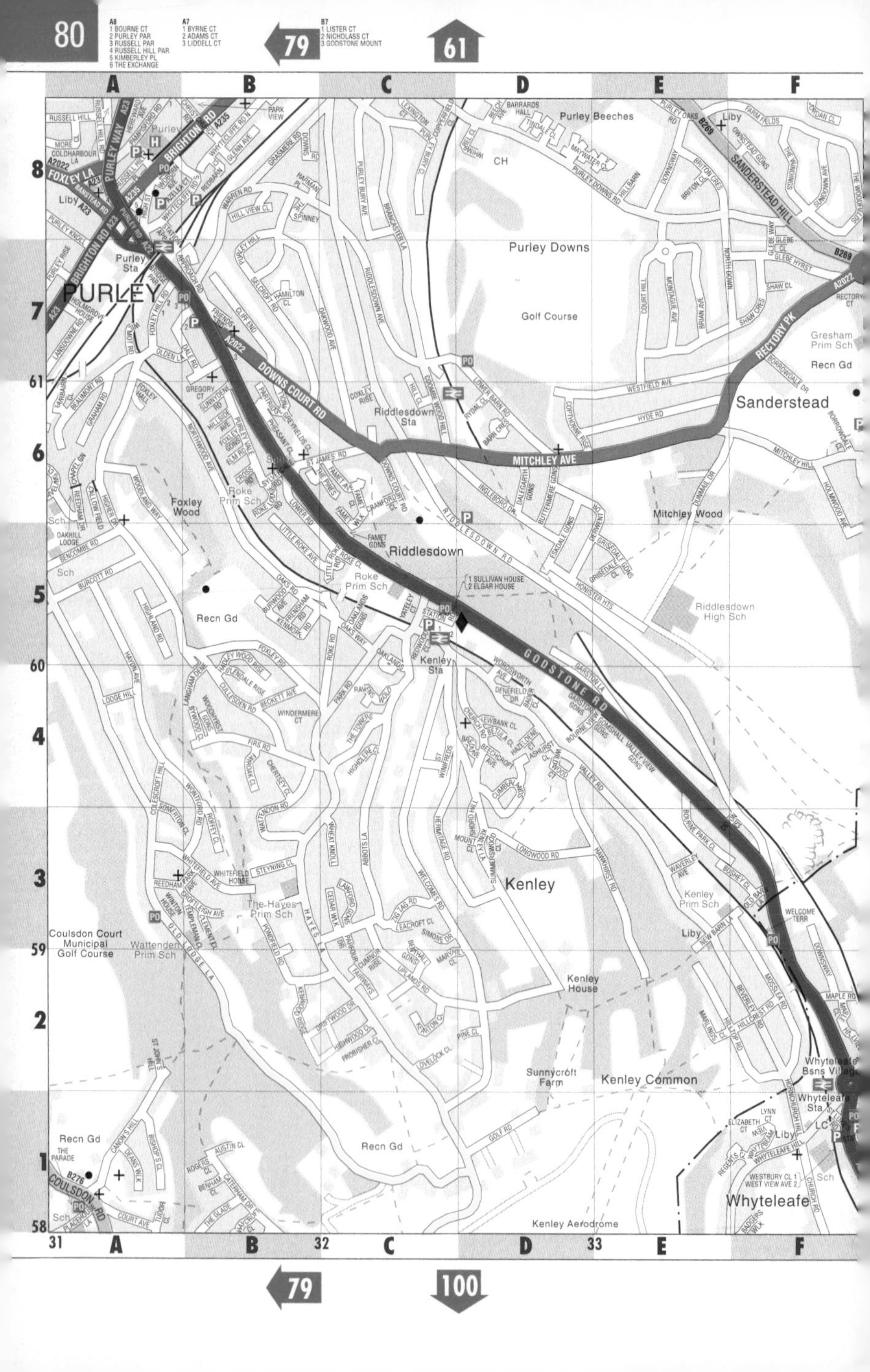
80
A8
1 BOURNE CT
2 PURLEY PAR
3 RUSSELL PAR
4 RUSSELL HILL PAR
5 KIMBERLEY PL
6 THE EXCHANGE
A7
1 BYRNE CT
2 ADAMS CT
3 LIDDELL CT
79
B7
1 LISTER CT
2 NICHOLASS CT
3 GODSTONE MOUNT
61
A
B
C
D
E
F
8
7
61
6
5
60
4
3
59
2
1
58
31
32
33
Purley
PURLEY
Purley Sta
Liby
FOXLEY LA
PURLEY WAY
BRIGHTON RD
RUSSELL HILL
COLDHARBOUR LA
PARK VIEW
Purley Beeches
CH
Purley Downs
Golf Course
SANDERSTEAD HILL
RECTORY PK
Gresham Prim Sch
Recn Gd
Sanderstead
MITCHLEY AVE
MITCHLEY HILL
Mitchley Wood
DOWNS COURT RD
Riddlesdown Sta
Riddlesdown
RIDDLESDOWN RD
Riddlesdown High Sch
Roke Prim Sch
Foxley Wood
Sch
1 SULLIVAN HOUSE
2 ELGAR HOUSE
GODSTONE RD
Kenley Sta
Kenley
Kenley Prim Sch
The Hayes Prim Sch
Wattenden Prim Sch
Coulsdon Court Municipal Golf Course
Kenley House
Sunnycroft Farm
Kenley Common
Whyteleafe Bsns Village
Whyteleafe Sta
Whyteleafe
Kenley Aerodrome
WELCOME TERR
WESTBURY CL 1
WEST VIEW AVE 2
COULSDON RD
GOLF RD
79
100

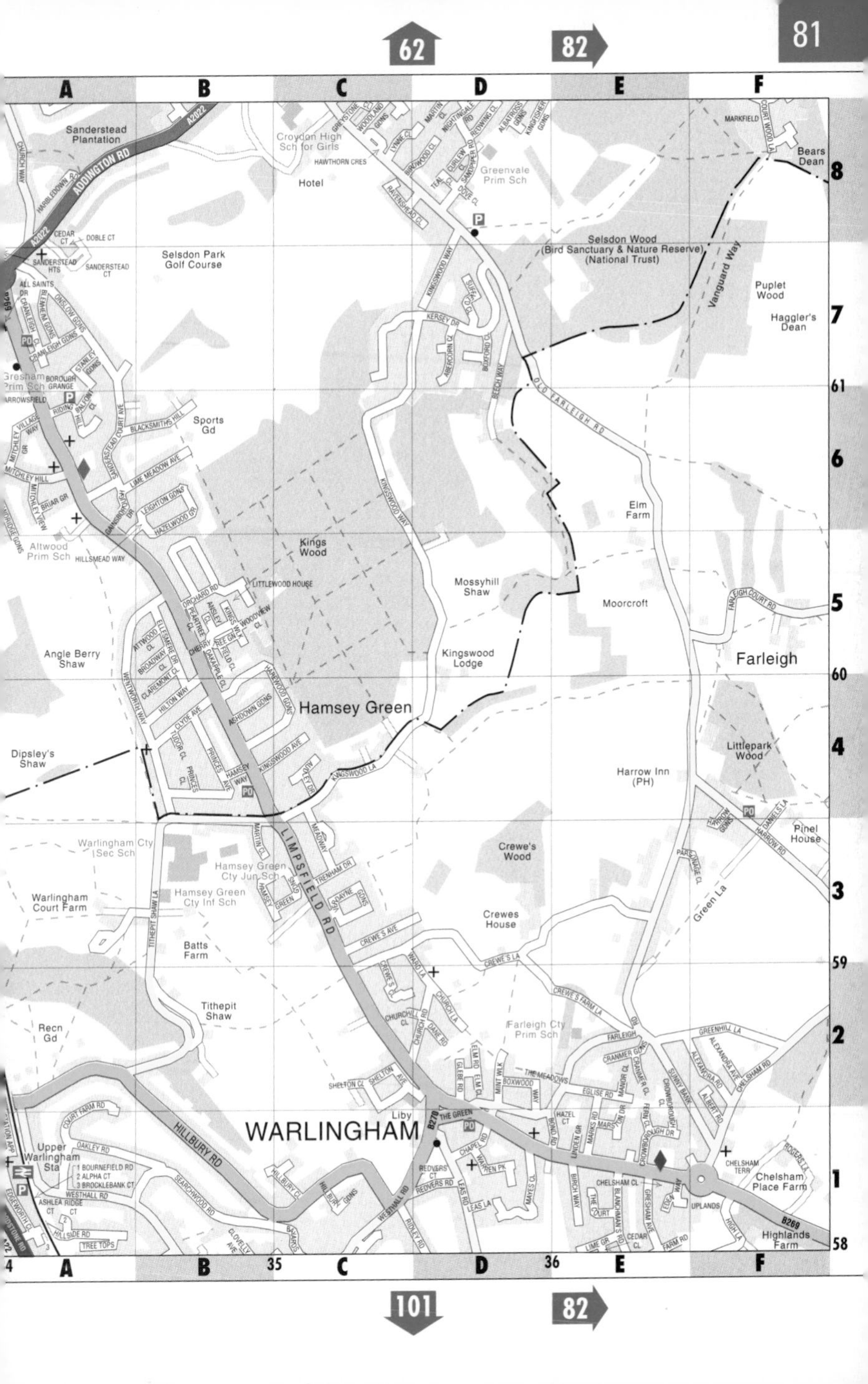
62
82
Sanderstead Plantation
ADDINGTON RD
Croydon High Sch for Girls
Hotel
Greenvale Prim Sch
Selsdon Park Golf Course
Selsdon Wood (Bird Sanctuary & Nature Reserve) (National Trust)
Vanguard Way
Bears Dean
Puplet Wood
Haggler's Dean
Gresham Prim Sch
Sports Gd
OLD FARLEIGH RD
Elm Farm
Altwood Prim Sch
Kings Wood
Mossyhill Shaw
Moorcroft
Angle Berry Shaw
Kingswood Lodge
Farleigh
Hamsey Green
Dipsley's Shaw
Littlepark Wood
Harrow Inn (PH)
Pinel House
Warlingham Cty Sec Sch
Hamsey Green Cty Jun Sch
Hamsey Green Cty Inf Sch
LIMPSFIELD RD
Crewe's Wood
Warlingham Court Farm
Crewes House
Green La
Batts Farm
Tithepit Shaw
Farleigh Cty Prim Sch
Recn Gd
WARLINGHAM
HILLBURY RD
Upper Warlingham Sta
Chelsham Place Farm
Highlands Farm
101
82

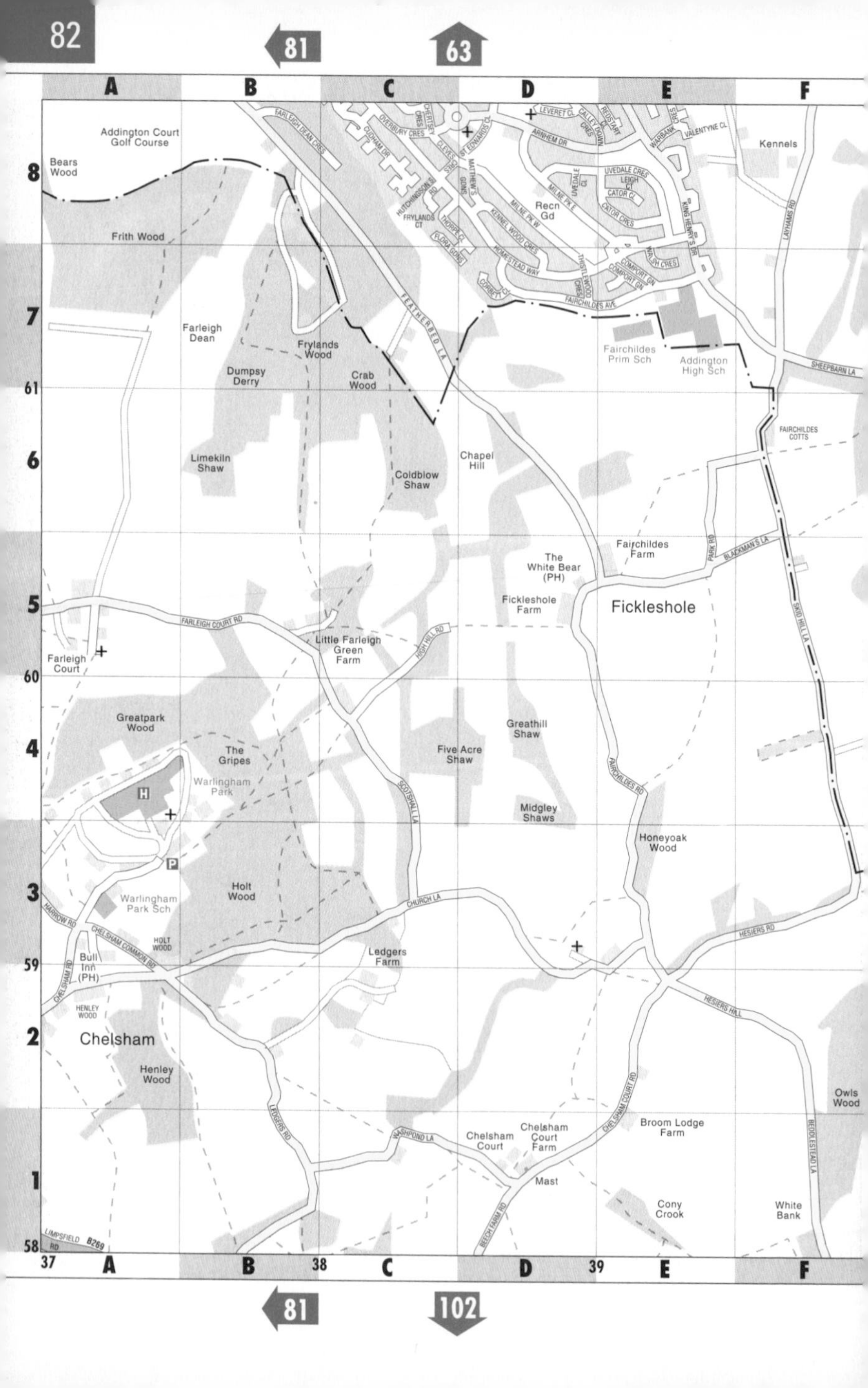
81
63
A
B
C
D
E
F
8
7
61
6
5
60
4
3
59
2
1
58
37
38
39
Addington Court
Golf Course
Bears
Wood
Frith Wood
Farleigh
Dean
Dumpsy
Derry
Frylands
Wood
Crab
Wood
Limekiln
Shaw
Coldblow
Shaw
Chapel
Hill
Kennels
Recn
Gd
Fairchildes
Prim Sch
Addington
High Sch
FAIRCHILDES
COTTS
SHEEPBARN LA
LAYHAMS RD
FEATHERBED LA
FARLEIGH DEAN CRES
OVERBURY CRES
CUDHAM DR
CHERTSEY CRES
CLEVES CRES
ST EDWARDS CL
MATTHEW'S GDNS
HUTCHINSON'S RD
FRYLANDS CT
THORPE CL
FLORA GDNS
LEVERET CL
CALLEY DOWN CRES
REDSTART CL
ARNHEM DR
WARBANK CRES
VALENTYNE CL
UVEDALE CL
UVEDALE CRES
LEIGH CT
CATOR CL
CATOR CRES
MILNE PK E
MILNE PK W
KENNEL WOOD CRES
HOMESTEAD WAY
THISTLEWOOD CRES
WALSH CRES
COMPORT GN
KING HENRY'S DR
CORBETT CL
FAIRCHILDES AVE
Fairchildes
Farm
The
White Bear
(PH)
PARK RD
BLACKMAN'S LA
Fickleshole
Farm
Fickleshole
SKID HILL LA
FARLEIGH COURT RD
Little Farleigh
Green
Farm
HIGH HILL RD
Farleigh
Court
Greatpark
Wood
The
Gripes
Warlingham
Park
Five Acre
Shaw
Greathill
Shaw
Midgley
Shaws
FAIRCHILDES RD
Honeyoak
Wood
SCOTSHALL LA
Holt
Wood
Warlingham
Park Sch
HARROW RD
CHELSHAM COMMON RD
HOLT
WOOD
CHURCH LA
Bull
Inn
(PH)
CHELSHAM RD
Ledgers
Farm
HESIERS RD
HESIERS HILL
HENLEY
WOOD
Chelsham
Henley
Wood
LEDGERS RD
WASHPOND LA
Chelsham
Court
Chelsham
Court
Farm
CHELSHAM COURT RD
Broom Lodge
Farm
Owls
Wood
BEDDLESTEAD LA
Mast
BEECH FARM RD
Cony
Crook
White
Bank
LIMPSFIELD
RD
B269
81
102

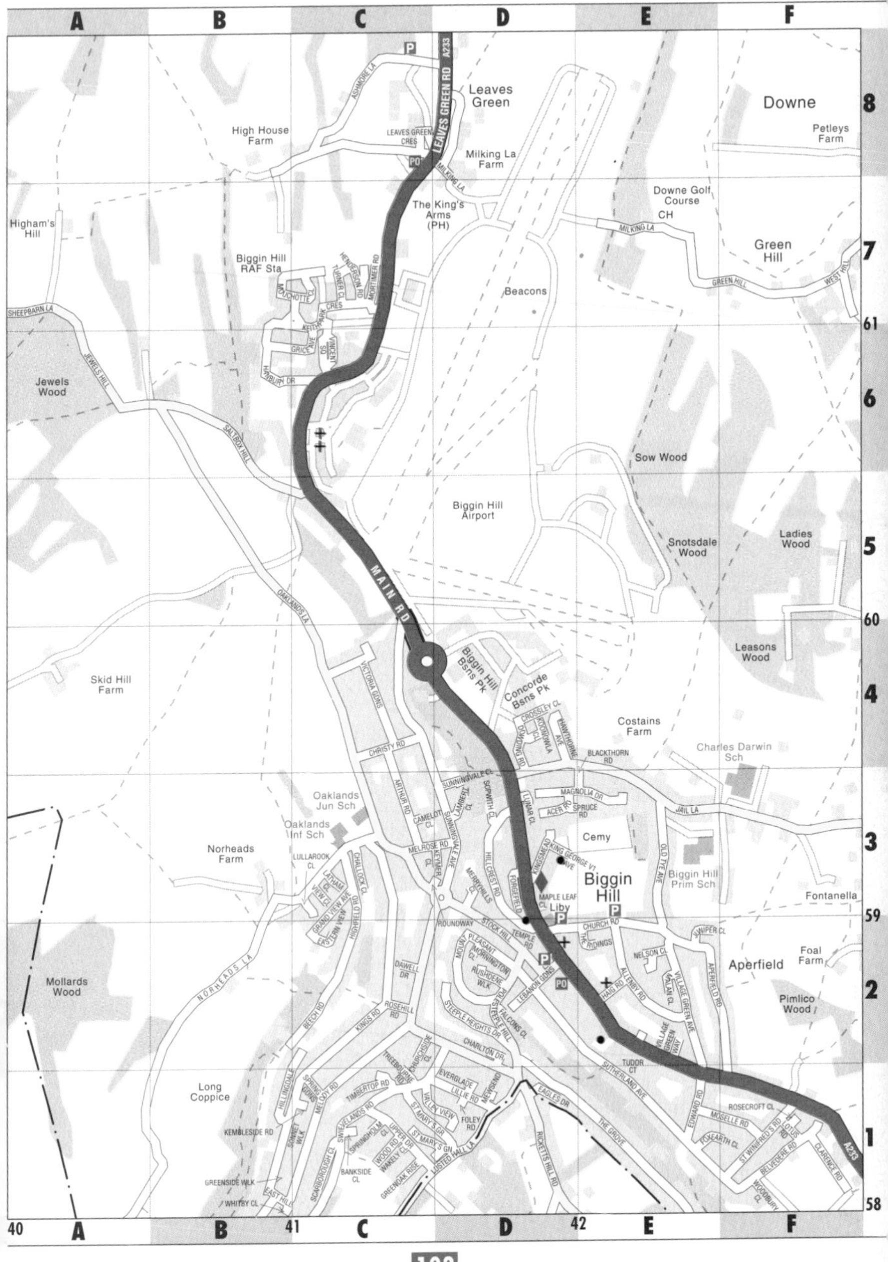

A
B
C
D
E
F
8
7
61
6
5
60
4
3
59
2
1
58
40
41
42
A233
LEAVES GREEN RD
Leaves Green
Downe
Petleys Farm
High House Farm
LEAVES GREEN CRES
Milking La Farm
MILKING LA
ASHMORE LA
The King's Arms (PH)
Downe Golf Course
CH
Higham's Hill
Green Hill
GREEN HILL
WEST HILL
Biggin Hill RAF Sta
HENDERSON RD
MORTIMER RD
TURNER CL
MOUCHOTTE CL
KEITH PARK CRES
GRICE AVE
VINCENT SQ
HANBURY DR
Beacons
SHEEPBARN LA
JEWELS HILL
Jewels Wood
SALTBOX HILL
Sow Wood
Biggin Hill Airport
Snotsdale Wood
Ladies Wood
MAIN RD
OAKLANDS LA
Leasons Wood
Biggin Hill Bsns Pk
Concorde Bsns Pk
Skid Hill Farm
VICTORIA GDNS
CROSSLEY CL
KOONOWLA CL
HAWTHORNE AVE
DOWDING RD
Costains Farm
BLACKTHORN RD
Charles Darwin Sch
CHRISTY RD
ARTHUR RD
SUNNINGVALE CL
SOPWITH CL
LUNAR CL
MAGNOLIA DR
ACER RD
SPRUCE RD
JAIL LA
Oaklands Jun Sch
Oaklands Inf Sch
CAMELOT CL
LAMBERT CL
SUNNINGVALE AVE
Cemy
OLD TYE AVE
Norheads Farm
LULLAROOK CL
LATHAM CL
CHALLOCK CL
MELROSE RD
KEYMER CL
HILLCREST RD
MERRYHILLS CL
FORGEFIELD
KINGSMEAD
KING GEORGE V1 AVE
Biggin Hill
Biggin Hill Prim Sch
Fontanella
VIEW CL
GRAND VIEW AVE
EASTERN VIEW
HIGHFIELD CL
MAPLE LEAF CL
Liby
ROUNDWAY
STOCK HILL
TEMPLE RD
CHURCH RD
THE RIDINGS
JUNIPER CL
MOUNT PLEASANT
MORNINGTON CL
NELSON CL
APERFIELD RD
Aperfield
Foal Farm
NORHEADS LA
Mollards Wood
DAWELL DR
RUSHDENE WLK
LEBANON GDNS
FALCONS CL
HAIG RD
ALLENBY RD
MILAN CL
VILLAGE GREEN AVE
Pimlico Wood
BEECH RD
KINGS RD
ROSEHILL RD
STEEPLE HEIGHTS DR
CHARLTON DR
VILLAGE GREEN WAY
TUDOR CT
SUTHERLAND AVE
Long Coppice
HILLINGDALE
SPRING GROVE
MELODY RD
TIMBERTOP RD
TREEBOURNE RD
CHURCHSIDE CL
EVERGLADE
LILLIE RD
NEWSEND
EAGLES DR
EDWARD RD
ROSECROFT CL
MOSELLE RD
LOTUS RD
KEMBLESIDE RD
SORRELL WLK
SWIEVELANDS RD
VALLEY VIEW
FOLEY RD
THE GROVE
FOXEARTH CL
ST WINIFRED'S RD
BELVEDERE RD
CLARENCE RD
A233
SPRINGHOLM CL
UPPER DR
ST MARY'S GR
ST MARY'S GN
WOOD RD
WAKELY CL
LUSTED HALL LA
RICKETTS HILL RD
BANKSIDE CL
GREENOAK RISE
SCARBOROUGH CL
GREENSIDE WLK
EAST HILL
WHITBY CL
WOODBURY CL

103

64

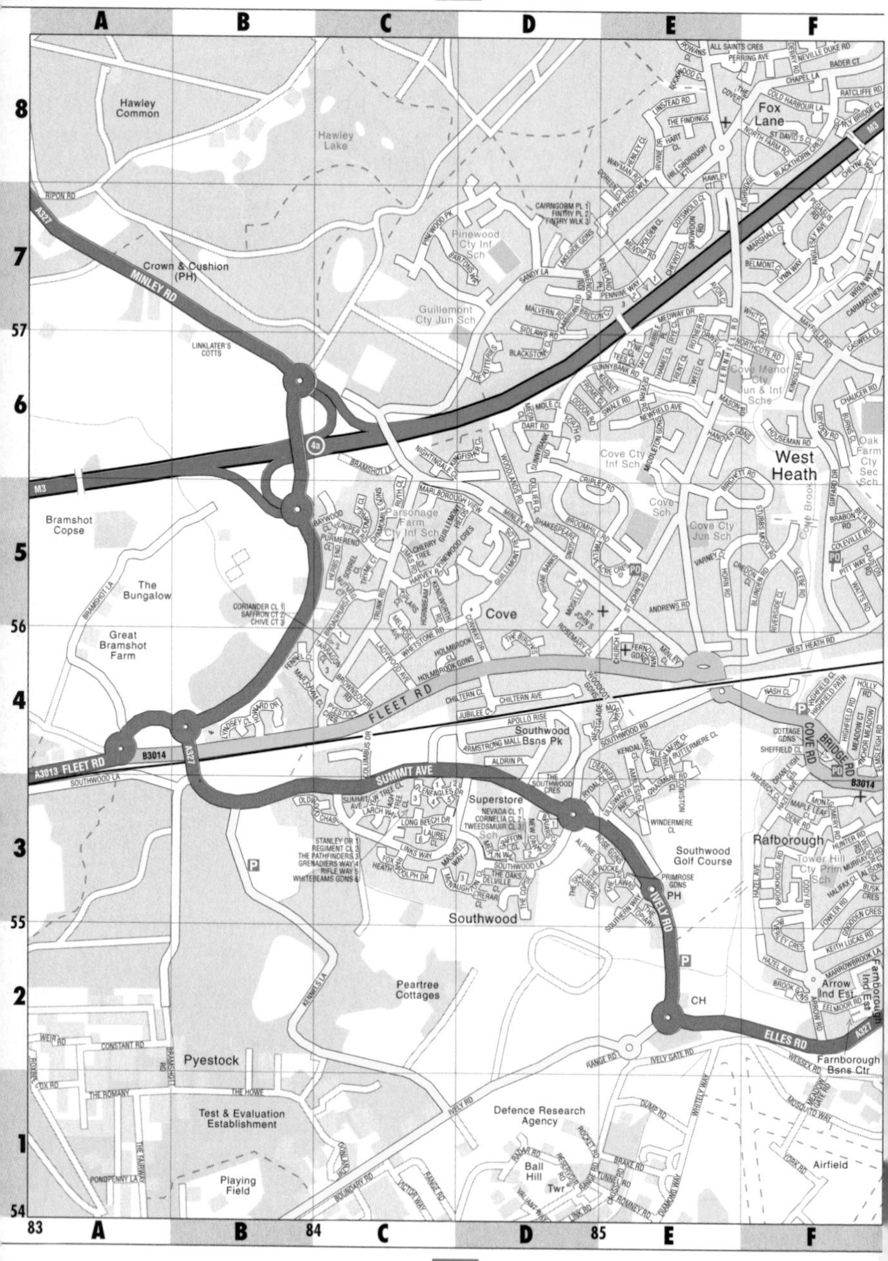
A
B
C
D
E
F
8
7
57
6
5
56
4
3
55
2
1
54
83
84
85
Hawley Common
Hawley Lake
Fox Lane
RIPON RD
A327
MINLEY RD
Crown & Cushion (PH)
Pinewood Cty Inf Sch
Guillemont Cty Jun Sch
LINKLATER'S COTTS
M3
4a
Bramshot Copse
The Bungalow
Great Bramshot Farm
BRAMSHOT LA
Parsonage Farm Cty Inf Sch
Cove
Cove Cty Inf Sch
Cove Sch
Cove Cty Jun Sch
Cove Manor Cty Jun & Inf Schs
West Heath
Oak Farm Cty Sec Sch
WEST HEATH RD
FLEET RD
A3013 FLEET RD
B3014
SOUTHWOOD LA
SUMMIT AVE
Southwood Bsns Pk
Superstore
Southwood Golf Course
Southwood
IVELY RD
PH
CH
Rafborough
Tower Hill Cty Prim Sch
COVE RD
BRIDGE RD
ELLES RD
Arrow Ind Est
Farnborough Ind Est
Farnborough Bsns Ctr
Peartree Cottages
KENNELS LA
Pyestock
Test & Evaluation Establishment
Playing Field
Defence Research Agency
Ball Hill
Twr
Airfield
IVELY GATE RD
RANGE RD
THE FAIRWAY
PONDPENNY LA
CONSTANT RD
WEIR RD
THE ROMANY
THE HOWE
BOUNDARY RD
VICTOR WAY
WHITELY WAY
MOSQUITO WAY
YORK RD
CORIANDER CL 1
SAFFRON CT 2
CHIVE CT 3
CAIRNGORM PL 1
FINTRY PL 2
FINTRY WLK 3
STANLEY DR 1
REGIMENT CL 2
THE PATHFINDERS 3
GRENADIERS WAY 4
RIFLE WAY 5
WHITEBEAMS GDNS 6
NEVADA CL 1
CORNELIA CL 2
TWEEDSMUIR CL 3

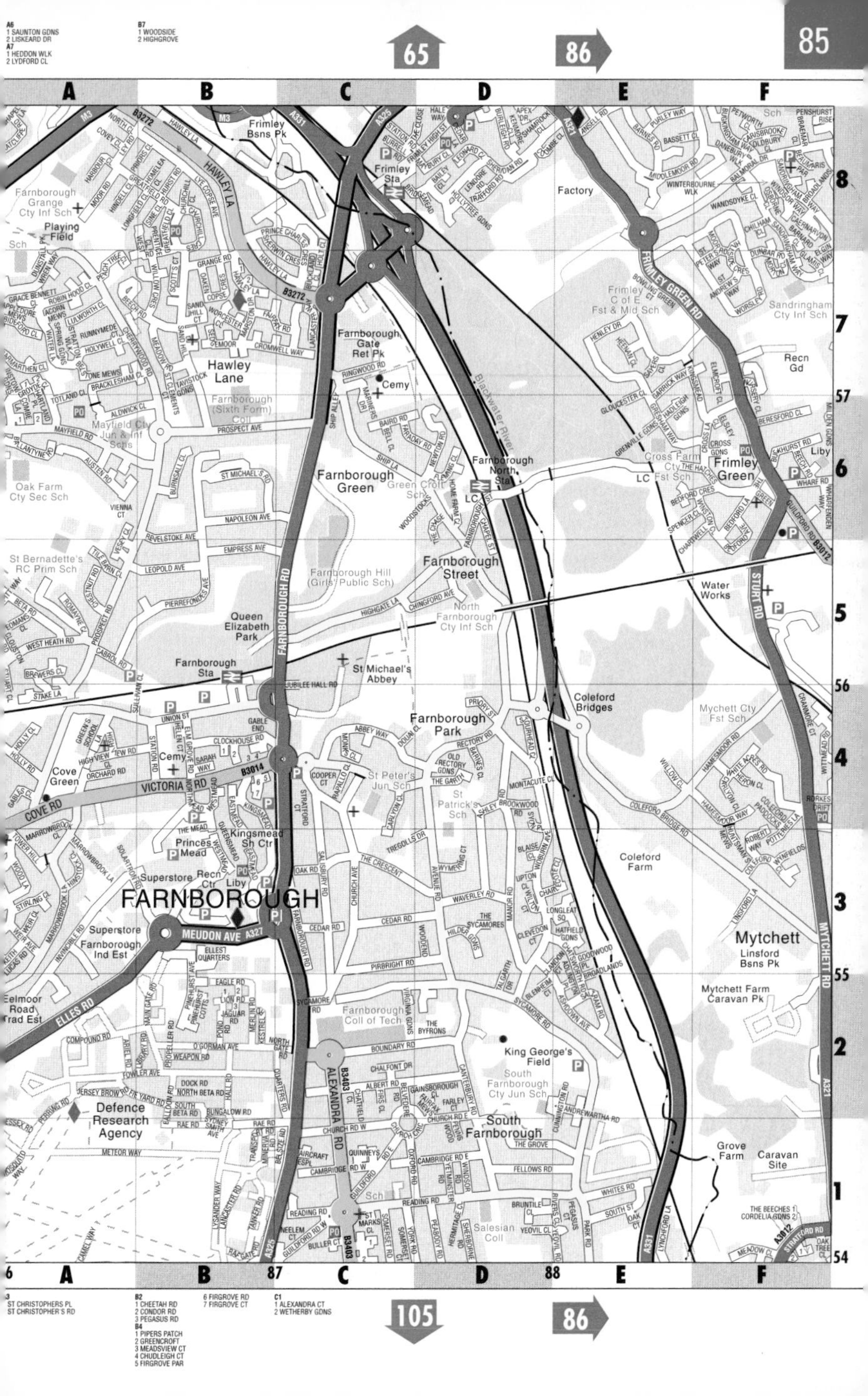
A6
1 SAUNTON GDNS
2 LISKEARD DR
A7
1 HEDDON WLK
2 LYDFORD CL
B7
1 WOODSIDE
2 HIGHGROVE
65
86
Frimley Bsns Pk
Frimley Sta
Factory
Farnborough Grange Cty Inf Sch
Playing Field
Hawley Lane
Farnborough (Sixth Form) Coll
Mayfield Cty Jun & Inf Schs
Frimley C of E Fst & Mid Sch
Sandringham Cty Inf Sch
Farnborough Gate Ret Pk
Cemy
Recn Gd
Oak Farm Cty Sec Sch
Farnborough Green
Green Croft Sch
Farnborough North Sta
Cross Farm Cty Fst Sch
Frimley Green
Blackwater River
St Bernadette's RC Prim Sch
Farnborough Hill (Girls' Public Sch)
Farnborough Street
Water Works
North Farnborough Cty Inf Sch
Queen Elizabeth Park
Farnborough Sta
St Michael's Abbey
Coleford Bridges
Mychett Cty Fst Sch
Farnborough Park
Cove Green
St Peter's Jun Sch
St Patrick's Sch
Kingsmead Sh Ctr
Princes Mead
Superstore
Recn Ctr
Liby
Coleford Farm
FARNBOROUGH
Farnborough Ind Est
Mytchett
Linsford Bsns Pk
Mytchett Farm Caravan Pk
Eelmoor Road Trad Est
Farnborough Coll of Tech
King George's Field
South Farnborough Cty Jun Sch
Defence Research Agency
South Farnborough
Grove Farm
Caravan Site
Salesian Coll
FARNBOROUGH RD
ALEXANDRA RD
VICTORIA RD
COVE RD
MEUDON AVE
ELLES RD
HAWLEY LA
FRIMLEY GREEN RD
STURT RD
MYTCHETT RD
105
86
3
ST CHRISTOPHERS PL
ST CHRISTOPHER'S RD
B2
1 CHEETAH RD
2 CONDOR RD
3 PEGASUS RD
B4
1 PIPERS PATCH
2 GREENCROFT
3 MEADSVIEW CT
4 CHUDLEIGH CT
5 FIRGROVE PAR
6 FIRGROVE RD
7 FIRGROVE CT
C1
1 ALEXANDRA CT
2 WETHERBY GDNS

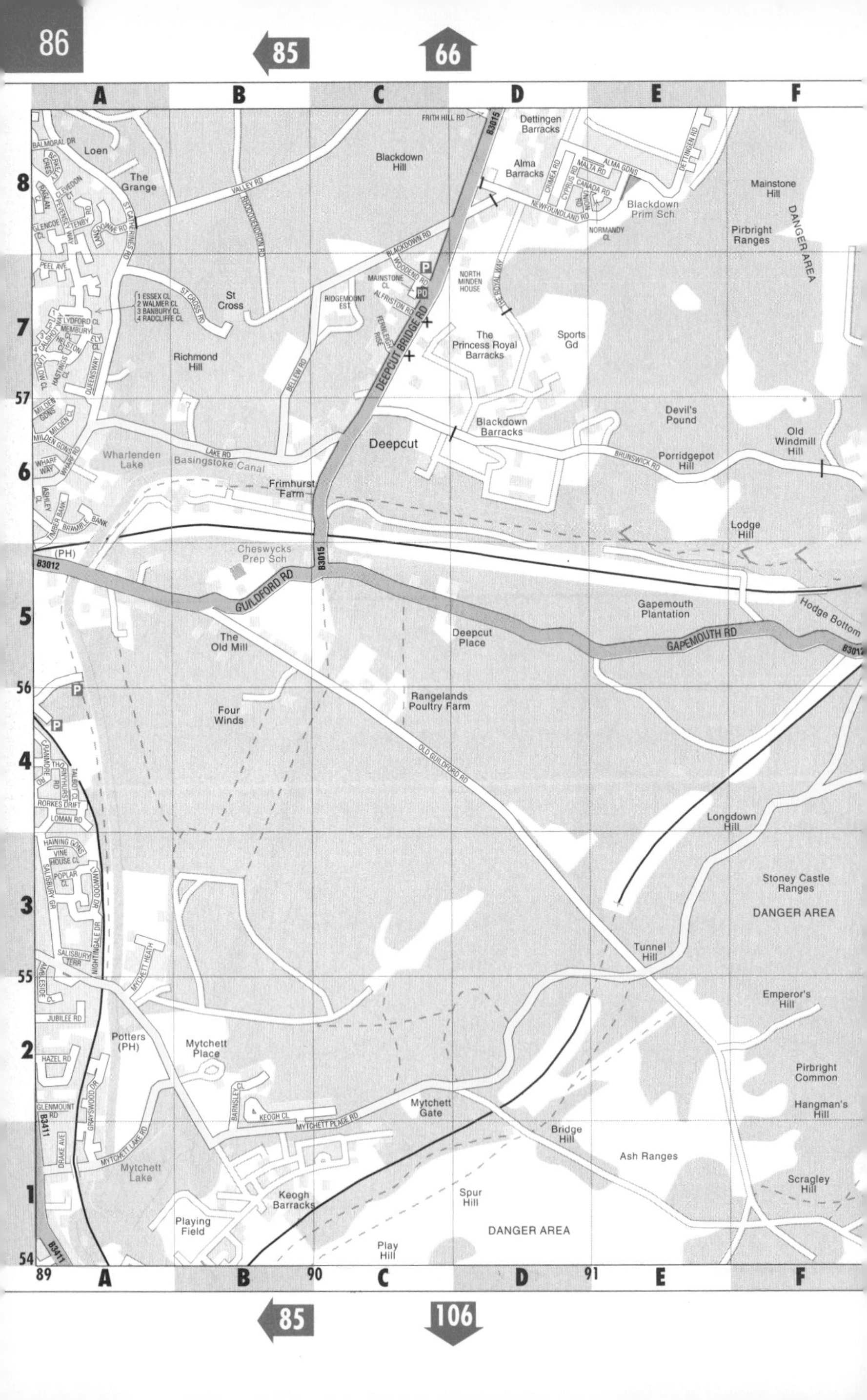
85
66
Loen
The Grange
Blackdown Hill
Dettingen Barracks
Alma Barracks
Blackdown Prim Sch
Mainstone Hill
Pirbright Ranges
DANGER AREA
St Cross
Richmond Hill
RIDGEMOUNT EST
NORTH MINDEN HOUSE
The Princess Royal Barracks
Sports Gd
Devil's Pound
Blackdown Barracks
Deepcut
Wharfenden Lake
Basingstoke Canal
Frimhurst Farm
Porridgepot Hill
Old Windmill Hill
Lodge Hill
Cheswycks Prep Sch
(PH)
GUILDFORD RD
Gapemouth Plantation
Hodge Bottom
GAPEMOUTH RD
The Old Mill
Deepcut Place
Four Winds
Rangelands Poultry Farm
OLD GUILDFORD RD
Longdown Hill
Stoney Castle Ranges
DANGER AREA
Tunnel Hill
Emperor's Hill
Potters (PH)
Mytchett Place
Pirbright Common
Hangman's Hill
Mytchett Gate
Bridge Hill
Ash Ranges
Mytchett Lake
Keogh Barracks
Spur Hill
Scragley Hill
Playing Field
DANGER AREA
Play Hill
DEEPCUT BRIDGE RD
B3015
B3012
B3411
VALLEY RD
RHODODENDRON RD
ST CATHERINES RD
ST CROSS RD
BLACKDOWN RD
WOODEND RD
MAINSTONE CL
ALFRISTON RD
FERNLEIGH RISE
BELLEW RD
LAKE RD
BRUNSWICK RD
FRITH HILL RD
THE ROYAL WAY
NEWFOUNDLAND RD
NORMANDY CL
CRIMEA RD
CYPRUS RD
MALTA RD
ALMA GDNS
CANADA RD
DETTINGEN RD
BALMORAL DR
BERKELEY CRES
CLEVEDON CT
RAGLAN CL
PEVENSEY WAY
TENBY RD
GLENCOE CL
LANSDOWNE RD
PEEL AVE
1 ESSEX CL
2 WALMER CL
3 BANBURY CL
4 RADCLIFFE CL
LYDFORD CL
MEMBURY CL
CALSHOT WAY
HELSTON CL
ELY CL
HASTINGS CL
LUDLOW CL
QUEENSWAY
MILDEN GDNS
MILDEN CL
WHARF WAY
WHARF RD
ASHLEY CL
TIMBER BANK
BRAMBLE BANK
CRANMORE RD
TALBOT CL
RORKES DRIFT
LOMAN RD
HAINING GDNS
VINE HOUSE CL
POPLAR CL
SALISBURY GR
LYNWOOD DR
NIGHTINGALE DR
SALISBURY TERR
AMBLESIDE CL
JUBILEE RD
MYTCHETT HEATH
HAZEL RD
GRAYSWOOD DR
GLENMOUNT RD
DRAKE AVE
MYTCHETT LAKE RD
BARNSLEY CL
KEOGH CL
MYTCHETT PLACE RD
A B C D E F
8 7 57 6 5 56 4 3 55 2 1 54
89 90 91
85
106

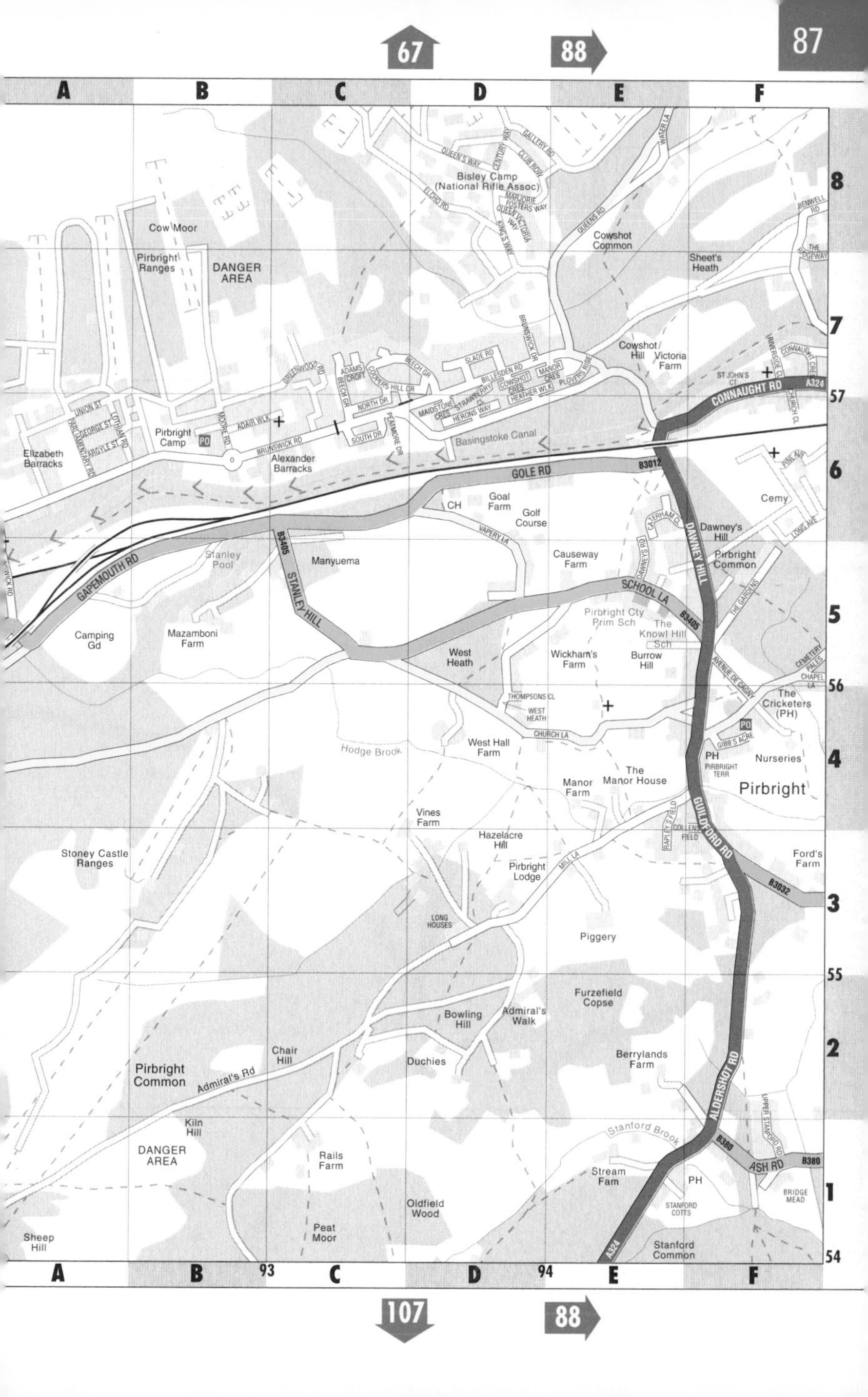

	A	B	C	D	E	F	

8

Bisley Camp
(National Rifle Assoc)

QUEEN'S WAY

CLUB RD

GALLERY RD

MAGELA

Cow Moor

Pirbright
Ranges

DANGER
AREA

Cowshot
Common

Sheet's
Heath

BENWELL
RD

THE
RIDGEWAY

7

Cowshot
Hill Victoria
Farm

St JOHN'S

BRIDLEWOOD

ADAMS
CROFT

SLADE RD

MANOR

OAKS

PLOVER'S

CONNAUGHT RD

A324

57

UNION ST

LOTHIAN RD

GEORGE RD

SAVILLE ST

Pirbright
Camp

PO

MOOR RD

ADAIR WLK

NORTH DR

SOUTH DR

BRUNSWICK RD

PENNYPOT LA

Alexander
Barracks

Basingstoke Canal

GOLE RD

B3012

6

Elizabeth
Barracks

GAPEMOUTH RD

B3406

CH

Goal
Farm

Golf
Course

VAPERY LA

Causeway
Farm

SCHOOL LA

Dawney's
Hill

Pirbright
Common

DAWNEY HILL

B3406

THE GARDENS

Cemy

VINE LA

LONG LA

56
5

Stanley
Pool

STANLEY HILL

Manyuema

Camping
Gd

Mazamboni
Farm

West
Heath

Wickham's
Farm

Pirbright City Prim Sch

The
Knowl Hill
Sch

Burrow
Hill

CEMETERY
PALES

CHAPEL
LA

The
Cricketers
(PH)

AVENUE DE CAGNY

THOMPSONS CL

WEST
HEATH

CHURCH LA

West Hall
Farm

The
Manor House

Manor
Farm

PH

PIRBRIGHT
TERR

GIBBS ACRE

PO

Nurseries

Pirbright

4

Hodge Brook

Vines
Farm

Hazelacre
Hill

Pirbright
Lodge

MILL LA

RAPLEY'S FIELD

GUILDFORD RD

COLLEGE
FIELDS

Ford's
Farm

B3032

3

Stoney Castle
Ranges

LONG
HOUSES

Piggery

55

Furzefield
Copse

2

Pirbright
Common

ADMIRAL'S RD

Chair
Hill

Duchies

Bowling
Hill

Admiral's
Walk

Berrylands
Farm

ALDERSHOT RD

Kiln
Hill

DANGER
AREA

Rails
Farm

Oldfield
Wood

Stanford Brook

Stream
Fam

PH

STANFORD
COTTS

B380

ASH RD

B380

BRIDGE
MEAD

1

Sheep
Hill

Peat
Moor

A324

Stanford
Common

54

	A	B	C	D	E	F	

87
68

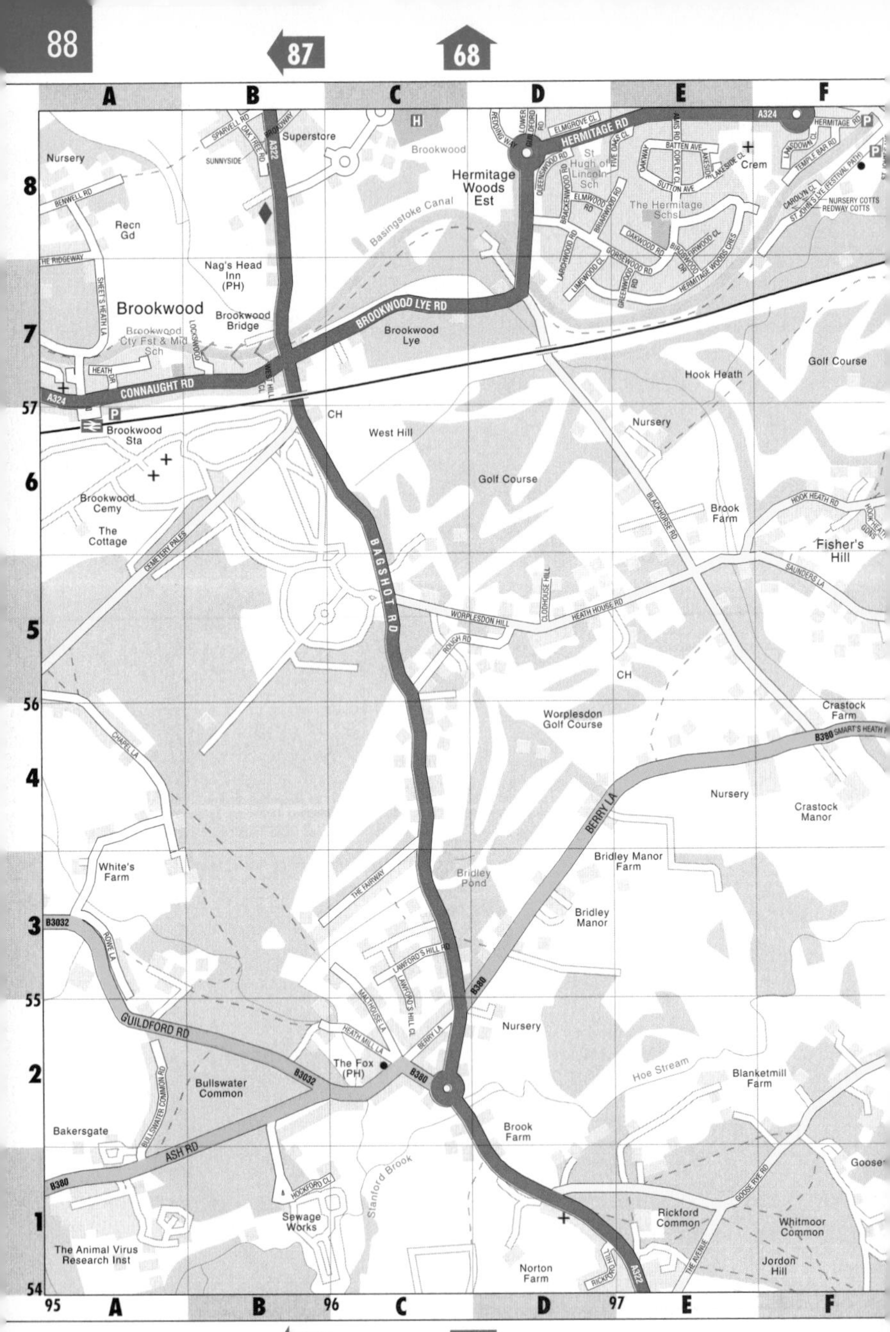
A
B
C
D
E
F
Nursery
Superstore
Brookwood
Hermitage Woods Est
St Hugh of Lincoln Sch
Crem
HERMITAGE RD
A324
Basingstoke Canal
Recn Gd
The Hermitage Schs
Nag's Head Inn (PH)
Brookwood
Brookwood Bridge
BROOKWOOD LYE RD
Brookwood Lye
Brookwood Cty Fst & Mid Sch
CONNAUGHT RD
Golf Course
Hook Heath
Brookwood Sta
CH
West Hill
Nursery
Golf Course
Brookwood Cemy
The Cottage
Brook Farm
Fisher's Hill
BAGSHOT RD
WORPLESDON HILL
HEATH HOUSE RD
CH
Worplesdon Golf Course
Crastock Farm
B380
BERRY LA
Nursery
Crastock Manor
White's Farm
Bridley Pond
Bridley Manor Farm
Bridley Manor
B3032
GUILDFORD RD
Nursery
The Fox (PH)
Bullswater Common
Hoe Stream
Blanketmill Farm
Bakersgate
ASH RD
Brook Farm
Stanford Brook
Sewage Works
Rickford Common
Whitmoor Common
The Animal Virus Research Inst
Norton Farm
Jordon Hill
A322
95
96
97
54
55
56
57

87
108

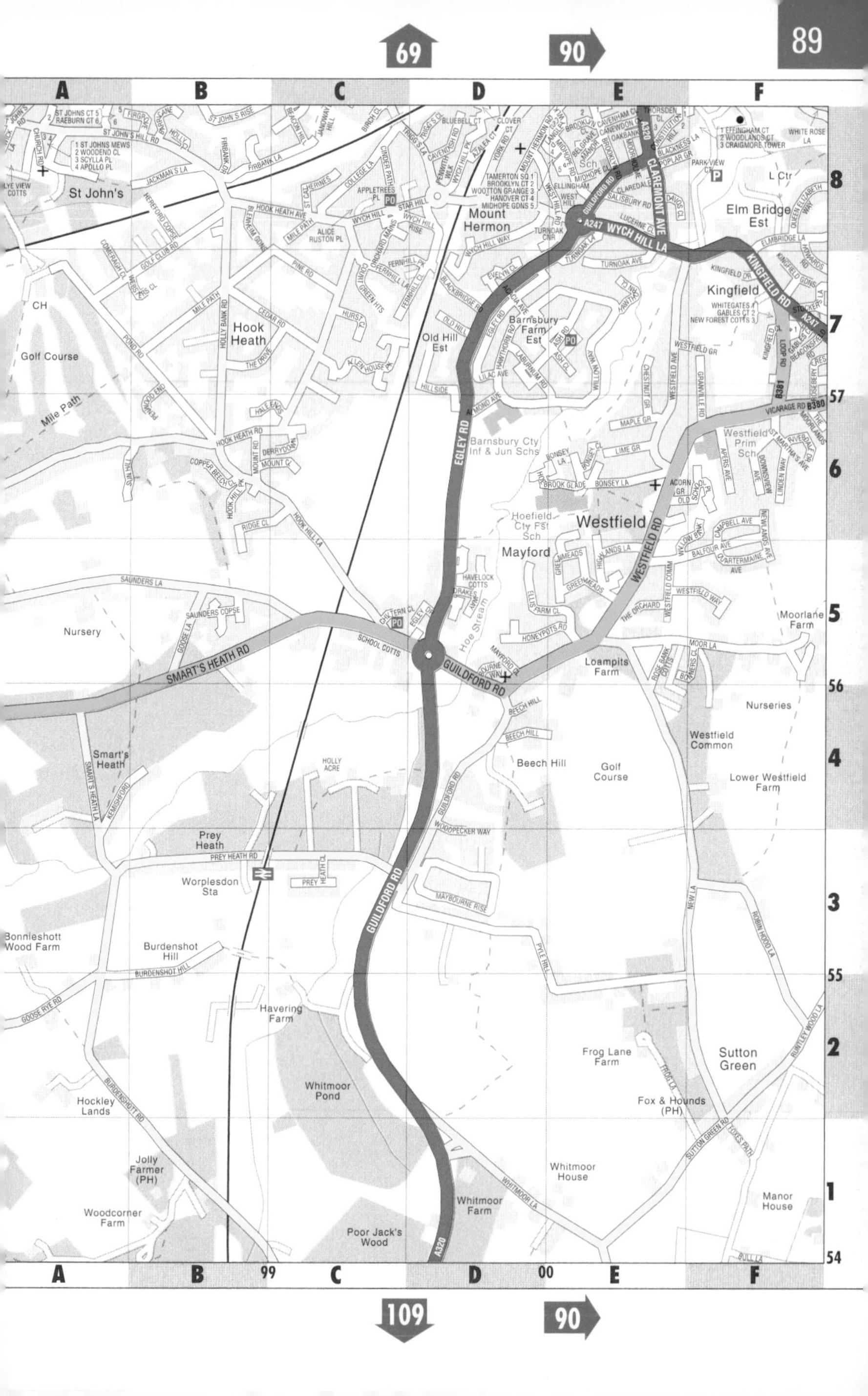
69
90
A
B
C
D
E
F
8
7
57
6
5
56
4
3
55
2
1
54
99
00
St John's
Mount Hermon
Elm Bridge Est
Kingfield
Hook Heath
Old Hill Est
Barnsbury Farm Est
Golf Course
Mile Path
CH
Barnsbury Cty Inf & Jun Schs
Westfield Prim Sch
Hoefield Cty Fst Sch
Westfield
Mayford
Moorlane Farm
Nursery
Loampits Farm
Nurseries
Westfield Common
Smart's Heath
Beech Hill
Golf Course
Lower Westfield Farm
Prey Heath
Worplesdon Sta
Bonnieshott Wood Farm
Burdenshot Hill
Havering Farm
Frog Lane Farm
Sutton Green
Fox & Hounds (PH)
Whitmoor Pond
Hockley Lands
Jolly Farmer (PH)
Whitmoor House
Woodcorner Farm
Whitmoor Farm
Poor Jack's Wood
Manor House
L Ctr
Hoe Stream
SMART'S HEATH RD
GUILDFORD RD
EGLEY RD
WESTFIELD RD
WYCH HILL LA
KINGFIELD RD
CLAREMONT AVE
HOOK HEATH RD
HOOK HEATH AVE
SAUNDERS LA
PREY HEATH RD
BURDENSHOT HILL
BURDENSHOT RD
GOOSE RYE RD
WHITMOOR LA
SUTTON GREEN RD
ROBIN HOOD LA
NEW LA
MOOR LA
PYLE HILL
BEECH HILL
WOODPECKER WAY
MAYBOURNE RISE
SCHOOL COTTS
VICARAGE RD
A320
A247
B380
B381
1 ST JOHNS MEWS
2 WOODEND CL
3 SCYLLA PL
4 APOLLO PL
1 EFFINGHAM CT
2 WOODLANDS CT
3 CRAIGMORE TOWER
TAMERTON SQ 1
BROOKLYN CT 2
WOOTTON GRANGE 3
HANOVER CT 4
MIDHOPE GDNS 5
WHITEGATES 1
GABLES CT 2
NEW FOREST COTTS 3

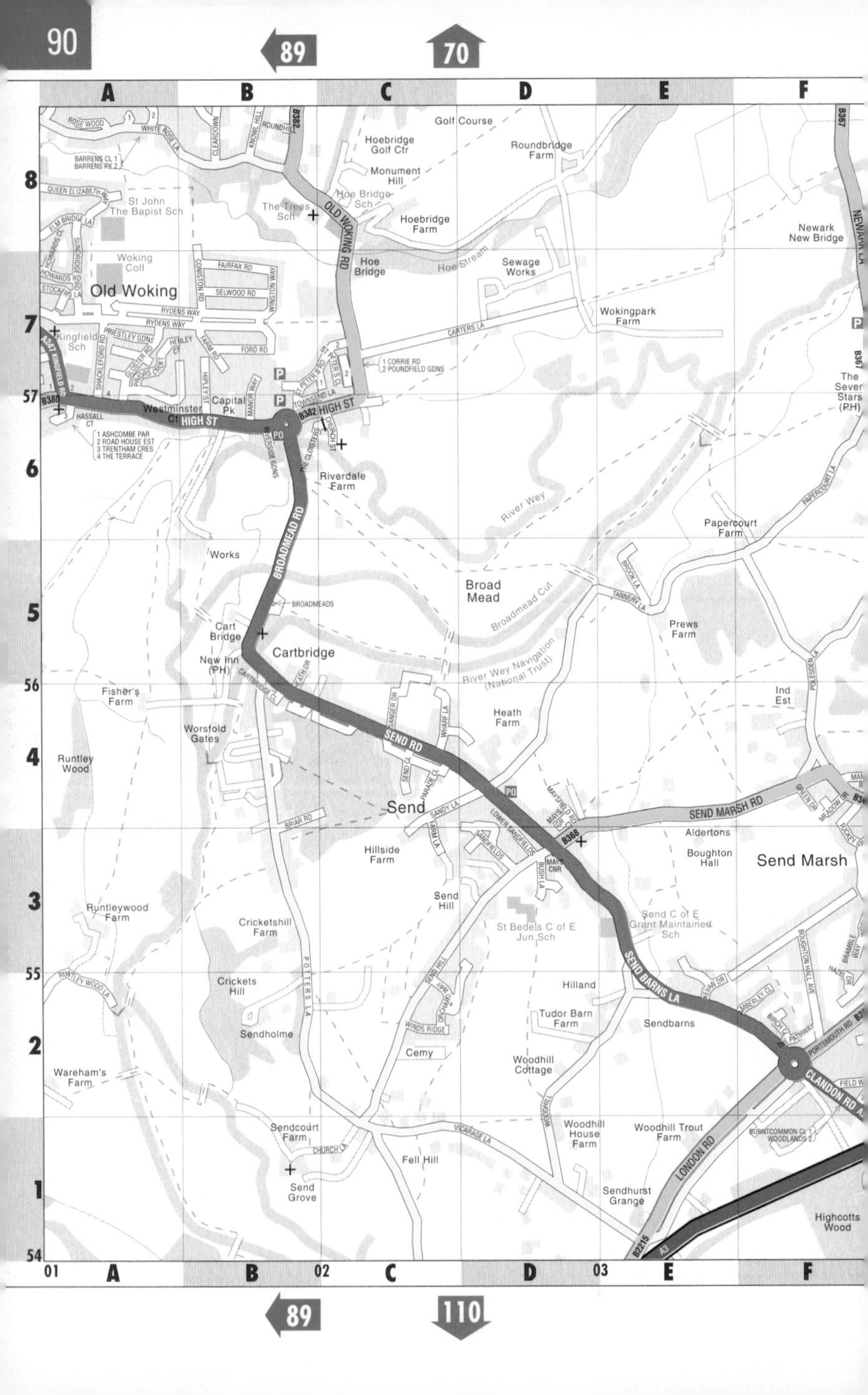
89
70
A
B
C
D
E
F
Golf Course
Hoebridge Golf Ctr
Roundbridge Farm
Monument Hill
St John The Bapist Sch
Hoe Bridge Sch
The Trees Sch
Hoebridge Farm
Newark New Bridge
Woking Coll
Old Woking
Hoe Bridge
Hoe Stream
Sewage Works
Wokingpark Farm
Kingfield Sch
Capital Pk
Westminster Ct
HIGH ST
OLD WOKING RD
CARTERS LA
1 CORRIE RD
2 POUNDFIELD GDNS
1 ASHCOMBE PAR
2 ROAD HOUSE EST
3 TRENTHAM CRES
4 THE TERRACE
The Seven Stars (PH)
Riverdale Farm
River Wey
Papercourt Farm
Works
BROADMEAD RD
Broad Mead
Broadmead Cut
BROADMEADS
Cart Bridge
Cartbridge
Prews Farm
New Inn (PH)
River Wey Navigation (National Trust)
Fisher's Farm
Heath Farm
Ind Est
Worsfold Gates
SEND RD
Runtley Wood
Send
SEND MARSH RD
Aldertons
Boughton Hall
Send Marsh
Hillside Farm
Send Hill
Runtleywood Farm
Cricketshill Farm
St Bede's C of E Jun Sch
Send C of E Grant Maintained Sch
SEND BARNS LA
Crickets Hill
Hilland
Tudor Barn Farm
Sendbarns
Sendholme
Cemy
Woodhill Cottage
Wareham's Farm
CLANDON RD
Sendcourt Farm
Woodhill House Farm
Woodhill Trout Farm
Fell Hill
LONDON RD
Send Grove
Sendhurst Grange
Highcotts Wood
01
02
03
54
55
56
57
1
2
3
4
5
6
7
8
89
110

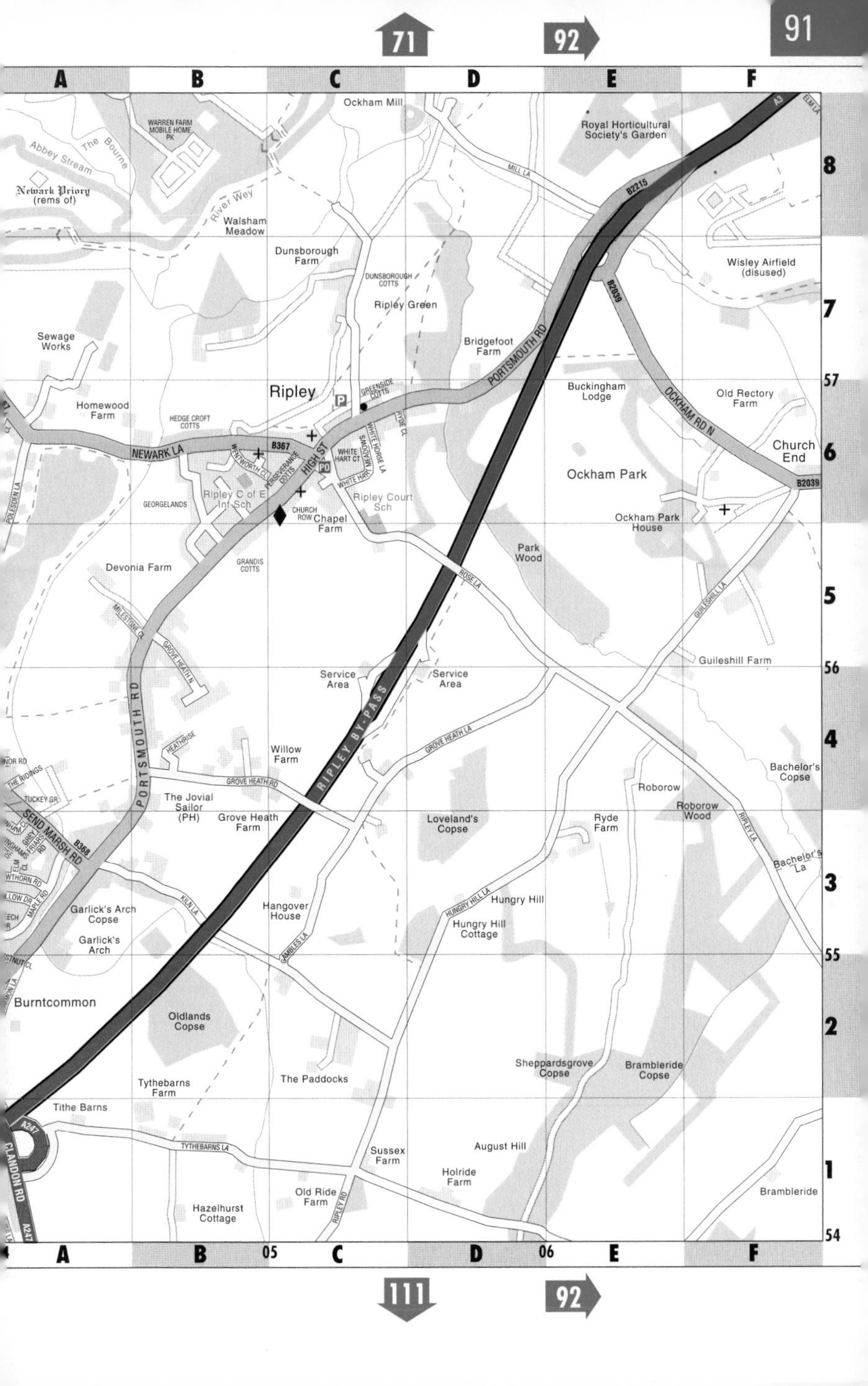

A   B   C   D   E   F

Ockham Mill

WARREN FARM
MOBILE HOME
PK
Abbey Stream
The Bourne
Royal Horticultural
Society's Garden

8

Newark Priory
(rems of)
River Wey
Walsham
Meadow
Dunsborough
Farm
Wisley Airfield
(disused)

7

Dunsborough
Farm
DUNSBOROUGH
COTTS
Ripley Green
Bridgefoot
Farm

57

Sewage
Works
Portsmouth Rd

Homewood
Farm
Ripley
GREENSIDE
COTTS
Buckingham
Lodge
Old Rectory
Farm

Newark La
HEDGE CROFT
COTTS
B367
HIGH ST
WHITE ROSE LA
Ockham Rd N
Church
End

6

GEORGELANDS
Ripley C of E
Inf Sch
WHITE HART CT
Ripley Court
Sch
Ockham Park
B2039

CHURCH
ROW
Chapel
Farm
GRANDIS
COTTS
Ockham Park
House

Devonia Farm

Park
Wood

5

MILESTONE RD
GROVE HEATH RD
ROSE LA
Service
Area
Service
Area
Guileshill Farm

56

Portsmouth Rd
GROVE HEATH RD
Willow
Farm
GROVE HEATH LA
Bachelor's
Copse

4

The Jovial
Sailor
(PH)
Grove Heath
Farm
Roborow
Roborow
Wood

RIPLEY BY-PASS
KILN LA
Hangover
House
Loveland's
Copse
Ryde
Farm
Bachelor's
La

3

SEND MARSH RD
Garlick's Arch
Copse
HUNGRY HILL LA
Hungry Hill
Hungry Hill
Cottage

55

Garlick's
Arch
Burntcommon
CAMBER LA

Oldlands
Copse
Sheppardsgrove
Copse
Brambleride
Copse

2

Tythebarns
Farm
The Paddocks

Tithe Barns
TYTHEBARNS LA
Sussex
Farm
August Hill
Brambleride

1

CLANDON RD
A247
Hazelhurst
Cottage
Old Ride
Farm
Holride
Farm

54

A   B   05   C   D   06   E   F

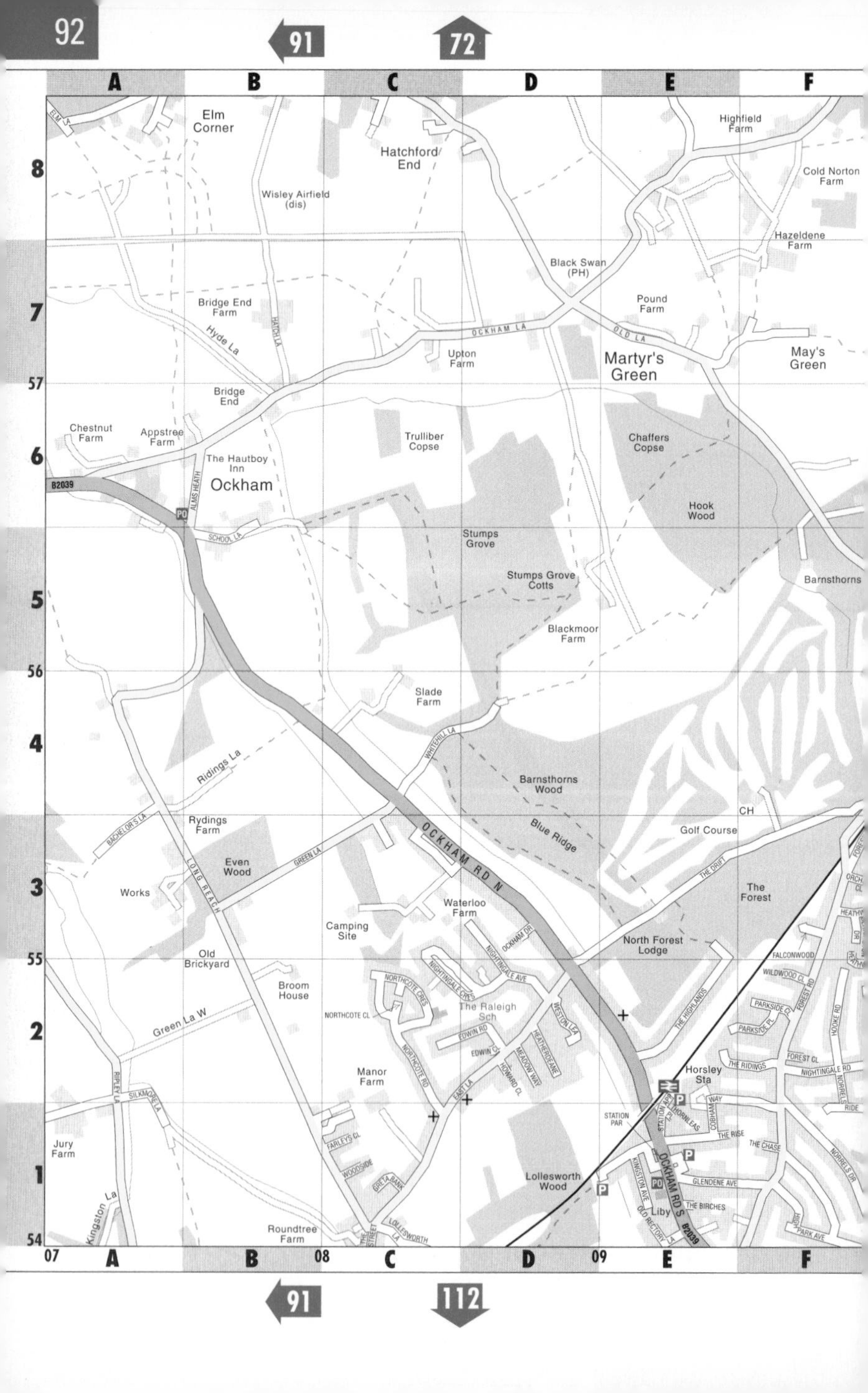
92
91
72
A
B
C
D
E
F
8
7
57
6
5
56
4
3
55
2
1
54
07
08
09
Elm Corner
Hatchford End
Highfield Farm
Cold Norton Farm
Wisley Airfield (dis)
Hazeldene Farm
Black Swan (PH)
Pound Farm
Bridge End Farm
Hyde La
Hatch La
Ockham La
Old La
Upton Farm
Martyr's Green
May's Green
Bridge End
Chestnut Farm
Appstree Farm
Trulliber Copse
Chaffers Copse
The Hautboy Inn
Ockham
B2039
PO
Alms Heath
School La
Hook Wood
Stumps Grove
Stumps Grove Cotts
Barnsthorns
Blackmoor Farm
Slade Farm
Whitehill La
Ridings La
Barnsthorns Wood
Blue Ridge
CH
Golf Course
Bachelor's La
Rydings Farm
Ockham Rd N
Long Reach
Even Wood
Green La
Works
The Drift
The Forest
Waterloo Farm
Camping Site
Ockham Dr
North Forest Lodge
Old Brickyard
Nightingale Ave
Falconwood
Wildwood Cl
Northcote Cres
Nightingale Cres
Broom House
Northcote Cl
The Raleigh Sch
Weston Lea
The Highlands
Parkside Cl
Parkside Pl
Forest Rd
Hooke Rd
Green La W
Edwin Rd
Edwin Cl
Heatherdene
Meadow Way
Howard Cl
Northcote Rd
Manor Farm
Horsley Sta
The Ridings
Forest Cl
Nightingale Rd
Norrels Ride
Ripley La
Silkmore La
East La
Station Par
Station App
Hornleas
Cobham Way
The Rise
The Chase
Jury Farm
Farleys Cl
Woodside
Greta Bank
P
Lollesworth Wood
Kingston Ave
Ockham Rd S
Glendene Ave
Norrels Dr
The Birches
Liby
Old Rectory La
Kingston La
Roundtree Farm
The Street
Lollesworth La
Park Ave
B2039
91
112

73
94

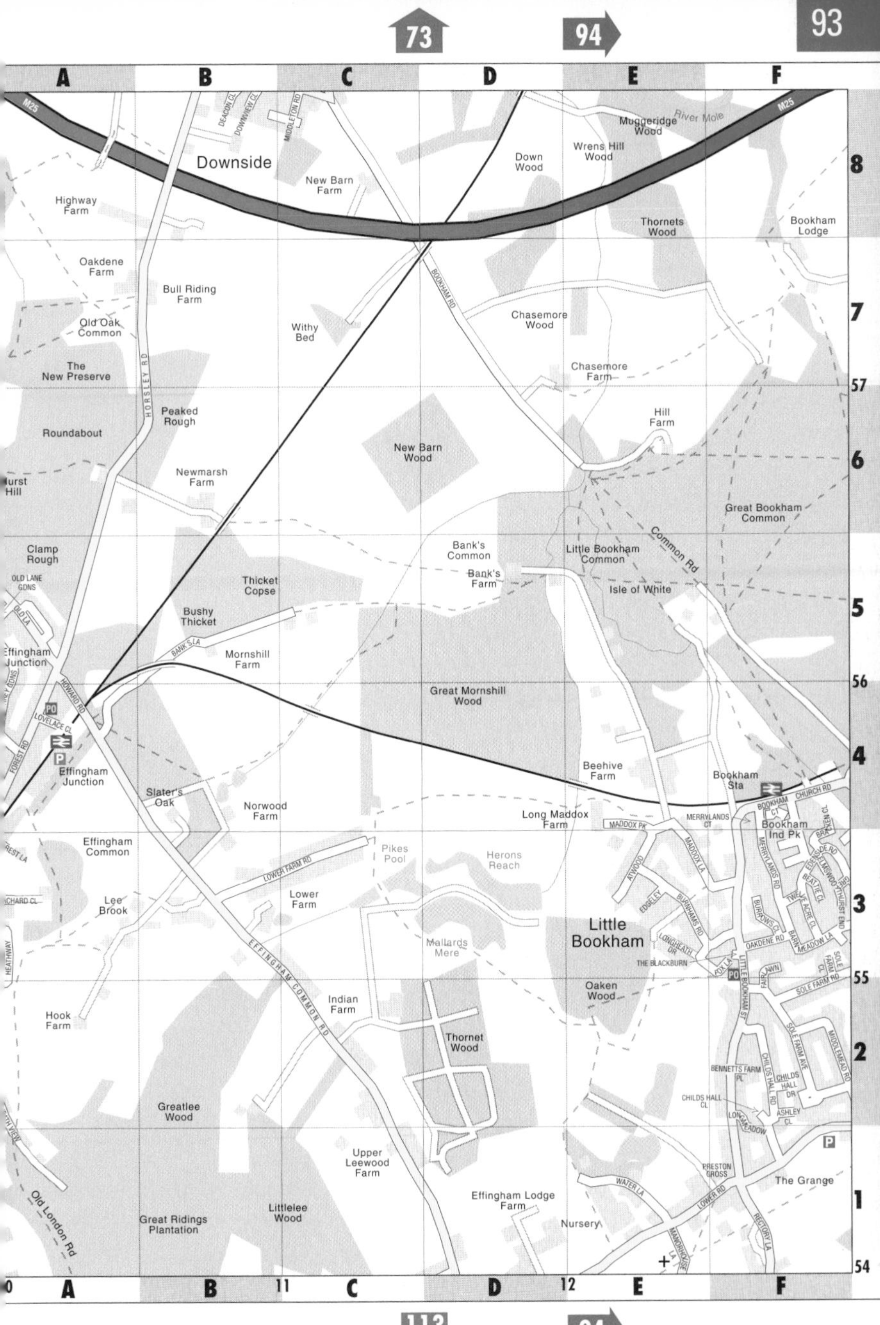
Downside
New Barn Farm
Down Wood
Wrens Hill Wood
Muggeridge Wood
River Mole
M25
Highway Farm
Thornets Wood
Bookham Lodge
Oakdene Farm
Bull Riding Farm
Chasemore Wood
Withy Bed
Old Oak Common
The New Preserve
Chasemore Farm
Peaked Rough
Roundabout
Hill Farm
New Barn Wood
Newmarsh Farm
Great Bookham Common
Clamp Rough
Bank's Common
Little Bookham Common
Common Rd
Bank's Farm
Thicket Copse
Isle of White
Bushy Thicket
Mornshill Farm
Effingham Junction
Great Mornshill Wood
Effingham Junction
Beehive Farm
Bookham Sta
Slater's Oak
Norwood Farm
Long Maddox Farm
Bookham Ind Pk
Effingham Common
Pikes Pool
Herons Reach
Lower Farm
Lee Brook
Little Bookham
Mallards Mere
Oaken Wood
Indian Farm
Hook Farm
Thornet Wood
Greatlee Wood
Upper Leewood Farm
The Grange
Effingham Lodge Farm
Nursery
Littlelee Wood
Great Ridings Plantation
Old London Rd
HORSLEY RD
BOOKHAM RD
EFFINGHAM COMMON RD
LOWER FARM RD
BANK'S LA
HOWARD RD
LOVELACE CL
FOREST RD
MADDOX PK
MERRYLANDS CT
MADDOX LA
CHURCH RD
MERRYLANDS RD
LITTLE BOOKHAM ST
SOLE FARM AVE
SOLE FARM RD
MIDDLEMEAD RD
OAKDENE RD
BURNHAMS RD
EDGELEY
ATWOOD
LONGHEATH DR
THE BLACKBURN
FOX LA
BENNETTS FARM PL
CHILDS HALL RD
CHILDS HALL DR
CHILDS HALL CL
ASHLEY CL
LONG MEADOW
PRESTON CROSS
WATER LA
LOWER RD
RECTORY LA
MANORHOUSE LA
DEACON CL
DOWNVIEW CL
MIDDLETON RD
OLD LANE GDNS
HEATHWAY
A B C D E F
8 7 57 6 5 56 4 3 55 2 1 54
11 12

113
94

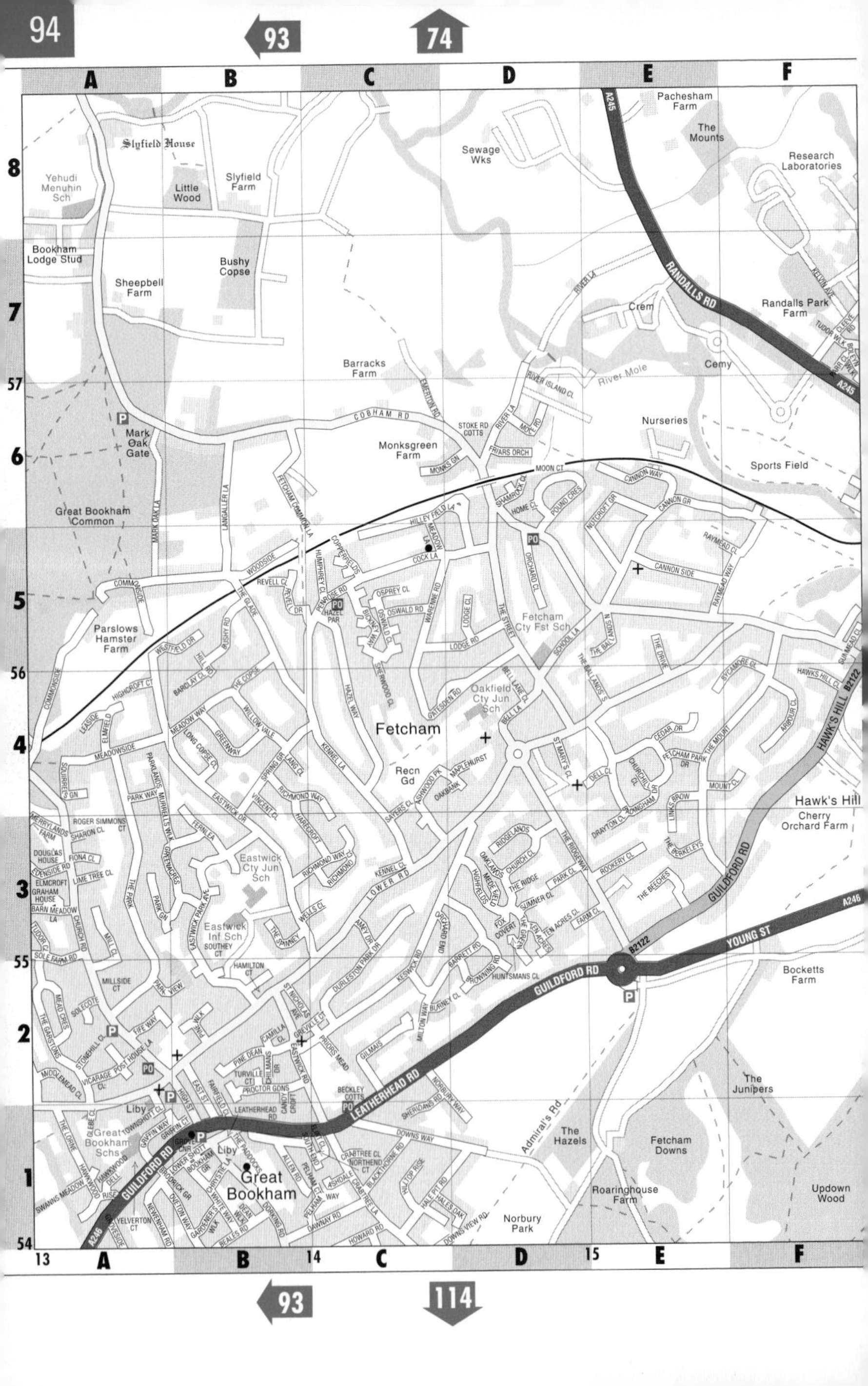

93
74
Slyfield House
Yehudi Menuhin Sch
Little Wood
Slyfield Farm
Sewage Wks
Pachesham Farm
The Mounts
Research Laboratories
Bookham Lodge Stud
Bushy Copse
Sheepbell Farm
Randalls Park Farm
Crem
Barracks Farm
Cemy
River Mole
Mark Oak Gate
Monksgreen Farm
Nurseries
Sports Field
Great Bookham Common
Parslows Hamster Farm
Fetcham Cty Fst Sch
Oakfield Cty Jun Sch
Fetcham
Recn Gd
Hawk's Hill
Cherry Orchard Farm
Eastwick Cty Jun Sch
Eastwick Inf Sch
Bocketts Farm
The Junipers
Liby
Great Bookham Schs
The Hazels
Fetcham Downs
Great Bookham
Roaringhouse Farm
Updown Wood
Norbury Park
RANDALLS RD
GUILDFORD RD
YOUNG ST
LEATHERHEAD RD
COBHAM RD
HAWK'S HILL
A245
A246
B2122
93
114

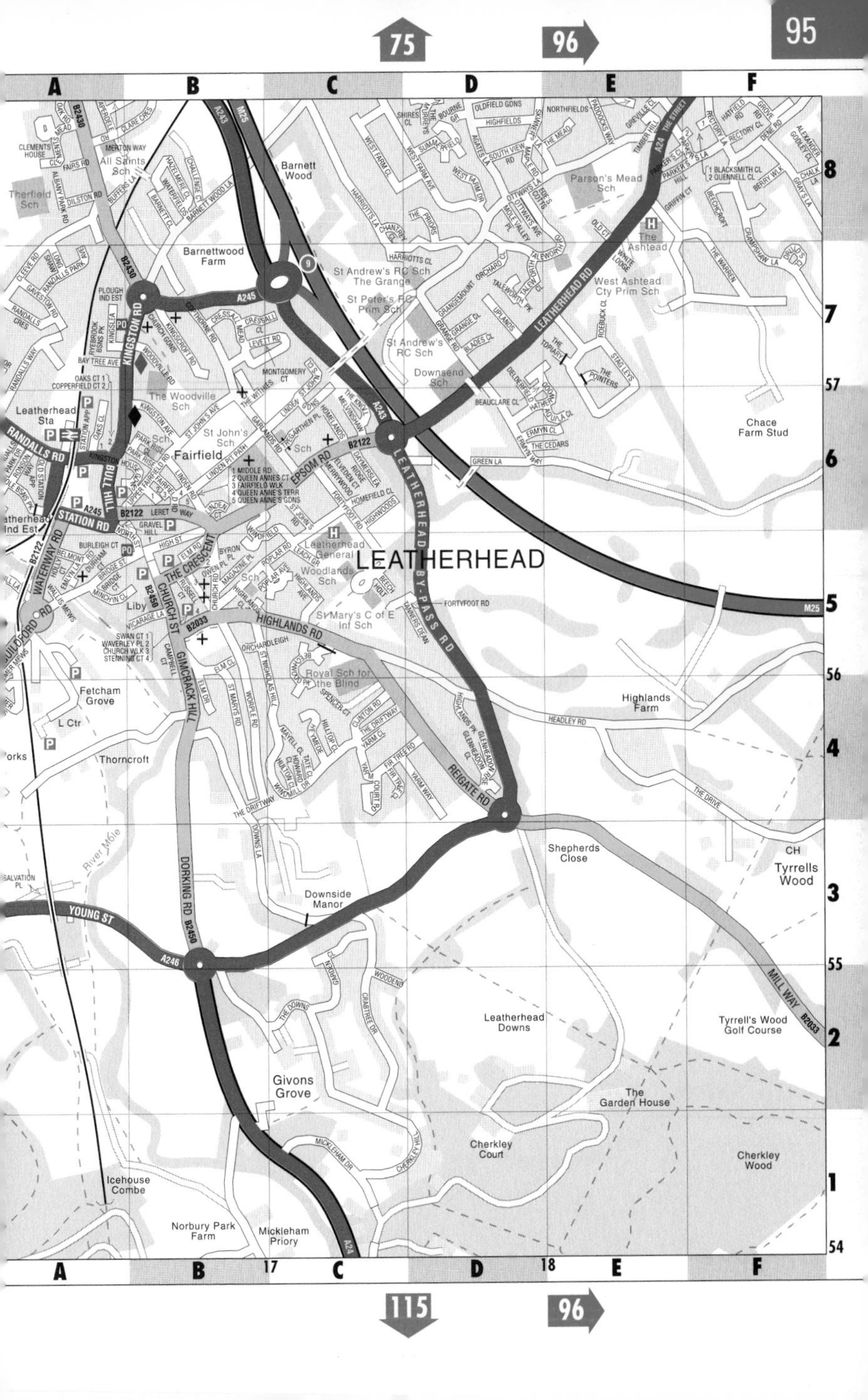

95
75
96
115
96
A
B
C
D
E
F
17
18
8
7
57
6
5
56
4
3
55
2
1
54
LEATHERHEAD
Barnett Wood
Barnettwood Farm
All Saints Sch
Therfield Sch
Clements House
St Andrew's RC Sch
The Grange
St Peter's RC Prim Sch
St Andrew's RC Sch
Downsend Sch
Parson's Mead Sch
The Ashtead
West Ashtead Cty Prim Sch
Chace Farm Stud
The Woodville Sch
Leatherhead Sta
St John's Sch
Fairfield
Leatherhead General
Woodlands Sch
St Mary's C of E Inf Sch
Royal Sch for the Blind
Liby
Fetcham Grove
L Ctr
Thorncroft
Highlands Farm
Shepherds Close
Tyrrells Wood
CH
Downside Manor
Leatherhead Downs
Tyrrell's Wood Golf Course
The Garden House
Givons Grove
Cherkley Court
Cherkley Wood
Icehouse Combe
Norbury Park Farm
Mickleham Priory
River Mole
M25
A243
A245
A24
A246
B2430
B2122
B2450
B2033
KINGSTON RD
LEATHERHEAD RD
LEATHERHEAD BY-PASS RD
EPSOM RD
HIGHLANDS RD
REIGATE RD
DORKING RD
GIMCRACK HILL
CHURCH ST
THE CRESCENT
STATION RD
RANDALLS RD
BULL HILL
WATERWAY RD
GUILDFORD RD
YOUNG ST
MILL WAY
HEADLEY RD
THE STREET
FORTYFOOT RD
GREEN LA
THE DRIVE

95
76

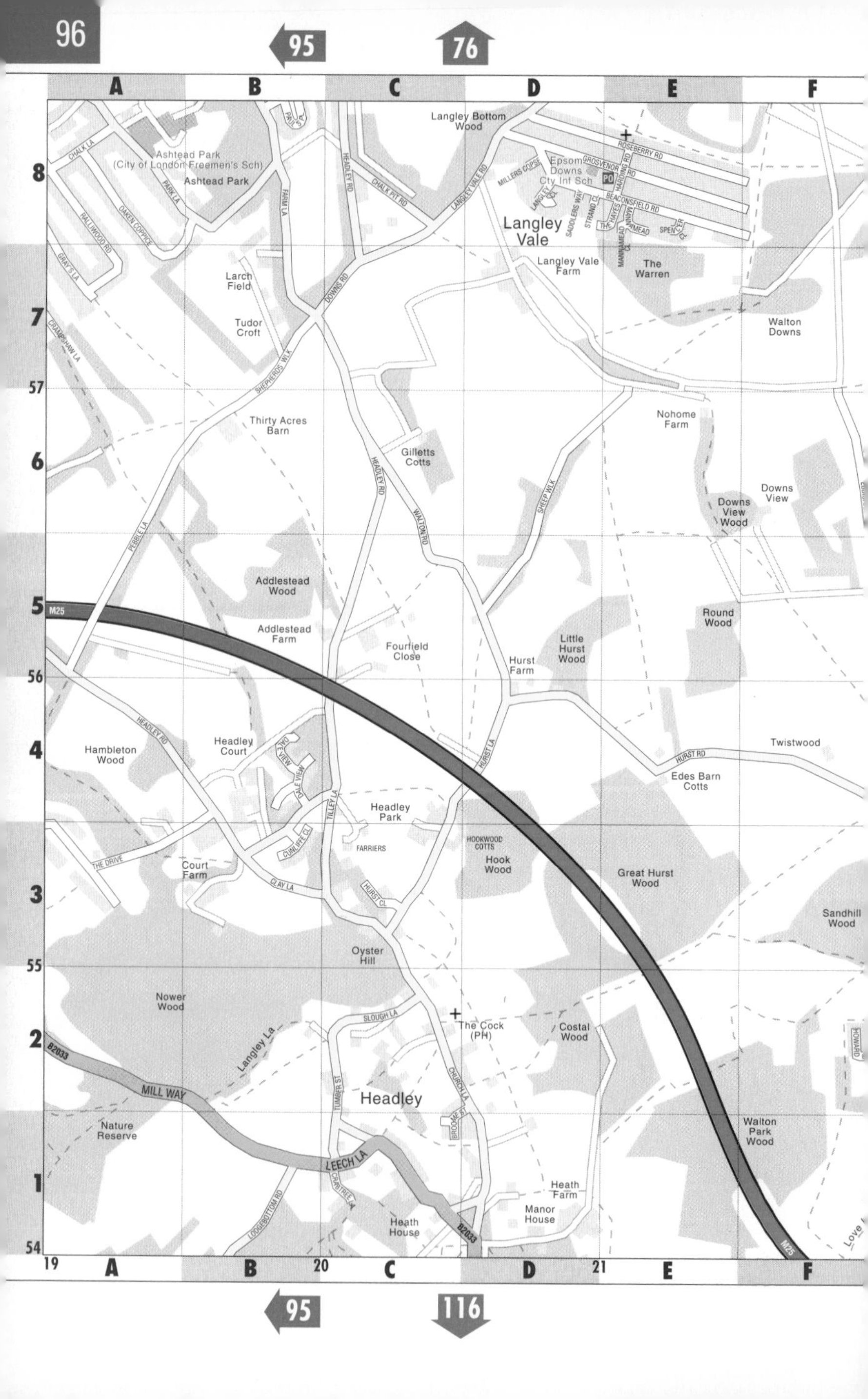
A
B
C
D
E
F
Langley Bottom Wood
Ashtead Park (City of London Freemen's Sch)
Ashtead Park
CHALK LA
PARK LA
OAKEN COPPICE
RALLIWOOD RD
GRAY'S LA
FARM LA
HEADLEY RD
CHALK PIT RD
LANGLEY VALE RD
ROSEBERRY RD
GROSVENOR RD
Epsom Downs City Inf Sch
PO
MILLERS COPSE
HARDING RD
BEACONSFIELD RD
SADDLERS WAY
STRAND CL
Langley Vale
SPENCER CL
Langley Vale Farm
The Warren
Larch Field
Tudor Croft
DOWNS RD
CRAMPSHAW LA
SHEPHERDS WLK
Walton Downs
Thirty Acres Barn
Nohome Farm
Gilletts Cotts
HEADLEY RD
WALTON RD
SHEEP WLK
Downs View Wood
Downs View
PEBBLE LA
Addlestead Wood
M25
Addlestead Farm
Fourfield Close
Round Wood
Hurst Farm
Little Hurst Wood
HEADLEY RD
Hambleton Wood
Headley Court
DALE VIEW
HURST LA
HURST RD
Twistwood
Edes Barn Cotts
TILLEY LA
Headley Park
CUNLIFFE CL
FARRIERS
HOOKWOOD COTTS
Hook Wood
THE DRIVE
Court Farm
CLAY LA
HURST CL
Great Hurst Wood
Sandhill Wood
Oyster Hill
Nower Wood
SLOUGH LA
The Cock (PH)
Costal Wood
Langley La
B2033
MILL WAY
HOWARD
TUMBER ST
CHURCH LA
Headley
BROOME ST
Nature Reserve
Walton Park Wood
LEECH LA
CRABTREE LA
LODGEBOTTOM RD
Heath Farm
Heath House
Manor House
B2033
Love
M25
8
7
57
6
5
56
4
3
55
2
1
54
19
20
21

95
116

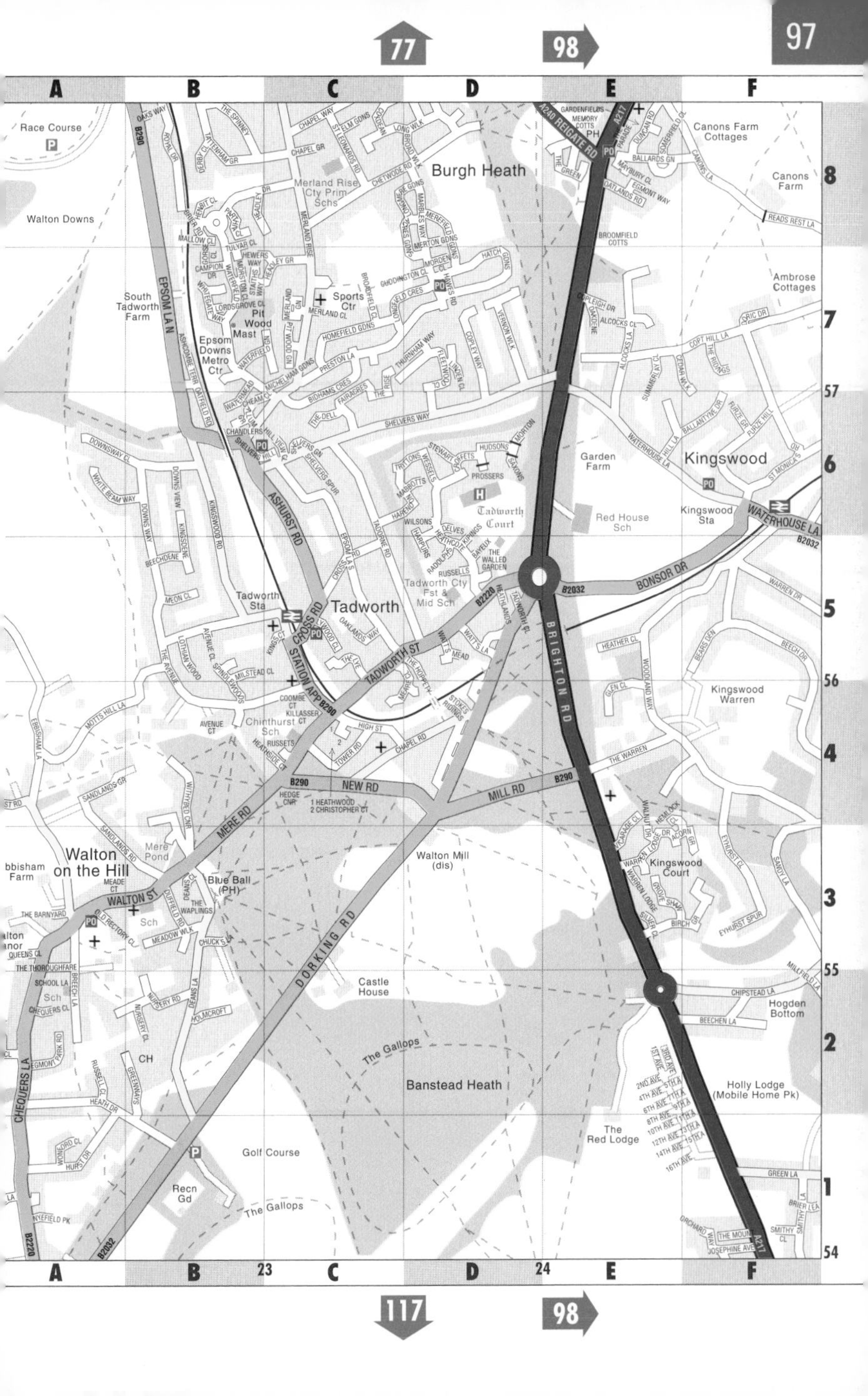
77
98
A
B
C
D
E
F
Race Course
Walton Downs
South Tadworth Farm
EPSOM LAN
Epsom Downs Metro Ctr
Pit Wood Mast
Merland Rise Cty Prim Schs
Burgh Heath
Sports Ctr
Canons Farm Cottages
Canons Farm
Ambrose Cottages
BROOMFIELD COTTS
A240 REIGATE RD
A217
Kingswood
Garden Farm
Red House Sch
Kingswood Sta
WATERHOUSE LA
B2032
BONSOR DR
Tadworth Court
Tadworth Sta
Tadworth
Tadworth Cty Fst & Mid Sch
ASHURST RD
CROSS RD
STATION APP
TADWORTH ST
BRIGHTON RD
Kingswood Warren
Chinthurst Sch
NEW RD
MILL RD
B290
MERE RD
1 HEATHWOOD
2 CHRISTOPHER CT
Walton on the Hill
Mere Pond
Walton Mill (dis)
Blue Ball (PH)
WALTON ST
Kingswood Court
DORKING RD
Castle House
Hogden Bottom
The Gallops
Banstead Heath
Holly Lodge (Mobile Home Pk)
The Red Lodge
Golf Course
Recn Gd
CHEQUERS LA
B2220
8
7
57
6
5
56
4
3
55
2
1
54
23
24
117
98

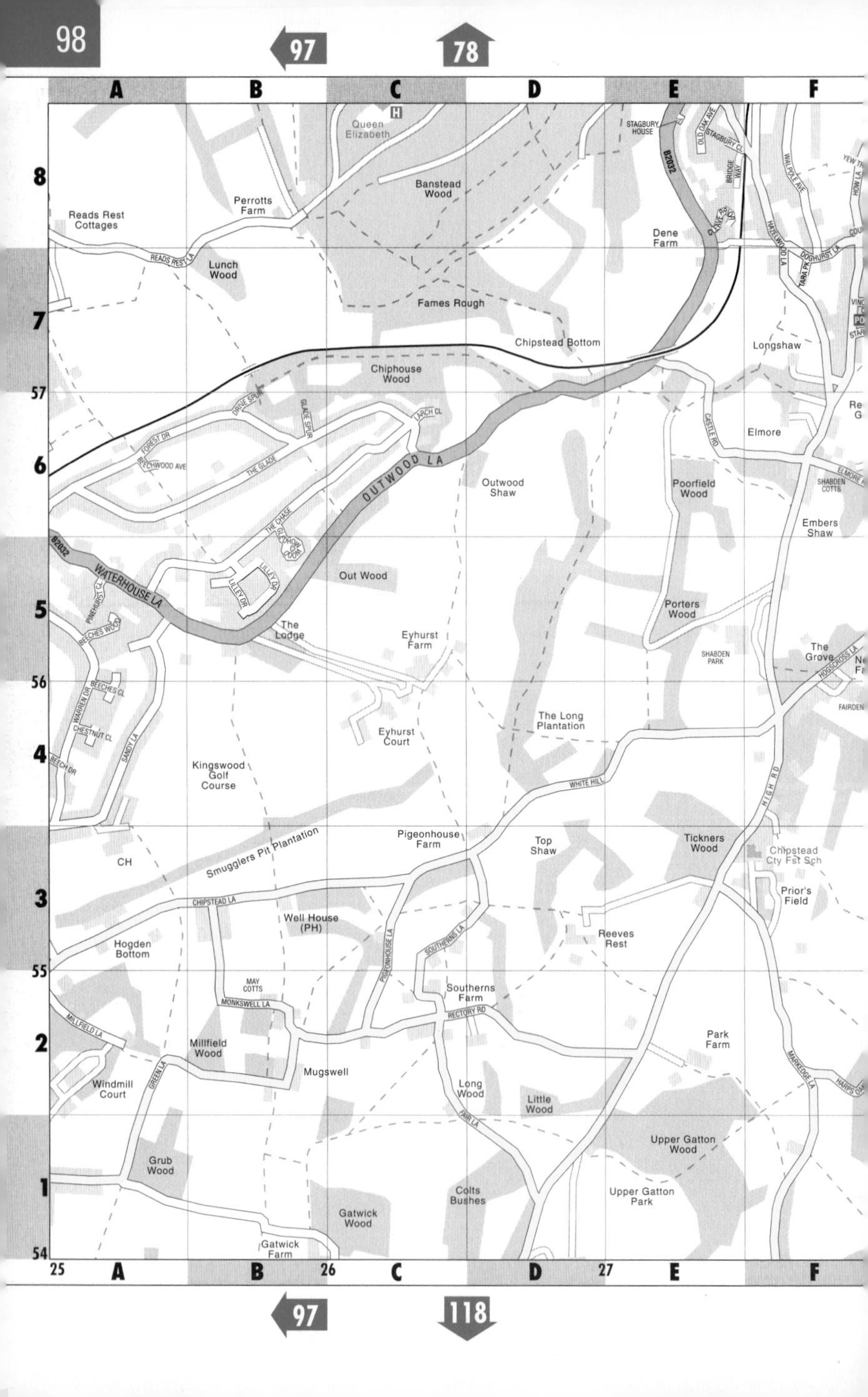

Map Labels

Queen Elizabeth H

Banstead Wood

Reads Rest Cottages

Perrotts Farm

READS REST LA

Lunch Wood

Fames Rough

Chipstead Bottom

Dene Farm

STAGBURY HOUSE

STAGBURY LA

OLD OAK AVE

BRIDGE LANE

HAZELWOOD LA

WALPOLE AVE

YEW TR

Longshaw

Re G

Chiphouse Wood

SPICE SPUR

GLADE SPUR

FOREST DR

BIRCHWOOD AVE

THE GLADE

LARCH CL

OUTWOOD LA

Outwood Shaw

Elmore

Poorfield Wood

SHADDEN COTTS

ELMORE R

Embers Shaw

THE CHASE

THE BECHINS

LILLEY LA

GLEN DR

Out Wood

The Lodge

WATERHOUSE LA

PINEHURST CL

BREECHES BEND

Eyhurst Farm

Porters Wood

SHADDEN PARK

The Grove

Ne F

HOLLYBUSH LA

FAIRDEN

BEECHES CL

CHESTNUT CL

BAKERS LA

DANE LA

BEECH DR

Kingswood Golf Course

Eyhurst Court

The Long Plantation

WHITE HILL

FELSH RD

Smugglers Pit Plantation

CH

Pigeonhouse Farm

Top Shaw

Tickners Wood

Chipstead Cty Fst Sch

CHIPSTEAD LA

Well House (PH)

SOUTHERNS LA

Prior's Field

Hogden Bottom

Reeves Rest

MILLFIELD LA

MAY COTTS

MONKSWELL LA

RECTORY RD

Southerns Farm

Park Farm

MARLPIT LA

HAPIS CRT

Millfield Wood

Mugswell

Windmill Court

GREEN LA

Long Wood

Little Wood

PARK LA

Upper Gatton Wood

Grub Wood

Upper Gatton Park

Gatwick Wood

Colts Bushes

Gatwick Farm

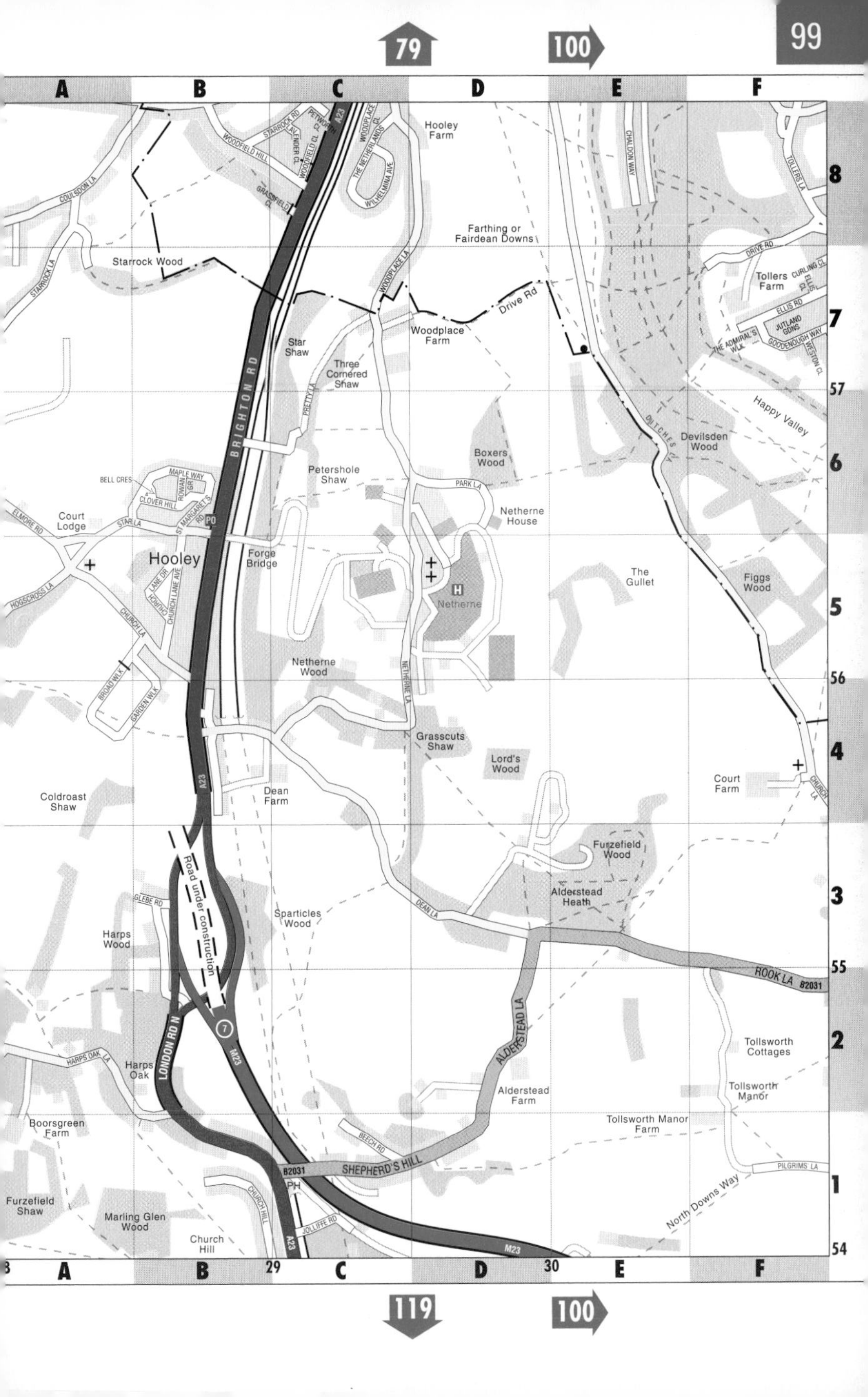
79
100
Hooley Farm
Farthing or Fairdean Downs
Starrock Wood
Drive Rd
Woodplace Farm
Star Shaw
Three Cornered Shaw
BRIGHTON RD
Petershole Shaw
Boxers Wood
Netherne House
Court Lodge
Hooley
Forge Bridge
Netherne
The Gullet
Figgs Wood
Devilsden Wood
Happy Valley
Tollers Farm
Netherne Wood
Grasscuts Shaw
Lord's Wood
Court Farm
Coldroast Shaw
Dean Farm
Road under construction
Furzefield Wood
Alderstead Heath
Sparticles Wood
Harps Wood
DEAN LA
ROOK LA
B2031
ALDERSTEAD LA
LONDON RD N
M23
A23
Harps Oak
Tollsworth Cottages
Tollsworth Manor
Alderstead Farm
Boorsgreen Farm
Tollsworth Manor Farm
SHEPHERD'S HILL
PILGRIMS LA
North Downs Way
Furzefield Shaw
Marling Glen Wood
Church Hill
119
100

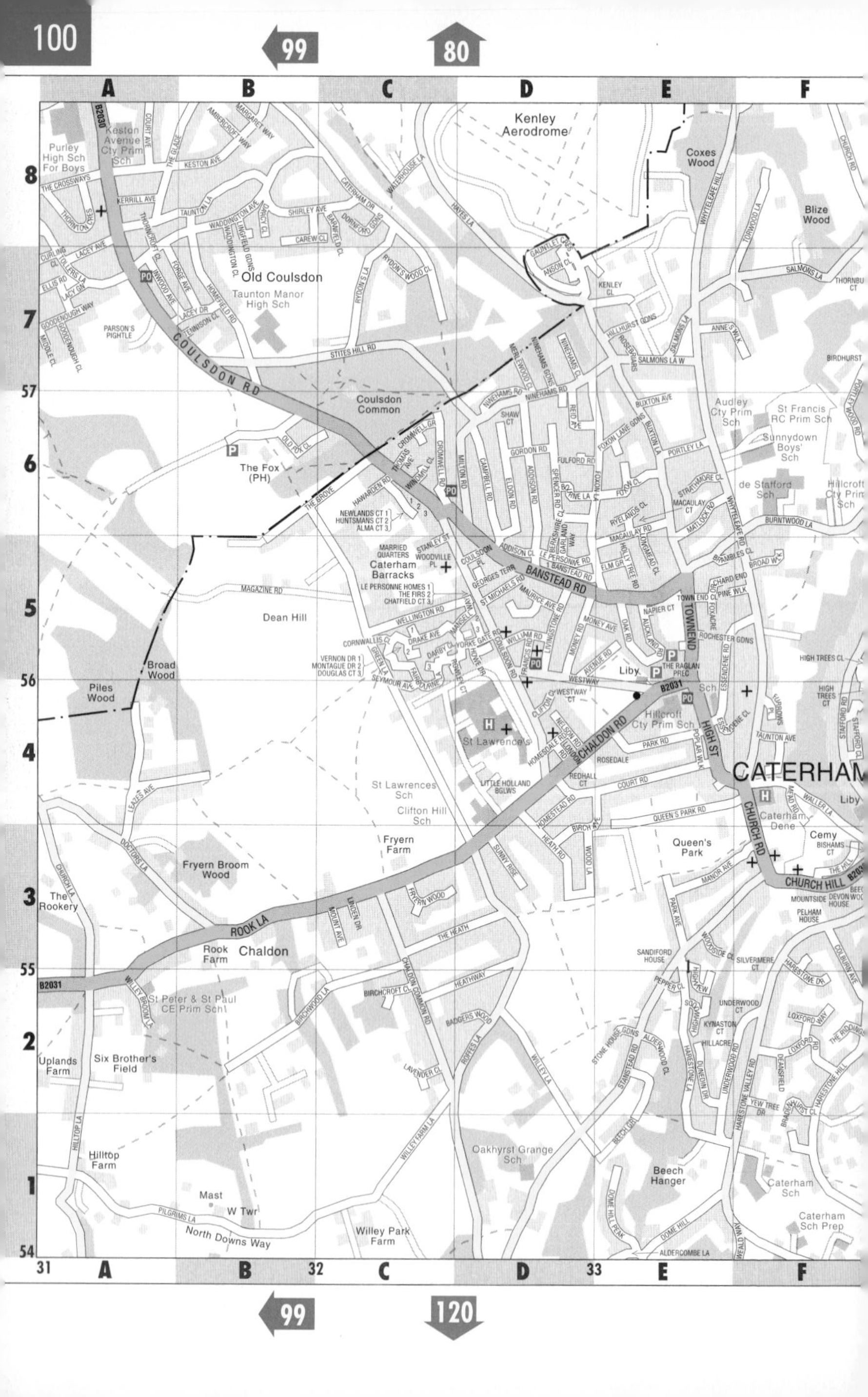
99
80
A
B
C
D
E
F
Kenley Aerodrome
Coxes Wood
Blize Wood
Purley High Sch For Boys
Keston Avenue Cty Prim Sch
Old Coulsdon
Taunton Manor High Sch
Parson's Pightle
COULSDON RD
Coulsdon Common
The Fox (PH)
Caterham Barracks
Married Quarters
Dean Hill
Broad Wood
Piles Wood
St Lawrence's
St Lawrences Sch
Clifton Hill Sch
Fryern Farm
Fryern Broom Wood
The Rookery
ROOK LA
Rook Farm
Chaldon
St Peter & St Paul CE Prim Sch
Uplands Farm
Six Brother's Field
Hilltop Farm
Mast
W Twr
North Downs Way
Willey Park Farm
Oakhyrst Grange Sch
Beech Hanger
Caterham Sch
Caterham Sch Prep
Queen's Park
Caterham Dene
Cemy
CATERHAM
Liby
Hillcroft Cty Prim Sch
Audley Cty Prim Sch
St Francis RC Prim Sch
Sunnydown Boys' Sch
de Stafford Sch
Hillcroft Cty Prim Sch
BANSTEAD RD
CHALDON RD
TOWNEND
HIGH ST
CHURCH RD
CHURCH HILL
B2030
B2031
8
7
57
6
5
56
4
3
55
2
1
54
31
32
33
99
120

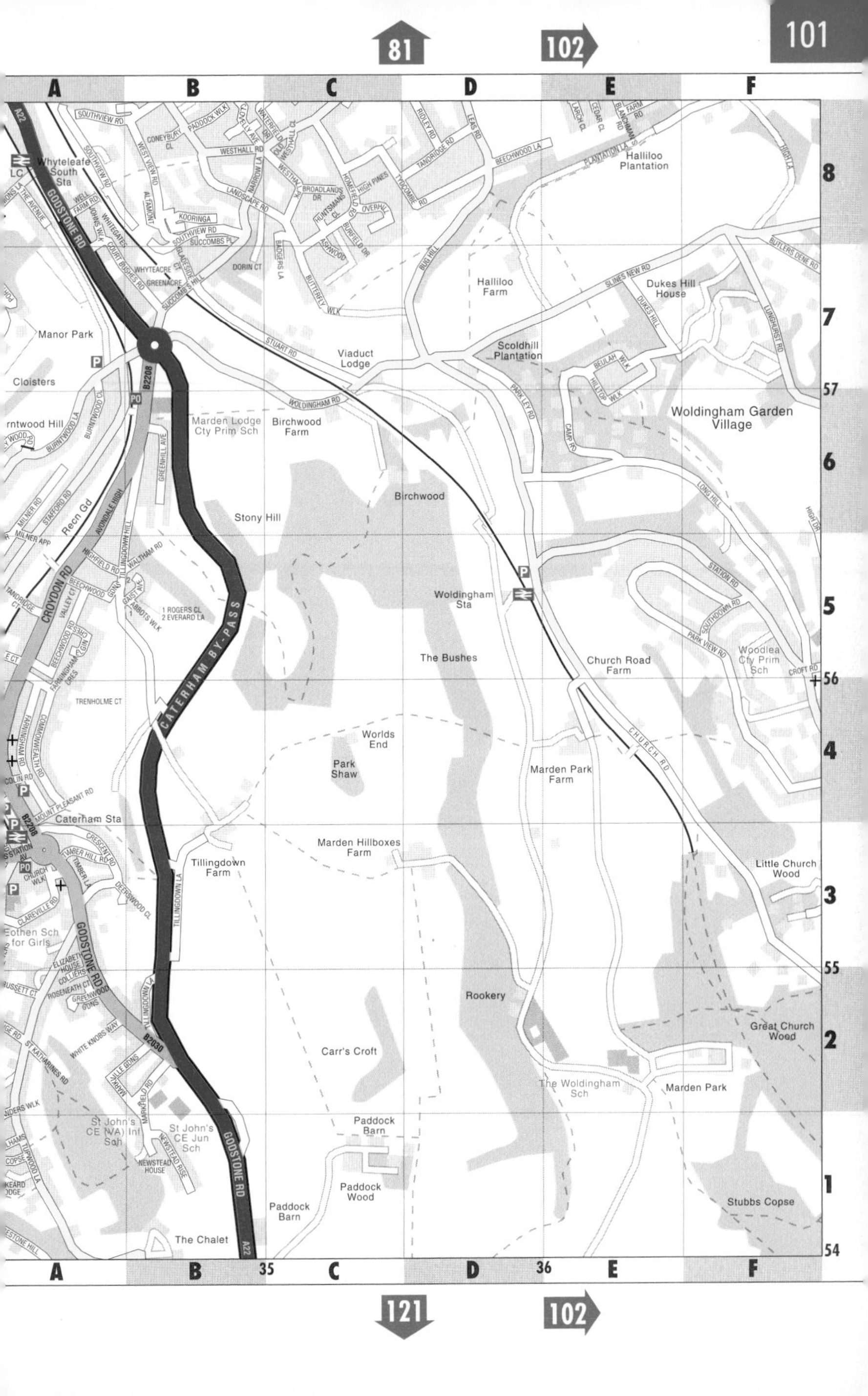

A   B   C   D   E   F

8

Whyteleafe
South Sta

Halliloo
Plantation

Southview Rd   Coneybury Cl   Paddock Wlk   Westhall Rd   Landscape Rd   Beechwood La

Kooringa   Broadlands   High Pines   Cedar Cl   Cherry Cl   Cedar La

Succombs Pl   Overn   Ridgewood Dr

Whyteacre   Greenacre   Dorin Ct   Badgers La   Butterfly Wlk

Halliloo
Farm

Slines New Rd   Dukes Hill
House

7

Manor Park

Cloisters

rntwood Hill

P   B2208

Stuart Rd   Viaduct
Lodge

Scoldhill
Plantation

Woldingham Garden
Village

57

Marden Lodge
Cty Prim Sch   Birchwood
Farm

Woldingham Rd

Birchwood

Stony Hill

6

Croydon Rd   Greenhill La   Beltham Rd

Reen Gd

Milner App

1 ROGERS CL
2 EVERARD LA

Camp Rd

Park Ley Rd

Blelham   Knoll Wlk   Long Hill   Station Rd

5

Woldingham
Sta   P

Church Road
Farm

Woodlea
Cty Prim
Sch

Croft Rd

The Bushes

TRENHOLME CT

Caterham Sta

P
P

Worlds
End   Park
Shaw

Marden Park
Farm

Caterham Rd

Little Church
Wood

56

4

3

Tillingdown
Farm   Marden Hillboxes
Farm

Eothen Sch
for Girls

Godstone Rd   55

Carr's Croft   Rookery   Great Church
Wood

2

The Woldingham
Sch   Marden Park

St John's
CE Inf
Sch   St John's
CE Jun
Sch   Paddock
Barn   Paddock
Wood

1

NEWSTEAD
HOUSE   Paddock
Barn

Stubbs Copse

The Chalet   R22   Godstone Rd

54

A   B   35   C   D   36   E   F

101
82

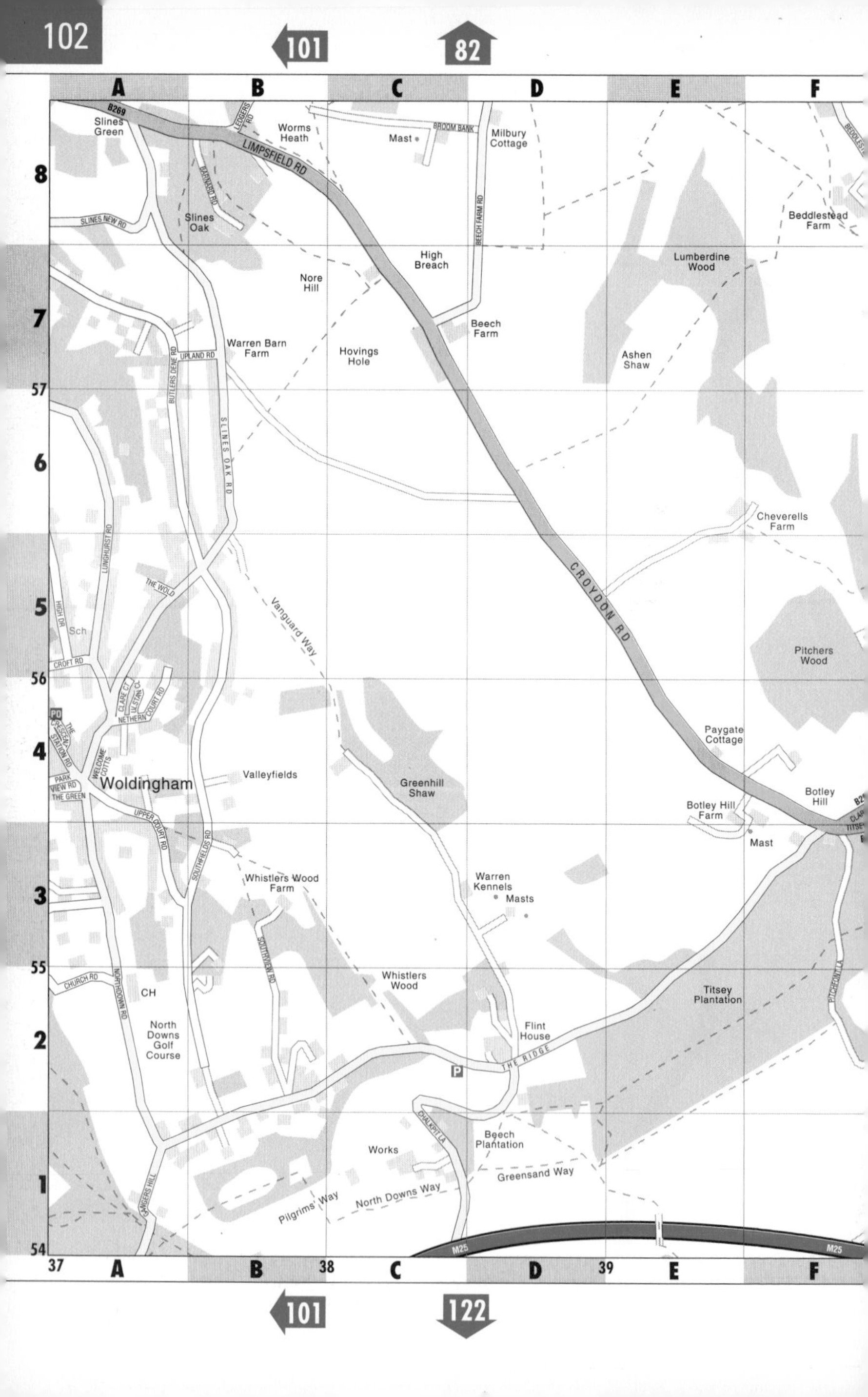
A
B
C
D
E
F
8
7
57
6
5
56
4
3
55
2
1
54
37
38
39
B269
Slines Green
LEDGERS RD
Worms Heath
LIMPSFIELD RD
Mast
BROOM BANK
Milbury Cottage
BEDDLESTEAD
BARNARD RD
Slines Oak
SLINES NEW RD
BEECH FARM RD
Beddlestead Farm
High Breach
Nore Hill
Lumberdine Wood
Beech Farm
Warren Barn Farm
UPLAND RD
BUTLERS DENE RD
Hovings Hole
Ashen Shaw
SLINES OAK RD
Cheverells Farm
LUNGHURST RD
THE WOLD
CROYDON RD
HIGH DR
Vanguard Way
Sch
Pitchers Wood
CROFT RD
CLARE CT
ULSTAN CL
NETHERN COURT RD
PO
THE CRESCENT
STATION RD
WELCOME COTTS
Paygate Cottage
Woldingham
Valleyfields
Greenhill Shaw
PARK VIEW RD
THE GREEN
Botley Hill
Botley Hill Farm
UPPER COURT RD
SOUTHFIELDS RD
Mast
Whistlers Wood Farm
Warren Kennels
Masts
SOUTHVIEW RD
CHURCH RD
NORTHDOWN RD
CH
Whistlers Wood
Titsey Plantation
PITCHFONT LA
North Downs Golf Course
Flint House
THE RIDGE
P
CHALKPIT LA
Beech Plantation
Works
Greensand Way
North Downs Way
Pilgrims' Way
GANGERS HILL
M25

101
122

83

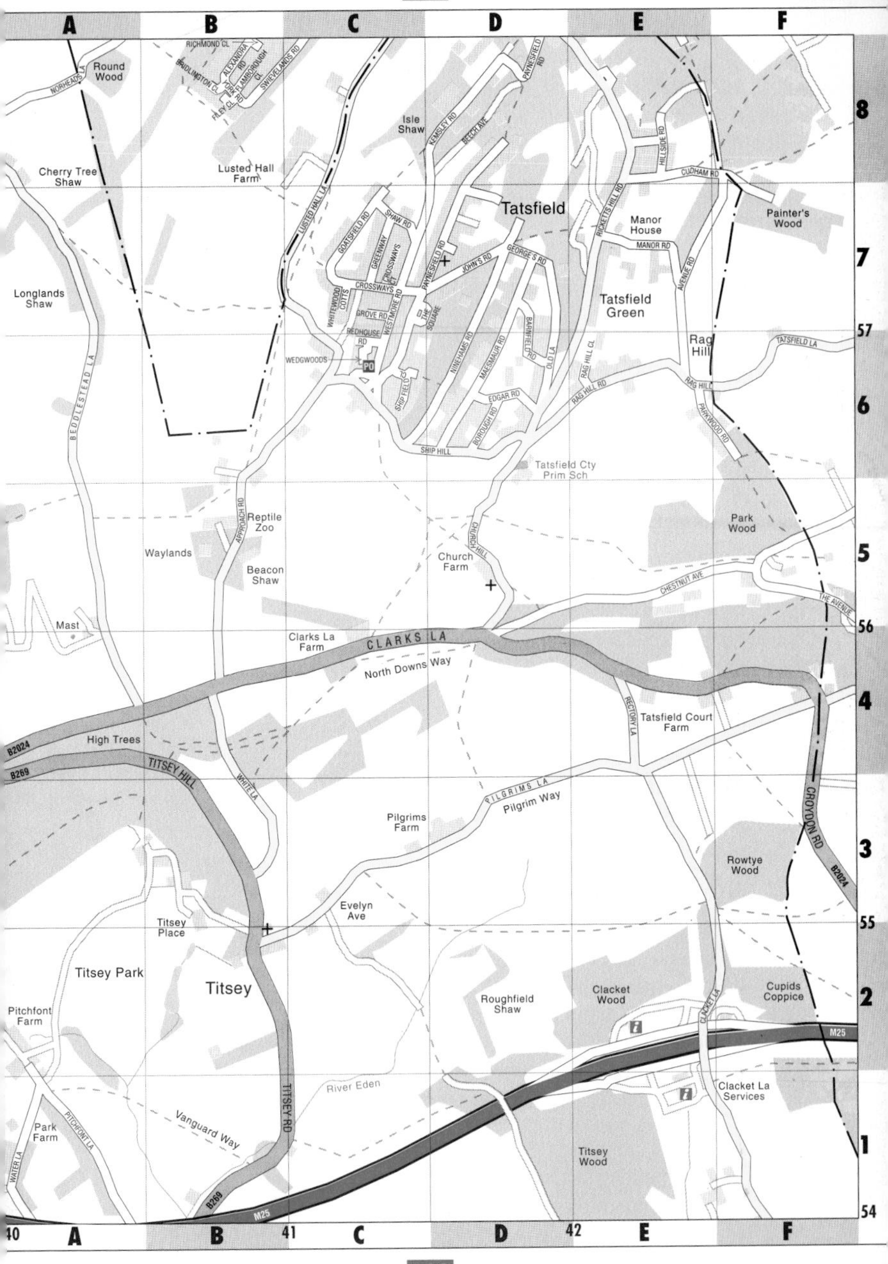

A
B
C
D
E
F
8
7
57
6
5
56
4
3
55
2
1
54
40
41
42
Round Wood
NORHEADS LA
RICHMOND CL
ALEXANDRA RD
BRIDLINGTON CL
FLAMBOROUGH CL
SWIEVELANDS RD
FILEY CL
Isle Shaw
KEMSLEY RD
BEECH AVE
PAYNESFIELD RD
Cherry Tree Shaw
Lusted Hall Farm
LUSTED HALL LA
HILLSIDE RD
CUDHAM RD
Tatsfield
Manor House
MANOR RD
Painter's Wood
GOATSFIELD RD
SHAW RD
GREENWAY
CROSSWAYS CT
JOHN'S RD
GEORGE'S RD
RICKETTS HILL RD
AVENUE RD
Longlands Shaw
CROSSWAYS
WHITEWOOD COTTS
GROVE RD
WESTMORE RD
THE SQUARE
REDHOUSE RD
WEDGWOODS
PO
Tatsfield Green
Rag Hill
TATSFIELD LA
BARNFIELD RD
OLD LA
NINEHAMS RD
MAESMAUR RD
RAG HILL CL
RAG HILL RD
RAG HILL
BEDDLESTEAD LA
SHIP FIELD CL
EDGAR RD
BOROUGH RD
PARKWOOD RD
SHIP HILL
Tatsfield Cty Prim Sch
APPROACH RD
Reptile Zoo
Park Wood
Waylands
Beacon Shaw
Church Farm
CHURCH HILL
CHESTNUT AVE
THE AVENUE
Mast
Clarks La Farm
CLARKS LA
North Downs Way
High Trees
B2024
RECTORY LA
Tatsfield Court Farm
B269
TITSEY HILL
WHITE LA
PILGRIMS LA
Pilgrim Way
Pilgrims Farm
CROYDON RD
B2024
Rowtye Wood
Evelyn Ave
Titsey Place
Titsey Park
Titsey
Pitchfont Farm
Roughfield Shaw
Clacket Wood
Cupids Coppice
CLACKET LA
M25
River Eden
Clacket La Services
TITSEY RD
Park Farm
PITCHFONT LA
Vanguard Way
WATER LA
Titsey Wood
B269
M25

123

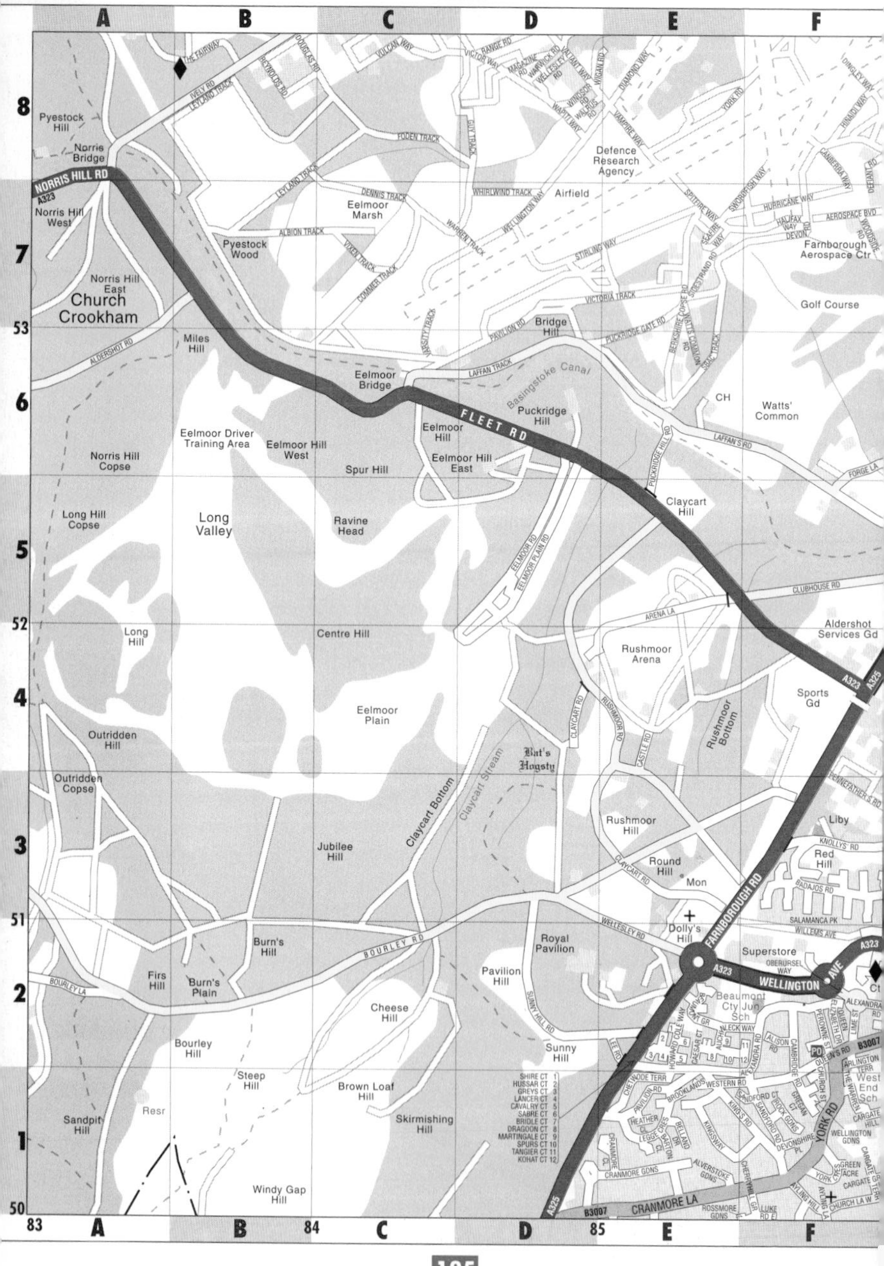

A   B   C   D   E   F

8

Pyestock Hill

Norris Bridge

NORRIS HILL RD
A323

Norris Hill West

7

Norris Hill East
Church Crookham

53

Miles Hill

Albershot RD

Eelmoor Marsh

Pyestock Wood

Dennis Track

Albion Track

Comber Track

Eelmoor Bridge

Defence Research Agency

Airfield

Bridge Hill

Basingstoke Canal

Laffan Track

FLEET RD

6

Eelmoor Driver Training Area

Eelmoor Hill West

Norris Hill Copse

Spur Hill

Eelmoor Hill

Eelmoor Hill East

Puckridge Hill

Claycart Hill

CH

Watts' Common

Farnborough Aerospace Ctr

Golf Course

5

Long Hill Copse

Long Valley

Ravine Head

52

Long Hill

Centre Hill

Arena La

Clubhouse Rd

Rushmoor Arena

Aldershot Services Gd

A323

4

Outridden Hill

Eelmoor Plain

Bat's Hogsty

Sports Gd

Rushmoor Bottom

Outridden Copse

Claycart Bottom

Claycart Stream

Rushmoor Hill

Liby

Red Hill

3

Jubilee Hill

Round Hill

Mon

FARNBOROUGH RD

Firs Hill

Burn's Hill

BOURLEY RD

Wellesley Rd

Dolly's Hill

Superstore

51

Burn's Plain

Royal Pavilion

WELLINGTON

A323

Bourley Hill

BOURLEY LA

Cheese Hill

Pavilion Hill

A323

2

Steep Hill

Sunny Hill

Beaumont Cty Jun Sch

Sandpit Hill

Resr

Brown Loaf Hill

Skirmishing Hill

B3007

YORK RD

1

Windy Gap Hill

SHIRE CT 1
RUSSAR CT 2
GREYS CT 3
LANCER CT 4
CAVALRY CT 5
SABRE CT 6
BRIDLE CT 7
DRAGOON CT 8
MARTINGALE CT 9
SPURS CT 10
TANGIER CT 11
KONAT CT 12

CRANMORE GDNS

CRANMORE LA

50

83   A   B   84   C   D   85   E   F

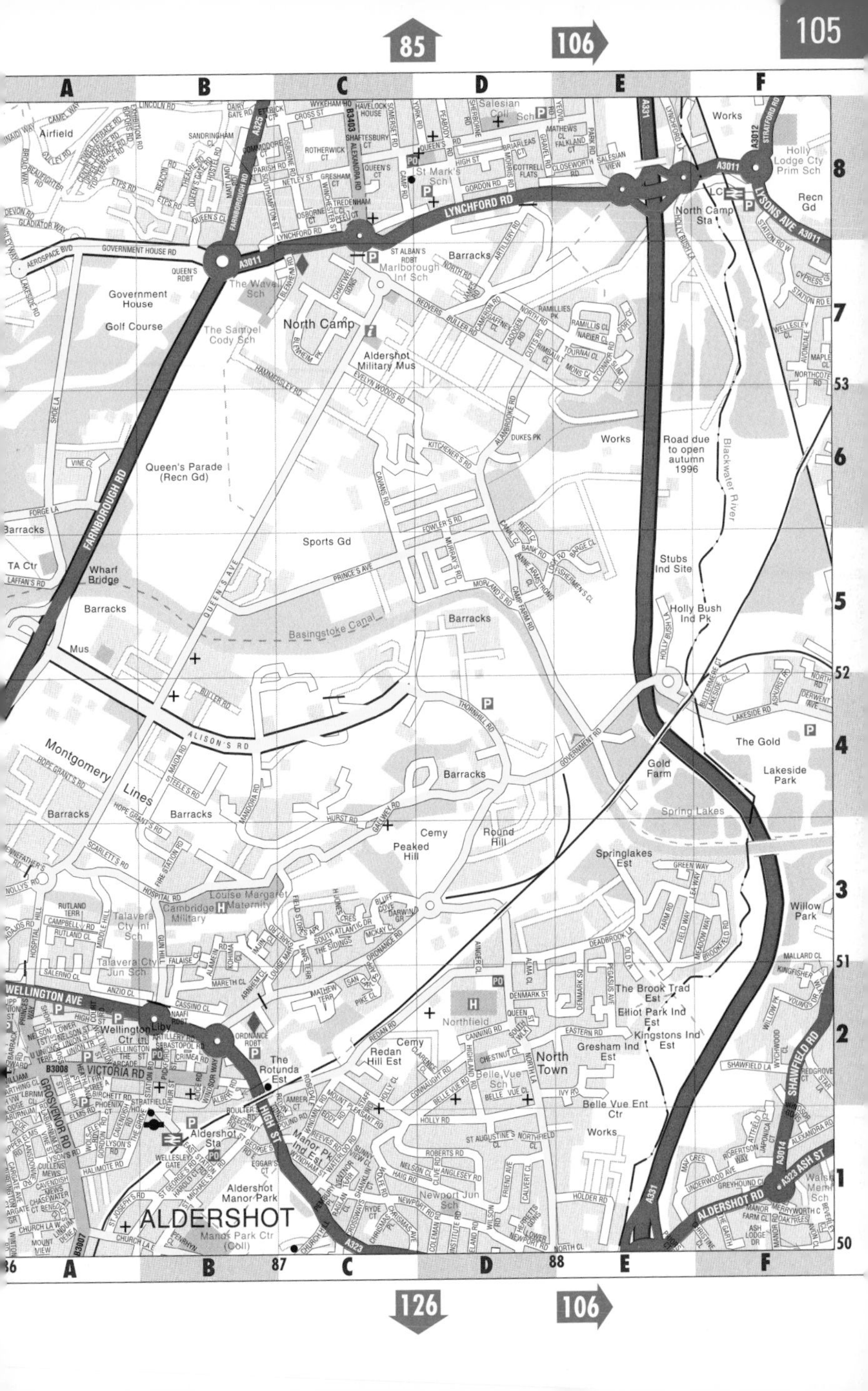
85
106
A
B
C
D
E
F
8
7
53
6
5
52
4
3
51
2
1
50
Airfield
Government House
Golf Course
FARNBOROUGH RD
A3011
LYNCHFORD RD
GOVERNMENT HOUSE RD
AEROSPACE BVD
The Wavell Sch
The Samuel Cody Sch
North Camp
Aldershot Military Mus
Marlborough Inf Sch
St Mark's Sch
Salesian Coll Sch
Barracks
Works
Holly Lodge Cty Prim Sch
Recn Gd
North Camp Sta
LYSONS AVE
A331
Queen's Parade (Recn Gd)
Sports Gd
Road due to open autumn 1996
Blackwater River
Stubs Ind Site
Holly Bush Ind Pk
Wharf Bridge
TA Ctr
Mus
Basingstoke Canal
QUEEN'S AVE
ALISON'S RD
Montgomery Lines
The Gold
Lakeside Park
Gold Farm
Spring Lakes
Springlakes Est
Cemy
Peaked Hill
Round Hill
Louise Margaret Maternity
Cambridge Military
Talavera Cty Inf Sch
Talavera Cty Jun Sch
Willow Park
WELLINGTON AVE
Wellington Ctr
Liby
VICTORIA RD
GROSVENOR RD
Aldershot Sta
The Rotunda Est
HIGH ST
Northfield
Redan Hill Est
Belle Vue Sch
North Town
Gresham Ind Est
The Brook Trad Est
Elliot Park Ind Est
Kingstons Ind Est
Belle Vue Ent Ctr
Manor Pk Ind Est
Aldershot Manor Park
ALDERSHOT
Manor Park Ctr (Coll)
Newport Jun Sch
ALDERSHOT RD
SHAWFIELD RD
A323 ASH ST
Walsh Meml Sch
A323
86
87
88
126
106

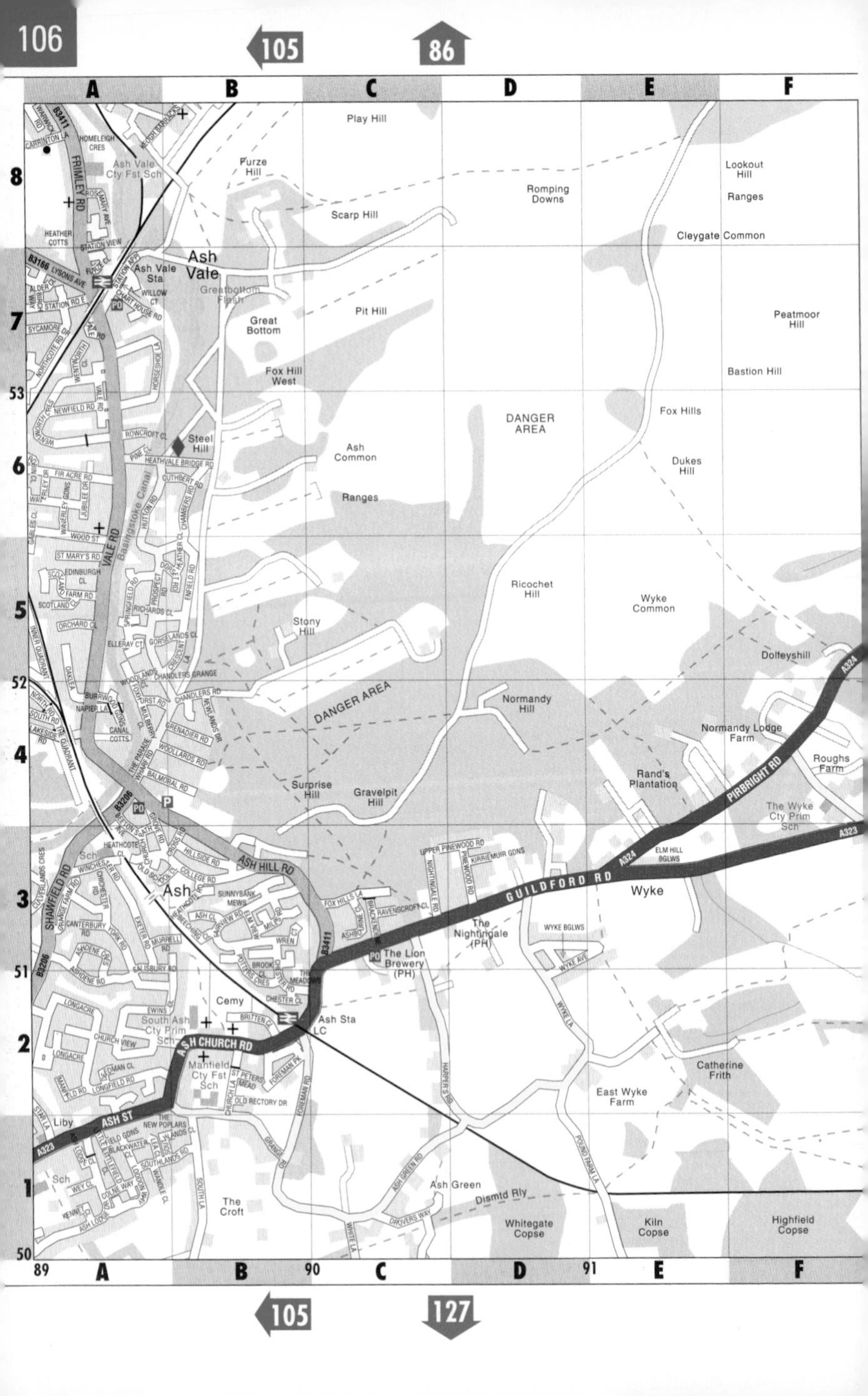
105
86
A
B
C
D
E
F
8
7
53
6
5
52
4
3
51
2
1
50
89
90
91
Play Hill
Furze Hill
Romping Downs
Lookout Hill
Ranges
Scarp Hill
Cleygate Common
Ash Vale
Ash Vale Sta
Ash Vale Cty Fst Sch
Greatbottom Flash
Great Bottom
Pit Hill
Peatmoor Hill
Fox Hill West
Bastion Hill
DANGER AREA
Fox Hills
Steel Hill
Ash Common
Ranges
Dukes Hill
Ricochet Hill
Wyke Common
Stony Hill
Dolleyshill
Normandy Hill
Normandy Lodge Farm
Roughs Farm
Rand's Plantation
Surprise Hill
Gravelpit Hill
The Wyke Cty Prim Sch
Ash
Wyke
The Nightingale (PH)
The Lion Brewery (PH)
Cemy
South Ash Cty Prim Sch
Ash Sta
LC
Manfield Cty Fst Sch
Catherine Frith
East Wyke Farm
Liby
Sch
Ash Green
Dismtd Rly
The Croft
Whitegate Copse
Kiln Copse
Highfield Copse
FRIMLEY RD
B3411
B3166
LYSONS AVE
STATION RD E
SYCAMORE DR
NORTHCOTE RD
WENTWORTH CRES
NEWFIELD RD
ROWCROFT CL
HEATHVALE BRIDGE RD
FIR ACRE RD
WAVERLEY GDNS
JUBILEE DR
WOOD ST
ST MARY'S RD
EDINBURGH CL
SCOTLAND FARM RD
SCOTLAND CL
ORCHARD CL
INNER QUADRANT
THE QUADRANT
VALE RD
Basingstoke Canal
HORSESHOE LA
CHART HOUSE RD
WILLOW CT
HUTTON RD
CUTHBERT RD
CHAMBERS RD
HEATHER CL
ENFIELD RD
DORSET RD
PROSPECT RD
SPRINGFIELD RD
RICHARDS CL
ELLERAY CT
GORSELANDS CL
CRESCENT LA
CHANDLERS GRANGE
CHANDLERS RD
NEWLANDS DR
GRENADIER RD
WOOLLARDS RD
BALMORAL RD
THE PARADE
WHARF RD
MULBERRY
B3206
ASH HILL RD
HILLSIDE RD
COLLEGE RD
SUNNYBANK MEWS
ASH CL
FAIRVIEW RD
ELM VIEW
MILLS RD
WREN CT
HEATHCOTE RD
BEECHING CL
FOX HILLS LA
RAVENSCROFT CL
BRACKENDENE
GUILDFORD RD
A324
A323
PIRBRIGHT RD
ELM HILL BGLWS
UPPER PINEWOOD RD
PINEWOOD RD
NIGHTINGALE RD
KIRRIEMUIR GDNS
WYKE BGLWS
WYKE AVE
WYKE LA
HARPERS RD
POUND FARM LA
SHAWFIELD RD
CULVERLANDS CRES
GRANGE FARM RD
WINCHESTER RD
CHICHESTER RD
CANTERBURY RD
YORK RD
EXETER RD
MURRELL RD
ASHDENE CRES
ASHDENE RD
SALISBURY RD
LONGACRE
CHURCH VIEW
ASH CHURCH RD
BRITTEN CL
CHESTER CL
POTTERS CRES
BROOK CL
THE MEADOWS
FOREMAN PK
FOREMAN RD
ST PETERS MEAD
OLD RECTORY DR
CHURCH LA
LONGFIELD RD
ASH ST
NEW POPLARS
BLACKWATER CL
SOUTHLANDS RD
WANDLE CL
LODDON WAY
COLNE WAY
WEY CL
KENNET CL
ASH LODGE DR
SOUTH LA
GRANGE RD
ASH GREEN RD
DROVERS WAY
WHITE LA
P
PO

105
127

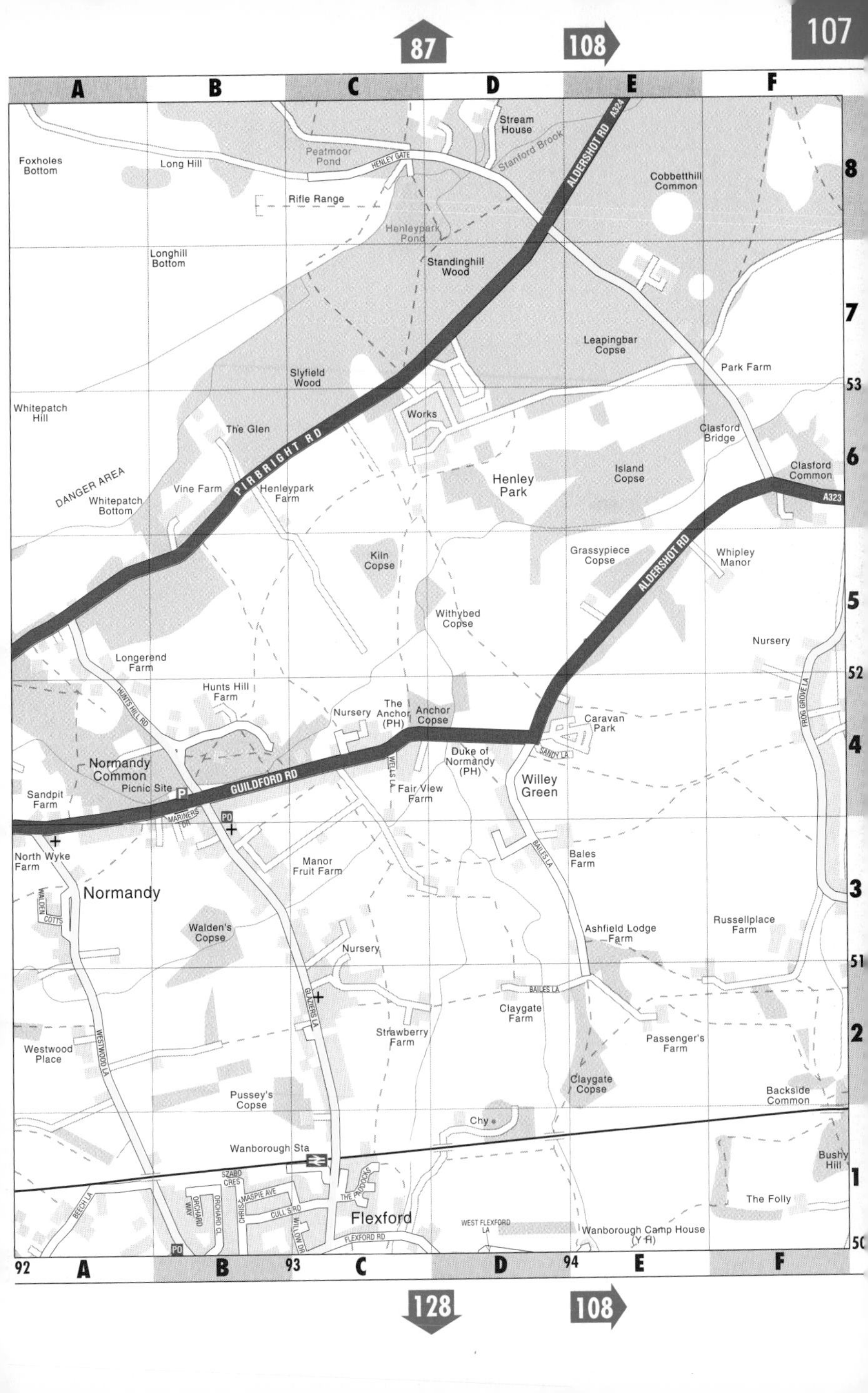
87
108
A
B
C
D
E
F
8
7
53
6
5
52
4
3
51
2
1
50
Stream House
Stanford Brook
ALDERSHOT RD A324
Foxholes Bottom
Long Hill
Peatmoor Pond
HENLEY GATE
Cobbetthill Common
Rifle Range
Henleypark Pond
Longhill Bottom
Standinghill Wood
Leapingbar Copse
Park Farm
Slyfield Wood
Whitepatch Hill
Works
The Glen
Clasford Bridge
PIRBRIGHT RD
Island Copse
Clasford Common
DANGER AREA
Henley Park
Vine Farm
Henleypark Farm
A323
Whitepatch Bottom
Kiln Copse
Grassypiece Copse
Whipley Manor
ALDERSHOT RD
Withybed Copse
Nursery
Longerend Farm
HUNTS HILL RD
Hunts Hill Farm
The Anchor (PH)
Anchor Copse
Nursery
Caravan Park
FROG GROVE LA
SANDY LA
Duke of Normandy (PH)
Normandy Common
WELLS LA
Willey Green
Picnic Site
GUILDFORD RD
Fair View Farm
Sandpit Farm
MARINERS DR
PO
North Wyke Farm
Bales Farm
BAILES LA
Manor Fruit Farm
Normandy
WALDEN COTTS
Walden's Copse
Ashfield Lodge Farm
Russellplace Farm
Nursery
BAILES LA
GLAZIERS LA
Claygate Farm
Westwood Place
WESTWOOD LA
Strawberry Farm
Passenger's Farm
Claygate Copse
Backside Common
Pussey's Copse
Chy
Wanborough Sta
Bushy Hill
SZABO CRES
THE PADDOCKS
BEECH LA
ORCHARD WAY
ORCHARD CL
CHRISTS
MASPIE AVE
CULL'S RD
The Folly
WILLOW DR
Flexford
WEST FLEXFORD LA
Wanborough Camp House (Y H)
FLEXFORD RD
PO
92
93
94
A
B
C
D
E
F
128
108

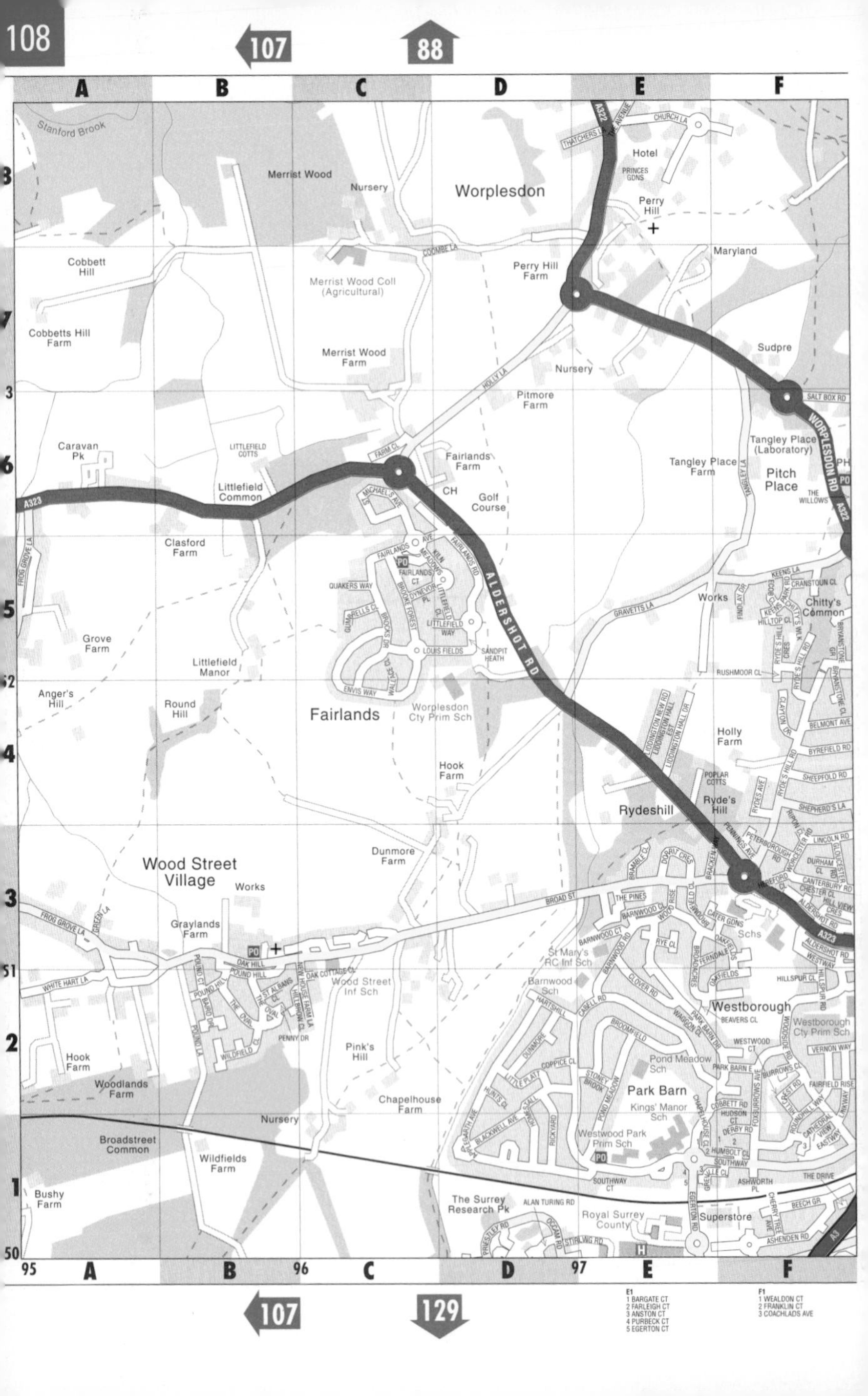

Stanford Brook

Merrist Wood

Nursery

Worplesdon

Hotel

PRINCES GDNS

Perry Hill +

Maryland

Cobbett Hill

Cobbetts Hill Farm

Merrist Wood Coll (Agricultural)

POUVRIE LA

Perry Hill Farm

Nursery

Sudpre

SALT BOX RD

Merrist Wood Farm

HOLLY LA

FARM ST

Pitmore Farm

WORPLESDON RD

Caravan Pk

LITTLEFIELD COTTS

Fairlands

Tangley Place (Laboratory)

PH

PO

Littlefield Common

CH

Golf Course

Tangley Place Farm

Pitch Place

THE WILLOWS

A323

MICHAEL

Clasford Farm

A323

FAIRLANDS

QUAKERS WAY

PO

FAIRLANDS CT

KEENS LA

CRANSTOUN CL

Works

Chitty's Common

GRAVETTS LA

Grove Farm

LITTLEFIELD WAY

LOUIS FIELDS

SANDPIT HEATH

RUSHMOOR CL

Littlefield Manor

ENVIS WAY

ALDERSHOT RD

Holly Farm

SHEPFOLD RD

Anger's Hill

Round Hill

Fairlands

Worplesdon Cty Prim Sch

POPLAR COTTS

Ryde's Hill

SHEPHERD'S LA

Hook Farm

Rydeshill

LINCOLN RD

Wood Street Village

Dunmore Farm

DURHAM CL

CANTERBURY RD

Works

BROAD ST

THE PINES

Schs

A323

ALDERSHOT RD

Graylands Farm

PO +

St Mary's RC Inf Sch

HILLSPUR CL

FROG GROVE LA

WHITE HART LA

Wood Street Inf Sch

Barnwood Sch

Westborough Cty Prim Sch

Hook Farm

Pink's Hill

VERNON WAY

FAIRFIELD RISE

Woodlands Farm

Pond Meadow Sch

Park Barn

Kings' Manor Sch

Broadstreet Common

Nursery

Chapelhouse Farm

Westwood Park Prim Sch

PO

THE DRIVE

Wildfields Farm

SOUTHWAY CT

ASHWORTH

BEECH GR

Bushy Farm

The Surrey Research Pk

ALAN TURING RD

Royal Surrey County

Superstore

STIRLING RD

H

ASHENDEN RD

A3

E1
1 BARGATE CT
2 FARLEIGH CT
3 ANSTON CT
4 PURBECK CT
5 EGERTON CT

F1
1 WEALDON CT
2 FRANKLIN CT
3 COACHLADS AVE

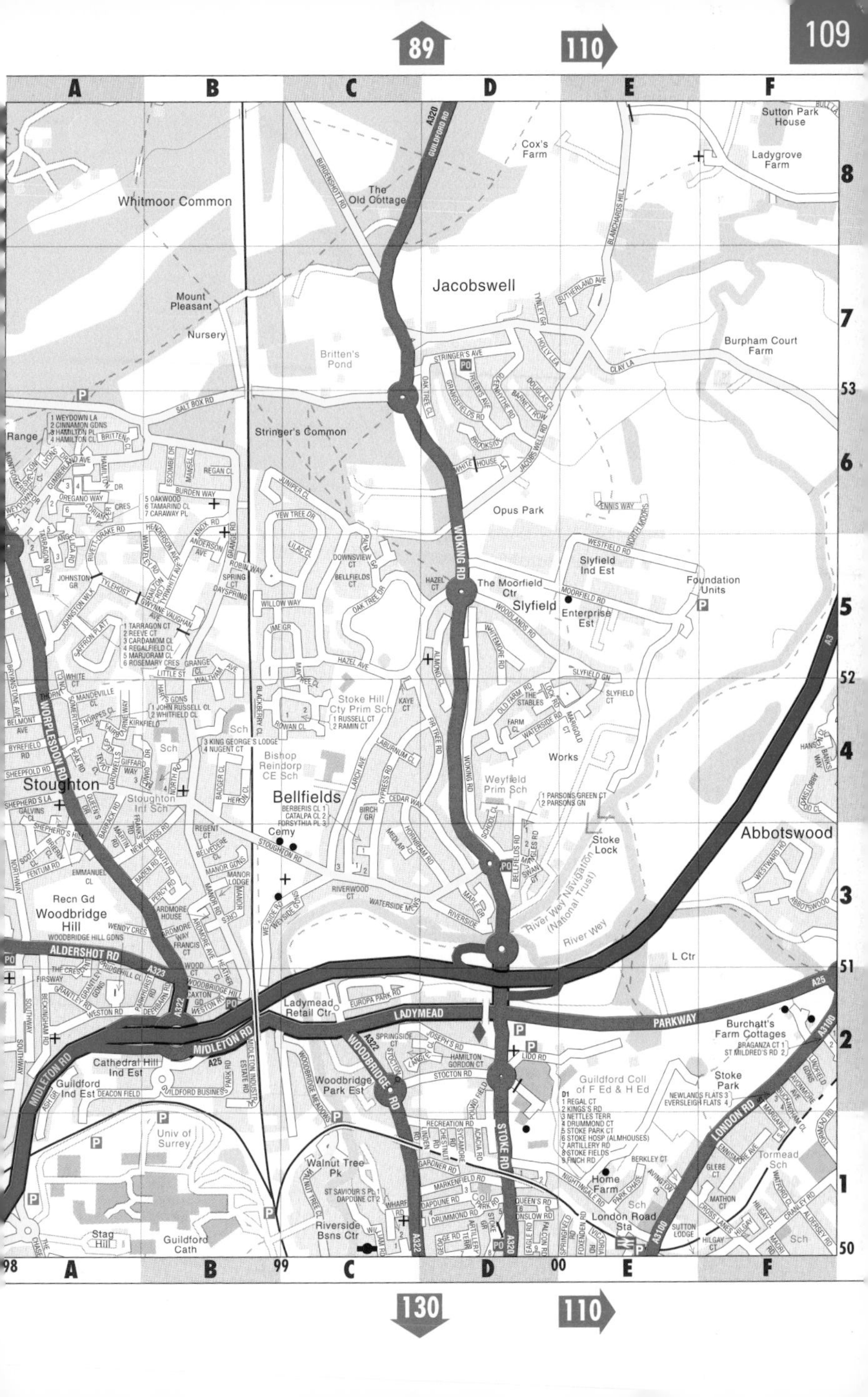
89
110
A
B
C
D
E
F
Sutton Park House
Ladygrove Farm
Cox's Farm
The Old Cottage
Whitmoor Common
Jacobswell
Mount Pleasant
Nursery
Britten's Pond
Burpham Court Farm
Stringer's Common
Range
Opus Park
Slyfield Ind Est
Foundation Units
The Moorfield Ctr
Slyfield
Enterprise Est
Stoke Hill Cty Prim Sch
Bishop Reindorp CE Sch
Bellfields
Cemy
Works
Weyfield Prim Sch
Stoke Lock
River Wey Navigation (National Trust)
River Wey
Abbotswood
Stoughton
Stoughton Inf Sch
Sch
Recn Gd
Woodbridge Hill
L Ctr
Ladymead Retail Ctr
Burchatt's Farm Cottages
Cathedral Hill Ind Est
Guildford Ind Est
Woodbridge Park Est
Guildford Coll of F Ed & H Ed
Stoke Park
Univ of Surrey
Walnut Tree Pk
Home Farm
Tormead Sch
Riverside Bsns Ctr
London Road Sta
Stag Hill
Guildford Cath
WORPLESDON RD
WOKING RD
ALDERSHOT RD
MIDLETON RD
LADYMEAD
PARKWAY
WOODBRIDGE RD
STOKE RD
LONDON RD
GUILDFORD RD
A320
A322
A323
A25
A3
A3100
8
7
6
5
4
3
2
1
53
52
51
50
98
99
00
130
110

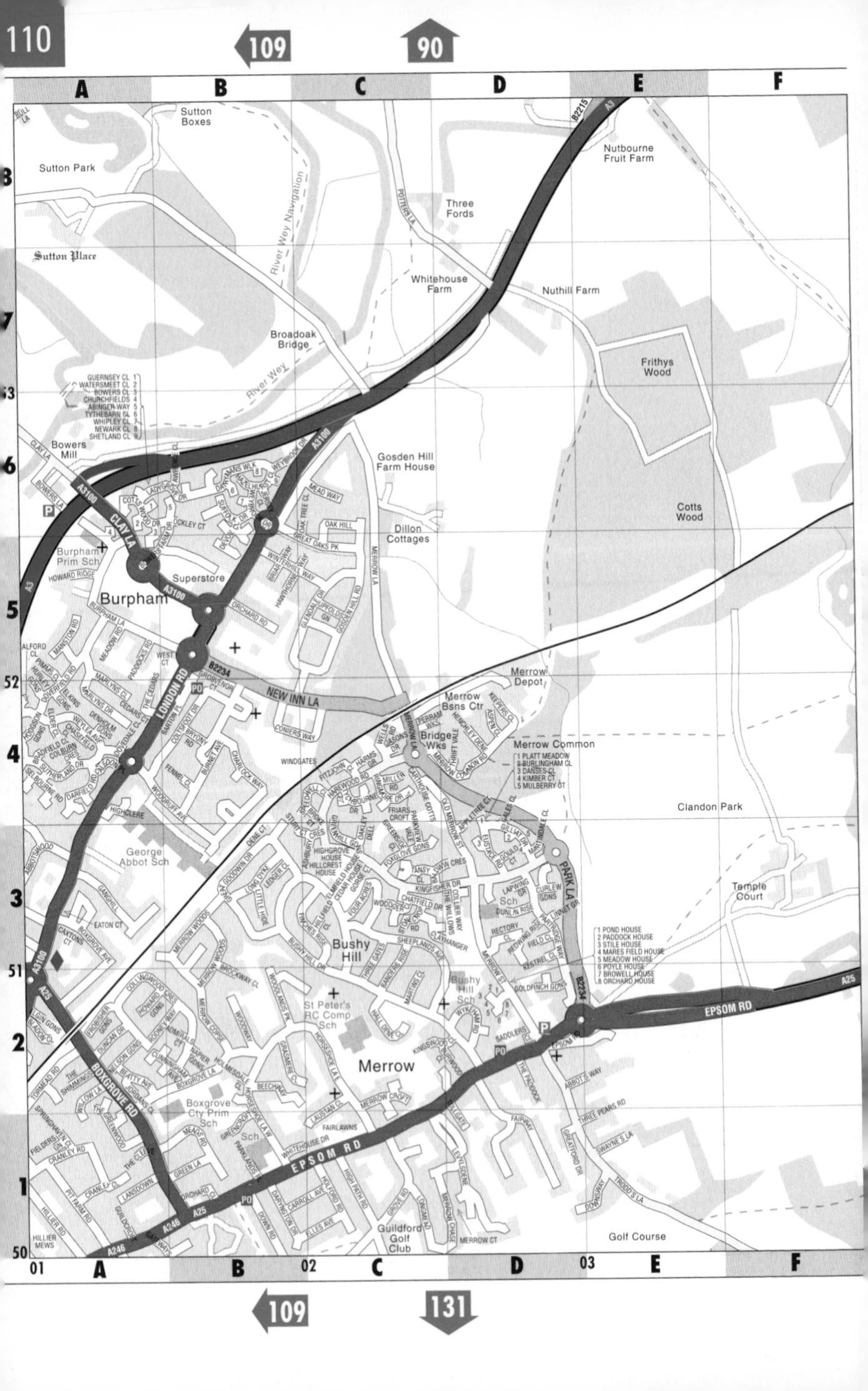

109
90
A
B
C
D
E
F
Sutton Boxes
Sutton Park
Sutton Place
River Wey Navigation
Three Fords
POTTERS LA
Nutbourne Fruit Farm
Whitehouse Farm
Nuthill Farm
Broadoak Bridge
River Wey
Frithys Wood
A3
B2215
GUERNSEY CL 1
WATERSMEET CL 2
BOWERS CL 3
CHURCHFIELDS 4
ABINGER WAY 5
TYTHEBARN CL 6
WHIPLEY CL 7
NEWARK CL 8
SHETLAND CL 9
Bowers Mill
CLAY LA
BOWERS LA
A3100
Gosden Hill Farm House
Cotts Wood
Dillon Cottages
MEAD WAY
OAK HILL
OAK TREE CL
GREAT OAKS PK
WINTERHILL WAY
BRIAR WAY
HAWTHORNE WAY
GLENDALE DR
UPFOLDS GN
GOSDEN HILL RD
MERROW LA
Burpham Prim Sch
HOWARD RIDGE
Burpham
Superstore
ORCHARD RD
BURPHAM LA
MANSTON RD
MEADOW RD
PADDOCKS RD
WEST CT
THE CEDARS
MARLYNS CL
MARLYNS DR
CEDARS CT
DENHOLM GDNS
LONDON RD
B2234
NEW INN LA
CONIERS WAY
WINDGATES
Merrow Depot
Merrow Bsns Ctr
KEEPERS CL
ASPEN CL
HENCHLEY DENE
THRIFT VALE
PERRAM WKS
Bridge Wks
MERROW COMMON RD
Merrow Common
1 PLATT MEADOW
2 BURLINGHAM CL
3 DANSES CL
4 KIMBER CT
5 MULBERRY CT
Clandon Park
BARTON PL
COLTSFOOT DR
BRYONY RD
BURNET AVE
CHARLOCK WAY
FENNEL CL
WOODRUFF AVE
HIGHCLERE
DOVEDALE CL
George Abbot Sch
ABBOTSWOOD
GANGHILL
EATON CT
CAXTONS CT
BOXGROVE AVE
FITZJOHN CL
HARMS GR
HAREWOOD RD
MILLER RD
FRIARS CROFT
OLD MERROW ST
APPLETREE CL
GALES CL
GILLIAT DR
EUSTACE RD
GOULD CT
MARTINDALE CL
PARK LA
Temple Court
HIGHGROVE HOUSE
HILLCREST HOUSE
LONG DYKE
LITTLE HIDE
LEDGER CL
DENE CT
GOODWIN DR
MERROW WOODS
FOUR ACRES
TANSY CL
KINGFISHER DR
CHATFIELD DR
COLLIER WAY
THE WILLOWS
LAPWING GR
CURLEW GDNS
DUNLIN RISE
LINNET GR
RECTORY CL
REDWING RISE
FIELD CL
KESTREL CL
PARTRIDGE WAY
1 POND HOUSE
2 PADDOCK HOUSE
3 STILE HOUSE
4 MARES FIELD HOUSE
5 MEADOW HOUSE
6 POYLE HOUSE
7 BROWELL HOUSE
8 ORCHARD HOUSE
Bushy Hill
BUSHY HILL DR
FINCHES RISE
THREE GATES
SANDERS RISE
MARTINS CL
SHEEPLANDS AVE
LAYHANGER
Bushy Hill Sch
MERROW ST
GOLDFINCH GDNS
B2234
A25
EPSOM RD
St Peter's RC Comp Sch
WOODLANDS PK
HALL DENE CL
WYKEHAM RD
SADDLERS
KINGSWOOD CT
BURWOOD CL
Merrow
ABBOT'S WAY
THREE PEARS RD
SWAYNE'S LA
GREATFORD DR
TRODD'S LA
DOWNSWAY
Golf Course
FAIRWAY
THE PADDOCK
COLLINGWOOD CRES
HOWARD GDNS
BROCKWAY CL
MERROW COPSE
WOODWAY
HORSESHOE LA E
GRASMERE CL
BEECHWAY
MERROW CROFT
LAUSTAN CL
FAIRLAWNS
Boxgrove Cty Prim Sch
BOXGROVE LA
BOXGROVE RD
FROBISHER GDNS
DUNCAN DR
NELSON GDNS
BEATTY AVE
JORDANS CL
CUNNINGHAM AVE
NAPIER GDNS
HOLMESDALE
HORSESHOE LA W
GREENCROFT
PARKLANDS PL
WHITEHOUSE DR
EPSOM RD
HIGH PATH RD
HOLFORD RD
CARROLL AVE
DARYNGTON DR
ELLES AVE
DOWN RD
GROVE RD
LONGMEAD
MEADOW CHASE
MERROW CT
Guildford Golf Club
LEYLSDENE
TORMEAD RD
THE SHIMMINGS
WILLOW LA
THE GREENWOOD
SPRINGHAVEN CL
FIELDERS GN
CRANLEY RD
CRANLEY CL
PIT FARM RD
LANSDOWN
THE CLEEVE
GREEN LA
MEADS RD
ORCHARD RD
A246
GUILDOWN
HILLIER RD
HILLIER MEWS
A25
01
02
03
50
51
52

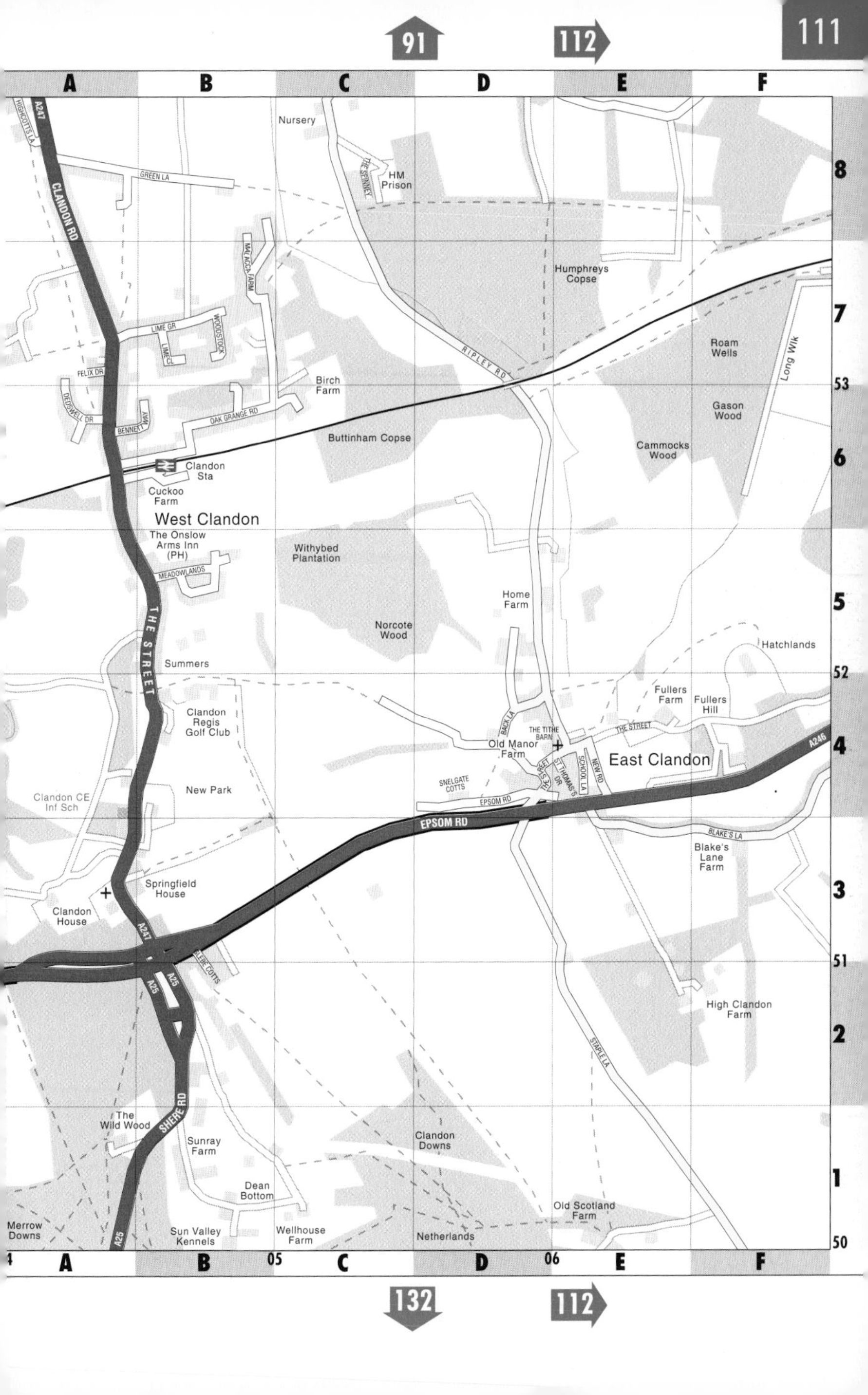
91
112
A
B
C
D
E
F
8
7
53
6
5
52
4
3
51
2
1
50
05
06
132
112
HIGHCOTTS LA
A247
CLANDON RD
GREEN LA
Nursery
THE SPINNEY
HM
Prison
MALACCA FARM
Humphreys
Copse
LIME GR
LIME CL
WOODSTOCK
FELIX DR
DEDSWELL DR
BENNETT WAY
OAK GRANGE RD
Birch
Farm
RIPLEY RD
Roam
Wells
Long Wlk
Gason
Wood
Buttinham Copse
Cammocks
Wood
Clandon
Sta
Cuckoo
Farm
West Clandon
The Onslow
Arms Inn
(PH)
MEADOWLANDS
Withybed
Plantation
Home
Farm
Norcote
Wood
THE STREET
Summers
Hatchlands
Clandon
Regis
Golf Club
Fullers
Farm
Fullers
Hill
THE STREET
BACK LA
THE TITHE
BARN
Old Manor
Farm
East Clandon
A246
SNELGATE
COTTS
THE STREET
ST THOMAS'S DR
SCHOOL LA
NEW RD
EPSOM RD
New Park
Clandon CE
Inf Sch
EPSOM RD
BLAKE'S LA
Blake's
Lane
Farm
Springfield
House
Clandon
House
A247
GLEBE COTTS
A25
A25
High Clandon
Farm
STAPLE LA
SHERE RD
The
Wild Wood
Sunray
Farm
Clandon
Downs
Dean
Bottom
Old Scotland
Farm
Merrow
Downs
A25
Sun Valley
Kennels
Wellhouse
Farm
Netherlands

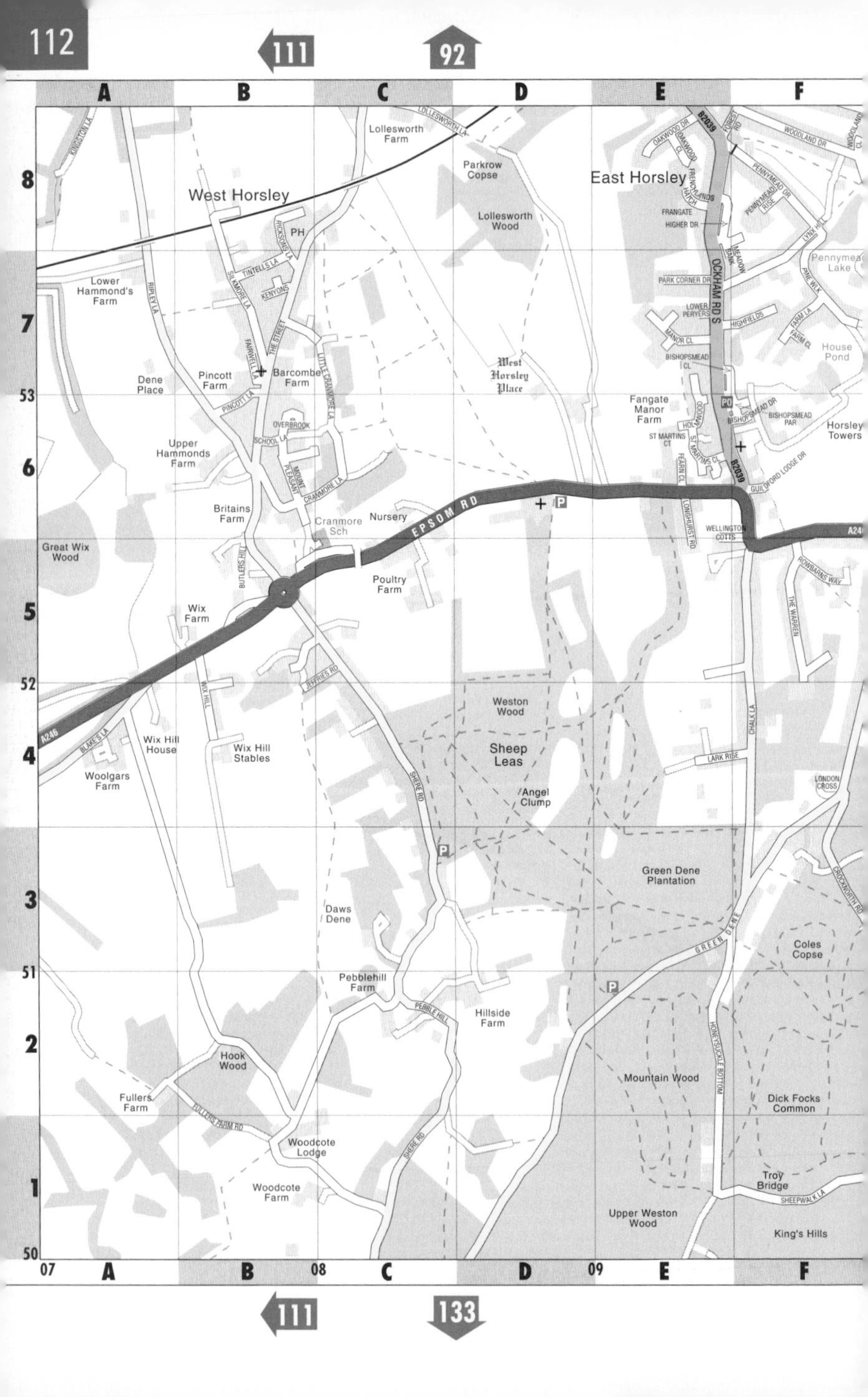

West Horsley

East Horsley

Lollesworth Farm

Parkrow Copse

Lollesworth Wood

PH

Lower Hammond's Farm

Dene Place

Pincott Farm

Barcombe Farm

Overbrook

West Horsley Place

Upper Hammonds Farm

Fangate Manor Farm

St Martins

Bishopsmead Par

Horsley Towers

Pennymead Lake

House Pond

Britains Farm

Cranmore Sch

Nursery

EPSOM RD

Wellington Cotts

A24

Great Wix Wood

Cranmore Sch

Poultry Farm

Wix Farm

A246

Wix Hill House

Wix Hill Stables

Woolgars Farm

Weston Wood

Sheep Leas

Angel Clump

Lark Rise

The Warren

LONDON CROSS

Daws Dene

Green Dene Plantation

Coles Copse

Pebblehill Farm

Hillside Farm

Hook Wood

Fullers Farm

Mountain Wood

Dick Focks Common

Woodcote Lodge

Troy Bridge

Woodcote Farm

Upper Weston Wood

King's Hills

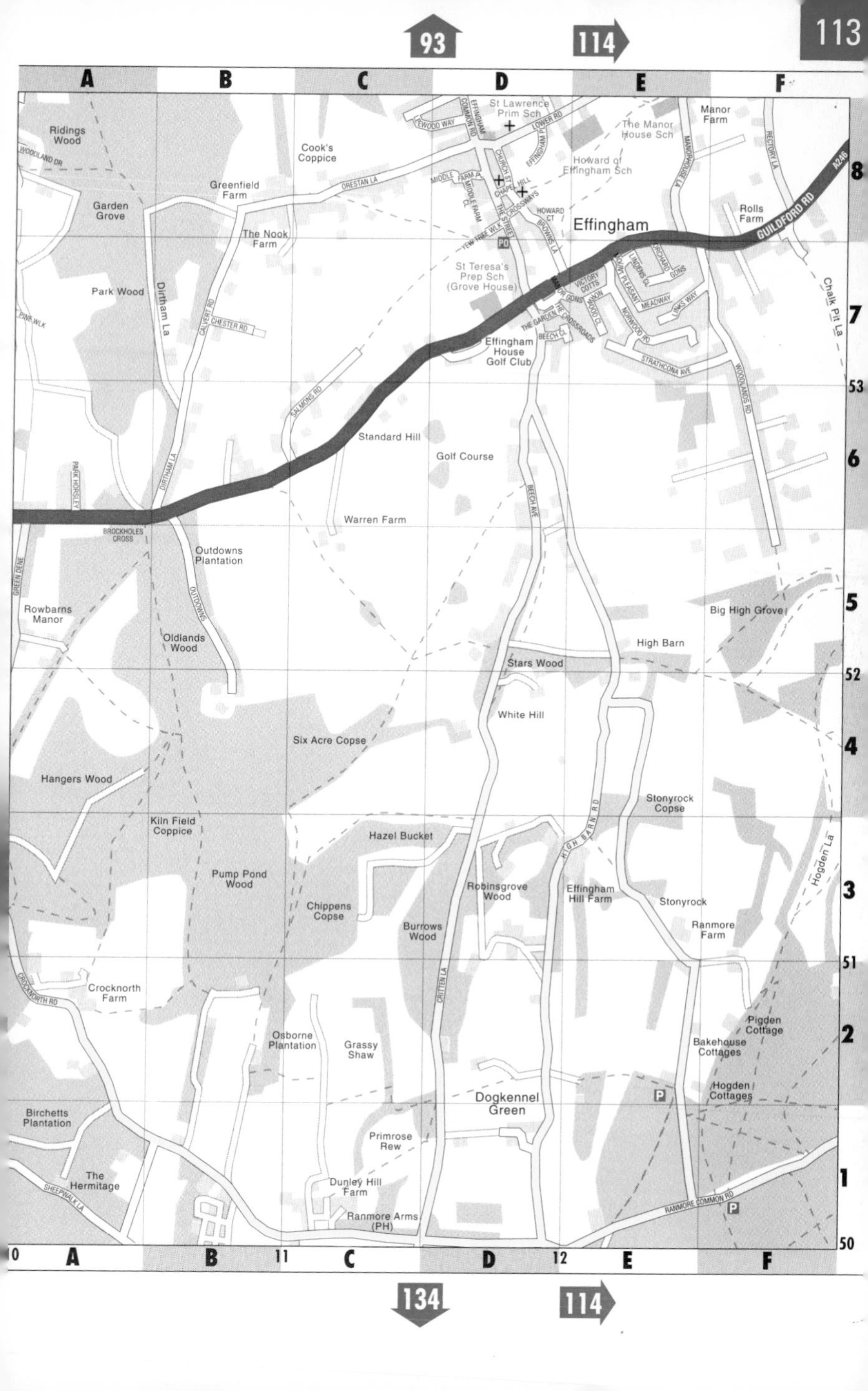
93
114
A
B
C
D
E
F
Ridings Wood
Woodland Dr
Cook's Coppice
St Lawrence Prim Sch
Effingham Common Rd
Lewood Way
Lower Rd
The Manor House Sch
Manor Farm
Rectory La
Manorhouse La
Howard of Effingham Sch
Effingham Pl
Church St
Chapel Hill
Crossways
Middle Farm Pl
Middle Farm Cl
Orestan La
Greenfield Farm
Garden Grove
The Nook Farm
Yew Tree Wlk
The Street
PO
Howard Ct
Browns La
Effingham
Guildford Rd
A246
Rolls Farm
St Teresa's Prep Sch (Grove House)
Victory Cotts
Lindens Cl
Orchard Gdns
Mount Pleasant
Meadway
Links Way
Manor Gdns
Woodlands Cl
Norwood Rd
The Garden
The Crossroads
Beech Cl
Strathcona Ave
Chalk Pit La
Park Wood
Dirtham La
Calvert Rd
Chester Rd
Pine Wlk
Effingham House Golf Club
Salmons Rd
Woodlands Rd
Standard Hill
Golf Course
Park Horsley
Beech Ave
Warren Farm
Brockholes Cross
Outdowns Plantation
Green Dene
Outdowns
Rowbarns Manor
Oldlands Wood
Big High Grove
High Barn
Stars Wood
White Hill
Six Acre Copse
Hangers Wood
Stonyrock Copse
Kiln Field Coppice
Hazel Bucket
High Barn Rd
Hogden La
Pump Pond Wood
Robinsgrove Wood
Effingham Hill Farm
Stonyrock
Chippens Copse
Burrows Wood
Ranmore Farm
Crocknorth Rd
Crocknorth Farm
Critten La
Pigden Cottage
Osborne Plantation
Grassy Shaw
Bakehouse Cottages
Hogden Cottages
P
Dogkennel Green
Birchetts Plantation
Primrose Rew
The Hermitage
Sheepwalk La
Dunley Hill Farm
Ranmore Common Rd
Ranmore Arms (PH)
8
7
53
6
5
52
4
3
51
2
1
50
10
11
12
134
114

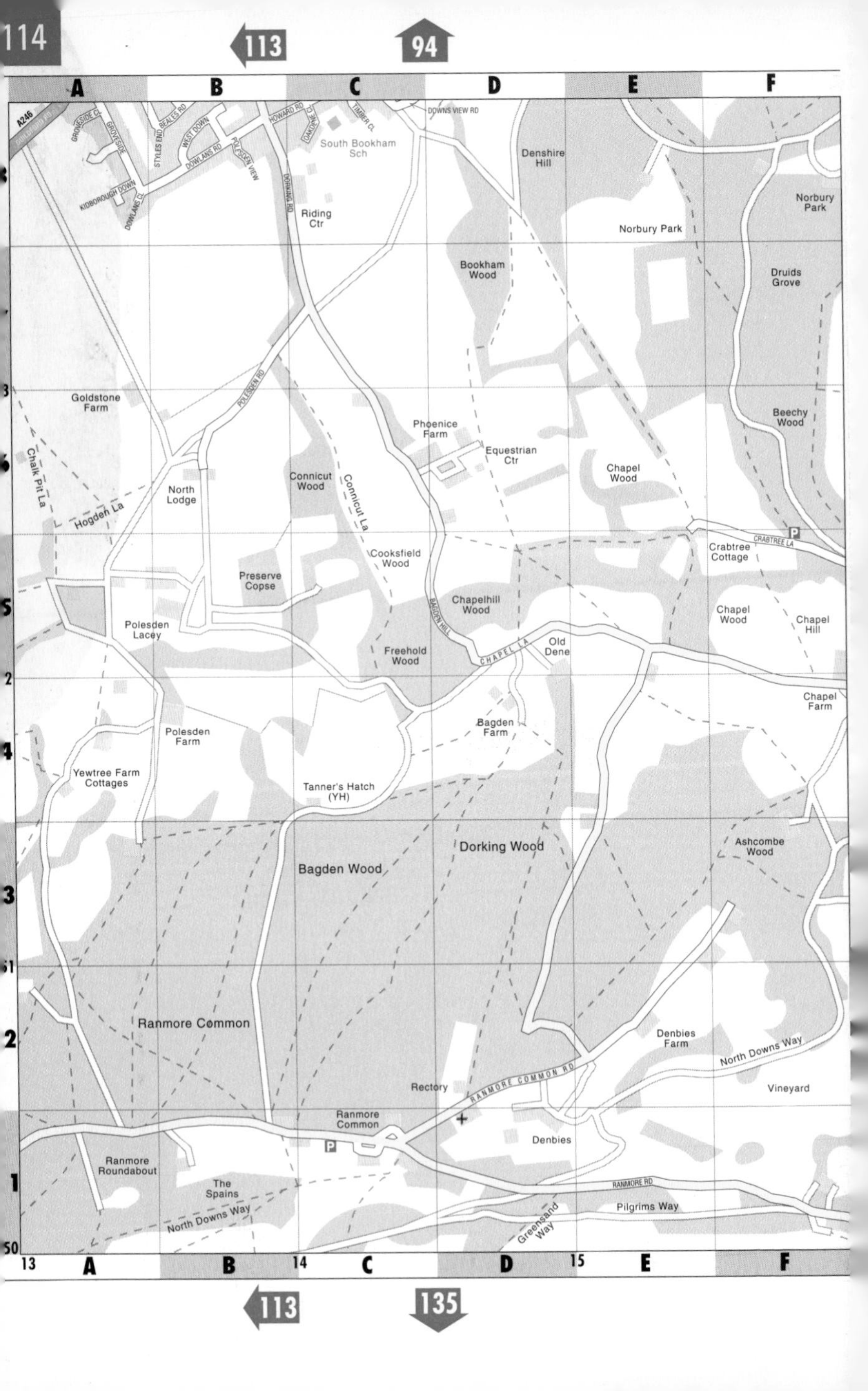
113
94
A
B
C
D
E
F
A246
South Bookham Sch
Riding Ctr
Denshire Hill
Norbury Park
Norbury Park
Bookham Wood
Druids Grove
Goldstone Farm
Phoenice Farm
Equestrian Ctr
Beechy Wood
Chalk Pit La
North Lodge
Connicut Wood
Connicut La
Chapel Wood
Hogden La
Cooksfield Wood
Crabtree Cottage
CRABTREE LA
Preserve Copse
Chapelhill Wood
Chapel Wood
Chapel Hill
Polesden Lacey
BAGDEN HILL
Freehold Wood
CHAPEL LA
Old Dene
Chapel Farm
Polesden Farm
Bagden Farm
Yewtree Farm Cottages
Tanner's Hatch (YH)
Dorking Wood
Bagden Wood
Ashcombe Wood
Ranmore Common
Denbies Farm
North Downs Way
Rectory
RANMORE COMMON RD
Vineyard
Ranmore Common
Denbies
Ranmore Roundabout
The Spains
RANMORE RD
Pilgrims Way
North Downs Way
Greensand Way
13
14
15
113
135

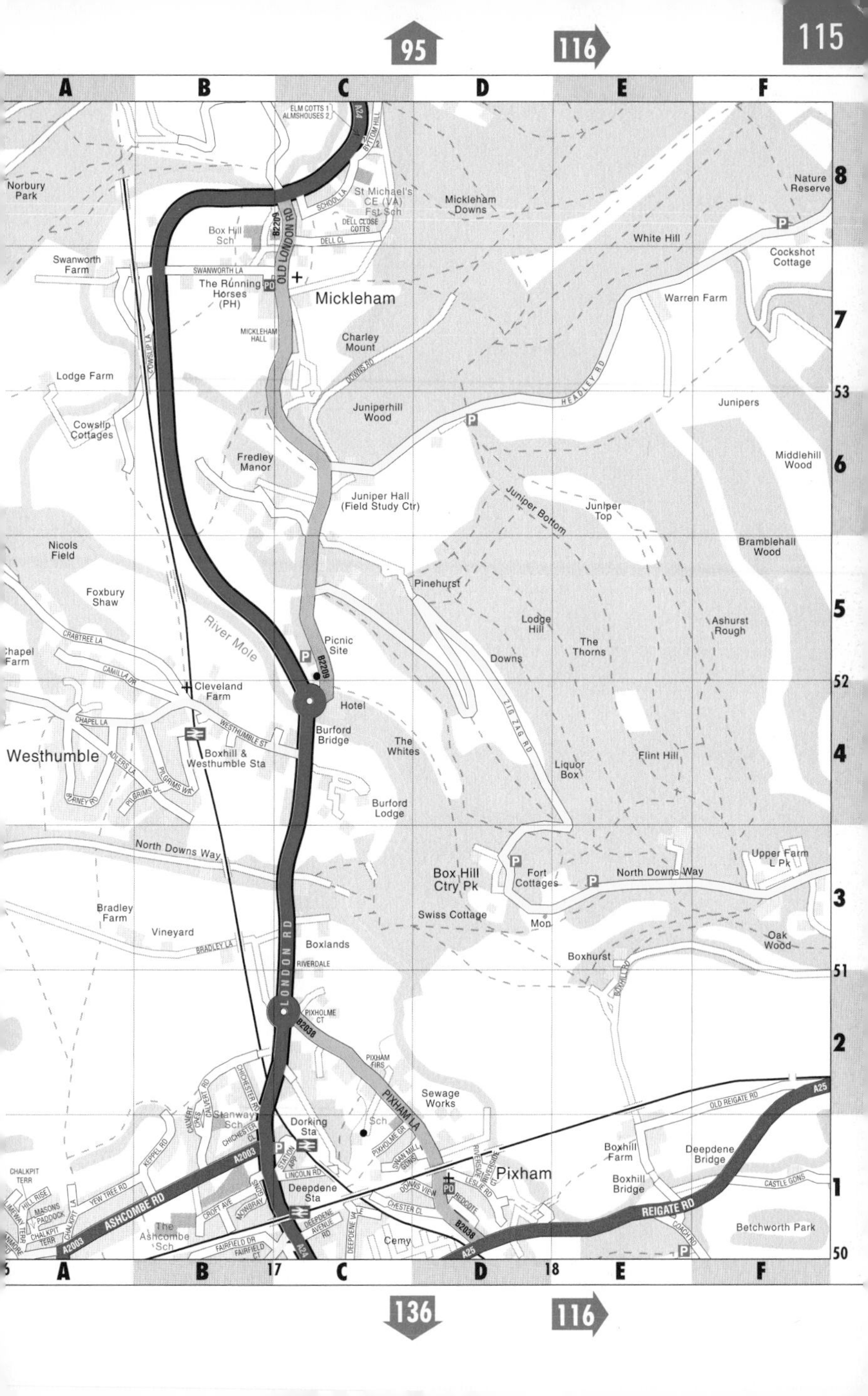
95
116
A
B
C
D
E
F
Norbury Park
Nature Reserve
St Michael's CE (VA) Fst Sch
Mickleham Downs
Box Hill Sch
White Hill
Cockshot Cottage
Swanworth Farm
The Running Horses (PH)
Mickleham
Warren Farm
Charley Mount
Lodge Farm
Junipers
Juniperhill Wood
Cowslip Cottages
Fredley Manor
Middlehill Wood
Juniper Hall (Field Study Ctr)
Juniper Bottom
Juniper Top
Nicols Field
Bramblehall Wood
Foxbury Shaw
Pinehurst
River Mole
Lodge Hill
Ashurst Rough
Picnic Site
The Thorns
Chapel Farm
Downs
Cleveland Farm
Hotel
Burford Bridge
The Whites
Westhumble
Boxhill & Westhumble Sta
Flint Hill
Liquor Box
Burford Lodge
North Downs Way
Upper Farm L Pk
Box Hill Ctry Pk
Fort Cottages
Bradley Farm
Swiss Cottage
Vineyard
Mon
Oak Wood
Boxlands
Boxhurst
Sewage Works
Stanway Sch
Dorking Sta
Sch
Boxhill Farm
Deepdene Bridge
Pixham
Deepdene Sta
Boxhill Bridge
The Ashcombe Sch
Cemy
Betchworth Park
ELM COTTS 1
ALMSHOUSES 2
BYTTOM HILL
SCHOOL LA
DELL CLOSE COTTS
DELL CL
SWANWORTH LA
OLD LONDON RD
B2209
MICKLEHAM HALL
COWSLIP LA
DOWNS RD
HEADLEY RD
CRABTREE LA
CAMILLA DR
CHAPEL LA
WESTHUMBLE ST
ADLERS LA
PILGRIMS WAY
PILGRIMS CL
BURNEY RD
ZIG ZAG RD
BRADLEY LA
LONDON RD
RIVERDALE
PIXHOLME CT
B2038
PIXHAM FIRS
PIXHAM LA
OLD REIGATE RD
A25
BOXHILL RD
CHICHESTER RD
CALVERT RD
CALVERT CRES
CHICHESTER CL
KEPPEL RD
STATION APP
LINCOLN RD
PIXHOLME GR
SWAN MILL GDNS
RIVERSIDE
LESLIE RD
DOWNS VIEW
REDCOTE
CHESTER CL
DEEPDENE AVENUE RD
DEEPDENE VALE
CHALKPIT TERR
HILL RISE
MASONS PADDOCK
CHALKPIT LA
YEW TREE RD
ASHCOMBE RD
A2003
CROFT AVE
MOWBRAY
FAIRFIELD DR
FAIRFIELD CT
A24
REIGATE RD
CASTLE GDNS
COACH RD
8
7
6
5
4
3
2
1
53
52
51
50
17
18
136
116

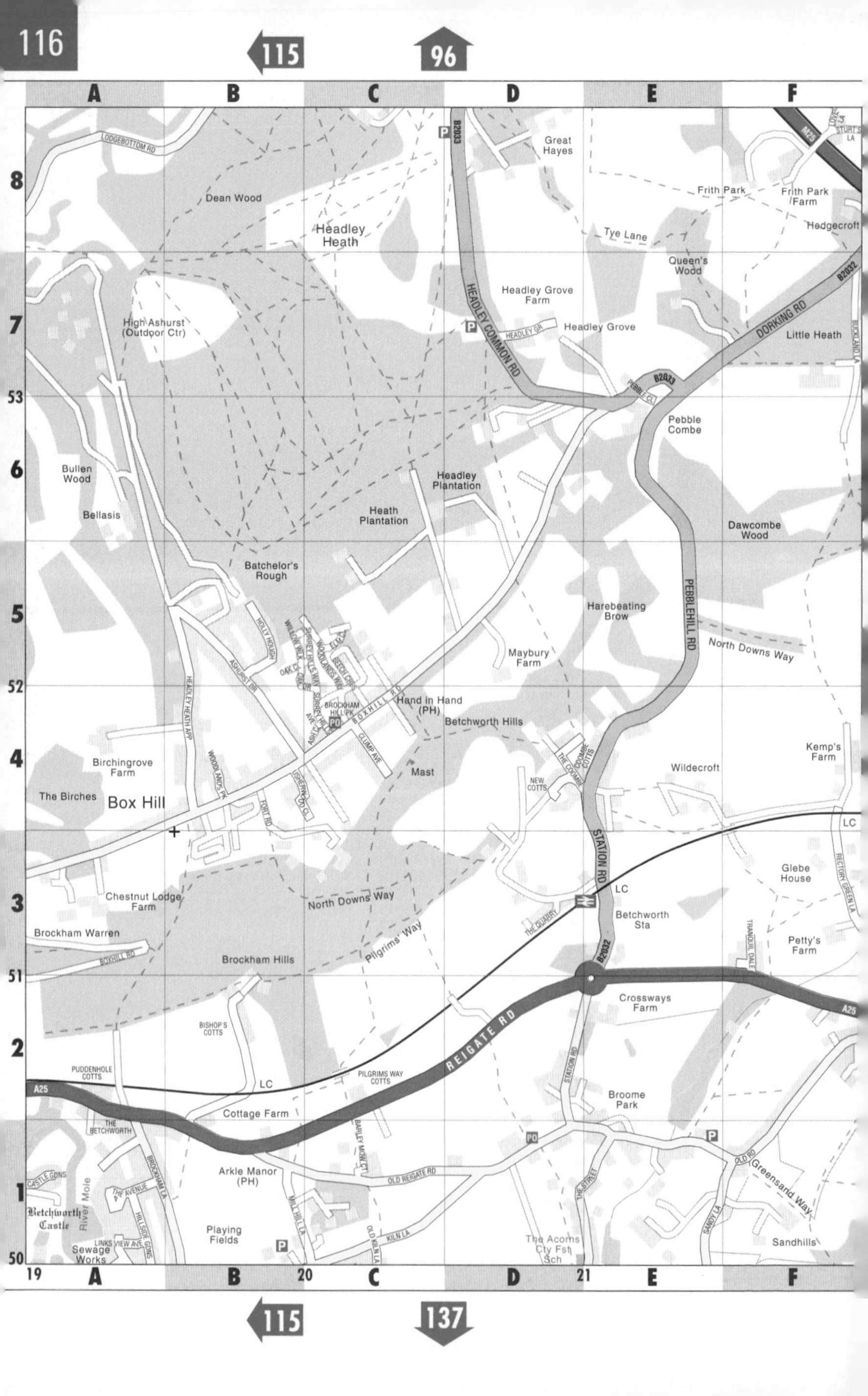
116
115
96
A
B
C
D
E
F
8
7
53
6
5
52
4
3
51
2
1
50
19
20
21
LODGEBOTTOM RD
Dean Wood
Headley Heath
B2033
Great Hayes
M25
Frith Park
Frith Park Farm
Hedgecroft
Tye Lane
Queen's Wood
B2032
High Ashurst (Outdoor Ctr)
HEADLEY COMMON RD
Headley Grove Farm
HEADLEY GR
Headley Grove
DORKING RD
Little Heath
BUCKLAND LA
PEBBLE CL
Pebble Combe
Bullen Wood
Headley Plantation
Bellasis
Heath Plantation
Dawcombe Wood
Batchelor's Rough
Harebeating Brow
PEBBLEHILL RD
HOLLY HOUGH
WILLOW WK
SURREY HILLS WAY
WOODLANDS WAY
ELM CL
BEECH CRES
OAK CL
ASHURST DR
North Downs Way
Maybury Farm
HEADLEY HEATH APP
BROCKHAM HILL PK
BOXHILL RD
Hand in Hand (PH)
Betchworth Hills
CLUMP AVE
Birchingrove Farm
WOODLANDS PK
Mast
THE COOMBE
COOMBE COTTS
NEW COTTS
Kemp's Farm
Wildecroft
The Birches
Box Hill
FORT RD
USHERWOOD CL
STATION RD
LC
Glebe House
RECTORY GREEN LA
Chestnut Lodge Farm
North Downs Way
Betchworth Sta
THE QUARRY
Brockham Warren
Pilgrims' Way
TRANQUIL DALE
Petty's Farm
BOXHILL RD
Brockham Hills
Crossways Farm
A25
BISHOP'S COTTS
REIGATE RD
PUDDENHOLE COTTS
PILGRIMS WAY COTTS
Broome Park
Cottage Farm
THE BETCHWORTH
BARLEY MOW CT
PO
OLD RD
Greensand Way
Arkle Manor (PH)
OLD REIGATE RD
CASTLE GDNS
THE AVENUE
BROCKHAM LA
River Mole
Betchworth Castle
HILLSIDE GDNS
MILL HILL LA
THE STREET
SANDY LA
Playing Fields
Sewage Works
LINKS VIEW AVE
OLD KILN LA
KILN LA
The Acorns Cty Fst Sch
Sandhills
137

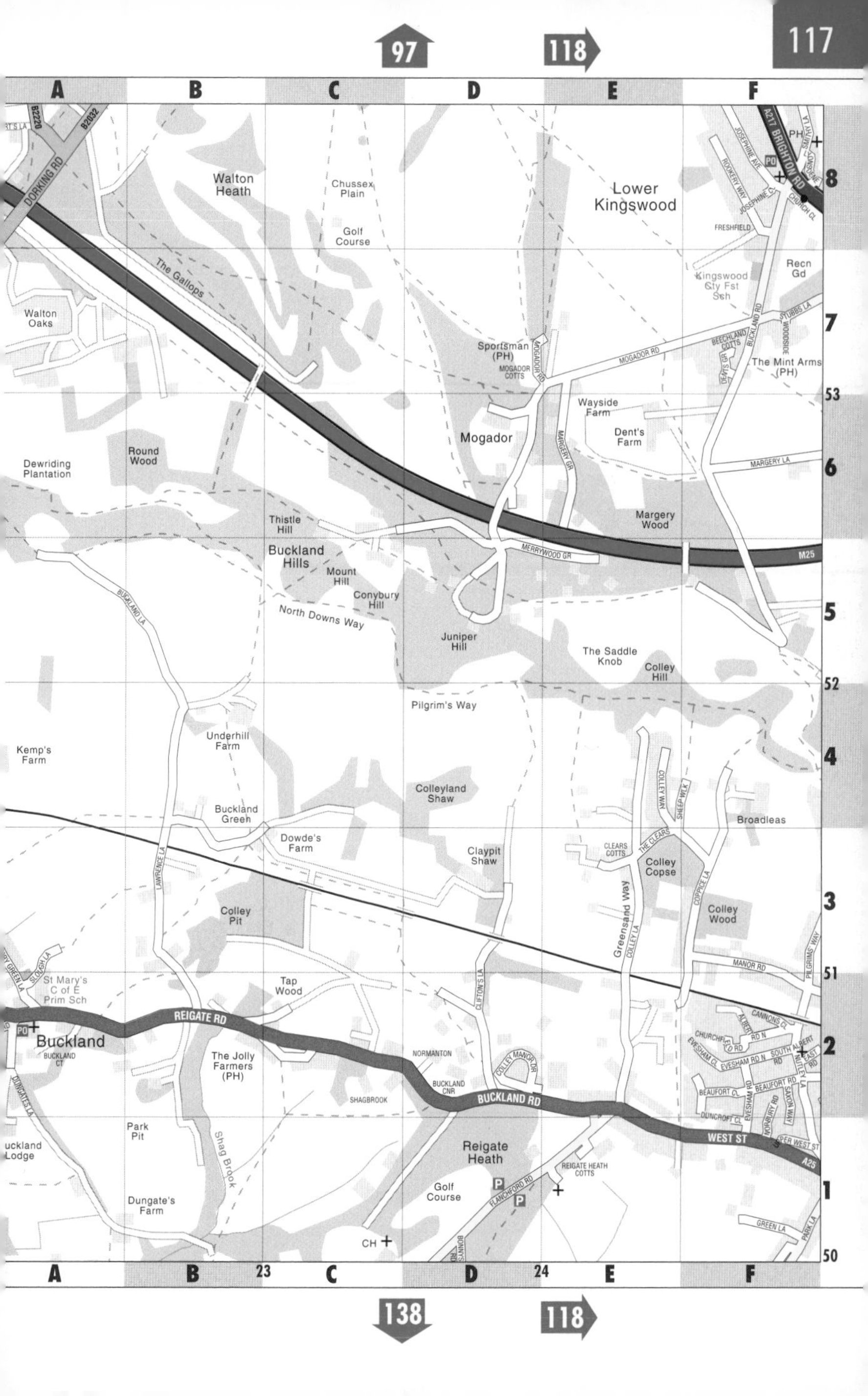
97
118
A
B
C
D
E
F
Walton Heath
Chussex Plain
Golf Course
Lower Kingswood
The Gallops
Walton Oaks
Kingswood Cty Fst Sch
Recn Gd
Sportsman (PH)
The Mint Arms (PH)
Wayside Farm
Dent's Farm
Mogador
Round Wood
Dewriding Plantation
Thistle Hill
Buckland Hills
Mount Hill
Conybury Hill
Margery Wood
North Downs Way
Juniper Hill
The Saddle Knob
Colley Hill
Pilgrim's Way
Underhill Farm
Kemp's Farm
Colleyland Shaw
Buckland Green
Dowde's Farm
Broadleas
Claypit Shaw
Colley Copse
Colley Pit
Colley Wood
Greensand Way
Tap Wood
St Mary's C of E Prim Sch
Buckland
The Jolly Farmers (PH)
Park Pit
Shag Brook
Reigate Heath
Golf Course
Dungate's Farm
Buckland Lodge
CH
DORKING RD
B2220
B2032
A217 BRIGHTON RD
M25
REIGATE RD
BUCKLAND RD
WEST ST
A25
8
7
53
6
5
52
4
3
51
2
1
50
23
24
138
118

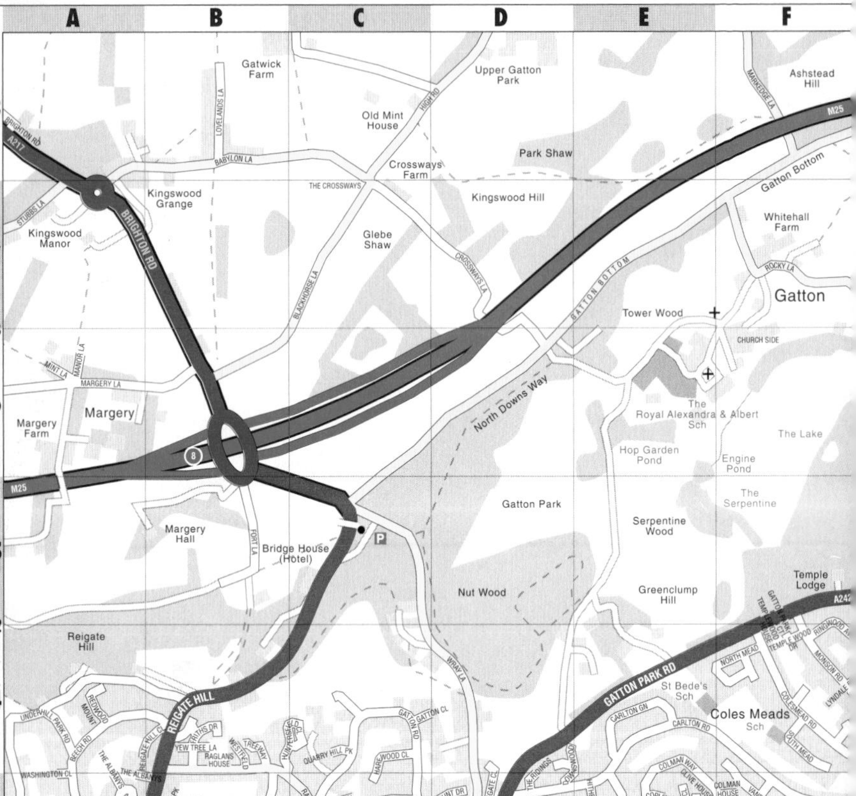

A B C D E F

8
7
53
6
5
52
4
3
51
2
1
50

25 A 26 B C 27 D E F

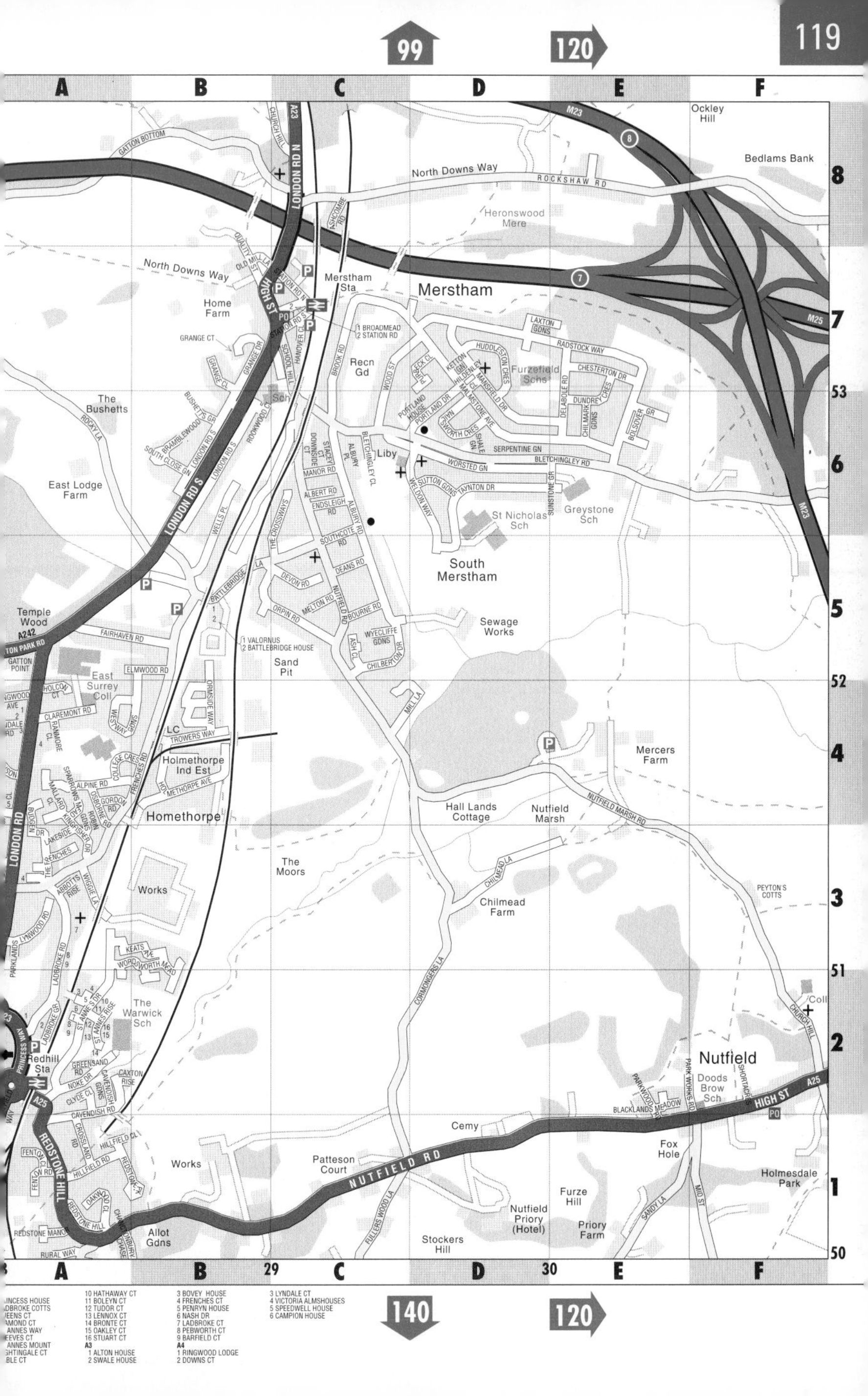

119
100

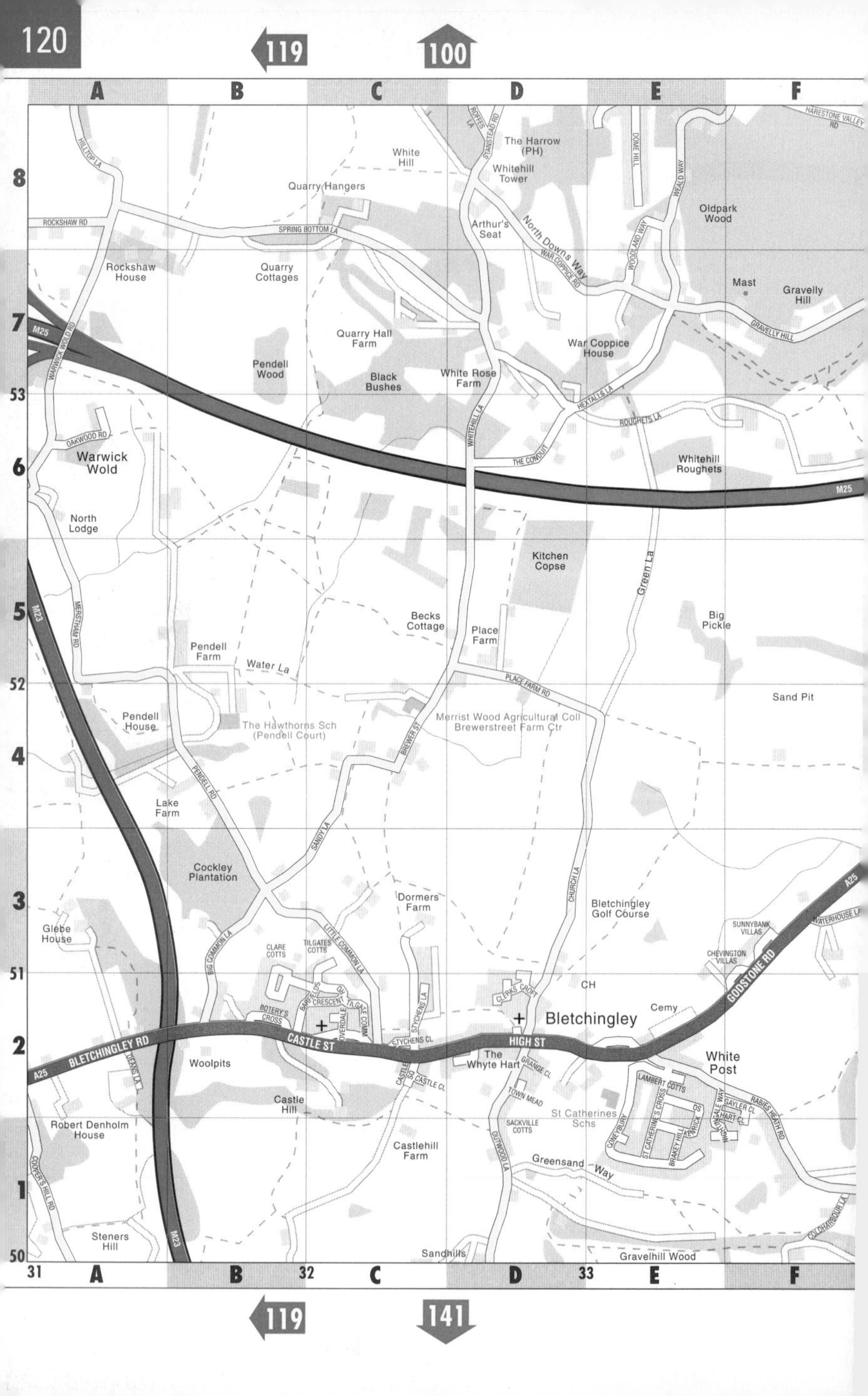
A
B
C
D
E
F
8
7
53
6
5
52
4
3
51
2
1
50
31
32
33
White Hill
The Harrow (PH)
Whitehill Tower
Quarry Hangers
ROCKSHAW RD
SPRING BOTTOM LA
Arthur's Seat
North Downs Way
WAR COPPICE RD
Oldpark Wood
Rockshaw House
Quarry Cottages
Mast
Gravelly Hill
GRAVELLY HILL
Quarry Hall Farm
War Coppice House
M25
WARWICK WOLD RD
Pendell Wood
Black Bushes
White Rose Farm
HEXTALLS LA
ROUGHETS LA
OAKWOOD RD
Warwick Wold
THE CONDUIT
WHITEHILL LA
Whitehill Roughets
North Lodge
Kitchen Copse
Green La
M23
MERSTHAM RD
Becks Cottage
Place Farm
Big Pickle
Pendell Farm
Water La
PLACE FARM RD
Sand Pit
Pendell House
The Hawthorns Sch (Pendell Court)
BREWER ST
Merrist Wood Agricultural Coll Brewerstreet Farm Ctr
PENDELL RD
Lake Farm
SANDY LA
Cockley Plantation
Dormers Farm
CHURCH LA
Bletchingley Golf Course
A25
Glebe House
BIG COMMON LA
CLARE COTTS
TILGATES COTTS
LITTLE COMMON LA
SUNNYBANK VILLAS
WATERHOUSE LA
CHEVINGTON VILLAS
GODSTONE RD
STYCHENS LA
CLERKS CROFT
CH
Cemy
BOTERY'S CROSS
BARFIELDS
CRESCENT
OVERDALE
TILGATE COMM
Bletchingley
BLETCHINGLEY RD
CASTLE ST
STYCHENS CL
HIGH ST
The Whyte Hart
White Post
DEAN'S LA
Woolpits
CASTLE SQ
CASTLE CL
GRANGE CL
LAMBERT COTTS
RABIES HEATH RD
TOWN MEAD
GAYLER CL
HART CL
Castle Hill
St Catherines Schs
SACKVILLE COTTS
CONEYBURY
ST CATHERINE'S CROSS
BRAKEY HILL
Robert Denholm House
Castlehill Farm
OUTWOOD LA
Greensand Way
COOPER'S HILL RD
COLDHARBOUR LA
Steners Hill
Sandhills
Gravelhill Wood
HARESTONE VALLEY RD
ROFFES LA
STANSTEAD RD
DOME HILL
WEALD WAY
WOODLAND WAY
HILLTOP LA

119
141

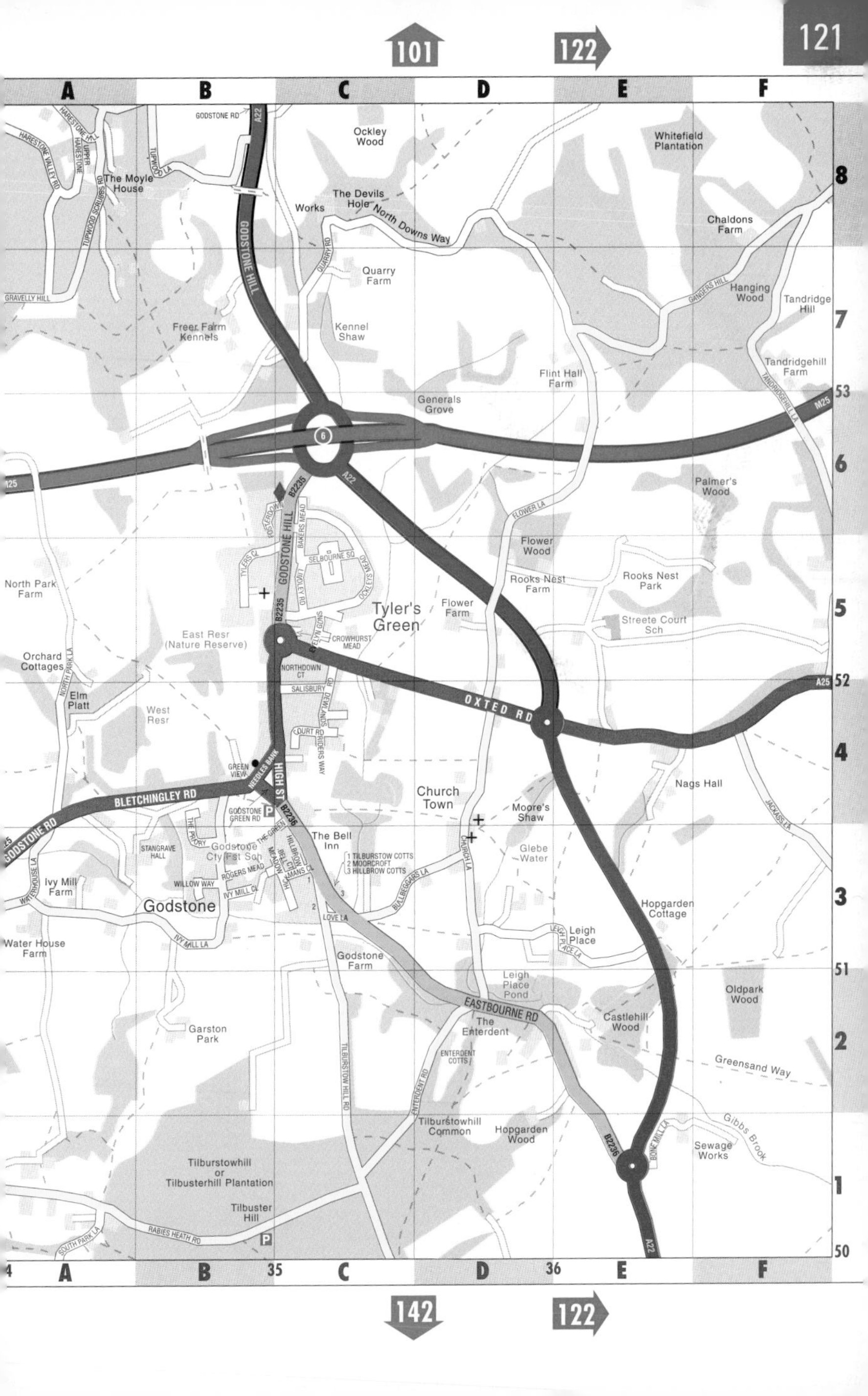

101
122
A
B
C
D
E
F
Ockley Wood
Whitefield Plantation
The Moyle House
The Devils Hole
Works
North Downs Way
Chaldons Farm
Quarry Farm
GODSTONE HILL
Hanging Wood
Tandridge Hill
Freer Farm Kennels
Kennel Shaw
Flint Hall Farm
Tandridgehill Farm
Generals Grove
M25
Palmer's Wood
Flower Wood
Rooks Nest Farm
Rooks Nest Park
North Park Farm
Tyler's Green
Flower Farm
Streete Court Sch
East Resr (Nature Reserve)
Orchard Cottages
Elm Platt
West Resr
OXTED RD
A25
BLETCHINGLEY RD
HIGH ST
Church Town
Moore's Shaw
Nags Hall
The Bell Inn
Glebe Water
Godstone Cty Fst Sch
Ivy Mill Farm
Godstone
Hopgarden Cottage
Leigh Place
Water House Farm
Godstone Farm
Leigh Place Pond
Oldpark Wood
EASTBOURNE RD
The Enterdent
Castlehill Wood
Garston Park
Greensand Way
Tilburstowhill Common
Hopgarden Wood
Gibbs Brook
Sewage Works
Tilburstowhill or Tilbusterhill Plantation
Tilbuster Hill
RABIES HEATH RD
A22
B2235
B2236
1 TILBURSTOW COTTS
2 MOORCROFT
3 HILLBROW COTTS
8
7
6
5
4
3
2
1
53
52
51
50
35
36
142
122

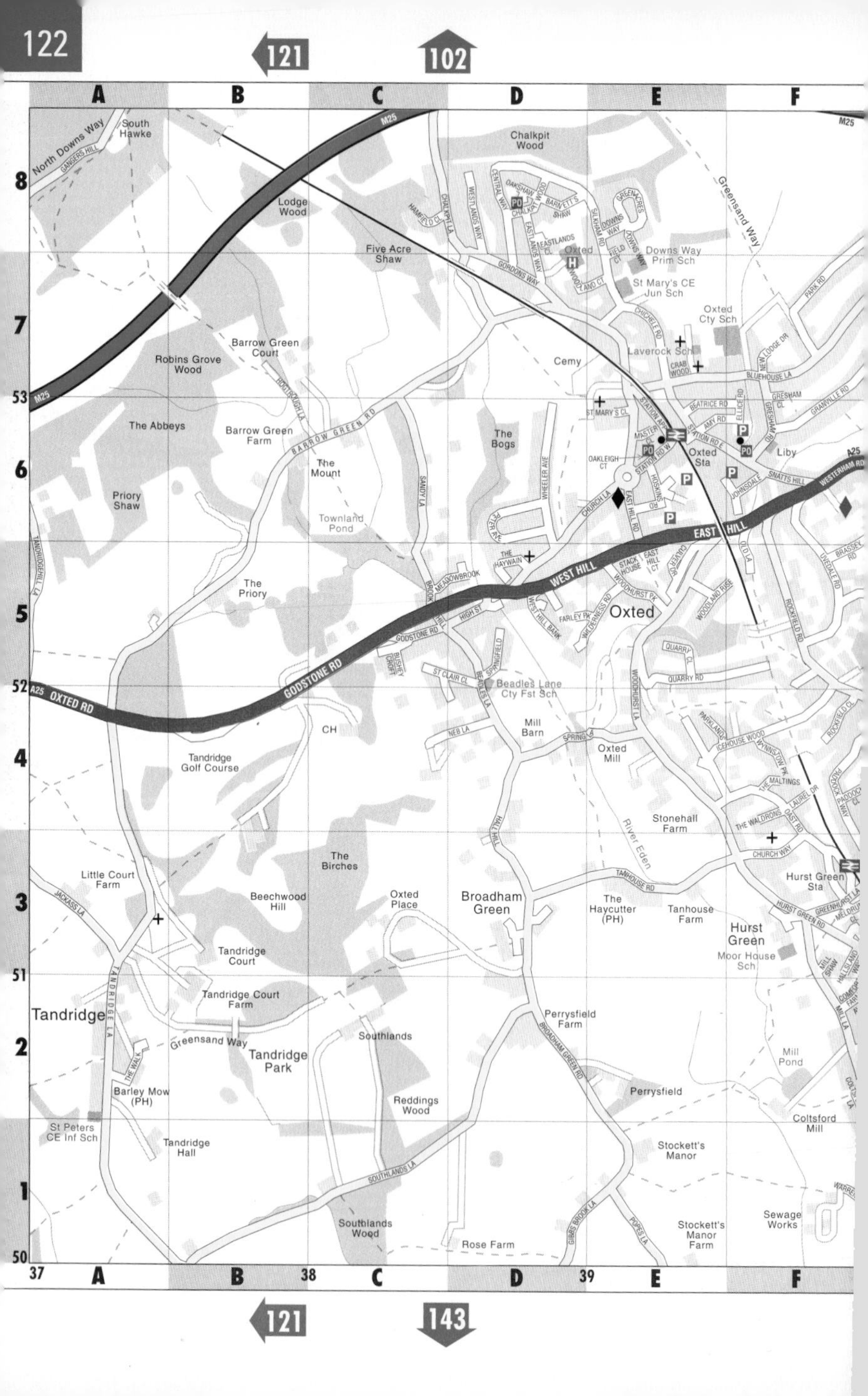
121
102
A
B
C
D
E
F
8
7
53
6
5
52
4
3
51
2
1
50
37
38
39
M25
North Downs Way
South Hawke
Gangers Hill
Lodge Wood
Chalkpit Wood
Five Acre Shaw
Oxted
Downs Way Prim Sch
St Mary's CE Jun Sch
Oxted Cty Sch
Greensand Way
Robins Grove Wood
Barrow Green Court
Cemy
Laverock Sch
Crab Wood
Bluehouse La
The Abbeys
Barrow Green Farm
Barrow Green Rd
The Bogs
St Mary's Cl
Oxted Sta
Liby
The Mount
Oakleigh Ct
Station Rd W
Station Rd E
Snatts Hill
Westerham Rd
A25
Priory Shaw
Townland Pond
Sandy La
Wheeler Ave
Church La
East Hill Rd
East Hill
The Haywain
West Hill
Stack House
Woodhurst Pk
Woodland Rise
The Priory
Brook Hill
Meadowbrook
Godstone Rd
High St
West Hill Bank
Farley Pk
Wilderness Rd
Rockfield Rd
Uvedale Rd
Brassey Rd
Bushey Croft
St Clair Cl
Beadles La
Springfield
Beadles Lane Cty Fst Sch
Quarry Cl
Quarry Rd
Woodhurst La
A25 Oxted Rd
Godstone Rd
CH
Mill Barn
Neb La
Spring La
Oxted Mill
Parkland
Icehouse Wood
Wynnstow Pk
Tandridge Golf Course
The Maltings
Laurel Dr
Paddock Way
Stonehall Farm
River Eden
The Waldrons
Oast Rd
Church Way
Hall Hill
Little Court Farm
Jackass La
The Birches
Beechwood Hill
Oxted Place
Broadham Green
Tanhouse Rd
The Haycutter (PH)
Tanhouse Farm
Hurst Green Sta
Hurst Green Rd
Greenhurst La
Hurst Green
Moor House Sch
Tandridge Court
Tandridge La
Tandridge Court Farm
Tandridge
Perrysfield Farm
Broadham Green Rd
Mill Shaw
Hallsland
Mill La
Greensand Way
Tandridge Park
Southlands
The Walk
Barley Mow (PH)
Reddings Wood
Perrysfield
Mill Pond
St Peters CE Inf Sch
Tandridge Hall
Stockett's Manor
Coltsford Mill
Southlands La
Southlands Wood
Gibbs Brook La
Popes La
Rose Farm
Stockett's Manor Farm
Sewage Works
Warren La
Coltsford La
121
143

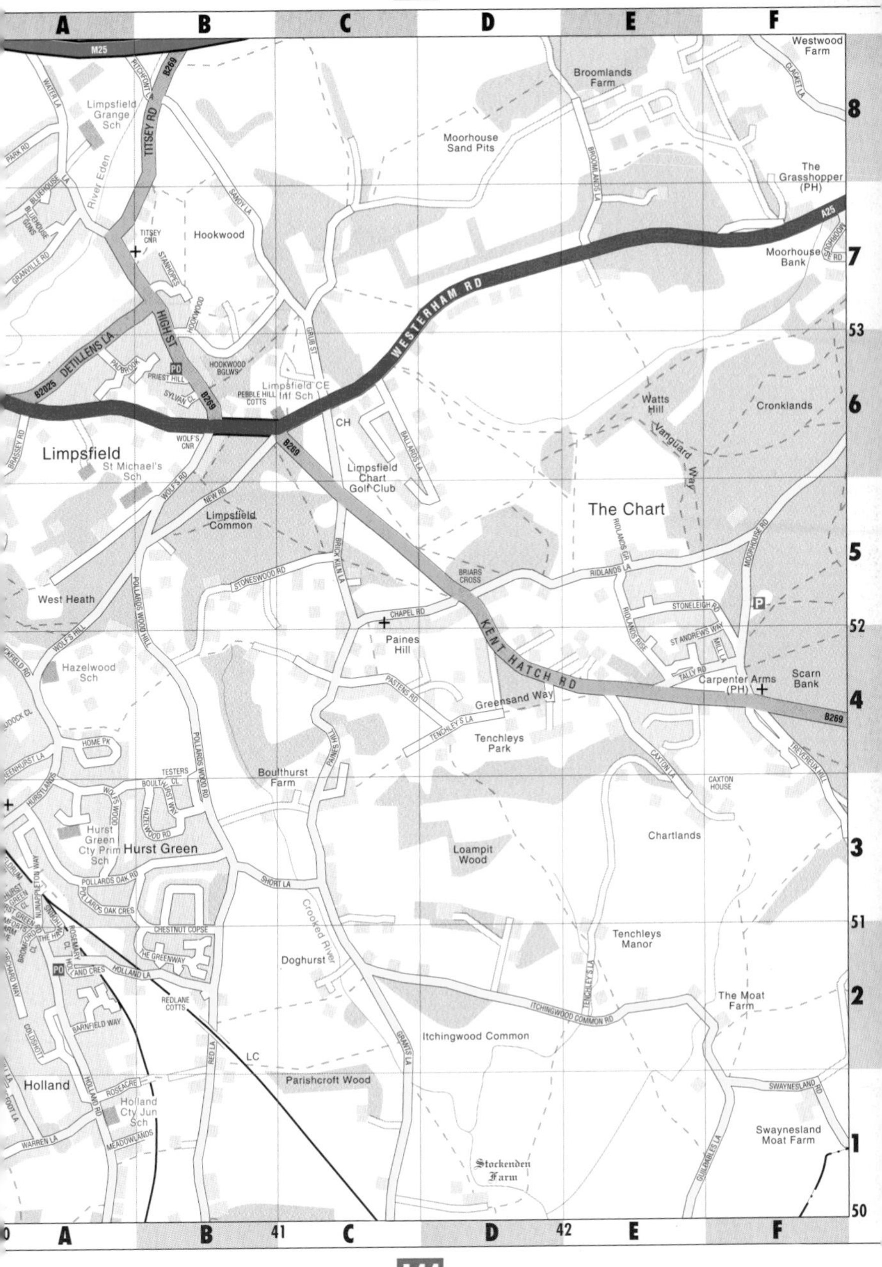

103

A B C D E F

M25

Westwood Farm

Limpsfield Grange Sch

Broomlands Farm

8

Moorhouse Sand Pits

The Grasshopper (PH)

A25

Hookwood

7

Moorhouse Bank

WESTERHAM RD

53

PRIEST HILL

Watts Hill

Cronklands

HIGH ST

DETILLENS LA

Hookwood Bglws

Vanguard Way

6

Limpsfield CE Inf Sch

B269

Pebble Hill Cotts

CH

Limpsfield

St Michael's Sch

WOLF'S CNR

Limpsfield Chart Golf Club

The Chart

Limpsfield Common

NEW RD

5

BRIARS CROSS

RIDLANDS LA

STONEWOOD RD

52

STONELEIGH AV

P

West Heath

CHAPEL RD

Paines Hill

St Andrews Wk

Carpenter Arms (PH)

Scarn Bank

Hazelwood Sch

KENT HATCH RD

B269

4

POLLARDS WOOD RD

Greensand Way

TENCHLEYS LA

Tenchleys Park

CAXTON HOUSE

Boulthurst Farm

HOME PK

TESTERS

Hurst Green Cty Prim Sch

Hurst Green

Chartlands

3

Loampit Wood

POLLARDS OAK RD

SHORT LA

51

POLLARDS OAK CRES

CHESTNUT COPSE

Crooked River

Tenchleys Manor

THE GREENWAY

Doghurst

ITCHINGWOOD COMMON RD

The Moat Farm

PO

2

REDLANE COTTS

BARNFIELD WAY

LC

Itchingwood Common

SWAYNESLAND RD

Holland

Parishcroft Wood

Holland Cty Jun Sch

ROSEACRE

MEADOWLANDS

Swaynesland Moat Farm

WARREN LA

1

Stockenden Farm

50

0 A B 41 C D 42 E F

144

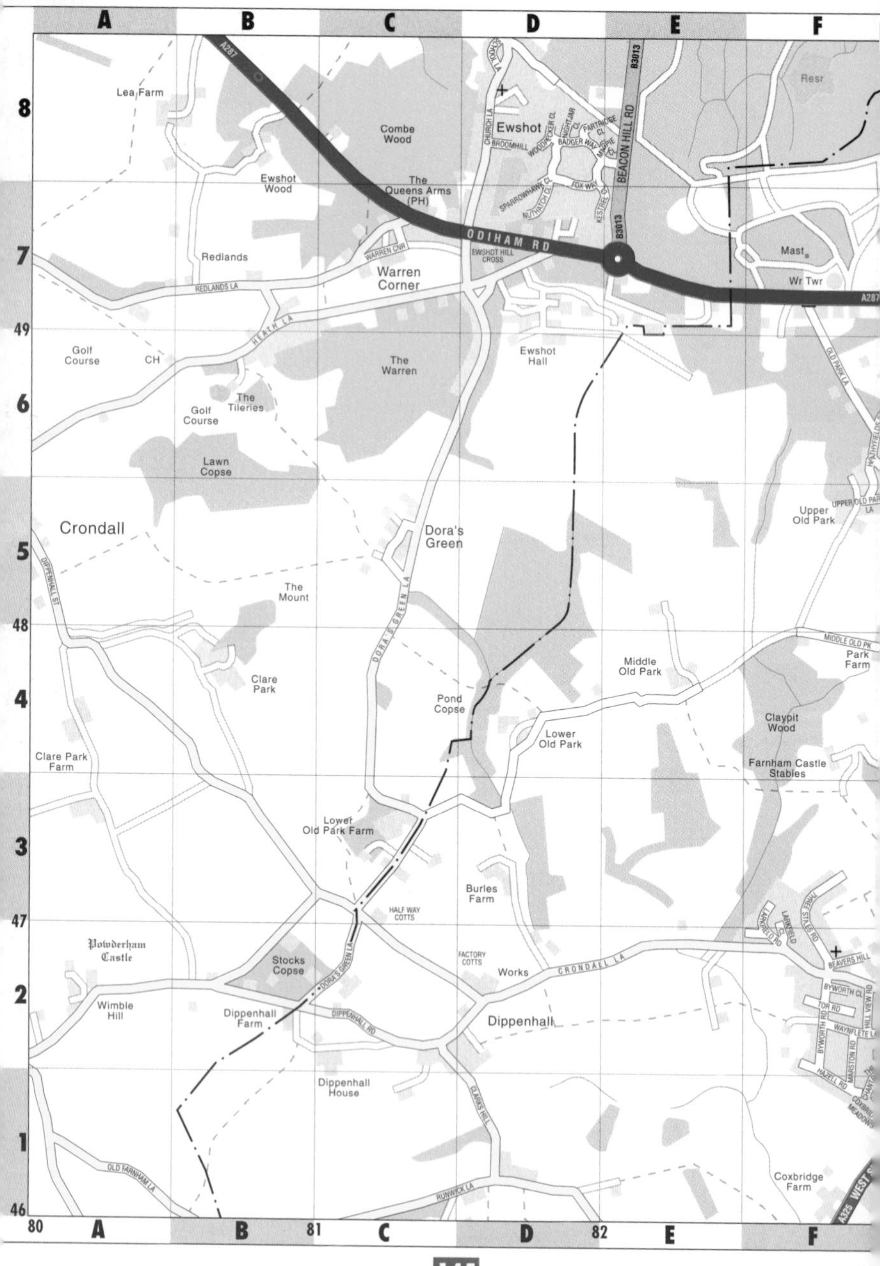

Lea Farm

A287

Combe
Wood

Ewshot

Ewshot
Wood

The Queens Arms
(PH)

ODIHAM RD

EWSHOT HILL
CROSS

BEACON HILL RD

B3013

B3013

Resr

Mast

Wr Twr

A287

8

Redlands

REDLANDS LA

HEATH LA

Warren
Corner

WARREN CNR

Ewshot
Hall

7

49

Golf
Course

CH

The Tileries

The
Warren

Dora's
Green

Upper
Old Park

UPPER OLD PARK LA

6

Golf
Course

Lawn
Copse

Crondall

The
Mount

DORA'S GREEN LA

Middle
Old Park

MIDDLE OLD PK

Park
Farm

5

DIPPENHALL ST

48

Clare
Park

Pond
Copse

Lower
Old Park

Claypit
Wood

Farnham Castle
Stables

4

Clare Park
Farm

Lower
Old Park Farm

Burles
Farm

BEAVERS HILL

3

47

Powderham
Castle

HALF WAY
COTTS

DIPPENHALL RD

Stocks
Copse

FACTORY
COTTS

Works

CRONDALL LA

BYWORTH CL

2

Wimble
Hill

Dippenhall
Farm

Dippenhall

HASTEL LA

Dippenhall
House

Coxbridge
Farm

A325 WEST ST

1

OLD KILN LA

RUNWICK LA

46

80 | A | B | 81 | C | D | 82 | E | F

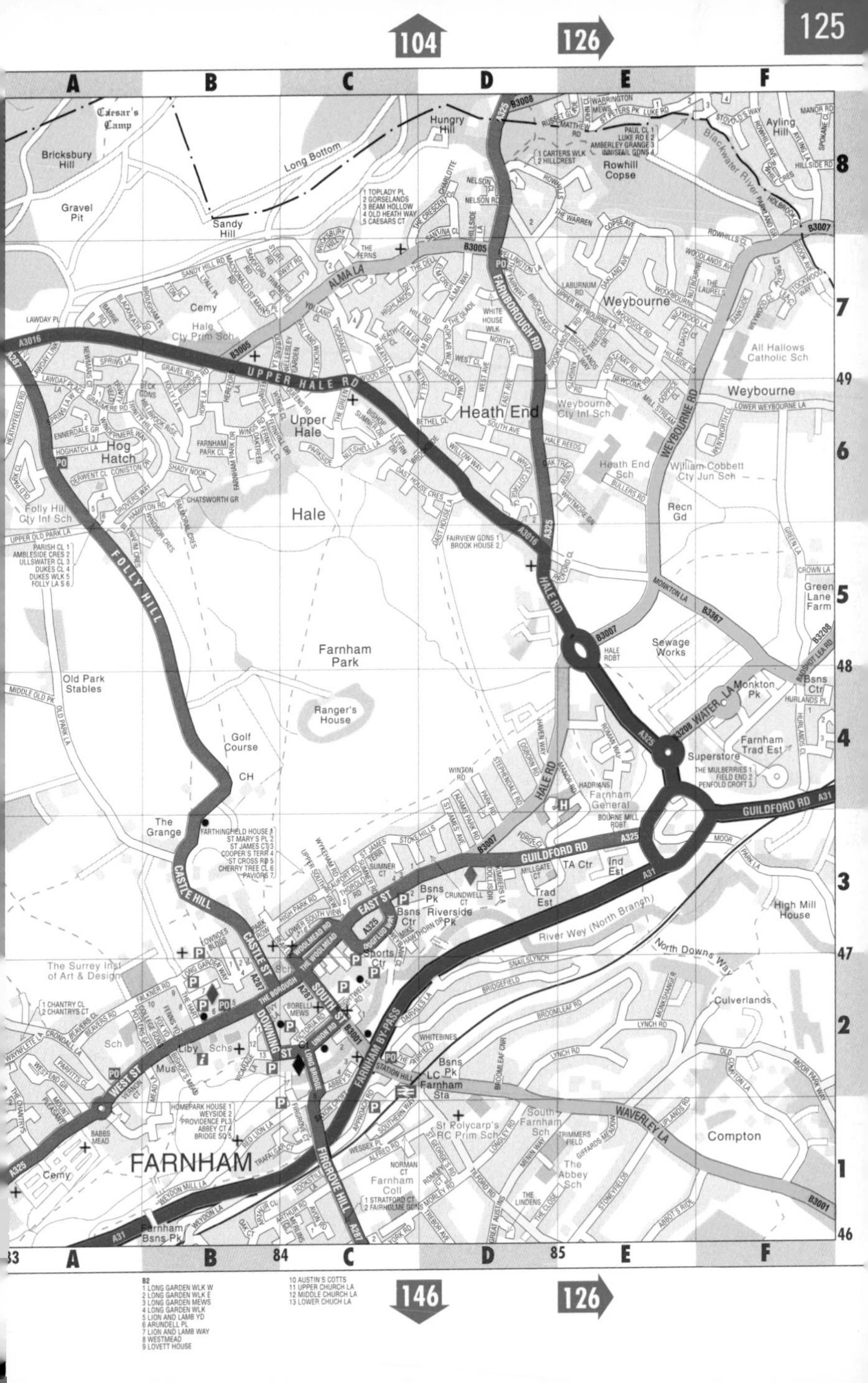

B2
1 LONG GARDEN WLK W
2 LONG GARDEN WLK E
3 LONG GARDEN MEWS
4 LONG GARDEN WLK
5 LION AND LAMB YD
6 ARUNDELL PL
7 LION AND LAMB WAY
8 WESTMEAD
9 LOVETT HOUSE

10 AUSTIN'S COTTS
11 UPPER CHURCH LA
12 MIDDLE CHURCH LA
13 LOWER CHUCH LA

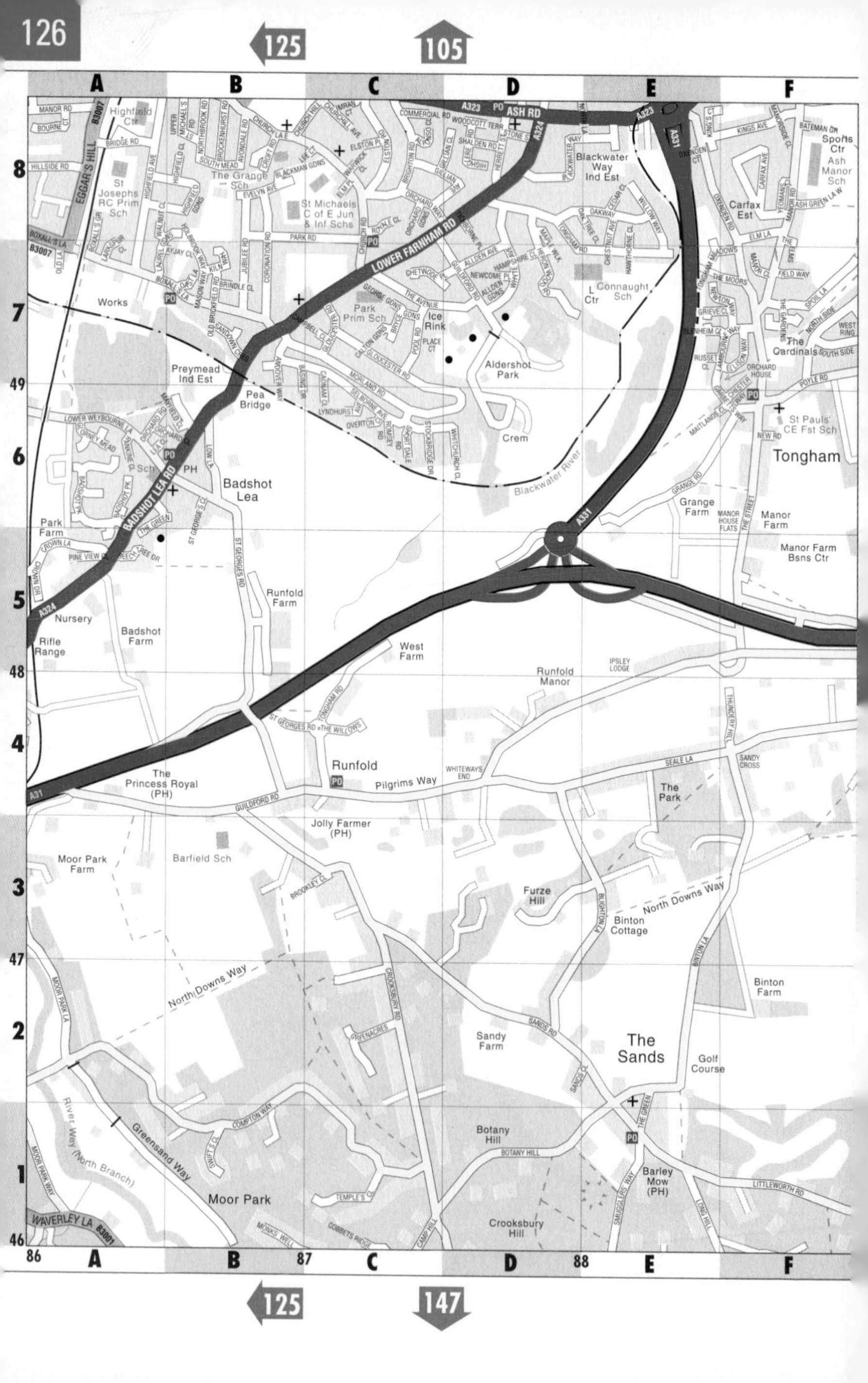

126
125
105
147
A
B
C
D
E
F
8
7
49
6
5
48
4
3
47
2
1
46
86
87
88
Highfield Ctr
St Josephs RC Prim Sch
The Grange Sch
St Michaels C of E Jun & Inf Schs
Blackwater Way Ind Est
Sports Ctr
Ash Manor Sch
Carfax Est
Works
Connaught Sch
L Ctr
Park Prim Sch
Ice Rink
Aldershot Park
Preymead Ind Est
Pea Bridge
Crem
Blackwater River
St Pauls' CE Fst Sch
Tongham
The Cardinals
Badshot Lea
P Sch
PH
Park Farm
Grange Farm
Manor Farm
Manor Farm Bsns Ctr
Nursery
Rifle Range
Badshot Farm
Runfold Farm
West Farm
Runfold Manor
Runfold
The Princess Royal (PH)
Pilgrims Way
Jolly Farmer (PH)
Moor Park Farm
Barfield Sch
The Park
Furze Hill
Binton Cottage
North Downs Way
Binton Farm
Sandy Farm
The Sands
Golf Course
Botany Hill
Barley Mow (PH)
Crooksbury Hill
Moor Park
Greensand Way
River Wey (North Branch)
ASH RD
A323
A324
A331
A31
B3007
B3001
LOWER FARNHAM RD
BADSHOT LEA RD
EGGAR'S HILL
GUILDFORD RD
SEALE LA
SANDS RD
BOTANY HILL
LITTLEWORTH RD
WAVERLEY LA
MOOR PARK LA
CROOKSBURY RD
BINTON LA
BLIGHTON LA
THUNDERY HILL
THE STREET
ST GEORGES RD
TONGHAM RD
COMPTON WAY

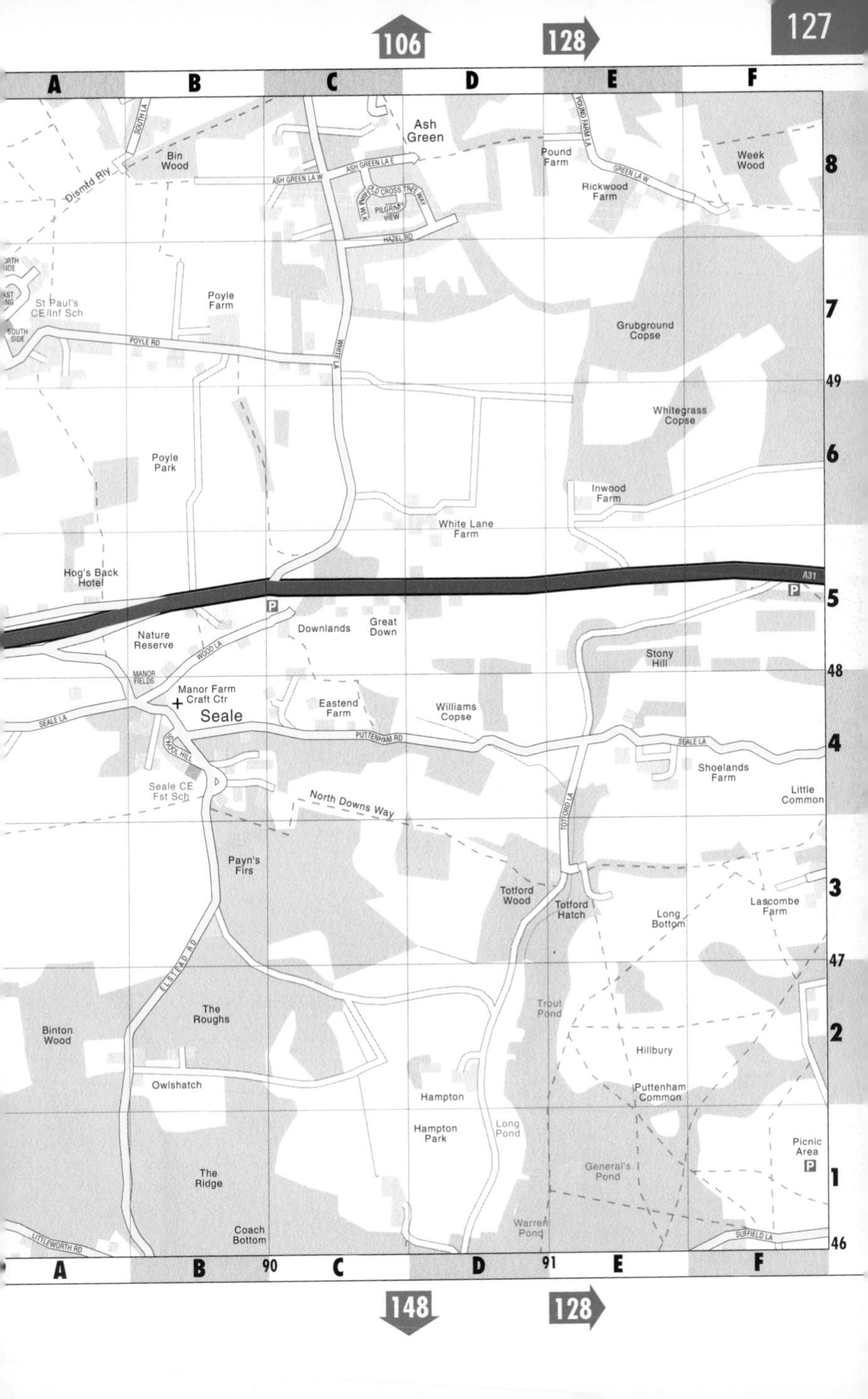
106
128
A
B
C
D
E
F
Ash Green
Bin Wood
Dismtd Rly
SOUTH LA
ASH GREEN LA W
ASH GREEN LA E
OLD CROSS TREE WAY
PILGRIMS VIEW
HAZEL RD
POUND FARM LA
Pound Farm
GREEN LA W
Rickwood Farm
Week Wood
8
St Paul's CE Inf Sch
Poyle Farm
POYLE RD
WHITE LA
Grubground Copse
7
49
Whitegrass Copse
Poyle Park
6
Inwood Farm
White Lane Farm
Hog's Back Hotel
A31
5
Nature Reserve
Downlands
Great Down
WOOD LA
MANOR FIELDS
Stony Hill
48
Manor Farm Craft Ctr
Seale
Eastend Farm
Williams Copse
SEALE LA
PUTTENHAM RD
SEALE LA
4
SCHOOL HILL
Shoelands Farm
Little Common
Seale CE Fst Sch
North Downs Way
TOTFORD LA
Payn's Firs
3
Totford Wood
Totford Hatch
Long Bottom
Lascombe Farm
ELSTEAD RD
47
The Roughs
Trout Pond
Binton Wood
2
Hillbury
Owlshatch
Puttenham Common
Hampton
Hampton Park
Long Pond
Picnic Area
The Ridge
General's Pond
1
Coach Bottom
Warren Pond
LITTLEWORTH RD
SUFFIELD LA
46
A
B
90
C
D
91
E
F
148
128

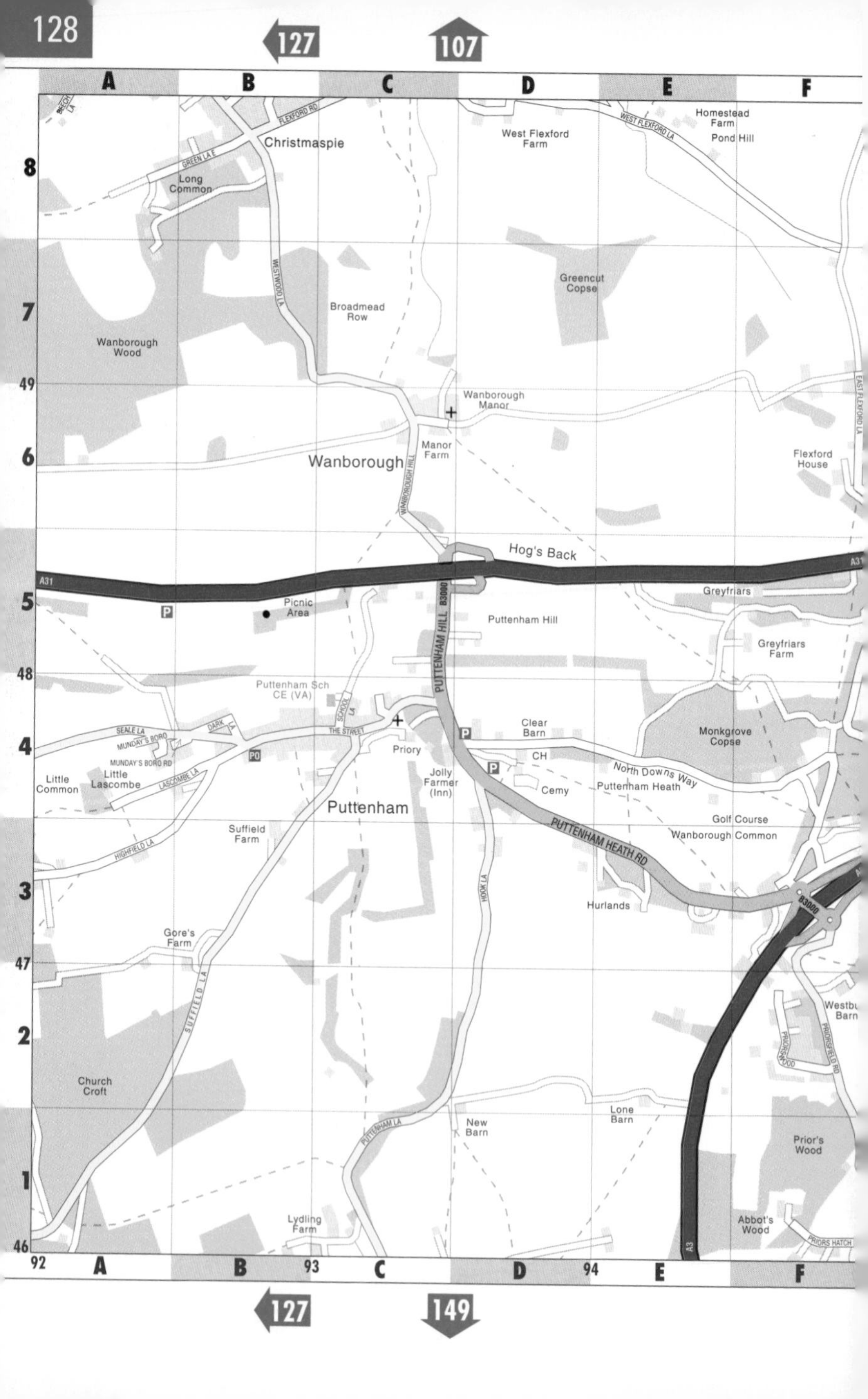
127
107
A
B
C
D
E
F
Christmaspie
FLEXFORD RD
GREEN LA E
Long Common
West Flexford Farm
WEST FLEXFORD LA
Homestead Farm
Pond Hill
8
WESTWOOD LA
Greencut Copse
Broadmead Row
7
Wanborough Wood
49
Wanborough Manor
Manor Farm
EAST FLEXFORD LA
Flexford House
6
Wanborough
WANBOROUGH HILL
Hog's Back
A31
B3000
Greyfriars
5
Picnic Area
Puttenham Hill
PUTTENHAM HILL
Greyfriars Farm
48
Puttenham Sch CE (VA)
SCHOOL LA
SEALE LA
MUNDAY'S BORO
DARK LA
THE STREET
Clear Barn
Monkgrove Copse
4
MUNDAY'S BORO RD
PO
Priory
CH
North Downs Way
Little Common
Little Lascombe
LASCOMBE LA
Jolly Farmer (Inn)
Cemy
Puttenham Heath
Puttenham
Golf Course
Suffield Farm
PUTTENHAM HEATH RD
Wanborough Common
HIGHFIELD LA
3
HOOK LA
Hurlands
B3000
Gore's Farm
47
SUFFIELD LA
Westbu Barn
2
PRIORSWOOD
PRIORSFIELD RD
Church Croft
PUTTENHAM LA
New Barn
Lone Barn
Prior's Wood
1
Lydling Farm
Abbot's Wood
PRIORS HATCH
A3
46
92
93
94
127
149

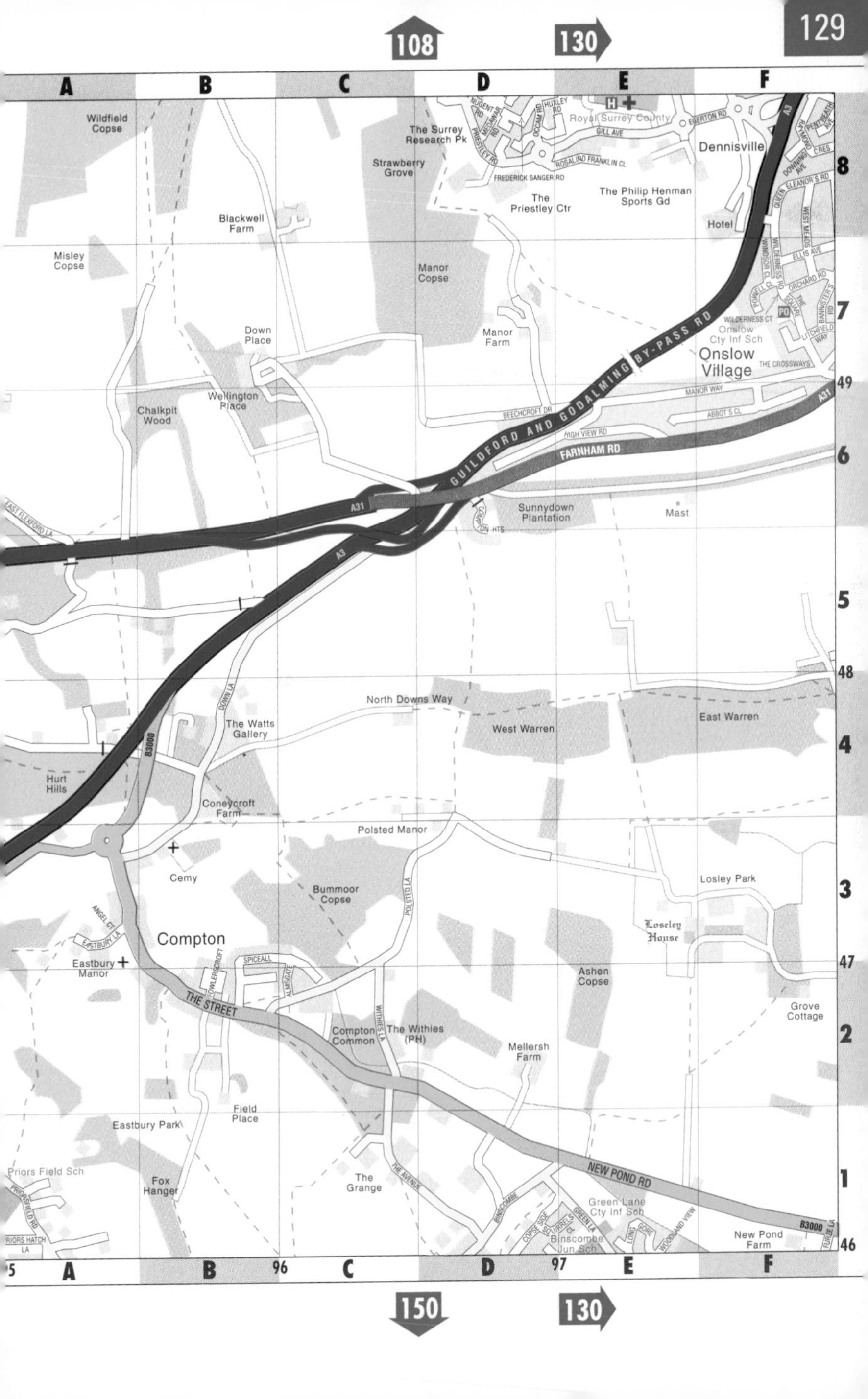
108
130
A
B
C
D
E
F
Wildfield Copse
Misley Copse
Blackwell Farm
Strawberry Grove
The Surrey Research Pk
Royal Surrey County
Dennisville
The Philip Henman Sports Gd
The Priestley Ctr
Hotel
Manor Copse
Manor Farm
Down Place
Wellington Place
Chalkpit Wood
Onslow Cty Inf Sch
Onslow Village
GUILDFORD AND GODALMING BY-PASS RD
FARNHAM RD
A3
A31
Sunnydown Plantation
Mast
North Downs Way
The Watts Gallery
West Warren
East Warren
Hurt Hills
Coneycroft Farm
Polsted Manor
Cemy
Bummoor Copse
Losley Park
Loseley House
Compton
Eastbury Manor
THE STREET
Compton Common
The Withies (PH)
Ashen Copse
Grove Cottage
Mellersh Farm
Field Place
Eastbury Park
Priors Field Sch
Fox Hanger
The Grange
NEW POND RD
Green Lane Cty Inf Sch
Binscombe Jun Sch
New Pond Farm
B3000
8
7
6
5
4
3
2
1
49
48
47
46
96
97
150
130

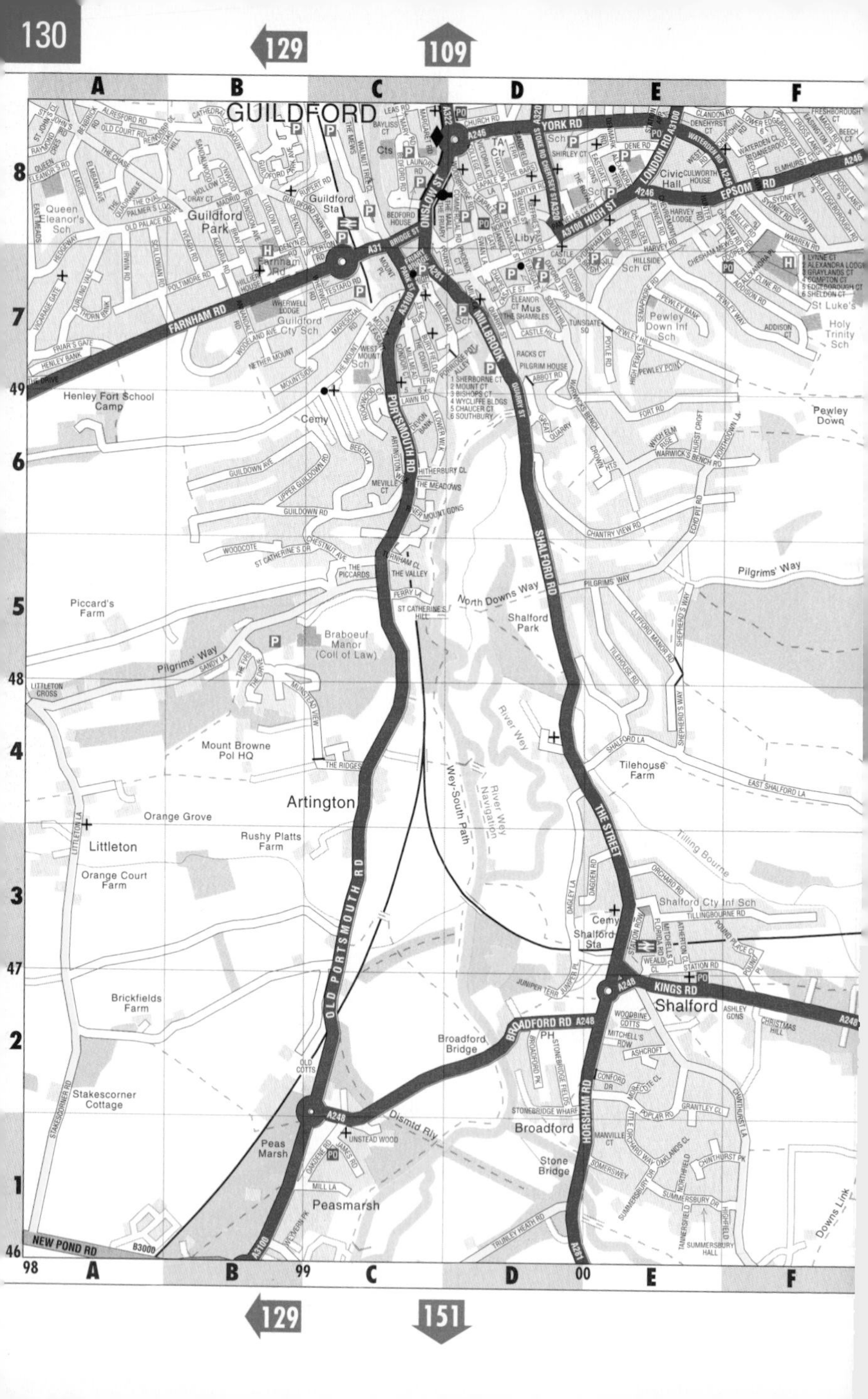
130
129
109
151
GUILDFORD
Guildford Park
Guildford Sta
Queen Eleanor's Sch
Guildford Cty Sch
Farnham Rd
FARNHAM RD
Henley Fort School Camp
Cemy
Civic Hall
YORK RD
EPSOM RD
LONDON RD
HIGH ST
ONSLOW ST
BRIDGE ST
MILLBROOK
PORTSMOUTH RD
SHALFORD RD
Pilgrims' Way
North Downs Way
Piccard's Farm
Braboeuf Manor (Coll of Law)
Shalford Park
Pewley Down
St Luke's
Holy Trinity Sch
Pewley Down Inf Sch
Mount Browne Pol HQ
Artington
Orange Grove
Littleton
Rushy Platts Farm
Orange Court Farm
Tilehouse Farm
River Wey
River Wey Navigation
Wey-South Path
Tilling Bourne
THE STREET
Shalford Cty Inf Sch
Shalford Sta
Shalford
KINGS RD
BROADFORD RD
Broadford Bridge
Brickfields Farm
OLD PORTSMOUTH RD
Stakescorner Cottage
Peas Marsh
Peasmarsh
Dismtd Rly
Broadford
Stone Bridge
HORSHAM RD
NEW POND RD
Downs Link
SUMMERSBURY HALL
1 SHERBORNE CT
2 MOUNT CT
3 BISHOPS CT
4 WYCLIFFE BLDGS
5 CHAUCER CT
6 SOUTHBURY
1 LYNNE CT
2 ALEXANDRA LODGE
3 GRAYLANDS CT
4 COMPTON CT
5 EDGEBOROUGH CT
6 SHELDON CT
A B C D E F
8 7 6 5 4 3 2 1
49 48 47 46
98 99 00

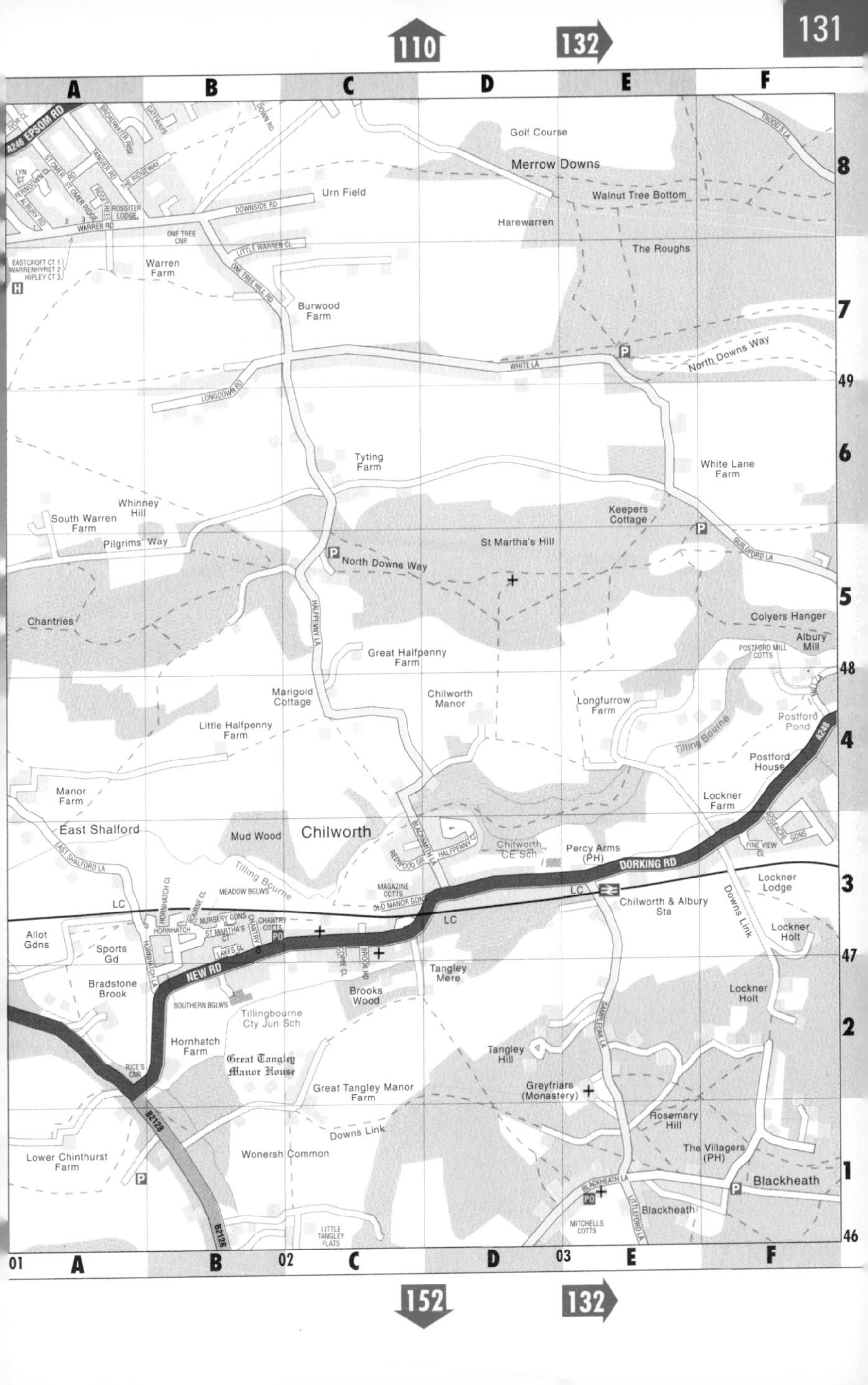
110
132
A
B
C
D
E
F
8
7
49
6
5
48
4
3
47
2
1
46
A246 EPSOM RD
BROADWATER RISE
GATEWAYS
DOWN RD
TANGIER RD
ST OMER RD
ST OMER RIDGE
THE RIDGEWAY
LYN CT
FERNDOWN CL
ALBURY RD
ROSETREES
ROSSITER LODGE
WARREN RD
DOWNSIDE RD
ONE TREE CNR
LITTLE WARREN CL
ONE TREE HILL RD
EASTCROFT CT 1
WARRENHYRST 2
HIPLEY CT 3
Golf Course
Merrow Downs
Walnut Tree Bottom
Urn Field
Harewarren
The Roughs
Warren Farm
Burwood Farm
WHITE LA
North Downs Way
LONGDOWN RD
TROOD'S LA
Tyting Farm
White Lane Farm
Whinney Hill
South Warren Farm
Pilgrims' Way
Keepers Cottage
St Martha's Hill
GUILDFORD LA
North Downs Way
Chantries
HALFPENNY LA
Colyers Hanger
Albury Mill
POSTFORD MILL COTTS
Great Halfpenny Farm
Marigold Cottage
Chilworth Manor
Longfurrow Farm
Little Halfpenny Farm
Postford Pond
Tilling Bourne
Postford House
A248
Manor Farm
Lockner Farm
East Shalford
Mud Wood
Chilworth
BLACKSMITH LA
HALFPENNY CL
REDWOOD GR
Chilworth CE Sch
Percy Arms (PH)
DORKING RD
ROSEACRE GDNS
PINE VIEW CL
EAST SHALFORD LA
Tilling Bourne
MEADOW BGLWS
MAGAZINE COTTS
OLD MANOR GDNS
Lockner Lodge
LC
HORNHATCH CL
BOURNE CL
NURSERY GDNS
CHANTRY COTTS
HORNHATCH
ST MARTHA'S CT
CHANTRY RD
LC
Chilworth & Albury Sta
Downs Link
Allot Gdns
Sports Gd
LAKES CL
PO
COPSE CL
BROOK RD
LC
Lockner Holt
HORNHATCH LA
NEW RD
Tangley Mere
Bradstone Brook
Brooks Wood
SOUTHERN BGLWS
Tillingbourne Cty Jun Sch
SAMPLEOAK LA
Lockner Holt
Hornhatch Farm
Great Tangley Manor House
Tangley Hill
RICE'S CNR
Great Tangley Manor Farm
Greyfriars (Monastery)
B2128
Rosemary Hill
Downs Link
Lower Chinthurst Farm
Wonersh Common
The Villagers (PH)
Blackheath
BLACKHEATH LA
PO
LITTLEFORD LA
Blackheath
MITCHELLS COTTS
LITTLE TANGLEY FLATS
B2128
01
02
03
152
132

131 111

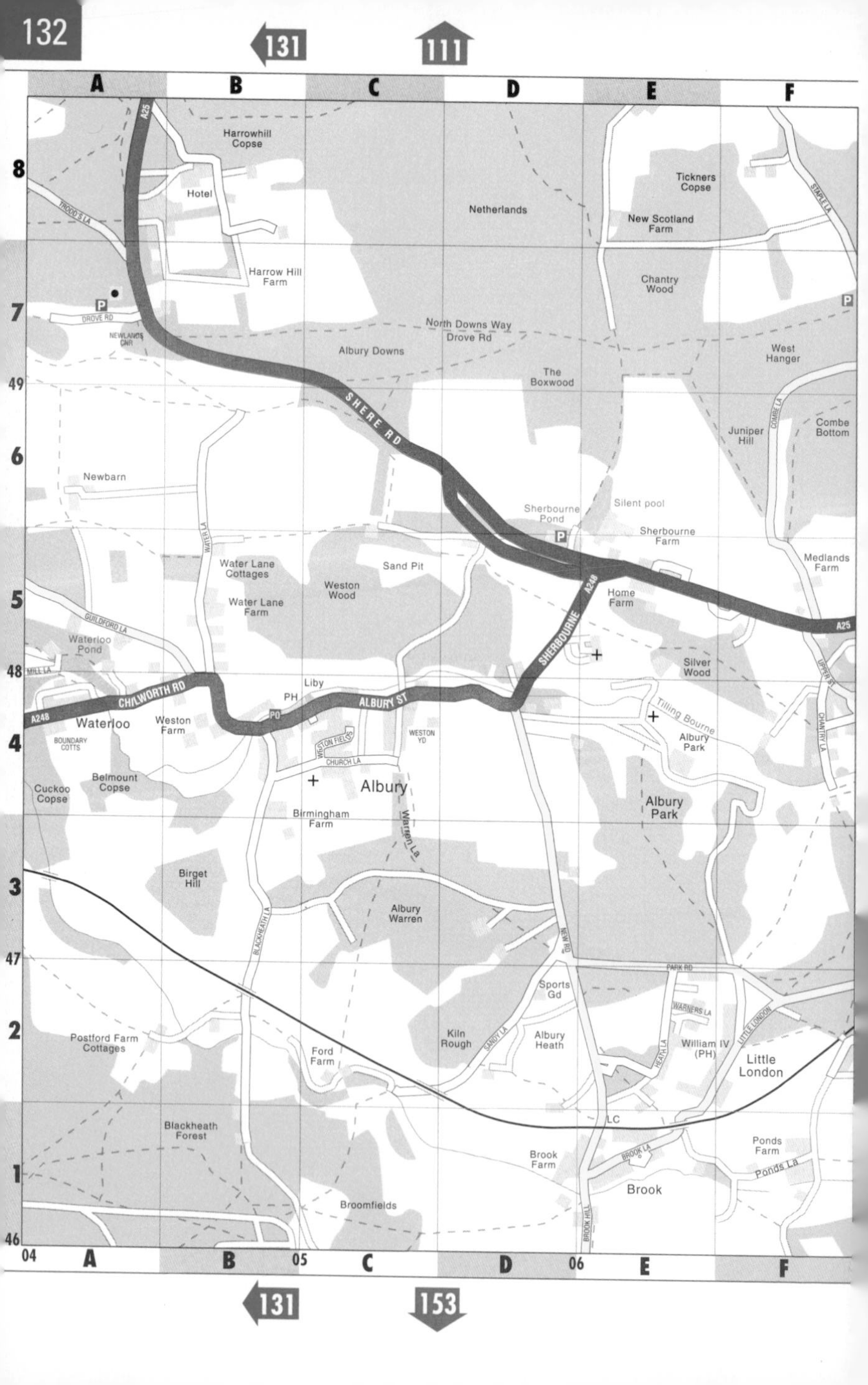
A
B
C
D
E
F
8
7
49
6
5
48
4
3
47
2
1
46
04
05
06
A25
Harrowhill Copse
Hotel
TROOD'S LA
Harrow Hill Farm
P
DROVE RD
NEWLANDS CNR
Netherlands
Tickners Copse
STAPLE LA
New Scotland Farm
Chantry Wood
North Downs Way
Drove Rd
Albury Downs
The Boxwood
West Hanger
SHERE RD
Juniper Hill
COMBE LA
Combe Bottom
Newbarn
Sherbourne Pond
Silent pool
Sherbourne Farm
Medlands Farm
WATER LA
Water Lane Cottages
Sand Pit
Weston Wood
Water Lane Farm
A248
Home Farm
SHERBOURNE
GUILDFORD LA
Waterloo Pond
MILL LA
Silver Wood
UPPER ST
Liby
PH
CHILWORTH RD
ALBURY ST
PO
Tilling Bourne
Waterloo
Weston Farm
WESTON FIELDS
WESTON YD
Albury Park
CHANTRY LA
BOUNDARY COTTS
CHURCH LA
Belmount Copse
Cuckoo Copse
Albury
Albury Park
Birmingham Farm
Warren La
Birget Hill
Albury Warren
BLACKHEATH LA
NEW RD
PARK RD
Sports Gd
WARNERS LA
Postford Farm Cottages
Kiln Rough
SANDY LA
Albury Heath
HEATH LA
William IV (PH)
LITTLE LONDON
Little London
Ford Farm
LC
Blackheath Forest
Ponds Farm
Brook Farm
BROOK LA
Ponds La
Brook
Broomfields
BROOK HILL

131 153

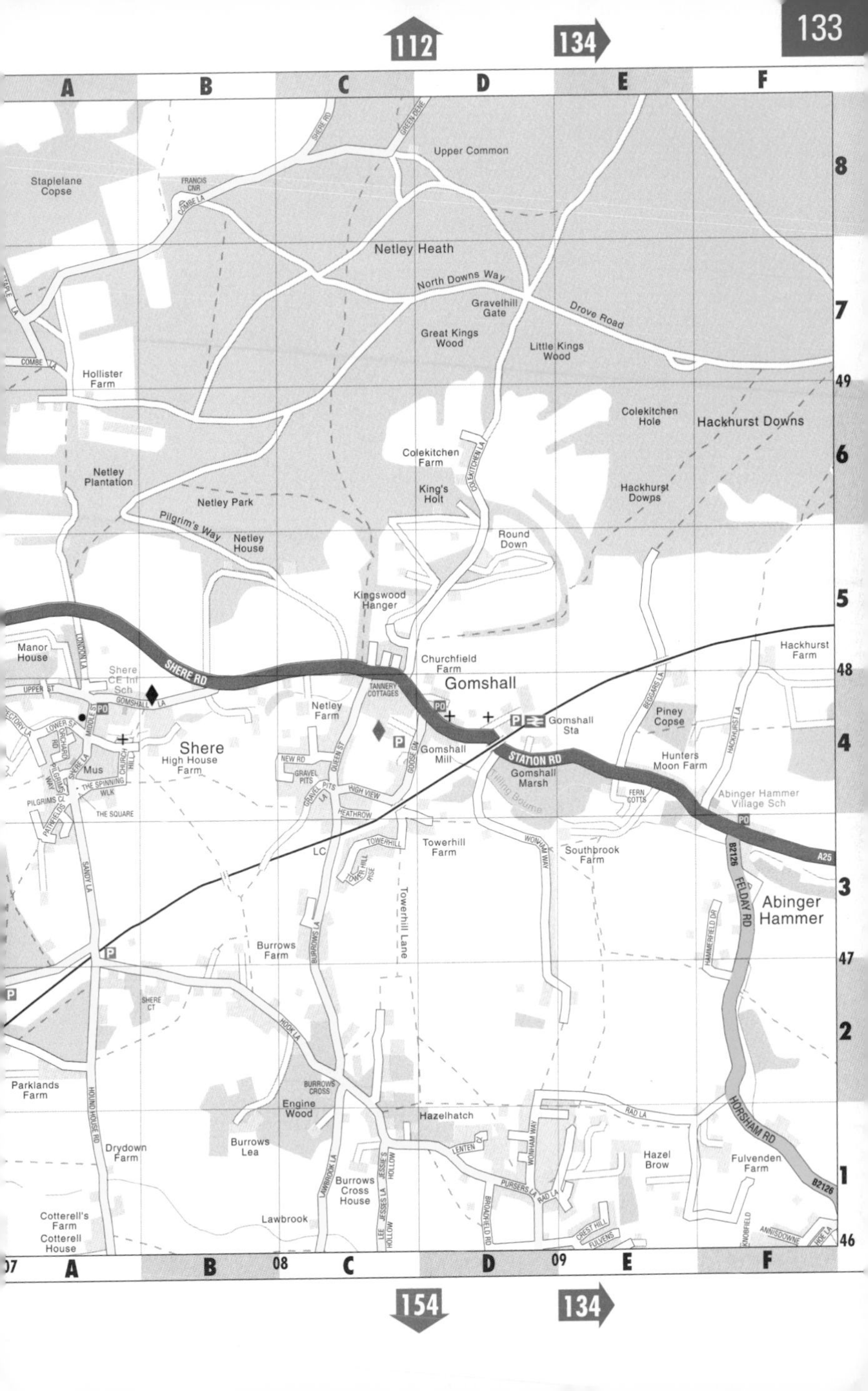
112
134
A
B
C
D
E
F
Upper Common
Staplelane Copse
FRANCIS CNR
COMBE LA
Netley Heath
North Downs Way
Gravelhill Gate
Drove Road
Great Kings Wood
Little Kings Wood
COMBE LA
Hollister Farm
Colekitchen Hole
Hackhurst Downs
Colekitchen Farm
COLEKITCHEN LA
Netley Plantation
King's Holt
Hackhurst Downs
Netley Park
Pilgrim's Way
Netley House
Round Down
Kingswood Hanger
Manor House
LONDON LA
SHERE RD
Churchfield Farm
Hackhurst Farm
Shere CE Inf Sch
Gomshall
UPPER ST
GOMSHALL LA
TANNERY COTTAGES
Netley Farm
PO
Gomshall Sta
Piney Copse
BEGGARS LA
Shere
High House Farm
Mus
NEW RD
GRAVEL PITS
QUEEN ST
GOOSE GN
Gomshall Mill
STATION RD
Gomshall Marsh
Tilling Bourne
Hunters Moon Farm
HACKHURST LA
FERN COTTS
Abinger Hammer Village Sch
THE SPINNING WLK
THE SQUARE
PILGRIMS CL
HIGH VIEW
HEATHROW
LC
TOWERHILL
TOWER HILL RISE
Towerhill Farm
WONHAM WAY
Southbrook Farm
A25
B2126
FELDAY RD
SANDY LA
Towerhill Lane
Abinger Hammer
HAMMERFIELD DR
Burrows Farm
BURROWS LA
P
SHERE CT
HOOK LA
Parklands Farm
HOUND HOUSE RD
BURROWS CROSS
Engine Wood
Hazelhatch
RAD LA
HORSHAM RD
Drydown Farm
Burrows Lea
LENTEN
Hazel Brow
Fulvenden Farm
Burrows Cross House
LAWBROOK LA
JESSIE'S HOLLOW
PURSERS LA
RAD LA
Cotterell's Farm
Cotterell House
Lawbrook
BROADFIELD RD
CREST HILL
FULVENS
ANNISDOWNE
HOE LA
KNOBFIELD
8
7
49
6
5
48
4
3
47
2
1
46
07
08
09
154
134

133
113

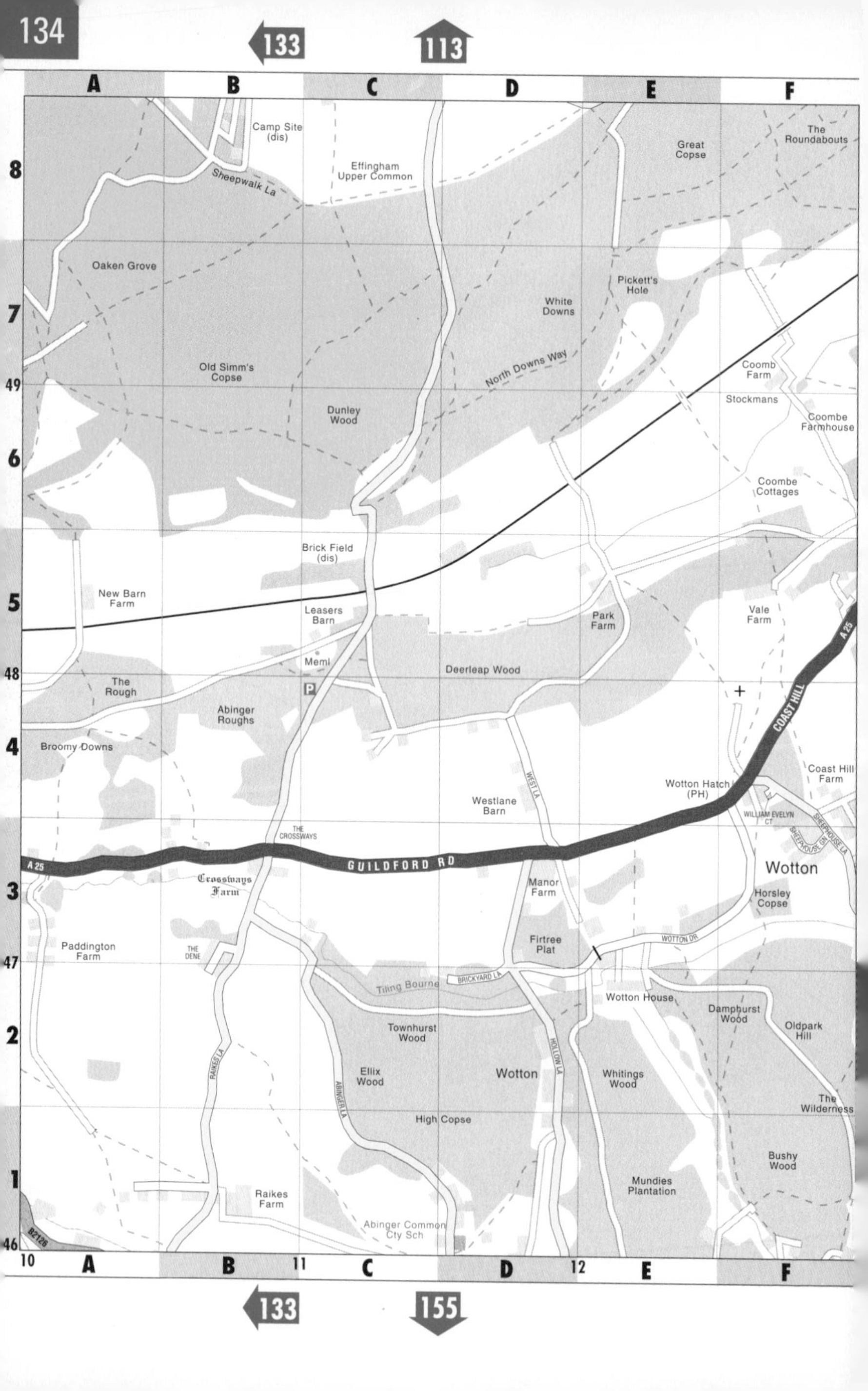
A
B
C
D
E
F
Camp Site (dis)
Effingham Upper Common
Great Copse
The Roundabouts
Sheepwalk La
Oaken Grove
Pickett's Hole
White Downs
Old Simm's Copse
North Downs Way
Coomb Farm
Stockmans
Dunley Wood
Coombe Farmhouse
Coombe Cottages
Brick Field (dis)
New Barn Farm
Leasers Barn
Park Farm
Vale Farm
A 25
Meml
Deerleap Wood
The Rough
Abinger Roughs
COAST HILL
Broomy Downs
WEST LA
Coast Hill Farm
Wotton Hatch (PH)
Westlane Barn
WILLIAM EVELYN CT
SHEEPHOUSE LA
SHEEPHOUSE GN
THE CROSSWAYS
A 25
GUILDFORD RD
Wotton
Crossways Farm
Manor Farm
Horsley Copse
Paddington Farm
THE DENE
Firtree Plat
WOTTON DR
BRICKYARD LA
Tiling Bourne
Wotton House
Damphurst Wood
Townhurst Wood
Oldpark Hill
RAIKES LA
HOLLOW LA
Ellix Wood
Wotton
Whitings Wood
ABINGER LA
High Copse
The Wilderness
Bushy Wood
Mundies Plantation
Raikes Farm
Abinger Common Cty Sch
B2126
8
7
49
6
5
48
4
3
47
2
1
46
10
11
12

133
155

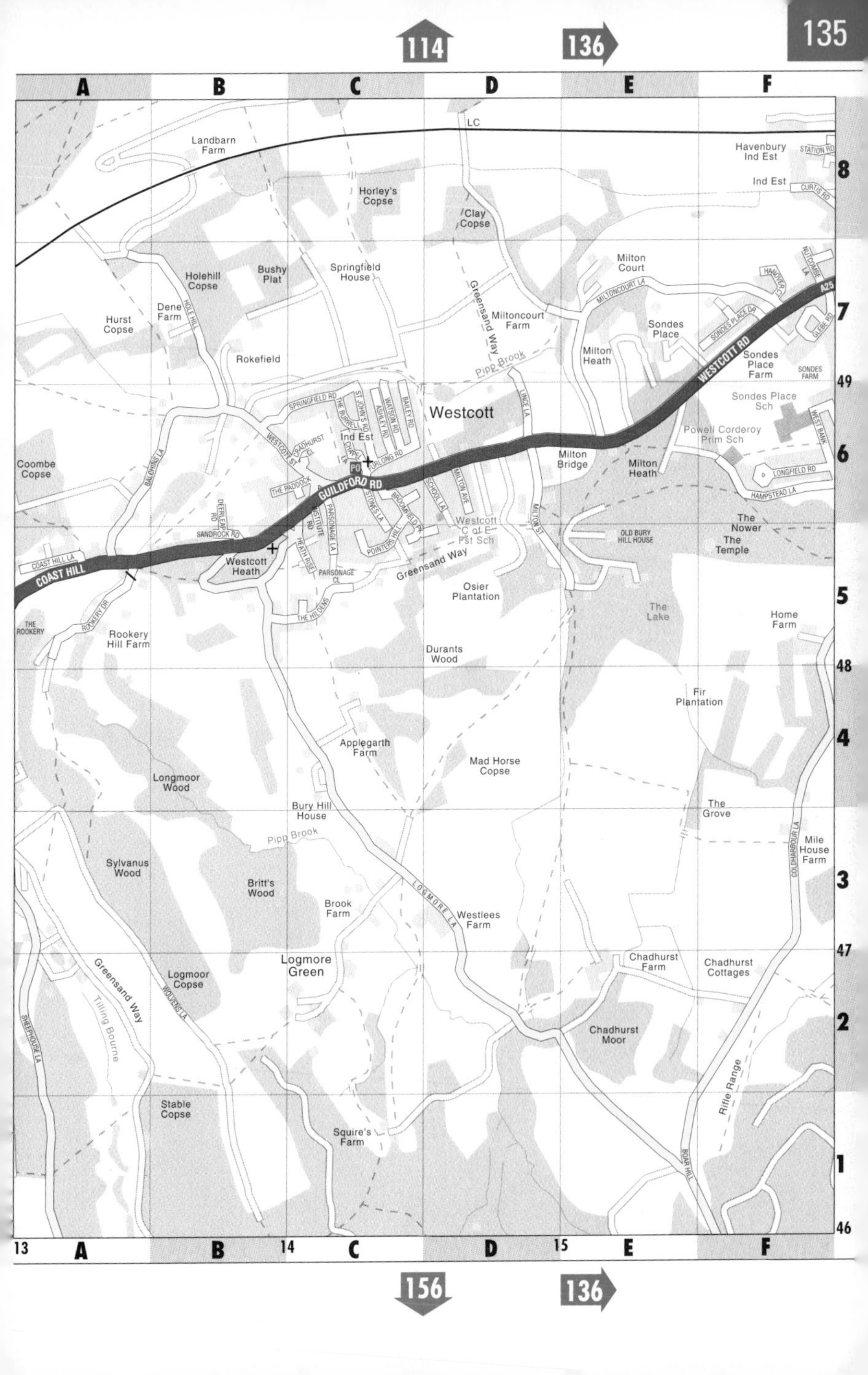
114
136
A
B
C
D
E
F
Landbarn Farm
Horley's Copse
Clay Copse
Havenbury Ind Est
Ind Est
Holehill Copse
Bushy Plat
Springfield House
Milton Court
Hurst Copse
Dene Farm
Miltoncourt Farm
Sondes Place
Greensand Way
Rokefield
Milton Heath
Sondes Place Farm
Pipp Brook
Westcott
Sondes Place Sch
Ind Est
Powell Corderoy Prim Sch
Coombe Copse
Milton Bridge
Milton Heath
GUILDFORD RD
WESTCOTT RD
COAST HILL
Westcott C of E Fst Sch
The Nower
The Temple
Westcott Heath
Greensand Way
Osier Plantation
The Lake
Home Farm
Rookery Hill Farm
Durants Wood
Fir Plantation
Applegarth Farm
Mad Horse Copse
Longmoor Wood
Bury Hill House
The Grove
Pipp Brook
Mile House Farm
Sylvanus Wood
Britt's Wood
Brook Farm
Westlees Farm
Logmore Green
Chadhurst Farm
Chadhurst Cottages
Logmoor Copse
Greensand Way
Tilling Bourne
Chadhurst Moor
Rifle Range
Stable Copse
Squire's Farm
13
14
15
156
136

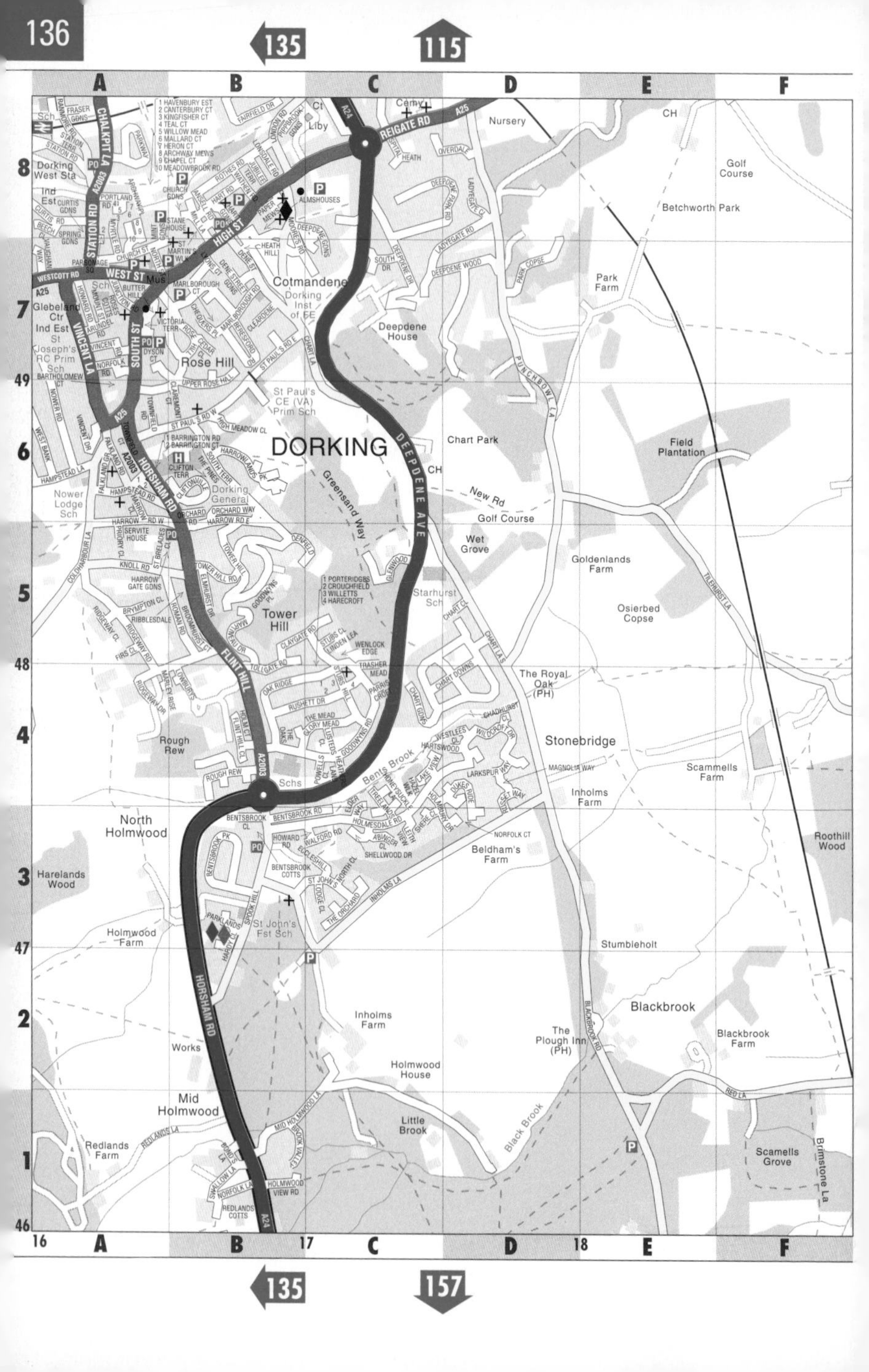
135
115
A
B
C
D
E
F
8
7
49
6
5
48
4
3
47
2
1
46
16
17
18
DORKING
Dorking West Sta
Ind Est
Cotmandene
Dorking Inst of FE
Deepdene House
Rose Hill
St Paul's CE (VA) Prim Sch
Chart Park
Greensand Way
DEEPDENE AVE
New Rd
Golf Course
Wet Grove
Nursery
Golf Course
Betchworth Park
Park Farm
Field Plantation
Goldenlands Farm
Osierbed Copse
Starhurst Sch
Tower Hill
The Royal Oak (PH)
Stonebridge
Scammells Farm
Inholms Farm
Beldham's Farm
Roothill Wood
North Holmwood
Harelands Wood
Holmwood Farm
St John's Fst Sch
Stumbleholt
Blackbrook
Blackbrook Farm
The Plough Inn (PH)
Inholms Farm
Holmwood House
Works
Mid Holmwood
Little Brook
Black Brook
Redlands Farm
Scammells Grove
Brimstone La
Rough Rew
Bents Brook
Nower Lodge Sch
Glebelands Ctr
Ind Est
St Joseph's RC Prim Sch
Dorking General
REIGATE RD
HIGH ST
WEST ST
WESTCOTT RD
STATION RD
CHALKPIT LA
VINCENT LA
SOUTH ST
HORSHAM RD
FLINT HILL
PUNCHBOWL LA
TILEHURST LA
BLACKBROOK RD
RED LA
A24
A25
A2003
1 HAVENBURY EST
2 CANTERBURY CT
3 KINGFISHER CT
4 TEAL CT
5 WILLOW MEAD
6 MALLARD CT
7 HERON CT
8 ARCHWAY MEWS
9 CHAPEL CT
10 MEADOWBROOK RD
1 BARRINGTON RD
2 BARRINGTON CT
1 PORTERIDGES
2 CROUCHFIELD
3 WILLETTS
4 HARECROFT
135
157

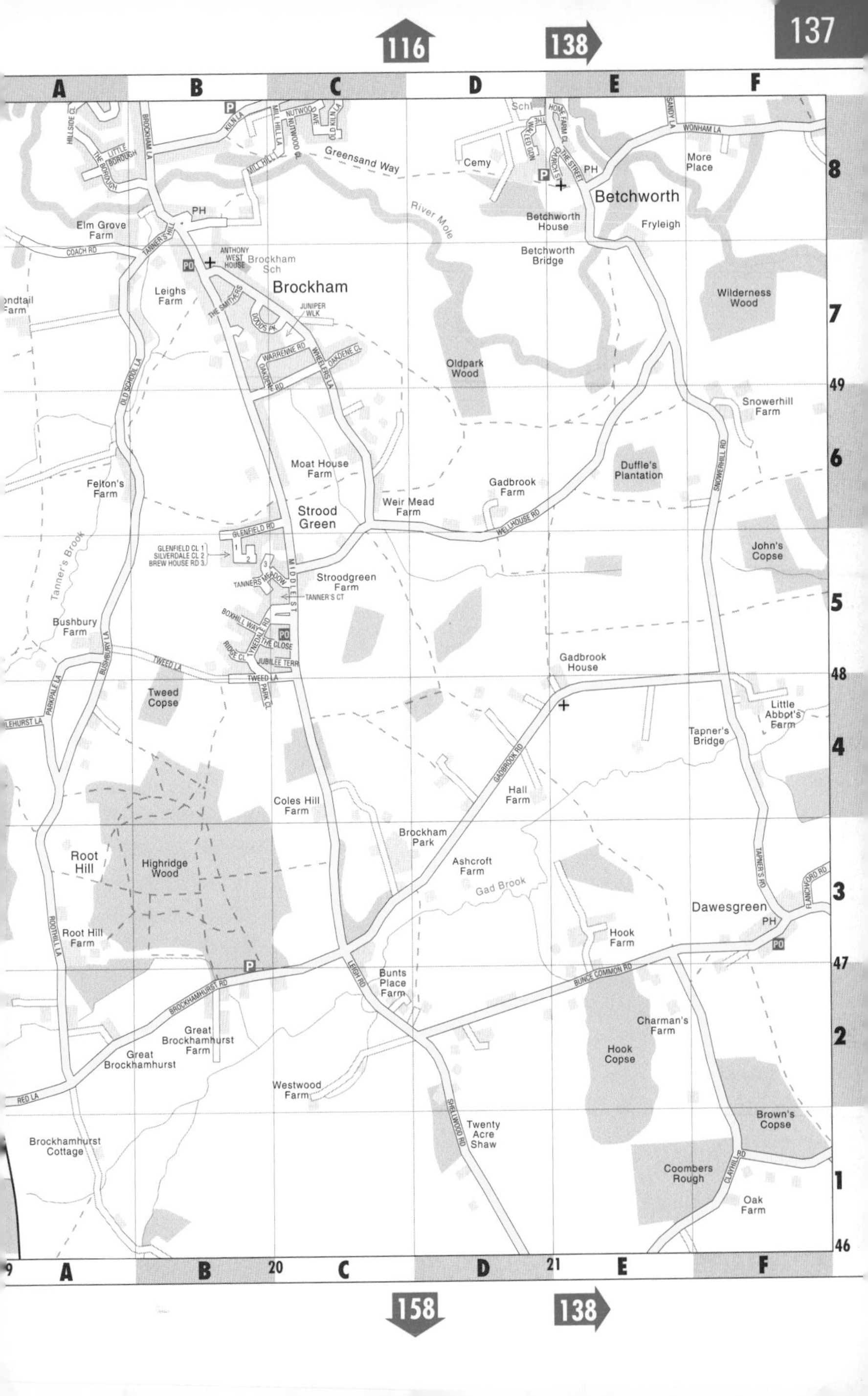
116
138
A
B
C
D
E
F
Greensand Way
Cemy
River Mole
Betchworth
Betchworth House
Betchworth Bridge
Fryleigh
More Place
Elm Grove Farm
Brockham
Brockham Sch
Leighs Farm
Wilderness Wood
Oldpark Wood
Snowerhill Farm
Moat House Farm
Duffle's Plantation
Felton's Farm
Gadbrook Farm
Weir Mead Farm
Strood Green
John's Copse
Tanner's Brook
Stroodgreen Farm
Bushbury Farm
Gadbrook House
Tweed Copse
Little Abbot's Farm
Tapner's Bridge
Coles Hill Farm
Hall Farm
Root Hill
Highridge Wood
Brockham Park
Ashcroft Farm
Gad Brook
Dawesgreen
Root Hill Farm
Hook Farm
Bunts Place Farm
Charman's Farm
Great Brockhamhurst Farm
Great Brockhamhurst
Hook Copse
Westwood Farm
Brown's Copse
Twenty Acre Shaw
Brockhamhurst Cottage
Coombers Rough
Oak Farm
158
138

137
117

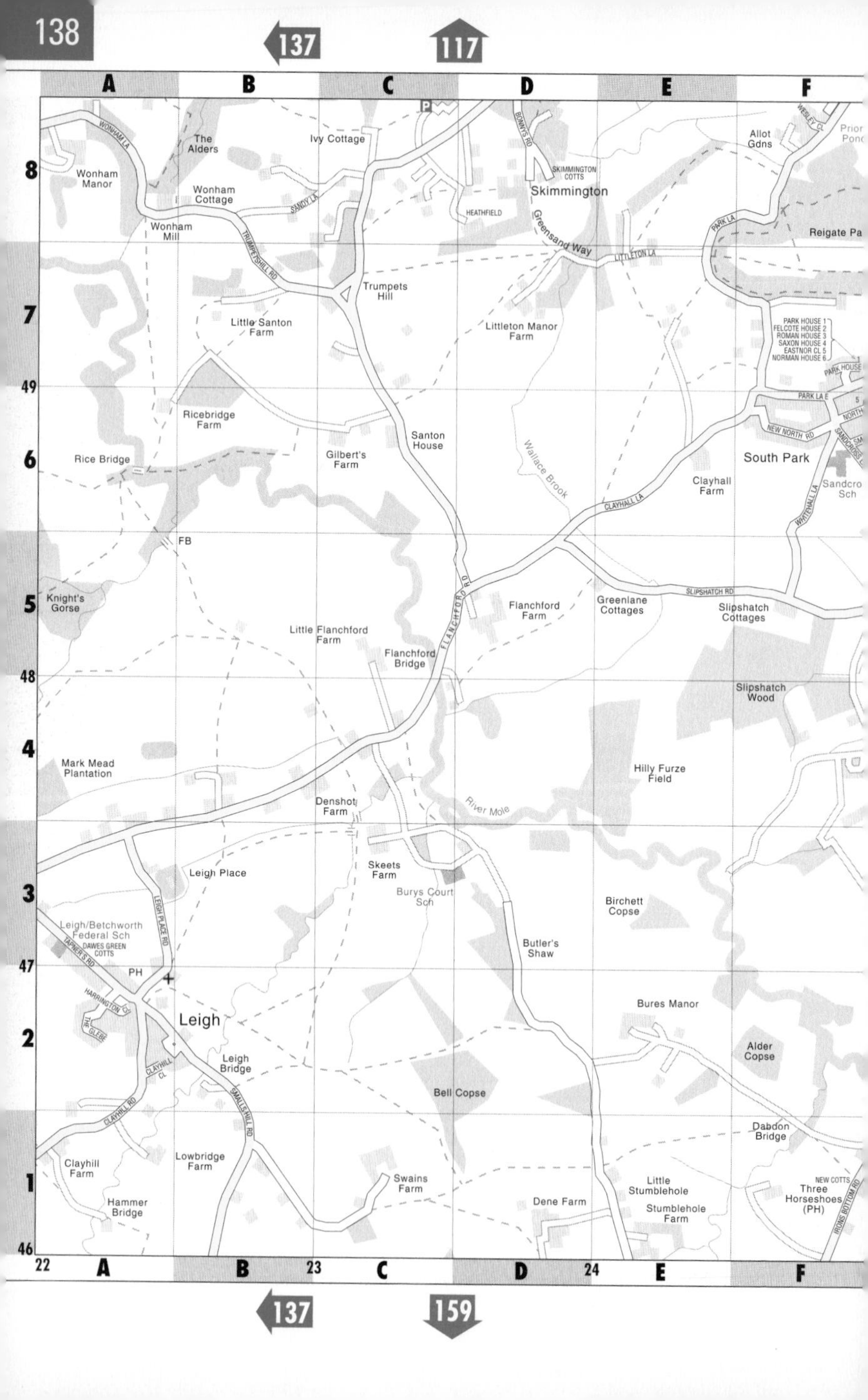
A
B
C
D
E
F
8
7
49
6
5
48
4
3
47
2
1
46
22
23
24
Wonham Manor
The Alders
Ivy Cottage
Wonham Cottage
Wonham Mill
SANDY LA
WONHAM LA
TRUMPETSHILL RD
Trumpets Hill
BONNY'S RD
SKIMMINGTON COTTS
Skimmington
HEATHFIELD
Greensand Way
LITTLETON LA
Allot Gdns
WESLEY CL
PARK LA
Reigate Pa
Little Santon Farm
Littleton Manor Farm
PARK HOUSE 1
FELCOTE HOUSE 2
ROMAN HOUSE 3
SAXON HOUSE 4
EASTNOR CL 5
NORMAN HOUSE 6
PARK HOUSE
PARK LA E
NEW NORTH RD
Ricebridge Farm
Santon House
Gilbert's Farm
Rice Bridge
Wallace Brook
South Park
Clayhall Farm
CLAYHALL LA
WHITEHALL LA
FB
FLANCHFORD RD
SLIPSHATCH RD
Knight's Gorse
Flanchford Farm
Greenlane Cottages
Slipshatch Cottages
Little Flanchford Farm
Flanchford Bridge
Slipshatch Wood
Mark Mead Plantation
Hilly Furze Field
River Mole
Denshot Farm
Skeets Farm
Burys Court Sch
Leigh Place
Leigh/Betchworth Federal Sch
DAWES GREEN COTTS
TAPNER'S RD
LEIGH PLACE RD
Birchett Copse
Butler's Shaw
PH
HARRINGTON CL
THE GLEBE
Leigh
Bures Manor
Leigh Bridge
CLAYHILL CL
SMALLSHILL RD
Alder Copse
Bell Copse
CLAYHILL RD
Dabdon Bridge
Clayhill Farm
Lowbridge Farm
Swains Farm
Little Stumblehole
Stumblehole Farm
Dene Farm
NEW COTTS
Three Horseshoes (PH)
IRONS BOTTOM RD
Hammer Bridge

137
159

118
140

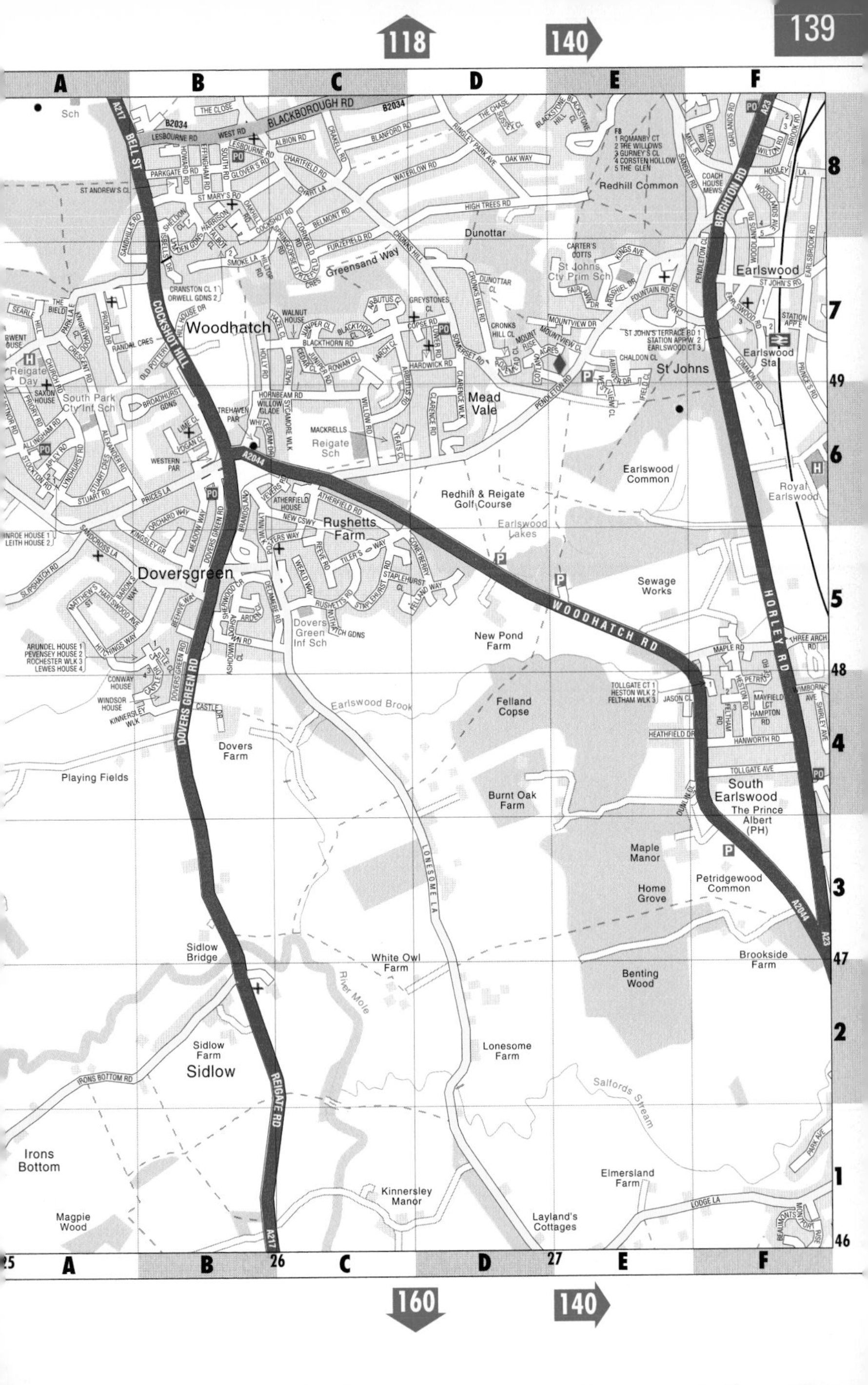
A
B
C
D
E
F
8
7
49
6
5
48
4
3
47
2
1
46
25
26
27
Woodhatch
Doversgreen
Sidlow
St Johns
Mead Vale
Earlswood
South Earlswood
Redhill Common
Dunottar
Rushetts Farm
Earlswood Common
Redhill & Reigate Golf Course
Earlswood Lakes
Sewage Works
New Pond Farm
Felland Copse
Burnt Oak Farm
Maple Manor
Home Grove
Petridgewood Common
The Prince Albert (PH)
Brookside Farm
Benting Wood
Lonesome Farm
White Owl Farm
Sidlow Bridge
Sidlow Farm
Irons Bottom
Magpie Wood
Kinnersley Manor
Layland's Cottages
Elmersland Farm
Dovers Farm
Playing Fields
Earlswood Brook
River Mole
Salfords Stream
Reigate Sch
Dovers Green Inf Sch
South Park Cty Inf Sch
St Johns Cty Prim Sch
Earlswood Sta
Royal Earlswood
Greensand Way
BELL ST
COCKSHOT HILL
DOVERS GREEN RD
REIGATE RD
WOODHATCH RD
HORLEY RD
BRIGHTON RD
BLACKBOROUGH RD
LONESOME LA
A217
A2044
A23
B2034
F8
1 ROMANBY CT
2 THE WILLOWS
3 GURNEY'S CL
4 CORSTEN HOLLOW
5 THE GLEN
CRANSTON CL 1
ORWELL GDNS 2
ST JOHN'S TERRACE RD 1
STATION APP W. 2
EARLSWOOD CT 3
ARUNDEL HOUSE 1
PEVENSEY HOUSE 2
ROCHESTER WLK 3
LEWES HOUSE 4
TOLLGATE CT 1
HESTON RD 2
FELTHAM WLK 3

160
140

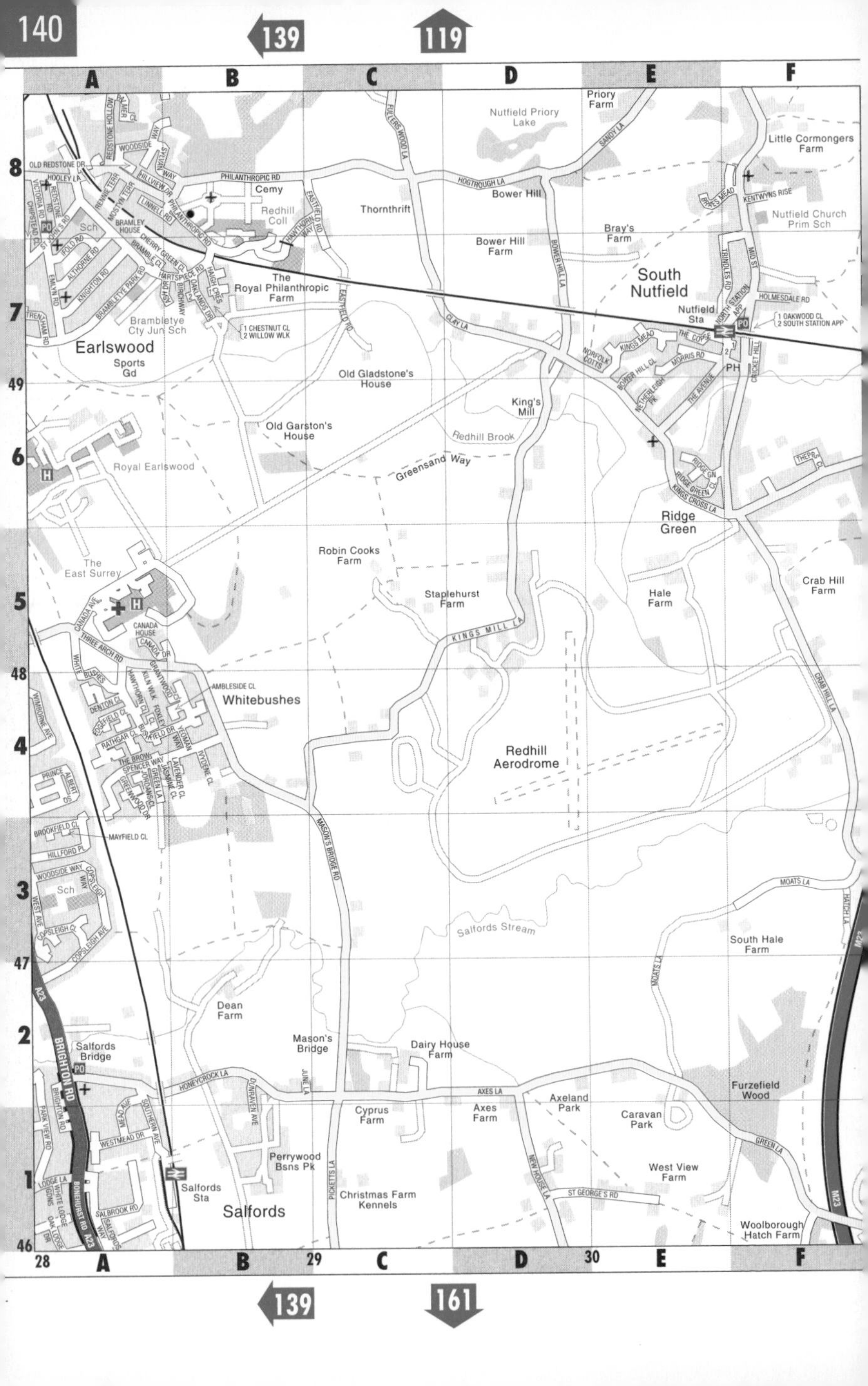
139
119
A
B
C
D
E
F
Priory Farm
Nutfield Priory Lake
Little Cormongers Farm
OLD REDSTONE DR
HOOLEY LA
PHILANTHROPIC RD
Cemy
Redhill Coll
HOGTROUGH LA
Bower Hill
Thornthrift
KENTWYNS RISE
Nutfield Church Prim Sch
Bray's Farm
Bower Hill Farm
South Nutfield
The Royal Philanthropic Farm
HOLMESDALE RD
Nutfield Sta
1 OAKWOOD CL
2 SOUTH STATION APP
1 CHESTNUT CL
2 WILLOW WLK
Brambletye Cty Jun Sch
Earlswood
Sports Gd
Old Gladstone's House
King's Mill
Old Garston's House
Redhill Brook
Greensand Way
Royal Earlswood
Ridge Green
KINGS CROSS LA
Robin Cooks Farm
The East Surrey
Staplehurst Farm
Hale Farm
Crab Hill Farm
KINGS MILL LA
CANADA HOUSE
AMBLESIDE CL
Whitebushes
Redhill Aerodrome
CRAB HILL LA
MAYFIELD CL
MASON'S BRIDGE RD
MOATS LA
Salfords Stream
South Hale Farm
Dean Farm
Salfords Bridge
Mason's Bridge
Dairy House Farm
BRIGHTON RD
HONEYCROCK LA
AXES LA
Axeland Park
Furzefield Wood
Cyprus Farm
Axes Farm
Caravan Park
GREEN LA
Perrywood Bsns Pk
West View Farm
Salfords Sta
Christmas Farm Kennels
ST GEORGE'S RD
Salfords
Woolborough Hatch Farm
M23
A23
28
29
30
46
47
48
49
1
2
3
4
5
6
7
8
161

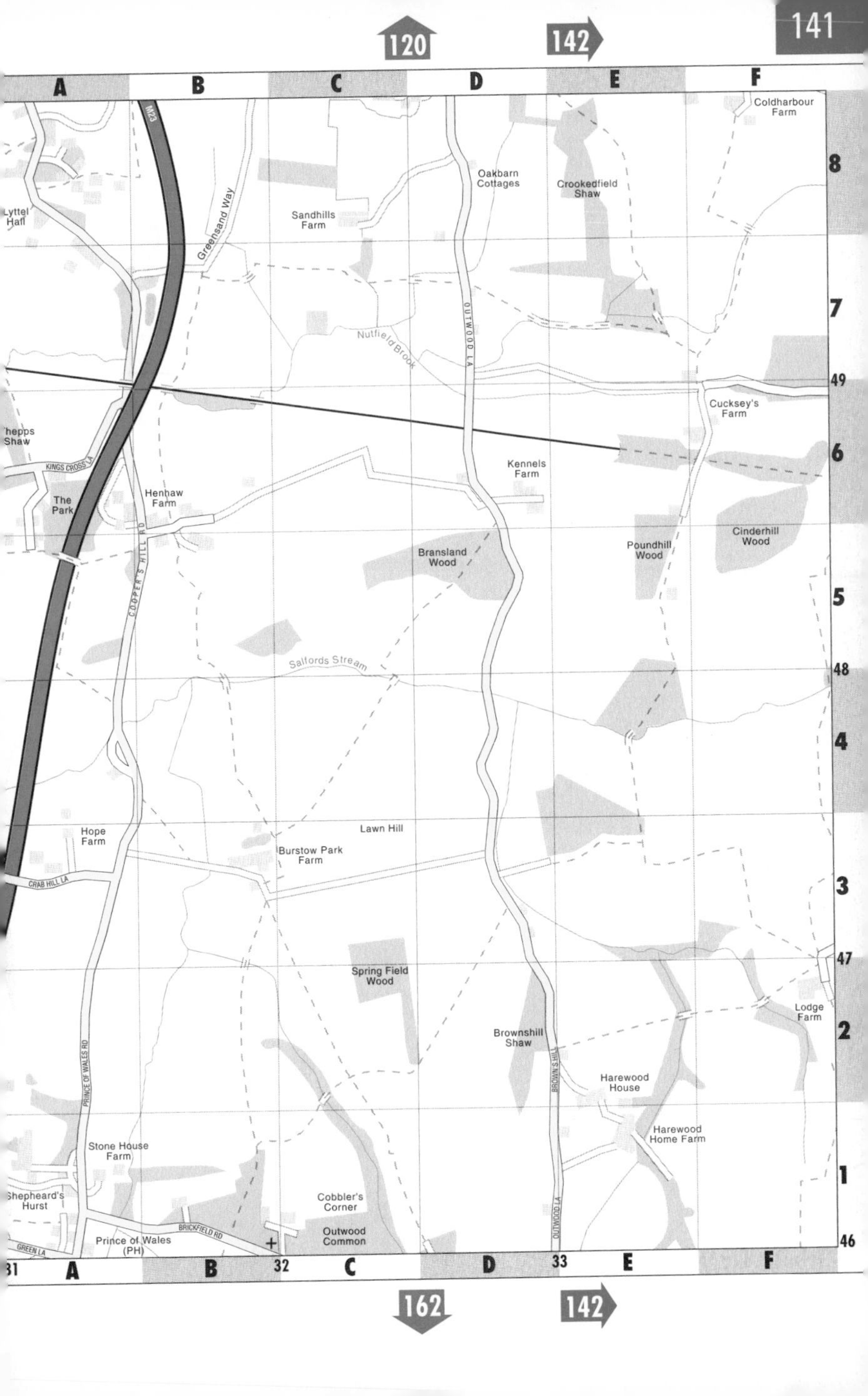

120
142
162
142

A   B   C   D   E   F

8
7
49
6
5
48
4
3
47
2
1
46

Coldharbour Farm

Lyttel Hall

Greensand Way

Sandhills Farm

Oakbarn Cottages

Crookedfield Shaw

Nutfield Brook

OUTWOOD LA

Cucksey's Farm

Shepps Shaw

KINGS CROSS LA

The Park

Henhaw Farm

Kennels Farm

COPPERS HILL RD

Bransland Wood

Poundhill Wood

Cinderhill Wood

Salfords Stream

Hope Farm

CRAB HILL LA

Lawn Hill

Burstow Park Farm

PRINCE OF WALES RD

Spring Field Wood

Brownshill Shaw

OUTWOOD LA

Harewood House

Stone House Farm

Harewood Home Farm

Shepheard's Hurst

BRICKFIELD RD

Prince of Wales (PH)

GREEN LA

Cobbler's Corner

Outwood Common

31   A   B 32 C   D 33 E   F

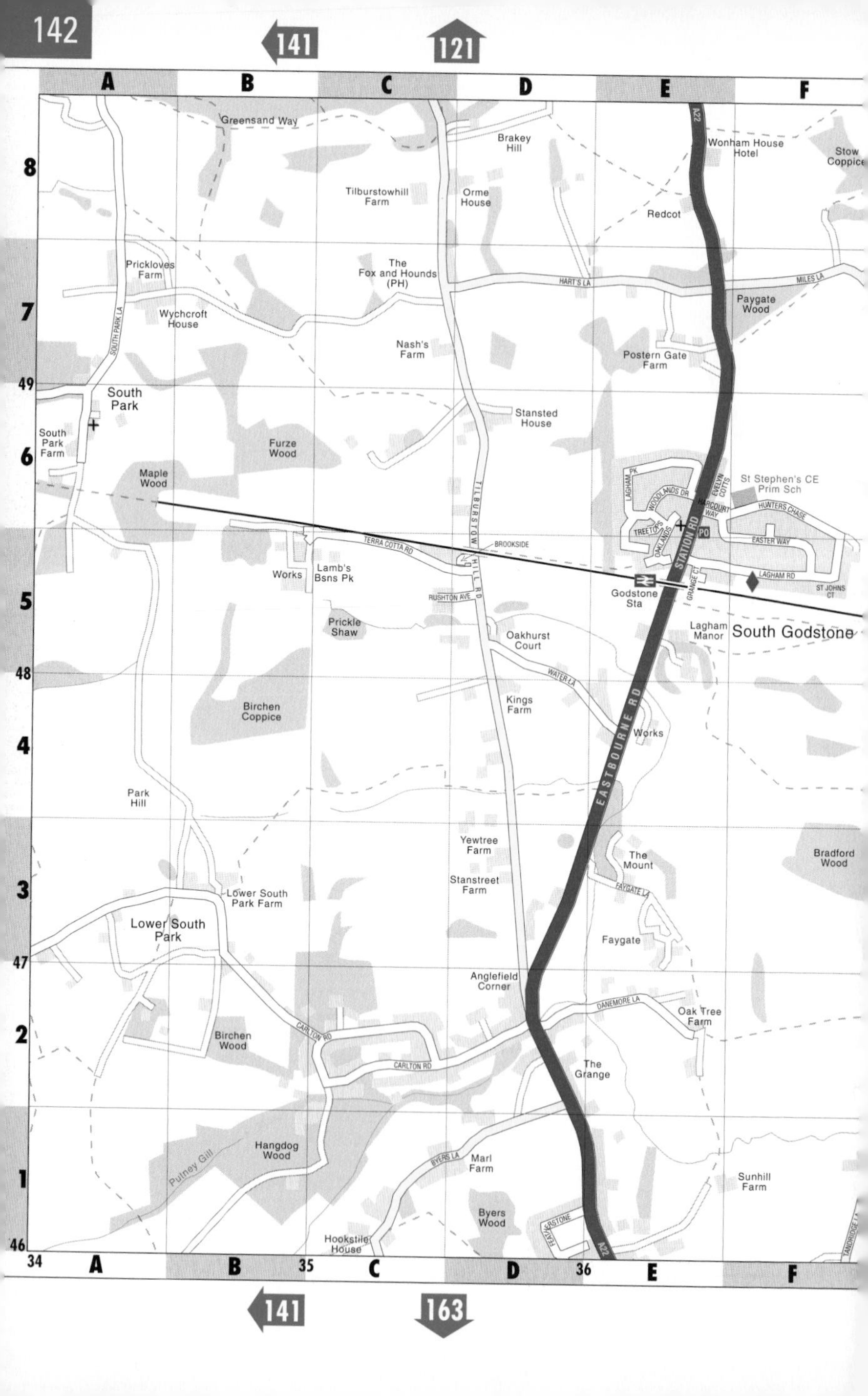
141
121
A
B
C
D
E
F
8
7
49
6
5
48
4
3
47
2
1
46
34
35
36
Greensand Way
Brakey Hill
Wonham House Hotel
Stow Coppice
Tilburstowhill Farm
Orme House
Redcot
Prickloves Farm
The Fox and Hounds (PH)
HART'S LA
MILES LA
Paygate Wood
Wychcroft House
SOUTH PARK LA
Nash's Farm
Postern Gate Farm
South Park
Stansted House
South Park Farm
Furze Wood
Maple Wood
St Stephen's CE Prim Sch
LAGHAM PK
WOODLANDS DR
EVELYN COTTS
HARCOURT WAY
HUNTERS CHASE
TREETOPS
OAKLANDS
STATION RD
PO
EASTER WAY
TILBURSTOW HILL RD
BROOKSIDE
TERRA COTTA RD
Works
Lamb's Bsns Pk
LAGHAM RD
GRANGE CT
Godstone Sta
ST JOHNS CT
RUSHTON AVE
Prickle Shaw
Lagham Manor
South Godstone
Oakhurst Court
WATER LA
Birchen Coppice
Kings Farm
EASTBOURNE RD
Works
Park Hill
Yewtree Farm
The Mount
Bradford Wood
Stanstreet Farm
FAYGATE LA
Lower South Park Farm
Lower South Park
Faygate
Anglefield Corner
DANEMORE LA
Oak Tree Farm
Birchen Wood
CARLTON RD
CARLTON RD
The Grange
Hangdog Wood
Pulney Gill
BYERS LA
Marl Farm
Sunhill Farm
Byers Wood
FEATHERSTONE
A22
TANDRIDGE LA
Hookstile House
141
163

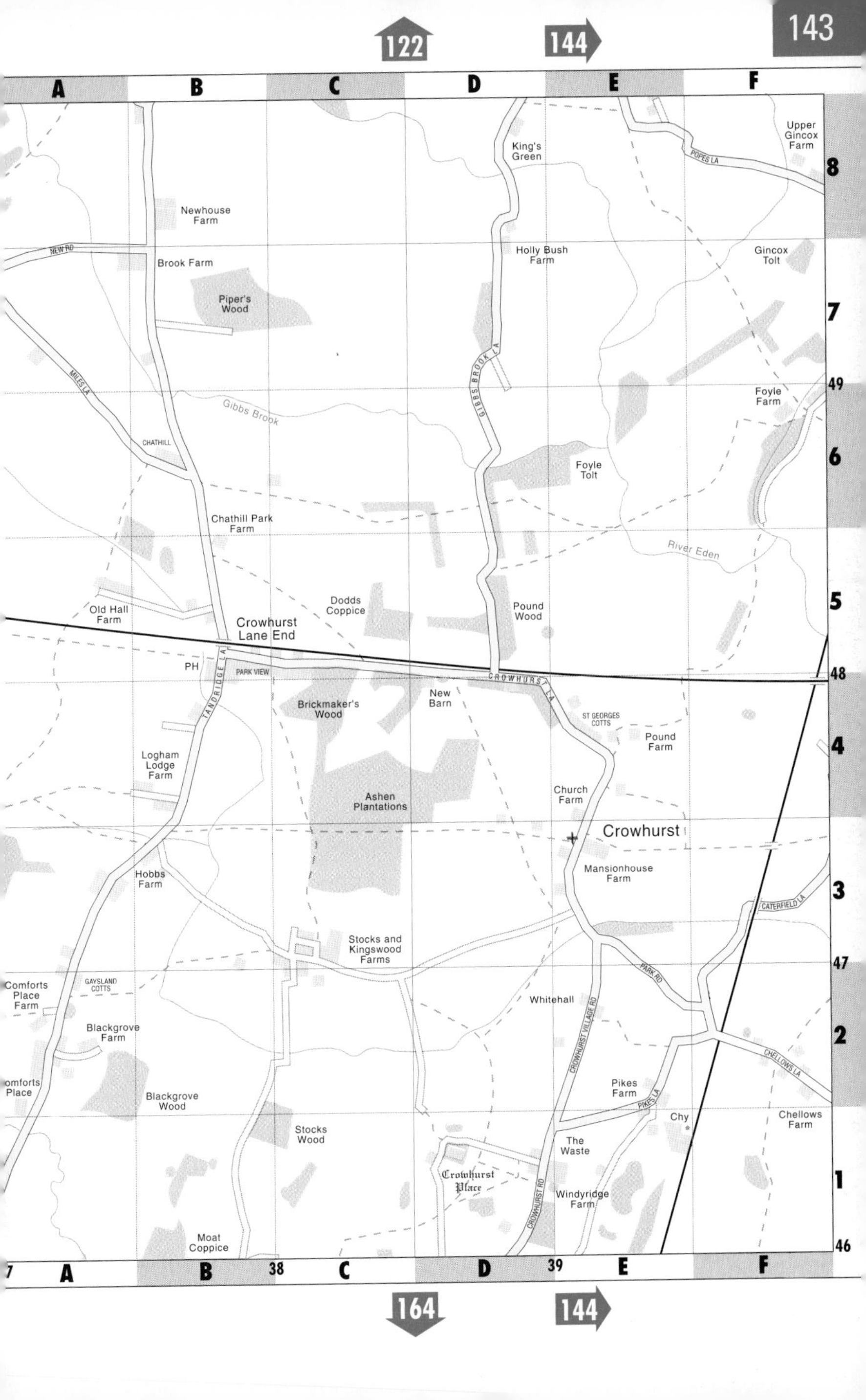

122
144
A
B
C
D
E
F
King's Green
POPES LA
Upper Gincox Farm
8
Newhouse Farm
NEW RD
Brook Farm
Holly Bush Farm
Gincox Tolt
Piper's Wood
7
MILES LA
GIBBS BROOK LA
49
Foyle Farm
Gibbs Brook
CHATHILL
Foyle Tolt
6
Chathill Park Farm
River Eden
Dodds Coppice
Pound Wood
5
Old Hall Farm
Crowhurst Lane End
PH
PARK VIEW
TANDRIDGE LA
CROWHURST LA
48
Brickmaker's Wood
New Barn
ST GEORGES COTTS
Pound Farm
4
Logham Lodge Farm
Church Farm
Ashen Plantations
Crowhurst
Mansionhouse Farm
Hobbs Farm
3
CATERFIELD LA
Stocks and Kingswood Farms
47
Comforts Place Farm
GAYSLAND COTTS
PARK RD
Whitehall
CROWHURST VILLAGE RD
Blackgrove Farm
2
CHELLOWS LA
omforts Place
Blackgrove Wood
Pikes Farm
PIKES LA
Chy
Chellows Farm
Stocks Wood
The Waste
Crowhurst Place
CROWHURST RD
Windyridge Farm
1
Moat Coppice
46
7
38
39
164
144

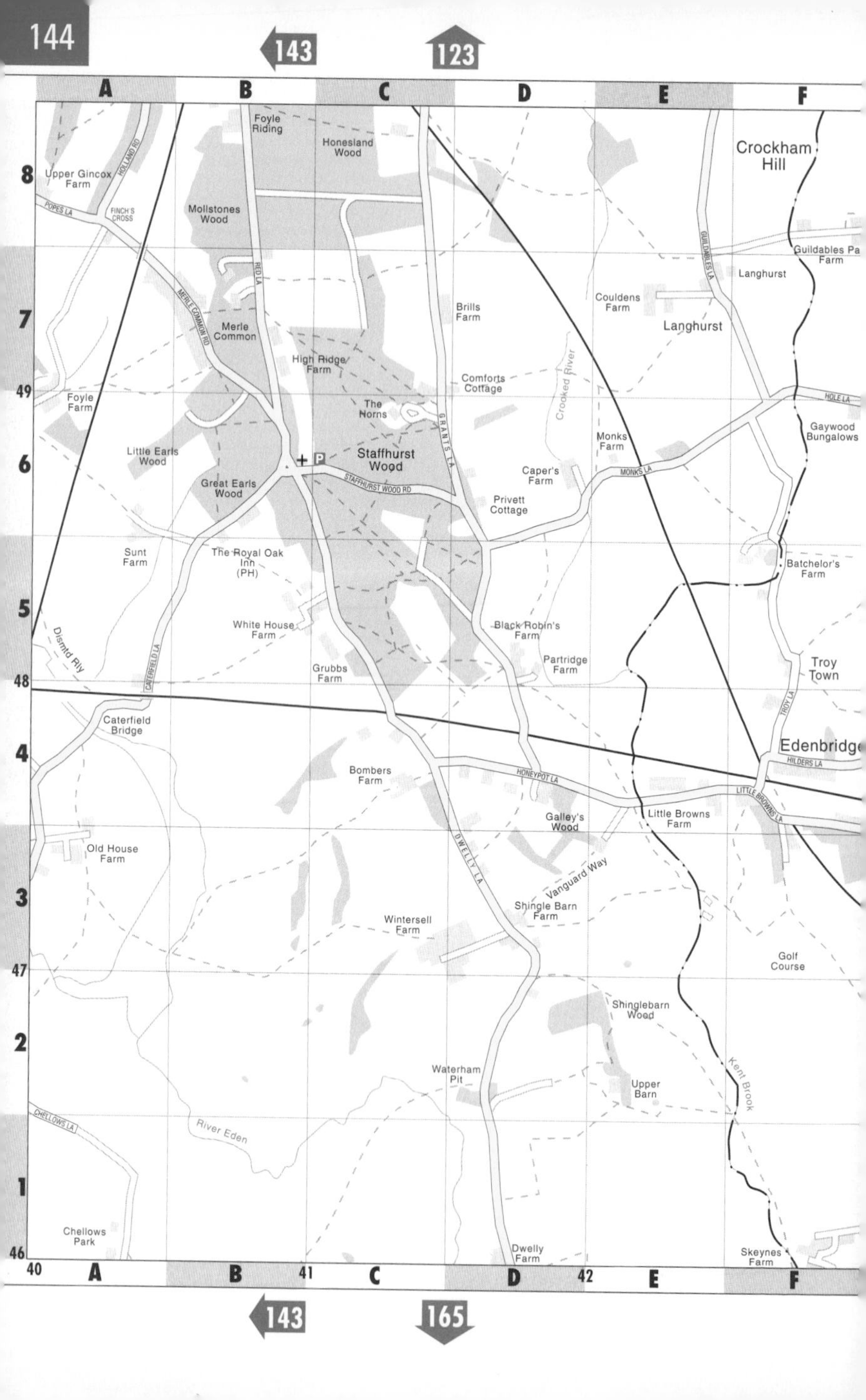

8

Upper Gincox Farm

FOYLE LA

FINCH'S CROSS

Foyle Riding

Honesland Wood

Mollstones Wood

Crockham Hill

Guildables Pa Farm

GUILDABLES LA

Langhurst

7

Merle Common

BELL COMMON RD

HOG LA

Brills Farm

Couldens Farm

Langhurst

High Ridge Farm

Comforts Cottage

Crooked River

HOLE LA

49

Foyle Farm

The Norns

GRANT'S LA

Gaywood Bungalows

6

Little Earls Wood

Great Earls Wood

Staffhurst Wood

STAFFHURST WOOD RD

Caper's Farm

Monks Farm

MONKS LA

5

Sunt Farm

The Royal Oak Inn (PH)

Privett Cottage

Batchelor's Farm

CAFFERDS LA

Dismd Rly

White House Farm

Black Robin's Farm

Troy Town

48

Grubbs Farm

Partridge Farm

Caterfield Bridge

4

Bombers Farm

HORSEPOT LA

Galley's Wood

Little Browns Farm

Edenbridge

HILDERS LA

LITTLE BROWNS LA

FLINT LA

3

Old House Farm

Wintersell Farm

DWELLY LA

Vanguard Way

Shingle Barn Farm

Golf Course

47

Shinglebarn Wood

2

CHELLOWS LA

River Eden

Waterham Pit

Upper Barn

Kent Brook

1

Chellows Park

Dwelly Farm

Skeynes Farm

46

124
146

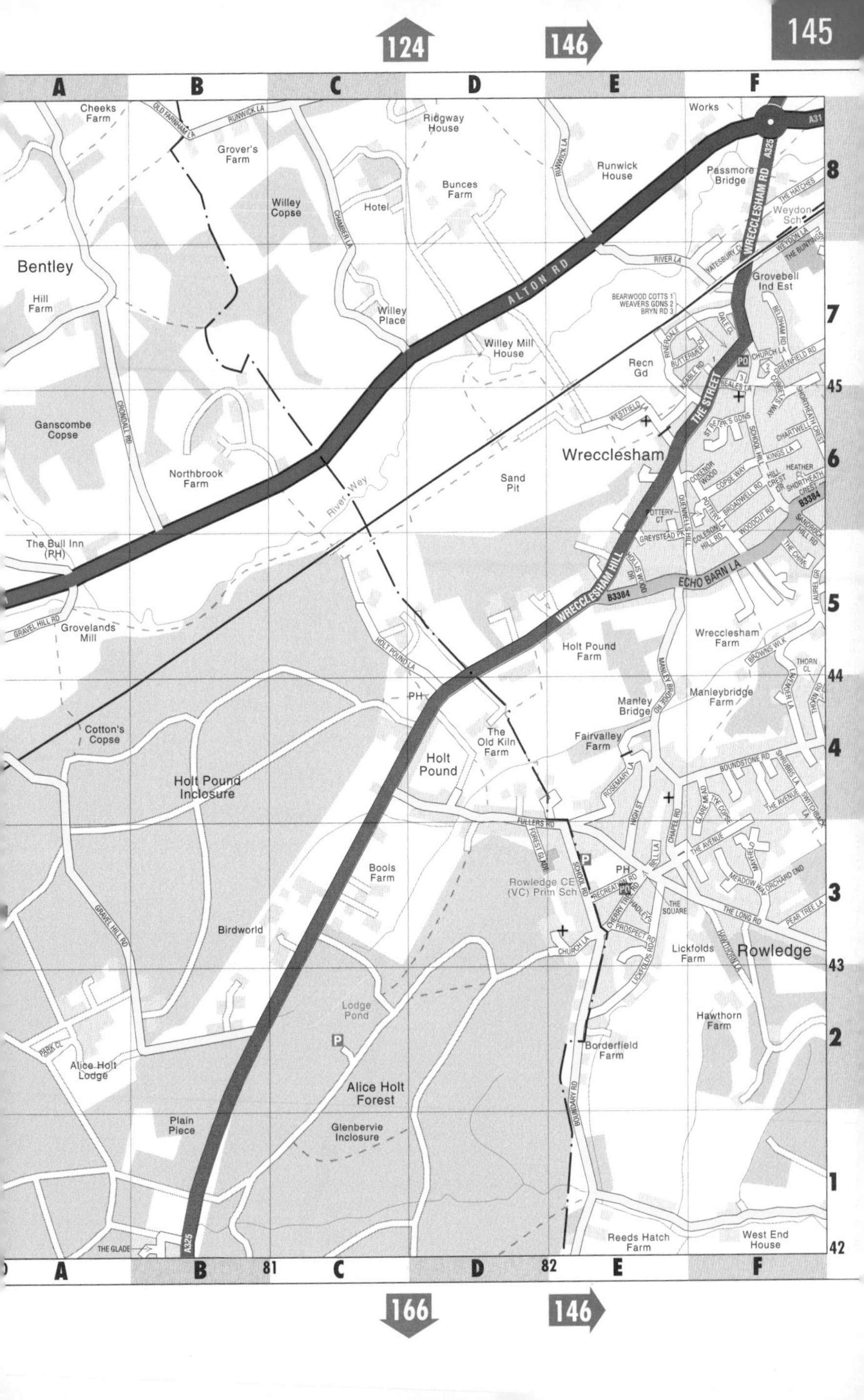
Cheeks Farm
Grover's Farm
Willey Copse
Hotel
Ridgway House
Bunces Farm
Runwick House
Works
Passmore Bridge
Weydon Sch
Bentley
Hill Farm
ALTON RD
Willey Place
Willey Mill House
Grovebell Ind Est
Recn Gd
Ganscombe Copse
Northbrook Farm
Wrecclesham
Sand Pit
River Wey
The Bull Inn (PH)
Grovelands Mill
ECHO BARN LA
WRECCLESHAM HILL
THE STREET
WRECCLESHAM RD
Wrecclesham Farm
Holt Pound Farm
Manley Bridge
Manleybridge Farm
Cotton's Copse
Fairvalley Farm
The Old Kiln Farm
Holt Pound
Holt Pound Inclosure
Bools Farm
Rowledge CE (VC) Prim Sch
Birdworld
Lickfolds Farm
Rowledge
Lodge Pond
Hawthorn Farm
Borderfield Farm
Alice Holt Lodge
Alice Holt Forest
Plain Piece
Glenbervie Inclosure
Reeds Hatch Farm
West End House
A325
A31
B3384

166
146

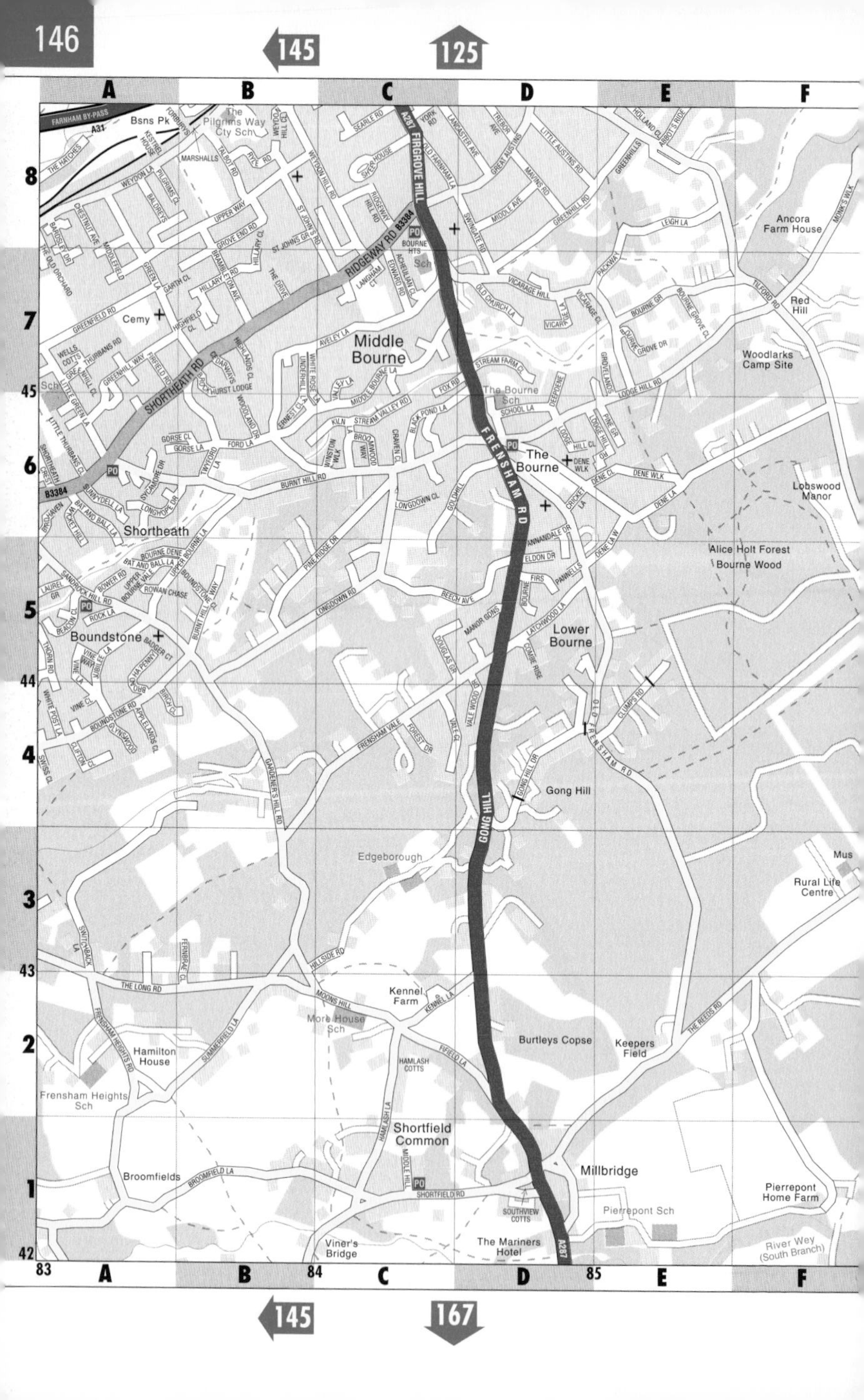
145
125
167
FARNHAM BY-PASS
A31
Bsns Pk
The Pilgrims Way Cty Sch
THE HATCHES
MARSHALLS
WEYDON LA
PILGRIMS CL
BALDREYS
CHESTNUT AVE
MIDDLEFIELD
THE OLD ORCHARD
UPPER WAY
GROVE END RD
BRAMBLETON AVE
HILLARY CL
HILLARY RD
GARTH CL
GREEN LA
ST JOHNS GR
ST JOHNS RD
THE DRIVE
WEYDON HILL RD
SEARLE RD
SHEPHOUSE
RIDGEWAY HILL RD
RIDGEWAY RD B3384
BOURNE HTS
Sch
LANGHAM CT
EDWARD RD
ACHEILLIAN CL
A287 FIRGROVE HILL
OLD FARNHAM LA
YORK RD
LANCASTER AVE
TREBOR AVE
GREAT AUSTINS
LITTLE AUSTINS RD
MAVINS RD
MIDDLE AVE
SWINGATE RD
GREENHILL RD
GREENHILLS
HOLLAND CL
ABBOT'S RIDE
LEIGH LA
PACKWAY
Ancora Farm House
MONK'S WLK
VICARAGE HILL
OLD CHURCH LA
VICARAGE CL
VICARAGE LA
BOURNE GR
BOURNE GROVE CL
GROVE DR
TILFORD RD
Red Hill
Woodlarks Camp Site
GREENFIELD RD
Cemy
HIGHFIELD CL
WELLS COTTS
THURBANS RD
GREENHILL WAY
FIFIELD RD
LITTLE GREEN LA
Sch
SHORTHEATH RD
HIGHLANDS CL
DARWIN'S CL
HURST LODGE
WOODLAND DR
AVELEY LA
Middle Bourne
UNDERHILL LA
WHITE ROSE LA
MIDDLE BOURNE LA
VALLEY LA
FOX RD
STREAM FARM CL
The Bourne Sch
SCHOOL LA
DEEPDENE
GROVELANDS
LODGE HILL RD
PINE GR
LODGE HILL CL
LITTLE THURBANS CL
SHORTHEATH CREST
GORSE CL
GORSE LA
FORD LA
TWYFORD LA
KILN LA
STREAM VALLEY RD
BLACK POND LA
WINSTON WLK
BROOM WAY
BROOMWOOD
CRAVEN CL
PO
The Bourne
DENE WLK
DENE CL
DENE LA
FRENSHAM RD
Lobswood Manor
B3384
SUNNYDELL LA
SYCAMORE DR
LONGHOPE DR
BURNT HILL RD
LONGDOWN CL
GOLDHILL
CRICKET LA
BRIGHAVEN
BAT AND BALL LA
CRICKET HILL
Shortheath
BOURNE DENE
UPPER BOURNE LA
PINE RIDGE DR
ANNANDALE DR
ELDON DR
DENE LA W
Alice Holt Forest
Bourne Wood
LAUREL GR
SANDROCK HILL RD
BOWER RD
UPPER BOURNE VALE
ROWAN CHASE
BOUNDSTONE CL
BURNT HILL WAY
LONGDOWN RD
BEECH AVE
BOURNE FIRS
PANNELLS
BEACON CL
ROCK LA
Boundstone
BADGER CT
MANOR GDNS
LATCHWOOD LA
Lower Bourne
DOUGLAS GR
COMBE RISE
THORN RD
VINE LA
VINE WAY
JUBILEE LA
HA'PENNY
BROOM
WHITE POST LA
VINE CL
BOUNDSTONE RD
APPLELANDS CL
BIRCH CL
CLIFTON CL
SWISS CL
GLYNSWOOD
FRENSHAM VALE
FOREST DR
VALE CL
VALE WOOD DR
CLUMPS RD
OLD FRENSHAM RD
GARDENER'S HILL RD
GONG HILL DR
Gong Hill
GONG HILL
Edgeborough
Mus
Rural Life Centre
SWITCHBACK LA
FERNBRAE CL
HILLSIDE RD
THE LONG RD
MOONS HILL
Kennel Farm
KENNEL LA
More House Sch
FRENSHAM HEIGHTS RD
Hamilton House
SUMMERFIELD LA
HAMLASH COTTS
FIFIELD LA
Burtleys Copse
Keepers Field
THE REEDS RD
Frensham Heights Sch
HAMLASH LA
Shortfield Common
MIDDLE HILL
Broomfields
BROOMFIELD LA
SHORTFIELD RD
Millbridge
Pierrepont Home Farm
SOUTHVIEW COTTS
Pierrepont Sch
Viner's Bridge
The Mariners Hotel
A287
River Wey (South Branch)
A B C D E F
8 7 6 5 4 3 2 1
45 44 43 42
83 84 85
145
167

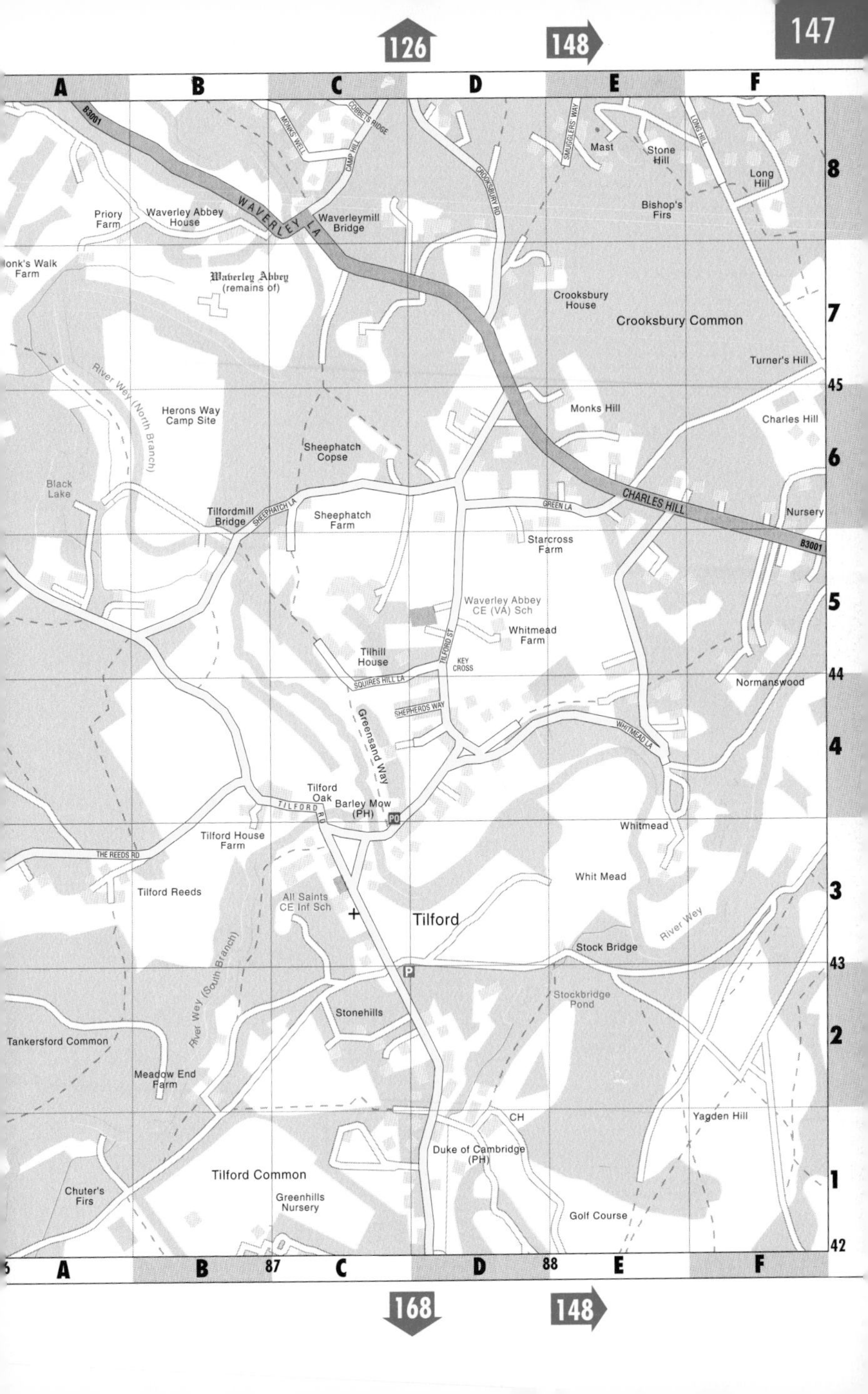
126
148
A
B
C
D
E
F
B3001
MONKS WELL
COBBETS RIDGE
CAMP HILL
CROOKSBURY RD
SMUGGLERS WAY
Mast
Stone Hill
LONG HILL
Long Hill
8
Priory Farm
Waverley Abbey House
WAVERLEY LA
Waverleymill Bridge
Bishop's Firs
Monk's Walk Farm
Waverley Abbey (remains of)
Crooksbury House
Crooksbury Common
7
Turner's Hill
45
River Wey (North Branch)
Herons Way Camp Site
Monks Hill
Charles Hill
Sheephatch Copse
6
Black Lake
CHARLES HILL
Nursery
Tilfordmill Bridge
SHEEPHATCH LA
Sheephatch Farm
GREEN LA
Starcross Farm
B3001
Waverley Abbey CE (VA) Sch
5
Whitmead Farm
TILFORD ST
Tilhill House
KEY CROSS
SQUIRES HILL LA
44
Normanswood
Greensand Way
SHEPHERDS WAY
WHITMEAD LA
4
Tilford Oak
Barley Mow (PH)
TILFORD RD
PO
Whitmead
Tilford House Farm
THE REEDS RD
Whit Mead
Tilford Reeds
3
All Saints CE Inf Sch
Tilford
River Wey
Stock Bridge
River Wey (South Branch)
43
P
Stockbridge Pond
Stonehills
2
Tankersford Common
Meadow End Farm
CH
Yagden Hill
Duke of Cambridge (PH)
1
Tilford Common
Chuter's Firs
Greenhills Nursery
Golf Course
42
A
B
87
C
D
88
E
F
168
148

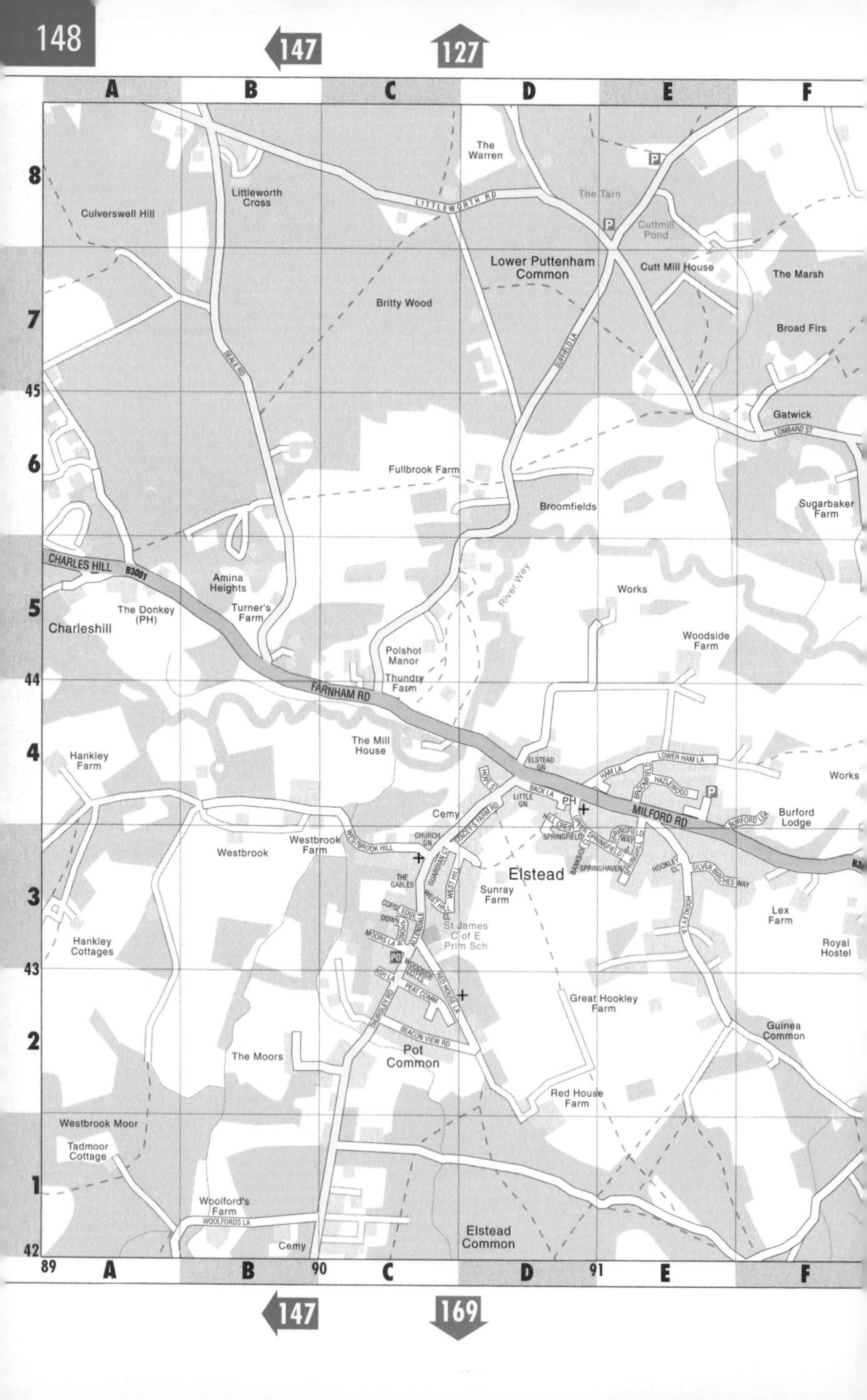
147
127
A
B
C
D
E
F
The Warren
Culverswell Hill
Littleworth Cross
LITTLEWORTH RD
The Tarn
Cuttmill Pond
Lower Puttenham Common
Cutt Mill House
The Marsh
Britty Wood
Broad Firs
SEALE RD
SUFFIELD LA
Gatwick
LOMBARD ST
Fullbrook Farm
Broomfields
Sugarbaker Farm
CHARLES HILL
B3001
Amina Heights
River Wey
Works
The Donkey (PH)
Turner's Farm
Charleshill
Woodside Farm
Polshot Manor
Thundry Farm
FARNHAM RD
The Mill House
Hankley Farm
ELSTEAD GN
LOWER HAM LA
HAM LA
HAZLEWOOD
BROOMFIELD
Works
HOPE ST
BACK LA
LITTLE GN
PH
MILFORD RD
BURFORD LEA
Burford Lodge
Cemy
STACEY'S FARM RD
HILL CREST
SPRINGFIELD
CHURCH GN
WESTBROOK HILL
Westbrook Farm
Westbrook
GUARDIAN CT
WEST HILL
Elstead
BANKSIDE CT
SPRINGHAVEN
SPRINGHILL
HOOKLEY CL
SILVER BIRCHES WAY
THE GABLES
Sunray Farm
Lex Farm
WEST HILL CL
COPSE EDGE
ALLENDALE
HOOKLEY LA
MOORS LA
St James C of E Prim Sch
Hankley Cottages
Royal Hostel
WOODSIDE COTTS
ASH LA
RED HOUSE LA
PEAT COMM
Great Hookley Farm
THURSLEY RD
BEACON VIEW RD
Guinea Common
The Moors
Pot Common
Red House Farm
Westbrook Moor
Tadmoor Cottage
Woolford's Farm
WOOLFORDS LA
Elstead Common
Cemy
8
7
45
6
5
44
4
3
43
2
1
42
89
90
91
147
169

128
150

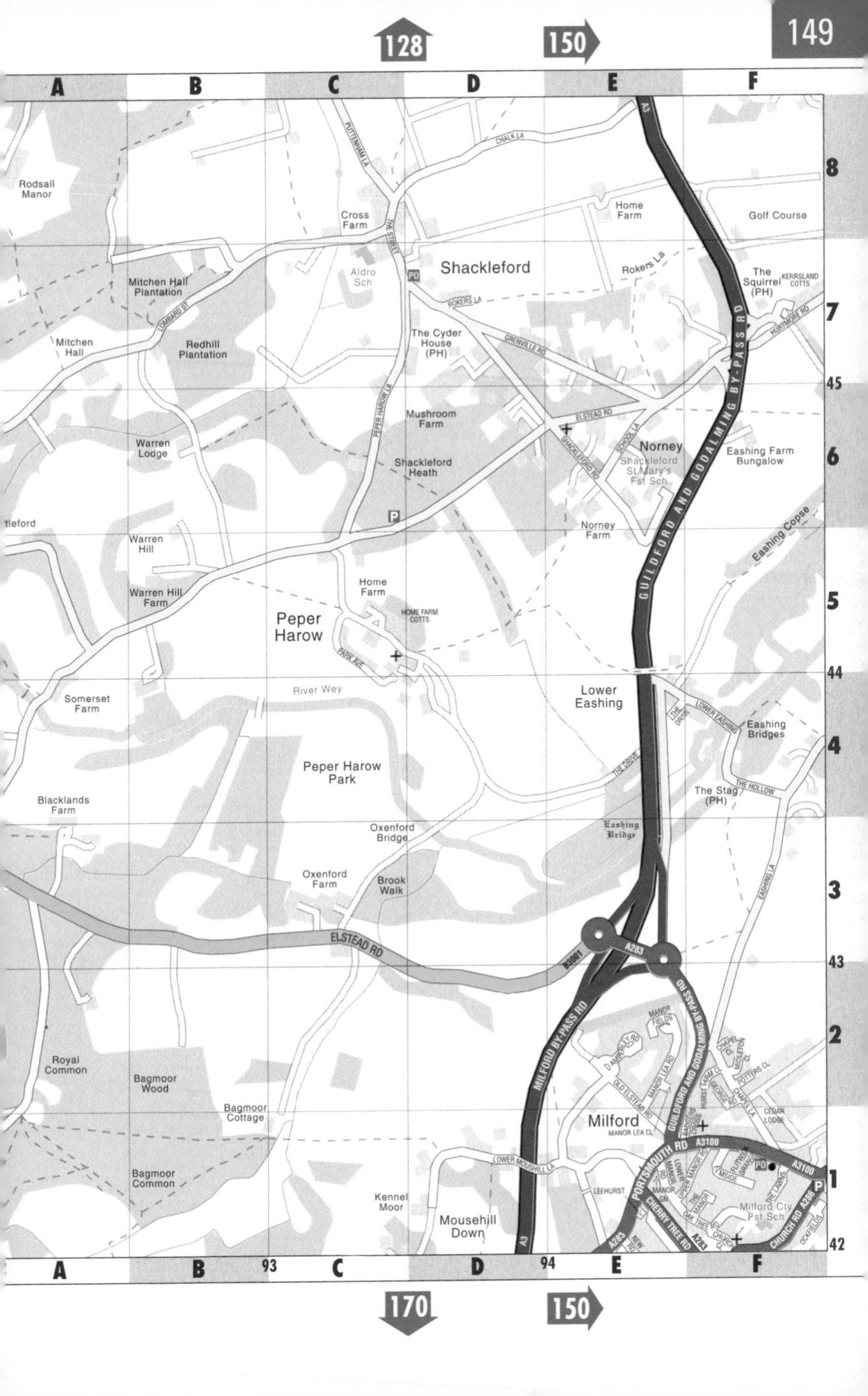
A
B
C
D
E
F
8
7
6
5
4
3
2
1
45
44
43
42
93
94
Rodsall Manor
Cross Farm
Home Farm
Golf Course
Shackleford
Aldro Sch
Rokers La
The Squirrel (PH)
KERRSLAND COTTS
Mitchen Hall Plantation
Mitchen Hall
Redhill Plantation
The Cyder House (PH)
Mushroom Farm
Norney
Shackleford St Mary's Fst Sch
Eashing Farm Bungalow
Warren Lodge
Shackleford Heath
Norney Farm
Eashing Copse
Warren Hill
Warren Hill Farm
Home Farm
HOME FARM COTTS
Peper Harow
Somerset Farm
River Wey
Lower Eashing
Eashing Bridges
Peper Harow Park
Blacklands Farm
The Stag (PH)
Eashing Bridge
Oxenford Bridge
Oxenford Farm
Brook Walk
ELSTEAD RD
B3001
A283
A3
GUILDFORD AND GODALMING BY-PASS RD
MILFORD BY-PASS RD
PUTTENHAM LA
CHALK LA
THE STREET
ROKERS LA
GRENVILLE RD
HURTMORE RD
LOMBARD ST
PEPER HAROW LA
ELSTEAD RD
SHACKLEFORD RD
SCHOOL LA
PARK AVE
THE DRIVE
LOWER EASHING
THE HOLLOW
EASHING LA
Royal Common
Bagmoor Wood
Bagmoor Cottage
Milford
MANOR LEA CL
MANOR FIELDS
AMBERLEY RD
MANOR LEA RD
OLD ELSTEAD RD
HURST FARM CL
CHAPEL CL
MIDLETON CL
POTTERS CL
CHAPEL LA
GEORGE RD
CEDAR LODGE
BADGERS CROSS
PORTSMOUTH RD
A3100
LOWER MOUSHILL LA
LEEHURST
Bagmoor Common
Kennel Moor
Mousehill Down
Milford Cty Fst Sch
CHERRY TREE RD
OAK TREE RD
CHURCH RD
CHURCH CL
NEW RD
FLITWICK GRANGE
THE LAWNS
OCKFIELDS
P
PO

170
150

149
129

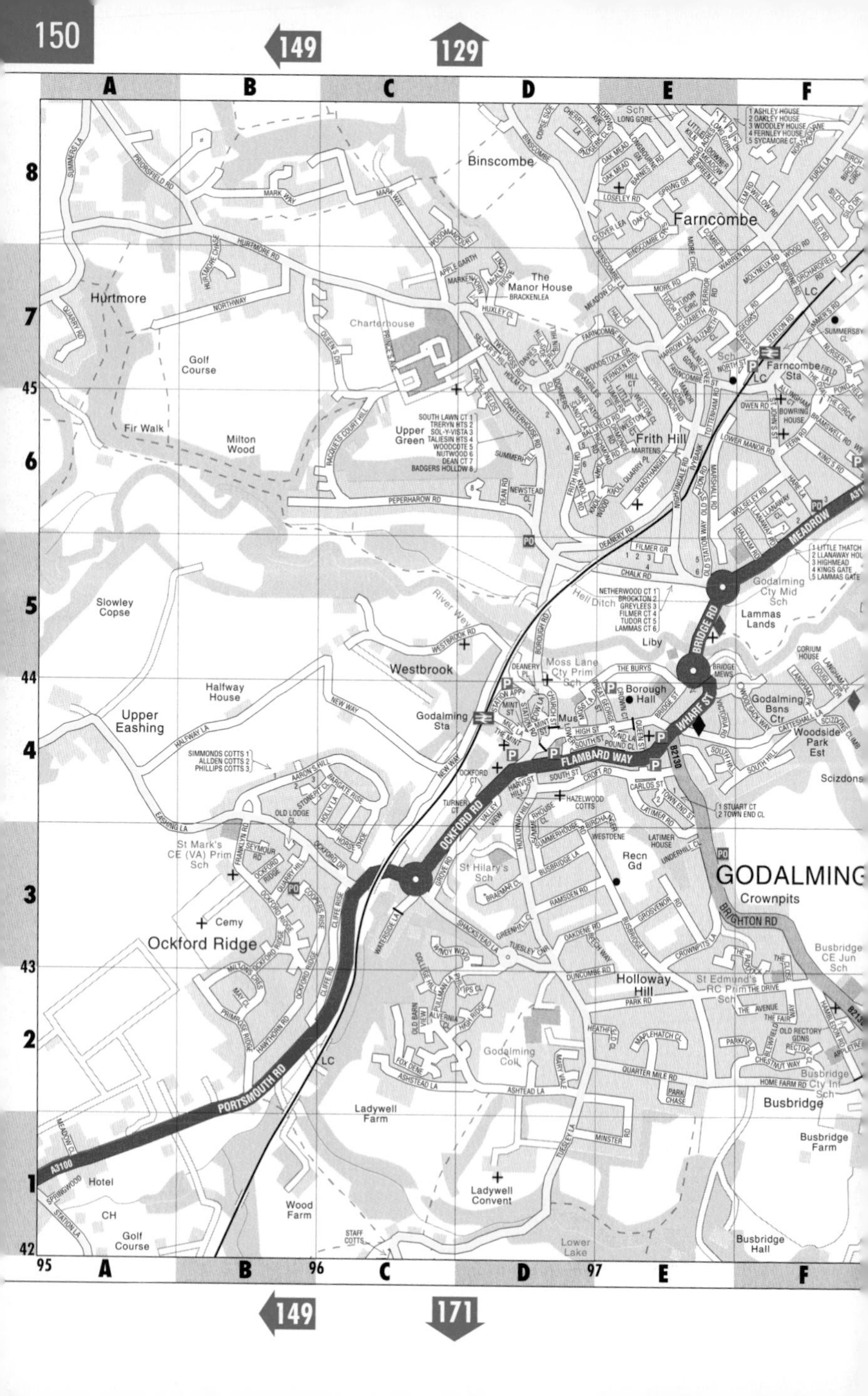
A
B
C
D
E
F
8
7
45
6
5
44
4
3
43
2
1
42
95
96
97
Binscombe
Farncombe
Hurtmore
The Manor House
Charterhouse
Golf Course
Fir Walk
Milton Wood
Upper Green
Frith Hill
Farncombe Sta
Slowley Copse
Hell Ditch
River Wey
Godalming Cty Mid Sch
Lammas Lands
Liby
Westbrook
Halfway House
Upper Eashing
Moss Lane Cty Prim Sch
Borough Hall
Godalming Sta
Mus
Godalming Bsns Ctr
Woodside Park Est
Scizdons
St Mark's CE (VA) Prim Sch
St Hilary's Sch
Recn Gd
GODALMING
Crownpits
Cemy
Ockford Ridge
Busbridge CE Jun Sch
Holloway Hill
St Edmund's RC Prim Sch
Godalming Coll
Busbridge Cty Inf Sch
Busbridge
Ladywell Farm
Busbridge Farm
Hotel
CH
Ladywell Convent
Wood Farm
Golf Course
Lower Lake
Busbridge Hall
PORTSMOUTH RD
A3100
FLAMBARD WAY
OCKFORD RD
BRIDGE RD
WHARF ST
MEADROW
B2130
BRIGHTON RD
HURTMORE RD
PEPERHAROW RD
CHALK RD
HIGH ST

149
171

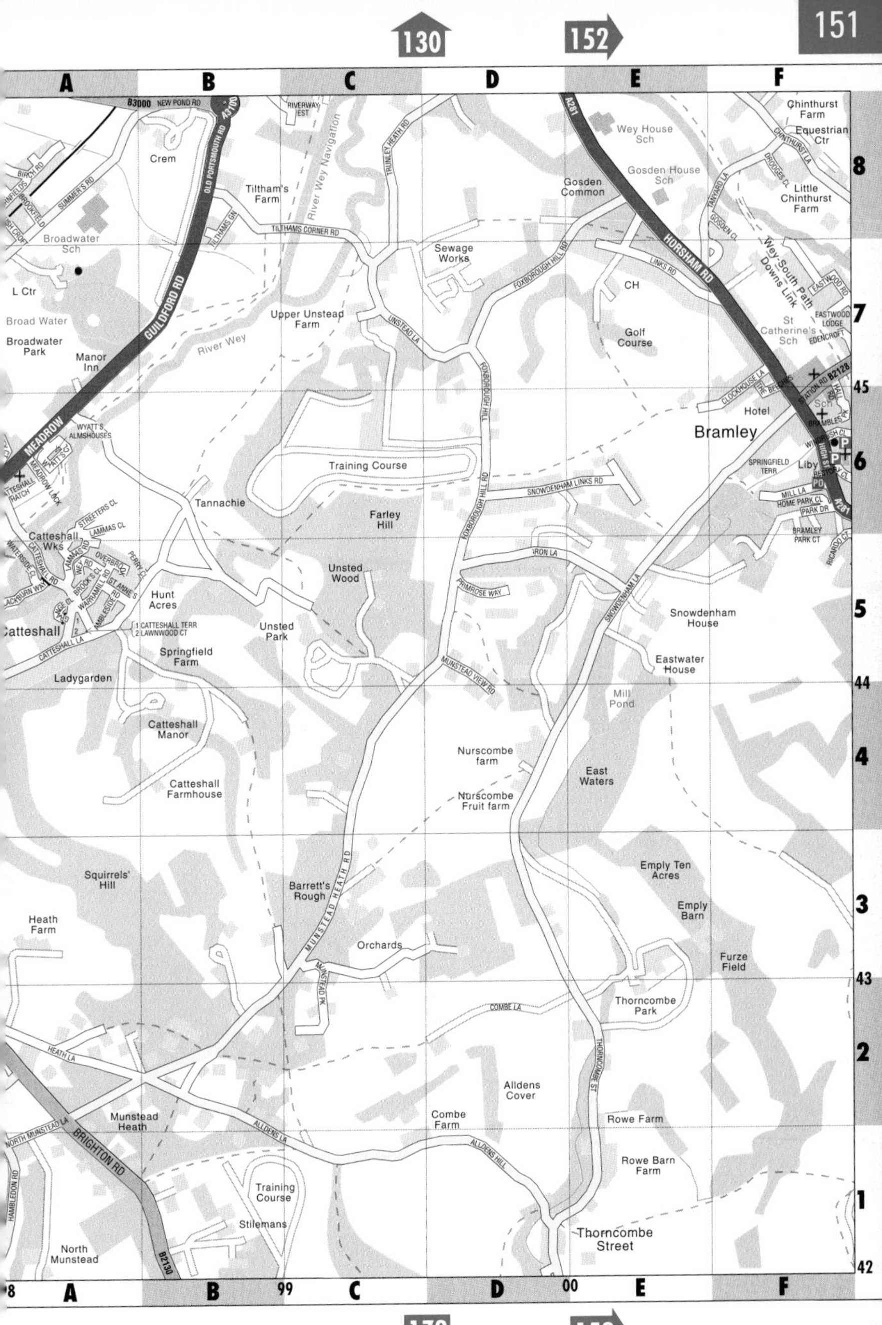

A B C D E F

8

7

45

6

5

44

4

3

43

2

1

42

B3000 NEW POND RD

Crem

Tiltham's Farm

RIVERWAY WEST

River Wey Navigation

THORLEY RD PETWS

Wey House Sch

Gosden House Sch

Chinthurst Farm

Equestrian Ctr

Little Chinthurst Farm

Broadwater Sch

SUMMER'S RD

L Ctr

Broad Water

Broadwater Park

Manor Inn

GUILDFORD RD

OLD PORTSMOUTH RD A3100

TILHAMS CORNER RD

Upper Unstead Farm

River Wey

UNSTEAD LA

Sewage Works

FOXBOROUGH HILL RD

Gosden Common

A281

LINKS RD

CH

Golf Course

HORSHAM RD

St Catherine's Sch

Wey South Path Downs Link

EASTWOOD LODGE

EDENCROFT

B2128

45

MEADROW

WYATT'S ALMSHOUSES

Catteshall Wks

Catteshall

STREETFRS CL

LARMAS CL

PERIDOT CT

Hunt Acres

Tannachie

Unsted Wood

Farley Hill

FOXENDOUGH HILL

OLD THORSHAM RD

SNOWDENHAM LINKS RD

IRON LA

SNOWDENHAM LA

Snowdenham House

Hotel

Bramley

SPRINGFIELD TERR

Lib

HIGH ST

HOME PARK CL

PARK DR

MILL LA

BRAMLEY PARK CT

Unsted Park

PRIMROSE WAY

MUNSTEAD VIEW RD

Eastwater House

Ladygarden

Catteshall Manor

Catteshall Farmhouse

Springfield Farm

Mill Pond

Nurscombe farm

Nurscombe Fruit farm

East Waters

Squirrels' Hill

Heath Farm

Barrett's Rough

MUNSTEAD HEATH RD

Orchards

Emply Ten Acres

Emply Barn

Furze Field

HEATH LA

BRIGHTON RD

NORTH MUNSTEAD LA

Munstead Heath

ALLDENS LA

COMBE LA

Thorncombe Park

THORNCOMBE ST

Combe Farm

Alldens Cover

ALLDENS HILL

Rowe Farm

Rowe Barn Farm

B2130

HAMBLEDON RD

Training Course

Stilemans

North Munstead

Thorncombe Street

1 CATTESHALL TERR
2 LAWNWOOD CT

8 A B 99 C D 00 E F

151
131

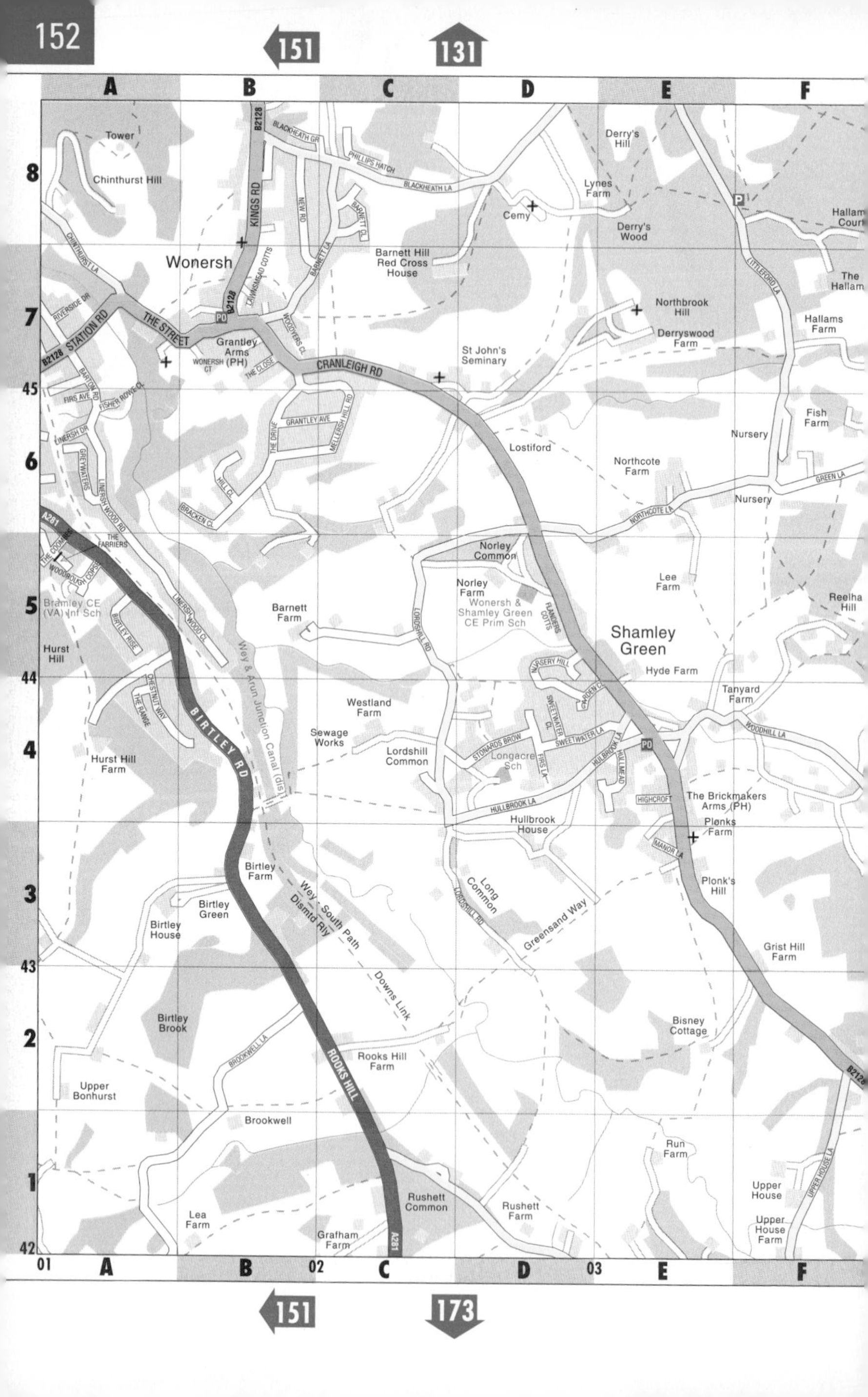
Tower
Chinthurst Hill
Wonersh
KINGS RD
B2128
BLACKHEATH GR
PHILLIPS HATCH
BLACKHEATH LA
NEW RD
BARNETT CL
BARNETT LA
LAWNSMEAD COTTS
CHINTHURST LA
RIVERSIDE DR
STATION RD
THE STREET
Grantley Arms (PH)
WONERSH CT
THE CLOSE
WOODYERS CL
CRANLEIGH RD
Barnett Hill Red Cross House
Cemy
Derry's Hill
Lynes Farm
Derry's Wood
Hallam Court
The Hallam
LITTLEFORD LA
Northbrook Hill
Derryswood Farm
Hallams Farm
St John's Seminary
BARTON RD
FIRS AVE
FISHER ROWE CL
LINERSH DR
GREYWATERS
LINERSH WOOD RD
GRANTLEY AVE
THE DRIVE
MELLERSH HILL RD
HILL CL
BRACKEN CL
Lostiford
Fish Farm
Nursery
Northcote Farm
NORTHCOTE LA
GREEN LA
A281
THE COOMBES
THE FARRIERS
WOODRUFF
BUSH COPSE
Bramley CE (VA) Inf Sch
BIRTLEY RISE
Hurst Hill
LINERSH WOOD CL
Norley Common
Norley Farm
Wonersh & Shamley Green CE Prim Sch
FLANNERS COTTS
Lee Farm
Reelhall Hill
Barnett Farm
LORDSHILL RD
Shamley Green
Hyde Farm
Wey & Arun Junction Canal (dis)
NURSERY HILL
GARDEN CL
SWEETWATER CL
SWEETWATER LA
CHESTNUT WAY
THE RANGE
BIRTLEY RD
Westland Farm
Sewage Works
Lordshill Common
STONARDS BROW
Longacre Sch
FIRS LA
HULLBROOK LA
HULLMEAD
Tanyard Farm
WOODHILL LA
Hurst Hill Farm
HULLBROOK LA
Hullbrook House
HIGHCROFT
The Brickmakers Arms (PH)
Plonks Farm
MANOR LA
Birtley Farm
Long Common
Plonk's Hill
Birtley Green
Birtley House
Wey - South Path
Dismtd Rly
Greensand Way
Grist Hill Farm
Downs Link
Birtley Brook
BROOKWELL LA
Bisney Cottage
Rooks Hill Farm
ROOKS HILL
Upper Bonhurst
Brookwell
Run Farm
Upper House
UPPER HOUSE LA
Rushett Common
Rushett Farm
Lea Farm
Grafham Farm
Upper House Farm
A
B
C
D
E
F
8
7
6
5
4
3
2
1
45
44
43
42
01
02
03

151
173

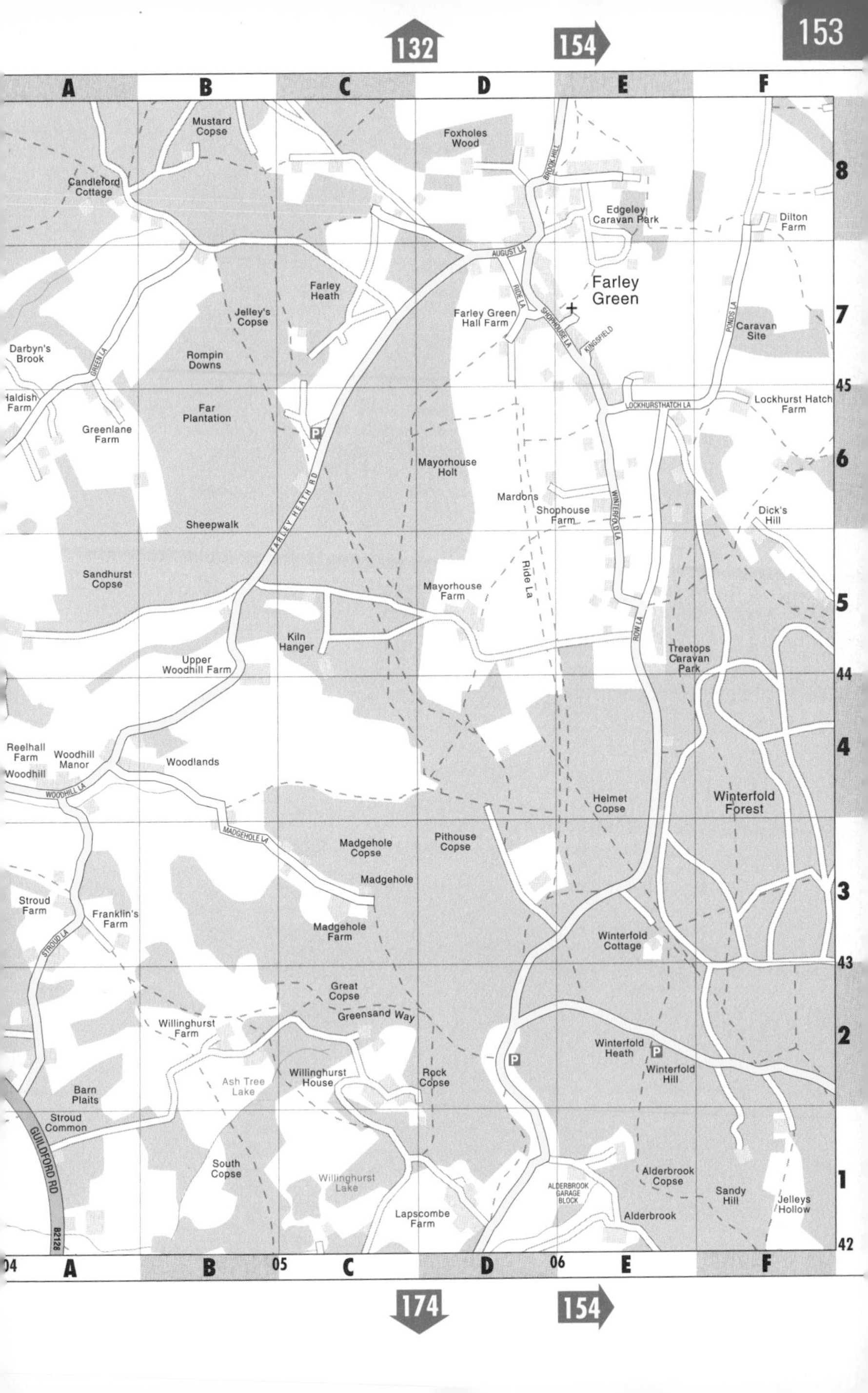

132
154
A
B
C
D
E
F
Mustard Copse
Foxholes Wood
BROOK HILL
Candleford Cottage
Edgeley Caravan Park
Dilton Farm
AUGUST LA
Farley Heath
Farley Green
RIDE LA
Jelley's Copse
Farley Green Hall Farm
SHOPHOUSE LA
KINGSFIELD
PONDS LA
Caravan Site
Darbyn's Brook
GREEN LA
Rompin Downs
Haldish Farm
Far Plantation
LOCKHURSTHATCH LA
Lockhurst Hatch Farm
Greenlane Farm
Mayorhouse Holt
Mardons
Shophouse Farm
WINTERFOLD LA
Dick's Hill
Sheepwalk
FARLEY HEATH RD
Sandhurst Copse
Mayorhouse Farm
Ride La
Kiln Hanger
ROW LA
Treetops Caravan Park
Upper Woodhill Farm
Reelhall Farm
Woodhill Manor
Woodlands
Woodhill
WOODHILL LA
Helmet Copse
Winterfold Forest
MADGEHOLE LA
Madgehole Copse
Pithouse Copse
Madgehole
Stroud Farm
Franklin's Farm
Madgehole Farm
Winterfold Cottage
STROUD LA
Great Copse
Greensand Way
Willinghurst Farm
Winterfold Heath
Winterfold Hill
Ash Tree Lake
Willinghurst House
Rock Copse
Barn Plaits
Stroud Common
GUILDFORD RD
South Copse
Willinghurst Lake
ALDERBROOK GARAGE BLOCK
Alderbrook Copse
Sandy Hill
Jelleys Hollow
Lapscombe Farm
Alderbrook
B2128
8
7
45
6
5
44
4
3
43
2
1
42
04
05
06
174
154

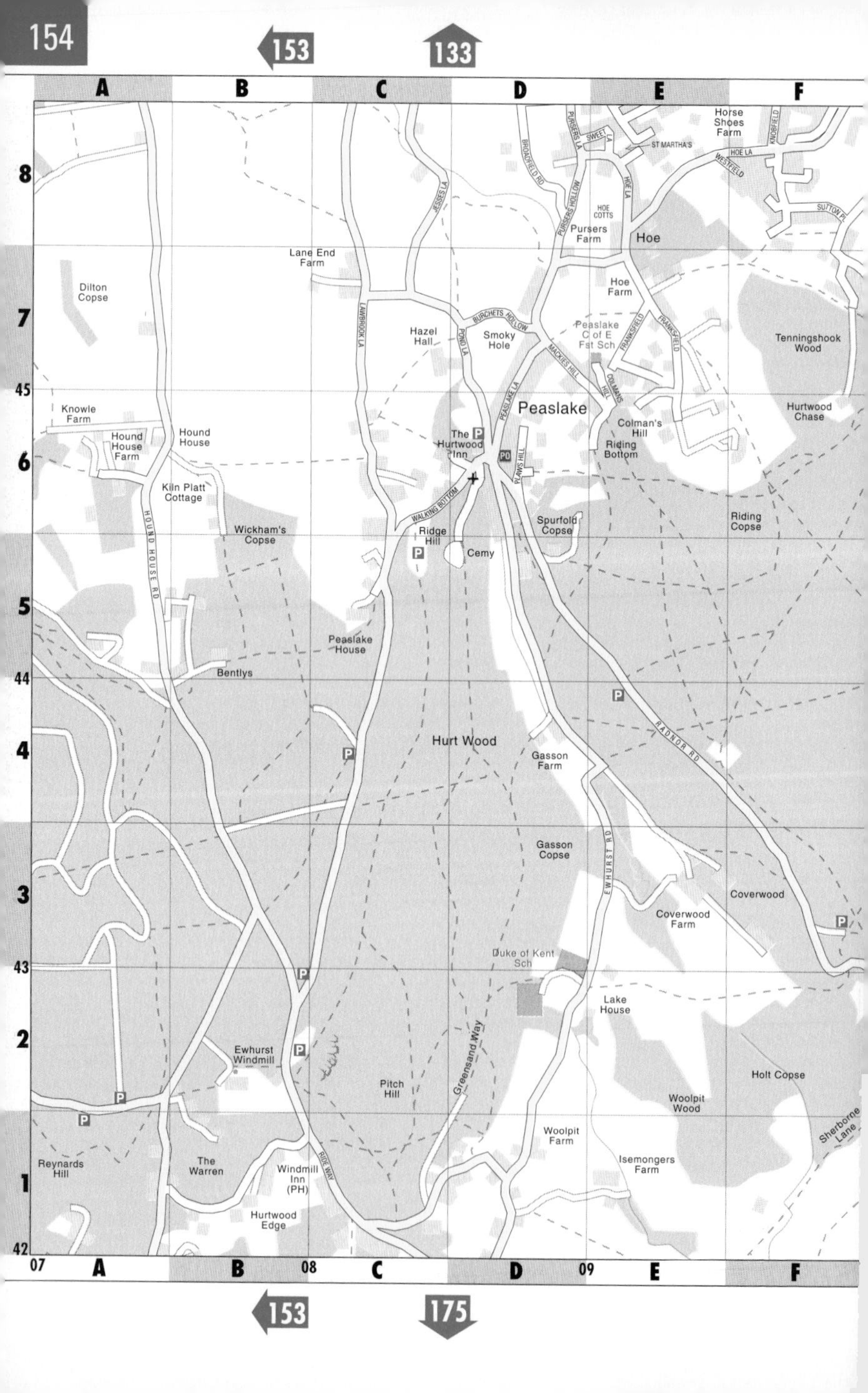
154
153
133
A
B
C
D
E
F
8
7
45
6
5
44
4
3
43
2
1
42
07
08
09
Horse Shoes Farm
KNOBFIELD
PURSERS LA
SWEET LA
ST MARTHA'S
HOE LA
WESTFIELD
BROADFIELD RD
JESSES LA
PURSERS HOLLOW
HOE LA
HOE COTTS
Pursers Farm
Hoe
SUTTON PL
Lane End Farm
Dilton Copse
Hoe Farm
LAWBROOK LA
BURCHETS HOLLOW
Hazel Hall
POND LA
Smoky Hole
Peaslake C of E Fst Sch
FRANKSFIELD
FRANKSFIELD
Tenningshook Wood
MACKIES HILL
COLMANS HILL
PEASLAKE LA
Peaslake
Knowle Farm
Hound House Farm
Hound House
The Hurtwood Inn
Colman's Hill
Riding Bottom
Hurtwood Chase
PO
PLAWS HILL
Kiln Platt Cottage
WALKING BOTTOM
HOUND HOUSE RD
Wickham's Copse
Ridge Hill
Spurfold Copse
Riding Copse
Cemy
Peaslake House
Bentlys
RADNOR RD
Hurt Wood
Gasson Farm
EWHURST RD
Gasson Copse
Coverwood
Coverwood Farm
Duke of Kent Sch
Lake House
Greensand Way
Ewhurst Windmill
Pitch Hill
Holt Copse
Woolpit Wood
Woolpit Farm
Sherborne Lane
Isemongers Farm
RIDE WAY
Reynards Hill
The Warren
Windmill Inn (PH)
Hurtwood Edge
153
175

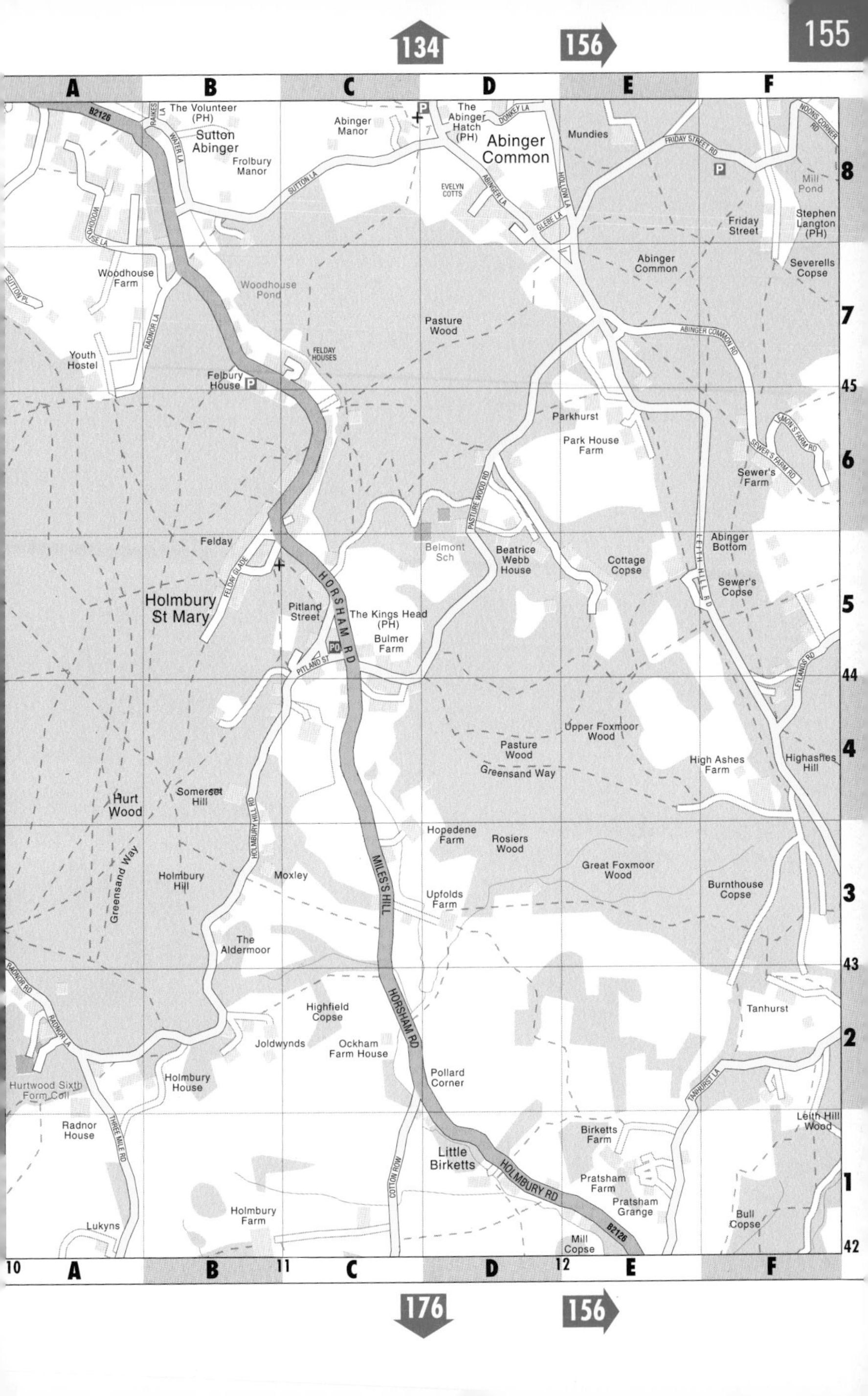

A   B   C   D   E   F

B2126

The Volunteer (PH)
Sutton Abinger
Frolbury Manor

Abinger Manor

The Abinger Hatch (PH)

Abinger Common

Mundies

DONKEY LA

FRIDAY STREET RD

Mill Pond

EVELYN COTTS

Friday Street

Stephen Langton (PH)

Severells Copse

Woodhouse Farm

Woodhouse Pond

Abinger Common

ABINGER COMMON RD

Pasture Wood

Youth Hostel

FELDAY HOUSES

Felbury House

Parkhurst

Park House Farm

Sewer's Farm

LADYE'S FARM RD

SEWERS FARM RD

Felday

Belmont Sch

Beatrice Webb House

Cottage Copse

Abinger Bottom

Sewer's Copse

Holmbury St Mary

HORSHAM RD

Pitland Street

The Kings Head (PH)

Bulmer Farm

PITLAND ST

PASTURE WOOD RD

LEITH HILL RD

LEITH HILL RD

Upper Foxmoor Wood

Pasture Wood

Greensand Way

High Ashes Farm

Highashes Hill

Hurt Wood

Somerset Hill

Greensand Way

OLD THE HAMMER LA

Hopedene Farm

Rosiers Wood

Great Foxmoor Wood

Burnthouse Copse

Holmbury Hill

Moxley

MILES'S HILL

Upfolds Farm

The Aldermoor

Highfield Copse

HORSHAM RD

Joldwynds

Ockham Farm House

Tanhurst

Hurtwood Sixth Form Coll

Holmbury House

Pollard Corner

Birketts Farm

Leith Hill Wood

Radnor House

THREE MILE RD

Holmbury Farm

Little Birketts

HOLMBURY RD

Pratsham Farm

Pratsham Grange

TANHURST LA

Bull Copse

Lukyns

COTTON MILL RD

Mill Copse

B2126

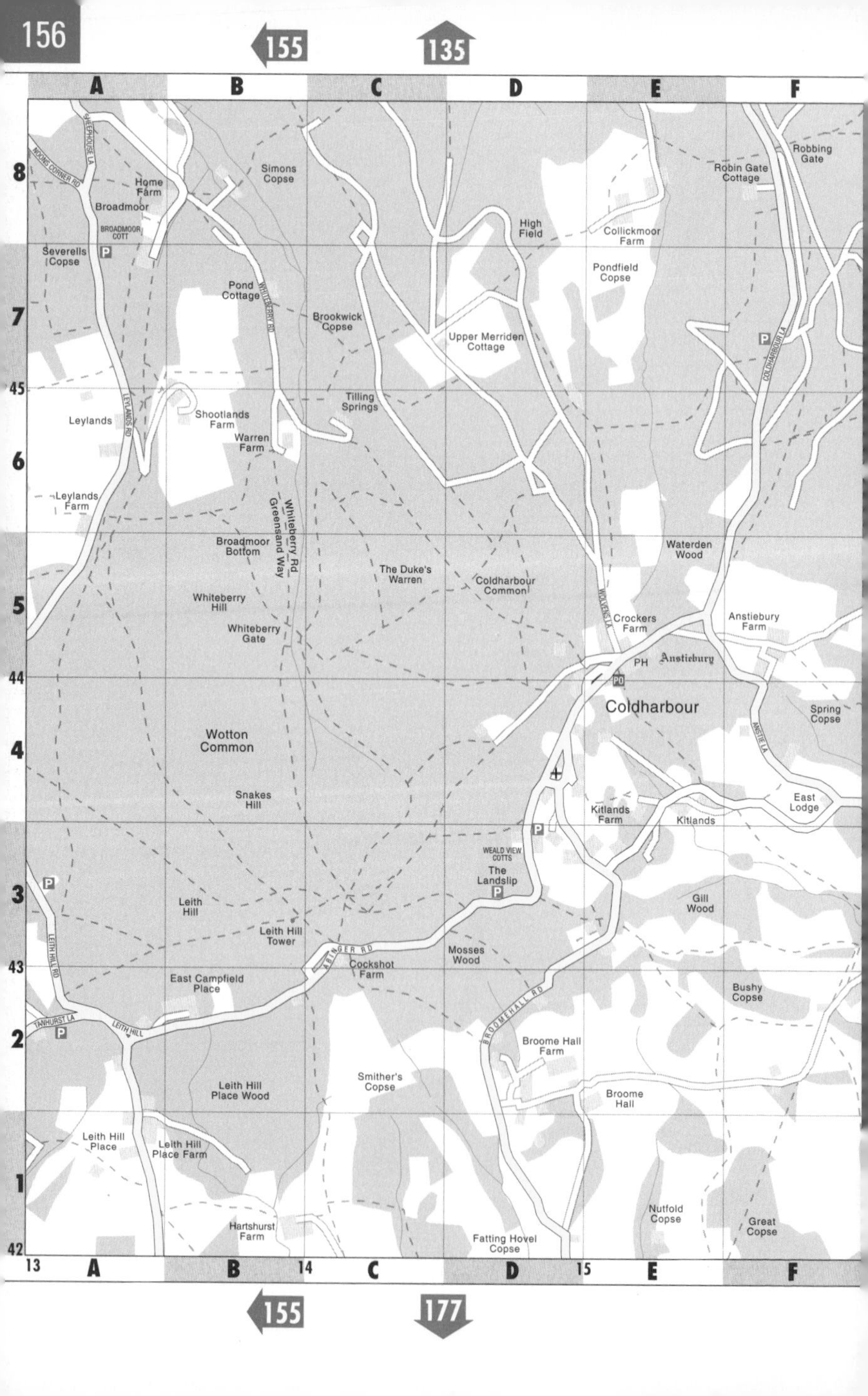

155
135
A
B
C
D
E
F
8
7
45
6
5
44
4
3
43
2
1
42
13
14
15
SHEEPHOUSE LA
MOONS CORNER RD
Home Farm
Broadmoor
BROADMOOR COTT
Severells Copse
Simons Copse
Robbing Gate
Robin Gate Cottage
High Field
Collickmoor Farm
Pondfield Copse
Pond Cottage
WHITEBERRY RD
Brookwick Copse
Upper Merriden Cottage
COLDHARBOUR LA
LEYLANDS RD
Leylands
Shootlands Farm
Tilling Springs
Warren Farm
Leylands Farm
Whiteberry Rd
Greensand Way
Broadmoor Bottom
The Duke's Warren
Coldharbour Common
Waterden Wood
Whiteberry Hill
WOLVENS LA
Crockers Farm
Anstiebury Farm
Whiteberry Gate
PH
Anstiebury
PO
Coldharbour
Spring Copse
ANSTIE LA
Wotton Common
Snakes Hill
Kitlands Farm
Kitlands
East Lodge
WEALD VIEW COTTS
The Landslip
Leith Hill
Gill Wood
Leith Hill Tower
LEITH HILL RD
ABINGER RD
Cockshot Farm
Mosses Wood
East Campfield Place
Bushy Copse
TANHURST LA
LEITH HILL
BROOMEHALL RD
Broome Hall Farm
Smither's Copse
Leith Hill Place Wood
Broome Hall
Leith Hill Place
Leith Hill Place Farm
Nutfold Copse
Hartshurst Farm
Great Copse
Fatting Hovel Copse
155
177

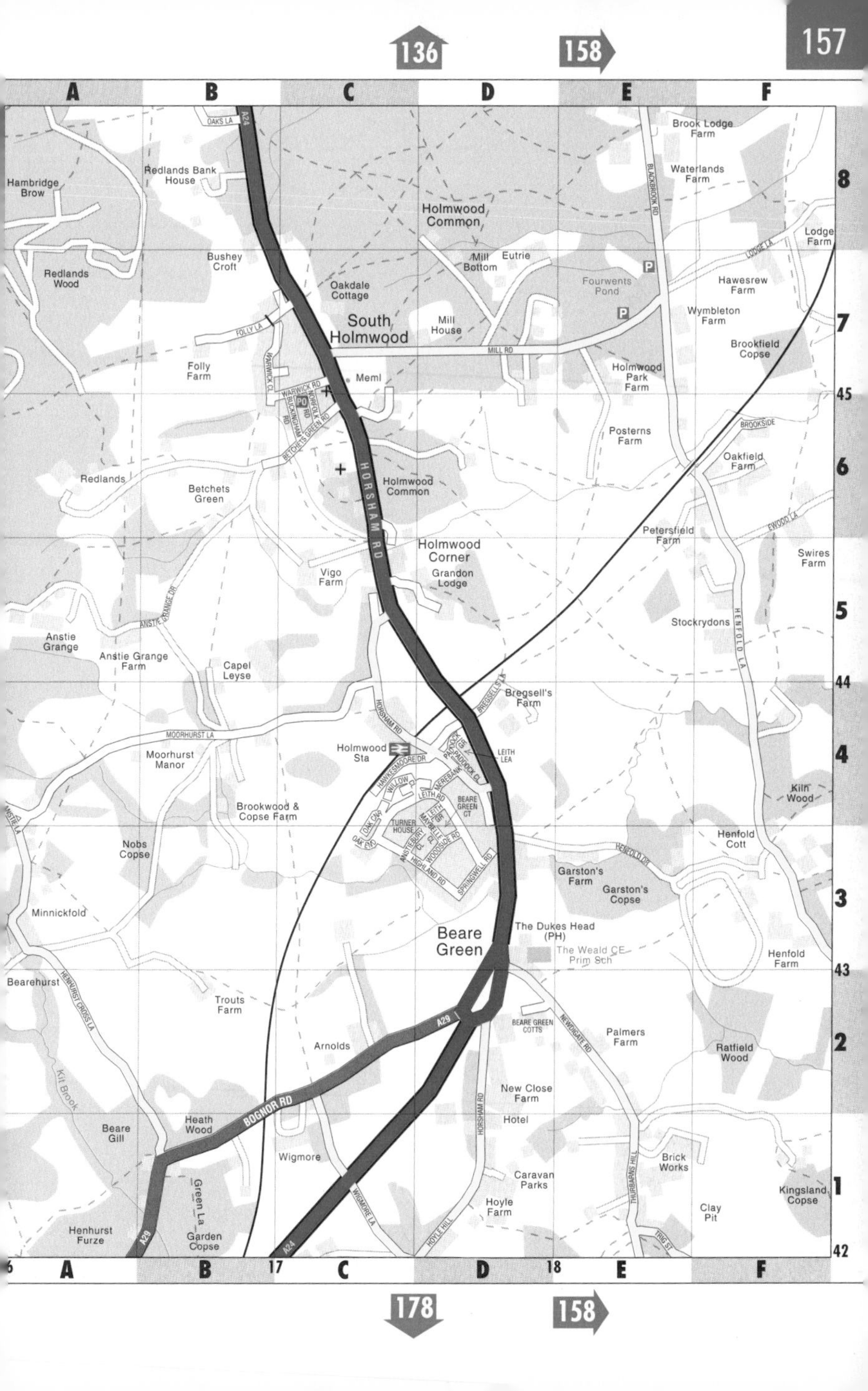
136
158
A
B
C
D
E
F
8
7
45
6
5
44
4
3
43
2
1
42
OAKS LA
A24
Redlands Bank House
Hambridge Brow
Holmwood Common
Brook Lodge Farm
Waterlands Farm
BLACKBROOK RD
Lodge Farm
LODGE LA
Bushey Croft
Redlands Wood
Mill Bottom
Eutrie
Fourwents Pond
Hawesrew Farm
Oakdale Cottage
South Holmwood
Mill House
Wymbleton Farm
Brookfield Copse
FOLLY LA
MILL RD
Folly Farm
WARWICK CL
WARWICK RD
Meml
PO
NORFOLK RD
BUCKINGHAM RD
BETCHETS GREEN RD
Holmwood Park Farm
Posterns Farm
BROOKSIDE
Oakfield Farm
Redlands
Betchets Green
HORSHAM RD
Holmwood Common
Petersfield Farm
EWOOD LA
Holmwood Corner
Swires Farm
Vigo Farm
Grandon Lodge
ANSTIE GRANGE DR
Stockrydons
HENFOLD LA
Anstie Grange
Anstie Grange Farm
Capel Leyse
BREGSELLS LA
Bregsell's Farm
MOORHURST LA
Moorhurst Manor
Holmwood Sta
HAWKESMOORE DR
PADDOCK CL
LEITH LEA
WILLOW CL
MEREBANK
LEITH RD
BEARE GREEN CT
Kiln Wood
ANSTIE LA
Brookwood & Copse Farm
OAK CNR
TURNER HOUSE
LEITH GR
MAYBELLE CL
OAK END
ANSTIEBURY CL
WOODSIDE RD
HIGHLAND RD
SPRINGWELL RD
Henfold Cott
HENFOLD DR
Nobs Copse
Garston's Farm
Garston's Copse
Minnickfold
Beare Green
The Dukes Head (PH)
The Weald CE Prim Sch
Henfold Farm
Bearehurst
HENHURST CROSS LA
Trouts Farm
A29
BEARE GREEN COTTS
NEWDIGATE RD
Palmers Farm
Arnolds
Ratfield Wood
Kit Brook
New Close Farm
BOGNOR RD
Beare Gill
Heath Wood
Hotel
HORSHAM RD
Wigmore
THURBARNS HILL
Brick Works
Green La
Caravan Parks
Kingsland Copse
WIGMORE LA
Hoyle Farm
Clay Pit
HOYLE HILL
Henhurst Furze
Garden Copse
TRIG ST
16
17
18
178
158

157 137

A B C D E F

8

Snellings Cottage
Shellwood Manor
Green La
Little Shellwood
Profits Farm

Fettercairn
Snelling Planted Field
Shellwood Cross
Brook Farm
Hilly Copse

7

Birch Platts
New Barn Shaw
Six Acre Copse
Furzefield Copse
Broadlane Rough
Parkhouse Copse

45

6

Ewood Cottages
Ewood Farm
Ewood La
Cowroom Copse
Hammond's Farm

Brook Copse
Ram Field
Parkgate Copse
Hammond's Copse
Parkhouse Farm

5

44

Cowless Field
Reffolds Copse
Reffolds Copse
Surrey Oaks (PH)
Parkgate
Partridge La
Collaroy Farm

4

Well Copse
Old St John's
Springfield Farm
Curls Copse
Blanks La
Batts La
Hales Bridge
Blank's Farm

3

Broadwood's Rough
Coombers Farm
Beam Brook

43

Gaterounds Farm
Mulberry Farm
Hound House Farm
The Red House
Sturtwood Farm

2

Henfold Cotts
Knowle
Brooklagg Farm
Woodpeckers La
Oak Lane Farm
Cudworth Rd

Knowle Copse
Newdigate
Newdigate Endowed CE Inf Sch
Hatchetts

1

Underhill Rd
Winfield Ct
PO
Kingsland
Northlands Bglws
PH
George Horley Pl
Old School La
Horsielands Farm

42

19 A B 20 C D 21 E F

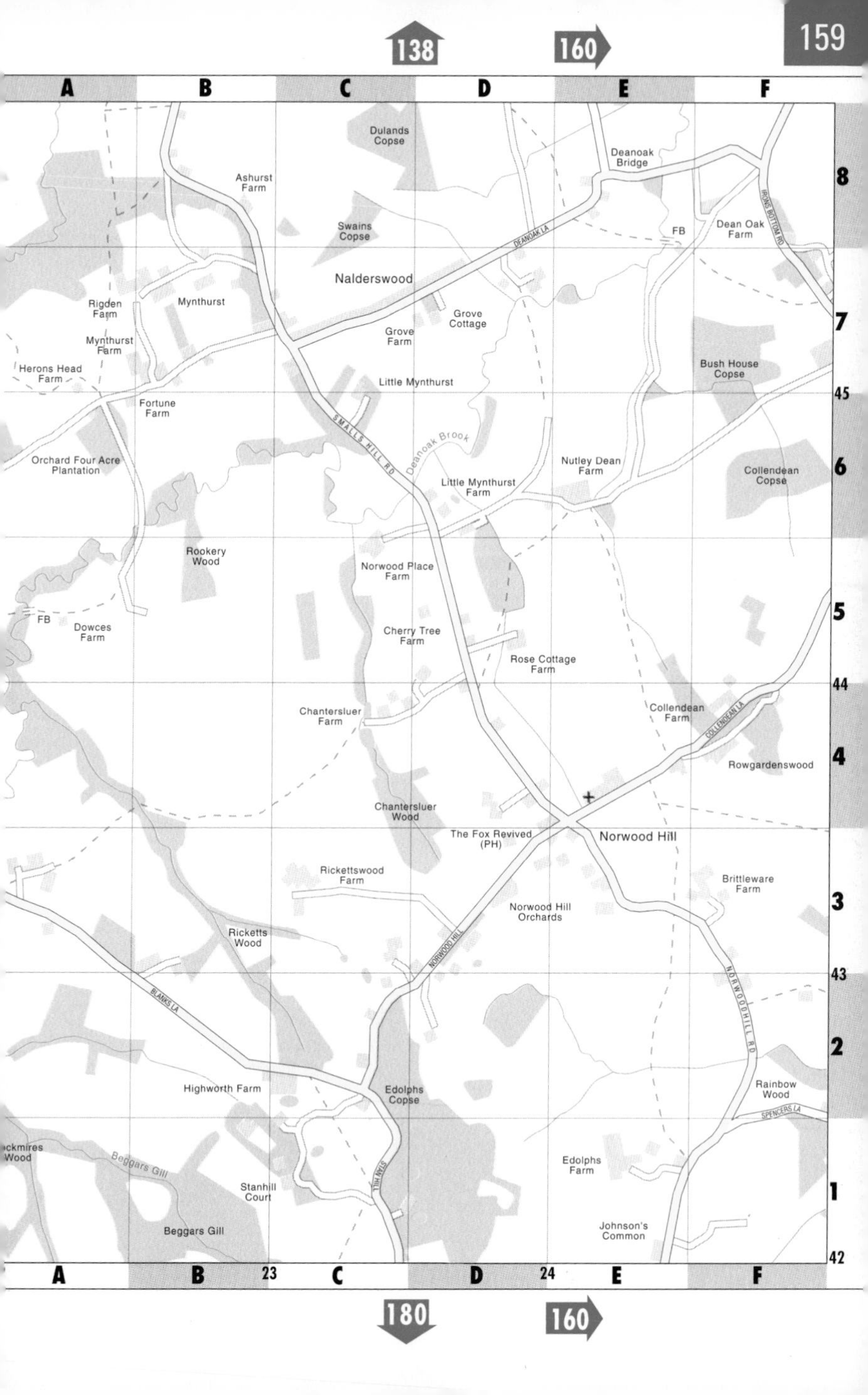

8

Dulands
Copse

Deanoak
Bridge

Ashurst
Farm

Swains
Copse

FB

Dean Oak
Farm

Nalderswood

7

Rigden
Farm

Mynthurst

Grove
Cottage

Bush House
Copse

Mynthurst
Farm

Grove
Farm

Herons Head
Farm

Little Mynthurst

45

Fortune
Farm

Deanoak Brook

Nutley Dean
Farm

Collendean
Copse

6

Orchard Four Acre
Plantation

Little Mynthurst
Farm

Rookery
Wood

Norwood Place
Farm

5

FB

Dowces
Farm

Cherry Tree
Farm

Rose Cottage
Farm

Collendean
Farm

44

Chantersluer
Farm

Rowgardenswood

4

Chantersluer
Wood

+

Norwood Hill

The Fox Revived
(PH)

Brittleware
Farm

3

Rickettswood
Farm

Norwood Hill
Orchards

Ricketts
Wood

43

BLARES LA

NORWOOD HILL

NORWOOD HILL RD

2

Highworth Farm

Rainbow
Wood

Edolphs
Copse

ckmires
Wood

Beggars Gill

Edolphs
Farm

1

Stanhill
Court

Johnson's
Common

Beggars Gill

42

159
139

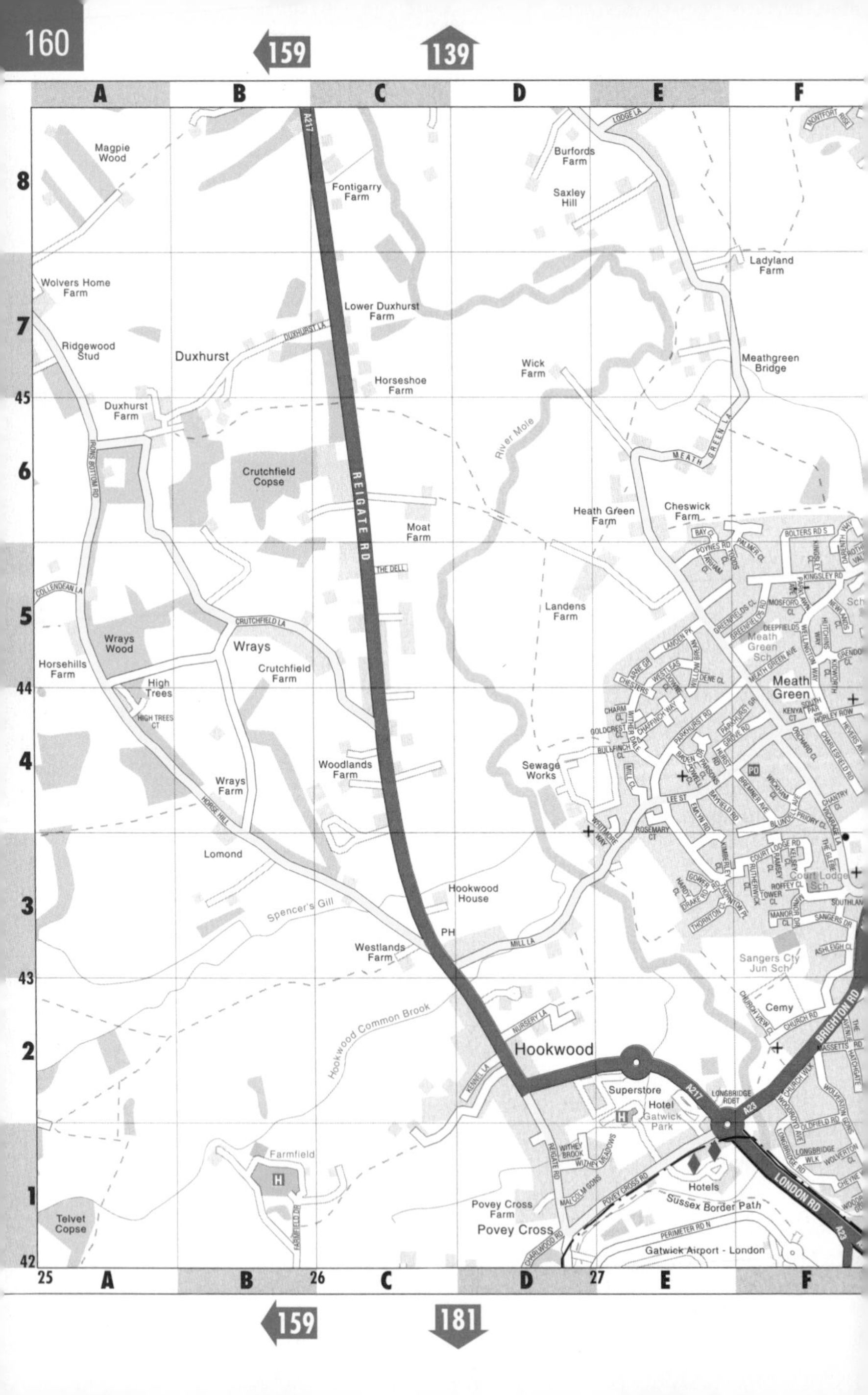
Magpie Wood
Fontigarry Farm
Burfords Farm
Saxley Hill
Ladyland Farm
Wolvers Home Farm
Lower Duxhurst Farm
Ridgewood Stud
Duxhurst
Horseshoe Farm
Wick Farm
Meathgreen Bridge
Duxhurst Farm
River Mole
Crutchfield Copse
REIGATE RD
Moat Farm
Heath Green Farm
Cheswick Farm
Landens Farm
Wrays Wood
Wrays
Crutchfield Farm
Horsehills Farm
High Trees
Meath Green
Meath Green Sch
Sewage Works
Woodlands Farm
Wrays Farm
Lomond
Hookwood House
Spencer's Gill
PH
Westlands Farm
Sangers Cty Jun Sch
Court Lodge Sch
Cemy
Hookwood Common Brook
Hookwood
Superstore
Hotel Gatwick Park
Farmfield
Hotels
Sussex Border Path
Telvet Copse
Povey Cross Farm
Povey Cross
Gatwick Airport - London
LONGBRIDGE RDBT
BRIGHTON RD
LONDON RD
A217
A23
MILL LA
HORSE HILL
IRONS BOTTOM RD
CRUTCHFIELD LA
DUXHURST LA
LODGE LA
MEATH GREEN LA
THE DELL
COLLENDEAN LA
HIGH TREES CT
NURSERY LA
KENNEL LA
CHARLWOOD RD
POVEY CROSS RD
PERIMETER RD N
WITHEY MEADOWS
MALCOLM GDNS
FARMFIELD DR
REIGATE RD
MONTFORT RISE
CHURCH RD
CHURCH VIEW CL
ROSEMARY CT
LEE ST
PARKHURST RD
A B C D E F
8 7 6 5 4 3 2 1
45 44 43 42
25 26 27

159
181

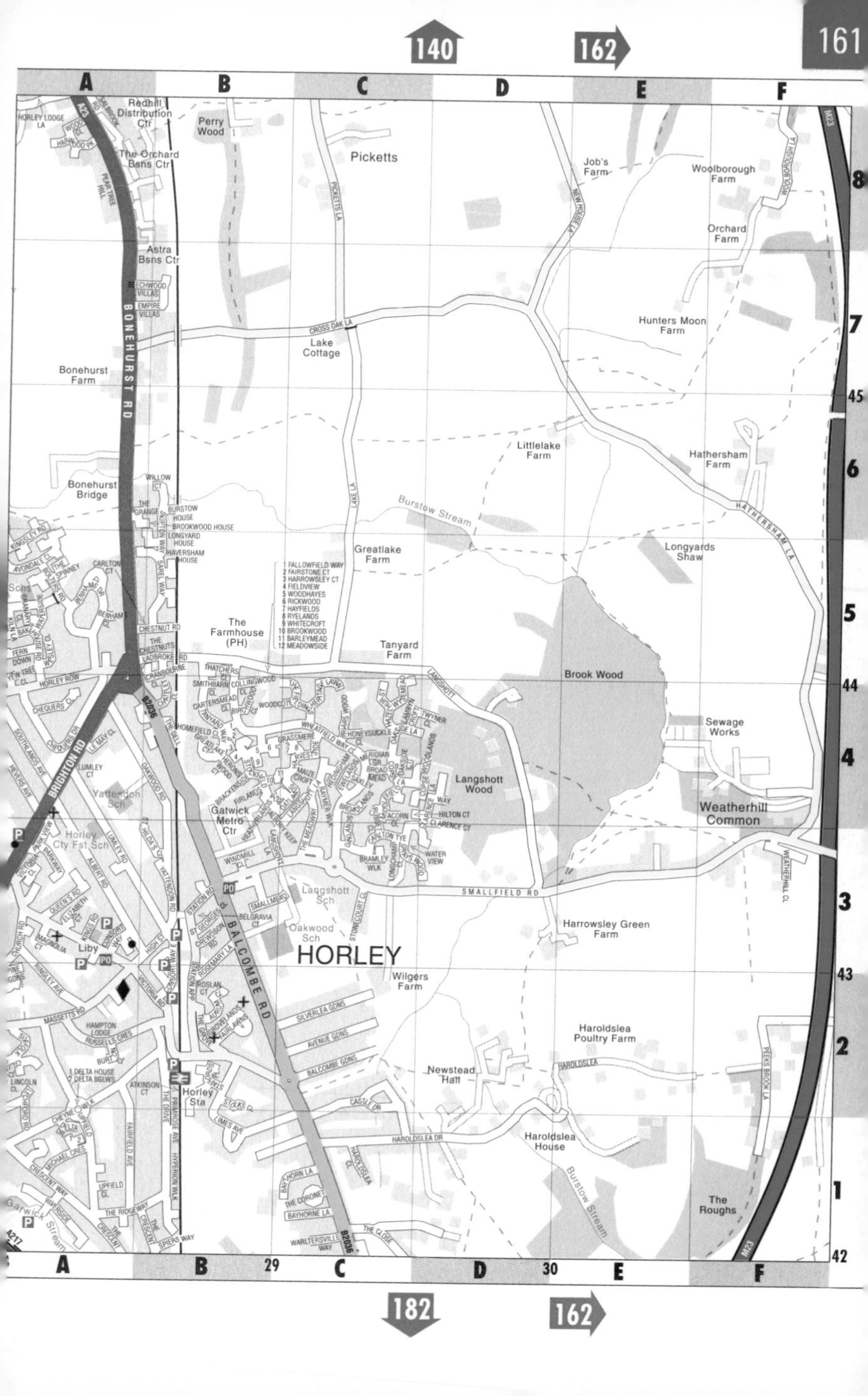

140
162

A **B** **C** **D** **E** **F**

8

7
45

6

5
44

4

3
43

2

1
42

HORLEY

Redhill Distribution Ctr
Perry Wood
Picketts
Job's Farm
Woolborough Farm
The Orchard Bsns Ctr
Orchard Farm
Astra Bsns Ctr
Hunters Moon Farm
Bonehurst Farm
Cross Oak La
Lake Cottage
Hathersham Farm
Bonehurst Bridge
Littlelake Farm
Burstow Stream
Longyards Shaw
Willow Ct
Burstow House
Brookwood House
Longyard House
Haversham House
The Grange
Greatlake Farm
Brook Wood
The Farmhouse (PH)

1 FALLOWFIELD WAY
2 FAIRSTONE CT
3 HARROWSLEY CT
4 FIELDVIEW
5 WOODHAYES
6 RICKWOOD
7 HAYFIELDS
8 RYELANDS
9 WHITECROFT
10 BROOKWOOD
11 BARLEYMEAD
12 MEADOWSIDE

Tanyard Farm
Langshott Wood
Sewage Works
Gatwick Metro Ctr
Weatherhill Common
Langshott Sch
Smallfield Rd
Oakwood Sch
Harrowsley Green Farm
Wilgers Farm
Silverlea Gdns
Avenue Gdns
Balcombe Gdns
Hampton Lodge
Haroldslea Poultry Farm
Newstead Hall
Haroldslea
1 DELTA HOUSE
2 DELTA MEWS
Horley Sta
Haroldslea Dr
Haroldslea House
Cass Cr
The Downs
Bayhorne La
Warltersville Way
The Close
Burston Stream
The Roughs

Bonehurst Rd
Brighton Rd
Balcombe Rd

A **B** 29 **C** **D** 30 **E** **F**

A B C D E F

8

Greenmeads Farm

Wasp Green Farm

Wasp Green

The Castle (PH)

Brightleigh Farm

LITTLE COLLINS

Outwood

7

M23

45

Rookery Farm

6

Drivers Green

Old Hall Farm

The Bell Inn

Gay House

Windmill

Marl House

Copsley Court

Hornecourt Wood

Hornecourt Manor Farm

Wilmot's Farm

Horne Grange

Maria Montessori Sch

Church Farm

Horne

5

Burstow Lodge Farm

Burstow Lodge

Hollesley Farm

Little Abbots Farm

Horne House Farm

44

Short Acre Farm

4

Weatherhill

WEATHERHILL COTTS

HAYES WLK

CAREY'S WOOD

CAREY'S COPSE

THE CRAVENS

COOPER CL

LARKFIELD CL

GRASSLANDS

CHURCH

HEATHER WLK

The Plough (PH)

Smallfield Place

3

NEW RD

PLOUGH RD

Rough Beech

Bysshe Court Farm

43

Burstow Prim Sch

BRIDGHAM WAY

Smallfield

Green Farm

Rough Beech Farm

2

Bridgeham Grange

RANELAGH COTTS

Redehall Prep Sch

Triddles Farm

Broadmead Farm

Saconnex Farm

Laburnum Court (Caravan Park)

1

Broadbridge Cottages

Broadbridge Farm

THE HOMESTEAD

Homestead Farm

Dowlands Wood

Roughbeech Wood

Chithurst Farm

42

CROSS LA

31 A B 32 C D 33 E F

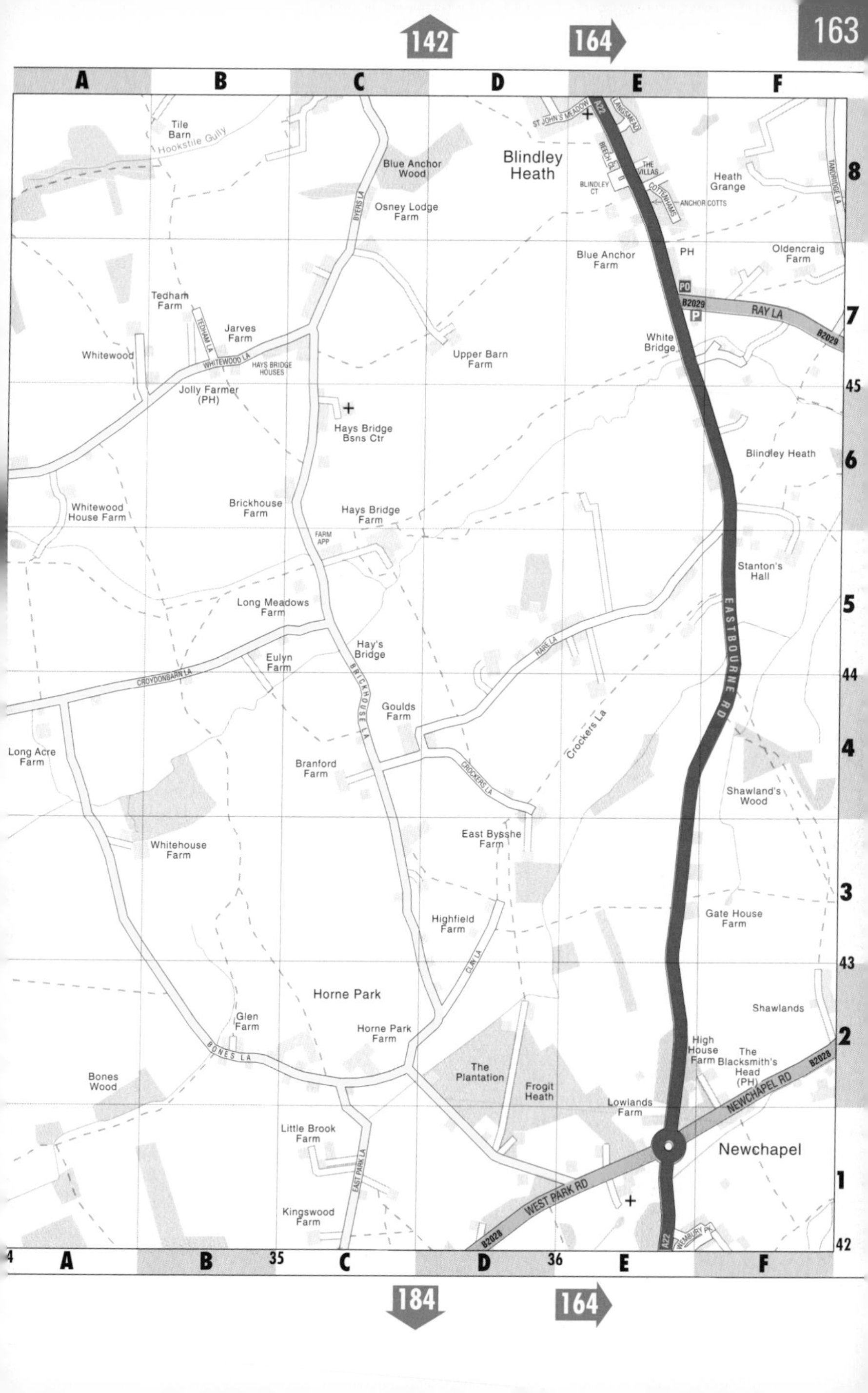
142
164
A
B
C
D
E
F
Tile Barn
Hookstile Gully
Blue Anchor Wood
Blindley Heath
ST JOHN'S MEADOW
A22
LANGSHAW
BEECH CT
THE VILLAS
BLINDLEY CT
COTTENHAMS
ANCHOR COTTS
Heath Grange
TANDRIDGE LA
8
BYERS LA
Osney Lodge Farm
Blue Anchor Farm
PH
Oldencraig Farm
PO
B2029
RAY LA
P
B2029
7
Tedham Farm
TEDHAM LA
Jarves Farm
Whitewood
WHITEWOOD LA
HAYS BRIDGE HOUSES
Upper Barn Farm
White Bridge
45
Jolly Farmer (PH)
Hays Bridge Bsns Ctr
Blindley Heath
6
Whitewood House Farm
Brickhouse Farm
Hays Bridge Farm
FARM APP
Stanton's Hall
EASTBOURNE RD
Long Meadows Farm
5
Hay's Bridge
HARE LA
Eulyn Farm
CROYDONBARN LA
BRICKHOUSE LA
44
Goulds Farm
Crockers La
Long Acre Farm
Branford Farm
CROCKERS LA
4
Shawland's Wood
Whitehouse Farm
East Bysshe Farm
3
Highfield Farm
Gate House Farm
CLIN LA
43
Horne Park
Shawlands
Glen Farm
Horne Park Farm
2
High House Farm
The Blacksmith's Head (PH)
B2028
BONES LA
The Plantation
Frogit Heath
NEWCHAPEL RD
Bones Wood
Lowlands Farm
Little Brook Farm
Newchapel
1
EAST PARK LA
WEST PARK RD
Kingswood Farm
B2028
A22
WEMBURY PK
42
4
A
B
35
C
D
36
E
F

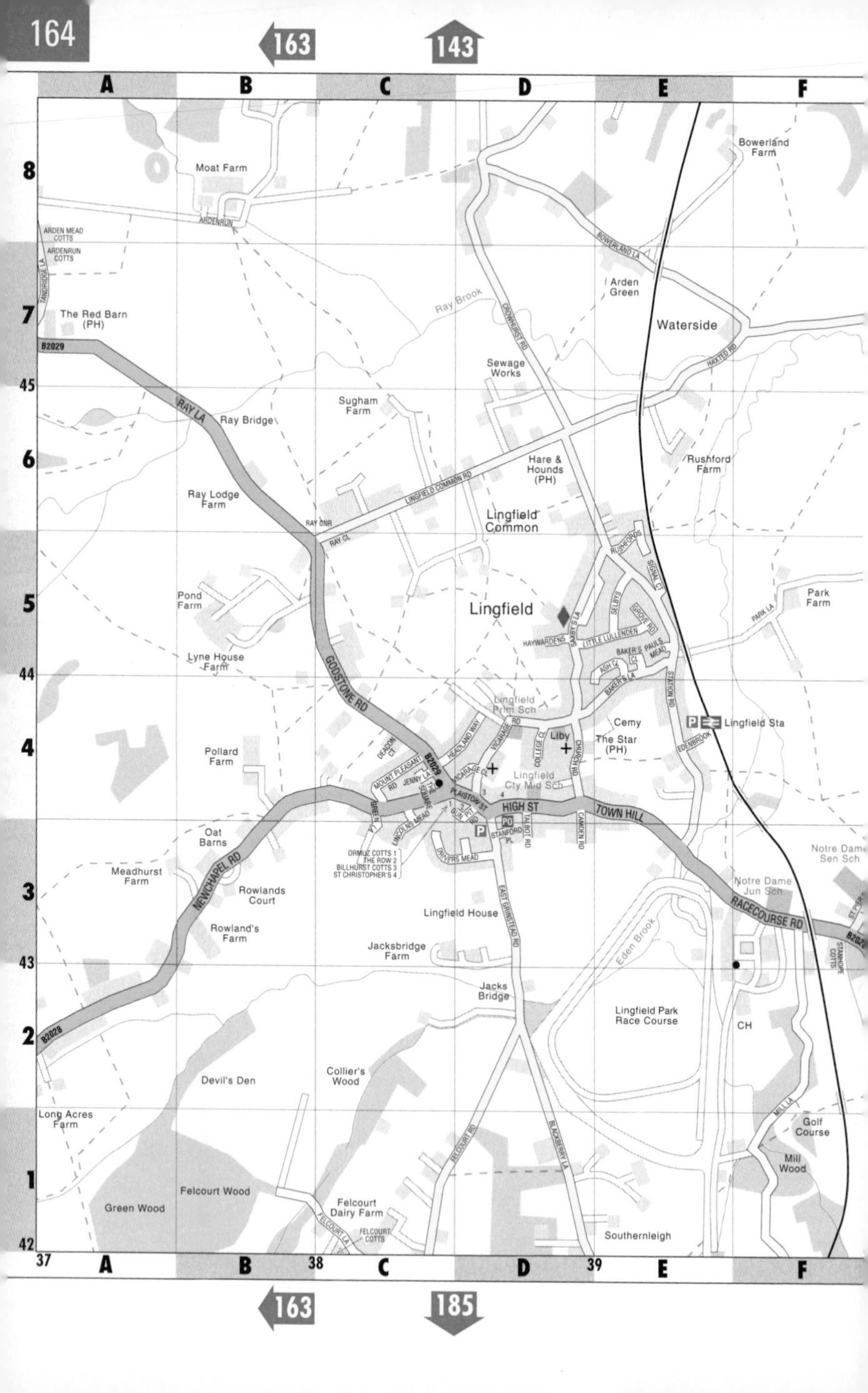
163
143
A
B
C
D
E
F
Moat Farm
ARDENRUN
ARDEN MEAD COTTS
ARDENRUN COTTS
TANDRIDGE LA
Bowerland Farm
BOWERLAND LA
Arden Green
Waterside
The Red Barn (PH)
B2029
Ray Brook
CROWHURST RD
HAXTED RD
Sewage Works
Sugham Farm
RAY LA
Ray Bridge
Hare & Hounds (PH)
Rushford Farm
Ray Lodge Farm
LINGFIELD COMMON RD
Lingfield Common
RAY CNR
RAY CL
RUSHFORDS
SIGNAL CT
Pond Farm
Lingfield
SELBYS
GROVE RD
PARK LA
Park Farm
HAYWARDENS
SAXBY'S LA
LITTLE LULLENDEN
BAKER'S CL
PAULS MEAD
ASH CL
BAKER'S LA
Lyne House Farm
GODSTONE RD
STATION RD
Lingfield Prim Sch
Cemy
Lingfield Sta
Liby
The Star (PH)
EDENBROOK
Pollard Farm
DEACON CT
HEADLAND WAY
VICARAGE RD
COLLEGE CL
CHURCH RD
MOUNT PLEASANT RD
JENNY LA
THE SQUARE
B2029
VICARAGE CL
Lingfield Cty Mid Sch
PLAISTOW ST
HIGH ST
TOWN HILL
GREEN LA
GUN PIT RD
PO
LINCOLNS MEAD
STANFORD PL
TALBOT RD
CAMDEN RD
Oat Barns
DRIVERS MEAD
ORMUZ COTTS 1
THE ROW 2
BILLHURST COTTS 3
ST CHRISTOPHER'S 4
Notre Dame Sen Sch
Meadhurst Farm
NEWCHAPEL RD
Rowlands Court
EAST GRINSTEAD RD
Notre Dame Jun Sch
RACECOURSE RD
Lingfield House
Rowland's Farm
Eden Brook
Jacksbridge Farm
STANHOPE COTTS
Jacks Bridge
Lingfield Park Race Course
CH
B2028
Devil's Den
Collier's Wood
Long Acres Farm
FELCOURT RD
BLACKBERRY LA
MILL LA
Golf Course
Mill Wood
Felcourt Wood
Green Wood
Felcourt Dairy Farm
FELCOURT LA
FELCOURT COTTS
Southernleigh
8
7
45
6
5
44
4
3
43
2
1
42
37
38
39
185

144

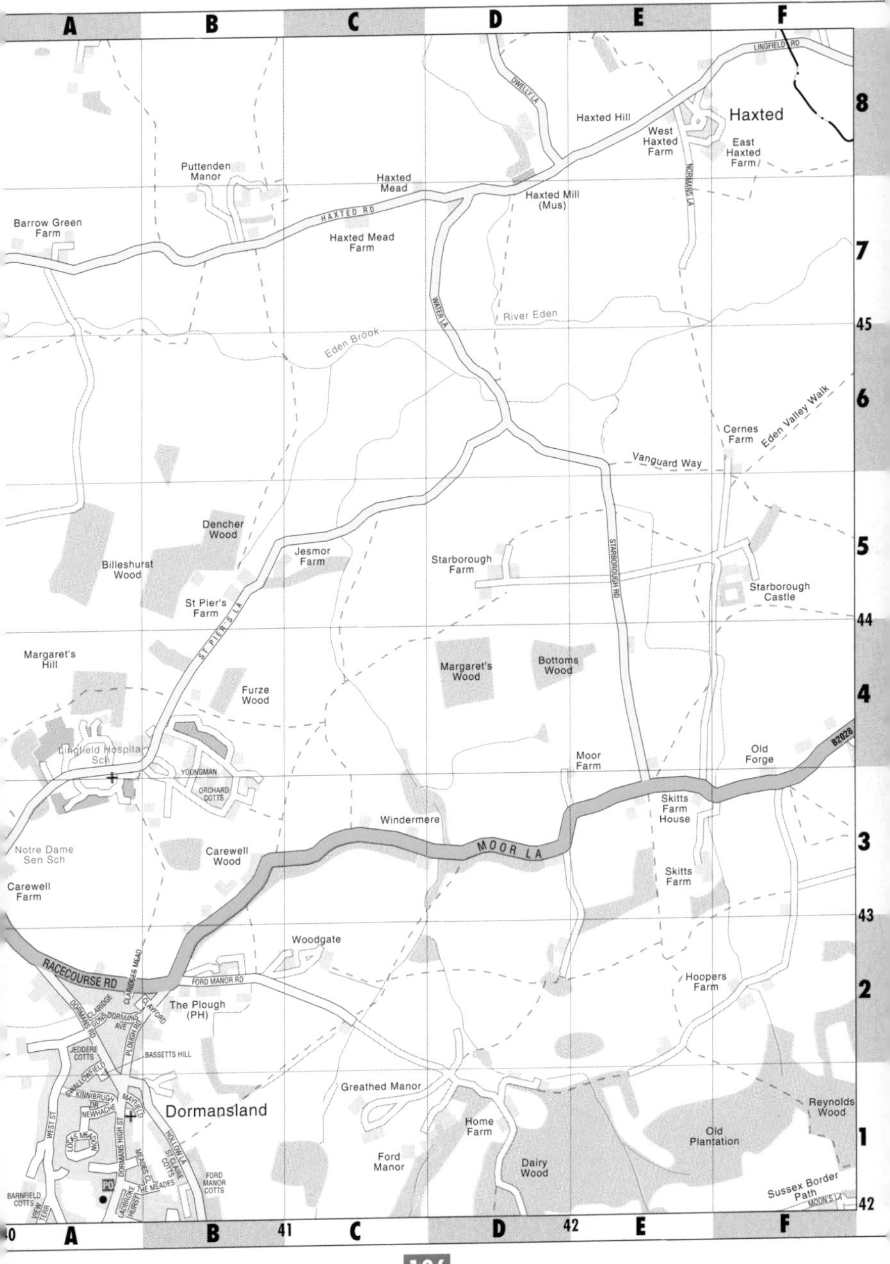

A
B
C
D
E
F
LINGFIELD RD
DWELLY LA
Haxted Hill
Haxted
West Haxted Farm
East Haxted Farm
Puttenden Manor
Haxted Mead
Haxted Mill (Mus)
NORMANS LA
Barrow Green Farm
HAXTED RD
Haxted Mead Farm
WATER LA
River Eden
Eden Brook
Cernes Farm
Eden Valley Walk
Vanguard Way
Dencher Wood
Jesmor Farm
Starborough Farm
STARBOROUGH RD
Starborough Castle
Billeshurst Wood
St Pier's Farm
ST PIER'S LA
Margaret's Hill
Margaret's Wood
Bottoms Wood
Furze Wood
Lingfield Hospital Sch
YOUNGMAN
ORCHARD COTTS
Moor Farm
Old Forge
B2028
Skitts Farm House
Windermere
MOOR LA
Notre Dame Sen Sch
Carewell Wood
Carewell Farm
Skitts Farm
Woodgate
RACECOURSE RD
CLARIDGES MEAD
FORD MANOR RD
Hoopers Farm
The Plough (PH)
DORMANS PARK
CLARIDGE GDNS
DORMANS AVE
PLOUGH RD
CLAYFORD
JEDDERE COTTS
BASSETTS HILL
SWALLOWFIELD
KINNIBRUGH DR
NEWHACHE
MAYFIELD
Greathed Manor
Dormansland
WEST ST
LOCKS MEADOW
DORMANS HIGH ST
HOLLOW LA
ST CLAIRE COTTS
MEADES CL
THE MEADES
Home Farm
Reynolds Wood
Old Plantation
Ford Manor
Dairy Wood
FORD MANOR COTTS
PO
BARNFIELD COTTS
VIEW TERR
LADBROKE HURST
Sussex Border Path
MOON'S LA
8
7
45
6
5
44
4
3
43
2
1
42
40
41
42

186

145

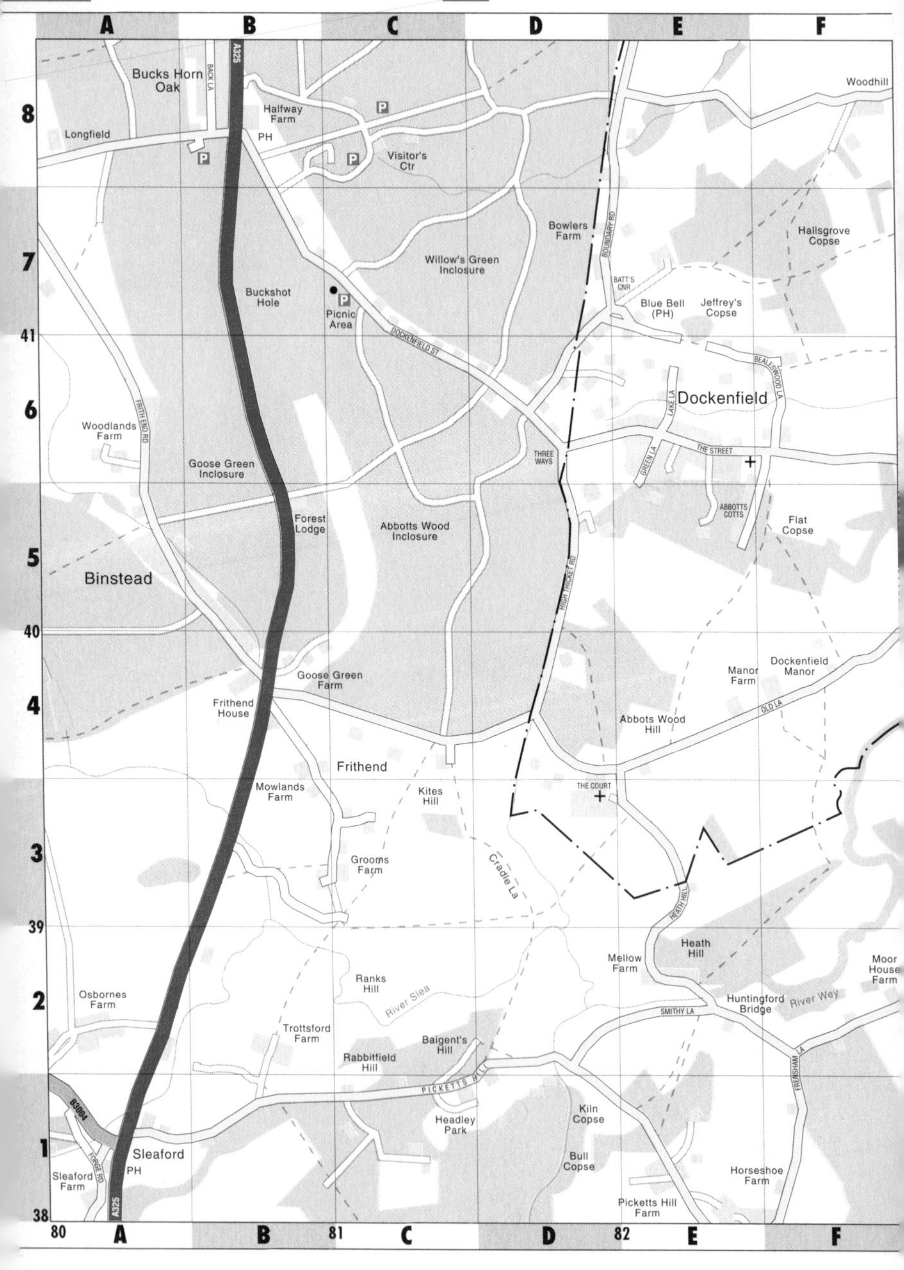
A
B
C
D
E
F
8
7
41
6
5
40
4
3
39
2
1
38
80
81
82
Bucks Horn Oak
BACK LA
A325
Halfway Farm
PH
Longfield
Visitor's Ctr
Woodhill
Bowlers Farm
BOUNDARY RD
Hallsgrove Copse
Willow's Green Inclosure
BATT'S CNR
Buckshot Hole
Picnic Area
Blue Bell (PH)
Jeffrey's Copse
DOCKENFIELD ST
BEALESWOOD LA
FRITH END RD
LAKE LA
Dockenfield
Woodlands Farm
THREE WAYS
GREEN LA
THE STREET
Goose Green Inclosure
ABBOTTS COTTS
Flat Copse
Forest Lodge
Abbotts Wood Inclosure
Binstead
HIGH THICKET RD
Dockenfield Manor
Manor Farm
Goose Green Farm
Frithend House
Abbots Wood Hill
OLD LA
Frithend
Mowlands Farm
Kites Hill
THE COURT
Grooms Farm
Cradle La
HEATH HILL
Heath Hill
Mellow Farm
Moor House Farm
Ranks Hill
Osbornes Farm
River Slea
Huntingford Bridge
River Wey
SMITHY LA
Trottsford Farm
Baigent's Hill
Rabbitfield Hill
FRENSHAM LA
PICKETTS HILL
B3004
Headley Park
Kiln Copse
Sleaford
PH
FORGE RD
Bull Copse
Sleaford Farm
Horseshoe Farm
Picketts Hill Farm

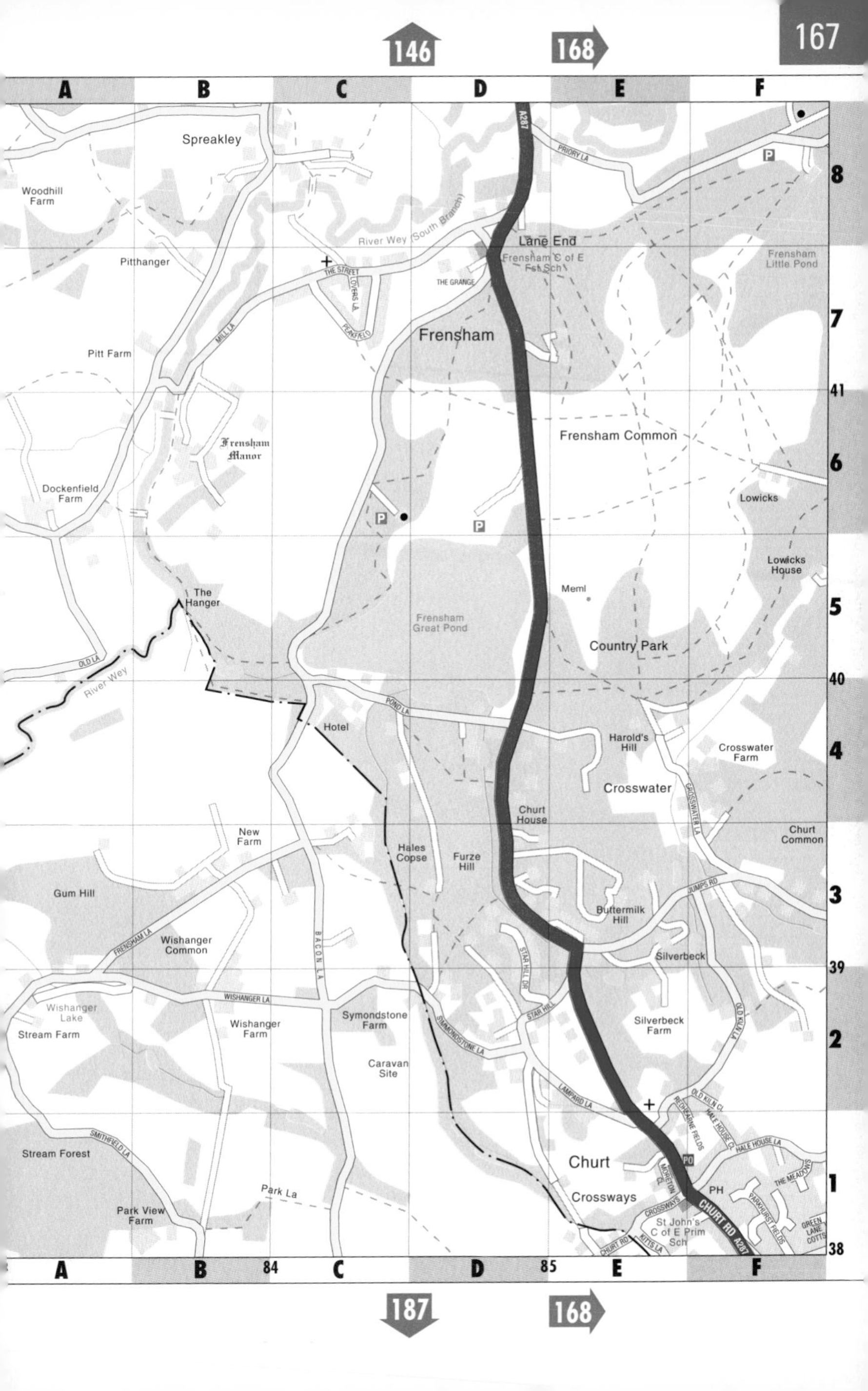

A   B   C   D   E   F

8

Woodhill Farm

Spreakley

River Wey (South Branch)

Lane End

Pitthanger

THE STREET
THE GRANGE
Frensham C of E
Fst Sch

Frensham
Little Pond

7

Pitt Farm

Frensham

41

Frensham Manor

Frensham Common

6

Dockenfield Farm

Lowicks

Lowicks House

The Hanger

OLD LA

River Wey

Frensham
Great Pond

Meml

Country Park

5

40

Hotel

POND LA

Harold's Hill

Crosswater Farm

4

New Farm

Hales Copse

Furze Hill

Churt House

Crosswater

Churt Common

Gum Hill

FRENSHAM LA

Wishanger Common

BACON LA

3

Wishanger Lake

WISHANGER LA

Wishanger Farm

Symondstone Farm

Buttermilk Hill

Silverbeck

39

Stream Farm

Caravan Site

SYMONDSTONE LA

STAR HILL DR

STAR HILL

Silverbeck Farm

2

Stream Forest

SMITHFIELD LA

Park La

Park View Farm

Churt

Crossways

CHURT RD

St John's
C of E Prim
Sch

PH

PO

THE MEADOW

GREEN LANE COTTS

1

38

A   B   84   C   D   85   E   F

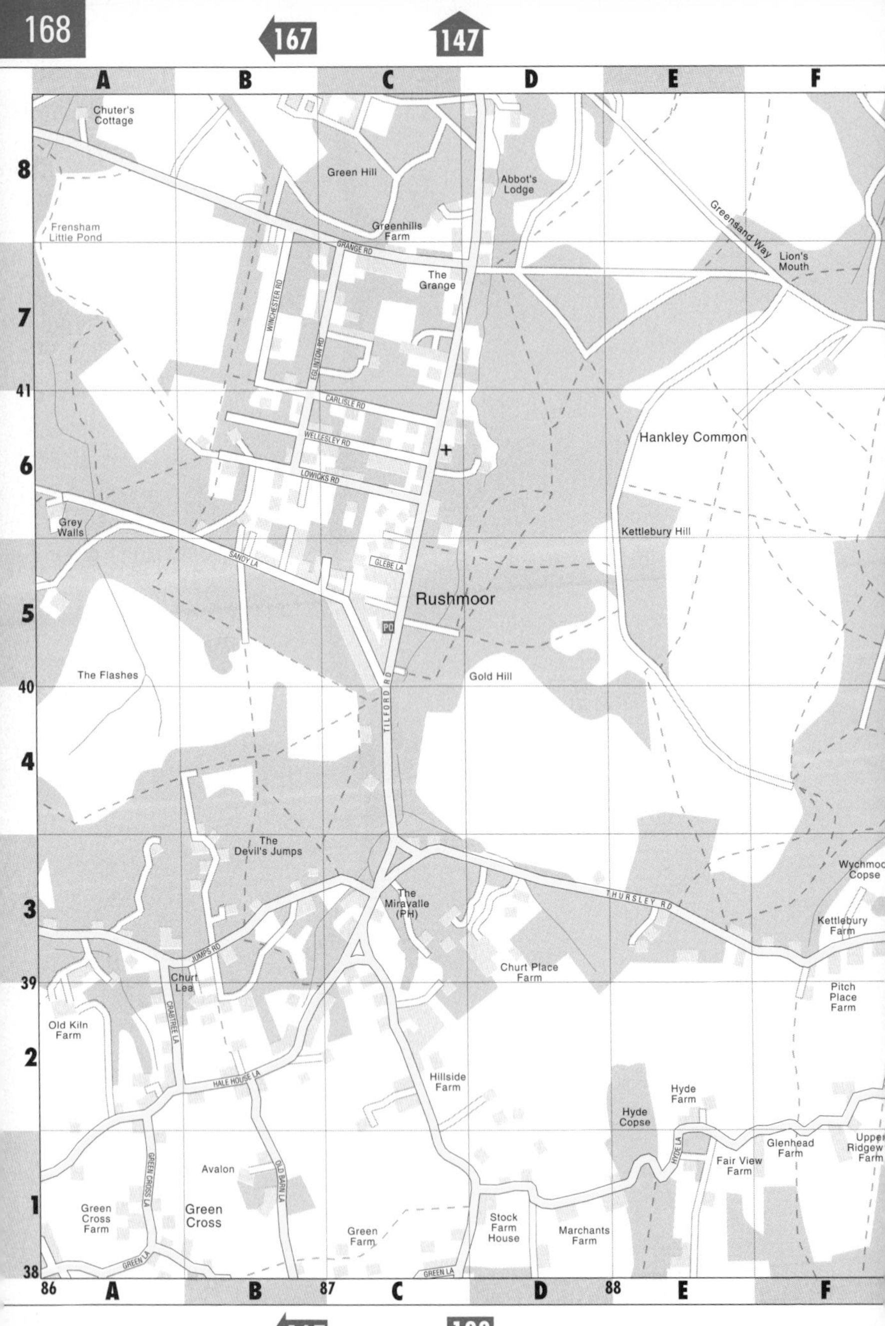

A B C D E F

Chuter's Cottage

8 Green Hill

Abbot's Lodge

Greenhills Farm

Frensham Little Pond

GRANGE RD

Greensand Way

Lion's Mouth

The Grange

7

WINCHESTER RD

GILSTON RD

41 CARLISLE RD

Hankley Common

WELLERLEY RD

6 LOWICKS RD

Kettlebury Hill

Grey Walls

SANDY LA

GLEBE LA

Rushmoor

5 P

TILFORD RD

The Flashes

40 Gold Hill

4

The Devil's Jumps

THURSLEY RD

Wychmoor Copse

The Miravalle (PH)

3

Kettlebury Farm

JUMPS RD

Churt Lea

Churt Place Farm

Pitch Place Farm

39

CHURT LA

Old Kiln Farm

2 HALE HOUSE LA

Hillside Farm

Hyde Farm

Hyde Copse

Glenhead Farm

Upper Ridgew Farm

GREEN CROSS LA

OLD BARN LA

Avalon

Fair View Farm

HYDE LA

1 Green Cross Farm

Green Cross

Green Farm

Stock Farm House

Marchants Farm

38

GREEN LA

GREEN LA

A 86 **B** 87 **C** **D** 88 **E** **F**

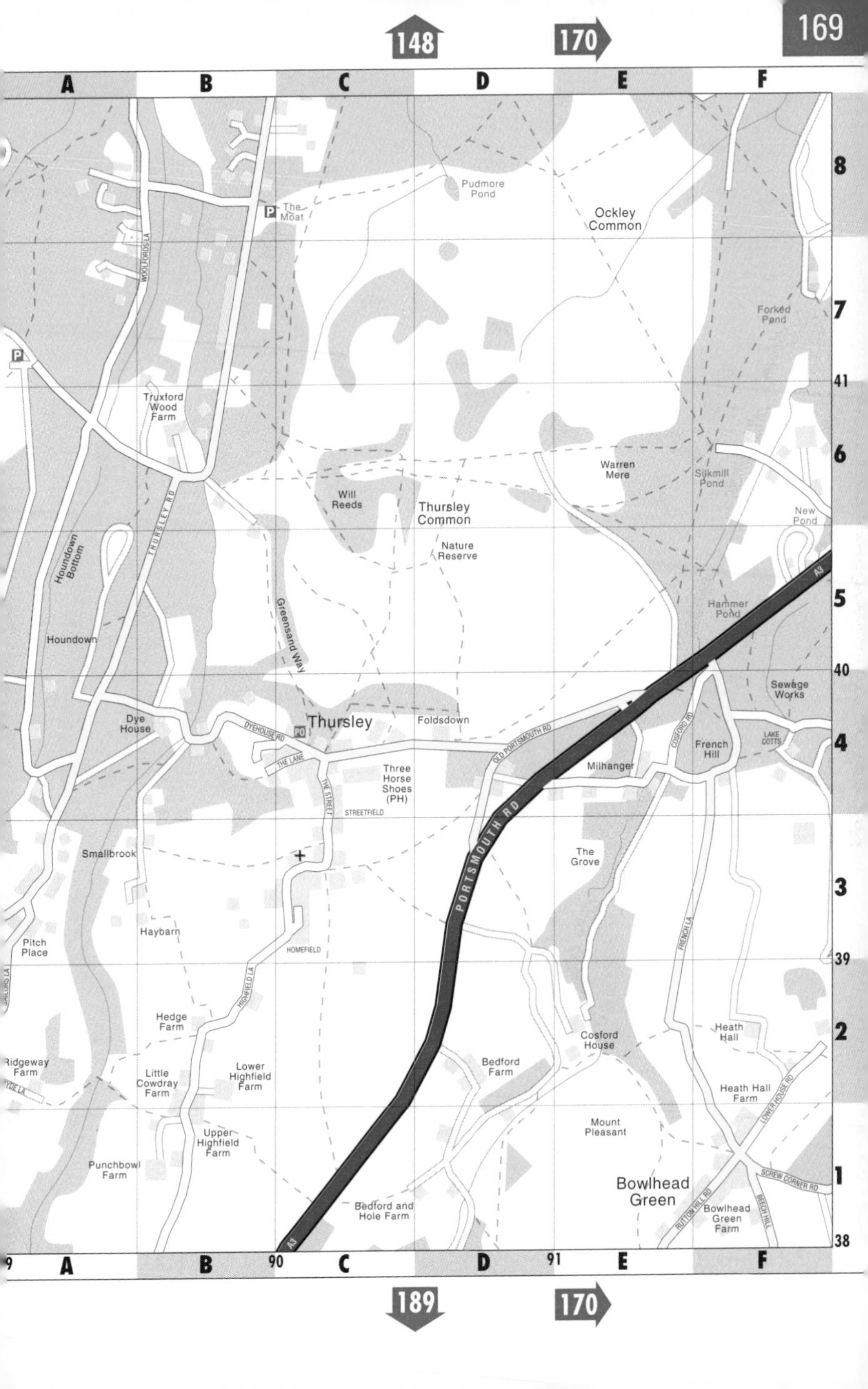
148
170
A
B
C
D
E
F
8
7
41
6
5
40
4
3
39
2
1
38
The Moat
Pudmore Pond
Ockley Common
Forked Pond
WOOLFORDS LA
Truxford Wood Farm
THURSLEY RD
Warren Mere
Silkmill Pond
New Pond
Will Reeds
Thursley Common
Nature Reserve
Houndown Bottom
Greensand Way
Hammer Pond
A3
Houndown
Sewage Works
Dye House
Thursley
Foldsdown
DYEHOUSE RD
PO
OLD PORTSMOUTH RD
COSFORD RD
French Hill
LAKE COTTS
THE LANE
THE STREET
Three Horse Shoes (PH)
Milhanger
STREETFIELD
PORTSMOUTH RD
Smallbrook
The Grove
Haybarn
HOMEFIELD
FRENCH LA
Pitch Place
HIGHFIELD LA
Hedge Farm
Heath Hall
Cosford House
Ridgeway Farm
Little Cowdray Farm
Lower Highfield Farm
Bedford Farm
Heath Hall Farm
LOWER HOUSE RD
Upper Highfield Farm
Mount Pleasant
Punchbowl Farm
Bowlhead Green
SCREW CORNER RD
RUTTON HILL RD
BEECH HILL
Bedford and Hole Farm
Bowlhead Green Farm
90
91
189
170

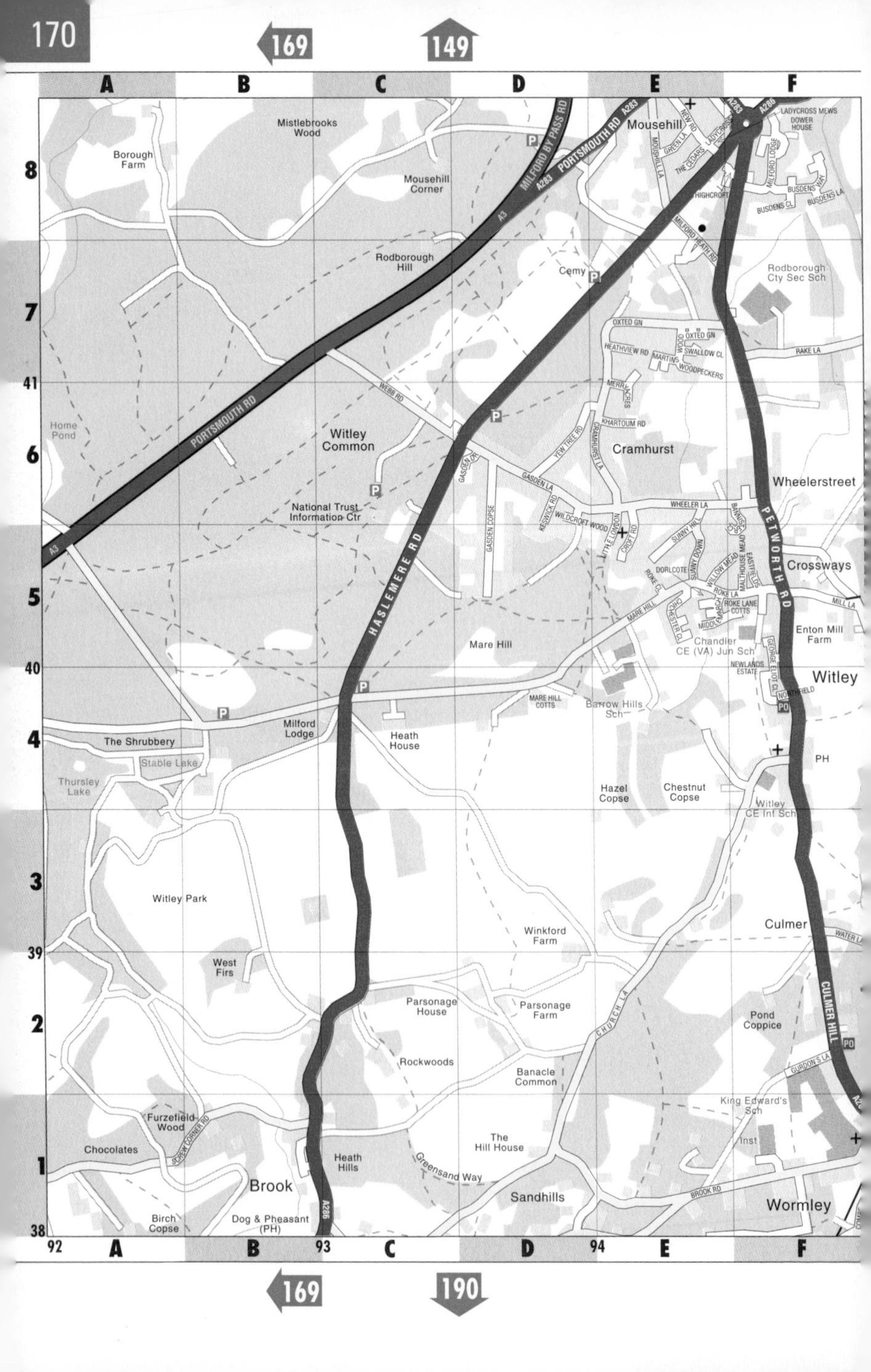
169
149
A B C D E F
8 7 41 6 5 40 4 3 39 2 1 38
92 93 94
Mistlebrooks Wood
Borough Farm
Mousehill Corner
Mousehill
MILFORD BY PASS RD
PORTSMOUTH RD
A3
A283
A286
LADYCROSS MEWS
DOWER HOUSE
MILFORD LODGE
BUSDENS WAY
BUSDENS CL
BUSDENS LA
HIGHCROFT
MILFORD HEATH RD
Rodborough Hill
Cemy
Rodborough Cty Sec Sch
OXTED GN
SWALLOW CL
HEATHVIEW RD
MARTINS
WOODPECKERS
RAKE LA
MERRYACRES
KHARTOUM RD
WEBB RD
Home Pond
Witley Common
Cramhurst
YEW TREE RD
CRAMHURST LA
GASDEN CR
GASDEN LA
GASDEN COPSE
Wheelerstreet
WHEELER LA
National Trust Information Ctr
KESWICK RD
WILDCROFT WOOD
LITTLE LONDON
CROFT RD
SUNNY HILL
SUNNY DOWN
WILLOW MEAD
MALTHOUSE MEAD
EASTFIELDS
PETWORTH RD
HASLEMERE RD
Crossways
DORLCOTE
ROKE CL
ROKE LA
ROKE LANE COTTS
MILL LA
MARE HILL
CHESTER CL
MIDDLEMARCH
Enton Mill Farm
Mare Hill
Chandler CE (VA) Jun Sch
GEORGE ELIOT CL
NEWLANDS ESTATE
NORTHFIELD
Witley
MARE HILL COTTS
Barrow Hills Sch
Milford Lodge
Heath House
The Shrubbery
Stable Lake
Thursley Lake
PH
Hazel Copse
Chestnut Copse
Witley CE Inf Sch
Witley Park
Culmer
WATER LA
Winkford Farm
West Firs
CULMER HILL
Parsonage House
Parsonage Farm
CHURCH LA
Pond Coppice
Rockwoods
Banacle Common
GURDON'S LA
King Edward's Sch
Furzefield Wood
SCREW CORNER RD
Chocolates
The Hill House
Inst
Heath Hills
Greensand Way
Brook
Sandhills
BROOK RD
Wormley
Birch Copse
Dog & Pheasant (PH)
169
190

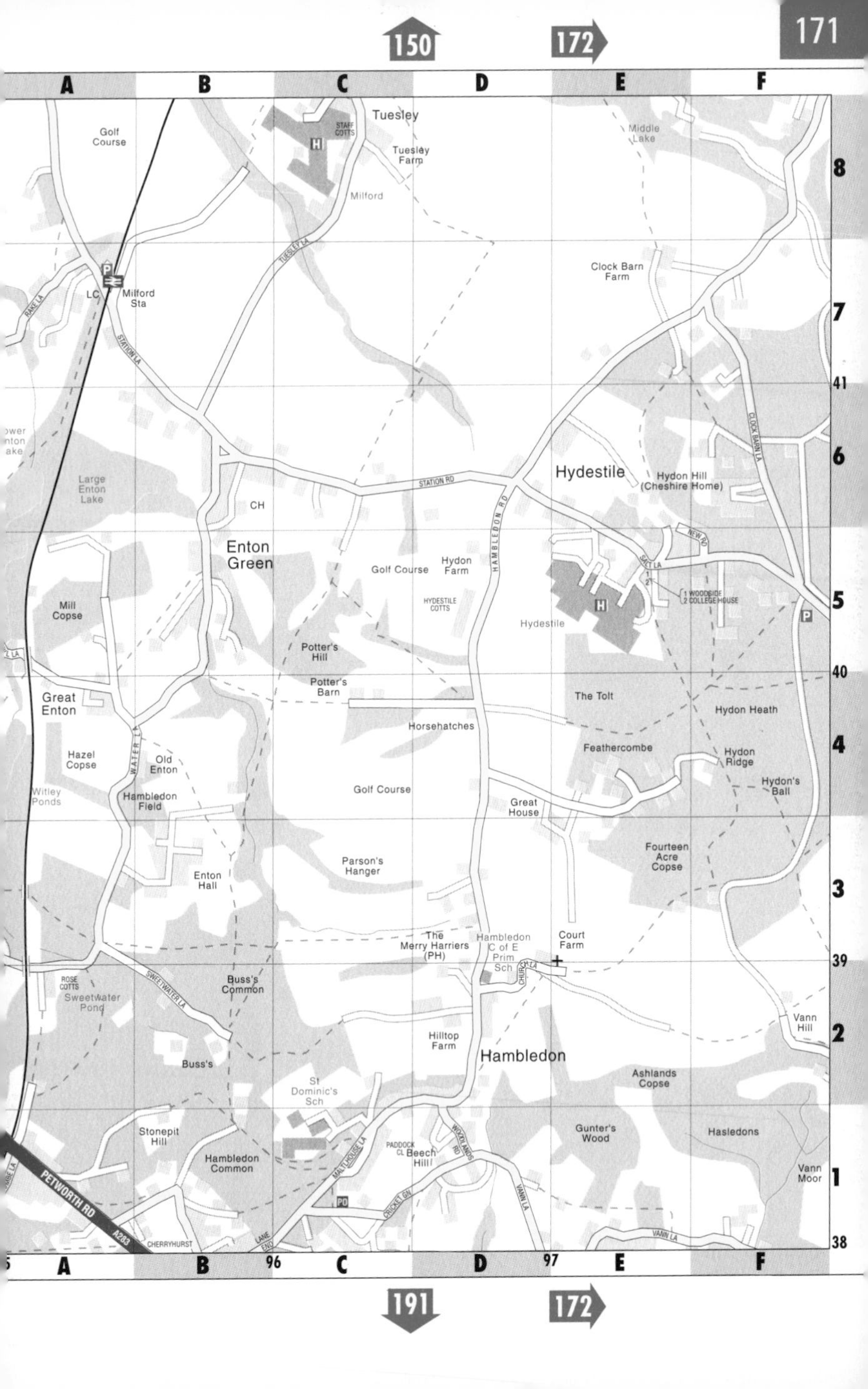

150
172

A   **B**   **C**   **D**   **E**   **F**

Golf
Course

Tuesley

Tuesley
Farm

Milford

STAFF
COTTS

H

8

Middle
Lake

Clock Barn
Farm

7

P

LC

Milford
Sta

TUESLEY LA

BEGUM LA

SQUIRREL LA

41

STATION RD

Large
Enton
Lake

CH

Enton
Green

Golf Course

Hydon
Farm

Hydestile

Hydon Hill
(Cheshire Home)

NEW RD

6

HYDESTILE
COTTS

Hydestile

H

WOODSIDE
COLLEGE HOUSE

P

5

HAMBLEDON RD

CLOCK BARN LA

SALT LA

Mill
Copse

Potter's
Hill

Potter's
Barn

The Tolt

Hydon Heath

40

Great
Enton

Horsehatches

Feathercombe

Hydon
Ridge

Hydon's
Ball

4

Hazel
Copse

Old
Enton

Hambledon
Field

Golf Course

Great
House

WITLEY LA

Witley
Ponds

Fourteen
Acre
Copse

Parson's
Hanger

Enton
Hall

3

The
Merry Harriers
(PH)

Hambledon
C of E
Prim
Sch

Court
Farm

+

39

ROSE
COTTS

Sweetwater
Pond

Buss's
Common

Hilltop
Farm

Hambledon

Vann
Hill

2

SALT LA

GREAT ENTON LA

CHURCH LA

Buss's

St
Dominic's
Sch

Ashlands
Copse

Hasledons

Stonepit
Hill

Hambledon
Common

PADDOCK
Gn

Beech
Hill

Gunter's
Wood

Vann
Moor

1

PO

PETWORTH RD
A283

VANN LA LANE

HALL HOUSE LA

LANE

CRICKET GN

BOXALL RD

VANN LA

Cherryhurst

38

A   **B**   **C**   **D**   **E**   **F**

96   97

191
172

171
151

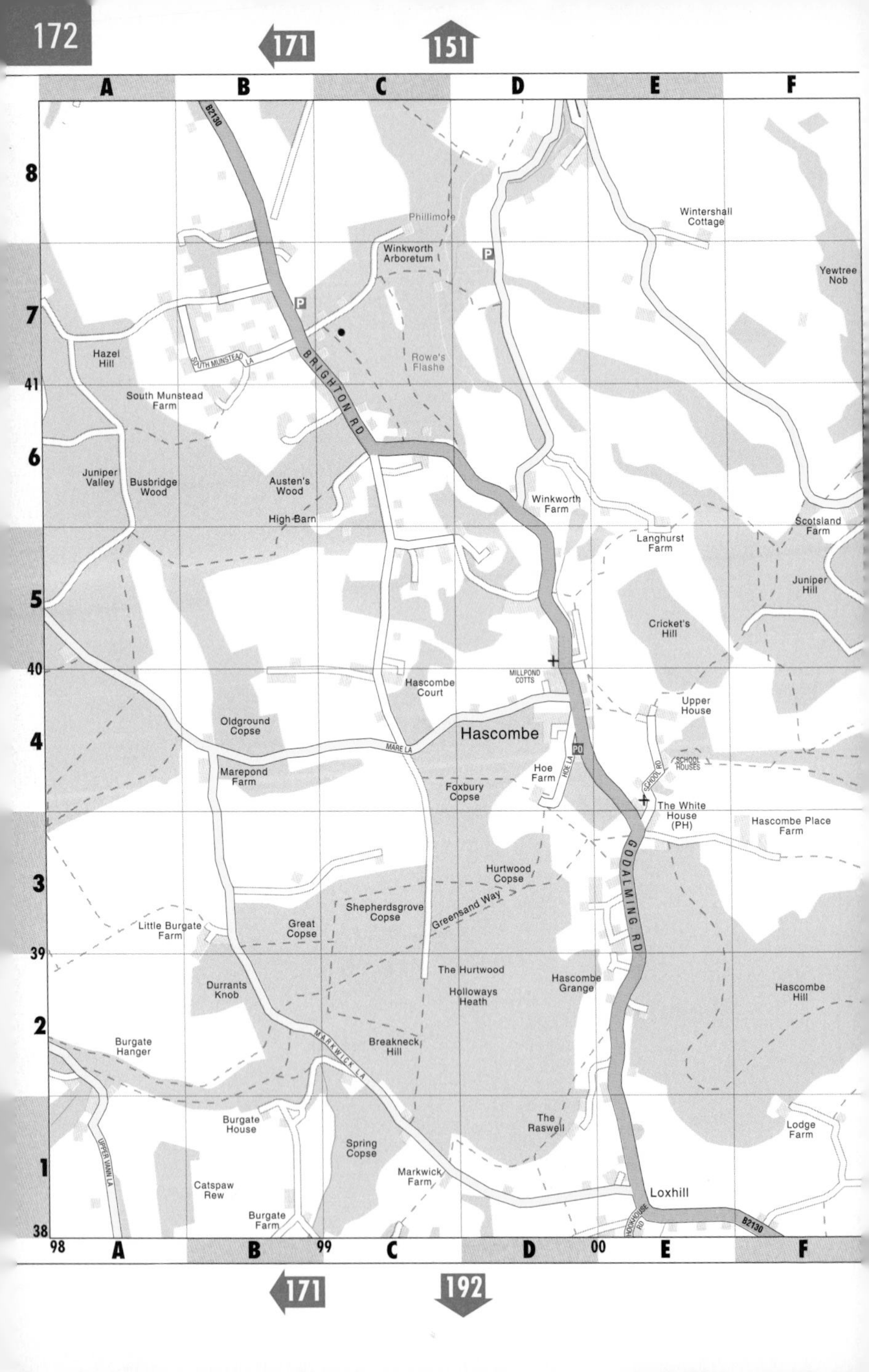
A
B
C
D
E
F
8
7
41
6
5
40
4
3
39
2
1
38
98
99
00
B2130
Phillimore
Winkworth
Arboretum
P
Wintershall
Cottage
Yewtree
Nob
Hazel
Hill
SOUTH MUNSTEAD LA
BRIGHTON RD
Rowe's
Flashe
South Munstead
Farm
Juniper
Valley
Busbridge
Wood
Austen's
Wood
High Barn
Winkworth
Farm
Langhurst
Farm
Scotsland
Farm
Juniper
Hill
Cricket's
Hill
MILLPOND
COTTS
Hascombe
Court
Upper
House
Oldground
Copse
Hascombe
MARE LA
PO
HOE LA
SCHOOL RD
SCHOOL
HOUSES
Marepond
Farm
Hoe
Farm
Foxbury
Copse
The White
House
(PH)
Hascombe Place
Farm
GODALMING RD
Hurtwood
Copse
Shepherdsgrove
Copse
Greensand Way
Little Burgate
Farm
Great
Copse
The Hurtwood
Hascombe
Grange
Hascombe
Hill
Durrants
Knob
Holloways
Heath
Burgate
Hanger
MARKWICK LA
Breakneck
Hill
Burgate
House
The
Raswell
Lodge
Farm
UPPER VANN LA
Spring
Copse
Catspaw
Rew
Markwick
Farm
Loxhill
Burgate
Farm
HOOKHOUSE RD
B2130

171
192

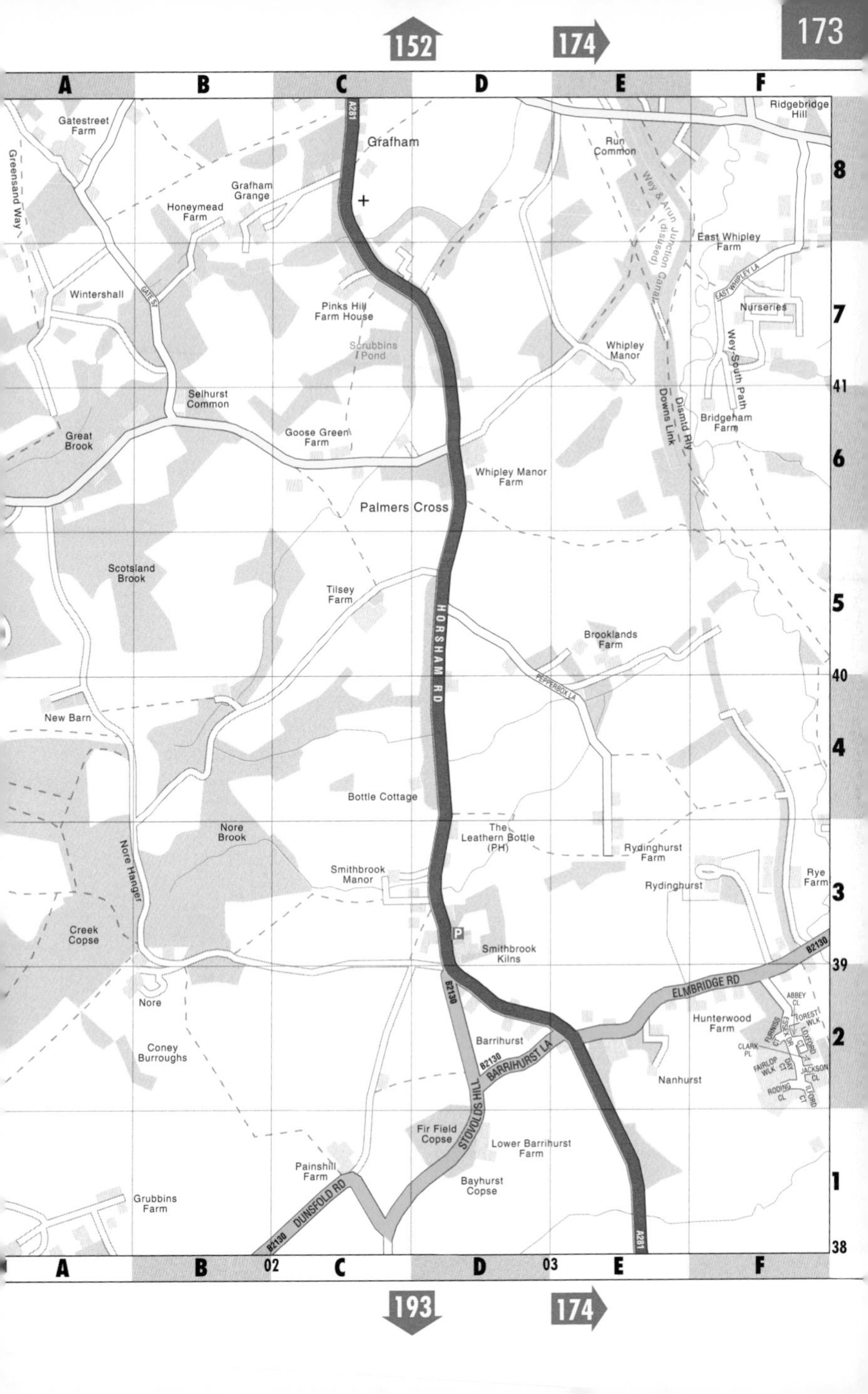
152
174
A
B
C
D
E
F
A281
Gatestreet Farm
Greensand Way
Grafham
Ridgebridge Hill
Run Common
Grafham Grange
Honeymead Farm
Wey & Arun Junction Canal (disused)
East Whipley Farm
EAST WHIPLEY LA
Wintershall
GATE ST
Pinks Hill Farm House
Nurseries
Scrubbins Pond
Whipley Manor
Wey-South Path
Selhurst Common
Dismtd Rly
Downs Link
Bridgeham Farm
Great Brook
Goose Green Farm
Whipley Manor Farm
Palmers Cross
Scotsland Brook
Tilsey Farm
HORSHAM RD
Brooklands Farm
PEPPERBOX LA
New Barn
Bottle Cottage
Nore Brook
Nore Hanger
The Leathern Bottle (PH)
Rydinghurst Farm
Smithbrook Manor
Rydinghurst
Rye Farm
Creek Copse
P
Smithbrook Kilns
B2130
ELMBRIDGE RD
Nore
ABBEY CL
FOREST WLK
Hunterwood Farm
FURNISS CT
ESSEX DR
CLARK PL
LOXFORD CT
FAIRLOP WLK
DAY CT
JACKSON CL
RODING CL
ILFORD CT
Barrihurst
BARRIHURST LA
Coney Burroughs
Nanhurst
Fir Field Copse
STOVOLDS HILL
Lower Barrihurst Farm
Painshill Farm
DUNSFOLD RD
Bayhurst Copse
Grubbins Farm
8
7
41
6
5
40
4
3
39
2
1
38
02
03
193
174

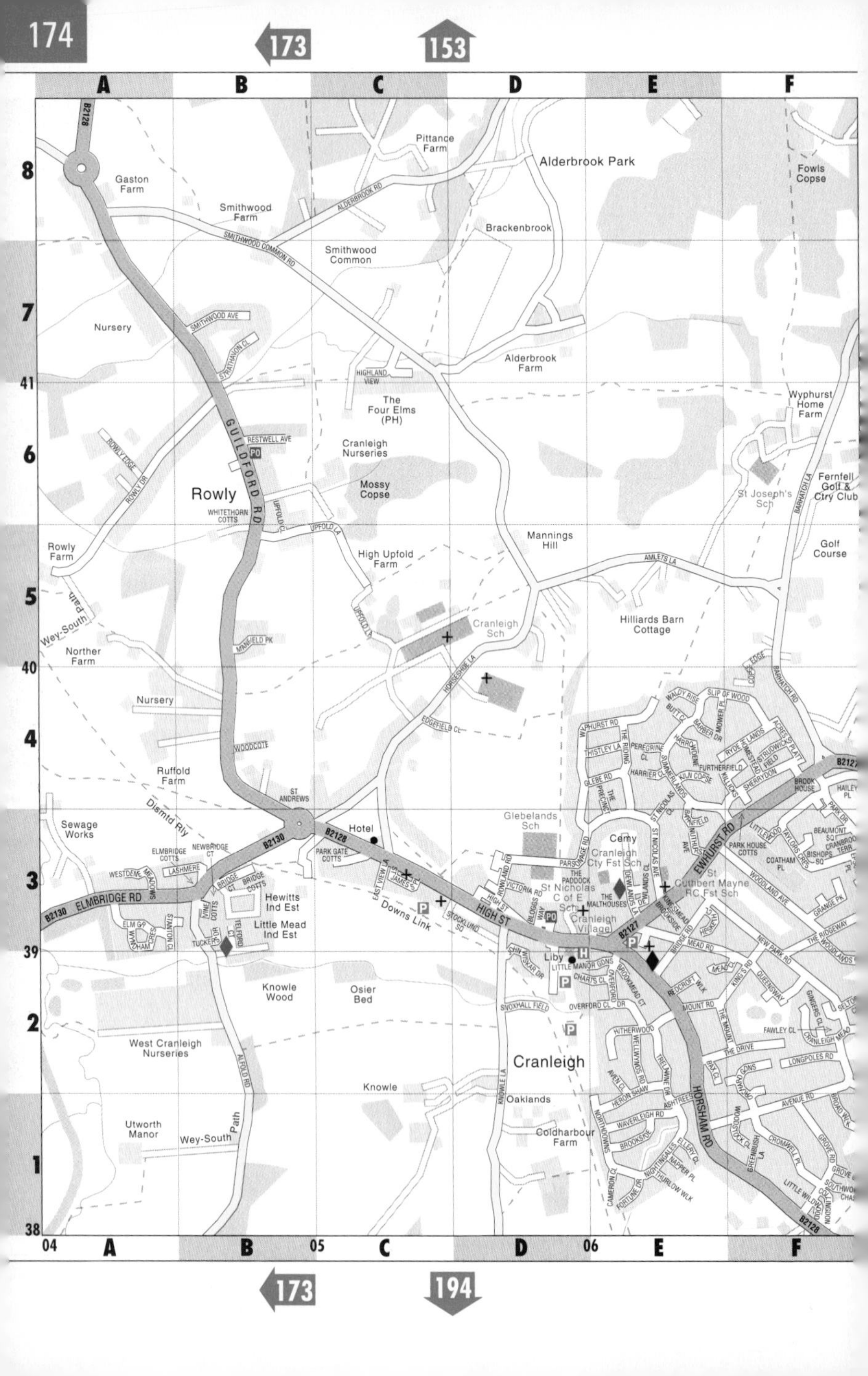
173
153
Pittance Farm
Alderbrook Park
Fowls Copse
Gaston Farm
Smithwood Farm
Brackenbrook
Smithwood Common
Nursery
Alderbrook Farm
The Four Elms (PH)
Wyphurst Home Farm
Cranleigh Nurseries
Mossy Copse
Rowly
St Joseph's Sch
Fernfell Golf & Ctry Club
Mannings Hill
Golf Course
Rowly Farm
High Upfold Farm
Wey-South Path
Cranleigh Sch
Hilliards Barn Cottage
Norther Farm
Nursery
Ruffold Farm
Dismtd Rly
Sewage Works
Hotel
Glebelands Sch
Cemy
Cranleigh Cty Fst Sch
St Cuthbert Mayne RC Fst Sch
St Nicholas C of E Sch
Hewitts Ind Est
Little Mead Ind Est
Downs Link
Cranleigh Village
Liby
Knowle Wood
Osier Bed
West Cranleigh Nurseries
Cranleigh
Knowle
Oaklands
Utworth Manor
Wey-South Path
Coldharbour Farm
GUILDFORD RD
HIGH ST
EWHURST RD
HORSHAM RD
ELMBRIDGE RD
ALDERBROOK RD
SMITHWOOD COMMON RD
AMLETS LA
HORSESHOE LA
173
194

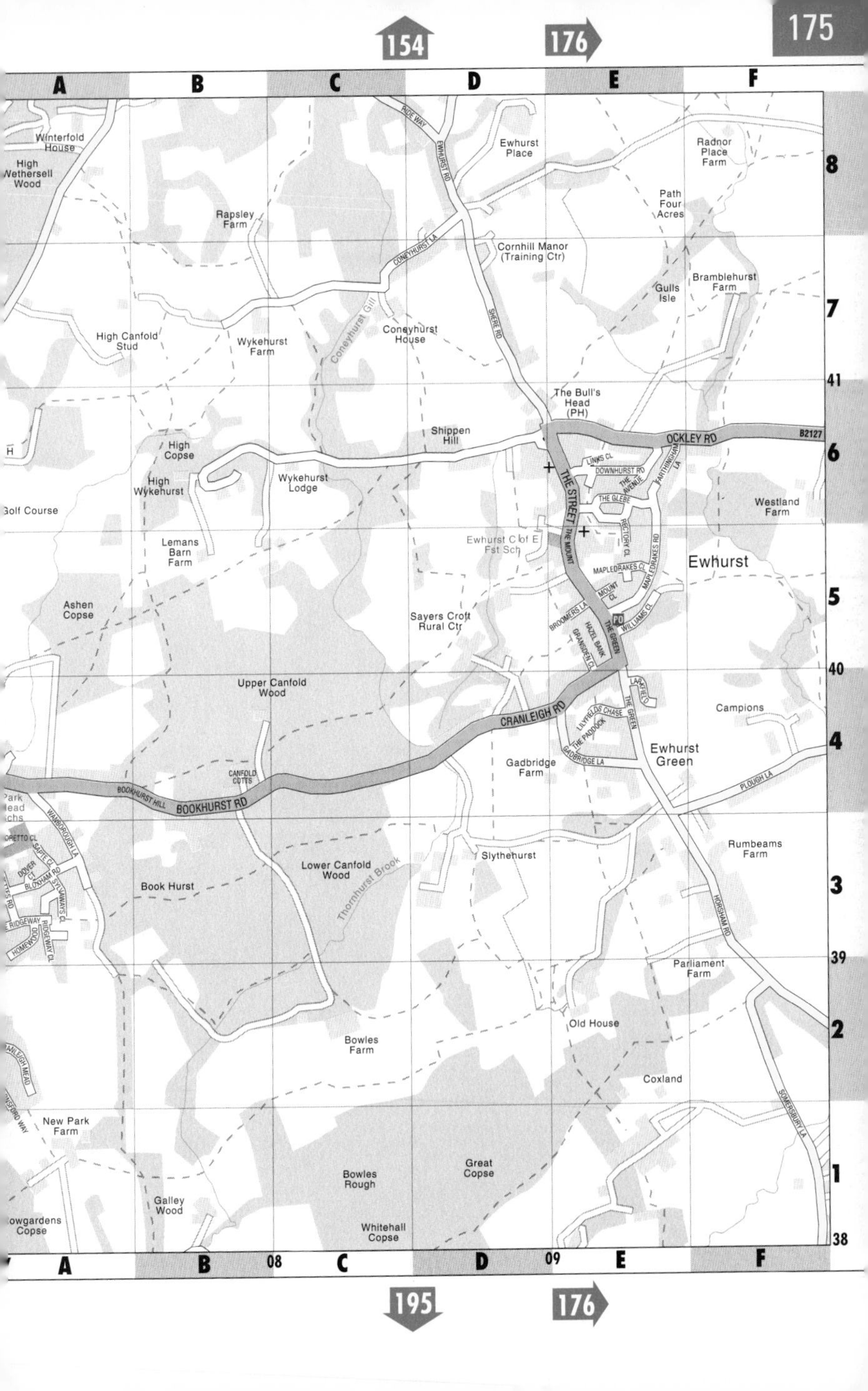
154
176
A
B
C
D
E
F
Winterfold House
High Wethersell Wood
Rapsley Farm
Ewhurst Place
Radnor Place Farm
Path Four Acres
Cornhill Manor (Training Ctr)
Gulls Isle
Bramblehurst Farm
High Canfold Stud
Wykehurst Farm
Coneyhurst House
Coneyhurst Gill
The Bull's Head (PH)
Shippen Hill
OCKLEY RD
B2127
High Copse
High Wykehurst
Wykehurst Lodge
Golf Course
Westland Farm
Lemans Barn Farm
Ewhurst C of E Fst Sch
Ewhurst
Ashen Copse
Sayers Croft Rural Ctr
THE STREET
THE MOUNT
THE GREEN
Upper Canfold Wood
Campions
CRANLEIGH RD
Ewhurst Green
Gadbridge Farm
BOOKHURST HILL
BOOKHURST RD
CANFOLD COTTS
PLOUGH LA
Rumbeams Farm
Slythehurst
Lower Canfold Wood
Thornhurst Brook
Book Hurst
HORSHAM RD
Parliament Farm
Old House
Bowles Farm
Coxland
New Park Farm
Great Copse
Bowles Rough
SOMERSBURY LA
Galley Wood
Whitehall Copse
8
7
41
6
5
40
4
3
39
2
1
38
08
09
195
176

175 155

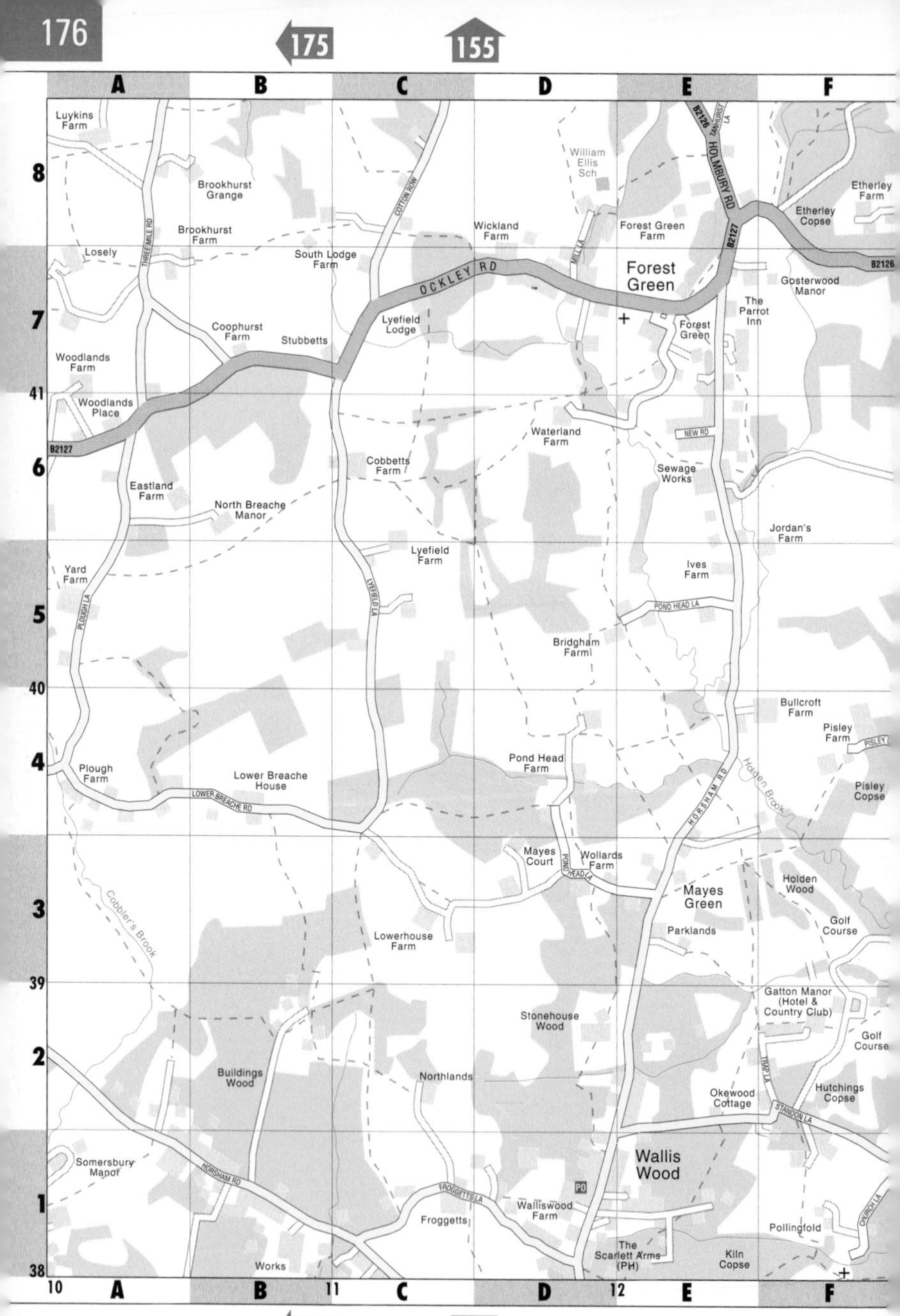
A
B
C
D
E
F
8
7
41
6
5
40
4
3
39
2
1
38
10
11
12
Luykins Farm
Brookhurst Grange
Brookhurst Farm
Losely
THREE MILE RD
South Lodge Farm
COTTON ROW
Wickland Farm
William Ellis Sch
MILL LA
Forest Green Farm
B2126
TANHURST LA
HOLMBURY RD
B2127
Etherley Farm
Etherley Copse
B2126
Gosterwood Manor
OCKLEY RD
Forest Green
The Parrot Inn
Coophurst Farm
Stubbetts
Lyefield Lodge
Forest Green
Woodlands Farm
Woodlands Place
B2127
Waterland Farm
NEW RD
Cobbetts Farm
Sewage Works
Eastland Farm
North Breache Manor
Jordan's Farm
Lyefield Farm
Ives Farm
Yard Farm
PLOUGH LA
LYEFIELD LA
POND HEAD LA
Bridgham Farm
Bullcroft Farm
Pisley Farm
PISLEY LA
Pond Head Farm
Plough Farm
Lower Breache House
LOWER BREACHE RD
HORSHAM RD
Holden Brook
Pisley Copse
Mayes Court
POND HEAD LA
Wollards Farm
Holden Wood
Mayes Green
Cobbler's Brook
Golf Course
Lowerhouse Farm
Parklands
Gatton Manor (Hotel & Country Club)
Stonehouse Wood
Golf Course
Buildings Wood
Northlands
TRAP LA
Okewood Cottage
Hutchings Copse
STANDON LA
Wallis Wood
Somersbury Manor
HORSHAM RD
PO
FROGGETTS LA
Walliswood Farm
CHURCH LA
Froggetts
Pollingfold
The Scarlett Arms (PH)
Kiln Copse
Works

175 196

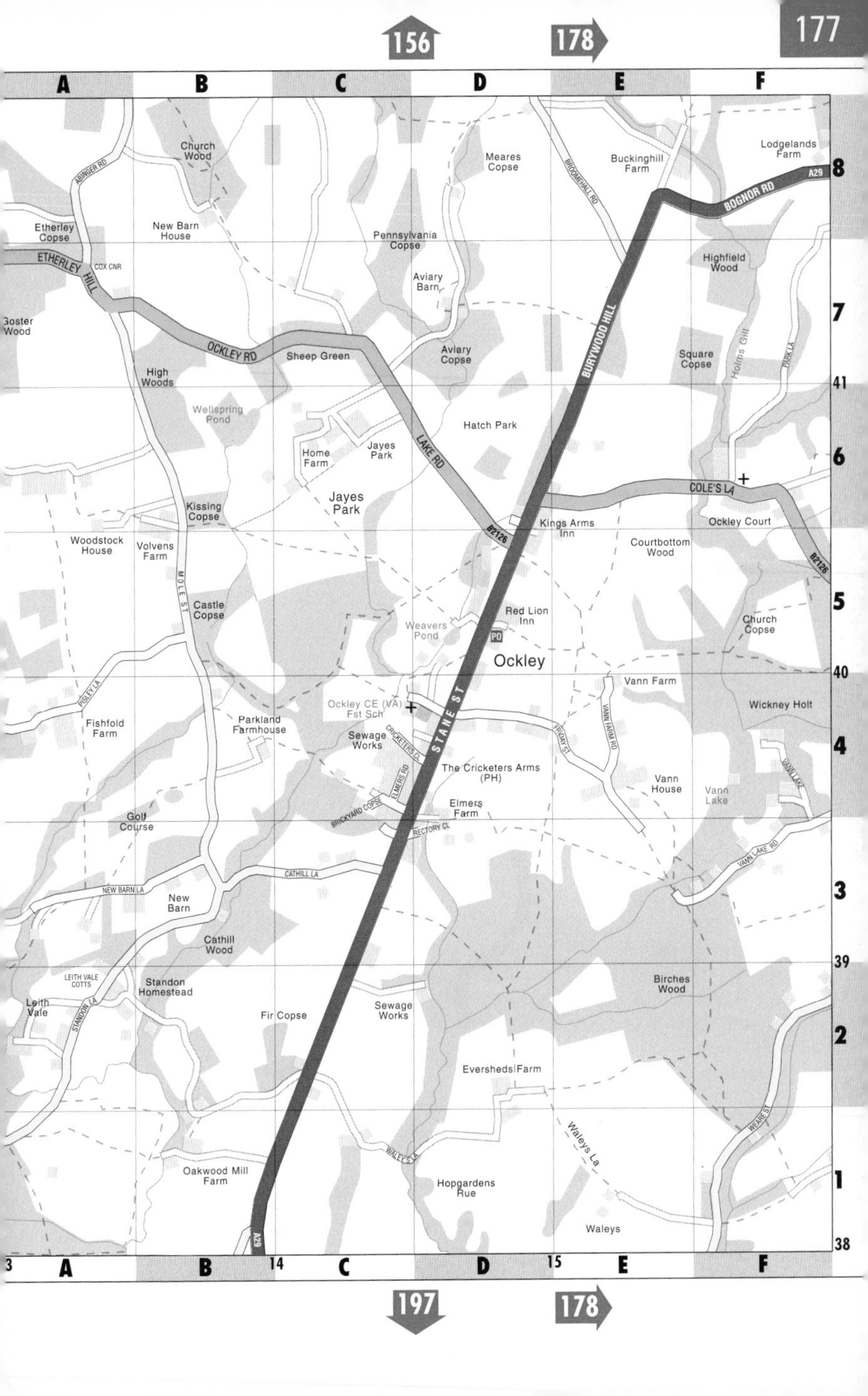
156
178
A
B
C
D
E
F
Church Wood
Meares Copse
Buckinghill Farm
Lodgelands Farm
ABINGER RD
BROOMEHALL RD
A29
BOGNOR RD
Etherley Copse
New Barn House
Pennsylvania Copse
Highfield Wood
ETHERLEY HILL
COX CNR
Aviary Barn
Goster Wood
BURYWOOD HILL
OCKLEY RD
Sheep Green
Aviary Copse
Square Copse
Holms Gill
PARK LA
High Woods
Wellspring Pond
Hatch Park
Home Farm
Jayes Park
LAKE RD
Jayes Park
COLE'S LA
Kissing Copse
Kings Arms Inn
Ockley Court
B2126
Woodstock House
Volvens Farm
Courtbottom Wood
MOLE ST
Castle Copse
Red Lion Inn
Weavers Pond
Church Copse
PO
Ockley
Vann Farm
PISLEY LA
Ockley CE (VA) Fst Sch
Wickney Holt
Fishfold Farm
Parkland Farmhouse
Sewage Works
CRICKETERS CL
STANE ST
FRIDAY ST
VANN FARM RD
VANN LAKE
ELMERS RD
The Cricketers Arms (PH)
Vann House
Vann Lake
Elmers Farm
BRICKYARD COPSE
RECTORY CL
Golf Course
CATHILL LA
NEW BARN LA
New Barn
VANN LAKE RD
Cathill Wood
LEITH VALE COTTS
Standon Homestead
Birches Wood
Leith Vale
STANDON LA
Fir Copse
Sewage Works
Eversheds Farm
WEARE ST
WALEYS LA
Waleys La
Oakwood Mill Farm
Hopgardens Rue
Waleys
A29
8
7
41
6
5
40
4
3
39
2
1
38
13
14
15
197
178

177
157

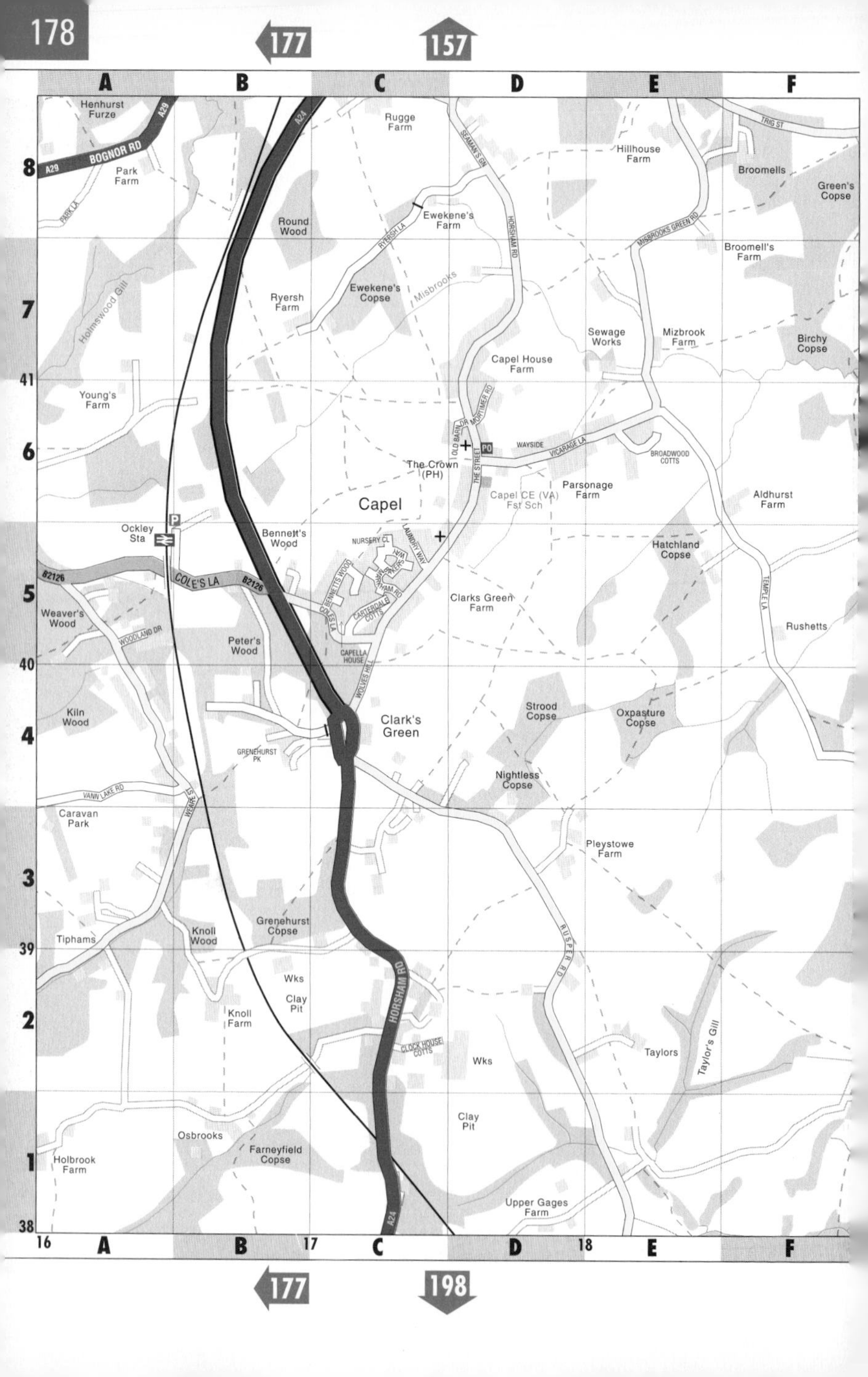
A
B
C
D
E
F
Henhurst Furze
A29
BOGNOR RD
A24
Rugge Farm
SEAMAN'S GN
TRIG ST
Hillhouse Farm
8
Park Farm
PARK LA
Broomells
Green's Copse
Round Wood
Ewekene's Farm
RYERSH LA
HORSHAM RD
MISBROOKS GREEN RD
Broomell's Farm
Holmswood Gill
Misbrooks
Ryersh Farm
Ewekene's Copse
7
Sewage Works
Mizbrook Farm
Birchy Copse
Capel House Farm
41
Young's Farm
MORTIMER RD
OLD BARN DR
6
PO
WAYSIDE
VICARAGE LA
BROADWOOD COTTS
The Crown (PH)
THE STREET
Parsonage Farm
Capel CE (VA) Fst Sch
Aldhurst Farm
Capel
P
Ockley Sta
Bennett's Wood
NURSERY CL
LAUNDRY WAY
Hatchland Copse
B2126
COLE'S LA
B2126
BENNETTS WOOD
5
Clarks Green Farm
TEMPLE LA
Weaver's Wood
COLES LA
CARTERDALE COTTS
Rushetts
WOODLAND DR
Peter's Wood
CAPELLA HOUSE
40
WOLVES HILL
Kiln Wood
Clark's Green
Strood Copse
Oxpasture Copse
4
GRENEHURST PK
Nightless Copse
VANN LAKE RD
Caravan Park
WEARE ST
Pleystowe Farm
3
Grenehurst Copse
RUSPER RD
Tiphams
Knoll Wood
39
Wks
Clay Pit
HORSHAM RD
2
Knoll Farm
CLOCK HOUSE COTTS
Taylors
Taylor's Gill
Wks
Clay Pit
Osbrooks
1
Holbrook Farm
Farneyfield Copse
Upper Gages Farm
A24
38
16
17
18

177
198

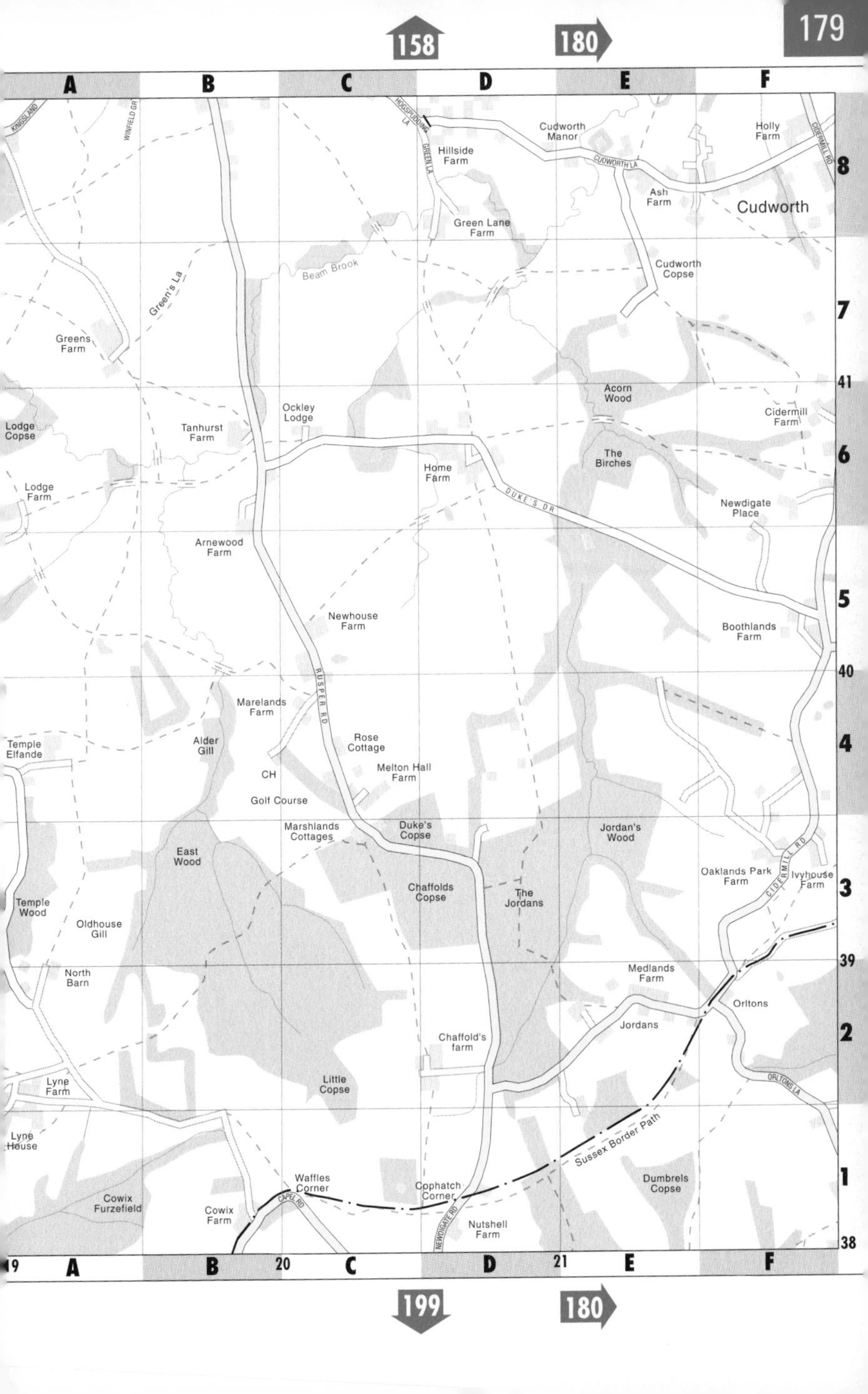
158
180
A
B
C
D
E
F
KINGSLAND
WINFIELD GR
HOGSPUDDING LA
GREEN LA
Hillside Farm
Cudworth Manor
CUDWORTH LA
Holly Farm
CIDERMILL RD
8
Ash Farm
Cudworth
Green Lane Farm
Beam Brook
Cudworth Copse
Green's La
7
Greens Farm
41
Acorn Wood
Ockley Lodge
Tanhurst Farm
Lodge Copse
Cidermill Farm
6
The Birches
Home Farm
Lodge Farm
DUKE'S DR
Newdigate Place
Arnewood Farm
5
Newhouse Farm
Boothlands Farm
40
RUSPER RD
Marelands Farm
Rose Cottage
4
Temple Elfande
Alder Gill
CH
Melton Hall Farm
Golf Course
Marshlands Cottages
Duke's Copse
Jordan's Wood
East Wood
Oaklands Park Farm
Ivyhouse Farm
CIDERMILL RD
3
Chaffolds Copse
The Jordans
Temple Wood
Oldhouse Gill
39
North Barn
Medlands Farm
Orltons
2
Jordans
Chaffold's farm
ORLTONS LA
Lyne Farm
Little Copse
Lyne House
Sussex Border Path
1
Dumbrels Copse
Waffles Corner
Cophatch Corner
CAPEL RD
Cowix Furzefield
Cowix Farm
NEWDIGATE RD
Nutshell Farm
38
19
A
B
20
C
D
21
E
F
199
180

179
159

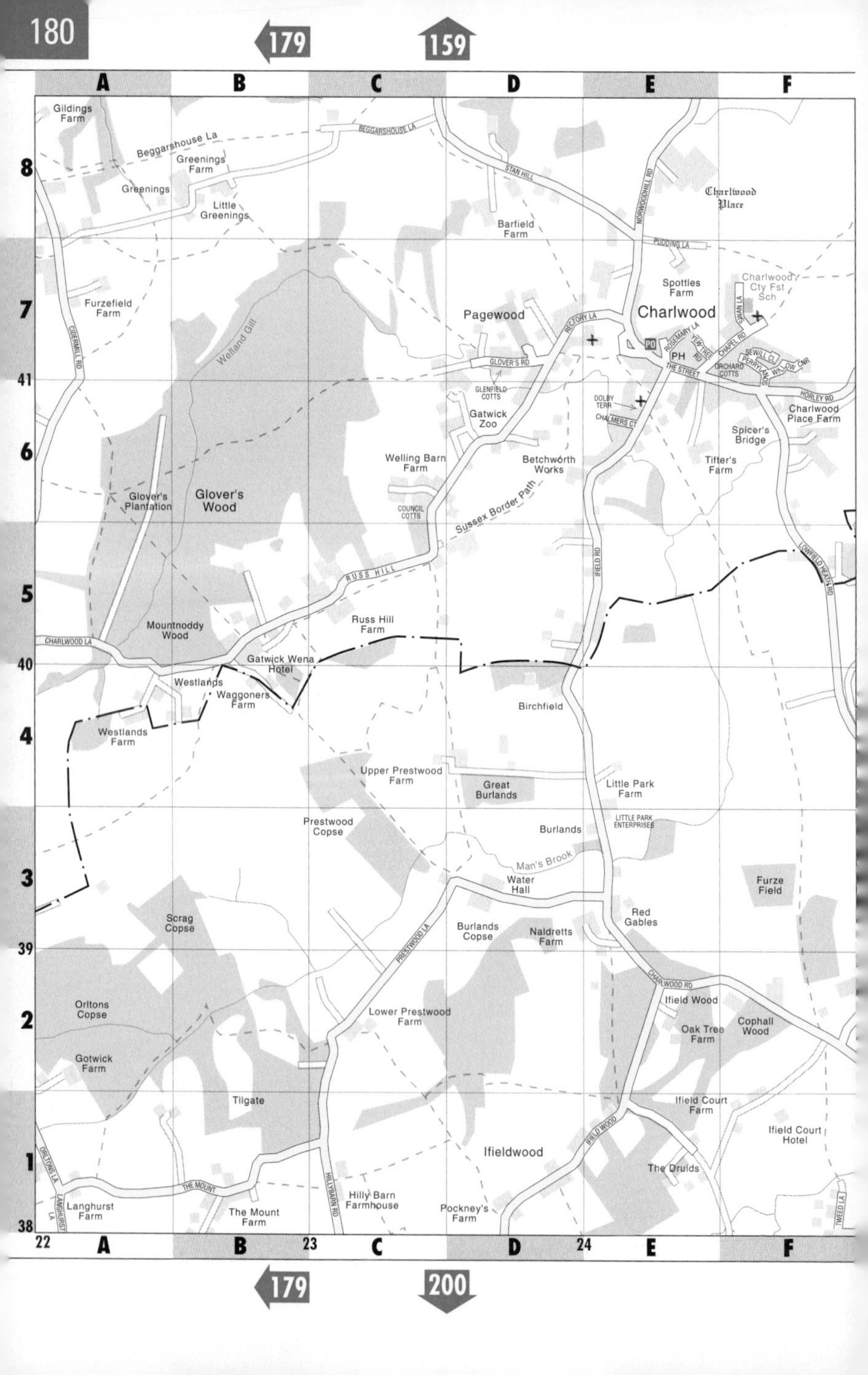
A
B
C
D
E
F
8
7
41
6
5
40
4
3
39
2
1
38
22
23
24
Gildings Farm
Beggarshouse La
BEGGARSHOUSE LA
Greenings Farm
Greenings
Little Greenings
STAN HILL
NORWOODHILL RD
Charlwood Place
Barfield Farm
PUDDING LA
Spottles Farm
Charlwood Cty Fst Sch
Furzefield Farm
Pagewood
Charlwood
Welland Gill
RECTORY LA
ROSEMARY LA
SWAN LA
CIDERMILL RD
GLOVER'S RD
PH
THE STREET
CHAPEL RD
SEWILL CL
PERRYLANDS
ORCHARD COTTS
WILLOW CNR
GLENFIELD COTTS
HORLEY RD
DOLBY TERR
Gatwick Zoo
CHALMERS CT
Charlwood Place Farm
Spicer's Bridge
Welling Barn Farm
Betchworth Works
Tifter's Farm
Glover's Plantation
Glover's Wood
COUNCIL COTTS
Sussex Border Path
IFIELD RD
LOWFIELD HEATH RD
RUSS HILL
Russ Hill Farm
Mountnoddy Wood
CHARLWOOD LA
Gatwick Wena Hotel
Westlands
Waggoners Farm
Birchfield
Westlands Farm
Upper Prestwood Farm
Great Burlands
Little Park Farm
LITTLE PARK ENTERPRISES
Prestwood Copse
Burlands
Man's Brook
Water Hall
Furze Field
Scrag Copse
Red Gables
Burlands Copse
Naldretts Farm
PRESTWOOD LA
CHARLWOOD RD
Ifield Wood
Orltons Copse
Lower Prestwood Farm
Oak Tree Farm
Cophall Wood
Gotwick Farm
Tilgate
Ifield Court Farm
Ifield Court Hotel
IFIELD WOOD
Ifieldwood
ORLTONS LA
The Druids
THE MOUNT
HILLYBARN RD
LANGHURST LA
Langhurst Farm
The Mount Farm
Hilly Barn Farmhouse
Pockney's Farm
TWEED LA

179
200

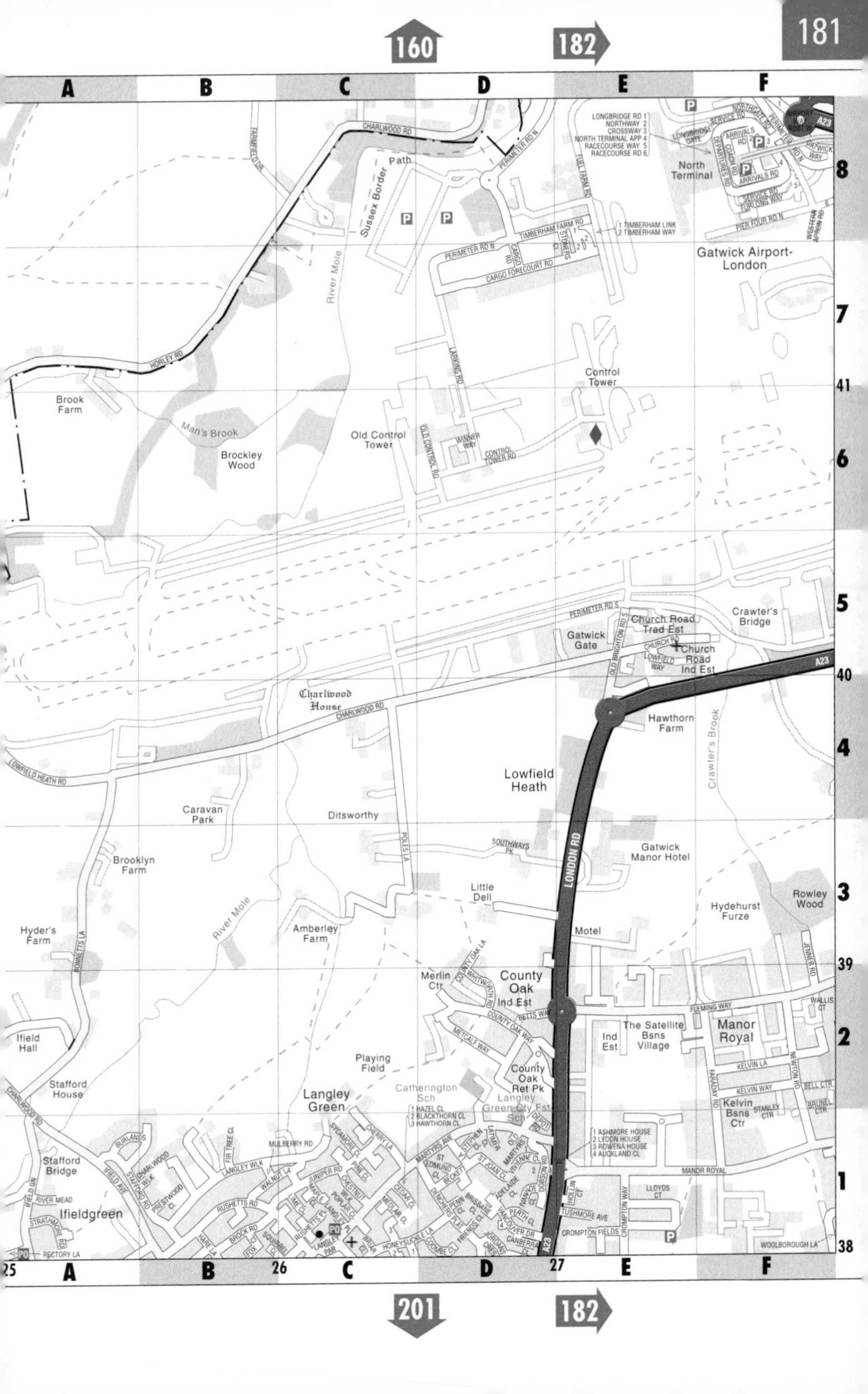
160
182
Gatwick Airport-London
North Terminal
Control Tower
Old Control Tower
Brook Farm
Brockley Wood
Man's Brook
Sussex Border Path
River Mole
Church Road Trad Est
Church Road Ind Est
Gatwick Gate
Crawter's Bridge
Charlwood House
Hawthorn Farm
Lowfield Heath
Caravan Park
Ditsworthy
Brooklyn Farm
Gatwick Manor Hotel
Little Dell
Hydehurst Furze
Rowley Wood
Hyder's Farm
Amberley Farm
Motel
Merlin Ctr
County Oak Ind Est
Manor Royal
The Satellite Bsns Village
Ind Est
Ifield Hall
Playing Field
County Oak Ret Pk
Stafford House
Langley Green
Catherington Sch
Langley Green City Est Sch
Kelvin Bsns Ctr
Stafford Bridge
Ifieldgreen
CHARLWOOD RD
HORLEY RD
PERIMETER RD N
TIMBERHAM FARM RD
CARGO FORECOURT RD
LARKINS RD
CONTROL TOWER RD
PERIMETER RD S
CHURCH RD
LOWFIELD HEATH RD
LONDON RD
POLES LA
BONNETTS LA
FLEMING WAY
KELVIN LA
KELVIN WAY
MANOR ROYAL
TUSHMORE AVE
CROMPTON WAY
CROMPTON FIELDS
WOOLBOROUGH LA
RUSHETTS RD
LANGLEY WLK
MULBERRY RD
IFIELD AVE
RECTORY LA
A23
1 LONGBRIDGE RD
2 NORTHWAY
3 CROSSWAY
4 NORTH TERMINAL APP
5 RACECOURSE WAY
6 RACECOURSE RD
1 TIMBERHAM LINK
2 TIMBERHAM WAY
1 HAZEL CL
2 BLACKTHORN CL
3 HAWTHORN CL
1 ASHMORE HOUSE
2 LYDDN HOUSE
3 ROWENA HOUSE
4 AUCKLAND CL
A B C D E F
8 7 6 5 4 3 2 1
41 40 39 38
25 26 27

181
161

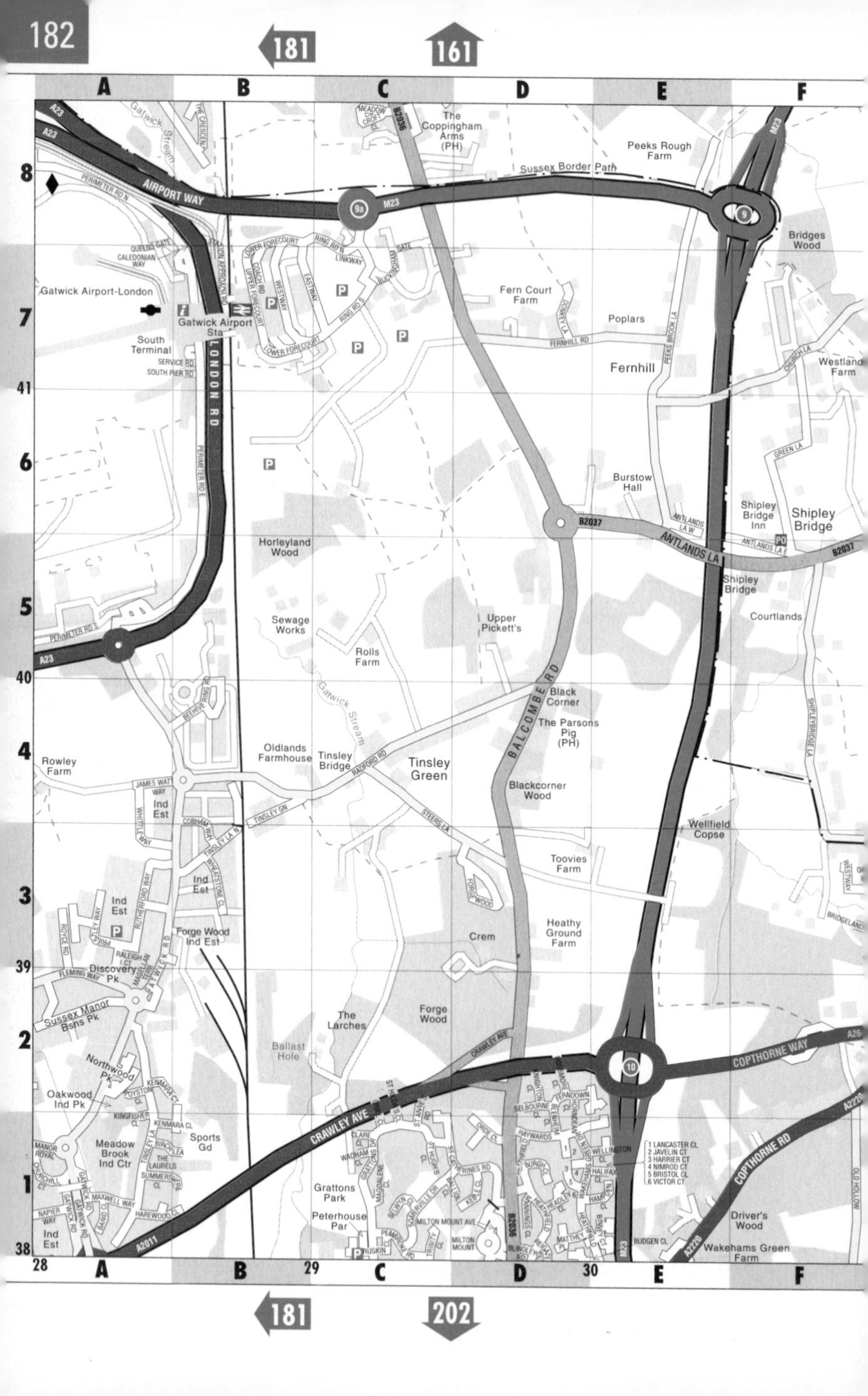
A
B
C
D
E
F
8
7
41
6
5
40
4
3
39
2
1
38
28
29
30
A23
AIRPORT WAY
M23
B2036
B2037
A2011
A2220
A26
Gatwick Stream
The Coppingham Arms (PH)
Peeks Rough Farm
Sussex Border Path
Bridges Wood
Gatwick Airport-London
Gatwick Airport Sta
South Terminal
Fern Court Farm
Poplars
Fernhill
Westland Farm
Burstow Hall
Shipley Bridge Inn
Shipley Bridge
ANTLANDS LA
Horleyland Wood
Sewage Works
Rolls Farm
Upper Pickett's
Courtlands
Black Corner
The Parsons Pig (PH)
BALCOMBE RD
Rowley Farm
Oldlands Farmhouse
Tinsley Bridge
Tinsley Green
Blackcorner Wood
Wellfield Copse
Ind Est
Toovies Farm
Forge Wood Ind Est
Crem
Heathy Ground Farm
Discovery Pk
Sussex Manor Bsns Pk
The Larches
Forge Wood
Ballast Hole
Northwood Pk
Oakwood Ind Pk
Sports Gd
Meadow Brook Ind Ctr
Grattons Park
Peterhouse Par
CRAWLEY AVE
COPTHORNE WAY
COPTHORNE RD
Driver's Wood
Wakehams Green Farm
1 LANCASTER CL
2 JAVELIN CT
3 HARRIER CT
4 NIMROD CT
5 BRISTOL CL
6 VICTOR CT

181
202

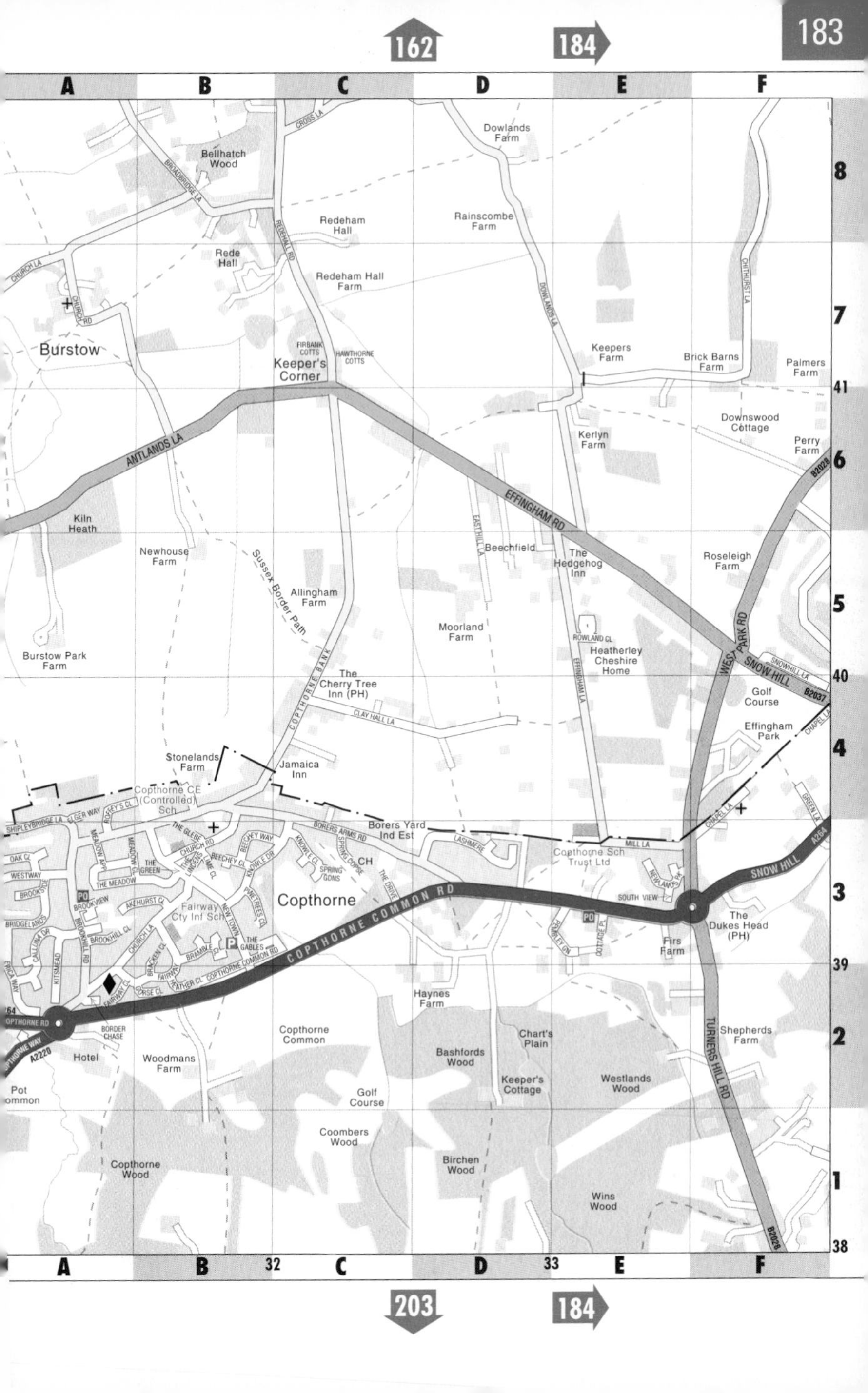

A   B   C   D   E   F

8

Dowlands
Farm

Bellhatch
Wood

Redeham
Hall

Rainscombe
Farm

BUCKNESTS LA

CROSS LA

REDEHALL RD

Rede
Hall

Redeham Hall
Farm

DING HARDS LA

7

Keepers
Farm

Brick Barns
Farm

Palmers
Farm

CHITHURST LA

CHURCH LA

Burstow

41

FIRBANK
COTTS
HAWTHORNE
COTTS

Keeper's
Corner

Downswood
Cottage

Perry
Farm

B2036

RAILANDS LA

Kerlyn
Farm

Roseleigh
Farm

6

EFFINGHAM RD

Kiln
Heath

Newhouse
Farm

Sussex Border Path

Allingham
Farm

EAST HILL

Beechfield

The
Hedgehog
Inn

WEST PARK RD

SNOW HILL

B2037

5

COPTHORNE BANK

Moorland
Farm

ROWLAND CL

SNOW HILL LA

Burstow Park
Farm

Heatherley
Cheshire
Home

Golf
Course

40

The
Cherry Tree
Inn (PH)

CLAY HALL LA

EFFINGHAM LA

Effingham
Park

CHAPEL LA

4

Stonelands
Farm

Jamaica
Inn

Copthorne CE
(Controlled
Sch)

BORERS ARMS RD

Borers Yard
Ind Est

LASHMERE

Copthorne Sch
Trust Ltd

MILL LA

COLE LA

A264

SHIPLEYBRIDGE LA

GREA WAY

OXLEY CL

THE GLEBE

COPSE LA

3

OAK CL

WESTWAY

THE MEADOW

CHURCH RD

BEECH CL

COLE CL

Copthorne

THE DRIVE

SOUTH VIEW

SNOW HILL

The
Dukes Head
(PH)

BROOKS

THE GREEN

BROOKVIEW

ARDHURST CL

COPTHORNE COMMON RD

PO

CLARKS

Firs
Farm

BRIDGELANDS

BROOK

Fairway
Cty Inf Sch

BRAMBLE

THE GABLES

CHURCH CL

FAIRWAY

FATHER CL

COPTHORNE COMMON RD

DOUBLE PL

PO

39

A2220

COPTHORNE RD

BORDER
CHASE

Hotel

Woodmans
Farm

Haynes
Farm

Chart's
Plain

Shepherds
Farm

TURNERS HILL RD

2

Copthorne
Common

Bashfords
Wood

Keeper's
Cottage

Westlands
Wood

Pot
Common

Golf
Course

Copthorne
Wood

Coombers
Wood

Birchen
Wood

Wins
Wood

1

38

B2028

A   B   C   D   E   F

32   33

183
163

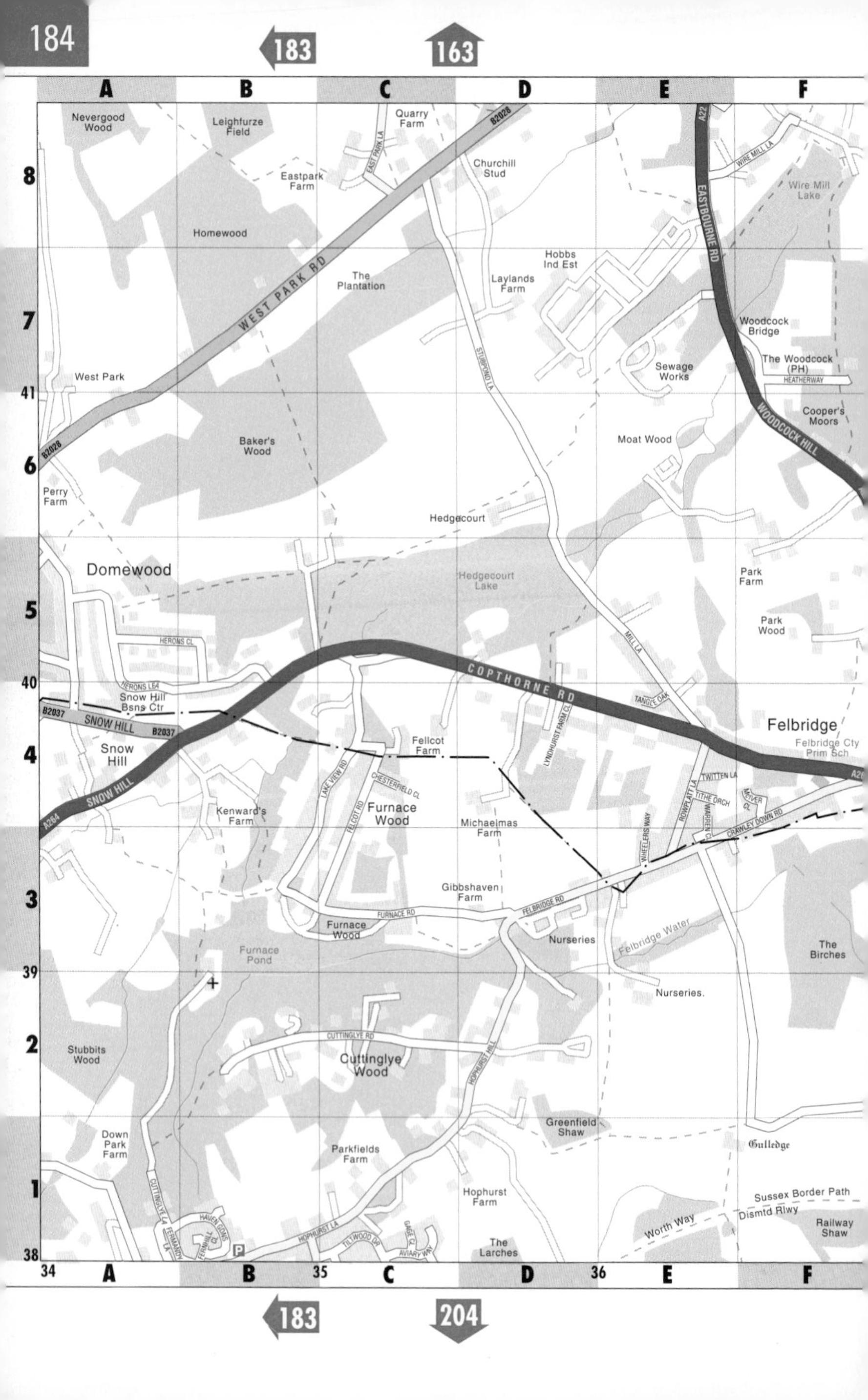
A
B
C
D
E
F
Nevergood Wood
Leighfurze Field
Quarry Farm
B2028
EAST PARK LA
A22
WIRE MILL LA
8
Eastpark Farm
Churchill Stud
EASTBOURNE RD
Wire Mill Lake
Homewood
Hobbs Ind Est
WEST PARK RD
The Plantation
Laylands Farm
7
Woodcock Bridge
Sewage Works
The Woodcock (PH)
STUBPOND LA
West Park
HEATHERWAY
41
Cooper's Moors
WOODCOCK HILL
Baker's Wood
Moat Wood
B2028
6
Perry Farm
Hedgecourt
Domewood
Hedgecourt Lake
Park Farm
5
Park Wood
HERONS CL
MILL LA
40
HERONS LEA
COPTHORNE RD
Snow Hill Bsns Ctr
TANGLE OAK
B2037
SNOW HILL
B2037
Felbridge
Felbridge Cty Prim Sch
Snow Hill
Fellcot Farm
LYNDHURST FARM CL
4
SNOW HILL
LAKE VIEW RD
CHESTERFIELD CL
TWITTEN LA
A264
Kenward's Farm
FELCOT RD
Furnace Wood
ROWPLATT LA
TITHE ORCH
MCIVER CL
WHEELERS WAY
WARREN CL
CRAWLEY DOWN RD
Michaelmas Farm
Gibbshaven Farm
3
FELBRIDGE RD
FURNACE RD
Furnace Wood
Nurseries
Felbridge Water
The Birches
Furnace Pond
39
Nurseries.
CUTTINGLYE RD
2
Stubbits Wood
Cuttinglye Wood
HOPHURST HILL
Greenfield Shaw
Down Park Farm
Parkfields Farm
Gulledge
1
CUTTINGLYE LA
Hophurst Farm
Sussex Border Path
Worth Way
Dismtd Rlwy
Railway Shaw
HAVEN GDNS
FERNHILL CL
HOPHURST LA
GAGE CL
TILTWOOD DR
AVIARY WAY
FERMANDY LA
The Larches
38
34
35
36
A
B
C
D
E
F

183
204

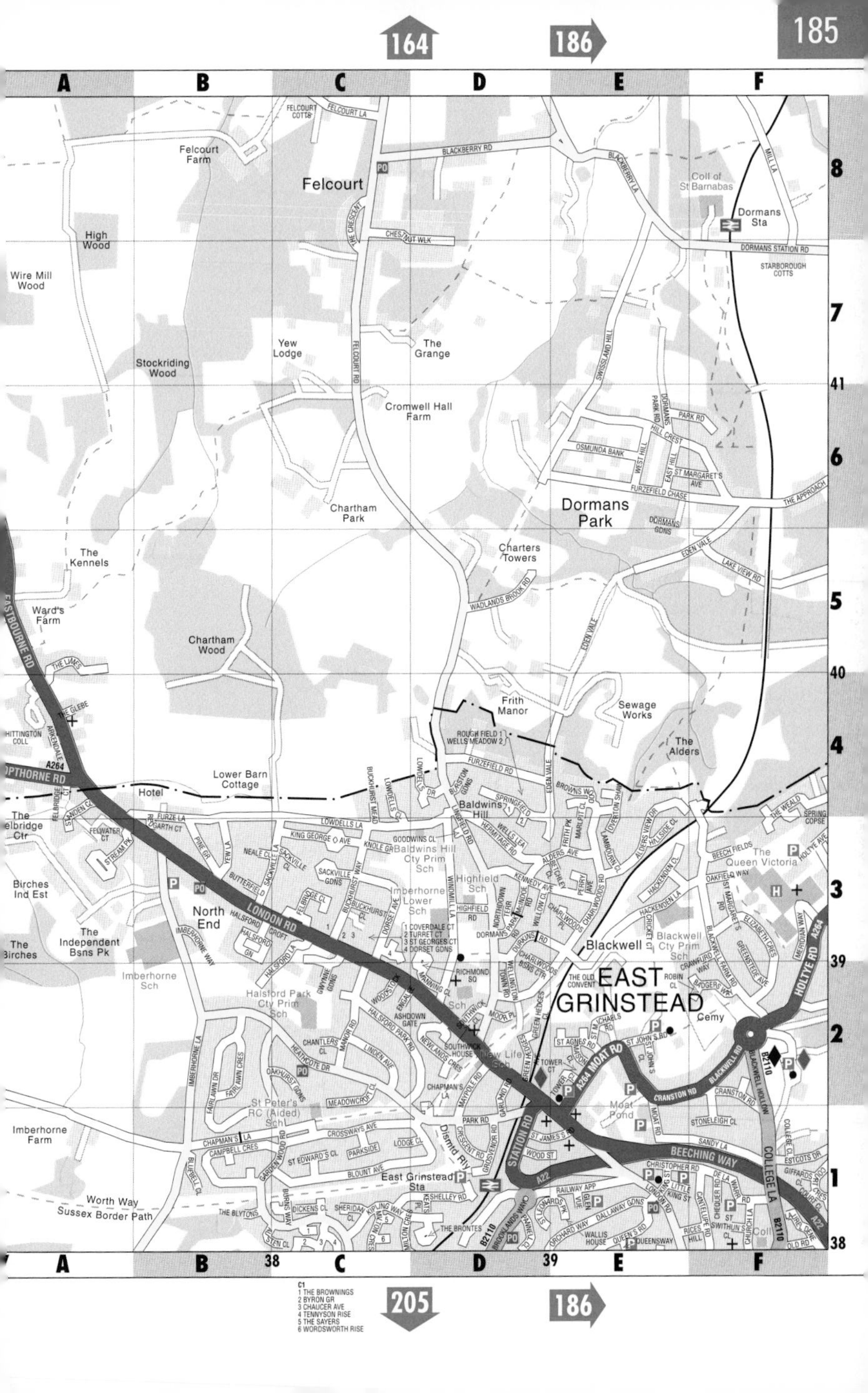
164
186
A
B
C
D
E
F
8
7
41
6
5
40
4
3
39
2
1
38
Felcourt Farm
Felcourt
FELCOURT COTTS
FELCOURT LA
BLACKBERRY RD
BLACKBERRY LA
Coll of St Barnabas
Dormans Sta
MILL LA
DORMANS STATION RD
STARBOROUGH COTTS
High Wood
Wire Mill Wood
THE CRESCENT
CHESTNUT WLK
Yew Lodge
The Grange
Stockriding Wood
FELCOURT RD
Cromwell Hall Farm
SWISSLAND HILL
PARK RD
HILL CREST
OSMUNDA BANK
WEST HILL
EAST HILL
ST MARGARET'S AVE
FURZEFIELD CHASE
THE APPROACH
Chartham Park
Dormans Park
DORMANS GDNS
The Kennels
Charters Towers
EDEN VALE
LAKE VIEW RD
WADLANDS BROOK RD
Ward's Farm
EASTBOURNE RD
Chartham Wood
THE LIMES
THE GLEBE
Frith Manor
Sewage Works
The Alders
ROUGH FIELD
WELLS MEADOW
FURZEFIELD RD
A264
COPTHORNE RD
Lower Barn Cottage
Hotel
Baldwins Hill
The Felbridge Ctr
Birches Ind Est
North End
LONDON RD
The Independent Bsns Pk
The Birches
Imberhorne Sch
Halsford Park Cty Prim Sch
Baldwins Hill Cty Prim Sch
Highfield Sch
Imberhorne Lower Sch
1 COVERDALE CT
2 TURRET CT
3 ST GEORGES CT
4 DORSET GDNS
Blackwell
Blackwell Cty Prim Sch
The Queen Victoria
EAST GRINSTEAD
THE OLD CONVENT
Cemy
HOLTYE RD
MOAT RD
CRANSTON RD
BLACKWELL HOLLOW
Moat Pond
New Life Sch
SOUTHWICK HOUSE
St Peter's RC (Aided) Sch
Imberhorne Farm
Dismtd Rly
East Grinstead Sta
STATION RD
BEECHING WAY
COLLEGE LA
A22
B2110
Worth Way
Sussex Border Path
THE BLYTONS
THE BRONTES
QUEENSWAY
A
B
38
C
D
39
E
F

C1
1 THE BROWNINGS
2 BYRON GR
3 CHAUCER AVE
4 TENNYSON RISE
5 THE SAYERS
6 WORDSWORTH RISE

185
165

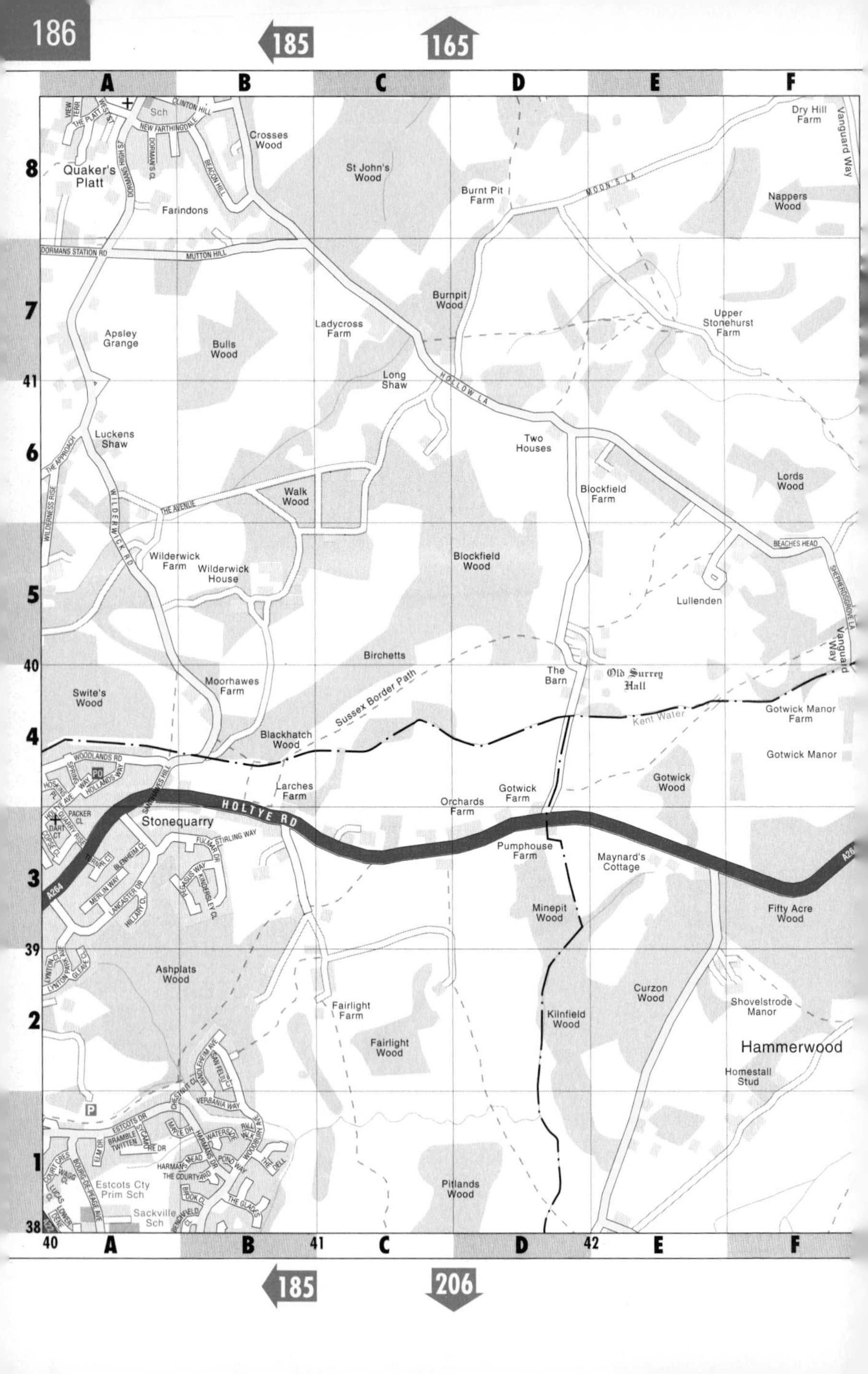
A
B
C
D
E
F
8
7
41
6
5
40
4
3
39
2
1
38
40
41
42
Quaker's Platt
Sch
CLINTON HILL
NEW FARTHINGDALE
VIEW TERR
THE PLATT
WEST ST
DORMANS HIGH ST
DORMAN'S CL
BEACON HILL
Crosses Wood
St John's Wood
Burnt Pit Farm
MOON'S LA
Dry Hill Farm
Vanguard Way
Nappers Wood
Farindons
DORMANS STATION RD
MUTTON HILL
Burnpit Wood
Ladycross Farm
Upper Stonehurst Farm
Apsley Grange
Bulls Wood
Long Shaw
HOLLOW LA
Luckens Shaw
THE APPROACH
Two Houses
Lords Wood
Blockfield Farm
Walk Wood
THE AVENUE
WILDERNESS RISE
WILDERWICK RD
BEACHES HEAD
Wilderwick Farm
Wilderwick House
Blockfield Wood
SHEPHERDSGROVE LA
Lullenden
Birchetts
Vanguard Way
The Barn
Old Surrey Hall
Swite's Wood
Moorhawes Farm
Sussex Border Path
Kent Water
Gotwick Manor Farm
Blackhatch Wood
Gotwick Manor
WOODLANDS RD
SPRING
HOSKINS PL
HOLLANDS WAY
PO
SANDHAWES HILL
Larches Farm
Gotwick Farm
Gotwick Wood
Orchards Farm
HOLTYE RD
Stonequarry
PACKER CL
DART CT
QUARRY RISE
COPSE CL
FULMAR DR
STIRLING WAY
BLENHEIM CL
PEGASUS WAY
KINDERSLEY CL
MERLIN WAY
LANCASTER DR
HILLARY CL
A264
Pumphouse Farm
Maynard's Cottage
Minepit Wood
Fifty Acre Wood
A264
LYNTON CL
LYNTON PARK AVE
GLEAVE CL
Ashplats Wood
Curzon Wood
Fairlight Farm
Kilnfield Wood
Shovelstrode Manor
Fairlight Wood
Hammerwood
Homestall Stud
P
CHESTNUT CL
VERBANIA WAY
ESTCOTS DR
BRAMBLE TWITTEN
SYCAMORE DR
ELM DR
HARMANS MEAD
HARMANS DR
THE COURTYARD
WATERSIDE
POND WAY
WOODBURY AVE
THE DELL
THE GLADES
BROOK CL
Estcots Cty Prim Sch
Sackville Sch
COURT CRES
WAGG CL
LUCAS CL
BOURG-DE-PEAGE AVE
LOWER DENE
Pitlands Wood

185
206

167
188

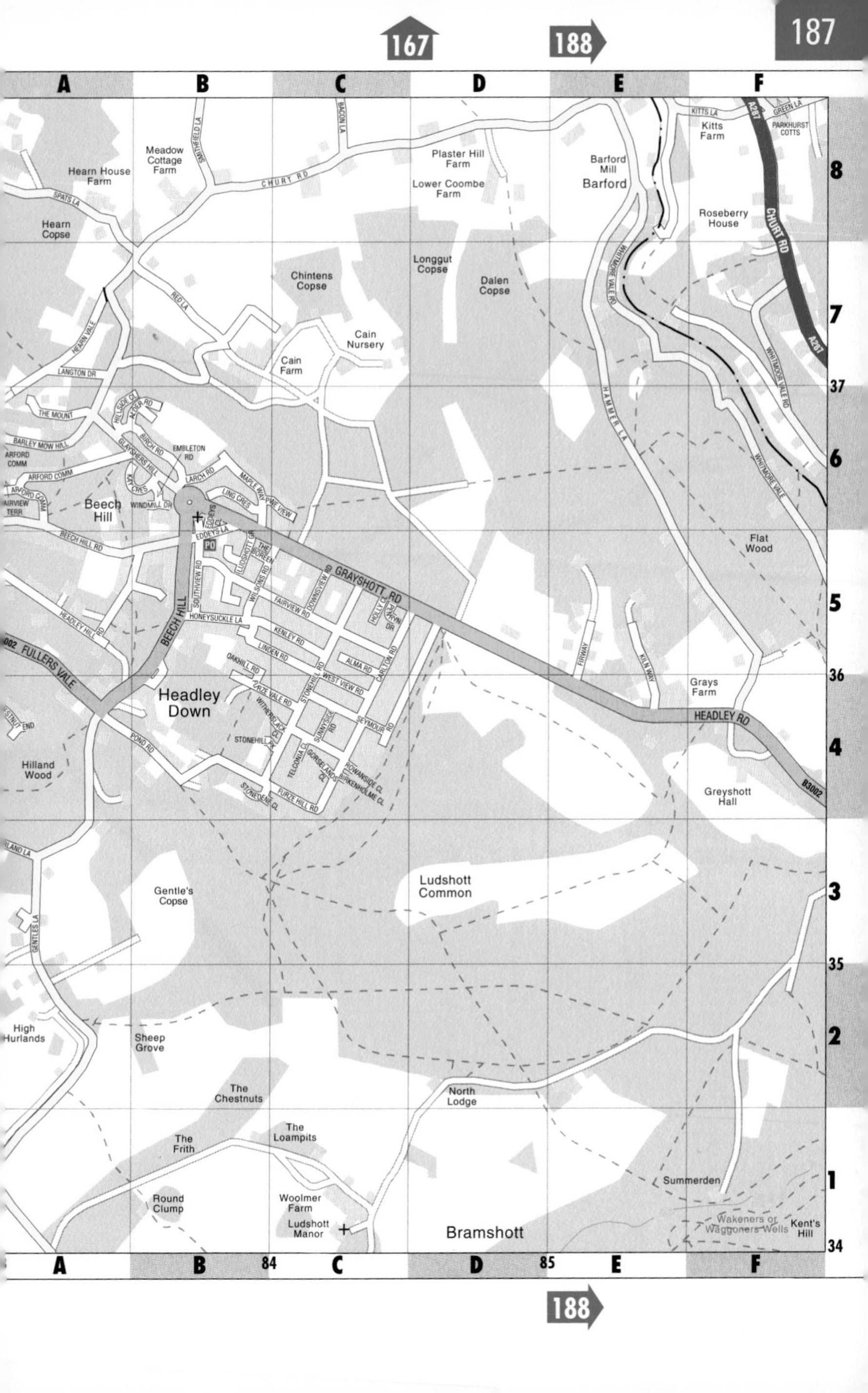
A
B
C
D
E
F
8
7
37
6
5
36
4
3
35
2
1
34
84
85
Hearn House Farm
Meadow Cottage Farm
Plaster Hill Farm
Lower Coombe Farm
Barford Mill
Barford
Kitts Farm
Parkhurst Cotts
Roseberry House
Hearn Copse
Chintens Copse
Longgut Copse
Dalen Copse
Cain Nursery
Cain Farm
Beech Hill
Headley Down
Flat Wood
Grays Farm
Greyshott Hall
Hilland Wood
Gentle's Copse
Ludshott Common
High Hurlands
Sheep Grove
The Chestnuts
North Lodge
The Frith
The Loampits
Summerden
Round Clump
Woolmer Farm
Ludshott Manor
Bramshott
Wakeners or Waggoners Wells
Kent's Hill
CHURT RD
SPATS LA
SMITHFIELD LA
BACON LA
KITTS LA
GREEN LA
A287
RED LA
HEARN VALE
LANGTON DR
THE MOUNT
HILLSIDE CL
ALDER RD
BIRCH RD
BARLEY MOW HILL
ARFORD COMM
GLAYSHERS HILL
EMBLETON RD
LARCH RD
MAPLE WAY
PINE VIEW
LING CRES
WINDMILL DR
FAIRVIEW TERR
BEECH HILL RD
EDDEYS LA
PO
LUDSHOTT GR
THE BUREEN
SOUTHVIEW RD
WILSONS RD
DOWNSVIEW RD
GRAYSHOTT RD
FAIRVIEW RD
HOLLY CL
HEADLEY HILL RD
BEECH HILL
HONEYSUCKLE LA
KENLEY RD
LINDEN RD
ALMA RD
CARLTON RD
OAKHILL RD
WEST VIEW RD
STONEHILL RD
FULLERS VALE
B3002
FURZE VALE RD
WITHERSLACK CL
SUNNYSIDE RD
SEYMOUR RD
STONEHILL PK
TELCONIA CL
GORSELANDS CL
ROWANSIDE CL
BIRKENHOLME CL
STONEDENE CL
FURZE HILL RD
POND RD
WHITMORE VALE RD
HAMMER LA
WHITMOORE VALE RD
WHITMORE VALE
FIRWAY
KILN WAY
HEADLEY RD
GENTLES LA

188

187
168

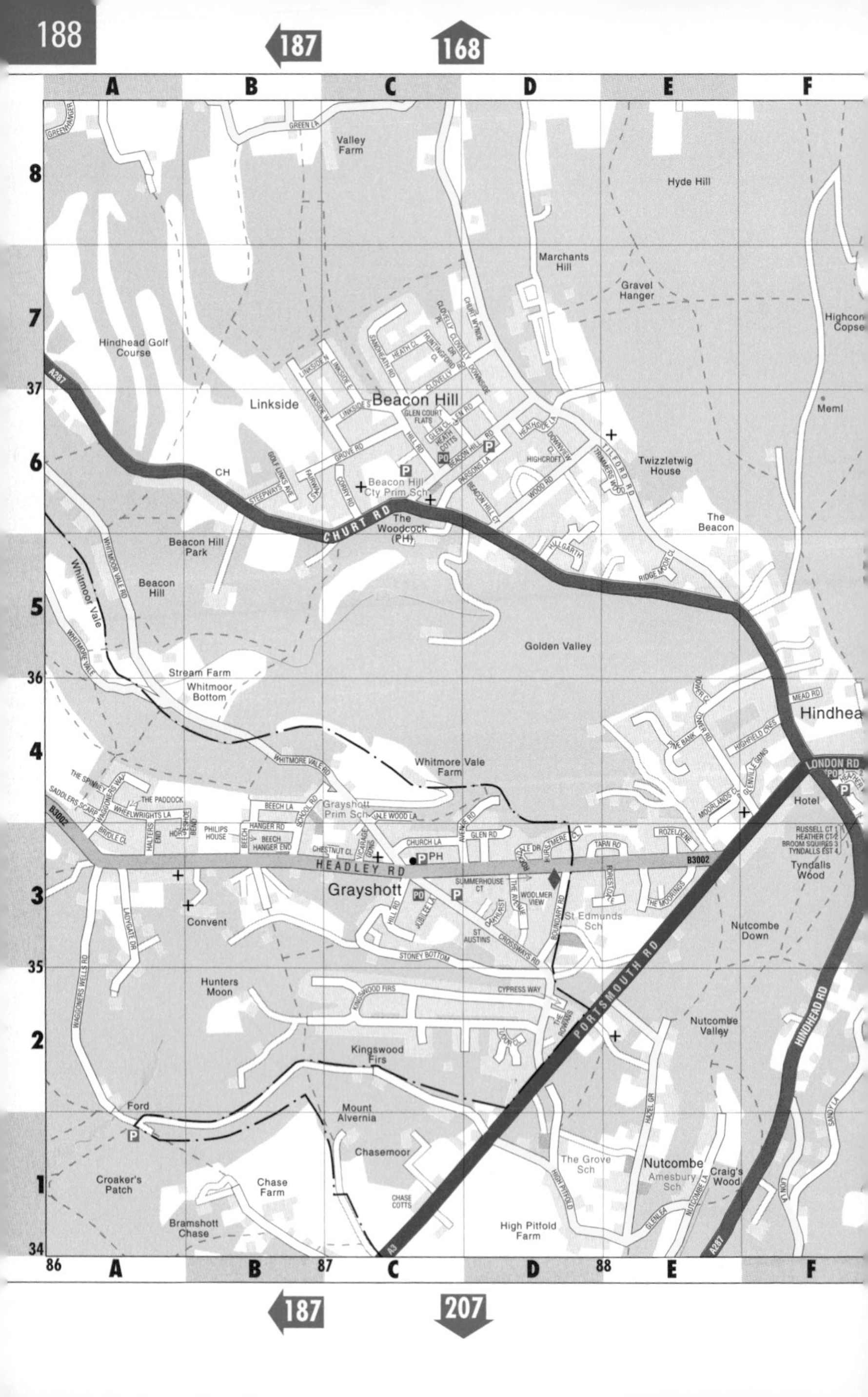
A
B
C
D
E
F
8
7
37
6
5
36
4
3
35
2
1
34
86
87
88
GREEN LA
Valley Farm
Hyde Hill
Marchants Hill
Gravel Hanger
Highcomb Copse
Hindhead Golf Course
A287
Linkside
Beacon Hill
LINKSIDE N
LINKSIDE E
LINKSIDE W
LINKSIDE S
SANDHEATH RD
HEATH CL
HUNTINGFORD CL
CLOVELLY RD
CHURT WYNDE
DOWNSIDE
GLEN COURT FLATS
GLEN RD
HEATH COTTS
HILL RD
BEACON HILL RD
GROVE RD
HEATHSIDE LA
DOWNVIEW CL
HIGHCROFT
TILFORD RD
TRIMMERS WOOD
PARSONS LA
WOOD RD
BEACON HILL CT
Meml
CH
GOLF LINKS AVE
STEEPWAYS
FAIRWAY
CORRY RD
Beacon Hill Cty Prim Sch
Twizzletwig House
CHURT RD
The Woodcock (PH)
The Beacon
HILL GARTH
RIDGEMOOR CL
Beacon Hill Park
Whitmoor Vale
WHITMOOR VALE RD
Beacon Hill
WHITMORE VALE
Golden Valley
Stream Farm
Whitmoor Bottom
MEAD RD
Hindhea
TOWER CL
TOWER RD
PINE BANK
HIGHFIELD CRES
Whitmore Vale Farm
WHITMORE VALE RD
LONDON RD
GLENVILLE GDNS
MOORLANDS CL
Hotel
THE SPINNEY
WAGGONERS WAY
THE PADDOCK
SADDLERS SCARP
WHEELWRIGHTS LA
BRIDLE CL
B3002
HALTERS END
HORSESHOE BEND
PHILIPS HOUSE
BEECH LA
SCHOOL RD
BEECH HANGER RD
BEECH HANGER END
Grayshott Prim Sch
VALE WOOD LA
AVENUE RD
GLEN RD
ROZELDENE
RUSSELL CT 1
HEATHER CT 2
BROOM SQUIRES 3
TYNDALLS EST 4
CHESTNUT CL
VICARAGE GDNS
CHURCH LA
PH
HURSTMERE CL
TARN RD
HEADLEY RD
Tyndalls Wood
Grayshott
SUMMERHOUSE CT
THE AVENUE
WOOLMER VIEW
FORESTSIDE
THE MOORINGS
LADYGATE DR
Convent
HILL RD
JUBILEE LA
OAKHURST
ST AUSTINS
CROSSWAYS RD
BOUNDARY RD
St Edmunds Sch
Nutcombe Down
STONEY BOTTOM
PORTSMOUTH RD
Hunters Moon
KINGSWOOD FIRS
CYPRESS WAY
WAGGONERS WELLS RD
THE ROWANS
Nutcombe Valley
HINDHEAD RD
TUDOR CL
Kingswood Firs
Ford
Mount Alvernia
HAZEL GR
SANDY LA
Chasemoor
The Grove Sch
Nutcombe
Amesbury Sch
Craig's Wood
Croaker's Patch
Chase Farm
HIGH PITFOLD
NUTCOMBE LA
LION LA
CHASE COTTS
Bramshott Chase
High Pitfold Farm
GLENLEA
A3
A287

187
207

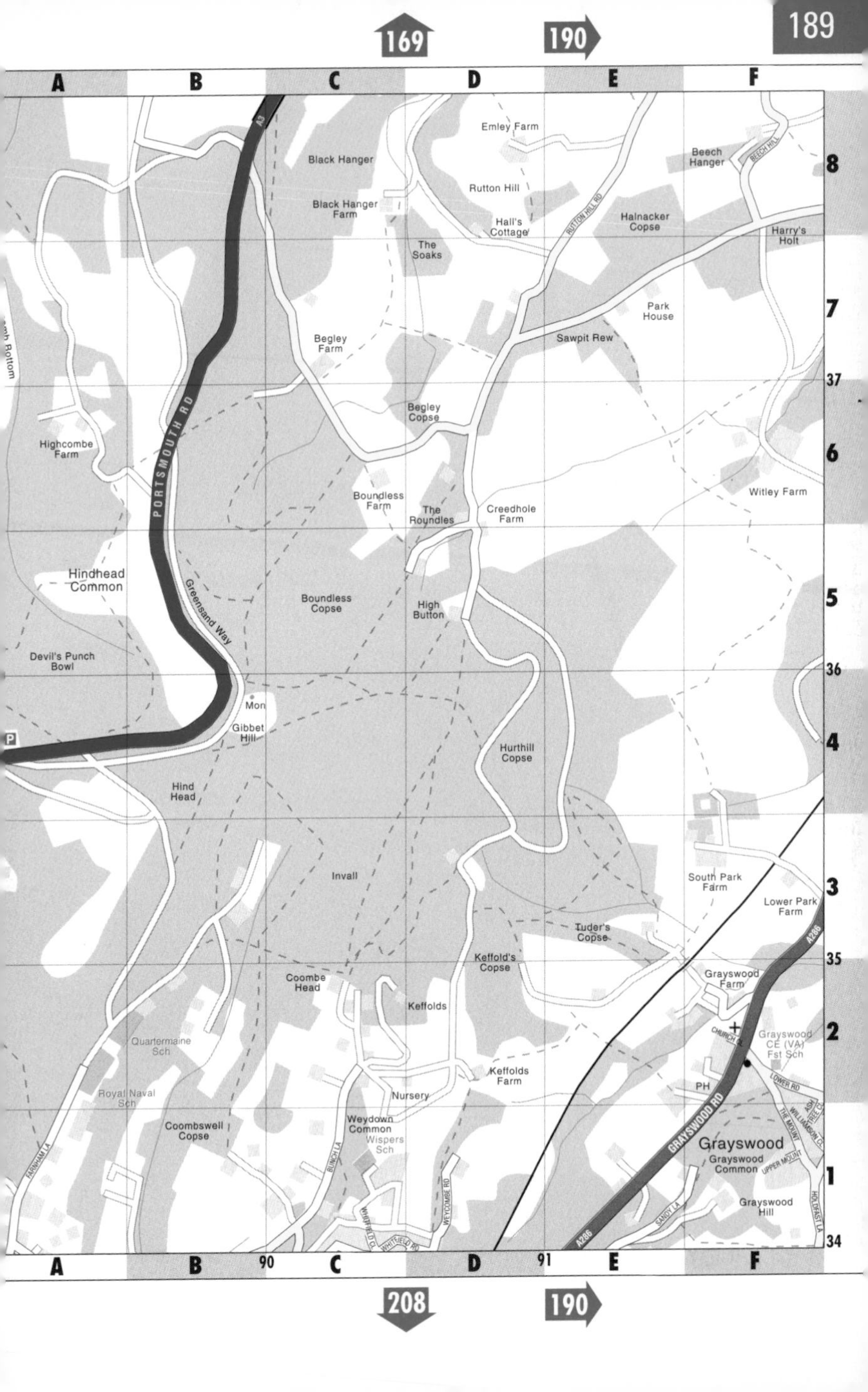
169
190
A
B
C
D
E
F
8
7
37
6
5
36
4
3
35
2
1
34
90
91
208
190
Emley Farm
Black Hanger
Beech Hanger
BEECH HILL
Rutton Hill
Black Hanger Farm
Hall's Cottage
RUTTON HILL RD
Halnacker Copse
Harry's Holt
The Soaks
A3
Park House
Begley Farm
Sawpit Rew
Begley Copse
Highcombe Farm
PORTSMOUTH RD
Boundless Farm
The Roundles
Creedhole Farm
Witley Farm
Hindhead Common
Greensand Way
Boundless Copse
High Button
Devil's Punch Bowl
Mon
Gibbet Hill
P
Hurthill Copse
Hind Head
Invall
South Park Farm
Lower Park Farm
Tuder's Copse
A286
Keffold's Copse
Grayswood Farm
Coombe Head
Keffolds
CHURCH GR
Grayswood CE (VA) Fst Sch
Quartermaine Sch
Keffolds Farm
LOWER RD
Royal Naval Sch
Nursery
PH
Coombswell Copse
Weydown Common
Wispers Sch
GRAYSWOOD RD
Grayswood
Grayswood Common
UPPER MOUNT
FARNHAM LA
BUNCH LA
WEYCOMBE RD
Grayswood Hill
SANDY LA
HOLDFAST LA
WHITFIELD CL
WHITFIELD RD
A286

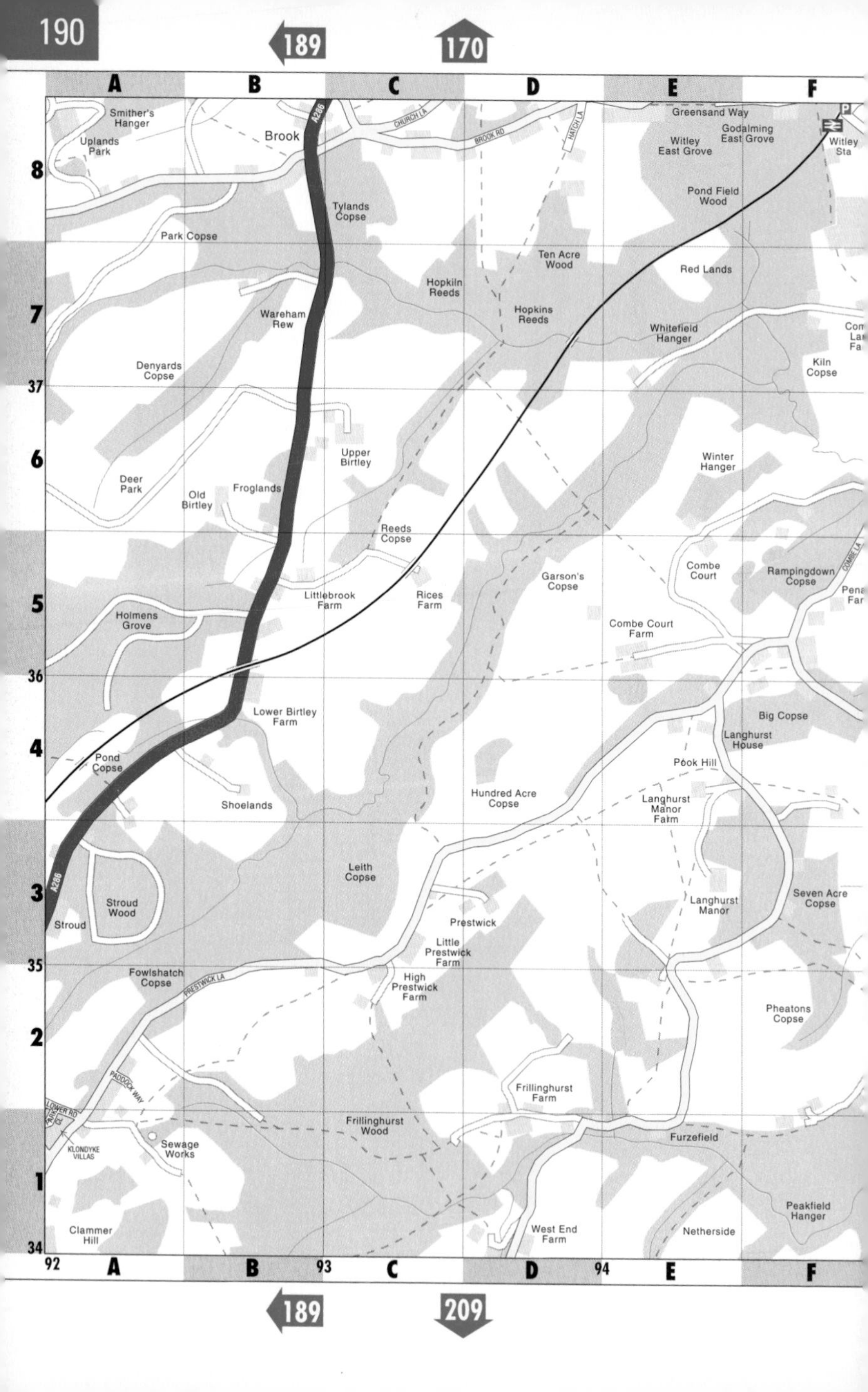
189
170
A
B
C
D
E
F
Smither's Hanger
Uplands Park
Brook
A286
CHURCH LA
BROOK RD
HATCH LA
Greensand Way
Witley East Grove
Godalming East Grove
Witley Sta
8
Tylands Copse
Pond Field Wood
Park Copse
Ten Acre Wood
Red Lands
Hopkiln Reeds
Hopkins Reeds
7
Wareham Rew
Whitefield Hanger
Denyards Copse
Kiln Copse
37
Upper Birtley
6
Winter Hanger
Deer Park
Old Birtley
Froglands
Reeds Copse
Combe Court
Garson's Copse
Rampingdown Copse
COMBE LA
5
Holmens Grove
Littlebrook Farm
Rices Farm
Combe Court Farm
36
Lower Birtley Farm
Big Copse
Langhurst House
4
Pond Copse
Pook Hill
Shoelands
Hundred Acre Copse
Langhurst Manor Farm
Leith Copse
3
Stroud Wood
Stroud
Prestwick
Langhurst Manor
Seven Acre Copse
Little Prestwick Farm
35
Fowlshatch Copse
PRESTWICK LA
High Prestwick Farm
Pheatons Copse
2
PADDOCK WAY
LOWER RD
Frillinghurst Farm
Frillinghurst Wood
Sewage Works
KLONDYKE VILLAS
Furzefield
1
Peakfield Hanger
Clammer Hill
West End Farm
Netherside
34
92
93
94
189
209

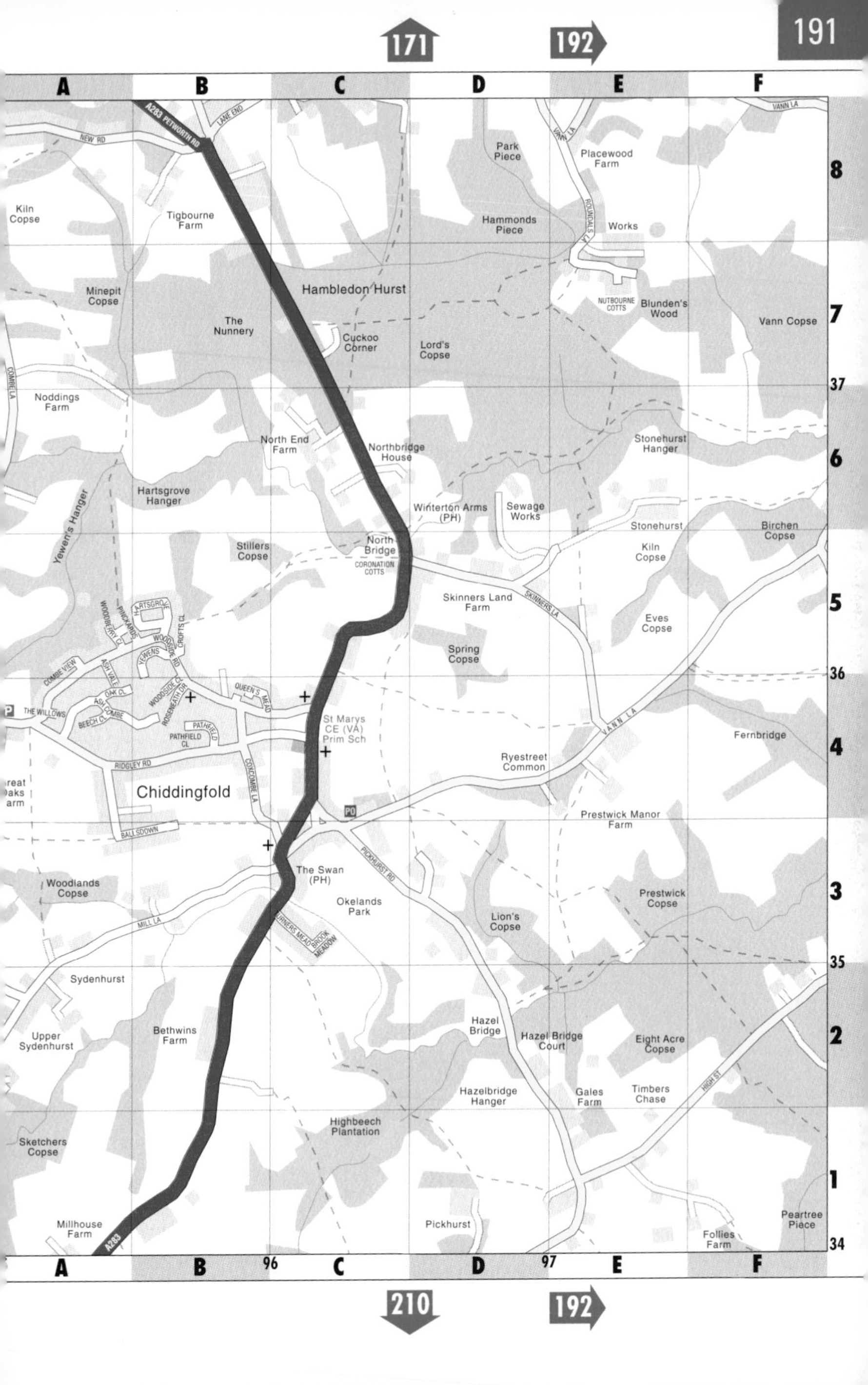

8

7

37

6

5

36

4

3

35

2

1

34

A B C D E F

NEW RD
A283 PETWORTH RD
LANE END

Kiln
Copse

Tigbourne
Farm

Park
Piece

Placewood
Farm

Hammonds
Piece

Works

Minepit
Copse

The
Nunnery

Hambledon Hurst

Cuckoo
Corner

Lord's
Copse

NUTBOURNE
COTTS

Blunden's
Wood

Vann Copse

Noddings
Farm

North End
Farm

Northbridge
House

Stonehurst
Hanger

Hartsgrove
Hanger

Yewen's Hanger

Winterton Arms
(PH)

Sewage
Works

Stonehurst

Birchen
Copse

Stillers
Copse

North
Bridge

CORONATION
COTTS

Skinners Land
Farm

Kiln
Copse

Eves
Copse

COMBE VIEW

THE WILLOWS

Spring
Copse

SKINNERS LA

reat
aks
arm

Chiddingfold

QUEEN'S MEAD

St Marys
CE (VA)
Prim Sch

PATHFIELD
CL

RIDGLEY RD

BALLSDOWN

Ryestreet
Common

VANN LA

Fernbridge

PO

Prestwick Manor
Farm

Woodlands
Copse

The Swan
(PH)

Okelands
Park

PICKHURST RD

Lion's
Copse

Prestwick
Copse

MILL LA

Sydenhurst

Upper
Sydenhurst

Bethwins
Farm

Hazel
Bridge

Hazel Bridge
Court

Eight Acre
Copse

HIGH ST

Hazelbridge
Hanger

Gales
Farm

Timbers
Chase

Sketchers
Copse

Millhouse
Farm

A283

Highbeech
Plantation

Pickhurst

Follies
Farm

Peartree
Piece

A B C D E F

96 97

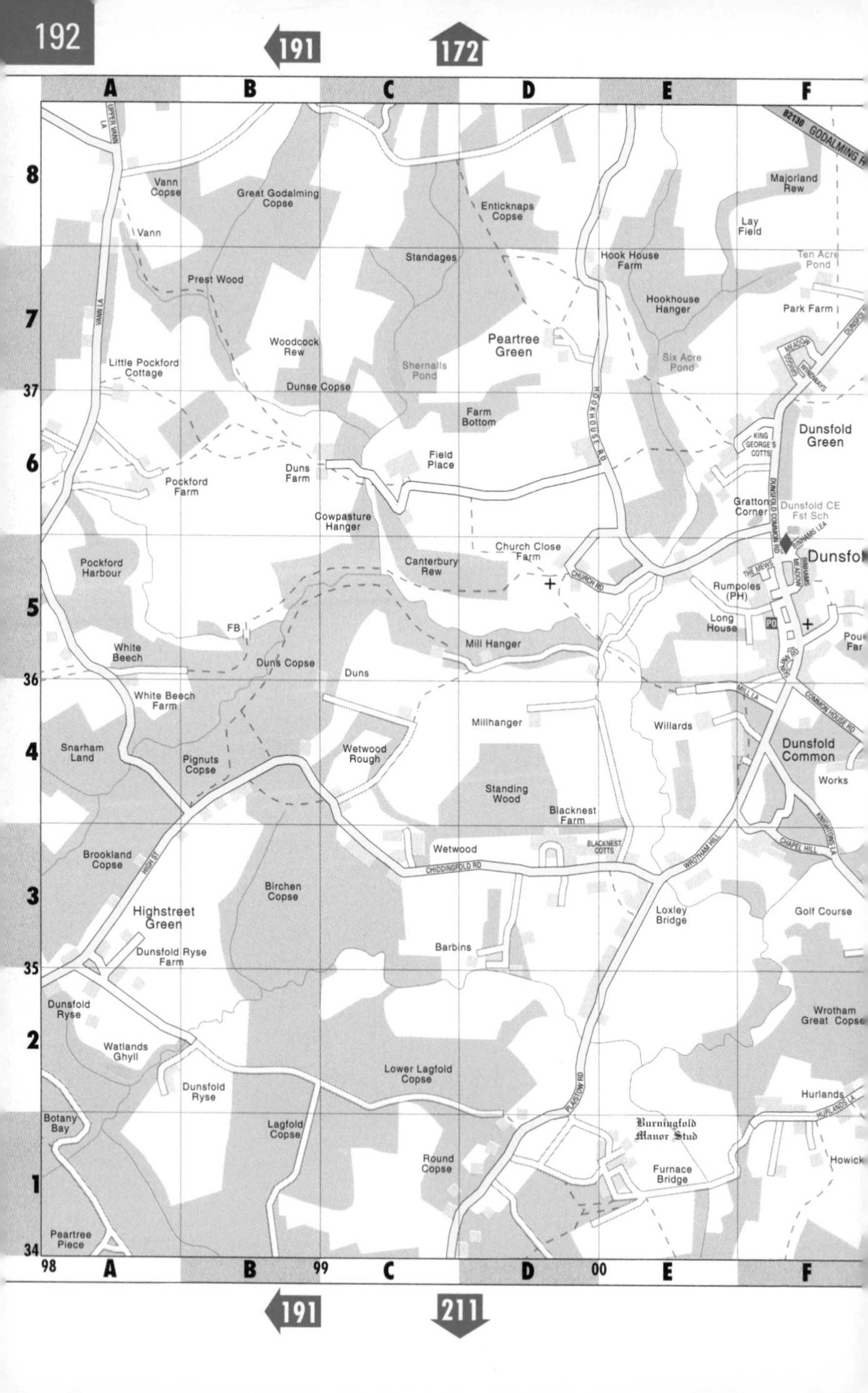
191
172
A
B
C
D
E
F
8
7
37
6
5
36
4
3
35
2
1
34
98
99
00
UPPER VANN LA
VANN LA
B2130 GODALMING R
Vann Copse
Great Godalming Copse
Enticknaps Copse
Majorland Rew
Lay Field
Vann
Prest Wood
Standages
Hook House Farm
Ten Acre Pond
Hookhouse Hanger
Park Farm
Woodcock Rew
Peartree Green
Little Pockford Cottage
Shernalls Pond
Six Acre Pond
Dunse Copse
Farm Bottom
HOOKHOUSE RD
Dunsfold Green
KING GEORGE'S COTTS
Field Place
Duns Farm
Pockford Farm
Gratton Corner
Dunsfold CE Fst Sch
Cowpasture Hanger
DUNSFOLD COMMON RD
Church Close Farm
Pockford Harbour
Canterbury Rew
Dunsfo
THE MEWS
CHURCH RD
Rumpoles (PH)
FB
Long House
PO
White Beech
Mill Hanger
Duns Copse
Duns
36
White Beech Farm
MILL LA
COMMON HOUSE RD
Millhanger
Willards
Snarham Land
Wetwood Rough
Dunsfold Common
Pignuts Copse
Works
Standing Wood
Blacknest Farm
Brookland Copse
Wetwood
BLACKNEST COTTS
CHAPEL HILL
WROTHAM HILL
CHIDDINGFOLD RD
HIGH ST
Birchen Copse
Highstreet Green
Loxley Bridge
Golf Course
Dunsfold Ryse Farm
Barbins
Dunsfold Ryse
Wrotham Great Copse
Watlands Ghyll
Lower Lagfold Copse
Dunsfold Ryse
Hurlands
HURLANDS LA
PLAISTOW RD
Botany Bay
Lagfold Copse
Burningfold Manor Stud
Round Copse
Furnace Bridge
Howick
Peartree Piece
191
211

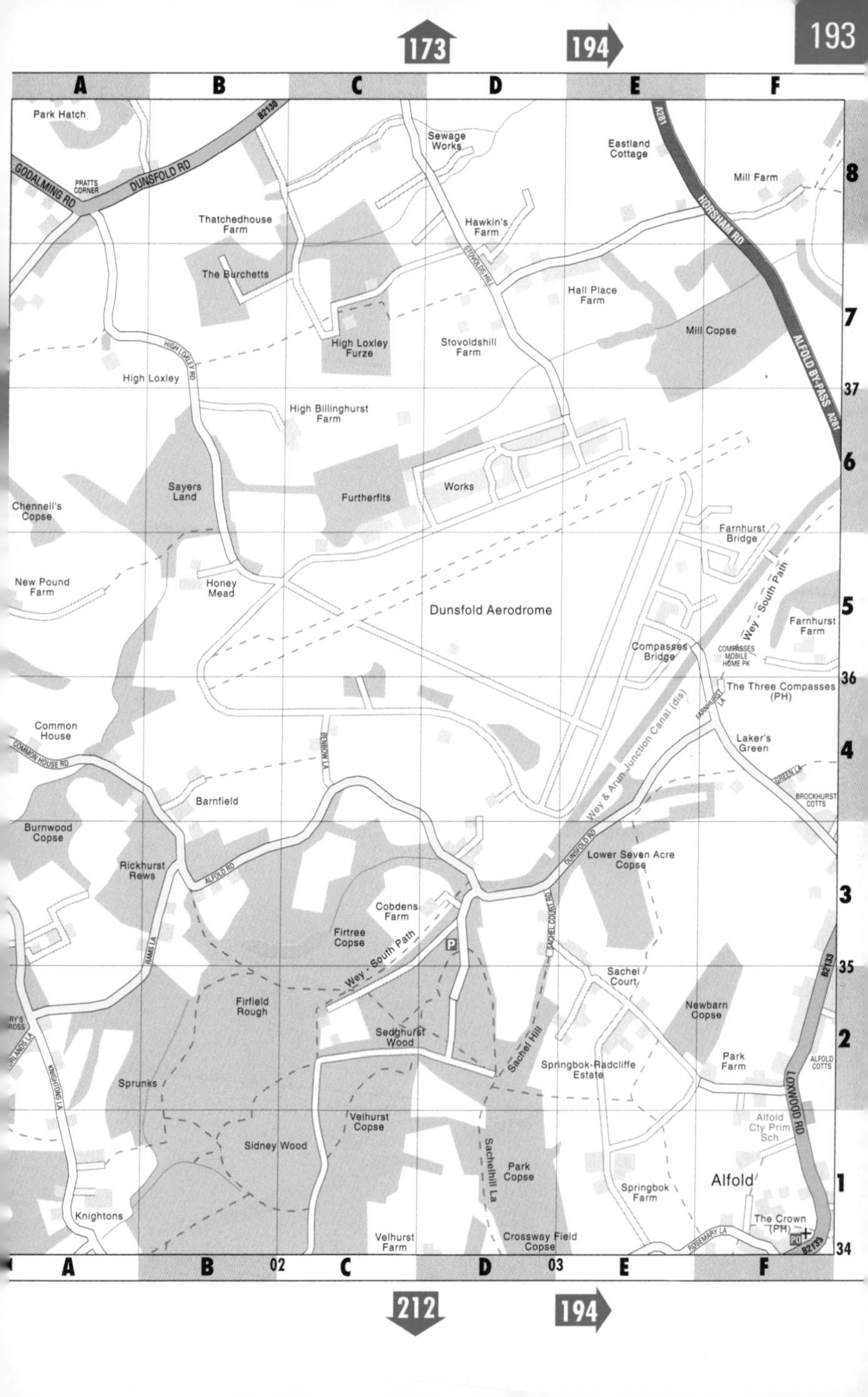

173
194

A   B   C   D   E   F

Park Hatch

GODALMING RD

PRATTS CORNER

DUNSFOLD RD

B2130

Sewage Works

Eastland Cottage

HORSHAM RD A281

Mill Farm

8

Thatchedhouse Farm

Hawkin's Farm

LOXLEY HILL

Hall Place Farm

Mill Copse

The Burchetts

ALFOLD BYPASS A281

7

High Loxley Furze

Stovoldshill Farm

HIGH LOXLEY RD

High Loxley

37

High Billinghurst Farm

Chennell's Copse

Sayers Land

Furtherfits

Works

6

Farnhurst Bridge

Wey - South Path

New Pound Farm

Honey Mead

Dunsfold Aerodrome

Farnhurst Farm

5

Compasses Bridge

COMPASSES MOBILE HOME PK

Common House

COMMON HOUSE RD

The Three Compasses (PH)

36

Wey & Arun Junction Canal (dis)

JARVIS LA

Laker's Green

4

Burnwood Copse

BENBOW LA

Barnfield

Lower Seven Acre Copse

GREEN LA

BROCKHURST COTTS

Rickhurst Rews

ALFOLD RD

DUNSFOLD RD

B2133

Cobdens Farm

Firtree Copse

P

SACHEL COURT RD

3

Wey - South Path

Sachel Court

35

Firfield Rough

SACHEL HILL

Newbarn Copse

LOXWOOD RD

Sedghurst Wood

Springbok-Radcliffe Estate

Park Farm

ALFOLD COTTS

2

Sprunks

RY'S CROSS

DUNSFOLD LA

KNIGHTONS LA

Sidney Wood

Velhurst Copse

SACHELHILL LA

Park Copse

Alfold Cty Prim Sch

1

Springbok Farm

Alfold

Knightons

Velhurst Farm

Crossway Field Copse

ROSEMARY LA

The Crown (PH)

B2133

34

A   B   02   C   D   03   E   F

212
194

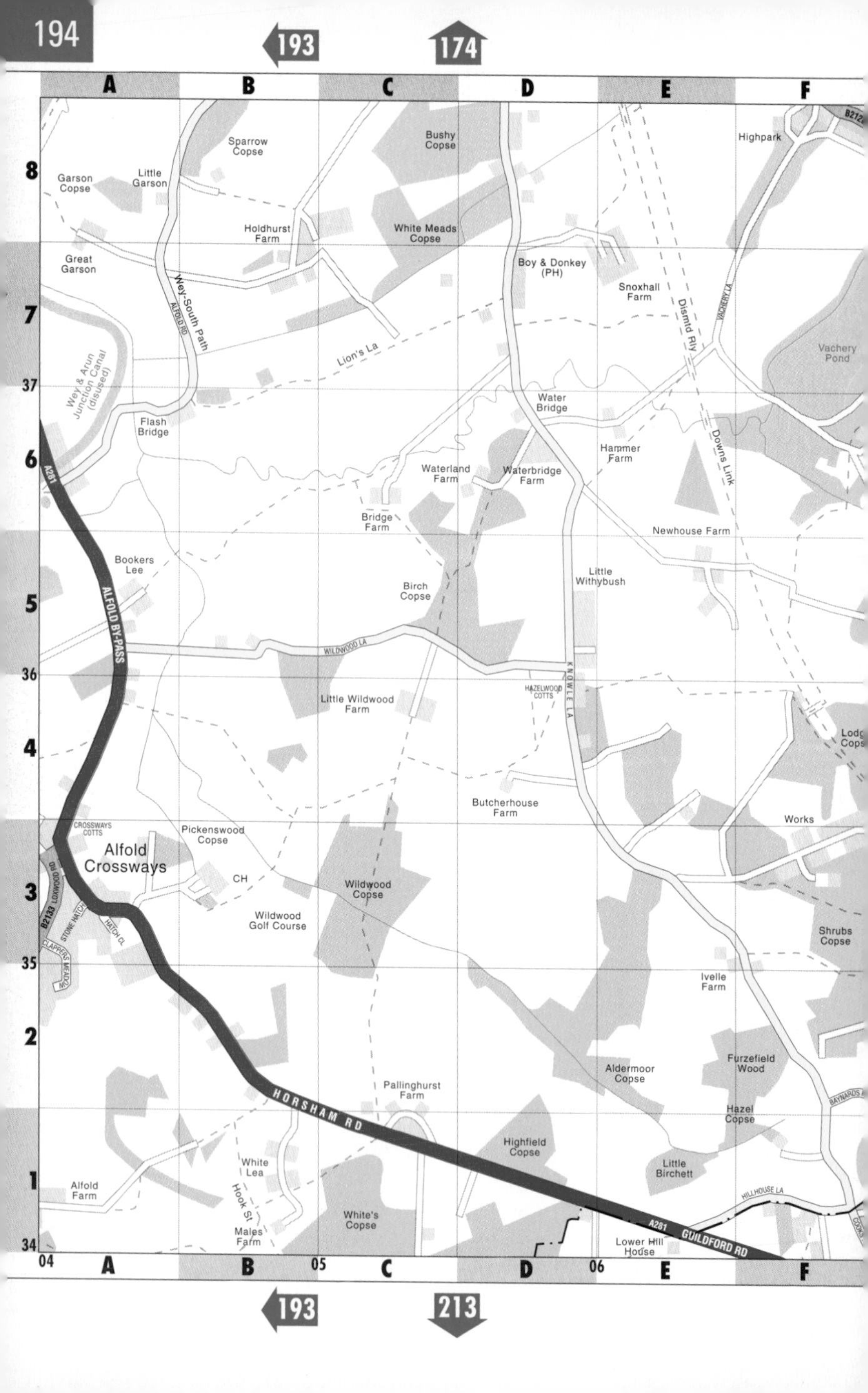
193
174
A
B
C
D
E
F
8
7
37
6
5
36
4
3
35
2
1
34
04
05
06
Sparrow Copse
Bushy Copse
Highpark
Garson Copse
Little Garson
Holdhurst Farm
White Meads Copse
Great Garson
Wey-South Path
ALFOLD RD
Boy & Donkey (PH)
Snoxhall Farm
Dismtd Rly
VACHERY LA
Lion's La
Vachery Pond
Wey & Arun Junction Canal (disused)
Water Bridge
Flash Bridge
Hammer Farm
Downs Link
A281
Waterland Farm
Waterbridge Farm
Bridge Farm
Newhouse Farm
Bookers Lee
Little Withybush
ALFOLD BY-PASS
Birch Copse
WILDWOOD LA
KNOWLE LA
HAZELWOOD COTTS
Little Wildwood Farm
Lodge Copse
Butcherhouse Farm
Works
CROSSWAYS COTTS
Pickenswood Copse
Alfold Crossways
CH
LOXWOOD RD
B2133
STONE HATCH
HATCH CL
Wildwood Copse
Wildwood Golf Course
CLAPPERS MEADOW
Shrubs Copse
Ivelle Farm
Furzefield Wood
Aldermoor Copse
Pallinghurst Farm
HORSHAM RD
Hazel Copse
BAYNARDS RD
Highfield Copse
White Lea
Little Birchett
Alfold Farm
Hook St
HILLHOUSE LA
White's Copse
Males Farm
Lower Hill House
GUILDFORD RD
193
213

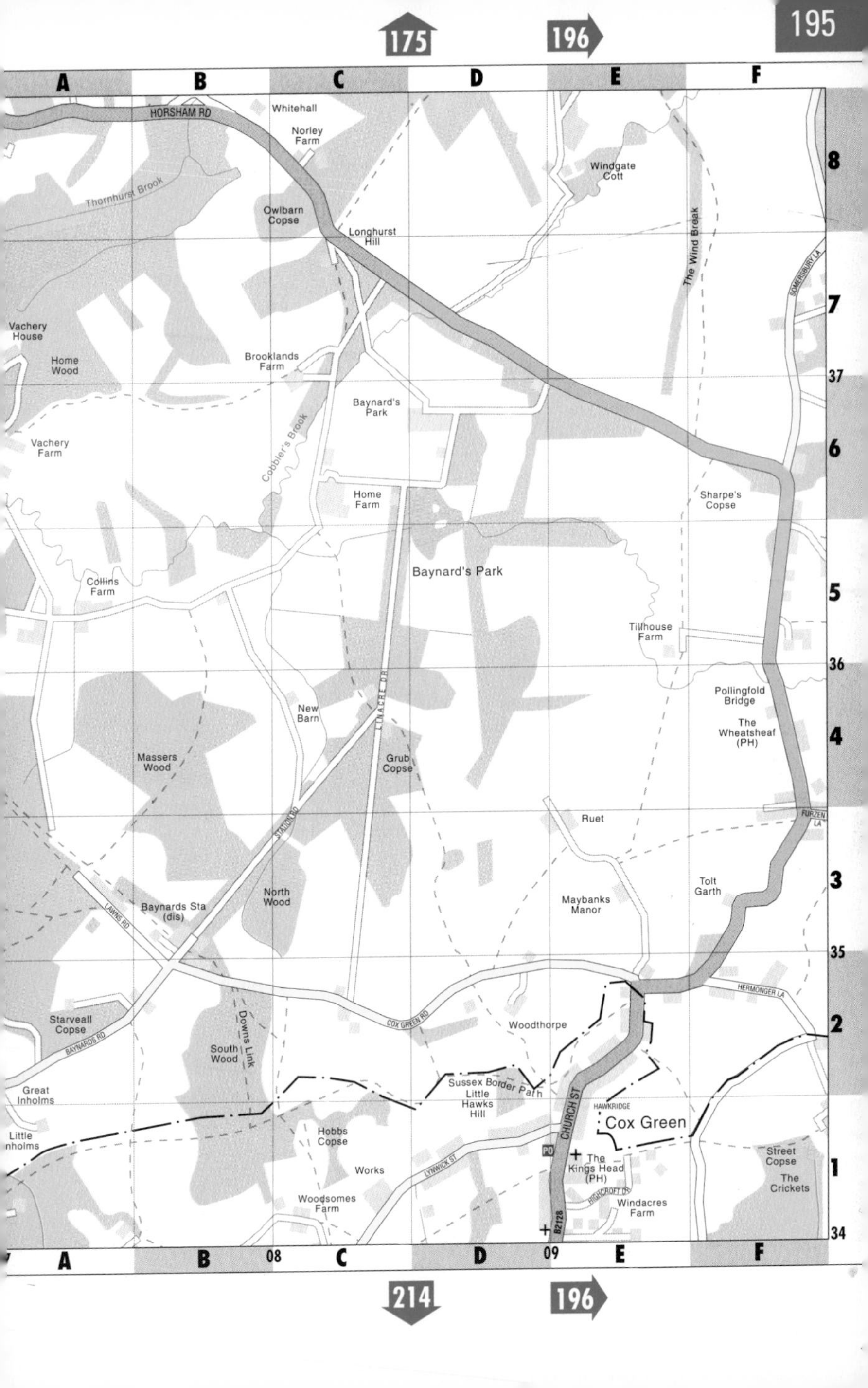

A B C D E F

8
7
37
6
5
36
4
3
35
2
1
34

HORSHAM RD
Whitehall
Norley Farm
Windgate Cott
Thornhurst Brook
Owlbarn Copse
Longhurst Hill
The Wind Break
Vachery House
Home Wood
Brooklands Farm
Baynard's Park
Cobbler's Brook
Sharpe's Copse
SOMERSBURY LA.
Vachery Farm
Home Farm
Collins Farm
Baynard's Park
Tilhouse Farm
Pollingfold Bridge
The Wheatsheaf (PH)
New Barn
LYNWICK RD
Grub Copse
Massers Wood
Ruet
FURZEN LA.
Tolt Garth
S'TONS RD.
Baynards Sta (dis)
North Wood
Maybanks Manor
LAKNE RD.
BAYNARDS RD.
Starveall Copse
Downs Link
South Wood
COX GREEN RD
Woodthorpe
HERMONGER LA.
Great Inholms
Hobbs Copse
Sussex Border Path
Little Hawks Hill
Works
CHURCH ST
HAWKRIDGE
Cox Green
Little Inholms
Woodsomes Farm
LYNWICK ST
PO
The Kings Head (PH)
HIGHCROFT DR
B2128
Windacres Farm
Street Copse
The Crickets

A B C D E F
08 09

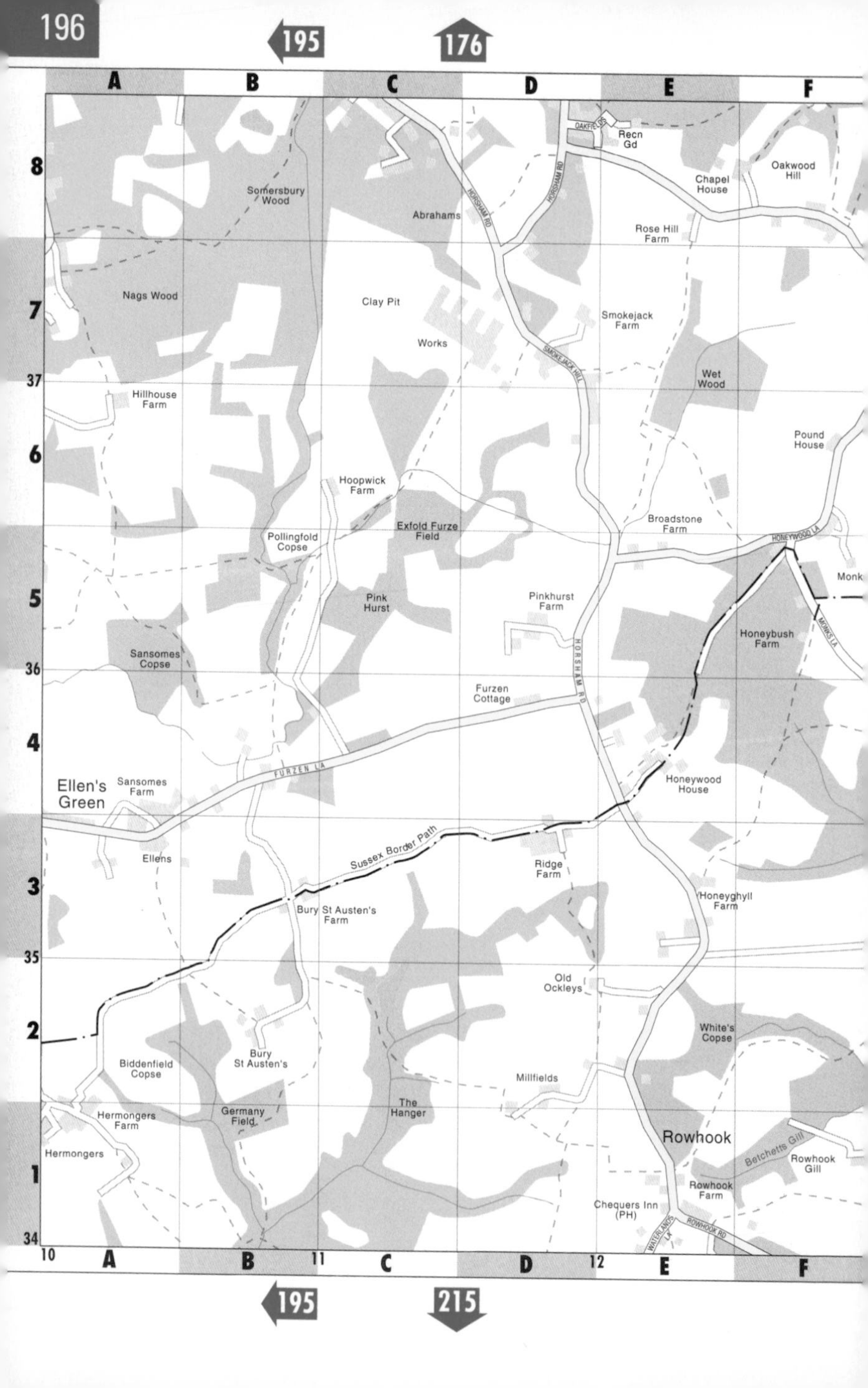
195
176
A
B
C
D
E
F
8
7
37
6
5
36
4
3
35
2
1
34
10
11
12
OAKFIELDS
Recn Gd
Chapel House
Oakwood Hill
Somersbury Wood
Abrahams
HORSHAM RD
Rose Hill Farm
Nags Wood
Clay Pit
Works
Smokejack Farm
SMOKEJACK HILL
Wet Wood
Hillhouse Farm
Pound House
Hoopwick Farm
Exfold Furze Field
Pollingfold Copse
Broadstone Farm
HONEYWOOD LA
Monk
Pink Hurst
Pinkhurst Farm
MONKS LA
Honeybush Farm
Sansomes Copse
Furzen Cottage
FURZEN LA
Ellen's Green
Sansomes Farm
Honeywood House
Ellens
Sussex Border Path
Ridge Farm
Bury St Austen's Farm
Honeyghyll Farm
Old Ockleys
White's Copse
Biddenfield Copse
Bury St Austen's
Millfields
Hermongers Farm
Germany Field
The Hanger
Rowhook
Betchetts Gill
Rowhook Gill
Hermongers
Rowhook Farm
Chequers Inn (PH)
WATERLANDS LA
ROWHOOK RD
195
215

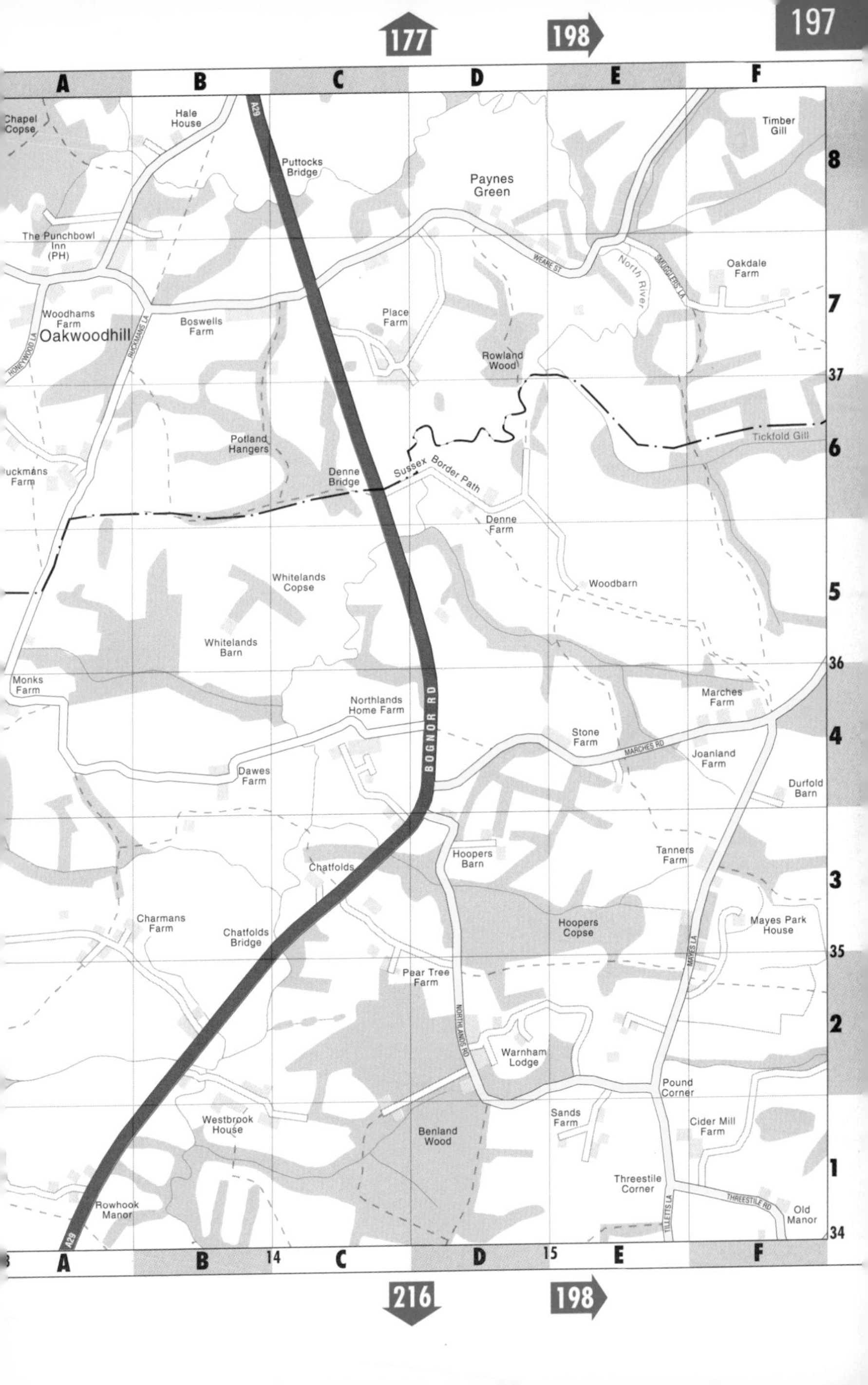
177
198
Chapel Copse
Hale House
Puttocks Bridge
Paynes Green
Timber Gill
The Punchbowl Inn (PH)
WEARE ST
North River
SMUGGLERS LA
Oakdale Farm
Woodhams Farm
Oakwoodhill
HONEYWOOD LA
RUCKMANS LA
Boswells Farm
Place Farm
Rowland Wood
Potland Hangers
Tickfold Gill
Ruckmans Farm
Denne Bridge
Sussex Border Path
Denne Farm
Whitelands Copse
Woodbarn
Whitelands Barn
Monks Farm
Northlands Home Farm
BOGNOR RD
Marches Farm
Stone Farm
MARCHES RD
Joanland Farm
Dawes Farm
Durfold Barn
Hoopers Barn
Tanners Farm
Chatfolds
Charmans Farm
Chatfolds Bridge
Hoopers Copse
Mayes Park House
MAYES LA
Pear Tree Farm
NORTHLANDS RD
Warnham Lodge
Pound Corner
Sands Farm
Westbrook House
Benland Wood
Cider Mill Farm
Threestile Corner
TILLETTS LA
THREESTILE RD
Rowhook Manor
Old Manor
A29
14
15
34
35
36
37
216
198

197
178

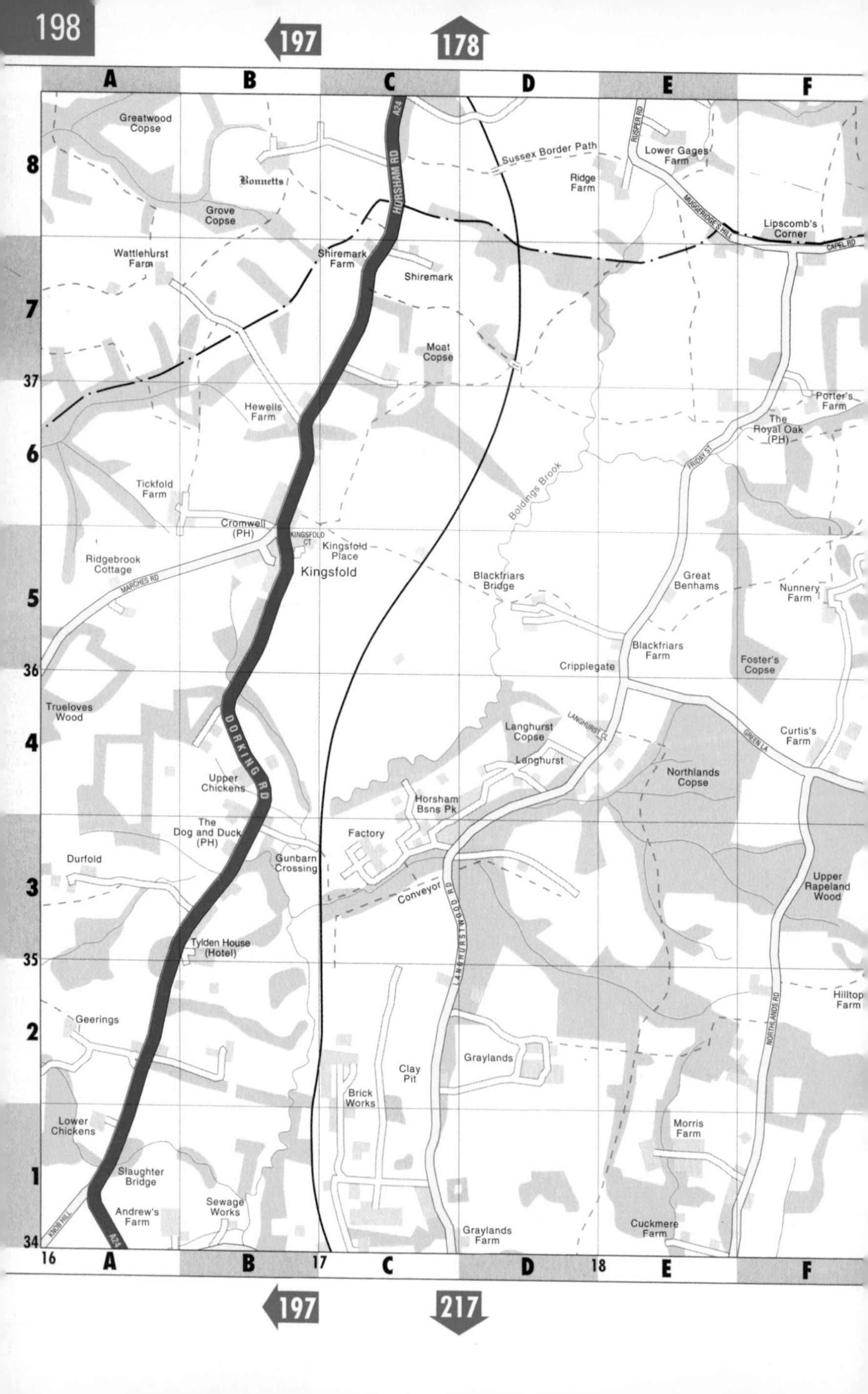
A
B
C
D
E
F
8
7
37
6
5
36
4
3
35
2
1
34
16
17
18
Greatwood Copse
Bonnetts
Grove Copse
A24
HORSHAM RD
Sussex Border Path
Ridge Farm
RUSPER RD
Lower Gages Farm
MUGGERIDGE'S HILL
Lipscomb's Corner
CAPEL RD
Wattlehurst Farm
Shiremark Farm
Shiremark
Moat Copse
Hewells Farm
Porter's Farm
The Royal Oak (PH)
FRIDAY ST
Boldings Brook
Tickfold Farm
Cromwell (PH)
KINGSFOLD CT
Kingsfold Place
Kingsfold
Ridgebrook Cottage
MARCHES RD
Blackfriars Bridge
Great Benhams
Nunnery Farm
Blackfriars Farm
Cripplegate
Foster's Copse
Trueloves Wood
DORKING RD
Langhurst Copse
LANGHURST CL
Langhurst
GREEN LA
Curtis's Farm
Northlands Copse
Upper Chickens
Horsham Bsns Pk
The Dog and Duck (PH)
Factory
Durfold
Gunbarn Crossing
Conveyor
LANGHURSTWOOD RD
Upper Rapeland Wood
Tylden House (Hotel)
Hilltop Farm
Geerings
NORTHLANDS RD
Graylands
Clay Pit
Brick Works
Lower Chickens
Morris Farm
Slaughter Bridge
KNOB HILL
Andrew's Farm
Sewage Works
Graylands Farm
Cuckmere Farm

197
217

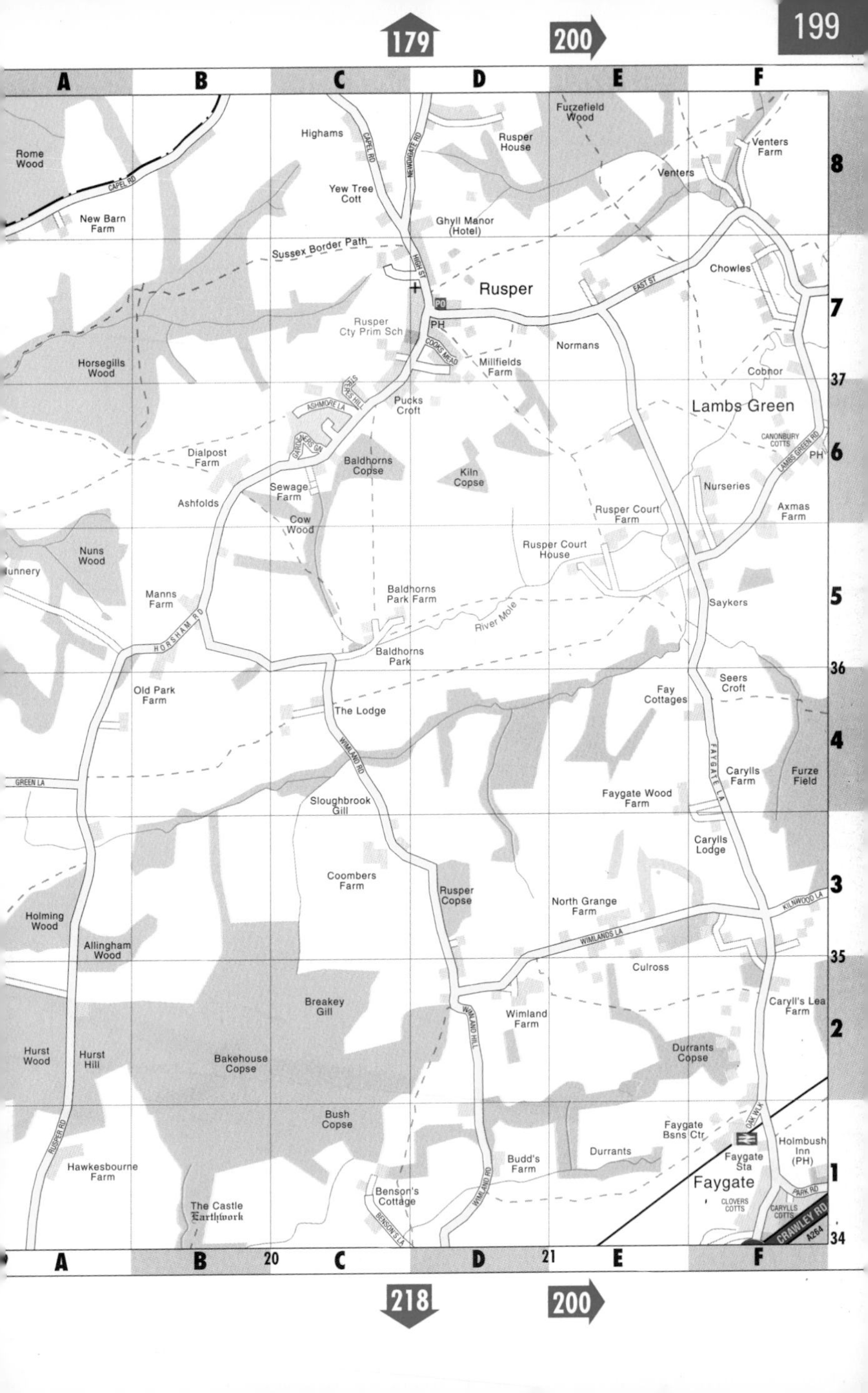
179
200
A
B
C
D
E
F
8
7
37
6
5
36
4
3
35
2
1
34
Rome Wood
New Barn Farm
CAPEL RD
Highams
CAPEL RD
NEWDIGATE RD
Yew Tree Cott
Rusper House
Furzefield Wood
Venters Farm
Venters
Ghyll Manor (Hotel)
Sussex Border Path
HIGH ST
Rusper
EAST ST
Chowles
PO
PH
Rusper Cty Prim Sch
COOKS MEAD
Millfields Farm
Normans
Horsegills Wood
Cobnor
Lambs Green
ASHMORE LA
Pucks Croft
CANONBURY COTTS
LAMBS GREEN RD
PH
Dialpost Farm
Baldhorns Copse
Kiln Copse
Sewage Farm
Ashfolds
Nurseries
Rusper Court Farm
Axmas Farm
Cow Wood
Nuns Wood
Rusper Court House
Manns Farm
HORSHAM RD
Baldhorns Park Farm
Saykers
River Mole
Baldhorns Park
Old Park Farm
Fay Cottages
Seers Croft
The Lodge
FAYGATE LA
Carylls Farm
Furze Field
WIMLAND RD
GREEN LA
Faygate Wood Farm
Sloughbrook Gill
Carylls Lodge
Coombers Farm
Rusper Copse
North Grange Farm
KILNWOOD LA
Holming Wood
WIMLANDS LA
Allingham Wood
Culross
Breakey Gill
Wimland Farm
Caryll's Lea Farm
WIMLAND HILL
Hurst Wood
Hurst Hill
Bakehouse Copse
Durrants Copse
Bush Copse
OAK WLK
Faygate Bsns Ctr
RUSPER RD
Holmbush Inn (PH)
Hawkesbourne Farm
Budd's Farm
Durrants
Faygate Sta
WIMLAND RD
Faygate
PARK RD
Benson's Cottage
CLOVERS COTTS
CARYLLS COTTS
The Castle
Earthwork
BENSON'S LA
CRAWLEY RD
A264
20
21
218
200

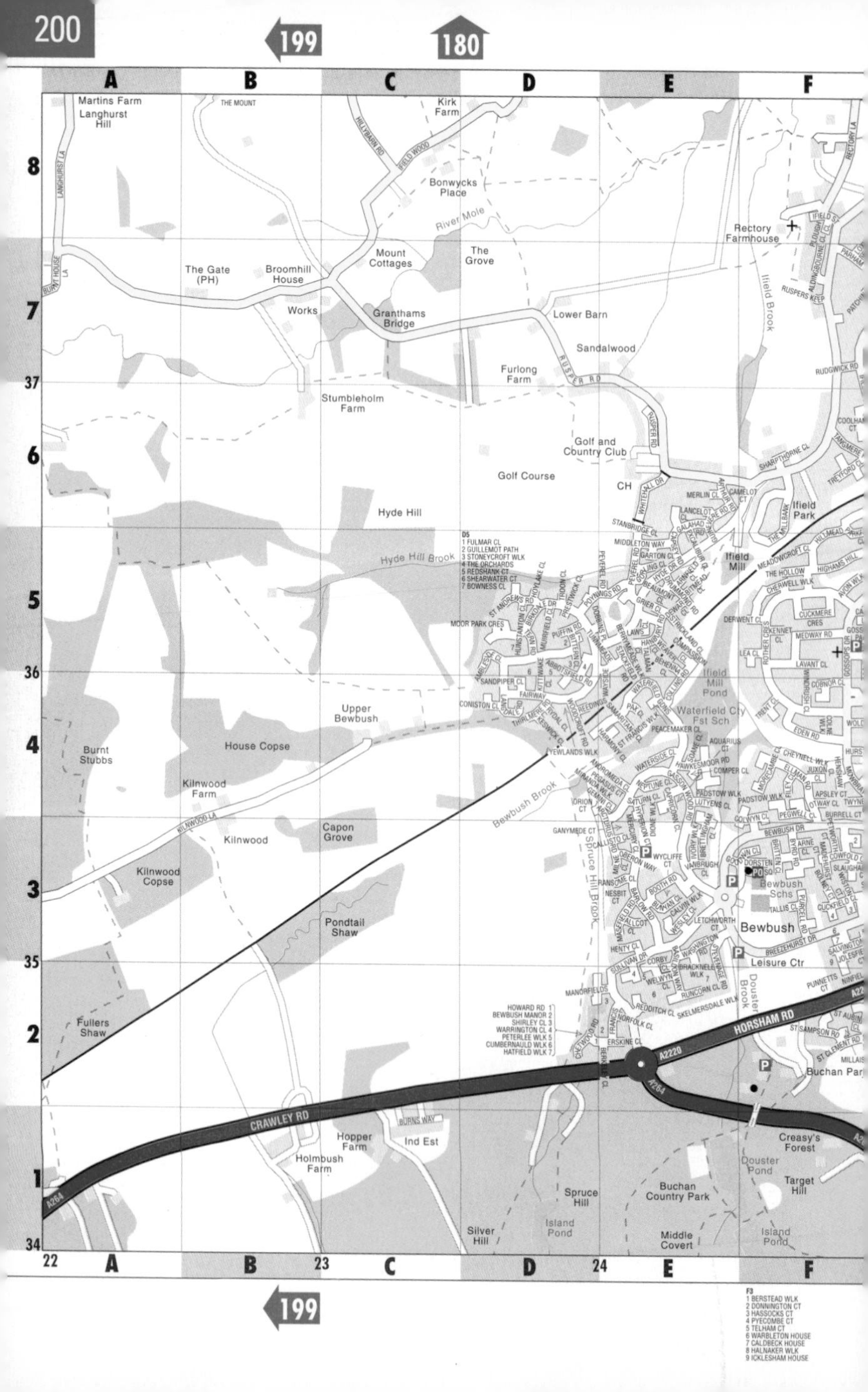
199
180
Martins Farm
Langhurst Hill
Kirk Farm
Bonwycks Place
River Mole
Rectory Farmhouse
The Gate (PH)
Broomhill House
Mount Cottages
The Grove
Works
Granthams Bridge
Lower Barn
Sandalwood
Ifield Brook
Furlong Farm
Stumbleholm Farm
Golf and Country Club
Golf Course
CH
Ifield Park
Hyde Hill
Hyde Hill Brook
D5
1 FULMAR CL
2 GUILLEMOT PATH
3 STONEYCROFT WLK
4 THE ORCHARDS
5 REDSHANK CT
6 SHEARWATER CT
7 BOWNESS CL
Ifield Mill
Ifield Mill Pond
Waterfield Cty Fst Sch
Upper Bewbush
Burnt Stubbs
House Copse
Kilnwood Farm
Bewbush Brook
Kilnwood
Capon Grove
Kilnwood Copse
Spruce Hill Brook
Bewbush Schs
Bewbush
Pondtail Shaw
Leisure Ctr
Douster Brook
HOWARD RD 1
BEWBUSH MANOR 2
SHIRLEY CL 3
WARRINGTON CL 4
PETERLEE WLK 5
CUMBERNAULD WLK 6
HATFIELD WLK 7
Fullers Shaw
HORSHAM RD
A2220
A264
Buchan Park
CRAWLEY RD
Hopper Farm
Ind Est
Holmbush Farm
Creasy's Forest
Douster Pond
Target Hill
Spruce Hill
Buchan Country Park
Island Pond
Silver Hill
Middle Covert
Island Pond
F3
1 BERSTEAD WLK
2 DONNINGTON CT
3 HASSOCKS CT
4 PYECOMBE CT
5 TELHAM CT
6 WARBLETON HOUSE
7 CALDBECK HOUSE
8 HALNAKER WLK
9 ICKLESHAM HOUSE

199

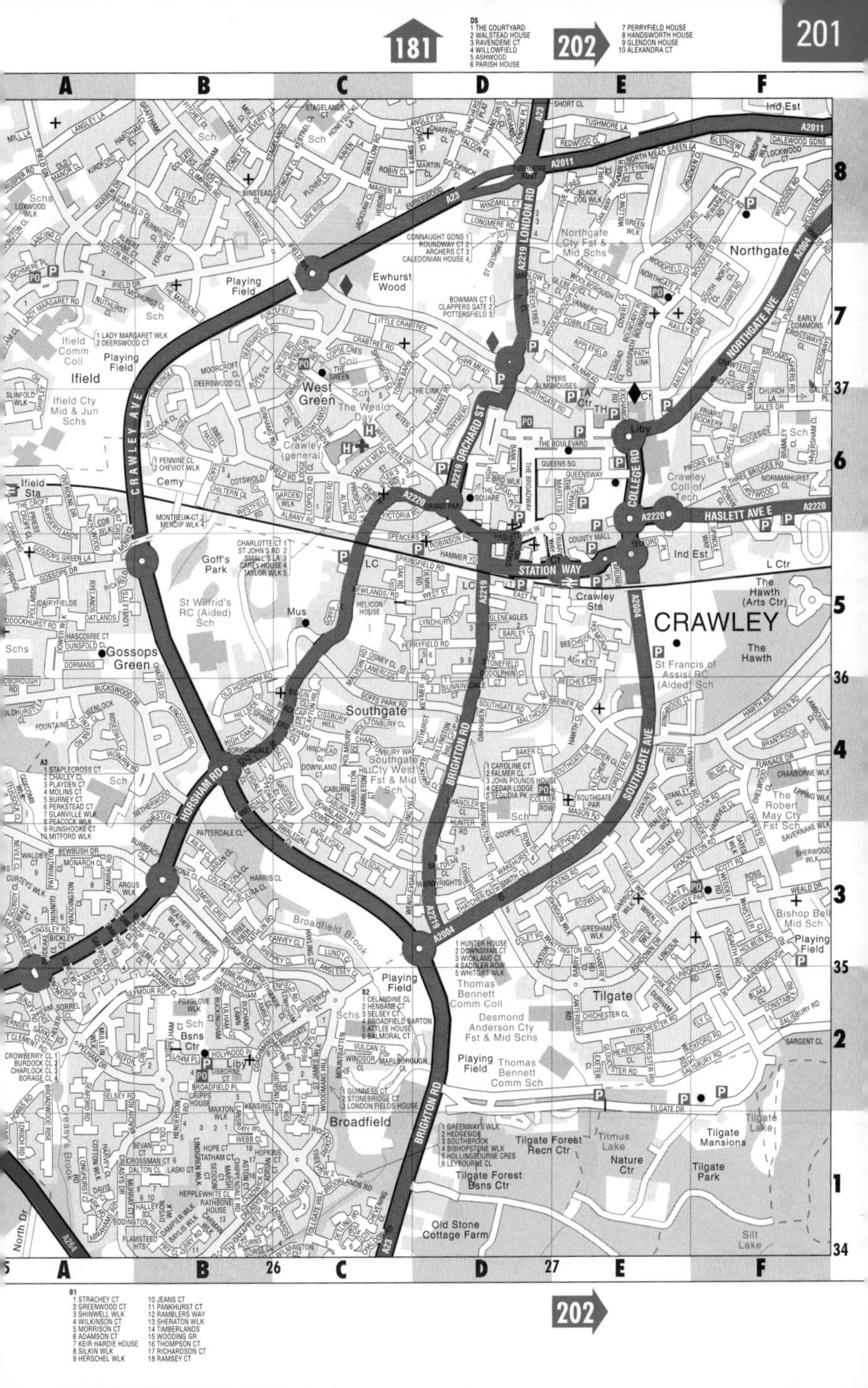

D5
1 THE COURTYARD
2 WALSTEAD HOUSE
3 RAVENDENE CT
4 WILLOWFIELD
5 ASHWOOD
6 PARISH HOUSE

7 PERRYFIELD HOUSE
8 HANDSWORTH HOUSE
9 GLENDON HOUSE
10 ALEXANDRA CT

B1
1 STRACHEY CT
2 GREENWOOD CT
3 SHINWELL WLK
4 WILKINSON CT
5 MORRISON CT
6 ADAMSON CT
7 KEIR HARDIE HOUSE
8 SILKIN WLK
9 HERSCHEL WLK
10 JEANS CT
11 PANKHURST CT
12 RAMBLERS WAY
13 SHERATON WLK
14 TIMBERLANDS
15 WOODING GR
16 THOMPSON CT
17 RICHARDSON CT
18 RAMSEY CT

Map

A **B** **C** **D** **E** **F**

A2011 · NORTHGATE AVE

Hazelwick Sch
Milton Mount Fst & Mid Sch
TRINITY CL
HOME CL
B2036
COPTHORNE RD
B2028 A2220
M23

1 HYDE HEATH CT
2 CHERRY TREE CL

Pound Hill
Burleys Wood

1 PENSHURST CL
2 THE PADDOCK
3 SHORT GALLOP
4 GREYHOUND SLIP
5 THE CACKSTONES

Three Bridges
WEST AVE
THE BIRCHES
WORTH PARK AVE
CHAUCER RD
TENNYSON
KIPLING
WORDSWORTH
SHELLEY
BYRON CL
BROWNING

8

7

Crabbet Park

37

PO Coll
GALES DR
Three Bridges Sta
Ind Est
BELVEDERE
NEW
PO

Pound Hill Fst & Mid Schs

1 ST IVES
2 ST NICHOLAS CT
3 ST BARNABAS CT

Notre Dame Intermediate Sch
BALCOMBE CT
TURNERS HILL RD
KELSO CL

Worth

1 GOUDHURST KEEP
2 GOUDHURST CL
3 CROWHURST KEEP

6

HASLETT AVE E
HAWTHORNE
A2220
Playing Field
Stockwell Works

Pound Hill Par
POUND
G & Worth Way
SPRING PLAT
BLACKWATER
SALEHURST RD
OSMOND RD
EDGAR RD
Worth Lodge Farm

5

LAMBERHURST WLK
STENNER CL
WANDLE CL
STIRLEY
BALCOMBE RD

1 TVLGTSON CL
2 MAYFLOWER CL
3 ALBION CL
4 WELLER CL
5 BETHUNE CL
6 THORNDYKE CL

Furnace Green
Sch
NORWICH RD
FURNACE
SHEYDON
SHEFFIELD CL
WEALD

Maidenbower Cty Fst Sch
ALDWYCH CL

36

Long Wood
ST LEONARDS
CHARLESTON
LEONARDSLEE CT

1 STRUGDATE CL
2 HAWKHURST WLK
3 LOWESTOFT WLK
4 BARTON WLK
5 HEMSBY WLK
6 ORMESBY WLK
7 WAVENEY WLK
8 WROXHAM WLK
9 OULTON WLK
10 HICKLING WLK

1 WALKER RD
2 RAWORTH CL
3 STEPNEY CL

STANLEY
Maidenbower

Worthlodge Forest

4

1 DONCASTER WLK
2 SHARON CL
3 GRAVETYE CL
4 FERRONERS CT
5 BRUNSWICK CT

Furnace Plain

MATTHEWS DR
STANFORD BRIDGE
CASPER DR
STONE CL
KERDALEGE
WORSTED RD

3

35

Tilgate Forest Golf Course
CH
TILGATE DR
Brick Field North

Flax Field

2

Brick Field South

Worth Forest

CUFFS HILL
B2036

1

Oldhouse Warren
Worth Forest

Whitely Hill
WHITELY HILL

34

M23

Rugs Corner

A **28** **B** **29** **C** **D** **30** **E** **F**

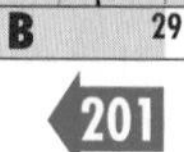

183
204

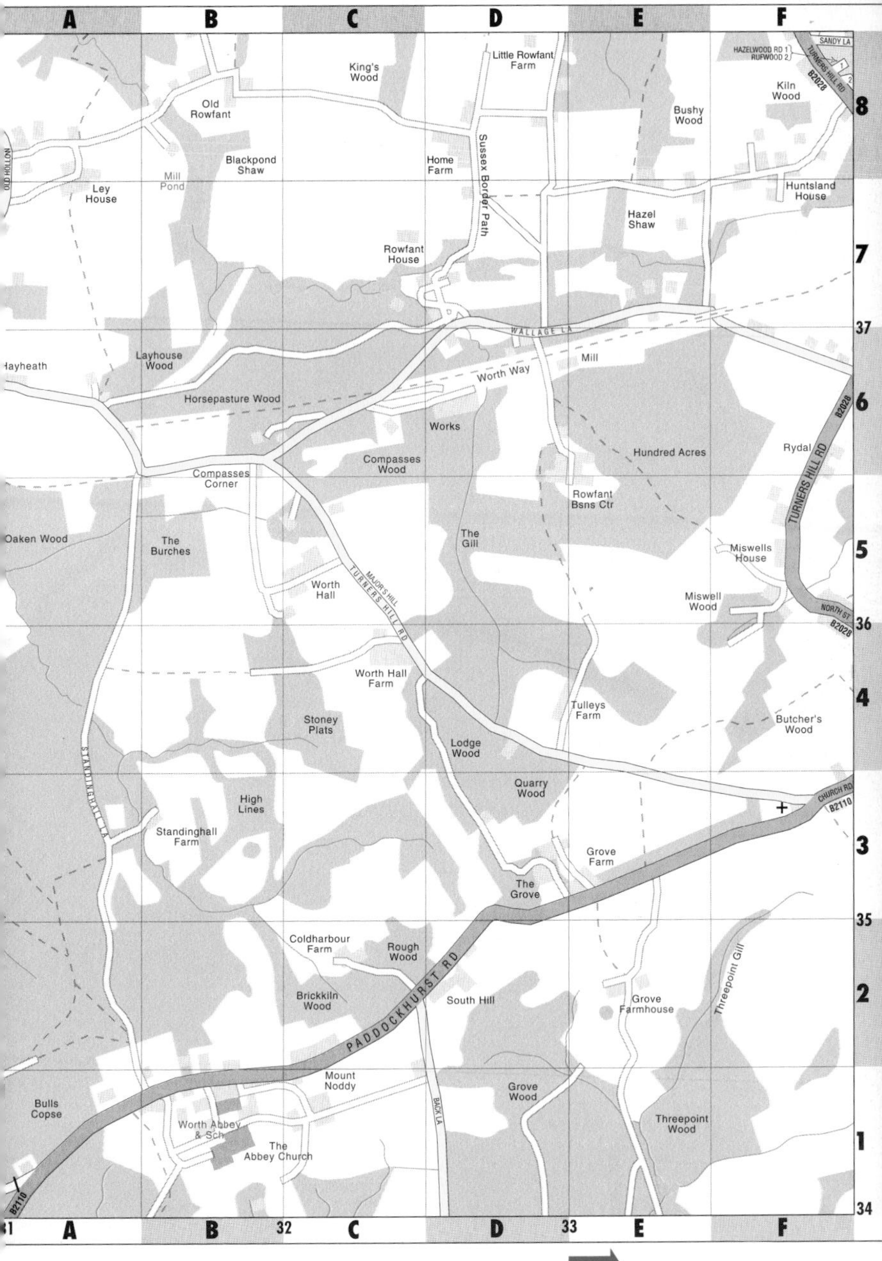

A
B
C
D
E
F
Little Rowfant Farm
King's Wood
Old Rowfant
HAZELWOOD RD 1
RUFWOOD 2
SANDY LA
TURNERS HILL RD
B2028
Kiln Wood
Bushy Wood
8
OLD HOLLOW
Blackpond Shaw
Home Farm
Sussex Border Path
Mill Pond
Ley House
Huntsland House
Hazel Shaw
Rowfant House
7
WALLAGE LA
37
Mill
Layhouse Wood
Hayheath
Worth Way
Horsepasture Wood
6
Works
Hundred Acres
Rydal
Compasses Wood
Compasses Corner
TURNERS HILL RD
Rowfant Bsns Ctr
Oaken Wood
The Burches
The Gill
Miswells House
5
MAJOR'S HILL
TURNERS HILL RD
Worth Hall
Miswell Wood
NORTH ST
B2028
36
Worth Hall Farm
4
Tulleys Farm
Butcher's Wood
Stoney Plats
STANDINGHALL LA
Lodge Wood
High Lines
Quarry Wood
CHURCH RD
B2110
Standinghall Farm
3
Grove Farm
The Grove
35
Coldharbour Farm
Rough Wood
PADDOCKHURST RD
Threepoint Gill
2
Brickkiln Wood
South Hill
Grove Farmhouse
Mount Noddy
BACK LA
Grove Wood
Bulls Copse
Threepoint Wood
Worth Abbey & Sch
The Abbey Church
1
B2110
34
31
32
33

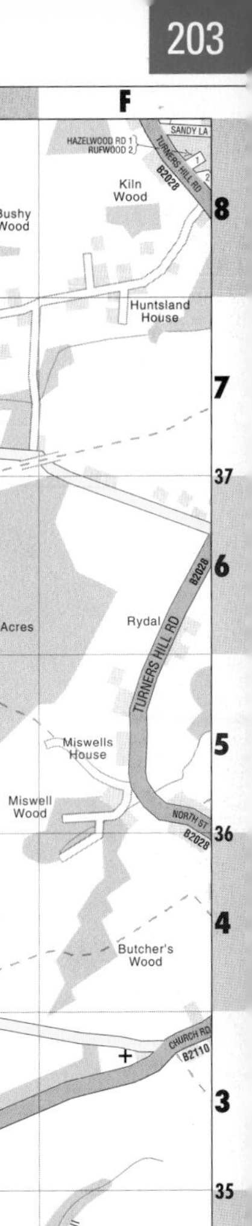

204

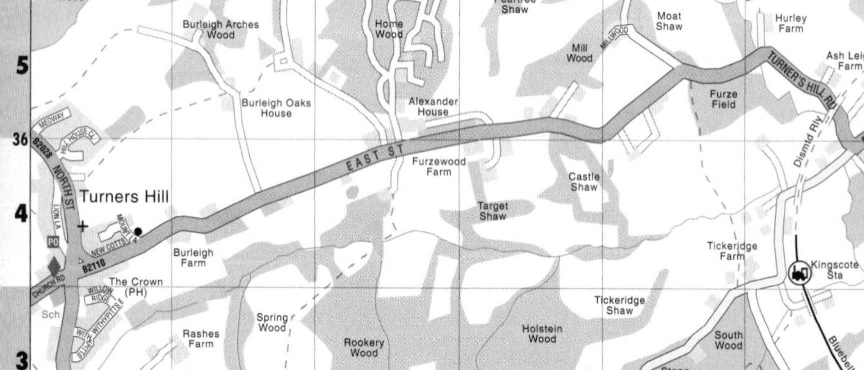

203
184

| A | B | C | D | E | F |

8

Sandy La
Sunnyhill Cl.
Schs
Buckley Pl.
Underwood
Front Wood
Scholars Ct.
Worth Way
Rushetts Wood
Gulledge Wood
French Wood

Crawley Down

7
Worth Way
Turners Hill Rd
Old Station Cl.
Grange Rd
Kiln Rd
Burleigh La
Sussex Border Path
Tilkhurst Farm

37
Sunnymead 1
Ridgedale 2
Auchinleck Ct 3
Royal Oak House 4
The Grange
Grange Farm
Burleigh House Farm

6
Sandhill
Rainbow Shaw
River Medway

Warren Wood
Little Nobs
Peartree Shaw
Fen Place Mill
Hurley Farm

5
Burleigh Arches Wood
Home Wood
Moat Shaw
Ash Leigh Farm
Burleigh Oaks House
Alexander House
Mill Wood
TURNER'S HILL RD

36
Midway
EAST ST
Furzewood Farm
Furze Field
Castle Shaw
Dismid Riv
B2110
NORTH ST

Turners Hill
New Cotts.
Target Shaw
Tickeridge Farm
Kingscote Sta

4
Burleigh Farm
Tickeridge Shaw
Church Rd
The Crown (PH)
Willow
Bluebell Rly

3
Sch
Withypitts
Rashes Farm
Spring Wood
Rookery Wood
Holstein Wood
Stone Wood
South Wood

35
Withy Pitts Farm
Coomberdean Wood
Great Wildgoose Wood
Minepit Wood
Vowels Gill
Mill Place Wood

2
The Punch Bowl (PH)
Thornhill Cottages
SELSFIELD RD
Selsfield Common
Selsfield Place
VOWELS LA
Drive Shaw
Bushy Wood

1
Bramblehill
Selsfield Common
Duckneil's Wood
Moatlands
Pine Wood
Warren's Wood
Home Farm
Hastings Wood

Selsfield House
West Hoathly
Gravetye Manor
Lower Lake

34

| A | B | C | D | E | F |
| 34 | 35 | | | 36 | |

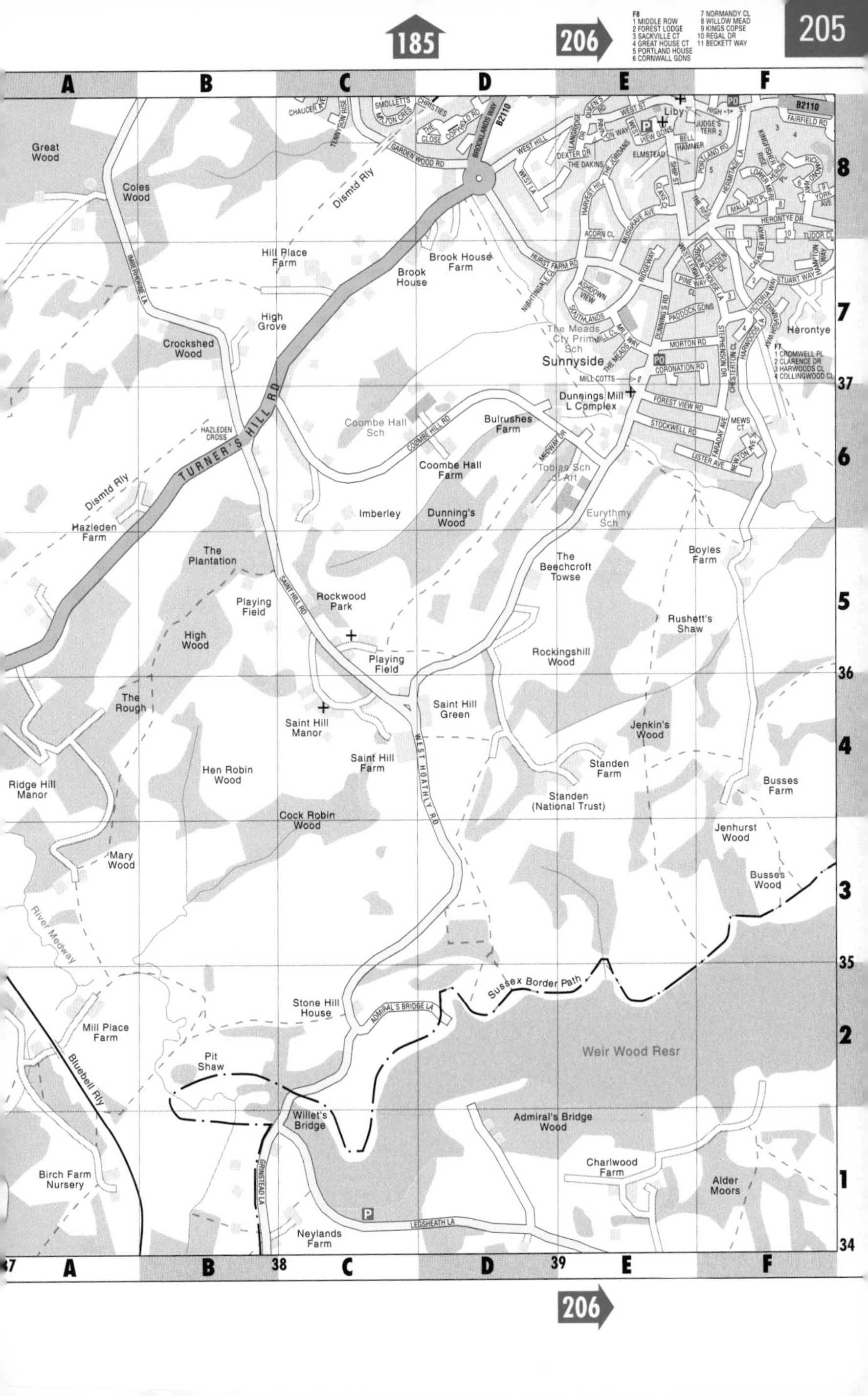
185
206
F8
1 MIDDLE ROW
2 FOREST LODGE
3 SACKVILLE CT
4 GREAT HOUSE CT
5 PORTLAND HOUSE
6 CORNWALL GDNS
7 NORMANDY CL
8 WILLOW MEAD
9 KINGS COPSE
10 REGAL DR
11 BECKETT WAY
Great Wood
Coles Wood
Dismtd Rly
Hill Place Farm
Brook House
Brook House Farm
High Grove
Crockshed Wood
Sunnyside
The Meads Cty Prim Sch
Dunnings Mill L Complex
Coombe Hall Sch
Bulrushes Farm
Coombe Hall Farm
Tobias Sch of Art
Eurythmy Sch
Herontye
F7
1 CROMWELL PL
2 CLARENCE DR
3 HARWOODS CL
4 COLLINGWOOD CL
TURNER'S HILL RD
HAZLEDEN CROSS
Hazleden Farm
Imberley
Dunning's Wood
The Plantation
The Beechcroft Towse
Boyles Farm
Rockwood Park
Playing Field
High Wood
Rushett's Shaw
Rockingshill Wood
The Rough
Saint Hill Manor
Saint Hill Green
Saint Hill Farm
Jenkin's Wood
Standen Farm
Standen (National Trust)
Busses Farm
Ridge Hill Manor
Hen Robin Wood
Cock Robin Wood
Jenhurst Wood
Mary Wood
Busses Wood
River Medway
Sussex Border Path
Stone Hill House
ADMIRAL'S BRIDGE LA
Mill Place Farm
Pit Shaw
Weir Wood Resr
Bluebell Rly
Willet's Bridge
Admiral's Bridge Wood
Charlwood Farm
Alder Moors
Birch Farm Nursery
Neylands Farm
LEGSHEATH LA
GRINSTEAD LA
WEST HOATHLY RD
SAINT HILL RD
IMBERHORNE LA
COOMBE HILL RD
B2110
BROOKLANDS WAY
GARDEN WOOD RD
WEST HILL
WEST LA
HURST FARM RD
NIGHTINGALE CL
MORTON RD
CORONATION RD
FOREST VIEW RD
STOCKWELL RD
LISTER AVE
FARADAY AVE
MEDWAY DR
A B C D E F
8 7 6 5 4 3 2 1
37 36 35 34 38 39

205
186

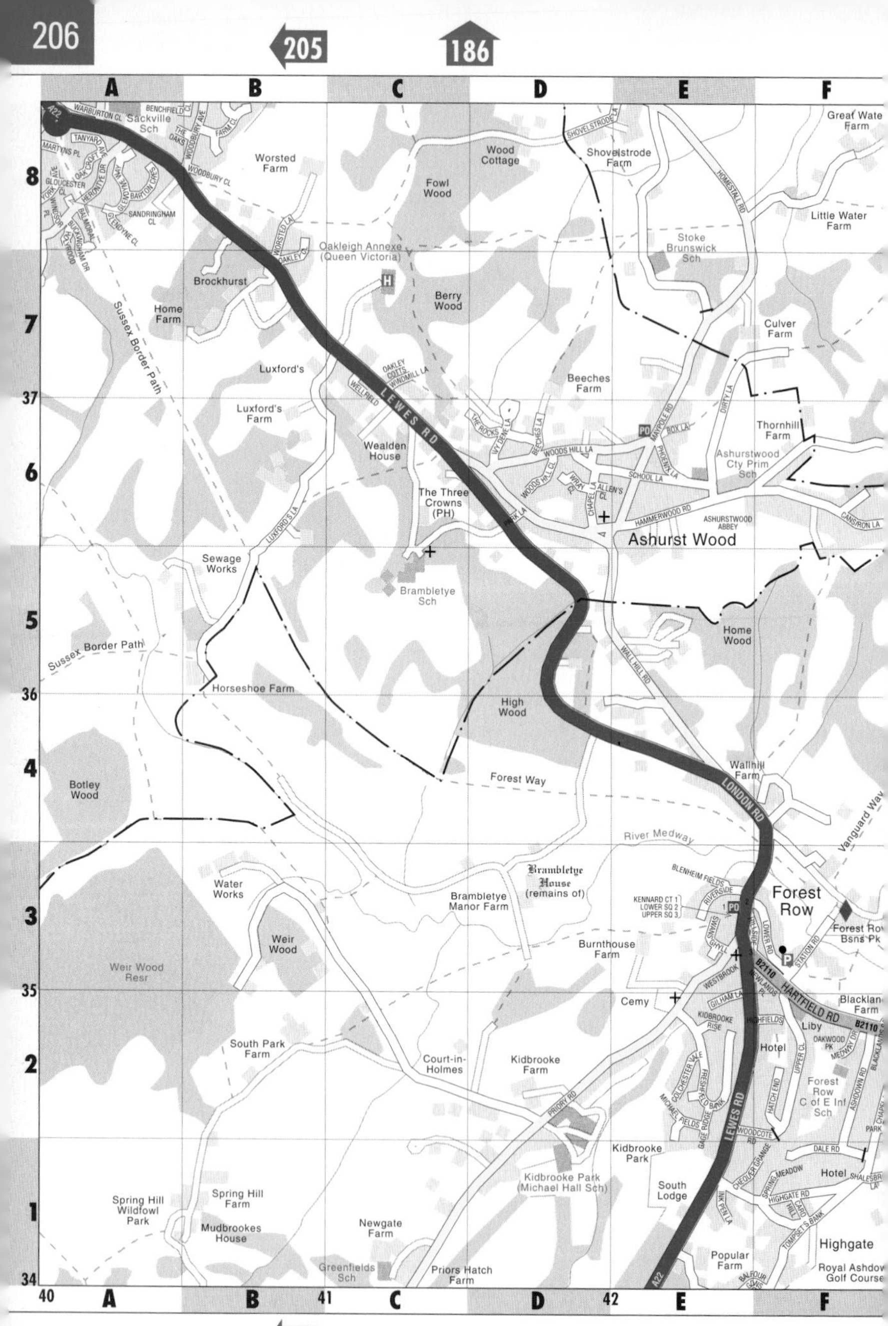

A B C D E F
8 7 6 5 4 3 2 1
37 36 35 34
40 41 42
Sackville Sch
Worsted Farm
Wood Cottage
Fowl Wood
Shovelstrode Farm
Great Water Farm
Little Water Farm
Stoke Brunswick Sch
Oakleigh Annexe (Queen Victoria)
Brockhurst
Berry Wood
Home Farm
Sussex Border Path
Culver Farm
Luxford's
Luxford's Farm
Beeches Farm
LEWES RD
Wealden House
Thornhill Farm
Ashurstwood Cty Prim Sch
The Three Crowns (PH)
Ashurst Wood
Sewage Works
Brambletye Sch
Home Wood
Horseshoe Farm
High Wood
Botley Wood
Forest Way
Wallhill Farm
LONDON RD
River Medway
Vanguard Way
Water Works
Brambletye House (remains of)
Brambletye Manor Farm
Forest Row
Weir Wood
Burnthouse Farm
Forest Row Bsns Pk
Weir Wood Resr
Cemy
Blackland Farm
HARTFIELD RD
B2110
South Park Farm
Liby
Hotel
Court-in-Holmes
Kidbrooke Farm
Forest Row C of E Inf Sch
Kidbrooke Park
Hotel
Kidbrooke Park (Michael Hall Sch)
South Lodge
Spring Hill Wildfowl Park
Spring Hill Farm
Mudbrookes House
Newgate Farm
Highgate
Popular Farm
Greenfields Sch
Priors Hatch Farm
Royal Ashdown Golf Course
A22

205

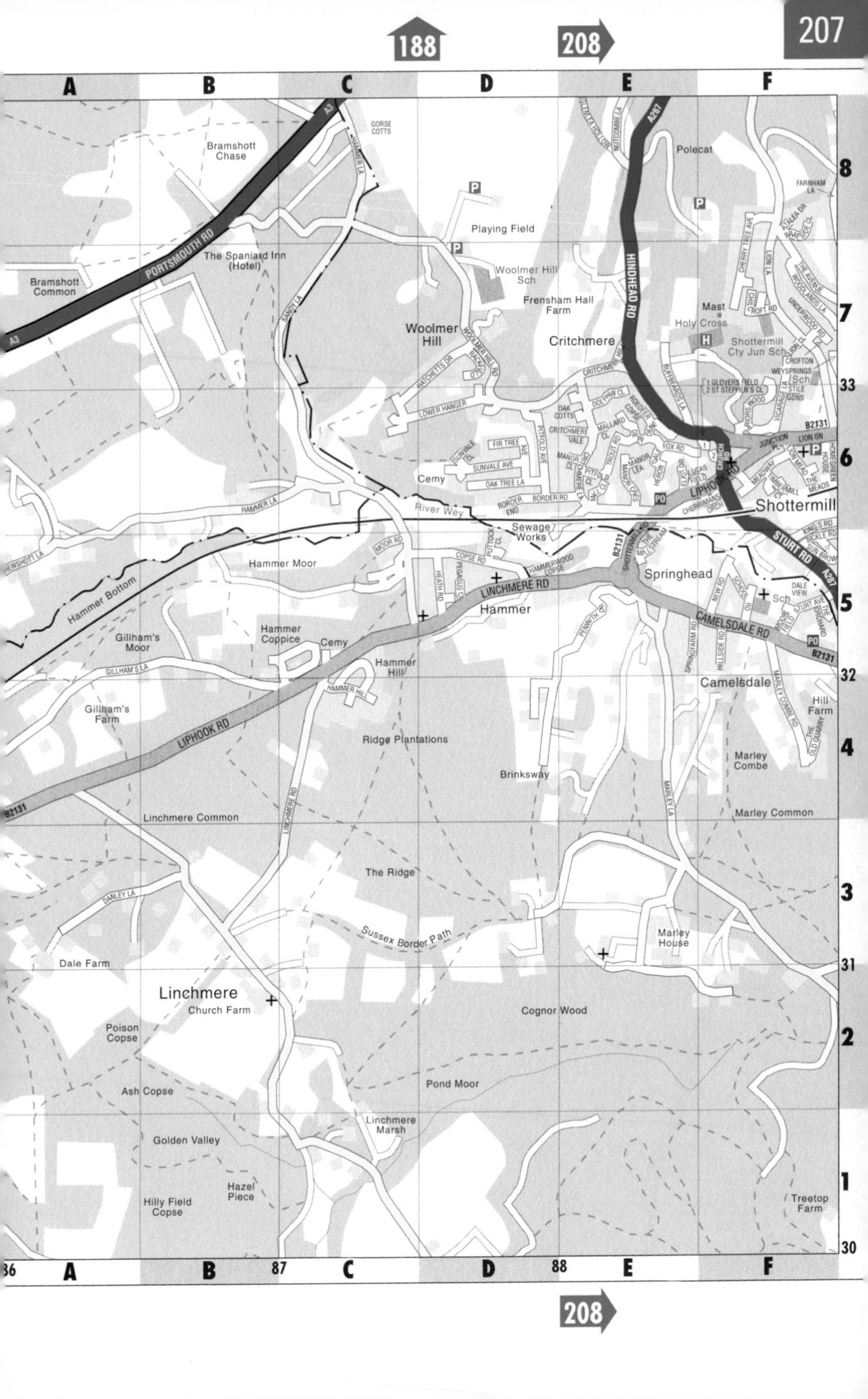
188
208
A
B
C
D
E
F
8
7
33
6
5
32
4
3
31
2
1
30
86
87
88
GORSE COTTS
Bramshott Chase
Polecat
Playing Field
The Spaniard Inn (Hotel)
PORTSMOUTH RD
Bramshott Common
A3
Woolmer Hill Sch
Frensham Hall Farm
Woolmer Hill
Critchmere
HINDHEAD RD
A287
Mast
Holy Cross
Shottermill Cty Jun Sch
LOWER HANGER
Cemy
SUNVALE AVE
OAK TREE LA
FIR TREE AVE
PITFOLD AVE
CRITCHMERE VALE
River Wey
BORDER RD
BORDER END
LIPHOOK RD
Shottermill
STURT RD
Sewage Works
HAMMER LA
Hammer Moor
MOOR RD
COPSE RD
HEATH RD
LINCHMERE RD
Hammer
Springhead
B2131
CAMELSDALE RD
SCHOOL RD
NEW RD
Hammer Bottom
Gillham's Moor
Hammer Coppice
Cemy
GILLHAM'S LA
Hammer Hill
HAMMER HILL
Gillham's Farm
Camelsdale
Hill Farm
MARLEY COMBE RD
Ridge Plantations
Brinksway
Marley Combe
MARLEY LA
Linchmere Common
Marley Common
LINCHMERE RD
The Ridge
DANLEY LA
Sussex Border Path
Marley House
Dale Farm
Linchmere
Church Farm
Cognor Wood
Poison Copse
Pond Moor
Ash Copse
Linchmere Marsh
Golden Valley
Hazel Piece
Hilly Field Copse
Treetop Farm
SANDY LA
HAMMER LA

208

207
189

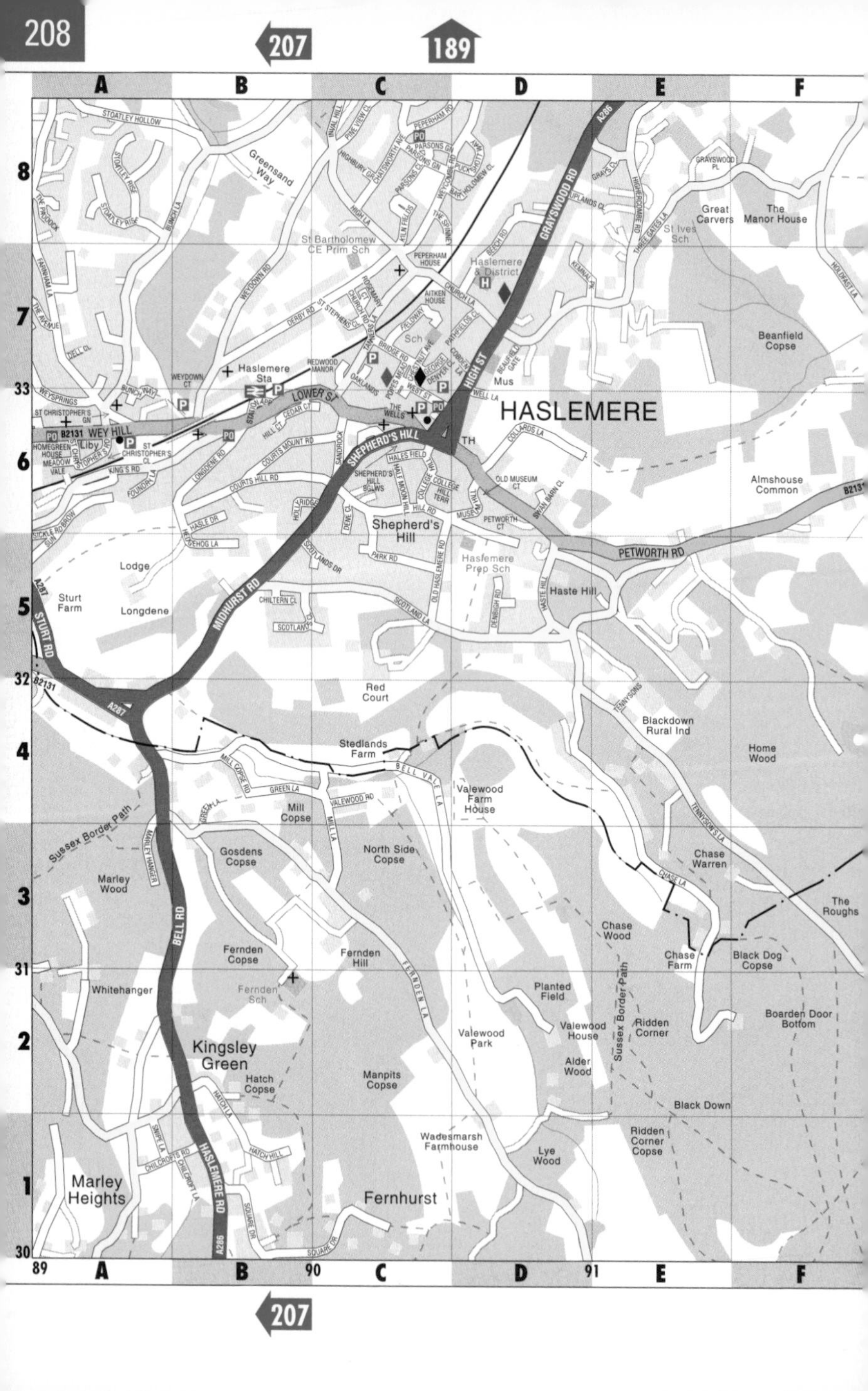
HASLEMERE
Haslemere Sta
St Bartholomew CE Prim Sch
Haslemere & District
Peperham House
Aitken House
Mus
Wey Hill
Liby
Greensand Way
Great Carvers
The Manor House
St Ives Sch
Beanfield Copse
Almshouse Common
Shepherd's Hill
Haslemere Prep Sch
Haste Hill
Lodge
Sturt Farm
Longdene
Red Court
Blackdown Rural Ind
Stedlands Farm
Home Wood
Valewood Farm House
Mill Copse
North Side Copse
Gosdens Copse
Marley Wood
Sussex Border Path
Chase Warren
The Roughs
Chase Wood
Chase Farm
Black Dog Copse
Fernden Copse
Fernden Hill
Fernden Sch
Whitehanger
Planted Field
Valewood House
Ridden Corner
Boarden Door Bottom
Valewood Park
Kingsley Green
Alder Wood
Hatch Copse
Manpits Copse
Black Down
Wadesmarsh Farmhouse
Ridden Corner Copse
Lye Wood
Marley Heights
Fernhurst
GRAYSWOOD RD
HIGH ST
PETWORTH RD
MIDHURST RD
SHEPHERD'S HILL
LOWER ST
STURT RD
BELL RD
HASLEMERE RD
A286
A287
B2131

207

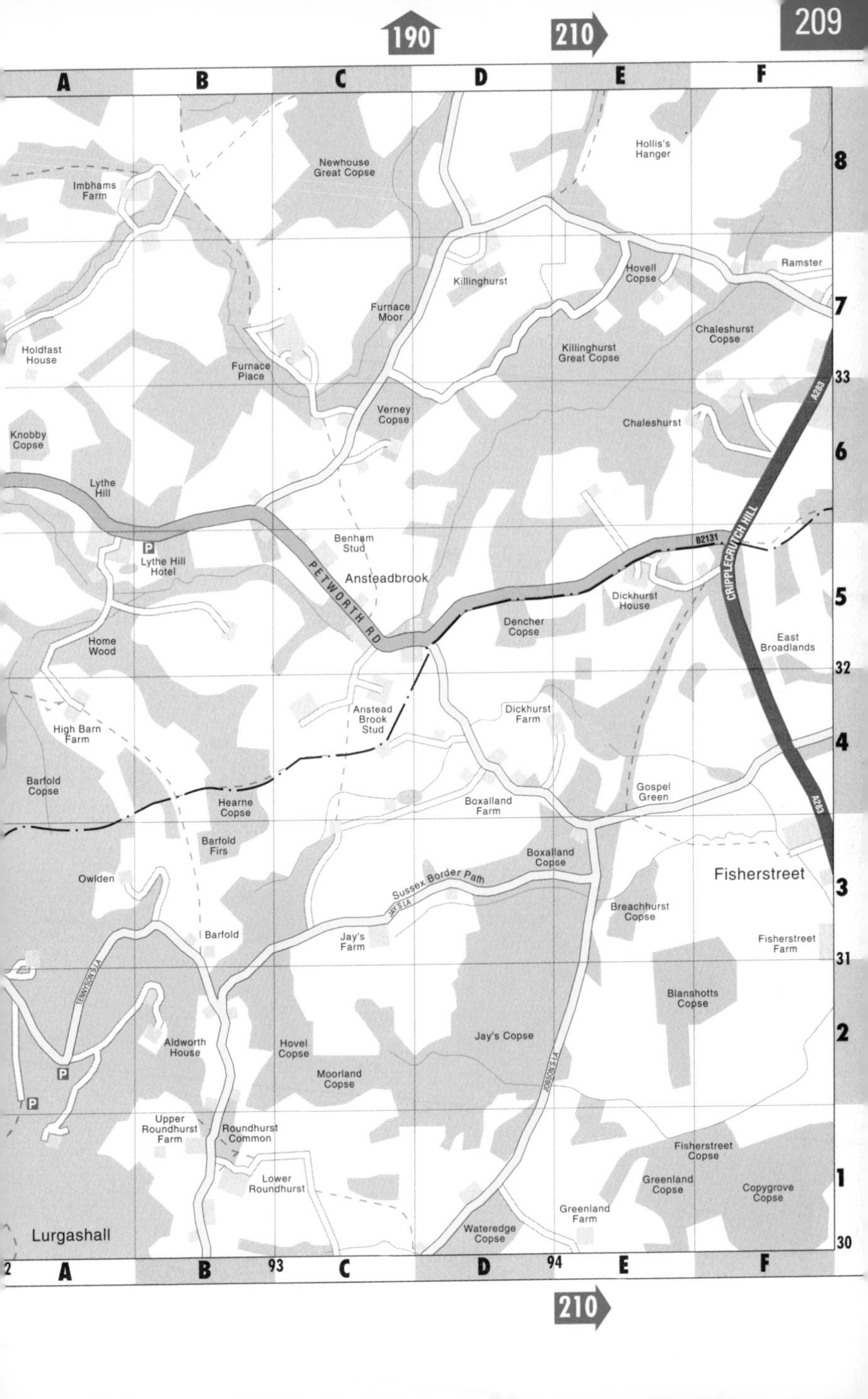
190
210
A
B
C
D
E
F
8
7
33
6
5
32
4
3
31
2
1
30
2
93
94
Hollis's Hanger
Newhouse Great Copse
Imbhams Farm
Ramster
Hovell Copse
Killinghurst
Furnace Moor
Holdfast House
Chaleshurst Copse
Killinghurst Great Copse
Furnace Place
A283
Verney Copse
Chaleshurst
Knobby Copse
Lythe Hill
CRIPPLECRUTCH HILL
Benham Stud
B2131
P
Lythe Hill Hotel
PETWORTH RD
Ansteadbrook
Dickhurst House
Dencher Copse
Home Wood
East Broadlands
Anstead Brook Stud
Dickhurst Farm
High Barn Farm
Barfold Copse
Gospel Green
Hearne Copse
Boxalland Farm
A283
Barfold Firs
Boxalland Copse
Owlden
Sussex Border Path
Fisherstreet
JAY'S LA
Breachhurst Copse
Barfold
Jay's Farm
Fisherstreet Farm
TENNYSON'S LA
Blanshotts Copse
Jay's Copse
Aldworth House
Hovel Copse
P
Moorland Copse
JOBSON'S LA
P
Upper Roundhurst Farm
Roundhurst Common
Fisherstreet Copse
Lower Roundhurst
Greenland Copse
Copygrove Copse
Greenland Farm
Wateredge Copse
Lurgashall

209
191

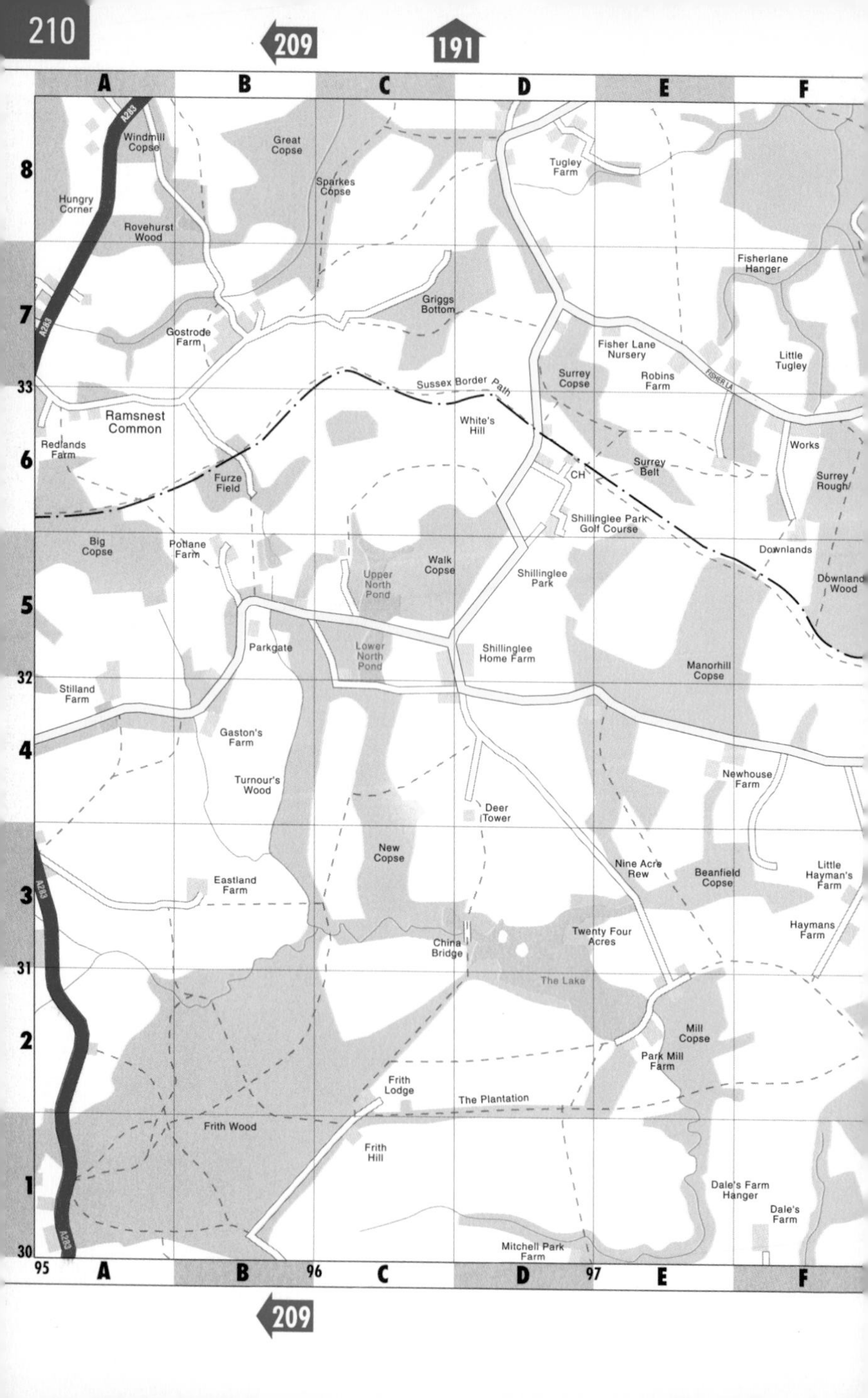
A
B
C
D
E
F
8
7
33
6
5
32
4
3
31
2
1
30
95
96
97
A283
Windmill Copse
Great Copse
Sparkes Copse
Tugley Farm
Hungry Corner
Rovehurst Wood
Fisherlane Hanger
Griggs Bottom
Gostrode Farm
Fisher Lane Nursery
Little Tugley
Surrey Copse
Robins Farm
FISHER LA
Sussex Border Path
Ramsnest Common
White's Hill
Redlands Farm
Works
Surrey Belt
CH
Furze Field
Surrey Rough
Shillinglee Park Golf Course
Big Copse
Pollane Farm
Downlands
Walk Copse
Shillinglee Park
Upper North Pond
Downland Wood
Parkgate
Lower North Pond
Shillinglee Home Farm
Manorhill Copse
Stilland Farm
Gaston's Farm
Newhouse Farm
Turnour's Wood
Deer Tower
New Copse
Nine Acre Rew
Beanfield Copse
Little Hayman's Farm
Eastland Farm
Haymans Farm
Twenty Four Acres
China Bridge
The Lake
Mill Copse
Park Mill Farm
Frith Lodge
The Plantation
Frith Wood
Frith Hill
Dale's Farm Hanger
Dale's Farm
Mitchell Park Farm

209

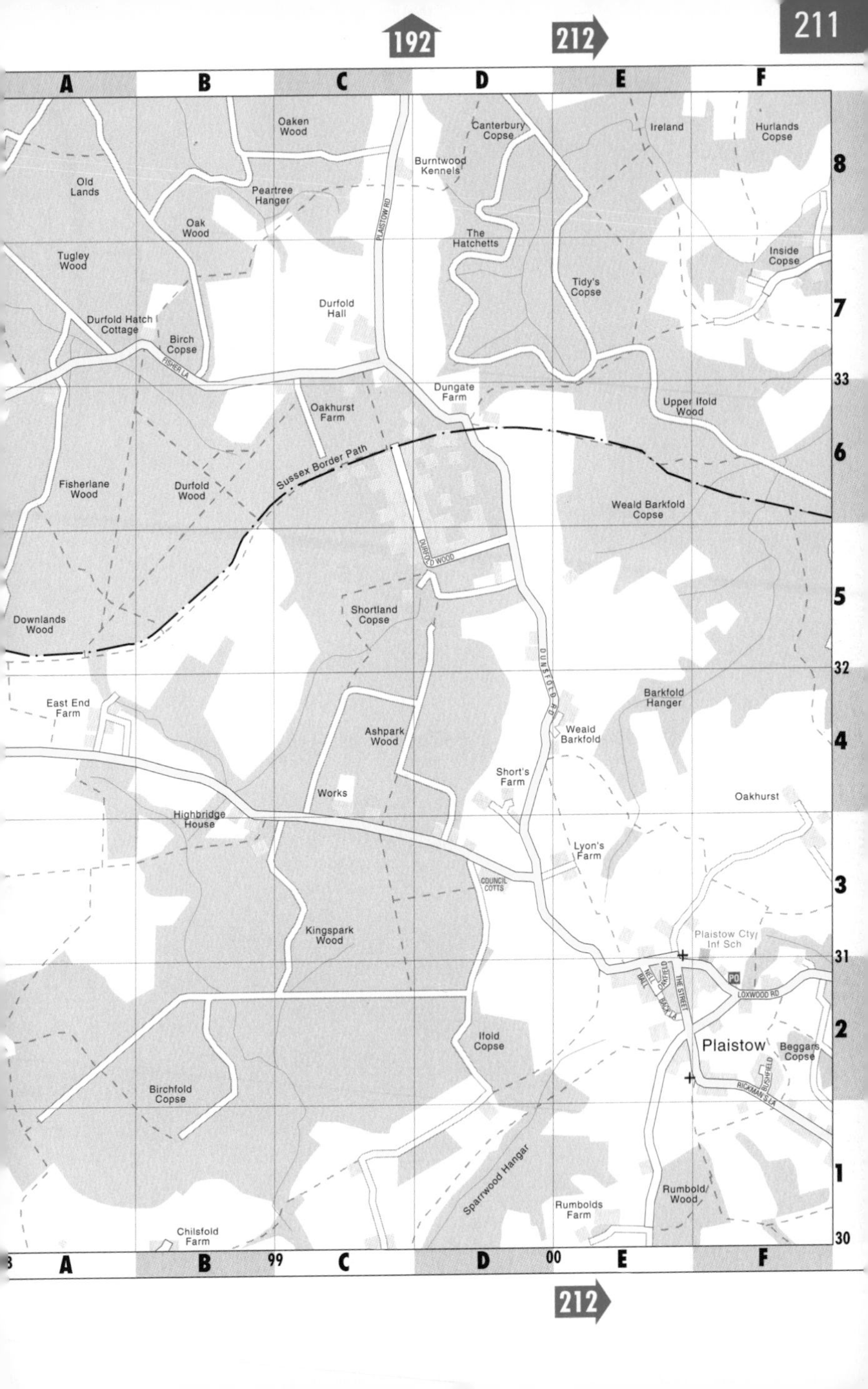

A B C D E F

8

Old Lands

Oaken Wood

Canterbury Copse

Ireland

Hurlands Copse

Burntwood Kennels

Peartree Hanger

7

Oak Wood

The Hatchetts

Inside Copse

Tugley Wood

Durfold Hall

Tidy's Copse

Durfold Hatch Cottage

Birch Copse

33

Oakhurst Farm

Dungate Farm

Upper Ifold Wood

6

Sussex Border Path

Fisherlane Wood

Durfold Wood

Weald Barkfold Copse

5

Downlands Wood

Shortland Copse

32

Barkfold Hanger

4

East End Farm

Ashpark Wood

Weald Barkfold

Oakhurst

Works

Short's Farm

Highbridge House

Lyon's Farm

3

COUNCIL COTTS

Plaistow Cty Inf Sch

Kingspark Wood

31

PO

THE STREET

LOXWOOD RD

2

Plaistow

Ifold Copse

Beggars Copse

Birchfold Copse

RICKMAN'S LA

1

Sparrwood Hangar

Rumbold Wood

Rumbolds Farm

Chilsfold Farm

30

B 99 C D 00 E F

A · B · C · D · E · F

8

Old Knightons

Upper Ifold Farm

Old Lock House

Glasshousa Copse

Priorswood

High Bridge

ROSEMARY LA

Turtles Farm

LOXWOOD RD

7

Sydney Wood Cott

Westland Copse

Sir Roger Tichbourne (PH)

Alfold Bars

PIGBUSH LA

Loxwood Hall

THE WALLED GARDEN

33

Gennets Wood

Oakhurst Farm

OAKHURST LA

Tokens Farm

6

Thirds Copse

Sydney Farm

Gennets Wood

The Rookery

Lee House Farm

Barberry Furze

Sussex Border Path

Barberry Bridge

Gennets Furze

Pawlies Farm

Pond Copse

5

Hog Wood

Oxoncroft Copse

Way South Path

LONG COPSE LA

32

Hog Copse

BRIDGE LA

Gennets Farm

Furzen Wood

Loxwood

4

Hogwood Farm

THE LANE

Barn Wood

Loxwood Place Farm

GUILDF. ROAD STATION

3

HOGWOOD RD

Devil's Hole

P

31

LOXWOOD RD

Charleshurst

CHALK RD

WILDACRE CL

THE CLOSE

THE RIDE

Ifold

Loxwoodhills Pond

THE DRIVE

2

Quennells Farm

Spring Copse

FOXBRIDGE LA

OLD CHURCH

Headfoldswood Farm

1

Flitchings Farm

RICHMER LA

FOXBRIDGE LA

Corner Copse

PLAISTOW RD

Foxbridge Hanger

Little Headfoldswood Copse

Woodlands Farm

LAKE LA

Foxbridge Farm

30

01 · A · B · 02 · C · D · 03 · E · F

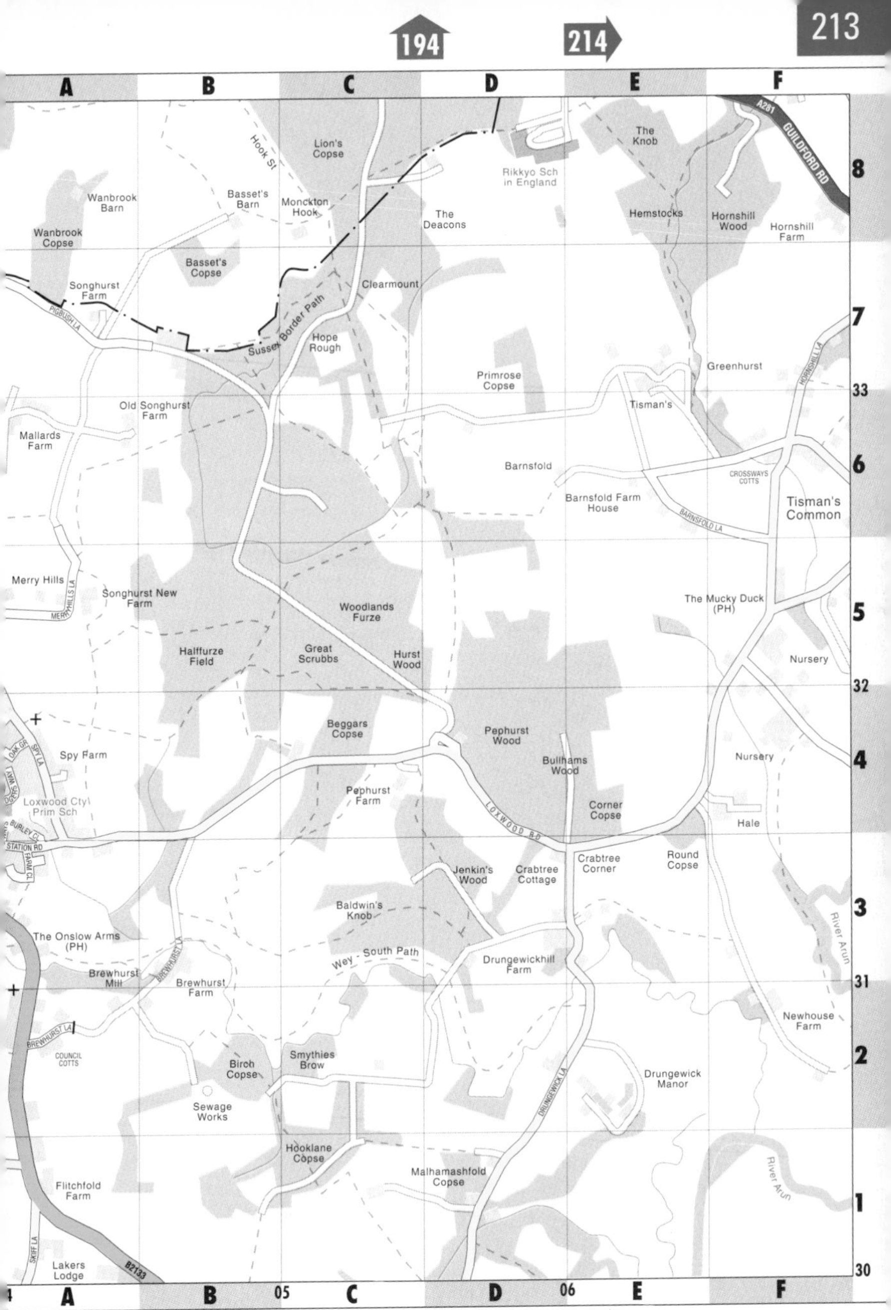

A B C D E F

8

The Knob

Rikkyo Sch in England

Hornshill Wood   Hornshill Farm

Lion's Copse

Hook St.

Basset's Barn

Monckton Hook

The Deacons

Hemstocks

Wanbrook Barn

Wanbrook Copse

Basset's Copse

Clearmount

7

Songhurst Farm

Sussex Border Path

Hope Rough

Greenhurst

Primrose Copse

Tisman's

33

Old Songhurst Farm

Mallards Farm

Barnsfold

6

Barnsfold Farm House

CROSSWAYS COTTS

Tisman's Common

Merry Hills

Songhurst New Farm

Woodlands Furze

The Mucky Duck (PH)

5

Halffurze Field

Great Scrubbs

Hurst Wood

Nursery

32

Beggars Copse

Pephurst Wood

Spy Farm

Loxwood Cty Prim Sch

Pephurst Farm

Bullhams Wood

Nursery

4

Corner Copse

Hale

Crabtree Cottage

Crabtree Corner

Round Copse

Jenkin's Wood

The Onslow Arms (PH)

Baldwin's Knob

Wey - South Path

Drungewickhill Farm

River Arun

3

31

Brewhurst Mill

Brewhurst Farm

Newhouse Farm

COUNCIL COTTS

Birch Copse

Smythies Brow

Drungewick Manor

2

Sewage Works

Hooklane Copse

Malhamashfold Copse

River Arun

1

Flitchfold Farm

Lakers Lodge

B2133

30

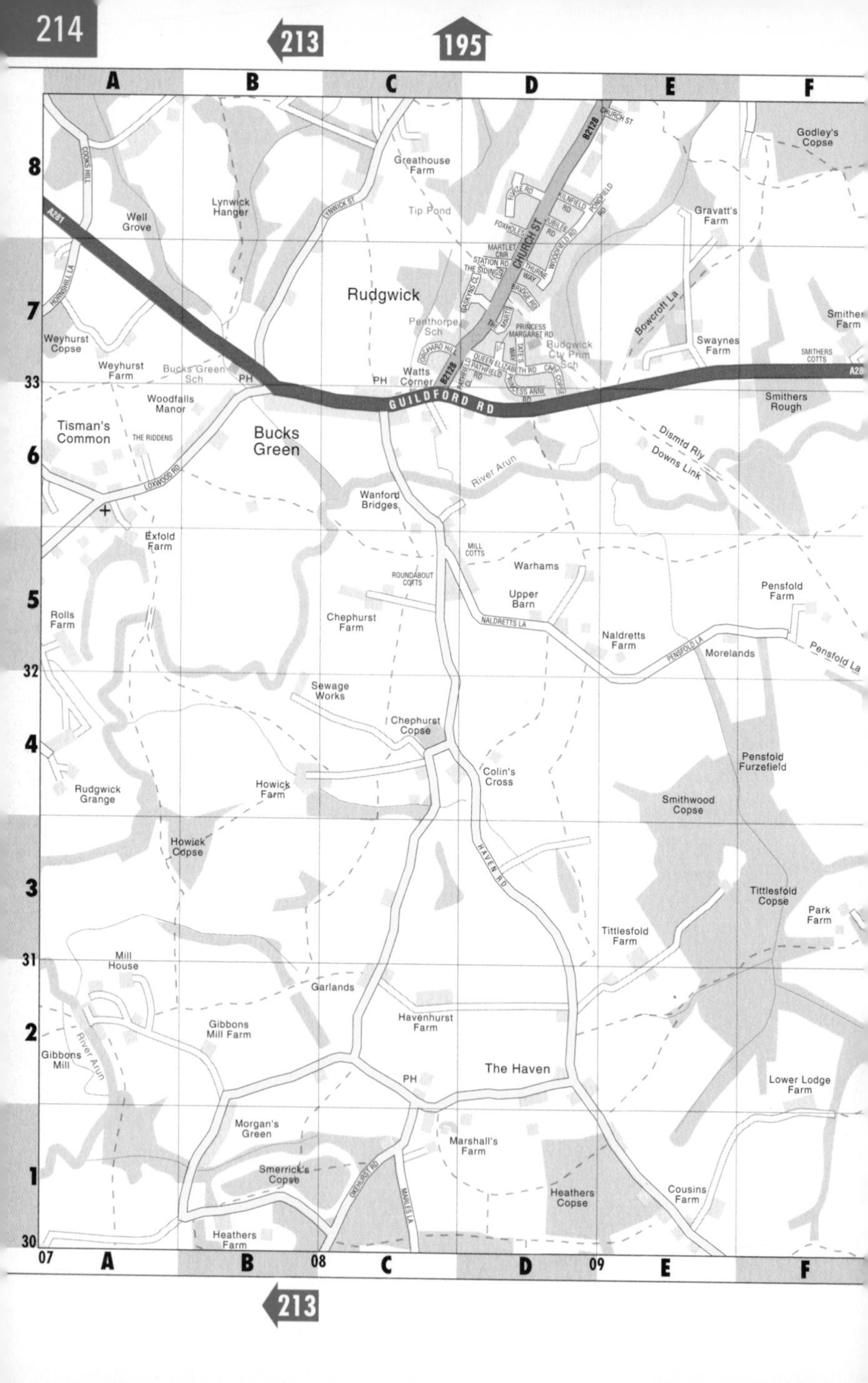
213
195
A
B
C
D
E
F
8
7
33
6
5
32
4
3
31
2
1
30
07
08
09
Godley's Copse
Greathouse Farm
Lynwick Hanger
Well Grove
Tip Pond
Gravatt's Farm
COOKS HILL
A281
LYNWICK ST
CHURCH ST
B2128
Rudgwick
Penthorpe Sch
Weyhurst Copse
Weyhurst Farm
Bucks Green Sch
PH
Watts Corner
Rudgwick Cty Prim Sch
Bowcroft La
Swaynes Farm
Smithers Farm
SMITHERS COTTS
GUILDFORD RD
Woodfalls Manor
Tisman's Common
THE RIDDENS
Bucks Green
Smithers Rough
Dismtd Rly
Downs Link
River Arun
LOXWOOD RD
Wanford Bridges
Exfold Farm
MILL COTTS
Warhams
ROUNDABOUT COTTS
Upper Barn
Pensfold Farm
Rolls Farm
Chephurst Farm
NALDRETTS LA
Naldretts Farm
PENSFOLD LA
Morelands
Pensfold La
Sewage Works
Chephurst Copse
Pensfold Furzefield
Rudgwick Grange
Howick Farm
Colin's Cross
Smithwood Copse
Howick Copse
HAVEN RD
Tittlesfold Copse
Park Farm
Tittlesfold Farm
Mill House
Garlands
Havenhurst Farm
Gibbons Mill Farm
Gibbons Mill
River Arun
The Haven
Lower Lodge Farm
Morgan's Green
Marshall's Farm
Smerrick's Copse
OKEHURST RD
MARLES LA
Heathers Copse
Cousins Farm
Heathers Farm
213

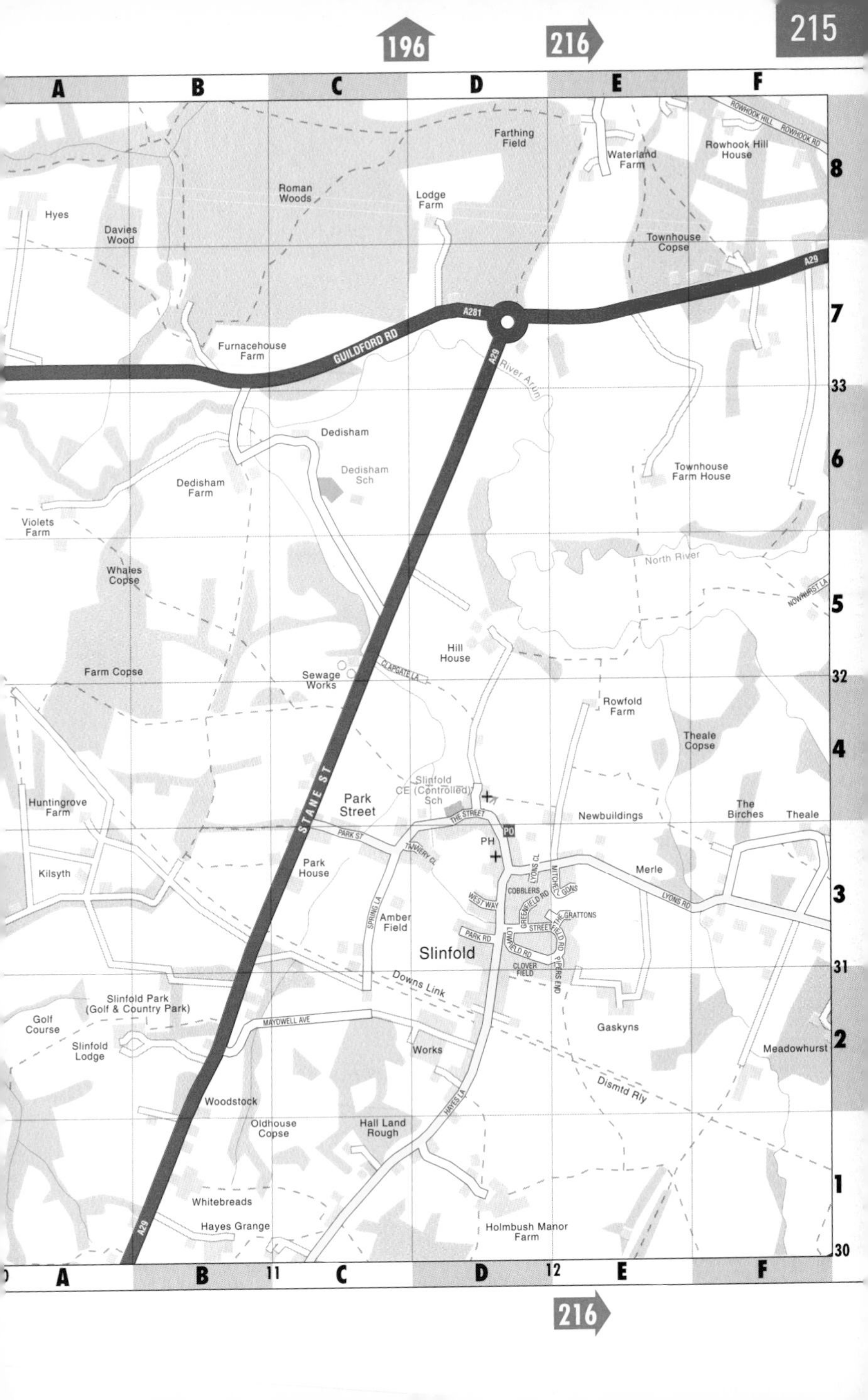

A B C D E F

8
7
33
6
5
32
4
3
31
2
1
30

ROWHOOK HILL
ROWHOOK RD
Rowhook Hill
House
Waterland
Farm
Farthing
Field
Townhouse
Copse
Roman
Woods
Lodge
Farm
A29
Hyes
Davies
Wood
GUILDFORD RD
A281
A29
Furnacehouse
Farm
River Arun
Townhouse
Farm House
Dedisham
Dedisham
Sch
Dedisham
Farm
Violets
Farm
North River
HOWINS LA
Whales
Copse
Farm Copse
FLAPGATE LA
Hill
House
Sewage
Works
Rowfold
Farm
Theale
Copse
The
Birches
Theale
STANE ST
Slinfold
CE (Controlled)
Sch
Newbuildings
Merle
Huntingrove
Farm
Park
Street
THE STREET
RD
PH
PARK ST
TANFURY CL
COBBLERS
KITCHEN CL
LYONS RD
Kilsyth
Park
House
SPRING LA
WEST WAY
STREET
CLOVER
FIELD
GRATTONS
PYCROFT RD
Amber
Field
PARK RD
Slinfold
Downs Link
Slinfold Park
(Golf & Country Park)
MAYDWELL AVE
Gaskyns
Golf
Course
Slinfold
Lodge
Meadowhurst
Works
Dismtd Rly
Woodstock
Oldhouse
Copse
Hall Land
Rough
GREYTILE LA
Whitebreads
Hayes Grange
Holmbush Manor
Farm

A 11 B C 12 D E F

215
197

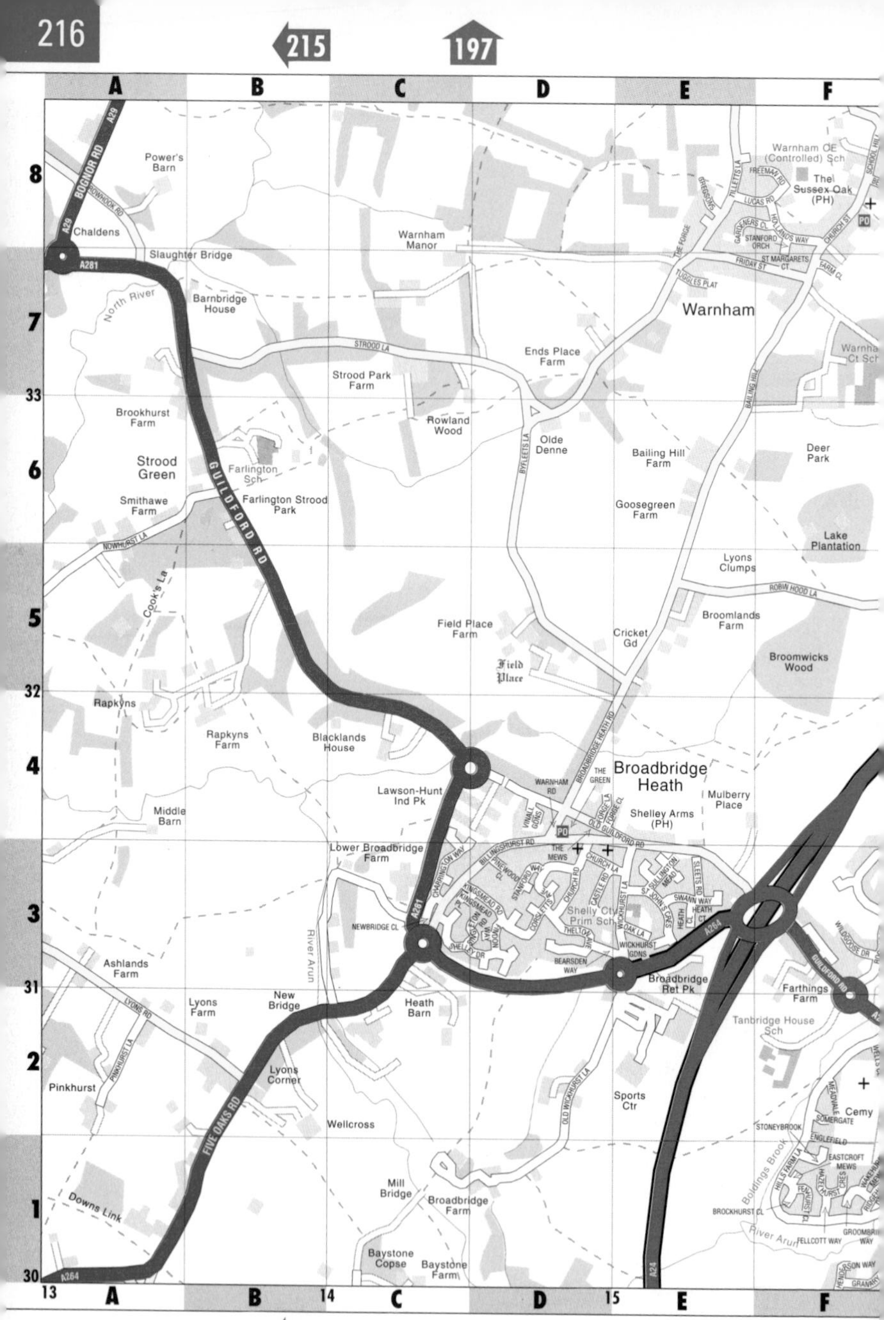
Power's Barn
Chaldens
Slaughter Bridge
Barnbridge House
North River
Warnham Manor
Strood Park Farm
Rowland Wood
Ends Place Farm
Warnham
Warnham CE (Controlled) Sch
The Sussex Oak (PH)
Brookhurst Farm
Strood Green
Farlington Sch
Smithawe Farm
Farlington Strood Park
Olde Denne
Bailing Hill Farm
Deer Park
Goosegreen Farm
Lake Plantation
Lyons Clumps
Broomlands Farm
Field Place Farm
Cricket Gd
Field Place
Broomwicks Wood
Rapkyns
Rapkyns Farm
Blacklands House
Broadbridge Heath
Lawson-Hunt Ind Pk
Mulberry Place
Shelley Arms (PH)
Middle Barn
Lower Broadbridge Farm
Shelly Cty Prim Sch
River Arun
Ashlands Farm
Broadbridge Ret Pk
Farthings Farm
Lyons Farm
New Bridge
Heath Barn
Tanbridge House Sch
Pinkhurst
Lyons Corner
Sports Ctr
Wellcross
Cemy
Mill Bridge
Broadbridge Farm
Downs Link
Boldings Brook
River Arun
Baystone Copse
Baystone Farm
BOGNOR RD
GUILDFORD RD
FIVE OAKS RD
STROOD LA
NOWHURST LA
Cook's La
BYFLEETS LA
ROBIN HOOD LA
BAILING HILL
BROADBRIDGE HEATH RD
OLD GUILDFORD RD
LYONS RD
PINKHURST LA
OLD WICKHURST LA
A29
A281
A264
A24

215

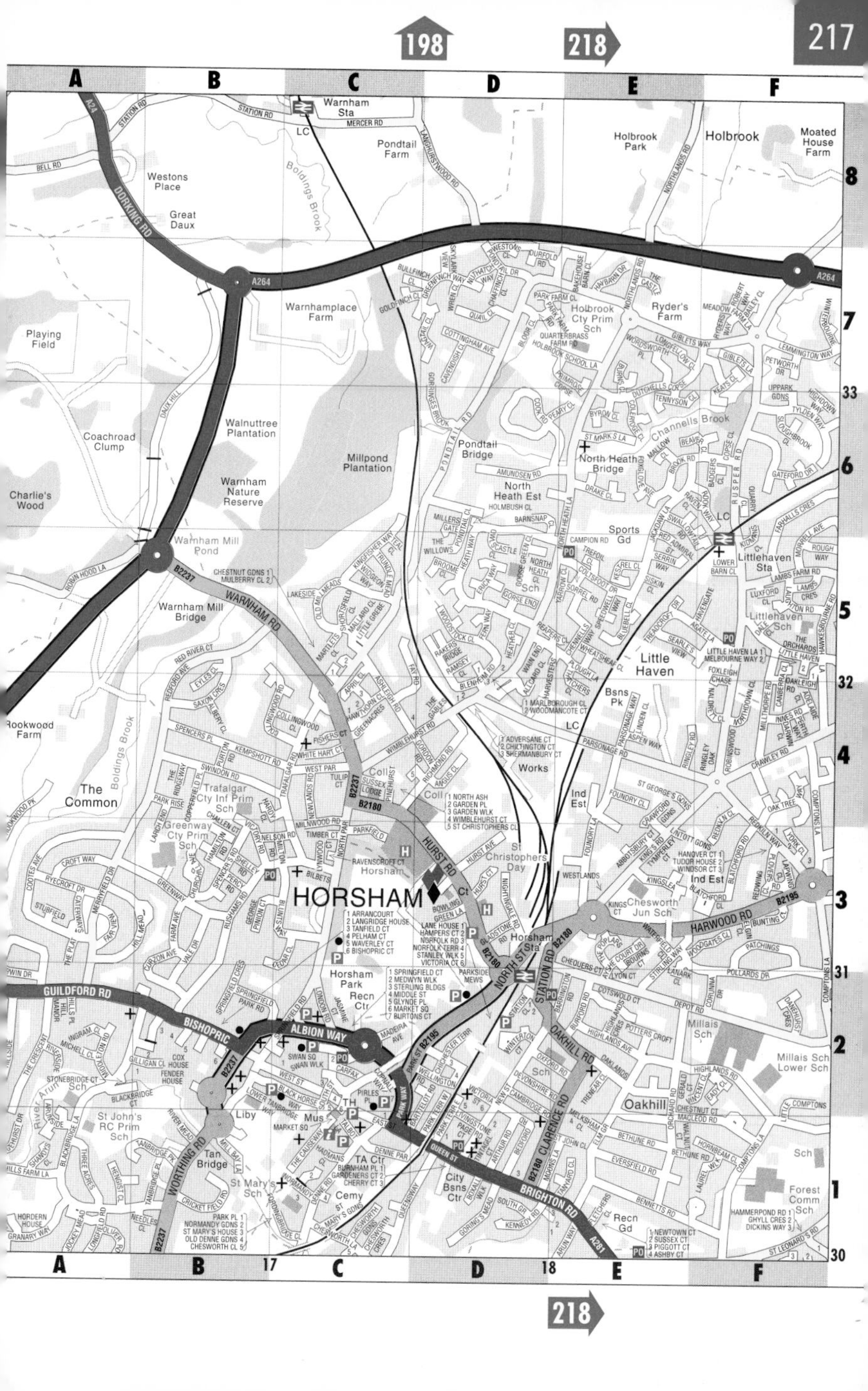
198
218
A
B
C
D
E
F
8
7
33
6
5
32
4
3
31
2
1
30
17
18
Warnham Sta
LC
STATION RD
MERCER RD
BELL RD
Pondtail Farm
Boldings Brook
Westons Place
Great Daux
DORKING RD
A264
A24
Holbrook Park
Holbrook
Moated House Farm
NORTHLANDS RD
Warnhamplace Farm
Holbrook Cty Prim Sch
Ryder's Farm
Playing Field
Walnuttree Plantation
Coachroad Clump
Millpond Plantation
Pondtail Bridge
North Heath Bridge
Channells Brook
Charlie's Wood
Warnham Nature Reserve
North Heath Est
Sports Gd
Warnham Mill Pond
ROBIN HOOD LA
B2237
WARNHAM RD
Warnham Mill Bridge
North Heath Sch
Littlehaven Sta
Littlehaven Sch
Little Haven
Bsns Pk
Rookwood Farm
Works
Ind Est
The Common
Trafalgar Cty Inf Prim Sch
Greenway Cty Prim Sch
Coll
HURST RD
B2180
St Christophers Day
HORSHAM
Horsham
Horsham Sta
Chesworth Jun Sch
HARWOOD RD
B2195
Ind Est
GUILDFORD RD
BISHOPRIC
ALBION WAY
Horsham Park
Recn Ctr
NORTH ST
STATION RD
OAKHILL RD
Millais Sch
Millais Sch Lower Sch
St John's RC Prim Sch
Liby
Mus
TH
Tan Bridge
WORTHING RD
TA Ctr
Cemy
St Mary's Sch
City Bsns Ctr
QUEEN ST
BRIGHTON RD
CLARENCE RD
Oakhill
Recn Gd
Sch
Forest Comm Sch
A281
CRAWLEY RD
PARSONAGE RD
RUSPER RD

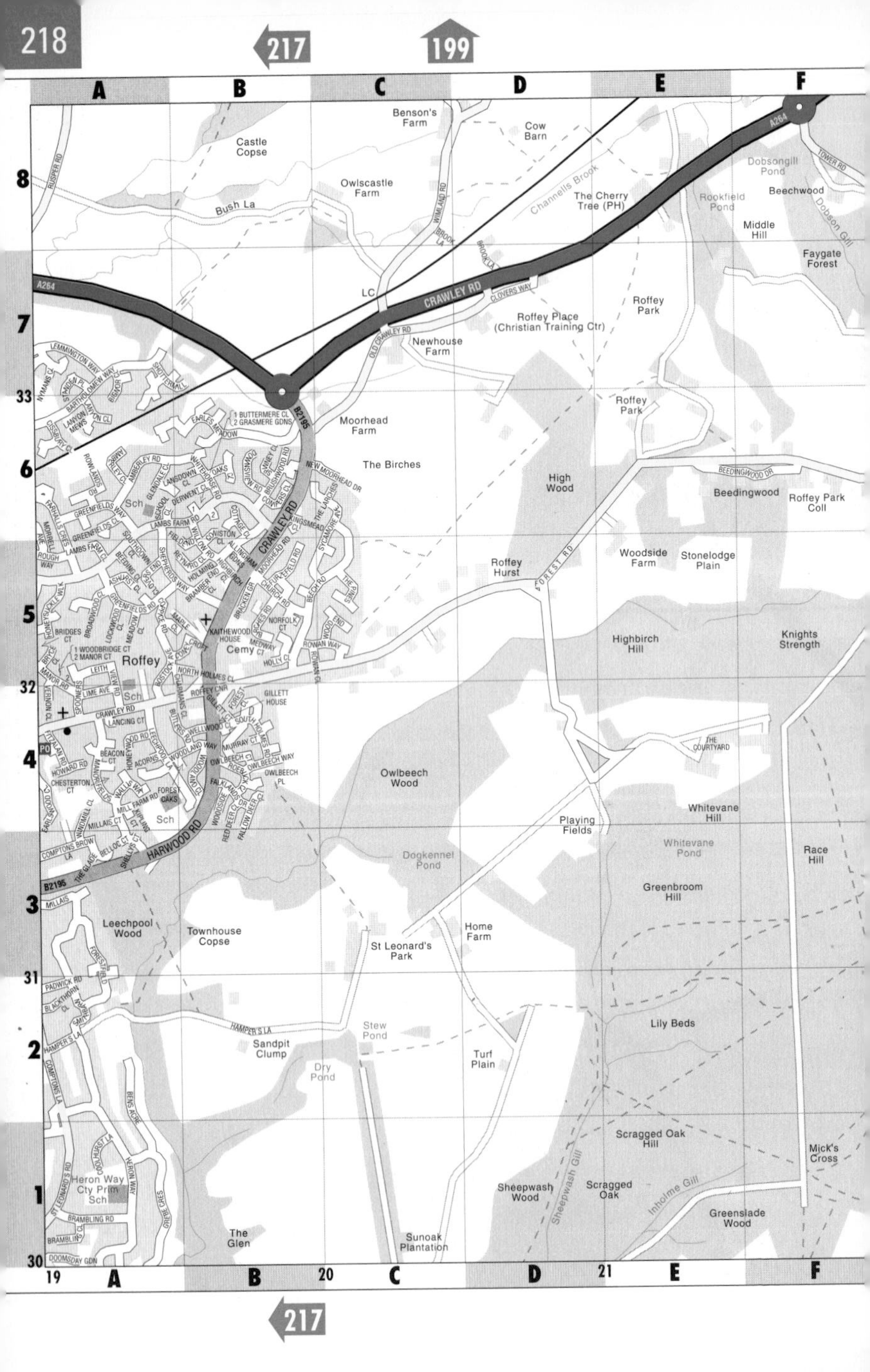
217
199
A
B
C
D
E
F
Benson's Farm
Cow Barn
Castle Copse
Owlscastle Farm
Bush La
Channells Brook
The Cherry Tree (PH)
Dobsongill Pond
Rookfield Pond
Beechwood
Dobson Gill
Middle Hill
Faygate Forest
A264
CRAWLEY RD
CLOVERS WAY
LC
Roffey Park
Roffey Place (Christian Training Ctr)
Newhouse Farm
OLD CRAWLEY RD
Moorhead Farm
The Birches
Roffey Park
High Wood
Beedingwood
BEEDINGWOOD DR
Roffey Park Coll
Woodside Farm
Stonelodge Plain
Roffey Hurst
FOREST RD
Highbirch Hill
Knights Strength
Roffey
Cemy
Sch
B2195
HARWOOD RD
THE COURTYARD
Owlbeech Wood
Whitevane Hill
Playing Fields
Whitevane Pond
Race Hill
Dogkennel Pond
Greenbroom Hill
Leechpool Wood
Townhouse Copse
Home Farm
St Leonard's Park
HAMPER'S LA
Stew Pond
Lily Beds
Sandpit Clump
Dry Pond
Turf Plain
Scragged Oak Hill
Mick's Cross
Heron Way Cty Prim Sch
Sheepwash Wood
Sheepwash Gill
Scragged Oak
Inholme Gill
Greenslade Wood
The Glen
Sunoak Plantation
8
7
33
6
5
32
4
3
31
2
1
30
19
20
21
217

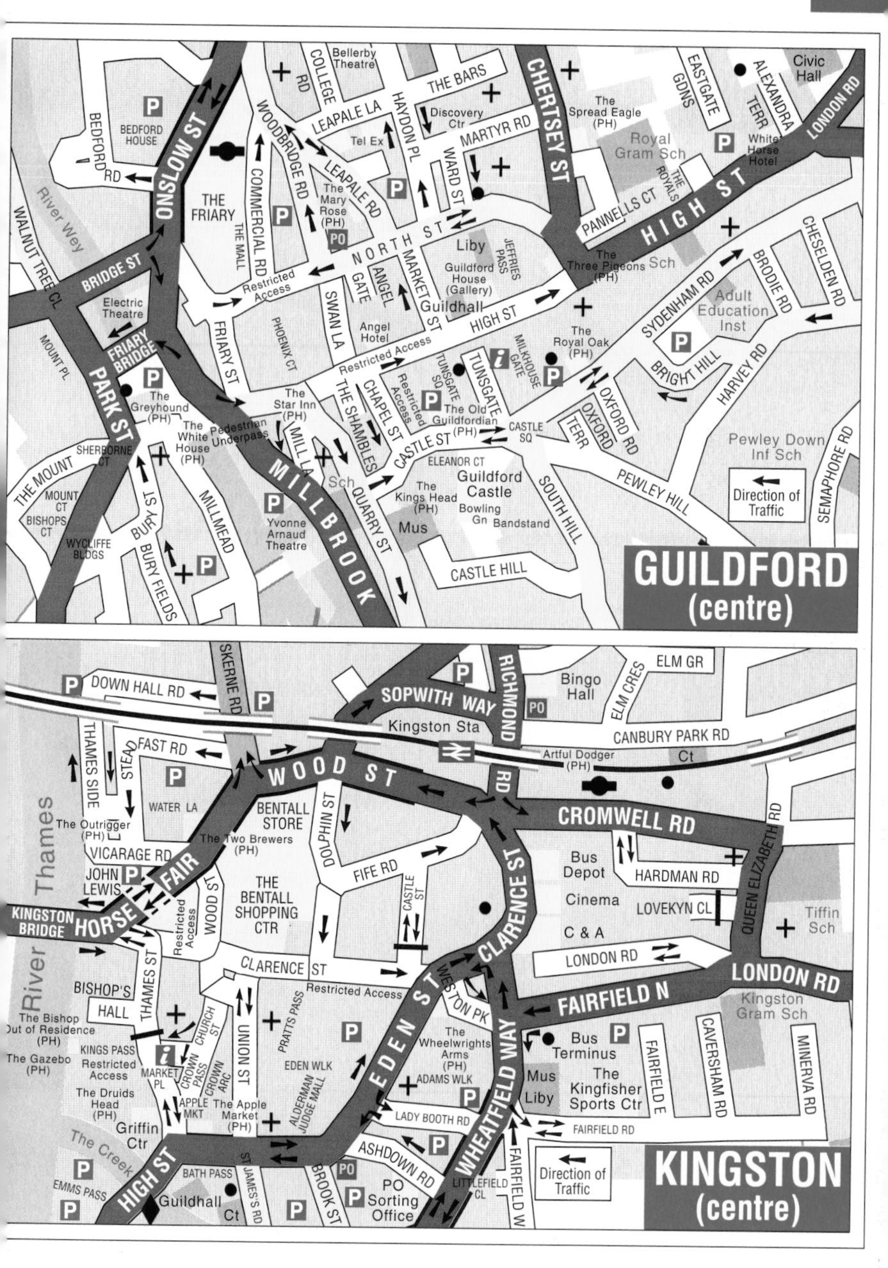
GUILDFORD
(centre)
ONSLOW ST
CHERTSEY ST
HIGH ST
LONDON RD
BRIDGE ST
FRIARY BRIDGE
PARK ST
MILLBROOK
THE FRIARY
COMMERCIAL RD
WOODBRIDGE RD
LEAPALE LA
LEAPALE RD
HAYDON PL
THE BARS
MARTYR RD
WARD ST
NORTH ST
MARKET ST
SWAN LA
ANGEL GATE
FRIARY ST
QUARRY ST
CASTLE ST
TUNSGATE
OXFORD RD
SYDENHAM RD
BRIGHT HILL
HARVEY RD
PEWLEY HILL
SOUTH HILL
CASTLE HILL
Guildford Castle
Guildhall
Direction of Traffic
KINGSTON
(centre)
WOOD ST
CROMWELL RD
SOPWITH WAY
RICHMOND RD
CLARENCE ST
EDEN ST
WHEATFIELD WAY
FAIRFIELD N
LONDON RD
HIGH ST
HORSE FAIR
KINGSTON BRIDGE
THAMES ST
UNION ST
ASHDOWN RD
QUEEN ELIZABETH RD
Kingston Sta
Bentall Shopping Ctr
River Thames
Direction of Traffic

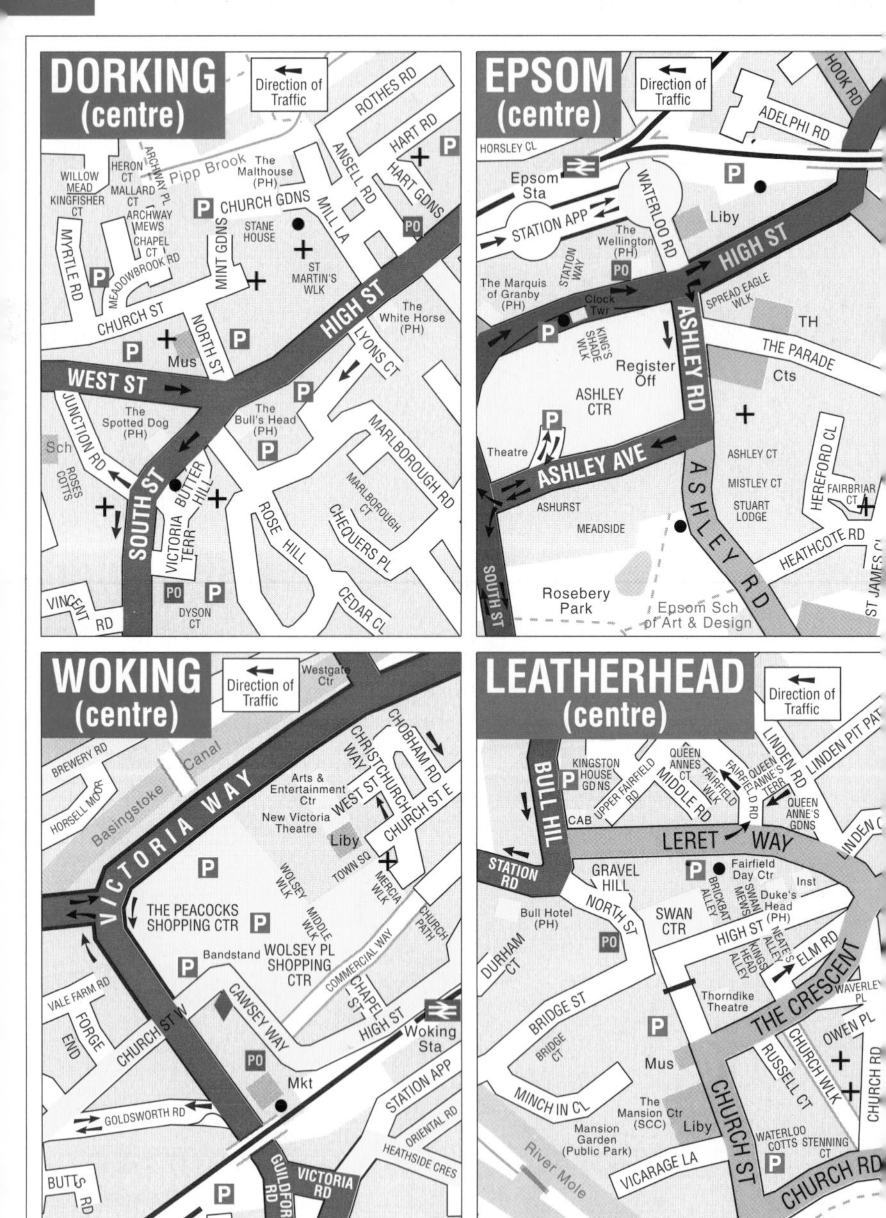

DORKING (centre)

Direction of Traffic

ROTHES RD
HART RD
HART GDNS
ANSELL RD
Pipp Brook
The Malthouse
HERON CT
ARCHWAY PL
CHURCH GDNS
WILLOW MEAD
KINGFISHER CT
MALLARD CT
ARCHWAY MEWS
CHAPEL CT
MILL A
STANE HOUSE
MYRTLE RD
MEADOWBROOK RD
MINT GDNS
ST MARTIN'S WLK
CHURCH ST
NORTH ST
HIGH ST
The White Horse (PH)
Mus
LYONS CT
WEST ST
The Spotted Dog (PH)
The Bull's Head (PH)
BUTTER HILL
MARLBOROUGH RD
JUNCTION RD
ROSES COTTS
Sch
SOUTH ST
VICTORIA TERR
ROSE HILL
MARLBOROUGH CT
CHEQUERS PL
VINCENT
PO
DYSON CT
CEDAR CL

EPSOM (centre)

Direction of Traffic

HOOK RD
ADELPHI RD
HORSLEY CL
Epsom Sta
Liby
STATION APP
WATERLOO RD
The Wellington (PH)
HIGH ST
The Marquis of Granby (PH)
STATION WAY
PO
SPREAD EAGLE WLK
Clock Twr
KING'S SHADE WLK
ASHLEY RD
TH
THE PARADE
Register Off
ASHLEY CTR
Cts
Theatre
ASHLEY AVE
ASHLEY CT
MISTLEY CT
STUART LODGE
HEREFORD CL
FAIRBRIAR CT
ASHURST
MEADSIDE
SOUTH ST
HEATHCOTE RD
ST JAMES CL
Rosebery Park
Epsom Sch of Art & Design
ASHLEY RD

WOKING (centre)

Direction of Traffic

Westgate Ctr
BREWERY RD
Canal
CHOBHAM RD
CHRISTCHURCH WAY
WEST ST
Arts & Entertainment Ctr
New Victoria Theatre
CHURCH ST E
HORSELL MOOR
Basingstoke
VICTORIA WAY
Liby
TOWN SQ
CAB
WOLSEY WLK
MEDIA WLK
P
THE PEACOCKS SHOPPING CTR
MIDDLE WLK
CHURCH PATH
Bandstand
WOLSEY PL SHOPPING CTR
COMMERCIAL WAY
VALE FARM RD
CAWSEY WAY
CHAPEL ST
HIGH ST
FORGE END
CHURCH ST W
Woking Sta
GOLDSWORTH RD
PO
Mkt
STATION APP
ORIENTAL RD
BUTTS RD
GUILDFORD RD
VICTORIA RD
HEATHSIDE CRES

LEATHERHEAD (centre)

Direction of Traffic

BULL HIL
KINGSTON HOUSE
QUEEN ANNES GDNS
FAIRFIELD RD
UPPER FAIRFIELD RD
MIDDLE RD
FAIRFIELD RD
QUEEN ANNE'S WLK
QUEEN ANNE'S TERR
LINDEN RD
LINDEN PIT PAT
QUEEN ANNE'S GDNS
LINDEN CL
CAB
LERET WAY
STATION RD
GRAVEL HILL
Fairfield Day Ctr
Inst
Bull Hotel (PH)
NORTH ST
SWAN CTR
Duke's Head (PH)
SWAN MEWS
BRICKBAT ALLEY
NEFE'S ALLEY
KINGS ALLEY
ELM RD
DURHAM CT
HIGH ST
PO
Thorndike Theatre
THE CRESCENT
WAVERLEY PL
BRIDGE ST
BRIDGE CT
Mus
RUSSELL CT
CHURCH WLK
OWEN PL
CHURCH RD
MINCH IN CL
The Mansion Ctr (SCC)
Mansion Garden (Public Park)
Liby
CHURCH ST
WATERLOO COTTS
STENNING CT
River Mole
VICARAGE LA
CHURCH RD

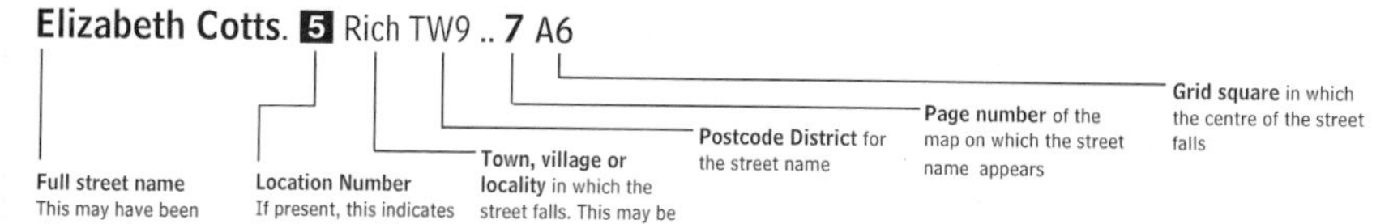

Street names are listed alphabetically and show the locality, the Postcode District, the page number and a reference to the square in which the name falls on the map page

Elizabeth Cotts. **5** Rich TW9 .. **7** A6

Grid square in which the centre of the street falls

Page number of the map on which the street name appears

Postcode District for the street name

Town, village or locality in which the street falls. This may be indicated by one of the abbreviations listed below

Location Number If present, this indicates the street's position on a congested area of the map instead of the name

Full street name This may have been abbreviated on the map

Schools, hospitals, sports centres, railway stations, shopping centres, industrial estates, public amenities and other places of interest are also listed.

App	Approach	Cl	Close	Espl	Esplanade	Orch	Orchard
Arc	Arcade	Comm	Common	Est	Estate	Par	Parade
Ave	Avenue	Cnr	Corner	Gdns	Gardens	Pk	Park
Bvd	Boulevard	Cotts	Cottages	Gn	Green	Pas	Passage
Bldgs	Buildings	Ct	Court	Gr	Grove	Pl	Place
Bsns Pk	Business Park	Ctyd	Courtyard	Hts	Heights	Prec	Precinct
Bsns Ctr	Business Centre	Cres	Crescent	Ind Est	Industrial Estate	Prom	Promenade
Bglws	Bungalows	Dr	Drive	Intc	Interchange	Ret Pk	Retail Park
Cswy	Causeway	Dro	Drove	Junc	Junction	Rd	Road
Ctr	Centre	E	East	La	Lane	Rdbt	Roundabout
Cir	Circus	Emb	Embankment	N	North	S	South

Sq	Square
Strs	Stairs
Stps	Steps
St	Street, Saint
Terr	Terrace
Trad Est	Trading Estate
Wlk	Walk
W	West
Yd	Yard

Abbots	Abbotswood 109 F3	Blind H	Blindley Heath 163 D8	Chobh	Chobham 49 F2
Abing C	Abinger Common .. 155 D8	Bowl Gn	Bowlhead Green 169 E1	Chur C	Church Crookham 104 A7
Abing H	Abinger Hammer 33 F3	Box H	Box Hill 116 A4	Churt	Churt 167 E1
Add	Addington .. 63 A5	Bra Hil	Brands Hill .. 1 A8	Clayg	Claygate 55 F3
Addl	Addlestone . 52 A6	Brack	Bracknell 27 D6	Cobham	Cobham 73 B5
Albury	Albury 132 C3	Bramly	Bramley 151 F6	Coldh	Coldharbour 156 E4
Alder	Aldershot .. 105 B1	Bramsh	Bramshott 187 D1	Coln	Colnbrook 1 D7
Alf Cr	Alfold Crossways 194 A3	Brent	Brentford 6 D7	Compt	Compton 129 B3
Alfold	Alfold 193 F1	Broad H	Broadbridge Heath 216 E4	Coney H	Coney Hall ... 63 F7
Arting	Artington .. 130 C4	Brock	Brockham .. 137 C7	Copth	Copthorne .. 183 C3
Ascot	Ascot 29 A6	Broml	Bromley 44 E8	Coulsd	Coulsdon 79 D3
Ash	Ash 106 B3	Brook	Brook 170 B1	Cox Gn	Cox Green .. 195 E1
Ash V	Ash Vale ... 106 B7	Brookw	Brookwood .. 88 A7	Cran	Cranleigh .. 174 D2
Ash W	Ashurst Wood 206 E6	Buck Gn	Bucks Green 214 B6	Cranf	Cranford 4 C6
Ashf	Ashford 13 F2	Buckl	Buckland .. 117 A2	Crawl	Crawley 201 F5
Ashtd	Ashstead 75 E1	Burgh H	Burgh Heath 97 D8	Crawl D	Crawley Down 204 C7
Bagsh	Bagshot 47 D3	Burph	Burpham .. 110 A5	Crock H	Crockham Hill 144 F8
Balham	Balham 21 A7	Burrh	Burrowhill .. 49 E3	Crond	Crondall 124 A5
Banstd	Banstead 78 B3	Burst	Burstow 183 A7	Crow	Crowhurst . 143 E3
Barnes	Barnes 7 F6	Byfl	Byfleet 71 D7	Crowth	Crowthorne .. 45 D5
Beac H	Beacon Hill 188 C6	Camb	Camberley .. 65 D6	Croy	Croydon 61 D8
Bear Gn	Beare Green 157 D3	Capel	Capel 178 C6	Cudw	Cudworth .. 179 F8
Beck	Beckenham .. 44 A7	Carsh	Carshalton .. 59 E6	Docken	Dockenfield 166 E6
Bellf	Bellfields .. 109 C4	Cater	Caterham .. 100 F4	Dome	Domewood 184 A5
Belm	Belmont 59 A2	Catf	Catford 24 A7	Dork	Dorking 136 C6
Bentl	Bentley 145 A7	Charl	Charlwood 180 E7	Dorm Pk	Dormans Park 185 E6
Betch	Betchworth 137 E8	Charlt	Charlton 34 D7	Dorman	Dormansland 165 B1
Bigg H	Biggin Hill .. 83 E3	Cheam	Cheam 58 F5	Dovgn	Doversgreen 139 B5
Binf	Binfield 26 C8	Chelsh	Chelsham .. 82 A2	Downe	Downe 83 F8
Binst	Binstead ... 166 A5	Chert	Chertsey 33 B2	Downs	Downside 93 B8
Bisley	Bisley 68 B3	Chess	Chessington 56 E4	Dulw	Dulwich 22 E5
Blckw	Blackwater .. 64 D4	Chidd	Chiddingfold 191 B4	Dunsf	Dunsfold ... 192 F5
Bletch	Bletchingley 120 D2	Chil	Chilworth . 131 C3	E Bed	East Bedfont 14 E7
		Chips	Chipstead .. 78 F1	E Clan	East Clandon 111 E4
		Chisw	Chiswick 7 D7	E Ewell	East Ewell .. 58 D1

E Grins	East Grinstead .. 185 E2	For Gn	Forest Green 176 E7
E Hors	East Horsley 112 C3	For Hil	Forest Hill .. 23 D7
E Mole	East Molesey 36 C4	For Row	Forest Row 206 F3
Earls	Earlswood 140 A7	Frensh	Frensham . 167 D7
Easth	Easthampstead ... 27 B5	Friml	Frimley 65 F2
Eden	Edenbridge 144 F4	G Book	Great Bookham 94 B1
Effing	Effingham .. 113 E8	Gatton	Gatton 118 F7
Egham	Egham 12 A3	Godal	Godalming 150 F3
Ell Gn	Ellen's Green 196 A4	Godst	Godstone .. 121 B3
Elst	Elstead 148 D3	Gomsh	Gomshall .. 133 D4
Eng Gn	Englefield Green 11 C2	Grays	Grayswood 189 F1
Ent Gn	Enton Green 171 B5	Graysh	Grayshott . 188 C3
Epsom	Epsom 76 C5	Guild	Guildford .. 130 B8
Esher	Esher 55 C6	Hackb	Hackbridge . 60 B8
Ewell	Ewell 58 A1	Hale	Hale 125 C6
Ewh	Ewhurst 175 F5	Hambl	Hambledon .. 171 D2
Fairl	Fairlands .. 108 C4	Hammer	Hammerwood ... 186 F2
Farl Gn	Farley Green 153 E7	Hampt	Hampton 36 A7
Farlgh	Farleigh 81 F5	Hams Gn	Hamsey Green 81 C4
Farnb	Farnborough 85 B3	Harl	Harlington 3 C8
Farnc	Farncombe 150 E8	Harm	Harmondsworth .. 2 E8
Farnh	Farnham ... 125 B1	Hasc	Hascombe 172 F4
Faygt	Faygate 199 F1	Haslem	Haslemere 208 D6
Felb	Felbridge .. 184 F4	Hatton	Hatton 3 F2
Felct	Felcourt ... 185 C8	Hawley	Hawley 64 E3
Felt	Feltham 15 A7	Haxted	Haxted 165 F8
Fern	Fernhurst . 208 C1	Hayes	Hayes 44 F3
Fetch	Fetcham 94 C4	Head	Headley 96 C2
Fickl	Ficklesholе .. 82 E5	Head Gn	Headley Down 157 B4
Fish	Fisherstreet 209 F3	Heath E	Heath End 125 C6
Flexf	Flexford 107 C1	Hersh	Hersham 54 D5
		Heston	Heston 4 F7
		Hinch W	Hinchley Wood 55 F7

Hind	Hindhead ..	188 F4
Hol St M	Holmbury St Mary	155 B5
Hookw	Hookwood	160 D2
Hooley	Hooley	99 B5
Horley	Horley	161 C3
Horne	Horne	162 F5
Horse	Horsell	69 D3
Horsh	Horsham ..	217 C3
Horton	Horton	1 A4
Hounsl	Hounslow	5 A5
Hyde	Hydestile ...	171 E6
Ifold	Ifold	212 D3
Islew	Isleworth	6 B4
Jacobs	Jacobswell	109 D7
Kenley	Kenley	80 D3
King Gn	Kingsley Green	208 B2
King U T	Kingston Upon Thames	37 C6
Kings	Kingswood ..	97 F6
Knaph	Knaphill	68 D1
L Book	Little Bookham ..	93 E3
L Kings	Lower Kingswood	117 E8
Laleh	Laleham	33 C6
Lamb Gn	Lambs Green	199 F6
Lang V	Langley Vale	96 D8
Leahd	Leatherhead	95 D5
Leigh	Leigh	138 B2
Lewish	Lewisham ...	24 C8
Lhtwat	Lightwater ...	66 F8
Limps	Limpsfield	123 A6
Linch	Linchmere .	207 B2
Lingf	Lingfield ...	164 D5
Littlt	Littleton	34 A6
Lo Hall	Lower Halliford	34 D2
Long D	Long Ditton	37 C1
Longc	Longcross ..	50 A7
Loxwd	Loxwood	212 F4
Lurg	Lurgashall	209 A1
Lyne	Lyne	32 B1
M Bourne	Middle Bourne ..	146 C7
Marl Ht	Marley Heights ..	208 A1
Mart Gn	Martyr's Green	92 E7
Mayb	Maybury	70 C2
Merrow	Merrow	110 C2
Merst	Merstham .	119 D7
Merton	Merton	39 F7
Mickle	Mickleham	115 C7
Milf	Milford	149 E1
Mitch	Mitcham ...	40 F5
Morden	Morden	40 B3
Mortl	Mortlake	7 C4
Mytch	Mytchett	85 F3
N Asct	North Ascot ..	28 E8
N Cheam	North Cheam	58 C8
New Add	New Addington ..	63 D3
New Gn	Newell Green	8 A1
New Haw	New Haw	52 C3
New Mal	New Malden	38 F5
Newch	Newchapel	163 F1
Newd	Newdigate .	158 B1
Nork	Nork	77 D4
Normdy	Normandy	107 A3
Nutf	Nutfield	119 F2
Oakwd	Oakwoodhill	197 A7
Oat Pk	Oatlands Park	53 E6
Ock Rid	Ockford Ridge	150 B3
Ockham	Ockham	92 B6
Ockley	Ockley	177 D5
Old W	Old Windsor ...	11 A8
Old Wok	Old Woking	90 A7
Onsl V	Onslow Village	129 F7
Ottsh	Ottershaw ..	51 D5
Outw	Outwood	162 B7
Oxsh	Oxshott	74 C6
Oxted	Oxted	122 E5
P Harow	Peper Harow	149 C5
Parkg	Parkgate ..	158 D4
Peasl	Peaslake ..	154 D6
Penge	Penge	23 D2
Pirb	Pirbright ...	87 F4
Pixham	Pixham	115 D1
Plaist	Plaistow ..	211 F2
Poyle	Poyle	1 B1
Purley	Purley	80 A7
Putney	Putney	19 D7
Putt	Puttenham	128 C4
Pyrf	Pyrford	70 E4
Redh	Redhill	118 E2
Reig	Reigate	118 B2
Rhampt	Roehampton .	7 F2
Rich	Richmond	6 D2
Ripley	Ripley	91 C6
Row Tn	Row Town	51 F4
Rowh	Rowhook	196 E1
Rowl	Rowledge ..	145 F3
Rowly	Rowly	174 B6
Rudg	Rudgwick .	214 C7
Rushm	Rushmoor	168 C5
Rusper	Rusper	199 D7
S Croy	South Croydon	61 D3
S Godst	South Godstone	14 F5
S Holm	South Holmwood	157 C7
S Norw	South Norwood	42 E5
S Nutf	South Nutfield	140 E7
Salfs	Salfords	140 B1
Sander	Sanderstead	80 F6
Sandh	Sandhurst ..	64 C7
Seale	Seale	127 B4
Selsd	Selsdon	62 D1
Send	Send	90 C4
Send M	Send Marsh .	90 F3
Shackl	Shackleford	149 D7
Shalf	Shalford ...	130 E2
Sham Gn	Shamley Green	152 E5
Sheer	Sheerwater	70 D6
Shep	Shepperton	34 C3
Shep Gn	Shepperton Green	34 B5
Shere	Shere	133 B4
Shottm	Shottermill	207 F6
Sidlow	Sidlow	139 B2
Slinf	Slinfold	215 D3
Smallf	Smallfield ..	162 B2
Stain	Staines	12 F4
Stan	Stanwell	13 C7
Stk D'A	Stoke D'Abernon ...	73 F3
Stonel	Stoneleigh .	58 A5
Stough	Stoughton	109 A4
Streat	Streatham ...	21 E2
Sunby	Sunbury	35 B6
Sunnin	Sunningdale	30 B4
Surb	Surbiton	37 E2
Sutton	Sutton	59 C5
Tadw	Tadworth	97 C5
Tand	Tandridge	122 A2
Tats	Tatsfield ...	103 D7
Tedd	Teddington .	17 B3
Thame D	Thames Ditton	37 B2
The Char	The Chart ..	123 E5
The San	The Sands .	126 E2
Thor L	Thorpe Lea ...	12 B1
Thorn H	Thornton Heath	42 B3
Thorpe	Thorpe	32 C6
Thursl	Thursley ...	169 C4
Tilf	Tilford	147 D3
Titsey	Titsey	103 B2
Tolw	Tolworth	57 B7
Tongh	Tongham ...	126 F6
Turn H	Turners Hill	204 A4
Twick	Twickenham	17 B8
Tyl Gn	Tyler's Green	121 C5
Up Hall	Upper Halliford	34 D5
UpToot	Upper Tooting	20 F5
Vir W	Virginia Water	31 C6
W Barn	West Barnes	39 C4
W Byfl	West Byfleet	71 B6
W Clan	West Clandon	111 B6
W End	West End	67 F6
W Ewell	West Ewell ..	57 E3
W Heath	West Heath .	84 F6
W Hoath	West Hoathly	204 D1
W Hors	West Horsley	112 B8
W Norw	West Norwood	22 C5
W Wick	West Wickham	44 E1
Wall W	Wallis Wood	176 E1
Wallin	Wallington .	60 A4
Walt O T	Walton-On-Thames	35 C2
Walt o t H	Walton on the Hill	97 A3
Wanb	Wanborough	128 C1
Wands	Wandsworth	20 C7
Warlgm	Warlingham	81 C1
Warn	Warnham ..	216 E7
Went	Wentworth ..	30 F3
Westc	Westcott ..	135 C4
Westfd	Westfield	89 E6
Westh	Westhumble	115 A4
Weyb	Weybridge .	53 A6
Whit V	Whiteley Village	53 E1
Whytlf	Whyteleafe ..	80 F1
Wimble	Wimbledon .	19 F2
Wind	Windsor	9 E8
Windl	Windlesham	48 C4
Wink	Winkfield	8 D4
Wisley	Wisley	71 E3
Witley	Witley	170 F4
Woki	Wokingham .	25 B5
Woking	Woking	69 E1
Wold	Woldingham	102 A4
Woner	Wonersh	152 B7
Wood S V	Wood Street Village	108 B3
Woodc	Woodcote ..	76 D3
Woodh	Woodhatch	139 B7
Woodhm	Woodham ..	52 A1
Woodm	Woodmansterne .	78 E4
Worc Pk	Worcester Park	57 F6
Wormly	Wormley ...	170 F1
Worpl	Worplesdon	108 D8
Worth	Worth	202 E6
Wotton	Wotton	134 F3
Wray	Wraysbury ...	11 E8
Wreccl	Wrecclesham	145 E6
Yatly	Yateley	64 A5

1st Ave. L Kings KT20 97 E2
2nd Ave. L Kings KT20 97 E2
3rd Ave. L Kings KT20 97 E2
4th Ave. L Kings KT20 97 E2
5th Ave. L Kings KT20 97 E2
6th Ave. L Kings KT20 97 E2
7th Ave. L Kings KT20 97 F2
8th Ave. L Kings KT20 97 E2
9th Ave. L Kings KT20 97 F2
10th Ave. Walt o t H KT20 97 A1
11th Ave. L Kings KT20 97 F1
12th Ave. L Kings KT20 97 F1
13th Ave. L Kings KT20 97 F1
14th Ave. L Kings KT20 97 F1
15th Ave. L Kings KT20 97 F1
16th Ave. L Kings KT20 97 F1
Aaron Ct. Beck BR3 44 B6
Aaron's Hill. Ock Rid GU7 150 B4
Abbess Cl. Streat SW2 22 B7
Abbetts La. Camb GU15 65 B3
Abbey Church The. Worth RH10 203 B1
Abbey Cl. Brack RG12 27 D4
Abbey Cl. Crawl GU6 173 F2
Abbey Cl. Pyrf GU22 70 E3
Abbey Cl. Woki RG11 25 C7
Abbey Ct. Camb GU15 65 D5
Abbey Ct. Chert KT16 33 B2
Abbey Ct. Farnh GU9 125 C2
Abbey Dr. Laleh TW18 33 C5
Abbey Dr. Up Toot SW17 21 A3
Abbey Gdns. Chert KT16 33 A3
Abbey Gn. Chert KT16 33 A3
Abbey Ind Est. Mitch CR4 40 F4
Abbey La. Beck BR3 24 A1
Abbey Lodge. Stain TW18 12 F3
Abbey Par. Merton SW19 20 C1
Abbey Pk. Beck BR3 24 A1
Abbey Rd. Chert KT16 33 B2
Abbey Rd. Croy CR0 & CR9 61 B7
Abbey Rd. Horse GU21 69 D2
Abbey Rd. Lo Hall TW17 34 A1
Abbey Rd. Merton SW19 40 C8
Abbey Rd. Selsd CR2 62 D1
Abbey Rd. Vir W GU25 31 D5
Abbey River Cotts. Chert KT16 33 C3
Abbey Sch The. M Bourn GU9 125 D1
Abbey St. Farnh GU9 125 C2
Abbey Way. Farnb GU14 85 C4
Abbey Wlk. E Mole KT8 36 B5
Abbey Wood. Sunnin SL5 30 A2
Abbeylands Sch. Addl KT15 52 A5
Abbot Cl. Byfl KT14 71 D8
Abbot Cl. Stain TW18 13 D1
Abbot Rd. Guild GU1 130 D7
Abbot's Cl. Onsl V GU2 129 F6
Abbot's Way. Merrow GU1 & GU4 110 D2
Abbots Ct. S Norw SE25 42 E6
Abbots Dr. Vir W GU25 31 C5
Abbots Gn. S Croy CR0 & CR2 62 D4
Abbots La. Kenley CR8 80 C3
Abbots Pk. Streat SW2 22 A7
Abbots Way. Beck BR3 43 E4
Abbots Wlk. Cater CR3 101 B5
Abbotsbury. Easth RG12 26 F4
Abbotsbury Ct. Horsh RH13 217 E3
Abbotsbury Fst Sch. Morden SM4 40 B4
Abbotsbury Rd. Coney H BR2 & BR4 63 F8
Abbotsbury Rd. Morden SM4 & SW19 40 B5
Abbotsfield Rd. Crawl RH11 200 D4
Abbotsford Cl. Woking GU22 70 A2
Abbotshall Rd. Catf SE6 24 D6
Abbotsleigh Cl. Belm SM2 59 B3
Abbotsleigh Rd. Streat SW16 21 C3
Abbotsmede Cl. Twick TW1 16 F6
Abbotswood. Abbots GU1 109 F3
Abbotswood. Walt O T KT13 53 F7
Abbotswood Cl. Burph GU1 109 F4
Abbotswood Dr. Whit V KT13 53 D1
Abbotswood Rd. Streat SW16 21 D5
Abbott Ave. Wimble SW20 39 D8
Abbott Cl. Hampt TW12 15 E2
Abbott House. Balham SW12 20 F8
Abbotts Cotts. Docken GU10 166 E5
Abbotts Rd. Cheam SM1 & SM3 58 E6
Abbotts Rd. Mitch CR4 & SW16 41 C5
Abbotts Rise. Redh RH1 119 A3
Abbotts Tilt. Hersh KT12 54 E7
Abelia Cl. W End GU24 67 E6
Abell Ct. Addl KT15 52 C6
Abercairn Rd. Streat SW16 21 C1
Aberconway Rd. Morden SM4 40 B5
Abercorn Cl. Selsd CR2 81 D7
Abercorn Way. Woking GU21 69 A1
Aberdare Cl. W Wick BR4 63 C8
Aberdeen Rd. Croy CR0 61 D6
Aberdour. Banstd KT20 77 F1
Aberfoyle Rd. Streat SW16 21 D2
Abingdon Cl. Brack RG12 27 E4
Abingdon Cl. Merton SW19 20 C2
Abingdon Cl. Woking GU21 69 C1
Abingdon Lodge. Broml BR2 44 F7
Abingdon Rd. Sandh GU15 & GU17 45 C1
Abingdon Rd. Thorn H SW16 41 E8
Abinger Ave. E Ewell SM2 58 D2
Abinger Cl. Dork RH5 136 C3
Abinger Cl. Wallin SM6 60 E5
Abinger Common Cty Sch. Abing C RH5 134 D1
Abinger Common Rd. Wotton RH5 155 F7
Abinger Ct. Wallin SM6 60 E5
Abinger Dr. Earls RH1 139 E7
Abinger Gdns. Islew TW7 5 E4
Abinger Hammer Village Sch. Abing H RH5 133 F4
Abinger House. 2 King U T KT2 18 B1
Abinger La. Abing C RH5 134 C2
Abinger Rd. Wotton RH5 156 C3
Abinger Way. Burph GU4 110 B6
Aboyne Dr. Wimble SW20 39 A7
Aboyne Rd. Wands SW17 20 D5
Abrahams Rd. Crawl RH11 201 A1
Acacia Ave. Brent TW8 6 B7
Acacia Ave. Sandh GU15 45 D1
Acacia Ave. Shep Gn TW17 34 A4
Acacia Ave. Woking GU22 89 D7
Acacia Cl. Penge SE20 43 A7
Acacia Cl. Woodhm KT15 51 F1
Acacia Ct. Easth RG12 27 B6
Acacia Ct. 5 W Norw SW16 22 A3
Acacia Dr. Cheam SM3 40 A1
Acacia Dr. Nork KT17 77 D5
Acacia Dr. Woodhm KT15 51 F1
Acacia Gdns. W Wick BR4 63 C8
Acacia Gr. Dulw SE21 22 D6
Acacia Gr. King U T KT3 38 E6
Acacia House. Reig RH2 118 A3
Acacia Mews. Harm UB7 2 D8
Acacia Rd. Beck BR3 43 F6
Acacia Rd. Guild GU1 109 D1
Acacia Rd. Hampt TW12 16 A2
Acacia Rd. Mitch CR4 41 B7
Acacia Rd. S Norw SW16 41 E8
Acacia Rd. Stain TW18 13 B3
Academy Cl. Camb GU15 65 E8
Academy Gdns. Croy CR0 42 F1
Accommodation La. Harm UB7 2 C8
Accommodation Rd. Longc KT16 50 E6
Ace Par. Chess KT9 56 E7
Acer Rd. Bigg H TN16 83 D3
Acheulian Cl. M Bourn GU9 146 C7
Achilles Pl. Horse GU21 69 C2
Ackroyd Rd. For Hil SE23 23 E8
Acorn Cl. E Grins RH19 205 E8
Acorn Cl. 1 Hampt TW12 16 B2
Acorn Cl. Horley RH6 161 C4
Acorn Dr. Woki RG11 25 C7
Acorn Gdns. S Norw SE19 42 F8
Acorn Gr. Harl UB3 3 F7
Acorn Gr. Kings KT20 97 F3
Acorn Gr. Westfd GU22 89 E6
Acorn Mews. W Heath GU14 85 A7
Acorn Rd. Blckw GU17 64 B5
Acorn Way. For Hil SE23 23 D5
Acorns. Horsh RH13 218 A4
Acorns Cty Fst Sch The. Betch RH3 116 D1
Acorns The. Crawl RH11 201 B1
Acorns The. 21 Putney SW19 19 D7
Acorns Way. Esher KT10 55 C5
Acre La. Wallin SM5 60 A6
Acre Rd. King U T KT2 37 E8
Acre Rd. Mitch SW19 20 D2
Acres Gdns. Burgh H KT20 97 D8
Acres Platt. Cran GU6 174 F4
Action Ct. Littlt TW15 34 C8
Acuba House. Wands SW18 20 B7
Acuba Rd. Wands SW18 20 B6
Adair Cl. Croy SE25 43 B6
Adair Wlk. Pirb GU24 87 B6
Adams Cl. Surb KT5 37 F3
Adams Croft. Pirb GU24 87 C7
Adams Ct. 2 Purley CR8 80 A7
Adams House. 3 Streat SW16 21 C3
Adams Park Rd. Farnh GU9 125 D3
Adams Rd. Beck BR3 43 E4
Adams Way. Croy SE25 & CR0 43 A3
Adams Wlk. 11 King U T KT1 37 E7
Adamson Ct. 6 Crawl RH11 201 B1
Adamsrill Prim Sch. For Hil SE26 23 E5
Adamsrill Rd. For Hil SE23 & SE26 23 E4
Adare Wlk. Streat SW16 & SW2 21 F6
Addington Bsns Ctr. New Add CR9 63 E1
Addington Court Golf Course. New Add CR0 63 A2
Addington Ct. 7 Mortl SW14 7 D4
Addington Golf Course. S Croy CR0 & CR9 62 E6
Addington Gr. For Hil SE26 23 E4
Addington High Sch. New Add CR0 82 E7
Addington Palace Golf Course. S Croy CR0 62 E5
Addington Palace (Royal Sch of . Church Music). S Croy CR9 62 F4
Addington Rd. Sander CR2 81 A8
Addington Rd. Selsd CR2 62 C1
Addington Rd. Thorn H CR0 42 A1
Addington Rd. W Wick BR4 & CR0 63 D6
Addington Rd. W Wick BR4 63 E8
Addington Village Rd. Add CR0 63 A5
Addiscombe Ave. Croy CR0 43 A2
Addiscombe Court Rd. Croy CR0 & CR9 61 E8
Addiscombe Rd. Crowth RG11 45 C4
Addiscombe Rd. Croy CR0 & CR9 61 E8
Addiscombe Rd. S Croy CR0 61 E8
Addiscombe Sta. Croy CR0 42 F1
Addison Ave. Hounsl TW3 5 C6
Addison Cl. Cater CR3 100 D5
Addison Ct. Guild GU1 130 F7
Addison Gdns. King U T KT5 37 F5
Addison Rd. Cater CR3 100 D6
Addison Rd. Croy SE25 43 A5
Addison Rd. Guild GU1 130 F7
Addison Rd. Tedd TW11 17 B2
Addison Rd. 8 Woking GU21 69 F2
Addison's Cl. Croy CR0 62 F8
Addlestone House. Addl KT15 52 B7
Addlestone Moor. Chert KT15 52 C8
Addlestone Pk. Addl KT15 52 B5
Addlestone Rd. Addl KT13 & KT15 52 E6
Addlestone Sta. Addl KT15 52 D6
Adecroft Way. E Mole KT8 36 C6
Adela Ave. W Barn KT3 39 B5
Adelaide Cl. Crawl RH11 181 D1
Adelaide Cl. Horsh RH12 217 F4
Adelaide Ct. 15 Beck BR3 24 A1
Adelaide Pl. Oat Pk KT13 53 D6
Adelaide Rd. Ashf TW15 13 D3
Adelaide Rd. Heston TW5 4 E6
Adelaide Rd. King U T KT6 37 E4
Adelaide Rd. Rich TW9 6 F3
Adelaide Rd. Tedd TW11 16 F2
Adelaide Rd. Walt O T KT12 54 B7
Adelina Mews. Streat SW12 21 D7
Adelphi Cl. Worth RH10 202 D4
Adelphi Rd. Ewell KT17 76 D6
Adenmore Rd. Catf SE6 24 A8
Adisham House. 7 Penge SE20 23 C1
Adlers La. Westh RH5 115 A4
Adlington Pl. Farnb GU14 85 E2
Admiral Ct. Carsh SM5 40 E1
Admiral Rd. Crawl RH11 201 A3
Admiral's Bridge La. E Grins RH19 205 C2
Admiral's Wlk The. Coulsd CR5 99 F7
Admirals Ct. Merrow GU1 110 B2
Admiralty Rd. Tedd TW11 16 F2
Admiralty Way. Camb GU15 64 F4
Adolf St. Catf SE6 24 B4
Adrian Ct. Crawl RH11 201 B1
Advance Rd. W Norw SE27 22 C4
Adversane Ct. Horsh RH12 217 D4
Aerodrome Way. Heston TW5 4 C8
Aerospace Bvd. Farnb GU11 105 A7
Agar Cl. Surb KT6 56 F8
Agar House. 6 King U T KT1 37 E6
Agate House. New Mal KT4 38 E1
Agate House. 12 Penge SE26 23 B3
Agate La. Horsh RH12 217 F5
Agates La. Ashtd KT21 95 D8
Agincourt Pl. Ascot SL5 29 C6
Agnes Scott Ct. 5 Weyb KT13 53 B7
Agnew Rd. For Hil SE23 23 D8
Agraria Rd. Guild GU2 130 B7
Ailsa Ave. Islew TW1 6 B2
Ailsa Cl. Crawl RH11 201 B3
Ailsa Rd. Islew TW1 6 B2
Ainger Cl. Alder GU12 105 D2
Ainsdale Way. Woking GU21 69 A1
Ainsworth Rd. Thorn H CR0 & CR9 61 B8
Aintree Cl. Poyle SL3 1 E6
Aintree House. Penge SE26 23 B2
Aintree Rd. Crawl RH10 202 A4
Airborne House. 10 Wallin SM6 60 B6
Aircraft Espl. Farnb GU14 85 C1
Airedale Rd. Balham SW12 20 F8
Airport Way. Horley RH6 182 B8
Airport Way. Stan TW19 2 A3
Airport Way Rdbt W. Crawl RH6 181 F8
Aisne Rd. Friml GU16 66 E1
Aitken Cl. Carsh CR4 40 F2
Aitken House. Haslem GU27 208 C7
Aitken Rd. Catf SE6 24 B6
Akabusi Cl. Croy SE25 43 A3
Akehurst Cl. Copth RH10 183 B3
Akehurst St. Putney SW15 19 A8
Akerman Rd. King U T KT6 37 C3
Alamein Rd. Alder GU11 105 B3
Alan Hilton Ct. Ottsh KT16 51 D4
Alan Rd. Wimble SW19 19 E3
Alan Turing Rd. Onsl V GU2 108 D1
Alanbrooke Cl. Knaph GU21 68 C1
Alanbrooke Rd. Farnb GU11 105 D6
Albain Cres. Stan TW15 13 E6
Albans Cl. Streat SW16 21 E5
Albany Cl. Esher KT10 55 A2
Albany Cl. Mortl SW14 7 B3
Albany Cres. Clayg KT10 55 E4
Albany Ct. King U T KT2 17 E2
Albany Ct. Oat Pk KT13 53 E8
Albany Ct. Rich TW10 17 B5
Albany Ct. 3 Weyb KT13 53 B6
Albany Ho. 6 Brent TW8 6 E8
Albany Mews. King U T KT2 17 D2
Albany Mews. Sutton SM1 59 B5
Albany Par. 4 Brent TW8 6 E8
Albany Pk Ind E. Friml GU16 65 C1
Albany Pk Rd. King U T KT2 17 E2
Albany Pk Rd. Leahd KT22 95 A8
Albany Pk. Camb GU16 65 B1
Albany Pk. Friml GU16 65 C1
Albany Pk. Poyle SL3 1 D7
Albany Pl. Brent TW8 6 E8
Albany Pl. Egham TW20 12 B4
Albany Rd. Brent TW8 6 D8
Albany Rd. Crawl RH11 201 C6
Albany Rd. Hersh KT12 54 D6
Albany Rd. New Mal KT3 38 D5
Albany Rd. Rich TW10 6 E2
Albany Rd. Wimble SW19 20 B3
Albany Reach. Thame D KT7 36 F4
Albany Terr. 5 Rich TW10 6 F2
Albanys The. Reig RH2 118 A3
Albatross Gdns. Selsd CR2 81 D8
Albemarle. Putney SW19 19 D6
Albemarle Ave. Twick TW2 15 F7
Albemarle Gdns. New Mal KT3 38 D5
Albemarle Lodge. For Hil SE26 23 E3
Albemarle Pk. Beck BR3 44 B8
Albemarle Rd.Beck BR2&BR3 44 C8
Albermarle Prim Sch. Putney SW19 19 E6
Albermarle Prim Sch (Annexe). Putney SW19 19 E7
Albert Ave. Thorpe KT16 33 A6
Albert Carr Gdns. Streat SW16 21 E3
Albert Crane Ct. Crawl RH11 201 A8
Albert Ct. 9 Putney SW19 19 E7
Albert Dr. Putney SW19 19 E6
Albert Dr. Sheer GU21 & KT14 70 D5
Albert Gr. Wimble SW20 39 D8
Albert Rd. Addl KT15 52 D6
Albert Rd. Alder GU11 105 B2
Albert Rd. Ashf TW15 13 F3
Albert Rd. Ashtd KT21 75 F1
Albert Rd. Bagsh GU19 47 E1
Albert Rd. Brack RG12 27 B8
Albert Rd. Camb GU15 65 C5
Albert Rd. Carsh SM1 59 D5
Albert Rd. Crowth RG11 45 B5
Albert Rd. Croy CR0 & SE25 43 B5
Albert Rd. Eng Gn TW20 11 D2
Albert Rd. Epsom KT17 76 F6
Albert Rd. Farnb GU14 85 C2
Albert Rd. Hampt TW12 16 C3
Albert Rd. Horley RH6 161 A3
Albert Rd. Hounsl TW3 5 A3
Albert Rd. King U T KT1 37 F7
Albert Rd. Merst RH1 119 C6
Albert Rd. Mitch CR4 40 F6
Albert Rd. New Mal KT3 38 F5
Albert Rd. Penge SE20 23 D2
Albert Rd. Rich TW10 6 F2
Albert Rd. Sutton SM1 59 D5
Albert Rd. Tedd TW11 16 F2
Albert Rd. Twick TW1 16 F7
Albert Rd. Warlgm CR6 81 F2
Albert Rd. Woki RG11 25 B5
Albert Rd N. Reig RH2 117 F2
Alberta Ave. Cheam SM1 58 F5
Alberta Dr. Smallf RH6 162 A3
Albertine Cl. Nork KT17 77 B3
Albery Cl. Horsh RH12 217 B4
Albion Cl. Worth RH10 202 D5
Albion Ct. Sutton SM2 59 D3
Albion Par. Knaph GU21 68 C2
Albion Pl. S Norw SE25 43 A6
Albion Rd. Hounsl TW3 5 A3
Albion Rd. King U T KT2 38 C8
Albion Rd. Reig RH2 139 C8
Albion Rd. Sandh GU17 64 B8
Albion Rd. Sutton SM2 59 D3
Albion Rd. Twick TW2 16 E7
Albion St. Thorn H CR0 & CR9 42 B1
Albion Track. Farnb GU14 104 B7
Albion Villas Rd. For Hil SE23 & SE26 23 C5
Albion Way. Horsh RH12 217 C2
Albury Ave. E Ewell SM2 58 C1
Albury Ave. Hounsl TW7 5 F7
Albury Cl. Hampt TW12 16 B2
Albury Cl. Longc KT16 50 A7
Albury Ct. 4 Croy CR0 61 C6
Albury Ct. Mitch CR4 40 D7
Albury Ct. Sutton SM1 59 C6
Albury Keep. Horley RH6 161 B4
Albury Lodge. 10 Streat SW2 21 F8
Albury Pl. Merst RH1 119 C6
Albury Rd. Chess KT9 56 E5
Albury Rd. Guild GU1 131 A8
Albury Rd. Merst RH1 119 C6
Albury Rd. Whit V KT12 53 F4
Albury St. Albury GU5 132 C4
Alcester Ct. 4 Wallin SM6 60 B6
Alcester Rd. Wallin SM6 60 B6
Alcock Cl. Wallin SM6 60 D3
Alcock Rd. Heston TW5 4 D7
Alcocks Cl. Kings KT20 97 E7
Alcocks La. Kings KT20 97 E7
Alcorn Cl. Cheam SM3 59 A8
Alcot Cl. Crowth RG11 45 B4
Alden Ct. S Croy CR0 61 D7
Aldenham Terr. Easth RG12 27 C3
Aldenholme. Whit V KT13 53 E4
Alder Cl. Ash V GU12 106 A7
Alder Cl. Crawl D RH10 204 B8
Alder Cl. Eng Gn TW20 11 E3
Alder Croft. Coulsd CR5 79 F3
Alder Ct. 3 W Norw SW16 22 A3
Alder Rd. Head Dn GU35 187 B6
Alder Rd. Mortl SW14 7 D4
Alderbrook Garage Block. Cran GU6 153 E1
Alderbrook Prim Sch. Balham SW12 21 B8
Alderbrook Rd. Balham SW12 21 B8
Alderbrook Rd. Cran GU6 174 C8
Aldergrove Gdns. Hounsl TW4 4 E5
Alderman Judge Mall. 6 King U T KT1 37 E7
Alderman Willey Cl. Woki RG11 25 B6
Aldermead. Hounsl TW3 5 B3

Aldermoor Rd. For Hil SE6 ... 23 F5
Alderney Ave. Hounsl TW5 .... 5 B7
Alders Ave. E Grins RH19 ... 185 E3
Alders Rd. Reig RH2 .... 118 B3
Alders The. Felt TW13 .... 15 E4
Alders The. Heston TW5 .... 4 F8
Alders The. Streat SW16 .... 21 C4
Alders The. W Wick BR4 ...... 63 B8
Alders View Dr. E Grins RH19 ...... 185 E3
Aldersbrook Dr. King U T KT2 17 F2
Aldersey Rd. Guild GU1 ...... 109 F1
Aldersgrove. E Mole KT8 ...... 36 D4
Aldershot Military Mus. Farnb GU11 ...... 105 C7
Aldershot Rd. Ash GU12 .... 105 F1
Aldershot Rd. Chur C GU13 104 A6
Aldershot Rd. Fairl GU3 .... 108 D5
Aldershot Rd. Pirb GU24 & GU3 ...... 87 F2
Aldershot Rd. Stough GU2 & GU3 ...... 108 D5
Aldershot Rd. Wood S V GU3 ...... 107 E5
Aldershot Sta. Alder GU11 105 B1
Alderside Wlk. Eng Gn TW20 11 E3
Aldersmead Ave. Croy CR0 .. 43 D3
Aldersmead Rd. Penge BR3 . 23 E1
Alderstead La. Hooley RH1 .. 99 D2
Alderton. King U T KT2 .... 38 B8
Alderton Ct. E Mole KT8 .... 35 F5
Alderton Rd. Croy CR0 .... 43 A2
Alderwick Dr. Hounsl TW3 .... 5 D4
Alderwood Cl. Cater CR3 ... 100 E2
Aldingbourne Cl. Crawl RH11 ...... 200 F7
Aldis Mews. Up Toot SW17 .. 20 E3
Aldis St. Up Toot SW17 .... 20 E3
Aldous House. Stain TW18 .. 12 E4
Aldren Rd. Wands SW17 ...... 20 C5
Aldrich Cres. New Add CR0 .. 63 C2
Aldrich Gdns. Cheam SM3 .... 58 F7
Aldrich Terr. Wands SW18 ... 20 C6
Aldridge Rise. New Mal KT3 38 E3
Aldrin Pl. Farnb GU14 .... 84 D4
Aldrington Rd. Streat SW16 21 C4
Aldro Sch. Shackl GU8 .... 149 C7
Aldwick Cl. W Heath GU14 .... 85 A6
Aldwick Rd. Wallin CR0 .... 60 F6
Aldworth Cl. Easth RG12 ...... 27 A5
Aldworth Gdns. Crowth RG11 ...... 45 A5
Aldwych Cl. Worth RH10 ... 202 D4
Aldwyn Ct. Eng Gn TW20 ...... 11 B2
Alexa Ct. Belm SM2 .... 59 A4
Alexander Cl. Twick TW2 ...... 16 F6
Alexander Ct. Beck BR3 .... 44 D8
Alexander Ct. 14 Surb KT6 .. 37 D2
Alexander Evans Mews. For Hil SE23 ...... 23 D6
Alexander Godley Cl. Ashtd KT21 ...... 95 F8
Alexander Rd. Coulsd CR5 .... 79 B4
Alexander Rd. Egham TW20 12 C3
Alexander Rd. Woodh RH2 139 A6
Alexander Wlk. Easth RG12 . 27 B4
Alexanders Wlk. Cater CR3 101 A1
Alexandra Ave. Camb GU15 . 65 A5
Alexandra Ave. Sutton SM1 . 59 A7
Alexandra Ave. Warlgm CR6 81 F2
Alexandra Cl. Ashf TW15 ...... 14 D1
Alexandra Cl. Stain TW18 ...... 13 D2
Alexandra Cl. Walt O T KT12 54 A8
Alexandra Cotts. Penge SE20 ...... 23 D2
Alexandra Cres. Broml BR1 . 24 F2
Alexandra Ct. Ashf TW15 ...... 14 D2
Alexandra Ct. 10 Crawl RH11 ...... 201 D5
Alexandra Ct. 1 Farnb GU14 ...... 85 C1
Alexandra Dr. Surb KT5 .... 38 A2
Alexandra Dr. W Norw SE19 22 E3
Alexandra Gdns. Chisw W4 ... 7 E7
Alexandra Gdns. Hounsl TW3 5 B5
Alexandra Gdns. Knaph GU21 ...... 68 C1
Alexandra Gdns. Wallin SM5 60 A2
Alexandra Inf Sch. King U T KT2 ...... 18 A1
Alexandra Inf Sch. Penge BR3 ...... 23 D1
Alexandra Jun & Inf Sch. Hounsl TW3 ...... 5 B5
Alexandra Jun Sch. Penge SE26 ...... 23 D2
Alexandra Lodge. Guild GU1 ...... 130 F8
Alexandra Lodge. 1 Weyb KT13 ...... 53 B6
Alexandra Pl. Croy CR0 .... 42 E1
Alexandra Pl. Guild GU1 ..... 130 F7
Alexandra Pl. S Norw SE25 .. 42 D4
Alexandra Rd. Addl KT15 ..... 52 D6
Alexandra Rd. Alder GU11 . 104 F2
Alexandra Rd. Ash GU12 .... 105 F1
Alexandra Rd. Ashf TW15 ..... 14 E2
Alexandra Rd. Bigg H TN16 103 B8
Alexandra Rd. 10 Brent TW8 . 6 D8
Alexandra Rd. Croy CR0 .... 42 E2
Alexandra Rd. Eng Gn TW20 11 C2
Alexandra Rd. Epsom KT17 .. 76 F6
Alexandra Rd. Farnb GU14 & GU11 ...... 85 C1
Alexandra Rd. Hounsl TW3 .... 5 B5
Alexandra Rd. King U T KT2 . 18 A1
Alexandra Rd. Mitch SW19 .. 20 E1
Alexandra Rd. Mortl SW14 .... 7 D4
Alexandra Rd. Penge SE26 ... 23 D2
Alexandra Rd. Rich TW9 .... 6 F5
Alexandra Rd. Thame D KT7 36 F4
Alexandra Rd. Twick TW1 .... 6 C1
Alexandra Rd. Warlgm CR6 . 81 F2
Alexandra Rd. Wimble SW19 20 A3
Alexandra Sq. Morden SM4 . 40 A4
Alexandra Terr. Guild GU1 . 130 E8
Alexandra Wlk. 8 W Norw SE19 ...... 22 E3
Alfold By-Pass. Alf Cr GU6 194 A5
Alfold By-Pass. Alfold GU6 . 193 F7
Alfold Cotts. Alf Cr GU6 ..... 193 F2
Alfold Cty Prim Sch. Alfold GU6 ...... 193 F1
Alfold La. Alf Cr GU6 .... 194 A7
Alfold Rd. Alfold GU8 .... 193 B3
Alfold Rd. Cran GU6 .... 194 B7
Alfold Rd. Dunsf GU8 .... 193 B3
Alfonso Cl. Alder GU12 .... 126 C8
Alford Cl. Burph GU4 .... 110 A4
Alford Ct. 5 Sutton SM2 .... 59 B3
Alford Gn. New Add CR0 ...... 63 D4
Alfred Butt House. Up Toot SW17 ...... 20 F5
Alfred Cl. Worth RH10 .... 202 E5
Alfred Hurley House. Up Toot SW17 ...... 20 C4
Alfred Mizen Prim Sch The. Mitch CR4 ...... 41 D6
Alfred Rd. Croy SE25 .... 43 A4
Alfred Rd. Felt TW13 .... 15 C6
Alfred Rd. King U T KT1 .... 37 F6
Alfred Rd. M Bourn GU9 ...... 125 C1
Alfred Rd. Sutton SM1 .... 59 C5
Alfreton Cl. Wimble SW19 ... 19 D5
Alfriston. Surb KT5 .... 37 F3
Alfriston Ave. Thorn H CR0 .. 41 E2
Alfriston Cl. Surb KT5 .... 37 F3
Alfriston Rd. Friml GU16 ...... 86 C7
Algar Cl. Islew TW7 .... 6 A4
Algar Rd. Islew TW7 .... 6 A4
Algarve Rd. Wands SW18 ..... 20 B7
Alice Gough Memorial Homes. Easth RG12 ...... 27 B6
Alice Mews. 8 Tedd TW11 .. 16 F3
Alice Rd. Alder GU11 .... 105 B2
Alice Ruston Pl. Woking GU22 ...... 89 C8
Alice Way. Hounsl TW3 .... 5 B3
Alicia Ave. Crawl RH10 .... 202 C6
Alington Gr. Wallin SM6 .... 60 D2
Alison Cl. Croy CR0 .... 43 D1
Alison Cl. Farnb GU14 .... 84 F3
Alison Cl. Horse GU21 .... 69 E4
Alison Dr. Camb GU15 .... 65 F5
Alison Rd. Alder GU11 .... 104 F2
Alison's Rd. Alder GU11 ...... 105 B4
All England Lawn Tennis & Croquet Club The. Wimble SW19 ...... 19 E5
All Hallows Catholic Sch. Heath E GU9 ...... 125 F7
All Saint's Prim Sch. S Norw SE19 ...... 42 E8
All Saints' Benhilton C of E Prim Sch. Sutton SM1 ...... 59 B7
All Saints C of E Inf Sch. Leahd KT22 ...... 95 A8
All Saints C of E Prim Sch. Merton SW19 ...... 20 C1
All Saints Carshalton CE Sch. Wallin SM5 ...... 60 A5
All Saints CE Inf Sch. Tilf GU10 ...... 147 C3
All Saints Cl. Woki RG11 .... 25 C7
All Saints Cres. W Heath GU14 ...... 64 E1
All Saints Ct. Heston TW5 ...... 4 D6
All Saints Dr. Sander CR2 ..... 81 A7
All Saints Rd. Lhtwat GU18 .. 48 C1
All Saints Rd. Merton SW19 . 20 C1
All Saints Rd. Sutton SM1 ..... 59 C7
All Souls' Rd. Ascot SL5 .... 29 A5
Allan Cl. New Mal KT3 .... 38 D4
Allbrook Cl. Tedd TW11 .... 16 E3
Allbrook House. 5 Rhampt SW15 ...... 19 A8
Allcard Cl. Horsh RH12 .... 217 D4
Allcot Cl. Crawl RH11 .... 200 E3
Allcot Cl. E Bed TW14 .... 14 F7
Allden Ave. Alder GU11 & GU12 ...... 126 D7
Allden Cotts. Ock Rid GU7 . 150 B4
Allden Gdns. Alder GU12 ... 126 D7
Alldens Hill. Bramly GU5 & GU8 ...... 151 D1
Alldens La. Godal GU8 .... 151 B1
Allen Cl. Sunby TW16 .... 35 B8
Allen House Pk. Woking GU22 ...... 89 C7
Allen Rd. G Book KT23 .... 94 B1
Allen Rd. Penge BR3 .... 43 D7
Allen Rd. Sunby TW16 .... 35 B7
Allen Rd. Thorn H CR0 .... 42 A1
Allen's Cl. Ash W RH19 .... 206 D6
Allenby Ave. S Croy CR2 .... 61 C2
Allenby Rd. Bigg H TN16 .... 83 E2
Allenby Rd. For Hil SE23 .... 23 E5
Allenby Rd. Sandh GU15 .... 65 A6
Allendale. Elst GU8 .... 148 C3
Allendale Cl. For Hil SE26 ..... 23 D3
Allendale Cl. Sandh GU17 ...... 45 A2
Allenford House. Rhampt SW15 ...... 7 F1
Allenswood. 12 Putney SW19 ...... 19 E7
Allerford Ct. Catf SE6 .... 24 B5
Allerford Rd. Catf SE6 .... 24 B4
Allerton Ct. N Cheam SM3 ... 58 D8
Allerton House. 4 Merton SW19 ...... 20 C1
Alleyn Cres. Dulw SE21 .... 22 D6
Alleyn Pk. Dulw SE21 .... 22 E5
Alleyn Rd. Dulw SE21 .... 22 E5
Allgood Cl. W Barn SM4 .... 39 D3
Alliance Ct. Ashf TW15 .... 14 C4
Allingham Ct. Farnc GU7 ... 150 F7
Allingham Gdns. Horsh RH12 ...... 218 B5
Allingham Rd. Woodh RH2 139 A6
Allington Ave. Up Hall TW17 34 E6
Allington Cl. Wimble SW19 .. 19 D3
Allington Ct. Croy CR0 .... 43 C3
Allison Gr. Dulw SE21 .... 22 E7
Alloway Cl. 4 Woking GU21 69 B1
Allsmoor La. Brack RG12 .... 27 F6
Allum Gr. Tadw KT20 .... 97 B6
Allwood Cl. For Hil SE26 .... 23 D4
Allyington Way. Worth RH10 ...... 202 D5
Allyn Cl. Stain TW18 .... 12 F2
Alma Cl. Alder GU12 .... 105 D2
Alma Cl. Knaph GU21 .... 68 E1
Alma Cres. Cheam SM1 .... 58 E5
Alma Ct. Cater CR3 .... 100 C6
Alma Gdns. Friml GU16 .... 86 E8
Alma Ho. 7 Brent TW8 .... 6 E8
Alma La. Heath E GU9 .... 125 C7
Alma Pl. Penge SE19 .... 22 F1
Alma Pl. Thorn H CR7 .... 42 A4
Alma Rd. Carsh SM5 .... 59 E5
Alma Rd. Head Dn GU35 ...... 187 C5
Alma Rd. Reig RH2 .... 118 B3
Alma Rd. Thame D KT10 & KT7 ...... 36 E1
Alma Terr. Wands SW18 .... 20 D8
Alma Way. Heath E GU9 ...... 125 D7
Almer Rd. Wimble SW20 .... 19 A1
Almners Rd. Chert KT16 .... 32 C2
Almners Rd. Lyne KT16 .... 32 B1
Almond Ave. Carsh SM5 .... 59 F8
Almond Ave. Woking GU22 .. 89 D6
Almond Cl. Bellf GU1 .... 109 D5
Almond Cl. Charlt TW17 .... 34 C7
Almond Cl. Crawl RH11 .... 201 A5
Almond Cl. Eng Gn TW20 ...... 11 B2
Almond Gr. Brent TW8 .... 6 B7
Almond Rd. Epsom KT19 .... 76 D8
Almond Way. Mitch CR4 .... 41 D5
Almorah Rd. Heston TW5 .... 4 D6
Alms Heath. Ockham GU23 .. 92 B6
Almsgate. Compt GU3 .... 129 C2
Almshouse La. Chess KT9 .... 56 D2
Almshouses. Dork RH4 .... 136 B8
Almshouses. Mickle RH5 ..... 115 C8
Almshouses. Sunby TW16 ..... 34 F8
Alnwick Gr. Morden SM4 .... 40 B5
Alpha Ct. Warlgm CR6 .... 81 A1
Alpha Rd. Chobh GU24 .... 49 F1
Alpha Rd. Crawl RH11 .... 201 C6
Alpha Rd. Croy CR0 .... 42 E1
Alpha Rd. Mayb GU22 .... 70 C4
Alpha Rd. Surb KT5 .... 37 F3
Alpha Rd. Tedd TW12 .... 16 D3
Alpha Way. Thorpe TW20 ...... 32 C8
Alphabet Gdns. Carsh SM5 .. 40 D3
Alphea Cl. Mitch SW19 .... 20 E1
Alphington Ave. Friml GU16 65 F1
Alphington Gn. Friml GU16 .. 65 F1
Alpine Ave. Tolw KT5 .... 57 C8
Alpine Cl. Farnb GU14 .... 84 D3
Alpine Cl. S Croy CR0 .... 61 E7
Alpine Rd. Redh RH1 .... 119 A4
Alpine Rd. Walt O T KT12 ...... 35 A2
Alpine View. Carsh SM1 .... 59 E5
Alresford Rd. Guild GU2 .... 130 A8
Alric Ave. King U T KT3 .... 38 F6
Alsace Wlk. Camb GU15 .... 65 B1
Alsford Cl. Lhtwat GU18 .... 66 F7
Alsom Ave. Worc Pk KT19 & KT4 ...... 58 A6
Alston Cl. Thame D KT7 .... 37 B2
Alston Rd. Up Toot SW17 ...... 20 D4
Alt Gr. Wimble SW19 .... 19 E1
Alterton Cl. Woking GU21 ..... 69 A2
Althorne Rd. Earls RH1 ...... 140 A7
Althorp Rd. Up Toot SW17 ... 20 F7
Alton Cl. Islew TW7 .... 5 F5
Alton Ct. 19 Beck BR3 .... 24 A1
Alton Ct. Egham TW18 .... 32 E8
Alton Gdns. Beck BR3 .... 24 A1
Alton Gdns. Twick TW2 .... 16 D8
Alton House. 1 Redh RH1 .. 119 A3
Alton Rd. Croy CR0 & CR9 .... 61 A7
Alton Rd. Farnh GU10 & GU9 ...... 145 D7
Alton Rd. Rhampt SW15 .... 19 A7
Alton Rd. Rich TW10 & TW9 ... 6 E3
Alton Ride. Blckw GU17 .... 64 C6
Altwood Prim Sch. Sander CR2 ...... 81 A6
Altyre Cl. Beck BR3 .... 43 F4
Altyre Rd. S Croy CR0 & CR9 61 D8
Altyre Way. Beck BR3 .... 43 F4
Alvernia Cl. Godal GU7 .... 150 C2
Alvernia Lodge. Sutton SM1 59 C8
Alverstoke Gdns. Alder GU11 ...... 104 E1
Alverston Gdns. S Norw SE25 ...... 42 E4
Alverstone Ave. Wimble SW18 & SW19 ...... 20 A6
Alverstone Rd. New Mal KT3 38 F5
Alvia Gdns. Sutton SM1 .... 59 C6
Alway Ave. W Ewell KT19 ...... 57 D5
Alway Ave. W Ewell KT19 ...... 57 D5
Alwyn Cl. New Add CR0 .... 63 B3
Alwyne Ct. Horse GU21 .... 69 E3
Alwyne Rd. Wimble SW19 ...... 19 F2
Alwyns Cl. Chert KT16 .... 33 A3
Alwyns La. Chert KT16 .... 33 A3
Amalgamated Dr. Brent TW8 6 B8
Amanda Ct. Ashf TW15 .... 13 F6
Ambassador. Easth RG12 ...... 26 F4
Ambassador Cl. Hounsl TW3 . 4 E5
Amber Ct. Alder GU12 .... 105 C2
Amber Ct. Mitch CR4 .... 40 E5
Amber Ct. Stain TW18 .... 12 F3
Amber Hill. Friml GU15 .... 66 B4
Ambercroft Way. Coulsd CR5 ...... 100 B8
Amberley Cl. Crawl RH10 ... 202 C6
Amberley Cl. Horsh RH12 . 218 A6
Amberley Cl. Send M GU23 .. 90 F2
Amberley Ct. Sutton SM2 ...... 59 C3
Amberley Dr. Woodhm KT15 70 F8
Amberley Gdns. Worc Pk KT19 ...... 57 F6
Amberley Gr. Croy CR0 .... 42 F2
Amberley Gr. For Hil SE26 ... 23 B3
Amberley Grange. Alder GU11 ...... 125 F8
Amberley Rd. Horsh RH12 218 A6
Amberley Rd. Milf GU8 .... 149 E2
Amberley Way. Heston TW4 . 4 C2
Amberley Way. Morden SM4 39 F2
Amberwood Dr. Camb GU15 65 F7
Amberwood Rise. New Mal KT3 ...... 38 E3
Amblecote. Cobham KT11 .... 73 E7
Ambleside. Catf BR1 .... 24 D2
Ambleside. Godal GU7 .... 151 A5
Ambleside. 13 Putney SW19 ...... 19 E7
Ambleside Ave. Beck BR3 .... 43 E4
Ambleside Ave. Streat SW16 ...... 21 D4
Ambleside Ave. Walt O T KT12 ...... 35 C1
Ambleside Cl. Crawl RH11 . 200 D5
Ambleside Cl. Earls RH1 ... 140 B4
Ambleside Cl. Farnb GU14 ... 84 E3
Ambleside Cl. Mytch GU16 .. 86 A2
Ambleside Cres. Hale GU9 125 A6
Ambleside Cty Jun Sch. Walt O T KT12 ...... 35 C1
Ambleside Dr. E Bed TW14 .. 14 F7
Ambleside Gdns. Selsd CR2 62 D1
Ambleside Gdns. Streat SW16 ...... 21 D3
Ambleside Gdns. Sutton SM2 ...... 59 C4
Ambleside Rd. Lhtwat GU18 67 B8
Ambleside Sch. Belm SM2 ... 58 E2
Ambleside Way. Thor L TW20 ...... 12 B1
Ambrey Way. Wallin CR8 & SM6 ...... 60 D2
Amen Cnr. Streat SW17 .... 21 A2
Amen Corner Bsns Pk. Binf RG12 ...... 26 D7
Amenity Way. W Barn SM4 . 39 C2
American Comm Sch. Esher KT11 ...... 54 C1
American Comm Sch. Vir W TW20 ...... 31 C7
American Comm Sch. Wimble SW19 ...... 19 C1
American Sch in Switzerland (English Branch) The. Thorpe TW20 ...... 32 C6
Amersham Rd. Thorn H CR0 42 D3
Amesbury Ave. Streat SW2 . 21 F6
Amesbury Cl. N Cheam KT4 . 39 C1
Amesbury Rd. Felt TW13 ...... 15 D6
Amesbury Sch. Shottm GU26 ...... 188 E1
Amey Dr. Fetch KT23 .... 94 C3
Amhurst Gdns. Islew TW7 ..... 6 A5
Amis Ave. Chess KT19 .... 57 B5
Amis Ave. Woodhm KT15 .... 52 A1
Amis Rd. Knaph GU21 .... 88 E8
Amity Gr. Wimble SW20 .... 39 C8
Amlets La. Cran GU6 .... 174 E5
Ampere Way. Croy CR0 & CR9 ...... 41 F1
Amroth Cl. For Hil SE23 .... 23 B7
Amstel Way. Knaph GU21 ..... 68 F1
Amundsen Rd. Horsh RH12 217 D6
Amy Johnson Prim Sch. Wallin SM6 ...... 60 E3
Amy Rd. Oxted RH8 .... 122 E6
Amyand Cotts. 12 Twick TW1 ...... 6 B1
Amyand Park Gdns. 3 Twick TW1 ...... 17 B8
Amyand Park Rd. Twick TW1 ...... 17 A8
Anarth Ct. Oat Pk KT13 .... 34 E1
Ancaster Cres. New Mal KT3 39 A3
Ancaster Dr. N Asct SL5 .... 28 E8
Ancaster Rd. Penge BR3 .... 43 D6
Anchor Cotts. Blind H RH7 . 163 E8
Anchor Cres. Knaph GU21 .... 68 D2
Anchor Hill. Knaph GU21 ...... 68 D2
Anchor Meadow. Farnb GU14 ...... 84 F4
Anchorage Cl. Wimble SW19 20 A3
Anderson Ave. Stough GU2 109 B5
Anderson Cl. Epsom KT19 ..... 76 B7
Anderson Dr. Ashf TW15 ...... 14 C4
Anderson House. Up Toot SW17 ...... 20 D3
Anderson Pl. Bagsh GU19 ..... 47 E4
Anderson Rd. Oat Pk KT13 ... 53 D7
Anderson's Pl. Hounsl TW3 .... 5 B3
Andhurst Ct. King U T KT2 ... 38 B8
Andon Ct. Beck BR3 .... 43 E6
Andover Cl. E Bed TW14 .... 14 F7
Andover Cl. Epsom KT19 .... 76 D8
Andover Ct. Stan TW19 .... 13 D8
Andover Rd. Blckw GU17 ...... 64 C6
Andover Rd. Twick TW2 .... 16 D7
Andover Way. Alder GU11 & GU9 ...... 126 B7
Andreck Ct. Beck BR3 .... 44 C7
Andrew Cl. Woki RG11 .... 25 E5
Andrew Ct. For Hil SE23 .... 23 D6
Andrew Ewing Prim Sch. Heston TW5 ...... 4 F7
Andrew Reed House. Putney SW18 ...... 19 E8
Andrew's Cl. Epsom KT17 ..... 76 F6
Andrewartha Rd. Farnb GU14 ...... 85 E2
Andrewes House. Sutton SM1 ...... 59 A6
Andrews Cl. N Cheam KT4 ..... 58 D8
Andrews Rd. W Heath GU14 84 E5
Andromeda Cl. Crawl RH11 200 E4
Anerley Ct. Penge SE20 .... 23 B1
Anerley Gr. Penge SE19 .... 22 F1
Anerley Hill. Penge SE19 .... 22 F2

Anerley Park Rd. Penge SE20 23 B1
Anerley Pk. Penge SE20 23 B1
Anerley Prim Sch. Penge SE20 43 A8
Anerley Rd. Penge SE20 & SE19 43 B8
Anerley Sch. Penge SE20 43 A8
Anerley Sta. Penge SE20 43 B8
Anerley Station Rd. Penge SE20 43 B8
Anerley Vale. Penge SE19 23 A1
Anfield Cl. Streat SW12 21 C8
Angas Ct. 4 Whit V KT13 53 C5
Angel Ct. Compt GU3 129 A3
Angel Gate. Guild GU1 130 D8
Angel Hill. Sutton SM1 59 B7
Angel Hill Dr. Sutton SM1 59 B7
Angel Rd. Thame D KT7 37 A1
Angela Ct. For Hil SE23 23 C7
Angelfield. Hounsl TW3 5 B2
Angelica Gdns. Croy CR0 43 D1
Angelica Rd. Bisley GU21 & GU24 68 A4
Angelica Rd. Stough GU2 109 A5
Anglers Reach. King U T KT6 37 D4
Angles Rd. Streat SW16 21 E4
Anglesea House. King U T KT1 37 D5
Anglesea Rd. King U T KT1 37 D5
Anglesey Ave. W Heath GU14 84 F7
Anglesey Cl. Ashf TW15 14 A5
Anglesey Cl. Crawl RH11 201 C2
Anglesey Court Rd. Wallin SM5 60 A4
Anglesey Gdns. Wallin SM5 60 A4
Anglesey Rd. Alder GU12 105 D1
Angus Cl. Chess KT9 57 A5
Angus Cl. Horsh RH12 217 D4
Angus House. 12 Streat SW12 21 D8
Anlaby Rd. Tedd TW11 16 E3
Ann Parkes Ct. Hounsl TW5 4 D5
Annandale Dr. M Bourn GU10 146 D6
Annandale Rd. Croy CR0 62 A8
Annandale Rd. Guild GU2 130 B7
Anne Armstrong Cl. Farnb GU11 105 D5
Anne Boleyn's Wlk. Cheam SM2 & SM3 58 E3
Anne Boleyn's Wlk. King U T KT2 17 E3
Anne Way. E Mole KT8 36 B5
Anne's Wlk. Whytlf CR3 100 E7
Anners Cl. Egham TW20 32 C6
Annesley Dr. Croy CR0 62 F7
Annett Cl. Up Hall TW17 34 E5
Annett Rd. Walt O T KT12 35 A2
Annie Brookes Cl. Stain TW18 12 D5
Anningsley Pk. Ottsh KT16 51 C1
Annisdowne. Peasl GU5 133 F1
Annsworthy Ave. S Norw CR7 & SE25 42 D6
Annsworthy Cres. S Norw CR7 42 D7
Ansell Gr. Carsh SM5 41 A1
Ansell Rd. Dork RH4 136 B8
Ansell Rd. Friml GU16 65 E1
Ansell Rd. Friml GU16 85 E8
Ansell Rd. Up Toot SW17 20 F5
Anselm Cl. S Croy CR0 61 F7
Ansford Rd. Catf BR1 & SE6 24 D4
Ansley Cl. Hams Gn CR2 81 B5
Anslie Wlk. 8 Balham SW12 21 B8
Anson Cl. Cater CR3 & CR8 100 D7
Anstice Cl. Chisw W4 7 E7
Anstie Grange Dr. S Holm RH5 157 B5
Anstie La. Coldh RH5 156 F4
Anstiebury Cl. Bear Gn RH5 157 C3
Anston Ct. 8 Stough GU2 108 E1
Anthony Rd. Croy CR0 & SE25 43 A3
Anthony West House. Brock RH3 137 B7
Antigua Wlk. W Norw SE19 22 D3
Antlands La. Burst RH6 183 B6
Antlands La. Crawl RH6 182 E5
Antlands La E. Burst RH6 182 F5
Antlands La W. Crawl RH6 182 E6
Anton Cres. Sutton SM1 59 A7
Antrobus Cl. Cheam SM1 58 F5
Anvil La. Cobham KT11 73 A5
Anvil Rd. Sunby TW16 35 A6
Anyards Rd. Cobham KT11 73 B5
Anzio Cl. Alder GU11 105 A2
Apeldoorn Dr. Wallin CR8 & SM6 60 E2
Aperdele Rd. Leahd KT22 75 A1
Aperfield Rd. Bigg H TN16 83 E2
Apers Ave. Westfd GU22 89 F6
Apex Cl. Beck BR3 44 B8
Apex Cl. Oat Pk KT13 53 D7
Apex Dr. Friml GU16 65 D1
Apley Rd. Woodh RH2 139 A6
Aplin Way. Hounsl TW7 5 E6
Aplin Way. Lhtwat GU18 48 A1
Apollo Pl. Woking GU21 89 A8
Apollo Rise. Farnb GU14 84 D4
Apple Garth. Farnc GU7 150 C7
Apple Gr. Chess KT9 56 E6
Apple Mkt. King U T KT1 37 D7
Apple Tree Way. Sandh GU15 45 D1
Appleby Cl. Twick TW2 16 D6
Appleby Ct. Camb GU15 65 B6
Appleby Gdns. E Bed TW14 14 F7
Appledore. Easth RG12 26 F3
Appledore Cl. Hayes BR2 44 F4
Appledore Cl. Up Toot SW12 & SW17 20 F6
Appledore Mews. W Heath GU14 85 A7
Appledown Rise. Coulsd CR5 79 C4
Applefield. Crawl RH10 201 E7
Applegarth. Clayg KT10 55 F5
Applegarth. New Add CR0 63 B3
Applegarth Ave. Stough GU2 108 D1
Applegarth Inf & Jun Sch. New Add CR0 63 B4
Applelands Cl. Rowl GU10 146 A4
Appleton Gdns. New Mal KT3 39 A3
Appleton Sq. Mitch CR4 40 E8
Appletree Cl. Godal GU7 150 F2
Appletree Cl. 6 Penge SE20 43 B8
Appletree Ct. Merrow GU4 110 D3
Appletree Pl. 4 Brack RG12 27 A8
Appletrees Pl. Woking GU22 89 C8
Appley Dr. Camb GU15 65 B6
Approach Rd. Ashf TW15 14 C2
Approach Rd. E Mole KT8 36 A4
Approach Rd. Farnh GU9 125 C1
Approach Rd. Merton SW20 39 C7
Approach Rd. Purley CR8 80 B7
Approach Rd. Tats CR6 & TN16 103 B5
Approach The. Dorman RH19 185 F6
April Cl. Ashtd KT21 75 F1
April Cl. Camb GU15 65 C2
April Cl. Felt TW13 15 A5
April Cl. Horsh RH12 217 C4
April Glen. For Hil SE23 23 D5
Aprilwood Cl. Woodhm KT15 70 F8
Apsley Ct. Crawl RH11 200 F4
Apsley Ct. Sutton SM2 59 C4
Apsley Rd. Croy SE25 43 B5
Apsley Rd. King U T KT3 38 C6
Aquarius. Twick TW1 17 B7
Aquarius Ct. Crawl RH11 200 E4
Aquila Cl. Ashtd KT21 95 E6
Arabella Dr. Rhampt SW15 7 E3
Aragon Ave. Ewell KT17 58 B2
Aragon Ave. Thame D KT7 36 F4
Aragon Cl. Ashf TW16 14 F1
Aragon Cl. New Add CR0 63 E1
Aragon Ct. Easth RG12 27 C5
Aragon Ct. Knaph GU21 68 D2
Aragon Rd. King U T KT2 17 E3
Aragon Rd. W Barn SM4 39 E2
Arbor Cl. Beck BR3 44 B7
Arbour Cl. Fetch KT22 94 F4
Arbrook La. Esher KT10 55 D4
Arbury Terr. For Hil SE26 23 B5
Arbutus Cl. Woodh RH2 139 C7
Arbutus Rd. Woodh RH1 & RH2 139 C6
Arcade The. Alder GU11 105 A2
Arch Rd. Hersh KT12 54 D7
Archbishop Lanfranc Sch The. Thorn H CR0 41 E3
Archbishop Tenison's Sch. S Croy CR0 61 F7
Archbishop's Pl. 3 Streat SW2 21 F8
Archdale Pl. King U T KT3 38 B6
Archdeacon Cambridge's Prim Sch (C of E). Twick TW2 16 E6
Archer Cl. King U T KT2 17 E1
Archer Rd. Croy SE25 43 B5
Archers Ct. Crawl RH11 201 D8
Archway Cl. Wallin SM6 60 E7
Archway Cl. Wimble SW19 20 B4
Archway Mews. Dork RH4 136 A8
Archway Pl. Dork RH4 136 A8
Archway St. Mortl SW13 & SW14 7 E4
Arcturus Rd. Crawl RH11 200 E3
Arcus Rd. Catf BR1 24 E2
Arden. 17 Putney SW19 19 D7
Arden Cl. Brack RG12 28 A7
Arden Cl. Dovgn RH2 139 B5
Arden Mead Cotts. Tand RH7 164 A8
Arden Rd. Crawl RH10 201 F4
Ardenrun. Tand RH7 164 B8
Ardenrun Cotts. Tand RH7 164 A7
Ardent Cl. S Norw SE25 42 E6
Ardesley Wood. Oat Pk KT13 53 E6
Ardfern Ave. Thorn H SW16 42 A6
Ardfillan Rd. Catf SE6 24 D6
Ardgowan Rd. Catf SE6 24 E7
Ardingly. Easth RG12 27 A4
Ardingly Cl. Crawl RH11 201 B8
Ardingly Cl. S Croy CR0 62 D7
Ardingly Ct. Epsom KT18 76 D5
Ardleigh Gdns. Cheam SM3 40 A2
Ardley Cl. For Hil SE23 & SE6 23 E5
Ardlui Rd. W Norw SE27 22 C6
Ardmay Gdns. King U T KT6 37 E4
Ardmore Ave. Stough GU2 109 B3
Ardmore House. Stough GU2 109 B3
Ardmore Way. Stough GU2 109 B3
Ardoch Rd. Catf SE6 24 D6
Ardrossan Ave. Friml GU15 66 A5
Ardrossan Gdns. Worc Pk KT4 58 A7
Ardshiel Dr. Earls RH1 139 E7
Ardwell Rd. Streat SW2 21 E6
Arena L Ctr. Camb GU15 65 C6
Arena La. Alder GU11 104 E5
Arenal Dr. Crowth RG11 45 C3
Arethusa Way. Bisley GU24 67 F3
Arford Comm. Head Dn GU35 187 A6
Argent Terr. Sandh GU15 64 E8
Argosy Gdns. Stain TW18 12 F2
Argosy La. Stan TW19 13 D8
Argus Wlk. Crawl RH11 201 A3
Argyle Ave. Islew TW2 & TW3 5 A1
Argyle Ave. Twick TW3 5 A1
Argyle House. Sutton SM2 59 C4
Argyle Rd. Hounsl TW3 5 B2
Argyle St. Pirb GU24 87 A6
Argyll Ct. 15 Streat SW2 21 E8
Ariel Rd. Farnb GU14 85 A2
Ariel Way. Hounsl TW4 4 B4
Arkell Gr. S Norw SW16 22 B1
Arkendale. Felb RH19 185 A4
Arkindale Rd. Catf SE6 24 C5
Arklow Mews. Surb KT6 56 E8
Arklow Mews. 3 Surb KT6 56 E8
Arkwright Dr. Binf RG12 26 D7
Arkwright House. 23 Streat SW2 21 E8
Arkwright Rd. Poyle SL3 1 E5
Arkwright Rd. S Croy CR2 61 F2
Arlington Cl. Brack RG12 27 A8
Arlington Cl. Sutton SM1 59 A8
Arlington Cl. Twick TW1 6 C1
Arlington Ct. Reig RH2 118 A3
Arlington Ct. 4 Twick TW1 6 C1
Arlington Dr. Carsh SM5 59 F8
Arlington Lodge. Weyb KT13 53 B6
Arlington Rd. Ashf TW15 13 F3
Arlington Rd. Rich TW10 17 D6
Arlington Rd. Surb KT6 37 D3
Arlington Rd. Tedd TW11 16 F4
Arlington Rd. Twick TW1 6 C1
Arlington Terr. Alder GU11 104 F2
Armadale Rd. Felt TW14 4 A2
Armadale Rd. Woking GU21 69 A2
Armeston. New Mal KT3 38 D2
Armfield Cl. E Mole KT8 35 F4
Armfield Cres. Mitch CR4 40 F7
Armitage Ct. Ascot SL5 29 C3
Armitage Dr. Friml GU16 65 F1
Armstrong Cl. Walt O T KT12 35 A3
Armstrong Mall. Farnb GU14 84 D4
Armstrong Rd. Eng Gn TW20 11 C2
Armstrong Rd. Felt TW13 15 E3
Armytage Rd. Heston TW5 4 D7
Arnal Cres. Putney SW18 19 E8
Arncliffe. Easth RG12 27 A4
Arndale Way. Egham TW20 12 A3
Arne Cl. Crawl RH11 200 F3
Arne Gr. Horley RH6 160 E5
Arnewood Cl. Oxsh KT22 74 B5
Arnewood Cl. Rhampt SW15 19 A7
Arney's La. Mitch CR4 41 A3
Arnfield Cl. Crawl RH11 200 E5
Arngask Rd. Catf SE6 24 D8
Arnhem Cl. Alder GU11 105 B2
Arnhem Dr. New Add CR0 82 D8
Arnison Rd. E Mole KT8 36 D5
Arnold Cres. Islew TW7 5 D2
Arnold Dr. Chess KT9 56 D4
Arnold Rd. Mitch SW17 20 F1
Arnold Rd. Sheer GU21 70 B4
Arnold Rd. Stain TW18 13 C1
Arnulf St. Catf SE6 24 B4
Arnull's Rd. S Norw SW16 22 B2
Arragon Gdns. Streat SW16 21 E1
Arragon Gdns. W Wick BR4 63 B7
Arragon Rd. 3 Twick TW1 17 A7
Arragon Rd. Twick TW1 17 A8
Arragon Rd. Wands SW18 20 A7
Arragon Wlk. Byfl KT14 71 F6
Arran Cl. Crawl RH11 201 B3
Arran Cl. Wallin SM6 60 C6
Arran Rd. Catf SE6 24 C6
Arran Way. Thame D KT10 55 B8
Arrancourt. Horsh RH12 217 B2
Arras Ave. Morden SM4 40 C4
Arrivals Rd. Crawl RH6 181 F8
Arrol Rd. Penge BR3 43 D6
Arrow Ind Est. Farnb GU14 84 F2
Arrow Rd. Farnb GU14 84 F2
Artel Croft. Crawl RH10 202 A6
Arterberry Rd. Wimble SW20 & SW19 39 D8
Arthur Cl. Bagsh GU19 47 E1
Arthur Cl. M Bourn GU9 125 B1
Arthur Ct. S Croy CR0 61 D7
Arthur Rd. Bigg H TN16 83 C3
Arthur Rd. Crawl RH11 200 E6
Arthur Rd. Horsh RH13 217 D1
Arthur Rd. 6 King U T KT2 18 A1
Arthur Rd. M Bourn GU9 125 C1
Arthur Rd. W Barn KT3 39 B4
Arthur Rd. Wimble SW19 20 A5
Arthur Rd. Woki RG11 25 A6
Arthur St. Alder GU11 105 B2
Arthur's Bridge Rd. Horse GU21 69 D2
Artillery Rd. Alder GU11 105 B2
Artillery Rd. Farnb GU11 & GU14 105 D8
Artillery Rd. 7 Guild GU1 109 D1
Artillery Terr. Guild GU1 109 D1
Artington Wlk. Guild GU2 130 C6
Arun Way. Horsh RH13 217 E1
Arundale. King U T KT1 37 D5
Arundel Ave. Ewell KT17 58 B1
Arundel Ave. Merton SM4 39 F5
Arundel Ave. S Croy CR2 62 A1
Arundel Cl. Crawl RH10 202 C6
Arundel Cl. Croy CR0 & CR9 61 B7
Arundel Cl. Hampt TW12 16 B3
Arundel Ct. Beck BR2 44 E7
Arundel House. Croy CR0 61 D5
Arundel House. Dovgn RH2 139 B5
Arundel Rd. Belm SM2 58 F3
Arundel Rd. Dork RH4 136 A7
Arundel Rd. Friml GU15 66 C4
Arundel Rd. Hounsl TW4 4 C4
Arundel Rd. King U T KT1 38 C7
Arundel Rd. Thorn H CR0 42 D3
Arundell Pl. 6 Farnh GU9 125 B2
Arunside. Horsh RH12 217 A1
Arunside Cty Prim Sch. Horsh RH12 217 A2
Ascalon Ct. 19 Streat SW2 21 F8
Aschurch Rd. Croy CR0 42 F2
Ascot Heath Cty Inf Sch. N Asct SL5 8 E1
Ascot Heath Jun Sch. N Asct SL5 8 E1
Ascot House. Penge SE26 23 B2
Ascot Mews. Wallin SM6 60 C2
Ascot Race Course. Ascot SL5 28 F6
Ascot Rd. E Bed TW14 & TW15 14 B6
Ascot Rd. Mitch SW17 21 A2
Ascot Sta. Ascot SL5 29 A5
Ascot Towers. N Asct SL5 28 F7
Ascot Wood. Ascot SL5 29 A6
Asford Gdns. Cobham KT11 73 D3
Ash Church Rd. Ash GU12 106 B2
Ash Cl. Ash GU12 106 B3
Ash Cl. Blckw GU17 64 C5
Ash Cl. Box H KT20 116 C4
Ash Cl. Carsh SM5 59 F8
Ash Cl. Crawl D RH10 204 C8
Ash Cl. King U T KT3 38 D7
Ash Cl. Lingf RH7 164 E5
Ash Cl. Merst RH1 119 C5
Ash Cl. Penge SE20 43 C7
Ash Cl. Pyrf GU22 71 A4
Ash Cl. Woking GU22 89 E7
Ash Combe. Chidd GU8 191 A4
Ash Ct. Ottsh KT16 51 C5
Ash Ct. W Ewell KT19 57 C6
Ash Ct. W Ewell KT19 57 C6
Ash Ct. 2 W Norw SW16 22 A3
Ash Dr. Earls RH1 140 B7
Ash Gr. E Bed TW14 14 E7
Ash Gr. Heston TW5 4 D7
Ash Gr. Penge SE20 43 C7
Ash Gr. Stain TW18 13 C2
Ash Gr. Stough GU2 109 A2
Ash Gr. W Wick BR4 44 C1
Ash Green La E. Ash GU12 127 C8
Ash Green La W. Ash GU12 126 F8
Ash Green La W. Ash GU12 127 C8
Ash Green Rd. Ash GU12 106 C1
Ash Hill Rd. Ash GU12 106 B3
Ash Keys. Crawl RH10 201 E5
Ash La. Elst GU8 148 C2
Ash Lodge. 2 Charlt TW16 14 F1
Ash Lodge Cl. Ash GU12 106 A1
Ash Lodge Dr. Ash GU12 106 A1
Ash Manor Sch. Ash GU12 126 F8
Ash Mews. Epsom KT18 76 E6
Ash Rd. Alder GU12 126 D8
Ash Rd. Cheam SM3 & SM4 39 F1
Ash Rd. Crawl RH10 202 A8
Ash Rd. Croy CR0 63 A8
Ash Rd. Pirb GU24 & GU3 88 A1
Ash Rd. Shep Gn TW17 34 A5
Ash Rd. Woking GU22 89 E7
Ash St. Ash GU12 106 A1
Ash Sta. Ash GU12 106 B2
Ash Tree Cl. Croy BR3 & CR0 43 E3
Ash Tree Cl. Farnb GU14 84 C3
Ash Tree Cl. Grays GU27 189 F1
Ash Tree Cl. 1 Surb KT6 37 E1
Ash Tree Way. Croy CR0 43 E3
Ash Vale. Chidd GU8 191 A5
Ash Vale Cty Fst Sch. Ash V GU12 106 A8
Ash Vale Sta. Ash V GU12 106 A7
Ashbourne. Easth RG12 26 F3
Ashbourne Cl. Ash GU12 106 C3
Ashbourne Cl. Coulsd CR5 79 C1
Ashbourne Rd. Mitch CR4 & SW17 21 A1
Ashbourne Terr. 1 Merton SW19 20 A1
Ashbrook Rd. Old W SL4 11 B8
Ashburnham Pk. Esher KT10 55 C6
Ashburnham Rd. Crawl RH10 202 A4
Ashburnham Rd. Rich TW10 17 B5
Ashburton Ave. Croy CR0 43 B1
Ashburton Cl. Croy CR0 43 A1
Ashburton Gdns. Croy CR0 62 A8
Ashburton Jun & Inf Sch. Croy CR0 43 B3
Ashburton Rd. Croy CR0 & CR9 62 A8
Ashburton Sch. Croy CR0 43 B2
Ashbury Cres. Merrow GU4 110 C3
Ashbury Dr. W Heath GU14 65 A1
Ashby Ave. Chess KT19 & KT9 57 A4
Ashby Ct. Horsh RH13 217 E1
Ashby Grange. 7 Wallin SM6 60 C4
Ashby Way. Harm UB7 3 A7
Ashby Wlk. Thorn H CR0 42 C3
Ashcombe Ave. Surb KT6 37 D2
Ashcombe Par. Old Wok GU22 90 A7
Ashcombe Rd. Dork RH4 115 A1
Ashcombe Rd. Merst RH1 119 C8
Ashcombe Rd. Wallin SM5 60 A4
Ashcombe Rd. Wimble SW19 20 A3
Ashcombe Sch. Dork RH4 115 B1
Ashcombe Sq. King U T KT3 38 C6
Ashcombe Terr. Burgh H KT20 97 B7
Ashcroft. Shalf GU4 130 E2
Ashcroft Pk. Cobham KT11 73 E6
Ashcroft Rd. Chess KT9 56 F7
Ashcroft Rise. Coulsd CR5 79 E3
Ashdale. G Book KT23 94 C1
Ashdale Cl. Stan TW19 13 E6
Ashdale Cl. Twick TW2 16 C8
Ashdale Way. Twick TW2 16 B8
Ashdene Cl. Littlt TW15 14 C1
Ashdene Cres. Ash GU12 106 A3
Ashdene House. Eng Gn TW20 11 C2
Ashdene Rd. Ash GU12 106 A2
Ashdown Ave. Farnb GU14 85 E2
Ashdown Cl. Beck BR3 44 B7
Ashdown Cl. Brack RG12 28 A7
Ashdown Cl. Dovgn RH2 139 B5
Ashdown Dr. Crawl RH10 201 E3
Ashdown Gate. E Grins RH19 185 D2
Ashdown Gdns. Hams Gn CR2 81 B4

Ashdown Pl. Thame D KT7 ... 37 A2
Ashdown Rd. Dovgn RH2 .. 139 B5
Ashdown Rd. Ewell KT17 ..... 77 A6
Ashdown Rd.For Row RH18 206 F2
Ashdown Rd. King U T KT1 .. 37 E7
Ashdown View. E Grins RH19 ..... 205 E7
Ashdown Way. Up Toot SW17 ..... 21 A6
Ashen Gr. Wimble SW19 ..... 20 A6
Ashen Vale. Selsd CR2 ..... 62 D2
Ashenden Rd. Stough GU2 . 108 F1
Ashfield Ave. Felt TW13 ..... 15 B7
Ashfield Cl. Beck BR3 ..... 24 A1
Ashfield Cl. Rich TW10 ..... 17 E7
Ashfields. Reig RH2 ..... 118 B3
Ashford Ave. Ashf TW15 ..... 14 B2
Ashford C of E Fst & Mid Sch. Ashf TW15 ..... 14 B2
Ashford Cl. Ashf TW15 ..... 13 E4
Ashford Cres. Ashf TW15 ..... 13 E5
Ashford High Sch The. Ashf TW15 ..... 13 E5
Ashford Hospl. Stan TW15 ... 13 E6
Ashford Ind Est. Felt TW15 . 14 C4
Ashford Manor Golf Club. Ashf TW15 ..... 13 F2
Ashford Park Cty Prim Sch. Ashf TW15 ..... 13 D4
Ashford Rd. Felt TW13 & TW15 ..... 14 E4
Ashford Rd. Littlt TW15 & TW17 ..... 14 C1
Ashford Rd. Stain TW18 ..... 33 D8
Ashford Rd. Stain TW18 ..... 33 D8
Ashford Sta. Ashf TW15 ..... 13 F5
Ashgrove Rd. Ashf TW15 ..... 14 D3
Ashgrove Rd. Catf BR1 ..... 24 D2
Ashlake Rd. Streat SW16 ..... 21 E4
Ashlea Ct. Warlgm CR6 ..... 81 A1
Ashleigh Ave. Thor L TW20 .. 12 C1
Ashleigh Cl. Horley RH6 ..... 160 F3
Ashleigh Ct. Penge SE26 ..... 23 B2
Ashleigh Gdns. Sutton SM1 . 59 B8
Ashleigh House. Mortl SW14 . 7 E4
Ashleigh Point. 8 For Hil SE26 ..... 23 D5
Ashleigh Rd. Horsh RH12 ... 217 C4
Ashleigh Rd. Mortl SW14 ..... 7 E4
Ashleigh Rd. Penge SE20 ..... 43 B6
Ashley Ave. Epsom KT18 ..... 76 D6
Ashley Ave. Morden SM4 ..... 40 A4
Ashley Cl. Friml GU16 ..... 86 A6
Ashley Cl. L Book KT23 ..... 93 F2
Ashley Cl. Oat Pk KT12 & KT13 ..... 34 F1
Ashley Ct. 5 Epsom KT18 ..... 76 D6
Ashley Ct. Knaph GU21 ..... 68 F1
Ashley Ctr. Epsom KT18 ..... 76 D6
Ashley Dr. Banstd SM7 ..... 78 A5
Ashley Dr. Blckw GU17 ..... 64 C4
Ashley Dr. Hounsl TW7 ..... 5 E8
Ashley Dr. Twick TW2 ..... 16 B7
Ashley Dr. Walt O T KT12 ..... 54 A7
Ashley Gdns. Rich TW10 ..... 17 D6
Ashley Gdns. Shalf GU4 ..... 130 F2
Ashley House. Farnc GU7 .. 150 E8
Ashley Inf Sch. Walt O T KT12 ..... 35 A1
Ashley La. Croy CR0 ..... 61 B6
Ashley Park Ave. Walt O T KT12 ..... 53 F8
Ashley Park Cres. Walt O T KT12 ..... 35 A1
Ashley Park Rd. Walt O T KT12 ..... 54 A7
Ashley Rd. Epsom KT18 ..... 76 E4
Ashley Rd. Farnb GU14 ..... 85 D4
Ashley Rd. Hampt TW12 ..... 36 A8
Ashley Rd. Knaph GU21 ..... 68 F1
Ashley Rd. Rich TW9 ..... 6 E4
Ashley Rd. Thame D KT7 ..... 36 F3
Ashley Rd. Thorn H CR7 ..... 41 F5
Ashley Rd. Walt O T KT12 ... 54 A8
Ashley Rd. Westc RH4 ..... 135 C6
Ashley Rd. Wimble SW19 ..... 20 B2
Ashley Rise. Walt O T KT12 .. 54 A7
Ashley Way. W End GU24 ..... 67 D6
Ashling Rd. Croy CR0 & CR9 . 43 A1
Ashlyn's Pk. Cobham KT11 ... 73 E6
Ashlyns Way. Chess KT9 ..... 56 D4
Ashmead Rd. E Bed TW14 ..... 15 A7
Ashmere Ave. Beck BR3 ..... 44 D7
Ashmere Cl. Cheam SM3 ..... 58 D5
Ashmill Ct. Thorn H CR0 ..... 42 C3
Ashmore Ct. Heston TW5 ..... 5 A8
Ashmore House. Crawl RH11 ..... 181 D1
Ashmore La. Bigg H BR2 & TN16 ..... 83 C8
Ashmore La. Rusper RH12 . 199 C6
Ashridge. W Heath GU14 ..... 84 F7
Ashridge Gn. 3 Brack RG12 27 B8
Ashridge Rd. Woki RG11 ..... 25 D8
Ashridge Way. Ashf TW16 ..... 15 A2
Ashridge Way. Merton SM4 & SW20 ..... 39 F5
Ashstead La. Godal GU7 ..... 150 C2
Ashstead Sta. Ashtd KT21 ..... 75 E3
Ashtead Ct. 15 Putney SW19 ..... 19 D7
Ashtead Hospl The. Ashtd KT21 ..... 95 E8
Ashtead La. Godal GU7 ..... 150 D2
Ashtead Park (London Freemen's Sch). Ashtd KT21 ..... 96 A8
Ashtead Woods Rd. Ashtd KT21 ..... 75 C3
Ashton Cl. Cheam SM1 ..... 59 A6
Ashton Cl. Hersh KT12 ..... 54 B4
Ashton Ct. Beck BR3 ..... 43 F8
Ashton Gdns. Hounsl TW4 ..... 4 F3
Ashton House. Rhampt SW15 ..... 19 B8
Ashton Rd. 2 Woking GU21 68 F2
Ashtree Ave. Mitch CR4 ..... 40 D7
Ashtree Ct. Ashf TW15 ..... 14 B3
Ashtrees. Cran GU6 ..... 174 E1
Ashurst. 3 Epsom KT18 ..... 76 D6
Ashurst Cl. Horsh RH12 ..... 218 A5
Ashurst Cl. Kenley CR8 ..... 80 D4
Ashurst Cl. Penge SE20 ..... 43 B8
Ashurst Dr. Box H KT20 ..... 116 B5
Ashurst Dr. Shep Gn TW17 ... 33 E5
Ashurst Dr. Worth RH10 ..... 202 D6
Ashurst Rd. Ash V GU12 ..... 105 F4
Ashurst Rd. Tadw KT20 ..... 97 C6
Ashurst Wlk. Croy CR0 ..... 62 B8
Ashurstwood Abbey. Ash W RH19 ..... 206 E6
Ashurstwood Cty Prim Sch. Ash W RH19 ..... 206 E6
Ashvale Rd. Up Toot SW17 .. 20 F3
Ashview Cl. Ashf TW15 ..... 13 E3
Ashview Gdns. Ashf TW15 ..... 13 E3
Ashville Way. Woki RG11 ..... 25 A5
Ashway Ctr. 3 King U T KT2 37 E8
Ashwell Ave. Camb GU15 ..... 65 F6
Ashwell Ct. Ashf TW15 ..... 13 E6
Ashwindam Ct. 1 Knaph GU21 ..... 68 F1
Ashwood. 5 Crawl RH11 . 201 D5
Ashwood. Warlgm CR6 ..... 101 C7
Ashwood Gdns. New Add CR0 ..... 63 C4
Ashwood Pk. 6 Belm SM2 .. 59 A3
Ashwood Pk. Fetch KT22 ..... 94 C4
Ashwood Pk. Woking GU22 .. 70 A1
Ashwood Rd. Eng Gn TW20 . 11 B2
Ashwood Rd. Woking GU22 . 70 A1
Ashworth Pl. Stough GU2 ... 108 F1
Aslett St. Wands SW18 ..... 20 C8
Asmar Cl. Coulsd CR5 ..... 79 E4
Aspen Cl. Merrow GU4 ..... 110 D4
Aspen Cl. Stain TW18 ..... 12 F5
Aspen Cl. Stk D'A KT11 ..... 73 E3
Aspen Ct. Rich TW9 ..... 7 A7
Aspen Gdns. Mitch CR4 ..... 41 A4
Aspen House Sch. Streat SW2 ..... 21 F8
Aspen Sq. Oat Pk KT13 ..... 53 D7
Aspen Way. Horsh RH12 ..... 217 E4
Aspen Way. Nork KT17 ..... 77 D5
Aspin Way. Blckw GU17 ..... 64 B5
Aspinall House. Streat SW12 21 E7
Asquith House. Banstd SM7 77 F4
Assembly Wlk. Carsh SM5 ... 40 E2
Assher Rd. Hersh KT12 ..... 54 E7
Assheton-Bennett House. 15 King U T KT6 ..... 37 E4
Astleham Way. Littlt TW17 .. 33 E6
Astley House. 8 W Norw SE27 ..... 22 C4
Aston Cl. Ashtd KT21 ..... 75 C1
Aston Ct. Crawl RH11 ..... 201 B1
Aston Gn. Cranf TW5 ..... 4 C5
Aston Rd. Clayg KT10 ..... 55 E5
Aston Rd. Merton SW20 ..... 39 C7
Aston Way. Epsom KT18 ..... 76 F3
Astonville St. Wands SW18 . 20 A7
Astor Cl. Addl KT15 ..... 52 D6
Astor Cl. King U T KT2 ..... 18 B2
Astoria Mansions. 18 Streat SW16 ..... 21 E5
Astoria Par. Streat SW16 ..... 21 E5
Astra Bsns Ctr. Salfs RH1 .. 161 A7
Astra Mead. Wink RG12 ..... 8 B2
Atalanta Cl. Purley CR8 ..... 61 A1
Atbara Ct. Tedd TW11 ..... 17 B2
Atbara Rd. Tedd TW11 ..... 17 B2
Atcham Rd. Islew TW3 ..... 5 C3
Atfield Gr. Windl GU20 ..... 48 D4
Atheldene Rd. Wands SW18 20 C7
Athelney Prim Sch. Catf SE6 24 A5
Athelney St. Catf SE6 ..... 24 A5
Athelstan Cl. Worth RH10 .. 202 E6
Athelstan House. King U T KT1 ..... 37 F5
Athelstan House Sch. Hampt TW12 ..... 36 A8
Athelstan Rd. King U T KT1 .. 37 F5
Athena Cl. King U T KT1 ... 37 F6
Atherfield Hse.Dovgn RH1 . 139 C6
Atherfield Rd. Woodh RH1 . 139 C6
Atherley Way. Twick TW4 ... 15 F8
Atherton Cl. Shalf GU4 ..... 130 E3
Atherton Cl. Stan TW19 ..... 2 D1
Atherton Dr. Wimble SW19 . 19 D4
Atherton House. S Croy CR2 61 E4
Athlone. Clayg KT10 ..... 55 E4
Athlone Rd. Streat SW2 ..... 22 A8
Atholl House. 7 Redh RH1 118 F1
Atkins Cl. Woking GU21 ..... 69 A1
Atkins Dr. W Wick BR4 ..... 63 D8
Atkins Rd. Streat SW4 & SW12 ..... 21 D8
Atkinson Ct. Horley RH6 ... 161 B2
Atkinson Morley's Hospl. Wimble SW20 ..... 19 B1
Atlanta Ct. S Norw CR7 ..... 42 C6
Atrebatti Rd. Sandh GU15 & GU17 ..... 45 C1
Attfield Cl. Ash GU12 ..... 105 F1
Attleborough Ct. Dulw SE21 23 B6
Attlee House. 5 Crawl RH11 ..... 201 B2
Attwood Cl. Hams Gn CR2 ... 81 B5
Atwater Cl. Streat SW2 ..... 22 A7
Atwood. L Book KT23 ..... 93 E3
Atwood Ave. Rich TW9 ..... 7 A5
Atwood House. Dulw SE21 .. 22 E5
Aubyn Hill. W Norw SE27 ... 22 D4
Auchinleck Ct. Crawl D RH10 ..... 204 B7
Auchinleck Way. Alder GU11 ..... 104 E2
Auckland Cl. Crawl RH11 .. 181 D1
Auckland Cl. S Norw SE19 ... 42 F8
Auckland Gdns. S Norw SE19 42 F8
Auckland Hill. W Norw SE27 22 C4
Auckland Rd. Cater CR3 ..... 100 E5
Auckland Rd. King U T KT1 .. 37 F5
Auckland Rd. S Norw SE19 & SE25 ..... 42 F8
Auckland Rise. S Norw SE19 42 E8
Audley Cl. Addl KT15 ..... 52 B5
Audley Ct. Surb KT5 ..... 37 F3
Audley Ct. Twick TW2 ..... 16 D5
Audley Cty Prim Sch. Whytlf CR3 ..... 100 F6
Audley Dr. Hams Gn CR2 & CR6 ..... 81 C4
Audley Firs. Hersh KT12 ..... 54 C6
Audley House. Addl KT15 ..... 52 B5
Audley Pl. Belm SM2 ..... 59 B3
Audley Rd. Rich TW10 ..... 6 F2
Audley Way. N Asct SL5 ..... 28 D6
Audrey Cl. W Wick BR3 ..... 44 B3
Audric Cl. King U T KT2 ..... 38 A8
Augur Cl. Stain TW18 ..... 12 F3
August La. Farl Gn GU5 ..... 153 D7
Augusta Cl. E Mole KT8 ..... 35 F6
Augusta Rd. Twick TW2 ..... 16 C6
Augustine Cl. Poyle SL3 ..... 1 E4
Augustus Cl. Brent TW8 ..... 6 D7
Augustus Ct. Hounsl TW3 ..... 5 C3
Augustus Ct. 8 Putney SW19 19 E7
Augustus Ct. S Norw SE19 ... 22 E1
Augustus Ct. Streat SW16 ... 21 D6
Augustus Gdns. Friml GU15 . 66 C5
Augustus Rd. Putney SW19 . 19 E7
Aultone Way. Carsh SM5 ..... 59 F7
Aultone Way. Sutton SM1 ..... 59 C8
Aurelia Gdns. Thorn H CR7 .. 41 F3
Aurelia Rd. Thorn H CR0 & CR7 & CR9 ... 41 F3
Auriol Cl. Worc Pk KT19 ..... 57 E7
Auriol Park Rd. Worc Pk KT19 & KT4 ..... 57 E7
Aurum Cl. Horley RH6 ..... 161 B2
Austen Cl. E Grins RH19 ..... 185 B1
Austen Rd. Guild GU1 ..... 130 F8
Austen Rd. W Heath GU14 ... 85 A6
Austin Cl. Coulsd CR8 ..... 80 B1
Austin Cl. For Hil SE23 & SE6 23 F8
Austin Cl. Twick TW1 ..... 6 C2
Austin House. 19 King U T KT6 ..... 37 E4
Austin's Cotts. 10 Farnh GU9 ..... 125 B2
Austyn Gdns. Tolw KT5 ..... 38 B1
Autumn Dr. Belm SM2 ..... 59 B2
Avalon Cl. Merton SW20 ..... 39 E7
Avarn Rd. Up Toot SW17 ..... 20 F2
Avebury. Easth RG12 ..... 27 A3
Avebury Rd. Merton SW19 ... 39 F8
Aveley La. M Bourn GU10 & GU9 ..... 146 C7
Aveling Cl. Purley CR8 ..... 79 F6
Aveling Cl. Worth RH10 ..... 202 C4
Aven Cl. Cran GU6 ..... 174 E2
Avening Rd. Wands SW18 ... 20 A8
Avening Terr. Wands SW18 . 20 A8
Avenue C. Chert KT15 ..... 52 E7
Avenue Cl. Cranf TW5 ..... 4 B6
Avenue Cl. Tadw KT20 ..... 97 B5
Avenue Cres. Cranf TW5 ..... 4 B7
Avenue Ct. Penge SE20 ..... 43 C8
Avenue Ct. Tadw KT20 ..... 97 B4
Avenue De Cagny. Pirb GU24 ..... 87 F5
Avenue Elmers. King U T KT6 37 E4
Avenue Gdns. Cranf TW5 ..... 4 B7
Avenue Gdns. Horley RH6 .. 161 C2
Avenue Gdns. Mortl SW14 ..... 7 E4
Avenue Gdns. S Norw SE25 . 43 A7
Avenue Gdns. Tedd TW11 ..... 16 F2
Avenue One. Addl KT15 ..... 52 E6
Avenue Park Rd. W Norw SE21 & SE27 ..... 22 B6
Avenue Prim Sch The. Belm SM2 ..... 59 A1
Avenue Rd. Banstd SM7 ..... 78 B4
Avenue Rd. Belm SM2 ..... 59 A1
Avenue Rd. Cater CR3 ..... 100 E5
Avenue Rd. Cobham KT11 .... 73 D3
Avenue Rd. Cran GU6 ..... 174 F1
Avenue Rd. Egham TW18 ..... 12 D3
Avenue Rd. Epsom KT18 ..... 76 D5
Avenue Rd. Farnb GU14 ..... 85 D3
Avenue Rd. Felt TW13 ..... 14 F5
Avenue Rd. Graysh GU26 ... 188 C3
Avenue Rd. Hampt TW12 ..... 36 B8
Avenue Rd. Hounsl TW7 ..... 5 F6
Avenue Rd. King U T KT1 ..... 37 E6
Avenue Rd. Mitch SW16 ..... 41 D7
Avenue Rd. New Mal KT3 ..... 38 E5
Avenue Rd. S Norw SE25 ..... 43 A7
Avenue Rd. S Norw BR3 & SE20 ..... 43 D8
Avenue Rd. Tats TN16 ..... 103 E7
Avenue Rd. Tedd TW11 ..... 17 A2
Avenue Rd. Wallin SM6 ..... 60 C3
Avenue Rd. Wimble SW20 ... 39 B7
Avenue South. Surb KT5 ..... 38 A2
Avenue Sucy. Camb GU15 .... 65 B4
Avenue Terr. King U T KT3 ... 38 C6
Avenue The. Alder GU11 & GU12 ..... 126 C7
Avenue The. Beck BR3 ..... 44 C8
Avenue The. Belm SM2 ..... 58 F2
Avenue The. Bigg H TN16 .. 103 F5
Avenue The. Brock RH3 & RH5 ..... 116 A1
Avenue The. Camb GU15 ..... 65 B5
Avenue The. Chobh GU24 ..... 50 A2
Avenue The. Clayg KT10 ..... 55 E5
Avenue The. Compt GU3 & GU7 ..... 129 C1
Avenue The. Coulsd CR5 ..... 79 D4
Avenue The. Cranf TW5 ..... 4 A6
Avenue The. Crowth RG11 ... 45 B5
Avenue The. Dorman RH19 186 B6
Avenue The. Egham TW20 ... 12 B4
Avenue The. Ewh GU6 ..... 175 E6
Avenue The. Godal GU7 ..... 150 F2
Avenue The. Graysh GU26 188 D3
Avenue The. Hampt TW12 ... 15 F2
Avenue The. Horley RH6 ..... 160 F2
Avenue The. Hounsl TW3 ..... 5 B2
Avenue The. Islew TW1 ..... 6 C2
Avenue The. Lhtwat GU18 ..... 48 A1
Avenue The. N Asct SL5 ..... 8 F1
Avenue The. 4 New Mal KT4 ..... 39 A1
Avenue The. Oxsh KT10 & KT22 ..... 74 F8
Avenue The. Rich TW9 ..... 6 F5
Avenue The. Rowl GU10 ..... 145 F3
Avenue The. S Croy CR0 ..... 61 E7
Avenue The. S Nutf RH1 ..... 140 E6
Avenue The. Shottm GU27 . 207 F7
Avenue The. Stain TW18 ..... 33 B8
Avenue The. Stonel KT17 & SM3 ..... 58 C3
Avenue The. Sunby TW16 .... 35 B7
Avenue The. Surb KT5 ..... 37 F3
Avenue The. Tadw KT20 ..... 97 B5
Avenue The. Twick TW1 ..... 6 B2
Avenue The. W Wick BR4 ..... 44 E2
Avenue The. Whytlf CR3 ... 101 A8
Avenue The. Woodhm KT15 . 52 A1
Avenue The. Worc Pk KT4 .... 57 F8
Avenue The. Worpl GU3 ..... 88 E1
Avenue Three. Chert KT15 ... 52 E7
Avenue Two. Addl KT15 ..... 52 E6
Averil Gr. S Norw SW16 ..... 22 B2
Avern Gdns. E Mole KT8 ..... 36 B5
Avern Rd. E Mole KT8 ..... 36 B5
Avery Ct. Penge SE20 ..... 23 B1
Aviary Rd. Pyrf GU22 ..... 71 A3
Aviary Way. Crawl D RH10 . 184 C1
Aviemore Cl. Beck BR3 ..... 43 F4
Aviemore Way. Beck BR3 .... 43 E4
Avington Cl. Guild GU1 ..... 109 E1
Avington Gr. Penge SE20 ..... 23 C1
Avoca Rd. Up Toot SW17 ..... 21 A4
Avocet Cres. Sandh GU15 .... 64 E8
Avon Cl. Ash GU12 ..... 105 F1
Avon Cl. Row Tn KT15 ..... 52 A4
Avon Cl. Sutton SM1 ..... 59 C6
Avon Cl. W Heath GU14 ..... 84 E7
Avon Cl. Worc Pk KT4 ..... 58 A8
Avon House. 9 Redh RH1 . 118 F2
Avon Rd. Ashf TW16 ..... 14 F1
Avon Rd. M Bourn GU9 ..... 125 C1
Avon Wlk. Crawl RH11 ..... 200 F5
Avondale. Ash V GU12 ..... 105 F7
Avondale Ave. Hinch W KT10 56 A7
Avondale Ave. New Mal KT4 38 F1
Avondale Ave. Stain TW18 ... 12 F1
Avondale Cl. Hersh KT12 ..... 54 C5
Avondale Cl. Horley RH6 ... 161 A5
Avondale Ct. Sutton SM2 ..... 59 C3
Avondale Gdns. Hounsl TW4 . 4 F2
Avondale High. Cater CR3 101 A6
Avondale House. 6 Mortl SW14 ..... 7 D4
Avondale Rd. Alder GU11 .. 126 B8
Avondale Rd. Ashf TW15 & TW19 ..... 13 D5
Avondale Rd. Broml BR1 ..... 24 F2
Avondale Rd. Catf BR1 ..... 24 F2
Avondale Rd. Mortl SW14 ..... 7 D4
Avondale Rd. S Croy CR2 ..... 61 C4
Avondale Rd. Wimble SW19 20 B3
Avonmore Ave. Guild GU1 . 109 F2
Avonwick Rd. Hounsl TW3 ..... 5 B5
Avro Way. Byfl KT13 ..... 52 E1
Avro Way. Wallin SM6 ..... 60 E3
Axbridge. Brack RG12 ..... 27 E4
Axes La. Salfs RH1 ..... 140 D2
Axford House. Streat SW2 ... 22 B7
Axwood. Woodc KT18 ..... 76 C4
Aycliffe Ct. King U T KT1 ..... 38 A7
Ayebridges Ave. Egham TW20 ..... 12 C1
Ayjay Cl. Alder GU11 ..... 126 A7
Aylesbury Ct. Sutton SM1 .... 59 C7
Aylesford Ave. Beck BR3 ..... 43 E4
Aylesworth Spur. Old W SL4 11 B8
Aylett Rd. Croy SE25 ..... 43 B5
Aylett Rd. Islew TW7 ..... 5 E5
Ayling Ct. Heath E GU9 ..... 125 F7
Ayling Hill. Alder GU11 ..... 104 F1
Ayling La. Alder GU11 ..... 125 F8
Aylward Rd. For Hil SE23 ..... 23 D6
Aylward Rd. Merton SW20 ... 39 F6
Aymer Cl. Egham TW18 ..... 32 E8
Aymer Dr. Egham TW18 ..... 32 E8
Aysgarth. Easth RG12 ..... 27 A3
Aysgarth Ct. Sutton SM1 ..... 59 B7
Aysgarth Rd. Dulw SE21 ..... 22 E8
Ayshe Court Dr. Horsh RH13 ..... 217 E3
Azalea Ct. Woking GU22 ..... 89 D8
Azalea Dr. Shottm GU27 ..... 207 F8
Azalea Way. Friml GU15 ..... 66 B6
Azelea Ct. Purley CR8 ..... 80 B8

Babbacombe Cl. Chess KT9 . 56 D5
Babbs Mead. Farnh GU9 .... 125 A1
Baber Dr. Felt TW14 ..... 4 C1
Babington Ct. Streat SW16 .. 21 D3
Babington Rd. Streat SW16 . 21 D3
Babylon La. L Kings KT20 & RH2 ..... 118 B8
Bachelor's La. Ockham GU23 92 A3
Back Gn. Hersh KT12 ..... 54 C4
Back La. Binst GU10 ..... 166 B8
Back La. Brent TW8 ..... 6 D8
Back La. E Clan GU4 ..... 111 D4
Back La. Elst GU8 ..... 148 D4
Back La. Plaist RH14 ..... 211 E2
Back La. Rich TW10 ..... 17 C6
Back La. Worth RH10 ..... 203 D1
Back Rd. Tedd TW11 ..... 16 E2
Bacon Cl. Sandh GU15 ..... 64 D6
Bacon La. Head Dn GU10 .... 167 C3
Badajos Rd. Alder GU11 ..... 104 F3
Baden Cl. Stain TW18 ..... 13 B1
Baden Dr. Horley RH6 ..... 160 E4

Baden Powell Cl. Surb KT6 ... 56 F8
Baden Rd. Stough GU2 ... 109 B3
Bader Cl. Kenley CR8 ... 80 D4
Bader Ct. W Heath GU14 ... 84 F8
Badger Cl. Felt TW13 ... 15 B5
Badger Cl. Hounsl TW4 ... 4 C4
Badger Cl. Stough GU2 ... 109 B4
Badger Ct. Rowl GU10 ... 146 A5
Badger Dr. Lhtwat GU18 ... 48 A1
Badger Way. Crond GU10 ... 124 D8
Badgers Cl. Ashf TW15 ... 13 F3
Badgers Cl. Farnc GU7 ... 150 D8
Badgers Cl. Horsh RH12 ... 217 F6
Badgers Cl. Woking GU21 ... 69 C1
Badgers Copse. Friml GU15 ... 65 E4
Badgers Copse. Worc Pk KT4 ... 57 F8
Badgers Cross. Milf GU8 ... 149 E1
Badgers Ct. [4] Epsom KT17 ... 76 E6
Badgers Hill. Vir W GU25 ... 31 C4
Badgers Hollow. Farnc GU7 ... 150 D6
Badgers La. Warlgm CR6 ... 101 C8
Badgers Lodge. [5] Epsom KT17 ... 76 E6
Badgers Way. Brack RG12 ... 27 F7
Badgers Way. E Grins RH19 ... 185 F2
Badgers Way. Loxwd RH14 ... 213 A4
Badgers Wlk. King U T KT3 ... 38 E7
Badgers Wlk. Purley CR8 ... 79 C8
Badgers Wlk. Whytlf CR3 ... 80 F1
Badgers Wood. Cater CR3 ... 100 D2
Badgerwood Dr. Friml GU16 ... 65 D2
Badingham Dr. Fetch KT22 ... 94 E4
Badminton Rd. Balham SW12 ... 21 A8
Badshot Lea Cty Inf Sch. Farnh GU9 ... 126 A6
Badshot Lea Rd. Farnh GU11 & GU9 ... 126 A6
Badshot Pk. Farnh GU9 ... 126 A6
Bagden Hill. G Book KT23 ... 114 D5
Bagot Cl. Ashtd KT21 ... 75 F3
Bagshot Cty Fst Sch. Bagsh GU19 ... 47 E2
Bagshot Gn. Bagsh GU19 ... 47 E3
Bagshot Rd. Ascot SL5 ... 29 C2
Bagshot Rd. Brack GU20 & SL5 ... 48 A8
Bagshot Rd. Brookw GU24 ... 88 C5
Bagshot Rd. Easth RG12 ... 27 C4
Bagshot Rd. Eng Gn TW20 ... 11 C2
Bagshot Rd. Knaph GU21 ... 88 C5
Bagshot Rd. Pirb GU3 ... 88 C5
Bagshot Rd. W End GU24 ... 68 B8
Bagshot Rd. Woking GU22 & GU24 ... 88 C5
Bagshot Sta. Bagsh GU19 ... 47 E4
Bahram Rd. Epsom KT19 ... 57 D1
Baigents La. Windl GU20 ... 48 D4
Bailes La. Flexf GU3 ... 107 D2
Bailes La. Normdy GU3 ... 107 D3
Bailey Cl. Friml GU16 ... 85 D8
Bailey Cl. Horsh RH12 ... 217 F7
Bailey House. [11] Penge SE26 ... 23 B3
Bailey Pl. Penge SE26 ... 23 D2
Bailey Rd. Westc RH4 ... 135 C6
Baileys Cl. Blckw GU17 ... 64 C4
Bailing Hill. Warn RH12 ... 216 E7
Baillie Rd. Guild GU1 ... 130 F8
Bain Ave. Camb GU15 ... 65 B2
Baines Cl. Croy CR0 ... 61 D5
Bainton Mead. Woking GU21 ... 69 A2
Baird Cl. Crawl RH10 ... 182 A1
Baird Dr. Wood S V GU3 ... 108 B2
Baird Gdns. Dulw SE19 & SE21 ... 22 E4
Baird Rd. Farnb GU14 ... 85 C6
Bakeham La. Eng Gn TW20 ... 11 D1
Bakehouse Barn Cl. Horsh RH12 ... 217 E7
Bakehouse Rd. Horley RH6 ... 161 A5
Baker Cl. Crawl RH10 ... 201 D4
Baker La. Mitch CR4 ... 41 A7
Baker St. Weyb KT13 ... 53 B6
Baker's Cl. Lingf RH7 ... 164 E5
Baker's La. Lingf RH7 ... 164 E4
Bakers Ct. S Norw SE25 ... 42 E6
Bakers End. Merton SW20 ... 39 E7
Bakers Mead. Tyl Gn RH9 ... 121 C6
Bakers Way. Capel RH5 ... 178 C5
Bakewell Dr. King U T KT3 ... 38 E7
Balaam House. Sutton SM1 ... 59 A6
Balaclava Rd. King U T KT6 ... 37 C2
Balchins La. Westc RH4 ... 135 B6
Balcombe Ct. Crawl RH10 ... 202 D7
Balcombe Gdns.Horley RH6 ... 161 C2
Balcombe House. [3] Streat SW2 ... 21 F7
Balcombe Rd. Crawl RH10 & RH6 ... 182 D5
Balcombe Rd. Horley RH6 ... 161 B2
Balcombe Rd. Worth RH10 ... 202 D5
Baldreys. M Bourn GU9 ... 146 A8
Baldry Gdns. Streat SW16 ... 21 F2
Baldwin Cres. Merrow GU4 ... 110 C3
Baldwin House. [15] Streat SW2 ... 22 A7
Baldwins Cty Prim Sch. E Grins RH19 ... 185 D3
Balfont Cl. Sander CR2 ... 81 A6
Balfour Ave. Westfd GU22 ... 89 F5
Balfour Cres. Easth RG12 ... 27 B4
Balfour Gdns. For Row RH18 ... 206 E1
Balfour Rd. Croy SE25 ... 43 A5
Balfour Rd. Hounsl TW3 ... 5 B4
Balfour Rd. Merton SW19 ... 20 B1
Balfour Rd. Wallin SM5 ... 59 F3
Balfour Rd. Weyb KT13 ... 53 A6
Balgowan Cl. New Mal KT3 ... 38 E5
Balgowan Prim Sch. Beck BR3 ... 43 E7
Balgowan Rd. Beck BR3 ... 43 F7
Balham Gr. Balham SW12 ... 21 A8
Balham High Rd. Balham SW12 & SW17 ... 21 A7
Balham High Rd. Up Toot SW12 ... 21 A7
Balham Hill. Balham SW12 ... 21 B8
Balham New Rd. Balham SW12 ... 21 B8
Balham Park Mansions. Up Toot SW12 ... 20 F7
Balham Park Rd. Balham SW12 & SW17 ... 21 A7
Balham Sta. Balham SW12 ... 21 B7
Balham Station Rd. Balham SW12 ... 21 B7
Balintore Ct. [8] Sandh GU15 ... 64 D8
Ball and Wicket La. Heath E GU9 ... 125 C7
Ballands N The. Fetch KT22 ... 94 E5
Ballands' S The. Fetch KT22 ... 94 E4
Ballantyne Dr. Kings KT20 ... 97 F6
Ballantyne Rd. W Heath GU14 ... 85 A6
Ballard Cl. King U T KT2 ... 18 D1
Ballard Ct. Camb GU15 ... 66 A8
Ballard Rd. Camb GU15 ... 66 A8
Ballards Farm Rd. S Croy CR2 ... 62 A4
Ballards Gn. Burgh H KT20 ... 97 E8
Ballards La. Limps RH8 ... 123 C6
Ballards Rise. S Croy CR2 ... 62 A4
Ballards Way. S Croy CR0 & CR2 ... 62 B4
Ballater Rd. S Croy CR2 ... 61 F5
Ballencrieff Rd. Sunnin SL5 ... 29 F2
Ballfield Rd. Farnc GU7 ... 150 E6
Ballina St. For Hil SE23 ... 23 D8
Balliol Cl. Crawl RH10 ... 182 D1
Balliol Way. Sandh GU15 ... 45 E1
Balloch Rd. Catf SE6 ... 24 D6
Balloon Rd. Farnb GU14 ... 85 B2
Ballsdown. Chidd GU8 ... 191 A3
Balmain Ct. Hounsl TW3 ... 5 B6
Balmoral. E Grins RH19 ... 206 A8
Balmoral Ave. Beck BR3 ... 43 E5
Balmoral Cres. E Mole KT8 ... 36 A6
Balmoral Cres. Hale GU9 ... 125 B6
Balmoral Ct. [11] Belm SM2 ... 59 A3
Balmoral Ct. [6] Crawl RH11 ... 201 B2
Balmoral Ct. N Cheam KT4 ... 58 B8
Balmoral Ct. W Norw SE27 ... 22 C4
Balmoral Dr. Friml GU16 ... 85 F8
Balmoral Dr. Mayb GU22 ... 70 C3
Balmoral Grange.Stain TW18 ... 33 B7
Balmoral Rd. Ash GU12 ... 106 B4
Balmoral Rd. King U T KT1 ... 37 F5
Balmoral Rd. N Cheam KT4 ... 58 B8
Balmoral Way. Belm SM2 ... 59 A1
Balquhain Cl. Ashtd KT21 ... 75 D2
Baltic Cl. Mitch SW19 ... 20 D1
Balvernie Gr. Wands SW18 ... 20 A8
Bamford Rd. Catf BR1 ... 24 D3
Bampfylde Cl. Wallin SM6 ... 60 C7
Bampton Rd. For Hil SE23 ... 23 D5
Bampton Way. Woking GU21 ... 69 A2
Banavie Gdns. Beck BR3 ... 44 C8
Banbury. Brack RG12 ... 27 E2
Banbury Cl. Friml GU16 ... 86 A7
Banbury Ct. [8] Belm SM2 ... 59 A3
Bancroft Cl. Ashf TW15 ... 14 A3
Bancroft Ct. Reig RH2 ... 118 B1
Bancroft Rd. Reig RH2 ... 118 B1
Bancroft Rd. Worth RH10 ... 202 D5
Band La. [1] Egham TW20 ... 12 A3
Banders Rise. Merrow GU1 ... 110 C2
Bandon Hill Prim Sch. Wallin SM6 ... 60 D4
Bandon Rise. Wallin SM6 ... 60 D5
Banfor Ct. Wallin SM6 ... 60 C4
Bank Ave. Mitch CR4 ... 40 D7
Bank La. Crawl RH11 ... 201 D6
Bank La. King U T KT2 ... 17 E1
Bank La. Rhampt SW15 ... 7 E2
Bank Mews. Sutton SM1 ... 59 C4
Bank Rd. Farnb GU11 ... 105 D5
Bank Willow. Rich TW10 ... 17 B5
Bank's La.Effing KT11 & KT24 ... 93 B5
Bankfoot Rd. Catf BR1 ... 24 E4
Bankhurst Rd. For Hil SE4 & SE6 ... 23 F8
Banks House. Hounsl TW7 ... 5 E5
Banks Rd. Crawl RH10 ... 202 C5
Banks Way. Burph GU1 ... 109 F4
Bankside. Heath E GU9 ... 125 F7
Bankside. S Croy CR2 ... 61 F4
Bankside. Woking GU21 ... 69 B1
Bankside Cl. Bigg H TN16 ... 83 C1
Bankside Cl. Carsh SM5 ... 59 E4
Bankside Cl. Elst GU8 ... 148 D3
Bankside Cl. Islew TW7 ... 5 F3
Bankside Dr. Hinch W KT7 ... 56 B8
Bankside Way. [6] W Norw SE19 ... 22 E2
Banning House. [4] Putney SW19 ... 19 D7
Bannister Cl. Streat SW2 ... 22 A7
Bannister Cl. Witley GU8 ... 170 F6
Bannister's Rd. Onsl V GU2 ... 129 F7
Banstead Cty Inf Sch. Banstd SM7 ... 77 F4
Banstead Cty Jun Sch. Banstd SM7 ... 77 F4
Banstead Downs Golf Club. Belm SM2 ... 78 A8
Banstead Rd. Belm SM7 ... 77 D7
Banstead Rd. Carsh SM2 & SM5 ... 59 E3
Banstead Rd. Cater CR3 ... 100 D5
Banstead Rd. E Ewell KT17 ... 77 D7
Banstead Rd. Nork SM7 ... 77 D7
Banstead Rd. Purley CR8 ... 80 A8
Banstead Rd. Sutton SM2 & SM5 ... 59 E3
Banstead Rd S. Sutton SM2 ... 59 D1
Banstead Sta. Banstd SM7 ... 77 F5
Banstead Way. Wallin SM6 ... 60 E5
Barbara Cl. Lo Hall TW17 ... 34 B4
Barber Dr. Cran GU6 ... 174 E4
Barberry Way. Hawley GU17 ... 64 F2
Barbon Cl. Friml GU15 ... 66 D3
Barclay Cl. Fetch KT23 ... 94 B4
Barclay Rd. Croy CR0 & CR9 ... 61 D7
Barcombe Ave. Streat SW2 ... 21 F6
Bardney Rd. Morden SM4 ... 40 B5
Bardolph Ave. New Add CR0 ... 62 F2
Bardolph Rd. Rich TW9 ... 6 F4
Bardon Wlk. Woking GU21 ... 69 B2
Bardsley Cl. S Croy CR0 ... 61 F7
Bardsley Dr. M Bourn GU9 ... 146 A8
Barfield Ct. [9] Redh RH1 ... 119 A3
Barfield Sch. Farnh GU10 ... 126 B3
Barfields. Bletch RH1 ... 120 C2
Barfreston Way. Penge SE20 ... 43 B8
Bargate Cl. New Mal KT3 ... 39 A2
Bargate Ct. [1] Stough GU2 ... 108 E1
Bargate Rise. Ock Rid GU7 ... 150 C4
Barge Cl. Farnb GU11 ... 105 E5
Bargery Rd. Catf SE6 ... 24 B7
Bargrove Cl. [8] Penge SE20 ... 23 A1
Bargrove Cres. For Hil SE6 ... 23 F6
Barham Cl. Weyb KT13 ... 53 C6
Barham Rd. Croy CR0 & CR2 ... 61 C5
Barham Rd. Wimble SW20 ... 19 A1
Barhatch La. Cran GU6 ... 174 F6
Barhatch Rd. Cran GU6 ... 174 F4
Baring Rd. Croy CR0 & CR9 ... 43 A1
Barker Gn. Easth RG12 ... 27 B4
Barker House. Dulw SE21 ... 22 E5
Barker Rd. Chert KT16 ... 32 F2
Barker Wlk. Streat SW16 ... 21 D5
Barkham Rd. Woki RG11 ... 25 A5
Barkhart Dr. Woki RG11 ... 25 C7
Barkhart Gdns. Woki RG11 ... 25 C7
Barkis Mead. Sandh GU15 ... 45 E2
Barley Cl. Crawl RH10 ... 201 D5
Barley Mow Cl. Knaph GU21 ... 68 D2
Barley Mow Ct. Brock RH3 ... 116 C1
Barley Mow Hill. Head Dn GU35 ... 187 A6
Barley Mow La. Knaph GU21 ... 68 D3
Barley Mow Rd. Eng Gn TW20 ... 11 C3
Barley Mow Way. Shep Gn TW17 ... 34 A5
Barleymead. Horley RH6 ... 161 B4
Barlow Cl. Wallin SM6 ... 60 E3
Barlow Rd. Crawl RH11 ... 200 E3
Barlow Rd. Hampt TW12 ... 16 A1
Barmeston Rd. Catf SE6 ... 24 B6
Barmouth Rd. Croy CR0 ... 62 D8
Barn Cl. Ashf TW15 ... 14 B3
Barn Cl. Brack RG12 ... 27 D7
Barn Cl. Camb GU15 ... 65 E6
Barn Cl. Oxsh KT22 ... 74 D4
Barn Cl. Woodc KT18 ... 76 C4
Barn Cl. Woodm SM7 ... 78 D4
Barn Cres. Sander CR8 ... 80 D6
Barn Field. Banstd SM7 ... 78 B5
Barn Meadow La.L Bk KT23 ... 93 F3
Barn Rd. Woodhm KT15 ... 52 B2
Barnard Cl. Friml GU16 ... 85 F8
Barnard Cl. Sunby TW16 ... 15 B1
Barnard Cl. Wallin SM6 ... 60 D3
Barnard Ct. [1] Knaph GU21 ... 68 E1
Barnard Ct. Streat SW16 ... 21 F5
Barnard Gdns. W Barn KT3 ... 39 A5
Barnard Rd. Chelsh CR6 ... 102 B8
Barnard Rd. Mitch CR4 ... 41 A7
Barnards Pl. S Croy CR2 ... 61 B2
Barnato Cl. Byfl KT14 ... 71 E7
Barnby Rd. Knaph GU21 ... 68 D2
Barnes Bridge Sta. Barnes SW13 ... 7 E5
Barnes Cl. Farnb GU14 ... 85 D4
Barnes Ct. S Norw CR7 ... 42 C6
Barnes End. W Barn KT3 ... 39 A4
Barnes High St. Barnes SW13 ... 7 F5
Barnes Hospl. Mortl SW14 ... 7 E4
Barnes Rd. Farnc GU7 ... 150 E8
Barnes Rd. Friml GU16 ... 85 E8
Barnes Wallis Dr. Byfl KT13 & KT14 ... 71 E8
Barnett Cl. Leahd KT22 ... 95 B8
Barnett Cl. Woner GU5 ... 152 C8
Barnett Ct. Brack RG12 ... 27 C7
Barnett Gn. Easth RG12 ... 27 B3
Barnett La. Lhtwat GU18 ... 66 F7
Barnett La. Woner GU5 ... 152 C7
Barnett Row. Jacobs GU4 ... 109 D6
Barnett Wood Cty Inf Sch. Ashtd KT21 ... 75 D2
Barnett Wood La. Ashtd KT21 & KT22 ... 75 D1
Barnett Wood La. Leahd KT22 ... 95 B8
Barnett's Shaw. Oxted RH8 ... 122 D8
Barnfield. Cran GU6 ... 174 E3
Barnfield. New Mal KT3 ... 38 E3
Barnfield Ave. Croy CR0 ... 62 C8
Barnfield Ave. King U T KT2 ... 17 E3
Barnfield Ave. Mitch CR4 ... 41 B6
Barnfield Cl. Coulsd CR5 ... 100 C8
Barnfield Cl. Wands SW17 ... 20 C5
Barnfield Cotts. Dorman RH7 ... 165 A1
Barnfield Gdns. King U T KT2 ... 17 E3
Barnfield Rd. Crawl RH10 & RH11 ... 201 E7
Barnfield Rd. S Croy CR2 ... 61 E2
Barnfield Rd. Tats TN16 ... 103 D6
Barnfield Way. Oxted RH8 ... 123 A2
Barnfield Wood Cl. W Wick BR3 ... 44 D3
Barnfield Wood Rd.Bck BR3 ... 44 D3
Barnhill Ave. Hayes BR2 ... 44 F4
Barnlea Cl. Felt TW13 ... 15 E6
Barnmead. Chobh GU24 ... 49 F1
Barnmead Rd. Penge BR3 ... 43 E8
Barnsbury Cl. New Mal KT3 ... 38 C5
Barnsbury Cres. Tolw KT5 ... 38 C1
Barnsbury Cty Inf & Jun Schs. Woking GU22 ... 89 D6
Barnsbury La. Tolw KT5 ... 38 C1
Barnscroft. W Barn SW20 ... 39 B6
Barnsfold La. Buck Gn RH12 & RH14 ... 213 E6
Barnsford Cres. W End GU24 ... 68 A6
Barnsley Cl. Mytch GU16 ... 86 B2
Barnsnap Cl. Horsh RH12 ... 217 D6
Barnway. Eng Gn TW20 ... 11 C3
Barnwood Cl. Crawl RH10 ... 202 C7
Barnwood Cl. Stough GU3 ... 108 E3
Barnwood Ct. Stough GU2 & GU3 ... 108 E3
Barnwood Rd. Stough GU2 & GU3 ... 108 E3
Barnwood Sch. Stough GU2 ... 108 E2
Barnyard The. Walt o t H KT20 ... 97 A3
Baron Ct. Mitch CR4 ... 40 E5
Baron Gr. Mitch CR4 ... 40 E5
Baron's Hurst. Woodc KT18 ... 76 C3
Baron's Way. Dovgn RH2 ... 139 A5
Baron's Wlk. Croy CR0 ... 43 E3
Barons Ct. Wallin SM6 ... 60 D7
Barons The. Twick TW1 ... 6 B1
Barons Way. Egham TW20 ... 12 D2
Baronsfield Rd. Twick TW1 ... 6 B1
Barossa Rd. Camb GU15 ... 65 D7
Barr Beacon. For Hil SE23 ... 23 C8
Barr's La. Knaph GU21 ... 68 D3
Barracane Dr. Crowth RG11 ... 45 B5
Barrack Path. Knaph GU21 ... 68 F1
Barrack Rd. Alder GU11 ... 105 A2
Barrack Rd. Hounsl TW4 ... 4 E3
Barrack Rd. Stough GU2 ... 109 A4
Barrards Hall. S Croy CR2 ... 80 D8
Barrens Brae. Mayb GU22 ... 70 A1
Barrens Cl. Mayb GU22 ... 90 A8
Barrens Pk. Mayb GU22 ... 90 A8
Barrett Cres. Woki RG11 ... 25 E6
Barrett Rd. Fetch KT22 & KT23 ... 94 D3
Barrhill Rd. Streat SW2 ... 21 E6
Barricane. Woking GU21 ... 89 B8
Barrie Cl. Coulsd CR5 ... 79 C3
Barrie Rd. Heath E GU9 ... 125 A7
Barrihurst La. Crawl GU6 ... 173 D2
Barringer Sq. Up Toot SW17 ... 21 A4
Barrington Ct. Dork RH4 ... 136 A6
Barrington Ct. Stain TW18 ... 12 F2
Barrington Lodge. Weyb KT13 ... 53 C5
Barrington Rd. Cheam SM3 ... 40 A1
Barrington Rd. Crawl RH10 ... 201 D3
Barrington Rd. Dork RH4 ... 136 A6
Barrington Rd. Horsh RH13 ... 217 E2
Barrington Rd. Purley CR8 ... 79 C7
Barrington Wlk. [8] S Norw SE19 ... 22 E2
Barrow Ave. Wallin SM5 ... 59 F3
Barrow Ct. Catf SE6 ... 24 F7
Barrow Green Rd. Oxted RH8 ... 122 C6
Barrow Green Rd. Tand RH9 ... 122 C6
Barrow Hedges Cl. Sutton SM5 ... 59 E3
Barrow Hedges Prim Sch. Sutton SM5 ... 59 E3
Barrow Hedges Way. Sutton SM2 & SM5 ... 59 E3
Barrow Hill. Worc Pk KT4 ... 57 E8
Barrow Hill Cl. Worc Pk KT4 ... 57 E8
Barrow Hills Sch. Witley GU8 ... 170 E4
Barrow Rd. Croy CR0 ... 61 A5
Barrow Rd. Streat SW16 ... 21 D2
Barrowsfield. Sander CR2 ... 81 A7
Barry Cl. Crawl RH10 ... 201 E3
Barry Terr. Ashf TW15 ... 13 F6
Bars The. Guild GU1 ... 130 D8
Barsons Cl. Penge SE20 ... 23 C1
Barston Rd. W Norw SE27 ... 22 C5
Barstow Cres. Streat SW2 ... 21 F7
Bartholomew Cl. Haslem GU27 ... 208 D8
Bartholomew Ct. Dork RH4 ... 136 A6
Bartholomew Way. Horsh RH12 ... 218 A7
Bartlett St. Croy CR0 & CR2 ... 61 D5
Barton Cl. Alder GU11 ... 104 E1
Barton Cl. Row Tn KT15 ... 52 A4
Barton Cl. Shep TW17 ... 34 B3
Barton Cres. E Grins RH19 ... 206 A8
Barton Ct. Beck BR2 ... 44 D6
Barton Gn. King U T KT3 ... 38 D7
Barton Pl. Burph GU1 ... 110 B4
Barton Rd. Bramly GU5 ... 152 A7
Barton The. Cobham KT11 ... 73 D7
Barton Wlk. Crawl RH10 ... 202 B4
Bartons Way. W Heath GU14 ... 84 D7
Barttelot Rd. Horsh RH12 ... 217 D2
Barwell Bsns Pk. Chess KT9 ... 56 D2
Barwood Ave. W Wick BR4 ... 44 B1
Basden Gr. Felt TW13 ... 16 A6
Basemoors. Brack RG12 ... 27 E7
Bashford Way. Crawl RH10 ... 202 D8
Basil Gdns. Croy CR0 ... 43 D1
Basildene Rd. Hounsl TW4 & TW5 ... 4 D4
Basildon Cl. Sutton SM2 ... 59 B2
Basildon Way. Crawl RH11 ... 200 E2
Basing Cl. Thame D KT7 ... 36 F2
Basing Dr. Alder GU11 ... 126 B7
Basing House. Catf SE6 ... 24 A4
Basing Rd. Banstd SM7 ... 77 F4
Basing Way. Thame D KT7 ... 36 F2
Basingfield Rd. Thame D KT7 ... 36 F2
Basinghall Gdns. Sutton SM2 ... 59 B2
Baskerville Rd. Wands SW18 ... 20 E8
Basset Cl. Woodhm KT15 ... 52 C1
Bassett Cl. Friml GU16 ... 85 E8
Bassett Cl. Sutton SM2 ... 59 B2
Bassett Gdns. Hounsl TW7 ... 5 C7
Bassett Rd. Mayb GU22 ... 70 C3
Bassetts Hill. Dorman RH7 ... 165 A2

Bassingham Rd.
Wands SW18 .... 20 C8
Bat and Ball La. Rowl GU10 146 A5
Bat and Ball La.
Wreccl GU10 & GU9 .... 146 A6
Batavia Cl. Sunby TW16 ...... 35 C8
Batavia Rd. Sunby TW16 ...... 35 B8
Batcombe Mead.Brack RG12 27 E2
Bateman Gr. Ash GU12 ...... 126 F8
Batemans Ct. Crawl RH10 .. 202 A3
Bates Cres. Croy CR0 .... 61 A5
Bates Cres. Streat SW16 ...... 21 C1
Bates Wlk. Haw Maw KT15 .... 52 C4
Bateson Way. Sheer GU21 ... 70 C5
Bath Ct. **3** For Hil SE26 ...... 23 A5
Bath House Rd.
Wallin CR0 & CR9 .... 41 E1
Bath Pas. King U T KT1 ...... 37 D7
Bath Rd. Camb GU15 .... 65 D6
Bath Rd.
Cranf TW3 & TW4 & TW5 ..... 4 E5
Bath Rd.
Harl TW6 & UB7 & TW5 ...... 3 D6
Bath Rd. Harm TW6 & UB7 .... 2 E6
Bath Rd.
Hounsl TW3 & TW4 & TW5 .... 4 F5
Bath Rd. Mitch CR4 .... 40 D6
Bath Rd.
Poyle SL3 & UB7 & TW6 ...... 1 E6
Bathgate Rd. Wimble SW19 . 19 D5
Bathurst Ave. Merton SW19 40 B8
Batsworth Rd. Mitch CR4 .... 40 D6
Batt's Cnr. Docken GU10 .... 166 E7
Batten Ave. Knaph GU21 ...... 88 E8
Battenberg Wlk. **10**
W Norw SE19 .... 22 E3
Battersby Rd. Catf SE6 ...... 24 D5
Battle Cl. Wimble SW19 ...... 20 C2
Battlebridge House.
Merst RH1 .... 119 B5
Battlebridge La. Merst RH1 119 B5
Batts Hill. Redh RH1 & RH2 118 E3
Batty's Barn Cl. Woki RG11 .. 25 D5
Baty House. Streat SW2 ...... 21 F7
Baudwin Rd. Catf SE6 .... 24 E6
Bavant Rd. Thorn H SW16 .... 41 F7
Bawtree Cl. Sutton SM2 ...... 59 C1
Bax Cl. Cran GU6 .... 174 E2
Baxter Ave. Redh RH1 ...... 118 F1
Baxter Cl. Worth RH10 ...... 202 D8
Bay Cl. Horley RH6 .... 160 E6
Bay Dr. Brack RG12 .... 27 E7
Bay Rd. Brack RG12 .... 27 E8
Bay Tree Ave. Leahd KT22 .... 95 A7
Bayards. Warlgm CR6 .... 81 C1
Baydon Ct. Beck BR2 .... 44 F6
Bayeux. Tadw KT20 .... 97 D5
Bayfield Ave.
Friml GU15 & GU16 .... 65 E2
Bayfield Rd. Horley RH6 .... 160 E4
Bayford Cl. W Heath GU14 .... 65 A1
Bayham Rd. Morden SM4 ...... 40 C5
Bayhorne La. Horley RH6 .... 161 C1
Bayleaf Cl. Tedd TW12 ...... 16 D3
Baylis Wlk. Crawl RH11 ..... 201 B1
Bayliss Ct. Guild GU1 ...... 130 C8
Baynards Rd. Cran RH12 .... 195 A2
Bays Cl. For Hil SE26 .... 23 C3
Baysfarm Ct.
Harm TW6 & UB7 .... 2 C2
Baywood Cl. W Heath GU14 . 84 C5
Bazalgette Cl. New Mal KT3 . 38 D4
Bazalgette Gdns.
New Mal KT3 .... 38 D4
Beach Gr. Felt TW13 .... 16 A6
Beachborough Rd. Catf BR1 24 C4
Beachy Rd. Crawl RH11 .... 201 A1
Beacon Cl. Nork SM7 .... 77 D3
Beacon Gr. Rowl GU10 ..... 146 A5
Beacon Cl. Horsh RH13 .... 218 A4
Beacon Rd. Carsh SM5 ...... 60 A6
Beacon Hill. Dorman RH7 .. 186 B8
Beacon Hill. Woking GU21 ... 89 C8
Beacon Hill Ct.
Beac H GU26 .... 188 D6
Beacon Hill Cty Prim Sch.
Beac H GU26 .... 188 C6
Beacon Hill Rd.
Beac H GU26 .... 188 D6
Beacon Hill Rd.
Crond GU10 .... 124 E8
Beacon House. **10**
Penge SE26 .... 23 B3
Beacon Rd. Farnb GU14 ..... 105 B8
Beacon Rd. Harl TW19 & TW6 3 A1
Beacon Sch The.
Burgh H KT20 .... 77 E2
Beacon View Rd. Elst GU8 . 148 C2

Beacon Way. Nork SM7 ...... 77 E3
Beaconsfield Pl. Ewell KT17 . 76 E7
Beaconsfield Rd. Clayg KT10 55 E3
Beaconsfield Rd.
King U T KT3 .... 38 D7
Beaconsfield Rd.
Lang Y KT18 .... 96 E8
Beaconsfield Rd.
Old Wok GU22 .... 89 F7
Beaconsfield Rd. Surb KT5 .. 37 F2
Beaconsfield Rd.
Thorn H CR0 .... 42 D3
Beaconsfield Rd. Twick TW1 .. 6 B1
Beaconshaw. Broml BR1 ...... 24 E1
Beadle Cl. Mitch CR4 .... 40 E6
Beadles La. Oxted RH8 ...... 122 D4
Beadles Lane Cty Fst Sch.
Oxted RH8 .... 122 D5
Beadlow Cl. Carsh SM4 ...... 40 D3
Beadman Pl. W Norw SE27 .. 22 B4
Beadman St. W Norw SE27 .. 22 B4
Beadnell Rd. For Hil SE23 .. 23 D7
Beafond Gr. Merton SW20 ... 39 F6
Beagle Cl. Felt TW13 .... 15 B4
Beale Cl. Woki RG11 .... 25 B7
Beale Ct. Crawl RH11 ...... 201 A3
Beale's La. Weyb KT13 ...... 53 B7
Beales La. Wreccl GU10 ..... 145 F7
Beales Rd. G Book KT23 ..... 94 B1
Bealeswood La.
Docken GU10 .... 166 F6
Beam Hollow. Heath E GU9 125 C7
Bean Oak Rd. Woki RG11 .... 25 F6
Bear La. Farnh GU9 .... 125 C3
Bear Rd. Felt TW13 .... 15 D4
Beard Rd. Rich TW10 .... 17 F3
Beard's Hill. Hampt TW12 ... 36 A8
Beard's Rd.
Ashf TW15 & TW16 .... 14 E2
Beardell St. W Norw SE19 ... 22 F2
Beards Hill Cl. Hampt TW12 36 A8
Beare Green Cotts.
Bear Gn RH5 .... 157 D2
Beare Green Ct.
Bear Gn RH5 .... 157 D4
Bearfield Rd. King U T KT2 .. 17 E1
Bears Den. Kings KT20 ...... 97 F5
Bearsden Way.
Broad H RH12 .... 216 D3
Bearwood Cl. Row Tn KT15 .. 52 A4
Bearwood Cotts.
Wreccl GU10 .... 145 F7
Beasley's Ait La.
Lo Hall TW16 & TW17 ...... 34 F3
Beatrice Ave. Thorn H SW16 41 F7
Beatrice Rd. Oxted RH8 .... 122 E6
Beatrice Rd. **1** Rich TW10 .... 6 F2
Beatrix Potter Prim Sch.
Wands SW18 .... 20 C7
Beattie Cl. E Bed TW14 ...... 14 F7
Beattie Cl. G Book KT23 ..... 93 F3
Beatty Ave. Merrow GU1 .... 110 A2
Beauchamp Rd. E Mole KT8 . 36 C4
Beauchamp Rd.
S Norw CR7 & SE25 .... 42 D8
Beauchamp Rd. Sutton SM1 59 A6
Beauchamp Rd. Twick TW1 .. 17 A8
Beauclare Cl. Ashtd KT21 .... 95 D6
Beauclerc Cty Inf Sch.
Sunby TW16 .... 35 C6
Beauclere House.
Sutton SM2 .... 59 C3
Beauclerk Cl. Felt TW13 .... 15 B7
Beauclerk House. **10**
Streat SW16 .... 21 E5
Beaufield Gate.
Haslem GU27 .... 208 D7
Beaufighter Rd.
Farnb GU14 .... 105 A8
Beaufort Cl. Mayb GU22 ..... 70 C3
Beaufort Cl. Putney SW19 ... 19 B8
Beaufort Cl. Reig RH2 ...... 117 F2
Beaufort Ct. Rich TW10 ..... 17 C4
Beaufort Gdns. Heston TW5 .. 4 E6
Beaufort Gdns. S Ascl SL5 .. 28 E8
Beaufort Gdns.S Norw SW16 21 F1
Beaufort Hse. Wimble SW20 39 D8
Beaufort Prim Sch.
Woking GU21 .... 68 F3
Beaufort Rd. Farnh GU9 .... 125 C3
Beaufort Rd.
King U T KT1 & KT5 & KT6 ... 37 E5
Beaufort Rd. Mayb GU22 .... 70 C3
Beaufort Rd. Reig RH2 ...... 117 F2
Beaufort Rd. Rich TW10 ..... 17 C4
Beaufort Rd. Twick TW1 ..... 17 C8
Beaufort Way. Stonel KT17 . 58 A3
Beauforts. Egh La Gu TW20 .. 11 C3
Beaufoys House. **3**
W Norw SE27 .... 22 B5
Beaufront Cl. Camb GU15 .... 66 A7

Beaufront Rd. Camb GU15 ... 66 B7
Beaulieu Ave. For Hil SE26 .. 23 B4
Beaulieu Cl. Brack RG12 ..... 28 A6
Beaulieu Cl. Hounsl TW4 ..... 4 F2
Beaulieu Cl. Mitch CR4 ...... 41 A8
Beaulieu Cl. **4** Twick TW1 .... 6 B1
Beaulieu Gdns. Blckw GU17 . 64 C5
Beaumaris Par. Friml GU16 .. 85 F8
Beaumont Ave. Rich TW9 .... 6 F4
Beaumont Cl. Crawl RH11 .. 200 E5
Beaumont Cl. Ascot SL5 ..... 28 F5
Beaumont Ct. Mitch CR4 ..... 41 A7
Beaumont Cty Jun Sch.
Beaumont Dr. Ashf TW15 .... 14 D3
Beaumont Gdns. Brack RG12 27 E4
Beaumont Gr. Aldr GU1 .... 104 E2
Beaumont House. **1**
Streat SW2 .... 21 E7
Beaumont House.
Wimble SW19 .... 20 A5
Beaumont Pl. Islew TW7 ...... 5 F2
Beaumont Prim Sch.
Purley CR8 .... 80 A5
Beaumont Rd. Purley CR8 ... 80 A6
Beaumont Rd.
Putney SW15 & SW19 ...... 19 E8
Beaumont Rd. S Norw SE19 . 22 C2
Beaumont Sq. Cran GU6 .... 174 F3
Beaumont Terr. **1**
Lewish SE13 .... 24 E8
Beaumonts. Salfs RH1 ...... 139 F1
Beaver Cl. Hampt TW12 ...... 36 B8
Beaver Cl. Horsh RH12 ..... 217 F6
Beaver Cl. **9** Penge SE20 ... 23 A1
Beavers Cl. Farnh GU9 ..... 125 A2
Beavers Cl. Stough GU2 .... 108 E2
Beavers Comm Prim Sch.
Hounsl TW4 .... 4 C4
Beavers Cres. Hounsl TW4 .... 4 D3
Beavers La. Hounsl TW4 ...... 4 C4
Beavers Rd. Farnh GU9 .... 124 F2
Beavers La. Hounsl TW4 ...... 4 C4
Beavers Rd. Farnh GU9 .... 125 A2
Beck Ct. Penge BR3 .... 43 D6
Beck Gdns. Hale GU9 ...... 125 A6
Beck La. Penge BR3 .... 43 D6
Beck River Pk. Beck BR3 .... 44 A8
Beck Way. Beck BR3 .... 44 A6
Beckenham Bsns Ctr.
Penge BR3 .... 23 E2
Beckenham Ct. Beck BR3 .... 44 A8
Beckenham Gr. Beck BR2 ... 44 D7
Beckenham Hill Rd.
Catf BR3 & SE6 .... 24 C3
Beckenham Hill Sta.
Catf SE6 .... 24 C3
Beckenham Hospl. Beck BR3 43 F7
Beckenham Junction Sta.
Beck BR3 .... 44 A8
Beckenham La.
Broml BR1 & BR2 .... 44 F7
Beckenham Place Pk.
Beck BR3 .... 24 B1
Beckenham Rd. Beck BR3 ... 43 E8
Beckenham Rd. Penge BR3 . 43 E8
Beckenham Rd.
W Wick BR3 & BR4 .... 44 C2
Beckenshaw Gdns.
Woodm SM7 .... 78 E4
Becket Cl. Croy SE25 .... 43 A3
Becket Cl. **2** Merton SW19 . 40 B8
Becket Wood. Parkg RH5 .. 158 C4
Beckett Ave. Purley CR8 .... 80 A4
Beckett Cl. Streat SW16 ..... 21 D6
Beckett Cl. Woki RG11 ...... 25 E6
Beckett La. Crawl RH11 .... 181 D1
Beckett Way. **11**
E Grins RH19 .... 205 F8
Beckett Wlk. Penge BR3 .... 23 E2
Becketts Cl. Felt TW14 ...... 4 B1
Becketts Pl. Tedd KT1 ...... 37 D8
Beckford Ave. Eastb RG12 .. 27 B3
Beckford Rd.
Croy SE25 & SE25 .... 42 F3
Beckingham Rd.
Stough GU2 .... 109 A2
Beckley Cotts. G Book KT23 . 94 C1
Beckmead Sch. Croy BR3 .... 44 A1
Beckway Rd. Mitch SW16 .... 41 D7
Beckworth Rd. Oat Pk KT13 . 53 E8
Beclands Rd. Streat SW17 ... 21 A2
Becmead Ave. Streat SW16 21 D4
Becondale Rd. W Norw SE19 22 E3
Bedale Cl. Crawl RH11 ..... 201 C4
Beddington Farm Rd.
Croy CR0 .... 60 F8
Beddington Farm Rd.
Wallin CR0 & CR9 .... 41 E1
Beddington Gdns.
Wallin SM5 & SM6 .... 60 A4
Beddington Gr. Wallin SM6 . 60 D5

Beddington Inf Sch.
Wallin SM6 .... 60 C6
Beddington La. Wallin CR0 .. 60 E8
Beddington Lane Sta.
Mitch CR4 .... 41 C3
Beddington Manor.
Sutton SM2 .... 59 D4
Beddington Park Cotts.
Wallin SM6 .... 60 D7
Beddington Park Prim Sch.
Wallin CR0 .... 60 D7
Beddlestead La. Titsey CR6 103 A6
Bedelsford Sch. King U T KT1 37 E6
Bedfont Cl. E Bed TW14 ...... 3 C1
Bedfont Cl. Mitch CR4 ...... 41 A7
Bedfont Cl. Harm TW19 ...... 2 B4
Bedfont Green Cl.
E Bed TW14 .... 14 C7
Bedfont Ind Pk N. Felt TW15 14 C5
Bedfont Jun Sch. Felt TW14 .. 3 E1
Bedfont La.
E Bed TW14 & TW13 ...... 14 F8
Bedfont Rd.
Felt TW13 & TW14 .... 14 D6
Bedfont Rd. Stan TW19 ...... 2 F1
Bedfont Rd. Harm GU16 ..... 85 F5
Bedford Cres. Friml GU16 ... 85 F6
Bedfont Ct. **6** Rich TW9 ...... 6 F3
Bedford Ct. S Norw SE19 .... 42 F8
Bedford Hill. Balham SW12 .. 21 B6
Bedford Hill. Streat SW16 ... 21 B6
Bedford Hill.
Up Toot SW12 & SW16 & SW17 21 B6
Bedford House. Guild GU1 . 130 C8
Bedford La. Friml GU16 ...... 85 F6
Bedford La. Sunnin SL5 ...... 30 B4
Bedford Pk. Croy CR0 .... 42 C1
Bedford Pl. Croy CR0 .... 42 D1
Bedford Rd. Guild GU1 ..... 130 C8
Bedford Rd. Horsh RH13 .. 217 D1
Bedford Rd. N Cheam KT4 .. 58 C8
Bedford Rd. Twick TW2 ..... 16 D5
Bedgebury Gdns.
Putney SW19 .... 19 E6
Bedlow Way. Wallin CR0 .... 60 F6
Bedser Cl. S Norw CR7 ...... 42 C6
Bedser Cl. E Mole KT8 ...... 36 B6
Bedwardine Rd.
S Norw SE19 .... 22 E1
Beech Ave. Brent TW8 .... 6 B7
Beech Ave. Camb GU15 ...... 65 D4
Beech Ave. Effing KT24 ..... 113 D6
Beech Ave. M Bourn GU10 . 146 C5
Beech Ave. S Croy CR2 ...... 61 D1
Beech Ave. Tats TN16 ..... 103 D8
Beech Cl. Ashf TW15 .... 14 D3
Beech Cl. Blind H RH7 ..... 163 E8
Beech Cl. Byfl KT14 .... 71 E7
Beech Cl. Carsh SM5 .... 59 F8
Beech Cl. Chidd GU8 ...... 191 A4
Beech Cl. Cobham KT11 .... 74 A8
Beech Cl. Dork RH4 .... 136 A8
Beech Cl. Effing KT24 ..... 113 D7
Beech Cl. Herst KT12 .... 54 C6
Beech Cl. Putney SW15 ...... 19 A8
Beech Cl. Stan TW19 .... 13 D8
Beech Cl. Sunby TW16 ...... 35 D7
Beech Cl. Wimble SW19 .... 19 C2
Beech Close Ct.
Cobham KT11 .... 73 F8
Beech Copse. S Croy CR2 ... 61 E5
Beech Cres. Box H KT20 .... 116 C5
Beech Ct. Beck BR3 .... 23 F1
Beech Ct. Guild GU1 ...... 130 F8
Beech Ct. Tedd TW11 .... 17 C2
Beech Ct. **4** W Norw SW16 22 A3
Beech Dr. Blckw GU17 ...... 64 D4
Beech Dr. Kings KT20 .... 97 F5
Beech Dr. Reig RH2 .... 118 D1
Beech Dr. Send M GU23 ..... 91 A3
Beech Farm Rd.
Chelsh CR6 .... 102 D8
Beech Fields. E Grins RH19 185 F3
Beech Gdns. Crawl D RH10 204 A8
Beech Gdns. Horse GU21 .... 69 E4
Beech Glen. Eastb RG12 .... 27 B5
Beech Gr. Addl KT15 .... 52 B6
Beech Gr. Burgh H KT18 .... 77 B2
Beech Gr. Cater CR3 ...... 100 E1
Beech Gr. King U T KT3 ..... 38 D6
Beech Gr. Mitch CR4 .... 41 D5
Beech Gr. Pirb GU24 .... 87 C7
Beech Gr. Pirb GU24 .... 87 D7
Beech Gr. Stough GU2 ..... 108 F1
Beech Hall. Ottsh KT16 ..... 51 C3
Beech Hanger End.
Grays GU26 .... 188 B3

Beech Hill. Bowl Gn GU8 ... 189 F8
Beech Hill. Head Dn GU35 . 187 B5
Beech Hill. Westfd GU22 .... 89 D4
Beech Hill Rd.
Head Dn GU35 .... 187 A5
Beech Hill Rd. Sunnin SL5 ... 29 F3
Beech Holme.
Crawl D RH10 .... 204 B8
Beech Holt. Leahd KT22 ..... 95 C5
Beech House. Heston TW5 ... 4 F7
Beech House. New Add CR0 63 B4
Beech House Rd.
Croy CR0 & CR9 .... 61 D7
Beech La. Flexf GU3 .... 107 A1
Beech La. Graysh GU26 .... 188 B4
Beech La. Guild GU2 ...... 130 C6
Beech Lodge. Egham TW18 . 12 E3
Beech Rd. Bigg H TN16 ..... 83 C2
Beech Rd. E Bed TW14 ...... 14 E8
Beech Rd. Epsom KT18 ...... 76 F4
Beech Rd. Friml GU16 .... 85 F6
Beech Rd. Haslem GU27 ... 208 D8
Beech Rd. Horsh RH12 .... 218 B5
Beech Rd. Merst RH1 .... 99 C1
Beech Rd. Oat Pk KT13 ..... 53 D6
Beech Rd. Reig RH2 .... 118 A4
Beech Rd. Thorn H SW16 .... 41 F6
Beech Rd. W Heath GU14 ... 85 A7
Beech Ride. Sandh GU17 .... 45 B1
Beech Tree Cl. Crawl RH11 201 D7
Beech Tree Dr. Farnh GU9 126 A5
Beech Tree La. Laleh TW18 . 33 B7
Beech Tree Pl. Sutton SM1 .. 59 B5
Beech Way. Epsom KT17 .... 76 F4
Beech Way. Godal GU2 .... 150 D3
Beech Way. Selsd CR2 ...... 81 D7
Beech Way. Twick TW13 .... 16 A5
Beech Wlk. Leatf KT17 ...... 77 A8
Beech Wood. Cater CR3 .... 100 F3
Beechcroft. Ashtd KT21 ..... 95 F8
Beechcroft. King U T KT2 ... 38 B8
Beechcroft Ave.
King U T KT1 & KT3 .... 38 C7
Beechcroft Cl. Ascot SL5 .... 29 D5
Beechcroft Cl. Heston TW5 .. 4 E7
Beechcroft Cl. Streat SW16 . 21 F3
Beechcroft Dr. Onsl V GU2 129 D6
Beechcroft Lodge.
Sutton SM2 .... 59 C3
Beechcroft Manor.
Oat Pk KT13 .... 53 D7
Beechcroft Mansions.
Streat SW16 .... 21 F3
Beechcroft Rd. Chess KT9 .. 56 F7
Beechcroft Rd. Mortl SW14 .. 7 C4
Beechcroft Rd.
Up Toot SW17 .... 20 E6
Beechdene. Tadw KT20 ...... 97 B5
Beechen Cliff Way.
Hounsl TW7 .... 5 F5
Beechen Pl. For Hil SE23 ... 23 C6
Beeches Ave The.
Sutton SM5 .... 59 E3
Beeches Cl. Kings KT20 .... 98 A4
Beeches Cl. Penge SE20 .... 43 C8
Beeches Cres. Crawl RH10 . 201 E4
Beeches Head.
Dorman RH19 .... 186 F5
Beeches La. Ash W RH19 .. 206 D6
Beeches Rd. Cheam SM3 .... 39 E1
Beeches Rd. Up Toot SW17 . 20 F5
Beeches The. Ash V GU12 ... 85 F1
Beeches The. Banstd SM7 .. 78 B3
Beeches The. Bramly GU5 . 151 F6
Beeches The. Fetch KT22 ... 94 E3
Beeches The. Hounsl TW3 ... 5 B6
Beeches The. Mitch CR4 .... 40 E4
Beeches The. Stain TW18 ... 13 A3
Beeches The.
Sutton SM2 & SM5 .... 59 E2
Beeches Wood. Kings KT20 . 98 A5
Beechey Cl. Copth RH10 ... 183 B3
Beechey Way. Copth RH10 183 B3
Beechfield. Banstd SM7 ..... 78 B6
Beechfield Cl. **7** Croy CR0 .. 61 C6
Beechfield Rd. For Hil SE6 .. 23 F7
Beeching Cl. Ash GU12 .... 106 B3
Beeching Way.E Grins RH19 185 E1
Beechland Cotts.
L Kings KT20 .... 117 F7
Beechlawn. Guild GU1 ..... 130 F8
Beechmeads. Cobham KT11 . 73 D6
Beechmont Ave. Went GU25 31 D4
Beechmont Cl. Catf BR1 .... 24 E3
Beechmore Gdns.
Cheam SM3 .... 58 D8

Beechnut Dr. Blckw GU17 64 B6
Beechnut Rd. Alder GU12 105 B1
Beecholme. Nork KT17 77 E5
Beecholme Ave. Mitch CR4 41 B8
Beecholme Fst Sch. Mitch CR4 41 B8
Beechrow. King U T KT2 17 E4
Beechside. Crawl RH10 201 E5
Beechtree Ave. Eng Gn TW20 11 B2
Beechvale. 3 Woking GU22 69 F1
Beechway. Merrow GU1 110 B2
Beechwood Ave. Ashf TW16 15 A2
Beechwood Ave. Kings KT20 98 A6
Beechwood Ave. Oat Pk KT13 53 E6
Beechwood Ave. Rich TW9 7 A6
Beechwood Ave. Stain TW18 13 B2
Beechwood Ave. Thorn H CR7 42 B5
Beechwood Ave. Wallin CR5 79 B4
Beechwood Cl. Knaph GU21 68 E2
Beechwood Cl. Long D KT6 37 D2
Beechwood Cl. N Asct SL5 8 F1
Beechwood Cl. Oat Pk KT13 53 E6
Beechwood Ct. Carsh SM5 59 F6
Beechwood Ct. Chisw W4 7 D8
Beechwood Ct. Sutton SM1 59 A5
Beechwood Ct. Walt O T KT12 54 A7
Beechwood Dr. Cobham KT11 74 A8
Beechwood Gdns. Cater CR3 101 A5
Beechwood La. Warlgm CR6 101 D8
Beechwood Manor. Oat Pk KT13 53 E6
Beechwood Pk. Leahd KT22 95 C5
Beechwood Rd. Cater CR3 101 A5
Beechwood Rd. Knaph GU21 68 D2
Beechwood Rd. S Croy CR2 61 E2
Beechwood Rd. Went GU25 31 B1
Beechwood Villas. Salfs RH1 161 A7
Beechwoods Ct. Dulw SE19 22 F3
Beecot La. Walt O T KT12 54 C8
Beeding Cl. Horsh RH12 218 A5
Beedingwood Dr. Crawl RH12 218 F6
Beedon Dr. Easth RG11 & RG12 26 E3
Beehive La. Binf RG12 26 C7
Beehive Rd. Binf RG12 26 D7
Beehive Rd. Stain TW18 12 F3
Beehive Ring Rd. Crawl RH10 & RH6 182 B4
Beehive Way. Dovgn RH2 139 B5
Beeleigh Rd. Morden SM4 40 B5
Beeston Way. Felt TW14 4 C1
Beeton's Ave. Ash GU12 106 A4
Beggar's Roost La. Cheam SM1 & SM2 59 A4
Beggars La. Chobh GU24 68 C8
Beggars La. Gomsh GU5 133 E4
Beggarshouse La. Charl RH6 180 C8
Begonia Pl. 1 Hampt TW12 16 A2
Behenna Cl. Crawl RH11 200 E5
Beira St. Balham SW12 21 B8
Belcroft Cl. Broml BR1 24 F1
Beldam Bridge Rd. W End GU24 68 A6
Beldham Gdns. E Mole KT8 36 B6
Beldham Rd. Wreccl GU10 & GU9 145 F7
Belenoyd Ct. Streat SW16 21 F5
Belfast Rd. Croy SE25 43 B5
Belfield Rd. W Ewell KT19 57 E3
Belfield Rd. W Ewell KT19 57 E3
Belfry The. Redh RH1 118 F2
Belgrade Rd. Hampt TW12 36 B8
Belgrave Cl. Hersh KT12 54 B6
Belgrave Cres. Sunby TW16 35 B8
Belgrave Ct. Hawley GU17 64 D3
Belgrave Manor. Woking GU22 89 E8
Belgrave Rd. Barnes SW13 7 F7
Belgrave Rd. Hounsl TW4 4 F4
Belgrave Rd. Mitch CR4 40 D6
Belgrave Rd. S Norw SE25 42 F5
Belgrave Rd. Sunby TW16 35 B8
Belgrave Wlk. Mitch CR4 40 D6
Belgravia Ct. Horley RH6 161 B3
Belgravia Gdns. Catf BR1 24 E2
Belgravia House. 1 Tedd TW11 17 C1
Belgravia Mews. King U T KT1 37 D5
Bell Bridge Rd. Chert KT16 32 F1
Bell Cl. Farnb GU14 85 C6
Bell Cnr. Chert KT16 32 F2
Bell Cres. Hooley CR5 99 B6
Bell Ct. Tolw KT5 57 B8
Bell Ctr. Crawl RH10 181 F2
Bell Dr. Putney SW18 19 E8
Bell Farm Cty Jun Sch. Hersh KT12 54 C6
Bell Foundry La. Woki RG11 25 C8
Bell Gn. For Hil SE6 23 F4
Bell Green La. For Hil BR3 & SE26 & SE6 23 F4
Bell Hammer. E Grins RH19 205 E8
Bell House. 15 Streat SW2 22 A8
Bell House Gdns. Woki RG11 25 B6
Bell La. Blckw GU17 64 C5
Bell La. Fetch KT22 94 D4
Bell La. Rowl GU10 145 E3
Bell La. Twick TW1 17 A7
Bell Lane Cl. Fetch KT22 94 D4
Bell Meadow. Dulw SE19 22 E4
Bell Meadow. Godst RH9 121 C3
Bell Pl. Bagsh GU19 47 F3
Bell Rd. E Mole KT8 36 D4
Bell Rd. Hounsl TW3 5 B3
Bell Rd. King Gn GU27 208 B3
Bell Rd. Warn RH12 217 A8
Bell St. Reig RH2 139 B8
Bell Vale La. Haslem GU27 208 C4
Bell Vale La. Lurg GU27 208 C4
Bell View. Beck BR3 23 F1
Bell Weir Cl. Wray TW19 12 B6
Bellamy House. Heston TW5 5 A8
Bellamy House. Up Toot SW17 20 D4
Bellamy St. Balham SW12 21 B8
Belland Dr. Alder GU11 104 E1
Bellasis Ave. Streat SW2 21 E6
Belle Vue Cl. Alder GU12 105 D2
Belle Vue Cl. Stain TW18 33 A8
Belle Vue Cty Inf Sch. Alder GU12 105 D2
Belle Vue Ent Ctr. Alder GU12 105 E2
Belle Vue Rd. Alder GU12 105 D2
Bellever Hill. Camb GU15 65 E5
Bellevue Pk. S Norw CR7 42 C5
Bellevue Rd. King U T KT1 37 E6
Bellevue Rd. Up Toot SW17 20 F7
Bellew Rd. Friml GU16 86 B7
Bellew St. Wands SW17 20 C5
Bellfield. New Add CR0 62 F3
Bellfields Ct. Bellf GU1 109 C5
Bellfields Rd. Bellf GU1 109 D3
Bellingham Cl. Friml GU15 66 C4
Bellingham Gn. Catf SE6 24 A5
Bellingham Rd. Catf SE6 24 C5
Bellingham Sta. Catf SE6 24 B5
Bellmarsh Rd. Addl KT15 52 B6
Bellmore Ct. 5 Croy CR0 42 F1
Bello Cl. Streat SE24 & SW2 22 B7
Belloc Cl. Crawl RH10 202 C7
Belloc Ct. Horsh RH13 218 A3
Bells La. Horton SL3 1 B4
Belltrees Gr. 1 Streat SW16 22 A3
Bellwether La. Outw RH1 162 B7
Belmont. Whit V KT13 53 C4
Belmont Ave. Stough GU2 108 F4
Belmont Ave. W Barn KT3 39 A5
Belmont Cl. W Heath GU14 84 F7
Belmont Mews. Camb GU15 65 C3
Belmont Rd. Beck BR3 43 F7
Belmont Rd. Belm SM2 59 A1
Belmont Rd. Camb GU15 65 C4
Belmont Rd. Crowth RG11 45 B6
Belmont Rd. Croy SE25 43 B4
Belmont Rd. Leahd KT22 95 A5
Belmont Rd. Reig RH2 139 C8
Belmont Rd. Twick TW2 16 D6
Belmont Rd. Wallin SM6 60 C5
Belmont Rise. Belm SM1 & SM2 58 F3
Belmont Sch. Abin C RH5 155 D6
Belmont Sta. Sutton SM2 59 B1
Belmore Ave. Mayb GU22 70 D3
Belsize Gdns. Sutton SM1 59 B6
Belsize Rd. Farnb GU14 85 C1
Belstone Mews. W Heath GU14 85 A7
Beltane Dr. Wimble SW19 19 D5
Belthorn Cres. Streat SW12 21 C8
Belton Rd. Camb GU15 65 E5
Belvedere Ave. Wimble SW19 19 E3
Belvedere Cl. Esher KT10 55 B5
Belvedere Cl. Stough GU2 109 B3
Belvedere Cl. Tedd TW11 16 E3
Belvedere Cl. Weyb KT13 53 A5
Belvedere Ct. Crawl RH10 202 B7
Belvedere Ct. Hawley GU17 64 D3
Belvedere Ct. 8 King U T KT2 18 A1
Belvedere Dr. Wimble SW19 19 E3
Belvedere Gdns. E Mole KT8 36 A4
Belvedere Gr. Wimble SW19 19 E3
Belvedere Rd. Bigg H TN16 83 F1
Belvedere Rd. Farnb GU14 85 C2
Belvedere Rd. Penge SE19 22 F1
Belvedere Sq. Wimble SW19 19 E3
Belvoir Cl. Friml GU16 65 F1
Belvoir Lodge. Dulw SE22 23 A8
Belvoir Rd. Dulw SE22 23 A8
Benbow La. Dunsf GU8 193 C4
Benbrick Rd. Guild GU2 130 A8
Benbury Cl. Catf BR1 24 C3
Bence The. Egham TW20 32 B6
Bench Field. S Croy CR2 61 F5
Benchfield Cl. E Grins RH19 186 B1
Bencombe Rd. Purley CR8 80 A5
Bencroft Rd. Streat SW16 21 C1
Bencurtis Pk. W Wick BR4 63 D8
Bendon Valley.Wands SW18 20 B8
Benedict Dr. E Bed TW14 14 D8
Benedict Fst Sch. Mitch CR4 40 D6
Benedict Prim Sch. Mitch CR4 40 D6
Benedict Rd. Mitch CR4 40 D6
Benedict Wharf. Mitch CR4 40 E6
Benen-Stock Rd. Stan TW19 2 A2
Benett Gdns. Thorn H SW16 41 E7
Benfleet Cl. Cobham KT11 73 E7
Benfleet Cl. Sutton SM1 59 C7
Benham Cl. Coulsd CR5 & CR8 80 B1
Benham Gdns. Hounsl TW3 & TW4 4 F2
Benhams Cl. Horley RH6 161 A5
Benhams Dr. Horley RH6 161 A5
Benhill Ave. Sutton SM1 59 B6
Benhill Ave. Sutton SM1 59 C6
Benhill Rd. Sutton SM1 59 D6
Benhill Wood Rd. Sutton SM1 59 C6
Benhilton Gdns. Sutton SM1 59 B7
Benhurst Cl. Selsd CR2 62 D1
Benhurst Ct. 13 Penge SE20 43 B8
Benhurst Ct. Streat SW16 22 A3
Benhurst Gdns. Selsd CR2 62 C1
Benhurst La. Streat SW16 22 A3
Benin St. Lewish SE13 24 D8
Benjamin Ct. Littlt TW15 14 C1
Benner La. W End GU24 68 A7
Bennet Cl. Tedd KT1 37 C8
Bennett Cl. Cobham KT11 73 A6
Bennett Cl. Crawl RH10 202 B2
Bennett Ct. Camb GU15 65 C5
Bennett House. 2 Streat SW4 21 D8
Bennett St. Chisw W4 7 E8
Bennett Way. W Clan GU4 111 B6
Bennetts Ave. Croy CR0 62 E8
Bennetts Cl. Mitch CR4 & SW16 41 B8
Bennetts Farm Pl. L Book KT23 93 F2
Bennetts Rd. Horsh RH13 217 E1
Bennetts Way. Croy CR0 62 F8
Bennetts Wood. Capel RH5 178 C5
Bens Acre. Horsh RH13 218 A2
Bensbury Cl. Putney SW15 19 C8
Bensham Cl. Thorn H CR7 42 C5
Bensham Gr. S Norw CR7 42 C7
Bensham La. Thorn H CR0 & CR7 42 B3
Bensham Manor Rd. Thorn H CR0 & CR7 42 C5
Bensham Manor Sch. Thorn H CR7 42 C4
Bensington Ct. E Bed TW14 3 D1
Benson Cl. Hounsl TW3 5 A3
Benson Prim Sch. Croy CR0 62 E7
Benson Rd. Croy CR0 & CR9 61 A7
Benson Rd. For Hil SE23 23 C7
Benson's La. Faygt RH12 199 C1
Bentall Sh Ctr The. 10 King U T KT2 37 E7
Benthall Gdns. Kenley CR8 80 C2
Bentham Ave. Sheer GU21 70 C4
Bentley Cl. Wimble SW19 20 A5
Bentley Copse. Friml GU15 66 B4
Bentley Dr. Whit V KT13 53 A2
Benton's La. W Norw SE27 22 C4
Benton's Rise. W Norw SE27 22 D3
Bentsbrook Cl. Dork RH5 136 B3
Bentsbrook Cotts. Dork RH5 136 B3
Bentsbrook Pk. Dork RH5 136 B3
Bentsbrook Rd. Dork RH5 136 B3
Benwell Ct. Sunby TW16 35 A8
Benwell Rd. Brookw GU24 88 A8
Benwick Ct. Penge SE20 43 C8
Benwood Ct. Sutton SM1 59 C7
Beomonds. Chert KT16 33 A2
Beomonds Row. Chert KT16 33 A2
Berberis Cl. Bellf GU1 109 C3
Bere Rd. Brack RG12 27 E3
Beresford Ave. Tolw KT5 38 C2
Beresford Ave. Twick TW1 6 C1
Beresford Cl. Friml GU16 85 F6
Beresford Ct. 11 Twick TW1 6 C1
Beresford Gdns. Hounsl TW4 4 F2
Beresford House. Dulw SE21 22 E5
Beresford Rd. Belm SM2 58 F3
Beresford Rd. Dork RH4 136 B7
Beresford Rd. King U T KT2 37 F8
Beresford Rd. King U T KT3 38 C5
Bergenia Ct. W End GU24 67 E6
Berkeley Ave. Cranf TW4 4 A5
Berkeley Cl. Crawl RH11 200 E2
Berkeley Cl. Stan TW19 12 D6
Berkeley Cres. Friml GU16 86 A8
Berkeley Ct. Ashtd KT21 75 F1
Berkeley Ct. Oat Pk KT13 53 E8
Berkeley Ct. 16 Streat SW2 22 A7
Berkeley Ct. Wallin SM6 60 C6
Berkeley Dr. E Mole KT8 36 A6
Berkeley Dr. Wink SL4 9 B7
Berkeley Gdns. Clayg KT10 56 A4
Berkeley Gdns. Pyrf KT14 70 F5
Berkeley Gdns. Walt O T KT12 34 F2
Berkeley House. 11 Brent TW8 6 D8
Berkeley Pl. Wimble SW19 19 D2
Berkeley Pl. Woodc KT18 76 D4
Berkeley Prim Sch. Heston TW5 4 D7
Berkeley Waye. Heston TW5 4 D7
Berkeleys The. Fetch KT22 94 E3
Berkley Cl. Twick TW2 16 E5
Berkley Ct. Guild GU1 109 E1
Berkley Ct. 7 Twick TW1 17 A8
Berkshire Cl. Cater CR3 100 D5
Berkshire Copse Rd. Farnb GU11 & GU14 104 E7
Berkshire House. Catf SE6 24 A4
Berkshire Rd. Camb GU15 65 F8
Berkshire Sq. Mitch CR4 41 E5
Berkshire Way. Binf RG12 26 D6
Berkshire Way. Brack RG12 26 D6
Berkshire Way. Mitch CR4 41 E5
Bernard Ct. Camb GU15 65 B4
Bernard Gdns. Wimble SW19 19 F3
Bernard Rd. Wallin SM5 & SM6 60 B6
Berne Rd. Thorn H CR7 42 C4
Bernel Dr. Croy CR0 62 F7
Bernersh Cl. Sandh GU15 & GU17 45 C1
Berney House. Beck BR3 43 E4
Berney Rd. Thorn H CR0 42 D2
Berridge Rd. W Norw SE19 22 E3
Berrington Dr. E Hors KT24 92 F3
Berry Ct. Hounsl TW4 4 F2
Berry La. Pirb GU3 88 C2
Berry La. W Norw SE21 & SE27 22 D4
Berry La. Woking GU22 & GU3 88 D4
Berry Meade. Ashtd KT21 75 F2
Berry Wlk. Ashtd KT21 95 F8
Berry's La. Byfl KT14 71 D8
Berrybank. Sandh GU15 64 E6
Berrycroft. Wink RG12 27 D8
Berrylands. Surb KT5 37 F3
Berrylands. W Barn SW20 39 C5
Berrylands Ct. 7 Sutton SM2 59 B3
Berrylands Rd. Surb KT5 37 F3
Berrylands Sta. Surb KT5 38 B5
Berryman's La. For Hil SE26 23 D4
Berrymeade Wlk. Crawl RH11 200 E5
Berryscourt. Byfl KT14 71 D8
Berryscroft Ct. Stain TW18 13 C1
Berryscroft Rd. Stain TW18 13 C1
Berstead Wlk. 1 Crawl RH11 200 F3
Bert Rd. Thorn H CR7 42 C4
Bertal Rd. Up Toot SW17 20 D4
Bertie Rd. Penge SE26 23 D2
Bertram Cotts. Merton SW19 20 A1
Bertram Rd. King U T KT2 18 A1
Bertrand House. 11 Streat SW16 21 E5
Berwyn Ave. Hounsl TW3 5 B6
Berwyn Rd. Mortl SW14 & TW10 7 B3
Berwyn Rd. Streat SE24 22 B7
Beryl Harding House. 3 Wimble SW19 19 D1
Berystede. King U T KT2 18 B1
Besley St. Streat SW16 21 C2
Bessborough Rd. Rhampt SW15 19 A7
Bessborough Wks. E Mole KT8 35 F4
Beswick Gdns. Brack RG12 27 F8
Beta Rd. Chobh GU24 49 F1
Beta Rd. Mayb GU22 70 B3
Beta Rd. W Heath GU14 85 A5
Beta Way. Thorpe TW20 32 C8
Betchets Green Rd. S Holm RH5 157 C6
Betchley Cl. E Grins RH19 185 E3
Betchworth Cl. Sutton SM1 59 D5
Betchworth Sta. Betch RH3 116 E3
Betchworth The. Brock RH4 116 A1
Betchworth Way. New Add CR0 63 C2
Betchworth Wks. Charl RH6 180 D6
Bethany Waye. E Bed TW14 14 E8
Bethel Cl. Heath E GU9 125 D6
Bethel La. Heath E GU9 125 D6
Bethersden Cl. Beck BR3 23 F1
Bethesda Ct. 8 Penge SE20 23 C1
Bethlem Royal Hospl The. Croy BR3 44 A2
Bethune Cl. Worth RH10 202 D5
Bethune Rd. Horsh RH13 217 E1
Betjeman Cl. Coulsd CR5 79 F2
Betley Ct. Walt O T KT12 54 B7
Betony Cl. Croy CR0 43 D1
Betts Cl. Penge BR3 43 E7
Betts Way. Crawl RH11 181 D2
Betts Way. Long D KT6 37 B1
Betts Way. Penge SE20 43 B8
Bettswood Ct. 16 Penge SE20 43 B8
Betula Cl. Kenley CR8 80 D4
Between Streets. Cobham KT11 73 A5
Beulah Ave. S Norw CR7 42 C7
Beulah Cres. S Norw CR7 42 C7
Beulah Gr. Thorn H CR0 42 C3
Beulah Hill. S Norw SE19 & SW16 22 C1
Beulah Inf Sch. S Norw CR7 42 C6
Beulah Jun Sch. S Norw CR7 42 C6
Beulah Rd. Merton SW19 19 F1
Beulah Rd. S Norw CR7 42 C6
Beulah Rd. Sutton SM1 59 A6
Beulah Wlk. Wold CR3 101 E7
Bevan Ct. Crawl RH11 201 B1
Bevan Ct. Croy CR0 61 A5
Beverley Ave. Hounsl TW4 4 F3
Beverley Ave. Wimble SW20 38 F8
Beverley Cl. Addl KT15 52 D5
Beverley Cl. Ash GU12 105 F1
Beverley Cl. Chess KT9 56 C6
Beverley Cl. E Ewell KT17 77 C8
Beverley Cl. Friml GU15 66 D6
Beverley Cl. Oat Pk KT13 53 E8
Beverley Cotts. King U T SW15 18 E5
Beverley Cres. Farnb GU14 84 F2
Beverley Ct. Hounsl TW4 4 F3
Beverley Ct. King U T SW20 38 F8
Beverley Gdns. Barnes SW13 7 F4
Beverley Gdns. 2 N Cheam KT4 39 A1
Beverley House. Catf BR1 24 D3
Beverley Hts. Reig RH2 118 B3
Beverley Hyrst. 7 Croy CR0 61 F8
Beverley La. King U T KT2 18 E1
Beverley Lodge. 6 Rich TW10 6 E2
Beverley Mansions. Hounsl TW4 4 F3
Beverley Rd. Barnes SW13 7 F4
Beverley Rd. Kenley CR3 80 F2
Beverley Rd. Mitch CR4 41 D5
Beverley Rd. N Cheam KT4 58 C8
Beverley Rd. New Mal KT3 39 A5
Beverley Rd. Penge SE20 43 B7
Beverley Rd. Sunby TW16 34 F8
Beverley Rd. Tedd KT1 37 C8
Beverley Sch. New Mal KT3 39 A4
Beverley Trad Est. W Barn SM4 39 D2
Beverley Way. King U T KT3 & SW20 & KT2 38 F8
Beverley Way. Wimble KT3 & SW20 39 A6
Beverley Way (Kingston By Pass). W Barn KT3 & SW20 39 A6
Beverley Way Kingston Bypass. King U T KT3 38 F8

Beverstone Rd. Thorn H CR7 42 B5
Bevill Allen Cl. Up Toot SW17 20 F3
Bevill Cl. Croy SE25 43 A6
Bevington Rd. Beck BR3 44 B7
Bew Ct. Dulw SE21 23 A8
Bewbush Dr. Crawl RH11 200 F3
Bewbush Fst Sch. Crawl RH11 200 F3
Bewbush Manor. Crawl RH11 200 E2
Bewbush Mid Sch. Crawl RH11 200 F3
Bewlys Rd. W Norw SE27 22 B3
Bexhill Cl. Felt TW13 15 E6
Bexhill Rd. For Hil SE4 23 F8
Bexhill Rd. Mortl SW14 7 C4
Beynon Rd. Wallin SM5 59 F5
Bicester Rd. Mortl TW9 7 B4
Bickersteth Rd. Up Toot SW17 20 F2
Bickley Ct. Crawl RH11 201 A3
Bickley St. Up Toot SW17 20 F3
Bicknell Rd. Friml GU16 65 E2
Bickney Way. Fetch KT22 94 C5
Bicknoller Cl. Sutton SM2 59 B1
Bidborough Cl. Hayes BR2 44 F4
Biddulph Rd. S Croy CR2 61 C2
Bideford Cl. Felt TW13 15 F5
Bideford Cl. W Heath GU14 85 A7
Bideford Rd. Catf BR1 24 F5
Bidhams Cres. Burgh H KT20 97 C6
Bidmead Ct. Surb KT6 56 E7
Bield The. Woodh RH2 139 A7
Bietigheim Way. 2 Camb GU15 65 C6
Big Common La. Bletch RH1 120 B3
Biggin Ave. Mitch CR4 40 F8
Biggin Cl. Crawl RH11 201 C4
Biggin Hill. S Norw SE19 & SW16 22 B1
Biggin Hill Airport. Bigg H TN16 83 D5
Biggin Hill Bsns Pk. Bigg H TN16 83 D4
Biggin Hill Prim Sch. Bigg H TN16 83 E3
Biggin Way. S Norw CR7 & SE19 & SW16 22 C1
Bigginwood Rd. S Norw SW16 42 B8
Bignor Cl. Horsh RH12 218 A7
Bilberry Cl. Crawl RH11 201 B3
Bilbets. Horsh RH12 217 C3
Billesden Rd. Pirb GU24 87 D7
Billet Rd. Stan TW18 & TW19 13 A5
Billhurst Cotts. Lingf RH7 164 D4
Billingshurst Rd. Broad H RH12 216 D3
Billinton Dr. Worth RH10 202 B5
Billockby Cl. Chess KT9 56 F4
Billsley Ct. S Norw SE25 42 E5
Bilton Ind Est. Easth RG12 26 E5
Binbury Row. Stain TW18 12 E4
Binfield Rd. Binf RG11 25 F7
Binfield Rd. Brack RG12 27 A8
Binfield Rd. Byfl KT14 71 E7
Binfield Rd. S Croy CR2 61 F5
Binfield Rd. Woki RG11 25 F7
Bingham Cnr. Croy CR0 43 A1
Bingham Dr. Knaph GU21 68 F1
Bingham Dr. Stain TW18 13 D1
Bingham Rd. Croy CR0 & CR9 43 B1
Bingley Rd. Ashf TW16 15 A1
Binhams Lea. Dunsf GU8 192 F5
Binhams Meadow. Dunsf GU8 192 F5
Binley House. Rhampt SW15 7 F1
Binney Ct. Crawl RH10 182 E1
Binscombe Cres. Farnc GU7 150 E8
Binscombe Jun Sch. Farnc GU7 129 E1
Binscombe La. Farnc GU7 150 E7
Binstead Cl. Crawl RH11 201 B8
Binsted Dr. Blckw GU17 64 D5
Binton La. The San GU10 126 E3
Birch Ave. Cater CR3 100 D3
Birch Circ. Farnc GU7 150 F8
Birch Cl. Brent TW8 6 B7
Birch Cl. Camb GU15 65 E8
Birch Cl. Crawl D RH10 204 C8
Birch Cl. Hounsl TW3 5 D5
Birch Cl. New Haw KT15 52 D2
Birch Cl. Rowl GU10 146 A4
Birch Cl. Send M GU23 90 F2
Birch Cl. Tedd TW11 17 A3
Birch Cl. Woking GU21 89 C8
Birch Ct. Ashtd KT21 75 D2
Birch Ct. Sutton SM1 59 C6
Birch Ct. 9 Wallin SM6 60 B6
Birch Dr. Hawley GU17 64 D3
Birch Gn. Stain TW18 13 A4
Birch Gr. Bellf GU1 109 C4
Birch Gr. Brack RG12 27 C5
Birch Gr. Kings KT20 97 F3
Birch Gr. Lewish SE12 24 F8
Birch Gr. Mayb GU22 70 D4
Birch Gr. Up Hall TW17 34 E7
Birch Hill. S Croy CR0 62 D5
Birch Hill Jun & Inf Sch. Easth RG12 27 B1
Birch Hill Rd. Easth RG12 27 B2
Birch La. Purley CR8 79 E8
Birch La. W End GU24 67 D7
Birch La. Wink RG12 & SL5 28 B8
Birch Lea. Crawl RH10 182 A1
Birch Platt. W End GU24 67 D6
Birch Rd. Farnc GU7 151 A8
Birch Rd. Felt TW13 15 D3
Birch Rd. Head Dn GU35 187 B6
Birch Rd. Windl GU20 48 E4
Birch Side. Crowth RG11 45 A6
Birch Tree Ave. Coney H BR4 63 F6
Birch Tree View. Lhtwat GU18 48 A1
Birch Tree Way. Croy CR0 62 B8
Birch Vale. Cobham KT11 74 A6
Birch Way. Ash V GU12 106 A7
Birch Way. Warlgm CR6 81 E1
Birch Wlk. Mitch CR4 41 B8
Birchanger. Godal GU7 150 E4
Birchanger Rd. Croy SE25 43 A4
Birchcroft Cl. Cater CR3 100 C2
Birchdale Cl. W Byfl KT14 71 C8
Birchend Cl. S Croy CR2 61 D4
Birches Cl. Epsom KT18 76 E4
Birches Cl. Mitch CR4 40 F6
Birches Ind Est. E Grins RH19 185 A3
Birches Rd. Horsh RH12 218 B5
Birches The. Beck BR2 44 F5
Birches The. Blckw GU17 64 B5
Birches The. Crawl RH10 202 A7
Birches The. E Hors KT24 92 E1
Birches The. S Norw SE25 42 F7
Birches The. Twick TW4 15 F8
Birches The. W Heath GU14 84 D4
Birches The. Woking GU22 69 F1
Birchett Rd. Alder GU11 105 A2
Birchett Rd. W Heath GU14 84 E6
Birchetts Cl. 2 Brack RG12 27 B8
Birchfield Cl. Addl KT15 52 B6
Birchfield Cl. Coulsd CR5 79 F3
Birchfield Gr. E Ewell KT17 58 C1
Birchfields. Camb GU15 65 C4
Birchgrove. Cobham KT11 73 D5
Birchington Rd. Surb KT5 37 F2
Birchlands. Sandh GU15 45 E2
Birchlands Ave. Balham SW12 20 F8
Birchway. Earls RH1 140 B7
Birchwood Ave. Beck BR3 43 F5
Birchwood Ave. Hackb SM5 & SM6 60 B7
Birchwood Cl. Horley RH6 161 B4
Birchwood Cl. Morden SM4 40 B5
Birchwood Dr. Lhtwat GU18 48 C1
Birchwood Dr. W Byfl KT14 71 A7
Birchwood Gr. Hampt TW12 16 A2
Birchwood La. Cater CR3 100 B2
Birchwood La. Oxsh KT10 & KT22 55 E1
Birchwood Rd. Streat SW17 21 B3
Birchwood Rd. W Byfl KT14 & KT15 71 A7
Bird Mews. Woki RG11 25 B6
Bird Wlk. Twick TW2 15 F7
Bird-In-Hand Pas. For Hil SE23 23 C6
Birdham Cl. Crawl RH11 201 B8
Birdhaven. Wreccl GU10 & GU9 146 A6
Birdhurst. Whytlf CR3 100 F7
Birdhurst Ave. S Croy CR2 61 D6
Birdhurst Ct. Wallin SM6 60 C3
Birdhurst Gdns. S Croy CR2 61 D6
Birdhurst Rd. Mitch SW19 20 E2
Birdhurst Rd. S Croy CR2 61 E5
Birdhurst Rise. S Croy CR2 61 E5
Birds Hill Dr. Oxsh KT22 74 D6
Birds Hill Rd. Oxsh KT22 74 D6
Birds Hill Rise. Oxsh KT22 74 D6
Birdsgrove. Knaph GU21 68 B1
Birdswood Dr. Knaph GU21 88 E7
Birdwood Cl. Selsd CR2 81 D8
Birdwood Cl. Tedd TW11 16 E4
Birdwood Rd. Sandh GU15 64 F6
Birdworld. Binst GU10 145 B3
Birkbeck Hill. W Norw SE21 22 B7
Birkbeck Pl. Sandh GU15 45 E1
Birkbeck Pl. W Norw SE21 22 C6
Birkbeck Rd. Penge BR3 43 D7
Birkbeck Rd. Wimble SW19 20 B2
Birkbeck Sta. Penge SE20 43 C6
Birkdale. Easth RG12 26 E2
Birkdale Ct. Ascot SL5 29 C4
Birkdale Dr. Crawl RH11 200 D5
Birkdale Gdns. S Croy CR0 62 D6
Birkenhead Ave. King U T KT2 37 F8
Birkenholme Cl. Head Dn GU35 187 C4
Birkhall Rd. Catf SE6 24 D6
Birkheads Rd. Reig RH2 118 A2
Birkwood Cl. Streat SW12 21 D8
Birling House. 4 Penge SE20 23 C1
Birnham Cl. Send M GU23 91 A3
Birtley Rd. Bramly GU5 152 B4
Birtley Rise. Bramly GU5 152 A5
Biscoe Cl. Heston TW5 5 A8
Bisenden Rd. Croy CR0 61 E8
Bisham Cl. Carsh CR4 40 F1
Bishams Ct. Cater CR3 100 F3
Bishop Bell Mid Sch. Crawl RH10 201 F3
Bishop Challoner Sch. Beck BR2 44 D7
Bishop David Brown Sch. Sheer GU21 70 D6
Bishop Duppa's Almshouses. 7 Rich TW10 6 E2
Bishop Duppas Pk. Oat Pk TW17 34 E2
Bishop Fox Way. E Mole KT8 35 F5
Bishop Gilpins Prim Sch. Wimble SW19 19 F3
Bishop Perrin (C of E) Sch. Twick TW2 16 B7
Bishop Reindorp CE Sch. Bellf GU1 109 C4
Bishop Sumner Dr. Hale GU9 125 C6
Bishop Thomas Grant Catholic Sec Sch. Streat SW16 21 F3
Bishop Wand C of E Sec Sch. Sunby TW16 34 F7
Bishop's Cl. Coulsd CR5 80 A1
Bishop's Cotts. Box H RH3 116 B2
Bishop's Hall. King U T KT1 37 D7
Bishop's La. Wink SL4 8 B7
Bishop's Mead. Farnh GU9 125 B2
Bishop's Pl. Sutton SM1 59 C5
Bishop's Rd. Thorn H CR0 42 B2
Bishopdale. Easth RG12 27 A5
Bishopric. Horsh RH12 217 B2
Bishopric Ct. Horsh RH12 217 B2
Bishops Cl. Sutton SM1 59 A7
Bishops Ct. 1 Ashf TW16 14 F1
Bishops Ct. Guild GU2 130 C7
Bishops Dr. E Bed TW14 3 D1
Bishops Dr. Woki RG11 25 C7
Bishops Gr. Hampt TW12 15 F4
Bishops Gr. Windl GU20 48 C4
Bishops Hill. Walt O T KT12 35 A2
Bishops Park Rd. Thorn H SW16 41 E8
Bishops Rd. Hale GU9 125 B7
Bishops Sq. Cran GU6 174 F3
Bishops Way. Egham TW20 12 D2
Bishops Wlk. S Croy CR0 & CR9 62 E5
Bishops Wood. Woking GU21 68 F2
Bishopscourt. 6 S Croy CR0 61 F8
Bishopsford Rd.Morden SM4 40 D3
Bishopsgate Rd. Eng Gn SL4 & TW20 11 B5
Bishopsmead C of E (Aided) Mid Sch. Epsom KT19 57 D1
Bishopsmead Cl. E Hors KT24 112 E7
Bishopsmead Dr. E Hors KT24 112 F6
Bishopsmead Par. E Hors KT24 112 F6
Bishopsthorpe Rd. For Hil SE26 23 D4
Bishopstone Wlk. Crawl RH11 201 C1
Bisley C of E Prim Sch. Bisley GU24 68 A3
Bisley Cl. N Cheam KT4 39 C1
Bisley House. Putney SW19 19 D6
Bitmead Cl. Crawl RH11 200 E5
Bittams La. Addl KT15 & KT16 51 E6
Bittern Cl. Crawl RH11 200 D5
Bittern Cl. Sandh GU15 64 D8
Bitterne Dr. Woking GU21 69 A2
Bittoms The. King U T KT1 37 D6
Black Dog Wlk. Crawl RH10 201 E8
Black Horse Way. Horsh RH12 217 C2
Black Lake Cl. Thorpe TW20 32 A8
Black Pond La. M Bourn GU10 146 C6
Black Prince Cl. Byfl KT14 71 F5
Blackberry Cl. Stough GU1 109 B4
Blackberry Cl. Up Hall TW17 34 E5
Blackberry Farm Cl. Heston TW5 4 E7
Blackberry La. Felct RH7 185 E8
Blackberry Rd. Felct RH19 & RH7 185 D8
Blackbird Cl. Sandh GU15 64 D8
Blackborough Cl. Reig RH2 118 C1
Blackborough Rd. Reig RH2 118 D1
Blackbridge Ct. Horsh RH12 217 B2
Blackbridge La. Horsh RH12 217 A1
Blackbridge Rd. Woking GU22 89 D7
Blackbrook Rd. Dork RH5 136 E2
Blackbrook Rd. S Holm RH5 157 E8
Blackburn The. L Book KT23 93 F3
Blackburn Trad Est. Stan TW19 2 F1
Blackburn Way. Godal GU7 151 A5
Blackbush Cl. Sutton SM2 59 B3
Blackcap Cl. Crawl RH11 201 C4
Blackcap Pl. Sandh GU15 64 E8
Blackdown Ave. Pyrf GU22 70 E4
Blackdown Cl. Mayb GU22 70 D3
Blackdown Prim Sch. Friml GU16 86 E8
Blackdown Rd. Friml GU16 86 C8
Blackdown Rural Ind. Haslem GU27 208 E4
Blackenham Rd. Up Toot SW17 20 F4
Blackett Cl. Egham TW18 & TW20 32 F7
Blackfold Rd. Crawl RH10 202 A5
Blackford Cl. S Croy CR2 61 B2
Blackham House. Wimble SW19 19 E2
Blackheath. Crawl RH10 202 D8
Blackheath Gr. Woner GU5 152 B8
Blackheath La. Albury GU5 132 B3
Blackheath La. Woner GU5 & GU4 152 C8
Blackheath Rd. Heath E GU9 125 A7
Blackhills. Esher KT10 55 A2
Blackhorse La. Croy CR0 43 A2
Blackhorse La. L Kings RH2 118 C7
Blackhorse Rd. Woking GU21 & GU22 88 E6
Blacklands Cres. For Row RH18 206 F2
Blacklands Meadow. Nutf RH1 119 E2
Blacklands Rd. Catf SE6 24 C4
Blackman Gdns. Alder GU11 126 B8
Blackman's La. Fickl CR6 82 F5
Blackmeadows. Easth RG12 27 C3
Blackmoor Cl. N Asct SL5 28 D7
Blackmoor Wood. N Asct SL5 28 D7
Blackmore Cres. Sheer GU21 70 C5
Blackmore House. For Hil SE23 23 F7
Blackmore's Gr. Tedd TW11 17 A2
Blackness La. Woking GU22 89 E8
Blacknest Cotts. Dunsf GU8 192 E3
Blacknest Rd. Went GU25 & SL5 30 E6
Blackshaw Rd. Up Toot SW17 20 D3
Blacksmith Cl. Ashtd KT21 95 F8
Blacksmith La. Chil GU4 131 D3
Blacksmith's La. Laleh TW18 33 C6
Blacksmiths Hill. Sander CR2 81 B6
Blacksmiths La. Chert KT16 33 A2
Blackstone Cl. Reig RH2 139 E8
Blackstone Cl.W Heath GU14 84 D6
Blackstone Hill. Reig RH1 & RH2 118 E1
Blackstone House. Dulw SE21 22 E5
Blackstroud La E. W End GU18 & GU24 67 E8
Blackstroud La W. Lhtwat GU18 67 D8
Blackthorn Cl. Crawl RH11 181 C1
Blackthorn Cl. Horsh RH13 218 A2
Blackthorn Cl. Woodh RH2 139 C7
Blackthorn Cres. W Heath GU14 84 F8
Blackthorn Ct. Heston TW5 4 E7
Blackthorn Ct. 6 W Norw SW16 22 A3
Blackthorn Dr. Lhtwat GU18 67 B7
Blackthorn Rd. Bigg H TN16 83 E3
Blackthorn Rd. Woodh RH2 139 C7
Blackthorne Ave. Croy CR0 43 C1
Blackthorne Cres. Poyle SL3 1 E5
Blackthorne Ind Pk. Poyle SL3 1 F5
Blackthorne Rd. G Book KT23 94 C1
Blackthorne Rd. Poyle SL3 1 E4
Blackwater Cl. Ash GU12 106 A1
Blackwater La. Crawl RH10 202 D6
Blackwater Sta. Blckw GU17 64 E4
Blackwater Way. Alder GU12 126 D8
Blackwater Way Ind Est. Alder GU12 126 E8
Blackwell Ave. Stough GU2 108 D1
Blackwell Cty Prim Sch. E Grins RH19 185 E3
Blackwell Farm Rd. E Grins RH19 185 F3
Blackwell Holl.E Grins RH19 185 F2
Blackwell Rd. E Grins RH19 185 F2
Blackwood Cl. W Byfl KT14 71 C7
Bladen Cl. Whit V KT13 53 E4
Blades Cl. Ashtd KT22 95 D7
Bladon Cl. Guild GU1 110 A2
Bladon Ct. Beck BR2 44 E7
Bladon Ct. Streat SW16 21 E2
Blagdon Rd. New Mal KT3 38 F5
Blagdon Wlk. Tedd TW11 17 C2
Blair Ave. Thame D KT10 55 C8
Blair Ct. Beck BR3 44 B8
Blair Ct. Catf SE6 24 F7
Blairderry Rd. Streat SW2 21 E6
Blaise Cl. Farnb GU14 85 D3
Blake Cl. Carsh SM5 40 E1
Blake Cl. Crawl RH10 201 F2
Blake Cl. Crowth RG11 45 C4
Blake Cl. Woki RG11 25 E8
Blake House. Beck BR3 24 B2
Blake Rd. Croy CR0 61 E8
Blake Rd. Mitch CR4 40 E6
Blake's Gn. W Wick BR4 44 C1
Blake's La. E Clan GU4 111 F3
Blake's La. W Hors GU4 111 F3
Blakeden Dr. Clayg KT10 55 F4
Blakehall Rd. Wallin SM5 59 F4
Blakemore Rd. Streat SW16 21 E5
Blakemore Rd. Thorn H CR7 41 F4
Blakeney Ave. Beck BR3 43 F8
Blakeney Cl. Epsom KT19 76 D8
Blakeney Rd. Beck BR3 43 F8
Blakes Ave. New Mal KT3 38 F3
Blakes La. New Mal KT3 38 F4
Blakes Terr. W Barn KT3 39 A4
Blakewood Cl. Felt TW13 15 C4
Blakewood Ct. Penge SE20 23 B1
Blanchards Hill. Westfd GU4 109 E8
Blanchland Rd. Morden SM4 40 B4
Blanchman's Rd. Warlgm CR6 81 E1
Blandfield Rd. Balham SW12 21 A8
Blandford Ave. Penge BR3 43 E7
Blandford Ave. Twick TW2 16 B7
Blandford Cl. Mayb GU22 70 B2
Blandford Cl. Wallin CR0 60 E7
Blandford Rd. Penge BR3 43 D7
Blandford Rd. Tedd TW11 16 E3
Blane's La. Brack SL5 28 C3
Blanford Rd. Reig RH2 139 C8
Blanks La. Charl RH5 & RH6 159 B2
Blanks La. Cudw RH5 & RH6 159 B2
Blashford St. Lewish SE13 24 D8
Blatchford Cl. Horsh RH13 217 F3
Blatchford Ct. Walt O T KT12 35 A1
Blatchford Rd. Horsh RH13 217 F3
Blay's La. Eng Gn TW20 11 B2
Blays Cl. Eng Gn TW20 11 C2
Blean Gr. Penge SE20 23 C1
Blegborough Rd. Streat SW16 21 C2
Blencarn Cl. Woking GU21 68 F3
Blendworth Point. 4 Rhampt SW15 19 B7
Blenheim. 26 Putney SW19 19 D7
Blenheim Bsns Ctr. Mitch CR4 40 F7
Blenheim Cl. Crawl RH10 182 D1
Blenheim Cl. E Grins RH19 186 A3
Blenheim Cl. Tongh GU10 126 E7
Blenheim Cl. W Barn SW20 39 C6

Blenheim Cl. W Byfl KT14 .... 70 F6
Blenheim Cl. Wallin SM6 ...... 60 C3
Blenheim Cres. Hale GU9 . 125 A5
Blenheim Cres. S Croy CR2 .. 61 C3
Blenheim Ct. Egham TW18 .. 12 D4
Blenheim Ct. Farnb GU14 .... 85 D2
Blenheim Ct. Rich TW9 .... 6 F4
Blenheim Ct. S Norw SE19 ... 42 E8
Blenheim Ct. Sutton SM2 ..... 59 C4
Blenheim Fields. For Row RH18 .... 206 E3
Blenheim Gdns. King U T KT2 .... 18 B1
Blenheim Gdns. Sander CR2 81 A7
Blenheim Gdns. Wallin SM6 60 C3
Blenheim Gdns. Woking GU22 .... 89 B8
Blenheim House. Hounsl TW3 5 A4
Blenheim Park Rd. S Croy CR2 .... 61 C2
Blenheim Pk. Farnb GU11 .. 105 C7
Blenheim Rd. Epsom KT19 ... 76 E8
Blenheim Rd. Farnb GU11 .. 105 C7
Blenheim Rd. Horsh RH12 217 D4
Blenheim Rd. Penge SE20 ... 23 C1
Blenheim Rd. Sutton SM1 .... 59 B7
Blenheim Rd. W Barn SW20 39 C6
Bleriot Rd. Heston TW5 .... 4 C7
Bletchingley Cl. Merst RH1 119 C6
Bletchingley Golf Course. Bletch RH1 .... 120 E3
Bletchingley Rd. Bletch RH1 & RH9 .... 121 B4
Bletchingley Rd. Godst RH1 & RH9 .... 121 B4
Bletchingley Rd. Merst RH1 119 E6
Bletchingley Rd. Nutf RH1 . 119 E6
Bletchingley Rd. Nutf RH1 120 A2
Bletchingly Cl. Thorn H CR7 . 42 B5
Bletchmore Cl. Harl UB3 .... 3 D8
Blewburton Wlk. Brack RG12 27 E5
Blewfield. Godal GU7 .... 150 F2
Bligh Cl. Crawl RH10 .... 201 F4
Bligh House. 4 W Norw SE27 .... 22 C4
Blighton La. The San GU10 . 126 E3
Blincoe Cl. Putney SW19 ...... 19 D6
Blind Cnr. Croy SE25 .... 43 B5
Blindley Ct. Blind H RH7 ..... 163 E8
Blindley Rd. Crawl RH10 ..... 182 D1
Bloggs Way. Cran GU6 .... 174 D3
Blomfield Dale. Binf RG12 .... 26 D7
Blondell Cl. Harm UB7 .... 2 D8
Bloom Gr. W Norw SE27 ...... 22 B5
Bloomfield Cl. Knaph GU21 .. 68 E1
Bloomfield Rd. King U T KT1 37 E6
Bloomsbury Cl. Epsom KT19 57 D1
Bloomsbury Ct. Cranf TW5 .... 4 B6
Bloomsbury Way. Hawley GU17 .... 64 D3
Bloor Cl. Horsh RH12 .... 217 D7
Blossom Cl. S Croy CR2 .... 61 F5
Blossom Waye. Heston TW5 . 4 E7
Blount Ave. E Grins RH19 ... 185 C1
Bloxham Cres. Hampt TW12 35 F8
Bloxham Rd. Cran GU6 ...... 175 A3
Bloxworth Cl. 9 Brack RG12 27 F5
Bloxworth Cl. Wallin SM6 .... 60 C7
Blue Anchor Alley. 3 Rich TW9 .... 6 E3
Blue Ball La. Egham TW20 .... 11 F3
Blue Barn Way. Whit V KT13 72 A8
Blue Cedars. Nork SM7 .... 77 D5
Blue Coat Wlk. Brack RG12 . 27 D4
Blue Sch The. Islew TW7 .... 6 A4
Bluebell Cl. Crawl RH11 .... 201 B3
Bluebell Cl. E Grins RH19 .. 185 B1
Bluebell Cl. For Hil SE19 & SE26 .... 22 F4
Bluebell Cl. Horsh RH12 ..... 217 E5
Bluebell Cl. Wallin CR4 .... 41 B1
Bluebell Ct. Woking GU22 .... 89 D8
Bluebell Hill. Brack RG12 .... 27 E8
Bluebell Rise. Lhtwat GU18 .. 67 B8
Blueberry Gdns. Coulsd CR5 79 F3
Bluefield Cl. Hampt TW12 .... 16 A3
Bluegates. Stonel KT17 .... 58 A3
Bluegates. Wimble SW19 ...... 19 E3
Bluehouse Gdns.Limps RH8 123 A7
Bluehouse La. Limps RH8 ... 122 F7
Bluethroat Cl. Sandh GU15 .. 64 E8
Bluff Cove. Alder GU11 .... 105 C3
Blundel La. Oxsh KT11 .... 74 B4
Blundel La. Stk D'A KT11 ...... 74 B4
Blundell Ave. Horley RH6 ... 160 F4
Blunden Rd. W Heath GU14 . 84 F5
Blunt Rd. Croy CR0 .... 61 D5
Blunts Ave. Harm UB7 .... 3 A7
Blunts Way. Horsh RH12 .... 217 C3
Blyth Cl. Twick TW1 .... 5 F1
Blyth Rd. Broml BR1 & BR2 .. 44 F8
Blythe Cl. For Hil SE23 .... 23 F8
Blythe Hill. For Hil SE23 & SE6 .... 23 F8
Blythe Hill La. For Hil SE23 & SE6 .... 23 F7
Blythe Vale. For Hil SE23 & SE6 .... 23 F7
Blythewood La. N Asct SL5 .. 28 E7
Blythwood Dr. Friml GU15 & GU16 .... 65 D2
Blythwood Pk. Broml BR1 .... 44 F8
Blytons The. E Grins RH19 185 B1
Boar Hill. Dork RH5 .... 135 E1
Board School Rd. Woking GU21 .... 69 F3
Bockhampton Rd. King U T KT2 .... 17 F1
Boddicott Cl. Putney SW19 .. 19 E6
Bodens Ride. Brack SL5 .... 28 F1
Bodiam Cl. Crawl RH10 ...... 202 C6
Bodiam Ct. Hayes BR2 .... 44 F5
Bodiam Rd. Streat SW16 ...... 21 D1
Bodley Cl. New Mal KT3 .... 38 E4
Bodley Manor Way. Streat SE24 .... 22 A8
Bodley Rd. New Mal KT3 ...... 38 E4
Bodmin Gr. Morden SM4 ...... 40 B4
Bodmin St. Wands SW18 ..... 20 A7
Bodnant Gdns. W Barn SW20 .... 39 B6
Bofors Rd. Farnb GU14 ...... 105 A8
Bog La. Brack RG12 .... 28 A5
Bognor Rd. Bear Gn RH5 ... 157 B2
Bognor Rd. Ockley RH5 ..... 157 B2
Bognor Rd. Warn RH12 & RH5 .... 197 D4
Bois Hall Rd. Addl KT15 .... 52 D5
Bolderwood Way. W Wick BR4 .... 63 B8
Bolding House La. W End GU24 .... 67 F7
Boleyn Ave. Ewell KT17 .... 58 B1
Boleyn Cl. Egham TW18 .... 12 E3
Boleyn Ct. E Mole KT8 .... 36 D5
Boleyn Ct. 11 Redh RH1 ..... 119 A2
Boleyn Dr. E Mole KT8 .... 35 F6
Boleyn Gdns. W Wick BR4 .... 63 B8
Boleyn Wlk. Leahd KT22 ...... 94 F7
Bolingbroke Gr. Balham SW11 .... 20 F8
Bolingbroke House.Catf BR3 24 B3
Bolney Ct. Crawl RH11 .... 200 F3
Bolney Ct. King U T KT6 .... 37 C4
Bolsover Gr. Merst RH1 ...... 119 E6
Bolstead Rd. Mitch CR4 .... 41 B8
Bolters La. Banstd SM7 .... 78 A4
Bolters Rd. Horley RH6 ...... 161 A5
Bolters Rd S. Horley RH6 ... 160 F6
Bolton Cl. Chess KT9 .... 56 E4
Bolton Cl. Penge SE20 .... 43 A7
Bolton Gdns. Broml BR1 ...... 24 F2
Bolton Gdns. Tedd TW11 ..... 17 A2
Bolton Rd. Chess KT9 .... 56 E4
Bolton Rd. Chisw W4 .... 7 C7
Bolton Rd. Worth RH10 ...... 202 C2
Bolton's La. Harl TW6 & UB7 . 3 C7
Bolton's La. Pyrf GU22 .... 71 A3
Boltons Cl. Pyrf GU22 .... 71 A3
Bomer Cl. Harm UB7 .... 3 A7
Bonchurch Cl. Sutton SM2 ... 59 B3
Bond Fst Sch. Mitch CR4 ...... 40 F7
Bond Gdns. Wallin SM6 .... 60 C6
Bond Rd. Mitch CR4 .... 40 F7
Bond Rd. Surb KT6 .... 56 F8
Bond Rd. Warlgm CR6 .... 81 E1
Bond St. Eng Gn TW20 .... 11 C3
Bond's La. Dork RH5 .... 136 B1
Bone Mill La. Godst RH9 .... 121 E1
Bonehurst Rd. Salfs RH1 & RH6 .... 161 A7
Bones La. Horne RH6 & RH7 & RH9 .. 163 B2
Bonner Hill Rd. King U T KT1 38 A6
Bonners Cl. Westfd GU22 ..... 89 F5
Bonnetts La. Rusper RH11 & RH6 .... 181 A3
Bonnys Rd. Reig RH2 .... 138 D8
Bonser Rd. Twick TW1 .... 16 F6
Bonsey Cl. Westfd GU22 ...... 89 E6
Bonsey La. Westfd GU22 ...... 89 E6
Bonsey's La. Chobh GU24 & KT16 .... 50 F2
Bonsor Dr. Kings KT20 .... 97 E5
Bonus Pastor RC Sch. Catf BR1 .... 24 E4
Bonville Rd. Broml BR1 .... 24 F3
Bookham Ct. L Book KT23 .... 93 F4
Bookham Ct. Mitch CR4 .... 40 D6
Bookham Gr. G Book KT23 ... 94 B1
Bookham Ind Pk. L Bk KT23 93 F4
Bookham Rd. Downs KT11 ... 93 D7
Bookham Sta. L Bk KT23 ...... 93 F4
Bookhurst Hill. Cran GU6 .. 175 A4
Bookhurst Rd. Cran GU6 ... 175 B4
Booth Dr. Stain TW18 .... 13 D2
Booth House. 2 Streat SW2 22 A8
Booth Rd. Crawl RH11 .... 200 E3
Booth Rd. Croy CR0 & CR9 ... 61 B8
Boothby House. 2 Streat SW16 .... 21 C3
Borage Cl. Crawl RH11 ...... 201 A3
Border Chase. Copth RH10 183 A2
Border Cres. Penge SE26 ..... 23 B3
Border End. Shottm GU27 . 207 D6
Border Gate. Mitch CR4 .... 40 F8
Border Gdns. Croy CR0 .... 63 B6
Border Rd. For Hil SE26 .... 23 B3
Border Rd. Shottm GU27 ... 207 D6
Bordesley Rd. Morden SM4 .. 40 B5
Bordon Wlk. 6 Rhampt SW15 .... 19 A8
Boreen The. Head Dn GU35 187 B5
Borelli Mews. Farnh GU9 ... 125 C2
Borers Arms Rd. Copth RH10 .... 183 C3
Borers Yard Ind Est. Copth RH10 .... 183 C3
Borland Rd. Tedd TW11 .... 17 B1
Borough Grange. Sander CR2 .... 81 A7
Borough Hill. Croy CR0 & CR9 .... 61 B7
Borough Rd. Farnc GU7 ..... 150 D5
Borough Rd. Godal GU7 .... 150 D5
Borough Rd. Hounsl TW7 .... 5 F6
Borough Rd. 7 King U T KT2 18 A1
Borough Rd. Mitch CR4 .... 40 E7
Borough Rd. Tats TN16 ..... 103 D6
Borough The. Brock RH3 & RH5 .... 137 A8
Borough The. Farnh GU9 .. 125 B2
Borrowdale Cl. Crawl RH11 201 B4
Borrowdale Cl. Sander CR2 . 80 F6
Borrowdale Cl. Thor L TW20 12 B1
Borrowdale Dr. Sander CR2 . 80 F7
Borrowdale Gdns. Friml GU15 .... 66 D4
Bosbury Rd. Catf SE6 .... 24 C5
Boscombe Cl. Thor L TW20 .. 32 C8
Boscombe Gdns. Streat SW16 .... 21 E2
Boscombe House. Croy CR0 42 D1
Boscombe Rd. Merton SW19 40 B8
Boscombe Rd. Mitch SW17 .. 21 A2
Boscombe Rd. N Cheam KT4 39 D1
Bosman Dr. Windl GU20 .... 48 B6
Bostock Ave. Horsh RH12 . 218 A5
Bostock House. Heston TW5 . 5 A8
Boston Ct. S Norw SE25 .... 42 F5
Boston Ct. Sutton SM2 .... 59 C3
Boston Gdns. Chisw W4 .... 7 E8
Boston Manor Rd. Brent TW8 6 C8
Boston Rd. Thorn H CR0 .... 42 A3
Boswell House. 5 Streat SW16 .... 21 C3
Boswell Rd. Crawl RH10 ..... 201 E3
Boswell Rd. Thorn H CR7 ...... 42 C5
Boswood Ct. Hounsl TW4 .... 4 F4
Botany Hill. The San GU10 126 D1
Botery's Cross. Bletch RH1 120 B2
Bothwell Rd. New Add CR0 .. 63 C1
Botsford Rd. Merton SW20 .. 39 E7
Boucher Cl. Tedd TW11 .... 16 F3
Boughton Ave. Hayes BR2 ... 44 F2
Boughton Hall Ave. Send M GU23 .... 90 F3
Bouldish Farm Rd. Ascot SL5 .... 29 A5
Boulevard The. Crawl RH10 & RH11 .... 201 E6
Boulevard The. 4 Up Toot SW17 .... 21 A6
Boullen Ct. Sutton SM1 .... 59 C6
Boulogne Rd. Thorn H CR0 .. 42 C3
Boulter's Rd. Alder GU11 & GU12 .... 105 B2
Boulters House. Brack RG12 27 E5
Boulthurst Way. Oxted RH8 123 B3
Boundaries Mansions. 4 Up Toot SW12 .... 21 A7
Boundaries Rd.Blham SW12 21 A7
Boundaries Rd. Felt TW13 ... 15 C7
Boundaries Rd. Up Toot SW12 & SW17 .... 21 A7
Boundary Bsns Ct.Mitch CR4 40 D6
Boundary Bsns Ctr. Woking GU21 .... 70 A4
Boundary Cl. Crawl RH10 ... 201 E7
Boundary Cl. King U T KT1 ... 38 B6
Boundary Cl. Penge SE20 ..... 43 A7
Boundary Cotts. Albury GU4 .... 132 A4
Boundary House. Twick TW1 . 6 B2
Boundary Rd. Binst GU10 ... 145 E2
Boundary Rd. Crawl RH10 .. 201 E7
Boundary Rd. Docken GU10 166 D7
Boundary Rd. Farnb GU14 ... 84 C1
Boundary Rd. Farnb GU14 .... 85 C2
Boundary Rd. Frensh GU10 145 E2
Boundary Rd. Graysh GU26 188 D3
Boundary Rd. Mitch SW19 ... 20 D2
Boundary Rd. Stain TW15 .... 13 C3
Boundary Rd. Wallin SM5 & SM6 .... 60 A3
Boundary Rd. Woking GU21 . 69 F3
Boundary Rd. Woking GU21 . 70 A4
Boundary Rd E. Woodhm KT15 .... 52 B2
Boundary Rd N. Woodhm KT15 .... 52 B2
Boundary Rd W. Woodhm KT15 .... 52 B2
Boundary Way. Add CR0 ...... 63 A5
Boundary Way. Woking GU21 .... 70 A4
Boundfield Rd. Catf SE6 .... 24 E6
Boundstone Cl. Rowl GU10 146 B5
Boundstone Rd. Rowl GU10 146 A4
Bourbon House. Catf SE6 .... 24 C4
Bourdon Rd. Penge SE20 ..... 43 C7
Bourg-De-Peage Ave. E Grins RH19 .... 186 A1
Bourke Hill. Chips CR5 .... 78 F1
Bourley La. Crond GU10 ..... 104 A2
Bourley Rd. Alder GU11 ...... 104 C2
Bourley Rd. Crond GU10 ..... 104 C2
Bourne Ave. Thorpe KT16 .... 33 A6
Bourne Cl. Chil GU4 .... 131 B3
Bourne Cl. W Byfl KT14 .... 71 B6
Bourne Ct. Alder GU11 ...... 126 A8
Bourne Ct. Chisw W4 .... 7 C8
Bourne Ct. 1 Purley CR8 .... 80 A8
Bourne Dene. Rowl GU10 .. 146 A5
Bourne Dr. Mitch CR4 .... 40 D7
Bourne Firs. M Bourn GU10 146 D5
Bourne Gr. Ashtd KT21 .... 95 D8
Bourne Gr. M Bourn GU10 & GU9 .... 146 E7
Bourne Grove Cl. M Bourn GU10 & GU9 .... 146 E7
Bourne Grove Dr. M Bourn GU10 .... 146 E7
Bourne Hall. Ewell KT17 ...... 57 F2
Bourne House. Ashf TW15 .... 14 A3
Bourne Hts. M Bourn GU9 .. 146 C8
Bourne La. Cater CR3 .... 100 D6
Bourne Meadow. Egham KT16 & TW20 .... 32 B5
Bourne Mill Ind Est. Farnh GU9 .... 125 E3
Bourne Mill Rdbt. Farnh GU10 & GU9 .... 125 E3
Bourne Park Cl. Kenley CR8 . 80 E3
Bourne Rd. Farnc GU7 .... 150 F7
Bourne Rd. Merst RH1 .... 119 C5
Bourne Rd. Went GU25 .... 31 D4
Bourne Rd. Woodhm KT15 ... 52 B2
Bourne Sch The. M Bourn GU10 .... 146 D6
Bourne St. Croy CR0 & CR9 ... 61 B8
Bourne Vale. Hayes BR2 ...... 44 F1
Bourne View. Kenley CR8 ..... 80 D4
Bourne Way. Addl KT15 .... 52 C5
Bourne Way. Cheam SM1 ..... 58 F5
Bourne Way. Coney H BR2 & BR4 .... 63 F8
Bourne Way. W Ewell KT19 .. 57 C6
Bourne Way. W Ewell KT19 .. 57 C6
Bourne Way. Westfd GU22 .. 89 D5
Bournefield Rd. Whytlf CR3 . 81 A1
Bournemouth Rd. Merton SW19 .... 40 A8
Bourneside. Went GU25 .... 31 A2
Bourneside Gdns. Catf SE6 .. 24 C3
Bourneside Rd. Addl KT15 ... 52 D5
Bournevale Rd. Streat SW16 21 E4
Bourns Ct. Horsh RH13 .... 217 E3
Bournville Rd. For Hil SE13 & SE6 .... 24 A8
Bousley Rise. Ottsh KT16 ..... 51 D4
Bouverie Rd. Chips CR5 .... 79 A1
Boveney House. Brack RG12 27 E5
Boveney Rd. For Hil SE23 ..... 23 D8
Bovey House. 3 Redh RH1 .... 119 A3
Bovill Rd. For Hil SE23 .... 23 D8
Bovingdon Sq. Mitch CR4 .... 41 E5
Bowater Rd. Worth RH10 ... 202 C3
Bowater Ridge. Whit V KT13 53 D1
Bowden Cl. E Bed TW14 .... 14 E7
Bowden Rd. Ascot SL5 .... 29 D4
Bowen Dr. Dulw SE19 & SE21 22 E5
Bower Ct. Mayb GU22 .... 70 B3
Bower Hill Cl. S Nutf RH1 ... 140 E6
Bower Hill La. Nutf RH1 .... 140 D7
Bower Rd. Rowl GU10 .... 146 A5
Bowerland La. Crow RH7 ... 164 E7
Bowers Cl. Burph GU4 .... 110 A5
Bowers Farm Dr. Burph GU4 .... 110 B5
Bowers La. Burph GU4 .... 110 A6
Bowers Pl. Crawl D RH10 .. 204 B8
Bowes Rd. Egham TW18 .... 12 E2
Bowes Rd. Walt O T KT12 ..... 54 B8
Bowie Cl. Streat SW4 .... 21 D8
Bowland Dr. Brack RG12 .... 27 E2
Bowley Cl. Dulw SE19 .... 22 F2
Bowley La. Dulw SE19 .... 22 F3
Bowling Green Cl. Putney SW19 .... 19 B8
Bowling Green Ct. Friml GU16 .... 85 E7
Bowling Green La. Horsh RH12 .... 217 D3
Bowling Green Rd. Burrh GU24 .... 49 E2
Bowlings The. Camb GU15 ... 65 C6
Bowman Ct. Crawl RH11 ... 201 D7
Bowman Mews. Wands SW18 .... 19 F7
Bowman's Meadow. Hackb SM6 .... 60 B7
Bowmans Lea. For Hil SE23 . 23 C8
Bowness Cl. 7 Crawl RH11 .... 200 D5
Bowness Cres. King U T KT2 & SW15 .... 18 E3
Bowness Dr. Hounsl TW4 .... 4 E3
Bowness Rd. Catf SE6 .... 24 B8
Bowring House. Farnc GU7 150 F6
Bowsley Ct. Felt TW13 .... 15 A6
Bowsprit The. Cobham KT11 73 C4
Bowyer Cres. Woki RG11 ..... 25 C8
Bowyers Cl. Ashtd KT21 .... 75 F1
Box Cl. Crawl RH11 .... 201 C1
Box Hill Ctry Pk. Mickle RH4 .... 115 D3
Box Hill Sch. Mickle RH5 ... 115 B8
Box La. Ash W RH19 .... 206 E6
Box Ridge Ave. Purley CR8 .. 79 F7
Boxall Rd. Dulw SE21 .... 22 E8
Boxall Wlk. Horsh RH13 .... 217 D1
Boxall's Gr. Alder GU11 ..... 126 A8
Boxall's La. Alder GU11 ..... 126 B7
Boxford Cl. Selsd CR2 .... 81 D7
Boxford Ridge. Easth RG12 .. 27 B6
Boxgrove Ave. Abbots GU1 110 A3
Boxgrove Cty Prim Sch. Merrow GU1 .... 110 B2
Boxgrove La. Merrow GU1 110 B2
Boxgrove Rd. Abbots GU1 . 110 A2
Boxgrove Rd. Merrow GU1 110 A2
Boxhill Rd. Box H RH4 .... 115 E3
Boxhill Way. Brock RH3 ..... 137 B5
Boxhill & Westhumble Sta. Westh RH5 .... 115 B4
Boxley Rd. Morden SM4 & SW19 .... 40 C5
Boxwood Way. Warlgm CR6 81 D2
Boyce House. Streat SW16 .. 21 C3
Boyd Cl. King U T KT2 .... 18 A1
Boyd Ct. Brack RG12 .... 27 A8
Boyd Rd. Mitch SW19 .... 20 D2
Boyland Rd. Broml BR1 .... 24 F3
Boyle Farm Rd. Thame D KT7 .... 37 A3
Brabazon Ave. Wallin SM6 ... 60 E3
Brabazon Rd. Heston TW5 ..... 4 D7
Braboeuf Manor (Coll of Law). Arting GU2 .... 130 C5
Brabon Rd. W Heath GU14 ... 84 F5
Brabourne Cl. 7 W Norw SE19 .... 22 E3
Brabourne Rise. Beck BR3 ... 44 D4
Brabrook Ct. Wallin SM6 ...... 60 B5
Bracebridge. Camb GU15 ..... 65 A5
Bracewood Gdns.S Croy CR0 61 F7
Bracken Ave. Balham SW12 . 21 A8
Bracken Ave. W Wick CR0 .... 63 B7
Bracken Bank. N Asct SL5 .... 28 C8
Bracken Cl. Ashf TW16 .... 14 F2
Bracken Cl. Copth RH10 ..... 183 B2
Bracken Cl. Crawl RH10 ..... 201 F8
Bracken Cl. L Book KT23 ...... 93 F3
Bracken Cl. Twick TW4 .... 16 A8
Bracken Cl. Woking GU22 ..... 69 F1
Bracken Cl. Woner GU5 ...... 152 B6
Bracken End. Islew TW7 .... 5 D2
Bracken Gr. Horsh RH12 .... 218 B5
Bracken Hill Cl. Broml BR1 .. 44 F8
Bracken Hill La. Broml BR1 .. 44 F8

Bracken Path. Epsom KT18 .. 76 B6
Bracken Way. Chobh GU24 .. 49 F1
Bracken Way. Stough GU3 . 108 E3
Brackendale. King U T KT1 ... 38 B7
Brackendale Cl. Friml GU15 . 65 E3
Brackendale Cl. Hounsl TW5 . 5 B6
Brackendale Ct. 2 Beck BR3 .... 24 A1
Brackendale Rd. Camb GU15 65 D4
Brackendene. Ash GU12 ..... 106 C3
Brackendene Cl. Horse GU21 .... 70 A4
Brackenhale Comp Sch. Easth RG12 .... 27 B5
Brackenhill. Oxsh KT11 .... 74 B7
Brackenlea. Farnc GU7 ...... 150 D7
Brackens. Beck BR3 .... 24 A1
Brackens The. Crowth RG11 45 A7
Brackenside. Horley RH6 ... 161 B4
Brackenwood. Friml GU15 ... 66 D5
Brackenwood. Sunby TW16 . 35 A8
Brackenwood Rd. Knaph GU21 .... 88 D8
Bracklesham Cl. W Heath GU14 .... 85 A7
Brackley. Whit V KT13 .... 53 D5
Brackley Cl. Wallin SM6 .... 60 E3
Brackley Rd. Beck BR3 .... 24 A1
Bracknell Beeches. Easth RG12 .... 27 B6
Bracknell Bsns Ctr The. Brack RG12 .... 26 F7
Bracknell Cl. Camb GU15 ..... 46 F1
Bracknell Coll. Brack RG12 .. 27 C7
Bracknell Coll. Brack RG12 .. 27 C8
Bracknell Coll (Annexe). Brack RG12 .... 27 A8
Bracknell Enterprise Ctr. Brack RG12 .... 27 A7
Bracknell Rd. Brack GU19 .... 47 E5
Bracknell Rd. Camb GU15 .... 47 A1
Bracknell Rd. Crowth RG11 .. 45 D6
Bracknell Rd. Wink RG12 & SL4 .... 8 A5
Bracknell Sports & L Ctr. Easth RG12 .... 27 C4
Bracknell Sta. Easth RG12 .... 27 B6
Bracknell Wlk. Crawl RH11 200 E3
Bracondale. Esher KT10 .... 55 C5
Bradbury Rd. Worth RH10 . 202 C3
Braddon Rd. Rich TW9 .... 6 F4
Bradenhurst Cl. Cater CR3 . 100 F2
Bradfield Cl. Burph GU1 .... 110 A4
Bradfield Cl. Woking GU22 ... 69 E1
Bradfields. Brack RG12 .... 27 D4
Bradford Cl. For Hil SE26 ..... 23 B4
Bradford Dr. W Ewell KT19 .. 57 F4
Bradford Dr. W Ewell KT19 .. 57 F4
Brading Rd. Streat SW2 .... 21 F8
Brading Rd. Thorn H CR0 ...... 41 F3
Bradley Ct. Croy CR0 .... 61 A6
Bradley La. Westh RH4 & RH5 .... 115 B3
Bradley Mews. Up Toot SW12 .... 20 F7
Bradley Rd. S Norw SE19 ..... 22 C2
Bradlord House. Dulw SE21 . 22 E5
Bradmore Way. Coulsd CR5 . 79 F1
Bradshaws Cl. Croy SE25 ..... 43 A6
Bradsole House. 13 Beck BR3 .... 24 A1
Bradstock Rd. Stonel KT17 ... 58 B5
Brae Ct. 2 King U T KT2 ...... 38 A8
Brae Ct. S Norw SE25 .... 42 E8
Braemar Ave. S Croy CR2 ..... 61 C2
Braemar Ave. Thorn H CR7 .. 42 B6
Braemar Ave. Wimble SW18 & SW19 .... 20 A6
Braemar Cl. Friml GU16 .... 85 F8
Braemar Cl. Godal GU7 ..... 150 D3
Braemar Ct. 5 Brent TW8 .... 6 D8
Braemar Ct. Catf SE6 .... 24 F7
Braemar Gdns. W Wick BR4 44 C1
Braemar House. Rich TW11 . 17 B3
Braemar Rd. Brent TW8 .... 6 D8
Braemar Rd. N Cheam KT4 ... 58 B7
Braes Mead. S Nutf RH1 ..... 140 E8
Braeside. Beck BR3 .... 24 B3
Braeside. Woodhm KT15 .... 71 B8
Braeside Ave. Merton SW19 39 E8
Braeside Cl. Shottm GU27 .. 207 F8
Braeside Rd. Streat SW16 ..... 21 C1
Brafferton Rd. Croy CR0 ...... 61 C6
Braganza Ct. Guild GU1 ...... 109 F2
Bragg Rd. Tedd TW11 .... 16 F2
Braid Cl. Felt TW13 .... 15 F6
Braidwood Rd. Catf SE6 .... 24 D7
Brailsford Cl. Mitch SW19 .... 20 E1
Brainton Ave. Felt TW14 ...... 15 C8
Brake Rd. Farnb GU14 .... 84 E1
Brakey Hill. Bletch RH1 .... 120 E1
Bramber Cl. Crawl RH10 .... 201 E8
Bramber Cl. Horsh RH12 ... 218 B5
Bramble Acres Cl. Belm SM2 59 A3
Bramble Bank. Friml GU16 ... 86 A6
Bramble Banks. Wallin SM5 . 60 A2
Bramble Cl. Copth RH10 ..... 183 B3
Bramble Cl. Croy CR0 .... 63 B6
Bramble Cl. Earls RH1 .... 140 A7
Bramble Cl. Stough GU3 .... 108 E3
Bramble Cl. Up Hall TW17 .... 34 D6
Bramble Hedge Farm (Ind Est). Whit V KT11 .... 72 C5
Bramble La. Hampt TW12 ..... 15 F2
Bramble Rise. Cobham KT11 73 C5
Bramble Twitten. E Grins RH19 .... 186 A1
Bramble Way. Send M GU23 90 F3
Bramble Wlk. Epsom KT18 ... 76 B6
Brambledene Cl. Woking GU21 .... 69 C1
Brambledown. Stain TW18 .. 33 B8
Brambledown Cl. Hayes BR2 & BR4 .... 44 E4
Brambledown Rd. S Croy CR2 .... 61 E3
Brambledown Rd. Wallin SM5 & SM6 .... 60 B3
Bramblegate. Crowth RG11 . 45 A6
Brambles Cl. Brent TW7 & TW8 .... 6 B7
Brambles Cl. Cater CR3 ...... 100 E5
Brambles Pk. Bramly GU5 .. 151 F6
Brambles The. Farnc GU7 . 150 D7
Brambles The. 8 Wimble SW19 .... 19 F3
Brambleton Ave. M Bourn GU9 .... 146 B7
Brambletye Cty Jun Sch. Earls RH1 .... 140 A7
Brambletye Park Rd. Earls RH1 .... 140 A7
Brambletye Rd. Crawl RH10 .... 202 A5
Brambletye Sch. Ash W RH19 .... 206 C5
Bramblewood. Merst RH2 . 119 B6
Bramblewood Cl. Carsh SM5 40 E1
Brambling Cl. Horsh RH13 218 A1
Brambling Rd. Horsh RH13 218 A1
Bramcote. Friml GU15 .... 66 C5
Bramcote Ave. Mitch CR4 .... 40 F5
Bramcote Ct. Mitch CR4 .... 40 F5
Bramerton Rd. Beck BR3 ..... 43 F6
Bramham Gdns. Chess KT9 . 56 D6
Bramley Ave. Coulsd CR5 ..... 79 C4
Bramley Ave. Sunby TW17 ... 34 E6
Bramley CE (VA) Inf Sch. Bramly GU5 .... 152 A5
Bramley Cl. Chert KT16 .... 33 B1
Bramley Cl. Crawl RH10 ...... 201 F6
Bramley Cl. Croy CR2 .... 61 C5
Bramley Cl. Stain TW18 .... 13 C2
Bramley Cl. Twick TW2 .... 5 C1
Bramley Ct. Mitch CR4 .... 40 D7
Bramley Ct. Redh RH1 .... 118 E3
Bramley Ct. Wallin SM6 .... 60 C5
Bramley Hill. Croy CR0 & CR2 .... 61 C6
Bramley House. Earls RH1 140 A8
Bramley House. 1 King U T KT2 .... 18 B1
Bramley House. Rhampt SW15 .... 7 F1
Bramley La. Blckw GU17 ...... 64 B5
Bramley Pk Ct. Bramly GU5 151 F6
Bramley Rd. Camb GU15 ...... 65 B2
Bramley Rd. Carsh SM1 .... 59 D5
Bramley Rd. E Ewell SM2 ..... 58 D2
Bramley Way. Ashtd KT21 .... 75 F2
Bramley Way. Hounsl TW4 .... 4 F2
Bramley Way. W Wick BR4 .. 63 B8
Bramley Wlk. Horley RH6 ... 161 C3
Bramleyhyrst. Croy CR2 .... 61 C5
Brampton Gdns. Hersh KT12 54 C5
Brampton Rd. Croy CR0 .... 42 F3
Bramshaw Rise. New Mal KT3 .... 38 E3
Bramshot La. Hawley GU14 . 84 A5
Bramshot La. W Heath GU14 84 C6
Bramshott Ct. 3 Surb KT6 .. 37 E3
Bramshott Rd. Farnb GU14 .. 84 A2
Bramston Rd. Wands SW17 . 20 C5
Bramswell Rd. Farnc GU7 .. 150 F6
Bramwell Cl. Sunby TW16 .... 35 D7
Brancaster La. Purley CR8 .... 80 C8
Brancaster Rd. Streat SW16 21 E5
Brancker Cl. Wallin SM6 .... 60 E3
Brandon Cl. Friml GU15 .... 66 D4
Brandon House. Catf BR3 .... 24 B3
Brandon Rd. Sutton SM1 ...... 59 B6
Brandreth Rd. Up Toot SW17 21 B6
Brandries The. Wallin SM6 .. 60 D7
Brands Rd. Bra Hil SL3 .... 1 B8
Brandsland. Dovgn RH2 ...... 139 B6
Brandy Way. Belm SM2 .... 59 A3
Brangbourne Rd. Catf BR1 ... 24 C3
Brangwyn Cres. Mitch SW19 40 D7
Branksome Cl. Camb GU15 .. 65 E6
Branksome Cl. Walt O T KT12 .... 54 D8
Branksome Hill Rd. Sandh GU15 .... 64 E8
Branksome Park Rd. Camb GU15 .... 65 E6
Branksome Rd. Merton SW19 .... 40 A8
Branksome Way. King U T KT3 .... 38 D8
Bransby Rd. Chess KT9 .... 56 E4
Branscombe Ct. Hayes BR2 . 44 E4
Branstone Ct. 9 Rich TW9 ... 6 F6
Branstone Rd. Rich TW9 .... 6 F6
Brantridge Rd. Crawl RH10 201 F4
Brants Bridge. Brack RG12 ... 27 E7
Brantwood Ave. Islew TW7 ... 6 A3
Brantwood Cl. 1 W Byfl KT14 .... 71 A6
Brantwood Ct. W Byfl KT14 . 70 F6
Brantwood Dr. W Byfl KT14 . 70 F6
Brantwood Gdns. W Byfl KT14 .... 71 A6
Brantwood Rd. S Croy CR2 .. 61 D2
Brassey Cl. E Bed TW14 .... 15 A7
Brassey Rd. Limps RH8 ...... 123 A6
Brasted Cl. Belm SM2 .... 59 A1
Brasted Cl. For Hil SE26 .... 23 C4
Brasted Lodge. 11 Beck BR3 .... 24 A1
Brathway Rd. Wands SW18 . 20 A8
Bratten Ct. Thorn H CR0 .... 42 D3
Bravington Cl. Shep Gn TW17 .... 33 F4
Braxted Pk. Streat SW16 ...... 21 F2
Bray Ct. Chess KT9 .... 56 F5
Bray Gdns. Pyrf GU22 .... 70 E3
Bray Rd. Guild GU2 .... 130 B8
Bray Rd. Stk D'A KT11 .... 73 E3
Braybourne Dr. Hounsl TW7 .. 5 F7
Braybrooke Gdns. S Norw SE19 .... 22 E1
Braycourt Ave. Walt O T KT12 .... 35 C2
Braye Cl. Sandh GU17 .... 45 C1
Braywick Ct. 9 King U T KT2 18 A1
Braywood Ave. Egham TW20 12 A2
Braziers La. Wink SL4 & SL5 ... 8 D4
Breakfield. Coulsd CR5 .... 79 E3
Breakspeare. Dulw SE21 .... 22 F5
Breamore Cl. Rhampt SW15 19 A7
Breamwater Gdns. Rich TW10 .... 17 B5
Brecon Cl. Mitch CR4 .... 41 E6
Brecon Cl. N Cheam KT4 .... 58 C8
Brecon Cl. W Heath GU14 .... 84 D7
Brecon House. Wands SW18 20 A8
Bredhurst Cl. Penge SE20 .... 23 C2
Bredinghurst. Dulw SE22 ..... 23 A8
Bredon Rd. Croy CR0 .... 42 F2
Bredune. Kenley CR8 .... 80 D4
Breech La. Walt o t H KT20 .. 97 A2
Breech The. Sandh GU15 ...... 64 E7
Breezehurst Dr. Crawl RH11 .... 200 F3
Bregsells La. Bear Gn RH5 157 D4
Bremer Rd.Stan TW18 & 19 13 A5
Bremner Ave. Horley RH6 .. 160 F4
Brenchley Cl. Hayes BR2 ...... 44 F3
Brenda Rd. Up Toot SW17 ... 20 F6
Brende Gdns. E Mole KT8 ..... 36 B5
Brendon Cl. Esher KT10 .... 55 C4
Brendon Cl. Harl UB7 .... 3 C7
Brendon Dr. Esher KT10 .... 55 C4
Brendon House. Sutton SM2 59 C4
Brendon Rd. W Heath GU14 . 84 D7
Brenley Cl. Mitch CR4 .... 41 A6
Brent House. Catf BR1 .... 24 D3
Brent Knoll Spec Sch. For Hil SE26 .... 23 D5
Brent Lea. Brent TW8 .... 6 C7
Brent Rd. Brent TW8 .... 6 C8
Brent Rd. S Croy CR2 .... 62 B2
Brent Way. Brent TW8 .... 6 D7
Brentford Bsns Ctr. Brent TW8 .... 6 C7
Brentford High St. Brent TW8 6 D8
Brentford House. 7 Twick TW1 .... 17 B8
Brentford Sch for Girls. Brent TW8 .... 6 D8
Brentford Sta. Brent TW8 ...... 6 C8
Brentmoor Rd. W End GU24 67 D6
Brentside. Brent TW8 .... 6 C8
Brentside Executive Ctr. Brent TW8 .... 6 B8
Brentwaters Bsns Pk. Brent TW8 .... 6 C7
Brentwood Ct. Addl KT15 ..... 52 B6
Brereton House. 4 Streat SW2 .... 22 A8
Breston Cross. G Book KT23 93 F1
Bret Harte Rd. Friml GU16 ... 65 E1
Bretherton Ct. S Croy CR2 ... 61 E4
Bretlands Rd. Addl KT16 ...... 51 E8
Brett House. 1 Putney SW15 .... 19 D8
Brett House Cl. 2 Putney SW15 .... 19 D8
Brettgrave. Epsom KT19 .... 57 C1
Brettingham Cl. Crawl RH11 .... 200 E3
Brew House Rd. Brock RH3 137 B5
Brewer Rd. Crawl RH10 ...... 201 E4
Brewer St. Bletch RH1 .... 120 C4
Brewers Cl. W Heath GU14 .. 85 A5
Brewers La. 11 Rich TW9 .... 6 D2
Brewery La. Byfl KT14 .... 71 E6
Brewery Mews Bsns Ctr. 1 Islew TW7 .... 6 A4
Brewery Rd. Horse GU21 ..... 69 E2
Brewhurst La. Loxwd RH14 213 A2
Breydon Wlk. Crawl RH10 . 202 B4
Brian Ave. Sander CR2 .... 80 E7
Briane Rd. Epsom KT19 .... 57 C1
Briar Ave. Lhtwat GU18 .... 67 A8
Briar Ave. S Norw SW16 .... 21 F1
Briar Banks. Wallin SM5 .... 60 A2
Briar Cl. Crawl RH11 .... 181 C1
Briar Cl. Hampt TW12 .... 15 F3
Briar Cl. Islew TW7 .... 5 F2
Briar Cl. W Byfl KT14 .... 71 C8
Briar Ct. Cheam SM3 .... 58 C6
Briar Ct. Hampt TW12 .... 16 B3
Briar Gdns. Hayes BR2 .... 44 F1
Briar Gr. Sander CR2 .... 81 A6
Briar Hill. Purley CR8 .... 79 E8
Briar La. Croy CR0 .... 63 B6
Briar La. Wallin SM5 .... 60 A2
Briar Patch. Farnc GU7 .... 150 D6
Briar Rd. Send GU23 .... 90 B4
Briar Rd. Shep Gn TW17 .... 34 A4
Briar Rd. Thorn H SW16 .... 41 F6
Briar Rd. Twick TW2 .... 16 E7
Briar Way. Burph GU4 .... 110 B5
Briar Wlk. W Byfl KT14 .... 71 A7
Briardale. Wands SW19 .... 19 F7
Briarleas Ct. Farnb GU14 ... 105 D8
Briars Cl. Farnb GU14 .... 84 D3
Briars Cross. The Char RH8 123 D5
Briars Ct. Oxsh KT22 .... 74 D5
Briars The. Stan TW19 .... 2 A2
Briars Wood. Horley RH6 ... 161 C4
Briarswood Cl. Crawl RH10 202 D8
Briarwood Cl. Felt TW13 ...... 14 E5
Briarwood Ct. 5 New Mal KT4 .... 39 A1
Briarwood Rd. Knaph GU21 . 88 D8
Briarwood Rd. Stonel KT17 .. 58 A4
Briary Lodge. Beck BR3 .... 44 C8
Briavels Ct. Epsom KT18 ...... 76 E4
Brick Farm Cl. Rich TW9 .... 7 B6
Brick Kiln La. Limps RH8 .... 123 C5
Brickfield Cl. Brent TW8 .... 6 C7
Brickfield La. Harl UB3 .... 3 D8
Brickfield Rd. Outw RH1 ..... 162 C8
Brickfield Rd. S Norw CR7 & SW16 .... 42 B8
Brickfield Rd. Wimble SW19 20 B4
Brickhouse La. Horne RH7 & RH9 .... 163 C4
Bricklands. Crawl D RH10 .. 204 B7
Bricksbury Hill. Heath E GU9 .... 125 C7
Brickwood Cl. For Hil SE26 .. 23 B5
Brickwood Rd. Croy CR0 ...... 61 E8
Brickyard Copse. Ockley RH5 .... 177 C4
Brickyard La. Crawl D RH10 204 B8
Brickyard La. Wotton RH5 . 134 D2
Brideake Cl. Crawl RH11 ... 201 A3
Bridge Barn La. Woking GU21 .... 69 D1
Bridge Cl. Byfl KT14 .... 71 F7
Bridge Cl. Horse GU21 .... 69 C2
Bridge Cl. Lo Hall KT12 .... 34 F1
Bridge Cl. Stain TW18 .... 12 E4
Bridge Cl. Tedd TW11 .... 16 F4
Bridge Cotts. Cran GU6 ..... 174 B3
Bridge Ct. Cran GU6 .... 174 B3
Bridge Ct. Horse GU21 .... 69 D2
Bridge Ct. Leahd KT22 .... 95 A5
Bridge Ct. 2 Weyb KT13 ..... 53 B6
Bridge End. Camb GU15 .... 65 B4
Bridge Gdns. E Mole KT8 ...... 36 D5
Bridge Gdns. Littlt TW15 ...... 14 C1
Bridge La. Longc GU25 & KT16 .... 31 F3
Bridge Mead. Pirb GU24 .... 87 F1
Bridge Mews. Godal GU7 ... 150 E4
Bridge Mews. Woking GU21 . 69 D2
Bridge Par. Purley CR8 .... 80 A7
Bridge Pl. Croy CR0 .... 42 D1
Bridge Rd. Alder GU11 .... 126 A8
Bridge Rd. Ascot SL5 .... 29 D4
Bridge Rd. Bagsh GU19 .... 47 E3
Bridge Rd. Beck BR3 .... 23 F1
Bridge Rd. Camb GU15 .... 65 B3
Bridge Rd. Chert KT16 .... 33 B2
Bridge Rd. Chess KT9 .... 56 E5
Bridge Rd. Cobham KT11 ...... 73 B4
Bridge Rd. Cran GU6 .... 174 E3
Bridge Rd. E Mole KT8 .... 36 E5
Bridge Rd. Epsom KT17 .... 76 F7
Bridge Rd. Farnb GU14 .... 84 F4
Bridge Rd. Farnc GU7 .... 150 E5
Bridge Rd. Haslem GU27 .... 208 C7
Bridge Rd. Hounsl TW3 .... 5 D4
Bridge Rd. Islew TW3 & TW7 . 5 D4
Bridge Rd. Penge BR3 .... 23 F1
Bridge Rd. Rudg RH12 .... 214 D7
Bridge Rd. Sutton SM2 .... 59 B4
Bridge Rd. Twick TW1 .... 6 B1
Bridge Rd. Wallin SM6 .... 60 C5
Bridge Rd. Weyb KT13 .... 52 F6
Bridge Row. Croy CR0 .... 42 D1
Bridge Sq. Farnh GU9 .... 125 C2
Bridge St. Coln SL3 .... 1 D7
Bridge St. Godal GU7 .... 150 E4
Bridge St. Guild GU1 .... 130 C8
Bridge St. Leahd KT22 .... 95 A5
Bridge St. Rich TW10 .... 6 D2
Bridge St. Stain TW18 .... 12 E4
Bridge St. Walt O T KT12 ...... 34 F2
Bridge View. Sunnin SL5 ...... 30 B2
Bridge Way. Chips CR5 .... 98 E8
Bridge Way. Twick TW2 .... 16 C8
Bridge Wks. Merrow GU4 ... 110 C4
Bridgefield. Farnh GU9 ...... 125 D2
Bridgefield Cl. Nork SM7 ...... 77 C4
Bridgefield Rd. Cheam SM1 & SM2 .... 59 A4
Bridgeham Cl. Weyb KT13 .... 53 A5
Bridgeham Way. Smallf RH6 .... 162 B2
Bridgehill Cl. Stough GU2 .. 109 A3
Bridgelands. Copth RH10 .. 183 A3
Bridgeman Rd. Tedd TW11 .. 17 A2
Bridgemead. Friml GU16 ...... 85 D8
Bridges Ct. Horsh RH12 ..... 218 A5
Bridges La. Wallin CR0 .... 60 E6
Bridges Rd. Wimble SW19 .... 20 B2
Bridges Road Mews. Wimble SW19 .... 20 B2
Bridgetown Cl. 5 W Norw SE19 .... 22 E3
Bridgewater Rd. Whit V KT13 .... 53 D4
Bridgewood Cl. Penge SE20 23 B1
Bridgewood Rd. N Cheam KT17 & KT4 .... 58 A6
Bridgewood Rd. Streat SW16 .... 21 D1
Bridgford St. Wands SW17 & SW18 .... 20 C5
Bridle Cl. Graysh GU26 ...... 188 A3
Bridle Cl. King U T KT1 .... 37 D5
Bridle Cl. Sunby TW16 .... 35 A6
Bridle Cl. W Ewell KT19 .... 57 D5
Bridle Cl. W Ewell KT19 .... 57 D5
Bridle Ct. Alder GU11 .... 104 E2
Bridle La. Oxsh KT11 & KT22 74 B4
Bridle Path. Wallin CR0 .... 60 E7
Bridle Path The. E Ewell KT17 .... 58 C1
Bridle Rd. Clayg KT10 .... 56 B4
Bridle Rd. Croy CR0 .... 63 A6
Bridle Rd. Croy CR0 .... 63 A7
Bridle Rd. Epsom KT17 .... 76 F6
Bridle Rd The. Purley CR8 .... 60 E1
Bridle Way. Crawl RH10 ..... 202 D7
Bridle Way. Croy CR0 .... 63 A6
Bridle Way The. Wallin SM6 60 C5
Bridlepath Way. E Bed TW14 14 E8
Bridleway Cl. E Ewell KT17 ... 58 C1
Bridlington Cl. Bigg H TN16 103 B8
Bridport Rd. Thorn H CR7 ..... 42 B6
Brier Lea. L Kings KT20 .... 97 F1
Brier Rd. Burgh H KT20 .... 97 B8
Brierley. New Add CR0 .... 63 B4
Brierley Cl. Croy SE25 .... 43 A5
Brierley Rd. Up Toot SW12 ... 21 C6
Brierly Cl. Stough GU2 .... 109 A3

Bright Hill. Guild GU1 .... 130 E7
Brightlands Rd. Reig RH2 .. 118 C3
Brightman Rd. Wands SW18 20 D7
Brighton Cl. Addl KT15 .... 52 C5
Brighton Rd. Addl KT15 .... 52 C5
Brighton Rd.
Alder GU11 & GU12 .... 126 C8
Brighton Rd. Banstd SM2 ..... 78 A7
Brighton Rd.
Burgh H KT20 & SM2 & SM7 77 F3
Brighton Rd.
Coulsd CR5 & CR8 .... 79 D4
Brighton Rd. Crawl RH11 .. 201 D4
Brighton Rd. Croy CR2 & CR8 61 C3
Brighton Rd. Earls RH1 ...... 139 F8
Brighton Rd.
Hooley CR5 & RH1 .... 99 B6
Brighton Rd. Horley RH6 .... 160 F2
Brighton Rd. Horsh RH13 ... 217 E1
Brighton Rd. King U T KT6 .... 37 D3
Brighton Rd. Kings KT20 ...... 97 E5
Brighton Rd. L Kings KT20 . 117 F8
Brighton Rd. Purley CR8 .... 80 B8
Brighton Rd. Redh RH1 ...... 139 F8
Brighton Rd. S Croy CR2 ..... 61 C3
Brighton Rd. Salfs RH1 ...... 140 A2
Brighton Rd. Sutton SM2 ...... 59 B2
Brightside Ave. Stain TW18 . 13 C1
Brightwell Cl. Thorn H CR0 .. 42 A1
Brightwell Cres.
Up Toot SW17 .... 20 F3
Brightwells Rd. Farnh GU9 125 C2
Brigstock Rd. Coulsd CR5 ..... 79 B3
Brigstock Rd. Thorn H CR7 ... 42 B5
Brimshot La. Burrh GU24 ...... 49 E2
Brindle Cl. Alder GU11 .... 126 B7
Brindles The. Burgh H SM7 .. 77 F2
Brindley House. 22
Streat SW12 .... 21 E8
Brine Ct. King U T KT6 .... 37 D4
Brinkley Rd. N Cheam KT4 ... 58 B8
Brinkworth Pl. Old W SL4 ..... 11 B8
Brinn's La. Blckw GU17 .... 64 C5
Brinsworth Cl. Twick TW2 .... 16 D6
Brisbane Ave. Merton SW19 40 B8
Brisbane Cl. Crawl RH11 ...... 181 D1
Briscoe Rd. Mitch SW19 .... 20 D2
Brisson Cl. Esher KT10 .... 54 F4
Bristol Cl. Crawl RH10 .... 182 D1
Bristol Cl. Stan TW19 .... 2 E1
Bristol Ct. 10 Stan TW19 .... 2 E1
Bristol Rd. Morden SM4 .... 40 C4
Bristow Cty Fst Sch.
Camb GU15 .... 65 B2
Bristow Rd. Camb GU15 .... 65 B3
Bristow Rd. Hounsl TW3 .... 5 C4
Bristow Rd. W Norw SE19 .... 22 E3
Bristow Rd. Wallin CR0 .... 60 E6
Britannia Ind Est. Poyle SL3 .. 1 E5
Britannia Rd. Surb KT5 .... 37 F2
Britannia Way. Stan TW19 ... 13 D8
British Home and Hospl for
Incurables. W Norw SE27 .... 22 B3
Briton Cl. S Croy CR2 .... 80 E8
Briton Cres. S Croy CR2 .... 80 E8
Briton Hill Rd. S Croy CR2 .... 61 F1
Brittain Ct. Sandh GU17 .... 64 C7
Brittain Rd. Hersh KT12 .... 54 D5
Britten Cl. Ash GU12 .... 106 B2
Britten Cl. Crawl RH11 .... 200 F3
Brittens Cl.
Stough GU2 & GU3 .... 109 A6
Britton Cl. Lewish SE6 .... 24 D8
Brixton Hill. Streat SW2 .... 21 E8
Brixton Hill Pl. Streat SW2 ... 21 E8
Broad Acres. Farnc GU7 ..... 150 E8
Broad Cl. Hersh KT12 .... 54 E7
Broad Green Ave.
Thorn H CR0 .... 42 B2
Broad Ha'penny.
Rowl GU10 .... 146 A5
Broad Highway.
Cobham KT11 .... 73 D5
Broad La. Brack RG12 .... 27 D6
Broad La. Hampt TW12 .... 16 A2
Broad La. Parkg RH2 & RH5 158 E6
Broad Oak. Ashf TW16 .... 14 F2
Broad Oaks. Tolw KT6 .... 57 B8
Broad Oaks Way. Hayes BR2 44 F4
Broad St. Stough GU3 .... 108 D3
Broad St. Tedd TW11 .... 16 F2
Broad St. W End GU24 .... 67 D6
Broad St. Woki RG11 .... 25 C6
Broad St. Wood S V GU3 .... 108 D3
Broad St Wlk. Woki RG11 .... 25 C6
Broad Way. Farnb GU14 .... 105 A8
Broad Wlk. Burgh H KT20 .... 97 D8
Broad Wlk. Cater CR3 .... 100 F5
Broad Wlk. Cran GU6 .... 174 F1
Broad Wlk.
Crawl RH10 & RH11 .... 201 D6
Broad Wlk. Friml GU16 .... 65 E2
Broad Wlk. Heston TW5 .... 4 D6
Broad Wlk. Heston TW5 .... 4 E6
Broad Wlk. L Kings CR5 .... 99 A4
Broad Wlk. Rich TW9 .... 6 F7
Broadacre. Stain TW18 .... 13 A3
Broadacres.
Stough GU2 & GU3 .... 108 E2
Broadbridge Heath Rd.
Broad H RH12 .... 216 D4
Broadbridge La. Burst RH6 183 B8
Broadbridge La. Smallf RH6 162 A2
Broadbridge Ret Pk.
Broad H RH12 .... 216 E3
Broadcoombe. S Croy CR2 ... 62 D3
Broadfield Barton. 4
Crawl RH11 .... 201 B2
Broadfield Cl. Burgh H KT20 97 C7
Broadfield Cl. Croy CR0 .... 60 F8
Broadfield Dr. Crawl RH11 201 B3
Broadfield East Cty Fst Sch.
Crawl RH11 .... 201 C2
Broadfield East Cty Mid Sch.
Crawl RH11 .... 201 C2
Broadfield North Cty Fst &
Mid Sch. Crawl RH11 .... 201 B2
Broadfield Pl. Crawl RH11 . 201 B2
Broadfield Rd. Catf SE6 .... 24 E7
Broadfield Rd. Peasl GU5 .. 154 D8
Broadfields. Thame D KT8 .... 36 E3
Broadford La. Chobh GU24 ... 68 E7
Broadford Pk. Shalf GU4 .... 130 D2
Broadford Rd. Shalf GU4 .... 130 D2
Broadgates Rd.
Wands SW18 .... 20 D7
Broadham Green Rd.
Oxted RH8 .... 122 D2
Broadhurst. Ashtd KT21 .... 75 E3
Broadhurst. W Heath GU14 .. 84 C5
Broadhurst Cl. 8 Rich TW10 6 F2
Broadhurst Gdns.
Woodh RH2 .... 139 B6
Broadlands. Farnb GU14 ...... 85 E2
Broadlands. Felt TW13 .... 16 A5
Broadlands. Friml GU16 .... 85 F8
Broadlands. Horley RH6 ..... 161 C4
Broadlands Ave. Shep TW17 34 C3
Broadlands Ave.
Streat SW16 .... 21 E6
Broadlands Cl. Streat SW16 21 E6
Broadlands Ct. Brack RG12 .. 26 E8
Broadlands Ct. Rich TW9 .... 7 A7
Broadlands Dr. Sunnin SL5 ... 29 D2
Broadlands Dr.Warlgm CR6 101 C8
Broadlands Mansions. 2
Streat SW16 .... 21 E6
Broadlands Way.
New Mal KT3 .... 38 F3
Broadley Gn. Windl GU20 ..... 48 D4
Broadmead. Ashtd KT21 .... 75 F2
Broadmead. Catf SE6 .... 24 A5
Broadmead. Horley RH6 ..... 161 C4
Broadmead. Merst RH1 ...... 119 C7
Broadmead Ave.
New Mal KT4 .... 39 A2
Broadmead Cl. Hampt TW12 16 A2
Broadmead Inf Sch.
Thorn H CR0 .... 42 D2
Broadmead Jun Sch.
Thorn H CR0 .... 42 D3
Broadmead Rd.
Send GU22 & GU23 .... 90 B5
Broadmeads. Send GU23 ..... 90 B5
Broadmere Sch. Sheer GU21 70 D6
Broadmoor Cott.
Wotton RH5 .... 156 A8
Broadmoor Cty Prim Sch.
Crowth RG11 .... 45 D4
Broadmoor Hospl.
Crowth RG11 .... 45 E5
Broadoaks Cres.
W Byfl KT14 .... 71 B6
Broadview Est. E Bed TW19 . 14 A8
Broadview Rd. Streat SW16 21 D1
Broadwater Cl. Sheer GU21 . 70 D7
Broadwater Cl. Whit V KT12 54 A5
Broadwater Cl. Wray TW19 . 11 E8
Broadwater House. 1
Weyb KT13 .... 53 B7
Broadwater Inf Sch.
Up Toot SW17 .... 20 E4
Broadwater Jun Sch.
Up Toot SW17 .... 20 E4
Broadwater Rd.
Up Toot SW17 .... 20 E4
Broadwater Rd N.
Whit V KT12 .... 54 A5
Broadwater Rd S.
Whit V KT12 .... 54 A5
Broadwater Rise.
Guild GU1 .... 131 A8
Broadwater Sch.
Farnc GU7 .... 151 A8
Broadway. Brack RG12 .... 27 C7
Broadway. Knaph GU21 .... 68 C1
Broadway. Stain TW18 .... 13 B2
Broadway. Stonel KT17 .... 58 A5
Broadway. Tolw KT6 .... 38 B1
Broadway. Wink SL4 .... 9 B7
Broadway Ave. Thorn H CR0 42 D4
Broadway Ave. Twick TW1 ..... 6 B1
Broadway Cl. Hams Gn CR2 . 81 B5
Broadway Ct. Beck BR3 .... 44 C6
Broadway Ct. Wimble SW19 19 F2
Broadway Gdns. Mitch CR4 . 40 E5
Broadway House.
Knaph GU21 .... 68 C1
Broadway Mkt.
Up Toot SW17 .... 20 F4
Broadway Rd. Lhtwat GU18 . 48 C2
Broadway Rd.
Windl GU18 & GU20 & GU24 48 C2
Broadway The. Cheam SM3 . 58 E4
Broadway The. Crawl RH10 201 D6
Broadway The. Laleh TW18 . 33 C7
Broadway The. Mortl SW13 ... 7 E5
Broadway The. Sandh GU17 64 B8
Broadway The. Sutton SM1 .. 59 C6
Broadway The.
Thame D KT10 .... 36 E1
Broadway The. Tolw KT6 ..... 38 A1
Broadway The. Wallin SM6 .. 60 E6
Broadway The.
Wimble SW19 .... 19 F2
Broadway The. Woking GU21 69 F2
Broadway The.
Woodhm KT15 .... 52 A1
Broadwell Ct. Heston TW5 ..... 4 D6
Broadwell Rd. Wreccl GU10 145 F6
Broadwood Cl. Horsh RH12 218 A5
Broadwood Cotts.
Capel RH5 .... 178 E6
Broadwood Rise.
Crawl RH11 .... 201 A2
Brock Rd. Crawl RH11 .... 181 B1
Brock Way. Vir W GU25 .... 31 C5
Brock's Cl. Godal GU7 .... 151 A5
Brockbridge House.
Rhampt SW15 .... 7 F1
Brockenhurst. E Mole KT8 .... 35 F3
Brockenhurst Ave.
New Mal KT4 .... 38 E1
Brockenhurst Cl.
Horse GU21 .... 69 F5
Brockenhurst Rd.
Alder GU11 .... 126 B8
Brockenhurst Rd. Ascot SL5 29 B3
Brockenhurst Rd.
Brack RG12 .... 28 A6
Brockenhurst Rd. Croy CR0 . 43 B2
Brockenhurst Way.
Mitch SW16 .... 41 D7
Brockham Cl. Wimble SW19 19 F3
Brockham Cres.
New Add CR0 .... 63 D3
Brockham Ct. 6 Sutton SM2 59 B3
Brockham Dr. Streat SW2 .... 21 F8
Brockham Hill Pk.
Box H KT20 .... 116 C4
Brockham House. 14
Streat SW2 .... 21 F8
Brockham La.
Brock RH3 & RH4 .... 116 A1
Brockham Sch. Brock RH3 137 B7
Brockhamhurst Rd.
Betch RH3 .... 137 B2
Brockholes Cross.
E Hors KT24 .... 113 A6
Brockhurst Cl. Horsh RH12 216 F1
Brockhurst Cotts.
Alf Cr GU6 .... 193 F4
Brockhurst Lodge.
M Bourn GU9 .... 146 B7
Brocklebank Ct. Whytif CR6 . 81 A1
Brocklebank Rd.
Wands SW18 .... 20 C8
Brocklesby Rd. Croy SE25 ... 43 B5
Brockley Combe.
Oat Pk KT13 .... 53 D6
Brockley Pk. For Hil SE23 ..... 23 E8
Brockley Rise. For Hil SE23 .. 23 E8
Brockley View. For Hil SE23 . 23 E8
Brockman Rise. Catf BR1 ..... 24 D4
Brocks Dr. Cheam SM3 .... 58 E7
Brocks Dr. Fairl GU3 .... 108 C5
Brockshot Cl. 1 Brent TW8 .. 6 D8
Brockton. Farnc GU7 .... 150 E5
Brockway Cl. Merrow GU1 110 B2
Brockwell Park Gdns.
Streat SE24 .... 22 B8
Brockworth. King U T KT2 .... 38 B8
Broderick House. Dulw SE21 22 E5
Brodie House. 7
Wallin SM6 .... 60 B6
Brodie Rd. Guild GU1 .... 130 E8
Brodrick Gr. G Book KT23 ..... 94 A1
Brodrick Rd. Up Toot SW17 .. 20 E6
Brograve Gdns. Beck BR3 .... 44 B7
Broke Ct. Merrow GU4 .... 110 C4
Brokes Cres. Reig RH2 .... 118 A3
Brokes Rd. Reig RH2 .... 118 A3
Bromford Cl. Oxted RH8 .... 123 A2
Bromleigh Ct.
Dulw SE21 & SE22 .... 23 B6
Bromley Ave. Broml BR1 ...... 24 E1
Bromley Cres. Broml BR2 ..... 44 F6
Bromley Ct. Broml BR1 .... 24 F1
Bromley Gdns. Broml BR2 .... 44 F6
Bromley Gr. Beck BR2 .... 44 D7
Bromley Hill. Catf BR1 .... 24 E2
Bromley Pk. Broml BR1 .... 44 F8
Bromley Rd. Beck BR3 .... 44 B8
Bromley Rd. Beck BR2 & BR3 44 D7
Bromley Rd. Catf SE6 & BR1 24 B5
Bromley Road Infs Sch.
Beck BR3 .... 44 B8
Brompton Cl. Hounsl TW4 ..... 4 F2
Brompton Cl. Penge SE20 .... 43 A7
Bromwich House. 3
Rich TW10 .... 6 E1
Bronson Rd. Merton SW20 ... 39 E7
Bronte Ct. 14 Redh RH1 ..... 119 A2
Brontes The. E Grins RH19 185 D1
Brook Ave. Heath E GU9 ..... 125 F7
Brook Cl. Ash GU12 .... 106 B3
Brook Cl. E Grins RH19 ...... 186 B1
Brook Cl. Epsom KT19 .... 57 E2
Brook Cl. Sandh GU15 .... 45 E1
Brook Cl. Stan TW19 .... 13 F8
Brook Cl. W Barn SW20 .... 39 B6
Brook Cl. Woki RG11 .... 25 A8
Brook Ct. Beck BR3 .... 43 F8
Brook Ct. 6 Brent TW8 .... 6 D8
Brook Ct. Cheam SM3 .... 58 C6
Brook Ct. Mortl SW14 .... 7 E4
Brook Dr. Ashf TW16 .... 14 E2
Brook Dr. Brack RG12 .... 27 E5
Brook Farm Rd.
Cobham KT11 .... 73 D4
Brook Gdns. Barnes SW13 ..... 7 F4
Brook Gdns. Farnb GU14 ...... 84 F2
Brook Gdns. King U T KT2 .... 38 C8
Brook Gn. Brack RG12 .... 26 F8
Brook Gn. Chobh GU24 .... 49 F1
Brook Hill. Farl Gn GU5 ..... 153 D8
Brook Hill. Oxted RH8 .... 122 C5
Brook House. Cran GU6 ..... 174 F4
Brook House. Heath E GU9 125 D6
Brook House. 4 Twick TW1 17 A8
Brook La. Chobh GU24 .... 68 D8
Brook La. Farl Gn GU5 .... 132 E1
Brook La. Faygt RH12 .... 218 C8
Brook La. Send GU23 .... 90 E5
Brook La Bns Ctr. 4
Brent TW8 .... 6 D8
Brook La N. 3 Brent TW8 ..... 6 D8
Brook Mead. W Ewell KT19 .. 57 E4
Brook Mead. W Ewell KT19 .. 57 E4
Brook Meadow. Chidd GU8 191 C3
Brook Rd. Bagsh GU19 .... 47 E2
Brook Rd. Brook GU8 .... 190 D8
Brook Rd. Camb GU15 .... 65 B4
Brook Rd. Chil GU4 .... 131 C3
Brook Rd. Horsh RH12 .... 217 E6
Brook Rd. Merst RH1 .... 119 C7
Brook Rd. Redh RH1 .... 139 F8
Brook Rd. Surb KT6 .... 56 E8
Brook Rd. Thorn H CR7 .... 42 C5
Brook Rd. Twick TW1 .... 6 A1
Brook Rd. Wormly GU8 ...... 170 E1
Brook Rd S. Brent TW8 .... 6 D8
Brook St. King U T KT1 .... 37 E7
Brook Trad Est The.
Alder GU12 .... 105 E2
Brook Valley. Dork RH5 ..... 136 B1
Brook Way. Leahd KT22 .... 75 A1
Brookdale Rd. Catf SE6 .... 24 B8
Brookdale Rd. 2
Lewish SE6 .... 24 B8
Brooke Ct. 7 King U T KT2 .. 17 D4
Brooke Forest. Fairl GU3 .... 108 C5
Brookehowse Rd. Catf SE6 .. 24 B5
Brookers Cl. Ashtd KT21 ...... 75 D2
Brookers Cnr. Crowth RG11 . 45 C5
Brookers House. Ashtd KT21 75 D2
Brookers Row. Crowth RG11 45 C6
Brookfield. Farnc GU7 .... 151 A8
Brookfield. Woking GU21 ..... 69 B3
Brookfield Ave.
Carsh SM1 & SM5 .... 59 E7
Brookfield Cl. Earls RH1 .... 140 A3
Brookfield Cl. Ottsh KT16 ..... 51 D4
Brookfield Gdns. Clayg KT10 55 F4
Brookfield Rd. Alder GU12 . 105 F3
Brookfields Ave. Mitch CR4 . 40 E4
Brookhill Cl. Copth RH10 ... 183 A3
Brookhill Rd. Copth RH10 .. 183 A3
Brookhouse Rd. Farnb GU14 84 F3
Brookhurst Rd. Addl KT15 .... 52 B4
Brooklands. Alder GU11 ..... 104 E1
Brooklands Ave.
Wimble SW18 .... 20 B6
Brooklands Cl. Charlt TW16 . 34 E8
Brooklands Cl. Cobham KT11 73 E4
Brooklands Cl.
Heath E GU9 .... 125 D7
Brooklands Coll. Weyb KT13 52 F4
Brooklands Ct. King U T KT1 37 D5
Brooklands Ct. Mitch CR4 .... 40 D7
Brooklands Ct.
New Haw KT15 .... 52 D1
Brooklands Ct. Reig RH2 ... 118 B3
Brooklands Ind Est.
Byfl KT13 .... 52 E1
Brooklands La. Weyb KT13 .. 52 F4
Brooklands Mus.
Whit V KT13 .... 53 A2
Brooklands Rd. Crawl RH11 201 C1
Brooklands Rd.
Heath E GU9 .... 125 E7
Brooklands Rd. Thame D KT7 37 A1
Brooklands Rd. Whit V KT13 53 B3
Brooklands Rd.
Whit V KT13 & KT14 .... 72 A8
Brooklands Sch. Reig RH2 118 B3
Brooklands The. Hounsl TW7 5 D6
Brooklands Way.
E Grins RH19 .... 205 D8
Brooklands Way.
Heath E GU9 .... 125 E7
Brooklands Way. Redh RH1 118 E3
Brookley Cl. Farnh GU10 .... 126 C3
Brookleys. Chobh GU24 .... 49 F1
Brooklyn. Penge SE20 .... 23 A1
Brooklyn Ave. Croy SE25 ...... 43 B5
Brooklyn Cl. Carsh SM5 .... 59 E8
Brooklyn Cl. Woking GU22 ... 89 E8
Brooklyn Ct. Woking GU22 ... 89 E8
Brooklyn Gr. Croy SE25 .... 43 B5
Brooklyn Rd. Croy SE25 .... 43 B5
Brooklyn Rd. Woking GU22 .. 89 E8
Brookmead. Mitch CR4 .... 41 C3
Brookmead Ct. Cran GU6 ... 174 E2
Brookmead Rd. Wallin CR0 .. 41 C3
Brooks Cl. Whit V KT13 .... 53 A1
Brooks House. 6
Streat SW2 .... 22 A7
Brooks La. Brent W4 .... 7 A8
Brooks Rd. Brent W4 .... 7 A8
Brooksby Cl. Blckw GU17 ..... 64 B5
Brookscroft. New Add CR0 ... 62 E1
Brookside. Bear Gn RH5 ..... 157 F6
Brookside. Chert KT16 .... 32 E2
Brookside. Coln SL3 .... 1 C7
Brookside. Copth RH10 ...... 183 A3
Brookside. Cran GU6 .... 174 E1
Brookside. Cran GU6 .... 174 E3
Brookside. Crawl RH10 .... 201 F7
Brookside. Hale GU9 .... 125 D6
Brookside. Jacobs GU4 ...... 109 D6
Brookside. S Godst RH9 ..... 142 D5
Brookside. Sandh GU17 .... 64 C8
Brookside. Wallin SM5 .... 60 A5
Brookside. Woki RG11 .... 25 A7
Brookside Ave. Stain TW15 . 13 D3
Brookside Cl. Felt TW13 .... 15 A5
Brookside Cres. 1
N Cheam KT4 .... 39 A1
Brookside Way. Croy CR0 .... 43 D3
Brookview. Copth RH10 ..... 183 A3
Brookview Rd.
Streat SW16 & SW17 .... 21 C3
Brookwell La. Bramly GU5 152 B2
Brookwood. Horley RH6 .... 161 B4
Brookwood Ave.
Barnes SW13 .... 7 F5
Brookwood Cl. Beck BR2 ..... 44 F5
Brookwood Cty Fst & Mid Sch.
Brookw GU24 .... 88 A7
Brookwood Hospl.
Knaph GU21 .... 68 C1
Brookwood Hospl.
Knaph GU21 .... 88 C8
Brookwood House.
Horley RH6 .... 161 B6
Brookwood Lye Rd.
Brookw GU21 & GU22 .... 88 C7
Brookwood Rd. Farnb GU14 85 D4
Brookwood Rd. Hounsl TW3 .. 5 B6
Brookwood Rd.
Wands SW18 .... 20 A7

Brookwood Sta. Brookw GU24 88 A6
Broom Acres. Sandh GU17 45 B1
Broom Bank. Chelsh CR6 102 C8
Broom Cl. Esher KT10 55 B5
Broom Cl. Hawley GU17 64 E4
Broom Cl. Tedd KT1 & TW11 17 D1
Broom Field. Lhtwat GU18 67 A7
Broom Gdns. Croy CR0 63 A7
Broom Hall. Oxsh KT22 74 D5
Broom La. Burrh GU24 49 E3
Broom Lock. Tedd TW11 17 C2
Broom Pk. Tedd KT1 17 D1
Broom Rd. Croy CR0 63 A7
Broom Rd. Rich TW11 17 C3
Broom Rd. Tedd KT1 & TW11 17 C2
Broom Squires. Hind GU26 188 F4
Broom Water. Tedd TW11 17 C3
Broom Water W. Tedd TW11 17 C3
Broom Way. Oat Pk KT13 53 E6
Broomcroft Dr. Mayb GU22 70 D3
Broomdashers Rd. Crawl RH10 201 F7
Broome Cl. Horsh RH12 217 D5
Broome Ct. 3 Rich TW9 7 A6
Broome Lodge. Stain TW18 13 B3
Broome Rd. Hampt TW12 35 F8
Broome St. Head KT18 96 C1
Broomehall Rd. Coldh RH5 156 D2
Broomehall Rd. Ockley RH5 177 E8
Broomers La. Ewh GU6 175 E5
Broomfield. Elst GU8 148 E4
Broomfield. Stain TW18 13 A2
Broomfield. Stough GU2 108 E2
Broomfield. Sunby TW16 35 A8
Broomfield Cl. Mayb GU22 70 D3
Broomfield Cl. Stough GU3 108 E3
Broomfield Cl. Sunnin SL5 30 B2
Broomfield Cotts. Burgh H KT20 97 E8
Broomfield Ct. Weyb KT13 53 B4
Broomfield Dr. Sunnin SL5 30 B3
Broomfield La. Frensh GU10 146 B1
Broomfield Pk. Sunnin SL5 30 B2
Broomfield Pk. Westc RH4 135 C6
Broomfield Rd. Beck BR3 43 F6
Broomfield Rd. Rich TW9 6 F6
Broomfield Rd. Surb KT5 37 F1
Broomfield Rd. Tedd TW11 17 C2
Broomfield Rd. Woodhm KT15 71 B8
Broomfield Ride. Oxsh KT22 74 D7
Broomfields. Esher KT10 55 C5
Broomhall Bldgs. Sunnin SL5 30 B2
Broomhall End. Horse GU21 69 E3
Broomhall La. Horse GU21 69 E3
Broomhall La. Sunnin SL5 30 A3
Broomhall Rd. Horse GU21 69 E3
Broomhall Rd. S Croy CR2 61 D2
Broomhill. Crond GU10 124 D8
Broomhill Rd. W Heath GU14 84 D5
Broomhurst Ct. Dork RH4 136 B5
Broomlands La. Titsey RH8 123 E8
Broomleaf Cnr. M Bourn GU9 125 D2
Broomleaf Rd. M Bourn GU9 125 E2
Broomleigh Bsns Pk. Beck SE6 23 F3
Broomloan La. Sutton SM1 59 A8
Broomsquires Rd. Bagsh GU19 47 F2
Broomwood Cl. Croy CR0 43 D4
Broomwood Way. M Bourn GU10 146 C6
Broseley Gr. For Hil SE26 23 E3
Broster Gdns. S Norw SE25 42 F6
Brough Cl. King U T KT2 17 D3
Brougham Pl. Heath E GU9 125 B7
Broughton Ave. Rich TW10 17 C4
Broughton Mews. Friml GU16 65 F1
Broughton Rd. Thorn H CR7 42 A3
Brow The. Earls RH1 140 A4
Browell House. Merrow GU4 110 D2
Browells La. Felt TW13 15 B6
Brown Bear Ct. Felt TW13 15 D4
Brown Cl. Wallin SM6 60 E3
Brown's Bldgs. Balham SW12 21 B7
Brown's Hill. Outw RH1 141 D2
Brown's Rd. Surb KT5 & KT6 37 F2
Browne House. 9 Penge SE26 23 B3
Browngraves Rd. Harl UB7 3 C7
Brownhill Rd. Catf SE6 24 C8
Browning Ave. Carsh SM1 59 E6
Browning Ave. N Cheam KT4 39 B1
Browning Cl. Crawl RH10 202 C7
Browning Cl. Friml GU15 66 C4
Browning Cl. Hampt TW12 15 F4
Browning Rd. Fetch KT22 94 D2
Browning Way. Heston TW5 4 D6
Brownings The. 1 E Grins RH19 185 C1
Brownlow Rd. Redh RH1 118 E1
Brownlow Rd. S Croy CR0 61 F6
Brownrigg Cres. Brack RG12 27 E8
Brownrigg Rd. Ashf TW15 14 A4
Browns La. Effing KT24 113 D8
Browns Wlk. Rowl GU10 145 F5
Browns Wood. E Grins RH19 185 E4
Brownsover Rd. W Heath GU14 84 C4
Brox La. Ottsh KT15 & KT16 51 D2
Brox La. Row Tn KT15 & KT16 51 D2
Brox La. Woodhm KT15 & 16 51 D2
Brox Rd. Ottsh KT16 51 D4
Broxholm Rd. W Norw SE27 & SW16 22 A5
Broxted Rd. For Hil SE23 & SE6 23 F6
Bruce Ave. Shep TW17 34 C3
Bruce Cl. Byfl KT14 71 E6
Bruce Dr. Selsd CR2 62 D2
Bruce Hall Mews. Up Toot SW17 21 A4
Bruce Lawns. Up Toot SW17 21 A4
Bruce Rd. Mitch CR4 21 A1
Bruce Rd. S Norw SE25 42 D5
Brudenell Rd. Up Toot SW17 21 A4
Brumana Cl. Weyb KT13 53 B4
Brumfield Rd. W Ewell KT19 57 C5
Brumfield Rd. W Ewell KT19 57 C5
Brunel Cl. Cranf TW5 4 B7
Brunel Cl. S Norw SE19 22 F2
Brunel Ct. Mortl SW13 7 F5
Brunel Ctr. Crawl RH10 181 F2
Brunel Dr. Crowth RG11 45 C8
Brunel House. 25 Streat SW2 21 E8
Brunel Pl. Crawl RH10 201 E5
Brunel Univ Coll Osterley Campus. Hounsl TW7 5 F7
Brunel Univ Coll (Twickenham Campus). Islew TW1 6 B3
Brunel Univ (Runnymede Campus). Eng Gn TW20 11 C5
Brunel Wlk. 3 Twick TW4 16 A8
Brunner Ct. Ottsh KT16 51 C5
Brunner House. Catf SE6 24 C4
Brunswick. Easth RG12 27 A2
Brunswick Cl. Crawl RH10 202 A4
Brunswick Cl. Thame D KT7 36 F1
Brunswick Cl. Twick TW2 16 D5
Brunswick Cl. Walt O T KT12 54 C8
Brunswick Ct. Crawl RH10 202 A4
Brunswick Ct. King U T KT2 17 D2
Brunswick Ct. 2 Penge SE19 23 A1
Brunswick Dr. Pirb GU24 87 D7
Brunswick Gr. Cobham KT11 73 C6
Brunswick Mews. Streat SW16 21 D2
Brunswick Pl. Penge SE19 23 A1
Brunswick Rd. King U T KT2 38 A8
Brunswick Rd. Pirb GU16 & GU24 86 E6
Brunswick Rd. Pirb GU24 87 C6
Brunswick Rd. Sutton SM1 59 B6
Bruntile Cl. Farnb GU14 85 D1
Brushwood Rd. Horsh RH12 218 B6
Bruton Rd. Morden SM4 40 C5
Bruton Way. Brack RG12 27 E2
Bryan Cl. Ashf TW16 15 A1
Bryanston Ave. Twick TW2 16 B7
Bryanstone Ave. Stough GU2 109 A4
Bryanstone Cl. Stough GU2 108 F4
Bryanstone Ct. Sutton SM1 59 C7
Bryanstone Gr. Stough GU2 108 F5
Bryce Cl. Horsh RH12 218 A5
Bryce Gdns. Alder GU11 126 C7
Bryden Cl. For Hil SE26 23 E3
Brympton Cl. Dork RH4 136 A5
Bryn Rd. Wreccl GU10 145 F7
Brynford Cl. Horse GU21 69 E4
Bryony House. Brack RG12 26 E8
Bryony Rd. Burph GU1 110 B4
Bryony Way. Ashf TW16 15 A2
Buchan The. Camb GU15 66 A8
Buchanan House. Dulw SE21 22 E5
Buchanan House. Wands SW18 20 A8
Buchans Lawn. Crawl RH11 201 B2
Bucharest Rd. Wands SW18 20 C8
Buckfast Rd. Morden SM4 40 B5
Buckhurst Ave. Carsh CR4 & SM5 40 F1
Buckhurst Cl. E Grins RH19 185 C3
Buckhurst Cl. Redh RH1 118 F3
Buckhurst Gr. Woki RG11 25 F5
Buckhurst Hill. Brack RG12 27 F5
Buckhurst La. Ascot SL5 30 A6
Buckhurst Mead. E Grins RH19 185 C4
Buckhurst Moors. Binf RG12 26 C6
Buckhurst Rd. Ascot SL5 29 F7
Buckhurst Rd. Friml GU16 85 F6
Buckhurst Way. E Grins RH19 185 C3
Buckingham Ave. E Mole KT8 36 B7
Buckingham Ave. Felt TW14 4 B1
Buckingham Ave. S Norw CR7 42 A8
Buckingham Cl. Guild GU1 109 F2
Buckingham Cl. Hampt TW12 15 F3
Buckingham Ct. Belm SM2 59 A2
Buckingham Ct. Crawl RH11 201 B2
Buckingham Ct. Stain TW18 13 A4
Buckingham Ct. Woki RG11 25 C6
Buckingham Dr. E Grins RH19 206 A8
Buckingham Gate. Crawl RH6 182 C7
Buckingham Gdns. Hampt KT8 36 B7
Buckingham Gdns. S Norw CR7 42 A7
Buckingham La. For Hil SE23 23 E8
Buckingham Prim Sch. Hampt TW12 15 F3
Buckingham Rd. Hampt TW12 & TW13 15 F3
Buckingham Rd. King U T KT1 37 F5
Buckingham Rd. Mitch CR4 41 E4
Buckingham Rd. Rich TW10 17 D6
Buckingham Rd. S Holm RH5 157 C6
Buckingham Way. Wallin SM6 60 C2
Buckland Cl. Farnb GU14 85 C7
Buckland Cnr. Reig RH2 117 D2
Buckland Ct. Buckl RH3 117 A2
Buckland Cty Inf Sch. Stain TW18 13 C1
Buckland Inf Sch. Chess KT9 56 F6
Buckland La. Buckl RH3 117 B5
Buckland Rd. Chess KT9 56 F5
Buckland Rd. E Ewell SM2 58 D2
Buckland Rd. L Kings KT20 117 F7
Buckland Rd. Reig RH2 117 D2
Buckland Way. N Cheam KT4 39 C1
Buckland Wlk. Morden SM4 40 C5
Bucklands Rd. Tedd TW11 17 C2
Bucklebury. Easth RG12 27 A2
Buckleigh Ave. Merton SW20 39 F6
Buckleigh Rd. Streat SW16 21 E1
Buckleigh Way. S Norw SE19 22 F1
Bucklers' Way. Carsh SM5 59 F7
Buckles Way. Nork SM7 77 E3
Buckley Pl. Crawl D RH10 204 A8
Buckmans Rd. Crawl RH11 201 D6
Bucknills Cl. Epsom KT18 76 C5
Bucks Cl. W Byfl KT14 71 B5
Bucks Green Sch. Buck Gn RH12 214 B7
Buckswood Dr. Crawl RH11 201 A4
Buckthorn Cl. Woki RG11 25 E7
Buddhapadipa Temple The. Wimble SW19 19 D4
Budebury Rd. Stain TW18 13 A3
Budge La. Carsh CR4 40 F2
Budge's Cotts. Woki RG11 25 E8
Budge's Gdns. Woki RG11 25 E7
Budge's Rd. Woki RG11 25 D7
Budgen Cl. Crawl RH10 182 D1
Budgen Dr. Redh RH1 119 A3
Budham Way. Easth RG12 27 B3
Buff Ave. Banstd SM7 78 B4
Buffbeards La. Shottm GU27 207 E6
Buffers La. Leahd KT22 95 A8
Bug Hill. Warlgm CR6 101 D7
Bugkingham Way. Friml GU16 65 F1
Bulbrook Row. Brack RG12 27 E7
Bulganak Rd. S Norw CR7 42 C5
Bulkeley Cl. Eng Gn TW20 11 C3
Bull Hill. Leahd KT22 95 A6
Bull La. Brack RG12 27 B8
Bull La. Westfd GU4 89 F1
Bullard Rd. Tedd TW11 16 F2
Bullbeggars La. Godst RH9 121 C3
Bullbeggars La. Horse GU21 69 B3
Bullbrook Dr. Brack RG12 27 F8
Buller Ct. Farnb GU14 85 C1
Buller Rd. Alder GU11 105 B4
Buller Rd. S Norw CR7 42 D6
Bullers Rd. Heath E GU9 125 E6
Bullfinch Cl. Horley RH6 160 E4
Bullfinch Cl. Horsh RH12 217 C7
Bullfinch Cl. Sandh GU15 64 E8
Bullfinch Ct. 3 W Norw SE21 22 D6
Bullfinch Rd. Selsd CR2 62 D1
Bulls Alley. Mortl SW14 7 D5
Bullswater Common Rd. Pirb GU24 & GU3 88 A2
Bulstrode Ave. Hounsl TW3 5 A4
Bulstrode Gdns. Hounsl TW3 5 A4
Bulstrode Rd. Hounsl TW3 5 A4
Bunbury Way. Nork KT17 77 B4
Bunce Common Rd. Leigh RH2 & RH3 137 E2
Bunch La. Haslem GU27 208 B8
Bunch La. Shottm GU27 208 B8
Bunch Way. Shottm GU27 208 A6
Bundy's Way. Egham TW18 12 F2
Bungalow Rd. Farnb GU14 85 B2
Bungalow Rd. S Norw SE25 42 E5
Bungalows The. Mitch SW16 21 B1
Bunting Cl. Horsh RH13 217 F3
Bunting Cl. Mitch CR4 40 F4
Buntings The. Wreccl GU9 145 F8
Bunyan Cl. Crawl RH11 200 E3
Bunyard Dr. Sheer GU21 70 C5
Burbage Gn. Brack RG12 27 F4
Burbage Rd. Dulw SE21 & SE24 22 D8
Burbeach Cl. Crawl RH11 201 B3
Burberry Cl. King U T KT3 38 E7
Burbidge Rd. Shep Gn TW17 34 A5
Burchets Hollow. Peasl GU5 154 D7
Burchetts Way. Shep TW17 34 B3
Burcote. 6 Whit V KT13 53 D4
Burcote Rd. Wands SW18 20 D8
Burcott Gdns. New Haw KT15 52 D4
Burcott Rd. Purley CR8 80 A5
Burden Way. Stough GU2 109 A5
Burdenshot Hill. Woking GU22 & GU3 89 B3
Burdenshott Ave. Mortl TW10 7 B3
Burdenshott Rd. Jacobs GU4 109 C8
Burdenshott Rd. Woking GU22 & GU3 & GU4 89 A2
Burdett Ave. Wimble SW20 39 A8
Burdett Cl. Worth RH10 202 D5
Burdett Rd. Rich TW9 6 F4
Burdett Rd. Thorn H CR0 42 D3
Burdock Cl. Crawl RH11 201 A2
Burdock Cl. Croy CR0 43 D1
Burdock Cl. Lhtwat GU18 67 B8
Burdon La. Belm SM2 58 F2
Burdon Pk. Belm SM2 58 F2
Burfield Cl. Up Toot SW17 20 D4
Burfield Dr. Warlgm CR6 101 C8
Burfield Rd. Old W SL4 & TW19 11 B8
Burford Ct. Woki RG11 25 E5
Burford La. E Ewell KT17 77 C8
Burford Lea. Elst GU8 148 E4
Burford Rd. Camb GU15 65 B4
Burford Rd. For Hil SE6 23 F6
Burford Rd. Horsh RH13 217 E2
Burford Rd. New Mal KT4 39 A2
Burford Rd. Sutton SM1 59 A8
Burford Way. New Add CR0 63 C4
Burges Way. Stain TW18 13 A3
Burgess Cl. Felt TW13 15 E4
Burgess Rd. Sutton SM1 59 B6
Burgh Cl. Crawl RH10 182 D1
Burgh Heath Rd. Epsom KT17 & KT18 76 F4
Burgh Mount. Nork SM7 77 F4
Burgh Wood. Nork SM7 77 F4
Burghead Cl. Sandh GU15 64 D7
Burghfield. Epsom KT17 76 F4
Burghill Rd. For Hil SE26 23 E4
Burghley Ave. King U T KT3 38 D8
Burghley Hse. Wimble SW19 19 E5
Burghley Pl. Mitch CR4 40 F5
Burghley Rd. Wimble SW19 19 E4
Burgoyne Rd. Ashf TW16 14 F2
Burgoyne Rd. Camb GU15 66 A6
Burgoyne Rd. S Norw SE25 42 F5
Burham Cl. Penge SE20 23 C1
Burhill Cty Inf Sch. Hersh KT12 54 D4
Burhill Rd. Hersh KT12 54 C3
Buriton House. 9 Rhampt SW15 19 B7
Burke Cl. Rhampt SW15 7 E3
Burlands. Crawl RH11 181 A1
Burlea Cl. Hersh KT12 54 B5
Burleigh Ave. Hackb SM6 60 B7
Burleigh Cl. Addl KT15 52 B5
Burleigh Cl. Crawl D RH10 204 B8
Burleigh Ct. Leahd KT22 95 A5
Burleigh Cty Inf Sch. Crawl D RH10 204 B8
Burleigh Gdns. Ashf TW15 14 C3
Burleigh La. Crawl D RH10 204 C7
Burleigh La. N Asct SL5 28 E8
Burleigh Pk. Cobham KT11 73 E7
Burleigh Rd. Addl KT15 52 B5
Burleigh Rd. Cheam SM3 & SM4 39 E1
Burleigh Rd. Friml GU16 85 D8
Burleigh Rd. N Asct SL5 28 E7
Burleigh Way. Crawl D RH10 204 B8
Burleigh Wlk. Catf SE6 24 C7
Burley Cl. Loxwd RH14 213 A4
Burley Cl. Mitch SW16 41 D7
Burley Orchard. Chert KT16 33 A3
Burley Way. Blckw GU17 64 C6
Burleys Rd. Crawl RH10 202 C6
Burlingham Cl. Merrow GU4 110 D3
Burlington Ave. Rich TW9 7 A6
Burlington Cl. E Bed TW14 14 D8
Burlington Ct. Alder GU11 105 A1
Burlington Ct. Chisw W4 7 C7
Burlington Ct. Hawley GU17 64 D3
Burlington Jun Sch. New Mal KT3 38 F5
Burlington La. Chisw W4 7 E8
Burlington Rd. Hounsl TW7 5 D6
Burlington Rd. New Mal KT3 38 F5
Burlington Rd. S Norw CR7 42 D7
Burlsdon Way. Brack RG12 27 E8
Burma Rd. Burrh GU24 49 F8
Burma Terr. 11 W Norw SE19 22 E3
Burmarsh Ct. Penge SE20 43 C8
Burmester House. Wands SW17 20 C5
Burmester Rd. Wands SW17 20 C5
Burn Cl. Addl KT15 52 D6
Burn Moor Chase. Brack RG12 27 E2
Burnaby Cres. Chisw W4 7 C8
Burnaby Gdns. Chisw W4 7 B8
Burnbury Rd. Streat SW12 21 C7
Burne-Jones Dr. Sandh GU15 64 D6
Burnell Ave. Rich TW10 17 C3
Burnell House. 19 Streat SW2 22 A7
Burnell Rd. Sutton SM1 59 B6
Burnet Ave. Burph GU1 & GU4 110 B4
Burnet Cl. W End GU24 67 E6
Burnet Gr. Epsom KT19 76 C6
Burney Ave. King U T KT5 37 F4
Burney Cl. Fetch KT22 94 C2
Burney Ct. 6 Crawl RH11 201 A3
Burney House. 4 Streat SW16 21 C3
Burney Rd. Westh RH5 115 A4
Burnham Cl. Knaph GU21 68 D1
Burnham Dr. N Cheam KT4 58 D8
Burnham Dr. Reig RH2 118 A2
Burnham Gdns. Cranf TW5 4 B6
Burnham Gdns. Croy CR0 42 F2
Burnham Manor. Camb GU15 66 A8
Burnham Pl. Horsh RH13 217 D1
Burnham Rd. Knaph GU21 68 D1
Burnham Rd. Morden SM4 40 B5
Burnham St. King U T KT2 38 A8
Burnhams Rd. L Book KT23 93 E3
Burnhill Rd. Beck BR3 44 A7
Burns Ave. Felt TW14 4 A1
Burns Cl. Horsh RH12 217 E7
Burns Cl. Mitch SW17 20 D2
Burns Cl. W Heath GU14 84 F6
Burns Ct. Wallin SM6 60 B3
Burns Dr. Nork SM7 77 E5
Burns Rd. Crawl RH10 202 C8
Burns Way. Crawl RH12 200 C1
Burns Way. E Grins RH19 185 C1
Burns Way. Heston TW5 4 D6
Burnsall Cl. Farnb GU14 85 B6
Burnside. Ashtd KT21 75 F1
Burnside Cl. Twick TW1 6 A1
Burnt Ash Jun Sch.Brml BR1 24 F3
Burnt Hill Rd. Rowl GU10 & GU9 146 B6

Burnt Hill Way. Rowl GU10 146 B5
Burnt House La. Rusper RH12 200 A7
Burnt Pollard La. Windl GU24 48 E1
Burntcommon Cl. Send M GU23 90 F2
Burntcommon La. Send M GU23 91 A2
Burntwood Cl. Cater CR3 .. 101 A6
Burntwood Cl. Wands SW18 20 E7
Burntwood Ct. Wands SW17 20 C5
Burntwood Grange Rd. Wands SW18 20 E7
Burntwood La. Cater CR3 . 101 A6
Burntwood La. Wands SW17 20 D6
Burntwood Sch. Wands SW17 20 D6
Burntwood View. Dulw SE19 22 F3
Burnwood Park Rd. Hersh KT12 54 B6
Burpham La. Burph GU4 .... 110 A5
Burpham Prim Sch. Burph GU4 110 A5
Burr Hill La. Burrh GU24 49 F2
Burr Rd. Wands SW18 20 A8
Burrell Cl. Croy CR0 43 E3
Burrell Ct. Crawl RH11 200 F4
Burrell House. 5 Twick TW1 17 B8
Burrell Rd. Friml GU16 85 C8
Burrell Row. Beck BR3 44 A7
Burrell The. Westc RH4 135 C6
Burrells. Beck BR3 44 B7
Burritt Rd. King U T KT1 38 A7
Burrow Hill Gn. Burrh GU24 49 E2
Burrow Hill Sch. Friml GU16 65 F1
Burrow Wlk. W Norw SE21 .. 22 C8
Burrows Cl. L Book KT23 93 F3
Burrows Cl. Stough GU2 108 F2
Burrows Cross. Gomsh GU5 133 C2
Burrows Hill Cl. Harm TW19 & TW6 2 C3
Burrows La. Gomsh GU5 133 C3
Burrwood Gdns. Ash V GU12 106 A4
Burstead Cl. Cobham KT11 ... 73 D7
Burston Gdns. E Grins RH19 185 D4
Burstow House. Horley RH6 161 B6
Burstow Prim Sch. Smallf RH6 162 B3
Burstow Rd. Wimble SW20 .. 39 E8
Burtenshaw Rd.Thme D KT7 37 A3
Burton Cl. Chess KT9 56 D3
Burton Cl. Horley RH6 161 A2
Burton Cl. Windl GU20 48 D4
Burton Ct. Thame D KT7 37 A3
Burton Gdns. Hounsl TW5 4 F6
Burton House. Penge SE26 .. 23 B3
Burton Rd. King U T KT2 17 E1
Burton's Rd. Hampt TW12 16 C4
Burtons Ct. Horsh RH12 217 C2
Burtwell La. W Norw SE21 & SE27 22 D4
Burwash Rd. Crawl RH10 .. 202 A5
Burway Cres. Thorpe KT16 ... 33 A5
Burwood Ave. Purley CR8 80 B5
Burwood Cl. Hersh KT12 54 C4
Burwood Cl. Merrow GU1 . 110 D2
Burwood Cl. Reig RH2 118 D1
Burwood Cl. Tolw KT6 38 A1
Burwood Ct. For Hil SE23 23 C8
Burwood Park Sch. Whit V KT12 53 F5
Burwood Rd. Hersh KT12 & KT13 54 B4
Burwood Rd. Hersh KT12 54 D5
Bury Cl. Horse GU21 69 D3
Bury Fields. Guild GU2 130 C7
Bury Gr. Morden SM4 40 B4
Bury La. Horse GU21 69 C3
Bury St. Guild GU2 130 C7
Burys Court Sch. Leigh RH2 138 C3
Burys The. Godal GU7 150 E5
Burywood Hill. Ockley RH5 177 E7
Busbridge CE Jun Sch. Godal GU7 150 F2
Busbridge Cty Inf Sch. Godal GU7 150 F2
Busbridge La. Godal GU7 .. 150 E3
Busby House. Streat SW16 .. 21 C4
Busch Cnr. Brent TW7 6 B6
Busdens Cl. Milf GU8 170 F8
Busdens La. Milf GU8 170 F8
Busdens Way. Milf GU8 170 F8
Bush Cl. Addl KT15 52 C5
Bush La. Send GU23 90 D3
Bush Rd. Rich TW9 6 F8
Bush Rd. Shep Gn TW17 33 F4
Bush Wlk. Woki RG11 25 C6
Bushbury La. Brock RH3 137 A5
Bushell Cl. Streat SW2 21 F6
Bushell House. 3 W Norw SE27 22 C4
Bushetts Gr. Merst RH1 & RH2 119 B6
Bushey Cl. Kenley CR3 & CR8 80 F3
Bushey Croft. Oxted RH8 ... 122 C5
Bushey Ct. W Barn SW20 39 B7
Bushey Down. Up Toot SW12 21 B6
Bushey La. Sutton SM1 59 A6
Bushey Mid Sch. W Barn SW20 39 B6
Bushey Prim Sch. W Barn KT3 39 B6
Bushey Rd. Croy CR0 63 A8
Bushey Rd. Merton SW20 39 D7
Bushey Rd. Sutton SM1 59 A6
Bushey Rd. Sutton SM1 59 B6
Bushey Rd. W Barn SW20 39 D7
Bushey Way. Beck BR3 44 D4
Bushfield. Plaist RH14 211 F2
Bushfield Dr. Earls RH1 140 A4
Bushnell Rd. Up Toot SW17 . 21 B5
Bushwood Rd. Rich TW9 7 A8
Bushy Ct. Tedd KT1 37 C8
Bushy Hill Dr. Merrow GU1 110 C3
Bushy Hill Sch. Merrow GU1 110 D2
Bushy Park Gdns. Tedd TW12 16 D3
Bushy Park Rd. Tedd TW11 . 17 B1
Bushy Rd. Fetch KT22 & KT23 94 B5
Bushy Rd. Tedd TW11 16 F1
Bushy Shaw. Ashtd KT21 75 C2
Business Ctr The. Woki RG11 25 B4
Busk Cres. Farnb GU14 84 F3
Bute Ave. Rich TW10 17 E6
Bute Ct. Wallin SM6 60 C5
Bute Gdns. Wallin SM6 60 C5
Bute Gdns W. Wallin SM6 60 C5
Bute Rd. Thorn H CR0 42 A1
Bute Rd. Wallin SM6 60 C6
Butler Rd. Bagsh GU19 47 F2
Butler Rd. Crowth RG11 45 B6
Butlers Dene Rd. Wold CR3 102 A7
Butlers Hill. W Hors KT24 . 112 B5
Butlers Rd. Horsh RH13 218 B4
Butt Cl. Cran GU6 174 E4
Butter Hill. Dork RH4 136 A7
Butter Hill. Hackb SM5 & SM6 60 A6
Buttercup Cl. Woki RG11 26 A6
Buttercup Sq. Stan TW19 13 D7
Butterfield. Camb GU15 65 B4
Butterfield. E Grins RH19 .. 185 B3
Butterfield Cl. Twick TW1 5 F1
Butterfly Wlk. Warlgm CR6 101 C7
Buttermer Cl. Wreccl GU10 145 F7
Buttermere Cl. E Bed TW14 . 14 F7
Buttermere Cl. Farnb GU14 . 84 E4
Buttermere Cl. Horsh RH12 218 B6
Buttermere Cl. W Barn SM4 39 D3
Buttermere Ct. Ash V GU12 105 F4
Buttermere Dr. Friml GU15 .. 66 D4
Buttermere Gdns. Brack RG12 27 C6
Buttermere Gdns. Sander CR8 80 D6
Buttermere Way. Thor L TW20 12 B1
Buttersteep Rise. Brack GU20 & SL5 28 C1
Butterworth Ct. Streat SW16 21 E5
Butts Cl. Crawl RH11 201 B7
Butts Cotts. Felt TW13 15 F5
Butts Cotts. 4 Woking GU21 69 A1
Butts Cres. Felt TW13 16 A5
Butts House. Felt TW13 16 A5
Butts Rd. Catf BR1 24 E3
Butts Rd. Woking GU21 69 E2
Butts The. Brent TW8 6 D8
Buxton Ave. Cater CR3 100 E6
Buxton Cres. Cheam SM3 58 E6
Buxton Dr. King U T KT3 38 D7
Buxton La. Cater CR3 100 E6
Buxton Rd. Ashf TW15 13 D3
Buxton Rd. Mortl SW14 7 E4
Buxton Rd. Thorn H CR7 42 B4
Byards Croft. Mitch SW16 41 D8
Byatt Wlk. Hampt TW12 15 E2
Bychurch End. 9 Tedd TW11 16 F3
Bycroft St. Penge SE20 23 D1
Bycroft Way. Crawl RH10 .. 202 B8
Bye Ways. Twick TW2 16 B5
Byerley Way. Crawl RH10 .. 202 E7
Byers La. Blind H RH7 & RH9 142 C1
Byeway The. Mortl SW14 7 C4
Byeways The. Surb KT5 38 B4
Byfield Ct. W Barn KT3 39 A5
Byfield Rd. Islew TW7 6 A4
Byfleet Cnr. W Byfl KT14 71 A6
Byfleet Cty Prim Sch. Byfl KT14 71 D8
Byfleet Ind Est. Byfl KT14 .... 71 D8
Byfleet & New Haw Sta. New Haw KT15 52 D1
Byfleet Rd. New Haw KT14 & KT15 52 D2
Byfleet Rd. Whit V KT11 & KT13 & KT14 72 C7
Byfleet Tech Ctr The. Byfl KT14 71 D8
Byfleets La. Warn RH12 ... 216 D6
Byfrons The. Farnb GU14 85 D2
Bygrove. New Add CR0 63 B3
Bygrove Ct. Mitch SW19 20 D2
Bygrove Rd. Mitch SW19 20 D2
Bylands. Woking GU22 70 A1
Byne Rd. Carsh SM5 59 E8
Byne Rd. Penge SE20 & SE26 23 C3
Bynes Rd. S Croy CR2 61 D3
Byrd Rd. Crawl RH11 200 F3
Byrefield Rd. Stough GU2 ... 108 F4
Byrne Ct. 1 Purley CR8 80 A7
Byrne Rd. Up Toot SW12 21 B6
Byron Ave. Carsh SM1 59 D6
Byron Ave. Coulsd CR5 79 F3
Byron Ave. Cranf TW4 4 B5
Byron Ave. Friml GU15 & GU16 66 B3
Byron Ave. W Barn KT3 39 A4
Byron Ave E. Carsh SM1 59 D6
Byron Cl. Crawl RH10 202 B7
Byron Cl. For Hil SE26 23 E4
Byron Cl. Hampt TW12 15 F4
Byron Cl. Horsh RH12 217 E6
Byron Cl. Knaph GU21 68 E2
Byron Cl. Walt O T KT12 35 E1
Byron Ct. Dulw SE21 23 A7
Byron Ct. 1 Rich TW10 17 D4
Byron Ct. S Norw CR7 42 C7
Byron Dr. Crowth RG11 45 B3
Byron Gdns. Carsh SM1 59 D6
Byron Gr. 2 E Grins RH19 . 185 C1
Byron House. Beck BR3 24 B2
Byron Inf Sch. Coulsd CR5 79 F2
Byron Jun Sch. Coulsd CR5 .. 79 F2
Byron Pl. Leahd KT22 95 B5
Byron Rd. Addl KT15 52 E6
Byron Rd. S Croy CR2 62 B1
Byron Rd. Up Toot SW17 20 F2
Byttom Hill. Mickle RH5 115 C8
Byward Ave. Felt TW14 4 C1
Byway The. Sutton SM2 59 D2
Byways The. Ashtd KT21 75 D1
Byways The. Worc Pk KT19 .. 57 F6
Bywood. Easth RG12 27 A2
Bywood Ave. Croy CR0 43 D3
Bywood Cl. Purley CR8 80 B4
Bywood Terr. Croy CR0 43 C3
Byworth Cl. Farnh GU9 124 F2
Byworth Rd. Farnh GU9 124 F2
Cabbell Pl. Addl KT15 52 C6
Cabell Rd. Stough GU2 108 E2
Cabin Moss. Brack RG12 27 E2
Cable House Sch. Horse GU21 69 E4
Cabrera Ave. Went GU25 31 D3
Cabrera Cl. Went GU25 31 D3
Cabrol Rd. Farnb GU14 85 A5
Caburn Ct. Crawl RH11 201 C4
Caburn Hts. Crawl RH11 201 C4
Cackstones The. Crawl RH10 202 D7
Cadbury Cl. Ashf TW16 14 E1
Cadbury Cl. Islew TW7 6 A6
Cadbury Rd. Ashf TW16 14 E2
Caddy Cl. 4 Egham TW20 ... 12 A3
Cadley Terr. For Hil SE23 23 C6
Cadmer Cl. New Mal KT3 38 E5
Cadnam Cl. Alder GU11 126 C6
Cadnam Point. 14 Rhampt SW15 19 B7
Cadogan Cl. Beck BR3 44 D7
Cadogan Cl. Tedd TW11 16 E3
Cadogan Ct. Sutton SM2 59 B4
Cadogan Rd. King U T KT6 ... 37 D4
Cadogen Rd. Farnb GU11 .. 105 D7
Caen Wood Rd. Ashtd KT21 75 C1
Caenshill Rd. Whit V KT13 ... 53 A3
Caenswood Hill. Whit V KT13 53 A1
Caenwood Cl. Weyb KT13 .... 53 A4
Caernarvon. Friml GU16 85 F8
Caernarvon Cl. Mitch CR4 .... 41 E6
Caernarvon Ct. 3 Surb KT5 37 F4
Caesar Ct. Alder GU11 104 E2
Caesar's Camp Rd. Camb GU15 66 A8
Caesar's Cl. Camb GU15 66 A8
Caesar's Way. Shep TW17 ... 34 D3
Caesars Ct. Heath E GU9 .... 125 C7
Caesars Wlk. Mitch CR4 40 F4
Caffins Cl. Crawl RH10 201 E8
Caillard Rd. Byfl KT14 71 E8
Cain Rd. Binf RG12 26 E7
Cain's La. Hatton TW14 3 E2
Cairn Cl. Friml GU15 & GU16 66 B3
Cairndale Cl. Broml BR1 24 F1
Cairngorm Pl. W Heath GU14 84 E7
Cairo New Rd. Croy CR0 & CR9 61 B8
Caister House. 10 Balham SW12 21 B8
Caistor Mews. Balham SW12 21 B8
Caistor Rd. Balham SW12 21 B8
Caithness Rd. Mitch CR4 21 B1
Calbourne Rd. Balham SW12 21 A8
Caldbeck Ave. N Cheam KT4 39 B1
Caldbeck House. 7 Crawl RH11 200 F3
Calder Rd. Morden SM4 40 C4
Calder Way. Poyle SL3 1 E4
Calderdale Cl. Crawl RH11 201 B4
Caldwell Rd. Windl GU20 48 D5
Caledon Pl. Burph GU1 110 A4
Caledon Rd. Hackb SM5 & SM6 60 A6
Caledonia Rd. Stan TW19 13 E7
Caledonian House. Crawl RH11 201 D8
Caledonian Way. Horley RH6 182 B8
Calfridus Way. Brack RG12 .. 27 F6
California Ct. Sutton SM2 59 B1
California Rd. King U T KT3 .. 38 C6
Callander Rd. Catf SE6 24 C6
Calley Down Cres. New Add CR0 & CR9 63 D1
Callis Farm Cl. Stan TW19 2 E1
Callisto Cl. Crawl RH11 200 E3
Callow Field. Purley CR8 80 A6
Callow Hill. Vir W GU25 & TW20 31 C7
Calluna Ct. Woking GU22 69 F1
Calluna Dr. Copth RH10 183 A3
Calmont Rd. Catf BR1 24 E2
Calonne Rd. Wimble SW19 .. 19 D4
Calshot Rd. Harl TW6 3 B5
Calshot Way. Friml GU16 86 A7
Calshot Way. Harl TW6 3 A5
Calthorpe Gdns. Sutton SM1 59 C7
Calton Gdns. Alder GU11 ... 126 C7
Calverley Cl. Beck BR3 24 B2
Calverley Rd. Stonel KT17 58 A4
Calvert Cl. Alder GU12 105 D1
Calvert Cres. Dork RH4 115 B1
Calvert Ct. 5 Rich TW9 6 F3
Calvert Rd. Dork RH4 115 B2
Calvert Rd. Effing KT24 113 B7
Calvin Cl. Friml GU15 66 B4
Calvin Wlk. Crawl RH11 200 E3
Camac Rd. Twick TW2 16 D7
Camber Cl. Crawl RH10 202 C6
Camberley Ave. Wimble SW20 39 B7
Camberley Cl. Cheam SM3 .. 58 D7
Camberley Ct. 8 Sutton SM2 59 B3
Camberley Cty Inf Sch. Camb GU15 65 C5
Camberley Heath Golf Course. Friml GU15 66 B5
Camberley Rd. Harl TW6 3 A4
Camberley Sta. Camb GU15 65 D5
Camberley Towers. Camb GU15 65 D5
Cambisgate. Wimble SW19 . 19 E3
Camborne Cl. Harm TW6 3 A4
Camborne Rd. Belm SM2 59 B3
Camborne Rd. Croy CR0 43 A2
Camborne Rd. Sutton SM2 .. 59 B3
Camborne Rd. W Barn SM4 . 39 D4
Camborne Rd. Wands SW18 20 A8
Camborne Rd S. Harm TW6 .. 3 A4
Camborne Way. Harm TW6 ... 3 A4
Camborne Way. Heston TW5 5 A6
Cambray Rd. Streat SW12 ... 21 C7
Cambria. Beck BR3 44 B7
Cambria Cl. Hounsl TW3 5 A3
Cambria Ct. Felt TW14 15 B8
Cambria Ct. Stain TW18 12 E4
Cambria Gdns. Stan TW19 ... 13 E8
Cambria House. For Hil SE26 23 A4
Cambrian Cl. Camb GU15 65 B5
Cambrian Cl. W Norw SE27 . 22 B5
Cambrian Rd. Rich TW10 6 F1
Cambrian Rd. W Heath GU14 84 D7
Cambridge Ave. King U T KT3 & SW20 38 F7
Cambridge Cl. Harm UB7 2 D8
Cambridge Cl. Hounsl TW4 ... 4 E3
Cambridge Cl. Knaph GU21 . 68 F1
Cambridge Cl. Wimble SW20 39 B8
Cambridge Cotts. Rich TW9 .. 7 A8
Cambridge Cres. Tedd TW11 17 A3
Cambridge Ct. Wimble SW20 39 B8
Cambridge Gdns. King U T KT1 38 A7
Cambridge Gr. Penge SE20 . 43 B8
Cambridge Grove Rd. King U T KT1 38 A6
Cambridge Grove Rd. 5 King U T KT1 38 A7
Cambridge House. 2 Tedd TW11 17 A3
Cambridge House Sch. Wimble SW20 39 C8
Cambridge Meadows. Farnh GU9 125 A1
Cambridge Military Hospl. Alder GU11 105 B3
Cambridge Park Ct. Twick TW1 17 D8
Cambridge Pk. Twick TW1 6 C1
Cambridge Rd. Alder GU11 104 F2
Cambridge Rd. Barnes SW13 7 F5
Cambridge Rd. Carsh SM5 .. 59 E5
Cambridge Rd. Crowth RG11 45 C4
Cambridge Rd. Croy SE20 & SE25 43 B6
Cambridge Rd. E Mole KT8 .. 35 F5
Cambridge Rd. Hampt TW12 15 F1
Cambridge Rd. Horsh RH13 217 D2
Cambridge Rd. Hounsl TW4 .. 4 E3
Cambridge Rd. King U T KT1 38 A7
Cambridge Rd. Littlt TW15 & TW17 14 C1
Cambridge Rd. Mitch CR4 41 C6
Cambridge Rd. New Mal KT3 38 E5
Cambridge Rd. Rich TW9 7 A7
Cambridge Rd. Sandh GU15 45 E1
Cambridge Rd. Tedd TW11 .. 17 A3
Cambridge Rd. Twick TW1 6 D1
Cambridge Rd. Walt O T KT12 35 B3
Cambridge Rd. Wimble SW20 39 B8
Cambridge Rd E. Farnb GU14 85 D1
Cambridge Rd W. Farnb GU14 85 C1
Cambridge Sq. Camb GU15 . 65 C6
Cambridge Wlk. 3 Camb GU15 65 C6
Camden Ave. Felt TW13 15 C7
Camden Gdns. S Norw CR7 . 42 B6
Camden Gdns. Sutton SM1 .. 59 B5
Camden Hill Rd. W Norw SE19 22 E2
Camden Jun Sch. Carsh SM5 59 F6
Camden Rd. Carsh SM5 59 F6
Camden Rd. Lingf RH7 164 D4
Camden Rd. Sutton SM1 59 B5
Camden Way. S Norw CR7 ... 42 B6
Cameford Ct. 20 Streat SW12 21 E8
Camel Way. Farnb GU14 ... 105 A8
Camellia Ct. 21 Beck BR3 24 A1
Camellia Ct. W End GU24 67 F6
Camellia Pl. Twick TW2 16 B8
Camelot Cl. Bigg H TN16 83 C3
Camelot Cl. Wimble SW19 ... 20 A4
Camelot Ct. Crawl RH11 200 E6
Camelsdale Cty Fst Sch. King Gn GU27 207 F5
Camelsdale Rd. King Gn GU27 207 F5
Camelsdale Rd. Linch GU27 207 F5
Cameron Cl. Cran GU6 174 E1
Cameron Ct. 3 Putney SW19 19 E7
Cameron House. Broml BR1 44 F8
Cameron Lodge. Hounsl TW3 5 C3
Cameron Rd. Farnb GU11 . 105 D7
Cameron Rd. For Hil SE6 23 F6
Cameron Rd. Thorn H CR0 ... 42 B3

Cameron Sq. Mitch CR4 ...... 40 E8
Camgate Est. Stan TW19 ...... 13 F8
Camilla Cl. Ashf TW16 .... 14 F2
Camilla Cl. G Book KT23 ...... 94 B2
Camilla Dr. Westh RH5 .... 115 A5
Camille Cl. Croy SE25 .... 43 A6
Camlan Rd. Catf BR1 .... 24 F4
Camm Gdns. 🗗
  King U T KT1 .... 37 F7
Camm Gdns. Thame D KT7 ... 36 F2
Camomile Ave. Mitch CR4 ...... 40 F8
Camp End Rd.
  Whit V KT11 & KT13 .... 72 C8
Camp Farm Rd.
  Farnb GU14 .... 105 D5
Camp Hill.
  Farnb GU10 & GU9 .... 147 C8
Camp Rd. Farnb GU14 .... 105 C8
Camp View. Wimble SW19 ... 19 C3
Camp Rd. Wold CR3 .... 101 E6
Camp View. Wimble SW19 ... 19 B3
Campbell Ave. Westfd GU22 89 F6
Campbell Cl. Alder GU11 ... 126 C7
Campbell Cl. Streat SW16 ... 21 D4
Campbell Cl. Twick TW2 ...... 16 D7
Campbell Cres.
  E Grins RH19 .... 185 B1
Campbell Cl. Dulw SE21 ...... 23 A7
Campbell Ct. Leahd KT22 ... 95 B5
Campbell House. 🗗
  Wallin SM6 .... 60 B6
Campbell Pl. Friml GU16 ...... 65 F3
Campbell Rd. Alder GU11 . 105 A3
Campbell Rd. Cater CR3 .... 100 D6
Campbell Rd. Thorn H CR0 .. 42 B3
Campbell Rd. Twick TW2 .... 16 D6
Campbell Rd. Whit V KT13 .. 53 A3
Campbell Rd. Worth RH10 . 202 C5
Campden Rd.
  S Croy CR0 & CR2 .... 61 E5
Campen Cl. Putney SW19 ... 19 E6
Camphill Ct. W Byfl KT14 ... 71 A7
Camphill Ind Est.
  W Byfl KT14 .... 71 B8
Camphill Rd.
  W Byfl KT14 & KT15 .... 71 B7
Campion Cl. Hawley GU17 .. 64 F3
Campion Cl. S Croy CR2 ..... 61 E6
Campion Dr. Burgh H KT20 .. 97 B7
Campion House. Brack RG12 26 E8
Campion House. 🗗
  Redh RH1 .... 119 A4
Campion House (Seminary).
  Hounsl TW7 .... 5 D6
Campion Rd. Horsh RH12 .. 217 E5
Campion Rd. Hounsl TW7 ..... 5 F6
Campion Way. Woki RG11 ... 25 E7
Camrose Ave. Felt TW13 .... 14 F5
Camrose Cl. Croy CR0 .... 43 E2
Camrose Cl. Morden SM4 .... 40 A5
Can Hatch. Burgh H KT20 .... 77 E1
Canada Ave. Earls RH1 ..... 140 A5
Canada Dr. Earls RH1 .... 140 A5
Canada House. Earls RH1 . 140 A5
Canada Rd. Byfl KT14 .... 71 C6
Canada Rd. Cobham KT11 ... 73 C6
Canada Rd. Friml GU16 ..... 66 B5
Canadian Ave. Catf SE6 ...... 24 B7
Canal Cl. Farnb GU11 .... 105 D5
Canal Cotts. Ash V GU12 ... 106 A4
Canal Wlk. Croy CR0 .... 42 F3
Canal Wlk. For Hil SE23 .... 23 C3
Canberra Cl. Crawl RH11 ... 181 D1
Canberra Cl. Horsh RH12 .. 217 F4
Canberra Pl. Horsh RH12 .. 217 F4
Canberra Rd. Harl TW6 .... 3 A4
Canberra Way. Farnb GU14 104 F8
Canbury Ave. King U T KT2 .. 37 F8
Canbury Bsns Pk. 🗗
  King U T KT2 .... 37 E8
Canbury Ct. King U T KT2 ... 17 E1
Canbury Mews. Dulw SE26 . 23 A5
Canbury Park Rd.
  King U T KT2 .... 37 E8
Candlerush Cl. Mayb GU22 .. 70 B2
Candover Cl. Harm UB7 .... 2 D7
Candy Croft. G Book KT23 ... 94 B2
Cane Cl. Wallin SM6 .... 60 E3
Cane Hill Hospl. Coulsd CR5 79 C2
Canewdon Cl. Woking GU22 89 E8
Canford Dr. Chert KT15 .... 52 B8
Canford Gdns. New Mal KT3 38 E3
Canham Rd. S Norw SE25 ... 42 E6
Canmore Gdns. Streat SW16 21 C1
Canning Rd. Alder GU12 ... 105 D2
Canning Rd. Croy CR0 & CR9 61 F8
Cannizaro Rd. Wimble SW19 19 D3
Cannon Cl. Hampt TW12 ..... 16 B2

Cannon Cl. Sandh GU15 ...... 64 F8
Cannon Cl. W Barn SW20 ... 39 C6
Cannon Cres. Chobh GU24 ... 68 E8
Cannon Gr. Fetch KT22 ...... 94 E6
Cannon Hill. Easth RG12 .... 27 C3
Cannon Hill La.
  Merton KT3 & SM4 & SW20 . 39 E5
Cannon Hill La.
  W Barn KT3 & SM4 & SW20 . 39 E5
Cannon House. Penge SE26 23 B2
Cannon Side. Fetch KT22 .... 94 E5
Cannon Way. E Mole KT8 ... 36 B5
Cannon Way. Fetch KT22 .... 94 E6
Cannons Cl. Reig RH2 ...... 117 F2
Canon's Hill.
  Coulsd CR5 & CR8 .... 80 A1
Canon's Wlk. Croy CR0 ...... 62 D7
Canonbie Rd. For Hil SE23 .. 23 C8
Canonbury Cotts.
  Lamb Gn RH12 .... 199 F6
Canons L Ctr The. Mitch CR4 40 F5
Canons La. Burgh H KT20 ... 97 F8
Canopus Way. Stan TW19 ... 13 E8
Cansiron La. Ash W RH19 .. 206 F6
Cantelupe Rd.
  E Grins RH19 .... 185 F1
Canter The. Crawl RH10 ... 202 E7
Canterbury Cl. Beck BR3 ..... 44 B8
Canterbury Ct. Ashf TW15 ... 13 F4
Canterbury Ct. Dork RH4 .. 136 A8
Canterbury Ct. S Croy CR2 . 61 C3
Canterbury Gr.
  W Norw SE27 & SW16 ...... 22 A5
Canterbury Mews.
  Oxsh KT22 .... 74 C6
Canterbury Rd. Ash GU12 . 106 A3
Canterbury Rd. Crawl RH10 201 E2
Canterbury Rd. Farnb GU14 85 B2
Canterbury Rd. Felt TW13 ... 15 E6
Canterbury Rd. Morden SM4 40 C3
Canterbury Rd. Stough GU2 108 F3
Canterbury Rd.
  Thorn H CR0 & CR7 .... 42 A2
Cantley Cres. Woki RG11 .... 25 A8
Cantley Gdns. S Norw SE19 42 F8
Canute Ct. W Norw SW16 ... 22 A5
Canvey Cl. Crawl RH11 ..... 201 C3
Cape Copse. Rudg RH12 ... 214 D7
Capel. Surb KT5 .... 37 F2
Capel Ave. Wallin SM6 .... 60 F5
Capel CE (VA) Fst Sch.
  Capel RH5 .... 178 D6
Capel Ct. Penge SE20 .... 43 C8
Capel La. Crawl RH11 ...... 200 F5
Capel Lodge. 🗗 Rich TW9 ..... 6 F6
Capel Lodge. 🗗 21 F8
  Streat SW20
Capel Rd. Rusper RH12 ..... 199 A8
Capella House. Capel RH5 . 178 C5
Capern Rd. Wands SW18 ... 20 C7
Capital Ind Est. Mitch CR4 . 40 F4
Capital Pk. Old Wok GU22 ... 90 B6
Caplan Est. Mitch CR4 .... 41 C8
Capper Rd. Sandh GU15 ..... 65 A7
Capri Rd. Croy CR0 .... 42 F2
Capricorn Cl. Crawl RH11 .. 200 E4
Capsey Rd. Crawl RH11 .... 200 E6
Capstans Wharf. Knaph GU21 68 F1
Capstone Rd. Catf BR1 .... 24 F4
Caradon Cl. Woking GU21 ... 69 B1
Caradon Ct. 🗗 Twick TW1 ...... 6 C1
Caraway Cl. Crawl RH11 .... 201 B2
Caraway Pl. Hackb SM6 ..... 60 B7
Caraway Pl. Stough GU2 ... 109 A6
Carberry Rd. 🗗
  S Norw SE19 .... 22 E2
Carbery La. Ascot SL5 .... 29 B6
Card Hill. For Row RH18 ... 206 F1
Cardamom Cl. Stough GU2 109 A5
Cardigan Cl. Knaph GU21 ... 68 E2
Cardigan Rd. Rich TW10 .... 6 E1
Cardigan Rd. Wimble SW19 . 20 C2
Cardinal Ave. King U T KT2 . 17 E2
Cardinal Ave. W Barn SM4 .. 39 E3
Cardinal Cl.
  Worc Pk KT19 & KT4 .... 58 A6
Cardinal Cres. King U T KT3 . 38 C7
Cardinal Dr. Walt O T KT12 .. 35 D1
Cardinal Newman RC Sch.
  Hersh KT12 .... 54 D7
Cardinal Rd. Felt TW13 .... 15 B7
Cardinal Road Inf Sch.
  Felt TW13 .... 15 B7
Cardinal's Wlk. Ashf TW16 . 14 E2
Cardinal's Wlk. Hampt TW12 16 C1
Cardingham. Woking GU21 .. 68 F2
Cardington Sq. Hounsl TW4 .. 4 D3
Cardwell Cres. Ascot SL5 ... 29 C4
Cardwells Keep.
  Stough GU2 .... 109 A4

Carew Cl. Coulsd CR5 .... 100 B8
Carew Ct. Sutton SM2 .... 59 B2
Carew House. Streat SW16 .. 22 A5
Carew Manor Sch.
  Wallin SM6 .... 60 D7
Carew Rd. Ashf TW15 .... 14 C2
Carew Rd. Mitch CR4 .... 41 A7
Carew Rd. Thorn H CR7 ...... 42 B5
Carew Rd. Wallin SM6 .... 60 C4
Carey House. Crawl RH11 . 201 C6
Carey Rd. Woki RG11 .... 25 C5
Carey's Copse. Smallf RH6 162 B3
Carey's Wood. Smallf RH6 162 B3
Carfax. Horsh RH12 .... 217 C2
Carfax Ave. Ash GU10 .... 126 F8
Cargate Ave. Alder GU11 .. 105 A1
Cargate Gr. Alder GU11 .... 105 A1
Cargate Hill. Alder GU11 ... 104 F1
Cargate Terr. Alder GU11 .. 104 F1
Cargill Rd. Wands SW18 .... 20 C7
Cargo Forecourt Rd.
  Crawl RH6 .... 181 D7
Cargo Rd. Crawl RH6 .... 181 D7
Cargreen Rd. S Norw SE25 . 42 F5
Carholme Rd. For Hil SE23 . 23 F7
Carisbrook Ct. 🗗
  Streat SW16 .... 21 F5
Carisbrooke. Friml GU16 .... 85 F8
Carisbrooke Ct. Belm SM2 . 58 F3
Carisbrooke Rd. Mitch CR4 . 41 C5
Carleton Ave. Wallin SM6 ... 60 D2
Carleton Cl. Thame D KT10 . 36 D1
Carlingford Gdns. Mitch CR4 21 A1
Carlingford Rd. W Barn SM4 39 D3
Carlinwark Dr. Camb GU15 . 65 F7
Carlisle Cl. King U T KT2 .... 38 A8
Carlisle Inf Sch.
  Hampt TW12 .... 16 B2
Carlisle Mews. King U T KT2 38 A8
Carlisle Rd. Cheam SM1 ..... 58 F4
Carlisle Rd. Hampt TW12 ... 16 B1
Carlisle Rd. Rushm GU10 .. 168 C6
Carlisle Way. Up Toot SW17 21 A3
Carlton Ave. Felt TW14 .... 4 C1
Carlton Ave. S Croy CR2 .... 61 E3
Carlton Cl. Chess KT9 .... 56 D4
Carlton Cl. Frml GU15 & 16 . 66 B3
Carlton Cl. Horse GU21 ...... 70 A5
Carlton Cres. Cheam SM3 .. 58 E6
Carlton Ct. Horley RG6 ..... 161 A5
Carlton Ct. 🗗 Penge SE20 .. 43 B8
Carlton Ct. S Norw SE19 .... 42 F8
Carlton Ct. Stain TW18 .... 13 A3
Carlton Gn. Redh RH1 ..... 118 E4
Carlton House. Cheam SM1 . 58 F4
Carlton House. Hounsl TW4 .. 5 A1
Carlton Park Ave.
  Merton SW20 .... 39 D7
Carlton Rd. Ashf TW16 .... 14 F1
Carlton Rd. Blind H RH9 ... 142 C2
Carlton Rd.
  Head On GU35 .... 187 C5
Carlton Rd. Horse GU21 ..... 70 A5
Carlton Rd. King U T KT3 ... 38 E7
Carlton Rd. Mortl SW14 .... 7 C3
Carlton Rd. Redh RH1 ...... 118 E4
Carlton Rd. S Croy CR2 ...... 61 D3
Carlton Rd. Walt O T KT12 .. 35 B2
Carlton Tye. For Hil SE26 ... 23 C5
Carlton Tye. Horley RH6 ... 161 C3
Carlwell St. Up Toot SW17 .. 20 E3
Carlyle Cl. E Mole KT8 .... 36 B7
Carlyle Cl. Fetch RH11 .... 45 C5
Carlyle Rd. Croy CR0 .... 62 A8
Carlyle Rd. Stain TW18 .... 13 A1
Carlyon Cl. Farnb GU14 ..... 85 C4
Carlyon Cl. Mytch GU16 ..... 85 F4
Carlys Cl. Penge BR3 .... 43 D7
Carmalt Gdns. Hersh KT12 . 54 C5
Carman Wlk. Crawl RH11 .. 201 B1
Carmarthen Cl.
  W Heath GU14 .... 85 A7
Carmel Cl. 🗗 Woking GU22 69 E1
Carmichael Ct. Barnes SW13 7 F5
Carmichael House. 🗗
  Dulw SE21 .... 22 E4
Carmichael Mews.
  Wands SW18 .... 20 D8
Carmichael Rd. Croy SE25 . 43 A5
Carminia Rd. Up Toot SW17 21 B6
Carnac St.
  W Norw SE21 & SE27 .... 22 D5
Carnation Dr. Wink RG12 ...... 8 B2
Carnegie Cl. Surb KT6 .... 56 F8
Carnegie Pl. Wimble SW19 . 19 D5
Carnforth Cl. W Ewell KT19 . 57 B4
Carnforth Rd. Streat SW16 . 21 D1
Carnoustie. Easth RG12 ...... 26 E2
Carole House. 🗗
  Penge SE20 .... 43 B8

Carolina Rd. S Norw CR7 .... 42 C8
Caroline Cl. Hounsl TW7 ...... 5 E7
Caroline Cl. S Croy CR0 ...... 61 E6
Caroline Cl. Streat SW16 .... 21 F5
Caroline Ct. Ashf TW15 ...... 14 B2
Caroline Ct. Catf SE6 .... 24 D4
Caroline Ct. Crawl RH11 .... 201 C6
Caroline Ct. 🗗 Surb KT6 ..... 37 D2
Caroline Dr. Woki RG11 ...... 25 A7
Caroline Pl. Harl UB3 .... 3 E7
Caroline Rd. Merton SW19 .. 19 F1
Carolyn Cl. Woking GU21 ... 88 F8
Carpenter Cl. Ewell KT17 ... 57 F2
Carpenters Ct. Twick TW2 .. 16 E6
Carrick Cl. Islew TW7 .... 6 A6
Carrick Gate. Esher KT10 ... 55 C7
Carrington Ave. Islew TW3 ... 5 B2
Carrington Cl. Croy CR0 ...... 43 E2
Carrington Cl. Redh RH1 ... 118 F2
Carrington Lodge. 🗗
  Rich TW10 .... 6 E2
Carrington Pl. Esher KT10 .. 55 C6
Carrington Rd. Rich TW10 .... 7 A3
Carrinton La. Ash V GU12 . 106 A8
Carroll Ave. Merrow GU1 ... 110 B1
Carroll Cres. Ascot SL5 ...... 28 F5
Carrow Rd. Walt O T KT12 .. 54 D7
Carshalton Beeches Sta.
  Wallin SM5 .... 59 F4
Carshalton Coll. Carsh SM5 . 59 F7
Carshalton Coll of FE (Elmwood
  Annexe). Hackb SM6 .... 60 B8
Carshalton Gr. Carsh SM1 .. 59 D5
Carshalton High Sch for Boys.
  Carsh SM5 .... 59 E8
Carshalton High Sch for Girls.
  Carsh SM5 .... 59 E7
Carshalton Lodge.
  Oat Pk KT13 .... 53 E7
Carshalton Park Rd.
  Wallin SM5 .... 59 F5
Carshalton Pl. Wallin SM5 .. 60 A5
Carshalton Rd. Camb GU15 . 47 A1
Carshalton Rd.
  Sutton SM1 & SM5 .... 59 D5
Carshalton Rd. Wallin SM7 . 78 B6
Carshalton Rd. Woodm SM7 78 F6
Carshalton Sta. Carsh SM5 . 59 F6
Carson Rd. W Norw SE21 ... 22 D6
Carstairs Rd. Catf SE6 .... 24 C5
Carswell Rd. Lewish SE6 .... 24 C8
Cartbridge Cl. Send GU23 ... 90 B4
Carter Cl. Wallin SM6 .... 60 D3
Carter Rd. Mitch SW19 ...... 20 D2
Carter's Cotts. Earls RH1 .. 139 E7
Carter's Rd. Epsom KT17 .... 76 F4
Carterdale Cotts.
  Capel RH5 .... 178 C5
Carters La. N Cheam KT4 ... 39 D1
Carters La. Mayb GU22 ...... 90 D7
Carters Wlk. Heath E Guy • 125 D8
Cartersmead Cl.
  Horley RH6 .... 161 B4
Carthouse Cotts.
  Merrow GU4 .... 110 C4
Carthouse La. Woking GU21 68 E5
Cartmel Cl. Redh RH1 .... 118 E3
Cartmel Ct. Beck BR2 .... 44 E7
Cartmel Gdns. Morden SM4 40 C4
Carwarden House Sch.
  Friml GU15 .... 66 A3
Caryl House. 🗗
  Putney SW19 .... 19 D7
Caryll Cotts. Faygt RH12 .. 199 F1
Cascades. New Add CR0 ..... 62 F1
Caselden Cl. Addl KT15 ...... 52 C5
Casewick Rd. W Norw SE27 22 B4
Casher Rd. Worth RH10 .... 202 C3
Cassel Hospl The.
  Rich TW10 .... 17 D4
Cassilis Rd. Twick TW1 .... 6 B1
Cassino Cl. Alder GU11 .... 105 B2
Cassiobury Ave. E Bed TW14 14 F8
Cassland Rd. S Norw CR7 .. 42 D5
Casslee Rd. For Hil SE6 ...... 23 F8
Cassocks Sq. Shep TW17 ... 34 D2
Castillon Rd. Catf SE6 .... 24 E6
Castlands Rd. For Hil SE6 .. 23 F6
Castle Ave. Ewell KT17 .... 58 B2
Castle Cl. Beck BR2 .... 44 E6
Castle Cl. Charl TW16 .... 14 E1
Castle Cl. Dovgn RH2 .... 139 B5
Castle Cl. Friml GU15 .... 65 F4
Castle Cl. Wimble SW19 .... 19 D5
Castle Cl. Sham M SM4 ...... 59 A4
Castle Ct. For Hil SE26 .... 23 E4
Castle Ct. Morden SM4 .... 40 D4

Castle Dr. Dovgn RH2 ...... 139 B4
Castle Dr. Horley RH6 .... 161 C2
Castle Gdns. Brock RH4 .... 115 F1
Castle Gn. Oat Pk KT13 ...... 53 E7
Castle Grove Rd.
  Chobh GU24 .... 68 E7
Castle Hill. Farnb GU9 ..... 125 B3
Castle Hill. Guild GU1 .... 130 D7
Castle Hill Ave.
  New Add CR0 .... 63 C2
Castle Hill Prim Sch.
  New Add CR0 .... 63 C4
Castle Hill Rd. Eng Gn TW20 11 C5
Castle House. 🗗
  Belm SM2 .... 59 A3
Castle Par. Stonel KT17 ...... 58 A3
Castle Rd. Alder GU11 ...... 104 E4
Castle Rd. Broad H RH12 .. 216 D3
Castle Rd. Camb GU15 .... 65 F4
Castle Rd. Epsom KT18 ...... 76 B4
Castle Rd. Horse GU21 .... 69 F5
Castle Rd. Islew TW7 .... 5 F5
Castle Rd. Kings CR5 .... 98 E6
Castle Rd. Oat Pk KT13 ...... 53 E7
Castle Sq. Bletch RH1 .... 120 C2
Castle St. Bletch RH1 .... 120 C2
Castle St. Farnb GU9 .... 125 B3
Castle St. Guild GU1 .... 130 D7
Castle St. King U T KT2 .... 37 E7
Castle The. Horsh RH12 .... 217 E7
Castle View. Epsom KT18 ... 76 B5
Castle View Rd. Weyb KT13 53 B6
Castle Way. Ewell KT17 ...... 58 A2
Castle Way. Felt TW13 .... 15 C4
Castle Way. Wimble SW19 .. 19 D5
Castle Wlk. Sunby TW16 .... 35 C6
Castle Yd. 🗗 Rich TW10 .... 6 D2
Castlecombe Dr.
  Putney SW19 .... 19 D8
Castlecraig Ct. Sandh GU15 . 64 D7
Castledine Rd. Penge SE20 23 B1
Castlefield Rd. Reig RH2 ... 118 A1
Castlegate. Rich TW9 .... 6 F4
Castlemaine Ave.
  Ewell KT17 .... 58 B2
Castlemaine Ave.
  S Croy CR0 & CR2 .... 61 F5
Castleman House. Ascot SL5 29 D4
Castleton Cl. Banstd SM7 ... 78 A4
Castleton Cl. Croy CR0 .... 43 E3
Castleton Ct. Surb KT5 .... 37 F4
Castleton Dr. Banstd SM7 ... 78 A5
Castleton Rd. Mitch CR4 .... 41 D5
Caswell Cl. W Heath GU14 .. 84 F6
Catalpa Cl. Belif GU1 .... 109 C3
Catena Rise. Lhtwat GU18 .. 48 B1
Cater Gdns.
  Stough GU2 & GU3 .... 108 F3
Caterfield La. Crow RH7 ... 143 F3
Caterfield La.
  Oxted RH7 & RH8 .... 144 A5
Caterham By-Pass.
  Cater CR3 .... 101 B4
Caterham Cl. Pirb GU24 ..... 87 E6
Caterham Dene Hospl.
  Cater CR3 .... 100 F4
Caterham Dr.
  Coulsd CR3 & CR5 & CR8 . 100 C8
Caterham Sch. Cater CR3 . 100 F1
Caterham Sch Prep.
  Cater CR3 .... 100 F1
Caterham Sta. Cater CR3 .. 101 A3
Caterways. Horsh RH12 .... 217 A3
Catford Bridge Sta. Catf SE6 24 A8
Catford Broadway. Catf SE6 24 A8
Catford Cty Sch. Catf SE6 .. 24 C5
Catford Cty Sch (Annexe).
  Catf BR1 .... 24 E4
Catford Hill. For Hil SE6 ..... 24 A7
Catford Rd. Catf SE6 .... 24 A7
Catford Rd. Catf SE6 .... 24 A8
Cathedral Cl. Guild GU2 ... 130 B8
Cathedral Hill Ind Est.
  Stough GU2 .... 109 A2
Cathedral View.
  Stough GU2 .... 108 F1
Catherine Baird Ct. 🗗
  Balham SW12 .... 21 B8
Catherine Cl. Byfl KT14 ...... 71 F5
Catherine Ct. 🗗
  Wimble SW19 .... 19 F3
Catherine Dr. Ashf TW16 ... 14 E2
Catherine Gdns. Islew TW3 . 5 D3
Catherine Howard Ct. 🗗
  Weyb KT13 .... 53 B7
Catherine Rd. King U T KT6 . 37 D4
Catherine Wheel Rd.
  Brent TW8 .... 6 D7
Catherington Sch.
  Crawl RH11 .... 181 D2

Cathill La. Ockley RH5 ... 177 C3
Cathles Rd. Balham SW12 ... 21 C8
Catlin Cres. Shep TW17 ... 34 D4
Catling Cl. For Hil SE23 ... 23 D5
Caton Ct. Beck BR2 ... 44 E7
Cator Cl. New Add CR0 ... 82 E8
Cator Cres. New Add CR0 ... 82 E8
Cator La. Beck BR3 ... 43 F8
Cator Park Girls Sch. Penge BR3 ... 23 E1
Cator Rd. Penge SE20 & SE26 ... 23 D2
Cator Rd. Wallin SM5 ... 59 F5
Catteshall Hatch. Farnc GU7 ... 151 A6
Catteshall La. Godal GU7 ... 150 F4
Catteshall Rd. Farnc GU7 ... 151 A5
Catteshall Terr. Godal GU7 151 A5
Causeway. Felt TW14 & TW4 . 4 B3
Causeway Ct. 2 Knaph GU21 ... 68 F1
Causeway Est. Egham TW20 12 C4
Causeway The. Carsh SM5 .. 60 A8
Causeway The. Clayg KT10 .. 55 F3
Causeway The. Egham TW18 & TW20 ... 12 D4
Causeway The. Horsh RH12 ... 217 C1
Causeway The. Sutton SM2 . 59 C2
Causeway The. Tedd TW11 . 16 F2
Causeway The. Wimble SW19 ... 19 C3
Cavalier Way. E Grins RH19 205 F7
Cavalry Cres. Hounsl TW4 ... 4 D3
Cavalry Ct. Alder GU11 ... 104 E2
Cavans Rd. Farnb GU11 ... 105 C6
Cave Rd. Rich TW10 ... 17 C4
Cavell Rd. Worth RH10 ... 202 C5
Cavendish Ave. W Barn KT3 39 B5
Cavendish Cl. Ashf TW16 ... 14 F2
Cavendish Cl. Horsh RH12 217 D7
Cavendish Ct. Ashf TW16 ... 14 F2
Cavendish Ct. Hawley GU17 64 D3
Cavendish Ct. Poyle SL3 ... 1 E6
Cavendish Dr. Clayg KT10 ... 55 E5
Cavendish Gdns. Earls RH1 119 A2
Cavendish House. Twick TW1 6 A1
Cavendish Jun & Inf Sch. Chisw W4 ... 7 E7
Cavendish Meads. Ascot SL5 ... 29 D3
Cavendish Mews. Alder GU11 ... 105 A1
Cavendish Rd. Alder GU11 105 A1
Cavendish Rd. Ashf TW16 ... 14 F2
Cavendish Rd. Balham SW12 21 B8
Cavendish Rd. Chisw W4 ... 7 C6
Cavendish Rd. Earls RH1 .. 119 A2
Cavendish Rd. Mitch SW19 .. 20 E1
Cavendish Rd. New Mal KT3 38 F5
Cavendish Rd. Sutton SM2 ... 59 C3
Cavendish Rd. Thorn H CR0 . 42 B1
Cavendish Rd. Whit V KT13 . 53 C3
Cavendish Rd. Woking GU22 89 D8
Cavendish Terr. Felt TW13 .. 15 A6
Cavendish Way. W Wick BR4 ... 44 B1
Cavenham Cl. Woking GU22 89 E8
Caverleigh Way. New Mal KT4 ... 39 B2
Caversham Ave. Cheam SM3 58 E8
Caversham House. 8 King U T KT1 ... 37 E7
Caversham Rd. King U T KT1 37 F7
Caves Farm Cl. Sandh GU17 64 A8
Cawnpore St. W Norw SE19 22 E3
Cawsey Way. Woking GU21 . 69 E2
Cawston Ct. Broml BR1 ... 24 F1
Caxton Ave. Row Tn KT15 ... 52 A4
Caxton Cl. Crawl RH10 ... 201 E3
Caxton Gdns. Stough GU2 . 109 B2
Caxton House. The Char RH8 ... 123 F3
Caxton La. The Char RH8 ... 123 E4
Caxton Rd. Wimble SW19 ... 20 C3
Caxton Rise. Earls RH1 ... 119 A2
Caxtons Ct. Abbots GU1 ... 110 A3
Caygill Cl. Beck BR2 ... 44 F5
Cayley Cl. Wallin SM6 ... 60 E3
Cearn Way. Coulsd CR5 ... 79 F4
Cecil Cl. Ashf TW15 ... 14 C1
Cecil Cl. Chess KT9 ... 56 D6
Cecil Ct. 9 Croy CR0 ... 61 F8
Cecil Lodge. Chess KT9 ... 56 D6
Cecil Mansions. 2 Up Toot SW17 ... 21 A6
Cecil Pl. Mitch CR4 ... 40 F4
Cecil Rd. Ashf TW15 ... 14 C2
Cecil Rd. Cheam SM1 & SM2 58 F4
Cecil Rd. Hounsl TW3 ... 5 C5
Cecil Rd. Merton SW19 ... 20 B1
Cecil Rd. Thorn H CR0 ... 41 F3
Cedar Ave. Blckw GU17 ... 64 D5
Cedar Ave. Cobham KT11 ... 73 C4
Cedar Ave. Twick TW2 ... 5 C1
Cedar Cl. Alder GU12 ... 126 E8
Cedar Cl. Bagsh GU19 ... 47 E3
Cedar Cl. Crawl RH11 ... 181 C1
Cedar Cl. Dork RH4 ... 136 B7
Cedar Cl. E Mole KT8 ... 36 E5
Cedar Cl. Epsom KT17 ... 76 F5
Cedar Cl. Esher KT10 ... 54 F3
Cedar Cl. Horsh RH12 ... 217 C3
Cedar Cl. King U T KT2 ... 18 D4
Cedar Cl. Laleh TW18 ... 33 C6
Cedar Cl. W Norw SE21 ... 22 C6
Cedar Cl. Wallin SM5 ... 59 F4
Cedar Cl. Warlgm CR6 ... 81 E1
Cedar Cl. Warlgm CR6 ... 101 E8
Cedar Cl. Woki RG11 ... 25 C6
Cedar Cl. Woodh RH2 ... 139 C7
Cedar Ct. 8 Brent TW8 ... 6 D8
Cedar Ct. Egham TW20 ... 12 A4
Cedar Ct. Haslem GU27 ... 208 B6
Cedar Ct. Mortl SW14 ... 7 C3
Cedar Ct. Ottsh KT16 ... 51 C5
Cedar Ct. Sander CR2 ... 81 A8
Cedar Ct. Sutton SM2 ... 59 C4
Cedar Ct. Wimble SW19 ... 19 D5
Cedar Dr. Fetch KT22 ... 94 E4
Cedar Dr. Sunnin SL5 ... 30 A2
Cedar Gdns. Sutton SM2 ... 59 C4
Cedar Gdns. Woking GU21 ... 69 B1
Cedar Gr. Bisley GU24 ... 68 A4
Cedar Gr. Weyb KT13 ... 53 C6
Cedar Hill. Woodc KT18 ... 76 C3
Cedar House. Charlt TW16 .. 14 F1
Cedar House. New Add CR0 . 63 B4
Cedar Hts. Rich TW10 ... 17 E7
Cedar La. Friml GU16 ... 85 D8
Cedar Lodge. Crawl RH11 . 201 D4
Cedar Lodge. Milf GU8 ... 149 F2
Cedar Rd. Cobham KT11 ... 73 B5
Cedar Rd. Cranf TW5 ... 4 C5
Cedar Rd. Croy CR0 & CR9 ... 61 E8
Cedar Rd. E Bed TW14 ... 14 D7
Cedar Rd. E Mole KT8 ... 36 E5
Cedar Rd. Farnb GU14 ... 85 C3
Cedar Rd. Sutton SM2 ... 59 C4
Cedar Rd. Tedd TW11 ... 17 A3
Cedar Rd. Weyb KT13 ... 53 A6
Cedar Rd. Woking GU22 ... 89 C7
Cedar Terr. Rich TW9 ... 6 E3
Cedar Tree Gr. W Norw SE27 ... 22 B3
Cedar Way. Bellf GU1 ... 109 C4
Cedar Way. Charlt TW16 ... 14 E1
Cedar Wlk. Kenley CR8 ... 80 C3
Cedar Wlk. Kings KT20 ... 97 E7
Cedarcroft Rd. Chess KT9 ... 56 F6
Cedars. 2 Brack RG12 ... 27 F5
Cedars. Woodm SM7 ... 78 F5
Cedars Ave. Mitch CR4 ... 41 A6
Cedars Ct. Burph GU1 ... 110 A4
Cedars House. 5 W Norw SW27 ... 22 B3
Cedars Prim Sch The. Cranf TW5 ... 4 A7
Cedars Rd. Barnes SW13 ... 7 F5
Cedars Rd. Beck BR3 ... 43 F7
Cedars Rd. Morden SM4 ... 40 A5
Cedars Rd. Tedd KT8 ... 37 C8
Cedars Rd. Wallin CR0 ... 60 E6
Cedars The. Ashtd KT21 & KT22 ... 95 D6
Cedars The. Burph GU1 ... 110 A4
Cedars The. Byfl KT14 ... 71 F7
Cedars The. Milf GU8 ... 170 E8
Cedars The. Reig RH2 ... 118 D1
Cedars The. Tedd TW11 ... 16 F2
Cedars The. Wallin SM6 ... 60 C6
Cedarville Gdns. Streat SW16 ... 21 F2
Cedarways. M Bourn GU9 . 146 B7
Celandine Cl. 1 Crawl RH11 ... 201 B2
Celandine Cl. Crowth RG11 .. 45 C6
Celandine Rd. Hersh KT12 ... 54 E6
Celia Cres. Stain TW15 ... 13 D2
Celia Ct. 7 Rich TW9 ... 6 F6
Celtic Ave. Beck BR2 ... 44 E6
Celtic Rd. Byfl KT14 ... 71 F5
Cemetery La. Lo Hall TW17 . 34 B2
Cemetery Pales. Brookw GU24 ... 88 A6
Cemetery Pales. Pirb GU24 . 87 F5
Centaurs Bsns Pk. Brent TW7 6 A8
Central Ave. E Mole KT8 ... 35 F4
Central Ave. Islew TW3 & TW7 ... 5 C3
Central Ave. Wallin SM6 ... 60 E5
Central Ct. Addl KT15 ... 52 B6
Central Hill. S Norw SE19 & SE27 ... 22 D2
Central La. Wink SL4 ... 9 B7
Central Par. Felt TW14 ... 15 C8
Central Par. Heston TW5 ... 5 A7
Central Par. King U T KT6 ... 37 E3
Central Par. New Add CR0 & CR9 ... 63 C1
Central Par. Penge SE20 ... 23 D1
Central Pk Est. Hounsl TW4 ... 4 D3
Central Rd. Morden SM4 ... 40 B4
Central Rd. N Cheam KT4 ... 58 A8
Central Sq. E Mole KT8 ... 35 F5
Central Terr. Penge BR3 ... 43 D6
Central Vet Lab Woodhm KT15 52B2
Central Way. Felt TW14 ... 4 B2
Central Way. Oxted RH8 ... 122 D8
Central Way. Sutton SM5 ... 59 E3
Central Way. Wink SL4 ... 9 B7
Central Wlk. Woki RG11 ... 25 C6
Centre Terrace Rd. Farnb GU14 ... 105 A8
Centre The. Felt TW13 ... 15 B6
Centre The. Felt TW13 ... 15 B7
Centre The. Walt O T KT12 .. 34 F1
Centurion Cl. 4 Sandh GU15 ... 64 D8
Century Rd. Egham TW20 ... 12 C3
Century Way. Pirb GU24 ... 87 D8
Cerne Rd. Morden SM4 ... 40 C3
Cerotus Pl. Chert KT16 ... 32 F2
Chadacre Rd. Stonel KT17 ... 58 B5
Chadhurst Cl. Dork RH5 ... 136 D4
Chadwick Cl. Crawl RH11 .. 201 B1
Chadwick Cl. Tedd TW11 ... 17 A2
Chadworth Way. Esher KT10 55 D5
Chaffers Mead. Ashtd KT21 . 75 F3
Chaffinch Ave. Croy CR0 ... 43 D3
Chaffinch Cl. Crawl RH11 .. 201 D8
Chaffinch Cl. Croy CR0 ... 43 D3
Chaffinch Cl. Horsh RH12 . 217 D7
Chaffinch Cl. 5 Sandh GU15 64 D8
Chaffinch Cl. Tolw KT6 ... 57 A7
Chaffinch Rd. Beck BR3 ... 43 E8
Chaffinch Way. Horley RH6 160 E4
Chagford Ct. Mitch SW19 ... 20 E1
Chailey Cl. 3 Crawl RH11 201 A3
Chailey Cl. Heston TW5 ... 4 D6
Chailey Pl. Hersh KT12 ... 54 E6
Chalcot Cl. Belm SM2 ... 59 A3
Chalcot Mews. Streat SW16 21 E5
Chalcott Gdns. Long D KT6 .. 37 C1
Chaldon Cl. Earls RH1 ... 139 E7
Chaldon Common Rd. Cater CR3 ... 100 C2
Chaldon Rd. Cater CR3 ... 100 D4
Chaldon Rd. Crawl RH11 ... 201 C1
Chaldon Way. Coulsd CR5 ... 79 E1
Chale Wlk. Sutton SM2 ... 59 B2
Chalet Ct. Thorn H CR7 ... 42 B4
Chalfont Dr. Farnb GU14 ... 85 C2
Chalfont Rd. S Norw SE25 ... 42 F6
Chalford Cl. E Mole KT8 ... 36 A5
Chalford Ct. Surb KT6 ... 37 F2
Chalford Rd. W Norw SE21 .. 22 D4
Chalgrove Ave. Morden SM4 40 A4
Chalgrove Rd. Sutton SM2 ... 59 D3
Chalice Cl. Wallin SM6 ... 60 D4
Chalk La. Ashtd KT21 ... 96 A8
Chalk La. E Hors KT24 ... 112 F4
Chalk La. Shackl GU8 ... 149 D8
Chalk La. Woodc KT18 ... 76 E3
Chalk Paddock. Woodc KT18 76 D4
Chalk Pit Rd. Banstd SM7 ... 78 A2
Chalk Pit Rd. Lang V KT18 & KT21 ... 96 C8
Chalk Pit Rd. Sutton SM1 ... 59 C5
Chalk Rd. Farnc GU7 ... 150 E5
Chalk Rd. Ifold RH14 ... 212 C3
Chalkenden Cl. Penge SE20 . 23 B1
Chalkley Cl. Mitch CR4 ... 41 A7
Chalkpit La. Dork RH4 ... 136 A8
Chalkpit La. Oxted RH8 ... 122 D8
Chalkpit La. Wold CR3 & RH8 ... 102 C1
Chalkpit Terr. Dork RH4 ... 115 A1
Chalkpit Wood. Oxted RH8 122 D8
Chalky La. Chess KT9 ... 56 D1
Challen Ct. Horsh RH12 ... 217 B3
Challenge Ct. Leahd KT22 ... 95 B8
Challenge Rd. Felt TW15 ... 14 D4
Challice Way. Streat SW2 ... 21 F7
Challin St. Penge SE20 ... 43 C8
Challis Pl. Binf RG12 ... 26 E8
Challock Cl. Bigg H TN16 ... 83 C3
Challoner Ct. Beck BR2 ... 44 D7
Challoners Cl. E Mole KT8 ... 36 D5
Chalmers Ct. Charl RH6 ... 180 E6
Chalmers Rd. Ashf TW15 ... 14 B3
Chalmers Rd. Banstd SM7 ... 78 C4
Chalmers Rd E. Ashf TW15 .. 14 C3
Chalmers Way. Felt TW14 ... 4 B2
Chalner House. 21 Streat SW2 ... 22 A7
Chamber La. Farnh GU10 ... 145 C7
Chamberlain Cres. W Wick BR4 ... 44 B2
Chamberlain Way. Surb KT6 37 E2
Chamberlain Wlk. Felt TW13 15 E4
Chambers House. 2 Streat SW16 ... 21 C4
Chambers Rd. Ash GU12 ... 106 B6
Chamomile Gdns. W Heath GU14 ... 84 C5
Champion Cres. For Hil SE26 23 E4
Champion Rd. For Hil SE26 .. 23 E4
Champness Cl. 9 W Norw SE27 ... 22 D4
Champneys Cl. Belm SM2 ... 58 F3
Chancellor Gdns. Croy CR2 . 61 B2
Chancellor Gr. W Norw SE21 22 C5
Chancery La. Beck BR3 ... 44 B7
Chanctonbury Chase. Earls RH1 ... 119 A1
Chanctonbury Dr. Sunnin SL5 ... 29 E1
Chanctonbury Gdns. Belm SM2 ... 59 B3
Chanctonbury Way. Crawl RH11 ... 201 C4
Chandler CE (VA) Jun Sch. Witley GU8 ... 170 F5
Chandler Cl. Crawl RH10 & RH11 ... 201 D4
Chandler Cl. Hampt TW12 ... 36 A8
Chandler Ct. 2 Tolw KT5 ... 38 B1
Chandler Ct. 8 Wallin SM6 60 B4
Chandlers. Tadw KT20 ... 97 B6
Chandlers Cl. E Bed TW14 ... 14 F8
Chandlers Field Sch. E Mole KT8 ... 36 A4
Chandlers Grange. Ash GU12 ... 106 A5
Chandlers Rd. Ash GU12 ... 106 B4
Chandlers Way. 11 Streat SE24 ... 22 A8
Chandon Lodge. Sutton SM2 59 C3
Chandos Rd. Egham TW18 ... 12 D3
Channel Cl. Heston TW5 ... 5 A6
Channings. Horse GU21 ... 69 E4
Channon Ct. 3 King U T KT6 37 E4
Chantlers Cl. E Grins RH19 185 C2
Chanton Dr. E Ewell SM2 ... 58 C1
Chantrey Cl. Ashtd KT21 ... 95 C8
Chantrey Rd. Crawl RH10 .. 201 E3
Chantry Cl. Farnh GU9 ... 125 A2
Chantry Cl. Horley RH6 ... 160 F4
Chantry Cotts. Chil GU4 ... 131 B3
Chantry Ct. Friml GU16 ... 65 D1
Chantry Hurst. Woodc KT18 76 D4
Chantry La. Shere GU5 ... 132 F4
Chantry Rd. Bagsh GU19 ... 47 D2
Chantry Rd. Chert KT16 ... 33 C2
Chantry Rd. Chess KT9 ... 57 A5
Chantry Rd. Chil GU4 ... 131 B3
Chantry View Rd. Guild GU1 & GU4 ... 130 E6
Chantry Way. Mitch CR4 ... 40 D6
Chantrys Ct. Farnh GU9 ... 125 A2
Chantrys The. Farnh GU9 .. 125 A1
Chapel Ave. Addl KT15 ... 52 B6
Chapel Cl. Brack RG12 ... 27 D6
Chapel Cl. Milf GU8 ... 149 F2
Chapel Ct. Dork RH4 ... 136 A7
Chapel Fields. Farnc GU7 .. 150 D7
Chapel Gn. Purley CR8 ... 80 A6
Chapel Gr. Addl KT15 ... 52 B6
Chapel Gr. Burgh H KT20 ... 97 C8
Chapel Hill. Dunsf GU8 ... 192 F3
Chapel Hill. Effing KT24 ... 113 D8
Chapel La. Ash W RH19 ... 206 D6
Chapel La. Bagsh GU19 ... 47 D2
Chapel La. Copth RH10 ... 183 F4
Chapel La. For Row RH18 ... 206 F2
Chapel La. G Book KT23 ... 114 D5
Chapel La. Milf GU8 ... 149 F2
Chapel La. Pirb GU24 ... 88 A4
Chapel La. W Heath GU14 ... 84 F8
Chapel La. Westc RH4 ... 135 C6
Chapel La. Westh RH5 ... 114 D5
Chapel Park Rd. Addl KT15 .. 52 B6
Chapel Rd. Camb GU15 ... 65 B5
Chapel Rd. Charl RH6 ... 180 F7
Chapel Rd. Hounsl TW3 ... 5 B4
Chapel Rd. Limps RH8 ... 123 C5
Chapel Rd. Redh RH1 ... 118 F1
Chapel Rd. Rowl GU10 ... 145 E3
Chapel Rd. Smallf RH6 ... 162 B4
Chapel Rd. Tadw KT20 ... 97 D4
Chapel Rd. Twick TW1 ... 17 B8
Chapel Rd. W Norw SE27 ... 22 B4
Chapel Rd. Warlgm CR6 ... 81 D1
Chapel Sq. Sandh GU15 ... 64 F6
Chapel St. Farnb GU14 ... 85 D6
Chapel St. Guild GU1 ... 130 D7
Chapel St. 6 Woking GU21 . 69 F2
Chapel View. S Croy CR2 ... 62 C3
Chapel Way. Burgh H KT18 & KT20 ... 77 C1
Chapelhouse Cl. Stough GU2 ... 108 E1
Chaplain's Hill. Crowth RG11 45 D4
Chaplin Cres. Ashf TW16 ... 14 E2
Chapman House. 2 W Norw SE27 ... 22 B5
Chapman Rd. Thorn H CR0 ... 42 A1
Chapman Rd. Worth RH10 . 202 C2
Chapman's La. E Grins RH19 ... 185 B1
Chapman's La. E Grins RH19 ... 185 D1
Chapter Way. Hampt TW12 . 16 A4
Chara Pl. Chisw W4 ... 7 D8
Charcot House. Rhampt SW15 7 F1
Chard Rd. Harl TW6 ... 3 B5
Chargate Cl. Whit V KT12 ... 54 A4
Charing Ct. Beck BR2 ... 44 E7
Charlbury Cl. 7 Brack RG12 27 F5
Charlecombe Ct. Stain TW18 ... 13 B3
Charlecote Cl. Farnb GU14 .. 85 D3
Charlecote Gr. For Hil SE26 . 23 B5
Charles Ct. 5 Tedd TW11 ... 16 E3
Charles Darwin Sch. Bigg H TN16 ... 83 F3
Charles Dickens Ct. Croy SE25 ... 43 A5
Charles Hill. Tilf GU10 ... 147 E6
Charles Mills Ct. Streat SW16 ... 21 E2
Charles Rd. Merton SW19 ... 40 A8
Charles Rd. Stain TW18 ... 13 D2
Charles Sq. Brack RG12 ... 27 C7
Charles St. Chert KT16 ... 32 F1
Charles St. Croy CR0 & CR9 . 61 C7
Charles St. Hounsl TW3 ... 4 F5
Charles St. Mortl SW13 & SW14 ... 7 E5
Charles Staunton House. 3 W Norw SE27 ... 22 D4
Charlesfield Rd. Horley RH6 ... 160 F4
Charleston Cl. Felt TW13 ... 15 A5
Charleston Ct. Crawl RH10 202 B3
Charleville Cir. Penge SE19 & SE26 ... 23 A3
Charlmont Rd. Up Toot SW17 ... 20 F2
Charlock Cl. Crawl RH11 ... 201 A2
Charlock Way. Burph GU1 110 B4
Charlotte Cl. Heath E GU9 . 125 D8
Charlotte Ct. Crawl RH11 ... 201 C6
Charlotte Gr. Smallf RH6 ... 162 A4
Charlotte Mews. 3 Esher KT10 ... 55 B6
Charlotte Rd. Barnes SW13 ... 7 F6
Charlotte Rd. Wallin SM6 ... 60 C4
Charlotte Sq. 5 Rich TW10 ... 6 F1
Charlton Ave. Hersh KT12 ... 54 B6
Charlton Ct. Sandh GU15 ... 45 D1
Charlton Dr. Bigg H TN16 ... 83 D2
Charlton Gdns. Coulsd CR5 .. 79 C1
Charlton Ho. 5 Brent TW8 ... 6 E8
Charlton Kings. Oat Pk KT13 53 E7
Charlton La. Up Hall TW17 ... 34 D5
Charlton Rd. Charlt TW17 ... 34 C7
Charlwood. New Add CR0 ... 62 F2
Charlwood Cty Fst Sch. Charl RH6 ... 180 F7
Charlwood Dr. Oxsh KT22 ... 74 D4
Charlwood House. 1 Streat SW2 ... 21 F7
Charlwood La. Charl RH5 .. 180 A5
Charlwood Rd. Crawl RH6 . 181 C4
Charlwood Rd. Hookw RH6 181 C8
Charlwood Rd. Rusper RH11 & RH6 ... 180 E2
Charlwood Sq. Mitch CR4 ... 40 D6
Charlwood Wlk.Crawl RH11 181 B1
Charlwoods Bsns Ctr. E Grins RH19 ... 185 D2
Charlwoods Pl. E Grins RH19 ... 185 E3
Charlwoods Rd. E Grins RH19 ... 185 E3
Charm Cl. Horley RH6 ... 160 E4
Charman Rd. Redh RH1 ... 118 E1
Charmans Cl. Horsh RH12 218 B5
Charminster Ave. Merton SW19 ... 40 B7

Charminster Ct. 3
Surb KT6 .... 37 D2
Charminster Rd.
N Cheam KT4 .... 39 D1
Charmouth Ct. Rich TW10 ..... 6 F2
Charnwood. Sunnin SL5 ..... 29 F3
Charnwood Ave.
Merton SW19 .... 40 B7
Charnwood Rd. New Mal KT3 38 E5
Charnwood Rd.
S Norw SE25 .... 42 D5
Charrington Rd. 2
Croy CR0 & CR9 .... 61 C8
Charrington Way.
Broad H RH12 .... 216 C3
Charsley Rd. Catf SE6 .... 24 B6
Chart Cl. Broml BR2 .... 44 E8
Chart Cl. Croy CR0 .... 43 C3
Chart Cl. Dork RH5 .... 136 D5
Chart Downs. Dork RH5 .... 136 D4
Chart Gdns. Dork RH5 ..... 136 C4
Chart House Rd.
Ash V GU12 .... 106 A7
Chart La. Dork RH4 & RH5 .. 136 C7
Chart La. Reig RH2 .... 139 C7
Chart La S. Dork RH5 ...... 136 D5
Charta Rd E. Egham TW20 .. 12 C2
Charta Rd S. Egham TW20 .. 12 C2
Charta Rd W. Egham TW20 . 12 C3
Charter Cres. Hounsl TW4 .... 4 E3
Charter Ct. King U T KT1 ... 38 A6
Charter Rd. King U T KT1 .... 38 B6
Charter Sq. King U T KT1 ... 38 B7
Charterhouse. Farnc GU7 .. 150 C7
Charterhouse Cl.
Brack RG12 .... 27 E4
Charterhouse Rd.
Farnc GU7 .... 150 D6
Charters Cl. W Norw SE19 ... 22 E3
Charters La. Ascot SL5 .... 29 E4
Charters Rd. Sunnin SL5 .... 29 E2
Charters Sch. Sunnin SL5 ... 29 F2
Charters Way. Sunnin SL5 .. 29 F2
Chartfield Rd. Reig RH2 .... 139 C8
Chartham Gr. W Norw SE27 .. 22 B5
Chartham Rd. Croy SE25 ..... 43 B6
Charts Cl. Cran GU6 .... 174 E2
Chartway. Reig RH2 .... 118 B1
Chartwell. Friml GU16 .... 85 F6
Chartwell. 25 Putney SW19 . 19 D7
Chartwell. Wreccl GU9 ..... 145 F6
Chartwell Cl. 2 Croy CR0 ... 42 D1
Chartwell Gdns. Cheam SM3 58 E6
Chartwell Gdns.
Farnb GU11 .... 105 C7
Chartwell Lodge. 5
Beck BR3 .... 24 A1
Chartwell Pl. Cheam SM3 ... 58 F6
Chartwell Pl. Epsom KT18 .. 76 E5
Chartwell Way. 4
Penge SE20 .... 43 B8
Charwood Rd. Woki RG11 ... 25 F7
Chase Bridge Inf Sch.
Twick TW2 .... 5 E1
Chase Bridge Jun Sch.
Twick TW2 .... 5 E1
Chase Cotts. Shottm GU26 . 188 C1
Chase Ct. Islew TW7 .... 6 A5
Chase Ct. Merton SW20 ...... 39 E7
Chase End. Epsom KT19 ...... 76 D7
Chase Gdns. Twick TW2 ...... 16 D8
Chase La. Haslem GU27 ... 208 E3
Chase Rd.
Epsom KT17 & KT19 .... 76 D7
Chase The. Ashtd KT21 ...... 75 C1
Chase The. Coulsd CR5 ...... 79 D5
Chase The. Crawl RH10 .... 202 A5
Chase The. Crowth RG11 ..... 48 A6
Chase The. E Hors KT24 ..... 92 F1
Chase The. Farnb GU14 ...... 85 D6
Chase The. Guild GU2 ...... 130 A8
Chase The. Kings KT20 ...... 98 B6
Chase The. Oxsh KT22 .... 74 C4
Chase The. Reig RH2 .... 139 D8
Chase The. S Norw SW16 .... 22 A1
Chase The. Sunby TW16 ..... 35 B8
Chase The.
Wallin CR0 & SM6 .... 60 F5
Chasefield Cl.
Burgh GU1 & GU4 ...... 110 A4
Chasefield Rd.
Up Toot SW17 .... 20 F4
Chaseley Cl. Oat Pk KT13 ... 34 E1
Chasemore Cl. Carsh CR4 ... 40 F2
Chasemore Gdns. Croy CR0 61 A5
Chaseside Ave.
Merton SW20 .... 39 E7
Chaseside Gdns. Chert TW16 33 B2

Chasewater Ct. Alder GU11 105 A1
Chatelet Cl. Horley RH6 .... 161 B4
Chatfield Cl. Farnb GU14 .... 85 C2
Chatfield Ct. Cater CR3 .... 100 D5
Chatfield Dr. Merrow GU4 .. 110 C3
Chatfield Rd. Thorn H CR0 ... 42 B1
Chatfields. Crawl RH11 ..... 201 B4
Chatham Ave. Hayes BR2 .... 44 F2
Chatham Cl. Cheam SM3 ..... 39 F2
Chatham Rd.
King U T KT1 & KT2 ...... 38 A7
Chathill. Tand RH8 .... 143 B6
Chatsfield. Ewell KT17 ...... 58 A1
Chatsworth Ave.
Haslem GU27 .... 208 C8
Chatsworth Ave.
Merton SW20 .... 39 E7
Chatsworth Cl.
Coney H BR2 & BR4 .... 63 F8
Chatsworth Cres.
Islew TW3 & TW7 .... 5 D3
Chatsworth Gdns.
New Mal KT3 .... 38 F4
Chatsworth Gr. Hale GU9 . 125 B6
Chatsworth House.
King U T KT6 .... 37 D4
Chatsworth Hts. Camb GU15 66 B7
Chatsworth Inf Sch.
Islew TW3 .... 5 C3
Chatsworth Jun Sch.
Islew TW3 .... 5 C3
Chatsworth Lodge.
W Wick BR4 .... 63 C8
Chatsworth Pl. Mitch CR4 .. 40 F6
Chatsworth Pl. Oxsh KT22 .. 74 D6
Chatsworth Pl. Tedd TW11 .. 17 A4
Chatsworth Rd. Cheam SM3 58 E6
Chatsworth Rd. Chisw W4 ... 7 C8
Chatsworth Rd.
Croy CR0 & CR9 .... 61 D7
Chatsworth Rd. Farnb GU14 85 E3
Chatsworth Way.
N Norw SE27 .... 22 C5
Chattern Hill. Ashf TW15 .... 14 B4
Chattern Rd. Ashf TW15 ..... 14 C4
Chatterton Ct. Rich TW9 ..... 6 F5
Chatton Row. Bisley GU24 .. 68 A2
Chaucer Ave. Croy CR4 .... 4 B5
Chaucer Ave. 3
E Grins RH19 .... 185 C1
Chaucer Ave. Rich TW9 .... 7 A5
Chaucer Ave. Whit V KT13 .. 53 A3
Chaucer Cl. Nork SM7 .... 77 F5
Chaucer Cl. Woki RG11 ...... 25 F6
Chaucer Ct. Guild GU2 ...... 130 C5
Chaucer Gdns. Sutton SM1 . 59 A7
Chaucer Gr. Camb GU15 ..... 65 D5
Chaucer House. Sutton SM1 59 A7
Chaucer House. 2
N Norw SE27 .... 22 C4
Chaucer Rd. Ashf TW15 ...... 13 F4
Chaucer Rd. Crawl RH10 ... 202 C8
Chaucer Rd. Crowth RG11 ... 45 B4
Chaucer Rd. Sutton SM1 .... 59 A6
Chaucer Rd. W Heath GU14 . 84 F6
Chaucer Way. Row Tn KT15 . 52 A4
Chavey Down Rd.
Wink RG2 & SL5 .... 8 B2
Chaworth Rd. Ottsh KT16 ... 51 C4
Chaworth Sch. Ottsh KT16 .. 51 C4
Chawridge La. Wink SL4 ...... 8 C7
Cheam Cl. Brack RG12 .... 27 D4
Cheam Cl. Burgh H KT20 .... 97 B6
Cheam Common Inf Sch.
N Cheam KT4 .... 58 B8
Cheam Common Jun Sch.
N Cheam KT4 .... 58 B8
Cheam Common Rd.
N Cheam KT4 .... 58 B8
Cheam Court Flats.
Cheam SM3 .... 58 C4
Cheam Fields Prim Sch.
Cheam SM3 .... 58 E5
Cheam High Sch.Cheam SM358 E6
Cheam Mansions. Belm SM3 58 E3
Cheam Park Farm Inf Sch.
Cheam SM3 .... 58 E7
Cheam Park Farm Jun Sch.
Cheam SM3 .... 58 E7
Cheam Park Way.
Cheam SM3 .... 58 E4
Cheam Rd. Belm SM2 .... 58 C1
Cheam Rd. Cheam SM1 ...... 59 A4
Cheam Rd.
E Ewell KT17 & SM2 .... 58 C1
Cheam Rd. Ewell SM2 ...... 58 C1
Cheam Sta. Belm SM2 .... 58 E3
Cheapside. Horse GU21 ..... 69 D5
Cheapside C of E Prim Sch.
Ascot SL5 .... 29 E8

Cheapside Rd. Ascot SL5 ..... 29 D7
Cheddar Rd. Harl TW6 .... 3 A1
Cheeseman Cl. Hampt TW12 15 E2
Cheeseman Cl. Woki RG11 .. 25 D7
Cheetah Rd. 1 Farnb GU14 85 B2
Chelford Rd. Catf BR1 & SE6 24 D3
Chellows La. Crow RH7 ...... 143 F2
Chelmsford Cl. Belm SM2 .... 59 A2
Chelsea Cl. Hampt TW12 ..... 16 C3
Chelsea Cl. New Mal KT4 .... 39 A2
Chelsea Fields. Mitch SW19 40 D8
Chelsea Gdns. Cheam SM3 .. 58 E6
Chelsfield Gdns.
For HSE26 .... 23 C5
Chelsham Common Rd.
Chelsh CR6 .... 82 A3
Chelsham Court Rd.
Chelsh CR6 .... 82 E2
Chelsham Rd. Croy CR2 ..... 61 D4
Chelsham Rd. Warlgm CR6 .. 81 F2
Chelsham Terr. Warlgm CR6 81 F1
Cheltenham Ave. 9
Twick TW1 .... 17 A8
Cheltenham Cl. King U T KT3 38 C6
Cheltenham Villas.
Thorn H CR7 .... 42 A3
Chelwood Cl. Crawl RH10 ... 201 F4
Chelwood Cl. Ewell KT17 .... 76 F7
Chelwood Gdns. Rich TW9 .... 7 A5
Cheney Ct. For Hil SE23 ..... 23 D7
Cheniston Cl. W Byfl KT14 .. 71 A6
Cheniston Cl. Sunnin SL5 .... 30 A2
Chennells Way.
Horsh RH12 .... 217 E5
Chennestone Cty Prim Sch.
Sunby TW16 .... 35 B7
Chepstow Cl. Crawl RH10 .. 202 E6
Chepstow Rd. S Croy CR0 .. 61 E6
Chequer Grange.
For Row RH18 .... 206 E1
Chequer Rd. E Grins RH19 . 185 F1
Chequer Tree Cl.
Woking GU21 .... 68 E3
Chequers Cl. Horley RH6 ... 161 A4
Chequers Cl.
Walt o t H KT12 .... 97 A2
Chequers Ct. 7 Croy CR0 ... 42 F1
Chequers Cl. Horsh RH13 .. 217 F2
Chequers Dr. Horley RH6 ... 161 A4
Chequers La.
Walt o t H KT12 .... 97 A2
Chequers Pl. Dork RH4 ..... 136 B7
Cherbury Cl. Brack RG12 .... 27 E5
Cherimoya Gdns.
E Mole KT8 .... 36 B6
Cherington Way. N Asct SL5 28 E7
Cheriton Ave. Hayes BR2 .... 44 F4
Cheriton Ct. S Norw SE25 .. 42 E4
Cheriton Ct. Walt O T KT12 . 35 C1
Cheriton Sq. Up Toot SW17 . 21 A6
Cheriton Way. Blckw GU17 .. 64 D5
Cherkley Hill.
Leahd KT22 & RH5 .... 95 D1
Cherrimans Orch.
Shottm GU27 .... 207 F6
Cherry Cl. Carsh SM5 .... 59 F8
Cherry Cl. 12 Streat SW2 ... 22 A8
Cherry Cres. Brent TW8 ...... 6 B7
Cherry Ct. Horsh RH13 ..... 217 D1
Cherry Green Cl. Earls RH1 140 B7
Cherry Hill Gdns. Croy CR0 . 60 F6
Cherry La. Crawl RH11 ...... 181 C1
Cherry Orch. Ashtd KT21 .... 76 B1
Cherry Orch. Stain TW18 .... 13 A3
Cherry Orchard Gdns. 6
Croy CR0 .... 61 D8
Cherry Orchard Gdns.
E Mole KT8 .... 35 F6
Cherry Orchard Rd.
Croy CR0 .... 61 D8
Cherry Orchard Rd.
E Mole KT8 .... 36 A6
Cherry St. Woking GU21 ..... 69 E1
Cherry Tree Ave.
Stain TW18 .... 13 B2
Cherry Tree Ave.
Stough GU2 .... 108 F1
Cherry Tree Cl.Crawl RH10 202 D8
Cherry Tree Cl. Farnh GU9 125 C3
Cherry Tree Cl. Sandh GU15 65 F5
Cherry Tree Cl.
W Heath GU14 .... 84 C5
Cherry Tree Ct. Coulsd CR5 . 79 F1
Cherry Tree Dr. Brack RG12 27 D4
Cherry Tree Dr. Streat SW16 21 E5
Cherry Tree Gn.
Hams Gn CR2 .... 81 B5

Cherry Tree La. Farnc GU7 150 D8
Cherry Tree Rd. Milf GU8 .. 149 E1
Cherry Tree Rd. Rowl GU10 145 E3
Cherry Tree Wlk. Beck BR3 . 43 F5
Cherry Tree Wlk.
Coney H BR4 .... 63 F6
Cherry Way. Horton SL3 ...... 1 C4
Cherry Way. Up Hall TW17 .. 34 E5
Cherry Way. W Ewell KT19 .. 57 D4
Cherry Way. W Ewell KT19 .. 57 D4
Cherrydale Rd. Friml GU15 .. 66 D5
Cherryhill Gr. Alder GU11 .. 104 F1
Cherryhurst. Hambl GU8 ... 171 B1
Cherrywood Ave.
Eng Gn TW20 .... 11 B1
Cherrywood Cl. King U T KT2 38 A1
Cherrywood Ct. 1
Tedd TW11 .... 17 A3
Cherrywood La.
Merton SM4 & SW20 .... 39 E5
Cherrywood Rd. Farnb GU14 85 B7
Chertsey Bridge Rd.
Laleh KT16 & TW18 .... 33 D2
Chertsey Bvd. Chert KT16 ... 32 F1
Chertsey Cl. Purley CR8 ..... 80 B4
Chertsey Cres. New Add CR0 63 C1
Chertsey Ct. Mortl SW14 ...... 7 B4
Chertsey Dr. Cheam SM3 .... 58 E8
Chertsey House. Felt TW13 . 16 A5
Chertsey La. Egham TW18 .. 12 F2
Chertsey Rd. Addl KT15 ..... 52 B8
Chertsey Rd.
Ashf TW15 & TW16 TWTW16 14 D2
Chertsey Rd.
Burrh GU20 & GU24 .... 49 C6
Chertsey Rd. Byfl KT14 ...... 71 D8
Chertsey Rd. Chert KT15 .... 52 B8
Chertsey Rd.
Chobh GU24 & KT16 & GU21 50 D1
Chertsey Rd.
Felt TW13 & TW16 .... 14 D2
Chertsey Rd.
Felt TW13 &TW16 TW16 .... 14 E4
Chertsey Rd. Lo Hall TW17 . 34 A2
Chertsey Rd. Shep TW17 .... 33 F2
Chertsey Rd. Twick TW2 .... 16 D7
Chertsey Rd. Windl GU20 ... 48 E5
Chertsey Rd. Woking GU21 .. 69 F3
Chertsey St. Guild GU1 .... 130 D8
Chertsey St. Up Toot SW17 . 21 A3
Chertsey Wlk. Chert KT16 .. 32 F1
Chervil Cl. Felt TW13 .... 15 A5
Cherwell Cl. Bra Hil SL3 ...... 1 B7
Cherwell Cl. Tedd KT1 ...... 17 D1
Cherwell Cl. W Ewell KT19 .. 57 C6
Cherwell Ct. W Ewell KT19 . 57 C6
Cherwell Wlk. Crawl RH11 . 200 F5
Cheselden Rd. Guild GU1 .. 130 E8
Cheseman St. For Hil SE26 .. 23 B5
Chesfield Rd. King U T KT2 .. 17 E1
Chesham Cl. Belm SM2 ...... 58 E1
Chesham Cres. Penge SE20 . 43 C8
Chesham Ct. Wands SW18 .. 20 D8
Chesham Mews. Guild GU1 130 F8
Chesham Rd. Guild GU1 .... 130 F8
Chesham Rd.
King U T KT1 & KT2 .... 38 A7
Chesham Rd. Penge SE20 ... 43 C8
Cheshire Cl.
Mitch CR4 & SW16 .... 41 E6
Cheshire Cl. Ottsh KT16 .... 51 D4
Cheshire Gdns. Chess KT9 .. 56 D4
Cheshire House.
Cheam SM4 .... 40 B2
Cheshire House. Ottsh KT16 51 D4
Chesney Cres. New Add CR0 63 C3
Chessholme Cl. Ashf TW15 . 14 E1
Chessholme Rd. Ashf TW15 . 14 C2
Chessington Cl.
W Ewell KT19 .... 57 C4
Chessington Cl.
W Ewell KT19 .... 57 C4
Chessington Comm Coll.
Chess KT9 .... 56 D3
Chessington Hall Gdns.
Chess KT9 .... 56 D4
Chessington Hill Pk.
Chess KT9 .... 57 A5
Chessington North Sta.
Chess KT9 .... 56 E5
Chessington Par. Chess KT9 56 D5
Chessington Park.
Chess KT9 .... 57 A6
Chessington Rd. Ewell KT19 57 D3
Chessington Rd.
W Ewell KT19 .... 57 D3
Chessington Rd.
W Ewell KT19 .... 57 D3
Chessington South Sta.
Chess KT9 .... 56 D3

Chessington Way.
W Wick BR4 .... 63 B8
Chester Ave. Rich TW10 ...... 6 F1
Chester Ave. Twick TW2 .... 15 F7
Chester Cl. Ash GU12 ...... 106 B2
Chester Cl. Ashf TW15 ...... 14 D3
Chester Cl. Pixham RH4 .... 115 C1
Chester Cl. 1 Rich TW10 ..... 6 F1
Chester Cl. Stough GU2 .... 108 F3
Chester Cl. Sutton SM1 ...... 59 A8
Chester Gdns. Morden SM4 . 40 C3
Chester House. King U T KT1 38 B7
Chester Rd. Ash GU12 ..... 106 B2
Chester Rd. Effing KT24 ... 113 B7
Chester Rd. Harl TW6 .... 3 A4
Chester Rd. Hounsl TW4 ..... 4 B4
Chester Rd.
Wimble SW19 & SW20 ..... 19 C2
Chester Way. Tongh GU10 . 126 F6
Chesterblade La.
Brack RG12 .... 27 E2
Chesterfield Cl.
Copth RH10 .... 184 C4
Chesterfield Ct. King U T KT6 37 E4
Chesterfield Dr.
Hinch W KT10 .... 56 A8
Chesterfield House. 6
Streat SW16 .... 21 C3
Chesterfield Rd. Ashf TW15 13 E3
Chesterfield Rd. Chisw W4 .. 7 C8
Chesterfield Rd.
W Ewell KT19 .... 57 D3
Chesterfield Rd.
W Ewell KT19 .... 57 D3
Chesters. Horley RH6 ...... 160 E5
Chesters Rd. Friml GU15 .... 66 B5
Chesters The. King U T KT3 . 38 E8
Chesterton Cl.
E Grins RH19 .... 205 F7
Chesterton Ct. Horsh RH13 218 A4
Chesterton Dr. Merst RH1 . 119 E7
Chesterton Dr. Stan TW19 .. 13 F7
Chesterton Terr.
King U T KT1 .... 38 A7
Chestnut Ave. Alder GU12 . 126 E8
Chestnut Ave. Camb GU15 .. 66 A6
Chestnut Ave. Coney H BR4 . 63 E6
Chestnut Ave. Guild GU2 .. 130 C5
Chestnut Ave. Hampt TW12 . 15 F7
Chestnut Ave.
Hampt KT8 &KT11 .... 36 F7
Chestnut Ave.
Haslem GU27 .... 208 C7
Chestnut Ave.
M Bourn GU9 .... 146 A8
Chestnut Ave. 11
Mortl SW14 .... 7 D4
Chestnut Ave. Tats TN16 ... 103 E5
Chestnut Ave.
Thame D KT10 .... 36 D1
Chestnut Ave. Went GU25 .. 30 F1
Chestnut Ave. Whit V KT13 . 53 C3
Chestnut Ave. Whit V KT12 . 53 E2
Chestnut Ave. Worc Pk KT19 57 E6
Chestnut Cl. Addl KT15 ..... 52 D5
Chestnut Cl. Alder GU12 ... 105 D2
Chestnut Cl. Ashf TW15 ..... 14 B4
Chestnut Cl. Ashf TW16 ..... 14 F2
Chestnut Cl. Blckw GU17 ... 64 E4
Chestnut Cl. Carsh SM5 .... 40 F1
Chestnut Cl. Catf SE6 .... 24 C4
Chestnut Cl. E Grins RH19 186 A1
Chestnut Cl. Earls RH1 .... 140 B7
Chestnut Cl. Eng Gn TW20 .. 11 C2
Chestnut Cl. Graysh GU26 . 188 C3
Chestnut Cl. Harl UB7 .... 3 B7
Chestnut Cl. Kings KT20 .... 98 A4
Chestnut Cl. Send M GU23 .. 91 A3
Chestnut Cl.
W Norw SE27 & SW16 ..... 22 A4
Chestnut Copse.
Oxted RH8 .... 123 B2
Chestnut Cres. Whit V KT12 53 E2
Chestnut Ct. Beck BR3 ...... 24 A1
Chestnut Ct. 5 Croy CR0 .... 61 C6
Chestnut Ct. Felt TW13 ..... 15 D2
Chestnut Ct. Horsh RH13 .. 217 E2
Chestnut Ct. Hounsl TW3 .... 5 A4
Chestnut Ct. King U T KT3 .. 38 E6
Chestnut Dr. Eng Gn TW20 . 11 D2
Chestnut End.
Head Dn GU35 .... 187 A4
Chestnut Gdns.
Horsh RH12 .... 217 C5
Chestnut Gr. Balham SW12 . 21 A7
Chestnut Gr. Islew TW7 .... 6 A3
Chestnut Gr. Kings U T KT3 . 38 E6
Chestnut Gr. Mitch CR4 ..... 41 D5
Chestnut Gr. S Croy CR2 .... 62 C3
Chestnut Gr. Stain TW18 ... 13 C2
Chestnut Gr. Westfd GU22 . 89 E7

Chestnut Grove Sch. Balham SW12 21 A7
Chestnut House. W Norw SE27 22 C5
Chestnut La. Burrh GU24 49 C4
Chestnut La. Weyb KT13 53 B5
Chestnut Manor Cl. Stain TW18 13 B3
Chestnut Mead. Redh RH1 118 E2
Chestnut Rd. Ashf TW15 14 B4
Chestnut Rd. Guild GU1 109 D1
Chestnut Rd. Horley RH6 161 B5
Chestnut Rd. King U T KT2 17 E1
Chestnut Rd. Merton SW20 39 D7
Chestnut Rd. Twick TW2 16 E6
Chestnut Rd. W Heath GU14 85 A5
Chestnut Rd. W Norw SE21 & SE27 22 C5
Chestnut Way. Bramly GU5 152 A4
Chestnut Way. Felt TW13 15 B5
Chestnut Way. Godal GU7 150 F2
Chestnut Wlk. Crawl RH11 181 C1
Chestnut Wlk. Felct RH19 185 C8
Chestnut Wlk. Up Hall TW17 34 E5
Chestnut Wlk. Whit V KT12 53 E2
Chestnuts The. Horley RH6 161 A5
Chestnuts The. Penge BR3 43 D6
Chestnuts The. Walt O T KT12 54 A8
Cheston Ave. Croy CR0 43 F1
Chesworth Cl. Horsh RH13 217 C1
Chesworth Cres. Horsh RH13 217 C1
Chesworth Gdns. Horsh RH13 217 C1
Chesworth Jun Sch. Horsh RH13 217 E3
Chesworth La. Horsh RH12 & RH13 217 C1
Cheswycks Prep Sch. Mytch GU16 86 B5
Chetwode Cl. Woki RG11 25 E6
Chetwode Dr. Burgh H KT20 77 D1
Chetwode Pl. Alder GU11 126 C7
Chetwode Rd. Burgh H KT20 97 C8
Chetwode Rd. Up Toot SW17 20 F5
Chetwode Terr. Alder GU11 104 E1
Chetwood Rd. Crawl RH11 200 D2
Chevening Cl. Crawl RH11 201 C1
Chevening Rd. S Norw SE19 22 D2
Chevington Villas. Bletch RH1 120 F3
Cheviot Cl. Banstd SM7 78 B4
Cheviot Cl. Friml GU15 66 C4
Cheviot Cl. Harl UB3 3 D7
Cheviot Cl. Sutton SM2 59 D2
Cheviot Cl. W Heath GU14 84 E7
Cheviot Gdns. W Norw SE27 22 B4
Cheviot Rd. W Norw SE27 22 B3
Cheviot Wlk. Crawl RH11 201 B6
Chevremont. Guild GU1 130 E8
Chewter Cl. Bagsh GU19 47 F3
Chewter La. Windl GU20 48 B6
Cheyham Gdns. E Ewell SM2 58 D1
Cheyham Way. Belm SM2 58 E1
Cheylesmore Dr. Friml GU16 66 D3
Cheyne Ave. Twick TW2 15 F7
Cheyne Ct. Banstd SM7 78 B4
Cheyne Ct. 4 Wallin SM6 60 B4
Cheyne Hill. King U T KT5 37 F5
Cheyne Rd. Ashf TW15 14 D2
Cheyne Way. W Heath GU14 84 F8
Cheyne Wlk. Croy CR0 62 A8
Cheyne Wlk. Horley RH6 161 A1
Cheynell Wlk. Crawl RH11 200 F4
Chichele Gdns. S Croy CR0 61 E6
Chichele Rd. Oxted RH8 122 E7
Chichester Cl. Crawl RH10 201 E2
Chichester Cl. Dork RH4 115 B1
Chichester Cl. Hampt TW12 15 F2
Chichester Cl. Witley GU8 170 E5
Chichester Ct. Ewell KT17 57 F2
Chichester Ct. Stan TW19 13 E7
Chichester Dr. Purley CR8 79 F7
Chichester Rd. Ash GU12 106 A3
Chichester Rd. Dork RH4 115 B2
Chichester Rd. S Croy CR0 61 E7
Chichester Terr. Horsh RH12 217 D2
Chichester Way. Felt TW14 15 C8
Chiddingfold Rd. Dunsf GU8 192 C3
Chiddingly Cl. Crawl RH10 202 B5
Chiddingstone Cl. Belm SM2 59 A1
Chilberton Dr. Merst RH1 119 C5
Chilbolton. Eng Gn TW20 11 E3
Chilbrook Rd. Downs KT11 73 A1
Chilchester Ct. Beck BR3 44 B6
Chilcombe House. 7 Rhampt SW15 19 A8
Chilcroft La. Marl Ht GU27 208 B1
Chilcroft Rd. Shottm GU27 207 F7
Chilcrofts Rd.Marl Ht GU27 208 A1
Childebert Rd. Up Toot SW17 21 B6
Childerly. King U T KT1 38 A6
Childs Hall Cl. L Book KT23 93 F2
Childs Hall Dr. L Book KT23 93 F2
Childs Hall Rd. L Book KT23 93 F2
Childs La. 10 S Norw SE19 22 E2
Chilham Cl. Friml GU16 85 F8
Chillerton Rd. Streat SW17 21 B3
Chillingford House. Up Toot SW17 20 C4
Chillingham Way. Camb GU15 65 C4
Chillingworth Gdns. Twick TW1 16 F5
Chilmans Dr. G Book KT23 94 B2
Chilmark Gdns. Merst RH1 119 E6
Chilmark Gdns. New Mal KT3 39 A3
Chilmark Rd. Mitch SW16 41 D8
Chilmead. 1 Redh RH1 118 F2
Chilmead La. Nutf RH1 119 D3
Chilsey Green Rd. Chert KT16 32 E2
Chiltern. Woking GU22 89 C5
Chiltern Ave. Twick TW2 16 A7
Chiltern Ave. W Heath GU14 84 D4
Chiltern Cl. Crawl RH11 201 B6
Chiltern Cl. Haslem GU27 208 B5
Chiltern Cl. N Cheam KT4 58 C8
Chiltern Cl. S Croy CR0 61 E7
Chiltern Cl. W Heath GU14 84 D4
Chiltern Dr. Surb KT5 38 B4
Chiltern Gdns. Beck BR2 44 F5
Chiltern Rd. Sandh GU17 45 A1
Chiltern Rd. Sutton SM2 59 C1
Chilterns The. Sutton SM2 59 B2
Chilthorne Cl. For Hil SE6 23 F8
Chiltington Ct. Horsh RH12 217 D4
Chilton Ct. Walt O T KT12 54 A6
Chilton Rd. Rich TW9 7 A4
Chiltons Cl. Banstd SM7 78 B4
Chilworth & Albury Sta. Chil GU4 131 C3
Chilworth CE Sch. Chil GU4 131 D3
Chilworth Ct. 8 Putney SW19 19 D7
Chilworth Ct. 13 Redh RH1 118 F2
Chilworth Gdns. Sutton SM1 59 C7
Chilworth Rd. Albury GU4 & GU5 132 A4
Chimneys Ct. Wimble SW19 19 C1
Chinchilla Dr. Hounsl TW4 4 C5
Chine The. Wreccl GU10 145 F5
Chingford Ave. Farnb GU14 85 D5
Chingley Cl. Catf BR1 24 E2
Chinthurst La. Shalf GU4 & GU5 130 F2
Chinthurst La. Woner GU5 152 A7
Chinthurst Pk. Shalf GU4 130 E1
Chinthurst Sch. Tadw KT20 97 C4
Chippendale Cl. Hawley GU17 64 E4
Chippendale Rd. Crawl RH11 201 B1
Chippenham. 4 King U T KT1 37 F7
Chipstead Ave. Thorn H CR7 42 B5
Chipstead Cl. Belm SM2 59 B2
Chipstead Cl. Coulsd CR5 79 A3
Chipstead Cl. Earls RH1 140 A7
Chipstead Cl. Penge SE19 22 F1
Chipstead Ct. Knaph GU21 68 E2
Chipstead Cty Fst Sch. L Kings CR5 98 F3
Chipstead House. 4 Streat SW2 21 E7
Chipstead La. Kings CR5 & KT20 98 B3
Chipstead Rd. Harl TW6 3 A4
Chipstead Sta. Chips CR5 78 F1
Chipstead Valley Prim Sch. Chips CR5 79 A3
Chipstead Valley Rd. Chips CR5 79 B3
Chipstead Valley Rd. Coulsd CR5 79 B3
Chipstead Way. Woodm CR5 & SM7 78 F3
Chirton Wlk. Woking GU21 69 A1
Chisbury Cl. Brack RG12 27 E3
Chisholm Rd. Croy CR0 61 E8
Chisholm Rd. 13 Rich TW10 6 F1
Chislehurst Rd. Rich TW10 6 E2
Chislet Cl. Beck BR3 24 A1
Chiswick Cl. Wallin CR0 60 F7
Chiswick Comm Sch. Chisw W4 7 D7
Chiswick La S. Chisw W4 7 F8
Chiswick Mall. Chisw W4 7 F8
Chiswick Quay. Chisw W4 7 C6
Chiswick Sq. Chisw W4 7 E8
Chiswick Sta. Chisw W4 7 C7
Chiswick Village. Brent W4 7 B8
Chithurst La. Horne RH6 & RH7 162 F2
Chittenden Cotts. Wisley GU23 & KT14 71 E3
Chitterfield Gate. Harm UB7 3 A7
Chitty's Wlk. Stough GU3 108 F5
Chive Ct. W Heath GU14 84 C4
Chivelston. 27 Putney SW19 19 D7
Chobham Cl. Ottsh KT16 51 B4
Chobham Gdns. Putney SW19 19 D6
Chobham Golf Course. Knaph GU21 68 C5
Chobham La. Went KT16 & GU24 50 A8
Chobham Park La. Chobh GU24 50 B2
Chobham Rd. Chobh GU21 69 E3
Chobham Rd. Friml GU16 66 A2
Chobham Rd. Horse GU21 & GU24 69 D5
Chobham Rd. Knaph GU21 68 B1
Chobham Rd. Knaph GU21 68 D3
Chobham Rd. Ottsh KT16 51 B4
Chobham Rd. 1 Woking GU21 69 F2
Choir Gn. Knaph GU21 68 E2
Cholmley Rd. Thame D KT7 37 B3
Cholmondeley Wlk. Rich TW9 6 C2
Chrislaine Cl. Stan TW19 2 D1
Chrismas Ave. Alder GU12 105 C1
Chrismas Pl. Alder GU12 105 C1
Christ Church C of E Mid Sch. Ottsh KT16 51 D4
Christ Church C of E Prim Sch. Purley CR8 61 B1
Christ Church C of E Prim Sch. Streat SW2 21 F7
Christ Church CE Inf Sch. King U T KT3 38 E6
Christ Church CE Jun Sch. King U T KT3 38 D6
Christ Church CE Prim Sch. Surb KT5 38 A3
Christ Church Mount. Epsom KT19 76 B7
Christ Church Prim Sch. For Hil SE23 23 D6
Christ Church Rd. Beck BR3 44 A7
Christ Church Rd. Epsom KT18 76 A6
Christ Church Rd. Surb KT5 37 F3
Christ the King RC Fst Sch. Stan TW19 2 E1
Christ's Sch (East Side). Mortl SW14 7 D4
Christ's Sch (West Side). Rich TW10 6 F2
Christabel Cl. Islew TW7 5 E4
Christchurch Ave. 4 Tedd TW11 17 A3
Christchurch C of E Fst Sch. Vir W GU25 31 B6
Christchurch Cl. Mitch SW19 20 D1
Christchurch Cotts. Vir W GU25 31 B6
Christchurch Dr. Blckw GU17 64 D6
Christchurch Gdns. Epsom KT19 76 B8
Christchurch House. 2 Streat SW2 21 E7
Christchurch Pk. Sutton SM2 59 C3
Christchurch Pl. Epsom KT19 76 B8
Christchurch Rd. Harl TW6 3 A4
Christchurch Rd.Mitch SW19 20 D1
Christchurch Rd. Mortl SW14 7 C2
Christchurch Rd. Purley CR8 80 B8
Christchurch Rd. Streat SW2 21 F7
Christchurch Rd. Vir W GU25 31 C5
Christchurch Way. 2 Woking GU21 69 F2
Christian Fields. S Norw SW16 22 A1
Christie Cl. Lhtwat GU18 48 C1
Christie Dr. Croy SE25 43 A4
Christie House. W Wick BR4 44 B1
Christies. E Grins RH19 205 D8
Christine Cl. Ash GU12 105 F1
Christmas Hill. Shalf GU4 130 F2
Christmaspie Ave. Flexf GU3 107 B1
Christopher Ct. Ashf TW15 13 E3
Christopher Ct. 6 Croy CR0 43 A1
Christopher Ct. Tadw KT20 97 C4
Christopher Rd. E Grins RH19 185 E1
Christy Rd. Bigg H TN16 83 C4
Chrystie La. G Book KT23 94 B1
Chuck's La. Walt o t H KT20 97 B3
Chudleigh Ct. 4 Farnb GU14 85 B4
Chudleigh Gdns. Sutton SM1 59 C7
Chudleigh Rd. Twick TW1 & TW2 16 F8
Chulsa Rd. For Hil SE26 23 B3
Chumleigh Wlk. King U T KT5 37 F5
Church Almshouses. 8 Rich TW9 6 F3
Church App. Dulw SE21 22 D5
Church App. Egham TW20 32 C6
Church Ave. Beck BR3 44 A8
Church Ave. Farnb GU14 85 C3
Church Ave. Mortl SW14 7 D4
Church Circ. Farnb GU14 85 C1
Church Cl. Addl KT15 52 B6
Church Cl. 6 Epsom KT17 76 E6
Church Cl. Fetch KT22 94 D3
Church Cl. Grays GU27 189 F2
Church Cl. Horse GU21 69 E3
Church Cl. Hounsl TW4 4 F5
Church Cl. L Kings KT20 117 F8
Church Cl. Laleh TW18 33 C6
Church Cl. Milf GU8 149 F1
Church Cl. Pirb GU24 87 F6
Church Ct. For Hil SE26 23 E3
Church Ct. Reig RH2 118 B1
Church Dr. Coney H BR4 63 E7
Church Farm La. Cheam SM3 58 E4
Church Field House. Cobham KT11 73 B5
Church Gdns. Dork RH4 136 B8
Church Gdns. Leahd KT22 95 B7
Church Gn. Elst GU8 148 C3
Church Gn. Hersh KT12 54 C4
Church Gr. Tedd KT1 37 C7
Church Hill. Alder GU11 & GU12 126 C8
Church Hill. Camb GU15 65 E5
Church Hill. Cater CR3 100 F3
Church Hill. Horse GU21 69 D3
Church Hill. Merst RH1 99 B1
Church Hill. Nutf RH1 119 F2
Church Hill. Purley CR8 60 E1
Church Hill. Shere GU5 133 A4
Church Hill. Tats TN16 103 D5
Church Hill. Wallin SM5 59 F5
Church Hill. Wimble SW19 19 F3
Church Hill House Hospl. Easth RG12 27 A3
Church Hill Rd. Cheam SM1 & SM3 58 E6
Church Hill Rd. King U T KT6 37 E4
Church La. Albury GU5 132 C4
Church La. Ascot SL5 29 D5
Church La. Ash GU12 106 B2
Church La. Binst GU10 145 E3
Church La. Bisley GU21 & GU24 68 A4
Church La. Bletch RH1 120 D3
Church La. Broad H RH12 216 D3
Church La. Brook GU8 190 C8
Church La. Burgh H KT18 & SM7 77 E2
Church La. Burst RH6 182 F7
Church La. Cater CR3 100 A3
Church La. Chelsh CR6 82 C3
Church La. Chess KT9 56 F4
Church La. Copth RH10 183 B3
Church La. Crawl RH10 201 F6
Church La. Crond GU10 124 D8
Church La. E Grins RH19 185 F1
Church La. Godst RH9 121 D3
Church La. Graysh GU26 188 C3
Church La. Hambl GU8 171 D2
Church La. Haslem GU27 208 D7
Church La. Head KT18 96 D2
Church La. Hooley CR5 99 B5
Church La. Merton SW19 39 F8
Church La. Oxted RH8 122 E6
Church La. Pirb GU24 87 D4
Church La. Send GU23 90 C1
Church La. Sunnin SL5 30 B4
Church La. Tedd TW11 16 F3
Church La. Thame D KT7 37 A3
Church La. Twick TW1 17 A7
Church La. Up Toot SW17 21 A3
Church La. Up Toot SW17 21 B4
Church La. W Heath GU14 84 E4
Church La. Wall W RH5 176 F1
Church La. Wallin SM6 60 D7
Church La. Warlgm CR6 81 D2
Church La. Witley GU8 170 E2
Church La. Wormly GU8 170 E2
Church La. Worpl GU3 108 E8
Church La. Wreccl GU10 145 F7
Church La E. Alder GU11 126 B8
Church La W. Alder GU11 105 A1
Church Lane Ave. Hooley CR5 99 B5
Church Lane Dr. Hooley CR5 99 B5
Church Meadow. Long D KT6 56 C8
Church Par. Ashf TW15 13 F4
Church Path. Ash GU12 106 A3
Church Path. Croy CR0 & CR9 61 C8
Church Path. Merton SW19 40 A7
Church Path. Mitch CR4 40 E6
Church Path. 7 Woking GU21 69 F2
Church Pl. Mitch CR4 40 E6
Church Rd. Addl KT15 52 B5
Church Rd. Alder GU11 126 C8
Church Rd. Ascot SL5 29 A5
Church Rd. Ashf TW15 13 F4
Church Rd. Ashf TW15 14 A3
Church Rd. Ashtd KT21 75 D1
Church Rd. Bagsh GU19 47 D3
Church Rd. Barnes SW13 7 F5
Church Rd. Beck BR2 44 E6
Church Rd. Bigg H TN16 83 E2
Church Rd. Brack RG12 27 C7
Church Rd. Broad H RH12 216 D3
Church Rd. Burst RH6 183 A7
Church Rd. Byfl KT14 71 E6
Church Rd. Cater CR3 100 F3
Church Rd. Cheam SM3 58 E4
Church Rd. Clayg KT10 55 F3
Church Rd. Copth RH10 183 B3
Church Rd. Crawl RH6 181 E5
Church Rd. Croy CR0 & CR9 61 C7
Church Rd. Dunsf GU8 192 D5
Church Rd. E Mole KT8 36 D6
Church Rd. Earls RH1 139 E7
Church Rd. Egham TW20 12 A3
Church Rd. Epsom KT17 76 E6
Church Rd. Felt TW13 15 D3
Church Rd. Fetch KT23 94 A3
Church Rd. Friml GU16 65 D1
Church Rd. Guild GU1 130 D8
Church Rd. Haslem GU27 208 C7
Church Rd. Heston TW5 4 B8
Church Rd. Heston TW5 5 A7
Church Rd. Horley RH6 160 F2
Church Rd. Horley RH6 161 A3
Church Rd. Horne RH6 162 F5
Church Rd. Horse GU21 69 E4
Church Rd. Horsh RH12 218 B5
Church Rd. Hounsl TW7 5 E7
Church Rd. Kenley CR8 80 D4
Church Rd. King U T KT1 37 F7
Church Rd. Leahd KT22 95 B5
Church Rd. Lingf RH7 164 D4
Church Rd. Lo Hall TW17 34 B2
Church Rd. Long D KT6 37 C1
Church Rd. Milf GU8 149 F1
Church Rd. Mitch CR4 & SW19 40 D7
Church Rd. New Mal KT4 38 E1
Church Rd. Purley CR8 60 E1
Church Rd. Rich TW10 & TW9 6 E2
Church Rd. Rich TW10 17 E4
Church Rd. S Norw SE19 22 E1
Church Rd. Sandh GU15 45 E1
Church Rd. Sandh GU15 64 F7
Church Rd. Shottm GU27 207 F6
Church Rd. Sunnin SL5 30 A3
Church Rd. Tedd TW11 16 F3
Church Rd. Turn H RH10 204 A3
Church Rd. W End GU24 67 F7
Church Rd. W Ewell KT19 57 D3
Church Rd. W Ewell KT19 57 D3
Church Rd. Wallin SM6 60 D7
Church Rd. Warlgm CR6 81 D2
Church Rd. Whytlf CR3 100 F8
Church Rd. Wimble SW19 19 E4
Church Rd. Windl GU20 48 C4
Church Rd. Wink SL4 8 C5
Church Rd. Wink SL5 28 B8
Church Rd. Woking GU21 89 A8
Church Rd. Wold CR3 & RH9 101 E4
Church Rd. Woodh RH2 139 A7
Church Rd. Worth RH10 202 E6
Church Rd E. Crowth RG11 45 B5
Church Rd E. Farnb GU14 85 D2
Church Rd W. Crowth RG11 45 B4
Church Rd W. Farnb GU14 85 C1
Church Rise. Chess KT9 56 F4

Church Rise. For Hil SE23 .... 23 D6
Church Road Ind Est.
Crawl RH6 .... 181 E5
Church Road Trad Est.
Crawl RH6 .... 181 E5
Church Row. Ripley GU23 .... 91 C6
Church Side. Epsom KT18 .... 76 B6
Church Side. Gatton RH2 .... 118 F6
Church Sq. Lo Hall TW17 ..... 34 B2
Church St. Alder GU11 .... 104 F2
Church St. Betch RH3 .... 137 E8
Church St. Chisw W4 .... 7 F8
Church St. Cobham KT11 ...... 73 B4
Church St. Cox Gn RH12 ...... 195 E1
Church St. Crawl RH11 .... 201 C6
Church St. Crowth RG11 .... 45 B4
Church St. Croy CR0 & CR9 .. 61 C8
Church St. Dork RH4 .... 136 A7
Church St. Effing KT24 ...... 113 D8
Church St.
Epsom KT17 & KT18 .... 76 E6
Church St. Esher KT10 .... 55 B6
Church St. Ewell KT17 .... 58 A2
Church St. Godal GU7 .... 150 D4
Church St. Hampt TW12 .... 36 C8
Church St. Islew TW7 .... 6 B5
Church St. King U T KT1 .... 37 D7
Church St. Leahd KT22 .... 95 B5
Church St. Old Wok GU22 .... 90 C6
Church St. Reig RH2 .... 118 B1
Church St. Rudg RH12 .... 214 E8
Church St. Stain TW18 .... 12 E4
Church St. Sunby TW16 .... 35 B6
Church St. Twick TW1 .... 17 A7
Church St. Walt O T KT12 ..... 35 A2
Church St. Warn RH12 .... 216 F8
Church St. Weyb KT13 .... 53 A6
Church St E. Woking GU21 .. 69 F2
Church St W. Woking GU21 . 69 E2
Church Stretton Rd.
Hounsl TW3 .... 5 C2
Church Terr. 20 Rich TW10 ... 6 D2
Church Vale. For Hil SE23 .... 23 D6
Church View. Ash GU12 .... 106 A2
Church View Cl.
Horley RH6 .... 160 F2
Church Villa. Sunby TW16 .... 35 B6
Church Way. Oxted RH8 ..... 122 F3
Church Way. S Croy CR2 ...... 81 A8
Church Wlk. Brent TW8 .... 6 C8
Church Wlk. Cater CR3 ..... 101 A3
Church Wlk. Chert KT16 .... 33 A3
Church Wlk. Horley RH6 .... 160 F2
Church Wlk. Leahd KT22 ...... 95 B5
Church Wlk. Mitch SW16 ..... 41 C7
Church Wlk. Reig RH2 .... 118 C1
Church Wlk. 15 Rich TW10 .... 6 D2
Church Wlk. Thame D KT7 ... 36 F3
Church Wlk. W Barn SW20 .. 39 C6
Church Wlk. Walt O T KT12 . 35 A1
Church Wlk. Weyb KT13 ...... 53 B8
Churchcroft Cl.
Balham SW12 .... 21 A8
Churchdown. Catf BR1 .... 24 E4
Churchfield Rd. Reig RH2 .. 117 F2
Churchfield Rd.
Walt O T KT12 .... 35 A1
Churchfield Rd. Weyb KT13 . 53 A6
Churchfields. Burph GU4 ... 110 A6
Churchfields. E Mole KT8 ..... 36 A6
Churchfields. Horse GU21 .... 69 E3
Churchfields Ave. Felt TW13 16 A5
Churchfields Ave.
Weyb KT13 .... 53 B6
Churchfields Prim Sch.
Penge BR3 .... 43 D6
Churchfields Rd. Penge BR3 43 E7
Churchill Ave. Alder GU12 . 126 C8
Churchill Ave. Horsh RH12 217 B3
Churchill Cl. E Bed TW14 ..... 14 F7
Churchill Cl. Farnb GU14 ...... 85 B8
Churchill Cl. Fetch KT22 .... 94 E4
Churchill Cl. Warlgm CR6 ..... 81 D2
Churchill Cres. Farnb GU14 . 85 B8
Churchill Ct. Crawl RH10 .. 182 A1
Churchill Ct. Stain TW18 ...... 13 C2
Churchill Dr. Weyb KT13 ...... 53 C6
Churchill Hse. Banstd SM7 .. 77 F4
Churchill Rd. Guild GU1 ...... 130 F8
Churchill Rd. N Asct SL5 ...... 28 F7
Churchill Rd. S Croy CR2 ...... 61 C3
Churchill Rd. Smallf RH6 .... 162 B3
Churchill Way. Ashf TW16 .... 15 A2
Churchley Rd. For Hil SE26 .. 23 B4
Churchley Villas.
For Hil SE26 .... 23 B4
Churchmore Rd.
Streat SW16 .... 41 D8
Churchside Cl. Bigg H TN16 . 83 C2
Churchview Rd. Twick TW2 . 16 D6
Churston Cl. 17
Streat SW2 .... 22 A7
Churston Dr. W Barn SM4 .... 39 E4
Churt Rd. Beac H GU26 ...... 188 C6
Churt Rd.
Head Dn GU10 & GU35 ...... 187 C8
Churt Wynde.
Beac H GU26 .... 188 D7
Chuters Cl. Byfl KT14 .... 71 F7
Chuters Gr. Ewell KT17 .... 76 F7
Cibber Rd. For Hil SE23 .... 23 D6
Cidermill Rd.
Cudw RH12 & RH5 .... 179 F3
Cidermill Rd.
Newd RH5 & RH12 .... 179 F3
Cinder Path. Woking GU22 .. 89 C8
Cinderford Way. Catf BR1 ... 24 E4
Cinnamon Gdns.
Stough GU2 .... 109 A6
Cintra Ct. Penge SE19 .... 22 F2
Cintra Pk. Penge SE19 .... 22 F1
Circle Gdns. Byfl KT14 .... 71 F6
Circle Gdns. Merton SW19 ... 40 A7
Circle Hill Rd. Crowth RG11 . 45 C5
Circle Rd. Whit V KT12 .... 53 E2
Circle The. Farnc GU7 .... 150 F6
Cissbury Cl. Horsh RH12 .... 218 A6
Cissbury Hill. Crawl RH11 .. 201 C4
Cissbury House. 6
For Hil SE26 .... 23 A5
City Bsns Ctr. Horsh RH13 217 D1
City Prospect. 5
W Norw SE19 .... 22 E2
City Wharf House.
Thame D KT7 .... 37 B3
Clacket La. Tats TN16 .... 103 E2
Clairvale Rd. Heston TW5 ...... 4 E6
Clairview Rd.
Streat SW16 & SW17 .... 21 B4
Clairville Ct. 1 Reig RH2 .. 118 D1
Clairville Point. 12
For Hil SE23 .... 23 D5
Clandon Ave. Thor L TW20 .. 12 C1
Clandon CE Inf Sch.
W Clan GU4 .... 111 A4
Clandon Cl. Stonel KT17 .... 58 A4
Clandon Ct. Farnb GU14 ...... 85 D3
Clandon House. 12
King U T KT2 .... 18 B2
Clandon Rd. Guild GU1 .... 130 E8
Clandon Rd.
Send M GU4 & GU23 .... 91 A1
Clandon Rd.
W Clan GU4 & GU23 .... 111 A8
Clandon Regis Golf Club.
W Clan GU4 .... 111 B4
Clandon Sta. W Clan GU4 . 111 B6
Clanfield House. 12
Rhampt SW15 .... 19 A7
Clanfield Ride. Blckw GU17 . 64 D5
Clapgate La. Slinfd RH13 .... 215 C5
Clappers Gate.
Crawl RH10 & RH11 .... 201 D7
Clappers La. Chobh GU24 ..... 68 D8
Clappers Meadow.
Alf Cr GU6 .... 194 A3
Clare Ave. Woki RG11 .... 25 C7
Clare Cl. Crawl RH10 .... 182 C1
Clare Cl. W Byfl KT14 .... 71 A6
Clare Cotts. Bletch RH1 ..... 120 B3
Clare Cres. Leahd KT22 .... 75 B1
Clare Ct. Wimble SW19 .... 19 E2
Clare Ct. Wold CR3 .... 102 A4
Clare Gdns. Egham TW20 .... 12 A3
Clare Hill. Esher KT10 .... 55 B5
Clare Hill Golf Course.
Esher KT10 .... 55 B4
Clare Hill (No 1).
Esher KT10 .... 55 B5
Clare Hill (No 2).
Esher KT10 .... 55 B5
Clare House Prim Sch.
Beck BR3 .... 44 C7
Clare Lawn Ave. Mortl SW14 . 7 D2
Clare Mead. Rowl GU10 ..... 145 F4
Clare Rd. Hounsl TW4 .... 4 F4
Clare Rd. Stan TW19 .... 13 E8
Clare Wood. Leahd KT22 ...... 75 B1
Claredale. Woking GU22 ...... 89 E8
Claredale Ct. Sutton SM2 ..... 59 C3
Clarefield Ct. Sunnin SL5 ..... 30 A2
Claremont. Shep TW17 .... 34 B3
Claremont Ave. Camb GU15 65 F5
Claremont Ave. Esher KT10 54 F4
Claremont Ave. Hersh KT12 54 D6
Claremont Ave. Sunby TW16 35 B8
Claremont Ave. W Barn KT3 39 B4
Claremont Ave.
Woking GU22 .... 89 E8
Claremont Cl. Hams Gn CR2 81 B4
Claremont Cl. Hersh KT12 ... 54 D5
Claremont Cl. 4
Streat SW2 .... 21 F7
Claremont Ct. Dork RH4 .... 136 B6
Claremont Dr. Esher KT10 ... 55 B4
Claremont Dr. Shep TW17 ... 34 B3
Claremont End. Esher KT10 55 B4
Claremont Fan Court Sch.
Esher KT10 .... 55 A3
Claremont Gdns.
King U T KT6 .... 37 E4
Claremont Gr. Chisw W4 .... 7 E7
Claremont Hospl.
King U T KT6 .... 37 D3
Claremont La. Esher KT10 ... 55 B5
Claremont Park Rd.
Esher KT10 .... 55 B4
Claremont Rd. Clayg KT10 ... 55 E3
Claremont Rd. Croy CR0 ...... 43 A1
Claremont Rd. Egham TW18 12 D3
Claremont Rd. King U T KT6 37 E4
Claremont Rd. Redh RH1 .. 119 A4
Claremont Rd. Tedd TW11 ... 16 F4
Claremont Rd. Twick TW1 ..... 6 C1
Claremont Rd. W Byfl KT14 . 71 A7
Claremont Terr.
Thame D KT7 .... 37 B2
Claremount Cl.
Burgh H KT18 .... 77 C2
Claremount Gdns.
Burgh H KT18 .... 77 D2
Clarence Ave. King U T KT3 . 38 D7
Clarence Ave. Streat SW4 .... 21 D8
Clarence Cl. Alder GU12 .... 105 D2
Clarence Cl. Hersh KT12 ...... 54 B6
Clarence Ct. Horley RH6 .... 161 D4
Clarence Dr. Camb GU15 ..... 66 B7
Clarence Dr. 2
E Grins RH19 .... 205 F7
Clarence Dr. Eng Gn TW20 ... 11 C4
Clarence House. Hersh KT12 54 B5
Clarence La. Rhampt SW15 .... 7 F1
Clarence Rd. Bigg H TN16 .... 83 F1
Clarence Rd. Hersh KT12 .... 54 B6
Clarence Rd. Horsh RH13 .. 217 E1
Clarence Rd. Rich TW9 .... 7 A6
Clarence Rd. Sutton SM1 ..... 59 B5
Clarence Rd. Tedd TW11 ...... 17 A2
Clarence Rd. Thorn H CR0 .... 42 D2
Clarence Rd. Wallin SM6 ...... 60 B5
Clarence Rd. Wimble SW19 . 20 B2
Clarence Rd. Woodh RH1 .. 139 D6
Clarence St. Egham TW20 ... 11 F2
Clarence St.
King U T KT1 & KT2 .... 37 E7
Clarence St. 4 Rich TW9 ...... 6 E3
Clarence St. Stain TW18 ...... 12 E4
Clarence Terr. Hounsl TW3 .... 5 B3
Clarence Way. Horley RH6 161 D4
Clarence Wlk. Woodh RH1 139 D6
Clarendon Cres. Twick TW2 16 D5
Clarendon Ct. Hawley GU17 64 D3
Clarendon Ct. 1 Rich TW9 ... 7 A6
Clarendon Cty Prim Sch.
Ashf TW15 .... 13 F5
Clarendon Gr. Mitch CR4 ..... 40 F6
Clarendon Prim Sch. Ashf TW15 .... 13 F4
Clarendon Rd.
Croy CR0 & CR9 .... 61 B8
Clarendon Rd. Mitch SW19 .. 20 E1
Clarendon Rd. Redh RH1 .... 118 F2
Clarendon Rd. Wallin SM6 ... 60 C4
Clarendon Sch. Hampt TW12 16 B2
Clarens St. For Hil SE6 .... 23 F6
Claret Gdns. S Norw SE25 ... 42 E5
Clareville Rd. Cater CR3 .... 101 A3
Clarewood Dr. Camb GU15 .. 65 E6
Clarice Way. Wallin SM6 ...... 60 E2
Claridge Gdns.
Dorman RH7 .... 165 A2
Claridges Mead.
Dorman RH7 .... 165 A2
Clark Pl. Crawl GU6 .... 173 F2
Clark Rd. Crawl RH11 .... 201 A1
Clark Way. Heston TW5 .... 4 D7
Clarke Cres. Sandh GU15 ..... 64 E7
Clarke's Ave.
N Cheam KT4 & SM3 .... 58 D8
Clarks Hill. Farnh GU10 ..... 124 D1
Clarks La.
Titsey CR6 & TN16 .... 103 C4
Claudia Pl. Putney SW19 ...... 19 E7
Claverdale Rd. Streat SW2 .. 22 A8
Claverdon. Easth RG12 .... 27 A2
Clavering Cl. Tedd TW1 .... 17 A4
Claverton. Ashtd KT21 .... 75 E2
Clay Ave. Mitch CR4 .... 41 B7
Clay Hall La. Burst RH10 .... 183 C4
Clay La. Burph GU4 .... 110 A5
Clay La. Head KT18 .... 96 B3
Clay La. Horne RH7 .... 163 D3
Clay La. Jacobs GU4 .... 109 E7
Clay La. Nutf RH1 .... 140 D7
Clay La. S Nutf RH1 .... 140 D7
Clay La. Woki RG11 .... 25 F5
Claycart Rd. Alder GU11 .... 104 D4
Claycart Rd. Alder GU11 .... 104 E3
Claydon Ct. Stain TW18 .... 13 A4
Claydon Dr. Wallin CR0 .... 60 E6
Claydon Gdns.
W Heath GU14 .... 65 A1
Claydon Rd. Woking GU21 ... 69 A3
Clayford. Dorman RH7 .... 165 B2
Claygate Cres. New Add CR0 63 D4
Claygate La. Hinch W KT10 .. 56 A8
Claygate La. Thame D KT7 ... 37 A1
Claygate Lodge Cl.
Clayg KT10 .... 55 E3
Claygate Prim Sch.
Clayg KT10 .... 55 E3
Claygate Rd. Dork RH4 ...... 136 B5
Claygate Sta. Clayg KT10 ..... 55 E4
Clayhall House. 3
Reig RH2 .... 118 A2
Clayhall La. Woodh RH2 ..... 138 E6
Clayhanger.
Merrow GU1 & GU4 .... 110 C3
Clayhill Cl. Brack RG12 .... 28 A6
Clayhill Cl. Leigh RH2 .... 138 A2
Clayhill Rd. Leigh RH2 .... 137 F1
Claylands Ct. W Norw SE19 . 22 D3
Claymore Cl.
Morden SM3 & SM4 .... 40 A2
Claypole Dr. Heston TW5 .... 4 E6
Clays Cl. E Grins RH19 .... 205 E8
Clayton Dr. Stough GU2 ..... 108 F4
Clayton Gr. Brack RG12 .... 27 E8
Clayton Hill. Crawl RH11 .... 201 C4
Clayton House. Long D KT7 . 37 B1
Clayton Rd.
Chess KT10 & KT9 .... 56 D6
Clayton Rd. Ewell KT17 .... 76 E6
Clayton Rd. Islew TW7 .... 5 E4
Clayton Rd. W Heath GU14 .. 64 F1
Cleardene. Dork RH4 .... 136 B7
Cleardown. Mayb GU22 .... 70 B1
Clears Cotts. Reig RH2 .... 117 E3
Clears The. Reig RH2 .... 117 E3
Clearsprings. Lhtwat GU18 .. 67 A8
Cleave Prior. Chips CR5 .... 98 E8
Cleave's Almshouses. 1
King U T KT2 .... 37 E7
Cleaveland Rd. King U T KT6 37 D4
Cleaverholme Cl. Croy SE25 43 B3
Cleeve Ct. E Bed TW14 .... 14 E7
Cleeve Hill. For Hil SE23 .... 23 B7
Cleeve House. Brack RG12 .. 27 E5
Cleeve Rd. Leahd KT22 .... 95 A7
Cleeve The. Guild GU1 .... 110 A1
Cleeves Ct. 6 Redh RH1 .. 119 A2
Clement Cl. Purley CR8 .... 80 B3
Clement Rd. Penge BR3 .... 43 D7
Clement Rd. Wimble SW19 .. 19 E3
Clements Ct. Hounsl TW4 ...... 4 D3
Clements Hse. Leahd KT22 .. 95 A8
Clements Mead. Leahd KT22 95 A8
Clements Rd. Walt O T KT12 54 B8
Clensham Ct. Sutton SM3 .... 59 A8
Clensham La. Sutton SM1 .... 59 A8
Clerics Wlk. Shep TW17 .... 34 D3
Clerks Croft. Bletch RH1 .... 120 D2
Clevedon. Whit V KT13 .... 53 D5
Clevedon Ct. Farnb GU14 ..... 85 D3
Clevedon Ct. Friml GU16 ..... 86 A8
Clevedon Ct. W Norw SE21 . 22 D5
Clevedon Gdns. Cranf TW5 ... 4 B6
Clevedon Rd. King U T KT1 .. 38 A7
Clevedon Rd. Penge SE20 .... 43 D8
Clevedon Rd. Twick TW1 .... 6 D1
Cleveland Ave. Hampt TW12 15 F1
Cleveland Ave.
Merton SW20 .... 39 F7
Cleveland Cl. Walt O T KT12 54 B7
Cleveland Dr. Stain TW18 .... 33 B8
Cleveland Gdns. Barnes SW13 7 F5
Cleveland Gdns.
Worc Pk KT4 .... 57 F8
Cleveland Pk. Stan TW19 .... 2 E1
Cleveland Rd. Barnes SW13 .. 7 F5
Cleveland Rd. Islew TW7 .... 6 A3
Cleveland Rd. New Mal KT3 . 38 E5
Cleveland Rd. Worc Pk KT4 . 57 E8
Cleveland Rise. W Barn SM4 39 D2
Cleves Ave. Ewell KT17 .... 58 B2
Cleves Cl. Cobham KT11 .... 73 B5
Cleves Cres. New Add CR0 ... 82 C8
Cleves Ct. Epsom KT17 .... 76 F7
Cleves Ct. King U T KT6 .... 37 E3
Cleves Ct. Knaph GU21 .... 68 D2
Cleves Cty Jun Sch.
Walt O T KT13 .... 53 F6
Cleves Rd. Rich TW10 .... 17 C5
Cleves Way. Ashf TW16 .... 14 F2
Cleves Way. Hampt TW12 .... 15 F1
Cleves Wood. Oat Pk KT13 .. 53 E6
Clewborough Dr.
Friml GU15 .... 66 B6
Clewborough House (Prep Sch).
Friml GU15 .... 66 B6
Clews La.
Bisley GU21 & GU24 .... 68 B3
Clifden Centre (Richmond Adult
& Comm Coll). Twick TW1 . 16 F7
Clifden House. 7 Brent TW8 6 D8
Clifden Rd. Brent TW8 .... 6 D8
Clifden Rd. Twick TW1 .... 16 F7
Cliff End. Purley CR8 .... 80 B7
Cliffe Rd. Croy CR2 .... 61 D5
Cliffe Rd. Ock Rid GU7 ...... 150 C2
Cliffe Rise. Ock Rid GU7 ...... 150 C3
Cliffe Wlk. Sutton SM1 .... 59 C5
Clifford Ave.
Mortl SW14 & TW10 & TW9 .. 7 B4
Clifford Ave. Wallin SM6 ...... 60 C6
Clifford Ct. Wands SW18 ...... 20 D8
Clifford Gr. Ashf TW15 .... 14 A4
Clifford House. Beck BR3 ..... 24 B2
Clifford Manor Rd.
Guild GU4 .... 130 E5
Clifford Rd. Croy SE25 .... 43 A5
Clifford Rd. Hounsl TW4 .... 4 D4
Clifford Rd. Rich TW10 .... 17 D6
Clifton Av. Sutton SM2 .... 78 B8
Clifton Ave. Felt TW13 .... 15 C5
Clifton Cl. Cater CR3 .... 100 D4
Clifton Cl. Chert KT15 .... 52 B8
Clifton Cl. Rowl GU10 .... 146 A4
Clifton Ct. Beck BR3 .... 44 B8
Clifton Ct. S Norw SE25 .... 42 E4
Clifton Ct. 8 Stan TW19 ...... 2 E1
Clifton Hill Sch. Cater CR3 100 D4
Clifton Lodge (Brunel Univ Coll
Twickenham Campus).
Islew TW1 .... 6 B2
Clifton Mews. S Norw SE25 . 42 E5
Clifton Par. Felt TW13 .... 15 C4
Clifton Park Ave.
Merton SW20 .... 39 C7
Clifton Pl. Banstd SM7 .... 78 A4
Clifton Rd. Coulsd CR5 .... 79 C4
Clifton Rd. Harl TW6 .... 3 B4
Clifton Rd. Hounsl TW7 .... 5 E5
Clifton Rd. King U T KT2 .... 37 F8
Clifton Rd. S Norw SE25 .... 42 E5
Clifton Rd. Tedd TW11 .... 16 E4
Clifton Rd. Wallin SM6 .... 60 B5
Clifton Rd. Wimble SW19 ..... 19 D2
Clifton Rd. Woki RG11 .... 25 A8
Clifton Rd. Worth RH10 ..... 202 C5
Clifton Terr. Dork RH4 .... 136 B6
Clifton Way. Woking GU21 ... 68 F2
Clifton Way. Woking GU21 ... 69 A2
Clifton's La. Reig RH2 .... 117 D2
Cliftonville. Dork RH4 .... 136 B6
Climping Rd. Crawl RH11 . 201 B8
Cline Rd. Guild GU1 .... 130 F7
Clinton Ave. E Mole KT8 ...... 36 C5
Clinton Cl. Knaph GU21 .... 68 D1
Clinton Hill. Dorman RH7 .. 186 A8
Clinton House. New Mal KT3 38 D1
Clinton House. 6 Surb KT6 37 D2
Clinton Rd. Leahd KT22 .... 95 C4
Clintons Gn. Brack RG12 ...... 27 A8
Clippesby Cl. Chess KT9 ...... 56 F4
Clipstone Rd. Hounsl TW3 ..... 5 A4
Clive Ct. Streat SW16 .... 21 D3
Clive Ct. Tolw KT6 .... 57 A8
Clive Gn. Easth RG12 .... 27 B4
Clive House. 3 Croy CR0 .... 42 F1
Clive House. Redh RH1 ...... 118 E3
Clive Rd. Alder GU12 .... 105 D1
Clive Rd. Esher KT10 .... 55 B6
Clive Rd. Felt TW14 .... 4 A1
Clive Rd. Mitch SW19 .... 20 E2
Clive Rd. Tedd TW1 .... 17 A4
Clive Rd. W Norw SE21 & 27 22 D5
Clive Way. Crawl RH10 ...... 202 C6
Cliveden Pl. Shep TW17 .... 34 C3
Cliveden Rd. Merton SW19 .. 39 F8
Clock Barn La. Hyde GU8 ... 171 F6
Clock House Cl. Byfl KT14 ... 71 F7
Clock House Cotts.
Capel RH5 .... 178 C2
Clock House Ct. Beck BR3 ... 43 E7
Clock House Mead.
Oxsh KT11 .... 74 B5
Clock House Rd. Beck BR3 .. 43 E7
Clock House Sta. Penge BR3 43 E8
Clock Tower Rd. Islew TW7 .. 5 F4
Clockhouse Cl. Putney SW19 19 C6
Clockhouse La.
Ashf TW14 & TW15 .... 14 B5

Clockhouse La. Bramly GU5 151 F7
Clockhouse La. E Bed TW14 & TW15 14 B5
Clockhouse La E. Thor L TW20 12 B1
Clockhouse La W. Thor L TW20 12 A1
Clockhouse Rd. Farnb GU14 85 B4
Clodhouse Hill. Woking GU22 88 D5
Cloister Cl. Rich TW11 17 B3
Cloister Gdns. Croy SE25 43 B3
Cloisters The. Friml GU16 65 D1
Cloisters The. Old Wok GU22 90 B6
Clone The. 5 King U T KT2 18 B1
Clonmel Rd. Tedd TW11 & TW12 & TW2 16 D4
Clonmore St. Wands SW18 19 F7
Close The. Beck BR3 43 E5
Close The. Brack RG12 27 C5
Close The. Brock RH3 137 B5
Close The. Cheam SM3 39 F2
Close The. Croy SE25 43 A3
Close The. E Grins RH19 205 D8
Close The. Esher KT10 55 B3
Close The. Friml GU16 85 C8
Close The. Godal GU7 150 F3
Close The. Horley RH6 161 C1
Close The. Hounsl TW7 5 D5
Close The. Ifold RH14 212 D3
Close The. King U T KT3 38 C7
Close The. Lhtwat GU18 48 A1
Close The. M Bourn GU9 125 D1
Close The. Mitch CR4 40 F5
Close The. Mortl TW9 7 B4
Close The. N Asct SL5 28 D7
Close The. Purley CR8 60 F1
Close The. Purley CR8 61 B1
Close The. Reig RH2 139 B8
Close The. Sandh GU15 64 E8
Close The. Surb KT6 37 E3
Close The. Vir W GU25 31 D4
Close The. W Byfl KT14 71 A6
Close The. Wallin SM5 59 E2
Close The. Woner GU5 152 B7
Closeworth Rd. Farnb GU14 105 E8
Cloudesdale Rd. Up Toot SW17 21 B6
Clouston Cl. Wallin SM6 60 E5
Clouston Rd. W Heath GU14 84 F5
Clovelly Ave. Warlgm CR6 101 B8
Clovelly Dr. Beac H GU26 188 D7
Clovelly Pl. Beac H GU26 188 C7
Clovelly Rd. Beac H GU26 188 C7
Clovelly Rd. Hounsl TW3 5 B5
Clover Cl. Woki RG11 25 E7
Clover Ct. Woking GU22 89 D8
Clover Field. Slinfd RH12 215 D4
Clover Hill. Hooley CR5 99 B6
Clover House. Hounsl TW3 5 C6
Clover Lea. Farnc GU7 150 E8
Clover Rd. Stough GU2 108 E2
Clover Way. Carsh CR4 41 A1
Clover Way. Smallf RH6 162 C3
Cloverlands. Crawl RH10 201 F8
Clovers Cotts. Faygt RH12 199 F1
Clovers End. Horsh RH12 218 A5
Clovers Way. Horsh RH12 218 D7
Clowders Rd. For Hil SE6 23 F5
Clowser Cl. Sutton SM1 59 C5
Club La. Crowth RG11 45 D5
Club Row. Pirb GU24 87 D8
Clubhouse Rd. Alder GU11 104 F5
Clump Ave. Box H KT20 116 C4
Clumps Rd. M Bourn GU10 146 E4
Clumps The. Felt TW15 14 D4
Clyde Ave. Hams Gn CR2 81 B4
Clyde Cl. Earls RH1 119 A2
Clyde Rd. Croy CR0 61 F8
Clyde Rd. Stan TW19 13 E7
Clyde Rd. Sutton SM1 59 A5
Clyde Rd. Wallin SM6 60 C4
Clyde Terr. For Hil SE23 23 C6
Clyde Vale. For Hil SE23 23 C6
Clydesdale Gdns. Mortl TW10 7 B3
Clymping Dene. Felt TW14 15 B8
Clytha Ct. W Norw SE27 22 C4
Clyve Way. Egham TW18 32 E8
Coach House Cl. Friml GU15 & GU16 65 E3
Coach House La. Wimble SW19 19 D5
Coach Rd. Brock RH4 & RH5 115 E1
Coach Rd. Brock RH3 & RH5 137 A7
Coach Rd. Crawl RH6 181 F8
Coach Rd. Crawl RH6 182 B7
Coach Rd. N Asct SL5 8 E1
Coach Rd. Ottsh KT16 51 C4
Coachlads Ave. 3 Stough GU2 108 F1
Coachmans Dr. Crawl RH11 201 B2
Coalbrook Mansions. Balham SW12 21 B7
Coaldale Wlk. W Norw SE21 22 C8
Coast Hill. Wotton RH4 & RH5 134 F4
Coast Hill La. Westc RH4 135 A5
Coates Wlk. 15 Brent TW8 6 E8
Coatham Pl. Cran GU6 174 F3
Cob Cl. Crawl D RH10 204 C8
Cob Wlk. Crawl RH11 201 A6
Cobb's Rd. Hounsl TW4 4 F3
Cobbets Ridge. Farnh GU10 147 C8
Cobbett Cl. Crawl RH10 202 C8
Cobbett Rd. Stough GU2 108 F2
Cobbett Rd. Twick TW2 16 A7
Cobbetts Cl. Woking GU21 69 B2
Cobbetts Farm. Bisley GU24 68 A4
Cobbetts Hill. Whit V KT13 53 B3
Cobbetts Way. Wreccl GU10 & GU9 145 F6
Cobbetts Wlk. Bisley GU24 68 A4
Cobbler's Wlk. Tedd TW11 16 F1
Cobblers. Slinfd RH12 215 D4
Cobbles Cres. Crawl RH10 201 E7
Cobden La. Haslem GU27 208 D7
Cobden Rd. Croy SE25 43 A4
Cobham Ave. W Barn KT3 39 A4
Cobham Cl. Wallin SM6 60 E4
Cobham Ct. Mitch CR4 40 D7
Cobham Gate. Cobham KT11 73 B5
Cobham Park Rd. Downs KT11 73 C2
Cobham Rd. Fetch KT11 & KT22 & KT23 94 C6
Cobham Rd. Heston TW5 4 C7
Cobham Rd. King U T KT1 & KT2 38 A7
Cobham Sta. Stk D'A KT11 73 E2
Cobham Way. Crawl RH10 182 B4
Cobham Way. E Hors KT24 92 E1
Cobnor Cl. Crawl RH11 200 F4
Cobs Way. Woodhm KT15 52 C1
Coburg Cres. Streat SW2 22 A7
Cochrane Pl. Windl GU20 48 D5
Cochrane Rd. Merton SW19 19 F1
Cock La. Fetch KT22 94 C5
Cock's La. New Gn SL4 8 A6
Cock's La. Wink RG12 8 A6
Cock-A-Dobby. Sandh GU17 45 A1
Cocks Cres. New Mal KT3 38 F5
Cockshot Hill. Woodh RH2 139 B7
Cockshot Rd. Reig RH2 139 C8
Codrington Ct. Knaph GU21 68 F1
Codrington Hill. For Hil SE23 & SE4 23 E8
Cody Cl. Wallin SM6 60 D3
Cody Rd. Farnb GU14 84 F3
Coe Ave. Croy SE25 43 A3
Coe Cl. Alder GU11 105 A1
Cogman's La. Smallf RH6 162 D4
Cokenor Wood. Wreccl GU10 145 F6
Cokers La. Dulw SE21 22 D7
Colborne Way. N Cheam KT4 58 C8
Colburn Ave. Cater CR3 100 F3
Colburn Cres. Burph GU1 110 A4
Colburn Way. Carsh SM1 59 D7
Colby Rd. Dulw SE19 22 E3
Colby Rd. Walt O T KT12 35 A1
Colchester Vale. For Row RH18 206 E2
Colchester Villas. Thorn H CR7 42 A3
Colcokes Rd. Banstd SM7 78 A3
Cold Harbour La. W Heath GU14 84 F8
Coldharbour Cl. Egham TW20 32 C6
Coldharbour La. Bletch RH1 120 F1
Coldharbour La. Dork RH4 & RH5 135 F3
Coldharbour La. Egham TW20 32 D6
Coldharbour La. Purley CR8 61 A1
Coldharbour La. Pyrf GU22 70 F4
Coldharbour La. S Holm RH5 156 F6
Coldharbour La. W End GU24 67 F8
Coldharbour Rd. Croy CR0 61 A5
Coldharbour Rd. Pyrf GU22 & KT14 70 F4
Coldharbour Sch. Croy CR9 61 A5
Coldharbour Way. Croy CR0 61 A5
Coldshott. Oxted RH8 123 A2
Cole Cl. Crawl RH11 201 B1
Cole Court Lodge. 8 Twick TW1 17 A8
Cole Gdns. Cranf TW5 4 A7
Cole Park Gdns. Twick TW1 6 A1
Cole Park Rd. Twick TW1 6 A1
Cole Park View. 2 Twick TW1 6 A1
Cole Rd. Twick TW1 6 A1
Cole's La. Ockley RH5 178 B5
Colebrook. Ottsh KT16 51 D4
Colebrook Cl. Putney SW19 19 D8
Colebrook Rd. Thorn H SW16 41 E8
Colebrook Rise. Beck BR2 44 E7
Colebrooke Pl. Ottsh KT16 51 C3
Colebrooke Rd. Redh RH1 118 E3
Coleford Bridge Rd. Farnb GU16 85 D4
Coleford Bridge Rd. Mytch GU14 & GU16 85 E4
Coleford Cl. Mytch GU16 85 F3
Coleford Paddocks. Mytch GU16 85 F4
Colekitchen La. Gomsh GU5 133 D6
Coleman Cl. S Norw SE25 43 A7
Coleman Ct. Wands SW18 20 A8
Coleman Rd. Alder GU12 105 D1
Coleridge Ave. Carsh SM1 59 E6
Coleridge Cl. Crowth RG11 45 C4
Coleridge Cl. Horsh RH12 217 E6
Coleridge Cres. Poyle SL3 1 E6
Coleridge Ct. 2 Rich TW10 17 D4
Coleridge Rd. Ashf TW15 13 F4
Coleridge Rd. Croy CR0 43 C2
Coles La. Capel RH5 178 C5
Colesburg Rd. Beck BR3 43 F7
Colescroft Hill. Purley CR8 80 A4
Coleshill Rd. Tedd TW11 16 E2
Colesmead Rd. Redh RH1 118 F4
Coleson Hill Rd. Wreccl GU10 145 F5
Colet Rd. Crawl RH10 201 D3
Coleville Rd. W Heath GU14 84 F5
Coley Ave. Woking GU22 70 A2
Colfe Rd. For Hil SE23 23 E7
Colgate Cl. Crawl RH11 201 B8
Colin Cl. Coney H BR4 63 F7
Colin Cl. Croy CR0 62 F7
Colin Ct. Streat SW16 21 D6
Colin Rd. Cater CR3 101 A4
Coliston Rd. Wands SW18 20 A8
Coll of Liberal Arts. Sutton SM1 59 B5
Coll of St Barnabas. Felct RH7 185 F8
Coll of Tech Three Bridges Outpost. Crawl RH10 202 A7
Collamore Ave. Wands SW18 20 E7
Collards La. Haslem GU27 208 D6
College Ave. Egham TW20 12 B2
College Ave. Epsom KT17 76 F5
College Cl. Addl KT15 52 D7
College Cl. Camb GU15 65 D7
College Cl. E Grins RH19 185 F1
College Cl. Lingf RH7 164 D4
College Cl. Twick TW2 16 D7
College Cres. Redh RH1 119 A4
College Cres. Sandh GU15 64 E8
College Ct. Croy CR0 62 A8
College Fields Bsns Ctr. Mitch SW19 40 E8
College Gdns. Dulw SE21 22 E7
College Gdns. Farnh GU9 125 B2
College Gdns. New Mal KT3 38 F4
College Gdns. Up Toot SW17 20 E6
College Gn. S Norw SE19 22 E1
College Hill. Godal GU7 150 C2
College Hill. Haslem GU27 208 C6
College Hill Terr. Haslem GU27 208 C6
College House. Hyde GU8 171 E5
College La. E Grins RH19 185 F1
College La. Woking GU22 89 C8
College Rd. Ash GU12 106 B3
College Rd. Brack RG12 27 D5
College Rd. Crawl RH10 201 E6
College Rd. Croy CR0 & CR9 61 D8
College Rd. Dulw SE19 & 21 22 E6
College Rd. Dulw SE19 22 F3
College Rd. Epsom KT17 76 F5
College Rd. Ewell KT17 77 B5
College Rd. Guild GU1 130 D8
College Rd. Hounsl TW7 5 F6
College Rd. Mayb GU22 70 B3
College Rd. Mitch SW19 20 D2
College Rd. Sandh GU15 64 E8
College Rdbt. 1 King U T KT1 37 E6
College Ride. Bagsh GU19 47 C2
College Ride. Camb GU15 65 D7
College Town Inf Sch. Sandh GU15 64 E8
College Town Jun Sch. Sandh GU15 64 E8
College Way. Ashf TW15 13 F4
College Wlk. King U T KT1 37 E6
Collendean La. Sidlow RH6 159 F4
Collens Field. Pirb GU24 87 F4
Collette Ct. S Norw SE25 42 E4
Colley La. Reig RH2 117 E3
Colley Manor Dr. Reig RH2 117 D2
Colley Way. Reig RH2 117 E4
Collier Cl. W Ewell KT19 57 B4
Collier Cl. W Ewell KT19 57 B4
Collier Cl. W Heath GU14 84 D5
Collier Row. Crawl RH10 201 D4
Collier Way. Merrow GU4 110 D3
Collier's Wood Sta. Mitch SW19 20 D1
Colliers. Cater CR3 101 A2
Colliers Cl. Woking GU21 69 B2
Colliers Water La. Thorn H CR7 42 A4
Collingdon. Cran GU6 174 F1
Collingsbourne. Addl KT15 52 B6
Collingtree Rd. For Hil SE26 23 C4
Collingwood Ave. Tolw KT5 38 C1
Collingwood Cl. 4 E Grins RH19 205 F7
Collingwood Cl. Horley RH6 161 B4
Collingwood Cl. Horsh RH12 217 C4
Collingwood Cl. 3 Penge SE20 43 B8
Collingwood Cl. Twick TW2 & TW4 16 A8
Collingwood Coll. Camb GU15 66 A8
Collingwood Cres. Merrow GU1 110 A2
Collingwood Mount. Camb GU15 66 A7
Collingwood Pl. Camb GU15 66 B8
Collingwood Pl. Walt O T KT12 54 B7
Collingwood Rd. Horsh RH12 217 B4
Collingwood Rd. Mitch CR4 40 E6
Collingwood Rd. Sutton SM1 59 A6
Collingwood Rd. Worth RH10 202 D5
Collingwood Rise. Camb GU15 66 A7
Collins Rd. Crawl RH11 200 E4
Collis Prim Sch. Tedd TW11 17 B2
Collyer Ave. Wallin CR0 60 E6
Collyer Rd. Wallin CR0 60 E6
Collyer's Sixth Form Coll. Horsh RH12 217 D4
Colman Cl. Burgh H KT18 77 C2
Colman House. Redh RH1 118 F3
Colman Way. Redh RH1 118 E4
Colmans Hill. Peasl GU5 154 E7
Colmer Rd. Streat SW16 21 E1
Coln Trad Est. Poyle SL3 1 F6
Colnbrook By-Pass. Bra Hil SL3 & UB7 1 D7
Colnbrook By-Pass. Coln SL3 & UB7 1 D7
Colnbrook By-Pass. Harm UB7 2 C7
Colnbrook C of E Comb Sch. Coln SL3 1 D7
Colnbrook Ct. Poyle SL3 1 F6
Colnbrook Ct. Up Toot SW17 20 D4
Colndale Rd. Poyle SL3 1 E5
Colne Bank. Horton SL3 & TW19 1 C4
Colne Ct. W Ewell KT19 57 C6
Colne Ct. W Ewell KT19 57 C6
Colne Dr. Walt O T KT12 54 D7
Colne House. 2 Redh RH1 118 F2
Colne Lodge. Walt O T KT12 54 D7
Colne Rd. Twick TW1 & TW2 16 E7
Colne Reach. Stan TW19 1 F2
Colne Way. Ash GU12 106 A1
Colne Way. Wray TW19 12 B6
Colne Wlk. Crawl RH11 200 F5
Colnebridge Cl. Stain TW18 12 E3
Coloma Convent Girls Sch. S Croy CR9 62 D7
Colonel's La. Chert KT16 33 A3
Colonial Ave. Twick TW2 5 C1
Colonial Rd. E Bed TW14 14 E8
Colonsay Rd. Crawl RH11 201 B3
Colony Gate. Friml GU16 66 D2
Colson Rd. Croy CR0 & CR9 61 E8
Colson Way. Streat SW16 21 C4
Colston Ave. Carsh SM1 & SM5 59 E6
Colston Ct. Carsh SM5 59 F6
Colston Rd. Mortl SW14 7 C3
Coltash Rd. Crawl RH10 202 A5
Coltsfoot Dr. Burph GU1 & GU4 110 B4
Coltsfoot Dr. Horsh RH12 217 E5
Coltsfoot La. Oxted RH8 123 A2
Columbia Ave. New Mal KT4 38 F2
Columbia Ct. New Mal KT3 38 F2
Columbine Ave. Croy CR2 61 B3
Columbus Dr. Farnb GU14 84 C4
Colville Gdns. Lhtwat GU18 67 C8
Colvin Cl. For Hil SE26 23 C3
Colvin Rd. Thorn H CR7 42 A4
Colwood Gdns. Mitch SW19 20 D1
Colworth Rd. Croy CR0 43 A1
Colwyn Cl. Crawl RH11 200 F4
Colwyn Cl. Streat SW16 21 C3
Colwyn Cres. Hounsl TW3 5 C6
Colyton Cl. Woking GU21 69 C1
Combe House. Mortl SW14 7 C5
Combe Hurst. King U T KT2 18 C3
Combe La. Bramly GU5 & GU8 151 D2
Combe La. Chidd GU8 191 A7
Combe La. Shere KT24 & GU4 133 B8
Combe La. W Heath GU14 85 A6
Combe La. Whit V KT12 53 F2
Combe La. Wormly GU8 170 F1
Combe Martin Coll. King U T KT2 18 C3
Combe Rd. Farnc GU7 150 E8
Combe Rise. M Bourn GU10 146 D5
Combe View. Chidd GU8 191 A5
Combemartin Rd. Putney SW18 19 E7
Combermere Rd. Morden SM4 40 B4
Comeragh Cl. Woking GU22 89 A7
Comet Rd. Stan TW19 13 D8
Comforts Farm Ave. Oxted RH8 123 A3
Comfrey Cl. W Heath GU14 84 C5
Comfrey Cl. Woki RG11 25 E8
Commer Track. Farnb GU14 104 C7
Commerce Rd. Brent TW8 6 C7
Commerce Way. Croy CR0 60 F8
Commercial Rd. Alder GU12 126 C8
Commercial Rd. Guild GU1 130 D8
Commercial Rd. Stain TW18 13 A2
Commercial Way. Woking GU21 69 F2
Commodore Ct. Farnb GU14 105 B8
Common Cl. Horse GU21 69 D5
Common House Rd. Dunsf GU8 192 F4
Common La. Clayg KT10 56 A3
Common La. New Haw KT15 52 C2
Common Rd. Clayg KT10 56 A3
Common Rd. Earls RH1 139 F7
Common Side. Epsom KT18 76 A4
Commonfield Rd. Banstd SM7 78 B6
Commonfields. W End GU24 67 F6
Commonfields. W End GU24 68 A7
Commonside. Fetch KT22 & KT23 94 A5
Commonside Cl. Sutton SM2 78 B8
Commonside Ct. Streat SW16 21 E2
Commonside E. Mitch CR4 41 B6
Commonweal Lodge Sch. Purley CR8 79 D7
Commonwealth Rd. Cater CR3 101 A4
Community Cl. Cranf TW5 4 B6
Como Rd. For Hil SE23 23 E6
Compass Hill. Rich TW10 6 D1
Compasses Mobile Home Pk. Alf Cr GU8 193 F5
Compassion Cl. Crawl RH11 200 E5
Comper Cl. Crawl RH11 200 E4
Comport Gn. New Add CR0 82 E7
Compound Rd. Farnb GU14 85 A2
Compton Cl. Easth RG12 26 E3
Compton Cl. Esher KT10 55 D5
Compton Cl. Sandh GU17 45 C1
Compton Cres. Chess KT9 56 E4
Compton Cres. Chisw W4 7 C8
Compton Ct. Guild GU1 130 F8

Compton Ct. Sutton SM1 59 C6
Compton Ct. 9 W Norw SE19 22 E3
Compton Hts. Compt GU3 129 D6
Compton Place Bsns Ctr. Camb GU15 65 A4
Compton Rd. Croy CR0 43 B1
Compton Rd. Wimble SW19 19 F2
Compton Way. Farnh GU10 126 B1
Comptons Brow La. Horsh RH13 218 A3
Comptons La. Horsh RH12 & RH13 217 F3
Comsaye Wlk. Easth RG12 27 C4
Conal Ct. Streat SW16 21 D3
Conaways Cl. Ewell KT17 58 A1
Concorde Bsns Pk. Bigg H TN16 83 D4
Concorde Cl. Hounsl TW3 5 B5
Concorde House. Addl KT15 52 B6
Condor Ct. Guild GU2 130 C7
Condor Rd. 2 Farnb GU14 85 B2
Condor Rd. Laleh TW18 33 C6
Conduit La. S Croy CR0 62 A5
Conduit The. Bletch RH1 120 D6
Coney Acre. W Norw SE21 22 C7
Coney Cl. Crawl RH11 201 B8
Coney Croft. Horsh RH12 218 B5
Coney Hall Par. Coney H BR4 63 E7
Coney Hill Rd. Coney H BR4 63 F8
Coney Hill Sch. Coney H BR2 63 F7
Coneyberry. Dovgn RH1 139 D5
Coneybury. Bletch RH1 120 E1
Coneybury Cl. Warlgm CR6 101 B8
Coneyhurst La. Ewh GU6 175 D7
Conford Dr. Shalf GU4 130 E2
Coniers Way. Burph GU1 & GU4 110 B4
Conifer Cl. Reig RH2 118 A3
Conifer Ct. 23 Putney SW19 19 D7
Conifer Dr. Camb GU15 66 A6
Conifer Gdns. Streat SW16 21 F5
Conifer Gdns. Sutton SM1 59 B8
Conifer La. Egham TW20 12 C3
Conifers. Oat Pk KT13 53 F6
Conifers Cl. Horsh RH12 218 B6
Conifers Cl. Tedd TW11 17 C1
Conifers The. Crowth RG11 45 A7
Coningsby. Easth RG12 27 C5
Coningsby Ct. Mitch CR4 41 A7
Coningsby Rd. S Croy CR2 61 C2
Conisborough Cres. Catf SE6 24 C5
Conista Ct. Woking GU21 68 F3
Coniston Cl. Barnes SW13 7 F7
Coniston Cl. Chisw W4 7 C7
Coniston Cl. Crawl RH11 200 D4
Coniston Cl. Farnb GU14 84 E3
Coniston Cl. Friml GU15 66 C3
Coniston Cl. Horsh RH12 218 B6
Coniston Cl. W Barn SM4 39 D3
Coniston Ct. Beck BR3 44 C8
Coniston Ct. Chess KT9 56 E7
Coniston Ct. Lhtwat GU18 48 B1
Coniston Ct. Penge SE26 23 B2
Coniston Ct. 3 Wallin SM6 60 B6
Coniston Ct. Whit V KT13 53 B4
Coniston Dr. Hale GU9 125 A6
Coniston Gdns. Sutton SM2 59 D4
Coniston Rd. Catf BR1 24 E2
Coniston Rd. Coulsd CR5 79 C3
Coniston Rd. Croy CR0 43 A2
Coniston Rd. Old Wok GU22 90 B7
Coniston Rd. Twick TW2 5 B1
Coniston Way. Chess KT9 56 E7
Coniston Way. Redh RH1 118 E2
Coniston Wlk. Thor L TW20 12 B1
Connaught Ave. Ashf TW15 13 E4
Connaught Ave. Hounsl TW4 4 E3
Connaught Ave. Mortl SW14 7 C3
Connaught Bsns Ctr. Mitch CR4 40 F4
Connaught Bsns Ctr. Wallin CR9 60 F4
Connaught Cl. Carsh SM1 59 D8
Connaught Cres. Brookw GU24 87 F7
Connaught Gdns. Crawl RH11 201 D8
Connaught Gdns. Morden SM4 40 C5
Connaught Rd. Alder GU12 105 D2
Connaught Rd. Bagsh GU19 47 C3
Connaught Rd. Brookw GU24 87 F7
Connaught Rd. Camb GU15 65 F5
Connaught Rd. Carsh SM1 59 D8
Connaught Rd. New Mal KT3 38 E5
Connaught Rd. 4 Rich TW10 6 F2
Connaught Rd. Tedd TW11 & TW12 16 D3
Connaught Sch. Alder GU12 126 E7
Connell House. 6 Wallin SM6 60 C4
Connington. 2 King U T KT1 38 A7
Connop Way. Friml GU16 65 F3
Conquest Rd. Addl KT15 52 A5
Conrad Dr. N Cheam KT4 39 D1
Consfield Ave. W Barn KT3 39 A4
Consort Dr. Camb GU15 66 C7
Consort Mews. Islew TW7 5 D2
Consort Way. Horley RH6 161 A3
Consort Way E. Horley RH6 161 B2
Constable Gdns. Islew TW7 5 D2
Constable Rd. Crawl RH10 201 F2
Constable Way. Sandh GU15 64 E6
Constable Wlk. Dulw SE21 22 E5
Constance Cres. Hayes BR2 44 F1
Constance Rd. Sutton SM1 59 C6
Constance Rd. Thorn H CR0 42 B2
Constance Rd. Twick TW2 16 B8
Constant Rd. Farnb GU14 84 A2
Constantine House. Streat SW2 22 B7
Constitution Hill. Woking GU22 89 E8
Contley House Hotel. Woki RG11 25 B8
Control Tower Rd. Crawl RH6 181 D6
Control Tower Rd. Harl TW6 3 B4
Convent Cl. Beck BR3 24 C1
Convent Hill. S Norw SE19 22 C2
Convent of the Sacred Heart Digby-Stuart Coll. Rhampt SW15 7 F2
Convent Rd. Ashf TW15 14 B3
Conway Cl. Friml GU16 65 F1
Conway Dr. Ashf TW15 14 C2
Conway Dr. Sutton SM2 59 B4
Conway Dr. W Heath GU14 84 D4
Conway Gdns. Mitch CR4 41 E5
Conway House. Dovgn RH2 139 A4
Conway House. 6 Streat SW2 21 E7
Conway Rd. Felt TW13 15 D3
Conway Rd. Harl TW6 3 B4
Conway Rd. Twick TW4 16 A8
Conway Rd. Wimble SW20 39 C8
Conway Wlk. Hampt TW12 15 F2
Conyer's Rd. Streat SW16 21 D3
Conyers Cl. Hersh KT12 54 D5
Cook Rd. Crawl RH10 201 F4
Cook Rd. Horsh RH12 217 D6
Cookes La. Cheam SM3 58 E4
Cookham Cl. Sandh GU17 45 C1
Cookham Rd. Binf RG12 26 E7
Cooks Hill. Buck Gn RH12 214 A8
Cooks Mead. Rusper RH12 199 D7
Coolarne Rise. Camb GU15 66 A6
Coolgardie Rd. Ashf TW15 14 C3
Coolham Ct. Crawl RH11 200 F6
Coolhurst La. Horsh RH13 218 A1
Coombe Ave. S Croy CR0 61 E6
Coombe Bank. King U T KT2 & KT3 38 E8
Coombe Cl. Crawl RH11 181 D1
Coombe Cl. Friml GU16 85 D8
Coombe Cl. Hounsl TW3 5 A3
Coombe Cotts. Betch RH3 116 D4
Coombe Cres. Hampt TW12 15 E1
Coombe Ct. Beck BR3 43 F8
Coombe Ct. Tadw KT20 97 C4
Coombe Dr. Row Tn KT15 51 F4
Coombe End. King U T KT2 18 D1
Coombe Gdns. New Mal KT3 38 F5
Coombe Gdns. Wimble SW20 39 A8
Coombe Girls Sch. King U T KT3 38 D7
Coombe Hall Sch. E Grins RH19 205 D6
Coombe Hill Glade. King U T KT2 18 E1
Coombe Hill Golf Course. King U T KT2 18 C1
Coombe Hill Inf Sch. King U T KT3 38 D8
Coombe Hill Jun Sch. King U T KT3 38 D8
Coombe Hill Rd. E Grins RH19 205 D6
Coombe Hill Rd. King U T KT2 18 E1
Coombe House Chase. King U T KT3 38 D8
Coombe La. S Croy CR0 62 B5
Coombe La. Wimble SW20 39 B7
Coombe La. Worpl GU3 108 D7
Coombe La W. King U T KT2 18 E1
Coombe Lane Flyover. King U T SW20 38 F8
Coombe Manor. Bisley GU24 68 B4
Coombe Neville. King U T KT2 18 D1
Coombe Pine. Brack RG12 27 D3
Coombe Pk. King U T KT2 18 D3
Coombe Rd. Croy CR0 61 E6
Coombe Rd. For Hil SE26 23 B4
Coombe Rd. Hampt TW12 15 F2
Coombe Rd. King U T KT2 38 A8
Coombe Rd. King U T KT3 38 E6
Coombe Rd. S Croy CR0 & CR2 61 E6
Coombe Ridings. King U T KT2 18 C3
Coombe Rise. King U T KT2 38 C8
Coombe The. Betch RH3 116 D4
Coombe Way. Byfl KT14 71 F7
Coombe Wlk. Sutton SM1 59 B7
Coombe Wood Golf Course. King U T KT2 18 C1
Coombe Wood Hill. Purley CR8 80 C6
Coombe Wood Rd. King U T KT2 18 C3
Coombefield Cl. New Mal KT3 38 E4
Coombelands Bsns Pk. Row Tn KT15 52 A4
Coombelands La. Row Tn KT15 52 A4
Coomber Way. Wallin CR0 & CR4 41 D2
Coombes The. Bramly GU5 152 A5
Cooper Cl. Smallf RH6 162 A3
Cooper Cres. Carsh SM5 59 F7
Cooper Ct. Farnb GU14 85 C4
Cooper House. Hounsl TW4 4 F4
Cooper House. 7 W Norw SW27 22 B3
Cooper Rd. Croy CR0 & CR9 61 B6
Cooper Rd. Guild GU1 130 F8
Cooper Rd. Windl GU20 48 D4
Cooper Row. Crawl RH10 201 D3
Cooper's Hill La. Eng Gn TW20 11 D4
Cooper's Hill Rd. Nutf RH1 120 A1
Cooper's Hill Rd. S Nutf RH1 120 A1
Cooper's Hill Rd. S Nutf RH1 141 B5
Cooper's Terr. Farnh GU9 125 C3
Cooper's Yd. W Norw SE19 22 E2
Coopers Cl. Egham TW18 12 E3
Coopers Hill Dr. Pirb GU24 87 C7
Coopers Rise. Ock Rid GU7 150 C3
Cootes Ave. Horsh RH12 217 A3
Copeland House. Up Toot SW17 20 D4
Copelands. Beck BR3 23 F1
Copelands Cl. Friml GU15 66 D4
Copeman Cl. For Hil SE26 23 C3
Copenhagen Way. Walt O T KT12 54 B7
Copenhagen Wlk. Crowth RG11 45 B4
Copers Cope Rd. Beck BR3 23 F1
Copleigh Dr. Kings KT20 97 E7
Copley Cl. Knaph GU21 88 E8
Copley Cl. Redh RH1 118 E3
Copley Pk. Streat SW16 21 F2
Copley Way. Tadw KT20 97 D7
Copnall Way. Horsh RH12 217 C2
Coppard Gdns. Chess KT9 56 C4
Copped Hall Dr. Friml GU15 66 C6
Copped Hall Way. Friml GU15 66 C6
Coppedhall. 1 Dulw SE21 22 D6
Copper Beech Cl. Woking GU22 89 B6
Copper Beeches. Hounsl TW7 5 D6
Copper Cl. S Norw SE19 22 F1
Copper Mill Dr. Islew TW7 5 F5
Copper Mill La. Wimble SW17 20 C4
Copperfield Ave. Sandh GU15 45 E2
Copperfield Cl. Purley CR2 & CR8 80 C8
Copperfield Ct. Leahd KT22 95 A6
Copperfield Pl. Horsh RH12 217 B4
Copperfield Rise. Row Tn KT15 51 F4
Copperfields. Beck BR3 44 C8
Copperfields. Fetch KT22 94 C5
Coppermill Rd. Horton TW19 1 B2
Coppice Cl. Heath E GU9 125 E6
Coppice Cl. Stough GU2 108 D2
Coppice Cl. W Barn SW20 39 C6
Coppice Dr. Wray TW19 11 D8
Coppice La. Reig RH2 117 F3
Coppice Rd. Horsh RH12 218 A5
Coppice The. Ashf TW15 14 B2
Coppice The. Crawl D RH10 204 B8
Coppice Wlk. Crawl RH10 202 A7
Coppin House. Streat SW2 22 B7
Copping Cl. S Croy CR0 61 E6
Coppins The. New Add CR0 63 B4
Coppsfield. E Mole KT8 36 A6
Copse Ave. Heath E GU9 125 E8
Copse Ave. W Wick BR4 63 B7
Copse Cl. Camb GU15 66 A6
Copse Cl. Chil GU4 131 C3
Copse Cl. Crawl D RH10 204 B8
Copse Cl. E Grins RH19 186 A3
Copse Cl. Horsh RH12 217 F6
Copse Cres. Crawl RH11 201 C7
Copse Dr. Woki RG11 25 A7
Copse Edge. Cran GU6 174 F4
Copse Edge. Elst GU8 148 C3
Copse Edge Ave. Epsom KT17 76 F6
Copse End. Camb GU15 66 A6
Copse Glade. Surb KT6 37 D1
Copse Hill. Purley CR8 79 E6
Copse Hill. Sutton SM2 59 B3
Copse Hill. Wimble SW20 19 B1
Copse La. Horley RH6 161 D4
Copse Rd. Cobham KT11 73 B6
Copse Rd. Knaph GU21 68 F1
Copse Rd. Linch GU27 207 D5
Copse Rd. Woodh RH2 139 D7
Copse Side. Farnc GU7 129 D1
Copse The. Cater CR3 101 A1
Copse The. Farnb GU14 84 D3
Copse The. Fetch KT22 & KT23 94 B4
Copse The. Rowl GU10 145 F4
Copse The. S Nutf RH1 140 E7
Copse View. S Croy CR2 62 E2
Copse Way. Wreccl GU10 145 F6
Copse Wood Ct. Redh RH1 118 E3
Copsem Dr. Esher KT10 55 B4
Copsem La. Esher KT10 55 C3
Copsem La. Oxsh KT22 55 C1
Copsem Way. Esher KT10 55 C4
Copsen Wood. Oxsh KT22 74 C8
Copsleigh Ave. Earls RH1 140 A3
Copsleigh Cl. Earls RH1 140 A3
Copsleigh Way. Earls RH1 140 A3
Copt Hill La. Kings KT20 97 F7
Copthall Gdns. Twick TW1 16 F7
Copthall Way. Woodhm KT15 52 A1
Copthorne Ave. Streat SW12 21 D8
Copthorne Bank. Burst RH10 & RH6 183 C4
Copthorne CE (Controlled) Sch. Copth RH10 183 B3
Copthorne Chase. Ashf TW15 13 F4
Copthorne Cl. Shep TW17 34 C3
Copthorne Common Rd. Copth RH10 183 C3
Copthorne Dr. Lhtwat GU18 48 B1
Copthorne Rd. Copth RH10 182 F1
Copthorne Rd. Crawl RH10 202 E8
Copthorne Rd. Dome RH10 & RH19 184 D4
Copthorne Rd. Felb RH10 & RH19 184 D4
Copthorne Rd. Leahd KT22 95 B7
Copthorne Rise. Sander CR8 80 D6
Copthorne Sch Trust Ltd. Copth RH10 183 E3
Copthorne Way. Copth RH10 182 F2
Copyhold Rd. E Grins RH19 205 D8
Corban Rd. Hounsl TW3 5 A4
Corbet Cl. Carsh CR4 & SM6 60 A8
Corbet Rd. Ewell KT17 57 E1
Corbett Cl. New Add CR0 82 D7
Corbett Ct. Catf SE6 23 F4
Corbett Dr. Lhtwat GU18 66 F7
Corbiere Ct. Wimble SW19 19 D2
Corby Cl. Crawl RH11 200 E3
Corby Dr. Eng Gn TW20 11 C2
Cordelia Croft. Wink RG12 27 E8
Cordelia Gdns. Ash V GU12 85 F1
Cordelia Gdns. Stan TW19 13 E8
Cordelia Rd. Stan TW19 13 E8
Corderoy Pl. Chert KT16 32 F3
Cordrey Gdns. Coulsd CR5 79 E4
Cordrey House. Chert KT15 52 B8
Cordwalles Cty Mid Sch. Camb GU15 65 F8
Cordwalles Rd. Camb GU15 65 F8
Corfe Cl. Ashtd KT21 75 C1
Corfe Gdns. Friml GU16 65 F1
Coriander Cl. W Heath GU14 84 C4
Coriander Cres. Stough GU2 109 A6
Corium House. Godal GU7 150 F5
Cork Tree House. 3 W Norw SW27 22 B3
Corkran Rd. Surb KT6 37 E2
Corkscrew Hill. W Wick BR4 63 D7
Cormongers La. Redh RH1 119 D2
Cormorant Ct. 12 W Norw SE21 22 D6
Cormorant Pl. Sandh GU15 64 E7
Cornbunting Cl. Sandh GU15 64 D8
Cornelia Cl. Farnb GU14 84 D3
Corner Fielde. Streat SW2 21 F7
Cornerside. Littlt TW15 14 C1
Cornerstone Sch The. Epsom KT18 76 C6
Corney Rd. Chisw W4 7 E8
Cornfield Rd. Reig RH2 139 C8
Cornfields. Farnc GU7 151 A8
Cornflower La. Croy CR0 43 D1
Cornford Gr. Up Toot SW12 21 B6
Cornhill Cl. Chert KT15 52 B8
Cornish Gr. Penge SE20 43 B8
Cornwall Ave. Byfl KT14 71 F5
Cornwall Ave. Clayg KT10 55 F3
Cornwall Cl. Camb GU15 65 F7
Cornwall Gdns. 6 E Grins RH19 205 F8
Cornwall Rd. Belm SM2 59 A2
Cornwall Rd. Thorn H CR0 & CR9 61 B8
Cornwall Rd. Twick TW1 17 A7
Cornwall Way. Egham TW18 12 E2
Cornwallis Cl. Cater CR3 100 C5
Coronation Cotts. Chidd GU8 191 C5
Coronation Rd. Alder GU11 126 B7
Coronation Rd. Ascot SL5 29 A2
Coronation Rd. Brack SL5 29 A2
Coronation Rd. E Grins RH19 205 E7
Coronation Sq. Woki RG11 25 D7
Coronet Cl. Crawl RH10 202 E7
Coronet The. Horley RH6 161 C1
Corporation Ave. Hounsl TW4 4 E3
Corpus Christi RC Prim Sch. King U T KT3 38 C6
Corrib Dr. Carsh SM1 59 E5
Corrie Gdns. Went GU25 31 C2
Corrie Rd. Addl KT15 52 D6
Corrie Rd. Old Wok GU22 90 C7
Corrigan Ave. Wallin CR5 79 A5
Corry Rd. Beac H GU26 188 C6
Corsair Cl. Stan TW19 13 E8
Corsair Rd. Stan TW19 13 E8
Corscombe Cl. King U T KT2 18 C3
Corsehill St. Streat SW16 21 C2
Corsham Way. Crowth RG11 45 B5
Corsletts Ave. Broad H RH12 216 D3
Corsten Hollow. 4 Earls RH1 139 F8
Corunna Dr. Horsh RH13 217 F2
Cosdach Ave. Wallin SM6 60 D3
Cosedge Cres. Croy CR0 & CR9 61 B5
Cosford Rd. Bowl Gn GU8 169 E4
Coteford St. Up Toot SW17 21 A4
Cotelands. S Croy CR0 61 E7
Cotford Rd. S Norw CR7 42 C5
Cotherstone. Epsom KT19 57 D2
Cotherstone Rd. Streat SW2 21 F7
Cotland Acres. Woodh RH1 139 D7
Cotsford Ave. New Mal KT3 38 D4
Cotswold Cl. Crawl RH11 201 B6
Cotswold Cl. King U T KT2 18 C2
Cotswold Cl. Stain TW18 13 A3
Cotswold Cl. W Heath GU14 84 E7
Cotswold Ct. Horsh RH13 217 E2
Cotswold Rd. Hampt TW12 16 A2
Cotswold Rd. Sutton SM2 59 B1
Cotswold St. W Norw SE27 22 B4
Cotswold Way. N Cheam KT4 58 C8
Cottage Cl. Horsh RH12 218 B6
Cottage Cl. Ottsh KT16 51 C4
Cottage Farm Way. Egham TW20 32 C6
Cottage Gdns. Farnb GU14 84 F4
Cottage Gr. King U T KT6 37 D3
Cottage Pl. Copth RH10 183 E3
Cottage Rd. W Ewell KT19 57 D3
Cottage Rd. W Ewell KT19 57 D3
Cottenham Dr. Wimble SW20 19 B1
Cottenham Par. Wimble SW20 39 B7

Cottenham Park C of E Prim Sch.
Wimble SW20 .... 39 A8
Cottenham Park Rd.
Wimble SW20 .... 39 B8
Cottenham Pl.
Wimble SW20 .... 19 B1
Cottenhams. Blind H RH7 . 163 E8
Cotterill Rd. Surb KT6 ...... 37 F1
Cottesbrooke Cl. Poyle SL3 ... 1 D6
Cottesmore. Easth RG12 ..... 27 A2
Cottimore Ave.
Walt O T KT12 .... 35 B1
Cottimore Cres.
Walt O T KT12 .... 35 B2
Cottimore La. Walt O T KT12 35 B2
Cottimore La. Walt O T KT12 35 D1
Cottimore Terr.
Walt O T KT12 .... 35 B2
Cottingham Ave.
Horsh RH12 .... 217 D7
Cottingham Rd. Penge SE20 23 D1
Cottington Rd. Felt TW13 ... 15 D4
Cotton Hill. Catf BR1 .... 24 D4
Cotton House. 18
Streat SW12 .... 21 E8
Cotton Row. For Gn RH5 ... 176 C8
Cotton Wlk. Crawl RH11 ... 201 A1
Cottongrass Cl. Croy CR0 ... 43 D1
Cottrell Flats. Farnb GU14 105 D8
Cotts Wood Dr. Burph GU4 110 A6
Couchmore Ave.
Hinch W KT10 .... 55 E8
Coulsdon C of E Prim Sch.
Coulsd CR5 .... 79 F1
Coulsdon Court Municipal Golf
Course. Purley CR5 ...... 79 F3
Coulsdon Court Rd.
Coulsd CR5 .... 79 F1
Coulsdon House. 6
Streat SW2 .... 21 E7
Coulsdon La. Chips CR5 ..... 99 A8
Coulsdon Pl. Cater CR3 .... 100 D5
Coulsdon Rd.
Cater CR3 & CR5 ...... 100 B7
Coulsdon Rd.
Coulsd CR3 & CR5 .... 100 B7
Coulsdon Rise. Coulsd CR5 . 79 E2
Coulsdon South Sta.
Coulsd CR5 .... 79 D3
Coulthurst Ct. Streat SW16 . 21 E1
Council Cotts. Charl RH6 ... 180 C6
Council Cotts. Loxwd RH14 213 A2
Council Cotts. Plaist RH14 211 D3
Council Cotts. W End GU24 . 67 F7
Countisbury Gdns.
Addl KT15 .... 52 B5
Countisbury House.
Dulw SE26 .... 23 A5
County Oak La.
Crawl RH11 .... 181 D3
County Oak Ret Pk.
Crawl RH11 .... 181 D2
County Oak Way.
Crawl RH11 .... 181 D3
County Rd. S Norw CR7 ..... 42 B7
Courier House. 17
Streat SW2 .... 22 A8
Courland Rd. Addl KT15 .... 52 B7
Course Rd. Ascot SL5 .... 29 A6
Court Ave. Coulsd CR5 .... 100 A8
Court Bushes Rd.
Whytlf CR3 .... 101 B7
Court Cl. E Grins RH19 .... 185 F1
Court Cl. Twick TW13 & TW2 16 B5
Court Close Ave.
Twick TW13 & TW2 .... 16 B5
Court Cres. Chess KT9 ...... 56 D4
Court Cres. E Grins RH19 .. 185 C1
Court Downs Rd. Beck BR3 . 44 B7
Court Dr. Carsh SM1 .... 59 E6
Court Dr. Croy CR0 .... 60 F6
Court Farm Ave.
W Ewell KT19 .... 57 D5
Court Farm Ave.
W Ewell KT19 .... 57 D5
Court Farm Gdns.
Epsom KT19 .... 76 C8
Court Farm Ind Est.
Stan TW19 .... 2 F1
Court Farm Rd. Warlgm CR6 81 A2
Court Gdns. Camb GU15 .... 65 D5
Court Green Hts.
Woking GU22 .... 89 C7
Court Haw. Wooden SM7 ... 78 E4
Court Hill. Sander CR2 ..... 80 E7
Court Hill. Wooden CR5 .... 78 F2
Court House Mansions.
Epsom KT19 .... 76 D7

Court La. Dulw SE21 .... 22 F8
Court La. Epsom KT19 ...... 76 C6
Court Lodge Cty Fst Sch.
Horley RH6 .... 160 F3
Court Lodge Rd.
Horley RH6 .... 160 F3
Court Rd. Alder GU11 ..... 105 A2
Court Rd. Banstd SM7 ...... 78 A4
Court Rd. Cater CR3 ...... 100 E8
Court Rd. S Norw SE25 ..... 42 F6
Court Rd. Tyl Gn RH9 ..... 121 C4
Court The. Docken GU10 ... 146 D2
Court The. Guild GU2 ..... 130 C7
Court The. Warlgm CR6 ..... 81 E1
Court Way.
Twick TW1 & TW2 ..... 16 F8
Court Wood La.
New Add CR0 .... 62 F1
Courtenay Ave. Belm SM2 .. 59 A2
Courtenay Ave. Beck BR3 ... 44 E7
Courtenay Mews.
Woking GU21 .... 70 A3
Courtenay Rd.
N Cheam KT4 & SM3 ... 58 C7
Courtenay Rd.
Penge BR3 & SE20 ..... 23 D2
Courtenay Rd. Woking GU21 70 A3
Courtfield Rd. Ashf TW15 .. 14 B2
Courtfield Rise. W Wick BR4 63 D7
Courthope Rd.
Wimble SW19 .... 19 E3
Courthope Villas.
Wimble SW19 .... 19 E1
Courtland Ave.
S Norw SW16 .... 21 F1
Courtlands. Beck BR3 ...... 44 B7
Courtlands. Rich TW10 ..... 7 A2
Courtlands. 10 Sutton SM2 . 59 B3
Courtlands. Walt O T KT12 .. 35 A2
Courtlands Ave. Esher KT10 55 A4
Courtlands Ave.
Hampt TW12 .... 15 F2
Courtlands Ave. Rich TW9 .. 7 B5
Courtlands Ave. W Wick BR4 44 F1
Courtlands Cl. S Croy CR2 .. 62 A1
Courtlands Cres.
Banstd SM7 .... 78 A3
Courtlands Dr. W Ewell KT19 57 F4
Courtlands Dr. W Ewell KT19 57 F4
Courtlands Rd. Surb KT5 ... 38 A2
Courtleas. Cobham KT11 .... 74 A6
Courtney Cl. S Norw SE19 .. 22 E2
Courtney Cres. Wallin SM5 . 59 F2
Courtney Pl. Croy CR0 ..... 61 A7
Courtney Rd.
Croy CR0 & CR9 .... 61 A7
Courtney Rd. Harl TW6 ..... 3 A4
Courtney Rd. Mitch SW19 .. 20 E1
Courts Hill Rd.
Haslem GU27 .... 208 B6
Courts Mount Rd.
Haslem GU27 .... 208 B6
Courts The. Streat SW16 ... 21 E1
Courtside. For Hil SE23 .... 23 C5
Courtwood Prim Sch.
New Add CR0 .... 62 F1
Courtyard The. 1
Crawl RH10 .... 201 D5
Courtyard The. Crawl RH13 218 E4
Courtyard The.
E Grins RH19 .... 186 B1
Coutts Ave. Chess KT9 ..... 56 E5
Coval Gdns. Mortl SW14 .... 7 B3
Coval La. Mortl SW14 ...... 7 B3
Coval Rd. Mortl SW14 ...... 7 C3
Cove Cty Inf Sch.
W Heath GU14 .... 84 E5
Cove Cty Jun Sch.
W Heath GU14 .... 84 E5
Cove Manor Cty Inf Sch.
W Heath GU14 .... 84 E6
Cove Manor Cty Jun Sch.
W Heath GU14 .... 84 E6
Cove Rd. Farnb GU14 ...... 84 F4
Cove Sch. W Heath GU14 ... 84 E5
Coveham Cres.
Cobham KT11 .... 73 A6
Coventry Rd. Croy SE25 .... 43 A5
Coverack Cl. Croy CR0 ..... 43 E2
Coverdale Ct. E Grins RH19 185 C3
Coverdale Gdns. S Croy CR0 61 F7
Covert Cl. Crawl RH10 .... 201 D7
Covert La. Brack RG12 ..... 27 C5
Covert The. Ascot SL5 ...... 29 B2
Covert The. W Heath GU14 . 84 E8
Coverton Rd. Up Tool SW17 20 D3
Coverts Rd. Clayg KT10 .... 55 F3
Covey Cl. Farnb GU14 ...... 85 A8

Covey The. Crawl RH10 .... 202 E8
Covington Gdns.
S Norw SW16 .... 22 B1
Covington Way.
S Norw SW16 .... 22 A1
Covington Way.
S Norw SW16 .... 22 B1
Streat SW16 .... 21 F2
Cow La. Goldal GU7 .... 150 D4
Cowden St. Catf SE6 .... 24 A4
Cowdray Cl. Crawl RH10 ... 202 C5
Cowdrey Rd. Wimble SW19 . 20 C3
Cowfold Cl. Crawl RH11 ... 200 F3
Cowick Rd. Up Tool SW17 .. 20 F4
Cowleaze Rd. King U T KT2 . 37 E8
Cowley Ave. Chert KT16 .... 32 F2
Cowley Cl. Selsd CR2 ...... 62 C2
Cowley Cres. Hersh KT12 .. 54 C6
Cowley La. Chert KT16 ..... 32 F2
Cowley Rd. Mortl SW14 ..... 7 E4
Coworth Cl. Sunnin SL5 .... 30 B4
Coworth Rd. Sunnin SL5 ... 30 A4
Cowper Ave. Carsh SM1 .... 59 D6
Cowper Cl. Chert KT16 ..... 32 F3
Cowper Gdns. Wallin SM6 .. 60 C4
Cowper Rd. Rich TW10 .... 17 F3
Cowper Rd. Wimble SW19 .. 20 C2
Cowshot Cres. Pirb GU24 .. 87 D7
Cowslip La. Mickle RH5 .... 115 B7
Cox Cnr. Ockley RH5 ...... 177 A7
Cox Green Rd. Cran RH12 . 195 C2
Cox Green Rd. Ewh RH12 .. 195 C2
Cox House. Horsh RH12 ... 217 B2
Cox La. Chess KT9 .... 56 F6
Cox La. W Ewell KT19 ..... 57 C5
Cox La. W Ewell KT19 ..... 57 C5
Coxbridge. Farnb GU9 .... 124 F1
Coxcombe Wlk. Crawl RH11 201 A4
Coxcombe La. Chidd GU8 . 191 B4
Coxdean. Burgh H KT20 .... 97 C8
Coxgreen. Sandh GU15 .... 64 D6
Coxley Rise. Purley CR8 ... 80 C6
Coxs Ave. Sunby TW17 ..... 34 E6
Coxwell Rd. S Norw SE19 .. 22 E1
Crab Hill. Beck BR3 .... 24 D1
Crab Hill La. S Nutf RH1 ... 140 F4
Crabbet Rd. Crawl RH10 ... 202 B6
Crabbs Croft Cl. Bcak KT23 . 94 C1
Crabtree Cnr. Thorpe TW20 . 32 B8
Crabtree Dr. Leakd KT22 ... 95 C2
Crabtree La. Churt GU10 ... 168 A2
Crabtree La. Bcak KT23 .... 94 C1
Crabtree La. Head KT22 .... 96 C1
Crabtree La. Westh RH5 ... 115 A3
Crabtree Office Village.
Thorpe TW20 .... 32 C8
Crabtree Rd. Camb GU15 ... 65 B2
Crabtree Rd. Crawl RH11 ... 201 C7
Crabtree Rd. Thorpe TW20 . 32 C7
Crabwood. Oxted RH8 .... 122 E7
Craddocks Ave. Ashtd KT21 . 75 F3
Craddocks Par. Ashtd KT21 . 75 F3
Cradhurst Cl. Westc RH4 .. 135 C6
Craig Rd. Rich TW10 ...... 17 C4
Craigans. Crawl RH11 ..... 201 A5
Craigen Ave. Croy CR0 ..... 43 B1
Craigmore Tower.
Woking GU22 .... 89 E8
Craignair Rd. Streat SW2 .. 22 A8
Craignish Ave.
Thorn H SW16 .... 41 F7
Craigside. King U T KT2 .... 38 B8
Craigside. Purley CR8 ...... 79 F5
Craigwell Ave. Felt TW13 .. 15 A5
Craigwell Cl. Egham TW18 . 32 E8
Crail Cl. Woki RG11 .... 25 A3
Crake Pl. Sandh GU15 ..... 64 D8
Crakell Rd. Reig RH2 ..... 139 C8
Cramhurst La. Witley GU8 . 170 E6
Cramond Ct. E Bed TW14 .. 14 E7
Crampshaw La. Ashtd KT21 . 95 F7
Crampton Rd. Penge SE20 . 23 C2
Cranborne Ave.
Tolw KT6 & KT9 .... 57 A7
Cranborne Wlk.
Crawl RH10 .... 201 F4
Cranbourne Cl. Horley RH6 161 B5
Cranbourne Cl.
Thorn H SW16 .... 41 E6
Cranbourne Cotts. Wink SL4 . 9 B5
Cranbourne Cty Prim Sch.
Wink SL5 .... 9 A4
Cranbrook Ct. 9 Brent TW8 . 6 D8
Cranbrook Dr.
Thame D KT10 .... 36 C1
Cranbrook Dr. Twick TW2 .. 16 B8
Cranbrook House.
S Norw SE19 .... 42 D8
Cranbrook Rd. Hounsl TW4 .. 4 F3
Cranbrook Rd. S Norw CR7 . 42 C7

Cranbrook Rd. Wimble SW19 19 E1
Cranbrook Terr. Cran GU6 . 174 F3
Crane Ave. Islew TW7 ...... 6 A2
Crane Ct. Sandh GU15 ..... 64 D8
Crane Ct. W Ewell KT19 .... 57 C6
Crane Ct. W Ewell KT19 .... 57 C6
Crane House. Catf BR1 ..... 24 D3
Crane Lodge Rd. Felt TW13 . 16 A5
Crane Inf Sch. Felt TW13 ... 15 F6
Crane Jun Sch. Felt TW13 .. 15 F6
Crane Lodge Rd. Heston TW5 4 B8
Crane Mead Ct. Twick TW1 . 16 F8
Crane Park Rd. Twick TW2 . 16 B6
Crane Rd. Stan TW19 .... 3 A1
Crane Rd. Twick TW2 ...... 16 E7
Crane Way. Twick TW2 ..... 16 C8
Cranebrook. Twick TW2 .... 16 F8
Craneford Cl. Twick TW2 ... 16 F8
Craneford Way.
Twick TW1 & TW2 ..... 16 F8
Cranes Dr. King U T KT5 ... 37 F5
Cranes Park Ave.
King U T KT5 & KT6 ... 37 F5
Cranes Park Cres.
King U T KT5 .... 37 F5
Cranes Pk.
King U T KT5 .... 37 E4
Craneswater. Harl TW6 ..... 3 F7
Cranfield Ct. 7
Woking GU21 .... 68 F1
Cranfield Rd E. Wallin SM5 . 60 A2
Cranfield Rd W. Wallin SM5 60 A2
Cranford Ave. Stan TW19 .. 13 F8
Cranford Cl. Purley CR8 ... 80 C6
Cranford Cl. Stan TW19 .... 13 E8
Cranford Cl. Wimble SW20 . 19 B1
Cranford Comm Sch.
Cranf TW5 .... 4 B8
Cranford Ct. Sutton SM1 ... 59 C6
Cranford Jun & Inf Schs.
Cranf TW4 .... 4 F8
Cranford La. Cranf UB3 ..... 4 A7
Cranford La. Harl UB3 ..... 3 E7
Cranford La. Hatton TW6 ... 3 F4
Cranford La. Hatton TW6 ... 3 F6
Cranford La. Heston TW5 ... 4 D7
Cranford Lodge.
Putney SW18 .... 19 E6
Cranford Rise. Esher KT10 . 55 C5
Cranleigh Cl. Penge SE20 .. 43 B7
Cranleigh Cl. Sander CR2 .. 81 A7
Cranleigh Ct. Farnb GU14 .. 84 F4
Cranleigh Ct. Mitch CR4 ... 40 D6
Cranleigh Ct. Rich TW9 ..... 7 A4
Cranleigh Cty Fst Sch.
Cran GU6 .... 174 E3
Cranleigh Gdns.
S Norw SE25 .... 42 E6
Cranleigh Gdns. Sander CR2 81 A7
Cranleigh Gdns. Sutton SM1 59 B8
Cranleigh House.
Wimble SW20 .... 39 B7
Cranleigh Mead. Cran GU6 174 F2
Cranleigh Rd. Ewh GU6 ... 175 D4
Cranleigh Rd. Felt TW13 ... 14 F4
Cranleigh Rd. Merton SW19 40 A6
Cranleigh Rd. Thame D KT10 36 A5
Cranleigh Rd. Woner GU5 . 152 C7
Cranleigh Sch. Cran GU6 . 174 C5
Cranleigh Village Hospl.
Cran GU6 .... 174 D3
Cranley Cl. Guild GU1 ..... 110 A1
Cranley Gdns. Wallin SM6 .. 60 C3
Cranley Pl. Knaph GU21 .... 68 D1
Cranley Rd. Guild GU1 .... 109 F1
Cranley Rd. W Hit V KT12 .. 53 F5
Cranmer Cl. Barn SM4 .... 39 E3
Cranmer Cl. Warlgm CR6 ... 81 E2
Cranmer Cl. W Hit V K13 ... 53 A3
Cranmer Cl. Hampt TW12 .. 16 B3
Cranmer Ct. King U T KT2 .. 17 D4
Cranmer Farm Cl. Mitch CR4 40 F5
Cranmer Gdns. Warlgm CR6 81 E2
Cranmer Mid Sch. Mitch CR4 40 F5
Cranmer Rd.
Croy CR0 & CR9 .... 61 C7
Cranmer Rd. Hampt TW12 . 16 B3
Cranmer Rd. King U T KT2 . 17 E3
Cranmer Rd. Mitch CR4 .... 40 F5
Cranmer Terr.
Up Toot SW17 .... 20 D3
Cranmer Wlk. Worth RH10 202 C5
Cranmore Ave. Hounsl TW7 . 5 C7
Cranmore Cl. Alder GU11 . 104 E1
Cranmore Gdns.
Alder GU11 .... 104 E1
Cranmore La. Alder GU11 . 104 E1
Cranmore La. W Hors KT24 112 C6
Cranmore Rd. Catf BR1 .... 24 F5

Cranmore Rd. Mytch GU16 .. 86 A4
Cranmore Sch.
W Hors KT24 .... 112 C6
Cranston Cl.
Hounsl TW3 & TW4 ..... 4 E5
Cranston Cl. Reig RH2 .... 139 B8
Cranston Rd. E Grins RH19 185 F2
Cranston Rd. For Hil SE23 . 23 E6
Cranstoun Cl. Stough GU3 . 108 F5
Crantock Rd. Catf SE6 ..... 24 C6
Cranwell Ct. Croy CR0 ..... 62 D8
Cranwell Gr. Lthwat GU18 .. 66 F8
Cranwell Gr. Shep W TW17 . 33 F5
Cranwell Rd. Harl TW6 ...... 3 B5
Craster Rd. Streat SW2 ..... 21 F8
Cravan Ave. Felt TW13 .... 15 A6
Craven Cl. M Bourn GU10 . 146 C6
Craven Gdns. Wimble SW19 20 B3
Craven House. 2
Mortl SW14 .... 7 D4
Craven Rd. Croy CR0 ...... 43 B1
Craven Rd. King U T KT2 ... 37 F8
Craven Rd. Worth RH10 ... 202 B5
Cravens The. Smallf RH6 .. 162 A3
Crawford Cl. Hounsl TW7 ... 5 E5
Crawford Gdns. Camb GU15 65 B5
Crawford Gdns.
Horsh RH13 .... 217 E4
Crawfurd Way.
E Grins RH19 .... 185 F3
Crawley Ave. Crawl RH10 . 182 C1
Crawley Ave.
Crawl RH10 & RH11 ... 201 A6
Crawley Chase. Wink RG12 . 8 B2
Crawley Coll of Tech.
Crawl RH10 .... 201 E6
Crawley Coll (West Green
Annexe). Crawl RH11 ... 201 C7
Crawley Down CE (Controlled)
Sch. Crawl D RH10 .... 204 B8
Crawley Down Rd.
E Grins RH19 .... 184 F4
Crawley Down Rd.
Felb RH19 .... 184 F4
Crawley Dr. Camb GU15 ... 65 F6
Crawley Hill. Camb GU15 .. 65 F5
Crawley Hospl (General).
Crawl RH11 .... 201 C6
Crawley La. Crawl RH10 ... 202 C7
Crawley Rd. Crawl RH12 .. 200 B1
Crawley Rd. Faygt RH12 .. 218 D7
Crawley Rd. Horsh RH12 .. 218 B5
Crawley Ridge. Camb GU15 . 65 F6
Crawley Ridge Cty Fst Sch.
Camb GU15 .... 65 F6
Crawley Ridge Cty Mid Sch.
Camb GU15 .... 65 F6
Crawley Sta. Crawl RH10 .. 201 E5
Crawley Wood Cl.
Camb GU15 .... 65 F5
Crawshaw Rd. Ottsh KT16 . 51 D4
Crawters Cl. Crawl RH10 .. 201 F7
Cray Ave. Ashtd KT21 ...... 75 F2
Crayke Hill. Chess KT9 ..... 56 E3
Crayonne Cl. Charlt TW16 .. 34 E8
Crealock St. Wands SW18 .. 20 B8
Creasys Dr. Crawl RH11 ... 201 B1
Credenhill St. Streat SW16 . 21 C2
Crediton Way. Clayg KT10 . 56 A5
Credon Cl. W Heath GU14 .. 84 F5
Cree's Meadow. Windl GU20 48 D3
Creek Rd. E Mole KT8 ...... 36 E5
Creek The. Sunby TW16 .... 35 A4
Creeland Gr. For Hil SE6 ... 23 F7
Cremorne Gdns.
Epsom KT19 .... 57 D2
Crerar Cl. Farnb GU14 ..... 84 D3
Crescent Ct. King U T KT6 .. 37 D4
Crescent Day Hospl.
New Add CR0 .... 63 C1
Crescent Gdns.
Wimble SW19 .... 20 A5
Crescent Gr. Mitch CR4 .... 40 E5
Crescent Cl. Ash GU12 .... 106 B5
Crescent Rd. Beck BR3 ..... 44 B7
Crescent Rd. Bletch RH1 .. 120 C2
Crescent Rd. Cater CR3 ... 101 A3
Crescent Rd. E Grins RH19 185 D1
Crescent Rd. Shep TW17 ... 34 C4
Crescent Rd. Wimble SW20 39 D8
Crescent Rd. Woki RG11 ... 25 C5
Crescent Rd. Woodh RH2 . 139 A7
Crescent The. Ashf TW15 .. 13 F3
Crescent The. Barnes SW13 . 7 F5
Crescent The. Beck BR3 .... 44 A8
Crescent The. Belm SM2 ... 78 A8
Crescent The. Brack RG12 . 27 C5

Crescent The. Carsh SM1 59 D5
Crescent The. E Mole KT8 36 A5
Crescent The. Egham TW20 11 F2
Crescent The. Epsom KT18 76 A4
Crescent The. Farnb GU14 85 C3
Crescent The. Felct RH19 185 C8
Crescent The. Harl UB7 3 D7
Crescent The. Heath E GU9 125 D8
Crescent The. Horley RH6 182 B8
Crescent The. Horsh RH12 217 A2
Crescent The. King U T KT6 37 E4
Crescent The. King U T KT3 38 C7
Crescent The. Leahd KT22 95 B5
Crescent The. Lo Hall TW17 34 F2
Crescent The. Reig RH2 118 B1
Crescent The. Stough GU2 109 A3
Crescent The. Thorn H CR0 & SE25 42 D3
Crescent The. Thorpe KT16 33 A6
Crescent The. W Wick BR4 44 E3
Crescent The. Weyb KT13 53 A7
Crescent The. Wimble SW19 20 A5
Crescent The. Wold CR3 102 A4
Crescent Way. Horley RH6 161 A1
Crescent Way. S Norw SW16 22 A1
Crescent Wood Rd. Dulw SE21 & SE26 23 A5
Cressage Ho. 9 Brent TW8 6 E8
Cressall Cl. Leahd KT22 95 B7
Cressall Mead. Leahd KT22 95 B7
Cressingham Gr. Sutton SM1 59 C6
Cresswell Rd. Croy SE25 43 A5
Cresswell Rd. Felt TW13 15 E4
Cresswell Rd. Twick TW1 6 D1
Crest Hill. Peasl GU5 133 E1
Crest Rd. S Croy CR2 62 B3
Crest Rd. W Wick BR2 44 F2
Crest The. Surb KT5 38 A4
Crest The. 10 W Norw SW27 22 B3
Cresta Dr. Woodhm KT15 51 F1
Creston Ave. Knaph GU21 68 E3
Creston Way. N Cheam KT4 39 D1
Crestwood Way. Hounsl TW4 4 E2
Creswell. Knaph GU21 68 D2
Crewdson Rd. Horley RH6 161 B3
Crewe's Ave. Warlgm CR6 81 C3
Crewe's Cl. Warlgm CR6 81 C2
Crewe's Farm La. Warlgm CR6 81 E2
Crewe's La. Warlgm CR6 81 D3
Crichton Ave. Wallin SM6 60 D6
Crichton Rd. Wallin SM5 59 F3
Cricket Ct. E Grins RH19 185 E3
Cricket Field Gr. Crowth RG11 45 D4
Cricket Field Rd. Horsh RH12 217 B1
Cricket Gn. Hambl GU8 171 C1
Cricket Gn. Mitch CR4 40 F5
Cricket Green Sch. Mitch CR4 40 E6
Cricket Hill. S Nutf RH1 140 F7
Cricket La. M Bourn GU10 146 D6
Cricket La. Penge BR3 23 E3
Cricket View. Weyb KT13 53 B5
Cricket Way. Oat Pk KT13 53 E8
Cricketers Cl. Chess KT9 56 D6
Cricketers Cl. Ockley RH5 177 C4
Cricketers La. Windl GU20 48 D4
Cricketers La. Wink RG12 8 A3
Cricklade Ave. Streat SW2 21 F6
Crieff Ct. 3 Tedd TW11 & KT8 17 C1
Criffel Ave. Streat SW2 21 D7
Crimea Rd. Alder GU11 105 B2
Crimea Rd. Friml GU16 86 D8
Crimp Hill. Eng Gn SL4 & TW20 11 A6
Crimp Hill. Old W SL4 & TW20 11 A6
Cripley Rd. W Heath GU14 84 D6
Cripplecrutch Hill. Chidd GU8 209 F5
Cripplecrutch Hill. Fish GU8 209 F5
Cripps House. Crawl RH11 201 B2
Crispen Rd. Felt TW13 15 E4
Crispin Cl. Ashtd KT21 75 F1
Crispin Cl. Wallin SM6 60 E8
Crispin Cres. Wallin SM6 60 D8
Critchmere Hill. Shottm GU27 207 E7
Critchmere La.Shottm GU27 207 E6
Critchmere Vale. Shottm GU27 207 E6
Critten La. Effing KT24 & RH5 113 D2
Crittenden Lodge. W Wick BR4 44 A1
Crocker Cl. N Asct SL5 28 F8
Crockers La. Horne RH7 163 D4
Crockerton Rd. Up Toot SW17 20 F6
Crockford Cl. Addl KT15 52 C6
Crockford Park Rd. Addl KT15 52 C5
Crockham Cl. Crawl RH11 201 C4
Crocknorth Rd. E Hors KT24 113 A2
Crocus Cl. Croy CR0 43 D1
Croffets. Tadw KT20 97 D6
Croft Ave. Dork RH4 115 B1
Croft Ave. W Wick BR4 44 C1
Croft Cl. Harl UB7 3 C7
Croft Cl. Woki RG11 25 A2
Croft Rd. Alder GU11 126 B8
Croft Rd. Carsh SM1 59 E5
Croft Rd. Godal GU7 150 E4
Croft Rd. Merton SW19 20 C1
Croft Rd. S Norw SW16 22 A1
Croft Rd. Witley GU8 170 E5
Croft Rd. Woki RG11 25 A1
Croft Rd. Wold CR3 102 A5
Croft The. Crawl RH11 201 A6
Croft The. Epsom KT17 76 F5
Croft The. Heston TW5 4 E7
Croft Way. Friml GU16 65 F2
Croft Way. Horsh RH12 217 A3
Croft Way. Rich TW10 17 B5
Crofter's Cl. Sandh GU17 64 A8
Crofters Cl. Islew TW7 5 D2
Crofters Mead. New Add CR0 62 F2
Croftleigh Ave. Purley CR8 80 B3
Crofton. Ashtd KT21 75 E1
Crofton Ave. Chisw W4 7 D7
Crofton Ave. Walt O T KT12 54 C7
Crofton Cl. Brack RG12 27 E4
Crofton Cl. Ottsh KT16 51 C3
Crofton Terr. Rich TW9 6 F3
Crofts Cl. Chidd GU8 191 B5
Crofts The. Up Hall TW17 34 E5
Croftside The. S Norw SE25 43 A6
Croham Cl. S Croy CR2 61 E4
Croham Hurst Golf Course. S Croy CR2 62 A3
Croham Hurst Sch. S Croy CR2 61 F5
Croham Manor Rd. S Croy CR2 61 E4
Croham Mount. S Croy CR2 61 E3
Croham Park Ave. S Croy CR0 & CR2 61 F5
Croham Rd. Croy CR0 & CR2 61 E5
Croham Rd. S Croy CR2 61 E5
Croham Valley Rd. S Croy CR2 62 B3
Croindene Rd. Thorn H SW16 41 E8
Cromer Ct. Streat SW16 21 E5
Cromer Rd. Croy SE25 43 B6
Cromer Rd. Harl TW6 3 A5
Cromer Rd. Mitch SW17 21 A2
Cromer Rd W. Harl TW6 3 A4
Cromford Way. King U T KT3 38 D8
Crompton Fields. Crawl RH10 181 E1
Crompton Way. Crawl RH10 181 E1
Cromwell Ave. New Mal KT3 38 F4
Cromwell Cl. Walt O T KT12 35 B1
Cromwell Ct. 15 King U T KT2 18 A1
Cromwell Gr. Cater CR3 100 C6
Cromwell House. Croy CR0 61 B7
Cromwell Pl. Cran GU6 174 F1
Cromwell Pl. 1 E Grins RH19 205 F7
Cromwell Pl. Mortl SW14 7 C4
Cromwell Rd. Ascot SL5 29 B4
Cromwell Rd. Beck BR3 43 E6
Cromwell Rd. Camb GU15 65 D7
Cromwell Rd. Cater CR3 100 C6
Cromwell Rd. Felt TW13 15 B7
Cromwell Rd. Hounsl TW3 5 A3
Cromwell Rd. King U T KT2 37 E8
Cromwell Rd. Redh RH1 118 F1
Cromwell Rd. Tedd TW11 17 A2
Cromwell Rd. Thorn H CR0 42 D2
Cromwell Rd. Wimble SW19 20 B3
Cromwell Rd. Worc Pk KT19 & KT4 57 E7
Cromwell St. Hounsl TW3 5 A3
Cromwell Way. Farnb GU14 85 C7
Cromwell Wlk. 1 Redh RH1 118 F1
Crondall Ct. Camb GU15 65 B4
Crondall House. Rhampt SW15 19 A7
Crondall La. Farnh GU10 & GU9 124 D2
Crondall Rd. Bentl GU10 145 A6
Cronks Hill. Woodh RH2 139 D7
Cronks Hill Cl. Woodh RH1 139 D7
Cronks Hill Rd. Woodh RH1 & RH2 139 D7
Crooksbury Rd. Farnh GU10 126 C2
Crooksbury Rd. Tilf GU10 147 D8
Crosby Cl. Felt TW13 15 E4
Crosby Hill Dr. Camb GU15 65 F7
Crosby Wlk. Streat SE24 22 A8
Cross Deep. Twick TW1 17 A6
Cross Deep Gdns. Twick TW1 16 F6
Cross Farm Cty Fst Sch. Friml GU16 85 E6
Cross Fell. Easth RG12 27 A5
Cross Gates Cl. Brack RG12 27 F6
Cross Gdns. Friml GU16 85 F6
Cross Keys. Crawl RH10 & RH11 201 D6
Cross La. Burst RH6 162 C1
Cross La. Friml GU16 85 F6
Cross La. Ottsh KT16 51 C4
Cross Lances Rd. Hounsl TW3 5 B3
Cross Lanes. Guild GU1 130 F8
Cross Oak La. Salfs RH1 & RH6 161 C7
Cross Rd. Ash GU12 106 B3
Cross Rd. Belm SM2 59 A1
Cross Rd. Carsh SM1 59 D5
Cross Rd. Croy CR0 42 D1
Cross Rd. Farnb GU14 84 E1
Cross Rd. Felt TW13 15 E4
Cross Rd. King U T KT2 17 F1
Cross Rd. Merton SW19 20 A1
Cross Rd. Oat Pk KT13 53 D7
Cross Rd. Purley CR8 80 B6
Cross Rd. Tadw KT20 97 C5
Cross Rd. Went SL5 30 A1
Cross St. Alder GU11 105 A2
Cross St. Farnb GU14 105 C8
Cross St. Hampt TW12 16 C3
Cross St. Mortl SW13 7 E4
Cross St. Woki RG11 25 C6
Crossacres. Pyrf GU22 70 E4
Crossfield Pl. Whit V KT13 53 B3
Crossland Rd. Earls RH1 119 A1
Crossland Rd. Thorn H CR7 42 B3
Crosslands. Addl KT16 51 E6
Crosslands Rd. W Ewell KT19 57 D4
Crosslands Rd. W Ewell KT19 57 D4
Crossley Cl. Bigg H TN16 83 D4
Crossman Ct. Crawl RH11 201 B1
Crossman Houses. 19 Streat SW12 21 E8
Crosspath. Crawl RH10 201 E7
Crossroads The. Effing KT24 113 D7
Crosswater La. Frensh GU10 167 F4
Crossway. Brack RG12 27 C7
Crossway. Crawl RH6 181 F8
Crossway. W Barn KT3 & SW20 39 C5
Crossway. Walt O T KT12 54 B8
Crossways. Alder GU12 105 C1
Crossways. Charlt TW16 14 F1
Crossways. Churt GU10 167 E1
Crossways. Crawl RH10 202 A7
Crossways. Effing KT24 113 D8
Crossways. Egham TW20 12 D2
Crossways. S Croy CR0 & CR2 62 F3
Crossways. Sutton SM2 59 D2
Crossways. Tats TN16 103 C7
Crossways Ave. E Grins RH19 185 C1
Crossways Cl. Crawl RH10 201 F7
Crossways Cotts. Alf Cr GU6 194 A3
Crossways Cotts. Buck Gn RH12 213 F6
Crossways Ct. Tats TN16 103 C7
Crossways La. L Kings RH2 118 D7
Crossways Rd. Beck BR3 44 A5
Crossways Rd. Graysh GU26 188 D3
Crossways Rd. Mitch CR4 41 B6
Crossways The. Abing H RH5 134 B3
Crossways The. Coulsd CR5 100 A8
Crossways The. Heston TW5 4 F7
Crossways The. L Kings RH2 118 C7
Crossways The. Merst RH1 119 C6
Crossways The. Onsl V GU2 129 F7
Crosswell Cl. Charlt TW17 34 C7
Crouch Cl. Beck BR3 24 A2
Crouch La. Wink SL4 8 F7
Crouch Oak La. Addl KT15 52 C6
Crouchfield. Dork RH4 136 C4
Crouchmans Cl. Dulw SE21 & SE26 23 A5
Crowberry Cl. Crawl RH11 201 A2
Crowborough Cl. Warlgm CR6 81 E1
Crowborough Dr. Warlgm CR6 81 E1
Crowborough Rd. Streat SW17 21 A3
Crowhurst. S Norw SE25 43 A6
Crowhurst Cl. Worth RH10 202 E6
Crowhurst Keep. Worth RH10 202 E6
Crowhurst La. Crow RH7 143 D5
Crowhurst La. Tand RH7 143 D5
Crowhurst Mead. Tyl Gn RH9 121 C5
Crowhurst Rd. Crow RH7 164 D7
Crowhurst Rd. Lingf RH7 164 D7
Crowhurst Village Rd. Crow RH7 143 E2
Crowland Rd. S Norw CR7 42 D5
Crowland Wlk. Morden SM4 40 C3
Crowley Cres. Croy CR0 61 A5
Crowmarsh Gdns. For Hil SE23 23 C8
Crown Arc. King U T KT1 37 D7
Crown Cl. Walt O T KT12 35 C2
Crown Cotts. Brack SL5 28 C4
Crown Cotts. Eng Gn TW20 11 A1
Crown Ct. Godal GU7 150 E4
Crown Ct. 4 Twick TW1 17 B8
Crown Dale. W Norw SE19 & SE27 22 C3
Crown Dr. Farnh GU9 126 A5
Crown Hill Ct. Ascot SL5 29 B4
Crown Hts. Guild GU1 130 E6
Crown La. Farnh GU9 126 A5
Crown La. Merton SM4 & SW19 40 A6
Crown La. S Norw SE19 & SW16 22 A3
Crown La. Went GU25 31 D3
Crown Lane Gdns. W Norw SE27 22 A3
Crown Lane Prim Sch. W Norw SE27 22 B3
Crown Meadow. Coln SL3 1 B7
Crown Par. Morden SM4 40 A5
Crown Par. S Norw SE19 22 B2
Crown Pas. King U T KT1 37 D7
Crown Pl. Sandh GU15 45 E1
Crown Point. S Norw SE19 22 B2
Crown Rd. King U T KT3 38 C8
Crown Rd. Morden SM4 & SW19 40 B5
Crown Rd. Sutton SM1 59 B6
Crown Rd. Twick TW1 6 B1
Crown Rd. Went GU25 31 C3
Crown Rise. Chert KT16 32 F1
Crown Row. Brack RG12 27 D3
Crown St. Egham TW20 12 A4
Crown Terr. Rich TW9 6 F3
Crown Wood Cty Prim Sch. Brack RG12 27 E3
Crown Yard. Hounsl TW3 5 C4
Crownbourne Ct. Sutton SM1 59 B6
Crownpits La. Godal GU7 150 E3
Crowntree Cl. Hounsl TW7 5 F8
Crowther Rd. Croy SE25 43 A5
Crowthorne C of E Sch. Crowth RG11 45 C5
Crowthorne Cl. Wands SW18 19 F7
Crowthorne Lodge. Easth RG12 27 B5
Crowthorne Rd. Easth RG11 & RG12 26 F2
Crowthorne Rd. Easth RG12 27 A5
Crowthorne Rd. Sandh GU17 & RG11 45 B2
Crowthorne Rd N. Easth RG12 27 B6
Croxall House. Walt O T KT12 35 C3
Croxden Wlk. Morden SM4 40 C3
Croxted Cl. W Norw SE21 22 C8
Croyde Cl. W Heath GU14 85 A7
Croydon Airport Ind Est. Wallin CR9 60 F4
Croydon Coll. Croy CR9 61 D8
Croydon Coll Annexe. Croy CR0 42 D1
Croydon Coll (Selhurst Tertiary Ctr). Thorn H SE25 42 D4
Croydon Flyover The. Croy CR0 & CR9 61 C7
Croydon General Hospl. Thorn H CR9 42 C1
Croydon Gr. Thorn H CR0 42 B1
Croydon High Sch for Girls. Selsd CR2 62 C1
Croydon La. Banstd SM7 78 D6
Croydon La. Wallin SM7 78 D6
Croydon La S. Banstd SM7 78 B5
Croydon Rd. Beck BR3 43 E6
Croydon Rd. Cater CR3 101 A5
Croydon Rd. Chelsh CR6 102 D5
Croydon Rd. Coney H BR2 & BR4 63 F7
Croydon Rd. Croy CR0 60 D7
Croydon Rd. Harl TW6 3 B4
Croydon Rd. Mitch CR0 & CR4 & CR9 41 C4
Croydon Rd. Penge SE20 43 C8
Croydon Rd. Reig RH2 118 C2
Croydon Rd. Tats TN16 103 F3
Croydon Rd. Titsey CR6 102 D5
Croydon Rd. Wallin CR0 & SM5 & SM6 60 D7
Croydon Rd Ind Est. Beck BR3 43 D5
Croydon Water Palace. Croy CR9 61 A4
Croydonbarn La. Horne RH6 & RH9 163 B4
Croylands Dr. Surb KT6 37 E2
Croysdale Ave. Sunby TW16 35 A6
Crozier Dr. S Croy CR2 62 B1
Cruikshank Lea. Sandh GU15 64 E6
Crunden Rd. S Croy CR2 61 D3
Crundwell Ct. Farnh GU9 125 D3
Crusader Gdns. S Croy CR0 61 E7
Crusoe Rd. Mitch CR4 20 F1
Crutchfield La. Sidlow RH6 160 B5
Crutchfield La. Walt O T KT12 54 B8
Crutchley Rd. Catf SE6 24 E6
Crutchley Rd. Woki RG11 25 D7
Crystal Palace National Sports Ctr. Penge SE19 23 A2
Crystal Palace Par. Dulw SE19 22 F3
Crystal Palace Park Rd. Penge SE19 & SE26 23 B3
Crystal Palace Sta. Penge SE19 23 A2
Crystal Palace Station Rd. Penge SE19 23 A2
Crystal Terr. S Norw SE19 22 D2
Crystal View Ct. Catf BR1 24 D4
Cty Inf Sch. Stain TW18 13 A3
Cubitt St. Croy CR0 60 F5
Cuckfield Cl. Crawl RH11 200 F3
Cuckmere Cres. Crawl RH11 200 F5
Cuckoo La. W End GU24 67 D6
Cuckoo Vale. W End GU24 67 D6
Cuda's Cl. Worc Pk KT19 57 F6
Cuddington Ave. Worc Pk KT19 & KT4 57 F7
Cuddington Cl. Burgh H KT20 97 D7
Cuddington Croft Cty Fst & Mid Sch. E Ewell SM2 58 D2
Cuddington Cty Prim Sch. Worc Pk KT4 57 F7
Cuddington Glade. Epsom KT19 76 A7
Cuddington Golf Course. Belm SM2 77 E7
Cuddington Hospl. Belm SM7 77 F6
Cuddington Way. Belm SM2 & SM7 77 D8
Cudham Dr. New Add CR0 82 C8
Cudham Rd. Tats TN16 103 E8
Cudham St. Lewish SE6 24 C8
Cudworth La. Cudw RH5 179 E8
Cuffs Hill. Worth RH10 202 E2
Culham House. Brack RG12 27 E5
Cull's Rd. Flexf GU3 107 B1
Cullens Mews. Alder GU11 105 A1
Cullerne Cl. Ewell KT17 57 F1
Cullesden Rd. Purley CR8 80 B4
Culmer Hill. Wormly GU8 170 F2
Culmington Rd. S Croy CR2 61 C2
Culmore Cross. Balham SW12 21 B7
Culsac Rd. 1 Surb KT6 56 E8
Culver Dr. Oxted RH8 122 E5
Culver Rd. Sandh GU15 45 D1
Culverden Ct. 5 Oat Pk KT13 53 D7
Culverden Rd. Up Toot SW12 21 C6
Culverden Terr. Oat Pk KT13 53 D7

Culverhay. Ashtd KT21 75 E3
Culverhouse Gdns. Streat SW16 21 F5
Culverlands Cres. Ash GU12 106 A3
Culverley Rd. Catf SE6 24 C7
Culvers Ave. Carsh SM5 & CR4 59 F8
Culvers Retreat. Carsh SM5 59 F8
Culvers Way. Carsh SM5 59 F8
Culverstone Cl. Hayes BR2 44 F4
Culworth House. Guild GU1 130 E8
Cumber House. Wands SW18 20 A7
Cumberland Ave. Stough GU2 & GU3 109 A6
Cumberland Cl. Epsom KT19 57 E1
Cumberland Cl. 2 Twick TW1 6 B1
Cumberland Cl. 6 Wimble SW20 19 D1
Cumberland Ct. 4 Croy CR0 42 D1
Cumberland Dr. Brack RG12 27 E8
Cumberland Dr. Chess KT9 56 F7
Cumberland Dr. Hinch W KT10 56 A8
Cumberland House. King U T KT2 18 B1
Cumberland Lodge. Old W SL4 10 D4
Cumberland Pl. Catf SE6 24 F7
Cumberland Pl. Sunby TW16 35 A5
Cumberland Rd. Ashf TW15 13 D5
Cumberland Rd. Barnes SW13 7 F6
Cumberland Rd. Beck BR2 44 F6
Cumberland Rd. Croy SE25 43 B3
Cumberland Rd. Friml GU15 66 C4
Cumberland Rd. Rich TW9 7 A7
Cumberland St. Egham TW18 12 D3
Cumberlands. Kenley CR8 80 D4
Cumberlow Ave. S Norw SE25 43 A6
Cumbernauld Gdns. Ashf TW16 14 F3
Cumbernauld Wlk. Crawl RH11 200 E2
Cumbrae Gdns. Long D KT6 56 D8
Cumnor Gdns. Stonel KT17 58 A4
Cumnor House Sch. S Croy CR2 61 B2
Cumnor Rd. Sutton SM2 59 C4
Cumnor Rise. Kenley CR8 80 C2
Cumnor Way. Brack RG12 27 E5
Cunliffe Cl. Head KT18 96 B3
Cunliffe Rd. Worc Pk KT19 57 F6
Cunliffe St. Streat SW16 21 C2
Cunningham Ave. Merrow GU1 110 B2
Cunningham Cl. W Wick BR4 63 B8
Cunningham Rd. Woodm SM7 78 D4
Cunnington Rd. Farnb GU14 85 E2
Cunworth Ct. Easth RG12 26 F3
Curfew Bell Rd. Chert KT16 32 F2
Curl Way. Woki RG11 25 A5
Curlew Cl. Selsd CR2 81 D8
Curlew Ct. Tolw KT6 57 A7
Curlew Gdns. Merrow GU4 110 D3
Curley Hill Rd. Lhtwat GU18 66 F7
Curling Cl. Coulsd CR5 100 A7
Curling Vale. Onsl V GU2 130 A7
Curly Bridge Cl. W Heath GU14 84 F8
Curnick's La. W Norw SE27 22 C4
Curran Ave. Hackb SM6 60 A7
Currie Hill Cl. Wimble SW19 19 F4
Currie House. 13 Streat SW12 21 D8
Curteys Wlk. Crawl RH11 201 A3
Curtis Cl. Camb GU15 66 C7
Curtis Field Rd. Streat SW16 22 A4
Curtis Gdns. Dork RH4 136 A8
Curtis Rd. Dork RH4 136 A8
Curtis Rd. Twick TW4 15 F8
Curtis Rd. W Ewell KT19 57 C6
Curtis Rd. W Ewell KT19 57 C6
Curvan Cl. Ewell KT17 57 F1
Curzon Ave. Horsh RH12 217 B3
Curzon Cl. Weyb KT13 53 A6
Curzon Rd. Thorn H CR7 42 A3
Curzon Rd. Weyb KT13 53 A5
Cusack Cl. Tedd TW1 16 F4
Cuthbert Gdns. S Norw SE25 42 E6
Cuthbert Rd. Ash GU12 106 B6
Cuthbert Rd. Thorn H CR0 & CR9 61 B8
Cuttinglye La. Crawl D RH10 184 A1
Cuttinglye Rd. Crawl D RH10 184 C2
Cutts Rd. Farnb GU11 105 D7
Cyclamen Cl. 4 Hampt TW12 16 A2
Cyclamen Way. W Ewell KT19 57 C5
Cyclamen Way. W Ewell KT19 57 C5
Cygnet Ave. Felt TW14 15 D8
Cygnets The. Felt TW13 15 E4
Cypress Ave. Twick TW2 16 C8
Cypress Ct. Sutton SM1 59 A4
Cypress Ct. Thorpe GU25 31 E5
Cypress Ct. 7 W Norw SW16 22 A3
Cypress Gr. Ash V GU12 105 F7
Cypress Inf Sch. S Norw SE25 42 E7
Cypress Jun Sch. S Norw SE25 42 E7
Cypress Lodge. S Norw SE25 42 E7
Cypress Rd. Bellf GU1 109 C4
Cypress Rd. S Norw SE25 42 E7
Cypress Way. Blckw GU17 64 B5
Cypress Way. Graysh GU26 188 D2
Cypress Way. Nork KT17 77 D5
Cypress Wlk. Eng Gn TW20 11 B2
Cyprus Rd. Friml GU16 86 D8

D'abernon Cl. Esher KT10 55 A6
D'Abernon Dr. Stk D'A KT11 73 E3
D'arcy Rd. Cheam SM3 58 D6
Dacre Rd. Thorn H CR0 41 E2
Dacres Rd. For Hil SE23 23 D5
Daffodil Cl. Croy CR0 43 D1
Daffodil Cl. 7 Hampt TW12 16 A2
Daffodil Dr. Bisley GU24 68 A3
Dafforne Rd. Up Toot SW17 21 A5
Dagden Rd. Shalf GU4 130 E3
Dagley La. Shalf GU4 130 D3
Dagmar Rd. 4 King U T KT2 18 A1
Dagmar Rd. S Norw SE25 42 E4
Dagnall Pk. Thorn H CR0 & SE25 42 E4
Dagnall Rd. S Norw SE25 42 E4
Dagnan Rd. Balham SW12 21 C8
Dahlia Gdns. Mitch CR4 41 D5
Dahomey Rd. Streat SW16 21 C2
Daimler Way. Wallin SM6 60 E3
Dainford Cl. Catf BR1 24 D3
Dairy Cl. S Norw CR7 42 C7
Dairy Gate Rd. Farnb GU14 105 B8
Dairyfields. Crawl RH11 201 A5
Dairymans Wlk. Burph GU4 110 B6
Daisy Cl. Croy CR0 43 D1
Dakin Cl. Worth RH10 202 C2
Dakins The. E Grins RH19 205 E8
Dalcross. Brack RG12 27 E3
Dalcross Rd. Hounsl TW4 & TW5 4 E5
Dale Ave. Hounsl TW4 4 E4
Dale Cl. Addl KT15 52 B5
Dale Cl. Horsh RH12 217 F5
Dale Cl. Sunnin SL5 30 A4
Dale Cl. Wreccl GU10 145 F7
Dale Ct. 3 King U T KT2 17 F1
Dale Gdns. Sandh GU17 64 A8
Dale Lodge Rd. Sunnin SL5 30 A4
Dale Park Ave. Carsh SM5 59 F8
Dale Park Rd. S Norw SE19 42 D8
Dale Rd. Ashf TW16 14 F1
Dale Rd. Cheam SM1 58 F6
Dale Rd. For Row RH18 206 F1
Dale Rd. Purley CR8 80 B7
Dale Rd. Walt O T KT12 34 F2
Dale View. Haslem GU27 207 F5
Dale View. Head KT18 96 B4
Dale View. Woking GU21 69 B1
Dalebury Rd. Up Toot SW17 20 F6
Dalegarth Gdns. Sander CR8 80 D6
Daleham Ave. Egham TW20 12 A2
Daleside Rd. Streat SW17 21 B3
Daleside Rd. W Ewell KT19 57 D4
Daleside Rd. W Ewell KT19 57 D4
Dalewood Gdns. Crawl RH10 201 F8
Dalewood Gdns. N Cheam KT4 58 B8
Dalkeith Rd. W Norw SE21 22 C8
Dallas Rd. Cheam SM3 58 E4
Dallas Rd. For Hil SE26 23 B5
Dallaway Gdns. E Grins RH19 185 E1
Dalley Ct. Sandh GU15 64 D7
Dallington Cl. Hersh KT12 54 C4
Dalmain Prim Sch. For Hil SE23 23 E7
Dalmain Rd. For Hil SE23 23 D7
Dalmally Rd. Croy CR0 43 A2
Dalmeny Ave. Thorn H SW16 42 A7
Dalmeny Cres. Islew TW3 5 D3
Dalmeny Rd. N Cheam KT4 58 B7
Dalmeny Rd. Wallin SM5 60 A3
Dalmore Ave. Clayg KT10 55 F4
Dalmore Rd. W Norw SE21 22 C6
Dalston Cl. Friml GU15 66 D3
Dalton Ave. Mitch CR4 40 E7
Dalton Cl. Crawl RH11 201 B1
Dalton House. 7 Balham SW12 21 B8
Dalton St. W Norw SE27 22 B5
Damascene Wlk. W Norw SE21 22 C7
Damask Cl. W End GU24 67 E6
Damer House. 9 Rich TW10 6 F1
Dampier Wlk. Crawl RH11 201 B1
Dan Bryant House. 5 Streat SW12 21 C8
Danbrook Rd. Streat SW16 21 E1
Danbury Mews. Wallin SM5 & SM6 60 B6
Dancer Rd. Rich TW9 7 A4
Dane Ct. Pyrf GU22 70 F4
Dane Rd. Ashf TW15 14 D2
Dane Rd. Merton SW19 40 C8
Dane Rd. Warlgm CR6 81 D2
Danebury. New Add CR0 63 B4
Danebury Prim Sch. Rhampt SW15 18 F8
Danebury Wlk. Friml GU16 85 F8
Daneby Rd. Catf SE6 24 C6
Danecourt Gdns. S Croy CR0 61 F7
Danehurst. Brent TW8 6 C7
Danehurst Cres. Horsh RH13 217 F2
Danehurst Ct. Ewell KT17 76 F6
Danemore La. Blind H RH9 142 E2
Danes Cl. Oxsh KT22 74 C5
Danes Hill. Mayb GU22 70 B1
Danes Hill Jun Sch. Oxsh KT22 74 C6
Danes Hill Sch. Oxsh KT22 74 D6
Danes Way. Oxsh KT22 74 D5
Danesbury Rd. Felt TW13 15 B7
Danescourt Cres. Sutton SM1 59 C8
Danesfield Sch. Walt O T KT12 54 C8
Daneshill. Redh RH1 118 E2
Daneshill Cl. Redh RH1 118 E2
Danesmead. Cobham KT11 74 A8
Danesrood. Guild GU1 130 F8
Daneswood Ave. Catf SE6 24 C5
Daneswood Cl. Weyb KT13 53 C5
Danetree Cl. W Ewell KT19 57 C3
Danetree Cl. W Ewell KT19 57 C3
Danetree Cty Mid Sch. W Ewell KT19 57 C4
Danetree Cty Mid Sch. W Ewell KT19 57 C4
Danetree Rd. W Ewell KT19 57 D3
Danetree Rd. W Ewell KT19 57 D3
Daniel Cl. Mitch SW17 & SW19 20 E2
Daniel Ct. 3 Beck BR3 24 A1
Daniel Way. Banstd SM7 78 B5
Daniell Way. Croy CR0 & CR9 41 F1
Daniels La. Warlgm CR6 81 F4
Danley La. Linch GU27 207 A3
Danses Cl. Merrow GU4 110 D3
Dapdune Ct. Guild GU1 109 C1
Dapdune Rd. Guild GU1 109 D1
Daphne Ct. Worc Pk KT4 57 E8
Daphne St. Wands SW18 20 C8
Darby Cl. Cater CR3 100 C5
Darby Cres. Sunby TW16 35 C7
Darby Gdns. Sunby TW16 35 C7
Darby Green La. Blckw GU17 64 B6
Darby Green Rd. Blckw GU17 64 B5
Darcy Ave. Wallin SM6 60 C6
Darcy Cl. Coulsd CR5 100 B8
Darcy Pl. Ashtd KT21 75 F2
Darcy Rd. Ashtd KT21 75 F2
Darcy Rd. Thorn H SW16 41 E7
Darell Prim Sch. Rich TW9 7 A4
Darell Rd. Rich TW9 7 A4
Darent House. Catf BR1 24 D3
Darenth Way. Horley RH6 160 F6
Darfield Rd. Burph GU1 110 A4
Dargate Cl. Penge SE19 22 F1
Dark La. Putt GU3 128 B4
Darlaston Rd. Wimble SW19 19 E1
Darley Cl. Addl KT15 52 C5
Darley Cl. Croy CR0 43 E3
Darley Dene Ct. Addl KT15 52 C6
Darley Dene Inf Sch. Addl KT15 52 C5
Darley Dr. King U T KT3 38 D7
Darley Gdns. Morden SM4 40 B3
Darleydale. Crawl RH11 201 C3
Darleydale Cl. Sandh GU15 45 D2
Darlington Ct. Catf SE6 24 F7
Darlington House. 2 Surb KT6 37 D2
Darlington Rd.W Norw SE27 22 B3
Darmaine Cl. S Croy CR2 61 C3
Darnley Pk. Weyb KT13 53 B7
Darracott Cl. Camb GU15 66 B8
Darrell Ct. Beck BR2 44 E6
Dart Cl. Bra Hil SL3 1 B8
Dart Ct. E Grins RH19 186 A3
Dart Rd. W Heath GU14 84 D6
Dartmouth Ave. Sheer GU21 70 D5
Dartmouth Cl. Brack RG12 27 E6
Dartmouth Gn. Sheer GU21 70 D5
Dartmouth House. Thorn H CR0 42 B2
Dartmouth Path. Sheer GU21 70 D5
Dartmouth Pl. Chisw W4 7 E8
Dartmouth Pl. For Hil SE23 23 C6
Dartmouth Rd. For Hil SE23 & SE26 23 C5
Dartnell Ave. W Byfl KT14 71 C7
Dartnell Cl. W Byfl KT14 71 B7
Dartnell Cres. W Byfl KT14 71 B7
Dartnell Ct. W Byfl KT14 71 C7
Dartnell Park Rd. W Byfl KT14 71 C8
Dartnell Pl. W Byfl KT14 71 B7
Dartnell Rd. Croy CR0 42 F2
Darvel Cl. Woking GU21 69 A3
Darvills La. Farnh GU9 125 C2
Darwall Dr. N Asct SL5 28 D7
Darwin Cl. Horsh RH12 217 F4
Darwin Gr. Alder GU11 105 C3
Daryngton Dr. Merrow GU1 110 B1
Dashwood Cl. Brack RG12 27 D8
Dashwood Cl. W Byfl KT14 71 C7
Dashwood Ct. Hounsl TW3 5 C3
Dashwood House. Dulw SE21 22 F5
Dassett Rd. W Norw SE27 22 B3
Datchet Rd. For Hil SE6 23 F6
Datchet Rd. Horton SL3 1 A4
Daux Hill. Warn RH12 217 B6
Davenant Rd. Croy CR0 & CR9 61 B6
Davenport Cl. Tedd TW11 17 A2
Davenport Lodge. Heston TW5 4 E7
Davenport Rd. Brack RG12 27 E8
Daventry Cl. Poyle SL3 1 F6
Daventry Ct. Brack RG12 27 B8
David Cl. Harl UB3 3 E7
David House. S Norw SE25 43 A6
David Livingstone Prim Sch. S Norw CR7 42 C8
David Rd. Poyle SL3 1 F5
David's Rd. For Hil SE23 23 C7
Davidson Inf Sch. Croy CR0 42 F2
Davidson Jun Sch. Croy CR0 42 F2
Davidson Lodge. Croy CR0 42 E2
Davidson Rd. Croy CR0 & SE25 42 F3
Davies Cl. Croy CR0 & SE25 43 A3
Davies Cl. Farnc GU7 150 D7
Davis Cl. Crawl RH11 201 A1
Davis Gdns. Sandh GU15 64 E7
Davis Rd. Chess KT9 57 A6
Davis Rd. Whit V KT13 52 F1
Davos Cl. Woking GU22 89 E8
Davy Cl. Woki RG11 25 C5
Dawell Dr. Bigg H TN16 83 C2
Dawes Ave. Islew TW7 6 A3
Dawes Ct. Esher KT10 55 B6
Dawes Green Cotts. Leigh RH2 138 A3
Dawley Ride. Poyle SL3 1 E6
Dawlish Ave. Wimble SW18 20 B6
Dawn Cl. Hounsl TW4 4 E4
Dawn Redwood Cl. Horton SL3 1 A4
Dawn Wlk. Beck BR2 44 D7
Dawnay Cl. N Asct SL5 28 F8
Dawnay Gdns. Wands SW18 20 D6
Dawnay Rd. Camb GU15 65 B7
Dawnay Rd. G Book KT23 94 C1
Dawnay Rd. Wands SW17 & SW18 20 D6
Dawney Hill. Pirb GU24 87 F5
Dawneys Rd. Pirb GU24 87 E5
Dawsmere Cl. Friml GU15 66 C5
Dawson Rd. Byfl KT14 71 E8
Dawson Rd. King U T KT1 37 F6
Dax Ct. Sunby TW16 35 C6
Day Ct. Crawl GU6 173 F2
Day's Acre. S Croy CR2 61 F1
Daybrook Rd. Merton SW19 40 B6
Daymerslea Ridge. Leahd KT22 95 C6
Daysbrook Rd. Streat SW2 21 F7
Dayseys Hill. Outw RH1 162 A8
Dayspring. Stough GU2 109 B5
Daytone House. Wimble SW20 39 D8
De Broome Rd. Felt TW13 15 C7
De Burgh House. 10 Merton SW19 20 C1
De Burgh Pk. Banstd SM7 78 B4
De Frene Rd. For Hil SE23 & SE26 23 E5
De Havilland Dr. Byfl KT13 52 E1
De Havilland Dr. Byfl KT13 71 E8
De Havilland Rd. Heston TW5 4 C7
De Havilland Rd. Wallin SM6 60 E3
De Havilland Way. Stan TW19 2 E1
De La Warr Rd. E Grins RH19 185 F1
De Lara Way. Woking GU21 69 D1
De Montfort Par. 1 Streat SW16 21 E5
De Montfort Rd.Streat SW16 21 E6
De Nederlandse Basis Sch. Mayb GU22 70 C2
De Ros Pl. Egham TW20 12 A2
De Stafford Sch.Whytlf CR3 100 F6
De'arn Gdns. Mitch CR4 40 E6
De-Vitre Gn. Woki RG11 25 F7
Deacon Cl. Downs KT11 93 B8
Deacon Cl. Wallin CR8 60 E2
Deacon Cl. Woki RG11 25 C8
Deacon Ct. Lingf RH7 164 C4
Deacon Field. Stough GU2 109 A2
Deacon Rd. King U T KT2 37 F8
Deacons Wlk. Hampt TW12 16 A4
Deadbrook La. Alder GU12 105 E3
Deal Rd. Mitch SW17 21 A2
Dean Cl. Pyrf GU22 70 E3
Dean Ct. Farnc GU7 150 D6
Dean Ct. 10 King U T KT2 18 A1
Dean Gr. Woki RG11 25 C7
Dean La. Hooley CR3 & CR5 & RH1 99 D3
Dean Par. Camb GU15 65 F8
Dean Rd. Croy CR0 61 D6
Dean Rd. Farnc GU7 150 D6
Dean Rd. Hampt TW12 16 A3
Dean Rd. Hampt TW12 16 A4
Dean Rd. Islew TW3 5 B2
Dean Wlk. G Book KT23 94 B1
Deanery Pl. Godal GU7 150 D4
Deanery Rd. Farnc GU7 150 E6
Deanfield Gdns. Croy CR0 61 D6
Deanhill Ct. Mortl SW14 7 B3
Deanhill Rd. Mortl SW14 7 B3
Deanoak La. Leigh RH2 159 D8
Deanoak La. Sidlow RH2 159 D8
Deans Cl. Chisw W4 7 B8
Deans Cl. S Croy CR0 61 F7
Deans Cl. Walt o t H KT20 97 B3
Deans Ct. Windl GU20 48 D4
Deans Gate Cl. For Hil SE23 23 D5
Deans La. Nutf RH1 120 A2
Deans La. Walt o t H KT20 97 B2
Deans Rd. Merst RH1 119 C5
Deans Rd. Sutton SM1 59 B7
Deans Wlk. Coulsd CR5 80 A1
Deansfield. Cater CR3 100 F2
Deansgate. Easth RG12 27 B2
Dearmer House. 6 Streat SW2 22 A8
Debden Cl. King U T KT2 17 D3
Deborah Cl. Hounsl TW7 5 E6
Deburgh Rd. Merton SW19 20 C1
Dedham House. Catf SE6 24 C4
Dedisham Cl. Crawl RH10 202 A5
Dedisham Sch. Slinfd RH12 215 C6
Dedswell Dr. W Clan GU4 111 A6
Dee Rd. Rich TW9 6 F3
Dee Way. Epsom KT19 57 E1
Deedman Cl. Ash GU12 106 A2
Deep Dene. Shottm GU27 207 E6
Deep Well Dr. Camb GU15 65 E5
Deepcut Bridge Rd. Friml GU16 86 C7
Deepdale. Easth RG12 27 A5
Deepdale. Wimble SW19 19 D4
Deepdale Ave. Hayes BR2 44 F5
Deepdene. M Bourn GU10 146 D7
Deepdene Ave. Dork RH4 & RH5 136 C6
Deepdene Ave. S Croy CR0 61 F7
Deepdene Avenue Rd. Dork RH4 115 C1
Deepdene Ct. Beck BR2 44 E6
Deepdene Dr. Dork RH5 136 C7
Deepdene Gdns. Dork RH4 & RH5 136 C8

Deepdene Gdns. Streat SW2 ... 21 F8
Deepdene Lodge. **8**
  Streat SW2 .... 21 F8
Deepdene Park Rd.
  For HIE SE26 .... 23 D5
Deepdene Point. **9**
  Dork RH5 .... 136 D8
Deepdene Sta. Dork RH4 ... 115 C1
Deepdene Wlk. Dork RH4 . 115 C1
Deepdene Wood.
  Dork RH5 .... 136 D7
Deepfield Rd. Brack RG12 ... 27 D7
Deepfield Way. Coulsd CR5 . 79 E3
Deepfields. Horley RH6 ... 160 F5
Deepwell Cl. Islew TW7 .... 6 A6
Deer Leap. Lthwd GU18 ...... 67 A8
Deer Park Cl. King U T KT2 ... 18 B1
Deer Park Gdns. Mitch CR4 . 40 D5
Deer Park Rd. Merton SW19 40 C7
Deer Park Way. Coney H BR4 63 F8
Deer Rock Hill. Easth RG12 . 27 C3
Deer Rock Rd. Camb GU15 ... 65 F8
Deerbarn Rd. Stough GU2 . 109 B2
Deerbrook Rd.
  Streat SE24 & SW2 .... 22 B7
Deerhurst. King U T KT2 ...... 38 B8
Deerhurst Cl. Felt TW13 ... 15 B4
Deerhurst Rd. Streat SW16 . 21 F3
Deerings Rd. Reig RH2 ...... 118 C1
Deerleap Rd. Westc RH4 ... 135 B6
Deers Farm.
  Wisley GU23 & KT14 .... 71 E3
Deerswood Cl. Cater CR3 . 101 A3
Deerswood Cl. Crawl RH11 201 B7
Deerswood Ct. Crawl RH11 201 B7
Deerswood Lower Sch.
  Crawl RH11 .... 201 A8
Deerswood Rd.
  Crawl RH11 .... 201 B7
Deerswood Upper Sch.
  Crawl RH11 .... 201 A8
Deeside Rd. Wands SW17 ... 20 D5
Defiant Rd. Farnb GU14 ... 104 F8
Defiant Way. Wallin SM6 ...... 60 E3
Defoe Ave. Rich TW9 .... 7 A7
Defoe Cl.
  Mitch SW17 & SW19 .... 20 E2
Delabole Rd. Merst RH1 ... 119 C6
Delamare Cres. Croy CR0 ... 43 C3
Delamere Rd. Dovgn RH2 . 139 C5
Delamere Rd. Wimble SW20 39 D8
Delaporte Cl. Ewell KT17 ... 76 E7
Delcombe Ave.
  N Cheam KT4 .... 39 C1
Delderfield. Ashtd KT21 ...... 95 D6
Delia St. Wands SW18 .... 20 B8
Dell Cl. Fetch KT22 .... 94 E4
Dell Cl. Mickle RH5 .... 115 C8
Dell Cl. Shotth GU27 .... 208 A7
Dell Cl. Wallin SM6 .... 60 D6
Dell Close Cotts.
  Mickle RH5 .... 115 C8
Dell Gr. Friml GU16 .... 65 F2
Dell House. S Croy CR2 ...... 61 C2
Dell La. Stonel KT17 .... 58 A5
Dell Rd. Stonel KT17 .... 58 A4
Dell The. Brent TW8 .... 6 C8
Dell The. Burgh H KT20 ...... 97 C6
Dell The. E Grins RH19 ..... 186 B1
Dell The. Eng Gn SL4 .... 11 A5
Dell The. Felt TW14 .... 15 B8
Dell The. Heath E GU9 ..... 125 D7
Dell The. Horley RH6 .... 161 B4
Dell The. Reig RH2 .... 118 C2
Dell The. S Norw SE19 .... 42 F8
Dell The. Sidlow RH6 .... 160 D5
Dell The. Woking GU21 .... 69 C1
Dell Wlk. King U T KT3 .... 38 E7
Dellbow Rd. Felt TW14 .... 4 B2
Dellfield Cl. Beck BR3 .... 44 C8
Delmey Cl. S Croy CR0 .... 61 F7
Delphian Ct. **5** Streat SW16 22 A4
Delta Bglws. Horley RH6 ... 161 A1
Delta Cl. Chobb GU24 .... 49 F1
Delta Cl. Worc Pk KT4 .... 57 E7
Delta Dr. Horley RH6 .... 161 A1
Delta House. Horley RH6 ... 161 A1
Delta Rd. Chobb GU24 .... 49 F1
Delta Rd. Woking GU21 .... 70 A3
Delta Rd.
  Worc Pk KT19 & KT4 .... 57 E7
Delta Way. Thorpe TW20 ... 32 C4
Delves. Tadw KT20 .... 97 D5
Delville Cl. Farnb GU14 ...... 84 D3
Demesne Rd. Wallin SM6 ... 60 E6
Dempster Cl. Long D KT6 ... 37 C1
Den Cl. Beck BR2 & BR3 ...... 44 D6
Den Rd. Beck BR2 .... 44 D6

Denbigh Cl. Cheam SM1 ...... 58 F5
Denbigh Gdns. Rich TW10 ... 6 F2
Denbigh Rd. Haslem GU27 208 D5
Denbigh Rd. Hounsl TW3 ...... 5 B5
Denby Rd. Cobham KT11 ... 73 C7
Denchers Plat. Crawl RH11 181 D1
Dencliffe. Ashf TW15 .... 14 A3
Dendy St. Balham SW12 .... 21 A7
Dene Ave. Hounsl TW3 .... 4 F4
Dene Cl. **2** Brack RG12 ...... 27 C8
Dene Cl. Haslem GU27 ...... 208 C6
Dene Cl. Hayes BR2 .... 44 F1
Dene Cl. Horley RH6 .... 160 F5
Dene Cl. Worc Pk KT4 .... 57 F8
Dene Ct. Merrow GU1 .... 110 B3
Dene Gdns. Hinch W KT7 ... 56 A8
Dene La. M Bourn GU10 ... 146 E6
Dene La. W Bourn GU10 ... 146 E6
Dene Pl. Woking GU21 .... 69 C1
Dene Rd. Ashtd KT21 .... 95 F8
Dene Rd. Farnb GU14 .... 84 F3
Dene Rd. Guild GU1 .... 130 E8
Dene St. Dork RH4 .... 136 B7
Dene Street Gdns.
  Dork RH4 .... 136 C5
Dene The. Abing H RH5 .... 134 B3
Dene The. Belm SM2 .... 77 F8
Dene The.
  E Mole KT12 & KT8 .... 35 F4
Dene The. S Croy CR0 .... 62 D6
Dene Tye. Crawl RH10 ...... 202 D7
Dene Wlk. M Bourn GU10 ... 146 E6
Denefield Dr. Kenley CR8 ... 80 D4
Denehurst Gdns. Mortl TW10 7 A3
Denehurst Gdns. Twick SW2 16 D8
Denehyrst Ct. Guild GU1 ... 130 E8
Denewood. **8** Epsom KT17 . 76 E6
Denfield. Dork RH4 .... 136 C5
Denham Cres. Mitch CR4 ... 40 F5
Denham Ct. For Hil SE26 ... 23 B5
Denham Gr. Easth RG12 ... 27 C2
Denham Rd. Egham TW20 ... 12 A4
Denham Rd. Ewell KT17 ...... 76 F7
Denham Rd. Felt TW14 ...... 15 C8
Denholm Gdns.
  Burph GU1 & GU4 .... 110 A4
Denison Rd. Felt TW13 ...... 14 F4
Denison Rd. Mitch SW19 ... 20 D2
Denleigh Gdns.
  Thame D KT7 .... 36 E3
Denly Way. Lhtwat GU18 ... 48 C1
Denman Dr. Ashf TW15 ...... 14 B2
Denman Dr. Clayg KT10 ...... 56 A5
Denmans. Crawl RH10 ...... 202 D7
Denmark Ave. Wimble SW19 19 E1
Denmark Ct. Morden SM4 ... 40 A4
Denmark Cl. **2** Weyb KT13 53 B7
Denmark Gdns. Cars SM5 ... 59 F7
Denmark Rd. Croy SE25 ...... 43 B4
Denmark Rd. Guild GU1 ... 130 E8
Denmark Rd. King U T KT1 ... 37 E6
Denmark Rd. Twick TW2 ... 16 D5
Denmark Rd. Wimble SW19 .19 D2
Denmark St. Alder GU12 ... 105 E2
Denmark St. Alder GU12 ... 105 D2
Denmark St. Woki RG11 .... 25 C5
Denmead Ct. Brack RG12 ... 27 E3
Denmead House.
  Rhampt SW15 .... 7 F1
Denmead Lower Sch.
  Hampt TW12 .... 16 B1
Denmead Rd. Thorn H CR0 . 42 B1
Denmead Upper Sch.
  Hampt TW12 .... 16 B1
Denmore Ct. Wallin SM6 ... 60 B5
Dennan Rd. Surb KT6 .... 37 F1
Denne Par.
  Horsh RH12 & RH13 .... 217 C1
Denne Rd. Crawl RH11 ...... 201 D5
Denne Rd. Horsh RH12 ...... 217 C1
Dennett Rd. Thorn H CR0 ... 42 A2
Denning Ave. Croy CR0 ...... 61 A5
Denning Cl. Hampt TW12 ... 15 F3
Denningtons The.
  Worc Pk KT4 .... 57 E8
Dennis Cl. Ashf TW15 .... 14 D1
Dennis Cl. Redh RH1 .... 118 E3
Dennis House. Sutton SM1 .. 59 A6
Dennis Pk Cres.WimbleSW20 39 E8
Dennis Rd. E Mole KT8 ...... 36 C5
Dennis Reeve Cl. Mitch CR4 40 F8
Dennis Track. Farnb GU14 . 104 C7
Dennis Way. Jacobs GU1 ... 109 E6
Dennistoun Cl. Camb GU15 . 65 D5
Densole Cl. Penge BR3 .... 43 E8
Denton Cl. Earls RH1 .... 140 A4
Denton Gr. Walt D T KT12 ... 54 E8
Denton Rd. Twick TW1 .... 6 D1
Denton Way. Woki RG11 ..... 25 C6

Denton Way. Friml GU16 ..... 65 D2
Denton Way. Woking GU21 . 69 A2
Dents Gr. L Kings KT20 .... 117 F7
Denvale Wlk. Woking GU21 . 69 A1
Denwood. For Hil SE23 ...... 23 D5
Denzil Rd. Guild GU2 .... 130 B8
Departures Rd. Crawl RH6 . 181 F8
Depot Rd. Crawl RH11 ...... 181 D1
Depot Rd. Epsom KT17 ...... 76 E6
Depot Rd. Horsh RH13 ...... 217 E2
Depot Rd. Hounsl TW3 & TW7 5 D4
Derby Arms Rd. Epsom KT18 76 F2
Derby Cl.
  Burgh H KT18 & KT20 .... 97 B8
Derby Hill. For Hil SE23 ...... 23 C6
Derby Hill Cres. For Hil SE23 23 C6
Derby Rd. Cheam SM1 & SM2 58 F4
Derby Rd. Haslem GU27 ... 208 B7
Derby Rd. Hounsl TW3 .... 5 B3
Derby Rd. Mortl SW14 .... 7 B3
Derby Rd. Stough GU2 ...... 108 F1
Derby Rd. Surb KT5 & KT6 ... 38 A1
Derby Rd. Thorn H CR0 ...... 42 B1
Derby Stables Rd.
  Epsom KT18 .... 76 F2
Derek Ave. Hackb SM6 .... 60 B6
Derek Ave. W Ewell KT19 ... 57 B5
Derek Ave. W Ewell KT19 ... 57 B5
Derek Cl. W Ewell KT19 ...... 57 B5
Derek Cl. W Ewell KT19 ...... 57 B5
Derek Horn Ct. Camb GU15 . 65 B6
Deri Denc Cl. **2** Stan TW19 ... 2 E1
Dering Pl. Croy CR0 .... 61 C6
Dering Rd. Croy CR0 & CR9 . 61 C6
Derinton Rd. Up Toot SW17 . 21 A4
Deronda Rd.
  Streat SE24 & SW2 .... 22 B7
Deroy Cl. Wallin SM5 .... 59 F4
Deroy Ct. Wallin SM5 .... 59 F4
Derrick Ave. S Croy CR2 ..... 61 C1
Derrick House. **13**
  Streat SW2 .... 22 A7
Derrick Rd. Beck BR3 .... 43 F5
Derry Rd. W Heath GU14 ..... 84 F8
Derry Rd. Wallin CR0 & SM6 . 60 E7
Derrydown. Woking GU22 ... 89 C6
Derwent Ave. Ash V GU12 . 105 F4
Derwent Ave. King U T SW15 18 E4
Derwent Cl. Addl KT15 .... 52 D5
Derwent Cl. Clayg KT10 ...... 55 F5
Derwent Cl. Crawl RH11 ... 200 F5
Derwent Cl. E Bed TW14 ... 14 F7
Derwent Cl. Farnb GU14 ..... 84 E4
Derwent Cl. Hale GU9 .... 125 A6
Derwent Cl. Horsh RH12 ... 218 B6
Derwent Dr. Sander CR8 ..... 80 E6
Derwent House. Penge SE20 43 B7
Derwent House.
  Woodh RH2 .... 139 A7
Derwent Lodge.
  N Cheam KT4 .... 57 E8
Derwent Rd. Lhtwat GU18 ... 67 B8
Derwent Rd. Penge SE20 ... 43 B7
Derwent Rd. Thor L TW20 ... 12 B1
Derwent Rd. Twick TW2 ...... 5 E1
Derwent Rd. W Barn SM4 ... 39 D3
Derwent Wlk. Wallin SM6 ... 60 B3
Desborough Cl.
  Lo Hall TW17 .... 34 A2
Desborough Ct. Croy SE25 . 43 B5
Desford Way. Ashf TW15 ... 13 F6
Desmond Anderson Cty Fst Sch.
  Crawl RH10 .... 201 E2
Desmond Anderson Cty Mid Sch.
  Crawl RH10 .... 201 E2
Despard House. Streat SW2 22 A6
Detherick Ct. Hounsl TW3 ... 5 A2
Detillens La. Limps RH8 ... 123 A6
Detling Rd. Crawl RH11 ... 201 C1
Dettingen Rd. Friml GU16 ... 86 C8
Deutsche Schule. Rich TW10 17 D7
Devana End. Carsh SM5 ...... 59 F7
Devas Rd. Wimble SW20 .... 39 C8
Devenish La.
  Sunnin GU20 & SL5 .... 29 D1
Devenish Rd.
  Ascot GU20 & SL5 .... 29 D2
Devenish Rd.
  Sunnin GU20 & SL5 .... 29 D2
Deverill Ct. Penge SE20 ...... 43 D8
Devil's La. Egham TW20 ...... 12 C2
Devitt Cl. Ashtd KT21 .... 76 A3
Devoil Cl. Burph GU4 .... 110 B5
Devoke Way. Walt D T KT12 54 D8
Devon Ave. Twick TW2 .... 16 C7
Devon Bank. Guild GU2 ... 130 C6
Devon Cl. Kenley CR8 .... 80 E3
Devon Cl. Sandh GU15 .... 64 D7
Devon Cres.
  Reig RH1 & RH2 .... 118 D1

Devon House. Cater CR3 ... 100 F3
Devon House. Knaph GU21 . 68 D2
Devon Ct. **6** Hampt GU1 ... 109 F4
Devon Rd. Belm SM2 .... 58 E2
Devon Rd.
  Farnb GU11 & GU14 .... 104 F7
Devon Rd. Hersh KT12 .... 54 C6
Devon Rd. Merst RH1 .... 119 C5
Devon Way. Chess KT9 .... 56 C6
Devon Way. W Ewell KT19 ... 57 B5
Devon Way. W Ewell KT19 ... 57 B5
Devoncroft Gdns.
  Twick TW1 .... 17 A8
Devonhurst Pl.
  Sheer GU21 .... 70 D6
Devonshire Ave. Sutton SM2 59 C3
Devonshire Ct. Croy CR0 ... 44 A1
Devonshire Ct. **6** Rich TW9 . 6 E6
Devonshire Dr. Camb GU15 . 65 F7
Devonshire Dr. Camb GU1 ... 65 F7
Devonshire Dr. Long D KT6 . 56 D8
Devonshire Gdns. Chisw W4 . 7 C7
Devonshire House. **14**
  Balham SW12 .... 21 B8
Devonshire House.
  Hounsl TW3 .... 5 C4
Devonshire Pl. Alder GU11 104 F1
Devonshire Prim Sch.
  Sutton SM2 .... 59 C3
Devonshire Rd. Chisw W4 ... 7 C8
Devonshire Rd. Felt TW13 ... 15 E4
Devonshire Rd. For Hil SE23 23 C8
Devonshire Rd.
  Hackb SM5 & SM6 .... 60 A6
Devonshire Rd.
  Horsh RH13 .... 217 D2
Devonshire Rd.
  Mitch SW17 & SW19 .... 20 E1
Devonshire Rd. Sutton SM2 . 59 C3
Devonshire Rd. Thorn H CR0 42 D2
Devonshire Rd. Weyb KT13 . 53 A6
Devonshire Way.
  Croy CR0 & CR9 .... 62 F8
Devonshires The.
  Epsom KT18 .... 76 F5
Dewar Cl. Crawl RH11 ...... 200 E5
Dewar House. Up Toot SW17 20 E3
Dewey St. Up Toot SW17 ... 20 F3
Dewlands. Tyl Gn RH9 ...... 121 C4
Dewlands Cl. Cran GU6 ..... 174 E3
Dewlands La. Cran GU6 .... 174 E3
Dewsbury Gdns.
  Worc Pk KT4 .... 58 A7
Dexter Dr. E Grins RH19 ... 205 E8
Diamedes Ave. Stan TW19 ... 13 D7
Diamond Cl. **4** Redh RH1 . 119 A2
Diamond Est. Up Toot SW17 20 E5
Diamond Hill. Camb GU15 ... 65 E7
Diamond Ridge. Camb GU15 65 E7
Diamond Way. Farnb GU14 104 E8
Diana Gdns. Surb KT6 .... 56 F8
Dianthus Cl. Chert KT16 ..... 32 E2
Dianthus Ct. Woking GU22 ... 69 D1
Dianthus Pl. Wink RG12 ...... 8 B2
Dibdin Cl. Sutton SM1 .... 59 A7
Dibdin Rd. Sutton SM1 ...... 59 A8
Diceland Rd. Banstd SM7 ... 77 F3
Dick Sheppard Sch.
  Streat SE24 .... 22 A8
Dick Turpin Way.
  Hatton TW14 .... 3 F3
Dickens Cl. E Grins RH19 ... 185 C1
Dickens Cl. Rich TW10 ...... 17 C6
Dickens Dr. Row Tn KT15 ... 51 F4
Dickens Rd. Crawl RH10 ... 201 E3
Dickenson's La. Croy SE25 . 43 A3
Dickenson's Pl. Croy SE25 . 43 A3
Dickerage Hill. King U T KT3 38 C6
Dickerage La. King U T KT3 . 38 C6
Dickerage Rd.
  King U T KT1 & KT2 & KT3 ... 38 D7
Dickins Way. Horsh RH13 ... 217 F1
Dickinson Rd. Felt TW13 ... 15 D3
Digby Pl. S Croy CR0 .... 61 F7
Digby Way. Byfl KT14 .... 71 F7
Digdens Rise. Woodc KT18 . 76 C4
Dillwyn Cl. For Hil SE26 ... 23 E4
Dilston Rd. Leahd KT22 ...... 95 A8
Dilton Gdns. Rhampt SW15 . 19 B7
Dingle Rd. Ashf TW15 .... 14 B3
Dingle The. Crawl RH11 ... 201 B6
Dingley La. Streat SW16 ... 21 D6
Dingley Way. Farnb GU14 . 104 F8
Dingwall Ave.
  Croy CR0 & CR9 .... 61 C8
Dingwall Rd.
  Croy CR0 & CR9 .... 61 D8

Dingwall Rd. Wallin SM5 ..... 59 F2
Dingwall Rd. Wands SW18 . 20 C8
Dinsdale Cl. Woking GU22 ... 70 A1
Dinsdale Gdns. S Norw SE25 42 E4
Dinsmore Rd. Balham SW12 21 B8
Dinton Rd. King U T KT2 ..... 17 F1
Dinton Rd.
  Mitch SW17 & SW19 .... 20 D2
Dione Wlk. Crawl RH11 ... 200 E4
Dippenhall Rd. Farnh GU10 124 C2
Dippenhall St. Crond GU10 124 A5
Dirdene Cl. Ewell KT17 .... 76 F7
Dirdene Gdns. Ewell KT17 ... 76 F7
Dirdene Gr. Ewell KT17 .... 76 F7
Dirtham La. Effing KT24 ... 113 B6
Dirty La. Ash W RH19 ...... 206 E7
Discovery Pk. Crawl RH10 182 A2
Disraeli Ct. Bra Hil SL3 .... 1 B8
Distillery Wlk. **14** Brent TW8 . 6 E8
Ditches La.
  Coulsd CR3 & CR5 .... 99 E6
Ditchling. Easth RG12 .... 27 A2
Ditchling Hill. Crawl RH11 . 201 C4
Ditton Cl. Thame D KT7 ...... 37 A2
Ditton Grange Cl.
  Long D KT6 .... 37 D1
Ditton Grange Dr.
  Long D KT6 .... 37 D1
Ditton Hill. Long D KT6 .... 56 D8
Ditton Hill Rd. Long D KT6 . 37 C1
Ditton Lawn. Thame D KT7 . 37 A1
Ditton Pl. **7** Penge SE20 ... 43 B8
Ditton Rd. Surb KT6 .... 37 E1
Ditton Reach. Thame D KT7 . 37 B3
Dixon Dr. Whit V KT13 .... 52 F1
Dixon Pl. W Wick BR4 .... 44 B1
Dixon Rd. S Norw SE25 ...... 42 F6
Dobbins Pl. Crawl RH11 ... 200 E5
Doble Ct. Sander CR2 .... 81 A8
Dobson Rd. Crawl RH11 ... 181 D1
Dock Rd. Brent TW8 .... 6 D7
Dock Rd. Farnb GU14 .... 85 B2
Dockenfield St. Binst GU10 166 C6
Dockett Eddy La.
  Lo Hall TW17 .... 33 F1
Docketts Mews.
  Chert KT16 .... 33 F1
Dockwell Cl. Hatton TW14 ... 4 A3
Dockwell's Ind Est.
  Felt TW14 .... 4 C2
Doctors Cl. For Hil SE26 ... 23 C3
Doctors La. Cater CR3 ..... 100 A3
Dodbrooke Rd.
  W Norw SE27 .... 22 B5
Dodd's La. W Byfl KT14 ...... 71 A5
Dodds Cres. W Byfl KT14 ... 71 A5
Dodds Pk. Brock RH3 .... 137 B7
Doel Cl. Merton SW19 .... 20 C1
Dogflud Way. Farnh GU9 ... 125 C3
Doggett Rd. Catf SE6 .... 24 A8
Doggett Rd. Lewish SE6 ..... 24 A8
Doghurst Ave. Harl UB7 .... 3 B7
Doghurst Dr. Harl UB7 .... 3 B7
Doghurst La. Chips CR5 ..... 98 F7
Doland Cl. Up Toot SW17 ... 20 F2
Dolby Terr. Chart RH6 ...... 180 E6
Dollis Cl. Worth RH10 ...... 202 C5
Dollis Dr. Farnh GU9 .... 125 D3
Dolphin Cl. King U T KT6 ... 37 D4
Dolphin Cl. Shotth GU27 ... 207 E6
Dolphin Ct. Merton SW19 ... 20 A1
Dolphin Ct. Stan TW19 .... 13 A5
Dolphin Ct. **2** Wallin SM6 ... 60 B4
Dolphin Ct N. Stan TW19 ... 13 A5
Dolphin Rd. Charlt TW16 ... 34 E8
Dolphin Rd N. Charlt TW16 . 34 E8
Dolphin Rd S. Charlt TW16 . 34 E8
Dolphin Rd W. Charlt TW16 . 34 E8
Dolphin Sq. Chisw W4 .... 7 E7
Dolphin St. King U T KT2 ... 37 E8
Doman Rd. Camb GU15 ...... 65 A4
Dome Hill. Cater CR3 .... 120 E8
Dome Hill Peak. Cater CR3 100 E1
Dome Hill Pk. For Hil SE26 . 22 F4
Dome Way. Redh RH1 ...... 118 F2
Dominion Rd. Croy CR0 ...... 42 F2
Donald Lynch House.
  Mitch CR4 .... 40 F7
Donald Rd.
  Thorn H CR0 & CR9 .... 41 F2
Doncaster Wlk. Crawl RH10 202 A4
Doncastle Rd. Easth RG12 ... 26 F6
Donkey La. Abin C RH5 .... 155 D8
Donkey La. Crawl RH6 ...... 182 D7
Donlan Dr. Farnb GU14 ...... 84 C1
Donne Cl. Crawl RH10 ...... 202 B8
Donne Gdns. Pyrf GU22 ...... 70 E4
Donne Pl. Mitch CR4 .... 41 B5
Donnington Cl. Camb GU15 . 65 B4
Donnington Ct. **2**
  Crawl RH11 .... 200 F3

Donnington Rd.
N Cheam KT4 .... 58 A8
Donnybrook. Easth RG12 ..... 27 A2
Donnybrook Rd.
Streat SW16 .... 21 D1
Donovan Cl. Epsom KT19 ..... 57 D1
Donyngs Place Recn Ctr.
Redh RH1 .... 118 E2
Doods Brow Sch. Nutf RH1 119 F2
Doods Park Rd. Reig RH2 .. 118 C1
Doods Pl. Reig RH2 .... 118 D2
Doods Rd. Reig RH2 .... 118 C2
Doods Way. Reig RH2 .... 118 D2
Doomsday Garden.
Horsh RH13 .... 218 A1
Doone Cl. Tedd TW11 .... 17 A2
Dora Rd. Wimble SW19 .... 20 A4
Dora's Green La.
Crond GU10 .... 124 C5
Doradus Ct. 20
Putney SW19 .... 19 D7
Doral Way. Wallin SM5 .... 59 F5
Doran Dr. Reig RH2 .... 118 D1
Doran Gdns. Reig RH2 .... 118 D1
Dorcas Ct. Camb GU15 .... 65 B3
Dorchester Ct. Mayb GU22 .. 70 A3
Dorchester Ct. Reig RH2 .... 118 C2
Dorchester Ct. Stain TW18 .. 13 A4
Dorchester Ct. 5
Streat SW16 .... 21 E6
Dorchester Dr. Felt TW14 ..... 3 E1
Dorchester Gr. Chisw W4 ...... 7 E8
Dorchester Mews.
New Mal KT3 .... 38 D5
Dorchester Mews. Twick TW1 6 C1
Dorchester Prim Sch.
N Cheam KT4 .... 39 C1
Dorchester Rd. Cheam SM4 . 40 C2
Dorchester Rd. Morden CR4 40 C2
Dorchester Rd.
N Cheam KT4 .... 39 C1
Dorchester Rd. Weyb KT13 .. 53 B7
Dore Gdns. Morden SM4 ...... 40 B2
Doreen Cl. W Heath GU14 .... 84 E7
Dorian Dr. Ascot SL5 .... 29 E8
Doric Dr. Kings KT20 .... 97 F7
Dorien Rd. Merton SW20 ..... 39 D7
Dorin Ct. Pyrf GU22 .... 70 E4
Dorin Ct. Warlgm CR6 .... 101 B7
Doris Rd. Ashf TW15 .... 14 D2
Dorking Cl. N Cheam KT4 ..... 58 D8
Dorking General Hospl.
Dork RH4 .... 136 B6
Dorking Inst of FE.
Dork RH4 .... 136 B7
Dorking Rd. Chil GU4 .... 131 E3
Dorking Rd. Epsom KT18 ..... 76 B4
Dorking Rd. G Book KT23 .... 114 C8
Dorking Rd. L Kings KT20 ... 116 F7
Dorking Rd. Leahd KT22 ...... 95 B3
Dorking Rd. Tadw KT20 .... 97 C3
Dorking Rd. Walt o t H KT20 97 C3
Dorking Rd.
Warn RH12 & RH5 .... 198 B4
Dorking Sta. Dork RH4 .... 115 C1
Dorking West Sta.
Dork RH4 .... 136 A8
Dorlcote. Witley GU8 .... 170 E5
Dorlcote Rd. Wands SW18 .. 20 E8
Dorling Dr. Ewell KT17 .... 76 F7
Dorly Cl. Up Hall TW17 .... 34 E4
Dorman's Cl. Dorman RH7 ... 186 A8
Dormans. Crawl RH11 .... 201 A5
Dormans Ave. Dorman RH7 165 A2
Dormans Gdns.
Dorm Pk RH19 .... 185 E6
Dormans High St.
Dorman RH7 .... 186 A8
Dormans Park Rd.
Dorm Pk RH19 .... 185 E6
Dormans Park Rd.
E Grins RH19 .... 185 D3
Dormans Rd. Dorman RH7 165 A2
Dormans Sta. Felct RH7 ..... 185 F8
Dormans Station Rd.
Dorman RH7 .... 185 F7
Dormans Station Rd.
Felct RH7 .... 185 F7
Dormansland Prim Sch.
Dorman RH7 .... 186 A8
Dormer Cl. Crowth RG11 ..... 45 A5
Dormers Cl. Farnc GU7 ..... 150 D7
Dormy House The.
Went GU25 .... 30 F3
Dorney Gr. Weyb KT13 .... 53 B8
Dorney Way. Hounsl TW4 ...... 4 E2
Dornford Gdns. Coulsd CR5 100 C8
Dornton Rd. S Croy CR2 .... 61 D5
Dornton Rd.
Up Toot SW12 & SW17 .... 21 C6
Dorrien Wlk. Streat SW16 .... 21 D6
Dorrington Ct. S Norw SE25 42 E7
Dorrit Cres. Stough GU3 ..... 108 E3
Dorryn Ct. For Hil SE26 .... 23 D3
Dorset Ave. E Grins RH19 .. 185 C3
Dorset Ct. Camb GU15 .... 65 F8
Dorset Ct. Epsom KT17 .... 76 F7
Dorset Dr. Mayb GU22 .... 70 B2
Dorset Gdns. E Grins RH19 185 C3
Dorset Gdns. Thorn H SW16 41 F5
Dorset House. 2
Penge SE20 .... 43 B8
Dorset Rd. Ash GU12 .... 106 B5
Dorset Rd. Ashf TW15 .... 13 D5
Dorset Rd. Belm SM2 .... 59 A1
Dorset Rd. Merton SW19 ...... 40 A7
Dorset Rd. Mitch CR4 .... 40 E7
Dorset Rd. Penge BR3 .... 43 D6
Dorset Sq. Epsom KT19 .... 57 D1
Dorset Way. Byfl KT14 .... 52 D1
Dorset Way. Twick TW2 .... 16 D7
Dorset Waye. Heston TW5 ..... 4 F7
Dorsten Sq. Crawl RH11 ..... 200 F3
Douai Cl. Farnb GU14 .... 85 C4
Douai Gr. Hampt TW12 .... 36 C8
Douglas Ave. W Barn KT3 .... 39 B5
Douglas Cl. Jacobs GU4 .... 109 D6
Douglas Cl. Wallin SM6 .... 60 E4
Douglas Ct. Cater CR3 .... 100 D5
Douglas Dr. Croy CR0 .... 63 A7
Douglas Dr. Godal GU7 ...... 150 F5
Douglas Gr. M Bourn GU10 146 C5
Douglas Gracey House.
Putney SW18 .... 19 E8
Douglas Houghton House. 11
Redh RH1 .... 118 F2
Douglas House. L Book KT23 94 A3
Douglas House. Twick TW1 ... 6 B2
Douglas Mews. Banstd SM7 77 F3
Douglas Rd. Addl KT15 .... 52 B7
Douglas Rd. Farnb GU14 .... 104 B8
Douglas Rd. Hounsl TW3 .... 5 B4
Douglas Rd. King U T KT1 ..... 38 B7
Douglas Rd. Stan TW19 .... 2 D1
Douglas Rd. Surb KT6 .... 37 F1
Douglas Rd. Thame D KT10 .. 55 B8
Douglas Robinson Ct.
Streat SW16 .... 21 E1
Douglas Sq. Morden SM4 ...... 40 A3
Doultons The. Stain TW18 ... 13 A2
Dounesforth Gdns.
Wands SW18 .... 20 B7
Dove Cl. Crawl RH11 .... 201 D8
Dove Cl. Selsd CR2 .... 81 D8
Dove Ct. Stan TW19 .... 13 E8
Dovecote Cl. Weyb KT13 ...... 53 B7
Dovecote Gdns. 8
Mortl SW14 .... 7 D4
Dovedale Cl. Burph GU1 ..... 110 A4
Dovedale Cl. Sandh GU15 .... 45 D2
Dovedale Cres. Crawl RH11 201 B4
Dovedale Rise. Mitch CR4 .... 20 F1
Dovehouse Gn. 1
Oat Pk KT13 .... 53 D6
Dover Ct. Cran GU6 .... 175 A3
Dover Gdns. Carsh SM5 .... 59 F7
Dover House. 7 Beck BR3 .. 24 A1
Dover House. 15
Penge SE20 .... 43 B8
Dover House Rd.
Putney SW15 .... 19 B8
Dover Rd. S Norw SE19 .... 22 D2
Dover Terr. Rich TW9 .... 7 A5
Dovercourt Ave. Thorn H CR7 42 A5
Dovercourt La. Sutton SM1 .. 59 C7
Dovercourt Rd.
Dulw SE21 & SE22 .... 22 E8
Doverfield Rd. Burph GU4 . 110 A4
Doverfield Rd. Streat SW2 ... 21 E8
Dovers Green Inf Sch.
Dovgn RH1 .... 139 C5
Dovers Green Rd.
Dovgn RH2 .... 139 B4
Doversmead. Knaph GU21 ... 68 E3
Doveton Rd. S Croy CR2 ...... 61 D5
Dowanhill Rd. Catf SE6 .... 24 D7
Dowdeswell Cl. Rhampt SW15 7 E3
Dowding Ct. Crowth RG11 .... 45 C6
Dowding Rd. Bigg H TN16 .... 83 D4
Dowell House. Dulw SE21 ... 22 F5
Dower Ave. Wallin SM6 .... 60 B2
Dower House. Milf GU8 ...... 170 F8
Dower Wlk. Crawl RH11 ...... 201 A5
Dowes House. 13
Streat SW16 .... 21 E5
Dowlands La.
Burst RH10 & RH6 .... 183 D7
Dowlans Cl. G Book KT23 .. 114 A8
Dowlans Rd. G Book KT23 . 114 B8
Dowler Ct. 2 King U T KT2 . 37 F8
Dowman Cl. 2
Merton SW19 .... 20 B1
Down Hall Rd. King U T KT2 . 37 D8
Down La. Compt GU3 .... 129 B4
Down Lodge Ct. Epsom KT18 76 E5
Down Rd. Merrow GU1 ...... 110 B1
Down Rd. Tedd TW11 .... 17 B2
Down St. E Mole KT8 .... 36 A4
Down Yhonda. Elst GU8 ..... 148 C3
Downderry Prim Sch.
Catf BR1 .... 24 E4
Downderry Rd. Catf BR1 ...... 24 E4
Downe Cl. Horley RH6 .... 160 E5
Downe Golf Course.
Downe BR6 .... 83 E7
Downe Rd. Mitch CR4 .... 40 F7
Downer Meadow.
Farnc GU7 .... 150 E8
Downes Cl. Twick TW1 .... 6 B1
Downfield. 7 New Mal KT4 39 A1
Downfield House.
New Mal KT3 .... 38 D1
Downham Enterprise Ctr.
Catf SE6 .... 24 F6
Downham Way. Catf BR1 .... 24 E4
Downhurst Rd. Ewh GU6 .... 175 E6
Downing Ave. Onsl V GU2 .. 129 F8
Downing House. 3
Merton SW19 .... 20 A1
Downing St. Farnh GU9 ..... 125 B2
Downland Cl. Burgh H KT18 . 77 B1
Downland Cl. Wallin CR5 ..... 79 B5
Downland Ct. Crawl RH11 .. 201 C4
Downland Dr. Crawl RH11 . 201 C3
Downland Gdns.
Burgh H KT18 .... 77 B1
Downland Pl. Crawl RH11 .. 201 C4
Downland Way.
Burgh H KT18 .... 77 B1
Downlands Rd. Purley CR8 .. 79 F6
Downmill Rd. Brack RG12 .... 26 F7
Downs Ave. Epsom KT18 ...... 76 F4
Downs Bridge Rd.
Beck BR2 & BR3 .... 44 D8
Downs Court Rd. Purley CR8 80 B6
Downs Ct. Purley CR8 .... 61 B1
Downs Ct. 2 Redh RH1 .... 119 A4
Downs Ct. 10 Wimble SW19 19 D1
Downs Est. Nork KT17 .... 77 C5
Downs Hill. Beck BR2 & BR3 44 D8
Downs Hill Rd. Epsom KT18 76 E5
Downs La. Leahd KT22 .... 95 B3
Downs Rd.
Ashtd KT18 & KT21 .... 96 C7
Downs Rd. Beck BR3 .... 44 B7
Downs Rd. Coulsd CR5 .... 79 D1
Downs Rd.
Epsom KT17 & KT18 .... 76 E3
Downs Rd. Mickle RH5 .... 115 C7
Downs Rd. Purley CR8 .... 80 B8
Downs Rd. S Norw CR7 .... 42 C8
Downs Rd. Sutton SM2 .... 78 C8
Downs Side. Belm SM2 .... 77 F8
Downs The. Leahd KT22 ...... 95 C2
Downs The.
Wimble SW19 & SW20 .... 19 D1
Downs View. Hounsl TW7 ...... 6 A6
Downs View. Pixham RH4 . 115 D1
Downs View. Tadw KT20 ...... 97 B6
Downs View Lodge. 9
Surb KT6 .... 37 E3
Downs View Rd.
G Book KT23 .... 114 C8
Downs Way. Epsom KT18 .... 76 F3
Downs Way. G Book KT23 .... 94 C1
Downs Way. Oxted RH8 ...... 122 E8
Downs Way. Tadw KT20 ...... 97 B6
Downs Way Prim Sch.
Oxted RH8 .... 122 E8
Downs Wood. Burgh H KT18 77 B2
Downsend Lodge Pre Prep Sch.
Leahd KT22 .... 95 B6
Downsend Lodge Sch.
Ewell KT17 .... 76 F7
Downsend Sch. Ashtd KT22 . 95 D7
Downshire Way. Easth RG12 27 B6
Downside. Beac H GU26 .... 188 D7
Downside. Epsom KT18 .... 76 E5
Downside. Twick TW1 .... 16 F5
Downside Bridge Rd.
Cobham KT11 .... 73 B4
Downside Cl. Wimble SW19 20 C2
Downside Common Rd.
Downs KT11 .... 73 C1
Downside Ct. Merst RH1 ..... 119 C6
Downside Orch.Woking GU22 70 A2
Downside Prep Sch.
Purley CR8 .... 79 D8
Downside Rd. Downs KT11 .. 73 B2
Downside Rd. Merrow GU4 131 B8
Downsman Ct. Crawl RH10 201 D3
Downsview Ave.
Westfd GU22 .... 89 F6
Downsview Ct. Bellf GU1 ... 109 C5
Downsview Gdns.
S Norw SE19 .... 22 C1
Downsview Prim Sch.
S Norw SE19 .... 22 C1
Downsview Rd.
Head Dn GU35 .... 187 C5
Downsview Rd.
Horsh RH12 .... 218 B6
Downsview Rd.
S Norw CR7 & SE19 .... 22 C1
Downsway. Merrow GU1 .... 110 E1
Downsway. S Croy CR2 .... 80 E8
Downsway. Whytlf CR3 .... 80 F2
Downsway Cl. Tadw KT20 .... 97 A6
Downsway The. Sutton SM2 59 C2
Downswood. Redh RH1 ...... 118 D4
Downton Ave. Streat SW2 ... 21 F6
Downview Cl. Beac H GU26 188 D6
Downview Cl. Downs KT11 .. 93 B8
Doyle Rd. Croy SE25 .... 43 A5
Dr Johnson Ave.
Up Toot SW17 .... 21 B5
Dragon La. Whit V KT13 .... 53 A1
Dragoon Ct. Alder GU11 ..... 104 E2
Drake Ave. Cater CR3 .... 100 C5
Drake Ave. Mytch GU16 .... 86 A1
Drake Ave. Stain TW18 .... 12 F3
Drake Cl. Easth RG12 .... 27 B4
Drake Cl. Horsh RH12 .... 217 E6
Drake Ct. Dulw SE19 .... 22 F3
Drake Ct. King U T KT5 .... 37 F5
Drake Rd. Chess KT9 .... 57 A5
Drake Rd. Crawl RH10 .... 201 E3
Drake Rd. Horley RH6 .... 160 E3
Drake Rd. Mitch CR4 .... 41 A3
Drake Rd.
Thorn H CR0 & CR9 .... 41 F2
Drake's Cl. Esher KT10 .... 55 A6
Drakefield Rd.
Up Toot SW17 .... 21 A5
Drakes Ct. For Hil SE23 .... 23 C7
Drakes Way. Woking GU22 .. 89 D5
Drakewood Rd. Streat SW16 21 D1
Drax Ave. Wimble SW20 .... 19 A1
Draxmont. Wimble SW19 ..... 19 E2
Dray Ct. Guild GU2 .... 130 B8
Draycot Rd. Tolw KT6 .... 38 A1
Draycott. Brack RG12 .... 27 E4
Drayhorse Dr. Bagsh GU19 .. 47 E2
Drayton Cl. Brack RG12 .... 27 D7
Drayton Cl. Fetch KT22 .... 94 E3
Drayton Cl. Hounsl TW4 .... 4 F2
Drayton Ct. Tolw KT5 .... 57 B8
Drayton Ct. W Byfl KT14 ...... 71 A6
Drayton Rd. Croy CR0 & CR9 61 B8
Dresden Way. Weyb KT13 ... 53 C5
Drew House. 12
Streat SW16 .... 21 E5
Drewstead Rd. Streat SW16 21 D6
Drift The.
E Hors KT11 & KT24 .... 92 E3
Drift The.
Mart Gn KT11 & KT24 .... 92 E3
Drift Way. Coln SL3 .... 1 C7
Driftway The. Leahd KT22 .... 95 C4
Driftway The. Mitch CR4 .... 41 A8
Driftway The. Nork SM7 .... 77 C4
Driftway (Worple Road) The.
Leahd KT22 .... 95 B4
Driftwood Dr. Kenley CR8 .... 80 C2
Drill Hall Rd. Chert KT16 .... 33 A2
Drive Rd. Coulsd CR5 .... 99 F7
Drive Spur. Kings KT20 .... 98 B6
Drive The. Arting GU3 .... 130 B5
Drive The. Ashf TW15 .... 14 D1
Drive The. Beck BR3 .... 44 A8
Drive The. Belm SM2 .... 77 F7
Drive The. Cobham KT11 ...... 73 F5
Drive The. Copth RH10 .... 183 C3
Drive The. Coulsd CR5 & CR8 79 E5
Drive The. Cran GU6 .... 174 F2
Drive The. Felt TW14 .... 15 C8
Drive The. Fetch KT22 .... 94 E5
Drive The. Godal GU7 .... 150 F2
Drive The.
Head KT18 & KT22 .... 96 A3
Drive The. Horley RH6 .... 161 B1
Drive The. Hounsl TW3 & TW7 5 D5
Drive The. Ifold RH14 .... 212 D2
Drive The. King U T KT2 .... 18 C1
Drive The.
Leahd KT22 & KT18 .... 95 F4
Drive The. M Bourn GU9 .... 146 B7
Drive The. Morden SM4 .... 40 D4
Drive The. Nork SM7 .... 77 E3
Drive The. Onsl V GU2 .... 108 F1
Drive The. Onsl V GU2 .... 130 A7
Drive The. S Norw CR7 .... 42 D5
Drive The.
Shackl GU7 & GU8 .... 149 E4
Drive The. Thame D KT10 ..... 36 C1
Drive The. Thorpe GU25 .... 31 F4
Drive The. W Ewell KT19 ...... 57 F4
Drive The. W Ewell KT19 ...... 57 F4
Drive The. W Wick BR4 .... 44 D2
Drive The. Wallin CR8 & SM6 60 D1
Drive The.
Wimble SW19 & SW20 .... 19 C1
Drive The. Woking GU22 ...... 89 B7
Drive The. Woner GU5 ...... 152 B6
Drivers Mead. Lingf RH7 ... 164 D3
Drodges Cl. Shalf GU5 .... 151 F8
Droitwich Cl. Brack RG12 ..... 27 E6
Droitwich Cl. For Hil SE26 ... 23 A5
Drove Rd. Albury GU4 .... 132 A7
Drovers Ct. 3 King U T KT1 37 E7
Drovers Rd. Croy CR2 .... 61 D5
Drovers Way. Ash GU12 .... 106 C1
Drovers Way. Brack RG12 .... 27 F6
Drovers Way. Hale GU9 .... 125 A6
Druid's Cl. Ashtd KT21 .... 95 F7
Druids Way. Beck BR2 .... 44 D5
Drumaline Ridge.
Worc Pk KT4 .... 57 E8
Drummond Cl. Brack RG12 .. 27 F8
Drummond Ct. 4
Guild GU1 .... 109 D1
Drummond Ctr. Croy CR9 .... 61 C8
Drummond Gdns.
Epsom KT19 .... 76 B8
Drummond Rd.
Crawl RH11 .... 200 E5
Drummond Rd.
Croy CR0 & CR9 .... 61 C8
Drummond Rd. Guild GU1 109 D1
Drummonds Pl. Rich TW9 ...... 6 E3
Drungewick La.
Loxwd RH14 .... 213 D2
Drury Cl. Worth RH10 .... 202 D4
Drury Cres. Croy CR0 & CR9 . 61 A8
Dry Arch Rd. Sunnin SL5 ...... 29 F3
Dryden. Easth RG12 .... 27 A2
Dryden Ct. 11 Rich TW10 ..... 17 D4
Dryden Rd. W Heath GU14 ... 84 F6
Dryden Rd. Wimble SW19 ... 20 C2
Drynham Pk. Oat Pk KT13 .... 53 E7
Du Cane Ct. Up Toot SW12 .. 21 A7
Ducavel House. Streat SW2 21 F7
Duck's Wlk. Twick TW1 .... 6 C2
Dudley Cl. Addl KT15 .... 52 C7
Dudley Dr. W Barn SM4 .... 39 E2
Dudley Gr. Epsom KT18 .... 76 C5
Dudley Rd. Ashf TW15 .... 13 F4
Dudley Rd. E Bed TW14 .... 14 D7
Dudley Rd. King U T KT1 .... 37 F6
Dudley Rd. Rich TW9 .... 7 A5
Dudley Rd. Walt O T KT12 .... 35 A2
Dudley Rd. Wimble SW19 ..... 20 A2
Dudset La. Cranf TW5 .... 4 A6
Duffield Rd. Walt o t H KT20 97 B3
Duffins Orch. Ottsh KT16 ..... 51 C3
Duke Of Cambridge Cl.
Twick TW2 .... 5 D1
Duke Of Cornwall Ave.
Camb GU15 .... 46 D1
Duke of Edinburgh Rd.
Carsh SM1 .... 59 D8
Duke of Kent Sch.
Ewh GU6 .... 154 D2
Duke St. Rich TW10 & TW9 .... 6 D2
Duke St. Sutton SM1 .... 59 D6
Duke St. Woking GU21 .... 69 F2
Duke's Ave. Chisw W4 .... 7 D8
Duke's Dr. Newd RH5 .... 179 D6
Duke's Hill. Windl GU19 .... 47 E5
Duke's La. Old W SL4 & SL5 . 10 B3
Duke's La. Wink SL5 .... 9 F1
Duke's Ride. Crowth RG11 ... 45 B5
Dukes Ave. Hounsl TW4 .... 4 E3
Dukes Ave.
King U T KT2 & TW10 .... 17 D4
Dukes Ave. King U T KT3 ...... 38 F6
Dukes Ave. Rich KT2 & TW10 17 D4
Dukes Cl. Ashf TW15 .... 14 C4
Dukes Cl. Cran GU6 .... 175 A2
Dukes Cl. Hale GU9 .... 125 A6
Dukes Cl. Hampt TW12 .... 15 F3
Dukes Covert. Brack GU19 .. 47 E6
Dukes Ct. Addl KT15 .... 52 C6
Dukes Ct. Beck BR3 .... 43 E6
Dukes Green Ave. Felt TW14 4 A2
Dukes Hill. Wold CR3 & CR6 101 E7
Dukes Pk. Farnb GU11 .... 105 D6
Dukes Rd. Hersh KT12 .... 54 D5
Dukes Ride. Dork RH5 .... 136 D4
Dukes Way. Coney H BR4 ..... 63 E7
Dukes Wlk. Hale GU9 .... 125 A6
Dukes Wood. Crowth RG11 .. 45 B5

Dukeshill Rd. Brack RG12 .... 27 B8
Dukesthorpe Rd. For Hil SE26 .... 23 D4
Dulverton Ct. 12 King U T KT6 .... 37 E4
Dulverton Rd. Selsd CR2 .... 62 C1
Dulwich and Sydenham Hill Golf Course. Dulw SE21 .... 22 F6
Dulwich Bsns Ctr. For Hil SE23 .... 23 D7
Dulwich Coll (Endowed). Dulw SE21 .... 22 E6
Dulwich Coll Picture Gal. Dulw SE21 .... 22 E8
Dulwich Coll Prep Sch. Dulw SE21 .... 22 E5
Dulwich Comm. Dulw SE21 . 22 E7
Dulwich Ct. Dulw SE22 .... 23 B7
Dulwich Oaks The. Dulw SE21 .... 22 F5
Dulwich Village. Dulw SE21 . 22 E8
Dulwich Wood Ave. Dulw SE19 .... 22 E3
Dulwich Wood Pk. Dulw SE21 & SE19 .... 22 E4
Dumbarton Ct. 16 Streat SW2 .... 21 E8
Dumbleton Cl. King U T KT2 38 B8
Dump Rd. Farnb GU14 .... 84 E1
Dumphreys House. 5 Streat SW4 .... 21 D8
Dunally Pk. Lo Hall TW17 .... 34 D2
Dunbar Ave. Beck BR3 .... 43 E5
Dunbar Ave. Thorn H CR7 & SW16 .... 42 A7
Dunbar Ct. Carsh SM1 .... 59 D5
Dunbar Ct. Walt O T KT12 .... 35 C1
Dunbar Rd. Friml GU16 .... 85 F7
Dunbar Rd. King U T KT3 .... 38 C5
Dunbar St. W Norw SE27 .... 22 C5
Dunboe Pl. Shep TW17 .... 34 C2
Dunbridge House. Rhampt SW15 .... 7 F1
Duncan Dr. Merrow GU1 .... 110 A2
Duncan Dr. Woki RG11 .... 25 E5
Duncan Rd. Burgh H KT20 .... 97 E8
Duncan Rd. Rich TW9 .... 6 E3
Duncombe Ct. Stain TW18 .. 12 F1
Duncombe Hill. For Hil SE23 23 E8
Duncombe House. 7 Putney SW19 .... 19 D7
Duncombe Rd. Godal GU7 150 D2
Duncroft Cl. Reig RH2 .... 117 F1
Dundaff Cl. Friml GU15 .... 66 A5
Dundas Cl. Easth RG12 .... 27 B5
Dundas Gdns. E Mole KT8 .... 36 B6
Dundee Rd. Croy SE25 .... 43 B4
Dundela Gdns. N Cheam KT17 & KT4 .... 58 B6
Dundonald Prim Sch. Merton SW19 .... 19 F1
Dundonald Rd. Merton SW19 .... 19 F1
Dundrey Cres. Merst RH1 .. 119 E6
Dundry House. 8 For Hil SE26 .... 23 A5
Dunedin Dr. Cater CR3 .... 100 E2
Dunelm Gr. W Norw SE27 .... 22 C5
Dunfee Way. Byfl KT14 .... 71 E7
Dunfield Gdns. Catf SE6 .... 24 B3
Dunfield Rd. Catf SE6 .... 24 B3
Dungates La. Buckl RH3 .... 117 A2
Dunheved Cl. Thorn H CR7 .. 42 A3
Dunheved Rd N. Thorn H CR7 .... 42 A3
Dunheved Rd S. Thorn H CR7 .... 42 A3
Dunheved Rd W. Thorn H CR7 .... 42 A3
Dunhill Point. 12 Rhampt SW15 .... 19 B7
Dunkeld Rd. S Norw SE25 .... 42 D5
Dunkirk St. 12 W Norw SE27 .... 22 C4
Dunleary Cl. Twick TW4 .... 15 F8
Dunley Dr. New Add CR0 .... 63 C4
Dunlin Cl. Earls RH1 .... 139 F4
Dunlin Ct. 11 W Norw SE21 .... 22 D6
Dunlin Rise. Merrow GU4 . 110 D3
Dunmail Dr. Sander CR2 & 8 80 E6
Dunmore. Stough GU2 .... 108 D2
Dunmore Rd. Wimble SW20 39 D8
Dunmow Cl. Felt TW13 .... 15 E4
Dunnets. Knaph GU21 .... 68 E2
Dunning's Rd. E Grins RH19 205 E7
Dunnings Mill L Complex. E Grins RH19 .... 205 E6
Dunnock Ct. 10 W Norw SE21 .... 22 D6
Dunnymans Rd. Banstd SM7 77 F4
Dunoon Gdns. For Hil SE23 .. 23 D8
Dunoon Rd. For Hil SE23 .... 23 C8
Dunottar Cl. Woodh RH2 .... 139 D7
Dunraven Ave. Salfs RH1 .. 140 B2
Dunraven House. 11 Rich TW9 .... 6 F6
Dunraven Lower Sch. Streat SW16 .... 21 F5
Dunraven Upper Sch. Streat SW16 .... 21 F5
Dunsborough Cotts. Ripley GU23 .... 91 C7
Dunsbury Cl. Sutton SM2 .... 59 B2
Dunsdon Ave. Guild GU2 .... 130 B8
Dunsfold CE Fst Sch. Dunsf GU8 .... 192 F6
Dunsfold Cl. Crawl RH11 .... 201 A5
Dunsfold Common Rd. Dunsf GU8 .... 192 F6
Dunsfold Ct. 9 Sutton SM2 59 B3
Dunsfold House. 10 King U T KT2 .... 18 B2
Dunsfold House. 7 Streat SW2 .... 21 F8
Dunsfold Rd. Alf Cr GU6 & GU8 .... 193 E3
Dunsfold Rd. Alfold GU6 & GU8 .... 193 E3
Dunsfold Rd. Bramly GU5 & GU8 .... 173 C1
Dunsfold Rd. Dunsf GU6 & GU8 .... 193 B8
Dunsfold Rd. Plaist GU8 & RH14 .... 211 D4
Dunsfold Rise. Coulsd CR5 .... 79 D6
Dunsfold Way. New Add CR0 63 C3
Dunsmore Rd. Walt O T KT12 .... 35 B3
Dunstable Rd. E Mole KT8 .... 35 F5
Dunstable Rd. Rich TW10 & TW9 .... 6 E3
Dunstall Pk. W Heath GU14 . 85 A7
Dunstall Rd. Wimble SW19 & SW20 .... 19 C2
Dunstall Way. E Mole KT8 .... 36 B6
Dunstan Ct. Stain TW18 .... 13 A4
Dunstan Rd. Coulsd CR5 .... 79 D2
Dunstan's Rd. Dulw SE22 .... 23 A8
Dunster Ave. W Barn SM4 .... 39 D1
Dunster House. Catf SE6 .... 24 B5
Dunton Cl. Surb KT6 .... 37 E1
Dunton Ct. Dulw SE26 .... 23 B6
Dunton House. 14 Streat SW16 .... 21 E5
Duntshill Rd. Wands SW18 .. 20 B7
Dunvegan Cl. E Mole KT8 .... 36 B5
Dunvegan House. 8 Redh RH1 .... 118 F1
Dupont Rd. Merton SW20 .... 39 D7
Duppas Ave. Croy CR0 .... 61 B6
Duppas Cl. Shep TW17 .... 34 D4
Duppas Ct. Croy CR0 .... 61 B7
Duppas Hill La. Croy CR0 .... 61 B6
Duppas Hill Rd. Croy CR0 .... 61 B6
Duppas Hill Terr. Croy CR0 & CR9 .... 61 B7
Duppas Jun Sch. Croy CR0 .. 61 B5
Duppas Rd. Croy CR0 & CR9 61 B7
Dura Den Cl. Beck BR3 .... 24 B1
Durand Cl. Carsh SM5 .... 40 F1
Durban Rd. Beck BR3 .... 43 F7
Durban Rd. W Norw SE27 .... 22 D4
Durbin Rd. Chess KT9 .... 56 F6
Durfold Dr. Reig RH2 .... 118 C1
Durfold Rd. Horsh RH12 .... 217 D7
Durfold Wood. Plaist RH14 211 D5
Durford Cres. Rhampt SW15 19 B7
Durham Ave. Beck BR2 .... 44 F5
Durham Cl. Crawl RH10 .... 201 E2
Durham Cl. Stough GU2 .... 108 F3
Durham Cl. Wimble SW20 .... 39 B7
Durham Ct. Leahd KT22 .... 95 A5
Durham Ct. Tedd TW11 .... 16 E4
Durham Hill. Catf BR1 .... 24 F4
Durham Rd. Beck BR2 .... 44 F6
Durham Rd. Felt TW14 .... 15 C8
Durham Rd. Sandh GU15 .... 45 E2
Durham Rd. Wimble SW20 .... 39 B8
Durkins Rd. E Grins RH19 .. 185 D3
Durleston Pk Dr. Fetch KT23 94 C2
Durley Mead. Brack RG12 .... 27 F4
Durlston Rd. King U T KT2 .... 17 E2
Durnford House. Catf SE6 .... 24 B5
Durning Rd. W Norw SE19 .... 22 D3
Durnsford Ave. Wimble SW18 & SW19 .... 20 A6
Durnsford Rd. Wimble SW18 & SW19 .... 20 B5
Durnsford Way. Cran GU6 175 A2
Durrell Way. Shep TW17 .... 34 D3
Durrington Ave. Wimble SW20 .... 19 C1
Durrington Park Rd. Wimble SW20 .... 39 C8
Dutch Barn Cl. Stan TW19 .... 2 D1
Dutch Gdns. King U T KT2 .... 18 B2
Dutchells Copse. Horsh RH12 .... 217 E7
Dutton House. Streat SW2 .. 22 B7
Duval Pl. Bagsh GU19 .... 47 E3
Duxford. 10 King U T KT1 .... 38 A7
Duxhurst La. Sidlow RH6 .... 160 B7
Dwelly La. Haxted TN8 .... 165 D8
Dwelly La. Limps RH7 & RH8 & TN8 .... 144 D3
Dyehouse Rd. Thursl GU8 .. 169 C4
Dyer House. Hampt TW12 .... 36 B8
Dyer's Field. Smallf RH6 .... 162 B3
Dyers Almshouses. Crawl RH10 .... 201 D7
Dykes Ct. 11 Streat SW2 .... 21 F7
Dykes Path. Sheer GU22 .... 70 C4
Dykes Way. Beck BR2 .... 44 F6
Dymes Path. Putney SW19 .. 19 D6
Dynevor Pl. Fairl GU3 .... 108 C5
Dynevor Rd. Rich TW10 .... 6 E2
Dysart Ave. King U T KT2 & TW10 .... 17 C4
Dysart Sch. King U T KT2 .... 17 D4
Dyson Ct. Dork RH4 .... 136 A7
Dyson Wlk. Crawl RH11 .... 201 B1
Eady Cl. Horsh RH13 .... 217 F2
Eagle Cl. Crowth RG11 .... 45 A7
Eagle Cl. Wallin SM6 .... 60 E4
Eagle Ct. 9 W Norw SE21 .... 22 D6
Eagle Hill. S Norw SE19 .... 22 D2
Eagle House Sch. Sandh GU17 .... 45 B2
Eagle Rd. Farnb GU14 .... 85 B2
Eagle Rd. Guild GU1 .... 109 D1
Eagle Trad Est. Mitch CR4 .... 40 F3
Eagles Dr. Bigg H TN16 .... 83 D1
Eagles Nest. Sandh GU17 .... 45 A1
Ealing Rd. Brent TW8 .... 6 E8
Eardley Prim Sch. Streat SW16 .... 21 C2
Eardley Rd. Streat SW16 .... 21 C2
Earl Rd. Mortl SW14 .... 7 C3
Earle Gdns. King U T KT2 .... 17 E1
Earles Meadow. Horsh RH12 .... 218 A6
Earles Meadow. Horsh RH12 .... 218 B6
Earleswood. Cobham KT11 .... 73 E7
Earleydene. Sunnin SL5 .... 29 B1
Earls Gr. Camb GU15 .... 65 E6
Earlsbrook Rd. Earls RH1 .... 139 F7
Earlsfield Prim Sch. Wands SW18 .... 20 C6
Earlsfield Rd. Wands SW18 . 20 C8
Earlsfield Sta. Wands SW18 20 C7
Earlsthorpe Rd. For Hil SE26 23 D4
Earlswood. Easth RG12 .... 27 B2
Earlswood Ave. Thorn H CR7 42 A4
Earlswood Cl. Horsh RH13 218 A4
Earlswood Ct. Earls RH1 .... 139 F7
Earlswood Cty Inf Sch. Earls RH1 .... 140 A8
Earlswood House. 2 Streat SW2 .... 21 F7
Earlswood Rd. Earls RH1 .... 139 F7
Earlswood Sta. Earls RH1 .... 139 F7
Early Commons. Crawl RH10 .... 201 F7
Easby Cres. Morden SM4 .... 40 B3
Easedale House. Islew TW7 .. 5 F2
Eashing La. Ock Rid GU7 & GU8 .... 150 A3
Eashing La. Shackl GU7 & GU8 .... 149 F3
Eashing Point. 5 Rhampt SW15 .... 19 B7
Easington Pl. Guild GU1 .... 130 F8
East Ave. Heath E GU9 .... 125 D6
East Ave. Wallin CR0 .... 60 F5
East Ave. Whit V KT12 .... 53 F1
East Croydon Sta. Croy CR9 61 D8
East Dr. Beck BR3 .... 44 C4
East Dr. Wallin SM5 .... 59 F2
East Dr. Went GU25 .... 31 B3
East Flexford La. Wanb GU3 .... 128 F6
East Gdns. Mayb GU22 .... 70 C2
East Gdns. Mitch SW17 & SW19 .... 20 E2
East Gn. Blckw GU17 .... 64 C4
East Grinstead Rd. Lingf RH7 .... 164 D3
East Grinstead Sta. E Grins RH19 .... 185 D1
East Hill. Bigg H TN16 .... 83 B1
East Hill. Dorm Pk RH19 .... 185 E6
East Hill. Mayb GU22 .... 70 C2
East Hill. Oxted RH8 .... 122 F6
East Hill. S Croy CR2 .... 61 E1
East Hill Ct. Oxted RH8 .... 122 E5
East Hill La. Burst RH10 .... 183 D5
East Hill Rd. Oxted RH8 .... 122 E6
East La. King U T KT1 .... 37 D6
East La. W Hors KT24 .... 92 D2
East Meads. Onsl V GU2 .... 130 A8
East Park La. Horne RH7 .... 163 C1
East Pk. Crawl RH10 & RH11 .... 201 D5
East Pl. W Norw SE27 .... 22 C4
East Ramp. Harl TW6 .... 3 B6
East Rd. E Bed TW14 .... 14 D8
East Rd. King U T KT2 .... 37 E8
East Rd. Merton SW19 .... 20 C2
East Rd. Reig RH2 .... 117 F2
East Rd. Whit V KT13 .... 53 D3
East Rd. Wimble SW19 .... 20 C2
East Resr (Nature Reserve). Tyl Gn RH9 .... 121 B5
East Ring. Tongh GU10 .... 127 A7
East Shalford La. Chil GU4 .. 131 A3
East Sheen Ave. Mortl SW14 . 7 D3
East Sheen Prim Sch. Mortl SW14 .... 7 E3
East St. Brent TW8 .... 6 C7
East St. Ewell KT17 .... 76 E7
East St. Farnh GU9 .... 125 C3
East St. G Book KT23 .... 94 B2
East St. Horsh RH12 .... 217 C1
East St. Rusper RH12 .... 199 E7
East St. Turn H RH10 & RH19 .... 204 C4
East Station Rd. Alder GU12 .... 105 B1
East Stratton Cl. Brack RG12 27 F4
East Surrey Coll. Redh RH1 119 A4
East Surrey Hospl. Redh RH1 .... 118 E1
East Surrey Hospl The. Earls RH1 .... 140 A5
East View La. Cran GU6 .... 174 C3
East Way. Croy CR0 .... 62 E7
East Whipley La. Rowly GU5 .... 173 F7
East Whipley La. Sham Gn GU5 .... 173 F8
East Wlk. Reig RH2 .... 118 B1
Eastbank Rd. Hampt TW12 .. 16 C3
Eastbourne Gdns. Mortl SW14 .... 7 C4
Eastbourne Rd. Blind H RH9 .... 142 E4
Eastbourne Rd. Chisw W4 .... 7 C8
Eastbourne Rd. Felb RH7 .. 184 E8
Eastbourne Rd. Felt TW13 .. 15 D6
Eastbourne Rd. Godst RH9 121 D2
Eastbourne Rd. Mitch SW17 21 A2
Eastbourne Rd. Newch RH7 & RH9 .... 163 F5
Eastbourne Rd. S Godst RH9 .... 142 E4
Eastbrook Cl. Woking GU21 . 70 A3
Eastbury Gr. Chisw W4 .... 7 E8
Eastbury La. Compt GU3 .... 129 A3
Eastbury Rd. King U T KT2 .. 17 E1
Eastchurch Rd. Hatton TW6 .. 3 E4
Eastcote Ave. E Mole KT8 .... 36 A4
Eastcroft Ct. Guild GU1 .... 131 A8
Eastcroft Mews. Horsh RH12 .... 216 F1
Eastcroft Rd. W Ewell KT19 . 57 E3
Eastcroft Rd. W Ewell KT19 . 57 E3
Eastdean Ave. Epsom KT18 . 76 B6
Easter Way. S Godst RH9 .... 142 F5
Eastern Ave. Thorpe KT16 .... 33 A6
Eastern Ind Area. Brack RG12 .... 27 D7
Eastern La. Crowth RG11 .... 45 F4
Eastern Perimeter Rd. Hatton TW14 .... 3 F5
Eastern Rd. Alder GU12 .... 105 E2
Eastern Rd. Brack RG12 .... 27 D7
Eastern View. Bigg H TN16 .. 83 C2
Eastfield Rd. Nutf RH1 .... 140 C8
Eastfields. Witley GU8 .... 170 F5
Eastfields High Sch. Mitch CR4 .... 41 B7
Eastfields Rd. Mitch CR4 .... 41 A7
Eastgate. Nork SM7 .... 77 F5
Eastgate Gdns. Guild GU1 .. 130 E8
Easthampstead Park Sch. Easth RG11 .... 26 D3
Easthampstead Rd. Brack RG12 .... 27 A7
Easthampstead Rd. Woki RG11 .... 25 E4
Eastheath Ave. Woki RG11 .. 25 A4
Eastheath Gdns. Woki RG11 25 B3
Eastlands Cl. Oxted RH8 .... 122 D8
Eastlands Cres. Dulw SE21 & SE22 .... 22 F8
Eastlands Way. Oxted RH8 122 D8
Eastleigh Cl. Sutton SM2 .... 59 B3
Eastleigh Rd. Hatton TW6 .... 3 F4
Eastleigh Way. E Bed TW14 15 A7
Eastleigh Wlk. 10 Rhampt SW15 .... 19 A8
Eastmead. Farnb GU14 .... 85 B3
Eastmead. Woking GU21 .... 69 B2
Eastmearn Rd. W Norw SE21 & SE27 .... 22 C6
Eastmont Rd. Hinch W KT10 55 F8
Eastney Rd. Thorn H CR0 .... 42 B1
Eastnor Cl. Woodh RH2 .... 138 F6
Eastnor Rd. Woodh RH2 .... 139 A6
Easton House. 4 W Norw SE27 .... 22 B5
Eastry Ave. Hayes BR2 .... 44 F3
Eastway. Crawl RH6 .... 182 B7
Eastway. Epsom KT19 .... 76 D8
Eastway. Merton SM4 & SW20 .... 39 E5
Eastway. Stough GU2 .... 108 F1
Eastway. Wallin SM6 .... 60 C6
Eastwell Cl. Penge BR3 .... 23 E1
Eastwick Ct. 2 Putney SW19 .... 19 D7
Eastwick Cty Jun Sch. Fetch KT23 .... 94 B3
Eastwick Dr. Fetch KT23 .... 94 B4
Eastwick Inf Sch. Fetch KT23 .... 94 B3
Eastwick Park Ave. Fetch KT23 .... 94 B3
Eastwick Rd. G Book KT23 .... 94 B2
Eastwick Rd. Whit V KT12 .... 54 B5
Eastwood. Crawl RH10 .... 201 F6
Eastwood. 3 Whit V KT13 .. 53 D4
Eastwood Lodge. Bramly GU5 .... 151 F7
Eastwood Rd. Bramly GU5 . 151 F7
Eastwood St. Streat SW16 .... 21 C2
Eastworth Rd. Chert KT15 & KT16 .... 33 A1
Eaton Ct. Abbots GU1 .... 110 A3
Eaton Ct. Sutton SM2 .... 59 D4
Eaton Dr. King U T KT2 .... 18 A1
Eaton Park Rd. Cobham KT11 .... 73 F5
Eaton Pk. Cobham KT11 .... 73 E5
Eaton Rd. Camb GU15 .... 65 B4
Eaton Rd. Islew TW3 & TW7 .. 5 D3
Eaton Rd. Sutton SM2 .... 59 D4
Eatonville Rd. Up Toot SW17 20 F6
Eatonville Villas. Up Toot SW17 .... 20 F6
Ebba's Way. Epsom KT18 .... 76 B4
Ebbage Ct. 5 Woking GU22 69 E1
Ebbisham Ct. Epsom KT18 .... 76 C4
Ebbisham La. Walt o t H KT20 & KT18 .... 97 A4
Ebbisham Rd. Epsom KT18 .. 76 B5
Ebbisham Rd. N Cheam KT4 58 C8
Ebenezer Wlk. Mitch CR4 .... 41 C8
Ebor Cotts. King U T SW15 .... 18 E5
Ebsworth St. For Hil SE23 .... 23 D8
Ecclesbourne Inf Sch. Thorn H CR7 .... 42 C4
Ecclesbourne Jun Sch. Thorn H CR7 .... 42 C4
Ecclesbourne Rd. Thorn H CR7 .... 42 C4
Eccleshill. Beck BR2 .... 44 F5
Eccleshill. Dork RH5 .... 136 C3
Echelford Cty Mid Sch. Ashf TW15 .... 14 B3
Echelforde Dr. Ashf TW15 .... 14 A4
Echo Barn La. Wreccl GU10 145 F5
Echo Pit Rd. Guild GU1 & GU4 .... 130 E6
Ecob Cl. Stough GU3 .... 108 F5
Ecton Rd. Addl KT15 .... 52 B6
Ector Rd. Catf SE6 .... 24 E6
Eddeys Cl. Head Dn GU35 . 187 B6
Eddeys La. Head Dn GU35 . 187 B6
Eddington Hill. Crawl RH11 201 B1
Eddington Rd. Easth RG12 .... 26 E3
Eddisbury House. 7 For Hil SE26 .... 23 A5
Eddy Rd. Alder GU12 .... 105 C1
Eddystone Wlk. Stan TW19 .. 13 E8
Ede Cl. Hounsl TW4 .... 4 F4
Ede Ct. Epsom KT17 .... 76 F7
Ede's Cotts. Ashtd KT21 .... 95 D8
Eden Cl. Woodhm KT15 .... 52 B1

Eden Grove Rd. Byfl KT14 71 E6
Eden Park Ave. Beck BR3 44 A4
Eden Park Sch. Beck BR3 43 F4
Eden Park Sta. Beck BR3 44 A4
Eden Rd. Crawl RH11 200 F4
Eden Rd. Croy CR0 61 D6
Eden Rd. Penge BR3 43 E8
Eden Rd. W Norw SE27 22 B3
Eden St. King U T KT1 & KT2 37 E7
Eden Vale. Dorm Pk RH19 185 E5
Eden Vale. E Grins RH19 185 E5
Eden Way. Beck BR3 44 A3
Eden Way. Warlgm CR6 81 E1
Eden Wlk. 5 King U T KT1 37 E7
Edenbrook. Lingf RH7 164 E4
Edencourt Rd. Streat SW16 21 B2
Edencroft. Bramly GU5 151 F7
Edenfield Gdns. Worc Pk KT4 57 F7
Edenham High Sch. Croy CR0 43 F2
Edenhurst Pl. Belm SM2 59 A4
Edenside Rd. L Book KT23 93 F3
Edensor Gdns. Chisw W4 7 E7
Edensor Rd. Chisw W4 7 E7
Edenvale Cl. Mitch CR4 21 A1
Edenvale Rd. Mitch CR4 21 A1
Ederline Ave. Thorn H SW16 42 A7
Edgar Cl. Worth RH10 202 E5
Edgar Ct. King U T KT3 38 E6
Edgar Rd. S Croy CR2 61 D2
Edgar Rd. Tats TN16 103 D6
Edgar Rd. Twick TW4 15 F8
Edgbarrow Rise. Sandh GU17 45 A2
Edgbarrow Sch.Crowth RG11 45 C3
Edgbarrowhill Star. Crowth RG11 45 A3
Edgcumbe Park Dr. Crowth RG11 45 A5
Edge Cl. Whit V KT13 53 A3
Edge Hill. Wimble SW19 19 D1
Edge Hill Ct. Wimble SW19 19 D1
Edgeborough. M Bourn GU10 146 C3
Edgeborough Ct. Guild GU1 130 F8
Edgecombe Cl. King U T KT2 18 D1
Edgecombe House. Putney SW19 19 E8
Edgecoombe. S Croy CR2 62 D2
Edgecumbe Ct. 2 Croy CR0 43 A1
Edgedale Cl. Crowth RG11 45 B5
Edgefield Cl. Cran GU6 174 C4
Edgefield Cl. Earls RH1 140 A4
Edgehill Ct. Walt O T KT12 35 C1
Edgehill House. 2 Redh RH1 118 F1
Edgehill Rd. Mitch CR4 41 B8
Edgehill Rd.Purly CR2 & CR8 61 B1
Edgeley. L Book KT23 93 E3
Edgell Cl. Thorpe GU25 31 F6
Edgell Rd. Stain TW18 12 F3
Edgemoor Rd. Friml GU15 & GU16 66 C3
Edgewood Cl. Crowth RG11 45 A7
Edgewood Gn. Croy CR0 43 D1
Edgeworth Cl. Whytlf CR3 81 A1
Edgington Rd. Streat SW16 21 D2
Edinburgh Cl. Ash V GU12 106 A5
Edinburgh Ct. Catf SE6 24 F7
Edinburgh Ct. 2 King U T KT1 37 E6
Edinburgh Ct. W Barn SM4 39 D4
Edinburgh Dr. Stain TW15 & TW18 13 D2
Edinburgh Rd. Sutton SM1 59 D8
Edinburgh Way. E Grins RH19 205 F7
Edith Gdns. Tolw KT5 38 B2
Edith Rd. Thorn H SE25 42 D4
Edith Rd. Wimble SW19 20 B2
Edmonds Ct. 4 Brack RG12 27 C8
Edmund Rd. Mitch CR4 40 E6
Edna Rd. Merton SW20 39 D7
Edrich Rd. Crawl RH11 201 A1
Edridge House. 9 W Norw SE27 22 B5
Edridge Rd. Croy CR0 & CR9 61 D7
Edward Alleyn House. Dulw SE21 22 E8
Edward Ave. Camb GU15 65 A5
Edward Ave. Morden CR4 & SM4 40 D4
Edward Cl. Hampt TW12 16 C3
Edward Ct. Stain TW18 13 C2
Edward II Ave. Byfl KT14 71 F5
Edward Pauling House. E Bed TW14 14 F8
Edward Pinner Ct. 5 Surb KT6 56 E8
Edward Rd. Bigg H TN16 83 E1
Edward Rd. Coulsd CR5 79 D4
Edward Rd. Croy CR0 42 E2
Edward Rd. Hampt TW12 16 C3
Edward Rd. Hatton TW14 3 E2
Edward Rd. M Bourn GU9 146 C7
Edward Rd. Penge SE20 23 D2
Edward Rd. Windl GU20 48 D4
Edward St. Alder GU11 105 A2
Edward Way. Ashf TW15 13 F6
Edwards Cl. N Cheam KT4 58 D8
Edwin Cl. W Hors KT24 92 D2
Edwin Rd. Twick TW1 & TW2 16 E7
Edwin Rd. W Hors KT24 92 D2
Edwin Stray House. Felt TW13 16 A5
Edwina Ct. Sutton SM1 59 B6
Eelmoor Plain Rd. Alder GU11 104 D5
Eelmoor Rd. Alder GU11 104 D5
Eelmoor Rd. Farnb GU14 84 F2
Eelmoor Road Trad Est. Farnb GU14 85 A2
Effingham Cl. Sutton SM2 59 B3
Effingham Common Rd. Effing KT24 93 C2
Effingham Ct. Mitch SW19 20 E1
Effingham Ct. Woking GU22 89 E8
Effingham House. 9 King U T KT2 18 B2
Effingham House Golf Club. Effing KT24 113 D7
Effingham Junction. E Hors KT24 93 A4
Effingham La. Burst RH10 183 E4
Effingham Lodge. 1 King U T KT6 37 E4
Effingham Pl. Effing KT24 113 D8
Effingham Rd. Burst RH10 & RH6 183 D6
Effingham Rd. Dome RH10 & RH6 183 D6
Effingham Rd. Reig RH2 139 B8
Effingham Rd. Thame D KT6 & KT7 37 C2
Effingham Rd. Thorn H CR0 41 F2
Effort St. Up Toot SW17 20 E3
Effra Ct. S Norw SE19 22 E1
Effra Rd. Wimble SW19 20 B2
Egbury House. Rhampt SW15 7 F1
Egerton Ct. 5 Rich TW10 6 E2
Egerton Ct. 5 Stough GU2 108 E1
Egerton House. Chisw W4 7 C8
Egerton Pl. Whit V KT13 53 C4
Egerton Rd. New Mal KT3 38 F5
Egerton Rd. Onsl V GU2 129 F8
Egerton Rd. S Norw SE25 42 E6
Egerton Rd. Sandh GU15 64 F7
Egerton Rd. Sandh GU15 65 A7
Egerton Rd. Twick TW2 16 E8
Egerton Rd. Whit V KT13 53 C4
Eggar's Ct. Alder GU12 105 B1
Eggar's Hill. Alder GU11 126 A8
Egham By-Pass. Egham TW20 12 A4
Egham Cl. Cheam SM3 58 E8
Egham Cl. Putney SW19 19 E6
Egham Cres. Cheam SM3 58 D8
Egham Ct. King U T KT6 37 D4
Egham Hill. Egham TW20 11 F3
Egham Hill. Eng Gn TW20 11 D2
Egham Hill Rdbt. Egham TW20 11 F3
Egham Sta. Egham TW20 12 A3
Egleston Rd. Morden SM4 40 B3
Egley Dr. Woking GU22 89 D5
Egley Rd. Woking GU22 89 D6
Eglinton Rd. Rushm GU10 168 B7
Eglise Rd. Warlgm CR6 81 E2
Egmont Ave. Surb KT6 37 F1
Egmont Park Rd. Walt o t H KT20 97 A2
Egmont Rd. New Mal KT3 38 F5
Egmont Rd. Surb KT6 38 A1
Egmont Rd. Sutton SM2 59 C3
Egmont Rd. Walt O T KT12 35 B2
Egmont Way. Burgh H KT20 97 E8
Egremont Rd. W Norw SE27 22 A5
Eighteenth Rd. Mitch CR4 41 E5
Eileen Rd. Thorn H SE25 42 D4
Eisenhower House. Tedd KT8 37 C8
Eland Pl. Croy CR9 61 B7
Eland Rd. Alder GU12 105 D1
Eland Rd. Croy CR0 & CR9 61 B7
Elberon Ave. Wallin CR0 41 C3
Elborough Rd. Croy SE25 43 A4
Elborough St. Wands SW18 20 A7
Elbow Meadow. Poyle SL3 1 F6
Elcho Rd. Pirb GU24 87 D8
Elder Cl. Burph GU1 & GU4 110 A4
Elder Gdns. 9 W Norw SE27 22 C4
Elder Oak Cl. Penge SE20 43 B8
Elder Rd. Bisley GU24 68 A4
Elder Rd. W Norw SE27 22 C3
Elder Way. Dork RH5 136 C3
Elderberry Gr. 10 W Norw SE27 22 C4
Eldersley Cl. Redh RH1 118 F3
Eldersley Gdns. Redh RH1 118 F3
Elderslie Cl. Beck BR3 44 B3
Elderton Rd. For Hil SE26 23 E4
Eldertree Pl. Mitch CR4 41 C8
Eldertree Way. Mitch CR4 41 C8
Elderwood. W Norw SE27 22 C3
Eldon Ave. Croy CR0 62 C8
Eldon Ave. Heston TW5 5 A7
Eldon Ct. Whit V KT13 53 C5
Eldon Dr. M Bourn GU10 146 D5
Eldon Pk. Croy SE25 43 B5
Eldon Rd. Cater CR3 100 D6
Eldrick Ct. E Bed TW14 14 D7
Eldridge Cl. E Bed TW14 15 A7
Eleanor Ave. Epsom KT19 57 D1
Eleanor Ct. Guild GU1 130 D7
Eleanor Gr. Mortl SW13 & SW14 7 E4
Eleanor House. 6 Merton SW19 40 B8
Elfin Gr. Tedd TW11 16 F3
Elfrida Cres. Catf SE6 24 A4
Elfrida Inf & Jun Sch. Catf SE6 24 A4
Elgar Ave. Crowth RG11 45 B7
Elgar Ave. Thorn H SW16 41 E6
Elgar Ave. Tolw KT5 & KT6 38 B2
Elgar House. Kenley CR8 80 C5
Elgar House. Twick TW2 5 D1
Elger Way. Copth RH10 183 A4
Elgin Ave. Ashf TW15 14 C2
Elgin Cl. Horsh RH13 217 F3
Elgin Cres. Cater CR3 101 A5
Elgin Cres. Harl TW6 3 E5
Elgin Ct. 6 Croy CR0 61 C6
Elgin Gdns. Guild GU1 110 A2
Elgin Rd. Croy CR0 61 F8
Elgin Rd. Sutton SM1 59 C7
Elgin Rd. Wallin SM6 60 C4
Elgin Rd. Weyb KT13 53 B5
Elgin Way. Friml GU16 85 F8
Eliot Bank. For Hil SE23 & SE26 23 B6
Eliot Bank Prim Sch. For Hil SE23 23 B6
Eliot Cl. Camb GU15 66 B7
Eliot Dr. Shottm GU27 207 E6
Eliot House. 10 Rich TW10 6 F1
Elizabeth Ave. Bagsh GU19 47 F2
Elizabeth Ave. Stain TW18 13 D2
Elizabeth Cl. Brack RG12 27 C5
Elizabeth Cl. Farnc GU7 150 E7
Elizabeth Cotts. 5 Rich TW9 7 A6
Elizabeth Cres. E Grins RH19 185 F3
Elizabeth Ct. Horley RH6 161 A3
Elizabeth Ct. Sunby TW16 35 C6
Elizabeth Ct. Tedd TW11 16 E3
Elizabeth Ct. W Barn SM4 39 E2
Elizabeth Ct. Whytlf CR3 80 F1
Elizabeth Gdns. Ascot SL5 29 B4
Elizabeth Gdns. Sunby TW16 35 C6
Elizabeth Hart Ct. Weyb KT13 52 F5
Elizabeth House. Cater CR3 101 A3
Elizabeth Rd. Farnc GU7 150 E7
Elizabeth Rd. Woki RG11 25 D6
Elizabeth Way. Felt TW13 15 C4
Elizabeth Way. S Norw SE19 22 D1
Elizabethan Cl. Stan TW19 13 D8
Elizabethan Way. Stan TW19 13 D8
Elizabethan Way. Worth RH10 202 C5
Elkins Gdns. Burph GU4 110 A4
Ellacombe House. 1 Streat SW2 22 A8
Elland Rd. Walt O T KT12 54 D8
Ellenborough Cl. Brack RG12 27 D8
Ellenbridge Way. S Croy CR2 61 E2
Elleray Ct. Ash GU12 106 A5
Elleray Rd. Tedd TW11 16 F2
Ellerdine Rd. Islew TW3 5 D3
Ellerker Gdns. Rich TW10 6 E1
Ellerman Ave. Twick TW2 & TW4 15 F7
Ellerslie Ct. 6 Wallin SM6 60 B4
Ellerton Rd. Surb KT6 37 F1
Ellerton Rd. Wands SW17 & SW18 20 D7
Ellerton Rd. Wimble SW20 19 A1
Ellery Cl. Cran GU6 174 E1
Ellery Rd. S Norw SE19 22 D1
Elles Ave. Merrow GU1 110 C1
Elles Quarters. Farnb GU14 85 B3
Elles Rd. Farnb GU14 84 F2
Ellesfield Ave. Easth RG12 26 E5
Ellesmere Ave. Beck BR3 44 B7
Ellesmere Ct. Chisw W4 7 D8
Ellesmere Ct. Penge SE20 43 B7
Ellesmere Ct. Whit V KT12 53 E4
Ellesmere Dr. Hams Gn CR2 81 B5
Ellesmere Hospl. Whit V KT13 53 E5
Ellesmere Rd. Twick TW1 6 C1
Ellesmere Rd. Whit V KT13 53 E4
Ellice Rd. Oxted RH8 122 F6
Ellingham. Woking GU22 89 E8
Ellingham Prim Sch. Chess KT9 56 D3
Ellingham Rd. Chess KT9 56 D4
Ellington Rd. Felt TW13 14 F4
Ellington Rd. Hounsl TW3 5 B5
Ellington Way. Burgh H KT18 77 B2
Elliot Cl. Worth RH10 202 C4
Elliot Park Ind Est. Alder GU12 105 E2
Elliot Rise. N Asct SL5 28 D7
Elliott Ct. Woking GU21 70 A3
Elliott Gdns. Shep Gn TW17 34 A5
Elliott Rd. Thorn H CR7 42 B5
Ellis Ave. Onsl V GU2 129 F7
Ellis Cl. Coulsd CR5 99 F7
Ellis Farm Cl. Westfd GU22 89 D5
Ellis Rd. Coulsd CR5 99 F7
Ellis Rd. Crowth RG11 45 B6
Ellis Rd. Mitch CR4 40 F3
Ellisfield Dr. Rhampt SW15 18 F8
Ellisfield Dr. Rhampt SW15 19 A8
Ellison Rd. Barnes SW13 7 F5
Ellison Rd. Streat SW16 21 E1
Ellison Way. Tongh GU10 126 F7
Ellison Way. Woki RG11 25 B6
Ellman Rd. Crawl RH11 200 F4
Ellora Rd. Streat SW16 21 D3
Ellson Cl. Worth RH10 202 C4
Ellswood Ct. 18 Surb KT6 37 D2
Elm Bank Gdns. Mortl SW13 7 E5
Elm Bank Mansions. Mortl SW13 7 E5
Elm Bridge La. Old Wok GU22 90 A8
Elm Cl. Box H KT20 116 C5
Elm Cl. Carsh SM5 40 F1
Elm Cl. Horse GU21 69 D4
Elm Cl. Leahd KT22 95 B5
Elm Cl. S Croy CR2 61 E4
Elm Cl. Send M GU23 91 A3
Elm Cl. Stan TW19 13 D7
Elm Cl. Tolw KT5 38 C2
Elm Cl. Twick TW13 & TW2 16 B6
Elm Cl. W Barn SW20 39 C5
Elm Cl. Warlgm CR6 81 D2
Elm Cotts. Mickle RH5 115 C8
Elm Court Sch. W Norw SE27 22 C6
Elm Cres. Heath E GU9 125 D7
Elm Cres. King U T KT2 37 E8
Elm Ct. Catf SE6 24 B7
Elm Ct. 5 Charlt TW16 14 F1
Elm Ct. Knaph GU21 68 D2
Elm Ct. Mitch CR4 40 F7
Elm Ct. Sandh GU15 45 E2
Elm Dr. Chobh GU24 49 F1
Elm Dr. E Grins RH19 186 A1
Elm Dr. Leahd KT22 95 B4
Elm Dr. Sunby TW16 35 C7
Elm Dr. Wink SL4 9 B7
Elm Gdns. Burgh H KT20 97 C8
Elm Gdns. Clayg KT10 55 F4
Elm Gdns. Mitch CR4 41 D5
Elm Gr. Bisley GU24 68 A3
Elm Gr. Cater CR3 100 E5
Elm Gr. Cran GU6 174 A3
Elm Gr. Epsom KT18 76 C5
Elm Gr. Heath E GU9 125 C7
Elm Gr. Horsh RH13 217 E1
Elm Gr. King U T KT2 37 E8
Elm Gr. Sutton SM1 59 B6
Elm Gr. Wimble SW19 19 E1
Elm Grove Par. Hackb SM6 60 A7
Elm Grove Rd. Cobham KT11 73 D3
Elm Grove Rd. Farnb GU14 85 B4
Elm Hill Bglws. Normdy GU3 106 E3
Elm House. 2 King U T KT2 17 F1
Elm La. Ash GU10 126 F8
Elm La. For Hil SE6 23 F6
Elm La. Ockham GU23 92 A8
Elm Park Rd. S Norw SE25 42 F6
Elm Pk. Streat SW2 21 F8
Elm Pk. Sunnin GU20 & SL5 29 E1
Elm Pl. Alder GU11 126 C8
Elm Rd. Beck BR3 43 F7
Elm Rd. Carsh CR4 & SM6 41 A1
Elm Rd. Chess KT9 56 E6
Elm Rd. Clayg KT10 55 F4
Elm Rd. E Bed TW14 14 D8
Elm Rd. Farnc GU7 150 F8
Elm Rd. Heath E GU9 125 D7
Elm Rd. Horse GU21 69 F4
Elm Rd. King U T KT2 37 F8
Elm Rd. King U T KT3 38 D6
Elm Rd. Leahd KT22 95 B5
Elm Rd. Mortl SW14 7 C3
Elm Rd. Purley CR8 80 B6
Elm Rd. Redh RH1 118 E1
Elm Rd. S Norw CR7 42 D5
Elm Rd. Stonel KT17 57 F4
Elm Rd. Warlgm CR6 81 D2
Elm Rd. Woking GU21 69 D1
Elm Rd W. Cheam SM4 39 F2
Elm Tree Ave. Thame D KT10 36 E2
Elm Tree Cl. Addl KT16 51 E8
Elm Tree Cl. Ashf TW15 14 B3
Elm View. Ash GU12 106 B3
Elm Way. N Cheam KT4 58 C7
Elm Way. W Ewell KT19 57 D5
Elm Way. W Ewell KT19 57 D5
Elm Wlk. W Barn SW20 39 D5
Elm Wood Prim Sch. W Norw SE27 22 D5
Elmbank Ave. Eng Gn TW20 11 B2
Elmbank Ave. Guild GU2 130 A8
Elmbourne Rd. Up Toot SW17 21 B5
Elmbridge Ave. Tolw KT5 38 C3
Elmbridge Cotts. Cran GU6 174 B3
Elmbridge La. Old Wok GU22 89 F8
Elmbridge Rd. Crawl GU6 173 F2
Elmbrook Cl. Sunby TW16 35 B8
Elmbrook Cty Fst Sch. Sunby TW16 35 B8
Elmbrook Rd. Cheam SM1 58 F6
Elmcourt Rd. W Norw SE21 & SE27 22 B6
Elmcroft. L Book KT23 94 A3
Elmcroft. 12 Woking GU22 69 E1
Elmcroft Cl. Chess KT9 56 E7
Elmcroft Cl. Felt TW14 3 F1
Elmcroft Cl. Friml GU16 85 F7
Elmcroft Dr. Ashf TW15 14 A3
Elmcroft Dr. Chess KT9 56 E7
Elmdene. Tolw KT5 38 C1
Elmdene Cl. Beck BR3 43 F4
Elmdon Rd. Hatton TW6 3 F4
Elmdon Rd. Hounsl TW5 4 E5
Elmer Cotts. Fetch KT22 95 A4
Elmer Gdns. Islew TW7 5 D4
Elmer Mews. Fetch KT22 95 A5
Elmer Rd. Catf SE6 24 C8
Elmer's Dr. Tedd TW11 17 B2
Elmers End Rd. Beck BR3 43 D5
Elmers End Rd. Penge BR3 & SE20 43 C6
Elmers End Sta. Beck BR3 43 D5
Elmers Rd. Croy CR0 & SE25 43 A2
Elmers Rd. Ockley RH5 177 C4
Elmerside Rd. Beck BR3 43 E5
Elmfield. Fetch KT23 94 A4
Elmfield Ave. Mitch CR4 41 A8
Elmfield Ave. Tedd TW11 16 F3
Elmfield House. Merrow GU4 110 C3
Elmfield Mansions. 5 Up Toot SW17 21 A6
Elmfield Rd. Up Toot SW17 21 B6
Elmfield Way. S Croy CR2 61 F2
Elmgate Ave. Felt TW13 15 C5
Elmgrove Cl. Knaph GU21 88 D8
Elmgrove Rd. Croy CR0 43 B2
Elmgrove Rd. Weyb KT13 53 A7
Elmhurst Ave. Mitch CR4 21 B1
Elmhurst Ballet Sch. Camb GU15 65 D5
Elmhurst Ct. Croy CR0 61 D5
Elmhurst Ct. Guild GU1 130 F8
Elmhurst Dr. Dork RH4 136 B5
Elmhurst Lodge. Sutton SM2 59 C3
Elmhurst Sch for Boys. S Croy CR2 61 D5
Elmore Rd. Chips CR5 99 A6
Elmpark Gdns. Selsd CR2 62 C1
Elms Cotts. Mitch CR4 40 F7
Elms Ct. Merton SW19 20 B1
Elms Rd. Alder GU11 105 A2
Elms Rd. Woki RG11 25 B5
Elms The. Ash GU10 126 F8
Elms The. Ashf TW15 14 A3
Elms The. Clayg KT10 55 F3

Elms The. Croy CR0 42 C1
Elms The. Mortl SW13 7 F4
Elmscott Rd. Catf BR1 24 F3
Elmshorn. Nork KT17 77 C3
Elmside. Guild GU2 130 A8
Elmside. Milf GU8 149 F1
Elmside. New Add CR0 63 B4
Elmsleigh Ct. Sutton SM1 59 B7
Elmsleigh Ctr The. Stain TW18 12 F4
Elmsleigh House. Twick TW2 16 D6
Elmsleigh Rd. Farnb GU14 84 F4
Elmsleigh Rd. Stain TW18 12 F3
Elmsleigh Rd. Twick TW2 16 D6
Elmslie Cl. Epsom KT18 76 C5
Elmstead. E Grins RH19 205 E8
Elmstead Cl. W Ewell KT19 57 E5
Elmstead Cl. W Ewell KT19 57 E5
Elmstead Gdns. Worc Pk KT4 58 A7
Elmstead Rd. W Byfl KT14 71 A5
Elmsway. Ashf TW15 14 A3
Elmswood. L Book KT23 93 F3
Elmsworth Ave. Hounsl TW3 5 B5
Elmtree Cl. Byfl KT14 71 E6
Elmtree Rd. Tedd TW11 16 E3
Elmwood Ave. Felt TW13 15 B5
Elmwood Cl. Ashtd KT21 75 D2
Elmwood Cl. Hackb SM6 60 B8
Elmwood Cl. Stonel KT17 58 A3
Elmwood Ct. Ashtd KT21 75 D2
Elmwood Dr. Stonel KT17 58 A3
Elmwood Inf Sch. Thorn H CR0 42 B3
Elmwood Jun Sch. Thorn H CR0 42 B2
Elmwood Rd. Chisw W4 7 C8
Elmwood Rd. Knaph GU21 88 D8
Elmwood Rd. Mitch CR4 40 F6
Elmwood Rd. Redh RH1 119 B5
Elmwood Rd. Thorn H CR0 42 B2
Elmworth Gr. W Norw SE21 22 D6
Elphinstone Ct. Streat SW16 21 E2
Elsdon Rd. Woking GU21 69 A1
Elsenham St. Wands SW18 & SW19 19 F6
Elsenwood Cres.Camb GU15 66 A6
Elsenwood Dr. Camb GU15 66 A7
Elsinore Ave. Stan TW19 13 E8
Elsinore Rd. For Hil SE23 23 E7
Elsinore Way. Mortl TW9 7 B4
Elsley Cl. Friml GU16 85 F6
Elsrick Ave. Morden SM4 40 A4
Elstan Way. Croy CR0 43 E2
Elstead Ct. Cheam SM4 39 E1
Elstead Gn. Elst GU8 148 D4
Elstead House. 12 Streat SW2 21 F8
Elstead Rd. Milf GU8 149 C3
Elstead Rd. Seale GU10 127 B3
Elstead Rd. Shackl GU7 & GU8 149 E6
Elstead Rd. The San GU10 127 A2
Elsted Cl. Crawl RH11 201 B8
Elston Pl. Alder GU12 126 C8
Elston Rd. Alder GU11 & GU12 126 C8
Elstree Hill. Catf BR1 24 E1
Elsworth Cl. E Bed TW14 14 E7
Elsworthy. Thame D KT7 36 E3
Elthorne Ct. Felt TW13 15 C7
Elton Rd. King U T KT2 38 A8
Elton Rd. Purley CR8 79 C7
Elveden Cl. Mayb GU22 71 B2
Elveden Ct. Leahd KT22 95 C6
Elveden Rd. Esher KT11 73 C8
Elvington Gn. Hayes BR2 44 F4
Elvino Rd. For Hil SE26 23 E3
Elwell Cl. Egham TW20 12 A2
Elwill Way. Beck BR3 44 D5
Ely Cl. Crawl RH10 201 F2
Ely Cl. Friml GU16 86 A7
Ely Cl. King U T SW20 38 F7
Ely Ct. King U T KT1 38 A6
Ely House. 6 Redh RH1 118 F1
Ely Rd. Hatton TW6 3 F5
Ely Rd. Hounsl TW4 4 C4
Ely Rd. Thorn H CR0 42 D4
Elystan Cl. Wallin SM6 60 C2
Embankment The. Twick TW1 17 A7
Embankment The. Wray TW19 11 C7
Embassy Ct. King U T KT6 37 D4
Embassy Ct. 7 Wallin SM6 60 B4
Embassy Gdns. Beck BR3 43 F8
Ember Cl. Addl KT15 52 D5
Ember Ctr. Walt O T KT12 54 E8
Ember Farm Ave. Thame D KT8 36 D3
Ember Farm Way. E Mole KT8 36 D4
Ember Gdns. Thame D KT10 & KT8 36 E2
Ember House. Catf BR1 24 D3
Ember La. Thame D KT10 & KT8 36 D2
Embercourt Rd. Thame D KT10 & KT7 & KT8 36 E3
Emberwood. Crawl RH11 201 D8
Embleton Rd. Head Dn GU35 187 B6
Embleton Wlk. Hampt TW12 15 F3
Emerton Rd. Fetch KT22 94 C6
Emery Down Cl. Brack RG12 28 A6
Emley Rd. Addl KT15 52 B6
Emlyn La. Leahd KT22 95 A5
Emlyn Rd. Earls RH1 140 A7
Emlyn Rd. Horley RH6 160 E4
Emmanuel Cl. Stough GU2 109 A4
Emmanuel House. W Norw SE21 22 D5
Emmanuel Rd. Streat SW12 21 D7
Emmbrook Rd. Woki RG11 25 A8
Emmbrook Sch The. Woki RG11 25 A8
Emmeline Ct. Walt O T KT12 35 C2
Emmetts Cl. Horse GU21 69 D2
Empire Villas. Salfs RH1 161 B7
Empress Ave. Farnb GU14 85 B5
Emsworth St. Streat SW2 21 F6
Ena Rd. Thorn H SW16 41 E6
Endale Cl. Carsh SM5 59 F8
Endeavour Way. Wallin CR0 41 E2
Endeavour Way. Wimble SW19 20 B4
Enderley House. S Norw SE19 42 F8
Endlesham Ct. 3 Balham SW12 21 A8
Endlesham Rd. Balham SW12 21 A8
Endsleigh Cl. Selsd CR2 62 C1
Endsleigh Gdns. Hersh KT12 54 C5
Endsleigh Gdns. King U T KT6 37 C3
Endsleigh Mansions. 4 Streat SW16 21 E5
Endsleigh Rd. Merst RH1 119 C6
Endway. Tolw KT5 38 B2
Enfield Rd. Ash GU12 106 B5
Enfield Rd. Crawl RH11 201 C2
Enfield Rd. Harl TW6 3 E5
Engadine Cl. S Croy CR0 61 F7
Engadine St. Wands SW18 20 A7
Engalee. E Grins RH19 185 C2
Englefield. Horsh RH12 216 F2
Englefield Cl. Eng Gn TW20 11 C2
Englefield Cl. Thorn H CR0 42 C3
Englefield Green Cty Inf Sch. Eng Gn TW20 11 C3
Englefield Rd. Knaph GU21 68 D2
Engleheart Dr. Felt TW14 3 F1
Engleheart Rd. Catf SE6 24 C8
Englehurst. Eng Gn TW20 11 C2
Englemere Pk. Ascot SL5 28 D5
Englemere Pond Nature Reserve. Ascot SL5 28 F6
Englesfield. Friml GU15 66 D5
Engliff La. Pyrf GU22 71 A3
Enid Wood House. Brack RG12 27 C7
Enmore Ave. Croy SE25 43 A4
Enmore Gdns. Mortl SW14 7 D2
Enmore Rd. Croy SE25 43 A4
Ennerdale. Easth RG12 27 A5
Ennerdale Cl. Cheam SM1 58 F6
Ennerdale Cl. Crawl RH11 201 B4
Ennerdale Cl. E Bed TW14 14 F7
Ennerdale Gr. Hale GU9 125 A6
Ennerdale Rd. Rich TW9 6 F5
Ennismore Ave. Guild GU1 109 F1
Ennismore Gdns. Thame D KT7 36 E3
Ennor Ct. Cheam KT4 58 C6
Ensham Sch. Up Toot SW17 20 F3
Ensham Sec Sch (Annexe). Up Toot SW17 20 E4
Ensign Cl. Purley CR8 61 A1
Ensign Cl. Stan TW19 13 D7
Ensign Way. Stan TW19 13 D7
Enterdent Cotts. Godst RH9 121 D2
Enterdent Rd. Godst RH9 121 D2
Enterprise Cl. Thorn H CR0 42 A1
Enterprise Est. Stough GU1 109 E5
Enterprise House. Walt O T KT12 35 B2
Enterprise Way. Tedd TW11 16 F2
Envis Way. Fairl GU3 108 C4
Eothen Sch for Girls. Cater CR3 101 A3
Epping Way. Brack RG12 27 F5
Epping Wlk. Crawl RH10 201 F4
Epsom Bsns Pk. Ewell KT17 76 E8
Epsom Cl. Camb GU15 65 C8
Epsom Coll. Epsom KT17 77 A5
Epsom Cty Jun & Inf Schs. Epsom KT19 76 D8
Epsom District Hospl. Woodc KT18 76 C4
Epsom Downs Cty Inf Sch. Lang V KT18 96 D8
Epsom Downs Metro Ctr. Burgh H KT20 97 B7
Epsom Downs Sta. Epsom KT17 77 B4
Epsom & Ewell Cottage Hospl. Epsom KT19 75 E8
Epsom & Ewell High Sch. W Ewell KT19 57 C5
Epsom La N. Burgh H KT18 & KT20 97 B7
Epsom La S. Tadw KT20 97 C5
Epsom Pl. Cran GU6 174 F3
Epsom Rd. Ashtd KT18 & KT21 76 A2
Epsom Rd. Cheam SM4 39 F2
Epsom Rd. Crawl RH10 202 A4
Epsom Rd. Croy CR0 61 A6
Epsom Rd. E Clan GU4 111 D3
Epsom Rd. Ewell KT17 76 F8
Epsom Rd. Guild GU1 130 F8
Epsom Rd. Leahd KT22 95 C6
Epsom Rd. Merrow GU1 & GU4 110 C1
Epsom Rd. Merrow GU4 110 F2
Epsom Rd. Morden SM4 39 F2
Epsom Rd. W Clan GU4 111 D3
Epsom Rd. W Hors GU4 & KT24 112 C6
Epsom Sch of Art & Design. Epsom KT18 76 D5
Epsom Sq. Hatton TW6 3 F5
Epsom Sta. Epsom KT18 76 D6
Epworth Rd. Brent TW7 & TW8 6 B7
Eresby Dr. Croy BR3 44 A1
Erica Cl. W End GU24 67 E6
Erica Ct. Woking GU22 69 D1
Erica Dr. Woki RG11 25 D5
Erica Gdns. W Wick CR0 63 B7
Erica Way. Copth RH10 183 A2
Erica Way. Horsh RH12 217 D5
Eridge Cl. Crawl RH10 202 C6
Erin Cl. Catf BR1 24 E1
Erindale Ct. Beck BR3 44 A8
Eriswell Cres. Whit V KT12 53 F4
Eriswell Rd. Whit V KT12 53 F5
Erkenwald Cl. Chert KT16 32 E3
Ermine Cl. Hounsl TW4 4 C5
Ermyn Cl. Ashtd KT21 95 D6
Ermyn Way. Ashtd KT21 & KT22 95 D6
Erncroft Way. Twick TW1 5 F1
Ernest Ave. W Norw SE27 22 B4
Ernest Bevin Sch. Up Toot SW17 20 E6
Ernest Cl. Beck BR3 44 A4
Ernest Cl. M Bourn GU10 & GU9 146 B6
Ernest Cotts. Ewell KT17 57 F3
Ernest Gdns. Chisw W4 7 B8
Ernest Gr. Beck BR3 43 F4
Ernest Rd. King U T KT1 38 B7
Ernest Sq. King U T KT1 38 B7
Ernle Rd. Wimble SW20 19 C1
Erridge Rd. Merton SW19 40 A7
Errol Gdns. W Barn KT3 39 A5
Erskine Cl. Carsh SM1 59 E7
Erskine Cl. Crawl RH11 200 E2
Erskine Rd. Carsh SM1 & SM5 59 D7
Esam Way. W Norw SE27 & SW16 22 A3
Escombe Dr. Stough GU2 & GU3 109 B6
Escot Rd. Charlt TW16 14 E1
Escott Pl. Ottsh KT16 51 D4
Esher Ave. Cheam SM3 58 D7
Esher Ave. Walt O T KT12 35 A1
Esher C of E Fst & Mid Sch. Esher KT10 55 B6
Esher Church Sch. Esher KT10 55 C5
Esher Cl. Esher KT10 55 B5
Esher Coll. Thame D KT7 36 E2
Esher Cres. Hatton TW6 3 F5
Esher Gdns. Putney SW19 19 D6
Esher Gn. Esher KT10 55 B6
Esher Green Dr. Esher KT10 55 B7
Esher Mews. Mitch CR4 40 F6
Esher Park Ave. Esher KT10 55 C5
Esher Place Ave. Esher KT10 55 B6
Esher Rd. Camb GU15 47 A1
Esher Rd. E Mole KT8 36 D4
Esher Rd. Hersh KT10 & KT12 54 E6
Esher Sta. Esher KT10 55 D8
Eskdale Gdns. Sander CR8 80 D5
Eskdale Way. Friml GU15 66 D4
Eskmont Ridge. S Norw SE19 22 E1
Esme House. Rhampt SW15 7 F3
Esparto St. Wands SW18 20 B8
Essenden Rd. S Croy CR2 61 E3
Essendene Cl. Cater CR3 100 E4
Essendene Lodge Sch. Cater CR3 100 E4
Essendene Rd. Cater CR3 100 E5
Essex Ave. Islew TW7 5 E4
Essex Cl. Addl KT15 52 C6
Essex Cl. Friml GU16 86 A7
Essex Cl. W Barn SM4 39 D2
Essex Ct. Barnes SW13 7 F5
Essex Ct. S Norw SE19 22 D2
Essex Dr. Crawl GU6 173 F2
Essex Gr. S Norw SE19 22 D2
Essex House. 5 Croy CR0 61 D8
Essex Tower. 5 Penge SE20 43 B8
Estcots Cty Prim Sch. E Grins RH19 186 A1
Estcots Dr. E Grins RH19 186 A1
Estcourt Rd. Croy CR0 & SE25 43 B3
Estella Ave. W Barn KT3 & SW20 39 B5
Estreham Rd. Streat SW16 21 D2
Estridge Cl. Hounsl TW3 5 A3
Eswyn Rd. Up Toot SW17 20 F3
Ethel Rd. Ashf TW15 13 E3
Ethelbert Rd. Wimble SW20 39 D8
Ethelbert St. Balham SW12 21 B7
Ethelworth Ct. 4 Streat SW2 22 A7
Etherley Hill. Wotton RH5 177 A7
Etherow St. Dulw SE22 23 A8
Etherstone Gn. Streat SW16 22 A4
Etherstone Rd. Streat SW16 22 A4
Eton Ave. Heston TW5 5 A8
Eton Ave. New Mal KT3 38 D5
Eton Cl. Wands SW18 20 B8
Eton Ct. Stain TW18 12 F3
Eton Pl. Heath E GU9 125 B7
Eton Rd. Harl UB3 3 F7
Eton St. Rich TW10 6 E2
Etps Rd. Farnb GU14 105 B8
Ettrick Ct. Farnb GU14 105 B8
Etwell Pl. Surb KT5 37 F3
Eureka Rd. King U T KT1 38 A7
Europa Park Rd. Guild GU1 109 C2
Eurythmy Sch. E Grins RH19 205 E6
Eustace Cres. Woki RG11 25 D8
Eustace Rd. Merrow GU4 110 D3
Euston Rd. Thorn H CR0 42 A1
Evans Cl. Worth RH10 202 D5
Evans Gr. Felt TW13 16 A6
Evans Rd. Catf SE6 24 E6
Eve Rd. Islew TW7 6 A3
Eve Rd. Sheer GU21 70 B4
Evedon. Easth RG12 27 B2
Evelina Rd. Penge SE20 23 D1
Eveline Rd. Mitch CR4 40 F8
Evelyn Ave. Alder GU11 126 B8
Evelyn Cl. Twick TW2 16 B8
Evelyn Cl. Woking GU22 89 D7
Evelyn Cotts. Abin C RH5 155 D8
Evelyn Cotts. S Godst RH9 142 E6
Evelyn Cres. Sunby TW16 34 F8
Evelyn Ct. Croy CR0 43 A2
Evelyn Gdns. Rich TW9 6 E3
Evelyn Gdns. Tyl Gn RH9 121 C5
Evelyn Rd. Rich TW9 6 E4
Evelyn Rd. Rich TW10 17 C5
Evelyn Rd. Wimble SW19 20 B2
Evelyn Terr. Rich TW9 6 E4
Evelyn Way. Stk D'A KT11 73 F3
Evelyn Way. Sunby TW16 34 F8
Evelyn Way. Wallin SM6 60 D6
Evelyn Woods Rd. Farnb GU11 105 C7
Evendon's Cl. Woki RG11 25 A3
Evendon's La. Woki RG11 25 A3
Evening Hill. Beck BR3 24 C1
Evenlode Way. Sandh GU15 & GU17 64 D8
Everard La. Cater CR3 101 B5
Everest Ct. S Norw SE19 42 E8
Everest Ct. Woking GU21 68 E3
Everest Rd. Camb GU15 65 D8
Everest Rd. Crowth RG11 45 B6
Everest Rd. Stan TW19 13 E8
Everglade. Bigg H TN16 83 D1
Everglades. Beck BR2 44 E6
Evergreen Ct. Stan TW19 13 D8
Evergreen Rd. Friml GU16 66 A3
Evergreen Way. Stan TW19 13 D8
Everlands Cl. 6 Woking GU22 69 E1
Eversfield Ct. 2 Reig RH2 118 C1
Eversfield Rd. Horsh RH13 217 E1
Eversfield Rd. Reig RH2 118 B1
Eversfield Rd. Rich TW9 6 F5
Eversley Cres. Hounsl TW7 5 D6
Eversley Pk. Wimble SW19 19 B3
Eversley Rd. King U T KT5 37 F4
Eversley Rd. S Norw SE19 22 D1
Eversley Way. Croy CR0 63 A7
Eversley Way. Thorpe TW20 32 C7
Everton Rd. Croy CR0 43 A1
Evesham Cl. Belm SM2 59 A3
Evesham Cl. Reig RH2 117 F2
Evesham Gn. Morden SM4 40 B3
Evesham Rd. Morden SM4 40 B3
Evesham Rd. Reig RH2 117 F2
Evesham Rd N. Reig RH3 117 F2
Evesham Wlk. Sandh GU15 45 D1
Ewart Rd. For Hil SE23 23 D8
Ewelands. Horley RH6 161 C4
Ewell By-Pass. Ewell KT17 58 A2
Ewell Castle Sch. Ewell KT17 58 A2
Ewell Court Ave. W Ewell KT19 57 E5
Ewell Court Ave. W Ewell KT19 57 E5
Ewell Downs Rd. Ewell KT17 77 A7
Ewell East Sta. Ewell KT17 58 B1
Ewell Grove Cty Inf Sch. Ewell KT17 57 F1
Ewell House. Ewell KT17 57 F1
Ewell House Gr. Ewell KT17 57 F1
Ewell Park Way. Stonel KT17 58 A3
Ewell Rd. Cheam SM2 & SM3 58 D4
Ewell Rd. Surb KT5 & KT6 37 F2
Ewell Rd. Thame D KT6 & KT7 37 B2
Ewell Rd. Tolw KT6 38 B1
Ewell West Sta. W Ewell KT19 57 E2
Ewell West Sta. W Ewell KT19 57 E2
Ewelme Rd. For Hil SE23 23 C7
Ewen Cres. Streat SW2 22 A8
Ewhurst Ave. S Croy CR2 61 F2
Ewhurst C of E Fst Sch. Ewh GU6 175 E5
Ewhurst Cl. Crawl RH11 201 C6
Ewhurst Cl. E Ewell SM2 58 C2
Ewhurst Ct. Mitch CR4 40 D6
Ewhurst Rd. Cran GU6 174 E3
Ewhurst Rd. Crawl RH11 201 C7
Ewhurst Rd. Ewh GU5 & GU6 154 E3
Ewins Cl. Ash GU12 106 A2
Ewood La. Bear Gn RH5 157 F6
Ewood La. Parkg RH5 158 C6
Ewshot Hill Cross. Crond GU10 124 D7
Exbury Rd. For Hil SE6 24 A6
Excalibur Cl. Crawl RH11 200 E5
Excelsior Cl. King U T KT1 38 A7
Exchange Rd. Ascot SL5 29 C4
Exchange Rd. Crawl RH10 201 E6
Exchange The. 6 Purley CR8 80 A8
Exeforde Ave. Ashf TW15 14 A4
Exeter Cl. Crawl RH10 201 E2
Exeter Ct. King U T KT6 37 E4
Exeter Ct. Mitch SW19 20 E1
Exeter House. Felt TW13 16 A6
Exeter Rd. Ash GU12 106 A3
Exeter Rd. Croy CR0 42 F2
Exeter Rd. Felt TW13 15 F5
Exeter Rd. Harl TW6 3 E4
Exeter Way. Harl TW6 3 E5
Exhibition Rd. Farnb GU14 105 A8
Explorer Ave. Stan TW19 13 E7
Eyebright Cl. Croy CR0 43 D1
Eyhurst Cl. Kings KT20 97 F3
Eyhurst Spur. Kings KT20 97 F3
Eyles Cl. Horsh RH12 217 B4
Eylewood Rd. W Norw SE27 22 C3
Eynella Rd. Dulw SE21 22 F8
Eyston Dr. Whit V KT13 53 A1

Fabyc House. Rich TW9 7 A7
Factory Cotts. Farnh GU10 124 D2
Factory La. Thorn H CR0 & CR9 61 B8

Fagg's Rd. Felt TW14 .... 4 A2
Fagg's Rd. Hatton TW14 .... 4 A2
Fair Green Ct. **1** Mitch CR4 40 F6
Fair La. L Kings CR5 & RH2 .... 98 D1
Fair Oak Cl. Oxsh KT22 .... 74 D7
Fair St. Hounsl TW3 .... 5 C4
Fair View. Horsh RH12 .... 217 A3
Fairacre. Hounsl TW7 .... 5 D6
Fairacre. King U T KT3 .... 38 E6
Fairacres. Burgh H KT20 .... 97 C6
Fairacres. Cobham KT11 .... 73 E7
Fairacres. New Add CR0 .... 62 F2
Fairbairn Cl. Purley CR8 .... 80 A6
Fairbourne. Cobham KT11 ...... 73 D6
Fairbourne Cl. Woking GU21 69 A1
Fairbourne La. Cater CR3 .... 100 C4
Fairbourne Way.
  Stough GU2 .... 109 A4
Fairbriar Ct. **9** Epsom KT18 76 E6
Fairchildes Ave.
  New Add CR0 .... 82 D7
Fairchildes Cotts.
  W Wick CR6 .... 82 F6
Fairchildes PrimSch.
  New Add CR0 .... 82 E7
Fairchildes Rd. Fickl CR6 .... 82 E4
Faircroft. For Hil SE26 .... 23 C4
Faircross. Easth RG12 .... 27 B6
Fairdene. Kings CR5 .... 98 F6
Fairdene Rd. Coulsd CR5 .... 79 D2
Fairfax. Brack RG12 .... 27 A8
Fairfax Ave. Ewell KT17 .... 58 B2
Fairfax Ave. Redh RH1 .... 118 F2
Fairfax Cl. Walt O T KT12 .... 35 B1
Fairfax Mews. Farnb GU14 ..... 85 D2
Fairfax Rd. Old Wok GU22 ...... 90 B7
Fairfax Rd. Tedd TW11 .... 17 B1
Fairfield App. Wray TW19 ...... 11 D8
Fairfield Ave. Horley RH6 .... 161 A1
Fairfield Ave. Stain TW18 ...... 12 F4
Fairfield Ave. Twick TW2 .... 16 B7
Fairfield Cl. G Book KT23 .... 94 B1
Fairfield Cl. Mitch SW19 .... 20 E1
Fairfield Cl. W Ewell KT19 ...... 57 E5
Fairfield Ct. Dork RH4 .... 115 B1
Fairfield Dr. Dork RH4 .... 136 B8
Fairfield Dr. Friml GU16 .... 65 E3
Fairfield E. King U T KT1 .... 37 E7
Fairfield Ind Est.
  King U T KT1 .... 37 F6
Fairfield La. W End GU24 .... 68 A7
Fairfield N.
  King U T KT1 & KT2 .... 37 E7
Fairfield Path.
  S Croy CR0 & CR9 .... 61 D7
Fairfield Pk. Cobham KT11 .... 73 D5
Fairfield Pl. King U T KT1 .... 37 E6
Fairfield Rd. Beck BR3 .... 44 A7
Fairfield Rd. E Grins RH19 .. 205 F8
Fairfield Rd. King U T KT1 ...... 37 E7
Fairfield Rd. Leahd KT22 .... 95 B6
Fairfield Rd.
  S Croy CR0 & CR9 .... 61 E7
Fairfield Rise. Stough GU2 .. 108 F2
Fairfield S. King U T KT1 .... 37 F7
Fairfield The. Farnh GU9 ...... 125 C2
Fairfield W. King U T KT1 .... 37 E7
Fairfield Way. Coulsd CR5 ..... 79 D5
Fairfield Way. W Ewell KT19 57 E5
Fairfield Wlk. Leahd KT22 ...... 95 B6
Fairfields. Lewish SE6 .... 24 B8
Fairfields Rd. Hounsl TW3 .... 5 C4
Fairford. For Hil SE6 .... 24 A7
Fairford Ave. Croy CR0 .... 43 D4
Fairford Cl. Croy CR0 .... 43 E4
Fairford Cl. Pyrf KT14 .... 70 F5
Fairford Ct. Reig RH2 .... 118 C3
Fairford Ct. Sutton SM2 .... 59 B3
Fairford Gdns. Worc Pk KT4 .. 57 F7
Fairgreen Rd. Thorn H CR7 .... 42 B4
Fairhaven. Egham TW20 .... 11 F3
Fairhaven Ave. Croy CR0 .... 43 D3
Fairhaven Ct. Croy CR2 .... 61 C5
Fairhaven Ct. **1**
  Egham TW20 .... 11 F3
Fairhaven Rd. Redh RH1 .... 119 A5
Fairholme. Bed TW14 .... 14 E8
Fairholme. **2** New Mal KT3 38 B5
Fairholme Cres. Ashtd KT21 75 C2
Fairholme Gdns.
  M Bourn GU9 .... 125 C1
Fairholme Jun & Inf Schs.
  E Bed TW14 .... 14 D7
Fairholme Rd. Ashf TW15 ...... 13 F3
Fairholme Rd. Cheam SM1 .... 58 F4
Fairholme Rd. Thorn H CR0 ... 42 A2
Fairings The. Hersh KT12 ...... 54 C6
Fairlands Ave. Fairl GU3 ...... 108 C5

Fairlands Ave. Sutton SM1 .... 59 A8
Fairlands Ave. Thorn H CR7 .. 42 A4
Fairlands Ct. Fairl GU3 .... 108 C5
Fairlands Ct. Fairl GU3 .... 108 D5
Fairlawn. L Book KT23 .... 93 F3
Fairlawn. Whit V KT13 .... 53 E5
Fairlawn Cl. Clayg KT10 .... 55 F4
Fairlawn Cl. Felt TW13 .... 15 F4
Fairlawn Cl. King U T KT2 ...... 18 C2
Fairlawn Cres.
  E Grins RH19 .... 185 B2
Fairlawn Dr. E Grins RH19 . 185 B2
Fairlawn Dr. Earls RH1 .... 139 E7
Fairlawn Dr. Woodh RH1 ..... 139 E7
Fairlawn Gr. Banstd SM7 .... 78 D6
Fairlawn Pk. For Hil SE26 ...... 23 E3
Fairlawn Pk. Horse GU21 ...... 69 E4
Fairlawn Prim Sch.
  For Hil SE23 .... 23 C8
Fairlawn Prim Sch Annexe.
  For Hil SE23 .... 23 C7
Fairlawn Rd. Merton SW19 . 19 F1
Fairlawn Rd.
  Sutton SM3 & SM5 .... 78 C8
Fairlawns. Wallin SM6 .... 60 B5
Fairlawns. Addl KT15 .... 52 B5
Fairlawns. Horley RH6 .... 161 B2
Fairlawns. Merrow GU1 .... 110 C1
Fairlawns. Sunby TW16 .... 35 A6
Fairlawns. Twick TW1 .... 6 C1
Fairlawns. Woodhm KT15 ...... 70 F8
Fairlawns. Wray TW19 .... 11 F8
Fairlea. Beck BR3 .... 44 B7
Fairlie Gdns. For Hil SE23 ..... 23 C8
Fairlight. Hampt TW12 .... 16 B3
Fairlight Cl. N Cheam KT4 ..... 58 C6
Fairlight Rd. Up Toot SW17 .. 20 D4
Fairline Ct. Beck BR3 .... 44 C7
Fairlop Wlk. Crawl GU6 .... 173 F2
Fairmead. Tolw KT5 & KT6 .... 38 B1
Fairmead. Woking GU21 .... 69 C1
Fairmead Cl. Heston TW5 .... 4 D7
Fairmead Cl. King U T KT3 .... 38 D6
Fairmead Cl. Sandh GU15 ...... 64 E7
Fairmead Rd. Thorn H CR0 .. 42 A2
Fairmile Ave. Cobham KT11 .. 73 F6
Fairmile Ave. Street SW16 .... 21 D3
Fairmile Hts. Cobham KT11 .. 74 A6
Fairmile La. Cobham KT11 .... 73 E5
Fairmile Park Copse.
  Cobham KT11 .... 73 F6
Fairmile Park Rd.
  Cobham KT11 .... 73 F6
Fairoak Cl. Purley CR8 .... 80 B4
Fairoak La.
  Chess KT9 & KT22 & KT10 .. 75 B8
Fairoak La.
  Oxsh KT10 & KT22 & KT9 ... 74 E8
Fairoaks Airport.Chbh GU24 50 E1
Fairoaks Ct. Addl KT15 .... 52 B5
Fairs Rd. Leahd KT22 .... 95 A8
Fairstone Ct. Horley RH6 .... 161 B4
Fairview. E Ewell KT17 .... 77 C8
Fairview Ave. Woking GU22 .. 69 F1
Fairview Cl. Woking GU22 ...... 69 F1
Fairview Cotts. Went GU25 .. 31 D3
Fairview Ct. Ashf TW15 .... 14 A3
Fairview Ct. King U T KT2 ...... 38 B8
Fairview Ct. Stain TW18 .... 13 A2
Fairview Dr. Shep Gn TW17 .. 33 F4
Fairview Gdns.
  Heath E GU9 .... 125 D6
Fairview House. **17**
  Street SW2 .... 21 F8
Fairview Pl. Street SW2 .... 21 F8
Fairview Rd. Ash GU12 .... 106 B3
Fairview Rd.
  Carsh SM1 & SM5 .... 59 E5
Fairview Rd. Ewell KT17 .... 76 F8
Fairview Rd. Head Dn GU35 187 C5
Fairview Rd. Thorn H SW16 .. 41 F8
Fairview Rd. Woki RG11 .... 25 C5
Fairview Terr.
  Head Dn GU35 .... 187 A6
Fairwater Dr.
  New Haw KT15 .... 52 D2
Fairwater House.
  Tedd TW11 .... 17 A4
Fairway. Chert KT16 .... 33 B1
Fairway. Copth RH10 .... 183 B2
Fairway. Crawl RH11 .... 200 D4
Fairway. Merrow GU1 .... 110 D1
Fairway. Sutton SM5 .... 78 C8
Fairway. W Barn SW20 .... 39 C6
Fairway Cl. E Grins RH19 .... 183 A2
Fairway Cl. Croy BR3 & CR0 .. 43 E4
Fairway Cl. W Ewell KT19 ...... 57 C6
Fairway Cl. W Ewell KT19 ...... 57 C6
Fairway Cty Inf Sch.
  Copth RH10 .... 183 B3

Fairway Est. Hounsl TW4 .... 4 C2
Fairway Gdns. Beck BR3 .... 44 D3
Fairway Hts. Frml GU15 .... 66 B6
Fairway The. E Mole KT8 .... 36 B6
Fairway The. Farnb GU14 ...... 84 A1
Fairway The.
  Frml GU15 & GU16 .... 66 A3
Fairway The. Godal GU7 ..... 150 F2
Fairway The. Heath E GU9 . 125 D7
Fairway The. King U T KT3 .... 38 D8
Fairway The. Leahd KT22 ...... 75 A1
Fairway The.
  Pirb GU22 & GU24 .... 88 C3
Fairway The. Whit V KT13 .... 72 A8
Fairways. Ashf TW15 .... 14 B3
Fairways. Beac H GU26 .... 188 B6
Fairways. Kenley CR8 .... 80 C2
Fairways. Tedd TW11 .... 17 D1
Fairwell La. W Hors KT24 .. 112 B7
Fairwyn Rd. For Hil SE26 ...... 23 E4
Fakenham Way.
  Sandh GU15 .... 45 D2
Falaise. Egham TW20 .... 11 F3
Falaise Cl. Alder GU11 .... 105 B3
Falcon Cl. Chisw W4 .... 7 C8
Falcon Cl. Crawl RH11 .... 201 D8
Falcon Cl. Lhtwat GU18 .... 66 F8
Falcon Cl. Friml GU16 .... 65 D1
Falcon Ct. Sheer GU21 .... 70 C6
Falcon Ct. **8** W Norw SE21 . 22 D6
Falcon Dr. Stan TW19 .... 2 E1
Falcon Rd. Guild GU1 .... 109 D1
Falcon Rd. Hampt TW12 .... 15 F1
Falcon Way. Sunby TW16 ...... 34 E7
Falcon Wood. King U T KT6 37 E4
Falconhurst. Oxsh KT22 ...... 74 D4
Falconry Ct. King U T KT1 ..... 37 E6
Falcons Cl. Bigg H TN16 .... 83 D2
Falconwood. E Hors KT24 .... 92 F3
Falconwood. Egm Gn TW20 .. 11 E3
Falconwood Rd.
  New Add CR0 .... 63 A3
Falcourt Cl. Sutton SM1 .... 59 B5
Falkland Ct. Farnb GU14 .... 105 E8
Falkland Gr. Dork RH4 .... 136 A6
Falkland House. Catf SE6 ..... 24 C4
Falkland Park Ave.
  S Norw SE25 .... 42 E7
Falkland Rd. Dork RH4 .... 136 A6
Falklands Dr. Horsh RH13 . 218 B4
Falkner Rd. Farnh GU9 .... 125 B2
Fallow Deer Cl.
  Horsh RH13 .... 218 B4
Fallowfield Way.
  Horley RH6 .... 161 B4
Fallsbrook Rd. Street SW16 . 21 C2
Falmer Cl. Crawl RH11 .... 201 D4
Falmouth Cl. Friml GU15 ...... 66 A4
Falmouth Rd. Hersh KT12 .... 54 C6
Falstone. Woking GU21 .... 69 B1
Fambridge Cl. For Hil SE26 .. 23 F4
Famet Ave. Purley CR8 .... 80 C6
Famet Cl. Purley CR8 .... 80 C6
Famet Gdns. Purley CR8 .... 80 C6
Famet Rd. Purley CR8 .... 80 C6
Fanchford Rd. Reig RH2 ..... 117 E1
Fanes Cl. Brack RG12 .... 26 F8
Fanfare The. Sheer GU22 ...... 70 C4
Faraday Ave. Rich TW10 .... 17 C4
Faraday Ave. S Croy CR0 & 9 41 F1
Faraday Ct. Sandh GU17 .... 64 C8
Fareham House. **13**
  Rhampt SW15 .... 19 A7
Fareham Rd. Felt TW14 .... 15 C8
Farewell Pl. Mitch CR4 .... 40 E8
Farhalls Cres. Horsh RH12 . 217 F6
Faringdon Cl. Sandh GU17 ... 45 C1
Faringdon Dr. Brack RG12 .... 27 D4
Farington Acres.
  Oat Pk KT15 .... 53 D7
Faris Barn Dr. Woodhm KT15 70 F8
Faris La. Woodhm KT15 .... 70 F8
Farleigh Ave. Hayes BR2 ...... 44 F2
Farleigh Court Rd.
  Farlgh CR6 .... 82 B5
Farleigh Ct. Croy CR2 .... 61 C5
Farleigh Ct. **2** Stough GU2 108 E1
Farleigh Cty Prim Sch.
  Warlgm CR6 .... 81 E2
Farleigh Dean Cres.
  New Add CR0 .... 82 B8

Farleigh House. **7**
  King U T KT2 .... 18 B2
Farleigh Rd. Warlgm CR6 ..... 81 E2
Farleigh Rd. Woodhm KT15 .. 71 A8
Farleton Cl. Whit V KT13 ...... 53 D4
Farley Copse. Binf RG12 ...... 26 E8
Farley Croft. Beck BR2 .... 44 E7
Farley Ct. Farnb GU14 .... 85 D2
Farley Heath Rd.
  Farl Gn GU5 .... 153 C6
Farley House. For Hil SE26 .. 23 B5
Farley Moor. Binf RG12 .... 26 D8
Farley Pk. Oxted RH8 .... 122 D5
Farley Pl. Croy SE25 .... 43 A5
Farley Rd. Lewish SE6 .... 24 C8
Farley Rd. S Croy CR2 .... 62 B2
Farleycroft. **1** Croy CR0 ...... 43 A1
Farley's Cl. W Hors KT24 ...... 92 C1
Farlington Pl. Rhampt SW15 19 B8
Farlington Sch. Slinfd RH12 216 B6
Farlton Rd. Wands SW18 ...... 20 B8
Farm App. Blind H RH9 .... 163 C5
Farm Ave. Horsh RH12 .... 217 B3
Farm Ave. Street SW16 .... 21 E4
Farm Cl. Ascot SL5 .... 29 C4
Farm Cl. Bellf GU1 .... 109 D4
Farm Cl. Brack RG12 .... 26 F8
Farm Cl. Byfl KT14 .... 71 F7
Farm Cl. Chert KT16 .... 32 A3
Farm Cl. Coney H BR4 .... 63 F7
Farm Cl. Crawl RH10 .... 202 A7
Farm Cl. Crowth RG11 .... 45 C7
Farm Cl. E Grins RH19 .... 206 B8
Farm Cl. E Hors KT24 .... 112 F7
Farm Cl. Egham TW18 .... 12 E3
Farm Cl. Fairl GU3 .... 108 C6
Farm Cl. Fetch KT22 .... 94 E3
Farm Cl. Lo Hall TW17 .... 34 A2
Farm Cl. Loxwd RH14 .... 213 A3
Farm Cl. Sutton SM2 .... 59 D3
Farm Cl. Wallin SM6 .... 60 C1
Farm Cl. Warn RH12 .... 216 F7
Farm Cl. Woking GU21 .... 69 C8
Farm Dr. Croy CR0 .... 62 F8
Farm Dr. Purley CR8 .... 79 D8
Farm Fields. S Croy CR2 .... 80 F8
Farm La. Ashtd KT21 & KT18 76 B2
Farm La. Croy CR0 .... 62 F8
Farm La. E Hors KT24 .... 112 F7
Farm La. Purley CR8 .... 60 C1
Farm La. Row Tn KT15 .... 52 A3
Farm La. Send GU23 .... 90 C3
Farm La. Wallin CR8 .... 60 C1
Farm Rd. Alder GU12 .... 105 E3
Farm Rd. Friml GU16 .... 65 F2
Farm Rd. Morden SM4 .... 40 B4
Farm Rd. Old Wok GU22 .... 90 B7
Farm Rd. Stain TW18 .... 13 B2
Farm Rd. Sutton SM2 .... 59 D3
Farm Rd. Thame D KT10 .... 55 B8
Farm Rd. Twick TW4 .... 15 E7
Farm Way. N Cheam KT4 ...... 58 C7
Farm Way. Stan TW19 .... 1 F1
Farm Wlk. Ash GU12 .... 127 C8
Farmdale Rd.
  Sutton SM2 & SM5 .... 59 E3
Farmer's Rd. Egham TW18 ... 12 E3
Farmfield Dr. Hookw RH6 . 160 B1
Farmfield Dr. Hookw RH6 . 160 B1
Farmfield Hospl.
  Hookw RH6 .... 160 B1
Farmfield Rd. Catf BR1 .... 24 E3
Farmhouse Cl. Mayb GU22 .. 70 D4
Farmhouse Rd. Street SW16 21 C1
Farmington Ave. Carsh SM1 59 D7
Farmleigh Cl. Crawl RH10 . 202 C8
Farmleigh Gr. Whit V KT12 .. 53 F5
Farmstead Rd. Catf SE6 .... 24 B4
Farmview. Cobham KT11 .... 73 D3
Farnaby Rd.
  Broml BR1 & BR2 .... 44 E8
Farnan Rd. Street SW16 .... 21 E3
Farnborough Ave.S Croy CR2 62 E3
Farnb GU14 .... 84 F2
Farnborough Bsns Ctr.
  Farnb GU14 .... 85 C2
Farnborough Cres.
  Coney H BR2 .... 44 F1
Farnborough Cres.
  S Croy CR2 .... 62 E2
Farnborough Gate Ret Pk.
  Farnb GU14 .... 85 B6
Farnborough Grange Cty Inf Sch.
  Farnb GU14 .... 85 A3
Farnborough Grange Cty Jun
  Sch. W Heath GU14 .... 85 A3
Farnborough Hill (Girls' Public
  Sch). Farnb GU14 .... 85 C5
Farnborough House. **1**
  Rhampt SW15 .... 19 A7

Farnborough Ind Est.
  Farnb GU14 .... 85 A3
Farnborough North Sta.
  Farnb GU14 .... 85 D6
Farnborough Rd.
  Alder GU11 .... 104 E3
Farnborough Rd.
  Farnh GU14 .... 85 C5
Farnborough Rd.
  Heath E GU11 & GU9 .... 125 D7
Farnborough (Sixth Form) Coll.
  W Heath GU14 .... 85 B6
Farnborough St.
  Farnb GU14 .... 85 D6
Farnborough Sta.
  Farnb GU14 .... 85 B5
Farnc C of E Inf Sch.
  Farnc GU7 .... 150 E7
Farncombe Hill. Farnc GU7 150 E7
Farncombe St. Farnc GU7 .. 150 E7
Farncombe Sta. Farnc GU7 150 F7
Farnell Rd. Islew TW7 .... 5 D4
Farnell Rd. Stan TW18 .... 13 A5
Farnell's Almshouses.
  Islew TW7 .... 5 F5
Farnham Bsns Ctr.
  Farnh GU9 .... 125 E1
Farnham Bsns Pk.
  Farnh GU9 .... 125 B1
Farnham By-Pass.
  Farnh GU10 & GU9 .... 125 C2
Farnham Cl. Brack RG12 .... 27 D7
Farnham Coll.
  M Bourn GU9 .... 125 C1
Farnham Ct. Cheam SM3 ..... 58 E4
Farnham Gdns.
  W Barn SW20 .... 39 B7
Farnham General Hospl.
  Farnh GU9 .... 125 B1
Farnham La. Shottm GU27 208 A7
Farnham Park Cl. Hale GU9 125 B6
Farnham Park Dr.
  Hale GU9 .... 125 B6
Farnham Rd.
  Elst GU10 & GU8 .... 148 C4
Farnham Rd.
  Guild GU1 & GU2 & GU3 .. 130 B7
Farnham Rd.
  Onsl V GU2 & GU3 .... 129 E6
Farnham Rd Hospl.
  Guild GU2 .... 130 B7
Farnham Sch of Art.
  Farnh GU9 .... 125 B2
Farnham Sta. Farnh GU9 ... 125 C2
Farnham Trad Est.
  Farnh GU9 .... 125 F4
Farnhurst La.
  Alf Cr GU6 & GU8 .... 193 F4
Farningham. Brack RG12 ...... 27 E3
Farningham Cres.
  Cater CR3 .... 101 A4
Farningham Ct.
  Streat SW16 .... 21 D1
Farningham Rd. Cater CR3 101 A4
Farnley. Woking GU21 .... 68 F2
Farnley Rd.
  S Norw CR7 & SE25 .... 42 D5
Farnsworth House. **8**
  W Norw SW27 .... 22 B3
Farquhar Rd. Dulw SE19 ...... 22 F3
Farquhar Rd. Wimble SW19 . 20 A5
Farquharson Rd.
  Thorn H CR0 .... 42 C1
Farrell Cl. Camb GU15 .... 65 C3
Farren Rd. For Hil SE23 .... 23 E6
Farrer's Pl. S Croy CR0 .... 62 D6
Farriers. Head KT18 .... 96 C3
Farriers Cl. Ewell KT17 .... 76 E7
Farriers Ct. Belm SM2 .... 58 E3
Farriers Ct. Wimble SW19 .... 19 E1
Farriers Rd. Ewell KT17 .... 76 E8
Farriers The. Bramly GU5 .. 152 A5
Farthingfield House.
  Reig RH2 .... 118 B2
Farthingham La. Ewh GU6 . 175 E6
Farthings. Woking GU21 .... 68 E2
Farthings The. **1**
  King U T KT2 .... 38 A8
Farwig La. Broml BR1 .... 44 F8
Fassett Rd. King U T KT1 ...... 37 E5
Fauconberg Ct. Chisw W4 ...... 7 C8
Fauconberg Rd. Chisw W4 ...... 7 C8
Faulkner Pl. Bagsh GU19 ...... 47 F4
Faulkner's Rd. Hersh KT12 ... 54 C5
Faversham Rd. Beck BR3 ...... 43 F7
Faversham Rd. For Hil SE6 ... 23 F7
Faversham Rd. Morden SM4 40 B3
Faversham Rd. Sandh GU15 45 D1

Fawcett Rd. Croy CR0 & CR9 61 C7
Fawcus Cl. Clayg KT10 55 E4
Fawler Mead. Brack RG12 27 F5
Fawley Cl. Cran GU6 174 F2
Fawns Manor Cl.E Bed TW14 14 C7
Fawns Manor Rd. E Bed TW14 14 D7
Fawsley Cl. Poyle SL3 1 E7
Fay Rd. Horsh RH12 217 C5
Faygate Bsns Ctr. Faygt RH12 199 F1
Faygate La. Blind H RH9 142 E3
Faygate La. Faygt RH12 199 F4
Faygate La. Rusper RH12 199 F4
Faygate Rd. Streat SW2 21 F6
Faygate Sta. Faygt RH12 199 F1
Fayland Ave. Streat SW16 21 C3
Fearn Cl. E Hors KT24 112 E6
Fearnley Cres. Hampt TW12 15 F2
Featherbed La. New Add CR0 63 A1
Feathers La. Wray TW19 12 A6
Featherstone. Blind H RH7 142 D1
Featherstone Ave. For Hil SE23 23 C6
Fee Farm Rd. Clayg KT10 55 F3
Felbridge Ave. Crawl RH10 202 D7
Felbridge Cl. E Grins RH19 185 C3
Felbridge Cl. Friml GU16 65 F1
Felbridge Cl. Streat SW16 22 A4
Felbridge Cl. Sutton SM2 59 B2
Felbridge Ct. E Grins RH19 185 A4
Felbridge Ct. Harl UB3 3 D8
Felbridge Ctr The. E Grins RH19 185 A3
Felbridge Cty Prim Sch. Felb RH19 184 F4
Felbridge Rd. Copth RH19 184 D3
Felcot Rd. Copth RH10 184 C4
Felcote House. Woodh RH2 138 F7
Felcott Cl. Hersh KT12 54 C7
Felcott Rd. Hersh KT12 54 C7
Felcourt Cotts. Felct RH19 185 C8
Felcourt La. Felct RH19 & RH7 164 C1
Felcourt Rd. Dorm Pk RH19 & RH7 185 C7
Felcourt Rd. Felct RH19 & RH7 185 C7
Felday Glade. Hol St M RH5 155 B5
Felday Houses. Hol St M RH5 155 C7
Felday Rd. Abing H RH5 133 F3
Felix Dr. W Clan GU4 111 A7
Felix La. Lo Hall TW17 34 F3
Felix Rd. Walt O T KT12 35 A3
Fell Rd. Croy CR0 & CR9 61 C7
Felland Way. Dovgn RH1 139 D5
Fellbrook. Rich TW10 17 B5
Fellcott Way. Horsh RH12 216 F1
Fellow Gn. W End GU24 67 F6
Fellow Green Rd. W End GU24 67 F6
Fellowes Ct. Harl UB3 3 D8
Fellowes Rd. Carsh SM1 & SM5 59 E8
Fellows Rd. Farnb GU14 85 D1
Felmingham Rd. Penge SE20 43 C7
Felnex Trad Est. Hackb SM6 60 A8
Felsberg Rd. Streat SW2 21 E8
Felside Ct. Weyb KT13 53 A5
Felstead Rd. Epsom KT19 76 D8
Feltham Arena. Felt TW14 15 A8
Feltham Ave. E Mole KT8 36 E5
Feltham Comm Sch. Felt TW13 15 C6
Feltham Corporate Ctr. Felt TW13 15 B5
Feltham Hill Jun & Inf Schs. Felt TW13 14 F5
Feltham Hill Rd. Ashf TW15 14 C2
Feltham Rd. Ashf TW15 14 C4
Feltham Rd. Earls RH1 139 F4
Feltham Rd. Mitch CR4 41 A7
Feltham Sta. Felt TW13 15 B7
Feltham Wlk. Earls RH1 139 F4
Felthambrook Ind Ctr. Felt TW13 15 B5
Felthambrook Way. Felt TW13 15 B3
Felthamhill Rd. Felt TW13 15 B4
Feltonfleet Sch. Whit V KT11 72 E6
Felwater Ct. E Grins RH19 185 A3
Fenchurch Rd. Worth RH10 202 B4
Fencote. Brack RG12 27 D3
Fendall Rd. W Ewell KT19 57 C5
Fendall Rd. W Ewell KT19 57 C5
Fender House. Horsh RH12 217 B2
Fengates Rd. Redh RH1 118 E1
Fenhurst Cl. Horsh RH12 216 F1
Fenn's Way. Horse GU21 69 E4
Fennel Cl. Burph GU1 110 B4
Fennel Cl. Croy CR0 43 D1
Fennel Cl. W Heath GU14 84 B4
Fennel Cres. Crawl RH11 201 B2
Fennells Mead. Ewell KT17 57 F2
Fenner House. Hersh KT12 54 A6
Fenning Ct. Mitch CR4 40 E5
Fenns La. W End GU24 67 E5
Fenns Yd. Farnh GU9 125 B2
Fennscombe Ct. W End GU24 67 F6
Fenstanton Prim Sch. Streat SW2 22 A7
Fenton Ave. Stain TW18 13 C3
Fenton Cl. Earls RH1 119 A1
Fenton House. Heston TW5 5 A8
Fenton Rd. Earls RH1 119 A1
Fentum Rd. Stough GU2 109 A3
Fenwick Cl. Woking GU21 69 B1
Ferguson Ave. King U T KT5 37 F4
Ferguson Cl. Beck BR2 & BR3 44 D6
Fermandy La. Crawl D RH10 184 A1
Fermor Rd. For Hil SE23 23 E7
Fern Ave. Mitch CR4 41 D5
Fern Cl. Crowth RG11 45 A7
Fern Cl. Friml GU16 66 C3
Fern Cl. Warlgm CR6 81 E1
Fern Cotts. Gomsh GU5 133 E4
Fern Gr. Felt TW14 15 B8
Fern Lodge. 13 W Norw SW16 22 A3
Fern Rd. Farnc GU7 150 F6
Fern Towers. Cater CR3 101 A2
Fern Way. Horsh RH12 217 D5
Fern Wlk. Ashf TW15 13 D3
Fernbank Ave. Walt O T KT12 35 E2
Fernbank Cres. N Asct SL5 28 D8
Fernbank Pl. N Asct SL5 28 D7
Fernbank Rd. Addl KT15 52 A5
Fernbank Rd. N Asct SL5 28 D8
Fernbrae Cl. Rowl GU10 146 B3
Ferndale. Stough GU2 108 E3
Ferndale Ave. Addl KT16 51 E7
Ferndale Ave. Hounsl TW4 4 E4
Ferndale Rd. Ashf TW15 13 E3
Ferndale Rd. Banstd SM7 77 F3
Ferndale Rd. Croy SE25 43 B4
Ferndale Rd. Woking GU21 69 F3
Fernden La. Fern GU27 208 C2
Fernden Rise. Farnc GU7 150 E7
Fernden Sch. Fern GU27 208 B2
Ferndown. Crawl RH10 182 D2
Ferndown. Horley RH6 161 A5
Ferndown. 5 King U T KT6 37 E4
Ferndown Cl. Guild GU1 131 A8
Ferndown Cl. Sutton SM2 59 D4
Ferndown Gdns. Cobham KT11 73 C6
Ferndown Gdns. W Heath GU14 84 E4
Fernery The. Egham TW18 12 E3
Ferney Ct. Byfl KT14 71 D8
Ferney Rd. Byfl KT14 71 D7
Fernfell Golf & Ctry Club. Cran GU6 174 F6
Fernham Rd. S Norw CR7 42 C6
Fernhill. Oxsh KT22 74 D5
Fernhill Cl. Crawl D RH10 184 B1
Fernhill Cl. Hale GU9 125 B6
Fernhill Cl. W Heath GU14 64 F1
Fernhill Cl. Woking GU22 89 D7
Fernhill Comp Sch. W Heath GU14 64 F1
Fernhill Ct. King U T KT2 17 D3
Fernhill Cty Prim Sch. W Heath GU14 64 F1
Fernhill Dr. Hale GU9 125 B6
Fernhill Gdns. King U T KT2 17 E3
Fernhill La. Hale GU9 125 B6
Fernhill La. W Heath GU14 64 F1
Fernhill La. Woking GU22 89 C7
Fernhill Pk. Woking GU22 89 D7
Fernhill Rd. Crawl RH6 182 D7
Fernhill Rd. Hawley GU14 & GU17 64 E2
Fernhill Rd. W Heath GU14 & GU17 64 E2
Fernhill Rd. W Heath GU14 & GU17 84 E6
Fernhill Wlk. W Heath GU14 64 F1
Fernhurst Cl. Crawl RH11 201 B8
Fernhurst Rd. Ashf TW15 14 C4
Fernhurst Rd. Croy CR0 43 B1
Ferniehurst. Camb GU15 65 F4
Fernihough Cl. Whit V KT13 72 A8
Fernlands Cl. Addl KT16 51 E7
Fernlea. Fetch KT23 94 B3
Fernlea Rd. Balham SW12 21 B7
Fernlea Rd. Mitch CR4 41 A8
Fernleigh Cl. Croy CR0 61 A6
Fernleigh Cl. Walt O T KT12 54 B7
Fernleigh Rise. Friml GU16 86 C7
Fernley House. Farnc GU7 150 E8
Ferns Cl. S Croy CR2 62 B1
Ferns The. Heath E GU9 125 C7
Fernside Ave. Felt TW13 15 B4
Fernside Rd. Balham SW12 21 A8
Fernthorpe Rd. Streat SW16 21 C2
Fernwood. New Add CR0 & CR2 62 E2
Fernwood. Putney SW19 19 F7
Fernwood Ave. Streat SW16 21 D4
Feroners Cl. Crawl RH10 202 A4
Ferrard Cl. N Asct SL5 28 D8
Ferraro Cl. Heston TW5 5 A8
Ferrers Ave. Wallin SM6 60 D6
Ferrers Rd. Streat SW16 21 D3
Ferriby Ct. Brack RG12 27 C7
Ferring Cl. Crawl RH11 201 B8
Ferrings. Dulw SE21 22 E5
Ferris Ave. Croy CR0 62 F7
Ferroners Ct. Crawl RH10 202 A4
Ferry Ave. Egham TW18 12 E1
Ferry La. Barnes SW13 7 F8
Ferry La. Brent TW8 6 E8
Ferry La. Chert KT16 33 A3
Ferry La. Guild GU2 & GU3 130 C5
Ferry La. Laleh TW18 33 C6
Ferry La. Lo Hall TW17 34 A1
Ferry La. Rich TW9 6 F8
Ferry La. Wray TW19 12 B5
Ferry Rd. E Mole KT8 36 A6
Ferry Rd. Rich TW11 17 B3
Ferry Rd. Thame D KT7 37 B3
Ferry Rd. Twick TW1 17 B7
Ferry Sq. 1 Brent TW8 6 E8
Ferry Wks. Lo Hall TW17 34 A1
Ferrymoor. Rich TW10 17 B5
Fetcham Common La. Fetch KT22 94 B6
Fetcham Cty Fst Sch. Fetch KT22 94 D5
Fetcham Park Dr. Fetch KT22 94 E4
Fettes Rd. Cran GU6 175 A3
Fiddicroft Ave. Banstd SM7 78 C5
Fie Yard Rd. Farnb GU14 85 B2
Field Cl. Chess KT9 56 C5
Field Cl. Cranf TW4 4 B6
Field Cl. E Mole KT8 36 B4
Field Cl. Hams Gn CR2 81 B5
Field Cl. Harl UB7 3 C7
Field Cl. Merrow GU4 110 D3
Field Ct. Oxted RH8 122 E8
Field End. Coulsd CR5 79 D5
Field End. Farnh GU9 125 F4
Field End. W End GU24 67 F6
Field House Cl. Brack SL5 29 A1
Field La. Brent TW8 6 C7
Field La. Farnc GU7 150 F7
Field La. Friml GU16 65 E1
Field La. Tedd TW11 17 A3
Field Pk. Wink RG12 27 D8
Field Pl. New Mal KT3 38 F3
Field Rd. Felt TW14 4 B1
Field Rd. W Heath GU14 64 F1
Field Stores App. Alder GU11 105 C3
Field View. Egham TW20 12 C3
Field View. Felt TW13 14 D5
Field Way. Alder GU12 105 E3
Field Way. New Add CR0 63 B4
Field Way. Send M GU23 90 F2
Field Way. Tongh GU10 126 F7
Field Wlk. Smallf RH6 162 C4
Fieldcommon La. Walt O T KT12 35 F1
Fielden Pl. Brack RG12 27 D7
Fieldend. Horsh RH12 218 B5
Fieldend. Tedd TW11 16 F4
Fieldend Rd. Streat SW16 41 C8
Fielders Gn. Guild GU1 110 A1
Fieldhouse Rd. Streat SW12 21 C7
Fieldhouse Villas. Woodm SM7 78 E4
Fieldhurst Cl. Addl KT15 52 B5
Fielding Ave. Twick TW2 16 C5
Fielding Gdns. Crowth RG11 45 B4
Fielding House. Chisw W4 7 E8
Fielding Rd. Sandh GU15 64 C6
Fieldings The. For Hil SE23 23 C7
Fieldings The. Horley RH6 161 C4
Fieldings The. Woking GU21 68 F3
Fieldsend Rd. Cheam SM3 58 E5
Fieldside Rd. Catf BR1 24 D3
Fieldview. Horley RH6 161 B4
Fieldview. Wands SW17 & SW18 20 D7
Fieldway. Haslem GU27 208 C7
Fife Rd. King U T KT2 37 E7
Fife Rd. Mortl SW14 7 C2
Fife Way. Fetch KT23 94 A2
Fifehead Cl. Ashf TW15 13 E2
Fifield La. Frensh GU10 146 C2
Fifield Path. For Hil SE23 23 D5
Fifth Cross Rd. Twick TW2 16 D6
Figge's Rd. Mitch CR4 21 A1
Filbert Cres. Crawl RH11 201 A6
Filby Rd. Chess KT9 56 F4
Filey Cl. Bigg H TN16 103 B8
Filey Cl. Crawl RH11 200 F4
Filey Cl. Sutton SM2 59 C3
Filmer Ct. Farnc GU7 150 E5
Filmer Gr. Farnc GU7 150 E5
Finborough Rd. Mitch SW17 20 F2
Finch Ave. W Norw SE27 22 D4
Finch Cl. Knaph GU21 68 C2
Finch Dr. Felt TW14 15 D8
Finch Rd. 9 Guild GU1 109 D1
Finch's Cross. Oxted RH8 144 A8
Finchampstead Rd. Woki RG11 25 B3
Finchdean House. Rhampt SW15 18 F8
Finches Rise. Merrow GU1 110 C3
Findhorn Cl. Sandh GU15 64 D7
Findings The. W Heath GU14 84 E8
Findlay Dr. Stough GU3 108 F5
Findon Ct. Row Tn KT15 51 F5
Findon Rd. Crawl RH11 201 B8
Findon Way. Broad H RH12 216 D3
Finlay Gdns. Addl KT15 52 C6
Finlays Cl. Chess KT9 57 A5
Finmere. Easth RG12 27 C2
Finnart Cl. Weyb KT13 53 C6
Finney Dr. Windl GU20 48 D4
Finsbury Cl. Crawl RH11 201 C2
Finstock Gn. Brack RG12 27 F5
Finton House Sch. Up Toot SW17 20 F6
Fintry Pl. W Heath GU14 84 E7
Fintry Wlk. W Heath GU14 84 E7
Finucane Ct. Rich TW9 6 F4
Fiona Cl. Fetch KT23 94 A3
Fir Acre Rd. Ash V GU12 106 A6
Fir Cl. Walt O T KT12 35 A2
Fir Dr. Hawley GU17 64 D3
Fir Gr. New Mal KT3 38 F3
Fir Grange Ave. Weyb KT13 53 B5
Fir Rd. Cheam SM3 39 F1
Fir Rd. Felt TW13 15 D3
Fir Tree Alley. Alder GU11 105 A2
Fir Tree Ave. Shottm GU27 207 D6
Fir Tree Cl. Ascot SL5 29 A2
Fir Tree Cl. Crawl RH11 181 B1
Fir Tree Cl. Esher KT10 55 C5
Fir Tree Cl. Leahd KT22 95 C4
Fir Tree Cl. Nork KT17 77 C4
Fir Tree Cl. Streat SW16 21 C3
Fir Tree Cl. Worc Pk KT19 57 F6
Fir Tree Gdns. Croy CR0 63 A6
Fir Tree Gr. Wallin SM5 59 F3
Fir Tree Rd. Bellf GU1 109 D4
Fir Tree Rd. Hounsl TW4 4 E3
Fir Tree Rd. Leahd KT22 95 C4
Fir Tree Rd. Nork KT17 & SM7 77 D5
Fir Tree Wlk. Reig RH2 118 D1
Fir Wlk. Cheam KT17 & SM3 58 D4
Firbank Cotts. Burst RH6 183 C7
Firbank Dr. Woking GU21 89 B8
Firbank La. Woking GU21 89 B8
Firbank Pl. Eng Gn TW20 11 B2
Fircroft Cl. Woking GU22 69 F1
Fircroft Ct. 9 Woking GU22 69 F1
Fircroft Prim Sch. Up Toot SW17 20 F5
Fircroft Rd. Chess KT9 56 F6
Fircroft Rd. Up Toot SW17 20 F5
Firdene. Tolw KT5 38 C1
Fire Bell Alley. Surb KT6 37 E3
Fire Station Cotts. Purley CR8 79 F6
Fire Station Flats. 3 Epsom KT17 76 E6
Fire Station Rd. Alder GU11 105 B3
Fireball Hill. Sunnin SL5 29 D2
Firefly Cl. Wallin SM6 60 E3
Firfield Rd. Addl KT15 52 A6
Firfield Rd. M Bourn GU9 146 A7
Firfields. Whit V KT13 53 B4
Firgrove. Woking GU21 89 B8
Firgrove Ct. 7 Farnb GU14 85 B4
Firgrove Ct. Farnh GU9 125 C1
Firgrove Hill. Farnh GU9 125 C1
Firgrove Hill. M Bourn GU9 125 C1
Firgrove Par. 5 Farnb GU14 85 B4
Firgrove Rd. 6 Farnb GU14 85 B4
Firhill Rd. Catf SE6 24 A5
Firlands. Brack RG12 27 C4
Firlands. Horley RH6 161 B4
Firlands. Whit V KT13 53 E4
Firlands Ave. Camb GU15 65 D5
Firle Cl. Crawl RH10 201 E8
Firmston House. 9 Mortl SW14 7 D4
Firs Ave. Bramly GU5 152 A6
Firs Ave. Mortl SW14 7 C3
Firs Cl. Clayg KT10 55 E4
Firs Cl. Dork RH4 136 A5
Firs Cl. Farnb GU14 85 C2
Firs Cl. For Hil SE23 23 E8
Firs Cl. Mitch CR4 41 B8
Firs Dr. Cranf TW5 4 B7
Firs La. Sham Gn GU5 152 D4
Firs Rd. Purley CR8 80 B4
Firs The. Arting GU3 130 B5
Firs The. Bisley GU24 68 A3
Firs The. 6 Brack RG12 27 F5
Firs The. Cater CR3 100 D5
Firs The. Clayg KT10 55 E4
Firs The. 2 For Hil SE26 23 B3
Firs The. For Hil SE26 23 C3
Firs The. Sutton SM2 59 B3
Firs The. Wimble SW20 19 A1
Firsby Ave. Croy CR0 43 E1
Firsdene Cl. Ottsh KT16 51 D4
First Ave. E Mole KT8 36 A5
First Ave. Mortl SW14 7 E4
First Ave. W Ewell KT19 57 E2
First Ave. W Ewell KT19 57 E2
First Ave. Walt O T KT12 35 B3
First Ave. Woodhm KT15 52 B2
First Cl. E Mole KT8 36 C6
First Cross Rd. Twick TW2 16 E6
First Quarter Bsns Pk. Epsom KT19 76 E8
Firstway. W Barn SW20 39 C7
Firsway. Stough GU2 109 A2
Firswood Ave. Worc Pk KT19 57 F5
Firtree Ave. Mitch CR4 41 A7
Firtree Ct. Beck BR2 44 F6
Firway. Graysh GU26 187 E5
Firwood Cl. Knaph GU21 88 E8
Firwood Ct. Camb GU15 65 C5
Firwood Dr. Camb GU15 65 C5
Firwood Rd. Went GU25 30 E3
Fisher Cl. Crawl RH10 201 E4
Fisher Cl. Croy CR0 42 F1
Fisher Cl. Hersh KT12 54 B6
Fisher La. Chidd GU8 210 E7
Fisher La. Dunsf GU8 211 B7
Fisher Rowe Cl. Bramly GU5 152 A6
Fisherdene. Clayg KT10 56 A3
Fisherman Cl. Rich TW10 17 C4
Fishermen's Cl. Farnb GU11 105 E5
Fishers Ct. Horsh RH12 217 C4
Fishers Ct. 4 Tedd TW11 16 F3
Fishers Wood. Sunnin SL5 30 C1
Fishponds Cl. Woki RG11 25 A4
Fishponds Est. Woki RG11 25 A4
Fishponds Rd. Up Toot SW17 20 F4
Fishponds Rd. Woki RG11 25 A4
Fiske Ct. 1 Merton SW19 20 C1
Fiske Ct. Sutton SM2 59 C3
Fitch Ct. Mitch CR4 41 A7
Fitchet Cl. Crawl RH11 201 B8
Fitz Wygram Cl. Hampt TW12 16 C3
Fitzalan Rd. Clayg KT10 55 E3
Fitzalan Rd. Horsh RH12 & RH13 218 A4
Fitzgeorge Ave. King U T KT2 & KT3 38 D8
Fitzgerald Ave. Mortl SW14 7 E4
Fitzgerald Rd. Mortl SW14 7 D4
Fitzgerald Rd. Thame D KT7 37 A3
Fitzherbert House. 11 Rich TW10 6 F1
Fitzjames Ave. S Croy CR0 62 A8
Fitzjohn Cl. Merrow GU4 110 C4
Fitzrobert Pl. Egham TW20 12 A2
Fitzroy Cres. Chisw W4 7 D7
Fitzroy Gdns. S Norw SE19 22 E1
Fitzwilliam Ave. Rich TW9 6 F5
Fitzwilliam House. Rich TW9 6 D3
Fitzwilliam Hts. For Hil SE23 23 C6
Five Acres. Crawl RH10 201 E8
Five Oaks Cl. Knaph GU21 88 E8
Five Oaks Rd. Broad H RH12 & RH13 216 B2
Five Oaks Rd. Slinfd RH12 & RH13 216 B2
Fiveacre Cl. Thorn H CR7 42 A3
Flag Cl. Croy CR0 43 D1

Flambard Way. Godal GU7 150 D4
Flamborough Cl. Bigg H TN16 103 B8
Flamsteed Hts. Crawl RH11 201 B1
Flanchford House. 2 Reig RH2 118 A2
Flanchford Rd. Dovgn RH2 138 D5
Flanchford Rd. Leigh RH2 . 138 D5
Flanchford Rd. Reig RH2 138 D5
Flanders Cotts. Sham Gn GU5 152 D5
Flanders Cres. Mitch SW17 & SW19 20 F2
Flanders Ct. Egham TW20 12 C3
Flatford House. Catf SE6 24 C4
Flats The. Blckw GU17 64 C4
Flaxley Rd. Morden SM4 40 B2
Flaxmore Ct. S Norw CR7 42 D7
Fleece Rd. Long D KT6 37 C1
Fleet Cl. E Mole KT8 35 F4
Fleet Rd. Alder GU11 104 D6
Fleet Rd. Chur C GU13 & GU14 104 D6
Fleet Rd. Hawley GU14 84 A4
Fleet Rd. W Heath GU14 84 C4
Fleet Terr. Catf SE6 24 C8
Fleetside. E Mole KT8 36 A4
Fleetway. Egham TW20 32 C6
Fleetwood Cl. Chess KT9 56 D3
Fleetwood Cl. S Croy CR0 61 F7
Fleetwood Cl. Tadw KT20 97 D7
Fleetwood Ct. 7 Stan TW19 2 E1
Fleetwood Ct. 2 W Byfl KT14 71 A6
Fleetwood Rd. King U T KT3 38 B6
Fleetwood Sq. King U T KT3 38 B6
Fleming Cl. Farnb GU14 85 D6
Fleming Ct. Croy CR0 61 A5
Fleming Mead. Mitch CR4 & SW19 20 F1
Fleming Way. Crawl RH10 & RH11 181 F2
Fleming Way. Islew TW7 5 F3
Flemish Fields. Chert KT16 33 A2
Fletcher Cl. Crawl RH10 201 E4
Fletcher Cl. Ottsh KT15 & KT16 51 E4
Fletcher Gdns. Binf RG12 26 D8
Fletcher Rd. Ottsh KT16 51 D4
Fletchers Cl. Horsh RH13 217 E1
Fleur Gates. 7 Putney SW19 19 D8
Flexford Gn. Easth RG12 26 E3
Flexford Rd. Flexf GU3 107 C1
Flexlands Sch. Chobh GU24 . 68 F8
Flimwell Cl. Catf BR1 24 E3
Flint Cl. G Book KT23 94 C1
Flint Cl. Redh RH1 118 F2
Flint Cl. Worth RH10 202 B3
Flint Hill. Dork RH4 & RH5 . 136 B5
Flint Hill Cl. Dork RH4 136 B4
Flintgrove. Brack RG12 27 D8
Flintlock Cl. Stan TW19 2 A3
Flitwick Grange. Milf GU8 149 F1
Flood La. 4 Twick TW1 17 A7
Flora Gdns. New Add CR0 82 C8
Floral Ct. Ashtd KT21 75 C1
Floral House. Chert KT16 33 A2
Florence Ave. Morden SM4 40 C4
Florence Ave. Woodhm KT15 71 A8
Florence Cl. Walt O T KT12 35 B2
Florence Cotts. King U T SW15 18 E5
Florence Cotts. Wink SL4 8 C7
Florence Ct. Wimble SW19 19 E2
Florence Gdns. Chisw W4 7 C8
Florence Gdns. Stain TW18 13 B1
Florence House. 5 King U T KT2 17 F1
Florence Rd. Felt TW13 15 B7
Florence Rd. 6 King U T KT2 17 F1
Florence Rd. Penge BR3 43 E7
Florence Rd. S Croy CR2 61 D2
Florence Rd. Sandh GU15 64 E7
Florence Rd. Walt O T KT12 . 35 B2
Florence Rd. Wimble SW19 . 20 B2
Florence Terr. King U T SW15 18 E5
Florian Ave. Carsh SM1 59 D6
Florida Ct. Beck BR2 44 F5
Florida Ct. Stain TW18 13 A3
Florida Rd. S Norw CR7 42 B8
Florida Rd. Shalf GU4 130 E3
Florys Ct. 7 Putney SW19 19 E7
Flower Cres. Ottsh KT16 51 C4
Flower La. Tyl Gn RH9 121 D6
Flower La. Wold RH9 121 D6
Flower Wlk. Guild GU2 130 C6
Flowersmead. Up Toot SW17 21 A6
Floyd's La. Pyrf GU22 71 A3
Foden Track. Farnb GU14 104 C8
Foley Mews. Clayg KT10 55 E4
Foley Rd. Bigg H TN16 83 D1
Foley Rd. Clayg KT10 55 E3
Folly Hill. Farnh GU9 125 A5
Folly Hill. Hale GU9 125 A5
Folly Hill Cty Inf Sch. Hale GU9 125 A6
Folly La. S Holm RH5 157 B7
Folly La N. Hale GU9 125 B6
Folly La S. Hale GU9 125 A6
Follyfield Rd. Banstd SM7 78 A5
Fontaine Ct. Beck BR3 43 F8
Fontaine Rd. Streat SW16 21 F1
Fontenoy Rd. Up Toot SW12 & SW17 21 C6
Fonthill Cl. Penge SE20 43 A7
Fonthill Ct. For Hil SE23 23 C8
Fontley Way. Rhampt SW15 19 A8
Fontmell Cl. Ashf TW15 14 A3
Fontmell Pk. Ashf TW15 14 A3
Fontwell Rd. Crawl RH10 202 A3
Forbes Chase. Sandh GU15 64 D7
Forbes Ct. Dulw SE19 22 E3
Forburys. M Bourn GU9 146 B8
Ford Cl. Ashf TW15 13 E2
Ford Cl. Shep Gn TW17 34 A4
Ford Cl. Thorn H CR7 42 B4
Ford La. M Bourn GU10 & GU9 146 B6
Ford Manor Cotts. Dorman RH7 165 B1
Ford Manor Rd. Dorman RH7 165 B2
Ford Rd. Ashf TW15 13 F4
Ford Rd. Bisley GU24 67 F4
Ford Rd. Burrh GU24 49 C1
Ford Rd. Chert KT16 33 B1
Ford Rd. Old Wok GU22 90 B7
Fordbridge Ct. Ashf TW15 13 E2
Fordbridge Rd. Ashf TW15 13 F3
Fordbridge Rd. Sunby TW16 35 A5
Fordbridge Rd. Up Hall TW16 & TW17 34 F3
Fordel Rd. Catf SE6 24 D7
Fordingbridge Cl. Chert KT16 33 B1
Fordingbridge Cl. Horsh RH12 217 C1
Fordington Hse. For Hil SE26 23 B5
Fordmill Rd. Catf SE6 24 A6
Fordwater Rd. Chert KT15 & KT16 33 B1
Fordwater Trad Est. Chert KT16 33 C1
Fordwells Dr. Brack RG12 27 F5
Fordyce House. 3 Streat SW16 21 C4
Foreman Pk. Ash GU12 106 B2
Foreman Rd. Ash GU12 106 B2
Forest Cl. Brack SL5 28 C6
Forest Cl. Crawl D RH10 204 B8
Forest Cl. E Hors KT24 92 F2
Forest Cl. Horsh RH12 218 B4
Forest Cl. Mayb GU22 70 D4
Forest Comm Sch. Horsh RH13 217 F1
Forest Cres. Ashtd KT21 76 A3
Forest Croft. For Hil SE23 23 B6
Forest Dene Ct. Sutton SM2 59 C4
Forest Dr. Charlt TW16 14 F1
Forest Dr. Kings KT20 98 A6
Forest Dr. M Bourn GU10 146 C4
Forest End Rd. Sandh GU17 . 64 A8
Forest Glade. Binst GU10 145 D3
Forest Gn. Brack RG12 27 D7
Forest Hill Bsns Ctr. For Hil SE23 23 C6
Forest Hill Ct. For Hil SE26 . 23 B5
Forest Hill Ind Est. For Hil SE23 23 C6
Forest Hill Rd. For Hil SE23 . 23 C8
Forest Hill Sec Sch. For Hil SE23 23 D5
Forest Hill Sta. For Hil SE23 23 C6
Forest Hills. Camb GU15 65 B4
Forest La. E Hors KT24 92 F3
Forest Lodge. 2 E Grins RH19 205 F8
Forest Lodge. For Hil SE23 . 23 C5
Forest Oaks. Horsh RH13 218 B4
Forest Rd. Cheam SM3 & SM4 40 A2
Forest Rd. Crawl RH12 218 D5
Forest Rd. Crowth RG11 45 C5
Forest Rd. E Hors KT24 92 F2
Forest Rd. Felt TW13 15 C6
Forest Rd. Mayb GU22 70 D4
Forest Rd. N Asct RG12 8 D2
Forest Rd. Rich TW9 7 A7
Forest Rd. Wind SL4 9 E7
Forest Rd. Wink RG12 & SL5 . 8 D2
Forest Ridge. Beck BR3 44 A6
Forest Row Bsns Pk. For Row RH18 206 F4
Forest Row C of E Inf Sch. For Row RH18 206 F2
Forest Side. New Mal KT4 38 F1
Forest View. Crawl RH10 202 A3
Forest View Rd. E Grins RH19 205 E6
Forest Way. Ashtd KT21 76 A3
Forest Wlk. Crawl GU6 173 F2
Forestdale. Hind GU26 188 E3
Forestdale Ctr The. New Add CR0 62 F3
Forestdale Prim Sch. New Add CR0 62 F2
Forester Rd. Crawl RH10 201 E4
Foresters Cl. Knaph GU21 68 F1
Foresters Cl. Wallin SM6 60 D3
Foresters Dr. Wallin CR8 & SM6 60 D2
Foresters Prim Sch. Wallin SM6 60 D4
Foresters Sq. Brack RG12 27 E6
Foresters Way. Crowth RG11 45 E8
Forestfield. Crawl RH10 202 B3
Forestfield. Horsh RH13 218 A3
Forestholme Cl. For Hil SE23 23 C6
Forge Ave. Coulsd CR5 100 B7
Forge Cl. Broad H RH12 216 D4
Forge Cl. Farnh GU9 125 D3
Forge Dr. Clayg KT10 56 A3
Forge End. Woking GU21 69 E2
Forge La. Broad H RH12 216 D4
Forge La. Cheam SM2 & SM3 58 E3
Forge La. Crawl RH10 202 A7
Forge La. Farnb GU11 105 A6
Forge La. Felt TW13 15 E3
Forge La. Sunby TW16 35 A6
Forge Lane Inf Sch. Felt TW13 15 E3
Forge Lane Jun Sch. Felt TW13 15 E3
Forge Rd. Crawl RH10 202 A7
Forge Rd. Headly GU35 166 A1
Forge Steading. Banstd SM7 78 B4
Forge The. Harl UB3 3 D8
Forge The. Warn RH12 216 E7
Forge Wood. Crawl RH10 . 182 D3
Forge Wood Ind Est. Crawl RH10 182 B3
Forgefield. Bigg H TN16 83 D3
Forman Ct. Twick TW1 16 F7
Forrest Gdns. Thorn H SW16 41 F6
Forrester Path. For Hil SE26 23 C4
Forster House. Catf SE6 24 D5
Forster Park Sch. Catf SE6 . 24 E5
Forster Rd. Beck BR3 43 E6
Forster Rd. Streat SW2 21 E8
Forster Rd. Thorn H CR0 42 C2
Forsyte Cres. S Norw SE19 . 42 E8
Forsyte Ct. King U T KT2 38 B8
Forsyth Path. Sheer GU21 70 D6
Forsyth Rd. Sheer GU21 70 C5
Forsythe Shades. Beck BR3 . 44 C8
Forsythia Pl. Bellf GU1 109 C3
Fort La. Reig RH2 118 B5
Fort Narrien. Sandh GU15 64 F7
Fort Rd. Box H KT20 116 B4
Fort Rd. Guild GU1 130 E6
Fortescue Ave. Twick TW2 . 16 C5
Fortescue Rd. Mitch SW19 20 D1
Fortescue Rd. Weyb KT13 52 F6
Forth Cl. W Heath GU14 84 D6
Fortrose Cl. Sandh GU15 64 D7
Fortrose Gdns. Streat SW12 & SW2 21 E7
Fortune Dr. Cran GU6 174 E1
Fortyfoot Rd. Leahd KT22 95 C6
Forum The. E Mole KT8 36 B5
Forval Cl. Mitch CR4 40 F4
Foss Ave. Croy CR0 & CR9 61 A5
Foss Rd. Up Toot SW17 20 D4
Fosse Way. W Byfl KT14 70 F6
Fosseway. Crowth RG11 45 A5
Fossewood Dr. Camb GU15 . 65 D7
Fosterdown. Tyl Gn RH9 121 B6
Fosters Gr. Windl GU20 48 B6
Fosters La. Knaph GU21 68 C2
Foulser Rd. Up Toot SW17 21 A5
Foulsham Rd. S Norw CR7 42 D6
Foundation Units. Bellf GU1 109 F5
Founders Gdns. S Norw SE19 22 C1
Foundry Cl. Horsh RH13 217 E4
Foundry Ct. Chert KT16 33 A2
Foundry La. Haslem GU27 . 208 A6
Foundry La. Horsh RH12 & RH13 217 E3
Foundry La. Horton SL3 1 B4
Foundry Mews. Chert KT16 . 33 A2
Fountain Ct. New Mal KT3 38 C5
Fountain Ct. Penge SE26 23 C2
Fountain Dr. Dulw SE19 22 F4
Fountain Dr. Wallin SM5 59 F2
Fountain Rd. Earls RH1 139 E7
Fountain Rd. S Norw CR7 42 C7
Fountain Rd. Up Toot SW17 . 20 D4
Fountains Ave. Felt TW13 15 F5
Fountains Cl. Crawl RH11 . 201 A4
Fountains Cl. Felt TW13 15 F5
Fountains Garth. Easth RG12 27 A6
Four Acres. Cobham KT11 73 E6
Four Acres. Merrow GU1 & GU4 110 C3
Four Seasons Cres. Cheam SM3 58 F8
Four Square Ct. Twick TW4 5 A1
Four Wents. Cobham KT11 73 C5
Fourth Cross Rd. Twick TW2 16 D6
Fourth Dr. Coulsd CR5 79 D3
Fowler Ave. Farnb GU14 85 B2
Fowler Cl. Worth RH10 202 C4
Fowler Rd. Farnb GU14 84 F3
Fowler Rd. Mitch CR4 41 A7
Fowler's Rd. Farnb GU11 105 D6
Fowlers La. Brack RG12 27 B8
Fowlers Mead. Burrh GU24 49 E2
Fowlerscroft. Compt GU3 129 B2
Fox Cl. Crawl RH11 181 B1
Fox Cl. Mayb GU22 70 D4
Fox Cl. Whit V KT13 53 D5
Fox Covert. Fetch KT22 94 D3
Fox Covert. Lhtwat GU18 67 A8
Fox Covert Cl. Ascot SL5 29 C4
Fox Dene. Godal GU7 150 C2
Fox Gr. Walt O T KT12 35 B2
Fox Heath. Farnb GU14 84 C3
Fox Hill. S Norw SE19 22 F1
Fox Hill Gdns. S Norw SE19 . 22 F1
Fox Hill Prim Sch. Easth RG12 27 B4
Fox Hills La. Ash GU12 106 C3
Fox Hills Rd. Ottsh KT16 51 B5
Fox La. L Book KT23 93 F3
Fox La N. Chert KT16 32 F1
Fox La S. Chert KT16 32 F1
Fox Rd. Brack RG12 27 C5
Fox Rd. M Bourn GU10 146 C7
Fox Rd. Shottm GU27 207 E6
Fox Way. Crond GU10 124 D8
Fox Yd. Farnh GU9 125 B2
Foxacre. Cater CR3 100 E5
Foxborough Hill. Bramly GU5 151 D6
Foxborough Hill Rd. Bramly GU5 151 D6
Foxbourne Rd. Up Toot SW17 21 A6
Foxbridge La. Ifold RH14 212 C1
Foxburrows Ave. Stough GU2 108 F2
Foxcombe. New Add CR0 63 B4
Foxcombe Rd. 6 Rhampt SW15 19 A7
Foxdown Cl. Camb GU15 65 C5
Foxearth Cl. Bigg H TN16 83 E1
Foxearth Rd. S Croy CR2 62 C2
Foxearth Spur. S Croy CR2 62 C2
Foxenden Rd. Guild GU1 109 E1
Foxes Dale. Beck BR2 44 D6
Foxes Path. Westfd GU4 89 F1
Foxglove Ave. Beck BR3 24 B1
Foxglove Ave. Horsh RH12 217 E6
Foxglove Cl. Stan TW19 13 D7
Foxglove Gdns. Merrow GU4 110 C3
Foxglove Gdns. Purley CR8 79 F8
Foxglove La. Chess KT9 57 A6
Foxglove Way. Carsh CR4 41 B1
Foxglove Wlk. Crawl RH11 201 B3
Foxgrove Dr. Horse GU21 70 A4
Foxgrove Rd. Beck BR3 24 C1
Foxhanger Gdns. Woking GU22 70 A3
Foxheath. Brack RG12 27 E4
Foxhill Cres. Camb GU15 66 B8
Foxhills. Woking GU21 69 C2
Foxhills Cl. Ottsh KT16 51 C4
Foxholes. Rudg RH12 214 D8
Foxholes. Whit V KT13 53 D5
Foxhurst Rd. Ash GU12 106 A4
Foxlake Rd. Byfl KT14 71 F7
Foxleigh Chase. Horsh RH12 217 F5
Foxley Cl. Blckw GU17 64 C5
Foxley Cl. Earls RH1 140 A4
Foxley Ct. Sutton SM2 59 C3
Foxley Gdns. Purley CR8 80 B6
Foxley Hall. Purley CR8 80 A6
Foxley Hill Rd. Purley CR8 80 A7
Foxley La. Purley CR8 60 E1
Foxley Rd. Purley CR8 80 B5
Foxley Rd. Thorn H CR7 42 B5
Foxoak Hill. Whit V KT12 & KT13 53 E1
Foxon Cl. Cater CR3 100 E6
Foxon La. Cater CR3 100 E6
Foxon Lane Gdns. Cater CR3 100 E6
Foxtail House. Hounsl TW3 5 C6
Foxton. King U T KT1 38 A6
Foxwarren. Clayg KT10 55 F2
Foxwood Cl. Felt TW13 15 B5
Frailey Cl. Mayb GU22 70 B3
Frailey Hill. Mayb GU22 70 B3
Framfield Cl. Crawl RH11 201 A8
Framfield Rd. Mitch CR4 21 A1
Frampton Cl. Belm SM2 59 A3
Frampton Rd. Hounsl TW4 4 E2
France Hill Dr. Camb GU15 65 C5
France Hill Sch. Camb GU15 65 C2
Frances Ct. S Norw SE25 42 F7
Franche Court Rd. Wands SW17 20 C5
Francis Ave. Felt TW13 15 A5
Francis Barber Cl. Streat SW16 21 F4
Francis Chichester Cl. Ascot SL5 29 B4
Francis Cl. Shep Gn TW17 34 A5
Francis Cl. W Ewell KT19 57 D6
Francis Cl. W Ewell KT19 57 D6
Francis Cnr. Shere KT24 133 B8
Francis Ct. King U T KT5 37 E5
Francis Ct. Stough GU2 109 B3
Francis Edwards Way. Crawl RH11 200 E2
Francis Gr. Wimble SW19 19 F2
Francis Rd. Cater CR3 100 D5
Francis Rd. Hounsl TW4 4 D5
Francis Rd. Thorn H CR0 42 B2
Francis Rd. Wallin SM6 60 C4
Francis Way. Friml GU15 66 C4
Franciscan Prim Sch. Up Toot SW17 21 A3
Franciscan Rd. Up Toot SW17 21 A4
Frangate. E Hors KT24 112 E8
Frank Dixon Cl. Dulw SE21 22 E7
Frank Dixon Way. Dulw SE21 22 E7
Frank Towell Ct. E Bed TW14 15 A7
Frankland House. 4 Balham SW12 21 B8
Franklands Dr. Row Tn KT15 51 F3
Franklin Cl. King U T KT1 38 A6
Franklin Cl. W Norw SE27 22 B5
Franklin Cres. Mitch CR4 41 C5
Franklin Ct. 2 Stough GU2 108 F1
Franklin House. Beck BR2 44 E7
Franklin Ind Est. Penge SE20 43 C8
Franklin Rd. Penge SE20 23 C1
Franklin Rd. Penge SE20 43 C8
Franklin Rd. Walt O T KT12 . 35 A3
Franklin Rd. Worth RH10 202 C5
Franklin Way. Croy CR0 & CR9 41 E2
Franklyn Rd. Ock Rid GU7 150 B3
Franklyn Rd. Walt O T KT12 . 35 B3
Franks Ave. New Mal KT3 38 C5
Franks House. Islew TW7 6 B3
Franks Rd. Stough GU2 109 A3
Franksfield. Peasl GU5 154 E7
Fransfield Gr. For Hil SE26 23 B5
Frant Cl. Penge SE20 23 C1
Frant Rd. Thorn H CR0 & CR7 42 B4
Franthorne Way. Catf SE6 24 B5
Fraser Gdns. Dork RH4 136 A8
Fraser Mead. Sandh GU15 64 E6
Fraser Rd. Brack RG12 27 B8
Frederick Cl. Cheam SM1 58 F5
Frederick Gdns. Cheam SM1 58 F5
Frederick Pl. Woki RG11 25 A6
Frederick Rd. Cheam SM1 58 F5
Frederick Sanger Rd. Onsl V GU2 129 D8
Frederick St. Alder GU11 105 A2
Free Prae Rd. Chert KT16 33 A1
Freeborn Way. Brack RG12 27 E7
Freedown La. Banstd SM2 78 C6
Freehold Ind Ctr. Hounsl TW4 4 C2
Freelands Ave. S Croy CR2 62 D2
Freelands Rd. Cobham KT11 73 B5
Freeman Cl. Up Hall TW17 34 E5
Freeman Dr. E Mole KT8 35 F5
Freeman House. 13 Streat SW2 21 E8

Freeman Rd.
Morden CR4 & SM4 .... 40 D4
Freeman Rd. Warn RH12 ... 216 F8
Freemantle Rd. Bagsh GU19 47 C8
Freemantles Sch.
Windl GU20 .... 48 C5
Freemason's Rd. Croy CR0 .. 42 E1
Freesia Dr. Bisley GU24 ...... 68 A3
Freethorpe Cl. S Norw SE19 42 E8
French Gdns. Cobham KT11 .. 73 C5
French Gdns. Hawley GU17 .. 64 D4
French La. Bowl Gn GU8 .... 169 E3
French St. Sunby TW16 ...... 35 C7
Frenchaye. Addl KT15 .... 52 C5
Frenches Ct. 4 Redh RH1 . 119 A3
Frenches Rd. Redh RH1 ..... 119 B4
Frenches The. Redh RH1 ... 119 A3
Frenchlands Hatch.
E Hors KT24 .... 112 E8
Frensham. Brack RG12 .... 27 D3
Frensham Ct. E of Est Sch.
Frensh GU10 .... 167 D7
Frensham Ct. Mitch CR4 .... 40 D6
Frensham Dr. New Add CR0 . 63 C3
Frensham Dr. Rhampt SW15 19 A6
Frensham Heights Rd.
Rowl GU10 .... 146 A2
Frensham Heights Sch.
Rowl GU10 .... 146 A2
Frensham House. 7
King U T KT6 .... 37 E4
Frensham La.
Head Dn GU35 .... 166 F2
Frensham Rd. Crowth RG11 . 45 B7
Frensham Rd.
M Bourn GU10 & GU9 ..... 146 D6
Frensham Rd. Purley CR8 .... 80 B5
Frensham Vale.
M Bourn GU10 .... 130 F8
Frensham Way. Nork KT17 .. 77 C3
Fresham House. Beck BR2 ... 44 F6
Freshborough Ct.
Guild GU1 .... 130 F8
Freshfield. L Kings KT20 ... 117 E8
Freshfield Bank.
For Row RH18 .... 206 E2
Freshfield Cl. Crawl RH10 . 202 A5
Freshfields. Croy CR0 .... 43 F1
Freshford St.
Wands SW17 & SW18 ...... 20 C5
Freshmount Gdns.
Epsom KT19 .... 76 B8
Freshwater Cl. Streat SW17 21 A2
Freshwater Rd. Streat SW17 21 A2
Freshwood Cl. Beck BR3 ..... 44 B8
Freshwood Way. Wallin SM6 60 C2
Frewin Rd. Wands SW18 ..... 20 D7
Friar Mews. W Norw SE27 ... 22 B5
Friar's Gate. Onsl V GU2 ... 130 A7
Friars Ave. Rhampt SW15 .... 18 F5
Friars Croft. Merrow GU4 .. 110 C4
Friars Ct. 5 Wallin SM6 ..... 60 B6
Friars Keep. Farnb RG12 .... 27 B5
Friars La. Rich TW9 .... 6 D2
Friars Orch. Fetch KT22 ..... 94 D6
Friars Rd. Vir W GU25 .... 31 D5
Friars Rise. Mayb GU22 ...... 70 A1
Friars Rookery. Crawl RH10 201 F6
Friars Stile Pl. 9 Rich TW10 . 6 E1
Friars Stile Rd. Rich TW10 .... 6 E1
Friars Way. Chert KT16 .... 33 A3
Friars Wood. New Add CR0 .. 62 E2
Friary Bridge. Guild GU1 .... 130 C7
Friary Ct. Knaph GU21 .... 68 F1
Friary Pas. Guild GU1 .... 130 C7
Friary Rd. Ascot SL5 .... 29 B3
Friary Rd. Wray TW19 .... 11 C8
Friary St. Guild GU1 & GU2 . 130 C7
Friary The. Guild GU1 .... 130 C8
Friary Way. Crawl RH10 ..... 201 E5
Friday Rd. Mitch CR4 .... 20 F1
Friday St. Faygt RH12 .... 198 E6
Friday St. Ockley RH5 .... 177 E4
Friday St. Rusper RH12 ..... 198 E6
Friday St. Warn RH12 .... 216 E7
Friday Street Rd.
Abin C RH5 .... 155 E8
Friend Ave. Alder GU12 ..... 105 D1
Friends Cl. Crawl RH11 ...... 181 D1
Friends' Rd. Croy CR0 & CR9 61 D7
Friends Rd. Purley CR8 .... 80 B7
Friendship Way. Eastn RG12 27 B6
Friern Rd. Dulw SE22 .... 23 A8
Frimley Ave. Wallin SM6 ..... 60 F5
Frimley Bsns Pk.
Farnb GU16 .... 85 B8
Frimley C of E Est & Mid Sch.
Friml GU16 .... 85 E7

Frimley Cl. New Add CR0 ..... 63 C3
Frimley Cl. Putney SW19 ..... 19 E6
Frimley Cres. New Add CR0 . 63 C3
Frimley Gdns. Mitch CR4 ..... 40 E6
Frimley Green Rd.
Friml GU16 .... 85 E7
Frimley Grove Gdns.
Friml GU16 .... 65 E1
Frimley Hall Dr. Camb GU15 65 F6
Frimley High St. Friml GU16 85 D8
Frimley House. Mitch CR4 .... 40 E6
Frimley Park Hospl.
Friml GU16 .... 65 D2
Frimley Rd. Ash V GU12 .... 106 A8
Frimley Rd. Camb GU15 ...... 65 B3
Frimley Rd. Chess KT9 .... 56 E5
Frimley Rd.
Friml GU15 & GU16 .... 65 C1
Frinton Rd. Mitch SW17 ...... 21 A2
Friston Wlk. Crawl RH11 .... 201 A7
Frith End Rd.
Binst GU34 & GU35 .... 166 A6
Frith Hill Rd. Farnc GU7 .... 150 D6
Frith Hill Rd. Friml GU16 .... 66 B1
Frith Knowle. Hersh KT12 ... 54 B5
Frith Pk. E Grins RH19 ...... 185 E3
Frith Rd. Croy CR0 & CR9 .... 61 C8
Fritham Cl. New Mal KT3 ..... 38 E3
Friths Dr. Reig RH2 .... 118 B4
Frithwald Rd. Chert KT16 .... 32 F2
Frobisher. Eastn RG12 .... 27 C2
Frobisher Cl. Kenley CR8 .... 80 C2
Frobisher Cres. Stan TW19 . 13 E8
Frobisher Ct. Belm SM2 ...... 58 F3
Frobisher Ct. For Hil SE23 ... 23 B6
Frobisher Gdns.
Merrow GU1 .... 110 A2
Frobisher Gdns. Stan TW19 . 13 E8
Frodsham Way. Sandh GU15 45 E2
Frog Grove La.
Wood S V GU3 .... 107 F4
Frog Hall. Woki RG11 .... 25 F5
Frog Hall Dr. Woki RG11 ..... 25 E5
Frog La. Eastn RG12 .... 27 A6
Frog La. Westfd GU4 .... 89 E2
Froggetts La.
Wall W GU6 & RH5 .... 176 C1
Frogmore Cl. Cheam SM3 .... 58 E7
Frogmore Comm Sch.
Yatly GU17 .... 64 A5
Frogmore Ct. Blckw GU17 ... 64 A4
Frogmore Cty Inf Sch.
Blckw GU17 .... 64 B5
Frogmore Cty Jun Sch.
Blckw GU17 .... 64 B5
Frogmore Gdns. Cheam SM3 58 E6
Frogmore Gr. Blckw GU17 ... 64 C4
Frogmore Park Dr.
Blckw GU17 .... 64 D4
Frogmore Rd. Blckw GU17 ... 64 C5
Frome Cl. W Heath GU14 ..... 84 D6
Fromondes Rd. Cheam SM3 . 58 E5
Fromow Gdns. Windl GU20 .. 48 D4
Froxfield Down. 6
Brack RG12 .... 27 F4
Fruen Rd. E Bed TW14 .... 14 F8
Fry Cl. Crawl RH11 .... 201 B1
Fry's Cross. Dunsf GU8 ..... 193 A2
Fryern Wood. Cater CR3 .... 100 C3
Frylands Ct. New Add CR0 ... 82 C8
Fryston Ave. Croy CR0 .... 62 A8
Fryston Ave. Wallin CR5 ...... 79 B5
Fuchsia Way. W End GU24 ... 67 E6
Fuel Farm Rd. Crawl RH6 .. 181 E8
Fulbourn. 4 King U T KT1 ... 38 A7
Fulbourne Cl. Redh RH1 .... 118 E3
Fulford Rd. Cater CR3 .... 100 D6
Fulford Rd. W Ewell KT19 ... 57 D3
Fulford Rd. W Ewell KT19 ... 57 D3
Fulham Cl. Crawl RH11 ...... 201 B2
Fullbrook Ave.
Woodhm KT15 .... 71 A8
Fullbrook Sch.
Woodhm KT15 .... 71 A8
Fullbrooks Ave.
New Mal KT4 .... 38 F1
Fuller's Wood. Croy CR0 ..... 63 A6
Fullers Ave. Surb KT6 .... 56 F8
Fullers Farm Rd.
Shere KT24 .... 112 B1
Fullers Rd. Binst GU10 ...... 145 D3
Fullers Rd. Rowl GU10 ...... 145 D3
Fullers Vale. Head Dn GU35 187 A5
Fullers Way N. Surb KT6 ..... 56 F7
Fullers Way S. Chess KT9 ... 56 E7
Fullers Wood La. Earls RH1 119 C1
Fullerton Cl. Byfl KT14 .... 71 F5
Fullerton Ct. Byfl KT14 .... 71 E5
Fullerton Ct. Tedd TW11 ..... 16 E5
Fullerton Dr. Byfl KT14 .... 71 E5
Fullerton Rd. Byfl KT14 ...... 71 E5
Fullerton Rd. Croy CR0 .... 42 F2
Fullerton Rd. Sutton SM5 .... 59 E2

Fullerton Way. Byfl KT14 ..... 71 E5
Fullmer Way. Woodhm KT15 51 F1
Fulmar Cl. 1 Crawl RH11 ... 200 D5
Fulmar Ct. 5 W Norw SE21 22 D6
Fulmar Dr. E Grins RH19 ... 186 B3
Fulmar Cl. Hampt TW12 ...... 15 E3
Fulstone Cl. Hounsl TW4 ...... 4 F3
Fulvens. Peasl GU5 .... 133 E1
Fulwell Golf Course.
Hampt TW12 .... 16 C4
Fulwell Park Ave. Twick TW2 16 C6
Fulwell Rd.
Tedd TW11 & TW12 .... 16 D4
Fulwell Sta. Tedd TW11 ...... 16 D4
Fulwood Gdns. Twick TW1 .... 6 A1
Fulwood Wlk. Putney SW19 . 19 E7
Furlong Cl. Carsh CR4 .... 41 B1
Furlong Rd. Westc RH4 ..... 135 C6
Furlong Way. Crawl RH6 ... 181 F8
Furlough The. Woking GU22 70 A2
Furmage St. Wands SW18 ... 20 B8
Furnace Dr. Crawl RH10 ... 201 F4
Furnace Farm Rd.
Crawl RH10 .... 202 A4
Furnace Par. Crawl RH10 ... 202 A4
Furnace Pl. Crawl RH10 .... 202 A4
Furnace Rd.
Copth RH10 & RH19 ...... 184 C3
Furneaux Ave. W Norw SE27 22 B3
Furness Rd. Morden SM4 .... 40 B3
Furniss Ct. Crawl GU6 .... 173 F2
Furnival Cl. Went GU25 .... 31 D3
Furrows Pl. Cater CR3 .... 100 F4
Furrows The. Walt O T KT12 54 C8
Furse Cl. Friml GU15 .... 66 C4
Further Green Rd. Catf SE6 . 24 E7
Furtherfield. Cran GU6 ...... 174 E4
Furtherfield Cl. Thorn H CR0 42 A3
Furze Cl. Ash V GU12 .... 106 A7
Furze Cl. Horl RH6 .... 118 F2
Furze Cl. Croy CR0 .... 62 A8
Furze Field. Oxsh KT22 .... 74 E6
Furze Gr. Kings KT20 .... 97 F6
Furze Hill. Kings KT20 .... 97 F6
Furze Hill. Purley CR8 .... 79 F8
Furze Hill Cres.
Crowth RG11 .... 45 C4
Furze Hill Rd.
Head Dn GU35 .... 187 C4
Furze La. E Grins RH19 .... 185 B4
Furze La. Farnc GU7 & GU3 150 F8
Furze La. Purley CR8 .... 79 F8
Furze Rd. Row Tn KT15 ...... 51 F4
Furze Rd. Rudg RH12 .... 214 D8
Furze Rd. S Norw CR7 .... 42 C6
Furze Vale Rd.
Head Dn GU35 .... 187 B4
Furzebank. Ascot SL5 .... 29 D5
Furzedown Dr. Streat SW17 21 B3
Furzedown Prim Sch.
Mitch SW17 .... 21 A2
Furzedown Rd. Streat SW17 21 B3
Furzedown Rd. Sutton SM2 . 78 C8
Furzefield. Crawl RH11 ..... 201 C7
Furzefield Chase.
Dorm Pk RH19 .... 185 E6
Furzefield Cres. Reig RH2 . 139 C7
Furzefield Cty Fst Sch.
Merst RH1 .... 119 D7
Furzefield Cty Mid Sch.
Merst RH1 .... 119 D7
Furzefield Rd.
E Grins RH19 .... 185 D4
Furzefield Rd. Horsh RH12 218 B5
Furzefield Rd. Reig RH2 .... 139 C7
Furzehill. Redh RH1 .... 118 E2
Furzeland House. 2
New Mal KT3 .... 38 E2
Furzemoors. Eastn RG12 .... 27 B4
Furzen La.
Ell Gn RH12 & RH5 .... 196 B4
Furzen La.
Wall W RH12 & RH5 ...... 196 B4
Furzewood. Sunby TW16 .... 35 A8
Fyfield Cl. Beck BR2 & BR3 . 44 D5
Fyfield Cl. Blckw GU17 .... 64 D5

Gable Ct. For Hil SE26 .... 23 B4
Gable Ct. 8 Redh RH1 ...... 119 A2
Gable End. Farnb GU14 ...... 85 B8
Gable Lodge. W Wick BR4 ... 44 C1
Gables Ave. Ashf TW15 ...... 13 F3
Gables Cl. Ash V GU12 ..... 106 A5
Gables Cl. Farnb GU14 .... 85 A4
Gables Cl. Old Wok GU22 .... 89 F7
Gables Cl. Old Wok GU22 .... 89 F7
Gables The. Banstd SM7 .... 77 F2
Gables The. Copth RH10 ... 183 B3
Gables The. Elst GU8 .... 148 C3
Gables The. Horsh RH12 ... 217 D4
Gables The. Oxsh KT22 .... 74 C7

Gables The. Whit V KT13 ..... 53 C5
Gabriel Cl. Felt TW13 .... 15 D4
Gabriel Dr. Friml GU15 .... 66 B4
Gabriel St. For Hil SE23 ...... 23 E8
Gadbridge La. Ewh GU6 .... 175 E4
Gadbrook Rd. Betch RH3 ... 137 D4
Gadesden Rd. W Ewell KT19 57 C4
Gadesden Rd. W Ewell KT19 57 C4
Gaffney Cl. Farnb GU11 .... 105 D7
Gage Cl. Crawl D RH10 .... 184 C1
Gage Ridge. For Row RH18 206 E2
Gainsborough. Eastn RG12 . 27 C2
Gainsborough Cl. Beck BR3 . 24 A1
Gainsborough Cl.
Camb GU15 .... 65 F7
Gainsborough Cl.
Farnb GU14 .... 85 D2
Gainsborough Cl.
Thame D KT10 .... 36 E1
Gainsborough Cl. Dulw SE21 22 E6
Gainsborough Ct.
Walt O T KT12 .... 54 A6
Gainsborough Dr.
N Asct SL5 .... 28 D7
Gainsborough Dr.
Sander CR2 .... 81 A6
Gainsborough Gdns.
Islew TW7 .... 5 D2
Gainsborough Rd.
Crawl RH10 .... 201 F3
Gainsborough Rd.
Epsom KT19 .... 57 C1
Gainsborough Rd.
New Mal KT3 .... 38 D2
Gainsborough Rd. Rich TW9 . 6 F4
Gaist Ave. Cater CR3 .... 101 B5
Galahad Rd. Crawl RH11 ... 200 E6
Galba Ct. 1 Brent TW8 .... 6 D7
Gale Cl. Hampt TW12 .... 15 E2
Gale Cl. Mitch CR4 .... 40 D6
Gale Cres. Banstd SM7 .... 78 A2
Gale Dr. Lhead GU18 .... 48 A1
Gales Dr. Crawl RH10 .... 201 F6
Gales Dr. Crawl RH10 .... 201 F6
Gales Pl. Crawl RH10 .... 201 F6
Galgate Cl. 4 Putney SW19 19 E7
Gallery Rd. Dulw SE21 .... 22 D7
Gallery Rd. Pirb GU24 ...... 87 D8
Galleymead Rd. Poyle SL3 ... 1 F6
Gallop The. S Croy CR2 ...... 62 B3
Gallop The. Sutton SM2 ..... 59 D2
Gallwey Rd. Alder GU11 ... 105 C3
Galpin's Rd.
Thorn H CR4 & CR7 .... 41 F5
Galsworthy Rd. Chert KT16 . 33 A2
Galsworthy Rd. King U T KT2 38 B8
Galton Rd. Sunnin SL5 .... 29 F3
Galvani Way.
Croy CR0 & CR9 .... 41 F1
Galvins Cl. Stough GU2 .... 109 A4
Gambles La. Ripley GU23 ... 91 C2
Gambole Rd. Up Toot SW17 20 E4
Gander Green La.
Cheam KT4 & SM1 & SM3 ... 58 F7
Gangers Hill. Wold RH9 .... 121 F7
Ganghill. Abbots GU1 .... 110 A3
Gannet Ct. 4 W Norw SE22 22 D6
Ganymede Ct. Crawl RH11 200 E3
Gap Rd. Wimble SW19 .... 20 B3
Gapemouth Rd.
Pirb GU16 & GU24 .... 86 E5
Garbetts Way. Tongh GU10 126 F6
Garbrand Wlk. Ewell KT17 ... 57 F2
Garden Ave. Mitch CR4 ...... 21 B1
Garden Cl. Addl KT15 .... 52 D6
Garden Cl. Ashf TW15 .... 14 C2
Garden Cl. Banstd SM7 ...... 78 A4
Garden Cl. E Grins RH19 .. 205 F7
Garden Cl. Hampt TW12 ..... 15 F3
Garden Cl. Leatd KT22 .... 95 C3
Garden Cl. Putney SW15 ..... 19 B8
Garden Cl. Sham Gn GU5 .. 152 D4
Garden Cl. Wallin SM6 .... 60 E5
Garden Cl. Belm SM2 .... 59 A3
Garden Cl. 4 Rich TW9 .... 6 F6
Garden Cl. S Croy CR0 .... 61 F7
Garden Flats. Streat SW16 .. 21 E5
Garden House La.
E Grins RH19 .... 205 F7
Garden La. Streat SW2 .... 21 F7
Garden Pl. Horsh RH12 .... 217 C4
Garden Rd. Mortl TW9 .... 7 A4
Garden Rd. Penge SE20 ..... 43 C8
Garden Rd. Walt O T KT12 ... 35 B2
Garden The. Effing KT24 ... 113 D7
Garden Wlk. Beck BR3 .... 43 F8
Garden Wlk. Crawl RH11 ... 201 C6
Garden Wlk. Hooley CR5 .... 99 B4
Garden Wlk. Horsh RH12 ... 217 C4
Garden Wood Rd.
E Grins RH19 .... 205 C8

Gardener's Hill Rd.
Rowl GU10 .... 146 B4
Gardener's Wlk.
G Book KT23 .... 94 B1
Gardeners Cl. Warn RH12 .. 216 E8
Gardeners Ct. Horsh RH13 217 D1
Gardeners Gn.
Rusper RH12 .... 199 C6
Gardeners Rd. Thorn H CR0 . 42 B1
Gardenfields. Burgh H KT20 . 97 E8
Gardenia Cl. 1 Beck BR3 .... 24 A1
Gardenia Dr. W End GU24 ... 67 F6
Gardens The. Beck BR3 ...... 44 D7
Gardens The. Esher KT10 .... 55 A6
Gardens The. Hatton TW14 ... 3 D1
Gardens The. Pirb GU24 ..... 87 F5
Gardens The. Tongh GU10 . 126 F7
Gardner House. Felt TW13 .. 15 F6
Gardner Ind Est.
Penge SE26 .... 23 F3
Gardner La. Crawl D RH10 204 A8
Gardner Rd. Guild GU1 .... 109 D1
Garendon Gdns.
Morden SM4 .... 40 B2
Garendon Rd. Cheam SM4 ... 40 B2
Gareth Cl. N Cheam KT4 ..... 58 D8
Gareth Ct. Streat SW16 ...... 21 D5
Garfield Prim Sch.
Wimble SW19 .... 20 C2
Garfield Rd. Addl KT15 .... 52 C6
Garfield Rd. Camb GU15 ..... 65 C5
Garfield Rd. 2 Twick TW1 .... 17 A7
Garfield Rd. Wimble SW19 .. 20 C2
Garibaldi Rd. Redh RH1 ... 139 F8
Garland Rd. E Grins RH19 . 185 D2
Garland Way. Cater CR3 .... 100 D5
Garlands Rd. Leahd KT22 ... 95 C6
Garlands Rd. Redh RH1 .... 118 F1
Garlichill Rd.
Burgh H KT17 & KT18 .... 77 B2
Garlies Rd. For Hil SE23 ..... 23 E5
Garnet House. New Mal KT4 38 D1
Garnet Rd. S Norw CR7 ...... 42 D5
Garrad's Rd. Streat SW16 ... 21 D4
Garrard Rd. Banstd SM7 .... 78 A3
Garrat La.
Up Toot SW17 & SW18 ..... 20 C5
Garratt Cl. Wallin CR0 .... 60 E6
Garratt Green Sch.
Wands SW17 .... 20 D5
Garratt La.
Wands SW17 .... 20 D5
Garratt Park Sec Sch.
Wands SW17 .... 20 C5
Garratt Terr. Up Toot SW17 . 20 E4
Garratts La. Banstd SM7 .... 78 A3
Garraway House. Dulw SE21 22 F5
Garrett Cl. Worth RH10 .... 202 C4
Garrett Cl. Hersh KT12 .... 54 B6
Garrick Cl. 1 Rich TW9 .... 6 D2
Garrick Cl. Stain TW18 .... 13 A1
Garrick Cres. S Croy CR0 ... 61 E8
Garrick Gdns. E Moke KT8 .. 36 A6
Garrick House. Chisw W4 ...... 7 E8
Garrick House. 2
King U T KT1 .... 37 E5
Garrick House. 7
Streat SW16 .... 21 C3
Garrick Rd. Rich TW9 .... 7 A5
Garrick Wlk. Friml GU16 ..... 85 E7
Garrick Wlk. Crawl RH10 .. 201 E3
Garrick's Ait. E Mole KT8 ... 36 C7
Garrison La. Chess KT9 ...... 56 E3
Garrones The. Crawl RH10 202 E7
Garside Cl. Hampt TW12 .... 16 B2
Garson La. Wray TW19 ...... 11 D8
Garson Rd. Esher KT10 ...... 54 F2
Garson's La. New Gn SL4 ..... 8 A7
Garston Gdns. Kenley CR8 .. 80 D4
Garston La. Kenley CR8 ...... 80 D4
Garstons The. L Book KT23 . 94 A2
Garswood. Brack RG12 .... 27 D3
Garth Cl. King U T KT2 .... 17 F3
Garth Cl. Morden SM4 ...... 146 A7
Garth Cl. W Barn SM4 .... 39 D2
Garth Cl. Chisw W4 .... 7 D8
Garth High Sch.
Morden SM4 .... 40 D3
Garth Hill Sch. Brack RG12 . 27 D8
Garth Rd. Chisw W4 .... 7 D8
Garth Rd. King U T KT2 ...... 17 F3
Garth Rd. W Barn SM4 .... 39 D2
Garth The.
Ash GU10 & GU12 .... 105 F1
Garth The. Cobham KT11 .... 73 E6
Garth The. Farnb GU14 ...... 85 D4
Garth The. Hampt TW12 ..... 16 B2
Garthorne Rd. For Hil SE23 . 23 D8
Garthside. Rich TW10 .... 17 E3
Gartmoor Gdns.
Wands SW19 .... 19 F7

Garton Cl. Crawl RH11 200 E5
Garvens. Dulw SE19 22 E3
Gascoigne Rd. New Add CR0 63 C2
Gascoigne Rd. Weyb KT13 53 B7
Gasden Copse. Witley GU8 170 D5
Gasden Dr. Witley GU8 170 D6
Gasden La. Witley GU8 170 D6
Gaskyns Cl. Rudg RH12 214 D7
Gassiot Rd. Up Toot SW17 20 F4
Gassiot Way. Carsh SM1 59 D7
Gasson Wood Rd. Crawl RH11 200 E4
Gaston Bell Cl. Rich TW9 6 F4
Gaston Bridge Rd. Shep TW17 34 D3
Gaston Bridge Rd. Up Hall TW17 34 E4
Gaston Rd. Mitch CR4 41 A6
Gaston Way. Shep TW17 34 D4
Gatcombe Ct. Beck BR3 24 A1
Gate Ct. 4 Weyb KT13 53 B7
Gate House. 4 Surb KT6 37 E1
Gate St. Bramly GU5 173 B7
Gateford Dr. Horsh RH12 217 F6
Gatehouse Cl. King U T KT2 18 C1
Gates Green Rd. Coney H BR4 63 F7
Gatesden Rd. Fetch KT22 94 C4
Gateside Rd. Up Toot SW17 20 F5
Gatestone Ct. 9 S Norw SE19 22 E2
Gatestone Rd. S Norw SE19 22 E2
Gateway The. Sheer GU21 70 C5
Gateways. Guild GU1 131 B8
Gateways. King U T KT6 37 E4
Gateways Ct. Wallin SM6 60 B5
Gateways The. Rich TW9 6 D3
Gatfield Gr. Felt TW13 16 A6
Gatfield House. Felt TW13 16 A6
Gatley Ave. W Ewell KT19 57 B5
Gatley Ave. W Ewell KT19 57 B5
Gatton Bottom. Gatton RH2 & RH1 118 E7
Gatton Bottom. L Kings RH1 & RH2 119 B8
Gatton Bottom. Merst RH1 & RH2 119 B8
Gatton Cl. Reig RH2 118 C4
Gatton Cl. Sutton SM2 59 B2
Gatton Park Ct. Redh RH1 118 F4
Gatton Park Rd. Redh RH1 & RH2 118 E4
Gatton Point. Redh RH1 119 A5
Gatton Prim Sch. Up Toot SW17 20 F4
Gatton Rd. Reig RH2 118 C4
Gatton Rd. Up Toot SW17 20 E4
Gatwick Airport Sta. Crawl RH6 182 B7
Gatwick Airport-London. Crawl RH6 181 F7
Gatwick Gate. Crawl RH6 181 E5
Gatwick Metro Ctr. Horley RH6 161 B4
Gatwick Park Hospl. Hookw RH6 160 E2
Gatwick Rd. Crawl RH10 & RH6 182 A3
Gatwick Rd. Wands SW18 19 F8
Gatwick Way. Crawl RH6 181 F8
Gatwick Zoo. Charl RH6 180 D6
Gauntlet Cres. Cater CR3 & CR8 100 D7
Gauntlett Rd. Carsh SM1 59 D5
Gavell Rd. Cobham KT11 73 A6
Gaveston Cl. Byfl KT14 71 F6
Gaveston Rd. Leahd KT22 95 A7
Gavina Cl. Morden SM4 40 E4
Gayfere Rd. Stonel KT17 58 A5
Gayhouse La. Horne RH1 162 E8
Gayler Cl. Bletch RH1 120 F2
Gaynesford Rd. For Hil SE23 23 D6
Gaynesford Rd. Wallin SM5 59 F3
Gaysland Cotts. Tand RH7 143 A2
Gayton Ct. New Mal KT3 38 F4
Gayton Ct. Reig RH2 118 A2
Gaywood Cl. Streat SW2 22 A7
Gaywood Rd. Ashtd KT21 75 F1
Geary Cl. Burst RH6 162 B1
Gedge Ct. Mitch CR4 40 E5
Geffers Ride. N Asct SL5 28 E7
Gemini Cl. Crawl RH11 200 E4
Gemma Ct. Beck BR3 43 F7
Genesis Bsns Pk. Sheer GU21 70 C4
Geneva Cl. Up Hall TW17 34 E7
Geneva Rd. King U T KT1 37 E5
Geneva Rd. Thorn H CR7 42 C4
Genoa Rd. Penge SE20 43 C8
Gentles La. Head Dn GU30 & GU35 187 A3
Genyn Rd. Guild GU2 130 B8
George Abbot Sch. Abbots GU1 110 A3
George Denyer Cl. Haslem GU27 208 C7
George Eliot Cl. Witley GU8 170 F5
George Gdns. Alder GU11 126 C7
George Groves Rd. Penge SE20 43 A8
George Horley Pl. Newd RH5 158 B1
George House. 8 Penge SE26 23 B3
George Pinion Ct. Horsh RH12 217 B3
George Rd. Farnc GU7 150 F7
George Rd. Guild GU1 109 D1
George Rd. King U T KT2 18 C1
George Rd. Milf GU8 149 F2
George Rd. New Mal KT3 38 F4
George Sq. Merton SW19 40 A6
George St. Croy CR0 & CR9 61 D8
George St. Hounsl TW3 & TW5 4 F5
George St. Pirb GU24 87 A6
George St. Rich TW10 6 D2
George St. Stain TW18 12 F4
George Wyver Cl. Putney SW18 19 E8
George's Rd. Tats TN16 103 D7
Georgeham Rd. Sandh GU15 45 D2
Georgelands. Ripley GU23 91 B6
Georges Terr. Cater CR3 100 D5
Georgetown Cl. 4 W Norw SE19 22 E3
Georgia Rd. King U T KT3 38 C5
Georgia Rd. S Norw CR7 42 B8
Georgian Cl. Camb GU15 65 E7
Georgian Cl. Stain TW18 13 B4
Georgian Cl. Worth RH10 202 D5
Georgian Ct. Croy CR0 & CR9 42 D1
Georgina Ct. 5 Twick TW1 6 C1
Gerald Ct. Horsh RH13 217 E2
Gerald's Gr. Nork SM7 77 D5
Geraldine Rd. Brent W4 7 A8
Gerard Ave. Twick TW4 16 A8
Gerard Rd. Barnes SW13 7 F6
Germander Dr. Bisley GU24 68 A4
Gerrards Mead. Banstd SM7 77 F3
Ghent St. Catf SE6 24 A6
Ghyll Cres. Horsh RH13 217 F1
Gibb's Acre. Pirb GU24 87 F4
Gibbet La. Camb GU15 66 A7
Gibbon Rd. King U T KT2 17 F1
Gibbons Cl. Sandh GU17 64 C8
Gibbs Ave. W Norw SE19 22 D3
Gibbs Brook La. Crow RH7 & RH8 143 D7
Gibbs Brook La. Oxted RH7 & RH8 143 D7
Gibbs Cl. W Norw SE19 22 D3
Gibbs House. 6 Balham SW12 21 B8
Gibbs House. Broml BR1 44 F8
Gibbs Sq. W Norw SE19 22 D3
Giblets La. Horsh RH12 217 F7
Giblets Way. Horsh RH12 217 E7
Gibraltar Cres. Epsom KT19 57 E1
Gibson Cl. Chess KT9 56 C5
Gibson Cl. Islew TW7 5 D4
Gibson Ct. Hinch W KT10 55 F7
Gibson House. Sutton SM1 59 A6
Gibson Pl. Stan TW19 2 C1
Gibson Rd. Sutton SM1 59 B5
Gibson's Hill. S Norw SW16 22 A1
Gibson's Hill. S Norw SW16 22 A2
Gidd Hill. Coulsd CR5 79 A3
Giffard Dr. W Heath GU14 84 F5
Giffard Way. Stough GU2 109 A4
Giffards Cl. E Grins RH19 185 F1
Giffards Meadow. M Bourn GU9 125 E1
Giggs Hill Rd. Thame D KT7 37 A2
Giggshill Gdns. Thame D KT7 37 A1
Gilbert Cl. 1 Merton SW19 40 B8
Gilbert Rd. Friml GU16 65 C2
Gilbert Rd. Merton SW19 20 C1
Gilbert Scott Jun & Inf Sch. S Croy CR2 62 E3
Gilbert St. Hounsl TW3 5 C4
Gilbey Rd. Up Toot SW17 20 E3
Gilders Rd. Chess KT9 56 F4
Giles Coppice. Dulw SE19 22 F4
Giles Travers Cl. Egham TW20 32 C6
Gilesmead. Epsom KT18 76 E5
Gilham La. For Row RH18 206 E2
Gilham's Ave. Belm SM7 77 E7
Gill Ave. Onsl V GU2 129 E8
Gillett Ct. Horsh RH13 218 B4
Gillett House. Horsh RH13 218 B4
Gillett Rd. S Norw CR7 42 D5
Gillette Cnr. Brent TW7 6 A7
Gillham's La. Linch GU27 207 A5
Gilliam Gr. Purley CR8 61 A1
Gillian Ave. Alder GU11 & GU12 126 D8
Gillian Cl. Alder GU12 126 D8
Gillian Park Rd. Cheam SM3 39 F1
Gilliat Dr. Merrow GU4 110 D3
Gilligan Cl. Horsh RH12 217 B2
Gilmais. Fetch KT23 94 C2
Gilmore Cres. Ashf TW15 14 A2
Gilpin Ave. Mortl SW14 7 D3
Gilpin Cl. Mitch CR4 40 E7
Gilpin Cres. Twick TW2 16 B8
Gilpin Way. Harl UB3 3 D7
Gilsland Rd. S Norw CR7 42 D5
Gilton Rd. Catf SE6 24 E5
Gimcrack Hill. Leahd KT22 95 B5
Gingers Cl. Cran GU6 174 F2
Ginhams Rd. Crawl RH11 201 B6
Gipsy Hill. W Norw SE19 & SE27 22 E3
Gipsy Hill Sta. W Norw SE19 22 E3
Gipsy La. Brack RG12 27 D7
Gipsy La. Woki RG11 25 C4
Gipsy Rd. W Norw SE21 & SE27 22 D4
Gipsy Road Gdns. W Norw SE27 22 C4
Girdwood Rd. Putney SW18 & SW19 19 E8
Girling Way. Hatton TW14 4 A4
Girton Cl. Sandh GU15 45 E1
Girton Gdns. Croy CR0 63 A7
Girton Rd. For Hil SE26 23 D3
Gittens Cl. Catf BR1 24 F4
Glade Cl. Long D KT6 56 D8
Glade Gdns. Croy CR0 43 E2
Glade House. Ascot SL5 29 D4
Glade Spur. Kings KT20 98 B6
Glade The. Ascot SL5 29 C4
Glade The. Belm SM2 58 E2
Glade The. Binst GU10 145 B1
Glade The. Coulsd CR5 & CR8 100 A8
Glade The. Crawl RH10 202 A4
Glade The. Croy CR0 43 D3
Glade The. Fetch KT22 94 B5
Glade The. Heath E GU9 125 D7
Glade The. Horsh RH13 218 A3
Glade The. Kings KT20 98 B6
Glade The. Sheer KT14 70 E6
Glade The. Stain TW18 13 B2
Glade The. Stonel KT17 58 A4
Glade The. W Wick BR4 63 B7
Glades The. E Grins RH19 186 B1
Gladeside. Croy CR0 43 D3
Gladeside Ct. Warlgm CR6 101 B7
Gladiator St. For Hil SE23 23 E8
Gladiator Way. Farnb GU11 & GU14 105 A8
Gladioli Cl. 6 Hampt TW12 16 A2
Gladsmuir Cl. Walt O T KT12 54 C8
Gladstone Ave. Felt TW14 4 B1
Gladstone Ave. Felt TW14 15 B8
Gladstone Ave. Twick TW2 16 D8
Gladstone Ct. 5 Merton SW19 20 A1
Gladstone Mews. 3 Penge SE20 23 C1
Gladstone Pl. Thame D KT8 36 E4
Gladstone Rd. Ashtd KT21 75 D1
Gladstone Rd. Croy CR0 42 D2
Gladstone Rd. Horsh RH12 217 D3
Gladstone Rd. King U T KT1 38 A6
Gladstone Rd. Merton SW19 20 A1
Gladstone Rd. Surb KT6 56 E8
Glamis Cl. Friml GU16 85 F7
Glamorgan Cl. Mitch CR4 & SW16 41 E6
Glamorgan Rd. Tedd KT1 17 C1
Glanfield Rd. Beck BR3 43 F5
Glanty The. Egham TW20 12 B4
Glanville House. 4 Streat SW12 21 C8
Glanville Wlk. 8 Crawl RH11 201 A3
Glasbrook Ave. Twick TW2 15 F7
Glasford St. Up Toot SW17 20 F2
Glassmill La. Broml BR2 44 F7
Glassonby Wlk. Friml GU15 66 C5
Glastonbury Prim Sch. Cheam SM4 40 B2
Glastonbury Rd. Cheam CR4 40 A2
Glastonbury Rd. Morden SM4 40 A2
Glayshers Hill. Head Dn GU35 187 B6
Glazebrook Cl. Dulw SE21 22 D6
Glazebrook Rd. Tedd TW11 16 F1
Glaziers La. Flexf GU3 107 C2
Gleave Cl. E Grins RH19 186 A2
Glebe Ave. Mitch CR4 40 E7
Glebe Cl. Crawl RH10 201 E7
Glebe Cl. G Book KT23 94 A1
Glebe Cl. Lhtwat GU18 48 C1
Glebe Cl. Sander CR2 80 F8
Glebe Cotts. Felt TW13 16 A5
Glebe Cotts. W Clan GU4 111 B3
Glebe Ct. Guild GU1 109 F1
Glebe Ct. Mitch CR4 40 F6
Glebe Gdns. Byfl KT14 71 E5
Glebe Gdns. New Mal KT3 38 E2
Glebe House. Felt TW13 16 A5
Glebe Hyrst. Sander CR2 80 F7
Glebe La. Abin C RH5 155 D8
Glebe La. Rushm GU10 168 C5
Glebe Path. Mitch CR4 40 F6
Glebe Rd. Ashtd KT21 75 D1
Glebe Rd. Belm SM2 58 E2
Glebe Rd. Cran GU6 174 E4
Glebe Rd. Dork RH4 135 F7
Glebe Rd. Egham TW20 12 C2
Glebe Rd. Merst CR5 99 B3
Glebe Rd. Stain TW18 13 B3
Glebe Rd. W Heath GU14 84 F5
Glebe Rd. Wallin SM5 59 F4
Glebe Rd. Warlgm CR6 81 D2
Glebe Sch. W Wick BR4 63 D8
Glebe Side. Twick TW1 5 F1
Glebe Sq. Mitch CR4 40 F6
Glebe The. Copth RH10 183 B3
Glebe The. Ewh GU6 175 E6
Glebe The. Felb RH19 185 A4
Glebe The. Hawley GU17 64 E3
Glebe The. Hawley GU17 64 E4
Glebe The. Horley RH6 160 F3
Glebe The. Leigh RH2 138 A2
Glebe The. New Mal KT4 38 F1
Glebe The. Streat SW16 21 D4
Glebe Way. Coney H BR4 63 E7
Glebe Way. Felt TW13 16 A5
Glebe Way. Sander CR2 80 F8
Glebe Way. W Wick BR4 63 D8
Glebeland Ctr. Dork RH4 136 A7
Glebeland Gdns. Shep TW17 34 C3
Glebeland Rd. Camb GU15 64 F4
Glebelands. Clayg KT10 55 F2
Glebelands. Crawl D RH10 204 A7
Glebelands. E Mole KT8 36 B5
Glebelands. Loxwd RH14 212 F4
Glebelands Rd. E Bed TW14 15 A8
Glebelands Rd. Woki RG11 25 C7
Glebelands Sch. Cran GU6 174 D3
Glebewood. Easth RG12 27 C4
Gledhow Wood. Kings KT20 98 B5
Glen Albyn Rd. Putney SW19 19 D6
Glen Ave. Ashf TW15 14 A4
Glen Cl. Beac H GU26 188 C6
Glen Cl. Kings KT20 97 E4
Glen Cl. Shep Gn TW17 34 A5
Glen Court Flats. Beac H GU26 188 C6
Glen Ct. Broml BR1 24 F1
Glen Ct. 10 Penge SE20 43 B8
Glen Ct. Row Tn KT15 51 F5
Glen Ct. Stain TW18 12 F1
Glen Dale Mews. Beck BR3 44 B8
Glen Gdns. Croy CR0 & CR9 61 A6
Glen Innes. Sandh GU15 45 E1
Glen Rd. Beac H GU26 188 C6
Glen Rd. Chess KT9 56 E7
Glen Rd. Graysh GU26 188 D3
Glen Road End. Wallin SM6 60 B2
Glen The. Ascot SL5 29 D5
Glen The. Beck BR2 44 E7
Glen The. Croy CR0 62 D7
Glen The. Earls RH1 139 F8
Glen The. Row Tn KT15 51 F5
Glen Vue. E Grins RH19 185 E1
Glena Mount. Sutton SM1 59 C6
Glenalmond Hse. Ashf TW15 13 E5
Glenavon Cl. Clayg KT10 56 A4
Glenavon Ct. N Cheam KT4 58 B8
Glenbow Rd. Catf BR1 24 E3
Glenbuck Ct. 6 Surb KT6 37 E3
Glenbuck Rd. Surb KT6 37 E3
Glenburnie Rd. Up Toot SW17 20 F5
Glencairn Rd. Streat SW16 21 E1
Glencoe Cl. Friml GU16 86 A8
Glencoe Rd. Weyb KT13 53 A7
Glendale Cl. Horsh RH12 218 A6
Glendale Cl. Woking GU21 69 C1
Glendale Dr. Burph GU4 110 C5
Glendale Rise. Purley CR8 80 B4
Glendene Ave. E Hors KT24 92 E1
Glendon House. 9 Crawl RH11 201 D5
Glendower Gdns. 10 Mortl SW14 7 D4
Glendower Rd. Mortl SW14 7 D4
Glendyne Cl. E Grins RH19 206 A8
Glendyne Way. E Grins RH19 206 A8
Gleneagle Lodge. Beck BR3 44 A8
Gleneagle Mews. Streat SW16 21 D3
Gleneagle Rd. Streat SW16 21 D3
Gleneagles Cl. Stan TW19 2 D1
Gleneagles Ct. Crawl RH10 & RH11 201 D5
Gleneagles Ct. 3 Tedd TW11 17 A3
Gleneagles Dr. Farnb GU14 84 C3
Gleneagles House. Easth RG12 26 E3
Gleneldon Mews. Streat SW16 21 E4
Gleneldon Rd. Streat SW16 21 E4
Glenfarg Rd. Catf SE6 24 D7
Glenfield Cl. Brock RH3 137 B5
Glenfield Cotts. Charl RH6 180 D7
Glenfield House. Easth RG12 27 C5
Glenfield Rd. Ashf TW15 14 C2
Glenfield Rd. Banstd SM7 78 B4
Glenfield Rd. Brock RH3 137 B6
Glenfield Rd. Streat SW12 21 C7
Glenhaven Dr. Stan TW19 2 A2
Glenheadon Cl. Leahd KT22 95 D4
Glenheadon Rise. Leahd KT22 95 D4
Glenhurst. Beck BR3 44 C8
Glenhurst Cl. Hawley GU17 64 E4
Glenhurst Ct. Dulw SE19 22 F3
Glenhurst Rd. Brent TW8 6 C8
Glenhurst Rise. S Norw SE19 22 C1
Glenister Park Rd. Streat SW16 21 D1
Glenlea. Shottm GU26 188 E1
Glenlea Hollow. Shottm GU26 & GU27 207 E8
Glenlion Ct. 2 Oat Pk KT13 53 D7
Glenmill. Hampt TW12 15 F3
Glenmore Cl. Addl KT15 52 B7
Glenmore House. 6 Rich TW10 6 E1
Glenmount Rd. Mytch GU16 86 A2
Glenn Ave. Purley CR8 80 B8
Glennie Ct. Dulw SE21 23 A7
Glennie Rd. W Norw SE27 & SW16 22 A5
Glentanner Way. Wands SW17 20 D5
Glenthorne Ave. Croy CR0 & CR9 43 C1
Glenthorne Cl. Cheam SM3 40 A1
Glenthorne Gdns. Cheam SM3 40 A1
Glenthorne High Sch. Cheam SM3 40 A1
Glenthorne Rd. King U T KT1 37 F5
Glenthorpe Rd. W Barn SM4 39 D4
Glenview Cl. Crawl RH10 201 F8
Glenville Gdns. Hind GU26 188 F4
Glenville Mews. Wands SW18 20 A8
Glenville Rd. King U T KT2 38 A8
Glenwood. Brack RG12 27 D5
Glenwood. Dork RH4 & RH5 136 C5
Glenwood. Vir W GU25 31 C8
Glenwood Rd. For Hil SE6 24 A7
Glenwood Rd. Hounsl TW3 5 D4
Glenwood Rd. Stonel KT17 58 A4
Glenwood Way. Croy CR0 43 D3
Globe Farm La. Blckw GU17 64 B5
Glorney Mead. Farnh GU9 126 A6
Glory Mead. Dork RH4 & 5 136 C4
Glossop Rd. S Croy CR2 61 D2
Gloster Rd. New Mal KT3 38 E5
Gloster Rd. Old Wok GU22 90 A7
Gloucester Cl. E Grins RH19 206 A8
Gloucester Cl. Friml GU16 85 E6
Gloucester Cl. Thame D KT7 37 A1
Gloucester Cres. Stain TW18 13 D2
Gloucester Ct. Rich TW9 7 A7
Gloucester Ct. 8 Surb KT6 37 D2
Gloucester Dr. Wray TW18 & TW19 12 D5
Gloucester Gdns. Bagsh GU19 47 E3
Gloucester Gdns. Sutton SM1 59 B8
Gloucester Lodge. 5 Croy CR0 61 F8

Gloucester Rd. Alder GU11 126 C7
Gloucester Rd. Bagsh GU19 47 E3
Gloucester Rd. Crawl RH10 201 E2
Gloucester Rd. Croy CR0 42 E2
Gloucester Rd. Felt TW13 15 C7
Gloucester Rd. Hampt TW12 16 B1
Gloucester Rd. Hounsl TW4 4 E3
Gloucester Rd. King U T KT1 & KT2 38 B7
Gloucester Rd. Redh RH1 118 F2
Gloucester Rd. Rich TW9 7 A7
Gloucester Rd. Stough GU2 108 F3
Gloucester Rd. Tedd TW11 16 E3
Gloucester Rd. Thorn H CR0 42 E2
Gloucester Rd. Twick TW2 16 C7
Glover's Rd. Charl RH6 180 D7
Glover's Rd. Reig RH2 139 B8
Glovers Field. Shottm GU27 207 F6
Gloxinia Wlk. Hampt TW12 16 A2
Glyn Cl. Ewell KT17 58 A2
Glyn Cl. S Norw SE19 & SE25 42 E8
Glyn Ct. W Norw SE27 22 A5
Glyn Rd. N Cheam KT4 & SM3 58 D8
Glyn Sch. Ewell KT17 76 F8
Glyndale Grange. Sutton SM2 59 B4
Glynde Pl. Horsh RH12 217 C2
Glynswood. Friml GU15 65 F3
Glynswood. Rowl GU10 146 A4
Glynwood Ct. For Hil SE23 23 C6
Goat Rd. Carsh CR4 40 F2
Goat Wharf. Brent TW8 6 E8
Goaters Rd. N Asct SL5 28 C7
Goatsfield Rd. Tats TN16 103 C7
Godalming Ave. Wallin SM6 60 F5
Godalming Bsns Ctr. Godal GU7 150 F4
Godalming Coll. Godal GU7 150 D2
Godalming Cty Mid Sch. Farnc GU7 150 F5
Godalming Rd. Dunsf GU8 193 A8
Godalming Rd. Hasc GU8 172 E3
Godalming Sta. Godal GU7 150 D4
Goddard Cl. Littlt TW17 33 F6
Goddard Cl. Worth RH10 202 B3
Goddard House. Putney SW19 19 D6
Goddard Rd. Beck BR3 43 E5
Goddards La. Camb GU15 65 B3
Godfrey Ave. Twick TW2 16 D8
Godfrey Way. Twick TW4 15 F8
Godley Rd. Byfl KT14 71 F6
Godley Rd. Wands SW18 20 D7
Godolphin Cl. Belm SM2 77 F8
Godolphin Ct. Crawl RH10 & RH11 201 D5
Godolphin House. 7 Streat SW2 22 A7
Godolphin Rd. Whit V KT13 53 D4
Godric Cres. New Add CR0 63 D1
Godson Rd. Croy CR0 & CR9 61 A7
Godstone Cty Fst Sch. Godst RH9 121 B3
Godstone Green Rd. Godst RH9 121 B4
Godstone Hill. Tyl Gn RH9 121 C5
Godstone Hill. Wold CR3 & RH9 121 B7
Godstone House. 1 King U T KT2 18 B2
Godstone Mount. 3 Purley CR8 80 B7
Godstone Rd. Bletch RH1 120 F2
Godstone Rd. Cater CR3 101 A3
Godstone Rd. Kenley CR3 & CR8 80 D4
Godstone Rd. Lingf RH7 164 C4
Godstone Rd. Oxted RH8 & RH9 122 C5
Godstone Rd. Purley CR8 80 D4
Godstone Rd. Sutton SM1 59 C6
Godstone Rd. Twick TW1 6 B1
Godstone Rd. Whytlf CR3 80 D4
Godstone Rd. Whytlf CR3 101 A3
Godstone Sta. S Godst RH9 142 E5
Godwin Cl. W Ewell KT19 57 C4
Godwin Cl. W Ewell KT19 57 C4
Goffs Cl. Crawl RH11 201 C5
Goffs La. Crawl RH11 201 B6
Goffs Park Rd. Crawl RH11 201 C4
Goffs Rd. Ashf TW15 14 D2
Gogmore Farm Cl. Chert KT16 32 F2
Gogmore La. Chert KT16 33 A2
Goidel Cl. Wallin SM6 60 D6
Gold Cup La. N Asct SL5 28 D8
Goldcliff Cl. Morden SM4 40 A2
Goldcrest Cl. Horley RH6 160 E4
Goldcrest Way. New Add CR0 63 D3
Goldcrest Way. Wallin CR8 60 D1
Golden Ct. 10 Rich TW9 6 D2
Golden Mews. Penge SE20 43 C8
Golden Orb Wood. Binf RG12 26 D8
Goldfinch Cl. Crawl RH11 201 D8
Goldfinch Cl. Horsh RH12 217 C7
Goldfinch Gdns. Merrow GU4 110 D2
Goldfinch Rd. Selsd CR0 & CR2 62 E1
Goldfort Wlk. Woking GU21 68 E3
Goldhill. M Bourn GU10 146 C6
Goldings The. Woking GU21 68 F3
Goldney Rd. Friml GU15 66 C4
Goldrings Rd. Oxsh KT22 74 C6
Goldsmith Way. Crowth RG11 45 B4
Goldsmiths Cl. Woking GU21 69 C1
Goldsworth Cty Fst Sch. Woking GU21 69 D2
Goldsworth Cty Mid Sch. Woking GU21 69 D2
Goldsworth Orch. 6 Woking GU21 69 A1
Goldsworth Park Ctr. Woking GU21 69 A2
Goldsworth Park Trad Est. Woking GU21 69 B3
Goldsworth Rd. Woking GU21 69 D2
Goldwell Rd. Thorn H CR7 41 F5
Gole Rd. Pirb GU24 87 D6
Golf Cl. Pyrf GU22 70 E5
Golf Club Dr. King U T KT2 18 D1
Golf Club Rd. Whit V KT13 53 C1
Golf Club Rd. Woking GU22 89 B7
Golf Dr. Friml GU15 65 F4
Golf Links Ave. Beac H GU26 188 B6
Golf Rd. Kenley CR8 80 D1
Golf Side. Belm SM2 77 E8
Golf Side. Twick TW2 16 D5
Golf Side Cl. King U T KT3 38 E7
Goliath Cl. Wallin SM6 60 E3
Gomer Gdns. Tedd TW11 17 A2
Gomer Pl. Tedd TW11 17 A2
Gomshall Ave. Wallin SM6 60 E5
Gomshall Gdns. Kenley CR8 80 E4
Gomshall La. Shere GU5 133 B4
Gomshall Rd. E Ewell KT17 & SM2 58 C1
Gomshall Sta. Gomsh GU5 133 E4
Gong Hill Dr. M Bourn GU10 146 D4
Gong Hill Frensham Rd. M Bourn GU10 146 D4
Gonston Cl. Putney SW19 19 E6
Gonville Prim Sch. Thorn H CR7 41 F4
Gonville Rd. Thorn H CR7 41 F4
Good Shepherd RC Prim Sch. Catf BR1 24 F4
Good Shepherd RC Prim Sch. New Add CR0 63 B3
Goodbehere House. 7 W Norw SE27 22 C4
Goodchild Rd. Woki RG11 25 D6
Goodden Cres. Farnb GU14 84 F3
Goodenough Rd. Merton SW19 19 F1
Goodenough Way. Coulsd CR5 99 F7
Goodhart Way. W Wick BR4 44 E3
Goodhew Rd. Croy CR0 & SE25 43 A3
Gooding Cl. New Mal KT3 38 C4
Goodings Gn. Woki RG11 25 F6
Goodland House. 1 New Mal KT3 38 E2
Goodman Cres. Streat SW2 21 D6
Goodman Pl. Stain TW18 12 F4
Goodson House. Morden SM4 40 C2
Goodways Dr. Brack RG12 27 D7
Goodwin Cl. Crawl RH11 200 F3
Goodwin Cl. Mitch CR4 40 D6
Goodwin Gdns. Croy CR0 & CR2 61 B4
Goodwin Rd. Croy CR0 61 B5
Goodwins Cl. E Grins RH19 185 D3
Goodwood Cl. Camb GU15 65 C8
Goodwood Cl. Crawl RH10 202 A3
Goodwood Cl. Morden SM4 40 A5
Goodwood House. Penge SE26 23 B2
Goodwood Par. Beck BR3 43 E5
Goodwood Pl. Farnb GU14 85 E3
Goodwood Rd. Redh RH1 118 F3
Goodwyns Pl. Dork RH4 136 B5
Goodwyns Rd. Dork RH4 & RH5 136 C4
Goose Gn. Gomsh GU5 133 C4
Goose Green Cl. Horsh RH12 217 D5
Goose La. Woking GU22 89 B5
Goose Rye Rd. Woking GU3 89 A2
Goose Rye Rd. Worpl GU3 88 E1
Goossens Cl. Sutton SM1 59 C5
Gordon Ave. Camb GU15 65 C4
Gordon Ave. Islew TW1 6 B2
Gordon Ave. Mortl SW14 7 E3
Gordon Ave. S Croy CR2 & CR8 61 C1
Gordon Cl. Addl KT16 51 E7
Gordon Cl. Stain TW18 13 B2
Gordon Cres. Camb GU15 65 C4
Gordon Cres. Croy CR0 42 F1
Gordon Dr. Addl KT16 51 E7
Gordon Dr. Shep TW17 34 D2
Gordon Rd. Alder GU11 105 A1
Gordon Rd. Ashf TW15 13 E5
Gordon Rd. Beck BR3 43 F6
Gordon Rd. Camb GU15 65 C5
Gordon Rd. Cater CR3 100 D6
Gordon Rd. Chisw W4 7 B8
Gordon Rd. Clayg KT10 55 E3
Gordon Rd. Crowth RG11 45 D3
Gordon Rd. Farnb GU14 105 D8
Gordon Rd. Horsh RH12 217 D4
Gordon Rd. Hounsl TW3 5 C3
Gordon Rd. King U T KT2 37 F8
Gordon Rd. Redh RH1 119 A4
Gordon Rd. Rich TW9 6 F5
Gordon Rd. Shep TW17 34 D3
Gordon Rd. Surb KT5 37 F2
Gordon Rd. Wallin SM5 59 F4
Gordon's Sch. W End GU24 67 E7
Gordondale Rd. Wimble SW18 & SW19 20 A6
Gordons Way. Oxted RH8 122 D7
Gore Rd. Merton SW20 39 C7
Goring Rd. Egham TW18 12 E3
Goring's Mead. Horsh RH13 217 D1
Gorling Cl. Crawl RH11 200 E5
Gorrick Sq. Woki RG11 25 B3
Gorringe Park Ave. Mitch CR4 & SW17 21 A1
Gorringe Park Mid Sch. Mitch CR4 41 A8
Gorringes Brook. Horsh RH12 217 D6
Gorse Bank. Lhtwat GU18 67 A8
Gorse Cl. Burgh H KT20 97 B7
Gorse Cl. Copth RH10 183 B2
Gorse Cl. Crawl RH11 201 B1
Gorse Cl. Wreccl GU10 146 B6
Gorse Cotts. Bramsh GU27 207 C8
Gorse Ct. Merrow GU4 110 C3
Gorse Dr. Smallf RH6 162 C3
Gorse End. Horsh RH12 217 D5
Gorse Hill La. Vir W GU25 31 D5
Gorse Hill Rd. Vir W GU25 31 D5
Gorse La. Burrh GU24 49 E3
Gorse La. Wreccl GU10 146 B6
Gorse Pl. Wink RG12 8 B1
Gorse Rd. Croy CR0 63 A7
Gorse Rd. Friml GU16 65 E2
Gorse Rise. Streat SW17 21 A3
Gorselands. Heath E GU9 125 C7
Gorselands Cl. Ash GU12 106 A5
Gorselands Cl. Head Dn GU35 187 C4
Gorselands Cl. W Byfl KT14 71 C8
Gorsewood Rd. Knaph GU21 88 E7
Gort Cl. Farnb GU11 105 E7
Gosberton Rd. Balham SW12 21 A7
Gosbury Hill. Chess KT9 56 E6
Gosden Cl. Crawl RH10 202 A5
Gosden Cl. Shalf GU5 151 F8
Gosden Hill Rd. Burph GU4 110 C5
Gosden House Sch. Shalf GU5 151 E8
Gosden Rd. W End GU24 67 F6
Gosfield Rd. Epsom KT19 76 D7
Gosnell Cl. Friml GU16 66 D3
Gosport House. 9 Rhampt SW15 19 A7
Gossops Dr. Crawl RH11 201 A5
Gossops Green Cty Fst Sch. Crawl RH11 201 A5
Gossops Green Cty Mid Sch. Crawl RH11 201 A5
Gossops Green La. Crawl RH11 201 A5
Gossops Par. Crawl RH11 200 F5
Gostling Rd. Twick TW2 16 A7
Goston Gdns. Thorn H CR7 42 A6
Gothic Ct. Harl UB3 3 D8
Gothic Ct. Sandh GU17 64 B7
Gothic Rd. Twick TW2 16 D6
Goudhurst Cl. Worth RH10 202 E6
Goudhurst House. 10 Penge SE20 23 C1
Goudhurst Keep. Worth RH10 202 E6
Goudhurst Rd. Catf BR1 24 F3
Gough House. 4 King U T KT1 37 E7
Gough's La. Brack RG12 27 D8
Gough's Meadow. Sandh GU17 64 B7
Gould Ct. Dulw SE19 22 E3
Gould Ct. Merrow GU4 110 D3
Gould Rd. E Bed TW14 14 E8
Gould Rd. Twick TW2 16 E7
Government House Rd. Farnb GU11 105 B7
Government Rd. Alder GU11 105 E4
Government Rd. Farnb GU11 105 E4
Governor's Rd. Sandh GU15 64 F6
Govett Ave. Shep TW17 34 C4
Govett Gr. Windl GU20 48 D5
Gower Pk. Sandh GU15 64 D7
Gower Rd. Horley RH6 160 E3
Gower Rd. Hounsl TW7 5 F8
Gower Rd. Whit V KT13 53 D4
Gower The. Egham TW20 32 C6
Gowland Pl. Beck BR3 43 F7
Graburn Way. E Mole KT8 36 D6
Grace Bennett Cl. W Heath GU14 85 A7
Grace Bsns Ctr. Mitch CR4 40 F3
Grace House. Penge SE26 23 B3
Grace Path. For Hil SE26 23 C4
Grace Rd. Crawl RH11 201 A1
Grace Rd. Thorn H CR0 42 C3
Grace Reynolds Wlk. 4 Camb GU15 65 C6
Gracedale Rd. Streat SW16 & SW17 21 B3
Gracefield Gdns. Streat SW16 21 E5
Gracious Pond Rd. Burrh GU24 50 B4
Gradient The. For Hil SE26 23 A4
Graemesdyke Ave. Mortl SW14 7 B3
Graffham Cl. Crawl RH11 201 B8
Grafton Cl. Twick TW4 15 F7
Grafton Cl. W Byfl KT14 70 F6
Grafton Cl. Worc Pk KT4 57 E7
Grafton Ct. E Bed TW14 14 D7
Grafton Park Rd. Worc Pk KT4 57 E8
Grafton Rd. King U T KT3 38 E6
Grafton Rd. Thorn H CR0 42 A1
Grafton Rd. Worc Pk KT19 & KT4 57 E7
Grafton Way. E Mole KT8 35 F5
Graham Ave. Mitch CR4 41 A8
Graham Cl. Croy CR0 63 A8
Graham Gdns. Surb KT6 37 E1
Graham House. 5 Balham SW12 21 B8
Graham House. L Book KT23 94 A3
Graham House. Redh RH1 118 E3
Graham Rd. Hampt TW12 16 A4
Graham Rd. Merton SW19 19 F1
Graham Rd. Mitch CR4 41 A8
Graham Rd. Purley CR8 80 A6
Graham Rd. Windl GU20 48 C4
Grainford Ct. Woki RG11 25 C5
Grainger Rd. Islew TW7 5 F5
Grampian Cl. Harl UB3 3 D7
Grampian Rd. Sandh GU17 45 A2
Granada St. Up Toot SW17 20 F3
Granard Rd. Balham SW11 & SW12 20 F8
Granary Cl. Horley RH6 161 A5
Granary Way. Horsh RH12 217 A1
Grand Ave. Camb GU15 65 C6
Grand Ave. Tolw KT5 38 B3
Grand Avenue Prim Sch. Tolw KT5 38 C3
Grand Avenue Prim Sch (Upper Sch). Tolw KT5 38 C3
Grand Dr. W Barn KT3 & SM4 & SW20 39 C5
Grand Par. Crawl RH11 201 D6
Grand Par. Mortl SW14 7 C3
Grand Par. Tolw KT6 38 A1
Grand Stand Rd. Epsom KT17 & KT18 77 A2
Grand View Ave. Bigg H TN16 83 C3
Granden Rd. Thorn H SW16 41 E7
Grandfield Ct. Chisw W4 7 D8
Grandis Cotts. Ripley GU23 91 B5
Grandison Rd. N Cheam KT4 58 C7
Grange Ave. Crowth RG11 45 B6
Grange Ave. S Norw SE25 42 E7
Grange Ave. Twick TW2 16 E6
Grange Cl. Ashtd KT22 95 D7
Grange Cl. Bletch RH1 120 D2
Grange Cl. Crawl RH10 202 A8
Grange Cl. E Mole KT8 36 B5
Grange Cl. Godal GU7 151 A5
Grange Cl. Heston TW5 4 F8
Grange Cl. Merst RH1 & RH2 119 B7
Grange Cl. Stough GU2 109 B5
Grange Cres. Crawl D RH10 204 B7
Grange Ct. Egham TW20 11 F3
Grange Ct. Hackb SM6 60 B7
Grange Ct. Merst RH2 119 B7
Grange Ct. S Godst RH9 142 E5
Grange Ct. Shep Gn TW17 34 A5
Grange Ct. Stain TW18 13 A3
Grange Ct. Sutton SM2 59 B3
Grange Ct. Walt O T KT12 54 A8
Grange Cty Inf Sch The. Woodhm KT15 52 A1
Grange Dr. Horse GU21 69 E4
Grange Dr. Merst RH1 119 B7
Grange End. Smallf RH6 162 A3
Grange Farm Rd. Ash GU12 106 A3
Grange Gdns. Banstd SM7 78 B6
Grange Gdns. S Norw SE25 42 E7
Grange Hill. S Norw SE25 42 E7
Grange La. Dulw SE21 22 F6
Grange Lodge. Wimble SW19 19 D2
Grange Mansions. Ewell KT17 57 F3
Grange Meadow. Banstd SM7 78 B6
Grange Mills. Streat SW12 21 C7
Grange Park Pl. Wimble SW20 19 B1
Grange Park Rd. S Norw CR7 42 D6
Grange Pk. Cran GU6 174 F3
Grange Pk. Horse GU21 69 F5
Grange Pl. Laleh TW18 33 C7
Grange Rd. Ash GU12 106 B1
Grange Rd. Ashtd KT21 & KT22 95 D7
Grange Rd. Belm SM2 59 A3
Grange Rd. Brack RG12 27 C8
Grange Rd. Camb GU15 65 E5
Grange Rd. Cater CR3 101 A2
Grange Rd. Chess KT9 56 E6
Grange Rd. Crawl D RH10 204 A7
Grange Rd. E Mole KT8 36 B5
Grange Rd. Egham TW20 11 F3
Grange Rd. Farnb GU14 85 B7
Grange Rd. Hersh KT12 54 E6
Grange Rd. Horse GU21 69 E5
Grange Rd. King U T KT1 37 E6
Grange Rd. Rushm GU10 168 C7
Grange Rd. S Croy CR2 61 C2
Grange Rd. S Norw SE19 & SE25 42 D7
Grange Rd. Stough GU2 & GU3 109 B5
Grange Rd. Sutton SM2 59 A3
Grange Rd. Tongh GU10 126 E6
Grange Rd. Woodhm KT15 52 B1
Grange Sch The. Alder GU11 126 B8
Grange The. Chobh GU24 49 E1
Grange The. Croy CR0 62 F8
Grange The. Frensh GU10 167 D7
Grange The. Horley RH6 161 A6
Grange The. New Mal KT3 39 A4
Grange The. Walt O T KT12 54 B8
Grange The. Wimble SW19 19 D2
Grange The. Worc Pk KT19 57 D6
Grange Vale. Sutton SM2 59 B3
Grangecliffe Gdns. S Norw SE25 42 E7
Grangefields Rd. Jacobs GU4 109 D6
Grangemill Rd. Catf SE6 24 A6
Grangemill Way. Catf SE6 24 A6
Grangemount. Ashtd KT22 95 D7
Grangeway. Smallf RH6 162 A3
Grangewood La. Beck BR3 23 F2
Gransden Cl. Ewh GU6 175 E5
Granston Way. Crawl D RH10 204 C8
Grant Cl. Shep TW17 34 B3
Grant Pl. 2 Croy CR0 42 F1
Grant Rd. Crowth RG11 45 C4
Grant Rd. Croy CR0 42 F1

Grant Way. Brent TW7 & TW8 6 A8
Grant Wlk. Sunnin SL5 29 E1
Grantchester. 3
King U T KT1 38 A7
Grantham Cl. Sandh GU15 45 E1
Grantham House.
Charlt TW16 14 E1
Grantham Rd. Chisw W4 7 E7
Grantley Ave. Woner GU5 152 B6
Grantley Cl. Shalf GU4 130 E2
Grantley House.
Putney SW19 19 D7
Grantley Rd.
Cranf TW4 & TW5 4 C5
Grantley Rd. Stough GU2 109 A2
Granton Rd. Streat SW16 41 C8
Grants Cotts. Esher KT10 55 D8
Grants La.
Limps RH7 & RH8 144 C6
Grantwood Cl. Earls RH1 140 B4
Granville Ave. Felt TW13 15 A6
Granville Ave.
Hounsl TW3 & TW4 5 A2
Granville Cl. Byfl KT14 71 F6
Granville Cl. S Croy CR0 61 E8
Granville Cl. Whit V KT13 53 C4
Granville Gdns.
S Norw SW16 21 F1
Granville Rd. Limps RH8 123 A7
Granville Rd. Merton SW19 20 A1
Granville Rd. Wands SW18 19 F8
Granville Rd. Westfd GU22 89 F7
Granville Rd. Whit V KT13 53 C4
Granwood Ct. 5 Hounsl TW7 5 E6
Grasmere Ave.
King U T SW15 18 E4
Grasmere Ave.
Merton SW19 40 A6
Grasmere Ave. Twick TW3 5 B1
Grasmere Cl. E Bed TW14 14 F7
Grasmere Cl. Merrow GU1 110 B2
Grasmere Cl. Thor L TW20 12 B1
Grasmere Ct. For Hil SE26 23 A3
Grasmere Gdns.
Horsh RH12 218 B6
Grasmere Rd. Broml BR1 24 F1
Grasmere Rd. Croy SE25 43 B4
Grasmere Rd. Farnb GU14 84 E4
Grasmere Rd. Hale GU9 125 A6
Grasmere Rd. Lhtwat GU18 48 B1
Grasmere Rd. Purley CR8 80 B8
Grasmere Rd. Streat SW16 21 F3
Grasmere Way. Byfl KT14 71 F7
Grassfield Cl. Coulsd CR5 99 C8
Grasslands. Smallf RH6 162 A3
Grassmere. Horley RH6 161 C4
Grassmount. For Hil SE23 23 B6
Grassmount. Wallin CR8 60 C1
Grassway. Wallin SM6 60 C6
Grately House. 10
Rhampt SW15 19 B7
Grattons Dr. Crawl RH10 182 C1
Grattons The. Slinfd RH13 215 E3
Gravel Hill. Leahd KT22 95 B6
Gravel Hill. S Croy CR0 & 2 62 E4
Gravel Hill Rd. Binst GU10 145 A3
Gravel Pits. Gomsh GU5 133 C4
Gravel Pits La. Gomsh GU5 133 C4
Gravel Rd. Farnb GU14 105 D8
Gravel Rd. Hale GU9 125 B7
Gravel Rd. Twick TW2 16 E7
Graveley. 7 King U T KT1 38 A7
Gravelly Hill.
Cater RH1 & RH9 120 F7
Gravenel Gdns.
Up Toot SW17 20 E3
Graveney Gr. Penge SE20 23 C1
Graveney Rd. Up Toot SW17 20 E4
Graveney Rd. Worth RH10 202 C5
Graveney Sch. Streat SW17 21 B3
Gravetts La. Worpl GU3 108 E5
Gravetye Cl. Crawl RH10 202 A4
Gray Ct. 8 King U T KT2 17 D4
Gray's La. Ashtd KT21 95 F8
Grayham Cres. New Mal KT3 38 D5
Grayham Rd. New Mal KT3 38 D5
Graylands. Horse GU21 69 E3
Graylands Cl. Horse GU21 69 E3
Graylands Ct. Guild GU1 130 F8
Grays Cl. Haslem GU27 208 E8
Grays La. Ashf TW15 14 B4
Grays Rd. Farnc GU7 150 F7
Grays Wood. Horley RH6 161 C3
Grayscroft Rd. Streat SW16 21 D1
Grayshot Dr. Blckw GU17 64 C5
Grayshott Prim Sch.
Graysh GU26 188 D3
Grayshott Rd.
Head Dn GU26 & GU35 187 C5
Grayswood CE (VA) Fst Sch.
Grays GU27 189 F2
Grayswood Dr. Mytch GU16 86 A2
Grayswood Gdns.
W Barn SW20 39 B7
Grayswood Pl.
Haslem GU27 208 E8
Grayswood Point. 14
Rhampt SW15 19 A7
Grayswood Rd. Grays GU27 189 F1
Grayswood Rd.
Haslem GU27 189 F1
Grazely Ct. W Norw SE19 22 E3
Great Austins.
M Bourn GU9 146 D8
Great Bookham Cty Inf Sch.
G Book KT23 94 A1
Great Bookham Cty Mid Sch.
G Book KT23 94 A1
Great Brownings. Dulw SE21 22 F4
Great Chertsey Rd.
Chisw SW14 & W4 7 D6
Great Chertsey Rd.
Felt TW13 & TW2 16 A5
Great Elshams. Banstd SM7 78 A3
Great George St.
Godal GU7 150 E4
Great Goodwin Dr.
Merrow GU1 110 B3
Great Hollands Cty Inf Sch.
Easth RG12 26 F4
Great Hollands Cty Jun Sch.
Easth RG12 26 E4
Great Hollands Rd.
Easth RG12 26 F3
Great Hollands Sq.
Easth RG12 26 F3
Great House Ct. 4
E Grins RH19 205 F8
Great Oaks Pk. Burph GU4 110 C5
Great Quarry. Guild GU1 130 D6
Great South-West Rd.
E Bed TW4 & 5 & 6 & 14 3 D2
Great South-West Rd.
Felt TW6 & TW14 3 D2
Great South-West Rd.
Hatton TW6 & TW14 3 D2
Great South-West Rd.
Hounsl TW5 4 B4
Great Tattenhams.
Burgh H KT18 77 C1
Great West Rd. Brent TW8 6 B8
Great West Rd. Cranf TW5 4 F6
Great West Rd. Heston TW5 4 F6
Great West Rd.
Hounsl TW5 & TW7 5 C6
Great West Road Cedars Rd.
Chisw W4 7 C8
Great West Road Chiswick.
Chisw W4 7 F8
Great West Road Ellesmere Rd.
Chisw W4 7 D8
Great West Road Hogarth La.
Chisw W4 7 E8
Great West Trad Est.
Brent TW8 6 B8
Great Woodcote Dr.
Wallin CR8 60 D1
Great Woodcote Pk.
Wallin CR8 & SM6 60 E1
Greatfield Cl. Farnb GU14 85 B8
Greatfield Rd. Farnb GU14 85 B8
Greatford Dr. Merrow GU1 110 D1
Greatham Wlk. 8
Rhampt SW15 19 A7
Greathurst End. L Book KT23 93 F3
Greatlake Ct. Horley RH6 161 B4
Greatstone House. 13
Penge SE20 23 C1
Greatwood Cl. Ottsh KT16 51 C2
Greaves Pl. Up Toot SW17 20 E4
Grebe Cres. Horsh RH13 218 A1
Grebe Terr. 4 King U T KT1 37 E6
Grecian Cres.
S Norw SE19 & SW16 22 B2
Green Acre. Alder GU11 104 F1
Green Acres. S Croy CR0 61 F7
Green Bsns Ctr The.
Egham TW20 12 C4
Green Cl. Beck BR2 44 E6
Green Cl. Carsh SM5 59 F8
Green Cl. Felt TW13 15 E3
Green Court Ave. Croy CR0 62 B8
Green Court Gdns. Croy CR0 62 B8
Green Croft. Woki RG11 25 E8
Green Croft Sch.
Farnb GU14 85 D6
Green Cross La.Churt GU10 168 A1
Green Ct. Ashf TW16 14 F2
Green Curve. Nork SM7 77 F4
Green Dene. E Hors KT24 112 E3
Green Dene. W Hors KT24 112 E3
Green Dr. Send M GU23 90 F4
Green Dr. Woki RG11 25 E4
Green Dragon Jun & Inf Sch.
Brent TW8 6 E8
Green End. Chess KT9 56 E6
Green Farm Rd. Bagsh GU19 47 F3
Green Finch Cl.
Crowth RG11 45 A6
Green Hedges. 8 Twick TW1 6 C1
Green Hedges Ave.
E Grins RH19 185 D2
Green Hedges Cl.
E Grins RH19 185 D2
Green Hill. Downe BR6 83 F7
Green Hill Cl. Friml GU15 66 C6
Green Hill Rd. Friml GU15 66 C6
Green House The. 5
Putney SW19 19 E7
Green La. Addl KT15 & KT16 51 E7
Green La. Alf Cr GU6 193 F4
Green La. Ascot SL5 29 E8
Green La. Ashf TW16 14 F2
Green La. Ashtd KT21 75 D1
Green La. Ashtd KT22 95 D6
Green La. Bagsh GU19 47 F2
Green La. Blckw GU17 64 B4
Green La. Burst RH6 182 F6
Green La. Byfl KT14 71 F7
Green La. Cater CR3 100 C5
Green La. Cheam SM4 40 B3
Green La. Chert KT15 & KT16 51 E7
Green La. Chess KT9 56 E3
Green La. Chobh GU24 49 F1
Green La. Churt GU10 168 A1
Green La. Cobham KT11 73 E7
Green La. Copth RH10 183 F4
Green La. Crawl RH10 201 E8
Green La. Cudw RH5 179 D8
Green La. Docken GU10 166 E6
Green La. E Mole KT8 36 B4
Green La. Earls RH1 140 A4
Green La. Egham TW20 12 B3
Green La. Egham TW18 32 E8
Green La. Farnc GU7 & GU3 150 E8
Green La. Farnh GU9 125 F5
Green La. Faygt RH12 198 F4
Green La. Felt TW13 15 E3
Green La. Fern GU27 208 B4
Green La. Hawley GU17 64 E4
Green La. Heath E GU9 125 F5
Green La. Hersh KT12 54 B5
Green La. Hounsl TW4 4 C3
Green La. L Kings KT20 97 F1
Green La. Leahd KT22 95 D6
Green La. Leigh RH2 158 E8
Green La. Lingf RH7 164 C4
Green La. M Bourn GU9 146 A7
Green La. Merrow GU1 110 B1
Green La. Milf GU8 170 E8
Green La. Morden SM4 40 B3
Green La. N Cheam KT4 39 A1
Green La. New Mal KT3 38 C4
Green La. Penge SE20 23 D1
Green La. Purley CR8 60 D1
Green La. Redh RH1 118 E3
Green La. Reig RH2 117 F1
Green La.
S Norw CR7 & SW16 42 B8
Green La. S Nutf RH1 140 F1
Green La. Sandh GU17 64 C7
Green La.
Sham Gn GU4 & GU5 153 A7
Green La. Shep TW17 34 C4
Green La. Streat SW16 21 F1
Green La. Tilf GU10 147 E6
Green La. W Clan GU4 111 B8
Green La.
W Hors GU23 & KT24 92 B3
Green La. Wood S V GU3 108 A3
Green La. Worth RH10 202 D6
Green La E. Flexf GU3 128 B8
Green La W. Normdy GU12 127 E8
Green Lane Ave. Hersh KT12 54 C5
Green Lane Cl. Addl KT16 51 E8
Green Lane Cl. Byfl KT14 71 F7
Green Lane Cl. Camb GU15 65 C7
Green Lane Cotts.
Churt GU10 167 F1
Green Lane Cty Inf Sch.
Farnc GU7 129 E1
Green Lane Gdns.
S Norw CR7 42 C7
Green Lane Prim Sch.
N Cheam KT4 39 B2
Green Lanes. W Ewell KT19 57 E2
Green Lanes. W Ewell KT19 57 E2
Green Leaf Ave. Wallin SM6 60 D6
Green Leas. Ashf TW16 14 F2
Green Leas. King U T KT1 37 E6
Green Leas Cl. Ashf TW16 14 F2
Green Man La. Hatton TW14 4 A3
Green Mead. Esher KT10 54 F4
Green Pk. Stain TW18 12 E5
Green Rd.
Egham KT16 & TW20 32 B5
Green Sch for Girls The.
Islew TW7 6 A6
Green St. Sunby TW16 35 A7
Green The. Broad H RH12 216 D4
Green The. Burgh H KT20 97 E8
Green The. Carsh SM6 60 A8
Green The. Clayg KT10 55 F4
Green The. Copth RH10 183 B3
Green The. Crawl RH11 201 C7
Green The. Easth RG12 27 B5
Green The. Ewell KT17 77 A7
Green The. Ewh GU6 175 E4
Green The. Farnh GU9 126 A6
Green The. Felt TW13 15 B6
Green The. Fetch KT22 94 D3
Green The. Friml GU16 85 F6
Green The. Hale GU9 125 C6
Green The. Heston TW5 5 A8
Green The. King U T KT3 38 C7
Green The. Merton SM4 39 E5
Green The. New Add CR0 62 F2
Green The. 7 Rich TW9 6 D2
Green The. Stain TW18 13 D3
Green The. Sutton SM1 59 B7
Green The. The San GU10 126 E1
Green The. Twick TW2 16 E6
Green The. Tyl Gn RH9 121 C4
Green The. Warlgm CR6 81 D1
Green The. Whit V KT12 53 E1
Green The. Wimble SW19 19 D3
Green The. Wold CR3 102 A4
Green View. Chess KT9 56 F3
Green View. Godst RH9 121 B4
Green Way. Alder GU12 105 E3
Green Way. Redh RH1 118 E3
Green Way. Sunby TW16 35 A5
Green Wlk. Crawl RH10 201 E8
Green Wlk. Hampt TW12 15 F2
Green Wood. N Asct SL5 28 C8
Green Wrythe Cres.
Carsh SM5 40 E1
Green Wrythe La.
Carsh SM4 & SM5 40 E2
Green Wrythe Prim Sch.
Carsh SM5 40 D3
Green's School La.
Farnb GU14 85 A4
Greenacre. Knaph GU21 68 E3
Greenacre. Whytlf CR3 101 B7
Greenacre Ct. Eng Gn TW20 11 C2
Greenacre Sch for Girls.
Banstd SM7 78 B6
Greenacres. Crawl RH10 202 A5
Greenacres. Farnh GU10 126 C2
Greenacres. Fetch KT23 94 A3
Greenacres. Horsh RH12 217 C4
Greenacres. Oxted RH8 122 E8
Greenaway Terr. Stan TW19 13 E7
Greenbank Way. Friml GU16 65 D2
Greenbush La. Cran GU6 174 F1
Greencroft. 2 Farnb GU14 85 B4
Greencroft. Merrow GU1 110 B1
Greencroft Rd. Heston TW5 4 F6
Greene Fielde End.
Stain TW18 13 D1
Greenfield Ave. Tolw KT5 38 B3
Greenfield House. 28
Putney SW19 19 D7
Greenfield Link. Coulsd CR5 79 E4
Greenfield Rd.
M Bourn GU9 & GU10 146 A7
Greenfield Rd. Slinfd RH13 215 D3
Greenfield Rd. Wreccl GU9 145 F7
Greenfield Sch.
Woking GU22 89 E8
Greenfield Way.
Crowth RG11 45 A7
Greenfields Cl. Horley RH6 160 E5
Greenfields Cl.
Horsh RH12 218 A6
Greenfields Rd.
Horley RH6 160 F5
Greenfields Rd.
Horsh RH12 218 A5
Greenfields Sch.
For Row RH18 206 C1
Greenfields Way.
Horsh RH12 218 A6
Greenfinch Way.
Horsh RH12 217 D7
Greenford Rd. Sutton SM1 59 B6
Greenham House.
Hounsl TW7 5 D4
Greenham Wlk.
Woking GU21 69 C1
Greenham Wood.
Easth RG12 27 C3
Greenhanger. Churt GU10 188 A8
Greenhayes Ave.
Banstd SM7 78 A4
Greenhayes Cl. Reig RH2 118 C1
Greenhayes Gdns.
Banstd SM7 78 A4
Greenhayes Sch.
W Wick BR4 63 C8
Greenheys Pl. Woking GU22 69 F1
Greenhill. Sutton SM1 59 C8
Greenhill Ave. Cater CR3 101 B6
Greenhill Cl. Godal GU7 150 D3
Greenhill Cl. Wreccl GU9 146 A7
Greenhill Gdns.
Merrow GU4 110 C3
Greenhill La. Warlgm CR6 81 F2
Greenhill Rd. M Bourn GU9 146 D8
Greenhill Way.
M Bourn GU9 146 A7
Greenhill Way.
Wreccl GU9 146 A7
Greenhills. M Bourn GU9 146 E8
Greenholme. Friml GU15 66 D5
Greenhow. Easth RG12 27 A6
Greenhurst La. Oxted RH8 123 A3
Greenhurst Rd.
W Norw SE27 22 A3
Greenlake Terr. Stain TW18 13 A1
Greenlands Rd. Camb GU15 65 B1
Greenlands Rd. Stain TW18 13 A4
Greenlands Rd. Weyb KT13 53 C7
Greenlaw Gdns.
New Mal KT3 38 F2
Greenlea Pk. Mitch SW19 40 E8
Greenleaf Cl. 8
Streat SW2 22 A8
Greenleas. Friml GU16 65 E2
Greenleaves Ct. Ashf TW15 14 B2
Greenmeads. Westfd GU22 89 E5
Greeno Cres. Shep Gn TW17 34 A4
Greenoak Rise. Bigg H TN16 83 C1
Greenoak Way.
Wimble SW19 19 D4
Greenock Rd. Streat SW16 41 D8
Greensand Rd. Earls RH1 119 A2
Greenside Cl. Catf SE6 24 D6
Greenside Cl. Merrow GU4 110 C3
Greenside Cotts.
Ripley GU23 91 C6
Greenside Rd. Thorn H CR0 42 A2
Greenside Wlk. Bigg H TN16 83 B1
Greensleeves Manor.
Sutton SM2 59 B4
Greenstede Ave.
E Grins RH19 185 F2
Greenvale Prim Sch.
Selsd CR2 81 D8
Greenvale Rd. Knaph GU21 68 D1
Greenvale Spec Sch.
For Hil SE23 23 E5
Greenview Ave. Beck CR0 43 E3
Greenview Ct. Ashf TW15 13 F4
Greenway. Fetch KT23 94 B4
Greenway. Horsh RH12 217 B3
Greenway. Tats TN16 103 C7
Greenway. W Barn SW20 39 C5
Greenway. Wallin SM6 60 C6
Greenway Cl. W Byfl KT14 71 A6
Greenway Cty Prim Sch.
Horsh RH12 217 B3
Greenway Dr. Stain TW18 33 D8
Greenway Gdns. Croy CR0 62 F7
Greenway The. Epsom KT18 76 A5
Greenway The. Hounsl TW4 4 F3
Greenway The. Oxted RH8 123 B2
Greenways. Beck BR3 44 A7
Greenways. Egham TW20 11 E3
Greenways. For Hil SE26 23 C4
Greenways. Hinch W KT10 55 E6
Greenways. Sandh GU17 45 B1
Greenways. Walt o t H KT20 97 B2
Greenways Dr. Sunnin SL5 29 E1
Greenways The. 1
Twick TW1 6 A1
Greenways Wlk.
Crawl RH11 201 C1
Greenwich Cl. Crawl RH11 201 C2
Greenwood. 4 Brack RG12 27 F5
Greenwood. 8
Putney SW19 19 D8
Greenwood Cl. Hinch W KT7 37 A1
Greenwood Cl. Merton SM4 39 E5
Greenwood Cl.
Woodhm KT15 70 F8
Greenwood Ct. 2
Crawl RH11 201 B1
Greenwood Dr. Earls RH1 140 A4
Greenwood Gdns.Cater CR3 101 A2
Greenwood La. Hampt TW12 16 B3

Greenwood Pk. King U T KT2 18 E1
Greenwood Prim Sch. Mitch CR4 41 D6
Greenwood Rd. Crowth RG11 45 B6
Greenwood Rd. Hinch W KT7 56 A8
Greenwood Rd. Islew TW7 5 F4
Greenwood Rd. Knaph GU21 88 E7
Greenwood Rd. Mitch CR4 41 D6
Greenwood Rd. Pirb GU24 87 C7
Greenwood Rd. Thorn H CR0 & CR9 42 C2
Greenwood The. Guild GU1 110 A1
Gregan Ct. Alder GU11 104 F1
Gregory Cl. Worth RH10 202 C2
Gregory Ct. Purley CR8 80 B6
Gregsons. Warn RH12 216 E8
Grena Gdns. Rich TW9 6 F3
Grena Rd. Rich TW10 & TW9 6 F3
Grenaby Ave. Croy CR0 42 D2
Grenaby Rd. Croy CR0 42 D2
Grenadier Rd. Ash GU12 106 B4
Grenadiers Way. Farnb GU14 84 C3
Grendon Cl. Horley RH6 160 F5
Grenehurst Pk. Capel RH5 178 B4
Grenfell Rd. Mitch CR4 & SW17 20 F2
Grennell Cl. Sutton SM1 59 D8
Grennell Rd. Sutton SM1 59 C8
Grenside Rd. Weyb KT13 53 B7
Grenville Cl. Cobham KT11 73 E6
Grenville Cl. Tolw KT5 38 C1
Grenville Ct. Dulw SE19 22 F3
Grenville Gdns. Friml GU16 85 E6
Grenville Mews. Hampt TW12 16 B3
Grenville Rd. New Add CR0 63 C2
Grenville Rd. Shackl GU8 149 D7
Gresham Ave. Warlgm CR6 81 E1
Gresham Cl. Limps RH8 122 F7
Gresham Ct. Farnb GU14 105 C8
Gresham Ct. Hounsl TW3 5 C6
Gresham Ct. Stain TW18 13 A3
Gresham House. [2] Tedd TW11 16 F3
Gresham House. [3] Thame D KT7 37 A2
Gresham Ind Est. Alder GU12 105 E2
Gresham Prim Sch. Sander CR2 81 A8
Gresham Rd. Croy SE25 43 A5
Gresham Rd. Hampt TW12 16 A2
Gresham Rd. Hounsl TW3 & TW5 5 C6
Gresham Rd. Limps RH8 122 F6
Gresham Rd. Penge BR3 43 E7
Gresham Rd. Stain TW18 13 A3
Gresham Way. Friml GU16 85 E6
Gresham Way. Wimble SW19 20 A5
Gresham Way Est. Wimble SW19 20 B5
Gresham Wlk. Crawl RH10 201 E3
Gressenhall Rd. Wands SW18 19 F8
Greta Bank. W Hors KT24 92 C1
Greville Ave. Selsd CR2 62 D1
Greville Cl. Ashtd KT21 95 E8
Greville Cl. Stough GU2 108 E1
Greville Cl. Twick TW1 17 B8
Greville Ct. Ashtd KT21 75 E1
Greville Ct. Fetch KT23 94 C2
Greville Cty Prim Sch The. Ashtd KT21 75 F2
Greville Park Ave. Ashtd KT21 75 E1
Greville Park Rd. Ashtd KT21 75 E1
Greville Rd. Rich TW10 6 F1
Grey Alders. Nork KT17 77 C5
Grey Court Sch. Rich TW10 17 C5
Greycot Rd. Beck BR3 24 A3
Greyfields Cl. Purley CR8 80 B6
Greyfriars. [16] For Hil SE26 23 A5
Greyfriars Dr. Ascot SL5 29 B3
Greyfriars Dr. Bisley GU24 68 A4
Greyfriars Rd. Send M GU23 91 A3
Greyhound Cl. Ash GU12 105 F1
Greyhound La. Streat SW16 21 D2
Greyhound Rd. Sutton SM1 59 C5
Greyhound Slip. Crawl RH10 202 D7
Greyhound Terr. Mitch SW16 41 C8
Greylees. Farnc GU7 150 E5
Greys Ct. Alder GU11 104 E2
Greystead Pk. Wreccl GU10 145 E5
Greystead Rd. For Hil SE23 23 C8
Greystoke Ct. Crowth RG11 45 A4
Greystone Cl. Selsd CR2 81 C8
Greystone Sch. Merst RH1 119 E6
Greystones Cl. Woodh RH1 & RH2 139 D7
Greystones Dr. Reig RH2 118 C3
Greyswood St. Streat SW16 21 B2
Greythorne Rd. Woking GU21 69 A1
Greywaters. Bramly GU5 152 A6
Grice Ave. Bigg H TN16 83 C6
Grier Cl. Crawl RH11 200 E5
Grierson Hse. Streat SW16 21 C4
Grierson Rd. For Hil SE23 23 D8
Grieve Cl. Tongh GU10 126 E7
Griffin Ct. Ashtd KT21 95 E8
Griffin Ct. [8] Brent TW8 6 E8
Griffin Ct. G Book KT23 94 B1
Griffin Ctr. King U T KT1 37 D7
Griffin Ctr The. Felt TW14 4 B1
Griffin Pk (Brentford FC). Brent TW8 6 D8
Griffin Way. G Book KT23 94 A1
Griffin Way. Sunby TW16 35 A7
Griffiths Cl. N Cheam KT4 58 B8
Griffiths Rd. Merton SW19 20 B1
Griffon Cl. Farnb GU14 84 D3
Griggs Meadow. Dunsf GU8 192 F7
Grimwade Ave. S Croy CR0 62 A7
Grimwood Rd. Twick TW1 16 F8
Grindall Cl. Croy CR0 61 B6
Grindley Gdns. Croy CR0 42 F3
Grindstone Cres. Knaph GU21 68 B1
Grindstone Handle Cnr. Knaph GU21 68 C1
Grinstead La. E Grins RH19 205 B1
Grisedale Cl. Crawl RH11 201 C4
Grisedale Cl. Sander CR8 80 E5
Grisedale Gdns. Sander CR8 80 E5
Grizedale Terr. For Hil SE23 23 B6
Grobars Ave. Horse GU21 69 C4
Groom Cres. Wands SW18 20 D8
Groombridge Cl. Hersh KT12 54 B5
Groombridge House. Penge SE20 23 D1
Groombridge Way. Horsh RH12 216 F1
Groomfield Cl. Up Toot SW17 21 A4
Grooms The. Crawl RH10 202 D8
Grosslea. Morden SM4 40 D4
Grosvenor Ave. Mortl SW14 7 E4
Grosvenor Ave. Rich TW10 6 E2
Grosvenor Ave. Wallin SM5 & SM6 60 A4
Grosvenor Ct. Burph GU4 110 B4
Grosvenor Ct. Hawley GU17 64 D3
Grosvenor Ct. Morden SM4 40 A5
Grosvenor Ct. Penge SE19 22 F2
Grosvenor Ct. [2] Rich TW10 6 F1
Grosvenor Ct. [1] Sutton SM2 59 C4
Grosvenor Ct. Tedd TW11 17 A2
Grosvenor Ct. Wimble SW19 19 E2
Grosvenor Gdns. King U T KT2 17 D2
Grosvenor Gdns. Mortl SW14 7 E4
Grosvenor Gdns. Wallin SM6 60 C3
Grosvenor Hill. Wimble SW19 19 E2
Grosvenor Pl. [1] Oat Pk KT13 53 D7
Grosvenor Rd. Alder GU11 105 A1
Grosvenor Rd. Brent TW8 6 D8
Grosvenor Rd. Croy SE25 43 A5
Grosvenor Rd. E Grins RH19 185 D1
Grosvenor Rd. Godal GU7 150 E3
Grosvenor Rd. Hounsl TW3 & TW4 4 F4
Grosvenor Rd. Lang V KT18 & KT21 96 E8
Grosvenor Rd. Rich TW10 6 E2
Grosvenor Rd. Stain TW18 13 A1
Grosvenor Rd. Twick TW1 17 A7
Grosvenor Rd. W End GU24 68 D6
Grosvenor Rd. W Wick BR4 63 B8
Grosvenor Rd. Wallin SM6 60 B5
Groton Rd. Wands SW18 20 B6
Grotto Rd. Twick TW1 16 F6
Grotto Rd. Weyb KT13 53 B7
Grove Ave. Epsom KT17 76 E6
Grove Ave. Sutton SM1 & SM2 59 A4
Grove Ave. Twick TW1 16 F7
Grove Cl. Cran GU6 174 F1
Grove Cl. For Hil SE23 23 E7
Grove Cl. [8] King U T KT1 37 F5
Grove Cl. Old W SL4 11 B8
Grove Cnr. G Book KT23 94 B1
Grove Cres. Felt TW13 15 E4
Grove Cres. King U T KT1 37 E6
Grove Cres. Walt O T KT12 35 B2
Grove Cross Rd. Friml GU16 65 D1
Grove Ct. E Mole KT8 36 D4
Grove Ct. Egham TW20 12 A3
Grove Ct. For Hil SE26 23 E4
Grove Ct. Hounsl TW3 5 B4
Grove Ct. [8] King U T KT1 37 E6
Grove Ct. King U T KT3 38 E6
Grove Ct. Penge SE20 23 B1
Grove Cty Prim Sch The. Friml GU16 65 E2
Grove End. Windl GU19 47 F5
Grove End La. Thame D KT10 36 D1
Grove End Rd.M Bourn GU9 146 B8
Grove Farm Ct. Mitch CR4 40 F4
Grove Gdns. Tedd TW11 17 A4
Grove Heath La. Ripley GU23 91 D4
Grove Heath N. Ripley GU23 91 B5
Grove Heath Rd. Ripley GU23 91 B4
Grove House. [7] Epsom KT17 76 E6
Grove House. Old W SL4 11 C8
Grove House. [5] Redh RH1 118 F1
Grove House. Walt O T KT12 35 B2
Grove House Froebel Ed Inst. Rhampt SW15 7 F1
Grove House Prim Sch. W Norw SE27 22 B6
Grove Jun & Inf Sch. Chisw W4 7 C8
Grove La. King U T KT1 37 E5
Grove La. Wallin CR5 79 B5
Grove La. Wink RG12 8 B4
Grove Park Bridge. Chisw W4 7 C7
Grove Park Gdns. Chisw W4 7 C7
Grove Park Rd. Chisw W4 7 B7
Grove Park Terr. Chisw W4 7 B8
Grove Pl. Weyb KT13 53 C5
Grove Rd. Ash GU12 106 A3
Grove Rd. Ashtd KT21 95 F8
Grove Rd. Barnes SW13 7 F5
Grove Rd. Beac H GU26 188 C6
Grove Rd. Camb GU15 65 F5
Grove Rd. Cheam SM2 59 A4
Grove Rd. Chert KT16 32 F3
Grove Rd. Cran GU6 174 F1
Grove Rd. E Mole KT8 36 D5
Grove Rd. Epsom KT17 & KT18 76 E6
Grove Rd. Godal GU7 150 C3
Grove Rd. Horley RH6 160 F4
Grove Rd. Hounsl TW3 5 A3
Grove Rd. Hounsl TW7 5 E6
Grove Rd. King U T KT6 37 D4
Grove Rd. Lingf RH7 164 E5
Grove Rd. Merrow GU1 110 C1
Grove Rd. Merton SW19 20 C1
Grove Rd. Mitch CR4 41 B7
Grove Rd. Rich TW10 6 F1
Grove Rd. [9] Rich TW10 6 F2
Grove Rd. Shep TW17 34 C3
Grove Rd. Sutton SM2 59 A4
Grove Rd. Tats TN16 103 C7
Grove Rd. Thorn H CR7 42 A5
Grove Rd. Twick TW2 16 D5
Grove Rd. Woking GU21 69 F3
Grove Rd Prim Sch. Hounsl TW3 5 A3
Grove Sch The. Shottm GU26 188 D1
Grove Shaw. Kings KT20 97 E3
Grove Terr. Tedd TW11 17 A4
Grove The. Addl KT15 52 B5
Grove The. Alder GU11 105 A1
Grove The. Bigg H TN16 83 E1
Grove The. Cater CR3 100 C6
Grove The. Coulsd CR5 79 D5
Grove The. Crawl RH11 201 C6
Grove The. Egham TW20 12 A3
Grove The. Epsom KT17 76 E6
Grove The. Farnb GU14 85 D1
Grove The. Friml GU16 65 D1
Grove The. Horley RH6 161 B2
Grove The. Hounsl TW7 5 E6
Grove The. N Asct SL5 28 C8
Grove The. Tedd TW11 17 A4
Grove The. [1] Twick TW1 6 B1
Grove The. W Wick BR4 63 C7
Grove The. Walt O T KT12 35 B2
Grove The. Woking GU21 69 F3
Grove Way. Thame D KT10 36 C1
Grove Wood Hill. Coulsd CR5 79 D5
Grovebarns. Stain TW18 13 A2
Grovebell Ind Est. Wreccl GU9 145 F7
Grovefields Ave. Friml GU16 65 D1
Grovehill Ct. Catf BR1 24 F2
Grovehill Rd. Redh RH1 118 F1
Groveland Ave. S Norw SW16 21 F1
Groveland Rd. Beck BR3 43 F6
Groveland Way. New Mal KT3 38 D4
Grovelands. E Mole KT8 36 A5
Grovelands. Horley RH6 161 B2
Grovelands. King U T KT1 37 D5
Grovelands. M Bourn GU10 146 E7
Grovelands Rd. Purley CR8 79 F7
Grovelands Sch. Walt O T KT12 35 B3
Groveley Rd. Ashf TW13 & 16 14 F3
Groveside. G Book KT23 114 A8
Groveside Cl. Carsh SM5 59 E8
Groveside Cl. G Book KT23 114 A8
Grovestile Waye. E Bed TW14 14 D8
Grovewood. [9] Rich TW9 7 A6
Grovewood Ct. [6] Hounsl TW7 5 E6
Grub St. Limps RH8 123 C6
Guardian Ct. Elst GU8 148 C3
Guards Ct. Sunnin SL5 30 B2
Guernsey Cl. Burph GU4 110 A6
Guernsey Cl. Crawl RH11 201 A2
Guernsey Cl. Heston TW5 5 A7
Guernsey Farm Dr. Horse GU21 69 D4
Guernsey Gr. Streat SE24 22 C8
Guildables La. Limps RH8 & TN8 144 E7
Guildcroft. Guild GU1 110 A1
Guildersfield Rd. Streat SW16 21 E1
Guildford Ave. Felt TW13 15 A6
Guildford Business Park Rd. Stough GU2 109 B2
Guildford Cath. Guild GU2 109 B1
Guildford Coll Markenfield House. Guild GU1 109 D1
Guildford Cty Sch. Guild GU2 130 B7
Guildford & Godalming By-Pass Rd. Compt GU3 129 E6
Guildford & Godalming By-Pass Rd. Onsl V GU2 129 E6
Guildford & Godalming By-Pass Rd. Shackl GU7 149 F6
Guildford Golf Club. Merrow GU1 110 C1
Guildford High Sch for Girls. Guild GU1 109 E1
Guildford Ind Est. Stough GU2 109 A2
Guildford Lodge Dr. E Hors KT24 112 F6
Guildford Park Ave. Guild GU2 130 B8
Guildford Park Rd. Guild GU2 130 C8
Guildford Rd. Abing H RH5 134 C3
Guildford Rd. Addl KT16 51 C5
Guildford Rd. Alder GU11 & GU12 126 D7
Guildford Rd. Ash GU12 & GU3 106 D3
Guildford Rd. Bagsh GU19 47 E3
Guildford Rd. Bisley GU24 67 F7
Guildford Rd. Broad H RH12 216 B6
Guildford Rd. Buck Gn RH12 214 C6
Guildford Rd. Chert KT16 32 F1
Guildford Rd. Cran GU6 174 B6
Guildford Rd. Farnc GU7 151 B7
Guildford Rd. Farnh GU10 & GU9 125 F4
Guildford Rd. Farnh GU10 126 B4
Guildford Rd. Fetch KT22 94 F3
Guildford Rd. Friml GU16 85 F6
Guildford Rd. G Book KT23 94 A1
Guildford Rd. Horsh RH12 217 A2
Guildford Rd. Lhtwat GU18 & GU19 48 B1
Guildford Rd. Mytch GU16 86 B5
Guildford Rd. Normdy GU3 107 B4
Guildford Rd. Ottsh KT16 51 C5
Guildford Rd. Pirb GU3 88 C2
Guildford Rd. Rowhk RH12 215 C7
Guildford Rd. Rowly GU6 174 B6
Guildford Rd. Rudg RH12 214 C6
Guildford Rd. Sham Gn GU5 153 A1
Guildford Rd. Slinfd RH12 215 C7
Guildford Rd. Thorn H CR0 42 D3
Guildford Rd. W End GU24 67 F7
Guildford Rd. W End GU21 & GU24 68 D6
Guildford Rd. Westc RH4 135 C6
Guildford Rd. Westfd GU22 & GU4 89 D4
Guildford Rd. Windl GU19 47 F2
Guildford Rd. Woking GU22 & GU4 89 E8
Guildford Rd. Wotton RH5 134 C3
Guildford Rd E. Farnb GU14 85 C1
Guildford Rd W. Farnb GU14 85 C1
Guildford Road Trad Est. Farnh GU9 125 D3
Guildford Sch of Acting. Guild GU2 130 D7
Guildford St. Chert KT16 33 A2
Guildford St. Stain TW18 13 A2
Guildford Sta. Guild GU1 130 C8
Guildford Way. Wallin SM6 60 E5
Guildown Ave. Guild GU2 130 B6
Guildown Rd. Guild GU2 130 C6
Guileshill La. Ockham GU23 91 F5
Guilford Ave. King U T KT5 37 F4
Guillemont Cty Jun Sch. W Heath GU14 84 D7
Guillemont Fields. W Heath GU14 84 D5
Guillemot Path. [2] Crawl RH11 200 D5
Guinevere Rd. Crawl RH11 200 E6
Guinness Ct. Crawl RH11 201 C2
Guinness Ct. [5] Knaph GU21 68 F1
Guinness Ct. [3] S Croy CR0 61 F8
Gull Cl. Wallin SM6 60 E3
Gulley Rd. Farnb GU14 105 A8
Gulliver Ct. Croy CR0 61 B3
Gumbrells Cl. Fairl GU3 108 C5
Gumley Gdns. Islew TW7 6 A4
Gumley House Convent Sch for Girls. Islew TW7 6 A4
Gun Hill. Alder GU11 105 B3
Gun Pit Rd. Lingf RH7 164 D4
Gunnell Cl. Croy SE25 43 A3
Gunnell Ct. Mitch CR4 40 E8
Gunners Rd. Wands SW18 20 D6
Gunning Cl. Crawl RH11 201 A3
Gunters Mead. Oxsh KT22 74 C8
Gunton Rd. Mitch SW17 21 A2
Gurdon's La. Wormly GU8 170 F2
Gurney Cres. Thorn H CR0 41 F1
Gurney Rd. Carsh SM5 60 A6
Gurney's Cl. [3] Redh RH1 139 F8
Guy Rd. Wallin CR0 & SM6 60 D7
Guy Track. Farnb GU14 104 D8
Guyatt Gdns. Mitch CR4 41 A7
Gwydor Rd. Penge BR3 43 D6
Gwydyr Rd. Broml BR2 44 F6
Gwynne Ave. Croy CR0 43 D2
Gwynne Gdns. E Grins RH19 185 C2
Gwynne House. [6] Streat SW2 21 F7
Gwynne Vaughan Ave. Stough GU2 109 B5

H. Jones Cres. Alder GU11 105 C3
Habershon Dr. Friml GU16 66 D2
Haccombe Rd. Wimble SW19 20 C2
Hackbridge Inf Sch. Hackb SM6 41 A1
Hackbridge Jun Sch. Hackb SM5 41 A1
Hackbridge Park Gdns. Carsh SM5 59 F8
Hackbridge Rd. Hackb SM5 & SM6 60 A8
Hackbridge Sta. Hackb SM6 60 B8
Hackenden Cl. E Grins RH19 185 E3
Hackenden La. E Grins RH19 185 E3
Hacketts La. Pyrf GU22 70 F4
Hackhurst La. Abing H RH5 133 F4
Hackington Cres. Beck BR3 24 A2
Haddenham Ct. Up Toot SW17 20 D4
Haddington Rd. Catf BR1 24 D4
Haddon Cl. New Mal KT3 38 F4
Haddon Cl. Oat Pk KT13 53 D6
Haddon Rd. Sutton SM1 59 B6
Hadfield Rd. Stan TW19 2 D1
Hadleigh Cl. Merton SW20 39 F7
Hadleigh Dr. Belm SM2 59 B2
Hadleigh Gdns. Friml GU16 85 E6
Hadley Ct. Poyle SL3 1 E6
Hadley Pl. Whit V KT13 53 A3
Hadley Rd. Mitch CR4 41 D5
Hadley Wood Rise. Purley CR8 80 B5

Hadleys. Rowl GU10 .... 145 E3
Hadlow Pl. Penge SE19 .... 23 A1
Hadmans Cl. Horsh RH12 ... 217 C1
Hadrian Cl. Stan TW19 .... 13 E8
Hadrian Cl. Wallin SM6 .... 60 E3
Hadrian Ct. 1 Belm SM2 ..... 59 B3
Hadrian Way. Stan TW19 ..... 13 D8
Hadrian Way. Stan TW19 ..... 13 E8
Hadrians. Farnh GU9 .... 125 E4
Hafton Rd. Catf SE6 .... 24 E6
Haggard Rd. Twick TW1 .... 17 B8
Haig Pl. Morden SM4 .... 40 A3
Haig Rd. Alder GU12 .... 105 C1
Haig Rd. Bigg H TN16 .... 83 E2
Haig Rd. Sandh GU15 .... 64 F6
Haigh Cres. Earls RH1 .... 140 B7
Hailes Cl. Wimble SW19 .... 20 C2
Hailey Pl. Cran GU6 .... 174 F4
Hailsham Ave. Streat SW2 ... 21 F6
Hailsham Cl. Sandh GU15 ..... 45 D1
Hailsham Cl. Surb KT6 .... 37 D2
Hailsham Rd. Mitch SW17 ... 21 A2
Haines Ct. Whit V KT13 .... 53 D5
Haines Wlk. Cheam SM4 ...... 40 B2
Haining Gdns. Mytch GU16 .. 86 A3
Hainthorpe Rd.
W Norw SE27 .... 22 B4
Halcyon Ct. Stain TW18 .... 33 B7
Haldane Pl. Wands SW18 ..... 20 B7
Hale Cty Prim Sch.
Heath E GU9 .... 125 B7
Hale End. Brack RG12 .... 27 F5
Hale Ends. Woking GU22 ...... 89 B6
Hale House Cl. Churt GU10 167 F1
Hale House La. Churt GU10 168 B2
Hale Pit Rd. G Book KT23 ..... 94 C1
Hale Rd. Farnh GU9 .... 125 D4
Hale Rd. Hale GU9 .... 125 D5
Hale Rdbt. Hale GU9 .... 125 E5
Hale Reeds. Heath E GU9 ... 125 E6
Hale St. Stain TW18 .... 12 E4
Hale Way. Friml GU16 .... 85 D8
Halebourne La. W End GU24 49 A2
Hales Ct. 5 Tedd TW11 ...... 17 A3
Hales Field. Haslem GU27 .. 208 C6
Hales Hse. 3 Balham SW12 21 B8
Hales Oak. G Book KT23 .... 94 C1
Halesowen Rd. Cheam SM4 . 40 B2
Haleswood. Cobham KT11 .... 73 C5
Halewood. Easth RG12 .... 26 F3
Half Acre. Brent TW8 .... 6 D8
Half Acre Mews. Brent TW8 .. 6 D8
Half Moon Hill.
Haslem GU27 .... 208 C6
Half Moon St. Bagsh GU19 .. 47 E3
Half Way Cotts.
Farnh GU10 .... 124 C3
Halford Rd. Rich TW10 .... 6 E2
Halfpenny Cl. Chil GU4 ...... 131 D3
Halfpenny Cross.
Downs KT11 .... 73 A2
Halfpenny Ct. Sunnin SL5 ..... 30 B2
Halfpenny La. Merrow GU4 131 C5
Halfpenny La. Sunnin SL5 ..... 30 A2
Halfway La. Shackl GU7 ..... 150 B4
Haliburton Rd.
Islew TW1 & TW7 .... 6 A3
Halifax Cl. Crawl RH10 .... 182 E1
Halifax Cl. Farnb GU14 .... 84 F3
Halifax St. For Hil SE26 .... 23 B5
Halifax Way. Farnb GU14 ... 104 F7
Halimote Rd. Alder GU11 .. 105 A1
Haling Down Pas.
Purley CR8 .... 61 C1
Haling Gr. S Croy CR2 .... 61 C3
Haling Manor High Sch.
Croy CR2 .... 61 B3
Haling Manor High Sch
(Pampisford Wing).Croy CR2 61 B2
Haling Park Gdns. Croy CR2 61 B4
Haling Park Rd. Croy CR2 .... 61 C4
Haling Rd. Croy CR2 .... 61 D4
Hall Cl. Camb GU15 .... 65 E6
Hall Cl. Farnc GU7 .... 150 E7
Hall Ct. Tedd TW11 .... 16 F3
Hall Dene Cl. Merrow GU1 . 110 C2
Hall Dr. For Hil SE26 .... 23 C3
Hall Farm Dr. Twick TW2 ..... 16 D8
Hall Grove (Sch).
Windl GU19 .... 48 A5
Hall Hill. Oxted RH8 .... 122 D4
Hall La. Harl UB3 .... 3 D7
Hall Pl. Woking GU21 .... 70 A3
Hall Place Dr. Whit V KT13 ... 53 E5
Hall Rd. Bramly GU5 .... 151 F6
Hall Rd. Farnb GU14 .... 85 B2
Hall Rd. Islew TW7 .... 5 D2
Hall Rd. Wallin SM6 .... 60 B2
Hall Sch Wimbledon.
Rhampt SW15 .... 19 A5
Hallam Rd. Farnc GU7 .... 150 F5
Halland Cl. Crawl RH10 ..... 202 A7
Hallane House.
W Norw SE27 .... 22 C3
Halley Cl. Crawl RH11 .... 201 B1
Halley Dr. N Asct SL5 .... 28 D7
Halley's App. Woking GU21 . 69 A1
Halley's Ct. 1 Woking GU21 69 A1
Halley's Wlk. New Haw KT15 52 C3
Hallgrove Bottom.
Windl GU19 .... 47 F5
Halliards The. Walt O T KT12 35 A3
Halliford Cl. Up Hall TW17 ... 34 E6
Halliford Rd. Sunby TW16 .... 35 A5
Halliford Rd.
Up Hall TW16 & TW17 .... 34 F5
Halliford Sch. Shep TW17 .... 34 C2
Hallington Cl. Woking GU21 69 B2
Hallmark Cl. Sandh GU15 ..... 64 E8
Hallmead Rd. Sutton SM1 .... 59 B7
Hallowell Ave. Wallin CR0 ... 60 E6
Hallowell Cl. Mitch CR4 .... 41 A6
Hallowfield Way. Mitch CR4 40 E6
Halls Farm Cl. Knaph GU21 .. 68 D2
Hallsland. Crawl D RH10 .... 204 C8
Hallsland Way. Oxted RH8 . 122 F3
Halnaker Wlk. 9
Crawl RH11 .... 200 F3
Halsford Croft.
E Grins RH19 .... 185 B3
Halsford Gn. E Grins RH19 185 B3
Halsford La. E Grins RH19 .. 185 C3
Halsford Park Cty Prim Sch.
E Grins RH19 .... 185 C2
Halsford Park Rd.
E Grins RH19 .... 185 C2
Halters End. Graysh GU26 188 A3
Ham Cl. Rich TW10 .... 17 C5
Ham Comm. Rich TW10 .... 17 D5
Ham Farm Rd.
Rich KT2 & TW10 .... 17 E4
Ham Gate Ave. Rich TW10 ... 17 E4
Ham Gate Ave. Rich TW10 ... 18 A4
Ham La. Elst GU8 .... 148 E4
Ham La. Eng Gn TW20 .... 11 B4
Ham Ridings. Rich TW10 ..... 17 F3
Ham St. Rich TW10 .... 17 C5
Ham St. Rich TW10 .... 17 C6
Ham The. Brent TW8 .... 6 C7
Ham View. Croy CR0 .... 43 E3
Hamble Ave. Blckw GU17 .... 64 D5
Hamble Cl. Woking GU21 ..... 69 A2
Hamble Ct. Tedd KT1 .... 17 D1
Hamble Wlk. Woking GU21 .. 69 A2
Hambleden Ct. Brack RG12 . 27 E5
Hambledon C of E Prim Sch.
Hambl GU8 .... 171 D2
Hambledon Ct. 9
Wallin SM6 .... 60 B4
Hambledon Gdns.
S Norw SE25 .... 42 F6
Hambledon Hill.Woodc KT18 76 C3
Hambledon House. 2
King U T KT2 .... 18 B2
Hambledon Pl. Dulw SE21 ... 22 F7
Hambledon Rd.
Godal GU8 & GU7 .... 171 D5
Hambledon Rd.
Hambl GU8 & GU7 .... 171 D5
Hambledon Rd.
Hyde GU8 & GU7 .... 171 D5
Hambledon Rd.Wands SW18 19 F8
Hambledon Vale.
Woodc KT18 .... 76 C3
Hambleton Cl.
Friml GU15 & GU16 .... 66 B3
Hambleton Cl. N Cheam KT4 58 C8
Hambleton Ct. Crawl RH11 201 C4
Hambleton Hill.
Crawl RH11 .... 201 C4
Hambridge Way.
Streat SW2 .... 22 A8
Hambro Rd. Streat SW16 ..... 21 D3
Hambrook Rd. Croy SE25 .... 43 B6
Hamers House. 19
Streat SW2 .... 22 A8
Hamesmoor Rd. Mytch GU16 85 F4
Hamesmoor Way.
Mytch GU16 .... 85 F4
Hamfield Cl. Oxted RH8 ..... 122 C8
Hamhaugh Island.
Lo Hall TW17 .... 53 A8
Hamilton Ave. Cheam SM3 ... 58 E8
Hamilton Ave. Cobham KT11 73 A6
Hamilton Ave. Pyrf GU22 ..... 70 E3
Hamilton Ave.Tolw KT6 &SM3 57 A8
Hamilton Cl. Ashf TW13 .... 14 F3
Hamilton Cl. Chert KT16 ...... 32 F1
Hamilton Cl. Epsom KT19 .... 76 C7
Hamilton Cl. Purley CR8 .... 80 B7
Hamilton Cl. Stough GU2 .. 109 A6
Hamilton Cres. Hounsl TW3 .. 5 B2
Hamilton Ct. Catf SE6 .... 24 F7
Hamilton Ct. Cobham KT11 .. 73 A6
Hamilton Ct. Croy CR0 .... 43 A1
Hamilton Ct. Fetch KT23 ...... 94 B2
Hamilton Ct. W Heath GU14 64 E1
Hamilton Dr. Stough GU2 .. 109 A6
Hamilton Dr. Sunnin SL5 ...... 29 E2
Hamilton House. Chisw W4 .. 7 E8
Hamilton House. 10
Rich TW9 .... 7 A6
Hamilton Mws.Cobham KT11 73 A6
Hamilton Mws. Weyb KT13 . 53 A6
Hamilton Par. Felt TW13 ...... 15 A4
Hamilton Pl. Stough GU2 .. 109 A6
Hamilton Pl. Sunby TW16 .... 15 B1
Hamilton Rd. Brent TW8 .... 6 D8
Hamilton Rd. Felt TW13 .... 14 F4
Hamilton Rd. Horsh RH12 . 217 B3
Hamilton Rd. Merton SW19 . 20 B1
Hamilton Rd. S Norw CR7 .... 42 D6
Hamilton Rd. Twick TW2 ...... 16 E7
Hamilton Rd. W Norw SE27 . 22 D4
Hamilton Road Ind Est.
W Norw SE27 .... 22 D4
Hamilton Road Mews. 1
Merton SW19 .... 20 B1
Hamilton Way. Wallin SM6 .. 60 D2
Hamlash Cotts.
Frensh GU10 .... 146 C2
Hamlash La. Frensh GU10 .. 146 C1
Hamlet Rd. Penge SE19 .... 23 A1
Hamlet St. Wink RG12 .... 27 E8
Hamlyn Gdns. S Norw SE19 . 22 E1
Hamm Court Est.
Lo Hall KT13 .... 52 F8
Hamm Moor La. Addl KT15 .. 52 E6
Hammelton Ct. Broml BR1 ... 44 F8
Hammelton Rd. Broml BR1 .. 44 F8
Hammer Hill. Linch GU27 ... 207 C4
Hammer La.
Bramsh GU27 & GU30 .... 207 B6
Hammer La. Bramsh GU26 207 C8
Hammer La. Graysh
GU10 & GU26 & GU35 .... 187 E6
Hammer Yd. Crawl RH11 .. 201 D5
Hammerfield Dr.
Abing H RH5 .... 133 F3
Hammerpond Rd.
Horsh RH13 .... 217 F1
Hammersley Rd.
Farnb GU11 .... 105 C7
Hammerwood Copse.
Linch GU27 .... 207 D5
Hammerwood Rd.
Ash W RH19 .... 206 E6
Hammond Ave. Mitch CR4 ... 41 B7
Hammond Cl. Hampt TW12 . 36 A8
Hammond Cl. Horse GU21 ... 69 C4
Hammond Cty Mid Sch.
Lhtwat GU18 .... 48 A1
Hammond Rd. Horse GU21 . 69 C4
Hammond Way.
Lhtwat GU18 .... 48 B1
Hampden Ave. Beck BR3 ..... 43 E7
Hampden Cl. Crawl RH10 .. 182 E1
Hampden Rd. Beck BR3 .... 43 E7
Hampden Rd. King U T KT1 .. 38 A6
Hamper's La. Horsh RH13 . 218 A2
Hampers Ct. Horsh RH13 .. 217 D2
Hampshire Cl. Alder GU12 126 D7
Hampshire Ct. Addl KT15 ..... 52 C5
Hampshire Ct. Barnes SW13 . 7 F5
Hampshire Rd. Camb GU15 . 65 F8
Hampstead La. Dork RH4 ... 135 F6
Hampstead La. Dork RH4 .. 136 A6
Hampstead Rd. Dork RH4 . 136 A6
Hampton Cl. Wimble SW20 . 19 C1
Hampton Court Ave.
Thame D KT8 .... 36 E3
Hampton Court Cres.
E Mole KT8 .... 36 D6
Hampton Court Palace.
Hampt KT8 .... 36 F6
Hampton Court Par.
E Mole KT8 .... 36 E5
Hampton Court Rd.
Hampt KT1 & KT8 .... 37 B6
Hampton Court Sta.
E Mole KT8 .... 36 E5
Hampton Court Way.
Thame D KT10 & KT7 & KT8 36 E3
Hampton Farm Ind Est.
Felt TW13 .... 15 E5
Hampton Gr. Ewell KT17 ..... 76 F8
Hampton Hill Jun Mix Sch.
Felt TW12 .... 16 C3
Hampton Inf Sch.
Hampt TW12 .... 16 A1
Hampton Jun Sch.
Hampt TW12 .... 36 A8
Hampton La. Felt TW13 .... 15 E4
Hampton Lodge.
Horley RH6 .... 161 A2
Hampton Rd. Earls RH1 ..... 139 F4
Hampton Rd. Hale GU9 ..... 125 B6
Hampton Rd. N Cheam KT4 . 58 B8
Hampton Rd.
Tedd TW11 & TW12 .... 16 E3
Hampton Rd. Thorn H CR0 ... 42 C3
Hampton Rd. Twick TW2 ..... 16 D5
Hampton Rd E. Felt TW13 .... 15 F5
Hampton Rd W. Felt TW13 .. 15 E5
Hampton Road Ind Pk.
Thorn H CR0 .... 42 C3
Hampton Sch. Hampt TW12 16 A3
Hampton Sta. Hampt TW12 . 36 A8
Hampton Way.
E Grins RH19 .... 205 F7
Hampton Wick Inf Sch.
Tedd KT1 .... 17 D1
Hampton Wick Sta.
Tedd KT1 .... 37 C8
Hamsey Green Cty Inf Sch.
Warlgm CR6 .... 81 B3
Hamsey Green Cty Jun Sch.
Warlgm CR6 .... 81 B3
Hamsey Green Gdns.
Warlgm CR6 .... 81 C3
Hamsey Way. Hams Gn CR2 81 B4
Hanbury Dr. Bigg H TN16 ..... 83 B6
Hanbury Path. Sheer GU21 .. 70 D5
Hanbury Rd. Crawl RH11 ... 200 E5
Hanbury Way. Camb GU15 .. 65 C3
Hancock Rd. S Norw SE19 .... 22 D2
Hancocks Mount. Ascot SL5 29 D3
Hancombe Rd. Sandh GU17 . 45 A1
Handcroft Rd. Thorn H CR0 . 42 B1
Handel House. Twick TW2 ..... 5 D1
Handside Cl. N Cheam KT4 .. 39 D1
Handsworth House. 8
Crawl RH11 .... 201 D5
Hanford Cl. Wands SW18 ..... 20 A7
Hanger Hill. Weyb KT13 .... 53 B5
Hanley Pl. Beck BR3 .... 24 A1
Hannah Cl. Beck BR3 .... 44 C6
Hannah Ct. Wimble SW19 ..... 19 D1
Hannay Wlk. Streat SW16 .... 21 D6
Hannen Rd. W Norw SE27 .... 22 B5
Hannibal Rd. Stan TW19 ...... 13 E8
Hannibal Way. Wallin CR0 ... 60 F4
Hanning Lodge. Hounsl TW3 . 5 C3
Hanover Ave. Felt TW13 ...... 15 A6
Hanover Cl. Cheam SM3 ...... 58 F6
Hanover Cl. Crawl RH10 ..... 201 F3
Hanover Cl. Eng Gn TW20 .... 11 B2
Hanover Cl. Friml GU16 .... 65 E1
Hanover Cl. Merst RH1 ...... 119 C7
Hanover Cl. Rich TW9 .... 7 A7
Hanover Ct. Dork RH4 .... 135 F7
Hanover Ct. Horsh RH13 .... 217 F3
Hanover Ct. 1 Penge SE19 . 23 A1
Hanover Ct. Woking GU22 ... 89 E8
Hanover Gdns. Easth RG12 .. 26 F2
Hanover Gdns.
W Heath GU14 .... 84 E6
Hanover House. Tolw KT6 .... 38 A1
Hanover Rd. Merton SW19 .. 20 C1
Hanover St. Croy CR0 & CR9 61 B7
Hanover Terr. Islew TW7 ...... 6 A6
Hanover Wlk. Oat Pk KT13 ... 53 E7
Hansler Gr. E Mole KT8 .... 36 D5
Hanson Cl. Balham SW12 ..... 21 B8
Hanson Cl. Beck BR3 .... 24 B2
Hanson Cl. Burph GU1 .... 109 F4
Hanson Cl. Camb GU15 .... 66 B7
Hanson Cl. Mortl SW14 .... 7 C4
Hanworth Cl. Easth RG12 ..... 27 C3
Hanworth La. Chert KT16 ..... 32 F1
Hanworth Rd. Earls RH1 .... 139 F4
Hanworth Rd. Easth RG12 ... 27 A2
Hanworth Rd. Felt TW13 ..... 15 B7
Hanworth Rd. Hampt TW12 . 16 A3
Hanworth Rd.
Hounsl TW3 & TW4 .... 5 B2
Hanworth Rd. Sunby TW16 .. 15 A1
Hanworth Rd. Twick TW4 .... 15 F8
Hanworth Terr. Hounsl TW3 .. 5 B3
Hanworth Trad Est.
Chert KT16 .... 32 F1
Hanworth Trad Est.
Felt TW13 .... 15 E5
Harberson Rd. Balham SW12 21 B7
Harbin House. 5
Streat SW2 .... 22 A7
Harbledown Rd. S Croy CR2 81 A8
Harborough Rd. Streat SW16 21 F4
Harbour Cl. Farnb GU14 .... 85 A8
Harbourfield Rd.
Banstd SM7 .... 78 B4
Harbridge Ave.
Rhampt SW15 .... 19 A8
Harbury Rd. Sutton SM5 .... 59 E3
Harcourt Ave. Wallin SM6 .... 60 B6
Harcourt Cl. Egham TW20 .... 12 C2
Harcourt Cl. Islew TW7 .... 6 A4
Harcourt Field. Wallin SM6 .. 60 B6
Harcourt Lodge. 2
Wallin SM6 .... 60 B6
Harcourt Rd. Camb GU15 ..... 65 B5
Harcourt Rd. Easth RG12 ..... 27 B4
Harcourt Rd. Merton SW19 .. 20 A1
Harcourt Rd. Thorn H CR7 ... 42 A3
Harcourt Rd. Wallin SM6 ..... 60 B6
Harcourt Way. S Godst RH9 142 E6
Hardcastle Cl. Croy SE25 ..... 43 A3
Hardcourts Cl. W Wick BR4 . 63 B7
Hardel Rise. Streat SW2 ...... 22 B7
Hardel Wlk.
Streat SE24 & SW2 .... 22 A8
Hardell Cl. Egham TW20 ...... 12 A3
Hardham Cl. Crawl RH11 .. 201 A8
Harding Ct. S Norw SE25 ..... 42 F7
Harding House. Wallin SM6 . 60 C2
Harding Pl. For Hil SE23 .... 23 E8
Harding Rd. Lang V KT18 ..... 96 E8
Hardings La. Penge SE20 ..... 23 D2
Hardman Rd. King U T KT2 .. 37 E7
Hardwell Way. Brack RG12 .. 27 E5
Hardwick Cl. Oxsh KT22 .... 74 C4
Hardwick La. Lyne KT16 .... 32 D1
Hardwick Rd.
Woodh RH1 & RH2 .... 139 D7
Hardwicke Ave. Heston TW5 . 5 A6
Hardwicke Rd. Reig RH2 ... 118 A2
Hardwicke Rd. Rich TW10 ... 17 C4
Hardy Cl. Crawl RH10 .... 202 C7
Hardy Cl. Dork RH5 .... 136 B3
Hardy Cl. Horley RH6 .... 160 E3
Hardy Cl. Horsh RH12 .... 217 B4
Hardy Gn. Crowth RG11 .... 45 B4
Hardy Rd. Merton SW19 .... 20 B1
Hardys Cl. E Mole KT8 .... 36 E5
Hare Hill. Row Tn KT15 .... 51 F4
Hare Hill Cl. Pyrf GU22 .... 71 A4
Hare La. Clayg KT10 .... 55 E4
Hare La. Crawl RH11 .... 201 B8
Hare La. Farnc GU7 .... 150 F6
Hare La. Horne RH7 .... 163 D5
Harebell Hill. Cobham KT11 . 73 E5
Harecroft. Dork RH4 & RH5 136 C4
Harecroft. Fetch KT23 .... 94 C3
Haredon Cl. For Hil SE23 ...... 23 D8
Harefield. Hinch W KT10 .... 55 E7
Harefield Ave. E Ewell SM2 .. 58 E2
Harefield Rd. S Norw SW16 .. 21 F1
Harelands Cl. Horse GU21 ... 69 C2
Harelands La. Horse GU21 ... 69 C2
Harendon. Tadw KT20 .... 97 D6
Hares Bank. New Add CR0 .... 63 D1
Harestone Dr. Cater CR3 .... 100 F2
Harestone Hill. Cater CR3 .. 100 F2
Harestone La. Cater CR3 .... 100 E2
Harestone Valley Rd.
Cater CR3 .... 100 F2
Harewood Cl. Crawl RH10 182 A1
Harewood Cl. Reig RH2 ..... 118 C4
Harewood Gdns.Hams Gn CR2 82 C4
Harewood Rd. Hounsl TW7 .... 5 F6
Harewood Rd. Merrow GU4 110 C4
Harewood Rd. Mitch SW19 .. 20 E2
Harewood Rd. S Croy CR2 .... 61 E4
Harfield Rd. Sunby TW16 ..... 35 D7
Harkness Cl. Nork KT17 .... 77 C3
Harland Ave. S Croy CR0 ...... 62 A7
Harland Fst Sch. Mitch CR4 . 40 D7
Harlech Ct. For Hil SE23 .... 23 C7
Harlech Gdns. Heston TW5 .... 4 C7
Harlech Rd. Hawley GU17 .... 64 D4
Harlequin Ave. Brent TW8 ..... 6 A8
Harlequin Cl. Islew TW7 .... 5 E2
Harlequin Rd. Tedd TW11 ... 17 B1
Harlington Cl. Harl UB7 .... 3 C7
Harlington Cnr. Harl UB3 .... 3 D6
Harlington Lower Sch.
Harl UB7 .... 3 C7
Harlington Rd E.
Felt TW13 & TW14 .... 15 C7
Harlington Rd W. Felt TW14 . 4 B1
Harlow Ct. 4 Reig RH2 ..... 118 D1
Harman Pl. Purley CR8 .... 80 B8
Harmans Dr. E Grins RH19 186 B1
Harmans Mead.
E Grins RH19 .... 186 B1
Harmans Water Cty Jun Sch.
Brack RG12 .... 27 E4
Harmans Water Rd.
Brack RG12 .... 27 D4
Harmar Cl. Woki RG11 .... 25 E6
Harmondsworth La.
Harm UB7 .... 2 E8

Harmondsworth Prim Sch. Harm UB7 ... 2 D8
Harmony Cl. Crawl RH11 ... 200 E4
Harmony Cl. Wallin SM6 ... 60 E2
Harms Gr. Merrow GU4 ... 110 C4
Harold Ct. Alder GU12 ... 105 B1
Harold Rd. Carsh SM1 ... 59 D6
Harold Rd. S Norw SE19 ... 22 D1
Harold Rd. Worth RH10 ... 202 E5
Haroldslea. Horley RH6 ... 161 E2
Haroldslea Cl. Horley RH6 . 161 C1
Haroldslea Dr. Horley RH6 161 D1
Harpenden Rd. W Norw SE27 & SW16 ... 22 B6
Harper Dr. Worth RH10 ... 202 C2
Harper's Rd. Ash GU12 ... 106 C2
Harpesford Ave. Vir W GU25 31 C4
Harps Oak La. L Kings RH1 & RH2 ... 99 A2
Harpurs. Tadw KT20 ... 97 D5
Harrier Cl. Cranl GU6 ... 174 E4
Harrier Ct. Crawl RH10 ... 182 D1
Harriet Gdns. Croy CR0 ... 62 A8
Harrington Cl. Leigh RH2 .. 138 A2
Harrington Cl. Wallin CR0 ... 60 E8
Harrington Ct. 7 Croy CR0 . 61 D8
Harrington Rd. Croy SE25 ... 43 B5
Harriotts Cl. Ashtd KT22 ... 95 C7
Harriotts La. Ashtd KT21 & KT22 ... 95 C8
Harris City Tech Coll. S Norw SE19 ... 42 F8
Harris Cl. Crawl RH11 ... 201 B3
Harris Cl. Hounsl TW5 ... 5 A6
Harris Lodge. Catf SE6 ... 24 C7
Harris Way. Charlt TW16 ... 34 E8
Harrison Cl. Reig RH2 ... 139 B8
Harrison Ct. Shep Gn TW17 . 34 B4
Harrison's Rise. Croy CR0 & CR9 ... 61 B7
Harrodian Sch. Barnes SW13 7 F7
Harrogate Ct. 2 For Hil SE26 ... 23 A5
Harrow Bottom Rd. Longc GU25 ... 31 F3
Harrow Cl. Chert KT15 ... 52 B8
Harrow Cl. Chess KT9 ... 56 D3
Harrow Cl. Dork RH4 ... 136 A6
Harrow Gate Gdns. Dork RH4 ... 136 A5
Harrow Gdns. Warlgm CR6 .. 81 F3
Harrow La. Farnc GU7 ... 150 E7
Harrow Lodge. Sutton SM2 .. 59 D4
Harrow Rd. Ashf TW15 ... 14 A6
Harrow Rd. Carsh SM1 & SM2 & SM5 ... 59 E4
Harrow Rd. Warlgm CR6 ... 81 F3
Harrow Rd E. Dork RH4 ... 136 B6
Harrow Rd W. Dork RH4 ... 136 A6
Harrow Way. Charlt TW17 ... 34 C7
Harrowdene. Cran GU6 ... 174 E4
Harrowdene Ct. Wimble SW19 ... 19 E3
Harrowdene Gdns. Tedd TW11 ... 17 A1
Harrowlands Pk. Dork RH4 136 B6
Harrowsley Ct. Horley RH6 161 B4
Hart Cl. Bletch RH1 ... 120 E2
Hart Cl. 1 Brack RG12 ... 27 B8
Hart Cl. W Heath GU14 ... 84 E8
Hart Dyke Cl. Woki RG11 ... 25 B2
Hart Gdns. Dork RH4 ... 136 B8
Hart House. Streat SW2 ... 22 A7
Hart Rd. Byfl KT14 ... 71 E6
Hart Rd. Dork RH4 ... 136 B8
Hart The. Farnh GU9 ... 125 B2
Hart's La. S Godst RH9 ... 142 D7
Harte Rd. Hounsl TW3 ... 4 F5
Hartfield Cres. Merton SW19 19 F1
Hartfield Gr. Penge SE20 ... 43 C8
Hartfield Rd. Chess KT9 ... 56 D5
Hartfield Rd. For Row RH18 206 F2
Hartfield Rd. Merton SW19 .. 20 A1
Hartford Rd. W Ewell KT19 .. 57 B4
Hartford Rd. W Ewell KT19 .. 57 B4
Hartford Rise. Camb GU15 ... 65 D6
Hartham Cl. Islew TW7 ... 6 A6
Hartham Rd. Islew TW7 ... 6 A6
Harting Ct. Crawl RH11 ... 200 F3
Hartington Ct. Chisw W4 ... 7 B7
Hartington Pl. Reig RH2 ... 118 A3
Hartington Rd. Chisw W4 ... 7 C6
Hartington Rd. Twick TW1 ... 6 B1
Hartland Cl. Woodhm KT15 .. 52 C2
Hartland Pl. W Heath GU14 . 85 A7
Hartland Rd. Cheam SM4 ... 40 B2
Hartland Rd. Hampt TW12 ... 16 B4
Hartland Rd. Islew TW7 ... 6 A4
Hartland Rd. Row Tn KT15 ... 52 A3
Hartland Way. Croy CR0 ... 62 E8
Hartland Way. Morden SM4 39 F2
Hartlands The. Heston TW5 .. 4 B8
Hartley Cl. Blckw GU17 ... 64 B5
Hartley Down. Coulsd CR5 & CR8 ... 79 F5
Hartley Farm. Coulsd CR8 ... 79 F4
Hartley Hill. Coulsd CR8 ... 79 F4
Hartley Old Rd. Coulsd CR8 . 79 F5
Hartley Rd. Thorn H CR0 ... 42 C2
Hartley Way. Coulsd CR5 & CR8 ... 79 F4
Harts Gdns. Stough GU2 ... 109 B4
Harts Leap Cl. Sandh GU17 .. 45 B1
Harts Leap Rd. Sandh GU17 . 64 A8
Hartscroft. New Add CR0 ... 62 E2
Hartsgrove. Chidd GU8 ... 191 B5
Hartshill. Stough GU2 ... 108 D2
Hartshill Wlk. Woking GU21 69 B3
Hartspiece Rd. Earls RH1 . 140 B7
Hartswood. Dork RH5 ... 136 D4
Hartswood Ave. Dovgn RH2 ... 139 A5
Hartswood House. 10 Streat SW2 ... 21 E7
Harvard Hill. Chisw W4 ... 7 B8
Harvard Rd. Hounsl TW7 ... 5 E6
Harvard Rd. Sandh GU15 ... 45 E1
Harvest Bank Rd. Coney H BR4 ... 63 F7
Harvest Ct. Beck BR3 ... 24 A1
Harvest Ct. Shep Gn TW17 ... 34 A5
Harvest Hill. E Grins RH19 . 205 E8
Harvest Hill. Godal GU7 ... 150 D4
Harvest La. Thame D KT7 ... 37 A3
Harvest Rd. Eng Gn TW20 ... 11 D2
Harvest Rd. Felt TW13 ... 15 A5
Harvest Rd. Worth RH10 ... 202 C4
Harvester Rd. Epsom KT19 .. 57 D1
Harvesters. Horsh RH12 ... 217 D5
Harvesters Cl. Islew TW7 ... 5 D2
Harvestside. Horley RH6 ... 161 C4
Harvey Cl. Crawl RH11 ... 201 A1
Harvey Lodge. Guild GU1 ... 130 E8
Harvey Rd. Guild GU1 ... 130 E8
Harvey Rd. Twick TW4 ... 15 F8
Harvey Rd. W Heath GU14 ... 84 C5
Harvey Rd. Walt O T KT12 ... 35 A2
Harwarden Cl. Crawl D RH10 ... 204 C8
Harwood Ave. Mitch CR4 ... 40 E6
Harwood Gdns. Old W SL4 .. 11 B8
Harwood Pk. Salfs RH1 ... 161 A8
Harwood Rd. Horsh RH13 .. 217 F3
Harwood Rd. Horsh RH12 & RH13 ... 218 A3
Harwoods Cl. 3 E Grins RH19 ... 205 F7
Harwoods La. E Grins RH19 205 F7
Hascombe Ct. Crawl RH11 201 A5
Hascombe House. 11 Rhampt SW15 ... 19 B7
Haseley End. For Hil SE23 ... 23 C8
Haseltine Prim Sch. For Hil SE6 ... 23 F4
Haseltine Rd. For Hil SE26 ... 23 F4
Haslam Ave. Cheam SM3 & SM4 ... 39 E1
Hasle Dr. Haslem GU27 ... 208 B6
Haslemere Ave. Cranf TW5 ... 4 C5
Haslemere Ave. Mitch CR4 & SW19 ... 40 D7
Haslemere Ave. Wimble SW18 ... 20 B6
Haslemere Cl. Friml GU16 ... 66 C3
Haslemere Cl. Hampt TW12 15 F3
Haslemere Cl. Wallin SM6 ... 60 E5
Haslemere & District Hospl. Haslem GU27 ... 208 D7
Haslemere Fst Sch. Mitch CR4 ... 40 D7
Haslemere & Heathrow Est The. Cranf TW4 ... 4 B4
Haslemere Ind Est. Felt TW14 ... 4 A2
Haslemere Ind Est. Wimble SW18 ... 20 B6
Haslemere Prep Sch. Haslem GU27 ... 208 D5
Haslemere Rd. Brook GU8 . 170 C5
Haslemere Rd. Marl Ht GU27 ... 208 B1
Haslemere Rd. Thorn H CR7 42 B4
Haslemere Rd. Witley GU8 170 C5
Haslemere Sta. Haslem GU27 ... 208 B6
Haslett Ave E. Crawl RH10 202 A6
Haslett Ave W. Crawl RH10 & RH11 ... 201 D5
Haslett Rd. Up Hall TW17 ... 34 E7
Hassall Ct. Old Wok GU22 ... 90 A6
Hassocks Cl. For Hil SE23 & SE26 ... 23 B5
Hassocks Ct. 3 Crawl RH11 ... 200 F3
Hassocks Rd. Mitch SW16 ... 41 D8
Haste Hill. Haslem GU27 ... 208 D5
Hastings Cl. Friml GU16 ... 86 A7
Hastings Dr. King U T KT6 ... 37 C3
Hastings Pl. 1 Croy CR0 ... 42 F1
Hastings Rd. Crawl RH10 ... 202 C6
Hastings Rd. Croy CR0 ... 42 F1
Hatch Cl. Addl KT15 ... 52 B7
Hatch Cl. Alf Cr GU6 ... 194 A3
Hatch End. For Row RH18 .. 206 F2
Hatch End. Windl GU20 ... 48 C4
Hatch Gdns. Burgh H KT20 .. 97 D7
Hatch Hill. Marl Ht GU27 ... 208 B1
Hatch La. Harm TW6 & UB7 ... 2 D7
Hatch La. Marl Ht GU27 ... 208 B2
Hatch La. Ockham GU23 ... 72 B1
Hatch La. Ockham GU23 ... 92 B7
Hatch La. S Nutf RH1 ... 140 F3
Hatch La. Wormly GU8 ... 190 D8
Hatch Pl. Rich TW10 ... 17 F3
Hatch Rd. Thorn H SW16 ... 41 E7
Hatch Ride. Crowth RG11 ... 45 B7
Hatch Ride Cty Prim Sch. Crowth RG11 ... 45 B7
Hatches The. Farnh GU9 ... 145 F8
Hatches The. Friml GU16 ... 85 F6
Hatchet La. Wink SL4 & SL5 ... 9 B5
Hatchett Rd. E Bed TW14 ... 14 C7
Hatchetts Dr. Shottm GU27 207 D7
Hatchford Park Sch. Downs KT11 ... 72 E1
Hatchgate. Horley RH6 ... 160 F2
Hatchgate Copse. Easth RG12 ... 26 E3
Hatchlands Rd. Redh RH1 .. 118 E1
Hatfield Cl. Belm SM2 ... 59 B2
Hatfield Cl. Mitch CR4 ... 40 D5
Hatfield Gdns. Farnb GU14 .. 85 E3
Hatfield House. 16 King U T KT6 ... 37 E4
Hatfield Mead. Morden SM4 40 A4
Hatfield Prim Sch. W Barn SM4 ... 39 E3
Hatfield Rd. Ashtd KT21 ... 95 F8
Hatfield Wlk. Crawl RH11 .. 200 E2
Hathaway Ct. 10 Redh RH1 ... 119 A2
Hathaway Rd. Thorn H CR0 .. 42 B2
Hatherleigh Cl. Chess KT9 .. 56 D5
Hatherleigh Cl. Morden SM4 40 A5
Hatherleigh House. Morden SM4 ... 40 A5
Hatherley Rd. Rich TW9 ... 6 F6
Hatherop Rd. Hampt TW12 .. 15 F1
Hathersham Cl. Smallf RH6 162 A4
Hathersham La. S Nutf RH1 & RH6 ... 161 F6
Hathersley House. 3 Streat SW2 ... 22 A8
Hatherwood. Ashtd KT21 ... 95 E6
Hatton Cross Sta. Hatton TW6 3 F3
Hatton Gdns. Mitch CR4 ... 40 F4
Hatton Gn. Hatton TW14 ... 4 A3
Hatton Hill. Windl GU20 ... 48 C5
Hatton Rd. E Bed TW14 ... 14 D8
Hatton Rd. Hatton TW14 & TW6 ... 3 E2
Hatton Rd. Thorn H CR0 ... 42 A1
Havana Rd. Wimble SW18 & SW19 ... 20 A6
Havelock Cotts. Woking GU22 ... 89 D5
Havelock Hall. 8 Croy CR0 . 42 F1
Havelock House. 4 Croy CR0 ... 42 F1
Havelock House. Farnb GU14 ... 105 C8
Havelock House. For Hil SE23 ... 23 C7
Havelock Rd. Croy CR0 ... 61 F8
Havelock Rd. Wimble SW19 20 C3
Havelock Rd. Woki RG11 ... 25 A6
Havelock St. Woki RG11 ... 25 A6
Havelock Wlk. For Hil SE23 . 23 C6
Haven Cl. Wimble SW19 ... 19 D5
Haven Ct. Beck BR3 ... 44 C7
Haven Gdns. Crawl D RH10 184 B1
Haven Rd. Ashf TW15 ... 14 B5
Haven Rd. Rudg RH12 & RH14 ... 214 D3
Haven The. Rich TW9 ... 7 A4
Haven Way. Farnh GU9 ... 125 D4
Havenbury Est. Dork RH4 . 136 A8
Havenbury Ind Est. Dork RH4 ... 135 F8
Havengate. Horsh RH12 ... 217 F5
Haverfield Gdns. Rich TW9 ... 7 A7
Haverhill Rd. Streat SW12 ... 21 C7
Havers Ave. Hersh KT12 ... 54 D5
Haversham Cl. Crawl RH10 201 F6
Haversham Cl. Twick TW1 ... 6 D1
Haversham Dr. Easth RG12 . 27 B3
Haversham House. Horley RH6 ... 161 B5
Havisham Pl. S Norw SW16 . 22 B1
Hawarden Gr. Streat SE24 ... 22 C8
Hawarden Rd. Cater CR3 ... 100 C6
Hawes Down Schs. W Wick BR4 ... 44 D1
Hawes La. W Wick BR4 ... 63 E8
Hawes Rd. Burgh H KT20 ... 97 D7
Haweswater House. Islew TW1 ... 5 F2
Hawk La. Brack RG12 ... 27 D5
Hawk's Hill. Fetch KT22 ... 94 F4
Hawke Rd. W Norw SE19 ... 22 E2
Hawkedale Fst Sch. Sunby TW16 ... 34 F6
Hawker Cl. Wallin SM6 ... 60 E3
Hawker Ct. 14 King U T KT2 ... 18 A1
Hawkes Cl. Woki RG11 ... 25 A7
Hawkes Leap. Windl GU20 ... 48 B6
Hawkes Rd. Mitch CR4 ... 40 F8
Hawkesbourne Rd. Horsh RH12 ... 217 F5
Hawkesfield Rd. For Hil SE23 & SE6 ... 23 F6
Hawkesley Cl. Tedd TW1 ... 17 A4
Hawkesmoor Rd. Crawl RH11 ... 200 E4
Hawkesmoore Dr. Bear Gn RH5 ... 157 C4
Hawkesworth Dr. Bagsh GU19 ... 47 E1
Hawkewood Rd. Sunby TW16 ... 35 A6
Hawkfield Ct. Islew TW7 ... 5 E5
Hawkhirst Rd. Kenley CR8 ... 80 E3
Hawkhurst. Cobham KT11 ... 74 A5
Hawkhurst Gdns. Chess KT9 56 E6
Hawkhurst Rd. Streat SW16 41 D8
Hawkhurst Way. New Mal KT3 ... 38 D4
Hawkhurst Way. W Wick BR4 ... 63 B8
Hawkhurst Wlk. Crawl RH10 ... 202 B4
Hawkins Cl. Brack RG12 ... 28 A7
Hawkins Rd. Crawl RH10 ... 201 E4
Hawkins Rd. Tedd TW11 ... 17 B2
Hawkins Way. Catf SE6 ... 24 A3
Hawkins Way. Woki RG11 ... 25 E6
Hawkley Gdns. W Norw SE27 ... 22 B6
Hawkridge. Cox Gn RH12 ... 195 E1
Hawkridge Ct. Brack RG12 .. 27 E6
Hawks Hill Cl. Fetch KT22 ... 94 F4
Hawks Rd. King U T KT1 ... 37 F7
Hawksbrook La. Beck BR3 ... 44 C3
Hawkshead Cl. Broml BR1 ... 24 E1
Hawkshill Cl. Esher KT10 ... 55 A4
Hawkshill Way. Esher KT10 . 55 A4
Hawksview. Cobham KT11 ... 73 F6
Hawksway. Stain TW18 ... 12 F5
Hawkswell Cl. Woking GU21 68 F2
Hawkswell Wlk. Woking GU21 ... 68 F3
Hawkswood Ave. Friml GU16 65 F2
Hawkswood House. Brack RG12 ... 26 E8
Hawkwood Dell. G Book KT23 ... 94 A1
Hawkwood Rise. G Book KT23 ... 94 A1
Hawley Cl. Hampt TW12 ... 15 F2
Hawley Ct. W Heath GU14 ... 84 E8
Hawley Cty Prim Sch. Hawley GU17 ... 64 E3
Hawley Garden Cotts. Hawley GU17 ... 64 D4
Hawley La. Farnb GU14 ... 85 B8
Hawley Lodge. Hawley GU14 64 F2
Hawley Place Sch. Hawley GU17 ... 64 E1
Hawley Rd. Hawley GU14 & GU17 ... 64 F3
Hawley Way. Ashf TW15 ... 14 B3
Hawmead. Crawl D RH10 ... 204 C8
Hawth (Arts Ctr) The. Crawl RH10 ... 201 F5
Hawth Ave. Crawl RH10 ... 201 F4
Hawth Cl. Crawl RH10 ... 201 E4
Hawthorn Ave. S Norw CR7 . 42 B8
Hawthorn Cl. Brack RG12 ... 27 A8
Hawthorn Cl. Cranf TW5 ... 4 B7
Hawthorn Cl. Crawl RH11 .. 181 C1
Hawthorn Cl. Earls RH1 ... 140 A4
Hawthorn Cl. Hampt TW12 .. 16 A3
Hawthorn Cl. Horsh RH12 .. 217 C4
Hawthorn Cl. Nork SM7 ... 77 E5
Hawthorn Cl. Woking GU22 . 89 E7
Hawthorn Cres. Selsd CR2 ... 81 C8
Hawthorn Cres. Up Toot SW17 ... 21 A3
Hawthorn Ct. Rich TW9 ... 7 B6
Hawthorn Ct. 8 W Norw SW16 ... 22 A3
Hawthorn Dr. Coney H BR4 .. 63 E6
Hawthorn Gr. Penge SE20 ... 43 B8
Hawthorn Hatch. Brent TW8 . 6 B7
Hawthorn La. New Gn SL4 ... 8 A7
Hawthorn La. Rowl GU10 ... 145 F3
Hawthorn Rd. Brent TW8 ... 6 B7
Hawthorn Rd. Carsh SM1 & SM2 & SM5 ... 59 E4
Hawthorn Rd. Friml GU16 ... 65 F2
Hawthorn Rd. Ock Rid GU7 150 B2
Hawthorn Rd. Send M GU23 91 A3
Hawthorn Rd. Wallin SM5 & SM6 ... 60 B3
Hawthorn Rd. Woking GU22 89 D7
Hawthorn Way. Bisley GU24 68 A3
Hawthorn Way. Earls RH1 140 B8
Hawthorn Way. Up Hall TW17 ... 34 D5
Hawthorn Way. Woodhm KT15 ... 52 C1
Hawthorndene Cl. Coney H BR2 ... 63 F8
Hawthorndene Rd. Coney H BR2 ... 63 F8
Hawthorne Ave. Bigg H TN16 ... 83 D4
Hawthorne Ave. Mitch CR4 .. 40 D7
Hawthorne Ave. Wallin SM5 60 A3
Hawthorne Ave. Wink SL4 ... 9 B6
Hawthorne Cl. Alder GU12 . 126 E7
Hawthorne Cl. Sutton SM1 .. 59 C8
Hawthorne Cotts. Burst RH6 ... 183 C7
Hawthorne Cres. Hawley GU17 ... 64 E4
Hawthorne Ct. Stan TW19 ... 13 D8
Hawthorne Dr. Wink SL4 ... 9 B7
Hawthorne Pl. Ewell KT17 ... 76 E7
Hawthorne Rd. Egham TW20 12 C4
Hawthorne Way. Burph GU4 ... 110 B5
Hawthorne Way. Stan TW19 13 D8
Hawthorne Way. Wink SL4 ... 9 B7
Hawthorns Sch (Pendell Court) The. Bletch RH1 ... 120 B4
Hawthorns The. Belm SM2 .. 59 A4
Hawthorns The. Ewell KT17 . 58 A3
Hawthorns The. Oxted RH8 123 A2
Hawthorns The. Poyle SL3 ... 1 F6
Haxted Mill (Mus). Haxted TN8 ... 165 D8
Haxted Rd. Haxted RH7 & TN8 ... 165 C7
Haxted Rd. Lingf RH7 & TN8 ... 165 C7
Haybarn Dr. Horsh RH12 ... 217 E7
Haycroft Cl. Coulsd CR8 ... 80 B1
Haycroft Rd. Surb KT6 ... 56 E7
Hayden Ct. Woodhm KT15 ... 71 B8
Haydn Ave. Purley CR8 ... 80 A4
Haydon House. 2 Tedd TW11 ... 17 C1
Haydon Pk Rd.Wimble SW19 20 B3
Haydon Pl. Guild GU1 ... 130 D8
Haydon's Rd. Merton SW19 . 20 C2
Haydon's Rd. Wimble SW19 20 C2
Haydons Road Sta. Wimble SW19 ... 20 C3
Hayes Barton. Mayb GU22 ... 70 D3
Hayes Chase. W Wick BR4 ... 44 E3
Hayes Cres. Cheam SM3 ... 58 D6
Hayes Ct. Streat SW12 ... 21 E7
Hayes Ct. Wimble SW19 ... 19 E2
Hayes Hill. W Wick BR2 ... 44 E1
Hayes Hill Rd. Hayes BR2 ... 44 F1
Hayes La. Beck BR2 & BR3 ... 44 D5
Hayes La. Kenley CR8 & CR3 80 B3
Hayes La. Purley CR8 ... 80 B3
Hayes La. Slinfd RH13 ... 215 D2
Hayes Mead Rd. W Wick BR2 44 E1
Hayes Prim Sch The. Purley CR8 ... 80 B3
Hayes Sta. Coney H BR2 ... 44 F1
Hayes The. Lang V KT18 ... 96 E8
Hayes Way. Beck BR3 ... 44 D5
Hayes Wlk. Smallf RH6 ... 162 A4
Hayesend House. Up Toot SW17 ... 20 C4
Hayesford Park Dr. Hayes BR2 ... 44 F4

Hayfields. Horley RH6 .... 161 C4
Haygarth Pl. Wimble SW19 .. 19 D3
Haygreen Cl. King U T KT2 ... 18 B2
Haylett Gdns. King U T KT1 .. 37 D5
Hayling Ave. Felt TW13 .... 15 A5
Hayling Ct. Cheam SM3 .... 58 C6
Hayling Ct. Crawl RH11 ...... 201 C3
Haymeads Dr. Esher KT10 ... 55 C4
Haymer Gdns. N Cheam KT4 58 A7
Hayne Rd. Beck BR3 .... 43 F8
Haynes La. S Norw SE19 ...... 22 E2
Haynt Wlk. Merton SW20 ..... 39 E6
Hays Bridge Bsns Ctr.
Blind H RH9 .... 163 C6
Hays Bridge Houses.
Horne RH9 .... 163 B7
Hays Wlk. E Ewell SM2 .... 58 D1
Haysleigh Gdns. Penge SE20 43 A7
Haysleigh House.
Penge SE20 .... 43 B7
Haywain The. Oxted RH8 .. 122 D5
Hayward Cl. Merton SW19 ... 40 B8
Haywardens. Lingf RH7 ..... 164 D5
Haywards. Crawl RH10 ...... 182 D1
Haywood. Easth RG12 .... 27 C2
Hazel Ave. Bellf GU1 .... 109 C5
Hazel Ave. Farnb GU14 .... 84 F3
Hazel Bank. Ewh GU6 .... 175 E5
Hazel Bank. S Norw SE25 ..... 42 E7
Hazel Bank. Tolw KT5 .... 38 C1
Hazel Cl. Brent TW8 .... 6 B7
Hazel Cl. Crawl RH11 .... 181 C1
Hazel Cl. Crawl D RH10 ...... 204 C8
Hazel Cl. Croy CR0 .... 43 D1
Hazel Cl. Eng Gn TW20 .... 11 B2
Hazel Cl. Mitch CR4 .... 41 D5
Hazel Cl. Twick TW2 .... 16 C8
Hazel Cl. Woodh RH2 .... 139 C7
Hazel Ct. Bellf GU1 .... 109 D5
Hazel Ct. 9 W Norw SW16 . 22 A3
Hazel Ct. Warlgm CR6 .... 81 E1
Hazel Dr. Send M GU23 .... 90 F2
Hazel Gr. For Hil SE26 .... 23 D4
Hazel Gr. Shottm GU26 .... 188 E2
Hazel Gr. Stain TW18 .... 13 C2
Hazel Mead. Ewell KT17 .... 58 A1
Hazel Par. Fetch KT22 .... 94 C5
Hazel Rd. Ash GU12 .... 127 C8
Hazel Rd. Mytch GU16 .... 86 A2
Hazel Rd. Woodh RH2 .... 139 C7
Hazel Way. Crawl D RH10 .. 204 C8
Hazel Way. Fetch KT22 .... 94 C4
Hazel Wlk. Dork RH5 .... 136 C4
Hazelbank Ct. Chert KT16 .... 33 C1
Hazelbank Rd. Catf SE6 .... 24 E6
Hazelbank Rd. Chert KT16 .... 33 C2
Hazelbury Cl. Merton SW19 . 40 A7
Hazeldene. Addl KT15 .... 52 C5
Hazeldene Ct. Kenley CR8 .... 80 D4
Hazelhurst. Beck BR3 .... 44 D8
Hazelhurst. Horley RH6 ...... 161 C4
Hazelhurst Cl. Burph GU4 . 110 B6
Hazelhurst Cres.
Horsh RH12 .... 216 F1
Hazelhurst Ct. Catf SE6 .... 24 C3
Hazelhurst Dr. Worth RH10 202 E6
Hazelhurst Rd.
Up Toot SW17 .... 20 D4
Hazelhurst Sch.
Wimble SW20 .... 39 D8
Hazell Hill. Brack RG12 .... 27 C6
Hazell Rd. Farnh GU9 .... 124 F1
Hazelmere Cl. Hatton TW14 .. 3 E1
Hazelmere Cl. Leahd KT22 ... 95 B8
Hazelmere Ct. 10
Streat SW2 .... 21 F7
Hazelwick Ave. Crawl RH10 202 B8
Hazelwick Mill La.
Crawl RH10 .... 202 A8
Hazelwick Rd. Crawl RH10 202 A7
Hazelwick Sch. Crawl RH10 202 A8
Hazelwood. Crawl RH11 .... 201 A5
Hazelwood Ave.
Morden SM4 .... 40 B5
Hazelwood Cl.
Crawl D RH10 .... 203 F8
Hazelwood Cotts.
Cran GU6 .... 194 D4
Hazelwood Cotts.
Godal GU7 .... 150 D4
Hazelwood Ct. Surb KT6 ...... 37 E3
Hazelwood Gr. Sander CR2 .. 81 B6
Hazelwood House. Beck BR2 44 E6
Hazelwood La. Chips CR5 .... 98 F8
Hazelwood Lodge.
W Wick BR4 .... 44 C2
Hazelwood Rd. Knaph GU21 68 E1
Hazelwood Rd. Oxted RH8 123 B3
Hazelwood Sch. Limps RH8 123 A4
Hazledean Rd.
Croy CR0 & CR9 .... 61 D8
Hazleden Cross.
E Grins RH19 .... 205 B6
Hazledene Rd. Chisw W4 .... 7 C8
Hazlemere Gdns.
N Cheam KT4 .... 39 A1
Hazlewood. Elst GU8 .... 148 E4
Hazlitt Cl. Felt TW13 .... 15 E4
Hazon Way. Epsom KT19 ..... 76 C7
Headcorn Pl. Thorn H CR7 .... 41 F5
Headcorn Rd. Broml BR1 ..... 24 F3
Headcorn Rd. Thorn H CR7 .. 41 F5
Headington Cl. Woki RG11 .. 25 D8
Headington Dr. Woki RG11 .. 25 D8
Headington Rd.
Wands SW18 .... 20 C6
Headlam Rd. Streat SW4 ..... 21 D8
Headland Way. Lingf RH7 . 164 D4
Headley Ave.
Wallin CR0 & SM6 .... 60 F5
Headley Cl. Chess KT19 .... 57 A4
Headley Cl. Crawl RH10 .... 182 D1
Headley Common Rd.
Head KT18 & KT20 .... 116 D7
Headley Ct. For Hil SE26 ...... 23 C3
Headley Dr. Burgh H KT20 ... 97 B8
Headley Dr. New Add CR0 .... 63 C3
Headley Gr. Burgh H KT20 ... 97 C7
Headley Gr. Head KT20 ..... 116 D7
Headley Heath App.
Box H KT20 .... 116 B4
Headley Hill Rd.
Head Dn GU35 .... 187 A5
Headley Rd. Ashtd KT18 .... 96 C6
Headley Rd. Graysh GU26 .. 188 C3
Headley Rd. Head KT18 .... 96 A4
Headley Rd. Hind GU26 ...... 188 C3
Headley Rd. Lang V KT21 ..... 96 C8
Headley Rd.
Leahd KT18 & KT22 .... 95 E4
Headley Rd. Mickle RH5 ..... 115 E7
Headway Cl. Rich TW10 .... 17 C4
Headway The. Ewell KT17 .... 57 F2
Hearn Vale. Head Dn GU35 187 A7
Hearn Wlk. Brack RG12 .... 27 E8
Hearne Rd. Brent W4 .... 7 A8
Hearnville Prim Sch.
Balham SW12 .... 21 A7
Hearnville Rd. Balham SW12 21 A7
Hearsey Gdns. Blckw GU17 . 64 B6
Hearsey Gdns. Blckw GU17 . 64 C6
Heath Bsns Ctr The.
Hounsl TW3 .... 5 C3
Heath Cl. Banstd SM7 .... 78 B5
Heath Cl. Beac H GU26 .... 188 C7
Heath Cl. Broad H RH12 ..... 216 E3
Heath Cl. Harl UB3 .... 3 D7
Heath Cl. Heath E GU9 .... 125 C7
Heath Cl. Stan TW19 .... 2 C1
Heath Cl. Vir W GU25 .... 31 D5
Heath Cl. Woki RG11 .... 25 B4
Heath Clark Tertiary Ctr.
Croy CR9 .... 61 A6
Heath Cotts. Beac H GU26 . 188 C6
Heath Ct. Broad H RH12 . 216 E3
Heath Dr. Brookw GU24 .... 88 A7
Heath Dr. Send GU23 .... 90 B5
Heath Dr. Sutton SM2 .... 59 C2
Heath Dr. W Barn SW20 .... 39 C5
Heath Dr. Walt o t H KT20 .... 97 A2
Heath End Sch.Heath E GU9 125 E6
Heath Gdns. Twick TW1 .... 16 F6
Heath Gr. Ashf TW16 .... 14 F1
Heath Gr. Penge SE20 .... 23 C1
Heath Hill. Docken GU10 .... 166 E3
Heath Hill. Dork RH4 .... 136 B7
Heath Hill Rd N.
Crowth RG11 .... 45 B5
Heath Hill Rd S.
Crowth RG11 .... 45 B4
Heath House. Thorn H CR7 .. 42 A4
Heath House. Weyb KT13 .... 53 A6
Heath House Rd.
Woking GU22 .... 88 D5
Heath La. Albury GU5 .... 132 E2
Heath La. Crond GU10 .... 124 B7
Heath La. Godal GU7 & GU8 151 A2
Heath La. Heath E GU9 .... 125 C7
Heath Mead. Wimble SW19 . 19 D5
Heath Mill La. Pirb GU3 .... 88 C2
Heath Rd. Bagsh GU19 .... 47 E3
Heath Rd. Cater CR3 .... 100 D3
Heath Rd. Horse GU21 .... 69 F4
Heath Rd. Islew TW3 & TW7 . 5 C3
Heath Rd. Linch GU27 .... 207 D5
Heath Rd. Oxsh KT22 .... 74 C7
Heath Rd. S Norw CR7 .... 42 C6
Heath Rd. Twick TW1 .... 16 F7
Heath Rd. Weyb KT13 .... 53 A5
Heath Ridge Gn.
Cobham KT11 .... 74 A6
Heath Rise. Camb GU15 .... 65 D5
Heath Rise. Hayes BR2 .... 44 F3
Heath Rise. Vir W GU25 .... 31 D5
Heath Rise. Westc RH4 ...... 135 C5
Heath The. Cater CR3 .... 100 C3
Heath View. E Hors KT24 ..... 92 F2
Heath Way. Horsh RH12 ... 217 D5
Heathacre. Poyle SL3 .... 1 E6
Heatham Pk. Twick TW2 ...... 16 F8
Heathbridge. Whit V KT13 ... 53 A4
Heathcote. Tadw KT20 .... 97 D5
Heathcote Cl. Ash GU12 ... 106 A3
Heathcote Dr. E Grins RH19 185 C2
Heathcote Rd. Ash GU12 ... 106 B3
Heathcote Rd. Camb GU15 .. 65 D5
Heathcote Rd. Epsom KT18 . 76 E6
Heathcote Rd. Twick TW1 ..... 6 B2
Heathcroft Ave. Ashf TW16 . 14 F1
Heathdale Ave. Hounsl TW4 .. 4 E4
Heathdene. Burgh H KT20 .... 77 E1
Heathdene Rd. Streat SW16 21 F1
Heathdene Rd.
Wallin SM5 & SM6 .... 60 B3
Heathdown Rd. Mayb GU22 70 D4
Heathedge.
For Hil SE23 & SE26 .... 23 B6
Heather Cl. Alder GU11 ...... 104 E1
Heather Cl. Ash GU12 .... 106 B5
Heather Cl. Copth RH10 .... 183 B2
Heather Cl. Hampt TW12 ..... 35 F8
Heather Cl. Horse GU21 .... 69 C4
Heather Cl. Horsh RH12 .... 217 D5
Heather Cl. Islew TW7 .... 5 D2
Heather Cl. Kings KT20 .... 97 E5
Heather Cl. Stough GU2 ..... 109 B3
Heather Cl. Woodhm KT15 ... 52 B1
Heather Cl. Wreccl GU9 ..... 145 F6
Heather Cotts. Ash V GU12 106 A8
Heather Ct. Hind GU26 .... 188 F4
Heather Dr. Sunnin SL5 .... 30 B2
Heather Gdns. Belm SM2 ..... 59 A4
Heather Mead. Friml GU16 .. 65 F2
Heather Mead Ct.Friml GU16 65 F2
Heather Pl. 4 Esher KT10 .... 55 B6
Heather Ridge Arc.
Friml GU15 .... 66 C4
Heather Ridge Fst Sch.
Friml GU15 .... 66 D4
Heather Way. Burrh GU24 .... 49 E3
Heather Way. Hind GU26 .... 188 F4
Heather Way. S Croy CR2 ..... 62 D2
Heather Wlk. Crawl RH11 . 201 B3
Heather Wlk. Pirb GU24 .... 87 D7
Heather Wlk. Smallf RH6 ... 162 C3
Heather Wlk. Twick TW4 ...... 16 A8
Heather Wlk. Whit V KT12 .... 53 F1
Heatherdale Cl. King U T KT2 18 B1
Heatherdale Rd. Camb GU15 65 D4
Heatherdeane. W Hors KT24 92 D2
Heatherdene Cl. Mitch CR4 . 40 E5
Heatherdene Mansions. 2
Twick TW1 .... 6 D1
Heatherlands. Ashf TW16 .... 15 A2
Heatherlands. Horley RH6 161 B4
Heatherley Cl. Camb GU15 .. 65 B5
Heatherley Rd. Camb GU15 . 65 B5
Heathermount. Brack RG12 . 27 E5
Heathermount Dr.
Crowth RG11 .... 45 A6
Heathermount Sch.
Ascot SL5 .... 29 D3
Heathers Land. Dork RH5 . 136 C4
Heathers The. Stan TW19 .... 13 F8
Heatherset Gdns.
S Norw SW16 .... 21 F1
Heatherside Dr. Went GU25 31 A3
Heatherside Rd.
W Ewell KT19 .... 57 D3
Heatherside Rd.
W Ewell KT19 .... 57 D3
Heathervale Rd.
Woodhm KT15 .... 52 B1
Heatherway. Crowth RG11 ... 45 A5
Heatherway.
Felb RH19 & RH7 .... 184 F7
Heatherwood Hospl.
Ascot SL5 .... 28 E6
Heathfield. Cobham KT11 ..... 74 A5
Heathfield. Crawl RH10 ...... 202 D8
Heathfield. Reig RH2 .... 138 D8
Heathfield Ave. Ascot SL5 .... 29 E4
Heathfield Ave.Wands SW18 20 D8
Heathfield Cl. Godal GU7 ... 150 E2
Heathfield Cl. Woking GU22 70 A1
Heathfield Ct. Ashf TW15 .... 13 E5
Heathfield Ct. Penge SE20 ... 23 C1
Heathfield Ct. Wands SW18 20 D8
Heathfield Dr. Earls RH1 .... 139 E4
Heathfield Dr. Mitch SW19 .. 20 E1
Heathfield Gdns. Croy CR0 .. 61 D6
Heathfield Inf Sch.
Twick TW2 .... 16 A7
Heathfield Jun Sch.
Twick TW2 .... 16 A7
Heathfield N.
Twick TW1 & TW2 .... 16 F8
Heathfield Rd. Broml BR1 .... 24 F1
Heathfield Rd. Croy CR0 ...... 61 D6
Heathfield Rd. Hersh KT12 .. 54 E6
Heathfield Rd. Wands SW18 20 D8
Heathfield Rd. Woking GU22 70 A1
Heathfield S.
Twick TW1 & TW2 .... 16 F8
Heathfield Sch. Wink SL5 ..... 28 B7
Heathfield Sq. Wands SW18 20 D8
Heathfield Vale. S Croy CR2 62 E2
Heathhurst Rd. S Croy CR2 .. 61 E2
Heathland Sch The.
Hounsl TW4 .... 4 F1
Heathland St. Alder GU11 . 105 A2
Heathlands. Tadw KT20 .... 97 D5
Heathlands. Up Toot SW12 .. 21 B6
Heathlands. Weyb KT13 .... 53 C5
Heathlands Cl. Horse GU21 . 69 E5
Heathlands Cl. Sunby TW16 35 A7
Heathlands Cl. Twick TW1 ... 16 F7
Heathlands Country Mkt.
Woki RG11 .... 25 E1
Heathlands Ct. Hounsl TW4 ... 4 E2
Heathlands Ct. Mitch CR4 .... 41 A6
Heathlands Rd. Woki RG11 .. 25 E2
Heathlands Sch.
Wimble SW19 .... 19 C5
Heathlands Way. Hounsl TW4 4 E2
Heathmere Prim Sch.
Rhampt SW15 .... 19 A7
Heathmoors. Easth RG12 ..... 27 C4
Heathpark Dr. Windl GU20 .. 48 E4
Heathrise. Ripley GU23 .... 91 B4
Heathrow. Gomsh GU5 .... 133 C4
Heathrow Airport London.
Harm TW6 .... 3 A5
Heathrow Bvd. Harm UB7 ...... 2 F7
Heathrow Causeway Est.
Hounsl TW4 .... 4 B4
Heathrow Central Sta.
Harl TW6 .... 3 B4
Heathrow Cl. Harm TW6 .... 2 B6
Heathrow International Trad Est.
Hounsl TW4 .... 4 B4
Heathrow Prim Sch.
Harm UB7 .... 2 F8
Heathrow Terminal 4 Sta.
E Bed TW6 .... 3 C1
Heathshot. 8 Rich TW10 ...... 6 E1
Heathside. Hinch W KT10 ..... 55 E7
Heathside. Twick TW4 .... 15 F8
Heathside. Weyb KT13 .... 53 B5
Heathside Cl. Hinch W KT10 55 E7
Heathside Cres.
Woking GU22 .... 69 F2
Heathside Ct. Tadw KT20 .... 97 C4
Heathside Gdns.
Woking GU22 .... 70 A2
Heathside La. Beac H GU26 188 D6
Heathside Park Rd.
Woking GU22 .... 70 A1
Heathside Rd. Woking GU22 69 F1
Heathside Sch. Weyb KT13 .. 52 F4
Heathvale Bridge Rd.
Ash V GU12 .... 106 A6
Heathview Ct. Putney SW19 19 D6
Heathview Gdns.
Putney SW15 .... 19 C8
Heathview Rd. Thorn H CR7 42 A5
Heathview Rd. Witley GU8 170 E7
Heathway. Camb GU15 .... 65 D5
Heathway. Cater CR3 .... 100 D2
Heathway. Croy CR0 .... 62 F7
Heathway. E Hors KT24 .... 93 A3
Heathway. N Asct SL5 .... 28 E8
Heathway Cl. Camb GU15 .... 65 D5
Heathwood. Tadw KT20 .... 97 C4
Heathwood Ct. Hounsl TW3 .. 5 B3
Heathwood Ct. Streat SW12 21 C7
Heathwood Point. 7
For Hil SE26 .... 23 D5
Heathyfields Rd. Hale GU9 125 A6
Heaton Rd. Mitch CR4 .... 21 A1
Heavers Farm Prim Sch.
S Norw SE25 .... 42 F4
Hebdon Rd. Up Toot SW17 .. 20 F5
Heddon Cl. Islew TW7 .... 6 A3
Heddon Wlk. 1
W Heath GU14 .... 85 A7
Hedge Cnr. Tadw KT20 .... 97 C4
Hedge Croft Cotts.
Ripley GU23 .... 91 B6
Hedge Wlk. Catf SE6 .... 24 B4
Hedgehog La.
Haslem GU27 .... 208 B5
Hedgerley Ct. Horse GU21 ... 69 C2
Hedgeside. Crawl RH11 ..... 201 C1
Hedgeway. Onsl V GU2 ...... 130 A7
Hedingham Cl. Horley RH6 161 C4
Hedley Rd. Twick TW4 .... 16 A8
Heelas Rd. Woki RG11 .... 25 A5
Heenan Cl. Friml GU16 .... 85 E7
Heighton Gdns. Croy CR0 .... 61 B5
Heights Cl. Nork SM7 .... 77 E3
Heights Cl. Wimble SW20 .... 19 B1
Heights The. Beck BR3 .... 24 C1
Helder Gr. Lewish SE12 .... 24 F8
Helder St. Croy CR2 .... 61 D4
Heldmann Cl. Islew TW7 .... 5 D3
Helen Ave. Felt TW14 .... 15 B8
Helen Cl. E Mole KT8 .... 36 B5
Helen Ct. Farnb GU14 .... 85 B4
Helena Cl. Wallin SM6 .... 60 E3
Helford Wlk. 3
Woking GU21 .... 69 A1
Helgiford Gdns. Ashf TW16 . 14 E1
Helicon House. Crawl RH11 201 C5
Helix Ho. Islew TW7 .... 6 B5
Helksham Cl. Sandh GU15 ... 45 D1
Helme Cl. Wimble SW19 ...... 19 F3
Helmsdale. Brack RG12 .... 27 E4
Helmsdale. 3 Woking GU21 69 B1
Helmsdale Rd. Streat SW16 21 D1
Helston Cl. Friml GU16 .... 86 A7
Helvellyn Cl. Thor L TW20 .... 12 C1
Helvetia St. For Hil SE6 .... 23 F6
Hemingford Rd. Cheam SM3 58 C6
Hemlock Cl. Kings KT20 .... 97 E4
Hemming Cl. 7
Hampt TW12 .... 36 A8
Hempshaw Ave.
Woodm SM7 .... 78 F3
Hemsby Rd. Chess KT9 .... 56 F4
Hemsby Wlk. Crawl RH10 . 202 B4
Henage Cnr. Burrh GU24 ..... 49 E2
Henbane Ct. 2
Crawl RH11 .... 201 B2
Henbit Cl. Burgh H KT20 ...... 97 B8
Henchley Dene.
Merrow GU4 .... 110 D4
Henderson Ave.
Stough GU2 .... 109 B5
Henderson Hospl. Belm SM2 59 B2
Henderson Rd. Bigg H TN16 83 C7
Henderson Rd. Crawl RH11 201 B1
Henderson Rd. Thorn H CR0 42 D3
Henderson Rd. Wands SW18 20 E8
Henderson Way.
Horsh RH12 .... 216 F1
Hendfield Ct. 5 Wallin SM6 60 B4
Hendham Rd. Up Toot SW17 20 F6
Hendon Terr. Ashf TW15 ..... 14 D2
Hendon Way. Stan TW19 ...... 2 D1
Hendrick Ave. Balham SW12 20 F8
Heneage Cres. New Add CR0 63 C1
Henfield Rd.
Merton SW19 & SW20 .... 39 F8
Henfold Cotts.
Bear Gn RH5 .... 158 A2
Henfold Dr. Bear Gn RH5 .... 157 E3
Henfold La. Bear Gn RH5 .... 157 F5
Hengelo Gdns. Mitch CR4 .... 40 D5
Hengist Cl. Horsh RH12 ..... 217 A1
Hengist Way.
Beck BR2 & BR3 .... 44 E5
Hengrave Rd. For Hil SE23 ... 23 D8
Hengrove Cres. Ashf TW15 . 13 D5
Henhurst Cross La.
Coldh RH5 .... 157 A2
Henley Ave. Cheam SM3 ...... 58 E7
Henley Bank. Onsl V GU2 .. 130 A7
Henley Cl. Hounsl TW7 .... 5 F6
Henley Cl. W Heath GU14 .... 84 E8
Henley Ct. Mitch CR4 .... 41 A6
Henley Ct. Old Wok GU22 .... 90 A7
Henley Dr. Friml GU16 .... 85 E7
Henley Dr. King U T KT2 .... 18 F1
Henley Gate.
Pirb GU24 & GU3 .... 107 C8
Henley Lodge. S Norw SE25 42 F5
Henley Way. Felt TW13 .... 15 D3
Henley Wood. Chelsh CR6 ... 82 A2
Hennel Cl. For Hil SE23 .... 23 C5
Hennessy Ct. Sheer GU21 .... 70 C6
Henry Cavendish Prim Sch.
Streat SW12 .... 21 C7
Henry Hatch Ct. Sutton SM2 59 C3
Hensford Gdns. For Hil SE26 23 B4
Henshaw Cl. Crawl RH11 ... 200 F4
Henslow Way. Sheer GU21 .. 70 D5
Henson Rd. Crawl RH10 .... 202 B7
Hensworth Rd. Stain TW15 . 13 D3
Henty Cl. Crawl RH11 .... 200 E3
Hepburn Gdns. W Wick BR2 44 F1
Hepple Cl. Islew TW7 .... 6 B5

Hepplewhite Cl.
Crawl RH11 ... 201 B1
Hepworth Croft.
Sandh GU15 ... 64 E6
Hepworth Ct. Cheam SM3 ... 40 A1
Hepworth Rd. Streat SW16 . 21 E1
Hepworth Way.
Walt O T KT12 ... 34 F1
Heracles Cl. Wallin SM6 ... 60 E3
Herald Gdns. Hackb SM6 ... 60 B7
Herbert Cl. Easth RG12 ... 27 B4
Herbert Cres. Knaph GU21 .. 68 E1
Herbert Gdns. Chisw W4 ... 7 B8
Herbert Rd. King U T KT1 ... 37 F6
Herbert Rd. Merton SW19 ... 19 F1
Herbs End. W Heath GU14 ... 84 C5
Hereford Cl. Crawl RH10 ... 201 E2
Hereford Cl. Epsom KT18 ... 76 D6
Hereford Cl. Stain TW18 ... 33 B8
Hereford Cl. Stough GU2 ... 108 F3
Hereford Copse.
Woking GU22 ... 89 B8
Hereford Ct. 6 Croy CR0 ... 42 F1
Hereford Gdns. Twick TW2 .. 16 C7
Hereford La. Hale GU9 ... 125 B7
Hereford Rd. Felt TW13 ... 15 C7
Hereford Way. Chess KT9 ... 56 D5
Hereward Ave. Purley CR8 ... 61 A1
Hereward Rd. Up Toot SW17 20 F4
Heriot Rd. Chert KT16 ... 33 A2
Heritage Ct. 2
Egham TW20 ... 12 A3
Heritage House. 22
Putney SW19 ... 19 D7
Heritage Lawn. Horley RH6 161 C4
Herlwyn Gdns.
Up Toot SW17 ... 20 F4
Herm Cl. Crawl RH11 ... 201 A2
Hermes House. Penge BR3 .. 43 E8
Hermes Way. Wallin SM6 ... 60 D3
Hermitage Cl. Clayg KT10 ... 56 A4
Hermitage Cl. Farnb GU14 ... 85 D1
Hermitage Cl. Friml GU16 ... 65 F1
Hermitage Cl.
Shep Gn TW17 ... 34 A5
Hermitage Ct. Stain TW18 ... 12 F3
Hermitage Cty Fst Sch The.
Knaph GU21 ... 88 E8
Hermitage Cty Jun Sch The.
Knaph GU21 ... 88 E8
Hermitage Dr. N Asct SL5 ... 28 E7
Hermitage Gdns.
S Norw SE19 ... 22 C1
Hermitage La. Croy CR0 ... 43 A3
Hermitage La.
E Grins RH19 ... 205 F8
Hermitage La. Streat SW16 . 21 F1
Hermitage Par. Ascot SL5 ... 29 A6
Hermitage Rd.
E Grins RH19 ... 185 D3
Hermitage Rd. Kenley CR8 .. 80 C3
Hermitage Rd. Knaph GU21 . 88 D8
Hermitage Rd. Knaph GU21 . 88 F8
Hermitage Rd. S Norw SE19 22 D2
Hermitage The. Barnes SW13 7 F6
Hermitage The. Felt TW13 .. 14 F5
Hermitage The. For Hil SE23 23 C7
Hermitage The.
King U T KT1 ... 37 D5
Hermitage The. Rich TW10 ... 6 E2
Hermitage Woods Cres.
Knaph GU21 ... 88 E7
Hermits Rd. Crawl RH10 ... 201 F7
Hermonger La. Ell Gn RH12 195 F2
Herndon Cl. Egham TW20 ... 12 A4
Herne Rd. Surb KT6 ... 56 E8
Heron Cl. Crawl RH11 ... 201 C8
Heron Cl. Mytch GU16 ... 85 F4
Heron Cl. N Asct SL5 ... 28 D8
Heron Cl. Stough GU2 ... 109 B4
Heron Ct. Dork RH4 ... 136 A8
Heron Ct. 5 King U T KT1 ... 37 E6
Heron Ct. Stan TW19 ... 13 E7
Heron Ct. 6 W Norw SE21 .. 22 D6
Heron Dale. Addl KT15 ... 52 D5
Heron House. Tedd KT1 ... 37 C8
Heron Pl. E Grins RH19 ... 205 F8
Heron Rd. Croy CR0 ... 61 E8
Heron Rd. Islew TW1 ... 6 B3
Heron Shaw. Cran GU6 ... 174 E1
Heron Sq. 25 Rich TW10 ... 6 D2
Heron Way. Horsh RH13 ... 218 A1
Heron Way Cty Prim Sch.
Horsh RH13 ... 218 A1
Heron Wlk. Sheer GU21 ... 70 C5
Heron Wood Rd.
Alder GU12 ... 126 D7
Heron's Way. Woki RG11 ... 25 E7
Herondale. Easth RG12 ... 27 C2
Herondale. Selsd CR2 ... 62 D2
Herondale. Shottm GU27 ... 207 E6
Herondale Ave.
Wands SW18 ... 20 E7
Heronfield. Eng Gn TW20 ... 11 C2
Heronry The. Whit V KT12 ... 54 A4
Herons Cl. Dome RH10 ... 184 B5
Herons Croft. Whit V KT13 ... 53 D4
Herons Lea. Dome RH10 ... 184 A4
Herons Pl. Islew TW7 ... 6 B4
Herons Way. Pirb GU24 ... 87 D6
Herons Wood Ct.
Horley RH6 ... 161 B4
Heronscourt. Lhtwat GU18 .. 67 C8
Herontye Dr. E Grins RH19 206 A8
Herrett St. Alder GU12 ... 126 D8
Herretts Gdns. Alder GU12 105 D1
Herrick Cl. Crawl RH10 ... 202 C8
Herrick Cl. Friml GU16 ... 66 C3
Herrick Ct. 4 Rich TW10 ... 17 D4
Herrings La. Windl GU20 ... 48 D4
Herschel Wlk. 9
Crawl RH11 ... 201 B1
Herschell Rd. For Hil SE23 ... 23 E8
Hersham Cl. Rhampt SW15 .. 19 A8
Hersham Gdns. Hersh KT12 54 C6
Hersham Rd. Hersh KT12 ... 54 D6
Hersham Rd. Walt O T KT12 54 B7
Hersham Sta. Hersh KT12 ... 54 E7
Hersham Trad Est.
Walt O T KT12 ... 54 E8
Hershell Ct. Mortl SW14 ... 7 B3
Hertford Ave. Mortl SW14 ... 7 E3
Hertford Lodge. 10
Putney SW19 ... 19 E7
Hertford Sq. Mitch CR4 ... 41 E5
Hertford Way. Mitch CR4 ... 41 E5
Hesiers Hill. Chelsh CR6 ... 82 E2
Hesiers Rd. Chelsh CR6 ... 82 F3
Hesketh Cl. Cran GU6 ... 174 E3
Heslop Ct. 2 Up Toot SW12 21 A7
Heslop Rd. Up Toot SW12 ... 20 F7
Hessle Gr. Ewell KT17 ... 76 F8
Hester Terr. Rich TW9 ... 7 A4
Hesterman Way.
Croy CR0 & CR9 ... 41 F1
Heston Ave. Heston TW5 ... 4 E7
Heston Comm Sch.
Heston TW5 ... 5 A7
Heston Grange. Heston TW5 . 4 F8
Heston Grange La.Heston TW5 4 F8
Heston Ind Mall. Heston TW5 4 F7
Heston Inf Sch. Heston TW5 . 5 A7
Heston Jun Sch. Heston TW5 5 A7
Heston Phoenix Distribution Pk.
Heston TW5 ... 4 C8
Heston Rd. Earls RH1 ... 139 F4
Heston Rd. Heston TW5 ... 5 A7
Heston Wlk. Earls RH1 ... 139 F4
Hetherington Rd.
Charlt TW17 ... 34 C7
Hetley Gdns. 1
S Norw SE19 ... 22 F1
Hevers Ave. Horley RH6 ... 161 A4
Hewers Way. Burgh H KT20 . 97 C7
Hewitt Cl. Croy CR0 ... 63 A7
Hewitts Ind Est. Cran GU6 174 B3
Hewlett Pl. Bagsh GU19 ... 47 F3
Hewshott La. Linch GU30 .. 207 A5
Hexal Rd. Catf SE6 ... 24 E5
Hexham Cl. Crawl RH10 ... 202 E6
Hexham Cl. Sandh GU15 ... 45 D2
Hexham Gdns. Hounsl TW7 ... 6 A7
Hexham Rd. Cheam SM4 ... 40 B1
Hexham Rd. W Norw SE27 ... 22 C6
Hextalls La. Bletch RH1 ... 120 E6
Heybridge Ave. Streat SW16 21 F2
Heydon Ct. W Wick BR4 ... 63 E8
Heyford Ave. Merton SW20 . 39 F6
Heyford Rd. Mitch CR4 ... 40 E7
Heymede. Leahd KT22 ... 95 C4
Heythorp St. Wands SW18 .. 19 F6
Heythorpe Cl. Woking GU21 68 F2
Heyward Ct. Belm SM2 ... 59 A4
Hibernia Gdns. Hounsl TW3 .. 5 A2
Hibernia Rd. Hounsl TW3 ... 5 A3
Hickey's Almshouses. 7
Rich TW9 ... 6 F3
Hickling Wlk. Crawl RH10 . 202 B4
Hickmans Cl. Godst RH9 ... 121 C3
Hicks La. Blckw GU17 ... 64 B5
Hidaburn Ct. 7
Streat SW16 ... 21 C4
Hidcote Gdns. W Barn SW20 39 B6
Hidcote House. Sutton SM2 . 59 C3
Hidecote Cl. Mayb GU22 ... 70 B3
Higgins Wlk. Hampt TW12 ... 15 E2
Higgs La. Bagsh GU19 ... 47 D3
High Ashton. 11
King U T KT2 ... 18 B1
High Ashurst (Outdoor Ctr).
Head RH5 ... 116 A7
High Barn Rd.
Wotton KT24 & RH5 ... 113 E3
High Beech. Brack RG12 ... 27 F5
High Beech. S Croy CR2 ... 61 E3
High Beeches. Friml GU16 ... 65 D2
High Beeches.
Nork KT17 & SM7 ... 77 D5
High Beeches Cl. Wallin CR8 60 D1
High Broom Cres.
W Wick BR4 ... 44 B2
High Cedar Dr.
Wimble SW20 ... 19 B1
High Close Sch. Woki RG11 . 25 C7
High Coombe Pl.
King U T KT2 ... 18 D1
High Down Rd. Sutton SM2 . 78 B8
High Dr. King U T KT2 & KT3 38 C7
High Dr. Oxsh KT22 ... 74 D5
High Dr. Wold CR3 ... 102 A5
High Fields. Sunnin SL5 ... 29 F4
High Foleys. Clayg KT10 ... 56 B3
High Gables. Beck BR2 ... 44 E7
High Garth. Esher KT10 ... 55 C4
High Hill Rd. Farlgh CR6 ... 82 C5
High Hill Rd. Fickl CR6 ... 82 C5
High La. Haslem GU27 ... 208 C8
High La. Warlgm CR3 & CR6 101 F8
High Level Dr. For Hil SE26 .. 23 A4
High Limes. 2
W Norw SE19 ... 22 E2
High Loxley Rd. Dunsf GU8 193 B7
High Mead. W Wick BR4 ... 63 E8
High Meadow Cl. Dork RH4 136 B6
High Oaks. Crawl RH11 ... 201 B4
High Par The. Streat SW16 .. 21 E5
High Park Ave. E Hors KT24 92 F1
High Park Ave. Rich TW9 ... 7 A6
High Park Rd. Farnh GU9 ... 125 C3
High Park Rd. Rich TW9 ... 7 A6
High Path. Merton SW19 ... 40 C8
High Path Rd. Merrow GU1 110 C1
High Pewley. Guild GU1 ... 130 E7
High Pine Cl. Weyb KT13 ... 53 C5
High Pines. Warlgm CR6 ... 101 C8
High Pitfold. Shottm GU26 188 D1
High Rd. Byfl KT14 ... 71 E6
High Rd. Chips CR5 & RH2 ... 98 F4
High Rd. Kings CR5 & RH2 ... 98 F4
High Rd. L Kings CR5 & RH2 . 98 F4
High Ridge. Godal GU7 ... 150 D2
High St. Addl KT15 ... 52 B6
High St. Alder GU11 ... 105 A2
High St.
Alder GU11 & GU12 ... 105 B1
High St. Ascot SL5 ... 29 A6
High St. Ascot SL5 ... 29 D4
High St. Bagsh GU19 ... 47 E3
High St. Banstd SM7 ... 78 B4
High St. Beck BR3 ... 44 A7
High St. Bletch RH1 ... 120 D2
High St. Brack RG12 ... 27 B7
High St. Brack RG12 ... 27 C7
High St. Bramly GU5 ... 151 F6
High St. Brent TW8 ... 6 D7
High St. Brent TW8 ... 6 E8
High St. Camb GU15 ... 65 D6
High St. Carsh SM5 ... 60 A6
High St. Cater CR3 ... 100 E4
High St. Cheam SM1 & SM3 . 58 E4
High St. Chidd GU8 ... 191 F2
High St. Chobh GU24 ... 68 E8
High St. Clayg KT10 ... 55 F4
High St. Cobham KT11 ... 73 B4
High St. Coln SL3 ... 1 C7
High St. Cran GU6 ... 174 D3
High St. Cranf TW5 ... 4 B7
High St. Crawl RH11 ... 201 D6
High St. Crowth RG11 ... 45 C4
High St. Croy SE25 ... 43 A5
High St. Croy CR0 & CR9 ... 61 C7
High St. Dork RH4 ... 136 B8
High St. E Grins RH19 ... 205 F8
High St. E Mole KT8 ... 36 A5
High St. Egham TW20 ... 11 F3
High St. Epsom KT17 & KT18 76 D6
High St. Esher KT10 ... 55 B6
High St. Esher KT10 ... 55 C6
High St. Ewell KT17 ... 58 A2
High St. Farnb GU14 ... 105 D8
High St. Felt TW13 ... 15 A6
High St. G Book KT23 ... 94 B2
High St. Godal GU7 ... 150 D4
High St. Godst RH9 ... 121 C4
High St. Guild GU1 & GU2 .. 130 D7
High St. Hampt TW12 ... 16 C2
High St. Harl UB3 ... 3 D8
High St. Harm UB7 ... 2 D8
High St. Haslem GU27 ... 208 D7
High St. Heston TW5 ... 4 B7
High St. Horley RH6 ... 161 B3
High St. Horse GU21 ... 69 C3
High St. Hounsl TW3 ... 5 B4
High St. King U T KT1 ... 37 D6
High St. Knaph GU21 ... 68 C2
High St. Leahd KT22 ... 95 B5
High St. Limps RH8 ... 123 B7
High St. Lingf RH7 ... 164 D4
High St. Merst RH1 ... 119 B7
High St. New Mal KT3 ... 38 E5
High St. Nutf RH1 ... 119 F2
High St. Old Wok GU22 ... 90 B6
High St. Oxsh KT22 ... 74 D5
High St. Oxted RH8 ... 122 D5
High St.
Penge SE19 & SE20 & BR3 ... 23 C1
High St. Purley CR8 ... 80 A8
High St. Redh RH1 ... 118 F2
High St. Reig RH2 ... 118 A1
High St. Ripley GU23 ... 91 C6
High St. Rowl GU10 ... 145 E4
High St. Rusper RH12 ... 199 D7
High St. S Norw CR7 & SE25 42 D5
High St. S Norw SE25 ... 43 A6
High St. Sandh GU17 ... 45 A1
High St. Sandh GU17 ... 64 A8
High St. Shep TW17 ... 34 C3
High St. Stain TW18 ... 12 F4
High St. Stan TW19 ... 2 D1
High St. Sunnin SL5 ... 30 A4
High St. Sutton SM1 & SM2 .. 59 B5
High St. Sutton SM1 ... 59 B6
High St. Tadw KT20 ... 97 C4
High St. Tedd TW12 ... 16 C2
High St. Tedd TW11 ... 17 A3
High St. Tedd KT1 ... 37 D8
High St. Thame D KT7 ... 37 A3
High St. Twick TW2 ... 16 C8
High St. Tyl Gn RH9 ... 121 C4
High St. W End GU24 ... 67 F7
High St. W Wick BR4 ... 44 B1
High St. Walt O T KT12 ... 35 A1
High St. Weyb KT13 ... 53 A6
High St. Wimble SW19 ... 19 D3
High St. Woking GU21 ... 69 F2
High St Mews.
Wimble SW19 ... 19 E3
High Street Collier's Wood.
Mitch SW17 & SW19 ... 20 D2
High Street Harlington.
Harl TW6 ... 3 D7
High The. Streat SW16 ... 21 E5
High Thicket Rd.
Docken GU10 ... 166 D5
High Tree Cl. Row Tn KT15 .. 52 A5
High Trees. Croy CR0 ... 43 E1
High Trees. Streat SW2 ... 22 A7
High Trees Cl. Cater CR3 ... 100 F5
High Trees Ct. Cater CR3 ... 100 F4
High Trees Ct. Sidlow RH6 160 A4
High Trees Rd. Reig RH2 .. 139 D8
High View. Belm SM2 ... 77 F8
High View. Gomsh GU5 ... 133 C4
High View. 5 Penge SE19 ... 22 F1
High View Ave.
Wallin CR0 & SM6 ... 60 F5
High View Cl. Farnb GU14 ... 85 A4
High View Cl.
S Norw SE19 & SE25 ... 42 F7
High View Lodge.
Alder GU11 ... 105 A2
High View Prim Sch.
Wallin SM6 ... 60 E5
High View Rd. Farnb GU14 .. 85 A4
High View Rd. Lhtwat GU18 66 F8
High View Rd. Onsl V GU2 . 129 E6
High View Rd. S Norw SE19 . 22 D2
Highams Hill. Crawl RH11 .. 200 F5
Highams La.
Burrh GU20 & GU24 ... 49 A5
Highbarrow Rd. Croy CR0 ... 43 A1
Highbirch Cl. Horsh RH12 . 218 B5
Highbury Ave. S Norw CR7 .. 42 B7
Highbury Cl. New Mal KT3 ... 38 C4
Highbury Cl. W Wick BR4 ... 63 B8
Highbury Cres. Camb GU15 . 66 A8
Highbury Gr. Haslem GU27 208 C8
Highbury Rd. Wimble SW19 19 E3
Highclere. Ascot SL5 ... 29 D4
Highclere. Burph GU1 ... 110 A4
Highclere Cl. Brack RG12 ... 27 E7
Highclere Cl. Kenley CR8 ... 80 C4
Highclere Ct. Knaph GU21 ... 68 C2
Highclere Dr. Camb GU15 ... 66 A7
Highclere Gdns.
Knaph GU21 ... 68 D2
Highclere Rd. Alder GU12 . 126 D8
Highclere Rd. King U T KT3 .. 38 D6
Highclere Rd. Knaph GU21 .. 68 C2
Highclere St. For Hil SE26 ... 23 E4
Highcliffe. Beck BR3 ... 44 B8
Highcliffe Dr. Rhampt SW15 .. 7 F1
Highcotts La.
Send M GU4 & GU23 ... 91 A1
Highcroft. Beac H GU26 ... 188 D6
Highcroft. Milf GU8 ... 170 F8
Highcroft. Purley CR8 ... 79 F5
Highcroft. Sham Gn GU5 ... 152 E4
Highcroft. 2 Surb KT5 ... 37 F4
Highcroft Ct. Fetch KT23 ... 94 A4
Highcroft Dr. Rudg RH12 ... 195 E1
Highcross Way. 4
Rhampt SW15 ... 19 A7
Highdaun Dr. Thorn H SW16 41 F5
Highdene. 6 Woking GU22 . 69 F1
Highdown. New Mal KT4 ... 57 F8
Highdown Ct. Crawl RH10 202 B3
Highdown Way.
Horsh RH12 ... 217 F6
Higher Alham. Brack RG12 .. 27 E2
Higher Dr. Belm KT17 & SM7 77 D6
Higher Dr. E Hors KT24 ... 112 E8
Higher Dr. Purley CR8 ... 80 A6
Higher Gn. Ewell KT17 ... 77 A6
Highercombe Rd.
Haslem GU27 ... 208 E8
Highfield. Easth RG12 ... 26 F3
Highfield. Felt TW14 ... 15 A7
Highfield. Shalf GU4 ... 130 F1
Highfield. Woodm SM7 ... 78 E2
Highfield Ave. Alder GU11 126 A8
Highfield Cl. Alder GU11 ... 126 B8
Highfield Cl. Eng Gn TW20 ... 11 C2
Highfield Cl. Farnb GU14 ... 84 F4
Highfield Cl. Long D KT6 ... 37 C1
Highfield Cl. M Bourn GU9 146 B7
Highfield Cl. Oxsh KT22 ... 74 D8
Highfield Cl. Woki RG11 ... 25 B6
Highfield Cres. Hind GU26 . 188 F4
Highfield Ct. Eng Gn TW20 .. 11 D2
Highfield Ct. Mitch CR4 ... 40 E5
Highfield Ctr (Farnborough Coll
of Tech Annexe).
Alder GU11 ... 126 A8
Highfield Dr. Beck BR2 ... 44 F5
Highfield Dr. W Ewell KT19 .. 57 F4
Highfield Dr. W Ewell KT19 .. 57 F4
Highfield Dr. W Wick BR4 ... 63 C7
Highfield Gdns. Alder GU11 126 B8
Highfield Hill. S Norw SE19 . 22 E1
Highfield Inf Sch. Beck BR2 44 E5
Highfield Jun Sch. Beck BR2 44 E5
Highfield La. Putt GU3 ... 128 A3
Highfield La. Thursl GU8 ... 169 B2
Highfield Path. Farnb GU14 . 84 F4
Highfield Rd. Bigg H TN16 ... 83 C3
Highfield Rd. Carsh SM1 ... 59 E5
Highfield Rd. Cater CR3 ... 101 A5
Highfield Rd. Chert KT16 ... 33 A1
Highfield Rd. E Grins RH19 185 D3
Highfield Rd. Farnb GU14 ... 84 F4
Highfield Rd. Felt TW13 ... 15 A7
Highfield Rd. Hounsl TW7 ... 5 F6
Highfield Rd. Purley CR8 ... 61 A1
Highfield Rd. Tolw KT5 ... 38 C2
Highfield Rd. Up Hall TW16 . 34 F4
Highfield Rd. W Byfl KT14 ... 71 A6
Highfield Rd. Walt O T KT12 35 A1
Highfield Sch.
E Grins RH19 ... 185 D3
Highfield Sch. Wands SW18 20 E8
Highfields. Ashtd KT21 ... 95 D8
Highfields. E Hors KT24 ... 112 F7
Highfields. Fetch KT22 ... 94 D3
Highfields. For Row RH18 .. 206 F2
Highfields. Sutton SM1 ... 59 A8
Highgate Ct. Crawl RH11 ... 201 C2
Highgate House. 11
For Hil SE26 ... 23 A5
Highgate La. Farnb GU14 ... 85 C5
Highgate Rd.
For Row RH18 ... 206 F1
Highgrove. 2 Farnb GU14 .. 85 B7
Highgrove Ct. Beck BR3 ... 24 A1
Highgrove House.
Merrow GU4 ... 110 C3
Highland Cotts. Wallin SM6 . 60 C6
Highland Croft. Catf BR3 ... 24 B2
Highland Lodge. 2
S Norw SE19 ... 22 F1
Highland Pk. Felt TW13 ... 14 F4
Highland Rd. Alder GU12 .. 105 D2
Highland Rd. Bear Gn RH5 157 D3
Highland Rd.
Broml BR1 & BR2 ... 44 F8
Highland Rd. Camb GU15 ... 65 E8
Highland Rd. Purley CR8 ... 80 A5
Highland Rd. W Norw SE19 . 22 E2
Highland View. Cran GU6 .. 174 C7
Highlands Ave. Horsh RH13 217 E2
Highlands Ave. Leahd KT22 . 95 C5
Highlands Cl. Hounsl TW3 ... 5 B6

Highlands Cl. Leahd KT22 .... 95 B5
Highlands Cl. M Bourn GU9 146 B7
Highlands Cres. Horsh RH13 .... 217 E2
Highlands Ct. W Norw SE19 22 E2
Highlands Heath. Putney SW15 .... 19 C8
Highlands La. Westfd GU22 . 89 E5
Highlands Pk. Leahd KT22 ... 95 D4
Highlands Rd. Heath E GU9 125 C7
Highlands Rd. Horsh RH13 217 F2
Highlands Rd. Leahd KT22 ... 95 C5
Highlands Rd. Reig RH1 & RH2 .... 118 D2
Highlands The. W Hors KT24 92 E2
Highmead. Farnc GU7 .... 150 F6
Highpoint. Weyb KT13 .... 53 A5
Highridge Cl. Epsom KT18 ... 76 E5
Highridge Ct. Epsom KT18 ... 76 E5
Highview. Cater CR3 .... 100 E2
Highview Cres. Camb GU15 . 46 F1
Highview Ct. 2 Putney SW19 .... 19 E7
Highview Ct. 2 Reig RH2 118 D1
Highview High Sch. Wallin SM6 .... 60 E5
Highway. Crowth RG11 .... 45 A5
Highway The. Sutton SM2 .... 59 C2
Highwayman's Ridge. Windl GU20 .... 48 B6
Highwold. Chips CR5 .... 79 A1
Highwood Cl. Kenley CR8 .... 80 C2
Highwoods. Cater CR3 .... 100 E2
Highwoods. Leahd KT22 .... 95 C6
Hilary Ave. Mitch CR4 .... 41 A6
Hilary Dr. Crowth RG11 .... 45 B6
Hilbert Rd. Cheam SM3 .... 58 D7
Hilborough Cl. Merton SW19 20 C1
Hildenborough Gdns. Catf BR1 .... 24 F2
Hildenborough House. Beck BR3 .... 23 F1
Hildenlea Pl. Beck BR2 .... 44 E7
Hildenley Cl. Merst RH1 .... 119 D7
Hildens The. Westc RH4 .... 135 C5
Hilder Gdns. Farnb GU14 .... 85 D3
Hilders La. Eden TN8 .... 144 F4
Hilders The. Ashtd KT21 .... 76 B2
Hilditch House. 7 Rich TW10 6 F1
Hildreth St. Balham SW12 ... 21 B7
Hilgay. Guild GU1 .... 109 F1
Hilgay Cl. Guild GU1 .... 109 F1
Hilgay Ct. Guild GU1 .... 109 F1
Hill Cl. Horse GU21 .... 69 D3
Hill Cl. Purley CR8 .... 80 C6
Hill Cl. Woner GU5 .... 152 B6
Hill Copse View. Brack RG12 27 E8
Hill Cres. King U T KT5 .... 37 F4
Hill Cres. N Cheam KT4 .... 58 C8
Hill Crest. Dorm Pk RH19 ... 185 E6
Hill Crest. Elst GU8 .... 148 D4
Hill Crest Dr. Wreccl GU10 145 F6
Hill Ct. Farnc GU7 .... 150 E6
Hill Ct. Haslem GU27 .... 208 B6
Hill Ct. 8 King U T KT2 .... 18 B1
Hill Ct. 14 King U T KT6 .... 37 E4
Hill Dr. Thorn H SW16 .... 41 F6
Hill Field Rd. Hampt TW12 ... 35 F8
Hill Gr. Felt TW13 .... 15 F6
Hill House Cl. Turn H RH10 204 A5
Hill House Dr. Whit V KT13 .. 72 A8
Hill House Dr. Woodh RH2 139 B7
Hill House Rd. Streat SW16 . 21 F3
Hill La. Kings KT20 .... 97 E6
Hill Manor. Horsh RH12 .... 217 A2
Hill Mead. Horsh RH12 .... 217 B3
Hill Rd. Beac H GU26 .... 188 C6
Hill Rd. Carsh SM5 .... 59 E4
Hill Rd. Fetch KT23 .... 94 B5
Hill Rd. Graysh GU26 .... 188 C3
Hill Rd. Haslem GU27 .... 208 C6
Hill Rd. Heath E GU9 .... 125 D7
Hill Rd. Mitch CR4 .... 21 B1
Hill Rd. Purley CR8 .... 79 F7
Hill Rd. Sutton SM1 .... 59 B5
Hill Rise. Dork RH4 .... 115 A1
Hill Rise. Hinch W KT10 .... 56 B8
Hill Rise. Rich TW10 .... 6 D2
Hill St. Rich TW10 .... 6 D2
Hill The. Cater CR3 .... 100 F3
Hill Top. Cheam SM3 & SM4 . 39 F2
Hill View. Mitch CR4 .... 41 E5
Hill View Cl. Purley CR8 .... 80 B8
Hill View Cl. Tadw KT20 .... 97 C6
Hill View Cres. Stough GU2 108 F3
Hill View Ct. 15 Woking GU22 .... 69 E1
Hill View Rd. Clayg KT10 .... 56 A3
Hill View Rd. Farnh GU9 .... 124 F2
Hill View Rd. Twick TW1 .... 6 A1
Hill View Rd. Woking GU22 .. 69 F1
Hillacre. Cater CR3 .... 100 E2
Hillard Ct. Wallin SM6 .... 60 D4
Hillars Heath Rd. Coulsd CR5 79 E4
Hillary Cl. E Grins RH19 .... 186 A3
Hillary Cl. M Bourn GU9 .... 146 B7
Hillary Cres. Walt O T KT12 .. 35 C1
Hillary Ct. Stan TW19 .... 13 E7
Hillary Hse. 10 Redh RH1 ... 118 F2
Hillary Rd. M Bourn GU9 .... 146 B7
Hillbarn. S Croy CR2 .... 80 E8
Hillberry. Easth RG12 .... 27 C2
Hillbrook Gdns. Whit V KT13 53 A3
Hillbrook Prim Sch & Hillcroft Sch Annexe. Up Toot SW17 21 A4
Hillbrook Rd. Up Toot SW17 21 A4
Hillbrook Rise. Hale GU9 .. 125 B6
Hillbrow. New Mal KT3 .... 38 F6
Hillbrow. 3 Reig RH2 .... 118 C1
Hillbrow. 7 Rich TW10 .... 6 E1
Hillbrow Cl. Wood S V GU3 108 B2
Hillbrow Cotts. Godst RH9 . 121 C3
Hillbrow Ct. Godst RH9 .... 121 C3
Hillbrow Rd. Catf BR1 .... 24 E2
Hillbrow Rd. Esher KT10 .... 55 C6
Hillbury Cl. Warlgm CR6 .... 81 C1
Hillbury Gdns. Warlgm CR6 . 81 C1
Hillbury Rd. Up Toot SW17 .. 21 B5
Hillbury Rd. Warlgm CR3 & CR6 .... 81 B1
Hillcote Ave. S Norw SW16 .. 22 A1
Hillcrest. Heath E GU9 .... 125 D8
Hillcrest. Weyb KT13 .... 53 B6
Hillcrest Ave. Addl KT16 .... 51 E6
Hillcrest Cl. Beck BR3 .... 43 F3
Hillcrest Cl. Crawl RH10 .... 202 D6
Hillcrest Cl. Epsom KT18 .... 76 F4
Hillcrest Cl. For Hil SE26 .... 23 A4
Hillcrest Cl. Sutton SM2 .... 59 D4
Hillcrest Ct. Weyb KT13 .... 53 B6
Hillcrest Gdns. Hinch W KT10 .... 55 F7
Hillcrest House. Merrow GU4 .... 110 C3
Hillcrest Par. Wallin CR5 .... 79 B5
Hillcrest Rd. Bigg H TN16 .... 83 D3
Hillcrest Rd. Camb GU15 .... 66 B7
Hillcrest Rd. Kenley CR3 .... 80 F2
Hillcrest Rd. Stough GU2 .... 108 F2
Hillcrest Rd. Wallin CR8 .... 60 F1
Hillcrest View. Beck BR3 .... 43 F3
Hillcroft Ave. Purley CR5 & CR8 .... 79 D6
Hillcroft Coll. Surb KT6 .... 37 E3
Hillcroft Cty Prim Sch. Cater CR3 .... 100 E4
Hillcroft Cty Prim Sch. Whytlf CR3 .... 100 F6
Hillcroome Rd. Sutton SM2 . 59 D4
Hillcross Ave. Merton SM4 ... 39 E4
Hillcross Ave. W Barn SM4 .. 39 E4
Hillcross Mid Sch. Merton SM4 .... 39 F5
Hilldale Rd. Cheam SM1 .... 58 F6
Hilldeane Rd. Wallin CR8 .... 61 A1
Hilldown Ct. Streat SW16 .... 21 E1
Hilldown Rd. Streat SW16 .... 21 F1
Hilldown Rd. W Wick BR2 .... 44 F1
Hilley Field La. Fetch KT22 .. 94 C6
Hillfield Ave. Carsh SM4 .... 40 E4
Hillfield Cl. Earls RH1 .... 119 A1
Hillfield Cl. Merrow GU1 .... 110 C3
Hillfield Rd. Earls RH1 .... 119 A1
Hillford Pl. Earls RH1 .... 140 A3
Hillgarth. Beac H GU26 .... 188 D5
Hillgate Pl. Balham SW12 .... 21 B8
Hillhouse La. Cran RH12 & RH14 .... 194 F1
Hillhurst Gdns. Cater CR3 .. 100 E7
Hillier Gdns. Croy CR0 .... 61 A5
Hillier House. Guild GU2 .... 130 B7
Hillier Lodge. Tedd TW12 .... 16 D3
Hillier Mews. Guild GU1 .... 110 A1
Hillier Pl. Chess KT9 .... 56 C4
Hillier Rd. Guild GU1 .... 110 A1
Hillier's La. Wallin CR0 & SM6 .... 60 E7
Hillingdale. Bigg H TN16 .... 83 B1
Hillingdale. Crawl RH11 .... 201 C1
Hillingdon Ave. Stan TW19 .. 13 E7
Hillmead. Crawl RH11 .... 200 F6
Hillmont Rd. Hinch W KT10 . 55 E7
Hillmore Gr. For Hil SE26 .... 23 E3
Hillmount. 13 Woking GU22 .... 69 E1
Hillrise. Bra Hil SL3 .... 1 A8
Hillrise. Walt O T KT12 .... 34 F2
Hills Farm La. Horsh RH12 . 216 F1
Hills Pl. Horsh RH12 .... 217 A2
Hillsborough Ct. W Heath GU14 .... 84 E8
Hillsborough Pk. Friml GU15 66 C5
Hillside. Ascot SL5 .... 29 C4
Hillside. Crawl D RH10 .... 204 B8
Hillside. For Row RH18 .... 206 E3
Hillside. Horsh RH12 .... 217 A2
Hillside. Nork SM7 .... 77 E4
Hillside. Sandh GU15 .... 64 F7
Hillside. Went GU25 .... 31 C3
Hillside. Wimble SW19 .... 19 D2
Hillside. Woking GU22 .... 89 D7
Hillside Ave. Purley CR8 .... 80 B6
Hillside Cl. Brock RH3 & RH5 .... 137 A8
Hillside Cl. Crawl RH11 .... 201 B4
Hillside Cl. E Grins RH19 .... 185 E3
Hillside Cl. Head Dn GU35 . 187 A6
Hillside Cl. Knaph GU21 .... 68 D2
Hillside Cl. Merton SM4 .... 39 E5
Hillside Cl. Nork SM7 .... 77 E3
Hillside Cres. Friml GU16 .... 85 F7
Hillside Ct. Guild GU1 .... 130 E8
Hillside Ct. 7 King U T KT2 . 18 B1
Hillside Gdns. Brock RH3 & RH5 .... 116 A1
Hillside Gdns. Row Tn KT15 . 51 F5
Hillside Gdns. Streat SW2 .... 22 A6
Hillside Gdns. Wallin SM6 .... 60 C3
Hillside La. Coney H BR2 .... 63 F8
Hillside La. Heath E GU9 ... 125 D8
Hillside Pk. Sunnin SL5 .... 29 F1
Hillside Rd. Alder GU11 .... 126 A8
Hillside Rd. Ash GU12 .... 106 B3
Hillside Rd. Ashtd KT21 .... 75 F2
Hillside Rd. Beck BR2 .... 44 F6
Hillside Rd. Belm SM2 .... 58 F3
Hillside Rd. Coulsd CR5 .... 79 F1
Hillside Rd. Croy CR0 .... 61 B6
Hillside Rd. E Ewell KT17 .... 58 C1
Hillside Rd. Heath E GU9 .... 125 E7
Hillside Rd. King U T KT5 .... 38 A4
Hillside Rd. Linch GU27 .... 207 F5
Hillside Rd. M Bourn GU10 . 146 C3
Hillside Rd. Streat SW2 .... 22 A6
Hillside Rd. Tats TN16 .... 103 E8
Hillside Rd. Warlgm CR3 & CR6 .... 81 A1
Hillside Rd. Whytlf CR3 & CR6 .... 81 A1
Hillside Way. Farnc GU7 ... 150 D7
Hillsmead Way. Sander CR2 81 B6
Hillspur Cl. Stough GU2 .... 108 F2
Hillspur Rd. Stough GU2 .... 108 F2
Hilltop Cl. Ascot SL5 .... 29 E7
Hilltop Cl. Leahd KT22 .... 95 C4
Hilltop Cl. Stough GU3 .... 108 F5
Hilltop Ct. S Norw SE19 .... 42 D8
Hilltop La. Cater CR3 & RH1 100 A1
Hilltop Rd. Kenley CR3 .... 80 F2
Hilltop Rd. Reig RH2 .... 139 B7
Hilltop Rise. G Book KT23 .... 94 C1
Hilltop Wlk. Wold CR3 .... 101 E6
Hillview. Whytlf CR3 .... 80 F2
Hillview. Wimble SW20 .... 19 B1
Hillview Ct. W Norw SE19 .... 22 E4
Hillview Dr. Earls RH1 .... 140 A8
Hillview Rd. Sutton SM1 .... 59 D7
Hillworth. Beck BR3 .... 44 B7
Hillworth Rd. Streat SW2 .... 22 A8
Hilly Mead. Wimble SW19 .... 19 E1
Hillybarn Rd. Rusper RH11 180 C1
Hilsea Point. 7 Rhampt SW15 .... 19 B7
Hilton Ct. Horley RH6 .... 161 C4
Hilton Way. Hams Gn CR2 ... 81 B4
Himley Rd. Up Toot SW17 .... 20 F2
Hinchcliffe Cl. Wallin SM6 .... 60 F3
Hinchley Cl. Hinch W KT10 .. 55 F7
Hinchley Dr. Hinch W KT10 .. 55 F7
Hinchley Way. Hinch W KT10 .... 56 A7
Hinchley Wood Prim Sch. Hinch W KT10 .... 56 A8
Hinchley Wood Sch. Hinch W KT10 .... 56 A8
Hinchley Wood Sta. Hinch W KT10 .... 55 F7
Hindell Cl. Farnb GU14 .... 85 A8
Hindhead Cl. Crawl RH11 ... 201 C4
Hindhead Point. 6 Rhampt SW15 .... 19 B7
Hindhead Rd. Shottm GU26 & GU27 .... 188 F2
Hindhead Way. Wallin SM6 . 60 E5
Hindsley's Pl. For Hil SE23 ... 23 C6
Hinkler Cl. Wallin SM6 .... 60 E3
Hinstock Cl. Farnb GU14 .... 85 A3
Hinton Ave. Hounsl TW4 .... 4 D3
Hinton Cl. Crowth RG11 .... 45 B7
Hinton Dr. Crowth RG11 .... 45 B7
Hinton Rd. Wallin SM6 .... 60 C4
Hipley Ct. Guild GU1 .... 131 A8
Hipley St. Old Wok GU22 .... 90 B7
Hitchcock Cl. Littlt TW17 .... 33 F6
Hitchings Way. Dovgn RH2 139 A5
Hither Green Hospl. Lewish SE13 .... 24 D8
Hither Green La. Lewish SE13 24 E8
Hitherbury Cl. Guild GU2 ... 130 C6
Hitherfield Prim Sch. Streat SW2 .... 22 A6
Hitherfield Rd. Streat SW16 & SW27 .... 22 A5
Hitherhooks Hill. Binf RG12 . 26 E8
Hithermoor Rd. Stan TW19 ... 2 A2
Hitherwood. Cran GU6 .... 174 E2
Hitherwood Cl. Redh RH1 .. 118 E3
Hitherwood Ct. Dulw SE21 .. 22 F4
Hitherwood Dr. Dulw SE19 & SE21 .... 22 F4
Hoadly Rd. Streat SW16 .... 21 D6
Hobart Gdns. S Norw CR7 .... 42 D6
Hobart Pl. 14 Rich TW10 .... 6 F1
Hobart Rd. N Cheam KT4 .... 58 B7
Hobbs Cl. W Byfl KT14 .... 71 B6
Hobbs Ind Est. Felb RH7 ... 184 D7
Hobbs Rd. Crawl RH11 .... 201 A2
Hobbs Rd. 5 W Norw SE27 .. 22 C4
Hobill Wlk. Surb KT5 .... 37 F3
Hocken Mead. Crawl RH10 202 D8
Hockering Gdns. Mayb GU22 70 B1
Hockering Rd. Mayb GU22 ... 70 B1
Hockford Cl. Pirb GU3 .... 88 B1
Hodge La. Wink SL5 .... 9 A3
Hodges Cl. Bagsh GU19 .... 47 E1
Hodgson Gdns. Burph GU1 & GU4 .... 110 A4
Hoe Bridge Sch. Mayb GU22 90 C8
Hoe Cotts. Peasl GU5 .... 154 E8
Hoe La. Hasc GU8 .... 172 D4
Hoe La. Peasl GU5 .... 154 F8
Hoebridge Golf Ctr. Mayb GU22 .... 90 C8
Hoebrook Glade. Westfd GU22 .... 89 E6
Hoebrook Glade. Woking GU22 .... 89 D6
Hoefield Cty Fst Sch. Westfd GU22 .... 89 E6
Hogarth Ave. Ashf TW15 .... 14 C2
Hogarth Bsns Pk. Chisw W4 .. 7 E8
Hogarth Cl. Sandh GU15 .... 64 E6
Hogarth Cres. Mitch CR4 & SW19 .... 40 D8
Hogarth Cres. Thorn H CR0 . 42 C2
Hogarth Ct. Dulw SE19 .... 22 F4
Hogarth Ct. Heston TW5 .... 4 E7
Hogarth Gdns. Heston TW5 ... 5 A7
Hogarth House. 6 W Norw SE27 .... 22 C4
Hogarth La. Chisw W4 .... 7 E8
Hogarth Rd. Crawl RH10 .... 201 F3
Hogarth Roundabout. Chisw W4 .... 7 E8
Hogarth Way. Hampt TW12 . 36 C8
Hoghatch La. Hale GU9 .... 125 A6
Hogoak La. New Gn SL4 .... 8 A8
Hogscross La. Kings CR5 .... 98 F5
Hogshill La. Cobham KT11 ... 73 C5
Hogsmill Way. W Ewell KT19 57 C6
Hogsmill Way. W Ewell KT19 57 C6
Hogspudding La.Newd RH5 158 C1
Hogtrough La. Nutf RH1 ... 140 D8
Hogtrough La. Oxted RH8 . 122 B6
Hogwood Rd. Ifold RH14 ... 212 C3
Holbeach Mews. Balham SW12 .... 21 B7
Holbeach Prim Sch. Lewish SE6 .... 24 A8
Holbeach Rd. Lewish SE6 .... 24 B8
Holbeck. Easth RG12 .... 26 F3
Holbeck Pl. Woking GU22 .... 69 F1
Holbein Rd. Crawl RH10 .... 201 F3
Holberry House. 5 Dulw SE21 .... 22 E4
Holborn Way. Mitch CR4 .... 40 F7
Holbrook Cl. Heath E GU9 .. 125 F8
Holbrook Ct. Egham TW20 ... 12 C3
Holbrook Cty Prim Sch. Horsh RH12 .... 217 E7
Holbrook House. 5 Streat SW2 .... 21 F7
Holbrook School La. Horsh RH12 .... 217 E7
Holbrook Way. Alder GU11 126 B7
Holcon Ct. Redh RH1 .... 119 A4
Holder Rd. Alder GU12 .... 105 E1
Holder Rd. Worth RH10 .... 202 B3
Holderness Way. W Norw SE27 .... 22 B3
Holdernesse Rd. 6 Up Toot SW17 .... 21 A6
Holdsworth House. 5 Streat SW2 .... 22 A8
Hole Hill. Westc RH4 .... 135 B7
Holford Rd. Merrow GU1 .... 110 C1
Holland Ave. Belm SM2 .... 59 A2
Holland Ave. Wimble SW20 . 38 F8
Holland Cl. Coney H BR2 .... 63 F8
Holland Cl. M Bourn GU9 .... 146 E8
Holland Cl. Redh RH1 .... 118 F1
Holland Cres. Oxted RH8 .. 123 A2
Holland Cty Jun Sch. Oxted RH8 .... 123 A1
Holland Dr. For Hil SE23 .... 23 E5
Holland Gdns. Egham TW20 32 F7
Holland La. Oxted RH8 .... 123 A2
Holland Pines. Easth RG12 .. 26 F2
Holland Rd. Croy SE25 .... 43 A4
Holland Rd. Oxted RH8 .... 123 A1
Holland Way. Coney H BR2 .. 63 F8
Hollands The. Felt TW13 .... 15 D4
Hollands The. New Mal KT4 . 38 F1
Hollands Way. E Grins RH19 .... 186 A4
Hollands Way. Warn RH12 216 F8
Holles Cl. Hampt TW12 .... 16 A3
Hollies Ave. W Byfl KT14 .... 70 F6
Hollies Cl. S Norw SW16 .... 22 A2
Hollies Cl. Twick TW1 .... 16 F6
Hollies Ct. Addl KT15 .... 52 C5
Hollies Way. 2 Balham SW12 .... 21 A8
Hollin Ct. Crawl RH10 & RH11 .... 181 E1
Hollingbourne Cres. Crawl RH11 .... 201 C1
Hollingsworth Rd. S Croy CR0 & CR2 .... 62 B4
Hollington Cres. New Mal KT3 .... 39 A3
Hollingworth Cl. E Mole KT8 35 F5
Hollingworth Ct. 7 Surb KT6 .... 37 D2
Hollis Wood Dr. Wreccl GU10 .... 145 E5
Hollman Gdns. S Norw SW16 .... 22 B2
Hollow Cl. Guild GU2 .... 130 B8
Hollow La. Dorman RH19 & RH7 .... 186 D6
Hollow La. Vir W GU25 .... 31 C6
Hollow La. Wotton RH5 .... 134 D2
Hollow The. Crawl RH11 .... 200 F5
Hollow The. Shackl GU7 .... 149 F4
Holloway Hill. Godal GU7 .. 150 D4
Holloway Hill. Lyne KT16 .... 51 D8
Holloway La. Harm UB7 .... 2 E8
Holloway St. Hounsl TW3 .... 5 B4
Holly Acre. Woking GU22 .... 89 C4
Holly Ave. Friml GU16 .... 66 B3
Holly Ave. Walt O T KT12 .... 35 D1
Holly Ave. Woodhm KT15 .... 52 A1
Holly Bank Rd. Woking GU22 89 B7
Holly Bush Ind Pk. Farnb GU12 .... 105 E5
Holly Bush La. Farnb GU11 105 E5
Holly Bush La. Farnb GU11 105 E7
Holly Bush La. Hampt TW12 15 F1
Holly Cl. Alder GU12 .... 105 C2
Holly Cl. Crawl RH10 .... 202 A8
Holly Cl. Eng Gn TW20 .... 11 B2
Holly Cl. Farnb GU14 .... 85 A4
Holly Cl. Felt TW13 .... 15 E3
Holly Cl. Head Dn GU35 .... 187 C5
Holly Cl. Horsh RH12 .... 218 B5
Holly Cl. Longc KT16 .... 50 A7
Holly Cl. Woking GU21 .... 89 B8
Holly Cott. Thame D KT7 .... 37 A1
Holly Cres. Beck BR3 .... 43 F4
Holly Ct. 9 Belm SM2 .... 59 A3
Holly Ct. Leahd KT22 .... 95 A5
Holly Gn. Oat Pk KT13 .... 53 D6
Holly Hedge Cl. Friml GU16 . 65 E2
Holly Hedge Rd. Cobham KT11 .... 73 B5
Holly Hedge Rd. Friml GU16 65 E2
Holly Hill Dr. Banstd SM7 .... 78 A3
Holly Hock. Bisley GU24 .... 68 A4
Holly Hough. Box H KT20 .. 116 B5
Holly House. Brent TW8 .... 6 C8
Holly House. Easth RG12 .... 27 B3
Holly La. Banstd SM7 .... 78 C2
Holly La. Ock Rid GU7 .... 150 C4
Holly La. Woodm SM7 .... 78 C2
Holly La. Worpl GU3 .... 108 D7
Holly La E. Banstd SM7 .... 78 B3
Holly La W. Banstd SM7 .... 78 B2
Holly Lea. Jacobs GU4 .... 109 D7
Holly Lodge Cty Prim Sch. Ash V GU12 .... 105 F8
Holly Rd. Alder GU12 .... 105 D1

Holly Rd. Farnb GU14 85 A4
Holly Rd. Hampt TW12 16 C2
Holly Rd. Hounsl TW3 5 B3
Holly Rd. Twick TW1 17 A7
Holly Rd. Woodh RH2 139 B7
Holly Ridge. W End GU24 67 E6
Holly Spring Cty Inf Sch. Brack RG12 27 E7
Holly Spring Cty Jun Sch. Brack RG12 27 E7
Holly Spring La. Brack RG12 27 D8
Holly Tree Rd. Cater CR3 100 E5
Holly Way. Blckw GU17 64 D4
Holly Way. Mitch CR4 41 D6
Holly Wlk. Wink SL4 9 E4
Hollybank. W End GU24 67 F6
Hollybank Cl. Hampt TW12 16 A3
Hollybank Rd. Pyrf KT14 71 A5
Hollybush Rd. Crawl RH10 201 E8
Hollybush Rd. King U T KT2 17 E2
Hollybush Ride. Windl GU19 & GU20 47 F6
Hollycombe. Eng Gn TW20 11 D4
Hollycroft Cl. Harm UB7 3 A8
Hollycroft Gdns. Harm UB7 3 A8
Hollydene. Broml BR1 44 F8
Hollyfield Rd. Surb KT5 37 F2
Hollyfield Sch. King U T KT6 37 E4
Hollyfields Cl. Camb GU15 65 B5
Hollymead. Carsh SM5 59 F7
Hollymead Rd. Chips CR5 79 A1
Hollymeoak Rd. Coulsd CR5 79 B1
Hollymoor La. Epsom KT19 57 D1
Hollymount Prim Sch. Wimble SW20 39 C8
Hollyridge. Haslem GU27 208 B6
Hollytree Cl. Putney SW19 19 D7
Hollytree Gdns. Friml GU16 85 D8
Hollywoods. New Add CR0 62 F2
Holm Cl. Woodhm KT15 70 E7
Holm Ct. Dork RH4 136 B4
Holm Ct. Farnc GU7 150 D7
Holman Ct. Ewell KT17 58 A2
Holman Rd. W Ewell KT19 57 C5
Holman Rd. W Ewell KT19 57 C5
Holmbank Dr. Up Hall TW17 34 E5
Holmbrook Cl. W Heath GU14 84 C4
Holmbrook Gdns. W Heath GU14 84 C4
Holmbury Ave. Crowth RG11 45 A7
Holmbury Cl. Crawl RH11 201 C4
Holmbury Cl. Mitch SW19 20 E1
Holmbury Ct. Up Toot SW17 20 F5
Holmbury Dr. Dork RH5 136 C4
Holmbury Gr. New Add CR0 62 F3
Holmbury Hill Rd. Hol St M RH5 155 B3
Holmbury Rd. For Gn RH5 155 D1
Holmbush Cl. Horsh RH12 217 D6
Holmcroft. Crawl RH10 201 E5
Holmcroft. Walt o t H KT20 97 B2
Holmdene Cl. Beck BR3 44 C7
Holme Chase. Whit V KT13 53 C4
Holme Cl. Crowth RG11 45 A7
Holmes Cl. Ascot SL5 29 C3
Holmes Cl. Woki RG11 25 A4
Holmes Cres. Woki RG11 25 A4
Holmes Rd. Merton SW19 20 C1
Holmes Rd. Twick TW1 16 F6
Holmesdale. 2 Whit V KT13 53 D4
Holmesdale Ave. Mortl SW14 7 B3
Holmesdale Cl. Merrow GU1 110 B2
Holmesdale Cl. S Norw SE25 42 F6
Holmesdale Rd. Dork RH5 136 C3
Holmesdale Rd. Reig RH2 118 B2
Holmesdale Rd. Rich TW9 6 F6
Holmesdale Rd. S Norw SE25 42 E5
Holmesdale Rd. S Nutf RH1 140 F7
Holmesdale Rd. Tedd TW11 17 C2
Holmesdale Rd. Thorn H CR0 42 D4
Holmesdale Sch. Reig RH2 118 B2
Holmethorpe Ave. Redh RH1 119 B4
Holmethorpe Ind Est. Redh RH1 119 B4
Holmewood Cl. Woki RG11 25 A2
Holmewood Gdns. Streat SW2 21 F8
Holmewood Rd. S Norw SE25 42 E6
Holmewood Rd. Streat SW2 21 F8
Holmgrove Hse. Purley CR8 80 A7
Holming End. Horsh RH12 218 B5
Holmoaks House. Beck BR3 44 C7
Holmshaw Cl. For Hil SE26 & SE6 23 E4
Holmsley Cl. New Mal KT3 38 F2
Holmsley House. Rhampt SW15 18 F8
Holmwood. 2 Surb KT5 37 F3
Holmwood Ave. Sander CR2 80 F6
Holmwood Cl. Addl KT15 52 A5
Holmwood Cl. Cheam SM2 58 D3
Holmwood Cl. E Hors KT24 112 E6
Holmwood Gdns. Wallin SM6 60 B4
Holmwood Rd. Chess KT9 56 E5
Holmwood Rd. E Ewell KT17 & SM2 58 C2
Holmwood Sta. Bear Gn RH5 157 C4
Holmwood View Rd. Dork RH5 136 B1
Holne Chase. Morden SM4 40 A3
Holroyd Rd. Clayg KT10 55 F2
Holstein Ave. Weyb KT13 53 A6
Holsworthy Way. Chess KT9 56 C5
Holt Cl. Farnb GU14 85 C7
Holt La. Woki RG11 25 B7
Holt Pound La. Binst GU10 145 C5
Holt Sch The. Woki RG11 25 B7
Holt The. Morden SM4 40 A5
Holt The. Wallin SM6 60 C6
Holt Wood. Chelsh CR6 82 A3
Holton Heath. 8 Brack RG12 27 F5
Holtwood Rd. Oxsh KT22 74 C6
Holtye Ave. E Grins RH19 186 A3
Holtye Rd. E Grins RH19 186 B3
Holtye Wlk. Crawl RH10 202 A4
Holy Cross Catholic Prim Sch. Catf SE6 24 C7
Holy Cross Hospl. Shottm GU27 207 F7
Holy Cross RC Convent Sch. New Mal KT3 38 E4
Holy Cross RC Prep Sch. King U T KT2 18 C1
Holy Family RC Prim Sch The. Row Tn KT15 52 A5
Holy Ghost RC Prim Sch. Balham SW12 21 A8
Holy Trinity C of E Inf Sch. Up Toot SW17 20 F6
Holy Trinity C of E Prim Sch. For Hil SE23 23 C6
Holy Trinity C of E Prim Sch. Streat SW2 21 F8
Holy Trinity C of E Prim Sch. W End GU24 68 A7
Holy Trinity C of E Prim Sch. Wimble SW19 20 B2
Holy Trinity CE (Aided) Sch The. Crawl RH11 201 A4
Holy Trinity CE Jun Sch. Mortl TW10 7 A3
Holy Trinity C of E Jun Sch. Wallin SM6 60 C6
Holy Trinity Prim Sch. Sunnin SL5 30 A3
Holy Trinity Sch. Guild GU1 130 F7
Holybourne Ave. Rhampt SW15 19 A8
Holyhead Ct. King U T KT1 37 D5
Holyhook Cl. Crowth RG11 45 A6
Holyoake Ave. Horse GU21 69 C2
Holyoake Cres. Horse GU21 69 C2
Holyrood. E Grins RH19 206 A8
Holyrood Pl. Crawl RH11 201 B2
Holywell Cl. Stan TW19 13 E7
Holywell Cl. W Heath GU14 85 A7
Holywell Way. Stan TW19 13 E7
Homan House. 6 Streat SW4 21 D8
Hombrook Dr. Binf RG12 26 E8
Hombrook House. Brack RG12 26 E8
Home Cl. Carsh SM5 59 F8
Home Cl. Crawl RH10 202 C8
Home Cl. Fetch KT22 94 D6
Home Ct. King U T KT6 37 D4
Home Farm Cl. Betch RH3 137 E8
Home Farm Cl. Burgh H KT18 77 D2
Home Farm Cl. Esher KT10 55 B4
Home Farm Cl. Farnb GU14 85 D6
Home Farm Cl. Ottsh KT16 51 A3
Home Farm Cl. Thame D KT7 36 F2
Home Farm Cl. Up Hall TW17 34 E5
Home Farm Cotts. P Harow GU8 149 C5
Home Farm Gdns. Walt O T KT12 54 C8
Home Farm Rd. Godal GU7 150 F2
Home Meadow. Banstd SM7 78 A3
Home Park Cl. Bramly GU5 151 F6
Home Park Rd. Wimble SW19 19 F4
Home Park Wlk. King U T KT1 37 D5
Home Pk. Oxted RH8 123 A4
Homebeech House. 7 Woking GU22 69 E1
Homecoppice House. 1 Broml BR1 24 F1
Homecourt. Felt TW14 15 A7
Homecroft Rd. For Hil SE26 23 C3
Homefield. Morden SM4 40 A5
Homefield. Thursl GU8 169 C3
Homefield Cl. Horley RH6 161 B4
Homefield Cl. Leahd KT22 95 C6
Homefield Cl. Woodhm KT15 70 E7
Homefield Gdns. Burgh H KT20 97 C7
Homefield Gdns. Mitch CR4 & SW19 40 D7
Homefield House. For Hil SE23 23 D5
Homefield Pk. Sutton SM1 & SM2 59 B4
Homefield Prep Sch. Sutton SM1 59 A5
Homefield Rd. Coulsd CR3 & CR5 100 B7
Homefield Rd. Walt O T KT12 35 E2
Homefield Rd. Warlgm CR6 101 C8
Homefield Rd. Wimble SW19 19 E3
Homegreen House. Shottm GU27 208 A6
Homeland Dr. Belm SM2 59 B2
Homelands. Leahd KT22 95 C6
Homelands Dr. S Norw SE19 22 E1
Homelea Cl. Farnb GU14 85 B8
Homeleigh Cres. Ash V GU12 106 A8
Homeleigh Ct. 8 Streat SW16 21 E5
Homemead. Up Toot SW12 21 B6
Homemead Rd. Wallin CR0 41 C3
Homepark House. Farnh GU9 125 C2
Homer Rd. Croy CR0 43 D3
Homersham Rd. King U T KT1 38 B7
Homesdale Rd. Cater CR3 100 D4
Homestall. Stough GU2 108 D2
Homestall Rd. Hammer RH19 206 E8
Homestead. Cran GU6 174 F4
Homestead Gdns. Clayg KT10 55 E5
Homestead Rd. Cater CR3 100 D4
Homestead Rd. Stain TW18 13 B2
Homestead Way. New Add CR0 82 D7
Homesteads The. Catf BR3 24 B2
Homewalk House. For Hil SE26 23 C4
Homewater House. 1 Epsom KT17 76 E6
Homewaters Ave. Sunby TW16 34 F8
Homewood. Cran GU6 175 A3
Homewood Cl. Hampt TW12 15 F2
Homewood Gdns. S Norw SE25 42 E4
Homewood (NHS Trust) Hospl. Addl KT16 51 C6
Homewoods. 2 Streat SW12 21 C8
Homeworth House. 8 Woking GU22 69 E1
Homildon House. 10 For Hil SE26 23 A5
Homington Ct. King U T KT2 17 E1
Homstead The. Burst RH6 162 B1
Hone Hill. Sandh GU17 64 B8
Hones Yard Bsns Pk. M Bourn GU9 125 D2
Honey Hill. Woki RG11 26 A1
Honeybrook Rd. Streat SW12 & SW4 21 C8
Honeycrock La. Salfs RH1 140 B2
Honeyhill Rd. Brack RG12 27 A8
Honeypot La. Limps RH7 & TN8 144 D4
Honeypots Rd. Westfd GU22 89 D5
Honeysuckle Bottom. E Hors KT24 112 E2
Honeysuckle Cl. Crowth RG11 45 A7
Honeysuckle Cl.Horley RH6 161 C4
Honeysuckle Gdns. Croy CR0 43 D1
Honeysuckle La. Crawl RH11 181 C1
Honeysuckle La. Dork RH5 136 C4
Honeysuckle La. Head Dn GU35 187 B5
Honeysuckle Wlk. Horsh RH12 218 A5
Honeywood La. Oakwd RH5 196 F5
Honeywood La. Rowhk RH5 196 F5
Honeywood Rd. Horsh RH13 218 A4
Honeywood Rd. Islew TW7 6 A3
Honeywood Wlk. Carsh SM5 59 F6
Honister Hts. Sander CR8 80 E5
Honister Wlk. Friml GU15 66 D4
Honley Rd. Lewish SE6 24 B8
Honnor Rd. Stain TW18 13 D1
Honor Oak Rd. For Hil SE23 23 C8
Hood Ave. Mortl SW14 7 C2
Hood Cl. Thorn H CR0 & CR9 42 B1
Hood Rd. Wimble SW20 18 F1
Hook Heath Ave. Woking GU22 89 C8
Hook Heath Gdns. Woking GU22 88 F6
Hook Heath Rd. Woking GU22 89 B6
Hook Hill. S Croy CR2 61 E1
Hook Hill La. Woking GU22 89 C6
Hook Hill Pk. Woking GU22 89 B6
Hook House. 9 W Norw SW27 22 B3
Hook La. Gomsh GU5 133 C2
Hook La. Putt GU3 128 D3
Hook La. W End GU24 67 C6
Hook Mill La. Windl GU24 48 D2
Hook Rd. Chess KT6 56 E7
Hook Rd. Epsom KT19 & KT17 57 C2
Hook Rd. Ewell KT19 76 D8
Hook Rd. Surb KT6 & KT9 56 E7
Hook Rise N. Tolw KT6 & KT9 57 B8
Hook Rise North. Surb KT6 56 E7
Hook Rise S. Tolw KT6 & KT9 57 B8
Hook Rise South. Chess KT6 56 E7
Hook Underpass. Surb KT6 56 E7
Hooke Rd. E Hors KT24 92 F2
Hookfield. Epsom KT18 & KT19 76 C6
Hookfield Mews. Epsom KT19 76 C6
Hookhouse Rd. Dunsf GU8 192 D6
Hookley Cl. Elst GU8 148 E3
Hookley La. Elst GU8 148 E3
Hookstile La. M Bourn GU9 125 C1
Hookstone La. W End GU24 67 F8
Hookwood Bglws. Limps RH8 123 B6
Hookwood Cnr. Limps RH8 123 B7
Hookwood Cotts. Head KT18 96 C3
Hooley La. Earls RH1 139 F8
Hoover House. Catf SE6 24 C4
Hope Ave. Brack RG12 27 E2
Hope Cl. Sutton SM1 59 C5
Hope Ct. Crawl RH11 201 B1
Hope Fountain. Friml GU15 65 F4
Hope Grant's Rd. Alder GU11 105 A4
Hope La. Hale GU9 125 B6
Hope Pk. Broml BR1 24 F1
Hope St. Elst GU8 148 D4
Hopeman Cl. Sandh GU15 64 D7
Hopes Cl. Heston TW5 5 A8
Hopfield. Horse GU21 69 E3
Hopfield Ave. Byfl KT14 71 E6
Hophurst Cl. Crawl D RH10 204 B8
Hophurst Dr. Crawl D RH10 204 B8
Hophurst Hill. Crawl D RH10 & RH19 184 D2
Hophurst La. Crawl D RH10 184 B1
Hopkins Ct. Crawl RH11 201 B1
Hoppety The. Tadw KT20 97 D5
Hoppingwood Ave. King U T KT3 38 E6
Hopton Gdns. New Mal KT3 39 A3
Hopton Rd. Streat SW16 21 E3
Horace Rd. King U T KT1 37 F6
Horatio Ave. Wink RG12 27 E8
Horatius Way. Wallin CR0 60 F4
Hordern House. Horsh RH12 217 A1
Horewood Rd. Easth RG12 27 B3
Horley Cty Fst Sch. Horley RH6 161 A3
Horley Lodge La. Salfs RH1 161 A8
Horley Rd. Crawl RH6 181 B7
Horley Rd. Earls RH1 139 F5
Horley Rd. Hookw RH6 181 B7
Horley Row. Horley RH6 161 A4
Horley Sta. Horley RH6 161 B2
Hormer Cl. Sandh GU15 45 D1
Horn Rd. W Heath GU14 84 E5
Hornbeam Cl. Horsh RH13 217 F1
Hornbeam Cl. Sandh GU15 45 D1
Hornbeam Cl. W Heath GU14 84 C5
Hornbeam Cres. Brent TW8 6 B7
Hornbeam Rd. Bellf GU1 109 C3
Hornbeam Rd. Woodh RH2 139 C6
Hornbeam Terr. Carsh SM5 40 E1
Hornbeam Wlk. Whit V KT12 53 F2
Hornchurch Cl. King U T KT2 17 D3
Hornchurch Hill. Whytlf CR3 80 F1
Horndean Cl. Crawl RH10 182 D2
Horndean Cl. 3 Rhampt SW15 19 A7
Horndean Rd. Brack RG12 27 F3
Horne Rd. Shep Gn TW17 34 A5
Hornecourt Hill. Horne RH1 & RH6 & RH9 162 F7
Horner La. Mitch CR4 40 D7
Hornhatch. Chil GU4 131 B3
Hornhatch Cl. Chil GU4 131 B3
Hornhatch La. Chil GU4 131 B2
Horniman Dr. For Hil SE23 23 C8
Horniman Prim Sch. For Hil SE23 23 B7
Hornshill La. Buck Gn RH12 213 F7
Horsa Cl. Wallin SM6 60 E3
Horse Fair. King U T KT1 37 D7
Horse Gate Ride. Ascot SL5 29 A3
Horse Hill. Horley RH6 160 B4
Horsebrass Dr. Bagsh GU19 47 E2
Horsecroft. Banstd SM7 77 F2
Horsell Birch. Horse GU21 69 B4
Horsell Birch. Woking GU21 69 A4
Horsell C of E Sch. Horse GU21 69 C3
Horsell Common Rd. Horse GU21 69 C5
Horsell Ct. Chert KT16 33 B2
Horsell Cty Fst Sch. Horse GU21 69 D4
Horsell High Sch. Horse GU21 69 D4
Horsell Moor. Horse GU21 69 D2
Horsell Park Cl. Horse GU21 69 D3
Horsell Pk. Horse GU21 69 E3
Horsell Rise. Horse GU21 69 E4
Horsell Rise Cl. Horse GU21 69 D4
Horsell Vale. Horse GU21 69 E3
Horsell Way. Horse GU21 69 C3
Horseshoe Bend. Graysh GU26 188 B3
Horseshoe Cl. Camb GU15 65 F8
Horseshoe Cl. Crawl RH10 202 D7
Horseshoe Cres. Camb GU15 65 F8
Horseshoe La. Ash V GU12 106 A7
Horseshoe La. Cran GU6 174 D4
Horseshoe La E. Merrow GU1 110 C2
Horseshoe La W. Merrow GU1 110 B1
Horseshoe Ridge. Whit V KT13 72 C8
Horseshoe The. Banstd SM7 77 F4
Horseshoe The. Coulsd CR5 & CR8 79 D6
Horseshoe The.Ock Rid GU7 150 C3
Horsham Bsns Pk. Faygt RH12 198 C4
Horsham Hospl. Horsh RH12 217 C3
Horsham Rd. Alfold GU6 193 F8
Horsham Rd. Bear Gn RH5 157 C4
Horsham Rd. Bear Gn RH5 157 C6
Horsham Rd. Bramly GU5 & GU4 151 E7
Horsham Rd. Bramly GU5 & GU6 173 D5
Horsham Rd. Capel RH5 178 C2
Horsham Rd. Capel RH5 178 D8
Horsham Rd. Cran GU6 174 E1
Horsham Rd. Cran GU6 & RH14 194 C1
Horsham Rd. Crawl GU5 & GU6 173 D5
Horsham Rd. Crawl RH11 201 B4
Horsham Rd. Dork RH4 136 A6
Horsham Rd. Dork RH5 136 B2
Horsham Rd. E Bed TW14 3 C1
Horsham Rd. Ell Gn GU6 176 B1
Horsham Rd. Ewh GU6 175 F3
Horsham Rd. Hol St M GU5 & RH5 & GU6 155 C5
Horsham Rd. Rowhk RH5 & RH12 196 D5
Horsham Rd. Rusper RH12 199 B5
Horsham Rd. S Holm RH5 157 C6
Horsham Rd. Sandh GU15 45 D1
Horsham Rd. Shalf GU4 130 E3

Horsham Rd. Wall W RH5 & GU6 176 E4
Horsham Rd. Wall W RH12 & RH5 196 D5
Horsham Sta. Horsh RH13 217 D2
Horsley Cl. Epsom KT19 76 D6
Horsley Dr. King U T KT2 17 D3
Horsley Dr. New Add CR0 63 C3
Horsley Rd. Downs KT11 & KT24 93 B7
Horsley Sta. W Hors KT24 92 E2
Horsneile La. Brack RG12 27 B8
Horton Hill. Epsom KT19 76 C8
Horton Hospl. Epsom KT19 76 B8
Horton La. Epsom KT19 & KT18 57 B2
Horton Rd. Coln SL3 1 A6
Horton Rd. Horton SL3 1 A6
Horton Rd. Poyle SL3 & TW19 1 E4
Horton Rd. Stan TW19 2 A2
Horton Trad Est. Horton SL3 1 C4
Horton Way. Croy CR0 43 D4
Horvath Cl. Oat Pk KT13 53 D6
Hosack Rd. Up Toot SW12 & SW17 21 A6
Hoskins Pl. E Grins RH19 186 A4
Hoskins Rd. Oxted RH8 122 E6
Hospital Bridge Rd. Twick TW2 16 B7
Hospital Hill. Alder GU11 105 A3
Hospital of the Holy Trinity (Almshouses). 5 Croy CR9 61 C8
Hospital Rd. Alder GU11 105 B3
Hospital Rd. Hounsl TW3 5 A4
Hostel Rd. Farnb GU14 105 B8
Hotham Cl. E Mole KT8 36 A6
Hotham Rd. Merton SW19 20 C1
Houblon Rd. Rich TW10 6 E2
Houghton Cl. Hampt TW12 15 E2
Houlder Cres. Croy CR0 61 B4
Houlton Ct. Bagsh GU19 47 F2
Hound House Rd. Shere GU5 154 A5
Hounslow Ave. Islew TW3 5 B2
Hounslow Bsns Pk. Hounsl TW3 5 B3
Hounslow Central Sta. Hounsl TW3 5 B4
Hounslow East Sta. Hounsl TW3 5 C5
Hounslow Gdns. Islew TW3 5 B2
Hounslow Heath Jun & Inf Schs. Hounsl TW4 4 E4
Hounslow Manor Sch. Hounsl TW3 5 C4
Hounslow Rd. Felt TW14 4 B1
Hounslow Rd. Felt TW13 & TW14 15 B8
Hounslow Rd. Felt TW13 15 D4
Hounslow Rd. Twick TW2 & TW3 5 C1
Hounslow Sta. Islew TW3 5 B2
Hounslow Town Prim Sch. Hounsl TW3 5 D4
Hounslow West Sta. Hounsl TW3 4 E5
Houseman Rd. W Heath GU14 84 F6
Houston Ct. 3 Croy CR0 42 E1
Houston Ct. Heston TW5 4 F7
Houston Rd. For Hil SE23 & SE6 23 E5
Hove Gdns. Cheam SM1 40 B1
Hovenden House. 6 Dulw SE21 22 E4
How La. Chips CR5 79 A1
Howard Ave. Ewell KT17 58 A1
Howard Cl. Ashf TW16 14 F2
Howard Cl. Ashtd KT21 75 F1
Howard Cl. Hampt TW12 16 C2
Howard Cl. Leahd KT22 95 C4
Howard Cl. W Hors KT24 92 D2
Howard Cl. Walt o t H KT20 97 A2
Howard Cole Way. Alder GU11 104 E2
Howard Ct. Beck BR3 44 C7
Howard Ct. Effing KT24 113 D8
Howard Ct. Reig RH2 118 B2
Howard Dr. W Heath GU14 84 B4
Howard Gdns. Merrow GU1 110 A2
Howard House. Penge SE20 43 C8
Howard House. Reig RH2 118 B2
Howard of Effingham Sch. Effing KT24 113 E8
Howard Prim Sch. Croy CR0 61 C6
Howard Rd. Coulsd CR5 79 D5
Howard Rd. Crawl RH11 200 D2
Howard Rd. Croy SE25 43 A3
Howard Rd. Dork RH4 136 A7
Howard Rd. Dork RH5 136 C3
Howard Rd. E Hors KT24 93 A4
Howard Rd. G Book KT23 114 C8
Howard Rd. Horsh RH13 218 A4
Howard Rd. Islew TW7 5 F4
Howard Rd. New Mal KT3 38 F5
Howard Rd. Penge SE20 43 C8
Howard Rd. Reig RH2 139 B8
Howard Rd. Surb KT5 37 F3
Howard Rd. Woki RG11 25 C5
Howard Ridge. Burph GU4 110 A5
Howard St. Thame D KT7 37 B3
Howards Cl. Old Wok GU22 90 A7
Howards Crest Cl. Beck BR3 44 C7
Howards La. Row Tn KT15 51 F3
Howards Rd. Old Wok GU22 89 F7
Howberry Rd. S Norw CR7 42 D7
Howden Ct. S Norw SE25 42 F7
Howden Rd. S Norw SE25 42 F7
Howe Dr. Cater CR3 100 D5
Howe The. Farnb GU14 84 B1
Howell Hill Cl. E Ewell KT17 77 C8
Howell Hill Gr. E Ewell KT17 58 C1
Howgate Rd. Mortl SW14 7 D4
Howland House. 9 Streat SW16 21 E5
Howley Rd. Croy CR0 & CR9 61 C7
Howmic Ct. 1 Twick TW1 6 C1
Howorth Ct. Brack RG12 27 E5
Howson Terr. Rich TW10 6 E1
Hoylake Cl. Crawl RH11 200 D5
Hoylake Gdns. Mitch CR4 41 C6
Hoyle Hill. Bear Gn RH5 157 D1
Hoyle Rd. Up Toot SW17 20 E3
Hubbard Rd. W Norw SE27 22 C4
Hubberholme. Easth RG12 27 A6
Huddleston Cres. Merst RH1 119 D7
Hudson Ct. 4 Merton SW19 40 B8
Hudson Ct. Stough GU2 108 F1
Hudson Rd. Crawl RH10 201 E4
Hudson Rd. Harl UB7 3 D8
Hudsons. Tadw KT20 97 D6
Hugh Herland. King U T KT1 37 E6
Hughenden Rd. New Mal KT4 39 A2
Hughes Ct. Thorn H CR0 42 A1
Hughes Rd. Ashf TW15 14 C2
Hughes Rd. Woki RG11 25 E7
Hughes Wlk. Thorn H CR0 42 C2
Hullbrook La. Sham Gn GU5 152 D4
Hullmead. Sham Gn GU5 152 E4
Hulton Cl. Leahd KT22 95 C4
Hulverston Cl. Sutton SM2 59 B2
Humber Way. Sandh GU15 64 D8
Humbolt Cl. Stough GU2 108 F1
Hummer Rd. Egham TW20 12 A4
Humphrey Cl. Fetch KT22 94 C5
Humphries Yd. Easth RG12 27 C5
Hungerford Cl. Sandh GU17 64 C8
Hungerford Sq. 3 Oat Pk KT13 53 D6
Hungry Hill La. Ripley GU23 91 D3
Hunstanton Cl. Crawl RH11 200 D5
Hunston Rd. Cheam SM4 40 B1
Hunter Cl. Up Toot SW12 21 A7
Hunter House. Crawl RH10 201 D3
Hunter Rd. Crawl RH10 & RH11 201 D4
Hunter Rd. Farnb GU14 84 F3
Hunter Rd. Guild GU1 130 E8
Hunter Rd. S Norw CR7 42 D6
Hunter Rd. Wimble SW20 39 C8
Hunters Chase. S Godst RH9 142 F6
Hunters Cl. Epsom KT19 76 C6
Hunters Ct. 5 Rich TW9 6 D2
Hunters Meadow. Dulw SE19 22 E4
Hunters Rd. Chess KT9 56 E6
Hunters The. Beck BR3 44 C8
Hunters Way. S Croy CR0 61 E6
Huntersfield Cl. Reig RH2 118 B4
Hunting Cl. Esher KT10 55 A6
Hunting Gate Dr. Chess KT9 56 E3
Hunting Gate Mews. Sutton SM1 59 B7
Hunting Gate Mews. Twick TW2 16 E7
Huntingdon Cl. Mitch CR4 & SW16 41 E5
Huntingdon Ct. Mortl SW14 7 C4
Huntingdon Gdns. Chisw W4 7 C7
Huntingdon Gdns. N Cheam KT4 58 C7
Huntingdon Rd. Redh RH1 118 F1
Huntingdon Rd. Woking GU21 68 F2
Huntingfield. New Add CR0 62 F3
Huntingfield Way. Egham TW20 12 D2
Huntingford Cl. Beac H GU26 188 C7
Huntley House. 7 Dulw SE21 22 E4
Huntley Way. Wimble SW20 39 A7
Huntly Rd. S Norw SE25 42 E5
Hunts Cl. Stough GU2 108 D2
Hunts Hill Rd. Normdy GU3 107 A4
Hunts Slip Rd. Dulw SE21 22 E6
Huntsgreen Ct. Brack RG12 27 C7
Huntsman Cl. Felt TW13 15 B4
Huntsman's Mews. Mytch GU16 85 F3
Huntsmans Cl. Fetch KT22 94 D3
Huntsmans Cl. Warlgm CR6 101 C8
Huntsmans Ct. Cater CR3 100 C6
Huntsmans Meadow. N Asct SL5 28 F8
Huntsmoor Rd. W Ewell KT19 57 D5
Huntsmoor Rd. W Ewell KT19 57 D5
Huntspill St. Wands SW17 20 C5
Huntsworth Ct. Catf SE6 24 A7
Hurlands Bsns Ctr. Farnh GU9 125 F4
Hurlands Cl. Farnh GU10 & GU9 125 F4
Hurlands La. Dunsf GU8 192 F2
Hurlands Pl. Farnh GU9 125 F4
Hurley Cl. Walt O T KT12 54 B8
Hurley Ct. Brack RG12 27 E5
Hurley Gdns. Burph GU4 110 A4
Hurlford. Woking GU21 69 A2
Hurlstone Rd. S Norw SE25 42 E4
Hurn Court Rd. Hounsl TW5 4 D5
Hurn Ct. Hounsl TW5 4 D5
Hurnford Cl. S Croy CR2 61 E1
Huron Rd. Up Toot SW17 21 A5
Hurricane Way. Farnb GU14 104 F7
Hursley Ct. 11 Surb KT6 37 D2
Hurst Ave. Horsh RH12 217 D3
Hurst Cl. Chess KT9 57 A5
Hurst Cl. Crawl RH11 200 F4
Hurst Cl. Hayes BR2 44 F1
Hurst Cl. Head KT18 96 C3
Hurst Cl. Woking GU22 89 C7
Hurst Croft. Guild GU1 130 E6
Hurst Ct. Beck BR3 24 A1
Hurst Ct. Horsh RH12 217 D3
Hurst Ct. S Norw SE25 42 F5
Hurst Dr. Walt o t H KT20 97 A1
Hurst Farm Cl. Milf GU8 149 F2
Hurst Farm Rd. E Grins RH19 205 D7
Hurst Gr. Walt O T KT12 34 F1
Hurst Green Cl. Oxted RH8 123 A3
Hurst Green Cty Prim Sch. Oxted RH8 123 A3
Hurst Green Rd. Oxted RH8 122 F3
Hurst Green Sta. Oxted RH8 122 F3
Hurst Hill Cotts. Bramly GU5 152 B4
Hurst House. 7 Penge SE26 23 B3
Hurst La. E Mole KT8 36 C6
Hurst La. Head KT18 96 D4
Hurst La. Thorpe TW20 32 A7
Hurst Lodge. 4 Whit V KT13 53 D4
Hurst Lodge Sch. Sunnin SL5 29 F2
Hurst Park Cty Prim Sch. E Mole KT8 36 A6
Hurst Rd. Alder GU11 105 C4
Hurst Rd. Croy CR0 61 D5
Hurst Rd. E Mole KT8 & KT12 36 C6
Hurst Rd. Epsom KT19 76 D8
Hurst Rd. Farnb GU14 85 B8
Hurst Rd. Horley RH6 160 E4
Hurst Rd. Horsh RH12 217 D3
Hurst Rd. Walt O T KT8&KT12 35 D5
Hurst View Rd. S Croy CR2 61 E3
Hurst Way. Pyrf GU22 70 E5
Hurst Way. S Croy CR2 61 E4
Hurstbourne. Clayg KT10 55 F4
Hurstbourne House. Rhampt SW15 7 F1
Hurstbourne Priors. S Croy CR2 61 E4
Hurstbourne Rd. For Hil SE23 23 E7
Hurstcourt Rd. Sutton SM1 59 B8
Hurstdene Ave. Hayes BR2 44 F1
Hurstdene Ave. Stain TW18 13 B2
Hurstfield Rd. E Mole KT8 36 A6
Hurstlands. Oxted RH8 123 A3
Hurstleigh Cl. Redh RH1 118 F3
Hurstleigh Dr. Redh RH1 118 F3
Hurstmere Cl. Graysh GU26 188 D3
Hurstview Grange. Croy CR0 61 B3
Hurstwood. Ascot SL5 29 A3
Hurtmore Chase. Farnc GU7 150 B7
Hurtmore Rd. Farnc GU7 150 B7
Hurtmore Rd. Shackl GU7 150 B7
Hurtwood Rd. Walt O T KT12 35 F2
Hurtwood Sixth Form Coll. Ewh GU6 155 A2
Hussar Ct. Alder GU11 104 E2
Hussars Cl. Hounsl TW4 4 E4
Hutchingson's Rd. New Add CR0 82 C8
Hutchins House. 8 Streat SW4 21 D8
Hutchins Way. Horley RH6 160 F5
Hutsons Cl. Woki RG11 25 D8
Hutton Cl. Windl GU20 48 D3
Hutton Rd. Ash V GU12 106 A6
Huxley Cl. Farnc GU7 150 D7
Huxley Rd. Onsl V GU2 129 D8
Hyacinth Cl. 3 Hampt TW12 16 A2
Hyacinth Rd. Rhampt SW15 19 A7
Hyde Cl. Ashf TW16 14 E2
Hyde Dr. Crawl RH11 200 E5
Hyde Farm Sch. Streat SW12 21 D7
Hyde Heath Ct. Crawl RH10 202 D8
Hyde La. Beac H GU10 & GU8 168 E1
Hyde La. Thursl GU8 169 A2
Hyde Rd. Rich TW10 6 F2
Hyde Rd. Sander CR2 & CR8 80 E6
Hyde Terr. Ashf TW15 & TW16 14 E2
Hyde Wlk. Morden SM4 40 A2
Hydestile Cotts. Hyde GU8 171 D5
Hydestile Hospl. Hyde GU8 171 E5
Hydethorpe Rd. Streat SW12 21 C7
Hylands Cl. Crawl RH10 202 A5
Hylands Cl. Woodc KT18 76 C4
Hylands Mews. Woodc KT18 76 C4
Hylands Rd. Woodc KT18 76 C4
Hylton Lodge. Hersh KT12 54 C5
Hyndewood. 14 For Hil SE23 23 D5
Hyperion Ct. Crawl RH11 200 E4
Hyperion House. 1 Streat SW2 21 F8
Hyperion Pl. Epsom KT19 57 D2
Hyperion Wlk. Horley RH6 161 B1
Hyrstdene. Croy CR0 61 B6
Hythe Cl. Brack RG12 27 E4
Hythe End Rd. Wray TW19 12 A5
Hythe Field Ave. Egham TW20 12 D2
Hythe Park Rd. Egham TW20 12 D2
Hythe Rd. Egham TW18 12 D3
Hythe Rd. S Norw CR7 & SE25 42 D7
Hythe Sch The. Egham TW18 12 D3
Hythe The. Egham TW18 12 E3

Ian Ct. For Hil SE23 23 C6
Iberian Ave. Wallin CR0 & SM6 60 E6
Iberian Way. Camb GU15 66 B6
Ibis La. Chisw W4 7 C6
Ibotson Ct. Poyle SL3 1 E6
Ibsley Gdns. Rhampt SW15 19 A7
Ibstock Place Sch. Rhampt SW15 7 E1
Icehouse Wood. Oxted RH8 122 F4
Icklesham House. 9 Crawl RH11 200 F3
Icklingham Gate. Cobham KT11 73 C7
Icklingham Rd. Cobham KT11 73 D6
Iden Cl. Beck BR2 44 E6
Idlecombe Rd. Streat SW17 21 A2
Idmiston Rd. New Mal KT4 38 F2
Idmiston Rd. W Norw SE21 & SE27 22 C6
Idmiston Sq. New Mal KT4 38 F2
Ifield Ave. Crawl RH11 201 C7
Ifield Cl. Earls RH1 139 E7
Ifield Comm Sch. Crawl RH11 201 A7
Ifield Cty Jun Sch. Crawl RH11 201 A6
Ifield Cty Mid Sch. Crawl RH11 201 A6
Ifield Fst Sch. Crawl RH11 201 A8
Ifield Gn. Crawl RH11 181 A1
Ifield Rd. Charl RH6 180 E5
Ifield Rd. Crawl RH11 201 C6
Ifield St. Crawl RH11 200 F8
Ifield Sta. Crawl RH11 201 A6
Ifield Wood. Rusper RH11 180 E1
Ifold Bridge La. Ifold RH14 212 D4
Ifold Rd. Earls RH1 140 A7
Ifoldhurst. Ifold RH14 212 C2
Ightham House. Beck BR3 23 F1
Ikona Ct. Whit V KT13 53 C5
Ildersly Gr. Dulw SE21 22 D6
Ilex Cl. Eng Gn TW20 11 B1
Ilex Cl. Sunby TW16 35 C7
Ilex House. Woodhm KT15 52 A1
Ilex Way. W Norw SW16 22 A3
Ilford Ct. Crawl GU6 173 F2
Ilfracombe Rd. Catf BR1 24 F5
Ilkley Cl. S Norw SE19 22 D2
Illingworth Cl. Mitch CR4 40 D6
Illingworth Gr. Brack RG12 27 F8
Imber Cl. Thame D KT7 36 D1
Imber Court Trad Est. Thame D KT8 36 D3
Imber Cross. Thame D KT7 36 F3
Imber Gr. Thame D KT10 36 D2
Imber Park Rd. Thame D KT10 36 D1
Imberhorne La. E Grins RH19 185 B2
Imberhorne Lower Sch. E Grins RH19 185 D3
Imberhorne Sch. E Grins RH19 185 B3
Imberhorne Way. E Grins RH19 185 B3
Imjin Cl. Alder GU11 105 B3
Immanuel & St Andrew C of E Prim Sch. Streat SW16 21 E2
Impact Ct. Penge SE20 43 B7
Imperial Gdns. Mitch CR4 41 B6
Imperial House. Vir W GU25 31 E4
Imperial Rd. E Bed TW14 14 E8
Imperial Way. Croy CR0 & CR9 61 A4
Impington. 8 King U T KT1 38 A7
Imran Ct. Alder GU12 126 C8
Ince Rd. Whit V KT12 53 E4
Inchmery Rd. Catf SE6 24 C7
Inchwood. Croy BR4 & CR0 63 B6
Inchwood. Easth RG12 27 C1
Independent Bsns Pk The. E Grins RH19 185 A3
Ingatestone Rd. Croy SE25 43 B5
Ingham Cl. S Croy CR2 62 D2
Ingham Rd. S Croy CR2 62 D2
Ingle Dell. Camb GU15 65 D4
Ingle House. Streat SW12 21 D7
Ingleboro Dr. Sander CR8 80 D6
Ingleby Way. Wallin SM6 60 D3
Inglehurst. Woodhm KT15 52 B1
Inglemere Ct. Mitch CR4 & SW17 20 F1
Inglemere Rd. For Hil SE23 23 D5
Inglemere Rd. Mitch CR4 & SW17 20 F1
Ingleside. Poyle SL3 1 F6
Ingleside Cl. Beck BR3 24 A1
Ingleton. Easth RG12 27 A6
Ingleton Rd. Sutton SM5 59 E2
Inglewood. Addl KT16 51 F7
Inglewood. New Add CR0 62 E2
Inglewood. Woking GU21 69 B1
Inglewood Ave. Friml GU15 66 D5
Inglewood Ct. 2 Broml BR1 24 F1
Inglis Rd. Croy CR0 42 F1
Ingram Cl. Horsh RH12 217 A2
Ingram High Sch for Boys. S Norw CR7 42 C8
Ingram House. Tedd KT8 37 C8
Ingram Rd. S Norw CR7 42 C8
Ingrams Almshouses. Islew TW7 6 A5
Ingrams Cl. Hersh KT12 54 C5
Ingrebourne Hse. Catf BR1 24 D3
Inholms La. Dork RH5 136 C3
Ink Pen La. For Row RH18 206 E1
Inkerman Rd. Knaph GU21 68 E1
Inkerman Way. Knaph GU21 68 E1
Inman Rd. Wands SW18 20 C8
Inner Park Rd. Putney SW19 19 D6
Inner Quadrant. Ash V GU12 106 A5
Inner Ring E. Harl TW6 3 B4
Inner Ring W. Harl TW6 3 A4
Inner Staithe. Chisw W4 7 C6
Innes Cl. Merton SW20 39 E7
Innes Lodge. For Hil SE23 23 D5
Innes Rd. Horsh RH12 217 F4
Innes Yd. Croy CR0 & CR9 61 C7
Innings La. Wink RG12 27 E8

Innisfail Gdns. Alder GU11 125 F8
Inst of Oceanographic Sciences. Wormly GU8 170 F1
Institute Rd. Alder GU12 .. 105 D1
Institute Rd. Westc RH4 .... 135 C6
Instone Cl. Wallin SM6 .... 60 E3
Instow Gdns. W Heath GU14 85 A7
Inval Hill. Haslem GU27 ..... 208 C8
Inveresk Gdns. Worc Pk KT4 58 A7
Inverness Ct. Catf SE6 .... 24 F7
Inverness Rd. Hounsl TW3 .... 5 A3
Inverness Rd. N Cheam KT4 39 D1
Inverness Way. Sandh GU15 64 D7
Invicta Cl. E Bed TW14 .... 14 F7
Invicta Ct. Chess KT9 .... 56 F5
Invincible Rd. Farnb GU14 ... 85 A3
Inwood Ave. Coulsd CR5 ... 100 A7
Inwood Ave. Hounsl TW3 ...... 5 C4
Inwood Bsns Pk. Hounsl TW3 5 B3
Inwood Cl. Croy CR0 .... 62 E8
Inwood Ct. 1 Walt O T KT12 .... 54 C8
Inwood Rd. Hounsl TW3 .... 5 C3
Iona Cl. Crawl RH11 .... 201 B3
Iona Cl. For Hil SE13 & SE4 & SE6 .... 24 A8
Ipsley Lodge. Tongh GU10 . 126 E5
Ipswich Rd. Mitch SW17 ...... 21 A2
Irene Rd. Oxsh KT11 .... 74 B5
Ireton Ave. Oat Pk KT13 ...... 53 F8
Iris Cl. Croy CR0 .... 43 D1
Iris Cl. Surb KT6 .... 37 F2
Iris Rd. Bisley GU24 .... 68 A4
Iris Rd. W Ewell KT19 .... 57 B5
Iris Rd. W Ewell KT19 .... 57 B5
Iron La. Bramly GU5 .... 151 D5
Irons Bottom Rd. Sidlow RH2 .... 159 F8
Irvine Ct. Thorn H CR7 .... 42 A3
Irvine Dr. W Heath GU14 ..... 84 E8
Irvine Pl. Thorpe GU25 .... 31 E4
Irving Wlk. Crawl RH10 ...... 201 E3
Irwin Dr. Horsh RH12 .... 217 A2
Irwin Rd. Guild GU2 .... 130 A7
Isabel Cotts. Epsom KT18 .... 76 B5
Isabella Ct. 8 Rich TW10 ..... 6 F1
Isbells Dr. Reig RH2 .... 139 B7
Isham Rd. Thorn H SW16 ..... 41 E7
Isis Ct. Chisw W4 .... 7 B7
Isis St. Wands SW18 .... 20 C6
Isis Way. Sandh GU15 & GU17 .... 64 D8
Island Cl. Stain TW18 .... 12 E4
Island Cotts The. Downs KT11 .... 73 B1
Island Farm Ave. E Mole KT8 35 F4
Island Farm Rd. E Mole KT8 36 A4
Island House. Morden SW19 40 C5
Island Rd. Mitch CR4 & SW19 .... 20 F1
Islay Gdns. Hounsl TW4 .... 4 D2
Isleworth Bsns Complex. Islew TW7 .... 5 F5
Isleworth Sta. Hounsl TW7 .... 5 F5
Isleworth & Syon Sch for Boys. Hounsl TW7 .... 5 E7
Isleworth Town Sch. Islew TW7 .... 6 A5
Itchingwood Common Rd. Limps RH8 .... 123 E2
Ivanhoe Cl. Crawl RH11 .... 181 D1
Ivanhoe House. 11 Balham SW12 .... 21 B8
Ivanhoe Rd. Hounsl TW4 .... 4 D4
Iveagh Cl. Crawl RH11 .... 201 C1
Iveagh Ct. Beck BR3 .... 44 B6
Iveagh Ct. Brack RG12 .... 27 C4
Iveagh Rd. Guild GU2 .... 130 B7
Ively Gate Rd. Farnb GU14 .. 84 E2
Ively Rd. Farnb GU14 .... 84 D1
Iverna Gdns. Hatton TW14 .... 3 D2
Ivers Way. New Add CR0 ..... 63 B3
Ivestor Terr. For Hil SE23 .... 23 C8
Ivor Cl. Guild GU1 .... 131 A8
Ivory Ct. Felt TW13 .... 15 A7
Ivory Wlk. Crawl RH11 .... 200 E3
Ivy Cl. Sunby TW16 .... 35 C7
Ivy Dene La. Ash W RH19 . 206 D6
Ivy Dr. Lhtwat GU18 .... 67 A7
Ivy Gdns. Mitch CR4 .... 41 D6
Ivy House. Croy CR0 .... 43 D1
Ivy La. Farnh GU9 .... 125 B2
Ivy La. Hounsl TW4 .... 4 F3
Ivy La. Mayb GU22 .... 70 B1
Ivy Mill Cl. Godst RH9 .... 121 B3
Ivy Mill La. Bletch RH1 & 9 121 B3
Ivy Mill La. Godst RH1 & RH9 .... 121 B3
Ivy Rd. Alder GU12 .... 105 E2
Ivy Rd. Hounsl TW3 .... 5 B3
Ivy Rd. Tolw KT6 .... 38 A1
Ivy Rd. Up Toot SW17 .... 20 E3
Ivybank. Farnc GU7 .... 150 E6
Ivybridge Cl. 3 Twick TW1 17 A8
Ivybridge Jun & Inf Sch. Islew TW1 .... 5 F1
Ivychurch Cl. Penge SE20 .... 23 C1
Ivydale Rd. Carsh SM5 .... 59 F8
Ivyday Gr. Streat SW16 .... 21 F5
Ivydene. E Mole KT12 & KT8 35 F4
Ivydene. Knaph GU21 .... 68 B1
Ivydene Cl. Earls RH1 .... 140 B4
Ivydene Cl. Sutton SM1 .... 59 C6
Ivymount Rd. W Norw SE27 22 A5
Jackass La. Tand RH9 .... 121 F4
Jackdaw Cl. Crawl RH11 .... 201 C8
Jackdaw La. Horsh RH12 .... 217 E6
Jackman's La. Woking GU21 89 B8
Jackson Cl. Crawl GU6 .... 173 F2
Jackson Cl. Easth RG12 .... 27 B4
Jackson Cl. Epsom KT18 .... 76 D5
Jackson's Pl. Croy CR0 .... 42 E1
Jackson's Way. W Wick CR0 63 B7
Jacob Cl. Binf RG12 .... 26 D7
Jacob Rd. Sandh GU15 .... 65 A7
Jacobean Cl. Worth RH10 .. 202 C5
Jacobs Well Rd. Jacobs GU4 .... 109 D6
Jaggard Way. Balham SW12 20 F8
Jaguar Rd. Farnb GU14 .... 85 B2
Jail La. Bigg H TN16 .... 83 E3
Jamaica Rd. Thorn H CR7 .... 42 B3
James Boswell. 1 Streat SW16 .... 22 A4
James Dixon Prim Sch. Penge SE20 .... 23 B1
James Est. Mitch CR4 .... 40 F7
James Rd. Camb GU15 .... 65 B2
James Rd. Farnb GU11 ...... 105 D7
James Rd. Shalf GU3 .... 130 C1
James St. Hounsl TW3 .... 5 D4
James Watt Way. Crawl RH10 .... 182 A4
James Way. Camb GU15 ...... 65 B2
Jameston. Easth RG12 .... 27 C1
Jamieson House. Twick TW4 15 F8
Jamnagar Cl. Stain TW18 ..... 12 F2
Janoway Hill. Woking GU21 . 89 C8
Japonica Cl. Woking GU21 .. 69 C1
Japonica Ct. Ash GU12 ...... 105 F1
Jarrett Cl. Streat SW2 .... 22 B7
Jarrow Cl. Morden SM4 .... 40 B4
Jarvis Rd. S Croy CR2 .... 61 D4
Jasmin Rd. W Ewell KT19 ..... 57 B5
Jasmin Rd. W Ewell KT19 ..... 57 B5
Jasmine Cl. Earls RH1 .... 140 A4
Jasmine Cl. Woking GU21 .... 68 F3
Jasmine Ct. Horsh RH12 .... 217 C2
Jasmine Ct. 11 Wallin SM6 . 60 B4
Jasmine Gdns. W Wick CR0 63 B7
Jasmine Gr. Penge SE20 ...... 43 B8
Jasmine Way. Thame D KT7 36 E5
Jason Cl. Earls RH1 .... 139 E4
Jason Cl. Weyb KT13 .... 53 C5
Jasons Dr. Merrow GU4 ..... 110 C4
Jasper House. New Mal KT4 38 D1
Jasper Rd. Dulw SE19 .... 22 F2
Jasper Rd. W Norw SE19 ..... 22 F2
Javelin Ct. Crawl RH10 ...... 182 D1
Jawahar Bagh. S Norw SW16 22 B2
Jay Ave. Chert KT15 .... 52 E7
Jay's La. Fish GU27 .... 209 C3
Jay's La. Lurg GU27 .... 209 C3
Jays Nest Cl. Blckw GU17 ... 64 D4
Jayson Ct. 7 Croy CR0 ...... 43 A1
Jeal Oakwood Ct. Epsom KT18 .... 76 E5
Jean House. Up Toot SW17 . 20 E3
Jean Humbert House. 2 W Norw SE27 .... 22 D4
Jeans Ct. 10 Crawl RH11 .. 201 B1
Jeddere Cotts. Dorman RH7 .... 165 A2
Jeffries Pas. Guild GU1 ...... 130 D8
Jeffries Rd. W Hors KT24 ... 112 C5
Jeffs Cl. Hampt TW12 .... 16 B2
Jeffs Rd. Cheam SM1 .... 58 F6
Jefton Ct. Wallin SM6 .... 60 C4
Jengar Cl. Sutton SM1 .... 59 B6
Jenkins' Hill London Rd. Bagsh GU19 .... 47 D2
Jenner Dr. W End GU24 .... 68 A6
Jenner Rd. Crawl RH10 ...... 181 F3
Jenner Rd. Guild GU1 .... 130 E8
Jennett Rd. Croy CR0 & CR9 61 A7
Jennifer Rd. Catf BR1 .... 24 F5
Jennings Cl. New Haw KT15 52 C2
Jenny La. Lingf RH7 .... 164 C4
Jenson Way. S Norw SE19 ... 22 F1
Jeppo's La. Mitch CR4 .... 40 F5
Jersey Brow Rd. Farnb GU14 85 A2
Jersey Cl. Addl KT16 .... 51 F7
Jersey Cl. Burph GU4 .... 110 B6
Jersey Rd. Crawl RH11 ...... 201 A2
Jersey Rd. Hounsl TW5 & TW7 5 D7
Jersey Rd. Mitch SW17 .... 21 B2
Jerviston Gdns. S Norw SW16 .... 22 A2
Jesmond Cl. Mitch CR4 .... 41 B6
Jesmond Rd. Croy CR0 .... 42 F2
Jessamy Rd. Weyb KT13 ...... 53 B8
Jesses La. Gomsh GU5 .... 154 C8
Jessie's Hollow. Gomsh GU5 .... 133 C1
Jessiman Terr. Shep Gn TW17 .... 34 A4
Jessops Way. Mitch CR0 & CR4 .... 41 C3
Jeston House. 10 W Norw SE27 .... 22 B5
Jevington. Easth RG12 .... 27 C1
Jewell House. 3 Streat SW12 .... 21 C8
Jewels Hill. Bigg H TN16 ...... 83 A6
Jewels Hill. W Wick CR6 ...... 83 A6
Jews Wlk. For Hil SE26 .... 23 B4
Jeypore Rd. Wands SW18 .... 20 C8
Jig's La S. Wink RG12 .... 27 E8
Jillian Cl. Hampt TW12 .... 16 A1
Jobson's La. Fish GU27 ..... 209 D2
Jobson's La. Lurg GU27 .... 209 D1
Jocelyn Rd. Rich TW9 .... 6 E4
Jock's La. Brack RG12 .... 26 E8
Jockey Mead. Horsh RH12 217 A1
Joe Hunte Ct. 2 W Norw SW27 .... 22 B3
John Baird Ct. For Hil SE26 . 23 D4
John Baird House. 14 Penge SE20 .... 23 C1
John Barter House. Hounsl TW3 .... 4 F5
John Busch Sch. Brent TW7 .. 6 B6
John Cl. Alder GU11 & GU9 125 E8
John Cobb Rd. Whit V KT13 53 A3
John Dee House. 3 Mortl SW14 .... 7 D4
John Fisher Sch The. Purley CR8 .... 60 E1
John Gale Ct. Ewell KT17 ..... 57 F2
John Kaye Ct. Shep Gn TW17 .... 34 A4
John Kirk House. 5 Streat SW16 .... 21 E5
John Nightingale Sch. E Mole KT8 .... 35 F6
John Nike Way. Binf RG12 ... 26 C7
John Paul II RC Sec Sch. Putney SW19 .... 19 D8
John Pounds House. Crawl RH11 .... 201 D4
John Ruskin Sixth Form Coll. S Croy CR2 .... 62 E3
John Russell Cl. Stough GU2 .... 109 A4
John St. Croy SE25 .... 43 A5
John St. Hounsl TW3 & TW5 .. 4 E5
John Wesley Ct. 5 Twick TW1 .... 17 A7
John Wiskar Dr. Cran GU6 174 D2
John's Cl. Ashf TW15 .... 14 C4
John's Rd. Tats TN16 .... 103 D7
John's Terr. Croy CR0 .... 42 E1
Johns La. Morden SM4 .... 40 C4
Johns Wlk. Whytlf CR3 ...... 101 A8
Johnsdale. Oxted RH8 .... 122 F6
Johnson Rd. Heston TW5 ...... 4 C7
Johnson Rd. Thorn H CR0 ... 42 D2
Johnson Wlk. Crawl RH10 . 201 E3
Johnson's Cl. Carsh SM5 ...... 59 F7
Johnsons Dr. Hampt TW12 .. 36 C8
Johnston Gr. Stough GU2 . 109 A5
Johnston Wlk. Stough GU2 109 A5
Joinville Pl. Addl KT15 .... 52 D6
Jolesfield. Crawl RH11 .... 200 F3
Jolliffe Rd. Merst RH1 .... 99 C1
Jones Wlk. 6 Rich TW10 ...... 6 F1
Jonquil Gdns. 5 Hampt TW12 .... 16 A2
Jonson Cl. Mitch CR4 .... 41 B6
Jordan Cl. S Croy CR2 .... 80 F8
Jordans Cl. Crawl RH11 ..... 201 D8
Jordans Cl. Earls RH1 .... 140 A4
Jordans Cl. Merrow GU1 ... 110 A2
Jordans Cl. Stan TW19 .... 13 C8
Jordans Cres. Crawl RH11 181 D1
Jordans The. E Grins RH19 205 E8
Josef Perrin House. 1 W Norw SE27 .... 22 D4
Joseph Hood Fst Sch. Merton SW20 .... 39 E6
Joseph Locke Way. Thame D KT10 .... 55 A8
Joseph's Rd. Guild GU1 ..... 109 D2
Josephine Ave. L Kings KT20 .... 117 F8
Josephine Cl. L Kings KT20 117 F8
Jubilee Ave. N Asct SL5 .... 28 E8
Jubilee Ave. Twick TW2 .... 16 C7
Jubilee Ave. Woki RG11 .... 25 B7
Jubilee Cl. N Asct SL5 .... 28 E8
Jubilee Cl. Stan TW19 .... 13 C8
Jubilee Cl. Tedd KT1 .... 37 C8
Jubilee Cl. W Heath GU14 .... 84 D4
Jubilee Cres. Addl KT15 .... 52 D5
Jubilee Ct. Brack RG12 .... 27 C6
Jubilee Ct. Hounsl TW3 .... 5 B4
Jubilee Ct. Stain TW18 .... 13 A4
Jubilee Ct. Thorn H CR7 ...... 42 A5
Jubilee Dr. Ash V GU12 ...... 106 A6
Jubilee Hall Rd. Farnb GU14 85 C4
Jubilee House. 5 Hampt TW12 .... 36 A8
Jubilee La. Graysh GU26 .... 188 C3
Jubilee La. Rowl GU10 ...... 146 A5
Jubilee Rd. Alder GU11 ...... 126 B7
Jubilee Rd. Cheam SM3 .... 58 D3
Jubilee Rd. Mytch GU16 .... 86 A2
Jubilee Rd. Rudg RH12 ...... 214 D8
Jubilee Terr. Brock RH3 ..... 137 C5
Jubilee Terr. Dork RH4 ...... 136 B8
Jubilee Villas. Thame D KT10 36 E1
Jubilee Way. Chess KT4 & KT9 .... 57 B7
Jubilee Way. E Bed TW14 .... 15 A7
Jubilee Way. Merton SW19 . 40 B8
Jubilee Way. Tolw KT4 & 9 .. 57 B7
Jubilee Wks. Merton SW19 . 40 C7
Jubilee Wlk. Crawl RH10 .. 202 A6
Judge Wlk. Clayg KT10 .... 55 E4
Judge's Terr. E Grins RH19 205 E8
Julian Cl. Woking GU21 .... 69 C1
Julian Hill. Whit V KT13 .... 53 B3
Julian House. Dulw SE21 ...... 22 E4
Julian Taylor Path. For Hil SE23 .... 23 B6
Julians Prim Sch. Streat SW16 .... 22 A4
Julien Rd. Coulsd CR5 .... 79 D4
Juliet Gdns. Wink RG12 .... 27 F8
Julius Ct. Brent TW8 .... 6 E7
Julius Hill. Wink RG12 .... 27 F8
Jumps Rd. Churt GU10 ...... 168 B3
Junction Pl. Shottm GU27 .. 207 F6
Junction Rd. Ashf TW15 ...... 14 C3
Junction Rd. Croy CR2 .... 61 D5
Junction Rd. Dork RH4 ...... 136 A7
Junction Rd. Lhtwat GU18 .... 48 B1
June Cl. Wallin CR5 .... 79 B5
June La. Salfs RH1 .... 140 B2
Junewood Cl. Woodhm KT15 70 F8
Juniper. Easth RG12 .... 27 C1
Juniper Cl. Bellf GU1 .... 109 C6
Juniper Cl. Bigg H TN16 .... 83 E2
Juniper Cl. Chess KT9 .... 56 F5
Juniper Cl. Woodh RH2 ...... 139 C7
Juniper Ct. Belm SM2 .... 59 A4
Juniper Dr. Bisley GU24 .... 68 A4
Juniper Gdns. Ashf TW16 ..... 14 F2
Juniper Gdns. Mitch CR4 ..... 41 C8
Juniper Hall (Field Study Ctr). Mickle RH5 .... 115 C6
Juniper Pl. Shalf GU4 .... 130 D2
Juniper Rd. Crawl RH11 ..... 181 C1
Juniper Rd. W Heath GU14 .. 84 C5
Juniper Rd. Woodh RH2 ..... 139 C7
Juniper Terr. Shalf GU4 .... 130 D2
Juniper Wlk. Brock RH3 ..... 137 C7
Jura Cl. Crawl RH11 .... 201 B3
Justin Cl. Brent TW8 .... 6 D7
Jutland Gdns. Coulsd CR5 .... 99 F7
Jutland Pl. Egham TW20 .... 12 C3
Jutland Rd. Catf SE6 .... 24 C8
Juxon Cl. Crawl RH11 .... 200 F4

Kaithwood House. Horsh RH12 .... 218 B5
Kangley Bridge Ctr. Penge SE26 .... 23 F3
Kangley Bridge Rd. For Hil SE26 .... 23 F3
Kangley Bridge Rd. Penge SE26 .... 23 F3
Karen Ct. Broml BR1 .... 44 F8
Kashmir Cl. New Haw KT15 . 52 D2
Katharine Rd. 1 Twick TW1 17 A7
Katharine St. Croy CR0 & CR9 .... 61 C7
Katherine Cl. Row Tn KT15 .. 52 A4
Katherine Ct. For Hil SE23 ... 23 C7
Kathleen Moore Ct. W Wick BR4 .... 63 C8
Kay Ave. Chert KT15 .... 52 E7
Kay Cres. Head Dn GU35 ... 187 B6
Kaye Ct. Bellf GU1 .... 109 C5
Kaye Don Way. Whit V KT13 53 A1
Kayemoor Rd. Sutton SM2 ... 59 E4
Kaynes Pk. N Asct SL5 .... 28 E8
Keable Rd. Wreccl GU10 .... 145 E7
Kearton Cl. Kenley CR8 .... 80 C2
Keates Gn. Brack RG12 .... 27 B8
Keats Ave. Redh RH1 .... 119 B3
Keats Cl. Horsh RH12 .... 217 F7
Keats Cl. Mitch SW17 & SW19 .... 20 D2
Keats House. Beck BR3 .... 24 B2
Keats Pl. E Grins RH19 .... 185 D1
Keats Way. Crowth RG11 ..... 45 B6
Keats Way. Croy CR0 .... 43 C3
Keble Cl. Crawl RH10 .... 182 D1
Keble Cl. New Mal KT4 .... 38 F1
Keble St. Wands SW17 .... 20 C4
Keble Way. Sandh GU15 .... 45 E2
Kedeston Ct. Sutton SM3 ..... 40 B1
Keedonwood Rd. Broml BR1 24 F3
Keedonwood Rd. Catf BR1 .. 24 F3
Keeley Rd. Croy CR0 & CR9 .. 61 C8
Keeling House. 2 Tedd TW11 .... 16 E3
Keen's Rd. Croy CR0 .... 61 C6
Keens Cl. Streat SW16 .... 21 D3
Keens La. Stough GU2 & GU3 .... 108 F5
Keens Park Rd. Stough GU3 108 F5
Keep Hatch Cty Inf Sch. Woki RG11 .... 25 D7
Keep Hatch Cty Jun Sch. Woki RG11 .... 25 D7
Keep The. Catf SE6 .... 24 B7
Keep The. King U T KT2 .... 17 F1
Keepers Cl. Merrow GU4 .... 110 D4
Keepers Combe. Brack RG12 27 D3
Keepers Mews. Tedd TW11 . 17 C2
Keepers Terr. Went GU25 .... 31 B4
Keepers Wlk. Vir W GU25 .... 31 D4
Keephatch Rd. Woki RG11 ... 25 E7
Keevil Dr. Putney SW19 .... 19 E8
Keir Hardie House. 7 Crawl RH11 .... 201 B1
Keith Lucas Rd. Farnb GU14 84 F2
Keith Park Cres. Bigg H TN16 .... 83 C7
Keldholme. Easth RG12 .... 27 A6
Kelling Gdns. Thorn H CR0 ... 42 B2
Kellino St. Up Toot SW17 ..... 20 F4
Kelly Cl. Up Hall TW17 .... 34 E7
Kelmscott. 5 For Hil SE23 .. 23 D5
Kelsey Cl. Horley RH6 .... 160 F3
Kelsey Gate. Beck BR3 .... 44 B7
Kelsey La. Beck BR3 .... 44 A6
Kelsey Park Ave. Beck BR3 .. 44 B7
Kelsey Park Rd. Beck BR3 .... 44 A7
Kelsey Park Sch. Beck BR3 .. 44 A6
Kelsey Sq. Beck BR3 .... 44 A7
Kelsey Way. Beck BR3 .... 44 A6
Kelso Cl. Crawl RH10 .... 202 E7
Kelso Ct. Penge SE20 .... 23 B1
Kelso Rd. Carsh SM5 .... 40 C2
Kelvedon Ave. Whit V KT12 . 53 F3
Kelvedon Cl. King U T KT2 .... 18 A2
Kelvin Ave. Leahd KT22 .... 94 F7
Kelvin Bsns Ctr. Crawl RH10 .... 181 F2
Kelvin Cl. Chess KT19 .... 57 A4
Kelvin Ct. Chisw W4 .... 7 C7
Kelvin Ct. Islew TW7 .... 5 E5
Kelvin Ct. 8 Penge SE20 ...... 43 B8
Kelvin Ct. 8 Twick TW1 .... 6 B1
Kelvin Dr. Twick TW1 .... 6 B1
Kelvin Gdns. Croy CR0 .... 41 E2
Kelvin Gr. Chess KT6 .... 56 E7
Kelvin Gr. For Hil SE26 .... 23 B5
Kelvin Grove Prim Sch. For Hil SE26 .... 23 B5
Kelvin Grove Prim Sch. For Hil SE23 .... 23 E7
Kelvin La. Crawl RH10 .... 181 F2
Kelvin Way. Crawl RH10 ..... 181 F2
Kelvinbrook. E Mole KT8 ...... 36 B6
Kelvington Cl. Croy CR0 ...... 43 E2
Kelyway House. 20 Streat SW2 .... 22 A8
Kemble Cl. Oat Pk KT13 .... 53 D6
Kemble Cotts. Addl KT15 ...... 52 A6
Kemble Rd. Croy CR0 & CR9 61 B7
Kemble Rd. For Hil SE23 ...... 23 D7
Kembleside Rd. Bigg H TN16 83 C1
Kemerton Rd. Beck BR3 .... 44 B7
Kemerton Rd. Croy CR0 .... 42 F2
Kemishford. Woking GU22 ... 89 A4
Kemnal Pk. Haslem GU27 .. 208 D7
Kemp Ct. Bagsh GU19 .... 47 F2
Kemp Gdns. Thorn H CR0 ..... 42 C3

Kempshott Rd. Horsh RH12 217 B4
Kempshott Rd. Streat SW16 21 E1
Kempston House. Sutton SM2 59 B2
Kempton Ave. Sunby TW16 35 B8
Kempton Ct. Sunby TW16 35 B8
Kempton Park Race Course. Sunby TW16 15 C1
Kempton Park Sta. Sunby TW16 15 B1
Kempton Rd. Hampt TW12 35 F7
Kempton Wlk. Croy CR0 43 E3
Kemsing Cl. Coney H BR2 63 F8
Kemsing Cl. Thorn H CR7 42 C5
Kemsley Rd. Tats TN16 103 D8
Kendal Cl. E Bed TW14 14 F7
Kendal Cl. Farnb GU14 84 E4
Kendal Cl. Redh RH1 118 D2
Kendal Ct. 7 Croy CR0 42 E1
Kendal Gdns. Sutton SM1 59 C8
Kendal Gr. Friml GU15 66 D4
Kendal House. 5 Croy CR0 42 E1
Kendal House. Penge SE20 43 B7
Kendale Rd. Lewish BR1 24 E3
Kendall Ave. Penge BR3 43 E7
Kendall Ave. S Croy CR2 61 D2
Kendall Ave S. S Croy CR2 61 D1
Kendall Ct. 4 Penge SE19 22 F1
Kendall House. Lewish SE12 24 F8
Kendall Rd. Islew TW7 6 A5
Kendall Rd. Penge BR3 43 E7
Kendor Ave. Epsom KT19 76 C8
Kendra Hall Rd. Croy CR2 61 B3
Kendrey Gdns. Twick TW2 16 E8
Kendrick Cl. Woki RG11 25 C5
Kenilford Rd. Balham SW12 21 B8
Kenilworth Ave. Brack RG12 27 D8
Kenilworth Ave. Oxsh KT11 74 B5
Kenilworth Ave. Wimble SW19 20 A4
Kenilworth Cl. Banstd SM7 78 B3
Kenilworth Cl. Crawl RH11 201 B2
Kenilworth Ct. Twick TW2 16 E6
Kenilworth Dr. Walt O T KT12 54 D7
Kenilworth Gdns. Stain TW18 13 C3
Kenilworth Rd. Ashf TW15 & TW19 13 D5
Kenilworth Rd. Penge SE20 43 D8
Kenilworth Rd. Stonel KT17 58 A5
Kenilworth Rd. W Heath GU14 84 C5
Kenilworth Terr. 3 Belm SM2 59 A3
Kenley Cl. Cater CR3 100 E7
Kenley Gdns. Thorn H CR7 42 B5
Kenley House. 5 Croy CR0 43 A1
Kenley La. Kenley CR8 80 D3
Kenley Prim Sch. Kenley CR3 80 E3
Kenley Rd. Head Dn GU35 187 C5
Kenley Rd. King U T KT1 & KT3 38 B7
Kenley Rd. Merton SW19 40 A6
Kenley Rd. Twick TW1 6 B1
Kenley Sta. Kenley CR8 80 C5
Kenley Wlk. Cheam SM3 58 D6
Kenlor Rd. Up Toot SW17 20 D3
Kenmara Cl. Crawl RH10 182 A1
Kenmara Ct. Crawl RH10 182 A2
Kenmare Dr. Mitch CR4 20 F1
Kenmare Rd. Thorn H CR7 42 A3
Kenmore Cl. Friml GU16 85 D8
Kenmore Cl. Rich TW9 7 A7
Kenmore Rd. Purley CR8 80 B5
Kennard Ct. For Row RH18 206 E3
Kennedy Ave. E Grins RH19 185 D3
Kennedy Ct. Ashf TW15 14 C3
Kennedy Rd. Horsh RH13 217 D1
Kennel Ave. N Asct SL5 28 F8
Kennel Cl. Fetch KT22 & KT23 94 C3
Kennel Cl. N Asct SL5 8 F2
Kennel Gn. N Asct SL5 28 E8
Kennel La. Fetch KT22 94 C4
Kennel La. Frensh GU10 146 C2
Kennel La. Hookw RH6 160 D2
Kennel La. Windl GU20 48 C5
Kennel Ride. N Asct SL5 8 F1
Kennel Wood. N Asct SL5 28 F8
Kennel Wood Cres. New Add CR0 82 D8
Kennels La. Farnb GU14 84 C2
Kennet Cl. Ash GU12 106 A1
Kennet Cl. Crawl RH11 200 F5
Kennet Cl. W Heath GU14 84 E6
Kennet House. 6 Redh RH1 118 F2
Kennet Rd. Islew TW7 5 F4
Kennet Sq. Mitch CR4 40 E8
Kenneth Rd. Woodm SM7 78 D4
Kennoldes. Dulw SE21 22 D6
Kenrick Sq. Bletch RH1 120 E1
Kensington Ave. S Norw CR7 42 A8
Kensington Avenue Inf Sch. S Norw CR7 42 A8
Kensington Avenue Jun Sch. S Norw CR7 42 A8
Kensington Rd. Crawl RH11 201 C2
Kensington Terr. S Croy CR2 61 D3
Kent Cl. Mitch CR4 & SW16 41 E5
Kent Cl. Stain TW18 13 D2
Kent Dr. Tedd TW11 16 E3
Kent Gate Way. Add CR0 63 B5
Kent Gate Way. New Add CR0 & CR2 62 F4
Kent Hatch Rd. Limps RH8 & TN8 123 D4
Kent Hatch Rd. The Char RH8 & TN8 123 D4
Kent House La. Penge BR3 23 E3
Kent House Rd. For Hil SE26 & BR3 23 E2
Kent House Rd. Penge SE26 & BR3 23 E2
Kent House Sta. Penge BR3 43 E8
Kent Lodge. 9 Putney SW19 19 D7
Kent Rd. E Mole KT8 36 C5
Kent Rd. King U T KT1 37 D6
Kent Rd. Mayb GU22 70 C3
Kent Rd. Rich TW9 7 A7
Kent Rd. W Wick BR4 44 B1
Kent Rd. Windl GU20 48 D5
Kent Tower. Penge SE20 23 B1
Kent Way. Surb KT6 56 F8
Kentigern Dr. Crowth RG11 45 E5
Kenton Ave. Sunby TW16 35 E7
Kenton Cl. Brack RG12 27 D7
Kenton Cl. Friml GU16 65 F1
Kenton Ct. For Hil SE26 23 E4
Kenton Way. Woking GU21 68 F2
Kentwyns Rise. S Nutf RH1 140 F8
Kenwood Cl. Harm UB7 3 A8
Kenwood Dr. Beck BR3 44 C6
Kenwood Dr. Whit V KT12 54 B5
Kenwood Pk. Whit V KT13 53 D4
Kenwood Ridge. Kenley CR8 80 B2
Kenwyn Rd. Wimble SW20 39 C8
Kenya Ct. Horley RH6 160 F4
Kenyngton Dr. Ashf TW16 15 A3
Kenyngton Manor Prim Sch. Ashf TW16 15 A2
Kenyons. W Hors KT24 112 B7
Keogh Barracks. Ash GU16 86 B1
Keogh Cl. Mytch GU16 86 B2
Keppel Rd. Dork RH4 115 B1
Keppel Spur. Old W SL4 11 B8
Kepple Pl. Bagsh GU19 47 F3
Kerdale Cl. Worth RH10 202 C2
Kerria Way. W End GU24 67 F6
Kerrill Ave. Coulsd CR5 100 A8
Kerrsland Cotts. Shackl GU7 149 F7
Kerry Terr. Woking GU21 70 B3
Kersey Dr. Selsd CR2 81 D7
Kershaw House. 7 W Norw SE27 22 B5
Keston Ave. Coulsd CR5 & CR8 100 B8
Keston Ave. Woodhm KT15 71 A8
Keston Avenue Cty Prim Sch. Coulsd CR5 100 A8
Keston Rd. Thorn H CR7 42 A3
Kestrel Ave. Stain TW18 12 F5
Kestrel Cl. Crawl RH11 201 C8
Kestrel Cl. Crond GU10 124 D7
Kestrel Cl. Horsh RH12 217 E5
Kestrel Cl. Merrow GU4 110 D3
Kestrel House. M Bourn GU9 146 A8
Kestrel Rd. Farnb GU14 85 B2
Kestrel Way. New Add CR0 63 D2
Keswick Ave. King U T KT2 & SW15 18 E3
Keswick Ave. Merton SW19 40 A7
Keswick Ave. Up Hall TW17 34 E6
Keswick Cl. Crawl RH11 200 D4
Keswick Cl. Friml GU15 66 D4
Keswick Cl. Sutton SM1 59 C6
Keswick Dr. Lhtwat GU18 67 B8
Keswick Rd. Fetch KT22 & KT23 94 C2
Keswick Rd. Thor L TW20 12 B1
Keswick Rd. Twick TW2 5 C1
Keswick Rd. W Wick BR4 63 E8
Keswick Rd. Witley GU8 170 D6
Kettering Ct. S Norw CR7 42 C5
Kettering St. Streat SW16 21 C2
Kettlewell Cl. Horse GU21 69 E4
Kettlewell Dr. Horse GU21 69 E5
Kettlewell Hill. Horse GU21 69 E4
Ketton Gn. Merst RH1 119 D7
Kevan Dr. Send M GU23 90 E2
Kevin Cl. Hounsl TW4 4 D5
Kew Bridge Rd. Brent TW8 6 F8
Kew Cres. Cheam SM3 58 F7
Kew Foot Rd. Rich TW9 6 E4
Kew Gardens Rd. Rich TW9 7 A6
Kew Gardens Sta. Rich TW9 7 A6
Kew Gn. Rich TW9 6 F8
Kew Lodge. 10 Rich TW9 6 F6
Kew Observatory. Rich TW9 6 C4
Kew Rd. Rich TW9 & W4 6 F5
Key Cross. Tilf GU10 147 D5
Keymer Cl. Bigg H TN16 83 D3
Keymer Rd. Crawl RH11 201 D4
Keymer Rd. Streat SW2 21 F6
Keynsham Rd. Cheam SM4 40 B1
Keynsham Way. Sandh GU15 45 D2
Keynsham Wlk. Cheam SM4 40 B1
Keysham Ave. Cranf TW5 4 A6
Keywood Dr. Ashf TW16 15 A2
Khama Rd. Up Toot SW17 20 E4
Khartoum Rd. Up Toot SW17 20 D4
Khartoum Rd. Witley GU8 170 E6
Kibble Gn. Easth RG12 27 C3
Kidborough Down. G Book KT23 114 A8
Kidborough Rd. Crawl RH11 200 F4
Kidbrooke Park (Michael Hall Sch). For Row RH18 206 D1
Kidbrooke Rise. For Row RH18 206 E2
Kidderminster Rd. Thorn H CR0 42 C2
Kidmans Cl. Horsh RH12 217 F5
Kidworth Cl. Horley RH6 160 F5
Kielder Wlk. Friml GU15 66 C4
Kier Pk. Ascot SL5 29 C6
Kilberry Cl. Hounsl TW7 5 D6
Kilcorral Cl. Ewell KT17 77 A5
Killasser Ct. Tadw KT20 97 C4
Killearn Rd. Catf SE6 24 D7
Killester Gdns. N Cheam KT17 & KT4 58 B6
Killick House. Sutton SM1 59 B6
Killicks. Cran GU6 174 F4
Killieser Ave. Streat SW2 21 E6
Killigrew House. Charlt TW16 14 E1
Killross Rd. E Bed TW14 14 D7
Kilmarnock Pk. Reig RH2 118 B2
Kilmartin Ave. Thorn H SW16 42 A6
Kilmartin Gdns. Friml GU16 65 F1
Kilmington Cl. Brack RG12 27 E2
Kilmiston Ave. Shep TW17 34 C3
Kilmiston House. Shep TW17 34 C3
Kilmore Dr. Friml GU15 66 B4
Kilmorey Gdns. Islew TW1 6 B3
Kilmorey Rd. Islew TW1 6 B3
Kilmorie Prim Sch. For Hil SE23 23 E6
Kilmorie Rd. For Hil SE23 23 E6
Kilmuir Cl. Sandh GU15 64 D7
Kiln Cl. Harl UB3 3 D8
Kiln Copse. Cran GU6 174 E4
Kiln Fields. Haslem GU27 208 C8
Kiln La. Brack RG12 27 A7
Kiln La. Brock RH3 116 C1
Kiln La. Ewell KT17 76 E8
Kiln La. Horley RH6 161 A5
Kiln La. M Bourn GU10 & GU9 146 C6
Kiln La. Ripley GU23 91 B3
Kiln La. Sunnin SL5 30 A4
Kiln Meadows. Fairl GU3 108 C5
Kiln Rd. Crawl D RH10 204 B7
Kiln Way. Alder GU11 126 B7
Kiln Way. Graysh GU26 187 E5
Kiln Wlk. Earls RH1 140 A4
Kilnfield Rd. Rudg RH12 214 D8
Kilnmead. Crawl RH10 & RH11 201 E7
Kilnmead Cl. Crawl RH10 201 E7
Kilnside. Clayg KT10 56 A3
Kilnwood La. Crawl RH12 200 B3
Kilnwood La. Faygt RH12 199 F3
Kilross Rd. E Bed TW14 14 E7
Kilrue La. Whit V KT12 53 F6
Kilrush Terr. Woking GU21 70 A3
Kilsha Rd. Walt O T KT12 35 C3
Kimber Ct. Merrow GU4 110 D3
Kimber Ctr The. Wands SW18 20 A8
Kimber Rd. Wands SW18 20 B8
Kimberley. Easth RG12 27 C1
Kimberley Cl. Horley RH6 160 E3
Kimberley Pl. 5 Purley CR8 80 A8
Kimberley Rd. Crawl RH10 202 B7
Kimberley Rd. Penge BR3 43 D7
Kimberley Rd. Thorn H CR0 & CR7 42 B3
Kimberley Ride. Cobham KT11 74 B6
Kimberley Wlk. Walt O T KT12 35 B2
Kimbers La. Farnh GU9 125 D3
Kimble Rd. Mitch SW17 & SW19 20 D2
Kimbolton Cl. Lewish SE12 24 F8
Kimmeridge. Brack RG12 27 E3
Kimpton Bsns Ctr. Cheam SM3 58 F8
Kimpton House. Rhampt SW15 19 A8
Kimpton Ind Est. Cheam SM3 58 F8
Kimpton Rd. Cheam SM3 58 F8
Kinburn Dr. Eng Gn TW20 11 E3
Kindell House. 4 Mortl SW14 7 D4
Kindersley Cl. E Grins RH19 186 B3
Kinfauns Rd. Streat SW2 22 A6
King Acre Ct. Stain TW18 12 E5
King Alfred Ave. Catf SE6 24 A4
King Athelstan Prim Sch. King U T KT1 37 F6
King Charles Cres. Surb KT5 37 F2
King Charles' Rd. Surb KT5 & KT6 37 F3
King Charles Wlk. 6 Putney SW19 19 E7
King Edward Dr. Chess KT6 56 E7
King Edward VII (Old Windsor Unit). Old W SL4 10 F8
King Edward's Gr. Tedd TW11 17 C2
King Edward's Sch. Wormly GU8 170 F1
King Edwards Rd. N Asct SL5 28 E8
King Edwards Rise. N Asct SL5 28 E8
King Garth Mews. For Hil SE23 23 C6
King Gdns. Croy CR0 61 B5
King George Ave. E Grins RH19 185 C3
King George Ave. Walt O T KT12 35 D1
King George Cl. Ashf TW16 14 E3
King George Sq. Rich TW10 6 F1
King George V1 Ave. Bigg H TN16 83 D3
King George VI Ave. Mitch CR4 40 F5
King George's Cotts. Dunsf GU8 192 F6
King George's Dr. Woodhm KT15 52 A1
King George's Lodge. Stough GU2 109 A4
King George's Trad Est. Chess KT9 57 A6
King Henry's Dr. New Add CR0 82 E8
King Henry's Dr. W Wick CR0 82 E8
King Henry's Rd. King U T KT1 & KT3 38 B6
King St. Chert KT16 33 A1
King St. E Grins RH19 185 E1
King St. Rich TW10 & TW9 6 D2
King St. Twick TW1 17 A7
King Street Par. 6 Twick TW1 17 A7
King William IV Gdns. Penge SE20 23 C2
King's Ave. Ashf TW16 14 F2
King's Ave.Hounsl TW3 & TW5 5 B6
King's Cl. Stain TW18 13 D1
King's Cl. Thame D KT7 37 A2
King's Coll Sch. Wimble SW19 19 D2
King's Court Cty Fst Sch. Old W SL4 11 B8
King's Ct. Alder GU10 & GU12 126 E8
King's Ct. Beck BR3 44 B6
King's Ct. Wimble SW19 20 A2
King's Dr. Thame D KT7 37 B2
King's Head La. Byfl KT14 71 D8
King's House Jun Sch. Rich TW10 6 F2
King's House Sch. Rich TW10 6 F2
King's Keep. Sandh GU17 45 B1
King's La. Carsh SM1 & SM2 59 D5
King's Paddock. Hampt TW12 36 C8
King's Pas. King U T KT2 37 D8
King's Rd. Alder GU11 104 F1
King's Rd. Ascot SL5 29 D4
King's Rd. Cran GU6 174 F2
King's Rd. Crowth RG11 45 C5
King's Rd. Croy SE25 43 A6
King's Rd. Egham TW20 12 A4
King's Rd. Farnc GU7 150 F6
King's Rd. Haslem GU27 208 A6
King's Rd. Horsh RH12 & RH13 217 E3
King's Rd. King U T KT2 18 E1
King's Rd. Long D KT6 37 C1
King's Rd. Mortl SW14 7 D4
King's Rd. Tedd TW11 & TW12 16 D3
King's Rd. Twick TW1 6 B1
King's Rd. Wimble SW19 20 A2
King's Ride. Brack SL5 28 D5
King's Ride. Camb GU15 65 D7
King's Shade Wlk. 1 Epsom KT18 76 D6
King's Terr. 8 Islew TW7 6 A4
King's Way. Pirb GU24 87 D8
King's Wlk. Sandh GU15 64 F6
Kingcup Cl. Croy CR0 43 D1
Kingcup Dr. Bisley GU24 68 A4
Kingfield Cl. Old Wok GU22 89 F7
Kingfield Dr. Old Wok GU22 89 F7
Kingfield Gdns. Old Wok GU22 89 F7
Kingfield Rd. Old Wok GU22 89 F7
Kingfield Sch. Old Wok GU22 90 A7
Kingfisher Cl. Crawl RH10 182 A1
Kingfisher Cl. Hersh KT12 54 E5
Kingfisher Cl. Putney SW19 19 E6
Kingfisher Cl. W Heath GU14 84 D6
Kingfisher Ct. Dork RH4 136 A8
Kingfisher Ct. E Mole KT8 36 E5
Kingfisher Ct. Islew TW3 5 B2
Kingfisher Ct. Sheer GU21 70 C5
Kingfisher Dr. Merrow GU4 110 C3
Kingfisher Dr. Redh RH1 119 A3
Kingfisher Dr. Stain TW18 12 F4
Kingfisher Dr. Tedd TW10 17 B4
Kingfisher Gdns. Selsd CR2 62 D1
Kingfisher Lodge. Tedd TW11 17 A4
Kingfisher Rise. E Grins RH19 205 F8
Kingfisher Sports Ctr The. 12 King U T KT1 37 E7
Kingfisher Way. Beck CR0 43 D4
Kingfisher Way. Horsh RH12 217 C5
Kingfisher Wlk. Alder GU12 105 F2
Kingham Cl. Wands SW18 20 C8
Kings Ave. Ash GU10 & GU12 126 F8
Kings Ave. Broml BR1 24 F2
Kings Ave. Byfl KT14 71 D7
Kings Ave. Earls RH1 139 E7
Kings Ave. New Mal KT3 38 F5
Kings Ave. Streat SW12 & SW4 21 D8
Kings Ave. Wallin SM5 59 F3
Kings Chase. E Mole KT8 36 C6
Kings Cl. Walt O T KT12 35 B1
Kings Copse. 9 E Grins RH19 205 F8
Kings Cres. Camb GU15 65 C8
Kings Cross La. S Nutf RH1 140 E6
Kings Ct. Horsh RH13 217 E3
Kings Ct. 16 King U T KT2 18 A1
Kings Ct. 11 Rhampt SW15 19 A8
Kings Ct. Tadw KT20 97 C5
Kings Ct. 3 Wallin SM6 60 B4
Kings Dr. Surb KT5 38 A3
Kings Dr The. Whit V KT12 53 F2
Kings Farm Ave. Rich TW10 7 A3
Kings Gate. Farnc GU7 150 F6
Kings Hall Rd. Penge BR3 43 E8
Kings Keep. King U T KT6 37 E5
Kings La. Eng Gn TW20 11 A2
Kings La. Windl GU20 48 E5
Kings La. Wreccl GU10 & GU9 145 F6
Kings' Manor Sch. Stough GU2 108 E1
Kings Mead. S Nutf RH1 140 E7
Kings Mead. Smallf RH6 162 B3
Kings Mead Pk. Clayg KT10 55 E3
Kings Mill La. S Nutf RH1 140 D5
Kings Mill La. Salfs RH1 140 D5
Kings Rd. Belm SM2 59 A1
Kings Rd. Bigg H TN16 83 C2
Kings Rd. Felt TW13 15 C7
Kings Rd. Horley RH6 161 A3

Kings Rd. Mitch CR4 .... 41 A6
Kings Rd. Rich TW10 & TW9 .. 6 F2
Kings Rd. Shalf GU4 .... 130 E2
Kings Rd. W End GU24 .... 68 A6
Kings Rd. Walt O T KT12 .... 35 B1
Kings Rd. Woking GU21 .... 70 A3
Kings Rd. Woner GU5 .... 152 B8
Kings Rd. Woodhm KT15 ...... 71 B8
Kings Way. Croy CR0 .... 60 F5
Kings Wlk. Hams Gn CR2 ...... 81 B5
Kings's Rd. 2 Guild GU1 .. 109 D1
Kingsbridge House. 11 Penge SE20 .... 43 B8
Kingsbridge Rd. W Barn SM4 39 D2
Kingsbridge Rd. Walt O T KT12 .... 35 B2
Kingsbrook. Leahd KT22 .... 75 A1
Kingsbury Cres. Egham TW18 .... 12 D4
Kingsbury Dr. Old W SL4 ...... 11 B8
Kingsclear Pk. Camb GU15 ... 65 D4
Kingsclere Cl. Rhampt SW15 19 A8
Kingscliffe Gdns. Wands SW19 .... 19 F7
Kingscote Hill. Crawl RH11 201 B4
Kingscote Rd. Croy CR0 & CR9 .... 43 B2
Kingscote Rd. King U T KT3 . 38 D6
Kingscote Sta. E Grins RH19 .... 204 F4
Kingscourt Rd. Streat SW16 21 E5
Kingscroft Cty Mid Sch. Stain TW18 .... 13 A2
Kingscroft La. New Gn RG12 & SL4 .... 8 A6
Kingscroft Rd. Leahd KT22 ... 95 B7
Kingscroft Rd. Woodm SM7 . 78 E4
Kingsdale Rd. Penge SE20 ... 23 D1
Kingsdale Sch. Dulw SE21 ... 22 E5
Kingsdene. Tadw KT20 .... 97 B5
Kingsdown. 1 Wimble SW19 .... 19 D1
Kingsdown Ave. S Croy CR2 & CR8 .... 61 C2
Kingsdown Rd. Cheam SM3 . 58 E5
Kingsdown Rd. Ewell KT17 .. 77 A6
Kingsdowne Rd. Surb KT6 ... 37 F2
Kingsfield. Farl Gn GU5 ...... 153 E7
Kingsfold Ct. Warn RH12 .. 198 B5
Kingsford Ave. Wallin SM6 .. 60 E3
Kingsgate Bsns Ctr. King U T KT2 .... 37 E8
Kingsgate Rd. King U T KT2 . 37 E8
Kingshill Ave. New Mal KT4 . 39 B2
Kingslake Ct. 2 Knaph GU21 .... 68 E1
Kingsland. Newd RH5 .... 158 A1
Kingslea. Horsh RH13 .... 217 E3
Kingslea. Leahd KT22 .... 95 A7
Kingslee Ct. 12 Sutton SM2 . 59 B3
Kingsleigh Pl. Mitch CR4 ...... 40 F6
Kingsleigh Wlk. Hayes BR2 .. 44 F5
Kingsley Ave. Banstd SM7 ... 78 A4
Kingsley Ave. Camb GU15 .... 65 D3
Kingsley Ave. Carsh SM1 ..... 59 D6
Kingsley Ave. Eng Gn TW20 . 11 B2
Kingsley Ave. Hounsl TW3 ..... 5 C5
Kingsley Cl. Crowth RG11 .... 45 B3
Kingsley Cl. Horley RH6 ..... 160 F5
Kingsley Ct. Walt O T KT12 .. 54 A7
Kingsley Ct. Worc Pk KT4 ..... 57 F8
Kingsley Dr. Worc Pk KT4 .... 57 F8
Kingsley Gr. Dovgn RH2 .... 139 B5
Kingsley House. 8 King U T KT6 .... 37 E4
Kingsley Inf Sch. Thorn H CR9 .... 42 A1
Kingsley Jun Sch. Thorn H CR9 .... 42 A1
Kingsley Rd. Crawl RH11 ... 201 A3
Kingsley Rd. Horley RH6 .... 160 F5
Kingsley Rd. Hounsl TW3 .... 5 C5
Kingsley Rd. Thorn H CR0 .... 42 A1
Kingsley Rd. W Heath GU14 . 84 F6
Kingsley Rd. Wimble SW19 .. 20 B3
Kingslyn Cres. S Norw SE19 42 E8
Kingsmead. Bigg H TN16 ...... 83 D3
Kingsmead. Cran GU6 .... 174 E3
Kingsmead. Farnb GU14 .... 85 B4
Kingsmead. Friml GU16 .... 85 E7
Kingsmead. Rich TW10 .... 6 F1
Kingsmead. Whit V KT13 ...... 53 D4
Kingsmead. Woking GU21 .... 70 A3
Kingsmead Ave. Mitch CR4 .. 41 C6
Kingsmead Ave. N Cheam KT4 .... 58 B7
Kingsmead Ave. Sunby TW16 .... 35 C7
Kingsmead Ave. Tolw KT6 ... 57 A8
Kingsmead Cl. Horsh RH12 218 B6
Kingsmead Cl. Tedd TW11 ... 17 B2
Kingsmead Cl. W Ewell KT19 57 D3
Kingsmead Cl. W Ewell KT19 57 D3
Kingsmead Ct. Broml BR1 .... 24 F1
Kingsmead Lodge. Sutton SM2 .... 59 D4
Kingsmead Pl. Broad H RH12 .... 216 C3
Kingsmead Rd. Broad H RH12 .... 216 D3
Kingsmead Rd. Streat SW2 . 22 A6
Kingsmead Sh Ctr. Farnb GU14 .... 85 B3
Kingsmere. Catf SE6 .... 24 B7
Kingsmere Rd. Brack RG12 .. 26 F8
Kingsmere Rd. Putney SW19 19 D6
Kingsnympton Pk. King U T KT2 .... 18 B2
Kingsthorpe Rd. For Hil SE26 .... 23 D4
Kingston Ave. Cheam SM3 ... 58 E7
Kingston Ave. E Hors KT24 .. 92 E1
Kingston Ave. Felt TW14 .... 3 F1
Kingston Ave. Leahd KT22 .... 95 B6
Kingston Bsns Ctr. Chess KT9 .... 56 F7
Kingston By - Pass. Tolw KT6 .... 57 B8
Kingston By-Pass. Surb KT6 & KT7 & KT9 .... 56 C7
Kingston Cl. Tedd TW11 .... 17 B2
Kingston Coll of F Ed. King U T KT1 .... 37 D6
Kingston Coll of F Ed (M V Annex). King U T KT2 . 37 E8
Kingston Cres. Beck BR3 ...... 43 F8
Kingston Cres. Stain TW15 .. 13 D2
Kingston Gdns. Wallin CR0 .. 60 E7
Kingston Gram Sch. King U T KT2 .... 37 F7
Kingston Hall Rd. King U T KT1 .... 37 D6
Kingston Hill. King U T KT2 .. 18 C2
Kingston Hill Pl. King U T KT2 & TW10 .... 18 C4
Kingston Hospl. King U T KT2 .... 38 B8
Kingston House Gdns. Leahd KT22 .... 95 B6
Kingston La. Tedd TW11 ...... 17 B2
Kingston La. W Hors KT24 .. 112 A8
Kingston Lodge. 1 New Mal KT3 .... 38 E5
Kingston Poly (Gipsy Hill Ctr). King U T KT2 .... 18 D3
Kingston Rd. Ashf TW15 & TW17 .... 13 F2
Kingston Rd. Ashtd KT22 & KT9 .... 75 A3
Kingston Rd. Camb GU15 ..... 47 A1
Kingston Rd. Ewell KT17 ...... 57 D6
Kingston Rd. King U T KT1 & KT3 .... 38 C5
Kingston Rd. Leahd KT22 ..... 75 A1
Kingston Rd. Merton SW19 & SW20 .... 39 E7
Kingston Rd. New Mal KT3 ... 38 C5
Kingston Rd. Putney SW15 & SW19 .... 19 B7
Kingston Rd. Rhampt SW15 & SW19 .... 19 B7
Kingston Rd. Stain TW15 & TW18 .... 13 B2
Kingston Rd. Tedd TW11 ..... 17 B2
Kingston Rd. Tolw KT4 & KT5 & KT6 .... 57 D6
Kingston Rd. Worc Pk KT19 . 57 D6
Kingston Rise. Woodhm KT15 .... 52 A1
Kingston Sq. W Norw SE19 .. 22 D3
Kingston Sta. King U T KT2 .. 37 E8
Kingston Univ. King U T KT2 18 D3
Kingston Univ. King U T KT1 37 E6
Kingston Univ Annex. King U T KT1 .... 37 F7
Kingston Univ Roehampton Vale Ctr. Rhampt SW15 .... 18 F5
Kingston Vale. King U T KT2 & SW15 .... 18 E4
Kingston Vale. King U T SW15 .... 18 E5
Kingstons Ind Est. Alder GU12 .... 105 E2
Kingsway. Alder GU11 .... 104 E1
Kingsway. Blckw GU17 .... 64 E5
Kingsway. Coney H BR4 .... 63 F7
Kingsway. Mortl SW14 & TW9 7 B4
Kingsway. Stan TW19 .... 13 E7
Kingsway. W Barn KT3 .... 39 C4
Kingsway. Woking GU21 .... 69 D1
Kingsway Ave. Selsd CR2 ..... 62 D2
Kingsway Ave. Woking GU21 69 D1
Kingsway Bsns Pk The. Hampt TW12 .... 35 F8
Kingsway Rd. Cheam SM3 .... 58 E3
Kingsway Terr. Whit V KT13 53 A2
Kingsway The. Ewell KT17 ... 57 F1
Kingswear House. For Hil SE23 .... 23 C6
Kingswick Cl. Ascot SL5 .... 29 D5
Kingswick Dr. Ascot SL5 .... 29 D5
Kingswood Ave. Beck BR2 & BR3 .... 44 E5
Kingswood Ave. Hampt TW12 .... 16 B2
Kingswood Ave. Hams Gn CR2 .... 81 C4
Kingswood Ave. Hounsl TW3 & TW5 .... 4 F5
Kingswood Ave. Thorn H CR7 .... 42 A4
Kingswood Cl. Eng Gn TW20 11 D4
Kingswood Cl. Merrow GU1 110 C2
Kingswood Cl. New Mal KT3 38 F3
Kingswood Cl. Surb KT6 .... 37 E2
Kingswood Cl. Whit V KT13 . 53 B3
Kingswood Ct. Horse GU21 69 E3
Kingswood Ct. 6 Rich TW10 6 F2
Kingswood Cty Fst Sch. L Kings KT20 .... 117 F7
Kingswood Dr. Belm SM2 .... 59 B2
Kingswood Dr. Carsh SM5 ... 40 F1
Kingswood Dr. Dulw SE19 & SE21 .... 22 F4
Kingswood Firs. Graysh GU26 .... 188 C2
Kingswood Golf Course. Kings KT20 .... 98 A3
Kingswood Hall of Residence. Eng Gn TW20 .... 11 D4
Kingswood House. 3 King U T KT2 .... 18 B2
Kingswood House Sch. Epsom KT18 .... 76 C6
Kingswood La. Warlgm CR6 81 C4
Kingswood Prim Sch. W Norw SE27 .... 22 D3
Kingswood Rd. Beck BR2 ..... 44 E6
Kingswood Rd. Merton SW19 .... 39 F8
Kingswood Rd. Penge SE20 .. 23 C2
Kingswood Rd. Streat SW2 .. 21 E8
Kingswood Rd. Tadw KT20 .. 97 B6
Kingswood Rise. Eng Gn TW20 .... 11 D4
Kingswood Sta. Kings KT20 . 97 F6
Kingswood Way. Hams Gn CR2 .... 81 C6
Kingswood Way. Selsd CR2 . 81 D7
Kingswood Way. Wallin SM6 60 E5
Kingsworth Cl. Beck BR3 ..... 43 E4
Kingsworthy Cl. King U T KT1 .... 37 F6
Kinloss Rd. Carsh SM5 .... 40 C2
Kinnaird Ave. Broml BR1 ...... 24 F2
Kinnaird Ave. Chisw W4 .... 7 C7
Kinnaird Cl. Broml BR1 .... 24 F2
Kinnear Ct. Wimble SW20 .... 39 D8
Kinnersley Wlk. Dovgn RH2 139 B4
Kinnibrugh Dr. Dorman RH7 .... 165 A1
Kinross Ave. Ascot SL5 .... 28 F4
Kinross Ave. Worc Pk KT4 .... 58 A8
Kinross Cl. Ashf TW16 .... 14 F3
Kinross Ct. Ascot SL5 .... 28 F4
Kinross Dr. Ashf TW16 .... 14 F3
Kinsey House. Dulw SE21 ..... 22 E4
Kintyre Cl. Thorn H SW16 ..... 41 F6
Kintyre Ct. 17 Streat SW2 ..... 21 E8
Kinver Rd. For Hil SE26 .... 23 C4
Kipings. Tadw KT20 .... 97 D5
Kipling Cl. Crawl RH10 .... 202 C8
Kipling Ct. Horsh RH13 ...... 218 A4
Kipling Dr. Mitch SW17 .... 20 D2
Kipling Way. E Grins RH19 . 185 C1
Kirby Cl. Worc Pk KT19 .... 57 F5
Kirby Rd. Horse GU21 .... 69 D2
Kirby Way. Walt O T KT12 .... 35 C3
Kirdford Cl. Crawl RH11 ..... 201 A8
Kirk Rise. Sutton SM1 .... 59 B7
Kirkby Ct. Friml GU16 .... 65 E1
Kirkdale. For Hil SE26 .... 23 B5
Kirkfield. Stough GU2 .... 109 A4
Kirkgate The. 2 Epsom KT17 .... 76 E6
Kirkham Cl. Sandh GU15 ...... 45 D2
Kirkland Ave. Woking GU21 . 68 F3
Kirkleas Rd. Surb KT6 .... 37 E1
Kirklees Rd. Thorn H CR7 ..... 42 A4
Kirkley Rd. Merton SW19 ..... 40 A8
Kirkly Cl. S Croy CR2 .... 61 E2
Kirkstall Gdns. Streat SW2 .. 21 E7
Kirkstall Rd. Streat SW2 .... 21 E7
Kirksted Rd. Cheam SM4 ...... 40 B1
Kirkstone Cl. Friml GU15 ...... 66 D4
Kirkstone Way. Catf BR1 ...... 24 E1
Kirrane Cl. New Mal KT3 ...... 38 F4
Kirriemuir Gdns. Normdy GU12 .... 106 D3
Kirtley Rd. For Hil SE26 .... 23 E4
Kitchener Rd. S Norw CR7 ... 42 D6
Kitchener's Rd. Farnb GU11 .... 105 D6
Kitchenride Cnr. Longc KT16 51 A6
Kites Cl. Crawl RH11 .... 201 C6
Kithurst Cl. Crawl RH11 ...... 201 D4
Kitley Gdns. S Norw SE19 ..... 42 F8
Kitsmead. Copth RH10 .... 183 A2
Kitsmead La. Longc KT16 ..... 50 D8
Kittiwake Cl. Crawl RH11 .. 200 D4
Kittiwake Cl. Selsd CR0 & CR2 .... 62 E1
Klondyke Villas. Grays GU27 .... 190 A1
Knaggs House. 1 Tedd TW11 .... 16 E3
Knapdale Cl. For Hil SE23 .... 23 B6
Knaphill Cty Jun Sch. Knaph GU21 .... 68 C1
Knaphill Lower Sch The. Knaph GU21 .... 68 B1
Knapmill Rd. Catf SE6 .... 24 B6
Knapmill Way. Catf SE6 .... 24 B6
Knapp Rd. Ashf TW15 .... 13 F4
Knapton Mews. Mitch SW17 21 A2
Knaresborough Dr. Wands SW18 .... 20 B7
Kneller Gdns. Islew TW7 .... 5 D1
Kneller Rd. New Mal KT3 ...... 38 E2
Kneller Rd. Twick TW2 .... 5 D1
Knepp Cl. Crawl RH10 .... 202 C6
Knight's Hill. W Norw SE19 & SE27 .... 22 B4
Knight's Hill Sq. W Norw SE27 .... 22 B4
Knight's Pk. King U T KT1 ..... 37 E6
Knighton Cl. Crawl RH10 ... 182 D2
Knighton Cl. Croy CR2 .... 61 B2
Knighton Park Rd. For Hil SE26 .... 23 D3
Knighton Rd. Earls RH1 .... 140 A7
Knightons La. Dunsf GU8 .. 193 A2
Knights Cl. Egham TW20 ...... 12 D2
Knights Ct. King U T KT1 ...... 37 E6
Knights Ct. Penge BR3 .... 43 E8
Knights Rd. Heath E GU9 .... 125 E7
Knights Way. Friml GU15 ..... 66 C4
Knightsbridge Cres. Stain TW18 .... 13 B2
Knightsbridge Rd. Camb GU15 .... 65 E7
Knightswood. Easth RG12 .... 27 B1
Knightswood. Woking GU21 68 F1
Knightwood Cl. Woodh RH2 .... 139 A7
Knightwood Cres. New Mal KT3 .... 38 E3
Knipp Hill. Cobham KT11 ...... 73 F6
Knob Hill. Warn RH12 .... 198 A1
Knobfield. Peasl GU5 .... 133 F1
Knobfield. Peasl GU5 .... 154 F8
Knole Cl. Crawl RH10 .... 202 D7
Knole Cl. Croy CR0 .... 43 C3
Knole Gr. E Grins RH19 .... 185 C3
Knole Wood. Sunnin SL5 ...... 29 C1
Knoll Ct. Dulw SE19 .... 22 F3
Knoll Park Rd. Chert KT16 .... 32 F1
Knoll Quarry. Farnc GU7 ..... 150 E6
Knoll Rd. Camb GU15 .... 65 D6
Knoll Rd. Dork RH4 .... 136 A5
Knoll Rd. Farnc GU7 .... 150 E6
Knoll The. Beck BR3 .... 44 B8
Knoll The. Cobham KT11 ...... 74 A6
Knoll The. Leahd KT22 .... 95 C6
Knoll Wood. Farnc GU7 ..... 150 D6
Knollmead. Tolw KT4 & KT5 . 38 C1
Knollmead Prim Sch. Tolw KT4 .... 57 C8
Knolls Cl. N Cheam KT4 .... 58 B7
Knolls The. Nork KT17 .... 77 C3
Knolly's Cl. W Norw SE27 & SW16 .... 22 A5
Knolly's Rd. W Norw SE27 & SW16 .... 22 A5
Knollys' Rd. Alder GU11 ..... 104 F3
Knott Park House. Oxsh KT22 .... 74 C4
Knowl Hill. Mayb GU22 .... 70 B1
Knowl Hill Sch The. Pirb GU24 .... 87 E5
Knowle Cl. Copth RH10 .... 183 C3
Knowle Dr. Copth RH10 ..... 183 B3
Knowle Gdns. W Byfl KT14 ... 70 F6
Knowle Gn. Stain TW18 .... 13 A3
Knowle Gr. Went GU25 .... 31 C2
Knowle Grove Cl. Went GU25 .... 31 C2
Knowle Hill. Went GU25 ...... 31 C2
Knowle La. Cran GU6 & RH12 .... 194 D4
Knowle Lodge. Cater CR3 101 A4
Knowle Park Ave. Stain TW18 .... 13 B3
Knowle Pk. Cobham KT11 .... 73 E4
Knowle Rd. Twick TW2 .... 16 E7
Knowlton Gn. Hayes BR2 ..... 44 F4
Knox Rd. Stough GU2 .... 109 B6
Kohat Ct. Alder GU11 .... 104 F2
Kohat Rd. Wimble SW19 ...... 20 B3
Kohima Cl. Alder GU11 .... 105 B3
Koonowla Cl. Bigg H TN16 ... 83 D4
Kooringa. Warlgm CR6 ...... 101 B8
Korda Cl. Littlt TW17 .... 33 F6
Kreisel Wlk. Rich TW9 .... 6 F8
Kristina Ct. Belm SM2 .... 59 A4
Krooner Rd. Camb GU15 ...... 65 B3
Kuala Gdns. S Norw SW16 ... 41 F8
Kyle Cl. Easth RG12 .... 27 B6
Kynaston Ave. Thorn H CR7 . 42 C4
Kynaston Cres. Thorn H CR0 & CR7 .... 42 C4
Kynaston Ct. Cater CR3 ...... 100 E2
Kynaston House. 7 Streat SW2 .... 21 F7
Kynaston Rd. Thorn H CR0 & CR7 .... 42 C4
Kynersley Cl. Carsh SM5 ...... 59 F7

La Retraite RC Girls Sch. Streat SW12 .... 21 C8
Laburnam Ct. 12 W Norw SW16 .... 22 A3
Laburnam Rd. Chert KT16 .... 33 A1
Laburnum Ave. Carsh SM1 .. 59 E7
Laburnum Cl. Alder GU11 . 105 A1
Laburnum Cl. Bellf GU1 ..... 109 C4
Laburnum Cres. Sunby TW16 .... 35 B8
Laburnum Ct. Mitch CR4 ...... 41 A7
Laburnum Gdns. Croy CR0 .. 43 D1
Laburnum Gr. Bra Hil SL3 ..... 1 B8
Laburnum Gr. Hounsl TW3 ..... 4 F3
Laburnum Gr. King U T KT3 . 38 D7
Laburnum Pas. Alder GU11 105 A1
Laburnum Pl. Eng Gn TW20 . 11 B2
Laburnum Rd. Alder GU11 105 A2
Laburnum Rd. Epsom KT18 . 76 E6
Laburnum Rd. Heath E GU9 125 E7
Laburnum Rd. Merton SW19 20 C1
Laburnum Rd. Mitch CR4 ..... 41 A7
Laburnum Rd. Woking GU22 89 D7
Laburnum Way. Stan TW19 . 13 F7
Laburnums The. Blckw GU17 64 B5
Lacey Ave. Coulsd CR5 ...... 100 A7
Lacey Cl. Egham TW20 .... 12 D1
Lacey Dr. Coulsd CR5 .... 100 B7
Lacey Dr. Hampt TW12 .... 35 F8
Lackford Rd. Chips CR5 .... 78 F1
Lacock Cl. Wimble SW19 ...... 20 C2
Lacy Gn. Coulsd CR5 .... 100 A7
Ladas Rd. W Norw SE27 .... 22 C3
Ladbroke Cotts. 2 Redh RH1 .... 119 A2
Ladbroke Ct. 7 Redh RH1 119 A3
Ladbroke Gr. Redh RH1 ..... 119 A2
Ladbroke Hurst. Dorman RH7 .... 165 A1
Ladbroke Rd. Epsom KT18 ... 76 D5
Ladbroke Rd. Horley RH6 .. 161 B5
Ladbroke Rd. Redh RH1 ..... 119 A3
Ladbrook Rd. S Norw SE25 .. 42 D5
Ladderstile Ride. King U T KT2 .... 18 C3
Ladderstile Ride. Rich KT2 & TW10 .... 18 B3
Ladlands. Dulw SE22 .... 23 A8
Lady Booth Rd. 7 King U T KT1 .... 37 E7
Lady Eleanor Holles Sch The (Jun Girls). Hampt TW12 ... 16 B3
Lady Eleanor Holles Sch The (Senior Girls). Hampt TW12 16 B3
Lady Hay. New Mal KT4 .... 57 F8
Lady Margaret Rd. Crawl RH11 .... 201 A7
Lady Margaret Rd. Sunnin SL5 .... 29 F2
Lady Margaret Wlk. Crawl RH11 .... 201 A7
Ladybank. Easth RG12 .... 27 B1
Ladycross. Milf GU8 .... 170 E8
Ladycross Mews. Milf GU8 170 E8

Ladyegate Cl. Dork RH5 136 D8
Ladyegate Rd. Dork RH5 136 D8
Ladygate Dr. Graysh GU26 188 A3
Ladygrove. Selsd CR2 62 D2
Ladygrove Dr. Burph GU4 110 B6
Ladymead. Guild GU1 109 C2
Ladymead Retail Ctr. Guild GU1 109 E2
Ladythorpe Cl. Addl KT15 52 B6
Ladywood Ave. W Heath GU14 84 C4
Ladywood Rd. Tolw KT6 57 A8
Laffan Track. Farnb GU11 104 D6
Laffan's Rd. Farnb GU11 104 E6
Lafone Ave. Felt TW13 15 C6
Lafone House. 11 Streat SW2 21 E8
Lagham Pk. S Godst RH9 142 E6
Lagham Rd. S Godst RH9 142 F5
Laglands Cl. Reig RH2 118 C3
Laings Ave. Mitch CR4 40 F7
Laings Cnr. Mitch CR4 40 F8
Lainlock Pl. Hounsl TW3 5 B6
Lainson St. Wands SW18 20 A8
Laird Ct. Bagsh GU19 47 E1
Lairdale Cl. W Norw SE21 22 C8
Laitwood Rd. Balham SW12 21 B7
Lake Cl. Byfl KT14 71 D7
Lake Cl. 6 Wimble SW19 19 F3
Lake Cotts. Bowl Gn GU8 169 F4
Lake End Way. Crowth RG11 45 A4
Lake Gdns. Hackb SM6 60 B7
Lake Gdns. Rich TW10 17 B6
Lake House. 4 W Norw SW27 22 B3
Lake La. Docken GU10 166 E6
Lake La. Horley RH1 & RH6 161 C6
Lake Rd. Croy CR0 62 F8
Lake Rd. Friml GU16 86 B6
Lake Rd. Ockley RH5 177 D6
Lake Rd. Vir W GU25 31 B5
Lake Rd. Wimble SW19 19 F3
Lake Side The. Blckw GU17 64 D4
Lake View. Dork RH5 136 C4
Lake View Rd. Copth RH10 184 C4
Lake View Rd. Dome RH10 184 C4
Lake View Rd. Dorm Pk RH19 185 F5
Lake View Rd. Dorman RH19 185 F5
Lakehall Gdns. Thorn H CR7 42 B4
Lakehall Rd. Thorn H CR7 42 B4
Lakehurst Rd. W Ewell KT19 57 E5
Lakehurst Rd. W Ewell KT19 57 E5
Lakeland Dr. Friml GU16 65 E1
Lakeman Ct. S Norw CR7 42 C7
Lakers Lea. Loxwd RH14 212 F1
Lakers Rise. Woodm SM7 78 E3
Lakes Cl. Chil GU4 131 B3
Lakeside. Beck BR3 44 B6
Lakeside. 3 Brack RG12 27 C8
Lakeside. Hackb SM6 60 B6
Lakeside. Horsh RH12 217 C5
Lakeside. 10 King U T KT2 18 B1
Lakeside. Knaph GU21 88 E8
Lakeside. Oat Pk KT13 53 E8
Lakeside. Redh RH1 119 A3
Lakeside. W Ewell KT19 57 E4
Lakeside. W Ewell KT19 57 E4
Lakeside Cl. Ash V GU12 105 F4
Lakeside Cl. Knaph GU21 88 E8
Lakeside Cl. S Norw SE25 43 A7
Lakeside Cty Prim Sch. Friml GU16 65 F1
Lakeside Dr. Esher KT10 55 C4
Lakeside Est. Harm SL3 2 A8
Lakeside Gdns. W Heath GU14 84 D7
Lakeside Grange. Weyb KT13 53 C7
Lakeside Mid Sch. Friml GU16 65 F1
Lakeside Rd. Ash V GU11 & GU12 105 F4
Lakeside Rd. Coln SL3 1 F7
Lakeside Rd. Farnb GU11 105 A7
Lakeview Rd. W Norw SE27 22 B3
Laleham C of E Prim Sch. Laleh TW18 33 C7
Laleham Ct. Horse GU21 69 E3
Laleham Lea Prep Sch. Purley CR8 60 E1
Laleham Rd. Catf SE6 24 C8
Laleham Rd. Lewish SE6 24 C8
Laleham Rd. Shep TW17 34 B3
Laleham Rd. Shep Gn TW17 34 A4
Laleham Rd. Stain TW18 12 F2
Lamb's Bsns Pk. S Godst RH9 142 C5
Lamberhurst Rd. W Norw SE27 22 A3
Lamberhurst Wlk. Crawl RH10 202 A5
Lambert Ave. Mortl TW9 7 B4
Lambert Cl. Bigg H TN16 83 D3
Lambert Cotts. Bletch RH1 120 E2
Lambert Cres. Blckw GU17 64 C4
Lambert Rd. Banstd SM7 78 B5
Lambert's Pl. Croy CR0 42 D1
Lambert's Rd. King U T KT6 37 F4
Lambeth Cl. Crawl RH11 201 B2
Lambeth Inst Strand Ctr. Streat SW2 21 F8
Lambeth Prospect. W Norw SE19 22 D2
Lambeth Rd. Thorn H CR0 42 B1
Lambly Hill. Thorpe GU25 31 E6
Lamborne Cl. Sandh GU17 45 A1
Lambourn Cl. E Grins RH19 185 E3
Lambourne Ave. Wimble SW19 19 F4
Lambourne Cl. Crawl RH10 201 F4
Lambourne Cres. Sheer GU21 70 D6
Lambourne Dr. Bagsh GU19 47 D2
Lambourne Dr. Cobham KT11 73 D4
Lambourne Gr. Brack RG12 27 E7
Lambourne Gr. King U T KT1 38 B7
Lambourne Way. Tongh GU10 126 F7
Lambs Cres. Horsh RH12 217 F5
Lambs Farm Cl. Horsh RH12 218 A5
Lambs Farm Rd. Horsh RH12 218 A6
Lambs Green Rd. Lamb Gn RH12 199 F6
Lambton Rd. Wimble SW20 39 C8
Lambyn Croft. Horley RH6 161 C4
Lamerock Rd. Catf BR1 24 F4
Lammas Ave. Mitch CR4 41 A7
Lammas Cl. Godal GU7 151 A6
Lammas Ct. Farnc GU7 150 E5
Lammas Ct. Stan TW19 12 D5
Lammas Dr. Wray TW18 12 D4
Lammas Gate. Farnc GU7 150 F6
Lammas Gn. For Hil SE26 23 B5
Lammas Hill. Esher KT10 55 A5
Lammas La. Esher KT10 55 A6
Lammas Rd. Godal GU7 151 A5
Lammas Rd. Rich TW10 17 C4
Lammermoor Rd. Balham SW12 21 B8
Lampard La. Churt GU10 167 E2
Lampeter Cl. 4 Woking GU22 69 E1
Lampton Ave. Hounsl TW5 5 B6
Lampton Ct. Hounsl TW5 5 B6
Lampton House Cl. Wimble SW19 19 D4
Lampton Park Rd. Hounsl TW3 5 B5
Lampton Rd. Hounsl TW3 & TW5 5 B5
Lampton Sch. Hounsl TW5 5 A6
Lanain Ct. Lewish SE12 24 F8
Lanark Cl. Friml GU16 65 E2
Lanark Cl. Horsh RH13 217 E2
Lancaster Ave. M Bourn GU9 146 D8
Lancaster Ave. Mitch CR4 41 E4
Lancaster Ave. W Norw SE21 & SE27 22 C6
Lancaster Ave. Wimble SW19 19 D3
Lancaster Cl. Beck BR2 44 F5
Lancaster Cl. Crawl RH10 182 D1
Lancaster Cl. Eng Gn TW20 11 D3
Lancaster Cl. King U T KT2 17 D3
Lancaster Cl. Stan TW19 2 E1
Lancaster Cl. Woking GU21 70 A3
Lancaster Cotts. 1 Rich TW10 6 E1
Lancaster Ct. 1 Belm SM2 59 A3
Lancaster Ct. 1 Nork SM7 77 F5
Lancaster Ct. Stan TW19 13 E7
Lancaster Ct. Walt O T KT12 35 B2
Lancaster Dr. E Grins RH19 186 A3
Lancaster Gdns. King U T KT2 17 D3
Lancaster Gdns. Wimble SW19 19 E3
Lancaster House. Easth RG12 27 B4
Lancaster House. Wands SW18 20 B8
Lancaster Mews. 2 Rich TW10 6 E1
Lancaster Pk. Rich TW10 6 E2
Lancaster Pl. Hounsl TW5 4 D5
Lancaster Pl. Twick TW1 17 A8
Lancaster Pl. Wimble SW19 19 D3
Lancaster Rd. Farnb GU14 85 B1
Lancaster Rd. S Norw SE25 43 A6
Lancaster Rd. Wimble SW19 19 E3
Lancaster Way. Farnb GU14 85 C7
Lancelot Cl. Crawl RH11 200 E6
Lancer Ct. Alder GU11 104 E2
Lanchester Dr. Crowth RG11 45 C7
Lancing Cl. Crawl RH11 201 A8
Lancing Ct. Horsh RH12 218 A4
Lancing Rd. Felt TW13 14 F6
Lancing Rd. Thorn H CR0 41 F2
Landen Ct. Woki RG11 25 B4
Landen Pk. Horley RH6 160 E5
Landgrove Rd. Wimble SW19 20 A3
Landon Way. Ashf TW15 14 B2
Landscape Rd. Warlgm CR6 101 B8
Landsdowne Cl. Tolw KT5 57 B8
Landseer Cl. Mitch SW19 40 D8
Landseer Cl. Sandh GU15 64 E6
Landseer Rd. Cheam SM1 & SM2 59 A4
Landseer Rd. New Mal KT3 38 D2
Lane Cl. Addl KT15 52 B5
Lane Ct. Balham SW11 20 F8
Lane End. Epsom KT18 76 B5
Lane End. Hambl GU8 191 B8
Lane End Dr. Knaph GU21 68 C2
Lane House. Horsh RH13 217 D2
Lane The. Ifold RH14 212 C4
Lane The. Thorpe GU25 31 E6
Lane The. Thorpe KT16 33 A6
Lane The. Thursl GU8 169 C4
Lanercost Rd. Crawl RH11 201 C5
Lanercost Rd. Streat SW2 22 A6
Lanesborough Prep Sch. Guild GU1 109 F1
Lang Cl. Fetch KT23 94 B4
Langaller La. Fetch KT22 94 B6
Langborough Rd. Woki RG11 25 C5
Langbourne Prim Sch. Dulw SE21 22 E5
Langbourne Way. Clayg KT10 56 A4
Langcroft Cl. Carsh SM5 59 F7
Langdale Ave. Mitch CR4 40 F6
Langdale Cl. Farnb GU14 84 E4
Langdale Cl. Horse GU21 69 C3
Langdale Cl. Mortl SW14 7 B3
Langdale Dr. N Asct SL5 28 E7
Langdale Rd. Crawl RH11 200 D4
Langdale Rd. Thorn H CR7 42 A5
Langdon Cl. Friml GU15 66 C4
Langdon Pl. Mortl SW14 7 C4
Langdon Rd. Morden SM4 40 C4
Langdon Wlk. Morden SM4 40 C4
Langham Cl. Godal GU7 150 F4
Langham Ct. M Bourn GU9 146 C7
Langham Ct. 12 Twick TW1 6 C1
Langham Ct. Wimble SW20 39 C7
Langham Dene. Purley CR8 80 B4
Langham Gdns. Rich TW10 17 C4
Langham House Cl. Rich TW10 17 D4
Langham Pk. Godal GU7 150 F4
Langham Pl. Chisw W4 7 E8
Langham Pl. Egham TW20 11 F3
Langham Rd. Tedd TW11 17 B2
Langham Rd. Wimble SW20 39 C8
Langholm Cl. Streat SW12 21 D8
Langhurst Cl. Faygt RH12 198 E4
Langhurst La. Rusper RH12 200 A8
Langhurstwood Rd. Faygt RH12 198 D3
Langland Gdns. Croy CR0 62 F8
Langlands Rise. Epsom KT19 76 C6
Langley Ave. N Cheam KT4 & SM3 58 D8
Langley Ave. Surb KT6 37 E1
Langley Cl. Guild GU1 109 D2
Langley Cl. Lang V KT18 96 D8
Langley Cres. Harl UB3 3 F7
Langley Ct. Reig RH2 118 B2
Langley Dr. Camb GU15 65 D6
Langley Dr. Crawl RH11 201 D8
Langley Gr. King U T KT3 38 E7
Langley Green Cty Fst Sch. Crawl RH11 181 D1
Langley Green Cty Mid Sch. Crawl RH11 201 C8
Langley La. Crawl RH11 201 A8
Langley Oaks Ave. S Croy CR2 62 A1
Langley Par. Crawl RH11 181 C1
Langley Park Golf Course. W Wick BR3 44 C2
Langley Park Rd. Sutton SM1 & SM2 59 C3
Langley Park Sch for Boys. Beck BR3 44 B3
Langley Park Sch for Girls. Beck BR3 44 C3
Langley Pl. Crawl RH11 181 C1
Langley Rd. Beck BR3 43 E5
Langley Rd. Islew TW7 5 F5
Langley Rd. Merton SW19 40 A8
Langley Rd. Selsd CR2 62 D2
Langley Rd. Stain TW18 12 F2
Langley Rd. Surb KT6 37 E2
Langley Vale Rd. Lang V KT18 & KT21 76 E1
Langley Way. W Wick BR4 44 E2
Langley Wlk. Crawl RH11 181 B1
Langley Wlk. Woking GU22 89 E8
Langmans Way. Woking GU21 68 E3
Langmead St. W Norw SE27 22 C4
Langport Ct. Walt O T KT12 35 C1
Langridge Dr. E Grins RH19 205 E8
Langridge House. Horsh RH12 217 B2
Langridge Mews. Hampt TW12 15 F2
Langroyd Rd. Up Toot SW17 20 F6
Langshott. Horley RH6 161 D4
Langshott Cl. Woodhm KT15 70 F8
Langshott La. Horley RH6 161 C4
Langshott Sch. Horley RH6 161 C3
Langsmead. Blind H RH7 163 E8
Langstone Cl. Worth RH10 202 C3
Langthorne Ct. Catf SE6 24 C4
Langton Ave. Ewell KT17 76 F8
Langton Cl. Addl KT15 52 B7
Langton Cl. Woking GU21 68 F2
Langton Dr. Head Dn GU35 187 A7
Langton House. 5 Streat SW16 21 C4
Langton Rd. E Mole KT8 36 C5
Langton Rise. For Hil SE22 & SE23 23 B8
Langton Way. Egham TW20 12 C2
Langton Way. S Croy CR0 61 E6
Langwood Chase. Tedd TW11 17 C2
Lanherne House. 5 Wimble SW19 19 D1
Lanigan Dr. Islew TW3 5 B2
Lankton Cl. Beck BR3 44 C8
Lansbury Ave. Felt TW14 4 B1
Lansbury Rd. Crawl RH11 201 B1
Lansdell Rd. Mitch CR4 41 A7
Lansdown. Guild GU1 110 A1
Lansdown Cl. Horsh RH12 218 B6
Lansdown Cl. Knaph GU21 88 F8
Lansdown Cl. Walt O T KT12 35 C1
Lansdowne Cl. Twick TW1 16 F7
Lansdowne Cl. Wimble SW20 19 D1
Lansdowne Ct. Purley CR8 61 B1
Lansdowne Ct. Worc Pk KT4 58 A8
Lansdowne Hill. W Norw SE27 22 B5
Lansdowne Pl. S Norw SE19 22 F1
Lansdowne Rd. Alder GU11 105 A1
Lansdowne Rd. Croy CR0 42 D1
Lansdowne Rd. Friml GU16 86 A8
Lansdowne Rd. Hounsl TW3 5 B4
Lansdowne Rd. Purley CR8 80 A7
Lansdowne Rd. Stain TW18 13 B1
Lansdowne Rd. W Ewell KT19 57 D3
Lansdowne Rd. W Ewell KT19 57 D3
Lansdowne Rd. Wimble SW19 & SW20 19 C1
Lansdowne Wood. 11 W Norw SE27 22 B5
Lantern Ct. Wimble SW20 39 D8
Lanyon Cl. Horsh RH12 218 A6
Lanyon Mews. Horsh RH12 218 A6
Lapse Wood Wlk. Dulw SE22 23 B7
Lapwing Cl. Horsh RH13 217 F3
Lapwing Cl. Selsd CR0 & CR2 62 E1
Lapwing Ct. Tolw KT6 57 A7
Lapwing Gr. Merrow GU4 110 D3
Lara Cl. Chess KT9 56 E3
Larbert Rd. Streat SW16 21 C1
Larby Pl. Ewell KT17 57 E1
Larch Ave. Ascot SL5 29 E4
Larch Ave. Bellf GU1 109 C4
Larch Ave. Woki RG11 25 A7
Larch Cl. Camb GU15 65 E8
Larch Cl. Kings KT20 98 C6
Larch Cl. Up Toot SW12 21 B6
Larch Cl. Warlgm CR6 101 E8
Larch Cl. Woodh RH2 139 C7
Larch Cres. W Ewell KT19 57 B4
Larch Cres. W Ewell KT19 57 B4
Larch End. Horsh RH12 217 B4
Larch Rd. Head Dn GU35 187 B6
Larch Tree Way. Croy CR0 63 A7
Larch Way. Farnb GU14 84 C3
Larches Ave. Mortl SW14 7 D3
Larches The. Horse GU21 69 E3
Larches The. Horsh RH12 218 C6
Larches Way. Blckw GU17 64 B5
Larches Way. Crawl D RH10 204 C8
Larchvale Ct. 4 Sutton SM2 59 B3
Larchwood. 5 Brack RG12 27 F5
Larchwood Cl. Nork SM7 77 E4
Larchwood Dr. Eng Gn TW20 11 B2
Larchwood Glade. Camb GU15 66 A7
Larchwood Rd. Knaph GU21 88 D8
Larcombe Cl. S Croy CR0 61 F6
Larges Bridge Dr. Brack RG12 27 D6
Larges La. Brack RG12 27 C7
Largewood Ave. Tolw KT6 57 A8
Lark Ave. Stain TW18 12 F5
Lark Rise. Crawl RH11 201 C8
Lark Rise. E Hors KT24 112 E4
Larkbere Rd. For Hil SE26 23 E4
Larkfield. Cobham KT11 73 A6
Larkfield. Ewh GU6 175 E4
Larkfield Cl. Coney H BR2 63 F8
Larkfield Cl. Farnh GU9 124 F2
Larkfield Ct. Smallf RH6 162 A3
Larkfield Rd. Farnh GU9 124 F2
Larkfield Rd. Rich TW9 6 E3
Larkhall Cl. Hersh KT12 54 C4
Larkham Cl. Felt TW13 14 E5
Larkin Cl. Coulsd CR5 79 F2
Larkins Rd. Crawl RH6 181 D7
Larks Way. Knaph GU21 68 C3
Larksfield. Eng Gn TW20 11 C1
Larkspur Cl. Alder GU11 126 A7
Larkspur Ct. Wallin SM6 60 B3
Larkspur Way. Dork RH5 136 D4
Larkspur Way. W Ewell KT19 57 C5
Larkspur Way. W Ewell KT19 57 C5
Larkswood Cl. Sandh GU17 45 A1
Larkswood Dr. Crowth RG11 45 B5
Lascombe La. Putt GU3 128 B4
Lashmere. Copth RH10 183 D3
Lashmere. Cran GU6 174 B3
Laski Ct. Crawl RH11 201 B1
Lasswade Ct. Chert KT16 32 F2
Lasswade Rd. Chert KT16 32 F2
Lastingham Ct. Stain TW18 13 A2
Latchmere Cl. King U T KT2 & TW10 17 E3
Latchmere Jun & Inf Schs. King U T KT2 17 F2
Latchmere La. King U T KT2 & TW10 17 F3
Latchmere La. Rich KT2 & TW10 17 F3
Latchmere Rd. King U T KT2 17 F2
Latchwood La. M Bourn GU10 146 D5
Lateward Rd. Brent TW8 6 D8
Latham Ave. Friml GU16 65 E2
Latham Cl. Bigg H TN16 83 C3
Latham Cl. 5 Twick TW1 17 A8
Latham Rd. Twick TW1 16 F8
Latham's Way. Croy CR0 60 F8
Lathwood House. 6 Penge SE26 23 B3
Latimer. Easth RG12 27 B1
Latimer Cl. Crawl RH11 181 D1
Latimer Cl. Mayb GU22 70 B3
Latimer Cl. N Cheam KT4 58 B6
Latimer House. Godal GU7 150 E3
Latimer Rd. Croy CR0 & CR9 61 B7
Latimer Rd. Godal GU7 150 E4
Latimer Rd. Tedd TW11 16 F3
Latimer Rd. Wimble SW19 20 B2
Latimer Rd. Woki RG11 25 B5
Latton Cl. Esher KT10 55 B6
Latton Cl. Walt O T KT12 35 E2
Latymer Cl. Weyb KT13 53 C6
Laud Dr. Worth RH10 202 D5
Laud St. Croy CR0 & CR9 61 C7
Laud Way. Woki RG11 25 E6
Lauder Cl. Friml GU16 65 E2
Lauderdale Dr. Rich TW10 17 D5
Lauderdale House. Stain TW18 12 F3
Laughton Rd. Horsh RH12 217 F5
Launceston Ct. Thorn H CR7 42 A3
Laundry La. Sandh GU15 64 E5
Laundry Rd. Guild GU1 130 C8
Laundry Way. Capel RH5 178 C5
Lauradale. Easth RG12 27 A5
Laurel Ave. Eng Gn TW20 11 B3

Laurel Ave. Twick TW1 ... 16 F7
Laurel Cl. Camb GU15 ... 65 D4
Laurel Cl. Crawl RH10 ... 202 A3
Laurel Cl. Farnb GU14 ... 84 C3
Laurel Cl. Poyle SL3 ... 1 E7
Laurel Cl. Up Toot SW17 ... 20 E3
Laurel Cres. Croy CR0 ... 63 A7
Laurel Cres. Sheer GU21 ... 70 D6
Laurel Ct. S Norw SE25 ... 42 E4
Laurel Dene. E Grins RH19 . 185 F1
Laurel Dr. Oxted RH8 ... 122 F4
Laurel Gdns. Alder GU11 ... 126 A7
Laurel Gdns. Hounsl TW4 ... 4 E3
Laurel Gr. For Hil SE26 ... 23 E4
Laurel Gr. Penge SE20 ... 23 C1
Laurel Gr. Rowl GU10 ... 145 F5
Laurel Gr. Wreccl GU10 ... 146 A5
Laurel House. Morden SM4 . 40 B4
Laurel Manor. Sutton SM2 ... 59 C3
Laurel Rd. Tedd TW12 ... 16 D3
Laurel Rd. Wimble SW20 ... 39 B8
Laurel Wlk. Horsh RH13 ... 217 F1
Laurels The. Banstd SM7 ... 77 F2
Laurels The. Cobham KT11 ... 73 E4
Laurels The. Crawl RH10 ... 182 A1
Laurels The. Heath E GU9 ... 125 F7
Laurels The. 6 Oat Pk KT13 53 D7
Laurier Rd. Croy CR0 ... 42 F2
Lauriston Cl. Knaph GU21 ... 68 D2
Lauriston Rd. Wimble SW19 19 D2
Lauser Rd. Stan TW19 ... 13 C8
Laustan Cl. Merrow GU1 ... 110 C2
Lavant Cl. Crawl RH11 ... 200 F5
Lavender Ave. Mitch CR4 ... 40 F8
Lavender Ave.
N Cheam KT4 & SM3 ... 58 C7
Lavender Cl. Cater CR3 ... 100 C2
Lavender Cl. Coulsd CR5 ... 99 C8
Lavender Cl. Earls RH1 ... 140 B4
Lavender Cl. Wallin SM5 ... 60 B6
Lavender Ct. E Mole KT8 ... 36 B6
Lavender Gr. Mitch CR4 ... 40 E8
Lavender La. Rowl GU10 ... 145 F4
Lavender Park Rd.
W Byfl KT14 ... 71 A6
Lavender Pk. Brack SL5 ... 28 C6
Lavender Rd. Carsh SM1 ... 59 D6
Lavender Rd. Mayb GU22 ... 70 B3
Lavender Rd. Thorn H CR0 ... 41 F3
Lavender Rd. W Ewell KT19 . 57 B4
Lavender Rd. W Ewell KT19 . 57 B4
Lavender Rd. Wallin SM5 ... 60 A6
Lavender Vale. Wallin SM6 .. 60 D4
Lavender Way. Croy CR0 ... 43 D3
Lavengro Rd. W Norw SE27 . 22 C6
Laverock Sch. Oxted RH8 ... 122 E7
Laverstoke Gdns.
Rhampt SW15 ... 19 A8
Lavington Cl. Crawl RH11 . 201 A7
Lavington Rd. Wallin CR0 ... 60 F6
Lavinia Ct. Broml BR1 ... 24 E1
Lawbrook La. Gomsh GU5 .. 154 C7
Lawbrook La. Peasl GU5 ... 154 C7
Lawday Link. Hale GU9 ... 125 A7
Lawday Pl. Hale GU9 ... 125 A7
Lawday Place La. Hale GU9 125 A7
Lawdon Gdns. Croy CR0 ... 61 B6
Lawford Cl. Wallin SM6 ... 60 E2
Lawford Gdns. Kenley CR8 ... 80 C3
Lawford Rd. Chisw W4 ... 7 C7
Lawford's Hill Cl. Pirb GU3 .. 88 C3
Lawford's Hill Rd. Pirb GU3 . 88 C3
Lawman Ct. 2 Rich TW9 ... 6 F6
Lawn Cl. King U T KT3 ... 38 E7
Lawn Cres. Rich TW9 ... 7 A5
Lawn Rd. Beck BR3 ... 23 F1
Lawn Rd. Guild GU2 ... 130 C6
Lawns Rd. Cran RH12 ... 195 A3
Lawns The. Belm SM2 ... 58 E3
Lawns The. Farnb GU14 ... 84 E3
Lawns The. Milf GU8 ... 149 F1
Lawns The. N Asct SL5 ... 28 D6
Lawns The. Purley CR8 ... 61 B1
Lawns The. S Norw SE19 ... 42 D8
Lawns The. 1 Wimble SW19 19 F3
Lawnsmead Cotts.
Woner GU5 ... 152 B7
Lawnwood Ct. Godal GU7 . 151 A5
Lawrence Ave. New Mal KT3 38 E2
Lawrence Cl. Burph GU4 ... 110 B6
Lawrence Cl. Woki RG11 ... 25 D6
Lawrence Cres. Windl GU20 48 D4
Lawrence Est. Hounsl TW4 ... 4 C3
Lawrence Gr. Binf RG12 ... 26 D8
Lawrence La. Buckl RH3 ... 117 B3
Lawrence Lodge.
Camb GU15 ... 65 D7
Lawrence Rd. Hampt TW12 . 15 F1
Lawrence Rd. Hounsl TW4 ... 4 C3
Lawrence Rd. Rich TW10 ... 17 C4
Lawrence Rd. S Norw SE25 .. 42 F5
Lawrence Way. Camb GU15 64 F4
Lawrence Weaver Cl.
Morden SM4 ... 40 A3
Lawrie Park Ave.For Hil SE26 23 B3
Lawrie Park Cres.
Penge SE26 ... 23 B3
Lawrie Park Gdns.
For Hil SE26 ... 23 B3
Lawrie Park Rd.
For Hil SE19 & SE26 ... 23 C3
Lawrie Park Rd.
Penge SE19 & SE26 ... 23 C3
Laws Cl. Crawl RH11 ... 200 E5
Laws Terr. Alder GU11 ... 105 C3
Lawson Cl. Wimble SW19 ... 19 D5
Lawson Ct. 13 Surb KT6 ... 37 D2
Lawson Way. Sunnin SL5 ... 30 B3
Lawson-Hunt Ind Pk.
Slinfd RH12 ... 216 C4
Laxton Ct. S Norw CR7 ... 42 C5
Laxton Gdns. Merst RH1 ... 119 D7
Layard Rd. S Norw CR7 ... 42 D7
Layburn Cres. Bra Hil SL3 ... 1 B8
Layhams Rd.
Coney H BR2 & BR4 & CR6 .. 63 F5
Layhams Rd. W Wick BR2 ... 63 F1
Layton Cres. Croy CR0 ... 61 B5
Layton Ct. Weyb KT13 ... 53 B6
Layton Rd. Hounsl TW3 ... 5 B3
Layton's La. Sunby TW16 ... 34 F7
Le Chateau. Croy CR0 ... 61 D7
Le Marchant Rd.
Friml GU15 & GU16 ... 65 F3
Le May Cl. Horley RH6 ... 161 A4
Le Personne Rd. Cater CR3 100 D5
Lea Cl. Ash GU12 ... 106 A1
Lea Cl. Crawl RH11 ... 200 F5
Lea Cl. Farnh GU9 ... 126 A6
Lea Croft. Crowth RG11 ... 45 B6
Lea Ct. Heath E GU9 ... 125 F7
Lea Rd. Beck BR3 ... 44 A7
Lea Rd. Camb GU15 ... 65 B2
Lea The. Thor L TW20 ... 12 C1
Lea Way. Alder GU12 ... 105 F3
Leach Gr. Leahd KT22 ... 95 C5
Leacroft. Stain TW18 ... 13 B4
Leacroft. Sunnin SL5 ... 30 A4
Leacroft Ave. Balham SW12 ... 20 F8
Leacroft Cl. Kenley CR8 ... 80 C3
Leacroft Cl. Stain TW18 ... 13 B4
Leaf Cl. Thame D KT7 & KT8 . 36 E4
Leaf Gr.
W Norw SE27 & SW16 ... 22 A3
Leafield Cl. S Norw SW16 ... 22 B2
Leafield Cl. Woking GU21 ... 69 B1
Leafield Copse. Brack RG12 27 F5
Leafield Rd.
Merton SW19 & SW20 ... 39 F6
Leafield Rd. Sutton SM1 ... 59 A8
Leafy Way. S Croy CR0 ... 61 F8
Leamington Ave.
Merton SM4 ... 39 F5
Leamington Cl. Islew TW3 ... 5 C2
Leamington Ct. 4
For Hil SE26 ... 23 A5
Leander Ct. 5 Surb KT6 ... 37 D2
Leander Rd. 4 Streat SW2 . 21 F8
Leander Rd. Thorn H CR7 ... 41 F5
Leapale La. Guild GU1 ... 130 D8
Leapale Rd. Guild GU1 ... 130 D8
Leas Cl. Chess KT9 ... 56 F3
Leas La. Warlgm CR6 ... 81 D1
Leas Rd. Guild GU1 ... 130 C8
Leas Rd. Warlgm CR6 ... 81 D1
Leaside. Fetch KT23 ... 94 A4
Leather Cl. Mitch CR4 ... 41 A7
Leatherhead By-Pass Rd.
Leahd KT22 ... 95 D5
Leatherhead General Hospl.
Leahd KT22 ... 95 C5
Leatherhead Golf Club.
Ashtd KT22 ... 75 A3
Leatherhead Ind Est.
Leahd KT22 ... 95 A6
Leatherhead Rd.
Ashtd KT21 & KT22 ... 95 E7
Leatherhead Rd. Chess KT9 75 C6
Leatherhead Rd.
Fetch KT22 & KT23 ... 94 C2
Leatherhead Rd.
G Book KT22 & KT23 ... 94 C2
Leatherhead Rd. Oxsh KT22 74 D4
Leatherhead Sta.
Leahd KT22 ... 95 A6
Leaveland Cl. Beck BR3 ... 44 A5
Leaves Gn. Brack RG12 ... 27 D3
Leaves Green Cres.
Bigg H BR2 ... 83 C8
Leaves Green Rd.
Bigg H BR2 ... 83 D8
Leavesden Rd. Weyb KT13 .. 53 B5
Leazes Ave. Cater CR3 ... 100 A4
Lebanon Ave. Felt TW13 ... 15 D3
Lebanon Ct. 11 Twick TW1 ... 17 B8
Lebanon Dr. Cobham KT11 ... 74 A6
Lebanon Gdns. Bigg H TN16 83 D2
Lebanon Pk. Twick TW1 ... 17 B8
Lebanon Rd. Croy CR0 ... 42 E1
Lechford Rd. Horley RH6 ... 161 A1
Leckford Rd. Wands SW18 .. 20 C7
Leconfield Ave.
Mortl SW13 & SW15 ... 7 F4
Ledbury Pl. Croy CR0 ... 61 C6
Ledbury Rd. Croy CR0 & CR9 61 D6
Ledbury Rd. Reig RH2 ... 118 A2
Ledger Cl. Merrow GU1 ... 110 B3
Ledger Dr. Row Tn KT15 ... 51 F4
Ledgers Rd. Chelsh CR6 ... 82 B1
Ledrington Rd. Penge SE19 . 23 A2
Lee Ct. Alder GU11 ... 126 C8
Lee Hollow. Gomsh GU5 ... 133 C1
Lee Rd. Alder GU11 ... 104 E2
Lee Rd. Merton SW19 ... 40 B8
Lee St. Horley RH6 ... 160 E4
Leech La. Head KT18 & KT22 96 C1
Leechcroft Rd. Hackb SM6 .. 60 A7
Leechpool La.
Horsh RH12 & RH13 ... 218 A4
Leechpool Lane Cty Prim Sch.
Horsh RH13 ... 218 A4
Leeds Ct. Carsh SM5 ... 59 F7
Leeds Ct. Catf SE6 ... 24 B5
Leehurst. Milf GU8 ... 149 E1
Lees The. Croy CR0 ... 62 F8
Leeson House. 8
Twick TW1 ... 17 B8
Leeward Gdns.
Wimble SW19 ... 19 F2
Leewood Way. Effing KT24 113 D8
Legge Cres. Alder GU11 ... 104 E1
Legion Ct. Morden SM4 ... 40 A3
Legrace Ave.
Hounsl TW4 & TW5 ... 4 D5
Legsheath La.
For Row RH19 ... 205 D1
Leicester. Brack RG12 ... 27 E2
Leicester Ave. Mitch CR4 ... 41 E5
Leicester Cl. N Cheam KT4 ... 58 C6
Leicester House. 2
Thame D KT7 ... 37 A2
Leicester Rd. Croy CR0 ... 42 E2
Leigh Cl. New Mal KT3 ... 38 D5
Leigh Cl. Row Tn KT15 ... 51 F3
Leigh Court Cl.
Cobham KT11 ... 73 D5
Leigh Cres. New Add CR0 ... 63 C3
Leigh Ct. New Add CR0 ... 82 E8
Leigh Hill Rd. Cobham KT11 73 D5
Leigh House. 4
King U T KT2 ... 18 B2
Leigh La. M Bourn GU9 ... 146 E8
Leigh Orchard Cl.
Streat SW16 ... 21 F5
Leigh Pl. Cobham KT11 ... 73 C5
Leigh Place La. Godst RH9 . 121 E3
Leigh Place Rd. Leigh RH2 138 A3
Leigh Rd. Betch RH3 ... 137 C2
Leigh Rd. Cobham KT11 ... 73 B5
Leigh Rd. Islew TW3 ... 5 D3
Leigh/Betchworth Federal Sch.
Leigh RH2 ... 138 A3
Leigham Ave. Streat SW16 .. 21 E5
Leigham Court Rd.
Streat SE27 & SW16& SW21 22 A4
Leigham Dr. Hounsl TW7 ... 5 E7
Leigham Hall. 3
Streat SW16 ... 21 E5
Leigham Hall Par. 2
Streat SW16 ... 21 E5
Leigham Vale.
Streat SW16 & SW2 ... 22 A6
Leighlands. Crawl RH10 ... 202 C8
Leighton Gdns. Sander CR2 . 81 B6
Leighton Gdns. Thorn H CR0 42 B1
Leighton House. 7
Surb KT6 ... 37 E3
Leighton St. Thorn H CR0 ... 42 B1
Leighton Way. Epsom KT18 . 76 D5
Leinster Ave. Mortl SW14 ... 7 C3
Leisure La. W Byfl KT14 ... 71 B7
Leith Cl. Crowth RG11 ... 45 A7
Leith Gr. Bear Gn RH5 ... 157 D4
Leith Hill Rd. Abin C RH5 ... 155 F5
Leith Hill Rd. Wotton RH5 . 156 A3
Leith House. 16
Streat SW2 ... 21 F8
Leith House. Woodh RH2 ... 139 A6
Leith Lea. Bear Gn RH5 ... 157 D4
Leith Rd. Bear Gn RH5 ... 157 D4
Leith Rd. Ewell KT17 ... 76 E7
Leith Towers. 11
Sutton SM2 ... 59 B3
Leith Vale Cotts.
Wall W RH5 ... 177 A2
Leith View. Dork RH5 ... 136 C3
Leith View Rd. Horsh RH12 218 A5
Leithcote Gdns. Streat SW16 21 F4
Leithcote Path. Streat SW16 21 F5
Lela Ave. Hounsl TW4 & TW5 . 4 C5
Lemington Gr. Easth RG12 .. 27 B3
Lemmington Way.
Horsh RH12 ... 218 A7
Lemon's Farm Rd.
Abin C RH5 ... 155 F6
Lendore Rd. Friml GU16 ... 85 D8
Lenelby Rd. Tolw KT6 ... 38 A1
Leney Cl. Woki RG11 ... 25 D8
Lenham Rd. S Norw CR7 ... 42 D7
Lenham Rd. Sutton SM1 ... 59 C5
Lennard Ave. W Wick BR4 ... 63 E8
Lennard Cl. W Wick BR4 ... 63 E8
Lennard Rd.
Penge BR3 & SE20 & SE26 ... 23 E2
Lennard Rd. Thorn H CR0 ... 42 C1
Lennox Ct. 13 Redh RH1 ... 119 A2
Lennox Gdns. Croy CR0 ... 61 B6
Lenten Cl. Peasl GU5 ... 133 D1
Lentmead Rd. Catf BR1 ... 24 F5
Lenton Rise. Rich TW9 ... 6 E4
Leo Ct. 4 Brent TW8 ... 6 D7
Leof Cres. Catf SE6 ... 24 B3
Leominster Rd. Morden SM4 40 C3
Leominster Wlk.
Morden SM4 ... 40 C3
Leonard Ave. Morden SM4 ... 40 C4
Leonard Cl. Friml GU16 ... 85 D8
Leonard Rd.
Mitch CR4 & SW16 ... 41 C8
Leonardslee Ct.
Crawl RH10 ... 202 B3
Leopold Ave. Farnb GU14 ... 85 B5
Leopold Ave. Wimble SW19 . 19 F3
Leopold Rd. Crawl RH11 ... 201 C6
Leopold Rd. Wimble SW19 .. 19 F4
Leopold Terr. Wimble SW19 20 A3
Leppington. Easth RG12 ... 27 B2
Leret Way. Leahd KT22 ... 95 B6
Lesbourne Rd. Reig RH2 ... 139 B8
Lescombe Cl. For Hil SE23 ... 23 E5
Lescombe Rd.
For Hil SE23 & SE6 ... 23 E5
Lesley Ct. 8 Wallin SM6 ... 60 B6
Leslie Gdns. Belm SM2 ... 59 A3
Leslie Gr. Croy CR0 ... 42 E1
Leslie Park Rd. Croy CR0 ... 42 E1
Leslie Rd. Chobh GU24 ... 49 E1
Leslie Rd. Pixham RH4 ... 115 D1
Lessing St. For Hil SE23 ... 23 E8
Lessingham Ave.
Up Toot SW17 ... 21 A4
Lessness Rd. Morden SM4 ... 40 C4
Letchworth Ave.
E Bed TW14 ... 14 F8
Letchworth Ct. Crawl RH11 200 E3
Letchworth St.
Up Toot SW17 ... 20 F4
Letcombe Sq. Brack RG12 ... 27 F5
Levana Cl. Putney SW19 ... 19 E7
Levehurst House.
W Norw SE27 ... 22 C3
Levendale Rd.
For Hil SE23 & SE6 ... 23 F6
Leveret Cl. New Add CR0 ... 82 D8
Leveret La. Crawl RH11 ... 201 B8
Leverkusen Rd. Easth RG12 . 27 B6
Levern Dr. Hale GU9 ... 125 C6
Leverson St. Streat SW16 ... 21 C2
Levett House. 8
Streat SW16 ... 21 C3
Levett Rd. Leahd KT22 ... 95 B7
Levylsdene. Merrow GU1 .. 110 D1
Lewes Cl. Crawl RH10 ... 202 C6
Lewes Ct. 3 Mitch CR4 ... 40 F6
Lewes House. Dovgn RH2 . 139 B5
Lewes Rd. Ash W RH19 ... 206 C6
Lewes Rd. E Grins RH19 ... 206 C6
Lewes Rd. For Row RH18 ... 206 C6
Lewes Rd. For Row RH18 ... 206 E2
Lewesdon Cl. 13
Putney SW19 ... 19 D7
Lewin Ct. Streat SW16 ... 21 E2
Lewin Rd. Mortl SW14 ... 7 D4
Lewin Rd. Streat SW16 ... 21 D2
Lewins Rd. Epsom KT18 ... 76 B5
Lewis Cl. Addl KT15 ... 52 C6
Lewis Rd. Mitch CR4 ... 40 E7
Lewis Rd. 18 Rich TW10 ... 6 D2
Lewis Rd. Sutton SM1 ... 59 B6
Lewis Sports & L Ctr.
S Norw SE19 ... 42 F8
Lewisham Cl. Crawl RH11 .. 201 C2
Lewisham Coll. Beck SE6 ... 23 F3
Lewisham Coll Downham Branch.
Catf BR1 ... 24 E3
Lewisham Way. Sandh GU15 45 D2
Lexden Rd. Mitch CR4 ... 41 D5
Lexington Ct. Purley CR8 ... 80 C8
Lexton Gdns. Streat SW12 ... 21 D7
Ley Rd. Farnb GU14 ... 85 A8
Leyborne Pk. Rich TW9 ... 7 A6
Leybourne Ave. Byfl KT14 ... 71 F6
Leybourne Cl. Byfl KT14 ... 71 F6
Leybourne Cl. Crawl RH11 . 201 C1
Leyburn Gdns. S Croy CR0 ... 61 E8
Leycester Cl. Windl GU20 ... 48 B6
Leyfield. New Mal KT4 ... 38 F1
Leyland Track. Farnb GU14 104 B8
Leylands La. Stan TW19 ... 2 A2
Leylands Rd. Abin C RH5 ... 155 F5
Leylands Rd. Wotton RH5 . 156 A6
Leys Rd. Oxsh KT22 ... 74 D7
Leys The. Hersh KT12 ... 54 E6
Leyside. Crowth RG11 ... 45 A5
Leyton Rd. Merton SW19 ... 20 C1
Liberty Ave. Mitch SW19 ... 40 D8
Liberty Hall Rd. Addl KT15 ... 52 A5
Liberty La. Addl KT15 ... 52 B5
Liberty Mid Sch. Mitch CR4 . 40 E7
Liberty Rise. Row Tn KT15 ... 52 A4
Library Rd. Farnb GU14 ... 85 B2
Licensed Victualers Sch.
Wink SL5 ... 28 C6
Lichfield Ct. King U T KT6 ... 37 E4
Lichfield Ct. Rich TW9 ... 6 E3
Lichfield Gdns.
Rich TW10 & TW9 ... 6 E2
Lichfield Rd. Hounsl TW4 ... 4 C4
Lichfield Rd. Rich TW9 ... 6 F6
Lichfield Terr. 1 Rich TW9 ... 6 E2
Lichfield Way. Selsd CR2 ... 62 D2
Lichfields. Brack RG12 ... 27 E7
Lickfolds Rd. Rowl GU10 ... 145 E3
Liddel Way. Ascot SL5 ... 28 F5
Liddell Ct. 3 Purley CR8 ... 80 A7
Liddington Hall Dr.
Stough GU3 ... 108 E4
Liddington Hall Est.
Stough GU3 ... 108 E4
Liddington New Rd.
Stough GU3 ... 108 E4
Lidiard Rd. Wands SW18 ... 20 C6
Lido Rd. Guild GU1 ... 109 D2
Lidstone Cl. Woking GU21 ... 69 B2
Lightwater Meadow.
Lhtwat GU18 ... 67 B8
Lightwater Rd. Lhtwat GU18 67 C8
Lightwater Village Sch.
Lhtwat GU18 ... 48 A1
Lightwood. Brack RG12 ... 27 D3
Lilac Ave. Woking GU22 ... 89 D7
Lilac Cl. Bellf GU1 ... 109 C5
Lilac Gdns. Croy CR0 ... 63 A7
Lilian Rd. Mitch CR4 & SW16 41 C8
Lilian Rolfe House. 5
W Norw SE27 ... 22 D4
Lilleshall Rd. Morden SM4 ... 40 D3
Lilley Dr. Kings KT20 ... 98 B5
Lillie Rd. Bigg H TN16 ... 83 D1
Lilliput Childrens Ctr.
Hersh KT12 ... 54 C5
Lily Hill Dr. Brack RG12 ... 27 E7
Lily Hill Rd. Brack RG12 ... 27 F7
Lilyfields Chase. Ewh GU6 . 175 E4
Lime Ave. Camb GU15 ... 66 A6
Lime Ave. Horsh RH12 ... 218 A4
Lime Ave. Wink SL4 ... 9 F5
Lime Cl. Carsh SM5 ... 59 F8
Lime Cl. Copth RH10 ... 183 B3
Lime Cl. Crawl RH11 ... 181 C1
Lime Cl. W Clan GU4 ... 111 B7
Lime Cl. Woodh RH2 ... 139 B6
Lime Cres. Sunby TW16 ... 35 C7
Lime Ct. Mitch CR4 ... 40 D7
Lime Gr. Addl KT15 ... 52 A6
Lime Gr. King U T KT3 ... 38 E6
Lime Gr. Stough GU1 ... 109 B5
Lime Gr. Twick TW1 ... 6 A1
Lime Gr. W Clan GU4 ... 111 B7
Lime Gr. Warlgm CR6 ... 81 E1
Lime Gr. Westfd GU22 ... 89 E6
Lime Lodge. 3 Charlt TW16 14 F1
Lime Meadow Ave.
Sander CR2 ... 81 B6
Lime St. Alder GU11 ... 104 F2
Lime Tree Ave.
Thame D KT10 & KT7 ... 36 E1
Lime Tree Cl. Fetch KT23 ... 94 A3
Lime Tree Ct. Ashtd KT21 ... 75 E1
Lime Tree Gr. Croy CR0 ... 62 F7
Lime Tree Rd. Hounsl TW5 ... 5 B6
Lime Tree Wlk. Coney H BR4 63 F6

Lime Tree Wlk. Thorpe GU25 31 E5
Lime Wlk. Brack RG12 27 C5
Limebush Cl. New Haw KT15 52 C2
Limecroft Cl. W Ewell KT19 57 D3
Limecroft Cl. W Ewell KT19 57 D3
Limecroft Rd. Knaph GU21 68 B2
Limerick Cl. Brack RG12 27 A8
Limerick Cl. Streat SW12 21 C8
Limerick Ct. 1 Streat SW12 21 C8
Limerick Hse. Woking GU22 70 A1
Limes Ave. Barnes SW13 7 F5
Limes Ave. Carsh SM5 40 F1
Limes Ave. Croy CR0 & CR9 61 A7
Limes Ave. Horley RH6 161 B1
Limes Ave. Penge SE20 23 B1
Limes Cl. Ashf TW15 14 A3
Limes Ct. Beck BR3 44 B7
Limes Field Rd. Mortl SW14 7 E4
Limes Rd. Beck BR3 44 B7
Limes Rd. Egham TW20 11 F3
Limes Rd. Thorn H CR0 42 D2
Limes Rd. W Heath GU14 84 C5
Limes Rd. Weyb KT13 53 A6
Limes The. Belm SM2 59 A4
Limes The. Dorm Pk RH19 185 A5
Limes The. E Mole KT8 36 B5
Limes The. Horse GU21 69 D4
Limes The. Woking GU21 70 A3
Limetree Cl. Streat SW2 21 F7
Limetree Pl. Mitch CR4 41 B8
Limetree Wlk. 2 Up Toot SW17 21 A3
Limeway Terr. Dork RH4 115 A1
Limewood Cl. Knaph GU21 88 D7
Limpsfield Ave. Putney SW19 19 D6
Limpsfield Ave. Thorn H CR7 41 F4
Limpsfield CE Inf Sch. Limps RH8 123 C6
Limpsfield Chart Golf Club. Limps RH8 123 C6
Limpsfield Grange Sch. Limps RH8 123 A8
Limpsfield Rd. Chelsh CR6 102 B8
Limpsfield Rd. Hams Gn CR2 & CR6 81 C3
Limpsfield Rd. Sander CR2 & CR6 81 C3
Limpsfield Rd. Warlgm CR2 & CR6 81 C3
Linacre Dr. Cran GU6 & RH12 195 C4
Linacre Dr. Ewh GU6 & RH12 195 C4
Lince La. Westc RH4 135 D6
Linchmere Pl. Crawl RH11 201 A7
Linchmere Rd. Lewish SE12 24 F8
Linchmere Rd. Linch GU27 207 C4
Linchmere Rd. Linch GU27 207 D5
Lincoln Ave. Twick TW2 16 C6
Lincoln Ave. Wimble SW19 19 D5
Lincoln Cl. Crawl RH10 201 E3
Lincoln Cl. Croy SE25 43 B3
Lincoln Cl. Friml GU15 66 B4
Lincoln Cl. Horley RH6 161 A2
Lincoln Ct. Hampt TW12 15 F3
Lincoln Dr. Pyrf GU22 70 E3
Lincoln Lodge. Beck BR3 44 B7
Lincoln Rd. Croy SE25 43 B6
Lincoln Rd. Dork RH4 115 C1
Lincoln Rd. Farnb GU14 105 B8
Lincoln Rd. Felt TW13 15 F5
Lincoln Rd. King U T KT3 38 C6
Lincoln Rd. Mitch CR4 41 E4
Lincoln Rd. N Cheam KT4 39 B1
Lincoln Rd. Stough GU2 108 F3
Lincoln Terr. 4 Belm SM2 59 A3
Lincoln Way. Charlt TW16 34 E8
Lincoln Wlk. Epsom KT19 57 D1
Lincolns Mead. Lingf RH7 164 C4
Lincombe Rd. Catf BR1 24 F5
Lind Rd. Sutton SM1 59 C5
Linda Ct. Chess KT9 56 D6
Lindale. Putney SW19 19 E6
Lindale Cl. Went GU25 30 F5
Lindbergh Rd. Wallin SM6 60 E3
Linden. 3 Brack RG12 27 F4
Linden Ave. Coulsd CR5 79 B3
Linden Ave. E Grins RH19 185 C2
Linden Ave. Hounsl TW3 5 B2
Linden Ave. Thorn H CR7 42 B5
Linden Bridge Sch The. Worc Pk KT4 57 E7
Linden Cl. Crawl RH10 202 A3
Linden Cl. Horsh RH12 217 E4
Linden Cl. Tadw KT20 97 D7
Linden Cl. Thame D KT7 37 A2
Linden Cl. Woodhm KT15 71 A8
Linden Cres. King U T KT1 37 F7
Linden Ct. Beck BR3 44 B6
Linden Ct. Camb GU15 65 F7
Linden Ct. Eng Gn TW20 11 B2
Linden Ct. Leahd KT22 95 B6
Linden Ct. Penge SE20 23 B1
Linden Dr. Cater CR3 100 C3
Linden Gdns. Leahd KT22 95 C6
Linden Gr. King U T KT3 38 E6
Linden Gr. Penge SE20 23 C2
Linden Gr. Tedd TW11 16 F3
Linden Gr. Walt O T KT12 53 F8
Linden Gr. Warlgm CR6 81 E1
Linden Lea. Dork RH4 136 C5
Linden Leas. W Wick BR4 63 D8
Linden Lodge Sch. Putney SW19 19 E7
Linden Pit Path. Leahd KT22 95 B6
Linden Pl. Ewell KT17 76 E7
Linden Pl. Mitch CR4 40 E5
Linden Pl. Stain TW18 13 A4
Linden Rd. Guild GU1 109 D1
Linden Rd. Hampt TW12 36 A8
Linden Rd. Head Dn GU35 187 C5
Linden Rd. Leahd KT22 95 B6
Linden Rd. Whit V KT13 53 C2
Linden Way. Send M GU23 90 F3
Linden Way. Shep TW17 34 C4
Linden Way. Wallin CR8 60 C1
Linden Way. Westfd GU22 89 F6
Lindenhill Rd. Brack RG12 26 F8
Lindens Cl. Effing KT24 113 E7
Lindens The. Chisw W4 7 D6
Lindens The. Copth RH10 183 B3
Lindens The. M Bourn GU9 125 D1
Lindens The. New Add CR0 63 C4
Lindfield Gdns. Guild GU1 109 F2
Lindfield Rd. Croy CR0 42 F3
Lindgren Wlk. Crawl RH11 201 B1
Lindisfarne Rd. Wimble SW20 19 A1
Lindley Ct. Tedd KT1 37 C8
Lindley Ct. W Byfl KT14 71 B7
Lindley Rd. Tyl Gn RH9 121 C5
Lindley Rd. Walt O T KT12 54 D7
Lindon Bennett Sch. Felt TW13 15 D3
Lindores Rd. Carsh SM5 40 C1
Lindsay Cl. Chess KT9 56 E3
Lindsay Cl. Epsom KT18 76 C6
Lindsay Cl. Stan TW19 2 D2
Lindsay Dr. Shep TW17 34 D3
Lindsay Rd. Hampt TW12 16 B4
Lindsay Rd. N Cheam KT4 58 B8
Lindsay Rd. Woodhm KT15 71 B8
Lindsey Cl. Mitch CR4 & SW16 41 E5
Lindsey Gdns. E Bed TW14 14 D8
Lindum Dene. Alder GU11 105 A1
Lindum Rd. Tedd TW11 17 C1
Lindums The. Beck BR3 23 F2
Lindway. W Norw SE27 22 B3
Linersh Dr. Bramly GU5 152 A6
Linersh Wood Cl. Bramly GU5 152 B5
Linersh Wood Rd. Bramly GU5 152 A6
Linfield Cl. Hersh KT12 54 B5
Linford Ct. Mitch CR4 40 E8
Ling Cres. Head Dn GU35 187 B6
Ling Dr. Lhtwat GU18 66 F7
Ling's Coppice. W Norw SE21 22 D6
Lingfield Ave. King U T KT1 & KT5 37 F5
Lingfield Common Rd. Lingf RH7 164 C6
Lingfield Ct. Wimble SW19 19 D2
Lingfield Cty Mid Sch. Lingf RH7 164 D4
Lingfield Dr. Crawl RH10 202 E7
Lingfield Gdns. Coulsd CR5 100 B8
Lingfield Hospital Sch. Lingf RH7 165 A4
Lingfield House. Penge SE26 23 B2
Lingfield Park Race Course. Felct RH7 164 E2
Lingfield Prim Sch. Lingf RH7 164 D4
Lingfield Rd. Dorm Pk RH19 185 D3
Lingfield Rd. E Grins RH19 185 D3
Lingfield Rd. Eden TN8 165 F8
Lingfield Rd. Haxted TN8 165 F8
Lingfield Rd. N Cheam KT4 58 C7
Lingfield Rd. Wimble SW19 19 D2
Lingfield Sta. Lingf RH7 164 E4
Lingwell Rd. Up Toot SW17 20 E5
Lingwood. Easth RG12 27 C3
Lingwood Gdns. Hounsl TW7 5 E7
Link La. Wallin SM6 60 E4
Link Prim Day Sch The. Wallin CR0 60 E6
Link Rd. Addl KT15 52 E6
Link Rd. Carsh CR4 & SM6 41 A1
Link Rd. E Bed TW14 14 F8
Link Rd. Farnb GU14 84 D1
Link Sec Day Sch The. Wallin CR0 60 F6
Link The. Crawl RH11 201 D6
Link The. Tedd TW11 16 F2
Link Way. Rich TW10 17 B6
Link Way. Stain TW18 13 B2
Link's Rd. Ewell KT17 77 A5
Linkfield. E Mole KT8 36 B6
Linkfield Cnr. Redh RH1 118 E2
Linkfield Gdns. Redh RH1 118 E1
Linkfield La. Redh RH1 118 F3
Linkfield Rd. Islew TW7 5 F5
Linkfield St. Redh RH1 118 E1
Linklater's Cotts. Hawley GU14 84 B6
Links Ave. Morden SM4 40 A5
Links Brow. Fetch KT22 94 E4
Links Cl. Ashtd KT21 75 C2
Links Cl. Ewh GU6 175 E6
Links Gdns. S Norw SW16 22 A1
Links Green Way. Cobham KT11 74 A5
Links Pl. Ashtd KT21 75 D2
Links Prim Sch. Mitch SW17 21 A2
Links Rd. Ashf TW15 13 E3
Links Rd. Ashtd KT21 75 C2
Links Rd. Bramly GU5 151 E7
Links Rd. Mitch SW16 & SW17 21 A2
Links Rd. W Wick BR4 44 C1
Links The. N Asct SL5 28 E7
Links The. Walt O T KT12 54 A8
Links View Ave. Brock RH3 & RH5 116 A1
Links View Rd. Croy CR0 63 A7
Links View Rd. Hampt TW12 16 C4
Links Way. Beck BR3 44 A3
Links Way. Effing KT24 113 E7
Links Way. Farnb GU14 84 C3
Links Way. Mitch SW17 21 A2
Linkscroft Ave. Ashf TW15 14 B2
Linkside. King U T KT3 38 E7
Linkside E. Beac H GU26 188 C7
Linkside N. Beac H GU26 188 B7
Linkside S. Beac H GU26 188 C6
Linkside W. Beac H GU26 188 B6
Linkway. Camb GU15 65 C4
Linkway. Crawl RH6 182 C7
Linkway. Crowth RG11 45 A5
Linkway. Mayb GU22 70 C2
Linkway. Stough GU2 108 F2
Linkway. W Barn SW20 39 B5
Linkway. W Barn KT3 & SW20 39 B6
Linkway The. Sutton SM2 59 C2
Linley Ct. 1 Dulw SE21 22 E4
Linley Ct. Sutton SM1 59 C6
Linnell Rd. Earls RH1 140 B8
Linnet Cl. Selsd CR2 62 D1
Linnet Gr. Merrow GU4 110 D3
Linnet Mews. Balham SW12 21 A8
Linsford Bsns Pk. Mytch GU16 85 F3
Linsford La. Mytch GU16 85 F3
Linslade Cl. Hounsl TW4 4 E2
Linstead Rd. W Heath GU14 84 E8
Linstead Way. Putney SW18 & SW19 19 E8
Linton Cl. Carsh CR4 & SM5 40 F2
Linton Glade. New Add CR0 62 E1
Linton Gr. W Norw SE27 22 C3
Linton's La. Ewell KT17 76 E7
Lintott Ct. Stan TW19 2 D1
Lintott Gdns. Horsh RH13 217 E3
Lion and Lamb Way. 7 Farnh GU9 125 B2
Lion and Lamb Yd. 5 Farnh GU9 125 B2
Lion Ave. Twick TW1 16 F7
Lion Cl. Littlt TW17 33 E6
Lion Cl. Shottm GU27 207 F7
Lion Ctr The. Felt TW13 15 E5
Lion Gate Gdns. Rich TW9 6 F4
Lion Gn. Shottm GU27 207 F6
Lion Green Rd. Coulsd CR5 79 D3
Lion La. Shottm GU27 207 F7
Lion La. Turn H RH10 204 A4
Lion Mead. Shottm GU27 207 F6
Lion Park Ave. Chess KT9 57 A6
Lion Rd. Farnb GU14 85 B2
Lion Rd. Thorn H CR0 42 C4
Lion Rd. Twick TW1 & TW2 16 F7
Lion Way. Brent TW8 6 D7
Lion Wharf Rd. Islew TW7 6 B4
Liphook Cres. For Hil SE23 23 C8
Liphook Rd. Linch GU27 207 B4
Liphook Rd. Shottm GU27 207 F6
Lipsham Cl. Banstd SM7 78 D6
Lisbon Ave. Twick TW2 16 C6
Liscombe. Easth RG12 27 B2
Liscombe Hse. Easth RG12 27 B2
Liskeard Dr. 2 W Heath GU14 85 A6
Lismore. 9 Wimble SW19 19 F3
Lismore Cl. Islew TW7 6 A5
Lismore Cres. Crawl RH11 201 B3
Lismore Rd. S Croy CR2 61 E4
Lissoms Rd. Chips CR5 79 A1
Lister Ave. E Grins RH19 205 F6
Lister Cl. Mitch SW19 40 E8
Lister Ct. 1 Purley CR8 80 B7
Litchfield Ave. Morden SM4 39 F2
Litchfield Rd. Sutton SM1 59 C6
Litchfield Way. Onsl V GU2 129 F7
Lithgow's Rd. Hatton TW14 & TW6 3 F3
Little Acre. Beck BR3 44 A6
Little Austins Rd. M Bourn GU9 146 D8
Little Birch Cl. New Haw KT15 52 D2
Little Bookham St. L Book KT23 93 F2
Little Bornes. Dulw SE21 22 E4
Little Borough. Brock RH3 137 A8
Little Brownings. For Hil SE23 23 B6
Little Browns La. Eden TN8 144 F4
Little Collins. Outw RH1 162 B7
Little Common La. Bletch RH1 120 C3
Little Comptons. Horsh RH13 217 F2
Little Crabtree. Crawl RH11 201 C7
Little Cranmore La. W Hors KT24 112 C6
Little Ct. W Wick BR4 63 E8
Little Dimocks. Up Toot SW12 21 B6
Little Elms. Harl UB3 3 D7
Little Ferry Rd. Twick TW1 17 B7
Little Gn. Elst GU8 148 D4
Little Grebe. Horsh RH12 217 C5
Little Green La. Addl KT16 51 E7
Little Green La. Wreccl GU9 146 A6
Little Halliards. Walt O T KT12 35 A3
Little Haven La. Horsh RH12 217 F5
Little Heath La. Cobham KT11 74 A5
Little Heath Rd. Burrh GU24 49 E2
Little Hide. Merrow GU1 110 B3
Little Holland Bglws. Cater CR3 100 D4
Little Kiln. Farnc GU7 150 E8
Little King St. E Grins RH19 185 E1
Little London. Shere GU5 132 F2
Little London. Witley GU8 170 E5
Little Lullenden. Lingf RH7 164 E5
Little Manor Gdns. Cran GU6 174 E2
Little Mead. Woking GU21 68 F3
Little Mead Ind Est. Cran GU6 174 B3
Little Moor. Sandh GU17 45 C1
Little Orch. Horse GU21 70 A5
Little Orch. Woodhm KT15 71 A8
Little Orchard Way. Shalf GU4 130 E1
Little Orchards. Epsom KT18 76 E5
Little Paddock. Camb GU15 66 A8
Little Park Dr. Felt TW13 15 E6
Little Park Ent. Rusper RH6 180 E3
Little Platt. Stough GU2 108 D2
Little Queens Rd. Tedd TW11 16 F2
Little Ringdale. Brack RG12 27 E5
Little Roke Ave. Purley CR8 80 B5
Little Roke Rd. Purley CR8 80 C5
Little St. Stough GU2 109 B5
Little St Leonards. Mortl SW14 7 C4
Little Sutton La. Bra Hil SL3 1 B8
Little Tangley Flats. Woner GU5 131 C1
Little Thatch. Farnc GU7 150 F6
Little Thurbans Cl. Wreccl GU9 146 A6
Little Tumners Ct. Farnc GU7 150 E6
Little Warren Cl. Merrow GU4 131 B7
Little Wellington St. Alder GU11 105 A2
Little Wildwood. Cran GU6 174 F1
Little Woodcote La. Wallin CR8 & SM5 & SM6 79 B8
Littlebourne. 2 Lewish SE13 24 E8
Littlebrook Cl. Croy CR0 43 D3
Littlecote Cl. Putney SW19 19 E8
Littlecroft Rd. Egham TW20 11 F3
Littledale Cl. Brack RG12 27 E6
Littlefield Cl. Ash GU12 106 A1
Littlefield Cl. Fairl GU3 108 D5
Littlefield Cl. 9 King U T KT1 37 E7
Littlefield Cotts. Worpl GU3 108 B6
Littlefield Ct. Harm UB7 2 D7
Littlefield Gdns. Ash GU12 106 A1
Littlefield Way. Fairl GU3 108 D5
Littleford La. Woner GU4 & GU5 152 F7
Littlehaven Sch. Horsh RH12 217 F5
Littleheath Rd. S Croy CR2 62 B2
Littlemead. Esher KT10 55 D6
Littlers Cl. Mitch SW19 40 D8
Littlestone Cl. Beck BR3 24 A2
Littleton C of E Fst Sch. Littlt TW17 34 A6
Littleton Cross. Arting GU3 130 A4
Littleton House. 4 Reig RH2 118 A2
Littleton La. Arting GU3 130 A3
Littleton La. Reig RH2 138 E7
Littleton La. Shep Gn TW17 & TW18 33 E4
Littleton Rd. Littlt TW15 & TW17 14 C1
Littleton St. Wands SW18 20 C6
Littlewick Cotts. Woking GU21 68 F4
Littlewick Rd. Woking GU21 68 E3
Littlewood. Cran GU6 174 F3
Littlewood Hse. Hams Gn CR2 81 B5
Littleworth Ave. Esher KT10 55 D5
Littleworth Common Rd. Esher KT10 55 D7
Littleworth La. Esher KT10 55 D6
Littleworth Pl. Esher KT10 55 D6
Littleworth Rd. Hinch W KT10 55 E6
Littleworth Rd. Putt GU10 & GU8 148 C8
Littleworth Rd. The San GU10 126 F1
Liverpool Rd. King U T KT2 18 A1
Liverpool Rd. S Norw CR7 42 C6
Livesey Cl. King U T KT1 37 F6
Livingstone Ct. Stan TW19 13 E7
Livingstone Rd. Cater CR3 100 D5
Livingstone Rd. Crawl RH10 201 E4
Livingstone Rd. Horsh RH13 217 D1
Livingstone Rd. Hounsl TW3 5 C3
Livingstone Rd. S Norw CR7 42 D7
Llanaway Cl. Farnc GU7 150 F6
LLanaway House. Farnc GU7 150 F6
Llanaway Rd. Farnc GU7 150 F6
Llangar Gr. Crowth RG11 45 A5
Llanthony Rd. Morden SM4 40 D4
Llanvair Cl. Ascot SL5 29 A3
Llanvair Dr. Ascot SL5 28 F3
Llewellyn Ct. Penge SE20 43 C8
Lloyd Ave. Thorn H SW16 41 E8
Lloyd Ave. Wallin CR5 79 B5
Lloyd Ct. 6 W Norw SE27 22 B5
Lloyd House. Beck BR3 24 B2
Lloyd Park Ave. S Croy CR0 61 F6
Lloyd Rd. N Cheam KT4 & SM3 58 D7
Lloyds Ct. Crawl RH10 181 E1
Lloyds Way. Beck BR3 43 F4
Lobelia Rd. Bisley GU24 68 A4
Lochinvar St. Balham SW12 21 B8
Lochinver. Easth RG12 27 B2
Lock Cl. Sheer GU21 & KT15 70 E7
Lock La. Ockham GU22 & GU23 & KT14 71 C3
Lock Rd. Bellf GU1 109 D4
Lock Rd. Farnb GU11 105 D5
Lock Rd. Rich TW10 17 C4
Lock's La. Mitch CR4 41 A7
Locke King Rd. Whit V KT13 53 A3
Locke-King Cl. Whit V KT13 53 A3
Lockesley Sq. Surb KT6 37 D3
Lockfield Dr. Woking GU21 68 F2
Lockhart Rd. Cobham KT11 73 C6
Lockhursthatch La. Farl Gn GU5 153 E6

Locks Meadow.
Dorman RH7 .... 165 A1
Locks Ride. Wink SL5 .... 8 C2
Locksley Dr. Knaph GU21 ..... 68 F2
Locksmeade Rd. Rich TW10 17 C4
Lockswood. Brookw GU24 .... 88 B7
Lockton Chase. N Asct SL5 .. 28 D6
Lockton House. Woki RG11 . 25 C6
Lockwood Cl. For Hil SE26 ... 23 D4
Lockwood Cl. Horsh RH12 218 A5
Lockwood Cl. W Heath GU14 84 E8
Lockwood Ct. Crawl RH10 .. 201 F8
Lockwood Path. Sheer GU21 70 E6
Lockwood Way. Chess KT9 .. 57 A5
Lodden Lodge. Sutton SM1 .. 59 C3
Loddon Cl. Camb GU15 ...... 66 A6
Loddon Way. Ash GU12 .... 106 A1
Loder Cl. Sheer GU21 .... 70 D6
Lodge Ave. Croy CRO & CR9 . 61 A7
Lodge Cl. Brent TW7 .... 6 B6
Lodge Cl. Crawl CR4 .... 41 A1
Lodge Cl. Crawl RH11 ...... 201 C6
Lodge Cl. Dork RH5 .... 136 C3
Lodge Cl. E Ewell KT17 .... 58 C1
Lodge Cl. E Grin RH19 ...... 185 D1
Lodge Cl. Eng Gn TW20 ..... 11 D3
Lodge Cl. Fetch KT22 .... 94 D5
Lodge Cl. Stk D'A KT11 ...... 73 F3
Lodge Gdns. Beck BR3 .... 43 F4
Lodge Hill. Purley CR8 .... 80 A4
Lodge Hill Cl.
  M Bourn GU10 .... 146 D6
Lodge Hill Rd.
  M Bourn GU10 .... 146 E7
Lodge La. Beck BR3 .... 44 B5
Lodge La.
  New Addl CRO & CR9 ..... 63 B3
Lodge La. S Croy CRO 63 A4
Lodge La. S Holm RH5 ..... 157 F8
Lodge La. Salfs RH1 .... 139 F1
Lodge Pl. Sutton SM1 .... 59 B5
Lodge Rd. Fetch KT22 .... 94 D5
Lodge Rd. Sutton SM1 .... 59 B5
Lodge Rd. Thorn H CRO 42 B2
Lodge Rd. Wallin SM6 .... 60 B5
Lodge Way. Ashf TW15 ...... 13 C6
Lodge Way. Charl TW17 ..... 34 C7
Lodgebottom Rd.
  Head KT22 & RH5 .... 116 A8
Logan Cl. Hounsl TW4 .... 4 F4
Logmore La.
  Westc RH4 & RH5 .... 135 D3
Lois Dr. Shep TW17 .... 34 B4
Lollesworth La.
  W Hors KT24 .... 112 C8
Loman Rd. Mytch GU16 .... 86 A4
Lomas Cl. New Addl CRO ... 63 C3
Lombard Bsns Pk.
  Merton SW19 .... 40 C8
Lombard Bsns Pk.
  Thorn H CR9 .... 41 F2
Lombard Rd. Merton SW19 . 40 B7
Lombard St. Shackl GU8 ... 149 B7
Lombardy Cl. Woking GU21 . 68 F2
Lomond Gdns. S Croy CR2 ... 62 E3
Loncin Mead Ave.
  New Haw KT15 .... 52 C2
London Cross. E Hors KT24 112 F4
London Fields House.
  Crawl RH11 .... 201 C2
London Inst The.
  Streat SW17 .... 21 B3
London La. Broml BR1 .... 24 F1
London La. Shere GU5 ..... 133 A5
London Rd.
  Abbots GU1 & GU4 ...... 110 B4
London Rd. Ascot SL5 .... 29 D5
London Rd.
  Blckw GU15 & GU17 ...... 64 E4
London Rd. Bra Hil SL3 .... 1 B8
London Rd.
  Brack RG12 & SL5 .... 28 C6
London Rd. Brent TW7 & TW8 6 B6
London Rd. Broml BR1 ...... 24 F1
London Rd.
  Burgh GU1 & GU4 .... 110 B4
London Rd. Camb GU15 .... 65 C6
London Rd. Cater CR3 ..... 100 D4
London Rd. Cheam KT17 ... 58 C6

London Rd. Crawl RH11 ..... 181 E3
London Rd. Dork RH4 ...... 115 C3
London Rd. E Grins RH19 .. 185 C3
London Rd. Eng Gn TW20 .... 11 C1
London Rd. Ewell KT17 ...... 58 C6
London Rd.
  For Hil SE22 & SE23 ...... 23 C7
London Rd. For Row RH18 . 206 E4
London Rd. Guild GU1 ..... 109 F1
London Rd.
  Hackb SM6 & CR4 .... 60 B7
London Rd. Hind GU26 .... 188 F4
London Rd. Horsh RH12 ... 217 C2
London Rd.
  Hounsl TW1 & 3 & 7 & 8 .... 5 D5
London Rd. Islew TW7 & 8 .... 6 B6
London Rd.
  King U T KT1 & KT2 .... 37 F7
London Rd.
  Mitch CR4 & SW17 .... 40 F6
London Rd. Morden SM4 .... 40 A5
London Rd.
  N Cheam KT4 & SM3 & SM4 58 C6
London Rd. Redh RH1 ...... 119 A3
London Rd. Reig RH2 .... 118 A2
London Rd. Send M GU23 ... 90 E1
London Rd.
  Stonel KT17 & KT4 & SM3 ... 58 C6
London Rd. Sunnin SL5 ...... 30 B4
London Rd. Sunnin SL5 ...... 30 C4
London Rd.
  Thorn H CR0 & CR7 & SW16 42 A3
London Rd. Twick TW1 .... 17 A7
London Rd. Vir W GU25 ...... 31 B7
London Rd.
  Went SL5 & GU25 .... 30 C4
London Rd. Westh RH4 ..... 115 C3
London Rd.
  Windl GU19 & GU20 .... 48 C7
London Rd. Woki RG11 SL5 . 25 C6
London Rd. N Merst RH1 .... 99 B2
London Rd. S Merst RH1 ... 119 B6
London Rd. S Redh RH1 ... 119 B6
London Road Sta.
  Guild GU1 .... 109 E1
London St. Chert KT16 ...... 33 A2
Lone Oak. Burst RH6 .... 162 B1
Loneacre. Windl GU20 ...... 48 E4
Lonesome Fst Sch.
  Mitch CR4 .... 41 B7
Lonesome La.
  Dovgn RH1 & RH2 .... 139 D3
Lonesome La.
  Salfs RH1 & RH2 .... 139 D3
Long Acre. Crawl D RH10 .. 204 A8
Long Beech Dr. Farnb GU14 84 C3
Long Bridge. Farnh GU9 ... 125 C2
Long Cl. Crawl RH10 .... 202 D6
Long Copse Cl. Fetch KT23 .. 94 B4
Long Ditton Cty Inf Sch.
  Long D KT6 .... 37 C1
Long Dyke. Merrow GU1 ... 110 B3
Long Garden Mews.
  Farnh GU9 .... 125 B2
Long Garden Way.
  Farnh GU9 .... 125 B2
Long Garden Wlk.
  Farnh GU9 .... 125 B2
Long Garden Wlk E.
  Farnh GU9 .... 125 B2
Long Garden Wlk W.
  Farnh GU9 .... 125 B2
Long Gore. Farnc GU7 .... 150 E8
Long Grove Rd. Epsom KT19 57 B1
Long Hill. The San GU10 ... 126 E1
Long Hill. Wold CR3 .... 101 F6
Long Hill Rd.
  Wink RG12 & SL5 .... 28 A7
Long Houses. Pirb GU24 ... 87 D3
Long La. Croy CRO 43 C3
Long La. Stan TW15 & TW19 13 F7
Long Lodge Dr.
  Walt O T KT12 .... 54 C7
Long Meadow Cl.
  W Wick BR3 & BR4 .... 44 C2
Long Mickle. Sandh GU47 .. 45 B1
Long Rd The. Rowl GU10 .. 146 A2
Long Reach. Ockham GU23 . 92 B3
Long Reach. W Hors KT24 .. 92 B3
Long Shaw. Leahd KT22 ..... 95 A7
Long Wlk. Burgh H KT20 .... 97 D8
Long Wlk. King U T KT3 ..... 38 A6
Long Wlk The. Old W SL4 .. 10 D7
Long's Way. Woki RG11 .... 25 E7
Longacre. Ash GU12 .... 106 A2
Longacre Pl. Wallin SM5 ... 60 A4
Longacre Sch.
  Sham Gn GU5 .... 152 D4
Longbourne Rd. Farnc GU7 150 E8
Longbourne Way.
  Chert KT16 .... 32 F3

Longboyds. Cobham KT11 ... 73 B4
Longbridge Gate.
  Crawl RH6 .... 181 E8
Longbridge Rd. Crawl RH6 181 F8
Longbridge Rd. Horley RH6 160 F1
Longbridge Rdbt.
  Hookw RH6 .... 160 E2
Longbridge Wlk.
  Horley RH6 .... 160 F1
Longchamp Cl. Horley RH6 161 C3
Longcroft Ave. Banstd SM7 . 78 C5
Longcross Rd.
  Longc KT16 & GU24 .... 50 C7
Longcross Sta. Went GU24 .. 30 F1
Longdene House.
  Haslem GU27 .... 208 B6
Longdown Cl.
  M Bourn GU10 .... 146 C6
Longdown La N. Ewell KT17 77 A6
Longdown La S.
  Epsom KT17 & KT18 .... 77 A4
Longdown Lodge.
  Sandh GU17 .... 64 B8
Longdown Rd. Catf SE6 ...... 24 A4
Longdown Rd. Ewell KT17 .. 77 A4
Longdown Rd.
  M Bourn GU10 .... 146 D6
Longdown Rd.
  Merrow GU4 .... 131 B6
Longdown Rd. Sandh GU17 . 45 B1
Longfellow Cl. Horsh RH12 217 E7
Longfellow Rd.N Cheam KT4 39 B1
Longfield. Broml BR1 .... 44 F8
Longfield Ave.
  Carsh CR4 & SM6 .... 41 A1
Longfield Cl. Farnb GU14 ... 85 B8
Longfield Cres.
  Burgh H KT20 .... 97 C7
Longfield Cres.
  For Hil SE23 & SE26 ...... 23 C5
Longfield Dr. Mitch SW19 ... 40 E8
Longfield Dr. Mortl SW14 ... 7 B2
Longfield Rd. Ash GU12 ... 106 A2
Longfield Rd. Dork RH4 ... 135 F6
Longfield Rd. Horsh RH12 217 A1
Longfield St. Wands SW18 .. 20 A8
Longford Ave. Felt TW14 ..... 3 F1
Longford Ave. Stan TW19 .. 13 E7
Longford Cl. Camb GU15 .... 65 D4
Longford Cl. Hampt TW12 .. 16 A4
Longford Ct. W Ewell KT19 . 57 C6
Longford Ct. W Ewell KT19 . 57 C6
Longford Gdns. Sutton SM1 . 59 C8
Longford House. Catf BR1 .. 24 D3
Longford House.
  Hampt TW12 .... 16 A4
Longford Ind Est.
  Hampt TW12 .... 16 B2
Longford Rd. Twick TW2 ... 16 B7
Longford Rdbt.
  Harm TW6 & GU7 .... 2 A6
Longford Sch. E Bed TW14 . 14 F8
Longford Way. Stan TW19 .. 13 E7
Longford Wlk.
  Streat SW2 .... 22 A8
Longheath Dr. L Book KT23 . 93 E3
Longheath Gdns. Croy CR0 . 43 C4
Longhedge House.
  For Hil SE26 .... 23 A3
Longhill Rd. Catf SE6 .... 24 D5
Longhope Dr. Wreccl GU10 146 A6
Longhurst Rd. Crawl RH11 201 A1
Longhurst Rd. Croy CR0 ..... 43 B3
Longhurst Rd. E Hors KT24 112 E6
Longlands Ave. Wallin CR5 .. 79 A5
Longlands Ct. Mitch CR4 .... 41 A8
Longlands Way. Frrml GU15 .. 66 D5
Longleat Sq. Farnb GU14 ... 85 E3
Longleat Way. E Bed TW14 . 14 D8
Longley Rd. M Bourn GU9 . 125 D1
Longley Rd. Thorn H CR0 ... 42 B2
Longley Rd. Up Toot SW17 .. 20 F2
Longmead. Merrow GU1 ... 110 C1
Longmead Bsns Ctr.
  Epsom KT19 .... 76 D8
Longmead Cl. Cater CR3 ... 100 E5
Longmead House.
  W Norw SE27 .... 22 C3
Longmead Rd. Epsom KT19 . 57 E1
Longmead Rd. Thame D KT7 36 F2
Longmead Rd.
  Up Toot SW17 .... 20 F3
Longmeadow.
  Friml GU15 & GU16 .... 65 F3
Longmeadow. L Book KT23 . 93 F2
Longmere Gdns.
  Burgh H KT20 .... 97 C8
Longmere Rd. Crawl RH11 201 D8
Longmoors. Brack RG12 ..... 26 E8
Longmore Rd. Hersh KT12 .. 54 E6
Longpoles Rd. Cran GU6 .. 174 F2

Longridge Gr. Pyrf GU22 .... 70 E5
Longs Cl. Pyrf GU22 .... 71 A3
Longs Ct. 2 Rich TW9 .... 6 E3
Longshot Ind Est. Binf RG12 26 E7
Longshot La. Binf RG12 ...... 26 E7
Longside Cl. Thorpe TW20 .. 32 C8
Longstaff Cres.
  Wands SW18 .... 20 A8
Longstaff Rd. Wands SW18 . 20 A8
Longstone Rd. Streat SW17 21 B3
Longthornton Rd.
  Mitch SW16 .... 41 D7
Longton Ave. For Hil SE26 .. 23 A4
Longton Gr. For Hil SE26 .... 23 B4
Longwater Rd. Easth RG12 . 27 C3
Longwood Dr. Putney SW15 19 B8
Longwood Rd. Kenley CR8 .. 80 D3
Longwood View.
  Crawl RH10 .... 202 A3
Longyard House.
  Horley RH6 .... 161 B5
Lonsdale Gdns.
  Thorn H CR7 & SW16 ...... 41 F5
Lonsdale Mews. 4 Rich TW9 7 A6
Lonsdale Rd. Barnes SW13 .. 7 F7
Lonsdale Rd. Croy SE25 .... 43 B5
Lonsdale Rd. Dork RH4 ... 136 B8
Lonsdale Rd. Whit V KT13 .. 53 A3
Look Out (Heritage Ctr) The.
  Crowth RG11 .... 27 D1
Loop Rd. Old Wok GU22 ..... 89 F7
Loop Rd. Woodc KT18 .... 76 C3
Loppets Rd. Crawl RH10 ... 201 F3
Loraine Gdns. Ashtd KT21 .. 75 E2
Loraine House. 1
  Wallin SM5 .... 60 B6
Loraine Rd. Chisw W4 .... 7 B8
Lord Chancellor Wlk.
  King U T KT2 .... 38 C8
Lord Knyvett Cl. Stan TW19 . 2 E1
Lordell Pl. Wimble SW19 ... 19 C2
Lords Cl. Felt TW13 .... 15 E6
Lords Cl. W Norw SE21 ..... 22 C6
Lordsbury Field. Wallin SM6 60 C1
Lordsgrove Cl. Burgh H KT20 97 B7
Lordshill Rd. Sham Gn GU5 152 C5
Lordship La.
  Dulw SE21 & SE22 .... 23 A8
Loretto Cl. Cran GU6 .... 175 A3
Lorian Dr. Reig RH2 .... 118 C2
Loriners. Crawl RH10 ...... 201 D3
Loring Rd. Islew TW7 .... 5 F5
Lorne Ave. Croy CR0 .... 43 D2
Lorne Gdns. Croy CR0 .... 43 D2
Lorne Rd. 2 Rich TW10 .... 6 F2
Lorne The. G Book KT23 .... 94 A1
Lorraine Ct. Beck BR3 .... 44 C8
Lorraine Cty Fst Sch.
  Camb GU15 .... 65 E8
Lorraine Rd. Camb GU15 ... 65 F8
Lory Ridge. Bagsh GU19 .... 47 E4
Loseberry Rd. Esher KT10 .. 55 D5
Loseley Rd. Farnc GU7 .... 150 E8
Lothian Rd. Pirb GU24 .... 87 A6
Lothian Wood. Tadw KT20 .. 97 B5
Lotus Rd. Bigg H TN16 .... 83 F1
Loubet St. Up Toot SW17 ... 20 F2
Loudwater Cl. Sunby TW16 . 35 A5
Loudwater Rd. Sunby TW16 . 35 A5
Loughborough. Brack RG12 . 27 E3
Louis Fields. Fairl GU3 ..... 108 C5
Louisa Ct. Twick TW2 .... 16 E6
Louisa House. Rhampt SW15 . 7 F3
Louise Margaret Maternity Hospl.
  Alder GU11 .... 105 B3
Louise Margaret Rd.
  Alder GU11 .... 105 C3
Louisville Rd. Up Toot SW17 21 A5
Lovat Wlk. Heston TW5 .... 4 E7
Love La. Cheam SM3 .... 58 E4
Love La. Croy SE25 .... 43 B6
Love La. Godst RH9 .... 121 C3
Love La. Long D KT6 .... 56 D8
Love La. Mitch CR4 .... 40 E6
Love La. Morden SM4 .... 40 B2
Love La. Sutton CR4 .... 40 B2
Love La. Walt o t H KT20 .... 97 A1
Loveday House. 2
  Streat SW2 .... 22 A7
Lovedean Ct. Brack RG12 ... 27 E3
Lovekyn Cl. King U T KT2 ... 37 F7
Lovel La. Wink SL5 .... 9 B3
Lovel Rd. Wink SL5 .... 9 A4
Lovelace Cl. E Hors KT24 ... 93 A4
Lovelace Dr. Pyrf GU22 ..... 70 F3
Lovelace Dr. Pyrf GU22 ..... 70 F3
Lovelace Gdns. Hersh KT12 . 54 C5
Lovelace Gdns. Surb KT6 ... 37 D2
Lovelace Prim Sch.
  Chess KT9 .... 56 C5
Lovelace Rd. Easth RG12 ... 26 E5

Lovelace Rd. Surb KT6 .... 37 D2
Lovelace Rd. W Norw SE21 . 22 C7
Lovelands La. L Kings KT20 118 B8
Lovelands La. W End GU24 . 68 C6
Loveletts. Crawl RH11 ...... 201 A5
Lovell House. 4
  Merton SW19 .... 40 C8
Lovell Rd. Rich TW10 .... 17 C5
Lovells Cl. Lhtwat GU18 ..... 48 B1
Lovelock Cl. Kenley CR8 ..... 80 C2
Lovers La. Frensh GU10 ... 167 C7
Lovett Dr. Carsh SM5 .... 40 D2
Lovett House. 9
  Farnh GU9 .... 125 B2
Lovett Rd. Egham TW20 .... 12 C4
Low Cross Wood La.
  Dulw SE21 .... 22 F5
Low La. Farnh GU9 .... 126 B6
Lowburn. Brack RG12 .... 27 E5
Lowburys. Dork RH4 .... 136 B4
Lowdells Cl. E Grins RH19 . 185 C4
Lowdells Dr. E Grins RH19 185 D4
Lowdells La. E Grins RH19 . 185 C3
Lower Addiscombe Rd.
  Croy CR0 .... 42 E1
Lower Barn Cl. Horsh RH12 217 F5
Lower Barn Rd. Sander CR8 80 D6
Lower Breache Rd.
  Ewh GU6 .... 176 B4
Lower Bridge Rd. Redh RH1 118 F1
Lower Broadmoor Rd.
  Crowth RG11 .... 45 D4
Lower Charles St.
  Camb GU15 .... 65 C6
Lower Church La. 13
  Farnh GU9 .... 125 B2
Lower Church St.
  Croy CR0 & CR9 .... 61 B8
Lower Coombe St.
  Croy CR0 & CR9 .... 61 C6
Lower Ct Rd. Epsom KT19 ... 76 C8
Lower Ct. Epsom KT19 ...... 76 D8
Lower Dene. E Grins RH19 186 A1
Lower Downs Rd.
  Wimble SW20 .... 39 D8
Lower Dunnymans. 4
  Banstd SM7 .... 77 F5
Lower Eashing. Shackl GU7 149 F4
Lower Edgeborough Rd.
  Guild GU1 .... 130 F8
Lower Farm Rd.
  Effing KT23 & KT24 .... 93 C3
Lower Farnham Rd.
  Alder GU11 & GU12 ...... 126 C7
Lower Forecourt.
  Crawl RH6 .... 182 B7
Lower George St. 13
  Rich TW10 .... 6 D2
Lower Gn. Hersh KT12 ...... 54 D5
Lower Gn W. Mitch CR4 ..... 40 E6
Lower Green Rd. Esher KT10 55 C8
Lower Green Rd.
  Thame D KT10 .... 55 C8
Lower Grove Rd. Rich TW10 . 6 F2
Lower Guildford Rd.
  Knaph GU21 .... 68 D1
Lower Ham La. Elst GU8 ... 148 E4
Lower Ham Rd. King U T KT2 17 D2
Lower Hampton Rd.
  Sunby TW12 & TW16 ...... 35 D7
Lower Hanger.
  Bramsh GU27 .... 207 C6
Lower Hanger.
  Shottm GU27 .... 207 D6
Lower Hill Rd. Epsom KT19 . 76 B7
Lower House Rd.
  Bowl Gn GU8 .... 169 F2
Lower Manor Rd.
  Farnc GU7 .... 150 F6
Lower Manor Rd. Milf GU8 149 E1
Lower Marsh La.
  King U T KT1 & KT5 .... 38 A5
Lower Mere. E Grins RH19 . 205 F8
Lower Mill Field.
  Bagsh GU19 .... 47 D2
Lower Moorden La.
  W Barn SM4 .... 39 E3
Lower Mortlake Rd. Rich TW9 6 F4
Lower Moushill La.
  Milf GU8 .... 149 D1
Lower Nelson St.
  Alder GU11 .... 105 A2
Lower Northfield. 5
  Banstd SM7 .... 77 F5
Lower Park Rd. Woodm CR5 78 E1
Lower Peryers. E Hors KT24 112 E7
Lower Pillory Down.
  Wallin SM5 .... 79 B7
Lower Rd. Effing KT24 ..... 113 D8
Lower Rd.
  Fetch KT22 & KT23 & KT24 .. 94 C3

Lower Rd. For Row RH18 ... 206 F3
Lower Rd.
G Book KT22 & KT23 & KT24 94 C3
Lower Rd. Grays GU27 .... 189 F2
Lower Rd. Purley CR8 .... 80 B6
Lower Rd. Sutton SM1 .... 59 C6
Lower Rd.
Woodh RH1 & RH2 .... 139 D7
Lower Richmond Rd.
Mortl SW14 & TW9 .... 7 B4
Lower Sandfields.
Send GU23 .... 90 D3
Lower Sawleywood. 2
Banstd SM7 .... 77 F5
Lower Shott. G Book KT23 ... 94 B1
Lower South St. Godal GU7 150 D4
Lower South View.
Farnh GU9 .... 125 C3
Lower Sq. For Row RH18 .... 206 E3
Lower St. Haslem GU27 ...... 208 C6
Lower St. Shere GU5 .... 133 A4
Lower Staithe. Chisw W4 .... 7 C6
Lower Sunbury Rd.
Hampt TW12 .... 36 A7
Lower Sydenham Sta.
Beck SE6 .... 23 F3
Lower Tanbridge Way.
Horsh RH12 .... 217 B2
Lower Teddington Rd.
Tedd KT1 .... 37 D8
Lower Terrace Rd.
Farnb GU14 .... 105 A8
Lower Village Rd. Ascot SL5 29 C4
Lower Weybourne La.
Farnh GU9 .... 126 A6
Lower Weybourne La.
Heath E GU9 .... 125 F6
Lower Wood Rd. Clayg KT10 56 B4
Lowestoft Wlk. Crawl RH10 202 B4
Loweswater Wlk.
Friml GU15 .... 66 D4
Lowfield Cl. Lhtwat GU18 ..... 67 A8
Lowfield Heath Rd.
Charl RH6 .... 180 F5
Lowfield Heath Rd.
Crawl RH6 .... 180 F5
Lowfield Rd. Slinfd RH13 ... 215 D3
Lowfield Way. Crawl RH6 .. 181 E5
Lowicks Rd. Rushm GU10 ... 168 C6
Lowlands Rd. Blckw GU17 ... 64 C6
Lowlands Rd. Stan TW19 .... 2 D2
Lowndes Bldgs. Farnh GU9 125 B3
Lowood Ct. Dulw SE19 .... 22 F3
Lowry Cl. Sandh GU15 .... 64 D6
Lowry Cres. Mitch CR4 .... 40 E7
Lowther Hill. For Hil SE23 .... 23 E8
Lowther Rd. Barnes SW13 ..... 7 F6
Lowther Rd. King U T KT2 .... 37 F8
Lowthorpe. 5 Woking GU21 69 A1
Loxford Ct. Crawl GU6 .... 173 F2
Loxford Rd. Cater CR3 .... 100 F2
Loxford Way. Cater CR3 ..... 100 F2
Loxley Cl. For Hil SE26 .... 23 D3
Loxley Rd. Hampt TW12 .... 15 F4
Loxley Rd. Wands SW18 ...... 20 D7
Loxton Rd. For Hil SE23 .... 23 E7
Loxwood Cl. E Bed TW14 ..... 14 E7
Loxwood Cty Prim Sch.
Loxwd RH14 .... 213 A4
Loxwood Rd. Alf Cr GU6 ...... 193 F2
Loxwood Rd. Alfold GU6 ..... 193 F2
Loxwood Rd. Buck Gn RH12 214 A6
Loxwood Rd. Ifold RH14 ..... 212 A2
Loxwood Rd.
Loxwd GU6 & RH14 .... 212 F8
Loxwood Rd.
Loxwd RH12 & RH14 .... 213 D4
Loxwood Rd. Plaist RH14 .. 212 A2
Loxwood Wlk. Crawl RH11 201 A8
Lucan Dr. Stain TW18 .... 13 D1
Lucas Cl. E Grins RH19 ...... 186 A1
Lucas Ct. For Hil SE26 .... 23 E3
Lucas Field. Shottm GU27 .. 207 E6
Lucas Green Rd.
W End GU24 .... 67 E5
Lucas Rd. Penge SE20 .... 23 C2
Lucas Rd. Warn RH12 .... 216 F8
Lucerne Cl. Woking GU22 .... 89 E8
Lucerne Ct. 8 Beck BR3 ...... 24 A1
Lucerne Rd. Thorn H CR7 .... 42 C5
Lucie Ave. Ashf TW15 .... 14 B2
Lucien Rd. Up Toot SW17 .... 21 A4
Lucien Rd. Wimble SW18 ..... 20 B6
Lucille House. Penge SE26 .. 23 B2
Luckley Oakfield Sch.
Woki RG11 .... 25 B3
Luckley Path. Woki RG11 ..... 25 C6
Luckley Rd. Woki RG11 .... 25 B3
Luckley Wood. Woki RG11 ... 25 B3
Lucraft House. 12
Streat SW2 .... 21 E8
Luddington Ave.
Thorpe GU25 & TW20 .... 31 F7
Ludford Cl. Croy CR0 .... 61 B6
Ludgrove Sch. Woki RG11 ... 25 D3
Ludlow. Easth RG12 .... 27 B2
Ludlow Cl. Friml GU16 .... 86 A7
Ludlow Rd. Felt TW13 .... 15 A4
Ludlow Rd. Guild GU2 .... 130 B8
Ludovick Wlk. Rhampt SW15 . 7 E3
Ludshott Gr. Head Dn GU35 187 B5
Luke Rd. Alder GU11 .... 125 E8
Luke Rd E. Alder GU11 .... 125 F8
Lullarook Cl. Bigg H TN16 .... 83 C3
Lullington Rd. Penge SE20 .. 23 A1
Lulworth Ave.
Hounsl TW5 & TW7 .... 5 C7
Lulworth Cl. W Heath GU14 . 85 A7
Lulworth Cres. Mitch CR4 .... 40 E7
Lumley Ct. Horley RH6 .... 161 A4
Lumley Gdns. Cheam SM3 ... 58 E5
Lumley House. New Mal KT3 38 D1
Lumley Rd.
Cheam SM1 & SM3 .... 58 E5
Lumley Rd. Horley RH6 ...... 161 A3
Luna Rd. S Norw CR7 .... 42 C6
Lunar Cl. Bigg H TN16 .... 83 D3
Lundy Cl. Crawl RH11 .... 201 C3
Lunghurst Rd. Wold CR3 ... 102 A5
Lunham Rd. W Norw SE19 ... 22 E2
Lupin Cl. Bagsh GU19 .... 47 C1
Lupin Cl. Croy CR0 .... 43 D1
Lupin Cl. Streat SW2 .... 22 B6
Lupin Ride. Crowth RG11 ..... 45 B7
Lupus Ct. S Norw SE19 .... 42 D8
Luscombe Ct. Beck BR2 .... 44 E7
Lushington Dr.
Cobham KT11 .... 73 B5
Lushington House.
Walt O T KT12 .... 35 C3
Lushington Rd. Catf SE6 ...... 24 B3
Lusted Hall La.
Bigg H TN16 .... 103 C7
Lusted Hall La. Tats TN16 .. 103 C7
Lusteds Cl.
Dork RH4 & RH5 .... 136 C4
Lutea House. Sutton SM2 ..... 59 C3
Luther Rd. Tedd TW11 .... 16 F3
Lutwyche Rd.
For Hil SE23 & SE6 .... 23 F6
Lutyens Cl. Crawl RH11 ...... 200 E4
Luxford Cl. Horsh RH12 ...... 217 F5
Luxford's La. Ash W RH19 . 206 B6
Luxford's La. For Row RH19 206 B6
Lyall Ave. Dulw SE21 .... 22 F4
Lyall Pl. Heath E GU9 .... 125 B7
Lycett House. 10
Streat SW2 .... 21 E8
Lych Way. Horse GU21 .... 69 D3
Lyconby Gdns. Croy CR0 ...... 43 E2
Lydbury. Brack RG12 .... 27 F6
Lydden Gr. Wands SW18 ..... 20 B8
Lydden Rd. Wands SW18 ..... 20 B8
Lydele Cl. Horse GU21 .... 69 F4
Lydford Cl. Friml GU16 .... 86 A7
Lydford Cl. 2
W Heath GU14 .... 85 A7
Lydhurst Ave. Streat SW2 .... 21 F6
Lydney. Easth RG12 .... 27 B2
Lydney Cl. Putney SW19 ...... 19 E6
Lydon House. Crawl RH11 ... 181 D1
Lye Copse Ave. Farnb GU14 85 B8
Lye The. Tadw KT20 .... 97 C5
Lye View Cotts.
Woking GU21 .... 89 A8
Lyefield La.
For Gn GU6 & RH5 .... 176 C5
Lyfield. Oxsh KT11 & KT22 .... 74 B5
Lyford Rd. Wands SW18 ...... 20 E7
Lyham Rd. Streat SW2 .... 21 E8
Lyle Cl. Carsh CR4 .... 41 A2
Lymbourne Cl. Belm SM2 ..... 59 A1
Lymden Gdns. Woodh RH2 139 B7
Lyme Regis Rd. Banstd SM7 77 F2
Lymer Ave. Dulw SE19 .... 22 F3
Lymescote Gdns.
Sutton SM1 .... 59 A8
Lyminge Gdns.
Wands SW17 & SW18 .... 20 E7
Lymington Cl. Mitch SW16 .. 41 D7
Lymington Ct. Sutton SM1 ... 59 C7
Lymington Gdns.
Worc Pk KT19 .... 57 F5
Lyn Ct. Guild GU1 .... 131 A8
Lynch Rd. M Bourn GU9 ..... 125 E2
Lynchen Cl. Cranf TW5 .... 4 B6
Lynchford La.
Farnb GU11 & GU14 .... 105 E8
Lynchford Rd.
Farnb GU11 & GU14 .... 105 D8
Lyncroft Gdns. Ewell KT17 ... 57 F2
Lyncroft Gdns. Islew TW3 ..... 5 C2
Lyndale Ct. 3 Redh RH1 .. 119 A4
Lyndale Rd. Redh RH1 .... 119 A4
Lynde House. Walt O T KT12 35 C3
Lynden Gate. Putney SW15 . 19 B8
Lynden Hurst. Croy CR0 .... 61 F8
Lyndhurst Ave. Alder GU11 126 C6
Lyndhurst Ave. Blckw GU17 64 C6
Lyndhurst Ave. Mitch SW16 41 D7
Lyndhurst Ave. Sunby TW16 35 A6
Lyndhurst Ave. Tolw KT5 ..... 38 B1
Lyndhurst Ave.
Twick TW2 & TW4 .... 16 A7
Lyndhurst Cl. Brack RG12 .... 28 A6
Lyndhurst Cl. Crawl RH11 .. 201 D5
Lyndhurst Cl. Horse GU21 .... 69 D4
Lyndhurst Cl. S Croy CR0 .... 61 F7
Lyndhurst Ct. 7 Belm SM2 . 59 A3
Lyndhurst Dr. New Mal KT3 . 38 F2
Lyndhurst Farm Cl.
Felb RH19 .... 184 D4
Lyndhurst House. 2
Rhampt SW15 .... 19 A8
Lyndhurst Rd. Ascot SL5 ...... 29 A5
Lyndhurst Rd. Coulsd CR5 ... 79 A3
Lyndhurst Rd. Thorn H CR7 . 42 A5
Lyndhurst Rd. Woodh RH2 139 A6
Lyndhurst Sch. Camb GU15 . 65 B5
Lyndhurst Way. Addl KT16 ... 51 E8
Lyndhurst Way. Belm SM2 .. 59 A2
Lyndon Ave. Hackb SM6 ...... 60 A7
Lyndon Yd. Wimble SW17 .... 20 B4
Lyndsey Cl. W Heath GU14 .. 84 B4
Lyne Cl. Longc GU25 .... 31 F3
Lyne Crossing Rd.
Chert KT16 & TW20 .... 32 B3
Lyne Ct. Longc GU25 .... 31 F2
Lyne La. Chert KT16 & TW20 32 A3
Lyne La. Lyne KT16 .... 32 A2
Lyne & Longcross C of E Fst Sch.
Lyne KT16 .... 51 B8
Lyne Place Manor.
Longc GU25 .... 31 F2
Lyne Rd. Longc GU25 .... 31 E3
Lynegrove Ave. Ashf TW15 . 14 C3
Lyneham Rd. Crowth RG11 .. 45 B5
Lynfield Ct. For Hil SE23 ..... 23 D8
Lynmouth Ave. W Barn SM4 39 D2
Lynmouth Gdns. Heston TW5 4 D6
Lynn Cl. Ashf TW15 .... 14 D3
Lynn Ct. Streat SW16 .... 21 D3
Lynn Ct. Whytlf CR3 .... 80 F1
Lynn Rd. Balham SW12 .... 21 B8
Lynn Way. W Heath GU14 .... 84 F7
Lynn Wlk. Dovgn RH2 .... 139 B6
Lynne Cl. Selsd CR2 .... 81 C8
Lynne Ct. For Hil SE23 .... 23 F8
Lynne Ct. Guild GU1 .... 130 F8
Lynne Ct. S Croy CR2 .... 61 E6
Lynne Ct. Wimble SW20 .... 39 B8
Lynne Wlk. Esher KT10 .... 55 C5
Lynscott Way. Croy CR2 ...... 61 B2
Lynsted Ct. Penge BR3 .... 43 E7
Lynton. Thame D KT7 .... 37 A2
Lynton Cl. Chess KT9 .... 56 E6
Lynton Cl. E Grins RH19 .... 186 A2
Lynton Cl. Islew TW7 .... 5 F3
Lynton Ct. Sutton SM2 .... 59 C4
Lynton Pk Ave. E Grins RH19 186 A2
Lynton Prep Sch. Ewell KT17 76 F8
Lynton Rd. New Mal KT3 ...... 38 D4
Lynton Rd.
Thorn H CR0 & CR7 .... 42 A3
Lynwick St. Buck Gn RH12 . 214 C8
Lynwick St. Cox Gn RH12 .. 195 D1
Lynwick St. Rudg RH12 ...... 214 C8
Lynwood. Guild GU2 .... 130 B8
Lynwood Ave. Egham TW20 11 E2
Lynwood Ave. Epsom KT17 .. 76 F5
Lynwood Ave. Wallin CR5 .... 79 B4
Lynwood Chase. 1
Brack RG12 .... 27 C8
Lynwood Cl. Sheer GU21 ..... 70 D6
Lynwood Cres. Sunnin SL5 ... 29 E3
Lynwood Ct. Horsh RH12 ... 217 C3
Lynwood Dr. Mytch GU16 .... 86 A3
Lynwood Dr. N Cheam KT4 .. 58 A8
Lynwood Flats. Ascot SL5 .... 29 E4
Lynwood Gdns. Croy CR0 .... 60 F6
Lynwood Rd. Epsom KT17 .... 76 F5
Lynwood Rd. Redh RH1 ..... 119 A3
Lynwood Rd. Thame D KT7 .. 36 F1
Lynwood Rd. Up Toot SW17 20 F4
Lynx Hill. E Hors KT24 .... 112 F8
Lyon Ct. Horsh RH13 .... 217 E2
Lyon Rd. Crowth RG11 .... 45 C6
Lyon Rd. Merton SW19 .... 40 C8
Lyon Rd. Walt O T KT12 .... 54 E8
Lyon Way. Friml GU16 .... 65 C1
Lyon Way Ind Est.
Friml GU16 .... 65 C1
Lyons Cl. Slinfd RH13 .... 215 D3
Lyons Ct. Dork RH4 .... 136 B7
Lyons Dr. Stough GU2 .... 109 A6
Lyons Rd. Slinfd RH13 .... 215 E3
Lyonsdene. L Kings KT20 .... 117 F8
Lyric Cl. Worth RH10 .... 202 D4
Lyric Rd. Barnes SW13 .... 7 F6
Lysander Rd. Wallin CR0 ...... 60 F4
Lysander Way. Farnb GU14 . 85 B1
Lysias Rd. Balham SW12 ...... 21 B8
Lyson's Rd. Alder GU11 ..... 105 A1
Lysons Ave. Ash V GU12 .... 105 F8
Lytchet Minster Cl. 4
Brack RG12 .... 27 F4
Lytchgate Cl. S Croy CR2 ..... 61 E3
Lytcott Dr. E Mole KT8 .... 35 F6
Lytham. Easth RG12 .... 26 E3
Lytham Ct. Ascot SL5 .... 29 C4
Lytton Dr. Crawl RH10 .... 202 D7
Lytton Gdns. Wallin SM6 ...... 60 D6
Lytton House. 3
Hampt TW12 .... 16 B2
Lytton Rd. Mayb GU22 .... 70 B3
Lyveden Rd.
Mitch SW17 & SW19 .... 20 F2
Lywood Cl. Tadw KT20 .... 97 C5

Mabbotts. Tadw KT20 .... 97 D6
Mabel St. Woking GU21 .... 69 D2
Maberley Cres. Penge SE19 . 23 A1
Maberley Ct. Penge SE19 ..... 23 A1
Maberley Rd. Penge SE19 .... 23 A1
Maberley Rd. Penge BR3 ..... 43 D6
Macadam Ave. Crowth RG11 45 C7
MacArthur House. 4
Streat SW2 .... 21 E8
Macaulay Ave. Hinch W KT10 55 E8
Macaulay Ct. Cater CR3 ..... 100 E6
Macaulay Rd. Cater CR3 .... 100 E6
Macbeth Ct. Wink RG12 .... 27 E8
Macclesfield Rd.
Croy CR0 & SE25 .... 43 C4
Macdonald Ct. Hounsl TW3 ... 5 C3
Macdonald Rd.
Heath E GU9 .... 125 B7
Macdonald Rd. Lhtwat GU18 67 A8
MacGregor House.
Streat SW12 .... 21 D7
Mackenzie Rd. Penge BR3 ... 43 D7
Mackie House. Streat SW2 .. 22 A8
Mackie Rd. 18 Streat SW2 ... 22 A8
Mackies Hill. Peasl GU5 .... 154 D7
Macklin House. For Hil SE23 23 B6
Mackrells. Woodh RH1 .... 139 C6
Macleod Rd. Horsh RH13 ... 217 F1
Macmillan House.Bnstd SM7 77 F4
Macphail Cl. Woki RG11 .... 25 E8
Maddison Cl. Tedd TW11 ..... 16 F2
Maddox La. L Book KT23 ...... 93 E3
Maddox Pk. L Book KT23 ...... 93 E4
Madehurst Ct. Crawl RH11 200 F3
Madeira Ave. Broml BR1 ...... 24 E1
Madeira Ave. Horsh RH12 .. 217 C2
Madeira Cl. W Byfl KT14 .... 71 A6
Madeira Cres. W Byfl KT14 .. 70 F6
Madeira Rd. Mitch CR4 .... 40 F5
Madeira Rd. Streat SW16 ..... 21 E3
Madeira Rd. W Byfl KT14 ..... 71 A6
Madeira Wlk.
Reig RH1 & RH2 .... 118 D2
Madeline Rd. Penge SE20 .... 23 A1
Madgehole La.Shm Gn GU5 153 B3
Madingley. Easth RG12 .... 27 B1
Madingley Ct. Twick TW1 ...... 6 C2
Madison Gdns. Beck BR2 ...... 44 F6
Madox Brown End.
Sandh GU15 .... 64 E6
Madrid Rd. Guild GU2 .... 130 B8
Maesmaur Rd. Tats TN16 . 103 D6
Mafeking Ave. Brent TW8 ...... 6 E8
Mafeking Rd. Wray TW19 .... 12 B6
Magazine Cotts. Chil GU4 .. 131 C3
Magazine Pl. Leahd KT22 ..... 95 B5
Magazine Rd. Cater CR3 .... 100 B5
Magazine Rd. Farnb GU14 104 D8
Magdala Rd. Islew TW7 .... 6 A4
Magdala Rd. S Croy CR2 .... 61 D3
Magdalen Cl. Byfl KT14 .... 71 E5
Magdalen Cres. Byfl KT14 .... 71 E5
Magdalen Ct. Croy SE25 ...... 43 A4
Magdalen Rd. Wands SW18 20 D7
Magdalene Cl. Crawl RH10 182 C1
Magdalene Rd. Littlt TW17 .. 33 F6
Magdalene Rd.
Sandh GU15 & RG11 .... 45 F2
Magellan Terr. Crawl RH10 182 A2
Magna Carta La. Wray TW19 11 E7
Magna Carta Sch The.
Egham TW20 .... 12 D2
Magna Rd. Eng Gn TW20 ...... 11 B2
Magnolia Cl. King U T KT2 .... 18 B2
Magnolia Cl. Sandh GU15 ..... 45 D1
Magnolia Ct. 3 Belm SM2 .. 59 B3
Magnolia Ct. Horley RH6 .... 161 A3
Magnolia Ct. Penge SE26 ..... 23 C3
Magnolia Ct. Rich TW9 .... 7 B6
Magnolia Ct. Wallin SM6 ...... 60 B5
Magnolia Dr. Bigg H TN16 .... 83 E3
Magnolia Rd. Chisw W4 .... 7 B8
Magnolia Way. Dork RH5 .. 136 D4
Magnolia Way.
W Ewell KT19 .... 57 C5
Magnolia Way.
W Ewell KT19 .... 57 C5
Magnolia Wharf. Brent W4 .... 7 B8
Magpie Cl. Coulsd CR5 .... 79 C1
Magpie Cl. Crond GU10 ..... 124 D8
Magpie Wlk. Crawl RH10 ... 201 F8
Maguire Dr. Friml GU16 .... 66 C3
Maguire Dr. Rich TW10 .... 17 C4
Mahonia Cl. W End GU24 ..... 67 F6
Maida Rd. Alder GU11 .... 105 B4
Maiden La. Crawl RH11 ...... 201 C8
Maiden's Gn. Wink SL4 .... 8 B6
Maidenbower Cty Fst Sch.
Worth RH10 .... 202 C4
Maidenbower Dr.
Worth RH10 .... 202 D4
Maidenbower La.
Worth RH10 .... 202 C4
Maidenshaw Rd.
Epsom KT19 .... 76 D7
Maids of Honour Row. 4
Rich TW9 .... 6 D2
Maidstone Cres. Pirb GU24 . 87 D6
Main Dr. Wink RG12 & SL5 .... 28 B8
Main Dr. Wink RG12&SL5 ..... 28 B8
Main Gate Rd. Farnb GU14 .. 85 B2
Main Rd. Bigg H TN16 .... 83 C5
Main St. Chert KT15 .... 52 E7
Main St. Felt TW13 .... 15 D3
Mainprize Rd. Brack RG12 .... 27 E7
Mainstone Cl. Friml GU16 .... 86 C7
Mainstone Rd. Bisley GU24 . 67 F3
Mainwaring Ct. Mitch CR4 ... 41 A7
Mais House. For Hil SE26 ..... 23 B6
Maise Webster Cl.
Stan TW19 .... 13 D8
Maisonettes The.
Cheam SM1 .... 58 F5
Maitland Cl. Hounsl TW4 .... 4 F4
Maitland Cl. W Byfl KT14 ...... 71 A6
Maitland Rd. Farnb GU14 .. 105 B8
Maitland Rd. Penge SE26 ..... 23 D2
Maitlands Cl. Tongh GU10 .. 126 F6
Maizecroft. Horley RH6 ...... 161 C4
Majestic Way. Mitch CR4 ..... 40 F7
Major's Farm Rd. Bra Hil SL3 1 A8
Major's Hill. Worth RH10 ... 203 C5
Malacca Farm. W Clan GU4 111 B7
Malan Cl. Bigg H TN16 .... 83 E2
Malcolm Cl. Penge SE20 ...... 23 C1
Malcolm Dr. Surb KT6 .... 37 E1
Malcolm Gdns. Hookw RH6 160 D1
Malcolm Prim Sch.
Penge SE20 .... 23 C1
Malcolm Rd. Coulsd CR5 ...... 79 D4
Malcolm Rd.
Croy CR0 & SE25 .... 43 A3
Malcolm Rd. Penge SE20 ..... 23 C1
Malcolm Rd. Wimble SW19 . 19 E2
Malden Ave. Croy SE25 .... 43 B6
Malden Ct. W Barn KT3 .... 39 B6
Malden Golf Course.
King U T KT3 .... 38 F7
Malden Green Ave.
New Mal KT4 .... 39 A1
Malden Hill. New Mal KT3 .... 38 F6
Malden Hill Gdns.
New Mal KT3 .... 38 F6
Malden Manor Prim Sch.
New Mal KT3 .... 38 E2
Malden Manor Sta.
New Mal KT3 .... 38 E2
Malden Parochial CE Prim Sch.
New Mal KT4 .... 38 E1
Malden Pk. New Mal KT3 ..... 38 F3
Malden Rd.
Cheam KT4 & SM3 .... 58 D5
Malden Rd.
New Mal KT3 & KT4 .... 38 F2
Malden Way. W Barn KT3 .... 39 A5
Malden Way (Kingston By Pass).
New Mal KT3 & KT5 .... 38 E4
Maldon Ct. Wallin SM6 .... 60 C5
Maldon Rd. Wallin SM6 .... 60 B5
Malet Cl. Egham TW20 .... 12 D2
Maley Ave. W Norw SE27 ..... 22 B6
Malham Fell. Easth RG12 ..... 27 A5
Malham Rd. For Hil SE23 ..... 23 D7

Malham Road Ind Est.
For Hil SE23 23 D7
Mall The. Brent TW8 6 D8
Mall The. Croy CR9 61 C8
Mall The. Guild GU1 130 C8
Mall The. Hersh KT12 54 D5
Mall The. King U T KT6 37 D4
Mall The. Mortl SW14 7 C2
Mall The (Prep Sch).
Twick TW2 16 D5
Mallard Cl. Alder GU12 105 F2
Mallard Cl. Horsh RH12 217 C5
Mallard Cl. Redh RH1 119 A4
Mallard Cl. Shottm GU27 207 E6
Mallard Cl. Twick TW4 16 A8
Mallard Ct. Dork RH4 136 A8
Mallard Ct. 6 Rich TW10 6 D1
Mallard Pl. E Grins RH19 205 F8
Mallard Pl. Twick TW1 17 A5
Mallard Rd. Selsd CR2 62 D1
Mallard Way. Wallin SM6 60 C2
Mallard Wlk. Beck BR3 & CR0 43 D4
Mallard's Reach.
Oat Pk KT13 53 D8
Mallards The. Laleh TW18 33 B7
Mallards Way. Lhtwat GU18 *67 A8
Malling Cl. Croy CR0 43 C3
Malling Gdns. Morden SM4 40 C3
Malling House. 9 Beck BR3 24 A1
Malling Way. Hayes BR2 44 F2
Mallinson Rd. Wallin SM6 60 D7
Mallow Cl. Burgh H KT20 97 B8
Mallow Cl. Croy CR0 43 D1
Mallow Cl. Horsh RH12 217 E6
Mallowdale Rd. Brack RG12 27 E2
Malloy Ct. Woking GU21 70 A3
Malmains Cl. Beck BR3 44 D5
Malmains Way. Beck BR3 44 D5
Malmesbury Fst Sch.
Morden SM4 40 C2
Malmesbury Mid Sch.
Morden SM4 40 C3
Malmesbury Rd.
Morden SM4 40 C3
Malmstone Ave.
Merst RH1 119 D6
Malt Hill. Egham TW20 11 E3
Malt House. Old W SL4 11 B8
Malt House Cl. Old W SL4 11 B8
Malta Rd. Friml GU16 86 E8
Maltby Rd. Chess KT9 57 A4
Malthouse Dr. Felt TW13 15 D3
Malthouse La.
Pirb GU24 & GU3 88 C2
Malthouse La. W End GU24 67 F7
Malthouse Md. Witley GU8 170 F5
Malthouse Rd.
Crawl RH10 & RH11 201 D4
Malthouses The. Cran GU6 174 E3
Maltings Cl. Barnes SW13 7 E5
Maltings The. Byfl KT14 71 F6
Maltings The. Oxted RH8 122 F4
Maltings The. Stain TW18 12 E4
Maltlhouse La. Hambl GU8 171 C1
Malton House. S Norw SE25 42 E5
Malus Cl. Row Tn KT15 51 F3
Malus Dr. Row Tn KT15 51 F3
Malvern Cl. Mitch CR4 41 C6
Malvern Cl. Ottsh KT16 51 C4
Malvern Cl. Penge SE20 43 A7
Malvern Cl. Surb KT6 37 E1
Malvern Ct. Belm SM2 59 A3
Malvern Ct. Bra Hil SL3 1 A8
Malvern Ct. Epsom KT18 76 D5
Malvern Ct. 3 Surb KT6 37 E1
Malvern Dr. Felt TW13 15 D3
Malvern Rd. Crawl RH11 201 C5
Malvern Rd. Hampt TW12 16 A1
Malvern Rd. Harl UB3 3 E7
Malvern Rd. Surb KT6 37 E1
Malvern Rd. Thorn H CR7 42 A5
Malvern Rd. W Heath GU14 84 D7
Malyons The. Shep TW17 34 D3
Manchester Rd. S Norw CR7 42 C6
Mandeville Cl. Merton SW19 39 E8
Mandeville Cl. Stough GU2 109 A4
Mandeville Ct. Egham TW20 12 A4
Mandeville Dr. Surb KT6 37 D1
Mandeville Rd. Islew TW7 6 A5
Mandeville Rd.
Shep Gn TW17 34 A4
Mandora Rd. Alder GU11 105 B4
Mandrake Rd. Up Toot SW17 20 F5
Manfield Cty Fst Sch.
Ash GU12 106 B2
Manfield Pk. Rowly GU6 174 B5
Manfield Rd. Ash GU12 106 A2
Mangles Rd. Bellf GU1 109 D3
Manley Bridge Rd.
Rowl GU10 145 E4
Manley Bridge Rd.
Wreccl GU10 145 E4
Mann's Cl. Islew TW7 5 F2
Mannamead. Lang V KT18 96 E8
Mannamead Cl. Lang V KT18 96 E8
Manning Cl. E Grins RH19 185 D2
Manning Pl. Rich TW10 6 F1
Mannings Cl. Crawl RH10 182 D1
Manningtree Cl.
Putney SW19 19 E7
Manoel Rd. Twick TW2 16 C6
Manor Ave. Cater CR3 100 E3
Manor Ave. Hounsl TW4 4 D5
Manor Chase. Weyb KT13 53 B5
Manor Cl. E Hors KT24 112 E7
Manor Cl. Horley RH6 160 F3
Manor Cl. New Mal KT4 38 E1
Manor Cl. Pyrf GU22 70 F3
Manor Cl. Shottm GU27 207 E6
Manor Cl. Tongh GU10 126 F7
Manor Cl. Warlgm CR6 81 E2
Manor Cotts. Woking GU21 68 E5
Manor Cres. Byfl KT14 71 F6
Manor Cres. Pirb GU24 87 D7
Manor Cres. Shottm GU27 207 E6
Manor Cres. Stough GU2 109 B3
Manor Cres. Surb KT5 38 A3
Manor Ct. Horsh RH12 218 A5
Manor Ct. King U T KT2 38 A8
Manor Ct. Streat SW16 21 E5
Manor Ct. Twick TW2 16 C6
Manor Ct. Weyb KT13 53 B6
Manor Dr. Felt TW13 15 D3
Manor Dr. Hinch W KT10 56 A7
Manor Dr. Horley RH6 160 F3
Manor Dr. Sunby TW16 35 A7
Manor Dr. Surb KT5 38 A3
Manor Dr. W Ewell KT19 57 E4
Manor Dr. W Ewell KT19 57 E4
Manor Dr. Woodhm KT15 52 A1
Manor Dr N.
New Mal KT3 & KT4 38 D2
Manor Dr The. New Mal KT4 38 F1
Manor Farm Ave.
Shep TW17 34 B3
Manor Farm Bsns Ctr.
Tongh GU10 126 F5
Manor Farm Cl. Ash GU12 105 F1
Manor Farm Ct.
Egham TW20 12 A3
Manor Farm La.
Egham TW20 12 A3
Manor Farm Rd.
S Norw CR7 & SW16 42 A7
Manor Fields.
Horsh RH12 & RH13 218 A4
Manor Fields. Milf GU8 149 E2
Manor Fields. Seale GU10 127 B4
Manor Gdns. Effing KT24 113 D7
Manor Gdns. Farnc GU7 150 E7
Manor Gdns. Hampt TW12 16 C1
Manor Gdns.
M Bourn GU10 146 D5
Manor Gdns.
Merton SW19 & SW20 39 F7
Manor Gdns.
Rich TW10 & TW9 6 F3
Manor Gdns. S Croy CR2 61 F4
Manor Gdns. Stough GU2 109 B3
Manor Gdns. Sunby TW16 35 A7
Manor Gn. Milf GU8 149 E1
Manor Gr. Beck BR3 44 B7
Manor Gr. Rich TW9 7 A4
Manor Green Rd.
Epsom KT19 76 C7
Manor Hill. Woodm SM7 78 F4
Manor Hospl The.
Epsom KT19 76 A7
Manor House. Wallin SM6 60 B5
Manor House Ct.
Epsom KT18 76 C6
Manor House Dr. Ascot SL5 9 A1
Manor House Flats.
Tongh GU10 126 F6
Manor House Sch The.
Effing KT23 113 E8
Manor House The.
Camb GU15 65 D6
Manor House Way.
Islew TW7 6 B4
Manor La. Felt TW13 15 A6
Manor La. Harl UB3 3 D8
Manor La. L Kings KT20 118 A6
Manor La. Lewish SE12 24 F8
Manor La. Sham Gn GU5 152 E3
Manor La. Sunby TW16 35 B7
Manor La. Sutton SM1 59 C5
Manor Lea. Shottm GU27 207 E6
Manor Lea Cl. Milf GU8 149 E2
Manor Lea Rd. Milf GU8 149 E2
Manor Leaze. Egham TW20 12 B3
Manor Lodge. Stough GU2 109 B3
Manor Mead Sch.
Shep TW17 34 B4
Manor Mount. For Hil SE23 23 C7
Manor Park Cl. W Wick BR4 44 B1
Manor Park Ctr (Coll of Tech).
Alder GU11 105 B1
Manor Park Ind Est.
Alder GU12 105 C1
Manor Park Prim Sch.
Sutton SM1 59 C5
Manor Park Rd. Sutton SM1 59 C5
Manor Park Rd. W Wick BR4 44 B1
Manor Pk. Rich TW9 6 F3
Manor Pl. E Bed TW14 15 A7
Manor Pl. Mitch CR4 41 C6
Manor Pl. Stain TW18 13 B3
Manor Pl. Sutton SM1 59 B6
Manor Rd.
Alder GU11 & GU12 126 A8
Manor Rd.
Ash GU10 & GU12 126 F8
Manor Rd. Ashf TW15 14 A3
Manor Rd. Beck BR3 44 B7
Manor Rd. Belm SM2 58 F2
Manor Rd. Croy SE25 43 A6
Manor Rd. E Grins RH19 185 C2
Manor Rd. E Mole KT8 36 D5
Manor Rd. Farnb GU14 85 D3
Manor Rd. Farnh GU9 125 E4
Manor Rd. Horsh RH12 218 A5
Manor Rd. Merst RH1 119 C6
Manor Rd. Merton SW20 39 F7
Manor Rd.
Mitch CR4 & SW16 41 C6
Manor Rd. Reig RH2 117 F3
Manor Rd. Rich TW10 & TW9 6 F3
Manor Rd. Rich TW11 17 B3
Manor Rd. Send M GU23 90 F4
Manor Rd. Stough GU2 109 B3
Manor Rd. Tats TN16 103 E7
Manor Rd. Twick TW2 16 D6
Manor Rd. W Wick BR4 63 B8
Manor Rd.
Wallin SM5 & SM6 60 B5
Manor Rd. Walt O T KT12 34 F2
Manor Rd. Woki RG11 25 A2
Manor Rd N.
Hackb SM5 & SM6 60 B6
Manor Rd N. Hinch W KT7 56 A8
Manor Rd S. Hinch W KT10 55 E6
Manor Royal.
Crawl RH10 & RH11 181 E1
Manor Sch The. Byfl KT14 71 E5
Manor The. Milf GU8 149 F1
Manor Way. Bagsh GU19 47 F3
Manor Way. Beck BR3 44 A6
Manor Way. Egham TW20 11 F2
Manor Way.
Mitch CR4 & SW16 41 C6
Manor Way. New Mal KT4 38 F1
Manor Way. Old Wok GU22 90 B6
Manor Way. Onsl V GU2 129 F6
Manor Way. Oxsh KT22 74 C3
Manor Way. Purley CR8 79 E7
Manor Way. S Croy CR2 61 F4
Manor Way. Woodm SM7 78 F3
Manor Way The. Wallin SM6 60 B6
Manor Wlk. Weyb KT13 53 B5
Manor Wood Rd. Purley CR8 79 E6
Manorcroft Sch.
Egham TW20 12 A2
Manorcrofts Rd.
Egham TW20 12 A2
Manordene Cl. Hinch W KT7 37 A1
Manorfields. Crawl RH11 200 D2
Manorgate Rd. King U T KT2 38 A8
Manorhouse La.
Effing KT23 113 E8
Manorside Cl.
Ash GU10 & GU12 126 F8
Mansard Beeches.
Streat SW17 21 A3
Mansard Manor. Sutton SM2 59 C3
Manse Cl. Harl UB3 3 D8
Mansel Cl. Stough GU2 109 B6
Mansel Rd. Wimble SW19 19 F2
Mansell Way. Cater CR3 100 D5
Mansfield Cl. N Asct SL5 28 D7
Mansfield Cres. Easth RG12 27 B3
Mansfield Dr. Merst RH1 119 D6
Mansfield Pl. N Asct SL5 28 D8
Mansfield Rd. Chess KT9 56 D5
Mansfield Rd. S Croy CR2 61 D4
Mansfield Rd. Woki RG11 25 A5
Manship Rd. Mitch CR4 41 A8
Manston Cl. Penge SE20 43 C8
Manston Dr. Easth RG12 27 C3
Manston Gr. King U T KT2 17 D3
Manston Rd. Burph GU4 110 A5
Mantilla Rd. Up Toot SW17 21 A4
Mantlet Cl. Streat SW16 21 C1
Manville Ct. Shalf GU4 130 E1
Manville Gdns.
Up Toot SW17 21 B5
Manville Rd. Up Toot SW17 21 B5
Many Gates. Up Toot SW12 21 B6
Manygate La. Shep TW17 34 C3
Maori Rd. Guild GU1 130 F8
Mapel Ct. 3 Brack RG12 27 F5
Maple Cl. Ash V GU12 106 A7
Maple Cl. Blckw GU17 64 C5
Maple Cl. Crawl RH11 181 C1
Maple Cl. Hampt TW12 15 F2
Maple Cl. Horsh RH12 218 A5
Maple Cl. Mitch CR4 41 B8
Maple Cl. Whytlf CR3 80 F2
Maple Ct. Catf SE6 24 B7
Maple Ct. 2 Croy CR0 61 C6
Maple Ct. Eng Gn TW20 11 B2
Maple Ct. Horse GU21 69 C3
Maple Ct. King U T KT3 38 D6
Maple Ct. 11
W Norw SW16 22 A3
Maple Dr. Crowth RG11 45 C7
Maple Dr. E Grins RH19 186 A1
Maple Dr. Lhtwat GU18 66 F8
Maple Dr. Lhtwat GU18 67 A8
Maple Gdns.
Stan TW15 & TW19 13 E6
Maple Gr. Bellf GU1 109 D3
Maple Gr. Brent TW8 6 B7
Maple Gr. Westfd GU22 89 E6
Maple Gr Bsns Ctr.
Hounsl TW4 4 C3
Maple House. 2
King U T KT6 37 E4
Maple Ind Est. Felt TW13 15 A5
Maple Inf Sch. King U T KT6 37 D4
Maple Leaf Cl. Bigg H TN16 83 D3
Maple Leaf Cl. Farnb GU14 84 F3
Maple Mews. Streat SW16 21 F3
Maple Pl. Nork KT17 77 D5
Maple Rd. Ashtd KT21 95 D8
Maple Rd. Earls RH1 139 F5
Maple Rd. King U T KT6 37 D4
Maple Rd. Penge SE20 43 C8
Maple Rd. Send M GU23 91 A3
Maple Rd. Whytlf CR3 80 F2
Maple Way. Felt TW13 15 B5
Maple Way. Head Dn GU35 187 B6
Maple Way. Hooley CR5 99 B6
Maple Wlk. Alder GU12 126 D8
Maple Wlk. Sutton SM2 59 B1
Mapledale Ave. S Croy CR0 62 B7
Mapledrakes Cl. Ewh GU6 175 E5
Mapledrakes Rd. Ewh GU6 175 E5
Maplehatch Cl. Godal GU7 150 E2
Maplehurst. Beck BR2 44 E7
Maplehurst. Fetch KT22 94 D4
Maplehurst Cl. King U T KT1 37 E5
Maples The. Banstd SM7 78 B5
Maples The. Ottsh KT16 51 C4
Maples The. 4 Tedd KT8 17 C1
Maplestead Rd. Streat SW2 21 F8
Maplethorpe Rd.
Thorn H CR7 42 B5
Marble Hill Cl. Twick TW1 17 B8
Marble Hill Gdns.
Twick TW1 17 B8
Marbles Way. Burgh H KT20 97 D8
March Rd. 6 Twick TW1 17 A8
March Rd. Weyb KT13 53 A5
Marcheria Cl. Easth RG12 27 B3
Marches Rd. Warn RH12 197 E4
Marchmont House. 10
Streat SW16 21 C3
Marchmont Rd. Rich TW10 6 F2
Marchmont Rd. Wallin SM6 60 C3
Marchside Cl. Heston TW5 4 D6
Marcus Ct. Brent TW8 6 E7
Mardale. Friml GU15 66 C4
Mardell Rd. Croy CR0 43 D4
Marden Ave. Hayes BR2 44 F3
Marden Cres. Thorn H CR0 41 F3
Marden Lodge Cty Prim Sch.
Cater CR3 101 B6
Marden Rd. Thorn H CR0 41 F3
Mardens The. Crawl RH11 201 B7
Mare Hill. Witley GU8 170 E5
Mare Hill Cotts.
Witley GU8 170 D4
Mare La. Hasc GU8 172 C4
Mares Field House.
Merrow GU4 110 D2
Mareschal Rd. Guild GU2 130 C7
Maresfield. S Croy CR0 61 E7
Mareth Cl. Alder GU11 105 B2
Marfleet Cl. Carsh SM5 59 E8
Margaret Cl. Stain TW18 13 D2
Margaret Rd. Guild GU1 130 C8
Margaret Roper RC Prim Sch.
Purley CR8 61 A1
Margaret Way. Coulsd CR8 100 B8
Margery Gr. L Kings KT20 117 E6
Margery La.
L Kings KT20 & RH2 118 A6
Margin Dr. Wimble SW19 19 D4
Marham Gdns. Morden SM4 40 C3
Marham Gdns.
Wands SW17 & SW18 20 E7
Maria Montessori Sch.
Horne RH6 162 F5
Maria Theresa Cl.
New Mal KT3 38 D4
Marian Ct. Sutton SM1 59 B5
Marian Rd.
Mitch CR4 & SW16 41 C8
Marian Vian Prim Sch.
Beck BR3 43 E4
Mariette Way. Wallin SM6 60 E2
Marigold Cl. Crowth RG11 45 A6
Marigold Ct. Bellf GU1 109 E4
Marigold Dr. Bisley GU24 68 A4
Marigold Way. Croy CR0 43 D1
Marina Ave. W Barn KT3 39 B4
Marina Way. Tedd TW11 17 D1
Mariner Gdns. Rich TW10 17 C5
Mariners Dr. Farnb GU14 85 C6
Mariners Dr. Normdy GU3 107 B4
Marion Ave. Shep TW17 34 B4
Marion Ct. Up Toot SW17 20 E3
Marion Rd. Crawl RH10 202 B3
Marion Rd. Thorn H CR0 42 D4
Marist RC Prim Sch.
W Byfl KT14 70 F6
Marius Mansions. 3
Up Toot SW17 21 A6
Marius Rd. Up Toot SW17 21 A6
Marjoram Cl. Stough GU2 109 A5
Marjoram Cl. W Heath GU14 84 B4
Marjorie Fosters Way.
Pirb GU24 87 D8
Marjory Kinnon Sch.
Hatton TW14 3 E2
Mark Oak La. Fetch KT22 94 A6
Mark St. Reig RH2 118 B2
Mark Way. Farnc GU7 150 B8
Markedge La.
L Kings CR5 & RH2 98 F2
Markenfield Rd. Guild GU1 109 D1
Markenhorn. Farnc GU7 150 D7
Market Par. Croy SE25 43 A5
Market Par. Felt TW13 15 E6
Market Pl. Brent TW8 6 C7
Market Pl. King U T KT1 37 D7
Market Pl. Woki RG11 25 C5
Market Rd. Mortl TW9 7 A4
Market Sq. Horsh RH12 217 C1
Market Sq. Reig RH2 118 A1
Market Sq. Stain TW18 12 E4
Market St. Brack RG12 27 B7
Market St. Guild GU1 130 D8
Market The.
Carsh SM1 & SM4 & SM5 40 C1
Marketfield Way.
Earls RH1 119 A1
Markfield. New Add CR0 81 F8
Markfield Rd. Cater CR3 101 B2
Markham House. 9
Dulw SE21 22 E4
Markham Mews. Woki RG11 25 C6
Markham Rd. Capel RH5 178 C5
Markhole Cl. Hampt TW12 15 F1
Marks Rd. Warlgm CR6 81 E1
Marks Rd. Woki RG11 25 A8
Marksbury Ave. Rich TW9 7 A4
Markville Gdns. Cater CR3 101 A2
Markway The. Sunby TW16 35 C7
Markwell Cl. For Hil SE26 23 B4
Markwick La. Hasc GU8 172 C2
Marlang Ct. Beck BR3 44 D8
Marlborough Rd.
Brent TW7 & TW8 6 B7
Marlborough. 11
Putney SW19 19 D7
Marlborough Cl.
Crawl RH11 201 C2
Marlborough Cl. Hersh KT12 54 D7
Marlborough Cl.
Horsh RH12 217 D5
Marlborough Cl. Mitch SW19 20 E2
Marlborough Ct. Dork RH4 136 B7
Marlborough Ct. Woki RG11 25 D7
Marlborough Cty Inf Sch.
Farnb GU11 105 C7
Marlborough Dr. Weyb KT13 53 C7
Marlborough Gdns.
Surb KT6 37 D2
Marlborough House.
Wimble SW19 19 D5

Marlborough Jun & Inf Sch. Islew TW7 .... 6 A6
Marlborough Rd. Ashf TW15 13 E3
Marlborough Rd. Dork RH4 136 B7
Marlborough Rd. Felt TW13 15 D6
Marlborough Rd. Hampt TW12 .... 16 A2
Marlborough Rd. Mitch SW19 .... 20 E2
Marlborough Rd. Rich TW10 . 6 F1
Marlborough Rd. S Croy CR2 61 C3
Marlborough Rd. Sutton SM1 .... 59 A8
Marlborough Rd. Woking GU21 .... 70 A3
Marlborough Rise. Camb GU15 .... 65 E6
Marlborough Trad Est. Rich TW9 .... 7 B6
Marlborough View. W Heath GU14 .... 84 C5
Marld The. Ashtd KT21 .... 75 F1
Marler Rd. For Hil SE23 .... 23 F7
Marles La. Rudg RH14 .... 214 C1
Marlesford Ct. Wallin SM6 ... 60 C6
Marley Cl. Row Tn KT15 .... 51 F4
Marley Combe Rd. King Gn GU27 .... 207 F4
Marley Croft. Stain TW18 .... 12 E5
Marley Hanger. King Gn GU27 .... 208 A3
Marley La. Linch GU27 .... 207 E4
Marley Rise. Dork RH4 .... 136 A4
Marlfield Ct. New Mal KT3 ... 38 F2
Marling Ct. Hampt TW12 .... 15 F2
Marlingdene Cl. Hampt TW12 .... 16 A2
Marlings Cl. Kenley CR3 .... 80 E2
Marlins Cl. Sutton SM1 .... 59 C5
Marlow Cl. Penge SE20 .... 43 B6
Marlow Cres. Twick TW1 .... 5 F1
Marlow Ct. Crawl RH10 & RH11 .... 201 D7
Marlow Dr. Cheam SM3 .... 58 D7
Marlow House. Tedd TW11 . 17 A4
Marlow Rd. Penge SE20 & SE25 .... 43 B7
Marlowe Ct. Dulw SE19 .... 22 F3
Marlowe Ct. 6 King U T KT2 17 D4
Marlowe House. King U T KT1 .... 37 D5
Marlowe Lodge. Croy CR0 ... 62 E8
Marlowe Sq. Mitch CR4 .... 41 C5
Marlowe Way. Wallin CR0 ... 60 E8
Marlpit Ave. Coulsd CR5 .... 79 E2
Marlpit Cl. E Grins RH19 .... 185 E4
Marlpit La. Coulsd CR5 .... 79 E2
Marlyns Cl. Burph GU4 .... 110 A4
Marlyns Dr. Burph GU1 & GU4 .... 110 A4
Marmion House. 13 Balham SW12 .... 21 B8
Marmot Rd. Hounsl TW4 .... 4 D4
Marncrest Ct. Hersh KT12 ... 54 B5
Marnell Way. Hounsl TW4 .... 4 D4
Marneys Cl. Epsom KT18 .... 76 A4
Maroons Way. Catf SE6 .... 24 A3
Marqueen Towers. Streat SW16 .... 21 F1
Marquis Ct. 1 King U T KT1 37 E5
Married Quarters. Cater CR3 .... 100 C5
Marriott Cl. Hatton TW14 .... 3 D1
Marriott House. Catf SE6 .... 24 C4
Marriott Lodge Cl. Addl KT15 .... 52 C6
Marrowbrook Cl. Farnb GU14 .... 85 A4
Marrowbrook La. Farnb GU14 .... 85 A3
Marrowells. Walt O T KT13 .. 53 F7
Marryat Pl. Wimble SW19 .... 19 E4
Marryat Rd. Wimble SW19 .... 19 E3
Marsh Ave. Epsom KT19 .... 57 E1
Marsh Ave. Mitch CR4 .... 41 A7
Marsh Ct. Crawl RH11 .... 201 B1
Marsh Ct. 3 Merton SW19 . 40 C8
Marsh Farm Rd. Twick TW2 . 16 F7
Marsh La. Addl KT15 .... 52 B6
Marshall Cl. Friml GU16 .... 66 D2
Marshall Cl. Hounsl TW4 .... 4 F2
Marshall Cl. W Heath GU14 .. 84 F7
Marshall House. 3 New Mal KT3 .... 38 E5
Marshall Par. Pyrf GU22 .... 70 F4
Marshall Pl. New Haw KT15 . 52 C2
Marshall Rd. Farnc GU7 .... 150 E6
Marshall Rd. Sandh GU15 .... 64 D6
Marshall Rd. Worth RH10 .. 202 C4
Marshall's Rd. Sutton SM1 ... 59 B6
Marshalls. M Bourn GU9 .... 146 B8
Marshalls Cl. Epsom KT19 .... 76 C6
Marsham Ct. 19 Putney SW19 .... 19 D7
Marshfields C of E Fst Sch. Ottsh KT16 .... 51 E4
Marshwood Rd. Lhtwat GU18 .... 67 D8
Marston. Epsom KT19 .... 76 C8
Marston Ave. Chess KT9 .... 56 E4
Marston Ct. Walt O T KT12 .. 35 C1
Marston Dr. Farnb GU14 .... 85 B7
Marston Dr. Warlgm CR6 .... 81 E1
Marston House. Redh RH1 118 F2
Marston Rd. Farnh GU9 .... 124 F2
Marston Rd. Rich TW11 .... 17 B3
Marston Rd. Woking GU21 ... 69 B2
Marston Way. N Asct SL5 .... 28 E7
Marston Way. S Norw SE19 . 22 C1
Martel Cl. Camb GU15 .... 66 C7
Martell Rd. W Norw SE21 .... 22 D5
Martens Pl. Farnc GU7 .... 150 E6
Martin Cl. Crawl RH11 .... 201 D8
Martin Cl. Selsd CR2 .... 62 D1
Martin Cl. Warlgm CR6 .... 81 B3
Martin Cres. Thorn H CR0 .... 42 A1
Martin Ct. Merton SW19 .... 20 A1
Martin Gr. Merton SM4 & SW19 .... 40 A6
Martin House. 5 New Mal KT3 .... 38 E5
Martin Rd. Stough GU2 .... 109 A3
Martin Way. Friml GU16 .... 65 E2
Martin Way. Merton SW19 & SW20 & SM4 .... 39 E6
Martin Way. Woking GU21 ... 69 A1
Martin's Heron Sta. Brack RG12 .... 27 F5
Martin's Rd. Broml BR2 .... 44 F7
Martindale. Mortl SW14 .... 7 C2
Martindale Ave. Friml GU15 66 C4
Martindale Cl. Merrow GU4 110 D3
Martindale Rd. Balham SW12 .... 21 B8
Martindale Rd. Hounsl TW4 ... 4 E4
Martindale Rd. Woking GU21 .... 69 A1
Martindale Sch. Hounsl TW4 . 4 E4
Martineau Cl. Esher KT10 .... 55 D6
Martineau Dr. Dork RH4 .... 136 B5
Martingale Cl. Sunby TW16 . 35 A5
Martingale Ct. Alder GU11 . 104 E2
Martingales Cl. Rich TW10 .. 17 D5
Martins Cl. Blckw GU17 .... 64 D4
Martins Cl. Merrow GU1 .... 110 C2
Martins Cl. W Wick BR4 .... 63 D8
Martins Dr. Woki RG11 .... 25 B7
Martins La. Brack RG12 .... 27 E6
Martins The. Crawl D RH10 204 C8
Martins The. For Hil SE26 .... 23 B3
Martins Wood. Witley GU8 170 E7
Martinsyde. Mayb GU22 .... 70 C2
Martlet Cnr. Rudg RH12 .... 214 D7
Martlets Cl. Horsh RH12 .... 217 C5
Martlets The. Crawl RH10 .. 201 E6
Marton Cl. Catf SE6 .... 24 A5
Marts The. Rudg RH12 .... 214 D7
Martyns Pl. E Grins RH19 .. 206 A8
Martyr Rd. Guild GU1 .... 130 D8
Martyrs Ave. Crawl RH11 .. 181 D1
Martyrs La. Sheer GU21 .... 70 B7
Marvell Cl. Crawl RH10 .... 202 C8
Marwell Cl. Coney H BR4 .... 63 F8
Mary Adelaide Cl. King U T SW15 .... 18 E5
Mary Rd. Guild GU1 .... 130 C8
Mary Rose Cl. Hampt TW12 . 36 A8
Mary Rose Gdns. Chess KT9 56 E6
Mary Vale. Godal GU7 .... 150 D2
Mary's Terr. Twick TW1 .... 17 A8
Marygold House. Hounsl TW3 5 C6
Maryhill Cl. Kenley CR8 .... 80 C2
Maryland Ct. King U T KT1 ... 38 B7
Maryland Rd. S Norw CR7 .... 42 B8
Maryland Way. Sunby TW16 35 A7
Marymount International Sch. King U T KT2 .... 18 C1
Masefield Ct. 19 Surb KT6 ... 37 D2
Masefield Rd. Crawl RH11 . 200 E3
Masefield Rd. Hampt TW13 . 15 F4
Masefield Way. Stan TW19 .. 13 F7
Maskall Cl. Streat SW2 .... 22 A7
Maskani Wlk. Streat SW16 .. 21 C1
Maskell Rd. Wands SW17 .... 20 C5
Maskell Way. Farnb GU14 .... 84 D3
Mason Cl. E Grins RH19 .... 185 E2
Mason Cl. Hampt TW12 .... 35 F8
Mason Cl. Wimble SW20 .... 39 D8
Mason Ct. 3 Penge SE19 .... 22 F1
Mason Rd. Crawl RH10 .... 201 E4
Mason Rd. W Heath GU14 .... 84 E6
Mason Way. Alder GU11 ... 126 B7
Mason's Ave. Croy CR0 & CR9 .... 61 C7
Mason's Bridge Rd. Earls RH1 .... 140 C3
Mason's Bridge Rd. Salfs RH1 .... 140 C3
Mason's Pl. Mitch CR4 .... 40 F8
Masonic Hall Rd. Chert KT16 32 F3
Masons Paddock. Dork RH4 .... 115 A1
Massetts Rd. Horley RH6 .. 161 A2
Master Cl. Oxted RH8 .... 122 E6
Mastin House. Wands SW18 20 A7
Maswell Park Cres. Islew TW3 .... 5 C2
Maswell Park Rd. Islew TW3 . 5 C3
Matham Rd. E Mole KT8 .... 36 D4
Mathew Terr. Alder GU11 .. 105 C2
Mathews Cl. Farnb GU14 ... 105 E8
Mathias Cl. Epsom KT18 .... 76 C6
Mathisen Way. Poyle SL3 .... 1 E6
Mathon Ct. Guild GU1 .... 109 F1
Matlock Cres. Cheam SM3 ... 58 E6
Matlock Gdns. Cheam SM1 & SM3 .... 58 E6
Matlock Pl. Cheam SM1 & SM3 .... 58 E6
Matlock Rd. Cater CR3 .... 100 E6
Matlock Way. King U T KT3 .. 38 D8
Matthew Arnold Cl. Cobham KT11 .... 73 A5
Matthew Arnold Sch The . Stain TW18 .... 13 C2
Matthew Ct. Mitch CR4 .... 41 D4
Matthew Rd. Alder GU9 .... 125 E8
Matthew's Gdns. New Add CR0 .... 82 D8
Matthew's St. Dovgn RH2 . 139 A5
Matthews Ct. Ascot SL5 .... 29 D5
Matthews Dr. Worth RH10 . 202 C3
Matthews La. Stain TW18 .... 12 F4
Matthews Rd. Camb GU15 ... 65 C8
Matthewsgreen Rd. Woki RG11 .... 25 A8
Matthey Pl. Crawl RH10 .... 182 D1
Matthias Ct. 12 Rich TW10 .... 6 E1
Maultway Cl. Camb GU15 .... 66 B8
Maultway Cres. Camb GU15 66 B8
Maultway N. Camb GU15 .... 47 B1
Maultway The. Camb GU15 & GU16 .... 66 D6
Maultway The. Friml GU15 & GU16 .... 66 D6
Maunsell Pk. Crawl RH10 .. 202 B6
Maurice Ave. Cater CR3 .... 100 D5
Maurice Ct. 3 Brent TW8 .... 6 D7
Mavery Ct. Broml BR1 .... 24 F1
Mavins Rd. M Bourn GU9 .... 146 D8
Mavis Ave. Worc Pk KT19 .... 57 E5
Mavis Cl. Worc Pk KT19 .... 57 E5
Mawbey Rd. Ottsh KT16 .... 51 D4
Mawson Cl. Merton SW20 .... 39 E7
Mawson La. Chisw W4 .... 7 F8
Maxine Cl. Sandh GU17 .... 45 B1
Maxton Wlk. Crawl RH11 .. 201 B2
Maxwell Cl. Croy CR0 .... 41 E1
Maxwell Ct. Dulw SE21 .... 23 A7
Maxwell Dr. W Byfl KT14 .... 71 C8
Maxwell Rd. Ashf TW15 .... 14 C2
Maxwell Way. Crawl RH10 182 A1
May Cl. Chess KT9 .... 56 F4
May Cl. Ock Rid GU7 .... 150 B2
May Cl. 2 Sandh GU15 .... 64 D8
May Cotts. L Kings CR5 .... 98 B2
May Cres. Ash GU12 .... 105 E1
May Ct. 2 Merton SW19 .... 40 C8
May Rd. Twick TW2 .... 16 E7
May's Hill Rd. Beck BR2 .... 44 E6
Maybelle Cl. Bear Gn RH5 . 157 D3
Mayberry Pl. Surb KT5 .... 37 F2
Maybourne Grange. S Croy CR0 .... 61 E8
Maybourne Rise. Westfd GU22 .... 89 D3
Maybury Cl. Burgh H KT20 ... 97 E8
Maybury Cl. Friml GU16 .... 85 D8
Maybury Ct. Mayb GU22 .... 70 B2
Maybury Cty Inf Sch. Woking GU21 .... 70 A3
Maybury Hill. Mayb GU21 & GU22 .... 70 B2
Maybury Rd. Woking GU21 .. 70 A3
Maybury Rough. Mayb GU22 70 B2
Maybury St. Up Toot SW17 .. 20 E3
Maycroft. Coney H BR2 .... 44 F1
Maycross Ave. Morden SM4 40 A5
Mayday Hospl. Thorn H CR7 42 B3
Mayday Rd. Thorn H CR0 & CR7 .... 42 B3
Maydwell Ave. Slinfd RH13 215 C2
Mayefield Rd. Thorn H CR7 .. 41 F4
Mayell Cl. Leahd KT22 .... 95 C4
Mayes Cl. Warlgm CR6 .... 81 D1
Mayes La. Warn RH12 .... 197 F3
Mayfair Ave. New Mal KT4 ... 39 A1
Mayfair Ave. Twick TW2 .... 16 C8
Mayfair Cl. Beck BR3 .... 44 B8
Mayfair Cl. Surb KT6 .... 37 E1
Mayfair Ct. Beck BR3 .... 44 B8
Mayfair Ct. 4 S Croy CR0 .... 61 F8
Mayfield. Dorman RH7 .... 165 A1
Mayfield. Hersh KT12 .... 54 C6
Mayfield. Rowl GU10 .... 145 F3
Mayfield. Worth RH10 .... 202 D6
Mayfield Ave. Woodhm KT15 52 C1
Mayfield Cl. Ashf TW15 .... 14 B2
Mayfield Cl. Earls RH1 .... 140 A3
Mayfield Cl. Farnh GU9 .... 126 B6
Mayfield Cl. Hersh KT12 .... 54 A6
Mayfield Cl. Hinch W KT7 .... 37 B1
Mayfield Cl. Penge SE20 .... 43 B8
Mayfield Cl. Weyb KT15 .... 52 C1
Mayfield Cres. Thorn H CR7 . 41 F5
Mayfield Ct. Earls RH1 .... 139 F4
Mayfield Ct. Sutton SM2 .... 59 C3
Mayfield Cty Inf Sch. W Heath GU14 .... 85 B6
Mayfield Cty Jun Sch. W Heath GU14 .... 85 A6
Mayfield Gdns. Egham TW18 12 F2
Mayfield Gdns. Walt O T KT12 .... 54 A6
Mayfield Rd. Camb GU15 .... 65 B1
Mayfield Rd. Hersh KT12 .... 54 A6
Mayfield Rd. Merton SW19 .. 39 F8
Mayfield Rd. S Croy CR2 .... 61 D2
Mayfield Rd. Sutton SM2 .... 59 D4
Mayfield Rd. W Heath GU14 84 F7
Mayfield Rd. Weyb KT13 .... 52 F5
Mayflower Cl. Worth RH10 202 D5
Mayford Cl. Balham SW12 ... 20 F8
Mayford Cl. Penge BR3 .... 43 D6
Mayford Cl. Westfd GU22 .... 89 D5
Mayford Rd. Balham SW12 .. 21 A8
Mayhurst Ave. Mayb GU22 .. 70 C3
Mayhurst Cl. Mayb GU22 .... 70 C3
Mayhurst Cres. Mayb GU22 . 70 C3
Maynard Ct. Stain TW18 .... 13 A4
Maynooth Gdns. Carsh CR4 . 40 F2
Mayo Rd. Thorn H CR0 .... 42 D4
Mayo Rd. Walt O T KT12 .... 35 A2
Mayow Rd. For Hil SE23 & SE26 .... 23 D4
Maypole Rd. Ash W RH19 .. 206 E6
Maypole Rd. E Grins RH19 185 D2
Mayroyd Ave. Tolw KT6 .... 57 A8
Mays Cl. Whit V KT13 .... 52 F1
Mays Cnr. Send GU23 .... 90 D3
Mays Gr. Send GU23 .... 90 D4
Mays Rd. Tedd TW11 & TW12 .... 16 D3
Mays Rd. Woki RG11 .... 25 E6
Maysfield Rd. Send GU23 .... 90 D4
Maytree Cl. Bellf GU1 .... 109 C5
Maytree Ct. Mitch CR4 .... 41 A6
Maytree Wlk. Streat SW2 .... 22 A6
Maytrees. Knaph GU21 .... 68 C2
Maywater Cl. S Croy CR2 .... 80 D8
Maywood Cl. Beck BR3 .... 24 B1
Maywood Dr. Camb GU15 .... 66 A7
Maze Rd. Rich TW9 .... 7 A7
McAlmont Ridge. Farnc GU7 .... 150 D7
McCarthy Rd. Felt TW13 .... 15 D3
McCormick House. 9 Streat SW2 .... 22 A7
McDonald House. 1 King U T KT2 .... 17 F1
McDonough Cl. Chess KT9 .. 56 E6
McDougall Ct. Rich TW9 .... 7 A5
McIndoe Rd. E Grins RH19 185 D3
McIntosh Cl. Wallin SM6 .... 60 E3
McIver Cl. Felb RH19 .... 184 F4
McKay Cl. Alder GU11 .... 105 C3
McKay Rd. Wimble SW20 .... 19 C2
Mckay Trad Est. Poyle SL3 .... 1 E5
McKinlay Ct. Beck BR3 .... 43 F7
Mcleod Ct. Dulw SE21 .... 23 A7
McLeod House. For Hil SE23 23 C6
McMillan Ct. Catf SE6 .... 24 F7
McNaughton Cl. Farnb GU14 84 D3
McRae La. Carsh CR4 .... 40 F2
Meachen Ct. Woki RG11 .... 25 C6
Mead Ave. Salfs RH1 .... 140 A1
Mead Cl. Cran GU6 .... 174 E2
Mead Cl. Egham TW20 .... 12 B2
Mead Cl. Redh RH1 .... 119 A4
Mead Cres. Carsh SM1 .... 59 E6
Mead Cres. L Book KT23 .... 94 A2
Mead Ct. Woking GU21 .... 68 E3
Mead Dr. Coulsd CR5 .... 79 E5
Mead End. Ashtd KT21 .... 75 F3
Mead La. Chert KT16 .... 33 C1
Mead La. Farnh GU9 .... 125 B2
Mead Path. Mitch SW17 .... 20 D2
Mead Pl. Thorn H CR0 .... 42 C1
Mead Rd. Cater CR3 .... 100 F4
Mead Rd. Cran GU6 .... 174 E3
Mead Rd. Crawl RH10 .... 201 F7
Mead Rd. Hersh KT12 .... 54 E6
Mead Rd. Hind GU26 .... 188 F4
Mead Rd. Rich TW10 .... 17 C5
Mead The. Ashtd KT21 .... 95 E8
Mead The. Beck BR3 .... 44 C8
Mead The. Dork RH4 .... 136 C4
Mead The. Farnb GU14 .... 85 B4
Mead The. W Wick BR4 .... 44 D1
Mead The. Wallin SM6 .... 60 D4
Mead Way. Burph GU4 .... 110 C6
Mead Way. Coulsd CR5 .... 79 F1
Mead Way. Croy CR0 .... 62 E8
Mead Way. Hayes BR2 & BR4 44 F3
Meadcroft House. 4 New Mal KT3 .... 38 E2
Meade Cl. Brent W4 .... 7 A8
Meade Ct. Bagsh GU19 .... 47 F3
Meade Ct. Walt o t H KT20 ... 97 A3
Meades Cl. Dorman RH7 ... 165 B1
Meades The. Dorman RH7 165 A1
Meadfoot Rd. Streat SW16 .. 41 C8
Meadhurst Rd. Chert KT16 .. 33 B1
Meadhurst Sports Club. Ashf TW16 .... 14 F3
Meadlands Dr. Rich TW10 .... 17 D6
Meadlands Prim Sch. Rich TW10 .... 17 C4
Meadow App. Copth RH10 183 A3
Meadow Ave. Croy CR0 .... 43 D3
Meadow Bank. E Hors KT24 112 E8
Meadow Bglws. Chil GU4 .. 131 B3
Meadow Brook Ind Ctr. Crawl RH10 .... 182 A1
Meadow Cl. Ash V GU12 .... 85 F1
Meadow Cl. Catf SE6 .... 24 A3
Meadow Cl. Copth RH10 .... 183 A3
Meadow Cl. Farnc GU7 .... 150 E7
Meadow Cl. Hawley GU17 .... 64 D4
Meadow Cl. Hersh KT12 .... 54 F6
Meadow Cl. Hinch W KT10 ... 55 F7
Meadow Cl. Horsh RH12 .... 218 A5
Meadow Cl. Milf GU8 .... 150 A1
Meadow Cl. Purley CR8 .... 79 D6
Meadow Cl. Rich TW10 .... 17 E7
Meadow Cl. Sutton SM1 .... 59 C8
Meadow Cl. Twick TW4 .... 16 A8
Meadow Cl. W Barn SW20 ... 39 C5
Meadow Cotts. W End GU24 67 F7
Meadow Croft Cl. Horley RH6 .... 182 C8
Meadow Ct. Epsom KT18 .... 76 C6
Meadow Ct. Farnb GU14 .... 84 F4
Meadow Ct. Stain TW18 .... 12 E5
Meadow Dr. Send M GU23 ... 90 F4
Meadow Farm La. Horsh RH12 .... 217 F7
Meadow Gate Rd. Farnb GU14 .... 84 F1
Meadow Gdns. Egham TW18 12 D3
Meadow Hill. Coulsd CR5 & CR8 .... 79 C6
Meadow Hill. New Mal KT3 .. 38 E3
Meadow Hill. Purley CR5 & CR8 .... 79 C6
Meadow House. Merrow GU4 .... 110 D2
Meadow La. Fetch KT22 .... 94 C5
Meadow Pl. Chisw W4 .... 7 E7
Meadow Rd. Ashf TW15 .... 14 D3
Meadow Rd. Ashtd KT21 .... 75 E2
Meadow Rd. Broml BR2 .... 44 E7
Meadow Rd. Burph GU4 .... 110 A5
Meadow Rd. Carsh SM1 .... 59 E5
Meadow Rd. Clayg KT10 .... 55 E4
Meadow Rd. Farnb GU14 .... 85 B7
Meadow Rd. Felt TW13 .... 15 E6
Meadow Rd. Merton SW19 .. 20 C1
Meadow Rd. Went GU25 & SL5 .... 30 E4
Meadow Rd. Woki RG11 .... 25 A5
Meadow Rise. Coulsd CR5 ... 79 D6
Meadow Rise. Knaph GU21 .. 68 C2
Meadow Stile. Croy CR0 & CR9 .... 61 C7
Meadow The. Copth RH10 . 183 A3
Meadow Vale. Shottm GU27 .... 208 A6
Meadow Vale Cty Prim Sch. Brack RG12 .... 26 F8
Meadow View. Smallf RH6 .... 162 C3

Meadow View Rd.
  Thorn H CR7 .... 42 B4
Meadow Way. Addl KT15 ...... 52 B6
Meadow Way. Alder GU12 .. 105 F3
Meadow Way. Blckw GU17 .... 64 C5
Meadow Way. Brack RG12 .... 27 A8
Meadow Way. Burgh H KT20 77 E2
Meadow Way. Chess KT9 ...... 56 E5
Meadow Way. Dovgn RH2 . 139 B5
Meadow Way. Fetch KT23 .... 94 B4
Meadow Way. Rowl GU10 .. 145 F3
Meadow Way. W End GU4 .... 69 F2
Meadow Way. W Hors KT24 92 D2
Meadow Way. Woki RG11 .... 25 A5
Meadow Wlk. Heston TW5 ...... 4 E7
Meadow Wlk. Hackb SM6 .... 60 B7
Meadow Wlk.
  W Ewell KT17 & KT19 ...... 57 F3
Meadow Wlk.
  Walt o t H KT20 .... 97 B3
Meadow Wlk. Woki RG11 .... 25 A6
Meadowbank. Surb KT5 .... 37 F3
Meadowbank Gdns.
  Cranf TW4 & TW5 .... 4 D5
Meadowbank Rd.
  Lhtwat GU18 .... 48 C1
Meadowbrook.
  Oxted RH8 .... 122 D5
Meadowbrook Rd. CR Poyle SL3 .. 1 F6
Meadowcroft Rd.
  Dork RH4 .... 136 A7
Meadowcroft Cl.
  Crawl RH11 .... 200 F5
Meadowcroft Cl.
  E Grins RH19 .... 185 C2
Meadow Cty Sch.
  Addl KT16 .... 51 F7
Meadowlands. Cobham KT11 73 A6
Meadowlands. Crawl RH11 201 C6
Meadowlands. Oxted RH8 . 123 A1
Meadowlands. W Clan GU4 111 B5
Meadowlea Cl. Harm UB7 ..... 2 D8
Meadows End. Sunby TW16 35 A8
Meadows Leigh Cl.
  Weyb KT13 .... 53 C7
Meadows The. Ash GU12 .. 106 B2
Meadows The. Churt GU10 167 F1
Meadows The. Guild GU2 .. 130 C6
Meadows The. Sandh GU15 .. 64 E5
Meadows The. Warlgm CR6 . 81 E2
Meadowside. Fetch KT23 ..... 94 A4
Meadowside. Horley RH6 .. 161 B4
Meadowside. Twick TW1 .... 17 D8
Meadowside. Walt O T KT12 54 C8
Meadowside Rd. Belm SM2 . 58 E2
Meadowview. Stan TW19 ...... 1 F2
Meadowview Rd. Catf SE6 .. 24 A3
Meadowview Rd.
  W Ewell KT19 .... 57 E2
Meadrow. Farnc GU7 .... 150 F6
Meadrow Lock. Farnc GU7 151 A6
Meads Cty Prim Sch The.
  E Grins RH19 .... 205 E7
Meads Rd. Merrow GU1 .... 110 B1
Meads The. Cheam SM3 ...... 58 E7
Meads The. E Grins RH19 .. 205 E7
Meads The. Shottm GU27 .. 207 F6
Meads The. Whit V KT13 .... 53 D4
Meadside. Epsom KT18 ... 76 D6
Meadside. Woking GU22 .. 69 F1
Meadside Cl. Penge BR3 .... 43 E8
Meadsview Ct.
  Farnb GU14 .... 85 B4
Meadvale. Horsh RH12 .... 216 F2
Meadway. Croy CR0 .... 43 E3
Meadway. Ashf TW15 .... 14 A4
Meadway. Beck BR3 .... 44 C8
Meadway. Effing KT24 ...... 113 E7
Meadway. Epsom KT19 ...... 76 C7
Meadway. Friml GU16 .... 65 F2
Meadway. Oxsh KT22 .... 74 E5
Meadway. Shottm GU27 .. 207 F6
Meadway. Stain TW18 .... 13 A1
Meadway. Tolw KT5 .... 38 C1
Meadway. Twick TW2 .... 16 D7
Meadway. W Barn SW20 .... 39 C5
Meadway. Warlgm CR6 ...... 81 C3
Meadway Dr. New Haw KT15 52 C3
Meadway The. Horley RH6 161 C3
Meaford Way. Penge SE20 .. 23 B1
Meare Cl. Tadw KT20 .... 97 C4
Meath Green Ave.
  Horley RH6 .... 160 F5
Meath Green Cty Fst Sch.
  Horley RH6 .... 160 F5

Meath Green City Inf Sch.
  Horley RH6 .... 161 A5
Meath Green City Jun Sch.
  Horley RH6 .... 160 F5
Meath Green La.
  Horley RH1 & RH6 .... 160 E6
Meath Green La.
  Salfs RH1 & RH6 .... 160 E6
Meath Sch. Ottsh KT16 .... 51 D3
Medawar Rd. Onsl V GU2 .. 129 D8
Medcroft Gdns. Mortl SW14 .. 7 C3
Mede Cl. Wray TW19 .... 11 D7
Mede Ct. Stain TW18 .... 12 E5
Mede Field. Fetch KT22 ..... 94 D3
Medfield St. Putney SW15 .. 19 B8
Medhurst Cl. Chobb GU24 ... 49 F2
Medina Ave. Hinch W KT10 .. 55 E7
Medlake Rd. Egham TW20 .. 12 C2
Medlar Cl. Bellf GU1 .... 109 C3
Medlar Cl. Crawl RH11 .... 181 C1
Medlar Dr. Hawley GU17 .... 64 F3
Medora Rd. Streat SW2 .... 21 F8
Medway. Turn H RH10 .... 204 A5
Medway Cl. Horsh RH12 .. 218 B5
Medway Ct. S Norw SE25 .. 42 E4
Medway Dr. E Grins RH19 . 205 D6
Medway Dr. For Row RH18 206 F2
Medway Dr. W Heath GU14 . 84 E7
Medway Rd. Crawl RH11 .. 200 F5
Medwyn Wlk. Horsh RH12 .217 C2
Melbourne Cl. Wallin SM6 .. 60 C5
Melbourne Cl. Penge SE20 . 23 A1
Melbourne Cl. Twick TW2 .. 16 D7
Melbourne Mews.
  Lewish SE6 .... 24 C8
Melbourne Rd.
  Merton SW19 .... 40 A8
Melbourne Rd. Tedd TW11 .. 17 C2
Melbourne Rd. Wallin SM6 .. 60 C5
Melbourne Way.
  Horsh RH12 .... 217 F5
Melbury Cl. Chert KT16 ...... 33 A2
Melbury Cl. Clayg KT10 ..... 56 B4
Melbury Cl. W Byfl KT14 .... 71 A5
Melbury Gdns.
  Wimble SW20 .... 39 B8
Melbury House. Theat TW2 .16 D6
Meldone. New Mal KT3 ...... 38 D1
Meldone Cl. Tolw KT5 .... 38 B3
Meldrum Cl. Oxted RH8 .... 123 A3
Melfield Gdns. Catf SE6 ..... 24 C3
Melfont Ave. Thorn H CR7 ... 42 B6
Melford Cl. Chess KT9 .... 56 F5
Melford Ct. Dulw SE22 ...... 23 A8
Melford Ct. Sutton SM2 ..... 59 C3
Melford Rd.
  Dulw SE22 & SE23 .... 23 A7
Melfort Rd.
  Thorn H CR7 & SW16 .... 42 B6
Meliot Rd. Catf SE6 .... 24 D6
Melksham Cl. Horsh RH13 . 217 E1
Meller Cl. Wallin SM6 .... 60 E7
Mellersh Hill Rd.
  Woner GU5 .... 152 C6
Mellish Ct. Surb KT6 .... 37 E3
Mellison Rd. Up Toot SW17 . 20 E3
Mellor Cl. Walt O T KT12 .... 35 F2
Mellor Ct. Merton SW19 .... 20 C1
Mellor House. Dulw SE21 . 22 E4
Mellow Cl. Banstd SM7 ...... 78 C5
Mellows Rd. Wallin SM6 ..... 60 D5
Melody Rd. Bigg H TN16 .... 83 C1
Melrose. Easth RG12 .... 27 B1
Melrose Ave. Mitch CR4 ..... 21 B1
Melrose Ave. Thorn H SW16 42 A6
Melrose Ave. Twick TW2 .... 16 B8
Melrose Ave. W Heath GU14 84 C5
Melrose Ave. Wimble SW20 20 A5
Melrose Gdns. Hersh KT12 .. 54 C5
Melrose Gdns. King U T KT3 38 D6
Melrose Rd. Barnes SW13 .... 7 F5
Melrose Rd. Bigg H TN16 ... 83 C3
Melrose Rd. Coulsd CR5 .... 79 A4
Melrose Rd. Merton SW19 .. 40 A8
Melrose Rd. Weyb KT13 .... 53 A5
Melrose Sch. Mitch CR4 ..... 40 E6
Melrose Tudor. Wallin SM6 . 60 E5
Melsa Rd. Morden SM4 ...... 40 C3
Melton Cl. B Croy CR0 .... 61 F8
Melton Ct. ☑ Twick TW1 ... 17 B8
Melton Fields. Epsom KT19 . 57 D2
Melton Pl. Epsom KT19 ...... 57 D2
Melton Rd. Merst RH1 .... 119 C5
Melville Ave. Friml GU16 .... 65 F1
Melville Ave.
  S Croy CR0 & CR2 .... 61 F5
Melville Ave. Wimble SW20 . 19 A1
Melvin Cl. ☑ Rich TW9 .... 7 A4
Melvin Rd. Penge SE20 ...... 43 C8
Melvinshaw. Leahd KT22 .... 95 C6

Membury Cl. Friml GU16 .... 86 A7
Membury Wlk. Brack RG12 .. 27 F5
Memorial Cl. Heston TW5 .... 4 F8
Memory Cotts.
  Burgh H KT20 .... 97 E8
Mendip Cl. For Hil SE26 ..... 23 C4
Mendip Cl. Harl UB3 .... 3 D7
Mendip Cl. N Cheam KT4 .... 58 C8
Mendip Rd. Brack RG12 ..... 27 E4
Mendip Rd. W Heath GU14 . 84 E7
Mendip Wlk. Crawl RH11 .. 201 B6
Menin Way. M Bourn GU9 . 125 D1
Menlo Gdns. S Norw SE19 .. 22 D1
Meon Cl. Tadw KT20 .... 97 B5
Meon Cl. W Heath GU14 .... 84 D6
Meon Ct. Hounsl TW7 .... 5 E5
Meopham Rd.
  Mitch CR4 & SW16 .... 41 C8
Merantum Way.
  Merton SW19 .... 40 C8
Merantum Way. Mitch SW19 40 C8
Mercer Cl. Thame D KT7 .... 36 F2
Mercer Cl. Worth RH10 .... 202 C3
Mercer Rd. Faygt RH12 ... 217 C8
Merchiston Rd. Catf SE6 .... 24 D6
Merca Wlk. ☑ Woking GU21 69 F2
Mercury Cl. Crawl RH11 ... 200 E3
Mercury Ctr. Felt TW14 .... 4 B2
Merc Cl.
  Putney SW15 & SW19 .... 19 D8
Mere End. Croy CR0 .... 43 D2
Mere Rd. Oat Pk KT13 .... 53 D7
Mere Rd. Shep TW17 .... 34 B3
Mere Rd. Tadw KT20 .... 97 B4
Mere Rd. Walt o t H KT20 ... 97 B4
Merebank. Bear Gn RH5 ... 157 D4
Merebank La.
  Croy CR0 & SM6 .... 60 F5
Merefield Gdns.
  Burgh H KT20 .... 97 C8
Meretune Ct. Merton SM4 .. 39 F6
Merevale Cres. Morden SM4 40 C3
Mereway Industry.
  Twick TW2 .... 16 E7
Mereway Rd. Twick TW2 .... 16 E7
Mereworth Cl. Hayes BR2 .. 44 F4
Mereworth Dr. Crawl RH10 202 D8
Meridian. Dr. Catf SE6 .... 24 F7
Meridian Ct. Croy CR0 .... 61 A6
Meridian Ct. Sunnin SL5 .... 29 B1
Meridian Gr. Horley RH6 .. 161 C4
Meridian Way.
  E Grins RH19 .... 185 F3
Merland Cl. Burgh H KT20 .. 97 C7
Merland Gn. Burgh H KT20 . 97 C7
Merland Rise.
  Burgh H KT18 & KT20 .... 97 C8
Merland Rise Cty Prim Schs.
  Burgh H KT20 .... 97 C8
Merle Common Rd.
  Limps RH8 .... 144 B7
Merlewood. Brack RG12 .... 27 D4
Merlewood Cl. Cater CR3 .. 100 D7
Merlin Cl. Bra Hil SL3 .... 1 B8
Merlin Cl. Crawl RH11 ...... 200 E6
Merlin Cl. S Croy CR0 .... 61 E6
Merlin Clove. Wink RG12 .... 8 B2
Merlin Ct. Beck BR2 .... 44 F5
Merlin Ct. Friml GU16 .... 65 D1
Merlin Ctr. Crawl RH11 .... 181 D2
Merlin Gr. Beck BR3 .... 44 A4
Merlin Rd. Farnb GU14 ...... 85 B2
Merlin Way. E Grins RH19 . 186 A3
Merlin Way. Farnb GU14 .... 84 D3
Merlins Cl. M Bourn GU9 .. 125 C1
Merrick House. Reig RH2 .. 118 C1
Merricks Ct. Mortl SW14 ..... 7 B3
Merrilands Rd. N Cheam KT4 39 C1
Merrilyn Cl. Clayg KT10 ..... 56 A4
Merrist Wood Coll. Brewerstreet
  Farm Ctr. Bletch RH1 ...... 120 C4
Merrist Wood Coll (Agricultural).
  Worpl GU3 .... 108 C7
Merritt Gdns. Chess KT9 .... 56 C5
Merrivale Gdns. Horse GU21 69 C2
Merrow Bsns Ctr The.
  Merrow GU1 .... 110 D4
Merrow CE Inf Sch.
  Merrow GU1 .... 110 D3
Merrow Chase.
  Merrow GU1 .... 110 D1
Merrow Common Rd.
  Merrow GU1 .... 110 D4
Merrow Copse.
  Merrow GU1 .... 110 B2
Merrow Croft. Merrow GU1 110 C2
Merrow Ct. Merrow GU1 ... 110 D1
Merrow Ct. Mitch CR4 .... 40 D7
Merrow La. Burph GU4 ..... 110 C5

Merrow La. Merrow GU4 .... 110 C4
Merrow Rd. E Ewell SM2 .... 58 D2
Merrow St.
  Merrow GU1 & GU4 .... 110 D2
Merrow Way. New Add CR0 . 63 C4
Merrow Woods.
  Merrow GU1 .... 110 B3
Merryacres. Witley GU8 .... 170 E6
Merryfield Dr. Horsh RH12 217 A3
Merryhill Rd. Brack RG12 .... 27 B8
Merryhills Cl. Bigg H TN16 .. 83 D3
Merryhills La. Loxwd RH14 213 A5
Merrylands. Addl KT16 ...... 51 E7
Merrylands Ct. L Book KT23 . 93 F4
Merrylands Farm.
  Fetch KT23 .... 94 A3
Merrylands Rd. L Book KT23 93 F3
Merryman Dr. Crowth RG45 45 A7
Merrymeet. Woodm SM7 .... 78 F5
Merryweather Ct. ☑
  New Mal KT3 .... 38 E4
Merrywood. Leahd KT22 .... 95 C6
Merrywood Gr. Reig KT20 .. 117 E5
Merrywood Pk. Friml GU15 .. 65 F4
Merrywood Pk. Reig RH2 .. 118 B3
Merryworth Cl. Ash GU12 . 105 F1
Mersham Pl. Penge SE20 .... 43 B8
Mersham Pl. S Norw CR7 .... 42 D7
Mersham Rd. S Norw CR7 ... 42 D7
Merstham Cty Fst Sch.
  Merst RH1 .... 119 C6
Merstham Rd. Bletch RH1 . 120 A5
Merstham Sta. Merst RH1 . 119 C7
Merton SW19 .... 40 B8
Merton Cl. Sandh GU15 ...... 45 F2
Merton Gdns. Burgh H KT20 97 D8
Merton Hall Gdns.
  Merton SW20 .... 39 E8
Merton Hall Rd.
  Merton SW19 & SW20 .... 39 E8
Merton High St.
  Merton SW19 .... 20 C1
Merton Ind Pk.
  Merton SW19 .... 40 C8
Merton Mansions.
  Merton SW20 .... 39 D7
Merton Park Par.
  Merton SW19 .... 40 A8
Merton Park Prim Sch.
  Merton SW19 .... 39 F8
Merton Park Sta.Mrtn SW19 40 A8
Merton Pl. ☑ Merton SW19 20 C1
Merton Rd. Croy SE25 .... 43 A4
Merton Rd. Merton SW19 ... 20 B1
Merton Rd. Wands SW18 .... 20 A7
Merton Sixth Form Coll.
  Morden SM4 .... 40 A4
Merton Tech Coll.Mrdn SM4 39 F4
Merton Tech Coll (Annexe).
  Merton SW19 .... 40 A8
Merton Way. E Mole KT8 .... 36 C6
Merton Way. Leahd KT22 ... 95 A8
Merton Wlk. Leahd KT22 .... 75 A1
Merton Pk Par.
  Merton SW19 .... 40 A8
Metcalf Rd. Ashf TW15 ...... 14 B3
Metcalf Way. Crawl RH11 . 181 D2
Metcalfe Wlk. Felt TW13 .... 15 E4
Meteor Way. Farnb GU14 .... 85 A1
Meteor Way. Wallin SM6 .... 60 E3
Meteorological Off (HQ).
  Brack RG12 .... 27 D7
Metro Bsns Ctr The.
  Penge SE26 .... 23 F3
Metro Ctr. W Barn SM4 ...... 39 D2
Metro Ind Ctr. Hounsl TW7 ... 5 E5
Meudon Ave. Farnb GU14 .. 85 B3
Meudon Ct. King U T KT6 ... 37 D4
Meville Ct. Guild GU2 ...... 130 C6
Mews Ct. E Grins RH19 .... 205 F6
Mews The. Banstd SM7 ...... 78 B4
Mews The. Broad H RH12 . 216 D4
Mews The. Dunsf GU8 ...... 192 F5
Mews The. Guild GU1 ...... 130 C8
Mews The. Reig RH2 .... 118 A1
Meyer House. ☑
  Balham SW12 .... 21 B8
Meyrick Cl. Woking GU21 ... 68 E3
Mezel Hill Cotts. Old W SL4 . 10 C3
Miall Wlk. For Hil SE26 ...... 23 E4
Michael Cres. Horley RH6 . 161 A1
Michael Fields.
  For Row RH18 .... 206 E2
Michael Rd. S Norw SE25 ... 42 E6
Michaelson House. ☑
  Dulw SE21 .... 22 E4
Michel's Row. ☑ Rich TW9 ... 6 E3
Micheldever Way.
  Brack RG12 .... 27 F4
Michelet Cl. Lhtwat GU18 ... 48 B1

Micheham Gdns.
  Burgh H KT20 .... 97 C7
Michelham Gdns.
  Twick TW1 .... 16 F5
Michell Cl. Horsh RH12 .... 217 A2
Michels Almshouses. ☑
  Rich TW10 .... 6 E2
Mickle Hill. Sandh GU17 .... 45 A1
Micklefield Sch. Reig RH2 . 118 A2
Mickleham Dr.
  Leahd KT22 & RH5 .... 95 C1
Mickleham Gdns.
  Cheam SM3 .... 58 E4
Mickleham Hall.
  Mickle RH5 .... 115 C7
Mickleham Way.
  New Add CR0 .... 63 D3
Mid Holmwood La.
  Dork RH5 .... 136 B1
Mid St. Nutf RH1 .... 119 F1
Mid St. S Nutf RH1 .... 140 F7
Middle Ave. M Bourn GU9 . 146 D8
Middle Bourne La.
  M Bourn GU10 & GU9 ...... 146 C7
Middle Church La. ☑
  Farnh GU9 .... 125 B2
Middle Cl. Coulsd CR5 .... 100 A7
Middle Cl. Ewell KT17 .... 76 E7
Middle Cl. Friml GU15 .... 66 C6
Middle Farm Cl.
  Effing RH7 .... 113 D8
Middle Farm Pl.
  Effing KT24 .... 113 D8
Middle Gn. Stain TW18 ..... 13 D1
Middle Gordon Rd.
  Camb GU15 .... 65 D5
Middle Green Cl. ☑
  Surb KT5 .... 37 F3
Middle Hill. Alder GU11 ... 105 A3
Middle Hill. Eng Gn TW20 .. 11 D3
Middle La. Tedd TW11 .... 16 F2
Middle Old Pk. Farnh GU9 . 124 F4
Middle Rd. Leahd KT22 ..... 95 B6
Middle Rd. Mitch SW16 ..... 41 D7
Middle Row. ☑
  E Grins RH19 .... 205 F8
Middle St. Brock RH3 ...... 137 C5
Middle St. Croy CR0 & CR9 .. 61 C7
Middle St. Horsh RH12 .... 217 C2
Middle St. Shere GU5 .... 133 A4
Middle Way. Mitch SW16 ... 41 D7
Middlefield. Horley RH6 ... 161 C4
Middlefields. New Add CR0 .. 62 E2
Middlemarch. Witley GU8 . 170 E5
Middlemead Cl. L Book KT23 94 A2
Middlemead Rd.
  L Book KT23 .... 93 F2
Middlemoor Rd. Friml GU16 85 E8
Middlesex Ct. Addl KT15 .... 52 C6
Middlesex House. ☑
  Penge SE20 .... 23 C1
Middlesex Rd. Mitch CR4 ... 41 E4
Middleton Gdns.
  W Heath GU14 .... 84 E6
Middleton Rd. Camb GU15 . 65 F7
Middleton Rd.
  Carsh SM4 & SM5 .... 40 D2
Middleton Rd. Downs KT11 . 93 C3
Middleton Rd. Epsom KT19 . 57 D1
Middleton Rd. Horsh RH12 217 A2
Middleton Rd. Morden SM4 . 40 D2
Middleton Way.
  Crawl RH11 .... 200 E5
Midgarth Cl. Oxsh KT22 ..... 74 D6
Midgley Rd. Crawl RH10 .. 201 F8
Midholm Rd. Croy CR0 ...... 62 E8
Midhope Cl. Woking GU22 . 89 E8
Midhope Gdns.
  Woking GU22 .... 89 E8
Midhope Rd. Woking GU22 . 89 E8
Midhurst. Penge SE26 .... 23 C2
Midhurst Ave. Thorn H CR0 . 42 A2
Midhurst Cl. Crawl RH11 .. 201 A7
Midhurst Rd. Haslem GU27 208 B5
Midleton Cl. Milf GU8 ...... 149 F2
Midleton Industrial Estate Rd.
  Stough GU2 .... 109 B2
Midleton Rd. Guild GU2 ... 109 A2
Midleton Rd. King U T KT3 . 38 C7
Midleton Rd. Stough GU2 . 109 B2
Midmoor Rd. Streat SW12 .. 21 C7
Midmoor Rd. Wimble SW19 . 39 E8
Midsummer Ave. Hounsl TW4 4 F3
Midsummer Wlk.
  Horse GU21 .... 69 D3
Midway. Cheam SM3 & SM4 . 39 F2
Midway. Walt O T KT12 ...... 54 B8
Midway Ave. Egham TW20 .. 32 B6

Midway Ave. Thorpe KT16 ... 33 A6
Midway Ave. Thorpe KT16 ... 33 B6
Miena Way. Ashtd KT21 ... 75 D2
Mike Hawthorn Dr.
Farnh GU9 ... 125 C3
Milbanke Ct. Brack RG12 ... 26 F7
Milbanke Way. Brack RG12 ... 26 F7
Milborne Rd. Worth RH10 ... 202 C2
Milborough Cres.
Lewish SE12 ... 24 E8
Milbourne La. Esher KT10 ... 55 C5
Milbourne Lodge Jun Sch.
Esher KT10 ... 55 C4
Milbourne Lodge Sch.
Esher KT10 ... 55 D4
Milbrook. Esher KT10 ... 55 C4
Milburn House.
Wimble SW20 ... 39 B7
Milburn Wlk. Epsom KT18 ... 76 E4
Milden Cl. Friml GU16 ... 86 A6
Milden Gdns. Friml GU16 ... 85 F6
Mile Path. Woking GU22 ... 89 B7
Mile Rd. Carsh CR4 & SM6 ... 41 A1
Mile Rd. Wallin
CR0 & CR4 & CR9 & SM6 ... 41 C1
Miles Ct. Thorn H CR9 ... 61 B8
Miles La. Cobham KT11 ... 73 E6
Miles La. S Godst RH9 ... 142 F7
Miles La. Tand RH8 & RH9 ... 143 A7
Miles Pl. Lhtwat GU18 ... 66 F7
Miles Rd. Ash GU12 ... 106 B3
Miles Rd. Epsom KT19 ... 76 D7
Miles Rd. Mitch CR4 ... 40 E6
Miles's Hill. Hol St M RH5 ... 155 C3
Miles's Hill. Peasl RH5 ... 155 C3
Milestone Cl. Ripley GU23 ... 91 B5
Milestone Cl. Sutton SM2 ... 59 D3
Milestone Rd. Penge SE19 ... 22 F2
Milford By Pass Rd.
Milf GU8 ... 149 D2
Milford Gr. Sutton SM1 ... 59 C6
Milford Heath Rd. Milf GU8 170 E8
Milford Hospl. Godal GU7 ... 171 C8
Milford Lodge. Milf GU8 ... 170 F8
Milford Mews. Streat SW16 . 21 F5
Milford Rd. Elst GU8 ... 148 E4
Milford Sta. Milf GU8 ... 171 A7
Milking La. Bigg H BR2 ... 83 D8
Milking La. Downe BR6 ... 83 E7
Mill Bay La. Horsh RH12 ... 217 B1
Mill Cl. Carsh SM5 ... 60 A8
Mill Cl. E Grins RH19 ... 205 E7
Mill Cl. Fetch KT23 ... 94 A3
Mill Cl. Horley RH6 ... 160 E4
Mill Cl. Shottm GU27 ... 207 E6
Mill Cl. Woki RG11 ... 25 A7
Mill Copse Rd. Fern GU27 . 208 B4
Mill Cotts. E Grins RH19 ... 205 E7
Mill Cotts. Rudg RH12 ... 214 D5
Mill Farm Ave. Charlt TW16 . 14 E1
Mill Farm Cres. Twick TW4 .. 15 E7
Mill Farm Rd. Horsh RH13 218 A4
Mill Field. Bagsh GU19 ... 47 D3
Mill Gdns. For Hil SE26 ... 23 B5
Mill Gn. Carsh CR4 ... 41 A2
Mill Green Bsns Pk.
Carsh CR4 ... 41 A2
Mill Green Rd. Carsh CR4 ... 41 A2
Mill Hill. Brock RH3 ... 137 B8
Mill Hill La. Brock RH3 ... 116 B1
Mill House La. Egham KT16 . 32 B5
Mill La. Ascot SL5 ... 30 A7
Mill La. Bramly GU5 ... 151 F6
Mill La. Byfl KT14 ... 71 F6
Mill La. Carsh SM5 ... 60 A7
Mill La. Chidd GU8 ... 191 B3
Mill La. Chil GU4 & GU5 ... 131 F4
Mill La. Copth RH10 ... 183 E3
Mill La. Crawl RH11 ... 201 A8
Mill La. Croy CR0 ... 60 F7
Mill La. Croy CR0 ... 61 A7
Mill La. Dork RH4 ... 136 B8
Mill La. Dunsf GU8 ... 192 F4
Mill La. Easth RG12 ... 26 F5
Mill La. Egham KT16 & TW20 32 C5
Mill La. Ewell KT17 ... 57 F2
Mill La. Felb RH19 ... 184 E5
Mill La. Felct RH7 ... 164 F2
Mill La. Fern GU27 ... 208 C3
Mill La. Fetch KT22 ... 95 A5
Mill La. For Gn RH5 ... 176 D7
Mill La. Frensh GU10 ... 167 B7
Mill La. Godal GU7 ... 150 D4
Mill La. Guild GU1 & GU2 ... 130 D7
Mill La. Hookw RH6 ... 160 D3
Mill La. Horton SL3 ... 1 C4
Mill La. Merst RH1 ... 119 D4
Mill La. Ockham GU23 ... 91 D8
Mill La. Oxted RH8 ... 122 F2
Mill La. Parkg RH5 ... 158 D5
Mill La. Pirb GU24 ... 87 E3
Mill La. Shalf GU3 ... 130 C1
Mill La. The Char RH8 ... 123 F4
Mill La. Witley GU8 ... 170 F5
Mill Lane Trad Est. Croy CR0 60 F7
Mill Mead. Stain TW18 ... 12 F4
Mill Pl. King U T KT1 ... 37 F6
Mill Plat. Islew TW7 ... 6 A5
Mill Plat. Islew TW7 ... 6 B4
Mill Plat Ave. Islew TW7 ... 6 A5
Mill Pond Rd. Windl GU20 ... 48 B6
Mill Rd. Cobham KT11 ... 73 C4
Mill Rd. Crawl RH10 ... 202 B7
Mill Rd. Epsom KT17 ... 76 F7
Mill Rd. Ewell KT17 ... 76 F7
Mill Rd. Kings KT20 ... 97 D4
Mill Rd. Merton SW19 ... 20 C1
Mill Rd. S Holm RH5 ... 157 D7
Mill Rd. Thame D KT10 ... 55 A8
Mill Rd. Twick TW2 ... 16 C6
Mill Ride. N Asct SL5 ... 28 D8
Mill Shaw. Oxted RH8 ... 122 F3
Mill St. Coln SL3 ... 1 D7
Mill St. King U T KT1 ... 37 E6
Mill St. Redh RH1 ... 139 F8
Mill Stream. Heath E GU9 .. 125 E6
Mill Vale. Broml BR2 ... 44 F7
Mill View Cl. Ewell KT17 ... 57 F3
Mill View Gdns. S Croy CR0 . 62 D7
Mill Way. E Grins RH19 ... 205 E7
Mill Way. Felt TW14 ... 4 B2
Mill Way. Head KT22 ... 96 A2
Millais. Horsh RH13 ... 218 A3
Millais Cl. Crawl RH11 ... 200 F2
Millais Ct. Horsh RH13 ... 218 A4
Millais Rd. New Mal KT3 ... 38 E2
Millais Sch. Horsh RH13 ... 217 F2
Millais Sch Lower Sch.
Horsh RH13 ... 217 F2
Millais Way. W Ewell KT19 ... 57 C6
Millais Way. W Ewell KT19 ... 57 C6
Millan Cl. Woodhm KT15 ... 52 B1
Milland House. 11
Rhampt SW15 ... 19 A7
Millbank. Wallin SM6 ... 60 D5
Millbank The. Crawl RH11 . 200 F6
Millbourne Rd. Felt TW13 ... 15 E4
Millbrook. Guild GU1 & GU2 130 D7
Millbrook. Oat Pk KT13 ... 53 E6
Millbrook Way. Poyle SL3 ... 1 E5
Millcombe Cl. 5
Woking GU21 ... 69 B1
Millcroft House. Catf SE6 ... 24 B4
Miller House. 9 Streat SW2 21 E8
Miller Rd. Merrow GU4 ... 110 C4
Miller Rd. Mitch SW19 ... 20 D2
Miller Rd. Thorn H CR0 ... 42 A1
Miller's Ct. Egham TW20 ... 12 D2
Miller's La. Outw RH1 ... 162 C7
Millers Cl. Stain TW18 ... 13 B3
Millers Copse. Lang V KT18 . 96 D8
Millers Copse. Outw RH1 .. 162 B7
Millers Gate. Horsh RH12 .. 217 D6
Millfarm Bsns Pk. Twick TW4 15 E8
Millfield. Charlt TW16 ... 34 D8
Millfield. King U T KT1 ... 37 F6
Millfield La. L Kings KT20 ... 98 A2
Millfield Rd. Twick TW4 ... 15 F7
Millford. Woking GU21 ... 69 B2
Millford Cty Fst Sch.
Milf GU8 ... 149 F1
Millgate Ct. Farnh GU9 ... 125 D3
Millhedge Cl. Cobham KT11 . 73 E3
Millholme Wlk. Friml GU15 .. 66 C4
Millhouse Pl. W Norw SE27 . 22 B4
Millins Cl. Sandh GU15 ... 45 E1
Millmead. Byfl KT14 ... 71 F7
Millmead. Guild GU2 ... 130 C7
Millmead. Woki RG11 ... 25 A7
Millmead Terr. Guild GU2 .. 130 C7
Millpond Cotts. Hasc GU8 172 D4
Millpond Ct. Addl KT15 ... 52 E5
Mills Spur. Old W SL4 ... 11 B8
Mills's Rd. Hersh KT12 ... 54 C5
Millside. Carsh SM5 ... 59 F8
Millside Ct. Fetch KT23 ... 94 A2
Millside Pl. Islew TW7 ... 6 B5
Millstream The. Linch GU27 207 E5
Millthorpe Rd. Horsh RH12 217 F4
Millview Cl. Redh RH1 ... 118 D3
Millway. Reig RH2 ... 118 D1
Millwood. Turn H RH19 ... 204 E5
Millwood Rd.
Islew TW3 & TW7 ... 5 C2
Milman Cl. Brack RG12 ... 28 A7
Milne Cl. Crawl RH11 ... 200 E3
Milne Pk E. New Add CR0 ... 82 D8
Milne Pk W. New Add CR0 ... 82 D8
Milner App. Cater CR3 ... 101 A6
Milner Cl. Cater CR3 ... 101 A5
Milner Dr. Cobham KT11 ... 73 F7
Milner Dr. Twick TW2 ... 16 D8
Milner Rd. Cater CR3 ... 101 A6
Milner Rd. King U T KT1 ... 37 D6
Milner Rd. Merton SW19 ... 40 B8
Milner Rd.
Morden CR4 & SM4 ... 40 D4
Milner Rd. S Norw CR7 ... 42 D6
Milnthorpe Rd. Chisw W4 ... 7 D8
Milnwood Rd. Horsh RH12 . 217 C3
Milstead Cl. Tadw KT20 ... 97 B5
Milton Ave. Carsh SM1 ... 59 E6
Milton Ave. Croy CR0 ... 42 D2
Milton Ave. Westc RH4 ... 135 D6
Milton Cl. Carsh SM1 ... 59 D7
Milton Cl. Easth RG12 ... 27 B3
Milton Cl. Horton SL3 ... 1 A4
Milton Cres. E Grins RH19 .. 205 C8
Milton Ct. King U T KT2 ... 17 E4
Milton Ct. Twick TW2 ... 16 E5
Milton Ct. Woki RG11 ... 25 B7
Milton Dr. Shep Gn TW17 ... 33 E5
Milton Dr. Woki RG11 ... 25 B7
Milton Gdns. Epsom KT18 ... 76 E5
Milton Gdns. Stan TW19 ... 13 F7
Milton Gdns. Woki RG11 ... 25 B6
Milton House. 12 Beck BR3 . 24 A1
Milton House. 5
King U T KT2 ... 18 B2
Milton House. Sutton SM1 ... 59 A7
Milton Lodge. Twick TW1 ... 16 F8
Milton Mount. Crawl RH10 182 D1
Milton Mount Ave.
Crawl RH10 ... 202 D8
Milton Mount Fst & Mid Sch.
Crawl RH10 ... 202 C8
Milton Rd. Cater CR3 ... 100 D6
Milton Rd. Crawl RH10 ... 202 C7
Milton Rd. Croy CR0 ... 42 D2
Milton Rd. Egham TW20 ... 11 F3
Milton Rd. Hampt TW12 ... 36 B8
Milton Rd. Horsh RH12 ... 217 C3
Milton Rd. Mitch CR4 ... 21 A1
Milton Rd. Mortl SW14 ... 7 D4
Milton Rd. Row Tn KT15 ... 52 A4
Milton Rd. Sutton SM1 ... 59 A6
Milton Rd. Wallin SM6 ... 60 D4
Milton Rd. Walt O T KT12 ... 54 D7
Milton Rd. Wimble SW19 ... 20 C2
Milton Rd. Woki RG11 ... 25 B6
Milton St. Westc RH4 ... 135 D6
Milton Way. Fetch KT23 ... 94 C2
Miltoncourt La. Dork RH4 .. 135 E7
Miltons Cres. Ock Rid GU7 150 B2
Milverton House.
For Hil SE23 ... 23 E5
Milward Gdns. Binf RG12 ... 26 C7
Mina Rd. Merton SW19 ... 40 A8
Minard Rd. Catf SE6 ... 24 E7
Minchin Cl. Leahd KT22 ... 95 A5
Mincing La. Burrh GU24 ... 49 F2
Mincing La. Chobh GU24 ... 49 F2
Minden Rd. Cheam SM3 ... 58 F8
Minden Rd. Penge SE20 ... 43 B8
Mindleheim Ave.
E Grins RH19 ... 186 B2
Minehead Rd. Streat SW16 .. 21 F3
Minerva Cl. Stan TW19 ... 2 A2
Minerva Rd. Farnb GU14 ... 85 B1
Minerva Rd. King U T KT1 ... 37 F7
Mink Ct. Hounsl TW4 ... 4 C5
Minley Cl. W Heath GU14 ... 84 E4
Minley Rd. Hawley GU14 ... 84 A7
Minley Rd. W Heath GU14 ... 84 D5
Minniedale. King U T KT5 ... 37 F4
Minorca Ave. Friml GU16 ... 66 E2
Minorca Rd. Friml GU16 ... 66 E1
Minorca Rd. Weyb KT13 ... 53 A6
Minshull Pl. 24 Beck BR3 ... 24 A1
Minstead Cl. Brack RG12 ... 27 F6
Minstead Gdns.
Rhampt SW15 ... 18 F8
Minstead Way. New Mal KT3 38 E3
Minster Ave. Sutton SM1 ... 59 A8
Minster Ct. Camb GU15 ... 64 F4
Minster Ct. Camb GU15 ... 65 D7
Minster Dr. S Croy CR0 ... 61 E6
Minster Gdns. E Mole KT8 ... 35 F5
Minster Rd. Godal GU7 ... 150 E1
Minsterley Ave.
Up Hall TW16 & TW17 ... 34 E5
Minstrel Gdns. King U T KT5 37 F5
Mint Gdns. Dork RH4 ... 136 A8
Mint La. L Kings KT20 ... 118 A6
Mint Rd. Wallin SM5 & SM6 . 60 B6
Mint Rd. Woodm SM7 ... 78 C3
Mint St. Godal GU7 ... 150 D4
Mint The. Godal GU7 ... 150 D4
Mint Wlk. Croy CR0 & CR9 ... 61 C7
Mint Wlk. Knaph GU21 ... 68 E2
Mint Wlk. Warlgm CR6 ... 81 D2
Miranda Wlk. Crawl RH11 .. 200 E4
Mirfield Ct. Penge SE20 ... 43 A7
Misbrooks Green Rd.
Capel RH5 ... 178 E8
Missenden Cl. E Bed TW14 .. 14 F7
Missenden Gdns.
Morden SM4 ... 40 C3
Mission Sq. 13 Brent TW8 ... 6 E8
Mistletoe Cl. Croy CR0 ... 43 D1
Mistley Ct. 6 Epsom KT18 .. 76 D6
Misty's Field. Walt O T KT12 35 C1
Mitcham Garden Village.
Mitch CR4 ... 41 A4
Mitcham Ind Est. Mitch CR4 41 A8
Mitcham Junc. Mitch CR4 ... 41 A4
Mitcham La. Streat SW16 ... 21 C3
Mitcham Pk. Mitch CR4 ... 40 F5
Mitcham Rd. Camb GU15 ... 47 A1
Mitcham Rd.
Thorn H CR0 & CR9 ... 41 F3
Mitcham Rd. Up Toot SW17 . 20 F3
Mitcham Sta. Mitch CR4 ... 40 E5
Mitchell Gdns. Slinfd RH13 215 E3
Mitchell's Row. Shalf GU4 . 130 E2
Mitchells Cl. Shalf GU4 ... 130 E3
Mitchells Cotts.
Woner GU4 ... 131 E1
Mitchells Rd. Crawl RH10 .. 201 F6
Mitchley Ave.
Sander CR2 & CR8 ... 80 D6
Mitchley Gr. Sander CR2 ... 81 A6
Mitchley Hill. Sander CR2 ... 80 F6
Mitchley View. Sander CR2 . 81 A6
Mitford Wlk. 11
Crawl RH11 ... 201 A3
Mitre Cl. Shep TW17 ... 34 D3
Mitre Cl. Sutton SM2 ... 59 D3
Mixbury Gr. Whit V KT13 ... 53 D4
Mixnams La. Thorpe KT16 ... 33 A6
Mizen Cl. Cobham KT11 ... 73 D5
Mizen Way. Cobham KT11 ... 73 D4
Moat Ct. Ashtd KT21 ... 75 E2
Moat Ct. Ottsh KT16 ... 51 C4
Moat Rd. E Grins RH19 ... 185 E2
Moat Side. Felt TW13 ... 15 C4
Moat The. King U T KT3 ... 38 E8
Moat Wlk. Crawl RH10 ... 202 C7
Moats La. S Nutf RH1 ... 140 F3
Moberly Rd. Streat SW4 ... 21 D8
Model Cotts. Mortl SW14 ... 7 C4
Moffat Ct. Up Toot SW17 ... 20 E4
Moffat Ct. Wimble SW19 ... 20 A3
Moffat Rd. S Norw CR7 ... 42 D7
Moffat Rd. Up Toot SW17 ... 20 F4
Moffatts Cl. Sandh GU17 ... 64 A8
Mogador Cotts.
L Kings KT20 ... 117 D7
Mogador Rd. L Kings KT20 . 117 E7
Mogden La. Islew TW7 ... 5 F2
Moir Cl. S Croy CR2 ... 62 A2
Moira Ct. Up Toot SW17 ... 21 A6
Mole Abbey Gdns.
E Mole KT8 ... 36 B6
Mole Bsns Pk. Leahd KT22 ... 95 A6
Mole Cl. Crawl RH11 ... 201 B8
Mole Cl. W Heath GU14 ... 84 D6
Mole Ct. W Ewell KT19 ... 57 C6
Mole Ct. W Ewell KT19 ... 57 C6
Mole House. Hersh KT12 ... 54 E5
Mole Rd. Fetch KT22 ... 94 D6
Mole Rd. Hersh KT12 ... 54 D5
Mole St. Wall W RH5 ... 177 B5
Mole Valley Pl. Ashtd KT21 .. 95 D8
Molember Ct. E Mole KT7 ... 36 E5
Molember Rd. Thame D KT8 36 E4
Moles Cl. Woki RG11 ... 25 D5
Moles Hill. Oxsh KT22 ... 74 D8
Molesey Ave.
E Mole KT12 & KT8 ... 35 F4
Molesey Cl. Hersh KT12 ... 54 E6
Molesey Dr. Cheam SM3 ... 58 E7
Molesey Hospl. E Mole KT8 . 36 A4
Molesey Park Ave.
E Mole KT8 ... 36 B4
Molesey Park Cl. E Mole KT8 36 C4
Molesey Park Rd.
E Mole KT8 ... 36 C4
Molesey Rd. E Mole KT12 ... 35 E2
Molesey Rd. Hersh KT12 ... 54 D5
Molesham Cl. E Mole KT8 ... 36 B6
Molesham Way. E Mole KT8 36 B6
Molesley Rd. Hersh KT12 ... 54 E8
Molesley Rd. Walt O T KT12 54 E8
Molesworth Rd.
Cobham KT11 ... 73 A6
Moliner Ct. 4 Beck BR3 ... 24 A1
Molins Ct. 5 Crawl RH11 . 201 A3
Mollie Davis Ct. S Norw SE19 22 F2
Mollison Dr. Wallin SM6 ... 60 E3
Molly Huggins Cl.
Streat SW12 ... 21 C8
Molly Millar Bridge.
Woki RG11 ... 25 B4
Molly Millar's La. Woki RG11 25 A4
Molyneux Rd. Farnc GU7 ... 150 F7
Molyneux Rd. Weyb KT13 ... 53 A5
Molyneux Rd. Windl GU20 ... 48 D4
Monahan Ave. Purley CR8 ... 79 F8
Monarch Cl. Coney H BR4 ... 63 F6
Monarch Cl. Crawl RH11 ... 201 A3
Monarch Cl. E Bed TW14 ... 14 E8
Monarch Mews.
W Norw SE27 & SW16 ... 22 A3
Monarch Par. Mitch CR4 ... 40 F7
Monaveen Gdns. E Mole KT8 36 B6
Monby Lodge Inf Sch.
Whit V KT13 ... 53 C5
Mondial Way. Harl UB7 ... 3 C7
Money Ave. Cater CR3 ... 100 E5
Money Rd. Cater CR3 ... 100 D5
Monivea Rd. Beck BR3 ... 23 F1
Monk's Wlk.
M Bourn GU10 & GU9 ... 146 F8
Monk's Wlk. Reig RH2 ... 118 B1
Monkleigh Rd.
Merton SM4 & SW20 ... 39 E5
Monks Ave. E Mole KT8 ... 35 F4
Monks Cl. Ascot SL5 ... 29 B3
Monks Cl. Farnb GU14 ... 85 C4
Monks Cres. Addl KT15 ... 52 B5
Monks Cres. Walt O T KT12 . 35 B1
Monks Ct. Reig RH2 ... 118 B1
Monks Dr. Ascot SL5 ... 29 B3
Monks Gn. Fetch KT22 ... 94 D6
Monks La. Limps RH8 & TN8 144 E6
Monks La. Rowhk RH5 ... 196 F5
Monks Orchard Rd.
Beck BR3 & CR0 ... 44 A1
Monks Orchard Rd.
Croy BR3 & CR0 ... 44 A1
Monks Orchard Sch.
Croy CR0 ... 43 D4
Monks Rd. Banstd SM7 ... 78 A3
Monks Rd. Vir W GU25 ... 31 D5
Monks Way. Beck BR3 ... 44 A3
Monks Way. Harm UB7 ... 2 E8
Monks Way. Stain TW18 ... 13 D1
Monks' Well. Farnh GU10 .. 147 C8
Monks Wlk. Ascot SL5 ... 29 B3
Monksdene Gdns.
Sutton SM1 ... 59 B7
Monksfield. Crawl RH10 ... 201 F7
Monkshanger.
M Bourn GU9 ... 125 E2
Monkshood Cl. Woki RG11 .. 25 E7
Monkswell La. L Kings CR5 .. 98 B2
Monkton La. Farnh GU9 ... 125 E5
Monkton Pk. Farnh GU9 ... 125 F4
Monmouth Ave. Tedd KT1 ... 17 C1
Monmouth Cl.
Mitch CR4 & SW16 ... 41 E5
Monro Dr. Stough GU2 ... 109 B4
Monroe Dr. Mortl SW14 ... 7 B2
Mons Cl. Farnb GU11 ... 105 E7
Mons Wlk. Egham TW20 ... 12 C3
Monsell Gdns. Egham TW18 12 E3
Monson Rd. Redh RH1 ... 118 F4
Montacute Cl. Farnb GU14 .. 85 D4
Montacute Rd.
For Hil SE23 & SE6 ... 23 F8
Montacute Rd. Morden SM4 40 D3
Montacute Rd. New Add CR0 63 C2
Montagu Gdns. Wallin SM6 . 60 C6
Montague Ave. Sander CR2 . 80 E7
Montague Cl. Camb GU15 ... 65 B5
Montague Cl. Lhtwat GU18 .. 48 A1
Montague Cl. Walt O T KT12 35 A2
Montague Dr. Cater CR3 ... 100 C5
Montague House (Coll & Liby).
Woki RG11 ... 25 C6
Montague Rd. Hounsl TW3 ... 5 B4
Montague Rd. Merton SW19 20 B1
Montague Rd. Rich TW10 ... 6 E1
Montague Rd. Thorn H CR0 . 42 B1
Montana Cl. S Croy CR2 ... 61 D1
Montana Rd. Up Toot SW17 . 21 A5
Montana Rd. Wimble SW20 . 39 C8
Montem Rd. For Hil SE23 ... 23 F8
Montem Rd. New Mal KT3 ... 38 E5
Montford Rd. Sunby TW16 ... 35 A5
Montfort Pl. Putney SW19 ... 19 D7
Montfort Rise. Salfs RH1 ... 139 F1
Montgomerie Dr.
Stough GU2 ... 109 A6
Montgomery Ave.
Hinch W KT10 ... 55 E8
Montgomery Cl. Mitch CR4 . 41 E5
Montgomery Cl.
Sandh GU17 ... 64 B8
Montgomery Ct. Chisw W4 ... 7 C8
Montgomery Ct. Leahd KT22 95 C7

Montgomery House. **5**
Mortl SW14 .... 7 D4
Montgomery Rd.
Farnb GU14 .... 84 F3
Montgomery Rd. **2**
Woking GU22 .... 69 E1
Montpelier Ct. Beck BR2 ..... 44 F5
Montpelier Rd.
Purley CR2 & CR8 .... 61 B1
Montpelier Rd.
S Croy CR2 & CR8 .... 61 B1
Montpelier Rd. Sutton SM1 .. 59 C6
Montpelier Row. Twick TW1 17 C8
Montrave Rd. Penge SE20 ... 23 C1
Montrell Rd. Streat SW2 ...... 21 E7
Montreux Ct. Crawl RH11 . 201 B6
Montrose Ave. Twick TW2 ... 16 B8
Montrose Cl. Ashf TW15 ...... 14 C3
Montrose Cl. Friml GU16 ..... 65 E1
Montrose Gdns. Mitch CR4 .. 40 F7
Montrose Gdns. Oxsh KT22 .. 74 D7
Montrose Gdns. Sutton SM1 59 B8
Montrose Rd. E Bed TW14 ... 3 D1
Montrose Way. For Hil SE23 23 D7
Montrose Wlk. Weyb KT13 .. 53 B7
Montrouge Cres. Nork KT17 77 C3
Montserrat Cl. W Norw SE19 22 D3
Monument Bridge Ind Est W.
Woking GU21 .... 70 A4
Monument Hill. Weyb KT13 . 53 B6
Monument Hill Cty Prim Sch.
Mayb GU22 .... 70 A4
Monument Rd. Sheer GU21 . 70 B4
Monument Rd. Weyb KT13 .. 53 B7
Monument Way E.
Sheer GU21 .... 70 B4
Monument Way W.
Woking GU21 .... 70 A4
Moon Ct. Fetch KT22 .... 94 D6
Moon's La.
Dorman RH19 & RH7 & TN8 186 E8
Moons Hill. Bram GU10 ...... 146 C2
Moons La. Horsh RH13 ...... 217 E1
Moor Cl. Sandh GU15 .... 65 C1
Moor House Sch.
Oxted RH8 .... 122 F3
Moor La. Chess KT9 .... 56 E5
Moor La. Harm UB7 .... 2 C8
Moor La. Lingf RH7 & TN8 . 165 D3
Moor La. Stain TW18 .... 12 D6
Moor La. Stan TW19 .... 12 D6
Moor La. Westfd GU22 .... 89 F5
Moor Lane Jun Sch.
Chess KT9 .... 56 F5
Moor Mead Rd. Twick TW1 ... 6 A1
Moor Park Cres.
Crawl RH11 .... 200 D5
Moor Park Gdns.
King U T KT2 .... 18 E1
Moor Park Hse. Easth RG12 . 26 E3
Moor Park La.
Farnb GU10 & GU9 .... 126 A2
Moor Park La.
M Bourn GU9 .... 125 F2
Moor Pl. E Grins RH19 ...... 185 D2
Moor Pl. Windl GU20 .... 48 B5
Moor Rd. Farnb GU14 .... 85 A8
Moor Rd. Friml GU16 .... 85 F8
Moor Rd. Linch GU27 .... 207 C5
Moor Rdbt. Harm UB7 .... 2 B7
Moorcroft. Godst RH9 .... 121 C3
Moorcroft Cl. Crawl RH11 . 201 B7
Moorcroft Rd. Streat SW16 . 21 E5
Moordale Ave. Brack RG12 .. 26 E8
Moore Cl. Addl KT15 .... 52 B5
Moore Cl. Mitch CR4 .... 41 B7
Moore Cl. Mortl SW14 .... 7 C4
Moore Cl. Wallin SM6 .... 60 E3
Moore Ct. Horsh RH12 ...... 217 A1
Moore Grove Cres.
Egham TW20 .... 11 F1
Moore House. **1**
W Norw SE27 .... 22 C4
Moore Rd. Pirb GU24 .... 87 B6
Moore Rd. S Norw SE19 ..... 22 C2
Moore Way. Belm SM2 .... 59 A2
Moore's Rd.
Dork RH4 & RH5 .... 136 B8
Mooreland Rd. Broml BR1 ... 24 F8
Moores Gn. Woki RG11 .... 25 E8
Moorfield. King Gn GU27 ... 207 F5
Moorfield Ctr The.
Bellf GU1 .... 109 D5
Moorfield Rd. Chess KT9 .... 56 E5
Moorfield Rd. Stough GU1 . 109 E5
Moorfields Cl. Egham TW18 32 E8
Moorfields Ct. **6**
Streat SW16 .... 21 C4

Moorhayes Dr. Laleh TW18 . 33 C6
Moorhead Rd. Horsh RH12 218 B5
Moorholme. Woking GU22 ... 89 E8
Moorhouse Rd.
The Char RH8 .... 123 F5
Moorhurst La. Coldh RH5 .. 157 B4
Moorings The. Hind GU26 .. 188 E3
Moorland Cl. Twick TW4 ..... 16 A8
Moorland Ct. Worth RH10 . 202 C3
Moorland Rd. Harm UB7 .... 2 C8
Moorlands. Walt O T KT12 .. 54 A7
Moorlands Cl. Hind GU26 .. 188 E4
Moorlands Pl. Camb GU15 .. 65 B5
Moorlands Rd. Camb GU15 .. 65 B4
Moorlands The.
Westfd GU22 .... 89 F6
Moormead Dr.
Worc Pk KT19 .... 57 E5
Moormede Cres. Stain TW18 12 F4
Moors La. Elst GU8 .... 148 C3
Moors The. Tongh GU10 .... 126 F7
Moorside Cl. W Heath GU14 65 A1
Moorside Rd. Catf BR1 .... 24 F4
Moorsom Way. Coulsd CR5 . 79 D2
Moray Ave. Sandh GU15 ..... 64 D7
Moray House. **11**
King U T KT6 .... 37 E4
Mordaunt Dr. Crowth RG11 . 45 B3
Morden Cl. Brack RG12 ...... 27 F5
Morden Cl. Burgh H KT20 ... 97 D7
Morden Court Par.
Morden SM4 .... 40 A5
Morden Ct. Morden SM4 ..... 40 B5
Morden Farm Mid Sch.
W Barn SM4 .... 39 E2
Morden Fst Sch.
Morden SM4 .... 40 A4
Morden Gdns. Mitch CR4 .... 40 D5
Morden Hall Rd.
Morden SM4 & SW19 .... 40 C5
Morden Park. Morden SM4 40 A5
Morden Park Sch Sports Ctr.
Morden SM4 .... 39 F4
Morden Rd.
Mitch CR4 & SM4 & SW19 .. 40 D5
Morden Road Sta.
Merton SW19 .... 40 B7
Morden South Sta.
Morden SM4 .... 40 A4
Morden Sta. Merton SW19 .. 40 B6
Morden Way. Cheam SM3 ... 40 A2
Mordred Rd. Catf SE6 .... 24 E6
More Circ. Farnc GU7 .... 150 F7
More Cl. Purley CR8 .... 80 A8
More House Sch.
M Bourn GU9 .... 146 C2
More La. Esher KT10 .... 55 B7
More Rd. Farnc GU7 .... 150 E7
Morecambe Cl. Crawl RH11 200 F4
Morecoombe Cl.
King U T KT2 .... 18 B1
Morecote Cl. Shalf GU4 ..... 130 E2
Moreland Ave. Coln SL3 .... 1 C7
Moreland Cl. Coln SL3 .... 1 C7
Morella Cl. Vir W GU25 ...... 31 D5
Morella Rd.
Balham SW11 & SW12 .... 20 F8
Moremead Rd. Catf SE6 ...... 24 A4
Morena St. Lewish SE6 .... 24 B8
Moresby Ave. Tolw KT5 ...... 38 B2
Moreton Ave. Hounsl TW7 .... 5 E6
Moreton Cl. Churt GU10 .... 167 E1
Moreton Green Fst Sch.
Morden SM4 .... 40 D4
Moreton House.
Up Toot SW17 .... 20 D4
Moreton Rd. N Cheam KT4 .. 58 B8
Moreton Rd. S Croy CR2 ..... 61 D5
Morgan Ct. Ashf TW15 .... 14 B3
Moring Rd. Up Toot SW17 ... 21 A4
Morkyns Wlk. Dulw SE21 ... 22 E5
Morland Ave. Croy CR0 ...... 42 E1
Morland Cl. Hampt TW12 ... 15 F3
Morland Cl. Mitch CR4 .... 40 E6
Morland Rd. Alder GU11 .. 126 C6
Morland Rd. Croy CR0 .... 42 F2
Morland Rd. Penge SE20 ... 23 D2
Morland Rd. Sutton SM1 .... 59 C5
Morland's Rd. Farnb GU11 105 D5
Morley Cl. Bexl BR3 .... 44 D8
Morley Ct. Beck BR2 .... 44 F5
Morley Ct. Sunnin SL5 .... 29 F3
Morley House. Streat SW2 .. 21 E8
Morley Rd. Cheam SM3 ...... 39 F1
Morley Rd. M Bourn GU9 .. 125 D1
Morley Rd. S Croy CR2 .... 61 F1
Morley Rd. Twick TW1 .... 6 D1
Morningside Rd.
N Cheam KT4 .... 58 C8
Mornington Cl. Bigg H TN16 83 D2

Mornington Cres. Cranf TW5 4 B6
Mornington Rd. Ashf TW15 . 14 C3
Mornington Wlk. Rich TW10 17 C4
Morrell Ave. Horsh RH12 ... 217 F6
Morrell Rd. Horsh RH12 .... 218 A6
Morris Cl. Croy BR3 & CR0 .. 43 E4
Morris Gdns. Wands SW18 . 20 A8
Morris Rd. Farnb GU14 ...... 105 D8
Morris Rd. Islew TW7 .... 5 F4
Morris Rd. S Nutf RH1 ...... 140 E7
Morrish Rd. Streat SW2 ...... 21 E8
Morrison Cl. **5**
Crawl RH11 .... 201 B1
Morrison House. Streat SW2 22 A7
Morston Cl. Burgh H KT20 ... 97 B7
Mortaine Rd. Ashf TW15 ..... 13 D5
Mortimer Cl. Streat SW16 ... 21 D6
Mortimer Cres. Worc Pk KT4 57 D7
Mortimer Lodge. **11**
Putney SW19 .... 19 E7
Mortimer Rd. Bigg H TN16 .. 83 C7
Mortimer Rd. Capel RH5 .. 178 D6
Mortimer Rd. Mitch CR4 ..... 40 F8
Mortimer Sch. Streat SW16 . 21 D6
Mortlake Cl. Wallin CR0 ...... 60 E7
Mortlake Dr. Mitch CR4 ...... 40 E8
Mortlake High St.
Mortl SW14 .... 7 D4
Mortlake Rd.
Rich SW14 & TW9 .... 7 A6
Mortlake Sta. Mortl SW14 .... 7 C4
Morton. Tadw KT20 .... 97 D6
Morton Cl. Friml GU16 .... 85 F7
Morton Cl. Horse GU21 ...... 69 D4
Morton Gdns. Wallin SM6 ... 60 C5
Morton House.
W Norw SE27 .... 22 D3
Morton Rd. E Grins RH19 .. 205 E7
Morton Rd. Horse GU21 ..... 69 D4
Morton Rd.
Morden CR4 & SM4 .... 40 D4
Morval Cl. Farnb GU14 .... 84 E4
Morven Rd. Up Toot SW17 .. 20 F5
Moselle Cl. W Heath GU14 .. 84 D5
Moselle Rd. Bigg H TN16 ... 83 F1
Mosford Cl. Horley RH6 .... 160 F5
Mospey Cres. Epsom KT17 .. 76 F4
Moss Gdns. S Croy CR2 ..... 62 D3
Moss La. Godal GU7 .... 150 D4
Moss Lane Cty Prim Sch.
Godal GU7 .... 150 D4
Mossfield. Cobham KT11 .... 73 A6
Mosslea Rd. Kenley CR3 ..... 80 F2
Mosslea Rd. Penge SE20 ... 23 C2
Mossville Gdns.
Merton SM4 & SW20 .... 39 F5
Mostyn Rd. Merton SW19 ... 39 F7
Mostyn Terr. Earls RH1 ..... 140 A8
Motspur Park Sta.
W Barn KT3 .... 39 B4
Motspur Pk. New Mal KT3 ... 39 A3
Motts Hill La. Tadw KT20 ... 97 A4
Motts Hill La.
Walt o T H KT20 .... 97 A4
Mouchotte Cl. Bigg H TN16 . 83 C7
Moulton Ave.
Hounsl TW3 & TW5 .... 4 F5
Mount Adon Pk.
Dulw SE21 & SE22 .... 23 A8
Mount Angelus Rd.
Rhampt SW15 .... 18 F8
Mount Ararat Rd. Rich TW10 6 E2
Mount Arlington. Beck BR2 . 44 F7
Mount Ash Rd. For Hil SE26 23 B5
Mount Ave. Cater CR3 .... 100 C3
Mount Cl. Crawl RH10 ...... 202 D7
Mount Cl. Ewh Gu6 .... 175 E5
Mount Cl. Fetch KT22 .... 94 F4
Mount Cl. Kenley CR8 .... 80 D3
Mount Cl. Wallin SM5 .... 60 A2
Mount Cl. Woking GU22 ...... 89 C6
Mount Cl. Guild GU2 .... 130 C7
Mount Cl. **6** King U T KT2 .. 18 B1
Mount Cl. Wick GR4 .... 63 E8
Mount Dr The. Reig RH2 ... 118 D3
Mount Ephraim La.
Streat SW16 .... 21 D5
Mount Ephraim Rd.
Streat SW16 .... 21 D5
Mount Felix. Walt O T KT12 . 34 F7
Mount Gdns. For Hil SE26 .. 23 B5
Mount Hermon Cl.
Woking GU22 .... 69 E1
Mount Hermon Rd.
Woking GU22 .... 69 E1
Mount La. Brack RG12 .... 27 C7
Mount La. Turn H RH10 .... 204 A4
Mount Lee. Egham TW20 .... 11 F3
Mount Nod Rd.
Streat SW16 & SW2 .... 21 F5

Mount Park Ave. S Croy CR2 61 B2
Mount Pk. Wallin SM5 .... 60 A2
Mount Pl. Guild GU1 .... 130 C7
Mount Pleasant.
Bigg H TN16 .... 83 D2
Mount Pleasant. Brack RG12 27 C6
Mount Pleasant.
Effing KT24 .... 113 E7
Mount Pleasant.
Farnh GU9 .... 125 A1
Mount Pleasant. Guild GU2 130 C7
Mount Pleasant.
Sandh GU17 .... 45 A1
Mount Pleasant.
W Hors KT24 .... 112 B6
Mount Pleasant.
W Norw SE27 .... 22 C4
Mount Pleasant. Weyb KT13 53 A7
Mount Pleasant. Woki RG11 25 A6
Mount Pleasant Cl.
Lhtwat GU18 .... 48 A1
Mount Pleasant Rd.
Alder GU12 .... 105 C2
Mount Pleasant Rd.
Cater CR3 .... 101 A4
Mount Pleasant Rd.
King U T KT3 .... 38 C6
Mount Primary Sch The.
King U T KT3 .... 38 C6
Mount Rd. Chess KT9 .... 56 F5
Mount Rd. Chobh GU24 ...... 69 B7
Mount Rd. Cran Gu6 .... 174 E2
Mount Rd. Felt TW13 .... 15 E5
Mount Rd. King U T KT3 ..... 38 D6
Mount Rd. Mitch CR4 .... 40 E7
Mount Rd. S Norw SE19 ..... 22 D2
Mount Rd.
Wimble SW18 & SW19 .... 20 B6
Mount Rd. Woking GU22 ..... 89 B6
Mount Rise. For Hil SE23 ... 23 C6
Mount Rise. Woodh RH1 ... 139 D7
Mount St. Dork RH4 .... 136 A7
Mount The. Cran GU6 .... 174 E2
Mount The. Esher KT10 ..... 55 A4
Mount The. Ewell KT17 ...... 57 F1
Mount The. Ewh GU6 .... 175 E5
Mount The. Fetch KT22 ...... 94 F4
Mount The. Grays GU27 ... 189 F1
Mount The. Guild GU2 ...... 130 C7
Mount The. Head Dn GU35 187 A6
Mount The. L Kings KT20 ... 97 F1
Mount The. N Cheam KT4 ... 58 B6
Mount The. New Mal KT3 .... 38 F6
Mount The. Oat Pk KT13 ..... 53 E8
Mount The.
Rusper RH11 & RH12 .... 180 B1
Mount The. Rusper RH12 .. 200 B8
Mount The. Wallin CR5 .... 79 B5
Mount The. Went GU25 ...... 31 D3
Mount The.
Woking GU21 & GU22 .... 69 D1
Mount Villas. W Norw SE27 . 22 B5
Mount Way. Wallin SM5 ...... 60 A2
Mountacre Cl. For Hil SE26 . 23 A4
Mountbatten Cl.
Crawl RH11 .... 201 C2
Mountbatten Cl. **6**
W Norw SE19 .... 22 E2
Mountbatten Gdns.
Beck BR3 .... 43 E5
Mountbatten Rise.
Sandh GU17 .... 45 A1
Mountcombe Cl. Surb KT6 .. 37 E2
Mountearl Gdns.
Streat SW16 & SW2 .... 21 F5
Mounthurst Rd. Hayes BR2 . 44 F2
Mounts Hill. Wink SL4 & SL5 . 9 F2
Mountsfield Cl. Stan TW19 ... 2 A2
Mountside. Cater CR3 .... 100 F3
Mountside. Guild GU2 .... 130 C7
Mountview. **5** Streat SW16 21 F5
Mountview Cl. Woodh RH1 139 E7
Mountview Dr. Earls RH1 .. 139 E7
Mountwood. E Mole KT8 ..... 36 B6
Mountwood Cl. S Croy CR2 . 62 B1
Moushill La. Milf GU8 .... 170 E8
Mowat Ct. Worc Pk KT4 ...... 57 F7
Mowbray Ave. Byfl KT14 ..... 71 E6
Mowbray Cres. Egham TW20 12 A3
Mowbray Ct. S Norw SE19 .. 42 F8
Mowbray Dr. Crawl RH11 . 200 F4
Mowbray Gdns. Dork RH4 . 115 B1
Mowbray Rd. S Norw SE19 .. 42 F8
Mower Cl. Woki RG11 .... 25 F7
Mower Pl. Cran Gu6 .... 174 E4

Moyne Ct. **4** Knaph GU21 .. 68 F1
Moyne Rd. Crawl RH11 ...... 201 C2
Moyser Rd.
Streat SW16 & SW17 .... 21 B3
Muchelney Rd. Morden SM4 40 C3
Muckhatch La. Thorpe TW20 32 B7
Mudie House. **8** Streat SW2 21 E8
Muggeridge's Hill.
Capel RH12 & RH5 .... 198 E8
Muggeridge's Hill.
Rusper RH12 & RH5 .... 198 E8
Muirdown Ave. Mortl SW14 ... 7 D3
Muirfield Cl. Crawl RH11 ... 200 D5
Muirfield House. Easth RG12 26 E3
Muirfield Rd. Woking GU21 . 69 A1
Muirkirk Rd. Catf SE6 .... 24 C7
Mulberries The. Farnh GU9 125 F4
Mulberry Ave. Stan TW19 .. 13 E7
Mulberry Bsns Pk.
Woki RG11 .... 25 A4
Mulberry Cl. Ash GU12 ...... 106 A4
Mulberry Cl. Crowth RG11 .. 45 C4
Mulberry Cl. Horse GU21 ... 69 E5
Mulberry Cl. Hrsh RH12 .... 217 C5
Mulberry Cl. **1** Sandh GU15 64 D8
Mulberry Cl. Streat SW16 ... 21 C4
Mulberry Cl. Weyb KT13 ..... 53 B7
Mulberry Cres. Brent TW8 .... 6 C7
Mulberry Ct. Ashtd KT21 .... 75 D1
Mulberry Ct. **1** Brack RG12 27 F4
Mulberry Ct. Merrow GU4 . 110 D3
Mulberry Ct. **4** Surb KT6 ... 37 D2
Mulberry Ct. Twick TW1 ...... 16 F5
Mulberry Ct. Woki RG11 ..... 25 C6
Mulberry La. Croy CR0 .... 42 E2
Mulberry Mews. **2**
Wallin SM6 .... 60 C4
Mulberry Rd. Crawl RH11 . 181 B1
Mulberry Trees. Shep TW17 34 D2
Mulgrave Chambers.
Sutton SM2 .... 59 B4
Mulgrave Manor.
Sutton SM2 .... 59 B4
Mulgrave Rd. Belm SM2 ..... 59 A4
Mulgrave Rd.
Croy CR0 & CR9 .... 61 D7
Mulgrave Rd. Friml GU16 ... 65 F2
Mulgrave Rd. Sutton SM2 ... 59 A4
Mulgrave Way. Knaph GU21 68 E1
Mulholland Cl. Mitch CR4 ... 41 B7
Mullards Cl. Carsh CR4 ...... 40 F1
Mullein Wlk. Crawl RH11 .. 201 A2
Mullens Rd. Egham TW20 ... 12 C3
Mullins Path. Mortl SW14 .... 7 D4
Mulroy Dr. Camb GU15 ...... 66 A6
Multon Rd. Wands SW18 ... 20 D8
Muncaster Cl. Ashf TW15 ... 14 A4
Muncaster Rd. Ashf TW15 .. 14 B3
Muncies Mews. Catf SE6 ... 24 C6
Munday's Boro. Putt GU3 .. 128 A4
Munday's Boro Rd.
Putt GU3 .... 128 B4
Munnings Dr. Sandh GU15 . 64 E6
Munnings Gdns. Islew TW7 .. 5 D2
Munroe House.
Woodh RH2 .... 139 A6
Munstead Ct. Sutton SM2 .. 59 C3
Munstead Heath Rd.
Bramly GU5 & GU7 & GU8 151 C3
Munstead Heath Rd.
Godal GU5 & GU7 & Gu8 ... 151 C3
Munstead Heath Rd.
Bramly GU5 & GU7 & Gu8 . 151 C2
Munstead View.
Arting GU3 .... 130 C4
Munstead View Rd.
Bramly GU5 .... 151 D5
Munster Ave. Hounsl TW4 .... 4 E2
Munster Ct. Tedd TW11 ...... 17 C2
Munster Rd. Tedd TW11 ..... 17 C2
Murdoch Cl. Stain TW18 ..... 13 A3
Murdoch Rd. Woki RG11 .... 25 D5
Murfett Cl. Putney SW19 .... 19 E6
Murray Ave. Islew TW3 .... 5 B2
Murray Ct. Ascot SL5 .... 29 C3
Murray Ct. Crawl RH11 .... 201 A1
Murray Ct. Horsh RH13 .... 218 B4
Murray Gn. Sheer GU21 ..... 70 C5
Murray House. Ottsh KT16 . 51 D4
Murray Rd. Farnb GU14 ...... 84 F3
Murray Rd.
Ottsh KT15 & KT16 .... 51 D5
Murray Rd. Rich TW10 .... 17 C6
Murray Rd. Wimble SW19 .. 19 D2
Murray Rd. Woki RG11 .... 25 A4
Murray's La. Byfl KT14 .... 71 E5
Murray's Rd. Farnb GU11 . 105 D5
Murrell Rd. Ash GU12 .... 106 A3
Murrellhill La. Binf RG12 .... 26 C8
Murrells La. Camb GU15 .... 65 B3
Murrells Wlk. Fetch KT23 ... 94 A3
Murreys The. Ashtd KT21 ... 75 D1

Muschamp Inf Sch.
Carsh SM5 .... 59 E8
Muschamp Jun Sch.
Carsh SM5 .... 59 E8
Muschamp Rd.
Carsh SM1 & SM5 .... 59 E8
Museum Hill. Haslem GU27 208 D6
Musgrave Ave.
E Grins RH19 .... 205 E8
Musgrave Rd. Hounsl TW7 .... 5 F6
Mushroom Castle La.
Wink RG12 .... 8 B2
Musquash Way. Hounsl TW4 . 4 C5
Mustard Mill Rd. Stain TW18 12 E4
Mutton Hill. Dorman RH7 .. 186 B7
Mutton Oaks. Binf RG12 .... 26 D8
Muybridge Rd. King U T KT3 38 C7
Mychell House. 8
Merton SW19 .... 20 C1
Mychett Cty Fst Sch.
Mytch GU16 .... 85 F4
Mychett Heath. Mytch GU16 86 A3
Myers Way. Friml GU16 .... 66 D2
Mylis Cl. For Hil SE26 .... 23 B4
Mylne Sq. Woki RG11 .... 25 D6
Mylor Cl. Horse GU21 .... 69 E5
Mynn's Cl. Epsom KT18 .... 76 B5
Mynterne Ct. 16
Putney SW19 .... 19 D7
Myrna Cl. Mitch SW19 .... 20 E1
Myrtle Ave. Hatton TW14 .... 3 E2
Myrtle Cl. Lhtwat GU18 .... 67 B8
Myrtle Cl. Poyle SL3 .... 1 E6
Myrtle Dr. Blckw GU17 .... 64 D5
Myrtle Gr. King U T KT3 .... 38 C7
Myrtle Rd. Croy CR0 .... 63 A7
Myrtle Rd. Dork RH4 .... 136 A8
Myrtle Rd. Hampt TW12 .... 16 C2
Myrtle Rd. Hounsl TW3 .... 5 C5
Myrtle Rd. Sutton SM1 .... 59 C5
Mytchett Lake Rd.
Mytch GU16 .... 86 A1
Mytchett Place Rd.
Mytch GU16 .... 86 C1
Mytchett Place Rd.
Normdy GU12,GU16 & GU24 86 C1
Mytchett Rd.
Mytch GU12 & GU16 .... 85 F3
Myton Rd. W Norw SE21 ...... 22 D5

Naafi Rdbt. Alder GU11 ..... 105 B2
Nadine Ct. Wallin SM6 .... 60 C2
Nailsworth Cres.
Merst RH1 .... 119 D6
Nairn Cl. Friml GU16 .... 65 E2
Nairn Ct. 3 Wallin SM6 .... 60 C4
Nairn Ct. Wimble SW19 .... 20 B2
Naldrett Cl. Horsh RH12 ..... 217 F4
Naldretts La. Rudg RH12 ... 214 D5
Nallhead Rd. Felt TW13 .... 15 C3
Namton Dr.
Thorn H CR7 & SW16 .... 41 F5
Napier Cl. Crowth RG11 .... 45 D5
Napier Cl. Farnb GU11 .... 105 E7
Napier Ct. Cater CR3 .... 100 E5
Napier Ct. 10 Croy CR0 .... 61 F8
Napier Ct. Horse GU21 .... 69 E3
Napier Ct. 1 Surb KT6 .... 37 D2
Napier Dr. Camb GU15 .... 66 A8
Napier Gdns. Merrow GU1 110 B2
Napier Lodge. Ashf TW15 .... 14 D2
Napier Rd. Ashf TW15 .... 14 D1
Napier Rd. Crowth RG11 ...... 45 C4
Napier Rd. Croy SE25 .... 43 B5
Napier Rd. Harm TW6 .... 2 D6
Napier Rd. Islew TW7 .... 6 A3
Napier Rd. S Croy CR2 .... 61 D3
Napier Way. Crawl RH10 ... 182 A1
Napier Wlk. Ashf TW15 .... 14 D1
Napoleon Ave. Farnb GU14 . 85 B6
Napoleon Rd. Twick TW1 ...... 17 B8
Napper Cl. N Asct SL5 .... 28 D7
Napper Pl. Cran GU6 .... 174 E1
Narrow La. Warlgm CR6 .... 101 B8
Naseby. Easth RG12 .... 27 B1
Naseby Cl. Hounsl TW7 .... 5 E6
Naseby Rd. S Norw SE19 ...... 22 D2
Nash Cl. Farnb GU14 .... 84 F4
Nash Dr. 6 Redh RH1 .... 119 A3
Nash Gdns. N Asct SL5 .... 28 E7
Nash Gdns. Redh RH1 .... 118 F3
Nash Rd. Crawl RH10 .... 201 E3
Nassau Rd. Barnes SW13 .... 7 F6
Nasturtium Dr. Bisley GU24 . 68 A4
Natal Rd. S Norw CR7 .... 42 D6
Natal Rd. Streat SW16 .... 21 D2
Natalie Cl. E Bed TW14 .... 14 D8
Natalie Mews. Twick TW2 ... 16 D5
National Physical Laboratory.
Tedd TW11 .... 16 E2
National Wks. Hounsl TW4 .... 4 F4
Nayland House. Catf SE6 ..... 24 C4
Neale Cl. E Grins RH19 ...... 185 B3
Neath Gdns. Morden SM4 .... 40 C3
Neb La. Oxted RH8 .... 122 D4
Needles Bank. Godst RH9 . 121 B4
Needles Cl. Horsh RH12 .... 217 B1
Neelem Ct. Farnb GU14 .... 85 C1
Neil Cl. Ashf TW15 .... 14 C3
Neil Wates Cres. 18
Streat SW2 .... 22 A7
Nelgarde Rd. Catf SE6 .... 24 A8
Nelgarde Rd. Lewish SE6 ..... 24 A8
Nell Ball. Plaist RH14 .... 211 E2
Nell Gwynn Ave. Shep TW17 34 D3
Nell Gwynne Ave. Ascot SL5 29 D5
Nell Gwynne Cl. Ascot SL5 .. 29 D5
Nello James Gdns.
W Norw SE27 .... 22 D4
Nelson Cl. Alder GU12 .... 105 D1
Nelson Cl. Bigg H TN16 .... 83 E2
Nelson Cl. Brack RG12 .... 27 E7
Nelson Cl. E Bed TW14 .... 14 F7
Nelson Cl. Heath E GU9 ...... 125 D8
Nelson Cl. Thorn H CR0 .... 42 B1
Nelson Cl. Walt O T KT12 ..... 35 B1
Nelson Cl. Worth RH10 ...... 202 C5
Nelson Ct. Carsh SM5 .... 59 F7
Nelson Ct. Chert KT16 .... 33 A1
Nelson Gdns. Merrow GU1 110 A2
Nelson Gdns.Twick TW3 & 4 .. 5 A1
Nelson Grove Rd.
Merton SW19 .... 40 C8
Nelson Hospl. Merton SW20 39 F7
Nelson Prim Sch. Twick TW2 5 B1
Nelson Rd. Ashf TW15 .... 13 E3
Nelson Rd. Cater CR3 .... 100 D4
Nelson Rd. Harm TW6 .... 2 F6
Nelson Rd. Heath E GU9 .... 125 D8
Nelson Rd. Horsh RH12 ...... 217 C3
Nelson Rd. Merton SW19 ...... 20 C1
Nelson Rd. New Mal KT3 ...... 38 D4
Nelson Rd.
Twick TW2 & TW4 .... 16 B8
Nelson St. Alder GU11 .... 105 A2
Nelson Trad Est.
Merton SW19 .... 40 B8
Nelson Way. Camb GU15 ..... 64 F4
Nene Gdns. Felt TW13 .... 15 F6
Nene Rd. Harl TW6 & UB7 ...... 3 B6
Nepean St. 4 Putney SW15 19 A8
Neptune Cl. Crawl RH11 .... 200 E4
Neptune Rd. Harl TW6 .... 3 C6
Nesbit Ct. Crawl RH11 .... 200 E3
Nesbitt Sq. S Norw SE19 ...... 22 E1
NESCOT Epsom's Coll of FE & HE.
Ewell KT17 .... 77 A8
Nether Mount. Guild GU2 . 130 B7
Netheravon Rd S. Chisw W4 . 7 F8
Netherby Pk. Whit V KT13 .... 53 E5
Netherby Rd. For Hil SE23 ... 23 C8
Nethercote Ave.
Woking GU21 .... 68 F2
Netherfield Rd.
Up Toot SW17 .... 21 A5
Netherlands The.
Coulsd CR5 .... 99 C8
Netherleigh Pk. S Nutf RH1 140 E6
Nethern Court Rd.
Wold CR3 .... 102 A4
Netherne Hospl. Hooley CR5 99 D5
Netherne La. Hooley CR5 ..... 99 C5
Netherton. Easth RG12 .... 27 A5
Netherton Rd. Twick TW1 ...... 6 B2
Netherwood. Crawl RH11 . 201 B4
Netherwood Ct. Farnc GU7 150 E5
Netley Cl. Cheam SM3 .... 58 D5
Netley Cl. New Add CR0 .... 63 C3
Netley Dr. Walt O T KT12 ..... 35 F2
Netley Gdns. Morden SM4 ... 40 C2
Netley Rd. Brent TW8 .... 6 E8
Netley Rd. Harl TW6 .... 3 D6
Netley Rd. Morden SM4 .... 40 C2
Netley Rd (W). Harl TW6 .... 3 D6
Netley St. Farnb GU14 .... 105 C8
Nettlecombe. Brack RG12 .... 27 D3
Nettlecombe Cl. Sutton SM2 59 B2
Nettlefold Pl. W Norw SE27 . 22 B5
Nettles Terr. 3 Guild GU1 109 D1
Nettlestead Cl. Beck BR3 ..... 23 F1
Nettlestead Cl. Beck BR3 ..... 44 A8
Nettleton Rd. Harl TW6 .... 3 B6
Nettlewood Rd.
Streat SW16 .... 21 D1
Neuchatel Rd. For Hil SE6 .... 23 F6
Nevada Cl. Farnb GU14 .... 84 D3
Nevada Cl. King T KT3 .... 38 C5
Nevelle Cl. Binf RG12 .... 26 D8
Nevile Cl. Crawl RH11 .... 201 A3
Neville Ave. King U T KT3 ..... 38 D8
Neville Cl. Banstd SM7 .... 78 B5
Neville Cl. Esher KT10 .... 54 F4
Neville Cl. Hounsl TW3 .... 5 B5
Neville Ct. 10 Streat SW12 .. 21 C8
Neville Duke Rd.
W Heath GU14 .... 84 F8
Neville Rd. Croy CR0 .... 42 D2
Neville Rd. King U T KT1 .... 38 A7
Neville Rd. Rich TW10 .... 17 C6
Neville Wlk. Carsh SM5 .... 40 E2
Nevis Rd. Up Toot SW17 .... 21 A6
New Barn La. Kenley CR3 ..... 80 E3
New Barn La. Wall W RH5 . 177 A3
New Barns Ave. Mitch CR4 .. 41 D5
New Beckenham Sta.
Beck BR3 .... 23 F1
New Belmont House.
For Hil SE23 .... 23 C7
New Berry La. Hersh KT12 ... 54 D5
New Chapel Sq. Felt TW13 .. 15 B7
New Church Ct. 3
Penge SE19 .... 23 A1
New Cl. Felt TW13 .... 15 E3
New Cl. Mitch SW19 .... 40 C6
New Colebrooke Ct.
Wallin SM5 .... 60 A3
New Cotts. Betch RH3 .... 116 D4
New Cotts. Sidlow RH2 ...... 138 F1
New Cotts. Turn H RH10 ... 204 A4
New Cross Rd. Stough GU2 109 B3
New Cswy.
Dovgn RH1 & RH2 .... 139 C6
New Ct. Addl KT15 .... 52 C7
New Dawn Cl. Farnb GU14 .. 84 D3
New Farthingdale.
Dorman RH7 .... 186 B8
New Forest Cotts.
Old Wok GU22 .... 89 F7
New Forest Ride.
Brack RG12 .... 27 F4
New Haw Cty Jun Sch.
Woodhm KT15 .... 52 A1
New Haw Rd.
New Haw KT15 .... 52 C4
New Heston Rd. Heston TW5 4 F7
New House Farm La.
Wood S V GU3 .... 108 C2
New House La. Salfs RH1 .. 161 E8
New Inn La. Burph GU4 .... 110 B4
New Kelvin Ave. Tedd TW11 16 E2
New La. Westfd GU22 & GU4 89 F3
New Life Sch. E Grins RH19 185 D2
New Lodge Dr. Limps RH8 . 122 F7
New Malden Sta.
New Mal KT3 .... 38 E6
New Meadow. N Asct SL5 .... 28 D8
New Mile Rd. Ascot SL5 .... 29 C7
New Moorhead Dr.
Horsh RH12 .... 218 C6
New North Rd. Woodh RH2 138 F6
New Par . Ashf TW15 .... 13 F4
New Park Ct. 26 Streat SW2 21 E8
New Park Par. 14
Streat SW2 .... 21 E8
New Park Rd. Ashf TW15 ..... 14 C3
New Park Rd. Cran GU6 ..... 174 F2
New Park Rd.
Streat SW12 & SW2 .... 21 E7
New Park Rd. Streat SW2 .... 21 E8
New Pl. Add CR0 .... 63 A4
New Pond Rd. Arting GU3 .. 129 E1
New Pond Rd. Compt GU3 . 129 E1
New Poplars The.
Ash GU12 .... 106 A1
New Rd. Albury GU5 .... 132 D3
New Rd. Bagsh GU19 .... 47 F3
New Rd. Brack RG12 .... 27 D7
New Rd. Brent TW8 .... 6 D8
New Rd. Carsh CR4 .... 41 A1
New Rd. Chil GU4 .... 131 B3
New Rd. Crowth RG11 .... 45 C5
New Rd. E Bed TW14 .... 3 D1
New Rd. E Clan GU4 .... 111 E4
New Rd. E Mole KT8 .... 36 A6
New Rd. Egham TW18 .... 12 C4
New Rd. Esher KT10 .... 55 C6
New Rd. Felt TW14 .... 15 B7
New Rd. Felt TW13 .... 15 E3
New Rd. For Gn RH5 .... 176 E6
New Rd. Gomsh GU5 .... 133 C4
New Rd. Harl TW6 & UB7 .... 3 C7
New Rd. Hawley GU17 .... 64 E4
New Rd. Hounsl TW3 .... 5 B3
New Rd. Hyde GU8 .... 171 F5
New Rd. King U T KT2 .... 18 A1
New Rd. Limps RH8 .... 123 B5
New Rd. Linch GU27 .... 207 F5
New Rd. Littlt TW17 .... 34 B6
New Rd. Milf GU8 .... 170 E8
New Rd. N Asct SL5 .... 8 F1
New Rd. Oxsh KT10 & KT22 .. 55 F1
New Rd. Oxsh KT10 & KT22 .. 74 F8
New Rd. Rich TW10 .... 17 C4
New Rd. Sandh GU17 .... 64 A8
New Rd. Smallf RH6 .... 162 B3
New Rd. Tadw KT20 .... 97 C4
New Rd. Tand RH8 & RH9 .. 143 A7
New Rd. Tongh GU10 .... 126 F6
New Rd. Weyb KT13 .... 53 C5
New Rd. Windl GU19 & GU20 48 A4
New Rd. Woner GU5 .... 152 B8
New Rd. Wormly GU8 .... 191 A8
New Rd Units. Hounsl TW3 .... 5 B3
New Residences. Addl KT16 51 C7
New Scotland Hill Cty Prim Sch.
Sandh GU17 .... 45 A2
New Sq. E Bed TW14 .... 14 C7
New St. Crawl RH10 .... 202 A7
New St. Horsh RH13 .... 217 D2
New St. Stain TW18 .... 13 A4
New Town. Copth RH10 ..... 183 B3
New Victoria Hospl The.
King U T KT3 .... 38 E8
New Way. Ock Rid GU7 .... 150 C4
New Wickham La.
Thor L TW20 .... 12 B1
New Wokingham Rd.
Crowth RG11 .... 45 A6
New Woodlands Sch.
Catf BR1 .... 24 E4
New Zealand Ave.
Walt O T KT12 .... 34 F1
Newall Rd. Harl TW6 .... 3 C6
Newark Cl. Burph GU4 .... 110 B6
Newark Cl. Ripley GU23 .... 91 A6
Newark Ct. Walt O T KT12 .... 35 C1
Newark La. Mayb GU22 .... 90 F8
Newark La.
Ripley GU22 & GU23 .... 91 A6
Newark Rd. Crawl RH10 ..... 201 F8
Newark Rd. S Croy CR2 .... 61 D4
Newark Rd. Windl GU20 .... 48 B6
Newbolt Ave. Cheam SM3 .... 58 D5
Newborough Gn.
New Mal KT3 .... 38 D5
Newborough House.
Mitch SW19 .... 20 D1
Newbridge Cl.
Broad H RH12 .... 216 C3
Newbridge Ct. Cran GU6 ... 174 B3
Newbridge Ct.
Up Toot SW17 .... 20 C4
Newbridge Point. 3
For Hil SE23 .... 23 D5
Newbury Gdns.
Worc Pk KT19 .... 57 F6
Newbury Rd. Harm TW6 .... 2 F6
Newchapel Rd. Lingf RH7 . 164 B3
Newchapel Rd. Newch RH7 163 F2
Newcome Gdns.
Streat SW16 .... 21 E4
Newcome Pl. Alder GU12 .. 126 D7
Newcome Rd. Heath E GU9 125 E6
Newdigate Endowed CE Inf Sch.
Newd RH5 .... 158 B1
Newdigate House. 6
King U T KT2 .... 18 B2
Newdigate Rd.
Bear Gn RH5 .... 157 E2
Newdigate Rd.
Rusper RH12 .... 199 C8
Newenham Rd. G Book KT23 94 A1
Newent Cl. Carsh SM5 .... 40 F1
Newfield Ave.
W Heath GU14 .... 84 E6
Newfield Cl. Hampt TW12 .... 36 A8
Newfield Rd. Ash V GU12 .. 106 A6
Newfoundland Rd.
Friml GU16 .... 86 D8
Newgate. Croy CR0 .... 42 C1
Newgate Cl. Felt TW13 .... 15 E5
Newhache. Dorman RH7 ... 165 A1
Newhaven Cres. Ashf TW15 14 D3
Newhaven Rd. S Norw SE25 42 D4
Newhouse. 5 New Mal KT3 38 E2
Newhouse Cl. New Mal KT3 . 38 E2
Newhouse Wlk. Morden SM4 40 C2
Newland House Sch.
Tedd TW1 .... 16 F4
Newland House Sch Annex.
Tedd TW1 .... 16 F4
Newlands Ave. Thame D KT7 36 E1
Newlands Ave. Westfd GU22 89 F6
Newlands Cl. Hersh KT12 .... 54 E6
Newlands Cl. Horley RH6 .... 160 F5
Newlands Cnr. Albury GU4 132 A7
Newlands Cres.
E Grins RH19 .... 185 D2
Newlands Croft. Penge SE20 23 C2
Newlands Ct. Addl KT15 .... 52 B5
Newlands Ct. Cater CR3 ..... 100 C6
Newlands Ct. Streat SW16 .. 21 E3
Newlands Dr. Ash GU12 .... 106 B4
Newlands Dr. Poyle SL3 .... 1 E4
Newlands Estate.
Witley GU8 .... 170 F5
Newlands Flats. Guild GU1 109 F2
Newlands Pk. Copth RH10 .. 183 E3
Newlands Pk.
For Hil SE20 & SE26 .... 23 D3
Newlands Pk. Penge SE26 ... 23 D3
Newlands Pl. For Row RH18 206 F3
Newlands Rd. Camb GU15 ... 65 B1
Newlands Rd. Crawl RH11 . 201 C5
Newlands Rd. Horsh RH12 . 217 C4
Newlands Rd. Thorn H SW16 41 E7
Newlands The. Wallin SM6 .. 60 D3
Newlands Way. Chess KT9 .. 56 C5
Newlands Wood.
New Add CR0 .... 62 F2
Newman Cl. Worth RH10 ... 202 C4
Newman Rd. Thorn H CR0 ... 41 F1
Newmans Ct. Hale GU9 ..... 125 A7
Newmarket Rd.
Crawl RH10 .... 202 A4
Newminster Rd.
Morden SM4 .... 40 C3
Newnham Cl. S Norw CR7 .... 42 C7
Newnham House. Catf SE6 .. 24 C5
Newport Jun Sch.
Alder GU12 .... 105 D1
Newport Rd. Alder GU12 ... 105 D1
Newport Rd. Harm TW6 .... 3 A6
Newquay Rd. Catf SE6 .... 24 C6
Newry Rd. Islew TW1 .... 6 A2
Newsham Rd. 1
Woking GU21 .... 68 F2
Newstead Cl. Farnc GU7 ... 150 D6
Newstead House.
Cater CR3 .... 101 B1
Newstead Rd. Lewish SE12 .. 24 F8
Newstead Rise. Cater CR3 101 B1
Newstead Way.
Wimble SW19 .... 19 E4
Newstead Wlk.
Carsh SM4 & SM5 .... 40 C2
Newton Ave. E Grins RH19 205 F6
Newton Rd. Crawl RH10 ..... 181 F2
Newton Rd. Farnb GU14 ...... 85 D6
Newton Rd. Harm TW6 .... 2 E6
Newton Rd. Islew TW7 .... 5 F5
Newton Rd. Merton SW19 .... 19 E1
Newton Rd. Purley CR8 .... 79 C7
Newton Way. Tongh GU10 . 126 F7
Newton Wood Rd.
Ashtd KT21 .... 75 F3
Newtown Ct. Horsh RH13 ... 217 E1
Newtown Rd. Sandh GU17 ... 64 B8
Nicholas Gdns. Pyrf GU22 .... 70 F3
Nicholas House. Penge SE26 23 B2
Nicholas Lodge.
Thame D KT10 .... 55 A8
Nicholas Rd. Wallin CR0 ...... 60 E6
Nicholass Ct. 2 Purley CR8 80 B7
Nicholes Rd. Hounsl TW3 .... 5 A3
Nicholsfield. Loxwd RH14 .. 212 F4
Nicholson Rd. Croy CR0 .... 42 F1
Nicholson Wlk. 3
Egham TW20 .... 12 A3
Nicol Cl. 6 Twick TW1 .... 6 B1
Nicola Cl. Croy CR2 .... 61 C4
Nicosia Rd. Wands SW18 ..... 20 E8
Niederwald Rd. For Hil SE26 23 E4
Nightingale Ave.
W Hors KT24 .... 92 D2
Nightingale Cl. Carsh SM5 ... 60 A8
Nightingale Cl. Chisw W4 ...... 7 C8
Nightingale Cl.
Cobham KT11 .... 73 D8
Nightingale Cl. Crawl RH11 201 C8
Nightingale Cl.
E Grins RH19 .... 205 D7
Nightingale Cl.
W Heath GU14 .... 84 C6
Nightingale Cres.
Brack RG12 .... 27 D4
Nightingale Cres.
W Hors KT24 .... 92 C2
Nightingale Ct. 3
Knaph GU21 .... 68 F1
Nightingale Ct. Penge SE19 . 22 F2
Nightingale Ct. 8
Redh RH1 .... 119 A2
Nightingale Dr. Mytch GU16 86 A3
Nightingale Dr.
W Ewell KT19 .... 57 B4
Nightingale Dr.
W Ewell KT19 .... 57 B4
Nightingale Gdns.
Sandh GU17 .... 64 B8
Nightingale La.
Balham SW11 & SW12 .... 20 F8

Nightingale La. Rich TW10 .. 17 E8
Nightingale Rd. Ash GU12 . 106 C3
Nightingale Rd. Carsh SM5 . 60 A8
Nightingale Rd. E Hors KT24 92 F2
Nightingale Rd. E Mole KT8 . 36 B4
Nightingale Rd. Esher KT10 54 F4
Nightingale Rd. Farnc GU7 150 E6
Nightingale Rd. Guild GU1 . 109 E1
Nightingale Rd.Hampt TW12 16 A2
Nightingale Rd. Horsh RH12 217 D3
Nightingale Rd. Selsd CR2 ... 62 D1
Nightingale Rd. Walt O T KT12 35 B2
Nightingale Sq. Balham SW12 21 A8
Nightingale Way. Bletch RH1 120 E2
Nightingales. Cran GU6 174 E1
Nightingales The. Stan TW19 13 F7
Nightjar Cl. Crond GU10 124 D8
Nimbus Rd. Epsom KT19 57 D1
Nimrod Ct. Crawl RH10 182 D1
Nimrod Rd. Harm TW6 3 A6
Nimrod Rd. Streat SW16 & SW17 21 B3
Nimrod Way. Harm TW6 3 A6
Nine Elms Cl. E Bed TW14 ... 14 F7
Nine Mile Ride. Crowth RG12 & RG11 26 F1
Nine Mile Ride. Easth RG12 & RG11 26 F1
Nineacres Way. Coulsd CR5 . 79 E3
Ninehams Cl. Cater CR3 .... 100 D7
Ninehams Gdns. Cater CR3 100 D7
Ninehams Rd. Cater CR3 .. 100 D6
Ninehams Rd. Tats TN16 ... 103 D6
Nineteenth Rd. Mitch CR4 ... 41 E5
Ninfield Ct. Crawl RH11 200 F2
Niton Rd. Rich TW9 7 A4
Niven Cl. Worth RH10 202 D5
Nobel Dr. Harl TW6 3 E7
Noble Cnr. Heston TW5 5 A6
Noble Ct. Mitch CR4 40 D7
Noble St. Walt O T KT12 54 C7
Nobles Way. Egham TW20 ... 11 E2
Noel Ct. Hounsl TW4 4 F4
Noel Terr. For Hil SE23 23 C6
Noke Dr. Earls RH1 119 A2
Nonsuch Ct Ave. Ewell KT17 58 B1
Nonsuch Ct. Cheam SM3 58 E4
Nonsuch High Sch for Girls. Cheam SM3 58 D3
Nonsuch Ind Est. Ewell KT17 76 E8
Nonsuch Prim Sch. Stonel KT17 58 B5
Nonsuch Wlk. E Ewell SM2 .. 58 D1
Noons Corner Rd. Wotton RH5 156 A8
Norbiton Ave. King U T KT1 & KT2 38 A7
Norbiton Common Rd. King U T KT1 & KT3 38 B6
Norbiton Hall. King U T KT2 . 37 F7
Norbiton Sta. King U T KT1 .. 38 A8
Norbury Ave. Islew TW3 5 D3
Norbury Ave. S Norw CR7 & SW16 42 B7
Norbury Cl. S Norw SW16 .... 42 B8
Norbury Court Rd. Thorn H SW16 41 E7
Norbury Cres. Thorn H SW16 42 A7
Norbury Cross. Thorn H SW16 41 E6
Norbury Hill. S Norw SW16 . 22 B1
Norbury Manor High Sch for Girls. S Norw CR7 42 A8
Norbury Rd. Reig RH2 117 F1
Norbury Rd. S Norw CR7 42 C6
Norbury Rise. Thorn H SW16 41 E6
Norbury Sta. S Norw SW16 .. 41 F8
Norbury Trad Est. Thorn H SW16 41 F7
Norbury Way. G Book KT23 . 94 C2
Norcroft Gdns. Dulw SE22 ... 23 A8
Norcutt Rd. Twick TW2 16 E7
Norfolk Ave. S Croy CR2 62 A1
Norfolk Cl. Crawl RH11 200 E2
Norfolk Cl. Horley RH6 161 A2
Norfolk Cl. 5 Twick TW1 6 B1
Norfolk Cotts. S Nutf RH1 .. 140 E7
Norfolk Ct. Dork RH5 136 D3
Norfolk Ct. Horsh RH12 218 B5
Norfolk Ct. Surb KT5 37 F3
Norfolk Farm Cl. Mayb GU22 70 D3
Norfolk Farm Rd. Mayb GU22 70 D3
Norfolk House. 2 Croy CR0 61 D8
Norfolk House. 11 Merton SW19 20 C1
Norfolk House. Penge SE20 . 43 C8
Norfolk House Rd. Streat SW16 21 E5
Norfolk La. Dork RH5 136 B1
Norfolk Rd. Clayg KT10 55 E5
Norfolk Rd. Dork RH4 136 A7
Norfolk Rd. Felt TW13 15 C7
Norfolk Rd. Horsh RH12 & RH13 217 D2
Norfolk Rd. Mitch SW19 20 E2
Norfolk Rd. S Holm RH5 157 C6
Norfolk Rd. S Norw CR7 42 C6
Norfolk Terr. Horsh RH12 & RH13 217 D2
Norgrove St. Balham SW12 . 21 A8
Norheads La. Bigg H TN16 ... 83 B2
Norheads La. Chelsh TN16 ... 83 B2
Norheads La. Chelsh CR6 & TN16 103 A8
Norhyrst Ave. S Norw SE25 . 42 F6
Nork Gdns. Nork SM7 77 E5
Nork Rise. Nork SM7 77 D3
Nork Way. Nork KT17 & SM7 77 D4
Norlands La. Egham TW18 & TW20 32 E7
Norlands La. Thorpe TW18 & TW20 32 E7
Norley Vale. Rhampt SW15 .. 19 A7
Norman Ave. Ewell KT17 76 F7
Norman Ave. Felt TW13 15 F6
Norman Ave. S Croy CR2 & CR8 61 C1
Norman Ave. Twick TW1 17 C8
Norman Colyer Court. Epsom KT19 57 D1
Norman Cres. Heston TW5 4 D7
Norman Ct. 9 Hampt TW12 36 A8
Norman Ct. M Bourn GU9 .. 125 C1
Norman Ct. Streat SW16 22 A3
Norman House. Felt TW13 .. 15 F6
Norman House. Lo Hall TW17 34 A2
Norman House. Woodh RH2 138 F6
Norman Rd. Ashf TW15 14 D2
Norman Rd. Merton SW19 ... 20 C1
Norman Rd. Sutton SM1 59 A5
Norman Rd. Thorn H CR7 42 B4
Norman's Rd. Outw RH1 & RH6 162 C5
Normandy. Horsh RH12 217 C1
Normandy Cl. 7 E Grins RH19 205 F8
Normandy Cl. Friml GU16 86 E8
Normandy Cl. Worth RH10 202 C4
Normandy Gdns. Horsh RH12 217 C1
Normandy Wlk. Egham TW20 12 C3
Normanhurst. Ashf TW15 14 A3
Normanhurst Cl. Crawl RH10 201 F6
Normanhurst Dr. Twick TW1 . 6 B2
Normanhurst Rd. Streat SW2 21 F6
Normanhurst Rd. Walt O T KT12 54 D8
Normans La. Haxted TN8 ... 165 E7
Normansfield Ave. Tedd KT1 & KT8 17 C1
Normansfield Hospl. Tedd KT8 17 C1
Normanton. Reig RH2 117 D2
Normanton Ave. Wimble SW18 & SW19 20 A6
Normanton Rd. S Croy CR2 . 61 E4
Normanton St. For Hil SE23 23 D6
Normington Cl. Streat SW16 22 A3
Norrels Dr. E Hors KT24 92 F1
Norrels Ride. E Hors KT24 ... 92 F2
Norreys Ave. Woki RG11 25 D7
Norris Hill Rd. Chur C GU13 & GU14 104 A8
Norris Rd. Stain TW18 12 F4
Norstead Pl. Rhampt SW15 .. 19 A6
North Acre. Banstd SM7 77 F3
North Ash. Horsh RH12 217 C4
North Ave. Heath E GU9 125 D7
North Ave. 8 Rich TW9 7 A6
North Ave. Wallin SM5 60 A3
North Ave. Whit V KT12 53 E2
North Beta Rd. Farnb GU14 . 85 B2
North Camp Sta. Ash V GU12 105 F8
North Cl. Ash GU12 105 E1
North Cl. Crawl RH10 201 F7
North Cl. Dork RH5 136 C3
North Cl. E Bed TW14 3 D1
North Cl. Farnb GU14 85 A8
North Cl. Merton SM4 39 E5
North Comm. Weyb KT13 53 C6
North Crofts. Dulw SE21 23 B7
North Dene. Hounsl TW5 5 B6
North Down. Sander CR2 80 E7
North Downs Cres. New Add CR0 63 B1
North Downs Golf Course. Wold RH9 102 A2
North Downs Rd. New Add CR0 63 C1
North Dr. Beck BR3 44 B5
North Dr. Hounsl TW3 & TW7 5 C5
North Dr. Pirb GU24 87 C6
North Dr. Streat SW16 21 C4
North Dr. Went GU25 30 E4
North East Surrey Coll of Tech. Epsom KT19 57 D1
North End. Croy CR0 & CR9 .. 61 C8
North End La. Sunnin SL5 30 B2
North Farm Rd. W Heath GU14 84 F8
North Farnborough Cty Inf Sch. Farnb GU14 85 D5
North Feltham Trad Est. Felt TW14 4 B3
North Gate Rd. Farnb GU14 . 85 C2
North Gdns. Mitch SW19 20 D1
North Gn. Brack RG12 27 D8
North Gr. Chert KT16 32 F3
North Hatton Rd. Harl TW6 ... 3 D6
North Heath Cl. Horsh RH12 217 D5
North Heath Cty Prim Sch. Horsh RH12 217 D5
North Heath Est. Horsh RH12 217 D6
North Heath La. Horsh RH12 217 E6
North Holmes Cl. Horsh RH12 218 B5
North Hyde La. Heston TW5 .. 4 F8
North La. Alder GU11 & GU12 105 D2
North La. Tedd TW11 16 F2
North Lodge Dr. N Asct SL5 . 28 C7
North Mead. Crawl RH10 201 E8
North Mead. Redh RH1 118 F4
North Minden House. Friml GU16 86 D7
North Moors. Bellf GU1 109 E6
North Munstead La. Godal GU7 151 A1
North Par. Chess KT9 56 F5
North Par. Horsh RH12 217 C3
North Park La. Bletch RH9 121 A5
North Pl. Mitch SW19 20 F1
North Pl. Tedd TW11 16 F2
North Pole La. Coney H BR2 63 F4
North Rd. Ash V GU12 105 F4
North Rd. Brent TW8 6 E8
North Rd. Crawl RH10 202 A7
North Rd. E Bed TW14 3 D1
North Rd. Farnb GU11 105 D7
North Rd. Hersh KT12 54 C5
North Rd. Heston TW5 4 C8
North Rd. King U T KT6 37 D3
North Rd. Mitch SW17 & SW19 20 C2
North Rd. Rich TW9 7 A5
North Rd. Stough GU2 109 B4
North Rd. W Wick BR4 44 B1
North Rd. Wimble SW17 & SW19 20 C2
North Rd. Wink SL5 28 B8
North Rd. Woking GU21 70 A3
North Rd. Woodh RH2 138 F6
North Sheen Sta. Rich TW10 . 7 A3
North Side. Tongh GU10 126 F7
North St. Carsh SM5 59 F6
North St. Dork RH4 136 A7
North St. Egham TW20 11 F2
North St. Farnc GU7 150 E7
North St. Guild GU1 130 D8
North St. Horsh RH12 & 13 217 D3
North St. Islew TW7 6 A4
North St. Leahd KT22 95 A6
North St. Redh RH1 118 F2
North St. Turn H RH10 204 A4
North St. Wink SL4 9 A6
North Station App. S Nutf RH1 140 F7
North Terminal App. Crawl RH6 181 F8
North View. Wimble SW19 ... 19 C3
North View Cres. Burgh H KT18 77 C2
North Weald La.King U T KT2 17 D3
North Weylands Ind Est. Walt O T KT12 54 E8
North Wlk. New Add CR0 63 C5
North Worple Way. Mortl SW14 7 D4
Northampton Cl. Brack RG12 27 E6
Northampton Rd. Croy CR0 & CR9 62 A8
Northanger Rd. Streat SW16 21 E2
Northborough Rd. Thorn H SW16 41 E7
Northbourne. Farnc GU7 .... 150 F8
Northbrook Coll of Design & Tech. Horsh RH12 217 C4
Northbrook Copse. Brack RG12 27 F3
Northbrook Rd. Alder GU11 126 B8
Northbrook Rd. Thorn H CR0 42 D4
Northcliffe Cl. Worc Pk KT4 . 57 E7
Northcote. Addl KT15 52 D6
Northcote Ave. Islew TW7 ... 6 A2
Northcote Ave. Tolw KT5 38 B2
Northcote Cl. W Hors KT24 . 92 C2
Northcote Cres. W Hors KT24 92 C2
Northcote La. Sham Gn GU5 152 E6
Northcote Pk. Oxsh KT22 74 C4
Northcote Rd. Ash V GU12 106 A7
Northcote Rd. Islew TW1 & TW7 6 A2
Northcote Rd. King U T KT3 . 38 D6
Northcote Rd. Thorn H CR0 . 42 D3
Northcote Rd. W Heath GU14 84 F6
Northcote Rd. W Hors KT24 92 C2
Northcott. Easth RG12 27 A1
Northcroft Cl. Eng Gn TW20 11 B3
Northcroft Gdns. Eng Gn TW20 11 B3
Northcroft Rd. Eng Gn TW20 11 B3
Northcroft Rd. W Ewell KT19 57 E3
Northcroft Rd. W Ewell KT19 57 E3
Northcroft Villas. Eng Gn TW20 11 B3
Northdown Cl. Horsh RH12 217 F4
Northdown Ct. Tyl Gn RH9 . 121 C5
Northdown La. Guild GU1 .. 130 E6
Northdown Rd. Belm SM2 ... 59 A1
Northdown Rd. Wold CR3 & RH9 102 A2
Northdown Terr. E Grins RH19 185 D3
Northdowns. Cran GU6 174 E1
Northend Ct. G Book KT23 ... 94 C1
Northern Perimeter Rd. Harl TW6 3 E6
Northern Perimeter Rd. Hatton TW6 3 E6
Northern Perimeter Road (W). Harm TW6 2 D6
Northernhay Wlk. Merton SM4 39 E5
Northey Ave. Belm SM2 58 E1
Northey Ave. E Ewell SM2 .... 58 E1
Northfield. Lhtwat GU18 67 B8
Northfield. Shalf GU4 130 E1
Northfield. Witley GU8 170 F4
Northfield Cl. Alder GU12 . 105 D1
Northfield Cres. Cheam SM3 58 E6
Northfield Ct. Stain TW18 .... 33 B8
Northfield Hospl. Alder GU12 105 D2
Northfield Pl. Whit V KT13 ... 53 B3
Northfield Rd. Cobham KT11 73 B6
Northfield Rd. Heston TW5 .... 4 D7
Northfield Rd. Stain TW18 ... 33 B8
Northfields. Ashtd KT21 95 E8
Northgate Ave. Crawl RH10 201 F7
Northgate Cty Fst Sch. Crawl RH10 201 E7
Northgate Cty Mid Sch. Crawl RH10 201 E7
Northgate Dr. Camb GU15 ... 66 A7
Northgate Pl. Crawl RH10 .. 201 E7
Northgate Rd. Crawl RH6 .. 181 F8
Northgate Rd. Crawl RH10 & RH11 201 D6
Northington Cl. Brack RG12 27 F3
Northlands Bglws. Newd RH5 158 B1
Northlands Rd. Faygt RH12 198 F2
Northlands Rd. Horsh RH12 217 E7
Northlands Rd. Warn RH12 197 D2
Northmead. Farnb GU14 85 B4
Northmead Grant Maintained Jun Sch. Stough GU2 109 B4
Northmoor. 4 For Hil SE23 23 D5
Northolt Rd. Harm TW6 2 E6
Northover. Catf BR1 24 F5
Northrop Rd. Harl TW6 3 E6
Northspur Rd. Sutton SM1 ... 59 A7
Northstead Rd. Streat SW2 . 22 A6
Northumberland Ave. Hounsl TW7 6 A7
Northumberland Cl. Stan TW19 2 E1
Northumberland Cres. Felt TW14 3 E1
Northumberland Gdns. Hounsl TW7 6 A7
Northumberland Gdns. Mitch CR4 41 D4
Northumberland Pl. 26 Rich TW10 6 D2
Northway. Crawl RH6 181 F8
Northway. Farnc GU7 150 B7
Northway. Merton SM4 & SW20 39 E5
Northway. Stough GU2 109 A3
Northway. Wallin SM6 60 C6
Northway Rd. Croy CR0 42 F2
Northwood Ave. Knaph GU21 68 D1
Northwood Ave. Purley CR8 80 B6
Northwood Pk. Crawl RH10 182 A2
Northwood Rd. For Hil SE23 23 F7
Northwood Rd. Harm TW6 .... 2 D6
Northwood Rd. S Norw CR7 42 C7
Northwood Rd. Wallin SM5 . 60 A4
Northwood Way. 1 W Norw SE19 22 E2
Norton Ave. Tolw KT5 38 B2
Norton Ct. Beck BR3 43 F8
Norton Gdns. Thorn H SW16 41 E7
Norton House. 4 New Mal KT3 38 E5
Norton Pk. Ascot SL5 29 C4
Norton Rd. Friml GU15 66 C4
Norton Rd. Woki RG11 25 C5
Norwich Ave. Camb GU15 .... 65 E3
Norwich Rd. Crawl RH10 ... 202 B5
Norwich Rd. S Norw CR7 42 C6
Norwood Cl. Effing KT24 ... 113 E7
Norwood Cl. Twick TW2 16 D6
Norwood Cres. Harl TW6 3 C6
Norwood Farm La. Esher KT11 73 B8
Norwood Heights Sh Ctr. S Norw SE19 22 E2
Norwood High St. W Norw SE27 22 C4
Norwood Hill. Charl RH6 ... 159 D3
Norwood Hospl. S Norw SE19 22 D2
Norwood Junction Sta. Croy SE25 43 A5
Norwood Park Rd. W Norw SE27 22 C3
Norwood Rd. Effing KT24 ... 113 E7
Norwood Rd. Streat SE24 & SE27 22 B7
Norwood Rd. W Norw SE24 & SE27 22 B7
Norwood Sch. W Norw SE27 22 C3
Norwood Sch. W Norw SE27 22 C4
Norwoodhill Rd. Charl RH6 159 F2
Noseby Ct. Walt O T KT12 .... 54 C8
Notley End. Eng Gn TW20 .... 11 C1
Notre Dame Int Sch. Crawl RH10 202 D6
Notre Dame Jun Sch. Lingf RH7 164 F3
Notre Dame Sen Sch. Lingf RH7 164 F3
Notson Rd. Croy SE25 43 B5
Nottingham Cl. Knaph GU21 68 F1
Nottingham Ct. 6 Knaph GU21 68 F1
Nottingham Rd. Croy CR2 ... 61 C5
Nottingham Rd. Islew TW7 ... 5 F5
Nottingham Rd. Up Toot SW17 20 F7
Nova Mews. W Barn SM4 39 E2
Nova Rd. Thorn H CR0 42 C2
Nower Lodge Sch. Dork RH4 136 A6
Nower Rd. Dork RH4 136 A6
Nowhurst La. Slinfd RH12 . 216 A5
Noyna Rd. Up Toot SW17 20 F5
Nuffield Dr. Sandh GU15 45 E1
Nugee Ct. Crowth RG11 45 B5
Nugent Ct. Stough GU2 109 B4
Nugent Ct. Streat SW16 21 C4
Nugent Rd. Onsl V GU2 129 D8
Nugent Rd. S Norw SE25 42 F6
Numa Ct. Brent TW8 6 D7
Nunappleton Way. Oxted RH8 123 A3
Nuneaton. Brack RG12 27 E3
Nuneham. Streat SW16 21 D4
Nuns Wlk. Vir W GU25 31 D4
Nuptown La. New Gn SL4 8 A8

Nursery Ave. Croy CR0 .... 62 D8
Nursery Cl. Capel RH5 .... 178 C5
Nursery Cl. Croy CR0 .... 62 D8
Nursery Cl. Ewell KT17 .... 57 E1
Nursery Cl. Felt TW14 .... 15 B8
Nursery Cl. Friml GU16 .... 85 F7
Nursery Cl. Horse GU21 .... 69 C3
Nursery Cl. Walt o t H KT20 .. 97 B2
Nursery Cl. Woodfm KT15 .. 51 F1
Nursery Cotts. Woking GU21 88 F8
Nursery Gdns. Chil GU4 .... 131 B3
Nursery Gdns. Stain TW18 .. 13 B1
Nursery Gdns. Sunby TW16 .. 34 F7
Nursery Hill. Sham Gn GU5 152 D5
Nursery La. Hookw RH6 .... 160 D2
Nursery La. N Ascot SL5 ...... 28 E8
Nursery Rd. Farnc GU7 .... 150 F7
Nursery Rd. Knaph GU21 .... 68 D2
Nursery Rd. Merton SW19 ... 40 B7
Nursery Rd. Mitch CR4 .... 40 E6
Nursery Rd.
  S Norw CR7 & SE25 .... 42 D5
Nursery Rd. Sunby TW16 .... 34 F7
Nursery Rd. Sutton SM1 .... 59 C6
Nursery Rd. Walt o t H KT20 97 B2
Nursery Rd. Wimble SW19 ... 19 E1
Nurserylands. Crawl RH11 201 A6
Nutborn House.
  Wimble SW19 .... 19 D2
Nutbourne. Heath E GU9 ... 125 E7
Nutbourne Cotts.
  Hambl GU8 .... 191 E7
Nutbourne Ct. Stain TW18 ... 12 F1
Nutcombe La. Dork RH4 .... 135 F7
Nutcombe La.
  Shottm GU26 & GU27 ...... 188 E1
Nutcroft Gr. Fetch KT22 .... 94 E6
Nutfield Church Prim Sch.
  S Nutf RH1 .... 140 F8
Nutfield Cl. Carsh SM5 ...... 59 E7
Nutfield Ct. Camb GU15 .... 65 D7
Nutfield Marsh Rd.
  Nutf RH1 .... 119 E4
Nutfield Rd. Coulsd CR5 .... 79 A3
Nutfield Rd. Earls RH1 .... 119 C1
Nutfield Rd. Merst RH1 .... 119 C5
Nutfield Rd. Redh RH1 .... 119 C1
Nutfield Rd. Thorn H CR7 .... 42 B5
Nutfield Sta. S Nutf RH1 .. 140 E7
Nuthatch Cl. Crond GU10 .. 124 D7
Nuthatch Gdns. Dovgn RH2 139 C5
Nuthatch Way.
  Horsh RH12 .... 217 D7
Nuthurst. Brack RG12 ...... 27 E4
Nuthurst Ave. Cran GU6 .... 174 E3
Nuthurst Ave. Streat SW2 .. 21 F6
Nuthurst Cl. Crawl RH11 .... 201 A7
Nutley. Easth RG12 .... 27 A1
Nutley Ct. Reig RH2 .... 118 A1
Nutley La. Reig RH2 .... 117 F2
Nutmeg Ct. W Heath GU4 .. 84 C5
Nutshell La. Hale GU9 .... 125 C6
Nutty La. Littlt TW17 .... 34 C6
Nutwell St. Up Toot SW17 ... 20 E3
Nutwood. Farnc GU7 .... 150 D6
Nutwood Ave. Brock RH3 .. 137 C8
Nutwood Cl. Brock RH3 .... 137 C8
Nyefield Pk. Walt o t H KT20 97 A1
Nylands Ave. Rich TW9 .... 7 A5
Nymans Cl. Horsh RH12 .... 218 A7
Nymans Ct. Crawl RH10 .... 202 B3
Nymans Gdns.
  W Barn SW20 .... 39 B6
Nyon Gr. For Hil SE23 & SE6 23 F6

O'Connor Rd. Farnb GU11 .. 105 E7
O'Gorman Ave. Farnb GU14 85 B2
Oak Ave. Croy CR0 .... 43 E3
Oak Ave. Egham TW20 .... 12 D1
Oak Ave. Hampt TW12 & 13 . 15 E2
Oak Ave. Heston TW5 .... 4 E7
Oak Ave. Sandh GU15 .... 65 C1
Oak Bank. New Add CR0 .... 63 C4
Oak Cl. Box H KT20 .... 116 B5
Oak Cl. Chidd GU8 .... 191 A4
Oak Cl. Copth RH10 .... 183 A3
Oak Cl. Farnc GU7 .... 150 E8
Oak Cnr. Bear Gn RH5 ...... 157 C4
Oak Cottage Cl. Catf SE6 ... 24 F7
Oak Cottage Cl.
  Wood S V GU3 .... 108 C2
Oak Cotts. Shottm GU27 .... 207 E6
Oak Croft. E Grins RH19 .... 206 A8
Oak Ct. M Bourn GU9 .... 125 B1
Oak Dell. Crawl RH10 .... 202 C7
Oak Dr. Box H KT20 .... 116 B5
Oak End. Bear Gn RH5 .... 157 C3
Oak End Way. Woodhm KT15 70 F7
Oak Farm Cl. Bickw GU17 .. 64 C5
Oak Farm Cty Sec Sch.
  W Heath GU14 .... 84 F6

Oak Gdns. Croy CR0 .... 63 A8
Oak Glade. Epsom KT19 .... 76 A7
Oak Gr. Loxwd RH14 .... 213 A4
Oak Gr. Sunby TW16 .... 15 B1
Oak Gr. W Wick BR4 .... 44 C1
Oak Grange Rd.
  W Clan GU4 .... 111 B6
Oak Grove Cres. Sandh GU15 64 F6
Oak Grove Rd. Penge SE20 . 43 C7
Oak Hill. Burgh GU4 .... 110 C6
Oak Hill. Surb KT6 .... 37 E2
Oak Hill. Wood S V GU3 .... 108 B3
Oak Hill. Woodc KT18 .... 76 D3
Oak Hill Cres. Surb KT6 .... 37 E2
Oak Hill Gr. Surb KT6 .... 37 E3
Oak Hill Rd. Surb KT6 .... 37 E3
Oak House. Penge SE20 .... 43 B7
Oak La. Broad H RH12 .... 216 E3
Oak La. Eng Gn TW20 .... 11 C5
Oak La. Islew TW7 .... 5 E3
Oak La. Mayb GU22 .... 70 B3
Oak La. Twick TW1 .... 17 A8
Oak Leaf Cl. Epsom KT19 .. 76 C7
Oak Lodge. Crowth RG11 .... 45 C5
Oak Lodge. Cl. Hersh KT12 .. 54 C5
Oak Lodge Dr. Salfs RH1 .. 140 A1
Oak Lodge Dr. W Wick BR4 . 44 B2
Oak Lodge Prim Sch.
  W Wick BR4 .... 44 B2
Oak Lodge Sch.
  Balham SW12 .... 21 A8
Oak Mead. Farnc GU7 .... 150 E8
Oak Park Gdns.
  Putney SW19 .... 19 D7
Oak Pk. Sheer KT14 .... 70 E6
Oak Rd. Cater CR3 .... 100 E5
Oak Rd. Cobham KT11 .... 73 E4
Oak Rd. Crawl RH11 .... 201 C5
Oak Rd. Farnb GU14 .... 85 C3
Oak Rd. King U T KT3 .... 38 D7
Oak Rd. Leahd KT22 .... 95 A8
Oak Rd. Reig RH2 .... 118 B2
Oak Ridge. Dork RH4 .... 136 B4
Oak Row. Mitch CR4 .... 41 C7
Oak Tree Cl. Alder GU12 .. 126 E5
Oak Tree Cl. Belif GU4 .... 109 C6
Oak Tree Cl. Burgh GU4 .... 110 C6
Oak Tree Cl. Knaph GU21 .. 68 B1
Oak Tree Cl. Went GU25 .... 31 D3
Oak Tree Dr. Belif GU1 .... 109 C5
Oak Tree Dr. Eng Gn TW20 .. 11 C3
Oak Tree La. Shottm GU27 207 D6
Oak Tree Rd. Knaph GU21 .. 68 B1
Oak Tree Rd. Knaph GU21 .. 88 B8
Oak Tree Rd. Milf GU8 .... 149 F1
Oak Tree View.
  Heath E GU9 .... 125 E6
Oak Way. Ashtd KT21 .... 76 A3
Oak Way. Crawl RH10 .... 201 E8
Oak Way. Croy CR0 .... 43 D3
Oak Way. E Bed TW14 .... 14 E7
Oak Way. Reig RH2 .... 139 D8
Oak Wlk. Faygt RH12 .... 199 F1
Oakapple Cl. Crawl RH11 .. 201 B1
Oakapple Cl. Hams Gn CR2 . 81 B5
Oakapple Cl. Crawl RH11 .. 201 B1
Oakbank. Fetch KT22 .... 94 D4
Oakbank. Woking GU22 .... 89 E8
Oakbank Ave. Walt o T KT12 35 F2
Oakbrook. Beck BR3 .... 44 B7
Oakcombe Cl. King U T KT3 . 38 E8
Oakcroft Bsns Ctr.
  Chess KT9 .... 56 F6
Oakcroft Cl. W Byfl KT14 .... 70 F5
Oakcroft House.
  New Mal K3 .... 38 E2
Oakcroft Rd. Chess KT9 .... 56 F6
Oakcroft Rd. Pyrf KT14 .... 70 F5
Oakcroft Villas. Chess KT9 .. 56 F6
Oakdale. Beck BR3 .... 44 C7
Oakdale. Brack RG12 .... 27 D3
Oakdale Rd. Epsom KT19 .. 57 D2
Oakdale Rd. Streat SW16 ... 21 E3
Oakdale Rd. Weyb KT13 .... 53 A7
Oakdale Way. Carsh CR4 .... 41 A2
Oakdene. Chobh GU24 .... 49 F1
Oakdene. Kings KT20 .... 97 E7
Oakdene. Sandh SL5 .... 29 F3
Oakdene. ▮ N Worw SE19 .. 22 E3
Oakdene Ave. Thame D KT7 . 37 A1
Oakdene Cl. Brock RH3 .... 137 C7
Oakdene Cl. G Book KT23 .. 114 C8
Oakdene Cl. Walt O T KT12 . 54 B7
Oakdene Lodge. Penge SE20 23 B1
Oakdene Mews. Cheam SM3 39 F1
Oakdene Par. Cobham KT11 . 73 B5
Oakdene Rd. Brock RH3 .... 137 C7

Oakdene Rd. Cobham KT11 .. 73 B5
Oakdene Rd. Godal GU7 .... 150 D3
Oakdene Rd. L Book KT23 .... 93 F3
Oakdene Rd. Redh RH1 .... 118 F1
Oakdene Rd. Shalf GU3 .... 130 C1
Oaken Coppice. Ashtd KT21 96 A8
Oaken Copse Cres.
  Farnb GU14 .... 85 B7
Oaken Dr. Clayg KT10 .... 55 F4
Oaken La. Clayg KT10 .... 55 E5
Oakengates. Easth RG12 .... 27 A1
Oakenshaw Cl. Surb KT6 .... 37 E2
Oakfield. Plaist RH14 .... 211 E2
Oakfield. Woking GU21 .... 68 E3
Oakfield Cl. New Mal KT3 .. 38 F3
Oakfield Cl. Weyb KT13 .... 53 C6
Oakfield Ct. Croy CR2 .... 61 C4
Oakfield Ct. Woki RG11 .... 25 A5
Fetch KT22 .... 94 D4
Oakfield Dr. Reig RH2 .... 118 B3
Oakfield Gdns. Beck BR3 .... 44 A4
Oakfield Gdns. Carsh SM5 ... 40 F1
Oakfield Gdns. ▮ Dulw SE19 22 E3
Oakfield Glade. Weyb KT13 . 53 C6
Oakfield Rd. Ashf TW15 .... 14 B3
Oakfield Rd. Ashtd KT21 .... 75 E1
Oakfield Rd. Cobham KT11 .. 73 B5
Oakfield Rd. Hawley GU17 .. 64 F3
Oakfield Rd. Penge SE20 .... 23 B1
Oakfield Rd. Thorn H CR0 .... 42 C1
Oakfield Rd. Wimble SW19 . 19 D5
Oakfield Sch. Dulw SE21 .... 22 D7
Oakfield Way. E Grins RH19 185 F3
Oakfields. Camb GU15 .... 65 B5
Oakfields. Crawl RH10 .... 202 D7
Oakfields. Stough GU2 .... 108 F3
Oakfields. W Byfl KT14 .... 71 B5
Oakfields. Wall W RH5 .... 196 D8
Oakhall Ct. Ashf TW16 .... 14 F3
Oakhall Dr. Ashf TW16 .... 14 F3
Oakham Cl. For Hil SE6 .... 23 F6
Oakham Dr. Hayes BR2 .... 44 F5
Oakhaven.
  Crawl RH10 & RH11 .... 201 D4
Oakhill. Clayg KT10 .... 56 A4
Oakhill Cl. Ashtd KT21 .... 75 C1
Oakhill Ct. ▮ Surb KT6 .... 37 E3
Oakhill Ct. Wimble SW19 .. 19 D1
Oakhill Gdns. Oat Pk KT13 . 53 E8
Oakhill Lodge. Purley CR8 .. 80 A6
Oakhill Rd. Ashtd KT21 .... 75 C1
Oakhill Rd. Beck BR3 .... 44 C7
Oakhill Rd. Head Dn GU35 . 187 B5
Oakhill Rd. Horsh RH13 .... 217 F2
Oakhill Rd. Reig RH2 .... 139 B8
Oakhill Rd. Row Tn KT15 ... 51 F4
Oakhill Rd. Sutton SM1 .... 59 C7
Oakhill Rd. Thorn H SW16 .. 41 F8
Oakhurst. Burrh GU24 .... 49 E2
Oakhurst. Grayysh GU26 .... 188 D3
Oakhurst Cl. ▮ Tedd TW11 . 16 E3
Oakhurst Gdns.
  E Grins RH19 .... 185 C2
Oakhurst La. Loxwd RH14 .. 212 E7
Oakhurst Rd. W Ewell KT19 . 57 C4
Oakhurst Rd. W Ewell KT19 . 57 D4
Oakhurst Rise. Sutton SM5 . 59 E1
Oakhyrst Grange Sch.
  Cater CR3 .... 100 D1
Oakington. ▮ King U T KT1 38 A7
Oakington Dr. Sunby TW16 . 35 C7
Oakland Ave. Heath E GU9 . 125 E7
Oakland Way. W Ewell KT19 57 E4
Oakland Way. W Ewell KT19 57 E4
Oaklands. Croy CR0 .... 61 B5
Oaklands. Fetch KT22 .... 94 D3
Oaklands. Haslem GU27 .... 208 C7
Oaklands. Horley RH6 .... 161 C3
Oaklands. Horsh RH13 .... 217 E2
Oaklands. Purley CR8 .... 80 C5
Oaklands. S Godst RH9 .... 142 E5
Oaklands. Twick TW2 .... 16 C8
Oaklands Ave. Hounsl TW7 .. 5 F8
Oaklands Ave. Thame D KT10 36 D1
Oaklands Ave. Thorn H CR7 . 42 A5
Oaklands Ave. W Wick BR4 . 63 B7
Oaklands Cl. Ash V GU12 .. 106 B4
Oaklands Cl. Chess KT9 .... 56 C6
Oaklands Cl. N Asct SL5 .... 8 F1
Oaklands Cl. Shalf GU4 .... 130 E1
Oaklands Cl. Addl KT15 .... 52 B7
Oaklands Cty Jun Sch.
  Crowth RG11 .... 45 A6
Oaklands Dr. Earls RH1 .... 140 B7
Oaklands Dr. N Asct SL5 .... 8 F1
Oaklands Dr. Woki RG11 ... 25 A5
Oaklands Gdns. Purley CR8 . 80 C5
Oaklands Inf Sch.
  Bigg H TN16 .... 83 C3

Oaklands Inf Sch.
  Crowth RG11 .... 45 A6
Oaklands Jun Sch.
  Bigg H TN16 .... 83 C3
Oaklands La. Bigg H TN16 .. 83 C5
Oaklands La. Crowth RG11 .. 45 B7
Oaklands Pk. Woki RG11 .... 25 A5
Oaklands Pk. Woki RG11 .... 25 A4
Oaklands Rd. Broml BR1 .... 24 E1
Oaklands Rd. Mortl SW14 ... 7 D4
Oaklands Sch. Islew TW3 .... 5 D4
Oaklands Way. Tadw KT20 .. 97 C5
Oaklands Way. Wallin SM6 . 60 D3
Oaklawn Rd. Ashtd KT22 .... 74 E3
Oaklawn Rd. Leahd KT22 .... 74 E2
Oaklea. Ash V GU12 .... 106 A5
Oaklea Ct. S Croy CR2 .... 61 D2
Oakleigh. Epsom KT18 .... 76 E5
Oakleigh. Lhtwat GU18 .... 67 C8
Oakleigh Annexe (Queen Victoria
  Hospl). Ash W RH19 .... 206 C7
Oakleigh Ave. Tolw KT6 .... 57 B8
Oakleigh Ct. Oxted RH8 .... 122 E8
Oakleigh Ct. Penge SE20 ... 23 B1
Oakleigh Rd. Horsh RH12 .. 217 F4
Oakleigh Way. Mitch CR4 .. 41 B8
Oakleigh Way. ▮ Tolw KT6 38 B1
Oakley Ave. Wallin CR0 .... 60 C6
Oakley Cl. Addl KT15 .... 52 D6
Oakley Cl. E Grins RH19 ... 206 B7
Oakley Cl. Hounsl TW7 .... 5 C6
Oakley Cotts. Ash W RH19 . 206 C7
Oakley Ct. Carsh CR4 .... 40 D3
Oakley Dell. Merrow GU4 .. 110 C3
Oakley Gdns. Banstd SM7 .. 78 B4
Oakley House. Farnc GU7 . 150 E8
Oakley Rd. Camb GU15 .... 65 B4
Oakley Rd. Croy SE25 .... 43 B4
Oakley Rd. Whytif CR6 .... 81 A1
Oakman House.
  Putney SW19 .... 19 D7
Oakmead Gn. Woodc KT18 .. 76 C4
Oakmead Pl. Mitch CR4 .... 40 E8
Oakmead Rd. Up Toot SW12 21 B7
Oakmead Rd. Wallin CR0 ... 41 D3
Oakridge. W End GU24 .... 67 F6
Oakridge Rd. Catf BR1 .... 24 E4
Oaks Ave. Felt TW13 .... 15 E6
Oaks Ave. N Cheam KT4 .... 58 B6
Oaks Ave.
  N Norw SE19 & SE27 .... 22 E3
Oaks Cl. Horsh RH12 .... 218 B6
Oaks Cl. Leahd KT22 .... 95 A6
Oaks La. Croy CR0 .... 62 C7
Oaks La. S Holm RH5 .... 157 B8
Oaks Rd. Purley CR8 .... 80 B5
Oaks Rd. Reig RH2 .... 118 D2
Oaks Rd. Stan TW19 .... 2 D1
Oaks Sports Ctr. Wallin SM5 78 F8
Oaks The. Brack RG12 .... 27 C7
Oaks The. E Grins RH19 .... 206 B8
Oaks The. Epsom KT18 .... 76 F5
The Oaks. Farnb GU14 .... 84 D3
Oaks The. Stain TW18 .... 12 F4
Oaks The. W Byfl KT14 .... 71 A5
Oaks The. Wimble SW19 .... 19 E2
Oaks Track.
  Wallin SM5 & SM6 .... 60 B1
Oaks Way. Burgh H KT18 ... 97 B8
Oaks Way. Long D KT6 ...... 37 D1
Oaks Way. Purley CR8 .... 80 C5
Oaks Way. Wallin SM5 .... 59 F3
Oaksford Ave. For Hil SE26 .. 23 B5
Oakshade Rd. Catf BR1 .... 24 D4
Oakshade Rd. Oxsh KT22 ... 74 C5
Oakshaw. Oxted RH8 .... 122 D8
Oakshaw Rd. Wands SW18 . 20 B8
Oakside Ct. Horley RH6 .... 161 C4
Oakside La. Horley RH6 .... 161 C4
Oaktree Way. Sandh GU17 . 45 A1
Oaktrees. Ash GU12 .... 105 F1
Oaktrees. Hale GU9 .... 125 B6
Oakview Gr. Croy CR0 .... 43 E1
Oakview Rd. Catf SE6 .... 24 B3
Oakway. Alder GU12 .... 126 E8
Oakway. Beck BR2 .... 44 D7
Oakway. Knaph GU21 .... 88 E8
Oakway. W Barn SW20 .... 39 C5
Oakway. Dr. Friml GU16 .... 65 E1
Oakwood. Stough GU2 .... 109 A6
Oakwood. Wallin SM6 .... 60 B2
Oakwood Ave. Beck BR3 & 4 44 C7
Oakwood Ave. Mitch CR4 .... 40 D7
Oakwood Ave. Purley CR8 .. 80 C7
Oakwood Cl. E Hors KT24 .. 112 E8
Oakwood Cl. Earls RH1 .... 119 A1
Oakwood Cl. S Nutf RH1 .... 140 F7

Oakwood Ct. Beck BR3 .... 44 C7
Oakwood Ct. Bisley GU24 ... 68 A3
Oakwood Dr. E Hors KT24 . 112 E8
Oakwood Dr. W Norw SE19 . 22 E2
Oakwood Gdns. Knaph GU21 68 B1
Oakwood Gdns. Sutton SM1 59 A8
Oakwood Ind Pk.
  Crawl RH10 .... 182 A2
Oakwood Pk. For Row RH18 206 F2
Oakwood Pl. Thorn H CR0 ... 42 A3
Oakwood Rd. Bletch RH1 .. 120 A6
Oakwood Rd. Brack RG12 ... 27 E7
Oakwood Rd. Horley RH6 .. 161 B4
Oakwood Rd. Knaph GU21 .. 88 B8
Oakwood Rd.
  Thorn H CR0 & CR7 .... 42 A3
Oakwood Rd. Thorpe GU25 .. 31 C4
Oakwood Rd. Wimble SW20 39 A8
Oakwood Rd. Windl GU20 .. 48 E4
Oakwood Sch. Horley RH6 . 161 C3
Oareborough. Brack RG12 ... 27 E4
Oast House Cl. Wray TW19 . 11 E8
Oast House Cres. Hale GU9 125 D6
Oast House La. Hale GU9 .. 125 D6
Oast La. Alder GU11 .... 126 B7
Oast Rd. Oxted RH8 .... 122 F4
Oates Cl. Beck BR2 .... 44 D6
Oates Wlk. Crawl RH10 .... 201 F3
Oatfield Rd. Tadw KT20 .... 97 B6
Oatlands. Crawl RH11 .... 201 A5
Oatlands. Horley RH6 .... 161 C4
Oatlands Ave. Oat Pk KT13 . 53 E6
Oatlands Ave. Weyb KT13 .. 53 E6
Oatlands Chase.
  Oat Pk KT12 & KT13 .... 53 E7
Oatlands Cl. Weyb KT13 .... 53 D6
Oatlands Ct. ▮
  Putney SW19 .... 19 D7
Oatlands Cty Inf Sch.
  Oat Pk KT13 .... 53 D6
Oatlands Dr.
  Weyb KT13 & KT12 .... 53 D7
Oatlands Gn. Oat Pk KT13 .. 53 D7
Oatlands Mere. Oat Pk KT13 53 D7
Oatlands Rd. Burgh H KT20 . 97 E8
Oban Rd. S Norw SE25 .... 42 C5
Obelisk Way. Camb GU15 ... 65 C6
Oberon Way. Crawl RH11 .. 200 E3
Oberon Way. Littlt TW17 ... 33 E6
Oberursel Way. Alder GU11 104 F2
Observatory Rd. Mortl SW14 . 7 C3
Observatory Wlk. ▮
  Redh RH1 .... 118 F1
Occam Rd. Onsl V GU2 .... 129 D8
Ockenden Cl. Woking GU22 . 69 F1
Ockenden Gdns.
  Woking GU22 .... 69 F1
Ockenden Rd. Woking GU22 69 F1
Ockfields. Milf GU8 .... 149 F1
Ockford Ct. Godal GU7 .... 150 D4
Ockford Dr. Ock Rid GU7 .. 150 C3
Ockford Rd. Godal GU7 .... 150 D4
Ockford Ridge.
  Ock Rid GU7 .... 150 B2
Ockham Dr. W Hors KT24 ... 92 D3
Ockham La. Downs KT11 .... 92 D7
Ockham La. Mart Gn GU23 . 92 D7
Ockham Rd N. Ockham GU23 92 C3
Ockham Rd N. W Hors KT24 92 C3
Ockham Rd S. E Hors KT24 112 E7
Ockley CE (VA) Fst Sch.
  Ockley RH5 .... 177 D4
Ockley Ct. Burph GU4 .... 110 B6
Ockley House. ▮
  King U T KT2 .... 18 B2
Ockley Rd. Ewh GU6 .... 175 F6
Ockley Rd.
  For Gn GU6 & RH5 .... 176 C7
Ockley Rd. Ockley RH5 .... 177 B7
Ockley Rd. Rudg RH12 .... 196 E2
Ockley Rd.
  Thorn H CR0 & CR9 .... 41 F2
Ockley Rd.
  Wotton GU6 & RH5 .... 176 C7
Ockley Sta. Ockley RH5 .... 177 D4
Ockleys Mead. Tyl Gn RH9 . 121 C5
Octagon Rd. Whit V KT12 ... 53 E1
Octavia. Easth RG12 .... 27 A1
Octavia Cl. Mitch CR4 .... 40 E4
Octavia Rd. Islew TW7 .... 5 F4
Octavia Way. Stain TW18 ... 13 A2
October Ct. Beck BR2 .... 44 F6
Odard Rd. E Moles KT8 ...... 36 A5
Odette House. ▮
  W Norw SE27 .... 22 D4

Odiham Rd.Crond GU9 & 10 124 D7
Odiham Rd.
  Heath E GU10 & GU40 ..... 124 D7
Ogden House. Felt TW13 ...... 15 E4
Okeburn Rd. Up Toot SW17 . 21 A3
Okehurst Rd. Rudg RH14 ... 214 C1
Okingham Cl. Sandh GU15 ... 45 D1
Olaf Palme House.
  Felt TW13 .... 15 B5
Old Acre. Pyrf KT14 .... 71 A5
Old Ave. Sheer GU21 & KT14 70 E6
Old Ave. Whit V KT13 .... 53 C3
Old Avenue Cl. Sheer KT14 ... 70 E6
Old Barn Cl. Belm SM2 .... 58 E3
Old Barn Dr. Capel RH5 ..... 178 D6
Old Barn La. Churt GU10 ... 168 B1
Old Barn La. Kenley CR3 .... 80 F3
Old Barn Rd. Woodc KT18 ... 76 C2
Old Barn View. Godal GU7 . 150 C2
Old Bisley Rd. Friml GU16 ... 66 C3
Old Bracknell La E.
  Easth RG12 .... 27 B6
Old Bracknell La W.
  Easth RG12 .... 27 B6
Old Brickfield Rd.
  Alder GU11 .... 126 B7
Old Bridge St. Tedd KT1 ..... 37 D7
Old Brighton Rd S.
  Crawl RH11 & RH6 .... 181 E5
Old Bromley Rd. Catf BR1 ... 24 D3
Old Charlton Rd. Shep TW17 34 C4
Old Chertsey Rd.
  Chobh GU24 .... 50 C1
Old Chestnut Ave.
  Esher KT10 .... 55 B4
Old Church La.
  M Bourn GU9 .... 146 D7
Old Church Path.
  Esher KT10 .... 55 B6
Old Claygate La. Clayg KT10 56 A5
Old Common Rd.
  Esher KT11 .... 73 B7
Old Compton La.
  M Bourn GU9 .... 125 F2
Old Control Rd. Crawl RH6 181 D6
Old Convent The.
  E Grins RH19 .... 185 C2
Old Cote Dr. Heston TW5 ..... 5 A8
Old Cotts. Shalf GU3 .... 130 C2
Old Court Rd. Guild GU2 ... 130 A8
Old Crawley Rd.
  Crawl RH12 .... 218 C7
Old Cross Tree Way.
  Ash GU12 .... 127 C8
Old Ct. Ashtd KT21 .... 95 E8
Old Dean Rd. Camb GU15 .... 65 D7
Old Deer Park Gdns.
  Rich TW9 .... 6 E4
Old Denne Gdns.
  Horsh RH12 .... 217 C1
Old Devonshire Rd.
  Balham SW12 .... 21 B8
Old Dock Cl. Rich TW9 .... 7 A8
Old Elstead Rd. Milf GU8 .. 149 E2
Old Esher Cl. Hersh KT12 ... 54 D5
Old Esher Rd. Hersh KT12 ... 54 E5
Old Farleigh Rd.
  Farlgh CR0 & CR2 & CR6 ..... 81 E6
Old Farleigh Rd.
  Selsd CR0 & CR6 & CR22 ..... 81 E6
Old Farm Cl. Hounsl TW4 ..... 4 F3
Old Farm Rd. Bellf GU1 ..... 109 D4
Old Farm Rd. Hampt TW12 .. 15 F2
Old Farmhouse Dr.
  Oxsh KT22 .... 74 D4
Old Farnham La.Bentl GU10 124 A1
Old Farnham La.
  M Bourn GU9 .... 146 C8
Old Ford House. Wallin CR0 60 E7
Old Forge Cres. Shep TW17 34 B3
Old Fox Cl. Coulsd CR3 ..... 100 B6
Old Frensham Rd.
  Frensh GU10 .... 146 E4
Old Frensham Rd.
  M Bourn GU10 .... 146 E4
Old Green La. Camb GU15 ... 65 C7
Old Guildford Rd.
  Mytch GU12 & GU16 & GU24 86 C4
Old Guildford Rd.
  Warn RH12 .... 216 E4
Old Haslemere Rd.
  Haslem GU27 .... 208 C5
Old Heath Way.
  Heath E GU9 .... 125 C7
Old Hill. Woking GU22 .... 89 D7
Old Horsham Rd.
  Crawl RH11 .... 201 B4

Old Hospital Cl.
  Up Toot SW12 & SW17 ...... 20 F7
Old House Cl. Ewell KT17 ... 57 F1
Old House La. Wimble SW19 19 E3
Old House Gdns. **9**
  Twick TW1 .... 6 C1
Old Kiln Cl. Churt GU10 ... 167 F2
Old Kiln La. Brock RH3 .... 137 C8
Old Kiln La. Churt GU10 ... 167 F2
Old Kingston Rd. Tolw KT4 .. 57 C7
Old La. Alder GU12 .... 105 E3
Old La. Alder GU11 .... 126 A7
Old La. Docken GU10 .... 166 F4
Old La. E Hors KT11 .... 93 A5
Old La. Mart Gn KT11 .... 92 E7
Old La. Ockham GU23 & KT11 72 B1
Old La. Oxted RH8 .... 122 F5
Old La. Tats TN16 .... 103 D6
Old Lands Hill. Wink RG12 ... 27 D8
Old Lane Gdns. E Hors KT11 93 A5
Old Lodge Cl. Ock Rid GU7 150 B3
Old Lodge La. Purley CR8 .... 80 A3
Old Lodge Pl. **7** Twick TW1 . 6 B1
Old London Rd.
  Epsom KT17 & KT18 .... 77 A2
Old London Rd. Mickle RH5 115 C8
Old Malden La. Worc Pk KT4 57 E8
Old Malt Way. Horse GU21 .. 69 D2
Old Manor Cl. Crawl RH11 201 A8
Old Manor Dr. Twick TW7 ..... 5 C1
Old Manor Gdns. Chil GU4 . 131 C3
Old Martyrs. Crawl RH11 ... 181 D1
Old Merrow St.
  Merrow GU4 .... 110 D3
Old Mill La. Merst RH1 ..... 119 B7
Old Millmeads.
  Horsh RH12 .... 217 C5
Old Museum Ct.
  Haslem GU27 .... 208 D6
Old Nursery Pl. Ashf TW15 .. 14 B3
Old Oak Ave. Chips CR5 .... 98 E8
Old Orch. Byfl KT14 .... 71 F7
Old Orch. Sunby TW16 .... 35 C7
Old Orchard The.
  M Bourn GU9 .... 146 A8
Old Palace La. Rich TW9 .... 6 C2
Old Palace Rd.
  Croy CR0 & CR9 .... 61 C7
Old Palace Rd. Guild GU2 .. 130 A8
Old Palace Rd. Weyb KT13 .. 53 B7
Old Palace Sch. Croy CR9 .... 61 B7
Old Palace Terr. **8** Rich TW9 . 6 C2
Old Palace Yd. **2** Rich TW9 .. 6 D2
Old Park Cl. Hale GU9 .... 125 A4
Old Park La. Farnh GU9 .... 125 A4
Old Park La. Hale GU9 ...... 124 F6
Old Park Mews. Heston TW5 .. 4 F7
Old Parvis Rd. W Byfl KT14 .. 71 C7
Old Pasture Rd.
  Friml GU16 & GU15 .... 65 F3
Old Pharmacy Ct.
  Crowth RG11 .... 45 C4
Old Pond Cl. Friml GU15 .... 65 C1
Old Portsmouth Rd.
  Arting GU2 & GU3 & GU7 ... 130 C3
Old Portsmouth Rd.
  Friml GU15 .... 66 A5
Old Portsmouth Rd.
  Shalf GU2 & GU3 & GU7 ... 130 C3
Old Portsmouth Rd.
  Thursl GU8 .... 169 D4
Old Pottery Cl. Woodh RH2 139 B7
Old Quarry The.
  King Gn GU27 .... 207 F4
Old Rd. Buckl RH3 .... 116 F1
Old Rd. E Grins RH19 .... 185 F1
Old Rd. Row Tn KT15 .... 51 F3
Old Rectory Cl.
  Walt ct H KT20 .... 97 A3
Old Rectory Dr. Ash GU12 106 B2
Old Rectory Gdns.
  Farnb GU14 .... 85 D4
Old Rectory Gdns.
  Godal GU7 .... 150 F2
Old Rectory La. E Hors KT24 92 E1
Old Redstone Dr.
  Earls RH1 .... 140 A8
Old Reigate Rd. Brock RH3 116 C1
Old Reigate Rd.
  Pixham RH4 .... 115 F2
Old Sawmill La.
  Crowth RG11 .... 45 C6
Old School Cl. Ash GU12 .. 106 A3
Old School Cl. Merton SW19 40 A7
Old School Cl. Penge BR3 .... 43 E7
Old School Ct. Wray TW19 .. 11 E8
Old School La. Brock RH3 . 137 A7
Old School La. Newd RH5 .. 158 B1
Old School Mews.
  Oat Pk KT13 .... 53 D6
Old School Pl. Westfd GU22 89 F6

Old School Sq. Thame D KT7 36 F3
Old Schools La. Ewell KT17 . 57 F2
Old Station App. Leahd KT22 95 A6
Old Station Cl.
  Crawl D RH10 .... 204 B7
Old Station Rd. Farnc GU7 . 150 E6
Old Station Way.
  Farnc GU7 .... 150 E5
Old Swan Yd. Carsh SM5 .... 59 F6
Old Town. Croy CR0 & CR9 .. 61 B7
Old Tye Ave. Bigg H TN16 ... 83 E3
Old Westhall Cl.
  Warlgm CR6 .... 101 C8
Old Wickhurst La.
  Broad H RH12 .... 216 D2
Old Woking Rd. Mayb GU22 90 C8
Old Woking Rd.
  Old Wok GU22 .... 90 C8
Old Woking Rd.
  Pyrf GU22 & KT14 .... 70 D3
Old Woking Rd. W Byfl KT14 71 A6
Old Wokingham Rd.
  Crowth RG11 .... 45 C7
Old Wokingham Rd.
  Easth RG11 .... 45 C7
Oldacre. W End GU24 .... 67 F7
Oldbury. Easth RG12 .... 26 F6
Oldbury Cl. Friml GU16 ...... 85 F8
Oldbury Rd. Chert KT16 ..... 32 E2
Olde Farm Dr. Blckw GU17 .. 64 B5
Olden La. Purley CR8 .... 80 A7
Oldfield Gdns. Ashtd KT21 .. 95 D8
Oldfield House. Streat SW16 21 B4
Oldfield House Sch.
  Hampt TW12 .... 35 F8
Oldfield Rd. Hampt TW12 .... 35 F8
Oldfield Rd. Horley RH6 .... 160 F1
Oldfield Rd. Wimble SW19 .. 19 E2
Oldfields Rd.
  Sutton SM1 & SM3 .... 59 A8
Oldfields Trad Est.
  Sutton SM1 .... 59 A7
Oldfieldwood. Mayb GU22 ... 70 B2
Oldham House. **10**
  Dulw SE21 .... 22 E4
Oldhouse La. Bisley GU24 ... 68 A5
Oldhouse La. W End GU24 ... 68 A5
Oldhouse La.
  Windl GU18 & GU24 .... 48 C2
Olding House. **6**
  Streat SW12 .... 21 C8
Oldridge Rd. Balham SW12 .. 21 B8
Oldstead. Brack RG12 .... 27 D4
Oldstead Rd. Catf BR1 ...... 24 C8
Oldwood Chase. Farnb GU14 84 C3
Oleander Cl. Crowth RG11 ... 45 A7
Olive Rd. **3** Merton SW19 .. 20 C1
Oliver Ave. S Norw SE25 ..... 42 F6
Oliver Cl. Addl KT15 .... 52 B6
Oliver Cl. Brent W4 .... 7 B8
Oliver Gr. S Norw SE25 .... 42 F5
Oliver Rd. Ascot SL5 .... 29 B5
Oliver Rd. Horsh RH12 ..... 217 A1
Oliver Rd. King U T KT3 ...... 38 C7
Oliver Rd. Sutton SM1 .... 59 D6
Olivier Rd. Worth RH10 .... 202 D5
Ollerton. Easth RG12 .... 27 A1
Olley Cl. Wallin SM6 .... 60 E4
Olveston Wlk.
  Carsh SM4 & SM5 .... 40 D3
Olyffe Dr. Beck BR3 .... 44 C8
Omega Rd. Woking GU21 .... 70 A3
Omega Way. Thorpe TW20 .. 32 C8
One Tree Cnr. Merrow GU4 131 B8
One Tree Hill Rd.
  Merrow GU4 .... 131 B7
Ongar Cl. Row Tn KT15 .... 51 F4
Ongar Hill. Row Tn KT15 .... 52 A4
Ongar Pl. Row Tn KT15 .... 52 A4
Ongar Place Inf Sch.
  Row Tn KT15 .... 52 A4
Ongar Rd. Addl KT15 .... 52 A5
Onslow Ave. Belm SM2 .... 77 F8
Onslow Ave. Rich TW10 .... 6 E2
Onslow Avenue Mansions. **10**
  Rich TW10 .... 6 E2
Onslow Cl. Thame D KT7 .... 36 E1
Onslow Cl. Woking GU22 .... 70 A2
Onslow Cres. Woking GU22 . 70 A2
Onslow Cty Inf Sch.
  Onsl V GU2 .... 129 F7
Onslow Dr. Ascot SL5 .... 9 A1
Onslow Gdns. Sander CR2 .. 81 A7
Onslow Gdns. Thame D KT7 . 36 E1
Onslow Gdns. Wallin SM6 ... 60 C3
Onslow House. **1**
  King U T KT2 .... 37 F8
Onslow Lodge. Stain TW18 . 12 F1
Onslow Mews. Chert KT16 .. 33 A3
Onslow Rd. Guild GU1 ...... 109 D1
Onslow Rd. New Mal KT3 .... 39 A5

Onslow Rd. Rich TW10 .... 6 E1
Onslow Rd. Sunnin SL5 .... 30 B2
Onslow Rd. Thorn H CR0 ..... 42 A1
Onslow Rd. Whit V KT12 ...... 54 A5
Onslow St. Guild GU1 .... 130 C8
Onslow Way. Pyrf GU22 ...... 70 F4
Onslow Way. Thame D KT7 .. 36 E1
Ontario Cl. Smallf RH6 ..... 162 A2
Onyx House. New Mal KT4 .. 38 D1
Opal House. New Mal KT4 ... 38 D1
Openview.
  Wands SW17 & SW18 .... 20 D6
Opladen Way. Brack RG12 .. 27 E4
Opossum Dr. Hounsl TW4 ..... 4 C4
Opus Pk. Jacobs GU4 .... 109 D6
Oracle Ctr. Brack RG12 ...... 27 C7
Orangery The. Rich TW10 ... 17 C6
Orchard Ave. Ashf TW15 .... 14 C2
Orchard Ave. Carsh CR4 .... 41 A1
Orchard Ave. Croy CR0 ...... 43 E1
Orchard Ave. Hatton TW14 ... 3 D2
Orchard Ave. Heston TW5 ..... 4 E7
Orchard Ave. Hinch W KT7 .. 56 A8
Orchard Ave. King U T KT3 .. 38 E6
Orchard Ave. Woodhm KT15 70 F8
Orchard Bsns Ctr.
  Penge SE26 .... 23 F3
Orchard Bsns Ctr The.
  Salfs RH1 .... 139 E6
Orchard Cl. Ash V GU12 .... 106 A5
Orchard Cl. Ashf TW15 ...... 14 C2
Orchard Cl. Ashtd KT21 ..... 95 D7
Orchard Cl. Banstd SM7 .... 78 B5
Orchard Cl. E Hors KT24 .... 92 F3
Orchard Cl. Farnh GU9 ..... 126 A6
Orchard Cl. Fetch RG22 ..... 94 D5
Orchard Cl. Flexf GU3 ...... 107 B1
Orchard Cl. Horley RH6 .... 160 F4
Orchard Cl. Mayb GU22 ..... 70 B3
Orchard Cl. Merrow GU1 ... 110 B1
Orchard Cl. W Barn SW20 ... 39 C5
Orchard Cl. W End GU24 .... 67 D6
Orchard Cl. W Ewell KT19 .. 57 B4
Orchard Cl. W Ewell KT19 .. 57 B4
Orchard Cl. W Heath GU4 ... 64 F1
Orchard Cl. Walt O T KT12 .. 35 B2
Orchard Cl. Woki RG11 .... 25 D6
Orchard Cotts. Charl RH6 . 180 F7
Orchard Cotts. Leigh RH7 .. 165 B3
Orchard Ct. Barnes SW13 .... 7 F4
Orchard Ct. Brack RG12 ..... 27 C7
Orchard Ct. Croy BR3 .... 44 C1
Orchard Ct. Harm UB7 .... 2 C7
Orchard Ct. Hounsl TW7 ..... 5 D7
Orchard Ct. Walt O T KT12 .. 34 F1
Orchard Cty Fst Sch The.
  E Mole KT8 .... 36 D5
Orchard Dene. W Byfl KT14 . 71 A6
Orchard Dr. Horse GU21 ..... 69 F4
Orchard Dr. Sunby TW17 .... 34 E6
Orchard End. Cater CR3 .... 100 E5
Orchard End. Fetch KT22 .... 94 D5
Orchard End. Oat Pk KT13 .. 53 E8
Orchard End. Rowl GU10 ... 145 F3
Orchard Gate. Sandh GU17 . 64 B8
Orchard Gate.
  Thame D KT10 .... 36 D1
Orchard Gdns. Alder GU11 . 126 C8
Orchard Gdns. Chess KT9 ... 56 E6
Orchard Gdns. Cran GU6 .. 174 F2
Orchard Gdns. Effing KT24 . 113 E7
Orchard Gdns. Epsom KT18 . 76 E6
Orchard Gdns. Sutton SM1 . 59 A5
Orchard Gr. Croy CR0 .... 43 E2
Orchard Gr. Penge SE20 ..... 23 A1
Orchard Hill. Windl GU20 ... 48 D7
Orchard House.
  Merrow GU4 .... 110 D2
Orchard House.
  Tongh GU10 .... 126 F7
Orchard House Cheyne Ctr
  (Hospl). W Wick BR4 .... 63 C7
Orchard Jun & Inf Sch The.
  Hounsl TW5 .... 5 A3
Orchard La. Thame D KT8 ... 36 D3
Orchard La. Wimble SW20 ... 39 B8
Orchard Lea Cl. Pyrf GU22 .. 70 E4
Orchard Mains.
  Woking GU22 .... 89 C8
Orchard Pl. Woki RG11 ...... 25 C6
Orchard Rd. Brent TW8 .... 6 C8
Orchard Rd. Burgh GU4 .... 110 B5
Orchard Rd. Chess KT9 ...... 56 E6
Orchard Rd. Dork RH4 ...... 136 B6
Orchard Rd. Farnb GU14 .... 85 A4
Orchard Rd. Farnh GU9 .... 126 A6
Orchard Rd. Hampt TW12 ... 15 F1
Orchard Rd. Hams Gn CR2 .. 81 B5
Orchard Rd. Horsh RH13 .. 217 C2

Orchard Rd. Hounsl TW4 ...... 5 A2
Orchard Rd. King U T KT1 ... 37 E7
Orchard Rd. Mortl TW9 .... 7 F4
Orchard Rd. Onsl V GU2 ... 129 F7
Orchard Rd. Reig RH2 .... 118 B1
Orchard Rd. Shalf GU4 ..... 130 E3
Orchard Rd. Shere GU5 .... 133 A4
Orchard Rd. Smallf RH6 ... 162 C2
Orchard Rd. Sunby TW16 ... 15 B1
Orchard Rd. Sutton SM1 .... 59 A6
Orchard Rd. Twick TW1 .... 6 B2
Orchard Rise. Croy CR0 ..... 43 F1
Orchard Rise. King U T KT2 .. 38 C8
Orchard Rise. Mortl TW9 ..... 7 B3
Orchard School Sports Ctr.
  Penge SE20 .... 43 A8
Orchard St. Crawl RH11 .... 201 D6
Orchard St. Thame D KT7 ... 37 B2
Orchard The. Banstd SM7 .. 78 A4
Orchard The. Dork RH5 .... 136 C3
Orchard The.Ewell KT17 & 19 57 F3
Orchard The. Ewell KT17 .... 57 F1
Orchard The. Haslem GU27 207 F8
Orchard The. Hounsl TW3 .... 5 C5
Orchard The. Lhtwat GU18 .. 67 B8
Orchard The. Thorpe GU25 .. 31 E4
Orchard The. Westfd GU22 . 89 E5
Orchard The. Weyb KT13 .... 53 B6
Orchard Way. Addl KT15 .... 52 B4
Orchard Way.
  Alder GU11 & GU12 .... 126 C8
Orchard Way. Ashf TW15 ... 13 F6
Orchard Way.
  Beck BR3 & CR0 .... 43 E3
Orchard Way. Camb GU15 .. 65 B2
Orchard Way. Carsh SM1 ... 59 D6
Orchard Way.
  Croy BR3 & CR0 .... 43 E3
Orchard Way. Dork RH4 .... 136 B6
Orchard Way. Dovgn RH2 . 139 B6
Orchard Way. E Grins RH19 185 E1
Orchard Way. Esher KT10 ... 55 C4
Orchard Way. Flexf GU3 .... 107 B1
Orchard Way. L Kings KT20 . 97 F1
Orchard Way. Oxted RH8 .. 123 A2
Orchard Way. Send GU23 ... 90 C2
Orchard Way Prim Sch.
  Croy CR0 .... 43 E2
Orchardfield Rd. Farnc GU7 150 F7
Orchardleigh. Leahd KT22 ... 95 B5
Orchards Cl. W Byfl KT14 .... 71 A5
Orchards The. Ashf TW15 ... 14 D3
Orchards The. **4**
  Crawl RH11 .... 200 D5
Orchards The. Horsh RH12 217 F5
Orchid Dr. Bisley GU24 .... 68 A4
Orde Cl. Crawl RH10 .... 182 D1
Ordnance Cl. Felt TW13 ..... 15 A6
Ordnance Rd. Alder GU11 .. 105 C3
Ordnance Rdbt.
  Alder GU11 .... 105 B2
Oregano Way. Stough GU2 109 A6
Oregon Cl. King U T KT3 .... 38 C5
Orestan La. Effing KT24 .... 113 C8
Orford Ct. W Norw SE27 .... 22 B6
Orford Ct. Wallin SM6 .... 60 C5
Orford Gdns. Twick TW1 ..... 16 F6
Orford Rd. Catf SE6 .... 24 B5
Oriel Cl. Crawl RH10 .... 182 C1
Oriel Cl. Mitch CR4 .... 41 D6
Oriel Ct. **6** Croy CR0 .... 42 E1
Oriel Hill. Camb GU15 .... 65 D4
Oriel Jun & Inf Sch.
  Felt TW13 .... 15 E5
Oriental Cl. Woking GU22 ... 70 A2
Oriental Rd. Ascot SL5 .... 29 D5
Oriental Rd. Woking GU22 ... 70 A3
Orion. Easth RG12 .... 27 A1
Orion Ct. Crawl RH11 .... 200 D4
Orion Ctr The. Wallin CR0 .. 60 E8
Orlando Gdns. Epsom KT19 . 57 D1
Orlean Ct. Walt O T KT12 .... 54 C8
Orleans Cl. Esher KT10 .... 55 D8
Orleans Ct. **10** Twick TW1 .. 17 B8
Orleans Inf Sch. Twick TW1 17 B8
Orleans Park Sec Sch.
  Twick TW1 .... 17 B8
Orleans Rd. S Norw SE19 ... 22 D2
Orleans Rd. **10** Twick TW1 .. 17 B8
Orltons La. Rusper RH12 ... 179 F2
Ormanton Rd. For Hil SE26 . 23 A4
Orme Rd. King U T KT1 & KT3 38 B7
Ormeley Rd. Balham SW12 .. 21 B7
Ormerod Gdns. Mitch CR4 .. 41 A8
Ormesby Wlk. Crawl RH10 202 B4
Ormond Ave. Hampt TW12 .. 36 B8
Ormond Ave. **22** Rich TW10 . 6 D2
Ormond Cres. Hampt TW12 . 36 B8
Ormond Dr. Hampt TW12 ... 16 B1
Ormond Rd. Rich TW10 .... 6 D2
Ormonde Ave. Epsom KT19 . 57 D1

Ormonde Lodge (West London Ins of Higher Education). Islew TW1 6 B2
Ormonde Rd. Farnc GU7 150 E6
Ormonde Rd. Horse GU21 69 C3
Ormonde Rd. Mortl SW14 7 C4
Ormonde Rd. Woki RG11 25 A5
Ormsby. Sutton SM2 59 B3
Ormside Way. Redh RH1 119 B4
Ormuz Cotts. Lingf RH7 164 C4
Orpin Rd. Merst RH1 119 C5
Orpwood Cl. Hampt TW12 15 F2
Orwell Cl. W Heath GU14 84 E6
Orwell Gdns. Reig RH2 139 B7
Orwell House. 7 Redh RH1 118 F2
Osborn La. For Hil SE23 23 E8
Osborn Rd. Farnh GU9 125 D4
Osborne Ave. Stan TW19 13 F7
Osborne Cl. Beck BR3 43 E5
Osborne Cl. Felt TW13 15 D3
Osborne Cl. Friml GU16 85 F8
Osborne Ct. Crawl RH11 201 B2
Osborne Ct. Farnb GU14 105 C8
Osborne Ct. 10 Surb KT6 37 E3
Osborne Dr. Lhtwat GU18 67 A8
Osborne Gdns. S Norw CR7 42 C7
Osborne Pl. Carsh SM1 59 D5
Osborne Rd. Egham TW20 11 F2
Osborne Rd. Farnb GU14 105 C8
Osborne Rd. Hounsl TW3 & TW4 4 F4
Osborne Rd. King U T KT2 17 E1
Osborne Rd. Redh RH1 119 A4
Osborne Rd. S Norw CR7 42 C7
Osborne Rd. Walt O T KT12 35 A1
Osborne Rd. Woki RG11 25 C6
Osbourne Terr. 1 Up Toot SW17 21 A3
Osier Way. Mitch CR4 40 F4
Osier Way. Nork KT17 & SM7 77 E5
Oslac Rd. Catf SE6 24 B3
Oslo Ct. Mitch SW19 20 D1
Osman's Cl. Wink RG12 8 B1
Osmond Gdns. Wallin SM6 60 C5
Osmund Cl. Worth RH10 202 E6
Osmunda Bank. Dorm Pk RH19 185 E6
Osnaburgh Hill. Camb GU15 65 B5
Osney Cl. Crawl RH11 201 C5
Osney Wlk. Carsh SM4 & SM5 40 D3
Osprey Cl. Fetch KT22 94 C5
Osprey Gdns. Selsd CR0 & CR2 62 E1
Ospringe Cl. 9 Penge SE20 23 C1
Ostade Rd. Streat SW2 21 F8
Osterley Ave. Hounsl TW7 5 D7
Osterley Cl. Woki RG11 25 F5
Osterley Cres. Hounsl TW7 5 F6
Osterley Ct. Hounsl TW7 5 D6
Osterley Lodge. 1 Hounsl TW7 5 E6
Osterley Rd. Hounsl TW7 5 E6
Osterley Sta. Hounsl TW7 5 D7
Osterly Gdns. S Norw CR7 42 C7
Oswald Cl. Fetch KT22 94 C5
Oswald Rd. Fetch KT22 94 C5
Osward. New Add CR0 62 F1
Osward Rd. Up Toot SW12 & SW17 20 F6
Otford Cl. Penge SE20 43 C8
Othello Gr. Wink RG12 27 E8
Otho Ct. 5 Brent TW8 6 D7
Otter Cl. Crowth RG11 45 A7
Otter Cl. Ottsh KT16 51 B4
Otterbourne Rd. 1 Croy CR0 & CR9 61 C8
Otterburn Gdns. Hounsl TW7 6 A7
Otterburn St. Up Toot SW17 20 F2
Otterden St. Catf SE6 24 A4
Ottermead La. Ottsh KT16 51 C4
Ottershaw Hospl. Ottsh KT16 51 D4
Ottershaw House. Mitch CR4 40 D7
Ottershaw Pk. Ottsh KT16 51 A3
Ottways Ave. Ashtd KT21 95 D8
Ottways La. Ashtd KT21 & KT22 95 D8
Otway Cl. Crawl RH11 200 F4
Oulton Wlk. Crawl RH10 202 B4
Our Lady of the Rosary RC Sch. Stain TW18 13 A2
Our Lady Queen Of Heaven RC (Aided) Sch. Crawl RH11 201 B8
Our Lady Queen of Heaven RC Prim Sch. Putney SW19 19 D8
Our Lady & St Philip Neri Prim Sch. For Hil SE26 23 E4
Our Lady & St Philip Neri RC Sch. For Hil SE23 23 D5
Our Lady & St Philip Neri RC Sch. For Hil SE26 23 E4
Our Lady's Prep Sch. Crowth RG11 45 B5
Our Ladys RC First Sch. Chert KT16 33 A1
Ouseley Rd. Up Toot SW12 20 F7
Ouseley Rd. Wray TW19 11 D8
Outdowns. Effing KT24 113 B5
Outram Pl. Whit V KT13 53 C5
Outram Rd. Croy CR0 61 F8
Outwood House. 6 Streat SW2 21 F8
Outwood La. Bletch RH1 141 D7
Outwood La. Chips CR5 & KT20 98 C6
Outwood La. Kings CR5 & KT20 98 C6
Outwood La. Outw RH1 141 D1
Oval Prim Sch. Croy CR0 42 E1
Oval Rd. Croy CR0 42 E1
Oval The. Banstd SM7 78 A5
Oval The. Farnc GU7 150 F7
Oval The. Guild GU2 130 A8
Oval The. Wood S V GU3 108 B2
Overbrae. Beck BR3 24 A3
Overbrook. Godal GU7 151 A5
Overbrook. W Hors KT24 112 B6
Overbury Ave. Beck BR3 44 C6
Overbury Cres. New Add CR0 63 C1
Overbury Ct. Beck BR3 44 C6
Overdale. Ashtd KT21 75 E3
Overdale. Bletch RH1 120 C2
Overdale. Dork RH5 136 D8
Overdale Ave. King U T KT3 38 D7
Overdale Rise. Friml GU15 65 E3
Overdene Dr. Crawl RH11 201 A6
Overdown Rd. Catf SE6 24 B4
Overford Cl. Cran GU6 174 E2
Overford Dr. Cran GU6 174 E2
Overhill. Warlgm CR6 101 C8
Overhill Rd. Dulw SE21 & SE22 23 A8
Overhill Rd. Wallin CR8 61 A1
Overhill Way. Beck BR3 44 D4
Overlord Cl. Camb GU15 65 C8
Overstand Cl. Beck BR3 44 A4
Overstone Gdns. Croy CR0 43 F2
Overthorpe. Knaph GU21 68 E2
Overton Cl. Alder GU11 126 C6
Overton Cl. Hounsl TW7 5 F6
Overton House. Rhampt SW15 18 F8
Overton Rd. Belm SM2 59 A3
Overton Shaw. E Grins RH19 185 E4
Overton's Yd. Croy CR0 & CR9 61 C7
Oveton Way. G Book KT23 94 B1
Ovett Cl. S Norw SE19 22 E2
Ovington Ct. Woking GU21 68 F3
Owen Cl. Thorn H CR0 42 D3
Owen House. Felt TW14 15 A8
Owen House. 6 Twick TW1 17 B8
Owen Pl. Leahd KT22 95 B5
Owen Rd. Farnc GU7 150 F6
Owen Rd. Windl GU20 48 D5
Owen Wlk. 7 Penge SE20 23 A1
Owens Way. For Hil SE23 23 E8
Owl Cl. Selsd CR2 62 D1
Owlbeech Ct. Horsh RH13 218 B4
Owlbeech Pl. Horsh RH13 218 B4
Owlbeech Way. Horsh RH13 218 B4
Owletts. Crawl RH10 202 D7
Owlscastle Cl. Horsh RH12 217 D5
Owlsmoor Cty Prim Sch. Sandh GU15 45 E1
Owlsmoor Rd. Sandh GU15 45 D1
Ownstead Gdns. S Croy CR2 80 F8
Ownsted Hill. New Add CR0 63 D1
Oxdowne Cl. Oxsh KT11 74 B5
Oxenden Ct. Alder GU10 126 E8
Oxenden Rd. Ash GU10 & GU12 126 F8
Oxenhope. Easth RG12 27 A5
Oxford Ave. Harl TW6 3 F7
Oxford Ave. Heston TW5 5 A8
Oxford Ave. Merton SW20 39 E7
Oxford Cl. Littlt TW15 & TW17 14 C1
Oxford Cl. Mitch CR4 41 C6
Oxford Cres. New Mal KT3 38 D3
Oxford Ct. Epsom KT18 76 E5
Oxford Ct. 17 King U T KT6 37 E4
Oxford Gdns. Brent W4 7 A8
Oxford Rd. Carsh SM2 & SM5 59 E5
Oxford Rd. Crawl RH10 201 F2
Oxford Rd. Farnb GU14 85 C1
Oxford Rd. Guild GU1 130 D7
Oxford Rd. Horsh RH13 217 E2
Oxford Rd. Redh RH1 118 E2
Oxford Rd. S Norw SE19 22 D2
Oxford Rd. Sandh GU15 45 E2
Oxford Rd. Tedd TW11 & TW12 16 D3
Oxford Rd. Wallin SM6 60 C5
Oxford Rd. Woki RG11 25 A6
Oxford Terr. Guild GU1 130 D7
Oxford Way. Felt TW13 15 D4
Oxleigh Cl. New Mal KT3 38 E4
Oxlip Cl. Croy CR0 43 D1
Oxshott Rd. Ashtd KT22 74 F3
Oxshott Rd. Leahd KT22 75 A2
Oxshott Rise. Cobham KT11 73 E5
Oxshott Sta. Oxsh KT22 74 C6
Oxshott Way. Cobham KT11 73 E4
Oxted Cl. Mitch CR4 40 D6
Oxted Cty Sch. Limps RH8 122 F7
Oxted Gn. Witley GU8 170 E7
Oxted Hospl. Oxted RH8 122 D7
Oxted Rd. Tand RH9 121 D4
Oxted Rd. Tyl Gn RH9 121 D4
Oxted Sta. Oxted RH8 122 E6
Oxtoby Way. Mitch SW16 41 D8
Oyster La. Byfl KT14 71 E7

Pacific Cl. E Bed TW14 14 F7
Packer Cl. E Grins RH19 186 A3
Packham Ct. N Cheam KT4 58 C7
Packway. M Bourn GU9 146 E7
Padbrook. Limps RH8 123 A6
Padbury Cl. E Bed TW14 14 D7
Padbury Oaks. Harm UB7 2 B6
Paddock Cl. Bear Gn RH5 157 D4
Paddock Cl. Camb GU15 66 A6
Paddock Cl. Cobham KT11 73 C5
Paddock Cl. For Hil SE26 23 D4
Paddock Cl. Hambl GU8 171 C1
Paddock Cl. New Mal KT4 38 E1
Paddock Cl. Oxted RH8 122 F4
Paddock Ct. W Barn SW20 39 C5
Paddock Gdns. E Grins RH19 205 E7
Paddock Gdns. S Norw SE19 22 E2
Paddock Gr. Bear Gn RH5 157 D4
Paddock House. Merrow GU4 110 D2
Paddock Sch. Rhampt SW15 7 F3
Paddock The. Add CR0 63 A4
Paddock The. Brack RG12 27 C6
Paddock The. Cran GU6 174 D3
Paddock The. Crawl RH10 202 D7
Paddock The. Crowth RG11 45 A6
Paddock The. Ewh GU6 175 E4
Paddock The. Godal GU7 150 F3
Paddock The. Graysh GU26 188 A4
Paddock The. Merrow GU1 110 D2
Paddock The. Shottm GU27 208 A8
Paddock The. Westc RH4 135 C6
Paddock Way. Grays GU27 190 A2
Paddock Way. Oxted RH8 122 F4
Paddock Way. Sheer GU21 70 B5
Paddock Wlk. Warlgm CR6 101 B8
Paddockhurst Rd. Crawl RH11 201 A5
Paddockhurst Rd. Worth RH10 203 C2
Paddocks Cl. Ashtd KT21 75 E1
Paddocks Mead. Woking GU21 68 F3
Paddocks Rd. Burph GU4 110 A5
Paddocks The. Flexf GU3 107 C1
Paddocks The. G Book KT23 94 B1
Paddocks The. Oat Pk KT13 53 E7
Paddocks Way. Ashtd KT21 75 E1
Paddocks Way. Chert KT16 33 B1
Padstow Wlk. Crawl RH11 200 F4
Padstow Wlk. E Bed TW14 14 F7
Padua Rd. Penge SE20 43 C8
Padwick Rd. Horsh RH13 218 A2
Page Cl. Hampt TW12 15 E2
Page Cres. Croy CR0 61 B5
Page Croft. Chert KT15 52 B8
Page Ct. Horsh RH13 217 D1
Page Rd. E Bed TW14 3 D1
Page's Croft. Woki RG11 25 D5
Page's Yd. Chisw W4 7 E8
Pageant Wlk. S Croy CR0 61 E7
Pagehurst Rd. Croy CR0 43 B2
Paget Ave. Carsh SM1 59 D7
Paget Cl. Camb GU15 66 B7
Paget Cl. Hampt TW12 16 D4
Paget La. Islew TW7 5 E4
Paget Pl. King U T KT2 18 C2
Paget Pl. Thame D KT7 36 F1
Pagoda Ave. Rich TW9 6 F4
Paice Gn. Woki RG11 25 D7
Pain's Cl. Mitch CR4 41 B7
Paines Hill. Limps RH8 123 C4
Paisley Rd. Carsh SM5 40 D1
Pakenham Cl. Up Toot SW12 21 A7
Palace Ct. S Norw CR7 42 D5
Palace Ct. Streat SW2 22 A6
Palace Ct. Woking GU21 70 A3
Palace Dr. Weyb KT13 53 B7
Palace Gn. New Add CR0 62 F3
Palace Gr. Penge SE19 22 F1
Palace Rd. E Mole KT8 36 D6
Palace Rd. King U T KT1 37 D5
Palace Rd. Penge SE19 22 F1
Palace Rd. Streat SE27 & SW16 & SW2 22 A6
Palace Rd. Woodhm KT15 52 B2
Palace Sq. Penge SE19 22 F1
Palace View. Croy CR0 62 F6
Palestine Gr. Mitch SW19 40 D8
Palewell Common Dr. Mortl SW14 7 D2
Palewell Pk. Mortl SW14 7 D3
Palgrave House. 4 Twick TW2 16 C8
Pallingham Dr. Worth RH10 202 C3
Palm Ct. Beck BR3 43 F6
Palm Gr. Bellf GU1 109 C5
Palmer Ave. Cheam KT4 & SM3 58 C6
Palmer C of E Jun Sch The. Woki RG11 25 D7
Palmer Cl. Crowth RG11 45 A8
Palmer Cl. Earls RH1 140 A8
Palmer Cl. Heston TW5 5 A6
Palmer Cl. Horley RH6 160 F5
Palmer Cl. W Wick BR4 63 D8
Palmer Cres. King U T KT1 37 E6
Palmer Cres. Ottsh KT16 51 D4
Palmer Rd. Worth RH10 202 C3
Palmer School Rd. Woki RG11 25 C6
Palmer's Lodge. Guild GU2 130 B8
Palmers Gr. E Mole KT8 36 A5
Palmers Rd. Mortl SW14 7 C4
Palmers Rd. Thorn H SW16 41 F7
Palmersfield Rd. Banstd SM7 78 B5
Palmerston Cl. Horse GU21 70 A5
Palmerston Ct. 9 Surb KT6 37 D2
Palmerston Gr. 4 Merton SW19 20 A1
Palmerston House. Banstd SM7 77 F4
Palmerston Rd. Carsh SM5 60 A6
Palmerston Rd. Merton SW19 20 A1
Palmerston Rd. Mortl SW14 7 C3
Palmerston Rd. Sutton SM1 59 C5
Palmerston Rd. Thorn H CR0 42 D4
Palmerston Rd. Twick TW2 5 E1
Pampisford Rd.Croy CR2 & 8 61 B2
Pampisford Rd. Purley CR2 & CR8 61 B2
Pams Way. W Ewell KT19 57 D5
Pan's Gdns. Friml GU15 65 F4
Pandora Ct. 4 Surb KT6 37 E3
Pangbourne Ct. Up Toot SW17 20 C4
Pankhurst Ct. 11 Crawl RH11 201 B1
Pankhurst Dr. Brack RG12 27 D4
Pankhurst Rd. Walt O T KT12 35 C2
Panmuir Rd. Wimble SW20 39 B8
Panmure Rd. For Hil SE26 23 B5
Pannell Cl. E Grins RH19 185 D1
Pannells. M Bourn GU10 146 D5
Pannells Cl. Chert KT16 32 F1
Pannells Ct. Guild GU1 130 D8
Pantile Rd. Oat Pk KT13 53 D6
Pantiles Cl. Woking GU21 69 B1
Paper Mews. Dork RH4 136 B8
Papercourt La. Ripley GU23 90 F6
Papplewick Sch. N Asct SL5 29 A2
Papworth Way. Streat SW2 22 A8
Parade Cl. Send GU23 90 C4
Parade Mews. Streat SE27 & SW2 22 B6
Parade The. Ash GU12 106 A4
Parade The. Ashf TW16 14 F1
Parade The. Burgh H KT20 97 E8
Parade The. Clayg KT10 55 E4
Parade The. Coulsd CR5 80 A1
Parade The. Epsom KT18 76 D6
Parade The. 2 King U T KT2 37 E7
Parade The. Wallin CR0 60 F5
Parade The. Went GU25 31 D3
Paradise Rd. Rich TW10 6 E2
Paragon Gr. Surb KT5 37 F3
Parbury Rise. Chess KT9 56 E4
Parchmore Rd. S Norw CR7 42 C6
Parchmore Way. S Norw CR7 42 B7
Pares Cl. Horse GU21 69 D3
Parfew Ct. Dulw SE22 23 B6
Parfitts Cl. Farnh GU9 125 A2
Parfour Dr. Kenley CR8 80 C3
Parham Rd. Crawl RH11 200 F7
Parish Church C of E Inf & Jun Schs. Croy CR9 61 B7
Parish Cl. Hale GU9 125 A6
Parish Ct. King U T KT6 37 E3
Parish House. 6 Crawl RH11 201 D5
Parish La. Penge SE20 & SE26 23 D1
Parish Rd. Farnb GU14 105 B8
Park Ave. Broml BR1 24 F2
Park Ave. Camb GU15 65 D4
Park Ave. Cater CR3 100 E3
Park Ave. Egham TW20 12 C1
Park Ave. Islew TW3 5 B1
Park Ave. Mitch CR4 21 B1
Park Ave. Mortl SW14 7 D3
Park Ave. P Harow GU8 149 C5
Park Ave. Salfs RH1 139 F1
Park Ave. Stain TW18 13 A2
Park Ave. Up Hall TW17 34 E6
Park Ave. W Wick BR4 63 C8
Park Ave. Wallin SM5 60 A4
Park Ave. Woki RG11 25 B6
Park Ave E. Stonel KT17 58 A4
Park Ave W. Stonel KT17 58 A4
Park Barn Dr. Stough GU2 & GU3 108 E2
Park Barn E. Stough GU2 108 F2
Park Chase. Godal GU7 150 E2
Park Chase. Guild GU1 109 E1
Park Cl. Binst GU10 145 A2
Park Cl. Brock RH3 137 B4
Park Cl. Esher KT10 55 A4
Park Cl. Fetch KT22 94 D3
Park Cl. Grays GU27 190 A1
Park Cl. Hampt TW12 36 C8
Park Cl. Islew TW3 & TW7 5 C2
Park Cl. King U T KT2 38 A8
Park Cl. Oat Pk KT13 53 F8
Park Cl. Wallin SM5 59 F4
Park Cl. Woodhm KT15 52 C1
Park Close Cotts. Eng Gn TW20 10 F3
Park Copse. Dork RH5 136 D7
Park Corner Dr. E Hors KT24 112 E7
Park Cotts. 10 Twick TW1 6 B1
Park Cres. Sunnin SL5 29 F3
Park Cres. Twick TW2 16 D7
Park Ct. Beck BR3 44 B6
Park Ct. New Mal KT3 38 D5
Park Ct. Tedd KT1 37 C8
Park Ct. Up Toot SW12 21 A7
Park Ct. W Norw SE21 22 D5
Park Ct. Wallin SM6 60 E5
Park Ct. Woking GU22 69 F1
Park Dr. Bramly GU5 151 F6
Park Dr. Cran GU6 174 F3
Park Dr. Mortl SW14 7 D3
Park Dr. Sunnin SL5 29 F3
Park Dr. Weyb KT13 53 B5
Park Dr. Woking GU22 69 F1
Park End. Broml BR1 44 F8
Park Farm Cl. Horsh RH12 217 D7
Park Farm Ind Est. Friml GU16 65 C1
Park Farm Rd. Horsh RH12 217 D7
Park Farm Rd. King U T KT2 17 E1
Park Gate Cotts. Cran GU6 174 C3
Park Gate Ct. Tedd TW12 16 C3
Park Gate Ct. 11 Woking GU22 69 E1
Park Gdns. King U T KT2 17 F3
Park Gn. Fetch KT23 94 A3
Park Hall Rd. Dulw SE21 22 D5
Park Hall Rd. Reig RH2 118 A3
Park Hall Rd. W Norw SE21 22 D5
Park Hall Road Trad Est. W Norw SE27 22 D5
Park Hill. For Hil SE23 23 C7
Park Hill. Rich TW10 6 F1
Park Hill. Wallin SM5 59 F4
Park Hill Cl. Carsh SM5 59 E5
Park Hill Ct. S Croy CR0 61 E8
Park Hill Ct. Up Toot SW17 20 F5
Park Hill Inf Sch. S Croy CR0 61 E7
Park Hill Jun Sch. S Croy CR0 61 E7
Park Hill Rd. Beck BR2 44 E7
Park Hill Rd. Ewell KT17 76 F8
Park Hill Rd. S Croy CR0 & CR2 61 E7
Park Hill Rd. Wallin SM6 60 B3
Park Hill Rise. S Croy CR0 61 F7

Park Hill Sch. King U T KT2 ... 18 A1
Park Horsley. E Hors KT24 113 A6
Park House. Penge SE26 ... 23 A3
Park House. Woodh RH2 ... 138 F7
Park House Cotts.
Cran GU6 ... 174 F3
Park House Dr. Woodh RH2 138 F7
Park House Gdns. Twick TW1 6 C2
Park House Mid Sch.
Wimble SW19 ... 19 F4
Park La. Ash W RH19 ... 206 D6
Park La. Ashtd KT21 ... 96 A8
Park La. Camb GU15 ... 65 C5
Park La. Cheam SM3 ... 58 E4
Park La. Cranf TW5 ... 4 A7
Park La. Croy CR0 & CR9 ... 61 D7
Park La. Hooley CR5 ... 99 D6
Park La. Horton SL3 ... 1 A4
Park La. Lingf RH7 ... 164 F5
Park La. Merrow GU4 ... 110 D3
Park La. Ockley RH5 ... 177 F7
Park La. Reig RH2 ... 138 E8
Park La. Rich TW9 ... 6 D3
Park La. Tedd TW11 ... 16 F2
Park La. Wallin SM5 & SM6 .. 60 A5
Park La. Wink SL4 ... 9 B7
Park La E. Reig RH2 ... 139 A7
Park La E. Woodh RH2 ... 139 A7
Park Lawn. S Norw CR7 ... 42 C7
Park Lawn Rd. Weyb KT13 ... 53 C6
Park Ley Rd. Wold CR3 ... 101 D6
Park Mansions. For Hil SE26 23 C5
Park Mead Grant Maintd Jun Sch.
Cran GU6 ... 175 A3
Park Mead Inf Sch.
Cran GU6 ... 175 A3
Park Mews. Stan TW19 ... 13 F8
Park Pl. Hampt TW12 ... 16 C2
Park Pl. Horsh RH12 ... 217 C1
Park Pl. 4 Woking GU22 ... 69 F1
Park Prim Sch. Alder GU11 126 C7
Park Rd. Albury GU5 ... 132 E2
Park Rd. Alder GU11 ... 126 B8
Park Rd. Ashf TW15 ... 14 B3
Park Rd. Ashtd KT21 ... 75 E1
Park Rd. Banstd SM7 ... 78 C3
Park Rd. Beck BR3 ... 23 F1
Park Rd. Brack RG12 ... 27 D8
Park Rd. Burst RH6 ... 162 C1
Park Rd. Camb GU15 ... 65 C4
Park Rd. Cater CR3 ... 100 E4
Park Rd. Cheam SM3 ... 58 E4
Park Rd. Chisw W4 ... 7 D8
Park Rd. Crow RH7 ... 143 E2
Park Rd. Dorm Pk RH19 ... 185 F6
Park Rd. E Grins RH19 ... 185 D1
Park Rd. E Mole KT8 ... 36 C5
Park Rd. Egham TW20 ... 12 A4
Park Rd. Esher KT10 ... 55 B6
Park Rd.
Farnb GU11 & GU14 ... 105 E8
Park Rd. Farnh GU9 ... 125 D4
Park Rd. Faygt RH12 ... 199 F1
Park Rd. Felt TW13 ... 15 D4
Park Rd. Fickl CR6 ... 82 E5
Park Rd. For Row RH18 ... 206 F2
Park Rd. Godal GU7 ... 150 E2
Park Rd. Guild GU1 ... 109 D1
Park Rd. Hackb SM6 ... 60 B8
Park Rd. Hampt TW12 ... 16 C3
Park Rd. Haslem GU27 ... 208 C5
Park Rd. Islew TW3 & TW7 ... 5 C2
Park Rd. Islew TW7 ... 6 B5
Park Rd. Kenley CR8 ... 80 C4
Park Rd.
King U T KT2 & TW10 ... 18 A1
Park Rd. Limps RH8 ... 122 F7
Park Rd. Lo Hall TW17 ... 34 A1
Park Rd. Mayb GU22 ... 70 B2
Park Rd. Mitch SW19 ... 20 E2
Park Rd. New Mal KT3 ... 38 D5
Park Rd. Redh RH1 ... 118 F3
Park Rd. Rich TW10 ... 6 F1
Park Rd. S Norw SE25 ... 42 E5
Park Rd. Sandh GU17 ... 64 C8
Park Rd. Slinfd RH13 ... 215 D3
Park Rd. Stan TW19 ... 2 C1
Park Rd. Sunby TW16 ... 15 B1
Park Rd. Surb KT5 ... 37 C8
Park Rd. Tedd TW11 ... 16 F2
Park Rd. Tedd KT1 ... 37 C8
Park Rd. Twick TW1 ... 6 C1
Park Rd. Wallin SM6 ... 60 B5
Park Rd. Woki RG11 ... 25 B6
Park Rd. Woking GU22 ... 70 A2
Park Rd.
Woodm CR5 & KT20 & SM7 . 78 C3
Park Rise. For Hil SE23 ... 23 E7
Park Rise. Horsh RH12 ... 217 B4
Park Rise. Leahd KT22 ... 95 B6
Park Rise Cl. Leahd KT22 ... 95 B6
Park Rise Rd. For Hil SE23 ... 23 E7
Park Road House. 3
King U T KT2 ... 18 A1
Park Row. Farnh GU9 ... 125 B3
Park Sch The. Woking GU22 70 A2
Park Sheen. Mortl SW14 ... 7 B3
Park Side. Woodhm KT15 ... 52 C1
Park Sq. 1 Esher KT10 ... 55 B6
Park St. Bagsh GU19 ... 47 E3
Park St. Camb GU15 ... 65 C5
Park St. Croy CR0 & CR9 ... 61 C8
Park St. Guild GU1 & GU2 ... 130 C7
Park St. Horsh RH12 ... 217 D2
Park St. Poyle SL3 ... 1 D6
Park St. Slinfd RH13 ... 215 C3
Park St. Tedd TW11 ... 16 E2
Park Terr. Carsh SM5 ... 59 E7
Park Terr. New Mal KT4 ... 39 A1
Park Terr E. Horsh RH13 ... 217 D1
Park Terr W. Horsh RH13 .. 217 D1
Park The. Fetch KT23 ... 94 A3
Park The. For Hil SE23 ... 23 C7
Park The. Wallin SM5 ... 59 F5
Park View. Addl KT15 ... 52 C5
Park View. Bagsh GU19 ... 47 D3
Park View. Fetch KT23 ... 94 A2
Park View. Horley RH6 ... 161 A3
Park View. Morden CR4 ... 40 D4
Park View. New Mal KT3 ... 38 F6
Park View. Purley CR8 ... 80 B8
Park View. Tand RH8 ... 143 B5
Park View Ct. Woking GU22 . 89 F8
Park View Rd. Salfs RH1 ... 140 A1
Park View Rd. Wold CR3 ... 101 F5
Park Way. Crawl RH10 ... 202 C7
Park Way. E Mole KT8 ... 36 B6
Park Way. Felt TW14 ... 15 B8
Park Way. Fetch KT23 ... 94 A4
Park Way. Horsh RH12 ... 217 C2
Park Wood Cl. Nork SM7 ... 77 D4
Park Wood Rd. Nork SM7 ... 77 D4
Park Wood View. Nork SM7 77 D4
Park Works Rd. Nutf RH1 ... 119 E2
Parkcroft Rd. Lewish SE12 ... 24 F8
Parkdale Cres. Worc Pk KT4 57 D7
Parke Rd. Sunby TW16 ... 35 A5
Parker Cl. Worth RH10 ... 202 D5
Parker Ct. Wimble SW19 ... 19 E1
Parker Rd. Croy CR0 & CR9 .. 61 C6
Parker's Cl. Ashtd KT21 ... 95 E8
Parker's Hill. Ashtd KT21 ... 95 E8
Parker's La. Ashtd KT21 ... 95 F8
Parker's La. Wink RG12 & SL4 8 B5
Parkfield. Godal GU7 ... 150 F2
Parkfield. Horsh RH12 ... 217 C3
Parkfield. 3 Hounsl TW7 ... 5 E6
Parkfield Ave. Felt TW13 ... 15 A5
Parkfield Ave. Mortl SW14 ... 7 E3
Parkfield Cl. Crawl RH11 ... 200 F6
Parkfield Cres. Felt TW13 ... 15 A5
Parkfield Par. Felt TW13 ... 15 A5
Parkfield Rd. Felt TW13 ... 15 A5
Parkfields. Croy CR0 ... 43 F1
Parkfields. Oxsh KT22 ... 74 D8
Parkfields Ave.
Wimble SW20 ... 39 B7
Parkfields Cl. Hackb SM5 ... 60 A6
Parkfields Rd. King U T TW10 17 F3
Parkgate Cl. King U T KT2 ... 18 B2
Parkgate Gdns. Mortl SW14 .. 7 D2
Parkgate Rd. Newd RH5 ... 158 C3
Parkgate Rd. Parkg RH5 ... 158 C3
Parkgate Rd. Reig RH2 ... 139 B8
Parkgate Rd.
Wallin SM5 & SM6 ... 60 B5
Parkham Ct. Beck BR2 ... 44 E7
Parkhill Cl. Blckw GU17 ... 64 D4
Parkhill Rd. Blckw GU17 ... 64 D4
Parkhurst. Epsom KT19 ... 57 C1
Parkhurst Cotts.
Churt GU10 ... 187 F8
Parkhurst Fields.
Churt GU10 ... 167 F1
Parkhurst Gr. Horley RH6 ... 160 F4
Parkhurst Rd. Carsh SM1 ... 59 D6
Parkhurst Rd. Horley RH6 .. 160 E4
Parkhurst Rd. Stough GU2 ... 109 B2
Parkin House. Penge SE20 ... 23 D1
Parkland Dr. Brack RG12 ... 27 E8
Parkland Gdns. 12
Putney SW19 ... 19 D7
Parkland Gr. Ashf TW15 ... 14 A4
Parkland Gr. Heath E GU9 .. 125 F8
Parkland Rd. Ashf TW15 ... 14 A4
Parklands. Addl KT15 ... 52 C5
Parklands. Dork RH5 ... 136 B3
Parklands. Fetch KT23 ... 94 A4
Parklands. King U T KT5 ... 37 F4
Parklands. Oxted RH8 ... 122 E4
Parklands. Redh RH1 ... 119 A3
Parklands Cl. Mortl SW14 ... 7 C2
Parklands Ct. Heston TW5 ... 4 D5
Parklands Pl. Merrow GU1 ... 110 B1
Parklands Rd.
Streat SW16 & SW17 ... 21 B3
Parklands Way. Worc Pk KT4 57 E8
Parklawn Ave. Epsom KT18 . 76 B6
Parklawn Ave. Horley RH6 . 160 F5
Parkleigh Ct. Merton SW19 . 40 B7
Parkleigh Rd. Merton SW19 . 40 B7
Parkleys.
King U T KT2 & TW10 ... 17 D4
Parkleys. Rich KT2 & TW10 ... 17 D4
Parkpale La. Betch RH3 ... 137 A4
Parkshot. Rich TW9 ... 6 E3
Parkside. Beck BR3 ... 44 B7
Parkside. Cheam SM3 ... 58 E4
Parkside. Crawl RH10 ... 201 E6
Parkside. E Grins RH19 ... 185 C1
Parkside. Hale GU9 ... 125 C6
Parkside. Tedd TW12 ... 16 C3
Parkside. Wimble SW19 ... 19 D4
Parkside Ave. Wimble SW19 19 D3
Parkside Cl. E Hors KT24 ... 92 F2
Parkside Cl. Penge SE20 ... 23 C1
Parkside Cres. Tolw KT5 ... 38 C3
Parkside Ct. Weyb KT13 ... 53 A6
Parkside Gdns. Coulsd CR5 .. 79 B2
Parkside Gdns.
Wimble SW19 ... 19 D4
Parkside Hospl.
Wimble SW19 ... 19 D5
Parkside Mews.
Horsh RH12 ... 217 D2
Parkside Pl. E Hors KT24 ... 92 F2
Parkside Rd. Hounsl TW3 ... 5 B2
Parkside Rd. Sunnin SL5 ... 30 A4
Parkside Sch. Stk D'A KT11 .. 74 A1
Parkstone Dr. Camb GU15 ... 65 C4
Parkthorne Rd. Streat SW12 21 D8
Parkview Lodge. Beck BR3 .. 44 B6
Parkview Rd.
Croy CR0 & CR9 ... 43 A1
Parkview Vale.
Merrow GU4 ... 110 C3
Parkway. Camb GU15 ... 65 C3
Parkway. Crowth RG11 ... 45 A5
Parkway. Dork RH4 ... 136 A8
Parkway. Guild GU1 ... 109 E2
Parkway. Horley RH6 ... 161 A3
Parkway.
New Add CR0 & CR9 ... 63 C1
Parkway. Oat Pk KT13 ... 53 D6
Parkway.
W Barn SM4 & SW20 ... 39 D5
Parkway Sch The. Cranf TW5 4 A7
Parkway The. Cranf TW5 ... 4 B7
Parkway Trad Est.
Heston TW5 ... 4 C8
Parkwood. Beck BR3 ... 24 A1
Parkwood Ave.
Thame D KT10 ... 36 C1
Parkwood Gr. Sunby TW16 .. 35 A6
Parkwood Rd. Bigg H TN16 103 F6
Parkwood Rd. Hounsl TW7 ... 5 F6
Parkwood Rd. Nutf RH1 ... 119 E2
Parkwood Rd. Wimble SW19 19 F3
Parley Dr. Woking GU21 ... 69 C1
Parliament Mews.
Mortl SW14 ... 7 C5
Parliamentary Rd.
Pirb GU24 ... 87 A6
Parnall House. 11
Dulw SE19 ... 22 E4
Parnham Ave. Lhtwat GU18 . 67 D8
Parr Ave. Ewell KT17 ... 58 B2
Parr Cl. Leahd KT22 ... 94 F7
Parr Ct. Felt TW13 ... 15 C4
Parr's Pl. Hampt TW12 ... 16 A1
Parris Croft. Dork RH5 ... 136 C4
Parrs Cl. S Croy CR2 ... 61 D2
Parry Cl. Stonel KT17 ... 58 A3
Parry Dr. Whit V KT13 ... 53 A1
Parry Rd. S Norw SE25 ... 42 E6
Parsley Gdns. Croy CR0 ... 43 D1
Parson's Mead. Thorn H CR0 42 B1
Parson's Mead Sch.
Ashtd KT21 ... 95 E8
Parson's Pightle.
Coulsd CR5 ... 100 A7
Parsonage Bsns Pk.
Horsh RH12 ... 217 E4
Parsonage Cl. Warlgm CR6 .. 81 F3
Parsonage Cl. Westc RH4 .. 135 C5
Parsonage Farm Cty Inf Sch.
W Heath GU14 ... 84 C5
Parsonage La. Westc RH4 .. 135 C6
Parsonage Rd. Cran GU6 .. 174 D3
Parsonage Rd. Eng Gn TW20 11 D3
Parsonage Rd.
Horsh RH12 & RH13 ... 217 E4
Parsonage Sq. Dork RH4 ... 136 A7
Parsonage Way. Friml GU16 65 E1
Parsonage Way.
Horsh RH12 ... 217 E4
Parsons Cl. Haslem GU27 ... 208 C8
Parsons Cl. Horley RH6 ... 160 E4
Parsons Field. Sandh GU17 .. 64 B8
Parsons Gn. Haslem GU27 . 208 C8
Parsons Green Ct.
Bellf GU1 ... 109 D3
Parsons House. 21
Streat SW12 ... 21 E8
Parsons La. Beac H GU26 ... 188 D6
Parsons Mead. E Mole KT8 .. 36 C6
Parsonsfield Cl. Nork SM7 .. 77 D4
Parsonsfield Rd. Nork SM7 .. 77 D4
Parthia Cl. Burgh H KT20 ... 97 B8
Partridge Cl. Crond GU10 ... 124 D8
Partridge Cl. Friml GU16 ... 65 E1
Partridge Knoll. Purley CR8 . 80 B6
Partridge La. Parkg RH5 ... 158 D4
Partridge Mead. Nork SM7 .. 77 C4
Partridge Rd. 8
Hampt TW12 ... 16 A2
Partridge Way.
Merrow GU4 ... 110 D3
Parvis Rd. Byfl KT14 ... 71 D7
Parvis Rd. W Byfl KT14 ... 71 D7
Parvis Rd. W Byfl KT14 ... 71 F7
Paschal Rd. Camb GU15 ... 65 F8
Passfields. Catf SE6 ... 24 C5
Passingham House.
Heston TW5 ... 5 A8
Pastens Rd. Limps RH8 ... 123 C4
Pasture Rd. Catf SE6 ... 24 F7
Pasture The. Crawl RH10 ... 202 C6
Pasture Wood Rd.
Abin C RH5 ... 155 D6
Patching Cl. Crawl RH11 ... 200 F7
Patchings. Horsh RH13 ... 217 F3
Paterson Cl. Friml GU16 ... 66 C3
Pates Manor Dr.
E Bed TW14 ... 14 D8
Path Link. Crawl RH10 ... 201 E7
Path The. Merton SW19 ... 40 B8
Pathfield. Chidd GU8 ... 191 B4
Pathfield Cl. Chidd GU8 ... 191 B4
Pathfield Cl. Rudg RH12 ... 214 D7
Pathfield Rd. Rudg RH12 ... 214 D7
Pathfield Rd. Streat SW16 ... 21 D2
Pathfields. Shere GU5 ... 133 A4
Pathfields Cl. Haslem GU27 208 D7
Pathfinders The.
Farnb GU14 ... 84 C3
Pathway The. Send M GU23 . 90 F2
Patmore La. Whit V KT12 ... 53 F4
Patricia Gdns. Belm SM2 ... 78 A8
Patrington Cl. Crawl RH11 201 A3
Patten Ash Dr. Woki RG11 ... 25 E7
Patten Rd. Wands SW18 ... 20 E8
Pattenden Rd.
For Hil SE23 & SE6 ... 23 F7
Patterdale Cl. Catf BR1 ... 24 E2
Patterdale Cl. Crawl RH11 . 201 C4
Patterson Ct. Penge SE19 ... 22 F2
Patterson Rd. Penge SE19 ... 22 F2
Paul Cl. Alder GU11 ... 125 E8
Paul Gdns. S Croy CR0 ... 61 F8
Paul Vanson Ct. Hersh KT12 54 D4
Paul's Pl. Ashtd KT21 ... 96 B8
Pauline Cres. Twick TW2 ... 16 C7
Pauls Mead. Lingf RH7 ... 164 E5
Paved Ct. 9 Rich TW9 ... 6 D2
Pavement The. 11
W Norw SE27 ... 22 C4
Pavilion Gdns. Stain TW18 ... 13 B1
Pavilion Rd. Alder GU11 ... 104 E1
Pavilion Rd. Farnb GU11 ... 104 D6
Pavilion Way. E Grins RH19 205 E8
Pavilions End. Camb GU15 ... 65 D3
Paviors. Farnh GU9 ... 125 C3
Pawleyne Cl. Penge SE20 ... 23 C1
Pawson's Rd. Thorn H CR0 ... 42 C4
Pax Cl. Crawl RH11 ... 200 E4
Paxton Cl. Rich TW9 ... 6 F5
Paxton Cl. Walt O T KT12 ... 35 C2
Paxton Ct. For Hil SE26 ... 23 E4
Paxton Ct. Mitch CR4 ... 40 F7
Paxton Gdns. Sheer GU21 ... 70 E7
Paxton Pl. W Norw SE27 ... 22 E4
Paxton Prim Sch.
W Norw SE19 ... 22 E2
Paxton Rd. For Hil SE23 ... 23 E5
Payley Dr. Woki RG11 ... 25 E8
Payne Cl. Crawl RH10 ... 202 D8
Paynesfield Ave. Mortl SW14 7 D4
Paynesfield Rd. Tats TN16 103 D7
Paynesfield Rd. Tats TN16 103 D8
Peabody Est. Streat SE24 ... 22 C8
Peabody Hill. W Norw SE21 . 22 C7
Peabody Rd.
Farnb GU11 & GU14 ... 105 D8
Peacemaker Cl.
Crawl RH11 ... 200 E4
Peach St. Woki RG11 ... 25 C6
Peach Tree Cl.
W Heath GU14 ... 85 A7
Peaches Cl. Belm SM2 ... 58 E3
Peacock Ave. E Bed TW14 ... 14 D7
Peacock Cotts. Easth RG12 . 26 C5
Peacock Gdns.
Selsd CR0 & CR2 ... 62 E1
Peacock La. Woki RG12 ... 26 D6
Peacock Wlk. 9
Crawl RH11 ... 201 A3
Peacocks Sh Ctr The.
Woking GU21 ... 69 E2
Peak Hill. For Hil SE26 ... 23 C4
Peak Hill Ave. For Hil SE26 .. 23 C4
Peak Hill Gdns. For Hil SE26 23 C4
Peak Rd. Stough GU2 ... 109 A4
Peak The. For Hil SE26 ... 23 C5
Peakfield. Frensh GU10 ... 167 C7
Peaks Hill. Purley CR8 ... 60 E1
Peaks Hill Rise. Purley CR8 .. 60 E1
Peall Rd. Thorn H CR0 ... 41 F3
Pear Ave. Up Hall TW17 ... 34 E6
Pear Tree Cl. Addl KT15 ... 52 A5
Pear Tree Cl. Mitch CR4 ... 40 E7
Pear Tree Ct. Camb GU15 ... 66 B8
Pear Tree Hill. Salfs RH1 ... 161 A8
Pear Tree La. Rowl GU10 ... 145 F3
Pear Tree Rd. Addl KT15 ... 52 A5
Pear Tree Rd. Ashf TW15 ... 14 C3
Pearce House. 7
Streat SW2 ... 21 E8
Pearcefield Ave.
For Hil SE23 ... 23 C7
Pearfield Rd. For Hil SE23 ... 23 E5
Pearl Ct. Woking GU21 ... 68 E3
Pearmain Cl. Shep TW17 ... 34 B4
Pears Rd. Hounsl TW3 ... 5 C4
Pearson Ct. Morden SM4 ... 40 B4
Pearson Rd. Crawl RH10 ... 202 C6
Peartree Ave. Wands SW17 . 20 C5
Peartree Cl. Hams Gn CR2 ... 81 B5
Peary Cl. Horsh RH12 ... 217 D6
Peaslake C of E Fst Sch.
Peasl GU5 ... 154 E7
Peaslake La. Peasl GU5 ... 154 D6
Peat Comm. Elst GU8 ... 148 C2
Peatmore Ave. Pyrf GU22 ... 71 A3
Peatmore Cl. Pyrf GU22 ... 71 A3
Peatmore Dr. Pirb GU24 ... 87 C6
Pebble Cl. Box H KT20 ... 116 E6
Pebble Hill. W Hors KT24 ... 112 C2
Pebble Hill Cotts.
Limps RH8 ... 123 B6
Pebble La.
Ashtd KT18 & KT21 ... 96 A5
Pebblehill Rd.
Betch KT20 & RH3 ... 116 E5
Pebblehill Rd.
Box H KT20 & RH3 ... 116 E5
Pebworth Ct. 8 Redh RH1 119 A3
Pebworth Lodge.
S Norw SE25 ... 42 F5
Peckarmans Wood.
Dulw SE21 & SE26 ... 23 A5
Peek Cres. Wimble SW19 ... 19 D3
Peeks Brook La. Crawl RH6 182 E7
Peeks Brook La.
Horley RH6 ... 161 F2
Peel Ave. Friml GU16 ... 86 A7
Peel Ct. Farnb GU14 ... 105 C8
Peel Ctr The. Brack RG12 ... 27 B7
Pegasus Ave. Alder GU12 ... 105 E2
Pegasus Cl. Linch GU27 ... 207 D5
Pegasus Ct. Crawl RH11 ... 200 E4
Pegasus Ct. Farnb GU14 ... 85 E1
Pegasus Ct. King U T KT1 ... 37 D6
Pegasus Rd. Croy CR0 & CR9 61 A4
Pegasus Rd. 3 Farnb GU14 85 B2
Pegasus Rd. W Heath GU14 . 84 F7
Pegasus Way. E Grins RH19 186 B3
Pegg Rd. Heston TW5 ... 4 D7
Peggotty Pl. Sandh GU15 ... 45 E2
Pegwell Cl. Crawl RH11 ... 200 F4
Peket Cl. Egham TW18 ... 32 E8
Peldon Ct. Rich TW10 ... 6 F2
Pelham Ct. Crawl RH11 ... 201 B2
Pelham Ct. G Book KT23 ... 94 C1
Pelham Ct. Horsh RH12 ... 217 B2
Pelham Ct. Stain TW18 ... 13 B3
Pelham Dr. Crawl RH11 ... 201 A2
Pelham House. Cater CR3 . 100 F3
Pelham Pl. Crawl RH11 ... 201 B2
Pelham Prim Sch.
Merton SW19 ... 20 A1
Pelham Rd. Merton SW19 ... 20 A1

Pelham Rd. Penge BR3 & SE20 .... 43 C7
Pelham Way. G Book KT23 .. 94 C1
Pelhams Cl. Esher KT10 .... 55 A6
Pelhams Wlk. Esher KT10 .... 55 A6
Pelinore Rd. Catf SE6 .... 24 E6
Pelling Hill. Old W SL4 .... 11 B7
Pelton Ave. Sutton SM2 .... 59 B1
Pelton Ct. S Croy CR2 .... 61 C4
Pemberton House. For Hil SE26 .... 23 A4
Pemberton Pl. Esher KT10 ... 55 C7
Pemberton Rd. E Mole KT8 .. 36 C5
Pembley Gn. Copth RH10 .... 183 E3
Pembridge Ave. Twick TW4 . 15 F7
Pembroke. Easth RG12 .... 27 A1
Pembroke Ave. Hersh KT12 . 54 D6
Pembroke Ave. Surb KT5 ..... 38 B4
Pembroke Broadway. Camb GU15 .... 65 C5
Pembroke Cl. Ascot SL5 .... 29 D4
Pembroke Cl. Banstd SM7 .... 78 B2
Pembroke Gdns. Woking GU22 .... 70 A1
Pembroke Mews. Ascot SL5 29 D4
Pembroke Pl. Hounsl TW7 ..... 5 E5
Pembroke Rd. Crawl RH10 182 C1
Pembroke Rd. Mitch CR4 ..... 41 A7
Pembroke Rd. S Norw SE25 . 42 E5
Pembroke Rd. Woking GU22 70 A2
Pembroke Villas. Rich TW9 ... 6 D3
Pembrook Lodge. 2 Streat SW16 .... 21 F5
Pembury Ave. N Cheam KT4 39 A2
Pembury Ave. New Mal KT4 39 A2
Pembury Cl. Hayes BR2 .... 44 F2
Pembury Cl. Wallin CR5 .... 79 A5
Pembury Ct. Harl UB3 .... 3 D8
Pembury Pl. Alder GU12 .... 105 C1
Pembury Rd. Croy SE25 .... 43 A5
Pemdevon Rd. Thorn H CR0 42 A2
Penarth Ct. Sutton SM2 .... 59 C3
Penates. Esher KT10 .... 55 D6
Penberth Rd. Catf SE6 .... 24 C7
Penceat Ct. Penge SE20 .... 43 C7
Pendarves Rd. Wimble SW20 39 C8
Pendell Ave. Harl UB3 .... 3 F7
Pendell Rd. Bletch RH1 ..... 120 B4
Pendennis Cl. W Byfl KT14 ... 71 A5
Pendennis Rd. Streat SW16 . 21 E4
Penderel Rd. Hounsl TW3 ...... 5 A2
Penderry Rise. Catf SE6 .... 24 D6
Pendine Pl. Easth RG12 .... 27 B4
Pendle Hse. 13 For Hil SE26 23 A5
Pendle Rd. Streat SW16 .... 21 B3
Pendlebury. Easth RG12 .... 27 A2
Pendleton Cl. Earls RH1 ..... 139 F7
Pendleton Rd. Woodh RH1 139 E6
Pendragon Rd. Catf BR1 .... 24 F5
Pendragon Way. Friml GU15 66 D3
Penerley Rd. Catf SE6 .... 24 B7
Penfold Cl. Croy CR0 & CR9 . 61 A7
Penfold Croft. Farnh GU9 .. 125 F4
Penfold Ct. Mitch CR4 .... 41 A7
Penfold Rd. Crawl RH10 ... 202 B2
Penge East Sta. Penge SE20 23 C2
Penge La. Penge SE20 .... 23 D1
Penge Rd. Croy SE20 & SE25 43 A6
Penge West Sta. Penge SE20 .... 23 B2
Penhurst. Horse GU21 .... 69 F5
Peninsular Cl. Felt TW14 .... 3 E1
Penistone Rd. Streat SW16 . 21 E1
Penn Cl. Crawl RH11 .... 181 D1
Pennards The. Sunby TW16 . 35 C6
Pennefather's Rd. Alder GU11 .... 104 F3
Penner Cl. Putney SW19 ...... 19 E6
Pennine Cl. Crawl RH11 ..... 201 B6
Pennine Way. Harl UB7 .... 3 D7
Pennine Way. W Heath GU14 84 E7
Pennings Ave. Stough GU2 & GU3 .... 108 F3
Pennington Cl. 10 W Norw SE27 .... 22 D4
Pennington Dr. Oat Pk KT13 53 E7
Pennington Lodge. 18 King U T KT5 .... 37 E4
Penns Wood. Farnb GU14 .... 85 D1
Penny Dr. Wood S V GU3 ... 108 B2
Penny La. Oat Pk TW17 .... 34 E2
Penny Royal. Wallin SM6 ..... 60 D4
Pennycroft. New Add CR0 .... 62 E2
Pennyfield. Cobham KT11 .... 73 A6
Pennymead Dr. E Hors KT24 .... 112 F8
Pennymead Rise. E Hors KT24 .... 112 F8
Pennypot La. Chobh GU24 ... 68 C7
Penrhyn Cl. Alder GU11 ..... 105 B1
Penrhyn Cres. Mortl SW14 .... 7 C3
Penrhyn Gdns. King U T KT1 37 D5
Penrhyn Rd. King U T KT1 ..... 37 E6
Penrith Cl. Beck BR3 .... 44 B8
Penrith Cl. Redh RH1 .... 118 E2
Penrith Pl. W Norw SE27 ...... 22 B6
Penrith Rd. New Mal KT3 ...... 38 D5
Penrith Rd. S Norw CR7 .... 42 C7
Penrith St. Streat SW16 .... 21 C2
Penrose Ct. Eng Gn TW20 .... 11 C2
Penrose Rd. Fetch KT22 .... 94 C5
Penryn Dr. Head Dn GU35 .. 187 C5
Penryn House. 5 Redh RH1 .... 119 A3
Pensfold La. Rudg RH12 & RH13 .... 214 E5
Pensford Ave. Rich TW9 .... 7 A5
Pensford Cl. Crowth RG11 .... 45 B7
Penshurst Cl. Crawl RH10 . 202 D7
Penshurst Gn. Hayes BR2 ..... 44 F4
Penshurst Rd. Thorn H CR7 . 42 B4
Penshurst Rise. Friml GU16 . 85 F8
Penshurst Way. Belm SM2 .. 59 A3
Penshurst Wlk. Hayes BR2 .. 44 F4
Pentelow Gdns. Felt TW14 .... 4 A1
Penthorpe Sch. Rudg RH12 214 C7
Pentland Ave. Shep Gn TW17 .... 34 A4
Pentland Pl. W Heath GU14 . 84 E7
Pentlands. Beck BR3 .... 44 C8
Pentlands Cl. Mitch CR4 .... 41 B6
Pentney Rd. Streat SW12 ..... 21 C7
Pentney Rd. Wimble SW19 & SW20 .... 39 E8
Penton Ave. Stain TW18 .... 32 F8
Penton Ct. Stain TW18 .... 12 F2
Penton Hall. Stain TW18 ...... 33 A8
Penton Hall Dr. Stain TW18 . 33 A8
Penton Hook Marina. Egham TW18 .... 32 F7
Penton Hook Marina. Thorpe KT16 .... 33 A6
Penton Hook Rd. Stain TW18 .... 33 A8
Penton House. Sutton SM2 .. 59 C3
Penton Rd. Stain TW18 .... 12 F1
Pentreath Ave. Onsl V GU2 129 F8
Penwerris Ave. Hounsl TW5 & TW7 .... 5 C7
Penwerris Ct. Hounsl TW7 ..... 5 C7
Penwith Dr. Linch GU27 ..... 207 E5
Penwith Rd. Wands SW18 .... 20 B6
Penwith Wlk. Woking GU22 . 89 D8
Penwood End. Woking GU22 89 B6
Penwood Gdns. Easth RG11 & RG12 .... 26 D3
Penwood Hse. Rhampt SW15 7 F1
Penwortham Prim Sch. Streat SW17 .... 21 B2
Penwortham Rd. S Croy CR2 61 D1
Penwortham Rd. Streat SW16 .... 21 C2
Peper Harow La. P Harow GU8 .... 149 C6
Peperham House. Haslem GU27 .... 208 C7
Peperham Rd. Haslem GU27 .... 208 C8
Peperharow Rd. Farnc GU7 150 C6
Pepper Cl. Cater CR3 .... 100 E2
Pepperbox La. Crawl GU5 .. 173 E4
Peppermint Cl. Croy CR0 ..... 41 E2
Pepys Cl. Ashtd KT21 .... 76 A2
Pepys Cl. Bra Hil SL3 .... 1 B8
Pepys Rd. Wimble SW20 .... 39 C8
Perak Ct. Tolw KT5 .... 38 C2
Percheron Cl. Islew TW7 .... 5 F4
Percival Rd. Felt TW13 .... 14 F6
Percival Rd. Mortl SW14 .... 7 C3
Percival Way. W Ewell KT19 57 D6
Percival Way. W Ewell KT19 57 D6
Percy Ave. Ashf TW15 .... 14 A3
Percy Bilton Ct. Heston TW5 . 5 B6
Percy Bryant Rd. Charlt TW16 .... 14 E1
Percy Ct. 1 Surb KT5 .... 37 F3
Percy Gdns. 3 Islew TW7 ..... 6 A4
Percy Gdns. New Mal KT4 .... 38 E1
Percy House. 4 Streat SW16 .... 21 C4
Percy Rd. Carsh CR4 .... 41 A2
Percy Rd. Croy SE25 .... 43 A4
Percy Rd. Hampt TW12 .... 16 A1
Percy Rd. Horsh RH12 .... 217 B3
Percy Rd. Islew TW7 .... 6 A3
Percy Rd. Penge SE20 .... 43 D8
Percy Rd. Stough GU2 .... 109 B3
Percy Rd. Twick TW2 .... 16 C7
Percy Way. Twick TW2 .... 16 C7
Peregrine Cl. Cran GU6 ...... 174 E4
Peregrine Cl. Easth RG12 ..... 27 B4
Peregrine Gdns. Croy CR0 ... 62 E8
Peregrine Rd. Sunby TW16 .. 34 F7
Peregrine Way. Wimble SW19 & SW20 .... 19 C1
Performing Arts & Tech Sch. Thorn H SE25 .... 42 D3
Perifield. W Norw SE21 .... 22 C7
Perimeter Rd E. Crawl RH6 182 B6
Perimeter Rd N. Crawl RH6 160 F1
Perimeter Rd N. Crawl RH6 181 D7
Perimeter Rd N. Crawl RH6 182 A8
Perimeter Rd S. Crawl RH6 181 E5
Perkins Ct. Ashf TW15 .... 13 F3
Perkins Way. Woki RG11 ...... 25 A5
Perkstead Ct. 7 Crawl RH11 .... 201 A3
Perleybrooke La. Woking GU21 .... 69 A2
Perowne St. Alder GU11 .... 104 F2
Perram Wks. Merrow GU4 . 110 C4
Perran Rd. Streat SE24 & SW2 .... 22 B6
Perran Wlk. 16 Brent TW8 ..... 6 E8
Perrin Cl. Ashf TW15 .... 13 F3
Perrin Ct. Sheer GU21 .... 70 B4
Perring Ave. W Heath GU14 . 84 F8
Perring Rd. Farnb GU14 .... 85 A2
Perrior Rd. Farnc GU7 .... 150 E7
Perry Ave. E Grins RH19 ..... 185 E3
Perry Cl. Godal GU7 .... 151 B5
Perry Hill. For Hil SE23 & SE6 23 F5
Perry House. 24 Streat SW2 .... 21 E8
Perry How. New Mal KT4 ..... 38 F1
Perry Oaks. Brack RG12 .... 27 E7
Perry Oaks Dr. Harm TW6 & UB7 .... 2 C5
Perry Rise. For Hil SE23 & SE6 .... 23 E5
Perry Vale. For Hil SE23 ...... 23 D6
Perry Way. Brack RG12 .... 27 E7
Perry Way. Lhtwat GU18 ...... 66 F7
Perryfield House. 7 Crawl RH11 .... 201 D5
Perryfield Rd. Crawl RH11 201 D5
Perryfield Way. Rich TW10 .. 17 B6
Perrylands. Charl RH6 .... 180 F7
Perrylands La. Smallf RH6 . 162 A2
Perrymount Prim Sch. For Hil SE23 .... 23 D6
Perryn Ct. 2 Twick TW1 ..... 17 A8
Perrywood Bsns Pk. Salfs RH1 .... 140 B1
Persant Rd. Catf SE6 .... 24 E6
Perseverance Cotts. Ripley GU23 .... 91 C6
Persfield Mews. Ewell KT17 . 57 F1
Persfield Rd. Ewell KT17 ...... 58 A1
Pershore Gr. Carsh SM5 .... 40 D3
Perth Cl. Crawl RH11 .... 181 D1
Perth Cl. Wimble SW20 .... 39 A7
Perth Rd. Beck BR3 .... 44 C7
Perth Way. Horsh RH12 ..... 217 F4
Perystreete. For Hil SE23 ..... 23 C6
Petauel Rd. Tedd TW11 .... 16 E3
Petavel Rd. Tedd TW11 .... 16 E2
Peter Ave. Oxted RH8 .... 122 D6
Peter Kennedy Ct. Croy CR0 43 F3
Peter's Path. For Hil SE26 .... 23 B4
Peterborough Rd. Carsh CR4 & SM4 & SM5 ..... 40 E3
Peterborough Rd. Crawl RH10 .... 201 E2
Peterborough Rd. Stough GU2 .... 108 F3
Peterhouse Cl. Sandh GU15 . 45 F2
Peterhouse Par. Crawl RH10 .... 182 C1
Peterlee Wlk. Crawl RH11 .. 200 E2
Petersfield Ave. Stain TW15 & TW18 .... 13 C2
Petersfield Cres. Coulsd CR5 79 E4
Petersfield Rd. Stain TW18 .. 13 C3
Petersfield Rise. Rhampt SW15 .... 19 B7
Petersham Ave. Byfl KT14 ... 71 E7
Petersham Cl. Byfl KT14 ...... 71 E7
Petersham Cl. Cheam SM1 .. 59 A5
Petersham Cl. Rich TW10 .... 17 D6
Petersham Rd. Rich TW10 ... 17 E7
Peterstow Cl. Putney SW19 . 19 E6
Peterwood Pk. Croy CR9 ...... 60 F8
Peterwood Way. Croy CR0 .. 60 F8
Petrel Ct. 7 W Norw SE21 .. 22 D6
Petridge Rd. Earls RH1 ...... 139 F4
Petters Rd. Ashtd KT21 .... 75 F3
Petts La. Shep Gn TW17 ...... 34 A5
Petworth Cl. Coulsd CR5 ...... 99 C8
Petworth Cl. Friml GU16 ...... 85 F8
Petworth Ct. Crawl RH11 ... 200 F3
Petworth Ct. Haslem GU27 208 D6
Petworth Dr. Horsh RH12 .. 217 F7
Petworth Gdns. W Barn SW20 .... 39 B6
Petworth Rd. Chidd GU27 & GU8 .... 209 C5
Petworth Rd. Witley GU8 .... 170 F5
Petworth Rd. Wormly GU8 . 170 F5
Pevensey Cl. Crawl RH10 ... 202 C5
Pevensey Cl. Hounsl TW7 ...... 5 C7
Pevensey Ct. W Norw SW16 22 A5
Pevensey House. Dovgn RH2 .... 139 B5
Pevensey Rd. Felt TW13 ...... 15 E7
Pevensey Rd. Up Toot SW17 20 D4
Pevensey Way. Friml GU16 .. 86 A8
Peverel Rd. Crawl RH11 ..... 200 E5
Peveril Dr. Tedd TW11 .... 16 D3
Pewley Bank. Guild GU1 ..... 130 E7
Pewley Down Inf Sch. Guild GU1 .... 130 E7
Pewley Hill. Guild GU1 .... 130 E7
Pewley Point. Guild GU1 .... 130 E7
Pewley Way. Guild GU1 ...... 130 F7
Pewsey Vale. Brack RG12 .... 27 F4
Peyton's Cotts. Nutf RH1 ... 119 F3
Pharaoh Cl. Carsh CR4 .... 40 F2
Pheasant Cl. Purley CR8 .... 80 B6
Philanthropic Rd. Earls RH1 .... 140 B8
Philip Gdns. Croy CR0 .... 62 F8
Philip Rd. Stain TW18 .... 13 D2
Philip Southcote Sch. Chert KT15 .... 52 C8
Philips House. Graysh GU26 .... 188 B3
Phillips Cl. Godal GU7 .... 150 D2
Phillips Cotts. Ock Rid GU7 150 B4
Phillips Hatch. Woner GU5 152 C8
Philpot La. Chobh GU24 .... 69 C7
Phipp's Bridge Rd. Mitch CR4 & SW19 .... 40 D6
Phoenix Bsns Pk. Binf RG12 . 26 C7
Phoenix Cl. W Wick BR4 .... 63 E8
Phoenix Ct. Alder GU11 ..... 105 A2
Phoenix Ct. Croy SE25 .... 43 A4
Phoenix Ct. Guild GU1 .... 130 D7
Phoenix La. Ash W RH19 ... 206 E6
Phoenix Pl. Stain TW18 .... 13 A3
Phoenix Rd. Penge SE20 ...... 23 C2
Phoenix Way. Heston TW5 .... 4 D8
Phyllis Ave. W Barn KT3 ...... 39 B4
Phyllis House. Croy CR0 .... 61 B6
Piccards The. Guild GU2 .... 130 C5
Pickering. Easth RG12 .... 27 A5
Pickering Gdns. Croy SE25 .. 42 F3
Picket Post Cl. Brack RG12 .. 27 F6
Pickets St. Balham SW12 ..... 21 B8
Picketts Hill. Head Dn GU35 166 C1
Picketts La. Salfs RH1 .... 161 C8
Pickford St. Alder GU11 ..... 105 B2
Pickhurst Gn. Hayes BR2 ..... 44 F2
Pickhurst Inf Sch. Hayes BR2 .... 44 F3
Pickhurst Jun Sch. Hayes BR2 .... 44 F3
Pickhurst La. Hayes BR2 & BR3 & BR4 ...... 44 E2
Pickhurst Mead. Hayes BR2 44 F2
Pickhurst Pk. Hayes BR2 ..... 44 F4
Pickhurst Rd. Chidd GU8 .... 191 C3
Pickhurst Rise. W Wick BR4 44 D1
Pickins Piece. Horton SL3 ...... 1 A5
Pickwick Cl. Hounsl TW4 .... 4 E2
Pickwick Rd. Dulw SE21 .... 22 E8
Picquets Way. Burgh H KT20 & SM7 .... 77 F2
Picton Cl. Camb GU15 .... 66 B7
Picton House. 1 Streat SW4 .... 21 E8
Pier Rd. Felt TW14 .... 4 B2
Pierrefondes Ave. Farnb GU14 .... 85 B5
Pierrepoint. S Norw SE25 ..... 42 E6
Pierrepont Sch. Frensh GU10 .... 146 E1
Pierson House. 12 Dulw SE19 .... 22 E4
Pigbush La. Loxwd RH14 ... 213 A7
Pigeon La. Hampt TW12 .... 16 A4
Pigeonhouse La. L Kings CR5 98 C3
Pigeonhouse La. Wink SL4 & SL5 .... 8 E4
Piggott Ct. Horsh RH13 ...... 217 E1
Pigott Ct. Woki RG11 .... 25 D6
Pigott Rd. Woki RG11 .... 25 E8
Pike Cl. Alder GU11 .... 105 C2
Pikes Hill. Epsom KT17 .... 76 E6
Pikes La. Crow RH7 .... 143 F2
Pikethorne. For Hil SE23 ...... 23 D6
Pilgrim Cl. Morden SM4 .... 40 B2
Pilgrim Hill. W Norw SE27 ... 22 C4
Pilgrim House. Guild GU1 . 130 D7
Pilgrim's Way. S Croy CR2 ... 61 F5
Pilgrims Cl. M Bourn GU9 .. 146 A8
Pilgrims Cl. Shere GU5 ...... 133 A4
Pilgrims Cl. Westh RH5 ...... 115 B4
Pilgrims La. Cater CR3 ...... 100 B1
Pilgrims La. Tats TN16 ...... 103 D3
Pilgrims La. Titsey RH8 & TN16 .... 103 D3
Pilgrims Pl. Reig RH2 .... 118 A3
Pilgrims View. Ash GU12 ... 127 C8
Pilgrims Way. Bisley GU24 .. 68 A3
Pilgrims' Way. Guild GU4 ... 130 E5
Pilgrims' Way. Reig RH2 ... 118 A3
Pilgrims Way. Shere GU5 ... 133 A4
Pilgrims Way. Westh RH5 . 115 B4
Pilgrims Way Cotts. Betch RH3 .... 116 C2
Pilgrims Way Cty Sch The. M Bourn GU9 .... 146 B8
Pilsden Cl. Putney SW19 ...... 19 D7
Pilton Est The. Thorn H CR9 61 B8
Pimms Cl. Burph GU4 .... 110 A5
Pinckards. Chidd GU8 .... 191 B5
Pincott La. W Hors KT24 ... 112 B6
Pincott Rd. Merton SW19 ..... 40 C8
Pine Ave. Camb GU15 .... 65 D3
Pine Ave. W Wick BR4 .... 44 B1
Pine Bank. Hind GU26 .... 188 E4
Pine Cl. Ash V GU12 .... 106 A6
Pine Cl. Crawl RH11 .... 181 C1
Pine Cl. Horse GU21 .... 69 C3
Pine Cl. Kenley CR8 .... 80 D2
Pine Cl. Penge SE20 .... 43 C8
Pine Cl. Sandh GU15 .... 64 E7
Pine Cl. Woodhm KT15 .... 71 B8
Pine Coombe. S Croy CR0 .... 62 D6
Pine Cres. Sutton SM5 .... 78 D8
Pine Croft Rd. Woki RG11 .... 25 A2
Pine Ct. Brack RG12 .... 27 E5
Pine Ct. 2 Whit V KT13 .... 53 C5
Pine Dean. G Book KT23 .... 94 B2
Pine Dr. Hawley GU17 .... 64 E3
Pine Gdns. Horley RH6 ...... 161 A2
Pine Gdns. Surb KT5 .... 38 A3
Pine Gr. E Grins RH19 .... 185 B3
Pine Gr. M Bourn GU10 ...... 146 E6
Pine Gr. Weyb KT13 .... 53 C5
Pine Gr. Wimble SW19 .... 19 F3
Pine Gr. Windl GU20 .... 48 D4
Pine Grove Mews. 3 Whit V KT13 .... 53 C5
Pine Hill. Woodc KT18 .... 76 D4
Pine Mount Rd. Camb GU15 65 D4
Pine Pl. Nork KT17 .... 77 D5
Pine Rd. Woking GU22 .... 89 C7
Pine Ridge. Wallin SM5 .... 60 A2
Pine Ridge Cty Inf Sch. Camb GU15 .... 47 A1
Pine Ridge Dr. M Bourn GU10 .... 146 C5
Pine Ridge Golf Ctr. Friml GU16 .... 66 D2
Pine Shaw. Crawl RH10 .... 202 D7
Pine Tree Cl. Cranf TW5 .... 4 B6
Pine Tree Hill. Mayb GU22 ... 70 D3
Pine Trees Bsns Pk. Egham TW18 .... 12 E3
Pine View. Head Dn GU35 .. 187 C6
Pine View Cl. Chil GU4 .... 131 F3
Pine View Cl. Farnh GU9 .... 126 A5
Pine View Cl. Haslem GU27 208 C8
Pine Way. Eng Gn TW20 .... 11 B2
Pine Way Cl. E Grins RH19 . 205 E7
Pine Wlk. Cater CR3 .... 100 F5
Pine Wlk. Cobham KT11 .... 73 D5
Pine Wlk. E Hors KT24 .... 112 F7
Pine Wlk. Fetch KT23 .... 94 B2
Pine Wlk. Surb KT5 .... 38 A3
Pine Wlk. Sutton SM5 .... 59 D1
Pine Wlk. Woodm CR5 & SM7 78 F2
Pine Wood. Sunby TW16 ...... 35 A8
Pineacre Ct. Mayb GU22 ...... 70 B2
Pinecote Dr. Sunnin SL5 .... 29 F2
Pinefields. Addl KT15 .... 52 B6
Pinefields Cl. Crowth RG11 .. 45 B4
Pinehill Rd. Crowth RG11 ..... 45 C3
Pinehill Rise. Sandh GU17 .... 64 C8
Pinehurst. Ascot SL5 .... 29 D4
Pinehurst. Horsh RH12 .... 217 C4
Pinehurst. 8 Woking GU22 . 69 F1
Pinehurst Ave. Farnb GU14 .. 85 B2
Pinehurst Cl. Kings KT20 ...... 98 A5
Pinehurst Cotts. Farnb GU14 85 B2
Pines Ct. 14 Putney SW19 ... 19 D7
Pines Cty Inf Sch The. Easth RG12 .... 27 A2
Pines Cty Jun Sch The. Easth RG12 .... 27 A2

Pines The. Camb GU15 65 F7
Pines The. Dork RH4 136 B6
Pines The. Horsh RH12 218 C5
Pines The. Purley CR8 80 C6
Pines The. S Norw SE19 & SW16 22 B2
Pines The. Stough GU3 108 E3
Pines The. Sunby TW16 35 A6
Pinetrees Cl. Copth RH10 183 B3
Pinewood Ave. Crowth RG11 45 C6
Pinewood Ave. Woodhm KT15 52 C1
Pinewood Cl. Broad H RH12 216 D3
Pinewood Cl. Horse GU21 70 A4
Pinewood Cl. S Croy CR0 62 E7
Pinewood Cres. W Heath GU14 84 C5
Pinewood Ct. Addl KT15 52 D6
Pinewood Ct. Woking GU21 70 A3
Pinewood Cty Inf Sch. W Heath GU14 84 D7
Pinewood Dr. Stain TW18 13 A3
Pinewood Gdns. Bagsh GU19 47 C3
Pinewood Gr. Woodhm KT15 52 B1
Pinewood Mews. Stan TW19 2 D1
Pinewood Pk. W Heath GU14 84 C7
Pinewood Pk. Woodhm KT15 71 B8
Pinewood Pl. W Ewell KT19 57 D6
Pinewood Pl. W Ewell KT19 57 D6
Pinewood Rd. Felt TW13 15 B5
Pinewood Rd. Normdy GU12 106 D3
Pinewood Rd. Went GU25 31 A5
Pinfold Rd. Streat SW16 21 E4
Pinglestone Cl. Harm TW6 & UB7 2 E7
Pinkcoat Cl. Felt TW13 15 B5
Pinkerton Pl. Streat SW16 21 D4
Pinkhurst La. Slinfd RH13 216 A2
Pioneers Ind Pk. Wallin CR9 41 E1
Piper Rd. King U T KT1 38 A6
Piper's End. Vir W GU25 31 D6
Pipers Cl. Cobham KT11 73 D3
Pipers End. Slinfd RH13 215 E3
Pipers Gdns. Croy CR0 43 E2
Pipers Patch. 1 Farnb GU14 85 B4
Pipewell Rd. Carsh SM5 40 E3
Pippbrook Gdns. Dork RH4 136 B8
Pippin Cl. Croy CR0 43 F1
Pippins Ct. Ashf TW15 14 B2
Piquet Rd. Penge BR3 & SE20 43 C7
Pirbright Cres. New Add CR0 63 C4
Pirbright Cty Prim Sch. Pirb GU24 87 E5
Pirbright House. 11 King U T KT2 18 B2
Pirbright Rd. Farnb GU14 85 C3
Pirbright Rd. Normdy GU3 107 B6
Pirbright Rd. Wands SW18 20 A7
Pirbright Terr. Pirb GU24 87 F4
Pirles Pl. Horsh RH12 217 C2
Pisley La. Wall W RH5 177 A4
Pit Farm Rd. Guild GU1 110 A1
Pit Wood Gn. Burgh H KT20 97 C7
Pitcairn Rd. Mitch CR4 20 F1
Pitchfont La. Limps CR6 & RH8 102 F2
Pitfold Ave. Shottm GU27 207 D6
Pitfold Cl. Shottm GU27 207 E6
Pitlake. Thorn H CR0 & CR9 61 B8
Pitland St. Hol St M RH5 155 C5
Pitman's Coll. Wimble SW19 19 F3
Pitson Cl. Addl KT15 52 D6
Pitt Cres. Wimble SW19 20 B4
Pitt Pl. Epsom KT17 76 E5
Pitt Rd. Epsom KT17 76 E5
Pitt Rd. Thorn H CR0 & CR7 42 C4
Pitt Way. W Heath GU14 84 F5
Pittville Gdns. S Norw SE25 43 A6
Pixfield Ct. Broml BR2 44 F7
Pixham Firs. Pixham RH4 115 C2
Pixham La. Pixham RH4 115 C2
Pixholme Ct. Pixham RH4 115 C2
Pixholme Gr. Pixham RH4 115 C1
Pixton Way. New Add CR0 & CR2 62 E2
Place Ct. Alder GU11 126 C7
Place Farm Rd. Bletch RH1 120 D4
Placehouse La. Coulsd CR5 80 A1
Plaistow Cty Inf Sch. Plaist RH14 211 F3
Plaistow Rd. Dunsf GU8 192 D2
Plaistow Rd. Ifold RH14 212 D1
Plaistow Rd. Loxwd RH14 212 D1
Plaistow St. Lingf RH7 164 D4
Plane St. For Hil SE26 23 B5
Plane Tree Cres. Felt TW13 15 B5
Plane Tree Wlk. 2 W Norw SE19 22 E2
Planes The. Chert KT16 33 C2
Plantagenet Cl. Worc Pk KT19 57 D6
Plantain Cres. Crawl RH11 201 A2
Plantation La. Warlgm CR6 101 E8
Plantation Row. Camb GU15 65 B5
Plassy Rd. Catf SE6 24 B8
Plat The. Horsh RH12 217 A3
Platt Meadow. Merrow GU4 110 D3
Platt The. Dorman RH7 186 A8
Platt's Eyot. Hampt TW12 36 A7
Plaws Hill. Peasl GU5 154 D6
Plawsfield Rd. Penge BR3 43 D8
Playden Ct. 4 Crawl RH11 201 A3
Playgreen Way. Catf SE6 24 A4
Playground Cl. Penge BR3 43 D7
Pleasant Gr. Croy CR0 62 F7
Pleasant Pl. Hersh KT12 54 D4
Pleasure Pit Rd. Ashtd KT21 76 B1
Plesman Way. Wallin SM6 60 E2
Plevna Rd. Hampt TW12 36 B8
Pleydell Ave. Penge SE19 22 F1
Plough Cl. Crawl RH11 200 F8
Plough Ind Est. Leahd KT22 95 A7
Plough La. Downs KT11 73 A2
Plough La. Ewh GU6 176 A5
Plough La. Horsh RH12 217 E5
Plough La. Purley CR0 & CR8 & SM6 60 F1
Plough La. Wallin CR0 & SM6 60 E5
Plough La. Wallin SM6 60 F2
Plough La. Wimble SW17 & SW19 20 C4
Plough La. Woki RG11 25 F6
Plough Lane Cl. Wallin CR0 & SM6 60 E5
Plough Rd. Dorman RH7 165 A2
Plough Rd. Smallf RH6 162 C3
Plough Rd. W Ewell KT19 57 D3
Plough Rd. W Ewell KT19 57 D3
Ploughlands. Brack RG12 26 F8
Ploughmans End. Islew TW7 5 D2
Plover Cl. Crawl RH11 201 C8
Plover Cl. Stain TW18 12 F5
Plovers Rd. Horsh RH13 217 F3
Plovers Rise. Pirb GU24 87 E7
Plowman House. Putney SW19 19 D6
Plummer La. Mitch CR4 40 F7
Plummer Rd. Streat SW4 21 D8
Plumpton Way. Carsh SM5 59 E7
Plumtree Cl. Wallin SM6 60 D3
Pocklington Ct. Rhampt SW15 19 A7
Point The (L Ctr). Brack RG12 27 B7
Point Royal. Easth RG12 27 B4
Pointers Hill. Westc RH4 135 C5
Pointers Rd. Downs KT11 72 E2
Pointers The. Ashtd KT21 95 E7
Polden Cl. W Heath GU14 84 E7
Polecroft La. For Hil SE6 23 F6
Poles La. Rusper RH11 & 6 181 C3
Polesden Gdns. W Barn SW20 39 B7
Polesden La. Ripley GU23 91 A6
Polesden La. Send M GU23 90 F5
Polesden Rd. G Book KT23 114 B6
Polesden View. G Book KT23 114 B8
Polesteeple Hill. Bigg H TN16 83 D2
Police Station Rd. Hersh KT12 54 C4
Pollard Gr. Friml GU15 66 C4
Pollard House. Cheam KT4 58 C6
Pollard Rd. Mayb GU22 70 B3
Pollard Rd. Morden SM4 40 D4
Pollardrow Ave. Brack RG12 26 F8
Pollards. Crawl RH11 201 A5
Pollards Cres. Thorn H SW16 41 E6
Pollards Dr. Horsh RH13 217 F2
Pollards Hill E. Thorn H SW16 41 F6
Pollards Hill N. Thorn H SW16 41 F6
Pollards Hill S. Thorn H SW16 41 F6
Pollards Hill W. Thorn H SW16 41 F6
Pollards Oak Cres. Oxted RH8 123 A3
Pollards Oak Rd. Oxted RH8 123 A3
Pollards Wood Hill. Limps RH8 123 B5
Pollards Wood Rd. Limps RH8 123 B4
Pollards Wood Rd. Thorn H SW16 41 E6
Polsted La. Compt GU3 129 C3
Polsted Rd. For Hil SE6 23 F8
Poltimore Rd. Guild GU2 130 B7
Polworth Rd. Streat SW16 21 E3
Polyanthus Way. Crowth RG11 45 B8
Pond Cl. Loxwd RH14 212 F4
Pond Cl. Whit V KT12 54 A4
Pond Copse La. Loxwd RH14 212 F5
Pond Cottage La. Croy BR3 & BR4 44 A1
Pond Cotts. Dulw SE21 22 E7
Pond Head La. For Gn RH5 176 E5
Pond Head La. Wall W RH5 176 D3
Pond Hill Gdns. Cheam SM3 58 E4
Pond House. Merrow GU4 110 D2
Pond La. Frensh GU10 167 C5
Pond La. Peasl GU5 154 D7
Pond Meadow. Stough GU2 108 E2
Pond Meadow Sch. Stough GU2 108 E2
Pond Moor Rd. Easth RG12 27 B4
Pond Piece. Oxsh KT22 74 B6
Pond Rd. Egham TW20 12 C2
Pond Rd. Farnb GU14 85 B2
Pond Rd. Head Dn GU35 187 B4
Pond Rd. Woking GU22 89 B7
Pond Way. E Grins RH19 186 B1
Pond Way. Tedd TW11 17 C2
Pond Wood Rd. Crawl RH10 202 A8
Pondfield House. W Norw SE27 22 C3
Pondfield Rd. Farnc GU7 150 F7
Pondfield Rd. Kenley CR8 80 B3
Pondfield Rd. Rudg RH12 214 D8
Pondfield Rd. W Wick BR2 44 E1
Pondpenny La. Farnb GU14 84 A1
Ponds La. Farl Gn GU5 153 F8
Ponds The. Whit V KT13 53 E4
Pondside Cl. Harl UB3 3 D7
Pondtail Cl. Horsh RH12 217 D6
Pondtail Dr. Horsh RH12 217 D7
Pondtail Rd. Horsh RH12 217 D6
Ponsonby Rd. Putney SW15 19 B8
Pontefract Rd. Broml BR1 24 F3
Ponton House. Streat SW2 22 A7
Pony Chase. Cobham KT11 73 F6
Pool Cl. Beck BR3 24 A3
Pool Ct. Catf SE6 24 A6
Pool End Cl. Shep Gn TW17 34 A4
Pool Rd. Alder GU11 126 C7
Pool Rd. E Mole KT12 & KT8 35 F4
Poole Court Rd. Hounsl TW5 4 E5
Poole Ct. Hounsl TW5 4 E5
Poole Rd. W Ewell KT19 57 D4
Poole Rd. W Ewell KT19 57 D4
Poole Rd. Woking GU21 69 E1
Pooley Ave. Egham TW20 12 B3
Pooley Green Cl. Egham TW20 12 C3
Pooley Green Rd. Egham TW20 12 C3
Pope Cl. E Bed TW14 14 F7
Pope Cl. Mitch SW17 & SW19 20 D2
Pope Ct. 10 King U T KT2 17 D4
Pope's Ave. Twick TW2 16 E6
Pope's Gr. Twick TW1 & TW2 16 F6
Popes Cl. Coln SL3 1 C7
Popes Gr. Croy CR0 62 F7
Popes La. Oxted RH8 143 F8
Popes Mead. Haslem GU27 208 C7
Popeswood Rd. Binf RG12 26 D8
Popham Cl. Brack RG12 27 F4
Popham Cl. Felt TW13 15 F5
Popham Gdns. Rich TW9 7 B4
Poplar Ave. Leahd KT22 95 C5
Poplar Ave. Mitch CR4 40 F8
Poplar Ave. Windl GU20 48 B6
Poplar Cl. Crawl RH11 181 C1
Poplar Cl. Mytch GU16 86 A3
Poplar Cl. Poyle SL3 1 E6
Poplar Cotts. Stough GU3 108 E4
Poplar Cres. W Ewell KT19 57 C4
Poplar Cres. W Ewell KT19 57 C4
Poplar Ct. 4 Streat SW16 21 F5
Poplar Ct. 13 Twick TW1 6 C1
Poplar Ct. Wimble SW19 20 A3
Poplar Dr. Nork KT17 & SM7 77 D5
Poplar Farm Cl. W Ewell KT19 57 C4
Poplar Farm Cl. W Ewell KT19 57 C4
Poplar Fst Sch. Merton SW19 40 A6
Poplar Gdns. King U T KT3 38 D7
Poplar Gr. King U T KT3 38 D6
Poplar Gr. Woking GU22 89 E8
Poplar La. Beck BR3 44 B4
Poplar Rd. Ashf TW15 14 C3
Poplar Rd. Cheam SM3 39 F1
Poplar Rd. Leahd KT22 95 C5
Poplar Rd. Merton SW19 40 A7
Poplar Rd. Shalf GU4 130 E2
Poplar Rd S. Merton SM4 & SW19 40 A6
Poplar Road C of E Prim Sch. Leahd KT22 95 B5
Poplar Way. Felt TW13 15 B5
Poplar Wlk. Cater CR3 100 E4
Poplar Wlk. Croy CR0 42 C1
Poplar Wlk. Heath E GU9 125 D7
Poplars Cl. W Heath GU14 84 C5
Poplars The. Ascot SL5 29 A4
Poplars The. Horsh RH13 217 E3
Poppy La. Croy CR0 & CR9 43 C1
Poppy Pl. Woki RG11 25 B6
Poppyhills Rd. Camb GU15 65 F8
Porchester. Ascot SL5 29 A5
Porchester Mead. Beck BR3 24 B2
Porchester Rd. King U T KT1 38 B7
Porchfield Cl. Sutton SM2 59 B1
Porlock House. 5 For Hil SE26 23 A5
Porridge Pot Alley. Guild GU2 130 C7
Port Way. Bisley GU24 68 A3
Portal Cl. W Norw SE27 22 A5
Porteridges. Dork RH4 136 C4
Portesbery Hill Dr. Camb GU15 65 E6
Portesbery Rd. Camb GU15 65 E6
Portesbery Sch. Camb GU15 65 D6
Porthcawe Rd. For Hil SE26 23 F4
Portia Gr. Wink RG12 27 E8
Portland Ave. New Mal KT3 38 F2
Portland Cotts. Wallin CR0 41 D2
Portland Cres. Felt TW13 & TW15 14 D4
Portland Dr. Merst RH1 119 D6
Portland House. 5 E Grins RH19 205 F8
Portland House. Merst RH1 119 D6
Portland House. 20 Streat SW2 22 A7
Portland House Mews. Epsom KT18 76 D5
Portland Pl. Croy SE25 43 A5
Portland Pl. Ewell KT17 76 E7
Portland Rd. Ashf TW15 13 E5
Portland Rd. Croy SE25 43 B4
Portland Rd. Dork RH4 136 A8
Portland Rd. E Grins RH19 205 F8
Portland Rd. King U T KT1 37 F6
Portland Rd. Mitch CR4 40 E7
Portland Terr. Rich TW9 6 D3
Portley La. Cater CR3 100 E6
Portley Wood Rd. Whytlf CR3 101 A7
Portman Ave. Mortl SW14 7 D4
Portman Cl. 5 Brack RG12 27 A8
Portman Rd. King U T KT1 37 F7
Portmore Park Rd. Weyb KT13 53 A7
Portmore Quays. Weyb KT13 52 F6
Portmore Way. Weyb KT13 53 A7
Portnall Dr. Went GU25 30 F4
Portnall Rd. Went GU25 30 F4
Portnall Rise. Went GU25 30 F3
Portnalls Cl. Coulsd CR5 79 B3
Portnalls Rd. Coulsd CR5 79 B2
Portnalls Rise. Coulsd CR5 79 C3
Portobello House. 6 W Norw SW27 22 B3
Porton Ct. King U T KT6 37 C3
Portsea House. 3 Rhampt SW15 19 B7
Portsmouth Ave. Thame D KT7 37 A2
Portsmouth Rd. Bramsh GU26 207 C8
Portsmouth Rd. Camb GU15 66 A7
Portsmouth Rd. Cobham KT10 & KT11 73 C7
Portsmouth Rd. Esher KT10 55 A4
Portsmouth Rd. Esher KT10 55 D7
Portsmouth Rd. Guild GU2 130 C6
Portsmouth Rd. Hinch W KT10 & KT7 55 E8
Portsmouth Rd. Hind GU26 188 E2
Portsmouth Rd. King U T KT1 & KT6 37 C3
Portsmouth Rd. Milf GU8 149 E1
Portsmouth Rd. Ock Rid GU7 & GU8 150 B2
Portsmouth Rd. Ockham GU23 91 D7
Portsmouth Rd. Putney SW15 19 C8
Portsmouth Rd. Ripley GU23 91 B4
Portsmouth Rd. Send M GU23 91 B4
Portsmouth Rd. Shottm GU26 188 E2
Portsmouth Rd. Thame D KT6 & KT7 37 C3
Portsmouth Rd. Thursl GU8 169 D3
Portsmouth Rd. Whit V KT11 72 F6
Portsmouth Rd. Wisley GU23 & KT11 72 C3
Portsmouth Rd. Witley GU8 170 B6
Portswood Pl. Rhampt SW15 7 F1
Portugal Gdns. Twick TW2 16 C6
Portugal Rd. Woking GU21 69 F3
Portway. Ewell KT17 58 A2
Portway Cres. Ewell KT17 58 A2
Post House La. L Book KT23 94 A2
Post La. Twick TW2 16 D7
Postford Mill Cotts. Chil GU4 131 F5
Postmill Cl. S Croy CR0 & CR9 62 D7
Potley Hill Cty Prim Sch. Yatly GU17 64 A5
Potley Hill Rd. Yatly GU17 64 A5
Potter Cl. Mitch CR4 41 B7
Potter's La. Streat SW16 21 D2
Potterhill Ct. Tedd TW11 17 B1
Potteries La. Mytch GU16 85 F4
Potteries The. W Heath GU14 84 D6
Potterne Cl. 5 Putney SW15 & SW19 19 D8
Potters Cl. Croy CR0 43 E1
Potters Cl. Milf GU8 149 F2
Potters Cres. Ash GU12 106 B2
Potters Croft. Horsh RH13 217 E2
Potters Gate. Farnh GU9 125 A2
Potters Gate CE Prim Sch. Farnh GU9 125 A2
Potters Gr. New Mal KT3 38 C5
Potters La. Send GU23 90 B2
Potters Way. Dovgn RH2 139 C5
Pottersfield. Crawl RH10 201 D7
Pottery Ct. Wreccl GU10 145 F6
Pottery La. Wreccl GU10 145 F6
Pottery Rd. Brent TW8 6 E8
Poulett Gdns. Twick TW1 17 A7
Poullett House. Streat SW2 22 B7
Poulton Ave. Carsh SM1 & SM5 59 D7
Pound Cl. Godal GU7 150 E4
Pound Cl. Long D KT6 37 C1
Pound Cl. Loxwd RH14 212 F5
Pound Cres. Fetch KT22 94 D6
Pound Ct. Ashtd KT21 75 F1
Pound Ct. Wood S V GU3 108 B2
Pound Farm La. Normdy GU12 106 D1
Pound Field. Guild GU1 109 D1
Pound Hill. Wood S V GU3 108 B2
Pound Hill Cty Fst & Mid Schs. Crawl RH10 202 C7
Pound Hill Par. Crawl RH10 202 C7
Pound Hill Pl. Crawl RH10 202 C6
Pound La. Epsom KT19 76 D8
Pound La. Godal GU7 150 E4
Pound La. Windl GU20 48 C4
Pound La. Wood S V GU3 108 B2
Pound Pl. Shalf GU4 130 F3
Pound Place Cl. Shalf GU4 130 F3
Pound Rd. Alder GU12 105 C1
Pound Rd. Banstd SM7 78 A2
Pound Rd. Chert KT16 33 B2
Pound St. Wallin SM5 59 F5
Poundfield Gdns. Old Wok GU22 90 C7
Poundfield La. Ifold RH14 212 B3
Povey Cross Rd. Hookw RH6 160 E1
Powder Mill La. Twick TW2 & TW4 16 A7
Powderham Ct. Knaph GU21 68 D1
Powell Cl. Horley RH6 160 E4
Powell Cl. Onsl V GU2 129 F7
Powell Cl. Wallin SM6 60 E3
Powell Corderoy Prim Sch. Dork RH4 135 F6
Powell Ct. Croy CR0 61 C6
Powell's Wlk. Chisw W4 7 F8
Powells Cl. Dork RH5 136 C4
Powers Ct. Twick TW1 17 D8
Pownall Gdns. Hounsl TW3 5 B3
Pownall Rd. Hounsl TW3 5 B3

Poyle 14 Trad Est. Poyle SL3 . 1 E4
Poyle Cty Fst Sch. Poyle SL3 . 1 F6
Poyle Gdns. Wink RG12 .... 27 D8
Poyle House. Merrow GU4 110 D2
Poyle New Cotts. Poyle SL3 .. 1 F5
Poyle Rd. Guild GU1 .... 130 E7
Poyle Rd. Poyle SL3 .... 1 E5
Poyle Rd. Tongh GU10 ... 127 B7
Poyle Tech Ctr The. Poyle SL3 1 E5
Poynders Gdns. Streat SW12 21 C8
Poynders Rd.
    Streat SW12 & SW4 .... 21 D8
Poynes Rd. Horley RH6 ... 160 E5
Poynings Rd. Crawl RH11 .. 200 G5
Prairie Cl. Addl KT15 .... 52 B7
Prairie Rd. Addl KT15 .... 52 B7
Pratts Corner. Dunsf GU8 . 193 A8
Pratts La. Hersh KT12 .... 54 D6
Precinct The. Cran GU6 ..... 174 E4
Precinct The. E Mole KT8 ..... 36 B6
Precinct The. Egham TW20 .. 12 A3
Precincts The. Medm SM4 . 40 A3
Prendergast House. [7]
    Streat SW4 .... 21 D8
Prentice Cl. Farnb GU14 ..... 85 B8
Prentice Ct. [2]
    Wimble SW19 .... 19 F3
Prentis Rd. Streat SW16 ...... 21 D4
Presburg Rd. New Mal KT3 .. 38 E4
Presbury Ct. Woking GU21 ... 69 A1
Prescott. Easth RG2 .... 26 F2
Prescott Rd. Poyle SL3 .... 1 E5
Presentation Mews.
    Streat SW2 .... 21 F7
Prestbury Cres. Woodm SM7 78 F3
Preston Cl. Twick TW2 ...... 16 E5
Preston Cl. Walt O T KT12 ... 35 C1
Preston Dr. W Ewell KT19 ... 57 F4
Preston Dr. W Ewell KT19 ... 57 F4
Preston Gr. Ashtd KT21 ...... 75 C2
Preston La. Burgh H KT20 ... 97 C7
Preston Pl. Rich TW10 .... 6 E2
Preston Rd. S Norw SE19 .... 22 B2
Preston Rd. Shep Gn TW17 .. 34 A4
Preston Rd. Wimble SW20 ... 18 F1
Prestwick Cl. Crawl RH11 . 200 D5
Prestwick La. Chidd GU27 . 190 B2
Prestwick La. Grays GU27 . 190 B2
Prestwood Cl. Crawl RH11 . 181 B1
Prestwood Gdns.
    Thorn H CR0 .... 42 C2
Prestwood La. Rusper
    RH11 & RH12 & RH6 ...... 180 C3
Pretoria Rd. Chert KT16 ...... 32 F1
Pretoria Rd. Streat SW16 .... 21 C3
Pretty La. Hooley CR5 .... 99 C6
Prey Heath Cl. Woking GU22 89 C3
Prey Heath Rd.
    Woking GU22 .... 89 B3
Preymead Ind Est.
    Alder GU9 .... 126 B7
Price Cl. Up Toot SW17 ...... 20 F5
Price Rd. Croy CR0 .... 61 B5
Price Way. Hampt TW12 ..... 15 E2
Prices La. Woodh RH2 ...... 139 B6
Prickley Wood. Coney H BR2 44 F1
Priddy's Yd. [4] Croy CR9 .... 61 C8
Prides Crossing. Ascot SL5 ... 9 A1
Pridham Rd. S Norw CR7 .... 42 D5
Priest Ave. Woki RG11 .... 25 F5
Priest Croft Cl. Crawl RH11 201 A6
Priest Hill.
    Eng Gn TW19 & TW20 .... 11 C6
Priest Hill. Limps RH8 ...... 123 B6
Priest Hill Sch Sports Ctr.
    Ewell KT17 .... 77 B8
Priest La. W End GU24 .... 48 A4
Priestfield Rd. For Hil SE23 . 23 E5
Priestley Gdns.
    Old Wok GU22 .... 90 A7
Priestley Rd. Mitch CR4 ...... 41 A7
Priestley Rd. Onsl V GU2 .. 129 D8
Priestley Way. Crawl RH10 182 A3
Priests Bridge.
    Mortl SW14 & SW15 .... 7 E4
Priestwood Ave. Brack RG12 26 F8
Priestwood Court Rd.
    Brack RG12 .... 27 A8
Priestwood Sq. [1]
    Brack RG12 .... 27 A8
Prim Sch of Our Lady
    Immaculate. Tolw KT6 ..... 38 B1
Primrose Ave. Horley RH6 161 B1
Primrose Cl. Carsh CR4 ...... 41 B1
Primrose Cl. Catf SE6 .... 24 C3
Primrose Cl. Crawl RH11 ... 201 B3
Primrose Copse.
    Horsh RH12 .... 217 E7
Primrose Ct. New Mal KT4 .. 39 A2
Primrose Ct. [11]
    Streat SW12 .... 21 D8

Primrose Dr. Bisley GU24 .... 68 A4
Primrose Gdns. Farnb GU14 84 E3
Primrose House. [1] Rich TW9 6 F6
Primrose La. Croy CR0 .... 43 D1
Primrose Rd. Hersh KT12 .... 54 C5
Primrose Ridge.
    Ock Rd GU7 .... 150 B2
Primrose Way. Bramly GU5 151 D5
Primrose Way. Sandh GU17 . 45 B1
Primrose Wlk. Brack RG12 .. 27 C4
Primrose Wlk. Ewell KT17 ... 57 F3
Prince Albert Dr. Brack SL5 . 28 D4
Prince Albert Sq. Earls RH1 140 A4
Prince Andrew Way.
    N Asct SL5 .... 28 D7
Prince Charles Cres.
    Farnb GU14 .... 85 C8
Prince Charles Way.
    Hackb SM6 .... 60 B7
Prince Consort Dr.
    Brack SL5 .... 28 D7
Prince Consort's Dr.
    Old W SL4 .... 10 A6
Prince Consort's Dr. Wink SL4 9 F4
Prince Dr. Sandh GU17 .... 45 A1
Prince George's Ave.
    Merton SW20 .... 39 C7
Prince Georges Rd.
    Mitch SW19 .... 40 D8
Prince Of Wales' Rd.
    Carsh SM1 .... 59 D8
Prince Of Wales Rd.
    S Null RH1 .... 141 A2
Prince of Wales Wlk. [1]
    Camb GU15 .... 65 C6
Prince Rd. S Norw SE25 ..... 42 E4
Prince Regent Rd.
    Hounsl TW3 .... 5 C4
Prince William Ct.
    Ashf TW15 .... 13 F3
Prince's Ave. Farnb GU11 .. 105 C5
Prince's Ave. Wdmt SM5 .... 59 F2
Prince's Dr. Oxsh KT22 ...... 74 E7
Prince's Rd. Earls RH1 ...... 139 F7
Prince's Rd. Mortl SW14 ...... 7 D4
Prince's Rd. Tedd TW11 & 12 16 D4
Prince's Rd. Weyb KT13 ..... 53 C5
Prince's Rd. Wimble SW19 .. 20 A2
Prince's St. Rich TW10 & TW9 6 E2
Princes Ave. Hdns GU3 ..... 108 A6
Princes Ave. Tolw KT6 .... 57 A8
Princes Ave. Wallin SM5 .... 59 F2
Princes Cl. Bagsh GU19 ..... 47 E1
Princes Cl. Hams Gn CR2 ... 81 B4
Princes Cl. New Mal KT3 .... 38 F6
Princes Cl. Weyb KT13 .... 53 B5
Princes Gdns. Worpl GU3 . 108 E8
Princes Mead. Farnb GU14 . 85 B3
Princes Rd. Ashf TW15 .... 13 F3
Princes Rd. Egham TW20 ... 11 F2
Princes Rd. Felt TW13 .... 14 F5
Princes Rd. King U T KT2 ... 18 A1
Princes Rd. Penge SE20 .... 23 D2
Princes Rd. Rich TW10 .... 6 F2
Princes Rd. Rich TW9 .... 6 F4
Princes St. Sutton SM1 ...... 59 D6
Princes Way. Alder GU11 .. 105 A2
Princes Way. Coney H BR4 .. 63 F7
Princes Way. Croy CR0 ...... 60 F5
Princes Way.
    Putney SW15 & SW19 ...... 19 E7
Princess Anne Rd.
    Rudg RH12 .... 214 D6
Princess Ct. [9]
    Wimble SW19 .... 19 D1
Princess Gdns. Mayb GU22 . 70 B3
Princess House. [1]
    Redh RH1 .... 119 A2
Princess Margaret Rd.
    Rudg RH12 .... 214 D6
Princess Mary's Rd.
    Addl KT15 .... 52 C6
Princess Rd. Crawl RH11 .. 201 C6
Princess Rd. Mayb GU22 .... 70 B3
Princess Rd. Thorn H CR0 .. 42 C3
Princess Sq. Brack RG12 .... 27 B7
Princess Way. Camb GU15 .. 65 C5
Princess Way. Redh RH1 ... 119 A2
Princethorpe Rd.
    For Hil SE26 .... 23 D4
Princeton Mews. [3]
    King U T KT2 .... 38 A8
Pringle Gdns. Purley CR8 ... 60 F1
Pringle Gdns. Streat SW16 .. 21 C4
Prior Ave. Sutton SM2 & SM5 59 E3
Prior Croft Cl. Frml GU15 ... 66 A5
Prior End. Frml GU15 .... 66 A5
Prior Heath Cty Inf Sch.
    Frml GU15 .... 66 A5

Prior Rd. Frml GU15 .... 66 A5
Prior's La. Yatly GU17 .... 64 A5
Prioress Rd. W Norw SE27 .. 22 B5
Priors Cl. Farnb GU14 .... 85 B8
Priors Croft. Old Wok GU22 . 90 A7
Priors Ct. Ash GU12 .... 105 S1
Priors Ct. Woking GU21 ...... 69 A1
Priors Field Sch.
    Compt GU7 .... 129 A1
Priors Hatch La.
    Compt GU7 .... 128 F1
Priors Lodge. [4] Rich TW10 .. 6 E1
Priors Mead. Fetch KT23 .... 94 F2
Priors The. Ashtd KT21 ...... 95 D8
Priors Wlk. Crawl RH10 .... 201 F6
Priors Wood. Shottm GU27 207 F6
Priorsfield Rd. Compt GU7 129 A1
Priorswood. Compt GU3 ... 128 F2
Priory Ave. Cheam SM3 ...... 58 D6
Priory C of E Mid Sch.
    Wimble SW19 .... 20 B3
Priory Cl. Beck BR3 .... 43 E6
Priory Cl. Dork RH4 .... 136 A5
Priory Cl. Hampt TW12 .... 35 F8
Priory Cl. Horley RH6 .... Inset F4
Priory Cl. [3] Merton SW19 .. 40 B8
Priory Cl. Sheer GU21 ...... 70 D6
Priory Cl. Sunby TW16 .... 15 A1
Priory Cl. Walt O T KT12 .... 54 A7
Priory Cres. Cheam SM3 .... 58 D6
Priory Cres. S Norw SE19 ... 22 C1
Priory Ct. Camb GU15 .... 64 F5
Priory Ct. Cheam SM3 .... 58 D6
Priory Ct. Egham TW20 ...... 12 C2
Priory Ct. Hounsl TW3 .... 5 B4
Priory Ct. Rhampt SW15 ...... 7 F3
Priory Dr. Wodh RH2 .... 139 A7
Priory Gdns. Hampt TW12 ... 35 F8
Priory Gdns. Mortl SW13 ..... 7 F4
Priory Gn. Stain TW18 .... 13 B3
Priory Hospl The.
    Rhampt SW15 .... 7 F3
Priory House Sch. Catf SE6 . 24 B7
Priory La. E Mole KT8 .... 36 B5
Priory La. Frensh GU10 .... 167 E8
Priory La. Rhampt SW15 ...... 7 F2
Priory Lodge. Coney H BR4 .. 63 E7
Priory Mews. Stain TW18 ... 13 B3
Priory Pl. Walt O T KT12 .... 54 A7
Priory Rd. Cheam SM3 .... 58 D6
Priory Rd. Chess KT9 .... 56 E7
Priory Rd. For Row RH18 .. 206 D2
Priory Rd. Hamd TW12 .... 16 A1
Priory Rd. Islew TW3 .... 5 C2
Priory Rd. Mitch SW19 .... 20 D1
Priory Rd. Rich TW9 .... 7 A7
Priory Rd. Sunnin SL5 .... 30 A2
Priory Rd. Thorn H CR0 ...... 42 A2
Priory Sch. S Norw SE25 .... 42 F6
Priory Sch. The. Banstd SM7 78 A4
Priory St. Farnb GU14 .... 85 D4
Priory The. Croy CR0 .... 61 A7
Priory The. Godst RH9 ...... 121 B3
Priory The. [2] Hersh KT6 . 37 E4
Priory Way. Harm UB7 .... 2 E8
Priory Wlk. Brack RG12 ...... 27 F5
Priscilla House. [8]
    Charlt TW16 .... 14 F1
Probyn Rd. Streat SW2 ...... 22 B6
Proctor Gdns. G Book KT23 . 94 B2
Proctors Cl. E Bed TW14 .... 15 A7
Proctors Rd. Woki RG11 ..... 25 F6
Profumo Rd. Hersh KT12 .... 54 D6
Progress Bsns Pk. Croy CR9 60 F8
Progress Way. Croy CR0 ..... 60 F8
Promenade Approach Rd.
    Chisw W4 .... 7 E7
Promenade De Verdun.
    Purley CR8 .... 79 D8
Promenade The. Chisw W4 ... 7 F6
Propeller Rd. Farnb GU14 ... 85 B2
Prospect Ave. Farnb GU14 .. 85 B6
Prospect Cl. For Hil SE26 .... 23 B4
Prospect Cl. Hounsl TW5 ..... 4 F6
Prospect Cotts. Binf RG12 .. 26 D8
Prospect Cres. Twick TW2 .... 5 C1
Prospect La. Eng Gn TW20 .. 11 A3
Prospect Pl. Crawl RH11 ... 201 C6
Prospect Pl. Ewell KT17 ...... 76 E6
Prospect Pl. Stain TW18 .... 12 F3
Prospect Rd. Ash GU12 .... 106 A5
Prospect Rd. Farnb GU14 ... 85 B6
Prospect Rd. Rowl GU10 ... 145 E7
Prospect Rd. Thame D KT6 .. 37 C3
Prospect Rd. Wrath GU14 .. 85 A5
Prossers. Tadw KT20 .... 97 D6
Providence House.
    Bagsh GU19 .... 47 E3
Providence La. Harl UB3 ...... 3 D7

Providence Pl. Ewell KT17 .. 76 E7
Providence Pl. Horsh GU9 . 125 C2
Provincial Terr. Penge SE20 23 D1
Prune Hill. Egham TW20 .... 11 E1
Prunus Cl. W End GU24 ...... 67 E6
Public Record Office.
    Rich TW9 .... 7 B7
Puckridge Gate Rd.
    Farnb GU11 .... 104 E6
Puckridge Hill Rd.
    Alder GU11 .... 104 E6
Puckshill. Knaph GU21 .... 68 D2
Puckshott Way.
    Haslem GU27 .... 208 D8
Puddenhole Cotts.
    Brock RH4 .... 116 A2
Pudding La. Charl RH6 ..... 180 E7
Puffin Cl. Beck BR3 & CR0 .. 43 D4
Puffin Rd. Crawl RH11 ...... 200 D5
Pulborough Way. Hounsl TW4 4 C3
Pullman Cl. Streat SW2 ...... 21 F7
Pullman La. Godal GU7 .... 150 C2
Pump Alley. [8] Brent TW8 ... 6 D7
Pump La. Ascot SL5 .... 29 E8
Pump Pail N.
    Croy CR0 & CR9 .... 61 C7
Pump Pail S.
    Croy CR0 & CR9 .... 61 C7
Pumping Station Rd.
    Chisw W4 .... 7 E8
Punch Copse Rd.
    Crawl RH10 .... 201 F7
Punchbowl La.
    Dork RH4 & RH5 .... 136 D6
Punnetts Ct. Crawl RH11 .. 200 F2
Purbeck Ave. New Mal KT3 . 38 F3
Purbeck Cl. Merst RH1 ...... 119 D7
Purbeck Ct. [4] Stough GU2 108 E1
Purbeck Dr. Horse GU21 .... 69 F5
Purberry Gr. Ewell KT17 ..... 57 F1
Purberry Shot. Ewell KT17 .. 57 F1
Purbrook Ct. Brack RG12 ... 27 E3
Purbrook House. [2]
    Rhampt SW15 .... 19 B7
Purcell House. Twick TW2 ... 5 D1
Purcell Rd. Crawl RH11 .... 200 F3
Purcell Rd. Crowth RG11 .... 45 B7
Purcell's Cl. Ashtd KT21 .... 75 F1
Purdey Ct. [3] Worc Pk KT4 . 39 A1
Purley Bury Ave. Purley CR8 80 C8
Purley Bury Cl. Purley CR8 . 80 C8
Purley Ct. Purley CR8 .... 61 B1
Purley Downs Rd.
    S Croy CR2 .... 80 E8
Purley High Sch For Boys.
    Couldsd CR5 .... 100 A8
Purley Hill. Purley CR8 .... 80 B7
Purley Hospl. Purley CR8 ... 80 A8
Purley Knoll. Purley CR8 .... 80 A8
Purley Oaks Prim Sch.
    S Croy CR2 .... 61 D3
Purley Oaks Rd. S Croy CR2 61 D1
Purley Oaks Sta. S Croy CR2 61 D2
Purley Par. [2] Purley CR8 .. 80 A8
Purley Park Rd. Purley CR8 . 61 B1
Purley Rd. Purley CR8 .... 80 B7
Purley Rd. S Croy CR2 .... 61 D2
Purley Rise. Purley CR8 ...... 79 F7
Purley Sta. Purley CR8 .... 80 B7
Purley Vale. Purley CR8 ...... 80 B6
Purley View Terr.
    S Croy CR2 .... 61 D3
Purley Way. Croy CR0 & CR9 61 A4
Purley Way. Friml GU16 ..... 65 E8
Purley Way. Purley CR8 ...... 80 A8
Purley Way.
    Thorn H CR0 & CR9 .... 41 F1
Purmerend Cl.
    W Heath GU14 .... 84 C5
Pursers Hollow. Peasl GU5 154 D8
Pursers La. Peasl GU5 ...... 154 D8
Purslane. Woki RG11 .... 25 D3
Purton Rd. Horsh RH12 .... 217 B4
Putney Heath. Putney SW15 19 B8
Putney Heath La. Putney SW15 19 D8
Puttenham Heath Rd.
    Putt GU3 .... 128 E3
Puttenham Heath Rd.
    Wanb GU3 .... 128 E3
Puttenham Hill. Wanb GU3 128 C5
Puttenham La.
    Shack GU3 & GU8 .... 128 C1
Puttenham Rd. Seale GU10 127 C4
Puttenham Sch CE (VA).
    Putt GU3 .... 128 C4
Puttock Cl. Linch GU27 .... 207 D5
Pyecombe Ct. [4]
    Crawl RH11 .... 200 F3
Pyegrove Chase. Brack RG12 27 E2
Pyestock Cres.
    W Heath GU14 .... 84 C4

Pylbrook Rd. Sutton SM1 .... 59 B7
Pyle Hill.
    Westfd GU22 & GU4 .... 89 D3
Pymers Mead. Dulw SE21 ... 22 D7
Pymers Mead. W Norw SE21 22 C7
Pyne Rd. Tolw KT6 .... 38 A1
Pyrcroft Cty Fst Sch.
    Chert KT16 .... 32 E2
Pyrcroft Grange Prim Sch.
    Chert KT16 .... 32 E3
Pyrcroft La. Weyb KT13 ...... 53 B5
Pyrcroft Rd. Chert KT16 ..... 32 E2
Pyrford Common Rd.
    Mayb GU22 .... 70 E2
Pyrford Cty Prim Sch.
    Pyrf GU22 .... 70 F3
Pyrford Heath. Pyrf GU22 ... 70 F3
Pyrford Prim Sch. Pyrf GU22 71 A3
Pyrford Rd.
    Mayb GU22 & KT14 .... 71 A4
Pyrford Rd.
    Pyrf GU22 & KT14 .... 71 A4
Pyrford Rd.
    W Byfl GU22 & KT14 .... 71 A4
Pyrford Woods Cl.
    Pyrf GU22 .... 70 F4
Pyrford Woods Rd.
    Pyrf GU22 .... 70 F4
Pyrland Rd. Rich TW10 .... 6 F1
Pyrmont Gr. W Norw SE27 .. 22 B5
Pyrmont Rd. Brent W4 .... 7 A8
Pytchley Cres. S Norw SE19 22 C2

Quadrangle Lodge.
    Wimble SW19 .... 20 A2
Quadrangle The. Guild GU2 130 A8
Quadrant Ct. Brack RG12 ... 27 E6
Quadrant Rd. Rich TW9 .... 6 D3
Quadrant Rd. Thorn H CR7 . 42 B5
Quadrant The. Ash V GU12 106 A4
Quadrant The. Merton SW20 39 E8
Quadrant The. Rich TW9 ...... 6 E3
Quadrant The. Sutton SM2 . 59 C4
Quail Cl. Horsh RH12 .... 217 D7
Quail Gdns. Selsd CR0 .... 62 E1
Quakers Way. Fairl GU3 .... 108 C5
Qualitas. Easth RG12 .... 26 F1
Quality St. Merst RH1 .... 119 B7
Quantock Cl. Crawl RH11 .. 201 B6
Quantock Cl. Harl UB3 .... 3 D7
Quantock Dr. N Cheam KT4 . 58 C8
Quarr Rd. Carsh SM5 .... 40 E3
Quarry Bank. Lhtwat GU18 . 67 A8
Quarry Cl. Horsh RH12 ..... 217 F6
Quarry Cl. Oxted RH8 ...... 122 E3
Quarry Hill. Ock Rd GU7 ... 150 B3
Quarry Hill Pk. Reig RH2 ... 118 C4
Quarry Park Rd. Cheam SM1 58 F4
Quarry Rd. Oxted RH8 ...... 122 E5
Quarry Rd. Shackl GU7 ..... 150 A7
Quarry Rd. Wold RH9 .... 121 C7
Quarry Rise. Cheam SM1 .... 58 F4
Quarry Rise. E Grins RH19 186 A3
Quarry St. Guild GU1 & GU2 130 D7
Quarry The. Betch RH3 ..... 116 D3
Quarter Mile Rd.
    Godal GU7 .... 150 E2
Quarterbrass Farm Rd.
    Horsh RH12 .... 217 D7
Quartermaine Ave.
    Westfd GU22 .... 89 F5
Quartermaine Sch.
    Shottm GU27 .... 189 B2
Quarters Rd. Farnb GU14 ... 85 C2
Quay West. Rich TW11 .... 17 B3
Quebec Cl. Smallf RH6 ..... 162 A3
Quebec Gdns. Hawley GU17 64 D4
Queen Adelaide Ct.
    Penge SE20 .... 23 C1
Queen Adelaide Rd.
    Penge SE20 .... 23 C1
Queen Alexandra's Ct. [5]
    Wimble SW19 .... 19 F3
Queen Anne Ave. Beck BR2 . 44 F6
Queen Anne Dr. Clayg KT10 55 E3
Queen Anne's Cl. Old W SL4 10 B5
Queen Anne's Gdns.
    Leahd KT22 .... 95 B6
Queen Anne's Gdns.
    Mitch CR4 .... 40 F6
Queen Anne's Terr. [6]
    Leahd KT22 .... 95 B6
Queen Annes Cl. Twick TW2 16 D5
Queen Annes Ct. Leahd KT22 95 B6
Queen Eleanor's C of E Mid Sch.
    Onsl V GU2 .... 130 A8
Queen Eleanor's Rd.
    Onsl V GU2 .... 129 F8

Queen Elizabeth Dr.
Alder GU11 104 F2
Queen Elizabeth Gdns.
Morden SM4 40 A5
Queen Elizabeth Hospl.
Woodm SM7 78 C1
Queen Elizabeth II Jubilee Sch
The. Horsh RH13 217 F1
Queen Elizabeth Rd.
Camb GU15 46 D1
Queen Elizabeth Rd.
King U T KT2 37 F7
Queen Elizabeth Rd.
Rudg RH12 214 D7
Queen Elizabeth Way.
Old Wok GU22 90 A8
Queen Elizabeth's Dr.
New Add CR0 63 D1
Queen Elizabeth's Gdns.
New Add CR0 63 D1
Queen Elizabeth's Training Coll.
Ashtd KT22 74 D2
Queen Elizabeth's Wlk.
Wallin SM6 60 D6
Queen Mary Ave.
Camb GU15 65 A5
Queen Mary Ave.
W Barn SM4 39 D4
Queen Mary Ave.
W Barn SM4 & SW20 39 D4
Queen Mary Cl. Mayb GU22 . 70 C3
Queen Mary Rd.
Charlt TW17 34 C7
Queen Mary Rd.
S Norw SE19 22 B2
Queen Mary's Ave.
Wallin SM5 59 F3
Queen Mary's Dr.
Woodhm KT15 52 A1
Queen St. Alder GU12 105 D2
Queen St. Chert KT16 33 A1
Queen St. Croy CR0 & CR9 61 C6
Queen St. Godal GU7 150 E4
Queen St. Gomsh GU5 133 C4
Queen St. Horsh RH13 217 D1
Queen Victoria Cross Roads.
Sandh GU15 65 A6
Queen Victoria Hospl The.
E Grins RH19 185 F3
Queen Victoria Way.
Pirb GU24 87 D8
Queen's Ave. Alder GU11 105 B5
Queen's Ave. Farnb GU11 . 105 B5
Queen's C of E Jun Mix Sch The.
Rich TW9 7 A7
Queen's C of E Jun Sch The.
Rich TW9 7 A7
Queen's Cl. Farnb GU14 105 B8
Queen's Cl. N Asct SL5 28 E8
Queen's Cl. Wallin SM6 60 B5
Queen's Ct. Beck BR3 44 A8
Queen's Ct. Croy CR2 61 C5
Queen's Ct. Farnb GU14 105 C8
Queen's Ct. 1 King U T KT2 18 A1
Queen's Ct. 3 Rich TW10 6 F1
Queen's Ct. Stain TW18 13 D2
Queen's Ct. Thorn H CR7 42 A4
Queen's Dr. Farnc GU7 150 C7
Queen's Dr. Stough GU2 109 A4
Queen's Dr. Thame D KT7 37 A3
Queen's Gate Rd.
Farnb GU14 105 B8
Queen's Gdns. Heston TW5 4 E6
Queen's Hospl. Thorn H CR0 42 C3
Queen's House. Tedd TW11 16 F2
Queen's Mead. Chidd GU8 191 B4
Queen's Mead Rd.
Broml BR2 44 F7
Queen's Park Rd.
Cater CR3 100 E4
Queen's Pl. Ascot SL5 29 A6
Queen's Pl. Morden SM4 40 A5
Queen's Rd. Alder GU11 104 F2
Queen's Rd. Ascot SL5 29 D4
Queen's Rd. Beck BR3 43 E7
Queen's Rd. E Grins RH19 185 E1
Queen's Rd. Egham TW20 11 F2
Queen's Rd. Farnb GU14 105 D8
Queen's Rd.
Felt TW13 & TW14 15 B7
Queen's Rd. Guild GU1 109 D1
Queen's Rd. Hampt TW12 16 B4
Queen's Rd. Horley RH6 161 A3
Queen's Rd. Hounsl TW3 5 B4
Queen's Rd. King U T KT2 18 A1
Queen's Rd. Knaph GU21 68 D1
Queen's Rd. Mitch CR4 40 D6
Queen's Rd. Mortl SW14 7 D4
Queen's Rd. New Mal KT3 38 F4
Queen's Rd. Rich TW10 6 F1
Queen's Rd.
Rich KT2 & TW10 18 A3
Queen's Rd. Tedd TW11 16 F2
Queen's Rd. Thame D KT7 36 F4
Queen's Rd. Thorn H CR0 42 C3
Queen's Rd. Wallin SM6 60 B5
Queen's Rd. Wimble SW19 20 A2
Queen's Rdbt. Farnb GU11 105 B7
Queen's Rise. Rich TW10 6 F1
Queen's Terr. Islew TW7 6 A3
Queen's Way. Pirb GU24 87 D8
Queendale Ct. Woking GU21 68 F3
Queenhill Rd. S Croy CR2 62 B1
Queenhythe Rd.
Jacobs GU4 109 D7
Queens Acre.
Cheam SM2 & SM3 58 E3
Queens Ave. Byfl KT14 71 D7
Queens Ave. Felt TW13 15 C4
Queens Cl. Bisley GU24 68 A3
Queens Cl. Walt o t H KT20 97 A3
Queens Court Ride.
Cobham KT11 73 A6
Queens Cres. Rich TW10 6 F2
Queens Ct. 3 Redh RH1 119 A2
Queens Ct. Whit V KT13 53 E4
Queens Dr. Oxsh KT22 74 C8
Queens Dr. Surb KT5 38 A3
Queens Gate. Crawl RH6 182 A8
Queens Hill Rise. Ascot SL5 . 29 C6
Queens Keep. Camb GU15 65 D5
Queens Keep. 10 Twick TW1 . 6 C1
Queens La. Heath E GU9 125 B7
Queens Park Gdns.
Felt TW13 14 F5
Queens Pine. Brack RG12 27 E3
Queens Pl.
Whit V KT12 & KT13 53 E5
Queens Rd. Belm SM2 78 A8
Queens Rd. Bisley GU24 67 F1
Queens Rd. Camb GU15 65 B4
Queens Rd. Hale GU9 125 C6
Queens Rd. Hersh KT12 54 A6
Queens Rd. Morden SM4 40 A5
Queens Rd. Twick TW1 17 A7
Queens Rd. Weyb KT13 53 C5
Queens Rd. Whit V KT13 53 C5
Queens Reach. E Mole KT8 36 E5
Queens Sq. Crawl RH10 201 D6
Queens Way. Croy CR0 60 F5
Queens Way. Felt TW13 15 C4
Queens Wlk. Ashf TW15 13 D4
Queensberry House. 6
Rich TW9 6 D2
Queensbridge Pk. Islew TW7 5 E2
Queensbury Ct. S Norw CR7 42 C7
Queensbury Pl.
Hawley GU17 64 C3
Queensfield Ct. Cheam SM3 58 C6
Queensgate. Cobham KT11 73 D7
Queenshill Lodge. Ascot SL5 29 B6
Queensland Ave.
Merton SW19 40 B8
Queensmead. Farnb GU14 85 B3
Queensmead Ave.
E Ewell KT17 58 B1
Queensmere Cl.
Putney SW19 19 D6
Queensmere Rd.
Putney SW19 19 D6
Queensmere (Southlands Coll).
Putney SW19 19 D6
Queensthorpe Rd.
For Hil SE26 23 D4
Queensville Rd.
Streat SW12 & SW4 21 D8
Queensway. Coney H BR4 63 F6
Queensway. Cran GU6 174 F2
Queensway. Crawl RH10 201 E6
Queensway. E Grins RH19 185 E1
Queensway. Friml GU16 86 A7
Queensway. Hersh KT12 54 B5
Queensway. Horsh RH13 217 C1
Queensway. Redh RH1 118 F2
Queensway. Sunby TW16 35 B7
Queensway N. Hersh KT12 54 D6
Queensway S. Hersh KT12 54 C5
Queenswood Ave.
Hampt TW12 16 B2
Queenswood Ave.
Hounsl TW3 & TW5 4 F5
Queenswood Ave.
Thorn H CR7 42 A4
Queenswood Ave.
Wallin CR0 & SM6 60 D6
Queenswood Ct. 11
W Norw SE27 22 D4
Queenswood Rd.
For Hil SE23 23 E5
Queenswood Rd.
Knaph GU21 88 D8
Quennel House. 7
Streat SW12 21 C8
Quennell Cl. Ashtd KT21 95 F8
Quennells Hill.
Wreccl GU10 145 E6
Quentin Way. Vir W GU25 31 B5
Quicks Rd. Merton SW19 20 B1
Quiet Cl. Addl KT15 52 A6
Quillot The. Whit V KT12 53 F5
Quince Cl. Ascot SL5 29 D5
Quince Dr.
Bisley GU21 & GU24 68 B4
Quincy Rd. Egham TW20 12 A3
Quinneys. Farnb GU14 85 D1
Quintilis. Easth RG12 26 F1
Quintin Ave. Merton SW20 39 F8
Quintin Ct. Chisw W4 7 C7
Quintock House. 2 Rich TW9 7 A6
Quinton Cl. Beck BR3 44 C6
Quinton Cl. Hackb SM6 60 B6
Quinton Cl. Heston TW5 4 B7
Quinton Rd. Thame D KT7 37 A1
Quinton St. Wands SW18 20 C6
Quintrell Cl. Woking GU21 69 B2

Rabbit La. Whit V KT12 54 B3
Rabies Heath Rd.
Bletch RH1 120 F2
Rabies Heath Rd.
Godst RH1 & RH9 121 B1
Raby Rd. New Mal KT3 38 D5
Raccoon Way. Hounsl TW4 4 C5
Racecourse Rd. Crawl RH6 181 F8
Racecourse Rd.
Dorman RH7 165 A2
Racecourse Rd. Lingf RH7 . 164 F3
Racecourse Way.
Crawl RH6 181 F8
Rachel Ct. Sutton SM2 59 D3
Rackfield. Shottm GU27 207 D7
Rackham Cl. Crawl RH11 201 D4
Rackham Mews.
Streat SW16 21 C2
Racks Ct. Guild GU1 130 D7
Rackstraw Rd.
Sandh GU15 & RG11 45 D2
Racquets Court Hill.
Farnc GU7 150 C6
Rad La. Peasl GU5 133 D1
Rad La. Peasl GU5 133 E1
Radar Rd. Farnb GU14 84 D1
Radbourne Rd. Streat SW12 21 D7
Radcliff Mews. Hampt TW12 16 C3
Radcliffe Cl. Friml GU16 86 A7
Radcliffe Gdns. Sutton SM5 . 59 E3
Radcliffe Rd. S Croy CR0 61 F7
Radcliffe Way. Binf RG12 26 E8
Radcot Point. 2
For Hil SE23 23 D5
Radford Cl. Hale GU9 125 E5
Radford Rd.
Crawl RH10 & RH6 182 C4
Radius Pk. Hatton TW6 3 F3
Radlet Ave. For Hil SE23 23 B6
Radley Cl. E Bed TW14 14 F7
Radley Ct. Catf BR1 24 C4
Radley Lodge. 30
Putney SW19 19 D7
Radnor Cl. Mitch CR4 41 E5
Radnor Ct. 6 For Hil SE23 23 D5
Radnor Ct. Redh RH1 118 E1
Radnor Gdns. Twick TW1 16 F6
Radnor La.
Abin C GU5 & RH5 155 B7
Radnor La. Ewh GU6 155 A2
Radnor Rd. Brack RG12 27 F6
Radnor Rd.
Peasl GU5 & GU6 154 E4
Radnor Rd. Twick TW1 16 F6
Radnor Rd. Weyb KT13 53 A7
Radnor Wlk. Croy CR0 43 E3
Radolphs. Tadw KT20 97 D5
Radstock Way. Merst RH1 . 119 E7
Radstone Ct. 1
Woking GU22 69 F1
Rae Rd. Farnb GU14 85 B1
Raebarn Ct. 6 Streat SW16 21 E5
Raeburn Ave. Surb KT3 38 B3
Raeburn Ave.
Tolw KT5 & KT6 38 B3
Raeburn Cl. Tedd KT1 17 D1
Raeburn Ct. Woking GU21 89 A8
Raeburn Way. Sandh GU15 64 D6
Raf Gate Rd. Farnb GU14 85 B1
RAF Staff Coll. Brack RG12 27 D5
Rag Hill. Tats TN16 103 E6
Rag Hill Cl. Tats TN16 103 E6
Rag Hill Rd. Tats TN16 103 E6
Raglan Cl. Alder GU12 105 C1
Raglan Cl. Friml GU16 86 A8
Raglan Cl. Hounsl TW4 4 F2
Raglan Cl. Reig RH2 118 D3
Raglan Ct. Croy CR0 & CR2 61 B5
Raglan Prec The.
Cater CR3 100 E5
Raglan Rd. Knaph GU21 68 E1
Raglan Rd. Reig RH2 118 C3
Raglans House. Reig RH2 . 118 B4
Ragwort Ct. 1 For Hil SE26 23 B3
Raikes La. Abing C RH5 134 B2
Railey Rd. Crawl RH10 201 E7
Railshead Rd.
Islew TW1 & TW7 6 B3
Railton Rd. Stough GU2 109 B5
Railway App. Chert KT16 32 F1
Railway App. E Grins RH19 185 E1
Railway App. 10
Twick TW1 17 A8
Railway App. Wallin SM6 60 B5
Railway Cotts. Purley CR8 79 F6
Railway Rd. Tedd TW11 16 F4
Railway Side.
Mortl SW13 & SW14 7 E4
Railway Terr. Egham TW18 12 D3
Railway Terr.
Felt TW13 & TW14 15 A7
Rainbow Ct. Woking GU21 68 E3
Rainbow Ctr The.
Ewell KT17 76 E7
Rake La. Milf GU8 171 A7
Rake La. Witley GU8 170 F7
Rakers Ridge. Horsh RH12 217 D5
Raleigh Ave. Wallin SM6 60 D6
Raleigh Ct. Beck BR3 44 B8
Raleigh Ct. Crawl RH10 182 A3
Raleigh Ct. Dulw SE19 22 F3
Raleigh Ct. Stain TW18 13 A4
Raleigh Ct. Wallin SM6 60 B4
Raleigh Dr. Esher KT10 55 D5
Raleigh Dr. Smallf RH6 162 A3
Raleigh Dr. Tolw KT5 38 C1
Raleigh Gdns. Mitch CR4 40 F6
Raleigh House. 1
Thame D KT7 37 A2
Raleigh Rd.
Felt TW13 & TW14 14 F6
Raleigh Rd. Penge SE20 23 D1
Raleigh Rd. Rich TW9 6 F4
Raleigh Sch The.
W Hors KT24 92 C2
Raleigh Way. Felt TW13 15 C3
Raleigh Way.
Friml GU15 & GU16 65 F3
Raleigh Wlk. Crawl RH10 201 E4
Ralliwood Rd. Ashtd KT21 96 A8
Ralph Perring Ct. Beck BR3 . 44 A5
Ralphs Ride. Brack RG12 27 E6
Rambler Cl. Streat SW16 21 C4
Ramblers Way. 12
Crawl RH11 201 B1
Rame Cl. Up Toot SW17 21 A3
Ramillies Pk. Farnb GU11 105 E7
Ramillis Cl. Farnb GU11 105 E7
Ramin Ct. Bellf GU1 109 C4
Ramornie Cl. Hersh KT12 54 F6
Rams La. Dunsf GU8 193 B3
Ramsay Rd. Windl GU20 48 E5
Ramsbury Cl. Easth RG12 26 E3
Ramsdale Rd. Streat SW17 21 A3
Ramsdean House. 1
Rhampt SW15 19 B7
Ramsden Rd. Balham SW12 21 A8
Ramsden Rd. Godal GU7 150 D3
Ramsey Cl. Camb GU15 66 B8
Ramsey Cl. Horley RH6 160 F3
Ramsey Cl. Horsh RH12 217 D5
Ramsey Ct. 18
Crawl RH11 201 B1
Ramsey Ct. Croy CR9 61 B8
Ramsey House.
Merton SW19 40 B8
Ramsey Rd. Thorn H CR7 41 F3
Ramslade Rd. Brack RG12 27 D5
Rances La. Woki RG11 25 E5
Randal Cres. Woodh RH2 139 A7
Randall Schofield Ct.
Crawl RH10 202 A7
Randalls Cotts.
Cobham KT11 73 B7
Randalls Cres. Leahd KT22 95 A7
Randalls Park Ave.
Leahd KT22 95 A7
Randalls Park Dr.
Leahd KT22 95 A6
Randalls Rd. Leahd KT22 94 E7
Randalls Way. Leahd KT22 95 A7
Randell Cl. W Heath GU14 64 E1
Randisbourne Gdns.
Catf SE6 24 B5
Randle Rd. Rich TW10 17 C4
Randlesdown Rd. Catf SE6 24 B5
Randmore Ct. 6 Beck BR3 . 24 A1
Randolph Cl. King U T KT2 18 C3
Randolph Cl. Knaph GU21 68 E2
Randolph Cl. Oxsh KT11 74 A4
Randolph Dr. Farnb GU14 84 C3
Randolph Rd. Epsom KT17 76 F5
Ranelagh Cotts.
Smallf RH6 162 B2
Ranelagh Cres. N Asct SL5 28 D8
Ranelagh Dr. Brack RG12 27 C6
Ranelagh Dr. Islew TW1 6 B2
Ranelagh Gdns. Chisw W4 7 C7
Ranelagh Pl. New Mal KT3 38 E4
Ranelagh Rd. Redh RH1 118 E1
Ranelagh Sch. Brack RG12 27 C6
Ranfurly Rd. Sutton SM1 59 A8
Range Rd. Farnb GU14 84 D1
Range Ride. Sandh GU15 64 F7
Range The. Bramly GU5 152 A4
Range View. Sandh GU15 64 E8
Range Villas. Lo Hall TW17 33 E2
Range Way. Lo Hall TW17 34 A2
Rangefield Prim Sch.
Catf BR1 24 E3
Rangefield Rd. Broml BR1 24 F3
Rangefield Rd. Catf BR1 24 F3
Rankine Cl. Farnh GU9 126 A6
Ranmere St. Balham SW12 21 B7
Ranmore Ave. S Croy CR0 61 F7
Ranmore Cl. Redh RH1 119 A4
Ranmore Common Rd.
Wotton RH5 114 D2
Ranmore Ct. King U T KT6 37 D4
Ranmore Ct. Wimble SW20 . 39 D8
Ranmore Pl. Weyb KT13 53 C5
Ranmore Rd. Dork RH4 136 A8
Ranmore Rd. E Ewell SM2 58 D2
Ranmore Rd.
Wotton RH4 & RH5 114 E1
Rann House. 1 Mortl SW14 . 7 D4
Rannoch Ct. 9 King U T KT6 37 E4
Ransford House. 16
Dulw SE21 22 E4
Ransome Cl. Crawl RH11 200 E3
Ranyard Cl. Chess KT9 56 F7
Rapallo Cl. Farnb GU14 85 C4
Rapley Cl. Camb GU15 65 F8
Rapley Gn. Easth RG12 27 C3
Rapley's Field. Pirb GU24 87 E4
Rapsley La. Knaph GU21 68 B1
Rastell Ave. Streat SW12 21 D7
Ratcliffe Rd. Farnb GU14 85 A8
Rathbone House.
Crawl RH11 201 B1
Rathbone House. 8
Wimble SW19 19 D1
Rathfern Prim Sch.
For Hil SE23 23 F7
Rathfern Rd.
For Hil SE23 & SE6 23 F7
Rathgar Cl. Earls RH1 140 A4
Rathlin Rd. Crawl RH11 201 B3
Raven Cl. Horsh RH12 217 E6
Raven La. Crawl RH11 201 C8
Ravendale Rd. Sunby TW16 . 34 F7
Ravendene Ct. 3
Crawl RH11 201 D5
Ravenfield Rd.
Up Toot SW17 20 F5
Ravens Cl. Broml BR2 44 F7
Ravens Cl. Knaph GU21 68 C3
Ravens Cl. Redh RH1 118 F2
Ravens Wold. Kenley CR8 80 C4
Ravensbourne. 3 Twick TW1 6 C1
Ravensbourne Ave.
Broml BR2 & BR3 44 E8
Ravensbourne Ave.
Catf BR2 24 D1
Ravensbourne Ave.
Stan TW19 13 E7
Ravensbourne Ct.
For Hil SE6 24 A8
Ravensbourne House.
Catf BR1 24 D3
Ravensbourne Park Cres.
For Hil SE6 23 F8
Ravensbourne Pk.
For Hil SE4 & SE6 24 A8
Ravensbourne Rd.
For Hil SE23 23 F7
Ravensbourne Rd. Twick TW1 6 C1
Ravensbourne Sta. Catf BR3 24 D1
Ravensbury Ave.
Morden SM4 40 C4
Ravensbury Ct. Mitch CR4 40 D5
Ravensbury Gr. Mitch CR4 40 D5
Ravensbury La. Mitch CR4 40 D5
Ravensbury Rd.Wands SW18 20 B6
Ravensbury Terr.
Wands SW18 20 B6

Ravenscar Lodge. 🔢
Wimble SW19 .... 19 D1
Ravenscar Rd. Catf BR1 ..... 24 E4
Ravenscar Rd. Surb KT6 ..... 56 F8
Ravenscote Jun Sch.
Friml GU16 .... 66 A3
Ravenscourt. Sunby TW16 .. 34 F8
Ravenscroft Cl. Ash GU12 .. 106 C3
Ravenscroft.
Horsh RH12 .... 217 C3
Ravenscroft Rd. Penge BR3 . 43 D7
Ravenscroft.
Whit V KT13 .... 72 C8
Ravensdale Gdns.
S Norw SE19 .... 22 C1
Ravensdale Rd. Ascot SL5 ... 29 A4
Ravensdale Rd. Hounsl TW4 .. 4 E4
Ravensfield. Eng Gn TW20 ... 11 C2
Ravensfield Gdns.
Worc Pk KT19 .... 57 E6
Ravenshead Cl. Selsd CR2 ... 81 C8
Ravenside. King U T KT6 ..... 37 D4
Ravenslea Rd.
Balham SW11 & SW12 ...... 20 F8
Ravensmead Rd. Broml BR2 24 D1
Ravensroost. S Norw SE19 .. 42 D8
Ravenstone Jun & Inf Schs.
Up Toot SW12 .... 21 A6
Ravenstone Rd. Friml GU15 . 66 D5
Ravenstone St.
Up Toot SW12 .... 21 A7
Ravensview Ct. King U T KT6 37 D4
Ravenswood Ave. Tolw KT6 . 57 A8
Ravenswood Ave.
W Wick BR4 .... 44 C1
Ravenswood Cl.
Cobham KT11 .... 73 D4
Ravenswood Cres.
W Wick BR4 .... 44 C1
Ravenswood Ct.
Woking GU22 .... 69 F1
Ravenswood Dr. Friml GU15 66 A5
Ravenswood Gdns.
Hounsl TW7 .... 5 E6
Ravenswood Rd.
Balham SW12 .... 21 B8
Ravenswood Rd.
Croy CR0 & CR9 .... 61 B7
Rawlins Cl. S Croy CR2 .... 62 F3
Rawlinson Rd. Sandh GU15 . 64 F6
Rawnsley Ave. Mitch CR4 .... 40 E4
Raworth Cl. Worth RH10 ... 202 C4
Ray Cl. Lingf RH7 .... 164 C5
Ray Cnr. Lingf RH7 .... 164 B6
Ray La. Blind H RH7 .... 163 F7
Ray La. Lingf RH7 .... 164 B6
Ray La. Tand RH7 .... 164 B6
Ray Rd. E Mole KT8 .... 36 B4
Raybell Ct. Islew TW7 .... 5 F5
Rayford Ave. Lewish SE12 ... 24 F8
Rayleigh Ave. Tedd TW11 ... 16 E2
Rayleigh Cl. 🔢 King U T KT1 37 F7
Rayleigh Rd. Merton SW19 .. 39 F8
Rayleigh Rise. S Croy CR2 ... 61 E4
Raymead Ave. Thorn H CR7 . 42 A4
Raymead Cl. Fetch KT22 ..... 94 F5
Raymead Way. Fetch KT22 .. 94 F5
Raymer Wlk. Horley RH6 ... 161 C4
Raymond Cl. For Hil SE26 ... 23 C3
Raymond Cl. Poyle SL3 .... 1 E6
Raymond Cres. Onsl V GU2 129 F8
Raymond Rd. Beck BR3 ...... 43 E5
Raymond Rd. Wimble SW19 19 E2
Raymond Way. Clay KT10 .. 56 A4
Raynald House. 🔢
Street SW16 .... 21 E5
Rayners Cl. Coln SL3 .... 1 C7
Raynes Park High Sch.
W Barn KT3 .... 39 B6
Raynes Park Sta.
W Barn SW20 .... 39 C7
Raynesfield. W Barn SW20 .. 39 C6
Rays Rd. W Wick BR4 .... 44 C2
Raywood Cl. Harl UB7 .... 3 C7
Read Rd. Ashtd KT21 .... 75 D2
Readens The. Woodm SM7 .. 78 F3
Reading Arch Rd.
Redh RH1 .... 118 F1
Reading Rd. Blckw GU17 .... 64 B4
Reading Rd. Farnb GU14 ... 85 D1
Reading Rd. Sutton SM1 .... 59 C5
Reading Rd. Woki RG11 ...... 25 A7
Reading Rd. Yatly GU17 ...... 64 B4
Readman Ct. 🔢 Penge SE20 43 B8
Reads Rest La. Barstd KT20 98 A2
Reapers Cl. Horsh RH12 ... 217 D5
Reapers Way. Islew TW7 ...... 5 D2
Rebecca Ct. Beck BR3 .... 44 A8
Recovery St. Up Toot SW17 21 D3
Recreation Rd. Broml BR2 ... 44 F7
Recreation Rd. For Hil SE26 23 D4

Recreation Rd. Guild GU1 . 109 D1
Recreation Rd. Rowl GU10 145 E3
Recreation Way.
Mitch CR4 & SW16 .... 41 E6
Rectory Cl. Ashtd KT21 ...... 95 F8
Rectory Cl. Bramly GU5 .... 151 F6
Rectory Cl. Byfl KT14 .... 71 E6
Rectory Cl. Easth RG12 ...... 27 C5
Rectory Cl. Ewh GU6 .... 175 E5
Rectory Cl. Godal GU7 ..... 150 F2
Rectory Cl. Littlt TW17 ...... 34 A6
Rectory Cl. Long D KT6 ...... 37 C1
Rectory Cl. Merrow GU4 ... 110 D3
Rectory Cl. Ockley RH5 .... 177 C3
Rectory Cl. W Barn SW20 ... 39 C6
Rectory Cl. Woki RG11 .... 25 C6
Rectory Cl. Felt TW13 .... 15 C4
Rectory Cl. Sander CR2 ...... 80 F7
Rectory Cl. Wallin SM6 ...... 60 C6
Rectory Gdns. Beck BR3 ..... 44 A8
Rectory Gn. Beck BR3 .... 43 F8
Rectory Gr. Croy CR0 & CR9 . 61 B8
Rectory Gr.
Hampt TW12 & TW13 ...... 15 F4
Rectory Green La.
Buckl RH3 .... 116 F3
Rectory La. Ashtd KT21 ...... 95 F8
Rectory La. Byfl KT14 .... 71 E6
Rectory La. Charl RH6 ...... 180 D7
Rectory La. Crawl RH11 .... 200 F8
Rectory La. Easth RG12 ...... 27 B5
Rectory La. G Book KT23 .. 113 F8
Rectory La. Long D KT6 ...... 37 C1
Rectory La. Shere GU5 ..... 133 A4
Rectory La. Streat SW17 .... 21 A3
Rectory La. Titsey TN16 .... 103 E4
Rectory La. Wallin SM6 ...... 60 C6
Rectory La. Windl GU20 ..... 48 C4
Rectory La.
Woodm CR5 & SM7 .... 78 F3
Rectory Orch. Wimble SW19 19 E4
Rectory Pk. Sander CR2 ...... 80 F7
Rectory Rd. Beck BR3 .... 44 A8
Rectory Rd. Cranf TW5 .... 4 C5
Rectory Rd. Farnb GU14 ... 85 D4
Rectory Rd. L Kings CR5 .... 98 D2
Rectory Rd. Sutton SM1 ..... 59 B7
Rectory Rd. Woki RG11 ...... 25 C6
Rectory Row. Easth RG12 ... 27 B5
Rectory Sch. Hampt TW12 .. 16 A3
Red Admiral St.
Horsh RH12 .... 217 E5
Red Deer Cl. Horsh RH13 . 218 B4
Red Gables Dr. S Croy CR2 .. 61 D1
Red House La. Elst GU8 .... 148 C2
Red House La.
Walt O T KT12 .... 54 A8
Red House Rd.
Wallin CR0 & CR9 .... 41 D3
Red House Sch. Kings KT20 . 97 E6
Red La. Clayg KT10 .... 56 A4
Red La. Head Dn GU35 ..... 187 B7
Red La. Limps RH8 .... 144 B7
Red La. S Holm RH5 & RH3 . 136 A7
Red Lion Bsns Ctr. Surb KT6 56 F7
Red Lion La. Burrh GU24 .... 49 E2
Red Lion La. Farnh GU9 .... 125 B1
Red Lion Rd. Burrh GU24 .... 49 E2
Red Lion Rd. Surb KT6 .... 57 A8
Red Lion St. Rich TW10 ...... 6 D2
Red Lodge. W Wick BR4 ..... 44 C2
Red Lodge Rd.
W Wick BR3 & BR4 .... 44 C3
Red Rd. W End GU15,18 &24 67 C7
Red River Ct. Horsh RH12 . 217 B5
Redan Gdns. Alder GU12 ... 105 C2
Redan Hill Est. Alder GU11 105 C2
Redan Rd. Alder GU12 ...... 105 C2
Redbarn Cl. Purley CR8 ...... 80 B8
Redberry Gr.
For Hil SE23 & SE26 .... 23 C5
Redcar House. Penge SE26 .. 23 B2
Redcliffe Missionary Training
Coll. Chisw W4 .... 7 B7
Redclose Ave. Morden SM4 . 40 A4
Redclyffe Terr. 🔢 Belm SM2 59 A3
Redcote. Pixham RH4 ...... 115 D1
Redcourt. Maybi GU22 .... 70 D4
Redcourt. Pyrf GU22 .... 70 E4
Redcrest Gdns. Camb GU15 . 65 F5
Redcroft Wlk. Cran GU6 ... 174 E2
Redding Way. Knaph GU21 .. 68 C1
Reddington Cl. S Croy CR2 .. 61 D2
Redditch. Brack RG12 .... 27 D2
Redditch Cl. Crawl RH11 ... 200 E2
Reddons Rd. Penge BR3 ..... 23 E1
Reddown Rd. Coulsd CR5 ... 79 D2
Rede Ct. Weyb KT13 .... 53 B7
Redehall Prep Sch.
Smallf RH6 .... 162 B2

Redehall Rd. Burst RH6 ..... 183 C8
Redehall Rd. Smallf RH6 .... 162 B2
Redesdale Gdns. Hounsl TW7 6 A7
Redfern Ave.
Twick TW2 & TW4 .... 16 A8
Redfern Rd. Lewish SE6 ..... 24 C8
Redford Ave. Horsh RH12 . 217 B4
Redford Ave. Thorn H CR7 .. 41 F5
Redford Ave. Wallin SM6 .... 60 E4
Redford Ave. Wallin CR5 ..... 79 B4
Redford Cl. Felt TW13 .... 14 F6
Redgarth Ct. E Grins RH19 185 B3
Redgrave Ct. Croy SE25 ..... 42 F3
Redgrave Dr. Worth RH10 . 202 D5
Redgrove Ct. Alder GU12 .. 105 F2
Redhall Ctr. Cater CR3 ..... 100 D4
Redhearne Fields.
Churt GU10 .... 167 E2
Redhill Coll. Earls RH1 ..... 140 B8
Redhill Ct. Streat SW2 .... 22 A6
Redhill Distribution Ctr.
Salfs RH1 .... 161 A8
Redhill Rd. Whit V KT11 ..... 72 B5
Redhill Sta. Redh RH1 ..... 119 A2
Redhouse Rd. Tats TN16 ... 103 C6
Redkiln Cl. Horsh RH13 .... 217 F4
Redkiln Way.
Horsh RH12 & RH13 .... 217 F3
Rednap House. Rich TW10 . 17 C5
Redlake La. Woki RG11 ...... 25 F2
Redland Gdns. E Mole KT8 . 35 F5
Redlands. Coulsd CR5 .... 79 E3
Redlands. Tedd TW11 .... 17 A2
Redlands CE Fst Sch The.
Dork RH4 .... 136 B4
Redlands Cotts. Dork RH5 136 B1
Redlands Ct. Broml BR1 ..... 24 E1
Redlands Cty Jun Sch The.
Dork RH4 .... 136 B4
Redlands La. Crond GU10 . 124 B7
Redlands La. Dork RH5 ..... 136 A1
Redlands The. Beck BR3 ..... 44 B7
Redlands Way. Streat SW2 .. 21 F8
Redlane Cotts. Oxted RH8 123 B2
Redleaves Ave. Ashf TW15 . 14 B2
Redlees Cl. Islew TW7 .... 6 A3
Redlin Ct. Redh RH1 .... 118 F3
Redmayne. Friml GU15 ...... 66 C4
Redroofs Cl. Beck BR3 .... 44 B8
Redruth House. Sutton SM2 59 B3
Redshank Ct. 🔢
Earls RH1 .... 200 D5
Redstart Cl.
New Add CR0 & CR9 .... 63 D1
Redstone Hill. Earls RH1 ... 119 A1
Redstone Hollow.
Earls RH1 .... 140 A8
Redstone Manor.
Earls RH1 .... 119 A1
Redstone Pk. Earls RH1 ... 119 B1
Redstone Rd. Earls RH1 .... 140 A8
Redvers Buller Rd.
Farnb GU11 .... 105 D7
Redvers Rd. Warlgm CR6 ... 81 C1
Redvers Rd. Easth RG12 ..... 27 B4
Redvers Rd. Warlgm CR6 ... 81 D1
Redway Cotts. Woking GU21 88 F8
Redway Dr. Twick TW2 .... 16 C8
Redwing Ave. Farnc GU7 .. 150 E8
Redwing Cl. Horsh RH13 ... 217 F3
Redwing Cl. Selsd CR2 .... 81 D8
Redwing Rise.
Merrow GU4 .... 110 D3
Redwood. Egham TW20 ..... 32 E7
Redwood Cl. Crawl RH10 .. 201 E8
Redwood Cl. Kenley CR8 .... 80 D5
Redwood Cl. 🔟 Surb KT6 ... 37 D2
Redwood Dr. Friml GU15 .... 66 B4
Redwood Dr. Sunnin SL5 .... 30 B3
Redwood Est. Heston TW5 .... 4 B8
Redwood Gr. Chil GU4 ...... 131 C3
Redwood Manor.
Haslem GU27 .... 208 C7
Redwood Mount. Reig RH2 118 A4
Redwood Wlk. Surb KT6 ..... 37 D1
Redwoods. Rhampt SW15 .. 19 A7
Redwoods The. Tilf GU10 .. 147 A3
Reed Cl. Farnb GU11 ...... 105 D5
Reed Pl. Sheer GU21 & KT14 70 E6
Reed Place Bsns Park.
Lo Hail TW17 .... 33 F1
Reed's Sch. Cobham KT11 .. 74 A7
Reedham Dr. Purley CR8 .... 79 F6
Reedham Dr. Purley CR8 .... 80 A6
Reedham Park Ave.
Purley CR8 .... 80 A3
Reedham Sta. Purley CR8 ... 79 F6
Reedings. Crawl RH11 ..... 200 D4
Reeds Rd The.
Frensh GU10 .... 146 E2
Reeds Rd The. Tilf GU10 .. 147 A3

Reedsfield Cl. Ashf TW15 .... 14 B5
Reedsfield Rd. Ashf TW15 .. 14 B4
Rees Gdns. Croy CR0 .... 42 F3
Reeve Ct. Stough GU2 ...... 109 B6
Reeve Rd. Dovgn RH1 ...... 139 C5
Reeves Cnr. Croy CR0 & CR9 61 B8
Reeves Rd. Alder GU12 .... 105 C1
Reeves Way. Woki RG11 ..... 25 A4
Regal Cres. Hackb SM6 .... 60 B7
Regal Ct. 🔢 Guild GU1 ..... 109 D1
Regal Ct. 🔢 Mitch CR4 ...... 40 F6
Regal Dr. 🔟 E Grins RH19 205 F8
Regalfield Cl. Stough GU2 . 109 A5
Regan Cl. Stough GU2 ...... 109 B6
Regency Ct. Hampt TW12 ... 15 F3
Regency Ct. 🔢 Surb KT5 .... 37 F4
Regency Ct. Sutton SM1 .... 59 B6
Regency Dr. W Byfl KT14 .... 70 F6
Regency Gdns.
Walt O T KT12 .... 35 D1
Regency Lodge. Oat Pk KT13 53 E7
Regency Mews. Beck BR3 ... 44 C8
Regency Mews. Islew TW7 ... 5 E2
Regency Wlk. Croy CR0 ...... 43 F3
Regency Wlk. 🔢 Rich TW10 . 6 E2
Regent Cl. Cranf TW5 .... 4 B6
Regent Cl. New Haw KT15 .. 52 D2
Regent Cres. Redh RH1 .... 118 F3
Regent Cl. Bagsh GU19 ...... 47 F2
Regent Cl. Stough GU2 .... 109 B3
Regent Lodge. 🔢
Street SW2 .... 21 F7
Regent Pk. Leahd KT22 ...... 75 A1
Regent Pl. Croy CR0 .... 42 F1
Regent Pl. Wimble SW19 ... 20 C3
Regent Rd. Surb KT5 .... 38 A4
Regent St. Brent W4 .... 7 A8
Regent Way. Friml GU16 .... 66 A1
Regents Cl. Crawl RH11 .... 201 C2
Regents Cl. S Croy CR2 ...... 61 E4
Regents Cl. Whytlf CR3 ...... 80 F1
Regents Cl. 🔢 Beck BR3 ..... 24 A1
Regents Cl. Broml BR1 .... 24 F1
Regents Ct. Whit V KT13 .... 53 B4
Regents Pl. Sandh GU17 .... 64 C8
Regents Wlk. Sunnin SL5 ... 29 C2
Regiment Cl. Farnb GU14 .. 84 C3
Regina Coeli RC Prim Sch.
Croy CR2 .... 61 B3
Regina Rd. Croy SE25 .... 43 A6
Reginald Ct. Beck BR3 .... 44 C8
Regis Ct. E Bed TW14 .... 3 D1
Regis Ct. Mitch SW19 .... 40 E8
Regnolruf Ct. Walt O T KT12 35 A2
Reid Ave. Cater CR3 .... 100 D6
Reid Ct. Mortl SW14 .... 7 C5
Reidonhill Cotts.
Bisley GU21 .... 68 B1
Reigate Ave.
Cheam SM3 & SM4 .... 40 B1
Reigate Cl. Crawl RH10 .... 182 D1
Reigate Coll. Reig RH2 .... 118 B1
Reigate Day Hospl.
Woodh RH2 .... 139 A7
Reigate Gram Sch.
Reig RH1 .... 118 C1
Reigate Heath Cotts.
Reig RH2 .... 117 E1
Reigate Hill. Reig RH2 ..... 118 B4
Reigate Hill Cl. Reig RH2 .. 118 B4
Reigate Priory Prim Sch.
Reig RH2 .... 118 B1
Reigate Rd. Betch
RH2 & RH3 & RH4 & RH5 .. 116 C2
Reigate Rd. Brock
RH2 & RH3 & RH4 & RH5 .. 116 C2
Reigate Rd. Burgh H KT18 ... 77 C4
Reigate Rd. Catf BR1 .... 24 F5
Reigate Rd.
Dork RH4 & RH5 .... 136 C8
Reigate Rd. Ewell KT17 ...... 77 C4
Reigate Rd. Hookw RH6 ... 160 C4
Reigate Rd. Leat KT22 .... 95 D4
Reigate Rd. Nork KT17 ...... 77 C4
Reigate Rd. Pixham RH4 .. 115 E1
Reigate Rd. Reig RH7 ...... 118 C1
Reigate Rd.
Sidlow RH2 & RH6 .... 160 C4
Reigate Sch. Woodh RH1 .. 139 C6
Reigate Sch of Art & Design.
Reig RH2 .... 118 D1
Reigate St Mary's Prep Sch.
Reig RH2 .... 118 B1
Reigate Sta. Reig RH2 ...... 118 A2
Reigate Way. Wallin SM6 ... 60 E5
Reindorp Cl. Guild GU2 ... 130 A8
Relko Ct. Epsom KT19 .... 76 D8
Relko Gdns. Carsh SM1 ..... 59 D5
Rembrandt Way.
Walt O T KT12 .... 54 B8

Rendle Cl. Croy CR0 & SE25 . 43 A4
Renfree Way. Shep TW17 ... 34 A2
Renfrew Ct. Hounsl TW5 ...... 4 E5
Renfrew Rd. Hounsl TW5 ..... 4 E5
Renfrew Rd. King U T KT2 .. 18 C1
Renmans The. Ashtd KT21 .. 75 F3
Renmuir St. Up Toot SW17 . 20 F2
Rennie Cl. Ashf TW15 .... 13 D5
Rennie Terr. Earls RH1 ..... 140 A8
Renown Cl. Thorn H CR0 .... 42 B1
Renshaw House. 🔢
W Norw SW27 .... 22 B3
Replingham Rd.
Wands SW18 .... 20 A7
Repton Cl. Carsh SM1 & SM5 59 E5
Repton Ct. Beck BR3 .... 44 B8
Reservoir Rd. Farnb GU14 .. 84 D1
Restmor Way.
Hackb SM5 & SM6 .... 60 A8
Restormel Cl. Hounsl TW3 ... 5 A2
Restwell Ave. Rowly GU6 .. 174 B6
Retreat Rd. Rich TW9 .... 6 D2
Retreat The. Eng Gn TW20 .. 11 E3
Retreat The. Mortl SW14 ..... 7 E4
Retreat The. N Cheam KT4 . 58 B8
Retreat The. S Norw CR7 ... 42 D5
Retreat The. Surb KT5 .... 37 F3
Revell Cl. Fetch KT22 .... 94 B5
Revell Dr. Fetch KT22 .... 94 B5
Revell Rd. Cheam SM1 ...... 58 F4
Revell Rd. King U T KT1 ..... 38 B8
Revelstoke Ave.
Farnb GU14 .... 85 B6
Revelstoke Rd.
Wands SW18 & SW19 ...... 20 A6
Revesby Cl. W End GU24 .... 67 D6
Revesby Rd. Carsh SM5 ..... 40 E3
Rewley Rd. Carsh SM4 .... 40 D3
Rex Ave. Ashf TW15 .... 14 A3
Rex House. Felt TW13 .... 15 E5
Reynard Cl. Horsh RH12 ... 218 B5
Reynard Dr. S Norw SE19 ... 22 F1
Reynolds Ave. Chess KT9 ... 56 E3
Reynolds Cl.
Carsh CR4 & SM5 .... 40 F1
Reynolds Cl.
Mitch CR4 & SW19 .... 40 D8
Reynolds Gn. Sandh GU15 . 64 D6
Reynolds Pl. Crawl RH11 .. 201 C7
Reynolds Pl. 🔢 Rich TW10 ... 6 F1
Reynolds Rd. Crawl RH11 .. 201 C7
Reynolds Rd. Farnb GU14 . 104 B8
Reynolds Rd. New Mal KT3 . 38 D2
Reynolds Way. S Croy CR0 . 61 E6
Rheingold Way. Wallin SM6 60 E2
Rhine Banks. W Heath GU14 84 D5
Rhodes Cl. Egham TW20 .... 12 B3
Rhodes Ct. Egham TW20 .... 12 C3
Rhodes Way. Crawl RH10 . 201 F3
Rhodes-Moorhouse Ct.
Morden SM4 .... 40 A3
Rhododendron Cl. N Asct SL5 8 E1
Rhododendron Rd.
Friml GU16 .... 86 B8
Rhododendron Wlk.
Eng Gn SL4 & TW20 .... 10 F3
Rhododendron Wlk.
N Asct SL5 .... 8 E1
Rhodrons Ave. Chess KT9 .. 56 E5
Rialto Rd. Mitch CR4 .... 41 A7
Ribble Pl. W Heath GU14 .... 84 E7
Ribblesdale. Dork RH4 ..... 136 B5
Ribblesdale Rd.
Street SW16 .... 21 B3
Ricardo Ct. Bramly GU5 ... 151 F5
Ricards Lodge High Sch.
Wimble SW19 .... 19 F3
Ricards Rd. Wimble SW19 .. 19 F3
Rice's Cnr. Chil GU4 .... 131 A2
Rices Hill. E Grins RH19 ... 185 E1
Richard Atkins Prim Sch.
Streat SW2 .... 21 E8
Richard Challoner Sch.
New Mal KT3 .... 38 D2
Richard Thornton House.
Merton SW19 .... 40 A7
Richards Cl. Ash GU12 .... 106 A5
Richards Cl. Harl UB3 .... 3 D8
Richards Cl. Penge BR3 ..... 43 D8
Richards Field. Epsom KT19 57 D2
Richards Rd. Oxsh KT11 ..... 74 B5
Richardson Ct. 🔢
Crawl RH11 .... 201 B1
Richardson's Lawn Cotts.
Old W SL4 .... 10 B5
Richbell Ct. Ashtd KT21 ..... 75 D1
Richfield Ct. Beck BR3 .... 43 F8
Richland Ave. Wallin CR5 ... 79 A5

Richlands Ave. Worc Pk KT17 ... 58 A6
Richmond Adult Coll. Rich TW9 ... 6 D3
Richmond Athletic Gd. Rich TW9 ... 6 D3
Richmond Ave. Felt TW14 ... 3 E1
Richmond Ave. Merton SW20 ... 39 E8
Richmond Bridge. Twick TW1 6 D1
Richmond Bridge Mansions. 1 Twick TW1 ... 6 D1
Richmond Cl. Bigg H TN16 103 B8
Richmond Cl. Epsom KT18 ... 76 E5
Richmond Cl. Fetch KT23 ... 94 C3
Richmond Cl. Friml GU16 ... 65 F1
Richmond Coll. Rich TW10 .. 17 E8
Richmond Cres. Stain TW18 12 F3
Richmond Ct. 12 King U T KT2 ... 18 A1
Richmond Ct. Mitch CR4 ... 40 D6
Richmond Ct. Wimble SW20 39 B7
Richmond Dr. Shep TW17 ... 34 D3
Richmond Gn. Wallin CR0 ... 60 E7
Richmond Hill. Rich TW10 ... 6 E1
Richmond Hill Ct. 5 Rich TW10 ... 6 E1
Richmond House. 12 For Hil SE26 ... 23 A5
Richmond House. Sandh GU15 ... 64 E7
Richmond House (Annexe of Rectory Sch). Hampt TW12 15 F3
Richmond Mansions. 5 Twick TW1 ... 6 D1
Richmond Park Rd. King U T KT2 ... 17 E1
Richmond Park Rd. Mortl SW14 ... 7 D3
Richmond Rd. Coulsd CR5 ... 79 B4
Richmond Rd. Farnc GU7 .. 150 E6
Richmond Rd. Horsh RH12 217 D4
Richmond Rd. Islew TW7 ... 6 A4
Richmond Rd. King U T KT2 . 17 E2
Richmond Rd. Sandh GU15 .. 64 E8
Richmond Rd. Stain TW18 ... 12 F3
Richmond Rd. Thorn H CR7 . 42 B5
Richmond Rd. Twick TW1 ... 17 B8
Richmond Rd. Wallin CR0 ... 60 E7
Richmond Rd. Wimble SW20 39 B8
Richmond Sq. E Grins RH19 ... 185 D2
Richmond Sta. Rich TW9 ... 6 E3
Richmond Upon Thames Coll. Twick TW2 ... 16 E8
Richmond Way. E Grins RH19 ... 205 F8
Richmond Way. Fetch KT23 94 C3
Richmondwood. Sunnin SL5 30 B1
Rickard Cl. Streat SW2 ... 22 A7
Rickards Cl. Surb KT6 ... 56 E8
Ricketts Hill Rd. Tats TN16 103 E7
Rickfield. Crawl RH11 ... 201 A5
Rickford Hill. Worpl GU3 ... 88 D1
Rickman Cl. Easth RG12 ... 27 C3
Rickman Cres. Addl KT15 ... 52 B7
Rickman Ct. Addl KT15 ... 52 B7
Rickman Hill. Coulsd CR5 ... 79 B2
Rickman Hill Rd. Chips CR5 . 79 B1
Rickman's La. Plaist RH14 . 211 F2
Ricksons La. W Hors KT24 112 B8
Rickwood. Horley RH6 ... 161 B4
Rickyard. Stough GU2 ... 108 D1
Riddens The. Buck Gn RH12 214 A6
Riddings The. Cater CR3 ... 100 F2
Riddlesdown Ave. Purley CR8 ... 80 C7
Riddlesdown High Sch. Sander CR2 ... 80 E5
Riddlesdown Rd. Purley CR3 & CR8 ... 80 D5
Riddlesdown Sta. Sander CR8 ... 80 C6
Ride La. Farl Gn GU5 ... 153 D7
Ride The. Ifold RH14 ... 212 C2
Ride Way. Ewh GU5 & GU6 154 C1
Riders Way. Tyl Gn RH9 ... 121 C4
Rideway Cl. Camb GU15 ... 65 B4
Ridge Cl. Brock RH3 ... 137 B5
Ridge Cl. Woking GU22 ... 89 B6
Ridge Ct. Warlgm CR6 ... 81 A1
Ridge Gn. S Nutf RH1 ... 140 E6
Ridge Green Cl. S Nutf RH1 140 E6
Ridge House. 4 King U T KT2 ... 18 B1
Ridge Langley. S Croy CR2 .. 62 A2
Ridge Moor Cl. Beac H GU26 ... 188 E5
Ridge Mount Rd. Sunnin SL5 30 A1
Ridge Pk. Wallin CR8 & SM6 60 D1
Ridge Prim Sch. Cheam SM3 39 E1
Ridge Rd. Cheam SM3 & SM4 39 F1
Ridge Rd. Mitch CR4 ... 21 B1
Ridge The. Coulsd CR5 ... 79 E5
Ridge The. Fetch KT22 ... 94 D3
Ridge The. Limps CR3 & CR6 ... 102 D2
Ridge The. Mayb GU22 ... 70 B2
Ridge The. Surb KT5 ... 38 A4
Ridge The. Twick TW2 ... 16 D8
Ridge The. Wallin CR8 ... 60 D1
Ridge The. Wold CR3 & RH9 ... 102 D2
Ridge The. Woodc KT18 & KT21 ... 76 C1
Ridge Way. Felt TW13 ... 15 E5
Ridge Way The. S Croy CR2 . 61 E1
Ridgedale. Crawl D RH10 .. 204 B8
Ridgegate Cl. Reig RH2 ... 118 D3
Ridgehurst Dr. Horsh RH12 216 F1
Ridgelands. Fetch KT22 ... 94 D3
Ridgemead Rd. Eng Gn TW20 ... 11 B5
Ridgemount. Guild GU2 ... 130 B8
Ridgemount. Oat Pk KT13 ... 53 E8
Ridgemount Ave. Coulsd CR5 ... 79 B2
Ridgemount Ave. Croy CR0 . 62 D8
Ridgemount Cl. Penge SE20 23 B1
Ridgemount Est. Friml GU16 86 C7
Ridges The. Arting GU3 ... 130 C4
Ridgeside. Crawl RH10 ... 201 F6
Ridgeway. E Grins RH19 ... 205 E7
Ridgeway. Epsom KT19 ... 76 C7
Ridgeway. Horse GU21 ... 69 D4
Ridgeway. Pyrf GU22 ... 71 A4
Ridgeway. 11 Rich TW10 ... 6 E1
Ridgeway. Walt O T KT12 ... 34 F1
Ridgeway. Wimble SW19 & SW20 ... 19 D2
Ridgeway Cl. Cran GU6 ... 175 A3
Ridgeway Cl. Dork RH4 ... 136 A5
Ridgeway Cl. Horse GU21 ... 69 D4
Ridgeway Cl. Lhtwat GU18 ... 67 A8
Ridgeway Cl. Oxsh KT22 ... 74 C5
Ridgeway Ct. Redh RH1 ... 118 F1
Ridgeway Dr. Dork RH4 ... 136 A4
Ridgeway Gdns. Horse GU21 ... 69 D4
Ridgeway Hill Rd. M Bourn GU9 ... 146 C8
Ridgeway Inf Sch. S Croy CR2 ... 61 E1
Ridgeway Jun Sch. S Croy CR2 ... 61 E1
Ridgeway Rd. Dork RH4 ... 136 A5
Ridgeway Rd. Hounsl TW7 ... 5 E6
Ridgeway Rd. M Bourn GU9 146 C8
Ridgeway Rd. Redh RH1 ... 118 F1
Ridgeway Rd N. Hounsl TW7 . 5 E7
Ridgeway Sch The. M Bourn GU9 ... 146 C7
Ridgeway The. Brack RG12 . 27 C6
Ridgeway The. Brookw GU24 ... 88 A7
Ridgeway The. Cran GU6 ... 174 F3
Ridgeway The. Croy CR0 ... 60 F7
Ridgeway The. Fetch KT22 .. 94 D3
Ridgeway The. Guild GU1 .. 131 A8
Ridgeway The. Horley RH6 161 A1
Ridgeway The. Horsh RH12 217 B4
Ridgeway The. Lhtwat GU18 48 B1
Ridgeway The. Oxsh KT22 .. 74 C5
Ridgewood Ctr (Hospl). Friml GU16 ... 66 C3
Ridgley Rd. Chidd GU8 ... 191 B4
Ridgway Ct. Wimble SW19 .. 19 D2
Ridgway Gdns. Wimble SW19 ... 19 D1
Ridgway Pl. Wimble SW19 ... 19 E2
Ridgway Rd. Pyrf GU22 ... 70 F4
Ridgway The. Sutton SM2 ... 59 D2
Riding Hill. Sander CR2 ... 81 A6
Riding The. Cran GU6 ... 174 E4
Riding The. Sheer GU21 ... 70 B5
Ridings The. Ashtd KT21 ... 75 D2
Ridings The. Bigg H TN16 ... 83 E2
Ridings The. Cobham KT11 .. 74 A7
Ridings The. Crawl RH10 .. 202 D7
Ridings The. E Hors KT24 ... 92 F2
Ridings The. Epsom KT18 ... 76 F4
Ridings The. Ewell KT17 ... 57 F2
Ridings The. Friml GU16 ... 66 B3
Ridings The. Kings KT20 ... 97 F7
Ridings The. Redh RH1 ... 118 D3
Ridings The. Row Tn KT15 ... 51 E4
Ridings The. Send M GU23 .. 91 A4
Ridings The. Sunby TW16 ... 35 A8
Ridings The. Surb KT5 ... 38 A4
Ridlands Gr. The Char RH8 123 E5
Ridlands La. The Char RH8 . 123 E5
Ridlands Rise. The Char RH8 ... 123 E4
Ridley Ct. Streat SW16 ... 21 E2
Ridley Rd. Broml BR2 ... 44 F6
Ridley Rd. Merton SW19 ... 20 B1
Ridley Rd. Warlgm CR6 ... 81 D1
Ridsdale Rd. Penge SE20 ... 43 B8
Ridsdale Rd. Woking GU21 .. 69 B2
Riesco Dr. S Croy CR0 ... 62 C4
Rifle Way. Farnb GU14 ... 84 C3
Rigby Cl. Croy CR0 & CR9 ... 61 A7
Rigg House. 2 Streat SW4 . 21 E8
Riggindale Rd. Streat SW16 21 D4
Rikkyo Sch in England. Buck Gn RH14 ... 213 D8
Riley House. 1 Streat SW4 21 D8
Rill Wlk. E Grins RH19 ... 186 B1
Rillside. Crawl RH10 ... 202 A3
Rimbault Cl. Farnb GU11 ... 105 E7
Rinaldo Rd. Balham SW12 ... 21 B8
Ring Rd N. Horley RH6 ... 182 C8
Ring Rd S. Crawl RH6 ... 182 C7
Ring The. Brack RG12 ... 27 C7
Ringley Ave. Horley RH6 ... 161 A2
Ringley Oak. Horsh RH12 ... 217 F4
Ringley Park Ave. Reig RH2 ... 139 D8
Ringley Park Rd. Reig RH2 118 C1
Ringley Rd. Horsh RH12 ... 217 E4
Ringmead. Easth RG12 ... 26 E4
Ringmead. Easth RG12 ... 27 B2
Ringmore Dr. Merrow GU4 110 C4
Ringmore Rd. Walt O T KT12 54 C7
Ringmore Rise. For Hil SE23 23 B8
Ringstead Rd. Carsh SM1 ... 59 D5
Ringstead Rd. Lewish SE6 ... 24 B8
Ringwold Cl. Penge BR3 ... 23 E1
Ringwood. Easth RG12 ... 26 F2
Ringwood Ave. Redh RH1 .. 118 F4
Ringwood Ave. Thorn H CR0 & CR9 ... 41 E2
Ringwood Cl. Ascot SL5 ... 29 B5
Ringwood Cl. Crawl RH10 .. 201 E4
Ringwood Gdns. Rhampt SW15 ... 19 A7
Ringwood Lodge. 1 Redh RH1 ... 119 A4
Ringwood Rd. Blckw GU17 .. 64 C6
Ringwood Rd. Farnb GU14 .. 85 C7
Ringwood Way. Hampt TW12 ... 16 A4
Ripley Ave. Egham TW20 ... 11 E2
Ripley By-Pass. Ockham GU23 ... 91 C4
Ripley By-Pass. Ripley GU23 91 C4
Ripley C of E Inf Sch. Ripley GU23 ... 91 B6
Ripley Cl. New Add CR0 ... 63 C4
Ripley Court Sch. Ripley GU23 ... 91 C6
Ripley Ct. Mitch CR4 ... 40 D7
Ripley Gdns. Mortl SW14 ... 7 D4
Ripley Gdns. Sutton SM1 ... 59 C6
Ripley House. 13 King U T KT2 ... 18 B2
Ripley House. Mortl SW14 ... 7 E4
Ripley House. 5 Penge SE26 ... 23 B3
Ripley La. Ripley GU23 ... 91 F3
Ripley La. W Hors KT24 & GU23 ... 112 A7
Ripley Rd. E Clan GU4 ... 111 D6
Ripley Rd. Hampt TW12 ... 16 A1
Ripley Rd. Ripley GU23 & GU4 ... 111 D7
Riplington Ct. Putney SW15 19 B8
Ripon Cl. Friml GU15 ... 66 D3
Ripon Cl. Stough GU2 ... 108 F3
Ripon Gdns. Chess KT9 ... 56 D5
Ripon Rd. Hawley GU14 ... 84 A7
Ripplesmere. Brack RG12 ... 27 D5
Ripplesmore Cl. Sandh GU17 64 B8
Ripston Rd. Ashf TW15 ... 14 D3
Risborough Dr. New Mal KT4 39 A2
Rise Rd. Sunnin SL5 ... 29 F3
Rise The. Crawl RH10 ... 202 D6
Rise The. Crowth RG11 ... 45 A5
Rise The. E Grins RH19 ... 205 F8
Rise The. E Hors KT24 ... 92 E1
Rise The. Ewell KT17 ... 57 F1
Rise The. S Croy CR2 ... 62 C2
Rise The. Tadw KT20 ... 97 C6
Rise The. Woki RG11 ... 25 A7
Ritchie Rd. Croy CR0 ... 43 B3
Ritherdon Rd. Up Toot SW17 21 B6
River Ave. Thame D KT7 ... 37 A2
River Bank. Thame D KT7 ... 36 F4
River Crane Way. Felt TW13 15 F6
River Ct. King U T KT6 ... 37 D4
River Ct. Sheer GU21 ... 70 C5
River Gdns. Carsh SM5 ... 60 A7
River Gdns. Felt TW14 ... 4 B2
River Gdns Bsns Ctr. Felt TW14 ... 4 B3
River Grove Pk. Beck BR3 ... 43 F8
River Hill. Cobham KT11 ... 73 B4
River House. For Hil SE26 ... 23 B5
River House. Mortl SW13 ... 7 E5
River Island Cl. Fetch KT22 . 94 D7
River La. Cobham KT11 ... 73 E3
River La. Farnh GU10 & GU9 145 E7
River La. Fetch KT22 ... 94 D6
River La. Leahd KT22 ... 94 E7
River La. Rich TW10 ... 17 D7
River La. Wreccl GU10 & GU9 ... 145 E7
River Mead. Crawl RH11 ... 181 A1
River Mead. Horsh RH12 ... 217 B1
River Meads Ave. Twick TW13 & TW2 ... 16 B5
River Mount. Walt O T KT12 34 F2
River Mount Gdns. Guild GU2 ... 130 C6
River Park Ave. Egham TW18 ... 12 D4
River Rd. Stain TW18 ... 32 F8
River Reach. Tedd TW11 ... 17 C3
River View. Addl KT15 ... 52 C5
River View Gdns. Twick TW1 16 F6
River Way. Twick TW13 & TW2 ... 16 B6
River Way. W Ewell KT19 ... 57 E5
River Way. W Ewell KT19 ... 57 E5
River Wlk. Sunby TW16 ... 35 C6
River Wlk. Walt O T KT12 ... 35 A3
Riverbank. E Mole KT8 ... 36 E5
Riverbank. Stain TW18 ... 12 F2
Riverbank Way. Brent TW8 ... 6 C8
Riverdale. Pixham RH4 ... 115 C3
Riverdale. Wreccl GU10 ... 145 E7
Riverdale Dr. Wands SW18 .. 20 B7
Riverdale Dr. Westfd GU22 .. 89 F6
Riverdale Gdns. Twick TW1 ... 6 C2
Riverdale Rd. Felt TW13 ... 15 F4
Riverdale Rd. Twick TW1 ... 6 C1
Riverdene Ind Est. Hersh KT12 ... 54 D5
Riverfield Rd. Stain TW18 ... 12 F2
Riverhead Dr. Belm SM2 ... 59 B1
Riverholme Dr. W Ewell KT19 ... 57 E2
Riverholme Dr. W Ewell KT19 ... 57 E2
Rivermead. Byfl KT14 ... 71 F6
Rivermead. E Mole KT8 ... 36 C6
Rivermead. King U T KT6 ... 37 D4
Rivermead Cl. New Haw KT15 ... 52 C3
Rivermead Cl. Rich TW11 ... 17 B3
Rivermead House. Sunby TW16 ... 35 C6
Rivermead Rd. Camb GU15 . 65 B2
Rivernook Cl. Walt O T KT12 35 C4
Riverpark Gdns. Catf BR2 ... 24 D1
Rivers Cl. Farnb GU14 ... 85 E1
Riversdale Prim Sch. Wands SW18 ... 20 A7
Riversdale Rd. Thame D KT7 37 A3
Riversdell Cl. Chert KT16 ... 32 F2
Riverside. Bellf GU1 ... 109 D3
Riverside. Catf SE6 ... 23 F4
Riverside. Egham TW20 ... 12 A5
Riverside. For Row RH18 ... 206 E3
Riverside. Horley RH6 ... 161 A1
Riverside. Horsh RH12 ... 217 A2
Riverside. Oat Pk TW17 ... 34 E2
Riverside. Pixham RH4 ... 115 D1
Riverside. Sunby TW16 ... 35 D7
Riverside. Twick TW1 ... 17 B7
Riverside. Wray TW19 ... 11 C8
Riverside Ave. E Mole KT8 ... 36 D4
Riverside Ave. Lhtwat GU18 67 C8
Riverside Bsns Ctr. Guild GU1 ... 109 C1
Riverside Bsns Ctr. Wands SW18 ... 20 B7
Riverside Bsns Pk. Merton SW19 ... 40 C8
Riverside Cl. Brookw GU24 .. 87 F7
Riverside Cl. Hackb SM6 ... 60 B7
Riverside Cl. King U T KT1 ... 37 D5
Riverside Cl. Stain TW18 ... 32 F8
Riverside Cl. W Heath GU14 84 F5
Riverside Ct. Pixham RH4 . 115 D1
Riverside Ct. Tedd TW11 ... 17 C3
Riverside Dr. Bramly GU5 . 152 A7
Riverside Dr. Chisw W4 ... 7 E6
Riverside Dr. Egham TW18 .. 12 E3
Riverside Dr. Esher KT10 ... 55 A6
Riverside Dr. Mitch CR4 ... 40 E4
Riverside Dr. Rich TW10 ... 17 B5
Riverside Dr. Stain TW18 ... 32 F8
Riverside Gdns. Old Wok GU22 ... 90 B6
Riverside House. Morden SW19 ... 40 C5
Riverside L Ctr. Chisw W4 ... 7 E6
Riverside Pk. Farnh GU9 ... 125 D3
Riverside Pl. Stan TW19 ... 2 D1
Riverside Rd. Hersh KT12 ... 54 E6
Riverside Rd. Stain TW18 ... 12 F1
Riverside Rd. Stan TW19 ... 2 E1
Riverside Rd. Wands SW17 & SW19 ... 20 C5
Riverside The. E Mole KT8 ... 36 D6
Riverside Way. Camb GU15 . 65 A3
Riverside Wlk. Islew TW7 ... 5 E4
Riverside Wlk. W Wick BR4 . 44 B1
Riverstone Ct. King U T KT2 . 37 F8
Riverview. Shep TW17 ... 34 D2
Riverview Cty Fst Sch. W Ewell KT19 ... 57 D6
Riverview Gr. Chisw W4 ... 7 B8
Riverview Pk. For Hil SE6 ... 24 A6
Riverview Rd. Chisw W4 ... 7 B8
Riverview Rd. W Ewell KT19 57 D6
Riverway. Stain TW18 ... 33 B8
Riverway Est. Shalf GU7 ... 151 C8
Riverwood Ct. Bellf GU1 ... 109 C3
Rivett-Drake Rd. Stough GU2 ... 109 A5
Rivey Cl. Pyrf KT14 ... 70 F5
Road House Est. Old Wok GU22 ... 90 A7
Roakes Ave. Chert KT15 ... 52 B8
Robert Cl. Hersh KT12 ... 54 B5
Robert Gerard House. 7 W Norw SE27 ... 22 D4
Robert May Cty Fst Sch The. Crawl RH10 ... 201 F4
Robert St. Croy CR0 & CR9 ... 61 C7
Robert Way. Horsh RH12 ... 217 F7
Robert Way. Mytch GU16 ... 85 F3
Roberts Cl. Cheam SM3 ... 58 D3
Roberts Cl. Stan TW19 ... 2 C1
Roberts Ct. Penge SE20 ... 43 C8
Roberts House. 5 W Norw SE27 ... 22 B5
Roberts Rd. Alder GU12 ... 105 D1
Roberts Rd. Sandh GU15 ... 65 A6
Roberts Way. Eng Gn TW20 . 11 C1
Robertsbridge Rd. Carsh SM5 ... 40 D2
Robertson Ct. 5 Knaph GU21 ... 68 E1
Robertson House. Up Toot SW17 ... 20 E3
Robertson Way. Ash GU12 105 F1
Robin Cl. Addl KT15 ... 52 D5
Robin Cl. Ash V GU12 ... 106 A6
Robin Cl. Crawl RH11 ... 201 C8
Robin Cl. E Grins RH19 ... 185 F2
Robin Cl. Hampt TW12 ... 15 E3
Robin Ct. Wallin SM6 ... 60 C4
Robin Gdns. Redh RH1 ... 119 A3
Robin Gr. Brent TW8 ... 6 C8
Robin Hill. Farnc GU7 ... 150 D7
Robin Hill Dr. Friml GU15 ... 66 A3
Robin Hood Cl. Knaph GU21 68 F1
Robin Hood Cl. W Heath GU14 ... 85 A7
Robin Hood Cres. Knaph GU21 ... 68 E2
Robin Hood Ct. Sutton SM1 . 59 B5
Robin Hood Inf Sch. Sutton SM1 ... 59 A5
Robin Hood Jun Sch. Sutton SM1 ... 59 B5
Robin Hood La. King U T SW15 ... 18 E4
Robin Hood La. Sutton SM1 . 59 B5
Robin Hood La. Warn RH12 216 F5
Robin Hood La. Westfd GU4 89 F3
Robin Hood Prim Sch. King U T SW15 ... 18 E3
Robin Hood Rd. Knaph GU21 68 E2
Robin Hood Rd. Knaph GU21 68 F1
Robin Hood Rd. Wimble SW15 & SW19 ... 18 F3
Robin Hood Rdbt. King U T SW15 ... 18 E5
Robin Hood Way (Kingston By-Pass). King U T KT2 & SW15 & SW20 ... 18 E3
Robin Hood Works. Knaph GU21 ... 68 E2
Robin La. Sandh GU17 ... 45 C1
Robin Way. Stain TW18 ... 12 F5
Robin Way. Stough GU2 ... 109 B5
Robin's Bow. Camb GU15 ... 65 B4
Robin's Ct. Beck BR3 ... 44 D7

Robinhood Cl. Mitch CR4 ..... 41 C6
Robinhood La. Mitch CR4 .... 41 C6
Robins Ct. Rich TW10 .... 6 E1
Robins Dale. Knaph GU21 ..... 68 C2
Robinson Ct. 4 Rich TW9 ..... 6 F3
Robinson Rd. Crawl RH11 . 201 D5
Robinson Rd. Mitch SW19 ... 20 E2
Robinsway. Hersh KT12 .... 54 C6
Robinswood Ct. Horsh RH12 .... 217 F4
Robinwood Pl. King U T SW15 .... 18 D4
Robson Rd. W Norw SE21 & SE27 .... 22 C5
Rochdale. 7 S Norw SE19 .. 22 E2
Roche Rd. Thorn H SW16 ..... 41 F8
Roche Wlk. Carsh SM4 & SM5 .... 40 D3
Rochelle Ct. Beck BR3 .... 24 B1
Rochester Ave. Felt TW13 ... 14 F6
Rochester Cl. Streat SW16 .. 21 E1
Rochester Ct. S Norw SE25 .. 43 A7
Rochester Gdns. Cater CR3 100 E5
Rochester Gdns. S Croy CR0 61 E7
Rochester Par. Felt TW13 .... 15 A5
Rochester Rd. Carsh SM5 .... 59 F6
Rochester Rd. Egham TW20 12 D2
Rochester Wlk. Dovgn RH2 139 B5
Rochford Way. Thorn H CR0 41 E3
Rock Ave. 13 Mortl SW14 ...... 7 D4
Rock Gdns. Alder GU11 ...... 104 F1
Rock Hill. Dulw SE19 .... 22 F4
Rock La. Rowl GU10 .... 146 A5
Rockbourne Rd. For Hil SE23 .... 23 D7
Rockdale Dr. Graysh GU26 188 D3
Rockery The. Farnb GU14 .... 84 E3
Rocket Rd. Farnb GU14 .... 84 D1
Rockfield Cl. Oxted RH8 ..... 122 F4
Rockfield Rd. Oxted RH8 .... 122 F5
Rockfield Way. 7 Sandh GU15 .... 64 D8
Rockhampton Cl. 4 W Norw SE27 .... 22 A4
Rockhampton Rd. S Croy CR2 .... 61 E4
Rockhampton Rd. W Norw SE27 & SW16 .... 22 A4
Rockingham Cl. Rhampt SW15 .... 7 F3
Rockingham Ct. 20 Beck BR3 .... 24 A1
Rockmount Jun Mix & Inf Lower Schs. S Norw SE19 .... 22 D2
Rockmount Jun Mix & Inf Upper Schs. S Norw SE19 .... 22 D2
Rockmount Rd. S Norw SE19 .... 22 D2
Rocks The. Ash W RH19 .... 206 D6
Rockshaw Rd. Cater RH1 ... 119 E8
Rockshaw Rd. Merstt RH1 . 119 E8
Rockwell Gdns. Dulw SE19 .. 22 E4
Rocky La. Gatton RH1 & RH2 .... 119 A6
Rocombe Cres. For Hil SE23 23 C8
Rodborough Cty Sec Sch. Witley GU8 .... 170 F7
Rodd Est. Shep TW17 .... 34 D4
Roden Gdns. Thorn H CR0 & SE25 .... 42 E3
Rodenhurst Rd. Streat SW4 21 C8
Rodgers House. 4 Streat SW4 .... 21 D8
Roding Cl. Crawl GU6 .... 173 F2
Rodmill La. Streat SW2 .... 21 E8
Rodney Cl. New Mal KT3 ...... 38 E4
Rodney Cl. Thorn H CR0 .... 42 B1
Rodney Cl. Walt O T KT12 .... 35 C1
Rodney Gn. 2 Walt O T KT12 .... 54 C8
Rodney Pl. Merton SW19 ..... 40 C8
Rodney Rd. Mitch CR4 .... 40 E6
Rodney Rd. New Mal KT3 ..... 38 E4
Rodney Rd. Twick TW4 .... 16 A8
Rodney Rd. Walt O T KT12 ... 54 C8
Rodney Way. Merrow GU1 110 A2
Rodney Way. Poyle SL3 .... 1 E6
Rodona Rd. Whit V KT13 ...... 72 D8
Rodway Rd. Rhampt SW15 .. 19 A8
Rodwell Ct. Addl KT15 .... 52 C6
Rodwell Ct. Walt O T KT12 ... 54 B7
Roe Way. Wallin SM6 .... 60 E4
Roebuck Cl. Ashtd KT21 .... 95 E7
Roebuck Cl. Felt TW13 .... 15 B4
Roebuck Cl. Horsh RH13 ... 218 B4
Roebuck Cl. Reig RH2 .... 118 A1
Roebuck Ct. 2 New Mal KT3 38 E4
Roebuck Rd. Chess KT9 .... 57 A5
Roedean Cres. Rhampt SW15 7 E2
Roedeer Copse. Shottm GU27 .... 207 E6
Roehampton CE Prim Sch. Rhampt SW15 .... 19 B8
Roehampton Club Golf Course. Rhampt SW15 .... 7 F2
Roehampton Gate. Rhampt SW15 .... 7 E1
Roehampton Gate Cty Prim Sch. Rhampt SW15 .... 7 E1
Roehampton High St. Putney SW15 .... 19 A8
Roehampton La. Putney SW15 & SW19 .... 19 A8
Roehampton La. Rhampt SW15 & SW19 .... 19 A8
Roehampton Vale. Rhampt SW15 .... 18 F5
Roehampton Vale. Rhampt SW15 .... 18 F6
Roffes La. Cater CR3 .... 100 D2
Roffey Cl. Horley RH6 .... 160 F3
Roffey Cl. Purley CR8 .... 80 B3
Roffey Cnr. Horsh RH12 .... 218 B4
Roffey's Cl. Copth RH10 .... 183 A4
Roffords. Woking GU21 .... 69 B2
Roger Simmons Ct. L Book KT23 .... 94 A3
Rogers Cl. Cater CR3 .... 101 B5
Rogers Cl. Coulsd CR5 & CR8 80 B1
Rogers La. Chelsh CR6 .... 81 F1
Rogers Mead. Godst RH9 .. 121 B3
Rogers Rd. Up Toot SW17 .... 20 E4
Rogosa Rd. W End GU24 ...... 67 E6
Rojack Rd. For Hil SE23 .... 23 D7
Roke Cl. Purley CR8 .... 80 C5
Roke Cl. Witley GU8 .... 170 E5
Roke La. Witley GU8 .... 170 F5
Roke Lane Cotts. Witley GU8 .... 170 F5
Roke Lodge Rd. Purley CR8 . 80 B6
Roke Prim Sch. Purley CR8 .. 80 B6
Roke Prim Sch. Purley CR8 .. 80 C5
Roke Rd. Purley CR8 .... 80 C5
Rokeby Cl. Brack RG12 .... 27 D8
Rokeby Ct. Knaph GU21 .... 68 F2
Rokeby House. 9 Balham SW12 .... 21 B8
Rokeby Pl. Wimble SW20 ..... 19 B1
Rokeby Sch. King U T KT2 ... 18 C1
Rokell House. Catf BR3 .... 24 B3
Rokers La. Shackl GU8 .... 149 D7
Roland Ct. S Norw SE19 .... 42 F8
Roland Way. Worc Pk KT4 ... 57 F8
Rollesby Rd. Chess KT19 & KT9 .... 57 A4
Rolleston Rd. S Croy CR2 ..... 61 D3
Rollit Cres. Hounsl TW3 .... 5 A2
Roman Cl. Felt TW14 .... 4 C2
Roman House. Woodh RH2 138 F7
Roman Ind Est. Croy CR0 .... 42 E2
Roman Rd. Dork RH4 .... 136 B5
Roman Rise. W Norw SE19 .. 22 D2
Roman Way. Croy CR9 .... 61 B8
Roman Way. Farnh GU9 ...... 125 E4
Roman Way. Thorn H CR9 ... 61 B8
Roman Way. Wink RG12 ...... 27 F8
Romana Ct. Stain TW18 .... 13 A4
Romanby Ct. 1 Redh RH1 139 F8
Romanhurst Ave. Beck BR2 . 44 E5
Romanhurst Gdns. Beck BR2 & BR3 .... 44 E5
Romans Way. Pyrf GU22 ...... 71 A4
Romany Gdns. Cheam SM3 . 40 A2
Romany Prospect. W Norw SE19 .... 22 D2
Romany The. Farnb GU14 .... 84 A1
Romayne Cl. W Heath GU14 85 A5
Romberg Rd. Up Toot SW17 21 A5
Romeo Hill. Wink RG12 .... 27 F8
Romeyn Rd. Streat SW16 .... 21 F5
Romley Ct. M Bourn GU9 .. 125 D1
Rommany Ct. W Norw SE27 22 D4
Rommany Rd. W Norw SE27 22 D4
Romney Cl. Ashf TW15 .... 14 C3
Romney Cl. Chess KT9 .... 56 E6
Romney House. Brack RG12 27 E5
Romney Rd. Farnb GU14 ...... 84 E1
Romney Rd. New Mal KT3 .... 38 D3
Romola Rd. Streat SE24 & SW2 .... 22 B7
Romsey Cl. Alder GU11 ...... 126 C6
Romsey Cl. Blckw GU17 .... 64 C6
Romulus Ct. 6 Brent TW8 .... 6 D7
Rona Cl. Crawl RH11 .... 201 B3
Ronald Cl. Beck BR3 .... 43 F4
Ronald Ross Prim Sch. Putney SW19 .... 19 E8
Ronelean Rd. Surb KT6 .... 56 F7
Ronneby Cl. Oat Pk KT13 ..... 53 E7
Ronson Way. Leahd KT22 .... 95 A6
Ronver Rd. Lewish SE12 .... 24 F7
Rook La. Cater CR3 .... 100 B3
Rook Way. Horsh RH12 ...... 217 F6
Rookeries Cl. Felt TW13 .... 15 C5
Rookery Cl. Fetch KT22 .... 94 E3
Rookery Dr. Westc RH4 .... 135 A5
Rookery Hill. Ashtd KT21 ..... 76 A1
Rookery Hill. Outw RH1 & RH6 .... 162 B6
Rookery Rd. Stain TW18 ...... 13 B3
Rookery The. Westc RH4 .. 135 A5
Rookery Way. L Kings KT20 117 F8
Rookley Cl. Sutton SM2 .... 59 B2
Rooks Hill. Bramly GU5 ...... 152 C2
Rooksmead Rd. Sunby TW16 35 A7
Rookstone Rd. Up Toot SW17 .... 20 F3
Rookwood Ave. Sandh GU15 45 E2
Rookwood Ave. W Barn KT3 39 A5
Rookwood Ave. Wallin SM6 . 60 D6
Rookwood Cl. Merst RH1 .. 119 B6
Rookwood Ct. Guild GU2 ... 130 C6
Rookwood Pk. Horsh RH12 216 F3
Roothill La. Betch RH3 ...... 137 A3
Roper House. 13 Dulw SE19 & SE21 .... 22 E4
Roper Way. Mitch CR4 .... 41 A7
Ropers Wlk. 13 Streat SE24 .... 22 A8
Rorkes Drift. Mytch GU16 .... 86 A4
Rosa Ave. Ashf TW15 .... 14 A4
Rosalind Franklin Cl. Onsl V GU2 .... 129 E8
Rosamond St. For Hil SE26 .. 23 B5
Rosamund Cl. S Croy CR2 .... 61 D6
Rosamund Rd. Crawl RH10 202 B3
Rosary Cl. Hounsl TW3 & TW5 4 E5
Rosary Gdns. Ashf TW15 ..... 14 B4
Rosary RC Inf Sch. Heston TW5 .... 5 A8
Rosary RC Jun Sch. Heston TW5 .... 5 A8
Rose Ave. Mitch CR4 .... 40 F8
Rose Ave. Morden SM4 .... 40 C4
Rose Bank Cotts. Westfd GU22 .... 89 E5
Rose Bushes. Nork KT17 ...... 77 C3
Rose Cotts. Ent Gn GU8 ..... 171 A2
Rose Cotts. Esher KT10 .... 55 D5
Rose Ct. 10 Wimble SW19 ... 19 F3
Rose Ct. Woki RG11 .... 25 C6
Rose End. N Cheam KT4 .... 39 D1
Rose Gdns. Farnb GU14 .... 84 E3
Rose Gdns. Felt TW13 .... 15 A6
Rose Gdns. Stan TW19 .... 13 D8
Rose Hill. Dork RH4 .... 136 B7
Rose Hill. Sutton SM1 & SM4 40 B1
Rose Hill Pk W. Sutton SM1 . 59 C8
Rose La. Ripley GU23 .... 91 D5
Rose St. Woki RG11 .... 25 C6
Rose View. Addl KT15 .... 52 C5
Rose Wlk. Purley CR8 .... 79 D8
Rose Wlk. Surb KT5 .... 38 B4
Rose Wlk. W Wick BR4 .... 63 D8
Rose Wood. Woking GU22 .... 90 A8
Roseacre. Oxted RH8 .... 123 A1
Roseacre Cl. Shep Gn TW17 34 A4
Roseacre Gdns. Chil GU4 ... 131 F3
Rosebank. Epsom KT18 .... 76 C5
Rosebank. Penge SE20 .... 23 B1
Rosebank Cl. Tedd TW11 ..... 17 A2
Rosebay. Woki RG11 .... 25 E8
Roseberry Rd. Lang V KT18 & KT21 .... 96 E8
Rosebery Ave. Epsom KT17 . 76 E5
Rosebery Ave. King U T KT3 38 F6
Rosebery Ave. S Norw CR7 .. 42 C7
Rosebery Cl. W Barn SM4 ... 39 D3
Rosebery Cres. Old Wok GU22 .... 89 F7
Rosebery Gdns. Sutton SM1 59 B6
Rosebery Rd. Cheam SM1 & SM2 .... 58 F4
Rosebery Rd. Islew TW3 & TW7 .... 5 C2
Rosebery Rd. King U T KT1 .. 38 B7
Rosebery Sch. Epsom KT18 . 76 C5
Rosebery Sq. King U T KT1 .. 38 B7
Rosebine Ave. Twick TW2 .... 16 D8
Rosebriar Cl. Pyrf GU22 .... 71 A3
Rosebriars. Cater CR3 .... 100 E7
Rosebriars. Esher KT10 .... 55 C5
Rosebury Dr. Bisley GU24 .... 68 A4
Rosecourt Rd. Thorn H CR0 . 41 F3
Rosecroft Cl. Bigg H TN16 ... 83 F1
Rosecroft Gdns. Twick TW2 16 D7
Rosedale. Alder GU12 .... 105 C2
Rosedale. Ashtd KT21 .... 75 C1
Rosedale. Cater CR3 .... 100 E4
Rosedale Cl. Crawl RH11 .. 201 A4
Rosedale Gdns. Easth RG12 27 A4
Rosedale Rd. N Cheam KT17 58 A5
Rosedale Rd. Rich TW9 .... 6 E3
Rosedale Rd. Stonel KT17 .... 58 A5
Rosedene Ave. Morden SM4 40 A4
Rosedene Ave. Streat SW16 21 F5
Rosedene Ave. Thorn H CR0 41 E2
Rosedene La. Sandh GU15 ... 64 D7
Rosefield Cl. Carsh SM5 .... 59 E5
Rosefield Gdns. Ottsh KT16 . 51 D4
Rosefield Rd. Stain TW18 .... 13 A4
Roseheath Rd. Hounsl TW4 ... 4 F2
Rosehill. Clayg KT10 .... 56 A4
Rosehill. Hampt TW12 .... 36 A8
Rosehill Ave. Carsh SM1 & SM5 .... 40 C1
Rosehill Ave. Horse GU21 .... 69 C3
Rosehill Farm Meadow. Banstd SM7 .... 78 B4
Rosehill Gdns. Sutton SM1 ... 59 C8
Rosehill Rd. Bigg H TN16 ..... 83 C2
Roseleigh Cl. 3 Twick TW1 .. 6 D1
Rosemary Ave. Ash V GU12 106 A8
Rosemary Ave. E Mole KT8 .. 36 A5
Rosemary Ave. Hounsl TW4 .. 4 D5
Rosemary Cl. Oxted RH8 ... 123 A2
Rosemary Cl. W Heath GU14 84 D4
Rosemary Cotts. Wimble SW19 .... 19 C1
Rosemary Cres. Stough GU2 .... 109 A5
Rosemary Ct. Haslem GU27 208 C7
Rosemary Ct. Horley RH6 .. 160 E4
Rosemary Gdns. Blckw GU17 .... 64 D5
Rosemary Gdns. Mortl SW14 7 C4
Rosemary La. Alfold GU6 ... 212 E8
Rosemary La. Blckw GU17 ... 64 D5
Rosemary La. Charl RH6 .... 180 E7
Rosemary La. Egham TW20 . 32 B6
Rosemary La. Horley RH6 . 161 B3
Rosemary La. Mortl SW14 ..... 7 C4
Rosemary La. Rowl GU10 ... 145 E4
Rosemary Rd. Wands SW17 20 C5
Rosemead. Chert KT16 .... 33 B2
Rosemead Ave. Felt TW13 .. 14 F6
Rosemead Ave. Mitch CR4 & SW16 .... 41 C7
Rosemead Cl. Woodh RH1 139 D7
Rosemead Sch. W Norw SE27 .... 22 C6
Rosemont Rd. King U T KT3 . 38 C6
Rosemont Rd. Rich TW10 ...... 6 E1
Rosemount. 5 Wallin SM6 .. 60 C4
Rosemount Ave. W Byfl KT14 .... 71 A6
Rosemount Par. W Byfl KT14 .... 71 A6
Rosemount Point. 10 For Hil SE23 .... 23 D5
Rosendale Infs Sch. W Norw SE21 .... 22 C8
Rosendale Jun Sch. W Norw SE21 .... 22 C8
Rosendale Rd. Streat SE21 & SE24 .... 22 C7
Rosendale Rd. W Norw SE21 & SE24 .... 22 C7
Roseneath Ct. Cater CR3 .. 101 A2
Roseneath Dr. Chidd GU8 . 191 B4
Rosery The. Croy CR0 .... 43 D3
Roses Cotts. Dork RH4 .... 136 A7
Rosethorn Cl. Streat SW12 .. 21 D8
Rosetrees. Guild GU1 .... 131 A8
Rosetta Ct. S Norw SE19 ...... 22 E1
Roseville Ave. Hounsl TW3 & TW4 .... 5 A2
Rosevine Rd. Wimble SW20 . 39 C8
Rosewarne Cl. Woking GU21 69 A1
Rosewood Ct. King U T KT2 . 18 A1
Rosewood Dr. Shep Gn TW17 .... 33 F4
Rosewood Gr. Sutton SM1 ... 59 C8
Rosewood Way. W End GU24 .... 67 E6
Roskeen Ct. Wimble SW19 .. 19 C1
Roslan Ct. Horley RH6 .... 161 B2
Roslyn Cl. Mitch CR4 .... 40 D7
Ross Cl. Crawl RH10 .... 201 F3
Ross Ct. Croy CR2 .... 61 C4
Ross Ct. 4 Putney SW15 ..... 19 D8
Ross House. Twick TW2 .... 16 B6
Ross Par. Wallin SM6 .... 60 B4
Ross Rd. Cobham KT11 .... 73 C6
Ross Rd. S Norw SE25 .... 42 E6
Ross Rd. Twick TW2 .... 16 C7
Ross Rd. Wallin SM6 .... 60 C5
Rossal Ct. Penge SE20 .... 23 B1
Rossdale. Carsh SM1 .... 59 E5
Rossendon Ct. 1 Wallin SM6 .... 60 C4
Rossett Cl. Easth RG12 .... 27 B5
Rossetti Gdns. Coulsd CR5 ... 79 F1
Rossignol Gdns. Carsh SM5 60 A8
Rossindel Rd. Hounsl TW3 ..... 5 A2
Rossiter Lodge. Guild GU1 131 A8
Rossiter Rd. Balham SW12 .. 21 B7
Rosslyn Ave. Felt TW14 .... 4 A1
Rosslyn Ave. Mortl SW13 & SW14 .... 7 F4
Rosslyn Cl. Ashf TW16 .... 14 E2
Rosslyn Cl. Coney H BR4 ...... 63 F7
Rosslyn House. 8 Rich TW9 6 F6
Rosslyn Pk. Oat Pk KT13 ...... 53 D6
Rosslyn Rd. Twick TW1 .... 6 C1
Rossmore Cl. Crawl RH10 . 182 D2
Rossmore Gdns. Alder GU11 .... 104 F1
Rosswood Gdns. Wallin SM6 60 C4
Rostella Rd. Up Toot SW17 .. 20 D4
Rostrevor Rd. Wimble SW19 20 A3
Rothbury Gdns. Hounsl TW7 . 6 A7
Rothbury Wlk. Friml GU15 ... 66 C4
Rother Cl. Sandh GU17 .... 64 C8
Rother Cres. Crawl RH11 ... 200 F5
Rother House. 4 Redh RH1 .... 118 F2
Rother Rd. W Heath GU14 ... 84 E7
Rotherfield Ave. Woki RG11 25 A7
Rotherfield Rd. Wallin SM5 . 60 A5
Rotherhill Ave. Streat SW16 21 D2
Rothermere Rd. Croy CR0 ... 60 F5
Rothervale. Horley RH6 ...... 160 F5
Rotherwick Ct. Farnb GU14 105 C8
Rotherwood Cl. Wimble SW19 & SW20 .... 39 E8
Rothes Rd. Dork RH4 .... 136 B8
Rothesay Ave. Merton SW20 39 E7
Rothesay Ave. Mortl SW14 & TW10 .... 7 B3
Rothesay Rd. S Norw SE25 ... 42 E5
Rothschild St. W Norw SE27 22 C4
Rothwell House. Crowth RG11 .... 45 C4
Rothwell House. Heston TW5 5 A8
Rotunda Est The. Alder GU11 .... 105 B2
Rougemont Ave. Morden SM4 .... 40 A3
Rough Field. E Grins RH19 185 D4
Rough Rd. Woking GU22 ...... 88 C5
Rough Rew. Dork RH4 & RH5 .... 136 B4
Rough Way. Horsh RH12 ... 217 F5
Roughets La. Bletch RH1 ... 120 E6
Roughlands. Pyrf GU22 .... 70 E4
Rounce La. W End GU24 .... 67 D6
Round Gr. Croy CR0 .... 43 D2
Round Hill. For Hil SE23 .... 23 C5
Round Oak Rd. Weyb KT13 .. 52 F6
Roundabout Cotts. Rudg RH12 .... 214 C5
Roundacre. Putney SW19 ..... 19 D6
Roundals La. Hambl GU8 ..... 191 E8
Roundell House. 14 Dulw SE19 & SE21 .... 22 E4
Roundhay Cl. For Hil SE23 ... 23 D6
Roundhill. Mayb GU22 .... 90 B8
Roundhill Dr. Mayb GU22 .... 70 B1
Roundhill Way. Oxsh KT11 .. 74 B7
Roundhill Way. Stough GU2 108 F1
Roundshaw Ctr. Wallin SM6 60 E3
Roundtable Rd. Catf BR1 ..... 24 F5
Roundthorn Way. Woking GU21 .... 68 F3
Roundway. Bigg H TN16 .... 83 D4
Roundway. Egham TW20 ..... 12 C3
Roundway. Friml GU15 .... 66 C6
Roundway Cl. Friml GU15 .... 66 C6
Roundway Ct. Crawl RH11 201 D8
Roundway The. Clayg KT10 . 55 F4
Roundwood View. Nork SM7 .... 77 D4
Roundwood Way. Nork SM7 77 D4
Roupell House. 7 King U T KT2 .... 17 F1
Roupell Rd. Streat SW2 .... 21 F7
Rouse Gdns. Dulw SE21 .... 22 E4
Routh Ct. E Bed TW14 .... 14 D7
Routh Rd. Wands SW18 .... 20 E8
Row Hill. Row Tn KT15 .... 51 F4
Row La. Farl Gn GU5 .... 153 E5
Row The. Lingf RH7 .... 164 D4
Row Town. Row Tn KT15 ...... 51 F3
Rowallan Ct. Catf SE6 .... 24 F7
Rowan. 2 Brack RG12 .... 27 F4
Rowan Ave. Egham TW20 .... 12 C3
Rowan Chase. Rowl GU10 . 146 A5
Rowan Cl. Bellf GU1 .... 109 C4
Rowan Cl. Camb GU15 .... 65 F8
Rowan Cl. Crawl RH10 .... 201 F6
Rowan Cl. Horsh RH12 ...... 218 B5

Rowan Cl. King U T KT3 .... 38 E7
Rowan Cl. Mitch SW16 .... 41 C8
Rowan Cl. Woodh RH2 .... 139 C7
Rowan Cres. Mitch SW16 ..... 41 C8
Rowan Ct. For Hil SE26 .... 23 C4
Rowan Ct. 11 King U T KT2 .. 18 A1
Rowan Ct. Wimble SW20 ..... 39 B7
Rowan Dr. Crowth RG11 .... 45 C6
Rowan Gdns. S Croy CR0 ..... 61 F7
Rowan Gn. Oat Pk KT13 .... 53 D6
Rowan Gr. Hooley CR5 .... 99 B6
Rowan High Sch.
Mitch SW16 .... 41 C7
Rowan Prep Sch. Clayg KT10 55 F3
Rowan Rd. Brent TW8 .... 6 B7
Rowan Rd. Mitch SW16 .... 41 C7
Rowan Way. Horsh RH12 ... 218 C5
Rowans Cl. W Heath GU14 ... 64 E1
Rowans Cl. W Heath GU14 ... 84 E8
Rowans The. Ashf TW16 .... 14 F3
Rowans The. Graysh GU26 188 D2
Rowans The. 3
Woking GU22 .... 69 E1
Rowanside Cl.
Head Dn GU35 .... 187 C4
Rowbarns Way.
E Hors KT24 .... 112 F5
Rowbury. Farnc GU7 .... 151 A7
Rowcroft Cl. Ash V GU12 .. 106 A6
Rowden Rd. Penge BR3 .... 43 F8
Rowden Rd. W Ewell KT19 ... 57 C6
Rowdown Cres.
New Add CR0 .... 63 E2
Rowdown Inf & Jun Schs.
New Add CR0 .... 63 D1
Rowe La. Pirb GU24 .... 88 A3
Rowena House.
Crawl RH11 .... 181 D1
Rowfant Bsns Ctr.
Worth RH10 .... 203 E6
Rowfant Rd.
Up Toot SW12 & SW17 .... 21 A6
Rowhill Ave. Alder GU11 .... 125 F8
Rowhill Cres. Alder GU11 ... 125 F8
Rowhills. Heath E GU9 .... 125 E8
Rowhills Cl. Heath E GU9 ... 125 F7
Rowhook Hill. Warn RH12 . 215 F8
Rowhook Rd. Rowhk RH12 196 E1
Rowhook Rd. Slinfd RH12 . 216 A8
Rowhurst Ave. Addl KT15 .... 52 B4
Rowland Cl. Burst RH10 ..... 183 E5
Rowland Gr. For Hil SE26 .... 23 B5
Rowland Hill Almshouses.
Ashf TW15 .... 14 A3
Rowland Rd. Cran GU6 ...... 174 D3
Rowland Way. Littlt TW15 ... 14 D1
Rowland Way. Merton SW19 40 B8
Rowlands Rd. Horsh RH12 218 A6
Rowledge CE (VC) Prim Sch.
Binst GU10 .... 145 E3
Rowley Cl. Brack RG12 .... 27 E6
Rowley Cl. Pyrf GU22 .... 71 B3
Rowley Ct. Cater CR3 .... 100 C5
Rowlls Rd. King U T KT1 .... 37 F6
Rowly Dr. Rowly GU6 .... 174 A6
Rowly Edge. Rowly GU6 .... 174 A6
Rowntree Rd. Twick TW2 ..... 16 E7
Rowplatt La. Felb RH19 ...... 184 E4
Roxbee Cox Rd. Farnb GU14 84 A1
Roxborough Ave. Hounsl TW7 5 F7
Roxburgh Cl. Friml GU15 ..... 66 C4
Roxburgh Rd. W Norw SE27 22 B3
Roxeth Ct. Ashf TW15 .... 14 A3
Roxford Cl. Up Hall TW17 .... 34 E4
Roxton Gdns. Add CR0 .... 63 A5
Roy Gr. Hampt TW12 .... 16 B2
Royal Alexandra & Albert Sch
The. Gatton RH2 .... 118 E6
Royal Ascot Golf Club.
Ascot SL5 .... 29 B7
Royal Ave. Worc Pk KT4 .... 57 E8
Royal Cir. W Norw SE27 .... 22 B5
Royal Cl. Worc Pk KT4 .... 57 E8
Royal Ct. 9 King U T KT2 .... 18 B1
Royal Dr. Burgh H KT18 .... 77 B1
Royal Dr.
Burgh H KT18 & KT20 .... 97 B8
Royal Earlswood Hospl.
Earls RH1 .... 140 A6
Royal Grammar Sch.
Guild GU1 .... 130 D8
Royal Holloway Univ of London.
Eng Gn TW20 .... 11 D2
Royal Horticultural Society Cotts.
Wisley GU23 & KT14 .... 71 E3
Royal Horticultural Society's
Garden. Wisley GU23 .... 71 E1
Royal Hospl. Putney SW19 ... 19 E8
Royal Hospl. Rich TW9 .... 6 E4
Royal Kent Sch The.
Oxsh KT22 .... 74 C5
Royal Marsden Hospl The (Surrey
Branch). Sutton SM2 .... 59 C1
Royal Mews. Hampt KT8 ...... 36 E6
Royal Mid-Surrey Golf Club.
Rich TW9 .... 6 D4
Royal Military Acad.
Sandh GU15 .... 64 F6
Royal Military Acad Hospl.
Sandh GU15 .... 65 A8
Royal Military Sch of Music
(Kneller Hall). Twick TW2 .... 5 D1
Royal Naval Sch.
Shottm GU27 .... 189 A2
Royal Oak Ctr The.
S Croy CR2 .... 61 C1
Royal Oak House.
Crawl D RH10 .... 204 B7
Royal Oak Rd. Woking GU21 69 D1
Royal Orchard Cl.
Putney SW18 .... 19 E8
Royal Rd. Tedd TW11 .... 16 D3
Royal Russell Sch (Ballards).
S Croy CR9 .... 62 B5
Royal Sch for the Blind.
Leahd KT22 .... 95 C5
Royal School. Old W SL4 ...... 10 C4
Royal Surrey County Hospl.
Onsl V GU2 .... 129 E8
Royal Surrey County Hospl.
Stough GU2 .... 108 E1
Royal Victoria Gdns.
Ascot SL5 .... 29 A4
Royal Way The. Friml GU16 . 86 D7
Royal Wimbledon Golf Course.
Wimble SW19 .... 19 B2
Royal Wlk. Hackb SM6 .... 60 B7
Royale Cl. Alder GU11 .... 126 C8
Royals The. Guild GU1 .... 130 E8
Royce Rd. Crawl RH10 .... 182 A3
Roycroft Cl. Streat SW2 .... 22 A7
Roydon Ct. Hersh KT12 .... 54 A6
Roydon Lodge. Addl KT15 .... 52 D7
Roymount Ct. Twick TW2 .... 16 E5
Royston Ave. Byfl KT14 .... 71 E7
Royston Ave. Carsh SM1 ...... 59 D7
Royston Ave. Wallin SM6 ..... 60 D6
Royston Cl. Cranf TW5 .... 4 B6
Royston Cl. Crawl RH10 ...... 182 A2
Royston Cl. Walt O T KT12 ... 35 A1
Royston Ct. 3 Rich TW9 .... 6 F6
Royston Ct. Tolw KT6 .... 57 A8
Royston Prim Sch.
Penge SE20 .... 43 D8
Royston Rd. Byfl KT14 .... 71 E7
Royston Rd.
Penge BR3 & SE20 .... 43 D8
Royston Rd. Rich TW10 .... 6 E2
Roystons The. Surb KT5 .... 38 B4
Rozeldene. Hind GU26 .... 188 E3
Rubens St. For Hil SE6 .... 23 F6
Rubus Cl. W End GU24 .... 67 E6
Ruckmans La. Ockley RH5 ... 197 B7
Rudd Hall Rise. Camb GU15 . 65 E4
Ruden Way. Nork KT17 .... 77 B4
Rudge Rise. Row Tn KT15 .... 51 F5
Rudgwick Cty Prim Sch.
Rudg RH12 .... 214 D7
Rudgwick Rd. Crawl RH11 . 200 F7
Rudloe Rd. Streat SW12 .... 21 C8
Rudolph Ct. Dulw SE22 .... 23 B8
Rudsworth Cl. Coln SL3 .... 1 D7
Ruffetts Cl. S Croy CR2 .... 62 B3
Ruffetts The. S Croy CR2 ...... 62 B3
Ruffetts Way. Burgh H KT20 77 E1
Rufus Bsns Ctr.
Wimble SW18 .... 20 B6
Rufwood. Crawl D RH10 .... 204 A8
Rugby Cl. Sandh GU15 .... 45 E1
Rugby La. E Ewell SM2 .... 58 D2
Rugby Rd. Twick TW1 & 2 & 7 5 E1
Ruggles-Brise Rd.
Ashf TW15 .... 13 D3
Ruislip St. Up Toot SW17 ..... 20 F4
Rumsey Cl. Hampt TW12 ...... 15 F2
Runcorn Cl. Crawl RH11 ..... 200 E2
Runes Cl. Mitch CR4 .... 40 E5
Runnemede Rd.
Egham TW20 .... 12 A4
Running Horse Yd. 12
Brent TW8 .... 6 E8
Runnymeade Ctr The.
Chert KT15 .... 52 B8
Runnymede. Mitch SW19 ...... 40 D8
Runnymede Cl. Twick TW2 .. 16 B8
Runnymede Cotts.
Poyle TW19 .... 12 D7
Runnymede Cres.
Streat SW16 .... 41 E8
Runnymede Ct.
Egham TW20 .... 12 A4
Runnymede Ct.
W Heath GU14 .... 85 A7
Runnymede Ct. 1
Wallin SM6 .... 60 B4
Runnymede Gdns.
Twick TW2 .... 16 B8
Runnymede Hospl The.
Addl KT16 .... 51 D7
Runnymede Rd. Twick TW2 ... 5 B1
Runnymede Rdbt.
Egham TW20 .... 12 B4
Runshooke Ct. 10
Crawl RH11 .... 201 A3
Runtley Wood La.
Westfd GU4 .... 89 F2
Runwick La. Farnh GU10 ... 124 C1
Rupert Rd. Guild GU2 .... 130 C8
Rural Life Centre. Tilf GU10 146 F3
Rural Way. Earls RH1 .... 119 A1
Rural Way. Mitch SW16 .... 21 B1
Ruscoe Dr. Woking GU22 ..... 70 A2
Ruscoe House. 12
W Norw SW27 .... 22 B3
Ruscombe Way. E Bed TW14 14 F8
Rush Croft. Farnc GU7 ...... 151 A8
Rush The. Merton SW20 .... 39 F8
Rusham Park Ave.
Egham TW20 .... 12 A2
Rusham Rd. Balham SW12 .. 20 F8
Rusham Rd. Egham TW20 .... 11 F2
Rushams Rd. Horsh RH12 . 217 B3
Rushbury Ct. 6
Hampt TW12 .... 36 A8
Rushden Cl. S Norw SE19 .... 22 D1
Rushden Way.
Heath E GU9 .... 125 D7
Rushdene Wlk. Bigg H TN16 83 D2
Rushen Wlk. Carsh SM5 .... 40 D1
Rushett Cl. Thame D KT7 ..... 37 B1
Rushett Dr. Dork RH4 .... 136 C4
Rushett La. Chess KT9 .... 75 D7
Rushett Rd. Thame D KT7 .... 37 B2
Rushetts Pl. Crawl RH11 .... 181 C1
Rushetts Rd. Crawl RH11 .. 181 B1
Rushetts Rd.
Dovgn RH1 & RH2 .... 139 C5
Rushey Cl. New Mal KT3 ...... 38 D5
Rushey Gn. Lewish SE6 .... 24 B8
Rushey Green Prim Sch.
Catf SE6 .... 24 B7
Rushfords. Lingf RH7 .... 164 E5
Rushmead. Rich TW10 .... 17 B5
Rushmead Cl. S Croy CR0 .... 61 F6
Rushmere Ct. Worc Pk KT4 . 58 A8
Rushmere House. 2
Rhampt SW15 .... 19 A7
Rushmere Pl. Wimble SW19 19 D3
Rushmon Gdns.
Walt O T KT12 .... 54 B7
Rushmon Pl. Cheam SM3 ..... 58 E4
Rushmoor Cl. Stough GU2 . 108 F5
Rushmoor Independant Sch.
Farnb GU14 .... 85 C1
Rushmoor Rd. Alder GU11 . 104 E4
Rusholme Gr. Dulw SE19 ..... 22 E3
Rushton Ave. S Godst RH9 142 D5
Rushworth Rd. Reig RH2 .. 118 B2
Rushy House. Brack RG12 .... 27 E5
Rushy Meadow La.
Carsh SM5 .... 59 E7
Rushy Meadow Prim Sch.
Carsh SM5 .... 59 E7
Ruskin Ave. Felt TW14 .... 3 F1
Ruskin Ave. Rich TW9 .... 7 A7
Ruskin Cl. Crawl RH10 .... 182 C1
Ruskin Dr. N Cheam KT4 ...... 58 C8
Ruskin Par. Croy CR0 .... 61 D5
Ruskin Rd. Croy CR0 & CR9 .. 61 B8
Ruskin Rd. Islew TW7 .... 5 F4
Ruskin Rd. Stain TW18 .... 12 F2
Ruskin Rd. Wallin SM5 .... 60 A5
Ruskin Way. Mitch SW19 ..... 40 D8
Rusper Ct. Coulsd CR5 .... 79 D3
Rusper Cty Prim Sch.
Rusper RH12 .... 199 C7
Rusper Rd. Capel RH5 .... 178 D2
Rusper Rd. Crawl RH11 ...... 200 E6
Rusper Rd. Faygt RH12 ..... 199 A1
Rusper Rd. Horsh RH12 ..... 217 F6
Rusper Rd. Lamb Gn RH11 200 D7
Rusper Rd.
Newd RH12 & RH5 .... 179 C4
Rusper Rd.
Rusper RH11 & RH12 .... 200 D7
Ruspers Keep. Crawl RH11 200 F7
Russ Hill. Charl RH5 & RH6 180 C5
Russel Cl. Beck BR3 .... 44 C6
Russell Cl. Horse GU21 .... 69 C4
Russell Cl. Walt o t H KT20 ... 97 A2
Russell Ct. Bellf GU1 .... 109 C4
Russell Ct. Blckw GU17 .... 64 D5
Russell Ct. Broml BR1 .... 24 F1
Russell Ct. Hind GU26 .... 188 F4
Russell Ct. Leahd KT22 .... 95 B5
Russell Ct. Streat SW16 .... 21 F3
Russell Ct. Surb KT6 .... 37 E2
Russell Ct. Wallin SM6 .... 60 C5
Russell Dr. Stan TW19 .... 2 D1
Russell Gdns. Harm UB7 .... 3 A8
Russell Gdns. Rich TW10 ..... 17 C6
Russell Green Cl. Purley CR8 61 A1
Russell Hill. Wallin CR8 .... 60 F1
Russell Hill Par. 4
Purley CR8 .... 80 A8
Russell Hill Pl. Purley CR8 ... 80 A8
Russell Hill Rd. Purley CR8 .. 80 A8
Russell Kerr Cl. Chisw W4 ..... 7 C7
Russell Par. 3 Purley CR8 .. 80 A8
Russell Prim Sch The.
Rich TW10 .... 17 D7
Russell Rd. Horse GU21 .... 69 C4
Russell Rd. Lo Hall TW17 ...... 34 C2
Russell Rd. Merton SW19 ..... 20 A1
Russell Rd. Mitch CR4 .... 40 E6
Russell Rd. Twick TW1 & TW2 5 F1
Russell Rd. Walt O T KT12 .... 35 A3
Russell Sch The. Rich TW10 17 D6
Russell Way. Crawl RH10 .. 202 A5
Russell Way. Sutton SM1 ..... 59 B5
Russell Wlk. 4 Rich TW10 .... 6 F1
Russells. Tadw KT20 .... 97 D5
Russells Cres. Horley RH6 . 161 A2
Russet Ave.
Sunby TW16 & TW17 .... 34 E6
Russet Cl. Hersh KT12 .... 54 E7
Russet Cl. Horley RH6 .... 161 C3
Russet Cl. Stan TW19 .... 1 F1
Russet Cl. Tongh GU10 ...... 126 E7
Russet Dr. Croy CR0 .... 43 E1
Russet Gdns. Camb GU15 .... 65 D3
Russet Glade. Alder GU11 .. 125 E8
Russet Way. Dork RH5 ...... 136 D4
Russets. Tadw KT20 .... 97 C4
Russett Ct. Cater CR3 .... 101 A2
Russetts Cl. Horse GU21 ...... 69 F4
Russington Rd. Shep TW17 . 34 D3
Russley Gn. Woki RG11 .... 25 A1
Rusthall Cl. Croy CR0 .... 43 C3
Rustic Ave. Mitch SW16 .... 21 B1
Rustington Wlk.
Morden SM4 .... 39 F2
Ruston Ave. Tolw KT5 .... 38 B2
Ruston Way. N Asct SL5 .... 28 E7
Rutford Rd. Streat SW16 ..... 21 E3
Ruth Cl. W Heath GU14 .... 84 C5
Ruthen Cl. Epsom KT18 .... 76 B5
Rutherford Cl. Sutton SM2 ... 59 D4
Rutherford Way.
Crawl RH10 .... 182 A3
Rutherwick Cl. Horley RH6 160 F3
Rutherwick Rise. Coulsd CR5 79 E3
Rutherwyk Rd. Chert KT16 .. 32 E2
Rutherwyke Cl. Stonel KT17 58 A4
Rutland Cl. Alder GU11 ..... 105 A3
Rutland Cl. Epsom KT19 .... 57 D1
Rutland Cl. Mitch SW19 .... 20 E1
Rutland Cl. Mortl SW14 .... 7 C4
Rutland Cl. Redh RH1 .... 118 F2
Rutland Dr. Morden SM4 ...... 40 A2
Rutland Dr. Rich TW10 .... 17 E7
Rutland Gate. Hayes BR2 ..... 44 F5
Rutland Gdns. S Croy CR0 .... 61 E6
Rutland Lodge. For Hil SE6 .. 23 F6
Rutland Pk. For Hil SE6 .... 23 F6
Rutland Rd. Mitch SW19 ...... 20 E1
Rutland Rd. Twick TW2 .... 16 D6
Rutland Terr. Alder GU11 .. 105 A3
Rutland Wlk. For Hil SE6 ...... 23 F6
Rutlish Rd. Merton SW19 ..... 40 A8
Rutlish Sch (Boys).
Merton SW20 .... 39 F7
Rutson Rd. Byfl KT14 .... 71 F5
Rutter Gdns.
Mitch CR4 & SW19 .... 40 D5
Rutton Hill Rd.
Bowl Gn GU8 .... 189 E8
Ruxbury Ct. Ashf TW15 .... 13 E5
Ruxbury Rd. Chert KT16 .... 32 D3
Ruxley Cl. W Ewell KT19 ...... 57 B5
Ruxley Cres. Clayg KT10 ...... 56 B3
Ruxley Ct. W Ewell KT19 ...... 57 C5
Ruxley La. W Ewell KT19 ...... 57 C5
Ruxley Mews. W Ewell KT19 57 B5
Ruxley Ridge. Clayg KT10 .... 56 A3
Ryan Ct. Streat SW16 .... 21 E1
Ryan Dr. Brent TW8 .... 6 A8
Ryan Mount. Sandh GU17 .... 64 A8
Rycott Path. Dulw SE22 .... 23 A8
Rydal Cl. Crawl RH11 .... 200 D4
Rydal Cl. Farnb GU14 .... 84 D3
Rydal Cl. Friml GU15 .... 66 D5
Rydal Cl. Sander CR8 .... 80 D6
Rydal Dr. W Wick BR4 .... 63 E8
Rydal Gdns. King U T SW15 . 18 E3
Rydal Gdns.
Twick TW2 & TW3 .... 5 B1
Rydal Pl. Lhtwat GU18 .... 67 B8
Rydal Rd. Streat SW16 .... 21 D4
Rydal Way. Thor L TW20 ...... 12 B1
Ryde Cl. Ripley GU23 .... 91 C6
Ryde Ct. Alder GU12 .... 105 C1
Ryde Heron. Knaph GU21 ..... 68 E2
Ryde Lands. Cran GU6 .... 174 F4
Ryde Pl. Twick TW1 .... 6 D1
Ryde The. Stain TW18 .... 33 B8
Ryde Vale Rd. Up Toot SW12 21 C6
Ryde's Hill Cres.
Stough GU2 & GU3 .... 108 F5
Ryde's Hill Rd.
Stough GU2 & GU3 .... 108 F4
Rydens Ave. Walt O T KT12 . 54 C8
Rydens Cl. Walt O T KT12 .... 54 C8
Rydens Gr. Hersh KT12 .... 54 D6
Rydens Pk. Walt O T KT12 ... 54 D8
Rydens Rd. Walt O T KT12 ... 54 C8
Rydens Sch. Hersh KT12 ...... 54 C6
Rydens Way. Old Wok GU22 90 A7
Ryder House. 5
Merton SW19 .... 40 B8
Ryders Way. Horsh RH12 ... 217 F7
Rydes Ave. Stough GU2 ...... 108 F4
Rydes Hill Prep Sch.
Stough GU2 .... 108 F3
Rydon's La.
Coulsd CR3 & CR5 .... 100 C7
Rydon's Wood Cl.
Coulsd CR3 & CR5 .... 100 C7
Rye Ash. Crawl RH10 .... 202 A7
Rye Brook Rd. Leahd KT22 ... 75 A1
Rye Cl. Stough GU2 .... 108 E3
Rye Cl. W Heath GU14 .... 84 E7
Rye Cl. Wink RG12 .... 27 D8
Rye Ct. Beck BR3 .... 43 F8
Rye Gr. Windl GU24 .... 48 F2
Ryebridge Cl. Leahd KT22 .... 75 A1
Ryebrook Bsns Pk.
Leahd KT22 .... 95 A7
Ryecotes Mead. Dulw SE21 . 22 E7
Ryecroft Ave. Twick TW2 ...... 16 B7
Ryecroft Dr. Horsh RH12 ... 217 A3
Ryecroft Gdns. Blckw GU17 . 64 E4
Ryecroft Rd. S Norw SW16 .. 22 A2
Ryedale Ct. 8 Hampt TW12 36 A8
Ryefield Path. 7
Rhampt SW15 .... 19 A7
Ryefield Rd. S Norw SE19 .... 22 C2
Ryehill Ct. New Mal KT3 .... 38 F2
Ryelands. Crawl RH11 .... 201 A5
Ryelands. Horley RH6 .... 161 C4
Ryelands Cl. Cater CR3 ...... 100 E6
Ryelands Ct. Leahd KT22 ..... 75 A1
Ryelands Inf Sch. Croy SE25 43 B4
Ryelands Pl. Oat Pk KT13 ..... 53 E7
Ryemead La.
Wink RG12 & SL4 .... 8 C5
Ryersh La. Bear Gn RH5 ..... 178 C8
Ryfold Rd. Wimble SW19 ..... 20 A5
Ryland Cl. Felt TW13 .... 14 F4
Ryland House. 11
Streat SW16 .... 21 C3
Rylandes Rd. S Croy CR2 ...... 62 B1
Ryle Rd. M Bourn GU9 .... 146 B8
Rylton House.
Walt O T KT12 .... 35 A1
Rymer Rd. Croy CR0 .... 42 E2
Rythe Ct. Thame D KT7 .... 37 A2
Rythe House. Catf BR1 .... 24 D3
Rythe Rd. Esher KT10 .... 55 E5

Sabah Ct. Ashf TW15 .... 14 A4
Sable Cl. Hounsl TW4 .... 4 C4
Sable Ct. 3 New Mal KT3 ... 38 E4
Sabre Ct. Alder GU11 .... 104 E2
Sachel Court Rd.
Alfold GU6 & GU8 .... 193 D3
Sackville Cl. E Grins RH19 .. 185 C3
Sackville Coll. E Grins RH19 185 F1
Sackville Cotts. Bletch RH1 120 D1
Sackville Ct. 3
E Grins RH19 .... 205 F8
Sackville Gdns.
E Grins RH19 .... 185 C3
Sackville House. 16
Streat SW16 .... 21 E5
Sackville La. E Grins RH19 . 185 C3
Sackville Rd. Belm SM2 .... 59 A3
Sackville Sch. E Grins RH19 186 A1
Sacred Heart Catholic Prim Sch.
W Barn KT3 .... 39 A5
Sacred Heart Coll.
Sunnin SL5 .... 30 C3

Sacred Heart RC Prim Sch. Tedd TW11 17 B1
Saddleback Rd. Camb GU15 65 E8
Saddlebrook Pk. Ashf TW16 14 E1
Saddler Row. Crawl RH10 201 D3
Saddlers Cl. Merrow GU1 110 D2
Saddlers Scarp. Graysh GU26 188 A4
Saddlers Way. Lang V KT18 96 D8
Saddlewood. Camb GU15 65 C4
Sadler Cl. Mitch CR4 40 F7
Sadlers Ride. E Mole KT8 36 C7
Saffron Cl. Crawl RH11 201 A3
Saffron Ct. W Heath GU14 84 C4
Saffron Platt. Stough GU2 109 A5
Saffron Rd. Easth RG12 27 B5
Saffron Way. Surb KT6 37 D1
Sailors La. Thursl GU8 169 A2
Sainfoin Rd. Up Toot SW17 21 A6
Sainsbury Ctr The. Chert KT16 33 A2
Sainsbury Rd. W Norw SE19 22 E3
Saint Hill Rd. E Grins RH19 205 C5
Saints Cl. W Norw SE27 22 B4
SS Peter & Paul's RC Prim Sch. Mitch CR4 40 F5
St Agatha's Dr. King U T KT2 17 F2
St Agatha's Gr. Carsh CR4 & SM5 40 F1
St Agatha's RC Prim Sch. King U T KT2 17 F2
St Agatha's RC Sch. King U T KT2 17 F1
St Agnes Rd. E Grins RH19 185 E2
St Aidan's RC Prim Sch. Coulsd CR5 79 C3
St Alban's Gdns. Tedd TW11 17 A3
St Alban's Gr. Carsh SM5 40 E2
St Alban's RC Prim Sch. E Mole KT8 36 C4
St Alban's Rd. Reig RH2 118 A3
St Alban's Rdbt. Farnb GU14 105 C7
St Albans Ave. Felt TW13 15 D3
St Albans Ave. Weyb KT13 53 A7
St Albans Cl. Wood S V GU3 108 B2
St Albans House. 2 Streat SW16 22 A4
St Albans Rd. Cheam SM1 58 F6
St Albans Rd. King U T KT2 17 E2
St Amunds Cl. Catf SE6 24 A4
St Andrew's C of E Fst & Mid Sch. Crawl RH10 202 A4
St Andrew's C of E Sec Sch. Cobham KT11 73 C6
St Andrew's C of E Sec Sch. Croy CR0 61 B6
St Andrew's CE (VC) Inf Sch. Farnh GU9 125 B2
St Andrew's Cl. 2 Hounsl TW7 5 E6
St Andrew's Cl. Reig RH2 139 B8
St Andrew's Cl. Up Hall TW17 34 D5
St Andrew's Cl. Wray TW19 11 E8
St Andrew's Ct. Wands SW18 20 C6
St Andrew's RC Sch. Ashtd KT22 95 D7
St Andrew's RC Sch The Grange. Ashtd KT22 95 D7
St Andrew's Rd. Coulsd CR5 79 B4
St Andrew's Rd. 3 Croy CR0 & CR9 61 C6
St Andrew's Rd. King U T KT6 37 D3
St Andrew's Sch. Horse GU21 69 D3
St Andrew's Sq. King U T KT6 37 D3
St Andrew's & St Mark's Sch. King U T KT6 37 D4
St Andrew's Way. Friml GU16 85 F7
St Andrew's Wlk. Cobham KT11 73 B4
St Andrews. Cran GU6 174 B4
St Andrews. Easth RG12 26 E3
St Andrews Cl. Horse GU21 69 C2
St Andrews Ct. Ascot SL5 29 C4
St Andrews Ct. Chisw W4 7 C6
St Andrews RC Prim Sch. Streat SW16 21 E3
St Andrews Rd. Carsh SM5 59 E7
St Andrews Rd. Crawl RH11 200 D5
St Andrews Way. The Char RH8 123 F4
St Ann's Cl. Chert KT16 32 F3
St Ann's Heath Cty Mid Sch. Thorpe GU25 31 E4
St Ann's Hill. Wands SW18 20 C8
St Ann's Hill Rd. Chert KT16 32 D3
St Ann's Rd. Chert KT16 32 F3
St Ann's Sch. Morden SM4 40 B4
St Ann's Way. Croy CR2 61 B4
St Anne's Ave. Stan TW19 13 D8
St Anne's Dr. Redh RH1 119 A2
St Anne's Prim Sch. Stan TW19 13 E8
St Anne's RC Prim Sch. Chert KT16 33 A1
St Anne's RC (VA) Prim Sch. Banstd SM7 78 A3
St Anne's Rd. Crawl RH10 182 C2
St Anne's Rd. Godal GU7 151 A5
St Annes Glade. Bagsh GU19 47 D3
St Annes Mount. 7 Redh RH1 119 A2
St Annes Rise. Redh RH1 119 A2
St Annes Way. 5 Redh RH1 119 A2
St Anns Rd. Barnes SW13 7 F6
St Anselm's Ct. Streat SW16 21 E3
St Anselm's RC Prim Sch. Up Toot SW17 21 A5
St Anthony's Ct. 1 Balham SW12 21 A8
St Anthony's Ct. Up Toot SW17 21 A6
St Anthony's Hospl. N Cheam KT4 39 D1
St Anthony's Way. Hatton TW14 3 F3
St Anthonys Cl. Brack RG12 27 A8
St Anthonys Cl. Up Toot SW17 20 E6
St Antony's RC Prim Sch. Penge SE20 43 B8
St Arvans Cl. S Croy CR0 61 E7
St Aubin Cl. Crawl RH11 200 F2
St Aubyn's Ave. Hounsl TW3 & TW4 5 A2
St Aubyn's Ave. Wimble SW19 19 F3
St Aubyn's Ct. Wimble SW19 19 E2
St Aubyn's Rd. S Norw SE19 22 F2
St Augustine's Ave. Croy CR2 61 C3
St Augustine's Ave. S Croy CR2 61 C3
St Augustine's Cl. Alder GU12 105 D1
St Augustines Ct. Penge BR3 43 E7
St Augustines's RC Prim Sch. Catf SE6 24 C3
St Austins. Graysh GU26 188 D3
St Barnabas Cl. Beck BR3 44 C7
St Barnabas Ct. Crawl RH10 202 C7
St Barnabas' Gdns. E Mole KT8 36 A4
St Barnabas Rd. Mitch CR4 21 A1
St Barnabas Rd. Sutton SM1 59 D5
St Bartholomew CE Fst Sch. Haslem GU27 208 C7
St Bartholomew CE Prim Sch. Haslem GU27 208 C7
St Bartholomew's Cl. For Hil SE26 23 C4
St Bartholomew's Prim Sch. For Hil SE26 23 C4
St Bede's C of E Jun Sch. Send GU23 90 D3
St Bede's RC Inf Sch. Streat SW12 21 D7
St Bede's Sch. Redh RH2 118 E4
St Benedict's Cl. Alder GU11 105 A1
St Benedict's Cl. Up Toot SW17 21 A3
St Benet's Gr. Carsh SM4 & 5 40 C2
St Benets Cl. Up Toot SW17 20 E6
St Bernadette RC Jun Mix Sch. Streat SW12 21 C8
St Bernadette's RC Prim Sch. W Heath GU14 85 A5
St Bernards. S Croy CR0 61 E7
St Bernards Cl. 8 W Norw SE27 22 D4
St Boniface Catholic Prim Sch. Up Toot SW17 20 F3
St Brelades Cl. Dork RH4 136 A5
St Brelades Rd. Crawl RH11 200 F2
St Catherine's Convent Girls Prep & Senior Schs. Twick TW1 17 A6
St Catherine's Cross. Bletch RH1 120 E2
St Catherine's Dr. Arting GU2 130 B5
St Catherine's Hill. Arting GU2 130 C5
St Catherine's RC Mid Sch. W Barn KT3 39 C4
St Catherine's Sch. Bramly GU5 151 F7
St Catherine's Sch. Camb GU15 65 C4
St Catherines. Weyb KT13 53 B7
St Catherines. Woking GU22 89 C8
St Catherines Cl. Up Toot SW17 20 E6
St Catherines Ct. Felt TW13 15 A7
St Catherines Fst & Mid Schs. Bletch RH1 120 E2
St Catherines Rd. Crawl RH10 182 D1
St Catherines Rd. Friml GU16 86 A8
St Cecilia's RC Prim Sch. N Cheam SM3 58 D8
St Chad's RC Prim Sch. S Norw SE25 42 E4
St Chads Cl. Long D KT6 37 C2
St Charles Borromeo RC Prim Sch. Weyb KT13 53 A7
St Charles Pl. Weyb KT13 53 A5
St Christopher's. Lingf RH7 164 D4
St Christopher's Cl. Hounsl TW7 5 E6
St Christopher's Cl. Shottm GU27 208 A6
St Christopher's Ct. 3 Walt O T KT12 54 C8
St Christopher's Gn. Shottm GU27 208 A6
St Christopher's Hospice. Penge SE26 23 C3
St Christopher's Mews. Wallin SM6 60 C5
St Christopher's Rd. 2 Farnb GU14 85 A3
St Christopher's Rd. Shottm GU27 208 A6
St Christopher's Sch. Beck BR3 44 C7
St Christopher's Sch. Epsom KT18 76 E5
St Christophers Cl. Horsh RH12 217 D4
St Christophers Day Hospl. Horsh RH12 217 D3
St Christophers Gdns. N Asct SL5 28 D8
St Christophers Gdns. Thorn H CR7 42 A6
St Christophers Pl. 1 Farnb GU14 85 A3
St Clair Cl. Oxted RH8 122 D5
St Clair Cl. Reig RH2 118 C1
St Clair Dr. N Cheam KT4 58 B6
St Clair's Rd. S Croy CR0 61 E8
St Claire Cotts. Dorman RH7 165 B1
St Clare Bsns Pk. Hampt TW12 16 C2
St Clement Rd. Crawl RH11 200 F2
St Clements Ct. Farnb GU14 85 B7
St Clements RC Prim Sch. Ewell KT17 57 F2
St Cloud Rd. W Norw SE27 22 D4
St Crispin's Sch. Woki RG11 25 E6
St Crispins Way. Ottsh KT16 51 C2
St Cross Rd. Farnh GU9 125 C3
St Cross Rd. Friml GU16 86 B7
St Cuthbert Mayne RC Fst Sch. Cran GU6 174 E3
St Cuthbert's Cl. Eng Gn TW20 11 D2
St Cuthbert's RC Prim Sch. Eng Gn TW20 11 C1
St Cyprian's St.Up Toot SW17 20 F4
St David's. Coulsd CR5 79 F2
St David's Cl. Heath E GU9 125 E7
St David's Cl. Reig RH2 118 C2
St David's Cl. W Heath GU14 84 F8
St David's Cl. W Wick BR3 & BR4 44 B2
St David's Coll. W Wick BR4 44 B2
St David's Jun Sch. Ashf TW15 13 F5
St Denis Rd. W Norw SE27 22 D4
St Deny's Cl. Knaph GU21 68 D1
St Dominic's Sch. Hambl GU8 171 C1
St Dunstan's C of E Prim Sch. Belm SM3 58 E3
St Dunstan's Coll. For Hil SE6 24 A7
St Dunstan's Hill. Cheam SM1 & SM3 58 E5
St Dunstan's La. Beck BR3 44 C4
St Dunstan's RC Prim Sch. Woking GU22 70 A2
St Dunstan's Rd. Cranf TW5 4 B5
St Dunstan's Rd. Cranf TW5 4 C5
St Dunstan's Rd. Felt TW13 14 F5
St Dunstan's Rd. S Norw SE25 42 F5
St Ebba's Hospl. Epsom KT19 57 C2
St Edmund Cl. Crawl RH11 181 D1
St Edmund's Catholic Prim Sch. Twick TW2 16 B8
St Edmund's La. Twick TW2 16 B8
St Edmund's RC Prim Sch. Godal GU7 150 F2
St Edmunds Cl. Up Toot SW17 20 E6
St Edmunds Sch. Graysh GU26 188 D3
St Edward's Cl. E Grins RH19 185 C1
St Edwards Cl. New Add CR0 82 D8
St Elizabeth's RC Prim Sch. Rich TW10 6 F1
St Elphege's RC Prim Sch. Wallin SM6 60 E4
St Faith's Rd. Streat SE24 22 B7
St Fillans. Mayb GU22 70 B3
St Fillans Rd. Catf SE6 24 C8
St Francis of Assisi RC (Aided) Sch. Crawl RH10 201 E4
St Francis RC Fst Sch. Woking GU22 70 A2
St Francis RC Prim Sch. Whytlf CR3 100 F6
St Francis RC Sch. Ascot SL5 29 A3
St Francis Wlk. Crawl RH11 200 E4
St George's Ave. Whit V KT13 53 C4
St George's Bsns Ctr. Whit V KT13 53 A2
St George's Cl. Farnh GU9 126 B6
St George's Cl. Whit V KT13 53 C5
St George's Coll. Chert KT15 52 D7
St George's Gdns. Epsom KT17 76 F5
St George's Gdns. Horsh RH13 217 E4
St George's Gdns. Tolw KT6 57 B8
St George's Gr. Wands SW17 20 D5
St George's Hill Artisan Golf Club. Whit V KT13 53 C2
St George's Hill Golf Course. Whit V KT13 72 B8
St George's Hospl. Up Toot SW17 20 D3
St George's Ind Est. King U T KT2 17 D3
St George's La. Ascot SL5 29 B5
St George's Lodge. Whit V KT13 53 D5
St George's Rd. Alder GU11 & GU12 105 B1
St George's Rd. Beck BR3 44 B8
St George's Rd. Camb GU15 65 D6
St George's Rd. Felt TW13 15 D4
St George's Rd. Islew TW1 6 B2
St George's Rd. 2 King U T KT2 18 A1
St George's Rd. M Bourn GU9 125 D1
St George's Rd. Mitch CR4 41 B6
St George's Rd. Rich TW9 6 F4
St George's Rd. S Nutf RH1 140 E1
St George's Rd. Wallin SM6 60 B5
St George's Rd. Whit V KT13 53 D4
St George's Rd. Wimble SW19 19 F2
St George's Rd E. Alder GU12 105 B1
St George's Sch. Ascot SL5 29 B6
St George's Sch. Farnh GU9 125 B2
St George's Sq. New Mal KT3 38 E6
St George's Wlk. Croy CR0 & CR9 61 C7
St Georges Cl. Horley RH6 161 B3
St Georges Cotts. Crow RH7 143 E4
St Georges Ct. Addl KT15 52 C6
St Georges Ct. Crawl RH11 201 D8
St Georges Ct. E Grins RH19 185 C3
St Georges Ct. Penge SE20 43 B8
St Georges Rd. Addl KT15 52 C6
St Georges Rd. Farnh GU10 126 B4
St German's Rd. For Hil SE23 23 E7
St Giles C of E Inf Sch. Ashtd KT21 75 F1
St Giles' Sch. Croy CR2 61 B4
St Gothard Rd. W Norw SE21 & SE27 22 D4
St Gregory's RC Inf Sch. Camb GU15 65 B6
St Helen's Cres. Thorn H SW16 41 F8
St Helen's Rd. Thorn H SW16 41 F8
St Helena Terr. 23 Rich TW9 6 D2
St Helens. Thame D KT7 36 F2
St Helens Cres. Sandh GU17 64 B8
St Helier Ave. Morden SM4 40 C3
St Helier Cl. Crawl RH11 201 A2
St Helier Cl. Woki RG11 25 B3
St Helier Hospl. Carsh SM5 40 C1
St Helier Sta. Morden SM4 40 A3
St Heliers Ave. Hounsl TW3 & TW4 5 A2
St Hilary's Sch. Godal GU7 150 D3
St Hilda's Ave. Ashf TW15 13 E3
St Hilda's Cl. Crawl RH10 182 C1
St Hilda's Cl. Horley RH6 161 B3
St Hilda's Cl. Knaph GU21 68 D2
St Hildas Cl. Up Toot SW17 20 E6
St Hugh of Lincoln RC Prim Sch. Knaph GU21 88 D8
St Hugh's Cl. Crawl RH10 182 C1
St Hugh's Rd. Penge SE20 23 B1
St Hughes Cl. Up Toot SW17 20 E6
St Ignatius RC Fst & Mid Sch. Sunby TW16 35 A8
St Ives. Crawl RH10 202 C7
St Ives Sch. Haslem GU27 208 E8
St James Ave. Ewell KT17 77 A8
St James' Ave. Farnh GU9 125 D3
St James Ave. Sutton SM1 59 A5
St James C of E Prim Sch. Elst GU8 148 C3
St James C of E Prim Sch. Weyb KT13 53 C7
St James Cl. Epsom KT18 76 E5
St James' Cl. New Mal KT3 38 F4
St James Cl. Woking GU21 69 A1
St James Ct. Ashtd KT21 75 D2
St James Ct. Farnh GU9 125 C3
St James' Ct. 7 King U T KT1 37 E6
St James Ct. Thorn H CR0 42 B2
St James Mews. Weyb KT13 53 B6
St James Rd. Carsh SM5 59 E7
St James' Rd. King U T KT6 37 D3
St James' Rd. Mitch CR4 21 A1
St James' Rd. Purley CR8 80 C6
St James Rd. Sutton SM1 & SM2 59 A5
St James' Terr. Farnh GU9 125 C3
St James The Great RC (Aided) Sch. S Norw CR7 42 B7
St James Wlk. Crawl RH11 201 C2
St James's Ave. Beck BR3 43 E6
St James's Ave. Hampt TW12 16 C3
St James's Cl. Up Toot SW17 20 F6
St James's Cotts. 14 Rich TW10 6 D2
St James's Dr. Balham SW12 & SW17 20 F8
St James's Dr. Up Toot SW17 20 F7
St James's Lodge. 4 Croy CR0 42 E1
St James's Pk. Thorn H CR0 42 C2
St James's Pl. Cran GU6 174 C3
St James's Rd. Croy CR0 42 D2
St James's Rd. E Grins RH19 185 D1
St James's Rd. Hampt TW12 16 B3
St James's Rd. King U T KT1 37 D7
St James's Rd. Thorn H CR0 42 D2
St James's Sch. Twick TW2 16 E5
St James's Terr. 3 Up Toot SW12 21 A7
St Joan Cl. Crawl RH11 181 D1
St John Baptist C of E Prim Sch. Catf BR1 24 C4
St John Cl. Horsh RH13 217 E1
St John Fisher RC Prim Sch. W Barn KT3 39 D4
St John Rigby RC Coll. Coney H BR4 63 D6
St John The Bapist Sch. Old Wok GU22 90 A8
St John the Baptist C of E Jun Sch. Tedd KT1 17 D1
St John's. Dork RH5 136 C3
St John's Ave. Leahd KT22 95 B6

St John's Beamont Prep Sch.
Eng Gn TW20 .... 11 B6
St John's Beamont Sch.
Eng Gn TW19 .... 11 B6
St John's C of E Prim Sch.
Churt GU10 .... 167 E1
St John's C of E Prim Sch.
Penge SE20 .... 23 C1
St John's CE Jun Sch.
Cater CR3 .... 101 B2
St John's CE Prim Sch.
King U T KT1 .... 37 E6
St John's CE (VA) Inf Sch.
Cater CR3 .... 101 B2
St John's Cl. E Grins RH19 .185 E2
St John's Cl. Leahd KT22 .... 95 C7
St John's Cl. Onsl V GU2 .... 130 A8
St John's Cotts. 2
Penge SE20 .... 23 C1
St John's Court.
King U T KT1 .... 37 E5
St John's Cres.
Broad H RH12 .... 216 E3
St John's Ct. Brookw GU24 .. 87 F7
St John's Ct. Islew TW7 .... 5 F5
St John's Ct. W Heath GU14 84 D5
St John's Cty Prim Sch.
Knaph GU21 .... 68 E1
St John's Dr. Wands SW18 .. 20 B7
St John's Fst Sch.
Dork RH4 .... 136 B3
St John's Gr. Barnes SW13 .. 7 F5
St John's Gr. 1 Rich TW9 .... 6 E3
St John's Hill. Purley CR8 .... 80 A2
St John's Hill Rd.
Woking GU21 & GU22 ..... 89 B8
St John's Hospl. Twick TW1 17 A8
St John's Lye. Woking GU21 88 F8
St John's Lye (Festival Path).
Woking GU21 .... 88 F8
St John's Meadow.
Blind H RH7 .... 163 E8
St John's RC Prim Sch.
Horsh RH12 .... 217 A1
St John's Rd. Carsh SM5 .... 59 E7
St John's Rd. Crawl RH11 .. 201 C6
St John's Rd.
Croy CR0 & CR9 .... 61 B7
St John's Rd. E Grins RH19 185 E2
St John's Rd. E Mole KT8 .... 36 D5
St John's Rd. Earls RH1 .... 139 F7
St John's Rd. Felt TW13 .... 15 F4
St John's Rd. Islew TW7 .... 5 F5
St John's Rd. Leahd KT22 .... 95 C6
St John's Rd. M Bourn GU9 146 B8
St John's Rd. N Asct SL5 .... 8 F1
St John's Rd. Onsl V GU2 .. 130 A8
St John's Rd. Penge SE20 .. 23 C2
St John's Rd. Rich TW9 .... 6 E3
St John's Rd. Sandh GU17 .. 64 C7
St John's Rd. Sutton SM1 .. 59 B8
St John's Rd. Tedd KT1 .... 37 C7
St John's Rd. W Heath GU14 84 C5
St John's Rd. Westc RH4 .... 135 C6
St John's Rd. Wimble SW19 19 E2
St John's Rd. Woking GU21 .. 69 B2
St John's Rise. Woking GU21 69 B8
St John's Sch. Leahd KT22 .. 95 B6
St John's (Shirley) C of E Prim
Sch. Croy CR0 .... 62 D7
St John's St. Farnc GU7 .. 150 F6
St John's Terrace Rd.
Earls RH1 .... 139 F7
St Johns Ave. Ewell KT17 .... 77 A7
St Johns Ct. Egham TW20 .... 12 A3
St Johns Ct. S Godst RH9 .. 142 F5
St Johns Ct. Woking GU21 .. 89 A8
St Johns Cty Prim Sch.
Earls RH1 .... 139 E7
St Johns Dr. Walt O T KT12 .. 35 C1
St Johns Gr. M Bourn GU9 146 B8
St Johns Mews.
Woking GU21 .... 89 A8
St Johns Rd. King U T KT3 .. 38 C6
St Joseph's Convent Prep Sch.
E Mole KT8 .... 36 C4
St Joseph's RC Coll.
S Norw SW16 .... 22 B2
St Joseph's RC Inf Sch.
S Norw SE19 .... 22 C2
St Joseph's RC Jun Sch.
S Norw SE19 .... 22 C2
St Joseph's RC Prim Sch.
Brack RG12 .... 27 D7
St Joseph's RC Prim Sch.
Dork RH4 .... 136 A7
St Joseph's RC Prim Sch.
Epsom KT18 .... 76 C5

St Joseph's RC Prim Sch.
King U T KT1 .... 37 F7
St Joseph's RC Prim Sch.
Redh RH1 .... 118 E2
St Joseph's RC (VA) Jun Sch.
Stough GU22 .... 108 F3
St Joseph's Rd.
Alder GU11 & GU12 ..... 105 A1
St Joseph's Sch. Cran GU6 174 F6
St Josephs RC Prim Sch.
Alder GU11 .... 126 A8
St Jude's C of E Sch.
Eng Gn TW20 .... 11 C2
St Jude's CI. Eng Gn TW20 .. 11 C3
St Jude's Cotts.
Eng Gn TW20 .... 11 C3
St Jude's Rd. Eng Gn TW20 .. 11 C3
St Julian's Cl.
W Norw SE27 & SW16 ...... 22 A4
St Julian's Farm Rd.
W Norw SE27 & SW16 ...... 22 B4
St Katharines Rd.
Cater CR3 .... 101 A2
St Kitts Terr. W Norw SE19 .. 22 E3
St Lawrence C of E (Aided) Fst &
Mid Sch. Chobh GU24 ...... 68 E8
St Lawrence C of E Mid Sch.
E Mole KT8 .... 36 D5
St Lawrence Ct. Chobh GU24 68 E8
St Lawrence Prim Sch.
Effing KT24 .... 113 D8
St Lawrence RC Sch.
Felt TW13 .... 15 B6
St Lawrence's Hospl.
Cater CR3 .... 100 D4
St Lawrences Sch.
Cater CR3 .... 100 D4
St Lawrences Way.
Reig RH2 .... 118 A1
St Leonard's Gdns.
Heston TW5 .... 4 E6
St Leonard's Rd. Clayg KT10 55 F4
St Leonard's Rd.
Croy CR0 & CR9 .... 61 B7
St Leonard's Rd.
King U T KT6 .... 37 D4
St Leonard's Rd.
Thame D KT7 .... 37 A2
St Leonard's Rd. Wind SL4 .... 9 D8
St Leonard's Sq.
King U T KT6 .... 37 D4
St Leonard's Wlk.
Streat SW16 .... 21 F1
St Leonards C of E Prim Sch.
Streat SW16 .... 21 D3
St Leonards Ct. Mortl SW14 .. 7 C4
St Leonards Cty Inf Sch.
Horsh RH13 .... 217 E2
St Leonards Dr.
Crawl RH10 .... 202 A4
St Leonards Pk.
E Grins RH19 .... 185 E1
St Leonards Rd.
Burgh H KT20 .... 97 C8
St Leonards Rd.
Horsh RH13 .... 218 A1
St Leonards Rd. Mortl SW14 .. 7 C4
St Louis Rd. W Norw SE27 .. 22 D4
St Luke's C of E Prim Sch.
King U T KT2 .... 37 F8
St Luke's C of E Sch.
Rich TW9 .... 7 A6
St Luke's C of E Sch.
W Norw SE27 .... 22 C3
St Luke's Cl. Croy SE25 .... 43 B3
St Luke's Hospl. Guild GU1 130 F7
St Luke's Rd. Whytlf CR3 .... 80 F1
St Margaret Clitherow RC Prim
Sch. Easth RG12 .... 26 F2
St Margaret's. Guild GU1 .. 109 F1
St Margaret's Ave.
Cheam SM3 .... 58 E7
St Margaret's Ave.
Dorm Pk RH19 .... 185 F6
St Margaret's CE (Aided) Sch.
Crawl RH11 .... 201 B7
St Margaret's Ct. 9
Twick TW1 .... 6 B1
St Margaret's Dr. Islew TW1 .. 6 B2
St Margaret's Dr. Twick TW1 .. 6 A1
St Margaret's Rd.
E Grins RH19 .... 185 F3
St Margaret's Rd.
Hooley CR5 .... 99 B6
St Margaret's Rd. Islew TW1 .. 6 B2
St Margaret's Rd. Twick TW1 .. 6 B2
St Margaret's Sta. Twick TW1 .. 6 B1
St Margarets Ave.
Ashf TW15 .... 14 B3
St Margarets Bsns Ctr. 11
Twick TW1 .... 6 B1

St Margarets Ct.
Warn RH12 .... 216 F7
St Margaret's C of E Prim Sch.
Croy SE25 .... 43 A5
St Mark's C of E Prim Sch.
Farnb GU14 .... 105 D8
St Mark's Catholic Sch.
Hounsl TW3 .... 5 A4
St Mark's CE Prim Sch.
Beck BR2 .... 44 F6
St Mark's CE (VA) Prim Sch.
Ock Rid GU7 .... 150 B3
St Mark's Fst Sch. Mitch CR4 40 F7
St Mark's Hill. King U T KT6 . 37 E3
St Mark's La. Horsh RH12 .. 217 E6
St Mark's Pl. Wimble SW19 . 19 F2
St Mark's Prim Sch.
Binf RG12 .... 26 C8
St Mark's Rd. Croy SE25 .... 43 A5
St Mark's Rd. Tedd TW11 .... 17 B1
St Marks Cl. Farnb GU14 .... 85 C1
St Marks Pl. Heath E GU9 .. 125 B7
St Marks Rd.
Burgh H KT18 & KT20 ...... 77 C1
St Martha's. Peasl GU5 .... 154 E8
St Martha's Ave.
Westfd GU22 .... 89 F6
St Martha's Sch. Chil GU4 .. 131 B3
St Martin's Ave. Epsom KT18 76 E5
St Martin's C of E Inf Sch.
Woodc KT18 .... 76 D4
St Martin's C of E Jun Sch.
Woodc KT18 .... 76 D4
St Martin's C of E Prim Sch.
Dork RH4 .... 136 A8
St Martin's C of E Sch.
Pixham RH4 .... 115 C1
St Martin's CE Prim Sch.
Dork RH4 .... 136 A7
St Martin's Cl. Epsom KT17 . 76 E6
St Martin's Cl. E Hors KT24 112 E6
St Martins Cl. E Hors KT24 112 E6
St Martins Dr. Walt O T KT12 54 C7
St Mary Ave. Hackb SM6 .... 60 B7
St Mary Magdalene C of E Sec
Sch. Rich TW10 .... 7 A2
St Mary's. 4 Oat Pk KT13 .. 53 D7
St Mary's Ave. Beck BR2 .... 44 E6
St Mary's Ave. Stan TW19 .. 13 D8
St Mary's Ave. Tedd TW11 .. 16 F2
St Mary's C of E Prim Sch.
Leahd KT22 .... 95 C5
St Mary's C of E Prim Sch.
Buckl RH3 .... 117 A2
St Mary's C of E Prim Sch.
Chess KT9 .... 56 F4
St Mary's C of E Prim Sch.
Long D KT7 .... 37 B1
St Mary's C of E Prim Sch.
Wink RG12 .... 8 B2
St Mary's C of E Sch.
Stan TW19 .... 13 E8
St Mary's CE (Aided) Sch.
E Grins RH19 .... 185 D2
St Mary's CE Jun Sch.
Oxted RH8 .... 122 F7
St Mary's CE Prim Sch.
Byfl KT14 .... 71 E6
St Mary's Church Sch.
Twick TW1 .... 17 A8
St Mary's Cl. Chess KT9 .... 56 F3
St Mary's Cl. Ewell KT17 .... 57 F2
St Mary's Cl. Fetch KT22 .. 94 D4
St Mary's Cl. Oxted RH8 .... 122 E6
St Mary's Cl. Stan TW19 .... 13 D8
St Mary's Cl. Sunb TW16 .... 35 A5
St Mary's Cottage Hospl.
Hampt TW12 .... 16 B1
St Mary's Cres. Hounsl TW7 .. 5 E7
St Mary's Cres. Stan TW19 .. 13 D8
St Mary's Ct. King U T KT3 .. 38 E6
St Mary's Ct. Wallin SM6 .... 60 C6
St Mary's Dr. Crawl RH10 . 202 B8
St Mary's Dr. E Bed TW14 .. 14 C8
St Mary's Gdns. Bagsh GU19 47 E3
St Mary's Gdns.
Horsh RH12 .... 217 C1
St Mary's Gn. Bigg H TN16 .. 83 C1
St Mary's Gn. Bigg H TN16 .. 83 C1
St Mary's Gr. Chisw W4 ...... 7 B8
St Mary's Gr.
Rich TW10 & TW9 .... 6 F3
St Mary's High Sch.
Thorn H CR0 .... 42 C1
St Mary's Hill. Ascot SL5 .... 29 C4

St Mary's House.
Horsh RH12 .... 217 C1
St Mary's Pl. Farnh GU9 .... 125 C3
St Mary's RC Inf Sch.
Croy CR0 .... 42 D1
St Mary's RC Inf Sch.
Stough GU3 .... 108 E3
St Mary's RC Jun Sch.
Carsh SM5 .... 59 F5
St Mary's RC Jun Sch.
Croy CR0 .... 42 D1
St Mary's RC Prim Sch.
Beck BR3 .... 24 C1
St Mary's RC Prim Sch.
Chisw W4 .... 7 E8
St Mary's RC Prim Sch.
Islew TW7 .... 6 A4
St Mary's RC Prim Sch.
Merton SW19 .... 20 A1
St Mary's RC Sch. Islew TW7 .6 A4
St Mary's Rd. Ascot SL5 .... 29 B3
St Mary's Rd. E Mole KT8 .... 36 D4
St Mary's Rd. Camb GU15 .. 65 C6
St Mary's Rd. E Mole KT8 .... 36 D4
St Mary's Rd. Horse GU21 .. 69 C2
St Mary's Rd. King U T KT6 .. 37 D3
St Mary's Rd. Long D KT6 .... 37 C1
St Mary's Rd. Oat Pk KT13 .. 53 D6
St Mary's Rd. Reig RH2 .... 139 B8
St Mary's Rd. S Croy CR2 .... 61 D2
St Mary's Rd. S Norw SE25 .. 42 E6
St Mary's Rd. Wimble SW19 19 F2
St Mary's Rd. Worc Pk KT4 .. 57 E8
St Mary's RC Inf Sch.
Carsh SM5 .... 59 F5
St Mary's Sch. Ascot SL5 .... 29 B2
St Mary's Sch. Horsh RH12 217 C1
St Mary's Univ Coll.
Twick TW1 .... 16 F3
St Mary's CE (VA) Prim Sch.
Chidd GU8 .... 191 C4
St Marys Cl. Sandh GU17 .... 64 C8
St Marys La. Wink SL4 .... 8 D5
St Marys Rd. Leahd KT22 .... 95 B4
St Matthew's Ave. Surb KT6 .37 F1
St Matthew's C of E Prim Sch.
Redh RH1 .... 118 F3
St Matthew's CE Prim Sch.
Surb KT6 .... 37 E2
St Matthew's Cl. Ashf TW15 14 A3
St Matthew's Rd.
Redh RH1 .... 118 F2
St Matthews (C of E) Sch.
Downs KT11 .... 73 B1
St Merryn Ct. Beck BR3 .... 24 A1
St Michael's Ave. Fairl GU3 108 C6
St Michael's C of E Prim Sch.
Easth RG12 .... 27 A4
St Michael's CE (VA) Prim Sch.
Mickle RH5 .... 115 C8
St Michael's C of E Sch.
For Hil SE26 .... 23 E4
St Michael's Prim Sch.
Wands SW18 .... 19 F8
St Michael's RC Prim Sch.
Ashf TW15 .... 14 A3
St Michael's Rd.
Alder GU11 & GU12 ..... 105 B1
St Michael's Rd. Croy CR0 .. 42 C1
St Michael's Rd. Farnb GU14 85 B6
St Michael's Rd. Sheer GU21 70 D5
St Michael's Rd. Wallin SM6 60 C4
St Michael's Sch.
Limps RH8 .... 123 A6
St Michael's & St Martin's RC
Prim Sch. Hounsl TW4 ...... 4 F4
St Michaels C of E Inf Sch.
Alder GU11 .... 126 B8
St Michaels C of E Jun Sch.
Alder GU11 .... 126 C8
St Michaels Cl. Worc Pk KT4 57 F8
St Michaels Cotts.
Crowth RG11 .... 45 C8
St Michaels Ct. 1
Whit V KT13 .... 53 C5
St Michaels Rd. Ashf TW15 .. 14 A3
St Michaels Rd. Camb GU15 65 B5
St Michaels Rd. Cater CR3 100 D5
St Michaels Rd.
E Grins RH19 .... 185 E2
St Micheal's C of E Sch.
Ascot SL5 .... 29 D4
St Mildred's Rd. Guild GU1 109 F2
St Mildreds Rd.
Lewish SE12 & SE6 .... 24 F8
St Monica's Rd. Kings KT20 . 97 F6
St Nazaire Cl. Egham TW20 .. 12 C3

St Nicholas Ave. Fetch KT23 94 B2
St Nicholas C of E Prim Sch.
Shep TW17 .... 34 B3
St Nicholas C of E Sch.
Cran GU6 .... 174 D3
St Nicholas Ct. Crawl RH10 202 C7
St Nicholas Dr. Sutton SM1 . 59 B5
St Nicholas Dr. Lo Hall TW17 34 A2
St Nicholas Glebe.
Up Toot SW17 .... 20 F2
St Nicholas Hill. Leahd KT22 95 B5
St Nicholas Rd. Sutton SM1 . 59 B5
St Nicholas Rd.
Thame D KT7 .... 36 F3
St Nicholas Sch.
Merst RH1 .... 119 D6
St Nicholas Sch. Purley CR8 80 A6
St Nicholas Way.
Sutton SM1 .... 59 B5
St Nicolas Ave. Cran GU6 .. 174 E3
St Nicolas CE Inf Sch.
Guild GU2 .... 130 C7
St Nicolas Cl. Cran GU6 .... 174 E3
St Normans Way.
E Ewell KT17 .... 58 A1
St Olave's Cl. Stain TW18 .... 12 F1
St Olave's Wlk. Mitch SW16 41 D7
St Omer Rd. Guild GU1 .... 131 A8
St Omer Ridge. Guild GU1 . 131 A8
St Osmund's RC Prim Sch.
Barnes SW13 .... 7 F6
St Oswald's Rd.
S Norw SW16 .... 42 B8
St Paul's C of E Jun Sch.
King U T KT2 .... 18 A1
St Paul's C of E Jun Sch.
Woki RG11 .... 25 A6
St Paul's Catholic Sch.
Sunby TW16 .... 35 A8
St Paul's CE Inf Sch.
Tongh GU10 .... 127 A7
St Paul's CE Inf Sch.
Addl KT15 .... 52 A6
St Paul's CE (VA) Prim Sch.
Chess KT9 .... 56 E6
St Paul's CE (VA) Prim Sch.
Dork RH4 .... 136 B6
St Paul's Cl. Addl KT15 ...... 52 A5
St Paul's Cl. Ashf TW15 .... 14 C3
St Paul's Cl. Carsh SM5 .... 40 E1
St Paul's Cl. Chess KT9 .... 56 D6
St Paul's Cl.
Hounsl TW3 & TW4 .... 4 E5
St Paul's Ct. Hounsl TW4 .... 4 E4
St Paul's Gate. Woki RG11 .. 25 A6
St Paul's RC Prim Sch.
Thame D KT7 .... 36 E2
St Paul's Rd. Brent TW8 ..... 6 D8
St Paul's Rd. Egham TW18 .. 12 D2
St Paul's Rd. S Norw CR7 .... 42 C6
St Paul's Rd E.
Dork RH4 & RH5 .... 136 B7
St Paul's Rd W. Dork RH4 . 136 B6
St Pauls C of E Prim Sch.
Brent TW8 .... 6 D8
St Pauls' CE Fst Sch.
Tongh GU10 .... 126 F6
St Pauls Rd. Mayb GU22 .... 70 B2
St Pauls Rd. Rich TW9 .... 6 F3
St Peter & St Paul CE Prim Sch.
Cater CR3 .... 100 A2
St Peter's Cl. Old Wok GU22 90 C7
St Peter's Cl. Stain TW18 .... 12 F2
St Peter's Gdns.
W Norw SE27 .... 22 A5
St Peter's Gdns.
Wreccl GU10 .... 145 F6
St Peter's Hospl. Addl KT16 . 51 D7
St Peter's Jun Sch.
Farnb GU14 .... 85 C4
St Peter's Prim Sch.
S Croy CR2 .... 61 E4
St Peter's RC (Aided) Sch.
E Grins RH19 .... 185 C1
St Peter's RC Comp Sch.
Merrow GU1 .... 110 C2
St Peter's RC Prim Sch.
Ashtd KT22 .... 95 C7
St Peter's Rd. Crawl RH11 . 201 C6
St Peter's Rd.
Croy CR0 & CR2 .... 61 D6
St Peter's Rd. E Mole KT8 .... 36 A5
St Peter's Rd. Islew TW1 .... 6 B2
St Peter's Rd.
Old Wok GU22 .... 90 B7
St Peter's St.
Croy CR0 & CR2 .... 61 D5
St Peter's Way.
Addl KT15 & KT16 .... 51 F6
St Peter's Way.
Addl KT15 & KT16 .... 51 F7
St Peter's Way. Chert KT15 . 52 B8

St Peter's Way. Friml GU16 85 F7
St Peters CE Inf Sch. Tand RH8 122 A2
St Peters CE Prim Sch. Wreccl GU9 146 A7
St Peters Cl. Up Toot SW17 20 E6
St Peters Ct. E Mole KT8 36 A5
St Peters Mead. Ash GU12 106 B2
St Peters Pk. Alder GU11 & GU9 125 E8
St Peters Rd. King U T KT1 38 A7
St Peters Way. Harl UB3 3 D8
St Philip's Ave. N Cheam KT4 58 B8
St Philip's Rd. King U T KT6 37 D3
St Philips Sch. Chess KT9 56 D4
St Philomena's Sch. Carsh SM5 59 E5
St Pier's La. Lingf RH7 & TN8 165 B5
St Pinnock Ave. Stain TW18 33 A8
St Polycarp's RC Prim Sch. M Bourn GU9 125 D1
St Richard's with St Andrew's CE Prim Sch. Rich TW10 17 B5
St Richards Ct. Rich TW10 17 B5
St Robert Southwell RC Sch. Horsh RH12 218 A6
St Sampson Rd. Crawl RH11 200 F2
St Saviour's Coll. W Norw SE27 22 D4
St Saviour's Pl. Guild GU1 109 C1
St Saviour's Rd. Thorn H CR0 42 C3
St Stephen's C of E Jun Sch. Twick TW1 6 B1
St Stephen's CE Prim Sch. S Godst RH9 142 F6
St Stephen's Cl. Shottm GU27 207 F6
St Stephen's Cres. Thorn H CR7 42 A6
St Stephen's Gdns. Twick TW1 6 C1
St Stephen's Rd. Hounsl TW3 & TW4 5 A2
St Stephens Ave. Ashtd KT21 75 E3
St Stephens Cl. Haslem GU27 208 C7
St Swithun's Cl. E Grins RH19 185 F1
St Tarsisius RC Jun Sch. Camb GU15 65 D6
St Teresa's Prep Sch (Grove House). Effing KT24 113 D7
St Teresa's RC Prim Sch. Morden SM4 40 D3
St Theresa's RC Prim Sch. Woki RG11 25 D5
St Theresa's Rd. Hatton TW14 3 F3
St Thomas Cl. Horse GU21 69 C2
St Thomas' Cl. Surb KT6 37 F1
St Thomas More RC Sch. E Mole KT8 36 C4
St Thomas of Canterbury RC Mid Sch. Mitch CR4 41 A6
St Thomas of Canterbury Sch. Merrow GU1 110 B1
St Thomas' Rd. Chisw W4 7 C8
St Thomas Wlk. Coln SL3 1 D7
St Thomas's Dr. E Clan GU4 111 E4
St Vincent Cl. W Norw SE27 22 B3
St Vincent Cl. Worth RH10 202 D5
St Vincent Rd. Twick TW2 5 C1
St Vincent Rd. Walt O T KT12 54 B7
St Wilfrid's RC (Aided) Sch. Crawl RH11 201 B5
St William of York RC Prim Sch. For Hil SE23 23 E7
St Winifred's RC Prim Sch. Lewish SE12 24 F8
St Winifred's Rd. Bigg H TN16 83 F1
St Winifred's Rd. Tedd TW11 17 B2
St Winifreds. Kenley CR8 80 C4
Salamanca Pk. Alder GU11 104 F3
Salamander Quay. Tedd KT1 37 D8
Salbrook Rd. Salfs RH1 140 A1
Salcombe Dr. W Barn SM4 39 D1
Salcombe House. For Hil SE23 23 C6
Salcombe Rd. Ashf TW15 13 E5
Salcot Cres. New Add CR0 63 C1
Salcott Rd. Wallin CR0 60 F6
Sale Garden Cotts. Woki RG11 25 C5
Salehurst Rd. Worth RH10 202 E6
Salem Pl. Croy CR0 & CR9 61 C7
Salerno Cl. Alder GU11 105 A2
Salesian Catholic Comp Sch. Addl KT16 51 E8
Salesian Coll. Farnb GU14 85 D1
Salesian Sch. Chert KT16 33 A1
Salesian View. Farnb GU14 105 E8
Salford Rd. Streat SW12 & SW2 21 D7
Salfords Cty Prim Sch. Earls RH1 140 A3
Salfords Sta. Salfs RH1 140 B1
Salfords Way. Salfs RH1 140 A1
Salisbury Ave. Cheam SM1 & SM2 58 F4
Salisbury Cl. Woki RG11 25 A2
Salisbury Cl. Worc Pk KT4 57 F7
Salisbury Gdns. Wimble SW19 19 E1
Salisbury Gr. Mytch GU16 86 A3
Salisbury House. Wimble SW19 19 D5
Salisbury Pl. W Byfl KT14 71 C8
Salisbury Rd. Ash GU12 106 A3
Salisbury Rd. Banstd SM7 78 B5
Salisbury Rd. Blckw GU17 64 C5
Salisbury Rd. Crawl RH10 201 F2
Salisbury Rd. Croy CR0 & SE25 43 A3
Salisbury Rd. Farnb GU14 85 C3
Salisbury Rd. Felt TW13 15 C7
Salisbury Rd. Harl TW6 3 C1
Salisbury Rd. Hounsl TW4 4 C4
Salisbury Rd. King U T KT3 38 D6
Salisbury Rd. Rich TW9 6 E3
Salisbury Rd. Tyl Gn RH9 121 C4
Salisbury Rd. Wallin SM5 59 F4
Salisbury Rd. Wimble SW19 19 E1
Salisbury Rd. Woking GU22 89 E8
Salisbury Rd. Worc Pk KT19 & KT4 57 E7
Salisbury Terr. Mytch GU16 86 A3
Salix Cl. Sunby TW16 15 B1
Salliesfield. Twick TW2 5 D1
Salmons La. Whytlf CR3 100 F7
Salmons La W. Cater CR3 100 E7
Salmons Rd. Chess KT9 56 E4
Salmons Rd. Effing KT24 113 C6
Salt Box Rd. Jacobs GU3 & GU4 109 B6
Salt Box Rd. Worpl GU3 & GU4 109 B6
Salt La. Hyde GU8 171 E5
Saltash Cl. Cheam SM1 58 F6
Saltbox Hill. Bigg H TN16 83 B6
Saltdean Cl. Crawl RH10 & RH11 201 D3
Salter House. 8 Streat SW16 21 C4
Salter's Hill. W Norw SE19 & SE27 22 D3
Salterford Rd. Streat SW17 21 A2
Salterns Rd. Worth RH10 202 C3
Saltire Gdns. 2 Brack RG12 27 A8
Saltram Rd. Farnb GU14 85 E2
Salvador. Up Toot SW17 20 F3
Salvation Pl. Fetch KT22 95 A3
Salvington Rd. Crawl RH11 200 F3
Salwey Cl. Easth RG12 27 B3
Samaritan Cl. Crawl RH11 200 E4
Samarkand Cl. Friml GU15 66 B4
Samos Rd. Penge SE20 43 B7
Samphire Cl. Crawl RH11 201 A3
Sampleoak La. Chil GU4 131 E2
Sampleoak La. Woner GU4 131 E2
Sampson Ct. Shep TW17 34 C4
Sampson Pk. Binf RG12 26 D8
Samuel Cody Sch The. Farnb GU11 105 B7
Samuel Ct. Beck BR3 44 B6
Samuel Johnson Cl. Streat SW16 21 F4
San Carlos App. Alder GU11 105 C2
San Feliu Ct. E Grins RH19 186 B2
Sanctuary Rd. Harm TW19 & TW6 3 A1
Sanctuary The. Morden SM4 40 A3
Sand Hill. Farnb GU14 85 B7
Sand Hill Ct. Farnb GU14 85 B7
Sandal Rd. New Mal KT3 38 E5
Sandalwood. Guild GU2 130 B8
Sandalwood Ave. Addl KT16 51 E7
Sandalwood Rd. Felt TW13 15 B5
Sandbourne Ave. Merton SW19 40 B7
Sandcross La. Dovgn RH2 139 A5
Sandcross Sch. Woodh RH2 138 F6
Sandell's Ave. Ashf TW15 14 C3
Sanders Cl. Hampt TW12 16 C3
Sanders House. Streat SW16 21 E2
Sandersfield Rd. Banstd SM7 78 B4
Sanderstead Cl. Streat SW12 21 C8
Sanderstead Court Ave. Sander CR2 81 A6
Sanderstead Ct. Sander CR2 81 A7
Sanderstead Hill. S Croy CR2 80 F8
Sanderstead Hts. S Croy CR2 81 A8
Sanderstead Rd. S Croy CR2 61 D2
Sanderstead Sta. S Croy CR2 61 D2
Sandes Pl. Leahd KT22 75 A1
Sandfield Cty Prim Sch. Guild GU1 130 D8
Sandfield Gdns. S Norw CR7 42 B6
Sandfield Pl. S Norw CR7 42 C6
Sandfield Rd. S Norw CR7 42 B6
Sandfield Terr. Guild GU1 130 D8
Sandfields. Send GU23 90 D3
Sandford Ct. Alder GU11 104 F1
Sandford Down. Brack RG12 27 F4
Sandford Rd. Alder GU11 104 F1
Sandford Rd. Heath E GU9 125 B7
Sandgate House. 14 Beck BR3 24 A1
Sandgate La. Wands SW17 & SW18 20 E7
Sandhawes Hill. E Grins RH19 186 A4
Sandheath Rd. Beac H GU26 188 C7
Sandhill La. Crawl D RH10 204 B7
Sandhills. Wallin CR0 & SM6 60 D6
Sandhills Ct. Thorpe GU25 31 E4
Sandhills La. Thorpe GU25 & TW20 31 F4
Sandhills Meadow. Lo Hall TW17 34 C2
Sandhills Rd. Reig RH2 139 A7
Sandhurst Ave. Tolw KT5 38 B2
Sandhurst Cl. S Croy CR2 61 E2
Sandhurst La. Blckw GU17 64 B6
Sandhurst Prim Sch. Catf SE6 24 E7
Sandhurst Rd. Catf SE6 24 D7
Sandhurst Rd. Crowth RG11 45 B3
Sandhurst Rd. Woki RG11 25 A1
Sandhurst Sch. Sandh GU15 45 D1
Sandhurst Sta. Sandh GU17 64 A8
Sandhurst Way. S Croy CR2 61 E3
Sandiford House. Cater CR3 100 E3
Sandiford Rd. Cheam SM3 58 F8
Sandiland Cres. Coney H BR2 63 F8
Sandilands. S Croy CR0 62 A7
Sandlands Gr. Walt o t H KT20 97 A4
Sandlands Rd. Walt o t H KT20 97 A3
Sandon Cl. Thame D KT10 36 D1
Sandon House. 5 Streat SW2 21 E8
Sandown Ave. Esher KT10 55 C5
Sandown Cl. Blckw GU17 64 D5
Sandown Cl. Cranf TW5 4 A6
Sandown Cres. Alder GU11 104 F1
Sandown Ct. 2 Belm SM2 59 B3
Sandown Dr. Friml GU16 65 E2
Sandown Dr. Wallin SM5 60 A2
Sandown Gate. Esher KT10 55 D7
Sandown House. Penge SE26 23 B2
Sandown Ind Pk. Thame D KT10 55 A8
Sandown Lodge. Woodc KT18 76 D5
Sandown Park. Esher KT10 55 C8
Sandown Rd. Coulsd CR5 79 A3
Sandown Rd. Croy SE25 43 B4
Sandown Rd. Esher KT10 55 C6
Sandpiper Cl. Crawl RH11 200 D4
Sandpiper Rd. Selsd CR2 81 D8
Sandpit Hall Rd. Chobh GU24 69 A7
Sandpit Heath. Fairl GU3 108 D5
Sandpit Rd. Catf BR1 24 E3
Sandpit Rd. Redh RH1 139 F8
Sandpits Rd. Rich TW10 17 D6
Sandpits Rd. S Croy CR0 62 D6
Sandra Cl. Islew TW3 5 B2
Sandra House. E Mole KT8 36 D4
Sandringham Ave. Merton SW20 39 E7
Sandringham Cl. E Grins RH19 206 A8
Sandringham Cl. Farnb GU14 105 B8
Sandringham Cl. 1 Putney SW19 19 D7
Sandringham Cl. Pyrf GU22 71 A3
Sandringham Ct. Beck BR3 44 C8
Sandringham Ct. Belm SM2 59 A2
Sandringham Cty Inf Sch. Friml GU16 85 F7
Sandringham Dr. Ashf TW15 13 D4
Sandringham Gdns. Cranf TW5 4 A6
Sandringham Rd. Crawl RH11 201 B2
Sandringham Rd. N Cheam KT4 58 A7
Sandringham Rd. Stan TW19 & TW6 2 E2
Sandringham Rd. Thorn H CR0 42 C4
Sandringham Way. Friml GU16 85 F8
Sandrock. Haslem GU27 208 C6
Sandrock Hill Rd. Rowl GU10 146 A5
Sandrock Hill Rd. Wreccl GU10 146 A5
Sandrock Pl. S Croy CR0 62 D6
Sandrock Rd. Westc RH4 135 B5
Sandroyd Way. Cobham KT11 74 A6
Sands Cl. The San GU10 126 D2
Sands Rd. Farnh GU10 126 D2
Sands Rd. The San GU10 126 D2
Sandstone. Rich TW9 7 A7
Sandways. 6 Rich TW9 7 A6
Sandy Cl. Mayb GU22 70 C2
Sandy Croft. E Ewell KT17 58 C1
Sandy Cross. The San GU10 126 F4
Sandy Ct. Cobham KT11 73 F6
Sandy Dr. Cobham KT11 74 A8
Sandy Dr. E Bed TW14 14 E7
Sandy Hill Rd. Heath E GU9 125 B7
Sandy Hill Rd. Wallin SM6 60 C2
Sandy Holt. Cobham KT11 73 F6
Sandy La. Albury GU5 132 D2
Sandy La. Arting GU2 & GU3 130 B5
Sandy La. Belm SM2 58 E2
Sandy La. Betch RH3 116 E1
Sandy La. Bletch RH1 120 C3
Sandy La. Brack RG12 27 C8
Sandy La. Burrh GU24 49 E2
Sandy La. Camb GU15 65 E6
Sandy La. Cobham KT11 & KT22 74 B7
Sandy La. Crawl D RH10 204 A8
Sandy La. E Grins RH19 185 F1
Sandy La. Farnc GU7 150 D6
Sandy La. Grays GU27 189 E1
Sandy La. Kings KT20 98 A4
Sandy La. Limps RH8 123 B7
Sandy La. Mayb GU22 70 C2
Sandy La. Mitch CR4 41 A8
Sandy La. N Asct SL5 28 C8
Sandy La. Normdy GU3 107 D4
Sandy La. Nutf RH1 119 E1
Sandy La. Oxted RH8 122 C6
Sandy La. Pyrf GU22 71 A3
Sandy La. Reig RH2 138 B8
Sandy La. Rich TW10 17 D6
Sandy La. Rushm GU10 168 B5
Sandy La. S Nutf RH1 119 E1
Sandy La. Sandh GU17 45 A2
Sandy La. Send GU23 90 C4
Sandy La. Shere GU5 133 A3
Sandy La. Shottm GU26 188 F2
Sandy La. Shottm GU26 & GU27 207 C7
Sandy La. Sunnin SL5 30 A4
Sandy La. Tedd KT8 & TW11 17 B1
Sandy La. Thorpe GU25 31 E5
Sandy La. W Heath GU14 84 D7
Sandy La. Walt O T KT12 35 C3
Sandy La N. Wallin SM6 60 D5
Sandy La S. Wallin SM6 60 C3
Sandy Lane Cty Jun Sch. Brack RG12 27 C8
Sandy Rd. Row Tn KT15 52 A4
Sandy Ride. Ascot SL5 29 E5
Sandy Way. Cobham KT11 74 A7
Sandy Way. Croy CR0 62 F7
Sandy Way. Mayb GU22 70 C2
Sandy Way. Walt O T KT12 34 F1
Sandycombe Rd. E Bed TW14 15 A7
Sandycombe Rd. Rich TW9 7 A5
Sandycoombe Rd. Twick TW1 6 C1
Sanger Ave. Chess KT9 56 F6
Sanger Dr. Send GU23 90 C4
Sangers Cty Jun Sch. Horley RH6 160 F3
Sangers Dr. Horley RH6 160 F3
Sangley Rd. Catf SE6 24 C7
Sangley Rd. S Norw SE25 42 E5
Santina Cl. Heath E GU9 125 D8
Sanway Cl. Byfl KT14 71 E5
Sanway Rd. Byfl KT14 71 E5
Sappho Ct. Woking GU21 68 E3
Sapte Cl. Cran GU6 175 A3
Saracen Cl. Thorn H CR0 42 D3
Sarah House. Rhampt SW15 7 F3
Sarah Way. Farnb GU14 85 B4
Sardeson House. 13 W Norw SW27 22 B3
Sarel Way. Horley RH6 161 B5
Sargent Cl. Crawl RH10 201 F2
Sarjant Path. Putney SW19 19 D6
Sark Cl. Crawl RH11 201 A2
Sark Cl. Heston TW5 5 A7
Sarsby Dr. Wray TW19 12 A6
Sarsen Ave. Hounsl TW3 5 A5
Sarsfeld Rd. Up Toot SW12 & SW17 20 F7
Sarum. Easth RG12 26 F1
Sarum Cres. Woki RG11 25 D7
Sarum Gn. Oat Pk KT13 53 E7
Satellite Bsns Village The. Crawl RH10 181 E2
Satis Ct. Ewell KT17 76 F8
Saturn Cl. Crawl RH11 200 E4
Saturn Croft. Wink RG12 8 B2
Saunders Cl. Crawl RH10 202 B7
Saunders Copse. Woking GU22 89 B5
Saunders House. 11 Streat SW2 22 A7
Saunders La. Woking GU22 89 B5
Saundersfield House. Banstd SM7 78 B5
Saunton Ave. Harl UB3 3 F7
Saunton Gdns. 1 W Heath GU14 85 A6
Savernake Way. Brack RG12 27 F4
Savernake Wlk. Crawl RH10 201 F3
Savile Cl. New Mal KT3 38 E4
Savile Gdns. S Croy CR0 61 F8
Savill Gdns. W Barn SW20 39 A6
Saville Cres. Ashf TW15 14 D2
Saville Gdns. Friml GU15 66 B5
Saville Rd. Twick TW1 16 F7
Saville Row. Coney H BR2 44 F1
Savin Lodge. Sutton SM2 59 C3
Savona Cl. 12 Wimble SW19 19 D1
Savona Ct. Wimble SW20 39 D8
Savoy Gr. Hawley GU17 64 D3
Sawkins Cl. Putney SW19 19 E6
Sawtry Cl. Carsh SM5 40 E2
Sawyer House. 15 Dulw SE21 22 E4
Sawyer's Hill. Rich TW10 17 F8
Saxby Rd. Streat SW2 21 E8
Saxby's La. Lingf RH7 164 D5
Saxley. Horley RH6 161 C4
Saxon Ave. Felt TW13 15 F6
Saxon Bsns Ctr. Merton SW19 40 C8
Saxon Cl. Surb KT6 37 D3
Saxon Cres. Horsh RH12 217 B4
Saxon Croft. Farnh GU9 125 C1
Saxon Cty Jun Sch. Shep Gn TW17 34 A4
Saxon Dr. Wink RG12 27 F8
Saxon House. Felt TW13 15 F6
Saxon House. Woodh RH2 138 F6
Saxon House. Woodh RH2 139 A6
Saxon Rd. Ashf TW15 14 D2
Saxon Rd. Broml BR1 24 F1
Saxon Rd. Thorn H CR0 & SE25 42 D4
Saxon Rd. Walt O T KT12 54 D7
Saxon Rd. Worth RH10 202 E5
Saxon Way. Harm UB7 2 C8
Saxon Way. Reig RH2 117 F2
Saxonbury Ave. Sunby TW16 35 B7
Saxonbury Cl. Mitch CR4 40 D6
Saxonbury Gdns. Long D KT6 37 C1
Saxons. Tadw KT20 97 D6
Sayer Ct. 4 Knaph GU21 68 E1
Sayer's Wlk. Rich TW10 17 F8
Sayers Cl. Fetch KT22 94 C4
Sayers Cl. Friml GU16 85 E7
Sayers The. 5 E Grins RH19 185 C1
Sayes Court Cty Jun Sch. Addl KT15 52 B5
Sayes Court Farm Dr. Addl KT15 52 B5
Sayes Ct. Addl KT15 52 C5
Sbac Track. Farnb GU11 104 E6
Scaitcliffe Sch. Eng Gn TW20 11 A5

Scallows Cl. Crawl RH10 ...... 4 D7
Scallows Rd. Crawl RH10 ..... 202 A7
Scampton Rd. Stan TW6 .... 2 F1
Scania Wlk. Wink RG12 .... 8 B2
Scarborough Cl. Belm SM2 .. 77 F8
Scarborough Cl.
Bigg H TN16 .... 83 C1
Scarborough Rd. Harl TW6 ... 3 C1
Scarbrook Rd.
Croy CR0 & CR9 .... 61 C7
Scarlet Oaks. Friml GU15 ..... 65 E3
Scarlet Rd. Catf SE6 .... 24 E5
Scarlett Cl. Knaph GU21 .... 68 F1
Scarlett's Rd. Alder GU11 .. 105 A3
Scarlette Manor Wlk. 10
Streat SE24 .... 22 A8
Scarth Rd. Barnes SW13 .... 7 F4
Schiller International Univ.
Coney H BR4 .... 63 D6
Scholars Ct. Crawl RH10 .... 204 A8
Scholars Rd. Streat SW12 .... 21 C7
School Cl. Belf GU1 .... 109 D3
School Cl. Bisley GU24 .... 68 A4
School Cl. Horsh RH12 .... 218 A6
School Cotts. Woking GU22 .. 89 C5
School Hill. Crowth RG11 ..... 45 D4
School Hill. Merst RH1 .... 119 C7
School Hill. Sandh GU17 ...... 45 A1
School Hill. Seale GU10 ...... 127 B4
School Hill. Warn RH12 ...... 216 F8
School Hill. Wrecl GU10 .... 145 F6
School House La.
Tedd TW11 .... 17 C1
School Houses. Hasc GU8 . 172 E4
School La. Addl KT15 .... 52 A6
School La. Ash W RH19 ...... 206 E6
School La. Bagsh GU19 .... 47 E2
School La. Crond GU10 ...... 124 D8
School La. E Clan GU4 .... 111 E4
School La. Egham TW20 .... 12 A3
School La. Fetch KT22 .... 94 D5
School La. La Hall TW17 ...... 34 B2
School La. M Bourn GU10 .. 146 D6
School La. Mickle RH5 .... 115 C8
School La. Ockham GU23 ..... 92 B5
School La. Pirb GU24 .... 87 E5
School La. Putt GU3 .... 128 C4
School La. Shackl GU8 .... 149 E6
School La. Surb KT6 .... 38 A1
School La. Tedd KT1 .... 37 C8
School La. W Hors KT24 ..... 112 B6
School La. Walt o t h KT20 ... 97 A2
School La. Westc RH4 .... 135 D6
School La. Windl GU20 .... 48 D4
School of Art Pewley Annexe.
Guild GU1 .... 130 E7
School Pas. 3 King U T KT1 .. 37 F7
School Rd. Ascot SL5 .... 29 D4
School Rd. Ashf TW15 .... 14 B2
School Rd. Binst GU10 .... 145 E3
School Rd. E Mole KT8 .... 36 D5
School Rd. Graysh GU26 .... 188 B4
School Rd. Hampt TW12 .... 16 C2
School Rd. Harm UB7 .... 2 D8
School Rd. Hasc GU8 .... 172 E4
School Rd. Hounsl TW3 .... 5 C4
School Rd. Linch GU27 .... 207 F5
School Rd. Tedd KT1 .... 37 C8
School Rd. Windl GU20 .... 48 B5
School Rd. Woki RG11 .... 25 D6
School Road Ave.
Hampt TW12 .... 16 C2
School Wlk. Sunby TW16 .... 35 A6
Schroder Ct. Eng Gn TW20 .. 11 B3
Scillonian Rd. Guild GU2 .. 130 B7
Scilly Isles. Hinch W KT10 .. 55 E8
Scizdons Climb. Godal GU7 150 F4
Scoles Cres. Streat SW2 ..... 22 A7
Scoresdale. S Norw SE19 .... 42 E8
Scory Cl. Crawl RH11 .... 201 A3
Scotland Bridge Rd.
Woodhm KT15 .... 71 A8
Scotland Cl. Ash V GU12 ... 106 A5
Scotland Farm Rd.
Ash V GU12 .... 106 A5
Scotland Hill. Sandh GU17 ... 45 A1
Scotland Hill. Sandh GU17 ... 64 A8
Scotland La. Haslem GU27 . 208 C5
Scotlands Cl. Haslem GU27 208 B5
Scotlands Dr. Haslem GU27 208 C5
Scots Cl. Stan TW19 .... 13 D7
Scotsdale Cl. Cheam SM2 .... 58 E3
Scotshall La. Farlgh CR6 ...... 82 C4
Scott Cl. Stough GU2 .... 109 A3
Scott Cl. Thorn H SW16 .... 41 F8
Scott Cl. W Ewell KT19 .... 57 C5
Scott Cl. W Ewell KT19 .... 57 C5
Scott Farm Cl. Hinch W KT7 37 B1

Scott Gdns. Heston TW5 .... 4 D7
Scott House. Rich TW10 .... 17 C6
Scott Rd. Crawl RH10 .... 201 F3
Scott Terr. Brack RG12 .... 27 E8
Scott's Ave. Ashf TW16 .... 14 E1
Scott's Ave. Beck BR2 .... 44 D7
Scott's Ct. Farnb GU14 .... 85 B7
Scott's Grove Cl.
W End GU24 .... 68 D6
Scott's Grove Rd.
W End GU24 .... 68 C6
Scott's Hill.
Outw RH1 & RH6 .... 162 D5
Scott's La. Beck BR2 & BR3 .. 44 D7
Scott's Way. Ashf TW16 .... 14 E1
Scotts Dr. Hampt TW12 .... 16 B1
Scotts Farm Rd.
W Ewell KT19 .... 57 C4
Screw Corner Rd.
Bowl Gn GU8 .... 170 A1
Scrooby St. 3 Lewish SE6 .. 24 B8
Scrutton Cl. Streat SW12 .... 21 D8
Scylla Cres. E Bed TW6 .... 3 B1
Scylla Cres.
E Bed TW6&TW14 .... 14 B8
Scylla Pl. Woking GU21 .... 89 A8
Scylla Rd. E Bed TW14 & TW6 3 B1
Seabrook Dr. W Wick BR4 ... 63 E8
Seafire Way.
Farnb GU11 & GU14 .... 104 E7
Seaford Rd. Crawl RH11 .... 201 A2
Seaford Rd.
Stan TW19 & TW6 .... 2 D2
Seaford Rd. Woki RG11 .... 25 D6
Seaforth Ave. W Barn KT3 ... 39 B5
Seaforth Gdns.
Worc Pk KT19 .... 57 F5
Seaforth Lodge. Barnes SW13 7 F5
Sealand Rd. Harm TW6 .... 3 A1
Seale La.
The San GU10 & GU3 .... 126 E4
Seale Rd. Elst GU8 .... 148 B7
Seale Rd. The San GU8 ...... 148 B7
Seaman's Gn. Bear Gn RH5 178 D8
Searchwood Rd.
Warlgm CR6 .... 81 B1
Searle Ct. Mitch CR4 .... 40 E8
Searle Hill. Woodh RH2 ..... 139 A7
Searle Rd. M Bourn GU9 .. 146 C8
Searle's View. Horsh RH12 217 E5
Seath House. 4 Penge SE26 23 B3
Seaton Cl. Putney SW15 ...... 19 B8
Seaton Cl. Twick TW2 .... 5 D1
Seaton Dr. Ashf TW15 .... 13 E6
Seaton Rd. Camb GU15 .... 65 B5
Seaton Rd. Mitch CR4 .... 40 E7
Seaton Rd. Twick TW2 .... 5 C1
Sebastopol Rd. Alder GU11 105 B2
Second Ave. Mortl SW14 ...... 7 E4
Second Ave. Walt O T KT12 .. 35 B3
Second Ave. Woodhm KT15 .. 52 B2
Second Cl. E Mole KT8 .... 36 C5
Second Cross Rd.
Twick TW2 .... 16 E6
Seddon Ct. Crawl RH11 .... 201 B1
Seddon Rd. Morden SM4 .... 40 D4
Sedgefield Cl. Crawl RH10 . 202 E7
Sedgehill Rd. Catf SE6 .... 24 B3
Sedgehill Sch. Catf SE6 ...... 24 B3
Sedgemoor. Farnb GU14 ...... 85 B7
Sedgeway. Catf SE6 .... 24 F7
Sedgewick Cl. Crawl RH10 . 202 C6
Sedgwick House.
Putney SW15 .... 19 D6
Sedgewood Cl. Hayes BR2 .. 44 F2
Sedley Ct. For Hil SE26 .... 23 B6
Seebys Oak. Sandh GU15 .... 64 E6
Seeley Dr. Dulw SE21 .... 22 E4
Seely Rd. Mitch SW17 .... 21 A2
Seething Wells Halls Of
Residence. King U T KT6 .. 37 C3
Seething Wells La.
King U T KT6 .... 37 C3
Sefton Cl. W End GU24 .... 67 F6
Sefton Cl. Wrecl GU10 .... 5 B6
Sefton Lodge. 2 Twick TW1 .. 6 C1
Sefton Rd. Croy CR0 .... 43 A1
Sefton Rd. Epsom KT19 .... 57 D1
Segal Cl. For Hil SE23 .... 23 E8
Segrave Cl. Whit V KT13 ...... 53 A3
Segsbury Gr. Brack RG12 .... 27 F5
Sekhon Terr. Felt TW13 .... 16 A5
Selborne Ave. Alder GU11 . 126 C6
Selborne Cl. Bickw GU17 .... 64 C6
Selborne Rd. King U T KT3 .. 38 E7
Selborne Rd. S Croy CR0 ..... 61 F7
Selbourne Ave.
Woodhm KT15 .... 52 B2
Selbourne Cl. Crawl RH10 182 D2
Selbourne Cl. Woodhm KT15 52 B1
Selbourne Rd. Burph GU1 . 110 A4

Selbourne Sq. Tyl Gn RH9 .. 121 C5
Selby Cl. Chess KT9 .... 56 E3
Selby Ct. Twick TW2 .... 16 D6
Selby Gn. Carsh SM5 .... 40 E2
Selby Rd. Ashf TW15 .... 14 C2
Selby Rd. Carsh SM5 .... 40 E2
Selby Rd. Penge SE20 .... 43 A7
Selby Wlk. 1 Woking GU21 69 B1
Selbys. Lingf RH7 .... 164 E5
Selcroft Rd. Purley CR8 .... 80 B7
Selham Cl. Crawl RH11 ..... 201 A7
Selhurst Cl. Horse GU21 ...... 69 F4
Selhurst Cl. Putney SW19 ... 19 D7
Selhurst New Ct.
Thorn H SE25 .... 42 E3
Selhurst New Rd.
Thorn H SE25 .... 42 E3
Selhurst Park. S Norw SE25 . 42 E5
Selhurst Pl.
Thorn H CR0 & SE25 .... 42 E3
Selhurst Rd.
S Norw CR0 & SE25 .... 42 E4
Selhurst Rd.
Thorn H CR0 & SE25 .... 42 E4
Selhurst Sta. S Norw SE25 .. 42 E4
Selkirk Rd. Twick TW2 .... 16 C7
Selkirk Rd. Up Toot SW17 ... 20 E4
Sellar's Hill. Farnc GU7 ..... 150 D7
Sellincourt Inf Sch.
Up Toot SW17 .... 20 E2
Sellincourt Jun Sch.
Up Toot SW17 .... 20 E2
Sellincourt Rd.
Up Toot SW17 .... 20 E2
Sellindge Cl. Beck BR3 .... 23 F1
Selsdon Ave. S Croy CR2 ..... 61 D4
Selsdon Cres. S Croy CR2 ... 62 C1
Selsdon High Sch.
S Croy CR2 .... 62 D3
Selsdon Park Golf Course.
Sander CR2 .... 81 B7
Selsdon Park Rd.
New Add CR0 & CR2 .... 62 D2
Selsdon Rd. S Croy CR2 ...... 61 D4
Selsdon Rd. N Worw SE27 ... 22 B4
Selsdon Rd. Woodhm KT15 .. 71 A8
Selsdon Prim Sch.
S Croy CR2 .... 62 C2
Selsdon Rd. S Croy CR2 ...... 61 D4
Selsdon Rd. N Worw SE27 ... 22 B4
Selsdon Rd. Woodhm KT15 .. 71 A8
Selsey Ct. 3 Crawl RH11 .. 201 B2
Selsey Rd. Crawl RH11 ..... 201 A2
Selsfield Rd.
Turn H RH10 & RH19 .... 204 A2
Selsfield Rd.
W Hoath RH19 .... 204 B1
Seltops Cl. Cran GU6 .... 174 F2
Selwood Cl. Stan TW19 .... 2 C1
Selwood Gdns. Stan TW19 ... 2 C1
Selwood Rd. Cheam SM3 .... 39 F1
Selwood Rd. Chess KT9 .... 56 D6
Selwood Rd. Croy CR0 .... 43 B1
Selwood Rd. Old Wok GU22 . 90 B7
Selworthy Rd.
For Hil SE23 & SE6 .... 23 F5
Selwyn Ave. Rich TW9 .... 6 F4
Selwyn Cl. Crawl RH11 ..... 182 C1
Selwyn Cl. Hounsl TW4 .... 4 E3
Selwyn Rd. 7 Rich TW10 ...... 6 F2
Selwyn Rd. New Mal KT3 .... 38 D4
Semaphore Rd. Guild GU1 . 130 E7
Semley Rd. Thorn H SW16 ... 41 E7
Semper Cl. Knaph GU21 ...... 68 E2
Send Barns La. Send GU23 .. 90 E2
Send Cl. Send GU23 .... 90 E4
Send C of E Grant Maintnd Sch.
Send GU23 .... 90 E3
Send Cl. Send GU23 .... 90 C4
Send Hill. Send GU23 .... 90 C3
Send Marsh Rd. Send GU23 . 90 F4
Send Marsh Rd.
Send M GU23 .... 90 E4
Send Rd. Send GU23 .... 90 C4
Seneca Rd. Thorn H CR7 ..... 42 C5
Senga Rd. Carsh CR4 .... 41 A1
Senhouse Rd. Cheam SM3 .. 58 D7
Sequoia Pk. Crawl RH11 ... 201 D4
Serpentine Gn. Merst RH1 119 D6
Serrin Way. Horsh RH12 .... 217 E5
Service Rd. Crawl RH6 .... 181 F8
Service Rd. Crawl RH6 .... 182 B7
Servite House. Beck BR3 ..... 43 F8
Servite House. Dork RH4 .. 136 A5
Servite House. Knaph GU21 . 68 D2
Servius Ct. 2 Brent TW8 .... 6 D7
Setley Way. Brack RG12 ...... 27 F6

Seven Acres. Carsh SM5 ...... 59 E8
Seven Arches App.
Whit V KT13 .... 53 A3
Seven Hills Cl.
Whit V KT12 & KT13 .... 53 E2
Seven Hills Rd.
Whit V KT12 & KT13 .... 53 E3
Seven Hills Rd (South).
Whit V KT11 .... 72 E6
Sevenoaks Cl. Belm SM2 .... 59 B1
Sevenoaks Cl. Sutton GU7 ... 64 C8
Severn Cres. Bra Hil SL3 ...... 1 B8
Severn Dr. Hinch W KT10 .... 56 A8
Severn Dr. Walt O T KT12 .... 54 D8
Severn Rd. W Heath GU14 ... 84 E6
Severn Rd. Worth RH10 ..... 202 C5
Seward Rd. Penge BR3 .... 43 D7
Sewell Ave. Woki RG11 .... 25 A8
Sewer's Farm Rd.
Abin C RH5 .... 155 F6
Sewill Cl. Charl RH6 .... 180 F7
Seychelle Ct. Beck BR3 .... 24 B1
Seymour Ave. Cater CR3 ... 100 C4
Seymour Ave. Ewell KT17 ... 58 B2
Seymour Ave. W Barn SM4 . 39 D2
Seymour Cl. E Mole KT8 ...... 36 C4
Seymour Dr. Camb GU15 .... 66 B7
Seymour Gdns. Felt TW13 .. 15 C4
Seymour Gdns. King U T KT5 37 F4
Seymour Gdns. Twick SW1 .. 17 B8
Seymour Pl. Croy SE25 .... 43 B5
Seymour Rd. Carsh CR4 ...... 41 A2
Seymour Rd. Crawl RH11 .. 201 B2
Seymour Rd. E Mole KT8 ..... 36 C4
Seymour Rd. Hampt TW12 .. 16 C3
Seymour Rd.
Head Gn GU35 .... 187 C4
Seymour Rd. Ock Rid GU7 . 150 B3
Seymour Rd. Tedd KT1 .... 37 D8
Seymour Rd. Wallin SM5 ..... 60 A5
Seymour Rd. Wands SW18 .. 19 F8
Seymour Rd. Wimb SW19 ... 19 D5
Seymour Terr. Penge SE20 .. 43 B8
Seymour Villas. Penge SE20 43 A8
Seymour Way. Ashf TW16 ... 14 E1
Shabden Cotts. Chips CR5 .. 98 F6
Shabden Park. Kings CR5 ... 98 E5
Shabden Park Hospl.
Kings CR5 .... 98 E5
Shackleford Rd.
Old Wok GU22 .... 90 A7
Shackleford Rd.
Shackl GU8 .... 149 E5
Shackleford St Mary's Fst Sch.
Shackl GU8 .... 149 E6
Shacklegate La. Tedd TW11 16 E4
Shackleton Cl. For Hil SE23 . 23 B6
Shackleton Ct. 2
Dulw SE21 .... 22 D6
Shackleton Ct. 6 Stan TW19 2 E1
Shackleton Rd. Crawl RH10 201 F3
Shackstead La. Godal GU7 150 D3
Shackter La. Godal GU7 .... 150 C3
Shadbolt Cl. Worc Pk KT4 ... 57 F8
Shady Nook. Hale GU9 ...... 125 B6
Shadynager. Farnc GU7 .... 150 E6
Shaef Way. Tedd TW11 .... 17 A1
Shaftesbury Ave. Felt TW14 .. 4 A1
Shaftesbury Cres.
Stain TW18 .... 13 D1
Shaftesbury Ct.
Farnb GU14 .... 105 C8
Shaftesbury Ct. Woki RG11 . 25 D7
Shaftesbury House.
Croy SE25 .... 43 A3
Shaftesbury Independent Sch.
Purley CR8 .... 80 B6
Shaftesbury Mount.
Hawley GU17 .... 64 D3
Shaftesbury Rd. Beck BR3 .. 43 F7
Shaftesbury Rd. Bisley GU24 67 F3
Shaftesbury Rd. Carsh SM5 . 40 E2
Shaftesbury Rd. Mayb GU22 70 B2
Shaftesbury Rd. Rich TW9 .... 6 E4
Shaftesbury Rd.
Worth RH10 .... 202 D4
Shaftesbury Way.Twick TW2 16 D5
Shaftesbury Way.
Up Toot SW17 .... 20 F5
Shagbrook. Buckl RH2 .... 117 C2
Shakespeare Ave. Felt TW14 . 4 A1
Shakespeare Gdns.
W Heath GU14 .... 84 D5
Shakespeare Rd. Addl KT15 . 52 D6
Shakespeare Way.
Felt TW13 .... 15 C4
Shakespeare Way.
Wink RG12 .... 27 E8
Shalbourne Rise.
Camb GU15 .... 65 D5

Shalden House. Rhampt SW15 7 F1
Shalden Rd. Alder GU12 ... 126 D8
Shaldon Dr. Merton SM4 ..... 39 E4
Shaldon Way. Walt O T KT12 54 C7
Shale Gn. Merst RH1 .... 119 D6
Shalesbrook La.
For Row RH18 .... 206 F1
Shalford City Inf Sch.
Shalf GU4 .... 130 E3
Shalford La. Guild GU4 ...... 130 E4
Shalford Rd.
Guild GU1 & GU4 .... 130 D5
Shalford Sta. Shalf GU4 .... 130 E3
Shalston Villas.
Surb KT5 & KT6 .... 37 F3
Shalstone Rd.
Mortl SW14 & TW9 .... 7 B4
Shambles The. Guild GU1 . 130 D7
Shamrock Cl. Fetch KT22 .... 94 D6
Shamrock Cl. Friml GU16 ... 85 D8
Shamrock House.
For Hil SE26 .... 23 A3
Shamrock Rd. Thorn H CR0 . 41 F3
Shandys Cl. Horsh RH12 ... 217 A1
Shanklin Ct. Alder GU12 ... 105 C1
Shannon Commercial Ctr.
W Barn KT3 .... 39 A5
Shannon Cnr. W Barn KT3 .. 39 A5
Shannon Ct. S Croy CR0 ..... 42 C1
Shannon Way. Beck BR3 ..... 24 B2
Shap Cres. Carsh SM5 .... 40 F1
Sharon Cl. Crawl RH10 ...... 202 A4
Sharon Cl. Epsom KT19 ...... 76 C6
Sharon Cl. Fetch KT23 .... 94 A3
Sharon Cl. Long D KT6 .... 37 C1
Sharonelle Ct. Woki RG11 .. 25 B6
Sharpthorne Cl.
Crawl RH11 .... 200 F6
Shaw Cl. Ewell KT17 .... 76 F8
Shaw Cl. Ottsh KT16 .... 51 C4
Shaw Cl. Sander CR2 .... 80 F7
Shaw Cres. Sander CR2 ...... 80 F7
Shaw Ct. Cater CR3 .... 100 D6
Shaw Dr. Walt O T KT12 ..... 35 C2
Shaw Path. Catf BR1 .... 24 F5
Shaw Pk. Crowth RG11 .... 45 B3
Shaw Rd. Catf BR1 .... 24 F5
Shaw Rd. Tats TN16 .... 103 C7
Shaw Way. Wallin SM6 .... 60 E3
Shawfield Cty Fst Sch.
Ash GU12 .... 106 A3
Shawfield La. Alder GU12 .. 105 F2
Shawfield Rd. Ash GU12 ... 106 A3
Shawford Ct. 9
Rhampt SW15 .... 19 A8
Shawford Rd. W Ewell KT19 57 D4
Shawley Cres. Burgh KT18 . 77 C1
Shawley Cty Fst & Mid Schs.
Burgh KT18 .... 77 C1
Shawley Way. Burgh H KT18 77 C1
Shaws Rd. Crawl RH10 ..... 201 F7
Shaxton Cres. New Add CR0 63 C2
Shearing Dr. Carsh SM4 ..... 40 C2
Shears Ct. Charlt TW16 .... 14 E1
Shearwater Ct. 6
Crawl RH11 .... 200 D5
Sheath's La. Oxsh KT22 ...... 74 C6
Sheen Common Dr.
Rich SW4 & TW10 .... 7 A2
Sheen Court Rd. Mortl TW10 7 A3
Sheen Gate Gdns.
Mortl SW14 .... 7 C3
Sheen La. Mortl SW14 .... 7 C3
Sheen Mount Jun Mix & Inf Sch.
Mortl SW14 .... 7 B2
Sheen Pk. Rich TW10 & TW9 . 6 F3
Sheen Rd. Rich TW10 & TW9 . 6 F3
Sheen Way. Wallin SM6 ...... 60 F5
Sheen Wood. Mortl SW14 .... 7 C2
Sheendale Rd. Rich TW9 ...... 6 F3
Sheenewood. For Hil SE26 .. 23 B4
Sheep Wlk. Meins
Wimble SW19 .... 19 E2
Sheep Wlk. Lang V KT18 ..... 96 D6
Sheep Wlk. Reig RH2 .... 117 E4
Sheepbarn La. W Wick CR6 . 82 F7
Sheepcote Cl. Cranf TW5 ...... 4 A7
Sheepfold Rd. Stough GU2 108 F3
Sheephatch La. Tilf GU10 .. 147 C6
Sheephouse. M Bourn GU9 146 C8
Sheephouse Gn.
Wotton RH5 .... 134 F3
Sheephouse La.
Wotton RH4 .... 135 A2
Sheeplands Ave.
Merrow GU1 .... 110 C3
Sheeps Ditch Cl. Stain TW18 13 A1
Sheepwalk. Shep TW17 ...... 33 F3
Sheepwalk. Shep Gn TW17 . 34 A3

Sheepwalk La. Abing H GU5 113 A1
Sheerwater Ave. Woodhm KT15 70 F7
Sheerwater Bsns Ctr. Sheer GU21 70 C4
Sheerwater Cotts. W Byfl KT14 70 F6
Sheerwater Rd. Sheer KT14 & KT15 70 F6
Sheet Street Rd. Old W SL4 10 A7
Sheet Street Rd. Wind SL4 10 A7
Sheet's Heath La. Brookw GU24 88 A7
Sheffield Cl. Crawl RH10 202 B4
Sheffield Cl. Farnb GU14 84 F4
Sheffield Rd. Harl TW14 & TW6 3 C2
Sheffield Way. Harl TW14 & TW6 3 D2
Shefford Cres. Woki RG11 25 D8
Shelburne House. 9 Streat SW16 21 C3
Sheldon Cl. Penge SE20 43 B8
Sheldon Cl. Reig RH2 139 B8
Sheldon Cl. Worth RH10 202 D5
Sheldon Ct. Guild GU1 130 F8
Sheldon House. Tedd TW11 17 A2
Sheldon St. Croy CR0 & CR9 61 C7
Sheldrick Cl. Mitch CR4 40 D7
Shelford. 9 King U T KT1 38 A7
Shelford Rise. S Norw SE19 22 F1
Shelley Ave. Brack RG12 27 E7
Shelley Cl. Coulsd CR5 79 F2
Shelley Cl. Crawl RH10 202 C8
Shelley Cres. Heston TW5 4 D6
Shelley Ct. Camb GU15 65 C5
Shelley Ct. 9 King U T KT2 17 D4
Shelley Ct. W Barn KT3 39 A4
Shelley Dr. Broad H RH12 216 C3
Shelley Rd. E Grins RH19 185 D1
Shelley Rd. Horsh RH12 217 B3
Shelley Way. Mitch SW17 20 D2
Shellwood Dr. Dork RH5 136 C3
Shellwood Rd. Leigh RH2 & RH3 137 D1
Shelly Cl. Nork SM7 77 E4
Shelly Cty Prim Sch. Broad H RH12 216 E3
Shellys Ct. Horsh RH13 218 A3
Shelson Ave. Felt TW13 14 F4
Shelton Ave. Warlgm CR6 81 C2
Shelton Cl. Stough GU2 109 A6
Shelton Cl. Warlgm CR6 81 C2
Shelton Rd. Merton SW19 40 A8
Shelvers Gn. Tadw KT20 97 C6
Shelvers Hill. Tadw KT20 97 B6
Shelvers Spur. Tadw KT20 97 C6
Shelvers Way. Tadw KT20 97 D6
Shene Sec Sch. Mortl SW14 7 E3
Shenley Rd. Heston TW5 4 E6
Shenstone House. Streat SW16 21 C3
Shenstone Pk. Ascot SL5 29 E5
Shepherd Cl. Crawl RH10 201 E3
Shepherd's Hill. Haslem GU27 208 C6
Shepherd's Hill. Merst RH1 99 C1
Shepherd's Hill. Stough GU2 109 A3
Shepherd's Hill Bglws. Haslem GU27 208 C6
Shepherd's La. Stough GU2 108 F4
Shepherd's Way. Guild GU4 130 E5
Shepherds Chase. Bagsh GU19 47 E2
Shepherds Cl. Shep TW17 34 B3
Shepherds Hill. Brack RG12 27 C8
Shepherds La. Burrh GU20 49 A6
Shepherds Way. Horsh RH12 218 A5
Shepherds Way. S Croy CR2 62 D3
Shepherds Way. Tilf GU10 147 D4
Shepherds' Wlk. Ashtd KT18 & KT21 96 B7
Shepherds Wlk. W Heath GU14 84 E7
Shepherdsgrove La. Dorman RH19 186 F5
Shepley Cl. Carsh SM5 60 A7
Shepley Ct. Streat SW16 21 C4
Shepley Dr. Went SL5 30 D3
Shepley End. Went SL5 30 D4
Sheppard Cl. King U T KT6 37 E5
Sheppard House. 8 Streat SW2 22 A7
Shepperton Bsns Park. Shep TW17 34 C4
Shepperton Court Dr. Shep TW17 34 B4
Shepperton Ct. Shep TW17 34 B3
Shepperton Rd. Laleh TW17 & TW18 33 D5
Shepperton Sta. Shep TW17 34 C4
Shepperton Studios. Littlt TW17 33 F6
Sheppey Cl. Crawl RH11 201 C3
Sheraton Cl. Hawley GU17 64 E4
Sheraton Dr. Epsom KT19 76 C6
Sheraton The. 22 King U T KT6 37 E4
Sheraton Wlk. 13 Crawl RH11 201 B1
Sherborne Cl. Burgh H KT18 77 C2
Sherborne Cl. Poyle SL3 1 E6
Sherborne Cres. Carsh SM5 40 E2
Sherborne Ct. Guild GU2 130 C7
Sherborne Ct. Penge SE20 43 C7
Sherborne Rd. Cheam SM3 40 A1
Sherborne Rd. Chess KT9 56 E5
Sherborne Rd. E Bed TW14 14 D7
Sherborne Rd. Farnb GU14 85 D1
Sherbourne. Albury GU5 132 D5
Sherbourne Ct. 2 Hampt TW12 36 A8
Sherbourne Dr. Went GU25 30 D4
Sherbourne Gdns. Oat Pk TW17 34 E2
Shere Ave. E Ewell KT17 & SM2 58 C1
Shere CE Inf Sch. Shere GU5 133 A4
Shere Cl. Chess KT9 56 D5
Shere Cl. Dork RH5 136 C3
Shere Ct. Shere GU5 133 B2
Shere La. Shere GU5 133 A4
Shere Rd. Albury GU4 & GU5 132 C6
Shere Rd. Ewh GU6 175 D7
Shere Rd. Shere GU5 133 B5
Shere Rd. W Clan GU4 & KT24 111 B1
Shere Rd. W Hors KT24 112 C4
Sherfield Gdns. Rhampt SW15 7 F1
Sheridan Cl. E Grins RH19 185 C1
Sheridan Ct. Hounsl TW4 4 E2
Sheridan Dr. Reig RH2 118 B3
Sheridan Pl. Hampt TW12 36 C8
Sheridan Pl. Mortl SW13 7 F4
Sheridan Rd. Friml GU16 85 D8
Sheridan Rd. Merton SW19 39 F8
Sheridan Rd. Rich TW10 17 C5
Sheridan Way. Beck BR3 43 F8
Sheridans Rd. G Book KT23 94 C1
Sheringham Ave. Twick TW2 16 A7
Sheringham Prim Sch. Wands SW18 19 F7
Sheringham Rd. Penge SE20 43 C6
Sherland Rd. Twick TW1 16 F7
Shermanbury Ct. Horsh RH12 217 D4
Sherringham Ave. Felt TW13 15 A5
Sherrydon. Cran GU6 174 F4
Sherwin Cres. Farnb GU14 85 C7
Sherwood. Long D KT6 56 D8
Sherwood Ave. Streat SW16 41 D8
Sherwood Cl. Brack RG12 28 A7
Sherwood Cl. Fetch KT22 94 C4
Sherwood Cl. Knaph GU21 68 E2
Sherwood Cres. Dovgn RH2 139 B5
Sherwood Ct. W Wick BR4 44 B1
Sherwood Park Rd. Mitch CR4 41 D5
Sherwood Park Rd. Sutton SM1 59 A5
Sherwood Park Sch. Wallin SM6 60 D7
Sherwood Prim Sch. Mitch CR4 41 C5
Sherwood Rd. Coulsd CR5 79 C3
Sherwood Rd. Croy CR0 & CR9 43 B1
Sherwood Rd. Hampt TW12 16 C3
Sherwood Rd. Merton SW19 19 F1
Sherwood Way. W Wick BR4 63 C8
Sherwood Wlk. Crawl RH10 201 F3
Shetland Cl. Burph GU4 110 B6
Shetland Cl. Crawl RH10 202 E7
Shewens Rd. Oat Pk KT13 53 D6
Shey Copse. Mayb GU22 70 C2
Shield Dr. Brent TW8 6 A8
Shield Rd. Felt TW15 14 D4
Shifford Path. For Hil SE23 23 D5
Shilburn Way. Woking GU21 69 A1
Shildon Cl. Friml GU15 66 D3
Shillinglee Park Golf Course. Plaist GU8 210 D6
Shimmings The. Guild GU1 110 A2
Shinners Cl. Croy SE25 43 A4
Shinwell Wlk. 3 Crawl RH11 201 B1
Ship Alley. Farnb GU14 85 C6
Ship Field Cl. Tats TN16 103 C6
Ship Hill. Tats TN16 103 D6
Ship La. Farnb GU14 85 C6
Ship La. Mortl SW14 7 C5
Ship St. E Grins RH19 205 E8
Ship Yd. Weyb KT13 53 B7
Shipka Rd. Balham SW12 21 B7
Shiplake Ct. Up Toot SW17 20 D4
Shiplake House. Brack RG12 27 F5
Shipley Bridge La. Copth RH10 183 A3
Shipley Ct. Penge SE20 43 A7
Shipley Rd. Crawl RH11 201 A6
Shipleybridge La. Burst RH10 & RH6 182 F4
Shipman Par. For Hil SE23 23 E6
Shipman Rd. For Hil SE23 23 D6
Shirburn Cl. For Hil SE23 23 C8
Shire Cl. Bagsh GU19 47 E2
Shire Ct. Alder GU11 104 E2
Shire Ct. Ewell KT17 57 F3
Shire Par. Crawl RH10 202 D7
Shires Cl. Ashtd KT21 95 D8
Shires House. Byfl KT14 71 E6
Shires The. Rich TW10 17 E4
Shirley Ave. Belm SM2 58 F1
Shirley Ave. Carsh SM1 59 E6
Shirley Ave. Coulsd CR5 & CR8 100 B8
Shirley Ave. Croy CR0 & CR9 43 C1
Shirley Ave. Earls RH1 139 F4
Shirley Church Rd. Add CR0 62 E7
Shirley Church Rd. Croy CR0 62 E7
Shirley Cl. Crawl RH11 200 E2
Shirley Cl. Islew TW3 5 C2
Shirley Cres. Beck BR3 43 E5
Shirley Ct. Guild GU1 130 D8
Shirley Ct. Thorn H SW16 41 F6
Shirley Dr. Islew TW3 5 C2
Shirley High Sch. S Croy CR0 62 D7
Shirley Hills Rd. S Croy CR0 62 D5
Shirley Hts. Wallin SM6 60 C2
Shirley Hyrst. Whit V KT13 53 D4
Shirley Lodge. For Hil SE26 23 E4
Shirley Oaks Hospl. Croy CR0 43 C2
Shirley Oaks Rd. Croy CR0 & CR9 62 D8
Shirley Park Golf Course. S Croy CR0 62 C7
Shirley Park Rd. Croy CR0 43 C1
Shirley Pl. Knaph GU21 68 C2
Shirley Rd. Croy CR0 & CR9 43 B1
Shirley Rd. Wallin SM6 60 C2
Shirley Way. Croy CR0 62 F7
Shoe La. Farnb GU11 105 A6
Sholto Rd. Stan TW6 2 F2
Shop Cl. Rich TW10 17 D5
Shophouse La. Farl Gn GU5 153 E7
Shord Hill. Kenley CR8 80 D3
Shore Cl. Felt TW14 15 A8
Shore Cl. Hampt TW12 15 E3
Shore Gr. Felt TW13 16 A6
Shore's Rd. Horse GU21 69 F5
Shoreham Cl. Croy CR0 43 C3
Shoreham Rd. Worth RH10 202 C3
Shoreham Rd (E). Stan TW6 2 E2
Shoreham Rd (W). Stan TW6 2 E2
Shorndean St. Catf SE6 24 C7
Short Cl. Crawl RH11 201 D8
Short Dale Rd. Alder GU11 126 C6
Short Gallop. Crawl RH10 202 D7
Short La. Limps RH8 123 B3
Short La. Stan TW15 & TW19 13 F7
Short Rd. Chisw W4 7 E8
Short Rd. Stan TW19 2 E1
Short St. Alder GU11 105 A2
Short Way. Twick TW2 16 C8
Shortacres. Nutf RH1 119 F2
Shortcroft Rd. Ewell KT17 57 F3
Shortfield Rd. Frensh GU10 146 C1
Shortheath Crest. Wreccl GU9 145 F6
Shortheath Rd. M Bourn GU9 & GU10 146 A7
Shortheath Rd. Wreccl GU9 & GU10 146 A7
Shortlands. Harl UB3 3 D8
Shortlands Gdns. Broml BR1 & BR2 44 E7
Shortlands Gr. Beck BR2 44 D6
Shortlands Rd. Beck BR2 & BR3 44 E6
Shortlands Rd. King U T KT2 17 F1
Shortlands Sta. Beck BR2 44 E7
Shorts Rd. Carsh SM5 59 E5
Shortsfield Cl. Horsh RH12 217 C5
Shortwood Ave. Ashf TW18 13 B5
Shortwood Cty Inf Sch. Stan TW18 13 B5
Shotfield. Wallin SM6 60 B4
Shott Cl. Sutton SM1 59 C5
Shottermill. Horsh RH12 218 A7
Shottermill Cty Fst Sch. Shottm GU27 207 F7
Shottermill Cty Jun Sch. Shottm GU27 207 F7
Shottermill Rd. Linch GU27 207 E5
Shottfield Ave. Mortl SW14 7 E3
Shovelstrode La. Hammer RH19 206 D8
Shrewsbury Ave. Mortl SW14 7 D3
Shrewsbury Cl. Surb KT6 56 E8
Shrewsbury House Sch. Long D KT6 56 D8
Shrewsbury Rd. Beck BR3 43 E6
Shrewsbury Rd. Carsh SM5 40 E2
Shrewsbury Rd. Harl TW14 & TW6 3 D1
Shrewsbury Rd. Redh RH1 118 E1
Shrewsbury Wlk. 7 Islew TW7 6 A4
Shrewton Rd. Mitch SW17 20 F1
Shrivenham Cl. 3 Sandh GU15 64 D8
Shroffold Rd. Catf BR1 24 E4
Shropshire Cl. Mitch CR4 41 E5
Shrubbery Rd. Streat SW16 21 E4
Shrubbery The. Farnb GU14 84 D3
Shrubbery The. 2 Surb KT6 37 E1
Shrubbs Hill. Burrh GU24 49 C2
Shrubbs Hill La. Sunnin SL5 30 C3
Shrubbs La. Rowl GU10 145 F4
Shrubland Ct. Banstd SM7 77 F3
Shrubland Gr. N Cheam KT4 58 C7
Shrubland Rd. Banstd SM7 78 A3
Shrublands Ave. Croy CR0 63 A6
Shrublands Cl. For Hil SE26 23 C5
Shrublands Dr. Lhtwat GU18 67 B8
Shute End. Woki RG11 25 B6
Sibthorp Rd. Mitch CR4 40 F7
Sibton Rd. Carsh SM5 40 E2
Sickle Rd. Haslem GU27 208 A5
Sidbury Cl. Sunnin SL5 30 A4
Siddons Rd. Croy CR0 & CR9 61 B7
Siddons Rd. For Hil SE23 23 E6
Sidestrand Rd. Farnb GU11 104 E7
Sidings The. Alder GU11 105 C3
Sidings The. Rudg RH12 214 D7
Sidings The. Stain TW18 13 B4
Sidlaws Rd. W Heath GU14 84 D6
Sidmouth Ave. Hounsl TW7 5 E5
Sidney Gdns. Brent TW8 6 D8
Sidney Rd. Croy SE25 43 A4
Sidney Rd. Penge BR3 43 E7
Sidney Rd. Stain TW18 13 A4
Sidney Rd. Twick TW1 6 B1
Sidney Rd. Walt O T KT12 35 B1
Signal Ct. Lingf RH7 164 E5
Silbury Ave. Mitch CR4 40 E8
Silbury House. 9 For Hil SE26 23 A5
Silchester Ct. Thorn H CR7 42 A5
Silchester Dr. Crawl RH11 201 B4
Silkham Rd. Oxted RH8 122 E8
Silkin Wlk. 8 Crawl RH11 201 B1
Silkmore La. W Hors KT24 92 A2
Silkmore La. W Hors KT24 112 B7
Silo Cl. Farnc GU7 150 F8
Silo Dr. Farnc GU7 150 F8
Silo Rd. Farnc GU7 150 F8
Silver Birch Cl. Woodhm KT15 70 E7
Silver Birches Way. Elst GU8 148 E3
Silver Blades Ice Rink. Streat SW16 21 D3
Silver Cl. Kings KT20 97 E3
Silver Dr. Friml GU15 & GU16 66 C3
Silver Hill. Sandh GU15 64 E8
Silver Jubilee Way. Cranf TW4 4 B5
Silver La. Purley CR8 79 E7
Silver La. W Wick BR4 63 D8
Silver Tree Cl. Walt O T KT12 54 A6
Silverdale. For Hil SE23 & 26 23 C4
Silverdale Ave. Oxsh KT22 74 C5
Silverdale Ave. Walt O T KT12 & KT13 53 F7
Silverdale Cl. Brock RH3 137 B5
Silverdale Cl. Cheam SM1 58 F6
Silverdale Dr. Sunby TW16 35 B7
Silverglade. Chess KT9 75 C7
Silverhall St. Islew TW7 6 A4
Silverlea Gdns. Horley RH6 161 C2
Silverleigh Rd. Thorn H CR7 42 A4
Silvermere Ct. Cater CR3 100 F3
Silvermere Rd. 1 Lewish SE6 24 B8
Silversmiths Way. Woking GU21 69 C1
Silverstone Cl. Redh RH1 118 F3
Silverton Lodge. S Norw SE19 22 E1
Silverwood Cl. Beck BR3 24 A1
Silverwood Cl. New Add CR0 63 A2
Silverwood Dr. Camb GU15 66 A7
Silwood. Easth RG12 26 E1
Silwood Cl. Ascot SL5 29 D7
Silwood Park (Imperial Coll). Ascot SL5 29 F6
Silwood Rd. Ascot SL5 29 F5
Silwood Rd. Sunnin SL5 29 F5
Sim's Cotts. Clayg KT10 55 F4
Simkins Cl. Wink RG12 8 B2
Simmil Rd. Clayg KT10 55 E5
Simmonds Cl. Binf RG12 26 E8
Simmonds Cotts. Ock Rid GU7 150 B4
Simmondstone La. Churt GU10 167 D2
Simmons Pl. Egham TW18 12 E3
Simms Cl. Carsh SM5 59 E8
Simon Lodge. 31 Putney SW19 19 D7
Simone Dr. Kenley CR8 80 C3
Simons Cl. Ottsh KT16 51 C4
Simons Wlk. Eng Gn TW20 11 C1
Simplemarsh Ct. Addl KT15 52 B6
Simplemarsh Rd. Addl KT15 52 B6
Simpson Rd. Rich TW10 17 C4
Simpson Rd. Twick TW4 4 F1
Sinclair Cl. Worth RH10 202 C4
Sinclair Ct. 22 Beck BR3 24 A1
Sinclair Ct. 2 Croy CR0 61 F8
Sinclair Dr. Belm SM2 59 B2
Sinclair House. Streat SW12 21 D7
Sincots Rd. Redh RH1 118 F1
Sine Cl. Farnb GU14 85 B8
Singlegate Prim Sch. Mitch SW19 20 D1
Singleton Cl. Mitch SW17 & SW19 20 F1
Singleton Cl. Thorn H CR0 42 C2
Singleton Rd. Broad H RH12 216 D3
Sinhurst Rd. Camb GU15 65 B4
Sion Ct. Twick TW1 17 B7
Sion Rd. Twick TW1 17 B7
Sipson Cl. Harm UB7 3 A8
Sipson La. Harl UB7 3 B8
Sipson Rd. Harl UB7 3 A7
Sipson Rd. Harm UB7 3 A7
Sipson Way. Harm UB7 3 A7
Sir Cyril Black Way. 2 Merton SW19 20 A1
Sir William Perkin's Ind Sch for Girls. Chert KT16 32 F1
Sirdar Rd. Mitch CR4 21 A2
Sirl Cotts. Ascot SL5 29 C5
Siskin Cl. Horsh RH12 217 E5
Sissinghurst Cl. Crawl RH10 202 D7
Sissinghurst Rd. Croy CR0 43 A2
Sistova Rd. Balham SW12 21 B7
Siward Rd. Wands SW17 20 C5
Six Cross-Roads. Horse GU21 70 A5
Sixth Cross Rd. Twick TW2 16 C5
Skeena Hill. Putney SW18 & SW19 19 E8
Skelbrook St. Wands SW18 20 C6
Skelmersdale Wlk. Crawl RH11 200 E2
Skerne Rd. King U T KT2 37 D8
Skid Hill La. Bigg H CR6 82 F5
Skid Hill La. Fickl CR6 82 F5
Skiff La. Loxwd RH14 213 A1
Skiffington Cl. Streat SW2 22 A7
Skimmington Cotts. Reig RH2 138 D8
Skimpedhill La. Brack RG12 27 B7
Skinners La. Ashtd KT21 75 D1
Skinners La. Chidd GU8 191 D5
Skinners La. Heston TW5 5 B6
Skipton Way. Horley RH6 161 B5
Sky Bsns Pk. Thorpe TW20 32 C8
Skyes Dr. Stain TW18 13 B3
Skylark View. Horsh RH12 217 D7
Skyport Dr. Harm UB7 2 D7
Skyway 14 Trad Est. Poyle SL3 1 F4
Slade Ct. Ottsh KT16 51 D4
Slade House. Twick TW4 4 F1
Slade Rd. Ottsh KT16 51 D4
Slade Rd. Pirb GU24 87 D7
Slaidburn Gn. Brack RG12 27 E2
Slattery Rd. Felt TW13 15 C7
Slaugham Ct. Crawl RH11 200 F3
Sledmere Ct. E Bed TW14 14 E7

Sleets Rd. Broad H RH12 216 E3
Slim Cl. Farnb GU11 105 E7
Slim Rd. Camb GU15 65 C7
Slines New Rd. Wold CR3 & CR6 101 E7
Slines Oak Rd. Wold CR3 & CR6 102 B6
Slinfold CE (Controlled) Sch. Slinfd RH12 215 D4
Slinfold Park (Golf & Ctry Pk). Slinfd RH12 215 A2
Slinfold Wlk. Crawl RH11 201 A6
Slip Of Wood. Cran GU6 174 F4
Slipshatch Rd. Dovgn RH2 138 E5
Slipshoe St. Reig RH2 118 A1
Sloane Hospl. Beck BR3 44 D8
Sloane Wlk. Croy CR0 43 F3
Slocock Hill. Horse GU21 69 C2
Slough La. Buckl RH3 117 A3
Slough La. Head KT18 96 C2
Sloughbrook Cl. Horsh RH12 217 F6
Slyfield Ct. Bellf GU1 109 E4
Slyfield Gn. Stough GU1 109 E5
Slyfield Ind Est. Stough GU4 109 E5
Small's La. Crawl RH11 201 C6
Smallberry Ave. Islew TW7 5 F5
Smallfield Rd. Horley RH6 161 D3
Smallfield Rd. Horne RH6 162 E3
Smallmead. Horley RH6 161 B3
Smalls Hill Rd. Charl RH2 & RH6 159 C6
Smalls Hill Rd. Leigh RH2 & RH6 159 C6
Smalls Hill Rd. Sidlow RH2 & RH6 159 C6
Smalls Mead. Crawl RH11 201 C6
Smallwood Jun & Inf Schs. Up Toot SW17 20 D4
Smallwood Rd. Up Toot SW17 20 D4
Smart's Heath La. Woking GU22 89 A4
Smart's Heath Rd. Woking GU22 89 B5
Smeaton Rd. Wands SW18 20 A8
Smith Cl. Crawl RH10 201 D3
Smith Ct. Sheer GU21 70 D6
Smith Rd. Woodh RH2 138 F6
Smith Sq. Brack RG12 27 D7
Smith St. Surb KT5 37 F3
Smith's Yd. Wands SW18 20 C6
Smitham Bottom La. Purley CR5 & CR8 79 D7
Smitham Cty Prim Sch. Coulsd CR5 79 D4
Smitham Downs Rd. Purley CR5 & CR8 79 E6
Smitham Prim Sch. Coulsd CR5 79 C3
Smitham Sta. Coulsd CR5 79 E4
Smithbarn. Horsh RH13 218 A2
Smithbarn Cl. Horley RH6 161 B4
Smithers Cotts. Rudg RH12 214 F7
Smithers House. Penge SE20 23 D1
Smithers The. Brock RH3 137 B7
Smithfield La. Head Dn GU35 167 A1
Smithwood Ave. Rowly GU6 174 B7
Smithwood Cl. Putney SW19 19 E6
Smithwood Common Rd. Rowly GU5 & GU6 174 B7
Smithy Cl. L Kings KT20 97 F1
Smithy La. Head Dn GU10 & GU35 166 E2
Smithy La. L Kings KT20 97 F1
Smithy's Gn. Windl GU20 48 D4
Smock Wlk. Thorn H CR0 42 C3
Smoke La. Reig RH2 139 B7
Smokejack Hill.Wall W RH5 196 D7
Smolletts. E Grins RH19 205 C8
Smoothfield. Hounsl TW3 5 A3
Smugglers' La. Ockley RH12 & RH5 197 E7
Smugglers' Way. The San GU10 126 E1
Snailslynch. Farnh GU9 125 D2
Snatts Hill. Limps RH8 122 F6
Snelgate Cotts. E Clan GU4 111 D4
Snell Hatch. Crawl RH11 201 B6
Snellings Rd. Hersh KT12 54 C5
Snipe La. Marl Ht GU27 208 A1
Snow Hill. Copth RH10 183 F3
Snow Hill. Copth RH10 184 A4
Snow Hill. Dome RH10 183 F5
Snow Hill Bsns Ctr. Dome RH10 184 A4
Snow House. W Norw SE27 22 B5
Snowdenham La. Bramly GU5 151 E5
Snowdenham Links Rd. Bramly GU5 151 D6
Snowdon Rd. Harl TW6 3 C1
Snowdon Rd. W Heath GU14 84 E7
Snowdown Cl. Penge SE20 43 D8
Snowdrop Cl. Crawl RH11 201 A2
Snowdrop Cl. 2 Hampt TW12 16 A2
Snowdrop Way. Bisley GU24 68 A2
Snowerhill Rd. Betch RH2 & RH3 137 F6
Snowhill La. Dome RH10 183 F5
Snows Paddock. Windl GU20 48 B7
Snows Ride. Windl GU20 48 B6
Snowy Fielder Waye. Islew TW7 6 B5
Snoxhall Field. Cran GU6 174 D2
Soames Wlk. King U T KT3 38 E8
Soane Cl. Crawl RH11 200 E4
Soho Mills. Hackb SM6 41 B1
Sol-y-vista. Farnc GU7 150 D6
Solartron Rd. Farnb GU14 85 B3
Sole Farm Ave. L Book KT23 93 F2
Sole Farm Cl. L Book KT23 93 F3
Sole Farm Rd. L Book KT23 93 F2
Solecote. L Book KT23 94 A2
Solent Rd. Stan TW6 2 F1
Soloms Court Rd. Woodm CR5 & SM7 78 E2
Solway Cl. Hounsl TW4 4 E4
Somborne House. Rhampt SW15 19 A8
Somerfield Cl. Burgh H KT20 97 E8
Somergate. Horsh RH12 216 F2
Somers Cl. Reig RH2 118 A2
Somers Pl. 1 Reig RH2 118 A2
Somers Pl. Streat SW2 21 F8
Somers Rd. Reig RH2 118 A2
Somers Rd. 2 Streat SW2 21 F8
Somersbury La. Ell Gn GU6 & RH12 195 F7
Somersby Est. Penge SE20 23 C1
Somerset Ave. Chess KT9 56 D6
Somerset Ave.Wimble SW20 39 B7
Somerset Cl. Epsom KT19 57 E2
Somerset Cl. Hersh KT12 54 B5
Somerset Cl. New Mal KT3 38 E4
Somerset Ct. 3 Hampt TW12 36 A8
Somerset Gdns. Tedd TW11 16 E3
Somerset Gdns. Thorn H SW16 41 F6
Somerset House. Wimble SW19 19 E5
Somerset Rd. Brent TW8 6 C8
Somerset Rd. Farnb GU14 85 C1
Somerset Rd. King U T KT1 37 F7
Somerset Rd. Tedd TW11 16 E3
Somerset Rd. Wimble SW19 19 D5
Somerset Rd. Woodh RH1 & RH2 139 D7
Somerset Waye. Heston TW5 4 E7
Somerswey. Shalf GU4 130 E1
Somerton Ave. Mortl TW9 7 B4
Somerton Cl. Purley CR8 80 A3
Somertons Cl. Stough GU2 109 A4
Somerville Ct. Streat SW16 21 D2
Somerville Dr. Crawl RH10 182 C1
Somerville Rd. Cobham KT11 74 A5
Somerville Rd. Penge BR3 & SE20 23 D1
Sondes Farm. Dork RH4 135 F7
Sondes Place Dr. Dork RH4 135 F7
Sondes Place Sch. Dork RH4 135 F6
Sonia Gdns. Heston TW5 5 A7
Sonnet Wlk. Bigg H TN16 83 C1
Sonning Ct. Croy CR0 62 A8
Sonning Gdns. Hampt TW12 15 E2
Sonning Rd. Croy CR0 43 A3
Sonninge Cl. Sandh GU15 64 D8
Sopwith Ave. Chess KT9 56 E5
Sopwith Cl. Bigg H TN16 83 D3
Sopwith Cl. Rich TW10 17 F3
Sopwith Dr. Byfl KT13 & KT14 71 E7
Sopwith Rd. Heston TW5 4 C7
Sopwith Way. King U T KT2 37 E8
Sorbie Cl. Whit V KT13 53 D4
Sorrel Bank. New Add CR0 62 E2
Sorrel Cl. Crawl RH11 201 A2
Sorrel Cl. W Heath GU14 84 C5
Sorrel Cl. Woki RG11 25 E8
Sorrel Dr. Lhtwat GU18 66 F7
Sorrel House. Hounsl TW3 5 C6
Sorrel Rd. Horsh RH12 217 E5
Sorrento Rd. Sutton SM1 59 B7
South Albert Rd. Reig RH2 117 F2
South Ash Cty Prim Sch. Ash GU12 106 B2
South Atlantic Dr. Alder GU11 105 C3
South Ave. Egham TW20 12 C2
South Ave. Heath E GU9 125 D6
South Ave. Rich TW9 7 A5
South Ave. Wallin SM5 60 A3
South Ave. Whit V KT12 53 E1
South Bank. Surb KT6 37 E3
South Bank Lodge. 2 Surb KT6 37 E3
South Bank Terr. Surb KT6 37 E3
South Beta Rd. Farnb GU14 85 B2
South Bookham Sch. G Book KT23 114 C8
South Border The. Purley CR8 79 E8
South Cl. Crawl RH10 201 F7
South Cl. Horse GU21 69 C3
South Cl. Morden SM4 40 A3
South Cl. Twick TW13 16 A5
South Cl. Woki RG11 25 D4
South Close Gn. Merst RH1 & RH2 119 B6
South Croxted Rd. W Norw SE21 22 D4
South Croydon Sta. S Croy CR2 61 D5
South Dr. Banstd SM7 78 E6
South Dr. Beck BR3 44 C4
South Dr. Belm SM2 58 E2
South Dr. Coulsd CR5 79 D4
South Dr. Dork RH5 136 C7
South Dr. Pirb GU24 87 C6
South Dr. Went GU25 31 A2
South Dr. Woki RG11 25 C5
South Eden Park Rd. Beck BR3 44 B4
South Eden Park Rd. W Wick BR3 44 B2
South End. Croy CR0 & CR9 61 C6
South End. G Book KT23 94 B1
South Farm La. Windl GU19 48 A2
South Farnborough Cty Inf Sch. Farnb GU14 105 D8
South Farnborough Cty Jun Sch. Farnb GU14 85 D2
South Farnham Sch. M Bourn GU9 125 D1
South Gate Ave. Felt TW13 14 D4
South Gdns. Mitch SW19 20 D1
South Gr. Chert KT16 32 F3
South Gr. Horsh RH13 217 D1
South Hill. Godal GU7 150 F4
South Hill. Guild GU1 130 D7
South Hill Park. Easth RG12 27 C2
South Hill Rd. Beck BR2 44 E5
South Hill Rd. Easth RG12 27 B3
South Holmes Rd. Horsh RH13 218 B4
South La. Ash GU12 106 B1
South La. King U T KT1 37 D6
South La. New Mal KT3 38 D3
South La W. New Mal KT3 38 D5
South Lawn Ct. Farnc GU7 150 D6
South Lodge. Twick TW2 5 C1
South Lodge Ave. Mitch CR4 & CR7 & SW16 41 E5
South Lodge Rd. Whit V KT12 54 B2
South London Coll. W Norw SE27 22 B4
South Lynn Cres. Easth RG12 27 B4
South Mead. Redh RH1 118 F4
South Mead. W Ewell KT19 57 F3
South Mead Rd. Alder GU11 126 B8
South Meadow. Crowth RG11 45 D3
South Merton Sta. Merton SW20 39 F6
South Munstead La. Godal GU8 172 B7
South Norwood High Sch. Croy SE25 43 B4
South Norwood Hill. S Norw SE19 & SE25 42 F7
South Norwood Prim Sch. Croy SE25 43 A5
South Oak Rd. Streat SW16 21 F4
South Par. Horley RH6 160 F4
South Park Cres. Catf SE6 24 F7
South Park Ct. 25 Beck BR3 24 A1
South Park Cty Inf Sch. Woodh RH2 139 A6
South Park Gr. New Mal KT3 38 C5
South Park Hill Rd. S Croy CR2 61 D6
South Park La. Bletch RH1 142 A7
South Park Rd. Wimble SW19 20 B2
South Pier Rd. Crawl RH6 182 B7
South Pl. Surb KT5 37 F2
South Pl. Woki RG11 25 C6
South Rd. Ash V GU12 106 A4
South Rd. Bisley GU24 67 F3
South Rd. Crowth RG11 45 E3
South Rd. Easth RG11 & RG12 26 E1
South Rd. Eng Gn TW20 11 D2
South Rd. Felt TW13 15 D3
South Rd. For Hil SE23 23 D6
South Rd. Hampt TW12 15 F2
South Rd. Horse GU21 69 C4
South Rd. Merton SW19 20 D2
South Rd. Mitch SW19 20 D2
South Rd. Reig RH2 139 B8
South Rd. Stough GU2 109 B3
South Rd. Twick TW2 16 D5
South Rd. Weyb KT13 53 C5
South Rd. Whit V KT13 53 B2
South Ridge. Whit V KT13 72 B8
South Rise. Wallin SM5 59 E2
South Side. Tongh GU10 126 F7
South St. Dork RH4 136 A7
South St. Epsom KT18 76 D5
South St. Farnb GU14 85 E1
South St. Farnh GU9 125 C2
South St. Godal GU7 150 D4
South St. Horsh RH12 217 C2
South St. Islew TW7 6 A4
South St. Stain TW18 12 F3
South Station App. S Nutf RH1 140 F7
South Terr. Dork RH4 136 B6
South Terr. Surb KT6 37 E3
South Vale. S Norw SE19 22 E2
South Vale Rd. 4 Surb KT6 56 E8
South View. Copth RH10 183 E3
South View. Wimble SW19 19 D2
South View Ct. S Norw SE19 22 C1
South View Rd. Ashtd KT21 95 D8
South Way. Croy CR0 62 E7
South Way. Sutton SM5 59 D1
South Way. Sutton SM5 78 D8
South West London Coll. Streat SW16 21 D5
South West London Coll. Up Toot SW17 20 E3
South Western Rd. Twick TW1 6 B1
South Wimbledon Sta. Merton SW19 20 B1
South Wlk. Alder GU12 105 D2
South Wlk. Coney H BR4 63 E7
South Wlk. Reig RH2 118 B1
South Worple Way. Mortl SW14 7 D4
Southall La. Heston TW5 4 B8
Southam House. Addl KT15 52 B5
Southampton Cl. Blckw GU17 64 C6
Southampton Gdns. Mitch CR4 41 E4
Southampton Rd. Stan TW19 & TW6 2 F1
Southampton St. Farnb GU14 105 B8
Southampton Way. Stan TW19 & TW6 2 E1
Southbank. Thame D KT7 37 B2
Southborough Cl. Surb KT6 37 D1
Southborough Rd. Surb KT6 37 E1
Southborough Sch. Surb KT6 56 E7
Southbridge Pl. Croy CR0 & CR9 61 C6
Southbridge Rd. Croy CR0 & CR9 61 C6
Southbrook. Crawl RH11 201 C1
Southbrook Rd. Streat SW16 41 E8
Southbury. Guild GU2 130 C7
Southcote. Horse GU21 69 D3
Southcote Ave. Felt TW13 15 A6
Southcote Ave. Tolw KT5 38 B2
Southcote Dr. Friml GU15 66 A5
Southcote Rd. Croy SE25 43 B3
Southcote Rd. Merst RH1 119 C6
Southcote Rd. S Croy CR2 61 F1
Southcroft. Eng Gn TW20 11 B3
Southcroft Ave. W Wick BR4 63 C8
Southcroft Rd. Streat SW17 21 A2
Southdean Gdns. Putney SW19 19 F6
Southdown Cl. Horsh RH12 218 A5
Southdown Dr. Wimble SW20 19 D1
Southdown Rd. Hersh KT12 54 E6
Southdown Rd. Wallin SM5 60 A2
Southdown Rd. Wimble SW20 39 D8
Southdown Rd. Wold CR3 101 F5
Southend La. Catf SE6 24 B4
Southend La. For Hil SE26 & SE6 23 F4
Southend Rd. Beck BR3 44 A8
Southerland Cl. Weyb KT13 53 C6
Southern Ave. E Bed TW14 15 A7
Southern Ave. S Norw SE25 42 F6
Southern Ave. Salfs RH1 140 A1
Southern Bglws. Chil GU4 131 B2
Southern Cotts. Stan TW19 2 A2
Southern Ind Area. Easth RG12 26 F6
Southern Perimeter Rd. E Bed TW6 3 B1
Southern Perimeter Rd. Felt TW14 & TW6 3 D2
Southern Perimeter Rd. Harl TW14 & TW6 3 D2
Southern Perimeter Rd. Stan TW19 & TW6 2 D2
Southern Rd. Camb GU15 65 C6
Southern Way. Farnb GU14 84 E3
Southern Way. M Bourn GU9 125 C1
Southerns La. L Kings CR5 98 C3
Southey Ct. Fetch KT23 94 B3
Southey Rd. Merton SW19 20 A1
Southey St. Penge SE20 23 D1
Southfield Gdns. Tedd TW1 & TW2 16 F4
Southfield Pl. Whit V KT13 53 B3
Southfield Sta. Wands SW18 19 F7
Southfields. Thame D KT8 36 E3
Southfields Ave. Ashf TW15 14 B2
Southfields Ct. Sutton SM3 59 A8
Southfields Rd. Wold CR3 & RH9 102 B3
Southfields Sch. Wands SW18 20 A7
Southfields Special Sch. Woki RG11 25 D5
Southgate Ave. Crawl RH10 & RH11 201 E4
Southgate Cty Fst & Mid Sch. Crawl RH10 201 D4
Southgate Cty West Fst & Mid Sch. Crawl RH11 201 C4
Southgate Dr. Crawl RH10 & RH11 201 E4
Southgate Par. Crawl RH10 201 D4
Southgate Rd. Crawl RH10 & RH11 201 D4
Southholme Cl. S Norw SE19 42 E8
Southland Way. Islew TW7 5 D2
Southlands. E Grins RH19 205 E7
Southlands. Horley RH6 160 F3
Southlands Ave. Horley RH6 161 A4
Southlands Cl. Ash GU12 106 A1
Southlands Cl. Coulsd CR5 79 F2
Southlands Cl. Woki RG11 25 D5
Southlands Coll. Putney SW19 19 D6
Southlands La. Tand RH8 122 C1
Southlands Rd. Ash GU12 106 A1
Southlands Rd. Woki RG11 25 D4
Southmead Jun & Inf Sch. Putney SW19 19 E7
Southmead Rd. Putney SW19 19 E7
Southmont Rd. Hinch W KT10 55 E7
Southridge Pl. Wimble SW20 19 D1
Southsea Rd. King U T KT1 37 E5
Southside Comm. Wimble SW19 19 D2
Southview Cl. Up Toot SW17 21 A3
Southview Cotts. Frensh GU10 146 D1
Southview Ct. 14 Woking GU22 69 E1
Southview Gdns. Wallin SM6 60 C3
Southview Rd. Catf BR1 24 D4
Southview Rd. Head Dn GU35 187 B5
Southview Rd. Warlgm CR6 101 A8
Southview Rd. Wold CR3 102 B3
Southviews. Selsd CR2 62 D2
Southville Cl. E Bed TW14 14 E7
Southville Cl. W Ewell KT19 57 D2
Southville Cl. W Ewell KT19 57 D2
Southville Cres. E Bed TW14 14 E7

Southville Jun & Inf Schs.
E Bed TW14 .... 14 F7
Southville Rd. E Bed TW14 .. 14 E8
Southville Rd. Thame D KT7 37 B2
Southwark Cl. Crawl RH11 201 B2
Southwater Cl. Beck BR3 ...... 24 B1
Southway. Camb GU15 .... 65 A4
Southway. W Barn SW20 ...... 39 D5
Southway. Wallin SM6 .... 60 C6
Southway Ct. Stough GU2 .. 108 E1
Southways Pk. Crawl RH11 181 D3
Southwell Park Rd.
    Camb GU15 .... 65 C5
Southwell Rd.
    Thorn H CR0 & CR7 .... 42 A3
Southwick. Bagsh GU19 .... 47 E1
Southwick Cl. E Grins RH19 185 D2
Southwick Ct. Brack RG12 ... 27 E3
Southwick House.
    E Grins RH19 .... 185 D2
Southwold. Easth RG22 ...... 26 E1
Southwood. Woki RG11 ...... 25 D4
Southwood Ave. Coulsd CR5 79 C4
Southwood Ave.
    King U T KT2 & KT3 .... 38 D8
Southwood Ave.
    Knaph GU21 .... 68 D1
Southwood Ave. Ottsh KT16 51 C3
Southwood Bsns Pk.
    Farnb GU14 .... 84 D4
Southwood Chase.
    Cran GU6 .... 174 F1
Southwood Cl. N Cheam KT4 39 D1
Southwood Cres The.
    Farnb GU14 .... 84 D3
Southwood Ct. Weyb KT13 .. 53 B5
Southwood Dr. Tolw KT5 ..... 38 C1
Southwood Gdns.
    Hinch W KT10 .... 56 A7
Southwood Golf Course.
    Farnb GU14 .... 84 E3
Southwood Inf Sch.
    Farnb GU14 .... 84 D3
Southwood La. Farnb GU14 . 84 A3
Southwood La. Farnb GU14 . 84 D3
Southwood Rd. Farnb GU14 84 D3
Sovereign Cl. E Mole KT8 .... 35 F5
Sovereign Dr. S Rich TW9 .... 6 F2
Sovereign Dr. Camb GU15 ... 66 B7
Sovereign House.
    Ashf TW15 .... 13 E4
Sovereign House.
    Wimble SW19 .... 19 E2
Spa Cl. S Norw SE19 .... 42 E8
Spa Dr. Epsom KT18 .... 76 A5
Spa Hill. S Norw CR7 & SE19 42 D8
Spa View. 6 Streat SW16 ... 21 F5
Space Wale. Felt TW14 .... 4 B2
Spalding Rd. Streat SW17 ... 21 B3
Sparks Cl. Hampt TW12 ...... 15 E2
Sparrow Cl. Hampt TW12 .... 15 E2
Sparrow Farm Dr.
    Felt TW14 .... 15 D8
Sparrow Farm Inf Sch.
    Felt TW14 .... 15 C8
Sparrow Farm Jun Sch.
    Felt TW14 .... 15 C8
Sparrow Farm Rd.
    N Cheam KT17 & KT4 .... 58 B6
Sparrow Row. Burrh GU24 .. 49 B4
Sparrowhawk Cl.
    Crond GU10 .... 124 D8
Sparrows Mead. Redh RH1 119 A4
Sparvell Rd. Knaph GU21 .... 88 B8
Sparvell Way. Camb GU15 ... 65 C6
Spats La. Head D GU35 ...... 187 A8
Speaker's Ct. 3 Croy CR0 ... 42 D1
Speart La. Heston TW5 .... 4 F7
Speedwell Cl. Merrow GU4 110 C4
Speedwell House. 5
    Redh RH1 .... 119 A4
Speedwell Way.
    Horsh RH12 .... 217 E5
Speer Rd. Thame D KT7 ...... 36 F3
Speirs Cl. New Mal KT3 ...... 38 F3
Speke Rd. S Norw CR7 .... 42 D7
Speldhurst Cl. Hayes BR2 ... 44 F4
Spelthorne Coll. Ashf TW15 13 F4
Spelthorne Cty Inf Sch.
    Ashf TW15 .... 14 A4
Spelthorne Gr. Charlt TW16 14 F1
Spelthorne La.
    Charlt TW15 & TW17 .... 34 C8
Spelthorne Sports Club.
    Ashf TW15 .... 14 D1
Spence Ave. Byfl KT14 .... 71 F5
Spencer Cl. Friml GU16 ...... 85 E6
Spencer Cl. Lang V KT18 ..... 96 E8
Spencer Cl. Sheer GU21 ...... 70 D5
Spencer Ct. Leahd KT22 ...... 95 C4

Spencer Ct. Wimble SW20 ... 39 B8
Spencer Gdns. Eng Gn TW20 11 D3
Spencer Gdns. Mortl SW14 ... 7 C2
Spencer Hill. Wimble SW19 . 19 E1
Spencer Hill Rd.
    Wimble SW19 .... 19 E1
Spencer House. 24
    Putney SW19 .... 19 D7
Spencer House.
    Wimble SW19 .... 19 D5
Spencer Mews. Dulw SE21 .. 22 D7
Spencer Pl. Croy CR0 .... 42 D2
Spencer Rd. Brack RG12 ..... 26 F8
Spencer Rd. Bromi BR1 ...... 24 F1
Spencer Rd. Carsh CR4 ...... 41 A2
Spencer Rd. Cater CR3 ..... 100 D6
Spencer Rd. Chisw W4 .... 7 C7
Spencer Rd. Cobham KT11 .. 73 B4
Spencer Rd. E Mole KT8 ...... 36 C4
Spencer Rd.
    Hounsl TW3 & TW5 & TW7 .. 5 C6
Spencer Rd. Mitch CR4 .... 41 A6
Spencer Rd. S Croy CR2 ..... 61 E5
Spencer Rd. Twick TW2 ...... 16 E6
Spencer Rd. Wimble SW20 .. 39 B8
Spencer Way. Eatch RH1 ... 140 A4
Spencer's La. Charl RH6 .... 159 F2
Spencer Rd. Horsh RH12 217 B3
Spencers Ct. Horsh RH12 .. 217 B4
Spencers Rd. Crawl RH11 . 201 D5
Spenser Ave. Whit V KT13 ... 53 A2
Spenser Ct. 5 Rich TW10 ... 17 D4
Spiceall. Compt GU3 .... 129 B3
Spicer Cl. Walt O T KT12 .... 35 C3
Spicers Field. Oxsh KT22 .... 74 E6
Spices Yd. Croy CR0 .... 61 C6
Spiers Way. Horley RH6 .... 161 B1
Spindle Way. Crawl RH10 .. 201 F5
Spindlewood Gdns.
    S Croy CR0 & CR2 .... 61 E6
Spindlewoods. Tadw KT20 .. 97 B4
Spinis. Easth RG12 .... 26 F1
Spinnaker Ct. 2 Tedd KT1 .. 37 D8
Spinner Gn. Easth RG12 ..... 27 B4
Spinney Cl. Cobham KT11 .. 74 A8
Spinney Cl. Crawl D RH10 . 204 C8
Spinney Cl. Horsh RH12 .... 218 B6
Spinney Cl. New Mal KT3 .... 38 E4
Spinney Dr. E Bed TW14 ..... 14 C8
Spinney Gdns. Dulw SE19 .. 22 F3
Spinney Hill. Row Tn KT15 .. 51 F5
Spinney La. Wink SL4 .... 9 B7
Spinney The. Ascot SL5 ...... 29 E4
Spinney The.
    Burgh H KT18 & KT20 ...... 97 B8
Spinney The. Cheam SM3 ... 58 C6
Spinney The. Crawl RH11 .. 201 B4
Spinney The. Fetch KT23 .... 94 B3
Spinney The. Friml GU15 .... 66 C6
Spinney The. Graysh GU26 188 A4
Spinney The. Haslem GU27 208 C8
Spinney The. Horley RH6 ... 161 A5
Spinney The. Oxsh KT22 .... 74 C7
Spinney The. Purley CR8 .... 80 B8
Spinney The. Ripley GU23 . 111 C8
Spinney The. Streat SW16 .. 21 D5
Spinney The. Sunby TW16 .. 35 A8
Spinneycroft. Oxsh KT22 .... 74 D4
Spinning Wlk The.
    Shere GU5 .... 133 A4
Spire Ct. 10 Rich TW10 .... 6 E1
Spital Heath.
    Dork RH4 & RH5 .... 136 C8
Spitfire Way. Farnb GU14 .. 104 E7
Spoil La. Tongh GU10 .... 126 F7
Spokane Cl. Alder GU11 ... 125 F8
Spook Hill. Dork RH5 .... 136 B3
Spooner House. Heston TW5 . 5 A8
Spooner Wlk. Wallin SM6 ... 60 D5
Spooners Rd. Horsh RH12 218 A4
Sportsbank St. Catf SE6 ..... 24 C8
Spout Hill. Add CR0 .... 63 A5
Spout La. Stan TW19 .... 2 A3
Spout La N. Harm TW19 .... 2 B3
Spratts Alley. Ottsh KT16 ... 51 E4
Spratts La. Ottsh KT15 .... 51 E4
Spread Eagle Wlk. 2
    Epsom KT18 .... 76 D6
Spreighton Rd. E Mole KT8 .. 36 B6
Spring Ave. Egham TW20 .... 11 F2
Spring Bottom La.
    Cater RH1 .... 120 C8
Spring Cnr. Felt TW13 .... 14 F5
Spring Copse. Copth RH10 183 C3
Spring Copse.
    E Grins RH19 .... 185 D3
Spring Cotts. King U T KT6 .. 37 D4
Spring Ct. Ewell KT17 .... 57 F2
Spring Ct. Stough GU2 ..... 109 A5
Spring Gdns. Ascot SL5 ...... 29 B5
Spring Gdns. Bigg H TN16 .. 83 C1

Spring Gdns. Copth RH10 .. 183 C3
Spring Gdns. Dork RH4 ..... 136 A8
Spring Gdns. E Mole KT8 .... 36 C5
Spring Gdns. Friml GU15 .... 66 A5
Spring Gdns. W Heath GU47 65 A7
Spring Gdns. Wallin SM6 .... 60 C5
Spring Gr. Brent W4 .... 7 A8
Spring Gr. Farnc GU7 .... 150 E8
Spring Gr.
    Fetch KT22 & KT23 .... 94 B4
Spring Gr. Hampt TW12 ..... 36 B8
Spring Gr. Mitch CR4 .... 41 A8
Spring Grove Cres.
    Hounsl TW3 & TW5 .... 5 C6
Spring Grove Jun & Inf Sch.
    Hounsl TW7 .... 5 D5
Spring Grove Rd.
    Hounsl TW3 & TW5 & TW7 .... 5 C6
Spring Grove Rd. Rich TW10 . 6 F2
Spring Grove Rd. Rich TW10 17 E6
Spring Hill. For Hil SE26 ..... 23 C4
Spring Hill Wildfowl Park.
    For Row RH18 .... 206 A1
Spring House. Merton SW19 39 F8
Spring La. Croy CR0 & SE25 . 43 B3
Spring La. Hale GU9 .... 125 A7
Spring La. Oxted RH8 .... 122 D4
Spring La. Slinfd RH13 ...... 215 C3
Spring La. W Hale GU9 ...... 125 A6
Spring Meadow. Brack RG12 27 D8
Spring Meadow.
    For Row RH18 .... 206 F1
Spring Park Ave. Croy CR0 .. 62 D8
Spring Park Inf Sch.
    Croy CR0 .... 63 A7
Spring Park Jun Sch.
    Croy CR0 .... 63 A7
Spring Park Rd. S Croy CR0 . 62 D8
Spring Plat. Crawl RH10 .... 202 C6
Spring Plat Ct. Crawl RH10 202 C6
Spring Rd. Felt TW13 .... 14 F5
Spring Rise. Egham TW20 ... 11 E2
Spring Terr. Rich TW10 .... 6 E2
Spring Way. E Grins RH19 . 186 A4
Spring Woods. Sandh GU17 45 C1
Spring Woods. Vir W GU25 . 31 B5
Springbank Rd. Lewish SE13 24 E8
Springbourne Ct. Beck BR3 . 44 C8
Springclose La. Cheam SM3 58 E4
Springcopse Rd. Reig RH2 . 139 C7
Springcross Ave.
    Hawley GU17 .... 64 D4
Springfarm Rd. Linch GU27 207 E5
Springfield. E Grins RH19 .. 185 D4
Springfield. Elst GU8 .... 148 D3
Springfield. Lmwat GU18 .... 67 D8
Springfield. Oxted RH8 ..... 122 D5
Springfield. S Norw SE25 ... 43 A6
Springfield Ave.
    Hampt TW12 .... 16 B2
Springfield Ave.
    Merton SW20 .... 39 F6
Springfield Cl. Knaph GU21 . 68 E1
Springfield Cres.
    Horsh RH12 .... 217 B2
Springfield Ct. Horsh RH12 217 C2
Springfield Ct. 9
    King U T KT1 .... 37 E5
Springfield Ct. Wallin SM6 .. 60 B5
Springfield Cty Fst & Mid Schs.
    Sunby TW16 .... 34 F7
Springfield Gdns.
    W Brick BR4 .... 63 B8
Springfield Gr. Sunby TW16 35 A8
Springfield Hospl.
    Up Tnot SW17 .... 20 E5
Springfield La. Weyb KT13 .. 53 B6
Springfield Meadows.
    Weyb KT13 .... 53 B6
Springfield Park Rd.
    Horsh RH12 .... 217 B2
Springfield Pl. King U T KT3 . 38 C5
Springfield Rd. Add GU2 ... 106 A5
Springfield Rd. Ashf TW15 . 13 F3
Springfield Rd. Binf RG12 ... 26 C8
Springfield Rd. Bra Hil SL3 ... 1 B7
Springfield Rd. Crawl RH11 201 B6
Springfield Rd. E Ewell KT17 58 C1
Springfield Rd. Friml GU15 . 66 B5
Springfield Rd. Guild GU1 .. 109 E1
Springfield Rd. Horsh RH12 217 C2
Springfield Rd. King U T KT1 37 E6
Springfield Rd. Penge SE26 . 23 C3
Springfield Rd. S Norw CR7 . 42 C8
Springfield Rd. 6
    Tedd TW11 .... 17 A3
Springfield Rd. Twick TW2 .. 16 A7
Springfield Rd. Wallin SM6 . 60 B5
Springfield Rd. Westc RH4 135 C6
Springfield Rd.
    Wimble SW19 .... 20 A3

Springfield Rise.
    For Hil SE26 .... 23 B5
Springfield Terr.
    Bramly GU5 .... 151 F6
Springfield Way. Elst GU8 . 148 E3
Springfields Ct. Chert KT16 . 33 B1
Springhaven. Elst GU8 ..... 148 E3
Springhaven Cl. Guild GU1 110 A1
Springhill. Elst GU8 .... 148 F3
Springhill Ct. Easth RG12 .. 27 B5
Springholm Cl. Bigg H TN16 83 C1
Springhurst Cl. Croy CR0 ... 62 F6
Springlakes Est.
    Alder GU11 .... 105 E3
Springmead Ct. Sandh GU15 45 E1
Springpark Dr. Beck BR3 .... 44 C6
Springpark Wlk. Streat SW16 . 21 F4
Springside Cl. Hounsl TW5 ... 4 D5
Springwell Jun & Inf Schs.
    Heston TW5 .... 4 E7
Springwell Rd.
    Bear Gn RH5 .... 157 D3
Springwell Rd. Heston TW5 . 4 D6
Springwell Rd. Streat SW16 22 A3
Springwood. Milf GU8 ...... 150 A1
Springwood Ct. S Croy CR2 . 61 E6
Sprint Ind Est. Byfl KT14 .... 71 D8
Spruce Dr. Lhtwat GU18 ..... 67 A7
Spruce Pk. Beck BR2 .... 44 F5
Spruce Rd. Bigg H TN16 .... 83 D3
Sprucedale Gdns.
    S Croy CR0 .... 62 D6
Sprucedale Gdns.
    Wallin CR8 .... 60 E2
Spur Rd. Brent TW7 .... 6 B7
Spur Rd. Felt TW13 .... 4 B3
Spur The. Knaph GU21 .... 68 B1
Spurfield. E Mole KT8 .... 36 B6
Spurgeon Ave. S Norw SE19 42 D8
Spurgeon Cl. Crawl RH11 .. 201 C7
Spurgeon Rd. S Norw SE19 . 22 D1
Spurgeon's Coll.
    S Norw SE25 .... 42 E7
Spurs Ct. Alder GU11 .... 104 E2
Spy La. Loxwd RH14 .... 213 A4
Square Dr. Marl Ht GU27 .. 208 B1
Square The. Bagsh GU19 .... 47 E3
Square The. Brack RG12 ..... 27 E5
Square The. Crawl RH11 ... 201 D6
Square The. Harm TW6 .... 2 B6
Square The. Lhtwat GU18 .... 48 A1
Square The. Lingf RH7 ...... 164 C4
Square The. Onsl V GU2 ... 129 F7
Square The. 7 Rich TW10 ... 6 D2
Square The. Rowl GU10 .... 145 F3
Square The. Tats TN16 ..... 103 C7
Square The. Wallin SM5 .... 60 A5
Square The. Weyb KT13 .... 53 C5
Square The.
    Wisley GU23 & KT14 ...... 71 E3
Squarey St. Wands SW17 ... 20 C5
Squire Ct. 2 Croy CR0 .... 42 E1
Squire's Bridge Rd.
    Littlt TW17 .... 34 A5
Squire's Rd. Shep Gn TW17 . 34 A5
Squires Bridge Rd.
    Shep Gn KT17 .... 33 F5
Squires Cl. Crawl D RH10 .. 204 A8
Squires Ct. Chert KT16 ...... 33 B1
Squires Ct. Wimble SW19 ... 20 A4
Squires Hill La. Tilf GU10 .. 147 C4
Squirrel Cl. Crawl RH11 .... 181 B1
Squirrel Cl. Hounsl TW4 .... 4 C4
Squirrel Cl. Sandh GU17 .... 64 B8
Squirrel Dr. Wink SL4 .... 9 B7
Squirrel Wood. W Byfl KT14 71 B7
Squirrel's Way. Woodl KT18 76 D4
Squirrels Cl. Farnc GU7 ... 129 D1
Squirrels Cl. Fetch KT23 ..... 94 A4
Squirrels Gn. 12 Redh RH1 118 F2
Squirrels Gn. Worc Pk KT4 . 58 A8
Stable Croft. Bagsh GU19 ... 47 D2
Stable Ct. Crawl RH10 .... 24 E3
Stable Mews. N Worw SE27 22 C7
Stables The. Belif GU1 ...... 109 D4
Stables The. Cobham KT11 . 73 F5
Stacey Way. Crawl RH10 ... 202 E8
Stacey Ct. Merst RH1 ...... 119 C6
Stacey's Farm Rd. Elst GU8 148 D4
Stack House. Oxted RH8 ... 122 E5
Stackfield Rd. Crawl RH11 200 E5
Staddon Ct. Beck BR3 .... 43 E5
Staff Coll. Camb GU15 ...... 65 C7
Staff College Rd.
    Camb GU15 .... 65 B6
Staff Rd. Alder GU12 .... 105 C2
Staffhurst Wood Rd.
    Limps RH8 .... 144 C6
Stafford Cl. Cater CR3 ...... 100 F4

Stafford Cl. Cheam SM3 ..... 58 E4
Stafford Gdns. Croy CR0 .... 60 F5
Stafford Lake.
    Bisley GU21 & GU24 .... 68 A1
Stafford Pl. Rich TW10 .... 17 F8
Stafford Rd. Cater CR3 ..... 101 A6
Stafford Rd. Crawl RH11 ... 181 B1
Stafford Rd. Croy CR0 .... 61 A6
Stafford Rd. King U T KT3 ... 38 C5
Stafford Rd.
    Wallin CR0 & SM6 .... 60 E4
Stafford Sq. 8 Oat Pk KT13 53 D6
Staffords Pl. Horley RH6 ... 161 B2
Stag Hill. Guild GU2 .... 130 A8
Stag La. Rhampt SW15 .... 18 F5
Stag Leys. Ashtd KT21 .... 95 E7
Stag Leys Cl. Woodm SM7 . 78 E4
Stagbury Ave. Chips CR5 .... 78 E1
Stagbury Cl. Chips CR5 ...... 98 E8
Stagbury House. Chips CR5 . 98 E8
Stagelands. Crawl RH11 ... 201 C8
Stagelands Ct. Crawl RH11 201 C8
Stags Way. Hounsl TW7 .... 5 F8
Stainash Cres. Stain TW18 .. 13 B3
Stainash Par. Stain TW18 ... 13 B3
Stainbank Rd. Mitch CR4 ... 41 B6
Staines Ave. Cheam SM3 ... 58 D8
Staines By-Pass.
    Stain TW15 & TW18 .... 13 C3
Staines Central Trad Est.
    Stain TW18 .... 12 E4
Staines La. Chert KT16 ...... 33 A3
Staines Lane Cl. Chert KT16 32 F4
Staines Prep Sch The.
    Stain TW18 .... 13 A3
Staines Rd. Chert KT16 ...... 32 F3
Staines Rd. E Bed TW14 .... 14 D8
Staines Rd.
    Felt TW14 & TW3 & TW4 ..... 4 D2
Staines Rd.
    Hounsl TW4 & TW3 & TW4 .. 4 D2
Staines Rd. Laleh TW18 ..... 33 B7
Staines Rd. Stain TW18 ..... 13 B7
Staines Rd. Thorpe KT16 ... 33 A5
Staines Rd.
    Twick TW13 & TW2 .... 16 C6
Staines Rd. Wray TW19 ..... 11 F7
Staines Rd E.
    Sunby TW12 & TW16 .... 35 C8
Staines Rd W. Ashf TW15 ... 14 B4
Staines Sta. Stain TW18 ..... 13 A3
Stainford Cl. Ashf TW15 .... 14 D3
Stainton Rd. Lewish SE13 .. 24 D8
Stainton Wlk. Woking GU21 69 C1
Staiths Way. Burgh H KT20 . 97 B7
Stake La. Farnb GU14 .... 85 A4
Stakescorner Rd.
    Arting GU3 .... 130 A2
Stambourne Way.
    S Norw SE19 .... 22 E1
Stambourne Way.
    W Wick BR4 .... 63 C7
Stamford Ave. Friml GU16 .. 65 F1
Stamford Dr. Hayes BR2 ..... 44 F5
Stamford Green Cty Fst & Mid
    Sch. Epsom KT19 .... 76 B7
Stamford Green Rd.
    Epsom KT18 .... 76 B6
Stamford Rd. Walt O T KT12 54 D7
Stan Hill. Charl RH6 .... 180 D8
Stanborough Cl.
    Hampt TW12 .... 15 F2
Stanborough Rd.
    Hounsl TW3 & TW7 .... 5 D4
Stanbridge Cl. Crawl RH11 200 E6
Standard Rd. Hounsl TW4 .... 4 E4
Standen Cl. E Grins RH19 .. 185 A4
Standen (National Trust).
    E Grins RH19 .... 205 D4
Standen Pl. Horsh RH12 ... 218 A7
Standen Rd. Wands SW18 .. 20 A8
Standinghall La.
    Worth RH10 .... 203 A3
Standlake Point. 1
    For Hil SE23 .... 23 D5
Standon La. Wall W RH5 ... 176 F2
Stane Cl. Merton SW19 ...... 20 B1
Stane House. Dork RH4 .... 136 B8
Stane St. Ockley RH5 .... 177 D4
Stane St.
    Slinfd RH12 & RH13 .... 215 C4
Stane Way. Ewell KT17 ...... 58 A1
Stanedge Ct. Streat SW16 .. 21 E3
Stanford Cl. Hampt TW12 .. 15 F2
Stanford Cotts. Pirb GU24 .. 87 E1
Stanford Mdt Sch.
    Mitch SW16 .... 41 D8
Stanford Orch. Warn RH12 216 F8

Stanford Pl. Lingf RH7 .... 164 D3
Stanford Rd. Thorn H SW16 .. 41 E7
Stanford Way.
  Broad H RH12 .... 216 D3
Stanford Way. Mitch SW16 .... 41 D7
Stanfords The. Ewell KT17 .... 76 F7
Stangate Mansions.
  Twick TW1 .... 16 F5
Stanger Rd. Croy SE25 .... 43 A5
Stangrave Hall. Godst RH9 121 B3
Stanhope Ave. Hayes BR2 .... 44 F1
Stanhope Cotts. Lingf RH7 164 F3
Stanhope Gr. Beck BR3 .... 43 F5
Stanhope Heath. Stan TW19 . 2 C1
Stanhope Rd. Camb GU15 .... 64 F4
Stanhope Rd. S Croy CR0 .... 61 E7
Stanhope Rd. Wallin SM5 .... 60 A3
Stanhope Way. Stan TW19 .... 2 C1
Stanier Cl. Worth RH10 ...... 202 B5
Staniland Dr. Whit V KT13 .. 52 F1
Stanley Ave.
  Beck BR3 & BR3 .... 44 C6
Stanley Ave. W Barn KT3 .... 39 A4
Stanley Cl. Coulsd CR5 .... 79 F2
Stanley Cl. Crawl RH10 ...... 201 E4
Stanley Cotts. Knaph GU21 .. 68 D2
Stanley Ct. Belm SM2 .... 59 B3
Stanley Ct. Wallin SM5 .... 60 C3
Stanley Ctr. Crawl RH10 .... 181 F2
Stanley Cty Inf Sch.
  Tedd TW1 .... 16 E4
Stanley Cty Jun Sch.
  Tedd TW1 .... 16 E4
Stanley Dr. Farnb GU14 ...... 84 C3
Stanley Gardens Rd.
  Tedd TW11 .... 16 E3
Stanley Gdns. Hersh KT12 .. 54 C4
Stanley Gdns. Mitch CR4 .... 21 A2
Stanley Gdns. Sander CR2 .. 81 A7
Stanley Gdns. Wallin SM6 .... 60 C4
Stanley Gr.
  Thorn H CR0 & CR7 .... 42 A3
Stanley Hill. Pirb GU24 .... 87 C5
Stanley Mansions.
  Up Toot SW17 .... 20 F6
Stanley Park High Sch.
  Wallin SM5 .... 60 A4
Stanley Park Inf Sch.
  Wallin SM5 .... 59 F3
Stanley Park Jun Sch.
  Wallin SM5 .... 59 F3
Stanley Park Rd.
  Wallin SM5 & SM6 .... 60 A3
Stanley Rd. Asht TW15 .... 13 E3
Stanley Rd. Hounsl TW3 ...... 5 C3
Stanley Rd. Mitch CR4 .... 21 A1
Stanley Rd. Morden SM4 .... 40 A5
Stanley Rd. Mortl SW14 ...... 7 B3
Stanley Rd. Sutton SM2 ...... 59 B3
Stanley Rd.
  Tedd TW11 & TW2 .... 16 E3
Stanley Rd.
  Thorn H CR0 & CR7 .... 42 A3
Stanley Rd. Twick TW2 ...... 16 D5
Stanley Rd. Wallin SM5 .... 60 A3
Stanley Rd. Wimble SW19 .. 20 A2
Stanley Rd. Woking GU21 .... 69 F2
Stanley Sq. Wallin SM5 .... 59 F2
Stanley St. Cater CR3 .... 100 C5
Stanley Tech High Sch.
  S Norw SE25 .... 42 F4
Stanley Wlk. Horsh RH13 .. 217 D2
Stanleycroft Cl. Hounsl TW7 . 5 E6
Stanmore Cl. Ascot SL5 ...... 29 A5
Stanmore Gdns. Rich TW9 .... 6 F4
Stanmore Gdns. Sutton SM1 59 C7
Stanmore Rd. Rich TW9 ...... 6 F4
Stanmore Terr. Beck BR3 .... 44 A7
Stannet Way. Wallin SM6 .... 60 D5
Stansfield Rd.
  Cranf TW4 & TW5 .... 4 B5
Stanstead Cl. Hayes BR2 .... 44 F3
Stanstead Gr. For Hil SE23 .. 23 F7
Stanstead Manor.
  Sutton SM1 .... 59 A4
Stanstead Rd.
  For Hil SE23 & SE6 .... 23 E7
Stansted Rd. Stan TW6 .... 2 F1
Stanthorpe Cl. Streat SW16 21 E4
Stanthorpe Rd. Streat SW16 21 E4
Stanthorpe Rd. Streat SW16 21 E4
Stanton Ave. Tedd TW11 .... 16 E2
Stanton Cl. Cran GU6 .... 174 A3
Stanton Cl. N Cheam KT4 .... 39 D1

Stanton Cl. W Ewell KT19 .... 57 B5
Stanton Rd. Barnes SW13 .... 7 F5
Stanton Rd. Thorn H CR0 .... 42 C2
Stanton Rd. Wimble SW20 .. 39 D8
Stanton Sq. For Hil SE6 ...... 23 F4
Stanton Way.
  For Hil SE26 & SE6 .... 23 F4
Stanway Sch. Dork RH4 .... 115 B1
Stanwell Cl. Stan TW19 .... 2 D1
Stanwell Gdns. Stan TW19 .. 2 D1
Stanwell Moor Rd.
  Harm TW19 & TW6 & UB7 .... 2 B4
Stanwell Moor Rd. Stan TW19 2 B4
Stanwell New Rd.
  Stan TW18 & TW19 .... 13 B5
Stanwell Rd. Ashf TW15 .... 13 E4
Stanwell Rd. E Bed
  TW6 & TW14 & TW19 .... 14 B8
Stanwell Rd.
  Horton SL3 & TW19 .... 1 C4
Stanworth Ct. Heston TW5 .. 5 A7
Stanyhurst. For Hil SE23 .... 23 E7
Staple Hill.
  Burrh GU24 & KT16 .... 49 E6
Staple La. E Clan GU4 .... 111 E2
Staple La. Albury GU4 .... 132 F8
Staplecross Ct. 1
  Crawl RH11 .... 201 A3
Staplefield Cl. 3
  Streat SW2 .... 21 E7
Stapleford Cl. King U T KT1 .. 38 A6
Stapleford Cl. Putney SW19 19 E8
Staplehurst. Easth RG12 .... 26 E2
Staplehurst Cl. Dovgn RH1 139 C5
Staplehurst Rd.
  Dovgn RH1 .... 139 C5
Staplehurst Rd. Sutton SM5 59 E3
Stapleton Gdns. Croy CR0 .. 61 A5
Stapleton Rd. Up Toot SW17 21 A5
Star and Garter Hill.
  Rich TW10 .... 17 E8
Star Hill. Churt GU10 .... 167 D2
Star Hill. Woking GU22 ...... 89 D8
Star Hill Dr. Churt GU10 .... 167 D2
Star La. Alder GU12 .... 105 F2
Star La. Hooley CR5 .... 99 A6
Star Post Rd. Camb GU15 .. 65 F8
Star Rd. Hounsl TW7 .... 5 D5
Starborough Cotts.
  Dorman RH7 .... 185 F7
Starborough Rd. Lingf TN8 165 E5
Starhurst Sch. Dork RH5 .. 136 C5
Starling Wlk. Hampt TW12 .. 15 E3
Starmead Dr. Woki RG11 .... 25 E5
Starrock La. Chips CR5 .... 99 A7
Starrock Rd. Coulsd CR5 .... 99 C8
Starwood Cl. W Byfl KT14 .. 71 C8
Staten Gdns. Twick TW1 .... 16 F7
Statham Ct. Binf RG12 .... 26 E8
Station App. Ash V GU12 .. 106 A7
Station App. Ashf TW15 ...... 13 F4
Station App. Beck SE6 .... 23 F3
Station App. Beck BR3 .... 44 A8
Station App. Belm SM2 .... 58 D3
Station App. Chips CR5 ...... 78 F1
Station App. Coulsd CR5 .... 79 D4
Station App. 3 Croy CR0 .... 61 D8
Station App. Dork RH4 ...... 115 C1
Station App. E Hors KT24 .... 92 E1
Station App.
  Epsom KT17 & KT19 .... 76 D6
Station App. Godal GU7 .... 150 D4
Station App. Guild GU1 .... 130 E8
Station App. Hampt TW12 .. 36 A8
Station App. Haslem GU27 208 B6
Station App. Hinch W KT10 .. 55 F7
Station App. Horley RH6 .... 161 B2
Station App. 4
  King U T KT1 & KT2 .... 38 A8
Station App. Leahd KT22 .... 95 A6
Station App. 6
  New Mal KT3 .... 39 A1
Station App. Oxted RH8 .... 122 E6
Station App. Purley CR8 .... 80 A8
Station App. Rich TW9 .... 7 A6
Station App. S Croy CR2 .... 61 D2
Station App. Shep TW17 .... 34 C4
Station App. Stain TW18 .... 13 A3
Station App. Streat SW16 .. 21 D3
Station App. Sunby TW16 .. 35 A8
Station App. 1 Surb KT6 .... 37 E3
Station App. Sutton SM2 .... 59 B1
Station App. Tadw KT20 .... 97 C4
Station App. Vir W GU25 .... 31 D5
Station App. W Byfl KT14 .... 71 A7
Station App. Weyb KT13 .... 53 A4
Station App. Whytlf CR3 .... 80 A1
Station App. Woking GU22 .. 69 F2
Station App. Worc Pk KT19 58 A5
Station App E. Earls RH1 .. 139 F7
Station App W. Earls RH1 .. 139 F7

Station Approach Rd.
  Chisw W4 .... 7 C7
Station Approach Rd.
  Coulsd CR5 .... 79 D4
Station Approach Rd.
  Crawl RH6 .... 182 B7
Station Ave. Cater CR3 ...... 101 A3
Station Ave. King U T KT3 .. 38 E6
Station Ave. W Ewell KT19 .. 57 E2
Station Ave. W Ewell KT19 .. 57 E2
Station Ave. Walt O T KT12 .. 54 A6
Station Bldgs. Wimble SW20 39 C7
Station Cl. Hampt TW12 .... 36 B8
Station Cl. Horsh RH13 ...... 217 D2
Station Cres. Ashf TW15 .... 13 E4
Station Est. Beck BR3 .... 43 D5
Station Estate Rd.
  Felt TW14 .... 15 B7
Station Flats. Wimble SW20 30 B2
Station Gdns. Chisw W4 ...... 7 C7
Station Hill. Crawl RH10 .. 202 B7
Station Hill. Ascot SL5 .... 29 A5
Station Hill. Farnb GU9 .... 125 C2
Station Ind. Est. Woki RG11 25 B6
Station La. Ent Gn GU8 .... 171 A7
Station La. Milf GU8 .... 171 A7
Station Par. Ashf TW15 ...... 13 F4
Station Par. Chips CR5 .... 78 F1
Station Par. E Hors KT24 .... 92 E1
Station Par. Felt TW14 ...... 15 B8
Station Par. Rich TW9 .... 7 A6
Station Par. Sunnin SL5 .... 30 A2
Station Par. 5
  Up Toot SW12 .... 21 A7
Station Par. Vir W GU25 .... 31 E4
Station Path. Stain TW18 .... 12 F4
Station Rd. Addl KT15 .... 52 D6
Station Rd. Alder GU11 .... 105 B2
Station Rd. Ashf TW15 ...... 13 F4
Station Rd. Bagsh GU19 .... 47 E4
Station Rd. Belm SM2 .... 59 A1
Station Rd. Betch RH3 ...... 116 B1
Station Rd. Brack RG12 ...... 27 B7
Station Rd. Bramly GU5 .... 152 A4
Station Rd. Broml BR2 .... 44 E7
Station Rd. Carsh SM5 .... 59 F6
Station Rd. Chert KT16 ...... 33 A1
Station Rd. Chess KT9 .... 56 E5
Station Rd. Chobh GU24 .... 69 B6
Station Rd. Cran RH12 .... 195 C3
Station Rd.
  Crawl RH10 & RH11 .... 201 D5
Station Rd. Crawl D RH10 .. 204 B8
Station Rd. Croy CR0 .... 42 C1
Station Rd. Dork RH4 .... 136 A8
Station Rd. E Grins RH19 .. 185 D1
Station Rd. Egham TW20 .... 12 A3
Station Rd. Esher KT10 ...... 55 D8
Station Rd. Esher KT10 ...... 55 E5
Station Rd. Farnb GU14 .... 85 B4
Station Rd. Farnc GU7 ...... 150 F7
Station Rd. For Row RH18 .. 206 F3
Station Rd. Godal GU7 ...... 150 D4
Station Rd. Gomsh GU5 .... 133 D4
Station Rd. Hampt TW12 .. 36 B8
Station Rd. Horley RH6 .... 161 B3
Station Rd. Horsh RH13 .... 217 D2
Station Rd. Hounsl TW3 ...... 5 B3
Station Rd. Hyde GU8 ...... 171 D6
Station Rd. Kenley CR8 ...... 80 C5
Station Rd. King U T KT2 .... 38 A8
Station Rd. Leahd KT22 .... 95 A6
Station Rd. Lingf RH7 ...... 164 E4
Station Rd. Loxwd RH14 .. 213 A3
Station Rd. Merst RH1 ...... 119 C7
Station Rd. Merton SW19 .. 40 C8
Station Rd. Penge SE20 .... 23 C2
Station Rd. Redh RH1 ...... 118 F2
Station Rd. Rudg RH12 .... 214 D7
Station Rd. S Godst RH9 .. 142 E5
Station Rd. Shalf GU4 ...... 130 C3
Station Rd. Shep TW17 ...... 34 C4
Station Rd. Stk D'A KT11 .... 73 F3
Station Rd. Sunby TW16 .... 15 A1
Station Rd. Sunnin SL5 ...... 30 A4
Station Rd. Tedd TW11 ...... 17 A2
Station Rd. Tedd TW11 ...... 17 A2
Station Rd. Thame D KT7 .... 36 F2
Station Rd. Thame D KT10 .. 55 D8
Station Rd. Twick TW1 ...... 16 F8
Station Rd. W Barn KT3 .... 39 B4
Station Rd. W Byfl KT14 .... 71 A7
Station Rd. W Wick BR4 .... 44 C1
Station Rd. Warn RH12 .... 217 B8
Station Rd. Whytlf CR3 ...... 80 F1
Station Rd. Woki RG11 ...... 25 B6
Station Rd. Wold CR3 .... 101 F5
Station Rd. Wray TW19 .... 1 A1

Station Rd E. Oxted RH8 .... 122 E6
Station Rd N. Egham TW20 . 11 F3
Station Rd N. Merst RH1 .... 119 C7
Station Rd S. Merst RH1 .... 119 C7
Station Rd W. Ash V GU12 105 F8
Station Rd W. Oxted RH8 .. 122 E6
Station Rise. Streat SE27 .... 22 B6
Station Row. Shalf GU4 .... 130 E3
Station Terr. Dork RH4 ...... 136 A8
Station View. Ash V GU12 .. 106 A8
Station Way.
  Cheam SM2 & SM3 .... 58 E3
Station Way.
  Crawl RH10 & RH11 .... 201 D5
Station Yd. Twick TW1 .... 17 A8
Staunton Rd. King U T KT2 .. 17 F1
Staveley Gdns. Chisw W4 .... 7 D6
Staveley Rd. Ashf TW15 .... 14 D2
Staveley Rd. Chisw W4 .... 7 D7
Staveley Way. Knaph GU21 . 68 E2
Staverton Cl. Woki RG11 .... 25 F6
Stavordale Rd.
  Carsh SM4 & SM5 .... 40 C2
Stayne End. Went GU25 .... 31 A5
Stayton Rd. Sutton SM1 .... 59 A7
Steadfast Rd. King U T KT1 .. 37 D8
Steam Farm La. Hatton TW14 3 F3
Steel's La.
  Oxsh KT11 & KT22 .... 74 C5
Steele Rd. Islew TW7 .... 6 A3
Steele's Rd. Alder GU11 .... 105 B4
Steep Hill. Burrh GU24 ...... 49 C3
Steep Hill. S Croy CR0 ...... 61 E6
Steep Hill. Streat SW16 .... 21 D5
Steeple Cl. Wimble SW19 .. 19 E4
Steeple Heights Dr.
  Bigg H TN16 .... 83 D2
Steepways. Beac H GU26 .. 188 B6
Steeres Hill. Rusper RH12 .. 199 C6
Steerforth Copse.
  Sandh GU15 .... 45 E2
Steerforth St. Wands SW18 20 C6
Steers La. Crawl RH10 ...... 182 C4
Steers Mead. Mitch CR4 .... 40 F8
Steetley Ct. Sutton SM2 .... 59 C3
Stella Rd. Up Toot SW17 .... 20 F2
Stembridge Rd. Penge SE20 43 B7
Stenning Ct. Leahd KT22 .... 95 B5
Stepgates. Chert KT16 .... 33 B2
Stepgates Cl. Chert KT16 .. 33 B2
Stepgates Prim Sch.
  Chert KT16 .... 33 B2
Stephanie Chase Ct.
  Woki RG11 .... 25 D7
Stephen Cl. Crawl RH11 .... 181 D1
Stephen Cl. Egham TW20 .. 12 C2
Stephen Ct. 18
  Putney SW19 .... 19 D7
Stephendale Rd.
  Farnb GU9 .... 125 D4
Stephenson Ct. Belm SM2 .. 58 F3
Stephenson Dr.
  E Grins RH19 .... 205 F7
Stephenson Pl. Crawl RH10 202 B6
Stephenson Rd. Twick TW4 . 16 A8
Stephenson Way.
  Crawl RH10 .... 202 B6
Stepney Cl. Worth RH10 .... 202 C4
Sterling Ave. Up Hall TW7 . 34 E6
Sterling Bldgs. Horsh RH12 217 C2
Sternhold Ave.
  Streat SW12 & SW2 .... 21 E6
Sternhold Ave. Streat SW2 21 E6
Sterry Dr. Thame D KT7 ...... 36 E3
Sterry Dr. Worc Pk KT19 .... 57 E6
Steucers La. For Hil SE23 .. 23 F7
Steve Biko La. Catf SE6 ...... 24 A4
Steve Biko Way. Hounsl TW3 5 A4
Stevenage Rd. Crawl RH11 200 E3
Stevens Cl. Beck BR3 .... 24 A2
Stevens Cl. Epsom KT17 .... 76 E6
Stevens Cl. Hampt TW12 .. 15 F2
Stevens Cl. Beck BR3 .... 24 A2
Stevens' La. Clayg KT10 .... 56 A4
Stewart. Tadw KT20 .... 97 D6
Stewart Ave. Shep Gn TW17 34 A5
Stewart Cl. Hampt TW12 .. 15 E7
Stewart Cl. Woking GU21 .. 68 F2
Stewart Fleming Prim Sch.
  Penge SE20 .... 43 C6
Steyning Cl. Crawl RH10 .. 201 E8
Steyning Cl. Purley CR8 .... 80 B3
Steyning Way. Hounsl TW4 .. 4 C3
Sthrathbrook Rd.
  Streat SW16 .... 21 F1
Stile Gdns. Shottn GU27 .. 207 F6
Stile House. Merrow GU4 .. 110 D2
Stile Path. Sunby TW16 .... 35 A6
Stirling Cl. Banstd SM7 ...... 77 F2
Stirling Cl. Farnb GU14 ...... 85 A3
Stirling Cl. Friml GU16 ...... 65 E2

Stirling Cl. Mitch SW16 ...... 41 C8
Stirling Cl. Worth RH10 .... 202 C5
Stirling Gr. Hounsl TW3 ...... 5 C5
Stirling House. 9
  Redh RH1 .... 118 F1
Stirling Rd. Stan TW19 & TW6 2 F1
Stirling Rd. Stough GU2 .... 108 E1
Stirling Rd. Twick TW2 ...... 16 B8
Stirling Way. E Grins RH19 186 B3
Stirling Way. Farnb GU14 .. 104 D7
Stirling Way. Horsh RH13 .... 2 F3
Stirrup Way. Crawl RH10 .. 202 D7
Stites Hill Rd.
  Coulsd CR3 & CR5 .... 100 C7
Stoatley Hollow.
  Shottm GU27 .... 208 A8
Stoatley House. 10
  Rhampt SW15 .... 19 A7
Stoatley Rise. Shottm GU27 208 B8
Stoats Nest Rd. Coulsd CR5 . 79 E5
Stoats Nest Village.
  Coulsd CR5 .... 79 E4
Stock Hill. Bigg H TN16 .... 83 D2
Stockbridge Dr.
  Alder GU11 .... 126 C6
Stockbury Rd. Croy CR0 .... 43 C3
Stockfield. Horley RH6 ...... 161 B4
Stockfield Rd. Clayg KT10 .. 55 E5
Stockfield Rd. Streat SW16 . 21 F5
Stockhams Cl. S Croy CR2 .. 61 D1
Stocklund Sq. Cran GU6 .. 174 D3
Stockport Rd. Streat SW16 .. 41 D8
Stocks Cl. Horley RH6 ...... 161 B2
Stockton Rd. Woodh RH2 . 139 A6
Stockwell Rd. E Grins RH19 205 E6
Stockwell Wks.
  Crawl RH10 .... 202 A6
Stockwood Rise. Camb GU15 65 F5
Stockwood Way.
  Heath E GU9 .... 125 F7
Stocton Cl. Guild GU1 ...... 109 C2
Stocton Rd. Guild GU1 .... 109 D2
Stodart Rd. Penge SE20 .... 43 C8
Stoford Cl. Putney SW19 .... 19 E8
Stoke Brunswick Sch.
  Hammer RH19 .... 206 E7
Stoke Cl. Stk D'A KT11 ...... 73 F3
Stoke Fields. 8 Guild GU1 109 D1
Stoke Gr. Guild GU1 .... 109 D1
Stoke Hill City Prim Sch.
  Bellf GU1 .... 109 C4
Stoke Hills. Farnb GU9 .... 125 C3
Stoke Hosp (Almshouses). 6
  Guild GU1 .... 109 D1
Stoke Park Ct. 5
  Guild GU1 .... 109 D1
Stoke Rd. Guild GU1 .... 109 D1
Stoke Rd. King U T KT2 .... 18 C1
Stoke Rd. Stk D'A KT11 .... 73 E2
Stoke Rd. Walt O T KT12 .... 54 C7
Stoke Rd Cotts. Fetch KT22 . 94 D6
Stokeford Cl. 3 Brack RG12 27 F3
Stokes Rd. Croy CR0 .... 43 D3
Stokes Ridings. Tadw KT20 . 97 D4
Stokesby Rd. Chess KT9 .... 56 F4
Stokesheath Rd. Oxsh KT22 74 A6
Stompond La. Walt O T KT12 54 A8
Stoms Path. Catf SE6 .... 24 A3
Stonards Brow.
  Sham Gn GU5 .... 152 D4
Stondon Pk. For Hil SE23 .. 23 E8
Stone Cres. E Bed TW14 .... 14 F8
Stone Hatch. Alf Cr GU6 .. 194 A3
Stone House Gdns.
  Cater CR3 .... 100 E2
Stone Park Ave. Beck BR3 .. 44 B5
Stone Pl. Worc Pk KT4 .... 58 A8
Stone Rd. Hayes BR2 .... 44 F4
Stone St. Alder GU12 .... 126 D8
Stone St. Croy CR0 & CR9 .. 61 A5
Stone's Rd. Ewell KT17 ...... 76 F7
Stonebanks. Walt O T KT12 . 35 A2
Stonebridge Ct.
  Crawl RH11 .... 201 C2
Stonebridge Ct.
  Horsh RH12 .... 217 A2
Stonebridge Fields.
  Shalf GU4 .... 130 C3
Stonebridge Wharf.
  Shalf GU4 .... 130 D2
Stonecot Cl.
  Cheam SM3 & SM4 .... 39 E1
Stonecot Hill. Cheam SM4 .. 39 E1
Stonecourt Cl. Horley RH6 . 161 C3
Stonecroft Way.
  Thorn H CR0 .... 41 E2
Stonecrop Cl. Crawl RH11 201 B3
Stonecrop Rd.
  Merrow GU1 & GU4 .... 110 C3
Stonedene Cl.
  Head Dn GU35 .... 187 B4

Stonefield Cl. Crawl RH10 & RH11 .... 201 D5
Stonegate. Friml GU15 .... 66 C6
Stonehaven. Beck BR3 .... 44 B7
Stonehill Cl. L Book KT23 ..... 94 A2
Stonehill Cl. Mortl SW14 .... 7 D2
Stonehill Cres. Longc KT16 .. 50 E4
Stonehill Pk. Head Dn GU35 187 C4
Stonehill Rd. Chobh GU24 & KT16 .... 50 D3
Stonehill Rd. Head Dn GU35 .... 187 C4
Stonehill Rd. Lhtwat GU18 ... 48 A1
Stonehill Rd. Mortl SW14 ...... 7 D2
Stonehill Rd. Ottsh GU24 & KT16 .... 50 D3
Stonehill's Mansions. 3 Streat SW16 .... 21 E6
Stonehills Ct. Dulw SE21 ..... 22 E5
Stonehouse Rise. Friml GU16 .... 65 E1
Stoneleigh Ave. N Cheam KT17 & KT4 .... 58 A7
Stoneleigh Cl. E Grins RH19 185 F1
Stoneleigh Cres. Worc Pk KT19 .... 57 F5
Stoneleigh Ct. Friml GU16 ... 65 F1
Stoneleigh Fst Grant Maintd Sch. N Cheam KT4 .... 58 B6
Stoneleigh Lodge. 12 Rich TW9 .... 6 F6
Stoneleigh Park Ave. Croy CR0 .... 43 D3
Stoneleigh Park Rd. Worc Pk KT19 & KT4 .... 58 A5
Stoneleigh Pk. Whit V KT13 . 53 C4
Stoneleigh Rd. Carsh SM5 .... 40 E2
Stoneleigh Rd. The Char RH8 .... 123 E5
Stoneleigh Sta. Stonel KT19 58 A5
Stonepit Cl. Ock Rid GU7 .... 150 C4
Stoners Cl. Crawl RH6 .... 181 E7
Stones La. Westc RH4 .... 135 C6
Stoneswood Rd. Limps RH8 .... 123 B5
Stoneworth Ct. Croy SE25 ... 43 A3
Stoney Bottom. Graysh GU26 .... 188 C3
Stoney Brook. Stough GU2 . 108 E2
Stoney Deep. Tedd TW11 .... 17 A4
Stoney La. S Norw SE19 ...... 22 F2
Stoney Rd. Brack RG12 .... 27 A8
Stoneybrook. Horsh RH12 . 216 F1
Stoneycroft Cl. Lewish SE12 24 F8
Stoneycroft Wlk. 3 Crawl RH11 .... 200 D5
Stoneyfield Rd. Coulsd CR5 . 79 F2
Stoneyland Ct. Egham TW20 11 F3
Stoneylands Rd. Egham TW20 .... 11 F3
Stonny Croft. Ashtd KT21 .... 75 F2
Stony Hill. Esher KT10 .... 54 F3
Stoop Ct. W Byfl KT14 .... 71 B7
Stopham Rd. Worth RH10 . 202 C3
Stormont Way. Chess KT9 ... 56 C5
Storrington Rd. Croy CR0 ... 42 F1
Stoughton Ave. Cheam SM3 58 E5
Stoughton Cl. Rhampt SW15 19 A7
Stoughton Grange Cty Jun Sch. Stough GU2 .... 109 B4
Stoughton Inf Sch. Stough GU2 .... 109 B4
Stoughton Rd. Bellf GU1 & GU2 .... 109 B3
Stoughton Rd. Stough GU1 & GU2 .... 109 B3
Stourhead Cl. Farnb GU14 ... 85 D4
Stourhead Cl. 6 Putney SW19 .... 19 D8
Stourhead Gdns. W Barn SW20 .... 39 A6
Stourton Ave. Felt TW13 ..... 15 F4
Stovold's Way. Alder GU11 125 F8
Stovolds Hill. Alfold GU6 & GU8 .... 193 D7
Stowell Ave. New Add CR0 .. 63 D2
Stowford Coll. Sutton SM2 .. 59 C3
Strachan Pl. Wimble SW19 & SW20 .... 19 C2
Strachey Ct. 1 Crawl RH11 .... 201 B1
Strafford Rd. Hounsl TW3 ...... 4 F4
Strafford Rd. Twick TW1 ...... 17 A8
Straight Rd. Old W SL4 & TW19 .... 11 C8
Strand Cl. Lang V KT18 .... 96 D8
Strand Cl. Worth RH10 ...... 202 D4
Strand on the Green Inf Sch. Brent W4 .... 7 A8
Strand on the Green Jun Sch. Brent W4 .... 7 A8
Strand-on-the-Green. Brent W4 .... 7 A8
Stranraer Rd. Stan TW6 .... 2 E1
Stranraer Way. 1 Stan TW6 2 E1
Stratfield. Easth RG12 .... 26 E1
Stratfield House. Alder GU11 .... 105 A2
Stratford Ct. Farnb GU14 .... 85 C4
Stratford Ct. M Bourn GU9 . 125 C1
Stratford Ct. New Mal KT3 . 38 D5
Stratford Rd. Harl TW6 .... 3 C2
Stratford Rd. Thorn H CR7 ... 42 B6
Strathavon Cl. Rowly GU6 . 174 B7
Strathcona Ave. Effing KT24 .... 113 E7
Strathdale. Streat SW16 ...... 21 F3
Strathdon Dr. Wands SW17 . 20 D5
Strathearn Ave. Harl UB3 ...... 3 F7
Strathearn Ave. Twick TW2 . 16 C7
Strathearn Rd. Sutton SM1 .. 59 A5
Strathearn Rd. Wimble SW19 .... 20 A4
Strathmore Cl. Cater CR3 .. 100 E6
Strathmore Rd. Crawl RH11 .... 181 A1
Strathmore Rd. Tedd TW11 & TW2 .... 16 E4
Strathmore Rd. Thorn H CR0 42 D2
Strathmore Rd. Wimble SW19 .... 20 A5
Strathmore Sch. Rich TW10 17 D6
Strathville Rd. Wands SW18 20 B6
Strathyre Ave. Thorn H CR7 & SW16 .... 42 A6
Stratton Ave. Wallin SM6 ..... 60 D2
Stratton Cl. Heston TW5 .... 5 A6
Stratton Cl. Merton SW19 .... 40 A7
Stratton Cl. Walt O T KT12 ... 35 C1
Stratton Ct. 10 King U T KT6 .... 37 E4
Stratton Rd. Merton SW19 ... 40 A7
Stratton Rd. Sunby TW16 ..... 34 F7
Stratton Wlk. W Heath GU14 85 A7
Strawberry Cl. Pirb GU24 ..... 87 D7
Strawberry Fields. Bisley GU24 .... 68 A4
Strawberry Hill Cl. Twick TW1 .... 16 F5
Strawberry Hill Golf Course. Twick TW2 .... 16 E5
Strawberry Hill Rd. Twick TW1 .... 16 F5
Strawberry Hill Sta. Twick TW2 .... 16 F5
Strawberry La. Carsh SM5 ... 60 A7
Strawberry Rise. Bisley GU24 .... 68 A4
Strawberry Vale. Twick TW1 17 A5
Stream Cl. Byfl KT14 .... 71 E7
Stream Farm Cl. M Bourn GU10 & GU9 ...... 146 D7
Stream Pk. E Grins RH19 ... 185 A3
Stream Valley Rd. M Bourn GU10 .... 146 C6
Streatham Cl. Streat SW16 . 21 E6
Streatham Comm N. Streat SW16 .... 21 F3
Streatham Comm S. Streat SW16 .... 21 F2
Streatham Common Sta. Streat SW16 .... 21 D1
Streatham Ct. Streat SW16 . 21 E5
Streatham High Rd. Streat SW16 & SW2 .... 21 E3
Streatham Hill. Streat SW2 . 21 E7
Streatham Hill & Clapham High Sch. Streat SW2 .... 21 F7
Streatham Hill Sta. Streat SW2 .... 21 E6
Streatham Pl. Streat SW2 .... 21 E8
Streatham Rd. Mitch CR4 & SW16 .... 21 B1
Streatham Rd. Mitch CR4 .... 41 A8
Streatham Sta. Streat SW16 21 D3
Streatham & Tooting Adult Inst. Streat SW16 .... 21 F6
Streatham Vale. Streat SW16 .... 21 D1
Streathbourne Rd. Up Toot SW17 .... 21 A5
Streathem Wells Prim Sch. Streat SW2 .... 22 A6
Streatleigh Par. 4 Streat SW16 .... 21 E6
Street Hill. Worth RH10 ..... 202 E5
Street The. Ashtd KT21 .... 75 F1
Street The. Betch RH3 .... 116 E1
Street The. Capel RH5 .... 178 D6
Street The. Charl RH6 .... 180 E7
Street The. Compt GU3 ..... 129 B2
Street The. Docken GU10 ... 166 E6
Street The. E Clan GU4 .... 111 E4
Street The. Effing KT24 ...... 113 D8
Street The. Ewh GU6 .... 175 E5
Street The. Fetch KT22 .... 94 D5
Street The. Frensh GU10 .... 167 C7
Street The. Plaist RH14 ...... 211 E2
Street The. Putt GU3 .... 128 C4
Street The. Shackl GU8 ...... 149 C8
Street The. Shalf GU4 .... 130 E3
Street The. Slinfd RH13 ..... 215 D4
Street The. Thursl GU8 .... 169 C4
Street The. Tongh GU10 ..... 126 F6
Street The. W Clan GU4 ..... 111 B5
Street The. W Hors KT24 .. 112 B7
Street The. Woner GU5 ..... 152 A7
Street The. Wreccl GU10 ... 145 F6
Streete Court Sch. Tyl Gn RH9 .... 121 E5
Streeters Cl. Godal GU7 .... 151 A6
Streeters La. Wallin SM6 ..... 60 D7
Streetfield. Thursl GU8 .... 169 C4
Streetfield Rd. Slinfd RH13 215 E3
Streets Heath. W End GU24 . 67 F7
Stretton Rd. Croy CR0 .... 42 E2
Stretton Rd. Rich TW10 .... 17 C6
Strickland Cl. Crawl RH11 .. 200 E5
Strickland Row. Wands SW18 .... 20 D8
Stringer's Ave. Jacobs GU4 109 D7
Stringhams Copse. Send M GU23 .... 91 A3
Strode House. 3 Streat SW2 .... 22 A7
Strode St. Egham TW20 .... 12 A4
Strode's Coll. Egham TW20 . 11 F3
Strode's Cres. Stain TW18 .... 13 C3
Strodes College La. Egham TW20 .... 11 F3
Strood House. 12 Penge SE20 .... 23 C1
Strood La. Warn RH12 .... 216 C7
Strood La. Wink SL5 .... 9 C2
Stroud Cres. Rhampt SW15 . 19 A5
Stroud Green Gdns. Croy CR0 .... 43 C2
Stroud Green Way. Croy CR0 .... 43 C3
Stroud La. Sham Gn GU5 ... 153 A3
Stroud Rd. Croy SE25 .... 43 A3
Stroud Rd. Wimble SW19 ..... 20 A5
Stroud Way. Ashf TW15 ...... 14 B2
Stroude Rd. Egham TW20 .... 12 A1
Stroude Rd. Thorpe GU25 & TW20 .... 31 E6
Stroudes Cl. New Mal KT4 ... 38 F2
Stroudley Cl. Worth RH10 . 202 B5
Stroudwater Pk. Whit V KT13 .... 53 C4
Strudgate Cl. Crawl RH10 . 202 B4
Strudwicks Field. Cran GU6 174 F4
Stuart Ave. Walt O T KT12 ... 35 C1
Stuart Cl. W Heath GU14 ...... 85 A5
Stuart Cl. Worth RH10 .... 202 D5
Stuart Cres. Croy CR0 .... 62 F7
Stuart Cres. Woodh RH2 ... 139 A6
Stuart Ct. Godal GU7 .... 150 E4
Stuart Ct. 16 Redh RH1 ...... 119 A2
Stuart Gr. Tedd TW11 .... 16 E3
Stuart House. Brack RG12 ... 26 F8
Stuart Lodge. 7 Epsom KT18 .... 76 D6
Stuart Lodge. S Norw SE25 .. 42 E7
Stuart Pl. Mitch CR4 .... 40 F8
Stuart Rd. Rich TW10 .... 17 B5
Stuart Rd. S Norw CR7 .... 42 C5
Stuart Rd. Warlgm CR3 & CR6 .... 101 C7
Stuart Rd. Wimble SW19 ...... 20 A5
Stuart Rd. Woodh RH2 ...... 139 A6
Stuart Way. E Grins RH19 .. 205 F7
Stuart Way. Stain TW18 .... 13 B2
Stuart Way. Vir W GU25 ...... 31 A5
Stubbington House Sch. Sunnin SL5 .... 29 B1
Stubbs Folly. Sandh GU15 .... 64 D7
Stubbs La. L Kings KT20 .... 118 A7
Stubbs Moor Rd. W Heath GU14 .... 84 F5
Stubbs Way. Mitch SW19 ..... 40 D8
Stubfield. Horsh RH12 .... 217 A3
Stubpond La. Felb RH19 & RH7 .... 184 D7
Stubs Cl. Dork RH4 .... 136 C5
Stubs Hill. Dork RH4 & RH5 136 C4
Stubs Ind Site. Farnb GU12 105 E5
Stucley Rd. Hounsl TW5 & TW7 .... 5 C7
Studios Rd. Littlt TW17 .... 33 F6
Studland Rd. Byfl KT14 .... 71 F6
Studland Rd. King U T KT2 ... 17 E2
Studland Rd. Penge SE26 ..... 23 D3
Study Prep Sch The. Wimble SW19 .... 19 C3
Stumblets. Crawl RH10 ...... 202 C7
Stumps Hill La. Beck BR3 .... 24 A2
Sturdee Cl. Friml GU16 .... 65 E1
Sturges Rd. Woki RG11 .... 25 D5
Sturt Ave. King Gn GU27 .... 207 F5
Sturt Ct. Merrow GU4 .... 110 C3
Sturt Rd. Friml GU16 .... 85 F5
Sturt Rd. Haslem GU27 .... 207 F5
Sturt Rd. Heath E GU9 .... 125 B7
Sturt Rd. Shottm GU27 .... 207 F5
Sturt's La. Walt o t H KT20 117 A8
Stychens Cl. Bletch RH1 ..... 120 C2
Stychens La. Bletch RH1 ..... 120 C2
Styles End. G Book KT23 ... 114 B8
Styles Way. Beck BR3 .... 44 C5
Styventon Pl. Chert KT16 ..... 32 F2
Succomb's Hill. Whytlf CR3 & CR6 .... 101 B7
Succombs Pl. Warlgm CR6 101 B8
Sudbrook Gdns. Rich TW10 . 17 E5
Sudbrook La. Rich TW10 ...... 17 E6
Sudbrook Pk (Richmond Golf Club). Rich TW10 .... 17 E6
Sudbury Gdns. S Croy CR0 ... 61 E6
Suffield Cl. Selsd CR2 .... 81 D7
Suffield La. Putt GU3 & GU10 & GU8 ... 128 B2
Suffield Rd. Penge SE20 ...... 43 C7
Suffolk Cl. Bagsh GU19 .... 47 E2
Suffolk Cl. Horley RH6 .... 161 A2
Suffolk Ct. 3 Streat SW16 ... 22 A4
Suffolk Dr. Burph GU4 .... 110 B6
Suffolk House. 4 Croy CR0 61 D8
Suffolk House. Penge SE20 . 43 C8
Suffolk Rd. Barnes SW13 .... 7 F7
Suffolk Rd. S Norw SE25 ...... 42 F5
Suffolk Rd. Worc Pk KT4 ...... 57 F8
Sugden Rd. Hinch W KT7 ..... 37 B1
Sulina Rd. Streat SW2 .... 21 E8
Sullington Hill. Crawl RH11 .... 201 D4
Sullington Mead. Broad H RH12 .... 216 E3
Sullivan Cl. E Mole KT8 .... 36 B6
Sullivan Cl. Farnb GU14 .... 85 A4
Sullivan Ct. 4 Croy CR0 ...... 43 A1
Sullivan Dr. Crawl RH11 ..... 200 E3
Sullivan House. Kenley CR8 . 80 C5
Sullivan House. Twick TW2 ... 5 D1
Sullivan Rd. Camb GU15 ...... 65 A5
Sullivans Reach. Walt O T KT12 .... 35 A2
Sultan St. Penge BR3 .... 43 D7
Summer Ave. Thame D KT8 . 36 E4
Summer Gdns. Friml GU15 .. 66 C5
Summer Gdns. Thame D KT8 36 E4
Summer Rd. E Mole KT8 ...... 36 D4
Summer Rd. Thame D KT7 & KT8 .... 36 F4
Summer Trees. Sunby TW16 35 B8
Summer's Rd. Farnc GU3 & GU7 .... 151 A8
Summerene Cl. Streat SW16 21 C1
Summerfield. Ashtd KT21 .... 95 D8
Summerfield La. Long D KT6 56 D8
Summerfield La. Rowl GU10 .... 146 B2
Summerfield St. Lewish SE12 .... 24 F8
Summerfields Cl. Row Tn KT15 .... 51 F5
Summerhayes Cl. Horse GU21 .... 69 E5
Summerhays. Cobham KT11 73 D6
Summerhill. Farnc GU7 ..... 150 D6
Summerhill Way. Mitch CR4 41 A8
Summerhouse Ave. Heston TW5 .... 4 E6
Summerhouse Cl. Godal GU7 .... 150 D4
Summerhouse Ct. Graysh GU26 .... 188 D3
Summerhouse La. Harm UB7 2 D8
Summerhouse Rd. Godal GU7 .... 150 D3
Summerlands. Cran GU6 ... 174 E4
Summerlay Cl. Kings KT20 ... 97 E7
Summerleigh. 5 Whit V KT13 .... 53 D4
Summerley St. Wands SW18 20 B6
Summerly Ave. Reig RH2 .. 118 A2
Summers Cl. Belm SM2 .... 59 A3
Summers Cl. Whit V KT13 .... 72 A8
Summers La. Compt GU7 .. 150 A8
Summersbury Dr. Shalf GU4 .... 130 E1
Summersbury Hall. Shalf GU4 .... 130 E1
Summersby Cl. Farnc GU7 150 F7
Summersell House. W Norw SE27 .... 22 D3
Summerstown. Wands SW17 .... 20 C4
Summersvere Cl. Crawl RH10 .... 182 A1
Summerswood Cl. Kenley CR8 .... 80 D3
Summerville Gdns. Cheam SM1 .... 58 F4
Summerwood Rd. Islew TW1 & TW7 .... 5 F1
Summit Ave. Farnb GU14 .... 84 C3
Summit Ctr. Harm UB7 .... 2 D7
Summit Pl. Whit V KT13 ...... 53 A3
Summit The. Sunby TW16 ... 15 A1
Summit Way. S Norw SE19 .. 22 E1
Sumner Cl. Fetch KT22 .... 94 D3
Sumner Ct. Farnh GU9 .... 125 C3
Sumner Gdns. Thorn H CR0 . 42 A1
Sumner Pl. Addl KT15 .... 52 A5
Sumner Rd. Farnh GU9 ...... 125 C3
Sumner Rd. Thorn H CR0 ..... 42 B1
Sumner Rd S. Thorn H CR0 .. 42 A1
Sun Alley. 5 Rich TW9 .... 6 E3
Sun Brow. Haslem GU27 .... 208 A5
Sun Hill. Woking GU22 .... 89 A6
Sun Inn Rd. Dunsf GU8 ...... 192 F5
Sun Life Trad Est. Hatton TW14 .... 4 A4
Sun Ray Est. Sandh GU17 .... 64 A8
Sunbury Ave. Mortl SW14 ...... 7 D3
Sunbury Court Island. Sunby TW16 .... 35 D6
Sunbury Court Rd. Sunby TW16 .... 35 C7
Sunbury Cres. Felt TW13 ..... 14 F4
Sunbury Cross Centre. 9 Charlt TW16 .... 14 F1
Sunbury Ct. Sunby TW16 ...... 35 D7
Sunbury Ct (Con Ctr). Sunby TW16 .... 35 D7
Sunbury Int Bsns Ctr. Charlt TW16 .... 34 E8
Sunbury La. Walt O T KT12 .. 35 A3
Sunbury Manor Sch. Sunby TW16 .... 34 F8
Sunbury Rd. Cheam SM3 ..... 58 E7
Sunbury Rd. Felt TW13 .... 14 F4
Sunbury Sta. Sunby TW16 ... 35 A8
Sunbury Way. Felt TW13 ...... 15 C3
Suncroft Pl. For Hil SE26 ...... 23 C5
Sundale Ave. Selsd CR2 .... 62 C1
Sunderland Ct. Dulw SE22 ... 23 A8
Sunderland Ct. 11 Stan TW19 .... 2 E1
Sunderland Mount. For Hil SE23 .... 23 D6
Sunderland Rd. For Hil SE23 23 D6
Sundew Cl. Crawl RH11 .... 201 A2
Sundew Cl. Lhtwat GU18 ..... 67 D8
Sundew Cl. Woki RG11 .... 25 E7
Sundial Ave. S Norw SE25 ... 42 F6
Sundial Ct. Tolw KT5 .... 57 B8
Sundon Cres. Went GU25 .... 31 C4
Sundown Ave. S Croy CR2 ... 80 F8
Sundown Rd. Ashf TW15 ..... 14 C3
Sundridge Rd. Croy CR0 & CR9 .... 43 A1
Sundridge Rd. Old Wok GU22 .... 90 A7
Sunkist Way. Wallin SM6 ..... 60 E2
Sunmead Cl. Fetch KT22 ...... 94 F5
Sunmead Rd. Sunby TW16 ... 35 A6
Sunna Gdns. Sunby TW16 .... 35 B7
Sunniholme Ct. Croy CR2 .... 61 C5
Sunning Ave. Sunnin SL5 ..... 29 E2
Sunning House. Ascot SL5 ... 29 D5
Sunning House. Windl GU20 48 F8
Sunningdale Ave. Felt TW13 15 E6
Sunningdale Cl. 2 Surb KT6 56 E8
Sunningdale Ct. Crawl RH11 .... 201 D4
Sunningdale Ct. 13 King U T KT2 .... 18 A1
Sunningdale House. Mitch CR4 .... 40 D7
Sunningdale Park (Civil Service Coll). Sunnin SL5 .... 29 F4
Sunningdale Rd. Cheam SM1 58 F6
Sunningdale Sch. Sunnin SL5 .... 29 F3
Sunningdale Sta. Sunnin SL5 30 A2
Sunninghill Ct. Ascot SL5 ..... 29 D5
Sunninghill Lodge. Ascot SL5 .... 29 C7
Sunninghill Rd. Ascot SL5 .... 29 D5
Sunninghill Rd. Windl GU20 48 A7

Sunninghill Rd.
Wink SL4 & SL5 .... 9 E2
Sunningvale Ave.
Bigg H TN16 .... 83 D3
Sunningvale Cl. Bigg H TN16 83 D3
Sunny Ave. Crawl D RH10 .. 204 A8
Sunny Bank. Croy SE25 .... 43 A6
Sunny Bank. Warlgm CR6 .... 81 E2
Sunny Bank. Woodc KT18 .... 76 C3
Sunny Down. Witley GU8 .... 170 E5
Sunny Hill. Witley GU8 .... 170 E6
Sunny Hill Rd. Alder GU11 104 D2
Sunny Nook Gdns. Croy CR2 61 D4
Sunny Rise. Cater CR3 ...... 100 D3
Sunny View Cl. Alder GU12 105 C1
Sunnybank Mews.
Ash GU12 .... 106 B3
Sunnybank Rd.
W Heath GU14 .... 84 D6
Sunnybank Rd.
W Heath GU14 .... 84 E6
Sunnybank Villas.
Bletch RH1 .... 120 F3
Sunnycroft Rd. Croy SE25 .. 43 A6
Sunnycroft Rd. Hounsl TW3 .. 5 B5
Sunnydell La.
Wreccl GU10 & GU9 .... 146 A6
Sunnydene Rd. Purley CR8 .. 80 B6
Sunnydene St. For Hil SE26 . 23 E4
Sunnydown Boys' Sch.
Whytlf CR3 .... 100 F6
Sunnyhill Cl. Crawl D RH10 204 A8
Sunnyhill Prim Sch.
Streat SW16 .... 21 F4
Sunnyhill Rd. Streat SW16 .. 21 E4
Sunnyhurst Cl. Sutton SM1 . 59 A7
Sunnymead. Crawl RH11 .. 201 D6
Sunnymead. Crawl D RH10 204 B8
Sunnymead Ave.
Mitch CR4 & SW16 .... 41 D6
Sunnymede Ave.
Sutton SM5 .... 78 D8
Sunnymede Ave.
W Ewell KT19 .... 57 E3
Sunnymede Ave.
W Ewell KT19 .... 57 E3
Sunnyside. Knaph GU21 ...... 88 B8
Sunnyside. Walt O T KT12 .. 35 C4
Sunnyside. Wimble SW19 .... 19 E2
Sunnyside Pl. Wimble SW19 19 E2
Sunnyside Rd.
Head Dn GU35 .... 187 C4
Sunnyside Rd. Tedd TW11 .. 16 D4
Sunray Ave. Tolw KT5 .... 57 B8
Sunrise Cl. Felt TW13 .... 15 F5
Sunset Gdns. S Norw SE25 .. 42 F7
Sunset Rd. Wimble SW19 .... 19 B3
Sunshine Way. Mitch CR4 .... 40 F7
Sunstone Gr. Merst RH1 .... 119 E6
Sunvale Ave. Shottm GU27 207 D6
Sunvale Cl. Shottm GU27 .. 207 D6
Surbiton Cres.
King U T KT1 & KT6 .... 37 E5
Surbiton Ct. King U T KT6 .. 37 D3
Surbiton Hall Cl.
King U T KT1 .... 37 E5
Surbiton High Sch.
King U T KT1 .... 37 E5
Surbiton High Sch Jun Sch for
Girls. King U T KT1 .... 37 E5
Surbiton Hill Pk. Surb KT5 .. 38 A4
Surbiton Hill Rd.
King U T KT6 .... 37 E4
Surbiton Hospl. Surb KT6 .... 37 E3
Surbiton Prep Sch.
King U T KT6 .... 37 E4
Surbiton Rd. Camb GU15 .... 47 A1
Surbiton Rd. King U T KT1 .. 37 E5
Surbiton Sta. Surb KT6 .... 37 E3
Surrey Ave. Camb GU15 ...... 65 A4
Surrey Bsns Pk. Ewell KT17 . 76 E8
Surrey Gr. Carsh SM1 .... 59 D7
Surrey Hills Ave.
Box H KT20 .... 116 C4
Surrey Hills Way.
Box H KT20 .... 116 C5
Surrey Inst of Art & Design The.
Farnh GU9 .... 125 B2
Surrey Lodge. Hersh K T12 .. 54 B5
Surrey Mews. W Norw SE27 22 E4
Surrey Rd. W Wick BR4 .... 44 B1
Surrey Research Pk The.
Onsl V GU2 .... 129 D8
Surrey Tower. 5
Penge SE20 .... 23 C1
Surrey Towers. Addl KT15 .. 52 C5
Surridge Ct. Bagsh GU19 .... 47 E2

Surridge Gdns. S Norw SE19 22 D2
Sussex Ave. Islew TW7 .... 5 E4
Sussex Cl. Knaph GU21 .... 68 C1
Sussex Cl. New Mal KT3 ...... 38 E5
Sussex Cl. Reig RH2 .... 139 D8
Sussex Cl. 4 Twick TW1 ...... 6 B1
Sussex Ct. Addl KT15 .... 52 C5
Sussex Ct. Barnes SW13 .... 7 F5
Sussex Ct. Horsh RH13 ...... 217 E1
Sussex Ct. Knaph GU21 .... 68 C2
Sussex Gdns. Chess KT9 ...... 56 D4
Sussex Ho. Rich TW9 .... 6 F5
Sussex Lodge. Horsh RH12 217 C4
Sussex Manor Bsns Pk.
Crawl RH10 .... 182 A2
Sussex Pl. New Mal KT3 ...... 38 E5
Sussex Rd. Croy CR2 .... 61 D4
Sussex Rd. Knaph GU21 .... 68 C1
Sussex Rd. Mitch CR4 .... 41 E4
Sussex Rd. New Mal KT3 ...... 38 E5
Sussex Rd. S Croy CR2 .... 61 D4
Sussex Rd. W Wick BR4 .... 44 B1
Sussex Rd. Wallin SM5 .... 59 F4
Sutherland Ave. Bigg H TN16 83 E1
Sutherland Ave.
Jacobs GU4 .... 109 E7
Sutherland Ave.
Sunby TW16 .... 34 F7
Sutherland Chase.
N Asct SL5 .... 28 E7
Sutherland Dr.
Burgh GU1 & GU4 .... 110 A4
Sutherland Dr. Mitch SW19 . 40 D8
Sutherland Gdns.
N Cheam KT4 .... 39 B1
Sutherland Gdns.
Sunby TW16 .... 34 F7
Sutherland Gr.
Putney SW18 & SW19 ...... 19 F8
Sutherland Gr. Tedd TW11 .. 16 E3
Sutherland Hse. Rich TW10 . 17 C6
Sutherland Rd. Chisw W4 .... 7 E8
Sutherland Rd. Thorn H CR0 42 A2
Suttons Meadow.
G Book KT23 .... 94 A1
Swaby Rd.
Wands SW17 & SW18 .... 20 C6
Swaffield Prim Sch.
Wands SW18 .... 20 C8
Swaffield Rd. Wands SW18 . 20 C8
Swail House. 8
Epsom KT18 .... 76 D6
Swain Cl.
Streat SW16 & SW17 .... 21 B2

Swain Rd. Thorn H CR7 .... 42 C4
Swains Rd.
Mitch CR4 & SW17 & SW19 . 20 F1
Swale House. 2 Redh RH1 119 A3
Swale Rd. W Heath GU14 .... 84 E6
Swaledale. Easth RG12 .... 27 A4
Swaledale Cl. Crawl RH11 .. 201 C3
Swallands Rd. Catf SE6 .... 24 A5
Swallow Cl. Stain TW18 .... 12 F4
Swallow Cl. Witley GU8 ...... 170 E7
Swallow La. Dork RH5 .... 136 B1
Swallow Pk. Surb KT6 .... 56 F7
Swallow Rd. Crawl RH11 .... 201 C8
Swallow Rise. Knaph GU21 .. 68 C2
Swallowdale. New Add CR2 .. 62 D2
Swallowdale. Selsd CR2 ...... 62 D2
Swallowfield. Dorman RH7 165 A2
Swallowfield. Eng Gn TW20 . 11 B2
Swallowfield Ct. Penge SE20 . 23 D1
Swallowtail Rd.
Horsh RH12 .... 217 E6
Swan Barn Ct.
Haslem GU27 .... 208 D6
Swan Cl. Croy CR0 .... 42 E2
Swan Cl. Felt TW13 .... 15 E4
Swan Cl. Bellf GU1 .... 109 D3
Swan Ct. Leahd KT22 .... 95 B5
Swan Ct. Wands SW17 .... 20 C5
Swan House. Sandh GU47 .... 64 B7
Swan La. Charl RH6 .... 180 F7
Swan La. Guild GU1 .... 130 D7
Swan La. Sandh GU17 .... 64 B7
Swan Mill Gdns.
Pixham RH4 .... 115 D1
Swan Pl. Barnes SW13 .... 7 F5
Swan Rd. Felt TW13 .... 15 E4
Swan Sq. Horsh RH12 .... 217 C2
Swan St. Islew TW7 .... 6 B4
Swan Wlk. Horsh RH12 ...... 217 C2
Swan Wlk. Oat Pk TW17 ...... 34 E2
Swancote Gn. Easth RG12 .. 27 B4
Swandrift. Stain TW18 .... 12 F1
Swann Way. Broad H RH12 216 E3
Swans Ghyll. For Row RH18 206 E3
Swansea Rd.
Harl TW4 & TW6 .... 3 D1
Swansmere Sch.
Walt O T KT12 .... 35 C1
Swanton Gdns.
Putney SW19 .... 19 D7
Swanwick Cl. Rhampt SW15 18 F8
Swanworth La. Mickle RH5 115 B7
Swayne's La. Merrow GU1 . 110 E1
Swaynesland Rd.
Limps RH8 .... 123 F1
Swaything House.
Rhampt SW15 .... 7 F1
Swedish Sch. Barnes SW13 .. 7 F8
Sweeps Ditch Cl.
Stain TW18 .... 13 B1
Sweeps La. Egham TW20 .... 11 F3
Sweet La. Peasl GU5 .... 154 E8
Sweetbriar. Crowth RG11 .... 45 A7
Sweetwater Cl.
Sham Gn GU5 .... 152 D4
Sweetwater La. Ent Gn GU8 171 B2
Sweetwater La.
Sham Gn GU5 .... 152 D4
Swievelands Rd.
Bigg H TN16 .... 83 C1
Swift St. Sutton SM2 .... 59 B3
Swift La. Crawl RH11 .... 201 C8
Swift La. Windl GU19 .... 47 F3
Swift Rd. Felt TW13 .... 15 E4
Swift Rd. Heath E GU9 ...... 125 C7
Swift's Cl. Farnh GU10 ...... 126 B2
Swiftsden Way. Catf BR1 .... 24 E2
Swinburne Cres. Croy CR0 .. 43 C3
Swindon Rd. Harl TW6 .... 3 C2
Swindon Rd. Horsh RH12 .. 217 B4
Swinfield Cl. Felt TW13 .... 15 E4
Swingate Rd. H Bourn GU9 146 D8
Swinley County Prim Sch.
Ascot SL5 .... 29 A4
Swinley Forest Golf Club.
Brack SL5 .... 28 F2
Swinley Rd. Brack SL5 .... 28 D4
Swiss Cl. Rowl GU10 .... 146 A4
Swissland Hill.
Dorm Pk RH19 & RH7 ...... 185 E7
Switchback La. Rowl GU10 145 F4
Switchback La. Rowl GU10 146 A3
Swordfish Way.
Farnb GU14 .... 104 F7
Sycamore Ave. Horsh RH12 218 C6
Sycamore Cl. Carsh SM5 ...... 59 F6
Sycamore Cl. Crawl RH11 .. 181 C1
Sycamore Cl. Felt TW13 ...... 15 A5

Sycamore Cl. Fetch KT22 ...... 94 F5
Sycamore Cl. Friml GU16 ...... 65 E1
Sycamore Cl. Sandh GU17 .... 64 B8
Sycamore Ct. Farnc GU7 .... 150 E8
Sycamore Ct. For Hil SE26 .. 23 C4
Sycamore Ct. Hounsl TW4 ...... 4 E3
Sycamore Ct. Ottsh KT16 .... 51 C5
Sycamore Ct. 10
W Norw SW16 .... 22 A3
Sycamore Ct. Walt O T KT13 53 F7
Sycamore Dr. Ash V GU10 . 106 A7
Sycamore Dr. E Grins RH19 186 A1
Sycamore Dr. Friml GU16 .... 65 E1
Sycamore Dr. Wreccl GU10 146 A6
Sycamore Gdns. Mitch CR4 . 40 D7
Sycamore Gr. King U T KT3 .. 38 E6
Sycamore Gr. Penge SE20 .. 43 A8
Sycamore Lodge. 7
Charlt TW16 .... 14 F1
Sycamore Rd. Farnb GU14 .. 85 D2
Sycamore Rd. Guild GU1 .... 109 D1
Sycamore Rd.
Wimble SW19 & SW20 ...... 19 C2
Sycamore Rise. Brack RG12 27 D6
Sycamore Rise.
Nork KT17 & SM7 .... 77 D5
Sycamore Way. Tedd TW11 17 C2
Sycamore Wlk.
Eng Gn TW20 .... 11 B2
Sycamore Wlk.
Woodh RH2 .... 139 C6
Sycamores The. Blckw GU17 64 B5
Sycamores The. Farnb GU14 85 D3
Sydenham Ave. Penge SE26 23 B3
Sydenham High Sch For Girls.
For Hil SE26 .... 23 B4
Sydenham Hill. For Hil SE26 23 B5
Sydenham Hill Sta.
Dulw SE21 .... 22 F5
Sydenham House. 16
Surb KT6 .... 37 D2
Sydenham Ind Est.
Penge SE26 .... 23 F3
Sydenham Park Mansions.
For Hil SE26 .... 23 C5
Sydenham Park Rd.
For Hil SE23 & SE26 .... 23 C5
Sydenham Rd. Croy CR0 ...... 42 D2
Sydenham Rd.
For Hil SE26 & SE6 .... 23 D5
Sydenham Rd. Thorn H CR0 42 D2
Sydenham Rise.
For Hil SE23 .... 23 B6
Sydenham Sch. For Hil SE26 23 D5
Sydenham Sec Sch.
For Hil SE26 .... 23 B5
Sydenham Sta. For Hil SE26 23 C4
Sydenham Station App.
For Hil SE26 .... 23 C4
Sydmons Ct. For Hil SE23 .. 23 C8
Sydney Ave. Purley CR8 ...... 79 F7
Sydney Cl. Crowth RG11 ...... 45 C7
Sydney Cotts. Clayg KT10 .. 55 F4
Sydney Cres. Ashf TW15 .... 14 B2
Sydney Rd. E Bed TW14 ...... 15 A7
Sydney Rd. Guild GU1 .... 130 E8
Sydney Rd. Merton SW20 .... 39 C8
Sydney Rd. Rich TW10 & TW9 . 6 E3
Sydney Rd. Sutton SM1 .... 59 A6
Sydney Rd. Tedd TW11 .... 16 F3
Sydney Smith Ave.
Farnb GU14 .... 85 B1
Sydney Terr. Clayg KT10 ...... 55 F5
Sylva Ct. 3 Putney SW15 .... 19 D8
Sylvan Cl. Limps RH8 .... 123 B6
Sylvan Cl. Mayb GU22 .... 70 B2
Sylvan Cl. S Croy CR2 .... 62 B1
Sylvan Gdns. Surb KT6 .... 37 D3
Sylvan Rd. S Norw SE19 ...... 42 E8
Sylvan Rd. Crawl RH10 ...... 202 A4
Sylvan Rd. S Norw SE19 ...... 42 F8
Sylvan Ridge. Sandh GU47 .. 45 A1
Sylvan Way. Coney H BR4 .... 63 E6
Sylvan Way. Earls RH1 ...... 140 A8
Sylvanus. Easth RG12 .... 26 F2
Sylvaways Cl. Cran GU6 ...... 175 A3
Sylverdale Rd.
Croy CR0 & CR9 .... 61 B7
Sylverdale Rd. Purley CR8 .. 80 B6
Sylvia Cl. Bisley GU24 .... 68 A4
Syon Gate Way. Brent TW8 .. 6 A7
Syon Gate Way.
Hounsl TW7 & TW8 .... 6 A7
Syon Ho. Brent TW8 .... 6 C6
Syon La. Brent TW7 .... 6 B7
Syon La. Brent TW7 & TW8 .. 6 B7
Syon La. Hounsl TW7 .... 6 A7
Syon Lane Sta. Brent TW7 ...... 6 B7

Syon Lane Sta. Hounsl TW7 .. 6 A7
Syon Park Cotts. Brent TW8 . 6 C6
Syon Park Gdns. Hounsl TW7 . 5 F7
Syon Pl. Farnb GU14 .... 85 D4
Sythwood. Woking GU21 ...... 69 B2
Sythwood Cty Fst & Mid Sch.
Woking GU21 .... 69 B3
Szabo Cres. Flexf GU3 ...... 107 B1
Tabard House. Tedd KT1 ...... 37 C8
Tabarin Way. Nork KT17 ...... 77 C3
Tabor Ct. Cheam SM3 .... 58 E4
Tabor Gdns.
Cheam SM2 & SM3 .... 58 F3
Tabor Gr. Wimble SW19 ...... 19 F1
Tachbrook Rd. E Bed TW14 . 14 F8
Tadlow. King U T KT1 .... 38 A6
Tadmor Cl. Lo Hall TW16 .... 34 F5
Tadorne Rd. Tadw KT20 ...... 97 C5
Tadworth Ave. New Mal KT3 38 F4
Tadworth Cl. Tadw KT20 .... 97 D5
Tadworth Court Hospl.
Tadw KT20 .... 97 D6
Tadworth Cty Fst & Mid Sch.
Tadw KT20 .... 97 D5
Tadworth St. Tadw KT20 ...... 97 C5
Tadworth Sta. Tadw KT20 .... 97 C5
Taffy's How. Mitch CR4 .... 40 E6
Tait Rd. Croy CR0 & SE25 .... 42 E2
Talavera Cty Inf Sch.
Alder GU11 .... 105 B3
Talavera Cty Jun Sch.
Alder GU11 .... 105 B3
Talbot Cl. Mytch GU16 .... 86 A4
Talbot Cl. Reig RH2 .... 139 B8
Talbot La. Horsh RH12 ...... 217 C1
Talbot Lodge. Esher KT10 .... 55 A5
Talbot Pl. Bagsh GU19 .... 47 E4
Talbot Rd. Ashf TW15 .... 13 E3
Talbot Rd. Islew TW1 & TW7 .. 6 A3
Talbot Rd. Lingf RH7 .... 164 D4
Talbot Rd. M Bourn GU9 .... 146 B8
Talbot Rd. S Norw CR7 .... 42 D5
Talbot Rd. Twick TW2 .... 16 F7
Talbot Rd. Wallin SM5 .... 60 A5
Talcott Path. 12
Streat SW2 .... 22 A7
Taleworth Cl. Ashtd KT21 .... 95 D7
Taleworth Pk. Ashtd KT21 .... 95 D7
Taleworth Rd. Ashtd KT21 .... 95 E7
Talgarth Dr. Farnb GU14 ...... 85 D2
Taliesin Hts. Farnc GU7 .... 150 D6
Talisman Sq. For Hil SE26 .. 23 A4
Talisman Way. Nork KT17 .... 77 C3
Tall Elms Cl. Hayes BR2 ...... 44 F4
Tall Trees. Poyle SL3 .... 1 E6
Tall Trees. Thorn H SW16 .... 41 F6
Tallis Cl. Crawl RH11 .... 200 F3
Tally Rd. The Char RH8 ...... 123 E4
Talma Gdns. Twick TW2 ...... 16 E8
Talmage Cl. For Hil SE23 .... 23 C8
Talman Cl. Crawl RH11 ...... 200 E5
Tamar Cl. Worth RH10 ...... 202 C5
Tamarind Cl. Stough GU2 .. 109 A6
Tamarind Ct. 3
Egham TW20 .... 11 F3
Tamarisk Rise. Woki RG11 .. 25 C7
Tamerton Sq. Woking GU22 89 E8
Tamesa House.
Lo Hall TW17 .... 34 C5
Tamesis Gdns. New Mal KT4 57 E8
Tamian Ind Est. Hounsl TW4 . 4 C3
Tamian Way. Hounsl TW4 ...... 4 C3
Tamworth. Brack RG12 .... 27 D2
Tamworth La. Mitch CR4 ...... 41 B6
Tamworth Manor High Sch.
Mitch CR4 .... 41 D6
Tamworth Pk. Mitch CR4 .... 41 B6
Tamworth Pl. 3
Croy CR0 & CR9 .... 61 C8
Tamworth Rd.
Croy CR0 & CR9 .... 61 C8
Tandridge House Sch.
Horsh RH12 .... 216 F2
Tanbridge Pk. Horsh RH12 217 B1
Tanbridge Pl. Horsh RH12 217 B1
Tandridge Ct. Cater CR3 .... 101 A5
Tandridge Dr. Sutton SM2 .. 59 B4
Tandridge Gdns. Sander CR2 81 A6
Tandridge Golf Course.
Tand RH9 .... 122 B4
Tandridge La.
Tand RH7 & RH8 & RH9 .... 143 B4
Tandridge Rd. Warlgm CR6 101 D8
Tandridgehill La. Wold RH9 121 F6
Tanfield Ct. Horsh RH12 .... 217 B2
Tanfield Rd. Croy CR0 & CR9 61 C6
Tangier Ct. Alder GU11 ...... 104 F2
Tangier Rd. Guild GU1 .... 131 A8
Tangier Rd. Mortl TW10 .... 7 B4

Tangier Way. Burgh H KT20 77 E1
Tangier Wood. Burgh H KT20 77 E1
Tangle Oak. Felb RH19 184 E4
Tanglewood Cl. Longc KT16 50 B7
Tanglewood Cl. Mayb GU22 70 D3
Tanglewood Cl. S Croy CR0 62 C7
Tanglewood Ride. W End GU24 67 D7
Tanglewood Way. Felt TW13 15 B5
Tangley Dr. Woki RG11 25 B4
Tangley Gr. Rhampt SW15 18 F8
Tangley La. Worpl GU3 108 F6
Tangley Park Rd. Hampt TW12 15 F3
Tanglyn Ave. Shep Gn TW17 34 B4
Tangmere Gr. King U T KT2 17 D3
Tangmere Rd. Crawl RH11 200 F6
Tanhouse La. Woki RG11 25 A5
Tanhouse Rd. Oxted RH8 122 E3
Tanhurst House. 27 Streat SW2 21 E8
Tanhurst La. Wotton RH5 155 E2
Tank Rd. Sandh GU15 64 F5
Tanker Rd. Farnb GU14 85 B1
Tankerton Rd. Surb KT6 56 F8
Tankerton Terr. Thorn H CR0 41 F3
Tankerville Rd. Streat SW16 21 E1
Tanner House. 1 Merton SW19 40 C8
Tanner's Ct. Brock RH3 137 C5
Tanner's Hill. Brock RH3 137 B8
Tanners Cl. Walt O T KT12 35 B3
Tanners Dean. Leahd KT22 95 D5
Tanners La. Haslem GU27 208 C7
Tanners Meadow. Brock RH3 137 B5
Tanners Yd. Bagsh GU19 47 E3
Tannersfield. Shalf GU4 130 E1
Tannery Cl. Beck BR3 & CR0 43 D4
Tannery Cl. Slinfd RH13 215 D3
Tannery Cotts. Gomsh GU5 133 C4
Tannery La. Send GU23 90 E5
Tannery La. Send M GU23 90 E5
Tannery The. Redh RH1 118 F1
Tannsfeld Rd. For Hil SE26 23 D3
Tansy Cl. Merrow GU4 110 C3
Tantallon Rd. Balham SW12 21 A7
Tanyard Ave. E Grins RH19 206 A8
Tanyard Cl. Horsh RH13 217 E1
Tanyard La. Bramly GU5 151 F8
Tanyard Way. Horley RH6 161 B4
Tapestry Cl. Sutton SM2 59 B3
Taplow Ct. Mitch CR4 40 E5
Tapner's Rd. Leigh RH2 137 F3
Tapping Cl. 5 King U T KT2 18 A1
Tara Ct. Beck BR3 44 B7
Tara Pk. Chips CR5 98 F7
Taragon Ct. Stough GU2 109 A5
Tarbat Ct. 6 Sandh GU15 64 D8
Target Cl. Felt TW14 3 E1
Tarham Cl. Horley RH6 160 E5
Tarleton Gdns. For Hil SE23 23 B7
Tarmac Way. Harm UB7 2 B7
Tarn Rd. Hind GU26 188 E3
Tarnbrook Way. Brack RG12 27 E2
Tarquin House. For Hil SE26 23 A4
Tarragon Cl. W Heath GU14 84 C4
Tarragon Dr. Stough GU2 109 A5
Tarragon Gr. Penge SE26 23 D2
Tarrington Cl. Streat SW16 21 D5
Tartar Hill. Cobham KT11 73 B6
Tartar Rd. Cobham KT11 73 C6
Tasker Cl. Harl UB7 3 C7
Tasman Ct. Ashf TW16 14 E1
Tatchbury House. Rhampt SW15 7 F1
Tate Cl. Leahd KT22 95 C4
Tate Rd. Cheam SM1 59 A5
Tate's Way. Rudg RH12 214 D7
Tatham Ct. Crawl RH11 201 B1
Tatsfield Cty Prim Sch. Tats TN16 103 D6
Tatsfield La. Bigg H TN16 103 F6
Tattenham Cnr. Epsom KT18 77 A1
Tattenham Corner Rd. Lang V KT18 77 A1
Tattenham Corner Sta. Burgh H KT18 77 B1
Tattenham Cres. Burgh H KT18 77 B1
Tattenham Gr. Burgh H KT18 & KT20 97 B8
Tattenham Way. Burgh H KT18 & KT20 77 E2
Tattersall Cl. Woki RG11 25 E5
Taunton Ave. Cater CR3 100 F4
Taunton Ave. Hounsl TW3 5 C5
Taunton Ave. Wimble SW20 39 B7
Taunton Cl. Cheam SM3 40 A1
Taunton La. Coulsd CR5 100 B8
Taunton Manor High Sch. Coulsd CR5 100 B7
Tavistock Cl. Stain TW18 13 D1
Tavistock Cres. Mitch CR4 41 E5
Tavistock Ct. 1 Croy CR0 42 D1
Tavistock Gdns. Farnb GU14 85 B7
Tavistock Gr. Croy CR0 42 D2
Tavistock Rd. Beck BR2 44 F5
Tavistock Rd. Carsh SM5 40 D1
Tavistock Rd. Croy CR0 42 D1
Tavistock Wlk. Carsh SM5 40 D1
Tavy House. 3 Redh RH1 118 F2
Tawfield. Easth RG12 26 E2
Tawny Cl. Felt TW13 15 A5
Tay Cl. W Heath GU14 84 E6
Tayben Ave. Twick TW2 5 E1
Tayles Hill. Ewell KT17 57 F1
Taylor Ave. Rich TW9 7 B5
Taylor Cl. Hampt TW12 16 C3
Taylor Cl. Hounsl TW3 5 C6
Taylor Ct. Penge SE20 43 C7
Taylor House. 10 Streat SW2 22 A7
Taylor Rd. Ashtd KT21 75 D2
Taylor Rd. Mitch CR4 & SW19 20 E1
Taylor Rd. Wallin SM6 60 B5
Taylor Wlk. Crawl RH11 201 C6
Taylor's La. For Hil SE26 23 B4
Taylors Cres. Cran GU6 174 F3
Taylors Ct. Felt TW13 15 A6
Taymount Grange. For Hil SE23 23 C6
Taymount Rise. For Hil SE23 23 C6
Taynton Dr. Merst RH1 119 D6
Teal Cl. Horsh RH12 217 C5
Teal Cl. Selsd CR2 81 D8
Teal Ct. Dork RH4 136 A8
Teal Ct. Wallin SM6 60 C5
Tealing Dr. W Ewell KT19 57 D6
Teasel Cl. Crawl RH11 201 B3
Teasel Cl. Croy CR0 43 D1
Teazlewood Pk. Leahd KT22 75 A1
Tebbit Cl. Brack RG12 27 D7
Tebbs House. 14 Streat SW2 22 A8
Tedder Cl. Chess KT9 56 C5
Tedder Rd. S Croy CR2 62 D2
Teddington Cl. Epsom KT19 57 D1
Teddington Memorial Hospl. Tedd TW11 16 E2
Teddington Park Rd. Tedd TW11 16 F4
Teddington Pk. Tedd TW11 16 F3
Teddington Sch. Tedd TW11 17 C2
Teddington Sta. Tedd TW11 17 A2
Tedham La. Horne RH9 163 B7
Tees Cl. W Heath GU14 84 E6
Teesdale. Crawl RH11 201 C3
Teesdale Ave. Islew TW7 6 A6
Teesdale Gdns. Islew TW7 6 A6
Teesdale Gdns. S Norw SE25 42 E7
Teevan Cl. Croy CR0 43 A2
Teevan Rd. Croy CR0 & CR9 43 A2
Tegg's La. Pyrf GU22 70 F3
Tekels Ave. Camb GU15 65 D4
Tekels Ct. Camb GU15 65 E4
Tekels Way. Friml GU15 65 E3
Telconia Cl. Head Dn GU35 187 C4
Telegraph La. Clayg KT10 55 F5
Telegraph Rd. Putney SW15 19 C8
Telegraph Track. Wallin SM5 & SM6 60 A1
Telfei House. 8 Dulw SE21 22 E4
Telferscot Jun Mix & Inf Sch. Streat SW12 21 D7
Telferscot Rd. Streat SW12 21 D7
Telford Ave. Crowth RG11 45 C8
Telford Ave. Streat SW12 & SW2 21 E7
Telford Avenue Mansions. 7 Streat SW2 21 E7
Telford Cl. S Norw SE19 22 F2
Telford Ct. Guild GU1 130 F8
Telford Dr. Walt O T KT12 35 C2
Telford Parade Mansions. 8 Streat SW2 21 E7
Telford Pl. Crawl RH10 201 E5
Telford Rd. Twick TW4 16 A8
Telham Ct. 5 Crawl RH11 200 F3
Tellisford. Esher KT10 55 B6
Temperley Rd. Balham SW12 21 A8
Tempest Rd. Egham TW20 12 C2
Templar Cl. Sandh GU17 64 A8
Templar Ct. New Add CR0 62 E2
Templar Pl. Hampt TW12 16 A1
Temple Ave. Croy CR0 62 F7
Temple Bar Rd. Knaph GU21 88 F8
Temple Cl. Worth RH10 202 D5
Temple Ct. 9 Rich TW10 6 E2
Temple Field Cl. Addl KT15 52 B4
Temple Gdns. Egham TW18 32 F8
Temple La. Capel RH5 178 F5
Temple Market. Weyb KT13 53 B6
Temple Rd. Bigg H TN16 83 D2
Temple Rd. Croy CR0 61 D6
Temple Rd. Epsom KT19 76 D7
Temple Rd. Hounsl TW3 5 C3
Temple Rd. Rich TW9 6 F5
Temple Sheen. Mortl SW14 7 C2
Temple Sheen Rd. Mortl SW14 7 C3
Temple Way. Binf RG12 26 E8
Temple Way. Carsh SM1 59 D7
Temple Wood Dr. Redh RH1 118 F4
Temple's Cl. Farnh GU10 126 C1
Templecombe Mews. Mayb GU22 70 B3
Templecombe Way. Merton SM4 39 E4
Templecroft. Ashf TW15 14 D2
Templedene. Beck BR2 44 D7
Templedene Ave. Stain TW18 13 C2
Templeman Cl. Purley CR8 80 B3
Templemere. Oat Pk KT13 53 D7
Templeton Cl. S Norw CR7 & SE19 42 D8
Templewood House. Redh RH1 118 F4
Ten Acre. Woking GU21 69 A1
Ten Acre La. Thorpe TW20 32 C7
Ten Acres. Fetch KT22 94 D3
Ten Acres Cl. Fetch KT22 94 D3
Tenbury Ct. Streat SW12 21 D7
Tenby Dr. Ascot SL5 29 D4
Tenby Rd. Friml GU16 86 A8
Tenchley's La. Limps RH8 123 D4
Tenchley's La. The Char RH8 123 E2
Tenham Ave. Streat SW2 21 D6
Tennison Cl. Coulsd CR5 100 B7
Tennison Rd. Croy SE25 42 F4
Tennison Rd. S Norw SE25 42 F4
Tennyson Ave. Twick TW1 16 F7
Tennyson Ave. W Barn KT3 39 B4
Tennyson Cl. Crawl RH10 202 B8
Tennyson Cl. Felt TW14 4 A1
Tennyson Cl. Horsh RH12 217 E6
Tennyson Ct. 3 Rich TW10 17 D4
Tennyson Rd. Addl KT15 52 E6
Tennyson Rd. Ashf TW15 13 E3
Tennyson Rd. Hounsl TW3 5 C5
Tennyson Rd. Penge SE20 23 D1
Tennyson Rd. Wimble SW19 20 C2
Tennyson Rise. E Grins RH19 205 C8
Tennyson's La. Haslem GU27 208 E4
Tennyson's La. Lurg GU27 209 A2
Tennysons. Haslem GU27 208 E4
Tensing Ct. Stan TW19 13 E7
Tenterden Gdns. Croy CR0 43 A2
Tenterden Rd. Croy CR0 43 A2
Tern Rd. Crawl RH11 200 D5
Terra Cotta Rd. S Godst RH9 142 C5
Terrace Gdns. Barnes SW13 7 F5
Terrace La. Rich TW10 6 E1
Terrace Rd. Walt O T KT12 35 B3
Terrace The. Addl KT15 52 E5
Terrace The. Ascot SL5 29 D4
Terrace The. Barnes SW13 & SW14 7 E5
Terrace The. Camb GU15 65 A5
Terrace The. Crowth RG11 45 D5
Terrace The. Mortl SW13 & SW14 7 E5
Terrace The. Old Wok GU22 90 A6
Terrace The. Woki RG11 25 B6
Terrapin Ct. Up Toot SW17 21 B5
Terrapin Rd. Up Toot SW17 21 B5
Terrapins. Surb KT6 37 D2
Terry House. Streat SW2 22 A7
Terry Rd. Crawl RH11 201 B1
Testard Rd. Guild GU2 130 C7
Testers Cl. Oxted RH8 123 B3
Teviot Cl. Stough GU2 109 A4
Tewkesbury Ave. For Hil SE23 23 B8
Tewkesbury Cl. Byfl KT14 71 D8
Tewkesbury Rd. Carsh SM5 40 D1
Thackeray Cl. Wimble SW19 19 D1
Thackeray Manor. Sutton SM1 59 C5
Thackery Lodge. E Bed TW14 3 D1
Thakeham Cl. For Hil SE26 23 B3
Thames Ave. Thorpe KT16 33 A6
Thames Bank. Mortl SW14 7 C5
Thames Cl. Chert KT16 33 C2
Thames Cl. E Mole TW12 36 B7
Thames Cl. W Heath GU14 84 E6
Thames Ct. E Mole KT8 36 B7
Thames Ditton Cty Fst Sch. Thame D KT7 36 F3
Thames Ditton & Esher Golf Club. Esher KT10 55 D8
Thames Ditton Hospl. Thame D KT7 36 F2
Thames Ditton Island. Thame D KT7 37 A4
Thames Ditton Jun Sch. Thame D KT7 36 F2
Thames Ditton Sta. Thame D KT7 36 F2
Thames Eyot. 7 Twick TW1 17 A7
Thames Haven. King U T KT6 37 D4
Thames Link House. 6 Rich TW9 6 E3
Thames Mead. Walt O T KT12 35 A2
Thames Meadow. E Mole KT8 36 A6
Thames Meadow. Lo Hall KT12 & TW17 34 E1
Thames Rd. Brent W4 7 B8
Thames Rd. Chisw W4 7 B8
Thames Side. King U T KT1 37 D8
Thames Side. Laleh KT16 & TW18 33 C5
Thames Side. Stain TW18 12 F2
Thames Side. Thame D KT7 37 B3
Thames St. E Mole TW12 36 B7
Thames St. King U T KT1 & KT2 37 D7
Thames St. Stain TW18 12 F3
Thames St. Sunby TW16 35 B6
Thames St. Walt O T KT12 34 F2
Thames St. Weyb KT13 53 B7
Thames View House. Walt O T KT12 35 A3
Thames Village. Chisw W4 7 C6
Thamesfield Ct. Shep TW17 34 C2
Thamesgate Cl. Tedd TW10 17 B4
Thameside. Tedd TW11 17 D1
Thamesmead Sch. Shep TW17 34 D3
Thamespoint. Tedd TW11 17 D1
Thamesvale Cl. Hounsl TW3 5 A5
Thanescroft Gdns. S Croy CR0 61 E7
Thanet House. 1 W Norw SE27 22 B5
Thanet Pl. Croy CR0 61 C6
Tharp Rd. Wallin SM6 60 D5
Thatcher Cl. Crawl RH10 201 D3
Thatchers Cl. Horley RH6 161 B5
Thatchers Cl. Horsh RH12 217 E4
Thatchers La. Worpl GU3 108 E8
Thatchers Way. Islew TW7 5 D2
Thaxted Pl. 7 Wimble SW20 19 D1
Thayers Farm Rd. Penge BR3 43 E8
Theal Cl. Sandh GU15 64 D8
Theatre Rd. Farnb GU14 105 B8
Thelma Gr. Tedd TW11 17 A2
Thelton Ave. Broad H RH12 216 D3
Theobald Rd. Thorn H CR0 & CR9 61 B8
Theobalds Way. Friml GU16 66 C3
Thepps Cl. S Nutf RH1 140 F6
Therapia La. Thorn H CR0 41 E3
Therapia La. Wallin CR0 & CR4 41 D2
Therapia La. Wallin CR0 41 E2
Theresa's Wlk. S Croy CR2 61 D2
Therfield Sch. Leahd KT22 95 A8
Thesiger Rd. Penge BR3 & SE20 23 D1
Thetford Ct. Dulw SE21 23 B6
Thetford Rd. Ashf TW15 13 E5
Thetford Rd. New Mal KT3 38 E4
Thetis Terr. Rich TW9 7 A8
Theydon Cl. Crawl RH10 202 A4
Thibet Rd. Sandh GU17 64 C8
Thicket Cres. Sutton SM1 59 C6
Thicket Gr. Penge SE20 23 A1
Thicket Rd. Penge SE19 & SE20 23 B1
Thicket Rd. Sutton SM1 59 C6
Thickthorne La. Stain TW18 13 C1
Third Cl. E Mole KT8 36 C5
Third Cross Rd. Twick TW2 16 D6
Thirlmere Cl. Farnb GU14 84 E4
Thirlmere Cl. Thor L TW20 12 B1
Thirlmere House. Islew TW1 5 F2
Thirlmere Rd. Crawl RH11 200 D4
Thirlmere Rd. Streat SW16 21 D4
Thirlmere Rise. Broml BR1 24 F2
Thirlmere Wlk. Friml GU15 66 D4
Thirsk Rd. Mitch CR4 21 A1
Thirsk Rd. S Norw SE25 42 D5
Thistle Way. Smallf RH6 162 C3
Thistlecroft Rd. Hersh KT12 54 C6
Thistledene. Thame D KT7 36 E3
Thistledene. W Byfl KT14 70 F6
Thistlewood Cres. New Add CR0 82 D7
Thistleworth Cl. Hounsl TW7 5 D7
Thistley La. Cran GU6 174 E4
Thomas Ave. Cater CR3 100 C6
Thomas Becket Jun Mix & Inf Sch. Croy SE25 43 A3
Thomas Bennett Comm Coll. Crawl RH10 201 D3
Thomas Bennett Comm Sch. Crawl RH10 201 E2
Thomas' La. Catf SE6 24 A8
Thomas Moore House. Reig RH2 118 C1
Thomas More RC High Sch. Purley CR8 61 A1
Thomas Pooley Ct. Surb KT6 37 E2
Thomas Wall Cl. Sutton SM1 59 B5
Thompson Ave. Rich TW9 7 A4
Thompson Ct. 16 Crawl RH11 201 B1
Thompson's La. Burrh GU24 49 D2
Thompsons Cl. Pirb GU24 87 D4
Thomson Cres. Thorn H CR0 42 A1
Thorburn Chase. Sandh GU15 64 E6
Thorburn Way. Mitch SW19 40 D8
Thorkhill Gdns. Thame D KT7 37 B1
Thorkhill Rd. Thame D KT7 37 B2
Thorley Cl. Pyrf KT14 71 A5
Thorley Gdns. Pyrf KT14 71 A5
Thorn Bank. Onsl V GU2 130 A7
Thorn Cl. Rowl GU10 145 F4
Thorn Rd. Rowl GU10 146 A5
Thornash Cl. Horse GU21 69 C4
Thornash Rd. Horse GU21 69 C4
Thornash Way. Horse GU21 69 C4
Thornbank Cl. Stan TW19 2 A2
Thornbury Ave. Hounsl TW7 5 D7
Thornbury Cl. Crowth RG11 45 B5
Thornbury Ct. Hounsl TW7 5 E7
Thornbury Ct. Whytlf CR3 100 F7
Thornbury Rd. Hounsl TW7 5 D6
Thorncombe St. Bramly GU5 & GU8 151 E2
Thorncroft. Eng Gn TW20 11 C1
Thorncroft Cl. Coulsd CR5 100 A8
Thorncroft Rd. Sutton SM1 59 B6
Thorndean St. Wands SW18 20 C6
Thorndon Gdns. Worc Pk KT19 57 E6
Thorndown La. Windl GU20 48 D3
Thorndyke Cl. Worth RH10 202 D5
Thorne Cl. Crowth RG11 45 A7
Thorne Cl. Littlt TW15 14 C1
Thorne St. Mortl SW13 & SW14 7 E4
Thorne's Cl. Beck BR3 44 C6
Thorneloe Gdns. Croy CR0 & CR9 61 B5
Thorneycroft Cl. Walt O T KT12 35 C3
Thornfield Gn. Hawley GU17 64 F3
Thornfield Rd. Banstd SM7 78 A2
Thornhill. Brack RG12 27 E5
Thornhill Ave. Surb KT6 56 E8
Thornhill Rd. Alder GU11 105 D4
Thornhill Rd. Surb KT6 56 F8
Thornhill Rd. Thorn H CR0 42 C2
Thornhill Way. Shep Gn TW17 34 A4
Thornlaw Rd. W Norw SE27 22 B4
Thornleas Pl. E Hors KT24 92 E1
Thornsbeach Rd. Catf SE6 24 C6
Thornsett Pl. Penge SE20 43 B7
Thornsett Rd. Penge SE20 43 B7
Thornsett Rd. Wands SW18 20 B7
Thornsett Terr. Penge SE20 43 B7
Thornton Ave. Streat SW2 21 D7
Thornton Ave. Thorn H CR0 41 F3
Thornton Cl. Horley RH6 160 E3
Thornton Cl. Stough GU2 109 A4
Thornton Cres. Coulsd CR5 100 A8
Thornton Ct. W Barn SW20 39 D4
Thornton Dene. Beck BR3 44 A7
Thornton Gdns. Streat SW12 21 D7
Thornton Heath Sta. Thorn H CR7 42 C5

Thornton Hill. Wimble SW19 19 E1
Thornton Pl. Horley RH6 160 F3
Thornton Rd. Carsh SM5 40 D1
Thornton Rd. Mortl SW14 7 D4
Thornton Rd. Streat SW12 & SW2 21 D7
Thornton Rd. Thorn H CR0 & CR7 & CR9 41 F3
Thornton Rd. Wimble SW19 19 D1
Thornton Rd E. Wimble SW19 19 D2
Thornton Row. Thorn H CR7 42 A4
Thornycroft Ct. Rich TW9 6 F5
Thornyhurst Rd. Mytch GU16 86 A4
Thorold Cl. Selsd CR0 & CR2 62 D1
Thorold House. 6 Streat SW2 21 E8
Thorold Rd. Farnh GU9 125 C3
Thoroughfare The. Walt o t H KT20 97 A3
Thorpe By-Pass. Egham KT16 & TW20 32 B6
Thorpe C of E Fst Sch. Egham TW20 32 B6
Thorpe Cl. For Hil SE26 23 D4
Thorpe Cl. New Add CR0 82 C8
Thorpe Cl. Woki RG11 25 A3
Thorpe Ind Est. Thorpe TW20 32 C8
Thorpe Ind Pk. Thorpe TW20 32 C8
Thorpe Lea Prim Sch. Egham TW20 12 D2
Thorpe Lea Rd. Egham TW20 12 C2
Thorpe Lea Rd. Thor L TW20 12 C2
Thorpe Park. Thorpe TW20 32 E5
Thorpe Rd. Chert KT16 32 D4
Thorpe Rd. Egham TW18 & TW20 12 D3
Thorpe Rd. King U T KT2 17 E1
Thorpes Cl. Stough GU2 109 A4
Thorpeside Cl. Egham TW18 & TW20 32 E7
Thorpewood Ave. For Hil SE23 & SE26 23 B6
Thorsden Cl. Woking GU22 89 E8
Thorsden Ct. 10 Woking GU22 69 E1
Thorsden Way. 2 W Norw SE19 22 E3
Thrale Almhouses. Streat SW16 21 E3
Thrale Rd. Streat SW16 21 C3
Three Acres. Horsh RH12 217 A1
Three Arch Rd. Earls RH1 140 A5
Three Bridges Cty Fst Sch. Crawl RH10 202 A7
Three Bridges Cty Mid Sch. Crawl RH10 201 F6
Three Bridges Rd. Crawl RH10 202 A6
Three Bridges Sta. Crawl RH10 202 B6
Three Gates. Merrow GU1 110 C3
Three Gates La. Haslem GU27 208 E8
Three Mile Rd. Ewh GU6 & RH5 155 A2
Three Pears Rd. Merrow GU1 110 E1
Three Stiles Rd. Farnh GU9 124 F3
Three Ways. Binst GU10 166 D6
Threestile Rd. Warn RH12 197 F1
Threshfield. Easth RG12 27 A4
Thriffwood. For Hil SE23 & SE26 23 D5
Thrift Vale. Merrow GU4 110 D4
Thrigby Rd. Chess KT9 56 F4
Throat Handpost Cnr The. Woki RG11 25 A1
Throwley Rd. Sutton SM1 59 B5
Throwley Way. Sutton SM1 59 B5
Thrupp Cl. Mitch CR4 41 B7
Thrupps Ave. Hersh KT12 54 D5
Thrupps La. Hersh KT12 54 D5
Thundery Hill. The San GU10 126 F4
Thurbans Rd. M Bourn GU9 146 A7
Thurbarn Rd. Catf SE6 24 B3
Thurbarns Hill. Bear Gn RH5 157 E1
Thurlby Rd. W Norw SE27 22 A4
Thurleigh Rd. Balham SW11 & SW12 20 F8
Thurleston Ave. Merton SM4 39 E4
Thurlestone Cl. Shep TW17 34 C3
Thurlestone Par. Shep TW17 34 C3
Thurlestone Rd. W Norw SE27 22 A4
Thurlow Hill. W Norw SE21 22 C6
Thurlow House. 17 Streat SW16 21 E5
Thurlow Park Rd. Dulw SE21 & SE24 22 C6
Thurlow Park Rd. W Norw SE21 & SE24 22 C6
Thurlow Park Sch. W Norw SE27 22 B6
Thurlow Towers. W Norw SE27 22 A5
Thurlow Wlk. Cran GU6 174 E1
Thurlton Ct. Horse GU21 69 E3
Thurnby Ct. Twick TW2 16 E5
Thurne Way. Rudg RH12 214 D7
Thurnham Way. Tadw KT20 97 D7
Thursby Rd. Woking GU21 69 A1
Thursley Cres. New Add CR0 63 D3
Thursley Gdns. Putney SW19 19 D6
Thursley House. 3 King U T KT2 18 B1
Thursley House. 13 Streat SW2 21 F8
Thursley Rd. Churt GU10 & GU8 168 C3
Thursley Rd. Thursl GU8 & GU10 169 B6
Thurso St. Up Toot SW17 20 D4
Thurstan Rd. Wimble SW20 19 B1
Thurston House. Beck BR3 24 B2
Thurza Ct. Hounsl TW7 5 F5
Thyme Ct. W Heath GU14 84 C5
Tibbet's Cnr. Putney SW19 19 D8
Tibbet's Ride. Putney SW19 19 D8
Tibbets Cl. Putney SW19 19 D7
Ticehurst Cl. Worth RH10 202 E6
Ticehurst Rd. For Hil SE23 23 E6
Tichborne Cl. Blckw GU17 64 D5
Tichborne Pl. Alder GU12 126 D8
Tichbourne Cl. Friml GU16 65 F3
Tichmarsh. Epsom KT19 57 C1
Tidenham Gdns. S Croy CR0 61 E7
Tideswell Rd. Croy CR0 63 A7
Tideway Cl. Rich TW10 17 C4
Tideway Yd. Mortl SW13 7 E5
Tidwells Lea. Wink RG12 27 E8
Tiepigs La. Coney H BR2 & BR4 44 F1
Tiepigs La. Hayes BR2 & BR4 44 F1
Tierney Ct. 1 Croy CR0 61 F8
Tierney Rd. Streat SW2 21 E7
Tierney Terr. Streat SW2 21 E7
Tiffin Girls' Sch. King U T KT2 17 E2
Tiffin Sch. King U T KT2 37 F7
Tilburstow Cotts. Godst RH9 121 C3
Tilburstow Hill Rd. Blind H RH9 142 D5
Tilburstow Hill Rd. S Godst RH9 142 D5
Tile Barn Cl. W Heath GU14 85 A5
Tilehouse Rd. Guild GU4 130 E5
Tilehurst La. Betch RH3 & RH5 136 F5
Tilehurst La. Dork RH3 & RH5 136 F5
Tilehurst Rd. Cheam SM3 58 E5
Tilehurst Rd. Wands SW17 & SW18 20 D7
Tiler's Way. Dovgn RH1 139 C5
Tilford Ave. New Add CR0 63 C2
Tilford Gdns. Putney SW19 19 D7
Tilford House. 11 Streat SW2 21 F8
Tilford Rd. Beac H GU10 & GU26 188 E6
Tilford Rd. Hind GU10 & GU26 188 E6
Tilford Rd. M Bourn GU10 & GU9 146 F7
Tilford Rd. Rushm GU10 168 C4
Tilford Rd. Tilf GU10 147 C4
Tilford St. Tilf GU10 147 D5
Tilgate Comm. Bletch RH1 120 C2
Tilgate Dr. Crawl RH10 & RH11 201 E2
Tilgate Forest Bsns Ctr. Crawl RH11 201 D1
Tilgate Forest Golf Course. Crawl RH10 202 A2
Tilgate Forest Recn Ctr. Crawl RH10 201 D1
Tilgate Par. Crawl RH10 201 E3
Tilgate Pl. Crawl RH10 201 E3
Tilgate Way. Crawl RH10 201 E3
Tilgates Cotts. Bletch RH1 120 C3
Tilletts La. Warn RH12 216 E8
Tilley La. Head KT18 96 C4
Tillingbourne Cty Jun Sch. Chil GU4 131 B2
Tillingbourne Rd. Shalf GU4 130 E3
Tillingdown Hill. Cater CR3 101 A5
Tillingdown La. Cater CR3 101 B2
Tillingdown La. Wold CR3 101 B3
Tillman House. 8 Streat SW2 21 F7
Tillotson Cl. Worth RH10 202 D5
Tilly's La. Stain TW18 12 F4
Tilney Ct. King U T KT6 37 D4
Tilson Gdns. Streat SW2 & SW4 21 E8
Tilson House. Streat SW2 21 E8
Tilt Cl. Stk D'A KT11 73 E3
Tilt Meadow. Cobham KT11 73 E3
Tilt Rd. Cobham KT11 73 D3
Tilthams Corner Rd. Shalf GU7 & GU7 151 C8
Tilthams Gn. Shalf GU7 151 B8
Tiltview. Cobham KT11 73 C4
Tiltwood Dr. Crawl D RH10 204 C8
Timber Bank. Friml GU16 86 A6
Timber Cl. G Book KT23 114 C8
Timber Cl. Pyrf GU22 70 F5
Timber Ct. Horsh RH12 217 C3
Timber Hill. Ashtd KT21 95 E8
Timber Hill Rd. Cater CR3 101 A3
Timber La. Cater CR3 101 A3
Timbercroft. Worc Pk KT19 57 E6
Timberham Farm Rd. Hookw RH6 181 D8
Timberham Link. Crawl RH6 181 E8
Timberham Way. Crawl RH6 181 E8
Timberlands. 14 Crawl RH11 201 B1
Timberling Gdns. S Croy CR2 61 D1
Timbermill Ct. Shottm GU27 207 F6
Timberslip Dr. Wallin SM6 60 D2
Timbertop Rd. Bigg H TN16 83 C1
Times Sq. Sutton SM1 59 B5
Timline Gn. Brack RG12 27 F7
Timperley Ct. Redh RH1 118 E3
Timperley Gdns. Redh RH1 118 E3
Timsbury Wlk. 5 Rhampt SW15 19 A7
Timsway. Egham TW18 12 F3
Tina Ct. W Norw SW16 22 A5
Tindale Cl. S Croy CR2 80 D8
Tinsey Cl. Egham TW20 12 B3
Tinsley Gn. Crawl RH10 182 B4
Tinsley La. Crawl RH10 182 A1
Tinsley La N. Crawl RH10 182 B3
Tinsley La S. Crawl RH10 202 A8
Tintagel Cl. Epsom KT17 76 F5
Tintagel Ct. Horsh RH13 217 D1
Tintagel Dr. Friml GU16 65 F1
Tintagel Way. Woking GU22 70 A3
Tintells La. W Hors KT24 112 B7
Tintern Cl. Merton SW19 20 C2
Tintern Rd. Carsh SM5 40 D1
Tintern Rd. Crawl RH11 201 A4
Tippits Mead. Binf RG12 26 D8
Tipton Dr. S Croy CR0 61 E6
Tiree Path. Crawl RH11 201 B3
Tirlemont Rd. Croy CR2 61 C3
Tirrell Rd. Thorn H CR0 42 C3
Tisbury Rd. Thorn H SW16 41 E7
Titchfield Rd. Carsh SM5 40 D1
Titchfield Wlk. Carsh SM5 40 D2
Titchwell Rd. Wands SW18 20 D7
Tite Hill. Eng Gn TW20 11 D3
Tithe Barn Cl. King U T KT2 37 F8
Tithe Barn The. E Clan GU4 111 D4
Tithe La. Wray TW19 1 A1
Tithe Meadows. Went GU25 31 D3
Tithe Orch. Felb RH19 184 E4
Tithepit Shaw La. Warlgm CR2 & CR6 81 B3
Titlarks Hill Rd. Sunnin SL5 30 B1
Titmus Dr. Crawl RH10 201 F2
Titsey Cnr. Limps RH8 123 B7
Titsey Hill. Titsey CR6 & RH8 103 B4
Titsey Rd. Limps RH8 123 B8
Titsey Rd. Titsey RH8 103 B1
Tiverton Rd. Hounsl TW3 5 C5
Tiverton Way. Chess KT9 56 D5
Tiverton Way. Friml GU16 65 F1
Tivoli Rd. Hounsl TW4 4 E3
Tivoli Rd. W Norw SE19 & 27 22 C3
Toad La. Hawley GU17 64 E4
Tobias Sch of Art. E Grins RH19 205 E6
Toby Way. Tolw KT5 & KT6 57 B8
Todds Cl. Horley RH6 160 E5
Toftwood Cl. Crawl RH10 202 C5
Toll Bar Ct. Sutton SM2 59 B2
Toll Gdns. Brack RG12 27 F6
Tolldene Cl. Knaph GU21 68 E2
Tollers La. Coulsd CR5 99 F8
Tollgate. Merrow GU1 110 D1
Tollgate Ave. Earls RH1 139 F4
Tollgate Ct. Earls RH1 139 F4
Tollgate Dr. Dulw SE21 22 E6
Tollgate Hill. Crawl RH11 201 C1
Tollgate Jun Mix & Inf Sch. Croy CR0 43 C3
Tollgate Rd. Dork RH4 136 B4
Tollhouse La. Wallin SM6 60 C2
Tolson Ho. 2 Islew TW7 6 A4
Tolson Rd. Islew TW7 6 A4
Tolvaddon. Woking GU21 69 A2
Tolverne Rd. Wimble SW20 39 C8
Tolworth Cl. Tolw KT6 38 B1
Tolworth Girls' Sch. Surb KT6 56 F7
Tolworth Hospl. Tolw KT6 57 A8
Tolworth Inf Sch. Surb KT6 37 F1
Tolworth Jun Sch. Surb KT6 37 F1
Tolworth Park Rd. Surb KT6 56 F8
Tolworth Rd. Surb KT6 56 E8
Tolworth Rise N. Tolw KT5 38 B1
Tolworth Rise S. Tolw KT5 38 B1
Tolworth Sta. Tolw KT5 57 B8
Tolworth Underpass. Tolw KT5 & KT6 57 B8
Tomlin Cl. Epsom KT19 76 D8
Tomlin Ct. Epsom KT19 76 D8
Tomlins Ave. Friml GU16 65 F2
Tomlinscote Sch. Friml GU16 66 A1
Tomlinscote Way. Friml GU16 66 A2
Tompset's Bank. For Row RH18 206 F1
Tonbridge Cl. Woodm SM7 78 F5
Tonbridge Rd. E Mole KT12 & KT8 35 F5
Tonfield Rd. Cheam SM3 39 F1
Tonge Cl. Beck BR3 44 A4
Tongham Meadows. Tongh GU10 126 F7
Tongham Rd. Alder GU12 126 D8
Tongham Rd. Farnh GU10 126 C4
Tonstall Rd. Epsom KT19 76 D8
Tonstall Rd. Mitch CR4 41 A7
Tooting Bec Gdns. Streat SW16 21 D4
Tooting Bec Hospl. Up Toot SW17 21 B4
Tooting Bec Rd. Streat SW16 21 B4
Tooting Bec Rd. Up Toot SW17 21 B4
Tooting Bec Sta. Up Toot SW17 21 A5
Tooting Broadway. Up Toot SW17 20 F3
Tooting Broadway Sta. Up Toot SW17 20 E3
Tooting Gr. Up Toot SW17 20 E3
Tooting High St. Up Toot SW17 & SW19 20 E3
Tooting Mkt. Up Toot SW17 20 F4
Tooting Sta. Mitch SW17 20 F2
Tootswood Rd. Beck BR2 & BR3 44 E5
Top Pk. Beck BR3 44 E4
Top Terrace Rd. Farnb GU14 105 A8
Topaz House. New Mal KT4 38 D1
Topiary Sq. Rich TW9 6 F4
Topiary The. Ashtd KT21 95 E7
Topiary The. Farnb GU14 84 E3
Toplady Pl. Heath E GU9 125 C7
Topsham Rd. Up Toot SW17 21 A4
Tor La. Whit V KT13 72 D8
Tor Rd. Farnh GU9 124 F2
Torcross Dr. For Hil SE23 23 C6
Torin Ct. Eng Gn TW20 11 C3
Torland Dr. Oxsh KT22 74 D6
Tormead Cl. Sutton SM1 59 A4
Tormead Rd. Guild GU1 109 F1
Tormead Sch. Guild GU1 109 F1
Toronto Dr. Smallf RH6 162 A3
Torr Rd. Penge SE20 23 D1
Torre Wlk. Carsh SM5 40 E1
Torridge Rd. Bra Hil SL3 1 B8
Torridge Rd. Thorn H CR7 42 B4
Torridon Cl. Woking GU21 69 B2
Torridon Inf Sch. Catf SE6 24 D6
Torridon Jun Sch. Catf SE6 24 D6
Torridon Rd. Catf SE13 & SE6 24 D7
Torrington Cl. Clayg KT10 55 E4
Torrington Ct. Penge SE26 23 A3
Torrington Rd. Clayg KT10 55 E4
Torrington Sq. Croy CR0 42 D2
Torrington Way. Morden SM4 40 A3
Torwood La. Whytlf CR3 100 F8
Totford La. Putt GU10 127 E4
Totham Lodge. Wimble SW20 39 B8
Totland Cl. W Heath GU14 85 A6
Tottenham Rd. Farnc GU7 150 E6
Tottenham Wlk. Sandh GU15 45 D1
Totterdown St. Up Toot SW17 20 F3
Totton Rd. Thorn H CR7 42 A6
Tournai Cl. Farnb GU11 105 E7
Toutley Rd. Woki RG11 25 A8
Tovil Cl. Penge SE20 43 B7
Tower Cl. E Grins RH19 185 E2
Tower Cl. Hind GU26 188 E4
Tower Cl. Horley RH6 160 F3
Tower Cl. Horse GU21 69 D2
Tower Cl. Penge SE20 23 B1
Tower Cotts. Esher KT10 54 F1
Tower Ct. E Grins RH19 185 E2
Tower Gr. Oat Pk KT13 53 E8
Tower Hill. Dork RH4 136 B5
Tower Hill. Farnb GU14 85 A3
Tower Hill Cty Prim Sch. Farnb GU14 84 F3
Tower Hill Rd. Dork RH4 136 B5
Tower Hill Rise. Gomsh GU5 133 C3
Tower Rd. Crawl RH12 218 F8
Tower Rd. Hind GU26 188 E4
Tower Rd. Tadw KT20 97 C4
Tower Rd. Twick TW1 & TW2 16 F5
Tower Rise. Rich TW9 6 E4
Tower View. Croy CR0 43 E2
Towerhill. Gomsh GU5 133 C3
Towers Dr. Crowth RG11 45 B4
Towers Pl. Rich TW10 6 E2
Towers The. Kenley CR8 80 C4
Towers The. 1 Rich TW9 6 F3
Towers Wlk. Whit V KT13 53 B4
Towfield Ct. Felt TW13 15 F6
Towfield Rd. Felt TW13 15 F6
Town Barn Rd. Crawl RH11 201 C7
Town End Cl. Cater CR3 100 E5
Town End Cl. Godal GU7 150 E4
Town End St. Godal GU7 150 E4
Town Farm Cty Prim Sch . Stan TW19 13 D8
Town Farm Way. Stan TW19 13 D8
Town Hill. Lingf RH7 164 E4
Town La. Stan TW19 13 D7
Town Mead. Bletch RH1 120 D2
Town Mead. Crawl RH11 201 D7
Town Meadow. Brent TW8 6 D7
Town Quay. Laleh TW18 33 C6
Town Sq. Brack RG12 27 C7
Town Sq. Camb GU15 65 C6
Town Sq. 3 Woking GU21 69 F2
Town Tree Rd. Ashf TW15 14 A3
Townend. Cater CR3 100 E5
Townend Ct. Broml BR1 44 F8
Townfield Ct. Dork RH4 136 A6
Townfield Rd. Dork RH4 136 A6
Towngate. Cobham KT11 73 E4
Townmead Rd. Rich TW9 7 B5
Townsend Cl. Brack RG12 27 E4
Townsend La. Old Wok GU22 90 B6
Townsend Rd. Ashf TW15 13 E3
Townshend Rd. Rich TW9 6 F3
Townshend Terr. Rich TW9 6 F3
Townshott Cl. G Book KT23 94 A1
Towpath Way. Croy CR0 & SE25 42 F4
Towton Rd. W Norw SE27 22 C6
Toynbee Rd. Merton SW19 & SW20 39 E8
Toynbee Rd. Wimble SW19 & SW20 39 E8
Tracery The. Banstd SM7 78 B4
Tracious Cl. Horse GU21 69 B3
Traemore Ct. W Norw SW16 22 A5
Trafalgar Ave. N Cheam KT4 & SM3 & SM4 39 D1
Trafalgar Ct. Cobham KT11 73 A6
Trafalgar Ct. Farnh GU9 125 C1
Trafalgar Ct. Hounsl TW3 4 F4
Trafalgar Ct. W Barn KT3 39 B6
Trafalgar Cty Inf Prim Sch. Horsh RH12 217 B4
Trafalgar Dr. Walt O T KT12 54 B7
Trafalgar Inf Sch. Twick TW2 16 D6
Trafalgar Jun Sch. Twick TW2 16 D6

Trafalgar Rd. Horsh RH12 .... 217 C4
Trafalgar Rd. Merton SW19 .. 20 C1
Trafalgar Rd. Twick TW2 ...... 16 D6
Trafalgar Way. Camb GU15 .. 64 F4
Trafalgar Way.
Croy CR0 & CR9 .... 61 A8
Trafford Rd. Friml GU16 .... 85 D8
Trafford Rd. Thorn H CR7 ..... 41 F4
Traherne Lodge. 3
Tedd TW11 .... 16 F3
Tramway Path. Mitch CR4 .... 40 E5
Tranmere Ct. Sutton SM2 ..... 59 C3
Tranmere Rd. Twick TW2 ...... 16 B8
Tranmere Rd.
Wands SW17 & SW18 .... 20 C6
Tranquil Dale. Buckl RH3 ... 116 F3
Transport Ave. Brent TW8 ...... 6 B8
Transport Rd. Farnb GU14 ... 85 B1
Transport & Road Research Lab.
Crowth RG11 .... 45 C7
Trap La. Wall W RH5 .... 176 F2
Traps La. King U T KT2 & KT3 38 E8
Trasher Mead.
Dork RH4 & RH5 .... 136 C4
Travellers Way. Cranf TW5 ..... 4 C5
Travis La. Sandh GU17 .... 64 C7
Treadcroft Dr. Horsh RH12 217 E5
Treadwell Rd. Epsom KT18 .. 76 F4
Treaty Ctr. Hounsl TW3 .... 5 B4
Trebor Ave. M Bourn Gu9 . 146 D8
Tredenham Cl. Farnb GU14 105 C8
Tredown Rd. For Hill SE26 ... 23 C3
Tredwell Rd. W Norw SE27 .. 22 B4
Tree Ave. Shotto GU27 .... 207 F8
Tree Cl. Rich TW10 .... 17 D7
Tree Tops. Whytif CR6 .... 81 A1
Tree Tops Ave. Camb GU15 .. 66 B8
Tree View Cl. S Norw SE19 .. 42 E8
Treebourne Rd. Bigg H TN16 83 C1
Treebys Ave. Jacobs GU4 . 109 D7
Treelands. Dork RH5 .... 136 C4
Treemount Ct. Epsom KT17 . 76 E6
Treen Ave.
Mortl SW13 & SW14 .... 7 F4
Trees Sch The. Mayb GU22 .. 90 B8
Treeside Dr. Heath E Gu9 . 125 E7
Treetops. S Godst RH9 .... 142 E6
Treetops Ct. Thorn H CR7 ..... 42 C4
Treeview. Crawl RH11 .... 201 C1
Treeview Ct. 3 Reig RH2 . 118 D1
Treeway. Reig RH2 .... 118 B4
Trefoil Cl. Horsh RH12 .... 217 E5
Trefoil Cl. Woki RG11 .... 25 E7
Trefoil Cres. Crawl RH11 ... 201 A2
Trefusis Ct. Cranf TW5 .... 4 B6
Tregaron Gdns.
New Mal KT3 .... 38 E5
Tregarth Pl. Woking GU21 ... 68 F2
Tregarthen Pl. Leath KT22 ... 95 C6
Treglos Ct. Oat Pk KT13 ..... 53 E8
Tregolls Dr. Farnb GU14 ..... 85 D3
Trehaven Par. Woodh RH2 139 B6
Trehern Rd. 12 Mortl SW14 .... 7 D4
Treherne Ct. Up Tooot SW17 . 21 A4
Trelawn Cl. Ottsh KT16 .... 51 C3
Trelawne Dr. Cran GU6 ...... 174 E2
Trelawney Gr. Weyb KT13 ... 53 A4
Treloar Gdns. S Norw SE19 . 22 D2
Tremaine Rd. Penge SE20 ... 43 B7
Trematon Pl. Tedd TW11 ..... 17 C1
Tremayne Wlk. Friml GU15 .. 66 C4
Trenance. Woking GU21 .... 69 A2
Trenchard Cl. Hersh KT12 ... 54 C5
Trenchard Ct. Morden SM4 .. 40 A3
Trenear Cl. Horsh RH13 ...... 217 E2
Trenham Dr. Warlgm CR6 .... 81 C3
Trenholme Cl. Penge SE20 .. 23 B1
Trenholme Ct. Cater CR3 ... 101 A4
Trenholme Rd. Penge SE20 . 23 B1
Trenholme Terr. Penge SE20 23 B1
Trent Cl. Crawl RH11 .... 200 F4
Trent Cl. W Heath GU14 ...... 84 E6
Trent Rd. Bra Hill SL3 .... 1 B8
Trent Way. N Cheam KT4 ..... 58 C7
Trentham Cres.
Old Wok GU22 .... 90 A6
Trentham Rd. Earls RH1 ... 140 A7
Trentham St. Wands SW18 .. 20 A7
Trenton Cl. Friml GU16 .... 66 A1
Treport St. Wands SW18 ..... 20 B8
Treryn Hts. Farnc GU7 .... 150 D6
Tresco Cl. Catf BR1 .... 24 E2
Tresidder House. 10
Streat SW8 .... 21 D8
Tresillian Way.
Woking GU21 .... 69 B2
Tresta Wlk. Woking GU21 ... 69 A3
Trevanne Plat. Crawl RH10 202 D7
Trevelayan Rd.
Up Toot SW17 .... 20 F2
Trevelyan. Easth RG12 .... 26 E2

Trevelyan Ct. New Mal KT3 .. 38 F2
Trevelyan House. 6
Twick TW1 .... 6 C1
Trevenna House. 13
For Hil SE23 .... 23 D5
Trevereux Hill.
The Char RH8 .... 123 F4
Treversh Ct. Broml BR1 .... 44 F8
Treville St. Putney SW15 ..... 19 B8
Treviso Rd. For Hil SE23 .... 23 D6
Trevithick Cl. E Bed TW14 .. 14 F7
Trevor Cl. Hayes BR2 .... 44 F2
Trevor Ct. Islew TW7 .... 5 F2
Trevor Rd. Merton SW19 ..... 19 E1
Trevose Ave. W Byfl KT14 ... 70 F5
Trewenna Dr. Chess KT9 ..... 56 D5
Trewince Rd. Wimble SW20 39 C8
Trewint St. Wands SW18 ..... 20 C6
Trewsbury Rd. For Hil SE26 . 23 D3
Treyford Cl. Crawl RH11 .... 200 F6
Triangle The. King U T KT3 .. 38 C7
Triangle The. Woking GU21 . 69 C1
Trickett House. Sutton SM2 . 59 B2
Trident Ind Est. Poyle SL3 ... 1 E4
Trig St. Newd RH5 .... 178 F8
Trigg's Cl. Woking GU22 ..... 89 D8
Trigg's La.
Woking GU21 & GU22 .... 89 D8
Trigo Ct. Epsom KT19 .... 76 D8
Trilby Rd. For Hil SE23 .... 23 D6
Trimmer Wlk. 11 Brent TW8 . 6 E8
Trimmers Cl. Heath E Gu9 . 125 C7
Trimmers Field.
M Bourn GU9 .... 125 E1
Trimmers Wood.
Beac H GU26 .... 188 E6
Trindles Rd. S Nutf RH1 .... 140 F7
Tring Ct. Tedd TW1 .... 17 A4
Tringham Cl. Ottsh KT16 .... 51 C5
Trinity. Sandh GU15 .... 45 E2
Trinity C of E Sch.
Esher KT10 .... 55 A7
Trinity Cl. Crawl RH10 .... 202 C8
Trinity Cl. Hounsl TW4 .... 4 E3
Trinity Cl. S Croy CR2 .... 61 E2
Trinity Cl. Stan TW19 .... 2 C1
Trinity Cotts. Rich TW9 .... 6 F4
Trinity Cres. Sunnin SL5 ...... 30 A4
Trinity Cres. Up Toot SW17 . 21 A6
Trinity Ct. Croy CR9 .... 61 C8
Trinity Ct. For Hil SE23 .... 23 C5
Trinity Ct. Thorn H SE25 ..... 42 E3
Trinity Ct. Twick TW2 .... 16 E6
Trinity Fields. Hale GU9 ..... 125 A6
Trinity Hill. Hale GU9 .... 125 A6
Trinity Mews. Penge SE20 .. 43 B8
Trinity Par. Hounsl TW3 .... 5 B4
Trinity Rd. Knaph GU21 .... 68 B1
Trinity Rd. Rich TW9 .... 6 F4
Trinity Rd.
Up Toot SW17 & SW18 .... 20 E7
Trinity Rd.
Wands SW17 & SW18 .... 20 E7
Trinity Rd. Wimble SW19 .... 20 A2
Trinity Rise.
Streat SE24 & SW2 .... 22 B8
Trinity Sch. Croy CR9 .... 62 C8
Trinity St Mary's (C of E) Prim
Sch. Up Toot SW12 .... 21 A7
Tristram Rd. Catf BR1 .... 24 F4
Triton Ave. Wallin CR0 .... 60 E6
Tritton Rd.
W Norw SE21 & SE27 .... 22 D5
Trittons. Tadw KT20 .... 97 D6
Triumph Cl. Harl UB7 .... 3 C6
Trodd's La.
Merrow GU1 & GU4 .... 110 E1
Trojan Way. Croy CR0 .... 60 F7
Trone Ct. Crawl RH11 .... 200 D5
Troon Ct. Ascot SL5 .... 29 C4
Troston Ct. Stain TW18 .... 12 F3
Trotsworth Ave. Vir W GU25 31 E5
Trotsworth Ct. Vir W GU25 .. 31 D5
Trotters La. Chobh GU24 ..... 69 B7
Trotwood Cl. Sandh GU15 ... 45 E2
Trout Rd. Shottm GU27 ...... 207 E6
Troutbeck Wlk. Friml GU15 . 66 D3
Trowers Way. Redh RH1 .... 119 B4
Trowlock Ave. Tedd TW11 .. 17 C2
Trowlock Way. Tedd TW11 .. 17 D2
Troy La. Eden TN8 .... 144 F4
Troy Rd. S Norw SE19 .... 22 D2
Trumpeters Inn. Rich TW9 .... 6 C2
Trumpetfield Rd. Reig RH2 138 B7
Trumps Green Cl.
Thorpe GU25 .... 31 E4
Trumps Green Ct. Fst Sch.
Went GU25 .... 31 D3
Trumps Mill La.
Thorpe GU25 .... 31 F4

Trumpsgreen Ave.
Went GU25 .... 31 D3
Trumpsgreen Rd.
Vir W GU25 .... 31 D3
Trundle Mead. Horsh RH12 217 C5
Trunk Rd. W Heath GU14 .... 84 C5
Trunley Heath Rd.
Shalf GU5 .... 151 C8
Truslove Rd. W Norw SE27 .. 22 B3
Truss Hill Rd. Ascot SL5 ..... 29 C4
Trust Wlk. Streat SE21 .... 22 B7
Trys Hill. Longc KT16 .... 51 A8
Trystings Cl. Clayg KT10 ..... 56 A4
Tuckers Dr. Cran GU6 .... 174 B3
Tuckey Gr. Send M GU23 ..... 90 F3
Tudor Ave. Hampt TW12 ...... 16 A1
Tudor Ave. N Cheam KT4 ..... 58 B6
Tudor Circ. Farnc GU7 .... 150 E7
Tudor Cl. Ashf TW15 .... 13 E4
Tudor Cl. Cheam SM3 .... 58 E4
Tudor Cl. Chess KT9 .... 56 E5
Tudor Cl. Cobham KT11 .... 73 F6
Tudor Cl. Coulsd CR5 .... 80 A1
Tudor Cl. E Grins RH19 ..... 205 F8
Tudor Cl. Graysh GU26 ...... 188 D2
Tudor Cl. Hampt TW12 .... 16 C3
Tudor Cl. Hams Gn CR2 ...... 81 B4
Tudor Cl. E Book KT23 .... 94 A3
Tudor Cl. Nork SM7 .... 77 E4
Tudor Cl. Smallf RH6 .... 162 B3
Tudor Cl. Wallin SM6 .... 60 C3
Tudor Cl. Woki RG11 .... 25 F5
Tudor Cl. Woking GU22 .... 70 A2
Tudor Cl. Worth RH10 .... 202 D5
Tudor Cl. Bigg H TN16 .... 83 E2
Tudor Cl. Farnc GU7 .... 150 E5
Tudor Cl. Felt TW13 .... 15 C4
Tudor Cl. 12 Redh RH1 ...... 119 A2
Tudor Cl. Stan TW19 .... 2 E1
Tudor Cl. Tedd TW11 .... 16 F2
Tudor Dr. King U T KT2 .... 17 E3
Tudor Dr. W Barn SM4 .... 39 E3
Tudor Dr. Walt O T KT12 ..... 35 D1
Tudor Gdns.
Mortl SW13 & SW14 .... 7 E4
Tudor Gdns. Twick TW1 .... 16 F7
Tudor Gdns. W Wick BR4 .... 63 C7
Tudor House. Easth RG12 ... 27 B4
Tudor House. Horsh RH13 . 217 F3
Tudor House. Weyb KT13 .... 53 A4
Tudor La. Old W SL4 .... 11 C8
Tudor Par. Hounsl TW3 .... 5 D5
Tudor Pl. Mitch SW19 .... 20 E1
Tudor Prim Sch.
W Barn SM4 .... 39 D2
Tudor Rd. Ashf TW15 .... 14 D2
Tudor Rd. Beck BR3 .... 44 B8
Tudor Rd. Croy CR0 & SE25 . 43 B4
Tudor Rd. Farnc GU7 .... 150 E7
Tudor Rd. Hampt TW12 .... 16 A1
Tudor Rd. Islew TW3 .... 5 D3
Tudor Rd. King U T KT2 .... 18 A1
Tudor Rd. Penge SE19 .... 22 F1
Tudor Wlk. Leald KT22 .... 94 F7
Tudor Wlk. 3 Weyb KT13 .... 53 B7
Tudors The. Beck BR3 .... 44 B7
Tuesley Cnr. Godal GU7 .... 150 D3
Tuesley La.
Godal GU7 & GU8 .... 150 D1
Tufton Gdns. E Mole KT8 .... 36 B7
Tugela Rd. Thorn H CR0 ...... 42 D3
Tugela St. For Hil SE6 .... 23 F6
Tuggles Plat. Warn RH12 ... 216 E7
Tulip Cl. Croy CR0 .... 43 D1
Tulip Cl. Hampt TW12 .... 15 F2
Tulip Cl. Horsh RH12 .... 217 C4
Tull St. Carsh CR4 .... 40 F2
Tullett Rd. Crawl RH10 ...... 202 B2
Tulse Cl. Beck BR3 .... 44 C6
Tulse Hill.
Streat SW2 & SE24 .... 22 A8
Tulse Hill Sta. W Norw SE27 22 B6
Tulsemere Rd.
W Norw SE21 & SE27 .... 22 C6
Tulyar Cl. Burgh H KT20 ...... 97 B7
Tumber St.
Head KT18 & KT22 .... 96 C2
Tumblewood Rd. Nork SM7 77 E3
Tumbling Bay.
Walt O T KT12 .... 35 A3
Tummons Gdns.
S Norw SE25 .... 42 E7
Tunbridge Ct. 1
For Hil SE26 .... 23 A5
Tunley Rd.
Up Toot SW12 & SW17 .... 21 A6
Tunnel Link Rd. Harm TW6 .... 3 A2
Tunnel Rd. Farnb GU14 .... 84 E1
Tunnel Rd E. Harl TW6 .... 3 B6

Tunnel Rd W. Harm TW6 .... 3 B6
Tunnmeade. Crawl RH11 ... 200 E5
Tunsgate. Guild GU1 .... 130 D7
Tunsgate Sq. Guild GU1 .... 130 D7
Tunstall Ct. 13 Rich TW9 ...... 6 F6
Tunstall Rd. Croy CR0 .... 42 E1
Tunstall Wlk. 10 Brent TW8 .. 6 E8
Tunworth Cres. Rhampt SW15 7 F1
Tupwood La. Cater CR3 ..... 101 A1
Tupwood Scrubbs Rd.
Cater CR3 & RH9 .... 121 A8
Turf Hill Rd. Camb GU15 ..... 65 F8
Turfhouse La. Burrh GU24 ... 49 E2
Turkey Oak Cl. S Norw SE19 42 E8
Turle Rd. Thorn H SW16 ...... 41 E7
Turnberry. Easth RG12 .... 26 E2
Turner Ave. Mitch CR4 .... 20 F1
Turner Ave. Twick TW2 .... 16 C5
Turner Cl. Bigg H TN16 .... 83 C7
Turner Cl. E Grins RH19 .... 186 A3
Turner Cl. Godal GU7 .... 150 D4
Turner House. Bear Gn RH5 157 C4
Turner Lodge. 10
Putney SW19 .... 19 D7
Turner Pl. Sandh GU15 .... 64 D6
Turner Rd. New Mal KT3 ..... 38 D2
Turner's Hill Rd.
E Grins RH19 .... 205 B6
Turners Cl. Stain TW18 .... 13 B3
Turners Hill CE (Controlled) Sch.
Turn H RH10 .... 204 A3
Turners Hill Rd.Copth RH10 183 F2
Turners Hill Rd.
Crawl D RH10 .... 204 A7
Turners Hill Rd.
Turn H RH10 .... 203 F5
Turner's Hill Rd.
Worth RH10 .... 203 C5
Turners La. Whit V KT12 ...... 54 B3
Turners Mead. Chidd GU8 . 191 C3
Turners Meadow Way.
Beck BR3 .... 43 F8
Turners Way.
Croy CR0 & CR9 .... 61 A8
Turney Sch. W Norw SE21 .. 22 C8
Turnham Cl. Guild GU2 ..... 130 C5
Turnoak Ave. Woking GU22 . 89 E7
Turnoak Cnr. Woking GU22 . 89 E8
Turnoak La. Woking GU22 ... 89 E8
Turnpike La. Sutton SM1 .... 59 C5
Turnpike Link. S Croy CR0 .. 61 E8
Turnpike Pl. Crawl RH11 ... 201 D8
Turnpike Rd. Bird RG12 ...... 26 C7
Turnstone Cl.
Selsd CR0 & CR2 .... 62 E1
Turnville Cl. Lhtwat GU18 ... 48 A1
Turpin Rd. Felt TW14 .... 3 F1
Turpin Way. Wallin SM6 ...... 60 B3
Turpins Rise. Windl GU20 ... 48 B6
Turret Ct. E Grins RH19 .... 185 C3
Turret House. King U T KT2 . 17 E3
Turville Ct. E Book KT23 ..... 94 B2
Tuscam Way. Camb GU15 ... 64 F4
Tushmore Ave.
Crawl RH10 & RH11 .... 181 C1
Tushmore La.
Crawl RH10 & RH11 .... 201 C8
Tushmore Rdbt.
Crawl RH11 .... 201 D8
Tussock Cl. Crawl RH11 .... 201 A4
Tuttle Cl. W Heath GU14 ..... 84 E6
Tweed La. Brock RH3 .... 137 B5
Tweed La. Rusper RH11 ..... 180 F1
Tweed Rd. Bra Hill SL3 .... 1 B8
Tweeddale Inf Sch.
Carsh SM5 .... 40 D2
Tweeddale Jun Sch.
Carsh SM5 .... 40 D2
Tweeddale Rd. Carsh SM5 .. 40 D1
Tweedsmuir Cl. Farnb GU14 84 D3
Tweedy Rd. Broml BR1 .... 44 F8
Twelve Acre Cl. L Book KT23 93 F3
Twelve Acre Cres.
W Heath GU14 .... 84 E5
Twickenham Bridge.
Twick TW9 .... 6 C2
Twickenham Golf Course.
Hampt TW12 .... 16 B4
Twickenham Rd. Felt TW13 . 15 F5
Twickenham Rd.
Islew TW1 & TW7 .... 6 A4
Twickenham Rd.
Rich TW1 & TW9 .... 6 C3
Twickenham Rd. Tedd TW11 17 A4
Twickenham Rugby Football
Union Ground. Twick TW2 ... 5 E1
Twickenham Sta. Twick TW1 17 A8
Twickenham Trad Ctr.
Islew TW1 .... 5 F1

Twilley St. Wands SW18 ...... 20 B8
Twining Ave. Twick TW2 ...... 16 D5
Twinoaks. Cobham KT11 ..... 74 A6
Twitten La. Felb RH19 .... 184 E4
Two Oaks. Weyb KT13 .... 53 B6
Two Ways. Loxwd RH14 .... 213 A4
Twycross Rd. Farnc GU7 ... 150 D3
Twyford La. Wrecel GU10 . 146 B6
Twyford Par. Tolw KT6 .... 38 A1
Twyford Rd. Carsh SM5 ...... 40 D1
Twyford Rd. Woki RG11 ...... 25 B8
Twyne Cl. Crawl RH11 .... 200 F4
Twyner Cl. Horley RH6 ...... 161 D4
Tybenham Rd. Merton SW19 40 A6
Tychbourne Dr.
Merrow GU4 .... 110 C4
Tydcombe Rd.
Warlgm CR6 .... 101 D8
Tyers House. 1
Streat SW16 .... 21 C3
Tylden Way. Horsh RH12 ... 217 F6
Tylecroft Rd. Thorn H SW16 41 E7
Tylehost. Stough GU2 .... 109 A5
Tyler Gdns. Addl KT15 .... 52 C6
Tyler Rd. Crawl RH10 .... 201 D3
Tylers Cl. Tyl Gn RH9 .... 121 B5
Tylers Path. Carsh SM5 .... 59 F6
Tylney Ave. Dulw SE19 .... 22 F3
Tymperley Ct. Horsh RH13 217 E3
Tynamara. King U T KT1 ...... 37 D5
Tynan Cl. E Bed TW14 .... 15 A7
Tyndalls Estate. Hind GU26 188 F4
Tyne Cl. W Heath GU14 .... 84 E6
Tyne Cl. Worth RH10 .... 202 C5
Tynedale Rd. Brock RH3 ... 137 B5
Tynemouth Rd. Mitch CR4 .. 21 A1
Tynley Gr. Jacobs GU4 ...... 109 D7
Tynwald House. 14
For Hil SE26 .... 23 A5
Tyrell Ct. Carsh SM5 .... 59 F6
Tyrolean Ct. Banstd SM7 .... 78 B4
Tyrrell House. Catf BR3 .... 24 B3
Tyrrell Sq. Mitch CR4 .... 40 E8
Tyrrell's Wood Golf Course.
Head KT22 .... 95 F2
Tyrwhitt Ave. Stough GU2 . 109 B5
Tyson Rd. For Hil SE23 .... 23 C8
Tythbarn Cl. Burgh GU4 ... 110 B6
Tythebarns La. Ripley GU23 . 91 B1
Tythebarns La. Send M GU23 91 B1
Tytherton. Brack RG12 .... 27 C7

Uckfield Rd. Mitch CR4 .... 41 A8
Udney Park Rd. Tedd TW1 .. 17 A2
Uffington Dr. Brack RG12 ... 27 E5
Uffington Rd. W Norw SE27 22 A4
Ujima Ct. Streat SW16 .... 21 E4
Ujima House. Streat SW16 .. 21 E4
Ullathorne Rd. Streat SW16 21 C4
Ullswater. Easth RG22 .... 26 F2
Ullswater Ave. Farnb GU14 . 84 E3
Ullswater Cl. Broml BR1 ..... 24 E1
Ullswater Cl. Hale GU9 ..... 125 A6
Ullswater Cl.
King U T KT2 & SW15 .... 18 D4
Ullswater Cl. Lhtwat GU18 .. 48 B1
Ullswater Cres. Coulsd CR5 . 79 E3
Ullswater Cres.
King U T SW15 .... 18 D4
Ullswater Rd. Lhtwat GU18 . 48 B1
Ullswater Rd.
W Norw SE27 & SW16 .... 22 B6
Ulstan Cl. Wold CR3 .... 102 A4
Ulster Ct. King U T KT2 .... 17 D2
Ulverstone Rd.
W Norw SE27 .... 22 B6
Ulwyn Ave. Byfl KT14 .... 71 E5
Underhill Cl. Godal GU7 ... 150 E3
Underhill Park Rd.
Reig RH2 .... 118 A4
Underhill Rd.
Dulw SE21 & SE22 .... 23 B8
Underhill Rd. Newd RH5 ... 158 B1
Undershaw Rd. Catf BR1 .... 24 F5
Underwood. Easth RG12 ..... 26 E3
Underwood. New Add CR0 .. 63 C5
Underwood Ave. Ash GU12 105 F1
Underwood Cl.
Crawl D RH10 .... 204 B8
Underwood Ct. Cater CR3 . 100 F2
Underwood Ct. Cater CR3 . 100 E2
Underwood Rd.
Shottm GU27 .... 207 F7
Undine St. Up Toot SW17 ... 20 F3
Unicorn Sch. Rich TW9 .... 6 F6
Union Cl. Sandh GU15 .... 45 E2

Union Ct. **2** Rich TW10 .... 6 E2
Union Rd. Farnh GU9 .... 125 C2
Union Rd. Friml GU16 .... 86 D8
Union Rd. Thorn H CR0 .... 42 C2
Union St. Alder GU11 .... 105 A2
Union St. Farnb GU14 .... 85 B4
Union St. King U T KT1 .... 37 D7
Union St. Pirb GU24 .... 87 A6
Unity Cl. New Add CR0 .... 63 B2
Unity Cl. W Norw SE19 & 27 22 C3
Univ of Greenwich The.
 Rhampt SW15 .... 19 A8
University Rd. Mitch SW19 .. 20 D2
Unstead La. Shalf GU5 ...... 151 C7
Unstead Wood. Shalf GU3 . 130 C1
Unwin Ave. Hatton TW14 ...... 3 D2
Unwin Rd. Islew TW7 .... 5 E4
Upavon Gdns. Brack RG12 ... 27 F4
Upchurch Cl. Penge SE20 .... 23 B1
Updown Hill. Windl GU20 .... 48 D4
Upfield. Horley RH6 .... 161 A1
Upfield. S Croy CR0 & CR9 ... 62 B7
Upfield Cl. Horley RH6 ...... 161 A1
Upfold Cl. Wodly GU6 .... 174 B5
Upfold La. Cran GU6 .... 174 C5
Upfolds Gn. Burgh GU4 ...... 110 C5
Upgrove Manor Way. **12**
 Streat SE24 .... 22 A8
Upland Ct. For Hil SE23 ...... 23 C6
Upland Rd. Camb GU15 ...... 65 D7
Upland Rd. Croy CR2 .... 61 D5
Upland Rd.
 Dulw SE21 & SE22 .... 23 A8
Upland Rd. Sutton SM2 ...... 59 D3
Upland Rd. Wold CR3 .... 102 B7
Uplands. Ashtd KT21 & KT22 95 D7
Uplands. Beck BR3 .... 44 A7
Uplands. Warlgm CR6 .... 81 F1
Uplands Cl. Haslem GU27 . 208 D8
Uplands Cl. Mortl SW14 ...... 7 B2
Uplands Cl. Sandh GU17 ...... 64 B8
Uplands Dr. Oxsh KT22 ...... 74 D5
Uplands Prim Sch.
 Sandh GU17 .... 64 B8
Uplands Rd. Kenley CR8 ...... 80 C2
Uplands Rd. M Bourn GU9 . 125 E1
Uppark Gdns. Horsh RH12 . 217 F6
Upper Beulah Hill.
 S Norw SE19 .... 42 E8
Upper Bourne La.
 Rowl GU10 .... 146 B5
Upper Bourne Vale.
 Rowl GU10 .... 146 A5
Upper Bridge Rd. Redh RH1 118 F1
Upper Brighton Rd.
 Surb KT6 .... 37 E2
Upper Broadmoor Rd.
 Crowth RG11 .... 45 D5
Upper Butts. Brent TW8 ...... 6 C8
Upper Charles St.
 Camb GU15 .... 65 C6
Upper Chobham Rd.
 Friml GU15 & GU16 .... 66 B4
Upper Church La. **11**
 Farnh GU9 .... 125 B2
Upper Cl. For Row RH18 .... 206 F2
Upper College Ride.
 Camb GU15 .... 65 E8
Upper Court Rd.
 Epsom KT19 .... 76 C8
Upper Court Rd. Wold CR3 102 A3
Upper Dr. Bigg H TN16 .... 83 C1
Upper Dunnymans. **6**
 Banstd SM7 .... 77 F5
Upper Edgeborough Rd.
 Guild GU1 .... 130 F8
Upper Elmers End Rd.
 Beck BR3 .... 43 E4
Upper Elms Rd.
 Alder GU11 .... 105 A1
Upper Fairfield Rd.
 Leahd KT22 .... 95 B6
Upper Farm L Pk.
 Box H KT20 .... 115 F3
Upper Farm Rd. E Mole KT8 35 F5
Upper Forecourt.
 Crawl RH6 .... 182 B7
Upper Gn E. Mitch CR4 ...... 40 F6
Upper Gn E. Mitch CR4 ...... 41 A6
Upper Gn W. Mitch CR4 ...... 40 F7
Upper Gordon Rd.
 Camb GU15 .... 65 D5
Upper Gn. S Norw SE25 ...... 42 F5
Upper Grotto Rd. Twick TW1 16 F6
Upper Guildown Rd.
 Guild GU2 .... 130 C6
Upper Hale Rd. Hale GU9 .. 125 C6

Upper Halliford Halt.
 Up Hall TW16 .... 34 E7
Upper Halliford Rd.
 Up Hall TW17 .... 34 E5
Upper Halliford Rd.
 Up Hall TW17 .... 34 E6
Upper Ham Rd.
 Rich KT2 & TW10 .... 17 D4
Upper Harestone.
 Cater CR3 .... 121 A8
Upper High St. Epsom KT17 76 E6
Upper House La.
 Sham Gn GU5 .... 152 F1
Upper Manor Rd.
 Farnc GU7 .... 150 E6
Upper Manor Rd. Milf GU8 149 F1
Upper Mount. Grays GU27 . 189 F1
Upper Mulgrave Rd.
 Belm SM2 .... 58 E3
Upper Nursery. Sunnin SL5 .. 30 A4
Upper Old Park La.
 Hale GU9 .... 125 A5
Upper Park Rd. Camb GU15 . 65 E6
Upper Park Rd. King U T KT2 18 A2
Upper Pillory Down.
 Wallin SM5 .... 79 A7
Upper Pinewood Rd.
 Normdy GU12 .... 106 D3
Upper Rd. Wallin SM6 ...... 60 E5
Upper Richmond Rd.
 Mortl SW15 .... 7 F3
Upper Richmond Rd W.
 Mortl TW10 & SW14 & SW15 7 C3
Upper Rose Hill. Dork RH4 136 B6
Upper Sawleywood. **3**
 Banstd SM7 .... 77 F5
Upper Selsdon Rd.
 S Croy CR2 .... 62 A2
Upper Shirley Rd.
 S Croy CR0 & CR9 .... 62 D7
Upper South View.
 Farnh GU9 .... 125 C3
Upper Springfield.
 Elst GU8 .... 148 D3
Upper Sq. For Row RH18 .... 206 E3
Upper Sq. Islew TW7 .... 6 A4
Upper St. Shere GU5 .... 133 A4
Upper St Michael's Rd.
 Alder GU11 .... 126 B8
Upper Staithe. Chisw W4 ...... 7 C6
Upper Stanford Rd.
 Pirb GU24 .... 87 F1
Upper Sunbury Rd.
 Hampt TW12 .... 36 A8
Upper Sutton La. Heston TW5 5 A6
Upper Teddington Rd.
 Tedd KT1 & KT8 .... 37 C8
Upper Terrace Rd.
 Farnb GU14 .... 105 A8
Upper Tooting Ind High Sch.
 Up Toot SW17 .... 20 F6
Upper Tooting Park Mansions. **1**
 Up Toot SW17 .... 21 A6
Upper Tooting Pk.
 Up Toot SW17 .... 20 F7
Upper Tooting Rd.
 Up Toot SW17 .... 20 F5
Upper Tulse Hill. Streat SW2 21 F8
Upper Union St.
 Alder GU11 .... 105 A2
Upper Union Terr.
 Alder GU11 .... 105 A2
Upper Vann La. Hambl GU8 172 A1
Upper Vernon Rd.Carsh SM1 59 D5
Upper Verran Rd.
 Camb GU15 .... 65 D3
Upper Village Rd. Ascot SL5 29 A4
Upper Warlingham Sta.
 Warlgm CR6 .... 81 A1
Upper Way. M Bourn GU9 . 146 B8
Upper West St. Reig RH2 .. 117 F1
Upper Weybourne La.
 Heath E GU9 .... 125 E7
Upper Wlk. Thorpe GU25 .... 31 E5
Upper Woodcote Village.
 Purley CR8 .... 79 D7
Upperton Rd. Guild GU2 .. 130 C7
Upshire Gdns. Brack RG12 ... 27 F5
Upshott La. Mayb GU22 ...... 70 F2
Upton. Woking GU21 .... 69 B2
Upton Cl. Farnb GU14 ...... 85 D3
Upton Ct. Penge SE20 ...... 23 C1
Upton Ct. **4** Wimble SW19 19 D1
Upton Dene. Belm SM2 ...... 59 B3
Upton Rd. Hounsl TW3 .... 5 A4
Upton Rd. S Norw CR7 ...... 42 D7
Upwood Rd. Thorn H SW16 . 41 E8
Urmston Dr. Putney SW19 .. 19 E7
Urquhart Ct. Beck BR3 ...... 23 F1
Ursuline Convent Prep Sch.
 Wimble SW19 .... 19 D1

Ursuline Convent Sch.
 Wimble SW20 .... 39 D8
Usherwood Cl. Box H KT20 116 C4
Uvedale Cl. New Add CR0 ... 82 D8
Uvedale Cres. New Add CR0 82 E8
Uvedale Rd. Limps RH8 .... 122 F5
Uxbridge Rd. Felt TW13 .... 15 D6
Uxbridge Rd.
 Hampt TW12 & TW13 ...... 16 B3
Uxbridge Rd.
 King U T KT1 & KT6 .... 37 D4

Vachery La. Cran GU6 ...... 194 E7
Vaillant Rd. Weyb KT13 ...... 53 C6
Valan Leas. Beck BR2 .... 44 E6
Vale Cl. Coulsd CR5 .... 79 E5
Vale Cl. M Bourn GU10 .... 146 C4
Vale Cl. Oat Pk KT13 .... 53 D7
Vale Cl. Twick TW1 .... 17 A5
Vale Cres. King U T SW15 .. 18 E4
Vale Croft. Clayg KT10 .... 55 F2
Vale Ct. Oat Pk KT13 .... 53 D7
Vale Dr. Horsh RH12 .... 217 B3
Vale Farm Rd. Woking GU21 69 E2
Vale House. Woking GU21 .. 69 E2
Vale Lodge. For Hil SE23 .... 23 C6
Vale Rd. Ash V GU12 .... 106 A5
Vale Rd. Camb GU15 .... 65 A4
Vale Rd. Clayg KT10 .... 55 F3
Vale Rd. Mitch CR4 .... 41 D5
Vale Rd. Oat Pk KT13 .... 53 D7
Vale Rd. Sutton SM1 .... 59 B6
Vale Rd. Worc Pk KT19 & KT4 57 F7
Vale Rd N. Surb KT6 .... 56 E8
Vale The. Ashf TW16 .... 15 A2
Vale The. Coulsd CR5 & CR8 . 79 E5
Vale The. Croy CR0 .... 62 D8
Vale The. Felt TW14 .... 4 B1
Vale The. Heston TW5 .... 4 E8
Vale Wood Dr.
 M Bourn GU10 .... 146 D4
Vale Wood La.
 Graysh GU26 .... 188 C4
Valens House. **1**
 Streat SW2 .... 22 A7
Valentine Ct. For Hil SE23 .. 23 D6
Valentyne Cl. New Add CR0 . 82 E8
Valerie Ct. Sutton SM2 ...... 59 B3
Valeswood Rd. Catf BR1 .... 24 F3
Valewood Rd. Fern GU27 .. 208 C4
Valiant Way. Farnb GU14 .. 104 D8
Valley Cres. Woki RG1 ...... 25 A8
Valley Ct. Cater CR3 .... 101 A5
Valley End C of E Inf Sch.
 Burrh GU24 .... 49 A4
Valley End Rd. Burrh GU24 .. 49 B4
Valley Gdns. Mitch SW19 .... 20 D1
Valley Gdns. Woking GU22 20 C1
Valley Mews. Twick TW1 .... 17 A6
Valley Prim Sch. Broml BR2 44 F7
Valley Prospect. **3**
 W Norw SE19 .... 22 E2
Valley Rd. Beck BR2 .... 44 E7
Valley Rd. Friml GU16 .... 86 B8
Valley Rd. Kenley CR3 & CR8 80 D4
Valley Rd. Streat SW16 ...... 21 F4
Valley The. Guild GU2 ...... 130 C5
Valley Wlk. Croy CR0 .... 62 C8
Valleyfield Rd. Streat SW16 21 F3
Vallis Way. Chess KT9 .... 56 D6
Valnay St. Up Toot SW17 .... 20 F3
Valornus. Merst RH1 .... 119 B5
Valroy Cl. Camb GU15 ...... 65 D6
Vampire Way. Farnb GU14 104 E8
Van Dyck Ave. New Mal KT3 38 D2
Vanborough Ct. Sutton SM2 59 C4
Vanbrugh Cl. Crawl RH11 .. 200 E3
Vanbrugh Dr. Walt O T KT12 35 C2
Vancouver Cl. Epsom KT19 .. 76 C8
Vancouver Ct. Smallf RH6 . 162 A3
Vancouver Dr. Crawl RH11 181 D1
Vancouver Rd. For Hil SE23 23 E6
Vancouver Rd. Rich TW10 .. 17 C4
Vanderbilt Rd. Wands SW18 20 C7
Vandyke. Easth RG12 .... 26 E3
Vandyke Cl. Putney SW15 .. 19 D8
Vandyke Cl. Redh RH1 ...... 118 F3
Vanfame Ct. New Mal KT3 .. 38 F6
Vanguard Cl. Thorn H CR0 .. 42 B1
Vanguard House. **7**
 Merton SW19 .... 20 C1
Vanguard House. **5**
 Stan TW19 .... 2 E1
Vanguard Way. Wallin SM6 . 60 E3
Vann Farm Rd. Ockley RH5 177 E4

Vann La. Chidd GU8 .... 191 E4
Vann La. Hambl GU8 .... 171 D1
Vann Lake. Ockley RH5 ...... 177 F4
Vann Lake Rd. Ockley RH5 . 177 F3
Vann Lake Rd. Ockley RH5 . 178 A4
Vanners. Crawl RH10 .... 201 E7
Vant Rd. Up Toot SW17 ...... 20 F3
Vapery La. Pirb GU24 .... 87 D6
Varley Way. Mitch CR4 ...... 40 D7
Varna Rd. Hampt TW12 ...... 36 B8
Varney Cl. W Heath GU14 ... 84 E5
Varsity Dr. Islew TW1 & TW7 5 F1
Varsity Row. Mortl SW14 ...... 7 C5
Varsity Track. Farnb GU11 . 104 C7
Vaughan Almshouses.
 Ashf TW15 .... 14 B3
Vaughan Rd. Thame D KT7 .. 37 B2
Vaughan Way. Dork RH4 .. 136 A7
Vaux Cres. Hersh KT12 ...... 54 B4
Vauxhall Gdns. Croy CR2 .... 61 C4
Veals Mead. Mitch CR4 ...... 40 E8
Vectis Gdns. Mitch SW17 .... 21 B2
Vectis Rd. Mitch SW17 ...... 21 B2
Vegal Cres. Eng Gn TW20 ... 11 C3
Vellum Dr. Hackb SM5 ...... 60 A7
Venita Manor. W Norw SE27 22 A3
Venner Rd.
 For Hil SE20 & SE26 .... 23 C3
Venner Rd.
 Penge SE20 & SE26 .... 23 C3
Ventnor Rd. Sutton SM2 .... 59 B3
Ventnor Terr. Alder GU12 .. 105 C1
Venton Cl. Woking GU21 .... 69 B2
Verbania Way.
 E Grins RH19 .... 186 B1
Verdant Cl. **3** Catf SE6 .... 24 E8
Verdant La. Catf SE6 .... 24 E7
Verdayne Ave.
 Croy CR0 & CR9 .... 62 D8
Verdayne Gdns.
 Warlgm CR6 .... 81 C3
Vere Bank. Wands SW19 .... 19 F7
Vereker Dr. Sunby TW16 .... 35 A6
Vermont Rd. S Norw SE19 ... 22 E2
Vermont Rd. Sutton SM1 .... 59 B7
Verney House. Hounsl TW3 .. 5 C3
Vernon Ave. Merton SW20 .. 39 D7
Vernon Cl. Horsh RH12 .... 218 A4
Vernon Cl. Ottsh KT16 ...... 51 D4
Vernon Cl. W Ewell KT19 ... 57 C4
Vernon Cl. W Ewell KT19 ... 57 C4
Vernon Ct. Farnh GU9 ...... 125 A2
Vernon Dr. Cater CR3 ...... 100 C5
Vernon Dr. N Asct SL5 ...... 28 E7
Vernon Rd. Felt TW13 ...... 14 F6
Vernon Rd. Mortl SW14 ...... 7 D4
Vernon Rd. Sutton SM1 ...... 59 D5
Vernon Way. Stough GU2 .. 108 F2
Vernon Wlk. Tadw KT20 ...... 97 D7
Verona Dr. Surb KT6 .... 56 E8
Veronica Gdns.
 Mitch CR4 & SW16 .... 41 C8
Veronica Rd. Up Toot SW17 . 21 B6
Verralls. Mayb GU22 .... 70 B2
Verran Rd. Balham SW12 .. 21 B8
Verran Rd. Camb GU15 ...... 65 D3
Versailles Rd. Penge SE20 .. 23 A1
Verulam Ave. Purley CR8 .... 79 C7
Veryan. Woking GU21 .... 69 A2
Vesey Cl. W Heath GU14 .... 85 A5
Vestris Rd. For Hil SE23 .... 23 D6
Vevers Rd. Dovgn RH2 .... 139 C6
Vevey St. For Hil SE23 & SE6 23 F6
Viart Gdns. Streat SW2 ...... 21 F8
Viburnum Ct. W End GU24 ... 67 E6
Vicarage Ave. Egham TW20 . 12 B3
Vicarage Cl. Kings KT20 .... 97 E3
Vicarage Cl. L Book KT23 .... 94 A2
Vicarage Cl. M Bourn GU10 146 D7
Vicarage Cres. Egham TW20 12 B3
Vicarage Ct. Beck BR3 ...... 43 E6
Vicarage Ct. E Bed TW14 .... 14 C8
Vicarage Ct. Egham TW20 .. 12 B2
Vicarage Ct. **8**
 Rhampt SW15 .... 19 A8
Vicarage Dr. Beck BR3 ...... 44 A8
Vicarage Dr. Mortl SW14 ...... 7 D2
Vicarage Farm Ct.
 Heston TW5 .... 4 F7
Vicarage Farm Rd.
 Heston TW3 & TW4 & TW5 .. 4 E6
Vicarage Farm Rd.
 Hounsl TW3 & TW4 & TW5 .. 4 E6
Vicarage Fields.
 Walt O T KT12 .... 35 C3
Vicarage Gdns. Onsl V GU2 130 A7
Vicarage Gdns. Ascot SL5 ... 29 A4
Vicarage Gdns.
 Graysh GU26 .... 188 C3
Vicarage Gdns. Mitch CR4 .. 40 E6

Vicarage Gdns. Mortl SW14 ... 7 D2
Vicarage Hill.
 M Bourn GU10 & GU9 ...... 146 D7
Vicarage House. **1**
 King U T KT1 .... 37 F7
Vicarage La. Capel RH5 .... 178 D6
Vicarage La. Farnh GU9 .... 125 B2
Vicarage La. Heath E GU9 . 125 C7
Vicarage La. Horley RH6 .. 160 F4
Vicarage La. Laleh TW18 .... 33 C6
Vicarage La. Leahd KT22 .... 95 B5
Vicarage La. M Bourn GU9 146 D7
Vicarage La. Send GU23 ...... 90 D1
Vicarage La. Shottm GU27 . 207 F6
Vicarage La. Wray TW19 .... 11 F7
Vicarage Rd. Ashf TW16 .... 14 F2
Vicarage Rd.
 Bagsh GU8 & GU20 .... 47 C3
Vicarage Rd. Chobh GU24 ... 68 B8
Vicarage Rd. Crawl D RH10 204 A8
Vicarage Rd.
 Croy CR0 & CR9 .... 61 A7
Vicarage Rd. Egham TW20 .. 12 B3
Vicarage Rd. Hawley GU17 . 64 E4
Vicarage Rd.
 King U T KT1 & KT2 .... 37 D7
Vicarage Rd. Lingf RH7 .... 164 D4
Vicarage Rd. Mortl SW14 ...... 7 D2
Vicarage Rd. Stain TW18 .... 12 E5
Vicarage Rd. Sutton SM1 .... 59 B7
Vicarage Rd. Tedd TW11 .... 17 A3
Vicarage Rd.
 Tedd KT1 & KT8 .... 37 C8
Vicarage Rd. Twick TW2 ...... 5 C1
Vicarage Rd. Twick TW2 .... 16 E6
Vicarage Rd. Westfd GU22 .. 89 F6
Vicarage Way. Coln SL3 ...... 1 D7
Vicars Oak Rd. W Norw SE19 22 E2
Viceroy Ct. **5** Croy CR0 ...... 42 D1
Viceroy Lodge. **6**
 King U T KT6 .... 37 E4
Vickers Ct. **3** Stan TW19 ...... 2 E1
Vickers Dr N. Byfl KT13 ...... 52 E1
Vickers Dr S. Byfl KT13 ...... 71 E8
Victor Ct. Crawl RH10 ...... 182 D1
Victor Rd. Penge SE20 ...... 23 D1
Victor Rd. Tedd TW11 ...... 16 E4
Victor Seymour Inf Sch.
 Carsh SM5 .... 59 F6
Victor Way. Farnb GU14 .. 104 D8
Victoria Almshouses. **4**
 Redh RH1 .... 119 A4
Victoria Almshouses. **1**
 Reig RH2 .... 118 C1
Victoria Ave. Camb GU15 ... 65 A5
Victoria Ave. E Mole KT8 ... 36 B6
Victoria House.
 Hackb SM5 & SM6 .... 60 A7
Victoria Ave.
 Hounsl TW3 & TW4 .... 5 A2
Victoria Ave. King U T KT6 .. 37 D3
Victoria Ave. S Croy CR2 .... 61 C1
Victoria Cl. E Mole KT8 ...... 36 A6
Victoria Cl. Horley RH6 .... 161 A3
Victoria Cl. Oat Pk KT13 .... 53 D7
Victoria Cres. Merton SW19 19 F1
Victoria Cres. S Norw SE19 22 E2
Victoria Cl. Bagsh GU19 .... 47 E1
Victoria Ct. Guild GU1 .... 130 D8
Victoria Ct. Horsh RH13 .. 217 D2
Victoria Ct. Penge SE26 .... 23 C2
Victoria Dr. Blckw GU17 .... 64 C4
Victoria Dr.
 Putney SW15 & SW19 ...... 19 D7
Victoria Entertainments Ctr The.
 Woking GU21 .... 69 E2
Victoria Gdns. Bigg H TN16 . 83 C4
Victoria Gdns. Heston TW5 ... 4 E7
Victoria Jun Sch The.
 Felt TW13 .... 15 B7
Victoria La.
 Wimble SW19 .... 19 C1
Victoria Lodge.
 Wimble SW19 .... 19 C1
Victoria Pl. **5** Esher KT10 ... 55 B6
Victoria Pl. Ewell KT17 ...... 76 E7
Victoria Pl. **16** Horley RH6 ... 6 D2
Victoria Rd. Addl KT15 ...... 52 D6
Victoria Rd. Alder GU11 .... 105 A2
Victoria Rd. Ascot SL5 ...... 29 A4
Victoria Rd. Coulsd CR5 .... 79 D4
Victoria Rd. Cran GU6 .... 174 D3
Victoria Rd. Crawl RH11 .. 201 C6
Victoria Rd. Earls RH1 .... 140 A8
Victoria Rd. Farnb GU14 .... 85 B4
Victoria Rd. Farnh GU9 .... 125 C2
Victoria Rd. Felt TW13 ...... 15 B6
Victoria Rd. Godal GU7 .... 150 E4
Victoria Rd. Guild GU1 .... 109 E1
Victoria Rd. Horley RH6 .. 161 B2
Victoria Rd. King U T KT6 ... 37 D3

Victoria Rd. King U T KT1 ..... 37 F7
Victoria Rd. Knaph GU21 ...... 68 E1
Victoria Rd. Mitch CR4 & SW19 .... 20 F1
Victoria Rd. Mortl SW14 .... 7 D4
Victoria Rd. Oat Pk KT13 ...... 53 D7
Victoria Rd. Sandh GU15 .... 45 E1
Victoria Rd. Stain TW18 .... 12 E5
Victoria Rd. Sutton SM1 .... 59 D5
Victoria Rd. Tedd TW11 .... 17 A2
Victoria Rd. Twick TW1 .... 17 B8
Victoria Rd. Woking GU22 ..... 69 F2
Victoria St. Eng Gn TW20 ..... 11 C2
Victoria St. Horsh RH13 ..... 217 D2
Victoria Terr. Dork RH4 ..... 136 A7
Victoria Track. Farnb GU11 104 E7
Victoria Villas. Rich TW9 .... 6 F3
Victoria Way. E Grins RH19 205 F7
Victoria Way. Oat Pk KT13 ... 53 D7
Victoria Way. Woking GU21 & GU22 .... 69 E2
Victors Dr. Hampt TW12 ...... 15 E2
Victory Ave. Morden SM4 .... 40 C4
Victory Bsns Ctr The. Islew TW7 .... 5 F3
Victory Cotts. Effing KT24 .. 113 E7
Victory Park Rd. Addl KT15 .. 52 C6
Victory Pl. S Norw SE19 .... 22 E2
Victory Rd. Chert KT16 .... 33 A1
Victory Rd. Horsh RH12 ..... 217 B3
Victory Rd. Merton SW19 ..... 20 C1
Victory Road Mews. 5 Merton SW19 .... 20 C1
Vienna Ct. W Heath GU14 .... 85 A6
View Cl. Bigg H TN16 .... 83 C3
View Terr. Dorman RH7 ..... 165 A1
Viewfield Rd. Wands SW18 . 19 F8
Viggory La. Horse GU21 .... 69 C4
Vigilant Cl. For Hil SE26 .... 23 A4
Viking. Easth RG12 .... 26 E4
Viking Ct. Hampt TW12 .... 36 B8
Village Cl. 3 Oat Pk KT13 ... 53 D7
Village Ct. Ascot SL5 .... 29 C4
Village Gate. Shep TW17 ..... 34 B4
Village Gdns. Ewell KT17 ..... 57 F1
Village Green Ave. Bigg H TN16 .... 83 E2
Village Green Way. Bigg H TN16 .... 83 E2
Village Rd. Egham TW20 ...... 32 C6
Village Row. Belm SM2 .... 59 A3
Village St. Newd RH5 .... 158 B1
Village The. Old W SL4 .... 10 B5
Village Way. Ashf TW15 .... 14 A4
Village Way. Beck BR3 .... 44 A6
Village Way. Sander CR2 ..... 81 A6
Villas The. Blind H RH7 .... 163 E8
Villiers Ave. King U T KT5 ..... 37 F5
Villiers Ave. Twick TW2 .... 15 F7
Villiers Cl. King U T KT5 .... 37 F5
Villiers Gr. E Ewell SM2 .... 58 D2
Villiers Mead. Woki RG11 ..... 25 A6
Villiers Rd. Hounsl TW7 .... 5 E5
Villiers Rd. King U T KT1 .... 37 F6
Villiers Rd. Penge BR3 .... 43 D7
Villiers The. Whit V KT13 ...... 53 D4
Vinall Gdns. Broad H RH12 216 D4
Vincam Cl. Twick TW2 .... 16 A8
Vincent Ave. Sutton SM5 ...... 78 D8
Vincent Ave. 3 Tolw KT5 .... 38 B1
Vincent Cl. Chert KT16 .... 32 E2
Vincent Cl. Esher KT10 .... 55 B7
Vincent Cl. Fetch KT23 .... 94 B4
Vincent Cl. Harm UB7 .... 3 A8
Vincent Cl. Horsh RH13 ...... 217 F2
Vincent Dr. Dork RH4 .... 136 A6
Vincent Dr. Up Hall TW17 .... 34 E6
Vincent House. New Mal KT3 38 F5
Vincent La. Dork RH4 .... 136 A7
Vincent Rd. Chert KT16 .... 32 E2
Vincent Rd. Coulsd CR5 .... 79 C3
Vincent Rd. Croy CR0 .... 42 E2
Vincent Rd. Dork RH4 .... 136 A7
Vincent Rd. Hounsl TW4 .... 4 D4
Vincent Rd. Hounsl TW7 .... 5 D6
Vincent Rd. King U T KT1 ..... 38 A6
Vincent Rd. Stk D'A KT11 ..... 73 E3
Vincent Rise. Brack RG12 .... 27 E6
Vincent Row. Hampt TW12 .. 16 C3
Vincent Sq. Bigg H TN16 ...... 83 C6
Vincents Cl. Chips CR5 .... 98 F7
Vine Cl. Farnb GU11 .... 105 A6
Vine Cl. Rowl GU10 .... 146 A4
Vine Cl. Stan TW19 .... 2 A2
Vine Cl. Surb KT5 .... 37 F3
Vine Cl. Sutton SM1 .... 59 C7
Vine Cotts. Cran GU6 .... 174 B3
Vine Ct. Hersh KT12 .... 54 C4
Vine House Cl. Mytch GU16 . 86 A3
Vine La. Rowl GU10 .... 146 A5
Vine Pl. Hounsl TW3 .... 5 B3
Vine Rd. Barnes SW13 & SW15 .... 7 F4
Vine Rd. E Mole KT8 .... 36 C5
Vine Rd. Mortl SW13 & SW15 7 F4
Vine St. Alder GU11 .... 105 A1
Vine Way. Rowl GU10 .... 146 A5
Vineries Cl. Harm UB7 .... 3 A8
Viners Cl. Walt O T KT12 .... 35 C3
Viney Bank. New Add CR0 ..... 62 F2
Vineyard Cl. For Hil SE6 .... 24 A7
Vineyard Cl. King U T KT1 .... 37 F6
Vineyard Hill Rd. Wimble SW19 .... 20 A4
Vineyard Path. Mortl SW14 ... 7 D4
Vineyard Rd. Felt TW13 .... 15 A5
Vineyard Row. Tedd KT1 & KT8 .... 37 C8
Vineyard Sch The. Rich TW10 6 E1
Vineyard The. Rich TW10 .... 6 E2
Vineyards The. Felt TW13 .... 15 A5
Vinter Ct. Shep Gn TW17 ...... 34 A4
Viola Ave. Felt TW14 .... 4 C1
Viola Ave. Stan TW19 .... 13 E7
Viola Croft. Wink RG12 .... 27 F8
Violet Cl. Carsh CR4 .... 41 A1
Violet Gdns. Croy CR0 .... 61 B5
Violet La. Croy CR0 .... 61 B5
Violette Szabo House. 4 W Norw SE27 .... 22 D4
Virginia Ave. Vir W GU25 ..... 31 C4
Virginia Beeches. Vir W GU25 .... 31 C6
Virginia Cl. Ashtd KT21 .... 75 D1
Virginia Cl. King U T KT3 ...... 38 C5
Virginia Cl. Laleh TW18 .... 33 C6
Virginia Cl. Whit V KT13 .... 53 C4
Virginia Ct. Vir W GU25 .... 31 D5
Virginia Dr. Vir W GU25 .... 31 C5
Virginia Gdns. Farnb GU14 .. 85 C2
Virginia Gdns. W Byfl KT14 .. 71 B7
Virginia Rd. S Norw CR7 .... 42 B8
Virginia Water Prep Sch. Vir W GU25 .... 31 D5
Virginia Water Sta. Vir W GU25 .... 31 E4
Viscount Gdns. Byfl KT14 ..... 71 E7
Viscount Ind Est. Poyle SL3 .. 1 E4
Viscount Rd. Stan TW19 ...... 13 E7
Viscount Way. Hatton TW6 ... 3 E3
Vivien Cl. Chess KT9 .... 56 E3
Vivienne Cl. Crawl RH11 ... 181 D1
Vivienne Cl. Twick TW1 .... 6 D1
Vivienne House. Stain TW18 13 A3
Vixen Track. Farnb GU14 ... 104 C7
Voewood Cl. New Mal KT3 ... 38 F3
Vogan Cl. Woodh RH2 .... 139 B6
Volta Way. Croy CR0 & CR9 . 41 F1
Voltaire. 14 Rich TW9 .... 6 F6
Voss Ct. Streat SW16 .... 21 E2
Vowels La. W Hoath RH19 . 204 E2
Vulcan Bsns Ctr. New Add CR9 .... 63 E2
Vulcan Cl. Crawl RH11 .... 201 C2
Vulcan Cl. Sandh GU17 .... 64 A7
Vulcan Cl. Wallin SM6 .... 60 F3
Vulcan Way. Farnb GU14 ... 104 C8
Vulcan Way. New Add CR0 & CR9 .... 63 E1
Vulcan Way. Sandh GU17 ...... 64 B7

Waddington Ave. Coulsd CR5 & CR8 .... 100 B8
Waddington Cl. Coulsd CR5 100 B8
Waddington Cl.Crawl RH11 201 A3
Waddington Way. S Norw CR7 & SE19 .... 42 D8
Waddon Cl. Croy CR0 & CR9 61 A7
Waddon Court Rd. Croy CR0 & CR9 .... 61 A7
Waddon Inf Sch. Croy CR9 .. 61 A5
Waddon Marsh Sta. Croy CR0 .... 41 F1
Waddon Marsh Way. Croy CR0 & CR9 .... 41 F1
Waddon New Rd. Croy CR0 & CR9 .... 61 B8
Waddon Park Ave. Croy CR0 & CR9 .... 61 A7
Waddon Rd. Croy CR0 & CR9 61 B7
Waddon Sta. Croy CR0 .... 61 A6
Waddon Way. Croy CR0 & CR2 & CR9 .... 61 B4
Wade's La. Tedd TW11 .... 17 A3
Wadham. Sandh GU15 .... 45 F1
Wadham Cl. Crawl RH10 ... 182 C1
Wadham Cl. Shep TW17 .... 34 C2
Wadhurst Cl. Penge SE20 .... 43 B7
Wadlands Brook Rd. Dorm Pk RH19 .... 185 D5
Wagbullock Rise. Easth RG12 .... 27 C3
Wagg Cl. E Grins RH19 ...... 186 A1
Waggon Cl. Stough GU2 ..... 108 E2
Waggoners Hollow. Bagsh GU19 .... 47 E2
Waggoners Way. Graysh GU26 .... 188 A4
Waggoners Wells Rd. Graysh GU26 .... 188 A2
Wagtail Cl. Horsh RH12 ..... 217 D7
Wagtail Gdns. Selsd CR2 ..... 62 E1
Waights Ct. King U T KT2 ..... 37 E8
Wain End. Horsh RH12 ...... 217 D5
Wainford Cl. Putney SW19 .. 19 D7
Wainwright Gr. Islew TW7 ..... 5 D3
Wainwrights. Crawl RH11 . 201 D3
Waite Davies Rd. Lewish SE12 .... 24 F8
Wakefield Cl. Byfl KT14 .... 71 E7
Wakefield Gdns. S Norw SE19 .... 22 E1
Wakefield House. Dulw SE22 .... 23 B7
Wakefield Rd. 19 Rich TW10 . 6 D2
Wakehams Green Dr. Crawl RH10 .... 182 D1
Wakehurst Dr. Crawl RH10 & RH11 .... 201 D3
Wakehurst Mews. Horsh RH12 .... 216 F1
Wakehurst Path. Sheer GU21 .... 70 C5
Wakelin House. For Hil SE23 23 E8
Wakeling House. 8 W Norw SE27 .... 22 B5
Wakely Cl. Bigg H TN16 .... 83 C1
Walburton Rd. Purley CR8 ... 79 C7
Walbury. Brack RG12 .... 27 E5
Waldby Ct. Crawl RH11 ...... 201 A3
Waldeck Gr. W Norw SE27 ... 22 B5
Waldeck Rd. Brent W4 .... 7 A8
Waldeck Rd. Mortl SW14 .... 7 C4
Waldeck Terr. Mortl SW14 ..... 7 C4
Waldegrave Ct. 1 Tedd TW11 .... 16 F3
Waldegrave Gdns. Twick TW1 .... 16 F5
Waldegrave Pk. Tedd TW1 .. 16 F4
Waldegrave Rd. Penge SE19 22 F1
Waldegrave Rd. Tedd TW11 16 F4
Waldegrave Sch for Girls. Twick TW2 .... 16 D5
Waldegrove. S Croy CR0 ...... 61 F7
Waldemar Rd. Wimble SW19 .... 20 A3
Walden Cotts. Normdy GU3 107 A3
Walden Gdns. Thorn H CR7 & SW16 .... 41 F5
Waldens Park Rd. Horse GU21 .... 69 C3
Waldens Rd. Horse GU21 ..... 69 D2
Waldenshaw Rd. For Hil SE23 .... 23 C7
Waldo Pl. Mitch SW19 .... 20 E1
Waldorf Cl. Croy CR2 .... 61 B2
Waldorf Hts. Hawley GU17 .. 64 D3
Waldram Cres. For Hil SE23 23 C7
Waldram Park Rd. For Hil SE23 .... 23 D7
Waldram Pl. For Hil SE23 ..... 23 C7
Waldron Gdns. Beck BR2 ..... 44 D6
Waldron Hill. Brack RG12 ..... 27 F8
Waldron Rd. Wands SW17 & SW18 .... 20 C6
Waldronhyrst. Croy CR0 & 2 61 B6
Waldrons The. Croy CR0 ...... 61 C6
Waldrons The. Oxted RH8 . 122 F4
Waldy Rise. Cran GU6 .... 174 E4
Wales Ave. Carsh SM5 .... 59 E5
Walesbeech. Crawl RH10 .. 202 A5
Waleton Acres. Wallin SM6 . 60 C4
Waley's La. Ockley RH5 ...... 177 C1
Walford Rd. Dork RH5 .... 136 C3
Walham Rise. Wimble SW19 19 E2
Walk The. Ashf TW16 .... 14 F1
Walk The. Tand RH8 .... 122 A2
Walkden Hall (Hall of Residence). King U T KT2 .... 18 D4
Walker Cl. E Bed TW14 .... 14 F8
Walker Cl. Hampt TW12 .... 15 F2
Walker Rd. Worth RH10 ..... 202 C4
Walker's Ridge. Camb GU15 65 E5
Walkerscroft Mead. W Norw SE21 .... 22 C7
Walkfield Dr. Burgh H KT18 . 77 B2
Walking Bottom. Peasl GU5 .... 154 C6
Wall Hill Rd. For Row RH18 & RH19 .... 206 E5
Wallace Cl. Fairl GU3 .... 108 C4
Wallace Cl. Up Hall TW17 .... 34 D5
Wallace Cres. Wallin SM5 .... 59 F5
Wallace Fields. Ewell KT17 .. 77 A6
Wallace Fields Cty Inf Sch. Ewell KT17 .... 77 A6
Wallace Fields Cty Jun Sch. Ewell KT17 .... 77 A7
Wallace Wlk. Addl KT15 .... 52 C6
Wallage La. Worth RH10 ... 203 D6
Wallage La. Worth RH10 ... 203 D6
Wallbrook Bsns Ctr. Hounsl TW4 .... 4 B4
Walled Garden The. Loxwd RH14 .... 212 F7
Walled Garden The. Tadw KT20 .... 97 D5
Walled Gdn The. Betch RH3 .... 137 D8
Waller La. Cater CR3 .... 100 F4
Wallingford Cl. Brack RG12 . 27 E5
Wallington Ct. 10 Wallin SM6 .... 60 B4
Wallington High Sch for Boys. Wallin SM6 .... 60 B6
Wallington High Sch for Girls. Wallin SM6 .... 60 B2
Wallington Rd. Camb GU15 . 47 A1
Wallington Sq. 4 Wallin SM6 .... 60 C4
Wallington Sta. Wallin SM6 . 60 B4
Wallis Ct. Crawl RH10 .... 181 D2
Wallis House. E Grins RH19 185 E1
Wallis Mews. Fetch KT22 ..... 95 A5
Wallis Way. Horsh RH13 ... 218 A4
Wallner Way. Woki RG11 ..... 25 E5
Wallop Sch. Weyb KT13 .... 53 B5
Wallorton Gdns. Mortl SW14 7 D3
Walmer Cl. Crowth RG11 ..... 45 C5
Walmer Cl. Friml GU16 .... 86 A7
Walmer House. 11 Penge SE20 .... 23 C1
Walmsley House. 1 Streat SW16 .... 21 C4
Walnut Cl. Alder GU11 ...... 126 A8
Walnut Cl. Carsh SM5 .... 59 F5
Walnut Cl. Epsom KT18 .... 76 F4
Walnut Ct. Horsh RH13 .... 217 E1
Walnut Dr. Kings KT20 .... 97 E3
Walnut Gr. Nork SM7 .... 77 D5
Walnut House. Woodh RH2 139 C7
Walnut La. Crawl RH11 ..... 181 B1
Walnut Mews. Sutton SM2 ... 59 C3
Walnut Tree Ave. Mitch CR4 40 E6
Walnut Tree Cl. Barnes SW13 7 F6
Walnut Tree Cl. Belm SM7 ... 77 E7
Walnut Tree Cl. Guild GU1 . 130 C8
Walnut Tree Gdns. Farnc GU7 .... 150 E7
Walnut Tree La. Byfl KT14 ... 71 D7
Walnut Tree Rd. Brent TW8 .. 6 E8
Walnut Tree Rd. Charlt TW17 .... 34 C7
Walnut Tree Rd. Heston TW5 4 F8
Walpole Ave. Chips CR5 .... 98 F8
Walpole Ave. Rich TW9 .... 6 F5
Walpole Cres. 7 Tedd TW11 .... 16 F3
Walpole Ct. Twick TW2 .... 16 E6
Walpole Gdns. Twick TW2 ... 16 E5
Walpole Pl. 6 Tedd TW11 .. 16 F3
Walpole Rd. Croy CR0 & CR9 61 D8
Walpole Rd. Mitch SW19 ..... 20 D2
Walpole Rd. Old W SL4 .... 11 B8
Walpole Rd. Surb KT6 .... 37 E3
Walpole Rd. Tedd TW11 ...... 16 F3
Walpole Rd. Twick TW2 .... 16 E6
Walrus Rd. Farnb GU14 ...... 104 D8
Walsh Cres. New Add CR0 ... 82 E7
Walsh Meml C of E Mid Sch. Ash GU12 .... 106 A1
Walsh Memorial C of E Fst Sch. Ash GU12 .... 105 F1
Walsham Rd. Felt TW14 .... 15 B8
Walsingham Gdns. Worc Pk KT19 .... 57 F5
Walsingham Rd. Mitch CR4 . 40 F4
Walsingham Rd. New Add CR0 .... 63 C1
Walstead House. 2 Crawl RH10 .... 201 D5
Walter Cty Inf Sch. Woki RG11 .... 25 A6
Walter St. 1 King U T KT2 .. 37 E8
Walter's Mead. Ashtd KT21 . 75 E2
Walter's Rd. S Norw SE25 .... 42 E5
Waltham Ave. Stough GU2 109 B5
Waltham Cl. Sandh GU15 ..... 45 D1
Waltham Rd. Carsh SM5 ...... 40 E1
Waltham Rd. Cater CR3 ..... 101 B5
Walton Ave. Cheam SM3 ...... 58 F7
Walton Ave. New Mal KT3 ... 38 F5
Walton Bridge Rd. Oat Pk KT12 & TW17 .... 34 E2
Walton Comm Hospl. Walt O T KT12 .... 54 C8
Walton Ct. Woking GU21 ...... 70 A3
Walton Dr. N Asct SL5 .... 28 F8
Walton Gdns. Felt TW13 ...... 14 F4
Walton Gn. New Add CR0 ..... 63 C3
Walton Heath. Crawl RH10 202 D8
Walton La. Lo Hall TW17 ...... 34 D2
Walton La. Oat Pk KT12 .... 34 E1
Walton La. Weyb KT12 & KT13 .... 53 C8
Walton Leigh Special Trng Sch. Walt O T KT13 .... 53 F6
Walton on the Hill CE Jun Sch. Walt o t H KT20 .... 97 A2
Walton on the Hill Cty Prim Sch. Walt o t H KT20 .... 97 B3
Walton Park La. Walt O T KT12 .... 54 D8
Walton Pk. Walt O T KT12 .... 54 D8
Walton Rd. Ashtd KT18 .... 96 C6
Walton Rd. E Mole KT8 & KT12 .... 36 B5
Walton Rd. Walt O T KT12&KT8 .... 35 E4
Walton Rd. Woking GU21 ..... 70 A3
Walton St. Walt o t H KT20 .. 97 B3
Walton Terr. Woking GU21 .. 70 B4
Walton Way. Mitch CR4 .... 41 C5
Wanborough Dr. Rhampt SW15 .... 19 B7
Wanborough Hill. Wanb GU3 .... 128 C6
Wanborough La. Cran GU6 175 A3
Wanborough Sta. Flexf GU3 .... 107 C1
Wandle Bank. Merton SW19 20 D1
Wandle Bank. Wallin CR0 ..... 60 E7
Wandle Cl. Ash GU12 .... 106 A1
Wandle Cl. Worth RH10 ..... 202 C5
Wandle Court Gdns. Wallin CR0 .... 60 E7
Wandle Ct. W Ewell KT19 ..... 57 C6
Wandle Ct. W Ewell KT19 ..... 57 C6
Wandle Ct. Wallin CR0 .... 60 E7
Wandle House. Catf BR1 ...... 24 D3
Wandle House. 5 Redh RH1 .... 118 F2
Wandle House. Wands SW18 .... 20 B8
Wandle Lodge. Wallin CR0 .. 60 E7
Wandle Prim Sch. Wands SW18 .... 20 B7
Wandle Rd. Croy CR0 & CR9 61 C7
Wandle Rd. Hackb SM6 .... 60 B8
Wandle Rd. Morden CR4 & SM4 & SW19 40 D4
Wandle Rd. Up Toot SW17 ... 20 E6
Wandle Rd. Wallin CR0 .... 60 E7
Wandle Side. Croy CR0 .... 60 F7
Wandle Side. Hackb SM6 ..... 60 B7
Wandle Tech Pk. Carsh CR4 40 F2
Wandle Trad Est. Carsh CR4 40 F2
Wandle Valley Sch. Carsh SM5 .... 40 E2
Wandle Way. Mitch CR4 .... 40 F4
Wandle Way. Wands SW18 . 20 B7
Wandsdyke Cl. Friml GU16 .. 85 F8
Wandsworth Common Sta. Balham SW12 .... 20 F8
Wandsworth Sch. Putney SW18 .... 19 F8
Wansford Gn. 3 Woking GU21 .... 68 F2
Wanstraw Gr. Brack RG12 ... 27 E2
Wantage Cl. Brack RG12 ...... 27 E4
Wantage Rd. Sandh GU15 .... 64 D8
Wapiti Way. Farnb GU14 ... 104 D8
Waplings The. Walt o t H KT20 .... 97 B3
Wapshott Rd. Egham TW18 . 12 E3
War Coppice Rd. Cater RH1 .... 120 D7
War Memorial Homes. Chisw W4 .... 7 D7
War Memorial Hospl. Wallin SM5 .... 59 F4
Warbank Cl. New Add CR0 ... 63 E1
Warbank Cres. New Add CR0 63 E1
Warbank La. King U T KT2 .... 18 F1
Warblers Gn. Cobham KT11 . 73 F5
Warbleton House. 6 Crawl RH11 .... 200 F3
Warboys App. King U T KT2 . 18 B2
Warboys Rd. King U T KT2 ... 18 B2
Warburton Cl. E Grins RH19 .... 206 A8
Warburton Rd. Twick TW2 ... 16 B7

Warbury La. Knaph GU21 ..... 68 C3
Ward Cl. Woki RG11 .... 25 D8
Ward La. Warlgm CR6 .... 81 D2
Ward St. Guild GU1 .... 130 D8
Wardle Cl. Bagsh GU19 .... 47 E3
Wardley St. Wands SW18 ..... 20 B8
Wardrobe The. 3 Rich TW9 . 6 D2
Wards Stone Pk. Brack RG12 27 E2
Ware Ct. Cheam SM1 .... 58 F6
Wareham Cl. Hounsl TW3 ...... 5 B3
Wareham Rd. Brack RG12 .... 27 F4
Warenne Rd. Fetch KT22 ...... 94 C5
Warfield Rd. Brack RG12 ...... 27 C8
Warfield Rd. E Bed TW14 ..... 14 E8
Warfield Rd. Hampt TW12 ..... 36 B8
Wargrove Dr. Sandh GU15 ... 64 D8
Warham Rd. Croy CR0 & CR2 61 C5
Waring St. W Norw SE27 ...... 22 C4
Warkworth Gdns. Hounsl TW7 .... 6 A7
Warlingham Cty Sec Sch. Warlgm CR6 .... 81 A3
Warlingham Park Hospl. Chelsh CR6 .... 82 A4
Warlingham Park Sch. Chelsh CR6 .... 82 A3
Warlingham Rd. Thorn H CR7 .... 42 B5
Warltersville Way. Horley RH6 .... 161 C1
Warminster Gdns. S Norw SE25 .... 43 A7
Warminster Rd. S Norw SE25 .... 43 A7
Warminster Sq. S Norw SE25 .... 43 A7
Warminster Way. Mitch CR4 41 B7
Warner Ave. Cheam SM3 ..... 58 E8
Warner Cl. Harl UB3 .... 3 D7
Warner Ct. Cheam SM3 .... 58 E8
Warner House. Beck BR3 ...... 24 B2
Warner Rd. Broml BR1 .... 24 F1
Warners La. Albury GU5 ..... 132 E2
Warnford House. Rhampt SW15 .... 7 E1
Warnham CE (Controlled) Sch. Warn RH12 .... 216 F8
Warnham Court Rd. Wallin SM5 .... 59 F3
Warnham Ct Sch. Warn RH12 .... 216 F7
Warnham House. 9 Streat SW2 .... 21 F8
Warnham Nature Reserve. Horsh RH12 .... 217 B6
Warnham Rd. Broad H RH12 .... 216 D4
Warnham Rd. Crawl RH10 202 B4
Warnham Rd. Horsh RH12 217 B5
Warnham Sta. Faygt RH12 217 C8
Warpole Pk. Whit V KT13 ..... 53 A3
Warramill Rd. Godal GU7 .. 151 A5
Warren Ave. Belm SM2 .... 58 F1
Warren Ave. Broml BR1 .... 24 E1
Warren Ave. Mortl SW14 & TW10 .... 7 B3
Warren Ave. S Croy CR2 .... 62 D3
Warren Cl. Esher KT10 .... 55 B6
Warren Cl. Felb RH19 .... 184 E3
Warren Cl. Sandh GU17 .... 64 A8
Warren Cl. W Norw SE21 ..... 22 C8
Warren Cnr. Crond GU10 .... 124 C7
Warren Ct. 18 Beck BR3 ...... 24 A1
Warren Ct. 6 Croy CR0 .... 42 E1
Warren Ct. Weyb KT13 .... 53 A5
Warren Cutting. King U T KT2 .... 18 D1
Warren Down. Brack RG12 .. 26 E8
Warren Dr. Crawl RH11 ..... 201 A8
Warren Dr. Kings KT20 .... 98 A4
Warren Dr N. Tolw KT5 & KT6 .... 38 B1
Warren Dr S. Tolw KT5 .... 38 C1
Warren Farm Mobile Home Pk. Mayb GU23 .... 91 B8
Warren Hill. Woodc KT18 ..... 76 D3
Warren House Rd. Woki RG11 .... 25 D8
Warren La. Mayb GU22 & GU23 .... 71 B1
Warren La. Oxsh KT22 .... 74 C7
Warren La. Oxted RH8 .... 123 A1
Warren Lodge. Kings KT20 .. 97 E3
Warren Lodge Dr. Kings KT20 .... 97 E3
Warren Mead. Nork SM7 ..... 77 C4
Warren Mead Cty Inf Sch. Nork SM7 .... 77 D4
Warren Mead Cty Jun Sch. Nork SM7 .... 77 D4
Warren Park Rd. Carsh SM1 & SM2 .... 59 E4
Warren Pk. King U T KT2 ...... 18 C2
Warren Pk. Warlgm CR6 ...... 81 D1
Warren Rd. Ashf TW15 .... 14 E1
Warren Rd. Croy CR0 .... 42 F1
Warren Rd. Farnc GU7 .... 150 E7
Warren Rd. Guild GU1 & GU4 .... 131 A8
Warren Rd. King U T KT2 ...... 18 C2
Warren Rd. Mitch SW19 .... 20 E2
Warren Rd. Nork KT17 & SM7 .... 77 D5
Warren Rd. Purley CR8 .... 80 B8
Warren Rd. Reig RH2 .... 118 B2
Warren Rd. Twick TW2 .... 5 D1
Warren Rd. Woodhm KT15 ... 52 A1
Warren Rise. Friml GU16 ..... 65 F3
Warren Rise. King U T KT3 ... 38 D8
Warren Row. N Asct SL5 ...... 28 D7
Warren The. Alder GU11 ... 104 F1
Warren The. Ashtd KT21 ...... 95 F7
Warren The. E Hors KT24 ... 112 F5
Warren The. Heath E GU9 .. 125 E8
Warren The. Heston TW5 ...... 4 F7
Warren The. Kings KT20 ...... 97 E4
Warren The. Oxsh KT22 .... 74 D6
Warren The. Sutton SM2 & SM5 .... 59 E2
Warren The. Worc Pk KT19 & KT4 .... 57 D7
Warren Track. Farnb GU14 104 D7
Warren Way. Whit V KT13 .... 53 C4
Warren Wood Cl. Coney H BR2 .... 63 F8
Warreners La. Whit V KT13 .. 53 D3
Warrenhyrst. Guild GU1 .... 131 A8
Warrenne Rd. Brock RH3 ... 137 C7
Warrington Cl. Crawl RH11 200 E2
Warrington Mews. Alder GU11 .... 125 E8
Warrington Rd.Croy CR0 & 9 61 B7
Warrington Rd. 21 Rich TW10 .... 6 D2
Warrington Spur. Old W SL4 11 B8
Warwick. Brack RG12 .... 27 E3
Warwick Ave. Stain TW18 ..... 13 C2
Warwick Ave. Thor L TW20 .. 32 C8
Warwick Cl. Alder GU11 ..... 126 C8
Warwick Cl. Friml GU15 .... 66 B3
Warwick Cl. Hampt TW12 ..... 16 C1
Warwick Cl. S Holm RH5 .... 157 B7
Warwick Ct. Beck BR2 .... 44 E7
Warwick Ct. Weyb KT13 .... 53 A5
Warwick Deeping. Ottsh KT16 .... 51 C5
Warwick Gdns. Ashtd KT21 . 75 C2
Warwick Gdns. Thame D KT7 36 F4
Warwick Gdns. Thorn H CR7 42 A5
Warwick Gr. Surb KT5 .... 37 F2
Warwick House. 4 King U T KT2 .... 37 E8
Warwick La. Woking GU21 ... 89 A8
Warwick Lodge. Cheam SM1 58 F6
Warwick Rd. Ash V GU12 .. 106 A8
Warwick Rd. Ashf TW15 .... 13 E3
Warwick Rd. Coulsd CR5 ...... 79 D5
Warwick Rd. Farnb GU14 .. 104 D8
Warwick Rd. Hounsl TW4 ...... 4 B4
Warwick Rd. King U T KT3 .... 38 C6
Warwick Rd. Penge SE20 ..... 43 B6
Warwick Rd. Redh RH1 ...... 118 F2
Warwick Rd. S Holm RH5 ... 157 C7
Warwick Rd. Sutton SM1 ...... 59 C5
Warwick Rd. Tedd KT1 .... 37 C8
Warwick Rd. Thame D KT7 .... 36 F4
Warwick Rd. Thorn H CR7 .... 42 A6
Warwick Rd. Twick TW2 .... 16 E7
Warwick Sch The. Redh RH1 .... 119 A2
Warwick Villas. Thor L TW20 32 C8
Warwick Wold Rd. Bletch RH1 .... 120 A7
Warwick Wold Rd. Cater RH1 .... 120 A7
Warwick's Bench Rd. Guild GU1 .... 130 E6
Warwicks Bench. Guild GU1 .... 130 D6
Wasdale Cl. Sandh GU15 ...... 45 D2
Washington Cl. Reig RH2 . 118 A3
Washington Ct. Up Toot SW17 .... 20 F2
Washington Rd. Crawl RH11 .... 200 E3
Washington Rd. King U T KT1 .... 38 A7
Washington Rd. N Cheam KT4 .... 39 B1
Washpond La. Chelsh CR6 ... 82 C1
Wasp Green La. Outw RH1 162 C8
Wassand Cl. Crawl RH10 ... 202 A6
Wastdale Rd. For Hil SE23 ... 23 D7
Watchetts Cty Jun Sch. Camb GU15 .... 65 B2
Watchetts Dr. Camb GU15 ... 65 C2
Watchetts Lake Cl. Camb GU15 .... 65 D3
Watchetts Rd. Camb GU15 .. 65 B4
Watchmoor Rd. Camb GU15 65 A4
Watchmoor Trade Ctr. Camb GU15 .... 65 A3
Watcombe Cotts. Rich TW9 .. 7 A8
Watcombe Rd. Croy SE25 .... 43 B4
Water La. Abin C RH5 .... 155 B8
Water La. Albury GU4 & GU5 .... 132 B5
Water La. Bisley GU24 .... 87 E8
Water La. Cobham KT11 .... 73 F5
Water La. Ent Gn GU8 .... 171 B4
Water La. Farnh GU9 .... 125 F4
Water La. King U T KT1 .... 37 D8
Water La. L Book KT23 & KT24 .... 93 E1
Water La. Limps RH8 .... 123 A8
Water La. Lingf TN8 .... 165 D7
Water La. Rich TW10 & TW9 .. 6 D2
Water La. S Godst RH9 ...... 142 D5
Water La. Twick TW1 .... 17 A7
Water La. W Heath GU14 ..... 85 A7
Water La. Wormly GU8 .... 171 B4
Water Lea. Crawl RH10 ..... 202 A5
Water Mill Way. Felt TW13 . 16 A6
Water Splash La. Ascot SL5 . 29 E8
Water Tower Hill. S Croy CR0 & CR2 .... 61 D6
Water View. Horley RH6 .... 161 C3
Waterbank Rd. Catf SE6 ...... 24 C4
Watercress Way. Woking GU21 .... 69 B2
Waterden Cl. Guild GU1 ..... 130 F8
Waterden Rd. Guild GU1 .... 130 E8
Waterer Gdns. Burgh H KT20 77 E1
Waterer House. Catf SE6 ..... 24 C4
Waterer Rise. Wallin SM6 .... 60 D4
Waterers Rise. Knaph GU21 68 D2
Waterfall Cl. Vir W GU25 ..... 31 A6
Waterfall Cotts. Mitch SW19 20 D2
Waterfall Rd. Mitch SW19 ... 20 D2
Waterfall Terr. Up Toot SW17 .... 20 E2
Waterfield. Burgh H KT20 .... 97 B7
Waterfield Cl. Horsh RH13 . 217 E3
Waterfield Cty Fst Sch. Crawl RH11 .... 200 E4
Waterfield Dr. Warlgm CR6 101 C8
Waterfield Gdns. Crawl RH11 .... 200 E4
Waterfield Gdns. S Norw SE25 .... 42 E4
Waterfield Gn. Burgh H KT20 97 B7
Waterfields. Leahd KT22 ...... 95 B8
Waterford Way. Woki RG11 25 C6
Watergardens The. King U T KT2 .... 18 C2
Waterham Rd. Easth RG12 ... 27 B3
Waterhouse Ct. 5 Tedd TW11 .... 16 F3
Waterhouse La. Bletch RH1 121 A3
Waterhouse La. Coulsd CR8 100 C8
Waterhouse La. Kings KT20 . 97 E6
Waterhouse Mead. Sandh GU15 .... 64 D7
Waterlands La. Rowhk RH12 .... 196 E1
Waterloo Cl. Camb GU15 ..... 66 B7
Waterloo Cl. E Bed TW14 ..... 14 F7
Waterloo Cres. Woki RG11 .. 25 E4
Waterloo Pl. Rich TW9 .... 7 A8
Waterloo Rd. Alder GU12 ... 105 C1
Waterloo Rd. Carsh SM1 ...... 59 D5
Waterloo Rd. Crowth RG11 .. 45 B4
Waterloo Rd. Epsom KT17 & KT19 .... 76 D6
Waterloo Rd. Woki RG11 ...... 25 F5
Waterlow Rd. Reig RH2 ..... 139 D8
Watermans Bsns Pk The. Egham TW18 .... 12 E4
Watermans Ct. 12 Brent TW8 .... 6 D8
Watermans Ct. 2 Brent TW8 6 E8
Watermead. E Bed TW14 ...... 14 E7
Watermead. Tadw KT20 .... 97 B6
Watermead. Woking GU21 ... 68 F3
Watermead La. Carsh CR4 .... 40 F2
Watermead Rd. Catf SE6 ..... 24 C4
Watermeads High Sch. Morden SM4 .... 40 D3
Watermen's Sq. 1 Penge SE20 .... 23 C1
Watermill Cl. Rich TW10 ...... 17 C5
Watermill Way. Merton SW19 .... 40 C8
Waterperry La. Chobh GU24 49 F1
Waters Dr. Stain TW18 .... 12 F4
Waters Rd. Catf SE6 .... 24 E5
Waters Rd. King U T KT1 ...... 38 B7
Waters Sq. King U T KT1 ...... 38 B6
Watersedge. W Ewell KT19 .. 57 C6
Watersedge. W Ewell KT19 .. 57 C6
Waterside. Beck BR3 .... 44 A8
Waterside. E Grins RH19 ... 186 B1
Waterside. Horley RH6 ...... 161 A5
Waterside Cl. Crawl RH11 . 200 E4
Waterside Cl. Godal GU7 .. 151 A5
Waterside Cl. Surb KT6 .... 56 E8
Waterside La. Godal GU7 ... 150 C3
Waterside Mews. Bellf GU1 109 C3
Waterside Rd. Bellf GU1 ... 109 D4
Waterside Trad Est. Addl KT15 .... 52 E6
Waterside Way. Wimble SW17 .... 20 C3
Waterside Way. 2 Woking GU21 .... 69 B1
Waterslade. Redh RH1 .... 118 E1
Watersmeet Cl. Burph GU4 110 A6
Watersplash Cl. King U T KT1 .... 37 E6
Watersplash Rd. Shep Gn TW17 .... 34 A5
Waterway Rd. Fetch KT22 .... 95 A5
Waterway Rd. Leahd KT22 ... 95 A5
Watery La. Chobh GU24 .... 49 D1
Watery La. Merton SW19 & SW20 .... 39 F7
Wates Way. Mitch CR4 .... 40 F3
Watford Cl. Guild GU1 .... 109 F1
Wathen Rd. Dork RH4 .... 136 B8
Watlings Cl. Croy CR0 .... 43 E3
Watlington Gr. For Hil SE26 23 E3
Watney Cotts. Mortl SW14 .... 7 C4
Watney Rd. Mortl SW14 .... 7 C4
Watneys Rd. Mitch CR4 .... 41 D4
Watson Ave. Cheam SM3 ..... 58 E8
Watson Cl. Mitch SW19 .... 20 E1
Watson House. 3 Streat SW2 .... 21 E8
Watson Rd. Westc RH4 ...... 135 C6
Watt's La. Tadw KT20 .... 97 D5
Watt's La. Tedd TW11 .... 17 A3
Watt's Mead. Tadw KT20 ..... 97 D5
Wattenden Prim Sch. Purley CR8 .... 80 B3
Wattendon Rd. Purley CR8 .. 80 B3
Watts Common Rd. Farnb GU11 .... 104 E7
Watts Rd. Thame D KT7 .... 37 A2
Watts Rd. W Heath GU14 ..... 84 F5
Wavel Ct. 7 Streat SW16 ... 21 E5
Wavel Pl. Dulw SE19 & SE26 22 F4
Wavell Sch The. Farnb GU11 .... 105 B7
Wavendene Ave. Thor L TW20 .... 12 C1
Waveney House. 4 Redh RH1 .... 118 F1
Waveney Wlk. Crawl RH10 202 B4
Waverleigh Rd. Cran GU6 .. 174 E1
Waverley. Easth RG12 .... 26 E4
Waverley Abbey CE (VA) Sch. Tilf GU10 .... 147 D5
Waverley Ave. Kenley CR8 ... 80 E3
Waverley Ave. Sutton SM1 .. 59 C8
Waverley Ave. Tolw KT5 ...... 38 C3
Waverley Ave. Twick TW2 & TW4 .... 16 A7
Waverley Cl. Friml GU15 ...... 65 F4
Waverley Ct. Horsh RH12 . 217 B2
Waverley Ct. 1 Woking GU22 .... 69 E1
Waverley Dr. Addl KT16 .... 51 D7
Waverley Dr. Ash V GU12 . 106 A6
Waverley Dr. Camb GU15 .... 65 F5
Waverley Dr. Vir W GU25 ..... 31 A5
Waverley Gdns. Ash V GU12 .... 106 A6
Waverley La. Farnh GU10 & GU9 .... 147 C8
Waverley La. M Bourn GU9 125 E1
Waverley Pl. Leahd KT22 .... 95 B5
Waverley Rd. Bagsh GU19 .... 47 E3
Waverley Rd. Croy SE25 ...... 43 B6
Waverley Rd. Farnb GU14 ... 85 D3
Waverley Rd. Oxsh KT11 & KT22 .... 74 B5
Waverley Rd. Stonel KT17 & KT4 .... 58 B5
Waverley Rd. Weyb KT13 ..... 53 A5
Waverley Way. Sutton SM2 & SM5 .... 59 E4
Waverton Rd. Wands SW18 20 C8
Wavertree Ct. 9 Streat SW2 .... 21 E7
Wavertree Rd. Streat SW2 .. 21 F7
Way The. Reig RH2 .... 118 D2
Waye Ave. Cranf TW5 .... 4 A6
Wayland Cl. Brack RG12 ...... 27 F5
Waylands Mead. Beck BR3 .. 44 B8
Waylett Pl. W Norw SE27 ..... 22 B5
Wayman Rd. W Heath GU14 84 E8
Wayneflete Tower Ave. Esher KT10 .... 55 A7
Waynflete Ave.Croy CR0 & 9 61 B7
Waynflete La. Farnh GU9 .... 124 F2
Waynflete St. Wands SW18 . 20 C6
Ways End. Camb GU15 .... 65 E4
Wayside. Capel RH5 .... 178 D6
Wayside. Crawl RH11 .... 200 E4
Wayside. Mortl SW14 .... 7 C2
Wayside. New Add CR0 .... 63 B4
Wayside Ct. Hounsl TW7 .... 5 E5
Wayside Ct. Twick TW1 .... 6 C1
Wayside Ct. Woking GU21 .... 68 E3
WC Lee's Resthouses. Windl GU20 .... 48 D4
Weald CE Prim Sch The. Bear Gn RH5 .... 157 D3
Weald Cl. Shalf GU4 .... 130 E3
Weald Day Hospl The. Crawl RH11 .... 201 C6
Weald Dr. Crawl RH10 .... 202 A4
Weald The. E Grins RH19 ... 185 F4
Weald View Cotts. Coldh RH5 .... 156 D3
Weald Way. Cater CR3 & RH1 .... 120 E8
Weald Way. Dovgn RH2 ..... 139 C5
Wealdon Ct. 1 Stough GU2 .... 108 F1
Wealdstone Rd. Cheam SM3 58 F8
Weapon Rd. Farnb GU14 ...... 85 B2
Weare St. Capel RH5 .... 178 B4
Weare St. Ockley RH5 .... 177 F1
Weasdale Ct. Woking GU21 . 68 F3
Weatherall Cl. Addl KT15 ..... 52 B5
Weatherhill Cl. Horley RH6 161 F3
Weatherhill Cotts. Smallf RH6 .... 162 A4
Weatherhill Rd. Smallf RH6 162 A3
Weatherill Ct. Croy SE25 ..... 43 B3
Weaver Cl. Crawl RH11 ...... 200 E5
Weaver Wlk. W Norw SE27 .. 22 B4
Weavers Cl. Islew TW7 .... 5 E3
Weavers Gdns. Wreccl GU10 & GU9 .... 145 F7
Webb Cl. Bagsh GU19 .... 47 E1
Webb Cl. Crawl RH11 .... 201 B1
Webb Ct. Woki RG11 .... 25 E8
Webb House. Felt TW13 ...... 15 E5
Webb Rd. Witley GU8 .... 170 C6
Webster Cl. Oxsh KT11 & KT22 .... 74 B5
Websters Cl. Woking GU22 .. 89 B7
Weddell Rd. Crawl RH10 ..... 201 F3
Wedgewood Ct. Beck BR2 ... 44 F5
Wedgwood Way. S Norw SE19 .... 22 C1
Wedgwoods. Tats TN16 ..... 103 C6
Weeks House. Rich TW10 .... 17 C4
Weighbridge Rd. Woodhm KT15 .... 52 B2
Weighton Rd. Penge SE20 ... 43 B7
Weihurst Ct. Carsh SM1 .... 59 E5
Weihurst Gdns. Carsh SM1 .. 59 D5
Weir Ave. Farnb GU14 .... 85 A3
Weir Cl. Farnb GU14 .... 85 A3
Weir House. 8 Streat SW12 21 C8
Weir Pl. Egham TW18 .... 32 E8
Weir Rd. Chert KT16 .... 33 B2
Weir Rd. Farnb GU14 .... 84 A2
Weir Rd. Streat SW12 .... 21 C8
Weir Rd. Walt O T KT12 .... 35 A3
Weir Rd. Wimble SW18 & 19 20 B5
Weirbrook. Crawl RH10 ..... 202 A3
Welbeck. Easth RG12 .... 26 E4
Welbeck Cl. Ewell KT17 .... 58 A3
Welbeck Cl. Farnb GU14 ...... 84 F3
Welbeck Cl. New Mal KT3 .... 38 F4
Welbeck Rd. Carsh SM1 & SM5 .... 59 D8
Welbeck Wlk. Carsh SM5 ..... 40 D1
Welcome Cotts. Wold CR3 102 A4
Welcome Terr. Whytlf CR3 .. 80 F3
Welcomes Rd. Kenley CR8 ... 80 C3
Weldon Ct. Thorn H CR7 ...... 42 B4
Weldon Dr. E Mole KT8 .... 35 F5
Weldon Way. Merst RH1 ... 119 D6
Welford Pl. Wimble SW19 .... 19 E4
Welham Rd. Streat SW16 & SW17 .... 21 B2
Welhouse Rd. Carsh SM5 .... 59 E8

Well Cl. Camb GU15 .... 65 B4
Well Cl. Horse GU21 .... 69 C2
Well Cl. Streat SW16 .... 21 F4
Well Farm Rd. Whytlf CR3 & CR6 .... 101 A8
Well House. Banstd SM7 .... 78 B4
Well La. Haslem GU27 .... 208 D6
Well La. Horse GU21 .... 69 C2
Well La. Mortl SW14 .... 7 C2
Well Path. Horse GU21 .... 69 C2
Well Way. Epsom KT18 .... 76 A5
Welland Cl. Bra Hil SL3 .... 1 B8
Wellburn Cl. Sandh GU17 .... 64 B7
Weller Cl. Worth RH10 .... 202 D5
Weller Dr. Camb GU15 .... 65 C3
Wellesford Cl. Banstd SM7 .. 77 F2
Wellesley Cl. Ash V GU12 ... 105 F7
Wellesley Cl. Bagsh GU19 .... 47 C3
Wellesley Court Rd. [1] Croy CR0 & CR9 .... 61 D8
Wellesley Cres. Twick TW2 . 16 E5
Wellesley Ct. Cheam SM3 .... 39 E1
Wellesley Ct. Twick TW2 .... 16 E5
Wellesley Garden. Heath E GU9 .... 125 C7
Wellesley Gate. Alder GU12 .... 105 B1
Wellesley Gr. Croy CR0 & CR9 .... 61 D8
Wellesley Rd. Alder GU11 .. 104 E2
Wellesley Rd. Croy CR0 .... 42 C1
Wellesley Rd. Farnb GU14 104 D8
Wellesley Rd. Rushm GU10 168 C6
Wellesley Rd. Sutton SM2 .... 59 C4
Wellesley Rd. Twick TW2 .... 16 E5
Wellfield. Ash W RH19 .... 206 C7
Wellfield Rd. Streat SW16 ... 21 F4
Wellhouse Rd. Beck BR3 .... 44 A5
Wellhouse Rd. Betch RH3 . 137 D6
Wellington Ave. Alder GU11 .... 104 F2
Wellington Ave. Hounsl TW3 & TW4 .... 5 A2
Wellington Ave. N Cheam KT4 .... 58 C7
Wellington Ave. Vir W GU25 31 B4
Wellington Ave. Went GU25 31 B4
Wellington Cl. Crawl RH10 182 E1
Wellington Cl. Sandh GU17 . 64 C8
Wellington Cl. Walt O T KT12 .... 34 F1
Wellington Coll. Crowth RG11 .... 45 A3
Wellington Cotts. E Hors KT24 .... 112 E6
Wellington Cres. King U T KT3 .... 38 C6
Wellington Ct. Stan TW19 .... 13 E8
Wellington Ct. [5] Surb KT6 . 37 E3
Wellington Ct. Tedd TW12 .. 16 D3
Wellington Ctr. Alder GU11 105 A2
Wellington Dr. Brack RG12 .. 27 E4
Wellington Dr. Wallin CR8 ... 60 F1
Wellington Gdns. Alder GU11 .... 104 F1
Wellington Gdns. Tedd TW12 & TW2 .... 16 D4
Wellington La. Heath E GU9 .... 125 D7
Wellington Prim Sch. Hounsl TW3 .... 4 F5
Wellington Rd. Ashf TW15 .. 13 E3
Wellington Rd. Cater CR3 .. 100 C5
Wellington Rd. Crowth RG11 45 C4
Wellington Rd. Hatton TW14 . 3 E2
Wellington Rd. Horsh RH12 & RH13 .... 217 D2
Wellington Rd. Sandh GU15 & GU17 .... 64 C8
Wellington Rd. Tedd TW12 & TW2 .... 16 D4
Wellington Rd. Thorn H CR0 42 B2
Wellington Rd. Wimble SW19 .... 20 A6
Wellington Rd. Woki RG11 .. 25 B5
Wellington Rd N. Hounsl TW4 4 F4
Wellington Rd S. Hounsl TW4 4 F3
Wellington St. Alder GU11 105 A2
Wellington Terr. [6] Knaph GU21 .... 68 E1
Wellington Terr. Sandh GU15 .... 64 C8
Wellington Town Rd. E Grins RH19 .... 185 D2
Wellington Way. Byfl KT13 .. 52 F1
Wellington Way. Farnb GU14 .... 104 D7
Wellington Way. Horley RH6 .... 160 F5
Wellington Way. Whit V KT13 .... 52 F1
Wellingtonia House. Addl KT15 .... 52 A5
Wellmeadow Rd. Catf SE13 & SE6 .... 24 E7
Wellow Wlk. Carsh SM5 .... 40 D1
Wells Cl. Fetch KT23 .... 94 C3
Wells Cl. Horsh RH12 .... 216 F2
Wells Cotts. Wreccl GU9 ... 146 A7
Wells La. Ascot SL5 .... 29 B5
Wells La. Normdy GU3 .... 107 C4
Wells Lea. E Grins RH19 .... 185 D3
Wells Meadow. E Grins RH19 .... 185 D3
Wells Park Ct. For Hil SE26 .. 23 B4
Wells Park Rd. For Hil SE21 & SE26 .... 23 B4
Wells Pl. Merst RH1 .... 119 B6
Wells Rd. Crawl RH10 .... 201 E2
Wells Rd. Epsom KT18 .... 76 B4
Wells Rd. Merrow GU4 .... 110 C4
Wells The. Haslem GU27 .... 208 C6
Wellside Gdns. Mortl SW14 ... 7 C2
Wellwood Cl. Coulsd CR5 & CR8 .... 79 E5
Wellwood Cl. Horsh RH13 218 B4
Wellwynds Rd. Cran GU6 ... 174 E2
Welwyn Ave. Felt TW14 .... 3 F1
Welwyn Cl. Crawl RH11 .... 200 E2
Wembley Rd. Hampt TW12 . 36 A8
Wembury Pk. Newch RH7 .. 163 E1
Wend The. Coulsd CR5 .... 79 D5
Wendela Cl. Woking GU22 ... 69 F1
Wendley Dr. Woodhm KT15 . 51 F1
Wendling Rd. Carsh SM1 & SM5 .... 59 D8
Wendover Dr. Friml GU16 .... 66 C3
Wendover Dr. New Mal KT3 38 F3
Wendover Pl. Egham TW18 . 12 D3
Wendover Rd. Egham TW18 & TW20 .... 12 D3
Wendron Cl. [2] Woking GU21 .... 69 A1
Wendy Cres. Guild GU2 .... 109 A3
Wenlock Cl. Crawl RH11 .... 201 A4
Wenlock Edge. Dork RH4 ... 136 C5
Wensleydale. Crawl RH11 .. 201 C3
Wensleydale Dr. Friml GU15 66 D5
Wensleydale Gdns. Hampt TW12 .... 16 B1
Wensleydale Rd. Hampt TW12 .... 16 B1
Wentland Cl. Catf SE6 .... 24 D6
Wentland Rd. Catf SE6 .... 24 D6
Wentworth Ave. N Asct SL5 28 C7
Wentworth Cl. Ash V GU12 106 A7
Wentworth Cl. Ashf TW15 ... 14 B4
Wentworth Cl. Heath E GU9 .... 125 F6
Wentworth Cl. Long D KT6 .. 56 D8
Wentworth Cl. Morden SM4 40 A2
Wentworth Cl. Ripley GU23 . 91 B6
Wentworth Club. Went GU25 .... 31 A4
Wentworth Cres. Ash V GU12 .... 106 A6
Wentworth Ct. [20] King U T KT6 .... 37 E4
Wentworth Ct. Twick TW2 ... 16 E5
Wentworth Dr. Crawl RH10 202 D7
Wentworth Dr. Went GU25 .. 30 F5
Wentworth House. Addl KT15 .... 52 B6
Wentworth Rd. Thorn H CR0 42 A2
Wentworth Way. Hams Gn CR2 .... 81 A4
Wentworth Way. N Asct SL5 28 C7
Werndee Rd. Croy SE25 .... 43 A5
Wesco Ct. Woking GU21 .... 70 A3
Wescott Cty Inf Sch. Woki RG11 .... 25 D6
Wescott Rd. Woki RG11 .... 25 D6
Wesley Ave. Hounsl TW3 .... 4 F5
Wesley Cl. Crawl RH11 .... 200 E3
Wesley Cl. Horley RH6 .... 161 A5
Wesley Cl. Reig RH2 .... 138 F8
Wesley Dr. Egham TW20 .... 12 A2
Wesley Pl. Wink SL4 .... 9 B6
Wessels. Tadw KT20 .... 97 D6
Wessex Ave. Merton SW19 .. 40 A6
Wessex Cl. King U T KT1 & KT2 .... 38 B8
Wessex Ct. [4] Stan TW19 .... 2 E1
Wessex Pl. M Bourn GU9 ... 125 C1
Wessex Rd. Farnb GU14 .... 84 F2
Wessex Rd. Harm TW19 & TW6 .... 2 E4
Wesson House. [3] Croy CR0 43 A1
West Ashtead Cty Prim Sch. Ashtd KT21 .... 95 E7
West Ave. Crawl RH10 .... 202 A8
West Ave. Earls RH1 .... 140 A3
West Ave. Heath E GU9 .... 125 D7
West Ave. Wallin CR0 & SM6 60 E5
West Ave. Whit V KT12 & KT13 .... 53 E2
West Bank. Dork RH4 .... 136 A6
West Barnes La. W Barn KT3 & SW20 .... 39 B6
West Barnes La. Wimble KT3 & SW20 .... 39 E4
West Byfleet Cty Inf Sch. W Byfl KT14 .... 71 B7
West Byfleet Cty Jun Sch. W Byfl KT14 .... 71 B7
West Cl. Ashf TW15 .... 13 E4
West Cl. Heath E GU9 .... 125 D7
West Cross Ctr. Brent TW8 ... 6 B8
West Cross Way. Brent TW8 . 6 B8
West Croydon Sta. Thorn H CR9 .... 42 C1
West Ct. Burph GU4 .... 110 B5
West Ct. Hounsl TW7 .... 5 C7
West Down. G Book KT23 . 114 B8
West Dr. Belm SM2 .... 58 E2
West Dr. Burgh H KT20 .... 77 D1
West Dr. Streat SW16 & SW17 .... 21 C4
West Dr. Sutton SM5 .... 59 D1
West Dr. Went GU24 & GU25 & SL5 ... 30 E2
West Dr. Woodhm KT15 .... 52 B2
West Dulwich Sta. Dulw SE21 .... 22 D7
West End Cty Inf Sch. Alder GU11 .... 104 F2
West End Gdns. Esher KT10 54 F5
West End Gr. Farnh GU9 .... 125 A2
West End La. Esher KT10 .... 54 F4
West End La. Harl UB7 .... 3 C7
West Ewell Cty Inf Sch. W Ewell KT19 .... 57 D5
West Ewell Cty Jun Sch. W Ewell KT19 .... 57 D5
West Farm Ave. Ashtd KT21 95 D8
West Farm Cl. Ashtd KT21 ... 95 C8
West Farm Dr. Ashtd KT21 .. 95 D8
West Flexford La. Wanb GU3 .... 128 E8
West Gdns. Ewell KT17 .... 57 F1
West Gdns. Mitch SW19 .... 20 E2
West Gr. Hersh KT12 .... 54 B6
West Green Cty Fst Sch. Crawl RH11 .... 201 C7
West Green Dr. Crawl RH11 .... 201 C6
West Hall Rd. Rich TW9 .... 7 B6
West Heath. Pirb GU24 .... 87 D4
West Heath Rd. W Heath GU14 .... 84 F4
West Hill. Dorm Pk RH19 .... 185 E6
West Hill. Downe BR6 .... 83 F7
West Hill. E Grins RH19 .... 205 D8
West Hill. Elst GU8 .... 148 C3
West Hill. Epsom KT18 & KT19 .... 76 C6
West Hill. Oxted RH8 .... 122 D5
West Hill. Putney SW15 .... 19 D8
West Hill. S Croy CR2 .... 61 E2
West Hill. Woking GU22 .... 89 E8
West Hill Ave. Epsom KT19 .. 76 C7
West Hill Bank. Oxted RH8 122 D5
West Hill Cl. Brookw GU24 .. 88 B7
West Hill Cl. Elst GU8 .... 148 C3
West Hill Rd. Wands SW18 .. 20 A8
West Hill Rd. Woking GU22 . 89 E8
West Hill Sch. Leahd KT22 ... 75 A1
West Hoathly Rd. E Grins RH19 .... 205 D4
West House. Penge SE20 .... 23 D1
West House. [9] Streat SW12 .... 21 C8
West House Cl. Putney SW19 19 E7
West La. E Grins RH19 .... 205 D8
West La. Wotton RH5 .... 134 D4
West Leigh. E Grins RH19 .. 205 E7
West Mead. W Ewell KT19 ... 57 E4
West Mead Sch. Woki RG11 25 E6
West Meads. Onsl V GU2 ... 129 F8
West Middlesex Univ Hospl. Islew TW7 .... 6 A5
West Mount. Guild GU2 .... 130 C7
West Norwood Sta. W Norw SE27 .... 22 B5
West Oak. Beck BR3 .... 44 D8
West Palace Gdns. Weyb KT13 .... 53 B7
West Par. Horsh RH12 .... 217 C4
West Park Ave. Rich TW9 .... 7 B6
West Park Cl. Heston TW5 .... 4 F8
West Park Hospl. Epsom KT19 .... 75 E7
West Park Rd. Dome RH10 183 F5
West Park Rd. Epsom KT19 . 75 F7
West Park Rd. Horne RH7 & RH10 .... 184 B7
West Park Rd. Rich TW9 .... 7 A6
West Pl. Wimble SW19 .... 19 C3
West Ramp. Harm TW6 .... 3 A6
West Rd. Camb GU15 .... 65 D5
West Rd. Chess KT9 .... 75 C8
West Rd. E Bed TW14 .... 14 D8
West Rd. Easth RG11 & RG12 26 D2
West Rd. Farnb GU14 .... 85 B8
West Rd. Guild GU1 .... 130 E8
West Rd. King U T KT2 & KT3 38 C8
West Rd. Reig RH2 .... 139 B8
West Rd. Whit V KT13 .... 53 B3
West Ring. Tongh GU10 .... 126 F7
West Sheen Vale. Rich TW9 .. 6 F3
West Side Comm. Wimble SW19 .... 19 C3
West St. Carsh SM5 .... 59 F6
West St. Crawl RH11 .... 201 D5
West St. Croy CR0 & CR9 .... 61 C6
West St. Dork RH4 .... 136 A7
West St. Dorman RH7 .... 165 A1
West St. E Grins RH19 .... 205 E8
West St. Epsom KT18 & KT19 76 C6
West St. Ewell KT17 .... 57 F1
West St. Farnh GU9 .... 125 A2
West St. Haslem GU27 .... 208 C6
West St. Horsh RH12 .... 217 C2
West St. Reig RH2 .... 117 F1
West St. Sutton SM1 .... 59 B5
West St. Woking GU21 .... 69 F2
West Street La. Carsh SM5 . 59 F6
West Street Pl. [1] Croy CR0 & CR9 .... 61 C6
West Surrey Estates. Littlt TW15 .... 34 C8
West Sutton Sta. Sutton SM1 .... 59 A6
West Temple Sheen. Mortl SW14 .... 7 B2
West Thames Coll. Hounsl TW7 .... 5 E6
West Thornton Prim Sch. Thorn H CR0 .... 41 F3
West View. E Bed TW14 .... 14 C8
West View Ave. Whytlf CR3 . 80 F1
West View Gdns. E Grins RH19 .... 205 E8
West View Rd. Head Dn GU35 .... 187 C4
West View Rd. Warlgm CR6 .... 101 B8
West Way. Crawl RH10 .... 202 A7
West Way. Croy CR0 .... 62 E7
West Way. Heston TW5 .... 4 F6
West Way. Shep TW17 .... 34 D3
West Way. Slinfd RH13 .... 215 D3
West Way. Sutton SM2 & SM5 .... 59 D1
West Way. W Wick BR4 .... 44 E3
West Way Gdns. Croy CR0 .. 62 D8
West Wickham Sta. W Wick BR3 .... 44 C2
Westacres. Esher KT10 .... 54 F3
Westbank Rd. Hampt TW12 . 16 C2
Westborough Cty Prim Sch. Stough GU2 .... 108 F2
Westbourne Ave. Cheam SM3 .... 58 E8
Westbourne Dr. For Hil SE23 23 D6
Westbourne House. Heston TW5 .... 5 A8
Westbourne House. [9] Twick TW1 .... 17 B8
Westbourne Prim Sch. Sutton SM1 .... 59 A7
Westbourne Rd. Croy CR0 ... 42 F3
Westbourne Rd. Felt TW13 . 14 F5
Westbourne Rd. Penge SE26 23 D2
Westbourne Rd. Sandh GU15 64 E7
Westbourne Rd. Stain TW18 13 B1
Westbrook. For Row RH18 . 206 E3
Westbrook Ave. Hampt TW12 .... 15 F1
Westbrook Gdns. Brack RG12 .... 27 D8
Westbrook Hill. Elst GU8 ... 148 C3
Westbrook Rd. Heston TW5 .. 4 F7
Westbrook Rd. Ock Rid GU7 .... 150 C5
Westbrook Rd. S Norw CR7 . 42 D7
Westbrook Rd. Stain TW18 . 12 F3
Westbury Ave. Clayg KT10 ... 55 F4
Westbury Cl. Crowth RG11 .. 45 B6
Westbury Cl. Shep TW17 .... 34 B3
Westbury Cl. Whytlf CR3 .... 80 F1
Westbury Ct. Beck BR3 .... 44 B8
Westbury House Sch. New Mal KT3 .... 38 D4
Westbury Pl. [2] Brent TW8 ... 6 D8
Westbury Rd. Beck BR3 .... 43 E6
Westbury Rd. Felt TW13 .... 15 D6
Westbury Rd. New Mal KT3 . 38 D4
Westbury Rd. Penge SE20 ... 43 D8
Westbury Rd. Thorn H CR0 .. 42 D3
Westcar La. Hersh KT12 .... 54 B5
Westcombe Ave. Thorn H CR0 .... 41 F2
Westcombe Cl. Brack RG12 . 27 E2
Westcoombe Ave. Wimble SW20 .... 38 F8
Westcote Rd. Streat SW16 .. 21 C3
Westcott C of E Fst Sch. Westc RH4 .... 135 D5
Westcott Cl. New Add CR0 ... 63 B2
Westcott Rd. Dork RH4 .... 135 F7
Westcott St. Westc RH4 ... 135 B6
Westcott Way. E Ewell SM2 . 58 C1
Westcroft Gdns. Merton SM4 & SW20 .... 39 F5
Westcroft Rd. Hackb SM5 & SM6 .... 60 A6
Westdene. Godal GU7 .... 150 E3
Westdene Meadows. Cran GU6 .... 174 A3
Westdene Way. Oat Pk KT13 53 E7
Westdown Rd. For Hil SE13 & SE6 .... 24 A8
Westende. Woki RG11 .... 25 D6
Westende Cty Jun Sch. Woki RG11 .... 25 D6
Westerdale Dr. Friml GU16 .. 66 B3
Westerfolds Cl. Mayb GU22 . 70 C2
Westerham. [13] King U T KT6 .... 37 E4
Westerham Cl. Belm SM2 .... 59 A1
Westerham Cl. New Haw KT15 .... 52 C4
Westerham Lodge. [10] Beck BR3 .... 24 A1
Westerham Rd. Limps RH8 & TN16 .... 123 C6
Westerley Cres. For Hil SE26 & SE6 .... 23 F3
Westermain. Woodhm KT15 52 C1
Western Apron Rd. Crawl RH6 .... 181 F8
Western Ave. Egham TW20 . 32 B6
Western Ave. Thorpe KT16 .. 33 A6
Western Cl. Thorpe KT16 .... 33 A6
Western Ctr The. Brack RG12 .... 26 F7
Western Dr. Shep TW17 .... 34 D3
Western Ind Area. Brack RG12 .... 27 A7
Western La. Balham SW12 ... 21 A8
Western Perimeter Rd. Harm TW19 & TW6 & UB7 .... 2 B5
Western Rd. Alder GU11 .... 104 E1
Western Rd. Brack RG12 .... 26 F7
Western Rd. Mitch CR4 & SW19 .... 40 E7
Western Rd. Sutton SM1 .... 59 A5
Westfield. Ashtd KT21 .... 75 F1
Westfield. Peasl GU5 .... 154 E8
Westfield. Reig RH2 .... 118 B4
Westfield Ave. Sander CR2 & CR8 .... 80 E6
Westfield Ave. Westfd GU22 89 E7
Westfield Cl. Cheam SM1 .... 58 F6
Westfield Comm. Westfd GU22 .... 89 E5
Westfield Ct. King U T KT6 ... 37 D4
Westfield Ct. New Haw KT15 52 D1
Westfield Dr. Fetch KT23 .... 94 B5
Westfield Gr. Westfd GU22 .. 89 E7
Westfield La. Wreccl GU10 145 E6
Westfield Par. New Haw KT15 .... 52 D1
Westfield Prim Sch. Westfd GU22 .... 89 F6
Westfield Rd. Beck BR3 .... 43 F7
Westfield Rd. Camb GU15 ... 65 B2
Westfield Rd. Cheam SM1 ... 58 F6
Westfield Rd. Crawl RH11 201 B6
Westfield Rd. King U T KT6 .. 37 D4
Westfield Rd. Mitch CR4 .... 40 F7
Westfield Rd. Stough GU1 . 109 E5
Westfield Rd. Thorn H CR0 & CR9 .... 61 B8
Westfield Rd. Walt O T KT12 35 E2
Westfield Rd. Westfd GU22 .. 89 E5
Westfield Way. Westfd GU22 89 F5
Westfields. Mortl SW13 .... 7 F4
Westfields Ave. Mortl SW13 & SW14 .... 7 E4
Westfields Sch. Mortl SW13 . 7 F4

Westgate Rd. Beck BR3 .... 44 C8
Westgate Rd. Croy SE25 ...... 43 B5
Westglade. Farnb GU14 .... 84 D4
Westhall Pk. Warlgm CR6 .. 101 C8
Westhall Rd. Warlgm CR6 . 101 B8
Westhay Gdns. Mortl SW14 ... 7 B2
Westhumble St. Westh RH5 .... 115 B4
Westland Cl. Stan TW19 .... 2 E1
Westland Dr. Coney H BR2 & BR4 .... 63 F8
Westlands. Horsh RH13 ..... 217 E3
Westlands Ct. E Mole KT8 .... 36 E5
Westlands Ct. Epsom KT18 .. 76 C4
Westlands Way. Oxted RH8 122 D8
Westleas. Horley RH6 .... 160 E5
Westlees Cl. Dork RH5 ...... 136 D4
Westleigh Ave. Coulsd CR5 . 79 B3
Westmacott Dr. E Bed TW14 14 F7
Westmark Point. 13 Rhampt SW15 .... 19 B7
Westmead. Farnb GU14 .... 85 B3
Westmead. 8 Farnh GU9 125 B2
Westmead. Putney SW15 .... 19 B8
Westmead. Woking GU21 ..... 69 B2
Westmead Dr. Salfs RH1 .. 140 A1
Westmead Rd. Carsh SM1 ... 59 D6
Westminster Ave. S Norw CR7 .... 42 B7
Westminster Cl. E Bed TW14 15 A7
Westminster Cl. Tedd TW11 17 A3
Westminster Ct. Old Wok GU22 .... 90 B6
Westminster Ct. S Norw CR7 42 C7
Westminster Rd. Carsh SM1 & SM5 .... 59 D8
Westminster Rd. Worth RH10 .... 202 C5
Westmoat Cl. Beck BR3 .... 24 C1
Westmont Rd. Hinch W KT10 55 E8
Westmore Rd. Tats TN16 ... 103 C7
Westmoreland Dr. Sutton SM2 .... 59 B2
Westmoreland Rd. Barnes SW13 .... 7 F6
Westmoreland Rd. Beck BR2 & BR3 .... 44 F5
Westmorland Cl. Epsom KT19 .... 57 E2
Westmorland Cl. 3 Twick TW1 .... 6 B1
Westmorland Ct. 12 Surb KT6 .... 37 D2
Westmorland Dr. Friml GU15 & GU16 .... 66 B3
Westmorland Sq. Mitch CR4 41 E4
Westmorland Way. Mitch CR4 .... 41 E4
Weston Ave. Addl KT15 .... 52 B6
Weston Ave. E Mole KT8 ...... 35 F5
Weston Ave. Thame D KT10 & KT7 .... 36 E2
Weston Cl. Coulsd CR5 .... 99 F7
Weston Cl. Farnc GU7 .... 150 E6
Weston Ct. Farnc GU7 .... 150 E6
Weston Ct. 3 King U T KT1 37 E6
Weston Fields. Albury GU5 132 C4
Weston Gdns. Hounsl TW7 .... 5 E6
Weston Gdns. Pyrf GU22 .... 70 E3
Weston Gn. Thame D KT7 .... 36 E1
Weston Gr. Bagsh GU19 .... 47 F2
Weston Gr. Broml BR1 .... 44 F8
Weston Green Prep Sch. Thame D KT7 .... 36 E1
Weston Green Rd. Thame D KT7 .... 36 E2
Weston Lea. W Hors KT24 ... 92 D2
Weston Park Cl. Thame D KT7 .... 36 E1
Weston Pk. King U T KT1 ...... 37 E7
Weston Pk. Thame D KT10 & KT7 .... 36 E1
Weston Rd. Broml BR1 .... 24 F1
Weston Rd. Ewell KT17 .... 76 E8
Weston Rd. Stough GU2 ..... 109 A2
Weston Rd. Thame D KT7 .... 36 E1
Weston Way. Pyrf GU22 ...... 70 E3
Westons Cl. Horsh RH12 ... 217 D7
Westover Cl. Sutton SM2 ..... 59 B2
Westover Rd. Wands SW18 . 20 C8
Westow Hill. S Norw SE19 ... 22 F2
Westow St. S Norw SE19 ..... 22 E2
Westpoint. Beck BR2 .... 44 D6
Westview. 5 Woking GU22 69 F1
Westview Cl. Earls RH1 ..... 139 E6
Westville Rd. Thame D KT7 .. 37 A2
Westward Ho. Abbots GU1 109 F3
Westwates Cl. Wink RG12 ... 27 D8
Westway. Cater CR3 .... 100 D5
Westway. Copth RH10 .... 183 A3
Westway. Crawl RH6 .... 182 B7
Westway. Stough GU2 .... 108 F3
Westway. W Barn KT3 & SW20 .... 39 C5
Westway Cl. W Barn SW20 .. 39 B6
Westway Ct. Cater CR3 ..... 100 D4
Westway Gdns. Redh RH1 119 A4
Westways. Worc Pk KT19 ..... 57 F6
Westwell Rd. Streat SW16 ... 21 E2
Westwell Road App. Streat SW16 .... 21 E2
Westwick Gdns. Cranf TW4 & TW5 .... 4 B5
Westwood Ave. S Norw SE19 .... 42 C8
Westwood Ave. Woodhm KT15 .... 70 F7
Westwood Cl. Esher KT10 .... 55 C7
Westwood Ct. For Hil SE23 .. 23 C7
Westwood Ct. Stough GU2 108 F2
Westwood Ct. 7 Wimble SW19 .... 19 F3
Westwood Gdns. Mortl SW13 7 F4
Westwood Hill. For Hil SE19 & SE26 .... 23 B4
Westwood La. Flexf GU3 .... 107 A2
Westwood La. Normdy GU3 107 A2
Westwood La. Wanb GU3 . 128 B7
Westwood Park Prim Sch. Stough GU2 .... 108 E1
Westwood Pk. For Hil SE23 . 23 B8
Westwood Rd. Coulsd CR5 .. 79 D1
Westwood Rd. Mortl SW13 & SW15 .... 7 F4
Westwood Rd. Windl GU20 . 48 E6
Westwood Sch. S Norw SE19 .... 22 D1
Wetheral Ct. Up Toot SW17 . 20 D4
Wetherby Ct. S Norw SE25 .. 42 E7
Wetherby Gdns. 2 Farnb GU14 .... 85 C1
Wetherby House. Camb GU15 .... 65 D7
Wetherby Way. Chess KT9 .. 56 E3
Wettern Cl. S Croy CR2 .... 61 E1
Wetton Pl. Egham TW20 ...... 11 F3
Wexfenne Gdns. Pyrf GU22 . 71 B3
Wexford Rd. Balham SW12 .. 20 F8
Wey Ave. Thorpe KT16 .... 33 A6
Wey Cl. Ash GU12 .... 106 A1
Wey Cl. Camb GU15 .... 65 B5
Wey Cl. W Byfl KT14 .... 71 B6
Wey Ct. Farnc GU7 .... 151 A6
Wey Ct. New Haw KT15 .... 52 D2
Wey Ct. W Ewell KT19 .... 57 C6
Wey Ct. W Ewell KT19 .... 57 C6
Wey Hill. Shottm GU27 ...... 208 A6
Wey House Sch. Shalf GU5 151 E8
Wey Manor Rd. New Haw KT15 .... 52 D2
Wey Rd. Godal GU7 .... 151 A5
Wey Rd. Weyb KT13 .... 52 F7
Weybank. Wisley GU23 .... 71 E3
Weybank Cl. Farnh GU9 .... 125 C3
Weybarton. Byfl KT14 .... 71 F6
Weybourne Cty Inf Sch. Heath E GU9 .... 125 E6
Weybourne Pl. S Croy CR2 ... 61 D1
Weybourne Rd. Heath E GU11 & GU9 .... 125 E6
Weybourne St. Wands SW18 20 C6
Weybridge Bsns Pk. Addl KT15 .... 52 E6
Weybridge Hospl. Weyb KT13 .... 53 A6
Weybridge House. Whit V KT13 .... 53 D5
Weybridge Pk. Weyb KT13 .. 53 B5
Weybridge Rd. Addl KT15 & KT13 .... 52 E6
Weybridge Rd. Thorn H CR7 42 A5
Weybridge Rd. Weyb KT13 & KT15 .... 52 E6
Weybridge Sta. Weyb KT13 . 53 A4
Weybridge Trad Est. Addl KT15 .... 52 D6
Weybrook Dr. Burph GU4 .. 110 B6
Weycombe Rd. Haslem GU27 .... 208 C8
Weydon Hill Cl. M Bourn GU9 .... 146 B8
Weydon Hill Rd. M Bourn GU9 .... 146 C8
Weydon La. M Bourn GU9 . 146 A8
Weydon La. Wreccl GU9 ..... 145 F8
Weydon Mill La. Farnh GU9 125 B1
Weydon Sch. Wreccl GU9 .. 145 F7
Weydown Cl. Putney SW19 . 19 E7
Weydown Cl. Stough GU2 . 109 A6
Weydown Ct. Haslem GU27 208 B7
Weydown La. Stough GU2 109 A6
Weydown Rd. Haslem GU27 .... 208 B7
Weyfield Prim Sch. Bellf GU1 .... 109 D4
Weylands Pk. Whit V KT13 ... 53 D4
Weylea Ave. Burph GU1 & GU4 .... 110 A4
Weymead Cl. Chert KT16 ...... 33 C1
Weymede. Byfl KT14 .... 71 F7
Weymouth Ct. Belm SM2 ..... 59 A3
Weymouth Ct. 18 Streat SW2 .... 21 F8
Weyside. Farnh GU9 .... 125 C2
Weyside Cl. Byfl KT14 .... 71 F7
Weyside Gdns. Bellf GU1 ... 109 C3
Weyside Rd. Bellf GU1 .... 109 B3
Weysprings. Shottm GU27 208 A6
Weyvern Pk. Shalf GU3 ...... 130 B1
Weywood Cl. Heath E GU9 . 125 F7
Weywood La. Heath E GU9 125 E7
Whaley Rd. Woki RG11 .... 25 D8
Wharf Bridge Rd. Islew TW7 . 6 B4
Wharf La. Send GU23 .... 90 C4
Wharf La. Twick TW1 .... 17 A7
Wharf Rd. Ash GU12 .... 106 A4
Wharf Rd. Friml GU16 .... 86 A6
Wharf Rd. Guild GU1 .... 109 C1
Wharf Rd. Wray TW19 .... 11 D8
Wharf St. Godal GU7 .... 150 E4
Wharf Way. Friml GU16 .... 86 A6
Wharfedale Gdns. Thorn H CR7 & SW16 .... 41 F6
Wharfenden Way. Friml GU16 .... 85 F6
Wharncliffe Gdns. S Norw SE25 .... 42 E7
Wharncliffe Rd. S Norw SE25 .... 42 E7
Whateley Rd. Penge SE20 .... 23 D1
Whateley Rd. Stough GU2 . 109 B5
Whatley Ave. Merton SW20 . 39 E6
Whatley Gn. Easth RG12 ...... 27 B3
Whatman Rd. For Hil SE23 .. 23 D8
Whatmore Cl. Stan TW19 .... 2 A1
Wheat Knoll. Kenley CR8 ..... 80 C3
Wheatash Rd. Chert KT15 .... 33 B1
Wheatash Rd. Chert KT15 .... 52 B8
Wheatfield Way. Horley RH6 .... 161 C4
Wheatfield Way. King U T KT1 .... 37 E7
Wheathill House. Penge SE20 .... 43 B7
Wheathill Rd. Penge SE20 ... 43 B6
Wheatlands. Heston TW5 .... 5 A8
Wheatlands Rd. Up Toot SW17 .... 21 A5
Wheatley. Easth RG12 .... 26 E4
Wheatley House. 3 Rhampt SW15 .... 19 A8
Wheatley Rd. Islew TW7 .... 5 F4
Wheatley's Ait. Lo Hall TW16 .... 35 A4
Wheatley's Ait. Sunby TW16 35 A4
Wheatsheaf Cl. Horsh RH12 .... 217 E5
Wheatsheaf Cl. Ottsh KT16 .. 51 D4
Wheatsheaf Cl. Woking GU21 .... 69 F3
Wheatsheaf La. Stain TW18 12 F1
Wheatstone Cl. Crawl RH10 .... 182 B3
Wheatstone Cl. Mitch SW19 40 E8
Wheeler Ave. Oxted RH8 ... 122 D6
Wheeler La. Witley GU8 ..... 170 E6
Wheeler Rd. Worth RH10 .. 202 B4
Wheelers La. Brock RH3 .... 137 C7
Wheelers La. Epsom KT18 ... 76 C5
Wheelers La. Smallf RH6 ... 162 B3
Wheelers Way. Felb RH19 . 184 E3
Wheelwrights La. Graysh GU26 .... 188 A4
Wheelwrights Pl. Coln SL3 .... 1 C7
Whelan Way. Wallin SM6 ..... 60 D7
Wherwell Lodge. Guild GU2 130 C7
Wherwell Rd. Guild GU2 ..... 130 C7
Whetstone Rd. W Heath GU14 .... 84 C4
Whimbrel Cl. S Croy CR2 & CR8 .... 80 D8
Whinfell Cl. Streat SW16 ..... 21 D3
Whins Cl. Camb GU15 .... 65 B4
Whins Dr. Camb GU15 .... 65 B4
Whinshill Ct. Sunnin SL5 ...... 30 A1
Whipley Cl. Burph GU4 ...... 110 B6
Whirlwind Track. Farnb GU14 .... 104 D7
Whistler Cl. Crawl RH10 ..... 201 F3
Whistler Gr. Sandh GU15 ..... 64 D6
Whistley Cl. Brack RG12 ...... 27 E6
Whitby Cl. Bigg H TN16 .... 83 B1
Whitby Gdns. Carsh SM1 & SM5 .... 59 D8
Whitby Rd. Carsh SM1 & SM5 .... 59 D8
Whitchurch Cl. Alder GU11 126 D6
Whitchurch Ct. Up Toot SW17 .... 20 D4
Whitchurch House. Catf SE6 24 C5
White Acres Rd. Mytch GU16 85 F4
White Beam Way. Tadw KT20 .... 97 A6
White Bridge Cl. Felt TW14 .... 3 F1
White Bushes. Earls RH1 .... 140 A4
White City. Crowth RG11 ...... 45 D5
White Cottage Cl. Heath E GU9 .... 125 D6
White Ct. Stough GU2 .... 109 A4
White Hart Ct. Horsh RH12 217 C4
White Hart Ct. Ripley GU23 . 91 C6
White Hart Ind Est. Blckw GU17 .... 64 E4
White Hart La. Mortl SW14 .... 7 E4
White Hart La. Wood S V GU3 .... 108 A2
White Hart Lodge. Wimble SW19 .... 20 C2
White Hart Meadows. Ripley GU23 .... 91 C6
White Hart Row. Chert KT16 33 A2
White Heron Mews. Tedd TW11 .... 16 F2
White Hill. Kings CR5 .... 98 D4
White Hill. S Croy CR2 .... 61 D1
White Hill. Windl GU20 .... 48 B6
White Horse Dr. Epsom KT18 .... 76 C5
White Horse La. Ripley GU23 91 C6
White House. 3 Streat SW4 .... 21 D8
White House Ct. Beck BR3 ... 44 C8
White House La. Jacobs GU4 .... 109 D6
White House Prep Sch. Woki RG11 .... 25 A3
White House Wlk. Heath E GU9 .... 125 D7
White Knights Rd. Whit V KT13 .... 53 C3
White Knobs Way. Cater CR3 .... 101 A2
White La. Ash GU10 & GU12 127 C7
White La. Merrow GU4 ...... 131 D7
White La. Titsey RH8 & TN16 .... 103 B3
White La. Tongh GU10 & GU12 .... 127 C7
White Lodge. Ashtd KT21 .... 95 E7
White Lodge. S Norw SE19 .. 22 B1
White Lodge Cl. Sutton SM2 59 C3
White Lodge Gdns. Salfs RH1 .... 140 A1
White Lodge The Royal Ballet Sch. Rich TW10 .... 18 D7
White Oak Dr. Beck BR3 ...... 44 D7
White Post La. Rowl GU10 146 A4
White Rd. Sandh GU15 .... 64 F6
White Rose La. M Bourn GU9 .... 146 B7
White Rose La. Mayb GU22 . 90 A8
White Rose La. Woking GU22 .... 69 F1
White Way. G Book KT23 ..... 94 B1
Whitebeam Dr. Woodh RH2 .... 139 B6
Whitebeams Gdns. Farnb GU14 .... 84 C3
Whiteberry Rd. Wotton RH5 .... 156 B7
Whitebines. Farnh GU9 ..... 125 D2
Whitecroft Cl. Beck BR3 ...... 44 D5
Whitecroft Way. Beck BR3 .. 44 D5
Whitefield Ave. Purley CR8 . 80 B3
Whitefield House. Purley CR8 .... 80 B3
Whitefoot La. Catf BR1 & SE6 .... 24 D5
Whitefoot Terr. Catf BR1 ..... 24 F5
Whitegate Way. Burgh H KT20 .... 97 B7
Whitegates. Old Wok GU22 .. 89 F7
Whitegates. Whytlf CR3 .... 101 A8
Whitehall Cres. Chess KT9 .. 56 D5
Whitehall Dr. Crawl RH11 .. 200 E6
Whitehall Farm La. Thorpe GU25 .... 31 E6
Whitehall Gdns. Chisw W4 ..... 7 B8
Whitehall La. Egham TW20 .. 11 F1
Whitehall La. Horton TW19 ..... 1 A1
Whitehall La. Woodh RH2 .. 138 F6
Whitehall Park Rd. Chisw W4 7 B8
Whitehall Pl. Wallin SM5 ..... 60 B6
Whitehall Rd. Thorn H CR7 .. 42 A4
Whitehead Cl. Wands SW18 20 C8
Whitehill Cl. Camb GU15 ...... 65 D7
Whitehill La. Bletch RH1 .... 120 D6
Whitehill La. Mart Gn GU23 . 92 C4
Whitehill Pl. Thorpe GU25 .... 31 E4
Whitehorse La. S Norw SE25 42 E5
Whitehorse Manor Inf Sch. S Norw CR7 .... 42 D5
Whitehorse Manor Jun Sch. S Norw CR7 .... 42 D5
Whitehorse Rd. Horsh RH12 .... 218 B6
Whitehorse Rd. S Norw CR0 & CR7 & SE25 . 42 D3
Whitehorse Rd. Thorn H CR0 & CR7 & SE25 . 42 D3
Whitehouse Dr. Merrow GU1 .... 110 B1
Whitelands Coll. Putney SW18 .... 19 E8
Whitelands Dr. N Asct SL5 ... 28 D8
Whiteley House. 9 Streat SW4 .... 21 D8
Whiteley House & Hospl. Whit V KT12 .... 53 F2
Whiteley Rd. W Norw SE19 . 22 D3
Whiteleys House. Felt TW13 16 A5
Whiteleys Way. Felt TW13 .. 16 A5
Whitelocke Cty Inf Sch. Woki RG11 .... 25 D7
Whitely Hill. Worth RH10 ... 202 F1
Whitely Way. Farnb GU14 ..... 84 E1
Whitemore Rd. Bellf GU1 . 109 D5
Whiteoak House. S Norw SE19 .... 22 C1
Whiteoaks. Banstd SM7 .... 78 B6
Whitepost Hill. Redh RH1 .. 118 E1
Whitepost House. Redh RH1 .... 118 E1
Whites Dr. Hayes BR2 .... 44 F2
Whites Rd. Farnb GU14 .... 85 E1
Whitethorn Ave. Wallin CR5 79 B4
Whitethorn Cotts. Rowly GU6 .... 174 B6
Whitethorn Gdns. Croy CR0 62 B8
Whiteways Ct. Stain TW18 .. 13 B1
Whiteways End. Farnh GU10 .... 126 D4
Whitewood Cotts. Tats TN16 .... 103 C7
Whitewood La. Horne RH9 163 B7
Whitfield Cl. Haslem GU27 189 C1
Whitfield Cl. Stough GU2 .. 109 A4
Whitfield Ct. 3 Dulw SE21 . 22 E4
Whitfield Rd. Haslem GU27 189 C1
Whitford Gdns. Mitch CR4 ... 40 F6
Whitgift Ave. Croy CR2 .... 61 C5
Whitgift Ctr. Croy CR9 .... 61 C8
Whitgift House. Croy CR2 ... 61 C5
Whitgift Sch. Croy CR2 .... 61 C5
Whitgift St. Croy CR0 & CR9 61 C7
Whitgift Wlk. Crawl RH10 . 201 D3
Whitland Rd. Carsh SM5 ...... 40 D1
Whitley Cl. Stan TW19 .... 2 E1
Whitlock Dr. Putney SW19 ... 19 E7
Whitmead Cl. S Croy CR2 ... 61 E4
Whitmead La. Tilf GU10 ..... 147 E4
Whitmoor La. Westfd GU4 ... 89 D1
Whitmoor Rd. Bagsh GU19 .. 47 F2
Whitmoor Vale Rd. Beac H GU26 .... 188 A5
Whitmore Cl. Sandh GU15 ... 45 D1
Whitmore Gn. Heath E GU9 125 E6
Whitmore La. Sunnin SL5 ..... 30 A5
Whitmore Rd. Beck BR3 ...... 43 F6
Whitmore Vale. Graysh GU26 .... 187 F6
Whitmore Vale. Head Dn GU26 .... 187 F6
Whitmore Vale Rd. Graysh GU26 .... 188 A4
Whitmore Vale Rd. Head Dn GU10 & GU26 ...... 187 E7
Whitmore Way. Horley RH6 160 E3
Whitmores Cl. Woodc KT18 . 76 C4
Whitstable Cl. Beck BR3 ...... 43 F8
Whittaker Ave. Rich TW10 & TW9 .... 6 D2
Whittaker Ct. Ashtd KT21 ..... 75 D2
Whittaker Pl. 24 Rich TW10 .. 6 D2
Whittaker Rd. Cheam SM3 ... 58 F7
Whittam House. W Norw SE27 .... 22 C3
Whittell Gdns. For Hil SE26 . 23 C5
Whittingham Ct. Chisw W4 ... 7 E7
Whittington Coll. Felb RH19 .... 185 A4
Whittington Ct. Penge SE20 43 B7

Whittington Rd. Crawl RH10 201 E3
Whittle Cl. Sandh GU17 45 A1
Whittle Cres. W Heath GU14 84 F7
Whittle Rd. Heston TW5 4 C7
Whittle Way. Crawl RH10 182 A3
Whittlebury Cl. Wallin SM5 59 F3
Whitton Dene. Islew TW2 & TW3 & TW7 5 D2
Whitton Dene. Twick TW2 & TW7 5 D1
Whitton Manor Rd. Islew TW7 5 C1
Whitton Rd. Brack RG12 27 F6
Whitton Rd. Hounsl TW3 5 B2
Whitton Rd. Islew TW3 5 B2
Whitton Rd. Twick TW1 17 A8
Whitton Sch. Twick TW2 16 B6
Whitton Sta. Twick TW2 16 C8
Whitton Waye. Twick TW2 & TW3 5 A1
Whitworth Rd. Crawl RH11 181 D2
Whitworth Rd. S Norw SE25 42 F5
Whopshott Ave. Horse GU21 69 C3
Whopshott Cl. Horse GU21 69 C3
Whopshott Dr. Horse GU21 69 C3
Whynstones Rd. Ascot SL5 29 A4
Whyte Ave. Alder GU12 126 D7
Whyteacre. Whytlf CR3 101 B7
Whytebeam View. Whytlf CR3 80 F1
Whytecliffe Rd N. Purley CR8 80 B8
Whytecliffe Rd S. Purley CR8 80 B8
Whytecroft. Heston TW5 4 D7
Whyteleafe Bsns Village. Whytlf CR3 80 F2
Whyteleafe Hill. Whytlf CR3 80 F1
Whyteleafe Rd. Cater CR3 100 F6
Whyteleafe Rd. Whytlf CR3 100 F6
Whyteleafe Sch. Whytlf CR3 80 F1
Whyteleafe South Sta. Whytlf CR3 101 A8
Whyteleafe Sta. Whytlf CR3 80 F2
Wick House. 1 Tedd KT1 37 D8
Wick La. Eng Gn TW20 10 F3
Wick Rd. Eng Gn TW20 11 B1
Wick Rd. Tedd TW11 17 C1
Wicket Hill. Wreccl GU10 & GU9 146 A6
Wicket The. Add CR0 63 A5
Wickets The. Ashf TW15 13 E4
Wickham Ave. Cheam KT4 & SM3 58 C5
Wickham Ave. Croy CR0 43 E1
Wickham Chase. W Wick BR4 44 E2
Wickham Cl. Horley RH6 160 F4
Wickham Cl. New Mal KT3 38 F4
Wickham Court Rd. W Wick BR4 63 C8
Wickham Cres. W Wick BR4 63 C8
Wickham La. Thor L TW20 12 A1
Wickham Rd. Beck BR3 44 B6
Wickham Rd. Camb GU15 65 E8
Wickham Rd. Croy CR0 & CR9 62 E8
Wickham Vale. Easth RG11 & RG12 26 E3
Wickham Way. Beck BR3 44 C4
Wickhurst Gdns. Broad H RH12 216 E3
Wickhurst La. Broad H RH12 216 E3
Wickland Ct. Crawl RH10 201 D3
Wicklow Ct. Penge SE26 23 C3
Wide Way. Mitch CR4 & SW16 41 D6
Widgeon Way. Horsh RH12 217 C5
Widmen Ct. Hounsl TW5 4 E5
Wigan Rd. Farnb GU14 104 D8
Wiggie La. Redh RH1 119 A3
Wigley Rd. Felt TW13 15 D7
Wigmore La. Bear Gn RH5 157 C1
Wigmore Rd. Carsh SM5 40 E1
Wigmore Wlk. Carsh SM5 59 D8
Wilberforce Ct. Epsom KT18 76 D5
Wilberforce Way. Brack RG12 27 D4
Wilberforce Way. Wimble SW19 19 D2
Wilbury Ave. Belm SM2 58 F1
Wilbury Rd. Woking GU21 69 D2
Wilcot Cl. Bisley GU24 68 A3
Wilcot Gdns. Bisley GU24 68 A3
Wilcox Gdns. Littlt TW17 33 F6
Wilcox Rd. Sutton SM1 59 B6
Wilcox Rd. Tedd TW11 16 D4
Wild Acres. W Byfl KT14 71 C8
Wildacre Cl. Ifold RH14 212 D3
Wildbank Ct. 2 Woking GU22 69 F1
Wildcroft Dr. Dork RH5 136 D4
Wildcroft Dr. Woki RG11 25 A1
Wildcroft Manor. Putney SW15 19 C8
Wildcroft Rd. Putney SW15 19 C8
Wildcroft Wood. Witley GU8 170 D6
Wilde Theatre. Easth RG12 27 C2
Wilderness Ct. Onsl V GU2 129 F7
Wilderness Rd. Friml GU16 65 E2
Wilderness Rd. Onsl V GU2 129 F7
Wilderness Rd. Oxted RH8 122 E5
Wilderness Rise. Dorman RH19 186 A6
Wilderness The. E Mole KT8 36 C4
Wilderness The. Hampt TW12 16 B4
Wilders Cl. Friml GU15 65 E3
Wilders Cl. Woking GU21 69 C1
Wilderwick Rd. Dorman RH19 & RH7 186 A5
Wildfell Rd. Lewish SE6 24 B8
Wildfield Cl. Wood S V GU3 108 B2
Wildgoose Dr. Horsh RH12 216 F3
Wildridings Cty Prim Sch. Easth RG12 27 A5
Wildridings Rd. Easth RG12 27 A5
Wildridings Sq. Easth RG12 27 A5
Wildwood Cl. E Hors KT24 92 F2
Wildwood Cl. Lewish SE12 24 F8
Wildwood Cl. Pyrf GU22 70 F4
Wildwood Ct. Kenley CR8 80 D4
Wildwood La. Alf Cr GU6 194 C5
Wilford Rd. Thorn H CR0 42 C2
Wilfred Owen Cl. Wimble SW19 20 C2
Wilfred St. Woking GU21 69 D1
Wilhelmina Ave. Coulsd CR5 99 C8
Wilkes Rd. 3 Brent TW8 6 E8
Wilkins Cl. Mitch CR4 40 E8
Wilkinson Ct. 4 Crawl RH11 201 B1
Wilkinson Ct. Up Toot SW17 20 D4
Wilks Gdns. Croy CR0 43 E1
Will Miles Ct. 6 Merton SW19 20 C1
Willats Cl. Chert KT16 33 A3
Willcocks Cl. Chess KT9 56 E7
Willems Ave. Alder GU11 104 F2
Willerton Lodge. 1 Whit V KT13 53 D4
Willett Pl. Thorn H CR7 42 A4
Willett Rd. Thorn H CR7 42 A4
Willetts. Dork RH4 136 C4
Willey Broom La. Cater CR3 100 A2
Willey Farm La. Cater CR3 100 C1
Willey La. Cater CR3 100 D2
William Booth Rd. Penge SE20 43 A8
William Brown Ct. W Norw SE27 22 B6
William Byrd Sch. Harl UB7 3 D8
William Cobbett Cty Jun Sch. Heath E GU9 125 E6
William Ellis Sch. For Gn RH5 176 E8
William Evelyn Ct. Wotton RH5 134 F4
William Farthing Cl. Alder GU11 105 A2
William Harvey House. 1 Putney SW19 19 E7
William Lilly House. Hersh KT12 54 C5
William Morris Mid Sch. Mitch CR4 41 D6
William Morris Way. Crawl RH11 201 C1
William Rd. Cater CR3 100 D5
William Rd. Guild GU1 109 C1
William Rd. Merton SW19 19 E1
William Rd. Sutton SM1 59 C5
William Russell Ct. 3 Knaph GU21 68 E1
William Sim Wood. Wink RG12 8 B2
William St. Carsh SM5 59 F7
William Wood House. For Hil SE26 23 C5
Williams Cl. Addl KT15 52 B5
Williams Cl. Ewh GU6 175 E5
Williams House. 14 Streat SW2 22 A7
Williams La. Morden SM4 40 C4
Williams La. Mortl SW14 7 C5
Williams Terr. Croy CR0 61 A4
Williams Way. Crawl RH10 202 B5
Williamson Cl. Grays GU27 189 F1
Willingham Way. King U T KT1 38 A7
Willington Cl. Camb GU15 65 B6
Willis Ave. Sutton SM2 59 E4
Willis Cl. Epsom KT18 76 B5
Willis Rd. Thorn H CR0 42 C2
Willlows The. Croy CR0 62 E8
Willmore End. Merton SW19 40 B7
Willoughby Ave. Wallin CR0 60 F6
Willoughby Rd. Easth RG12 26 F6
Willoughby Rd. King U T KT2 37 F8
Willoughby Rd. Twick TW1 6 D2
Willoughbys The. Mortl SW15 7 E3
Willow Ave. Barnes SW13 7 F5
Willow Bank. Westfd GU22 89 F6
Willow Brean. Horley RH6 160 E5
Willow Cl. Bear Gn RH5 157 C4
Willow Cl. Brent TW8 6 C8
Willow Cl. Catf SE6 24 F7
Willow Cl. Coln SL3 1 C7
Willow Cl. Crawl RH10 201 E8
Willow Cl. E Grins RH19 185 D3
Willow Cl. Mytch GU16 85 E4
Willow Cl. Woodhm KT15 70 F8
Willow Cnr. Charl RH6 180 F7
Willow Cotts. Carsh CR4 40 F2
Willow Cotts. Rich TW9 7 A8
Willow Cres. Farnb GU14 85 B7
Willow Ct. Ash V GU12 106 A7
Willow Ct. Friml GU16 65 D1
Willow Ct. Horley RH6 161 B6
Willow Ct. 3 Streat SW16 21 F5
Willow Ct. Thorn H CR7 42 D4
Willow Ct. Woki RG11 25 B6
Willow Ctr The. Mitch CR4 40 F3
Willow Dr. Brack RG12 27 C8
Willow Dr. Flexf GU3 107 C1
Willow Dr. Send M GU23 91 A3
Willow End. Surb KT6 37 E1
Willow Gdns. Hounsl TW5 5 A6
Willow Glade. Woodh RH2 139 B6
Willow Gn. W End GU24 68 A6
Willow House. Felt TW14 4 B2
Willow La. Guild GU1 110 A2
Willow La. Hawley GU17 64 D4
Willow La. Mitch CR4 40 F3
Willow Lodge. 6 Charlt TW16 14 F1
Willow Manor. Cheam SM1 58 F6
Willow Mead. Dork RH4 136 A8
Willow Mead. 8 E Grins RH19 205 F8
Willow Mead. Witley GU8 170 E5
Willow Mount. S Croy CR0 61 E7
Willow Pk. Alder GU12 105 F2
Willow Rd. Farnc GU7 150 F8
Willow Rd. Horsh RH12 218 B5
Willow Rd. King U T KT3 38 C5
Willow Rd. Poyle SL3 1 E5
Willow Rd. Wallin SM6 60 B3
Willow Rd. Woodh RH1 & RH2 139 C6
Willow Ridge. Turn H RH10 204 A3
Willow Tree Cl. Wands SW18 20 B7
Willow Vale. Fetch KT23 94 B4
Willow View. Mitch SW19 40 D8
Willow Way. Alder GU12 126 E8
Willow Way. For Hil SE26 23 C5
Willow Way. Godst RH9 121 B3
Willow Way. Heath E GU9 125 D6
Willow Way. Stough GU1 109 B5
Willow Way. Sunby TW16 35 A5
Willow Way. Twick TW2 16 B6
Willow Way. W Byfl KT14 71 C8
Willow Way. W Ewell KT19 57 D4
Willow Way. W Ewell KT19 57 D4
Willow Way. Woking GU22 89 E7
Willow Wlk. Box H KT20 116 B5
Willow Wlk. Cheam SM1 & SM3 58 F7
Willow Wlk. Earls RH1 140 B7
Willow Wlk. Eng Gn TW20 11 C3
Willow Wood Cres. Thorn H SE25 42 E3
Willowbrook Rd. Stan TW19 13 E6
Willowdene Cl. Twick TW2 16 C8
Willowfield. 4 Crawl RH11 201 D5
Willowhayne Dr. Walt O T KT12 35 B2
Willowhayne Gdns. N Cheam KT4 58 C6
Willowherb Cl. Woki RG11 25 E7
Willowmead. Stain TW18 33 B8
Willowmead Cl. Woking GU21 69 A3
Willowmere. Esher KT10 55 C6
Willows Ave. Morden SM4 40 B4
Willows End. Sandh GU17 64 B8
Willows Path. Epsom KT18 76 B5
Willows The. Beck BR3 44 A8
Willows The. 1 Brack RG12 27 F5
Willows The. Byfl KT14 71 E6
Willows The. Chidd GU8 191 A4
Willows The. Clayg KT10 55 E4
Willows The. Farnh GU10 126 C4
Willows The. Horsh RH12 217 D5
Willows The. Lhtwat GU18 48 C1
Willows The. Merrow GU4 110 D3
Willows The. 2 Redh RH1 139 F8
Willows The. Stough GU2 108 F6
Willows The. Weyb KT13 53 A7
Wills Cres. Twick TW3 5 B1
Willson Rd. Eng Gn TW20 11 B3
Wilmar Gdns. W Wick BR4 44 B1
Wilmer Cl. King U T TW10 17 F3
Wilmer Cres. King U T KT2 & TW10 17 F3
Wilmerhatch La. Woodc KT18 & KT21 76 B2
Wilmington Ave. Chisw W4 7 D7
Wilmington Cl. Crawl RH11 201 C1
Wilmington Ct. Streat SW16 21 E1
Wilmot Rd. Purley CR8 80 A7
Wilmot Rd. Wallin SM5 59 F5
Wilmot Way. Banstd SM7 78 A5
Wilmot Way. Friml GU15 65 F3
Wilmot's La. Horne RH1 & RH6 162 E5
Wilmots Cl. Reig RH2 118 C2
Wilna Rd. Wands SW18 20 C8
Wilson Ave. Mitch CR4 & SW19 40 E8
Wilson Cl. Croy CR0 61 D5
Wilson Dr. Ottsh KT16 51 B5
Wilson Hospl. Mitch CR4 40 F5
Wilson Rd. Alder GU12 105 D1
Wilson Rd. Chess KT9 56 F4
Wilson Rd. Farnb GU14 84 F3
Wilson Way. Horse GU21 69 D3
Wilson's Sch. Wallin SM6 60 E4
Wilsons. Tadw KT20 97 D6
Wilsons Rd. Head Dn GU35 187 B5
Wilton Cl. Harm UB7 2 D8
Wilton Cres. Merton SW19 39 F8
Wilton Ct. Farnb GU14 85 D3
Wilton Ct. 4 Rich TW10 6 E2
Wilton Gdns. E Mole KT8 36 A6
Wilton Gdns. Walt O T KT12 35 D1
Wilton Gr. Merton SW19 39 F8
Wilton Gr. New Mal KT3 38 F3
Wilton Par. Felt TW13 15 B6
Wilton Pl. Beck BR3 44 C6
Wilton Pl. New Haw KT15 52 D2
Wilton Rd. Camb GU15 65 B3
Wilton Rd. Hounsl TW4 4 D4
Wilton Rd. Mitch SW19 20 E1
Wilton Rd. Redh RH1 139 F8
Wiltshire Ave. Crowth RG11 45 B5
Wiltshire Dr. Woki RG11 25 D7
Wiltshire Gdns. Twick TW2 16 C7
Wiltshire Rd. Thorn H CR7 42 A6
Wiltshire Rd. Woki RG11 25 C7
Wilverley Cres. New Mal KT3 38 E3
Wilwood Rd. Brack RG12 26 E8
Wimbart Rd. Streat SW2 21 F8
Wimbledon Bridge. Wimble SW19 19 F2
Wimbledon Chase Mid Sch. Merton SW20 39 E8
Wimbledon Chase Sta. Merton SW20 39 E7
Wimbledon Cl. Camb GU15 46 F1
Wimbledon Cl. 2 Wimble SW20 19 D1
Wimbledon Coll. Wimble SW19 19 D1
Wimbledon Common Prep Sch. Wimble SW19 19 D1
Wimbledon High Sch. Wimble SW19 19 E2
Wimbledon Hill Rd. Wimble SW19 19 F2
Wimbledon House Sch. Merton SW19 40 A8
Wimbledon Lawn Tennis Mus. Wimble SW19 19 E5
Wimbledon Park Ct. Putney SW19 19 F7
Wimbledon Park Prim Sch. Wimble SW19 20 B6
Wimbledon Park Rd. Putney SW18 & SW19 19 F7
Wimbledon Park Rd. Wands SW18 & SW19 19 F7
Wimbledon Park Side. Putney SW19 19 D7
Wimbledon Park Sta. Wimble SW19 20 A5
Wimbledon Rd. Camb GU15 46 F1
Wimbledon Rd. Wands SW17 20 C4
Wimbledon Sch of Art. Merton SW19 39 E8
Wimbledon Sch of Art Annexe. Merton SW19 20 A1
Wimbledon Sta. Wimble SW19 19 F2
Wimbledon Stadium. Wimble SW17 20 C4
Wimblehurst Ct. Horsh RH12 217 C4
Wimblehurst Rd. Horsh RH12 217 C4
Wimborne Ave. Earls RH1 139 F4
Wimborne Ave. Earls RH1 140 A4
Wimborne Cl. Epsom KT17 76 E6
Wimborne Cl. N Cheam KT4 39 C1
Wimborne House. Croy CR0 43 C4
Wimborne House. Up Toot SW12 21 C5
Wimborne Way. Beck BR3 43 E5
Wimbourne Ct. Mitch SW19 20 D1
Wimbourne Ct. S Croy CR2 61 E4
Wimland Hill. Faygt RH12 199 D2
Wimland Rd. Faygt RH12 199 D1
Wimland Rd. Rusper RH12 199 C4
Wimlands La. Rusper RH12 199 E3
Wimpole Cl. 1 King U T KT1 38 A7
Wimshurst Cl. Croy CR0 41 E1
Wincanton Rd. Wands SW18 19 F8
Winchcombe Rd. Carsh SM5 40 E1
Winchelsey Rise. S Croy CR2 61 F4
Winchendon Rd. Tedd TW11 & TW12 16 D4
Winchester Ave. Heston TW5 4 F8
Winchester Cl. Beck BR2 44 F6
Winchester Cl. Esher KT10 55 A7
Winchester Cl. King U T KT2 18 B1
Winchester Cl. Poyle SL3 1 E6
Winchester Pk. Beck BR2 44 F6
Winchester Rd. Ash GU12 106 A3
Winchester Rd. Beck BR2 44 F6
Winchester Rd. Crawl RH10 201 E2
Winchester Rd. Felt TW13 15 F5
Winchester Rd. Harl UB3 3 E7
Winchester Rd. Rushm GU10 168 B7
Winchester Rd. Twick TW1 6 B1
Winchester Rd. Walt O T KT12 35 A1
Winchester St. Farnb GU14 105 C8
Winchester Way. Blckw GU17 64 C6
Winchet Wlk. Croy CR0 43 C3
Winchfield House. Rhampt SW15 7 F1
Winchfield Rd. For Hil SE26 23 E3
Winchilsea Cres. E Mole KT8 36 C7
Winchstone Cl. Shep Gn TW17 33 F5
Windborough Rd. Wallin SM5 60 A3
Windermere Ave. Merton SM4 & SW19 40 B6
Windermere Cl. E Bed TW14 14 F7
Windermere Cl. Farnb GU14 84 E3
Windermere Cl. Stan TW19 13 D6
Windermere Cl. Thor L TW20 12 B1
Windermere Ct. Barnes SW13 7 F8
Windermere Ct. Purley CR8 80 B4
Windermere House. Islew TW1 5 F2
Windermere Rd. Coulsd CR5 79 E4
Windermere Rd. Croy CR0 42 F1
Windermere Rd. King U T SW15 18 E3
Windermere Rd. Lhtwat GU18 48 B1
Windermere Rd. Mitch SW16 41 D7
Windermere Rd. W Wick BR4 63 E8
Windermere Way. Hale GU9 125 A6
Windermere Way. Redh RH1 118 E2
Windermere Wlk. Friml GU15 66 D5
Windfield. Leahd KT22 95 B5
Windfield Cl. For Hil SE26 23 D4
Windgates. Merrow GU4 110 C4
Windham Ave. New Add CR0 63 D1
Windham Rd. Rich TW9 6 F4
Winding Wood Dr. Friml GU15 & GU16 66 B3
Windings The. S Croy CR2 80 F8
Windle Cl. Windl GU20 48 D4

Windlebrook Gn. 3 Brack RG12 ... 27 A8
Windlemere Golf Ctr. W End GU24 ... 67 E8
Windlesham Ct. Windl GU20 48 C6
Windlesham Gr. Putney SW19 ... 19 D7
Windlesham House. Mitch CR4 ... 40 D7
Windlesham Rd. Brack RG12 26 F8
Windlesham Rd. Burrh GU24 49 C3
Windlesham Rd. W End GU24 ... 67 F7
Windlesham Village Cty Inf Sch. Windl GU20 ... 48 B6
Windley Cl. For Hil SE23 ... 23 C6
Windmill Ave. Ewell KT17 ... 76 F8
Windmill Bridge House. 1 Croy CR0 ... 42 E1
Windmill Bsns Village. Charlt TW16 ... 34 E8
Windmill Cl. Cater CR3 ... 100 C6
Windmill Cl. Charlt TW16 ... 14 E1
Windmill Cl. Ewell KT17 ... 76 F7
Windmill Cl. Horley RH6 ... 161 B3
Windmill Cl. Horsh RH13 .. 218 B4
Windmill Cl. Long D KT6 ... 37 C2
Windmill Ct. Crawl RH11 .. 201 D8
Windmill Dr. Head Dn GU35 ... 187 B6
Windmill Dr. Leahd KT22 ... 95 C4
Windmill Dr. Redh RH1 ... 118 E3
Windmill End. Ewell KT17 ... 76 F7
Windmill Field. Windl GU20 . 48 D4
Windmill Gr. Thorn H CR0 ... 42 C3
Windmill La. Ash W RH19 .. 206 C7
Windmill La. E Grins RH19 185 D3
Windmill La. Ewell KT17 ... 76 F7
Windmill La. Thame D KT7 ... 37 B2
Windmill Lodge. Charlt TW16 ... 34 E8
Windmill Rd. Alder GU12 ... 105 C1
Windmill Rd. Brack RG12 ... 27 A8
Windmill Rd. Brent TW8 ... 6 D8
Windmill Rd. Charlt TW16 ... 34 E8
Windmill Rd. Hampt TW12 ... 16 C3
Windmill Rd. Mitch CR4 ... 41 C5
Windmill Rd. Rhampt SW19 . 19 B5
Windmill Rd. Thorn H CR0 ... 42 C2
Windmill Rd W. Charlt TW16 34 E8
Windmill Rise. King U T KT2 18 B1
Windmill Terr. Lo Hall TW17 34 E2
Windmill Trad Est. Charlt TW16 ... 34 E8
Windmill Way. Redh RH1 .. 118 D3
Windrush Cl. Bramly GU5 .. 151 F6
Windrush Cl. Chisw W4 ... 7 C7
Windrush Cl. Crawl RH11 .. 200 F4
Windrush House. 8 Redh RH1 ... 118 F2
Windrush Hts. Sandh GU17 . 64 B8
Windrush La. For Hil SE23 ... 23 D5
Winds Ridge. Send GU23 ... 90 C2
Windsor Ave. Cheam SM3 ... 58 E7
Windsor Ave. E Mole KT8 ... 36 A6
Windsor Ave. Merton SW19 40 C8
Windsor Ave. New Mal KT3 . 38 C4
Windsor Cl. Crawl RH11 ... 201 C2
Windsor Cl. Onsl V GU2 ... 129 F7
Windsor Cl. W Norw SE27 ... 22 C4
Windsor Cres. Hale GU9 ... 125 B6
Windsor Ct. Ashf TW16 ... 15 A1
Windsor Ct. Burrh GU24 ... 49 E2
Windsor Ct. Horsh RH13 ... 217 F3
Windsor Ct. S Norw SE19 ... 42 E8
Windsor Dr. Ashf TW15 ... 13 D4
Windsor Gdns. Ash GU12 .. 105 F1
Windsor Gdns. Wallin CR0 ... 60 E7
Windsor Gr. W Norw SE27 ... 22 C4
Windsor House. Dovgn RH2 ... 139 B4
Windsor Mews. For Hil SE23 23 E7
Windsor Park Rd. Harl UB3 ... 3 F7
Windsor Pk. Merton SW19 ... 40 C8
Windsor Pl. Chert KT16 ... 33 A3
Windsor Pl. E Grins RH19 .. 206 A8
Windsor Rd. Ashf TW16 ... 15 A2
Windsor Rd. Burrh GU24 ... 49 D3
Windsor Rd. Cranf TW4 & TW5 ... 4 C5
Windsor Rd. Eng Gn TW19 & TW20 ... 11 E6
Windsor Rd. Farnb GU14 ... 85 D1
Windsor Rd. Farnb GU14 .. 104 D8
Windsor Rd. King U T KT2 ... 17 E1
Windsor Rd. N Asct SL5 ... 29 A8
Windsor Rd. Rich TW9 ... 6 F5
Windsor Rd. S Norw CR7 ... 42 B7
Windsor Rd. Tedd TW11 ... 16 D3
Windsor Rd. Worc Pk KT4 ... 58 A8
Windsor Ride. Brack SL5 ... 28 C4
Windsor Ride. Sandh GU15 .. 65 A8
Windsor St. Chert KT16 ... 33 A3
Windsor Way. Alder GU11 105 B2
Windsor Way. Friml GU16 ... 85 F8
Windsor Way. Mayb GU22 ... 70 C3
Windsor Wlk. Walt O T KT12 35 D1
Windsor Wlk. Weyb KT13 ... 53 B5
Windways. Dunsf GU8 ... 192 F7
Windy Ridge Cl. Wimble SW19 ... 19 D3
Windy Wood. Godal GU7 ... 150 C3
Windycroft Cl. Coulsd CR5 & CR8 ... 79 D6
Windyridge. Crawl RH11 ... 201 A5
Winern Glebe. Byfl KT14 ... 71 D6
Winery La. King U T KT1 ... 37 F6
Winfield Ct. Newd RH5 ... 158 B1
Winfield Gr. Newd RH5 ... 158 B1
Winfrith Rd. Wands SW18 ... 20 C7
Wingate Cres. Thorn H CR0 . 41 E3
Wingfield Cl. Woodhm KT15 52 B1
Wingfield Gdns. Friml GU16 66 D3
Wingfield Rd. King U T KT2 .. 18 A2
Wingham House. 3 Penge SE26 ... 23 B3
Wingrove Rd. Catf SE6 ... 24 E6
Wings Cl. Hale GU9 ... 125 B6
Wings Cl. Sutton SM1 ... 59 A6
Wings Rd. Hale GU9 ... 125 B6
Winifred Rd. Coulsd CR5 ... 79 B4
Winifred Rd. Hampt TW12 ... 16 A4
Winifred Rd. Merton SW19 .. 40 A8
Winkfield Cl. Woki RG11 ... 25 B3
Winkfield La. Wink SL4 ... 8 D7
Winkfield Plain. Wink SL4 ... 9 B8
Winkfield Rd. Ascot SL5 ... 29 B7
Winkfield Rd. Wind SL4 ... 9 C8
Winkfield Row. Wink RG12 ... 8 B3
Winkfield St. Wink SL4 ... 8 C6
Winkworth Pl. Banstd SM7 .. 78 A5
Winkworth Rd. Banstd SM7 . 78 A5
Winlaton Rd. Catf BR1 & SE6 24 D4
Winner Way. Crawl RH6 ... 181 D6
Winnington Way. Woking GU21 ... 69 C1
Winscombe. Easth RG12 ... 26 E4
Winsford Rd. For Hil SE6 ... 23 F5
Winslade Way. Catf SE6 ... 24 B8
Winslow Way. Felt TW13 ... 15 E5
Winslow Way.Walt O T KT12 54 C7
Winstanley Cl. Cobham KT11 73 B5
Winstanley Wlk. Cobham KT11 ... 73 B5
Winston Churchill Sch The. Knaph GU21 ... 68 F1
Winston Cl. Friml GU16 ... 85 F6
Winston Dr. Stk D'A KT11 ... 73 E3
Winston Way. Old Wok GU22 ... 90 B7
Winston Wlk. M Bourn GU10 ... 146 C6
Winter Box Wlk. Rich TW10 .. 6 F2
Winterbourne. Horsh RH12 217 F7
Winterbourne Ct. Brack RG12 ... 27 D7
Winterbourne Gr. Whit V KT13 ... 53 C4
Winterbourne Inf Sch. Thorn H CR7 ... 42 A5
Winterbourne Jun Boys' Sch. Thorn H CR7 ... 42 A5
Winterbourne Jun Girls' Sch. Thorn H CR7 ... 42 A5
Winterbourne Rd. For Hil SE23 & SE6 ... 23 F7
Winterbourne Rd. Thorn H CR7 ... 42 A5
Winterbourne Wlk. Friml GU16 ... 85 F8
Winterdown Gdns. Esher KT10 ... 54 F4
Winterdown Rd. Esher KT10 54 F4
Winterfold. Crawl RH10 ... 202 A3
Winterfold Cl. Putney SW19 19 E6
Winterfold La. Farl Gn GU5 153 E6
Winterhill Way. Burph GU4 110 B5
Winters Rd. Thame D KT7 ... 37 B2
Wintersells Ind Est. Byfl KT14 ... 52 D1
Wintersells Rd. Byfl KT13 & KT14 ... 52 E1
Winterstoke Rd. For Hil SE23 & SE6 ... 23 F7
Winterton Ct. Horsh RH13 217 D2
Winton Ct. 15 Surb KT6 ... 37 D2
Winton House. Purley CR8 ... 80 A3
Winton House Sch. Croy CR0 ... 61 F8
Winton Rd. Alder GU11 ... 105 A1
Winton Rd. Farnh GU9 ... 125 D4
Winton Way. W Norw SW16 22 A3
Wire Mill La. Newch RH7 ... 184 F8
Wirrall House. 15 For Hil SE26 ... 23 A5
Wisbeach Rd. Thorn H CR0 .. 42 D4
Wisborough Ct. Crawl RH11 ... 200 F3
Wisborough Rd. S Croy CR2 61 F2
Wisdom Ct. 5 Islew TW7 ... 6 A4
Wiseman Ct. 12 W Norw SE19 ... 22 E3
Wiseton Rd. Up Toot SW17 .. 20 F7
Wishanger La. Head Dn GU10 & GU35 ... 167 B2
Wishbone Way. Woking GU21 ... 68 F3
Wishford Ct. Ashtd KT21 ... 75 F1
Wishmoor Cl. Camb GU15 ... 65 E8
Wishmoor Rd. Camb GU15 ... 65 E8
Wishmore Cross Sch. Chobh GU24 ... 49 F1
Wisley La. Wisley GU23 & KT14 ... 71 E3
Wispers Sch. Haslem GU27 189 C1
Wiston Ct. Crawl RH11 ... 200 F3
Witham Rd. Hounsl TW7 ... 5 D6
Witham Rd. Penge BR3 & SE20 ... 43 C6
Wither Dale. Horley RH6 ... 160 E4
Witherby Cl. S Croy CR0 & CR2 ... 61 E6
Witherslack Cl. Head Dn GU35 ... 187 C4
Withey Brook. Hookw RH6 160 D1
Withey Meadows. Hookw RH6 ... 160 D1
Witheygate Ave. Stain TW18 13 B2
Withies La. Compt GU3 ... 129 C2
Withies The. Knaph GU21 ... 68 E2
Withies The. Leahd KT22 ... 95 B6
Withy Cl. Lhtwat GU18 ... 48 C1
Withybed Cnr. Tadw KT20 ... 97 B4
Withypitts. Turn H RH10 ... 204 A3
Withypitts E. Turn H RH10 204 A3
Witley CE Inf Sch. Witley GU8 ... 170 F4
Witley Cres. New Add CR0 ... 63 C4
Witley House. 5 Streat SW2 ... 21 F8
Witley Point. 8 Rhampt SW15 ... 19 B7
Witley Sta. Wormly GU8 ... 190 F8
Witney Path. For Hil SE23 ... 23 D5
Witten House. New Mal KT3 38 D1
Wittenham Rd. Brack RG12 . 27 F8
Wittering Cl. King U T KT2 ... 17 D3
Wittersham Rd. Catf BR1 ... 24 F3
Wittmead Rd. Mytch GU16 .. 85 F4
Wivenhoe Ct. Hounsl TW4 ... 4 F3
Wiverton Rd. Penge SE20 & SE26 ... 23 C3
Wix Hill. W Hors KT24 ... 112 B4
Woburn Ave. Farnb GU14 ... 85 D3
Woburn Ave. Purley CR8 ... 80 A8
Woburn Cl. Friml GU16 ... 66 A1
Woburn Cl. Merton SW19 ... 20 C2
Woburn Ct. Croy CR0 ... 42 C1
Woburn Ct. Rich TW9 ... 6 F4
Woburn Hill. Addl KT15 ... 52 D7
Woburn Hill Pk. Chert KT15 . 52 D8
Woburn Hill Sch. Chert KT15 ... 52 D7
Woburn Rd. Carsh SM5 ... 40 E1
Woburn Rd. Crawl RH11 ... 201 A4
Woburn Rd. Croy CR0 ... 42 C1
Wodeland Ave. Guild GU2 . 130 B7
Woffington Cl. Tedd KT1 & KT8 ... 37 C8
Woking Bsns Pk. Sheer GU21 ... 70 B4
Woking Cl. Rhampt SW15 ... 7 F3
Woking Coll. Old Wok GU22 90 A7
Woking Comm Hospl. Woking GU22 ... 69 F1
Woking Nuffield Hospl The. Horse GU21 ... 69 E5
Woking Rd. Bellf GU1 & GU4 ... 109 D5
Woking Rd. Jacobs GU1 & GU4 ... 109 D5
Woking Sta. Woking GU22 ... 69 F2
Wokingham Hospl. Woki RG11 ... 25 A6
Wokingham Rd. Brack RG12 26 F8
Wokingham Sta. Woki RG11 25 B6
Wokingham Theatre. Woki RG11 ... 25 B8
Wold Cl. Crawl RH11 ... 200 F4
Wold The. Wold CR3 ... 102 A5
Woldhurstlea Cl. Crawl RH11 ... 201 A4
Woldingham Rd. Warlgm CR3 & CR6 ... 101 C7
Woldingham Sch The. Wold RH9 ... 101 E2
Woldingham Sta. Wold CR3 ... 101 D5
Wolf's Cnr. Limps RH8 ... 123 A5
Wolf's Hill. Limps RH8 ... 123 A4
Wolf's Rd. Limps RH8 ... 123 B5
Wolfe Rd. Alder GU12 ... 105 C1
Wolfington Rd. W Norw SE27 ... 22 B4
Wolfs Wood. Oxted RH8 ... 123 A3
Wolseley Ave. Wimble SW18 & SW19 ... 20 A6
Wolseley Gdns. Chisw W4 ... 7 B8
Wolseley Rd. Alder GU11 .. 105 A1
Wolseley Rd. Carsh CR4 ... 41 A2
Wolseley Rd. Farnc GU7 ... 150 F6
Wolsey Cl. Islew TW3 ... 5 C3
Wolsey Cl. King U T KT2 ... 38 B8
Wolsey Cl. Wimble SW20 ... 19 B1
Wolsey Cl. Worc Pk KT19 & KT4 ... 58 A6
Wolsey Cres. New Add CR0 . 63 C2
Wolsey Cres. W Barn SM4 ... 39 F2
Wolsey Ct. Broml BR1 ... 24 F1
Wolsey Dr. King U T KT2 ... 17 E2
Wolsey Dr. Walt O T KT12 ... 35 D1
Wolsey Gr. 2 Esher KT10 ... 55 B6
Wolsey House. 2 Hampt TW12 ... 16 B2
Wolsey Inf & Jun Schs. New Add CR0 ... 63 D3
Wolsey Pl Sh Ctr. Woking GU22 ... 69 E2
Wolsey Rd. Ashf TW15 ... 13 F4
Wolsey Rd. Ashf TW16 ... 14 F2
Wolsey Rd. E Mole KT8 ... 36 D5
Wolsey Rd. Esher KT10 ... 55 B6
Wolsey Rd. Hampt TW12 ... 16 C2
Wolsey Way. Chess KT9 ... 57 A5
Wolsey Wlk. 4 Woking GU21 ... 69 F2
Wolstonbury Cl. Crawl RH11 ... 201 C4
Wolvens La. Coldh RH5 ... 156 E5
Wolvens La. Westc RH4 & RH5 ... 135 B2
Wolverton Ave. King U T KT2 38 A8
Wolverton Cl. Horley RH6 .. 160 F1
Wolverton Gdns. Horley RH6 ... 160 F2
Wolves Hill. Capel RH5 ... 178 C4
Wonersh Ct. Woner GU5 ... 152 B7
Wonersh & Shamley Green CE Prim Sch. Sham Gn GU5 .. 152 D5
Wonersh Way. E Ewell SM2 . 58 D2
Wonford Cl. King U T KT2 & KT3 ... 38 E8
Wonford Cl. Walt o t H KT20 97 A1
Wonham La. Betch RH3 & RH2 ... 137 F8
Wonham Way. Gomsh GU5 133 D3
Wonham Way. Peasl GU5 . 133 D1
Wontford Rd. Purley CR8 ... 80 B4
Wontner Rd. Up Toot SW12 & SW17 ... 20 F6
Wood Cl. Salfs RH1 ... 161 A8
Wood Ct. Stough GU2 ... 109 B2
Wood End. Horsh RH12 ... 218 C5
Wood End The. Wallin SM6 . 60 B2
Wood La. Banstd KT20 ... 77 F2
Wood La. Binf RG12 ... 26 E8
Wood La. Cater CR3 ... 100 D3
Wood La. Farnb GU14 ... 85 A3
Wood La. Hounsl TW7 ... 5 F7
Wood La. Knaph GU21 ... 68 D1
Wood La. Seale GU10 ... 127 B5
Wood La. Whit V KT13 ... 53 C2
Wood Lodge La. W Wick BR4 ... 63 C7
Wood Rd. Beac H GU26 ... 188 D6
Wood Rd. Bigg H TN16 ... 83 C1
Wood Rd. Camb GU15 ... 65 B1
Wood Rd. Farnc GU7 ... 150 F7
Wood Rd. Heath E GU9 ... 125 C7
Wood Rd. Shep Gn TW17 ... 34 A5
Wood Riding. Pyrf GU22 ... 70 E4
Wood Rise. Stough GU3 ... 108 E3
Wood St. Ash V GU12 ... 106 A6
Wood St. Carsh CR4 ... 41 A2
Wood St. E Grins RH19 ... 185 D1
Wood St. King U T KT2 ... 37 E8
Wood St. Merst RH1 ... 119 C7
Wood Street Inf Sch. Wood S V GU3 ... 108 C3
Wood Vale. For Hil SE22 ... 23 B8
Woodbank Rd. Catf BR1 ... 24 F5
Woodbastwick Rd. Penge SE26 ... 23 E3
Woodberry Cl. Ashf TW16 ... 15 A2
Woodberry Cl. Chidd GU8 . 191 A5
Woodbine Cl. Sandh GU17 ... 64 C7
Woodbine Cl. Twick TW2 ... 16 D6
Woodbine Cotts. Shalf GU4 130 E2
Woodbine Gr. Penge SE20 ... 23 B1
Woodbine La. N Cheam KT4 58 C7
Woodbines Ave. King U T KT1 ... 37 D6
Woodbourne. Heath E GU9 125 E7
Woodbourne Ave. Streat SW16 ... 21 D5
Woodbourne Cl. Streat SW16 ... 21 E5
Woodbourne Dr. Clayg KT10 55 F4
Woodbourne Gdns. Wallin SM6 ... 60 B3
Woodbridge Ave. Leahd KT22 ... 75 A1
Woodbridge Ct. Horsh RH12 ... 218 A5
Woodbridge Dr. Camb GU15 65 D7
Woodbridge Gr. Leahd KT22 75 A1
Woodbridge Hill. Stough GU2 ... 109 B2
Woodbridge Hill Gdns. Stough GU2 ... 109 A2
Woodbridge Meadows. Guild GU1 ... 109 C2
Woodbridge Pk Est. Guild GU1 ... 109 C2
Woodbridge Rd. Blckw GU17 ... 64 B5
Woodbridge Rd. Guild GU1 & GU2 ... 109 C2
Woodbrook Sch. Beck BR3 .. 43 F8
Woodbury Ave. E Grins RH19 ... 186 B1
Woodbury Cl. Bigg H TN16 ... 83 F1
Woodbury Cl. E Grins RH19 206 B8
Woodbury Cl. S Croy CR0 ... 61 F8
Woodbury Dr. Sutton SM2 ... 59 C1
Woodbury Hse. For Hil SE26 23 B5
Woodbury St. Up Toot SW17 20 E3
Woodby Dr. Sunnin SL5 ... 29 F2
Woodcock Dr. Burrh GU24 .. 49 C3
Woodcock Hill. Felb RH19 & RH7 ... 184 F6
Woodcock La. Burrh GU24 ... 49 B3
Woodcombe Cres. For Hil SE23 ... 23 C7
Woodcot Gdns. W Heath GU14 ... 84 D4
Woodcote. Arting GU2 & GU3 ... 130 B5
Woodcote. Cran GU6 ... 174 B4
Woodcote. Farnc GU7 ... 150 D6
Woodcote. Horley RH6 ... 161 C4
Woodcote Ave. Thorn H CR7 42 B5
Woodcote Ave. Wallin SM6 . 60 B2
Woodcote Cl. Epsom KT18 .. 76 D5
Woodcote Cl. King U T KT2 .. 17 F3
Woodcote Dr. Purley CR8 ... 60 D1
Woodcote End. Woodc KT18 76 D4
Woodcote Gn. Wallin SM6 ... 60 C2
Woodcote Green Rd. Woodc KT18 ... 76 C4
Woodcote Grove Rd. Coulsd CR5 ... 79 D5
Woodcote Hall. Epsom KT18 76 D5
Woodcote Hall. Wallin SM6 . 60 B2
Woodcote High Sch. Coulsd CR5 ... 79 D6
Woodcote House. Woodc KT18 ... 76 D4
Woodcote House Ct. Woodc KT18 ... 76 D4
Woodcote House (Sch). Windl GU20 ... 48 B5
Woodcote Hurst. Woodc KT18 ... 76 C3
Woodcote Inf Sch. Coulsd CR5 ... 79 D5
Woodcote Jun Sch. Coulsd CR5 ... 79 D5
Woodcote La. Purley CR8 ... 79 D7
Woodcote Mews. Wallin SM6 ... 60 B4
Woodcote Park Ave. Purley CR5 & CR8 ... 79 C7
Woodcote Park Golf Club. Wallin CR5 ... 79 B5
Woodcote Park Golf Course. Woodc KT18 ... 76 D2
Woodcote Park Rd. Woodc KT18 ... 76 C4
Woodcote Pl. N Asct SL5 ... 28 F8
Woodcote Pl. 1 W Norw SE27 ... 22 B3

Woodcote Rd. Epsom KT18 . 76 D5
Woodcote Rd.
  For Row RH18 .... 206 F2
Woodcote Rd.
  Wallin CR8 & SM6 .... 60 C2
Woodcote Rd. Woodc KT18 . 76 D5
Woodcote Side.
  Woodc KT18 .... 76 B4
Woodcote Valley Rd.
  Purley CR5 & CR8 .... 79 E7
Woodcott House. 1
  Rhampt SW15 .... 19 A8
Woodcott Terr. Alder GU12 126 D8
Woodcourt. Crawl RH11 .... 201 C1
Woodcrest Rd. Purley CR8 .. 79 E6
Woodcrest Wlk. Redh RH1 118 E3
Woodcroft Rd. Crawl RH11 200 D4
Woodcroft Rd.
  Thorn H CR0 & CR7 .... 42 B3
Woodend. Farnb GU14 .... 85 D3
Woodend. Leahd KT22 .... 95 C2
Woodend. S Norw SE19 ...... 22 C2
Woodend. Sutton SM1 .... 59 C8
Woodend. Thame D KT10 ..... 55 C8
Woodend Cl. Crawl RH10 .. 202 A8
Woodend Cl. N Asct SL5 ..... 28 E8
Woodend Cl. Woking GU21 .. 89 A8
Woodend Dr. Ascot SL5 ...... 29 B4
Woodend Pk. Cobham KT11 . 73 D4
Woodend Rd. Friml GU16 .... 86 C7
Woodenhill. Eastb RG12 ..... 26 E1
Woodenhill Cty Prim Sch.
  Eastb RG12 .... 26 E2
Wooderson Cl. S Norw SE25 42 E5
Woodfield. Ashtd KT21 .... 75 D2
Woodfield Ave. Streat SW16 21 D5
Woodfield Ave. Wallin SM5 . 60 A3
Woodfield Cl. Ashtd KT21 ... 75 D2
Woodfield Cl. Coulsd CR5 ... 99 C8
Woodfield Cl. Crawl RH10 . 201 E7
Woodfield Cl. Redh RH1 .... 118 E3
Woodfield Cl. S Norw SE19 . 22 C1
Woodfield Gdns.
  New Mal KT3 .... 38 F4
Woodfield Gr. Streat SW16 . 21 D5
Woodfield Hill. Coulsd CR5 . 99 B8
Woodfield House. 11
  For Hil SE23 .... 23 D5
Woodfield House.
  New Mal KT3 .... 38 F4
Woodfield La. Ashtd KT21 ... 75 D2
Woodfield La. Ashtd KT21 ... 75 D2
Woodfield Rd.
  Cranf TW4 & TW5 .... 4 B5
Woodfield Rd. Crawl RH10 201 F7
Woodfield Rd.
  Hinch W KT10 & KT7 .... 55 F8
Woodfield Way. Redh RH1 118 E3
Woodfields Ct. Sutton SM1 . 59 C7
Woodfields The. S Croy CR2 80 F8
Woodford Gn. Brack RG12 ... 27 F5
Woodgate Ave. Chess KT9 .. 56 D5
Woodgates Cl. Horsh RH13 217 F3
Woodgavil. Nork SM7 .... 77 F3
Woodger Cl.
  Merrow GU4 & GU4 .... 110 C3
Woodgrange Ct.
  Coney H BR2 .... 44 F1
Woodhall Ave. Dulw SE21 ... 22 F5
Woodhall Dr. Dulw SE21 ..... 22 F5
Woodhall La. Windl GU20 ... 48 E8
Woodham La.
  New Haw KT15 .... 52 B1
Woodham La.
  Sheer GU21 & KT15 .... 70 D7
Woodham La. Woodhm KT15 52 B1
Woodham Park Rd.
  Woodhm KT15 .... 51 F1
Woodham Pk Way.
  Woodhm KT15 .... 70 F8
Woodham Rd. Catf SE6 ...... 24 C5
Woodham Rd. Horse GU21 .. 69 F4
Woodham Rise. Horse GU21 70 A4
Woodham Waye.
  Sheer GU21 .... 70 B5
Woodhatch Rd.
  Dovgn RH1 & RH2 .... 139 E5
Woodhatch Rd.
  Earls RH1 & RH2 .... 139 E5
Woodhatch Spinney.
  Coulsd CR5 .... 79 E3
Woodhaw. Egham TW20 ..... 12 B4
Woodhayes. Horley RH6 .... 161 B4
Woodhayes Rd.
  Wimble SW19 & SW20 ...... 19 C2
Woodhill. Send GU23 .... 90 D2
Woodhill La. Sham Gn GU5 152 F4
Woodhouse La.
  Peasl GU5 & RH5 .... 155 A8

Woodhouse St. Binf RG12 ... 26 E8
Woodhurst La. Oxted RH8 . 122 E4
Woodhurst Pk. Oxted RH8 . 122 E5
Woodhyrst Gdns.
  Purley CR8 .... 80 B4
Wooding Gr. 15
  Crawl RH11 .... 201 B1
Woodland Ave. Cran GU6 .. 174 F3
Woodland Cl. E Hors KT24 . 112 F8
Woodland Cl. Horsh RH13 218 B4
Woodland Cl. W Ewell KT19 57 E4
Woodland Cl. W Norw SE19 22 E2
Woodland Ct. Cheam SM1 ... 59 A4
Woodland Ct. Ewell KT17 ... 76 F7
Woodland Ct. Oxted RH8 ... 122 E7
Woodland Dr.
  Crawl D RH10 .... 204 B8
Woodland Dr. E Hors KT24 112 F8
Woodland Dr.
  M Bourn GU10 .... 146 B6
Woodland Dr. Ockley RH5 . 178 A5
Woodland Gdns. Islew TW7 . 5 E4
Woodland Gdns. Selsd CR2 . 81 C8
Woodland Gr. Weyb KT13 ... 53 D6
Woodland Hill.
  W Norw SE19 .... 22 E2
Woodland Rd. Thorn H CR7 . 42 A5
Woodland Rd. W Norw SE19 22 E2
Woodland Rise. Oxted RH8 122 E5
Woodland View. Farnc GU7 129 E1
Woodland Way. Cater RH1 120 E8
Woodland Way.
  Croy CR0 & CR9 .... 43 A2
Woodland Way.
  Horsh RH13 .... 218 B4
Woodland Way. Kings KT20 97 E4
Woodland Way.
  Merton SM4 .... 39 F5
Woodland Way. Mitch CR4 . 21 A1
Woodland Way. Purley CR8 . 80 A6
Woodland Way. Tolw KT5 ... 57 B8
Woodland Way. W Wick BR4 63 C7
Woodland Way.
  Whit V KT13 .... 53 D5
Woodlands. Beck BR3 .... 24 B1
Woodlands. Chert KT15 ...... 52 E7
Woodlands. Crawl RH10 .... 202 D8
Woodlands. Horley RH6 ..... 161 C4
Woodlands. Send M GU23 ... 90 F2
Woodlands. W Barn SW20 ... 39 D5
Woodlands Ave. Earls RH1 139 F8
Woodlands Ave.
  Heath E GU9 .... 125 F7
Woodlands Ave.
  King U T KT3 .... 38 D8
Woodlands Ave.
  W Byfl KT14 .... 70 F7
Woodlands Ave.
  W Byfl KT14 & KT15 .... 71 A7
Woodlands Ave.
  Worc Pk KT4 .... 58 A8
Woodlands Cl. Ascot SL5 .... 28 F3
Woodlands Cl. Ash GU12 .. 106 A5
Woodlands Cl. Clayg KT10 . 55 F3
Woodlands Cl. Cran GU6 .. 174 F2
Woodlands Cl.
  Crawl D RH10 .... 204 B7
Woodlands Cl. Ottsh KT16 . 51 B1
Woodlands Cl.
  W Heath GU14 .... 64 E1
Woodlands Ct. Bromll BR1 .. 44 F8
Woodlands Ct. Dulw SE22 .. 23 B8
Woodlands Ct. Sandh GU15 . 45 F1
Woodlands Dr. 7
  Woking GU21 .... 69 A1
Woodlands Ct. Woking GU21 89 E8
Woodlands Dr.
  S Godst RH9 .... 142 E6
Woodlands Dr. Sunby TW16 35 D7
Woodlands Gr. Coulsd CR5 . 79 B2
Woodlands Gr. Islew TW7 .... 5 E5
Woodlands House.
  Craw GU22 .... 70 C5
Woodlands La.
  Shotm GU27 .... 207 F7
Woodlands La. Stk D'A KT11 74 B2
Woodlands La.
  Windl GU20 & GU24 .... 48 E3
Woodlands Pk. Ashf TW15 . 14 C2
Woodlands Pk. Box H KT20 116 B4
Woodlands Pk.
  Merrow GU1 .... 110 B2
Woodlands Pk. Row Tn KT15 51 F5
Woodlands Pk. Sheer GU21 . 70 C5
Woodlands Rd.
  Ashtd KT11 & KT22 .... 74 D1
Woodlands Rd. Bellf GU1 . 109 D5
Woodlands Rd. Camb GU15 . 65 B5
Woodlands Rd.
  E Grins RH19 .... 186 A4
Woodlands Rd. Earls RH1 . 139 F7

Woodlands Rd.
  Effing KT23 & KT24 .... 113 F6
Woodlands Rd. Epsom KT18 76 A4
Woodlands Rd. Hambl GU8 171 D1
Woodlands Rd. Islew TW7 .... 5 F5
Woodlands Rd.
  Leahd KT11 & KT22 .... 74 D1
Woodlands Rd. Mortl SW13 .. 7 F4
Woodlands Rd. Pyrf KT14 ... 70 F5
Woodlands Rd. Surb KT6 .... 37 D2
Woodlands Rd. Vir W GU25 . 31 C5
Woodlands Rd.
  W Heath GU14 .... 84 D6
Woodlands Rd E.
  Vir W GU25 .... 31 C5
Woodlands Rd W.
  Vir W GU25 .... 31 C5
Woodlands Ride. Ascot SL5 . 29 A3
Woodlands St. Lewish KT22 . 95 C3
Woodlands The. Islew TW7 ... 5 F5
Woodlands The.
  Lewish SE13 .... 24 D8
Woodlands The. Mitch CR4 . 41 A6
Woodlands The.
  S Norw SE19 .... 22 C1
Woodlands The.
  Small RH6 .... 162 B3
Woodlands The.
  Thame D KT10 .... 55 C8
Woodlands The. Wallin SM6 60 B2
Woodlands Way.
  Ashtd KT21 .... 76 B2
Woodlands Way.
  Box H KT20 .... 116 C5
Woodlands Wlk.
  W Heath GU14 .... 64 E1
Woodlawn Cres. Twick TW2 16 B6
Woodlawn Dr. Felt TW13 .... 15 D6
Woodlawn Gr. Horse GU21 . 69 F4
Woodlea Cty Prim Sch.
  Wold CR3 .... 101 F5
Woodlea Dr. Hayes BR2 ...... 44 E4
Woodlee Cl. Vir W GU25 .... 31 C7
Woodleigh. 1 Surb KT5 ..... 37 F4
Woodleigh Gdns.
  Streat SW16 .... 21 E5
Woodley Cl. Mitch SW17 .... 20 F1
Woodley House. Farnc GU7 150 E8
Woodley La.
  Carsh SM1 & SM5 .... 59 E7
Woodlodge. Ashtd KT21 ...... 75 E2
Woodlodge. 4
  Wimble SW19 .... 19 F3
Woodman Rd. Coulsd CR5 .. 79 D4
Woodmancote Ct.
  Horsh RH12 .... 217 D5
Woodmancote Gdns.
  W Byfl KT14 .... 71 A6
Woodmancott Cl.
  Brack RG12 .... 27 F3
Woodmancourt. Farnc GU7 150 C8
Woodmans Hill.
  Crawl RH11 .... 201 C2
Woodmansterne Cty Prim Sch.
  Woodm SM7 .... 78 F5
Woodmansterne La.
  Banstd SM7 .... 78 D4
Woodmansterne La.
  Wallin SM5 & SM6 .... 79 A7
Woodmansterne La.
  Woodm SM7 .... 78 D4
Woodmansterne Prim Sch.
  Street SW16 .... 41 D8
Woodmansterne Rd.
  Coulsd CR5 .... 79 C4
Woodmansterne Rd.
  Street SW16 .... 41 D8
Woodmansterne Rd.
  Sutton SM5 & SM2 .... 59 E2
Woodmansterne Sta.
  Coulsd CR5 .... 79 B3
Woodmere. Brack RG12 ...... 27 E3
Woodmere Ave. Croy CR0 ... 43 D2
Woodmere Cl. Croy CR0 ..... 43 D2
Woodmere Gdns. Croy CR0 . 43 D2
Woodmere Way. Beck BR3 . 44 D4
Woodnook Rd. Streat SW16 21 B3
Woodpecker Cl.
  Cobham KT11 .... 73 E7
Woodpecker Cl.
  Crond GU10 .... 124 D8
Woodpecker La. Newd RH5 158 C2
Woodpecker Mount.
  New Add CR0 .... 62 F2
Woodpecker Way.
  Westfd GU22 .... 89 D3
Woodpeckers. Eastb RG12 . 27 B5
Woodpeckers. Witley GU8 . 170 E7

Woodplace Cl. Coulsd CR5 .. 79 C1
Woodplace La. Coulsd CR5 . 99 C7
Woodplace La. Hooley CR5 . 99 C7
Woodridge Cl. Brack RG12 .. 27 C6
Woodrough Copse.
  Bramly GU5 .... 152 A5
Woodrow Dr. Woki RG11 ... 25 F6
Woodroyd Ave. Horley RH6 160 F2
Woodroyd Gdns.
  Horley RH6 .... 160 F1
Woodruff Ave. Burph GU1 110 B4
Woods Hill Cl. Ash W RH19 206 D6
Woods Hill La.
  Ash W RH19 .... 206 D6
Woodshore Cl. Went GU25 .. 31 B3
Woodshore La. Went GU25 .. 31 C3
Woodside. 1 Farnb GU14 .. 85 B7
Woodside. Fetch KT22 .... 94 B5
Woodside. Hawley GU17 .... 64 C3
Woodside. Horsh RH13 ..... 218 B4
Woodside. Hyde GU8 .... 171 A5
Woodside. L Kings KT20 ... 117 F7
Woodside. Sandh GU15 ..... 64 F7
Woodside. W Hors KT24 .... 92 C1
Woodside. Walt O T KT12 ... 35 A1
Woodside. Wimble SW19 ... 19 F3
Woodside Ave. Croy SE25 .. 43 A3
Woodside Ave. Hersh KT12 . 54 B6
Woodside Ave.
  Thame D KT10 .... 36 E2
Woodside Cl. Cater CR3 .... 100 E3
Woodside Cl. Chidd GU8 ... 191 B4
Woodside Cl. Knaph GU21 .. 68 D2
Woodside Cl. Tolw KT5 ...... 38 C2
Woodside Cotts. Elst GU8 . 148 C3
Woodside Court Rd.
  Croy CR0 & CR9 .... 43 A2
Woodside Cres. Smallf RH6 162 A3
Woodside Gn.
  Croy CR0 & SE25 .... 43 A3
Woodside House.
  Wimble SW19 .... 19 F2
Woodside Jun & Inf Sch.
  Croy CR0 .... 43 A2
Woodside La. Wink SL4 & SL5 9 C3
Woodside Pk Est.
  Godal GU7 .... 150 F4
Woodside Pk. Croy SE25 .... 43 B3
Woodside Rd. Bear Gn RH5 157 D3
Woodside Rd. Chidd GU8 ... 191 B5
Woodside Rd. Cobham KT11 74 A6
Woodside Rd. Crawl RH10 . 201 F8
Woodside Rd. Croy SE25 .... 43 B3
Woodside Rd. Farnb GU11 . 104 F7
Woodside Rd. Heath E GU9 125 E7
Woodside Rd. King U T KT2 . 17 E1
Woodside Rd. King U T KT3 . 38 E7
Woodside Rd. Purley CR8 ... 79 E6
Woodside Rd. Stough GU2 . 108 F2
Woodside Rd. Sutton SM1 .. 59 C7
Woodside Sta. Croy CR0 .... 43 B3
Woodside Way. Croy CR0 ... 43 C3
Woodside Way. Earls RH1 140 A3
Woodside Way. Earls RH1 140 A8
Woodside Way. Streat CR4 . 41 C8
Woodside Way. Vir W GU25 31 B6
Woodsome Lodge.
  Whit V KT13 .... 53 C4
Woodspring Rd.
  Putney SW19 .... 19 E6
Woodstock. E Grins RH19 . 185 C2
Woodstock. W Clan GU4 ... 111 B7
Woodstock. Woki RG11 ...... 25 C6
Woodstock Ave.
  Cheam SM3 & SM4 .... 39 F2
Woodstock Ave. Islew TW7 .. 6 A2
Woodstock Cl. Cran GU6 .. 174 F1
Woodstock Cl. Horse GU21 . 69 E3
Woodstock Cl. Horsh RH12 217 D5
Woodstock Coll. Long D KT6 56 D8
Woodstock Ct. Ewell KT17 .. 76 D7
Woodstock Gdns. Beck BR3 24 B1
Woodstock La. N Long D KT6 56 C8
Woodstock La S.
  Clayg KT10 & KT6 .... 56 C6
Woodstock Rd. Coulsd CR5 . 79 B3
Woodstock Rd.
  Croy CR0 & CR9 .... 61 D7
Woodstock Rd.
  Wallin SM5 & SM6 .... 60 A5
Woodstock Rise.
  Cheam SM3 .... 39 F2
Woodstock Way. Mitch CR4 41 C7
Woodstocks. Farnb GU14 ... 85 D6
Woodstone Ave.
  Stonel KT17 & KT4 .... 58 A5
Woodsway. Oxsh KT22 .... 74 E5
Woodsyre. Dulw SE19 & 26 .. 22 F4
Woodthorpe Rd. Ashf TW15 13 D4
Woodthorpe Rd. Stain TW15 13 D4
Woodvale Ave. S Norw SE25 42 F7

Woodvale Ct. S Norw SE25 .. 42 F6
Woodvale Wlk.
  N Norw SE27 .... 22 C3
Woodview. Chess KT9 .... 75 C8
Woodview Cl. Hams Gn CR2 81 B5
Woodview Cl.
  King U T SW15 .... 18 D4
Woodview Cl. Weyb KT13 ... 53 C5
Woodville Cl. Blckw GU17 ... 64 B3
Woodville Cl. Tedd TW11 ... 17 A4
Woodville Gdns. Surb KT6 .. 37 D2
Woodville Pl. Cater CR3 .... 100 C5
Woodville Rd. Leahd KT22 ... 95 B7
Woodville Rd. Merton SM4 . 40 A5
Woodville Rd. Rich TW10 ... 17 C5
Woodville Rd. S Norw CR7 . 42 D6
Woodville Sch The.
  Leahd KT22 .... 95 B7
Woodward Cl. Clayg KT10 .. 55 F4
Woodwarde Rd. Dulw SE22 . 22 F8
Woodwards. Crawl RH11 ... 201 C1
Woodway. Camb GU15 ...... 65 B5
Woodway. Merrow GU1 .... 110 B2
Woodyard La. Dulw SE21 ... 22 E8
Woodyers Cl. Woner GU5 . 152 B7
Wool Rd. Wimble SW20 ..... 19 B2
Woolborough Cl.
  Crawl RH10 .... 201 E7
Woolborough La.
  Crawl RH10 .... 181 F1
Woolborough La.
  Crawl RH10 .... 202 A8
Woolborough La.
  S Nuff RH1 .... 161 F8
Woolborough Rd.
  Crawl RH10 .... 201 E7
Woolford Cl. Wink RG12 ...... 8 C1
Woolfords La. Elst GU8 .... 169 B7
Woolhampton Way.
  Brack RG12 .... 27 D4
Woolhams. Cater CR3 ...... 101 A1
Woollards Rd. Ash GU12 .. 106 B4
Woolmead Rd. Farnb GU9 . 125 C3
Woolmead The. Farnh GU9 125 C3
Woolmer Hill Rd.
  Shottm GU26 & GU27 ..... 207 D7
Woolmer Hill Sch.
  Shottm GU27 .... 207 D7
Woolmer View.
  Graysh GU26 .... 188 D3
Woolsack Way. Godal GU7 150 F4
Woolstone Rd.
  For Hil SE23 & SE6 .... 23 E6
Woosehill La. Woki RG11 ... 25 A5
Wootton Cl. Epsom KT18 ... 76 F3
Wootton Grange.
  Woking GU22 .... 89 E8
Worbeck Rd. Penge SE20 ... 43 C7
Worcester Cl. Croy CR0 ..... 63 A8
Worcester Cl. Farnb GU14 .. 85 B7
Worcester Cl. Mitch CR4 .... 41 A7
Worcester Ct. Ashf TW15 ... 14 B3
Worcester Ct. Walt O T KT12 35 C1
Worcester Ct. Worc Pk KT4 . 57 F7
Worcester Dr. Ashf TW15 ... 14 B3
Worcester Gdns.
  Worc Pk KT4 .... 57 E7
Worcester Park Rd.
  Worc Pk KT4 .... 57 D7
Worcester Park Sta.
  New Mal KT3 .... 39 A1
Worcester Rd. Belm SM2 ... 59 B3
Worcester Rd. Crawl RH10 201 E2
Worcester Rd. Reig RH2 ... 118 A2
Worcester Rd. Stough GU2 108 F3
Worcester Rd. Sutton SM2 . 59 B3
Worcester Rd. 11
  Wimble SW19 .... 19 F3
Wordsworth. Easth RG12 ... 26 F4
Wordsworth Ave.
  Kenley CR8 .... 80 D4
Wordsworth Cl.
  Crawl RH10 .... 202 B8
Wordsworth Dr.
  Cheam KT4 & SM3 .... 58 C6
Wordsworth Mead.
  Redh RH1 .... 119 B3
Wordsworth Pl.
  Horsh RH12 .... 217 E7
Wordsworth Rd. Addl KT15 . 52 D6
Wordsworth Rd.
  Hampt TW12 & TW13 .... 15 F4
Wordsworth Rd.
  Penge SE20 .... 23 D1
Wordsworth Rd. Wallin SM6 60 D4
Wordsworth Rise. 6
  E Grins RH19 .... 185 C1
Works Rd. Woodhm KT15 ... 52 B2

World of Adventures.
Chess KT9 .... 56 C1
Worlds End Hill. Brack RG12 27 F3
Worple Ave. Islew TW7 ...... 6 A2
Worple Ave. Stain TW18 ...... 13 B2
Worple Ave. Wimble SW19 ... 19 D1
Worple Ct. Wimble SW19 ..... 19 E2
Worple Prim Sch. Islew TW7 6 A3
Worple Rd. Epsom KT18 ...... 76 E5
Worple Rd. Islew TW7 .... 6 A3
Worple Rd. Leahd KT22 ...... 95 B4
Worple Rd. Stain TW18 .... 13 B1
Worple Rd.
Wimble SW19 & SW20 ...... 39 D8
Worple Rd. Woodc KT18 ..... 76 D4
Worple Road Mews.
Wimble SW19 .... 19 F2
Worple St. Mortl SW14 .... 7 D4
Worple Way. Rich TW10 ...... 6 E3
Worplesdon Cty Prim Sch.
Fairl GU3 .... 108 D4
Worplesdon Golf Course.
Woking GU22 .... 88 D4
Worplesdon Hill.
Woking GU22 .... 88 D5
Worplesdon Rd.
Stough GU2 .... 109 A4
Worplesdon Sta.
Woking GU22 .... 89 B3
Worslade Rd. Up Toot SW17 20 D4
Worsley Bridge Jun Sch.
Beck BR3 .... 24 A1
Worsley Bridge Rd.
Beck BR3 & SE6 .... 24 A2
Worsley Bridge Rd. Catf SE6 23 F3
Worsley House. For Hil SE23 23 B6
Worsley Rd. Friml GU16 ...... 85 F7
Worsted Gn. Mersf RH1 .... 119 D6
Worsted La. E Grins RH19 . 206 B8
Worth Abbey & Sch.
Worth RH10 .... 203 B1
Worth Park Ave.
Crawl RH10 .... 202 C7
Worth Rd. Crawl RH10 ...... 202 C6
Worth Way. Worth RH10 .... 202 E5
Worthfield Cl. W Ewell KT19 57 D3
Worthfield Rd. W Ewell KT19 57 D3
Worthing Rd. Heston TW5 .... 4 F8
Worthing Rd. Horsh RH12 217 B1
Worthington Cl. Mitch CR4 .. 41 B6
Worthington House. **16**
Streat SW2 .... 22 A8
Worthington Rd. Surb KT6 .. 37 F1
Wortley Rd. Thorn H CR0 .... 42 A2
Worton Cl. Islew TW7 .... 5 E3
Worton Gdns. Hounsl TW7 .... 5 D5
Worton Hall Est. Islew TW7 .. 5 E3
Worton Rd. Islew TW7 .... 5 E4
Worton Way.
Hounsl TW3 & TW7 .... 5 D5
Wotton Dr. Wotton RH5 ..... 134 E3
Wotton Way. E Ewell SM2 ... 58 C1
Wrabness Way.
Stain TW18 .... 33 B8
Wray Cl. Ash W RH19 .... 206 D6
Wray Common Cty Prim Sch.
Reig RH1 .... 118 D2

Wray Common Rd.
Reig RH2 .... 118 D2
Wray House. **11**
Streat SW2 .... 21 E7
Wray La. Reig RH2 .... 118 D4
Wray Mill House. Redh RH1 118 E3
Wray Mill Pk. Redh RH1 .... 118 E3
Wray Park Rd. Reig RH2 .... 118 C2
Wray Rd. Belm SM2 .... 58 F2
Wrayfield Ave. Reig RH2 ... 118 C2
Wrayfield Rd. Cheam SM3 ... 58 D7
Wraylands Dr.
Redh RH1 & RH2 .... 118 D3
Wraymead Pl. Reig RH2 .... 118 D2
Wraymill Ct. **4** Reig RH2 . 118 D1
Wraysbury Cl. Hounsl TW4 .... 4 E2
Wraysbury Rd. Stain TW18 . 12 C5
Wraysbury Rd. Wray TW19 . 12 C5
Wraysbury Sta. Wray TW19 .. 1 A1
Wrecclesham Hill.
Wreccl GU10 .... 145 E5
Wrecclesham Rd.
Farnh GU10 & GU9 .... 145 F8
Wrecclesham Rd.
Wreccl GU10 & GU9 .... 145 F8
Wren Cl. Horsh RH12 .... 217 D7
Wren Cl. Selsd CR2 .... 62 D2
Wren Cres. Addl KT15 .... 52 D5
Wren Ct. Ash GU12 .... 106 B3
Wren Ct. Crawl RH10 .... 201 E3
Wren Ct. S Croy CR0 .... 61 D6
Wren House. **4**
Hampt TW12 .... 16 B2
Wren Way. W Heath GU14 .. 84 F7
Wren's Ave. Ashf TW15 ...... 14 C4
Wren's Hill. Oxsh KT22 ...... 74 C4
Wrenthorpe Rd. Catf BR1 ... 24 E4
Wrekin Rd. Heston TW5 ...... 4 C7
Wright's Row. Walln SM5 .... 60 B6
Wrighton Ct. Cheam SM1 .... 58 F4
Wrights Rd. S Norw SE25 ... 42 E6
Wrotham Hill. Dunsf GU8 .. 192 E3
Wrotham House. Beck BR3 . 23 F1
Wroxham. Easth RG12 .... 26 F4
Wroxham Wlk. Crawl RH10 202 B4
Wrythe Green Rd.
Carsh SM5 .... 59 F7
Wrythe La.
Carsh SM1 & SM5 & SM4 ... 59 E7
Wyatt Cl. Felt TW13 .... 15 E7
Wyatt Park Mansions. **1**
Streat SW2 .... 21 E6
Wyatt Park Rd. Streat SW2 . 21 F6
Wyatt Rd. Stain TW18 .... 13 A3
Wyatt's Almshouses.
Farnc GU7 .... 151 A6
Wyatt's Cl. Farnc GU7 ...... 151 A6
Wych Elm Rise. Guild GU1 . 130 E6
Wych Hill. Woking GU22 ..... 89 C8
Wych Hill La. Woking GU22 . 89 E8
Wych Hill Rd. Woking GU22 . 89 D8
Wych Hill Rise.
Woking GU22 .... 89 D8
Wych Hill Way.
Woking GU22 .... 89 D8
Wyche Gr. S Croy CR2 .... 61 D2
Wychelm Rd. Lhtwat GU18 .. 67 B8
Wychwood Ave. Brack RG12 27 F5
Wychwood Ave. S Norw CR7 42 C6

Wychwood Cl. Alder GU12 . 105 F2
Wychwood Cl. Ashf TW16 ... 15 A2
Wychwood Pl. Camb GU15 .. 66 B8
Wychwood Way.
W Norw SE19 .... 22 D2
Wycliffe Bldgs. Guild GU2 . 130 C7
Wycliffe Cl. Crawl RH11 .... 200 E3
Wycliffe Rd. Merton SW19 . 20 B2
Wycliffe Rd. Wimble SW19 . 20 B2
Wydell Cl. W Barn SM4 ...... 39 D3
Wydenhurst Rd.
Croy CR0 & CR9 .... 43 B2
Wye Cl. Ashf TW15 .... 14 B4
Wyecliffe Gdns. Merst RH1 119 C5
Wyeth's Mews. Epsom KT17 76 F6
Wyeth's Rd. Epsom KT17 .... 76 F6
Wyke Ave. Normdy GU12 .. 106 E3
Wyke Bglws. Normdy GU22 106 D3
Wyke Cl. Hounsl TW7 .... 5 F8
Wyke Cty Prim Sch Thc.
Normdy GU2 .... 106 F4
Wyke Green Golf Course.
Hounsl TW7 .... 5 F8
Wyke La. Normdy GU12 .... 106 D7
Wyke Rd. Wimble SW20 ..... 39 C7
Wykeham Cl. Harm UB7 ...... 3 A8
Wykeham Hse.Farnb GU14 105 C8
Wykeham House.
Merton SW19 .... 40 A8
Wykeham Rd. Farnb GU .. 125 C3
Wykeham Rd. Merrow GU1 110 D2
Wylam. Easth RG12 .... 26 F4
Wyleu St. For Hil SE23 .... 23 E8
Wymering Ct. Farnb GU14 .. 85 D3
Wynash Gdns. Carsh SM5 ... 59 E5
Wynbourne Ct. Penge SE20 . 43 B7
Wyncote Way. Selsd CR2 .... 62 D2
Wyndham Ave.
Cobham KT11 .... 73 A6
Wyndham Cl. Belm SM2 ..... 59 A3
Wyndham Cres. Cran GU6 174 A3
Wyndham Cres. Twick TW4 ... 5 A1
Wyndham Rd. King U T KT2 . 17 F1
Wyndham Rd. Woking GU21 69 B1
Wyndham St. Alder GU12 .. 105 C1
Wynell Rd. For Hil SE23 ..... 23 D5
Wynfields. Mytch GU16 ...... 85 F3
Wynlea Cl. Crawl D RH10 .. 204 A8
Wynne Ct. **4** Islew TW7 ...... 6 A4
Wynnstow Pk. Oxted RH8 . 122 F4
Wynsham Way. Windl GU20 48 B6
Wynton Gdns. S Norw SE25 42 F4
Wynton Gr. Walt O T KT12 .. 54 A7
Wyphurst Rd. Cran GU6 .... 174 E4
Wyresdale. Brack RG12 ...... 27 F2
Wysemead. Horley RH6 .... 161 C4
Wythegate. Stain TW18 ...... 12 F1
Wyvern Cl. Easth RG12 ...... 27 A5
Wyvern Est The.
W Barn KT3 .... 39 A5
Wyvern Pl. Addl KT15 .... 52 B6
Wyvern Rd. Purley CR8 ...... 61 B1

Yaffle Rd. Whit V KT13 .... 53 C1
Yale Cl. Hounsl TW4 .... 4 F2
Yale Cl. Sandh GU15 .... 45 F2
Yarborough Rd.
Mitch SW19 .... 40 D8
Yarbridge Cl. Sutton SM2 .. 59 B1
Yard Mead. Egham TW20 ... 12 A5

Yardley. Easth RG12 .... 26 F4
Yardley Cl. Reig RH2 .... 118 B3
Yardley Ct. Cheam SM3 ..... 58 C6
Yarm Cl. Leahd KT22 .... 95 C4
Yarm Court Rd. Leahd KT22 95 C4
Yarm Way. Leahd KT22 ...... 95 D4
Yarmouth Cl. Crawl RH10 . 202 A4
Yarnold Cl. Woki RG11 ...... 25 F7
Yarrow Cl. Horsh RH12 .... 217 F3
Yateley Ct. Purley CR8 .... 80 C5
Yatesbury Cl. Farnh GU9 .. 145 F7
Yattendon Rd. Horley RH6 161 B3
Yattendon Sch. Horley RH6 161 A4
Yaverland Dr. Bagsh GU19 .. 47 D2
Ye Market. Croy CR0 .... 61 D5
Yeats Cl. Woodh RH1 .... 139 C6
Yehudi Menuhin Sch.
Fetch KT11 .... 94 A8
Yellowcress Dr. Bisley GU24 68 A3
Yelverton Ct. G Book KT23 .. 94 A1
Yelverton Rd. For Hil SE23 .. 23 A8
Yenston Cl. Morden SM4 .... 40 A3
Yeoman Cl. W Norw SE27 .. 22 B5
Yeoman Way. Earls RH1 ... 140 B4
Yeomanry Cl. Ewell KT17 ... 76 F7
Yeomans Cl.
Ash GU8 & GU12 .... 126 F8
Yeomans Cl. W Heath GU14 85 A5
Yeomans Way. Camb GU15 . 65 E5
Yeoveney Cl. Stan TW19 ... 12 D6
Yeovil Cl. Farnb GU14 .... 85 D1
Yeovil Rd. Farnb GU14 .... 85 E1
Yeovil Rd. Sandh GU15 ...... 45 E1
Yetminster Rd. Farnb GU14 85 D1
Yew La. E Grins RH19 .... 185 B3
Yew Pl. Walt O T KT13 .... 53 F7
Yew Tree Bottom Rd.
Nork KT17 & KT18 .... 77 C2
Yew Tree Cl. Chips CR5 ...... 98 F8
Yew Tree Cl. Farnb GU14 .... 84 C3
Yew Tree Cl. Horley RH6 ... 161 A4
Yew Tree Cl. New Mal KT4 .. 38 E1
Yew Tree Cotts. Esher KT10 55 D8
Yew Tree Ct. Sutton SM2 .... 59 C3
Yew Tree Dr. Belif GU1 .... 109 C6
Yew Tree Dr. Cater CR3 .... 100 F2
Yew Tree Gdns. Woodc KT18 76 C4
Yew Tree House.
New Mal KT4 .... 38 E1
Yew Tree La. Reig RH2 ...... 118 B4
Yew Tree Rd. Charl RH6 .... 180 E7
Yew Tree Rd. Dork RH4 .... 115 A1
Yew Tree Wlk. Effing KT24 113 D8
Yew Tree Wlk. Frimi GU16 .. 65 F1
Yew Tree Wlk. Hounsl TW4 .. 4 F2
Yew Tree Wlk. S Croy CR8 ... 61 C1
Yew Trees. Shep Gn TW17 .. 33 F5
Yewdale Cl. Catf BR1 .... 24 E2
Yewdale Cl. Catf BR1 .... 24 E2
Yewens. Chidd GU8 .... 191 B5
Yewlands Cl. Banstd SM7 ... 78 C4
Yewlands Wlk.
Crawl RH11 .... 200 D4
Yews The. Ashf TW15 .... 14 B8
Yewtree Rd. Beck BR3 .... 43 F6
Yewtrees. Egham TW20 ...... 32 C6
Yockley Cl. Frimi GU15 ...... 66 D3
Yolland Cl. Heath E GU9 ... 125 C7

York Ave. E Grins RH19 .... 206 A8
York Ave. Mortl SW14 .... 7 C2
York Cl. Byfl KT14 .... 71 E7
York Cl. Horsh RH13 .... 217 F3
York Cl. Morden SM4 .... 40 B5
York Cres. Alder GU11 ...... 104 F1
York Ct. Beck BR3 .... 44 D8
York Ct. King U T KT2 .... 17 D2
York Ct. Walln SM6 .... 60 C4
York Gdns. Walt O T KT12 ... 54 D8
York Hill.
W Norw SE27 & SW16 .... 22 B5
York House. Brack RG12 .... 26 F8
York House. For Hil SE26 .... 23 C3
York House. **4** King U T KT2 17 F1
York House. Rich TW9 .... 7 A6
York House. S Norw SE25 ... 42 E5
York Rd. Alder GU11 .... 104 F1
York Rd. Ash GU12 .... 106 A3
York Rd. Belm SM1 & SM2 .. 59 A3
York Rd. Bigg H TN16 .... 103 D8
York Rd. Byfl KT14 .... 71 F7
York Rd. Camb GU15 .... 65 D7
York Rd. Crawl RH10 .... 201 E2
York Rd. Farnb GU14 .... 85 C1
York Rd. Farnb GU14 .... 104 E8
York Rd. **3** Rich TW10 ...... 6 F2
York Rd. Selsd CR2 .... 62 D1
York Rd. Tedd TW11 .... 16 E4
York Rd. Thorn H CR0 .... 42 A2
York Rd. Weyb KT13 .... 53 C6
York Rd. Wimble SW19 ...... 20 C2
York Rd. Woking GU22 .... 69 E1
York St. Carsh SM4 .... 41 A2
York St. Twick TW1 .... 17 A7
York Town Ind Est.
Camb GU15 .... 65 A5
York Way. Chess KT9 .... 56 E3
York Way. Felt TW13 .... 15 F5
York Way. Sandh GU17 ...... 64 B8
Yorke Gate Rd. Cater CR3 100 D5
Yorke Gdns. Reig RH2 .... 118 A2
Yorke Rd. Reig RH2 .... 118 A2
Yorkshire Rd. Mitch CR4 .... 41 E5
Yorktown Rd.
Sandh GU15 & GU17 .... 64 C7
Yorktown Rd. Sandh GU15 .. 64 E7
Youlden Cl. Camb GU15 ..... 66 A5
Youlden Dr. Frimi GU15 ...... 66 B6
Young St. Fetch KT22 .... 94 F3
Young St. Leahd KT22 .... 95 A3
Youngman. Lingf RH7 .... 165 B4
Youngs Dr. Alder GU12 .... 105 F2
Youngstroat La. Chobh GU24 50 E1
Yukon Rd. Balham SW12 .... 21 B8

Zealand Ave. Harm UB7 ...... 2 E7
Zennor Rd. Streat SW12 ..... 21 C7
Zermatt Rd. Thorn H CR7 ... 42 C5
Zig Zag Rd. Kenley CR8 ...... 80 C3
Zig Zag Rd.
Mickle KT20 & RH4 & RH5 115 D4
Zinnia Dr. Bisley GU24 .... 68 A3
Zion Pl. S Norw CR7 .... 42 D5
Zion Rd. S Norw CR7 & SE25 42 D5
Zodiac Ct. Thorn H CR0 ...... 42 B1